MICROSOFT

Office 97

Introductory Concepts and Techniques

ENHANCED EDITION

Gary B. Shelly
Thomas J. Cashman
Misty E. Vermaat

Contributing Authors
Marvin M. Boetcher
Steven G. Forsythe
Sherry L. Green
Philip J. Pratt
James S. Quasney
Joy L. Starks

COURSE TECHNOLOGY
ONE MAIN STREET
CAMBRIDGE MA 02142

an International Thomson Publishing company 

CAMBRIDGE • ALBANY • BONN • CINCINNATI • LONDON • MADRID • MELBOURNE
MEXICO CITY • NEW YORK • PARIS • SAN FRANCISCO • TOKYO • TORONTO • WASHINGTON

COURSE TECHNOLOGY

Printed in the United States of America

For more information, contact:

Course Technology
One Main Street
Cambridge, Massachusetts 02142, USA

ITP GmbH
Konigswinterer Strasse 418
53227 Bonn, Germany

ITP Europe
Berkshire House
168-173 High Holborn
London, WC1V 7AA, United Kingdom

International Thomson Editores
Saneca, 53
Colonia Polanco
11560 Mexico D.F. Mexico

ITP Asia
60 Albert Street, #15-01
Albert Complex
Singapore 189969

ITP Australia
102 Dodds Street
South Melbourne
Victoria 3205 Australia

ITP Nelson Canada
1120 Birchmount Road
Scarborough, Ontario
Canada M1K 5G4

ITP Japan
Hirakawa-cho Kyowa Building, 3F
2-2-1 Hirakawa-cho, Chiyoda-ku
Tokyo 102, Japan

PHOTO CREDITS: Figure 1 Courtesy of Corel Professional Photos CD-ROM Image usage, KTP Metatools, Photo Disc, Inc., SoftKey; Figure 2 Courtesy of Photo Disc, Inc.; Figure 3 Courtesy of Scott Goodwin Photography; Figure 8 Courtesy of Intel Corporation, Photo Disc, Inc.; Figure 9 Courtesy of Scott Goodwin Photography; Figure 10 Courtesy of Eastman Kodak Company; Figure 14 Courtesy of Gateway 2000 Inc.; Figure 15 Courtesy of NEC Technologies, Inc.; Figure 16 Courtesy of Casino,Inc.; Figure 17 Courtesy of Scott Goodwin Photography; Figure 18 Courtesy of Scott Goodwin Photography; Figure 20 Courtesy of Seagate Technology; Figure 22 Courtesy of Pioneer Electronics; Figure 39 Courtesy of International Business Machines; Figure 40 Courtesy of Toshiba America, Inc.; Figure 41 Courtesy of Xircom Corporation; Figure 42 Courtesy of In Focus Corporation. Background images: COM1 Courtesy of Photo Disc, Inc.; COM2 Courtesy of Photo Disc, Inc.; COM5 Courtesy of Photo Disc, Inc.; COM9 Courtesy of Corel Professional Photos CD-ROM Image usage, Photo Disc, Inc.; COM10 Courtesy of Digital Stock, Photo Disc, Inc.; COM14 Courtesy of Photo Disc, Inc.; COM15 Courtesy of Photo Disc, Inc.; COM16 Courtesy of Digital Stock; COM17 Courtesy of Corel Professional Photos CD-ROM Image usage; COM18 Courtesy of Photo Disc, Inc.; COM20 Courtesy of Corel Professional Photos CD-ROM Image usage; COM21 Courtesy of Photo Disc, Inc., COM22 Courtesy of Photo Disc, Inc.; Courtesy of Corel Professional Photos CD-ROM Image usage; COM24 Courtesy of Photo Disc, Inc.; COM27 Courtesy of Photo Disc, Inc.; COM28 Courtesy of Corbis Images; COM29 Courtesy of Corel Professional Photos CD-ROM Image usage, Photo Disc, Inc. **Microsoft Windows 95** *Project 1, page WIN 1.4* Bill Gates, © Matthew McVay, Stock Boston; Seattle skyline, © Paul Conklin, PhotoEdit; *page WIN 1.5* International Business Machines Corporation; *Project 2, page WIN 2.3* Quantum Corp; **Microsoft Word 97** *Project 1, page WD 1.4-5* Pen and ink well, hieroglyphics, deers, hunters, book, mallet, Courtesy of Corel Professional Photos CD-ROM Image usage; Computer, monitor, keyboard, stone background, © Metatools, created by Photospin; Computer with CD-ROM provided by PhotoDisc, Inc. © 1996; *Project 2, pages W 2.2-3* Man with newspaper provided by PhotoDisc, Inc. © 1996; *Project 3, pages W 3.2-3*; Globe and street sign, Courtesy of Corel Professional Photos CD-ROM Image usage; **Microsoft Excel 97** *Project 1, pages E 1.4-5* Race car and laptop, Courtesy of Corel Professional Photos CD-ROM Image usage; Hot Lap and scope on tripod, Courtesy of Serena Industries; *Project 2, pages E 2.2-3* Runner, biker, watch, swimmer, soccer ball, skiing, cycling, bowling ball, and pins, Courtesy of Corel Professional Photos CD-ROM Image usage; *Project 3, pages E 3.2-3* Rings, Courtesy of Corel Professional Photos CD-ROM Image usage; Red and white flowers and cake, © Metatools, created by PhotoSpin; **Microsoft Access 97** *Project 1, pages A 1.4-5* James Smithson, Courtesy of Smithsonian Institute; American flag, © Metatools, created by PhotoSpin; *Project 2, pages A 2.2-3* Credit card and mail sign, Courtesy of Corel Professional Photos CD-ROM Image usage; David Janssen, provided by Motion Picture & Television Photo Archive; sign post and path, © Metatools, created by PhotoSpin; *Project 3, pages A 3.2-3* Dr. Thaddeus S. C. Lowe, provided by NorthWind Archives; Goodyear blimp photo, Courtesy of Goodyear Rubber and Tire Company; **Microsoft PowerPoint 97** *Project 1, pages PP 1.4-5* Man, money bag, and movie camera, Courtesy of Corel Professional Photos CD-ROM Image usage; food collage, © Metatools, created by PhotoSpin; *Project 2, pages PP 2.2-3* Iceberg, Courtesy of Corel Professional Photos CD-ROM Image usage; Titanic provided by Brown Brothers; Molly Brown provided by Colorado Historical Society; Euro-poster provided by PhotoDisc, Inc. © 1996; **Microsoft Outlook 97** *Project 1, page O 1.2* Globe and telephone, Courtesy of Corel Professional Photos CD-ROM Image usage; **Office 97 Integration** *Project 1, page I 1.3* Woman chef provided by PhotoDisc, Inc. © 1996.

ISBN 0-7895-5797-5 (Perfect bound) ISBN 0-7895-5798-3 (Spiral bound)

2 3 4 5 6 7 8 9 10 BC 04 03 02 01 00

MICROSOFT

Office 97

Introductory Concepts and Techniques

ENHANCED EDITION

CONTENTS

PROJECT THREE

Creating a Research Paper with a Table

INTEGRATION FEATURE

Creating Web Pages

Microsoft Excel 97 *E 1.1*

PROJECT ONE

Creating a Worksheet and Embedded Chart

PROJECT TWO

Formulas, Formatting, Charts, and Web Queries

Microsoft PowerPoint 97 PP 1.1

PROJECT ONE

Using a Design Template and Style Checker to Create a Presentation

PROJECT TWO

Using Outline View and Clip Art to Create an Electronic Slide Show

INTEGRATION FEATURE

Importing Clip Art from the Microsoft Clip Gallery Live Web Site

Preface

The Shelly Cashman Series® offers the finest textbooks in computer education. We are proud of the fact that our Microsoft Office 4.3, Microsoft Office 95, and Microsoft Office 97 textbooks have been runaway best-sellers. Each edition of our Office textbooks has included innovations, many based on comments made by the instructors and students who use our books.

Because of the delay in the release of Office 2000, the increased emphasis on the Microsoft Office User Specialist (MOUS) Certification, and many instructor requests for new laboratory exercises, we decided to publish an *Enhanced Edition* of our best-selling textbook, *Microsoft Office 97: Introductory Concepts and Techniques*. This *Enhanced Edition* continues with the innovation, quality, and reliability that you have come to expect from the Shelly Cashman Series. *Microsoft Office 97: Introductory Concepts and Techniques, Enhanced Edition* includes the following enhancements:

- Microsoft Office 2000 Preview
- New laboratory exercises for each project
- Quick Reference Summary that shows how to complete all the Office 97 tasks presented in the book using the mouse, menu, shortcut menu, and keyboard
- Microsoft Office User Specialist (MOUS) Certification information and tables that map the required skills to the book
- Completely updated *Introduction to Computers* section that presents the necessary computer concepts for success with the Office 97 applications

In this *Enhanced Edition*, you will find an educationally sound and easy-to-follow pedagogy that combines a step-by-step approach with corresponding screens. Every project and exercise in this book is designed to take full advantage of the Office 97 features. The popular Other Ways and More About features offer in-depth knowledge of Office 97. The project openers provide a fascinating perspective on the subject covered in the project. The project material is developed carefully to ensure that students will see the importance of learning Office 97 applications for future course work. This Shelly Cashman Series Office 97 textbook will help make your applications class the most interesting and popular on campus.

Objectives of This Textbook

Microsoft Office 97: Introductory Concepts and Techniques, Enhanced Edition is intended for a three-unit course that presents Microsoft Office 97 products: Microsoft Word 97, Microsoft Excel 97, Microsoft Access 97, Microsoft PowerPoint 97, Microsoft Outlook 97, integration among these products, and the power of the Internet. No experience with a computer is assumed, and no mathematics beyond the high school freshman level is required. The objectives of this book are:

- To teach the fundamentals of Microsoft Office 97.
- To help students demonstrate their proficiency in Microsoft Office applications. After completion of a two-course sequence with the companion textbook, *Microsoft Office 97: Advanced Concepts and Techniques*, this book prepares students to pass the Proficient level Microsoft Office User Specialist Exam for Microsoft Word 97 and Microsoft Excel 97 and the Expert level Microsoft Office User Specialist Exam for Microsoft Access 97 and Microsoft PowerPoint 97.
- To expose students to examples of the computer as a useful tool.
- To develop an exercise-oriented approach that allows students to learn by example.
- To augment learning with eleven new pages of laboratory exercises that have been added to this *Enhanced Edition.*
- To encourage independent study, and help those who are working alone in a distance education environment.

Approved by Microsoft as Courseware for the Microsoft Office User Specialist Program

Microsoft Office 97: Introductory Concepts and Techniques, Enhanced Edition and *Microsoft Office 97: Advanced Concepts and Techniques* used in combination in a two-course sequence have been approved by Microsoft as courseware for the Microsoft Office User Specialist (MOUS) program. After completing the projects and exercises in these two companion textbooks, students will be prepared to take the Proficient level Microsoft Office User Specialist Exam for Microsoft Word 97 and Microsoft Excel 97 and the Expert level Microsoft Office User Specialist Exam for Microsoft Access 97 and Microsoft PowerPoint 97. By passing the certification exam for a Microsoft software program, students demonstrate their proficiency in that program to employers. These exams are offered at participating test centers, participating corporations, and participating employment agencies. For more information about certification, please visit the Shelly Cashman Series MOUS Web page at www.scseries.com/off97/cert.htm.

The Shelly Cashman Approach

Features of the Shelly Cashman Series Office 97 books include:

- **Project Orientation:** Each project in the book uses the unique Shelly Cashman Series screen-by-screen, step-by-step approach.
- **Screen-by-Screen, Step-by-Step Instructions:** Each of the tasks required to complete a project is identified throughout the development of the project. The steps are accompanied by full-color screens.
- **Thoroughly Tested Projects:** Every screen in the book is correct because it is produced by the author only after performing a step, resulting in unprecedented quality.
- **Other Ways Boxes and Quick Reference:** Office 97 provides a wide variety of ways to carry out a given task. The Other Ways boxes displayed at the end of most of the step-by-step sequences specify the other ways to do the task completed in the steps. Thus, the steps and the Other Ways box make a comprehensive reference unit. In addition, a Quick Reference Summary at the end of the book summarizes the ways a task can be completed.
- **More About Feature:** These marginal annotations provide background information that complements the topics covered, adding interest and depth to the learning process.

Organization of This Textbook

Microsoft Office 97: Introductory Concepts and Techniques, Enhanced Edition consists of a brief introduction to computers, two projects on Microsoft Windows, an introduction to Microsoft Office 97, three projects each on Microsoft Word 97, Microsoft Excel 97, and Microsoft Access 97, two projects on Microsoft PowerPoint 97, one project on Microsoft Outlook 97, four short integration features following each application, one project on integrating Office 97 applications and the Internet, an Office 2000 Preview, new laboratory exercises, Microsoft Office User Specialist (MOUS) certification information, and a Quick Reference Summary. A short description of each follows.

Introduction to Computers

Many students taking a course in the use of Microsoft Office 97 will have little previous experience with computers. For this reason, the Office 97 book begins with a completely updated section titled *Introduction to Computers* that covers essential computer hardware and software concepts and information on how to purchase, install, and maintain a personal computer.

Microsoft Windows

To use the Microsoft Office 97 application software products effectively, students need a practical knowledge of Windows. Thus, two Windows projects are included as an introduction to the graphical user interface.

Project 1 – Fundamentals of Using Windows In Project 1, students learn about user interfaces and Windows. Topics include using the Windows desktop as a work area; using the mouse; the keyboard and keyboard shortcuts; using context-sensitive menus; sizing and scrolling windows; creating a document by starting an application program; saving a document on disk; printing a document; closing a program; modifying a document; using Windows Help; and shutting down Windows.

Project 2 – Using Windows Explorer In Project 2, students are introduced to Windows Explorer. Topics include displaying the contents of a folder; expanding and collapsing a folder; creating a folder; changing the view; selecting and copying a group of files; creating, renaming, and deleting a folder; and renaming and deleting a file.

Microsoft Office 97

The Microsoft Office 97 applications work alike and work together as if they were a single program. Microsoft Office 97 also allows you to interact in each application with the Internet in a seamless fashion. One brief project is included following the two projects on Windows to give students an overview of Office 97.

Project 1 – Introduction to Microsoft Office 97 In this project, students are introduced to each Office 97 application. A brief explanation of Word 97, Excel 97, Access 97, PowerPoint 97, and examples of how these applications take advantage of the Internet, World Wide Web, and intranets are presented. Outlook 97 and the applications within Outlook (Inbox, Calendar, Contacts, Tasks, Journal, and Notes) also are explained.

Microsoft Word 97

After presenting the basic computer concepts, Windows, and an introduction to the Office 97 products, this textbook provides detailed instruction on how to use Word 97. The material is divided into three projects followed by a section on creating Web pages.

Project 1 – Creating and Editing a Word Document In Project 1, students are introduced to Word terminology and the Word window by preparing an announcement. Topics include starting and quitting Word; entering text; adding bullets to paragraphs while typing; checking spelling while typing; saving a document; selecting characters, lines, and paragraphs; centering, bolding, italicizing, and changing the font and font size of selected text; importing a picture from the Web and then resizing the picture; printing a document; opening a document; correcting errors; and using Word Help.

Project 2 – Using Word's Wizards and Templates to Create a Cover Letter and Resume In Project 2, students create a resume using Word's Resume Wizard. Topics include personalizing the resume using Word's AutoFormat feature and print preview. Then, students create a cover letter using a Word letter template. Topics include personalizing the cover letter; creating and inserting an AutoText entry; dragging and dropping selected text; aligning text vertically with the TAB key; and checking spelling at once. Finally, students switch from one open Word document to another and then close all open Word documents.

Project 3 – Creating a Research Paper with a Table In Project 3, students use the MLA style of documentation to create a research paper. Topics include changing margins; adjusting line spacing; using a header to number pages; first-line indenting paragraphs; using Word's AutoCorrect features; creating a Word table, entering data into the table, and formatting the table; adding a footnote; inserting a manual page break; creating a hanging indent; creating a text hyperlink; sorting paragraphs; using the thesaurus; and counting the words in a document.

Integration Feature – Creating Web Pages In this section, students are introduced to creating Web pages. Topics include saving the resume created in Project 2 as an HTML file; creating a personal Web page using the Web Page Wizard; and personalizing the Web page using hyperlinks.

Microsoft Excel 97

Following the three projects on Word 97, this textbook presents three projects on Excel 97, followed by a section on linking a worksheet to a Word document.

Project 1 – Creating a Worksheet and Embedded Chart In Project 1, students are introduced to Excel terminology, the Excel window, and the basic characteristics of a worksheet and workbook. Topics include starting and quitting Excel; entering text and numbers; selecting a range; using the AutoSum button; copying using the fill handle; changing font size; bolding; centering across columns; using the AutoFormat command; charting using the Chart Wizard; saving and opening a workbook; editing a worksheet; using the AutoCalculate area; and obtaining Excel Help.

Project 2 – Formulas, Formatting, and Creating Charts In Project 2, students use formulas and functions to build a worksheet and learn more about formatting and printing a worksheet. Topics include entering formulas; using functions; formatting text; formatting numbers; drawing borders and adding colors; changing the widths of columns and rows; spell checking; creating a 3-D Pie chart on a separate sheet; previewing a worksheet; printing a section of a worksheet; and displaying and printing the formulas in a worksheet. This project also introduces students to accessing real-time data using Web queries.

Project 3 – What-If Analysis and Working with Large Worksheets In Project 3, students learn how to work with larger worksheets, how to create a worksheet based on assumptions, how to use the IF function and absolute cell references, and how to perform what-if analysis. Topics include assigning global formats; rotating text; using the fill handle to create a series; deleting, inserting, copying, and moving data on a worksheet; displaying and docking toolbars; adding drop shadows to ranges; freezing titles; changing the magnification of worksheets; displaying different parts of the worksheet using panes; and simple what-if analysis and goal seeking.

Integration Feature – Linking an Excel Worksheet to a Word Document In this section, students are introduced to linking a worksheet to a Word document. Topics include a discussion of the differences among copying and pasting, copying and embedding, and copying and linking; opening multiple applications; printing and saving a document with a linked worksheet; and editing a linked worksheet in a Word document.

Microsoft Access 97

Following Excel 97, this textbook provides detailed instruction on Access 97. The topics are divided into three projects followed by a section on integrating worksheet data into a database.

Project 1 – Creating a Database Using Design and Datasheet Views In Project 1, students are introduced to the concept of a database and shown how to use Access to create a database. Topics include creating a database; creating a table; defining the fields in a table; opening a table; adding records to a table; closing a table; and previewing and printing the contents of a table. Other topics in this project include using a form to view data; using the Report Wizard to create a report; and using Access Help. Students also learn how to design a database to eliminate redundancy.

Project 2 – Querying a Database Using the Select Query Window In Project 2, students learn to use queries to obtain information from the data in their databases. Topics include creating queries, running queries, and printing the results. Specific query topics include displaying only selected fields; using character data in criteria; using wildcards; using numeric data in criteria; using various comparison operators; and creating compound criteria. Other related topics include sorting, joining tables, and restricting records in a join. Students also use computed fields, statistics, and grouping.

Project 3 – Maintaining a Database Using the Design and Update Features of Access In Project 3, students learn the crucial skills involved in maintaining a database. These include using Datasheet view and Form view to add new records, to change existing records, and to delete records; and searching for a record. Students also learn the processes of changing the structure of a table; adding additional fields; changing characteristics of existing fields; creating a variety of validation rules; and specifying referential integrity. Students perform mass changes and deletions using queries and create single-field and multiple-field indexes.

Integration Feature – Integrating Excel Worksheet Data into an Access Database In this section, students learn how to create an Access table based on data stored in an Excel worksheet by using the Import Spreadsheet Wizard. Topics include creating a database and converting an Excel worksheet to an Access database.

Microsoft PowerPoint 97

Following Access 97, this textbook includes two projects on creating presentation graphics using PowerPoint 97 followed by a section showing how to access clip art from a Microsoft Web site.

Project 1 – Using a Design Template and Style Checker to Create a Presentation In Project 1, students are introduced to PowerPoint terminology, the PowerPoint window, and the basics of creating a multi-level bulleted list presentation. Topics include selecting a design template; changing font style; decreasing font size; saving a presentation; displaying slides in an electronic slide show; checking a presentation for spelling errors; identifying design inconsistencies using Style Checker; printing copies of the slides to make overhead transparencies; and using PowerPoint Help.

Project 2 – Using Outline View and Clip Art to Create an Electronic Slide Show In Project 2, students create a presentation in outline view, insert clip art, and add animation effects. Topics include creating a slide presentation by promoting and demoting text in outline view; changing slide layouts; inserting clip art; adding slide transition effects; adding text animation effects; animating clip art; running an animated slide show, and printing audience handouts from an outline.

Integration Feature – Importing Clip Art from the Microsoft Clip Gallery Live Web Site In this section, students are introduced to importing clip art from a source on the World Wide Web into a presentation. Topics include downloading clip art to the Microsoft Clip Gallery 3.0; importing clip art to a presentation; and applying an animation effect.

Microsoft Outlook 97

Following PowerPoint 97, students are introduced to Outlook 97, a useful desktop information management system.

Project 1 – Desktop Information Management Using Outlook In this project, students explore the benefits of desktop information management systems by using Outlook to create a schedule of work and classes. Students learn to enter both one-time and recurring appointments and events. Topics include starting and quitting the Inbox, Calendar, Contacts, Tasks, Journal, and Notes folders in Outlook. Other topics include generating and managing daily, weekly, and monthly schedules; printing and saving a calendar; generating a list of contacts; keeping track of tasks through completion; and adding a note to an appointment.

Office 97 Integration

Following Outlook 97, students are presented with a project on Office 97 Integration.

Project 1 – Introduction to Integrating Office 97 Applications In this project, students are introduced to the seamless partnership of the Microsoft Office 97 applications, which allows the sharing of information among Word, Excel, Access, Outlook, and the World Wide Web. Topics include editing a worksheet to incorporate 3-D references; updating a worksheet and chart by running a Web query; embedding an Excel chart and worksheet into a Word document; printing an Access report; sending a Word document to Outlook as a file attachment to send as an e-mail message over the Internet; inserting an Access database into an Outlook e-mail message; and printing an Outlook e-mail message.

Microsoft Office 2000 Preview

The Microsoft Office 2000 Preview special feature follows the Introduction to Integrating Office 97 Applications project. This section gives an overview of Office 2000. It describes the new features of Office 2000, paying particular attention to the new Web capabilities and the new applications, Publisher 2000, PhotoDraw 2000, and FrontPage 2000.

Office 97 Enhanced Exercises

Following the Microsoft Office 2000 Preview are eleven pages of new laboratory exercises. Included are two to three exercises per project for Word, Excel, Access, and PowerPoint. Samples of what the student creates in the exercises are available on the World Wide Web at www.scsite.com/off97enh/labs.htm.

Appendix A - MOUS Certification Program

Appendix A follows the Enhanced Exercises and includes information on the Microsoft Office User Specialist (MOUS) Certification program, including how to prepare for the exams, how to find and authorized testing center, and more than twenty links to Web sites for additional information. This section includes tables that map to the book the MOUS skill sets and activities with which you should be familiar.

Appendix B - Quick Reference Summary

In the Microsoft Office 97 applications, you can accomplish a task in a number of ways. The book concludes with a Quick Reference Summary in Appendix B made up of tables (one each for Word, Excel, Access, PowerPoint, and Outlook) that list how to complete a task using the mouse, menu, shortcut menu, and keyboard.

End-of-Project Student Activities

A notable strength of the Shelly Cashman Series Office 97 books is the extensive student activities at the end of each project. Well-structured student activities can make the difference between students merely participating in a class and students retaining the information they learn. The activities in the Shelly Cashman Series Office 97 books include the following.

- What You Should Know A listing of the tasks completed within a project together with the pages where the step-by-step, screen-by-screen explanations appear. This section provides a perfect study review for students.
- Test Your Knowledge Four pencil-and-paper activities designed to determine students' understanding of the material in the project. Included are true/false questions, multiple-choice questions, and two short-answer activities.
- Use Help Any user of Office 97 must know how to use Help. Therefore, this book contains two Help exercises per project. These exercises alone distinguish the Shelly Cashman Series from any other set of Office 97 instructional materials.
- Apply Your Knowledge This exercise requires students to open and manipulate a file on the Data Disk that accompanies the Office 97 books.
- In the Lab Three in-depth assignments per project require students to apply the knowledge gained in the project to solve problems on a computer. **Eleven pages of new laboratory exercises have been added to this *Enhanced Edition*.**
- Cases and Places Seven unique case studies require students to apply their knowledge to real-world situations.

Shelly Cashman Series Teaching Tools

A comprehensive set of Teaching Tools accompanies this textbook in the form of a CD-ROM. The CD-ROM includes an Instructor's Manual (ElecMan) and teaching and testing aids. The CD-ROM (ISBN 0-7895-5847-5) is available through your Course Technology representative or by calling one of the following telephone numbers: Colleges and Universities, 1-800-648-7450; High Schools, 1-800-824-5179; and Career Colleges, 1-800-477-3692. The contents of the CD-ROM are listed on the next page.

- **ElecMan** The electronic Instructor's Manual is made up of Microsoft Word files. The files include lecture notes, solutions to laboratory assignments, and a large test bank. The files allow you to modify the lecture notes or generate quizzes and exams from the test bank using your own word processor. Where appropriate, solutions to laboratory assignments are embedded as icons in the files. When an icon appears, double-click it and the application will start and the solution will display. Each project includes: project objectives; project overview; detailed lesson plans with page number references; teacher notes and activities; answers to the end-of-project exercises; test bank of 110 questions for every project (50 true/false, 25 multiple-choice, and 35 fill-in-the-blank) with page number references; and transparency references. The transparencies are available through the Figures on CD-ROM. The test bank questions are numbered the same as in Course Test Manager. Thus, you can print a copy of the project test bank and use the printout to select your questions in Course Test Manager.
- **Figures on CD-ROM** Illustrations for most of the figures in the textbook are available. Use this ancillary to create a slide show from the illustrations for lecture or to print transparencies.
- **Course Test Manager** Course Test Manager is a powerful testing and assessment package that enables instructors to create and print tests from the large test bank. Instructors with access to a networked computer lab (LAN) can administer, grade, and track tests online.
- **Lecture Success System** Lecture Success System files are for use with the application software, a personal computer, and projection device to explain and illustrate the step-by-step, screen-by-screen development of a project in the textbook without entering large amounts of data.
- **Instructor's Lab Solutions** Solutions and required files for all the In the Lab assignments at the end of each project and the new enhanced exercises are available.
- **Lab Tests/Test Outs** Tests that parallel the In the Lab assignments are supplied for the purpose of testing students in the laboratory on the material covered in the project or testing students out of the course.
- **Student Files** All the files that are required by students to complete the Apply Your Knowledge exercises are included.
- **Interactive Labs** Eighteen hands-on interactive labs that take students from ten to fifteen minutes each to step through help solidify and reinforce mouse and keyboard usage and computer concepts. Student assessment is available in each interactive lab.

Acknowledgments

The Shelly Cashman Series would not be the leading computer education series without the contributions of outstanding publishing professionals. First, and foremost, among them is Becky Herrington, director of production and designer. She is the heart and soul of the Shelly Cashman Series, and it is only through her leadership, dedication, and tireless efforts that superior products are made possible. Becky created and produced the award-winning Windows 95 series of books.

Under Becky's direction, the following individuals made significant contributions to these books: Doug Cowley, production manager; Ginny Harvey, series specialist and developmental editor; Ken Russo, senior Web designer; Mike Bodnar, associate production manager; Stephanie Nance, graphic artist, Mark Norton, Web designer; Nancy Lamm, Lyn Markowicz, and Cherilyn King, proofreaders; Cristina Haley, indexer; Sarah Evertson of Image Quest, photo researcher; and Peggy Wyman and Jerry Orton, Susan Sebok, and Nancy Lamm, contributing writers.

Special thanks go to Richard Keaveny, managing editor; Jim Quasney, series consultant; Lora Wade, product manager; Meagan Walsh, associate product manager; Erin Bennet, editorial assistant; Francis Schurgot, Web product manager; Tonia Grafakos, associate Web product manager; Scott Wiseman, online developer; and Rajika Gupta, marketing manager. Special mention must go to Suzanne Biron, Becky Herrington, and Michael Gregson for the outstanding book design; Becky Herrington for the cover design; and Stephanie Nance for the cover illustrations.

Gary B. Shelly
Thomas J. Cashman
Misty E. Vermaat

Essential

Introduction to Computers and How to Purchase, Install, and Maintain a Personal Computer

Objectives

After completing this material, you will be able to:

- Define the term computer and discuss the four basic computer operations: input, processing, output, and storage
- Define data and information
- Explain the principal components of the computer and their use
- Describe the use and handling of floppy disks and hard disks
- Discuss computer software and explain the difference between system software and application software
- Describe several types of personal computer application software
- Discuss computer communications channels and equipment and the Internet and World Wide Web
- Explain how to purchase, install, and maintain a personal computer

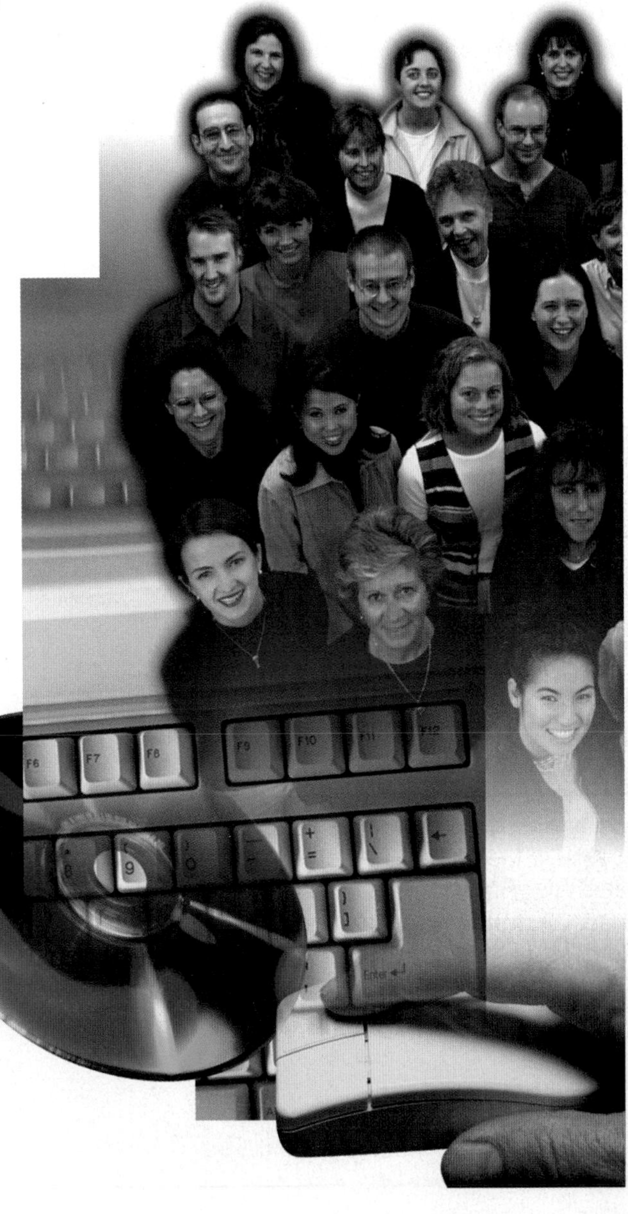

Every day, computers impact how individuals work and how they live. The use of personal computers continues to increase and has made computing available to almost anyone. In addition, advances in communications technology allow people to use personal computers to access and send information easily and quickly to other computers and computer users. At home, at work, and in the field, computers are helping people to do their work faster, more accurately, and in some cases, in ways that previously would not have been possible.

Why Study Computers and Application Software?

Today, many people believe that knowing how to use a computer is a basic skill necessary to succeed in business or to function effectively in society. As you can see in Figure 1, the use of computer technology is widespread in the world. It is important to understand that while computers are used in many different ways, there are certain types of common applications computer users need to know. It is this type of software that you will learn as you use this book. Given the widespread use and availability of computers, knowing how to use common application software on a computer is an essential skill for practically everyone.

Before you learn about application software, however, it will help if you understand what a computer is, the components of a computer, and the types of software used on computers. These topics are explained in this book. Also included is information that describes computer networks and a list of guidelines for purchasing, installing, and maintaining a personal computer.

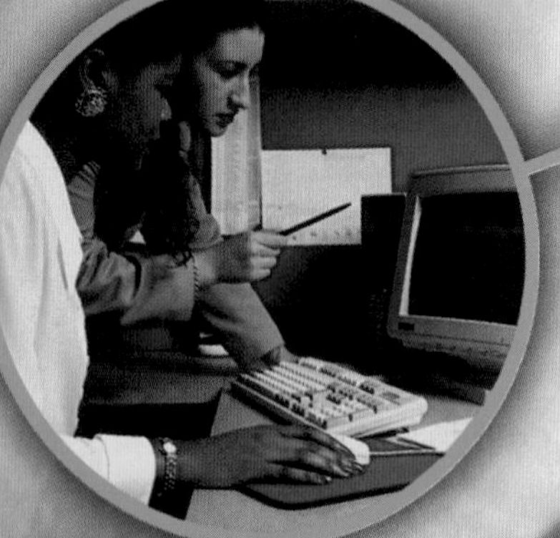

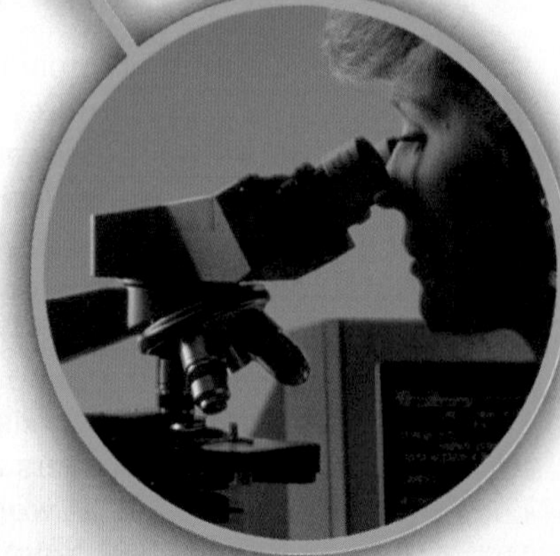

Figure 1
Computers are present in every aspect of daily living — in the workplace, at home, and in the classroom.

What Is a Computer?

The most obvious question related to understanding computers is, What is a computer? A **computer** is an electronic device, operating under the control of instructions stored in its own memory unit, that can accept data (input), manipulate the data according to specified rules (process), produce information (output) from the processing, and store the results for future use. Generally the term is used to describe a collection of devices that function together as a system. An example of the devices that make up a personal computer, or microcomputer, is shown in Figure 2.

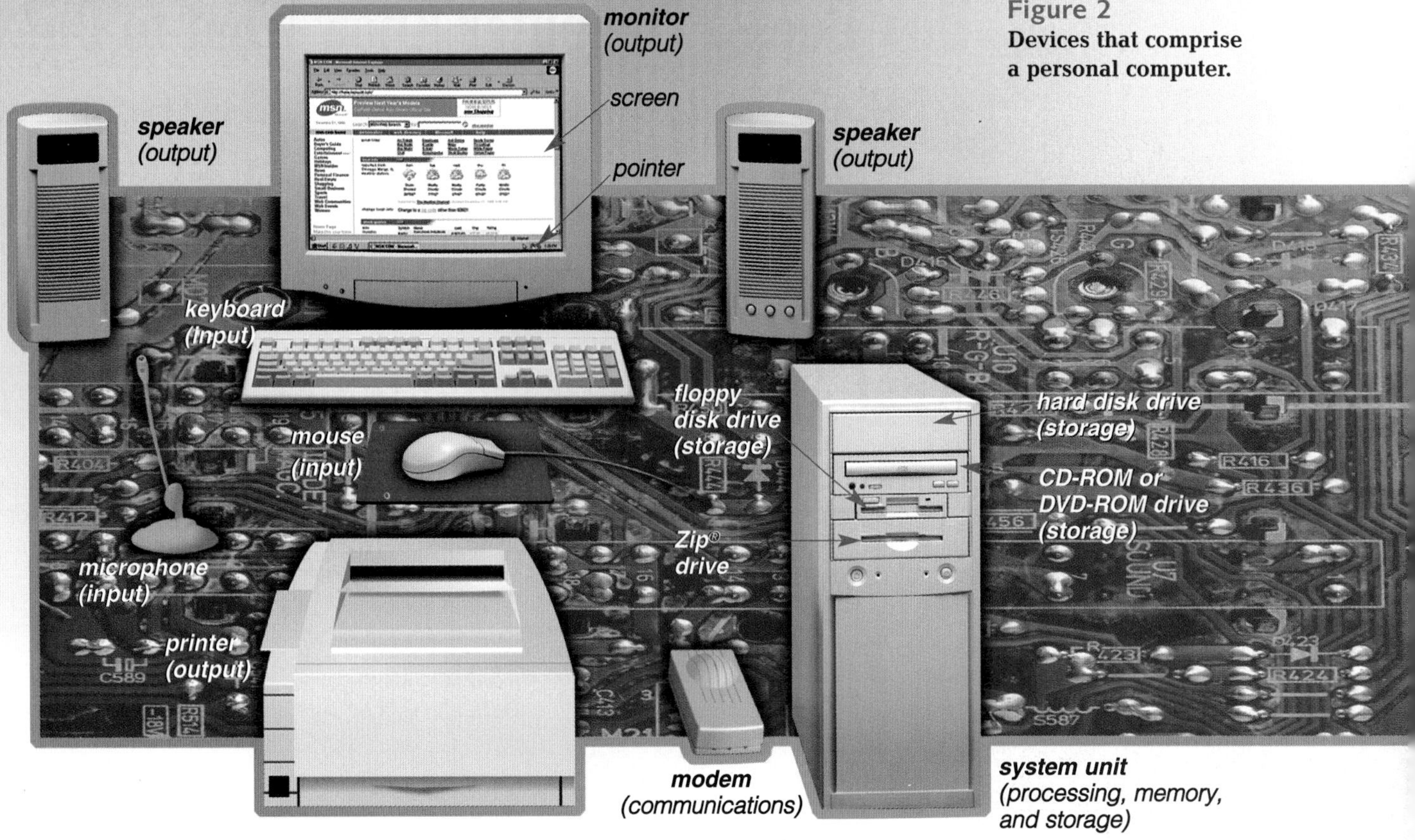

Figure 2
Devices that comprise a personal computer.

What Does a Computer Do?

Whether small or large, computers can perform four general operations. These operations comprise the **information processing cycle** and are input, process, output, and storage. Collectively, these operations describe the procedures a computer performs to process data into information and store it for future use.

All computer processing requires data. **Data** refers to the raw facts, including numbers, words, images, video, and sounds, given to a computer during the input operation. Computers manipulate data to create information. **Information** is data that is organized, has meaning, and is useful. During the output operation, the information that has been

Figure 3
Inside a computer are chips and other electronic components that process data in billionths of a second.

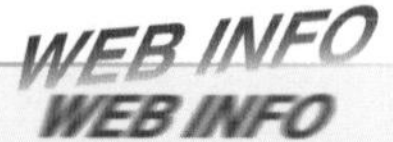

For more information on computers, visit the Introduction to Computers WEB INFO page **(www.scsite.com/IC/webinfo.htm)** and click Computers.

created is put into some form, such as a printed report, an invoice, a Web page, or a paycheck. The information also can be placed in computer storage for future use.

These operations occur through the use of electronic circuits contained on small silicon chips inside the computer (Figure 3 on the previous page). Because these electronic circuits rarely fail and the data flows along these circuits at close to the speed of light, processing can be accomplished in billionths of a second.

The people who either use the computer directly or use the information it provides are called **computer users**, **end users**, or sometimes, just **users**.

How Does a Computer Know What to Do?

For a computer to perform operations, it must be given a detailed set of instructions that tell it exactly what to do. These instructions are called a **computer program**, or **software**. Before processing for a specific job begins, the computer program corresponding to that job is stored in the computer. Once the program is stored, the computer can begin to operate by executing the program's first instruction. The computer executes one program instruction after another until the job is complete.

What Are the Components of a Computer?

To understand how computers process data into information, you need to examine the primary components of the computer. The four primary components of a computer are input devices, the central processing unit (control unit and arithmetic/ logic unit), output devices, and storage devices as shown in Figure 4.

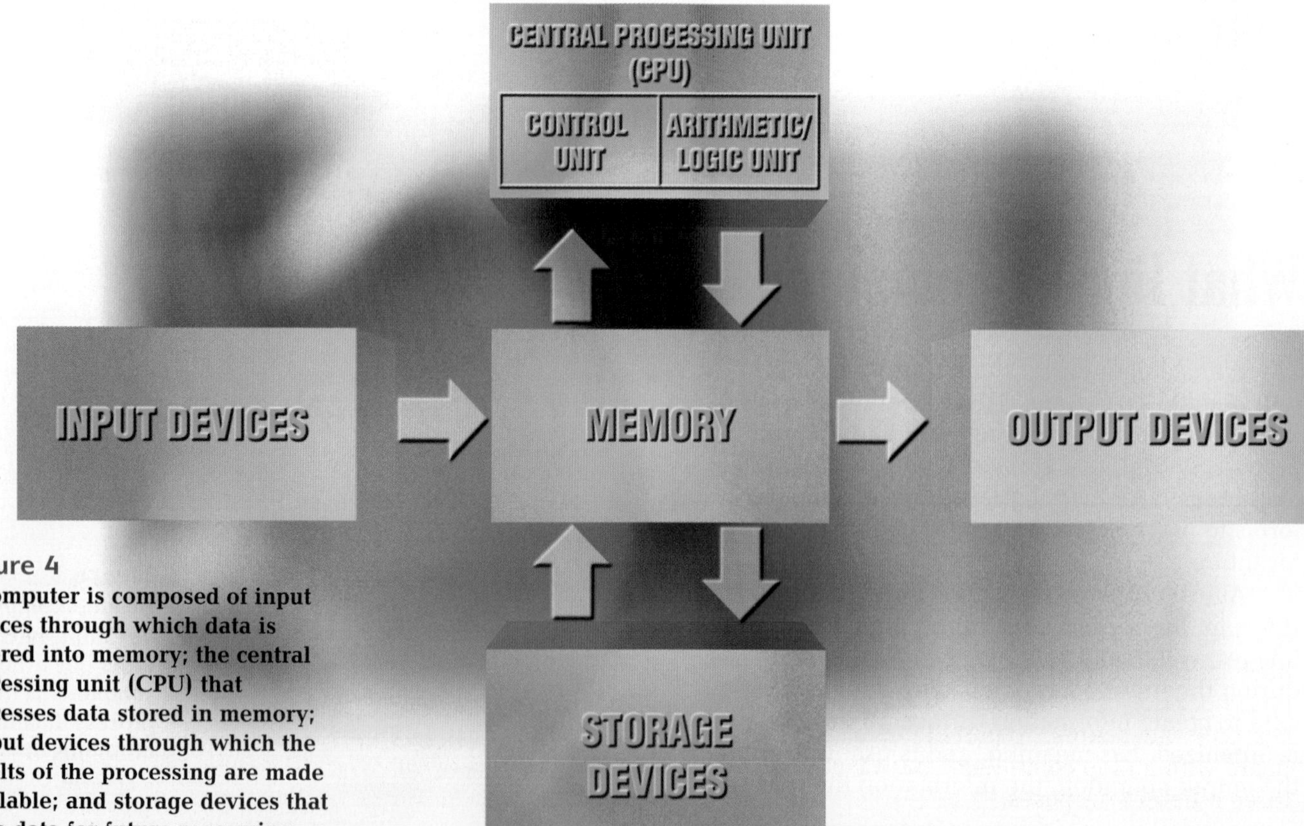

Figure 4
A computer is composed of input devices through which data is entered into memory; the central processing unit (CPU) that processes data stored in memory; output devices through which the results of the processing are made available; and storage devices that store data for future processing.

Input Devices

Input devices are any hardware components that allow you to enter data, programs, commands, and user responses into a computer. Input devices include the keyboard, the mouse, scanners and reading devices, digital cameras, audio and video input devices, and input devices for physically challenged users. The two primary input devices used are the keyboard and the mouse. This section discusses both of these input devices.

For more information on input devices, visit the Introduction to Computers WEB INFO page **(www.scsite.com/IC/webinfo.htm)** and click Input Devices.

The Keyboard

The most commonly used input device is the **keyboard**, on which data is entered by manually keying in or typing. The keyboard on most computers is laid out in much the same manner as the one shown in Figure 5. The alphabetic keys are arranged like those on a typewriter.

Most of today's desktop computer keyboards are **enhanced keyboards**, which means they consist of keys for letters of the alphabet, numbers, special characters, twelve function keys along the top, and a set of arrow and additional keys between the typing area and the numeric keypad.

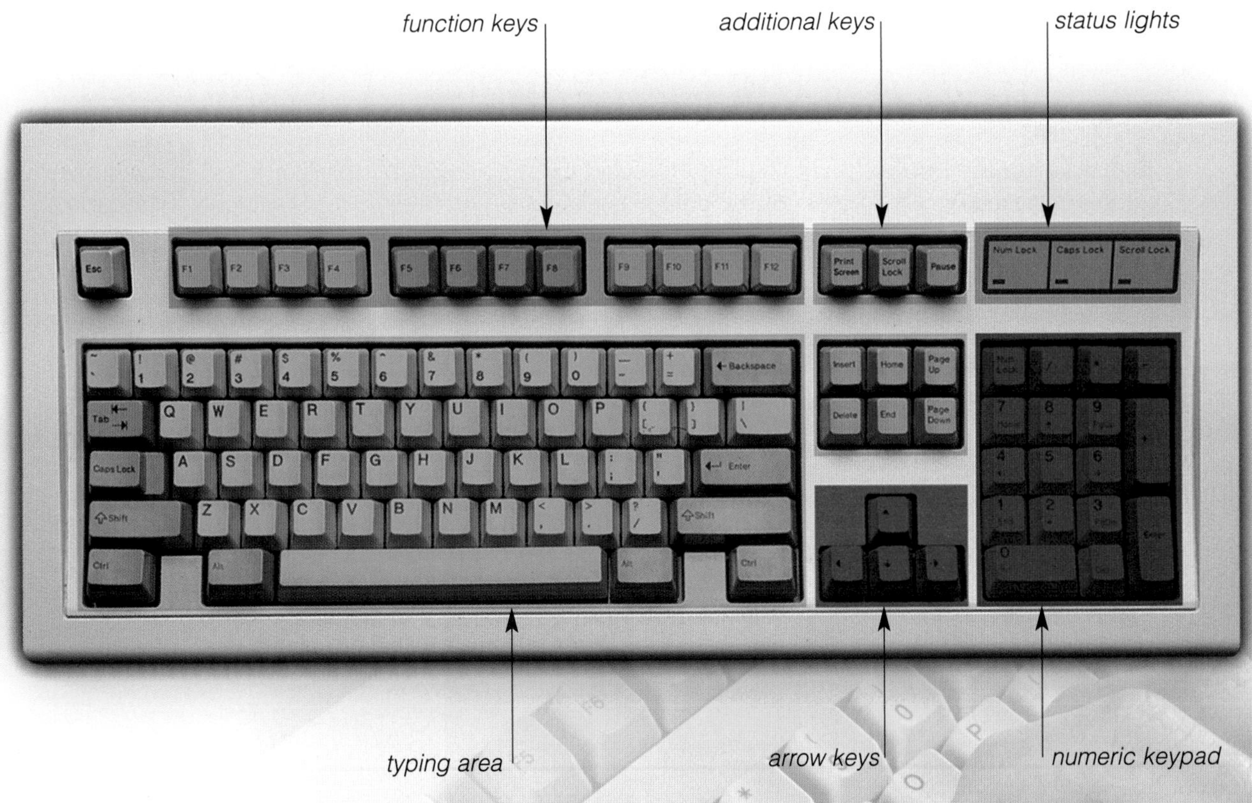

Figure 5
This keyboard represents the features found on most personal computer keyboards.

On laptops and many handheld computers, the keyboard is built into the top of the system unit (Figure 6 on the next page). To fit in these smaller computers, the keyboards usually are smaller and have fewer keys. A typical laptop computer keyboard, for example, has only 85 keys compared to the 105 keys on most desktop computer keyboards. To provide all of the functionality of a desktop computer keyboard with laptop computers, manufacturers design many of the keys to serve two or three different purposes.

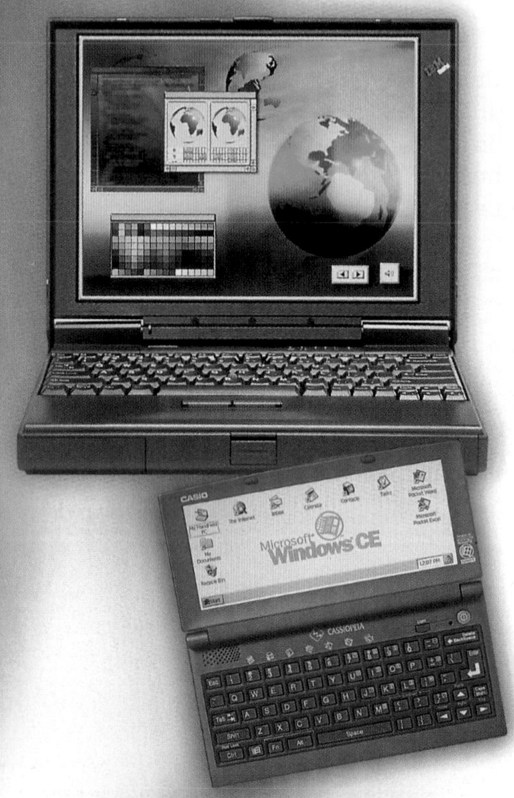

Figure 6
On laptop and many handheld computers, the keyboard is built into the top of the system unit.

Regardless of size, most keyboards have a rectangular shape with the keys aligned in rows. Users who spend a significant amount of time typing on these keyboards sometimes experience repetitive strain injuries of their wrists. For this reason, some manufacturers have redesigned their keyboards to minimize the chance of these types of workplace injuries. Keyboards such as these are called ergonomic keyboards. The goal of **ergonomics** is to incorporate comfort, efficiency, and safety into the design of items in the workplace.

The Mouse

A **mouse** (Figure 7) is a pointing device you can use instead of the keyboard keys. You lay the palm of your hand over the mouse and move it across the surface of a pad that provides traction for a rolling ball on the bottom of the mouse. The mouse detects the direction of the ball movement and sends this information to the screen to move a pointer that you use to make selections. You press buttons on top of the mouse to indicate your choice of actions from lists or icons displayed on the screen.

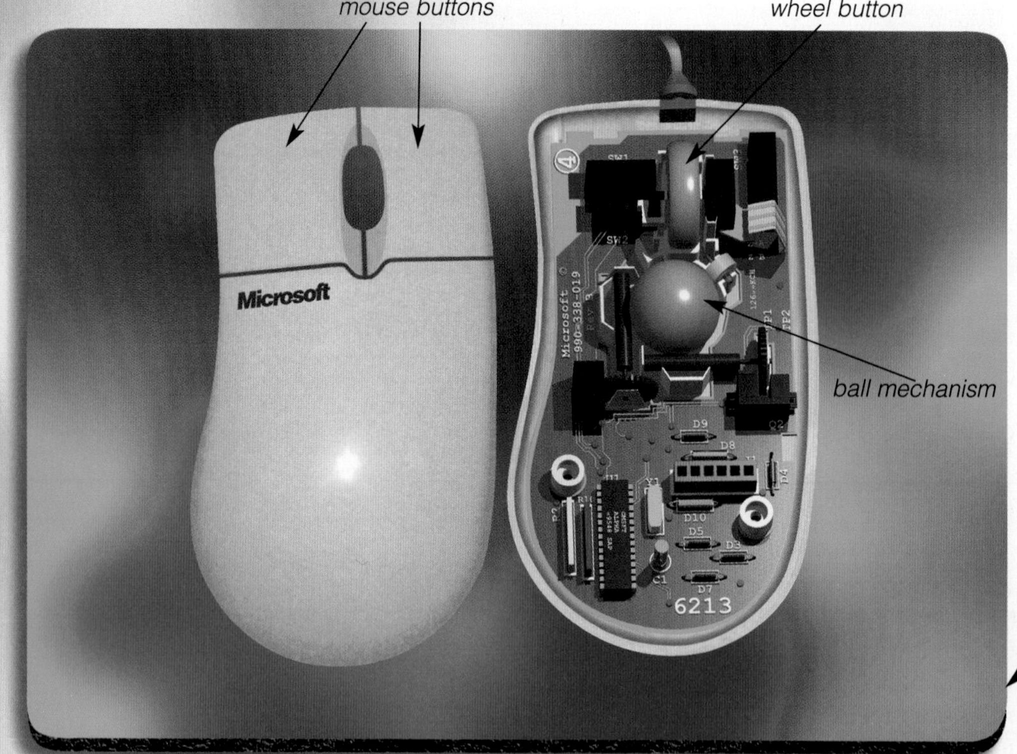

Figure 7
A mouse is used to control the movement of a pointer on the screen and make selections from the screen. Electronic circuits in a mouse translate the movement of the mouse into signals that are sent to the computer.

The Central Processing Unit

The **central processing unit** (**CPU**) contains the electronic circuits that cause processing to occur. The CPU is made up of the control unit and arithmetic/logic unit (see Figure 4 on page COM4). The **control unit** interprets the instructions. The **arithmetic/ logic unit** performs the logical and arithmetic processes. On personal computers, the CPU is designed into a chip called **a microprocessor** (Figure 8). The **microprocessors** shown in Figure 8 can fit in the palm of your hand. The high end microprocessors contain 7.5 million transistors and are capable of performing some operations 10 million times in a tenth of a second, or in the time it takes to blink your eye.

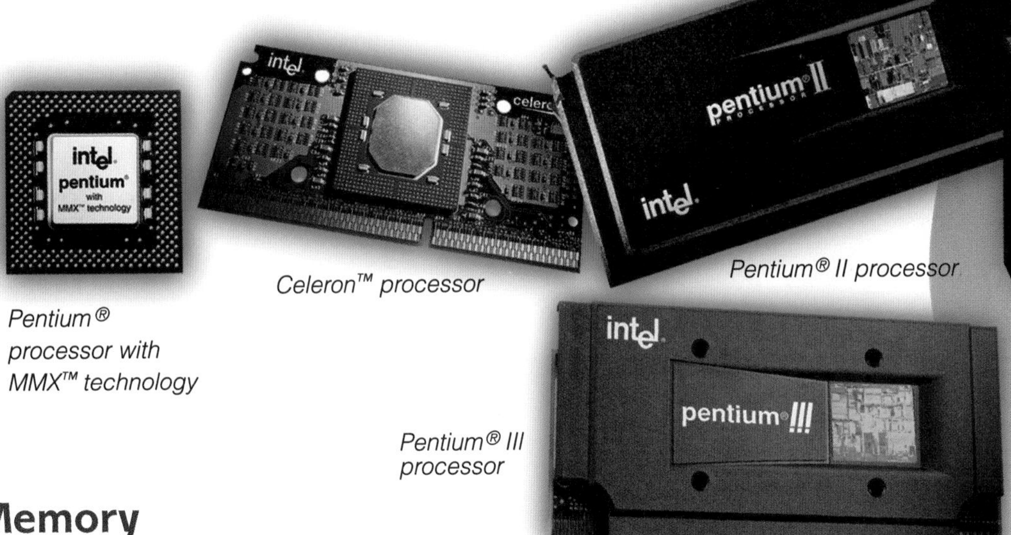

Figure 8
The Pentium® processors are designed for higher-performance PCs, while the Celeron™ processor is intended for the basic PCs that cost less than $1,000. The Xeon™ processor is geared toward servers and workstations.

Memory

Memory, also called **random access memory**, or **RAM**, consists of electronic components that store data including numbers, letters of the alphabet, graphics, and sound. Any data to be processed must be stored in memory. The amount of memory in computers typically is measured in kilobytes or megabytes. One **kilobyte** (**K** or **KB**) equals approximately 1,000 memory locations and one **megabyte** (**M** or **MB**) equals approximately one million memory locations. A memory location, or **byte**, usually stores one character. Therefore, a computer with 64 MB of memory can store approximately 64 million characters. One megabyte can hold approximately 500 pages of text information.

WEB INFO

For more information on CPUs, visit the Introduction to Computers WEB INFO page (**www.scsite.com/IC/webinfo.htm**) and click CPUs.

Output Devices

Output devices make the information resulting from processing available for use. The output from computers can be presented in many forms, such as a printed report or color graphics. When a computer is used for processing tasks such as word processing, spreadsheets, or database management, the two output devices more commonly used are the printer and the television-like display device called the **monitor**.

Printers

Printers used with computers either can be impact printers or nonimpact printers. An **impact printer** prints by striking an inked ribbon against the paper. One type of impact printer used with personal computers is the dot matrix printer (Figure 9 on the next page).

Nonimpact printers, such as ink-jet printers and laser printers (Figure 10 on the next page), form characters by means other than striking a ribbon against paper.

Figure 9
Dot matrix printers are capable of handling wide paper and printing multipart forms.

One advantage of using a nonimpact printer is that it can print higher-quality text and graphics than an impact printer, such as the dot matrix. **Nonimpact printers** also do a better job printing different fonts (Figure 11) and are quieter.

The popular and affordable **ink-jet printer** forms a character by using a nozzle that sprays drops of ink onto the page. Ink-jet printers produce excellent images.

The speed of an ink-jet printer is measured by the number of pages per minute (ppm) it can print. Most ink-jet printers print from one to eight pages per minute. Graphics and colors print at the slower rate.

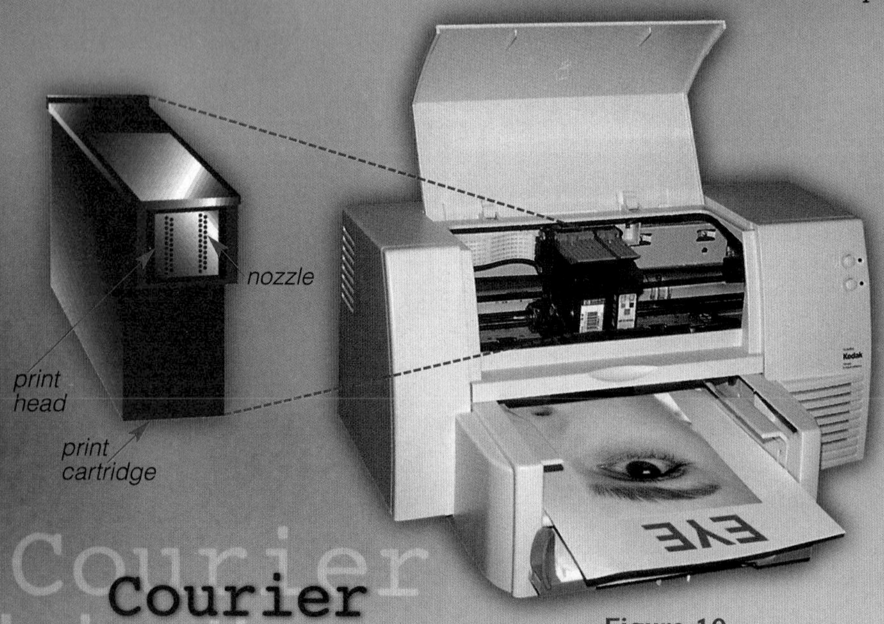

Figure 10
Two types of nonimpact printers are the laser printer (right) and the ink-jet printer (top). Nonimpact printers are excellent for printing work that includes graphics.

Courier
Helvetica
Script
Times New Roman

Figure 11
A varity of typefaces (fonts) are commonly available on personal computers.

Laser printers work similarly to a copying machine by converting data from the computer into a beam of light that is focused on a photoconductor drum, forming the images to be printed (Figure 12). The photoconductor attracts particles of toner that are fused by heat and pressure onto paper to produce an image. Laser printers produce high-quality black-and-white or color output and are used for applications that combine text and graphics such as **desktop publishing**. Laser printers for personal computers can cost from $300 to more than $10,000. The more expensive the laser printer, the more pages it can print per minute.

WEB INFO

For more information on output devices, visit the Introduction to Computers WEB INFO page **(www.scsite.com/IC/webinfo.htm)** and click Output Devices.

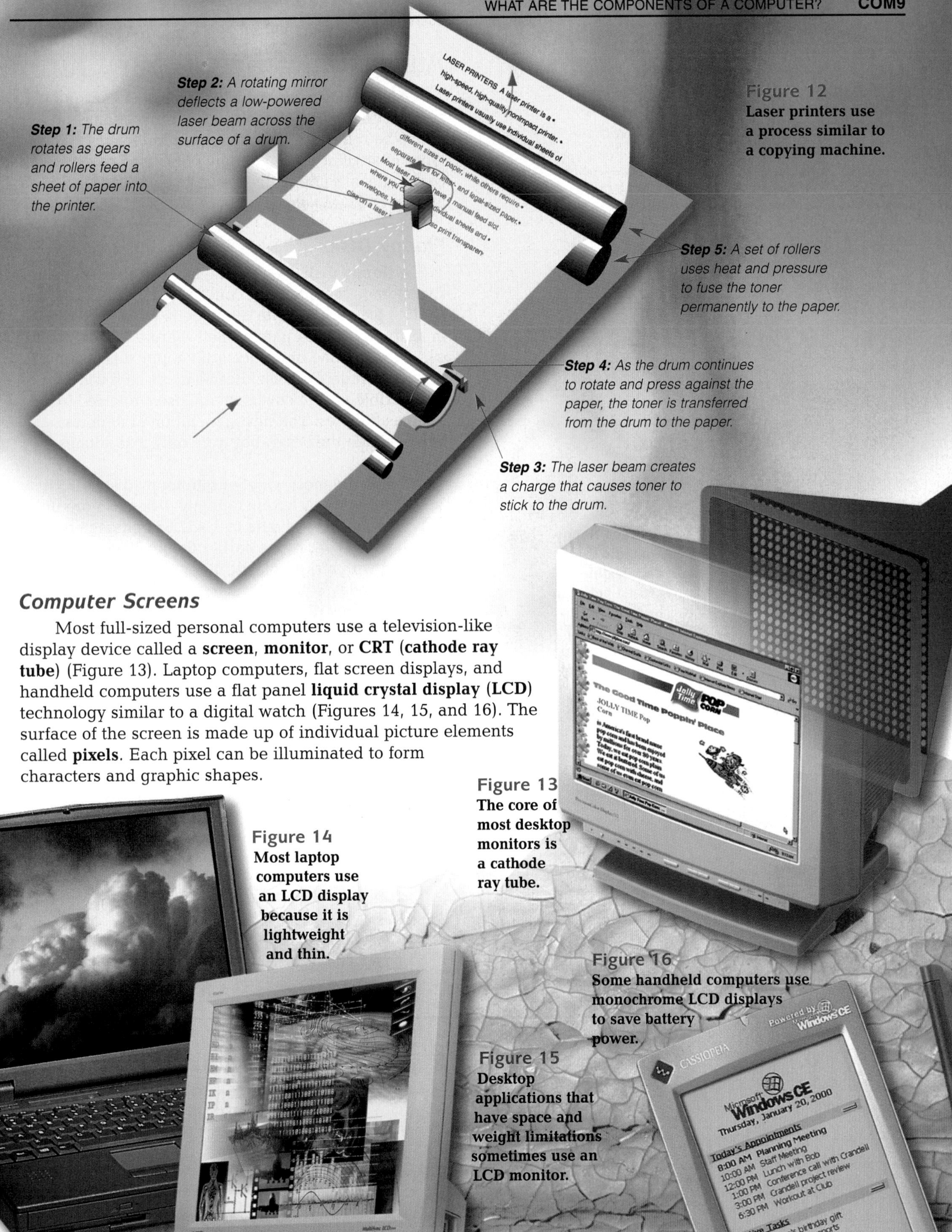

Figure 12
Laser printers use a process similar to a copying machine.

Computer Screens

Most full-sized personal computers use a television-like display device called a **screen**, **monitor**, or **CRT** (**cathode ray tube**) (Figure 13). Laptop computers, flat screen displays, and handheld computers use a flat panel **liquid crystal display** (**LCD**) technology similar to a digital watch (Figures 14, 15, and 16). The surface of the screen is made up of individual picture elements called **pixels**. Each pixel can be illuminated to form characters and graphic shapes.

Figure 13
The core of most desktop monitors is a cathode ray tube.

Figure 14
Most laptop computers use an LCD display because it is lightweight and thin.

Figure 16
Some handheld computers use monochrome LCD displays to save battery power.

Figure 15
Desktop applications that have space and weight limitations sometimes use an LCD monitor.

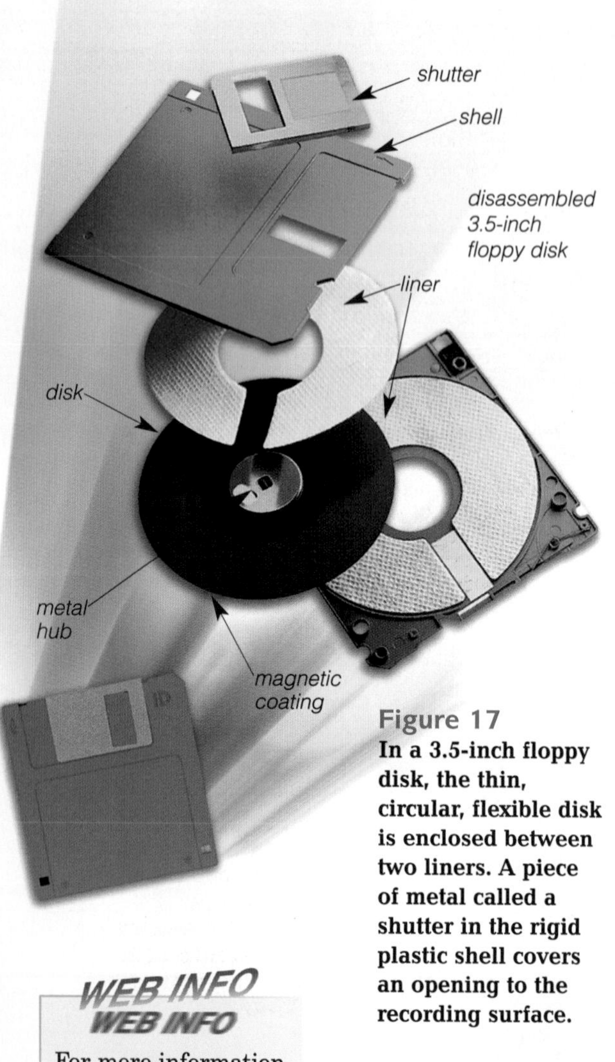

Figure 17
In a 3.5-inch floppy disk, the thin, circular, flexible disk is enclosed between two liners. A piece of metal called a shutter in the rigid plastic shell covers an opening to the recording surface.

Auxiliary Storage

Auxiliary storage devices, also called **secondary storage devices**, are used to store instructions and data when they are not being used in memory. Two types of auxiliary storage more often used on personal computers are floppy disks and hard disks. CD-ROMs and DVD-ROMs also are common.

Floppy Disks

A **floppy disk**, or **diskette**, is a portable, inexpensive storage medium that consists of a thin, circular, flexible plastic disk with a magnetic coating enclosed in a square-shaped plastic shell (Figure 17). In the early 1970s, IBM introduced the floppy disk as a new type of storage. Because these early 8-inch wide disks had flexible plastic covers, many users referred to them as floppies. The next generation of floppies looked much the same, but were only 5.25-inches wide.

Today, the most widely used floppy disk is 3.5-inches wide. A 3.5-inch floppy disk can store up to 1.44 megabytes of data or 1,457,664 characters. The flexible cover of the earlier floppy disks has been replaced with a rigid plastic outer cover. Thus, although today's 3.5-inch disks are not at all floppy, the term floppy disk still is used.

As noted, a floppy disk is a portable storage medium. When discussing a storage medium, the term **portable** means you can remove the medium from one computer and carry it to another computer. For example, you can insert a floppy disk into and remove it from a floppy disk drive on many types of computers (Figure 18). A **floppy disk drive** is a device that can read from and write to a floppy disk.

WEB INFO

For more information on floppy disks, visit the Introduction to Computers WEB INFO page **(www.scsite.com/IC/webinfo.htm)** and click Floppy Disks.

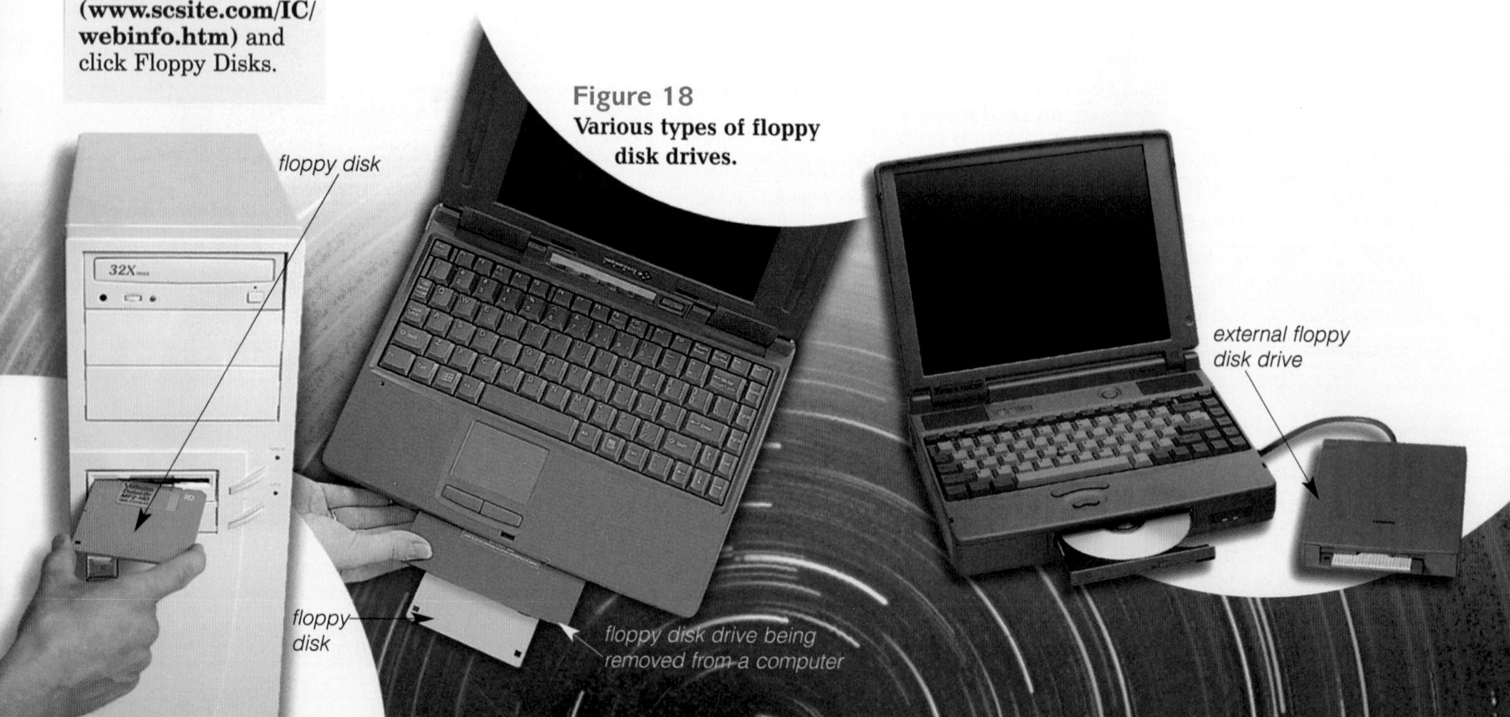

Figure 18
Various types of floppy disk drives.

A floppy disk is a type of a magnetic disk, which means it uses magnetic patterns to store items such as data, instructions, and information on the disk's surface. Most magnetic disks are **read/write** storage media; that is, you can access (read) data from and place (write) data on a magnetic disk any number of times, just as you can with an audiocassette tape.

A new, blank floppy disk has nothing stored on it. Before you can write on a new floppy disk, it must be formatted.

Formatting is the process of preparing a disk (floppy disk or hard disk) for reading and writing by organizing the disk into storage locations called tracks and sectors (Figure 19). A **track** is a narrow recording band that forms a full circle on the surface of the disk. The disk's storage locations then are divided into pie-shaped sections, which break the tracks into small arcs called sectors. A **sector** is capable of holding 512 bytes of data. A typical floppy disk stores data on both sides and has 80 tracks on each side of the recording surface with 18 sectors per track.

Figure 19
A track is a narrow recording band that forms a full circle on the surface of a disk. The disk's storage locations then are divided into pie-shaped sections, which break the tracks into small arcs called sectors. A sector can store 512 bytes of data.

Data stored in sectors on a floppy disk must be retrieved and placed into memory to be processed. The time required to access and retrieve data is called the **access time**. The access time for floppy disks varies from about 175 milliseconds (one millisecond equals 1/1000 of a second) to approximately 300 milliseconds. On average, data stored in a single sector on a floppy disk can be retrieved in approximately 1/15 to 1/3 of a second.

WEB INFO

For more information on storage devices, visit the Introduction to Computers WEB INFO page **(www.scsite.com/IC/webinfo.htm)** and click Storage Devices.

Hard Disks

Another form of auxiliary storage is a hard disk. A **hard disk** consists of one or more rigid metal platters coated with a metal oxide material that allows data to be recorded magnetically on the surface of the platters (Figure 20). Although hard disks are available in removable cartridge form, most disks cannot be removed from the computer. As with floppy disks, the data is recorded on hard disks on a series of tracks. The tracks are divided into sectors when the disk is formatted.

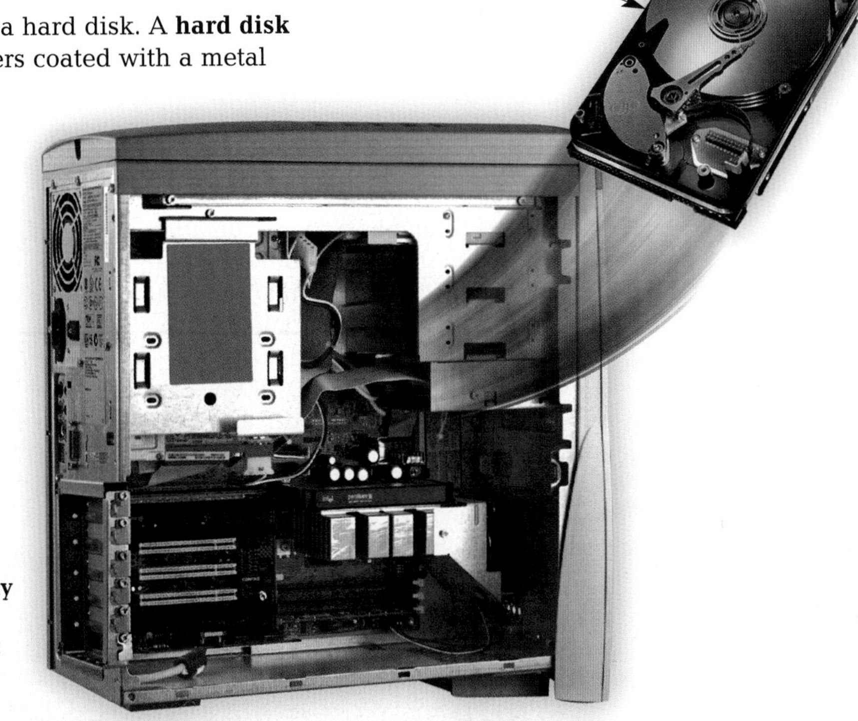

Figure 20
The hard disk in a desktop personal computer normally is housed permanently inside the system unit; that is, it is not portable.

The hard disk platters spin at a high rate of speed, typically 7,200 revolutions per minute. When reading data from the disk, the read head senses the magnetic spots that are recorded on the disk along the various tracks and transfers that data to memory. When writing, the data is transferred from memory and is stored as magnetic spots on the tracks on the recording surface of one or more of the disk platters. When reading or writing, the read/write heads on a hard disk drive do not actually touch the surface of the disk.

The number of platters permanently mounted on the spindle of a hard disk varies. On most drives, each surface of the platter can be used to store data. Thus, if a hard disk drive uses one platter, two surfaces are available for data. If the drive uses two platters, four sets of read/write heads read and record data from the four surfaces. Storage capacities of internally mounted fixed disks for personal computers range from one billion characters to more than ten billion characters. One billion bytes is called a **gigabyte (GB)**. Typical hard disk sizes range from 6 GB to 19 GB.

WEB INFO

For more information on CD-ROMs, visit the Introduction to Computers WEB INFO page **(www.scsite.com/IC/webinfo.htm)** and click CD-ROM.

CD-ROMs

Compact disc read-only memory (CD-ROM) are discs used to store large amounts of prerecorded information (Figure 21). CD-ROMs use the same laser technology as audio CDs for recording music. Each CD-ROM can store more than 600 million bytes of data — the equivalent of 300,000 pages of text. Because of their large storage capacity, CD-ROMs often are used for multimedia material. **Multimedia** combines text, graphics, animation, video, and audio (sound).

1. Push a button to slide out a tray.

2. Insert a compact disc, label side up.

Figure 21
CD-ROM drives allow the user to access tremendous amounts of pre-recorded information — more than 600 MB of data can be stored on one CD-ROM.

DVD-ROMs

Although CD-ROMs have huge storage capacities, even a CD-ROM is not large enough for many of today's complex programs. Some software, for example, is sold on five or more CD-ROMs. To meet these tremendous storage requirements, some software companies moved from CD-ROMs to the larger DVD-ROM format — a technology that can be used to store large amounts of text and even videos (Figure 22). A **DVD-ROM (digital video disc-ROM)** is a very high capacity compact disc capable of storing from 4.7 GB to 17 GB — more than enough to hold a telephone book containing every resident in the United States. Not only is the storage capacity of a DVD-ROM greater than a CD-ROM, a DVD-ROM's quality also far surpasses that of a CD-ROM. In order to read a DVD-ROM, you must have a DVD-ROM drive or DVD player. These drives also can read CD-ROMs.

DVD-ROM drive

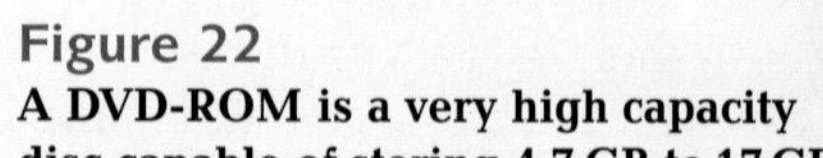

Figure 22
A DVD-ROM is a very high capacity disc capable of storing 4.7 GB to 17 GB.

WEB INFO

For more information on DVD-ROMs, visit the Introduction to Computers WEB INFO page **(www.scsite.com/IC/webinfo.htm)** and click DVD-ROM.

Computer Software

Computer software is the key to productive use of computers. With the correct software, a computer can become a valuable tool. Software can be categorized into two types: system software and application software.

For more information on operating systems, visit the Introduction to Computers WEB INFO page **(www.scsite.com/IC/webinfo.htm)** and click Operating System.

System Software

System software consists of programs to control the operations of computer equipment. An important part of system software is a set of programs called the **operating system**. Instructions in the operating system tell the computer how to perform the functions of loading, storing, and executing an application program and how to transfer data. For a computer to operate, an operating system must be stored in the computer's memory. When a computer is turned on, the operating system is loaded into the computer's memory from auxiliary storage. This process is called **booting**.

Today, most computers use an operating system that has a **graphical user interface (GUI)** that provides visual cues such as icon symbols to help the user. Each **icon** represents an application such as word processing, or a file or document where data is stored. Microsoft Windows (Figure 23) is a widely used graphical operating system. Apple Macintosh computers also have a graphical user interface operating system. **DOS** (**Disk Operating System**) is an older and seldom used operating system that is text-based.

Figure 23
A graphical user interface such as Microsoft Windows makes the computer easier to use. The small pictures, or symbols, on the screen are called icons. The icons represent a program, an instruction, or some other object the user can choose. A window is a rectangular area of the screen that is used to display a program, data, and/or information.

Application Software

Application software consists of programs that tell a computer how to produce information. The different ways people use computers in their careers or in their personal lives are examples of types of application software. Business, scientific, and educational programs are all examples of application software.

Personal Computer Application Software

WEB INFO

For more information on word processing software, visit the Introduction to Computers WEB INFO page **(www.scsite.com/IC/webinfo.htm)** and click Word Processing Software.

Personal computer users often use application software. Some of the more commonly used applications are word processing, electronic spreadsheet, presentation graphics, database, communications, and electronic mail software. Some software packages, such as Microsoft Office 2000, also include access to the World Wide Web as an integral part of the applications.

Word Processing

Word processing software (Figure 24) is used to create, edit, format, and print documents. A key advantage of word processing software is that users easily can make changes in documents, such as correcting spelling, changing margins, and adding, deleting, or relocating entire paragraphs. These changes would be difficult and time consuming to make using manual methods such as a typewriter. With a word processor, documents can be printed quickly and accurately and easily stored on a disk for future use. Word processing software is oriented toward working with text, but most word processing packages also can include numeric and graphic information.

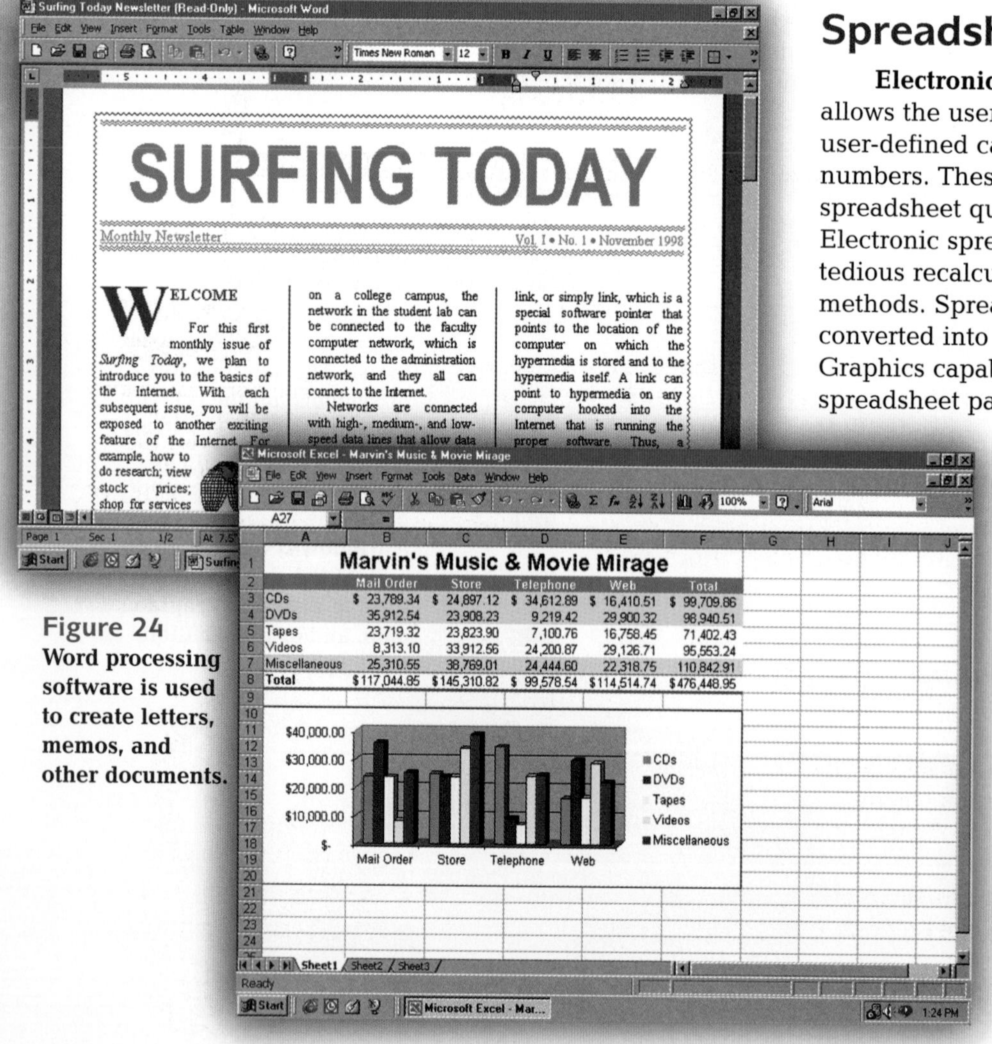

Marvin's Music & Movie Mirage

	Mail Order	Store	Telephone	Web	Total
CDs	$ 23,789.34	$ 24,897.12	$ 34,612.89	$ 16,410.51	$ 99,709.86
DVDs	35,912.54	23,908.23	9,219.42	29,900.32	98,940.51
Tapes	23,719.32	23,823.90	7,100.76	16,758.45	71,402.43
Videos	8,313.10	33,912.56	24,200.87	29,126.71	95,553.24
Miscellaneous	25,310.55	38,769.01	24,444.60	22,318.75	110,842.91
Total	$117,044.85	$145,310.82	$ 99,578.54	$114,514.74	$476,448.95

Figure 24
Word processing software is used to create letters, memos, and other documents.

Spreadsheet

Electronic spreadsheet software (Figure 25) allows the user to add, subtract, and perform user-defined calculations on rows and columns of numbers. These numbers can be changed and the spreadsheet quickly recalculates the new results. Electronic spreadsheet software eliminates the tedious recalculations required with manual methods. Spreadsheet information frequently is converted into a graphic form, such as charts. Graphics capabilities now are included in most spreadsheet packages.

Database

Database software (Figure 26) allows the user to enter, retrieve, and update data in an organized and efficient manner. These software packages have flexible inquiry and reporting capabilities that let users access the data in different ways and create custom reports that include some or all of the information in the database.

Figure 25
Electronic spreadsheet software frequently is used by people who work with numbers. The user enters the data and the formulas to be used on the data, and the computer calculates the results.

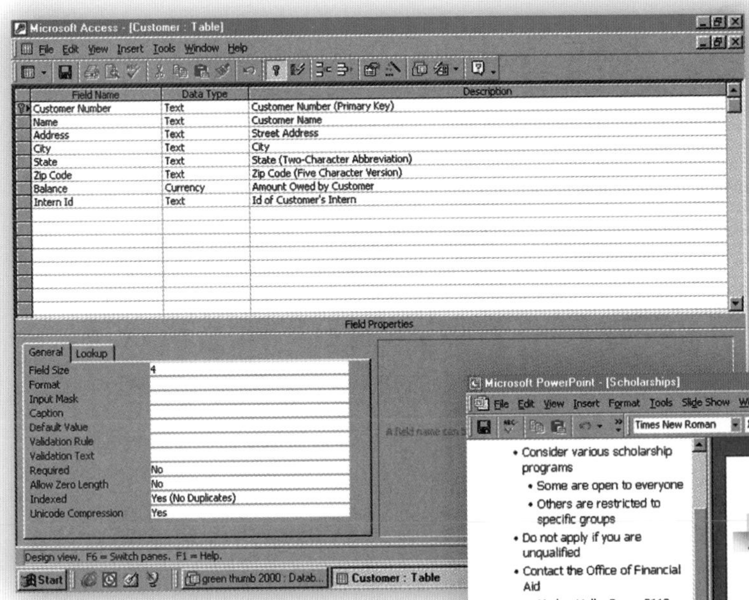

Figure 26
Database software allows the user to enter, retrieve, and update data in an organized and efficient manner.

WEB INFO

For more information on database software, visit the Introduction to Computers WEB INFO page **(www.scsite.com/IC/webinfo.htm)** and click Database Software.

Presentation Graphics

Presentation graphics software (Figure 27) allows the user to create documents called **slides** to be used in making presentations. Using special projection devices, the slides are projected directly from the computer. In addition, the **slides** can be printed and used as handouts, or converted into transparencies and displayed on overhead projectors. Presentation graphics software includes many special effects, color, and art that enhance information presented on a slide. Because slides frequently include numeric data, presentation graphics software includes the capability of converting the numeric data into many forms of charts.

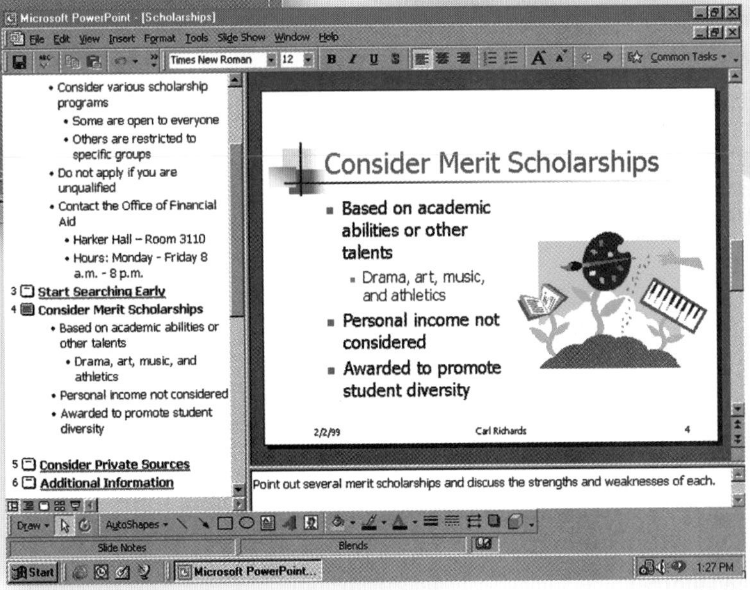

Figure 27
Presentation graphics software allows the user to create documents called slides for use in presentations.

WEB INFO

For more information on presentation graphics, visit the Introduction to Computers WEB INFO page **(www.scsite.com/IC/webinfo.htm)** and click Presentation Graphics.

Networks and the Internet

A **network** is a collection of computers and devices connected together via communications media and devices such as cables, telephone lines, modems, or other means.

Computers are networked together so users can share **resources**, such as hardware devices, software programs, data, and information. Sharing resources saves time and money. For example, instead of purchasing one printer for every computer in a company, the firm can connect a single printer and all computers via a network (Figure 28); the network enables all of the computers to access the same printer.

Figure 28
This local area network (LAN) enables two separate computers to share the same printer.

WEB INFO

For more information on the Internet, visit the Introduction to Computers WEB INFO page **(www.scsite.com/IC/webinfo.htm)** and click Internet.

Most business computers are networked together. These networks can be relatively small or quite extensive. A network that connects computers in a limited geographic area, such as a school computer laboratory, office, or group of buildings, is called a **local area network (LAN)**. A network that covers a large geographical area, such as one that connects the district offices of a national corporation, is called a **wide area network (WAN)** (Figure 29).

Figure 29
A network can be quite large and complex, connecting users in district offices around the country (WAN).

The Internet

The world's largest network is the **Internet**, which is a worldwide collection of networks that links together millions of computers by means of modems, telephone lines, and other communications devices and media. With an abundance of resources and data accessible via the Internet, more than 125 million users around the world are making use of the Internet for a variety of reasons, some of which include the following (Figure 30):

- Sending messages to other connected users (e-mail)
- Accessing a wealth of information, such as news, maps, airline schedules, and stock market data
- Shopping for goods and services
- Meeting or conversing with people around the world
- Accessing sources of entertainment and leisure, such as online games, magazines, and vacation planning guides

Figure 30
Users access the Internet for a variety of reasons: to send messages to other connected users, to access a wealth of information, to shop for goods and services, to meet or converse with people around the world, and for entertainment.

(a) e-mail

(b) stock market data

(c) shopping

(d) meeting people

(e) vacation planning

Most users connect to the Internet in one of two ways: through an Internet service provider or through an online service. An **Internet service provider (ISP)** is an organization that supplies connections to the Internet for a monthly fee. Like an ISP, an **online service** provides access to the Internet, but it also provides a variety of other specialized content and services such as financial data, hardware and software guides, news, weather, legal information, and other similar commodities. For this reason, the fees for using an online service usually are slightly higher than fees for using an ISP. Two popular online services are America Online and The Microsoft Network.

WEB INFO

For more information on the World Wide Web, visit the Introduction to Computers WEB INFO page **(www.scsite.com/IC/webinfo.htm)** and click World Wide Web.

The World Wide Web

One of the more popular segments of the Internet is the **World Wide Web**, also called the **Web**, which contains billions of documents called Web pages. A **Web page** is a document that contains text, graphics, sound, and/or video, and has built-in connections, or **hyperlinks**, to other Web documents. Web pages are stored on computers throughout the world. A **Web site** is a related collection of Web pages. You access and view Web pages using a software program called a **Web browser**.

A Web page has a unique address, called a **Uniform Resource Locator (URL)**. A browser retrieves a Web page by using its URL, which tells the browser where the document is located. URLs make it possible for you to navigate using **links** because a link is associated with a URL. When you click a link, you are issuing a request to display the Web site or the document specified by the URL.

If you know the URL of a Web page, you can type it into a text box at the top of the browser window. For example, if you type the URL, http://www.suntimes.com/index/business.html, in the Address text box and then press the ENTER key, the browser will download and display the Business Section of the *Chicago Sun-Times Online* newspaper (Figure 31).

As shown in Figure 31, a URL consists of a protocol, domain name, and sometimes the path to a specific Web page or location in a Web page. Most Web page URLs begin with **http://**, which stands for **hypertext transfer protocol**, the communications standard used to transfer pages on the Web. The **domain name** identifies the Web site, which is stored on a Web server. A **Web server** is a computer that delivers (serves) requested Web pages.

ONLINE SERVICE

Step 1: Use your computer and modem to make a local telephone call to an Internet service provider.

Step 2: With your browser on the screen, enter the address, or URL, of the Web site you want to visit.

Step 3: The Web browser locates the Web site for the entered address and displays a Web page on your screen.

protocol · domain name · path

http://www.suntimes.com/index/business.html ← URL

Figure 31
One method of connecting to the Web and displaying a Web page.

If you do not enter a URL exactly, your browser will not be able to locate the site or Web page you want to visit (view). To help minimize errors, most current browsers allow you to type URLs without the http:// portion. For example, you can type, www.suntimes.com/index/business.html instead of, http:// www.suntimes .com/index/ business.html. If you enter an incorrect address, some browsers search for similar addresses and provide a list from which you can select.

How to Purchase, Install, and Maintain a Personal Computer

The decision to buy a personal computer system is an important one – and finding and purchasing a personal computer system suited to your needs will require an investment of both time and money. In general, personal computer buyers fall into three categories: first-time buyers, replacement buyers, and upgrade buyers. A recent survey of North American consumers found that the largest of the three categories, first-time buyers, make up 40 percent of the PC market. Surprisingly, the survey also discovered that most first-time buyers have little computer experience. In fact, more than 70 percent of first-time home computer buyers do not even use a computer at work.

As with many buyers, you may have little computer experience and find yourself unsure of how to proceed. The following guidelines are presented to help you purchase, install, and maintain a computer system. These guidelines also apply to the purchase of a laptop computer. Purchasing a laptop also involves some additional considerations, which are addressed later in this section.

Type of System	Web Site	URL
PC	PC Comparison	www.computers.com/scoreboard
	Computer Shopper	www.zdnet.com/computershopper/edit/howtobuy/C0000001
	PC World Magazine	www.pcworld.com
	Tech Web Buyer's Guides	www.techweb.com/infoseek/shopper/bguides.html
	Byte Magazine	www.byte.com
	PC Computing Magazine	www.zdnet.com/pccomp
	PC Magazine	www.zdnet.com/pcmag
	Ziff-Davis	www.zdnet.com/product
	Yahoo! Computers	computers.yahoo.com
	Family PC Magazine	www.zdnet.com/familypc/filters/fpc.hardware.html
	Compare.Net	compare.net
	Tips on Buying a PC	www.css.msu.edu/pc-guide.html
Macintosh	Byte Magazine	www.techweb.com/wire/apple/
	Ziff-Davis	www.zdnet.com/mac
	Macworld Magazine	www.macworld.com
	Apple	www.apple.com

For an updated list of hardware and software reviews and their Web sites, visit www.scsite.com/IC.htm

Figure 32
Hardware and software reviews.

How to Purchase a Personal Computer

1. Determine what application software products you will use on your computer. Knowing what software applications you plan to use will help you decide on the type of computer to buy, as well as to define the memory, storage, and other requirements. Certain software products, for example, can run on only Macintosh computers, while others run on only a PC with the Windows operating system. Further, some software products require more memory and disk space than others, as well as additional input/output devices.

When you purchase a computer system, it may come bundled with several software products (although not all will). At the very least, you probably will want software for word processing and a browser to access the World Wide Web. If you need additional applications, such as a spreadsheet, database, or presentation graphics, consider purchasing a software suite that offers reduced pricing on several applications.

Before selecting a specific package, be sure the software contains the features necessary for the tasks you want to perform. Many Web sites and magazines, such as those listed in Figure 32, provide reviews of software products. These sites also frequently have articles that rate computer systems and software on cost, performance, and support.

2. Before buying a computer system, do some research. Talk to friends, coworkers, and instructors about prospective computer systems. What type of computer system did they buy? Why? Would they recommend their system and the company from which they bought it? You also should visit the Web sites or read reviews in the magazines listed in Figure 32. As you conduct your research, consider the following important criteria:

- Speed of the processor
- Size and types of memory (RAM) and storage (hard disk, floppy disk, CD-ROM, DVD-ROM, Zip® drive)
- Input/output devices included with the system (e.g., mouse, keyboard, monitor, printer, sound card, video card)
- Communications devices included with the system (modem, network interface card)
- Any software included with the system
- Overall system cost

3. Look for free software. Many system vendors include free software with their systems. Some sellers even let you choose which software you want. Remember, however, that free software has value only if you would have purchased the software even if it had not come with the computer.

4. If you are buying a new computer system, you have several purchasing options: buying from your school bookstore, a local computer dealer, a local large retail store; or ordering by mail via telephone or the World Wide Web. Each purchasing option has certain advantages. Many college bookstores, for example, sign exclusive pricing agreements with computer manufacturers and thus, can offer student discounts. Local dealers and local large retail stores, however, more easily can provide hands-on support. Mail-order companies that sell computer systems by telephone or online via the Web (Figure 33) often provide the lowest prices but extend less personal service. Some major mail-order companies, however, have started to provide next-business-day, onsite services.

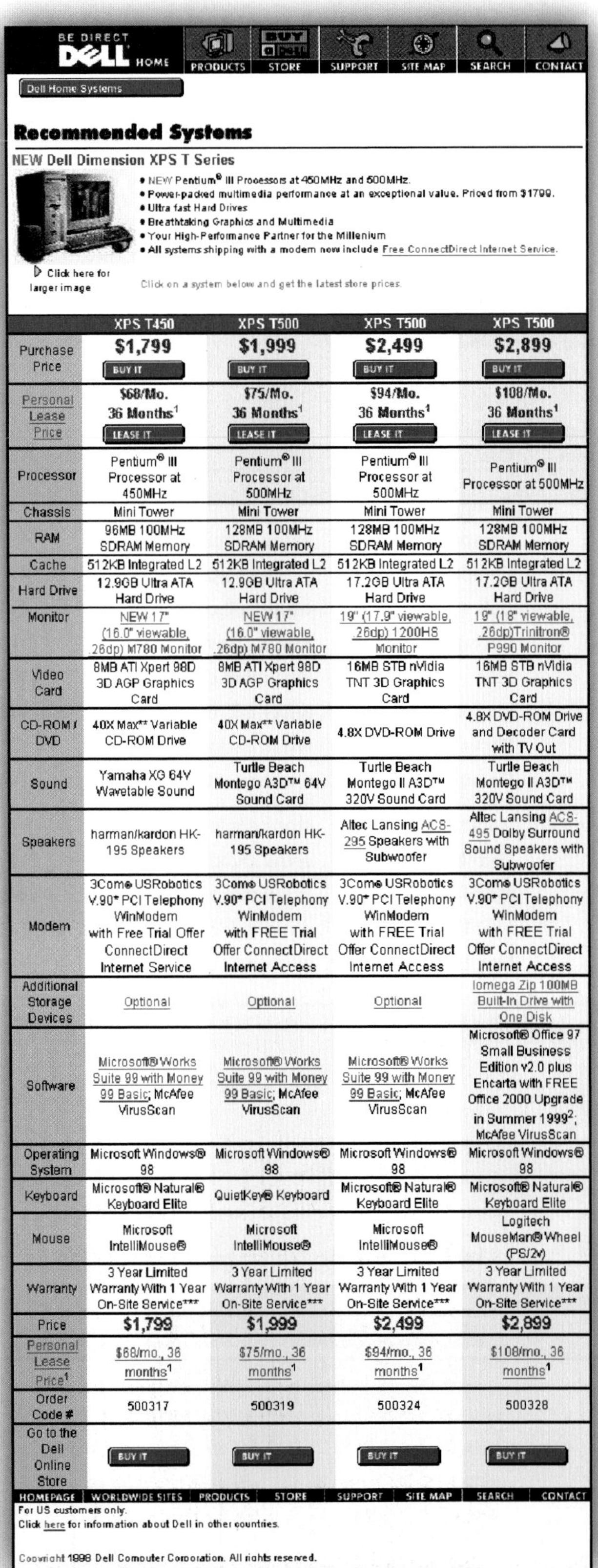
BE DIRECT DELL HOME | PRODUCTS | STORE | SUPPORT | SITE MAP | SEARCH | CONTACT

Dell Home Systems

Recommended Systems

NEW Dell Dimension XPS T Series

- NEW Pentium® III Processors at 450MHz and 600MHz.
- Power-packed multimedia performance at an exceptional value. Priced from $1799.
- Ultra fast Hard Drives
- Breathtaking Graphics and Multimedia
- Your High-Performance Partner for the Millenium
- All systems shipping with a modem now include Free ConnectDirect Internet Service.

Click here for larger image

Click on a system below and get the latest store prices.

	XPS T450	XPS T500	XPS T500	XPS T500
Purchase Price	$1,799 BUY IT	$1,999 BUY IT	$2,499 BUY IT	$2,899 BUY IT
Personal Lease Price	$68/Mo. 36 Months[1] LEASE IT	$75/Mo. 36 Months[1] LEASE IT	$94/Mo. 36 Months[1] LEASE IT	$108/Mo. 36 Months[1] LEASE IT
Processor	Pentium® III Processor at 450MHz	Pentium® III Processor at 500MHz	Pentium® III Processor at 500MHz	Pentium® III Processor at 500MHz
Chassis	Mini Tower	Mini Tower	Mini Tower	Mini Tower
RAM	96MB 100MHz SDRAM Memory	128MB 100MHz SDRAM Memory	128MB 100MHz SDRAM Memory	128MB 100MHz SDRAM Memory
Cache	512KB Integrated L2	512KB Integrated L2	512KB Integrated L2	512KB Integrated L2
Hard Drive	12.9GB Ultra ATA Hard Drive	12.9GB Ultra ATA Hard Drive	17.2GB Ultra ATA Hard Drive	17.2GB Ultra ATA Hard Drive
Monitor	NEW 17" (16.0" viewable, .26dp) M780 Monitor	NEW 17" (16.0" viewable, .26dp) M780 Monitor	19" (17.9" viewable, .26dp) 1200HS Monitor	19" (18" viewable, .26dp)Trinitron® P990 Monitor
Video Card	8MB ATI Xpert 98D 3D AGP Graphics Card	8MB ATI Xpert 98D 3D AGP Graphics Card	16MB STB nVidia TNT 3D Graphics Card	16MB STB nVidia TNT 3D Graphics Card
CD-ROM / DVD	40X Max** Variable CD-ROM Drive	40X Max** Variable CD-ROM Drive	4.8X DVD-ROM Drive	4.8X DVD-ROM Drive and Decoder Card with TV Out
Sound	Yamaha XG 64V Wavetable Sound	Turtle Beach Montego A3D™ 64V Sound Card	Turtle Beach Montego II A3D™ 320V Sound Card	Turtle Beach Montego II A3D™ 320V Sound Card
Speakers	harman/kardon HK-195 Speakers	harman/kardon HK-195 Speakers	Altec Lansing ACS-295 Speakers with Subwoofer	Altec Lansing ACS-495 Dolby Surround Sound Speakers with Subwoofer
Modem	3Com® USRobotics V.90* PCI Telephony WinModem with Free Trial Offer ConnectDirect Internet Service	3Com® USRobotics V.90* PCI Telephony WinModem with FREE Trial Offer ConnectDirect Internet Access	3Com® USRobotics V.90* PCI Telephony WinModem with FREE Trial Offer ConnectDirect Internet Access	3Com® USRobotics V.90* PCI Telephony WinModem with FREE Trial Offer ConnectDirect Internet Access
Additional Storage Devices	Optional	Optional	Optional	Iomega Zip 100MB Built-In Drive with One Disk
Software	Microsoft® Works Suite 99 with Money 99 Basic; McAfee VirusScan	Microsoft® Works Suite 99 with Money 99 Basic; McAfee VirusScan	Microsoft® Works Suite 99 with Money 99 Basic; McAfee VirusScan	Microsoft® Office 97 Small Business Edition v2.0 plus Encarta with FREE Office 2000 Upgrade in Summer 1999[2]; McAfee VirusScan
Operating System	Microsoft Windows® 98	Microsoft Windows® 98	Microsoft Windows® 98	Microsoft Windows® 98
Keyboard	Microsoft® Natural® Keyboard Elite	QuietKey® Keyboard	Microsoft® Natural® Keyboard Elite	Microsoft® Natural® Keyboard Elite
Mouse	Microsoft IntelliMouse®	Microsoft IntelliMouse®	Microsoft IntelliMouse®	Logitech MouseMan® Wheel (PS/2v)
Warranty	3 Year Limited Warranty With 1 Year On-Site Service***	3 Year Limited Warranty With 1 Year On-Site Service***	3 Year Limited Warranty With 1 Year On-Site Service***	3 Year Limited Warranty With 1 Year On-Site Service***
Price	$1,799	$1,999	$2,499	$2,899
Personal Lease Price[1]	$68/mo., 36 months[1]	$75/mo., 36 months[1]	$94/mo., 36 months[1]	$108/mo., 36 months[1]
Order Code #	500317	500319	500324	500328
Go to the Dell Online Store	BUY IT	BUY IT	BUY IT	BUY IT

HOMEPAGE | WORLDWIDE SITES | PRODUCTS | STORE | SUPPORT | SITE MAP | SEARCH | CONTACT

For US customers only.
Click here for information about Dell in other countries.

Figure 33
Some mail-order companies, such as Dell Computer, sell computers online.

A credit card usually is required to buy from a mail-order company. Figure 34 lists some of the more popular mail-order companies and their Web site addresses.

5. If you are buying a used computer system, stick with name brands. Although brand-name equipment can cost more, most brand-name systems have longer, more comprehensive warranties, are better supported, and have more authorized centers for repair services. As with new computer systems, you can purchase a used computer from local computer dealers, local large retail stores, or mail order via the telephone or the Web. Classified ads and used computer brokers offer additional outlets for purchasing used computer systems. Figure 35 lists several major used computer brokers and their Web site addresses.

6. Use a worksheet to compare computer systems, services, and other considerations. You can use a separate sheet of paper to take notes on each vendor's computer system and then summarize the information on a spreadsheet, such as the one shown in Figure 36. Most companies advertise a price for a base system that includes components housed in the system unit (processor, RAM, sound card, video card), disk drives (floppy disk, hard disk, CD-ROM, and DVD-ROM), a keyboard, mouse, monitor, printer, speakers, and modem. Be aware, however, that some advertisements list prices for systems with only some of these components. Monitors, printers, and modems, for example, often are not included in a base system price. Depending on how you plan to use the system, you may want to invest in additional or more powerful components. When you are comparing the prices of computer systems, make sure you are comparing identical or similar configurations.

Type of System	Company	URL	Telephone Number
PC	Computer Shopper	www.computershopper.com	
	Compaq	www.compaq.com	1-800-888-0220
	CompUSA	www.compusa.com	1-800-266-7872
	Dell	www.dell.com	1-800-678-1626
	Gateway	www.gateway.com	1-800-846-4208
	IBM	www.ibm.com	1-800-426-7235
	Micron	www.micron.com	1-800-964-2766
	Packard Bell	www.packardbell.com	1-888-474-6772
	Quantex	www.quantex.com	1-800-346-6685
Macintosh	Apple Computer	store.apple.com	1-800-795-1000
	Club Mac	www.clubmac.com	1-800-258-2622
	MacBase	www.macbase.com	1-800-951-1230
	Mac Wholesale	www.macwholesale.com	1-800-531-4622
	Mac Exchange	www.macx.com	1-888-650-4488

For an updated list of new computer mail-order companies and their Web sites, visit www.scsite.com/IC.htm

Figure 34
New computer mail-order companies.

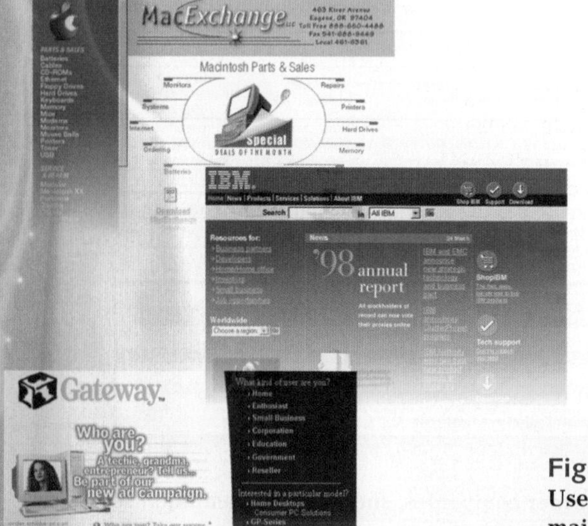

Company	URL	Telephone Number
American Computer Exchange	www.amcoex.com	1-800-786-0717
Boston Computer Exchange	www.bocoex.com	1-617-625-7722
United Computer Exchange	www.uce.com	1-800-755-3033
Used Computer Exchange	www.usedcomputer exchange.com	1-888-256-0481

For an updated list, visit www.scsite.com/IC.htm

Figure 35
Used computer mail-order companies.

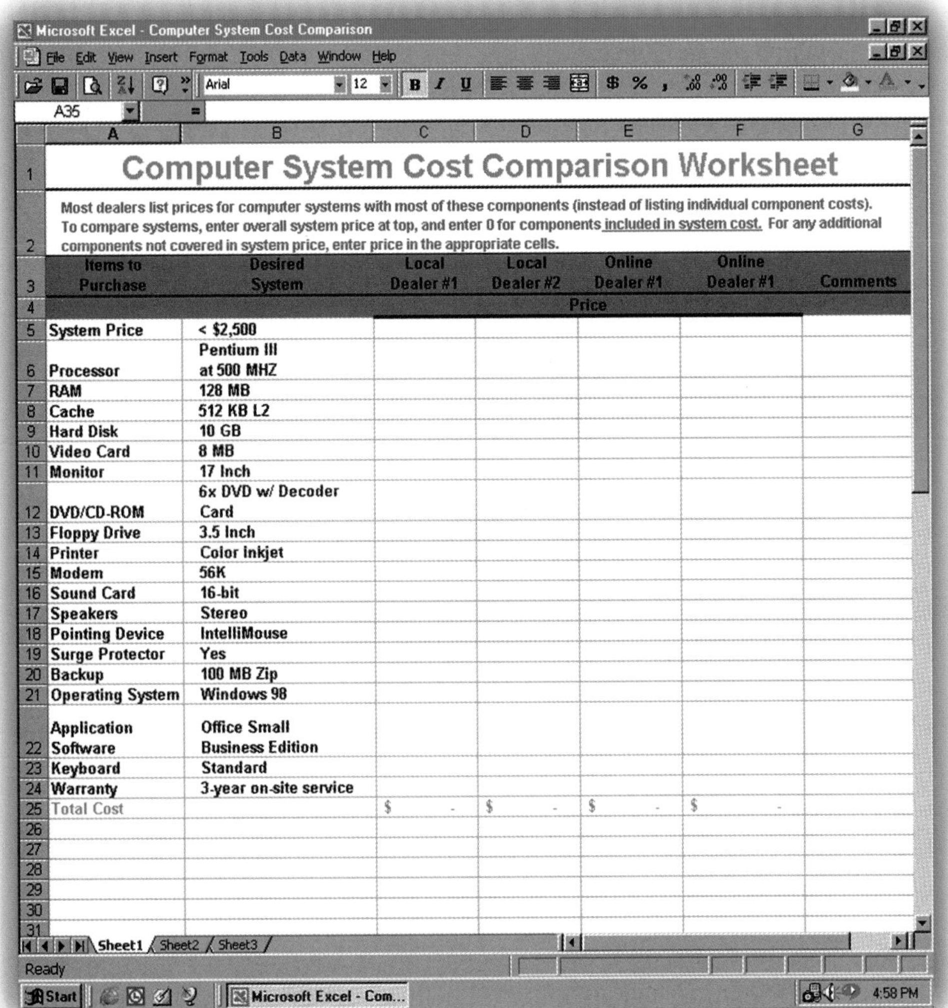
Microsoft Excel - Computer System Cost Comparison

Computer System Cost Comparison Worksheet

Most dealers list prices for computer systems with most of these components (instead of listing individual component costs). To compare systems, enter overall system price at top, and enter 0 for components included in system cost. For any additional components not covered in system price, enter price in the appropriate cells.

Items to Purchase	Desired System	Local Dealer #1	Local Dealer #2	Online Dealer #1	Online Dealer #1	Comments
		Price				
System Price	< $2,500					
Processor	Pentium III at 500 MHZ					
RAM	128 MB					
Cache	512 KB L2					
Hard Disk	10 GB					
Video Card	8 MB					
Monitor	17 Inch					
DVD/CD-ROM	6x DVD w/ Decoder Card					
Floppy Drive	3.5 Inch					
Printer	Color Inkjet					
Modem	56K					
Sound Card	16-bit					
Speakers	Stereo					
Pointing Device	IntelliMouse					
Surge Protector	Yes					
Backup	100 MB Zip					
Operating System	Windows 98					
Application Software	Office Small Business Edition					
Keyboard	Standard					
Warranty	3-year on-site service					
Total Cost		$ -	$ -	$ -	$ -	

Figure 36

A spreadsheet is an effective tool for summarizing and comparing the prices and components of different computer vendors.

7. Be aware of hidden costs. Before purchasing, be sure to consider any additional costs associated with buying a computer, such as an additional telephone line, an uninterruptible power supply (UPS), computer furniture, floppy disks and paper, or computer training classes you may want to take. Depending on where you buy your computer, the seller may be willing to include some or all of these in the system purchase price.

8. Consider more than just price. The lowest cost system may not be the best buy. Consider such intangibles as the vendor's time in business, the vendor's regard for quality, and the vendor's reputation for support. If you need to upgrade your computer often, you may want to consider a leasing arrangement, in which you pay monthly lease fees but upgrade or add on to your computer system as your equipment needs change. If you are a replacement buyer, ask if the vendor will buy your old system; an increasing number of companies are taking trade-ins. No matter what type of buyer you are, insist on a 30-day, no questions-asked return policy on your computer system.

9. Select an Internet service provider (ISP) or online service. You can access the Internet in one of two ways: via an ISP or an online service. Both provide Internet access for a monthly fee that ranges from $5 to $20. Local ISPs offer Internet access through local telephone numbers to users in a limited geographic region. National ISPs provide access for users nationwide (including mobile users), through local and toll-free telephone numbers. Because of their size, national ISPs

offer more services and generally have a larger technical support staff than local ISPs. Online services furnish Internet access as well as members-only features for users nationwide. Figure 37 lists several national ISPs and online services. Before you choose an Internet access provider, compare such features as the number of access hours, monthly fees, available services (e-mail, Web page hosting, chat), and reliability.

Company	Service	URL	Telephone Number
America Online	ONLINE	www.americaonline.com	1-800-827-6364
AT&T Network Commerce Services	ISP	www.att.com/work-net	1-800-467-8467
CompuServe	ONLINE	www.compuserve.com/gateway/default.asp	1-800-394-1481
Earthlink Network	ISP	www.earthlink.com	1-800-395-8425
GTE Internet	ISP	www.gte.net	1-888-GTE-SURF
IBM Internet Connection Services	ISP	www.ibm.net	1-800-455-5056
MCI	ISP	www.mciworldcom.com	1-800-888-0800
Prodigy/Prodigy Classic	ISP/ONLINE	www.prodigy.com	1-800-PRODIGY
The Microsoft Network	ONLINE	www.msn.com	1-800-386-5550
UUNet Technologies	ISP	www.uu.net	1-800-4UUNET4

For information on local ISPs or to learn more on any ISPs and online services listed here, visit The List™ atthelist.internet.com. The List™ — the most comprehensive and accurate directory of ISPs and online services on the Web — compares dial-up services, access hours, and fees for more than 5,000 access providers.

For an updated list of ISPs and online service providers, visit www.scsite.com/IC.htm.

Figure 37 **National ISPs and online services.**

10. Buy a system compatible with the ones you use elsewhere. If you use a personal computer at work or in some other capacity, make sure the computer you buy is compatible. For example, if you use a PC at work, you may not want to purchase a Macintosh for home use. Having a computer compatible with the ones at work or school will allow you to transfer files and spend time at home on work- or school-related projects.

11. Consider purchasing an onsite service agreement. If you use your computer for business or are unable to be without your computer, consider purchasing an onsite service agreement through a local dealer or third-party company. Most onsite service agreements state that a technician will come to your home, work, or school within 24 hours. If your system includes onsite service only for the first year, think about extending the service for two or three years when you buy the computer.

12. Use a credit card to purchase your system. Many credit cards now offer purchase protection and extended warranty benefits that cover you in case of loss of or damage to purchased goods. Paying by credit card also gives you time to install and use the system before you have to pay for it. Finally, if you are dissatisfied with the system and are unable to reach an agreement with the seller, paying by credit card gives you certain rights regarding withholding payment until the dispute is resolved. Check your credit card agreement for specific details.

13. Avoid buying the smallest system available. Computer technology changes rapidly, meaning a computer that seems powerful enough today may not serve your computing needs in a few years. In fact, studies show that many users regret they did not buy a more powerful system. Plan to buy a system that will last you for two to three years. You can help delay obsolescence by purchasing the fastest processor, the most memory, and the largest hard drive you can afford. If you must buy a smaller system, be sure you can upgrade it with additional memory and auxiliary devices as your system requirements grow. Figure 38 includes the minimum recommendations for the following categories of users: Home User, Small Business User, Mobile User, Large Business User, and Power User. The Home User category is divided into two groups, Application Home User and Game Home User.

BASE SYSTEM COMPONENTS

	Application Home User	Game Home User	Small Business User	Mobile User	Large Business User	Power User
HARDWARE						
Processor	Pentium III at 450 MHz	Pentium III at 500 MHz	Pentium III at 500 MHZ	Pentium II at 366 MHz	Pentium III at 500 MHz	Pentium III Xeon at 500 MHz
RAM	96 MB	128 MB	128 MB	96 MB	192 MB	256 MB
Cache	512 KB L2	512 KB L2	512 KB L2	512 KB L2	512 KB L2	512 KB L2
Hard Drive	12.9 GB	12.9 GB	17.2 GB	10 GB	17.2 GB	16.8 GB
Video Graphics Card	8 MB	16 MB	8 MB	8 MB	8 MB	16 MB
Monitor	17"	19"	17"	15" active matrix	19"	21"
DVD/CD-ROM Drive	40X CD-ROM	5X DVD with Decoder Card	40X CD-ROM	24X CD-ROM	40X CD-ROM	5X DVD with Decoder Card
Floppy Drive	3.5"	3.5"	3.5"	3.5"	3.5"	3.5"
Printer	Color ink-jet	Color ink-jet	8 ppm laser	Portable ink-jet	24 ppm laser	8 ppm laser
Fax/modem	56 K	56 K	56 K	56 K	ISDN	ISDN
Sound Card	16-bit	16-bit	16-bit	Built-In	16-bit	16-bit
Speakers	Stereo	Full-Dolby surround	Stereo	Stereo	Stereo	Full-Dolby surround
Pointing Device	IntelliMouse	IntelliMouse and Joystick	IntelliMouse	Touchpad or Pointing Stick and IntelliMouse	IntelliMouse	IntelliMouse and Joystick
Keyboard	Yes	Yes	Yes	Built-In	Yes	Yes
Backup Disk/Tape Drive	100 MB Zip	1 GB Jaz	1 GB Jaz and Tape	100 MB Zip	2 GB Jaz and Tape	2 GB Jaz and Tape
SOFTWARE						
Operating System	Windows 98	Windows 98	Windows 98	Windows 98	Windows NT	Windows NT
Application Software Suite	Office Standard	Office Standard	Office Small Business Edition	Office Small Business Edition	Office Professional	Office Professional
Internet Access	Online Service or ISP	Online Service or ISP	LAN (ISDN)	ISP	LAN/WAN (T1/T3)	LAN
OTHER						
Surge Protector	Yes	Yes	Yes	Portable	Yes	Yes
Warranty	3-year on-site service	3-year on-site service	3-year on-site service	3-year on-site service	3-year on-site service	3-year on-site service
Other		Headset		Docking Station		
				Carrying case		

Optional Components for all Categories
digital camera
multifunction device (MFD)
scanner
uninterruptable power supply
ergonomic keyboard
network interface card
TV/FM tuner
recordable CD-ROM
video camera
mouse pad/wrist rest

Figure 38
Base system components and optional components.

How to Purchase a Laptop Computer

If you need computing capability when you travel, you may find a laptop computer to be an appropriate choice. The guidelines mentioned in the previous section also apply to the purchase of a laptop computer (Figure 39). The following are additional considerations unique to laptops.

Figure 39
Laptop computer.

1. **Purchase a laptop with a sufficiently large active-matrix screen. Active-matrix screens** display high-quality color that is viewable from all angles. Less expensive, passive matrix screens sometimes are hard to see in low-light conditions and cannot be viewed from an angle. Laptop computers typically come with a 12.1-inch, 13.3-inch, or 14.1-inch display. For most users, a 13.3-inch display is satisfactory. If you intend to use your laptop as a desktop replacement, however, you may opt for a 14.1-inch display. If you travel a lot and portability is essential, consider that most of the lightest machines are equipped with a 12.1-inch display. Regardless of size, the resolution of the display should be at least 800 x 600 pixels.

2. **Experiment with different pointing devices and keyboards.** Laptop computer keyboards are far less standardized than those for desktop systems. Some laptops, for example, have wide wrist rests, while others have none. Laptops also use a range of pointing devices, including pointing sticks, touchpads, and trackballs. Before you purchase a laptop, try various types of keyboard and pointing devices to determine which is easiest for you to use. Regardless of the pointing device you select, you also may want to purchase a regular mouse unit to use when you are working at a desk or other large surface.

3. **Make sure the laptop you purchase has a CD-ROM or DVD-ROM drive.** Loading software, especially large software suites, is much faster if done from a CD-ROM or DVD-ROM. Today, most laptops come with either an internal or external CD-ROM drive; others have an internal and external unit that allows you to interchange the 3.5-inch floppy drive and the CD-ROM drive. An advantage of a separate CD-ROM drive is that you can leave it behind to save weight. Some users prefer a DVD-ROM drive to a CD-ROM drive. Although DVD-ROM drives are more expensive, they allow you to read CD-ROMs and to play movies using your laptop.

4. **If you plan to use your laptop both on the road and at home or in the office, consider a docking station.** A **docking station** usually includes a floppy disk drive, a CD-ROM or DVD-ROM drive, and a connector for a full-sized monitor. When you work both at home and in the office, a docking station is an attractive alternative to buying a full-sized system. A docking station essentially turns your laptop into a desktop, while eliminating the need to transfer files from one computer to another.

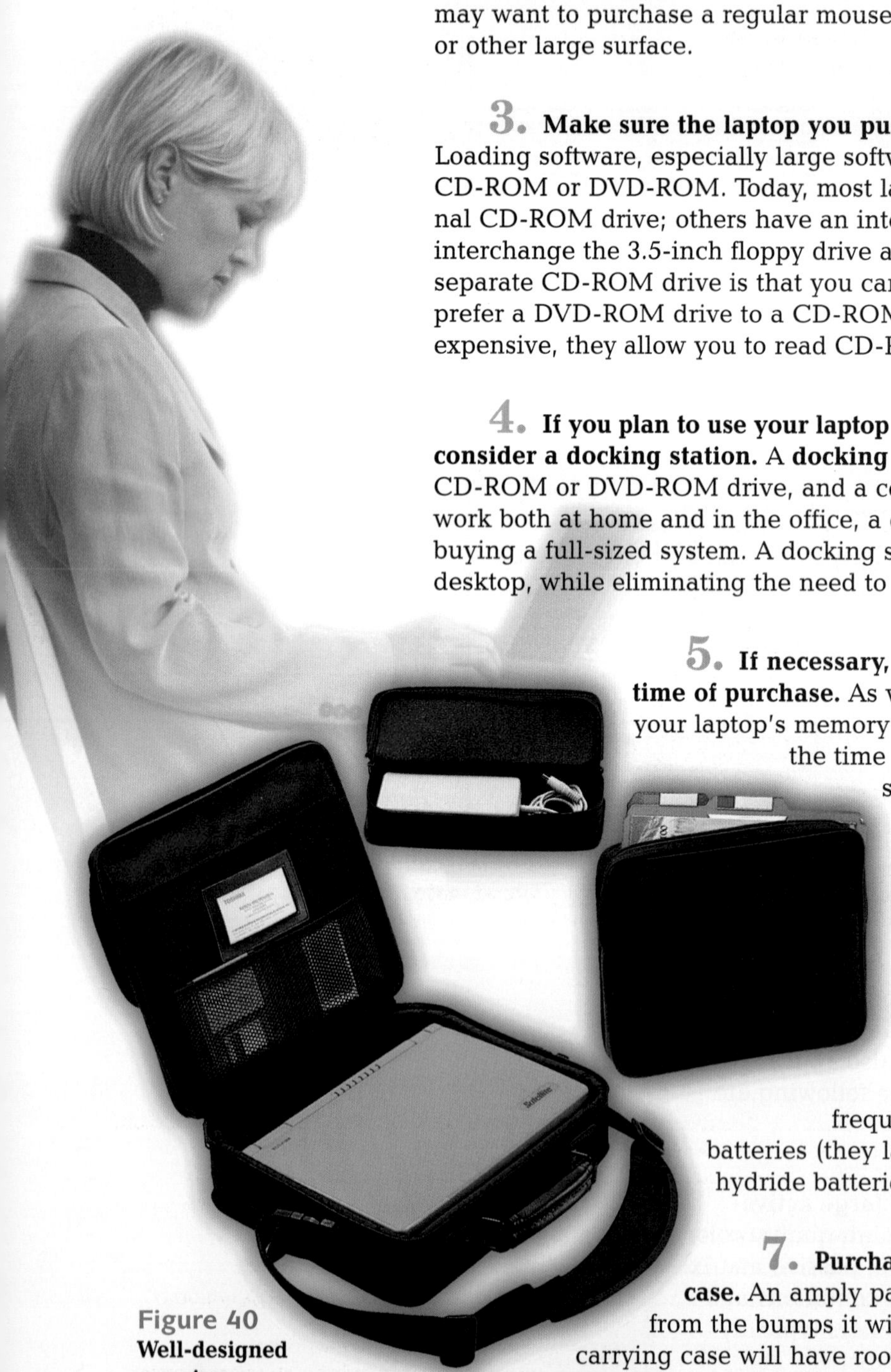

5. **If necessary, upgrade memory and disk storage at the time of purchase.** As with a desktop computer system, upgrading your laptop's memory and disk storage usually is less expensive at the time of the initial purchase. Some disk storage systems are custom designed for laptop manufacturers, meaning an upgrade might not be available two or three years after you purchase your laptop.

6. **If you are going to use your laptop on an airplane, purchase a second battery.** Two batteries should provide enough power to last through most airplane flights. If you anticipate running your laptop on batteries frequently, choose a system that uses lithium-ion batteries (they last longer than nickel cadmium or nickel hydride batteries).

7. **Purchase a well-padded and well-designed carrying case.** An amply padded carrying case will protect your laptop from the bumps it will receive while traveling. A well-designed carrying case will have room for accessories such as spare floppy disks; an external floppy disk, CD-ROM, or DVD-ROM drive; a user manual; pens; and paperwork (Figure 40).

Figure 40
Well-designed carrying case.

8. If you travel overseas, obtain a set of electrical and telephone adapters. Different countries use different outlets for electrical and telephone connections. Several manufacturers sell sets of adapters that will work in most countries (Figure 41).

Figure 41
Set of electrical and telephone adapters.

9. If you plan to connect your laptop to a video projector, make sure the laptop is compatible with the video projector (Figure 42). Some laptops will not work with certain video projectors; others will not allow you to display an image on the laptop and projection device at the same time. Either of these factors can affect your presentation negatively.

Figure 42
With a laptop connected to a video projector, an individual can deliver a professional presentation.

How to Install a Personal Computer

1. Read the installation manuals before you start to install your equipment. Many manufacturers include separate installation instructions with their equipment that contain important information. You can save a great deal of time and frustration if you make an effort to read the manuals.

2. Do some research. To locate additional instructions on installing your computer, review the computer magazines or Web sites listed in Figure 43 to search for articles on installing a computer system.

Web Site	URL
Getting Started/Installation Once You've Bought It	
newsday.com	www.newsday.com/plugin/c101main.htm
HelpTalk Online	www.helptalk.com
Ergonomics	
Ergonomic Computing	cobweb.creighton.edu/training/ergo.htm
Healthy Choices for Computer Users	www-ehs.ucsd.edu/vdttoc.htm
Video Display Health Guidelines	www.uhs.berkeley.edu/facstaff/ergonomics/ergguide.html

For an updated list of reference materials, visit www.scsite.com/IC.htm.

Figure 43
Web references on setting up and using your computer.

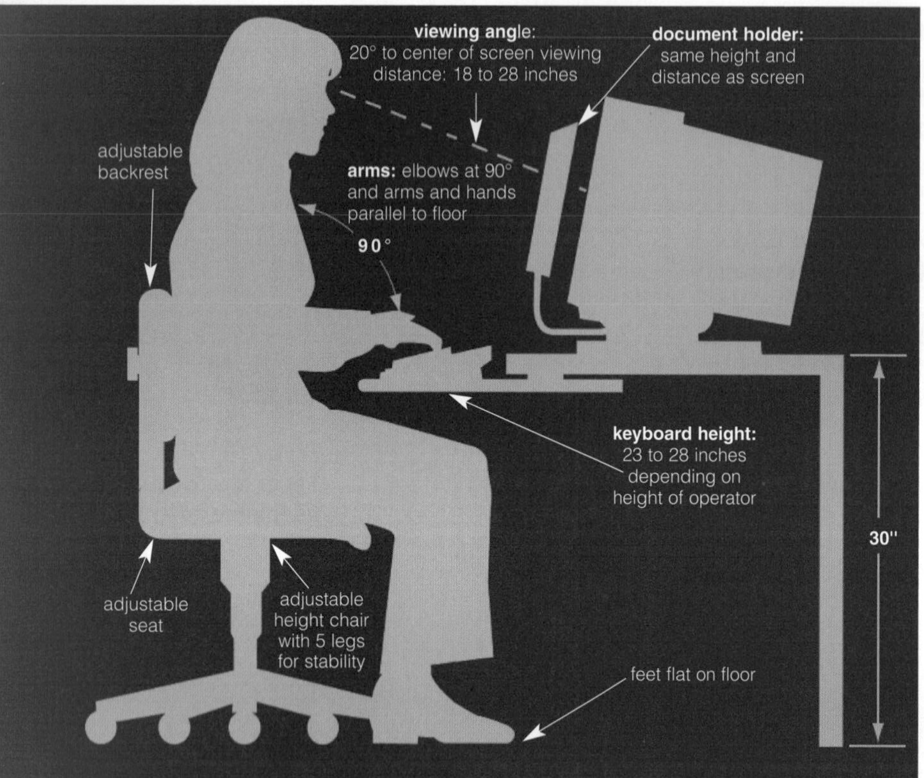

Figure 44
A well-designed work area should be flexible to allow adjustments to the height and build of different individuals. Good lighting and air quality also are important considerations.

3. Set up your computer in a well-designed work area, with adequate workspace around the computer. Ergonomics is an applied science devoted to making the equipment and its surrounding work area safer and more efficient. Ergonomic studies have shown that using the correct type and configuration of chair, keyboard, monitor, and work surface will help you work comfortably and efficiently, and help protect your health. For your computer workspace, experts recommend an area of at least two feet by four feet. Figure 44 illustrates additional guidelines for setting up your work area.

4. Install bookshelves. Bookshelves above and/or to the side of your computer area are useful for keeping manuals and other reference materials handy.

5. Have a telephone outlet and telephone near your workspace so you can connect your modem and/or place calls while using your computer. To plug in your modem to dial up and access the World Wide Web, you will need a telephone outlet close to your computer. Having a telephone nearby also helps if you need to place business or technical support calls while you are working on your computer. Often, if you call a vendor about a hardware or software problem, the support person can talk you through a correction while you are on the telephone. To avoid data loss, however, do not place floppy disks on the telephone or near any other electrical or electronic equipment.

6. While working at your computer, be aware of health issues. Working safely at your computer requires that you consider several health issues. To minimize neck and eye discomfort, for instance, obtain a document holder that keeps documents at the same height and distance as your computer screen. To provide adequate lighting that reduces eye strain, use non-glare light bulbs that illuminate your entire work area. Figure 45 lists additional computer user health guidelines.

Computer User Health Guidelines

1. Work in a well-designed work area.
2. Alternate work activities to prevent physical and mental fatigue. If possible, change the order of your work to provide some variety.
3. Take frequent breaks. Every fifteen minutes, look away from the screen to give your eyes a break. At least once per hour, get out of your chair and move around. Every two hours, take at least a fifteen-minute break.
4. Incorporate hand, arm, and body stretching exercises into your breaks. At lunch, try to get outside and walk.
5. Make sure your computer monitor is designed to minimize electromagnetic radiation (EMR). If it is an older model, consider adding EMR reducing accessories.
6. Try to eliminate or minimize surrounding noise. Noisy environments contribute to stress and tension.
7. If you frequently use the telephone and the computer at the same time, consider using a telephone headset. Cradling the telephone between your head and shoulder can cause muscle strain.
8. Be aware of symptoms of repetitive strain injuries: soreness, pain, numbness, or weakness in neck, shoulders, arms, wrists, and hands. Do not ignore early signs; seek medical advice.

Figure 45
Following these health guidelines will help computer users maintain their health.

7. Obtain a computer tool set. Computer tool sets include any screwdrivers and other tools you might need to work on your computer. Computer dealers, office supply stores, and mail-order companies sell these tool sets. To keep all the tools together, get a tool set that comes in a zippered carrying case.

8. Save all the paperwork that comes with your system. Keep the documents that come with your system in an accessible place, along with the paperwork from your other computer-related purchases. To keep different-sized documents together, consider putting them in a manila file folder, large envelope, or sealable plastic bag.

9. Record the serial numbers of all your equipment and software. Write the serial numbers of your equipment and software on the outside of the manuals packaged with these items. As noted in Figure 47, you also should create a single, comprehensive list that contains the serial numbers of all your equipment and software.

10. Complete and send in your equipment and software registration cards. When you register your equipment and software, the vendor usually enters you in its user database. Being a registered user not only can save you time when you call with a support question, it also makes you eligible for special pricing on software upgrades.

11. Keep the shipping containers and packing materials for all your equipment. Shipping containers and packing materials will come in handy if you have to return your equipment for servicing or must move it to another location.

12. Identify device connectors. At the back of your system, you will find a number of connectors for your printer, monitor, mouse, telephone line, and so forth (Figure 46). If the manufacturer has not identified them for you, use a marking pen to write the purpose of each connector on the back of the computer case.

13. Install your computer in an area where you can maintain the temperature and humidity. You should keep the computer in an area with a constant temperature between 60°F and 80°F. High temperatures and humidity can damage electronic components. Be careful when using space heaters, for example, as the hot, dry air they generate can cause disk problems.

14. Keep your computer area clean. Avoid eating and drinking around your computer. Also, avoid smoking. Cigarette smoke can cause damage to the floppy disk drives and floppy disk surfaces.

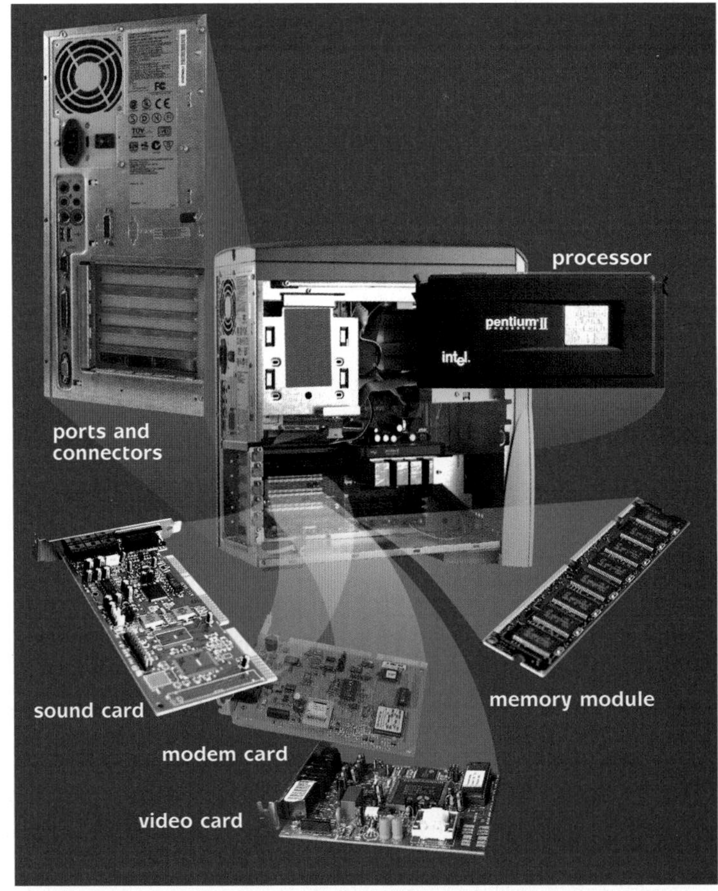

Figure 46
Inside the system unit and the connectors at the back.

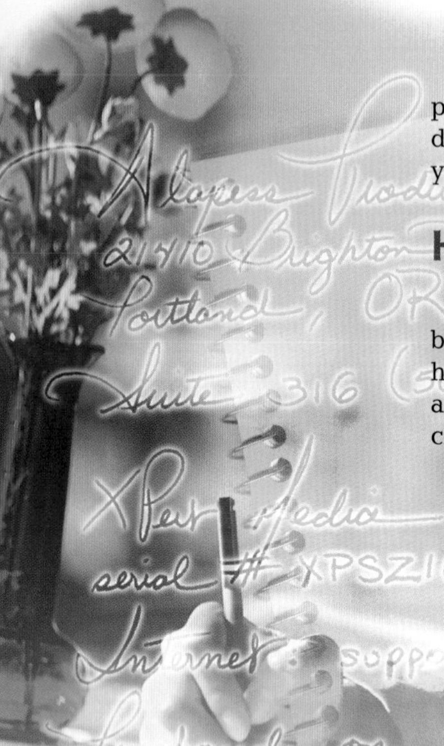

15. Check your home or renter's insurance policy. Some renter's insurance policies have limits on the amount of computer equipment they cover. Other policies do not cover computer equipment at all if it is used for business. In this instance, you may want to obtain a separate insurance policy.

How to Maintain a Personal Computer

1. Start a notebook that includes information on your system. Keep a notebook that provides a single source of information about your entire system, both hardware and software. Each time you make a change to your system, such as adding or removing hardware or software or altering system parameters, record the change in your notebook. Include the following items in your notebook.

- Vendor support numbers from your user manuals
- Serial numbers of all equipment and software
- User IDs, passwords, and nicknames for your ISP or online service, network access, Web sites, and so on
- Vendor and date of purchase for all software and equipment
- Trouble log that provides a chronological history of equipment or software problems
- Notes on any discussions with vendor support personnel

Figure 47 provides a suggested outline for the contents of your notebook.

PC OWNER'S NOTEBOOK OUTLINE

1. Vendors
   - Vendor
   - City/State
   - Product
   - Telephone #
   - URL
2. Internet and online services information
   - Service provider name
   - Logon telephone number
   - Alternate logon telephone number
   - Technical support telephone number
   - User ID
   - Password
3. Web site information
   - Web site name
   - URL
   - User ID
   - Password
   - Nickname
4. Serial numbers
   - Product
   - Manufacturer
   - Serial #
5. Purchase history
   - Date
   - Product
   - Manufacturer
   - Vendor
   - Cost
6. Software log
   - Date installed/uninstalled
7. Trouble log
   - Date
   - Time
   - Problem
   - Resolution
8. Support calls
   - Date
   - Time
   - Company
   - Contact
   - Problem
   - Comments
9. Vendor paperwork

Figure 47
To keep important information about your computer on hand and organized, use an outline such as this sample outline.

2. Before you work inside your computer, turn off the power and disconnect the equipment from the power source. Working inside your computer with the power on can affect both you and the computer adversely. Thus, you should turn off the power and disconnect the equipment from the power source before you open a computer to work inside. In addition, before you touch anything inside the computer, you should touch an unpainted metal surface such as the power supply. Doing so will help discharge any static electricity that could damage internal components.

3. Keep the area surrounding your computer dirt and dust free. Reducing the dirt and dust around your computer will reduce the need to clean the inside of your system. If dust builds up inside the computer, remove it carefully with compressed air and a small vacuum. Do not touch the components with the vacuum.

4. Back up important files and data. Use the operating system or utility program to create an emergency or rescue disk to help you restart your computer if it crashes. You also regularly should copy important data files to disks, tape, or another computer.

5. Protect your system from computer viruses. A **computer virus** is a potentially damaging computer program designed to infect other software or files by attaching itself to the software or files with which it comes in contact. Virus programs are dangerous because often they destroy or corrupt data stored on the infected computer. You can protect your computer from viruses by installing an **antivirus program**.

6. Keep your system tuned. Most operating systems include several system tools that provide basic system maintenance functions. One important system tool is the disk defragmenter. **Defragmenting** your hard disk reorganizes files so they are in contiguous (adjacent) clusters, making disk operations faster. Some programs allow you to schedule system maintenance tasks for times when you are not using your computer. If necessary, leave your computer on at night so the system can run the required maintenance programs. If your operating system does not provide the system tools, you can purchase a stand-alone utility program to perform basic system maintenance functions.

7. Learn to use system diagnostic tools. Diagnostic tools help you identify and resolve system problems, thereby helping to reduce your need for technical assistance. **Diagnostic tools** help you test system components, monitor system resources such as memory and processing power, undo changes made to system files, and more. As with basic maintenance tools, most operating systems include system diagnostic tools; you also can purchase or download many stand-alone diagnostic tools.

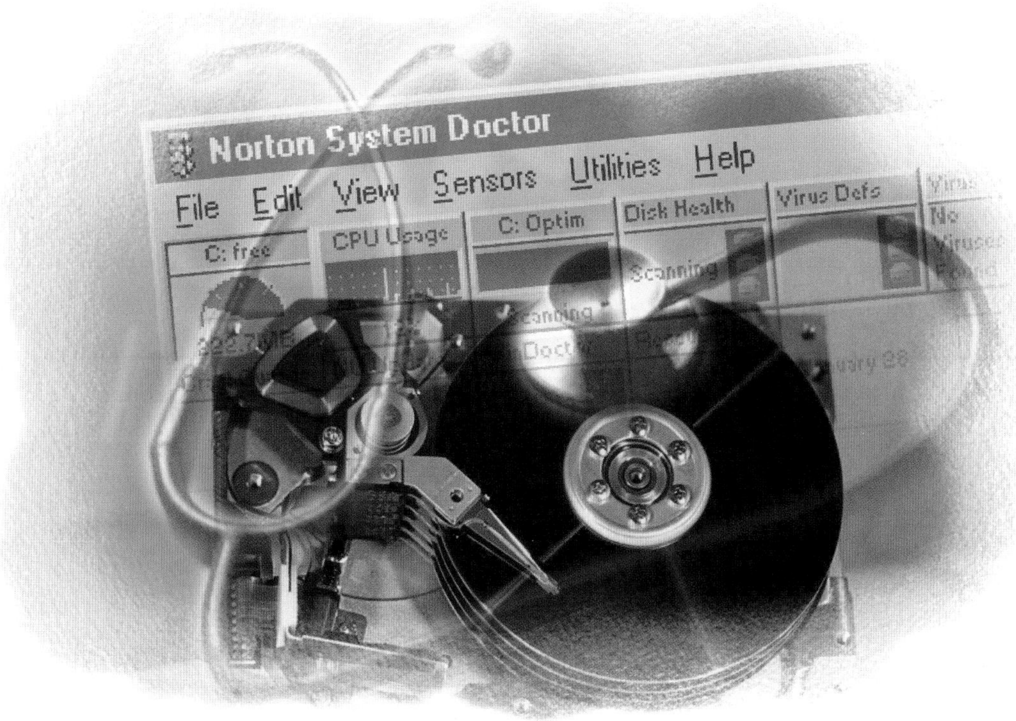

STUDENT ASSIGNMENTS

Student Assignment 1: True/False

Instructions: Circle T if the statement is true or F if the statement is false.

T F 1. A computer is an electronic device, operating under the control of instructions stored in its own memory unit, that can accept data (input), manipulate the data according to specified rules (process), produce information (output) from the processing, and store the results for future use.

T F 2. Information refers to data processed into a form that has meaning and is useful.

T F 3. A URL is a detailed set of instructions that tells a computer exactly what to do.

T F 4. A mouse is a communications device used to convert between digital and analog signals so telephone lines can carry data.

T F 5. The central processing unit contains the processor unit and memory.

T F 6. A laser printer is a nonimpact printer that provides high-quality output.

T F 7. Auxiliary storage is used to store instructions and data when they are not being used in memory.

T F 8. A floppy disk is considered to be a form of memory.

T F 9. CD-ROMs often are used for multimedia material that combines text, graphics, animation, video, and sound.

T F 10. The operating system tells the computer how to perform functions such as how to load, store, and execute an application program and how to transfer data.

T F 11. Programs such as database management, spreadsheet, and word processing software are called system software.

T F 12. The world's largest network is the World Wide Web.

T F 13. A communications network is a collection of computers and other equipment that use communications channels to share hardware, software, data, and information.

T F 14. Determining what applications you will use on your computer will help you purchase a computer that is the type and size that meets your needs.

T F 15. When purchasing a computer, consider only the price because one computer is no different from another.

Student Assignment 2: Multiple Choice

Instructions: Circle the correct response.

1. The four operations performed by a computer include __________.

   a. input, control, output, and storage
   b. interface, processing, output, and memory
   c. input, output, processing, and storage
   d. input, logical/rational, arithmetic, and output

2. A handheld input device that controls the insertion point location is ________.

   a. the keyboard
   b. a mouse
   c. a modem
   d. the CRT

3. A DVD-ROM is a type of __________.

   a. memory
   b. auxiliary storage
   c. communications equipment
   d. system software

4. An operating system is considered part of __________.
   a. word processing software
   b. database software
   c. system software
   d. spreadsheet software

5. The type of application software most commonly used to create and print documents is __________.
   a. word processing
   b. electronic spreadsheet
   c. database
   d. browser

Student Assignment 3: Visiting WEB INFO Sites

Instructions: Start your computer and then your browser. Visit each of the fourteen sites listed in the WEB INFOs found in the margins. The first WEB INFO is on page COM4 and the last WEB INFO is on page COM17. Print the main Web page for each of the fourteen sites you visit and hand them in to your instructor.

Student Assignment 4: Using the Shelly Cashman Series Web Guide

Instructions: Start you computer and then your browser. Enter the URL www.scsite.com/IC/webinfo.htm in the Address text box. Click Shelly Cashman Series Web Guide. Click Computers and Computing. Take a tour of the Computer Museum. When you are finished, close the window and then prepare a brief one-page report on your tour.

Student Assignment 5: Comparing Personal Computer Advertisements

Instructions: Obtain a copy of a recent computer magazine and review the advertisements for desktop personal computers and laptops. Compare ads for the least and most expensive desktop computers and the least and most expensive laptops you can find. Discuss the differences.

Student Assignment 6: Evaluating Online Information Services

Instructions: The Microsoft Network and America Online both offer consumer-oriented online information services. Contact each company (see Figure 37 on page COM22) and request each to send you information on the specific services it offers. Try to talk to someone who actually uses one or both of the services. Discuss how each service is priced and the differences between the two online services.

Student Assignment 7: Visiting Local Computer Retail Stores

Instructions: Visit local computer retail stores and compare the various types of computers and support equipment available. Ask about warranties, repair services, hardware setup, training, and related issues. Report on the knowledge of the sales staff assisting you and their willingness to answer your questions. Visit two of the new computer mail-order Web sites (Figure 34 on page COM20) and two used computer mail-order Web sites (Figure 35 on page COM20). Use the computer system described in Figure 36 on page COM21 to compare prices. List the four mail-order Web sites in sequence by cost.

Student Assignment 8: Understanding the Y2K Problem

Instructions: The computer-related Y2K (year 2000) problem has been called the most complex technological problem in history. Over the past 50 years, most governmental agencies and industries stored dates in computers using only the last two digits of the year. This method of storage works fine until a new century comes along. Then the last two digits of a new-century year are less then a year from the previous century. This can cause computers that use dates to make the wrong decision, and thus carry out an unexpected action. Start your computer and browser. Enter the URL www.scsite.com/cobol/index.htm in the Address text box. When the Web page displays, visit three links and write a one-page report on the Y2K problem.

INDEX

PHOTO CREDITS

Figure 1 Courtesy of Corel Professional Photos CD-ROM Image usage, KTP Metatools, Photo Disc, Inc., SoftKey; *Figure 2* Courtesy of Photo Disc, Inc.; *Figure 3* Courtesy of Scott Goodwin Photography; *Figure 8* Courtesy of Intel Corporation, Photo Disc, Inc.; *Figure 9* Courtesy of Scott Goodwin Photography; *Figure 10* Courtesy of Eastman Kodak Company; *Figure 14* Courtesy of Gateway 2000 Inc.; *Figure 15* Courtesy of NEC Technologies, Inc.; *Figure 16* Courtesy of Casino,Inc.; *Figure 17* Courtesy of Scott Goodwin Photography; *Figure 18* Courtesy of Scott Goodwin Photography; *Figure 20* Courtesy of Seagate Technology; *Figure 22* Courtesy of Pioneer Electronics; *Figure 39* Courtesy of International Business Machines; *Figure 40* Courtesy of Toshiba America, Inc.; *Figure 41* Courtesy of Xircom Corporation; *Figure 42* Courtesy of In Focus Corporation. *Background images: COM1* Courtesy of Photo Disc, Inc.; *COM2* Courtesy of Photo Disc, Inc.; *COM5* Courtesy of Photo Disc, Inc.; *COM9* Courtesy of Corel Professional Photos CD-ROM Image usage, Photo Disc, Inc.; *COM10* Courtesy of Digital Stock, Photo Disc, Inc.; *COM14* Courtesy of Photo Disc, Inc.; *COM15* Courtesy of Photo Disc, Inc.; *COM16* Courtesy of Digital Stock; *COM17* Courtesy of Corel Professional Photos CD-ROM Image usage; *COM18* Courtesy of Photo Disc, Inc.; *COM20* Courtesy of Corel Professional Photos CD-ROM Image usage; *COM21* Courtesy of Photo Disc, Inc., *COM22* Courtesy of Photo Disc, Inc.; Courtesy of Corel Professional Photos CD-ROM Image usage; *COM24* Courtesy of Photo Disc, Inc.; *COM27* Courtesy of Photo Disc, Inc.; *COM28* Courtesy of Corbis Images; *COM29* Courtesy of Corel Professional Photos CD-ROM Image usage, Photo Disc, Inc.

PROJECT ONE

Fundamentals of Using Windows 95

Objectives:

You will have mastered the material in this project when you can:

- Describe Microsoft Windows 95
- Describe a user interface
- Identify the objects on the Microsoft Windows 95 desktop
- Perform the basic mouse operations: point, click, right-click, double-click, drag, and right-drag
- Open a Windows 95 window
- Maximize, minimize, and restore a Windows 95 window
- Close a Windows 95 window
- Resize a window
- Scroll in a window
- Move a window on the Windows 95 desktop
- Understand keyboard shortcut notation
- Start an application program
- Create a written document
- Save a document on disk
- Print a document
- Close an application program
- Modify a document stored on disk
- Use Windows 95 Help
- Shut down Windows 95

PROJECT TWO

Using Windows Explorer

Objectives:

You will have mastered the material in this project when you can:

- Start Windows Explorer
- Understand the elements of the Exploring – My Computer window
- Display the contents of a folder
- Expand and collapse a folder
- Change the view
- Select and copy one file or a group of files
- Create, rename, and delete a folder
- Rename and delete a file

A $14 Billion Mistake

Digital Research officials would not yield to IBM's demands

Have you ever missed a meeting you should have attended but something else was more important? Did you lose $14 billion dollars because you were absent? Gary Kildall might have.

In the 1970s, Kildall's company, Digital Research, had developed an operating system called CP/M that was used on most microcomputers except the Apple II. Kildall was a leader in the microcomputer software business. Then, in 1980, IBM came calling.

Having decided to build a personal computer, IBM approached Bill Gates, president of a small company called Microsoft, in Redmond, Washington, to create the operating system. Gates demurred, suggesting IBM contact Kildall.

MICROSOFT

MS-DOS

Bill Gates

SEATTLE COMPUTER PRODUCTS

When IBM arrived for the meeting in Pacific Grove, California, Kildall was off flying his airplane. The reasons are not entirely clear. Some say Kildall was a free spirit and not inclined to do business with the monolithic IBM. Kildall claimed he was flying to another important meeting.

Without Kildall at the meeting, IBM insisted on knowing everything about CP/M while disclosing nothing about its new computer. Fearing IBM would steal their secrets, Digital Research officials would not yield to IBM's demands. Rebuffed, IBM scurried back to Gates.

Sensing an opportunity, Gates agreed to provide an operating system to IBM even though he had no idea how. It just so happened, however, that a small company named Seattle Computer Products, almost next door to Microsoft, was writing an operating system called QDOS v0.110 (QDOS stood for Quick and Dirty Operating System).

Gates learned of QDOS and approached Seattle Computer Products to ask if the operating system was for sale. For a few favors and a little money, Microsoft, in December 1980, acquired non-exclusive rights to QDOS. Later, Microsoft acquired all rights and renamed the operating system MS-DOS. Seattle Computer Products received about $1 million.

Microsoft made substantial changes to MS-DOS and when IBM announced its personal computer in August 1981, MS-DOS was the operating system. The IBM machine was an instant hit. Microsoft sold millions of copies of MS-DOS and grew to be the largest software company in the world. Bill Gates became the world's richest man, with assets in excess of $14 billion dollars.

And Gary Kildall? He continued to develop software at Digital Research. Eventually, Digital Research was sold to Novell, Inc. In the summer of 1994, Kildall died. He left a legacy as an early pioneer who made a significant contribution to microcomputing, but perhaps his most memorable act was missing a meeting.

QDOS

```
Enter today's date (m-d-y): 8-4-1981

The IBM Personal Computer DOS
Version 1.00 (C)Copyright IBM Corp 1981

A>
```

Courtesy of Tim Paterson,
reprinted by permission of Microsoft Corporation.

The Microsoft Disk Operating System, or MS-DOS, was shipped as PC-DOS on the original IBM Personal Computer and later with many IBM compatible machines. Like other operating systems, MS-DOS oversees all the functions of a computer. Various upgrades to MS-DOS and further product refinements led to the release of Windows, an operating system that uses a graphical user interface. Microsoft's current version of Windows, released in August of 1995, is called Windows 95.

CP/M GARY KILDALL IBM DIGITAL RESEARCH

Microsoft sold millions of copies of MS-DOS and grew to be the largest software company in the world

Microsoft
Windows 95

Fundamentals of Using Windows 95

Case Perspective

Need: Each day millions of Windows 95 users turn on their computers, whether at home, in the office, at school, on an airplane, or at the beach. When the computer starts, the first image on the monitor is the Windows 95 desktop. If these users did not know how to start application programs from the desktop, manipulate files and images on the desktop, and preserve the work accomplished, their computers would be useless. You have just acquired a computer containing Windows 95. Your task is to learn the basics of Windows 95 so your computer will be useful to you.

Introduction

An **operating system** is the set of computer instructions, called a computer program, that controls the allocation of computer hardware such as memory, disk devices, printers, and CD-ROM drives, and provides the capability for you to communicate with your computer. The most popular and widely used operating system for personal computers is **Microsoft Windows. Microsoft Windows 95** (called Windows 95 for the rest of this book), the newest version of Microsoft Windows, allows you to easily communicate with and control your computer. Windows 95 is easier to use and more efficient than previous versions of Windows and can be customized to fit individual needs. Windows 95 simplifies the process of working with documents and applications, transferring data between documents, and organizing the manner in which you interact with your computer.

In Project 1, you will learn about Windows 95 and how to use the Windows 95 user interface.

Microsoft Windows 95

Microsoft Windows 95 is an operating system that performs every function necessary for you to communicate with and use your computer. Unlike previous versions of Windows, no associated operating system is required. Windows 95 is called a **32-bit operating system** because it uses 32 bits for addressing and other purposes, which means the operating system can address more than four gigabytes of RAM and perform tasks faster than older operating systems.

Windows 95 is designed to be compatible with all existing **application programs**, which are programs that perform an application-related function such as word processing. To use the application programs that can be executed under Windows 95, you must know about the Windows 95 user interface.

What Is a User Interface?

A **user interface** is the combination of hardware and software that you use to communicate with and control your computer. Through the user interface, you are able to make selections on your computer, request information from your computer, and respond to messages displayed by your computer. Thus, a user interface provides the means for dialogue between you and your computer.

Hardware and software together form the user interface. Among the hardware devices associated with a user interface are the monitor, keyboard, and mouse (Figure 1-1). The monitor displays messages and provides information. You respond by entering data in the form of a command or other response using the keyboard or mouse. Among the responses available to you are responses that specify what application program to run, what document to open, when to print, and where to store data for future use.

The computer software associated with the user interface consists of the programs that engage you in dialogue (Figure 1-1). The computer software determines the messages you receive, the manner in which you should respond, and the actions that occur based on your responses.

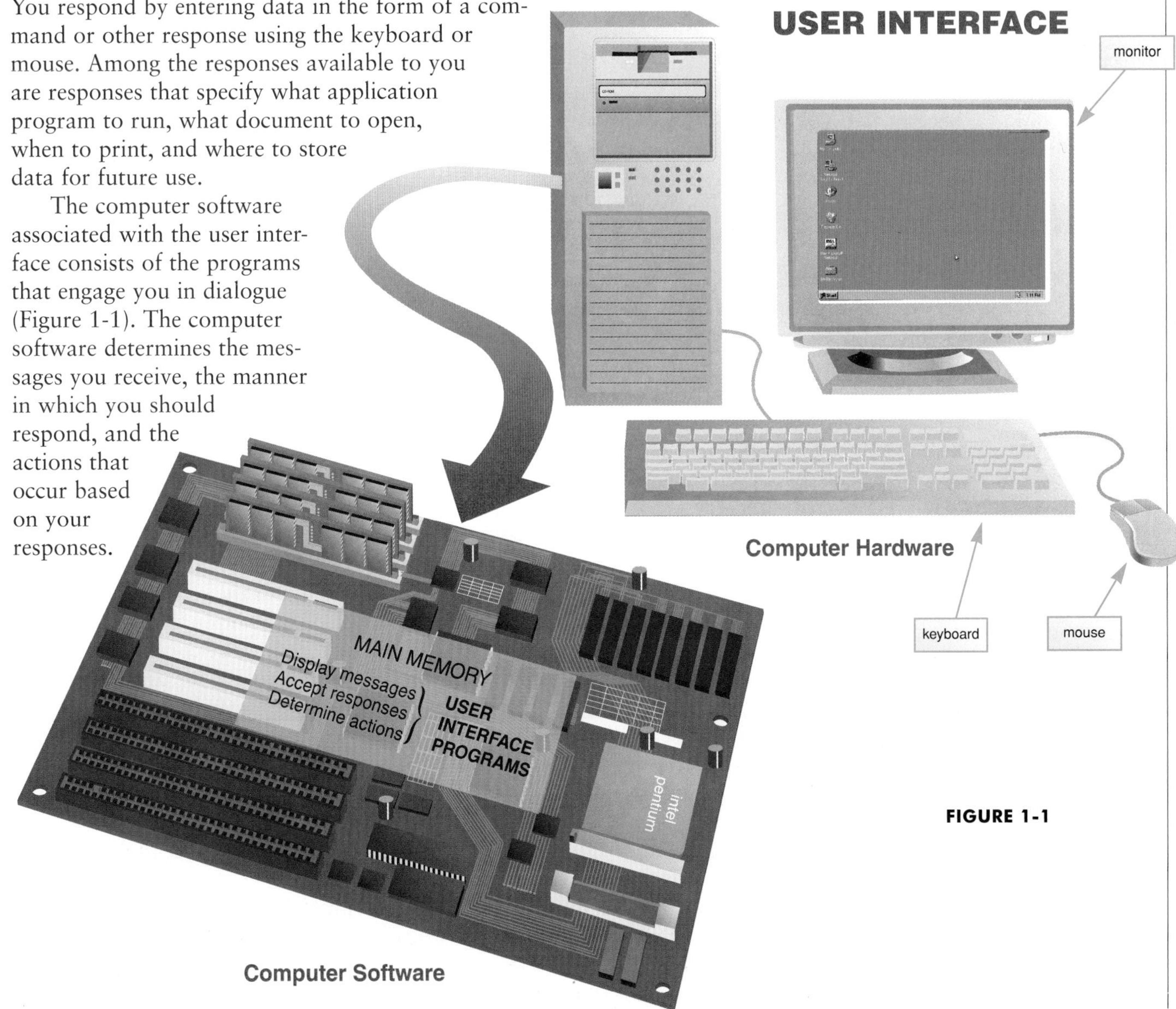

FIGURE 1-1

The goal of an effective user interface is to be **user friendly**, meaning that the software can be used easily by individuals with limited training. Research studies have indicated that the use of graphics can play an important role in aiding users to interact effectively with a computer. A **graphical user interface**, or **GUI** (pronounced gooey), is a user interface that displays graphics in addition to text when it communicates with the user.

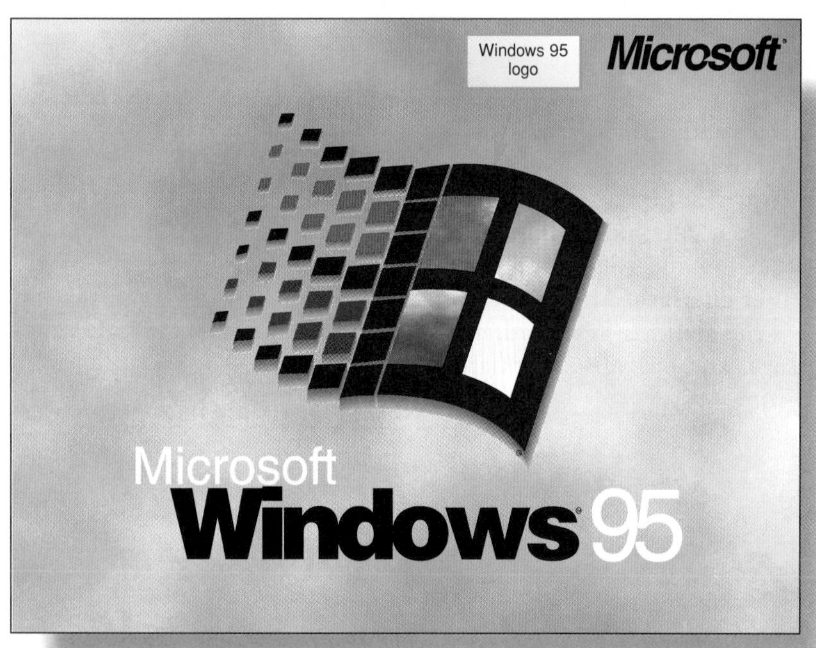

FIGURE 1-2

The Windows 95 graphical user interface was carefully designed to be easier to set up, simpler to learn, and faster and more powerful than previous versions of Microsoft Windows.

Starting Microsoft Windows 95

When you turn on your computer, an introductory screen consisting of the Windows 95 logo and the Microsoft Windows 95 name displays on a blue sky and clouds background (Figure 1-2).

The screen clears and several items display on a background called the **desktop**. The default color of the desktop background is green, but your computer may display a different color. Your screen might display as shown in Figure 1-3. It also might display without the Welcome screen shown in Figure 1-3.

The items on the desktop in Figure 1-3 include six icons and their names on the left of the desktop, the Welcome screen in the center of the desktop, and the taskbar at the bottom of the desktop. Through the use of the six **icons**, you can view the contents of your computer (**My Computer**), work with other computers connected to your computer (**Network Neighborhood**), receive and send electronic faxes and mail (e-mail) from or to other computers (**Inbox**), discard unneeded objects (**Recycle Bin**), connect to the Microsoft online service (**The Microsoft Network**), and transfer data to and from a portable computer (**My Briefcase**). Your computer's desktop might contain more, fewer, or some different icons because the desktop of your computer can be customized.

More *About* **the Windows 95 Interface**

Thousands of hours were spent developing the Windows 95 graphical user interface. Of tremendous importance in the development were Microsoft's usability labs, where everyone from raw beginners to experts interacted with many different versions of the interface. The taskbar and other significant features of the interface emerged from the experiences in these labs.

The Welcome screen that might display on your desktop is shown in Figure 1-3. The **title bar**, which is dark blue in color at the top of the screen, identifies the name of the screen (Welcome) and contains the Close button, which can be used to close the Welcome screen. In the Welcome screen, a welcome message (Welcome to Windows 95) displays together with a helpful tip for using Windows 95, a check box containing a check mark, and several command buttons. The **check box** represents an option to display the Welcome screen each time Windows 95 starts that you can turn on or turn off. The **command buttons** allow you to perform different operations such as displaying the next tip or closing the screen.

Below the screen is the mouse pointer. On the desktop, the **mouse pointer** is the shape of a block arrow. The mouse pointer allows you to point to items on the desktop.

The **taskbar** at the bottom of the screen in Figure 1-3 contains the Start button, the Welcome button, and the Tray status area. The **Start button** provides an entry point to begin using the features of Windows 95, the Welcome button indicates the Welcome screen is open on the desktop, and the current time (6:06 PM) displays in the Tray status area.

Nearly every item on the Windows 95 desktop is considered an object. Even the desktop itself is an object. Every **object** has properties. The **properties** of an object are unique to that specific object and may affect what can be done to the object or what the object does. For example, the properties of an object may be the color of the object, such as the color of the desktop.

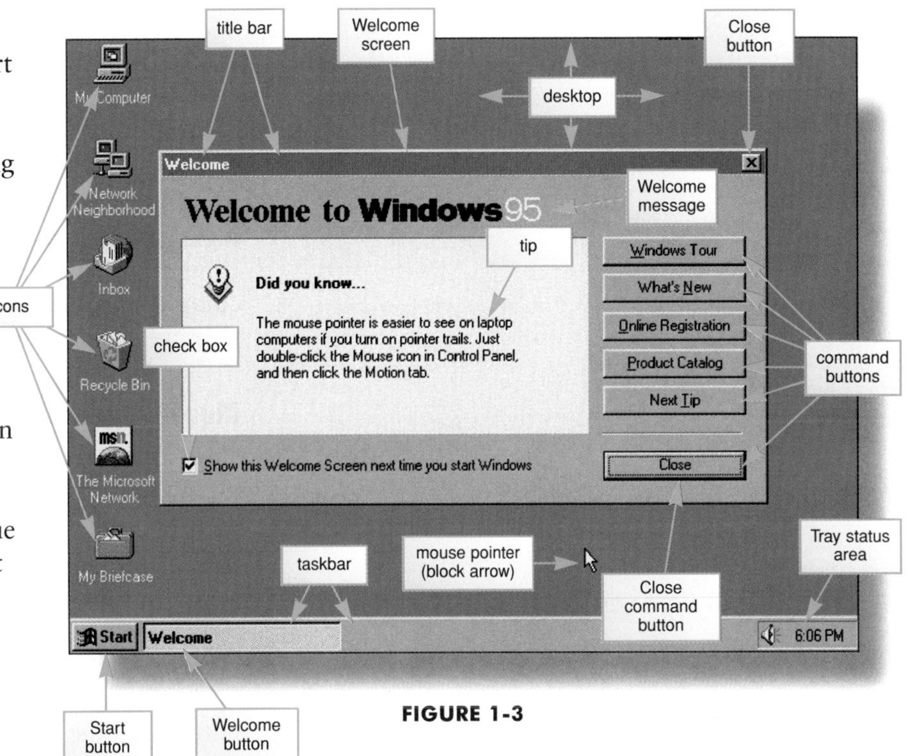

FIGURE 1-3

Closing the Welcome Screen

As noted, the Welcome screen might display when you start Windows 95. If the Welcome screen does display on the desktop, normally you should close it prior to beginning any other operations using Windows 95. To close the Welcome screen, complete the following step.

TO CLOSE THE WELCOME SCREEN

Step 1: Press the ESC key on the keyboard as shown in Figure 1-4.

The Welcome screen closes.

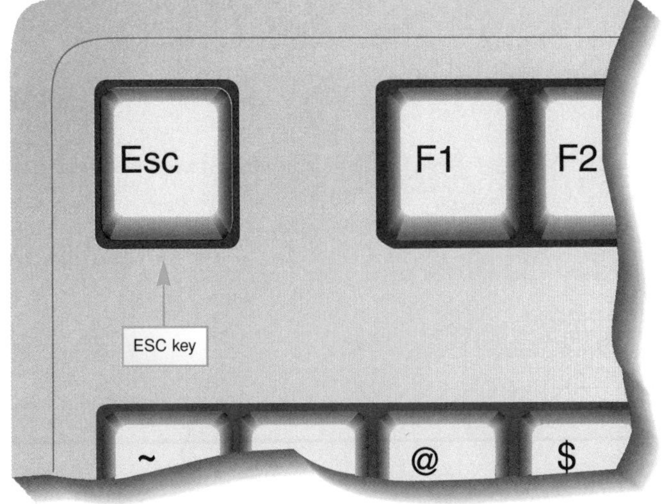

FIGURE 1-4

The Desktop as a Work Area

The Windows 95 desktop and the objects on the desktop were designed to emulate a work area in an office or at home. The Windows desktop may be thought of as an electronic version of the top of your desk. You can move objects around on the desktop, look at them and then put them aside, and so on. In Project 1, you will learn how to interact with and communicate with the Windows 95 desktop.

More About the Mouse

The mouse, though invented in the 1960's, was not widely used until the Apple Macintosh computer became available in 1984. Even then, some high-brows called mouse users "wimps." Today, the mouse is an indispensable tool for every computer user.

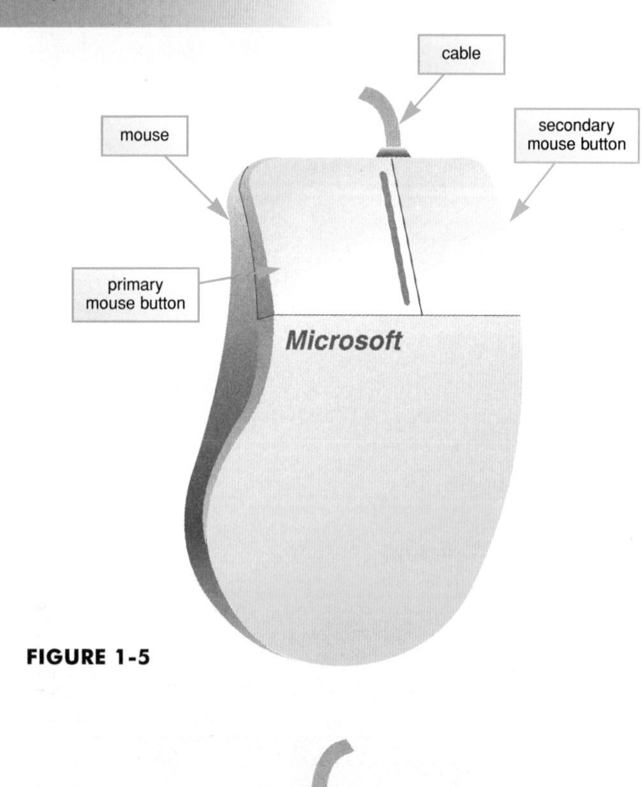

FIGURE 1-5

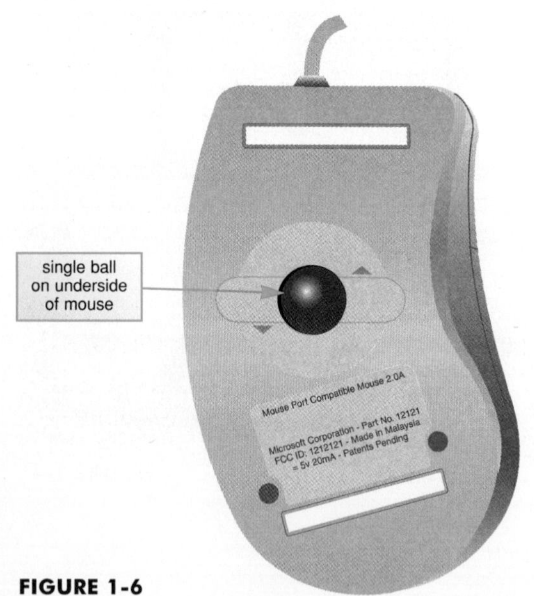

FIGURE 1-6

Communicating with Microsoft Windows 95

The Windows 95 interface provides the means for dialogue between you and your computer. Part of this dialogue involves your requesting information from your computer and responding to messages displayed by your computer. You can request information and respond to messages using either a mouse or a keyboard.

Mouse Operations

A **mouse** is a pointing device used with Windows 95 that is attached to the computer by a cable. It contains two buttons — the primary mouse button and the secondary mouse button (Figure 1-5). The **primary mouse button** is typically the left mouse button and the **secondary mouse button** is typically the right mouse button although Windows 95 allows you to switch them. In this book, the left mouse button is the primary mouse button and the right mouse button is the secondary mouse button.

Using the mouse, you can perform the following operations: (1) point; (2) click; (3) right-click; (4) double-click; (5) drag; and (6) right-drag. These operations are demonstrated on the following pages.

Point and Click

Point means you move the mouse across a flat surface until the mouse pointer rests on the item of choice on the desktop. As you move the mouse across a flat surface, the movement of a ball on the underside of the mouse (Figure 1-6) is electronically sensed, and the mouse pointer moves across the desktop in the same direction.

Click means you press and release the primary mouse button, which in this book is the left mouse button. In most cases, you must point to an item before you click. To become acquainted with the use of a mouse, perform the following steps to point to and click various objects on the desktop.

Steps To Point and Click

1 **Point to the Start button on the taskbar by moving the mouse across a flat surface until the mouse pointer rests on the Start button.**

The mouse pointer points to the Start button and a ***ToolTip*** *(Click here to begin) displays (Figure 1-7). The ToolTip, which provides instructions, displays on the desktop for approximately five seconds.*

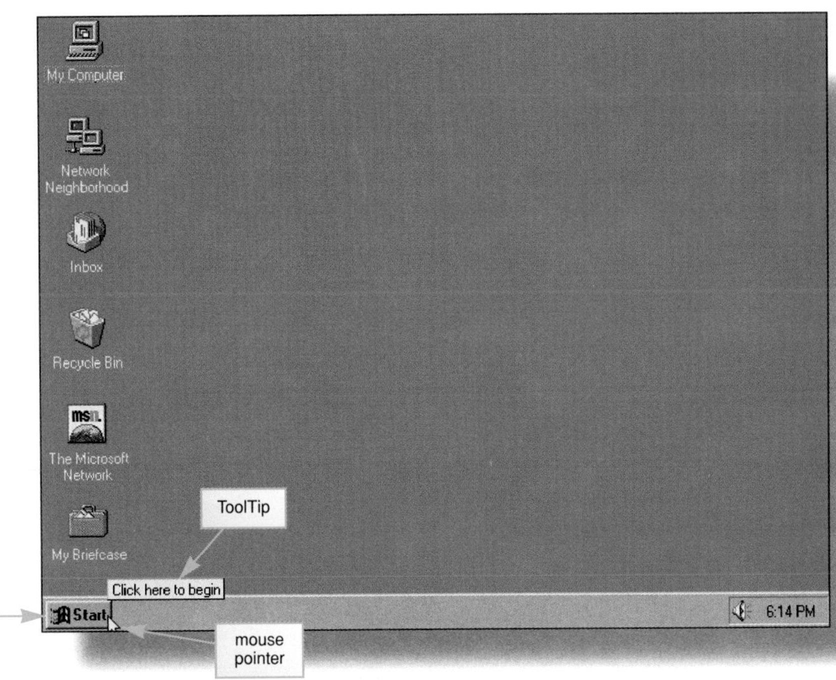

FIGURE 1-7

2 **Click the Start button on the taskbar by pressing and releasing the left mouse button.**

Windows 95 opens the ***Start menu*** *and indents the Start button (Figure 1-8). A* ***menu*** *is a list of related commands. Nine commands display on the Start menu. A* ***command*** *directs Windows 95 to perform a specific action such as opening another menu or shutting down the operating system. Each command consists of an icon and a command name. Some commands (Run and Shut Down) are followed by an* ***ellipsis*** *(...) to indicate Windows 95 requires more information before executing the command. Other commands (Programs, Documents, Settings, and Find) are followed by a* ***right arrow****. A right arrow indicates that pointing to the command will open a submenu containing more commands.*

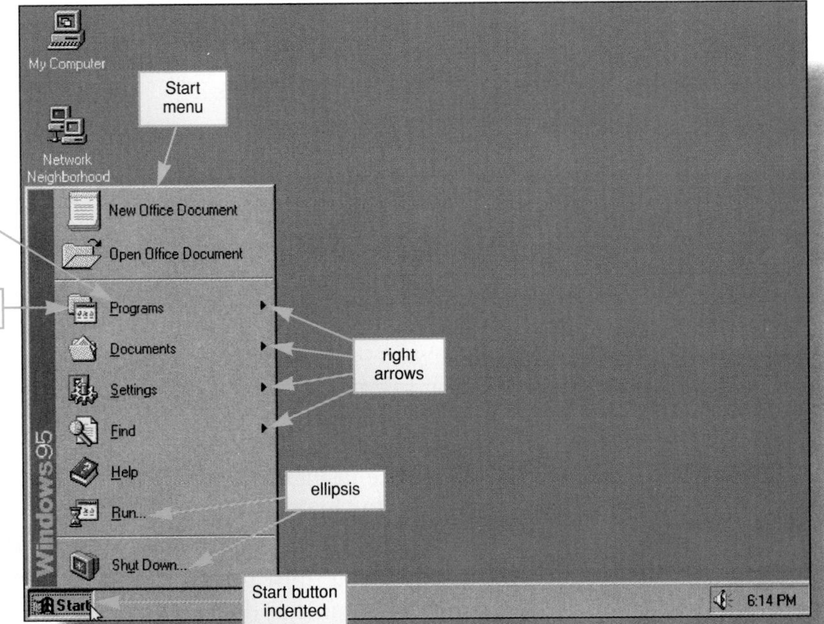

FIGURE 1-8

3 **Point to Programs on the Start menu.**

When you point to Programs, Windows 95 highlights the Programs command on the Start menu and opens the ***Programs submenu*** *(Figure 1-9). A* ***submenu*** *is a menu that displays when you point to a command that is followed by a right arrow.*

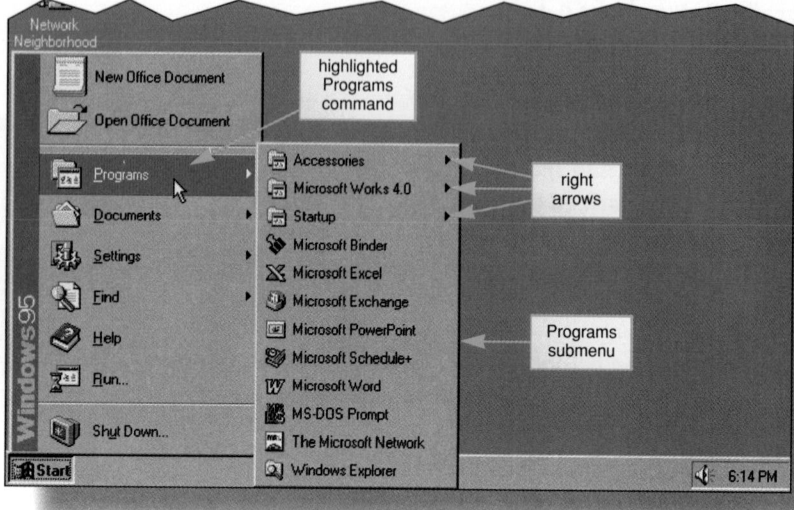

FIGURE 1-9

4 **Point to an open area of the desktop and then click the open area of the desktop.**

Windows 95 closes the Start menu and the Programs submenu (Figure 1-10). The mouse pointer points to the desktop. To close a menu anytime, click anywhere on the desktop except the menu itself. The Start button is not indented.

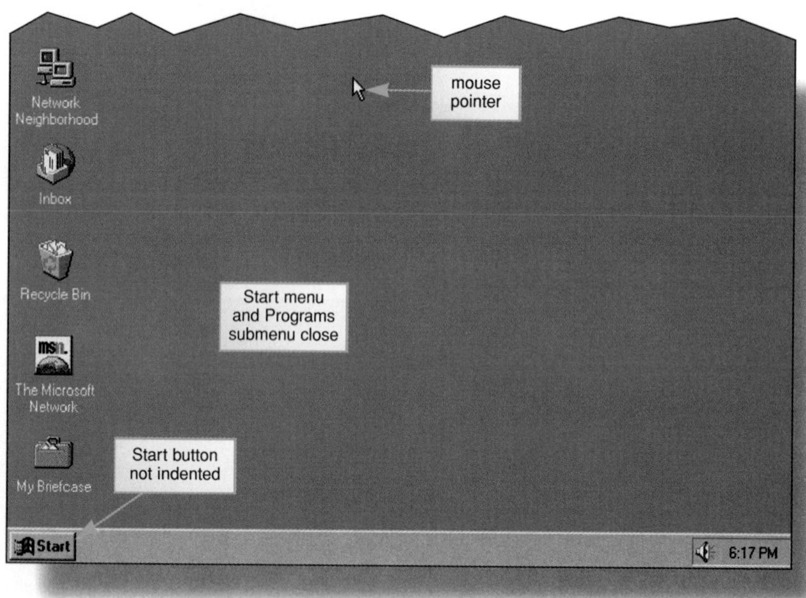

FIGURE 1-10

More ***About*** **Buttons**

Buttons on the desktop and in programs are in integral part of Windows 95. When you point to them, their function displays in a ToolTip. When you click them, they appear to indent on the screen to mimic what would happen if you pushed an actual button. All buttons in Windows 95 behave in the same manner.

Notice in Figure 1-9 that whenever you point to a command on a menu, the command is highlighted.

When you click an object such as the Start button in Figure 1-8 on the previous page, you must point to the object before you click. In the steps that follow, the instruction that directs you to point to a particular item and then click is, Click the particular item. For example, Click the Start button, means point to the Start button and then click.

Right-Click

Right-click means you press and release the secondary mouse button, which in this book is the right mouse button. As when you use the primary mouse button, normally you will point to an object on the screen prior to right-clicking. Perform the following steps to right-click the desktop.

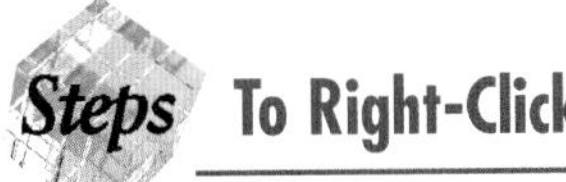

To Right-Click

1 Point to an open area on the desktop and press and release the right mouse button.

Windows 95 displays a context-sensitive menu containing six commands (Figure 1-11). Right-clicking an object, such as the desktop, opens a ***context-sensitive menu*** *(also referred to as a* ***shortcut menu*** *or an* ***object menu****) that contains a set of commands specifically for use with that object. The Paste command in Figure 1-11 is dimmed, meaning that command cannot be used at the current time.*

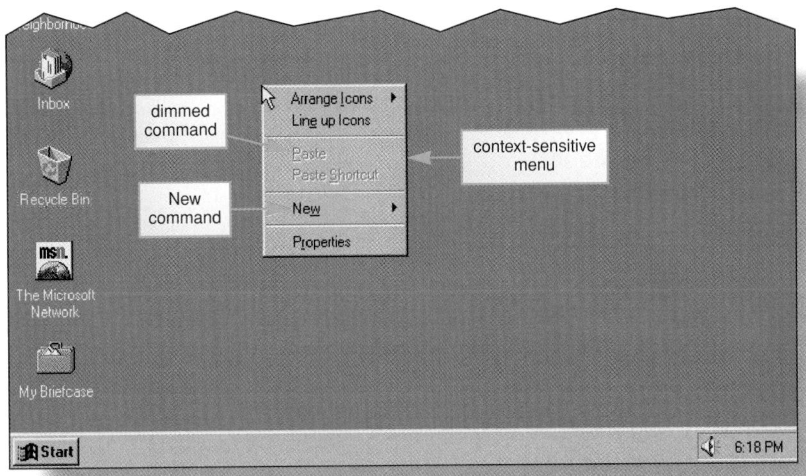

FIGURE 1-11

2 Point to New on the context-sensitive menu.

When you move the mouse pointer to the New command, Windows 95 highlights the New command and opens the ***New submenu*** *(Figure 1-12). The New submenu contains a variety of commands. The number of commands and the actual commands that display on your computer might be different.*

3 Point to an open area of the desktop and click the open area to remove the context-sensitive menu and the New submenu.

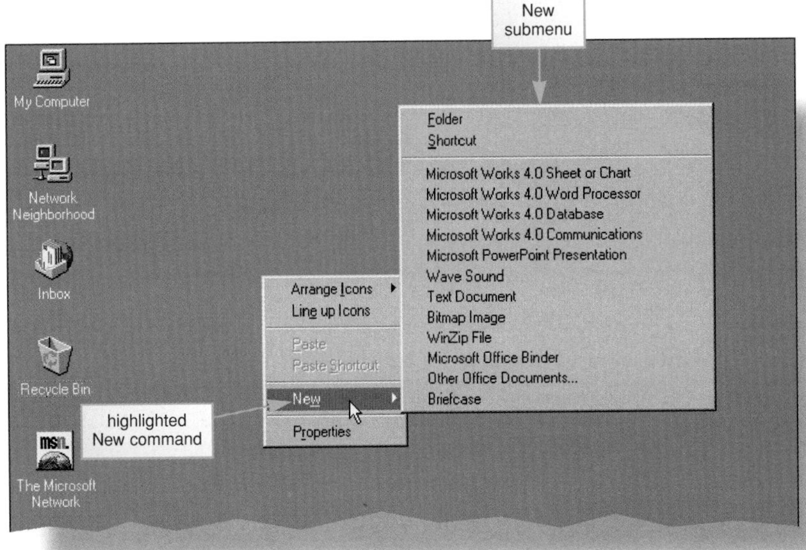

FIGURE 1-12

Whenever you right-click an object, a context-sensitive, or shortcut, menu will display. As you will see, the use of shortcut menus speeds up your work and adds flexibility to your interface with the computer.

Double-Click

Double-click means you quickly press and release the left mouse button twice without moving the mouse. In most cases, you must point to an item before you double-click. Perform the step on the next page to open the My Computer window on the desktop by double-clicking the My Computer icon.

Steps To Open a Window by Double-Clicking

1 Point to the My Computer icon on the desktop and double-click by quickly pressing and releasing the left mouse button twice without moving the mouse.

*Windows 95 opens the My Computer window and adds the My Computer button to the taskbar (Figure 1-13). The My Computer window is the active window. The **active window** is the window currently being used. Whenever you double-click an object that can be opened, Windows 95 will open the object; and the open object will be identified by a button on the taskbar. The active window is identified by the indented button.*

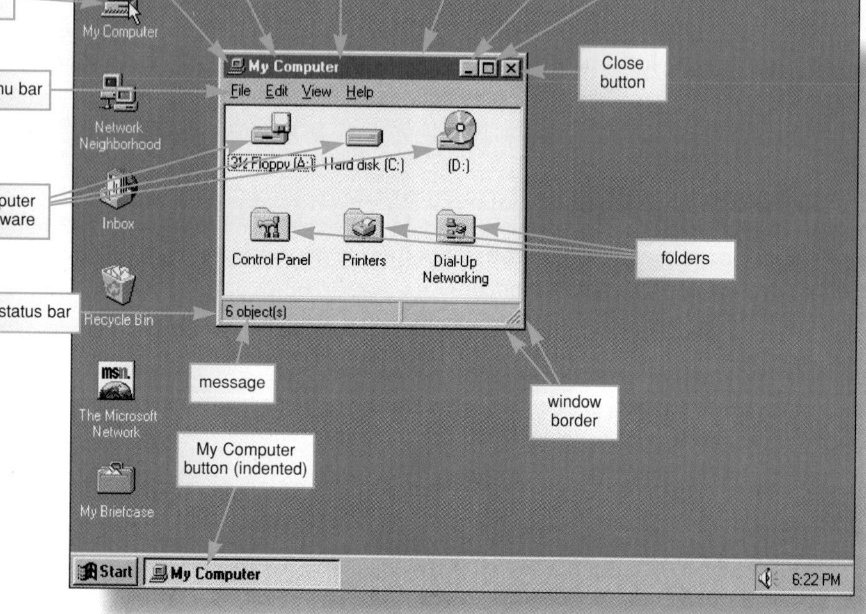

FIGURE 1-13

More About Double-Clicking

Double-clicking is the most difficult mouse skill to learn. Many people have a tendency to move the mouse before they click a second time, even when they do not want to move the mouse. You should find, however, that with a little practice double-clicking becomes quite natural.

More About My Computer

The trade press and media have poked fun at the icon name, My Computer. One wag said no one should use Windows 95 for more than five minutes without changing the name (which is easily done). Microsoft responds that in its usability labs, My Computer was the most easily understood name by beginning computer users.

My Computer Window

The thin line, or **window border**, surrounding the My Computer window in Figure 1-13 determines its shape and size. The **title bar** at the top of the window contains a small icon that is the same as the icon on the desktop and the **window title** (My Computer) that identifies the window. The color of the title bar (dark blue) and the indented My Computer button on the taskbar indicate the My Computer window is the active window. The color of the active window on your computer might be different from the dark blue color.

Clicking the icon at the left on the title bar will open the Control menu, which contains commands to carry out actions associated with the My Computer window. At the right on the title bar are three buttons, the Minimize button, the Maximize button, and the Close button, that can be used to specify the size of the window and can close the window.

The **menu bar**, a horizontal bar below the title bar of a window (see Figure 1-13), contains a list of menu names for the My Computer window: File, Edit, View, and Help. One letter in each menu name is underlined. You can open a menu by clicking the menu name on the menu bar.

Six icons display in the My Computer window. A name below each icon identifies the icon. The three icons in the top row represent a 3½ floppy disk drive (3½ Floppy [A:]), a hard disk drive (Hard disk [C:]), and a CD-ROM drive ([D:]). The contents of the My Computer window on your computer might be different than shown in Figure 1-13.

The icons in the second row are folders. A **folder** is an object created to contain related documents, applications, and other folders. A folder in Windows 95 contains items in much the same way a folder on your desk contains items. If you double-click a folder, the items within the folder display in a window. A message at the left of the **status bar** located at the bottom of the window indicates the window contains six objects (see Figure 1-13).

Minimize Button

Two buttons on the title bar of a window, the Minimize button and the Maximize button, allow you to control the way a window displays or does not display on the desktop. When you click the **Minimize button** (see Figure 1-13), the My Computer window no longer displays on the desktop and the indented My Computer button on the taskbar changes to a non-indented button. A minimized window or application program is still open but it does not display on the screen. To minimize and then redisplay the My Computer window, complete the following steps.

More *About* **Minimizing Windows**

Window management on the Windows 95 desktop is important in order to keep the desktop uncluttered. You will find yourself frequently minimizing windows, and then later reopening them with a click of a button on the taskbar.

Steps To Minimize and Redisplay a Window

1 Point to the Minimize button on the title bar of the My Computer window.

The mouse pointer points to the Minimize button on the My Computer window title bar (Figure 1-14). The My Computer button on the taskbar is indented.

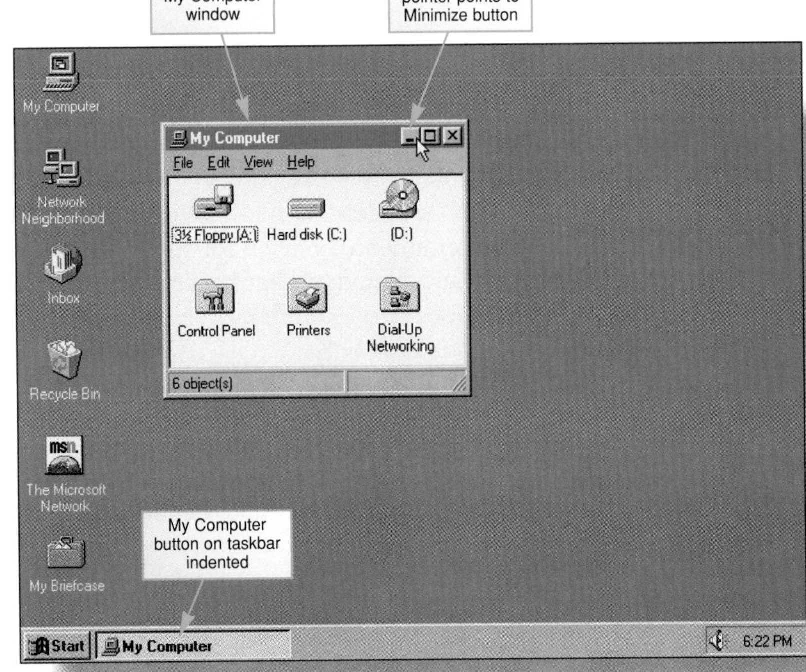

FIGURE 1-14

2 Click the Minimize button.

The My Computer window disappears from the desktop and the My Computer button on the taskbar changes to a non-indented button (Figure 1-15).

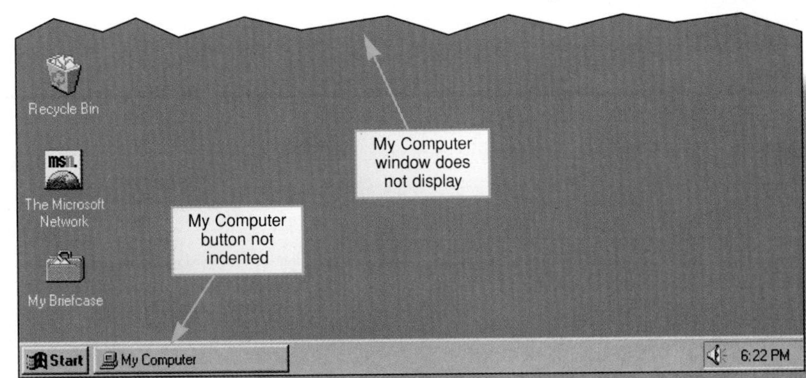

FIGURE 1-15

3 **Click the My Computer button on the taskbar.**

The My Computer window displays on the desktop in the same place and size as before it was minimized (Figure 1-16). In addition, the My Computer window is the active window because it contains the dark blue title bar and the My Computer button on the taskbar is indented.

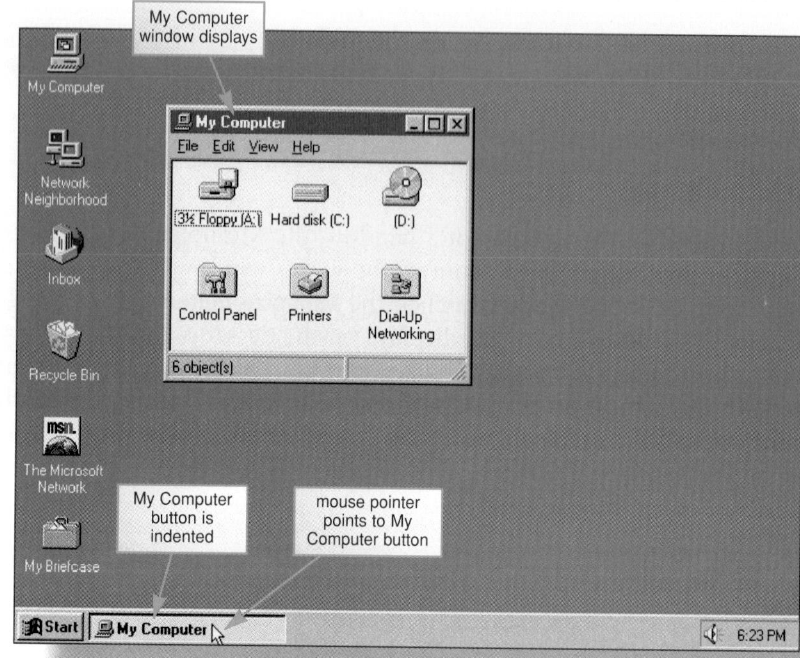

FIGURE 1-16

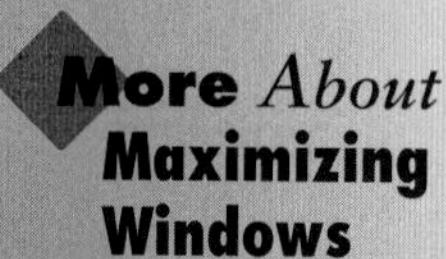

More About Maximizing Windows

Many application programs run in a maximized window by default. Often you will find that you want to work with maximized windows.

Whenever a window is minimized, it does not display on the desktop but a non-indented button for the window does display on the taskbar. Whenever you want a window that has been minimized to display and be the active window, click the window's button on the taskbar.

Maximize and Restore Buttons

The **Maximize button** maximizes a window so the window fills the entire screen, making it easier to see the contents of the window. When a window is maximized, the **Restore button** replaces the Maximize button on the title bar. Clicking the Restore button will return the window to its size before maximizing. To maximize and restore the My Computer window, complete the following steps.

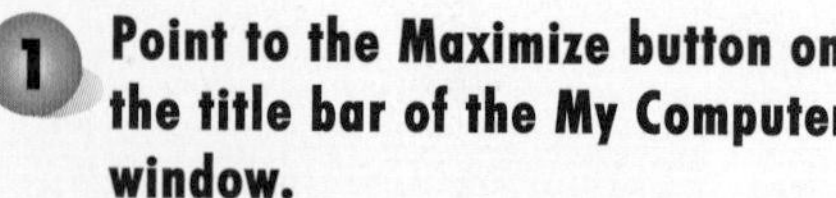

Steps To Maximize and Restore a Window

1 **Point to the Maximize button on the title bar of the My Computer window.**

The mouse pointer points to the Maximize button on the title bar of the My Computer window (Figure 1-17).

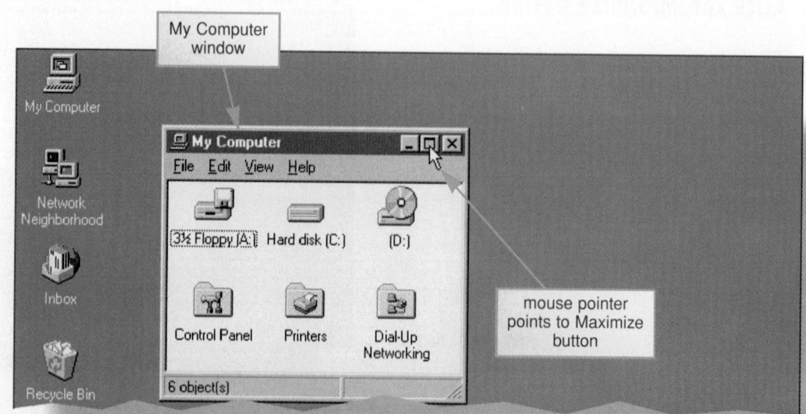

FIGURE 1-17

2 **Click the Maximize button.**

The My Computer window expands so it and the taskbar fill the entire screen (Figure 1-18). The Restore button replaces the Maximize button. The My Computer button on the taskbar does not change. The My Computer window is still the active window.

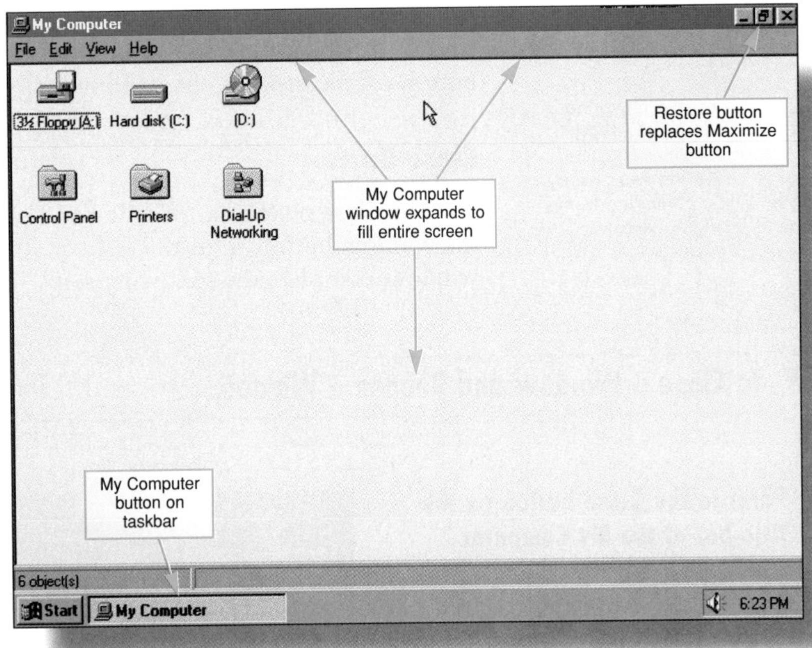

FIGURE 1-18

3 **Point to the Restore button on the title bar of the My Computer window.**

The mouse pointer points to the Restore button on the title bar of the My Computer window (Figure 1-19).

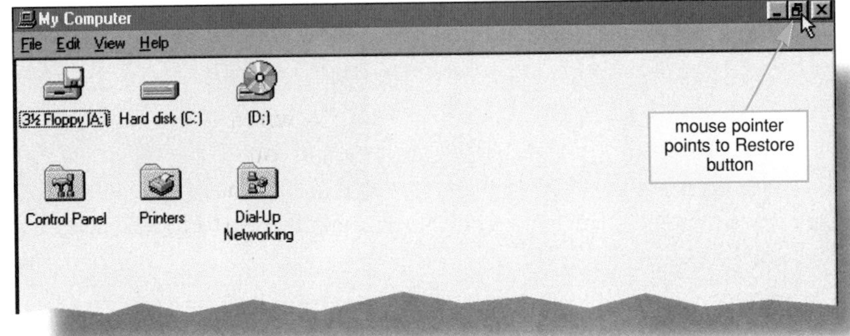

FIGURE 1-19

4 **Click the Restore button.**

The My Computer window returns to the size and position it occupied before being maximized (Figure 1-20). The My Computer button on the taskbar does not change. The Maximize button replaces the Restore button.

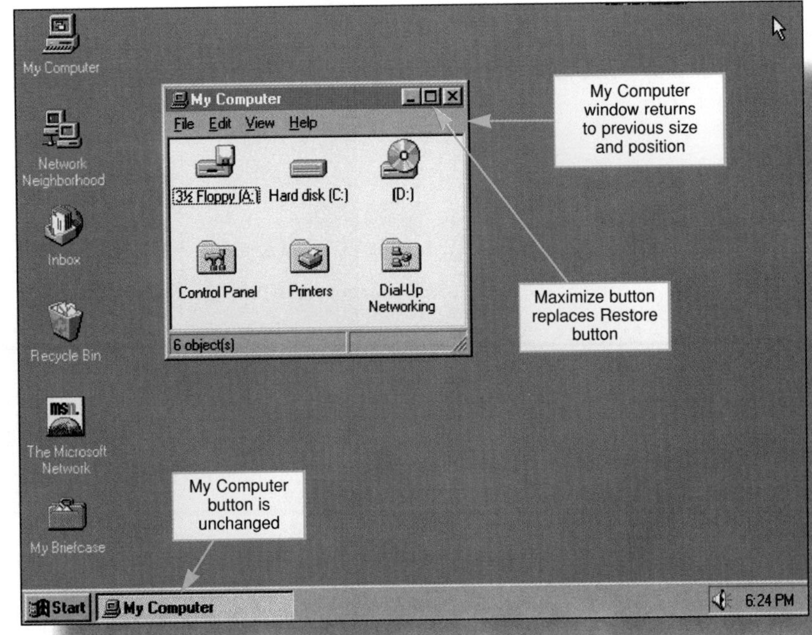

FIGURE 1-20

More About the Close Button

The Close button is a new innovation for Windows 95. In previous versions of Windows, the user had to either double-click a button or click a command from a menu to close the window.

When a window is maximized, you can also minimize the window by clicking the Minimize button. If, after minimizing the window, you click the window button on the taskbar, the window will return to its maximized size.

Close Button

The **Close button** on the title bar of a window closes the window and removes the window button from the taskbar. To close and then reopen the My Computer window, complete the following steps.

Steps To Close a Window and Reopen a Window

1 Point to the Close button on the title bar of the My Computer window.

The mouse pointer points to the Close button on the title bar of the My Computer window (Figure 1-21).

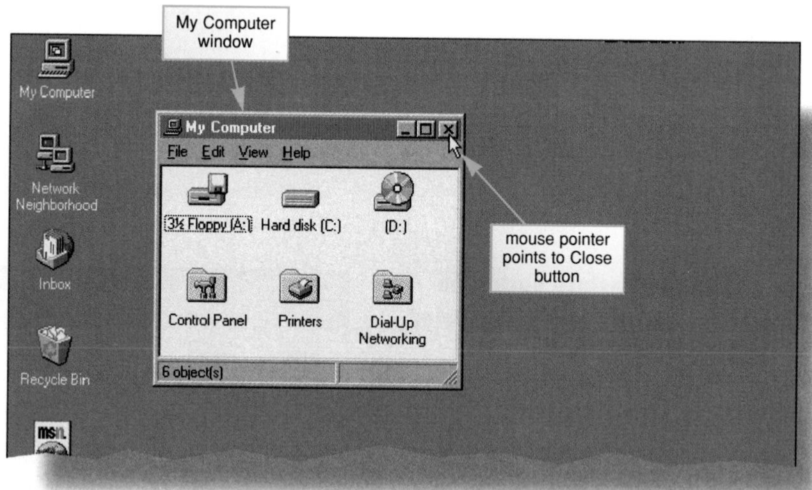

FIGURE 1-21

2 Click the Close button.

The My Computer window closes and the My Computer button no longer displays on the taskbar (Figure 1-22).

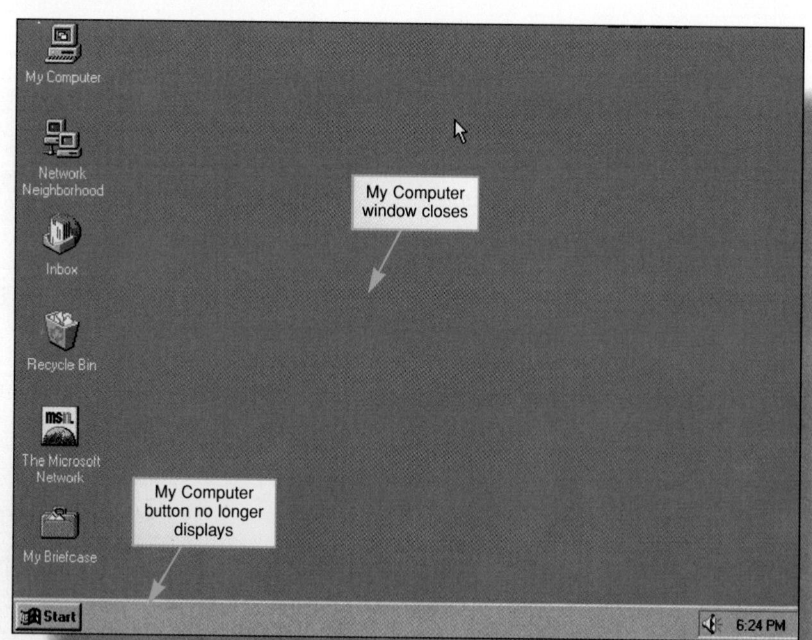

FIGURE 1-22

3 Point to and double-click the My Computer icon on the desktop.

The My Computer window opens and displays on the screen (Figure 1-23). The My Computer button displays on the taskbar.

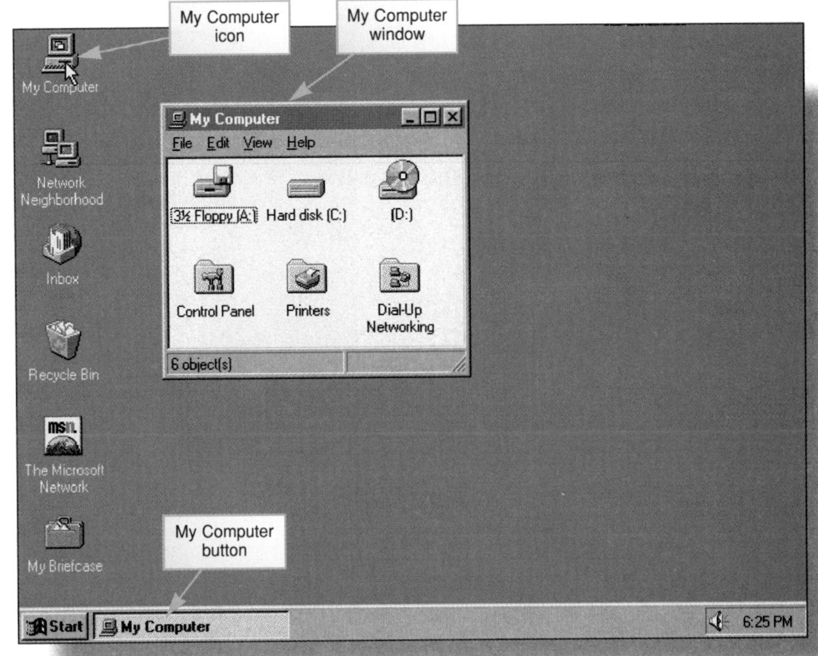

FIGURE 1-23

Drag

Drag means you point to an item, hold down the left mouse button, move the item to the desired location on the screen, and then release the left mouse button. You can move any open window to another location on the desktop by pointing to the title bar of the window and dragging the window. To drag the My Computer window, perform the following steps.

More About Dragging

Dragging is the second-most difficult skill to learn with a mouse. You may want to practice dragging a few times so you are comfortable with it.

Steps To Move an Object by Dragging

1 Point to the My Computer window title bar.

The mouse pointer points to the My Computer window title bar (Figure 1-24).

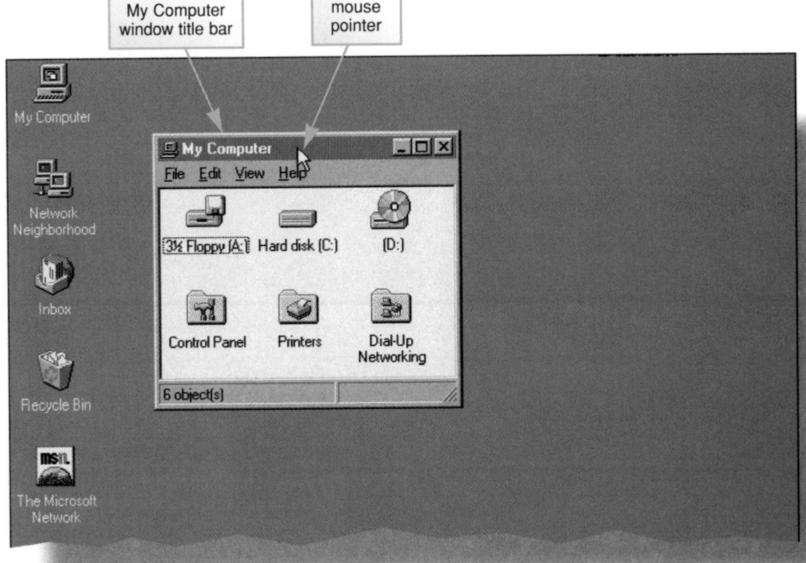

FIGURE 1-24

2 **Hold down the left mouse button and then move the mouse so the window outline moves to the center of the desktop (do not release the left mouse button).**

As you drag the My Computer window, Windows 95 displays an outline of the window (Figure 1-25). The outline, which can be positioned anywhere on the desktop, specifies where the window will display when you release the left mouse button.

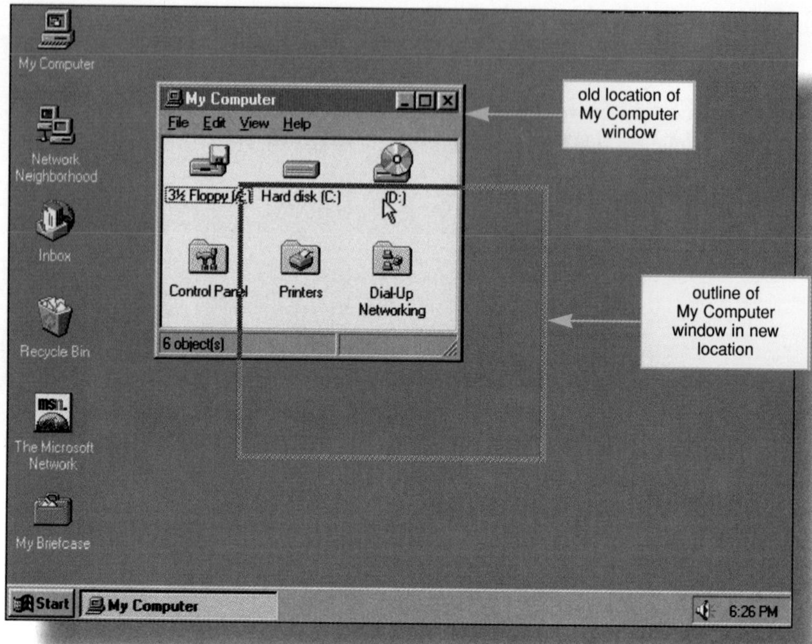

FIGURE 1-25

3 **Release the left mouse button.**

Windows 95 moves the My Computer window to the location the outline occupied prior to releasing the left mouse button (Figure 1-26).

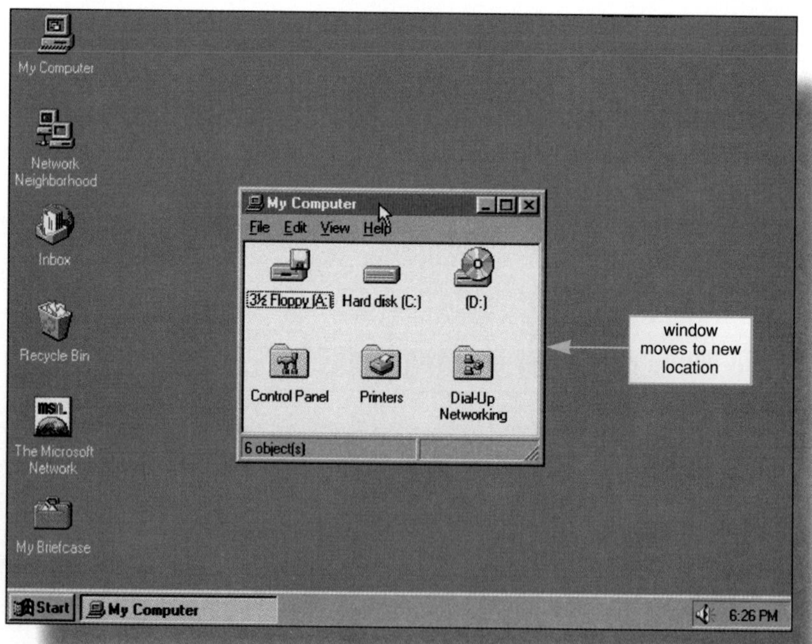

FIGURE 1-26

Sizing a Window by Dragging

You can use dragging for more than just moving an item or object. For example, you can drag the border of a window to change the size of the window. To change the size of the My Computer window, complete the following step.

More About Window Sizing

Windows 95 remembers the size of a window when you close the window. When you reopen the window, it will display in the same size as when you closed it.

To Size a Window by Dragging

1 Position the mouse pointer over the lower right corner of the My Computer window until the mouse pointer changes to a two-headed arrow. Drag the lower right corner upward and to the left until the window on your desktop resembles the window in Figure 1-27.

As you drag the lower right corner, the My Computer window changes size and a vertical scroll bar displays (Figure 1-27). A ***scroll bar*** *is a bar that displays at the right edge and/or bottom edge of a window when the window contents are not completely visible. A vertical scroll bar contains an* ***up scroll arrow****, a* ***down scroll arrow****, and a* ***scroll box****.*

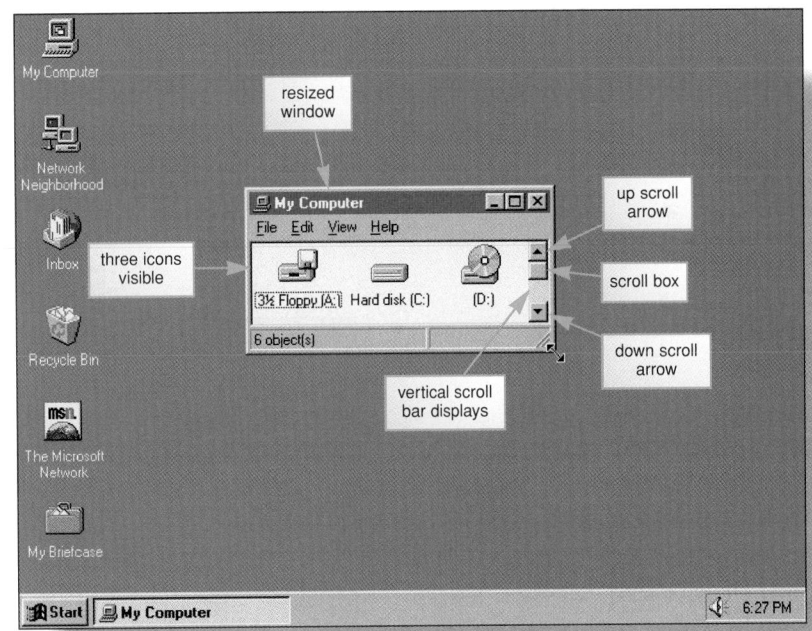

FIGURE 1-27

The size of the scroll box in any window is dependent on the amount of the window that is not visible. The smaller the scroll box, the more of the window that is not visible. In addition to dragging a corner of a window, you can also drag any of the borders of a window.

Scrolling in a Window

You can use the scroll bar to view the contents of a window that are not visible. Scrolling can be accomplished in three ways: click the scroll arrows; click the scroll bar; and drag the scroll box.

To display the contents of the My Computer window by scrolling using scroll arrows, complete the steps on the next page.

More About Scrolling

Most people will either maximize a window or size it so all the objects in the window are visible to avoid scrolling because scrolling takes time. It is more efficient not to have to scroll in a window.

Steps To Scroll a Window Using Scroll Arrows

Point to the down scroll arrow on the vertical scroll bar.

The mouse pointer points to the down scroll arrow on the scroll bar (Figure 1-28).

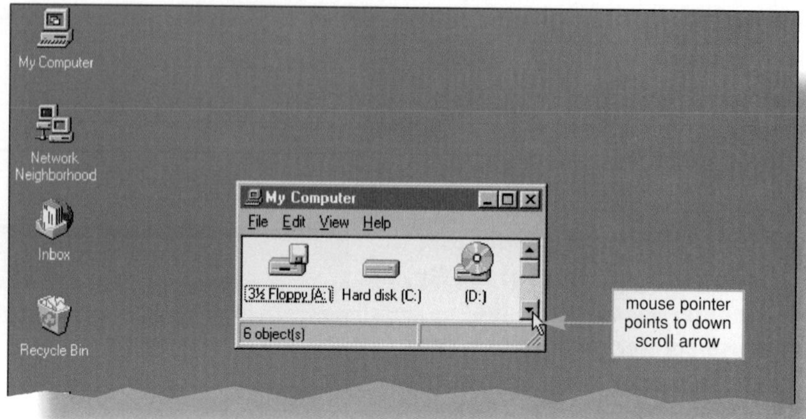

FIGURE 1-28

Click the down scroll arrow one time.

The window scrolls down (the icons move up in the window) and displays the tops of icons not previously visible (Figure 1-29). Because the window size does not change when you scroll, the contents of the window will change, as seen in the difference between Figure 1-28 and Figure 1-29.

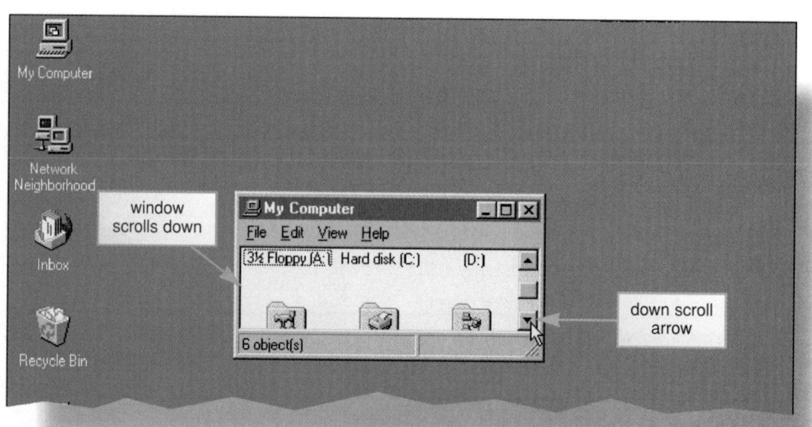

FIGURE 1-29

3 Click the down scroll arrow two more times.

The scroll box moves to the bottom of the scroll bar and the icons in the last row of the window display (Figure 1-30).

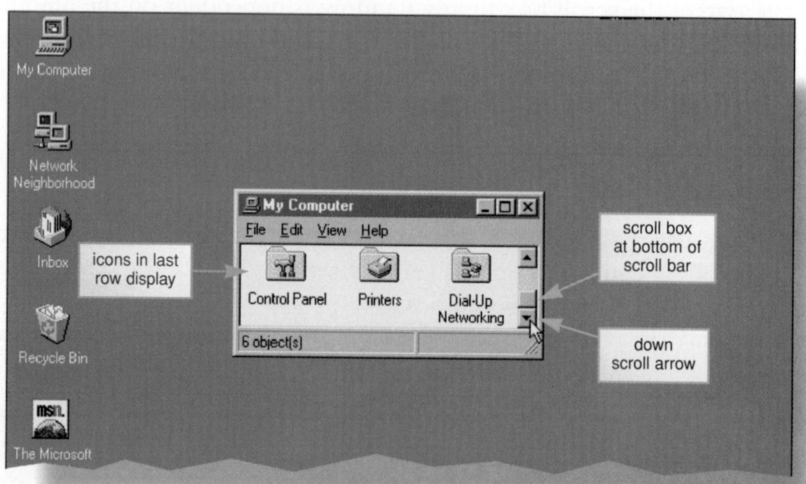

FIGURE 1-30

You can continuously scroll through a window using scroll arrows by clicking the up or down scroll arrow and holding down the left mouse button. The window continues to scroll until you release the left mouse button or you reach the top or bottom of the window.

You can also scroll by clicking the scroll bar itself. When you click the scroll bar, the window moves up or down a greater distance than when you click the scroll arrows.

A third way in which you can scroll through a window to view the window's contents is by dragging the scroll box. When you drag the scroll box, the window moves up or down as you drag.

Being able to view the contents of a window by scrolling is an important Windows 95 skill because the entire contents of a window may not be visible.

More *About* the Scroll Bar

In many application programs, clicking the scroll bar will move the window a full screen's worth of information up or down. You can step through a word processing document screen by screen, for example, by clicking the scroll bar.

More *About* the Scroll Box

Dragging the scroll box is the most efficient technique to scroll long distances. In many application programs, such as Microsoft Word 7, as you scroll using the scroll box, the page number of the document displays next to the scroll box.

More *About* Scrolling Guidelines

General scrolling guidelines: (1) To scroll short distances (line by line), click the scroll arrows; (2) To scroll one screen at a time, click the scroll bar; (3) To scroll long distances, drag the scroll box.

Resizing a Window

You might want to return a window to its original size. To return the My Computer window to about its original size, complete the following steps.

TO RESIZE A WINDOW

Step 1: Position the mouse pointer over the lower right corner of the My Computer window border until the mouse pointer changes to a two-headed arrow.

Step 2: Drag the lower right corner of the My Computer window until the window is the same size as shown in Figure 1-26 on page WIN 1.18, and then release the mouse button.

The My Computer window is about the same size as before you changed it.

Closing a Window

After you have completed your work in a window, normally you will close the window. To close the My Computer window, complete the following steps.

TO CLOSE A WINDOW

Step 1: Point to the Close button on the right of the title bar in the My Computer window.

Step 2: Click the Close button.

The My Computer window closes and the desktop contains no open windows.

Right-Drag

Right-drag means you point to an item, hold down the right mouse button, move the item to the desired location, and then release the right mouse button. When you right-drag an object, a context-sensitive menu displays. The context-sensitive menu contains commands specifically for use with the object being dragged. To right-drag the My Briefcase icon to the center of the desktop, perform the steps on the next page. If the My Briefcase icon does not display on your desktop, you will be unable to perform Step 1 through Step 3 on the next page.

To Right-Drag

1 Point to the My Briefcase icon on the desktop, hold down the right mouse button, drag the icon diagonally toward the center of the desktop, and then release the right mouse button.

The dragged My Briefcase ghosted icon and a context-sensitive menu display in the center of the desktop (Figure 1-31). The My Briefcase icon remains at its original location on the left of the screen. The context-sensitive menu contains four commands: Move Here, Copy Here, Create Shortcut(s) Here, and Cancel. The Move Here command in bold (dark) type identifies what happens if you were to drag the My Briefcase icon with the left mouse button.

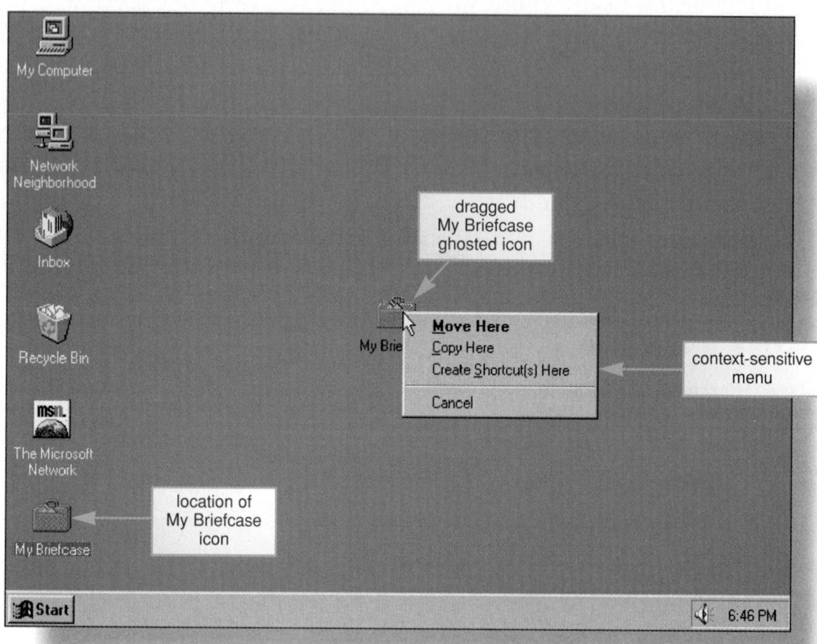

FIGURE 1-31

2 Point to Cancel on the context-sensitive menu.

The mouse pointer points to Cancel on the context-sensitive menu (Figure 1-32). The Cancel command is highlighted.

3 Click Cancel on the context-sensitive menu.

The context-sensitive menu and the dragged My Briefcase icon disappear from the screen.

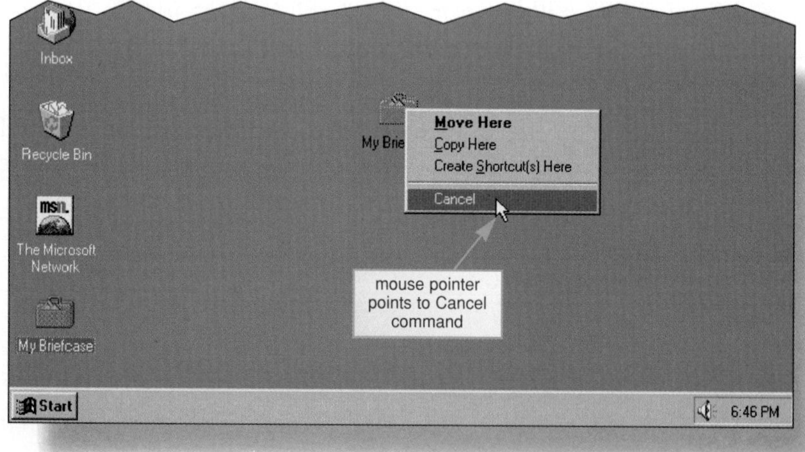

FIGURE 1-32

More About Right-Dragging

Right-dragging was not even available on earlier versions of Windows, so you might find people familiar with Windows not even considering right-dragging. Because it always produces a context-sensitive menu, however, right-dragging is the safest way to drag.

Whenever you begin an operation but do not want to complete the operation, click Cancel on a context-sensitive menu or click the Cancel button in a dialog box. The Cancel command will reset anything you have done.

If you click Move Here on the context-sensitive menu shown in Figure 1-31, Windows 95 will move the icon from its current location to the new location. If you click the Copy Here command, the icon will be copied to the new location and two icons will display on the desktop. Windows 95 automatically will give the second icon and the associated file a different name. If you click the Create Shortcut(s) Here command, a special object called a shortcut will be created.

Although you can move icons by dragging with the primary (left) mouse button and by right-dragging with the secondary (right) mouse button, it is strongly suggested you right-drag because a menu displays and you can specify the exact operation you want to occur. When you drag using the left mouse button, a default operation takes place and the operation may not do what you want.

The Keyboard and Keyboard Shortcuts

FIGURE 1-33a

The **keyboard** is an input device on which you manually key, or type, data. Figure 1-33a shows the enhanced IBM 101-key keyboard and Figure 1-33b shows a Microsoft keyboard designed specifically for use with Windows 95. Many tasks you accomplish with a mouse also can be accomplished using a keyboard.

To perform tasks using the keyboard, you must understand the notation used to identify which keys to press. This notation is used throughout Windows 95 to identify **keyboard shortcuts.**

Keyboard shortcuts consist of: (1) pressing a single key (example: press F1); or, (2) holding down one key and pressing a second key, as shown by two key names separated with a plus sign (example: press CTRL+ESC). For example, to obtain Help about Windows 95, you can press the F1 key. To open the Start menu, hold down the CTRL key and press the ESC key (press CTRL+ESC).

FIGURE 1-33b

Often, computer users will use keyboard shortcuts for operations they perform frequently. For example, many users find pressing the F1 key to start Windows 95 Help easier than using the Start menu as shown later in this project. As a user, you will likely find your own combination of keyboard and mouse operations that particularly suit you, but it is strongly recommended that generally you use the mouse.

More About the Microsoft Keyboard

The Microsoft keyboard in Figure 1-33(b) not only has special keys for Windows 95, but also is designed ergonomically so you type with your hands apart. It takes a little time to get used to, but several authors on the Shelly Cashman Series writing team report they type faster with more accuracy and less fatigue when using the keyboard.

Creating a Document by Starting an Application Program

A **program** is a set of computer instructions that carries out a task on your computer. An **application program** is a program that allows you to accomplish a specific task for which that program is designed. For example, a word processing program is an application program that allows you to create written documents, a spreadsheet program is an application program that allows you to create spreadsheets and charts, and a presentation graphics application program allows you to create graphic presentations for display on a computer or as slides.

More About Application Programs

Some application programs, such as Notepad, are part of Windows 95. Most application programs, however, such as Microsoft Office 95, Lotus SmartSuite 96, and others must be purchased separately from Windows 95.

The most common activity on a computer is to run an application program to accomplish tasks using the computer. You can start an application program by using the Start button on the taskbar.

To illustrate the use of an application program to create a written document, assume each morning you create a daily reminders list so you will remember the tasks you must accomplish throughout the day. You print the document containing the reminders for your use. On occasion, you must update the daily reminders list as events occur during the day. You have decided to use **Notepad**, a popular application program available with Windows 95, to create your list.

To create the list, one method you can use with Windows 95 is to start the Notepad application program using the Start button on the taskbar. After the Notepad program is started, you can enter your daily reminders.

To start the Notepad program, perform the following steps.

Steps To Start a Program

1 Click the Start button on the taskbar. Point to Programs on the Start menu. Point to Accessories on the Programs submenu. If you happen to point to another command on one of the menus or submenus, a different submenu might display. Merely move the mouse so it points to Programs and then Accessories to display the correct menu and submenus.

Windows 95 opens the Start menu, the Programs submenu, and the Accessories submenu (Figure 1-34). The mouse pointer points to Accessories on the Programs submenu. The Accessories submenu contains the Notepad command to start the Notepad program. Notice that whenever you point to a menu name that has a right arrow following it, a submenu displays. You might find more, fewer, or different commands on the submenus on your computer.

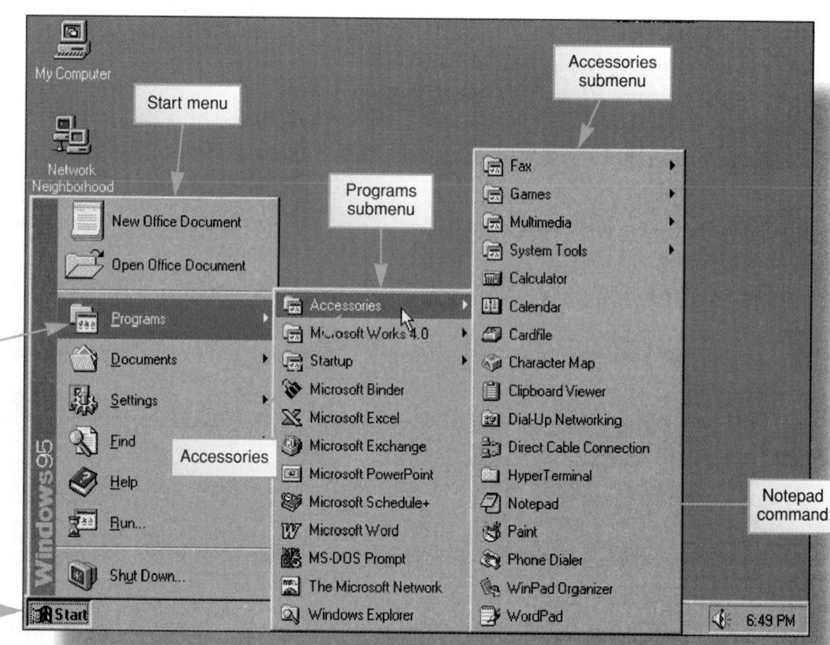

FIGURE 1-34

2 **Point to Notepad on the Accessories submenu.**

When the mouse pointer points to Notepad on the Accessories submenu, the Notepad command is highlighted (Figure 1-35).

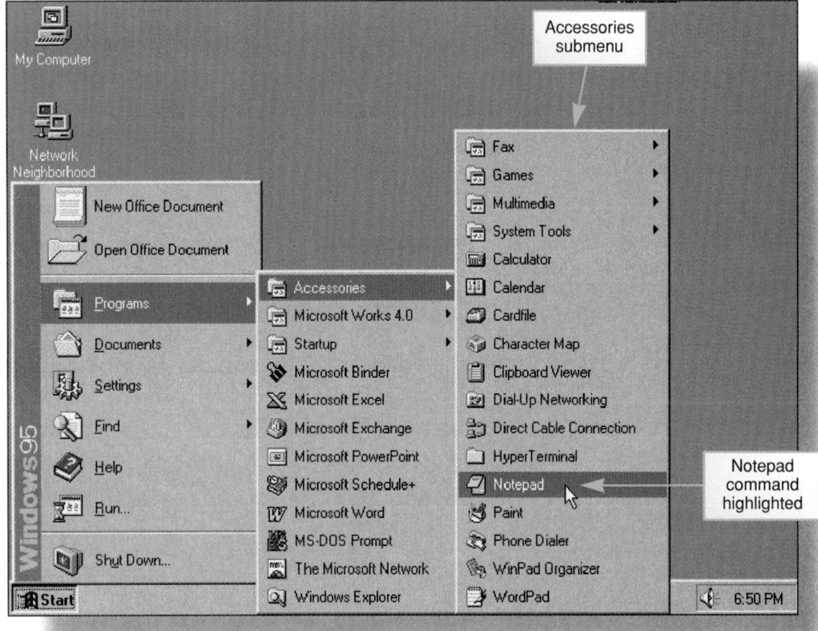

FIGURE 1-35

3 **Click Notepad.**

Windows 95 starts the Notepad program by opening the Notepad window on the desktop and adding an indented Notepad button to the taskbar (Figure 1-36). Notepad is the active window (dark blue title bar). The word Untitled in the window title (Untitled - Notepad) and on the Notepad button indicates the document has not been saved on disk. The menu bar contains the following menu names: File, Edit, Search, and Help. The area below the menu bar contains an insertion point and two scroll bars. The **insertion point** *is a flashing vertical line that indicates the point at which text typed on the keyboard will be displayed. The scroll bars do not contain scroll boxes, indicating the document is not large enough to allow scrolling.*

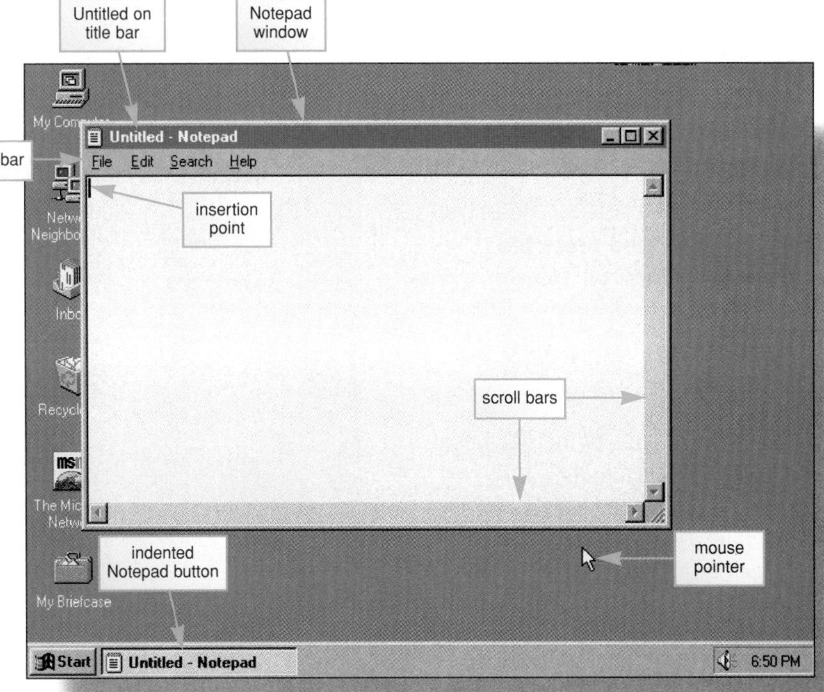

FIGURE 1-36

*Other*Ways

1. Right-click desktop, point to New, click Text Document, double-click the New Text Document icon
2. Click Start button, click Run, type `Notepad`, click OK button
3. Press CTRL+ESC, press R, type `Notepad`, press ENTER key

After you have started an application program such as Notepad, you can use the program to prepare your document.

Windows 95 provides a number of ways in which to accomplish a particular task. When a task is illustrated by a series of steps in this book, those steps may not be the only way in which the task can be done. If you can accomplish the same task using other methods, the Other Ways box specifies the other methods. In each case, the method shown in the steps is the preferred method, but it is important you are aware of all the techniques you can use.

Creating a Document

To create a document in Notepad, you must type the text you want in the document. After typing a line of text, press the ENTER key to indicate the end of the line. If you press the ENTER key when the insertion point is on a line by itself, Notepad inserts a blank line in the document. To create the Daily Reminders document, perform the following step.

Steps To Create a Document

1. **Type** `Daily Reminders - Wednesday` **and press the ENTER key twice. Type** `1. Call Tim Hoyle - Photoshop retouch due` **and press the ENTER key. Type** `2. Memo to Linda Tomms - Meeting next week` **and press the ENTER key. Type** `3. Lunch with Harris - Noon, Remmington's` **and press the ENTER key.**

   The first five lines of the document are entered (Figure 1-37). A blank line is inserted following the first line. The insertion point is positioned on the sixth line of the document.

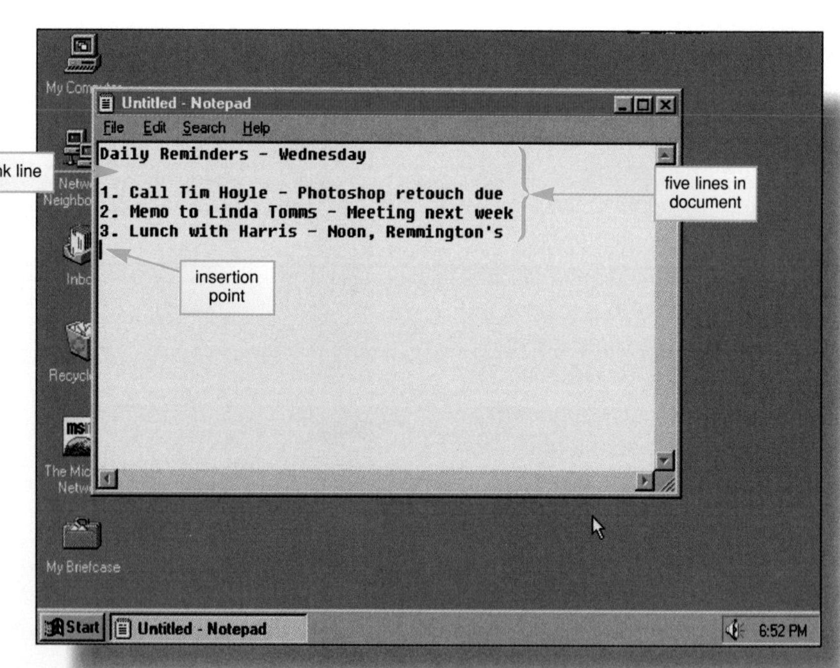

FIGURE 1-37

More About Saving a Document

Most people who have used a computer can tell at least one horror story of working on their computer for a long stretch of time and then losing the work because of some malfunction with the computer or even with the operating system or application program. Be Warned: Save and save often to protect the work you have completed on your computer.

Saving a Document on Disk

When you create a document using a program such as Notepad, the document is stored in the main memory (RAM) of your computer. If you close the program without saving the document or if your computer accidentally loses electrical power, the document will be lost. To protect against the accidental loss of a document and to allow you to easily modify the document in the future, you can save the document on disk.

When you save a document, you must assign a filename to the document. All documents are identified by a filename. Typical filenames are Daily Reminders - Wednesday, Mileage Log, and Automobile Maintenance. A filename can contain up to 255 characters, including spaces. Any uppercase or lowercase character is valid when creating a filename, except a backslash (\), slash (/), colon (:), asterisk (*), question mark (?), quotation mark ("), less than symbol (<), greater than symbol (>), or vertical bar (|). Filenames cannot be CON, AUX, COM1, COM2, COM3, COM4, LPT1, LPT2, LPT3, PRN, or NUL.

To associate a document with an application, Windows 95 assigns an extension of a period and up to three characters to each document. All documents created using the Notepad program, which are text documents, are saved with the .TXT extension. To save the document you created using Notepad on a floppy disk in drive A of your computer using the filename, Daily Reminders - Wednesday, perform the following steps.

More About Filenames

Because of restrictions with Microsoft DOS, previous versions of Windows allowed filenames of only eight or fewer characters. F56QPSLA, and similar indecipherable names, were common. Microsoft touts the long filename capability of Windows 95 as a significant breakthrough. Apple Macintosh users, however, shrug and ask what's the big deal. They have used long filenames for years.

Steps To Save a Document on Disk

1 **Insert a formatted floppy disk into drive A on your computer. Click File on the menu bar.**

Windows 95 highlights the File menu name on the menu bar and opens the File menu in the Notepad window (Figure 1-38). The mouse pointer points to File on the menu bar.

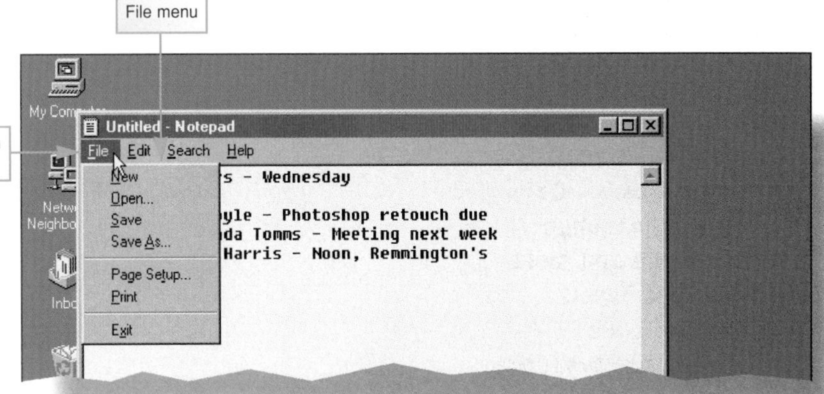

FIGURE 1-38

2 **Point to Save As on the File menu.**

The mouse pointer points to the Save As command on the File menu (Figure 1-39). The ellipsis (...) following the Save As command indicates Windows 95 requires more information to carry out the Save As command and will open a dialog box when you click Save As. A ***dialog box*** *displays whenever Windows 95 needs to supply information to you or wants you to enter information or select among several options.*

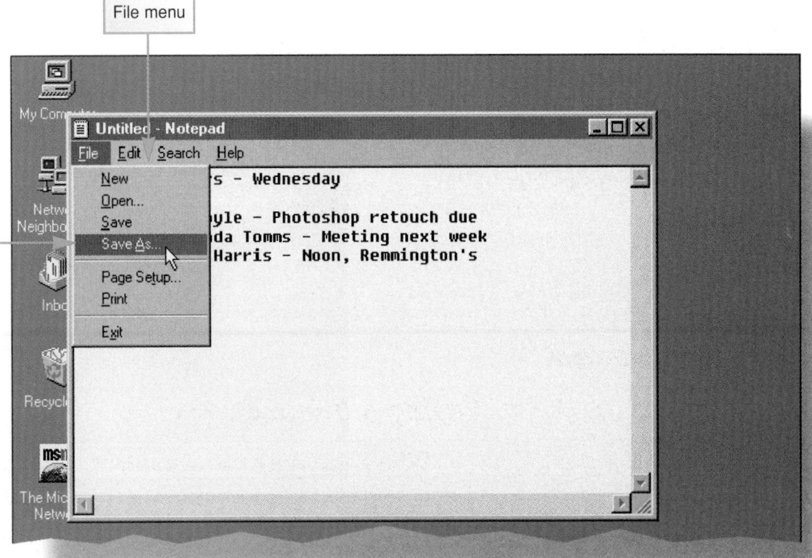

FIGURE 1-39

3 **Click Save As.**

Windows 95 displays the Save As dialog box (Figure 1-40). The Save As dialog box becomes the active window (dark blue title bar) and the Notepad window becomes the ***inactive window*** *(light blue title bar). The Save As dialog box contains the Save in drop-down list box. A* ***drop-down list box*** *is a rectangular box containing text and a down arrow on the right. The Save in drop-down list box displays the Desktop icon and Desktop name. The entry in the Save in drop-down list box indicates where the file will be stored. At the bottom of the dialog box is the File name text box. A* ***text box*** *is a rectangular area in which you can enter text. The File name text box contains the highlighted entry, Untitled. When you type the filename from the keyboard, the filename will replace the highlighted entry in the File name text box.*

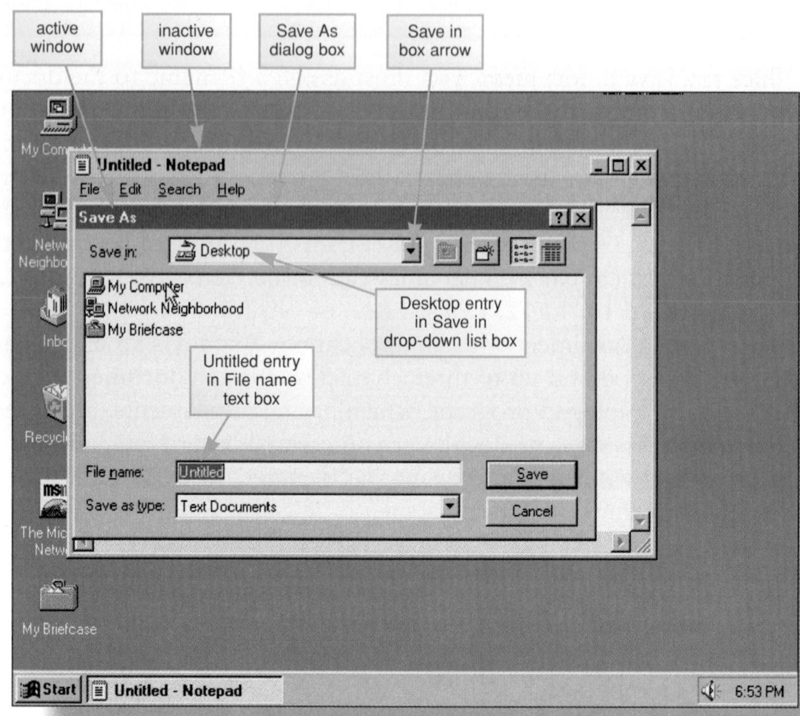

FIGURE 1-40

4 **Type** `Daily Reminders - Wednesday` **in the File name text box. Point to the Save in box arrow.**

The filename, Daily Reminders – Wednesday, and an insertion point display in the File name text box (Figure 1-41). When you save this document, Notepad will automatically add the .TXT extension. The mouse pointer points to the Save in box arrow.

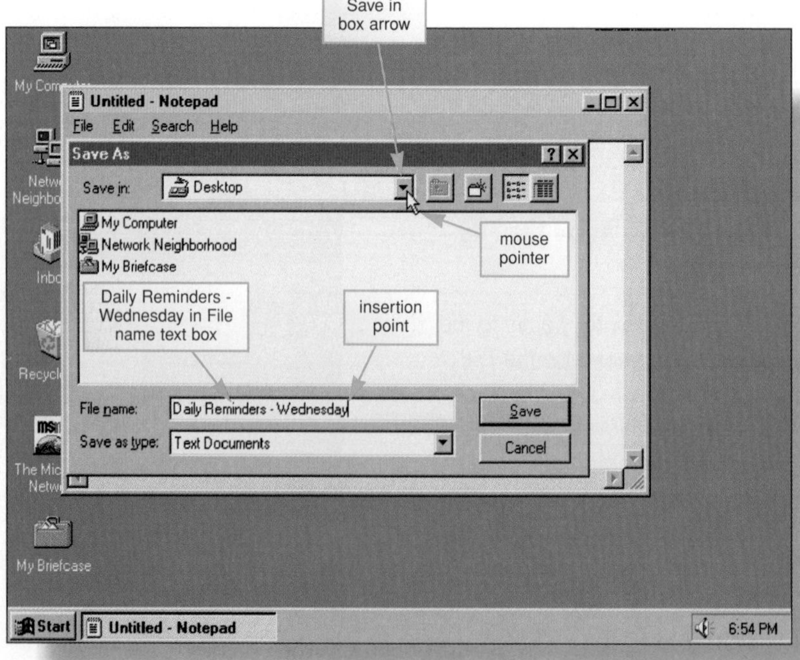

FIGURE 1-41

5 **Click the Save in box arrow and then point to the 3½ Floppy [A:] icon.**

Windows 95 displays the Save in drop-down list (Figure 1-42). The list contains various elements of your computer, including the Desktop, My Computer, Network Neighborhood, and My Briefcase. Within My Computer are 3½ Floppy [A:], Hard disk [C:], and [D:]. When you point to the 3½ Floppy [A:] icon, the entry in the list is highlighted.

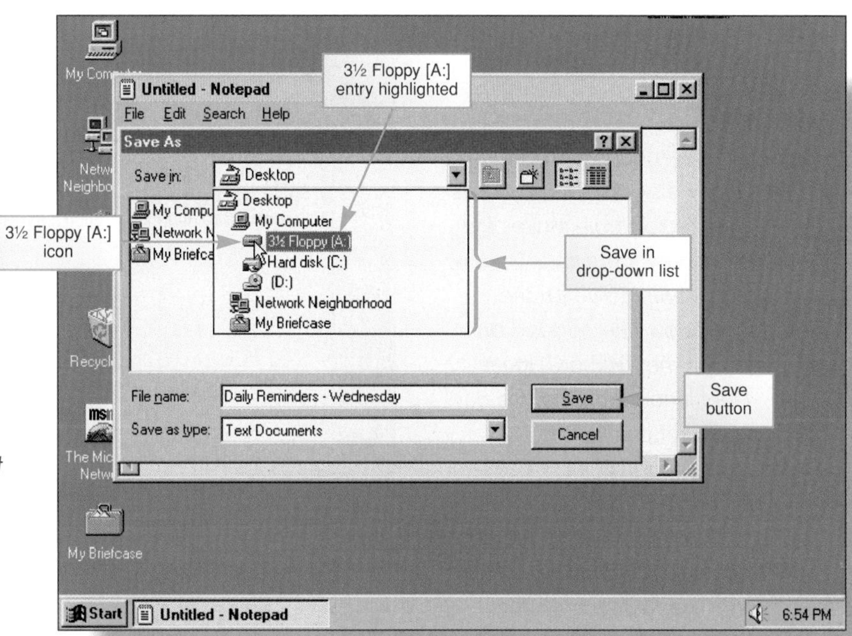

FIGURE 1-42

6 **Click the 3½ Floppy [A:] icon and then point to the Save button.**

The 3½ Floppy [A:] entry displays in the Save in drop-down list box (Figure 1-43). This specifies that the file will be saved on the floppy disk in drive A using the filename specified in the File name text box. The mouse pointer points to the Save button.

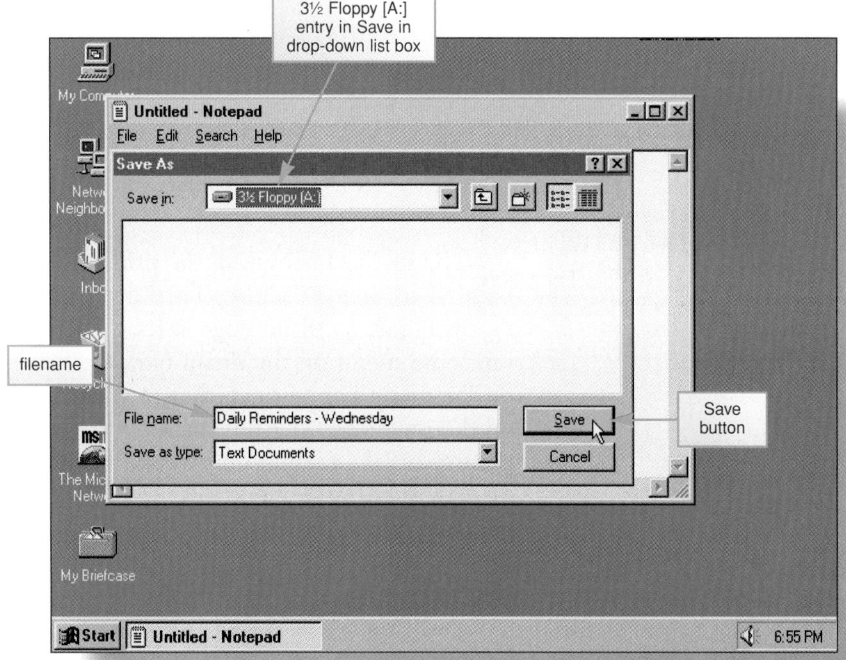

FIGURE 1-43

7 Click the Save button.

Windows 95 displays an **hourglass icon** *while saving the Daily Reminders - Wednesday document on the floppy disk in drive A, closes the Save As dialog box, makes the Notepad window the active window, and inserts the filename on the Notepad window title bar and on the button on the taskbar (Figure 1-44). The filename on the title bar may or may not display the .TXT extension, depending on the setting on your computer. The hourglass icon indicates Windows 95 requires a brief interval of time to save the document. The filename on the button on the taskbar (Daily Reminders - We...) contains an ellipsis to indicate the entire button name does not fit on the button. To display the entire button name for a button on the taskbar, point to the button.*

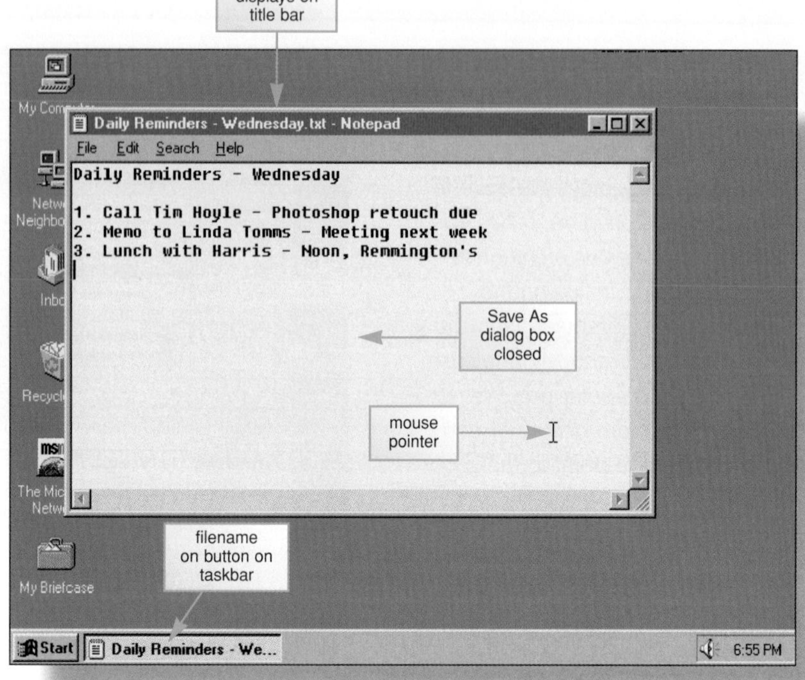

FIGURE 1-44

OtherWays

1. On File menu click Save, type filename, select drive and folder, click Save button
2. Press ALT+F, press A, type filename, select drive and folder, press S

The method shown in the previous steps for saving a file on a floppy disk can be used to save a file on a hard disk, such as drive C, or even on the desktop.

In Figure 1-38 on page WIN 1.27, the File menu displays. Once you have opened a menu on the menu bar, you need merely point to another menu name on the menu bar to open that menu. Thus, in Figure 1-38, if you point to Edit on the menu bar, the Edit menu will display. If you accidentally move the mouse pointer off the menu you want to display, point back to the menu name to display the desired menu. To close a menu without carrying out a command, click anywhere on the desktop except on the menu.

More *About* Printing

Printing is and will remain important for documents. Many sophisticated application programs, however, are extending the printing capability to include transmitting faxes, sending e-mail, and even posting documents on Web pages of the World Wide Web.

Printing a Document

Quite often, after creating a document and saving it, you will want to print it. Printing can be accomplished directly from an application program. To print the Daily Reminders – Wednesday document, perform the following steps.

To Print a Document

1 Click File on the menu bar and then point to Print on the File menu.

The File menu displays and the mouse pointer points to the Print command (Figure 1-45). As with all menu commands when you point to them, the Print command is highlighted.

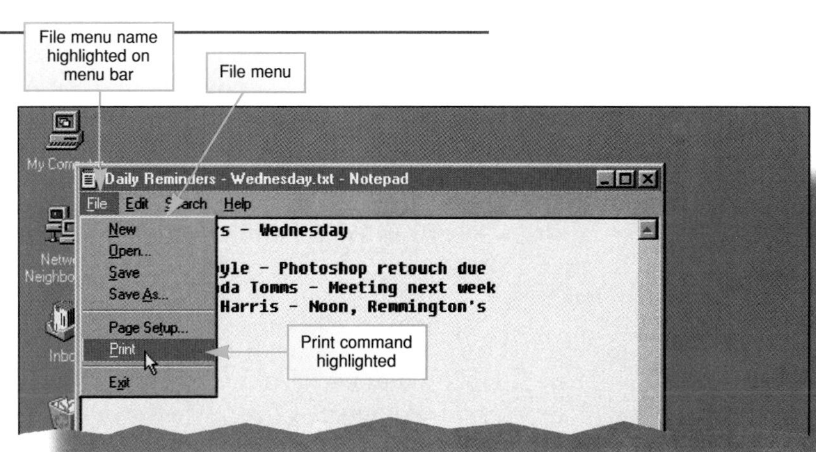

FIGURE 1-45

2 Click Print.

A Notepad dialog box briefly displays with a message that indicates the Daily Reminders document is being printed (Figure 1-46). The dialog box disappears after the report has been printed. To cancel printing, you can click the Cancel button. The printed report is shown in Figure 1-47. Notepad automatically places the filename at the top of the page and a page number at the bottom of the page.

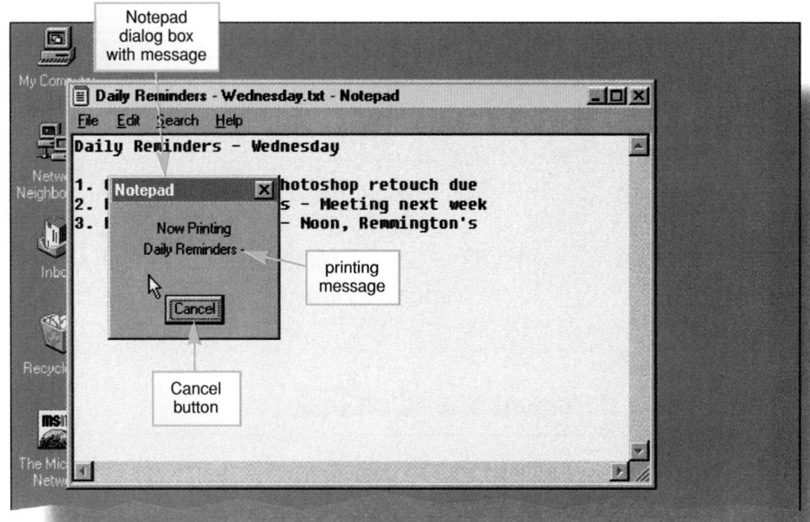

FIGURE 1-46

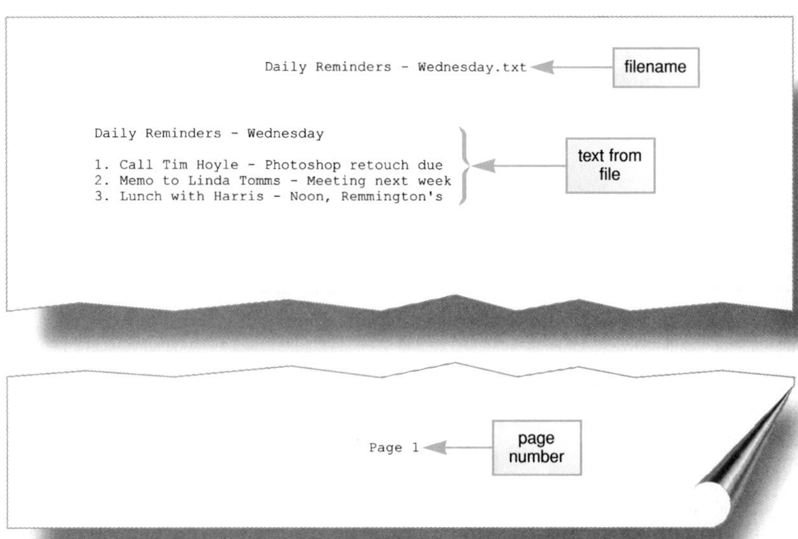

FIGURE 1-47

Other Ways

1. Press ALT+F, press P

Closing a Program

After creating the Daily Reminders – Wednesday document, saving the document on the floppy disk in drive A, and printing it, your use of the Notepad program is complete. Therefore, the Notepad program should be closed by performing the following steps.

OtherWays

1. Double-click Notepad logo on title bar
2. On File menu click Exit
3. Press ALT+F4

TO CLOSE A PROGRAM

Step 1: Point to the Close button on the Notepad title bar.
Step 2: Click the Close button.

Windows 95 closes the Daily Reminders – Wednesday.txt – Notepad window and removes the Daily Reminders – Wednesday.txt – Notepad button from the taskbar.

Modifying a Document Stored on Disk

Many documents you create will need to be modified at some point in time after you have created them. For example, the Daily Reminders - Wednesday document should be modified each time you determine another task to be done. To modify an existing document, you can start the application program and open the document. To start the Notepad program and open the Daily Reminders – Wednesday document, complete the following steps.

Steps To Open a Document Stored on Disk

1. **Click the Start button on the taskbar. Point to Programs. Point to Accessories. Point to Notepad.**

   The Start menu, Programs submenu, and Accessories submenu display (Figure 1-48). The mouse pointer points to the Notepad command.

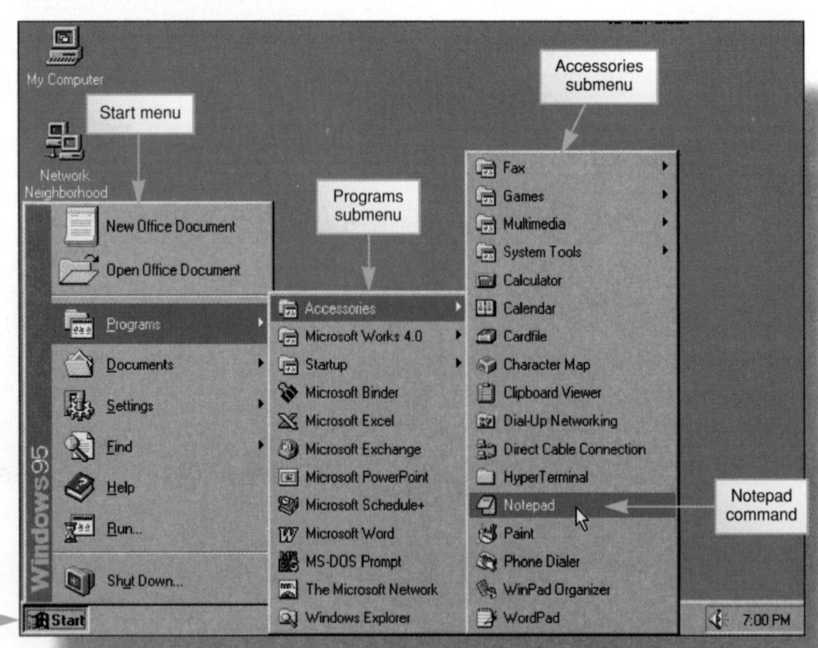

FIGURE 1-48

2 **Click Notepad. When the Notepad window opens, click File on the menu bar and then point to Open on the File menu.**

Windows 95 starts the Notepad program (Figure 1-49). The Untitled – Notepad button on the taskbar indicates no document has been opened. The File menu displays and the mouse pointer points to the Open command.

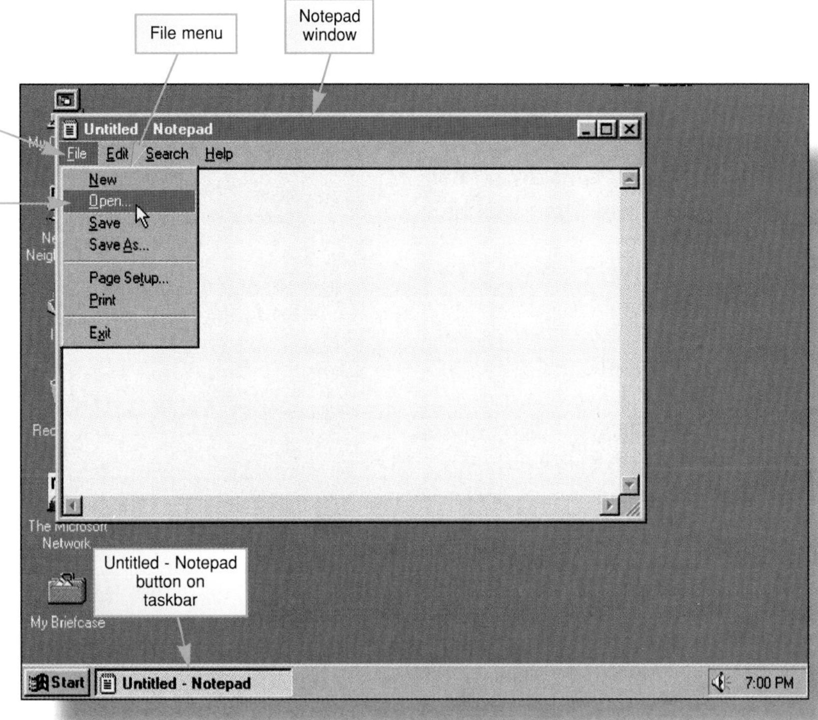

FIGURE 1-49

3 **Click Open. Click the Look in box arrow. Point to the 3½ Floppy [A:] icon.**

Windows 95 displays the Open dialog box (Figure 1-50). When you click the Look in box arrow, the Look in drop-down list displays. The mouse pointer points to the 3½ Floppy [A:] icon. The 3½ Floppy [A:] entry is highlighted.

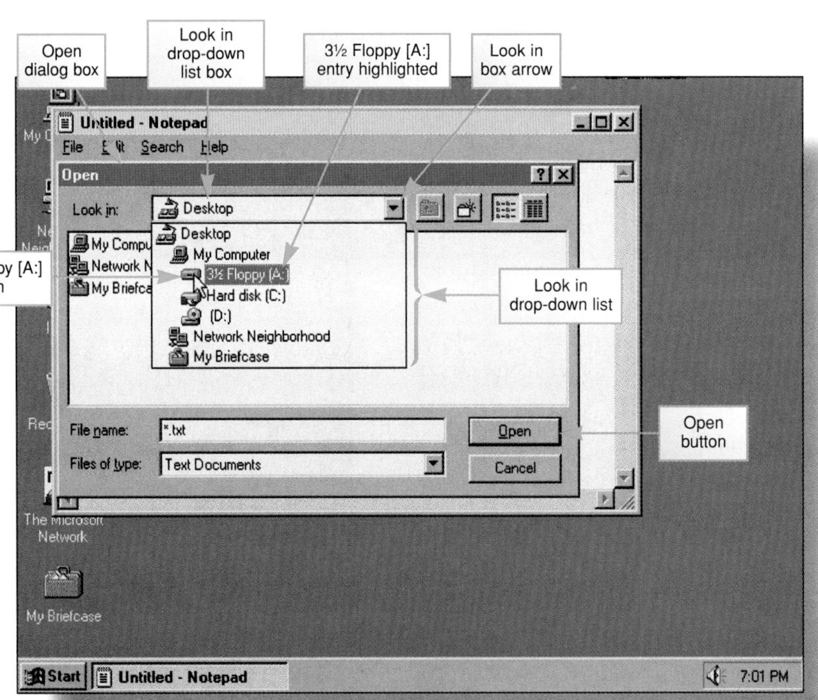

FIGURE 1-50

4 **Click the 3½ Floppy [A:] icon. When the filenames display in the window, click Daily Reminders – Wednesday.txt and then point to the Open button.**

Windows 95 places the 3½ Floppy [A:] icon and entry in the Look in drop-down list box, indicating that the file to be opened is found on the floppy disk in drive A (Figure 1-51). The names of folders and/or text document files stored on the floppy disk in drive A are displayed in the window below the Look in drop-down list box. The Daily Reminders - Wednesday.txt file is selected, as indicated by the highlight, and the mouse pointer points to the Open button. Notice that the Daily Reminders – Wednesday.txt filename displays in the File name text box, indicating this is the file that will be opened.

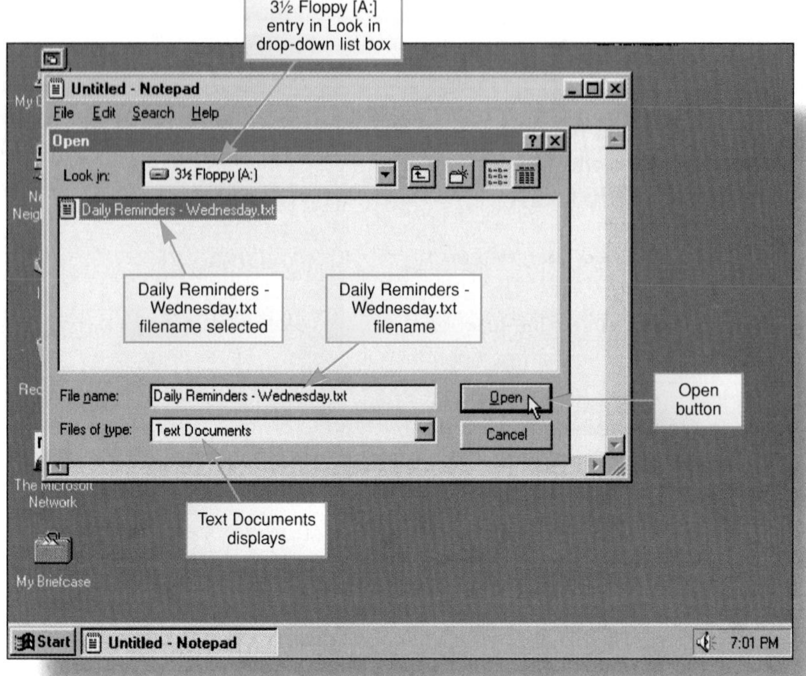

FIGURE 1-51

5 **Click the Open button.**

Windows 95 opens the Daily Reminders – Wednesday.txt file and displays it in the Notepad window (Figure 1-52). The filename displays on the title bar of the Notepad window and on the button on the taskbar.

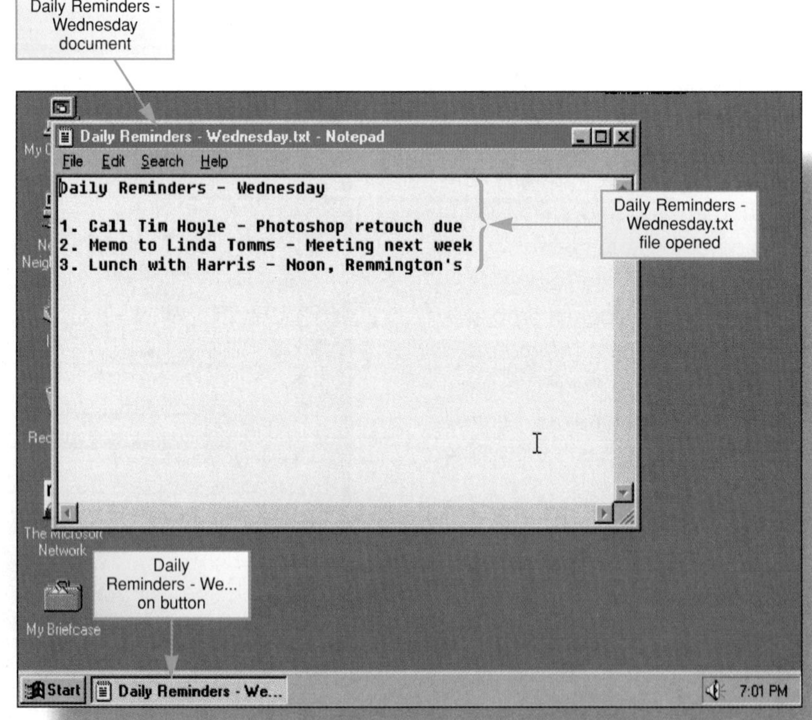

FIGURE 1-52

OtherWays

1. Double-click My Computer icon, double-click drive A icon, double-click file icon
2. Press ALT+F, press O, select drive and folder, type file-name, press O

After opening the Daily Reminders – Wednesday document, perform the following step to modify the document by adding another line.

TO MODIFY A DOCUMENT

Step 1: Press the DOWN ARROW key five times, type `4. E-Mail Sue Wells - Adobe Illustrator drawing` as the new line, and then press the ENTER key.

After modifying the Daily Reminders – Wednesday document, you should save the modified document on the floppy disk in drive A using the same filename. To save the modified document on the disk, complete the following steps.

To Save a Modified Document on Disk

1 Click File on the menu bar and then point to Save.

The File menu opens and the mouse pointer points to the Save command (Figure 1-53). The Save command is used to save a file that has already been created.

2 Click Save.

The modified document is stored on the floppy disk in drive A and the Notepad window remains open. Whenever you use the Save command, the document is stored using the same filename in the same location from which it was opened.

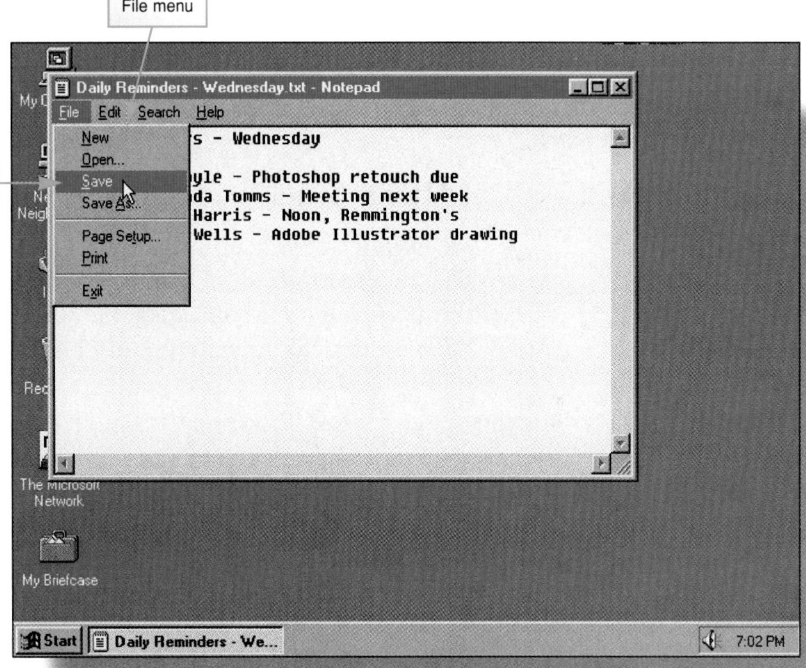

FIGURE 1-53

OtherWays

1. Press ALT+F, press S

If you want to print the modified document, click File on the menu bar and then click Print on the File menu in the same manner as shown in Figure 1-45 and Figure 1-46 on page WIN 1.31.

Closing the Notepad Program

After modifying the document and storing the modified document on the floppy disk in drive A, normally you will close the Notepad program. To close the Notepad program, complete the step on the next page.

TO CLOSE A PROGRAM

Step 1: Click the Close button on the right of the Notepad title bar.

The Notepad window closes and the Notepad button on the taskbar disappears.

Modifying an existing document is a common occurrence and should be well understood when using Windows 95.

Using Windows Help

One of the more powerful application programs for use in Windows 95 is Windows Help. Windows Help is available when using Windows 95, or when using any application program running under Windows 95, to assist you in using Windows 95 and the various application programs. It contains answers to virtually any question you can ask with respect to Windows 95.

More *About* Windows 95 Help

If you purchased an operating system or application program five years ago, you received at least one, and more often several, thick and heavy technical manuals that explained the software. With Windows 95, you receive a skinny manual less than 100 pages in length. The online Help feature of Windows 95 replaces reams and reams of printed pages in hard-to-understand technical manuals.

Contents Sheet

Windows 95 Help provides a variety of ways in which to obtain information. One method to find a Help topic involves using the Contents sheet to browse through Help topics by category. To illustrate this method, you will use Windows 95 Help to determine how to find a topic in Help. To start Help, complete the following steps.

To Start Help

1 Click the Start button on the taskbar. Point to Help on the Start menu.

Windows 95 opens the Start menu (Figure 1-54). Because the mouse pointer points to the Help command, the Help command is highlighted.

FIGURE 1-54

2 **Click Help on the Start menu. If the Contents sheet does not display, click the Contents tab.**

Windows 95 opens the Help Topics: Windows Help window (Figure 1-55). The window contains three ***tabs*** *(Contents, Index, and Find). The* ***Contents sheet*** *is visible in the window. Clicking either the Index tab or the Find tab opens the Index or Find sheet, respectively. The Contents sheet contains two* ***Help topics*** *preceded by a question mark icon and five books. Each book consists of a closed book icon followed by a book name. The first Help topic, Tour: Ten minutes to using Windows, is highlighted. Three command buttons (Display, Print, and Cancel) display at the bottom of the window.*

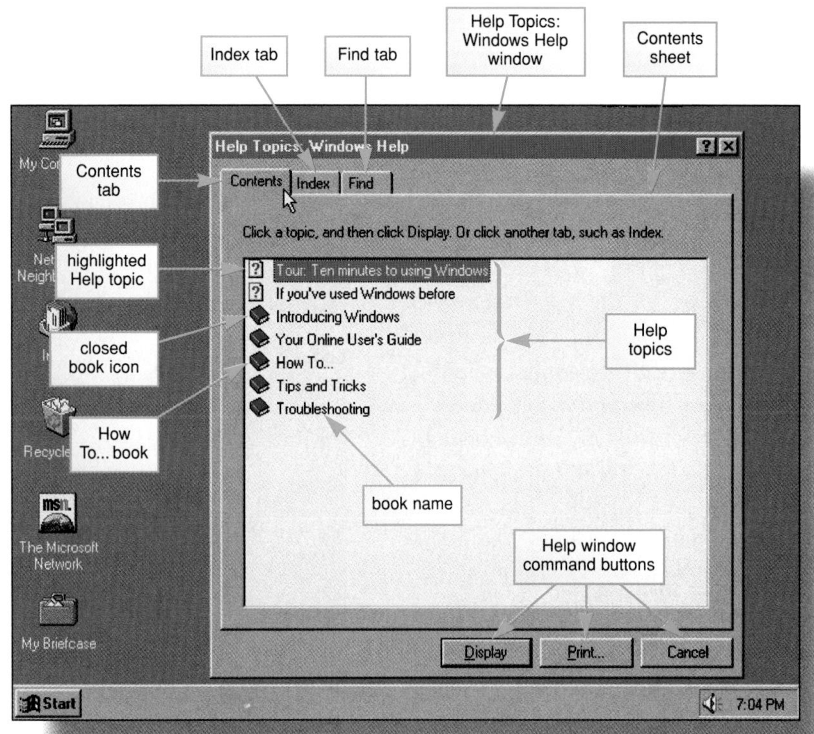

FIGURE 1-55

OtherWays

1. Press F1, press CTRL+TAB or CTRL+SHIFT+TAB to highlight desired sheet

In the Help window shown in Figure 1-55, the closed book icon indicates Help topics or more books are contained within the book. The question mark icon indicates a Help topic without any further subdivisions.

In addition to starting Help by using the Start button, you can also start Help by pressing the F1 key.

After starting Help, the next step is to find the topic in which you are interested. To find the topic that describes how to find a topic in Help, complete the steps on the next two pages.

To Use Help to Find a Topic in Help

1 Double-click How To... in the Help Topics: Windows Help window. Point to the Use Help closed book.

Windows 95 highlights the How To book and opens the How To book (Figure 1-56). The ellipsis following the How To book indicates additional books will display when you open the book. The list of closed book icons indicates more Help information is available. The mouse pointer points to the Use Help closed book icon. The Close button in Figure 1-56 replaces the Display button in Figure 1-55. If you click the Close button, the How To book will close and the list of books below the How To book disappears.

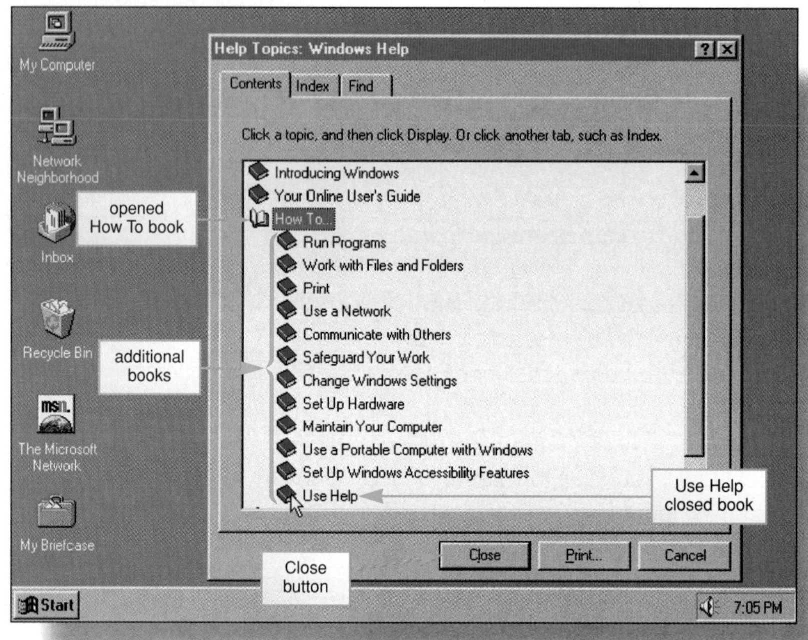

FIGURE 1-56

2 Double-click the Use Help closed book icon and then point to Finding a topic in Help in the opened Use Help book.

Windows 95 opens the Use Help book and displays several Help topics in the book (Figure 1-57). The mouse pointer points to Finding a topic in Help.

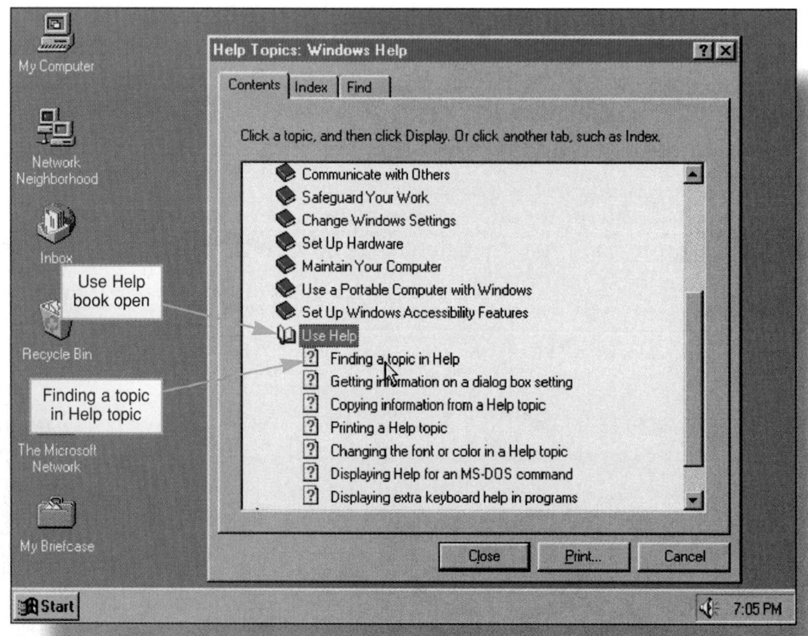

FIGURE 1-57

3 Double-click Finding a topic in Help.

Windows 95 closes the Help Topics: Windows Help window and opens the Windows Help window (Figure 1-58). The window contains three buttons (Help Topics, Back, and Options), steps to find a topic in Help, and a Tip. The Windows Help button displays on the taskbar.

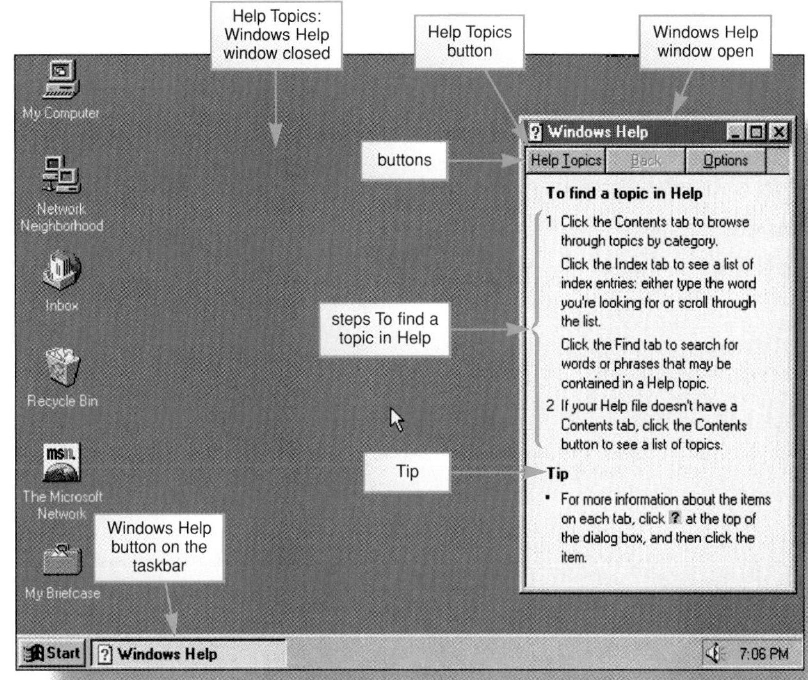

FIGURE 1-58

4 After reading the information in the Windows Help window, click the Help Topics button in the Windows Help window.

The Help Topics: Windows Help window displays together with the Windows Help window (Figure 1-59).

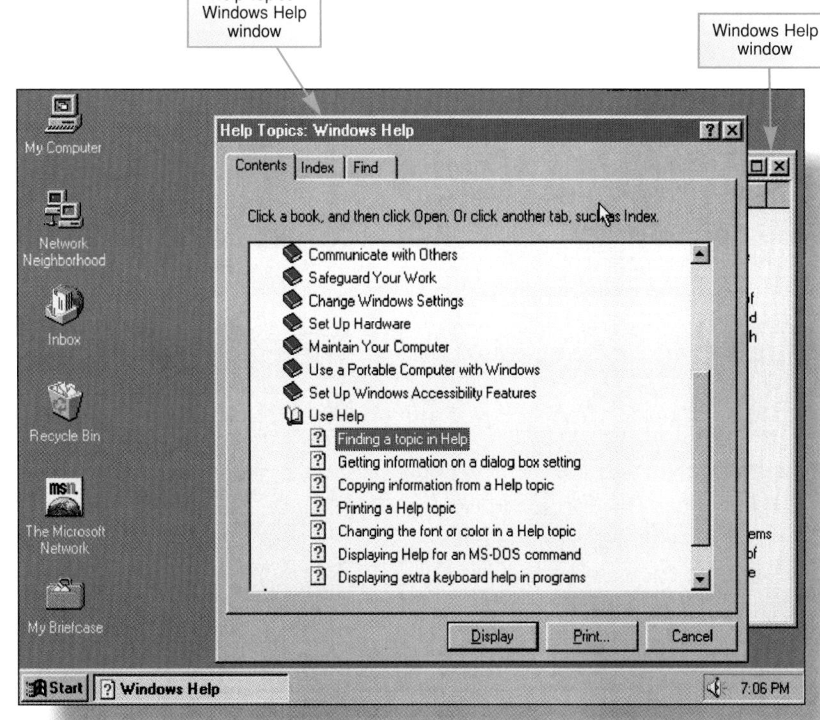

FIGURE 1-59

***Other*Ways**

1. Press DOWN ARROW until book or topic highlighted, press ENTER, continue until Help topic displays, read Help topic, press T

Clicking the Help Topics button in the Windows Help window will always display the Help Topics: Windows Help window.

In Figure 1-58 on the previous page, if you click the Back button in the Windows Help window (when the button is not dimmed), Windows 95 will display the previously displayed Help topic. Clicking the Options button in the Windows Help window allows you to annotate a Help topic, copy or print a Help topic, change the font and color scheme of Help windows, and control how Help windows display in relation to other windows on the desktop.

Notice also in Figure 1-58 that the Windows Help title bar contains a Minimize button, a Maximize button, and a Close button. You can minimize and maximize the Windows Help window, and you can also close the Windows Help window without returning to the Help Topics: Windows Help window.

More *About* the Index Sheet

The Index sheet is probably the best source of information in Windows Help because you can enter the subject you are interested in. Sometimes, however, you will have to be creative to discover the index entry that answers your question because the most obvious entry will not always lead to your answer.

Index Sheet

A second method to find answers to your questions about Windows 95 or application programs is the Index sheet. The **Index sheet** lists a large number of index entries, each of which references one or more Help screens. To learn more about Windows 95 basic skills by using the Index sheet, and to see an example of animation available with Help, complete the following steps.

Steps To Use the Help Index Sheet

1 Click the Index tab. Type basic skills **(the flashing insertion point is positioned in the text box). Point to the Display button.**

The Index sheet displays, including a list of entries that can be referenced (Figure 1-60). When you type an entry, the list automatically scrolls and the entry you type, such as basic skills, is highlighted. To see additional entries, use the scroll bar at the right of the list. To highlight an entry in the list, click the entry. On some computers, the basic skills entry may not be present. On those machines, select another topic of interest to you.

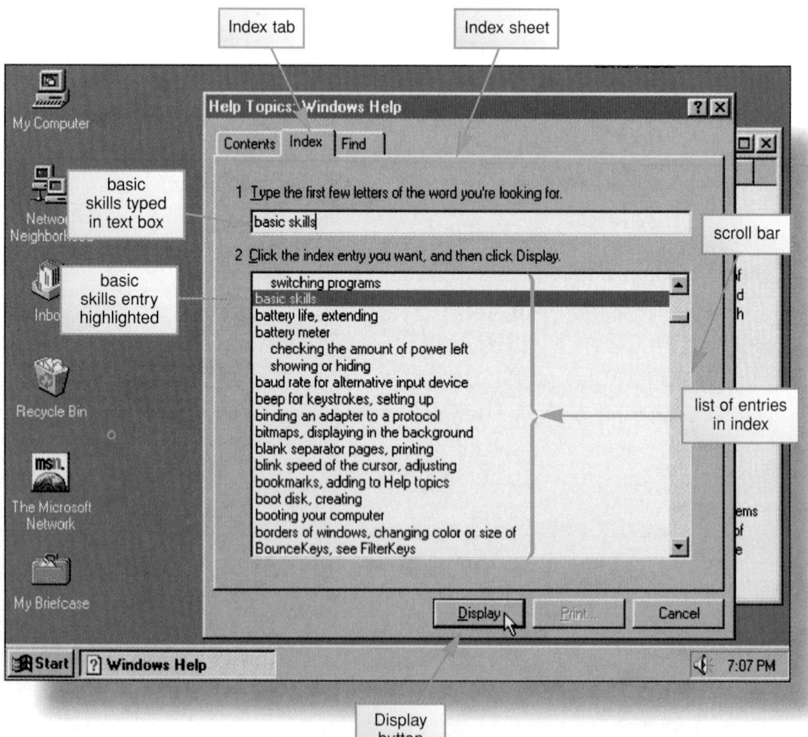

FIGURE 1-60

2 **Click the Display button. Click the Maximize button in the Windows Help title bar. Point to the Sizing windows button.**

The Windows Help window opens and a screen titled, The Basics, displays (Figure 1-61). The window is maximized and the Restore button displays in place of the Maximize button. The screen includes six buttons to learn Windows essentials and a picture of the Windows 95 desktop. When the mouse pointer is positioned on one of the buttons, it changes to a hand with a pointing finger. The Windows Help button displays on the taskbar.

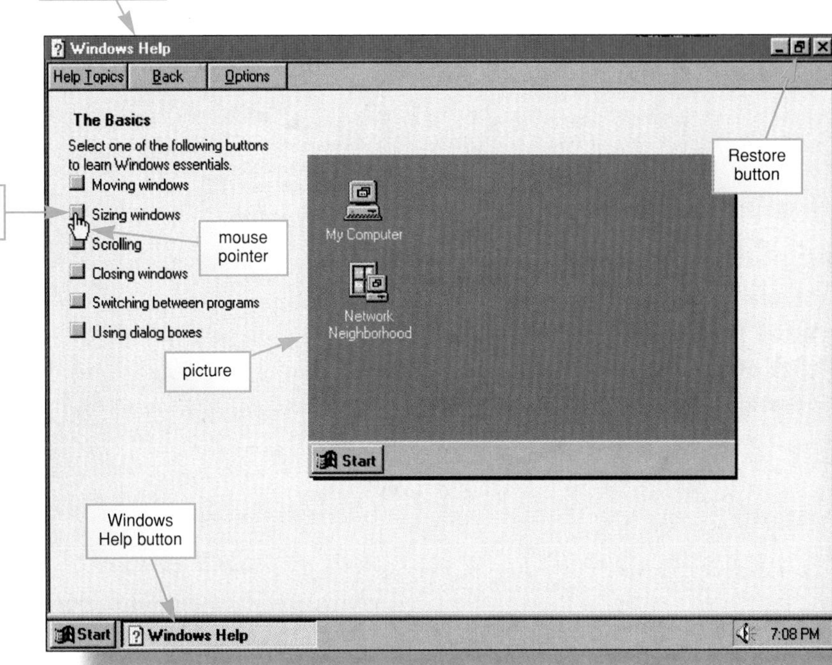

FIGURE 1-61

3 **Click the Sizing windows button. Point to the Play button (the button with the right arrow) below the picture on the right.**

The words, Sizing windows, display in bold, the My Computer window is added to the picture on the right, and the controls to play the animation display (Figure 1-62). The Play button will play the animation, the Option button displays a series of options regarding the animation, and the slide indicates progress when the animation plays. Text that explains how to accomplish the task, such as sizing windows, displays above the picture. On some computers, the animation might not be available. On those computers, instead of displaying the animation picture, the message, Unable to display graphic, will display on the screen. The text above the picture that explains how to perform the task still displays.

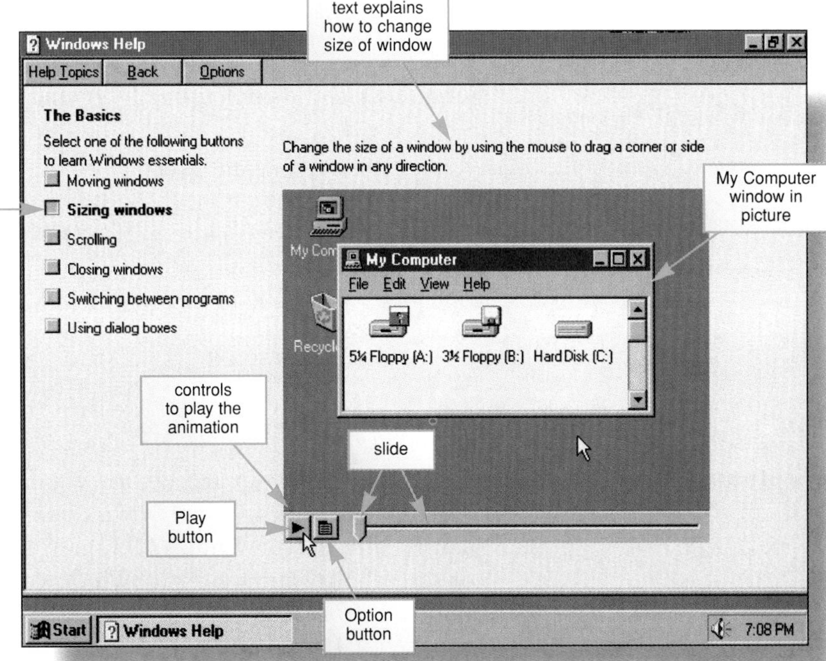

FIGURE 1-62

4 Click the Play button if it displays on the screen.

The Play button changes to a Stop button and the animation plays (Figure 1-63). The slide indicates the progress of the animation.

5 When the animation is complete, click any buttons you wish to view other animations.

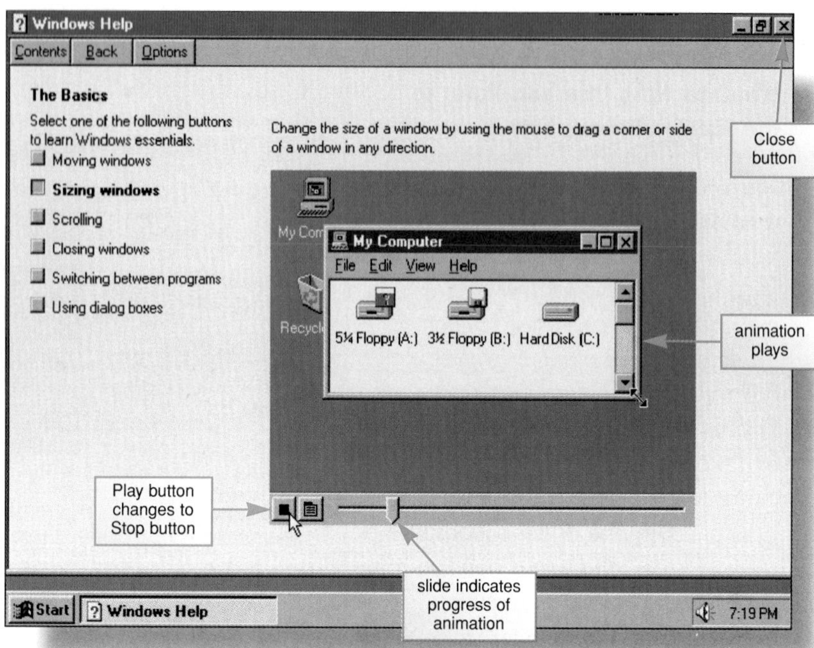

FIGURE 1-63

OtherWays

1. Press CTRL+TAB, type topic name, press ENTER, press ALT+SPACEBAR, press X, press TAB until topic highlighted, press ENTER, click Play button

After viewing Help topics, normally you will close Windows Help. To close Windows Help, complete the following step.

TO CLOSE WINDOWS HELP

Step 1: Click the Close button on the title bar of the Windows Help window.

Windows 95 closes the Windows Help window.

More About Shut Down Procedures

Some users of Windows 95 have turned off their computer without following the shut down procedure only to find data they thought they had stored on disk was lost. Because of the way Windows 95 writes data on the disk, it is important you shut down windows properly so you do not lose your work.

Shutting Down Windows 95

After completing your work with Windows 95, you might want to shut down Windows 95 using the **Shut Down command** on the Start menu. If you are sure you want to shut down Windows 95, perform the steps on the next page. If you are not sure about shutting down Windows 95, read the following steps without actually performing them.

To Shut Down Windows 95

1 Click the Start button on the taskbar and then point to Shut Down on the Start menu.

Windows 95 displays the Start menu (Figure 1-64). The Shut Down command is highlighted because the mouse pointer points to it.

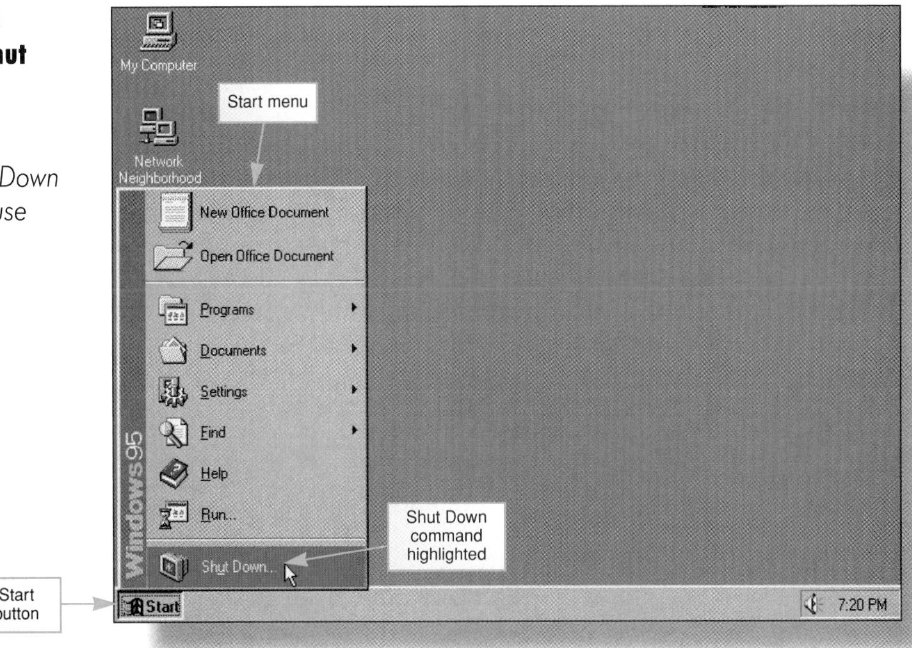

FIGURE 1-64

2 Click Shut Down. Point to the Yes button in the Shut Down Windows dialog box.

Windows 95 darkens the entire desktop and opens the Shut Down Windows dialog box (Figure 1-65). The dialog box contains four option buttons. The selected option button, Shut down the computer?, indicates that clicking the Yes button will shut down Windows 95.

3 Click the Yes button.

Two screens display while Windows 95 is shutting down. The first screen containing the text, Shutting down Windows, displays momentarily while Windows 95 is being shut down. Then, a second screen containing the text, It is okay to turn off your computer, displays. At this point you can to turn off your computer. When shutting down Windows 95, you should never turn off your computer before this last screen displays.

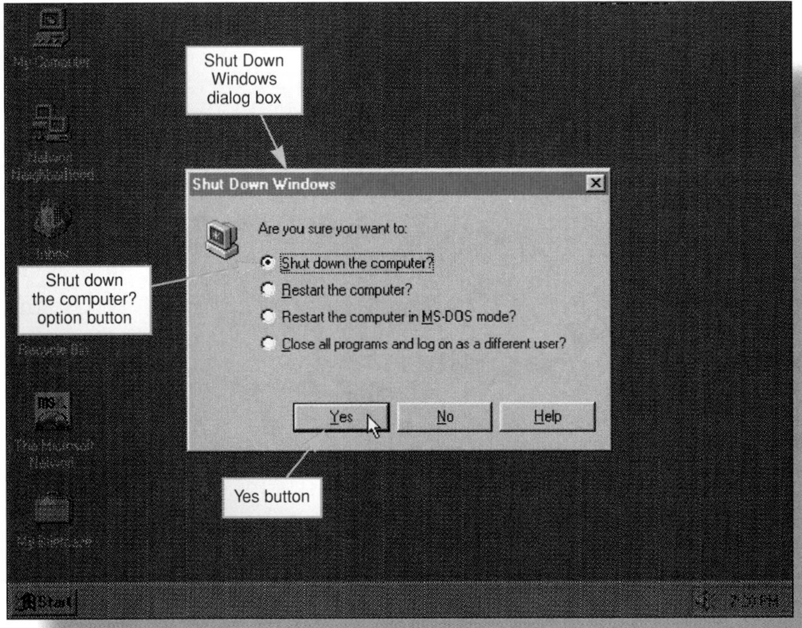

FIGURE 1-65

*Other*Ways

1. Press CTRL+ESC, press U, press UP ARROW or DOWN ARROW until option button selected, press ENTER
2. Press ALT+F4, press UP ARROW or DOWN ARROW until option button selected, press ENTER

If you accidentally click Shut Down on the Start menu and you do not want to shut down Windows 95, click the No button in the Shut Down Windows dialog box to return to normal Windows 95 operation.

Project Summary

Project 1 illustrated the Microsoft Windows 95 graphical user interface. You started Windows 95, learned the parts of the desktop, and learned to point, click, right-click, double-click, drag, and right-drag. You created a document by starting Notepad, entering text, saving the document on a floppy disk, and printing the document. You then modified the Notepad document and saved the modified document. Using both the Help Content and the Help Index sheets you obtained Help about Microsoft Windows 95. You shut down Windows 95 using the Shut Down command on the Start menu.

What You Should Know

Having completed this project, you should now be able to perform the following tasks:

- Close a Program *(WIN 1.32, WIN 1.36)*
- Close the Welcome Screen *(WIN 1.7)*
- Close a Window *(WIN 1.20)*
- Close a Window and Reopen a Window *(WIN 1.16)*
- Close Windows Help *(WIN 1.42)*
- Create a Document *(WIN 1.26)*
- Maximize and Restore a Window *(WIN 1.14)*
- Minimize and Redisplay a Window *(WIN 1.13)*
- Modify a Document *(WIN 1.35)*
- Move an Object by Dragging *(WIN 1.17)*
- Open a Document Stored on Disk *(WIN 1.32)*
- Open a Window by Double-Clicking *(WIN 1.12)*
- Point and Click *(WIN 1.9)*
- Print a Document *(WIN 1.31)*
- Resize a Window *(WIN 1.21)*
- Right-Click *(WIN 1.11)*
- Right-Drag *(WIN 1.22)*
- Save a Document on Disk *(WIN 1.27)*
- Save a Modified Document on Disk *(WIN 1.35)*
- Scroll a Window Using Scroll Arrows *(WIN 1.20)*
- Shut Down Windows 95 *(WIN 1.43)*
- Size a Window by Dragging *(WIN 1.19)*
- Start a Program *(WIN 1.24)*
- Start Help *(WIN 1.36)*
- Use Help to Find a Topic in Help *(WIN 1.38)*
- Use the Help Index Sheet *(WIN 1.40)*

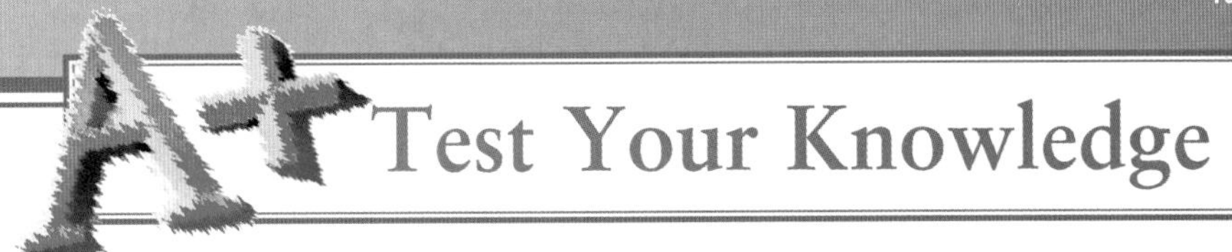

Test Your Knowledge

1 True/False

Instructions: Circle T if the statement is true or F if the statement is false.

T F 1. A user interface is a combination of computer hardware and computer software.
T F 2. Click means press the right mouse button.
T F 3. When you drag an object on the desktop, Windows 95 displays a context-sensitive menu.
T F 4. You can resize a window by dragging the title bar of the window.
T F 5. Daily Reminders - Friday and Mileage Log are valid filenames.
T F 6. To save a new document created using Notepad, click Save As on the File menu.
T F 7. To print a document, click Print on the File menu.
T F 8. To open a document stored on a floppy disk, click Open on the Start menu.
T F 9. You can start Help by clicking the Start button and then clicking Help on the Start menu.
T F 10. To find an item in the Windows Help Index, type the first few characters of the item in the text box on the Contents sheet.

2 Multiple Choice

Instructions: Circle the correct response.

1. Through a user interface, the user is able to __________.
   a. control the computer
   b. request information from the computer
   c. respond to messages displayed by the computer
   d. all of the above
2. A context-sensitive menu opens when you __________ a(n) __________.
   a. right-click, object
   b. click, menu name on the menu bar
   c. click, submenu
   d. double-click, indented button on the taskbar
3. In this book, a dark blue title bar and an indented button on the taskbar indicate a window is __________.
   a. inactive
   b. minimized
   c. closed
   d. active
4. To view contents of a window that are not currently visible in the window, use the __________.
   a. title bar
   b. scroll bar
   c. menu bar
   d. Restore button

(continued)

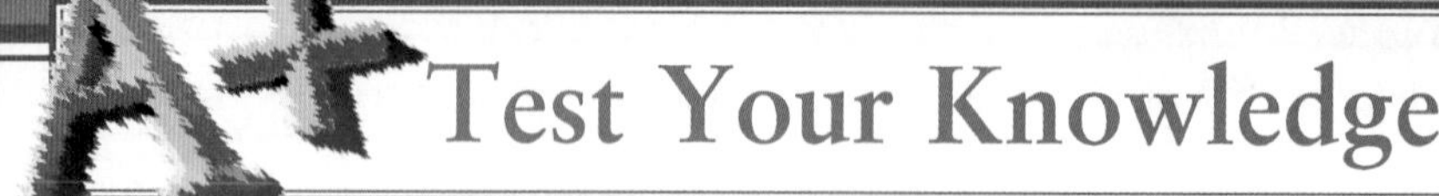

Test Your Knowledge

Multiple Choice *(continued)*

5. __________ is holding down the right mouse button, moving an item to the desired location, and then releasing the right mouse button.
   a. Double-clicking
   b. Right-clicking
   c. Right-dragging
   d. Pointing
6. The Notepad command used to start the Notepad application program is located on the __________ (sub)menu.
   a. Start
   b. Accessories
   c. Programs
   d. Help
7. To quit the Notepad application and close its window, __________.
   a. click the Close button on the Notepad title bar
   b. click File on the menu bar
   c. double-click the Notepad title bar
   d. click the Minimize button on the Notepad title bar
8. To save a Notepad document after modifying the document, __________.
   a. click the Close button on the Notepad title bar
   b. click the Minimize button on the Notepad title bar
   c. click Save on the File menu
   d. click Exit on the File menu
9. For information about an item on the Index sheet of the Help Topics: Windows Help window, __________.
   a. press the F1 key
   b. click the Question Mark button in the top right corner of the dialog box and then click the item
   c. click the Find tab in the Help Topics: Windows Help window
   d. press CTRL+F3
10. To shut down Windows 95, __________.
   a. click the Start button, click Shut Down on the Start menu, click the Shut down the computer? option button, and then click the Yes button
   b. click the Shut Down button on the Windows 95 File menu
   c. click the taskbar, click Close down Windows 95, and then click the Yes button
   d. press the F10 key and then click the Yes button

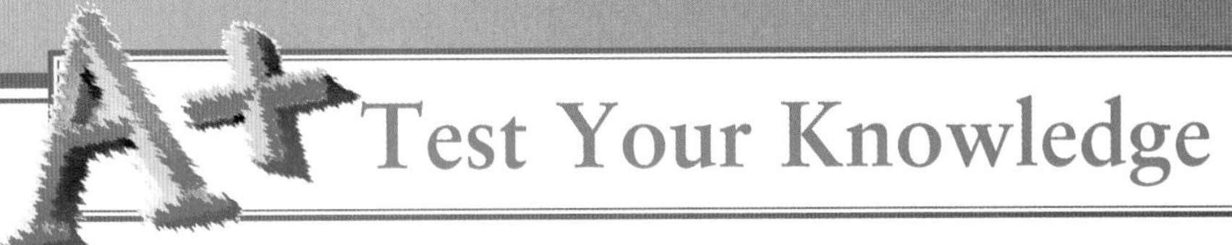

3 Identifying Objects on the Desktop

Instructions: On the desktop in Figure 1-66, arrows point to several items or objects on the desktop. Identify the items or objects in the spaces provided.

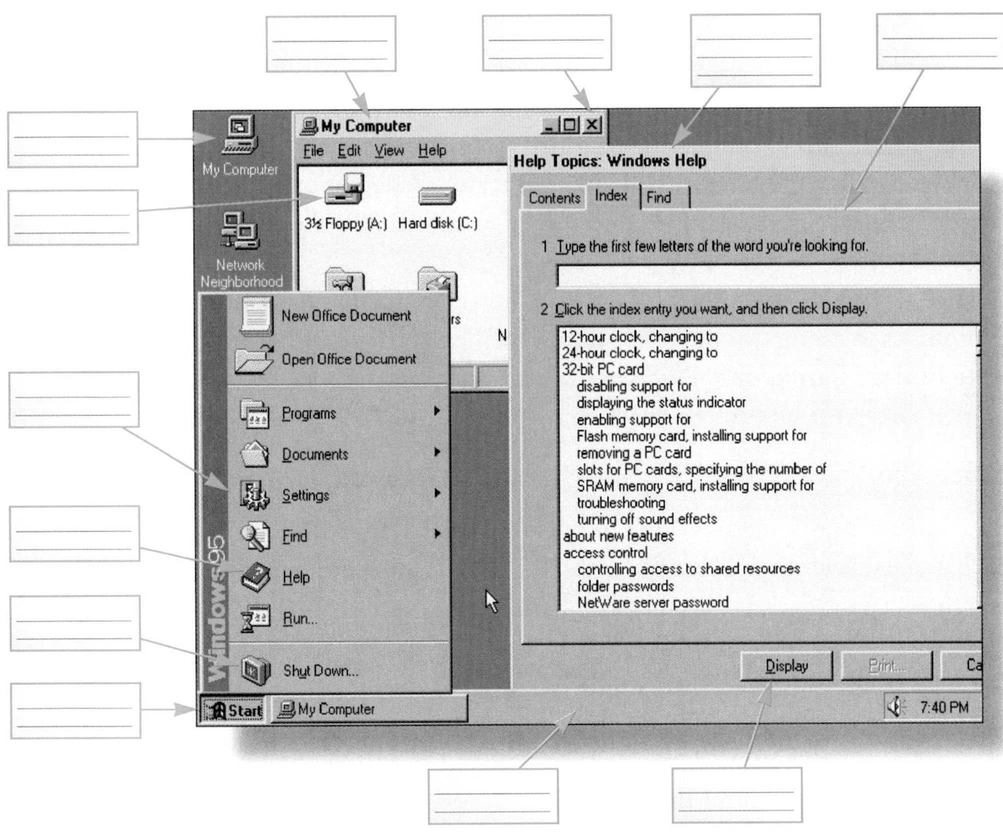

FIGURE 1-66

4 Saving a Document

Instructions: List the steps in the spaces provided to save a new Notepad file on a floppy disk in drive A using the filename, This is my file.

Step 1: ____________________

Step 2: ____________________

Step 3: ____________________

Step 4: ____________________

Step 5: ____________________

Step 6: ____________________

Step 7: ____________________

Use Help

1 Using Windows Help

Instructions: Use Windows Help and a computer to perform the following tasks.

Part 1: *Using the Question Mark Button*

1. Start Microsoft Windows 95 if necessary.
2. Click the Start button. Click Help on the Start menu to open the Help Topics: Windows Help window. If the Contents tab sheet does not display, click the Contents tab.
3. Click the Question Mark button on the title bar. The mouse pointer changes to a block arrow with question mark pointer. Click the list box containing the Help topics and Help books. A pop-up window explaining the list box displays. Click an open area of the list box to remove the pop-up window.
4. Click the Question Mark button on the title bar and then click the Display button.
5. Click the Question Mark button on the title bar and then click the Print button.
6. Click the Question Mark button on the title bar and then click the Cancel button.
7. Click an open area of the list box to remove the pop-up window.

Part 2: *Finding What's New with Windows 95*

1. Double-click the Introducing Windows book to open the book. Double-click the Welcome book to open the book. Double-click the A List of What's New book to open the book. Double-click the A new look and feel Help topic to open the Windows Help window. Click the first button (Start button and taskbar) and read the contents of the What's New window.
2. Click the Close button in the What's New window.
3. Click the Help Topics button in the Windows Help window to open the Help Topics: Windows Help window. Click the Print button in the Help Topics: Windows Help window. Click the OK button in the Print dialog box to print the Help topic (A new look and feel).
4. Click the Help Topics button in the Windows Help window.
5. Double-click the Welcome book to close the book.

Part 3: *Learning About Getting Your Work Done*

1. Double-click the Getting Your Work Done book to open the book. Double-click the Saving your work Help topic. Click the Save button and read the pop-up window.
2. Click other items in the Save As dialog box and read the pop-up windows.
3. Click the Help Topics button in the Windows Help window to open the Help Topics: Windows Help window. Click the Print button in the Help Topics: Windows Help window. Click the OK button in the Print dialog box to print the Saving your work Help topic.
4. Click the Close buttons in the Windows Help windows to close the windows.

Use Help

2 Using Windows Help to Obtain Help

Instructions: Use Windows Help and a computer to perform the following tasks.

1. Find Help about viewing the Welcome screen that displays when you start Windows 95 by looking in the Tips of the Day book within the Tips and Tricks book in the Help Topics: Windows Help window. Answer the following questions in the spaces provided.
   a. How can you open the Welcome screen? ______________________________
   b. How can you see the list of tips in the Welcome screen? ______________________________
   c. Open the Welcome screen. Cycle through the tips in the Welcome screen. How can you set your computer's clock? ______________________________
   d. Click the What's New button in the Welcome screen. According to Help, how do you start a program? ______________________________
   e. Close the Welcome screen. Click the Help Topics button in the Windows Help window.
2. Find Help about keyboard shortcuts by looking in the Keyboard Shortcuts book. Answer the following questions in the spaces provided.
   a. What keyboard shortcut is used to quit a program? ____________________
   b. What keyboard shortcut is used to display the Start menu? ____________________
   c. What keyboard shortcut is used to view the shortcut menu for a selected item? __________
   d. What keyboard shortcut is used to rename an item? ____________________
   e. What keyboard shortcut is used to open the Save in list box (drop-down list box)? __________
   f. Click the Help Topics button in the Windows Help window.
3. Find Help about Notepad by looking in the For Writing and Drawing book. Answer the following questions in the spaces provided.
   a. Can you create or edit a text file that requires formatting using Notepad? ______________
   b. What size file can you create using Notepad? ____________________
   c. Which program can you use to create a larger file? ____________________
   d. What is the only format used by Notepad to store a file? ____________________
4. Find Help about the Internet by looking in the Welcome to the Information Highway book. Answer the following questions in the spaces provided.
   a. List one source of online information available on the Internet. ____________________
   b. How do you use The Microsoft Network to sign up for the Internet?
   c. Where else can you find information about connecting to the Internet? ______________
5. Find Help about what to do if you have a problem starting Windows 95. The process of solving such a problem is called troubleshooting. Answer the following questions in the spaces provided.
   a. What size floppy disk do you need to create a startup disk? ____________________
   b. To start Windows in safe mode, what do you do when you see the message "Starting Windows 95?" ____________________
6. Answer the following questions in the spaces provided.
   a. List two ways you can get Help in a dialog box: ____________________; __________.
   b. How can you print information displayed in a Help pop-up window?
   ____

(continued)

Use Help

Use Help *(continued)*

7. You have been assigned to obtain information on software licensing. Answer the following questions, and find and print information from Windows Help that supports your answers.
   a. How is computer software protected by law?
   b. What is software piracy? Why should you be concerned?
   c. Can you use your own software on both your desktop and your laptop computers?
   d. How can you identify illegal software?
8. Close all open Windows Help windows.

In the Lab

1 Improving Your Mouse Skills

Instructions: Use a computer to perform the following tasks:

1. Start Microsoft Windows 95 if necessary.
2. Click the Start button on the taskbar, point to Programs on the Start menu, point to Accessories on the Programs submenu, point to Games on the Accessories submenu, and click Solitaire on the Games submenu.
3. Click the Maximize button in the Solitaire window.
4. Click Help on the Solitaire menu bar.
5. Click Help Topics on the Help menu.
6. If the Contents sheet does not display, click the Contents tab.
7. Review the How to play Solitaire and Scoring information Help topics on the Contents sheet.
8. After reviewing the topics, close all Help windows.
9. Play the game of Solitaire.
10. Click the Close button on the Solitaire title bar to close the game.

2 Starting an Application, Creating a Document, and Modifying a Document

Instructions: Perform the following steps to start the Notepad application and create and modify a document.

Part 1: *Creating a Document*

1. Start Microsoft Windows 95 if necessary.
2. Click the Start button. Point to Programs on the Start menu. Point to Accessories on the Programs submenu. Click Notepad on the Accessories submenu.

In the Lab

3. Enter the document shown in Figure 1-67 in the Notepad document.
4. Insert a formatted floppy disk in drive A of your computer.
5. Click File on the menu bar. Click Save As on the File menu.
6. Type `Office Supplies Shopping List - Tuesday` in the File name text box.
7. Click the Save in box arrow. Click the 3½ Floppy [A:] icon. Click the Save button.
8. Click File on the menu bar. Click Print on the File menu.
9. Click the Close button on the Notepad title bar.
10. If you are not completing Part 2 of this assignment, remove your floppy disk from drive A.

```
Office Supplies Shopping List - Tuesday

1. Staples
2. 2 boxes of copier paper
3. Toner for computer printer
4. Box of formatted floppy disks
```

FIGURE 1-67

Part 2: *Modifying a Document*

1. Click the Start button, point to Programs on the Start menu, point to Accessories on the Programs submenu, and then click Notepad on the Accessories submenu.
2. Click File on the menu bar and then click Open on the File menu. Click the Look in box arrow and then click the 3½ Floppy [A:] icon. Click Office Supplies Shopping List - Tuesday. Click the Open button.
3. Press the DOWN ARROW key six times. Type `5. Two boxes of black ink pens` and then press the ENTER key.
4. Click File on the menu bar and then click Save on the File menu.
5. Click File on the menu bar and then click Print on the File menu.
6. Click the Close button on the Notepad title bar.
7. Remove the floppy disk from drive A of your computer.

3 Creating a Document

Instructions: As a student, you would like to give a copy of your daily schedule to your parents and friends so you can be contacted in an emergency. To do this, you want to create a document for each weekday (Monday through Friday). Each document will have an appropriate title and contain your daily school and personal schedule. Each course in the document will contain the start and finish time for the course, course number, course title, room number, and instructor name. Other entries for extracurricular activities, sporting events, or personal events also will be included in the documents. Print the five documents on the printer and follow directions from your instructor for turning in this assignment. Store the five documents on a floppy disk.

200 MHz

Cases and Places

The difficulty of these case studies varies:

◗ Case studies preceded by a single half moon are the least difficult. You can complete these case studies using your own computer or a computer in the lab.
◗◗ Case studies preceded by two half moons are more difficult. You must research the topic presented using the Internet, a library, or another resource, and then prepare a brief written report.
◗◗◗ Case studies preceded by three half moons are the most difficult. You must visit a store or business to obtain the necessary information, and then use it to create a brief written report.

1 ◗ Your employer is concerned that some people in the company are not putting enough thought into software purchases. She has prepared a list of steps she would like everyone to follow when acquiring software (Figure 1-68).

Steps in Software Acquisition

1. *Summarize your requirements*
2. *Identify potential vendors*
3. *Evaluate alternative software packages*
4. *Make the purchase*

FIGURE 1-68

You have been asked to use WordPad to prepare a copy of this list that can be posted in every department. Use the concepts and techniques presented in this project to start WordPad and create, save, and print the document. After you have printed one copy of the document, try experimenting with different WordPad features to make the list more eye-catching. If you like your changes, save and print a revised copy of the document. If WordPad is not available on your machine, use Notepad.

2 ◗ The local community center has asked you to teach an introductory class on Windows 95 to a group of adults with little previous computer experience. The center director has sent you a note about one of his concerns (Figure 1-69).

Is online Help enough for this group?

These people are pretty traditional and are used to having a printed text. Do we need to buy some kind of "help resource book" for everyone? We don't have much money, but on the other hand we don't want people to be disappointed.

Please think about it and get back to me.

FIGURE 1-69

Think of two topics about which people in the class may have questions. Use online Help to find answers to the questions. Consider how you would find answers to the same questions using a book. Write a response to the center director describing the advantages and disadvantages of using online Help instead of a book. Explain why you feel the class does or does not need a resource book. To make the director aware of online Help's limitations, tell how you think Microsoft could improve Help in Windows 95.

Cases and Places

3 ▶▶ Early personal computer operating systems were adequate, but they were not user-friendly and had few advanced features. Over the past several years, however, personal computer operating systems have become increasingly easy to use, and some now offer features once available only on mainframe computers. Using the Internet, a library, or other research facility, write a brief report on four personal computer operating systems. Describe the systems, pointing out their similarities and differences. Discuss the advantages and disadvantages of each. Finally, tell which operating system you would purchase for your personal computer and explain why.

4 ▶▶ Many feel that Windows 95 was one of the most heavily promoted products ever released. Using the Internet, current computer magazines, or other resources, prepare a brief report on the background of Windows 95. Explain why Windows 95 was two years behind schedule and how it was promoted. Discuss the ways in which Windows 95 is different from earlier versions of Windows (such as Windows 3.1). Based on reviews of the new operating system, describe what people like and do not like about Windows 95. Finally, from what you have learned and your own experience, explain how you think Windows 95 could be improved.

5 ▶▶▶ Software must be compatible with (able to work with) the operating system of the computer on which it will be used. Visit a software vendor and find the five application packages (word processing programs, spreadsheet programs, games, and so on) you would most like to have. List the names of the packages and the operating system used by each. Make a second list of five similar packages that are compatible (meaning they use the same operating system). Using your two lists, write a brief report on how the need to purchase compatible software can affect buying application packages and even the choice of an operating system.

6 ▶▶▶ Because of the many important tasks it performs, most businesses put a great deal of thought into choosing an operating system for their personal computers. Interview people at a local business on the operating system they use with their personal computers. Based on your interviews, write a brief report on why the business chose that operating system, how satisfied they are with it, and under what circumstances they might consider switching to a different operating system.

7 ▶▶▶ In a recent television commercial from Apple Computers, a frustrated father tries to use Windows 95 to display pictures of dinosaurs for his young son. After waiting impatiently, the boy tells his father he is going next door to the neighbor's because they have a Mac. Visit a computer vendor and try an operating system with a graphical user interface other than Windows 95, such as Macintosh System 7.5 or OS/2. Write a brief report comparing the operating system to Windows 95, and explain which operating system you would prefer to have on your personal computer.

Putting the Squeeze on DATA

In 1994, a federal district court ruled that Microsoft violated the rights of Stac Electronics in the data compression software component of MS-DOS 6.2, Microsoft's operating system. In response, Microsoft paid Stac a royalty of $43 million and replaced MS-DOS 6.2 with version 6.21, which did not contain the offending code.

Why the lawsuit? Data compression software, which allows you to store more data on your hard disk, is an important component of your computer's software and is so valuable to its developers that they will sue to protect their rights.

Disk storage capacity has not always been critical. Indeed, the first personal computers did not have disk storage. Instead, they used slow, unreliable tape cassettes. Then, in 1978, Apple demonstrated its first working prototype of the Apple

1978

320K

floppy disk drive. The drive could store 320,000 bytes, or characters, on a floppy disk 5.25 inches in diameter. It was a marvel and, by the end of 1978, Apple had sold more than 270,000 floppy disk drives.

It was not long, however, before computer users craved more disk storage. Apple announced its first hard disk drive in 1981. The drive could store five megabytes, but cost $3,500 ($700 per megabyte). By 1983, a hard disk drive could store 44 megabytes. Clearly the race was on to build drives that, today, store upwards of one gigabyte (one billion characters) at a price of about 25 cents per megabyte.

The hardware manufacturers were not the only ones trying to squeeze more data onto disks. Software companies developed data compression schemes that increased the apparent capacity of hard disks by storing the contents in a compressed form. Compressing data occurs in two ways. First, the software restructures the files on your hard disk so the data is stored more efficiently. Second, data is coded so redundancies in the data are reduced.

Some personal computer applications could not occur without data compression. For example, an uncompressed ten-second video requires nearly 200 megabytes of storage. This means an entire gigabyte drive would be consumed by a one-minute video if the video data was not compressed.

Compression, using hardware, software, or a combination of the two, is big business, and millions of dollars are being spent to develop new compression schemes. In the future, whether you are retrieving a word processing file from your hard disk or conducting a video conference over your network, it is likely the data will be stored and transmitted as compressed data.

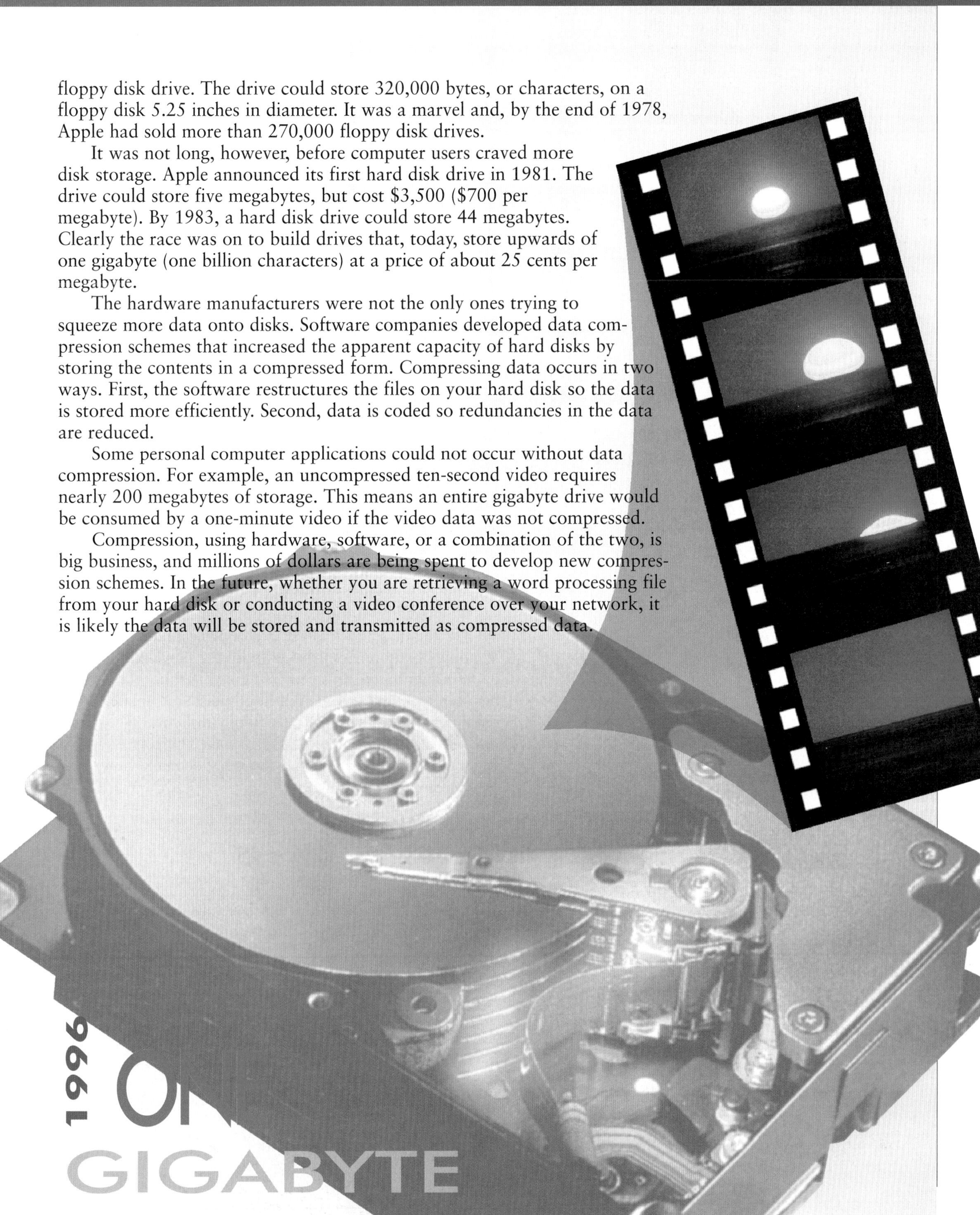

Microsoft
Windows 95

Using Windows Explorer

Case Perspective

Need: Your organization has finally made the decision to switch to Windows 95 from Windows 3.1. Although most everyone is excited about the change, many are apprehensive about file management. Few of them ever felt comfortable with Windows 3.1 File Manager and, as a result, hardly ever used it. Your boss has read in computer magazines that in order to effectively use Windows 95, people must learn Windows Explorer. She has asked you to teach a class with an emphasis on file management to all employees who will be using Windows 95. Your goal in Project 2 is to become competent using Windows Explorer so you can teach the class.

Introduction

Windows Explorer is an application program included with Windows 95 that allows you to view the contents of the computer, the hierarchy of folders on the computer, and the files and folders in each folder.

Windows Explorer also allows you to organize the files and folders on the computer by copying and moving the files and folders. In this project, you will use Windows Explorer to (1) work with the files and folders on your computer; (2) select and copy a group of files between the hard drive and a floppy disk; (3) create, rename, and delete a folder on floppy disk; and (4) rename and delete a file on floppy disk. These are common operations that you should understand how to perform.

Starting Windows 95

As explained in Project 1, when you turn on the computer, an introductory screen consisting of the Windows 95 logo and the Microsoft Windows 95 name displays on a blue sky and clouds background. The screen clears and Windows 95 displays several items on the desktop.

If the Welcome to Windows screen displays on your desktop, click the Close button on the title bar to close the screen. Six icons (My Computer, Network Neighborhood, Inbox, Recycle Bin, The Microsoft Network, and My Briefcase) display along the left edge of the desktop, the Microsoft Office Manager toolbar displays in the upper right corner of the desktop, and the taskbar displays along the bottom of the desktop (Figure 2-1).

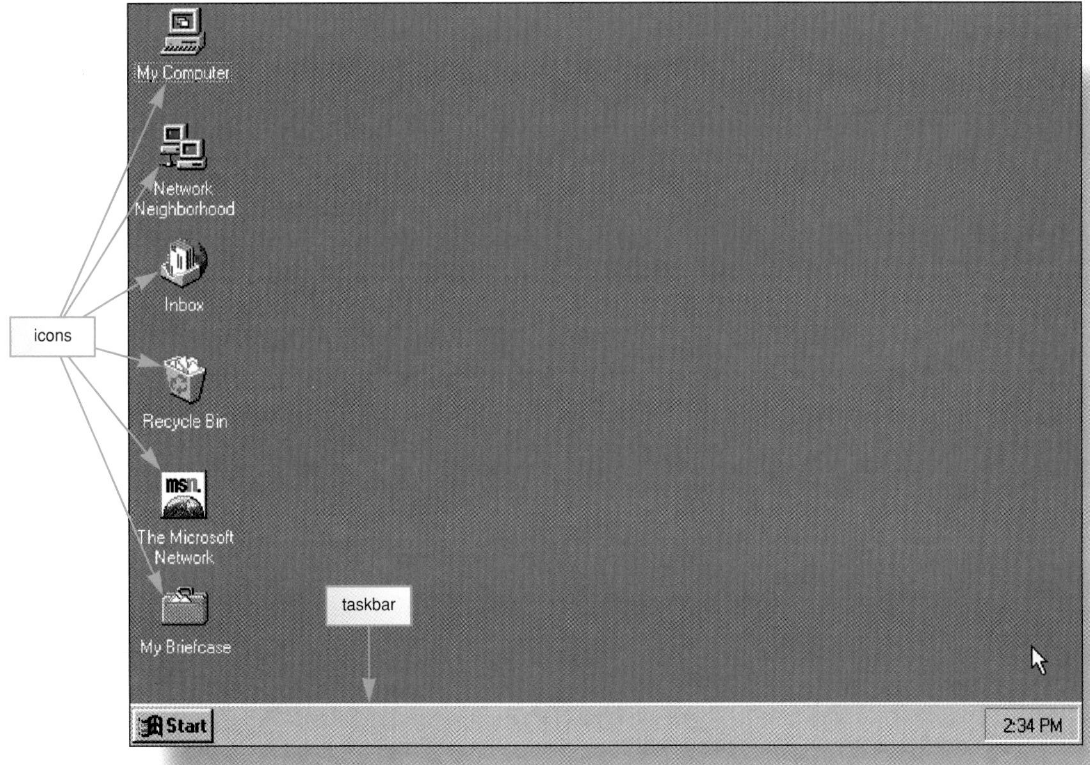

FIGURE 2-1

Starting Windows Explorer and Maximizing Its Window

To start Windows Explorer and explore the files and folders on the computer, right-click the My Computer icon on the desktop, which opens a context-sensitive menu, and then click the Explore command on the menu to open the Exploring – My Computer window. To maximize the Exploring – My Computer window, click the Maximize button on the title bar.

Steps To Start Windows Explorer and Maximize Its Window

1 Right-click the My Computer icon to open a context-sensitive menu, and then point to the Explore command on the menu.

Windows 95 highlights the My Computer icon, opens a context-sensitive menu, and highlights the Explore command on the menu (Figure 2-2). The mouse pointer points to the Explore command on the menu.

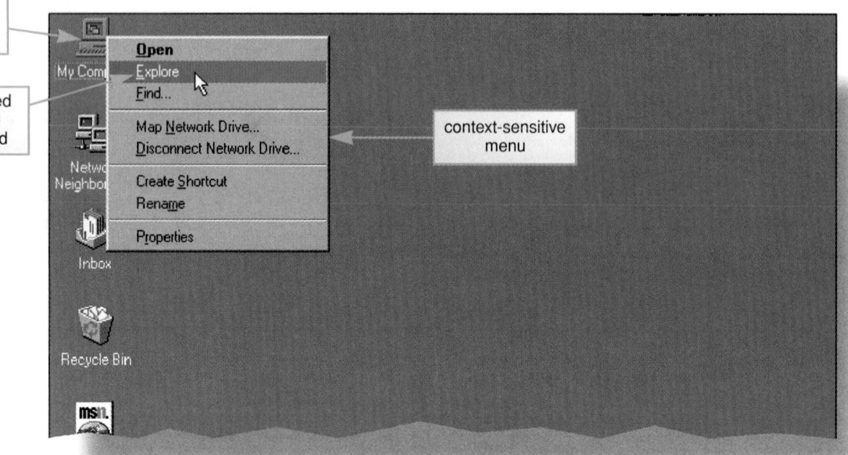

FIGURE 2-2

2 Click Explore on the context-sensitive menu, and then click the Maximize button on the Exploring – My Computer title bar.

Windows 95 opens and maximizes the Exploring – My Computer window and adds the indented Exploring – My Compu... button to the taskbar (Figure 2-3).

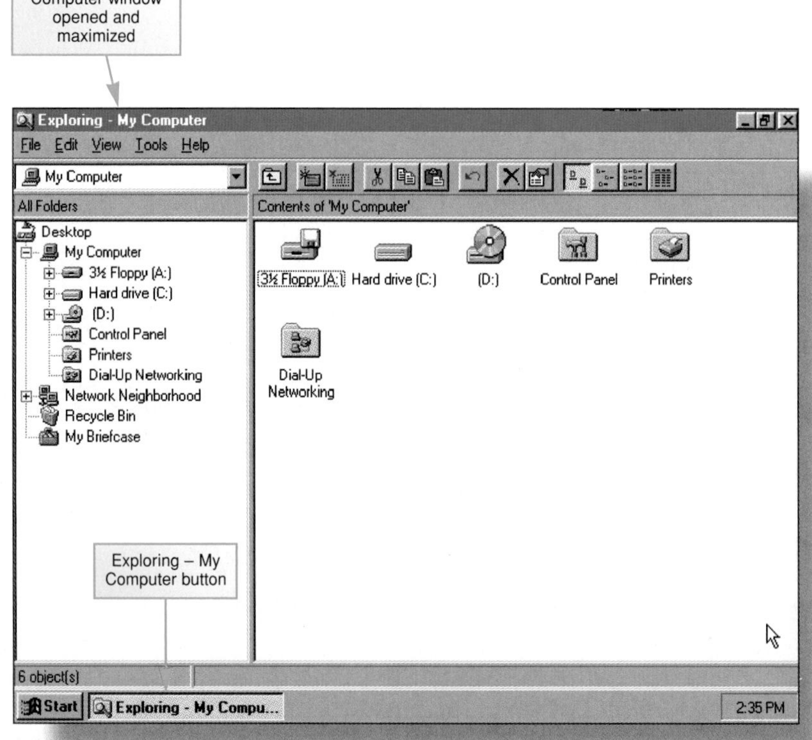

FIGURE 2-3

*Other*Ways

1. Right-click Start button, click Explore on context-sensitive menu
2. Click Start button, point to Programs, click Windows Explorer on the Programs submenu
3. Right-click Network Neighborhood icon, or Inbox icon, or Recycle Bin icon, or The Microsoft Network icon, or My Briefcase icon, click Explore on context-sensitive menu
4. Right-click Start button or any icons in 3 above, press E

Windows Explorer

When you start Windows Explorer by right-clicking the My Computer icon, Windows 95 opens the Exploring – My Computer window (Figure 2-4). The menu bar contains the File, Edit, View, Tools, and Help menu names.

These menus contain commands to organize and work with the drives on the computer and the files and folders on those drives.

Below the menu bar is a toolbar. The **toolbar** contains a drop-down list box and thirteen buttons. The drop-down list box contains an icon and the My Computer folder name. The entry in the drop-down list box, called the **current folder**, indicates Windows Explorer was started by right-clicking the My Computer icon. The buttons on the toolbar provide a quick way to perform commonly used tasks in Windows Explorer. Many of the buttons correspond to the commands available from the menu bar. Pointing to a button on the toolbar displays a ToolTip identifying the button. If the toolbar does not display in the Exploring – My Computer window on your computer, click View on the menu bar and then click Toolbar on the View menu.

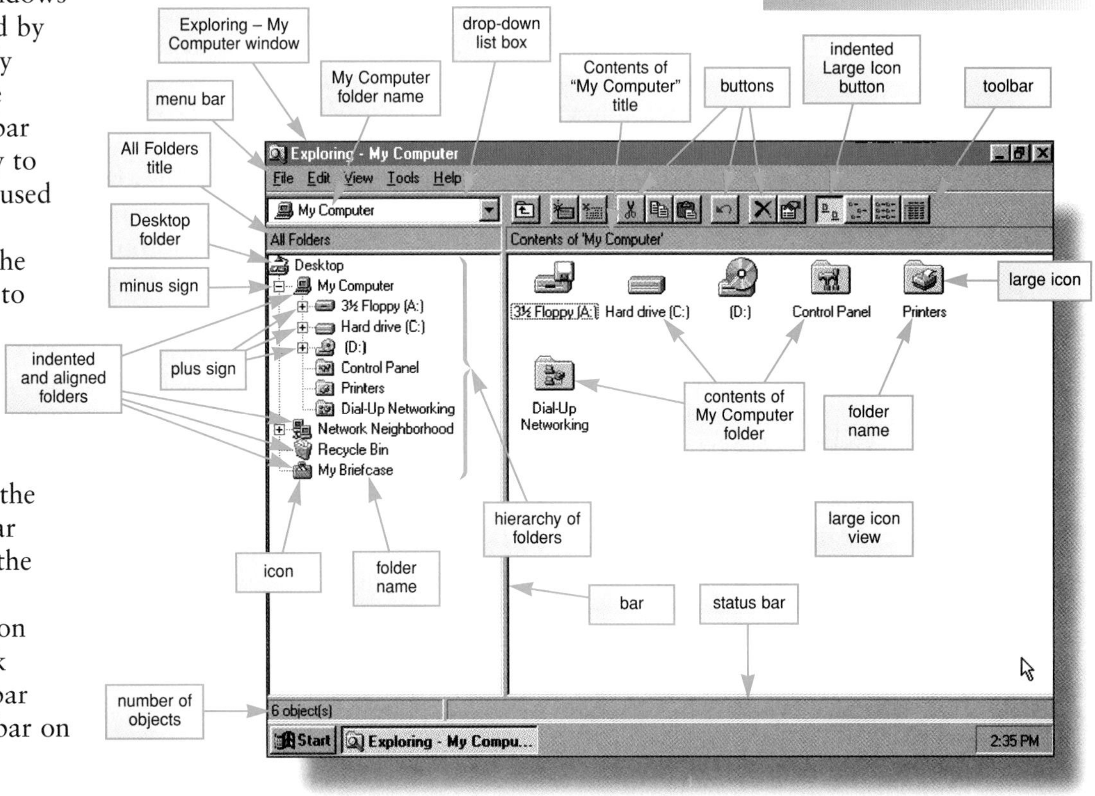

The window is divided into two areas separated by a bar. The left side of the window, identified by the All Folders title, contains a **hierarchy** of folders on the computer. The right side of the window, identified by the Contents of 'My Computer' title, displays the contents of the current folder (My Computer). In Figure 2-4, the Contents side contains the icons and folder names of six folders (3½ Floppy [A:], Hard drive [C:], and [D:], Control Panel, Printers, and Dial-Up Networking). These folders may be different on your computer. You change the size of the All Folders and Contents sides of the window by dragging the bar that separates the two sides.

Each folder in the All Folders side of the window is represented by an icon and folder name. The first folder, consisting of an icon and the Desktop folder name, represents the desktop of the computer. The four folders indented and aligned below the Desktop folder name (My Computer, Network Neighborhood,

FIGURE 2-4

More About Explorer

For those familiar with Windows 3.1, Windows 95 Explorer bears some resemblance to File Manager. Microsoft, however, made significant improvements and changed the basic way the program works. Those who passionately disliked File Manager might find Explorer a better way to perform file maintenance.

More About a Hierarchy

One definition of hierarchy in Webster's Ninth New Collegiate Dictionary is, "a division of angels." While no one would argue angels have anything to do with Windows 95, some preach that working with a hierarchical structure as presented by Explorer is less secular ("of or relating to the worldly") and more spiritual ("of or relating to supernatural phenomena") than the straight-forward showing of files in windows. What do you think?

Recycle Bin, and My Briefcase) are connected to the vertical line below the Desktop icon. These folders correspond to four of the six icons displayed on the left edge of the desktop (see Figure 2-1 on page WIN 2.5). These folders may be different on your computer.

Windows 95 displays a minus sign (–) in a box to the left of any icon in the All Folders side to indicate the corresponding folder contains one or more folders that are visible in the All Folders side. These folders, called **subfolders**, are indented and aligned below the folder name.

In Figure 2-4 on the previous page, a minus sign precedes the My Computer icon, and six subfolders are indented and display below the My Computer folder name. The six subfolders (3½ Floppy [A:], Hard drive [C:], [D:], Control Panel, Printers, and Dial-Up Networking) correspond to the six folders in the Contents side. Clicking the minus sign, referred to as **collapsing the folder**, removes the indented subfolders from the hierarchy of folders in the All Folders side and changes the minus sign to a plus sign.

Windows 95 displays a plus sign (+) in a box to the left of an icon to indicate the corresponding folder consists of one or more subfolders that are not visible in the All Folders side of the window. In Figure 2-4, a plus sign precedes the first three icons indented and aligned below the My Computer name (3½ Floppy [A:], Hard drive [C:], [D:]) and the Network Neighborhood icon. Clicking the plus sign, referred to as **expanding the folders**, displays a list of indented subfolders and changes the plus sign to a minus sign.

If neither a plus sign nor a minus sign displays to the left of an icon, the folder does not contain subfolders. In Figure 2-4, the Control Panel, Printers, Dial-Up Networking, Recycle Bin, and My Briefcase icons are not preceded by a plus or minus sign and do not contain subfolders.

The status bar at the bottom of the Exploring – My Computer window indicates the number of folders, or objects, displayed in the Contents side of the window (6 object(s)). Depending upon the objects displayed in the Contents side, the amount of disk space the objects occupy and the amount of unused disk space may also display on the status bar. If the status bar does not display in the Exploring – My Computer window on your computer, click View on the menu bar and then click Status Bar on the View menu.

In addition to using Windows Explorer to explore your computer by right-clicking the My Computer icon, you can also use Windows Explorer to explore different aspects of your computer by right-clicking the Start button on the taskbar and the Network Neighborhood, Inbox, Recycle Bin, The Microsoft Network, and My Briefcase icons on the desktop.

Displaying the Contents of a Folder

In Figure 2-4 on the previous page, the current folder (My Computer) displays in the drop-down list box on the toolbar and the Contents side of the window contains the subfolders in the My Computer folder. In addition to displaying the contents of the My Computer folder, the contents of any folder in the All Folders side can be displayed in the Contents side. Perform the following steps to display the contents of the Hard drive [C:] folder.

Steps To Display the Contents of a Folder

1 **Point to the Hard drive [C:] folder name in the All Folders side of the Exploring – My Computer window (Figure 2-5).**

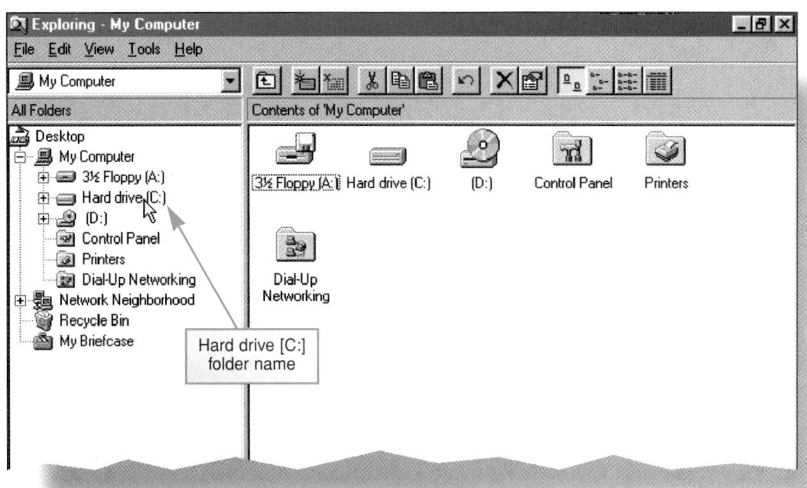

FIGURE 2-5

2 **Click the Hard drive [C:] folder name.**

Windows 95 highlights the Hard drive [C:] folder name in the All Folders side, changes the current folder in the drop-down list box to the Hard drive [C:] folder, displays the contents of the Hard drive [C:] folder in the Contents side, changes the window title to contain the current folder name (Exploring – Hard drive [C:]), changes the button on the taskbar to contain the current folder name, and changes the messages on the status bar (Figure 2-6). The status bar messages indicate there are 82 objects and 19 hidden objects in the Hard drive [C:] folder, the objects occupy 25.9MB of disk space, and the amount of unused disk space is 12.5MB. The contents of the Hard drive [C:] folder may be different on your computer.

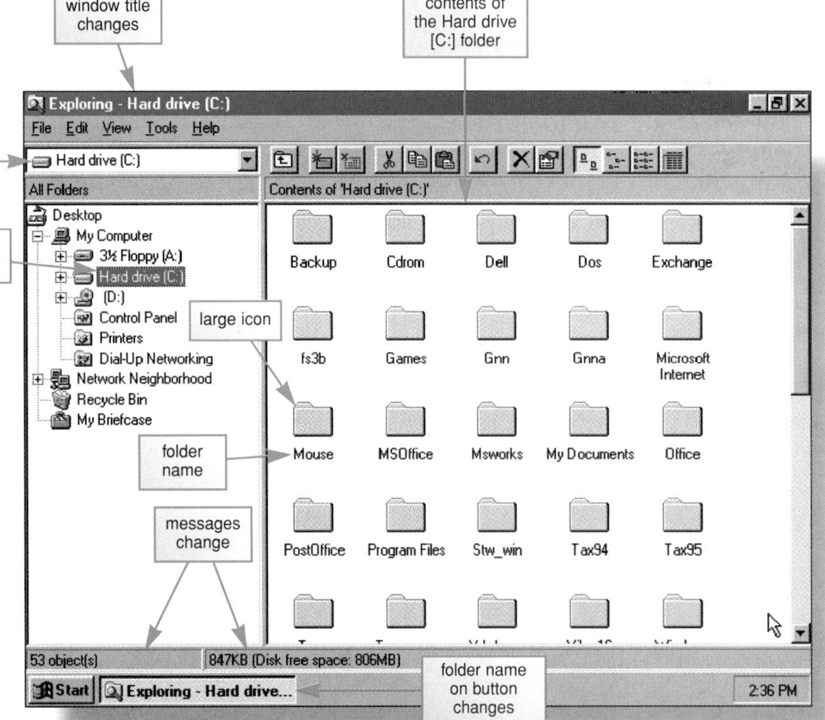

FIGURE 2-6

*Other*Ways

1. Double-click Hard disk [C:] icon in Contents side
2. Press TAB until any icon in All Folders side highlighted, press DOWN ARROW or UP ARROW until Hard disk [C:] highlighted in Contents side

In addition to displaying the contents of the Hard drive [C:] folder, you can display the contents of the other folders by clicking the corresponding icon or folder name in the All Folders side. The contents of the folder you click will then display in the Contents side of the window.

Expanding a Folder

Currently, the Hard drive [C:] folder is highlighted in the All Folders side of the Exploring – Hard drive [C:] window and the contents of the Hard drive [C:] folder display in the Contents side of the window. Windows 95 displays a plus sign (+) to the left of the Hard drive [C:] icon to indicate the folder contains subfolders that are not visible in the hierarchy of folders in the All Folders side of the window. To expand the Hard drive [C:] folder and display its subfolders, click the plus sign to the left of the Hard drive [C:] icon. Perform the following steps to expand the Hard drive [C:] folder.

To Expand a Folder

1 Point to the plus sign to the left of the Hard drive [C:] icon in the All Folders side of the Exploring – Hard drive [C:] window (Figure 2-7).

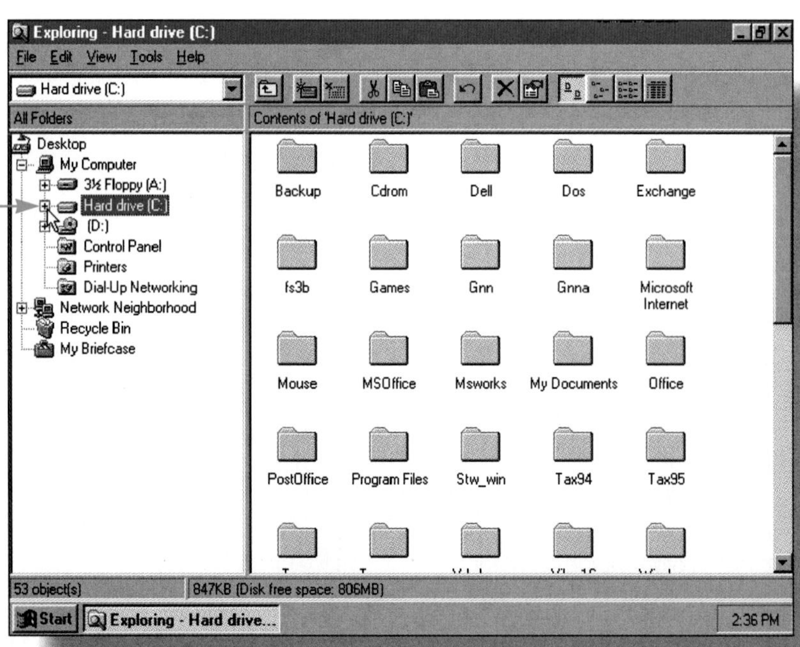

FIGURE 2-7

2 **Click the plus sign to display the subfolders in the Hard drive [C:] folder.**

Windows 95 replaces the plus sign preceding the Hard drive [C:] icon with a minus sign, displays a vertical scroll bar, and expands the Hard drive [C:] folder to include its subfolders, indented and aligned below the Hard drive [C:] folder name, (Figure 2-8). Each subfolder in the Hard drive [C:] folder is identified by a closed folder icon and folder name. The window title, current folder in the drop-down list box on the toolbar, and the files and folders in the Contents side of the window remain unchanged.

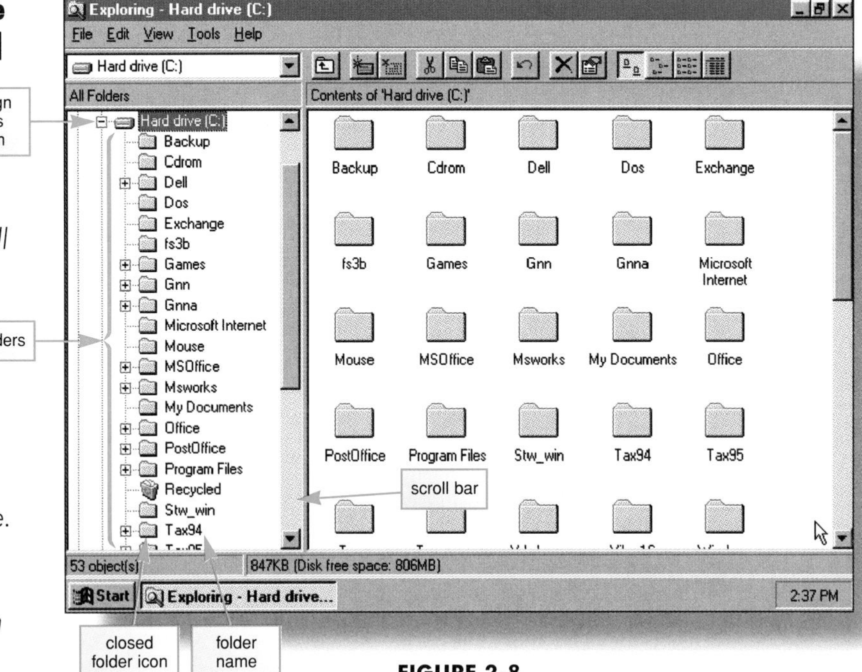

FIGURE 2-8

OtherWays

1. Double-click the folder icon
2. Select folder to expand, press PLUS on numeric keypad
3. Select folder to expand, press RIGHT ARROW

Collapsing a Folder

Currently, the subfolders in the Hard drive [C:] folder display indented and aligned below the Hard drive [C:] folder name (see Figure 2-8). Windows 95 displays a minus sign (–) to the left of the Hard drive [C:] icon to indicate the folder is expanded. To collapse the Hard drive [C:] folder and then remove its subfolders from the hierarchy of folders in the All Folders side, click the minus sign preceding the Hard drive [C:] icon. Perform the following steps to collapse the Hard drive [C:] folder.

Steps To Collapse a Folder

1 **Point to the minus sign preceding the Hard drive [C:] icon in the All Folders side of the Exploring – Hard drive [C:] window (Figure 2-9).**

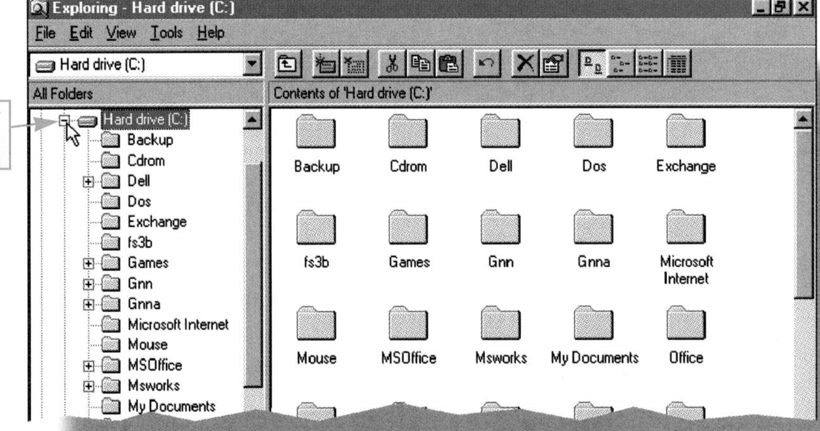

FIGURE 2-9

2 Click the minus sign to display the Hard drive [C:] folder without its subfolders.

Windows 95 replaces the minus sign preceding the Hard drive [C:] icon with a plus sign and removes the subfolders in the Hard drive [C:] folder from the hierarchy of folders (Figure 2-10).

plus sign replaces minus sign

subfolders do not display

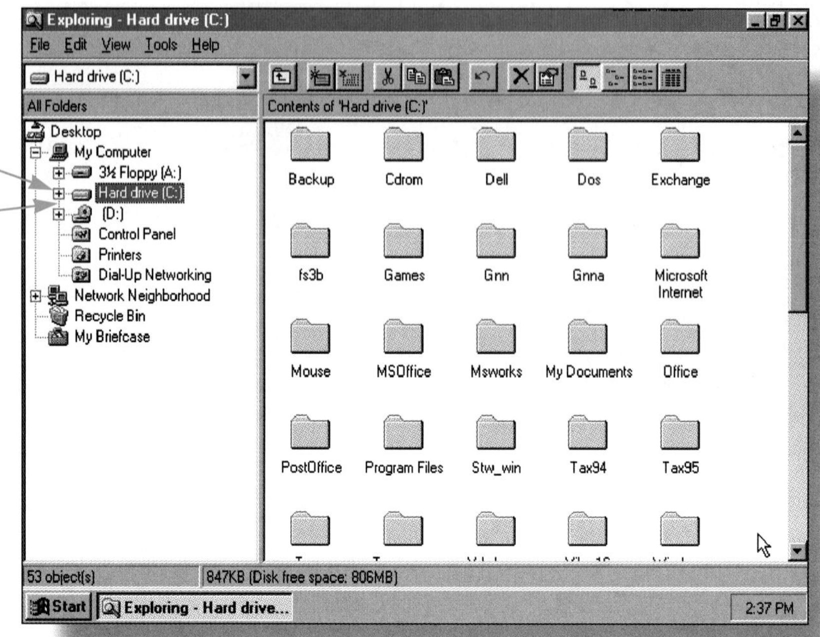

FIGURE 2-10

OtherWays

1. Highlight folder icon, press MINUS SIGN on numeric keypad
2. Double-click the folder icon
3. Select folder to collapse, press LEFT ARROW

Copying Files to a Folder on a Floppy Disk

One common operation that every student should understand how to perform is copying a file or group of files from one disk to another disk or from one folder to another folder. On the following pages, you will create a new folder, named My Files, on the floppy disk in drive A, select a group of files in the Windows folder on drive C, and copy the files from the Windows folder on drive C to the My Files folder on drive A.

When copying files, the drive and folder containing the files to be copied are called the **source drive** and **source folder**, respectively. The drive and folder to which the files are copied are called the **destination drive** and **destination folder**, respectively. Thus, the Windows folder is the source folder, drive C is the source drive, the My Files folder is the destination folder, and drive A is the destination drive.

Creating a New Folder

In preparation for selecting and copying files from a folder on the hard drive to a folder on the floppy disk in drive A, a new folder with the name of My Files will be created on the floppy disk. Perform the following steps to create the new folder.

Steps To Create a New Folder

1. **Insert a formatted floppy disk into drive A on your computer.**

2. **Click the 3½ Floppy [A:] folder name in the All Folders side of the Exploring – Hard drive [C:] window and then point to an open area of the Contents side of the window.**

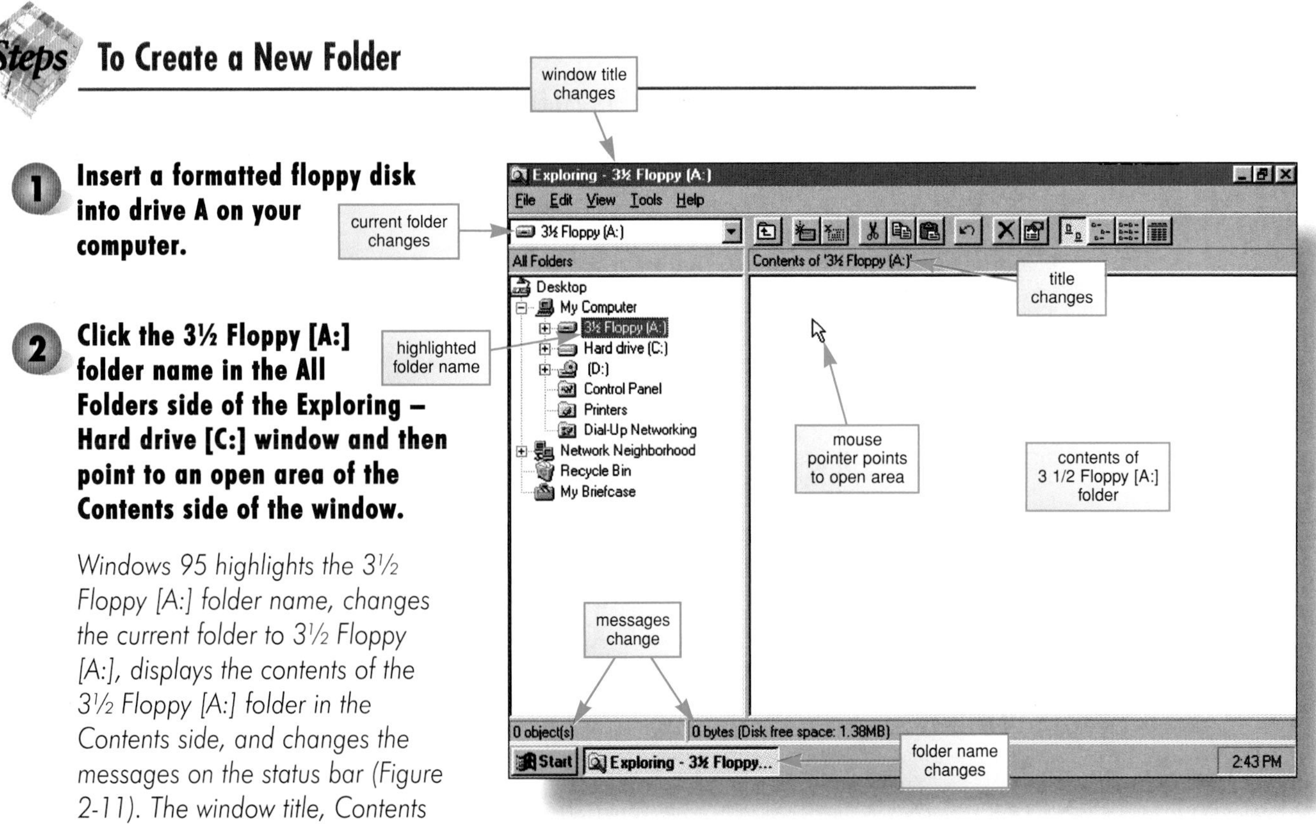

FIGURE 2-11

Windows 95 highlights the 3½ Floppy [A:] folder name, changes the current folder to 3½ Floppy [A:], displays the contents of the 3½ Floppy [A:] folder in the Contents side, and changes the messages on the status bar (Figure 2-11). The window title, Contents side title, and button on the taskbar change to include the 3½ Floppy [A:] folder name. Currently, no files or folders display in the Contents side. The files and folders may be different on your computer. The mouse pointer points to an open area of the Contents side.

3. **Right-click the open area of the Contents side of the window to open a context-sensitive menu and then point to New on the menu.**

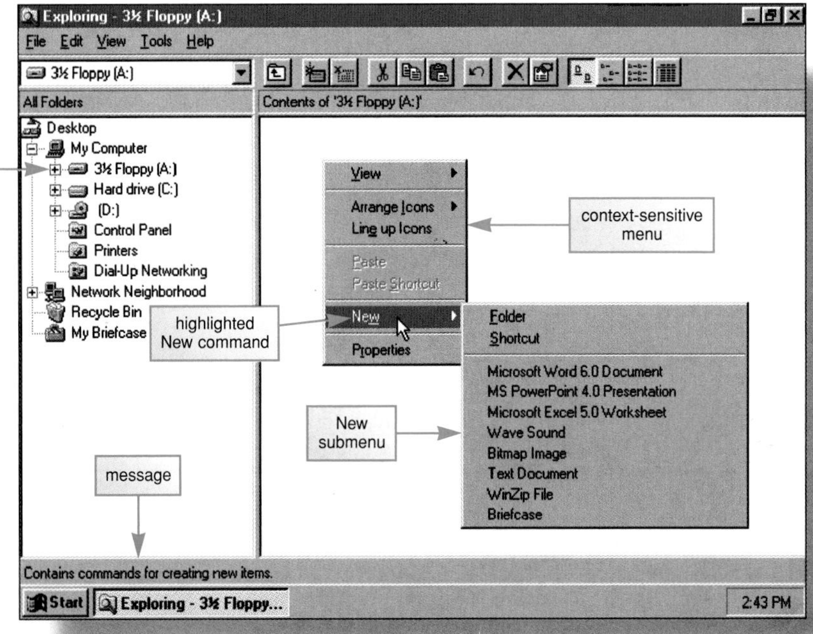

FIGURE 2-12

Windows 95 opens a context-sensitive menu and the New submenu, highlights the New command in the context-sensitive menu, and displays a message on the status bar (Figure 2-12). The message, Contains commands for creating new items., indicates the New submenu contains commands that allow you to create new items in the Contents side. The mouse pointer points to the New command. Although no subfolders display in the Contents side and no plus sign should precede the 3½ Floppy [A:] icon in the All Folders area, a plus sign precedes the icon.

4 Point to Folder on the New submenu.

Windows 95 highlights the Folder command on the New submenu and displays the message, Creates a new, empty folder., on the status bar (Figure 2-13). The mouse pointer points to the Folder command. Clicking the Folder command will create a folder in the Contents side of the window using the default folder name, New Folder.

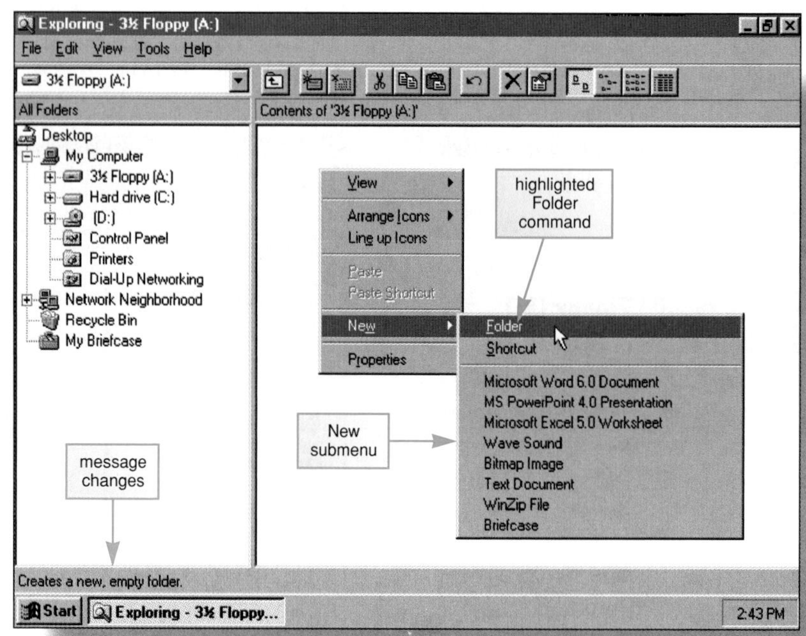

FIGURE 2-13

5 Click Folder on the New submenu.

Windows 95 closes the context-sensitive menu and New submenu, displays the highlighted New Folder icon in the Contents side, and changes the message on the status bar (Figure 2-14). The text box below the icon contains the highlighted default folder name, New Folder, followed by the insertion point. A plus sign continues to display to the left of the 3½ Floppy [A:] icon to indicate the 3½ Floppy [A:] folder contains the New Folder subfolder. The message on the status bar indicates one object is selected in the Contents side.

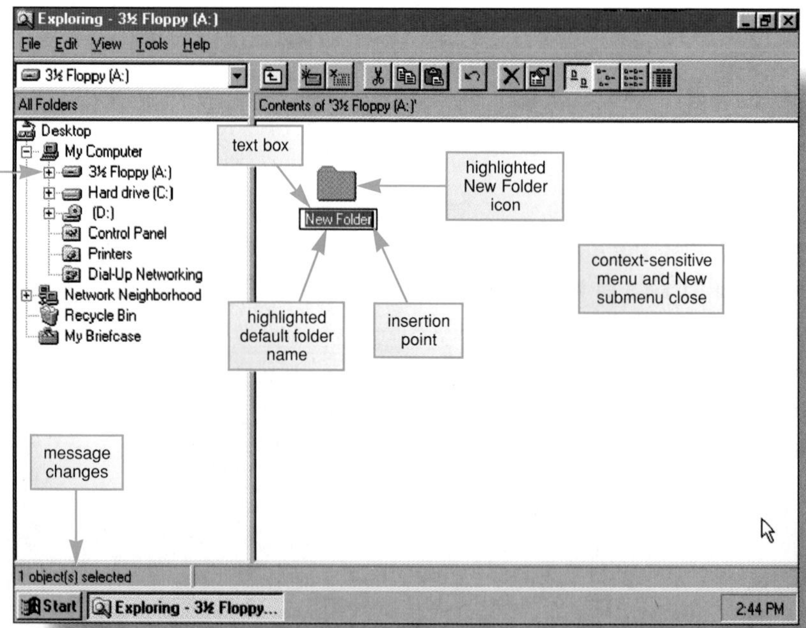

FIGURE 2-14

6 **Type** `My Files` **in the text box and then press the ENTER key.**

The new folder name, My Files, is entered and Windows 95 removes the text box (Figure 2-15).

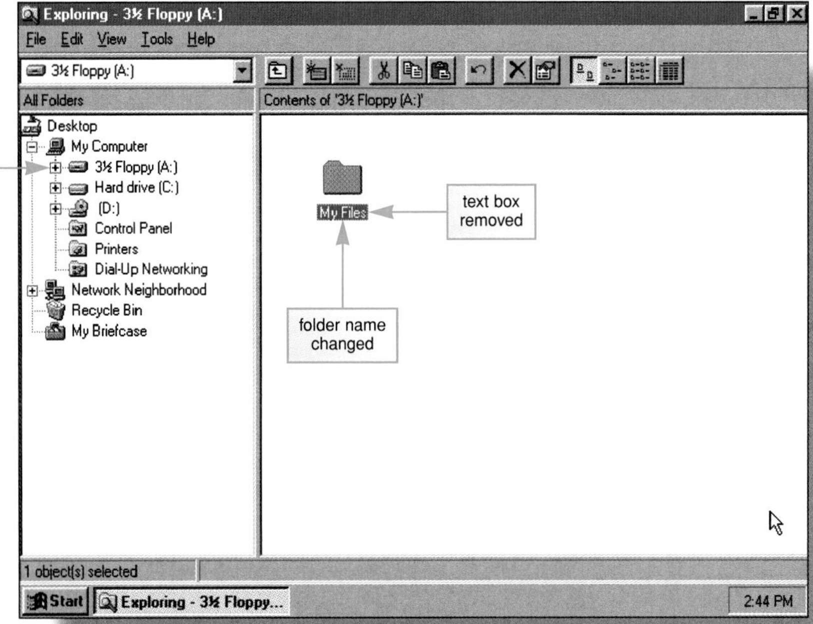

FIGURE 2-15

OtherWays

1. Select drive, click File on the menu bar, on File menu click New, click Folder on New submenu

After creating the My Files folder on the floppy disk in drive A, you can save files in the folder or copy files from other folders to the folder. On the following pages, you will copy a group of files consisting of the Black Thatch, Bubbles, and Circles files from the Windows folder on drive C to the My Files folder on drive A.

Displaying the Destination Folder

To copy the three files from the Windows folder on drive C to the My Files folder on drive A, the files to be copied will be selected in the Contents side and right-dragged to the My Files folder in the All Folders side. Prior to selecting or right-dragging the files, the destination folder (My Files folder on drive A) must be visible in the All Folders side and the three files to be copied must be visible in the Contents side.

Currently, the plus sign (+) to the left of the 3½ Floppy [A:] icon indicates the folder contains one or more subfolders that are not visible in the All Folders side (see Figure 2-15). Perform the steps on the next page to expand the 3½ Floppy [A:] folder to display the My Files subfolder.

TO EXPAND THE 3½ FLOPPY [A:] FOLDER

Step 1: Point to the plus sign to the left of the 3½ Floppy [A:] icon in the All Folders side of the Exploring – 3½ Floppy [A:] window.
Step 2: Click the plus sign to display the subfolders in the 3½ Floppy [A:] folder.

Windows 95 replaces the plus sign preceding the 3½ Floppy [A:] folder with a minus sign, highlights the 3½ Floppy [A:] folder name, and displays the subfolders in the 3½ Floppy [A:] folder, indented and aligned below the 3½ Floppy [A:] folder name (Figure 2-16). Currently, only one subfolder (My Files) displays.

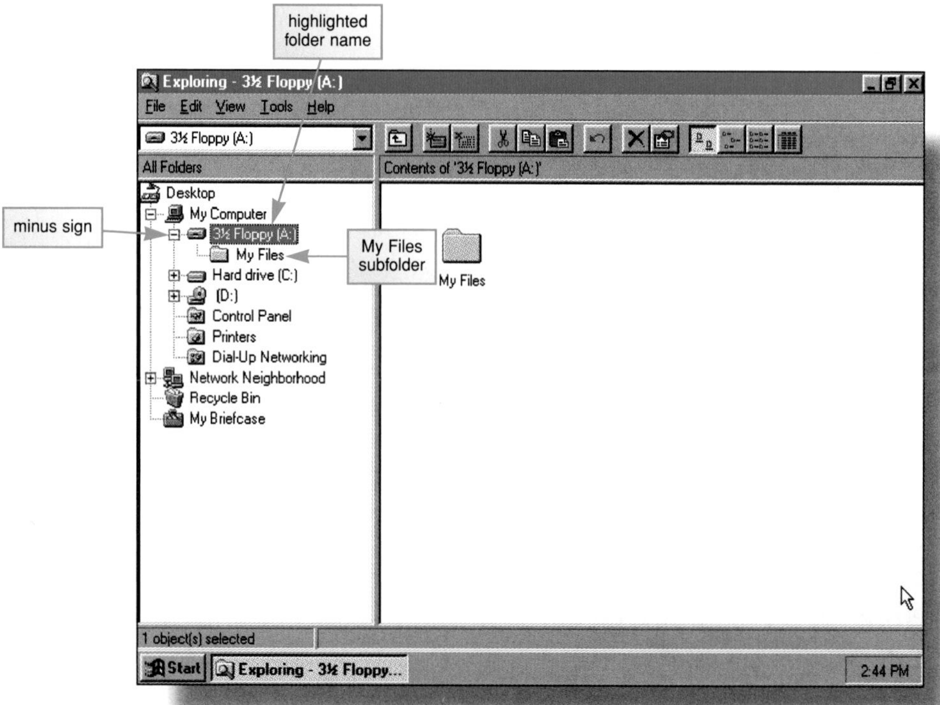

FIGURE 2-16

OtherWays

1. Right-click 3½ Floppy [A:] icon, click Explore

Displaying the Contents of the Windows Folder

Currently, the My Files folder displays in the Contents side of the Exploring – 3½ Floppy [A:] window. To copy files from the source folder (Windows folder on drive C) to the My Files folder, the Windows folder must be visible in the All Folders side. To make the Windows folder visible, you must expand the Hard drive [C:] folder, scroll the All Folders side to make the Windows folder name visible, and then click the Windows folder name to display the contents of the Windows folder in the Contents side. Perform the following steps to display the contents of the Windows folder.

Steps To Display the Contents of a Folder

1 **Click the plus sign to the left of the Hard drive [C:] icon in the All Folders side of the Exploring – 3½ Floppy [A:] window, scroll the All Folders side to make the Windows folder name visible, and then point to the Windows folder name.**

*Windows 95 replaces the plus sign to the left of the Hard drive [C:] icon with a minus sign, displays the subfolders in the Hard drive [C:] folder, and scrolls the hierarchy of folders in the All Folders side to make the Windows folder visible (Figure 2-17). In addition to folders and other files, the Windows folder contains a series of predefined graphics, called **clip art files**, that can be used with application programs. The mouse pointer points to the Windows folder name. The plus sign to the left of the Hard drive [C:] icon is not visible in Figure 2-17.*

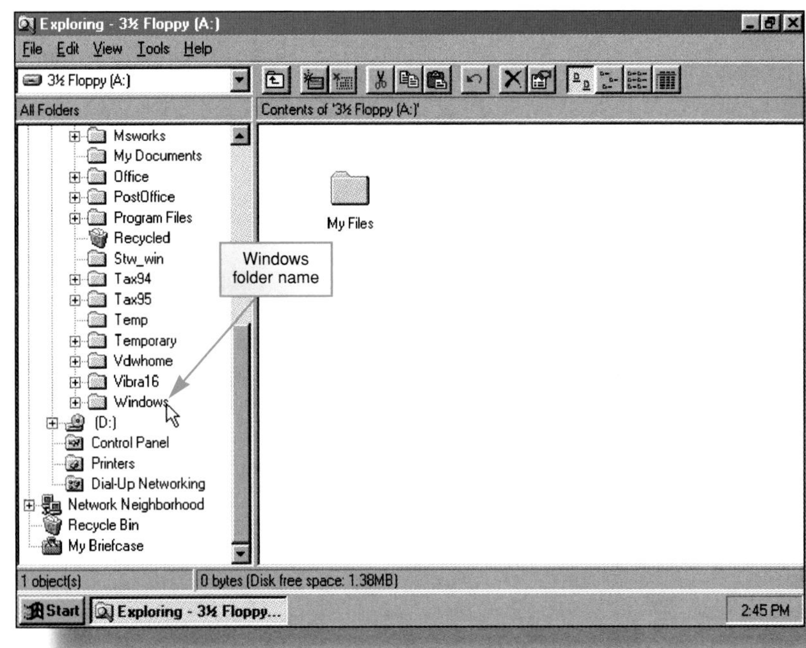

FIGURE 2-17

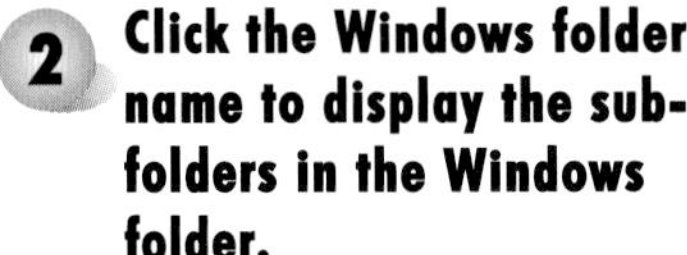

2 **Click the Windows folder name to display the subfolders in the Windows folder.**

Windows 95 highlights the Windows folder name in the All Folders side of the window, changes the closed folder icon to the left of the Windows folder name to an open folder icon, and displays the contents of the Windows folder in the Contents side (Figure 2-18).

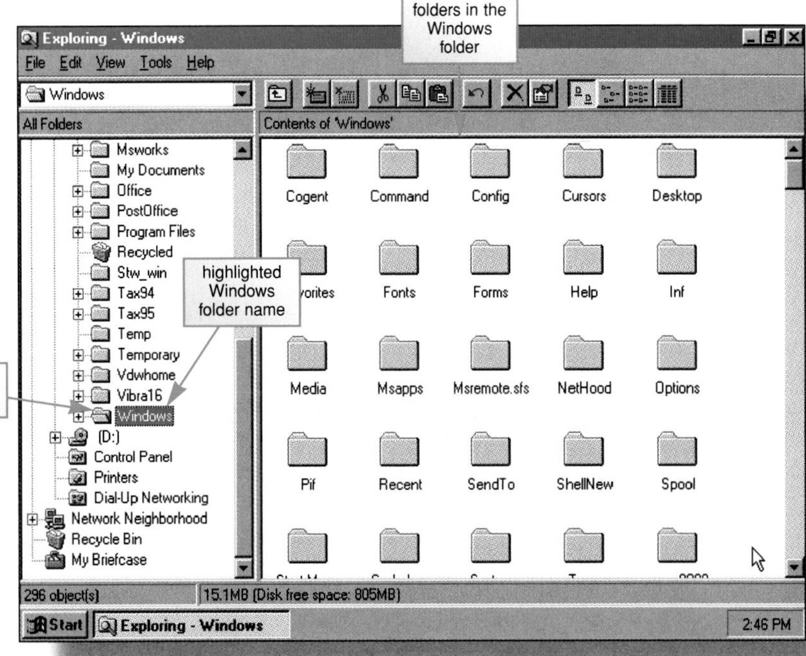

FIGURE 2-18

3 Scroll the Contents side to make the files in the Windows folder visible.

One folder (Wordview folder) and several files display in the Contents side of the window (Figure 2-19). Each file is identified by a large icon and a filename. The files and folders in the Windows folder may be different and the file extensions may not display on your computer.

FIGURE 2-19

Changing the View

In Figure 2-19, the files and folder in the Contents side of the Exploring – Windows window display in large icons view. In **large icons view**, each file and folder is represented by a large icon and a filename or folder name. Other views include the small icons, list, and details views. The list view is often useful when copying or moving files from one location to another location. In **list view**, each file or folder is represented by a smaller icon and name, and the files and folders are arranged in columns. Perform the following steps to change from large icons view to list view.

Steps To Change to List View

1 Right-click any open area in the Contents side of the Exploring – Windows window to open a context-sensitive menu, point to View on the context-sensitive menu, and then point to List on the View submenu.

Windows 95 opens a context-sensitive menu, highlights the View command on the context-sensitive menu, opens the View submenu, and highlights the List command on the View submenu (Figure 2-20). A large dot to the left of the Large Icons command on the View submenu indicates files and folders in the Contents side display in large icons view. The mouse pointer points to the List command. Clicking the List command will display the files and folders in the Contents side in list view.

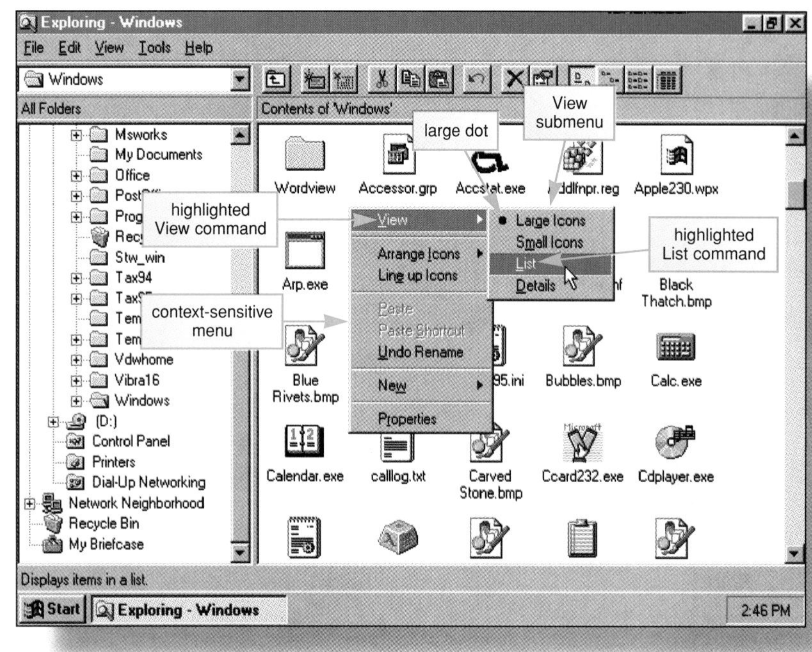

FIGURE 2-20

2 Click List on the View submenu.

Windows 95 displays the files and folders in the Contents side of the window in list view, indents the List button on the toolbar, and returns the Large Icons button to normal (Figure 2-21).

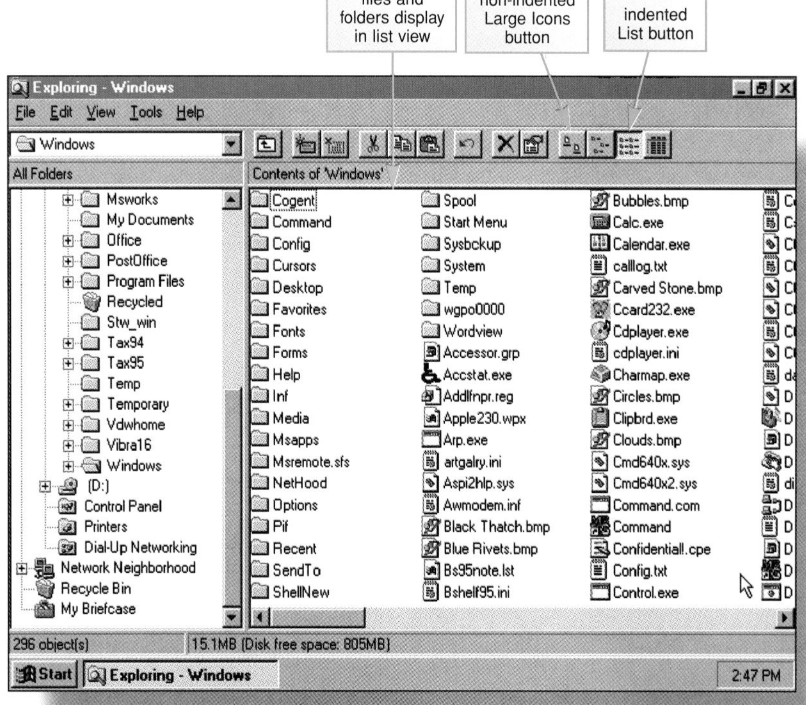

FIGURE 2-21

OtherWays

1. On View menu click List
2. Click List button on toolbar
3. Press ALT+V, press L

Selecting a Group of Files

You can easily copy a single file or group of files from one folder to another folder using Windows Explorer. To copy a single file, select the file in the Contents side of the window and right-drag the highlighted file to the folder in the All Folders side where the file is to be copied. Group files are copied in a similar fashion. Select the first file in a group of files by clicking its icon or filename. You select the remaining files in the group by pointing to each file icon or filename, holding down the CTRL key, and clicking the file icon or filename. Perform the following steps to select the group of files consisting of the Black Thatch.bmp, Bubbles.bmp, and Circles.bmp files.

To Select a Group of Files

1. **Select the Black Thatch.bmp file by clicking the Black Thatch.bmp filename, and then point to the Bubbles.bmp filename.**

Windows highlights the Black Thatch.bmp file in the Contents side and displays two messages on the status bar (Figure 2-22). The messages indicate that one file is selected (1 object(s) selected) and the size of the file (182 bytes). The mouse pointer points to the Bubbles.bmp filename.

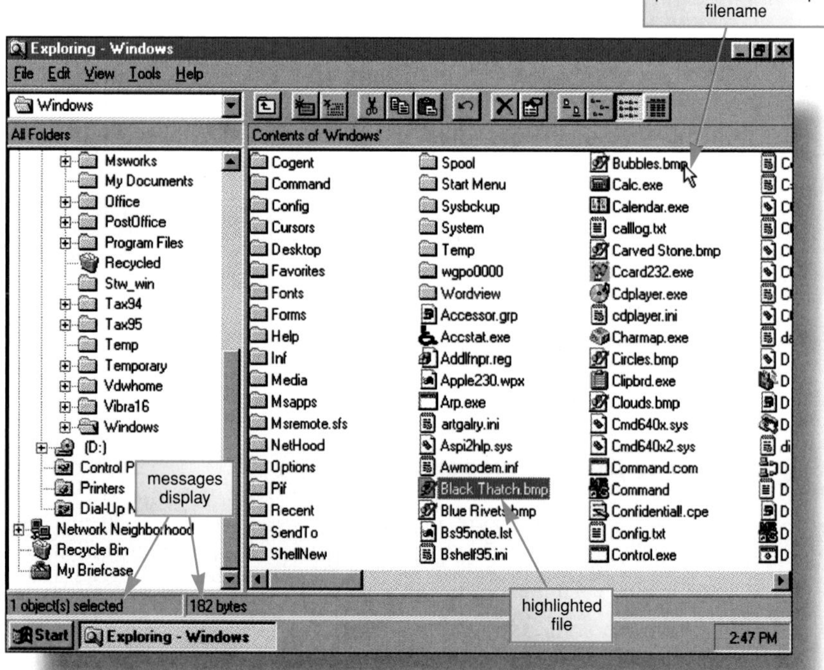

FIGURE 2-22

2 **Hold down the CTRL key, click the Bubbles.bmp filename, release the CTRL key, and then point to the Circles.bmp filename.**

The Black Thatch.bmp and Bubbles.bmp files are highlighted, and the two messages on the status bar change to reflect the additional file selected (Figure 2-23). The messages indicate that two files are selected (2 object(s) selected) and the size of the two files (2.24KB). The mouse pointer points to the Circles.bmp filename.

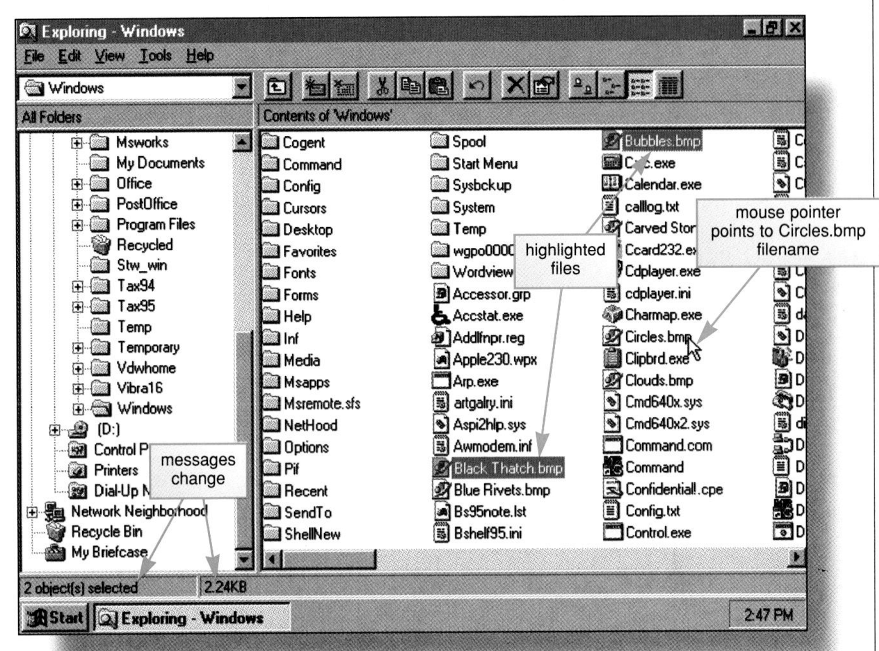

FIGURE 2-23

3 **Hold down the CTRL key, click the Circles.bmp filename, and then release the CTRL key.**

The group of files consisting of the Black Thatch.bmp, Bubbles.bmp, and Circles.bmp files is highlighted, and the messages on the status bar change to reflect the selection of a third file (Figure 2-24). The messages indicate that three files are selected (3 object(s) selected) and the size of the three files (2.43KB).

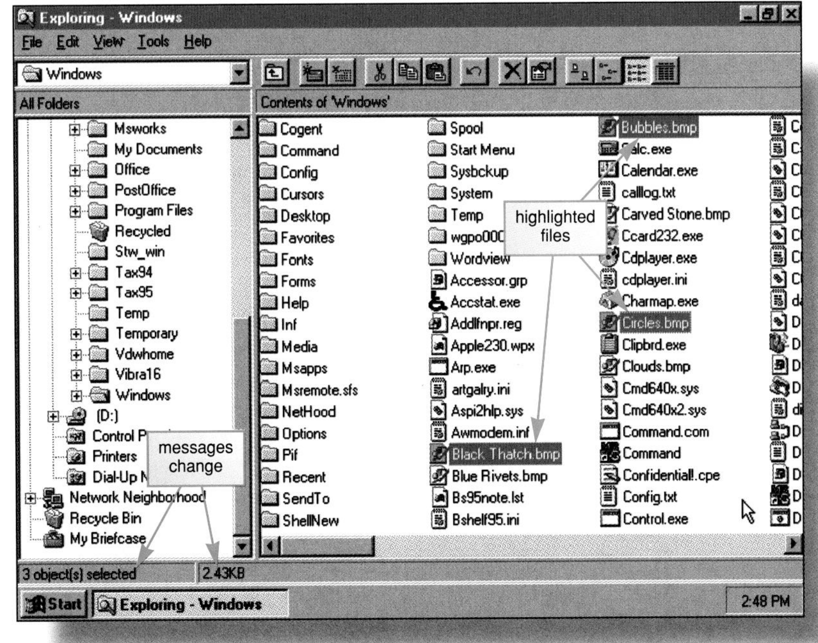

FIGURE 2-24

OtherWays

1. Use arrow keys to select first file, hold down SHIFT key to move to next file, press SPACEBAR
2. To select contiguous files, select first filename, hold down SHIFT key, click last filename
3. To select all files, click Edit on menu bar, click Select All

Copying a Group of Files

After selecting a group of files, copy the files to the My Files folder on drive A by pointing to any highlighted filename in the Contents side, and right-dragging the filename to the My Files folder in the All Folders side. Perform the following steps to copy a group of files.

Steps To Copy a Group of Files

1 Scroll the All Folders side of the Exploring – Windows window to make the My Files folder visible and then point to the highlighted Black Thatch.bmp filename in the Contents side.

Windows 95 scrolls the All Folders side to make the My Files folder visible (Figure 2-25). The mouse pointer points to the highlighted Black Thatch.bmp filename in the Contents side.

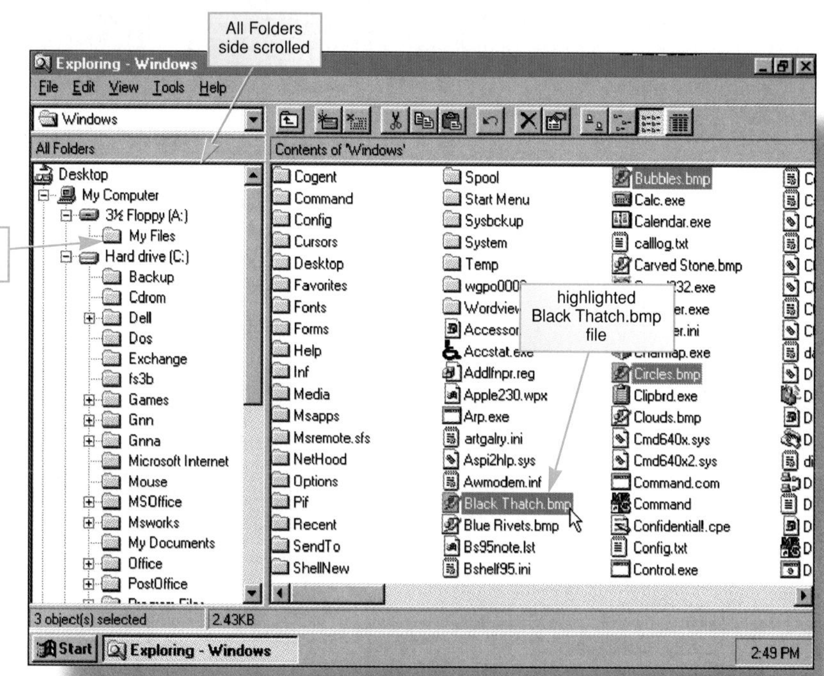

FIGURE 2-25

2 Right-drag the Black Thatch.bmp file over the My Files folder name in the All Folders side of the Exploring – Windows window.

As you drag the file, Windows 95 displays an outline of an icon and a horizontal line of one or more of the three files being copied and highlights the My Files folder name (Figure 2-26). The mouse pointer contains a plus sign to indicate the group of files is being copied, not moved.

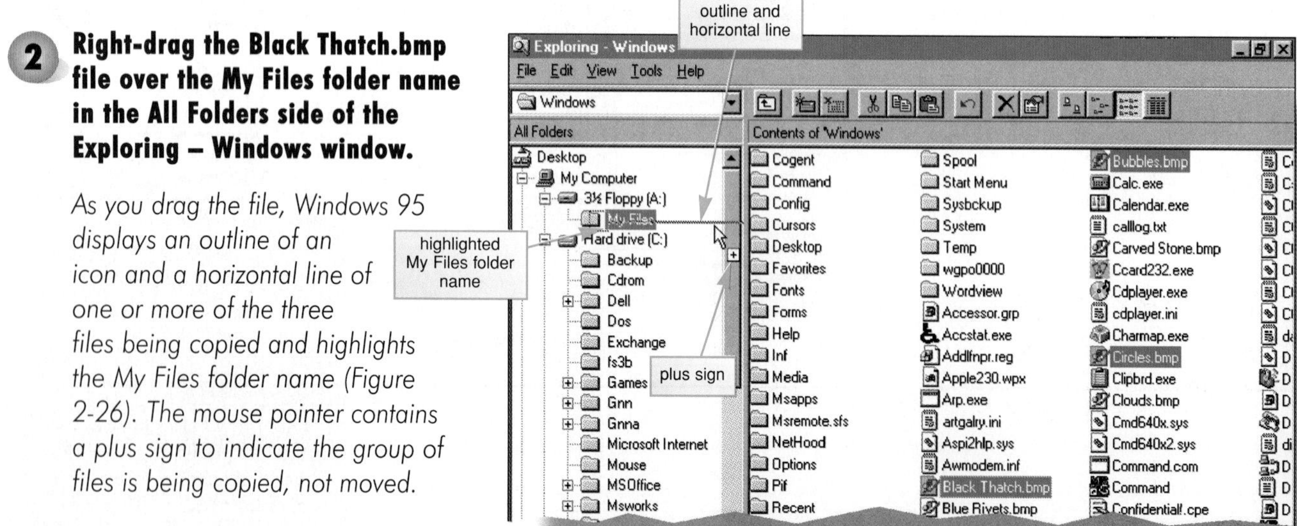

3 **Release the right mouse button to open a context-sensitive menu, and then point to the Copy Here command on the menu.**

Windows 95 opens a context-sensitive menu and highlights the Copy Here command on the menu (Figure 2-27). The mouse pointer points to the Copy Here command. Clicking the Copy Here command will copy the three files to the My Files folder.

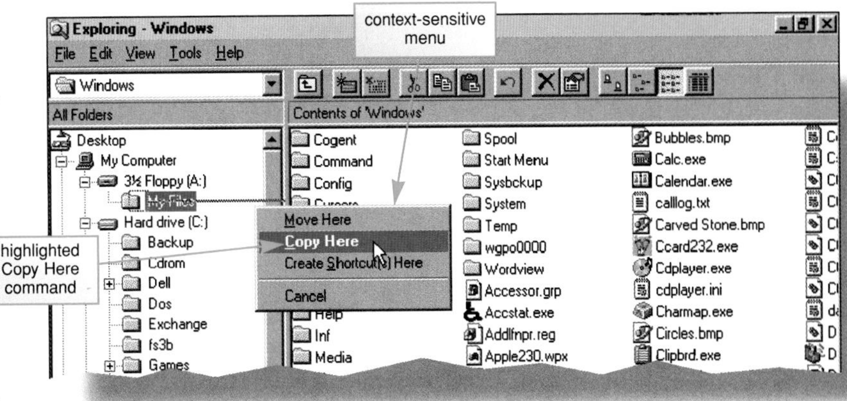

FIGURE 2-27

4 **Click Copy Here on the context-sensitive menu.**

Windows 95 opens the Copying dialog box, and the dialog box remains on the screen while Windows 95 copies each file to the My Files folder (Figure 2-28). The Copying dialog box shown in Figure 2-28 indicates the Black Thatch.bmp file is currently being copied.

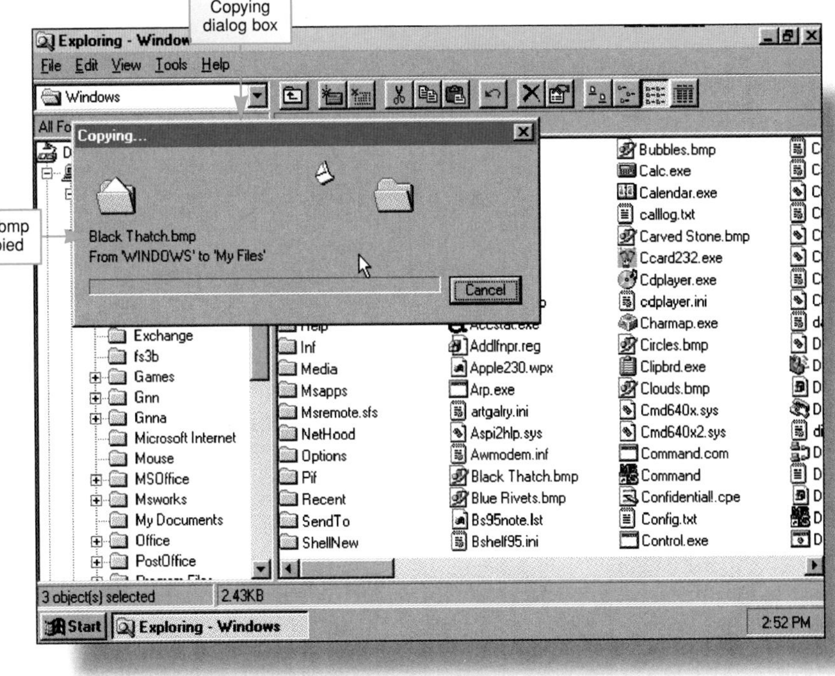

FIGURE 2-28

OtherWays

1. Right-drag file to copy from Contents side to folder icon in All Folders side, click Copy on context-sensitive menu
2. Select file to copy in Contents side, click Edit on menu bar, click Copy on Edit menu, select folder icon to receive copy, click Edit on menu bar, click Paste on Edit menu

Displaying the Contents of the My Files Folder

After copying a group of files, you should verify that the files were copied into the correct folder. To view the files that were copied to the My Files folder, click the My Files folder name in the All Folders side.

More About Copying and Moving

"Copying, moving, it's all the same to me," you might be tempted to say. They're not the same at all! When you copy a file, it will be located at two different places - the place it was copied to and the place it was copied from. When a file is moved, it will be located at only one place - where it was moved to. Many users have been sorry they did not distinguish the difference when a file they thought they had copied was moved instead.

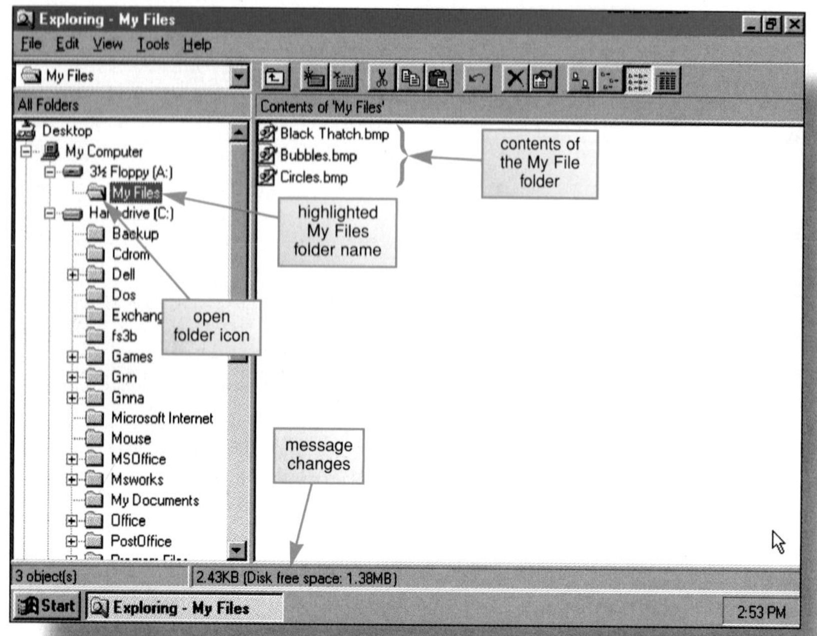

FIGURE 2-29

TO DISPLAY THE CONTENTS OF A FOLDER

Step 1: Point to the My Files folder name in the All Folders side of the Exploring – Windows window.

Step 2: Click the My Files folder name in the All Folders side.

Windows 95 highlights the My Files folder name in the All Folders side, replaces the closed folder icon to the left of the My Files folder name with an open folder icon, displays the contents of the My Files folder in the Contents side, and changes the message on the status bar (Figure 2-29). The status bar message indicates 1.38MB of free disk space on the disk in drive A.

More *About* **Renaming a File or Folder**

A file or folder name can contain up to 255 characters, including spaces. But, they cannot contain any of the following characters: \ /:*?"<>|.

Renaming a File or Folder

Sometimes, you may want to rename a file or folder on disk. You change the filename by clicking the filename twice, typing the new filename, and pressing the ENTER key. Perform the following steps to change the name of the Circles.bmp file on drive A to Blue Circles.bmp.

Steps To Rename a File

1 Point to the Circles.bmp filename in the Contents side.

The mouse pointer points to the Circles.bmp filename (Figure 2-30).

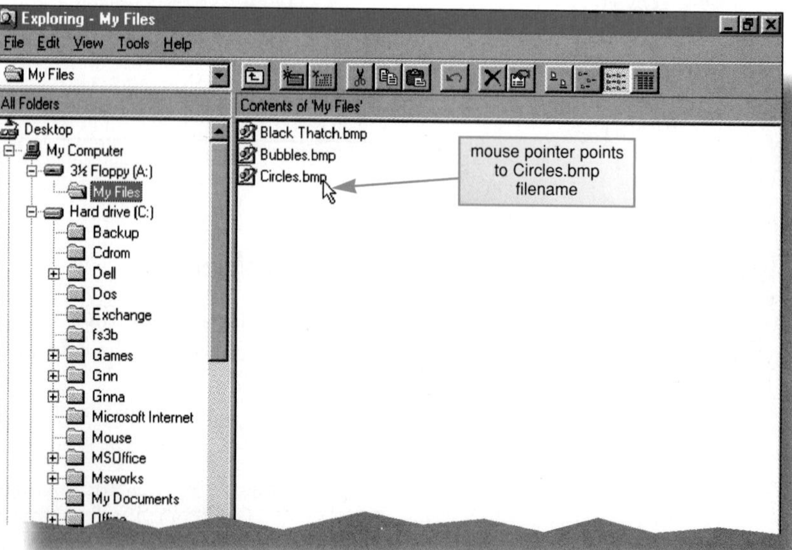

FIGURE 2-30

2 **Click the Circles.bmp filename twice (do not double-click the filename).**

Windows 95 displays a text box containing the highlighted Circles.bmp filename and insertion point (Figure 2-31).

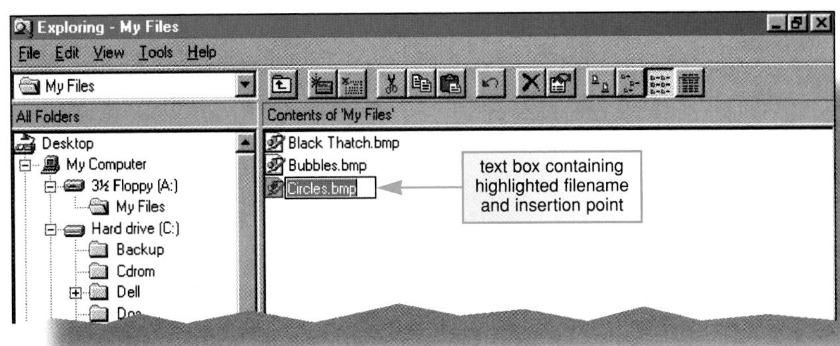

FIGURE 2-31

3 **Type** `Blue Circles.bmp` **and then press the ENTER key.**

Windows 95 changes the filename to Blue Circles.bmp and removes the box surrounding the filename (Figure 2-32).

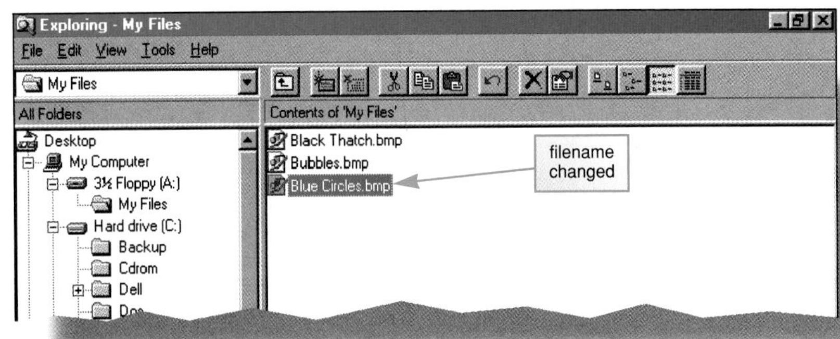

FIGURE 2-32

*Other*Ways

1. Right-click filename in Contents side, click Rename on context-sensitive menu, type name, press ENTER
2. Select filename in Contents side, click File on menu bar, click Rename on File menu, type name, press ENTER

To change a folder name, click the folder name twice, type the new folder name, and press the ENTER key. Perform the steps below and on the next page to change the name of the My Files folder to Clip Art Files.

Steps To Rename a Folder

1 **Point to the My Files folder name in the All Folders side of the Exploring – My Files window.**

The mouse pointer points to the My Files folder name (Figure 2-33).

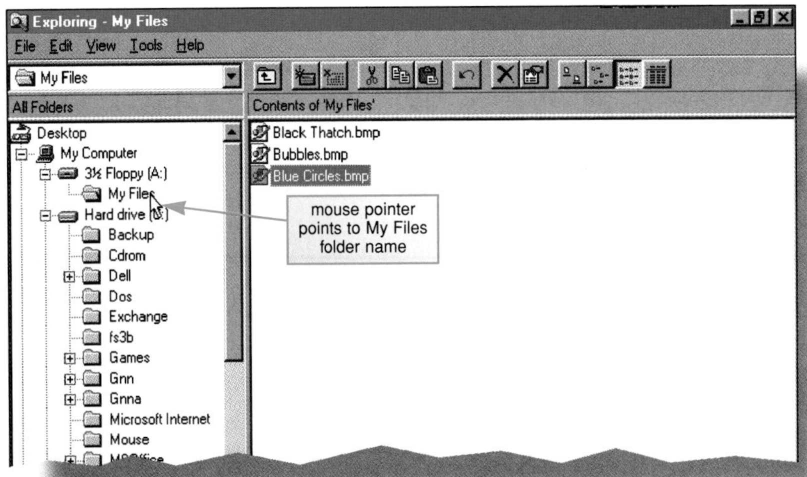

FIGURE 2-33

2 **Click the My Files folder name twice (do not double-click the folder name).**

Windows 95 displays a text box containing the highlighted My Files name and insertion point (Figure 2-34).

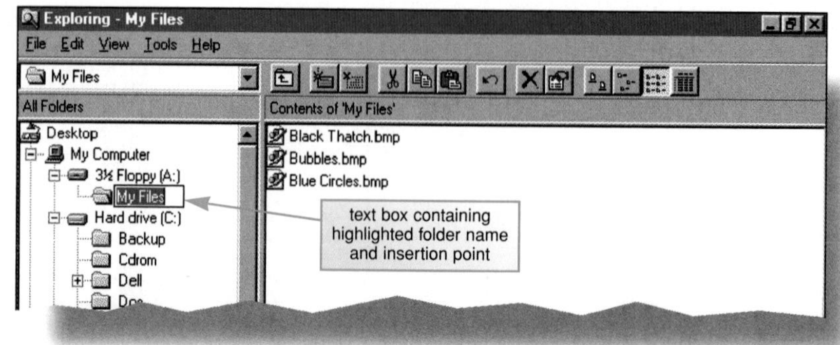

FIGURE 2-34

3 **Type** `Clip Art Files` **and then press the ENTER key.**

Windows 95 changes the folder name to Clip Art Files and removes the box surrounding the folder name (Figure 2-35). The new folder name replaces the old folder name in the window title, drop-down list box, Contents side title, and button on the taskbar.

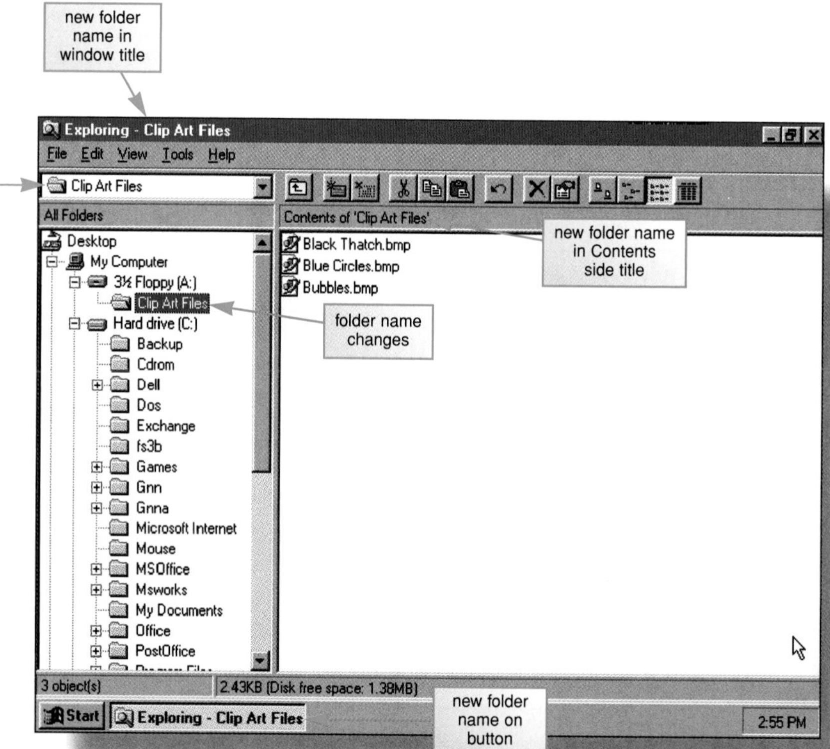

FIGURE 2-35

OtherWays

1. Click folder name, press F2, type new name, press ENTER
2. Click folder name, click File on menu bar, click Rename, type new name, press ENTER

Deleting a File or Folder

When you no longer need a file or folder, you can delete it. Two methods are commonly used to delete a file or folder. One method uses the Delete command on the context-sensitive menu that opens when you right-click the filename or folder name. Another method involves right-dragging the unneeded file or folder to the **Recycle Bin**. The Recycle Bin icon is located at the left edge of the desktop (see Figure 2-1 on page WIN 2.5).

When you delete a file or folder on the hard drive using the Recycle Bin, Windows 95 stores the deleted file or folder temporarily in the Recycle Bin until you permanently discard the contents of the Recycle Bin by emptying the Recycle Bin. Until the Recycle Bin is emptied, you can retrieve the files and folders you deleted in error. Unlike deleting files or folders on the hard drive, when you delete a file or folder located on a floppy disk, the file or folder is deleted immediately and not stored in the Recycle Bin.

On the following pages, you will delete the Bubbles.bmp and Black Thatch.bmp files. The Bubbles.bmp file will be deleted by right-clicking the Bubbles.bmp filename and then clicking the Delete command on a context-sensitive menu. Next, the Black Thatch.bmp file will be deleted by dragging the Black Thatch.bmp file to the Recycle Bin.

More *About* Deleting Files

A few years ago, someone proposed that the Delete command be removed from operating systems. It seems an entire database was deleted by an employee who thought he knew what he was doing, resulting in a company that could not function for more than a week while the database was rebuilt. Millions of dollars in revenue were lost. The Delete command is still around, but it should be considered a dangerous weapon.

Deleting a File by Right-Clicking Its Filename

To delete a file using the Delete command on a context-sensitive menu, right-click the filename in the Contents side to open a context-sensitive menu and then click the Delete command on the menu. To illustrate how to delete a file by right-clicking, perform the steps below and on the next page to delete the Bubbles.bmp file.

Steps To Delete a File by Right-Clicking

1 **Right-click the Bubbles.bmp filename in the Contents side of the Exploring – Clip Art Files window and then point to the Delete command on the context-sensitive menu.**

Windows 95 opens a context-sensitive menu and highlights the Bubbles.bmp filename (Figure 2-36). The mouse pointer points to the Delete command on the menu.

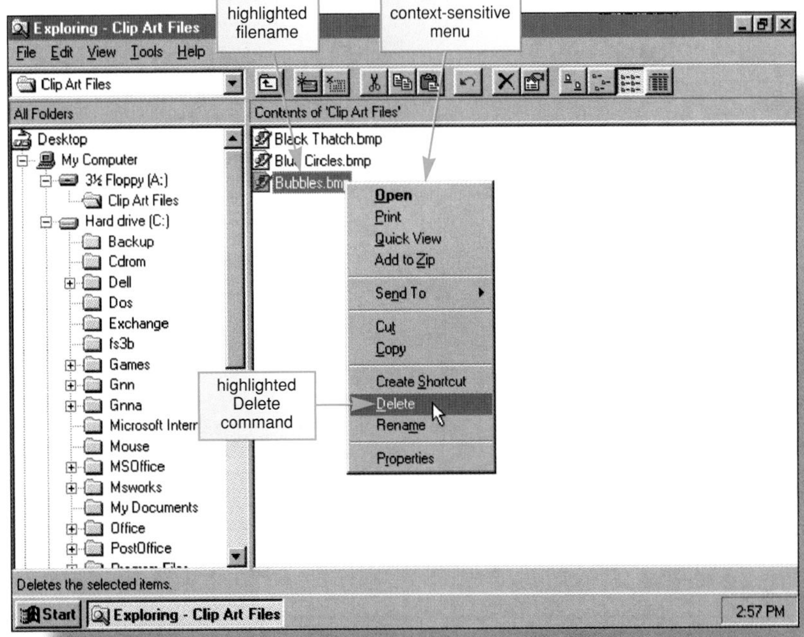

FIGURE 2-36

2 **Click Delete on the context-sensitive menu. When the Confirm File Delete dialog box opens, point to the Yes button.**

Windows 95 opens the Deleting dialog box and then opens a Confirm File Delete dialog box on top of the Deleting dialog box (Figure 2-37). The Confirm File Delete dialog box contains the message, Are you sure you want to delete 'Bubbles.bmp'?, and the Yes and No command buttons. The mouse pointer points to the Yes button. Clicking the Yes button confirms the deletion of the Bubbles.bmp file and causes the file to be deleted.

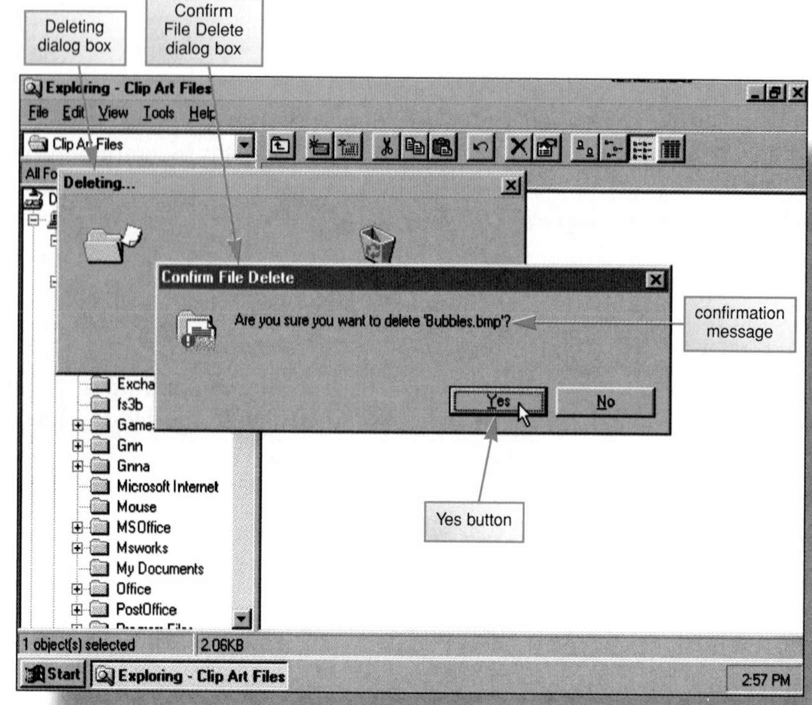

FIGURE 2-37

3 **Click the Yes button in the Confirm File Delete dialog box.**

Windows 95 closes the Confirm File Delete dialog box, displays the Deleting dialog box while the file is being deleted, and then removes the Bubbles.bmp file from the Contents side (Figure 2-38).

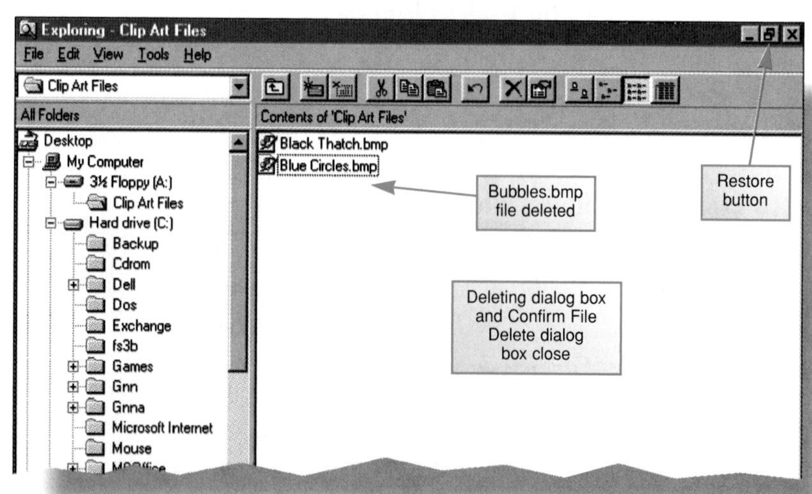

FIGURE 2-38

OtherWays

1. Click filename, press DELETE

More About Deleting Files

Warning! This is your last warning! Be EXTREMELY careful when deleting files. Hours and weeks of hard work can be lost with one click of a button. If you are going to delete files or folders from your hard disk, consider making a backup of those files so that if you inadvertently delete something you need, you will be able to recover.

Deleting a File by Right-Dragging Its Filename

Another method to delete a file is to right-drag the filename from the Contents side of the window to the Recycle Bin icon on the desktop to open a context-sensitive menu, and then click the Move Here command on the context-sensitive menu. Currently, the Exploring – Clip Art Files window is maximized and occupies the entire desktop. With a maximized window, you cannot right-drag a file to the Recycle Bin. To allow you to right-drag a file, restore the Exploring – Clip Art Files window to its original size by clicking the Restore button on the title bar. Perform the following steps to delete the Black Thatch.bmp file by right-dragging its filename.

To Delete a File by Right-Dragging

1 **Click the Restore button on the Exploring – Clip Art Files window title bar and then point to the Black Thatch.bmp filename in the Contents side of the window.**

Windows 95 restores the Exploring – Clip Art Files window to its original size before maximizing the window and replaces the Restore button on the title bar with the Maximize button (Figure 2-39). The mouse pointer points to the Black Thatch.bmp filename in the Contents side of the window.

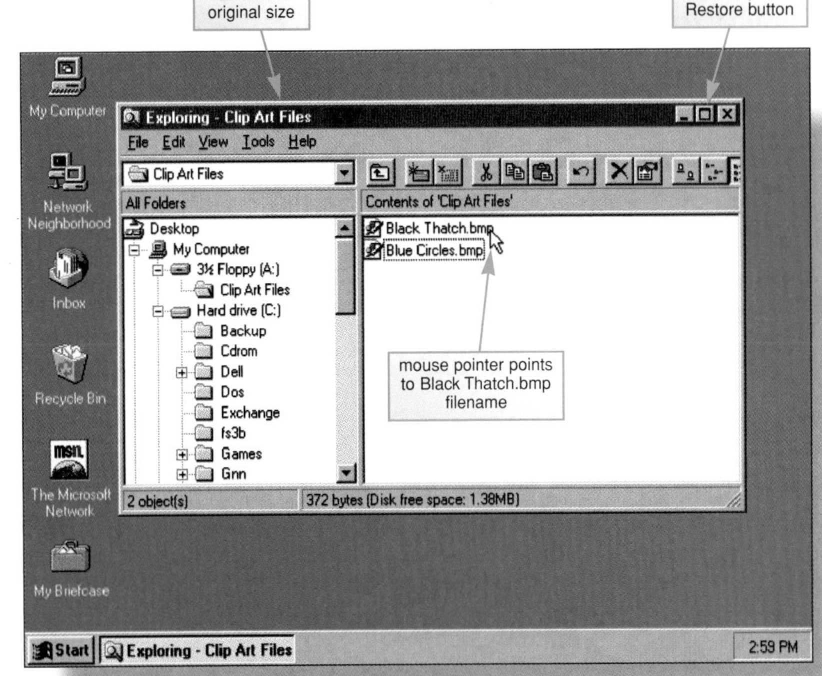

FIGURE 2-39

2 **Right-drag the Black Thatch.bmp filename over the Recycle Bin icon, and then point to the Move Here command on the context-sensitive menu.**

Windows 95 opens a context-sensitive menu and highlights the Move Here command on the menu (Figure 2-40). The Black Thatch.bmp filename displays on top of the Recycle Bin icon on the desktop and the mouse pointer points to the Move Here command on the menu.

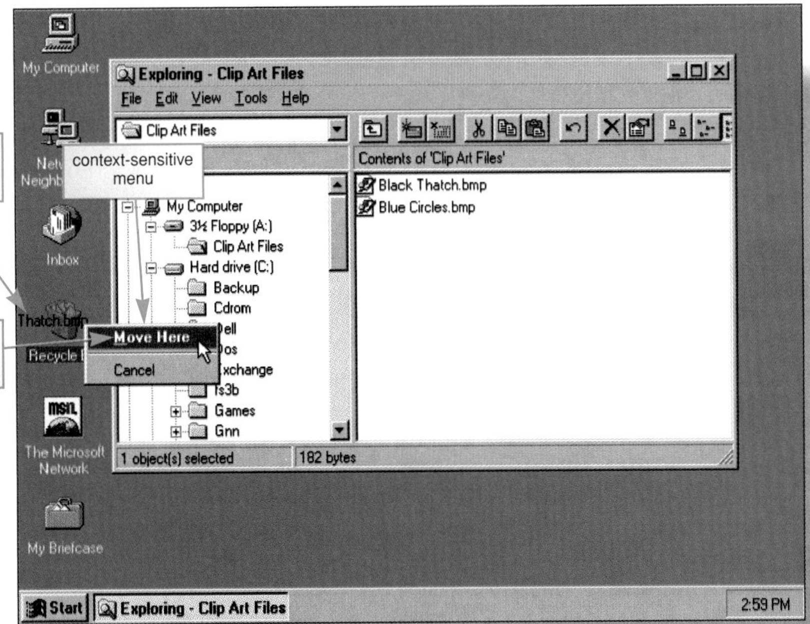

FIGURE 2-40

3 Click Move Here on the context-sensitive menu. When the Confirm File Delete dialog box opens, point to the Yes button.

Windows 95 opens the Deleting dialog box and then opens the Confirm File Delete dialog box on top of the Deleting dialog box (Figure 2-41). The Confirm File Delete dialog box contains the message, Are you sure you want to delete 'Black Thatch.bmp'?, and the Yes and No command buttons. The mouse pointer points to the Yes button. Clicking the Yes button confirms the deletion of the Black Thatch.bmp file and causes the file to be deleted.

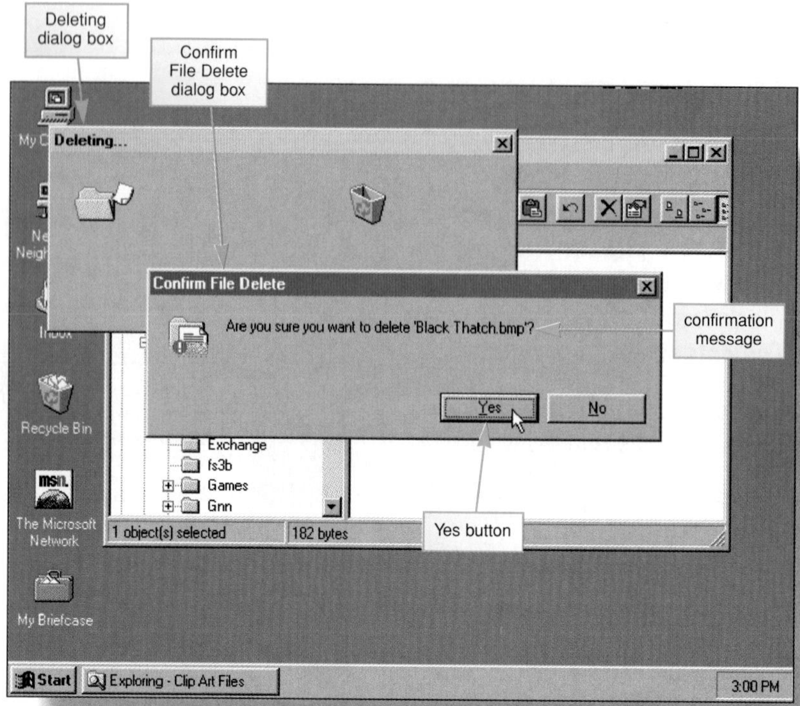

FIGURE 2-41

4 Click the Yes button in the Confirm File Delete dialog box.

Windows 95 closes the Confirm File Delete dialog box, displays the Deleting dialog box while the file is being deleted, and then removes the Black Thatch.bmp file from the Contents side (Figure 2-42).

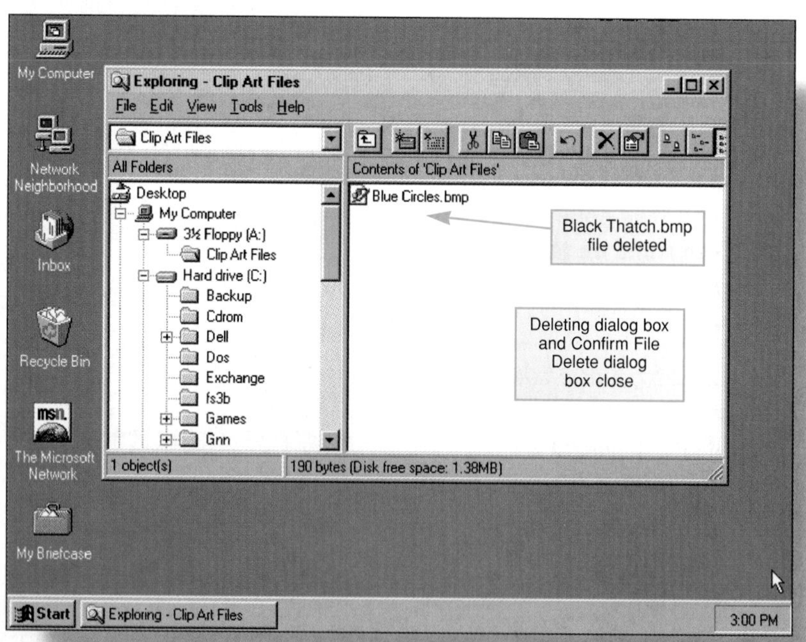

FIGURE 2-42

More *About* the Recycle Bin

Once you delete a file or folder, it's gone forever – True or False? Windows stores deleted files and folders in the Recycle Bin. You can recover files or folders you delete in error using the Recycle Bin.

Whether you delete a file by right-clicking or right-dragging, you can use the file selection techniques illustrated earlier in this project to delete a group of files. When deleting a group of files, click the Yes button in the Confirm Multiple File Delete dialog box to confirm the deletion of the group of files.

Deleting a Folder

When you delete a folder, Windows 95 deletes any files or subfolders in the folder. You can delete a folder using the two methods shown earlier to delete files (right-clicking or right-dragging). Perform the steps below and on the next page to delete the Clip Art Files folder on drive A by right-dragging the folder to the Recycle Bin.

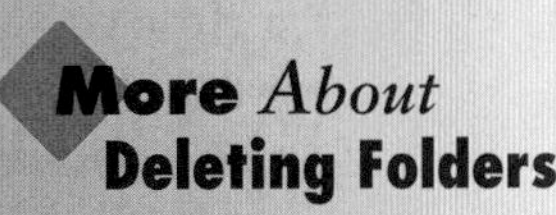

If you drag a folder to the Recycle Bin, only the files in that folder appear in the Recycle Bin. If you restore a file that was originally located in a deleted folder, Windows recreates the folder, and then restores the file to it.

Steps To Delete a Folder

1 **Point to the Clip Art Files folder name in the All Folders side of the Exploring – Clip Art Files window (Figure 2-43).**

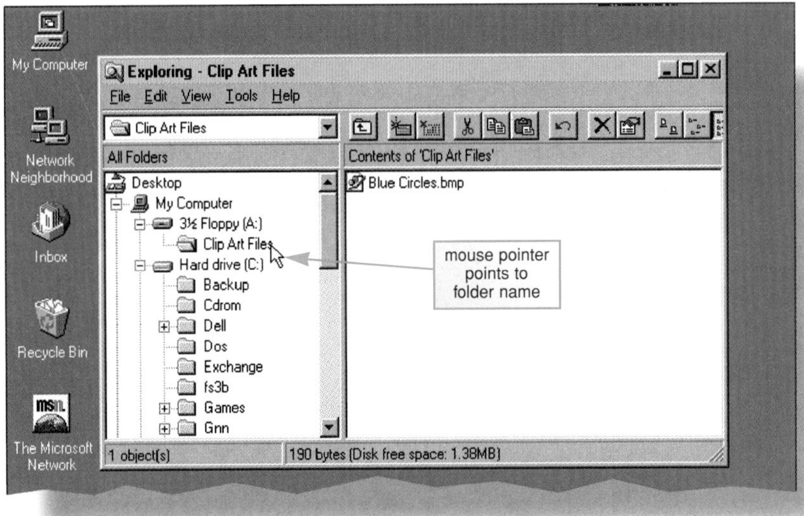

FIGURE 2-43

2 **Right-drag the Clip Art Files icon in the All Folders side to the Recycle Bin icon, and then point to the Move Here command on the context-sensitive menu.**

Windows 95 opens a context-sensitive menu (Figure 2-44). The mouse pointer points to the highlighted Move Here command on the menu.

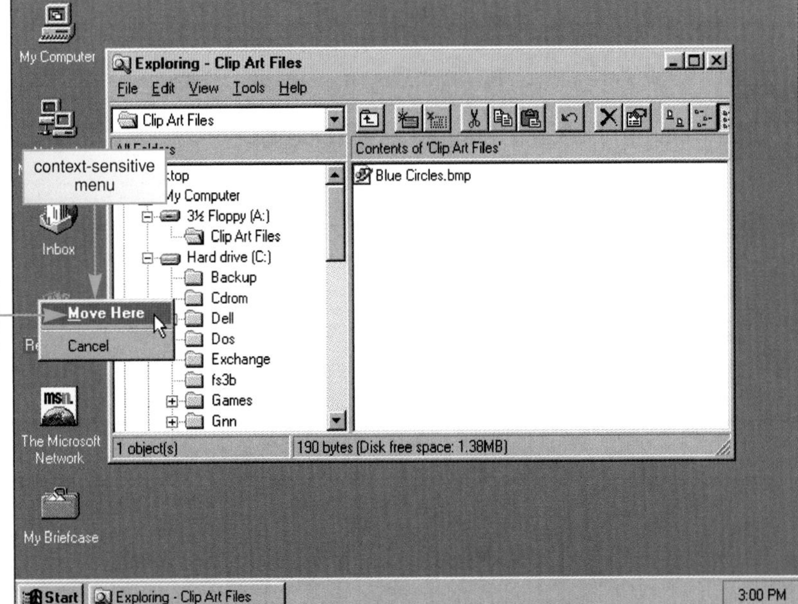

FIGURE 2-44

3 **Click Move Here on the context-sensitive menu. When the Confirm Folder Delete dialog box opens, point to the Yes button.**

Windows 95 opens the Deleting dialog box and then opens the Confirm Folder Delete dialog box on top of the Deleting dialog box (Figure 2-45). The Confirm Folder Delete dialog box contains the message, Are you sure you want to remove the folder 'Clip Art Files' and all its contents?, and the Yes and No command buttons. The mouse pointer points to the Yes button. Clicking the Yes button confirms the deletion of the Clip Art Files folder and causes the folder and its contents to be deleted.

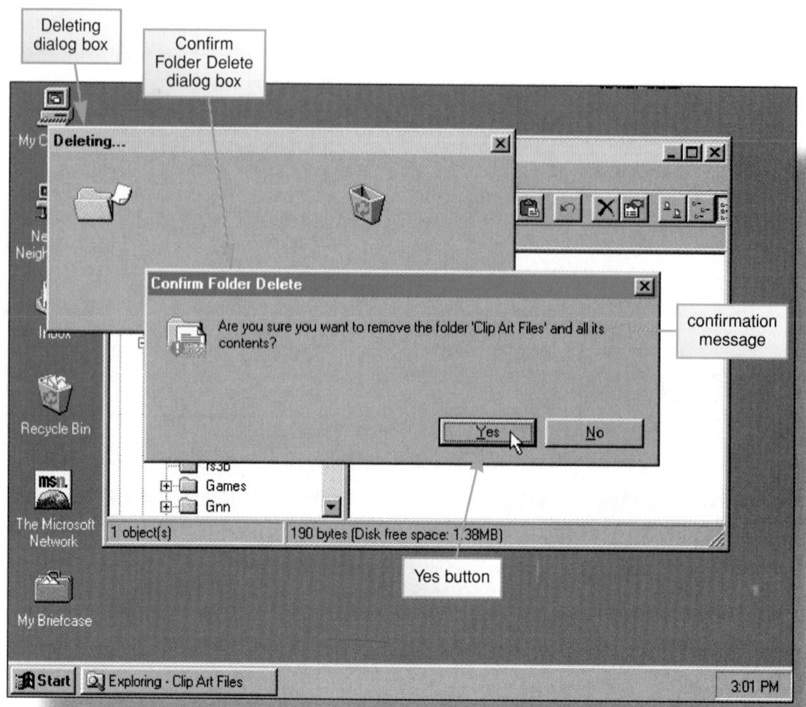

FIGURE 2-45

4 **Click the Yes button in the Confirm Folder Delete dialog box.**

Windows 95 closes the Confirm Folder Delete dialog box, displays the Deleting dialog box while the folder is being deleted, removes the Clip Art Files folder from the All Folders side, and replaces the minus sign preceding the 3½ Floppy [A:] icon with a plus sign (Figure 2-46).

5 **Remove the floppy disk from drive A.**

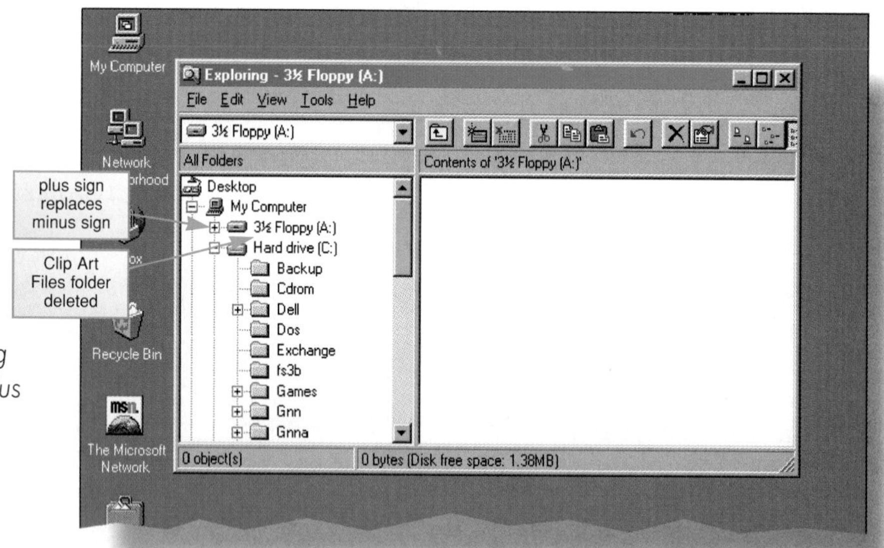

FIGURE 2-46

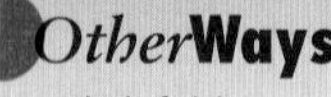

Other Ways

1. Click folder name, press DELETE

Quitting Windows Explorer and Shutting Down Windows 95

After completing work with Windows Explorer, quit Windows Explorer using the Close button on the Windows Explorer title bar, and then shut down Windows using the Shut Down command on the Start menu.

Perform the following steps to quit Windows Explorer.

TO QUIT AN APPLICATION

Step 1: Point to the Close button in the Exploring window.
Step 2: Click the Close button.

Windows 95 closes the Windows Explorer window and quits Windows Explorer.

Perform the following steps to shut down Windows 95.

TO SHUT DOWN WINDOWS 95

Step 1: Click the Start button on the taskbar.
Step 2: Click Shut Down on the Start menu.
Step 3: Click the Yes button in the Shut Down Windows dialog box.
Step 4: Turn off the computer.

Project Summary

In this project, you used Windows Explorer to select and copy a group of files, change views, display the contents of a folder, create a folder, expand and collapse a folder and rename and delete a file and a folder.

What You Should Know

Having completed this project, you should now be able to perform the following tasks:

- Change to List View *(WIN 2.19)*
- Collapse a Folder *(WIN 2.11)*
- Copy a Group of Files *(WIN 2.22)*
- Create a New Folder *(WIN 2.13)*
- Delete a File by Right-Clicking *(WIN 2.27)*
- Delete a File by Right-Dragging *(WIN 2.29)*
- Delete a Folder *(WIN 2.31)*
- Display the Contents of a Folder *(WIN 2.9, WIN 2.17, WIN 2.24)*
- Expand a Folder *(WIN 2.10)*
- Expand the 3½ Floppy [A:] Folder *(WIN 2.16)*
- Quit an Application *(WIN 2.33)*
- Rename a File *(WIN 2.24)*
- Rename a Folder *(WIN 2.25)*
- Select a Group of Files *(WIN 2.20)*
- Shut Down Windows 95 *(WIN 2.33)*
- Start Windows Explorer and Maximize Its Window *(WIN 2.6)*

Test Your Knowledge

1 True/False

Instructions: Circle T if the statement is true or F if the statement is false.

T F 1. Windows Explorer is an application you can use to organize and work with the files and folders on the computer.

T F 2. Double-clicking the My Computer icon is the best way to open Windows Explorer.

T F 3. The contents of the current folder are displayed in the All Folders side.

T F 4. To display the contents of drive C on your computer in the Contents side, click the plus sign in the small box next to the drive C icon.

T F 5. A folder that is contained within another folder is called a subfolder.

T F 6. To display the contents of a folder, right-click its folder name.

T F 7. Collapsing a folder removes the subfolders from the hierarchy of folders in the All Folders side.

T F 8. After you expand a drive or folder, the information in the Contents side is always the same as the information displayed below the drive or folder icon in the All Folders side.

T F 9. The source folder is the folder containing the files to be copied.

T F 10. You select a group of files in the Contents side by pointing to each icon or filename and clicking the left mouse button.

2 Multiple Choice

Instructions: Circle the correct response.

1. The drop-down list box in the Exploring - My Computer window contains the ______________.
   a. hierarchy of folders
   b. source folder
   c. files in the current folder
   d. current folder
2. The ______________ contains the hierarchy of folders on the computer.
   a. Contents side
   b. status bar
   c. All Folders side
   d. toolbar

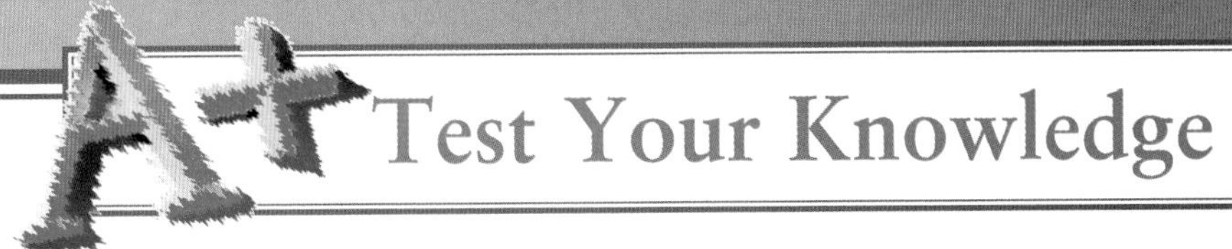

3. To display the contents of a folder in the Contents side, ______________________.
   a. double-click the plus sign next to the folder icon
   b. right-click the folder icon in the All Folders side
   c. click the folder icon in the Contents side
   d. click the folder icon in the All Folders side
4. You ______________________ the minus sign preceding a folder icon to expand a folder.
   a. click
   b. drag
   c. double-click
   d. point to
5. When an expanded file is collapsed in the All Folders side, ______________________.
   a. the expansion closes and the contents of the folder display in the Contents side
   b. the entire Exploring - My Computer window closes
   c. the computer beeps at you because you cannot perform this activity
   d. the My Computer window opens
6. To select multiple files in the Contents side, ______________________.
   a. right-click each file icon
   b. hold down the SHIFT key and then click each file icon you want to select
   c. hold down the CTRL key and then click each file icon you want to select
   d. hold down the CTRL key and then double-click each file icon you want to select
7. After selecting a group of files, you ______________________ the group to copy the files to a new folder.
   a. click
   b. right-drag
   c. double-click
   d. none of the above
8. In ______________________ view, each file or folder in the Contents side is represented by a smaller icon, and the files or folders are arranged in columns.
   a. large icons
   b. small icons
   c. list
   d. details
9. A file or folder can be renamed by ______________________.
   a. right-dragging its filename
   b. double-clicking its filename
   c. dragging its filename
   d. clicking its filename twice

(continued)

Test Your Knowledge

Multiple Choice *(continued)*

10. A file can be deleted by right-dragging the filename from the Contents side of the window to the ______________________ icon on the desktop.
    a. My Computer
    b. Network Neighborhood
    c. Recycle Bin
    d. My Briefcase

3 Understanding the Exploring - My Computer Window

Instructions: In Figure 2-47 arrows point to several items in the Exploring - My Computer window. Identify the items or objects in the spaces provided.

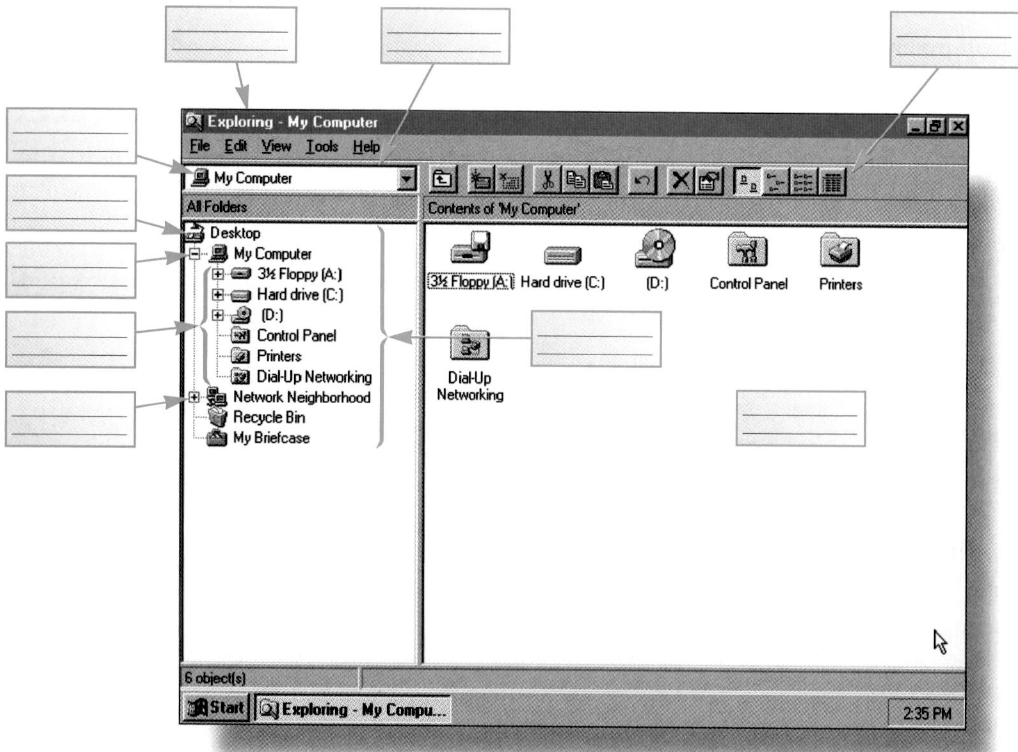

FIGURE 2-47

Use Help

1 Using Windows Help

Instructions: Use Windows Help and a computer to perform the following tasks.

1. Start Microsoft Windows 95 if necessary.
2. Answer the following questions about paths.
   a. What is a path? ______________________________
   b. What does a path include? ______________________________
   c. How do you specify a path? ______________________________
   d. What do you do if your filename contains more than eight characters? ____________________
3. Open the Help Topics: Windows Help window. Click the Index tab if necessary and then type `windows explorer` in the text box. Click demo in the Windows Explorer list and then click the Display button. In the Windows Help window, play the demonstration.
   a. How does the demonstration open Windows Explorer? ______________________________
   b. What folders are contained on drive C in the demonstration? ____________________________
4. How can you cause Explorer to start each time you start Windows 95? ____________________
5. You have recently written a business letter to a manager named Lori Hill. You explained CD-ROM drives to her. You want to see what else you said in the letter, but you can neither remember the name of the file nor where you stored the file on your computer. You read something in your Windows 95 manual that the Find command could be used to find lost files. Using Help, determine what you must do to find your letter. Write those steps in the spaces provided.

   ____

   ____

   ____
6. You and a friend both recently bought computers. She was lucky and received a color printer as her birthday gift. You would like to print some of your more colorful documents on her color printer. You have heard that for not too much money you can buy a network card and some cable and hook up your computers on a network. Then, you can print documents stored on your computer on her color printer. Using Windows Help, determine if you can share her printer. If so, what must you do in Windows 95 to make this become a reality. Print the Help pages that document your answer.
7. You can hardly believe that last week you won a laptop computer at a charity dance. The application programs on the laptop are the same as those on your desktop computer. The only trouble is that when you use your laptop computer to modify a file, you would like the same file on your desktop also to be modified. In that way, you can work on the file either on your desktop computer or on your laptop computer. A friend mentioned that the My Briefcase feature of Windows 95 allows you to do what you want to do. Using Windows Help, find out all you can about My Briefcase. Print the Help pages that specify how to keep files on both your desktop and laptop computers synchronized with each other.

1 File and Program Properties

Instructions: Use a computer to perform the following tasks and answer the questions.

1. Start Microsoft Windows 95 if necessary.
2. Open the My Computer window.
3. Open the drive C window on your computer.
4. Scroll until the Windows icon is visible in the drive C window.
5. Right-click the Windows icon.
6. Click Open on the context-sensitive menu.
7. Scroll until the Black Thatch icon is visible. If the Black Thatch icon does not display on your computer, find another Paint icon.
8. Right-click the Black Thatch icon.
9. Click Properties on the context-sensitive menu.
10. Answer the following questions about the Black Thatch file:
    a. What type of file is Black Thatch? ________________
    b. What is the path for the location of the Black Thatch file? (Hint: Point to the location of the file) ________________________________
    c. What is the size (in bytes) of the Black Thatch file? ________________
    d. What is the MS-DOS name of the Black Thatch file? ________________ The tilde (~) character is placed in the MS-DOS filename when the Windows 95 filename is greater than 8 characters. Windows 95 uses the first six characters of the long filename, the tilde character, and a number to distinguish the file from other files that might have the same first six characters.
    e. When was the file created? ________________
    f. When was the file last modified? ________________
    g. When was the file last accessed ? ________________
11. Click the Cancel button in the Black Thatch Properties dialog box.
12. Scroll in the Windows window until the Notepad icon displays.
13. Right-click the Notepad icon.
14. Click Properties on the context-sensitive menu.
15. Answer the following questions:
    a. What type of file is Notepad? ________________
    b. What is the path of the Notepad file? ________________
    c. How big is the Notepad file? ________________
    d. What is the file extension of the Notepad file? What does it stand for? ________________
    e. What is the file version of the Notepad file? ________________
    f. What is the file's description? ________________
    g. Who is the copyright owner of Notepad? ________________
    h. What language is Notepad written for? ________________
16. Click the Cancel button in the Notepad Properties dialog box.
17. Close all open windows.

In the Lab

2 Windows Explorer

Instructions: Use a computer to perform the following tasks:

1. Start Microsoft Windows 95.
2. Right-click the My Computer icon.
3. Click Explore on the context-sensitive menu.
4. Maximize the Exploring window.
5. Drag the bar between the All Folders side and the Contents side to the center of the Exploring window. What difference do you see in the Window? ____________________

    ____
6. Return the bar to its previous location.
7. Click Tools on the menu bar.
8. Click Go to on the Tools menu.
9. Type `c:\windows` and then click the OK button in the Go To Folder dialog box. What happened in the Exploring window? ____________________
10. Click View on the menu bar and then click Small Icons on the View menu.
11. Click View on the menu bar and then click Options on the View menu.
12. Drag the Options dialog box so you can see the Contents side of the Exploring window. Click Show all files. Click the Apply button. Do any more folders display? If so, what new folders display? Did more files display?

    ____

    ____
13. Click Hide files of these types. Click Hide MS-DOS file extensions for file types that are registered. Click the Apply button. Did the filenames displayed in the Contents area change? If so, what are the changes? Give three examples of filenames that are different:

    ____

    ____
14. Click Hide MS-DOS file extensions for file types that are registered. Click Hide files of these types. Click the OK button.
15. Click View on the menu bar and then click Details on the View menu.
    a. In the Contents side, scroll until you see only file icons and then click the Name button below the Contents of 'Windows' bar. Did the sequence of file icons change? How?

    ____

    b. Click the Size button. How did the sequence of file icons change? ____________________
    c. Click the Type button. How did the sequence of file icons change? ____________________
    d. Click the Modified button. How did the sequence of folder and file icons change?

    ____

    e. Click the Name button.

(continued)

In the Lab

Windows Explorer *(continued)*

16. Click Edit on the menu bar. Click Select All on the Edit menu. If the Select All dialog box displays, click the OK button. What happened? ______________________
17. Click Edit on the menu bar. Click Invert Selection on the Edit menu. Was there any change? ______________________
18. Click File on the menu bar. Point to New on the File menu and then click Bitmap Image on the New submenu. What happened? ______________________
19. Type `In the Lab Image` and then press the ENTER key. What is the name of the bitmap image? ______________________
20. Right-click the In the Lab Image icon. Click Delete on the context-sensitive menu. Click the Yes button in the Confirm File Delete dialog box.
21. Close the Exploring window.

3 Window Toolbars

Instructions: Use a computer to perform the following tasks:

1. Open the My Computer window.
2. Maximize the My Computer window.
3. Click View on the menu bar. Click Large icons on the View menu.
4. Click View on the menu bar. If a check does not display to the left of the Toolbar command, click Toolbar on the View menu. A toolbar displays in the My Computer window (Figure 2-48).
5. Click the down arrow next to the drop-down list box containing the My Computer icon and name.
6. Click the drive C icon in the drop-down list. How did the window change? ______________________
7. Double-click the Windows icon. What happened? ______________________
8. In the Windows window, if the toolbar does not display, click View on the menu bar and then click Toolbar on the View menu.
9. Scroll down if necessary until the Argyle icon displays in the window. If the Argyle icon does not display on your computer, find another Paint icon. Click the Argyle icon and then point to the Copy button on the toolbar (Hint: To determine the function of each button on the toolbar, point to the button).
10. Click the Copy button. Do you see any change? If so, what? ______________________

11. Insert a formatted floppy disk in drive A of your computer.
12. Click the down arrow next to the drop-down list box containing the Windows icon and name.
13. Click the 3½ Floppy [A:] icon in the drop-down list. What happened? ________________________
14. If the toolbar does not display in the 3½ Floppy [A:] window, click View on the menu bar and then click Toolbar on the View menu.
15. In the 3½ Floppy [A:] window, click the Paste button on the toolbar. The Argyle icon displays in the 3½ Floppy [A:] window.
16. With the Argyle icon highlighted in the 3½ Floppy [A:] window, click the Delete button on the toolbar and then click the Yes button in the Confirm File Delete dialog box.
17. In the 3½ Floppy [A:] window, return the toolbar status to what it was prior to step 8. Close the 3½ Floppy [A:] window.
18. In the drive C window, click the Small Icons button and then describe the screen. _______________ ____
19 Click the List button and then describe the screen. ____
20. Click the Details button and then describe the screen. _____________________________________
21. Click the Large Icons button on the toolbar
22. Click the Up One Level button on the toolbar. What is the difference between clicking the Up One Level button and clicking My Computer in the drop-down list box? __________________________
23. Return the toolbar status to what it was prior to step 4. Close the My Computer and drive C windows.

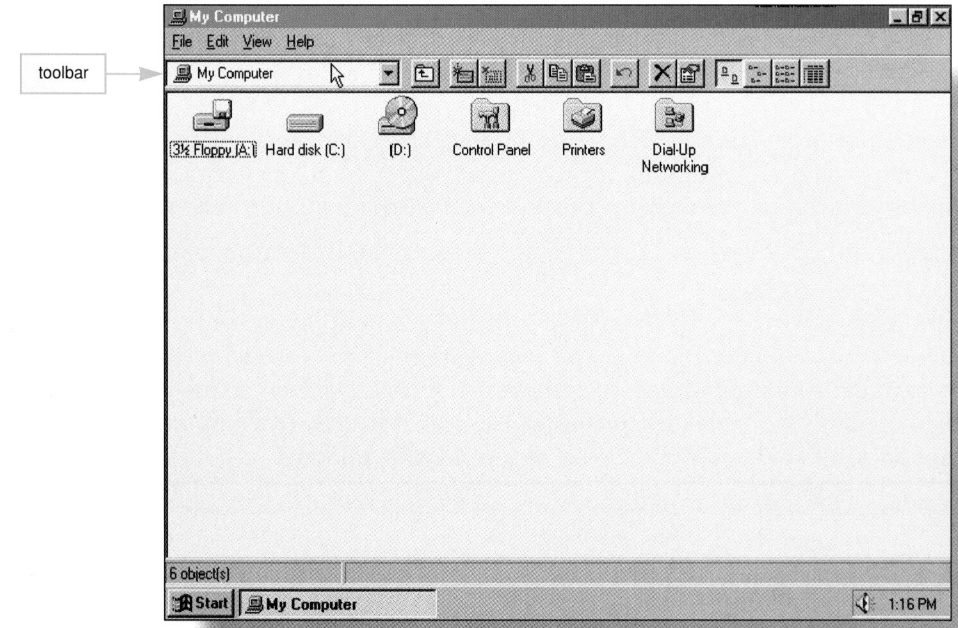

FIGURE 2-48

Cases and Places

The difficulty of these case studies varies:

◗ Case studies preceded by a single half moon are the least difficult. You can complete these case studies using your own computer in the lab.
◗◗ Case studies preceded by two half moons are more difficult. You must research the topic presented using the Internet, a library, or another resource, and then prepare a brief written report.
◗◗◗ Case studies preceded by three half moons are the most difficult. You must visit a store or business to obtain the necessary information, and then use it to create a brief written report.

1 ◗ A key feature of Windows 95 is the capability to modify the view of a window to suit individual preferences and needs. Using Windows Explorer, display the Hard drive [C:] folder in the Contents side and then experiment with the different commands on the View menu. Describe the effects of the Large Icons, Small Icons, List, and Details commands on the icons in the Contents side. When using details view, explain how clicking one of the buttons at the top of the Contents side (such as Name or Type) changes the window. Try out diverse arrangements of icons on the Contents side by pointing to the Arrange Icons command on the View menu and then clicking various commands on the Arrange Icons submenu. Finally, specify situations in which you think some of the views you have seen would be most appropriate.

2 ◗ When the Hard disk [C:] folder is displayed in the Contents side of the Exploring window, it is clear that an enormous number of folders and files are stored on your computer's hard disk. Imagine how hard it would be to manually search through all the folders and files to locate a specific file! Fortunately, Windows 95 provides the Find command to perform the search for you. Click Tools on the Exploring window menu bar, point to Find, and then click Files or Folders on the Find submenu. Learn about each sheet in the Find: All Files dialog box by clicking a tab (Name & Location, Date Modified, or Advanced), clicking the Help menu, clicking What's This? on the Help menu, and then clicking an item on a sheet. Try finding a file using each sheet. Finally, explain how the Find command is used and describe a circumstance in which each sheet would be useful. When you are finished, click the Close button on the window title bar to close the Find: All Files dialog box.

3 ◗◗ Backing up files is an important way to protect data and ensure it is not inadvertently lost or destroyed. File backup on a personal computer can use a variety of devices and techniques. Using the Internet, a library, personal computer magazines, or other resources, determine the types of devices used to store backed up data, the schedules, methods, and techniques for backing up data, and the consequences of not backing up data. Write a brief report of your findings.

Cases and Places

4 ▶▶ A hard disk must be maintained in order to be used most efficiently. This maintenance includes deleting old files, defragmenting a disk so it is not wasteful of space, and from time to time finding and attempting to correct disk failures. Using the Internet, a library, Windows 95 Help, or other research facilities, determine the maintenance that should be performed on hard disks, including the type of maintenance, when it should be performed, how long it takes to perform the maintenance, and the risks, if any, of not performing the maintenance. Write a brief report on the information you obtain.

5 ▶▶▶ The quest for more and faster disk storage continues as application programs grow larger and create sound and graphic files. One technique for increasing the amount of data that can be stored on a disk is disk compression. Disk compression programs, using a variety of mathematical algorithms, store data in less space on a hard disk. Many companies sell software you can load on your computer to perform the task. Windows 95 has disk compression capabilities as part of the operating system. Visit a computer store and find two disk compression programs you can buy. Write a brief report comparing the two packages to the disk compression capabilities of Windows 95. Discuss the similarities and differences between the programs and identify the program that claims to be the most efficient in compressing data.

6 ▶▶▶ Some individuals in the computer industry think both the Windows 3.1 and the Windows 95 operating systems are deficient when it comes to ease of file management. Therefore, they have developed and marketed software that augments the operating systems to provide different and, they claim, improved services for file management. Visit a computer store and inquire about products such as Symantec's Norton Navigator for Windows 95. Write a brief report comparing the products you tested with Windows 95. Explain which you prefer and why.

7 ▶▶▶ Data stored on disk is one of a company's more valuable assets. If that data were to be stolen, lost, or compromised so it could not be accessed, the company could literally go out of business. Therefore, companies go to great lengths to protect their data. Visit a company or business in your area. Find out how it protects its data against viruses, unauthorized access, and even against such natural disasters as fire and tornadoes. Prepare a brief report that describes the procedures. In your report, point out any areas where you see the company has not adequately protected its data.

Index

Microsoft Office 97

▶ **PROJECT ONE**

INTRODUCTION TO MICROSOFT OFFICE 97

Objectives:

You will have mastered the material in this project when you can:

- Identify each application in Microsoft Office 97
- Define World Wide Web, intranet, and Internet
- Explain how each Microsoft Office 97 application uses the Internet
- Identify the purpose of the Web toolbar
- View e-mail messages, appointments, contacts, tasks, journal entries, and notes using Microsoft Outlook
- Use the Office Assistant
- Identify hardware innovations useful with Microsoft Office 97

Microsoft
Office 97

Introduction to Microsoft Office 97

Case Perspective

Your organization recently installed Microsoft Office 97 on all computers. As the computer trainer for an upcoming seminar, you realize you should know more about Microsoft Office 97 but have had little time to learn about it. Since installing Office 97, many employees have come to you with questions about the Office applications and the World Wide Web. You have taken the time to answer their questions by sitting down with them in front of their computers and searching for the answers. From their questions, you have determined that a good starting place to learn about Office 97 would be to learn more about each Office application. Your goal in this project is to become familiar with the Microsoft Office 97 applications so you can teach the seminar.

Microsoft Office 97

Microsoft Office 97, the latest edition of the world's best-selling office suite, is a collection of the more popular Microsoft application software products that work alike and work together as if they were a single program. Microsoft Office 97 Professional Edition includes Microsoft Word 97, Microsoft Excel 97, Microsoft Access 97, Microsoft PowerPoint 97, and Microsoft Outlook 97. Microsoft Office 97 integrates these applications with the power of the Internet so you can move quickly among applications, transfer text and graphics easily among applications, and interact seamlessly with the World Wide Web. An explanation of each of the application software programs in Microsoft Office 97 is given in this project.

Microsoft Office 97 and the Internet

Every application in Microsoft Office 97 allows you to take advantage of the Internet, the World Wide Web, and intranets. The **Internet** is a worldwide network of thousands of computer networks and millions of commercial, educational, government, and personal computers. The **World Wide Web** is an easy-to-use graphical interface for exploring the Internet. The World Wide Web consists of many individual Web sites. A **Web site** can consist of a single **Web page** or multiple Web pages linked together. The first Web page in the Web site is called the **home page**. A unique address, called a **Uniform Resource Locator (URL)**, identifies each Web page.

A software tool, called a **browser**, allows you to locate and view a Web page. One method to view a Web page is to use the browser to enter a URL for the Web page. A widely used browser, called **Microsoft Internet Explorer**, is included with Microsoft Office 97. Another method of viewing Web pages allows you to click a hyperlink. A **hyperlink** is colored or underlined text or a graphic that, when clicked, connects to another Web page.

An **intranet** is a special type of Web that is available only to the users of a particular type of computer network, such as those used within a company or organization for internal communication. Like the Internet, hyperlinks are used within an intranet to access documents, pages, and other destinations on the intranet.

Microsoft Office 97 applications allow you to create hyperlinks to Web sites on the Internet easily, create Web pages for publication on an intranet or the Internet, and retrieve information from the Internet or an intranet into an Office document. Explanations of each of the application software programs in Microsoft Office 97 along with how they are used to access an intranet or the Internet are given on the following pages.

For more information about Office 97, click Help on the menu bar on any Office 97 application window, point to Microsoft on the Web, and click Microsoft Office Home Page. Explore a Web page by clicking a hyperlink. After clicking a hyperlink, click the Back button to display the last Web page.

Microsoft Word 97

Microsoft Word 97 is a full-featured word processing program that allows you to create many types of personal and business communications, including announcements, letters, memos, resumes, and business and academic reports, as well as other forms of written documents.

Figure 1-1 illustrates the top portion of the announcement that students create in one of the exercises in Project One of the Microsoft Word section of this book. The steps to create this announcement are shown in Project One of Word.

Microsoft Word AutoCorrect and Spelling and Grammar features allow you to proofread your documents for spelling and grammatical errors, identifying errors and offering corrections as you type. When you are creating specific documents, such as a business letter or resume, Word provides **wizards**, which ask questions and then use your answers to format the document prior to typing information into the document.

FIGURE 1-1

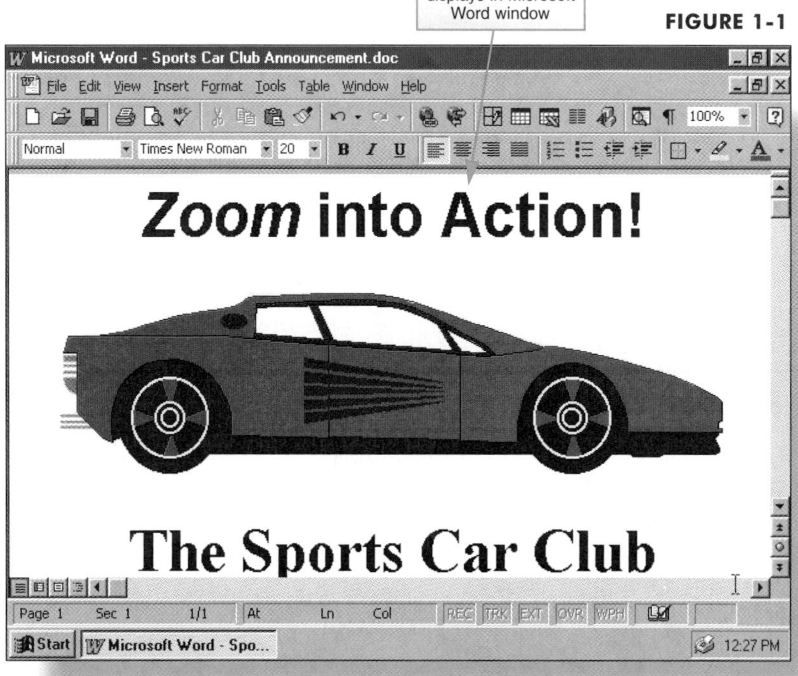

Microsoft Word automates many common tasks and provides you with powerful desktop publishing tools you can use to create professional looking brochures, advertisements, and newsletters. The Office drawing tools allow you to design impressive 3-D effects, shadows, textures, and curves. In addition, the CD-ROM that accompanies Microsoft Office 97 supplies approximately 3,000 clip art images, 150 fonts, and sounds, pictures, and movies that can be used to enhance the appearance of a document.

More About Microsoft Word 97

For more information about Word's tools and features, click Help on the menu bar, point to Microsoft on the Web, click Product News, and click a hyperlink. After clicking a hyperlink, click the Back button to display the last Web page.

Microsoft Word 97 and the Internet

Microsoft Word makes it possible to search for information and access Web pages, design and publish Web pages on an intranet or the Internet, and insert a hyperlink to a Web page in a word processing document. Figure 1-2 illustrates a memo that contains a hyperlink to a Web page on Microsoft Corporation's Web site on the Internet.

Clicking the hyperlink starts the Internet Explorer browser and displays the associated Web page in the Microsoft Internet Explorer window (Figure 1-3). The Web page contains tips for using Microsoft Outlook. The URL for the Web page displays in the Address text box.

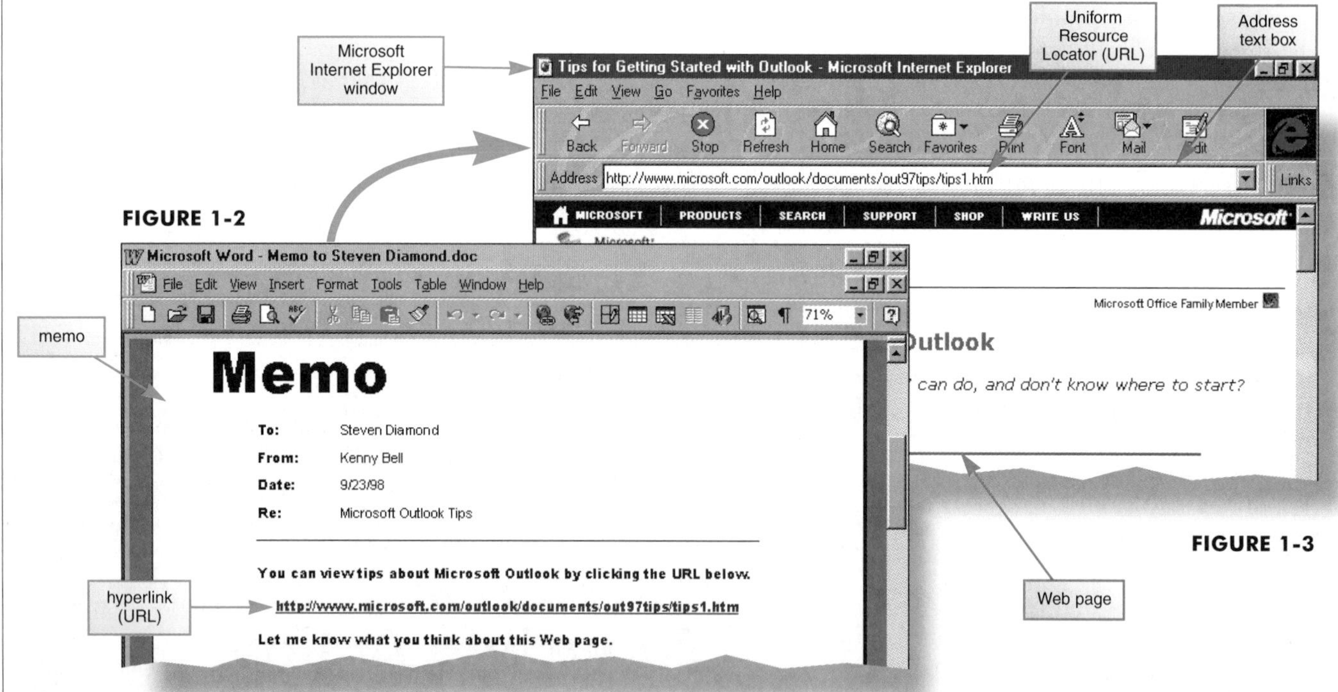

FIGURE 1-2

FIGURE 1-3

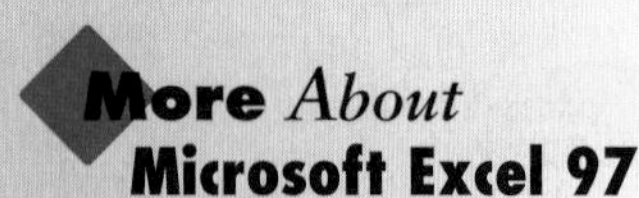

For more information about Excel's tools and features, click Help on the menu bar, point to Microsoft on the Web, click Product News, and click a hyperlink. After clicking a hyperlink, click the Back button to display the last Web page.

Microsoft Excel 97

Microsoft Excel 97 is a spreadsheet program that allows you to organize data, perform calculations, make decisions, graphically display data in charts, develop professional looking reports, convert Excel files for use on the Web, and access the Web. Figure 1-4 illustrates the worksheet and 3-D Column chart created in Project One of the Microsoft Excel section of this book as it displays in the Microsoft Excel window. The steps to create the worksheet and 3-D Column chart are shown in Project One of Excel.

Microsoft Excel's natural language formula capability simplifies the process of building formulas by allowing you to enter formulas using the English language and correcting common entry errors automatically. In addition, Microsoft Excel provides a Chart Wizard that allows you to create a variety of charts from the data in a worksheet. Other features allow multiple users to work with the same worksheet simultaneously.

worksheet and 3-D Column chart display in Microsoft Excel window

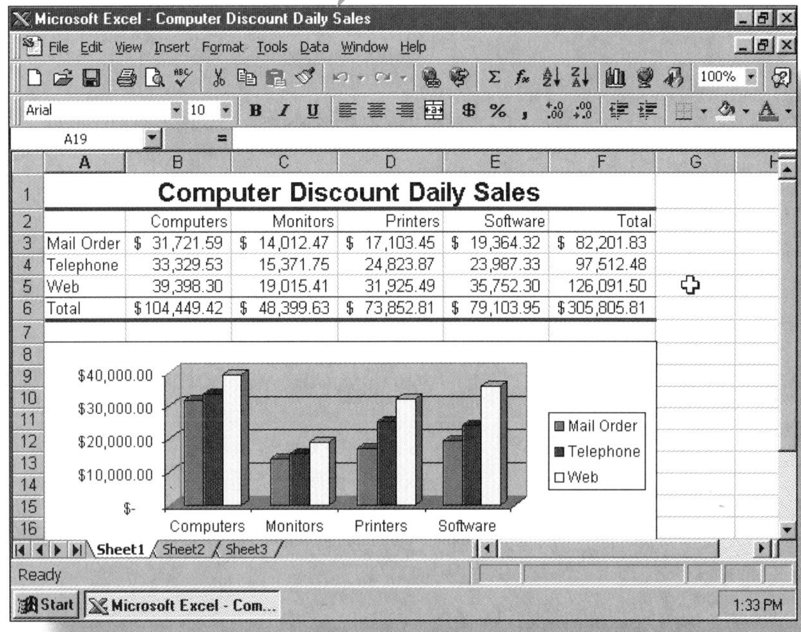

FIGURE 1-4

Microsoft Excel 97 and the Internet

Using Microsoft Excel, you can create hyperlinks within a worksheet to other Office 97 documents on your network, your organization's intranet, or the Internet. You can save worksheets and charts in a format that allows you to display them on a Web page. You also can create and run queries to retrieve information from a Web page directly into a worksheet.

Figure 1-5 illustrates a worksheet created by running a Web query to retrieve stock market information for two stocks (Boeing Corporation and Walt Disney Corporation). The two hyperlinks in the first column are created using the Insert HyperLink button on the Standard toolbar. The information in the worksheet was obtained from the PC Quote, Inc. Web site. The External Data toolbar containing the Refresh All button displays on the worksheet.

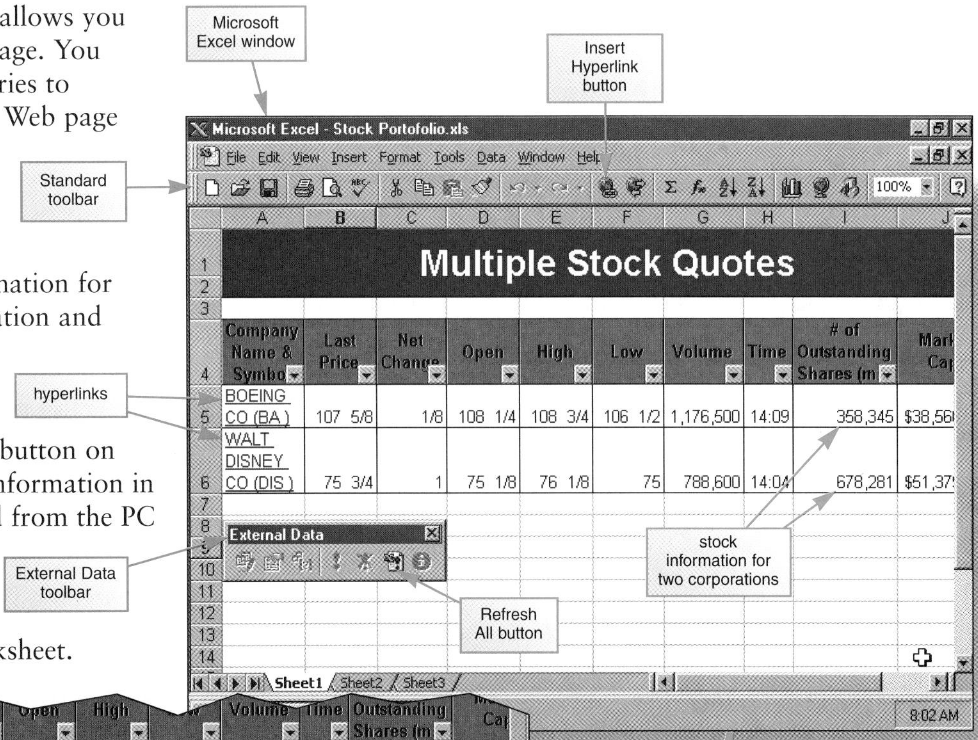

Microsoft Excel window

Insert Hyperlink button

Standard toolbar

hyperlinks

External Data toolbar

stock information for two corporations

Refresh All button

Microsoft Excel - Stock Portofolio.xls

Multiple Stock Quotes

FIGURE 1-5

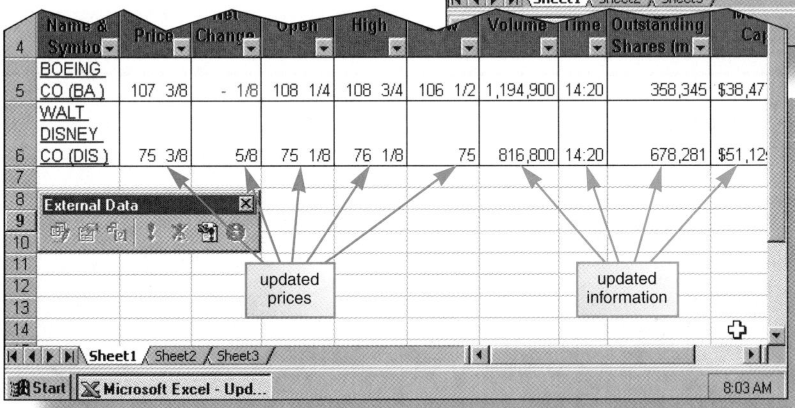

updated prices

updated information

FIGURE 1-6

Clicking the Refresh All button locates the PC Quote, Inc. Web site, retrieves current information for the stocks in the worksheet using the hyperlinks in the first column, and displays the updated information in the worksheet (see Figure 1-6 on the previous page). Notice that the stock prices and information in this worksheet are different from the worksheet in Figure 1-5 on the previous page.

Microsoft Access 97

Microsoft Access 97 is a comprehensive **database program**. A **database** is a collection of data organized in a manner that allows access, retrieval, and use of that data. Microsoft Access allows you to create a database; add, change, and delete data in the database; sort data in the database; retrieve data from the database; and create forms and reports using the data in the database.

Figure 1-7 illustrates the database created in Project One of the Microsoft Access section of this book as it displays in the Microsoft Access window. The steps to create this database are shown in Project One of Access.

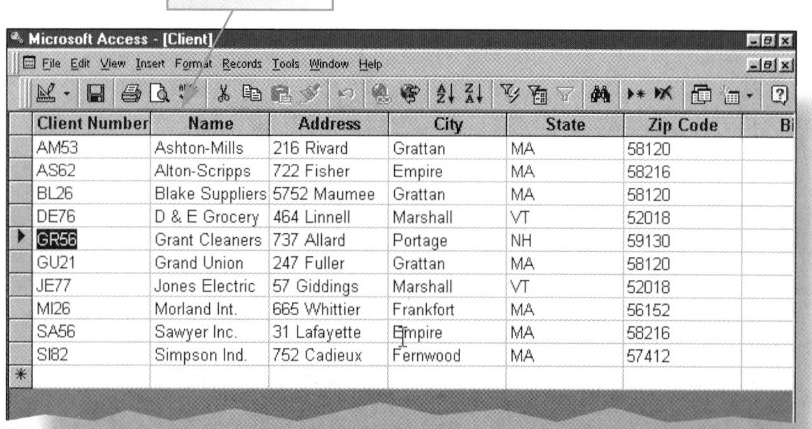

Client Number	Name	Address	City	State	Zip Code
AM53	Ashton-Mills	216 Rivard	Grattan	MA	58120
AS62	Alton-Scripps	722 Fisher	Empire	MA	58216
BL26	Blake Suppliers	5752 Maumee	Grattan	MA	58120
DE76	D & E Grocery	464 Linnell	Marshall	VT	52018
GR56	Grant Cleaners	737 Allard	Portage	NH	59130
GU21	Grand Union	247 Fuller	Grattan	MA	58120
JE77	Jones Electric	57 Giddings	Marshall	VT	52018
MI26	Morland Int.	665 Whittier	Frankfort	MA	56152
SA56	Sawyer Inc.	31 Lafayette	Empire	MA	58216
SI82	Simpson Ind.	752 Cadieux	Fernwood	MA	57412

FIGURE 1-7

Microsoft Access 97 and the Internet

Databases are used to provide a central location to store related pieces of information. Microsoft Access simplifies the creation of databases with the Database Wizard that can be used to build quickly one of more than twenty types of databases. You also can transform lists or worksheets into databases using Access wizards. As with the other Office applications, Access allows you to share a database with other computer users on your network,

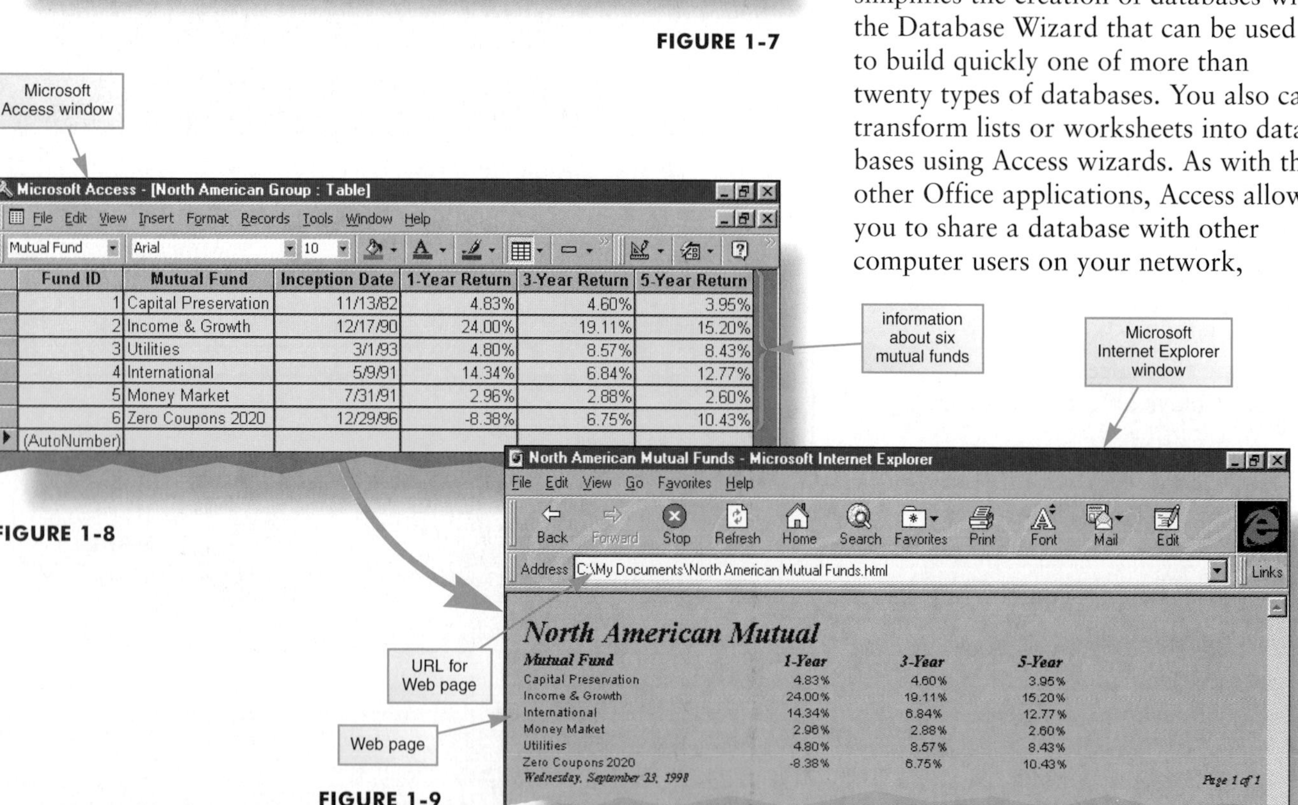

Fund ID	Mutual Fund	Inception Date	1-Year Return	3-Year Return	5-Year Return
1	Capital Preservation	11/13/82	4.83%	4.60%	3.95%
2	Income & Growth	12/17/90	24.00%	19.11%	15.20%
3	Utilities	3/1/93	4.80%	8.57%	8.43%
4	International	5/9/91	14.34%	6.84%	12.77%
5	Money Market	7/31/91	2.96%	2.88%	2.60%
6	Zero Coupons 2020	12/29/96	-8.38%	6.75%	10.43%
(AutoNumber)					

FIGURE 1-8

Mutual Fund	1-Year	3-Year	5-Year
Capital Preservation	4.83%	4.60%	3.95%
Income & Growth	24.00%	19.11%	15.20%
International	14.34%	6.84%	12.77%
Money Market	2.96%	2.88%	2.60%
Utilities	4.80%	8.57%	8.43%
Zero Coupons 2020	-8.38%	6.75%	10.43%

FIGURE 1-9

intranet, or over the Internet. The database in Figure 1-8 contains information (fund ID, mutual fund name, inception date, 1-year average return, 3-year average return, and 5-year average return) about six mutual stock funds.

Figure 1-9 illustrates a simple Web page created from information in the database in Figure 1-8. The Web page is displayed using the Microsoft Internet Explorer browser. The URL for the Web page displays in the Address text box in the window.

More *About* **Microsoft Access 97**

For more information about Access's tools and features, click Help on the menu bar, point to Microsoft on the Web, click Product News, and click a hyperlink. After clicking a hyperlink, click the Back button to display the last Web page.

Microsoft PowerPoint 97

Microsoft PowerPoint 97 is a complete **presentation graphics program** that allows you to produce professional looking presentations. PowerPoint gives you the flexibility to make informal presentations using overhead transparencies, make electronic presentations using a projection device attached to a personal computer, make formal presentations using 35mm slides, or run virtual presentations on the Internet.

Figure 1-10 illustrates the first slide in a presentation created in Project One of the Microsoft PowerPoint section of this book as it displays in the Microsoft PowerPoint window. The steps to create this presentation are shown in Project One of PowerPoint.

Microsoft PowerPoint allows you to create dynamic presentations easily with multimedia features including sounds, movies, and pictures. PowerPoint comes with Design templates and Content templates that assist you in designing a presentation that can be used to create a slide show.

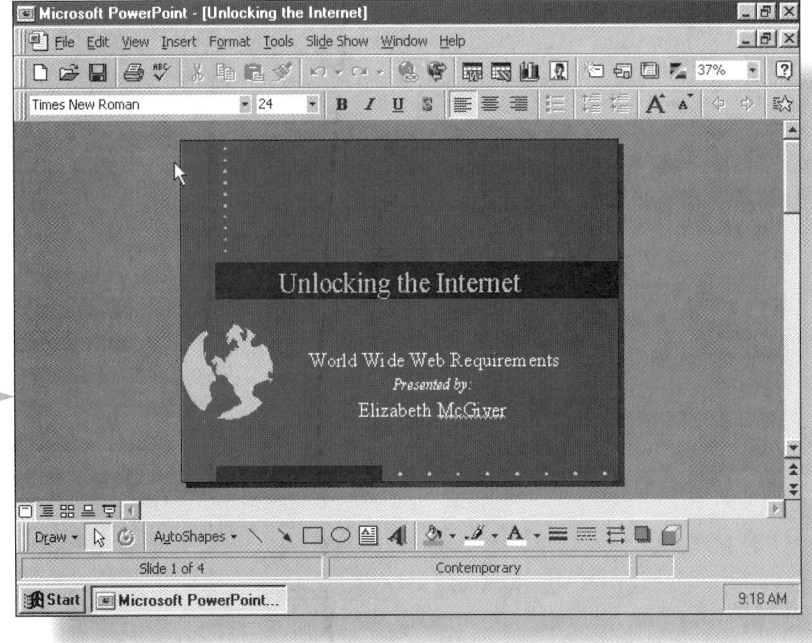

FIGURE 1-10

Microsoft PowerPoint 97 and the Internet

A clip art gallery that contains more than 1,000 clip art images, and sounds, pictures, and movies for use when creating a presentation is located on the Internet and is updated periodically by Microsoft Corporation. In addition, PowerPoint lets you publish your presentations on your intranet or the Internet using the HTML format. **HTML (HyperText Markup Language)** is a system of marking up, or tagging, a document so it can be published on the World Wide Web. Figure 1-11, on the next page, illustrates the first slide in a presentation to be published on the Internet. The slide was created using the Contemporary design, contains a clip art image (blue ribbon), title (Microsoft® Office 97), subtitle (Guide to Office Applications), and creation date (October 1998). Additional slides in this presentation are not visible in Figure 1-11.

More *About* **Microsoft PowerPoint 97**

For more information about PowerPoint's tools and features, click Help on the menu bar, point to Microsoft on the Web, click Product News, and click a hyperlink. After clicking a hyperlink, click the Back button to display the last Web page.

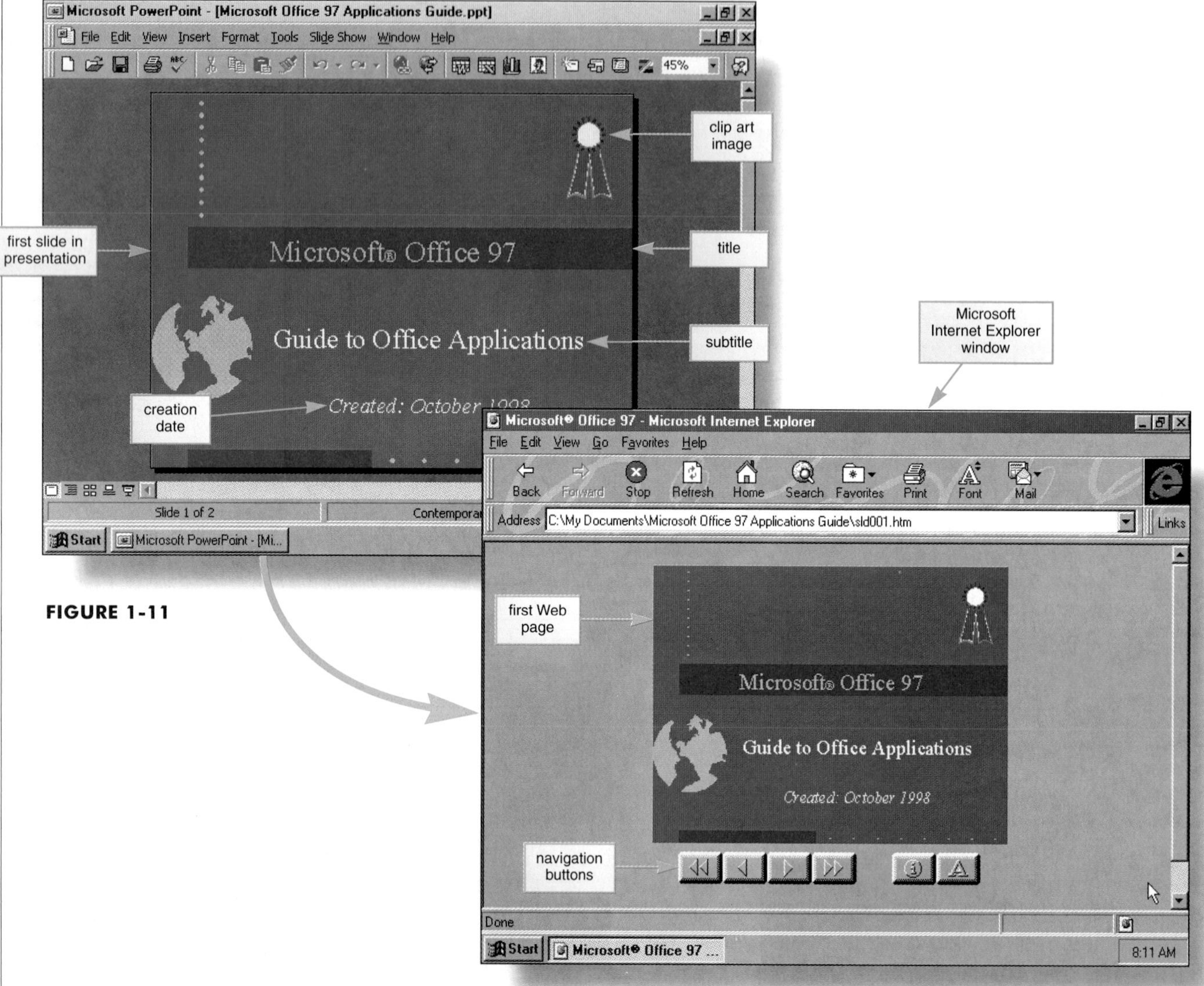

FIGURE 1-11

FIGURE 1-12

Figure 1-12 illustrates the first Web page in a series of Web pages created from the presentation in Figure 1-11. The Web page displays in the Microsoft Internet Explorer window. The navigation buttons at the bottom of the page allow you to view additional Web pages in the presentation.

The Web Toolbar

The easiest method to navigate an intranet or the Internet is to use the **Web toolbar**. The Web toolbar allows you to search for and open Microsoft Office 97 documents on your intranet or Web pages on the Internet. The Web toolbar shown in the Microsoft Word window in Figure 1-13 is available in all Microsoft Office 97 applications, except Microsoft Outlook. Currently, a Word document (a memorandum) displays in the window, and the path and file name of the document display in the text box on the Web toolbar.

The buttons and text box on the Web toolbar allow you to jump to Web pages you have previously viewed, cancel a jump to a Web page, update the contents of the current Web page, and replace all other toolbars with the Web toolbar. In addition, you can view the first Web page displayed, search the Web for new Web sites, and add Web pages you select to the Favorites folder so you can return to them quickly in the future.

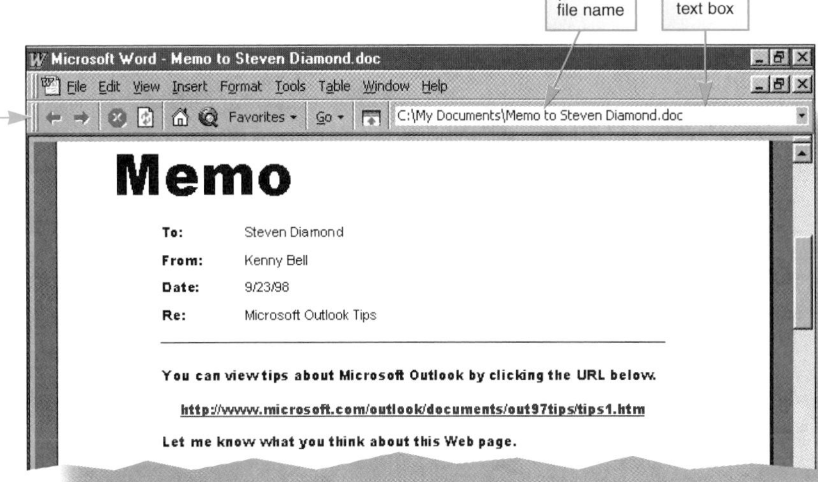

FIGURE 1-13

Microsoft Outlook 97

According to Microsoft Corporation's research, forty percent of the people who use software suites want their suites to include a software application that can manage tasks and appointments, organize and share information with others, and keep track of contacts. In response, Microsoft developed **Microsoft Outlook 97**, an integrated **desktop information management (DIM)** program that helps you organize information on your desktop and share information with others. Microsoft Outlook allows you to manage personal and business information such as e-mail, appointments, contacts, tasks, and documents, and keep a journal of your activities. Outlook organizes and stores this information in folders.

More *About* **Microsoft Outlook 97**

For more information about Outlook's tools and features, click Help on the menu bar, point to Microsoft on the Web, click Product News, and click a hyperlink. After clicking a hyperlink, click the Back button to display the last Web page.

Viewing Electronic Mail (E-Mail)

Electronic mail, or **e-mail**, is the fastest growing desktop application. With this in mind, Microsoft designed Microsoft Outlook to allow you to check for and read e-mail messages easily, compose and send a response to an e-mail message, or compose and send a new e-mail message. When you start Microsoft Outlook, the Inbox – Microsoft Outlook window displays and the contents of the Inbox folder (your e-mail messages) display in the window (Figure 1-14).

The Inbox icon, representing the Inbox folder, displays on the **Outlook Bar** on the left side of the window and the contents of

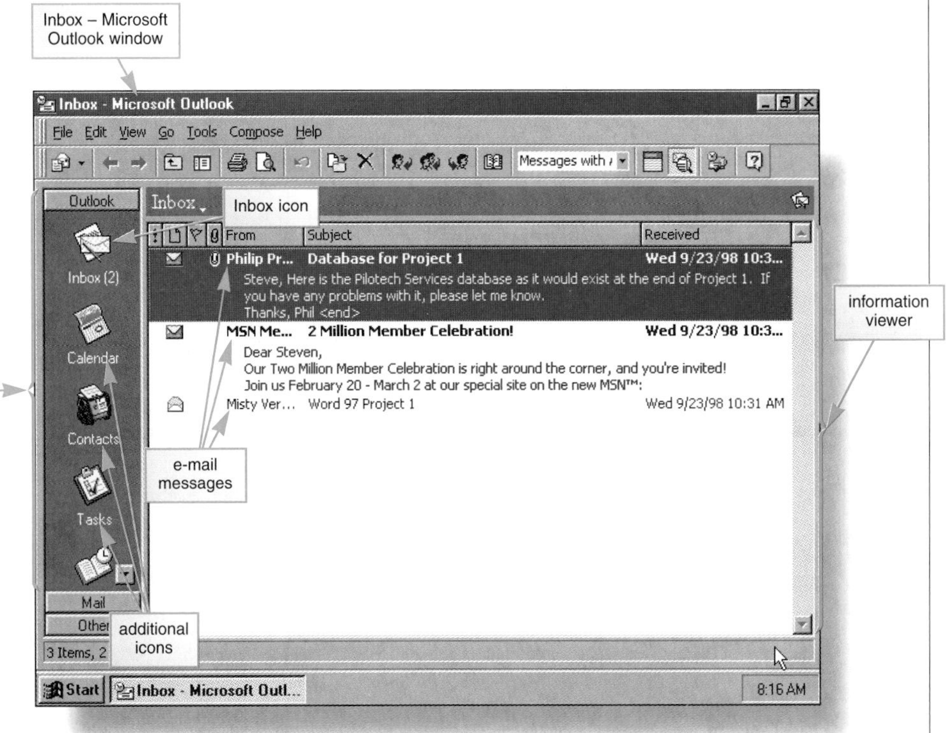

FIGURE 1-14

More About Inbox

To obtain more information about Inbox, click the Office Assistant button on the toolbar, type `inbox` in the text box, click the Search button, and click the Inbox option button. Click the hyperlinks on the screen to display Help topics.

the Inbox folder (three e-mail messages) display in the information viewer on the right side of the window. The **information viewer** displays the contents of the active folder (Inbox folder). Also visible on the Outlook Bar are the Calendar, Contacts, and Tasks icons. Clicking an icon on the Outlook Bar displays the contents of the associated folder in the information viewer.

Several Microsoft Outlook features enhance the performance and functionality of the Inbox. The AutoPreview feature displays the first three lines of the body of each e-mail message in the Subject column, allowing you to review the purpose of a message quickly and to read or delete messages without opening them. The AutoName Check feature helps to ensure that an e-mail message is sent to the correct recipient by checking the recipient's name against a list of valid names, quickly identifying invalid names, and resolving ambiguous names. The Voting feature allows you to poll multiple users by sending one or more questions and receiving answers. The Voting feature tallies the votes as they arrive, making individual and group responses available.

Viewing Appointments

Microsoft's research determined that personal and group scheduling is second in popularity only to e-mail. The most common scheduling activity is browsing the schedules of a group of users to find an available time for a group meeting. In response, Microsoft included the Calendar application in Microsoft Outlook. The **Calendar** application allows you to schedule activities (events, appointments, and meetings). An **event** is an activity that lasts 24 hours or longer (seminar, holiday, birthday, and so on), an **appointment** is an activity for which you block time that does not involve other people or resources, and a **meeting** is an appointment requiring resources and to which you invite people.

When you click the Calendar icon on the Outlook Bar, Microsoft Outlook displays the Calendar – Microsoft Outlook window, and the contents of the Calendar folder (today's events, appointments, and meetings) display in the window (Figure 1-15).

FIGURE 1-15

The Calendar – Microsoft Outlook window contains a **calendar** that lists the hours from 8:00 a.m. to 2:00 p.m. and the events, appointments, and meetings scheduled for the current day. In Figure 1-15, one event (Allan Preston's birthday), one appointment (Finish Marketing Plan), and one meeting (Weekly Sales Meeting) are scheduled.

To the right of the calendar and at the top of the information viewer is the date navigator. The **date navigator** contains a two-month calendar (September and October) and allows you to navigate through additional months. Bold dates in the date navigator indicate that an activity has been scheduled for that day.

The **TaskPad**, located below the date navigator, contains a list of tasks to be performed for the current day. A **task** is a personal or business-related activity you want to track from its inception to its completion.

Using Calendar, you can share information with other Office 97 programs, share information with groups of people, connect to and share information across the World Wide Web, and browse and find Office 97 files within your organization or around the world. Other features allow you to use your Outlook information when you leave your computer and use a portable or laptop computer.

More About Calendar

To obtain more information about Calendar, click the Office Assistant button on the toolbar, type `calendar` in the text box, click the Search button, and click the Calendar option button. Click the hyperlinks on the screen to display Help topics.

Viewing Contacts

The most commonly requested improvement by users of Microsoft Schedule+ (an application included with Office 95 that was enhanced and is included in Microsoft Outlook) is the addition of a contact address book that maintains a list of contacts and e-mail addresses. In response, Microsoft included the **Contacts** application in Microsoft Outlook.

When you click the Contacts icon on the Outlook Bar, the Contacts – Microsoft Outlook window displays and the contents of the Contacts folder (your contacts) display in the window (Figure 1-16).

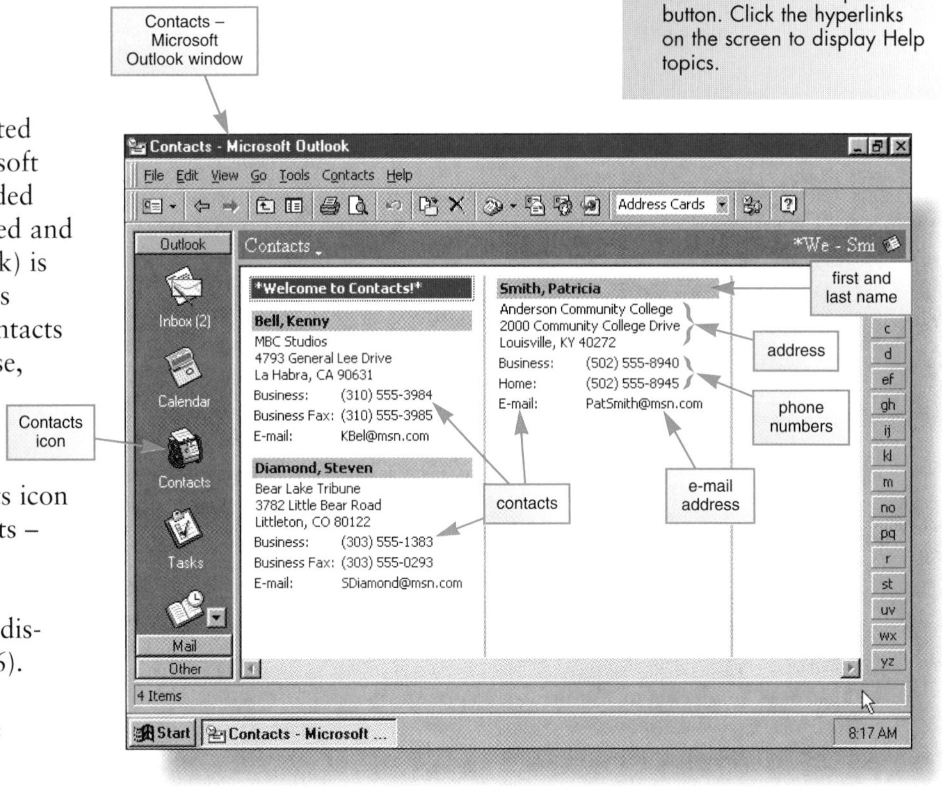

The Contacts – Microsoft Outlook window contains three contacts (Kenny Bell, Steven Diamond, and Patricia Smith). The contacts display in alphebetical order by last name. Each contact consists of the contact's last name and first name, an address, telephone and fax numbers, and an e-mail address.

FIGURE 1-16

Using Contacts, you can maintain an Internet address for each contact for faster access to a contact's home page, store up to 19 different telephone numbers for each contact, automatically dial a telephone number, and send e-mail messages.

More About Contacts

To obtain more information about Contacts, click the Office Assistant button on the toolbar, type `contacts` in the text box, click the Search button, and click the Contacts option button. Click the hyperlinks on the screen to display Help topics.

Viewing Tasks

As mentioned above, a task is a personal or business-related activity you want to track from its inception to its completion. A task can occur once or repeat at regular intervals (a recurring task). The TaskPad shown in Figure 1-15 contains a list of the tasks for the current day. When you click the Tasks icon on the Outlook Bar, a detailed list of the tasks in the Tasks folder displays in the Tasks – Microsoft Outlook window (see Figure 1-17 on the next page).

The Tasks – Microsoft Outlook window contains two tasks (Inventory Office Equipment and Hair Cut at Raffi's). The type of task, level of importance, whether or not it contains an attachment, subject, status, due date, percentage complete, and category display for each task.

More About Tasks

To obtain more information about Tasks, click the Office Assistant button on the toolbar, type `tasks` in the text box, click the Search button, and click the Tasks option button. Click the hyperlinks on the screen to display Help topics.

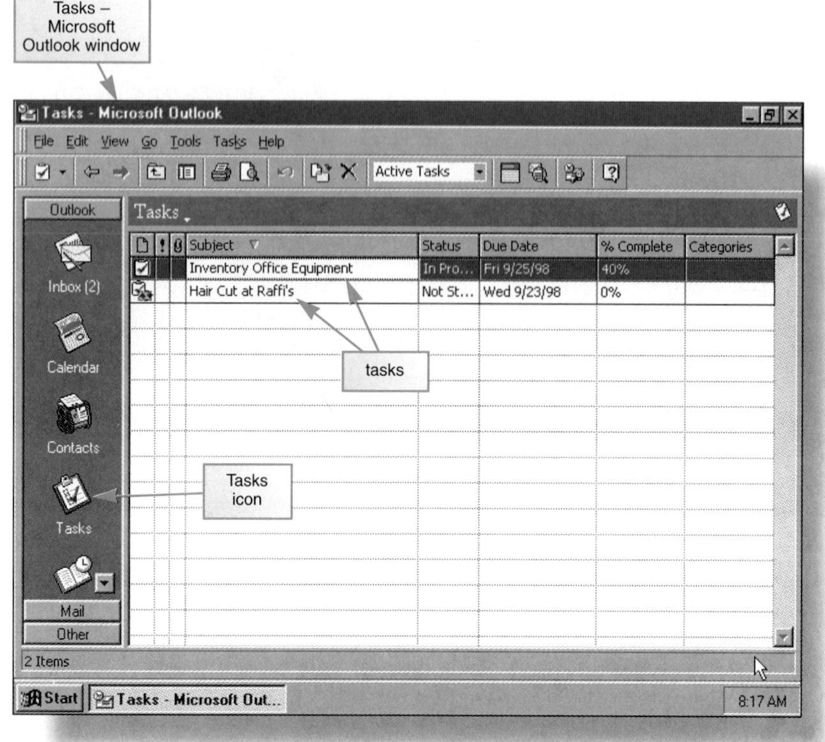

FIGURE 1-17

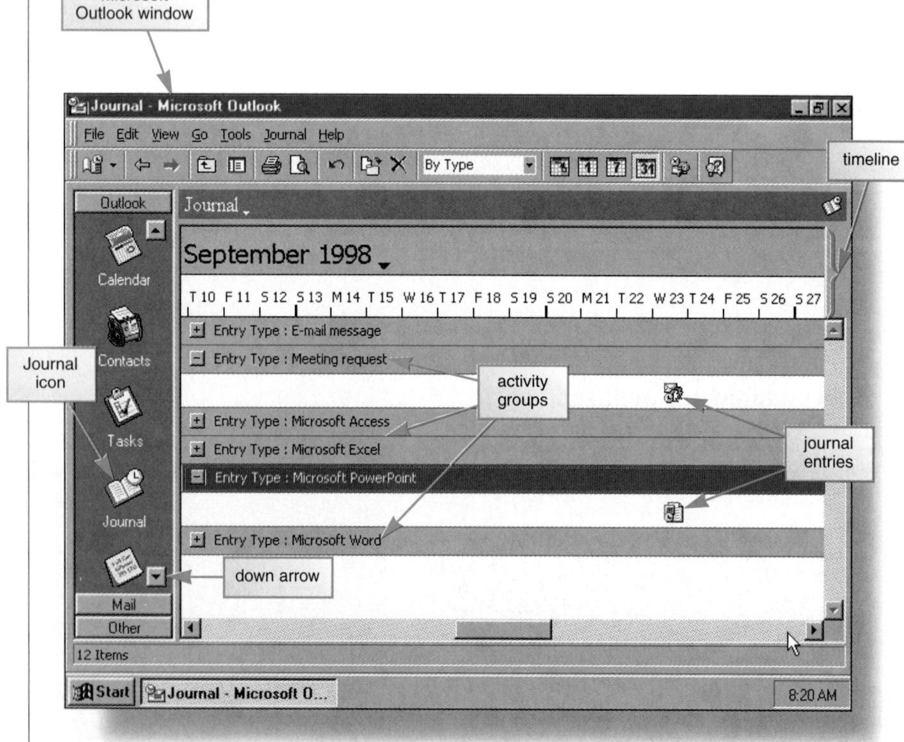

FIGURE 1-18

Viewing Journal Entries

The **Journal** application automatically maintains a journal of your activities. A **journal entry** is recorded based upon when an activity occurs. For example, you can tell Office 97 to record a journal entry automatically when you create an Office 97 document, record all e-mail messages for the contacts you specify, or record each telephone number you dial. Journal entries are organized into groups.

When you click the down arrow on the Outlook Bar and then click the Journal icon, Microsoft Outlook displays the Journal – Microsoft Outlook window and the contents of the Journal folder (Figure 1-18).

The Journal – Microsoft Outlook window contains a timeline and six activity groups. The **timeline** consists of a banner containing the current month and year (September 1998) and a banner containing several days in the current month. Below the timeline are six groups (E-mail message, Meeting request, Microsoft Access, Microsoft Excel, Microsoft PowerPoint, and Microsoft Word). The journal entries in two groups (Meeting request and Microsoft PowerPoint) are visible in the information viewer. Thus, a meeting was scheduled for the current day and a PowerPoint document was created, opened, or printed on that day.

Each journal entry is a shortcut to the activity it represents and is identified by the clock in the lower-left corner of the icon that represents the journal entry. Double-clicking the icon for the meeting request entry opens a window containing the details of the meeting. Double-clicking the icon for the PowerPoint document entry opens a window containing the details of the document and another icon. Double-clicking the icon starts Microsoft PowerPoint and displays the document in the PowerPoint window.

The shortcut allows you to find a document easily based on the date you created or worked on the document, without worrying about where you saved the document or what you named the document.

Viewing Notes

Notes are the electronic equivalent of paper *sticky notes*. The **Notes** application provides a location to store bits of information that are important to you that ordinarily would end up on stray scraps of paper. You can use Notes to record questions, lists, ideas, directions, reminders, or anything you would write on paper. When you click the Notes icon on the Outlook Bar, Microsoft Outlook displays the Notes – Microsoft Outlook window and the notes in the Notes folder (Figure 1-19). When you double-click a note, the contents of the note display in the information viewer.

Three notes and the contents of the Weekend Schedule note are visible in the information viewer. The notes contain directions to Anaheim Stadium, a grocery store shopping list, and a weekend schedule. The Weekend Schedule note contains a list of three weekend activities.

The Deleted Items icon on the Outlook Bar in Figure 1-19 represents the Deleted Items folder, which contains all the items (e-mail, appointments, and so on) that were deleted while using Microsoft Outlook.

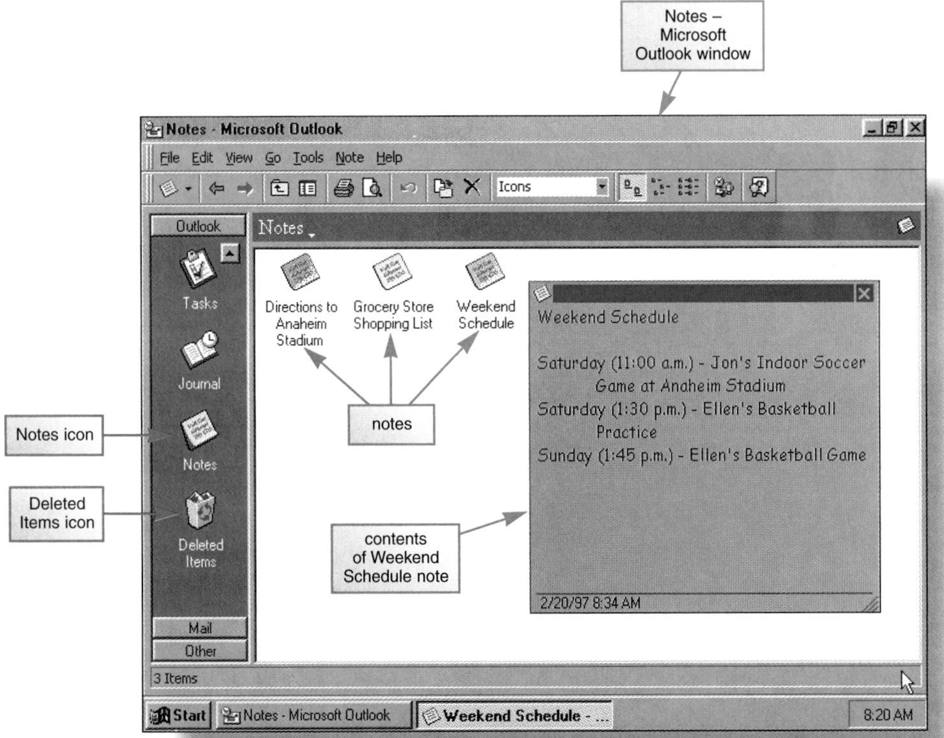

FIGURE 1-19

More About Journal

To obtain more information about Journal, click the Office Assistant button on the toolbar, type `journal` in the text box, click the Search button, and click the Journal option button. Click the hyperlinks on the screen to display Help topics.

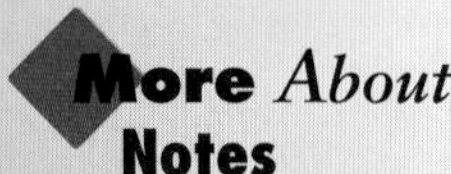

More About Notes

To obtain more information about Notes, click the Office Assistant button on the toolbar, type `notes` in the text box, click the Search button, and click the Notes option button. Click the hyperlinks on the screen to display Help topics.

More *About*
Office Assistant

To change the Office Assistant, right-click the Office Assistant window, click Options on the shortcut menu, if necessary click Gallery tab, click Next button to select Office Assistant, and click the OK button.

The Office Assistant

The **Office Assistant** answers your questions and suggests more efficient ways to complete a task. With the Office Assistant active, for example, you can type a word or phrase in a text box and the Office Assistant provides immediate Help on the subject. As you work with an Office 97 application, the Office Assistant accumulates tips that suggest more effective ways to perform the tasks you completed while using the application. This tip feature is part of the **IntelliSense technology** that is built into Microsoft Office 97. IntelliSense technology allows Office Assistant to understand what you are trying to do and suggest better ways to do it.

The Office Assistant and balloon display whenever you start a Microsoft Office 97 application. The Office Assistant and balloon that display when you start Microsoft Outlook are illustrated in Figure 1-20.

The Office Assistant (a two-dimensional, animated paper clip or other object in a window) is completely customizable so you can select one of nine Office Assistants and the options that best suit the way you work. Detailed instructions about using the Office Assistant will be explained in each section of this book.

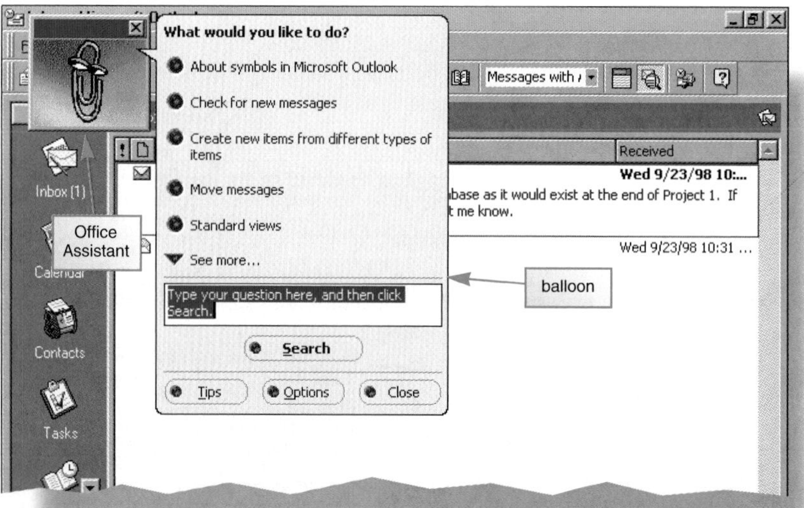

FIGURE 1-20

Hardware Innovations and Microsoft Office 97

Two hardware products from Microsoft Corporation, the Microsoft IntelliMouse and the Microsoft Natural keyboard, make working with Microsoft Office 97 faster and easier (Figure 1-21).

The **Microsoft IntelliMouse** was designed specifically for Office 97 and contains a wheel positioned between the two mouse buttons. The IntelliMouse allows you to scroll, zoom, and navigate through an Office 97 document without taking your hand off the mouse. You can rotate the IntelliMouse wheel to scroll through a document, press the wheel down and move the mouse to quickly scroll vertically or horizontally, or click the wheel once to read a document as it scrolls slowly up the screen.

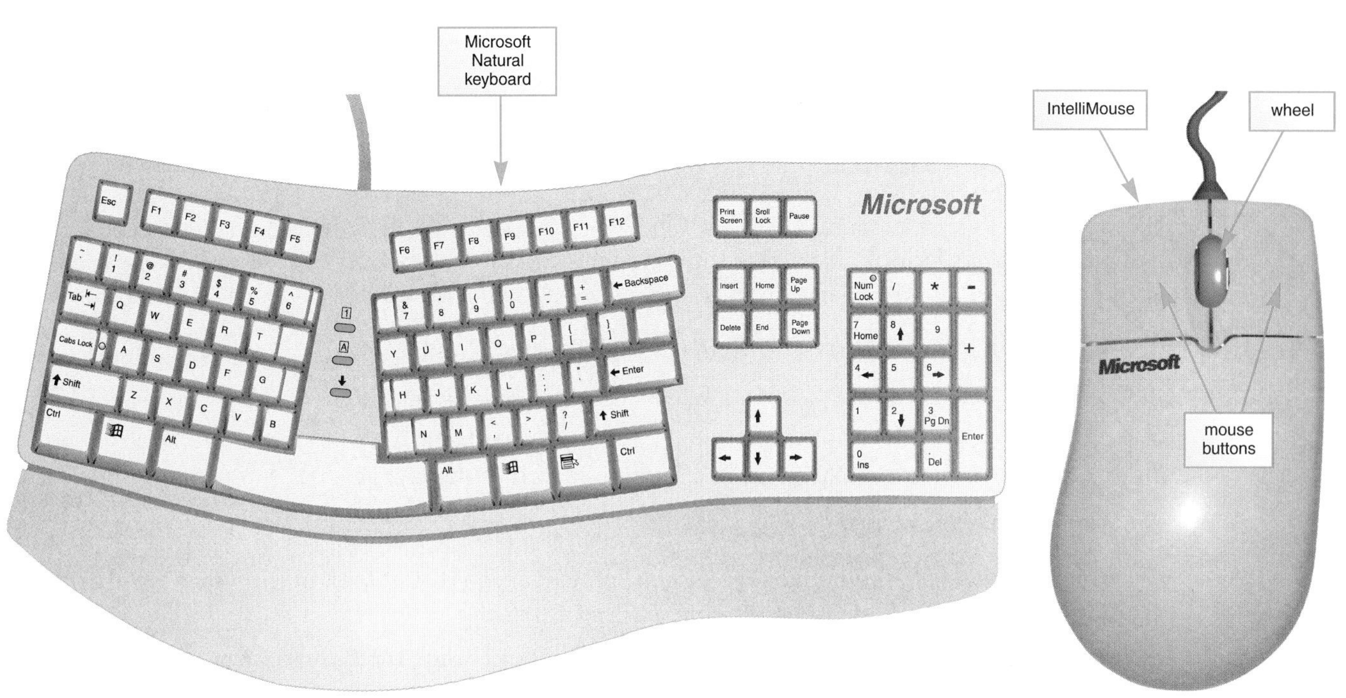

FIGURE 1-21

To zoom, or magnify, a document, hold down the CTRL key as you rotate the wheel to change the magnification within a document. To navigate a document, you can hold down the SHIFT key as you rotate the wheel to jump to a hyperlink, return to a previous Web page, expand or collapse a Microsoft Word document in outline form, or expand or collapse hierarchical structures in Windows Explorer.

Although not designed specifically for Microsoft Office 97, the **Microsoft Natural keyboard** allows you to work more comfortably by helping you place your hands, wrists, and forearms in a relaxed position.

Project Summary

The purpose of this project is to introduce you to the Microsoft Office 97 applications. Brief explanations of the Microsoft Word, Microsoft Excel, Microsoft Access, and Microsoft PowerPoint applications and examples of how these applications interact with the Internet, World Wide Web, and intranets were given. The Microsoft Outlook application and the applications within Outlook (Inbox, Calendar, Contacts, Tasks, Journal, and Notes) also were explained. In addition, the Microsoft IntelliMouse and Microsoft Natural keyboard were illustrated. With this introduction, you are ready to begin the study of each of the Microsoft Office 97 applications explained in this book.

In the Lab

1 Using Office Assistant

Instructions: To better understand Microsoft Outlook, you decide to use Office Assistant to get an overview of Microsoft Outlook. Complete the following steps to get an overview of the Calendar and Contacts applications. Submit your printouts and answers to your instructor.

Part 1: *Starting Microsoft Outlook and Office Assistant*

1. Click the Start button on the taskbar. Click Microsoft Outlook on the Start menu.
2. If the Office Assistant does not display, click the Office Assistant button on the toolbar at the top of the window. A question mark within a balloon identifies the button.

Part 2: *Using Office Assistant*

1. When the Office Assistant and balloon display, type `Microsoft Outlook` in the What would you like to do? text box.
2. Click the Search button. Click What is Microsoft Outlook? Click the Basics of Outlook topic to display the Basics of Outlook screen.
3. Click the Outlook Bar link (red and white box) to open a pop-up box containing information about the Outlook Bar. Read the information and then print the information by right-clicking the pop-up box, clicking Print Topic on the shortcut menu, and then clicking the OK button in the Print dialog box.
4. Click the Outlook Bar link again to remove the pop-up box. Click the other links on the screen and read about the other Help topics. Click the Back button in the Microsoft Outlook window.

Part 3: *Searching for Information about Calendar and Contacts*

1. Click the Calendar topic in the What is Microsoft Outlook? screen. Click the links in the Calendar screen and answer the following questions.
   a. What three activities can you record in the calendar? ____________
   b. How can you select nonadjacent days in the date navigator? ____________
   c. How do you schedule time to work on a task? ____________
2. Click the Back button in the Microsoft Outlook window.
3. Click the Contacts topic in the What is Microsoft Outlook? screen. Read about Contacts by clicking the links in the Contacts screen. Print the Contacts screen by right-clicking the screen, clicking Print Topic on the shortcut menu, and then clicking the OK button in the Print dialog box.
4. Click the Back button in the Microsoft Outlook window.

Part 4: *Closing Office Assistant and Microsoft Outlook*

1. Click the Close button in the Microsoft Outlook window.
2. Click the Close button in the Office Assistant window.
3. Click the Close button in the Inbox – Microsoft Outlook window.

PROJECT ONE

Creating and Editing a Word Document

PROJECT TWO

Using Word's Wizards and Templates to Create a Cover Letter and Resume

PROJECT THREE

Creating a Research Paper with a Table

INTEGRATION FEATURE

Creating Web Pages

Microsoft Word 97

Microsoft *Word 97*

Creating and Editing a Word Document

Objectives:

You will have mastered the material in this project when you can:

- Start Word
- Describe the Word screen
- Change the default font size of all text
- Enter text into a document
- Spell check as you type
- Save a document
- Select text
- Center a paragraph
- Change the font size of selected text
- Change the font of selected text
- Bold selected text
- Underline selected text
- Italicize selected text
- Import a picture from the Web
- Resize a picture
- Print a document
- Correct errors in a document
- Use Microsoft Word Help
- Quit Word

Letter Perfect

From Carved Tablets to Computerized Font Libraries

Longfellow speaks of the "footprints on the sands of time" left by great ancestors. Indeed, these recordings of events and accomplishments communicate messages of days long gone. In ancient times, thoughts were shared by making symbols in the sand, drawing on cave walls, and etching hieroglyphics and pictoral carvings on tombs. The Egyptians are credited with creating the first alphabet of symbols and pictures, which in approximately 1000 B.C., was modified when the Phoenicians added consonants and the Romans agreed upon 23 unique uppercase letters. The straight shapes of these Roman letters were created out of necessity, as artists had difficulty chiseling curves in stone.

The Roman alphabet influenced early Latin writing, but scribes developed additional lowercase letters. They handwrote on scrolls made from animal skins or on paper made from organic vegetable material. Their Carolingian script was adopted by the Emperor

Charlemagne as an educational standard during the tenth century. These scrolls evolved into folded manuscript books produced by monks in monasteries and lay people in universities.

Several centuries later, the developing European bourgeoisie longed for multiple copies of documents and reading materials. Thus, when Johann Gutenberg developed the printing press in the fifteenth century, he caused a European upheaval. In 1454, he printed Bibles, which were the first mass-produced books printed with moveable type. To make this type, he painstakingly punched a mirror image of a letter in a soft piece of metal, poured molten metal into this hole, and produced a letter. The letters were arranged in a matrix, inked, and pressed onto paper. By the end of the century, more than 1,000 printers worked in 200 European cities.

During the Industrial Revolution in the 1800s, steam presses cut the printing time by 85 percent. A machine eliminated the need to create punched type by hand. In the 1900s, the need for metal type ceased. Letters were created by the photocomposition process, which projects letters on photosensitive paper. In today's digital age, letters are created by the computer, and an abundance of font styles are available.

Microsoft Word 97 provides a font list that allows you to add variety to and enhance the appearance of your documents. Now, thousands of fonts are available from numerous sources including the Internet and for purchase on CD-ROM.

Each font has a unique name. Some are named after the designer. For example, the Baskerville font was developed by John Baskerville, a teacher turned printer in the seventeenth century. Other fonts named for their designers are Giambattista Bodoni, William Caslon, and Claude Garamond. Times New Roman resembles the letters inscribed on the base of Trajan's Column in the Roman Forum in A.D. 114. As you work through the projects in this book, recall that the letters you type are descendants of the footprints left by our printing forefathers.

Microsoft
Word 97

Creating and Editing a Word Document

Case Perspective

Tropical Travel, a local travel agency, specializes in customized vacation packages to locations around the world. One popular package is to Paradise Island. Surrounded by crystal-clear waters and lined with white-sand beaches, Paradise Island offers swimming, surfing, SCUBA diving, snorkeling, sailing, and scenic hiking.

Each month, Tropical Travel prepares a flier announcing exciting vacation packages. The announcement is posted in local retail stores, printed in magazines and newspapers, and mailed to the general public. You have been asked the prepare an announcement for the Paradise Island vacation packages. To add appeal to the announcement, you are asked to include a picture of Paradise Island in the announcement. When you are finished creating the announcement, you print it for distribution.

You surf the Internet for a picture of Paradise Island and locate one at the Web site of www.scsite.com/wd97/pr1.htm. Details for the announcement, such as information about Paradise Island, can be obtained from any travel agent at Tropical Travel.

What Is Microsoft Word?

Microsoft Word is a full-featured word processing program that allows you to create professional looking documents such as announcements, letters, resumes, and reports; and revise them easily. You can use Word's desktop publishing features to create high-quality brochures, advertisements, and newsletters. Word has many features designed to simplify the production of documents. For example, you can instruct Word to create a prewritten document for you, and then you can modify the document to meet your needs. Using its expanded **IntelliSense**™ technology, Word can perform tasks such as correcting text, checking spelling and grammar, and formatting text – *all while you are typing*. Using Word's thesaurus, you can add variety and precision to your writing. With Word, you easily can include tables, graphics, pictures, and live hyperlinks in your documents. From within Word, you can search the Web for documents or create your very own Web pages.

Project One – Paradise Island Announcement

To illustrate the features of Word, this book presents a series of projects that use Word to create documents similar to those you will encounter in the academic and business environments. Project 1 uses Word to produce the announcement shown in Figure 1-1. The announcement informs the public about exciting vacation packages at Paradise Island through the Tropical Travel agency. Below the headline, PARADISE ISLAND, is a picture of the breathtaking scenery at Paradise Island, designed to catch the attention of the reader. The picture is located at the Web page www.scsite.com/wd97/pr1.htm. Below the picture is the body title, Ready For A Vacation?, followed by a brief paragraph about Paradise Island. Next, a bulleted list identifies vacation package details. Finally, the last line of the announcement lists the telephone number of Tropical Travel.

Document Preparation Steps

Document preparation steps give you an overview of how the document in Figure 1-1 will be developed. The following tasks will be completed in this project:

1. Start Word.
2. Change the size of the displayed and printed characters.
3. Enter the document text.
4. Spell check as you type.
5. Add bullets as you type.
6. Save the document on a floppy disk.
7. Format the document text (center, enlarge, bold, underline, and italicize).
8. Insert the picture from a Web page.
9. Resize the picture.
10. Save the document again.
11. Print the document.
12. Quit Word.

FIGURE 1-1

The following pages contain a detailed explanation of each of these tasks.

Mouse Usage

In this book, the mouse is the primary way to communicate with Word. You can perform six operations with a standard mouse: point, click, right-click, double-click, drag, and right-drag. If you have a **Microsoft IntelliMouse™**, then you also have a wheel between the left and right buttons. This wheel can be used to perform three additional operations: rotate wheel, click wheel, or drag wheel.

Point means you move the mouse across a flat surface until the mouse pointer rests on the item of choice on the screen. As you move the mouse, the mouse pointer moves across the screen in the same direction. **Click** means you press and release the left mouse button. The terminology used in this book to direct you to point to a particular item and then click is, click the particular item. For example, *click the Bold button*, means point to the Bold button and then click.

Right-click means you press and release the right mouse button. As with the left mouse button, you normally will point to an item on the screen prior to right-clicking. In many cases, when you right-click, Word displays a **shortcut menu** that contains the commands most often used for the current activity. Thus, when these projects instruct you to display a shortcut menu, point to the item being discussed and then right-click.

Double-click means you quickly press and release the left mouse button twice without moving the mouse. In most cases, you must point to an item before double-clicking. **Drag** means you point to an item, hold down the left mouse button, move the item to the desired location on the screen, and then release the left mouse button. **Right-drag** means you point to an item, hold down the right mouse button, move the item to the desired location, and then release the right mouse button.

If you have a Microsoft IntelliMouse™, then you can use the **rotate wheel** to view parts of the document that are not visible. The wheel also can serve as a third button. When the wheel is used as a button, it is referred to as the **wheel button**. For example, dragging the wheel button causes Word to scroll in the direction you drag.

The use of the mouse is an important skill when working with Microsoft Word 97.

More *About* Mouse Usage

Some mouse users bend their wrists frequently while moving the mouse. To help prevent wrist injuries, place the mouse at least six inches from the edge of a workstation. In this location, the wrist is forced to be flat, which causes bending to occur at the elbow when the mouse is moved.

More *About* Microsoft IntelliMouse™

You can use the Microsoft IntelliMouse™ to pan (scroll continuously) through a document or zoom a document. To pan up or down, hold down the wheel button and drag the pointer above or below the origin mark (two triangles separated by a dot). To zoom in or out, hold down the CTRL key while rotating the wheel button forward or back.

Starting Word

Follow these steps to start Word, or ask your instructor how to start Word for your system.

To Start Word

1 Click the Start button on the taskbar and then point to New Office Document.

The programs in the Start menu display above the Start button (Figure 1-2). The New Office Document command is highlighted on the Start menu.

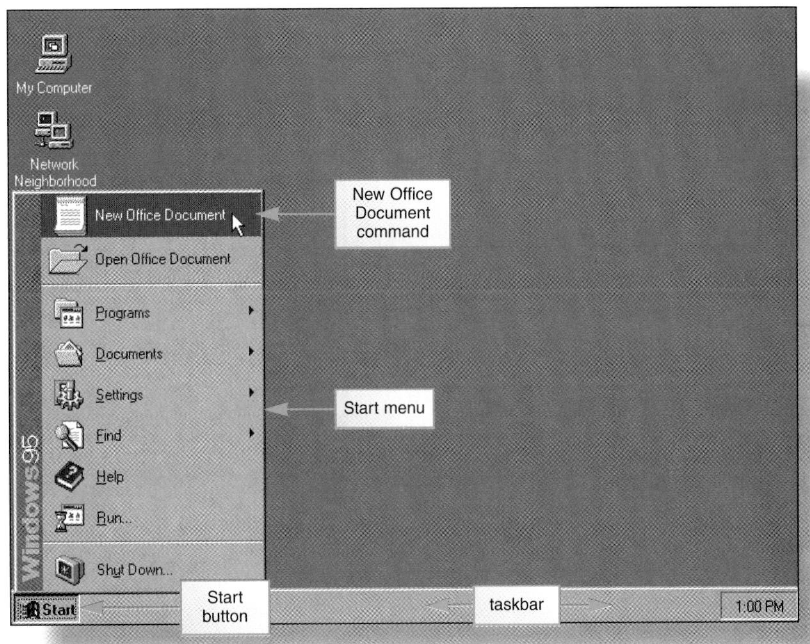

FIGURE 1-2

2 Click New Office Document. If necessary, click the General tab when the New Office Document dialog box first opens.

Office displays several icons on the General sheet in the New Office Document dialog box (Figure 1-3). Each icon represents a different type of document you can create in Microsoft Office. In this project, you are to create a new document using Microsoft Word 97.

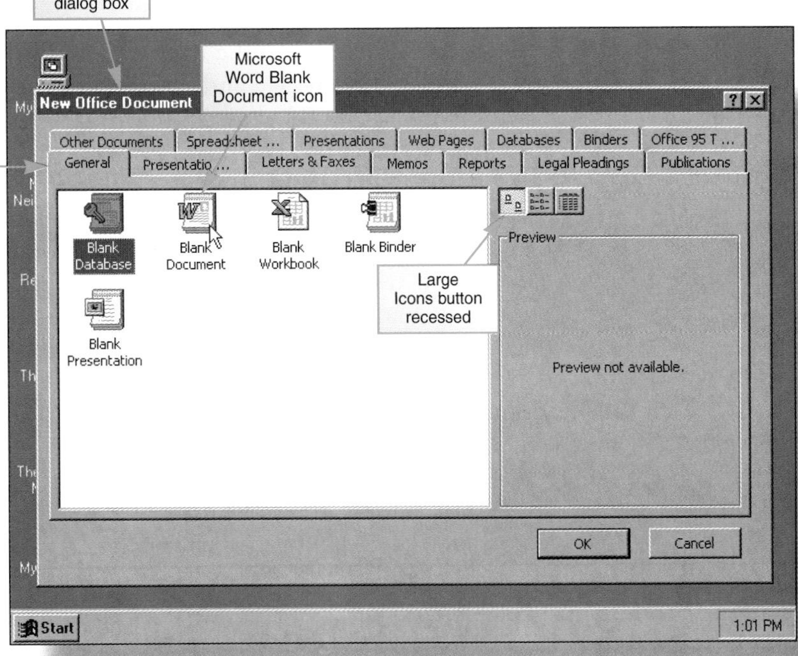

FIGURE 1-3

3 **Double-click the Blank Document icon.**

Office starts Word. While Word is starting, the mouse pointer changes to the shape of an hourglass. After a few moments, an empty document titled Document1 displays on the Word screen (Figure 1-4).

4 **If the Word screen is not maximized, double-click its title bar to maximize it. If the Office Assistant displays, click its Close button.**

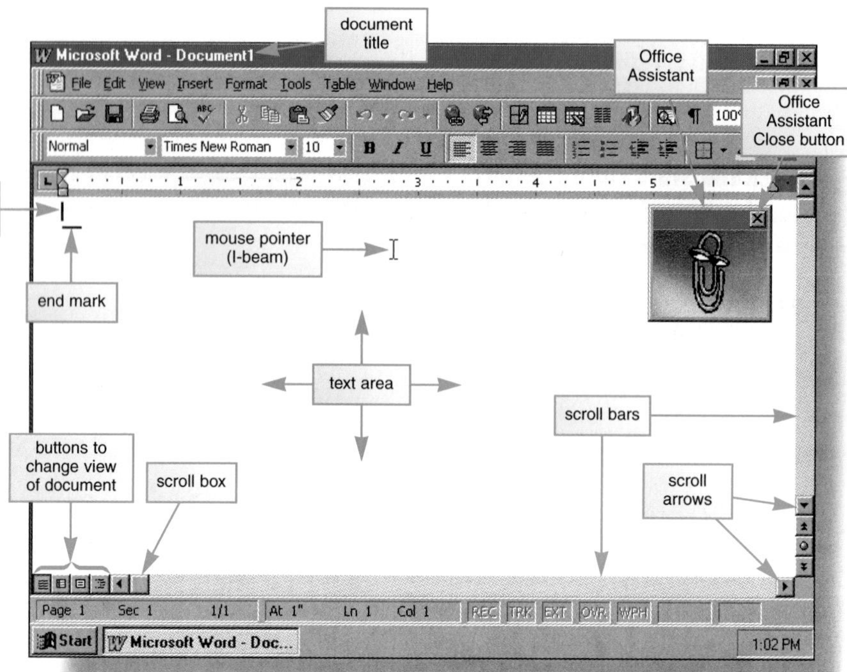

FIGURE 1-4

OtherWays

1. Right-click Start button, click Open, double-click New Office Document, click General tab, double-click Blank Document icon
2. Click Start a New Document button on Microsoft Office Shortcut Bar, click General tab, double-click Blank Document icon
3. On Start menu point to Programs, click Microsoft Word

The Word Screen

The **Word screen** (Figure 1-4) consists of a variety of features to make your work more efficient and the results more professional. If you are following along on a personal computer and your screen differs from Figure 1-4, click View on the menu bar and then click Normal.

Word Document Window

The Word document window contains several elements similar to the document windows in other applications, as well as some elements unique to Word. The main elements of the Word document window are the text area, insertion point, end mark, mouse pointer, and scroll bars (Figure 1-4).

TEXT AREA As you type or insert pictures, your text and graphics display in the **text area.**

INSERTION POINT The **insertion point** is a blinking vertical bar that indicates where text will be inserted as you type. As you type, the insertion point moves to the right and, when you reach the end of a line, it moves downward to the next line. You also insert graphics at the location of the insertion point.

END MARK The **end mark** indicates the end of your document. Each time you begin a new line as you type, the end mark moves downward.

MOUSE POINTER The **mouse pointer** becomes different shapes depending on the task you are performing in Word and the pointer's location on the screen. The mouse pointer in Figure 1-4 has the shape of an I-beam. The mouse pointer displays as an **I-beam** when it is in the text area. Other mouse pointer shapes are described as they appear on the screen during this and subsequent projects.

SCROLL BARS You use the **scroll bars** to display different portions of your document in the document window. At the right edge of the document window is a vertical scroll bar, and at the bottom of the document window is a horizontal scroll bar. On both scroll bars, the **scroll box** indicates your current location in the document. At the left edge of the horizontal scroll bar, Word provides three buttons you use to change the view of your document. These buttons are discussed as they are used in a later project.

Word is preset to use standard 8.5-by-11-inch paper, with 1.25-inch left and right margins and 1-inch top and bottom margins. Only a portion of your document, however, displays on the screen at one time. You view the portion of the document displayed on the screen through the **document window** (Figure 1-5).

More About Scroll Bars

You can use the vertical scroll bar to scroll through multi-page documents. As you drag the scroll box up or down the scroll bar, Word displays a page indicator to the left of the scroll box. The page indicator reflects the current page, if you were to release the mouse at that moment.

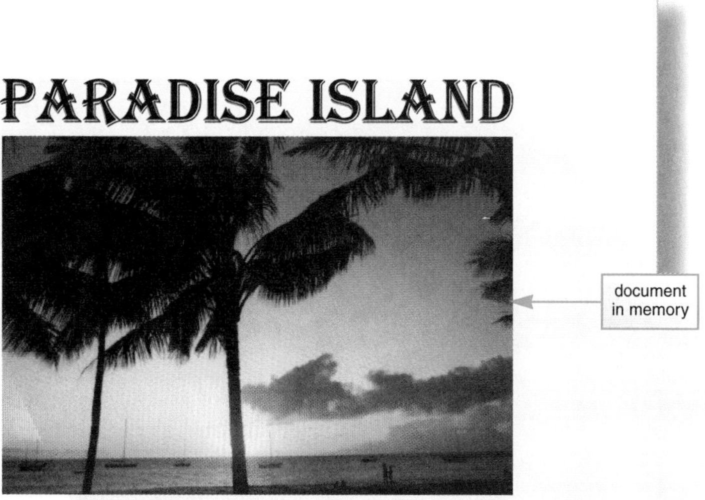

Ready For A Vacation?

Paradise Island offers glistening, white-sand beaches and swimming in crystal-clear waters. Recreational activities include surfing, SCUBA diving, snorkeling, sailing, and scenic hiking.

- Paradise Island vacation packages fit
- Cottages, suites, condos, and inns are

Call *Tropical Travel* at 555-

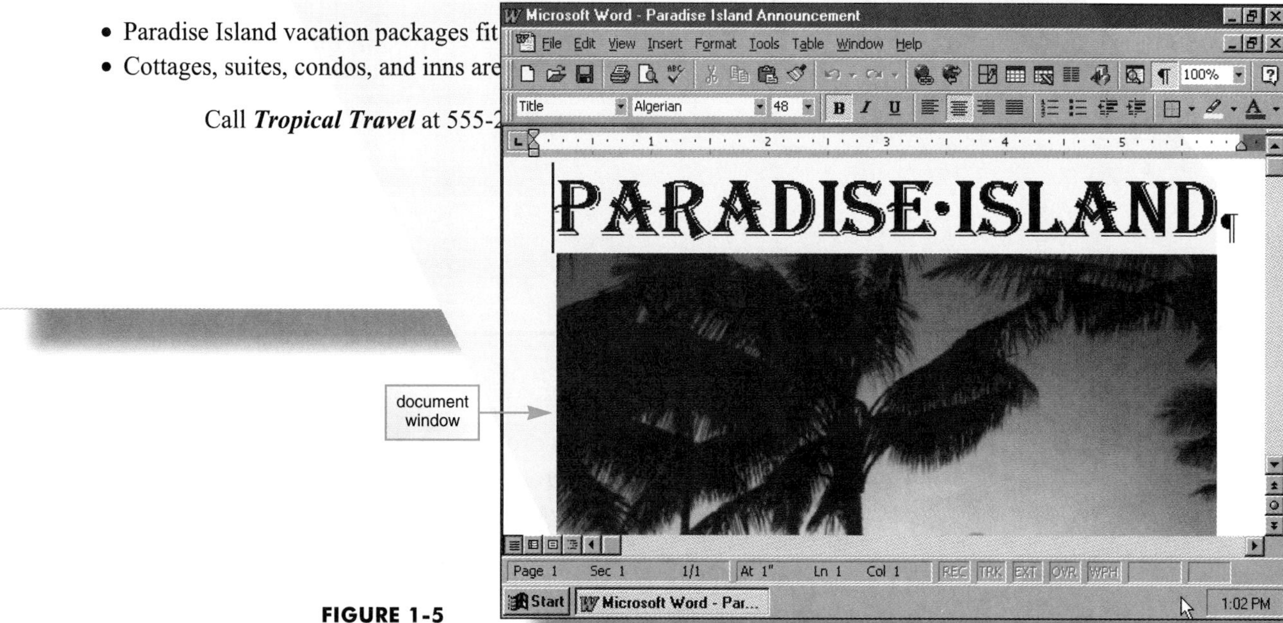

FIGURE 1-5

Menu Bar, Toolbars, Rulers, and Status Bar

The menu bar, toolbars, and horizontal ruler appear at the top of the screen just below the title bar (Figure 1-6). The status bar appears at the bottom of the screen.

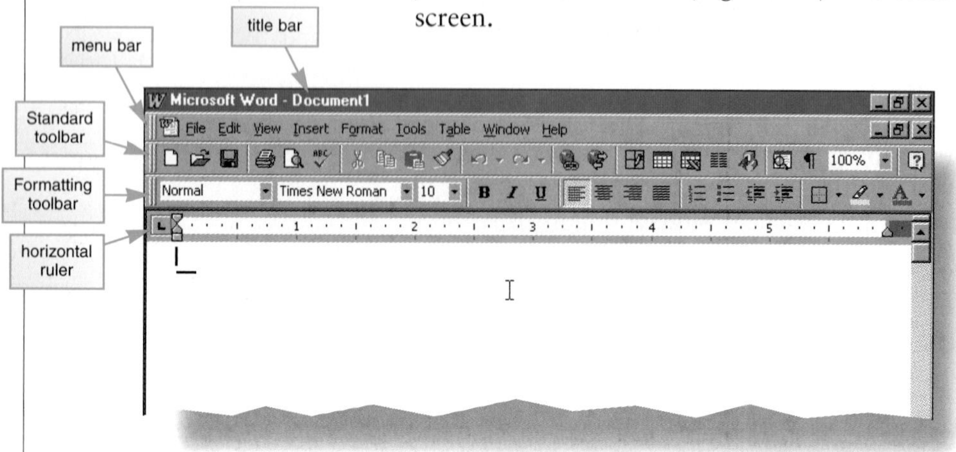

FIGURE 1-6

MENU BAR The **menu bar** displays the Word menu names. Each menu name contains a list of commands you can use to retrieve, store, print, and format data in your document and perform other tasks. Many of these commands have a picture beside them to help you quickly identify them. For example, the Save command on the File menu has a picture of a floppy disk beside it. To display a menu, such as the File menu, click the menu name on the menu bar.

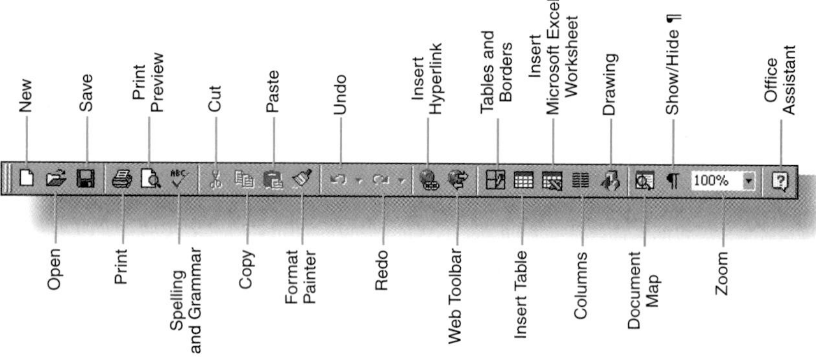

FIGURE 1-7

TOOLBARS The menu bar is actually the first toolbar on the Word screen. Just below the menu bar is the **Standard toolbar**. Immediately below the Standard toolbar is the **Formatting toolbar**.

Toolbars contain buttons, boxes, and menus that allow you to perform tasks more quickly than using the standard menu bar. For example, to print, click the Print button on the Standard toolbar. Each button has a picture on the face that helps you remember its function. Figure 1-7 illustrates the Standard toolbar and identifies its buttons and boxes; Figure 1-8 illustrates the Formatting toolbar. Each button and box is explained in detail as it is used in the projects.

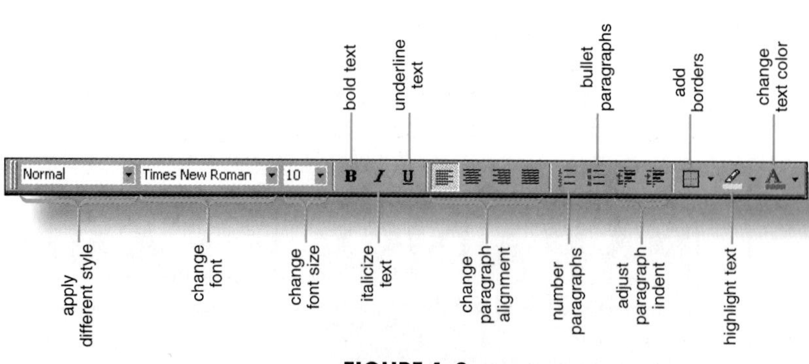

FIGURE 1-8

The Standard and Formatting toolbars initially display **docked**, or attached to top edge of the Word window directly below the menu bar. Additional toolbars may display automatically on the Word screen, depending on the task you are performing. These additional toolbars display either stacked below the Formatting toolbar or floating on the Word screen. A floating toolbar is not attached to an edge of the Word window. You can rearrange the order of **docked toolbars** and can move **floating toolbars** anywhere on the Word screen. Later in the book, steps are presented that show you how to float a docked toolbar or dock a floating toolbar.

RULERS Below the Formatting toolbar is the **horizontal ruler** (Figure 1-9). You use the horizontal ruler, sometimes simply called the **ruler**, to set tab stops, indent paragraphs, adjust column widths, and change page margins. An additional ruler, called the **vertical ruler**, displays at the left edge of the window when you are performing certain tasks. The vertical ruler is discussed as it displays on the screen in a later project.

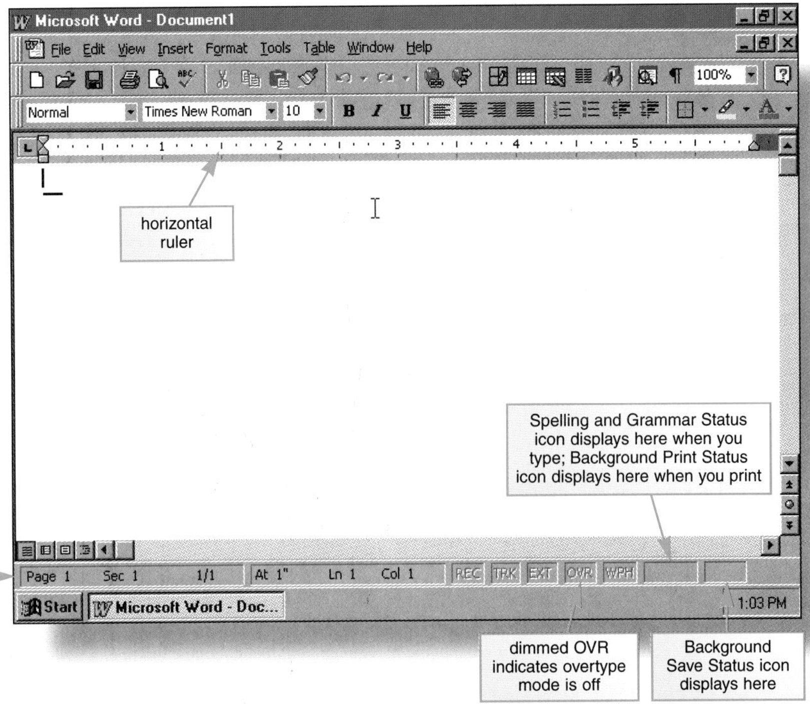

FIGURE 1-9

STATUS BAR The **status bar** is located at the bottom of the screen. From left to right, the following information displays about the page shown in Figure 1-9: the page number, the section number, the page visible in the document window followed by the total number of pages in the document, the position of the insertion point in inches from the top of the page, the line number and column number of the insertion point, and several **status indicators**. If the insertion point does not display in the document window, then no measurement displays on the status bar for the position of the insertion point, its line, and its column.

The right half of the status bar displays several status indicators. Five of these status indicators (REC, TRK, EXT, OVR, and WPH or WPN) appear darkened when on and dimmed when off. For example, the dimmed OVR indicates overtype mode is off. To turn most of these status indicators on or off, double-click the status indicator. These status indicators are discussed as they are used in the projects.

Other status indicators appear as you perform certain tasks. When you begin typing in the text area, a Spelling and Grammar Status icon appears at the right edge of the status bar. When Word is saving your document, a Background Save Status icon appears on the status bar. When you print a document, a Background Print Status icon appears. These status icons will be discussed later in this project.

Depending on how you installed Word and the status of certain keys on your keyboard, your status bar may have different status indicators on or off. For example, the dimmed WPH on the status bar indicates WordPerfect Help is off. If your WordPerfect Help status indicator is darkened, WordPerfect Help is active and you need to deactivate it. When WordPerfect Help is on, the keys you press on the keyboard work according to WordPerfect instead of Word. To deactivate the WordPerfect Help, ask for assistance from your instructor or do the following: Click Tools on the menu bar and then click Options; click the General tab; click Help for WordPerfect users and click Navigation keys for WordPerfect users to clear these check boxes; and then click the OK button in the Options dialog box.

If a task you select requires several seconds (such as saving a document), the status bar displays a message informing you of the progress of the task.

More *About* **Horizontal Ruler**

If the horizontal ruler does not display on your screen, click View on the menu bar and then click Ruler. This command is a toggle. That is, to hide the ruler, also click View on the menu bar and then click Ruler.

More About Font Sizes

Many people need to wear reading glasses. For this reason, you should increase the font size of characters in a document to at least 12 point. Because an announcement is usually posted on a bulletin board, its font size should be as large as possible so that the announcement can be seen easily by all potential readers.

Changing the Default Font Size

Characters that display on the screen are a specific shape, size, and style. The **font**, or typeface, defines the appearance and shape of the letters, numbers, and special characters. The preset, or default, font is Times New Roman (Figure 1-10 below). The **font size** specifies the size of the characters on the screen. Font size is gauged by a measurement system called **points**. A single point is about 1/72 of one inch in height. Thus, a character with a font size of ten is about 10/72 of one inch in height. The default font size in most versions of Word is 10. If more of the characters in your document require a larger font size, you easily can change the default font size before you type. In Project 1, many of the characters in the announcement are a font size of 20. Follow these steps to increase the font size before you begin entering text.

Steps To Increase the Default Font Size Before Typing

1. **Point to the Font Size box arrow on the Formatting toolbar.**

The mouse pointer changes to a left-pointing block arrow when positioned on a toolbar (Figure 1-10). When you point to a toolbar button or box, Word displays a ScreenTip *immediately below the button or box. The ScreenTip in this figure is Font Size.*

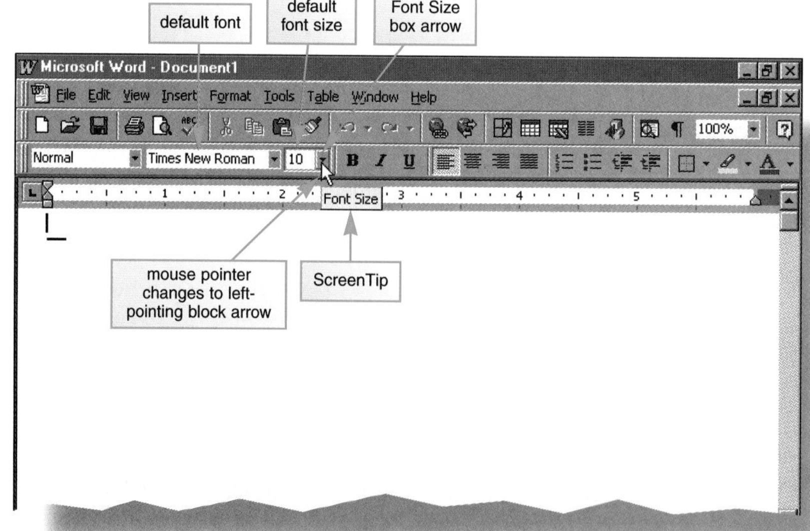

FIGURE 1-10

2. **Click the Font Size box arrow on the Formatting toolbar.**

A list of available font sizes displays in a Font Size list box (Figure 1-11). The font sizes displayed depend on the current font, which is Times New Roman.

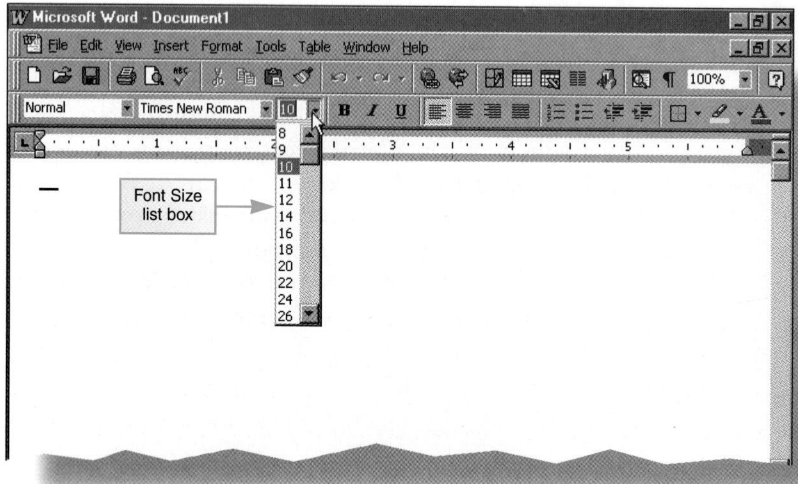

FIGURE 1-11

3 **Point to font size 20.**

Word highlights font size 20 in the list (Figure 1-12).

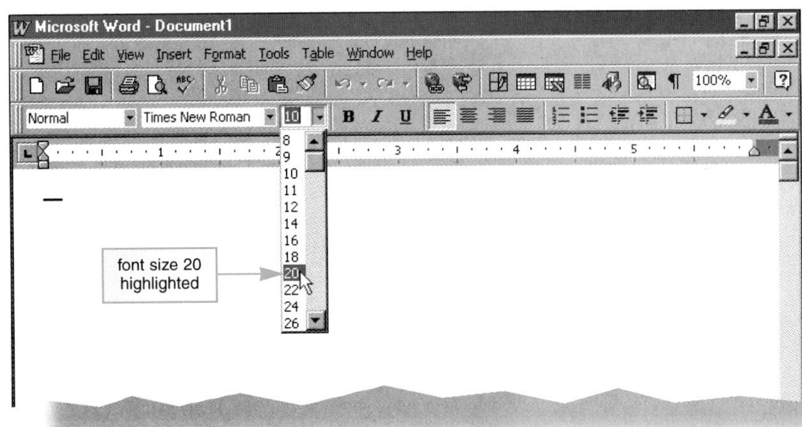

FIGURE 1-12

 **Click font size 20.**

The font size for this document changes to 20 (Figure 1-13). The size of the insertion point increases to reflect the current font size of 20.

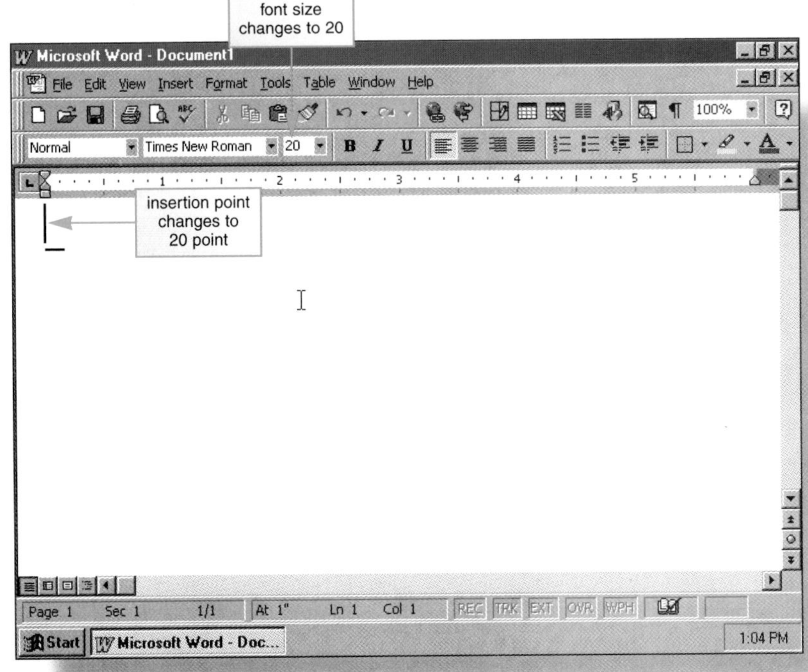

FIGURE 1-13

The new font size takes effect immediately in your document. Word uses this font size for the remainder of this announcement.

Entering Text

To prepare a document in Word, you enter text by typing on the keyboard. In Project 1, the headline (PARADISE ISLAND) is capitalized. The example on the next page explains the steps to enter the headline in all capital letters at the left margin. Later in the project, this headline will be centered across the top of the document, formatted in bold, and enlarged.

Other **Ways**

1. Right-click paragraph mark above end mark, click Font on shortcut menu, click Font tab, click desired point size in Size list box, click OK button
2. On Format menu click Font, click Font tab, select desired point size in Size list box, click OK button
3. Press CTRL+SHIFT+P, type desired point size, press ENTER
4. Press CTRL+SHIFT+>

Steps To Enter Text

1. **If the CAPS LOCK indicator is not lit on your keyboard, press the CAPS LOCK key. Type** PARADISE ISLAND **as the headline. If at any time during typing you make an error, press the BACKSPACE key until you have deleted the text in error and then retype the text correctly.**

Word places the P in PARADISE ISLAND at the location of the insertion point. As you continue typing this headline, the insertion point moves to the right (Figure 1-14). The insertion point is currently on line 1 in column 16.

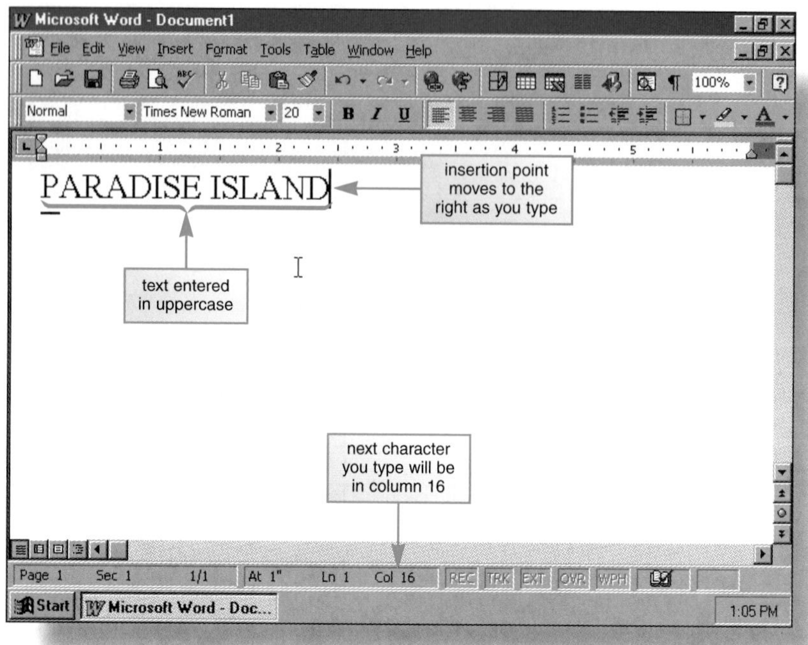

FIGURE 1-14

2. **Press the CAPS LOCK key and then press the ENTER key.**

Word creates a new paragraph by moving the insertion point to the beginning of the next line (Figure 1-15). Whenever you press the ENTER key, Word considers the previous line and the next line to be different paragraphs. Notice the status bar indicates the current position of the insertion point. That is, the insertion point is currently on line 2 column 1.

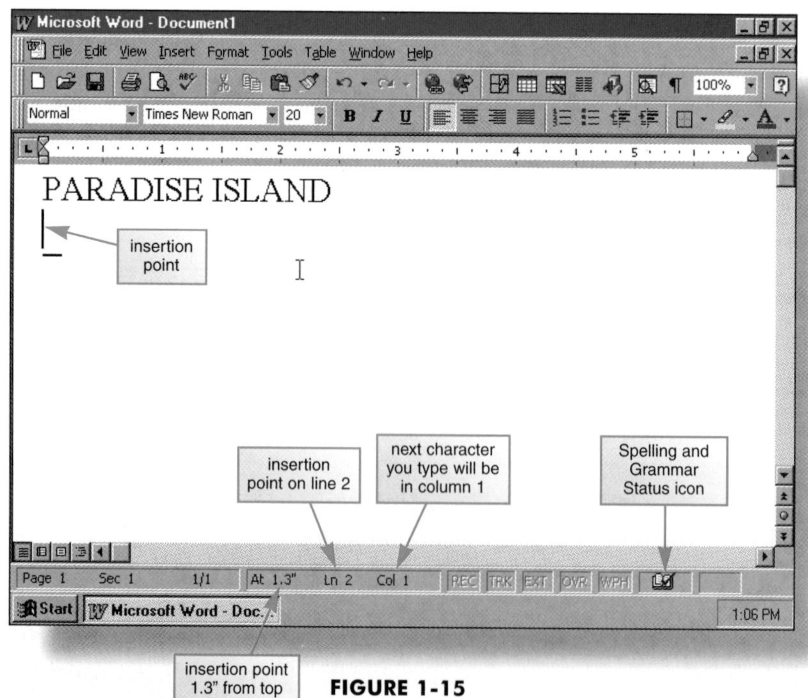

FIGURE 1-15

More About Headlines

Because the headline is the first item a reader notices, it should be effective. Headlines of fewer than four words are often typed in all-capital letters.

When you begin entering text into a document, the **Spelling and Grammar Status icon** displays at the right edge of the status bar (Figure 1-15). As you type, the spelling icon shows an animated pencil writing on paper, which indicates Word is checking for possible errors. When you stop typing, the pencil changes to either a red check mark or a red X. In Figure 1-15, the Spelling and Grammar Status icon displays a red check mark. In general, if all of the words you have typed are in Word's dictionary and your grammar is correct, a red check mark appears on the Spelling and Grammar Status icon. If you type a word not in the dictionary (because it is a proper name or misspelled), a red wavy underline appears below the word. If you type text that may be grammatically incorrect, a green wavy underline appears below the text. When Word underlines a possible spelling or grammar error, it also changes the red check mark on the Spelling and Grammar Status icon to a red X. As you enter text into the announcement, your Spelling and Grammar Status icon may show a red X, rather than a red check mark. Later in this project, you check the spelling of these words. At that time, the red X returns to a red check mark.

More About Entering Text

In the days of typewriters, the letter l was used for both the letter I and the number one. Keyboards, however, have both a number one and the letter l. Keyboards also have both a number zero and the letter o. Be careful to press the correct keyboard character when creating a word processing document.

Entering Blank Lines into a Document

To enter a blank line into a document, press the ENTER key without typing anything on the line. The following example explains how to enter two blank lines below the headline, PARADISE ISLAND.

Steps To Enter Blank Lines into a Document

1 Press the ENTER key two times.

Word inserts two blank lines into your document below the headline (Figure 1-16).

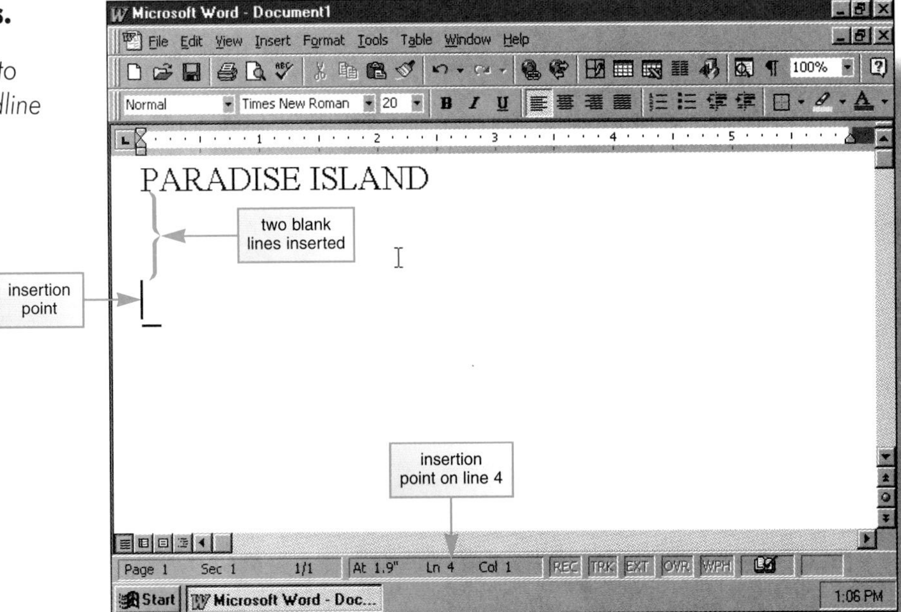

FIGURE 1-16

Displaying Nonprinting Characters

To indicate where in the document you press the ENTER key or SPACEBAR, you may find it helpful to display **nonprinting characters**. The paragraph mark (¶) is a nonprinting character that indicates where you pressed the ENTER key. A raised dot (•) shows where you pressed the SPACEBAR. Nonprinting characters display only on the screen. They do not appear in printed documents. Other nonprinting characters are discussed as they display on the screen in subsequent projects. The following steps illustrate how to display nonprinting characters, if they are not already displaying on your screen.

Steps To Display Nonprinting Characters

1 Point to the Show/Hide ¶ button on the Standard toolbar.

Word displays the ScreenTip for the button (Figure 1-17).

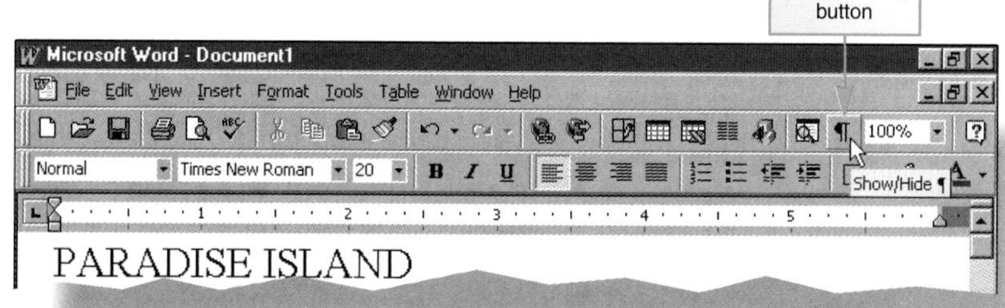

FIGURE 1-17

2 If it is not already recessed, click the Show/Hide ¶ button on the Standard toolbar.

Word displays nonprinting characters on the screen, and the Show/Hide ¶ button on the Standard toolbar is ***recessed****, or pushed in (Figure 1-18).*

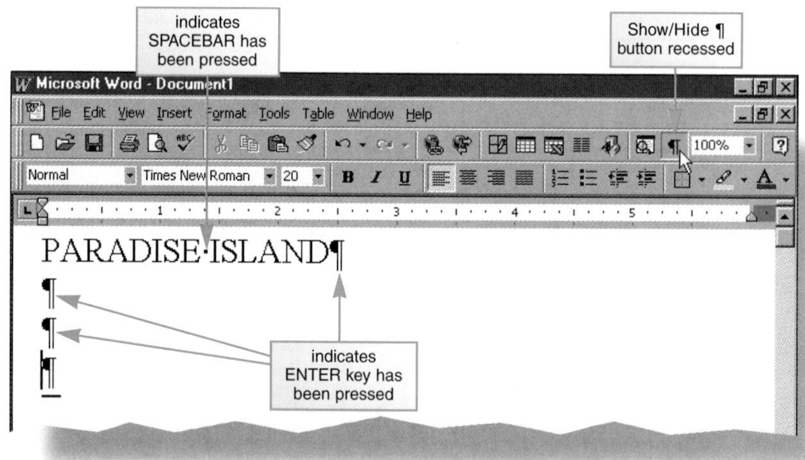

FIGURE 1-18

Other Ways

1. On Tools menu click Options, click View tab, click All, click OK button
2. Press CTRL+SHIFT+*

Notice several changes to your screen display (Figure 1-18). A paragraph mark appears at the end of each line to indicate you pressed the ENTER key. Recall that each time you press the ENTER key, Word creates a new paragraph. Because you changed the font size, the paragraph marks are 20 point. Notice the paragraph mark above the end mark – you cannot delete this paragraph mark. Between each word, a raised dot appears, indicating you pressed the SPACEBAR. Finally, the Show/Hide ¶ button is recessed to indicate it is selected.

If you feel the nonprinting characters clutter your screen, you can hide them by clicking the Show/Hide ¶ button again. It is recommended that you display nonprinting characters; therefore, the screens presented in this book show the nonprinting characters.

Entering More Text

The next step is to enter the body title, Ready For A Vacation?, into the document window as explained in the steps below.

TO ENTER MORE TEXT

Step 1: Type `Ready For A Vacation?` to enter the body title.
Step 2: Press the ENTER key twice.

The body title displays on line 4 as shown in Figure 1-19.

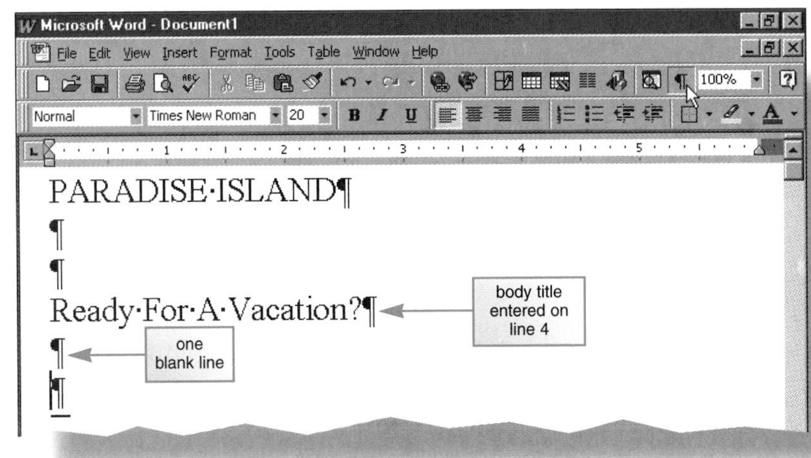

FIGURE 1-19

Using the Wordwrap Feature

Wordwrap allows you to type words in a paragraph continually without pressing the ENTER key at the end of each line. When the insertion point moves beyond the right margin, Word positions it automatically at the beginning of the next line. As you type, if a word extends beyond the right margin, Word also positions the word automatically on the next line with the insertion point. Thus, as you enter text using Word, do not press the ENTER key when the insertion point reaches the right margin. Because Word creates a new paragraph each time you press the ENTER key, press the ENTER key only in these circumstances:

1. To insert blank lines into a document
2. To begin a new paragraph
3. To terminate a short line of text and advance to the next line
4. In response to certain Word commands

Perform the following step to become familiar with the wordwrap feature.

More About Wordwrap

Your printer controls where wordwrap occurs for each line in your document. For this reason, it is possible that the same document could wordwrap on different words if printed on different printers.

Steps To Wordwrap Text as You Type

1 **Type** `Paradise Island offers glistening, white-sand beaches and swimming in crystal-clear waters.` **to enter the first sentence in the paragraph below the body title of the announcement.**

Word wraps the word, and, to the beginning of line 7 because it is too long to fit on line 6 (Figure 1-20). Your document may wordwrap on a different word depending on the type of printer you are using.

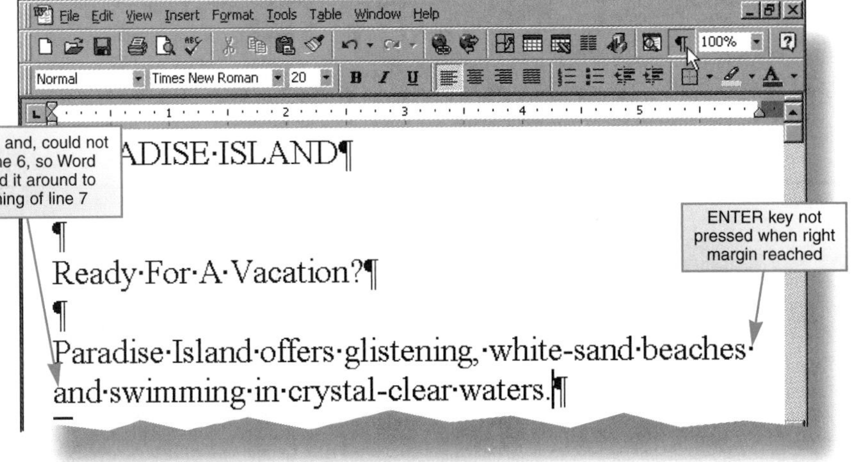

FIGURE 1-20

Checking Spelling Automatically as You Type

As you type text into the document window, Word checks your typing for possible spelling and grammar errors. If a word you type is not in the dictionary, a red wavy underline appears below it. Likewise, if text you type contains possible grammar errors, a green wavy underline appears below the text. In both cases, the Spelling and Grammar Status icon displays a red X, instead of a check mark. Although you can check the entire document for spelling and grammar errors at once, you also can check these errors immediately.

To verify that the spell check as you type feature is enabled, right-click the Spelling and Grammar Status icon on the status bar and then click Options on the shortcut menu. When the Spelling & Grammar dialog box displays, be sure Check spelling as you type is selected and Hide spelling errors in this document is not selected.

When a word is flagged with a red wavy underline, it is not in Word's dictionary. If a word is flagged, it is not necessarily misspelled. For example, many names, abbreviations, and specialized terms are not in the Word's main dictionary. In these cases, you tell Word to ignore the flagged word. As you type, Word also detects duplicate words. For example, if your document contains the phrase, to the the store, Word places a red wavy underline below the second occurrence of the word, the. To display a list of suggested corrections for a flagged word, you right-click it.

In the following example, the word, include, has been misspelled intentionally as incude to illustrate Word's spell check as you type feature. If you are doing this project on a personal computer, your announcement may contain different misspelled words, depending on the accuracy of your typing.

More *About* Entering Sentences

Word processing documents use variable character fonts; for example, the letter w takes up more space that the letter i. Thus, it is often difficult to count the number of spaces between sentences. For this reason, the two spaces after a period rule is not followed when using variable character fonts.

Steps To Spell Check as You Type

1 Press the SPACEBAR once. Type the beginning of the next sentence: `Recreational activities incude` **and then press the SPACEBAR.**

Word flags the misspelled word, incude, by placing a red wavy underline below it (Figure 1-21). Notice the Spelling and Grammar Status icon on the status bar now displays a red X, indicating Word has detected a possible spelling or grammar error.

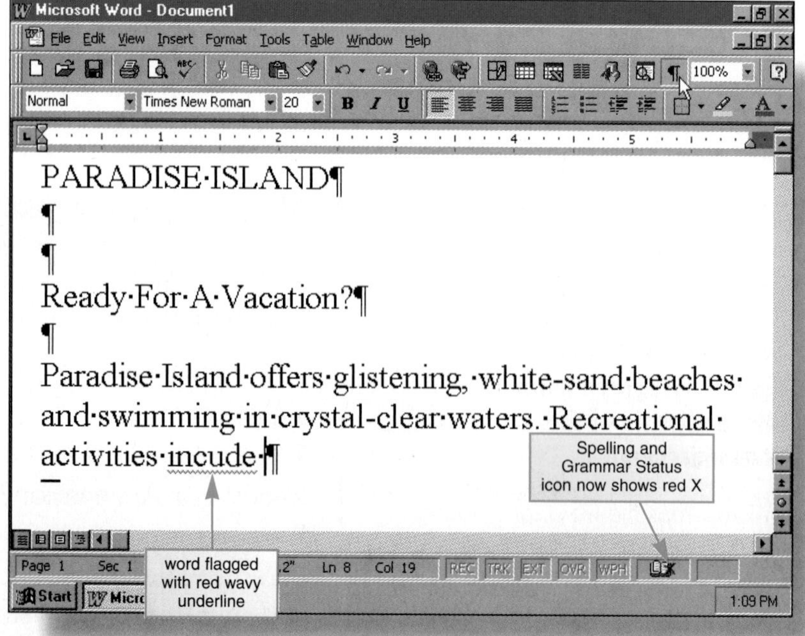

FIGURE 1-21

2 **Position the mouse pointer in the flagged word (incude, in this case).**

The mouse pointer's shape is an I-beam when positioned in a word (Figure 1-22).

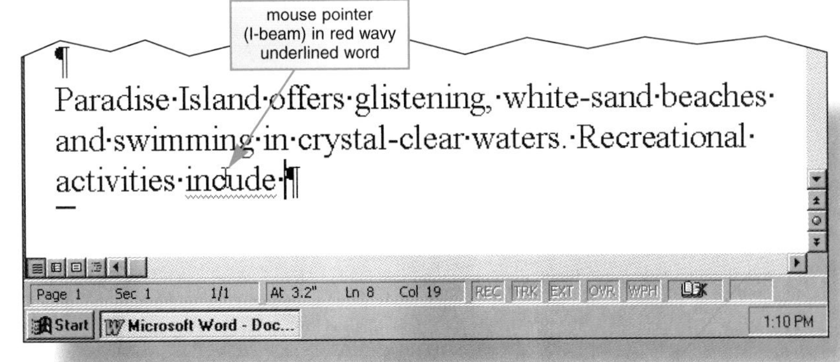

FIGURE 1-22

3 **Right-click the flagged word, incude. When the shortcut menu displays, point to include.**

Word displays a shortcut menu that lists suggested spelling corrections for the flagged word (Figure 1-23).

4 **Click include. Press the END key and then type** `surfing, SCUBA diving, snorkeling, sailing, and scenic hiking.` **to enter the remainder of the sentence.**

Word replaces the misspelled word with the selected word on the shortcut menu (Figure 1-24 on the next page). The Spelling and Grammar Status icon replaces the red X with a check mark.

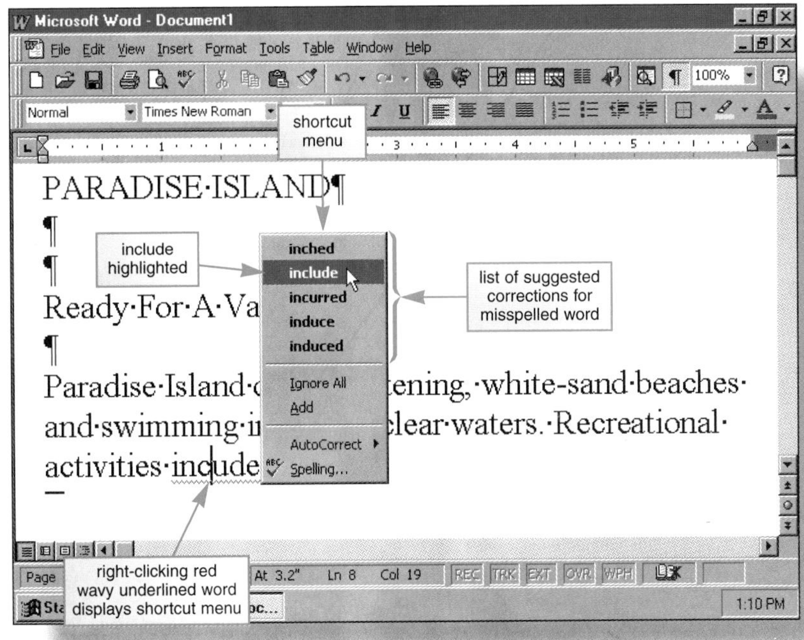

FIGURE 1-23

OtherWays

1. Click flagged word, double-click Spelling and Grammar Status icon, click correct word on shortcut menu

If your word actually is spelled correctly and, for example, is a proper name, you can right-click it and then click Ignore on the shortcut menu. If, when you right-click the misspelled word, your desired correction is not in the list (Figure 1-23), you can click outside the shortcut menu to make the menu disappear and then retype the correct word.

If you feel the wavy underlines clutter your document window, you can hide them temporarily until you are ready to check for spelling errors. To do this, you right-click the Spelling and Grammar Status icon on the status bar and then click Hide Spelling Errors on the shortcut menu.

Entering Documents that Scroll the Document Window

As you type more lines of text than Word can display in the text area, Word **scrolls** the top portion of the document upward off the screen. Although you cannot see the text once it scrolls off the screen, it remains in the document. Recall that the document window allows you to view only a portion of your document at one time (Figure 1-5 on page WD 1.11).

Follow this step to scroll the document window while entering text.

To Enter a Document that Scrolls the Document Window

Press the ENTER key twice.

Word scrolls the headline, PARADISE ISLAND, off the top of the screen (Figure 1-24). Your screen may scroll differently depending on the type of monitor you are using.

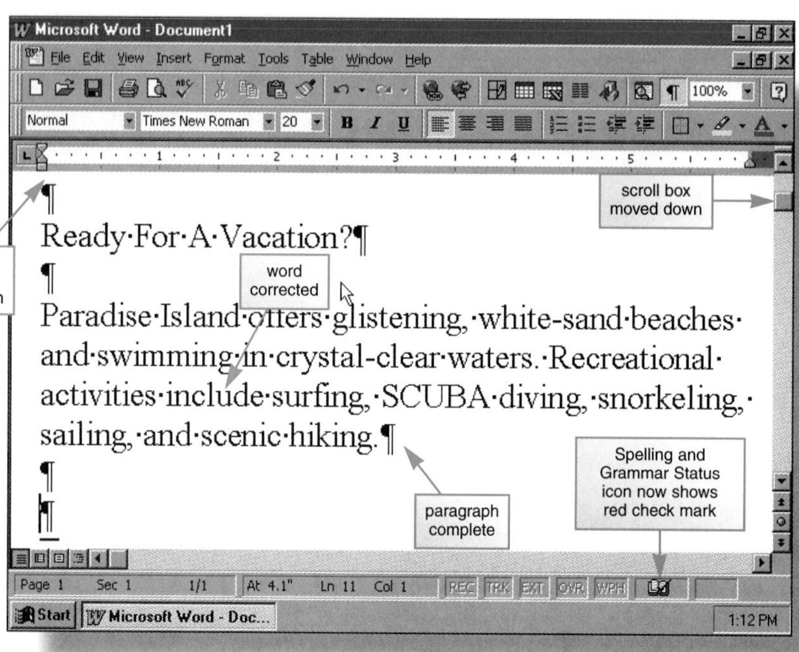

FIGURE 1-24

More About Scrolling

Computer users frequently switch between the keyboard and the mouse during a word processing session, which places strain on the wrist. To help prevent wrist injury, minimize switching. If your fingers are already on the keyboard, use keyboard keys to scroll; if your hand is already on the mouse, use the mouse to scroll.

When Word scrolls text off the top of the screen, the scroll box on the scroll bar at the right edge of the document window moves downward (Figure 1-24). The **scroll box** indicates the current relative location of the insertion point in the document. You may use either the mouse or the keyboard to move the insertion point to a different location in a document.

With the mouse, you use the scroll bars to bring a different portion of the document into the document window, and then click the mouse to move the insertion point to that location. Table 1-1 explains the techniques for scrolling with the mouse.

TABLE 1-1

SCROLL LOCATION	MOUSE USAGE
Up	Drag the scroll box upward.
Down	Drag the scroll box downward.
Up one screen	Click anywhere above the scroll box.
Down one screen	Click anywhere below the scroll box.
Up one line	Click the scroll arrow at the top of the scroll bar.
Down one line	Click the scroll arrow at the bottom of the scroll bar.

When you use the keyboard, the insertion point moves automatically when you press the appropriate keys. Table 1-2 outlines the various techniques to scroll through a document with the keyboard.

TABLE 1-2

SCROLL LOCATION	KEY(S) TO PRESS
Left one character	LEFT ARROW
Right one character	RIGHT ARROW
Left one word	CTRL+LEFT ARROW
Right one word	CTRL+RIGHT ARROW
Up one line	UP ARROW
Down one line	DOWN ARROW
To end of a line	END
To beginning of a line	HOME
Up one paragraph	CTRL+UP ARROW
Down one paragraph	CTRL+DOWN ARROW
Up one screen	PAGE UP
Down one screen	PAGE DOWN
Previous page	CTRL+PAGE UP
Next page	CTRL+PAGE DOWN
To the beginning of a document	CTRL+HOME
To the end of a document	CTRL+END

AutoFormat As You Type

The next step is to enter the bulleted list in the announcement. In Word, a **list** is a series of paragraphs. A **bullet** is a small circle positioned at the beginning of a paragraph. Bullets differ from the nonprinting character for the SPACEBAR because bullets print. You can type the list and then place the bullets on the paragraphs at a later time, or you can instruct word to place a bullet character automatically as you type the paragraphs. For example, you can type an asterisk (*) at the beginning of the first paragraph in the list. When you press the ENTER key to add another item to the list, Word automatically changes the asterisk to a bullet character.

This type of automatic change is one of the many **AutoFormat As You Type** features of Word. To be sure this feature is on, click Tools on the menu bar, click AutoCorrect, click the AutoFormat As You Type tab, be sure these two check boxes are selected: Automatic bulleted lists and Format beginning of list item like the one before it, and then click the OK button.

Perform the following steps to add bullets automatically to a list as you type.

Steps To Bullet a List as You Type

1 **Type an asterisk (*) and then press the SPACEBAR. Type** `Paradise Island vacation packages fit any budget` **as the first item in the list.**

The asterisk character must be followed by a SPACEBAR for the AutoFormat As You Type feature to work properly (Figure 1-25).

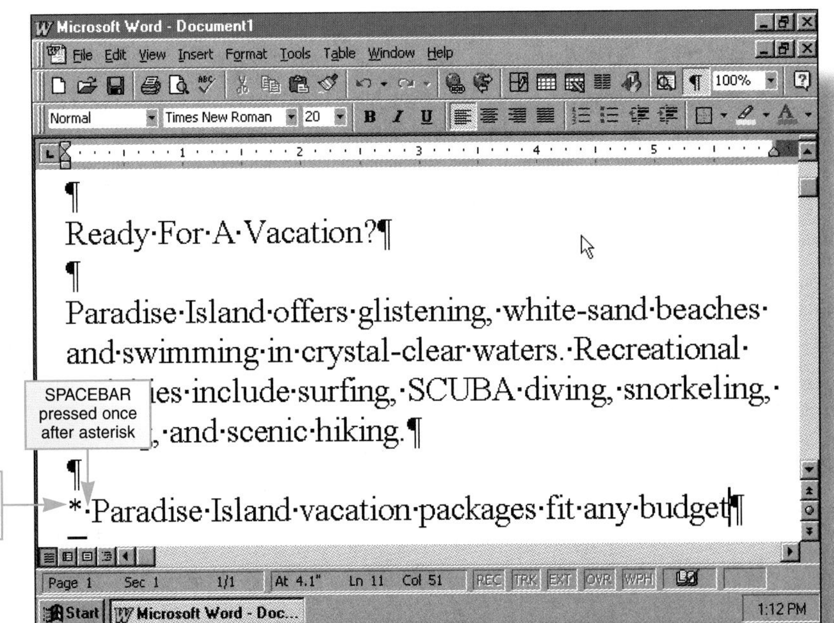

FIGURE 1-25

2 Press the ENTER key.

Word converts the asterisk on line 11 to a bullet character and places another bullet character on line 12 (Figure 1-26). Each time you press the ENTER key, Word considers the next line a new paragraph and places a bullet character automatically at the beginning of the line. The Bullets button on the Formatting toolbar is recessed, indicating the current paragraph is bulleted.

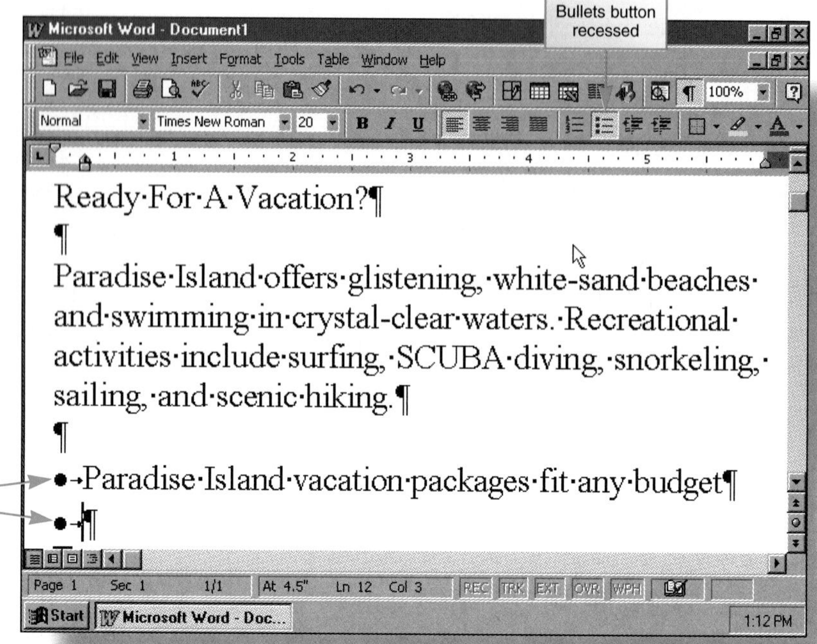

FIGURE 1-26

3 Type `Cottages, suites, condos, and inns are available` **and then press the ENTER key.**

Word places a bullet character on line 13 (Figure 1-27). Because you are finished with the list, you must instruct Word to stop bulleting paragraphs. To stop automatic bulleting, you press the ENTER key again.

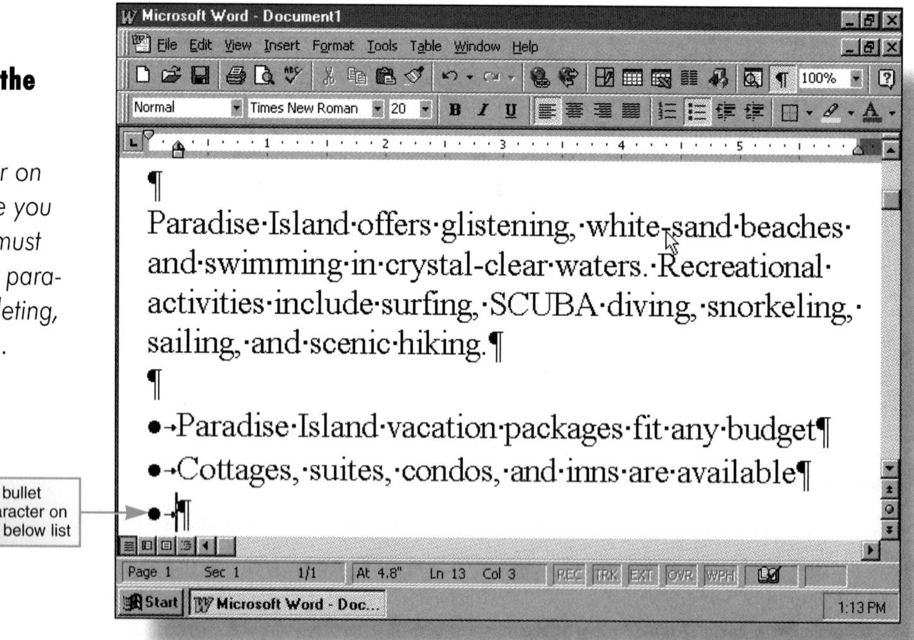

FIGURE 1-27

4 **Press the ENTER key. Type** `Call Tropical Travel at 555-2121` **as the last line in the announcement.**

Word removes the lone bullet character after the list because you pressed the ENTER key twice (Figure 1-28). The text of the announcement is completely entered.

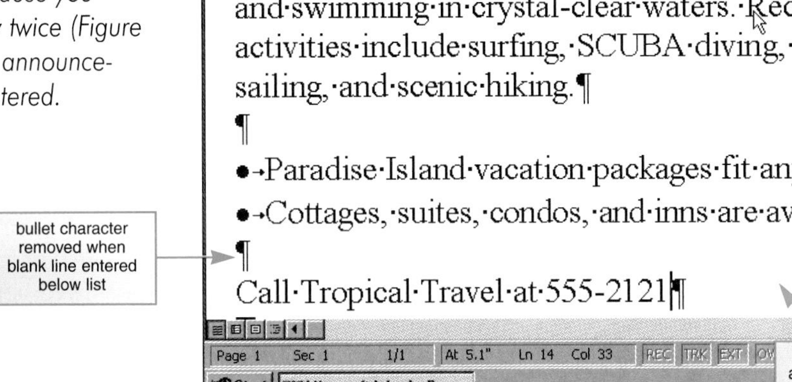

FIGURE 1-28

OtherWays

1. Type list, select list, click Bullets button on Formatting toolbar
2. Type list, select list, right-click selected list, click Bullets and Numbering on shortcut menu, click Bulleted tab, click desired bullet type, click OK button
3. Type list, select list, on Format menu click Bullets and Numbering, click Bulleted tab, click desired bullet type, click OK button

If you know before you type a list that it is to be numbered, you can add numbers as you type, just as you add bullets as you type. To add numbers, type the number one followed by a period and a space (1.) at the beginning of the first item and then type your text. When you press the ENTER key, Word places the number two (2.) at the beginning of the next line automatically. As with automatic bullets, to stop automatic numbering, press the ENTER key twice at the end of the list.

Saving a Document

When you are creating a document in Word, the computer stores it in memory. If the computer is turned off or if you lose electrical power, the document is lost. Hence, it is mandatory to save on disk any document that you will use later. The steps on the next page illustrate how to save a document on a floppy disk inserted in drive A using the Save button on the Standard toolbar.

More About Saving

When you save a document, you should create readable and meaningful filenames. A filename can be up to 255 characters, including spaces. The only invalid characters are backslash (\ ), slash (/), colon (:), asterisk (*), question mark (?), quotation mark ("), less than symbol (<), greater than symbol (>), and vertical bar (|).

To Save a New Document

1 **Insert a formatted floppy disk into drive A. Click the Save button on the Standard toolbar.**

Word displays the Save As dialog box with the insertion point blinking after the default file name, PARADISE ISLAND, in the File name text box (Figure 1-29). Notice that Word chooses the first line of the document as the default file name. Because the file name is selected initially when the Save As dialog box displays, you can change the file name by immediately typing the new name. If you do not enter a new file name, the document will be saved with the default file name, PARADISE ISLAND.

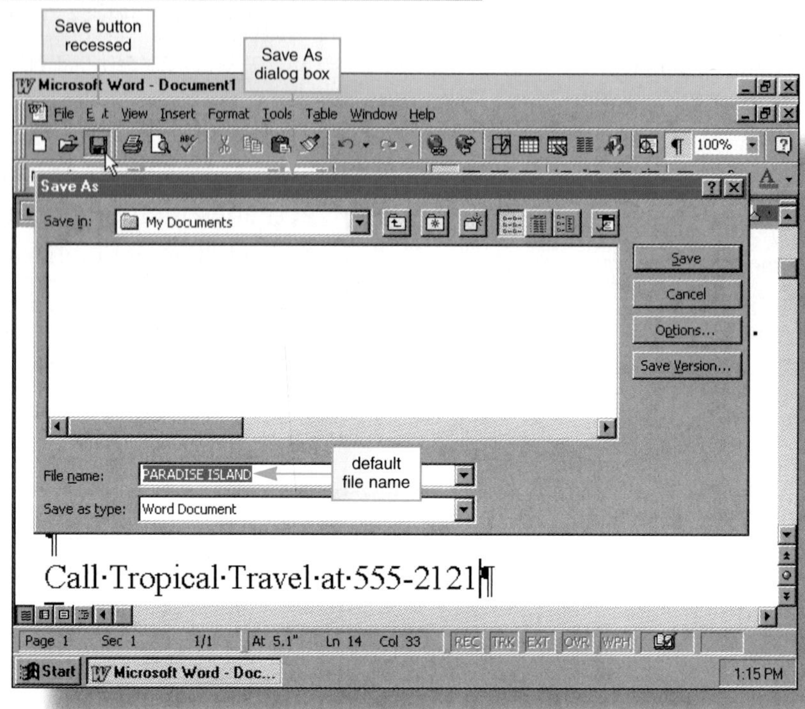

FIGURE 1-29

2 **Type the file name** `Paradise Island Announcement` **in the File name text box. Do not press the ENTER key after typing the file name.**

The file name, Paradise Island Announcement, displays in the File name text box (Figure 1-30). When creating file names, you should be as meaningful as possible. Thus, the first words in this file name (Paradise Island) relate to the nature of this document, and the last word (Announcement) relates to the category of this document. Using this technique, all files relating to Paradise Island, whether a letter, a memo, or an announcement, will be grouped together in a folder. A **folder** *is a specific location on a disk. Notice that the current folder is My Documents. To change to a different drive or folder, you must use the Save in box.*

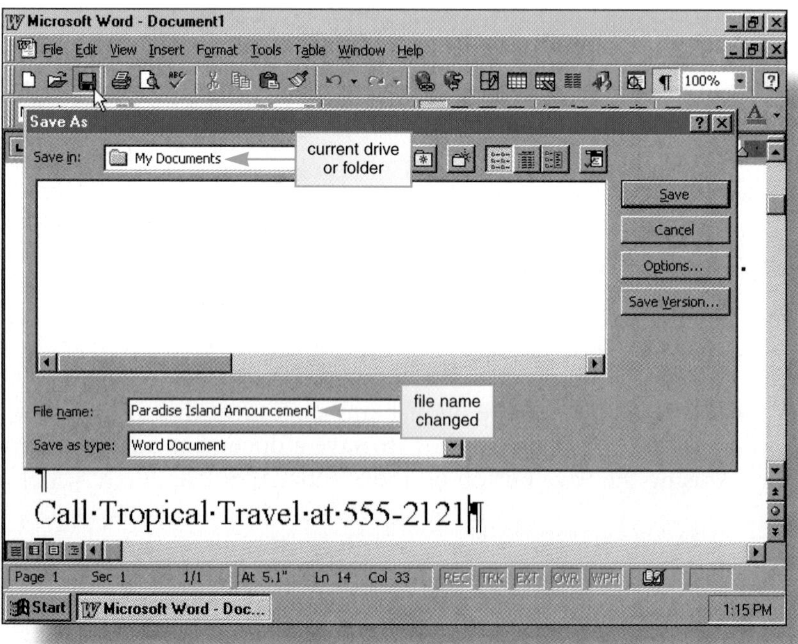

FIGURE 1-30

3 **Click the Save in box arrow and then point to 3½ Floppy (A:).**

A list of the available drives displays with 3½ Floppy (A:) highlighted (Figure 1-31). Your list may differ depending on your system configuration.

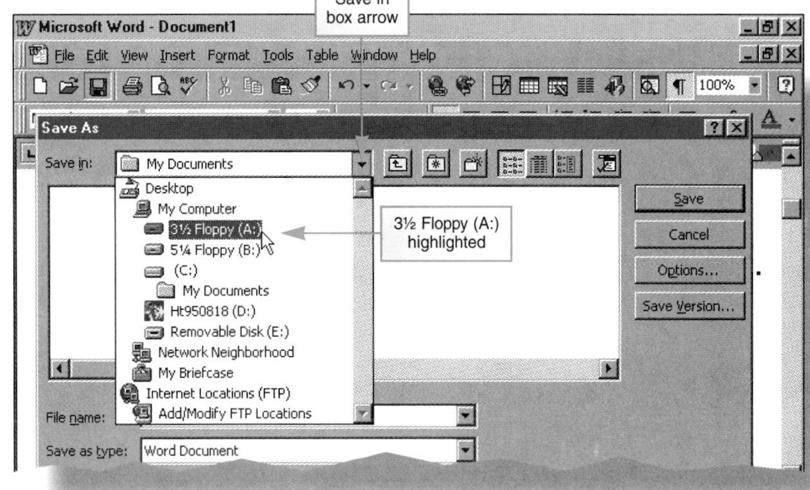

FIGURE 1-31

4 **Click 3½ Floppy (A:) and then point to the Save button in the Save As dialog box.**

The 3½ Floppy (A:) drive becomes the selected drive (Figure 1-32). The names of existing files stored on the floppy disk in drive A display. In Figure 1-32, no files currently are stored on the floppy disk in drive A.

FIGURE 1-32

5 **Click the Save button in the Save As dialog box.**

Word saves the document on the floppy disk in drive A with the file name Paradise Island Announcement (Figure 1-33). Although the announcement is saved on a floppy disk, it also remains in main memory and displays on the screen.

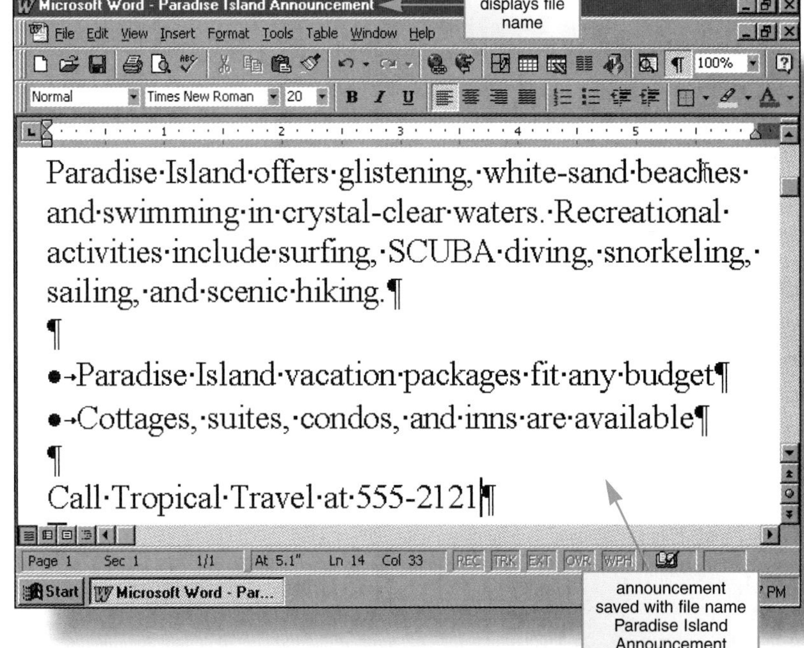

FIGURE 1-33

*Other*Ways

1. On File menu click Save, type file name, select location in Save in box, click Save button in dialog box
2. Press CTRL+S, type file name, select location in Save in box, click Save button in dialog box

Formatting Paragraphs and Characters in a Document

The text for Project 1 now is complete. The next step is to format the characters and paragraphs within the announcement. Paragraphs encompass the text up to and including the paragraph mark (¶). **Paragraph formatting** is the process of changing the appearance of a paragraph. For example, you can center or indent a paragraph.

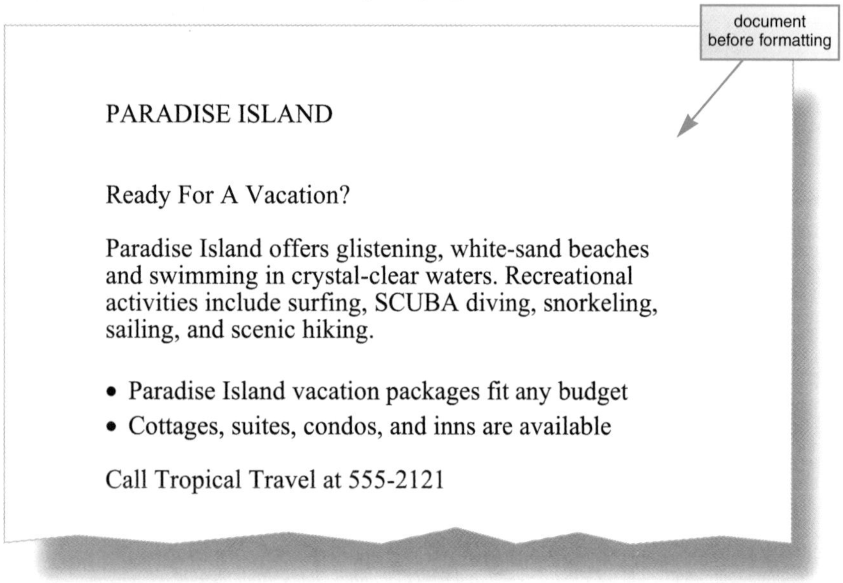

FIGURE 1-34

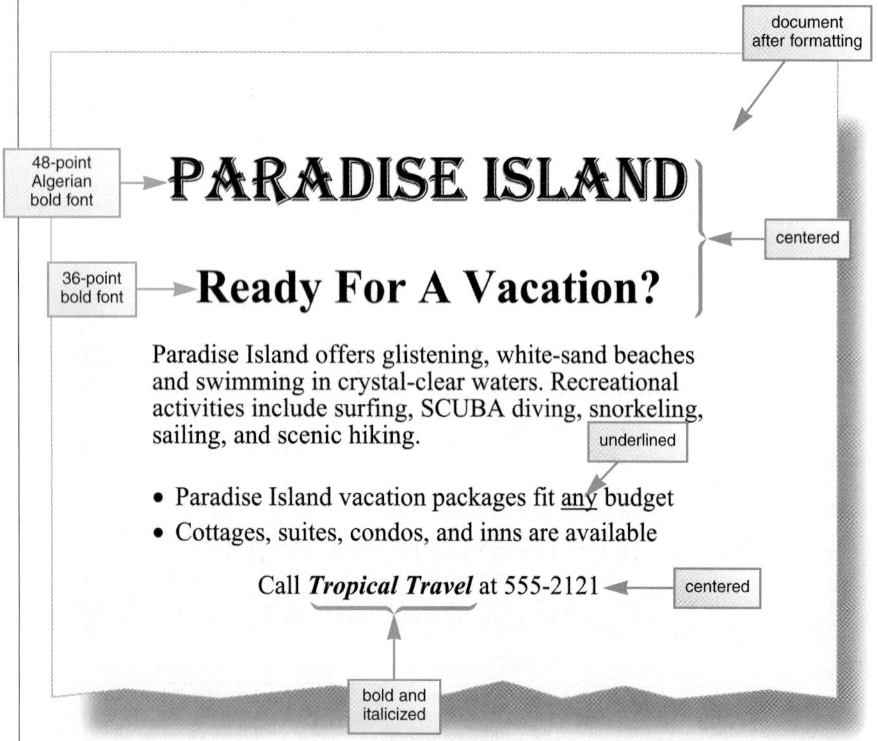

FIGURE 1-35

Characters include letters, numbers, punctuation marks, and symbols. **Character formatting** is the process of changing the way characters appear on the screen and in print. You use character formatting to emphasize certain words and improve readability of a document.

With Word, you can format before you type or apply new formats after you type. Earlier, you changed the font size before you typed any text, and then you entered the text. You also used AutoFormat to insert bullets as you typed the list in the announcement. In this section, you format existing text.

Figure 1-34 shows the announcement before formatting the paragraphs and characters in it. Figure 1-35 shows the announcement after formatting it. As you can see from the two figures, a document that is formatted not only is easier to read, but it looks more professional.

In the pages that follow, you will change the unformatted announcement in Figure 1-34 to the formatted announcement in Figure 1-35 using these steps:

1. Center the headline and body title across the page.
2. Enlarge the headline.
3. Change the font of the headline.
4. Bold the headline.
5. Bold and enlarge the body title.
6. Underline a word in the bulleted list.
7. Bold and italicize a series of words in the last line of the announcement.
8. Center the last line of the announcement.

The process required to format the announcement is explained on the following pages. The first formatting step is to center the first two lines of text between the margins. Recall that each line is considered a separate paragraph because each line ends with a paragraph mark.

Selecting and Formatting Paragraphs and Characters

To format a single paragraph, move the insertion point into the paragraph and then format it. To format multiple paragraphs in a document, however, the paragraphs you want to format first must be selected and then they can be formatted. In the same manner, to format characters, you first must select the characters to be formatted and then format your selection. Selected text is highlighted. For example, if your screen normally displays dark letters on a light background, then selected text appears as light letters on a dark background.

> **More *About* Formatting**
>
> Character formatting includes changing the font, font style, font size; adding an underline, color, strikethrough, shadow, outline; embossing; engraving; making a superscript or subscript; and changing the case of the letters. Paragraph formatting includes alignment; indentation; and spacing above, below, or in between lines.

Selecting Multiple Paragraphs

The headline (PARADISE ISLAND) and the body title (Ready For A Vacation?) are separated by two paragraph marks. Thus, the headline and the body title are actually four separate paragraphs. Recall that each time you press the ENTER key, Word creates a new paragraph.

To center the headline and body title in Project 1, you must first **select** all four paragraphs as shown in the following steps.

Steps To Select Multiple Paragraphs

1 **Press CTRL+HOME to position the insertion point at the top of the document; that is, press and hold the CTRL key, then press the HOME key, and then release both keys. Move the mouse pointer to the left of the first paragraph to be centered (the headline) until the mouse pointer changes to a right-pointing block arrow.**

The mouse pointer changes to a right-pointing block arrow when positioned to the left of a paragraph (Figure 1-36).

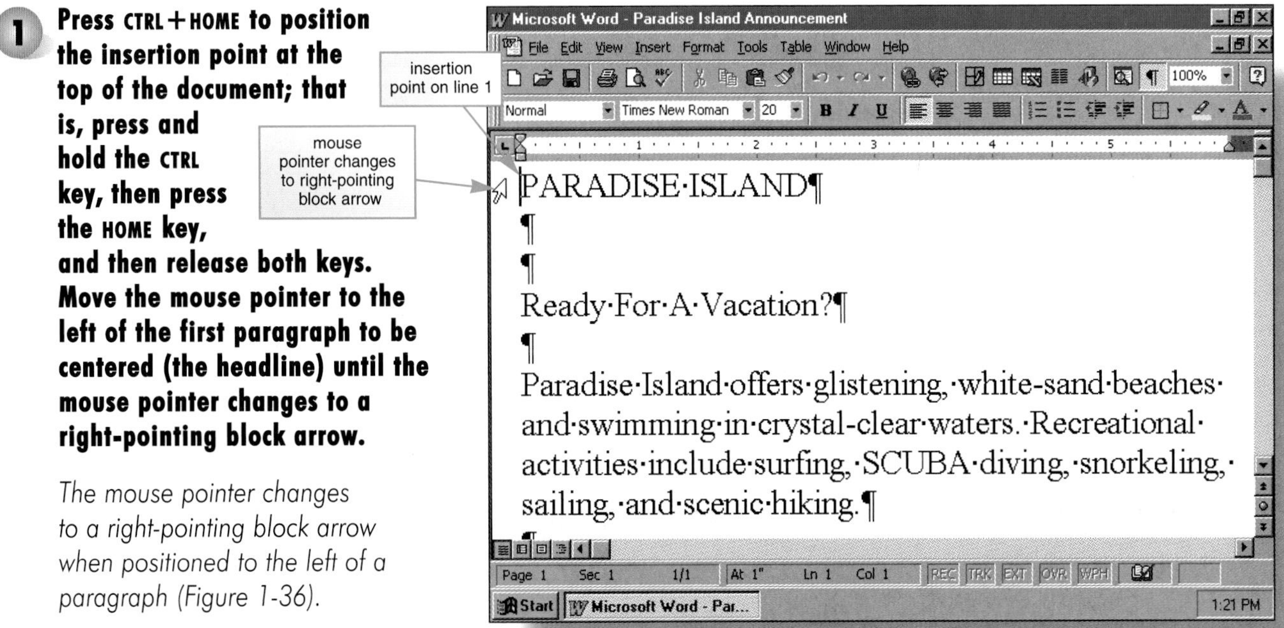

FIGURE 1-36

2 Drag downward to the last line of the last paragraph to be centered (the body title).

All of the paragraphs to be centered are selected; that is, light letters on a dark background (Figure 1-37). Recall that dragging is the process of holding down the mouse button while moving the mouse, and finally releasing the mouse button.

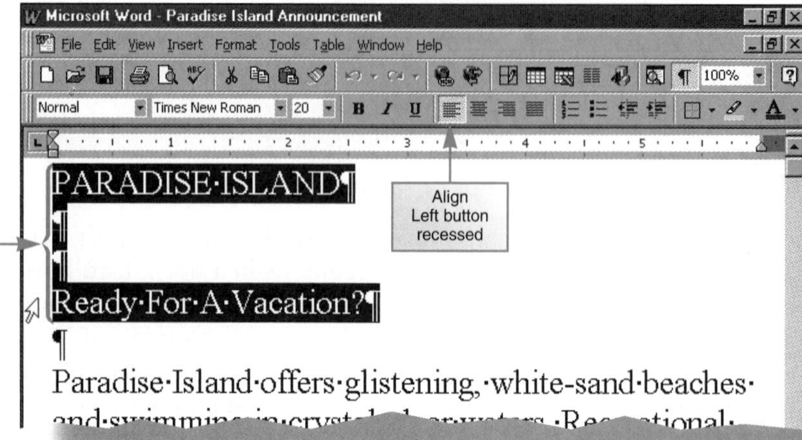

FIGURE 1-37

OtherWays

1. With insertion point at beginning of desired paragraph, press CTRL+SHIFT+DOWN ARROW

Centering Selected Paragraphs

The default alignment for paragraphs is **left-aligned**; that is, flush margins at the left edge, and jagged edges at the right edge. In Figure 1-37, the **Align Left button** is recessed to indicate the selected paragraphs currently are left-aligned. To center selected paragraphs, click the Center button as shown in the following step.

Steps To Center Selected Paragraphs

1 With the paragraphs still selected, click the Center button on the Formatting toolbar.

Word centers the headline and body title between the left and right margins (Figure 1-38). The Center button on the Formatting toolbar is recessed, which indicates the highlighted paragraphs are centered.

Align Left button no longer recessed
Center button recessed
selected paragraphs are centered

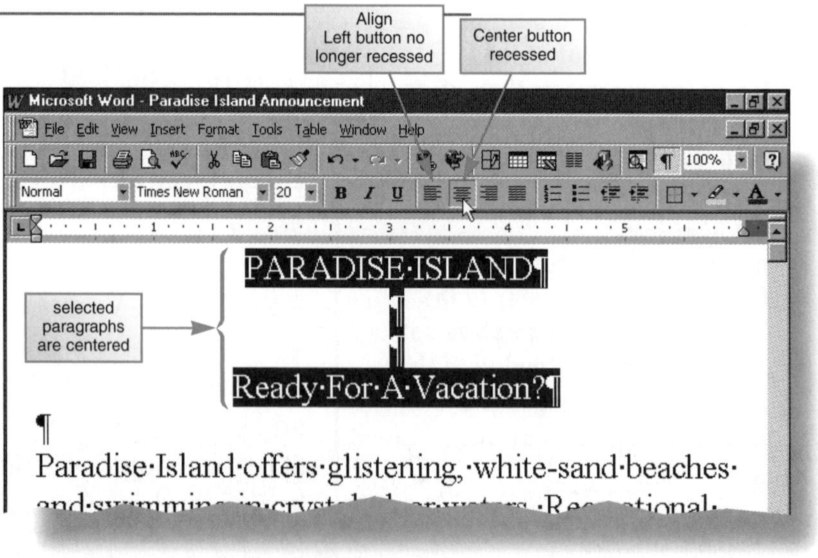

FIGURE 1-38

OtherWays

1. Right-click selected paragraph, click Paragraph on shortcut menu, click Indents and Spacing tab, click Alignment box arrow, click Centered, click OK button
2. On Format menu click Paragraph, click Indents and Spacing tab, click Alignment box arrow, click Centered, click OK button
3. Press CTRL+E

When a selected paragraph(s) is centered, the Center button on the Formatting toolbar is recessed. If, for some reason, you wanted to return the selected paragraphs to left-aligned, you would click the Align Left button on the Formatting toolbar.

The next series of steps selects the headline and formats the characters in it. In the pages that follow, you select the headline, increase the font size of the selected characters to 48, change the font of the selected characters to Algerian, and then bold the selected characters.

More About Headlines

Make a headline as large as possible without detracting from the body of the announcement. To attract attention, change the font of the headline.

Selecting a Single Line

To select the headline, the first line of the announcement, perform the following step.

Steps To Select a Single Line

1 Move the mouse pointer to the left of the line to be selected (the headline) until it changes to a right-pointing block arrow and then click.

The entire line to the right of the mouse pointer is selected (Figure 1-39).

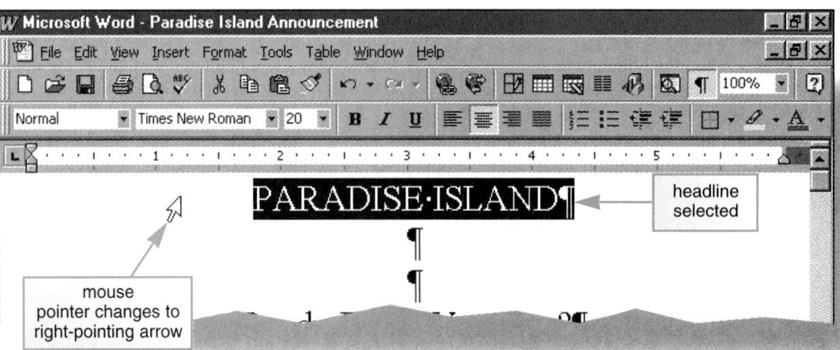

FIGURE 1-39

OtherWays

1. With insertion point at beginning of desired line, press SHIFT+DOWN ARROW

Changing the Font Size of Selected Text

The next step in formatting the headline is to increase its font size. Recall that the font size specifies the size of the characters on the screen. Earlier in this project, you changed the font size for the entire announcement from 10 to 20. The headline, however, requires a larger font size than the rest of the document. Follow these steps to increase the font size of the headline from 20 to 48 points.

Steps To Change the Font Size of Selected Text

1 While the text is selected, click the Font Size box arrow on the Formatting toolbar, and then point to the down arrow on the Font Size scroll bar.

Word displays a list of the available font sizes (Figure 1-40). Available font sizes vary depending on the font and printer driver.

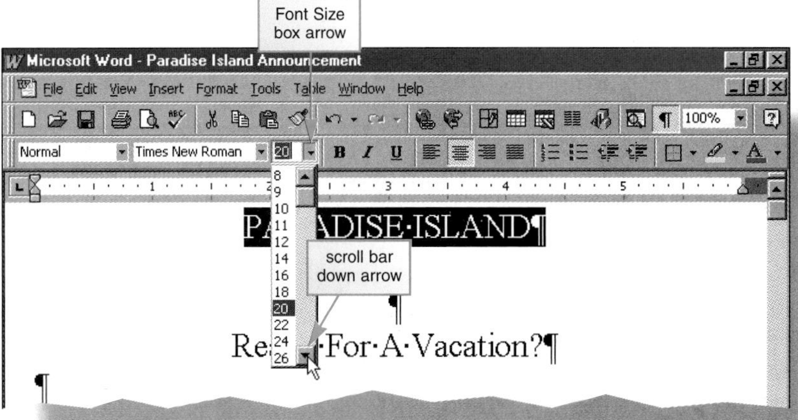

FIGURE 1-40

2 Click the down arrow on the scroll bar until the font size 48 displays in the list and then point to 48.

Font size 48 is highlighted (Figure 1-41).

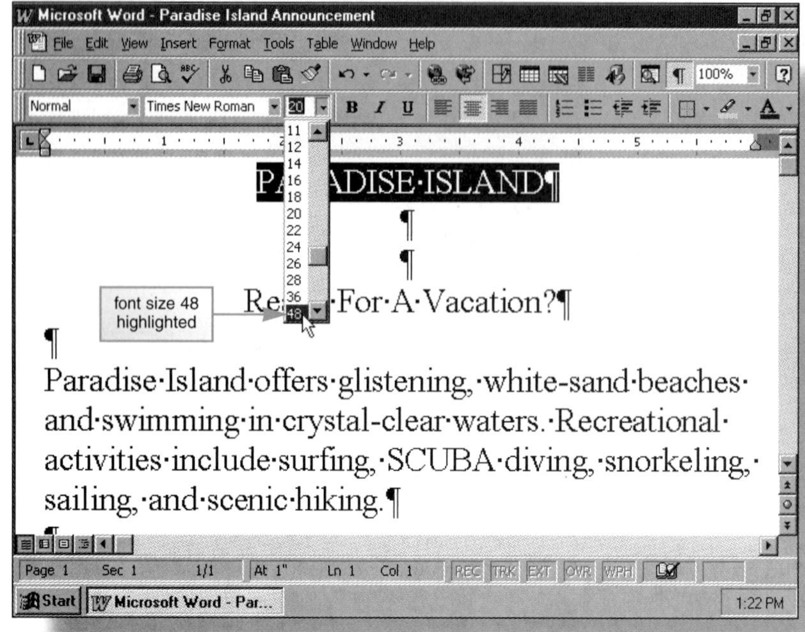

FIGURE 1-41

3 Click font size 48.

Word increases the font size of the headline from 20 to 48 (Figure 1-42). The Font Size box on the Formatting toolbar displays 48, indicating the selected text has a font size of 48.

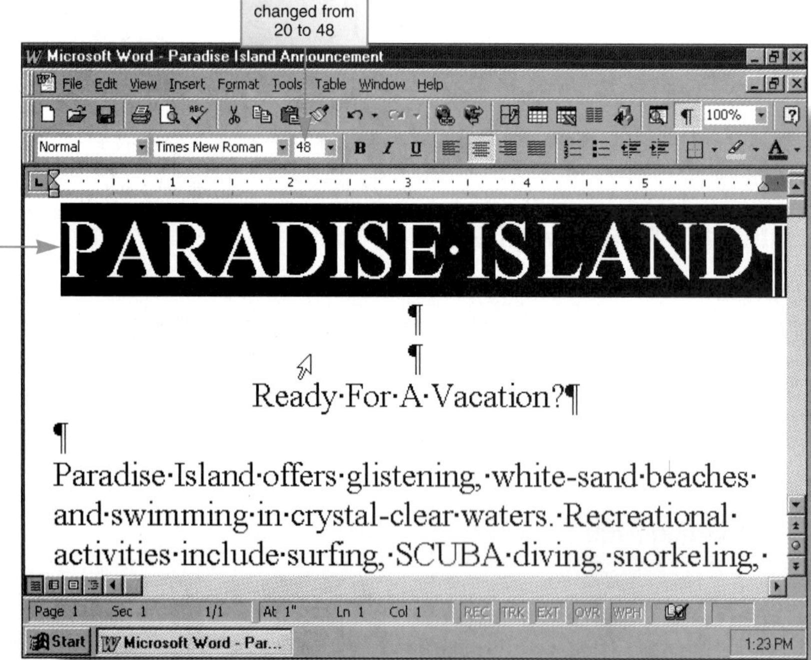

FIGURE 1-42

Other Ways

1. Right-click selected text, click Font on shortcut menu, click Font tab, select desired point size in Size list box, click OK button
2. On Format menu click Font, click Font tab, select desired point size in Size list box, click OK button
3. Press CTRL+SHIFT+P, type desired point size, press ENTER

Changing the Font of Selected Text

Recall that the default font is Times New Roman. Word, however, provides many other fonts to add variety to your documents. Thus, change the font of the headline in the announcement to Algerian as shown in these steps.

Steps To Change the Font of Selected Text

1 **While the text is selected, click the Font box arrow on the Formatting toolbar, scroll through the list until Algerian displays, and then point to Algerian.**

Word displays a list of available fonts (Figure 1-43). Your list of available fonts may be different, depending on the type of printer you are using.

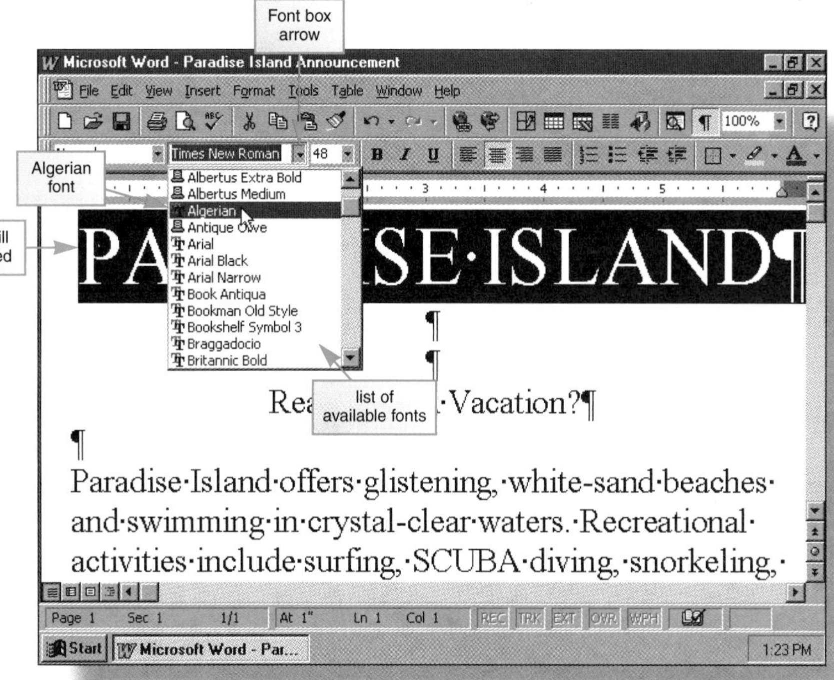

FIGURE 1-43

2 **Click Algerian.**

Word changes the font of the selected text to Algerian (Figure 1-44).

FIGURE 1-44

Other Ways

1. Right-click selected text, click Font on shortcut menu, click Font tab, select desired font in Font list box, click OK button
2. On Format menu click Font, click Font tab, select desired font in Font list box, click OK button
3. Press CTRL+SHIFT+F, press DOWN ARROW key until desired font displays, press ENTER

Bold Selected Text

To further emphasize the headline of the announcement, perform the step on the next page to make it bold.

To Bold Selected Text

1 While the text is selected, click the Bold button on the Formatting toolbar.

Word formats the headline in bold (Figure 1-45). The Bold button is recessed.

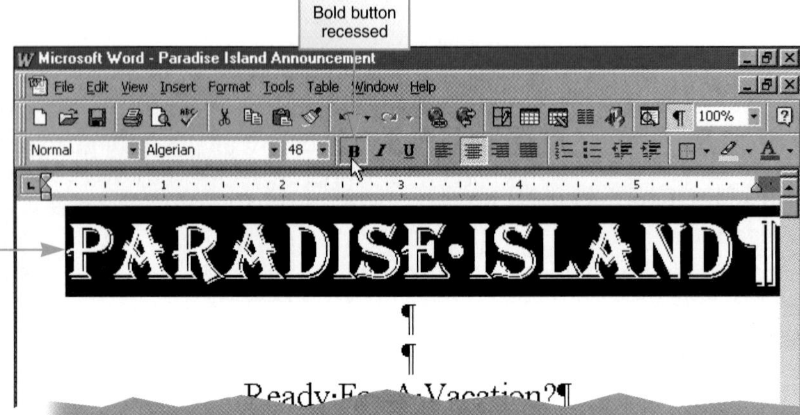

FIGURE 1-45

Other Ways

1. Right-click selected text, click Font on shortcut menu, click Font tab, click Bold in Font style list box, click OK button
2. On Format menu click Font, click Font tab, click Bold in Font style list box, click OK button
3. Press CTRL+B

When the selected text is bold, the Bold button on the Formatting toolbar is recessed. If, for some reason, you wanted to remove the bold format of the selected text, you would click the Bold button a second time.

Continuing to Format Text

The next step is to select the body title (Ready For A Vacation?), increase its font size, and bold it.

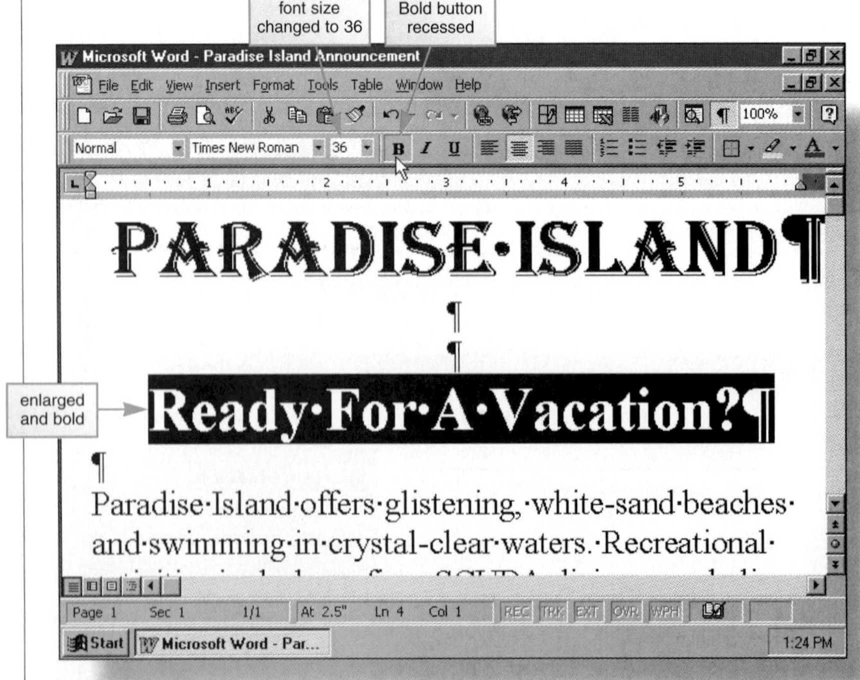

FIGURE 1-46

TO FORMAT A LINE OF TEXT

Step 1: Click to the left of the line to be formatted (the body title).
Step 2: Click the Font Size box arrow on the Formatting toolbar and scroll to the font size 36. Click font size 36.
Step 3: Click the Bold button on the Formatting toolbar.

The body title is enlarged and bold (Figure 1-46).

Scrolling

Continue formatting the document by scrolling down one screen so the bottom portion of the announcement displays in the document window.

To Scroll Through the Document

1 Position the mouse pointer below the scroll box on the vertical scroll bar (Figure 1-47).

2 Click below the scroll box on the vertical scroll bar.

Word scrolls down one screenful in the document (see Figure 1-48 below). Depending on your monitor type, your screen may scroll differently.

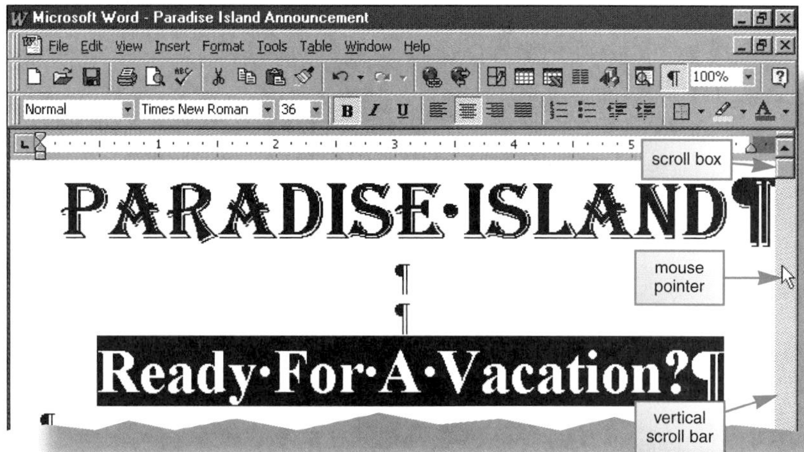

FIGURE 1-47

Other Ways

1. Drag scroll box on vertical scroll bar
2. Click scroll arrows on vertical scroll bar
3. Press PAGE DOWN or PAGE UP
4. See Tables 1-1 and 1-2 on pages WD 1.22 and WD 1.23

Selecting a Single Word

Follow these steps to select the word, any, so it can be underlined.

To Select a Single Word

1 Position the mouse pointer somewhere in the word to be formatted (any, in this case).

The mouse pointer's shape is an I-beam in a word that has not yet been selected (Figure 1-48).

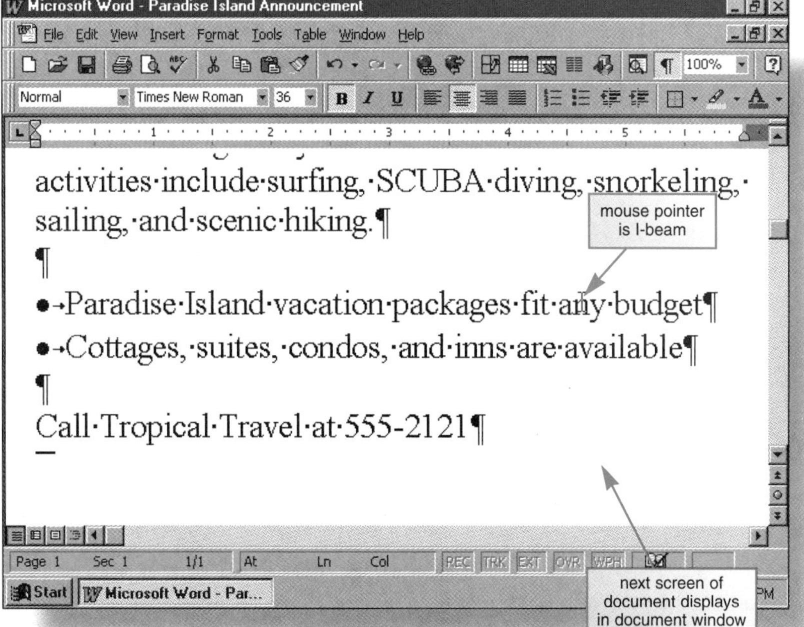

FIGURE 1-48

2 **Double-click the word to be formatted.**

The word, any, is selected (Figure 1-49). Notice that when the mouse pointer is positioned in a selected word, its shape is a left-pointing block arrow.

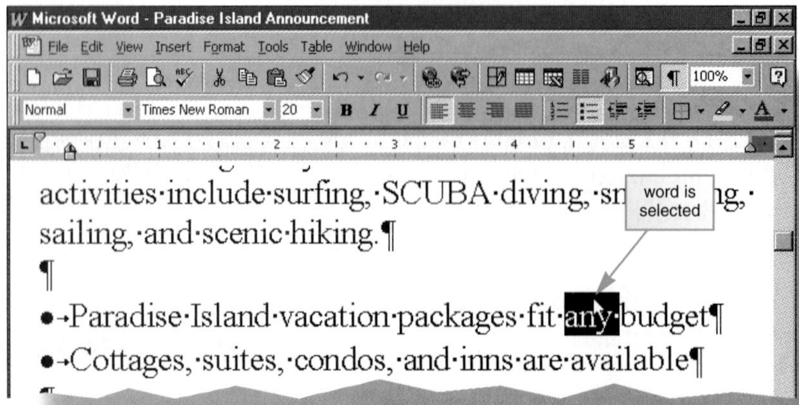

FIGURE 1-49

Other Ways

1. With insertion point at beginning of desired word, press CTRL+SHIFT+RIGHT ARROW

Underlining Selected Text

The next step is to underline the selected word, any.

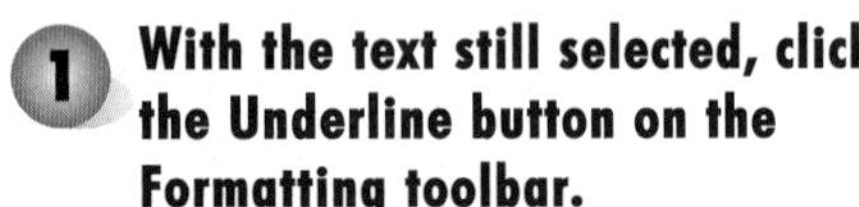

Steps To Underline Selected Text

1 **With the text still selected, click the Underline button on the Formatting toolbar.**

The word, any, is underlined (Figure 1-50). The Underline button is recessed.

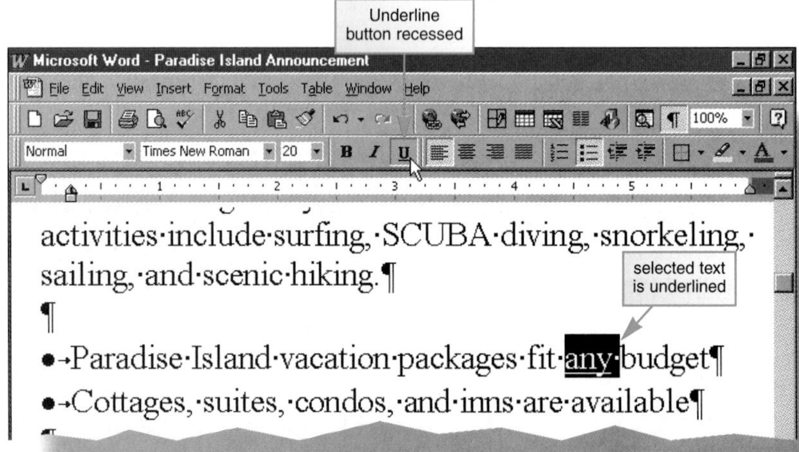

FIGURE 1-50

Other Ways

1. Right-click selected text, click Font on shortcut menu, click Font tab, click Underline box arrow, click Single, click OK button
2. On Format menu click Font, click Font tab, click Underline box arrow, click Single, click OK button
3. Press CTRL+U

When the selected text is underlined, the Underline button on the Formatting toolbar is recessed. If, for some reason, you wanted to remove the underline from the selected text, you would click the Underline button a second time.

Selecting a Group of Words and Formatting Them

The next formatting step is to italicize and bold the phrase, Tropical Travel, in the last line of the announcement. The first set of steps selects the text. Then perform the second set of steps to bold and italicize the selected text.

Steps To Select a Group of Words

1 **Position the mouse pointer on the first character of the first word to be selected.**

The mouse pointer, an I-beam, is at the beginning of the word, Tropical (Figure 1-51).

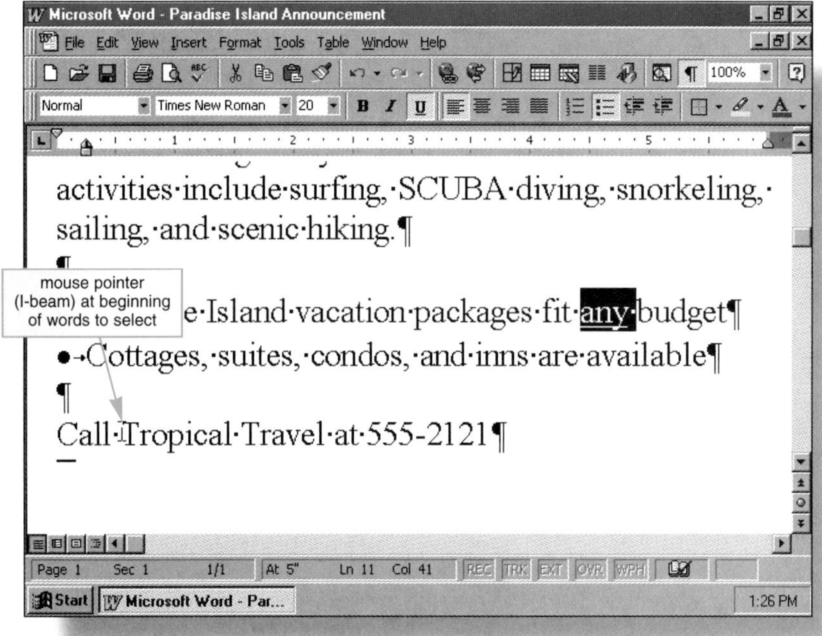

FIGURE 1-51

2 **Drag the mouse pointer through the last character of the last word to be selected.**

The phrase, Tropical Travel, is selected (Figure 1-52).

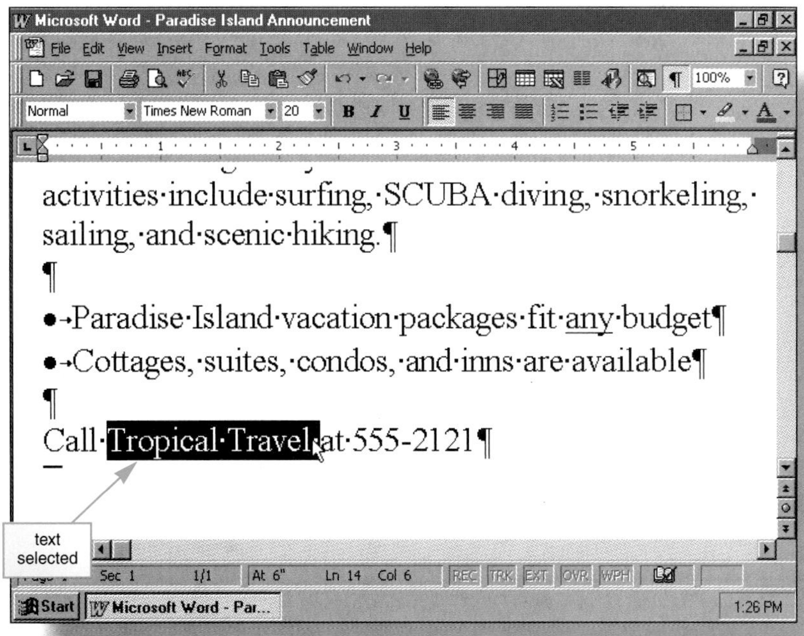

FIGURE 1-52

Other Ways

1. With insertion point at beginning of first word in the group, press CTRL+SHIFT+RIGHT ARROW until words are selected

To Italicize and Bold Selected Text

1 With the text still selected, click the Italic button on the Formatting toolbar. Click the Bold button on the Formatting toolbar. Click inside the selected text to remove the highlight.

Word italicizes and bolds the text and positions the insertion point inside the bold and italicized text (Figure 1-53). When the insertion point is inside the bold and italicized text, the Bold and Italic buttons on the Formatting toolbar are recessed.

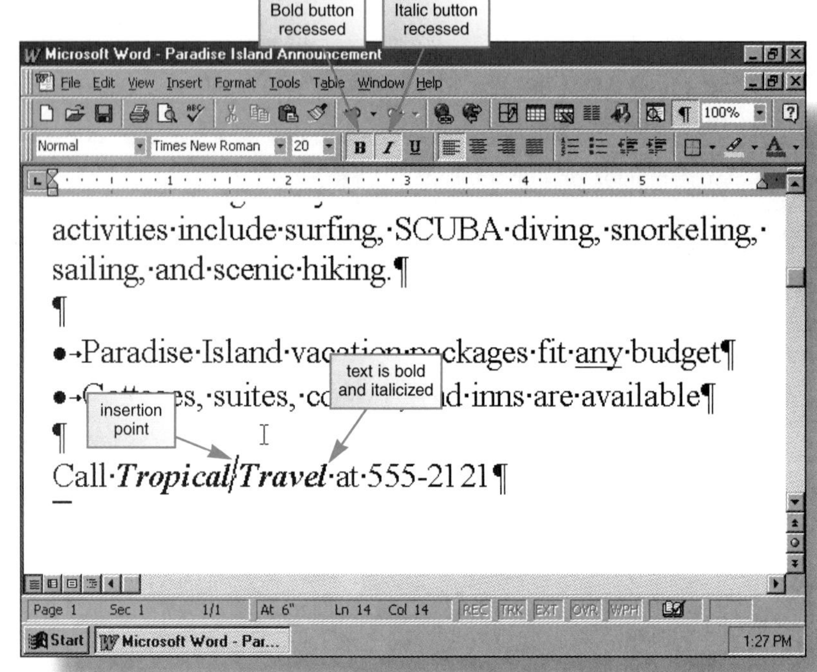

FIGURE 1-53

OtherWays

1. Right-click selected text, click Font on shortcut menu, click Font tab, click Italic in Font style list box, click OK button
2. On Format menu click Font, click Font tab, click Italic in Font style list box, click OK button
3. Press CTRL+I

To remove a highlight, click the mouse. If you click inside the highlight, the Formatting toolbar displays the formatting characteristics of the characters and paragraphs containing the insertion point.

Centering a Paragraph

The last step in formatting Project 1 is to center the last line of the announcement. Recall that paragraph formatting does not require you to select the paragraph. That is, just position the insertion point in the paragraph to be formatted and then format it accordingly.

Perform the following step to center the last line in the announcement.

More About the Formatting Toolbar

Many of the buttons on the Formatting toolbar are toggles; that is, click them once to format the selected text, and click them again to remove the format from the selected text. For example, clicking the Italic button italicizes selected text; clicking the Italic button again de-italicizes the selected text.

To Center a Single Paragraph

1 **Be sure the insertion point is still in the last line of the announcement. Click the Center button on the Formatting toolbar.**

The last line of the announcement is centered (Figure 1-54). Notice that you did not have to select the paragraph before centering; paragraph formatting requires only that the insertion point be somewhere in the paragraph.

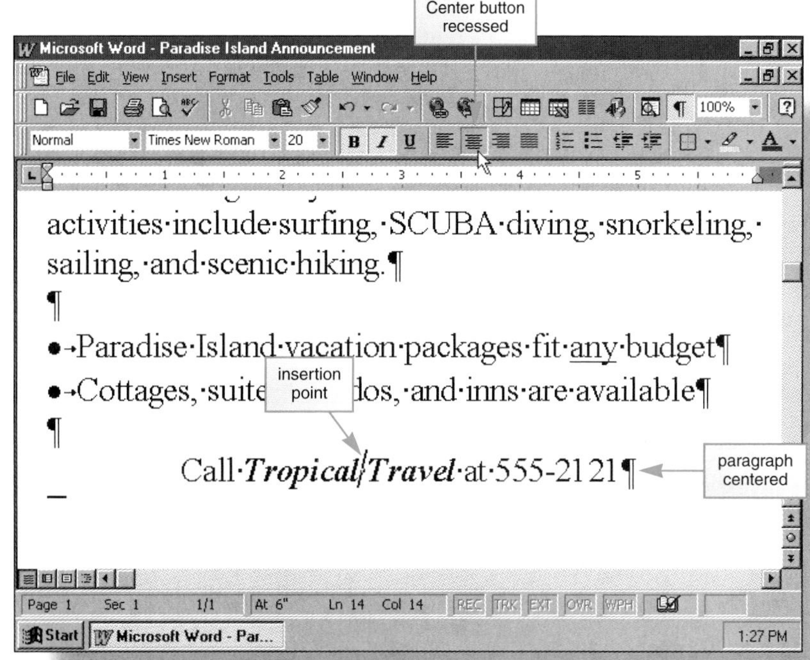

FIGURE 1-54

OtherWays

1. With insertion point in desired paragraph, click Paragraph on shortcut menu, click Indents and Spacing tab, click Alignment box arrow, click Centered, click OK button
2. With insertion point in desired paragraph, on Format menu click Paragraph, click Indents and Spacing tab, click Alignment box arrow, click Centered, click OK button
3. Press CTRL+E

The formatting for the announcement is now complete. The next step is to import a graphic from the Web and then resize it.

Inserting a Picture from the Web into a Word Document

Graphic files are available from a variety of sources. Word 97 includes a series of predefined graphic files called **clip art** that you can insert into a Word document. These clip art files are located in the Clip Gallery, which contains its own Help system to assist you in locating an image suited to your application. If you have a scanner attached to your system, Word can insert the scanned photograph directly from the scanner; or, you can scan the picture into a file and then insert the scanned file into the Word document at a later time. Instead of scanning your own pictures, you can purchase photographs from a local software retailer, usually on a CD-ROM, or you can locate a picture on the Internet.

Once you have a graphic file, you can then insert, or **import**, it into a Word document. If you locate the picture on the Web, some browsers require you to copy the picture to a file on a local drive and then import the picture from your own disk. Other browsers, such as Microsoft Internet Explorer, allow you to copy the picture to the Clipboard and paste it into your Word document – *without first having to copy the file to a local disk!*

In this project, you locate a picture of Paradise Island at the Web site of www.scsite.com/wd97/pr1.htm that you want to use in the announcement. If you do not have access to the Web, go to the steps on page WD 1.44 to insert the picture from the Data Disk that accompanies this book.

More About Using Graphics

Emphasize a graphic in an announcement by placing it at the optical center of the page. To determine optical center, divide the page in half horizontally and vertically. The optical center is located one third of the way up the vertical line from the point of intersection of the two lines.

NOTE: The following steps assume you are using Microsoft Internet Explorer as your browser. If you are not using Internet Explorer and your browser does not allow you to copy pictures to the Windows Clipboard, you will need to perform a different set of steps. Your browser's handling of pictures on the Web will be discovered in Step 6 on page WD 1.42. If necessary, you may be directed to follow the steps on page WD 1.44 to save the Paradise Island picture on a disk and then insert the picture into the announcement from the disk.

To Insert a Picture from the Web

1 **Press CTRL+HOME. Position the insertion point where you want the picture to be inserted. Click Insert on the menu bar.**

The insertion point is positioned on the paragraph mark immediately below the headline of the announcement (Figure 1-55). The Insert menu and its list of commands display.

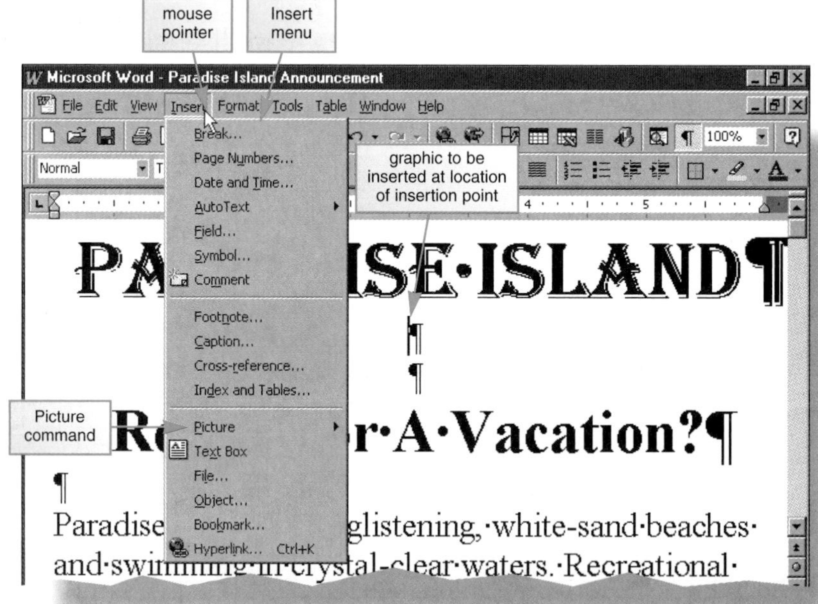

FIGURE 1-55

2 **Point to Picture on the Insert menu and then point to From File on the Picture submenu (Figure 1-56).**

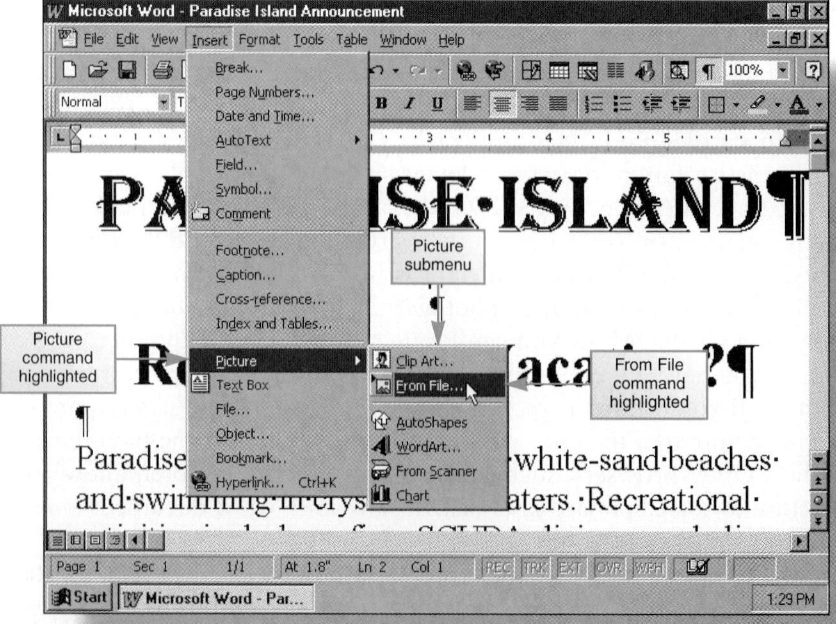

FIGURE 1-56

3 **Click From File. When the Insert Picture dialog box displays, point to the Search the Web button.**

Word displays the Insert Picture dialog box (Figure 1-57). The current folder is Clipart; graphic files supplied with Word are located in this folder. The Paradise Island picture is located on the Web.

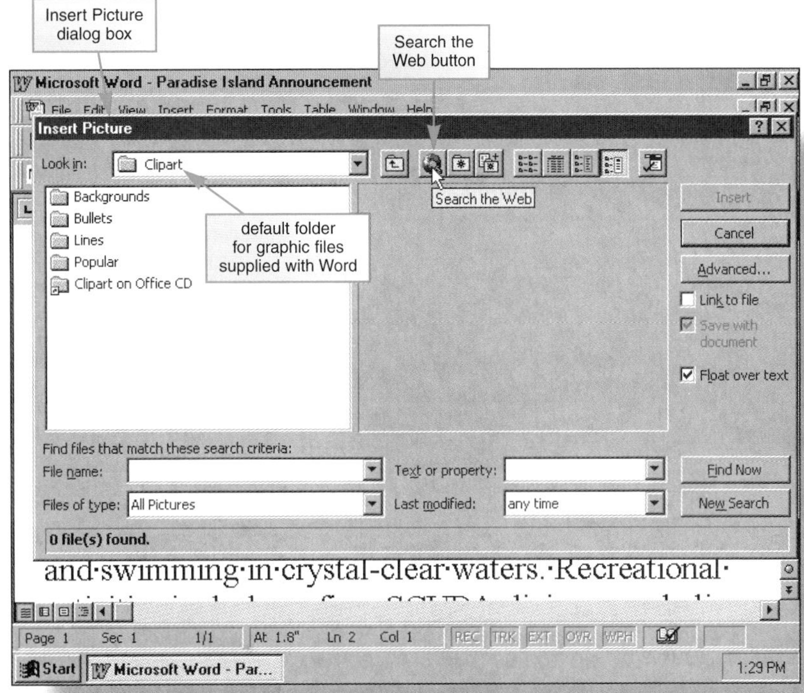

FIGURE 1-57

4 **Click the Search the Web button. When the Find it Fast – Microsoft Internet Explorer window displays, click the Address text box to select its contents and then type** `www.scsite.com/wd97/pr1.htm` **in the Address text box.**

If you currently are not connected to the Web, Word connects you using your default browser. Word displays the Find it Fast window (Figure 1-58). You can search by words or phrases in the Internet Searches text box; or if you know the exact address of the Web site containing the desired picture, you can enter the address in the Address text box.

FIGURE 1-58

5 **Press the ENTER key. If necessary, maximize the Web page window. Right-click the picture of Paradise Island. Point to Copy on the shortcut menu. (If you do not have a Copy command, go to the steps on page WD 1.44.)**

The http://www.scsite.com/wd97/pr1.htm Web page displays (Figure 1-59). This Web page displays several pictures used in this project. This announcement uses the picture of Paradise Island. Your browser displays a shortcut menu. If you do not have a Copy command on your shortcut menu, your browser requires that you save the picture on a disk and then insert the picture from the disk. Thus, if you do not have a Copy command on your shortcut menu, go to the steps on page WD 1.44 to copy the picture onto a disk and then insert the picture into the announcement from your disk.

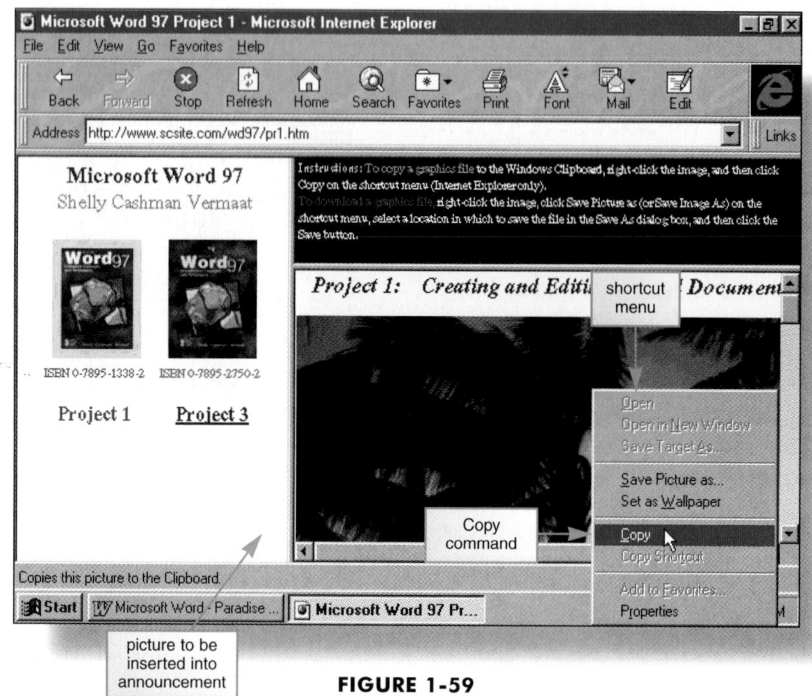

FIGURE 1-59

6 **Click Copy on the shortcut menu. Close the browser window. Be sure the insertion point is still on the paragraph mark below the headline in the announcement. Click Edit on the menu bar and then point to Paste Special (Figure 1-60).**

The picture of Paradise Island is copied to the ***Clipboard***, *which is a temporary Windows storage area. You will paste the picture into the announcement from the Clipboard.*

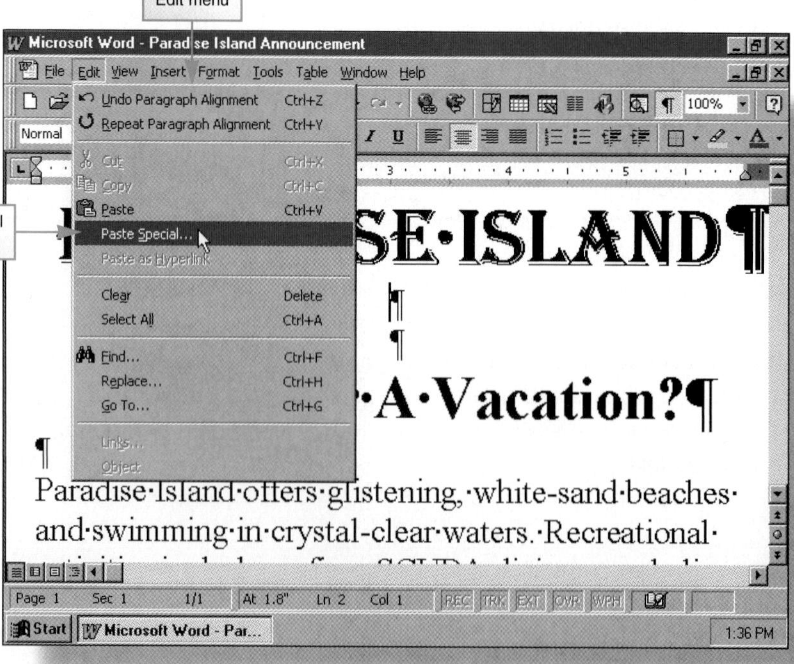

FIGURE 1-60

7 Click Paste Special. When the Paste Special dialog box displays, click Float over text to clear the check box. Point to the OK button.

Word displays the Paste Special dialog box (Figure 1-61). You want to clear the Float over text check box so the picture of Paradise Island is inserted as an inline picture, instead of a floating picture. A ***floating picture*** *is one inserted in a layer over the text; whereas, an* ***inline picture*** *is positioned directly in the text at the location of the insertion point. Floating pictures are discussed in a later project.*

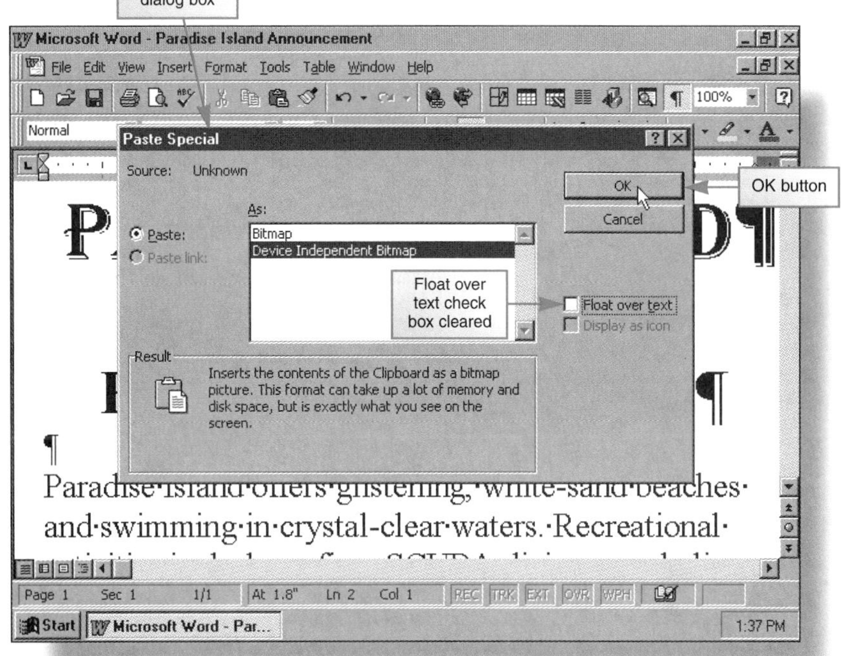

FIGURE 1-61

8 Click the OK button.

Word inserts the picture into your document at the location of the insertion point (Figure 1-62).

FIGURE 1-62

Because you inserted the picture as an inline picture, it is part of a paragraph. Therefore, you can use any of the paragraph alignment buttons on the Formatting toolbar to reposition the picture. Recall that earlier you formatted that paragraph mark to centered. Thus, the Paradise Island picture is centered across the page.

More About Shortcut Menus

Right-clicking an object opens a shortcut menu (also called a context-sensitive or object menu). Depending on the object, the commands in the shortcut menu vary. A dimmed command in a shortcut menu means the command cannot be used at the current time.

If, when you right-click the Paradise Island picture on the Web, you did not have a Copy command on the shortcut menu, you have to save the picture on a disk and then insert it from the disk. With the shortcut menu on the screen, proceed with these steps.

More *About* Graphic Files

Microsoft has graphic files you may download from its Web site. To do this, click Help on the menu bar, point to Microsoft on the Web, and then click Free Stuff. Follow the links to the Word 97 Free Stuff page and download any graphic files of interest to you.

TO SAVE A PICTURE ON THE WEB ON A DISK AND THEN INSERT IT IN THE DOCUMENT

Step 1: Click Save Image As (or a similar command) on the shortcut menu.
Step 2: Insert a formatted floppy disk into drive A.
Step 3: When the Save As dialog box displays, type `a:vacation` and then click the Save button. Close your browser.
Step 4: Be sure the insertion point is still positioned on the paragraph mark immediately below the headline. Click Insert on the menu bar, point to Picture, and then click From File.
Step 5: When the Insert Picture dialog box displays, click Float over text to clear the check box.
Step 6: Type `a:vacation` in the File name text box and then click the Insert button.
Step 7: If Word displays a ruler at the left edge of the screen, click View on the menu bar and then click Normal.

Word inserts the picture into your document at the location of the insertion point as shown in Figure 1-62 on the previous page.

If you do not have access to the Web, follow the steps below to insert the picture from the Data Disk that accompanies this book.

TO INSERT A PICTURE FROM THE DATA DISK THAT ACCOMPANIES THIS BOOK

Step 1: Press CTRL+HOME. Position the insertion point where you want the picture to be inserted (on the paragraph mark immediately below the headline of the announcement).
Step 2: Insert the Data Disk that accompanies this book into drive A.
Step 3: Click Insert on the menu bar, point to Picture, and then click From File.
Step 4: When the Insert Picture dialog box displays, click Float over text to clear the check box.
Step 5: Type `a:\Word\vacation` in the File name text box and then click the Insert button.
Step 6: Replace the Data Disk with your floppy disk.

Word inserts the picture into your document at the location of the insertion point as shown in Figure 1-62 on the previous page.

The picture in Figure 1-62 is a little too small for this announcement. The next step is to resize the imported graphic.

Resizing an Imported Graphic

Once a graphic has been imported into a document, you can easily change its size. **Resizing** includes both enlarging and reducing the size of a graphic. To resize a graphic, you first must select it. The following steps show how to select and then resize the picture you just imported from the Web.

Steps To Resize a Graphic

1 **Click anywhere in the graphic. If your screen does not display the Picture toolbar, right-click the Paradise Island picture and then click Show Picture Toolbar.**

Word selects the graphic (Figure 1-63). The Picture toolbar floats on the Word screen when a graphic is selected. Selected graphics display surrounded by a **selection rectangle** *with small squares, called* **sizing handles,** *at each corner and middle location of the selection rectangle. To resize the graphic, you drag the sizing handles until the graphic is the desired size. Dragging a corner sizing handle maintains the proportions of the graphic; whereas, dragging a middle sizing handle distorts the proportions of the graphic.*

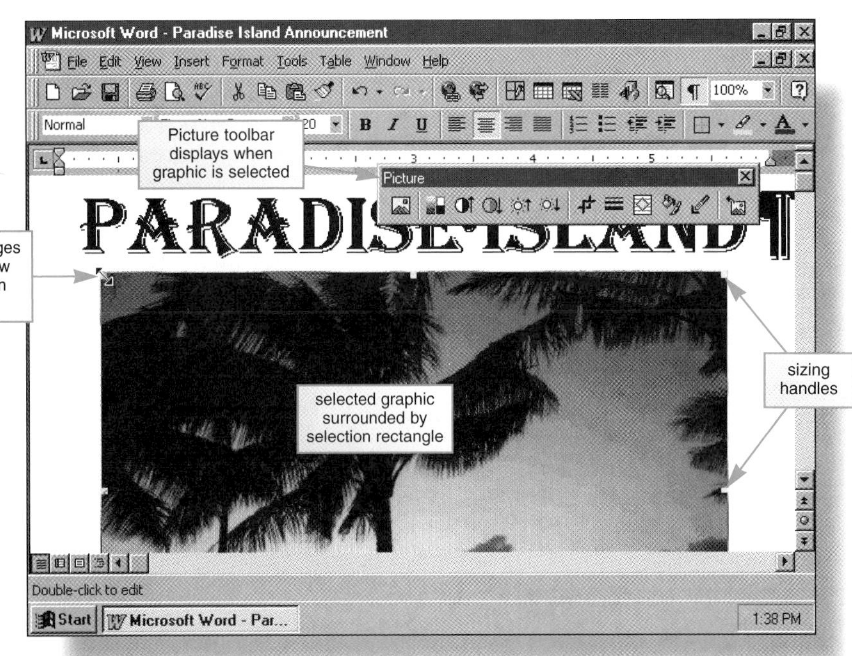

FIGURE 1-63

2 **Point to the upper-left corner sizing handle.**

The mouse pointer changes to a two-headed arrow when it is on a sizing handle.

3 **Drag the sizing handle outward until the selection rectangle is positioned approximately to the position shown in Figure 1-64.**

FIGURE 1-64

Release the mouse button. Click outside the graphic, above it or below it in the text, or to the right of it to deselect it.

Word resizes the graphic (Figure 1-65). The Picture toolbar disappears from the screen when you deselect the graphic.

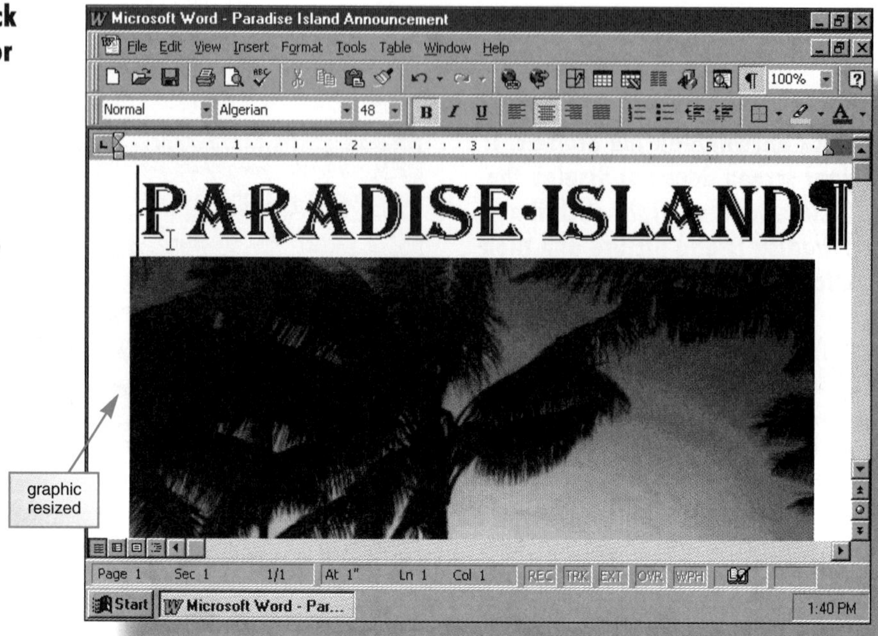

FIGURE 1-65

OtherWays

1. Click Format Picture button on Picture toolbar, click Size tab, enter desired width and height, click OK button
2. On Format menu click Picture, click Size tab, enter desired width and height, click OK button

Instead of resizing a selected graphic with the mouse, you also can use the Format Picture dialog box to resize a graphic by clicking the Format Picture button on the Picture toolbar and then clicking the Size tab. Using the Size sheet, you enter exact width and height measurements. If you have a precise measurement for the graphic, use the Format Picture dialog box; otherwise, drag the sizing handles to resize the graphic.

Restoring a Resized Graphic to Its Original Size

Sometimes you might resize a graphic and realize it is the wrong size. In these cases, you may want to return the graphic to its original size and start over. To return a resized graphic to its original size, click the graphic to select it and then click the Format Picture button on the Picture toolbar to display the Format Picture dialog box. Click the Size tab and then click the Reset button. Finally, click the OK button.

More *About* Saving

Through the Options button in the Save As dialog box, you can instruct Word to automatically save backup copies of your files in case your original becomes destroyed, or you can password protect files so only authorized users can access them. To access the Save As dialog box, click File on the menu bar and then click Save As.

Saving an Existing Document with the Same File Name

The announcement for Project 1 is now complete. To transfer the formatting changes and imported graphic to your floppy disk in drive A, you must save the document again. When you saved the document the first time, you assigned a file name to it (Paradise Island Announcement). Word assigns this same file name automatically to the document each time you subsequently save it if you use the following procedure.

Steps To Save an Existing Document with the Same File Name

1 Click the Save button on the Standard toolbar.

Word saves the document on a floppy disk inserted in drive A using the currently assigned file name, Paradise Island Announcement. When the save is finished, the document remains in memory and displays on the screen (Figure 1-66).

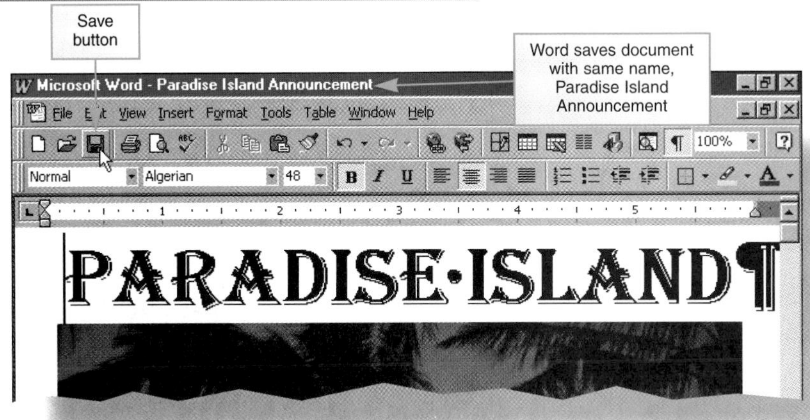

FIGURE 1-66

OtherWays

1. On File menu click Save
2. Press CTRL+S

If, for some reason, you want to save an existing document with a different file name, click Save As on the File menu to display the Save As dialog box. Then, fill in the Save As dialog box as discussed in Steps 2 through 5 on pages WD 1.26 and WD 1.27.

Printing a Document

The next step is to print the document you created. A printed version of the document is called a **hard copy** or **printout**. Perform the following steps to print the announcement created in Project 1.

Steps To Print a Document

1 Ready the printer according to the printer instructions. Click the Print button on the Standard toolbar.

The mouse pointer briefly changes to an hourglass shape, and then Word quickly displays a message on the status bar, indicating it is preparing to print the document. A few moments later, the document begins printing on the printer. The right edge of the status bar displays a printer icon while the document is printing (Figure 1-67).

FIGURE 1-67

2 **When the printer stops, retrieve the printout (Figure 1-68).**

PARADISE ISLAND

Ready For A Vacation?

Paradise Island offers glistening, white-sand beaches and swimming in crystal-clear waters. Recreational activities include surfing, SCUBA diving, snorkeling, sailing, and scenic hiking.

- Paradise Island vacation packages fit any budget
- Cottages, suites, condos, and inns are available

Call ***Tropical Travel*** at 555-2121

FIGURE 1-68

Other **Ways**

1. On File menu click Print, click OK button
2. Press CTRL+P, press ENTER

More *About* **Printing**

To print multiple copies of the same document, click File on the menu bar and then click Print. When the Print dialog box displays, type the desired number of copies in the Number of copies text box in the Copies area and then click the OK button.

When you use the Print button to print a document, Word prints the entire document automatically. You then may distribute the hard copy or keep it as a permanent record of the document.

If you wanted to cancel a job that is printing or waiting to be printed, double-click the printer icon on the status bar (Figure 1-67 on the previous page). In the printer window, click the job to be canceled and then click Cancel Printing on the Document menu.

Quitting Word

After you create, save, and print the announcement, Project 1 is complete. To quit Word and return control to Windows 95, perform the following steps.

Steps To Quit Word

1 Point to the Close button in the upper-right corner of the title bar (Figure 1-69).

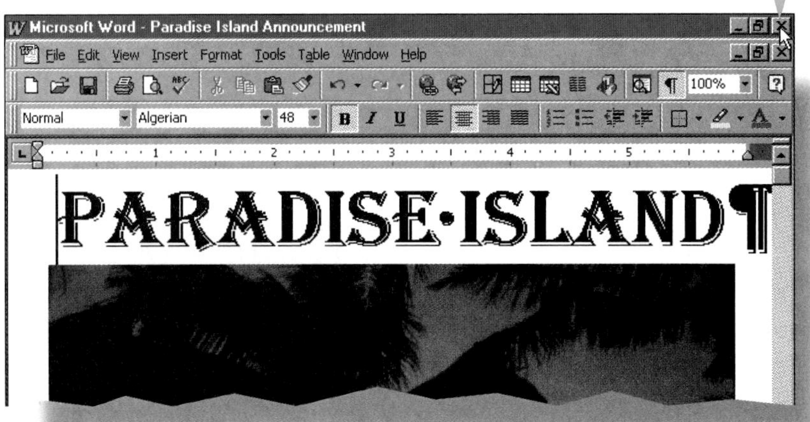

FIGURE 1-69

2 Click the Close button.

If you made changes to the document since the last save, Word displays a dialog box asking if you want to save the changes (Figure 1-70). Clicking the Yes button saves changes; clicking the No button ignores the changes; and clicking the Cancel button returns to the document. If you did not make any changes since you saved the document, this dialog box does not display.

FIGURE 1-70

OtherWays

1. On File menu click Exit
2. Press ALT+F4

Project 1 is now complete. You created and formatted the announcement, inserted a picture from the Web on it, printed it, and saved it as both a Word document and a Web document. You might decide, however, to change the announcement at a later date. To do this, you must start Word and then retrieve your document from the floppy disk in drive A.

Opening a Document

Earlier, you saved the Word document built in Project 1 on floppy disk using the file name Paradise Island Announcement. Once you have created and saved a document, you often will have reason to retrieve it from the disk. For example, you might want to revise the document. The following steps illustrate how to open the file Paradise Island Announcement.

Steps To Open a Document

1. **Click the Start button on the taskbar and then point to Open Office Document (Figure 1-71).**

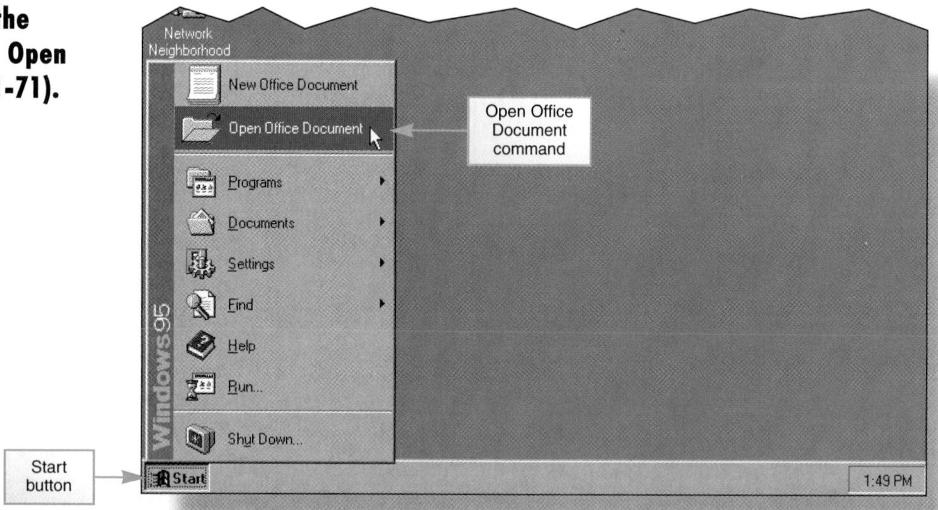

FIGURE 1-71

2. **Click Open Office Document. If necessary, click the Look in box arrow, and then click 3½ Floppy (A:). If it is not already selected, click the file name Paradise Island Announcement. Point to the Open button.**

Office displays the Open Office Document dialog box (Figure 1-72). Office displays the files on the floppy disk in drive A.

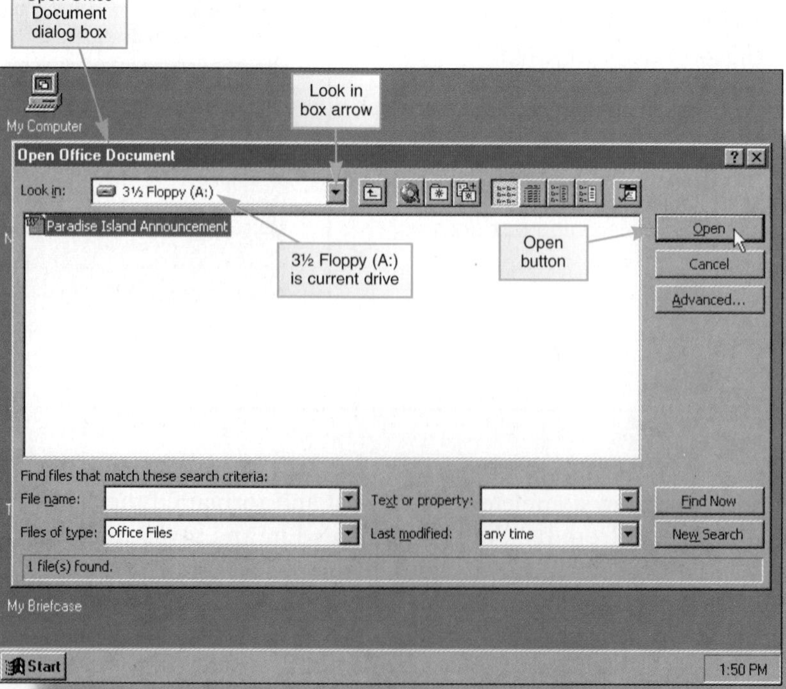

FIGURE 1-72

3 **Click the Open button.**

Office starts Word, and then Word opens the document, Paradise Island Announcement, from the floppy disk in drive A and displays the document on the screen (Figure 1-73).

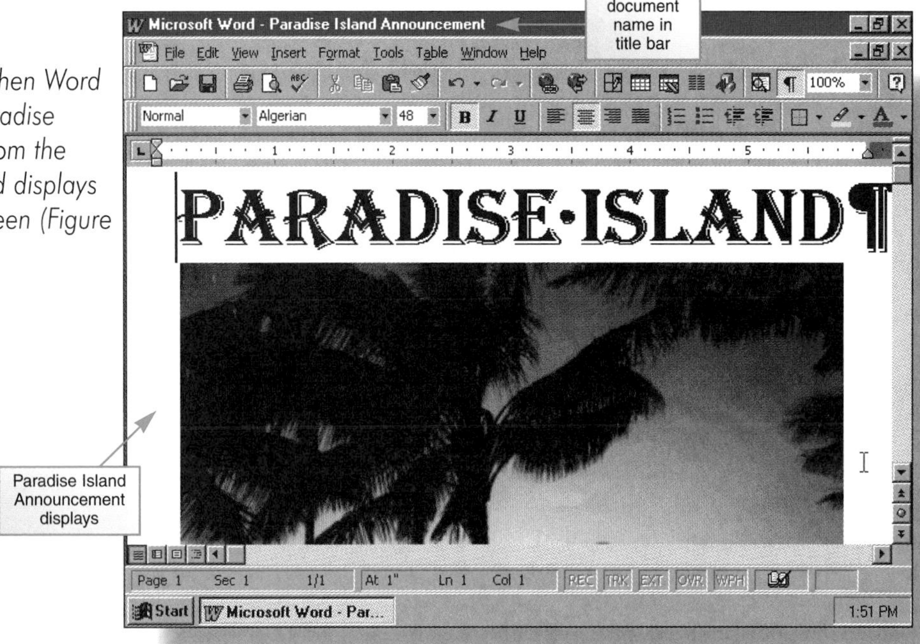

FIGURE 1-73

OtherWays

1. Right-click Start button, click Open, double-click Open Office Document, select file name, click Open button
2. Click Open a Document on Microsoft Office Shortcut Bar, select file name, click Open button in dialog box
3. In Microsoft Word, click Open button on Standard toolbar, select file name, click Open button in dialog box
4. In Microsoft Word, on File menu click Open, select file name, click Open button in dialog box
5. In Microsoft Word, press CTRL+O, select file name, press ENTER

Correcting Errors

After creating a document, you often will find you must make changes to the document. Changes can be required because the document contains an error or because of new circumstances.

Types of Changes Made to Documents

The types of changes made to documents normally fall into one of the three following categories: additions, deletions, or modifications.

ADDITIONS Additional words, sentences, or paragraphs may be required in the document. Additions occur when you omit text from a document and are required to add it later. For example, you accidentally may forget to put the telephone number in the last line of Project 1.

DELETIONS Sometimes, text in a document is incorrect or is no longer needed. For example, the agency might remove condos from their package deals. In this case, you would delete the word condos from the bulleted list.

MODIFICATIONS If an error is made in a document, you might have to revise the word(s) in the text. For example, SCUBA diving might be offered to only certified divers.

Word provides several methods for correcting errors in a document. For each of the error correction techniques, you first must move the insertion point to the error.

More About Opening Files

In Word, you can open a recently used file by clicking File on the menu bar and then clicking the file name on the File menu. To instruct Word to show the recently used documents on the File menu, click Tools on the menu bar, click Options, click the General tab, click Recently used file list, and then click the OK button.

Inserting Text into an Existing Document

If you leave a word or phrase out of a sentence, you can include it in the sentence by positioning the insertion point where you intend to insert the text. Word always inserts the text to the left of the insertion point. The text to the right of the insertion point moves to the right and downward to accommodate the new text. The following steps illustrate inserting the word, beautiful, before the word, crystal, in the first sentence of the paragraph below the body title in Project 1.

Steps To Insert Text into an Existing Document

1 **Scroll through the document and click immediately to the left of the letter c in the word, crystal.**

The insertion point displays immediately to the left of the letter c in crystal (Figure 1-74).

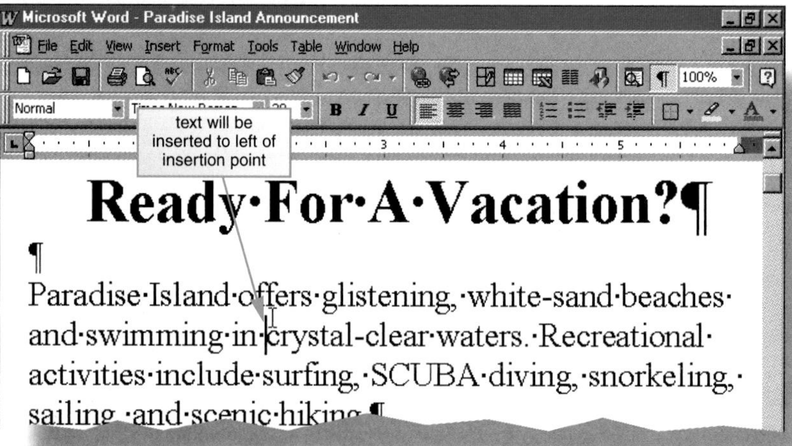

FIGURE 1-74

2 **Type** `beautiful,` **and then press the SPACEBAR.**

The word, beautiful, is inserted between the words, in and crystal, in the announcement for Project 1 (Figure 1-75). Be sure to include the comma after the word, beautiful, as shown in the figure.

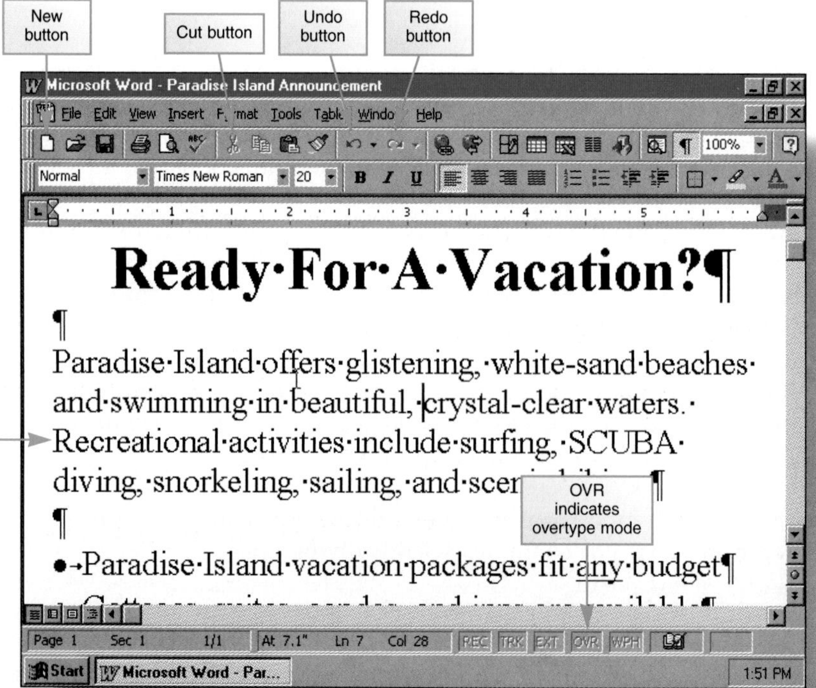

FIGURE 1-75

Notice in Figure 1-75 that the text to the right of the word, crystal, moved to the right and downward to accommodate the insertion of the word, beautiful. That is, the word, Recreational, moved down to line 8.

In Word, the default typing mode is insert mode. In **insert mode**, as you type a character, Word inserts the character and moves all the characters to the right of the typed character one position to the right. In the example just given, you used insert mode to add the word, beautiful. You can change to overtype mode by double-clicking the **OVR status indicator** on the status bar (Figure 1-75). In **overtype mode**, Word replaces characters to the right of the insertion point. Double-clicking the OVR status indicator a second time returns you to insert mode.

Deleting Text from an Existing Document

It is not unusual to type incorrect characters or words in a document. In such a case, to correct the error, you may want to delete certain letters or words.

TO DELETE AN INCORRECT CHARACTER IN A DOCUMENT

Step 1: Click next to the incorrect character.
Step 2: Press the BACKSPACE key to erase to the left of the insertion point; or press the DELETE key to erase to the right of the insertion point.

TO DELETE AN INCORRECT WORD OR PHRASE IN A DOCUMENT

Step 1: Select the word or phrase you want to erase.
Step 2: Right-click the selected word or phrase, and then click Cut on the shortcut menu; or click the Cut button on the Standard toolbar (Figure 1-75); or press the DELETE key.

Undoing Recent Actions

Word provides an **Undo button** on the Standard toolbar that you can use to cancel your recent command(s) or action(s). If you delete some text accidentally, you can bring it back. If you want to cancel your undo, you can use the **Redo button**. Some actions, such as saving or printing a document, cannot be undone or redone.

TO CANCEL YOUR MOST RECENT ACTION

Step 1: Click the Undo button (Figure 1-75) on the Standard toolbar.

TO CANCEL YOUR MOST RECENT UNDO

Step 1: Click the Redo button (Figure 1-75) on the Standard toolbar.

TO CANCEL A SERIES OF PRIOR ACTIONS

Step 1: Click the Undo button arrow to display the undo actions list.
Step 2: Drag through the actions to be undone.

Closing the Entire Document

Sometimes, everything goes wrong. If this happens, you may want to close the document entirely and start over. You also may want to close a document when you are finished with it so you can begin your next document. To close the document, follow these steps.

More About Help

If you purchased an application program five years ago, you received one or more thick technical manuals explaining the software. With Microsoft Word 97, you receive a small manual. The online Help feature of Microsoft Word 97 replaces the reams and reams of printed pages in hard-to-understand technical manuals.

TO CLOSE THE ENTIRE DOCUMENT AND START OVER

Step 1: Click File on the menu bar and then click Close.
Step 2: If Word displays a dialog box, click the No button to ignore the changes since the last time you saved the document.
Step 3: Click the New button (Figure 1-75 on page WD1.52) on the Standard toolbar.

You also can close the document by clicking the Close button at the right edge of the menu bar.

Microsoft Word Help

At any time while you are working in Word, you can answer your Word questions by using **Help**. Used properly, this form of online assistance can increase your productivity and reduce your frustrations by minimizing the time you spend learning how to use Word. Table 1-3 summarizes the five categories of Word Help available to you.

Table 1-3

HELP CATEGORY	DESCRIPTION	HOW TO ACTIVATE
Office Assistant	Answers your questions, offers tips, and provides Help for a variety of Word features.	Click the Office Assistant button on the Standard toolbar.
Contents Sheet	Groups Help topics by general categories. Similar to a table of contents in a book.	Click Contents and Index on the Help menu and then click the Contents tab.
Index Sheet	Accesses Help topics by subject. Similar to an index in a book.	Click Contents and Index on the Help menu and then click the Index tab.
Find Sheet	Searches the index for all phrases that include the term in question.	Click Contents and Index on the Help menu and then click the Find tab.
Question Mark button and What's This? command	Used to identify unfamiliar items on the screen.	In a dialog box, click the Question Mark button and then click an item in a dialog box. Click What's This? on the Help menu and then click an item on the screen.

The following sections show examples of the various types of Help described in Table 1-3.

Using the Office Assistant

The **Office Assistant** answers your questions and suggests more efficient ways to complete a task. With the Office Assistant active, for example, you can type a word or phrase in a text box, and the Office Assistant provides immediate Help on the subject. Also, as you create a document, the Office Assistant accumulates tips that suggest more efficient ways to complete a task you performed while creating the document, such as formatting, printing, or saving. This tip feature is part of the **IntelliSense™ technology** that is built into Word.

The following steps show how to use the Office Assistant to obtain information on saving a Word document as a Web page.

Steps To Obtain Help Using the Office Assistant

1. **If the Office Assistant is not on the screen, click the Office Assistant button on the Standard toolbar. If the Office Assistant is on the screen, click it. Type** `save Word document as a Web page` **in the What would you like to do? text box and then point to the Search button (Figure 1-76).**

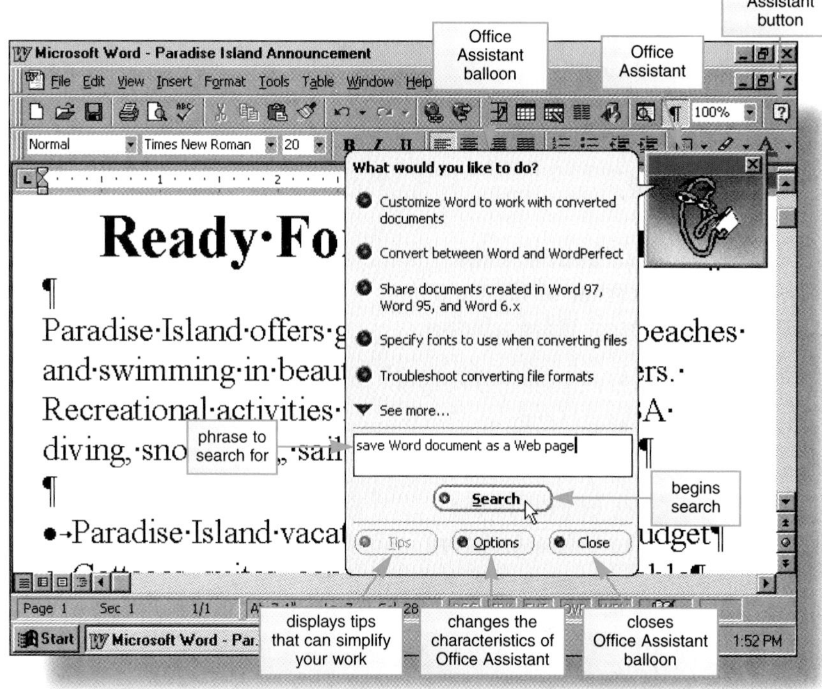

FIGURE 1-76

2. **Click the Search button and then point to the Learn what happens when you save a Word 97 document as a Web page topic.**

   The Office Assistant displays a list of topics relating to the phrase, save Word document as a Web page (Figure 1-77).

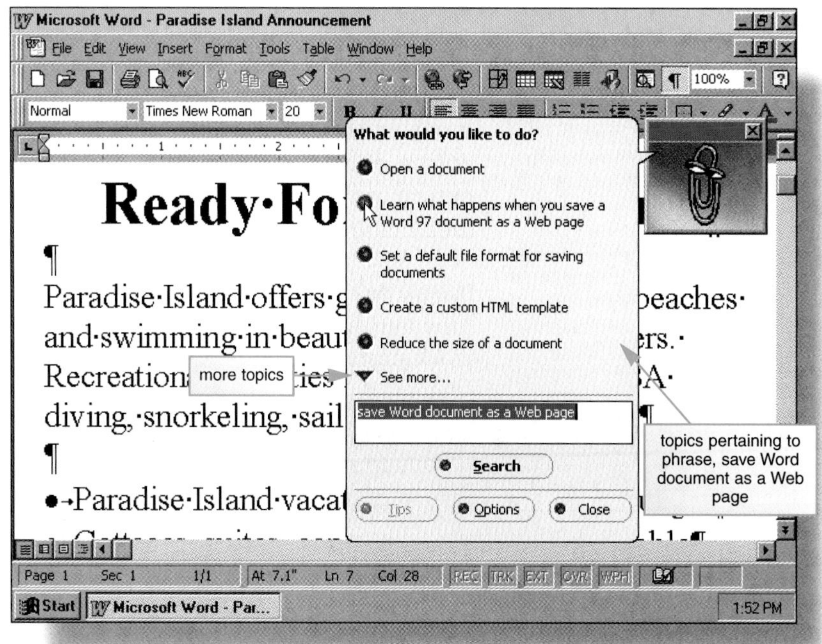

FIGURE 1-77

3 Click Learn what happens when you save a Word 97 document as a Web page.

The Office Assistant displays the Help Topics: Microsoft Word window (Figure 1-78). Word Help windows contain a variety of links, which include buttons and green underlined words. When you point to a link, the mouse pointer shape changes to a pointing hand.

4 Click the Close button in the upper-right corner of the Help Topics: Microsoft Word window.

The Help window closes and control returns to the Word window.

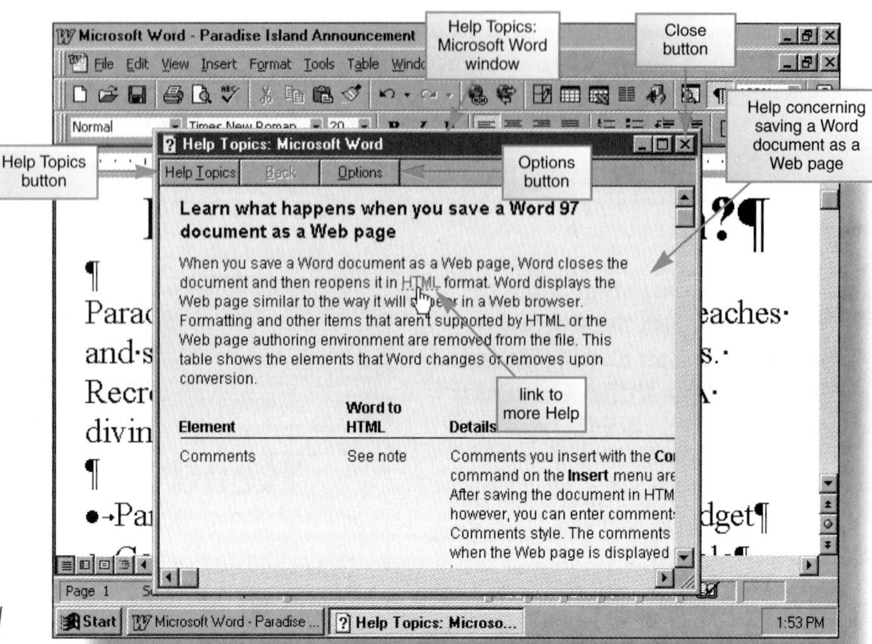

FIGURE 1-78

5 Click the Close button on the title bar of the Office Assistant window.

The Office Assistant disappears from the screen.

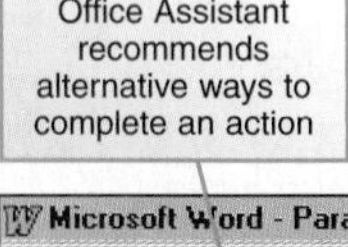

Other Ways

1. To display Office Assistant, press F1 or on Help menu click Microsoft Word Help
2. To hide Office Assistant, right-click Office Assistant window, click Hide Assistant on shortcut menu

You can use the Office Assistant to search for Help on any topic concerning Word. Once Help displays, you can read it, print it, or click one of its links to display a related Help topic. To print the Help information, click the Print button if one exists. If the window does not contain a Print button, click the Options button or right-click the window and then click Print Topic. The Help Topics button in the Help window allows you to obtain Help through the Contents, Index, and Find sheets.

DISPLAYING TIPS TO IMPROVE YOUR WORK HABITS If you click the Office Assistant Tips button (Figure 1-76 on the previous page), Word displays tips on how to work more efficiently. Once a tip displays (Figure 1-79), you can move backward or forward through the list of accumulated tips. As you work through creating a document, Word adds tips to the list. If the Office Assistant displays on the screen and it has a new tip for you, a light bulb appears in the Office Assistant window. If the Office Assistant does not display on the screen and it has a new tip for you, the light bulb appears on the Office Assistant button on the Standard toolbar.

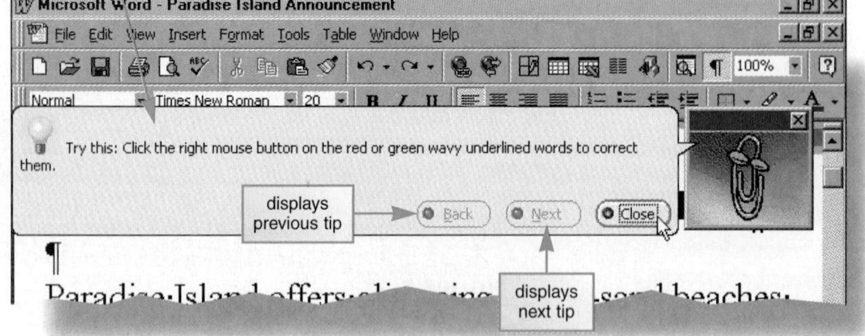

FIGURE 1-79

OFFICE ASSISTANT SHORTCUT MENU When you right-click the Office Assistant window, a shortcut menu displays, which allows you to change the characteristics of the Office Assistant. For example, you can hide the Office Assistant, display tips, change its appearance, select a different icon for the assistant, or view animation of the Office Assistant. These options also are available by clicking the Options button that displays when you click the Office Assistant.

Using the Contents and Index Command to Obtain Help

The Contents and Index command provides access to the Contents, Index, and Find sheets. The **Contents sheet** in the Help Topics: Microsoft Word dialog box offers you assistance when you know the general category of the topic in question, but not the specifics. Use the Contents sheet in the same manner you would use a table of contents at the front of a textbook. The following steps show how to use the Contents sheet to obtain information on getting assistance while you work.

Steps To Obtain Help Using the Contents Sheet

1 Click Help on the menu bar and then point to Contents and Index (Figure 1-80).

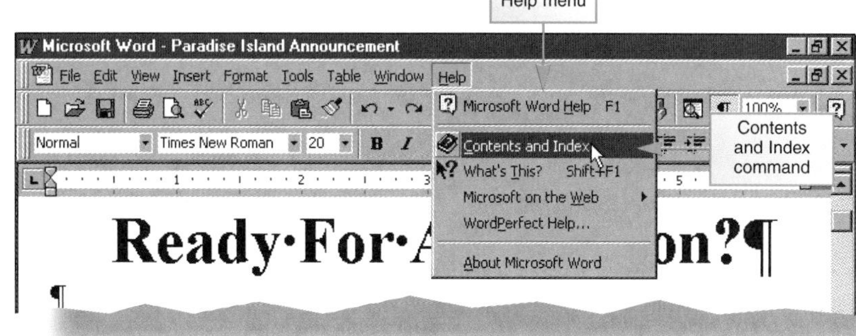

FIGURE 1-80

2 Click Contents and Index. If necessary, click the Contents tab. Double-click the Getting Help book. Point to the Ways to get assistance while you work topic.

The Help Topics: Microsoft Word dialog box displays (Figure 1-81). This dialog box contains three tabbed sheets: Contents, Index, and Find. In Figure 1-81, the Getting Help topic is preceded by a book icon. A ***book icon*** *means subtopics exist. To display the subtopics associated with a topic, you double-click its book icon. The subtopics are preceded by a* ***question mark icon****. To display information on a subtopic, you double-click the subtopic. A book icon opens when you double-click it.*

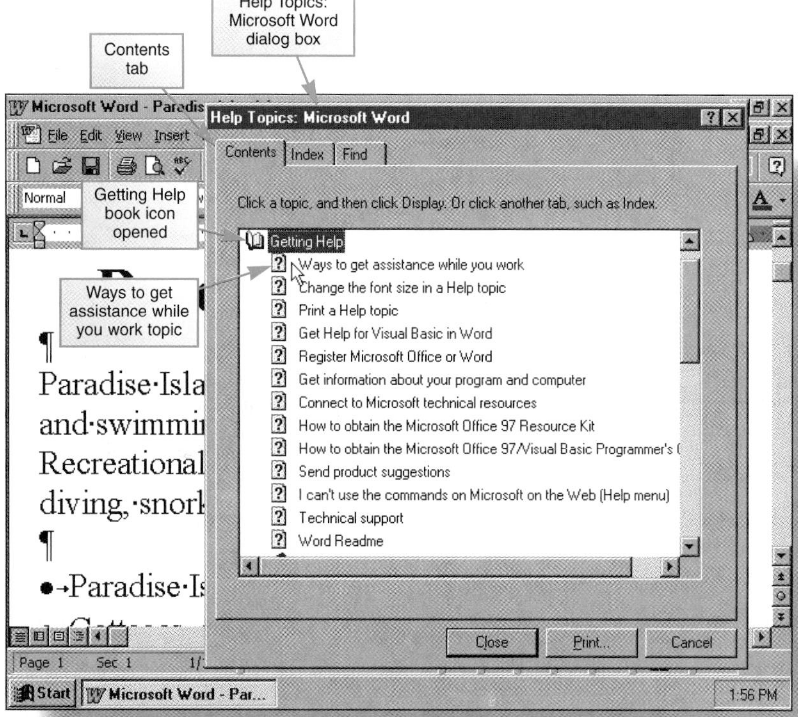

FIGURE 1-81

3 **Double-click the Ways to get assistance while you work topic.**

Word displays the Microsoft Word window containing tips on Word's Help (Figure 1-82). When you click a link, Word displays additional Help information.

4 **Click the Close button in the upper-right corner of the Microsoft Word Help window.**

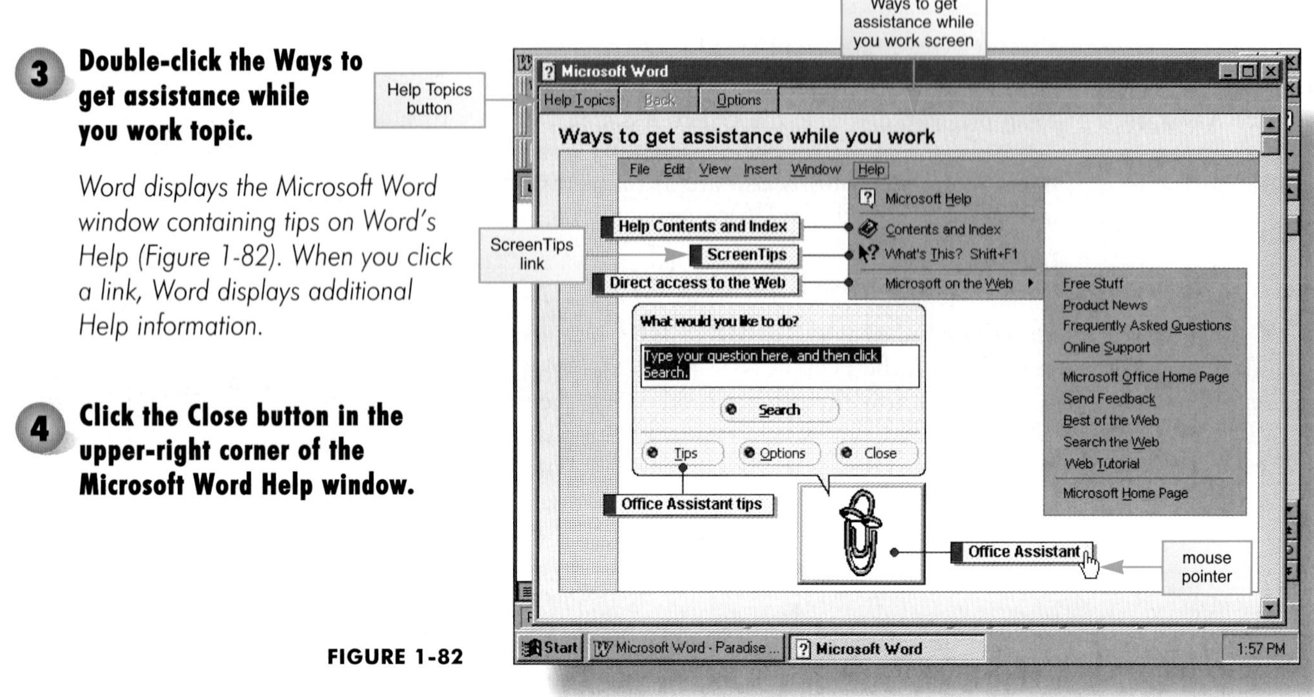

FIGURE 1-82

Instead of closing the Microsoft Word window in Step 3, you could click the Help Topics button in Figure 1-82 to return to the Contents sheet (Figure 1-81 on the previous page).

The Contents sheet in the Help Topics: Microsoft Word dialog box is much like a table of contents in the front of a book. The **Index sheet**, however, is similar to an index in the back of a book. For example, if you wanted help on formatting characters in bold, you would display the Index sheet, type `bold` (Figure 1-83) and then double-click the bold formatting topic to display Help information on formatting characters in bold. Then, click the Close button.

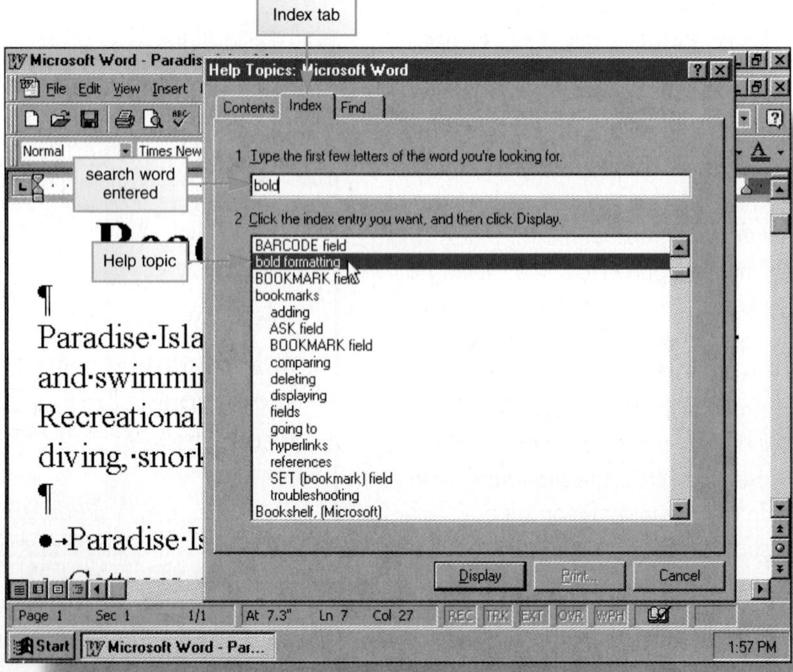

FIGURE 1-83

The **Find sheet** is used to locate a Help topic on a particular word or phrase. For example, if you wanted help on inserting an inline floating picture, you would display the Find sheet, type `insert picture` (Figure 1-84) and then double-click the Change a floating picture to an inline picture and vice-versa topic. Then, close the Help window.

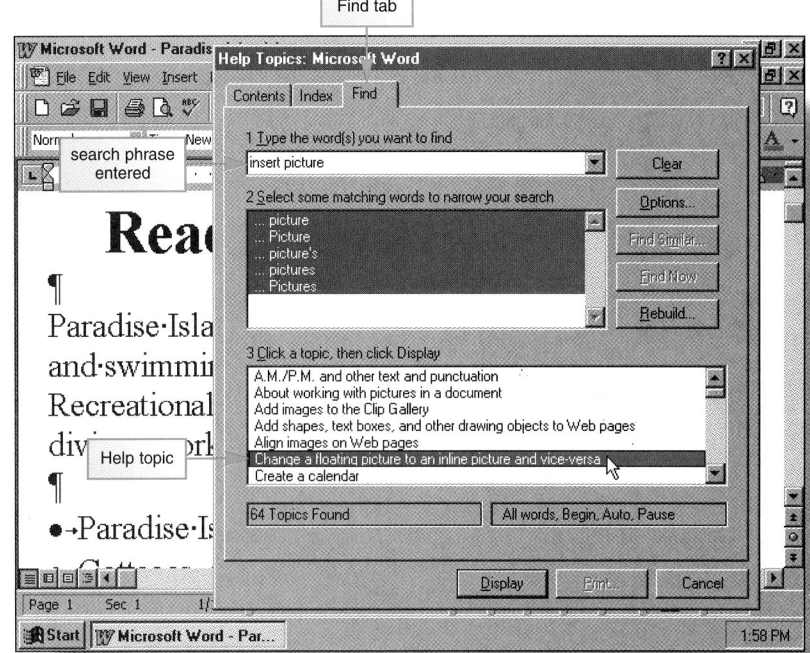

FIGURE 1-84

Obtaining Web Information

To obtain Web-related information, click Help on the menu bar and then point to Microsoft on the Web to display a submenu of Web-related commands. The Help window in Figure 1-82 shows this submenu. If you click any command on the submenu, your system will launch your browser and connect to a corresponding page on the World Wide Web. Use the commands on the Web submenu to obtain up-to-date information on a variety of topics.

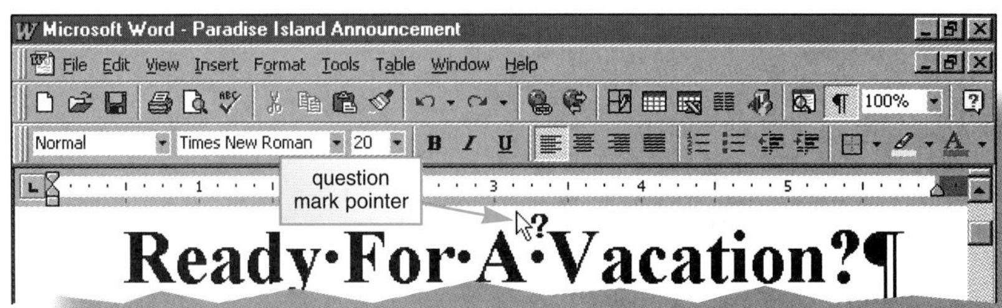

FIGURE 1-85

Using What's This? or the Question Mark Button

To obtain Help on an item on the Word screen, click Help on the menu bar and then click What's This? To obtain help on an item in a Word dialog box, click the **Question Mark button** that displays in the upper-right corner of a dialog box. Using either technique, the mouse pointer changes to an arrow and a question mark as shown in Figure 1-85. Move the **question mark pointer** to any item on the Word screen or in a dialog box, and then click to display a **ScreenTip**, which offers an explanation of the item on which you clicked. For example, clicking the Print button on the Standard toolbar displays the Help message shown in Figure 1-86.

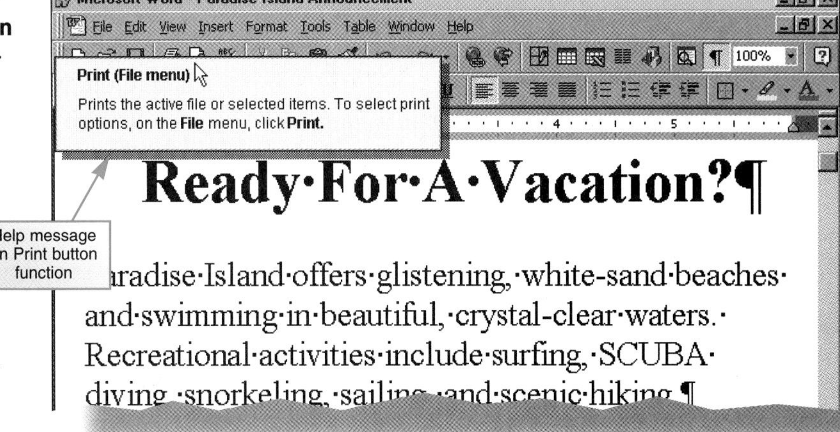

FIGURE 1-86

If you click text with the question-mark pointer, Word displays the paragraph and character formatting characteristics of the text on which you click.

Word Help has features that make it powerful and easy to use. The best way to familiarize yourself with Word Help is to use it.

Wizards

Word supplies **wizards** to assist you in creating common types of documents, such as letters, memos, resumes, and newsletters. To use a wizard, click File on the menu bar, click New, and then select the wizard you desire from the appropriate tabbed sheet. The wizard asks you a few basic questions, and then displays a formatted document on the screen for you to customize or fill in blanks. In Project 2, you will use a wizard.

Project Summary

Project 1 introduced you to starting Word and creating a document. Before entering any text in the document, you learned how to change the font size. You also learned how to save and print a document. You used Word's spell check as you type feature and automatically added bullets to paragraphs as you typed them into the document. Once you saved the document, you learned how to format its paragraphs and characters. Then, you imported a graphic file from the Web and resized it. With the technologies presented, you learned to move the insertion point so you could insert, delete, and modify text. Finally, you learned to use Word Help.

What You Should Know

Having completed this project, you now should be able to perform the following tasks:

- Bold Selected Text *(WD 1.34)*
- Bullet a List as You Type *(WD 1.23)*
- Cancel a Series of Prior Actions *(WD 1.53)*
- Cancel Your Most Recent Action *(WD 1.53)*
- Cancel Your Most Recent Undo *(WD 1.53)*
- Center a Single Paragraph *(WD 1.39)*
- Center Selected Paragraphs *(WD 1.30)*
- Change the Font of Selected Text *(WD 1.33)*
- Change the Font Size of Selected Text *(WD 1.31)*
- Close the Entire Document and Start Over *(WD 1.54)*
- Delete an Incorrect Character in a Document *(WD 1.53)*
- Delete an Incorrect Word or Phrase in a Document *(WD 1.53)*
- Display Nonprinting Characters *(WD 1.18)*
- Enter a Document that Scrolls the Document Window *(WD 1.22)*
- Enter Blank Lines into a Document *(WD 1.17)*
- Enter More Text *(WD 1.19)*
- Enter Text *(WD 1.16)*
- Format a Line of Text *(WD 1.34)*
- Increase the Default Font Size Before Typing *(WD 1.14)*
- Insert a Picture from the Data Disk that Accompanies this Book *(WD 1.44)*
- Insert a Picture from the Web *(WD 1.40)*
- Insert Text into an Existing Document *(WD 1.52)*
- Italicize and Bold Selected Text *(WD 1.38)*
- Obtain Help Using the Contents and Index Command *(WD 1.57)*
- Obtain Help Using the Office Assistant *(WD 1.55)*
- Open a Document *(WD 1.50)*
- Print a Document *(WD 1.47)*
- Quit Word *(WD 1.49)*
- Resize a Graphic *(WD 1.45)*
- Save a New Document *(WD 1.26)*
- Save a Picture on the Web on a Disk and Insert It in the Document *(WD 1.44)*
- Save an Existing Document with the Same File Name *(WD 1.47)*
- Scroll Through the Document *(WD 1.35)*
- Select a Group of Words *(WD 1.37)*
- Select a Single Line *(WD 1.31)*
- Select a Single Word *(WD 1.35)*
- Select Multiple Paragraphs *(WD 1.29)*
- Spell Check as You Type *(WD 1.20)*
- Start Word *(WD 1.9)*
- Underline Selected Text *(WD 1.36)*
- Wordwrap Text as You Type *(WD 1.19)*

Test Your Knowledge

1 True/False

Instructions: Circle T if the statement is true or F if the statement is false.

T F 1. Microsoft Word 97 is an operating system.
T F 2. The insertion point indicates where text will be inserted as you type.
T F 3. The Standard toolbar initially displays floating on the Word screen.
T F 4. To create a new paragraph, press the ENTER key.
T F 5. Double-click a red wavy underlined word to display a shortcut menu that lists suggested spelling corrections for the flagged word.
T F 6. To save a document with the same file name, click the Open button on the taskbar.
T F 7. Italicizing a word is an example of character formatting.
T F 8. To center selected paragraphs, click the Center button on the Formatting toolbar.
T F 9. A floating picture is one positioned directly in the text at the location of the insertion point.
T F 10. The Office Assistant button is on the Standard toobar.

2 Multiple Choice

Instructions: Circle the correct response.

1. __________ are used to display different portions of your document in the document window.
   a. Status indicators b. Toolbars c. Scroll bars d. Rulers
2. If a word you type is not in Word's dictionary, a __________ wavy underline appears below the word and a red __________ displays on the Spelling and Grammar Status icon.
   a. green, check mark b. green, X c. red, check mark d. red, X
3. To scroll down one entire screenful at a time, __________.
   a. click below the scroll box on the scroll bar b. click scroll arrow at bottom of the scroll bar
   c. press PAGE DOWN d. both a and c
4. To place a bullet automatically at the beginning of a paragraph, type a(n) __________ and then press the SPACEBAR.
   a. asterisk (*) b. plus (+) c. letter o d. exclamation point (!)
5. To select a single word, __________ the word.
   a. click b. right-click c. double-click d. drag
6. Selected graphics display __________ handles at the corner and middle locations.
   a. selection b. sizing c. picture d. resizing
7. To erase the character to the right of the insertion point, press the __________ key.
   a. DELETE b. INSERT c. BACKSPACE d. both a and c
8. __________ the OVR status indicator to toggle between overtype and insert mode.
   a. Click b. Right-click c. Double-click d. Drag
9. To close a document and start over, __________.
   a. click Close on File menu b. click Close button on menu bar
   c. click Close button on Standard toolbar d. both a and b
10. If Office Assistant has a new tip, a __________ displays in the Office Assistant button or window.
    a. light bulb b. flashlight c. paper clip d. magic wand

Test Your Knowledge

3 Understanding the Word Screen

Instructions: In Figure 1-87, arrows point to major components of the Word screen. Identify the various parts of the screen in the spaces provided.

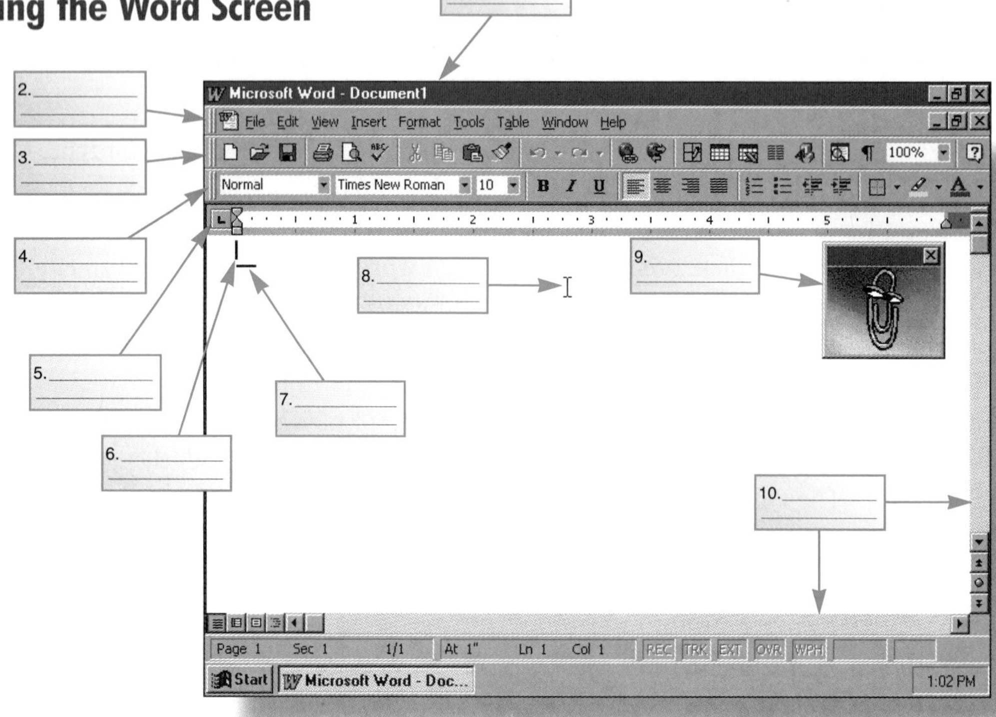

FIGURE 1-87

4 Understanding the Standard and Formatting Toolbars

Instructions: In Figure 1-88, arrows point to several of the buttons and boxes on the Standard and Formatting toolbars. In the spaces provided, briefly explain the purpose of each button and box.

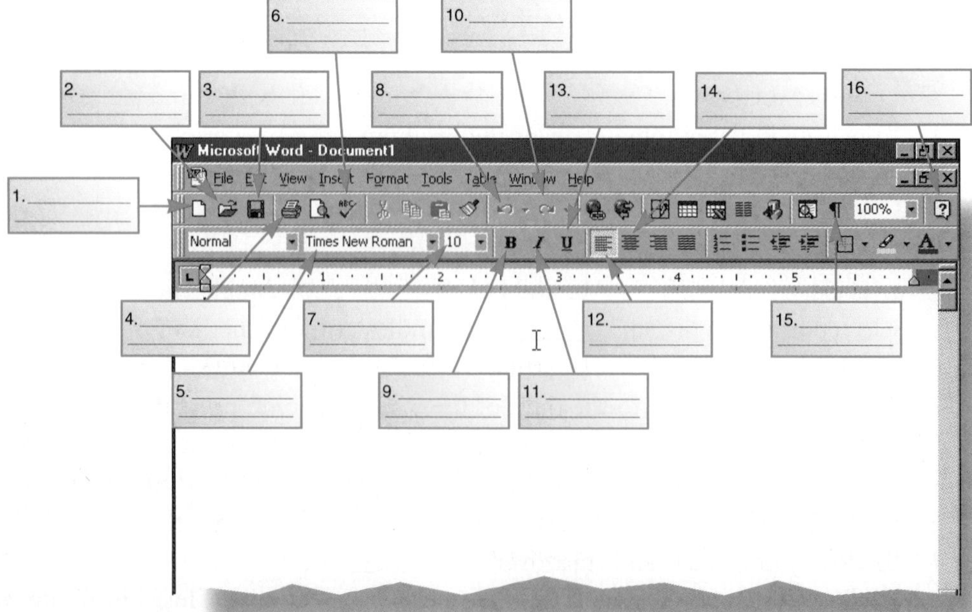

FIGURE 1-88

Use Help

1 Reviewing Project Activities

Instructions: Perform the following tasks using a computer.

1. Start Word.
2. If the Office Assistant is on your screen, click it to display its balloon. If the Office Assistant is not on your screen, click the Office Assistant button on the Standard toolbar.
3. Click Options in the Office Assistant balloon and then click the Gallery tab. Click the Next button repeatedly to view the various assistants. Display Mother Nature. Click the Options tab and then review the different options for the Office Assistant. Close the Office Assistant dialog box. Change the Office Assistant icon back to the original one.
4. Click the Office Assistant to display its balloon. Type `select text` in the What would you like to do? text box. Click the Search button. Click the Select text and graphics link.
5. Click Select text and graphics by using the mouse. Read the information. Use the shortcut menu or Options button to print the information. Click the Back button. Click Select text and graphics by using shortcut keys. Read and print the information. Click the Close button in the Help window. Close the Office Assistant window.
6. Click Help on the menu bar and then click Contents and Index. Click the Contents tab. Double-click the Key Information book. Double-click the For Customers Using Word for the First Time book. Double-click the What's new in Word 97 topic. Read and print the following help topics: Automating your tasks and getting assistance, Editing and proofing tools, Working with Web tools. Close any open Help window(s).

2 Expanding on the Basics

Instructions: Use Word Help to better understand the topics listed below. Answer the questions on your own paper or hand in the printed Help topic to your instructor.

1. In this project, you checked spelling as you typed. Use the Office Assistant to answer the following questions about checking spelling all at once.
   a. What button do you click to spell check the document all at once?
   b. If you want to do a grammar check with a spelling check, how do you turn on the grammar check feature?
   c. What are the readability scores? How do you turn them on?
2. In this project, you opened a single file from the Open dialog box. Use the Contents tab in the Help Topics: Microsoft Word dialog box to determine how to select multiple files in the Open dialog box.
3. In this project, you imported a Graphics Interchange Format (GIF) file from the Web into the announcement. Use the Index tab in the Help Topics: Microsoft Word dialog box to determine the complete list of graphic file types that may be inserted into a Word document.
4. In this project, you saved a Word document as a Web page. Use the Find tab in the Help Topics: Microsoft Word dialog box to learn how to use the Web wizard to create a Web page.
5. Use the What's This? command on the Help menu to display ScreenTips for five buttons that you are unfamiliar with on the Standard and Formatting toolbars. Print each ScreenTip by right-clicking it, clicking Print Topic on the shortcut menu, and then clicking the OK button.

Apply Your Knowledge

CAUTION: To ensure you have enough disk space to save your files, it is recommended that you create a copy of the Data Disk that accompanies this book. Then, delete folders from the copy of the Data Disk that are not needed for the application you are working on. Do the following: (1) Insert the Data Disk in drive A; (2) start Explorer; (3) right-click the 3½ Floppy (A:) folder in the All Folders side of the window; (4) click Copy Disk; (5) click Start and OK as required; (6) insert a floppy disk when requested; (7) delete all folders on the floppy disk you created except the Word folder; (8) remove the floppy disk from drive A and label it Word Data Disk.

1 Spell Checking a Document

Instructions: Start Word. Open the document, apply-1, from the Word folder on the Data Disk that accompanies this book. As shown in Figure 1-89, the document is an announcement for Computers Made Easy that contains many spelling and grammar errors. You are to right-click each of the errors and then click the desired correction on the shortcut menu. You may need to refer to your Use Help 2 responses to information on how to verify that the grammar checker is enabled.

spelling and grammar errors are circled to help you identify them

Feeling Frustrated?

WE CAN HELP!

Our goal at Computers Made Easy are to take the complexity out of comptuer programs. We offer three three levels of training in each of these application: word processing, electronic mail, spreadsheets, databases, ard presentation graphics. We also offering Internet training!

- Coarses are $99 eacxh for seven contact hours
- Each student is provided with a hands-on textbook

to sign up, call 555-9090

FIGURE 1-89

Perform the following tasks:

1. Position the insertion point at the beginning of the document. Scroll down until you encounter the first error.
2. Right-click the flagged phrase, goal at Computers Made Easy are. Change the incorrect verb in the flagged phrase by clicking the phrase, goal at Computers Made Easy is, on the shortcut menu.
3. Right-click the flagged word, comptuer. Change the incorrect word, comptuer, to computer by clicking computer on the shortcut menu.
4. Right-click the flagged word, three. Click Delete Repeated Word on the shortcut menu to remove the duplicate occurrence of the word, three.
5. Right-click the flagged word, ard. Because the correct word is not on the shortcut menu, click outside the shortcut menu to remove it from the screen. Correct the misspelled word, ard, to the correct word, and, by removing the letter r and replacing it with the letter n.
6. Right-click the flagged phrase, also offering. Change the phrase, also offering, to the correct phrase by clicking the phrase, also offer, on the shortcut menu.
7. Right-click the flagged phrase, these application. Change the word, application, to its plural form by clicking the phrase, these applications, on the shortcut menu.

Apply Your Knowledge

8. Right-click the flagged word, Coarses. Change the incorrect word, Coarses, to Courses by clicking Courses on the shortcut menu.
9. Right-click the incorrect word, eacxh. Change the incorrect word, eacxh, to each by clicking each on the shortcut menu.
10. Right-click the flagged word, to. Capitalize the word, to, by clicking To on the shortcut menu.
11. Click File on the menu bar and then click Save As. Save the document using Corrected apply-1 as the file name.
12. Print the revised document.

In the Lab

1 Creating an Announcement with an Imported Picture from the Web

Problem: You own the cutest golden retriever puppy named Pumpkin. The problem is that you cannot keep Pumpkin because you are moving to a condominium that does not allow pets. You have a picture of Pumpkin in a file called puppy. You decide to prepare an announcement for the sale of Pumpkin. The unformatted announcement is shown in Figure 1-90, and the formatted document is shown in Figure 1-91 on the next page.

unformatted document

PUPPY FOR SALE!

Pumpkin Needs a Home

Pumpkin is a two-month old, purebred, female golden retriever. A playful puppy with a sweet temperament, Pumpkin is current on all her shots. Owner has a three-generation pedigree.

- Owner is moving and must leave Pumpkin behind
- Take home this great family companion for $450

Interested? Please call (607) 555-0909

FIGURE 1-90

Instructions:

1. Change the font size from 10 to 20 by clicking the Font Size box arrow and then clicking 20.
2. If necessary, click the Show/Hide ¶ button on the Standard toolbar to display paragraph marks and spaces.
3. Create the unformatted announcement shown in Figure 1-90. Add the bullets to the list as you type by beginning the first item in the list with an asterisk followed by a space.
4. Save the document on a floppy disk with Puppy Announcement as the file name.
5. Select the headline and body title line. Center them.

(continued)

Creating an Announcement with an Imported Picture from the Web *(continued)*

6. Select the headline. Bold it. Change its font size from 20 to 48. Change its font to Comic Sans MS. If the headline wraps to the next line, adjust the font size so it fits on one line.
7. Select the body title line. Increase its font size from 20 to 36. Bold it.
8. Select the words, great family companion, in the bulleted list. Bold them.
9. Select the word, Please, in the last line of the announcement. Italicize it.
10. Click somewhere in the last line of the announcement. Center it.
11. Import the graphic file called Puppy on the paragraph mark below the headline. The picture is located on the Web page www.scsite.com/wd97/pr1.htm and also on the Data Disk that accompanies this book. Enlarge the picture of the puppy about 25%. If the last line of the announcement moves to another page when you resize the picture, make the picture smaller.
12. Check the spelling of the announcement.
13. Save the announcement again with the same file name.
14. Print the announcement (Figure 1-91).

48-point Comic Sans MS bold font

PUPPY FOR SALE!

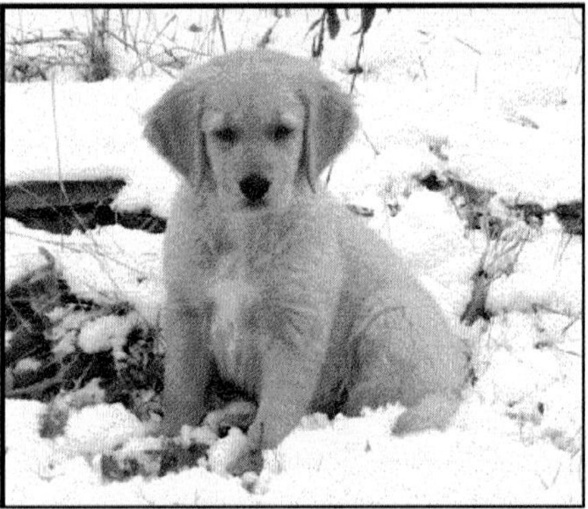

36-point bold

Pumpkin Needs a Home

Pumpkin is a two-month old, purebred, female golden retriever. A playful puppy with a sweet temperament, Pumpkin is current on all her shots. Owner has a three-generation pedigree.

- Owner is moving and must leave Pumpkin behind
- Take home this **great family companion** for $450

Interested? *Please* call (607) 555-0909

FIGURE 1-91

2 Creating an Announcement with Clip Art

Problem: You are the president of The Sports Car Club and you are preparing an announcement inviting new members (Figure 1-92). You decide to use the Sports Car Clip Art from the Clip Gallery supplied with Word.

Instructions:

1. Change the font size from 10 to 20 by clicking the Font Size box arrow and then clicking 20.
2. If it is not already selected, click the Show/Hide ¶ button on the Standard toolbar to display paragraph marks and spaces.
3. Create the announcement shown in Figure 1-92. Enter the document first without the graphic file and unformatted; that is, without any bolding, underlining, italicizing, or centering.
4. Save the document on a floppy disk with Sports Car Club Announcement as the file name.
5. Select the headline and body title line. Center them.
6. Select the headline. Bold it. Change its font size from 20 to 48. Change its font to Arial.
7. Select the body title line. Increase its font size from 20 to 48. Bold it.
8. Select the word, Zoom, in the headline and italicize it.
9. Select the following words one at a time in the paragraph and bold them: road rally, car shows, picnics, contests, and fund-raisers.
10. Click somewhere in the last line of the announcement. Center it.
11. Import the Sports Car clip art file located in the Transportation category of the Clip Gallery below the headline. That is, click Insert on the menu bar, point to Picture, and then click Clip Art. Scroll through the files, select the sports car, and then click the Insert button.

48-point Arial bold font

***Zoom* into Action!**

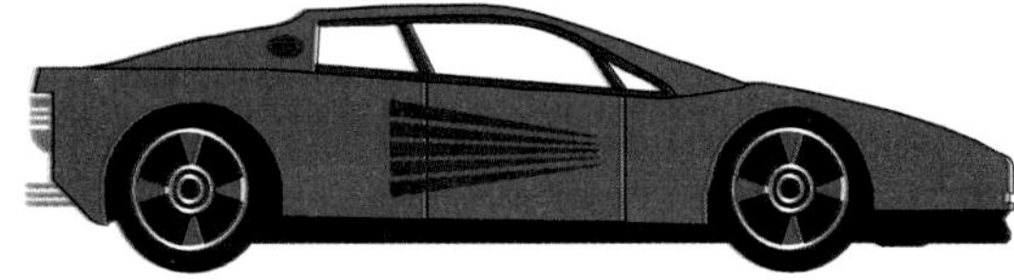

48-point bold

The Sports Car Club

Do you have a sports car? Do you wish you had a sports car? The Sports Car Club is just for you! At our monthly meetings, members share ideas and learn from knowledgeable guest speakers. Exciting events include an annual **road rally**, **car shows**, **picnics**, **contests**, **fund-raisers**, and a variety of members-only social activities.

- Individual membership dues are $30 per year; family membership dues are $50 per year
- Meetings are the first Saturday of each month from 3:00 p.m. to 6:00 p.m.

Call Dave at 555-4235 for all the details!

FIGURE 1-92

(continued)

Creating an Announcement with Clip Art *(continued)*

12. Change the clip art from a floating object to an inline object. To do so, click the picture, then click the Format Picture button on the Picture toolbar. Click the Position tab and then clear the Float over text check box. Click the OK button. Click View on the menu bar and then click Normal to return to normal view.
13. Enlarge the graphic if necessary. If the last line of the announcement moves to a second page, then make the graphic smaller.
14. Check the spelling of the announcement. Save the announcement again with the same file name.
15. Print the announcement.

3 Composing an Announcement from a Draft

Problem: You are the marketing director for Water World Park. You want to prepare an announcement of the park and its activities for the public. You have obtained a picture of one of the park's bears to use in the announcement.

Instructions: You are to create the unformatted announcement shown in Figure 1-93. The picture of the bear is located on Web page www.scsite.com/wd97/pr1.htm and also on the Data Disk that accompanies this book. Then, using the techniques presented in this project, format the announcement. Below are some general guidelines:

1. Center the headline and title.
2. Bullet short lists.
3. Use italics, bold, and underlining to emphasize words or phrases.
4. Change font to emphasize text.
5. Increase font size of headline and title.
6. Increase the size of the picture.

unformatted document

Polar Bear Show!

WATER WORLD PARK

Offering fun and entertainment for the whole family, Water World Park is both an amusement park and a water zoo. We have rides for children and adults of all ages. The water zoo has hundreds of aquariums and pools. Our arena has a water show every hour.

Admission is $15 per adult and $8 for children under 10 years
Park is open from 10:00 a.m. to 8:00 p.m. every day between March 1 and October 31

Call 555-0762 for more information

FIGURE 1-93

Cases and Places

The difficulty of these case studies varies: ◗ are the least difficult; ◗◗ are more difficult; and ◗◗◗ are the most difficult.

1 ◗ You have been assigned the task of preparing an announcement for World Wide Communications. The announcement contains a picture to be imported from the Web. Use the following text and picture: headline – Need a Second Phone Line?; picture located on Web site www.scsite.com/wd97/pr1.htm of a girl on the telephone; body title – World Wide Communications; paragraph text – For our current customers, we are offering a special promotion through the month of October. You can have a second telephone line installed into your home without charge. All you pay is $14 per month thereafter for the second telephone line. What a small price to pay for an available telephone line!; first bulleted item – We guarantee installation within four days of your order; second bulleted item – Select a telephone number of your choice; last line – To order, call us at (888) 555-9898. Use the concepts and techniques presented in this project to create and format this announcement.

2 ◗ You have been assigned the task of preparing an announcement for Buckley School of Business. The announcement contains a clip art image from the Clip Gallery. Use the following text and picture: headline – Registration Begins Today!; picture located in Business category of Clip Gallery; body title – Buckley School of Business; paragraph text – Our school offers the finest education in word processing, spreadsheets, databases, presentation graphics, electronic mail, the Internet, computer programming, systems analysis and design, and much more! We have the latest technology and the highest quality instructors, which enables us to provide a job-placement guarantee to all our graduates; first bulleted item – Classes cost $85 per credit hour and parking is $40 per semester; second bulleted item – Fall classes begin Monday, August 31, at 8:00 a.m.; last line – Call 555-8989 to register today. Use the concepts and techniques presented in this project to create and format this announcement.

3 ◗◗ Your Aunt Ruth, a graduate of Green Grove High School, will be celebrating her fortieth high school reunion this year. She has asked you to prepare an announcement that can be sent to each member of the graduating class. The reunion will feature dinner at Broadway Restaurant, live entertainment by The Bakers Band, and a special guest appearance by Joey Williams, a local comedian. The reunion will be held on Saturday, November 14, at 6:00 p.m. Guests will have the opportunity to reminisce about old times, catch up on current projects, and share future plans. Everyone is encouraged to take part in the food and fun. More information can be obtained by calling Mrs. Betty Travis at (576) 555-2223. Use the concepts and techniques presented in this project to create the announcement. Be sure to include at least two bulleted items in a list and insert an appropriate graphic from the Clip Gallery or the Web.

Cases and Places

4 ▶▶ You have just been hired by Nature Valley, a public nature park, as the marketing director. You decide to put together an announcement for the upcoming open house, which has been scheduled for the weekend of September 14 and 15 from 9:00 a.m. to 7:00 p.m. both days. Admission for the open house is $4 per person. Nature Valley offers breathtaking scenery with abundant, lush vegetation and friendly animals. Guests can take nature walks or hikes on trails; swim or boat in crystal-clear lakes; or fish in rippling rivers. More information can be obtained by calling John Gray at 555-9087. Use the concepts and techniques presented in this project to create the announcement. Be sure to include at least two bulleted items in a list and insert an appropriate graphic from the Clip Gallery or the Web.

5 ▶▶▶ Many organizations, such as schools, libraries, grocery stores, child-care centers, and so on, have a place where announcements are posted on a public bulletin board. Often, so many announcements are displayed that some go unnoticed. Find a posted announcement at one of the above mentioned organizations that you think might be overlooked. Copy the text from the announcement. Using this text, together with the techniques presented in this project, create an announcement that would be more likely to catch a reader's eye. Format the announcement effectively and include a bulleted list and suitable graphic from the Clip Gallery or the Web.

6 ▶▶▶ Both small and large companies advertise on the World Wide Web. Some of these advertisements are written as plain text without any formatting or graphics. Surf the Web for an advertisement that you feel lacks luster. Copy the text from the announcement. Using this text, together with the techniques presented in this project, create an announcement that would be more likely to catch a reader's eye. Format the announcement effectively and include a bulleted list and suitable graphic from the Clip Gallery or the Web.

7 ▶▶▶ Many retail stores post announcements throughout the store to promote new or unique products or products on sale. These announcements are designed to encourage consumers to purchase products they were not even considering when they first entered the store. Visit a local electronics store and select an item you believe could have greater sales with increased in-store advertising. Write the text for a promotional announcement and then, using the techniques presented in this project, create an announcement that could be posted around the store to enhance the sales of the item. Format the announcement effectively and include a bulleted list and suitable graphic from the Clip Gallery or the Web.

Microsoft Word 97

Using Word's Wizards and Templates to Create a Cover Letter and Resume

Objectives:

You will have mastered the material in this project when you can:

- Create a resume using Word's Resume Wizard
- Identify the Word screen in page layout view
- Use styles in a document
- Replace selected text with new text
- Insert a line break
- Use AutoFormat As You Type
- Select a table
- Change the font size of all characters in a table
- Use print preview to view and print a document
- Explain the components of a business letter
- Create a cover letter using Word's letter template
- Zoom a document
- Create an AutoText entry
- Select a paragraph
- Format characters using shortcut keys
- Insert an AutoText entry
- Select a sentence
- Drag and drop selected text
- Indent the left margin of a paragraph
- Use the TAB key to vertically align text
- Spell and grammar check a document at once
- Switch from one open Word document to another
- Close all open Word documents

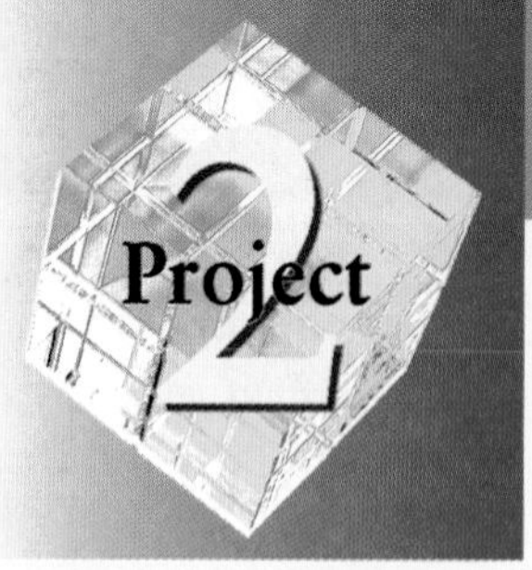

Resume Writing

Keywords Are the Key to Getting Noticed

In many European countries, the art of fine penmanship is one of the qualifications to land a job. In France, for example, job seekers handwrite their applications, and some companies spend as much as $30,000 analyzing the handwriting on these forms.

Not so in the United States. With downsizing affecting corporate human resources' staffs, companies have turned to a high-tech method of screening the volume of resumes. This "electronic applicant tracking" system uses an optical scanner to convert a typed page to electronic text, stores the resume in a database, and then uses artificial intelligence to select certain resumes matching the job qualifications. Thus, job applicants today must write a resume that the scanner can read and the computer will choose from the database.

Optical scanners work best when reading a clean, clear, concise document.

The artificial intelligence software screens the resumes, retrieves those matching keywords in up to 20 categories, and then ranks the selected documents according to the number of matching keyword terms, or *hits*. Thus, your goal is to include as many of these words or phrases as possible when describing your talents and qualifications. To do so, use simple, precise nouns instead of verbs. For example, use the phrase, project manager, instead of managed projects. Common keywords are writer, supervisor, production, fluent, analytical ability, assertive, college graduate, communication skills, organizational skills, creative, customer oriented, detail minded, flexible, industrious, innovative, open minded, results oriented, risk-taker, self-starter, supportive, and team player. Jargon is fine, but do not use abbreviations.

As you begin your job search, you may need two versions of your resume: one that is scannable electronically to send to large corporations, and a second, conventional document similar to the one you will create in this project for smaller companies. Both should have similar content. Each resume should be customized to meet the requirements of a specific job advertisement. The ease with which you can create resumes in Microsoft Word 97 makes it a value tool for the job seeker. The Resume Wizard helps you organize your skills, education, and experience in a format that is appropriate for the type of job you are pursuing. The wizard offers several built-in headings that you can place in any order, and you can add your own headings. The wizard also helps you create a cover letter and send the resume and cover letter to a prospective employer by e-mail or fax.

One researcher estimates that nearly 80 percent of resumes today are never seen by humans once they are scanned into the electronic system. Although this method seems impersonal and cold, unlike the European handwritten application style, it is a valuable step to help you land the job of your dreams.

Microsoft
Word 97

Using Word's Wizards and Templates to Create a Cover Letter and Resume

Case Perspective

Caroline Louise Schmidt has recently graduated from North Carolina University with a Bachelor of Arts degree in Technical Writing and an Associate of Science degree in Computer Technology. Because she now is ready to embark on a full-time career, Caroline decides to prepare a resume to send to prospective employers. She wants the resume to look professional while highlighting her education and experience. Once she prepares her resume, Caroline's next step is to prepare a personalized cover letter to send to each prospective employer. As she reads yesterday's edition of the *Charlotte News*, she locates a classified advertisement for a computer textbook proofreading position at International Markson Press, which sounds like a position suited just for her. Caroline immediately begins writing a cover letter to Mr. Samuel Parker at International Markson Press. In her cover letter, she emphasizes her first-hand experience with both computers and proofreading. As she places her cover letter and resume in the mail, Caroline dreams about a career at International Markson Press.

Caroline created her resume using Word's Resume Wizard, which is a tool designed to assist users in preparing a resume. Then, she composed her cover letter using a Word letter template, which produces a properly formatted business letter.

Introduction

At some time in your professional life, you will prepare a resume along with a personalized cover letter to send to a prospective employer(s). In addition to some personal information, a **resume** usually contains the applicant's educational background and job experience. Because employers review many resumes for each vacant position, you should design your resume carefully so it presents you as the best candidate for the job. You should attach a personalized cover letter to each resume you send. A **cover letter** enables you to elaborate on positive points in your resume; it also provides you with an opportunity to show the potential employer your written communication skills. Thus, it is important that your cover letter is well written and follows proper business letter rules.

Because composing letters and resumes from scratch is a difficult process for many people, Word provides **wizards** and **templates** to assist you in these document preparations. A template is like a blueprint; that is, Word prepares the requested document with text and/or formatting common to all documents of this nature. By asking you several basic questions, Word's wizards prepare and format a document for you based on your responses. Once Word creates a document from either a template or a wizard, you then fill in the blanks or replace prewritten words in the documents. Some wizards and templates are installed with Word; others are on Microsoft's Web page for you to download.

Project Two – Cover Letter and Resume

Project 2 uses Word to produce the cover letter shown in Figure 2-1 and resume shown in Figure 2-2 on the next page. Caroline Louise Schmidt, a recent college graduate, is seeking a full-time position as a computer textbook proofreader with a major publishing firm. In addition to her resume, she sends a personalized cover letter to Mr. Samuel Parker at International Markson Press detailing her work experience.

cover letter

Caroline Louise Schmidt 406 Hill Creek Road Charlotte NC 28215

December 9, 1998

Mr. Samuel Parker
International Markson Press
102 Madison Avenue
Chicago, IL 60606

Dear Mr. Parker:

I am interested in the computer textbook proofreading position you advertised in yesterday's edition of the *Charlotte News*. I have enclosed my resume highlighting my background and feel my accomplishments will be valuable to International Markson Press.

Through my part-time work at the university for the Information Systems Department and my volunteer work for the Tutoring Center, I have first-hand experience with both computers and proofreading. My course of study at North Carolina University has focused heavily on these skills. As shown in the following table, I have obtained exceptional grades in writing and computer courses.

GPA for Writing Courses	4.0/4.0
GPA for Computer Courses	3.8/4.0
Overall GPA	3.9/4.0

Given my extensive course work and experience, I feel I could be a definite asset to your organization. I look forward to hearing from you to schedule an interview and to discuss my career opportunities with International Markson Press.

Sincerely,

Caroline Louise Schmidt

FIGURE 2-1

Document Preparation Steps

Document preparation steps give you an overview of how the cover letter and resume in Figures 2-1 and 2-2 will be developed. The following tasks will be completed in this project:

1. Start Word.
2. Use the Resume Wizard to create a resume.
3. Personalize the resume.
4. View and print the resume in print preview.
5. Save the resume.
6. Use a letter template to create a cover letter.
7. Create an AutoText entry.
8. Type the cover letter using the AutoText entry.
9. Move a sentence in the cover letter.
10. Spell check the cover letter.
11. Save and print the cover letter.
12. Switch to the resume.
13. Spell check and save the resume.

The following pages contain a detailed explanation of each of these tasks.

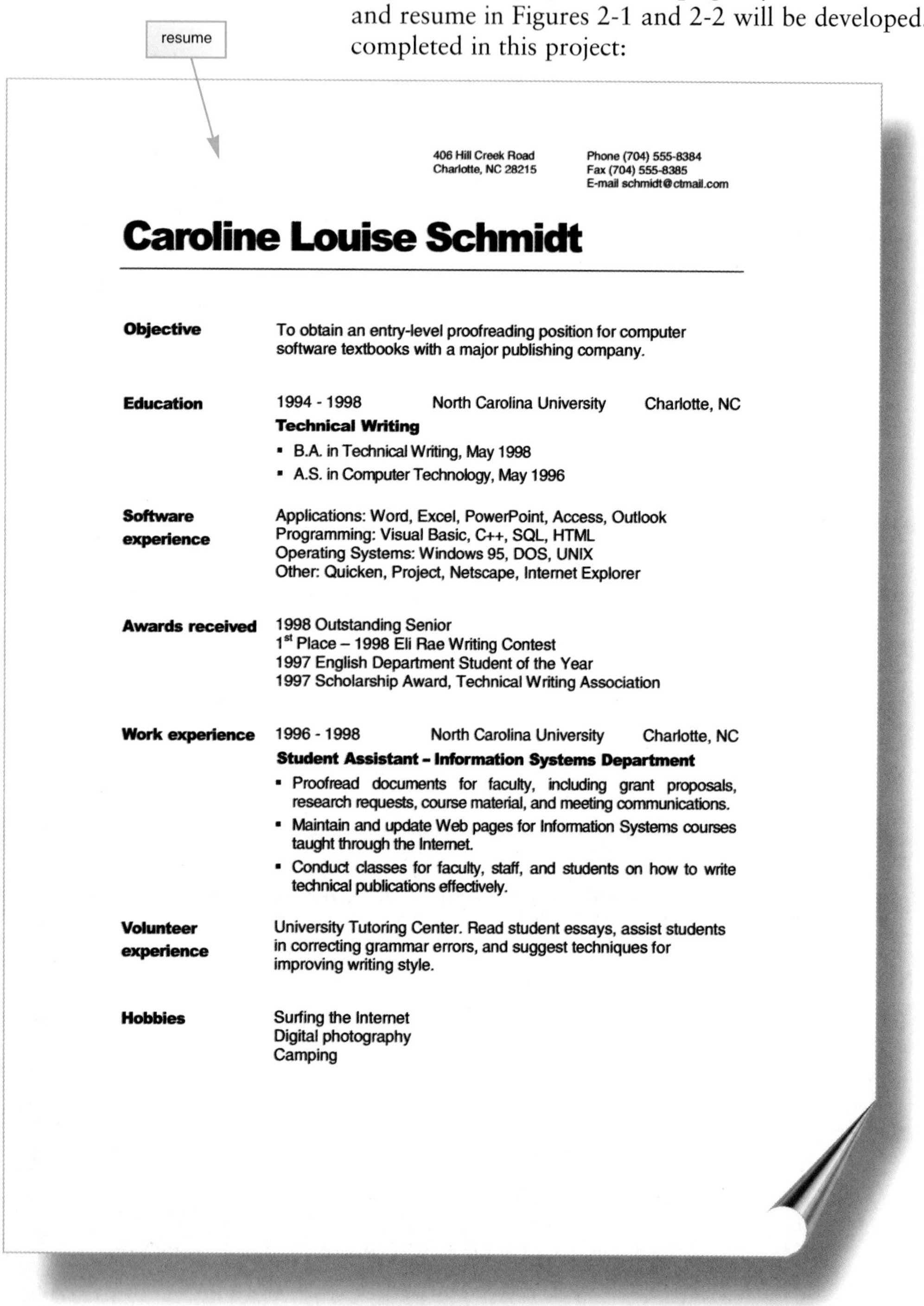

resume

406 Hill Creek Road
Charlotte, NC 28215

Phone (704) 555-8384
Fax (704) 555-8385
E-mail schmidt@ctmail.com

Caroline Louise Schmidt

Objective To obtain an entry-level proofreading position for computer software textbooks with a major publishing company.

Education 1994 - 1998 North Carolina University Charlotte, NC
Technical Writing
- B.A. in Technical Writing, May 1998
- A.S. in Computer Technology, May 1996

Software experience
Applications: Word, Excel, PowerPoint, Access, Outlook
Programming: Visual Basic, C++, SQL, HTML
Operating Systems: Windows 95, DOS, UNIX
Other: Quicken, Project, Netscape, Internet Explorer

Awards received
1998 Outstanding Senior
1st Place – 1998 Eli Rae Writing Contest
1997 English Department Student of the Year
1997 Scholarship Award, Technical Writing Association

Work experience 1996 - 1998 North Carolina University Charlotte, NC
Student Assistant - Information Systems Department
- Proofread documents for faculty, including grant proposals, research requests, course material, and meeting communications.
- Maintain and update Web pages for Information Systems courses taught through the Internet.
- Conduct classes for faculty, staff, and students on how to write technical publications effectively.

Volunteer experience University Tutoring Center. Read student essays, assist students in correcting grammar errors, and suggest techniques for improving writing style.

Hobbies
Surfing the Internet
Digital photography
Camping

FIGURE 2-2

Using Word's Resume Wizard to Create a Resume

You can type a resume from scratch into a blank document window, or you can use a wizard and let Word format the resume with appropriate headings and spacing. Then, you can customize the resulting resume by filling in the blanks or selecting and replacing text. Perform the following steps to create a resume using the **Resume Wizard**.

Steps To Create a Resume Using Word's Resume Wizard

1 Click the Start button on the taskbar and then click New Office Document. If necessary, click the Other Documents tab when the New Office Document dialog box first opens. Click the Resume Wizard icon.

Office displays several wizard and template icons in the Other Documents sheet in the New Office Document dialog box (Figure 2-3). Icons without the word, wizard, below them are templates. If you click an icon in the Other Documents sheet, a preview of the resulting document displays in the Preview area; thus, the Resume Wizard is selected and a preview of a resume displays in the Preview area.

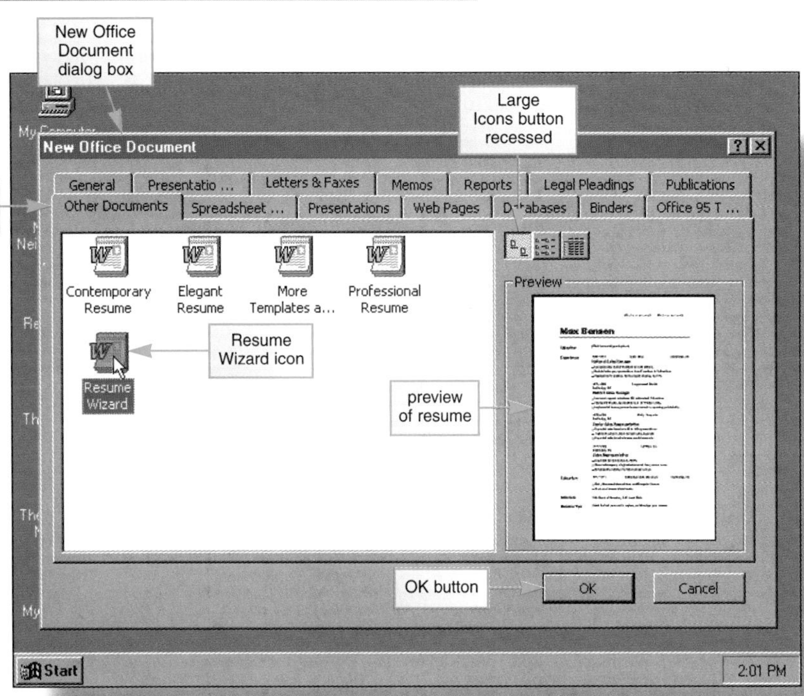

FIGURE 2-3

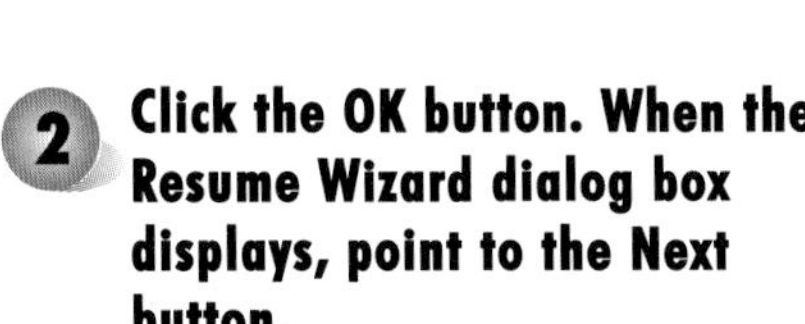

2 Click the OK button. When the Resume Wizard dialog box displays, point to the Next button.

After a few seconds, Word displays the Start panel *of the* Resume Wizard dialog box, *informing you the Resume Wizard has started (Figure 2-4). Notice this dialog box has an Office Assistant button you can click to obtain help while using this wizard. Depending on your system, the Word screen may or may not be maximized behind the Resume Wizard dialog box.*

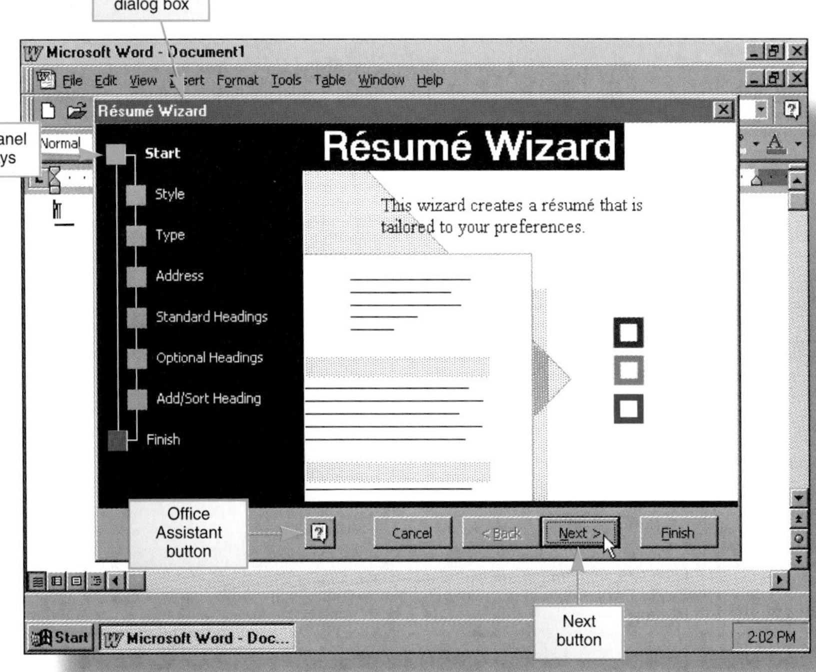

FIGURE 2-4

3 **Click the Next button. When the Style panel displays in the Resume Wizard dialog box, click Professional, if necessary, and then point to the Next button.**

Word displays the ***Style panel*** *in the Resume Wizard dialog box, requesting the style of your resume (Figure 2-5). Word provides three* ***styles****, or* ***families****, of wizards and templates: Professional, Contemporary, and Elegant. A preview of each style resume displays below each respective option button in this panel.*

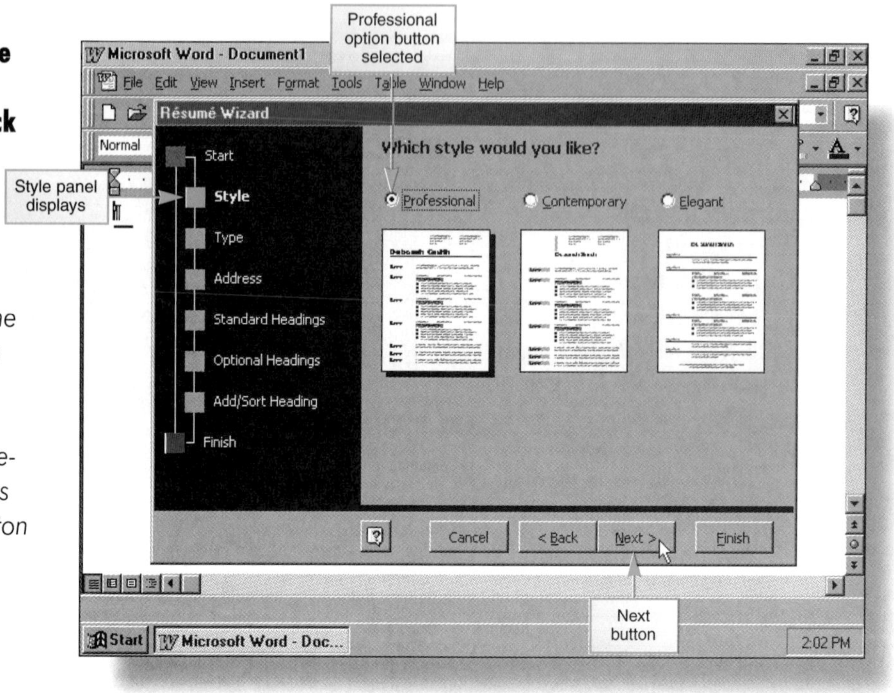

FIGURE 2-5

4 **Click the Next button. When the Type panel displays in the Resume Wizard dialog box, click Entry-level resume, if necessary, and then point to the Next button.**

Word displays the ***Type panel*** *in the Resume Wizard dialog box, asking for the type of resume that you want to create (Figure 2-6).*

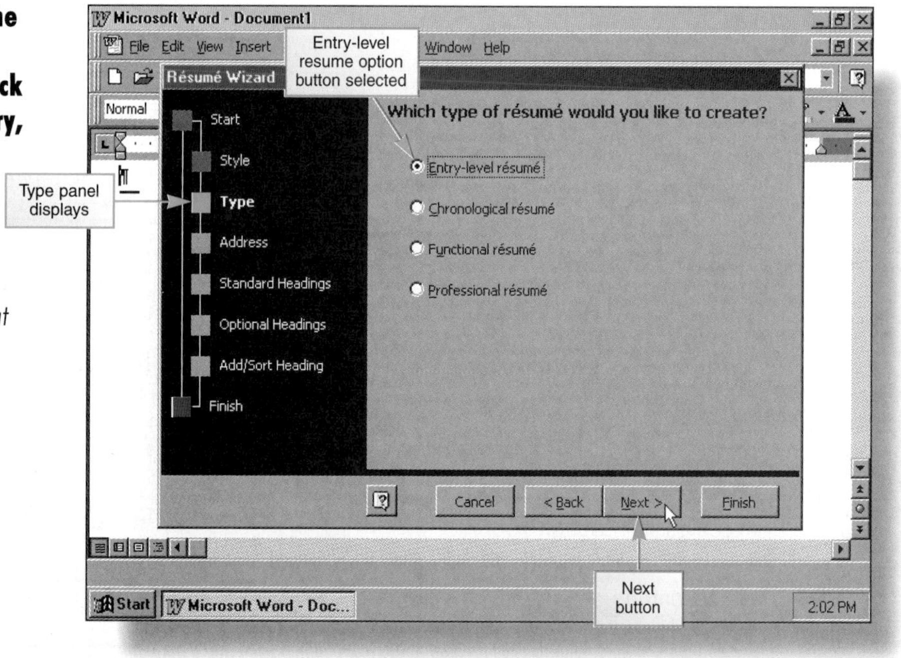

FIGURE 2-6

5 **Click the Next button.**

Word displays the **Address panel** *in the Resume Wizard dialog box, with the current name selected (Figure 2-7). The name displayed and selected in your Name text box will be different, depending on the name of the last person using the Resume Wizard.*

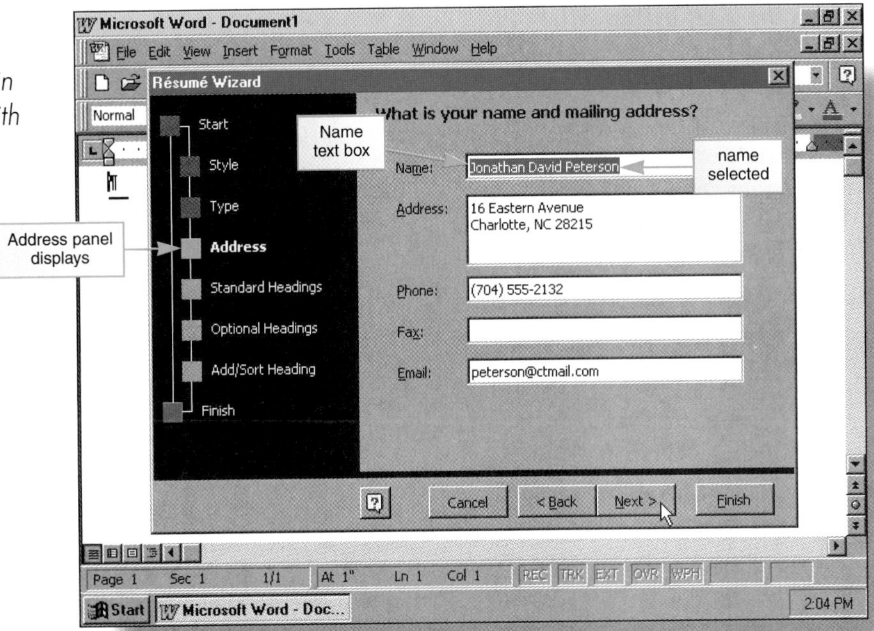

FIGURE 2-7

6 **With the name in the Name text box selected, type** `Caroline Louise Schmidt` **and then press the TAB key to advance to the Address text box. Type** `406 Hill Creek Road` **and then press the ENTER key. Type** `Charlotte, NC 28215` **and then press the TAB key to advance to the Phone text box. Type** `(704) 555-8384` **and then press the TAB key to advance to the Fax text box. Type** `(704) 555-8385` **and then press the TAB key to advance to the Email text box. Type** `schmidt@ctmail.com` **and then point to the Next button.**

The personal information is entered in the Address panel in the Resume Wizard dialog box (Figure 2-8). Notice that as you typed the name, Caroline Louise Schmidt, it automatically replaced the selected text in the Name text box. When you want to replace text in Word, select the text to be removed and then type the desired text.

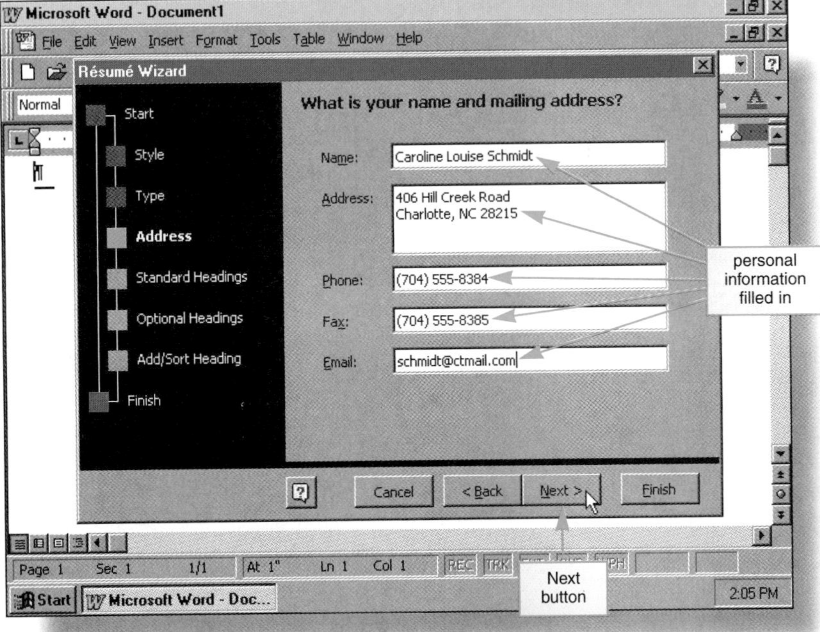

FIGURE 2-8

7 **Click the Next button. When the Standard Headings panel displays in the Resume Wizard dialog box, if necessary, click Interests and activities, Languages, and References to remove the check marks to clear the options. All other check boxes should be selected. Point to the Next button.**

*Word displays the **Standard Headings panel** in the Resume Wizard dialog box, which requests the headings you want on your resume (Figure 2-9). You want all headings, except for these three: Interests and activities, Languages, and References.*

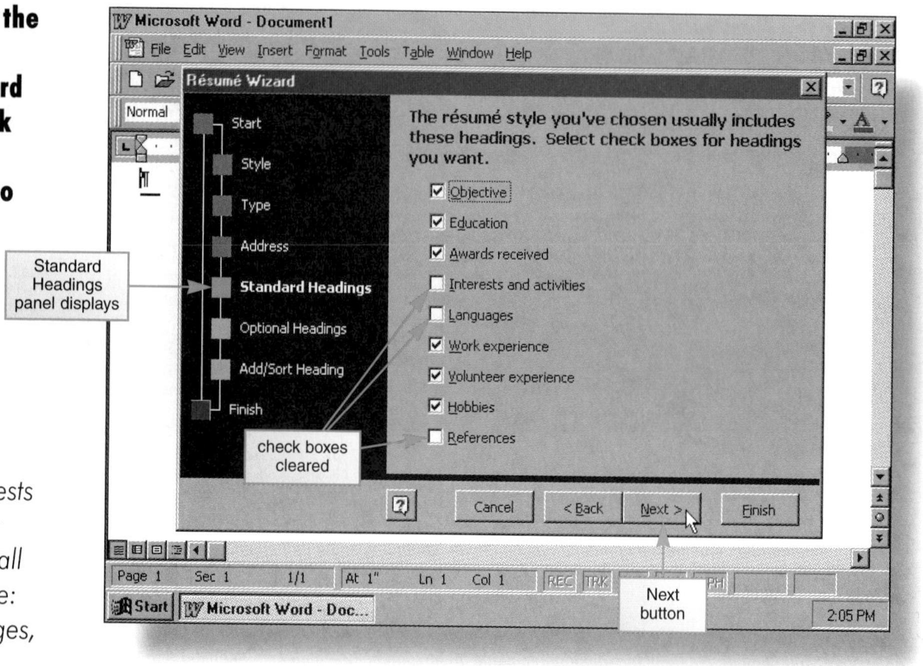

FIGURE 2-9

8 **Click the Next button. Point to the Next button in the Optional Headings panel in the Resume Wizard dialog box.**

*Word displays the **Optional Headings panel** in the Resume Wizard dialog box, which allows you to choose additional headings for your resume (Figure 2-10). All of these check boxes should be cleared because none of these headings is required on your resume.*

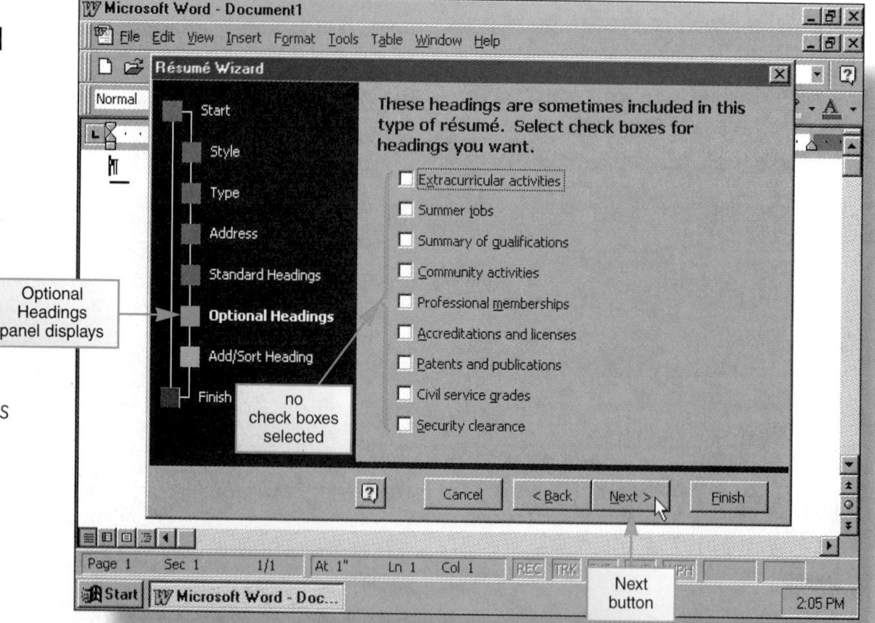

FIGURE 2-10

9 **Click the Next button. When the Add/Sort Heading panel displays in the Resume Wizard dialog box, type** `Software experience` **in the additional headings text box. Point to the Add button.**

Word displays the **Add/Sort Heading panel** *in the Resume Wizard dialog box, which allows you to enter any additional headings you want on your resume (Figure 2-11).*

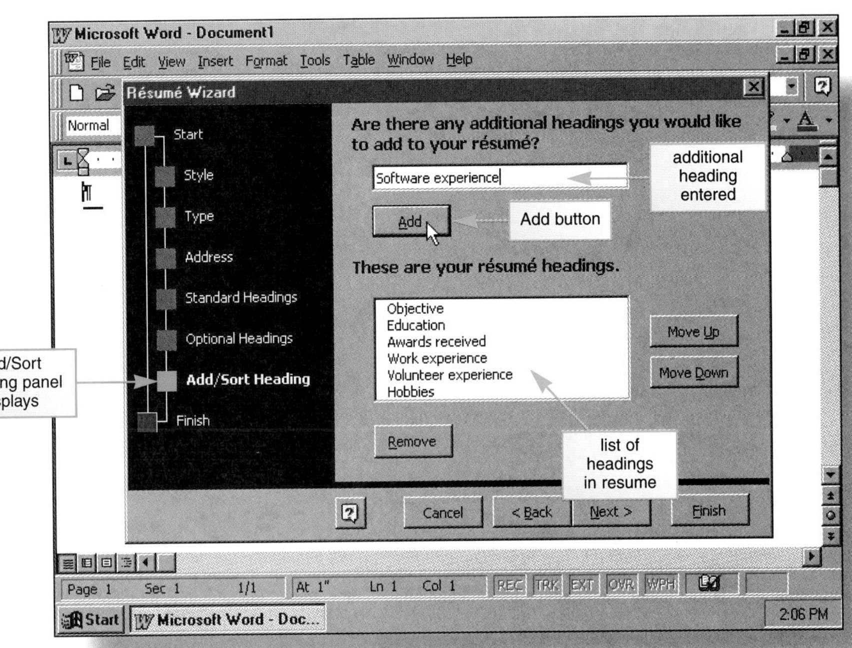

FIGURE 2-11

10 **Click the Add button. Scroll to the bottom of the list of resume headings and then click Software experience. Point to the Move Up button.**

*The Software experience heading is selected (Figure 2-12). You can rearrange the order of the headings on your resume by selecting a heading and then clicking the appropriate button (***Move Up button** *or* **Move Down button***). The headings will display on the resume in the order the names are displayed in this dialog box.*

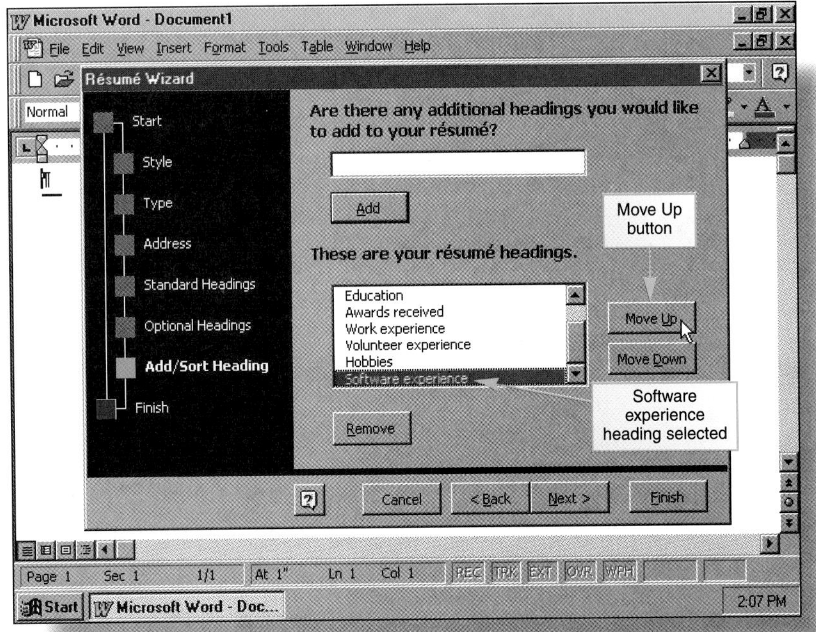

FIGURE 2-12

11 **Click the Move Up button four times.**

Word moves the heading, Software experience, up above the Awards received heading (Figure 2-13).

12 **If the last person using the Resume Wizard added headings, you may have some additional unwanted headings. Your heading list should be as follows: Objective, Education, Software experience, Awards received, Work experience, Volunteer experience, and Hobbies. If you have an additional heading(s), click the unwanted heading and then click the Remove button in the Add/Sort Heading panel.**

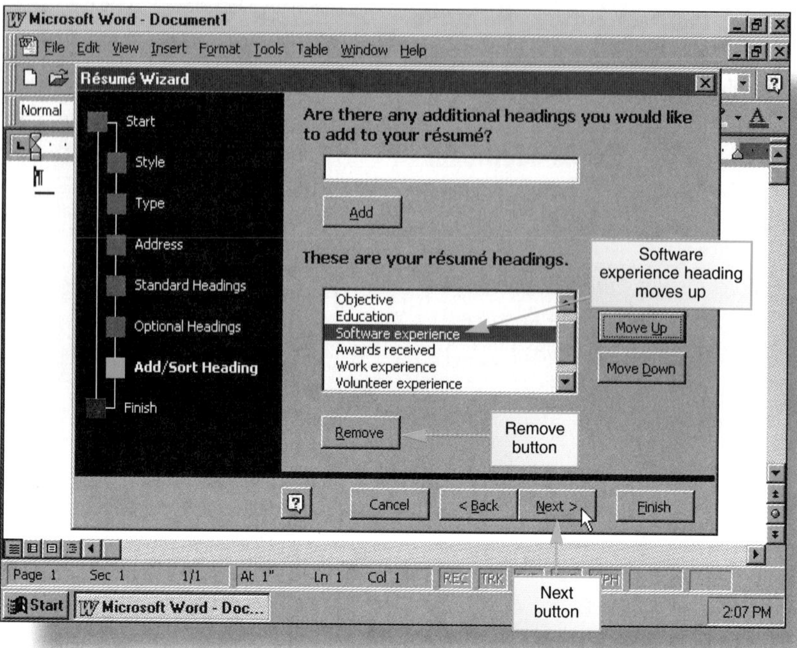

FIGURE 2-13

13 **Click the Next button. When the Finish panel displays in the Resume Wizard dialog box, point to the Finish button.**

Word displays the Finish panel in the Resume Wizard dialog box (Figure 2-14).

FIGURE 2-14

14 **Click the Finish button. If the Office Assistant displays, click its Cancel button.**

Word creates an entry-level professional style resume layout for you (Figure 2-15). You are to personalize the resume as indicated.

15 **If the Word screen is not maximized, double-click its title bar to maximize it.**

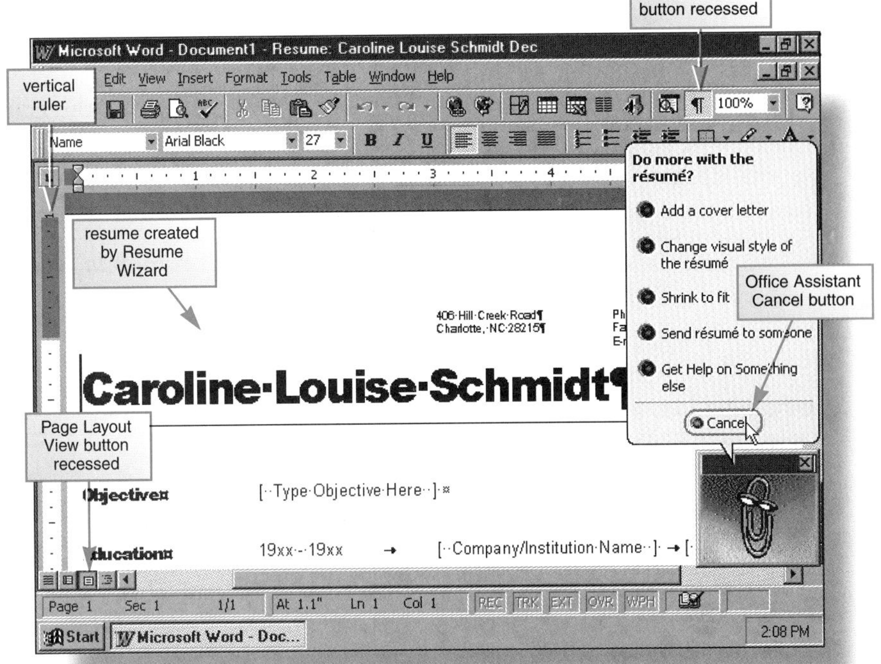

FIGURE 2-15

OtherWays

1. Click Start a New Document button on Microsoft Office Shortcut Bar, click Other Documents tab, double-click Resume Wizard icon
2. In Microsoft Word, on File menu click New, click Other Documents tab, double-click Resume Wizard icon

When you create a resume using the Resume Wizard, you can click the Back button in any panel of the Resume Wizard dialog box to change any of the previous options you selected. To exit the Resume Wizard and return to the document window without creating the resume, click the Cancel button in any panel of the Resume Wizard dialog box.

In addition to the Resume Wizard, Word provides many other wizards to assist you in creating documents: agenda for a meeting, award certificate, calendar, envelope, fax cover sheet, legal pleading, letter, mailing label, memorandum, newsletter, table, and Web page. These wizards either are installed with Word or may be downloaded from Microsoft's Web page.

When Word displays the resume in the document window, it switches from **normal view** to **page layout view**. The announcement you created in Project 1 was in normal view. In both normal and page layout views, you can type and edit text. The difference is that page layout view shows you exactly how the printed page will look.

You can tell you are in page layout view by looking at the Word screen (Figure 2-15). Notice that in page layout view, the **Page Layout View button** at the bottom of the Word screen is recessed. Also, notice that a **vertical ruler** now displays at the left edge of the document window, in addition to the horizontal ruler at the top of the window. In page layout view, the entire piece of paper is positioned in the document window, showing precisely the positioning of the text and margins on the printed page.

To see the entire resume created by the Resume Wizard, you should print the resume.

More About Resumes

Think of your resume as an advertisement about you. A good advertisement (and resume) doesn't tout negatives; rather it promotes positives. A resume should be accurate and truthful. It should also be up-to-date and customized for each job advertisement. List qualifications from most relevant to least, and be concise.

TO PRINT THE RESUME CREATED BY THE RESUME WIZARD

Step 1: Ready the printer and then click the Print button on the Standard toolbar.
Step 2: When the printer stops, retrieve the hard copy resume from the printer.

The printed resume is shown in Figure 2-16.

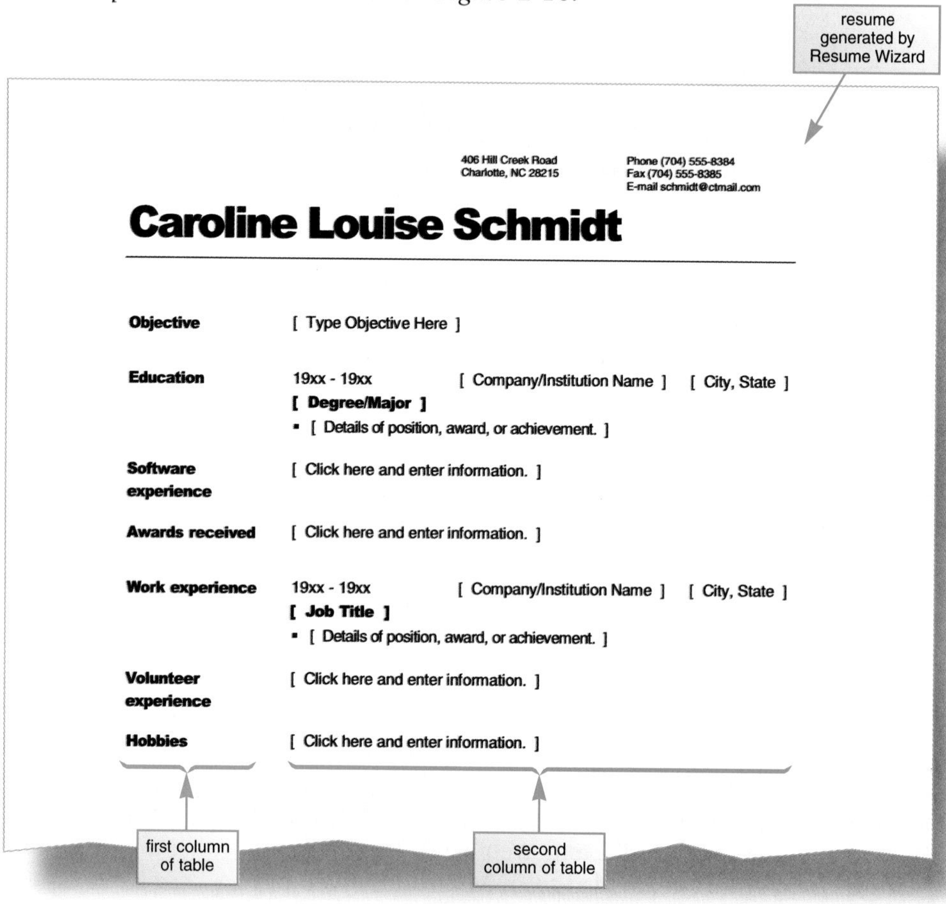

> **More About Resume Contents**
>
> Leave the following items off a resume: social security number, marital status, age, height, weight, gender, physical appearance, health, citizenship, references, reference of references, previous pay rates, reasons for leaving a prior job, current date, and high school information (if you are a college graduate).

resume generated by Resume Wizard

406 Hill Creek Road
Charlotte, NC 28215

Phone (704) 555-8384
Fax (704) 555-8385
E-mail schmidt@ctmail.com

Caroline Louise Schmidt

Objective	[Type Objective Here]
Education	19xx - 19xx [Company/Institution Name] [City, State] **[Degree/Major]** ▪ [Details of position, award, or achievement.]
Software experience	[Click here and enter information.]
Awards received	[Click here and enter information.]
Work experience	19xx - 19xx [Company/Institution Name] [City, State] **[Job Title]** ▪ [Details of position, award, or achievement.]
Volunteer experience	[Click here and enter information.]
Hobbies	[Click here and enter information.]

first column of table

second column of table

FIGURE 2-16

Personalizing the Resume

The next step is to **personalize the resume.** Where Word has indicated, you type the objective, education, software experience, awards received, work experience, volunteer experience, and hobbies next to the respective headings. In the education and work experience sections, you select and replace text to customize these sections. The following pages show how to personalize the resume generated by the Resume Wizard.

Displaying Nonprinting Characters

As discussed in Project 1, it is helpful to display **nonprinting characters** that indicate where in the document you pressed the ENTER key and SPACEBAR. If nonprinting characters do not already display on your screen, follow this step to display them.

TO DISPLAY NONPRINTING CHARACTERS

Step 1: If necessary, click the Show/Hide ¶ button on the Standard toolbar.

Word displays nonprinting characters in the document window, and the Show/Hide ¶ button on the Standard toolbar is recessed (Figure 2-15 on page WD 2.13).

Tables

When the Resume Wizard prepares a resume, it arranges the body of the resume as a table. A Word **table** is a collection of rows and columns. The section headings (Objective, Education, Software experience, Awards received, Work experience, Volunteer experience, and Hobbies) are placed in the first column of the table; and the detail for each of these sections is placed in the second column of the table (Figure 2-16). Thus, this table contains two columns. It also contains seven rows – one row for each section. To see clearly the rows and columns in a Word table, some users prefer to show gridlines. **Gridlines** are nonprinting characters; that is, they do not print in a hard copy. If you want to display gridlines in a table, position the insertion point somewhere in the table, click Table on the menu bar, and then click **Show Gridlines**. As illustrated in Figure 2-17, gridlines help identify the rows and columns in a table. The intersection of a row and a column is called a **cell**, and cells are filled with text. Each cell has an **end-of-cell mark**, which is another nonprinting character used to select and format cells. If you want to hide the gridlines, click somewhere in the table, click Table on the menu bar, and then click **Hide Gridlines**. Tables are discussed in more depth in a later project.

To select a single cell in a table, click the left of the cell. To select an entire row, click to the left of the row. To select an entire column, click the column's top border. To add a row or column to the middle of a table, select the row below or column to the right, right-click the selection, and then click Insert Row or Insert Column.

Styles

When you use a wizard to create a document, Word formats the document using styles. A **style** is a customized format applied to characters or paragraphs. The Style box on the Formatting toolbar displays the name of the style associated with the location of the insertion point. You can identify many of the characteristics assigned to a style by looking at the Formatting toolbar. In Figure 2-17, the insertion point is in a paragraph formatted with the Name style, which uses the 27-point Arial Black font for the characters.

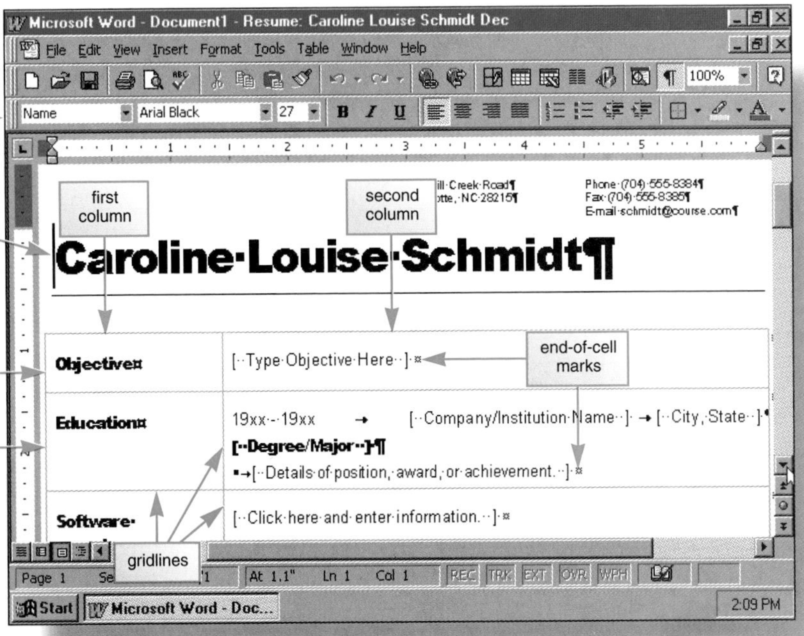

FIGURE 2-17

If you click the Style box arrow on the Formatting toolbar, the list of styles associated with the current document displays. Paragraph styles affect an entire paragraph, whereas character styles affect only selected characters. In the Style list, **paragraph style** names are followed by a proofreader's paragraph mark (¶), and **character style** names are followed by a bold underlined letter a (**a**).

More About Character Size

To adjust the size of the characters on the screen, you can increase or decrease the zoom percentage by clicking the Zoom box arrow on the Standard toolbar and then selecting the desired percentage. Zooming a document has no effect on the printed characters.

You can change a style applied to text. You also may select the appropriate style from the Style list box before entering the text so the text you type will be formatted according to the selected style.

Inserting a Blank Line above a Paragraph

The first step in formatting the resume is to insert a blank line between the e-mail address and the name. These two lines are too close to one another. Pressing the ENTER key will insert a 27-point blank line, which is too large. Perform the following step to insert a 12-point blank line above a paragraph.

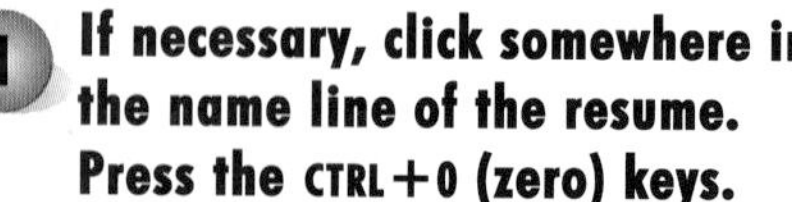

Steps To Insert a Blank Line above a Paragraph

1. **If necessary, click somewhere in the name line of the resume. Press the CTRL+0 (zero) keys.**

Word inserts a blank line above the name in the resume (Figure 2-18). The shortcut CTRL+0 is a **toggle**; *that is, the first time you press it, Word inserts a blank line, and the second time you press it, Word removes the blank line.*

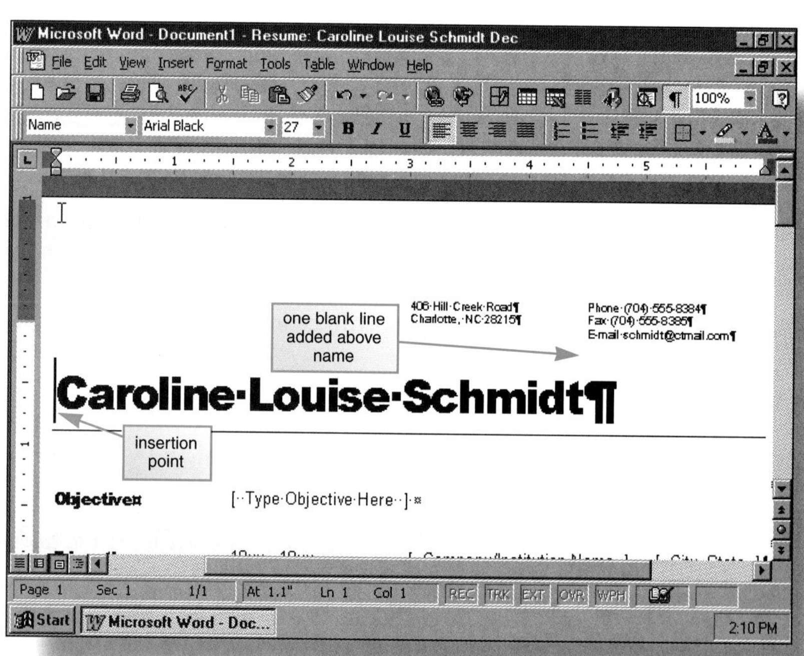

FIGURE 2-18

Other Ways

1. Right-click paragraph, click Paragraph on shortcut menu, click Indents and Spacing tab, type 12 in Spacing Before text box, click OK button
2. On Format menu click Paragraph, click Indents and Spacing tab, type 12 in Spacing Before text box, click OK button

Selecting and Replacing Text

The next step in personalizing the resume is to select the placeholder text that the Resume Wizard inserted into the resume and replace it with the personal information. The first heading on the resume is the objective. You enter the objective where the Resume Wizard inserted the words, Type Objective Here, which is called **placeholder text**. To do this, click the placeholder text, Type Objective Here, to select it. Then, you type the objective. As soon as you begin typing, the selected placeholder text is deleted; thus, you do not have to delete the selection before you begin typing. Perform the following steps to enter the objective into the resume.

Steps To Select and Replace Placeholder Text

1 **Click the placeholder text, Type Objective Here.**

Word highlights the placeholder text in the resume (Figure 2-19). Notice the new style is Objective in the Style box on the Formatting toolbar. The Objective style uses the 10-point Arial font for characters.

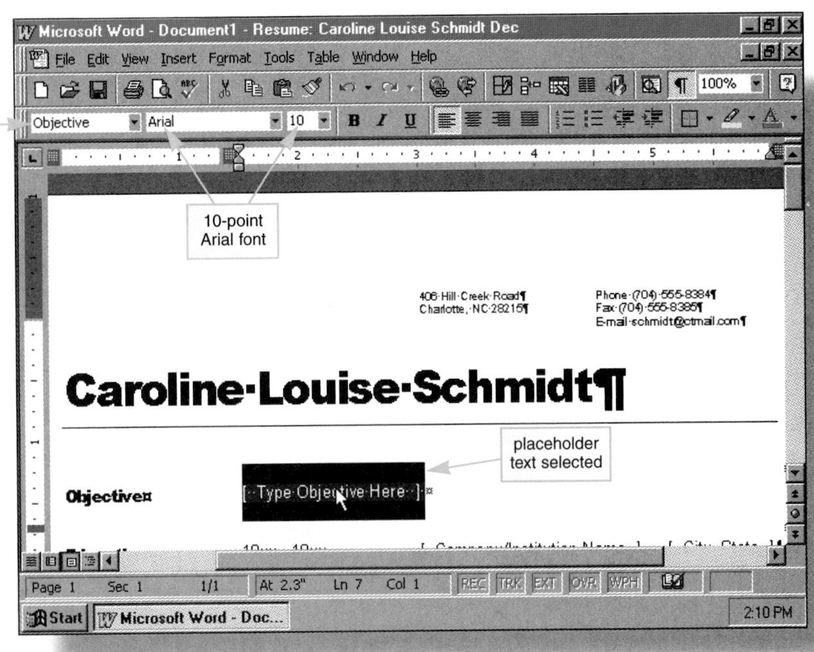

FIGURE 2-19

2 **Type** `To obtain an entry-level proofreading position for computer software textbooks with a major publishing company.`

Word replaces the highlighted placeholder text, Type Objective Here, with the objective you type (Figure 2-20). Your document may wordwrap on a different word depending on the type of printer you are using.

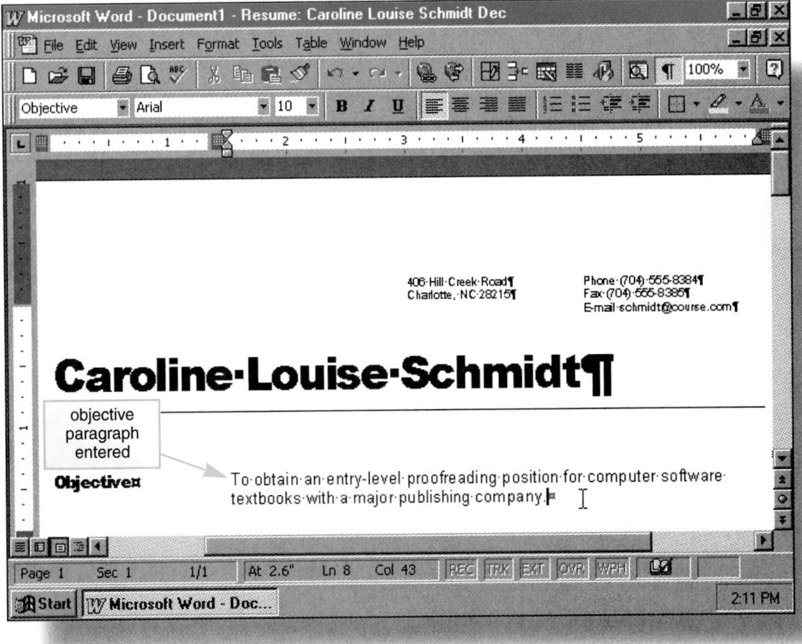

FIGURE 2-20

The next step in personalizing the resume is to replace the Wizard's words and phrases in the education section of the resume with your own words and phrases as shown in the steps on the next page.

To Select and Replace Resume Wizard Supplied Text

1 **If necessary, scroll down to display the entire education section of the resume. Drag through the xx in the first 19xx in the education section.**

Word selects the xx in the first year (Figure 2-21).

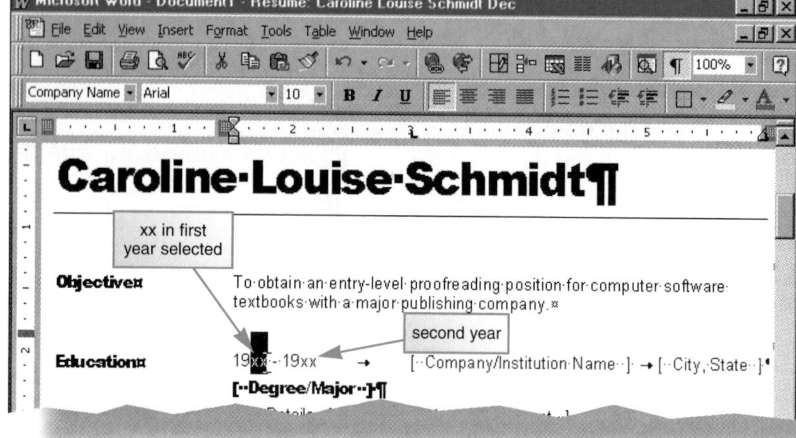

FIGURE 2-21

2 **Type** 94 **and then drag through the xx in the second year in the education section. Type** 98 **and then click the placeholder text, Company/Institution Name.**

Word highlights the placeholder text, Company/Institution Name (Figure 2-22). Notice the years now display as 1994 - 1998 in the education section.

FIGURE 2-22

3 **Type** North Carolina University **and then click the placeholder text, City, State. Type** Charlotte, NC **and then click the placeholder text, Degree/Major. Type** Technical Writing **and then click the placeholder text, Details of position, award, or achievement. Type** B.A. in Technical Writing, May 1998 **and then press the ENTER key. Type** A.S. in Computer Technology, May 1996 **as the second item in the list.**

The university name, city, state, major and degrees are entered (Figure 2-23).

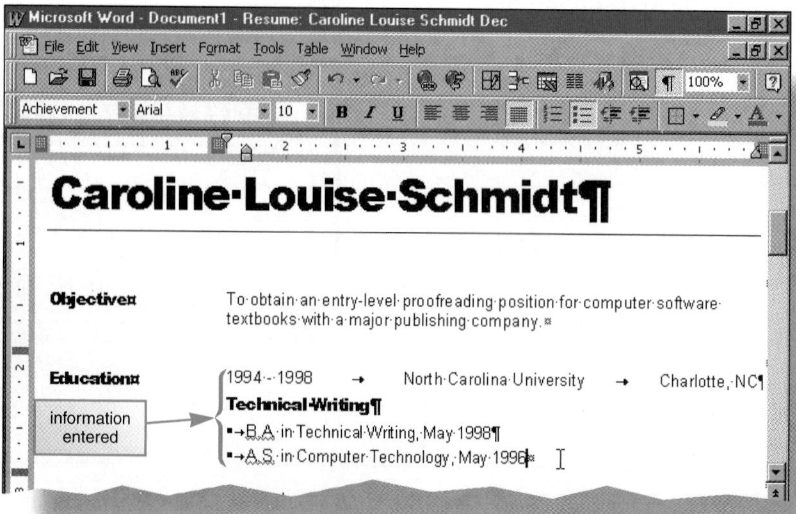

FIGURE 2-23

Entering a Line Break

The next step in personalizing the resume is to enter the software experience section. The style used for the characters in the software experience section is the same as for the objective section, that is, 10-point Arial font. A paragraph formatting characteristic of the Objective style is that when you press the ENTER key, the insertion point advances downward at least 11 points, which leaves nearly an entire blank line between each paragraph. Because you want the lines within the software experience section to be close to each other, you will not press the ENTER key between each type of software experience. Instead, you will create a **line break**, which advances the insertion point to the beginning of the next physical line – ignoring any paragraph formatting instructions. Perform the following steps to enter the software experience section using a line break, instead of a paragraph break, between each line.

More About Styles

To apply a different style to a paragraph, click the paragraph, click the Style box arrow on the Formatting toolbar, and then click the desired paragraph style. To apply a different character style, select the characters, click the Style box arrow on the Formatting toolbar, and then click the desired character style.

Steps To Enter a Line Break

1 **If necessary, scroll down to display the software experience section of the resume. In the software experience section, click the placeholder text, Click here and enter information. Type** `Applications: Word, Excel, PowerPoint, Access, Outlook` **and then press the SHIFT+ENTER keys.**

Word inserts a line break character after the software product names and moves the insertion point to the beginning of the next physical line (Figure 2-24). Because the ENTER key would create a new paragraph and advance the insertion point down nearly two lines due to the paragraph formatting created by the Resume Wizard, you do not want to create a new paragraph. Thus, you enter a line break to start a new line. The line break character is a nonprinting character that displays on the screen each time you create a line break.

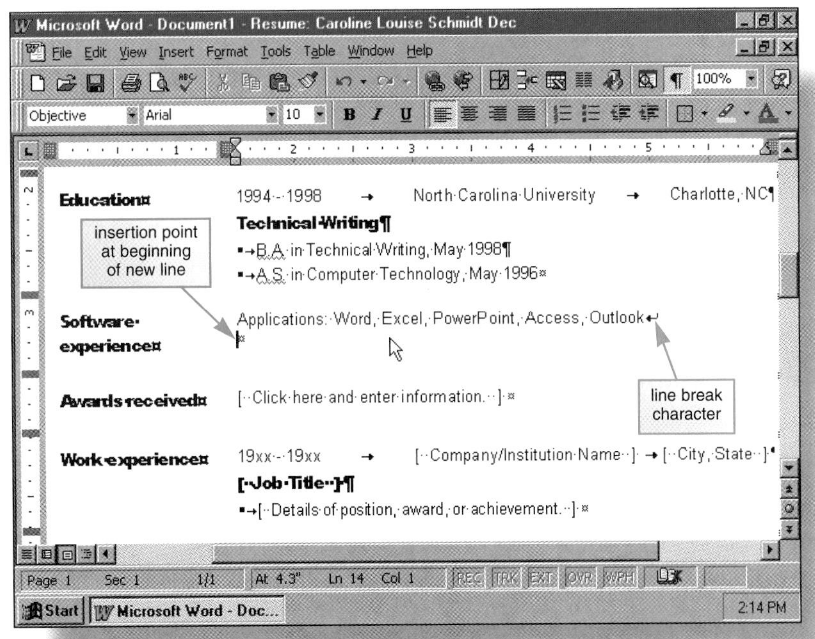

FIGURE 2-24

2 **Type** `Programming: Visual Basic, C++, SQL, HTML` **and then press the SHIFT+ENTER keys. Type** `Operating Systems: Windows 95, DOS, UNIX` **and then press the SHIFT+ENTER keys. Type** `Other: Quicken, Project, Netscape, Internet Explorer` **as the other software experience.**

The software experience section is entered (Figure 2-25).

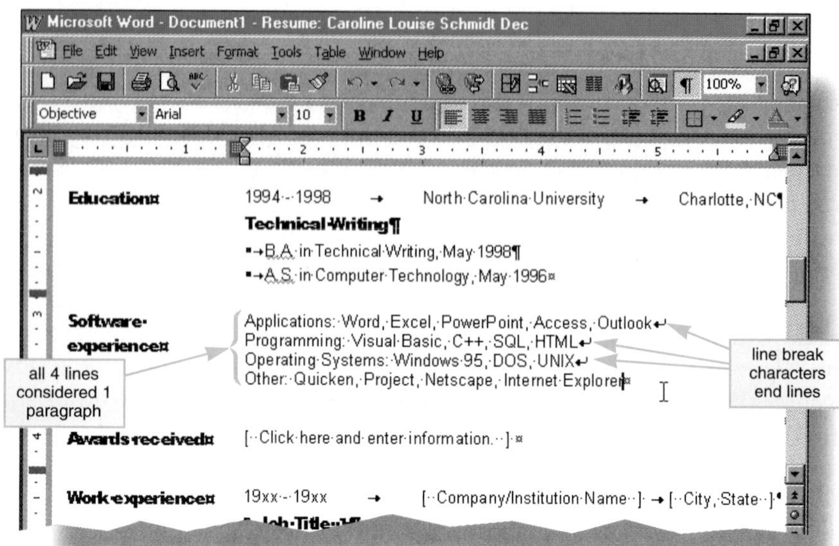

FIGURE 2-25

More *About* **As You Type**

Word has other As You Type features. For example, teh changes to the when you press the SPACEBAR. You can also add special symbols to your writing. For example, typing :) changes to ☺ when you press the SPACEBAR. To see a complete list, click Tools on the menu bar, click AutoCorrect, and then click the AutoCorrect tab.

AutoFormat As You Type

As you type text into a document, Word automatically formats it for you. Table 2-1 summarizes the types of AutoFormats available and their results. For the AutoFormat As You Type feature to work, it must be on. To check if AutoFormat is enabled, click Tools on the menu bar, click AutoCorrect, click the AutoFormat As You Type tab, select the appropriate check boxes, and then click the OK button.

Table 2-1

ENTRY	WORD AUTOFORMATTING	EXAMPLE
Number followed by a period, hyphen, or right parenthesis and then a space or tab followed by text	Creates a numbered list when you press the ENTER key	1. Numbered lists 2. are easy to 3. create with Word
Asterisk, hyphen, or dash and then a space or tab followed by text	Creates a bulleted list when you press the ENTER key	• Bulleted lists • make items • stand out
Three underscores, equal signs, or dashes and then press the ENTER key	Creates a border above the paragraph	Underscores converted to a solid line
Fraction and then a space or hyphen	Converts the entry to a fraction-like notation	½
Ordinal and then a space or hyphen	Makes the ordinal a superscript	2nd
Web address	Formats it as a hyperlink	http://www.scseries.com
Two hyphens followed by text	Converts hyphens to an em dash	Em dash – two hyphens

In the awards received section of the resume, you use two of Word's AutoFormat As You Type features, as shown in the following steps.

To AutoFormat As You Type

1 **If necessary, scroll down to display the awards received section of the resume. Click the placeholder text, Click here and enter information. Type** `1998 Outstanding Senior` **and then press the SHIFT+ENTER keys. Type** `1st` **as the beginning of the second award.**

The text and ordinal are entered (Figure 2-26).

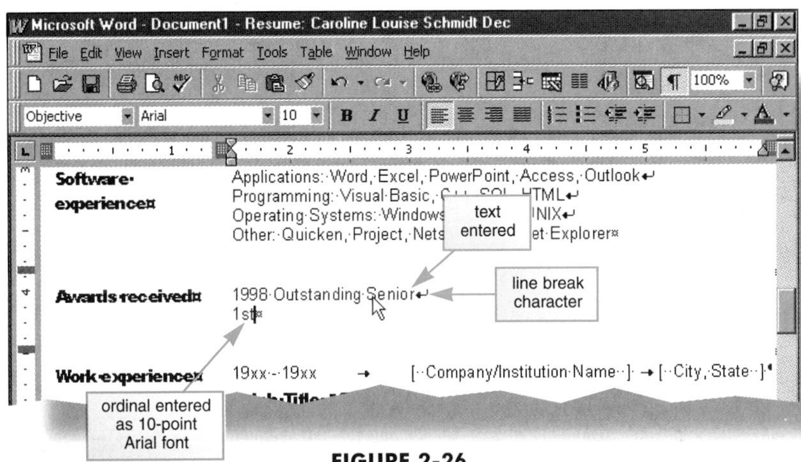

FIGURE 2-26

2 **Press the SPACEBAR. Type** `Place` **and then press the SPACEBAR. Type two hyphens (--).**

Word formats the ordinal as a superscript (Figure 2-27).

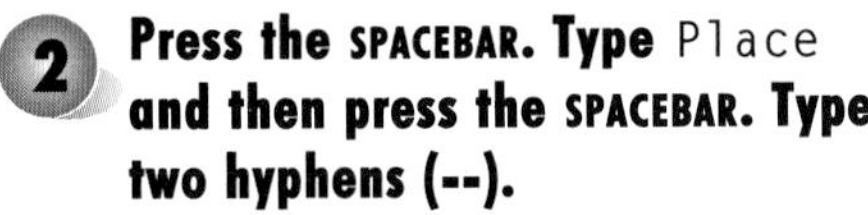

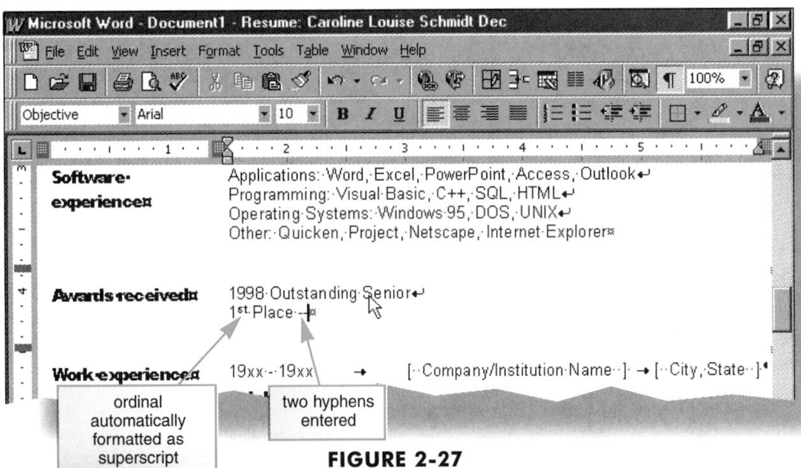

FIGURE 2-27

3 **Press the SPACEBAR. Type** `1998 Eli Rae Writing Contest` **and then press the SHIFT+ENTER keys. Type** `1997 English Department Student of the Year` **and then press the SHIFT+ENTER keys. Type** `1997 Scholarship Award, Technical Writing Association` **as the last award in the list.**

Word converts the two hyphens to an em dash (Figure 2-28). The awards received section is complete.

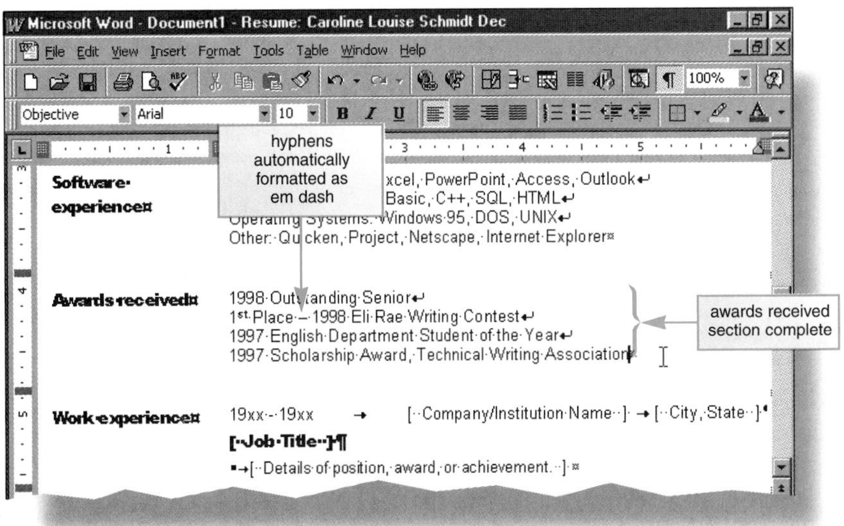

FIGURE 2-28

If, for some reason, you do not want Word to AutoFormat As You Type, you can turn off this feature. To do this, click Tools on the menu bar, click AutoCorrect, click the AutoFormat As You Type tab, turn off the check boxes, and then click the OK button.

Enter the remaining text for the resume as described in the following steps.

TO ENTER THE REMAINING SECTIONS OF THE RESUME

More About References

Do not state "References Available Upon Request" on your resume; nor should you list references on the resume. Employers assume you will give references, if asked, and this information simply clutters a resume. Often you are asked to list references on your application. Be sure to give your references a copy of your resume.

Step 1: If necessary, scroll down to display the work experience section of the resume. Drag through the xx in the first 19xx in the work experience section, type `96` and then drag through the xx in the second year. Type `98` as the year.

Step 2: Click the placeholder text, Company/Institution Name. Type `North Carolina University` as the college.

Step 3: Click the placeholder text, City, State. Type `Charlotte, NC` as the city and state.

Step 4: Click the placeholder text, Job Title. Type `Student Assistant – Information Systems Department` as the title.

Step 5: Click the placeholder text, Details of position, award, or achievement. Type `Proofread documents for faculty, including grant proposals, research requests, course material, and meeting communications.`

Step 6: Press the ENTER key. Type `Maintain and update Web pages for Information Systems courses taught through the Internet.`

Step 7: Press the ENTER key. Type `Conduct classes for faculty, staff, and students on how to write technical publications effectively.`

Step 8: If necessary, scroll down to display the volunteer experience section of the resume. Click the placeholder text, Click here and enter information. Type `University Tutoring Center. Read student essays, assist students in correcting grammar errors, and suggest techniques for improving writing style.`

Step 9: If necessary, scroll down to display the hobbies section of the resume. Click the placeholder text, Click here and enter information. Type `Surfing the Internet` and then press the SHIFT+ENTER keys. Type `Digital photography` and then press the SHIFT+ENTER keys. Type `Camping` as the last hobby.

The work experience, volunteer experience, and hobbies sections of the resume are complete (Figure 2-29).

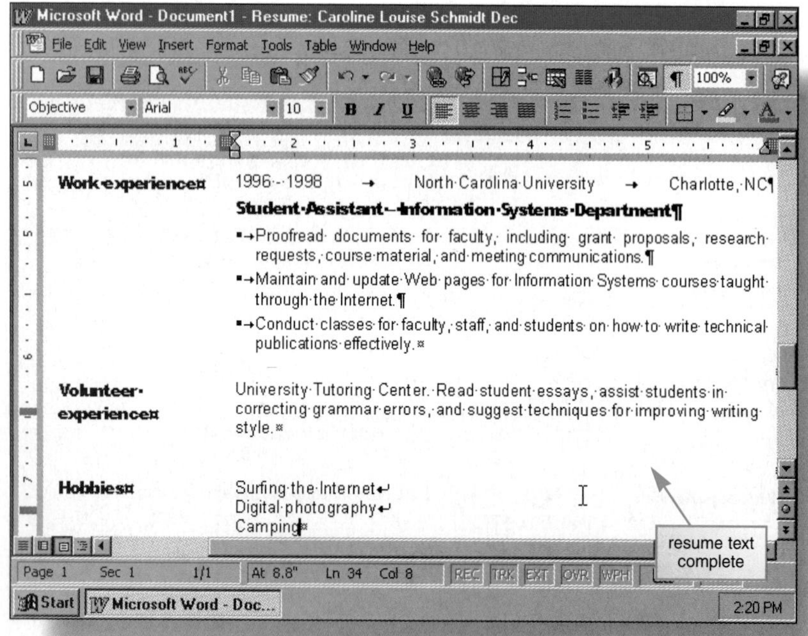

FIGURE 2-29

Changing the Font Size of Characters in the Resume

The next step in modifying the resume is to change the font size of all of the characters in the table of the resume, that is, all the text below the name. Currently, the characters are 10 point, which is difficult for most people to read comfortably. To change all the characters in the table to 11 point, you must select the entire table first and then change the font size as shown in the following steps.

More About Tables

If you use the keyboard shortcut to select a table, ALT+NUM5, you must press the 5 on the numeric keypad. You cannot use the 5 on the keyboard area. Also, be sure that NUM LOCK is off; otherwise, the keyboard shortcut will not work.

To Select a Table and Format Its Characters

1. **Be sure the insertion point is somewhere in the table. Click Table on the menu bar and then point to Select Table (Figure 2-30).**

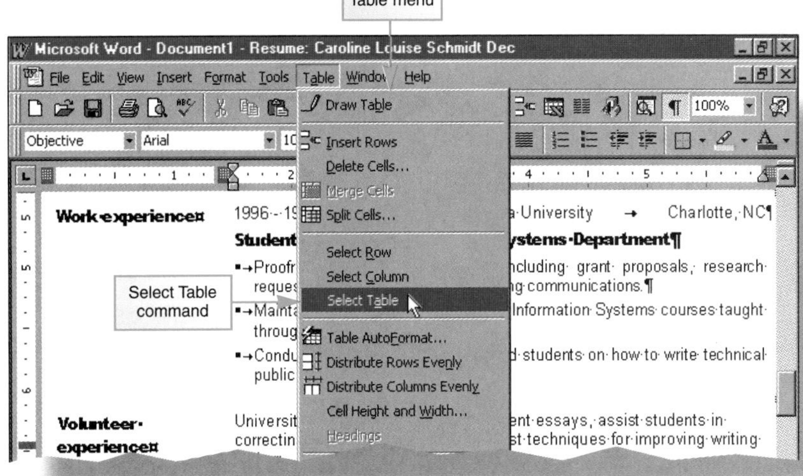

FIGURE 2-30

2. **Click Select Table.**

   Word highlights all of the characters in the table (Figure 2-31).

3. **Click the Font Size box arrow on the Formatting toolbar and then point to 11.**

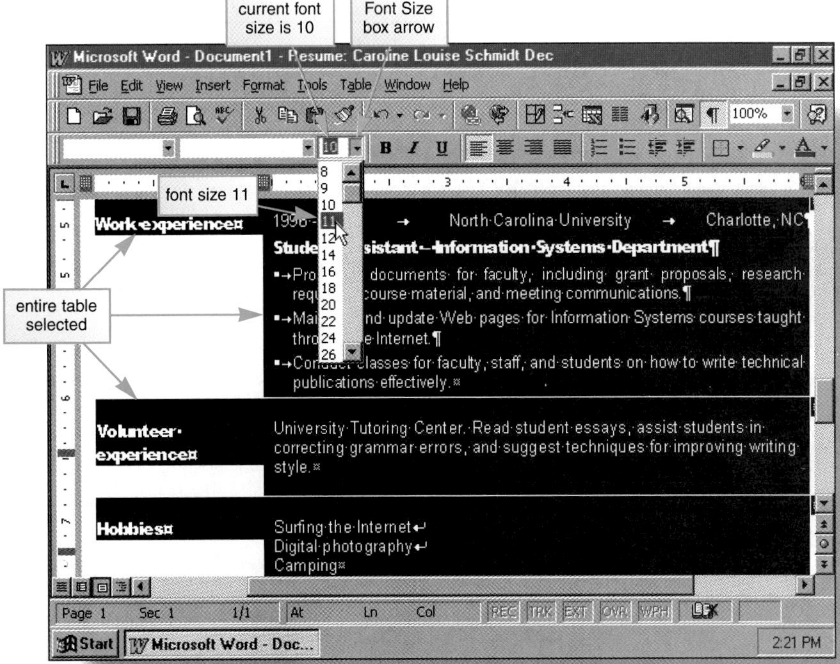

FIGURE 2-31

4 **Click 11.**

Word changes the font size of the selected text from 10 to 11 (Figure 2-32).

5 **Click anywhere in the document to remove the highlight.**

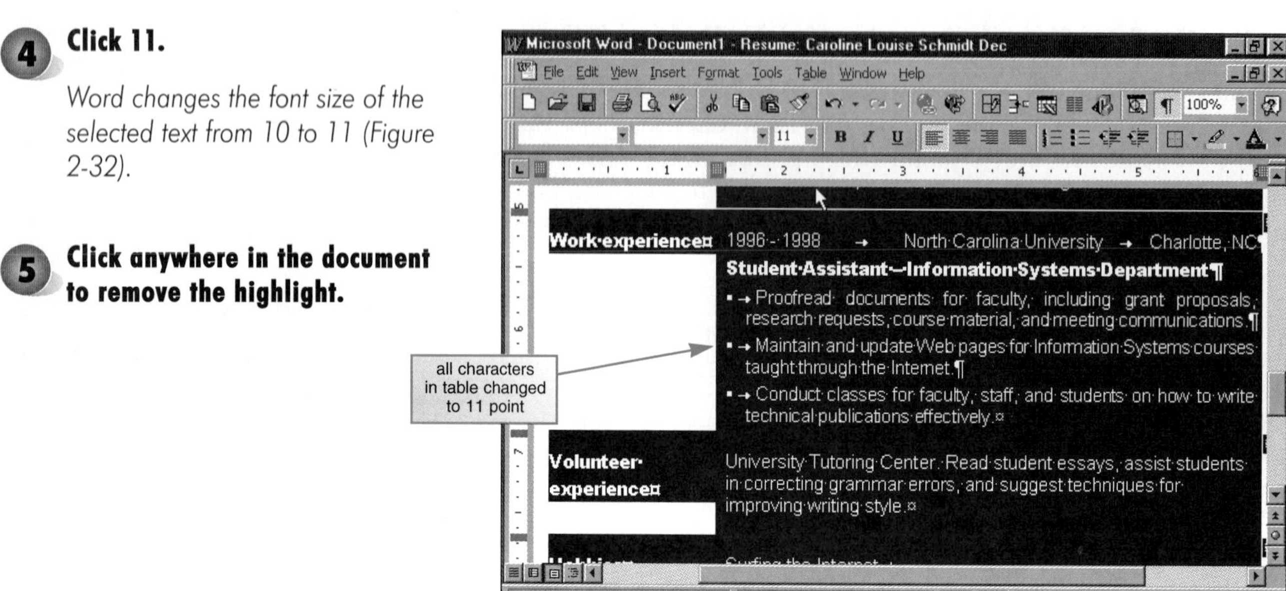

FIGURE 2-32

OtherWays

1. With insertion point somewhere in table, press ALT+5 (on numeric keypad with NUM LOCK off)

The next step is to increase the font size of the address and telephone information that the Resume Wizard placed at the top of the resume. To allow for these items to be positioned anywhere on the resume, Word placed the address information in one frame and the telephone and e-mail address in another frame. Currently, the text in each of these frames is 7 point, which you increase by one point as shown in the following steps.

To Increase the Font Size by One Point

1 **Press the CTRL+HOME keys to position the insertion point at the top of the document. Drag through the address above the name.**

Word surrounds the address information with a frame (Figure 2-33). A ***frame****, indicated with the crosshatched border, is an invisible container for text or graphics that can be positioned anywhere on the page.*

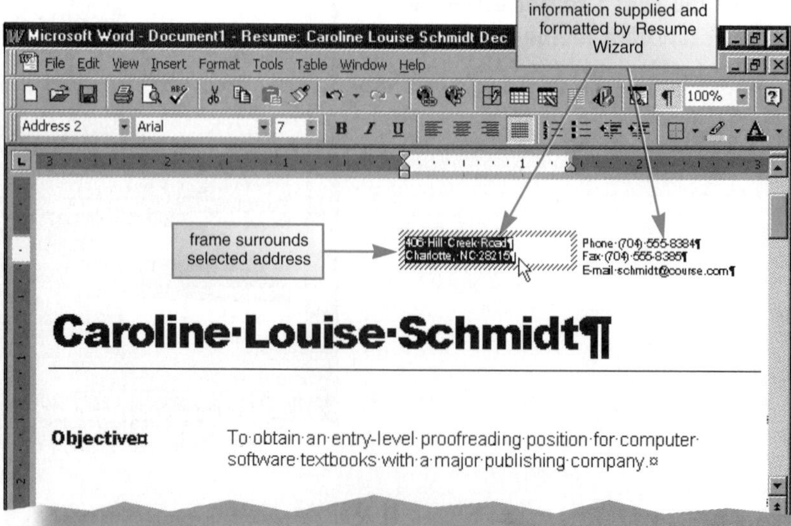

FIGURE 2-33

2 **Press the CTRL+] keys. Drag through the telephone and e-mail information to the right of the address.**

Word increases the font size of the selected text by one point, to 8 in this case (Figure 2-34). The telephone and e-mail information is surrounded by a frame.

3 **Press the CTRL+] keys. Click anywhere to remove the selection.**

Word increase the font size of the selected text by one point, to 8 in this case (see Figure 2-35).

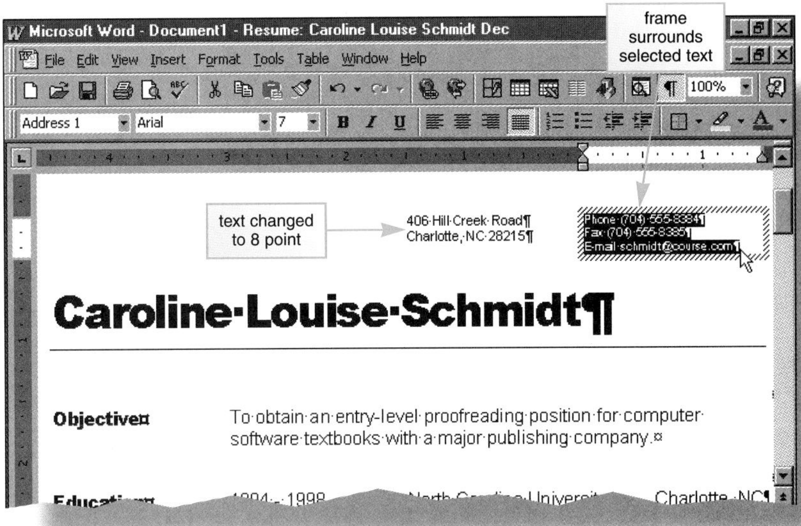

FIGURE 2-34

OtherWays

1. Click Font Size box arrow on Formatting toolbar, select desired point size in list
2. Right-click selected text, click Font on shortcut menu, click Font tab, select desired point size in Size list box, click OK button
3. On Format menu click Font, click Font tab, select desired point size in Size list box, click OK button
4. Press CTRL+SHIFT+P, type desired point size, press ENTER

The resume is completely entered and formatted.

Viewing and Printing the Resume in Print Preview

To see exactly how a document will look when you print it, you should display it in **print preview**. Print preview displays the entire document in reduced size on the Word screen. In print preview, you can edit and format text, adjust margins, and view multiple pages. Once you preview the document, you can print it directly from within print preview. Perform the following steps to use print preview.

Steps To Print Preview a Document

1 **Point to the Print Preview button on the Standard toolbar (Figure 2-35).**

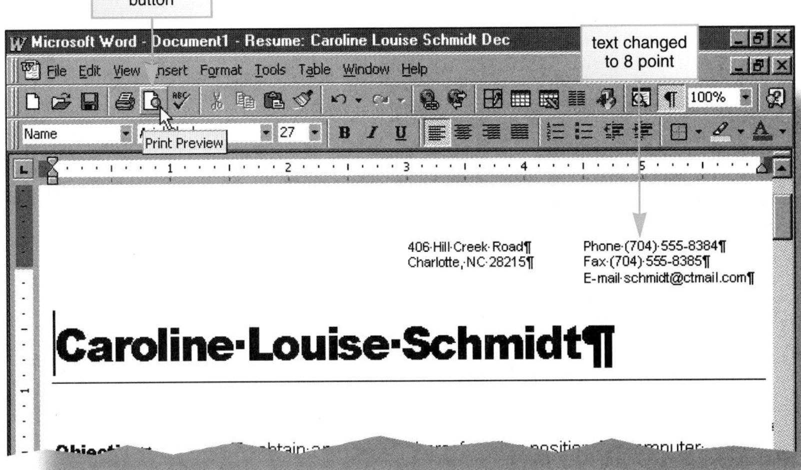

FIGURE 2-35

2 Click the Print Preview button. If your preview displays more than one page, click the One Page button on the Print Preview toolbar. Point to the Print button on the Print Preview toolbar.

*Word displays the document in print preview (Figure 2-36). The **Print Preview toolbar** displays below the menu bar; the Standard and Formatting toolbars have disappeared from the screen. You use the Print Preview toolbar to zoom and print the document.*

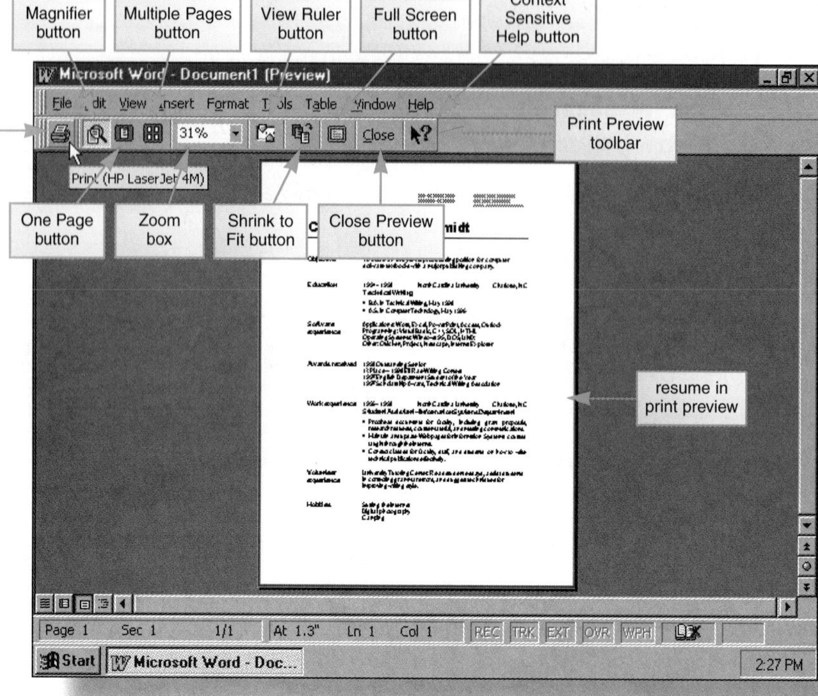

FIGURE 2-36

3 Ready the printer. Click the Print button on the Print Preview toolbar. When the printer stops, retrieve the printout.

Word prints the document on the printer (Figure 2-37).

4 Click the Close Preview button on the Print Preview toolbar.

Word returns to the document window (Figure 2-35 on the previous page).

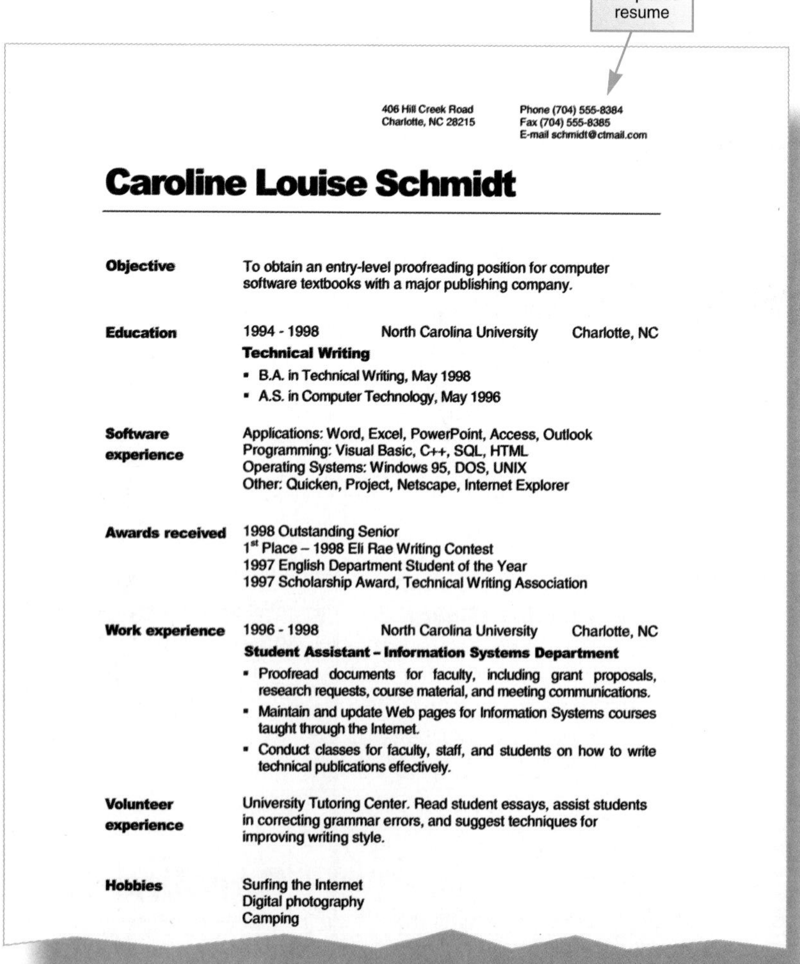

406 Hill Creek Road
Charlotte, NC 28215

Phone (704) 555-8384
Fax (704) 555-8385
E-mail schmidt@ctmail.com

Caroline Louise Schmidt

Objective To obtain an entry-level proofreading position for computer software textbooks with a major publishing company.

Education 1994 - 1998 North Carolina University Charlotte, NC
Technical Writing
- B.A. in Technical Writing, May 1998
- A.S. in Computer Technology, May 1996

Software experience Applications: Word, Excel, PowerPoint, Access, Outlook
Programming: Visual Basic, C++, SQL, HTML
Operating Systems: Windows 95, DOS, UNIX
Other: Quicken, Project, Netscape, Internet Explorer

Awards received 1998 Outstanding Senior
1st Place – 1998 Eli Rae Writing Contest
1997 English Department Student of the Year
1997 Scholarship Award, Technical Writing Association

Work experience 1996 - 1998 North Carolina University Charlotte, NC
Student Assistant – Information Systems Department
- Proofread documents for faculty, including grant proposals, research requests, course material, and meeting communications.
- Maintain and update Web pages for Information Systems courses taught through the Internet.
- Conduct classes for faculty, staff, and students on how to write technical publications effectively.

Volunteer experience University Tutoring Center. Read student essays, assist students in correcting grammar errors, and suggest techniques for improving writing style.

Hobbies Surfing the Internet
Digital photography
Camping

FIGURE 2-37

Other Ways

1. On File menu click Print Preview
2. Press CTRL+F2

Saving the Resume

Because the resume is now complete, you should save it. For a detailed example of the procedure summarized below, refer to pages WD 1.25 through WD 1.27 in Project 1.

TO SAVE A DOCUMENT

Step 1: Insert your floppy disk into drive A.
Step 2: Click the Save button on the Standard toolbar.
Step 3: Type `Schmidt Resume` in the File name text box. Do not press the ENTER key.
Step 4: Click the Save in box arrow and then click 3½ Floppy (A:).
Step 5: Click the Save button in the Save As dialog box.

Word saves the document on a floppy disk in drive A with the file name Schmidt Resume.

The resume now is complete. The next step in Project 2 is to create a cover letter to send with the resume to a potential employer. Do not close the Schmidt Resume. You will use it again later in this project when you spell check it.

More About Print Preview

If you want to read the contents of a page in print preview, you must magnify it. To magnify a page, be sure the Magnifier button is recessed on the Print Preview toolbar and then click in the document to zoom in or out. Magnifying a page has no effect on the printed document; it only changes the size of the characters on the screen.

Creating a Cover Letter

You have created a personalized resume to send to prospective employers. Along with the resume, you will attach a cover letter. The following pages outline how to use Word to create and personalize a cover letter.

More About Cover Letters

You should always send a personalized cover letter with every resume. A cover letter should highlight aspects of your background relevant to the position. Because it is often difficult to recall past achievements and activities, you should keep a personal personnel file containing documents that outline your accomplishments.

Components of a Business Letter

During your professional career, you will create many business letters. A **cover letter** is one type of a business letter. All business letters contain the same basic components. You should take care when preparing business letters to include all essential elements. **Essential business letter elements** include the date line, inside address, message, and signature block (Figure 2-38 on the next page). The **date line**, which consists of the month, day, and year, is positioned two to six lines below the letterhead. The **inside address**, placed three to eight lines below the date line, usually contains the addressee's courtesy title plus full name; business affiliation; and full geographical address. The **salutation**, if present, begins two lines below the last line of the inside address. The body of the letter, the **message**, begins two lines below the salutation. Within the message, paragraphs are single spaced with double-spacing between paragraphs. Two lines below the last line of the message, the **complimentary close** displays. You capitalize only the first word in a complimentary close. The **signature block** is typed at least four lines below the complimentary close, allowing room for the author to sign his or her name.

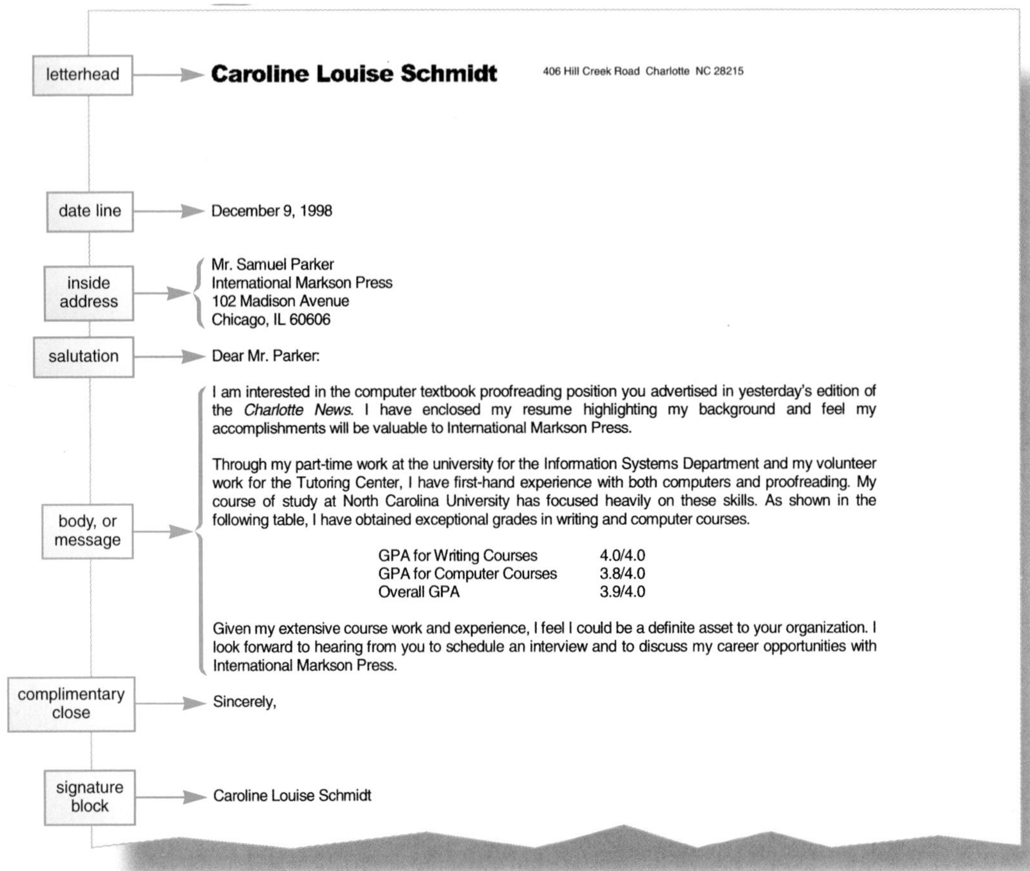
Caroline Louise Schmidt 406 Hill Creek Road Charlotte NC 28215

December 9, 1998

Mr. Samuel Parker
International Markson Press
102 Madison Avenue
Chicago, IL 60606

Dear Mr. Parker:

I am interested in the computer textbook proofreading position you advertised in yesterday's edition of the *Charlotte News*. I have enclosed my resume highlighting my background and feel my accomplishments will be valuable to International Markson Press.

Through my part-time work at the university for the Information Systems Department and my volunteer work for the Tutoring Center, I have first-hand experience with both computers and proofreading. My course of study at North Carolina University has focused heavily on these skills. As shown in the following table, I have obtained exceptional grades in writing and computer courses.

GPA for Writing Courses	4.0/4.0
GPA for Computer Courses	3.8/4.0
Overall GPA	3.9/4.0

Given my extensive course work and experience, I feel I could be a definite asset to your organization. I look forward to hearing from you to schedule an interview and to discuss my career opportunities with International Markson Press.

Sincerely,

Caroline Louise Schmidt

FIGURE 2-38

You can follow many different styles when you create business letters. The cover letter in this project (Figure 2-38) follows the **block style**. Table 2-2 outlines the differences between the common styles of business letters.

Table 2-2

LETTER STYLES	FEATURES
Block	**All components of the letter begin flush with the left margin.**
Modified Block	**The date, complimentary close, and signature block are positioned approximately five spaces to the right of center or at the right margin. All other components of the letter begin flush with the left margin.**
Modified Semi-Block	**The date, complimentary close, and signature block are positioned approximately five spaces to the right of center or at the right margin. The first line of each paragraph in the body of the letter is indented 5 or 10 spaces from the left margin. All other components of the letter begin flush with the left margin.**

More *About* Templates

When you create a new document by clicking the New button on the Standard toolbar, Word uses the Blank Document Template located on the General tab sheet in the New dialog box to format the document. If you want to use a different template or a wizard, you must use the New dialog box.

Using a Letter Template to Create a Resume Cover Letter

To create a resume cover letter, you can type a letter from scratch into a blank document window following the rules listed in the preceding paragraphs; you can use a wizard and let Word format the letter with appropriate spacing and layout as you did with the resume; or you can use a template. Recall that a template is like a blueprint; that is, Word prepares the requested document with text and/or formatting common to all documents of this nature. Then, you customize the letter by selecting and replacing text.

Recall that Word provides three styles, or families, of wizards and templates: Professional, Contemporary, and Elegant. If you want a related set of documents to have similar formatting, use wizards and templates from the same family. Because you used the Professional style for the resume, you should use the Professional style for the cover letter as shown in the following steps.

Steps To Create a Letter Using a Word Template

1 Click File on the menu bar and then point to New (Figure 2-39).

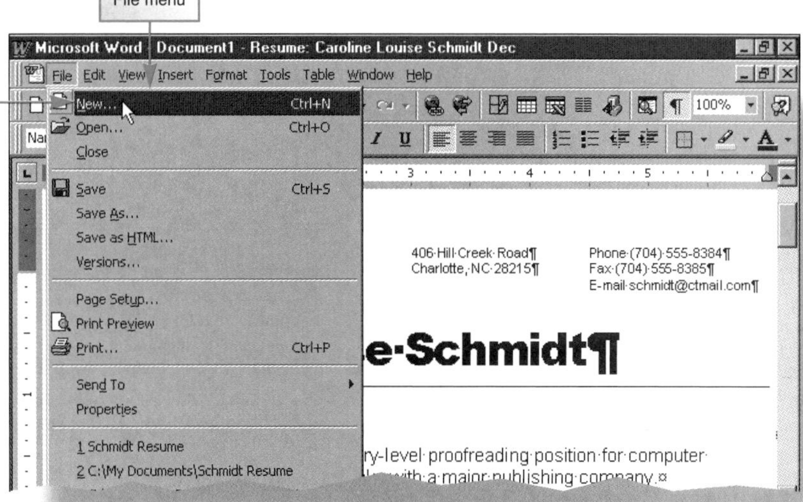

FIGURE 2-39

2 Click New. If necessary, click the Letters & Faxes tab when the New dialog box first opens. Click the Professional Letter icon.

Word displays the New dialog box (Figure 2-40). Recall that icons without the word, wizard, below them are templates. The Professional Letter icon is selected, and a preview of a professional letter displays in the Preview area. When you create a new document using the New button on the Standard toolbar, you use the **Blank Document template** *located on the General sheet in the New dialog box. If you want to use a different template or a wizard, you must use the New dialog box.*

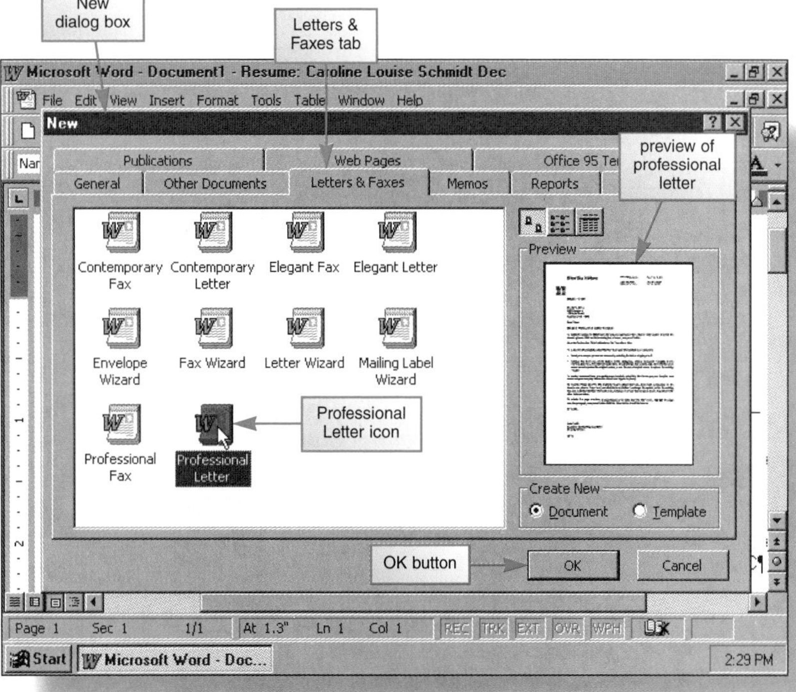

FIGURE 2-40

3 **Click the OK button.**

Word creates a Professional style letter layout for you and displays it in a document window (Figure 2-41). Because Word displays the current date in the letter, your date line probably will display a different date.

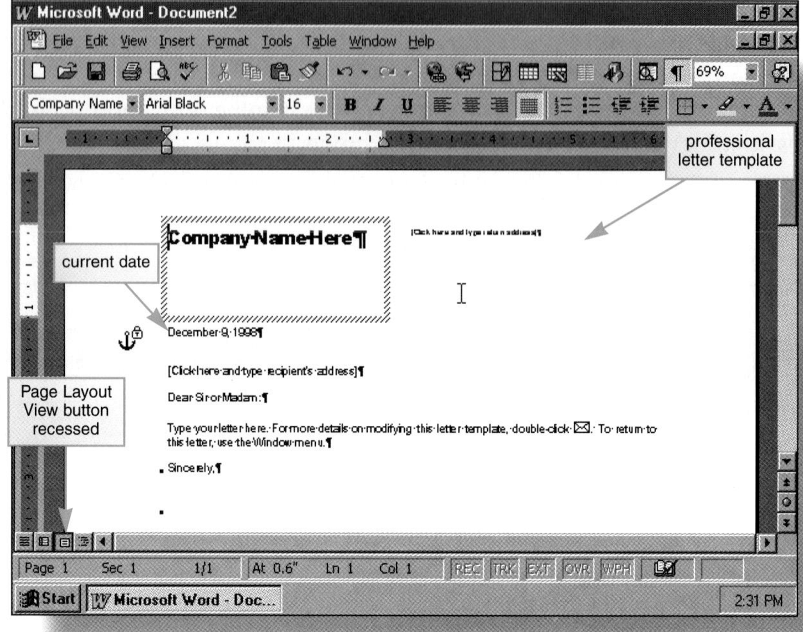

FIGURE 2-41

OtherWays

1. On Start menu click New Office Document, click Letters & Faxes tab, double-click Professional Letter icon
2. Click Start a New Document button on Microsoft Office Shortcut Bar, click Letters & Faxes tab, double-click Professional Letter icon
3. Click New button on Standard toolbar, on Tools menu click Letter Wizard, select options, click OK button

To see the entire letter created by Word, you should print it.

Printing the Cover Letter Generated Using Word's Professional Letter Template

To print the cover letter generated by Word, click the Print button on the Standard toolbar. The resulting printout is shown in Figure 2-42.

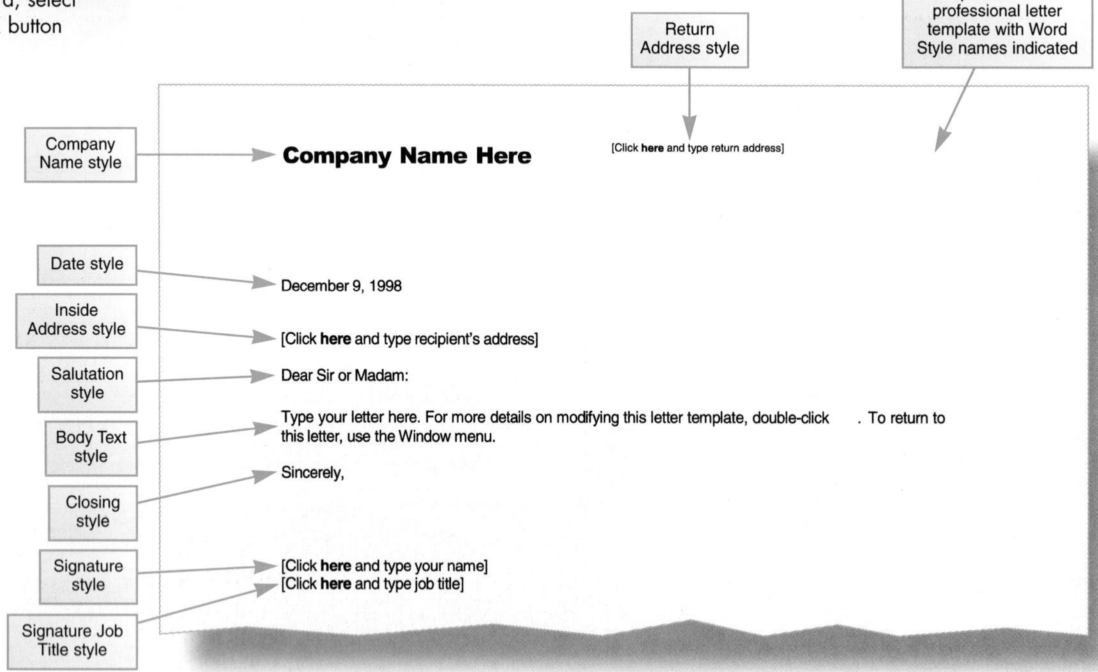

FIGURE 2-42

Recall that a **style** is a customized format Word applies to characters or paragraphs. The Style box on the Formatting toolbar displays the name of the style associated with the location of the insertion point. The styles used in the Professional Letter template are indicated in the printout of the cover letter in Figure 2-42. When you modify the cover letter, the style associated with the location of the insertion point will be applied to the text you type.

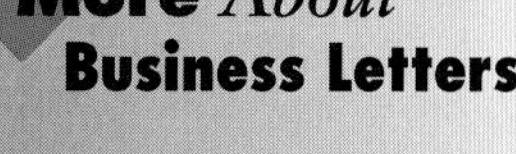

More About Business Letters

A finished business letter should look like a symmetrically framed picture with even margins, all balanced below an attractive letterhead. In addition, the contents of the letter should contain proper grammar, correct spelling, logically constructed sentences, flowing paragraphs, and sound ideas.

Personalizing the Cover Letter

If you compare the printout in Figure 2-42 to the cover letter in Figure 2-1 on page WD 2.5, you will notice several modifications are required. Notice how the template (Figure 2-42) creates the formatting for the business letter using the block style. The template uses proper spacing between lines for a business letter and indicates what you should type in the respective areas of the letter via placeholder text. You can see that using a template saves you formatting time when creating a business letter. The steps on the following pages illustrate how to personalize the cover letter.

More About Frames

The crosshatched border surrounding the company name in Figure 2-43 is called a frame. A frame is an invisible container for text or graphics that can be positioned anywhere on the page. To change the contents of the frame, select the words as you would any other text and then type.

Zooming a Document on the Screen

The document displayed in Figure 2-43 is displayed at 69% of its normal size. The characters and words are small and difficult to read. Depending on your settings, your zoom percentage may be different from that shown in Figure 2-43. To make the displayed characters larger or smaller on the screen, you change the zoom percentage, as shown in the following steps.

Steps To Zoom a Document

1 Click the Zoom box arrow on the Standard toolbar and then point to 100%.

A list of magnification percentages displays (Figure 2-43). Any number greater than the current percentage will increase the size of the characters on the screen, and any number smaller will decrease the size of the characters on the screen.

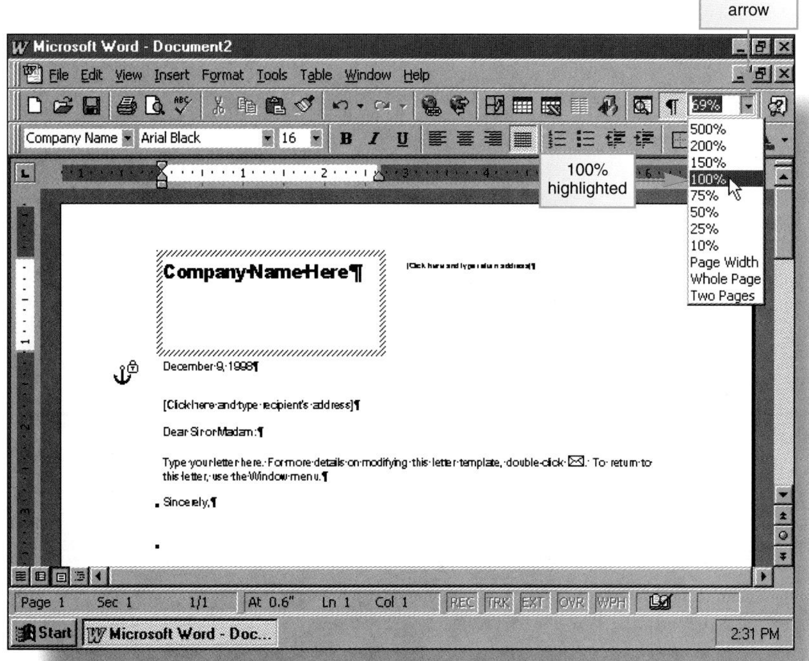

FIGURE 2-43

2 Click 100%.

The characters in the document window increase from 69% of their normal size to 100% (Figure 2-44). Notice that the characters are now easier to read. The larger the magnification, the easier the characters are to read.

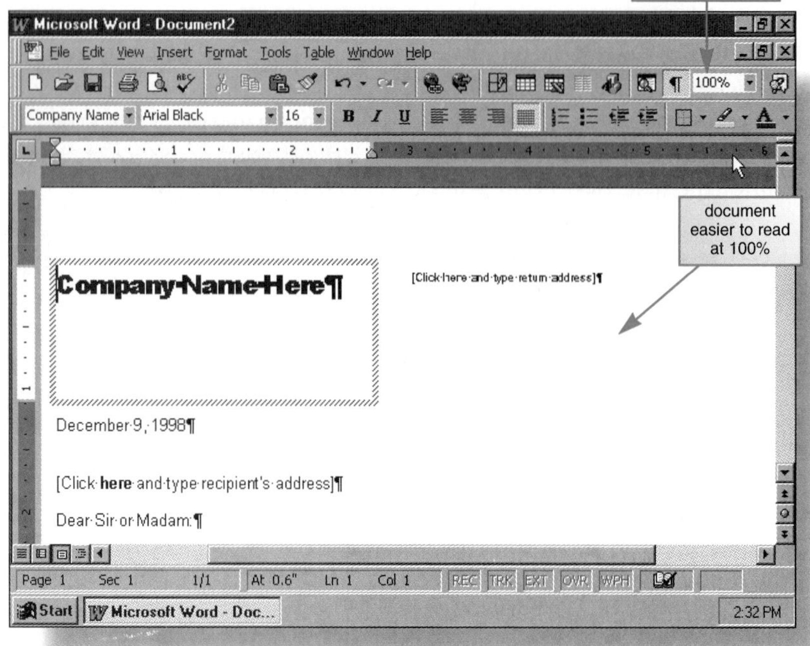

FIGURE 2-44

OtherWays

1. On View menu click Zoom, select desired percentage, click OK button

Selecting and Replacing Template Placeholder Text

The next step in personalizing the cover letter is to select the placeholder text in the letter template and replace it with the personal information. The first placeholder text on the cover letter is in the letterhead, Company Name Here. Select and then replace this text as described below.

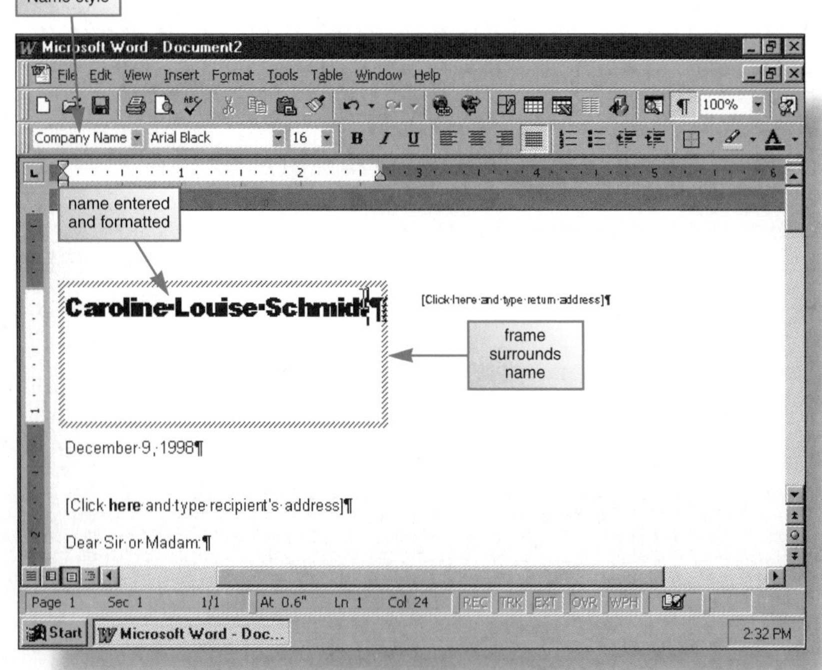

FIGURE 2-45

TO SELECT AND REPLACE PLACEHOLDER TEXT

Step 1: Drag through the placeholder text, Company Name Here.

Step 2: Type `Caroline Louise Schmidt` as the name.

The name displays surrounded by a frame on the first line of the letterhead (Figure 2-45). The Professional Letter template framed the name to provide flexibility in its location in the document. Notice the style is of this text is Company Name in the Style box. The Company Name style uses 16-point Arial Black font for characters.

The next step is to enter the return address to the right of the name as described in the steps below.

TO SELECT AND REPLACE MORE PLACEHOLDER TEXT

Step 1: Click the placeholder text, Click here and type return address, to select it.
Step 2: Type `406 Hill Creek Road, Charlotte, NC 28215` as the address.

The address displays surrounded by a frame to the right of the name (Figure 2-46). The Professional Letter template framed the return address to provide flexibility in its location in the document. Notice the style of this text is Return Address in the Style box. The Return Address style uses 7-point Arial font for characters.

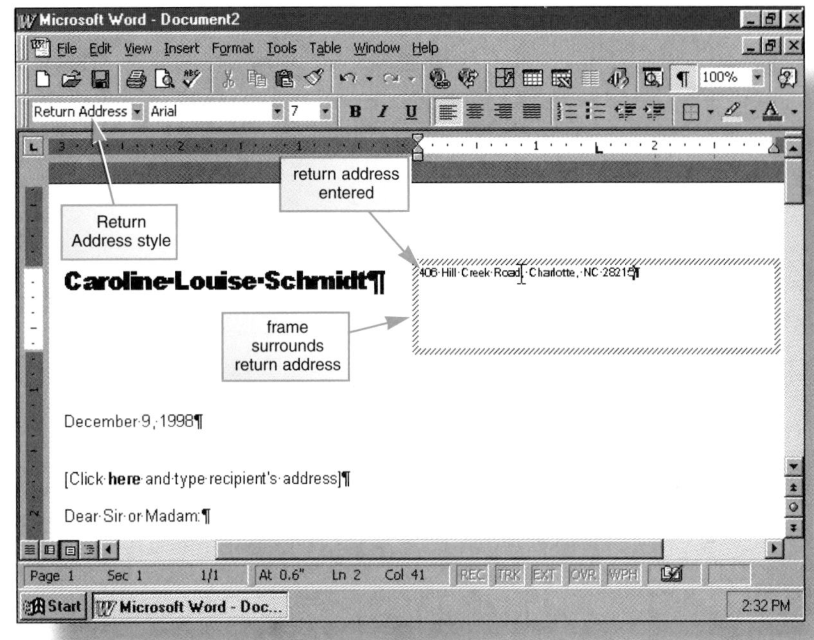

FIGURE 2-46

With the letterhead complete, the next step in personalizing the cover letter is to enter the recipient's address as described in the following steps.

TO SELECT AND REPLACE MORE PLACEHOLDER TEXT

Step 1: Click the placeholder text below the date, Click here and type recipient's address, to select it.
Step 2: Type `Mr. Samuel Parker` and then press the ENTER key.
Step 3: Type `International Markson Press` and then press the ENTER key.
Step 4: Type `102 Madison Avenue` and then press the ENTER key.
Step 5: Type `Chicago, IL 60606` as the city, state, and zip code.

The recipient's name, company, and address are entered (Figure 2-47). Notice the style is now Inside Address.

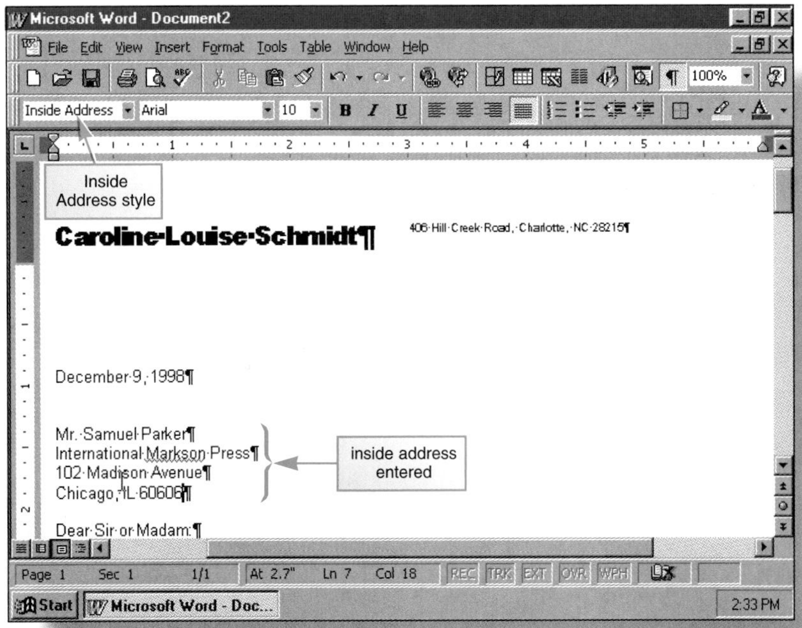

FIGURE 2-47

More *About* **the Inside Address**

Pay close attention to the spelling, punctuation, and official abbreviations of company names. For example, does the company name spell out the word and/or use the ampersand (&) character? Is the word Company spelled out?

Creating an AutoText Entry

If you use the same text frequently, you can store the text in an **AutoText entry** and then use the stored entry throughout this document, as well as future documents. That is, you need to type the entry only once, and for all future occurrences of the text, you access the stored entry as you need it. In this way, you avoid entering the text inconsistently or incorrectly in different places throughout the same document. Follow these steps to create an AutoText entry for the prospective employer's company name.

Steps To Create an AutoText Entry

1. **Drag through the text to be stored (International Markson Press, in this case). Be sure not to select the paragraph mark at the end of the text.**

   Word highlights the company name, International Markson Press, in the inside address (Figure 2-48). Notice the paragraph mark is not part of the selection.

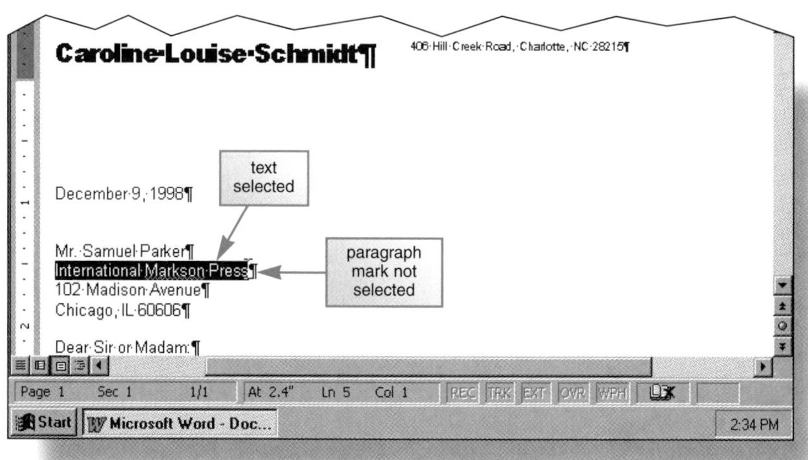

FIGURE 2-48

2. **Click Insert on the menu bar and then point to AutoText. Point to New on the AutoText submenu (Figure 2-49).**

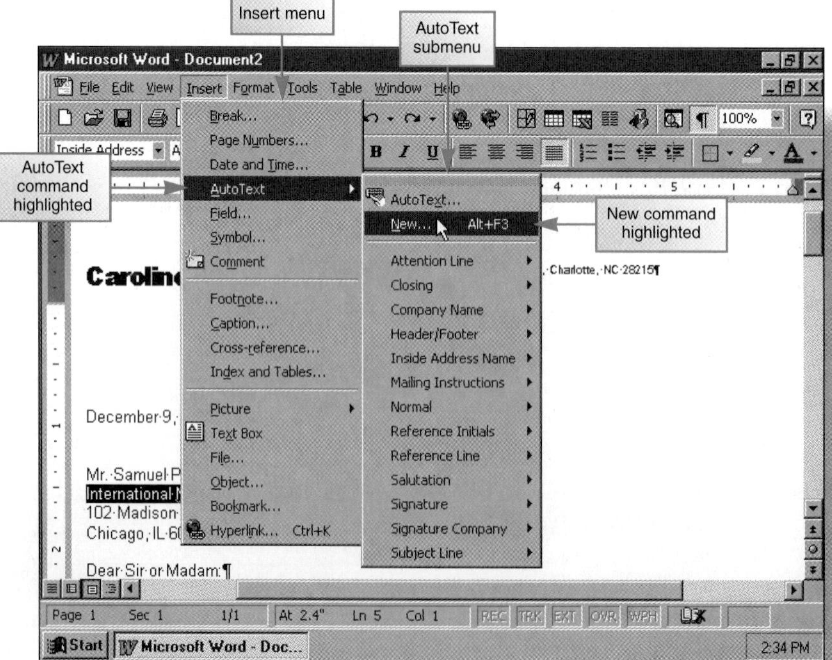

FIGURE 2-49

3 **Click New on the AutoText submenu. When the Create AutoText dialog box displays, type** `imp` **and then point to the OK button.**

Word displays the Create AutoText dialog box (Figure 2-50). In this dialog box, Word proposes a name for the AutoText entry, which usually is the first word(s) of the selection. In this case, the default AutoText entry's name is International. You change it to a shorter name, imp.

4 **Click the OK button.**

Word stores the entry, closes the AutoText dialog box, and returns to the document window.

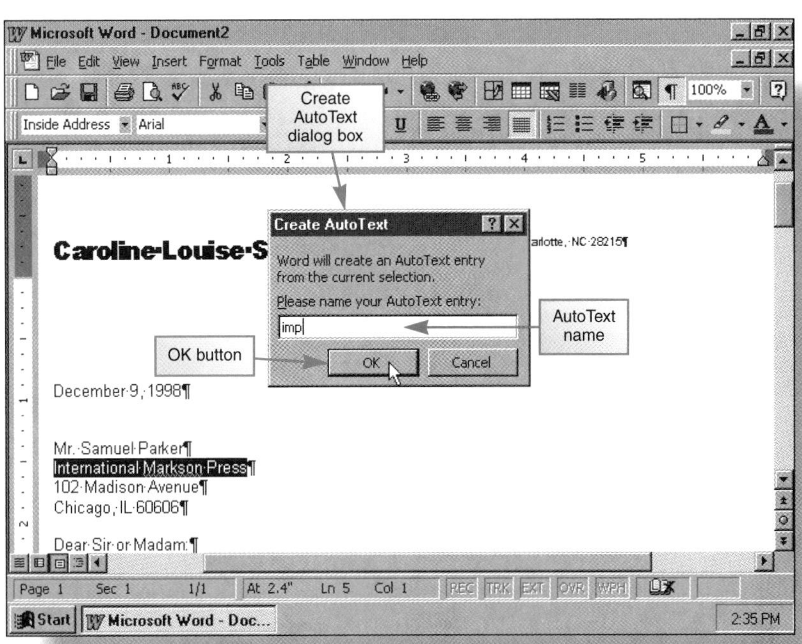

FIGURE 2-50

The name imp has been stored as an AutoText entry. Later in the project, you will use the AutoText entry (imp) instead of typing the company name (International Markson Press) again.

The next step is to enter the salutation as described in the steps below.

TO ENTER THE SALUTATION

Step 1: If necessary, scroll down to display the salutation.
Step 2: Drag through the text, Sir or Madam, in the salutation to select it.
Step 3: Type `Mr. Parker` as the recipient's name.

The salutation of the cover letter now displays as shown in Figure 2-51.

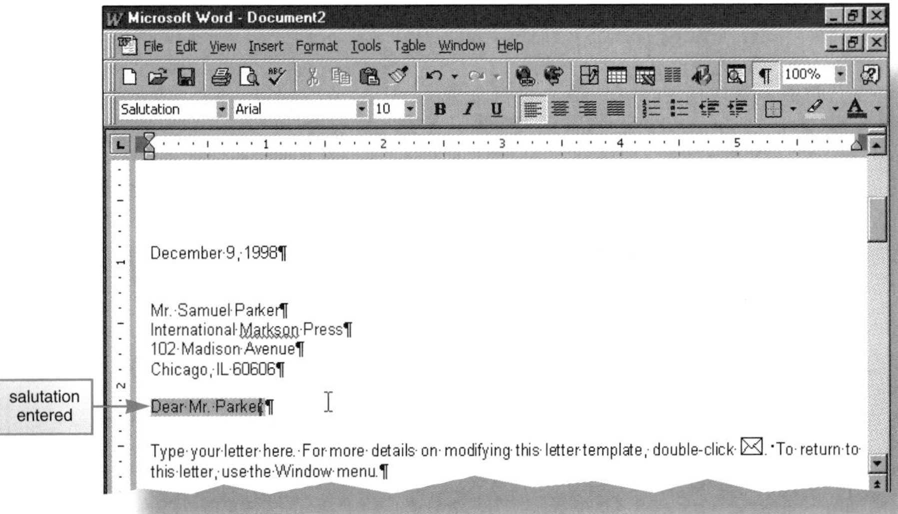

FIGURE 2-51

More About Salutations

The salutation "To whom it may concern" should be avoided – it is extremely impersonal. If you cannot obtain the name and gender of the company officer to whom you are addressing your letter, then use the recipient's title in the salutation, e.g., Dear Personnel Supervisor.

Saving the Cover Letter

Recall from Project 1 that it is prudent to save your work on disk at regular intervals. Because you have performed several tasks thus far, you should save your cover letter. For a detailed example of the procedure summarized below, refer to pages WD 1.25 through WD 1.27 in Project 1.

TO SAVE A DOCUMENT

Step 1: Insert your floppy disk into drive A.
Step 2: Click the Save button on the Standard toolbar.
Step 3: Type `Schmidt Cover Letter` in the File name text box. Do not press the ENTER key.
Step 4: Click the Save in box arrow and then click 3½ Floppy (A:).
Step 5: Click the Save button in the Save As dialog box.

Word saves the document on a floppy disk in drive A with the file name, Schmidt Cover Letter (Figure 2-52 below).

More About Formatting

Minimize strain on your wrist by switching between the mouse and keyboard as little as possible. If your fingers are already on the keyboard, then use shortcut keys on the keyboard to format text; if you fingers are already on the mouse, then use the mouse to format text.

Applying Formatting Using Shortcut Keys

The next step is to type the message, or body, of the letter below the salutation. As you type paragraphs of text, you may want to format characters within the paragraph as you type them, instead of formatting them later. In Project 1, you typed all characters in the document and then selected the ones to be formatted and applied the desired formatting. In this section, you will use **shortcut keys** to format text as you type.

First, you will select the placeholder text below the salutation and then you will enter the text.

Steps To Select a Paragraph

1 If necessary, scroll down to display the body of the letter. Position the mouse pointer in the paragraph to be selected and then triple-click.

Word selects the entire paragraph, which is placeholder text (Figure 2-52).

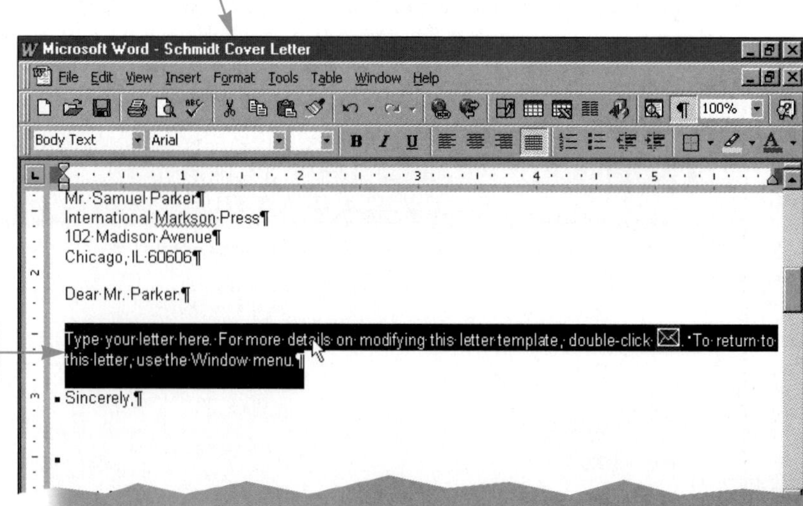

FIGURE 2-52

Other Ways

1. Double-click to left of paragraph to be selected

With the paragraph selected, you will begin typing the body of the letter. Recall that typing replaces selected text; thus, you do not have to delete the selected text. The following steps show how to format characters using the shortcut keys.

To Format Characters Using Shortcut Keys

1 **Type** `I am interested in the computer textbook proofreading position you advertised in yesterday's edition of the` **and then press the SPACEBAR. Press the CTRL+I keys.**

Word replaces the selection with the entered text (Figure 2-53). The next word to be typed is a newspaper name, which should be italicized. Because you pressed CTRL+I, the Italic button on the Formatting toolbar is recessed. When your fingers are on the keyboard, it sometimes is desirable to use a shortcut key to format text, instead of using the mouse to click a button.

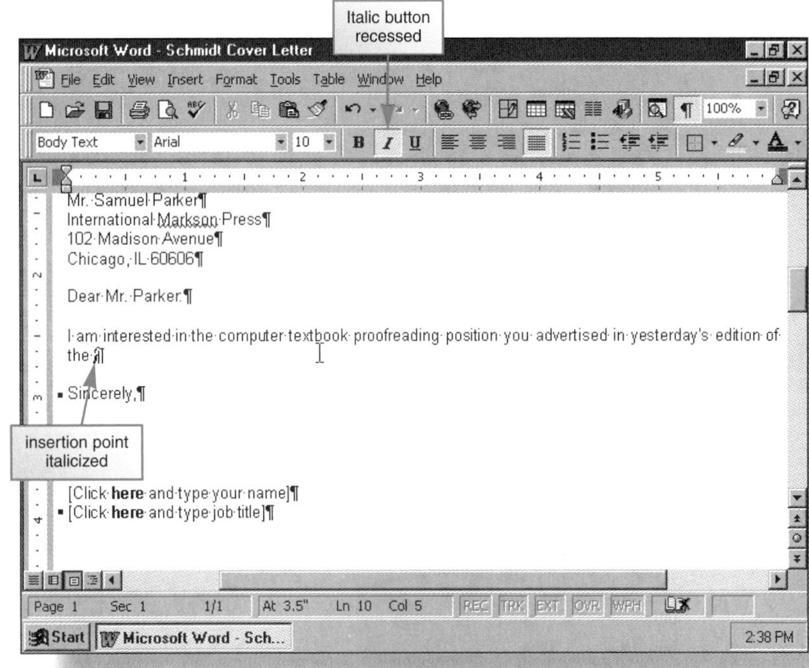

FIGURE 2-53

2 **Type** `Charlotte News` **and then press the CTRL+I keys. Type a period (.) and then press the SPACEBAR once.**

The newspaper name is entered in italics (Figure 2-54). The Italic button on the Formatting toolbar is no longer recessed. CTRL+I is a ***toggle****; that is, the shortcut key is used once to activate the button and used again to deactivate the button.*

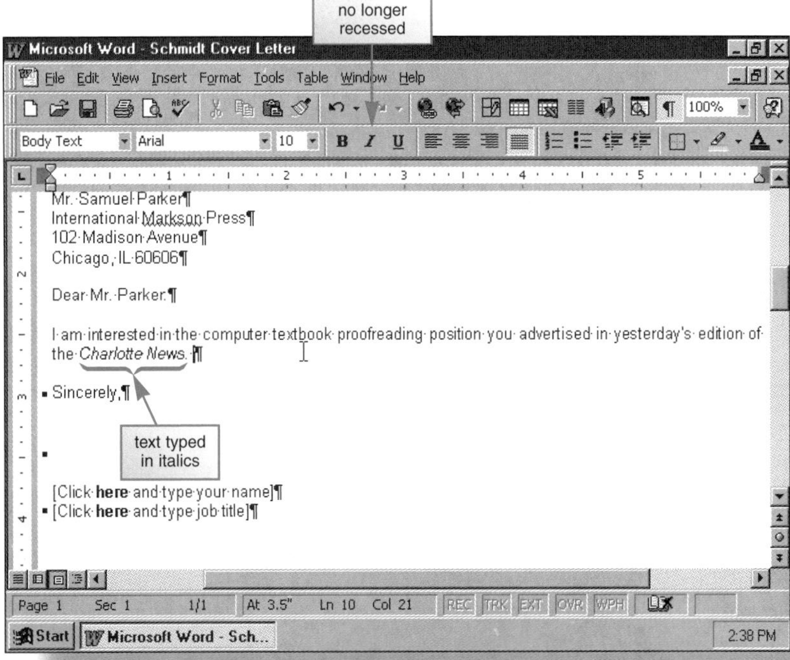

FIGURE 2-54

Many shortcut keys exist in Word for your convenience while typing. Table 2-3 lists the common shortcut keys used for formatting characters and their functions.

More About Shortcut Keys

To print a complete list of shortcut keys for formatting, click Help on the menu bar and then click Contents and Index, click the Index tab, type KEYS and then double-click shortcut keys. Click the Keys for formatting characters and paragraphs topic; right-click the Help window, click Print Topic on the shortcut menu, and then click the OK button.

Table 2-3

FUNCTION	SHORTCUT KEYS
Bold	CTRL+B
Capitalize letters	CTRL+SHIFT+A
Decrease font size	CTRL+SHIFT+<
Decrease font size one point	CTRL+[
Double-underline	CTRL+SHIFT+D
Increase font size	CTRL+SHIFT+>
Increase font size one point	CTRL+]
Italicize	CTRL+I
Remove formatting (plain text)	CTRL+SPACEBAR
Small capitals	CTRL+SHIFT+K
Subscript	CTRL+=
Superscript	CTRL+SHIFT+PLUS SIGN
Underline	CTRL+U
Underline words, not spaces	CTRL+SHIFT+W

Inserting an AutoText Entry

At the end of the next sentence in the body of the cover letter, you want to put the company name, International Markson Press. Recall that earlier in this project, you stored an AutoText entry name of imp for International Markson Press. Thus, you will type the AutoText entry's name and then instruct Word to replace the AutoText entry's name with the stored entry of International Markson Press. Perform the following steps to insert an AutoText entry.

Steps To Insert an AutoText Entry

1. **Type** `I have enclosed my resume highlighting my background and feel my accomplishments will be valuable to imp` **as the beginning of the AutoText entry's name.**

The AutoText entry name displays (Figure 2-55).

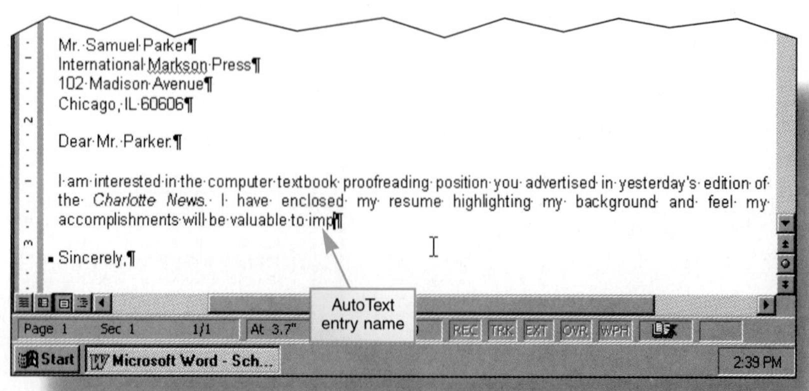

FIGURE 2-55

2 **Press F3. Type a period (.) and then press the ENTER key.**

Word replaces the characters, imp, in the cover letter with the stored AutoText entry, International Markson Press (Figure 2-56). Pressing F3 instructs Word to replace the AutoText entry name with the stored AutoText entry.

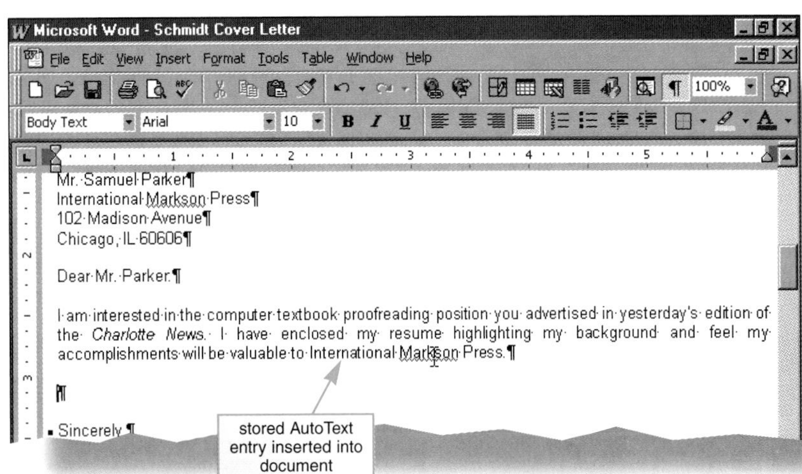

FIGURE 2-56

OtherWays

1. Type first few characters to display AutoComplete tip, press ENTER
2. On Insert menu point to AutoText, point to style linked to AutoText entry, click desired AutoText entry
3. On Insert menu point to AutoText, click AutoText, select desired AutoText entry name, click OK button

If you watch the screen as you type, you may discover that AutoComplete tips display on the screen. As you type, Word searches the list of AutoText entry names and if one matches your typing, Word displays its complete name above your typing as an **AutoComplete tip**. In addition to AutoText entries, Word proposes AutoComplete tips for the current date, a day of the week, a month, and so on. If your screen does not display AutoComplete tips, click Tools on the menu bar, click AutoCorrect, click the AutoText tab, click Show AutoComplete tip for AutoText and dates to select it, and then click the OK button. To view the complete list of entries, click Tools on the menu bar, click AutoCorrect, click the AutoText tab, and then scroll through the list of entries. To ignore an AutoComplete tip proposed by Word, simply continue typing to remove the AutoComplete tip from the screen.

Perform the following steps to enter the next paragraph into the cover letter.

TO ENTER A PARAGRAPH

Step 1: Type `Through my part-time work at the university for the Information Systems Department and my volunteer work for the Tutoring Center, I have first-hand experience with both computers and proofreading.`

Step 2: Press the SPACEBAR. Type `As shown in the following table, I have obtained exceptional grades in writing and computer courses.`

Step 3: Press the SPACEBAR. Type `My course of study at North Carolina University has focused heavily on these skills.`

The paragraph is entered (Figure 2-57).

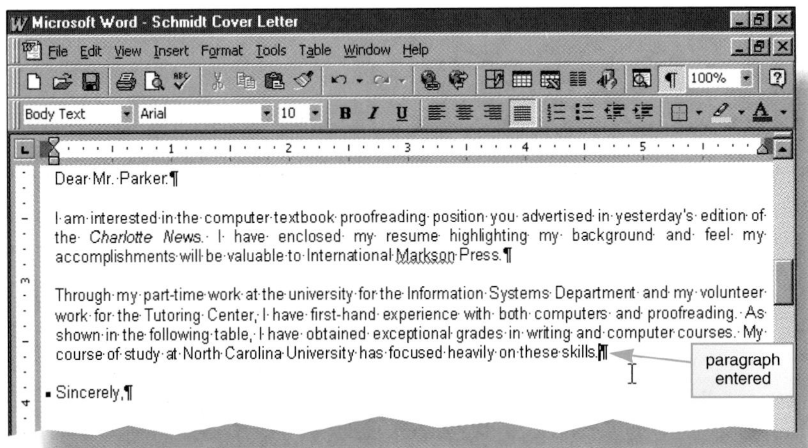

FIGURE 2-57

More *About* **Moving Text**

When moving text a short distance, you should use the drag-and-drop technique. To move text a longer distance, like across multiple pages, use the cut-and-paste technique or print preview. In print preview, click the Magnifier button on the Print Preview toolbar and then drag and drop or cut and paste the text as you would in normal view.

Switching Two Sentences in the Resume

After proofreading the paragraph you just entered, you might realize that the second and third sentences in the paragraph would flow better if they were reversed. That is, you must move the second sentence so it is positioned at the end of the paragraph.

To move any items, such as sentences, you can **drag and drop** one of them or you can **cut and paste** one of them. Both techniques require that you first select the item to be moved. With **dragging and dropping**, you drag the selected item to its new location and then insert, or drop, it there. **Cutting** involves removing the selected item from the document and then placing it on the **Clipboard**, which is a temporary Windows storage area. **Pasting** is the process of copying an item from the Clipboard into the document at the location of the insertion point. When you paste text into a document, the contents of the Clipboard are not erased.

You should use the drag and drop technique to move an item a short distance. When you are moving between several pages or documents, however, the cut and paste technique is more efficient. Thus, use the drag and drop technique to switch the second and third sentences. To do this, you first must select the sentence to be moved as shown below.

To Select a Sentence

1. **Position the mouse pointer (an I-beam) in the sentence to be moved. Press and hold the CTRL key. While holding the CTRL key, click the sentence. Release the CTRL key.**

   Word selects the entire sentence (Figure 2-58). Notice the space after the period is included in the selection.

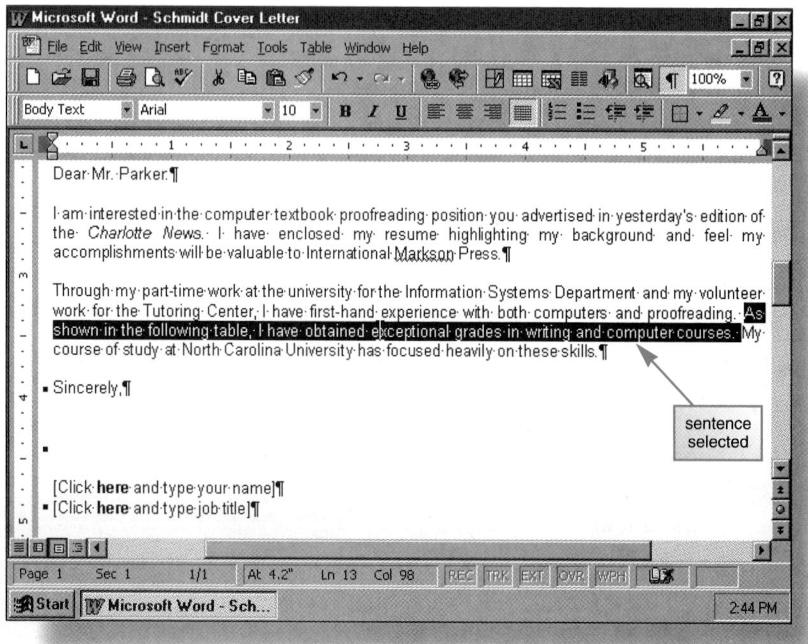

FIGURE 2-58

Throughout Projects 1 and 2, you have selected text and then formatted it. The text has ranged from characters to words to an entire document. Because selecting text is such a crucial function of Word, Table 2-4 summarizes the techniques used to select various forms of text with the mouse.

Table 2-4

ITEM TO SELECT	MOUSE ACTION
Block of text	Click at beginning of selection, scroll to end of selection, position mouse pointer at end of selection, hold down SHIFT key, then click
Character or Characters	Drag through character(s)
Document	Move mouse to left of paragraph until mouse pointer changes to a right-pointing arrow, then triple-click
Graphic	Click the graphic
Line	Move mouse to left of line until mouse pointer changes to a right-pointing arrow, then click
Lines	Move mouse to left of first line until mouse pointer changes to a right-pointing arrow, then drag up or down
Paragraph	Triple-click paragraph or move mouse to left of paragraph until mouse pointer changes to a right-pointing arrow, then double-click
Paragraphs	Move mouse to left of paragraph until mouse pointer changes direction, double-click, then drag
Sentence	Press and hold CTRL key, then click sentence
Word	Double-click the word
Words	Drag through words

With the sentence to be moved selected, you can drag and drop it as shown in the following steps.

Steps To Drag and Drop Selected Text

1 Move the mouse pointer into the selected text. Press and hold the mouse button.

When you begin to drag the selected text, the insertion point changes to a ***dotted insertion point*** *and the mouse pointer has a small dotted box below it (Figure 2-59).*

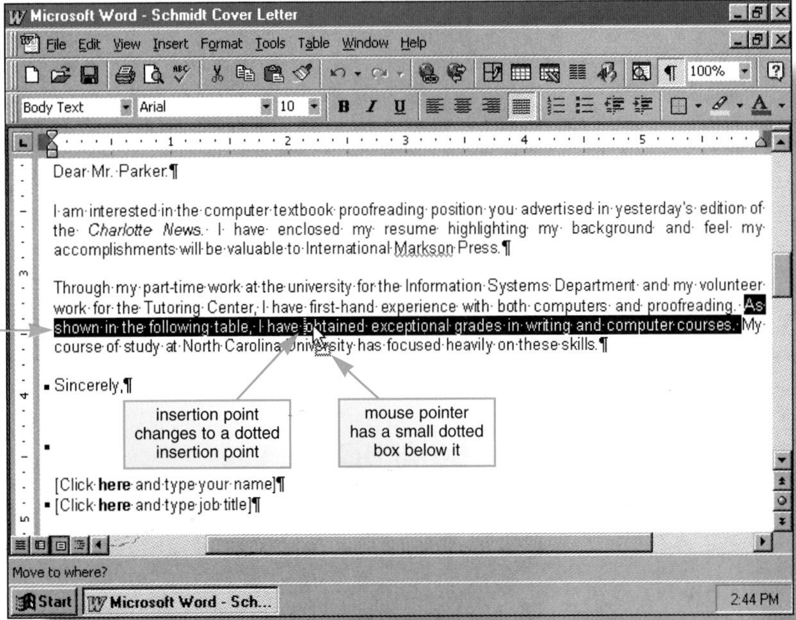

FIGURE 2-59

2 Drag the dotted insertion point to the location where the selected text is to be moved.

The dotted insertion point is at the end of the paragraph (Figure 2-60).

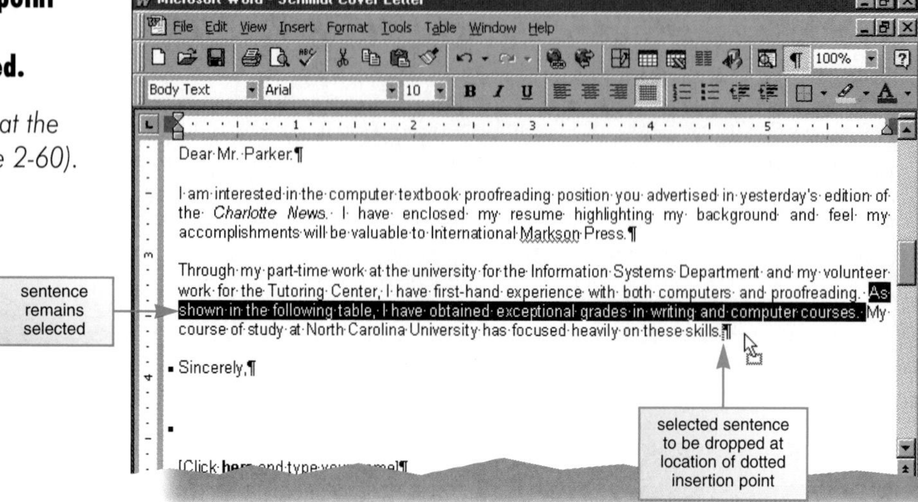

FIGURE 2-60

3 Release the mouse button. Click outside the selection to remove the highlight.

The selected text is moved to the location of the dotted insertion point in the document (Figure 2-61). The second and third sentences in the paragraph are switched.

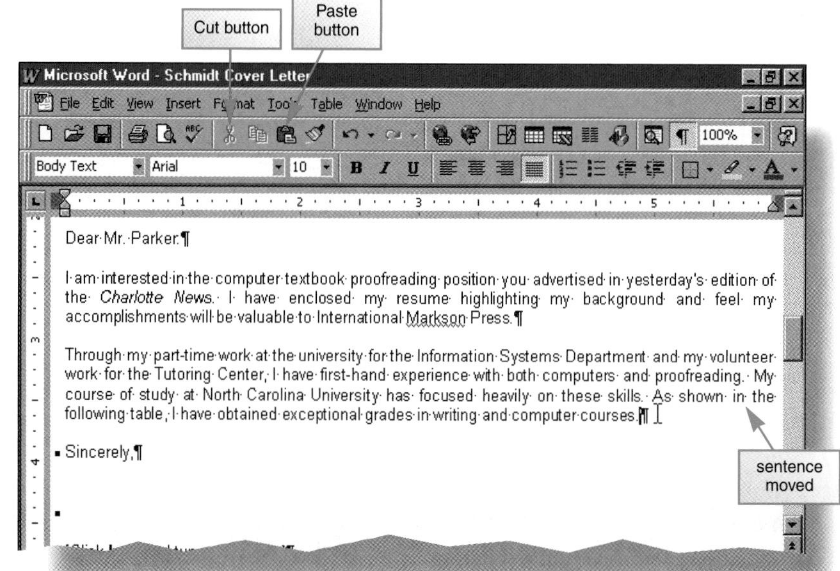

FIGURE 2-61

Other Ways

1. Click Cut button on Standard toolbar, position insertion point at location where text is to be pasted, click Paste button on Standard toolbar
2. On Edit menu click Cut, position insertion point at location where text is to be pasted, on Edit menu click Paste
3. Press CTRL+X, position insertion point at location where text is to be pasted, press CTRL+V

You can use the Undo button on the Standard toolbar if you accidentally drag and drop incorrectly or cut the wrong text.

You can use the drag and drop and cut and paste techniques to move any selected item. That is, you can move words, sentences, phrases, and graphics by selecting them and then dragging and dropping them or cutting and pasting them.

Using the TAB key

The next step is to create a small table to contain the GPAs you obtained. The table will contain two columns: one for a description and one for the GPA numbers. You want the GPA numbers to be aligned vertically; thus, you will use the TAB key to align the GPA numbers.

Word presets tab stops at every one-half inch. These preset, or **default**, tabs are indicated on the horizontal ruler by small **tick marks** (Figure 2-62). You want the first column of the table to begin at the 1.5-inch mark on the ruler and the second column to begin at the 3.5-inch mark. Instead of pressing the TAB key to move the insertion point from the 0-inch mark to the 1.5-inch mark, you will move the left margin inward to the 1.5-inch mark for this paragraph. Perform the following steps to increase the indent of the left margin.

More About Aligning Text

You may be tempted to vertically-align text by pressing the SPACEBAR. The problem is that word processors use variable character fonts. Thus, when you use the SPACEBAR to vertically-align text, the column has a wavy look because each character does not begin at the same location.

Steps To Increase the Indent of the Left Margin

1. **Be sure the insertion point is at the end of the second paragraph in the body of the cover letter and then press the ENTER key. Point to the Increase Indent button on the Formatting toolbar.**

   The insertion point is positioned at the 0-inch mark on the ruler (Figure 2-62).

FIGURE 2-62

2. **Click the Increase Indent button three times.**

   Word moves the Left Indent marker to the 1.5-inch mark on the ruler (Figure 2-63). That is, the Left Indent marker moves one-half inch to the right each time you click the Increase Indent button.

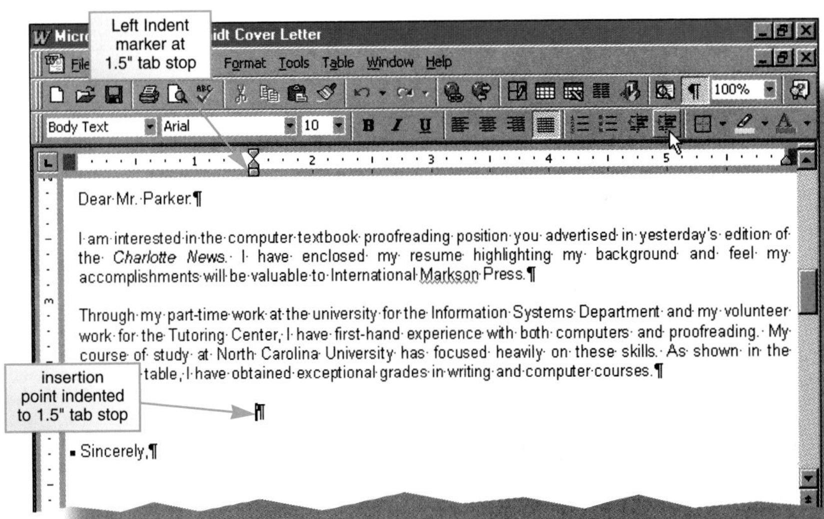

FIGURE 2-63

Other Ways

1. Drag Left Indent marker to desired location on ruler

With the left margin set for the first column of the table, the next step is to enter the table text as shown in the steps on the next page.

Steps To Align Information Vertically with the TAB Key

1 **Type** `GPA for Writing Courses` **and then press the TAB key twice.**

Word moves the insertion point two tab stops to the right (Figure 2-64). Thus, the GPA number will be entered at the 3.5-inch mark on the ruler. Notice the right-pointing arrows after the first column of text. A nonprinting character, the ***right-pointing arrow****, displays each time you press the TAB key. Recall nonprinting characters do not print; they only display in the document window*

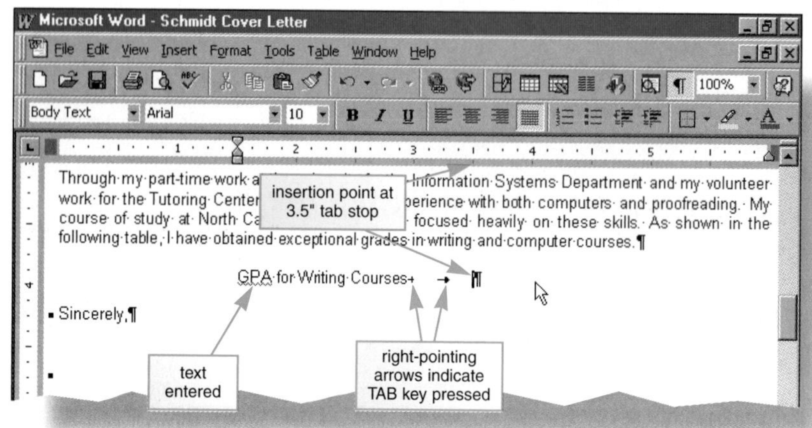

FIGURE 2-64

2 **Type** `4.0/4.0` **and then press the SHIFT+ENTER keys. Type** `GPA for Computer Courses` **and then press the TAB key. Type** `3.8/4.0` **and then press the SHIFT+ENTER keys.**

The first column of text is aligned at the 1.5-inch mark on the ruler, and the second column is aligned at the 3.5-inch mark (Figure 2-65).

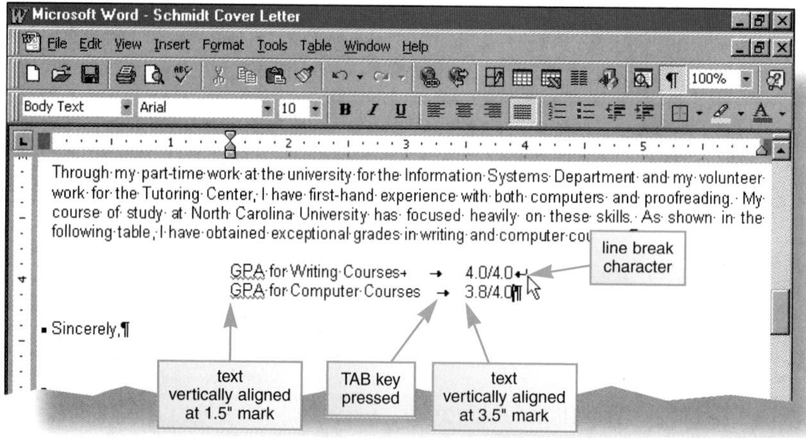

FIGURE 2-65

3 **Type** `Overall GPA` **and then press the TAB key three times. Type** `3.9/4.0` **as the last entry in the table.**

The table is complete (Figure 2-66).

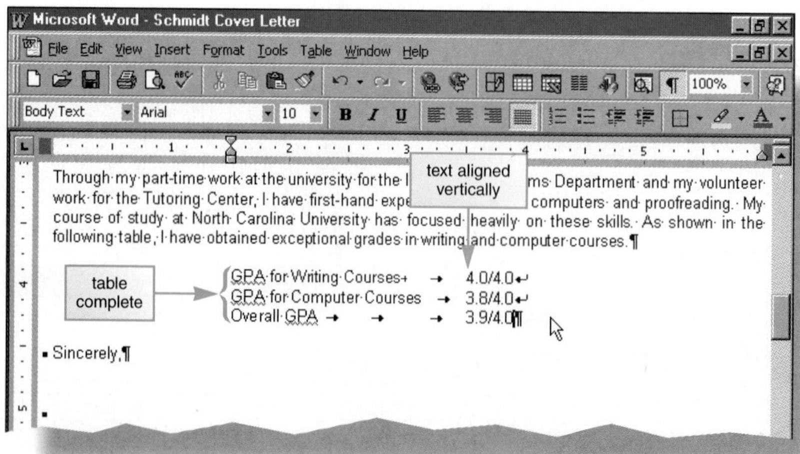

FIGURE 2-66

The next step is to enter the next paragraph in the cover letter. When you press the ENTER key to continue, however, the left margin will be indented 1.5 inches. Thus, you must reset the next paragraph to the left margin before you continue as shown in the following steps.

More About Tab Stops

To set a custom tab, click the paragraph to contain the tab and then click the ruler at the desired tab stop location. To remove a custom tab stop, drag the tab stop marker down and out of the ruler.

To Decrease the Indent in a Paragraph

1. **With the insertion point at the end of the table, press the ENTER key. Point to the Decrease Indent button on the Formatting toolbar.**

   The insertion point is indented 1.5 inches from the left margin (Figure 2-67). Paragraph formatting is carried forward each time you press the ENTER key.

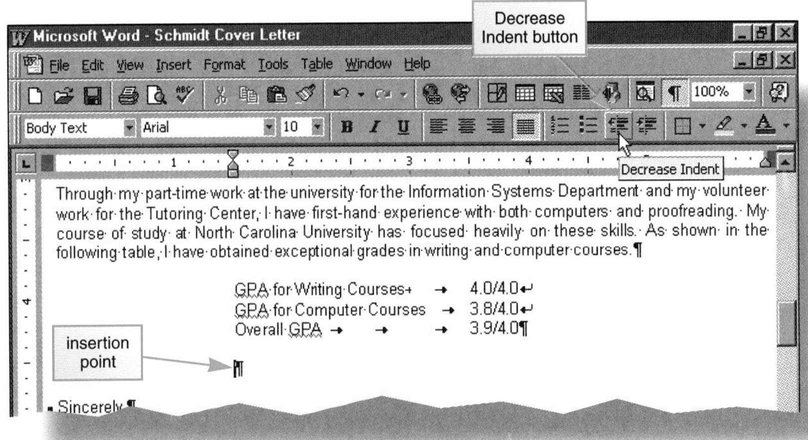

FIGURE 2-67

2. **Click the Decrease Indent button three times.**

   Word positions the insertion point at the left margin.

3. **Type** `Given my extensive course work and experience, I feel I could be a definite asset to your organization. I look forward to hearing from you to schedule an interview and to discuss my career opportunities with imp` **and then press F3. Type a period.**

   The paragraph is entered beginning at the left margin (Figure 2-68).

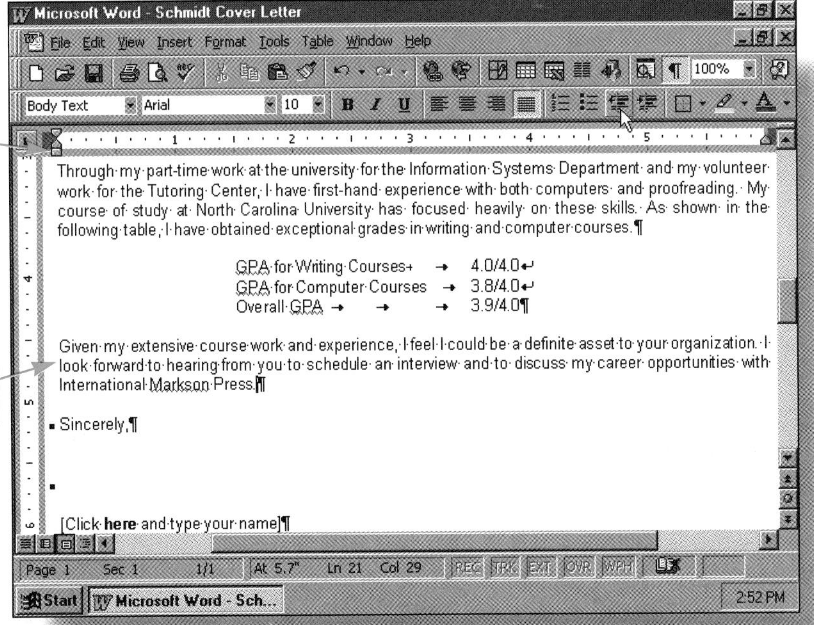

FIGURE 2-68

Other Ways

1. Drag Left Indent marker to desired location on ruler

The next step is to enter the signature block, which in this project contains just your name. Thus, you will delete the signature title line. Follow the steps on the next page to enter the signature block.

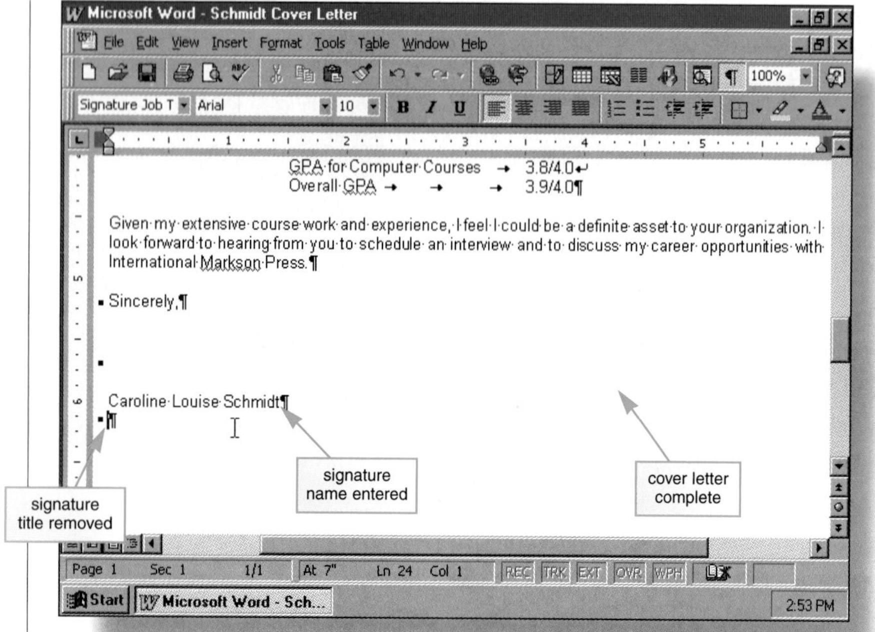

FIGURE 2-69

TO ENTER THE SIGNATURE BLOCK

Step 1: If necessary, scroll down to display the signature block.
Step 2: Click the first line of placeholder text in the signature block, Click here and type your name, to select it.
Step 3: Type `Caroline Louise Schmidt` as the name.
Step 4: Click the second line of placeholder text in the signature block, Click here and type job title, to select it.
Step 5: Right-click the selection to display a shortcut menu and then click Cut on the shortcut menu.

The signature block is entered (Figure 2-69).

More *About* **Flagged Words**

Recall that the commands in a shortcut menu differ depending on the object on which you right-click. If you select and then right-click a word, you can cut, copy, or paste it from the shortcut menu; however, if the selected word has a red wavy underline below it, you can only spell check it from the shortcut menu.

Checking Spelling at Once

As discussed in Project 1, Word checks your spelling and grammar as you type and places a wavy underline below possible spelling or grammar errors. You learned in Project 1 how to check these flagged words immediately. You also can wait and check the entire document for spelling or grammar errors at once.

The following steps illustrate how to spell check the Schmidt Cover Letter at once. Notice in the following example that the word, heavily, has been misspelled intentionally as heaviy to illustrate the use of Word's spell check at once feature. If you are doing this project on a personal computer, your cover letter may contain different misspelled words, depending on the accuracy of your typing.

Steps To Spell Check At Once

1. **Press the CTRL+HOME keys to position the insertion point at the top of the document. Point to the Spelling and Grammar button on the Standard toolbar.**

With the insertion point at line 1 and column 1, Word will begin the spelling and grammar check at the beginning of the document (Figure 2-70).

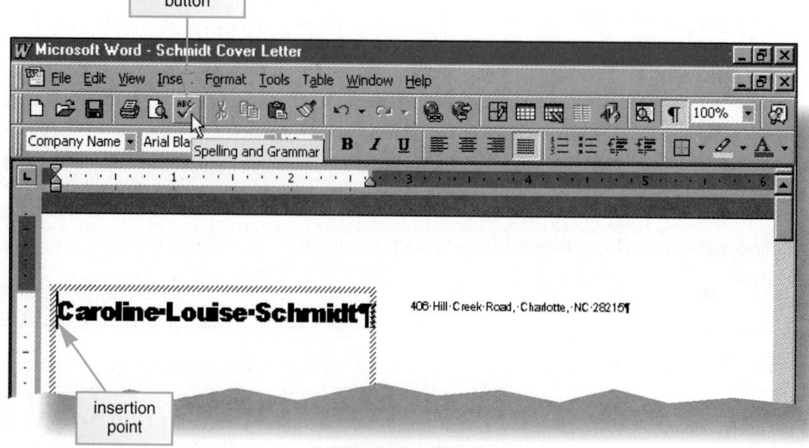

FIGURE 2-70

2 **Click the Spelling and Grammar button.**

Word displays the Spelling and Grammar: English (United States) dialog box (Figure 2-71). Word did not find Markson in its main dictionary because Markson is a company name. Markson is spelled correctly.

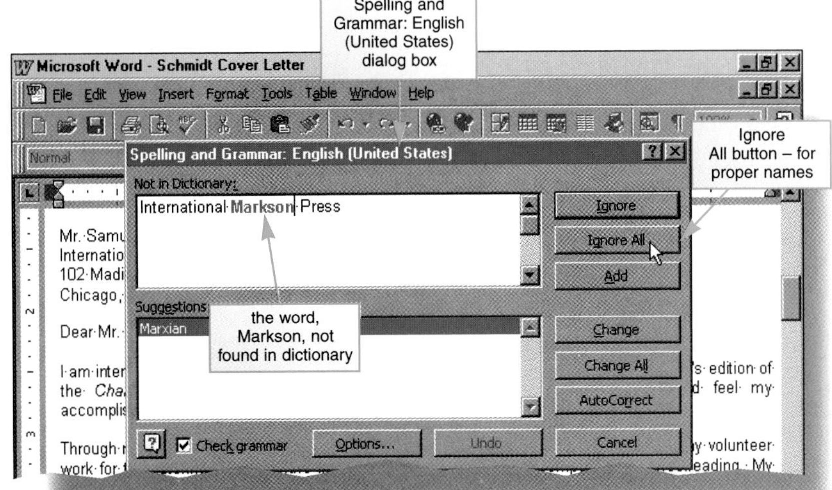

FIGURE 2-71

3 **Click the Ignore All button.**

The spelling and grammar check ignores all future occurrences of the word, Markson. Word continues the spelling and grammar check until it finds the next error or reaches the end of the document. The spelling and grammar check did not find the misspelled word, heaviy, in its main dictionary. The dialog box lists suggested corrections in the Suggestions list box, one of which you may select.

4 **Click heavily in the list (Figure 2-72).**

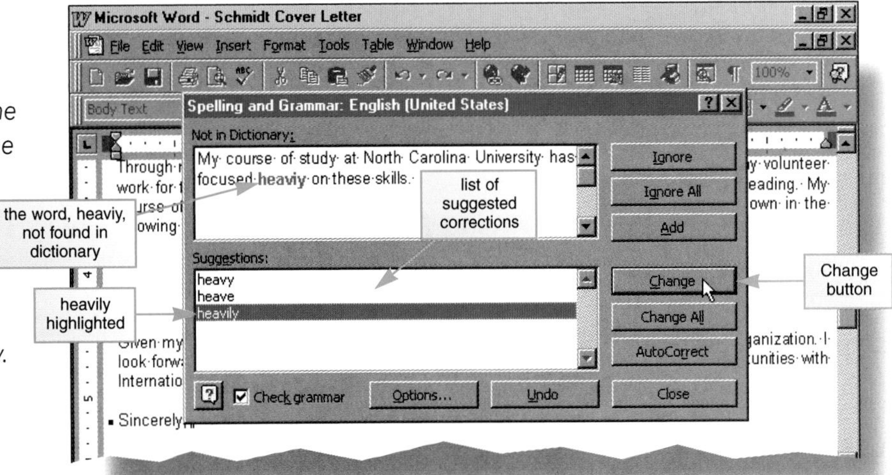

FIGURE 2-72

5 **Click the Change button.**

The spelling and grammar check changes the misspelled word (heaviy) to the selected word (heavily). Word continues to check spelling and grammar until it finds the next error or reaches the end of the document. Word did not find GPA in its main dictionary because it is an abbreviation (Figure 2-73).

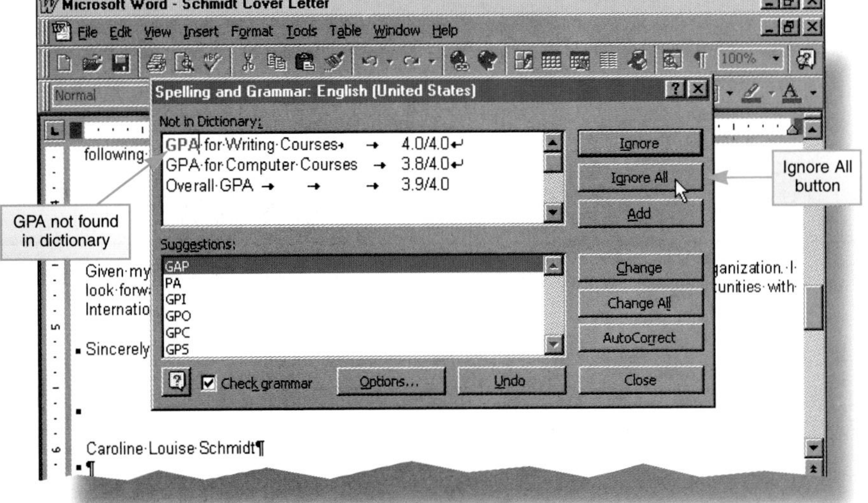

FIGURE 2-73

6 Click the Ignore All button.

Word continues to spell and grammar check until it finds the next error or reaches the end of the document. Word displays a message that is has checked the entire document (Figure 2-74).

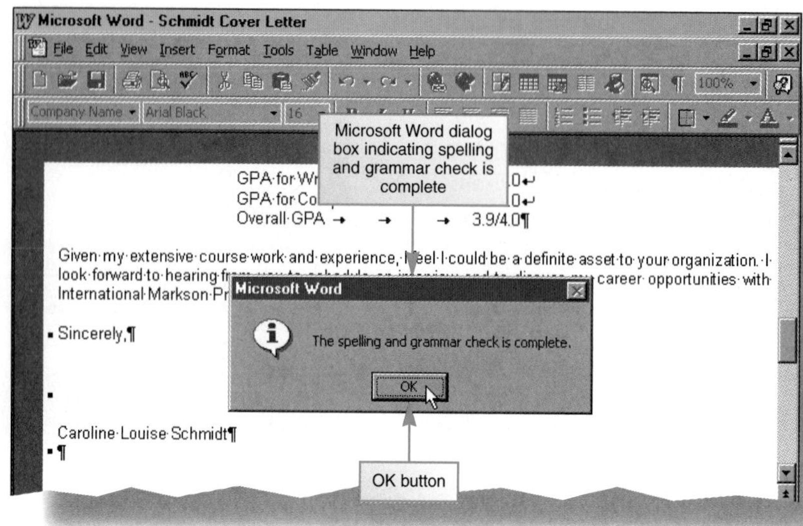

FIGURE 2-74

7 Click the OK button.

Word returns to your document. Your document no longer displays red and green wavy underlines below words and phrases. In addition, the red X on the Spelling and Grammar Status icon has returned to a red check mark.

Other Ways

1. On Tools menu click Spelling and Grammar
2. Press F7
3. Right-click flagged word, click Spelling on shortcut menu

Saving Again and Printing the Cover Letter

The cover letter for the resume is now complete. Because you have performed several tasks since the last save, you should save the cover letter again by clicking the Save button on the Standard toolbar. Finally, you should print the cover letter by clicking the Print button on the Standard toolbar. When you remove the document from the printer, the printout displays the finished cover letter (Figure 2-75).

More About Printing

Use a laser printer to print the resume and cover letter on standard letter-size white or ivory paper. Be sure to print a copy for yourself. And read it – especially before the interview. Most likely, the interviewer will have copies in hand, ready to ask you questions about the contents of both the resume and cover letter.

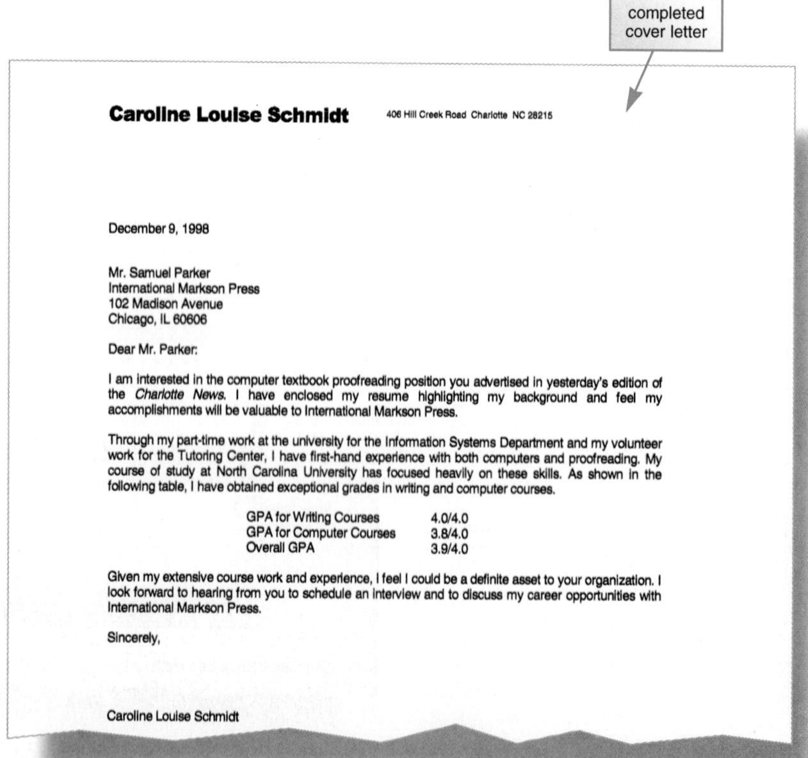

Caroline Louise Schmidt 406 Hill Creek Road Charlotte NC 28215

December 9, 1998

Mr. Samuel Parker
International Markson Press
102 Madison Avenue
Chicago, IL 60606

Dear Mr. Parker:

I am interested in the computer textbook proofreading position you advertised in yesterday's edition of the *Charlotte News*. I have enclosed my resume highlighting my background and feel my accomplishments will be valuable to International Markson Press.

Through my part-time work at the university for the Information Systems Department and my volunteer work for the Tutoring Center, I have first-hand experience with both computers and proofreading. My course of study at North Carolina University has focused heavily on these skills. As shown in the following table, I have obtained exceptional grades in writing and computer courses.

GPA for Writing Courses	4.0/4.0
GPA for Computer Courses	3.8/4.0
Overall GPA	3.9/4.0

Given my extensive course work and experience, I feel I could be a definite asset to your organization. I look forward to hearing from you to schedule an interview and to discuss my career opportunities with International Markson Press.

Sincerely,

Caroline Louise Schmidt

FIGURE 2-75

Working with Multiple Open Word Documents

You might realize at this time that you did not spell check the resume, or you might want to print another copy of the resume.

You currently have two documents open: the cover letter and the resume. Each is in a different document window. You can switch back and forth easily between the two documents. Perform the following steps to switch from the cover letter to the resume.

To Switch from One Open Word Document to Another

1 Click Window on the menu bar and then point to 1 Document1 – Resume: Caroline Louise Schmidt.

Two Word documents currently are open: 1 Document1 – Resume: Caroline Louise Schmidt and 2 Schmidt Cover Letter (Figure 2-76). If you have closed and opened the resume during this project, the resume name will appear as 1 Schmidt Resume.

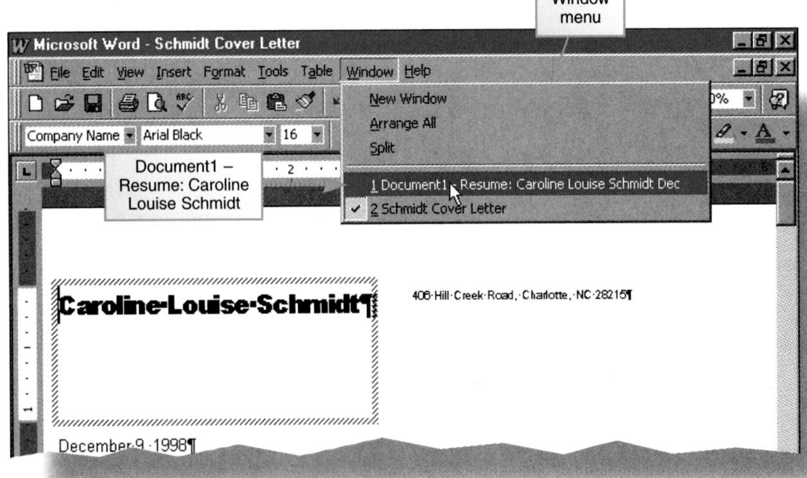

FIGURE 2-76

2 Click 1 Document1 – Resume: Caroline Louise Schmidt.

Word switches from the cover letter to the resume. The document window now displays the resume you created earlier in this project (Figure 2-77).

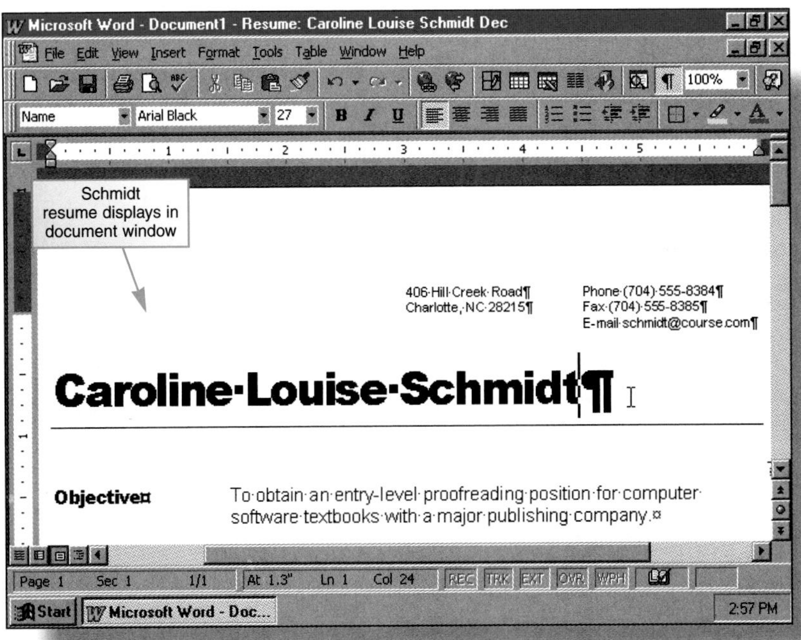

FIGURE 2-77

With the resume in the document window, you can spell and grammar check it, print it, or perform any other editing tasks you desire.

When you are finished with both documents, you may wish to close them. Instead of closing each one individually, you can close all open files at once as shown in these steps.

To Close All Open Word Documents

1 **Press and hold the SHIFT key and then click File on the menu bar. Release the SHIFT key. Point to Close All on the File menu.**

Word displays the Close All command, instead of a Close command, on the File menu because you used the SHIFT key when clicking the menu name (Figure 2-78).

2 **Click Close All.**

Word closes all open documents and displays a blank document window. If at this point you wanted to begin a new document, you would click the New button on the Standard toolbar.

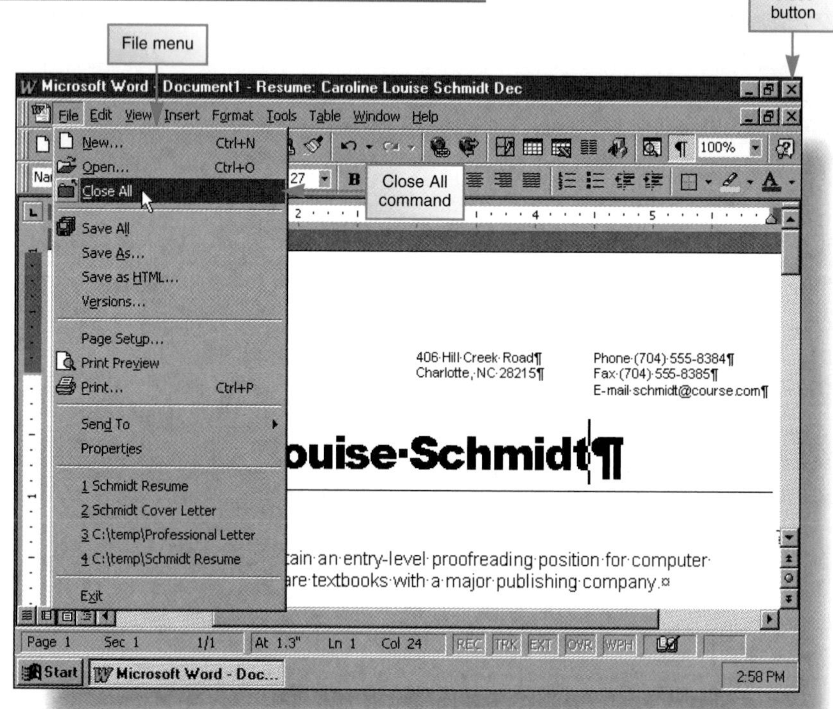

FIGURE 2-78

The final step in this project is to quit Word as described in the step below.

TO QUIT WORD

Step 1: Click the Close button in the Word window.

The Word window closes.

More About Proofreading

You should be absolutely certain that your resume and accompanying cover letter are error free. Use a spell checker! Proofread for grammar errors. Set the resume and cover letter aside for a couple of days, and then proofread them again. Ask others, like a friend or teacher, to proofread them also.

Project Summary

Project 2 introduced you to creating a cover letter and a resume using Word wizards and templates. You used the Resume Wizard to create a resume. Then, you used several formatting techniques to personalize the resume. You viewed and printed the resume in print preview. You used a letter template to create a cover letter and then personalized the cover letter. You created an AutoText entry, which you used when you personalized the cover letter. You learned how to move text using drag-and-drop editing. Finally, you learned how to switch between one open Word document to another and close multiple open Word documents.

What You Should Know

Having completed this project, you now should be able to perform the following tasks:

- Align Information Vertically with the TAB Key (*WD 2.44*)
- AutoFormat As You Type (*WD 2.21*)
- Close All Open Word Documents (*WD 2.50*)
- Create a Letter Using a Word Template (*WD 2.29*)
- Create a Resume Using Word's Resume Wizard (*WD 2.7*)
- Create an AutoText Entry (*WD 2.34*)
- Decrease the Indent in a Paragraph (*WD 2.45*)
- Display Nonprinting Characters (*WD 2.15*)
- Drag and Drop Selected Text (*WD 2.41*)
- Enter a Line Break (*WD 2.19*)
- Enter a Paragraph (*WD 2.39*)
- Enter the Remaining Sections of the Resume (*WD 2.22*)
- Enter the Salutation (*WD 2.35*)
- Enter the Signature Block (*WD 2.46*)
- Format Characters Using Shortcut Keys (*WD 2.37*)
- Increase the Indent of the Left Margin (*WD 2.43*)
- Increase the Font Size by One Point (*WD 2.24*)
- Insert a Blank Line above a Paragraph (*WD 2.16*)
- Insert an AutoText Entry (*WD 2.38*)
- Print Preview a Document (*WD 2.25*)
- Print the Resume Created by the Resume Wizard (*WD 2.14*)
- Quit Word (*WD 2.50*)
- Save a Document (*WD 2.27, WD 2.36*)
- Select a Paragraph (*WD 2.36*)
- Select a Sentence (*WD 2.40*)
- Select a Table and Format Its Characters (*WD 2.23*)
- Select and Replace Placeholder Text (*WD 2.17, WD 2.32*)
- Select and Replace Resume Wizard Supplied Text (*WD 2.18*)
- Spell and Grammar Check At Once (*WD 2.46*)
- Switch From One Open Word Document to Another (*WD 2.49*)
- Zoom a Document (*WD 2.31*)

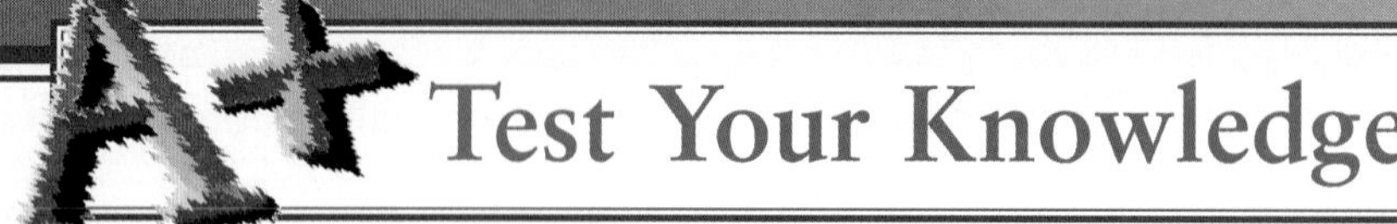

Test Your Knowledge

1 True/False

Instructions: Circle T if the statement is true or F if the statement is false.

T F 1. By asking you several basic questions, Word's templates prepare and format a document for you based on your responses.
T F 2. A cell is the intersection of a row and a column.
T F 3. Press the CTRL+B keys to insert a blank line above a paragraph.
T F 4. You can print a document from within print preview.
T F 5. Word provides three styles, or families, of wizards and templates: Gold, Silver, and Bronze.
T F 6. When you paste text into a document, the Clipboard contents are erased.
T F 7. The TAB key is used to align text vertically in a document.
T F 8. In Word, the default, or preset, tabs are spaced every inch on the ruler.
T F 9. To spell and grammar check at once, right-click the flagged word.
T F 10. To switch from one open Word document to another, click the Switch button on the Standard toolbar.

2 Multiple Choice

Instructions: Circle the correct response.

1. In the Style list box, style names followed by an underlined bold letter a (**a**) are called ___________.
   a. active styles
   b. inactive styles
   c. paragraph styles
   d. character styles
2. Press the ___________ key(s) to create a line break.
   a. ENTER
   b. CTRL+ENTER
   c. SHIFT+ENTER
   d. ALT+ENTER
3. To increase the font size of selected text by one point, press the ___________ keys.
   a. CTRL+]
   b. CTRL+>
   c. SHIFT+]
   d. SHIFT+>
4. In print preview, the Formatting toolbar ___________.
   a. displays above the Print Preview toolbar
   b. displays below the Print Preview toolbar
   c. displays above the Formatting toolbar
   d. does not display

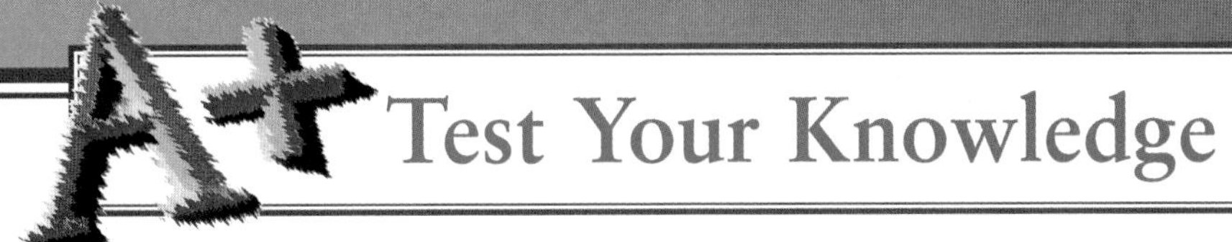

5. Which of the following is optional in a business letter?
   a. signature block b. inside address c. salutation d. complimentary close
6. To insert an AutoText entry, press the ___________ key(s) after you type the AutoText entry name.
   a. INSERT b. ENTER c. F3 d. CTRL+ENTER
7. To underline words, not spaces between words, press the ___________ keys.
   a. CTRL+U
   b. CTRL+W
   c. CTRL+SHIFT+U
   d. CTRL+SHIFT+W
8. To select an entire paragraph, ___________.
   a. double-click to the left of the paragraph
   b. triple-click the paragraph
   c. both a and b
   d. neither a nor b
9. When you press the TAB key, a ___________ displays on the screen.
   a. raised dot
   b. paragraph mark
   c. right-pointing arrow
   d. letter T
10. To display the Close All command on the File menu, ___________.
    a. double-click File on the menu bar
    b. right-click File on the menu bar
    c. press and hold the SHIFT key and then click File on the menu bar
    d. press and hold the ALT key and then click File on the menu bar

3 Understanding the Print Preview Toolbar

Instructions: In Figure 2-79, arrows point to several of the boxes and buttons on the Print Preview toolbar. In the spaces provided, briefly explain the purpose of each button or box.

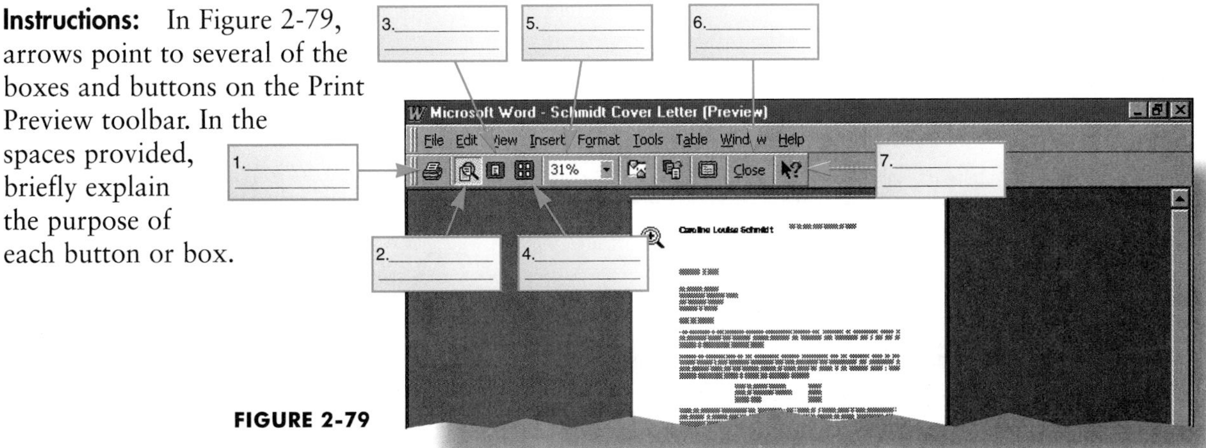

FIGURE 2-79

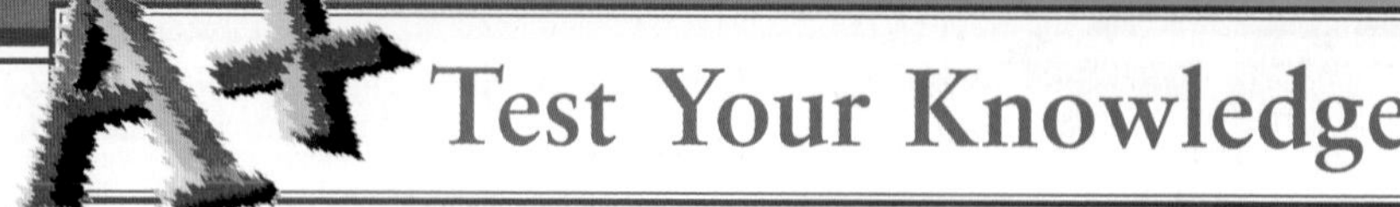

4 Understanding the Components of a Business Letter

Instructions: In Figure 2-80, arrows point to components a business letter. Identify the various elements of the letter in the spaces provided.

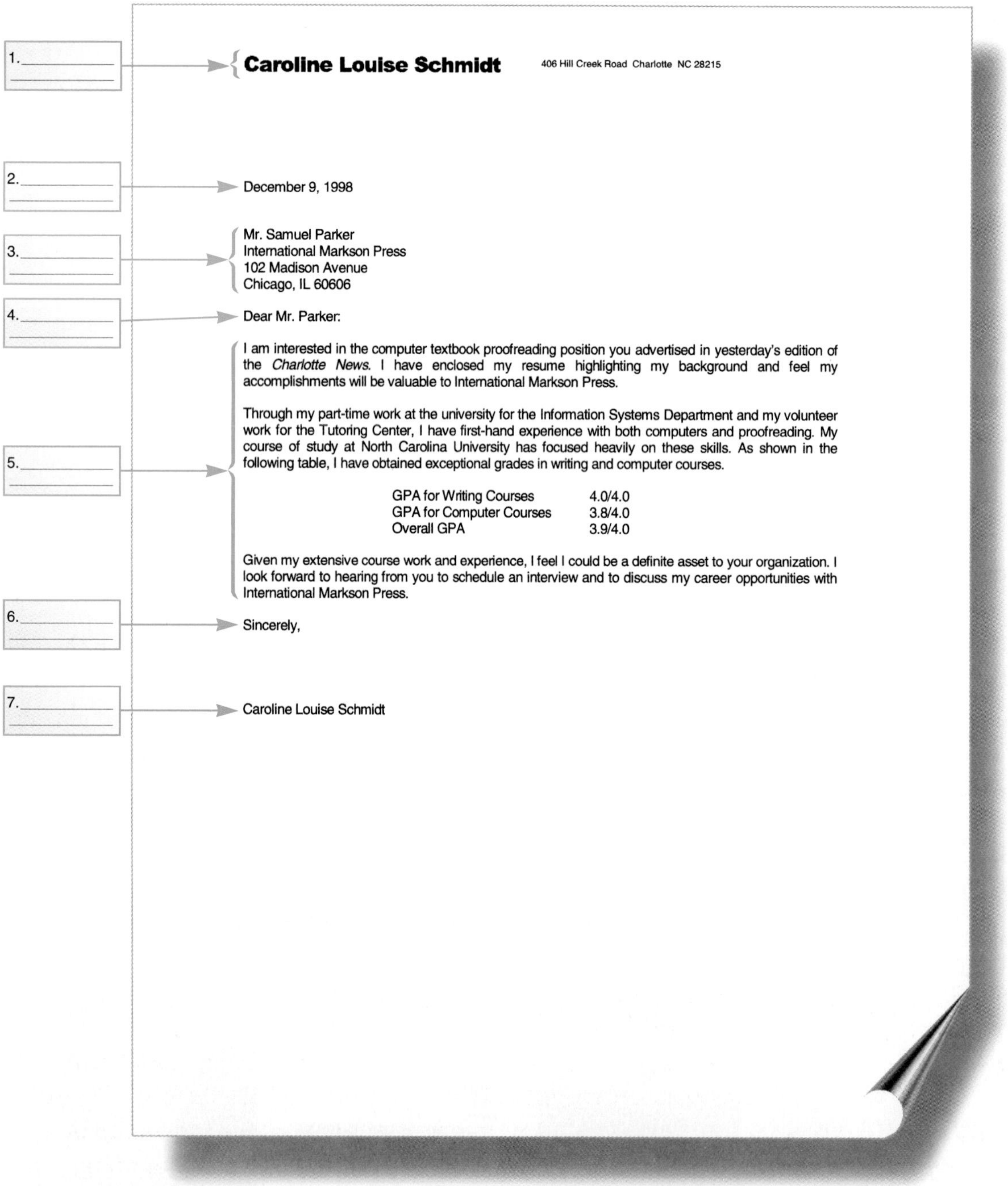

1. ____________

Caroline Louise Schmidt 406 Hill Creek Road Charlotte NC 28215

2. ____________

December 9, 1998

3. ____________

Mr. Samuel Parker
International Markson Press
102 Madison Avenue
Chicago, IL 60606

4. ____________

Dear Mr. Parker:

5. ____________

I am interested in the computer textbook proofreading position you advertised in yesterday's edition of the *Charlotte News*. I have enclosed my resume highlighting my background and feel my accomplishments will be valuable to International Markson Press.

Through my part-time work at the university for the Information Systems Department and my volunteer work for the Tutoring Center, I have first-hand experience with both computers and proofreading. My course of study at North Carolina University has focused heavily on these skills. As shown in the following table, I have obtained exceptional grades in writing and computer courses.

GPA for Writing Courses	4.0/4.0
GPA for Computer Courses	3.8/4.0
Overall GPA	3.9/4.0

Given my extensive course work and experience, I feel I could be a definite asset to your organization. I look forward to hearing from you to schedule an interview and to discuss my career opportunities with International Markson Press.

6. ____________

Sincerely,

7. ____________

Caroline Louise Schmidt

FIGURE 2-80

Use Help

1 Reviewing Project Activities

Instructions: Perform the following tasks using a computer.

1. Start Word. If the Office Assistant is on your screen, click it to display its balloon. If the Office Assistant is not on your screen, click the Office Assistant button on the Standard toolbar.
2. Type `templates and wizards` in the What would you like to do? text box. Click the Search button. Click the Quick ways to create letters, memos, and other documents link. Read the information. Use the shortcut menu or Options button to print the information.
3. Click the Help Topics button to display the Help Topics: Microsoft Word dialog box. Click the Contents tab. Double-click the Formatting book. Double-click the Formatting with Styles book. Double click the About styles topic. Read and print the information.
4. Click the Help Topics button. Click the Index tab. Type `AutoText` in the top box labeled 1 and then double-click the overview topic in the list box labeled 2. Double-click the Use shortcuts to insert frequently used text and graphics topic. Read and print the information.
5. Click the Help Topics button. Click the Find tab. Type `drag and drop` in the top box labeled 1 and then double-click the Move or copy text and graphics topic. Click the Move or copy text and graphics a short distance within a window link. Read and print the information.
6. Close any open Help dialog box or window by clicking its Close button. Close the Office Assistant.

2 Expanding on the Basics

Instructions: Use Word Help for a better understanding of the topics listed below. Answer the questions on your own paper or hand in the printed Help topic to your instructor.

1. In this project, you worked with a Word table in the resume. Use the Office Assistant to answer the following questions about Word tables.
   a. How do you create a simple Word table?
   b. How do you create a complex Word table?
   c. How to you convert existing text to a Word table?
2. In this project, you used print preview to view your document before printing it. Use the Contents tab in the Help Topics: Microsoft Word dialog box to answer the following questions about print preview.
   a. How do you edit text in print preview?
   b. In print preview, how can you prevent text from spilling onto a second page?
3. In this project, you used shortcut keys to format characters and paragraphs. Use the Index tab in the Help Topics: Microsoft Word dialog box to locate Help windows describing the keys used for the following tasks: editing and moving text and graphics, formatting characters and paragraphs, printing and previewing documents, and working with documents. Print each of the four Help topics.

(continued)

Use Help

Expanding on the Basics *(continued)*

4. In this project, you used the Professional Letter template to create the cover letter. Use the Find tab in the Help Topics: Microsoft Word dialog box to determine how to create a letter using the Letter Wizard, which is a command on a menu. Then, determine how to modify a letter created with the Letter Wizard.
5. Use the Microsoft on the Web command on the Help menu to connect to Microsoft's Free Stuff page on the Web. Print the pages associated with free items you may download that work with Word.

Apply Your Knowledge

1 Enhancing a Document

Instructions: Start Word. Open the document, apply-2, from the Word folder on the Data Disk that accompanies this book. The document, shown in Figure 2-81, is a cover letter for a resume. You are to switch two sentences and insert a table to the letter.

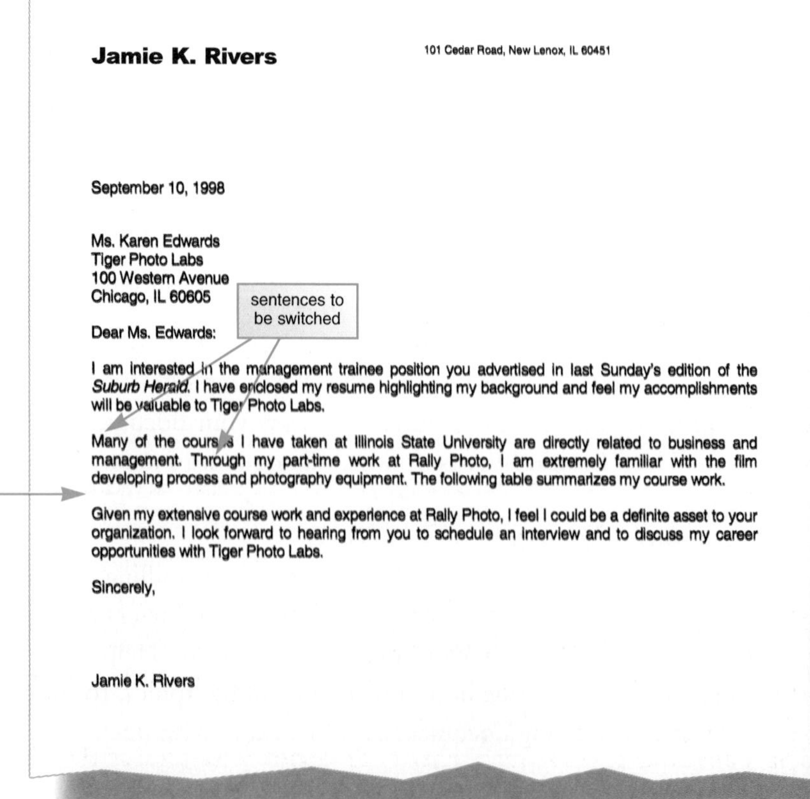

Jamie K. Rivers 101 Cedar Road, New Lenox, IL 60451

September 10, 1998

Ms. Karen Edwards
Tiger Photo Labs
100 Western Avenue
Chicago, IL 60605

Dear Ms. Edwards:

I am interested in the management trainee position you advertised in last Sunday's edition of the *Suburb Herald*. I have enclosed my resume highlighting my background and feel my accomplishments will be valuable to Tiger Photo Labs.

Many of the courses I have taken at Illinois State University are directly related to business and management. Through my part-time work at Rally Photo, I am extremely familiar with the film developing process and photography equipment. The following table summarizes my course work.

Given my extensive course work and experience at Rally Photo, I feel I could be a definite asset to your organization. I look forward to hearing from you to schedule an interview and to discuss my career opportunities with Tiger Photo Labs.

Sincerely,

Jamie K. Rivers

FIGURE 2-81

Apply Your Knowledge

Perform the following tasks:

1. Position the mouse pointer in the sentence that begins, Through my part-time work at Rally ...
2. Press and hold the CTRL key while clicking the sentence. Release the CTRL key.
3. With the mouse pointer in the selected sentence, press and hold down the left mouse button. Drag the insertion point to the left of the M in the sentence beginning, Many of the courses I have taken, ... and then release the mouse button.
4. Position the insertion point at the end of the second paragraph and then press the ENTER key.
5. Click the Increase Indent button on the Formatting toolbar to move the Left Indent marker to the 0.5-inch mark on the ruler.
6. Click the Align Left button on the Formatting toolbar to left align the paragraphs in the table.
7. Type `Business:` and then press the TAB key. Type `Accounting, Business Law, Finance, Marketing, Retailing, Sales` and then press the SHIFT+ENTER keys.
8. Type `Management:` and then press the TAB key. Type `Auditing, Forecasting, Information Systems, Investments, Operations` as the end of the table.
9. Click File on the menu bar and then click Save As. Use the file name, Revised Rivers Letter, and then save the document on your floppy disk.
10. Click the Print Preview button on the Standard toolbar. Print the revised document in print preview.

In the Lab

1 Using Word's Resume Wizard to Create a Resume

Problem: You are a student at Wisconsin University expecting to receive your Bachelor of Science degree in Business Management this May. As the semester end is approaching quickly, you are beginning a search for full-time employment upon graduation. You prepare the resume shown in Figure 2-82 using Word's Resume Wizard.

Instructions:

1. Use the Resume Wizard to create a resume. Use the name and address information in Figure 2-82 when the Resume Wizard requests it.
2. Personalize the resume as shown in Figure 2-82. When entering multiple lines in the Awards received, Software experience, Interests and activities, and Hobbies sections, be sure to enter a line break at the end of each line, instead of a paragraph break. Add an extra blank line above the name at the top of the resume. Increase the font size of the text as indicated in Figure 2-82.
3. Check the spelling of the resume.
4. Save the resume on a floppy disk with Peterson Resume as the file name.
5. Print the resume from within print preview.

(continued)

Using Word's Resume Wizard to Create a Resume *(continued)*

54 Seventh Place
Monroe, WI 53566

Phone (608) 555-1355
Fax (608) 555-4436
E-mail peterson@course.com

Mark Allan Peterson

Objective To obtain an entry-level accountant position.

Education 1994 - 1998 Wisconsin University Madison, WI

Business/Accounting

- B.S. in Business Management, May 1998
- A.S. in Business Practices, May 1996

Awards received 1st Place – 1998 Entrepreneur Society Challenge
1998 Outstanding Senior
1997 Top Student Award, Small Business Association

Relevant course work Financial Accounting I and II, Intermediate Accounting, Cost Accounting, Tax Accounting, Auditing, Federal Income Taxes, Managerial Statistics, Management Information Systems

Work experience 1996 - 1998 West Accounting Services Madison, WI

Accounting Assistant

- Assist CPAs in tax preparation activities for individuals, small businesses, and large companies.
- Post journal entries, prepare balance sheets and income statements, balance checkbook registers, generate payroll, pay bills for small businesses.

Software experience Accounting: Quicken, Money
Word Processing: Word, WordPerfect
Spreadsheet: Excel, Quattro Pro
Database: Access
Other: PowerPoint, Internet Explorer

Interests and activities Accounting Club, Treasurer, 1996-1998
Student Government Association, President, 1997-1998

Hobbies Surfing the Internet
Hiking
Antique Cars

FIGURE 2-82

2 Using the Letter Template to Create a Cover Letter

Problem: You have just prepared the resume shown in Figure 2-82 and now are ready to create a cover letter to send to a prospective employer. In yesterday's edition of the *Wisconsin Herald*, you noticed an advertisement for an entry-level accounting position at Lakeway Accounting. You prepare the cover letter shown in Figure 2-83 to send with your resume.

Instructions:

1. Create a professional style letter by clicking the Professional Letter icon on the Letters & Faxes sheet in the New dialog box.
2. Save the letter on a floppy disk with Peterson Cover Letter as the file name.
3. Enter the letterhead so it looks like the letterhead shown in Figure 2-83. Enter the inside address and then the salutation.
4. Create an AutoText entry for Lakeway Accounting that displays in the inside address.
5. Personalize the body of the cover letter so it matches Figure 2-83. Use the AutoText entry you created in Step 5 whenever you have to enter the company name, Lakeway Accounting. The first column of the table is indented 1.5-inches from the left margin, and the second column is positioned at the 3.5-inch mark on the ruler.
6. Enter the signature block as shown in Figure 2-83.
7. Check the spelling of the cover letter. Save the cover letter again with the same file name.
8. Print the cover letter.

Mark Allan Peterson 54 Seventh Place, Monroe, WI 53566

March 30, 1998

Ms. Rita Kramer
Lakeway Accounting
50 Randolph Street
Chicago, IL 60606

Dear Ms. Kramer:

I am interested in the entry-level accounting position you advertised in yesterday's edition of the *Wisconsin Herald*. I have enclosed my resume highlighting my background and feel my accomplishments will be valuable to Lakeway Accounting.

As a part-time employee at West Accounting Services and with my school club activities, I have first-hand experience with accounting practices. My course of study at Wisconsin University has focused heavily on accounting. As shown in the following table, I have obtained exceptional grades in my courses:

GPA for major courses	3.9/4.0
GPA for non-major courses	3.7/4.0
Total Accumulated GPA	3.8/4.0

With my extensive course work and experience, I feel I can be an asset to your organization. I look forward to hearing from you to schedule an interview and to discuss my career opportunities with Lakeway Accounting.

Sincerely,

Mark Allan Peterson

FIGURE 2-83

3 Using Word's Wizards to Compose a Cover Letter and Resume

Problem: You are looking for a new job and need to prepare a resume and cover letter.

Instructions: Obtain a copy of last Sunday's newspaper. Look through the classified section and cut out a want ad in an area of interest to you. Assume you are in the market for the position being advertised. Use the Resume Wizard to create a resume. Use the Letter Wizard to create the cover letter. Display the Letter Wizard by clicking Tools on the menu bar and then clicking Letter Wizard. You may need to refer to your Use Help 2 responses for assistance in using the Letter Wizard. Use the want ad for the inside address and your personal information for the return address. Try to be as accurate as possible when personalizing the resume and cover letter. Turn in the want ad with your cover letter and resume.

The difficulty of these case studies varies: ◗ are the least difficult; ◗◗ are more difficult; and ◗◗◗ are the most difficult.

1 ◗ To keep on schedule, you post a large calendar for the current month on your door or wall. As the end of this month approaches, you begin preparation for next month's calendar. Next month is your birthday! Use the Calendar Wizard, together with the concepts and techniques presented in this project, to create a calendar for your birthday month (the calendar should have a clip art graphic on it). Be sure to delete the default graphic and insert an appropriate clip art file for your birthday month. If the Calendar Wizard is not installed on your system, click Help on the menu bar, point to Microsoft on the Web, click Free Stuff, and then follow the instructions to download more wizards from the Web.

2 ◗ You have just completed Word Project 2. Congratulations! Your instructor decides to present you with an award. You are the recipient of the award; your instructor will sign the award; the award is a Certificate of Completion presented by your school; and the accomplishment is Completing Word Project 2. Use today's date. Use the Award Wizard, together with the concepts and techniques presented in this project to create the Certificate of Completion. If the Award Wizard is not installed on your system, click Help on the menu bar, point to Microsoft on the Web, click Free Stuff, and then follow the instructions to download more wizards from the Web.

Cases and Places

3 ▶▶ As book reviewer for Jameson Publishers, you have just reviewed the word processing chapter in a computer concepts book. Your review is five pages long. It must be faxed to E. P. Harding at Jameson Publishers (145 Western Avenue, Hammond, IN 46323; telephone 219-555-2063; fax 219-555-2064), with a copy faxed to B. T. Andrews at the same number. In the fax, write a message informing E. P. Harding that your review of the word processing chapter is attached and if she has any questions, she can contact you. Use your own name, address, and telephone information in the fax. Use the Fax Wizard, together with the concepts and techniques presented in this project, to create and format a cover sheet for the facsimile transmission.

4 ▶▶ David Brandy, your boss at Grover Electric, has just received last month's telephone bill. He is extremely concerned about the increasing number of personal long-distance calls being made by company employees. Mr. Brandy does not mind an occasional telephone call home, but conversations ranging from 20 minutes to more than an hour are unacceptable. Not only does it take the employees away from their job duties, but also it is costing the company hundreds of dollars each month. Mr. Brandy has asked you to prepare a confidential memorandum regarding this matter for Sara Reynolds, a department head. The memorandum should explain the problem and solicit solutions. Copies of the memo also should be sent to Julie Adams and Ed West, the other department heads. Use the Memo Wizard, together with the concepts and techniques presented in this project, to create and format the interoffice memorandum.

5 ▶▶ Your credit report is maintained by one or more credit bureaus or credit reporting agencies. Obtain the name, address, and telephone number of a credit bureau that maintains your information. Find out how much they charge for a copy of a credit report. Using Word's Letter Wizard, prepare a credit report request. Apply the concepts and techniques presented in this project to personalize the credit report request.

6 ▶▶▶ Many organizations distribute brochures to promote their products and/or services. Brochures present prospective customers with more information than posted or published advertisements, as well as provide written material they can take with them and review at their leisure. Visit a local company and learn as much as you can about their product(s) and/or service(s). Find out how the product(s) and/or service(s) is unique, what features it offers, and why it would be valuable to potential buyers. Then, use Word's Newsletter Wizard, along with the concepts and techniques presented in this project, to design a newsletter advertising the product(s) and/or service(s). When the newsletter is complete, take it to the company and ask for its comments, suggestions, or recommendations.

Cases and Places

7 ▶▶▶ Everyone, at one time or another, has attended a meeting that was so disorganized that very little was accomplished. Meetings often can be more effective with an agenda, which is a written plan that states when and where the meeting will take place, the subject of the meeting, the participants and their responsibilities, and the topics that will be discussed. An agenda helps the chairperson keep a meeting on track and helps attendees prepare for the meeting. Find out about an upcoming meeting at your school, such as a club or student government meeting. Use Word's Agenda Wizard, and the concepts and techniques presented in this project, to prepare a thorough agenda for the meeting. Distribute the agenda to the relevant participants, and then attend the meeting to see if the agenda helps the meeting run more efficiently. If the Agenda Wizard is not installed on your system, click Help on the menu bar, point to Microsoft on the Web, click Free Stuff, and then follow the instructions to download more wizards from the Web.

Microsoft *Word 97*

Creating a Research Paper with a Table

Objectives:

You will have mastered the material in this project when you can:

- Describe the MLA documentation style for research papers
- Change the margin settings in a document
- Adjust line spacing in a document
- Use a header to number pages of a document
- Indent paragraphs
- Use Word's AutoCorrect feature
- Add a footnote to a research paper
- Insert a Word table into a document
- Enter data into a Word table
- Format a Word table
- Insert a manual page break
- Create a hanging indent
- Create a text hyperlink
- Sort selected paragraphs
- Scroll by a page
- Find and replace text
- Use Word's thesaurus
- Display the number of words in a document
- Display the Web site associated with a hyperlink

Researching, Writing, and Referencing

Citing Sources in Style

Throughout your collegiate career, adhering to one or more styles from a number of established guidelines, you will write research papers and other reports on a diversity of topics covered in your courses of study. After you have researched your subjects, found your reference materials, and written your essays, the crucial step of documenting these resources remains. The citation procedure may seem tedious, but it is the way your readers know how to find additional information on the subjects and the way you ethically give credit to the individuals who have researched these topics before you.

Depending on the course you are taking and the type of document that is assigned, your method of presenting these sources will vary. In academia, three major style systems for writers of research and scientific papers generally are recognized. Your instructors likely will direct you to the required style and appropriate handbooks as assignments are given. The research paper you are to create in this project with Microsoft Word 97 uses the Modern Language Association (MLA) style, which is used by scholars in the humanities fields. Another popular citation style developed by the American Psychological Association (APA) is used by researchers in the social sciences. The third style is the number system used by writers in the applied sciences.

These writers consult standard style manuals that describe, in detail, how to acknowledge reference sources in the body of the paper and in a general list at the end of the report. The MLA style is explained in the *MLA Handbook for Writers of Research Papers*, and the APA style is documented in the *Publication Manual of the American Psychological Association*. The researchers also consult other style guides, such as the University of Chicago's *The Chicago Manual of Style*, the *American Chemical Society Handbook for Authors*, and *The Microsoft Manual of Style for Technical Publications*.

Teams of instructors and scholars develop the style guidelines in each of these publications. The *MLA Handbook,* for example, originated in 1951 for MLA members. In 1977, it was expanded to become a guide for undergraduate students and renamed the *MLA Handbook for Writers of Research Papers.* Subsequent editions were published in 1984, 1988, and 1995. Keeping up with necessary revisions, however, is a never-ending task, especially with the evolution of online references on the Internet. Researchers are challenged continually to keep methods of style and citation accurate and current.

Until scholars agree on a universal style of documentation, you can familiarize yourself with the numerous citation systems and style guides available. Writers of virtually all types of commentary find the guides essential in preparation of essays, research papers, reports, and manuscripts of every kind. Attention to style and detail is evident in the finished product and just may make the difference in an excellent grade.

Raymond Chandler, U.S. author, stated in his 1947 *Letter*, "The most durable thing in writing is style, and style is the most valuable investment a writer can make with his time . . . the writer who puts his individual mark on the way he writes will always pay off."

Microsoft
Word 97

Creating a Research Paper with a Table

Case Perspective

Anna L. Porter is a full-time student at Michigan State University, majoring in Information Systems and Computer Programming. The professor in one of her computer classes, CIS 201, has assigned a 500-word research paper. The paper must discuss some aspect of personal computers. Because Anna's computer at home recently was infected with a computer virus, Anna decides to write the research paper on computer viruses. The paper must be written according to the MLA documentation style, which specifies guidelines for report preparation. Professor Brown suggests students use the Internet to obtain the MLA guidelines. The paper also must contain one footnote, a table, and three references – one of which must be from the World Wide Web.

Anna will visit a library, surf the Internet, stop by a computer store, and interview the director of the Information Systems department at her school for information on computer viruses. She also plans to surf the Internet to obtain information and the guidelines for the MLA style of documentation.

Introduction

In both the academic and business environments, you will be asked to write reports. Business reports range from proposals to cost justifications to five-year plans to research findings. Academic reports focus mostly on research findings. Whether you are writing a business report or an academic report, you should follow a standard style when preparing it.

Many different styles of documentation exist for report preparation, depending on the nature of the report. Each style requires the same basic information; the differences among styles appear in the manner of presenting the information. For example, one documentation style may use the term *bibliography*, whereas another uses *references*, and yet a third prefers *works cited*. The **Modern Language Association (MLA)** presents a popular documentation style used today for research papers. Thus, this project uses the **MLA style of documentation**.

Project Three – Research Paper with a Table

Project 3 illustrates the creation of a short research paper describing computer viruses. A table at the end of the research paper outlines techniques for virus protection and system backup. As depicted in Figure 3-1, the paper follows the MLA style of documentation. The first two pages present the research paper and the third page lists the works cited alphabetically.

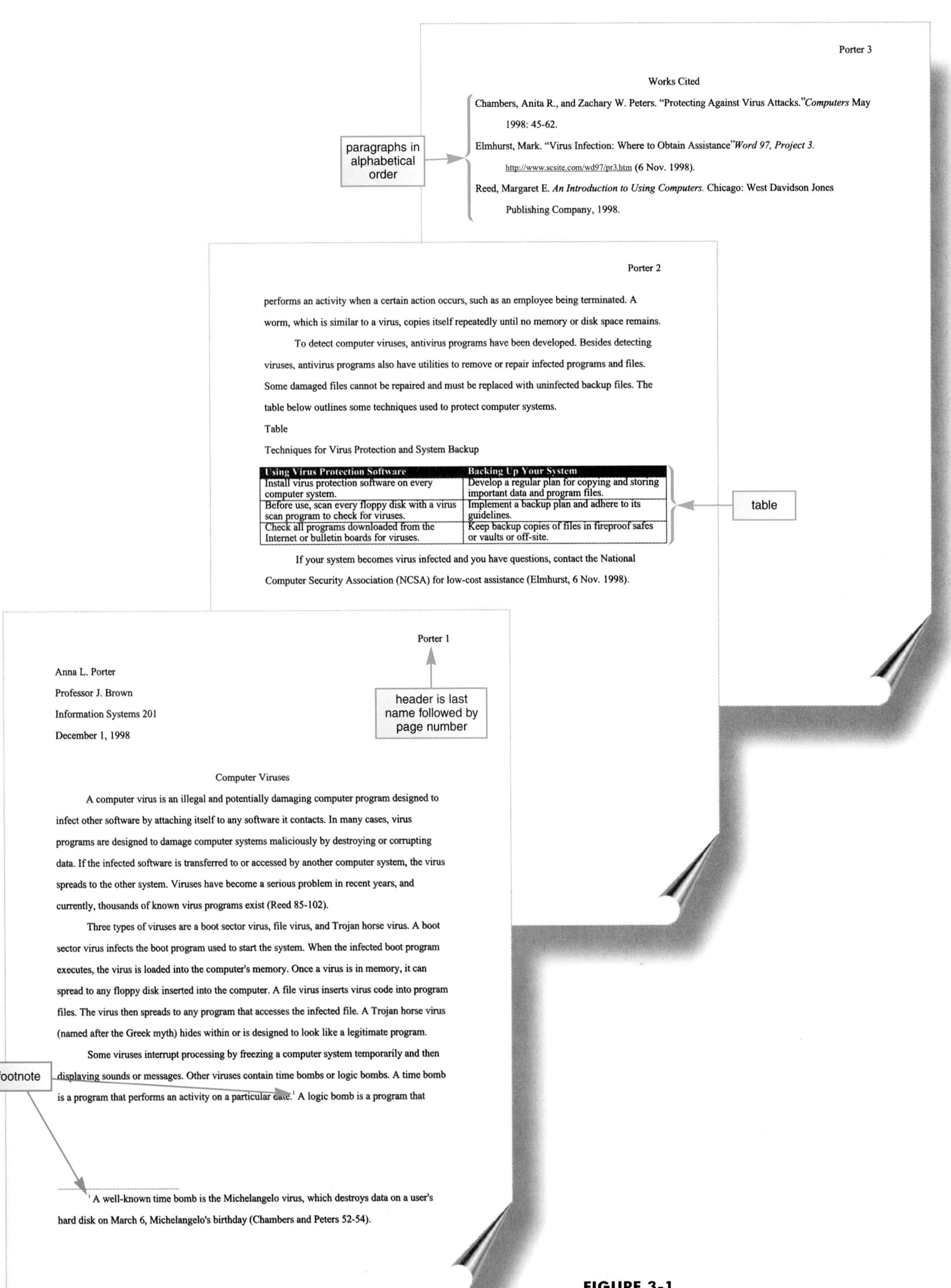

Porter 1

Anna L. Porter

Professor J. Brown

Information Systems 201

December 1, 1998

Computer Viruses

A computer virus is an illegal and potentially damaging computer program designed to infect other software by attaching itself to any software it contacts. In many cases, virus programs are designed to damage computer systems maliciously by destroying or corrupting data. If the infected software is transferred to or accessed by another computer system, the virus spreads to the other system. Viruses have become a serious problem in recent years, and currently, thousands of known virus programs exist (Reed 85-102).

Three types of viruses are a boot sector virus, file virus, and Trojan horse virus. A boot sector virus infects the boot program used to start the system. When the infected boot program executes, the virus is loaded into the computer's memory. Once a virus is in memory, it can spread to any floppy disk inserted into the computer. A file virus inserts virus code into program files. The virus then spreads to any program that accesses the infected file. A Trojan horse virus (named after the Greek myth) hides within or is designed to look like a legitimate program.

Some viruses interrupt processing by freezing a computer system temporarily and then displaying sounds or messages. Other viruses contain time bombs or logic bombs. A time bomb is a program that performs an activity on a particular date.[1] A logic bomb is a program that

[1] A well-known time bomb is the Michelangelo virus, which destroys data on a user's hard disk on March 6, Michelangelo's birthday (Chambers and Peters 52-54).

Porter 2

performs an activity when a certain action occurs, such as an employee being terminated. A worm, which is similar to a virus, copies itself repeatedly until no memory or disk space remains.

To detect computer viruses, antivirus programs have been developed. Besides detecting viruses, antivirus programs also have utilities to remove or repair infected programs and files. Some damaged files cannot be repaired and must be replaced with uninfected backup files. The table below outlines some techniques used to protect computer systems.

Table

Techniques for Virus Protection and System Backup

Using Virus Protection Software	Backing Up Your System
Install virus protection software on every computer system.	Develop a regular plan for copying and storing important data and program files.
Before use, scan every floppy disk with a virus scan program to check for viruses.	Implement a backup plan and adhere to its guidelines.
Check all programs downloaded from the Internet or bulletin boards for viruses.	Keep backup copies of files in fireproof safes or vaults or off-site.

If your system becomes virus infected and you have questions, contact the National Computer Security Association (NCSA) for low-cost assistance (Elmhurst, 6 Nov. 1998).

Porter 3

Works Cited

Chambers, Anita R., and Zachary W. Peters. "Protecting Against Virus Attacks."*Computers* May 1998: 45-62.

Elmhurst, Mark. "Virus Infection: Where to Obtain Assistance"*Word 97, Project 3.* http://www.scsite.com/wd97/pr3.htm (6 Nov. 1998).

Reed, Margaret E. *An Introduction to Using Computers.* Chicago: West Davidson Jones Publishing Company, 1998.

FIGURE 3-1

More *About* **Documentation Styles**

Another popular documentation style is by the American Psychological Association (APA). The MLA style is the standard in the humanities, whereas the APA style is preferred in the social sciences. Many differences exist between the two styles. For example, the APA style uses the term References for the bibliography.

MLA Documentation Style

When writing papers, you must be sure to adhere to some form of documentation style. The research paper in this project follows the guidelines presented by the MLA. To follow the MLA style, double-space all pages of the paper with one-inch top, bottom, left, and right margins. Indent the first word of each paragraph one-half inch from the left margin. At the right margin of each page, place a page number one-half inch from the top margin. On each page, precede the page number by your last name.

The MLA style does not require a title page; instead, it requires you to place your name and course information in a block at the left margin beginning one inch from the top of the page. Center the title two double-spaces below your name and course information. In the body of the paper, place author references in parentheses with the page number(s) where the referenced information is located. These in-text **parenthetical citations** are used instead of footnoting each source at the bottom of the page or at the end of the paper. In the MLA style, **footnotes** are used only for explanatory notes. In the body of the paper, use **superscripts** (raised numbers) to signal that an explanatory note exists.

According to the MLA style, explanatory notes are optional. **Explanatory notes** are used to elaborate on points discussed in the body of the paper. Explanatory notes may be placed either at the bottom of the page as footnotes or at the end of the paper as endnotes. Double-space the explanatory notes. Superscript each note's reference number, and indent it one-half inch from the left margin. Place one space following the note number before beginning the note text. At the end of the note text, you may list bibliographic information for further reference.

The MLA style uses the term **works cited** for the bibliographical references. The works cited page alphabetically lists works that are directly referenced in the paper by each author's last name. Place the works cited on a separate numbered page. Center the title, Works Cited, one inch from the top margin. Double-space all lines. Begin the first line of each work cited at the left margin; indent subsequent lines of the same work one-half inch from the left margin.

More *About* **Paper Topics**

When you are assigned a research paper, you should be sure to select a topic that really interests you, as well as presents a thought that will appeal to your audience. To research your topic, use the following sources: library catalog, the Internet, periodical indexes, computer databases, magazines and journals, and books.

Document Preparation Steps

Document preparation steps give you an overview of how the research paper in Figure 3-1 will be developed. The following tasks will be completed in this project:

1. Start Word.
2. Change the margin settings for the document.
3. Adjust the line spacing for the document.
4. Create a header to number pages.
5. Change the font size to 12.
6. Enter your name and course information.
7. Center the paper title.
8. Save the research paper.
9. First-line indent paragraphs in the paper.
10. Enter the research paper with footnotes and a table.
11. Insert a manual page break.
12. Enter the works cited page.
13. Sort the paragraphs on the works cited page.
14. Save the document again.

15. Use Word's thesaurus.
16. Check the number of words in the document.
17. Print the research paper.
18. Visit the Web site associated with a hyperlink in the document.
19. Quit Word.

The following pages contain a detailed explanation of each of these tasks.

Starting Word

Follow these steps to start Word or ask your instructor how to start Word for your system.

TO START WORD

Step 1: Click the Start button on the taskbar.
Step 2: Click New Office Document on the Start menu. If necessary, click the General tab when the New dialog box first opens.
Step 3: Double-click the Blank Document icon on the General sheet.
Step 4: If the Word screen is not maximized, double-click its title bar to maximize it.

Office starts Word. After a few moments, an empty document titled Document1 displays on the Word screen.

Displaying Nonprinting Characters

As discussed in the previous projects, it is helpful to display **nonprinting characters** that indicate where in the document you pressed the ENTER key, SPACEBAR, or TAB key. Follow this step to display nonprinting characters.

TO DISPLAY NONPRINTING CHARACTERS

Step 1: If the Show/Hide ¶ button on the Standard toolbar is not already recessed, click it.

Word displays nonprinting characters in the document window, and the Show/Hide ¶ button on the Standard toolbar is recessed (Figure 3-2 on the next page).

Changing the Margins

Word is preset to use standard 8.5-by-11-inch paper, with 1.25-inch left and right margins and 1-inch top and bottom margins. These margin settings affect every paragraph in the document. Often, you may want to change these default margin settings. For example, the MLA documentation style requires one-inch top, bottom, left, and right margins throughout the paper. The steps on the next page illustrate how to change the default margin settings for a document when your screen is in normal view.

More About Changing Margins

In page layout view, you can change the margins using the ruler. The current margins are shaded in gray, and the margin boundary is positioned where the gray meets the white. You drag the margin boundary to change the margin. Hold down the ALT key while dragging the margin boundary to display the margin settings.

To Change the Default Margin Settings

1 **Click File on the menu bar and then point to Page Setup (Figure 3-2).**

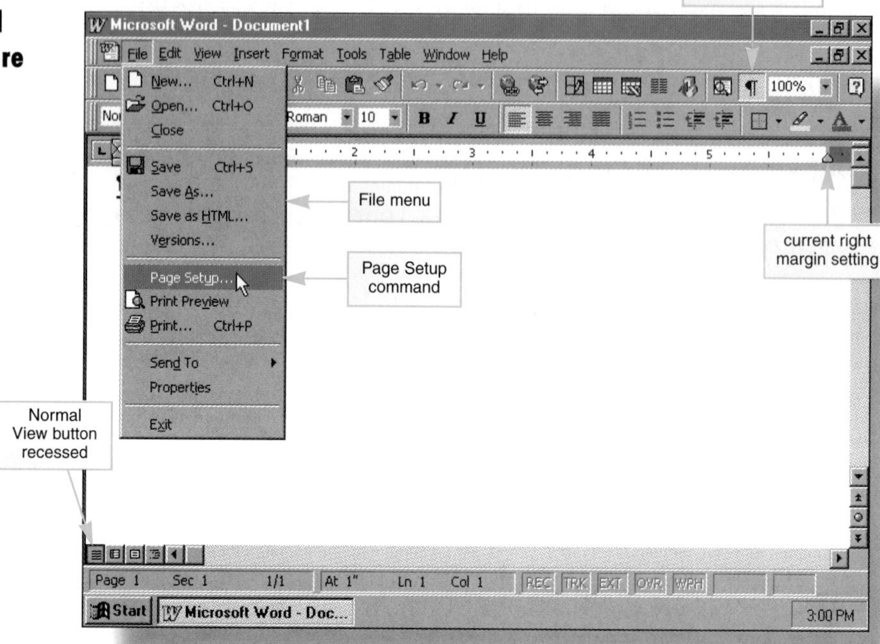

FIGURE 3-2

2 **Click Page Setup. If necessary, click the Margins tab when the Page Setup dialog box first opens.**

Word displays the Page Setup dialog box (Figure 3-3). Word lists the current margin settings in the respective text boxes and displays the settings graphically in the Preview area of the dialog box.

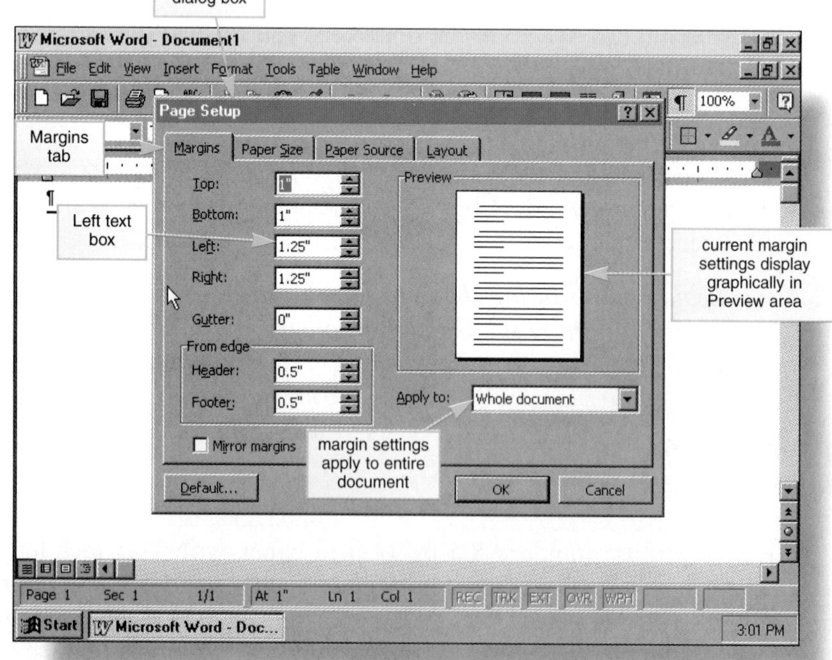

FIGURE 3-3

3 **Drag through the text in the Left text box to highlight 1.25". Type** 1 **and then press the TAB key. Type** 1 **and then point to the OK button.**

The new left and right margin settings are 1 inch (Figure 3-4). The Preview area in the Page Setup dialog box adjusts accordingly to reflect the new margin settings.

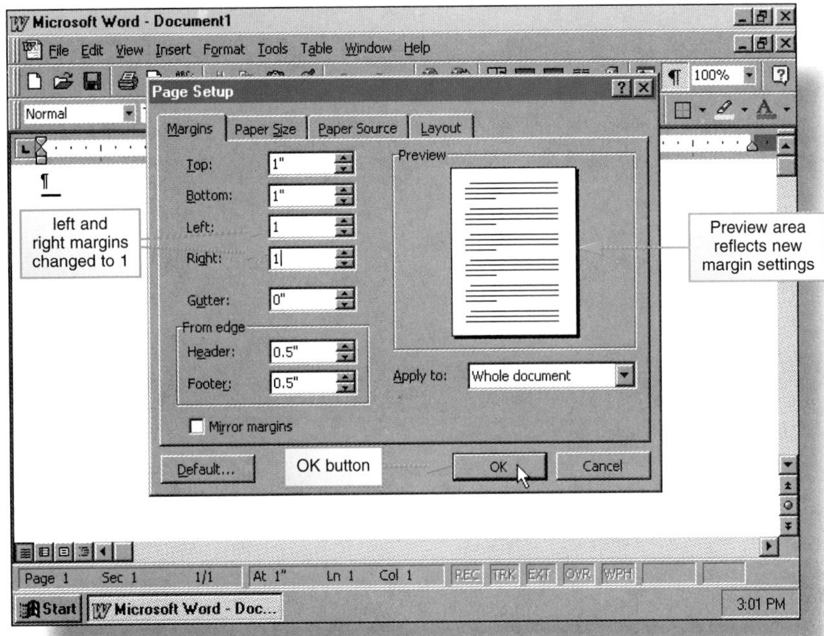

FIGURE 3-4

4 **Click the OK button.**

Word changes the left and right margins in the current document window (Figure 3-5).

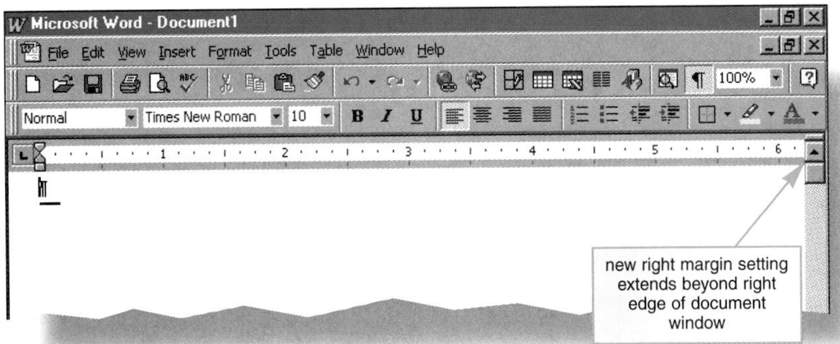

FIGURE 3-5

OtherWays

1. In page layout view, drag margin boundary(s) on ruler

Compare Figure 3-2 to Figure 3-5. Notice that the right margin does not display in the document window in Figure 3-5, as it did in Figure 3-2, because you increased the width of your typing area when you changed the margins. The new margin settings take effect in the document immediately, and Word uses these margins for the entire document.

Adjusting Line Spacing

Word, by default, single-spaces between lines of text and automatically adjusts line height to accommodate various font sizes and graphics. The MLA documentation style requires that you double-space the entire paper; that is, one blank line should display between each line of text. Thus, you must adjust the line spacing from single to double as described in the steps on the next page.

More About Line Spacing

Sometimes when you increase the font size of characters or import a graphic, the top of the characters or graphic is chopped off. If this happens, someone has set the line spacing in Word to Exactly. To correct it, change the line spacing to At least in the Paragraph dialog box, which accommodates the largest font or graphic.

To Double-Space a Document

1 **Right-click the paragraph mark above the end mark in the document window. Point to Paragraph on the shortcut menu.**

Word displays a shortcut menu in the document window (Figure 3-6).

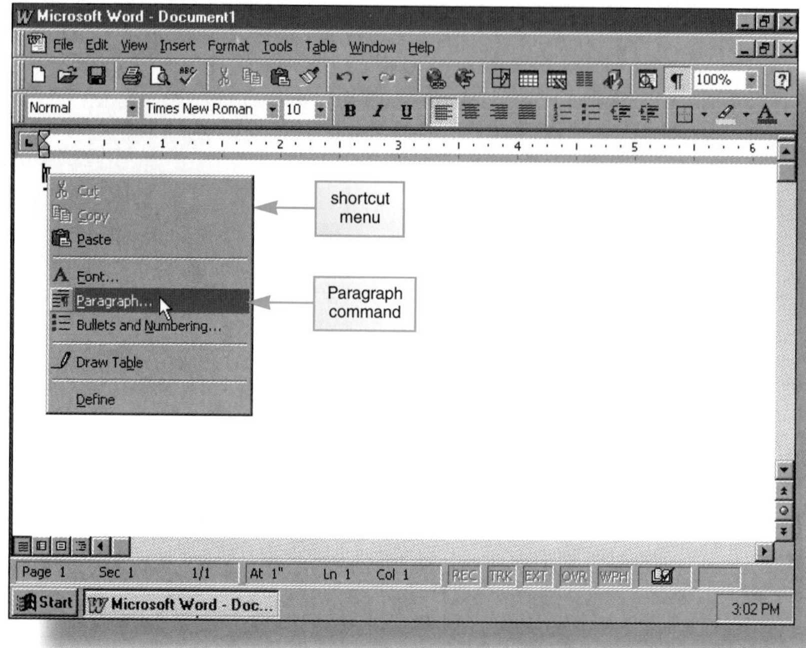

FIGURE 3-6

2 **Click Paragraph. If necessary, click the Indents and Spacing tab when the Paragraph dialog box first opens.**

Word displays the Paragraph dialog box, which lists the current settings in the text boxes and displays them graphically in the Preview area.

3 **Click the Line spacing box arrow and then point to Double.**

A list of available line spacing options displays (Figure 3-7).

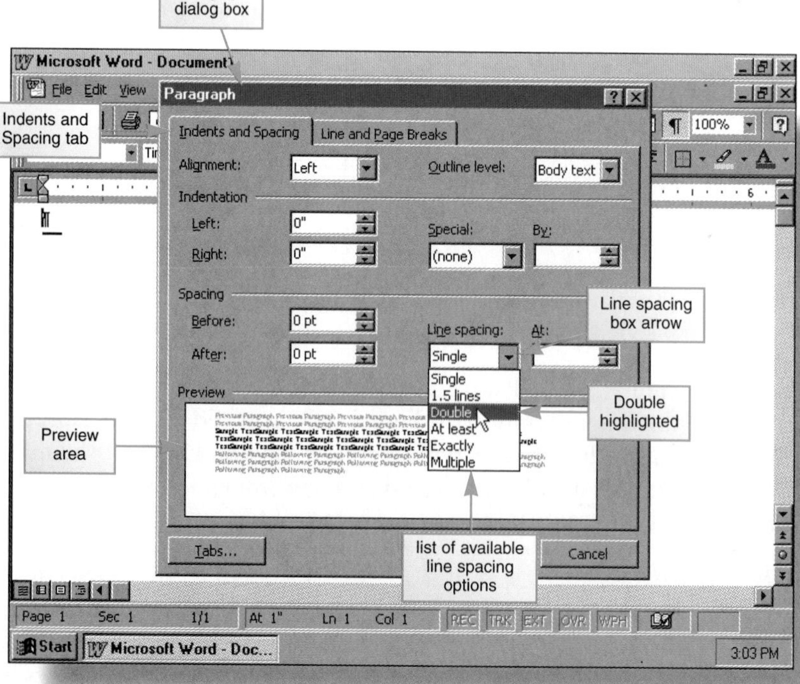

FIGURE 3-7

4 **Click Double. Point to the OK button.**

Word displays Double in the Line spacing text box and graphically portrays the new line spacing in the Preview area (Figure 3-8).

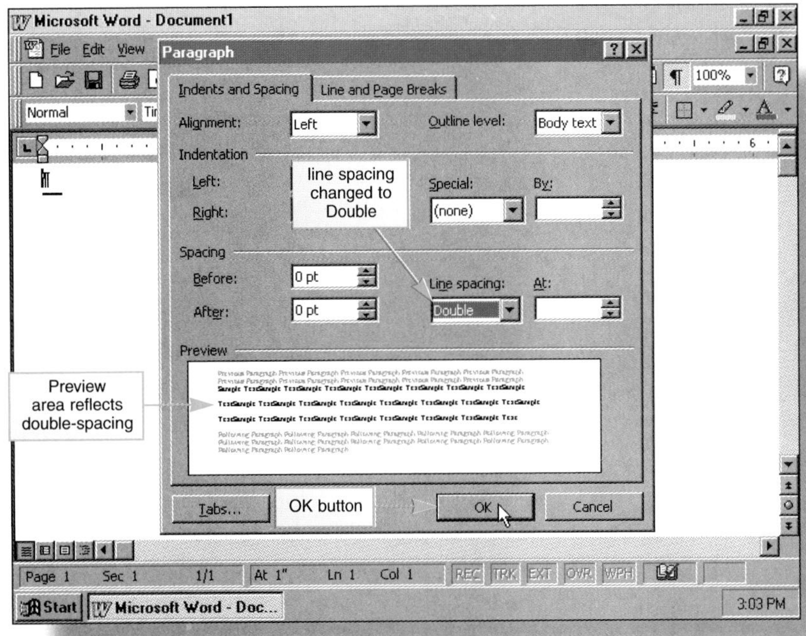

FIGURE 3-8

5 **Click the OK button.**

Word changes the line spacing to double in the current document (Figure 3-9). Notice that when line spacing is double, the end mark is positioned one blank line below the insertion point.

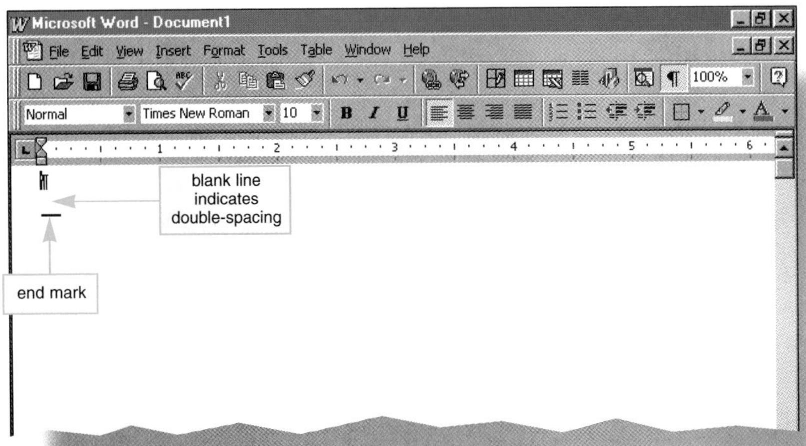

FIGURE 3-9

Other Ways

1. On Format menu click Paragraph, click Indents and Spacing tab, click Line spacing box arrow, click Double, click OK button
2. Press CTRL+2

The Line spacing list box contains a variety of settings for the line spacing (Figure 3-7). The default, Single, and the options 1.5 lines and Double instruct Word to adjust line spacing automatically to accommodate the largest font or graphic on a line. The next two options, At least and Exactly, enable you to specify a line spacing not provided in the first three options. The difference is that the At least option instructs Word to increase the designation if necessary; whereas, the Exactly option does not allow Word to increase the specification. With the last option, Multiple, you enter a multiple. For example, a multiple of 3 is the same as triple-spacing.

More *About* **APA Guidelines**

To follow the APA style, double-space all pages of the paper with 1.5" top, bottom, left, and right margins. Indent the first word of each paragraph one-half inch from the left margin. A running head is placed in the upper-right margin of each page; it consists of the page number double-spaced beneath a summary of the paper title.

Using a Header to Number Pages

In Word, you can number pages easily by clicking Insert on the menu bar and then clicking Page Numbers. Once you have clicked the Page Numbers command, it places page numbers on every page after the first. You cannot, however, place your name as required by the MLA style in front of the page number with the Page Numbers command. To place your name in front of the page number, you must create a header that contains the page number.

Headers and Footers

A **header** is text you want printed at the top of each page in the document. A **footer** is text you want printed at the bottom of every page. In Word, headers are printed in the top margin one-half inch from the top of every page, and footers are printed in the bottom margin one-half inch from the bottom of each page, which meets the MLA style. Headers and footers can include both text and graphics, as well as the page number, total number of pages, current date, and current time.

In this project, you are to precede the page number with your last name placed one-half inch from the top of each page. Your name and the page number should print **right-aligned**, that is, at the right margin. Use the procedures in the following steps to create the header with page numbers according to the MLA style.

Steps To Create a Header

1. **Click View on the menu bar and then point to Header and Footer (Figure 3-10).**

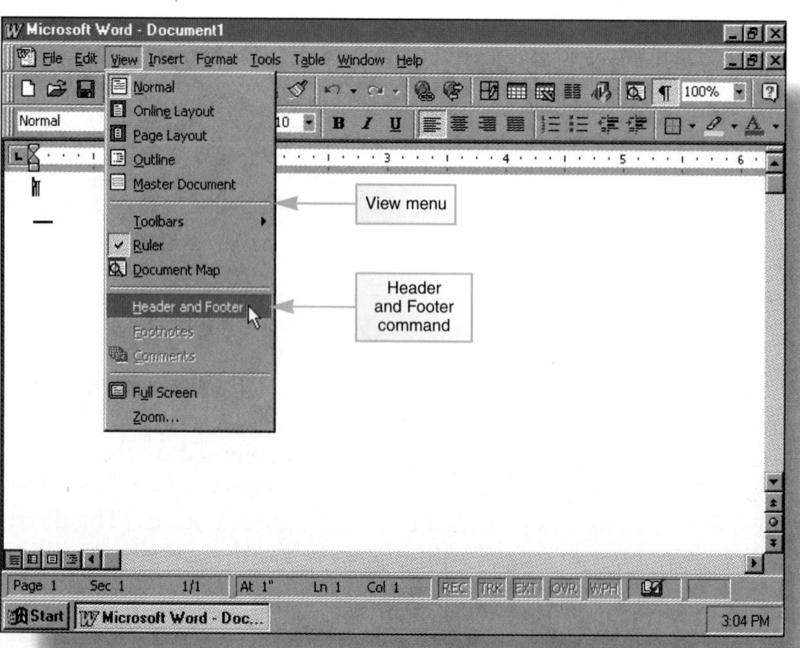

FIGURE 3-10

2 **Click Header and Footer. Point to the Align Right button on the Formatting toolbar.**

Word switches from normal view to page layout view and displays the ***Header and Footer toolbar*** *(Figure 3-11). The Header and Footer toolbar floats in the middle of the document window. You type header text in the* ***header area****, which displays enclosed by a nonprinting dashed rectangle above the Header and Footer toolbar. Notice that both the left and right margins display in the document window because Word switched to page layout view. Your zoom percentage may differ from this figure.*

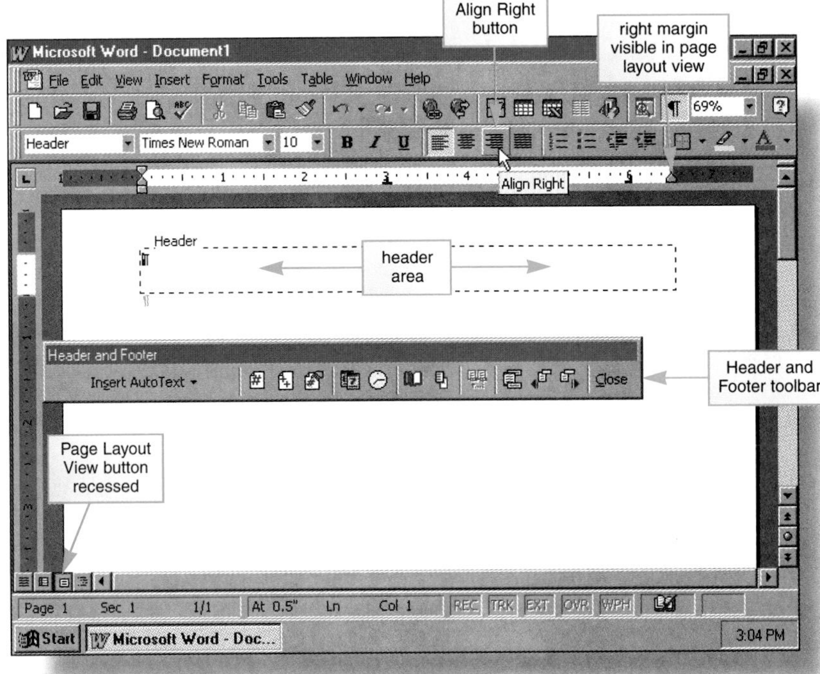

FIGURE 3-11

3 **Click the Align Right button on the Formatting toolbar. Type** `Porter` **and then press the SPACEBAR. Point to the Insert Page Number button on the Header and Footer toolbar.**

Word displays the last name, Porter, right-aligned in the header area (Figure 3-12). The Align Right button is recessed because the paragraph containing the insertion point is right-aligned.

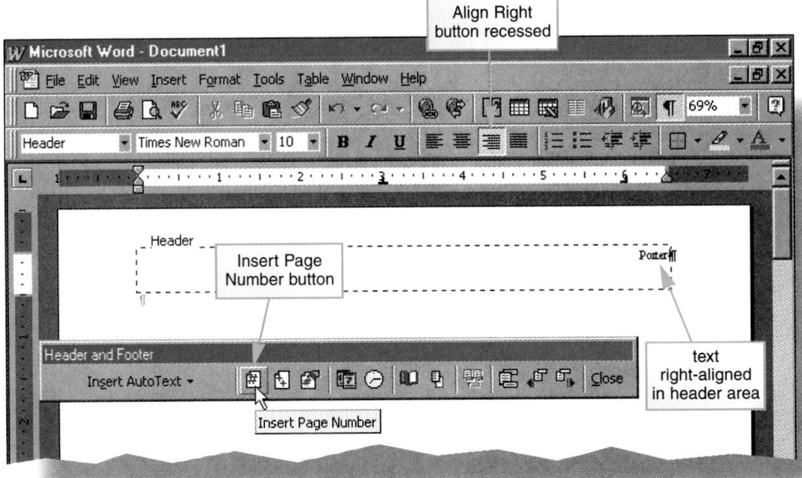

FIGURE 3-12

4 **Click the Insert Page Number button.**

Word displays the page number 1 in the header area (Figure 3-13). Notice that the header text is 10 point. You want all text in your research paper to be 12 point.

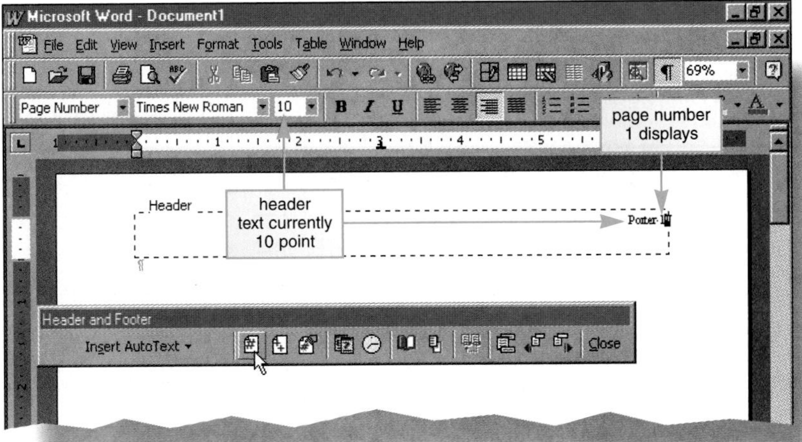

FIGURE 3-13

5 **Select the text, Porter 1, by clicking to its left. Click the Font Size box arrow on the Formatting toolbar and then point to 12.**

Word highlights the text, Porter 1, in the header area (Figure 3-14).

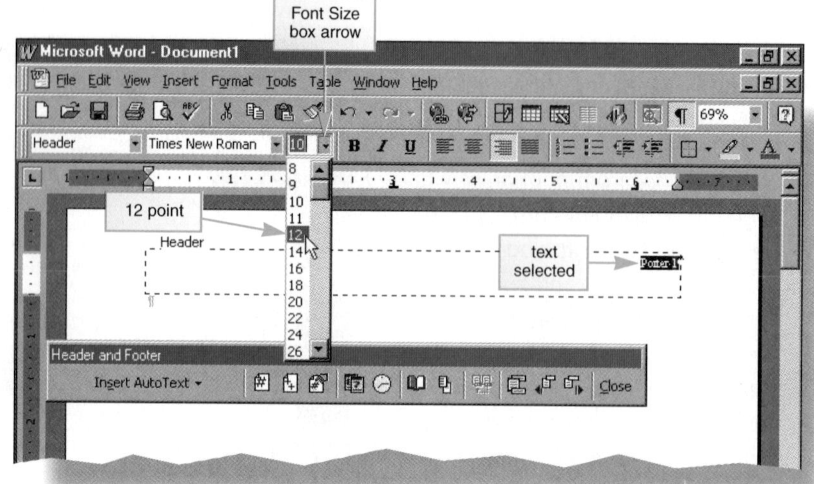

FIGURE 3-14

6 **Click font size 12. Point to the Close Header and Footer button on the Header and Footer toolbar.**

Word changes the font size of the selected text from 10 to 12 (Figure 3-15).

7 **Click the Close Header and Footer button.**

Word closes the Header and Footer toolbar and returns to normal view (Figure 3-16 on the opposite page).

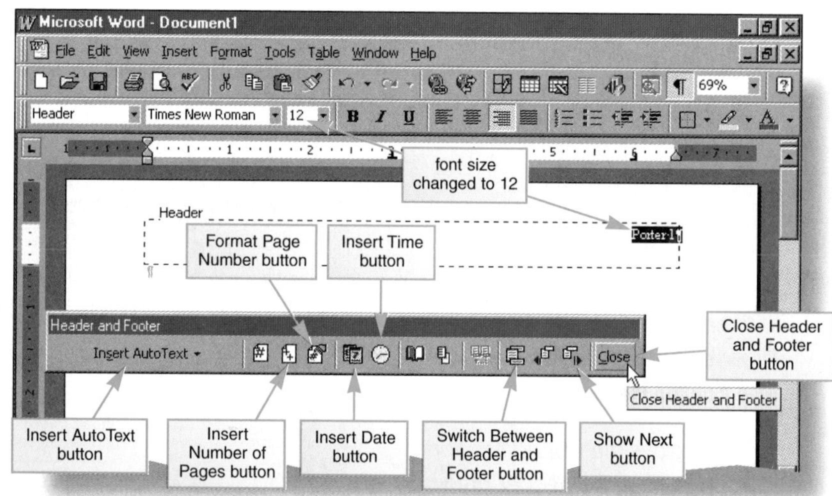

FIGURE 3-15

More About Page Layout View

To see the exact positioning of headers, footers, and notes, switch to page layout view. Headers and footers display dimmed in page layout view. Use the scroll bars to move around the pages of the document. To advance forward or backward an entire page, click the double arrows on the bottom of the vertical scroll bar.

The header does not display on the screen when the document window is in normal view because it tends to clutter the screen. You will, however, want to verify that the header will print correctly. To see the header in the document window, you must switch to page layout view or display the document in print preview. These views display the header on the screen with the rest of the text. You can edit header text in both these views.

Just as the Insert Page Number button on the Header and Footer toolbar inserts the page number into the document, three other buttons on the Header and Footer toolbar (Figure 3-15 above) insert items into the document. The Insert Number of Pages button inserts the total number of pages in the document; the Insert Date button inserts the current date into the document; and the Insert Time button inserts the current time.

To edit an existing header, you can follow the same procedure that you use to create a new header. That is, click View on the menu bar and then click Header and Footer to display the Header and Footer toolbar; or switch to page layout view and then double-click the dimmed header. If you have multiple headers, click the Show Next button on the Header and Footer toolbar (Figure 3-15) until the appropriate header displays in the header area. Edit the header as you would any Word text and then click the Close Header and Footer button on the Header and Footer toolbar.

To create a footer, click View on the menu bar, click Header and Footer, click the Switch Between Header and Footer button on the Header and Footer toolbar, and then follow the same procedure as to create a header.

Notice that the Header and Footer toolbar initially floats in the middle of the document window. You can **dock**, or anchor, the floating toolbar below the Formatting toolbar by double-clicking its title bar. To move a docked toolbar, point between two buttons or boxes or to the edge of the toolbar and then drag it to the desired location. If you drag it to an edge of the window, the toolbar snaps to the edge of the window. If you drag it to the middle of the window, the toolbar floats in the Word window. If you double-click between two buttons or boxes or the edge of the toolbar, it floats in its original floating position.

Typing the Body of the Research Paper

The body of the research paper encompasses the first two pages in Figure 3-1 on page WD 3.5. The steps on the following pages illustrate how to enter the body of the research paper.

> **More *About* Writing Papers**
>
> When beginning to write a paper, many students take notes to keep track of information. One method is to summarize, or condense, the information. Another is to paraphrase, or rewrite the information in your own words. And yet a third is to quote, or record the exact words of the original. Be sure to use quotation marks when directly quoting a source.

Changing the Default Font Size

As discussed in previous projects, a font size of 10 point is difficult for many people to read. In this project, all characters in all paragraphs should be a font size of 12. Perform the following steps to change the font size to 12.

TO CHANGE THE DEFAULT FONT SIZE

Step 1: Click the Font Size box arrow on the Formatting toolbar.
Step 2: Click font size 12.

Word changes the font size to 12 (Figure 3-16).

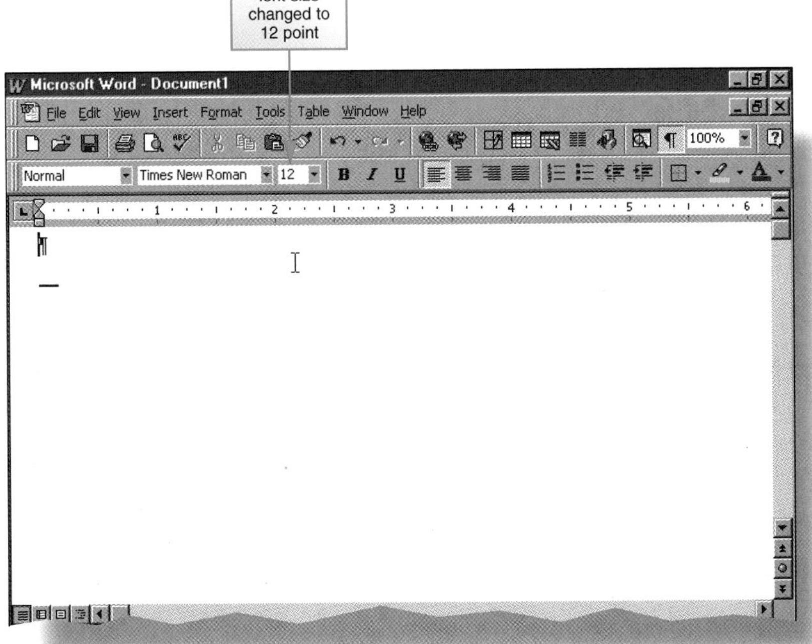

FIGURE 3-16

Entering Name and Course Information

Recall that the MLA style does not require a separate title page for research papers. Instead, you place your name and course information in a block at the top of the page at the left margin. Thus, follow the step below to begin the body of the research paper.

Steps To Enter Name and Course Information

1. **Type** `Anna L. Porter` **and then press the ENTER key. Type** `Professor J. Brown` **and then press the ENTER key. Type** `Information Systems 201` **and then press the ENTER key. Type** `December 1, 1998` **and then press the ENTER key twice.**

   The student name displays on line 1, the professor name on line 2, the course name on line 3, and the paper due date on line 4 (Figure 3-17). Each time you press the ENTER key, Word advances two lines on the screen, but increments the line counter on the status bar by only one because earlier you set line spacing to double.

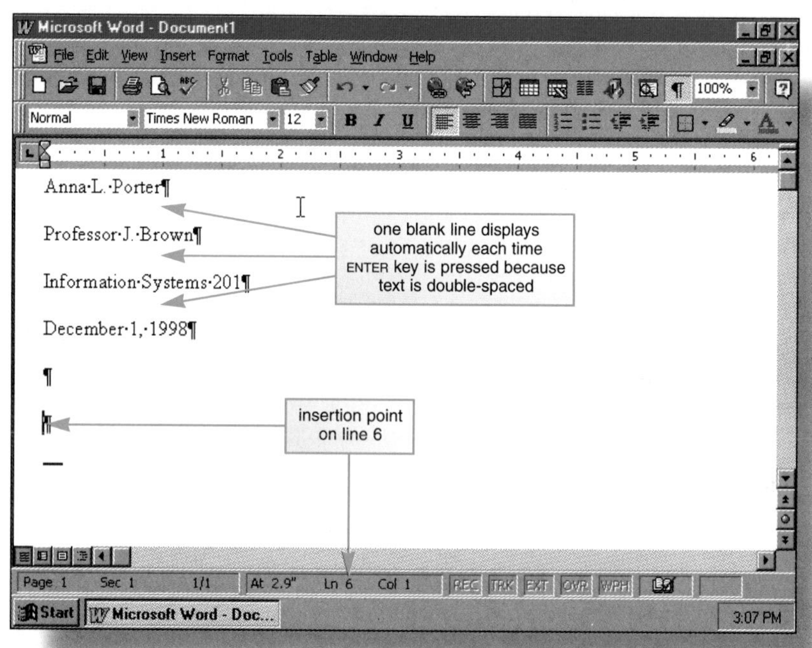

FIGURE 3-17

> **More About APA Guidelines**
>
> APA guidelines call for a title page as a separate page of a research paper, rather than entering name and course information on the first page of the paper. The running head (the brief summary of the title and the page number) should appear on the title page also, with the page number 1 on the title page.

If you watch the screen as you type, you may have noticed that as you typed the first few characters, Dece, Word displayed the **AutoComplete tip**, December, above the characters. To save typing, you could press the ENTER key while the AutoComplete tip displays, which instructs Word to place the text of the AutoComplete tip at the location of your typing.

Centering a Paragraph Before Typing

In Project 1, you learned how to center a paragraph after you typed it. You also can center a paragraph before you type it. Because your fingers are already on the keyboard, you will use shortcut keys to format the paragraph as shown in the following steps.

To Center a Paragraph Before Typing

1. **Position the insertion point on the paragraph mark to be centered and then press the CTRL+E keys. Type** `Computer Viruses` **and then press the ENTER key.**

Word centers the title between the left and right margins and the insertion point advances to line 7 (Figure 3-18). Notice that the paragraph mark and insertion point on line 7 are centered because the formatting specified in the prior paragraph (line 6) is carried forward to the next paragraph (line 7). Thus, the Center button on the Formatting toolbar remains recessed, indicating the next text you type will be centered. You do not, however, want the next line of text to be centered.

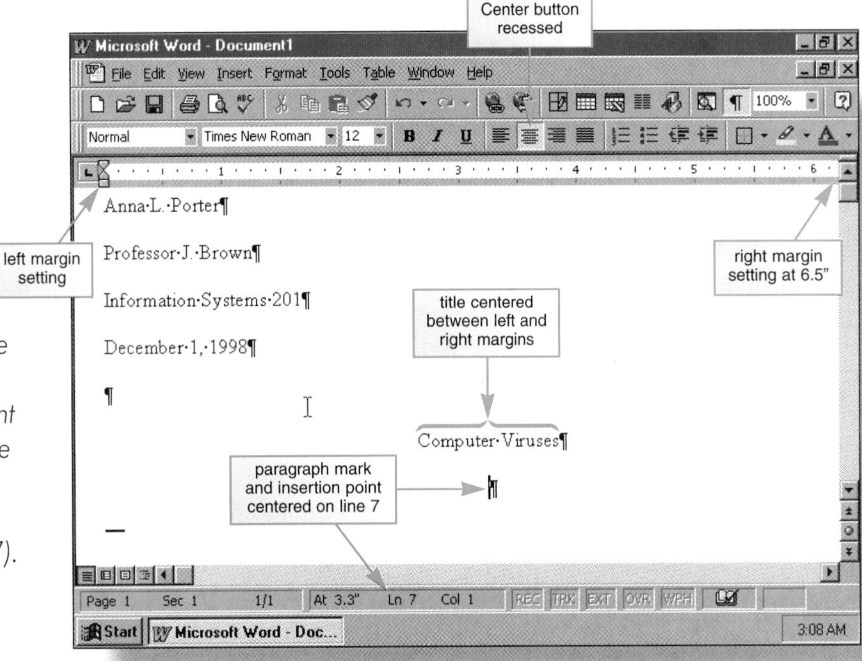

FIGURE 3-18

2. **Press the CTRL+L keys.**

Word positions the paragraph mark and the insertion point at the left margin (Figure 3-19). The next text you type will be left-aligned. CTRL+L *is the keyboard shortcut to left-align a paragraph.*

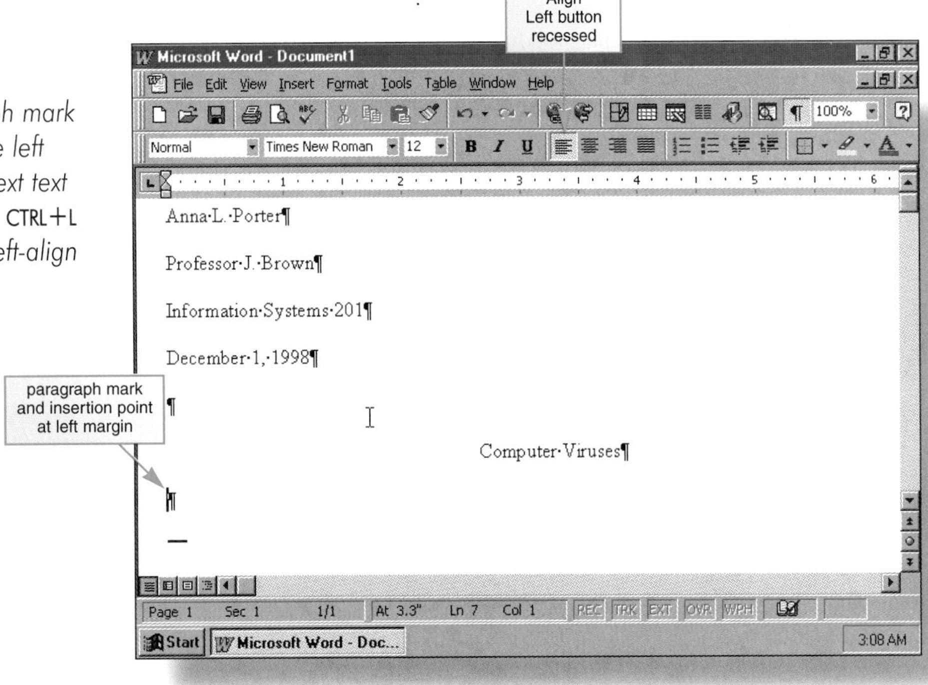

FIGURE 3-19

Other Ways

1. Click Center button
2. Right-click paragraph, click Paragraph on shortcut menu, click Indents and Spacing tab, click Alignment box arrow, click Centered, click OK button
3. On Format menu click Paragraph, click Indents and Spacing tab, click Alignment box arrow, click Centered, click OK button

Saving the Research Paper

Recall that it is prudent to save your work on disk at regular intervals. Because you have performed several tasks thus far, you should save your research paper. For a detailed example of the procedure summarized below, refer to pages WD 1.25 through WD 1.27 in Project 1.

TO SAVE A DOCUMENT

Step 1: Insert your floppy disk into drive A.
Step 2: Click the Save button on the Standard toolbar.
Step 3: Type the file name `Virus Research Paper` in the File name text box. Do not press the ENTER key after typing the file name.
Step 4: Click the Save in box arrow and then click 3½ Floppy (A:).
Step 5: Click the Save button in the Save As dialog box.

More About First Line Indent

You may be tempted to use the TAB key to indent the first line of each paragraph in your research paper. Using the TAB key for this task is inefficient because you must press it each time you begin a new paragraph. Because first-line indent is a paragraph format, it is automatically carried forward when you press the ENTER key.

Indenting Paragraphs

According to the MLA style, the first line of each paragraph in the research paper is to be indented one-half inch from the left margin. This procedure, called **first-line indent**, can be accomplished using the horizontal ruler as shown in the following steps.

Steps To First-Line Indent Paragraphs

1 Point to the First Line Indent marker on the ruler.

The First Line Indent marker is the top triangle at the 0" mark on the ruler (Figure 3-20). The small square at the 0" mark, called the Left Indent marker, is used to change the entire left margin, whereas the First Line Indent marker affects only the first line of the paragraph.

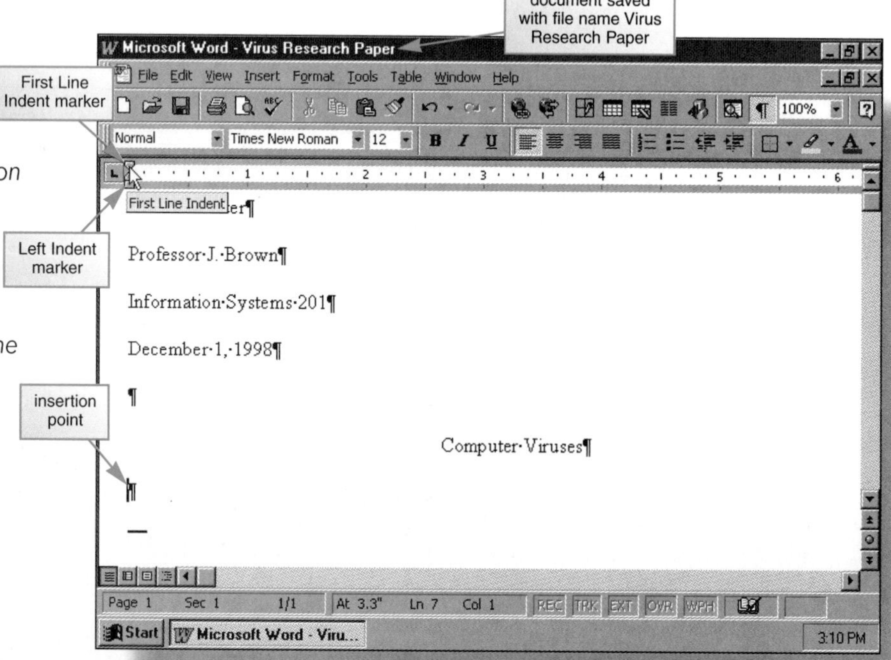

FIGURE 3-20

2 Drag the First Line Indent marker to the .5" mark on the ruler.

As you drag the mouse, a vertical dotted line displays in the document window, indicating the proposed location of the First Line Indent marker (Figure 3-21).

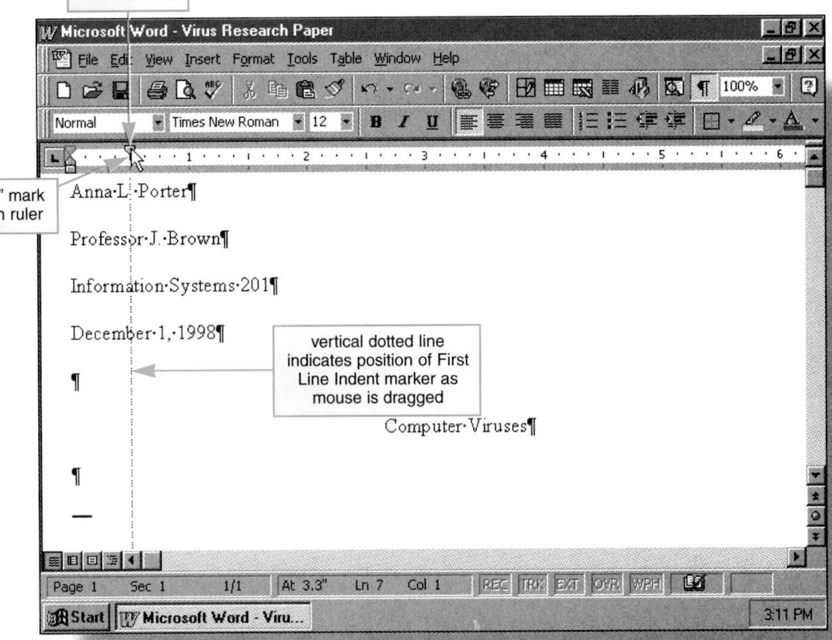

FIGURE 3-21

3 Release the mouse button.

The First Line Indent marker displays at the location of the first tab stop, which is one-half inch from the left margin (Figure 3-22). The paragraph mark containing the insertion point in the document window also moves one-half inch to the right.

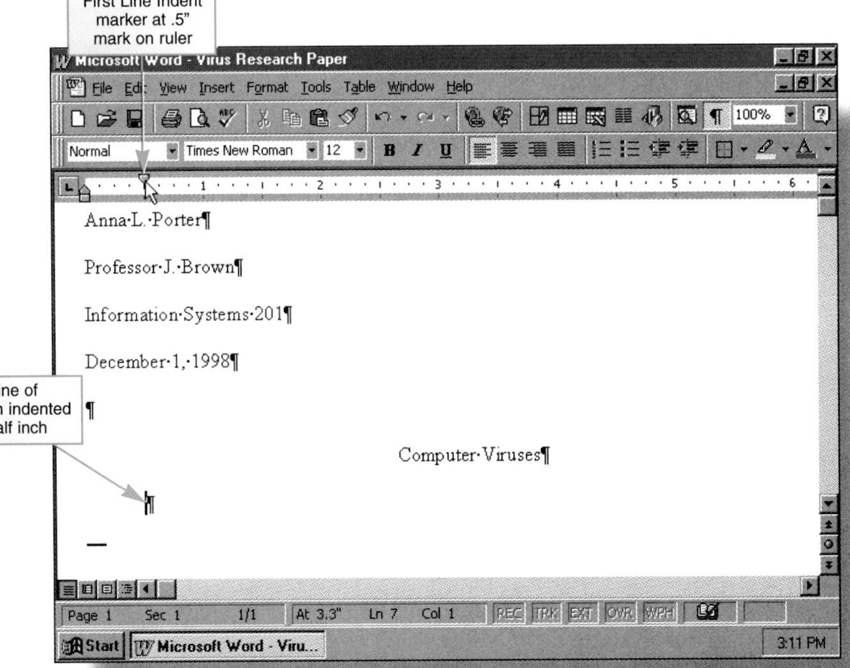

FIGURE 3-22

4 **Type the first paragraph of the research paragraph as shown in Figure 3-24 below. Press the ENTER key. Type the first sentence of the second paragraph:** `Three types of viruses are a boot sector virus, file virus, and Trojan horse virus.`

When you press the ENTER key at the end of the first paragraph of text, the insertion point automatically indents the first line of the second paragraph by one-half inch (Figure 3-23). Recall that each time you press the ENTER key, the paragraph formatting in the prior paragraph is carried forward to the next paragraph.

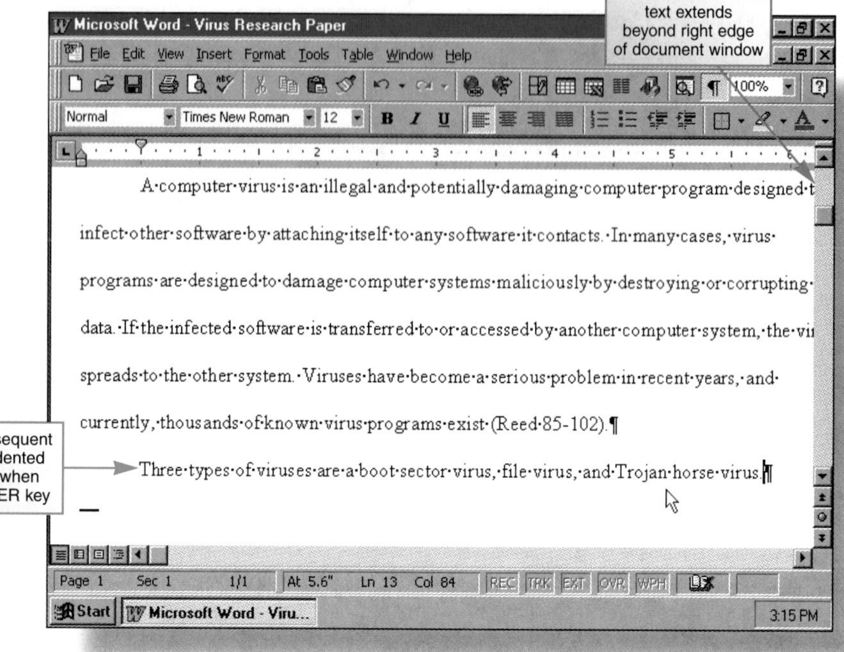

FIGURE 3-23

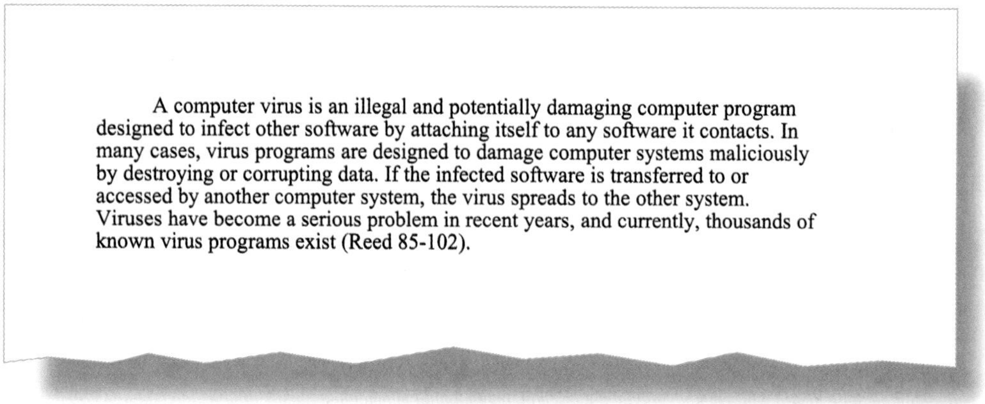

A computer virus is an illegal and potentially damaging computer program designed to infect other software by attaching itself to any software it contacts. In many cases, virus programs are designed to damage computer systems maliciously by destroying or corrupting data. If the infected software is transferred to or accessed by another computer system, the virus spreads to the other system. Viruses have become a serious problem in recent years, and currently, thousands of known virus programs exist (Reed 85-102).

FIGURE 3-24

Other Ways

1. Right-click paragraph, click Paragraph on shortcut menu, click Indents and Spacing tab, click Special box arrow, click First line, click OK button
2. On Format menu click Paragraph, click Indents and Spacing tab, click Special box arrow, click First line, click OK button

By setting the first-line indent with the ruler, the first-line indent format is carried automatically to each subsequent paragraph you type.

Zooming Page Width

When you changed the left and right margin settings earlier in this project, the right margin moved beyond the right edge of the document window. (Depending on your Word settings, your right margin may already display in the document window.) Thus, some of the text at the right edge of the document does not display in the document window (Figure 3-23 above). Recall in Project 2, you zoomed the cover letter and resume to make the characters appear larger on the screen. In this project, you want to make the characters smaller.

Because you often want to see both margins in the document window at the same time, Word provides a **page width zoom**, which brings both the left and right margins into view as shown in the following steps.

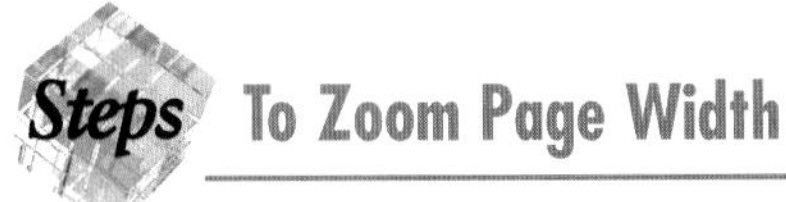

To Zoom Page Width

1 **Click the Zoom box arrow on the Standard toolbar and then point to Page Width.**

Word displays a list of available zoom percentages, as well as the Page Width zoom option (Figure 3-25).

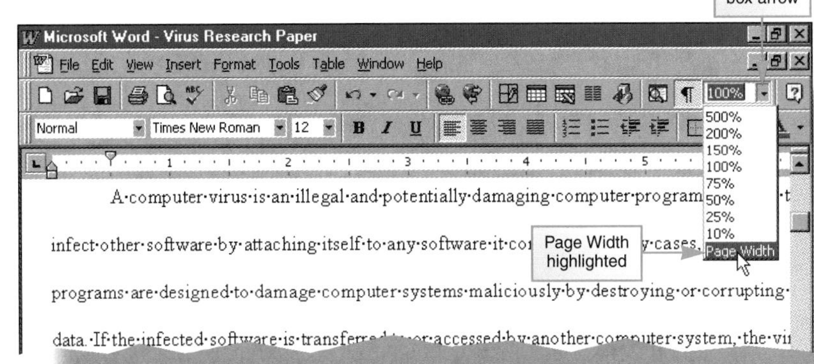

FIGURE 3-25

2 **Click Page Width.**

Word brings both the left and right margins into view in the document window (Figure 3-26). The Zoom box now displays 92%, which Word computes based on your margin settings. Your percentage may be different depending on your system configuration.

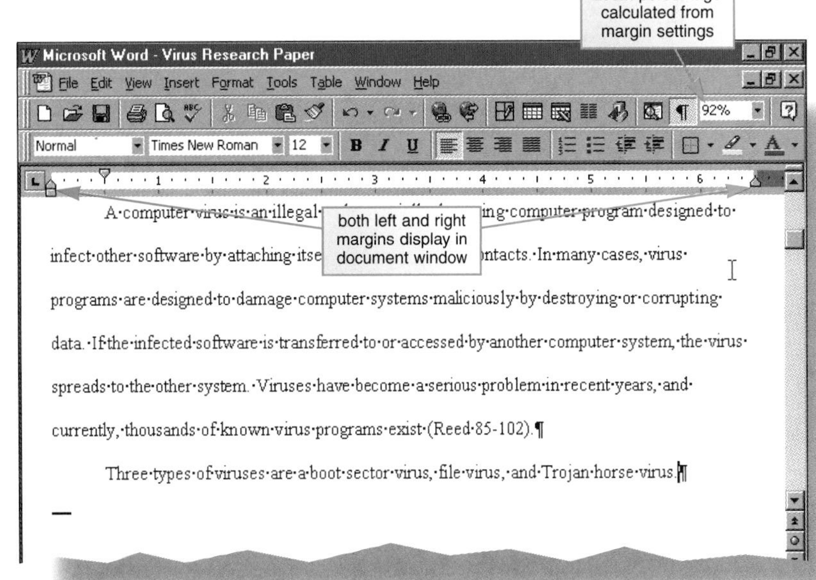

FIGURE 3-26

Other Ways

1. On View menu click Zoom, select desired zoom percentage, click OK button

If you want to zoom to a percentage not displayed in the Zoom list box, you can click View on the menu bar, click Zoom, and then enter any zoom percentage you desire.

More About AutoCorrect

In addition to correcting misspelled words, the AutoCorrect feature fixes other mistakes. If you type two capital letters at the beginning of a sentence, Word makes the second letter lower case. If you forget to capitalize the first letter of a sentence, Word capitalizes it for you. Word also capitalizes names of days of the week, if you forget to.

Using Word's AutoCorrect Feature

Because you may often misspell words or phrases when you type, Word provides an **AutoCorrect** feature, which automatically corrects your misspelled words as you type them into the document. For example, if you type *adn*, Word automatically changes it to *and* for you. Word has predefined many commonly misspelled words, which it automatically corrects for you as shown on the next page.

To AutoCorrect As You Type

1 **Press the SPACEBAR. Type the beginning of the second sentence in the second paragraph, and misspell the word, the, as follows:** `A boot sector virus infects teh` **(Figure 3-27).**

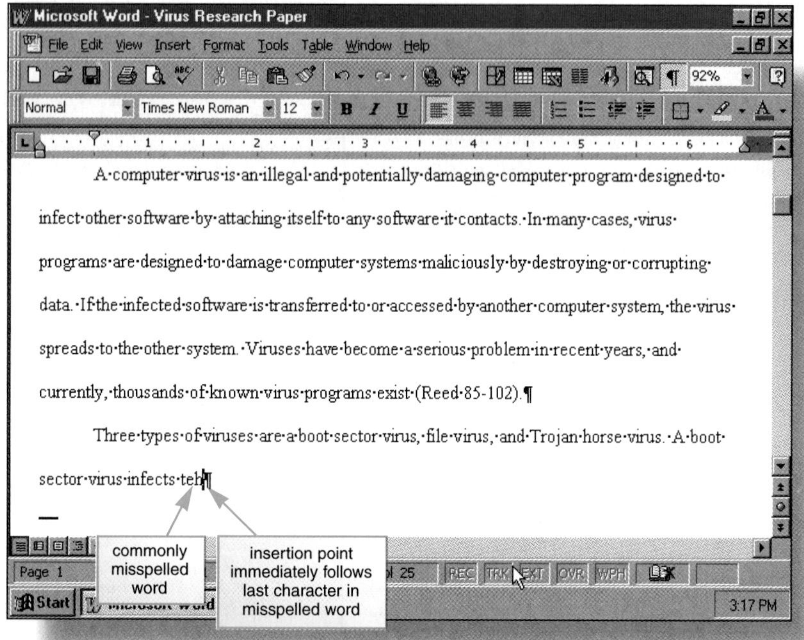

FIGURE 3-27

2 **Press the SPACEBAR.**

As soon as you press the SPACEBAR, Word's AutoCorrect feature detects the misspelling and corrects the misspelled word for you (Figure 3-28).

3 **Type** `boot program used to start the system.` **and then press the SPACEBAR.**

The second sentence of the second paragraph is complete.

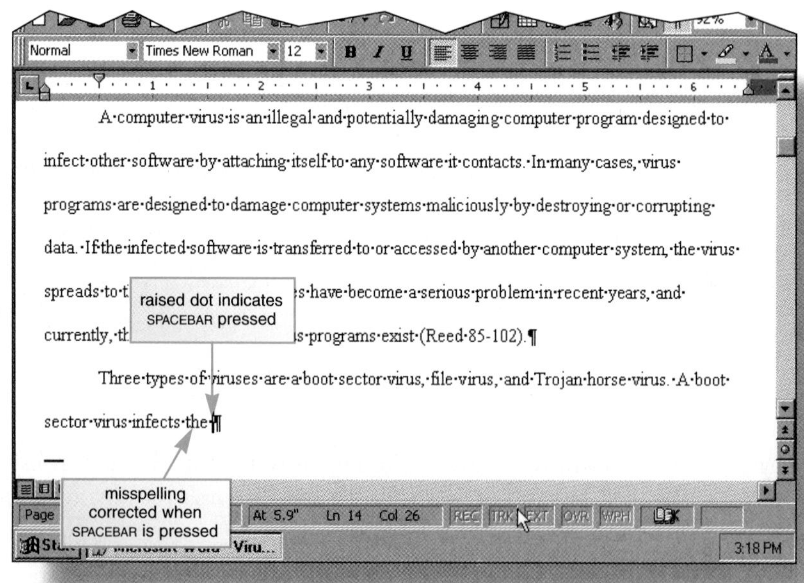

FIGURE 3-28

Word has a list of predefined misspelled words that AutoCorrect can detect and correct. In addition to the predefined list of commonly misspelled words, you can create your own AutoCorrect entries to add to the list. For example, if you often misspell the word *virus* as *vires*, you should make an AutoCorrect entry for it as shown in these steps.

To Create an AutoCorrect Entry

1 Click Tools on the menu bar and then point to AutoCorrect (Figure 3-29).

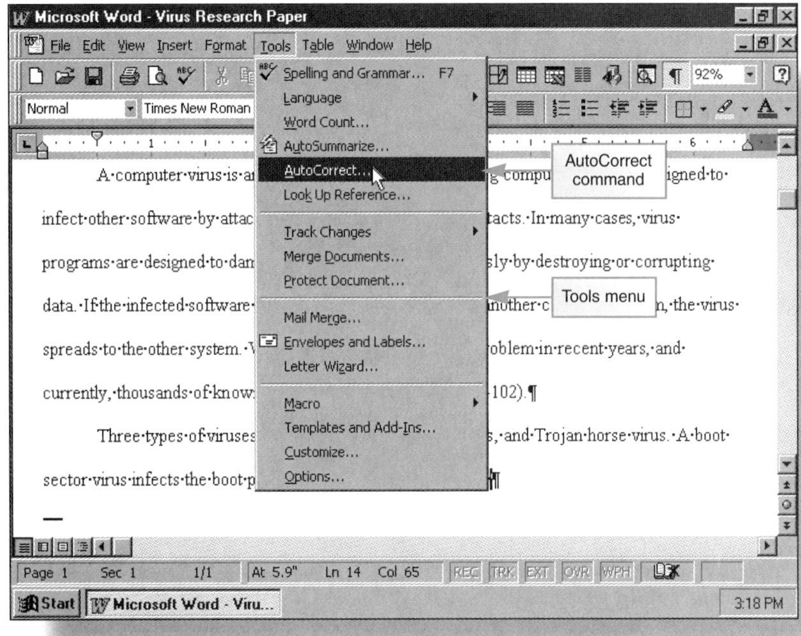

FIGURE 3-29

2 Click AutoCorrect.

Word displays the AutoCorrect dialog box (Figure 3-30). The insertion point blinks in the Replace text box, ready for you to create an AutoCorrect entry.

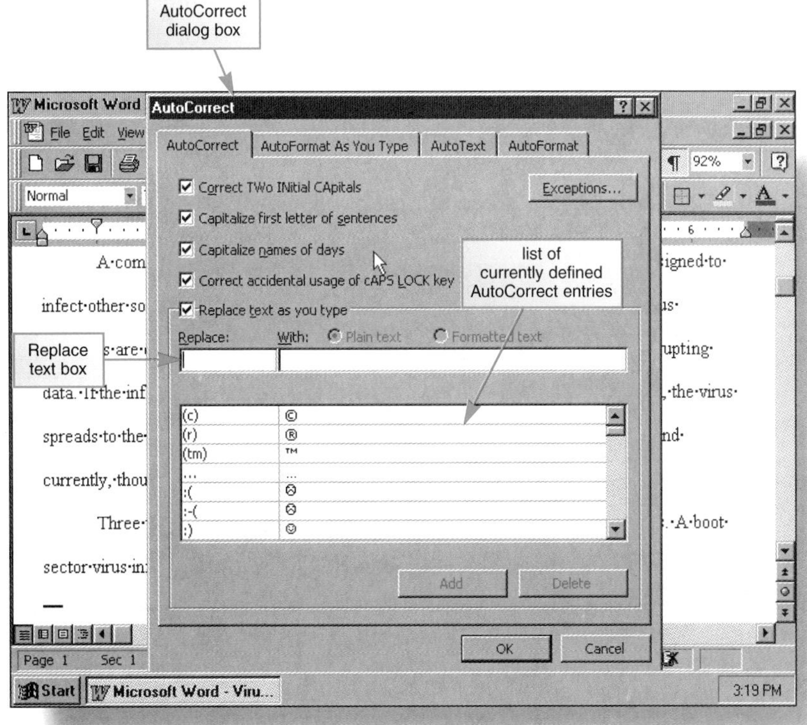

FIGURE 3-30

3 **Type** `vires` **in the Replace text box. Press the TAB key to advance to the With text box. Type** `virus` **in the With text box. Point to the Add button.**

The Replace text box contains the misspelled word, and the With text box contains its correct spelling (Figure 3-31).

4 **Click the Add button. (If your dialog box displays a Replace button instead, click it and then click the Yes button in the Microsoft Word dialog box.) Click the OK button.**

Word adds the entry alphabetically to the list of words to correct automatically as you type.

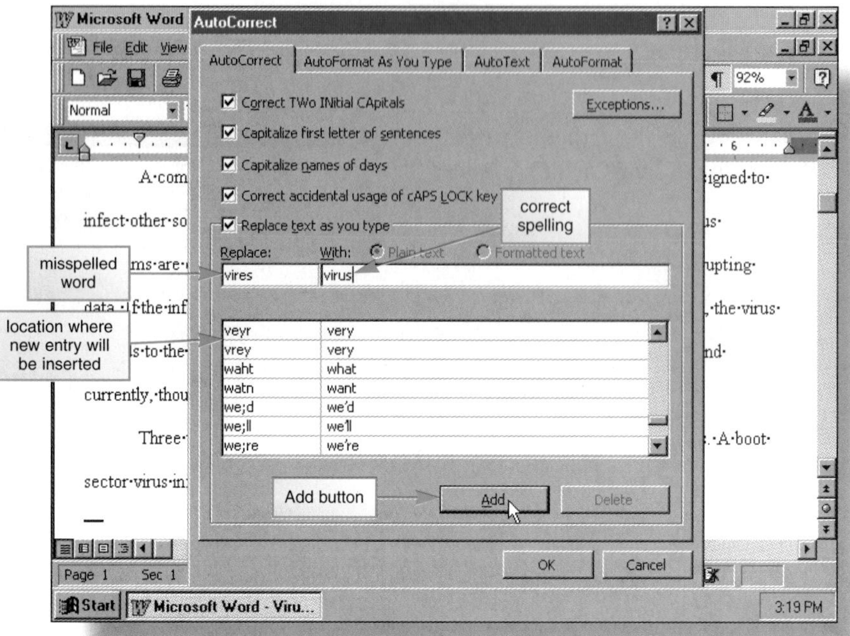

FIGURE 3-31

In addition to creating AutoCorrect entries for words you commonly misspell, you can create entries for abbreviations, codes, and so on. For example, you could create an AutoCorrect entry for *asap*, indicating that Word should replace this text with the phrase *as soon as possible*.

If you look at the list of AutoCorrect entries in the AutoCorrect dialog box (Figure 3-30 on the previous page), you will notice that Word also predefines commonly used symbols. For example, to insert a smiling face into a document, you type :) and word automatically changes it to ☺. Table 3-1 lists the characters you type to insert arrows, faces, and symbols into a Word document.

If, for some reason, you do not want Word to correct automatically as you type, you can turn off the replace as you type feature by clicking Tools on the menu bar, clicking AutoCorrect, clicking the AutoCorrect tab, clicking the Replace text as you type check box to deselect it, and then clicking the OK button.

The AutoCorrect sheet also contains four other check boxes that correct your typing if selected. If you type two capital letters in a row such as TH, Word will make the second letter lowercase, Th. If you begin a sentence with a lowercase letter, Word will capitalize the first letter of the sentence. If you type the name of a day in lowercase such as tuesday, Word will capitalize the first letter of the day, Tuesday. Finally, if you leave the CAPS LOCK key on and begin a new sentence such as aFTER, Word corrects the typing, After, and turns off the CAPS LOCK key.

In Project 2, you learned how to use the AutoText feature, which enables you to create entries (just as you did for the AutoCorrect feature) and then insert them into the document. The difference is that the AutoCorrect feature makes the corrections for you automatically as soon as you press the SPACEBAR, whereas you must press F3 or click the AutoText command before Word will make an AutoText correction.

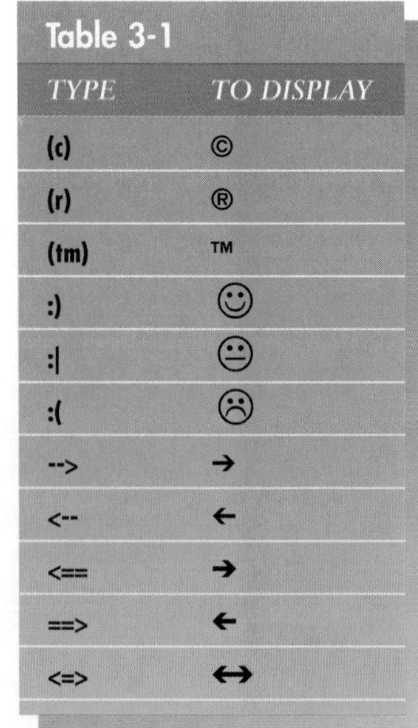
Table 3-1

TYPE	TO DISPLAY
(c)	©
(r)	®
(tm)	™
:)	☺
:|	😐
:(	☹
-->	→
<--	←
<==	→
==>	←
<=>	↔

Adding Footnotes

Recall that **explanatory notes** are optional in the MLA documentation style. They are used primarily to elaborate on points discussed in the body of the paper. The style specifies to use superscripts (raised numbers) to signal that an explanatory note exists either at the bottom of the page as a **footnote** or at the end of the document as an **endnote**.

Word, by default, places notes at the bottom of each page. In Word, **note text** can be any length and format. Word automatically numbers notes sequentially for you by placing a **note reference mark** in the body of the document and in front of the note text. If you rearrange, insert, or remove notes, the remaining note text and reference marks are renumbered according to their new sequence in the document. Perform the following steps to add a footnote to the research paper.

More *About* Footnotes

Both the MLA and APA guidelines suggest the use of in-text parenthetical citation, as opposed to footnoting each source of material in a paper. These parenthetical acknowledgments guide the reader to the end of the paper for complete information on the source, if the reader desires it.

To Add a Footnote

1 Type the text shown in Figure 3-33. Click Insert on the menu bar and then point to Footnote.

The insertion point is positioned immediately after the period following the word, date, in the research paper (Figure 3-32).

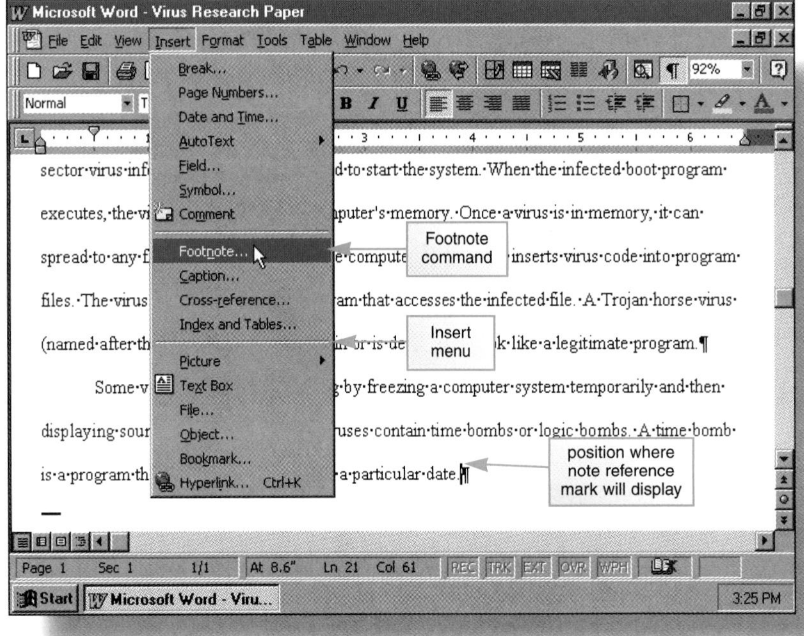

FIGURE 3-32

When the infected boot program executes, the virus is loaded into the computer's memory. Once a virus is in memory, it can spread to any floppy disk inserted into the computer. A file virus inserts virus code into program files. The virus then spreads to any program that accesses the infected file. A Trojan horse virus (named after the Greek myth) hides within or is designed to look like a legitimate program.

Some viruses interrupt processing by freezing a computer system temporarily and then displaying sounds or messages. Other viruses contain time bombs or logic bombs. A time bomb is a program that performs an activity on a particular date.

FIGURE 3-33

2 **Click Footnote. When the Footnote and Endnote dialog box displays, point to the OK button.**

Word displays the Footnote and Endnote dialog box (Figure 3-34). The selected Footnote option button indicates that footnotes are the default placement for notes.

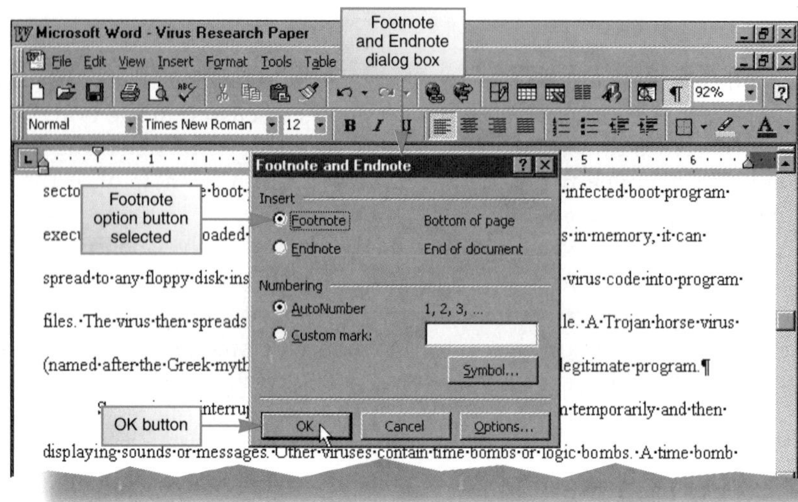

FIGURE 3-34

3 **Click the OK button.**

Word opens a **note pane** *in the lower portion of the window with the note reference mark (a superscripted 1) positioned at the left margin of the pane (Figure 3-35). A* **pane** *is an area at the bottom of the screen, which contains an* **option bar**, *a* **text area**, *and a* **scroll bar**. *The note reference mark also displays in the document window at the location of the insertion point. Note* **reference marks** *are, by default, superscripted; that is, raised above other letters. Notice that the default font size of footnote text is 10 point.*

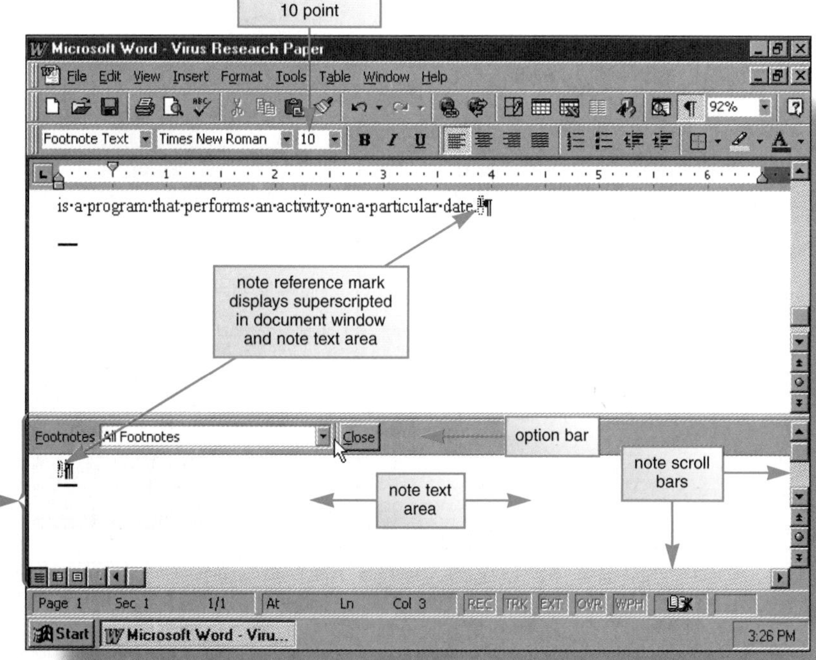

FIGURE 3-35

4 **Right-click to the right of the paragraph mark in the note pane. Point to Paragraph on the shortcut menu.**

Word displays a shortcut menu (Figure 3-36). Because you want to change both first-line indent and line spacing for the notes, you will use the Paragraph dialog box to perform both changes.

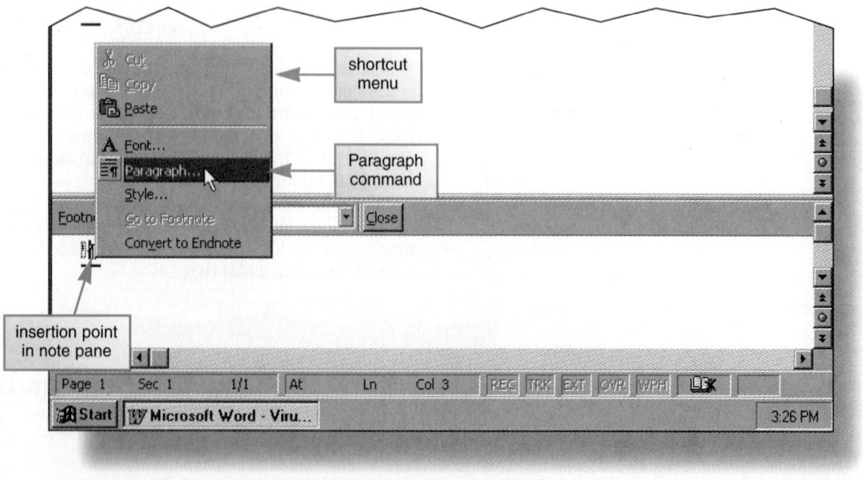

FIGURE 3-36

5 **Click Paragraph. If necessary, click the Indents and Spacing tab when the Paragraph dialog box first opens. Click the Special box arrow and then point to First line.**

Word displays the Paragraph dialog box (Figure 3-37). You can change the first-line indent in the Indents and Spacing sheet in the Paragraph dialog box.

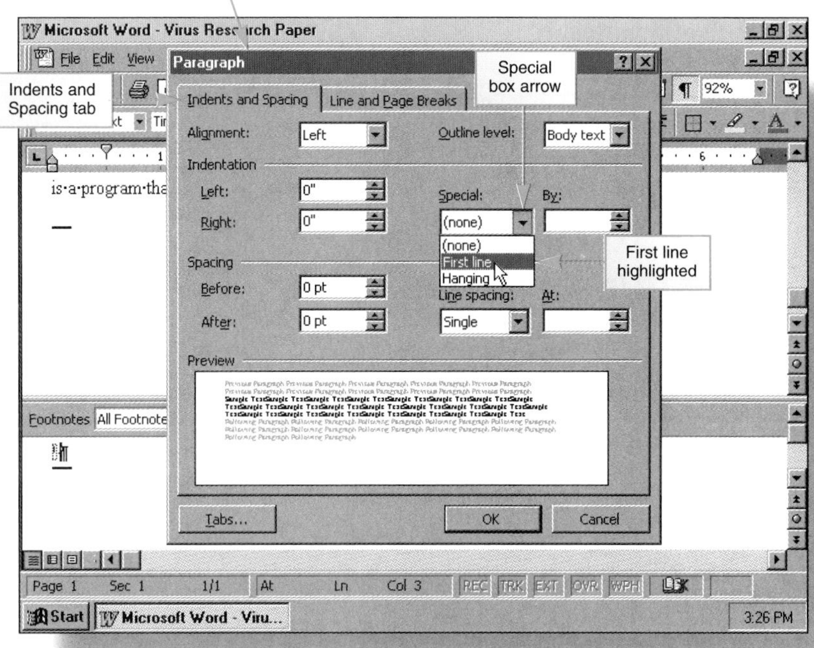

FIGURE 3-37

6 **Click First line. Click the Line spacing box arrow and then click Double. Point to the OK button.**

Word displays First line in the Special box and Double in the Line spacing box (Figure 3-38). The Preview area reflects the current settings in the Paragraph dialog box.

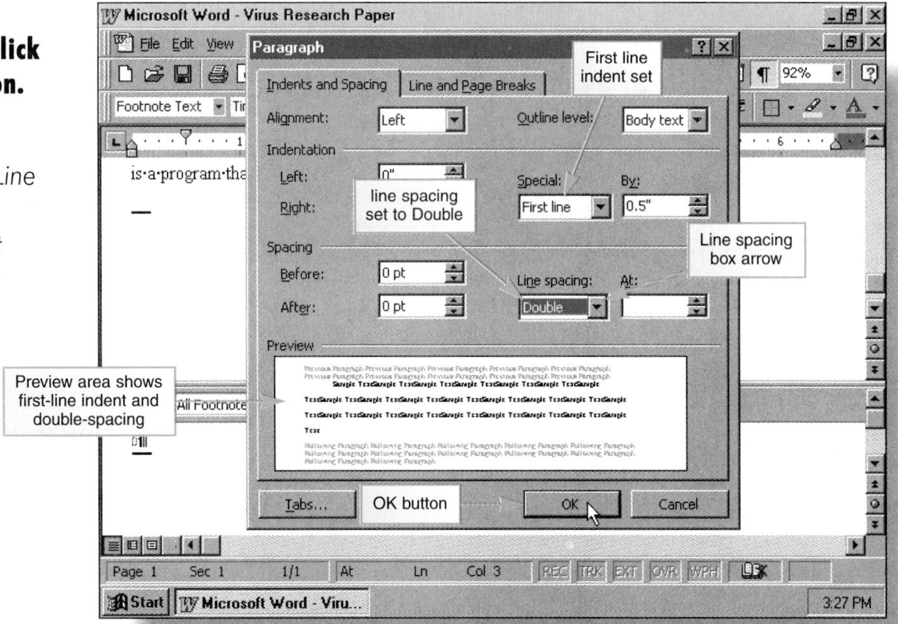

FIGURE 3-38

7 Click the OK button.

Word indents the first line of the note by one-half inch and sets the line spacing for the note to double.

8 Click the Font Size box arrow and then click 12. Type the note text: `A well-known time bomb is the Michelangelo virus, which destroys data on a user's hard disk on March 6, Michelangelo's birthday (Chambers and Peters 52-54).`

The note text is entered in the note pane in 12-point font (Figure 3-39).

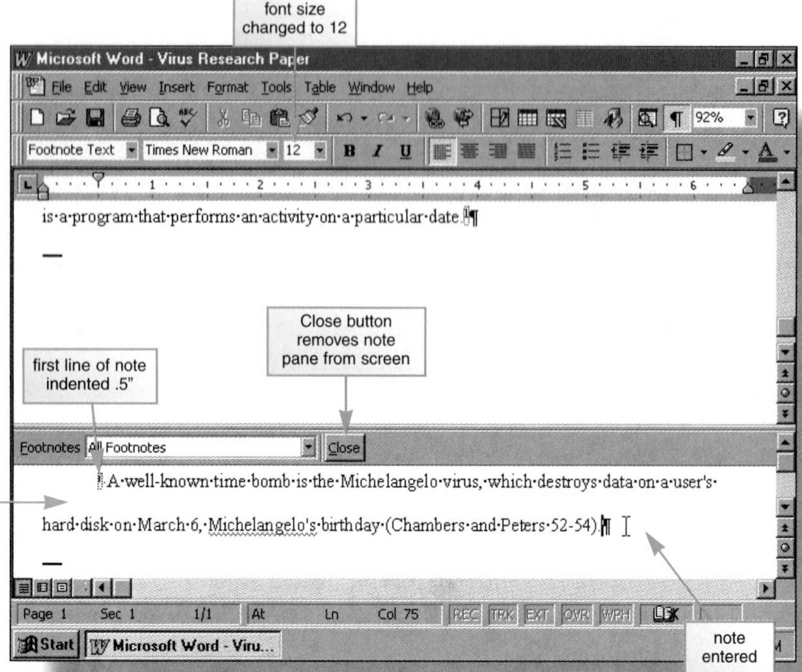

FIGURE 3-39

9 Click the Close button on the note pane option bar. Point to the note reference mark in the document window.

Word closes the note pane (Figure 3-40).

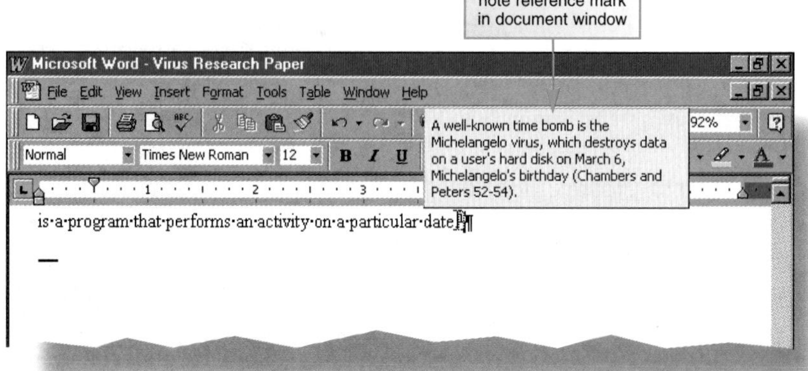

FIGURE 3-40

When Word closes the note pane and returns to the document, the note text disappears from the screen. Although the note text still exists, it is usually not visible as a footnote in normal view. If, however, you point to the note reference mark as shown in Figure 3-40, the note text appears above the note reference mark as a ScreenTip. To display footnotes in a note pane at the bottom of the screen, double-click the note reference mark in the document. If you want to verify that the note text is positioned correctly on the page, you must switch to page layout view or display the document in print preview.

To edit an existing footnote, click View on the menu bar and then click Footnotes or double-click the note reference mark in the document to display the note pane. Edit the footnote as you would any Word text and then click the Close button on the note pane option bar.

Automatic Page Breaks

As you type documents that exceed one page, Word automatically inserts page breaks, called **automatic page breaks** or **soft page breaks**, when it determines the text has filled one page according to paper size, margin settings, line spacing, and other settings. If you add text, delete text, or modify text on a page, Word recomputes the position of automatic page breaks and adjusts them accordingly. Word performs page recomputation between the keystrokes, that is, in between the pauses in your typing. Thus, Word refers to the automatic page break task as **background repagination**. In normal view, automatic page breaks appear on the Word screen as a single dotted horizontal line. Word's automatic page break feature is illustrated below.

More *About* Background Repagination

If background repagination has been deactivated on your system, Word stops all activities while repaginating the document. You can enable background repagination by clicking Tools on the menu bar, clicking Options, clicking the General tab, clicking the Background Repagination check box, and then clicking the OK button.

Steps To Page Break Automatically

Press the SPACEBAR and then type `A logic bomb is a program that performs an activity when a certain action occurs, such as an employee being terminated. A worm, which is similar to a virus, copies itself repeatedly until no memory or disk space remains.` **Press the ENTER key and then type the next paragraph of the research paper, as shown in Figure 3-42 below.**

As you begin typing the paragraph, Word places an automatic page break above line containing the note reference mark. When Word detects an additional line at the end of the paragraph, it moves the automatic page break down one line, below the line with the note reference mark (Figure 3-41). The status bar now displays Page 2 as the current page.

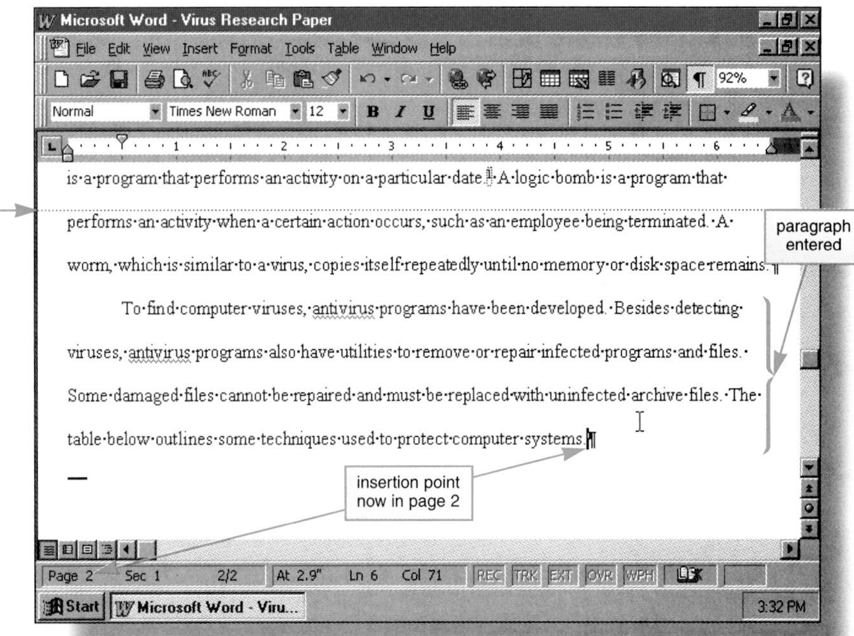

FIGURE 3-41

To find computer viruses, antivirus programs have been developed. Besides detecting viruses, antivirus programs also have utilities to remove or repair infected programs and files. Some damaged files cannot be repaired and must be replaced with uninfected archive files. The table below outlines some techniques used to protect computer systems.

FIGURE 3-42

Word, by default, prevents widows and orphans from occurring in a document. A **widow** is created when the last line of a paragraph displays by itself at the top of a page, and an **orphan** occurs when the first line of a paragraph displays by itself at the bottom of a page. When you typed the end of the third paragraph, Word placed the automatic page break above the line with the note reference mark to ensure that the last two lines of the paragraph would be at the top of the next page (avoiding a widow). When you continued typing the paragraph, however, Word recognized the multiple lines at the end of the paragraph and moved the automatic page break. If, for some reason, you wanted to allow a widow or an orphan in a document, you would right-click the paragraph in question, click Paragraph on the shortcut menu, click the Line and Page Breaks tab in the Paragraph dialog box, click Widow/Orphan control to deselect the check box, and then click the OK button.

Creating a Table with the Insert Table Button

At the end of the fourth paragraph of the research paper, you are to place a table outlining the techniques for virus protection and system archive (Figure 3-1 on page WD 3.5). In Project 2, you created a table of GPAs in the cover letter for the resume using the TAB key. In this project, you create a table using Word's table feature. A Word **table** is a collection of rows and columns. The intersection of a row and a column is called a **cell**.

Within a Word table, you easily can rearrange rows and columns, change column widths, sort rows and columns, and sum the contents of rows and columns. You can use the Table AutoFormat dialog box to make the table display in a professional manner. You also can chart table data. For these reasons, many Word users create tables with the Insert Table button, rather than using tabs as discussed in the previous project.

The first step in creating a table is to insert an empty table into the document. When inserting a table, you must specify the total number of rows and columns in the table, called the **dimension** of the table. The table in this project has two columns. Because you often do not know the total number of rows in a table, many Word users create two rows initially and then add rows as they need them. The first number in a dimension is the number of rows, and the second is the number of columns. Perform the following steps to insert a 2 x 2 table, that is, a table with two rows and two columns.

More *About* Word Tables

Although you can use the TAB key to create a table, many Word users prefer to use its table feature. With a Word table, you can arrange numbers in columns. For emphasis, tables can be shaded and have borders. Word tables can be sorted. And you can have Word add the contents of an entire row or column.

Steps To Insert an Empty Table

1 **With the insertion point at the end of the document, press the SHIFT+ENTER keys. Type** `Table` **and then press the SHIFT+ENTER keys. Type** `Techniques for Virus Protection and System Archive` **as the table title. Point to the Insert Table button on the Standard toolbar.**

Word places a line break character at the end of each line entered (Figure 3-43). Recall that a line break causes Word to ignore paragraph formatting when advancing the insertion point to the next line. Thus, Word does not first-line indent the table caption or title.

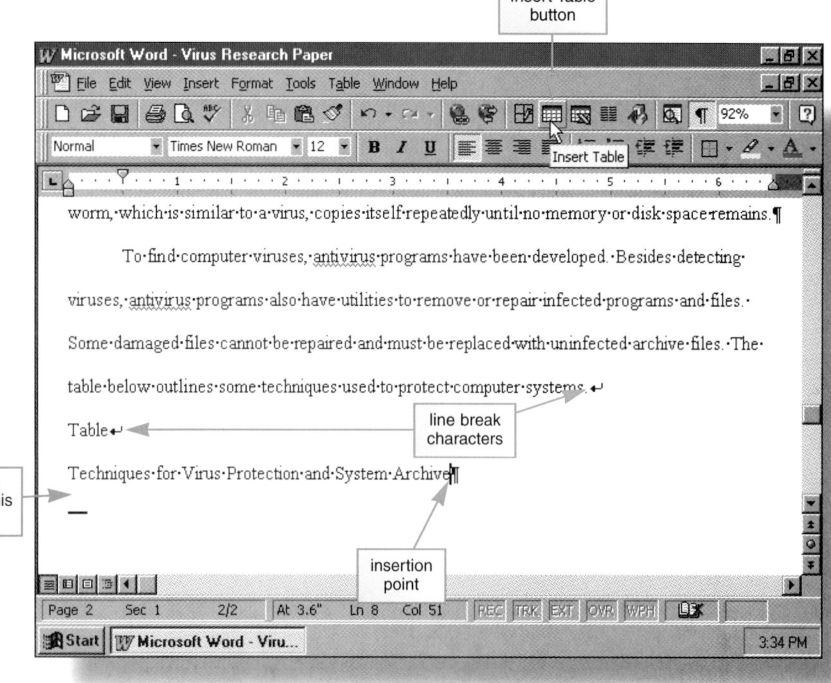

FIGURE 3-43

2 **Click the Insert Table button on the Standard toolbar. Point to the cell in the second row and second column of the grid.**

Word displays a ***grid*** *to define the dimensions of the desired table (Figure 3-44). The first two columns and first two rows in the grid are selected. The Insert Table button on the Standard toolbar is recessed. Word will insert the 2 × 2 table below the insertion point in the document window.*

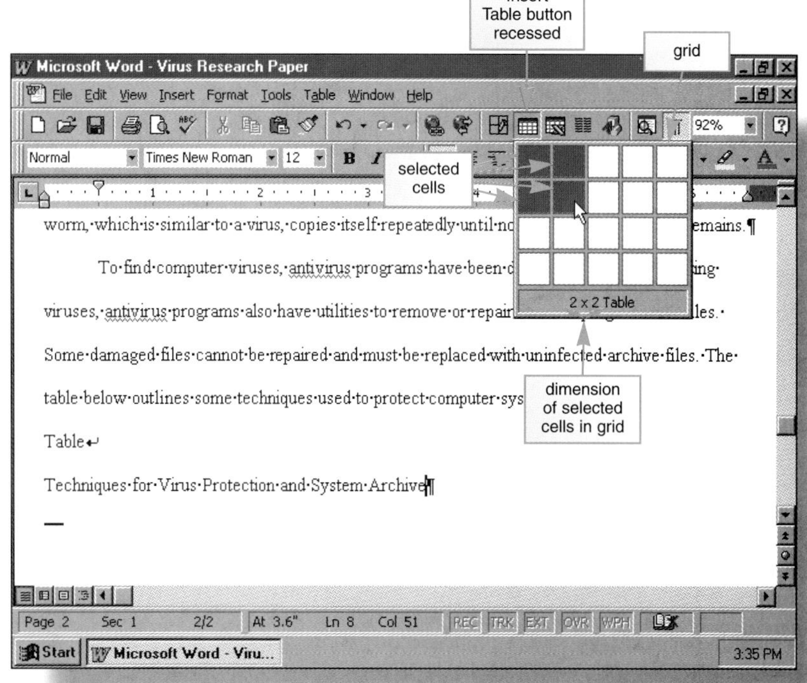

FIGURE 3-44

3 Click the cell in the second row and second column of the grid. If necessary, use the scroll bar to display the entire table in the document window.

Word inserts an empty 2 × 2 table into the document (Figure 3-45). The insertion point is in the first cell (row 1 and column 1) of the table.

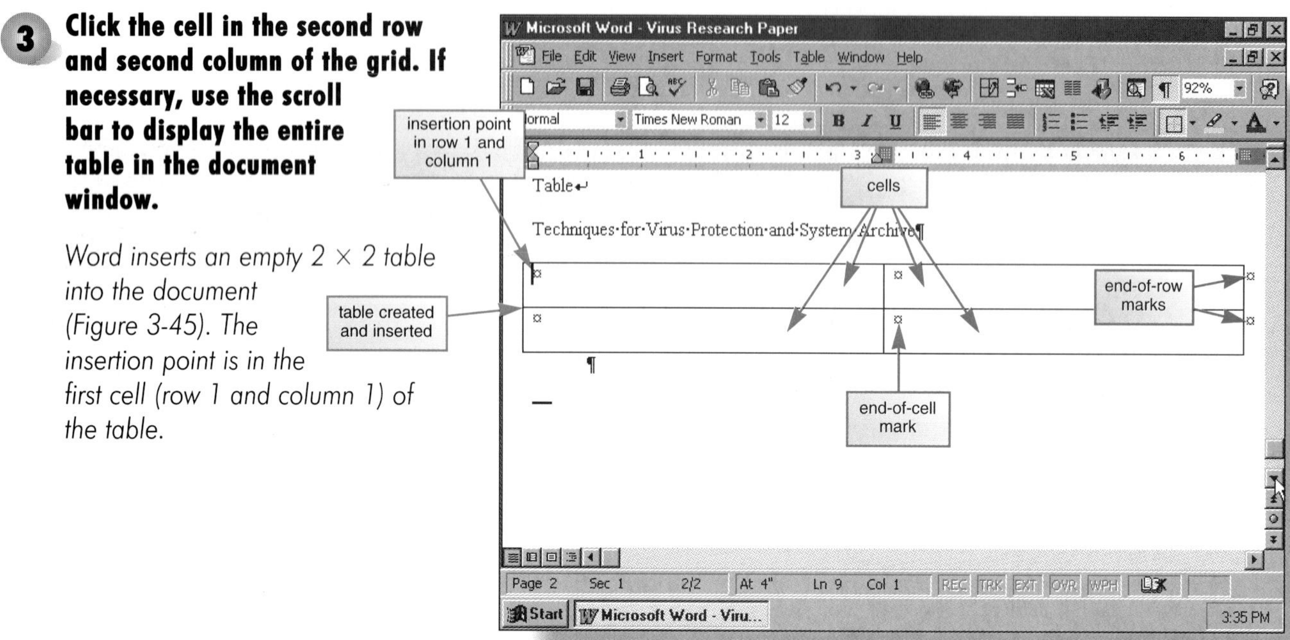

FIGURE 3-45

OtherWays

1. On Table menu click Insert Table, enter number of columns, enter number of rows, click OK button

Each row has an **end-of-row mark**, which is used to add columns to the right of a table. Each cell has an **end-of-cell mark**, which is used to select a cell. Notice the end-of-cell marks are currently left-aligned within each cell, which indicates the data will be left-aligned within the cells.

For simple tables, such as the one just created, Word users click the Insert Table button to create a table. For more complex tables, such as one with a varying number of columns per row, Word has a new Draw Table feature that allows you to use a pen pointer to draw the table on the screen. The Draw Table feature is discussed in Project 4.

More About Draw Table

To use Draw Table, click Tables and Borders button on the Standard toolbar to change the mouse pointer to a pen. Use the pen to draw from one corner to the opposite diagonal corner to define the perimeter of the table. Then, draw the column and row lines inside the perimeter. To remove a line, use the Eraser button on the Tables and Borders toolbar.

Entering Data into a Word Table

The next step is to enter data into the empty table. Cells are filled with data. The data you enter within a cell wordwraps just as text does between the margins of a document. To place data into a cell, you click the cell and then type. To advance rightward from one cell to the next, press the TAB key. When you are at the rightmost cell in a row, also press the TAB key to move to the first cell in the next row; do not press the ENTER key. The ENTER key is used to begin a new paragraph within a cell. Perform the following steps to enter the data into the table.

To Enter Data into a Table

1 **With the insertion point in the upper-left cell of the table, type** `Using Virus Protection Software` **and then press the TAB key. Type** `Backing Up Your System` **and then press the TAB key. Type** `Install virus protection software on every computer system.` **Press the TAB key. Type** `Develop a regular plan for copying and storing important data and program files.`

row 1 (header row) data entered

row 2 data entered

insertion point

FIGURE 3-46

The table data is entered into the header row and the second row of the table (Figure 3-46). When the first row of a table contains column titles, it is called the ***header row****.*

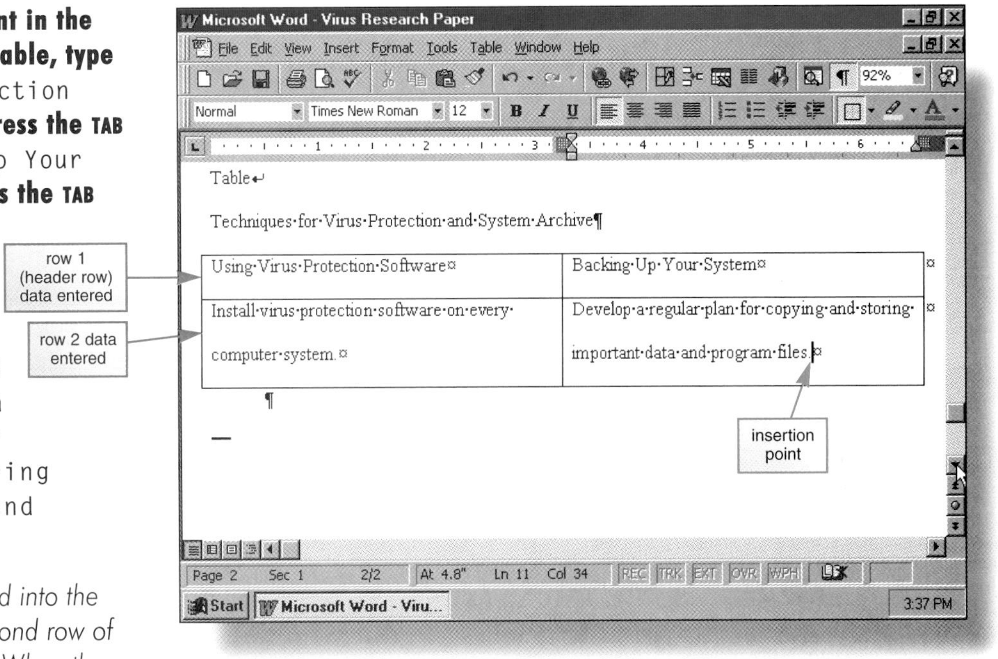

The insertion point currently is positioned at the cell intersecting row 2 and column 2. To create a new row at the bottom of a table, you press the TAB key while the insertion point is in the lower-right cell of the table.

2 **Press the TAB key. Type** `Before use, scan every floppy disk with a virus scan program to check for viruses.` **Press the TAB key. Type** `Implement a backup plan and adhere to its guidelines.` **Press the TAB key. Type** `Check all programs downloaded from the Internet or bulletin boards for viruses.` **Press the TAB key. Type** `Keep backup copies of files in fireproof safes or vaults or off-site.`

row 3 data entered

row 4 data entered

FIGURE 3-47

The table data is completely entered (Figure 3-47).

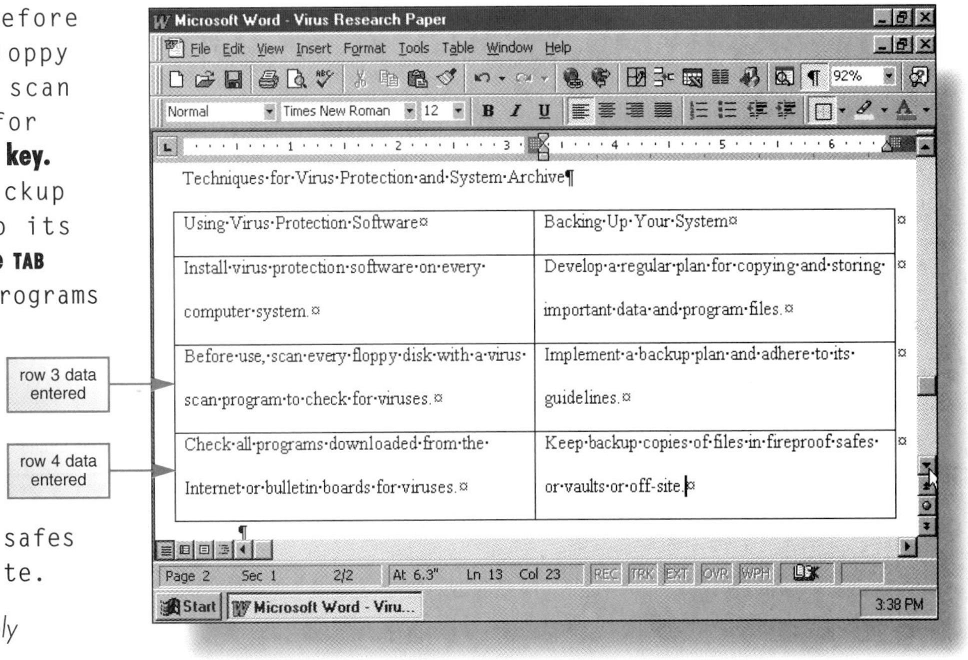

More About Tables

To select a single cell in a table, click to the left of the cell. To select an entire row, click to the left of the row. To select an entire column, click the column's top border. To add a row or column to the middle of a table, select the row below or column to the right, right-click the selection and then click Insert Row or Insert Column.

You modify the contents of cells just as you modify text in a document. To delete the contents of a cell, select the cell contents by pointing to the left edge of the cell and clicking when the mouse pointer changes direction, and then press the DELETE key. To modify text within a cell, click in the cell, and then correct the entry. You can double-click the OVR indicator on the status bar to toggle between insert and overtype modes. You also may drag and drop or cut and paste the contents of cells.

Because the TAB key advances you from one cell to the next in a table, press the CTRL+TAB keys to insert a tab character into a cell.

Formatting a Table

Although you can format each row, column, and cell of a table individually, Word provides a Table AutoFormat feature that contains predefined formats for tables. Perform the following steps to format the entire table using **Table AutoFormat**.

Steps To AutoFormat a Table

1 Right-click the table. Point to Table AutoFormat on the shortcut menu.

Word displays a shortcut menu for tables (Figure 3-48).

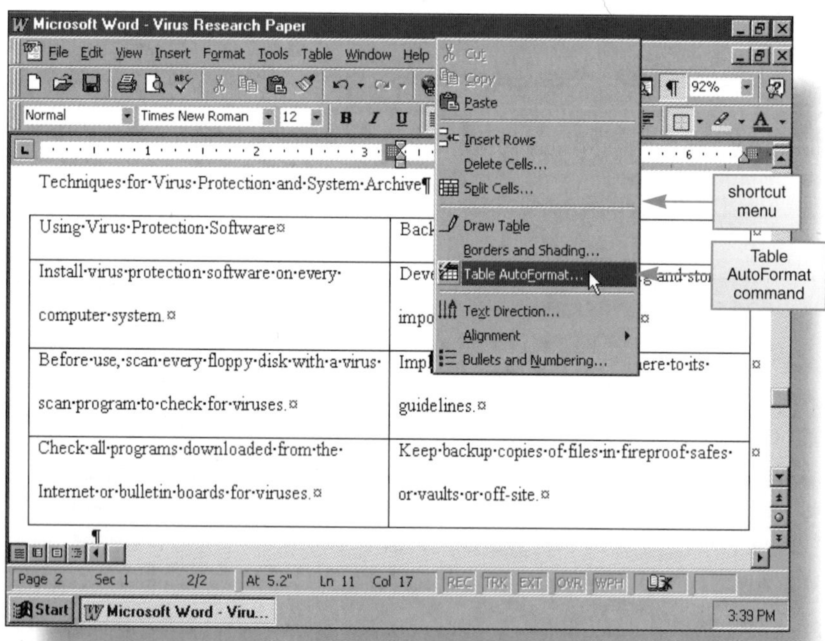

FIGURE 3-48

2 **Click Table AutoFormat. When the Table AutoFormat dialog box displays, if necessary, click Color in the Formats to apply area to turn color on for the table. Scroll through the Formats list and then click Grid 8. Point to the OK button.**

Word displays the Table AutoFormat dialog box (Figure 3-49). The Preview area shows the Grid 8 format. Because Heading rows is selected in the dialog box, the header row of the table has formatting different from the rest of the rows in the table.

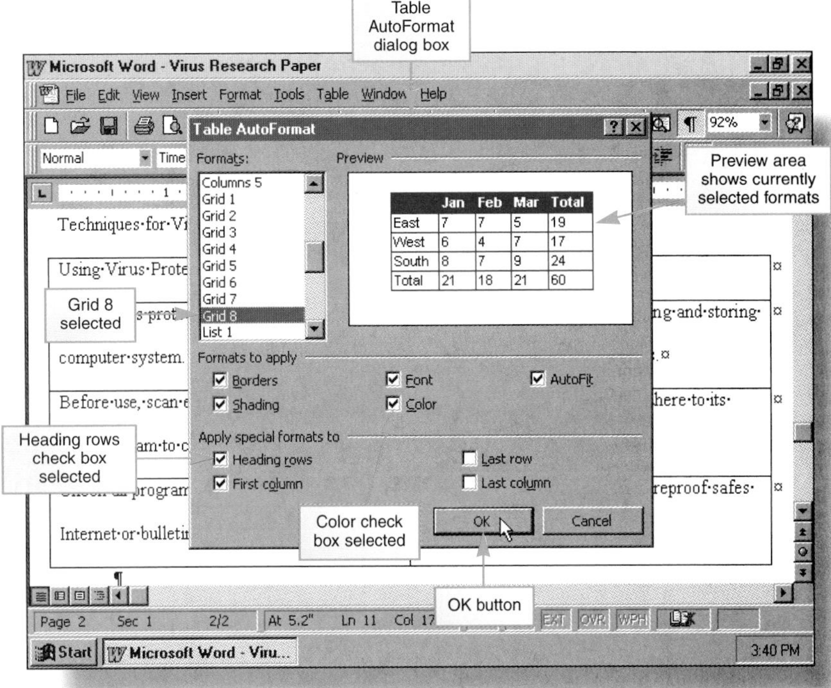

FIGURE 3-49

3 **Click the OK button.**

Word formats the table according to the Grid 8 format (Figure 3-50).

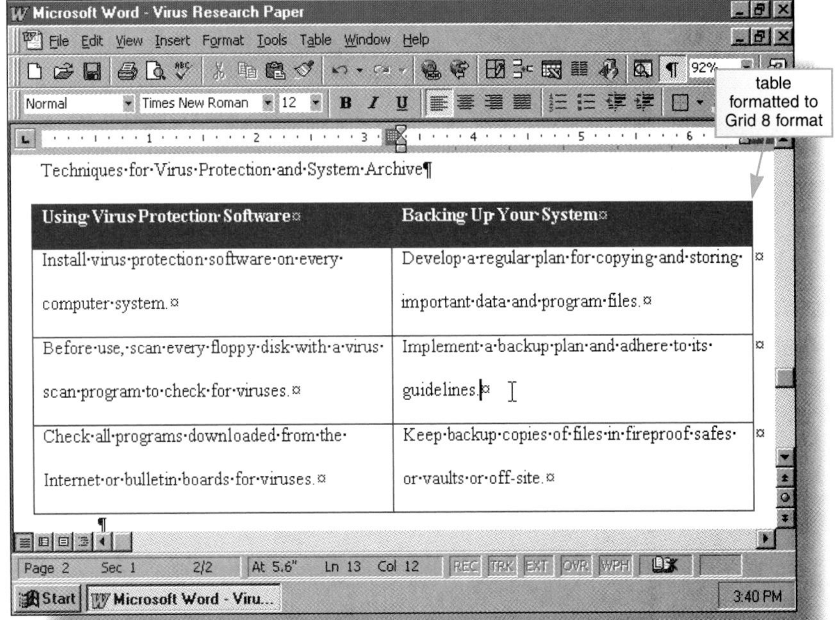

FIGURE 3-50

Other Ways

1. Click table, on Table menu click Table AutoFormat, click appropriate settings, click OK button

Changing the Line Spacing of the Table

Notice in Figure 3-50 that the cell contents are double-spaced; you want the paragraphs within the cells to be single-spaced. To change the line spacing of paragraphs in the table, you first must select the entire table and then format as shown in the steps on the next page.

To Select an Entire Table

1 **With the insertion point somewhere in the table, click Table on the menu bar and then point to Select Table (Figure 3-51).**

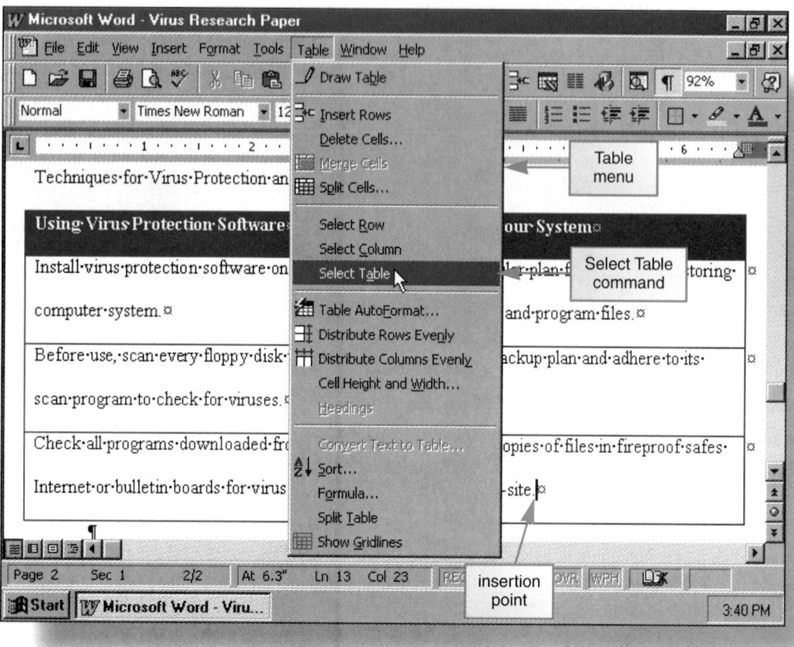

FIGURE 3-51

2 **Click Select Table.**

Word highlights the contents of the entire table.

3 **Press the CTRL+1 keys.**

Word single-spaces the contents of the table (Figure 3-52). CTRL+1 *is the keyboard shortcut for single-spacing paragraphs;* CTRL+2 *is the keyboard shortcut for double-spacing paragraphs.*

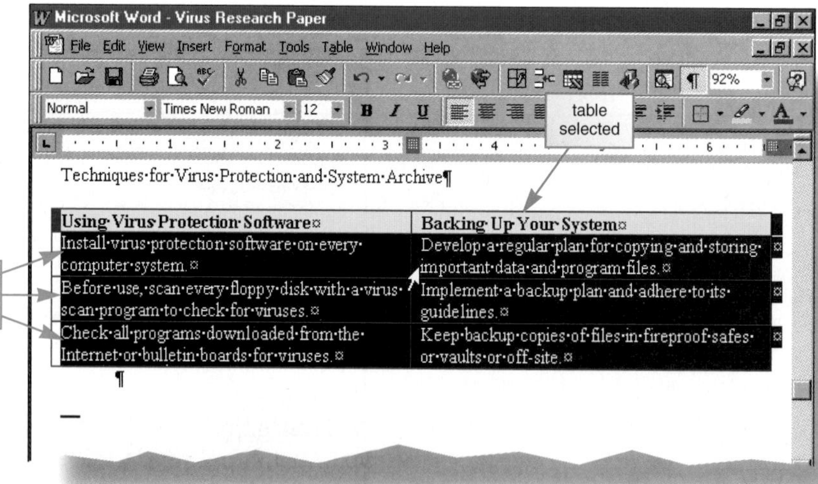

FIGURE 3-52

Other Ways

1. With insertion point somewhere in table, press ALT+5 (on numeric keypad with NUM LOCK off)

Changing Paragraph Formatting

When Word placed the table into the research paper, it placed a paragraph mark immediately below the table with no blank line between the paragraph mark and the table. Because the MLA style requires double-spacing of the entire document, you must change the line spacing above the paragraph mark. Perform the following step to insert a blank line above the paragraph mark below the table.

Steps To Insert a Blank Line above a Paragraph

1. **Position the insertion point on the paragraph mark directly below the table (Figure 3-53).**

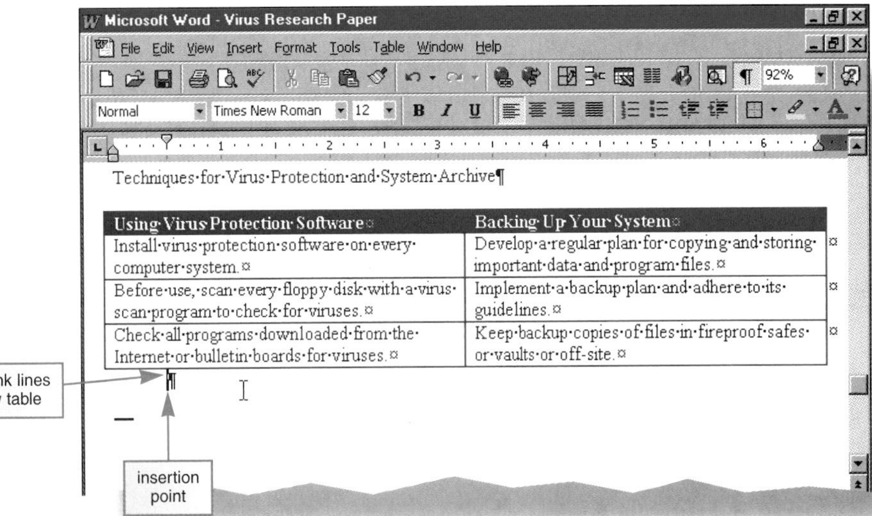

FIGURE 3-53

2. **Press the CTRL+0 (zero) keys.**

   Word inserts a blank line between the paragraph mark and the table.

3. **Type the last sentence of the research paper:** `If your system becomes virus infected and you have questions, contact the National Computer Security Association (NCSA) for low-cost assistance (Elmhurst, 6 Nov. 1998).`

   The body of the research paper is complete (Figure 3-54).

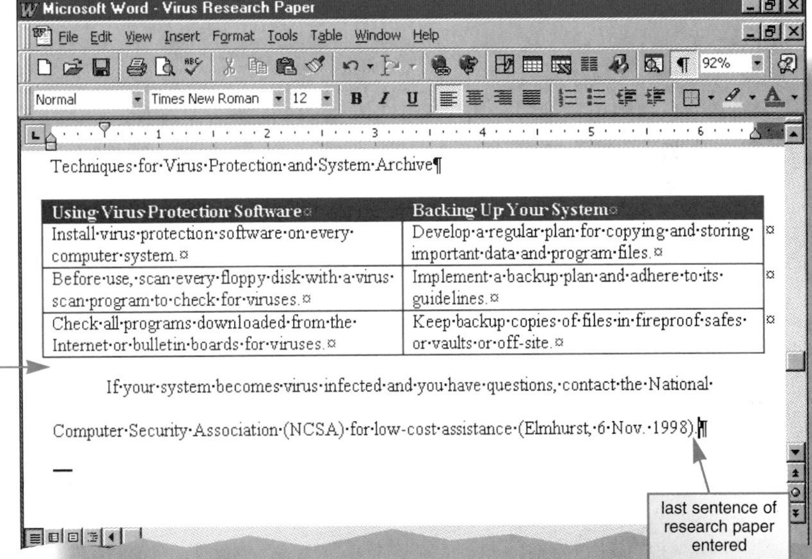

FIGURE 3-54

OtherWays

1. Right-click paragraph, click Paragraph on shortcut menu, click Indents and Spacing tab, type 12 in Spacing Before text box, click OK button
2. On Format menu click Paragraph, click Indents and Spacing tab, type 12 in Spacing Before text box, click OK button

Creating an Alphabetical Works Cited Page

According to the MLA style, the **works cited page** is a bibliographical list of works you reference directly in your paper. The list is placed on a separate page with the title, Works Cited, centered one inch from the top margin. The works are to be alphabetized by author's last name. The first line of each work begins at the left margin; subsequent lines of the same work are indented one-half inch from the left margin.

The first step in creating the works cited page is to force a page break so the works display on a separate page.

Manual Page Breaks

Because the works cited are to display on a separate numbered page, you must insert a manual page break following the body of the research paper. A **manual page break** or **hard page break** is one that you force into the document at a specific location. Manual page breaks display on the screen as a horizontal dotted line, separated by the words, Page Break. Word never moves or adjusts manual page breaks; however, Word does adjust any automatic page breaks that follow in the document. Word inserts manual page breaks just before the location of the insertion point. Perform the following steps to insert a manual page break after the body of the research paper.

To Page Break Manually

1 With the insertion point at the end of the research paper, press the ENTER key. Press the CTRL+0 (zero) keys. Click Insert on the menu bar and then point to Break.

Word removes the extra blank line above the paragraph mark (Figure 3-55). Recall that you inserted a blank line above the paragraph below the table. When you pressed the ENTER key, this paragraph formatting carried forward; thus, two blank lines displayed between these paragraphs (one for the double-spacing and one for the extra blank line). Pressing the CTRL+0 keys a second time removes one blank line from above a paragraph. The insertion point now is positioned one blank line below the body of the research paper.

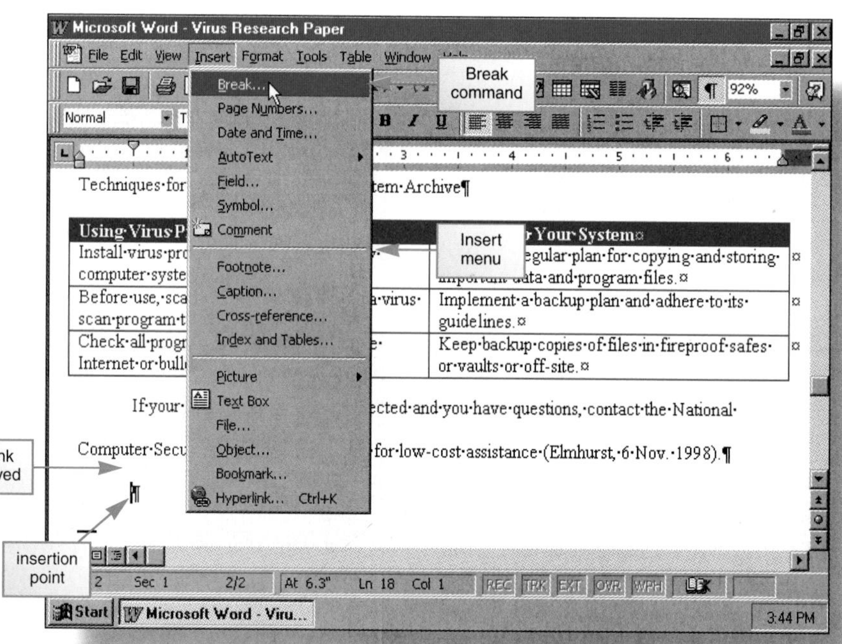

FIGURE 3-55

2 Click Break.

Word displays the Break dialog box (Figure 3-56). The default option is Page Break.

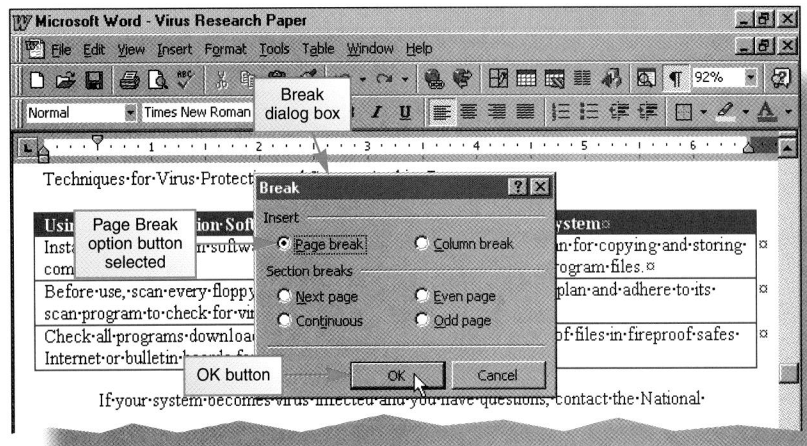

FIGURE 3-56

3 Click the OK button.

Word inserts a manual page break immediately above the insertion point and positions the insertion point immediately below the manual page break (Figure 3-57). The manual page break displays as a horizontal dotted line with the words, Page Break, in the middle of the line. The status bar indicates the insertion point is located on page 3.

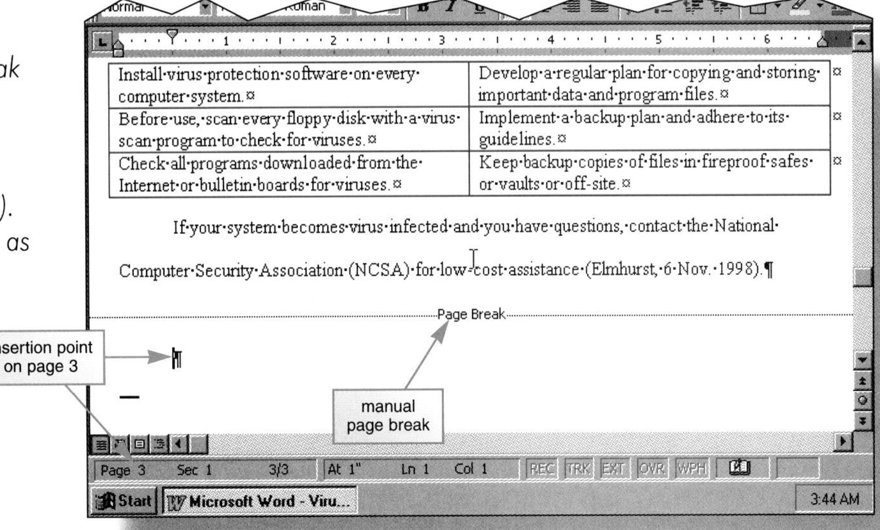

FIGURE 3-57

Other Ways

1. Press CTRL+ENTER

If, for some reason, you wanted to remove a manual page break from your document, you must first select it by double-clicking it. Then, right-click the selection and click Cut on the shortcut menu; or click the Cut button on the Standard toolbar; or press the DELETE key.

Centering the Title of the Works Cited Page

The works cited title is to be centered between the margins. If you simply click the Center button on the Formatting toolbar, the title will not be properly centered; instead, it will be one-half inch to the right of the center point because earlier you set first-line indent at the first tab stop. Thus, the first line of every paragraph is indented one-half inch. To properly center the title of the works cited page, you must move the First Line Indent marker back to the left margin before clicking the Center button as described on the next page.

More About Sources

When writing a research paper, you must acknowledge sources of information. Citing sources boils down to ethics and honesty. Caution must be used when summarizing or paraphrasing a source. Be sure to avoid plagiarism, which includes using someone else's words and ideas and claiming them as your own.

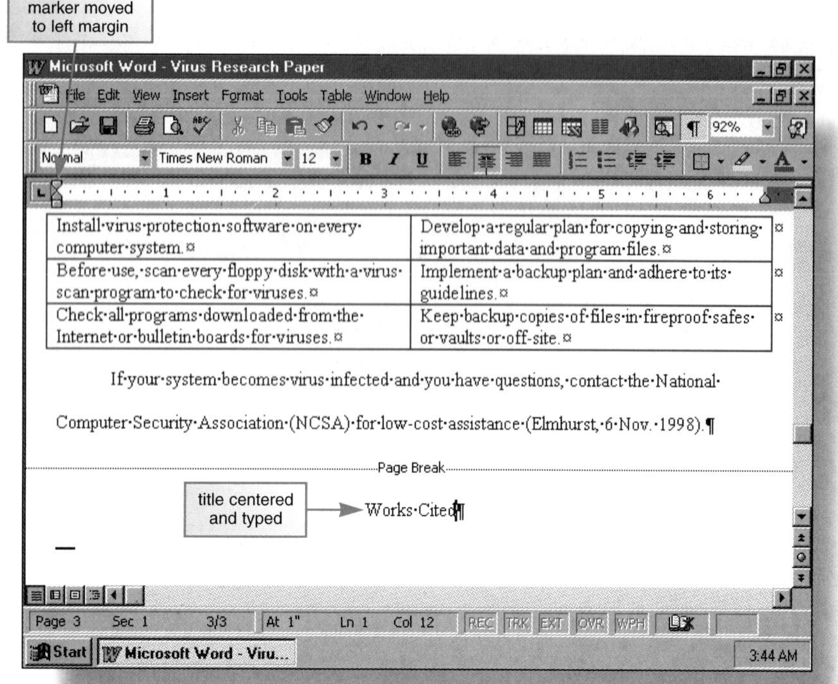

FIGURE 3-58

TO CENTER THE TITLE OF THE WORKS CITED PAGE

Step 1: Drag the First Line Indent marker to the 0" mark on the ruler.

Step 2: Click the Center button on the Formatting toolbar.

Step 3: Type `Works Cited` as the title.

The title displays centered properly (Figure 3-58).

Creating a Hanging Indent

On the works cited page, the works begin at the left margin. Subsequent lines in the same paragraph are indented one-half inch from the left margin. In essence, the first line *hangs* to the left of the rest of the paragraph; thus, this type of paragraph formatting is called a **hanging indent.** Perform the following steps to create a hanging indent.

To Create a Hanging Indent

1 **Press the ENTER key. Click the Align Left button on the Formatting toolbar. Point to the Hanging Indent marker on the ruler (Figure 3-59).**

*Recall that the small square at the 0" mark, called the Left Indent marker, is used to change the entire left margin, whereas the **Hanging Indent marker** affects only the subsequent lines of the same paragraph.*

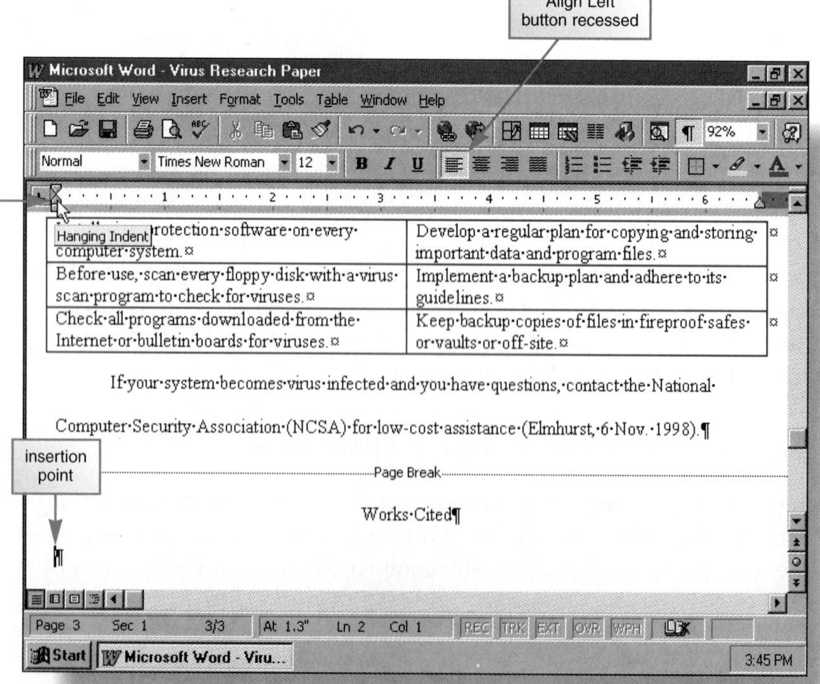

FIGURE 3-59

2 Drag the Hanging Indent marker to the .5-inch mark on the ruler.

The Hanging Indent marker and Left Indent marker display at the location of the first tab stop, one-half inch from the left margin (Figure 3-60). When you drag the Hanging Indent marker, the Left Indent marker moves with it. The paragraph containing the insertion point in the document window is positioned at the left margin because only subsequent lines in the paragraph are to be indented.

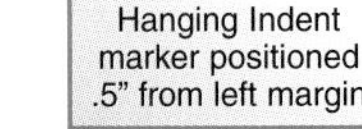

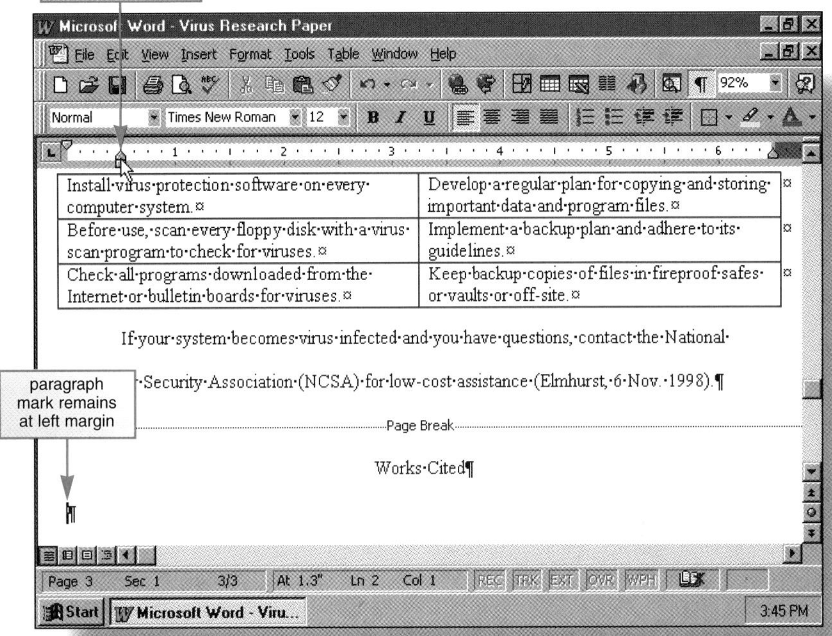

FIGURE 3-60

OtherWays

1. Right-click paragraph, click Paragraph on shortcut menu, click Indents and Spacing tab, click Special box arrow, click Hanging, click OK button
2. On Format menu click Paragraph, click Indents and Spacing tab, click Special box arrow, click Hanging, click OK button
3. Press CTRL+T

To drag both the First Line Indent and Hanging Indent markers at the same time, you drag the Left Indent marker on the ruler.

Creating a Hyperlink

A **hyperlink** is a shortcut that allows a user to jump easily and quickly to other documents, objects, or pages. **Jumping** is the process of following a hyperlink to its destination. For example, by clicking hyperlink text on the Word screen, you jump to another document on your computer, on your network, or on the World Wide Web. When you close the hyperlink destination page or document, you return to the original location in your Word document. When the hyperlink text displays initially, it is underlined and colored blue. Once you click a hyperlink, the hyperlink text color changes to purple. When you create a Word document and wish to create a hyperlink to a Web page, you do not have to be connected to the Internet.

Recall from Project 2 that Word has an AutoFormat As You Type feature. Using this feature, you can create a hyperlink simply by typing the address of the file or Web page to which you want to jump. Be sure this feature is enabled by clicking Tools on the menu bar, clicking AutoCorrect, clicking the AutoFormat As You Type tab, clicking the Internet and network paths with hyperlinks, and then clicking the OK button.

In this project, one of the works is from a Web page on the Internet. When someone displays your research paper on the screen, you want him or her to be able to click the Web address in the work and jump to the site for more information. Perform the steps on the next page to create a hyperlink as you type.

More About Citing Sources

Information that is commonly known or accessible to the audience constitutes common knowledge and does not have to be listed as a parenthetical citation or in the bibliography. If, however, you question whether certain information is common knowledge, you should document it – just to be safe.

To Create a Hyperlink As You Type

1 **Type the Works Cited paragraphs as shown in Figure 3-62 below.**

When Word wraps the text in each works cited paragraph, it automatically indents the second line of the paragraph by one-half inch (Figure 3-61). When you press the ENTER key at the end of the first paragraph of text, the insertion point returns automatically to the left margin for the next paragraph. Recall that each time you press the ENTER key, the paragraph formatting in the prior paragraph is carried forward to the next paragraph. The insertion point is positioned to the right of the Web address.

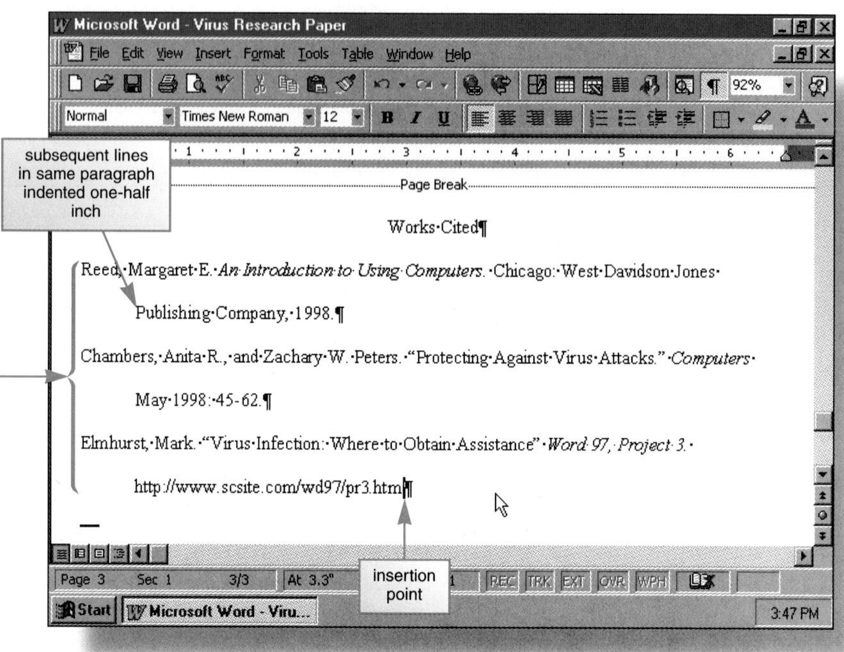

FIGURE 3-61

Reed, Margaret E. *An Introduction to Using Computers.* Chicago: West Davidson Jones Publishing Company, 1998.

Chambers, Anita R., and Zachary W. Peters. "Protecting Against Virus Attacks." *Computers* May 1998: 45-62.

Elmhurst, Mark. "Virus Infection: Where to Obtain Assistance" *Word 97, Project 3.* http://www.scsite.com/wd97/pr3.htm

FIGURE 3-62

2 **Press the SPACEBAR and then type** `(6 Nov. 1998).`

As soon as you press the SPACEBAR after typing the Web address, the address formats as a hyperlink (Figure 3-63).

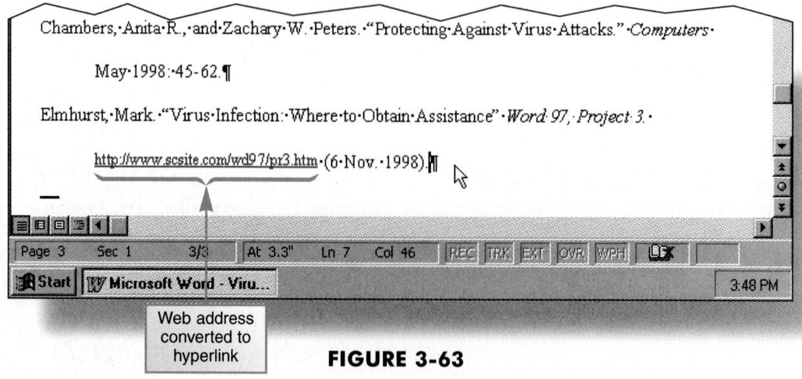

FIGURE 3-63

OtherWays

1. Click Insert Hyperlink button on Standard toolbar, type Web address in Link to file or URL text box, click OK button

Later in this project, you will jump to the hyperlink destination.

Sorting Paragraphs

The MLA style requires that the works cited be listed in alphabetical order by author's last name. With Word, you can arrange paragraphs in alphabetic, numeric, or date order based on the first character in each paragraph. Ordering characters in this manner is called **sorting**. Arrange the works cited paragraphs in alphabetical order as illustrated in the following steps.

More About Sorting

You can also sort the contents of a table. First, select the rows in the table to be sorted. Click Table on the menu bar, click Sort Text, click Ascending or Descending, and then click the OK button. Once a document has been saved with sorted paragraphs or tables, you cannot return to original order of the paragraphs or table.

Steps To Sort Paragraphs

1 Select all the works cited paragraphs by pointing to the left of the first paragraph and dragging down. Click Table on the menu bar and then point to Sort.

All of the paragraphs to be sorted are selected (Figure 3-64).

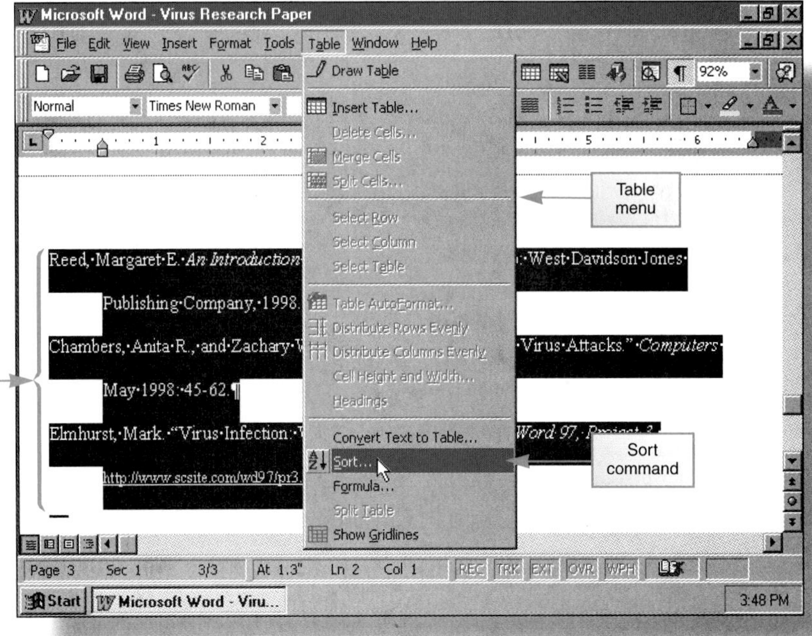

FIGURE 3-64

2 Click Sort.

Word displays the Sort Text dialog box (Figure 3-65). In the Sort by area, Ascending is selected. Ascending sorts in alphabetic or numeric order.

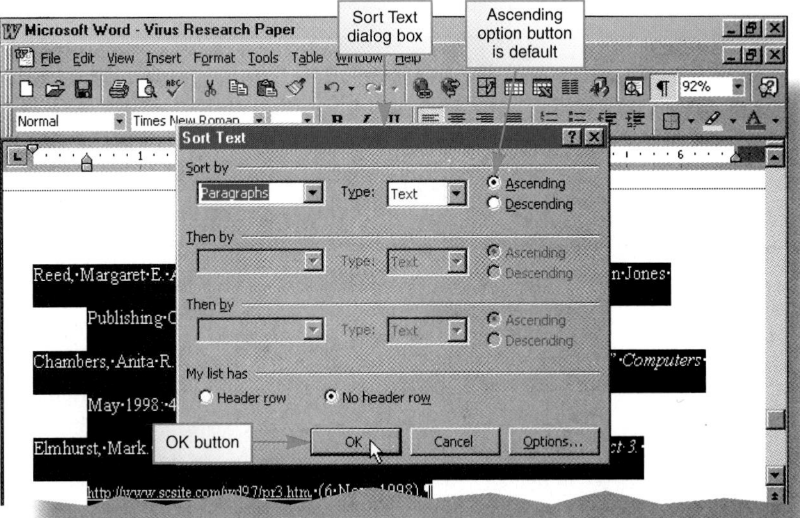

FIGURE 3-65

3 **Click the OK button. Click outside of the selection to remove the highlight.**

Word sorts the works cited paragraphs alphabetically (Figure 3-66).

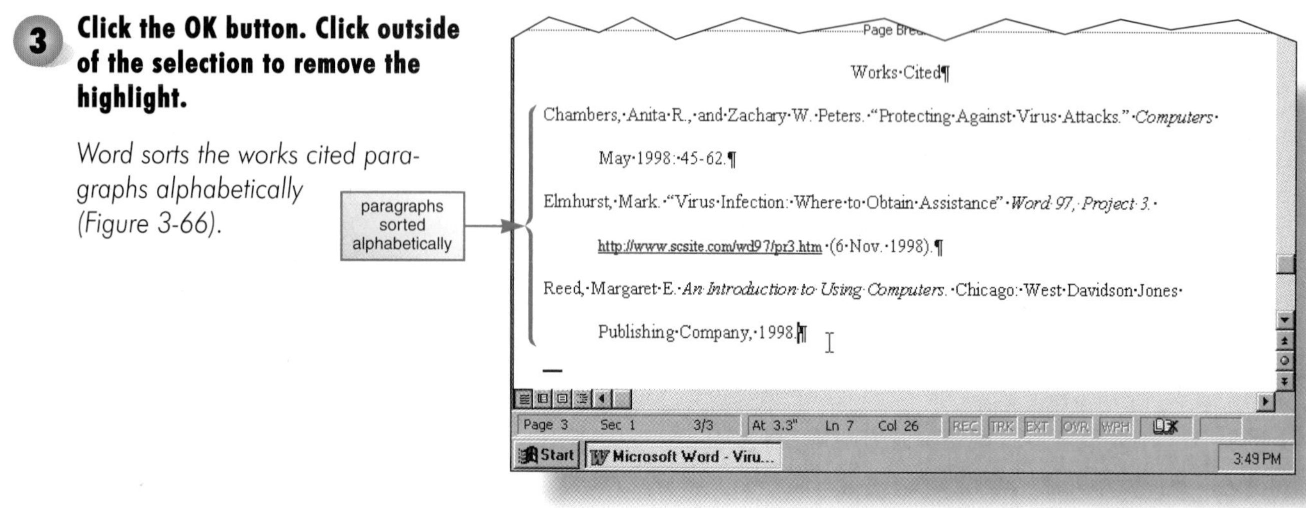

FIGURE 3-66

More *About* **APA Style**

The APA style requires that the working bibliography be on a separate page, like the MLA; however, the title should be References, rather than Works Cited. The running head should appear on the References page. Guidelines for preparing reference list entries differ significantly from the MLA style. Refer to an APA handbook for specifics.

If you accidentally sort the wrong paragraphs, you can undo a sort by clicking the Undo button on the Standard toolbar.

In the Sort Text dialog box (Figure 3-65 on the previous page), the default sort order is Ascending. If the first character of each paragraph to be sorted is a letter, Word sorts alphabetically on the first letter of the paragraphs. If the first character of each paragraph to be sorted is a number, Word sorts numerically on the first number of the paragraphs. Word by default, orders in **ascending sort order**, which means from the beginning of the alphabet, lowest number, or earliest date. If the first character of the paragraphs to be sorted contains a mixture of letters, numbers, and dates, then the numbers appear first and letters appear last once the paragraphs are sorted. Uppercase letters appear before lowercase letters. In case of ties, Word looks to the first character with a nonidentical character and sorts on that character for the paragraphs where the tie occurs.

You also can sort in descending order by clicking Descending in the Sort Text dialog box. **Descending sort order** begins sorting from the end of the alphabet, the highest number, or the most recent date.

The research paper is now complete and ready for proofing.

Proofing and Revising the Research Paper

As discussed in Project 1, once you complete a document, you might find it necessary to make changes to it. Before submitting a paper to be graded, you should proofread it. While proofreading, you look for grammatical errors and spelling errors. You want to be sure the transitions between sentences flow smoothly and the sentences themselves make sense. Very often, you may count the words in a paper to meet minimum word guidelines specified by an instructor. To assist you in this proofreading effort, Word provides several tools. You already have used the spell checker and grammar checker in previous projects. Other helpful tools are discussed in the following pages.

Going to a Specific Location in a Document

Often, you would like to bring a certain page or footnote into view in the document window. To do this, you could scroll though the document to find the desired page or note. Instead of scrolling though the document, Word provides an easier method of going to a specific location via the **Select Browse Object menu**. Perform the following steps to go to the top of page two in the research paper.

Steps To Browse by Page

1 Click the Select Browse Object button on the vertical scroll bar. When the Select Browse Object menu displays, point to Browse by Page.

Word displays the Select Browse Object menu (Figure 3-67). As you point to various commands in the Select Browse Object menu, Word displays the command name at the bottom of the menu. For example, you could browse by footnote, endnote, table, and so on.

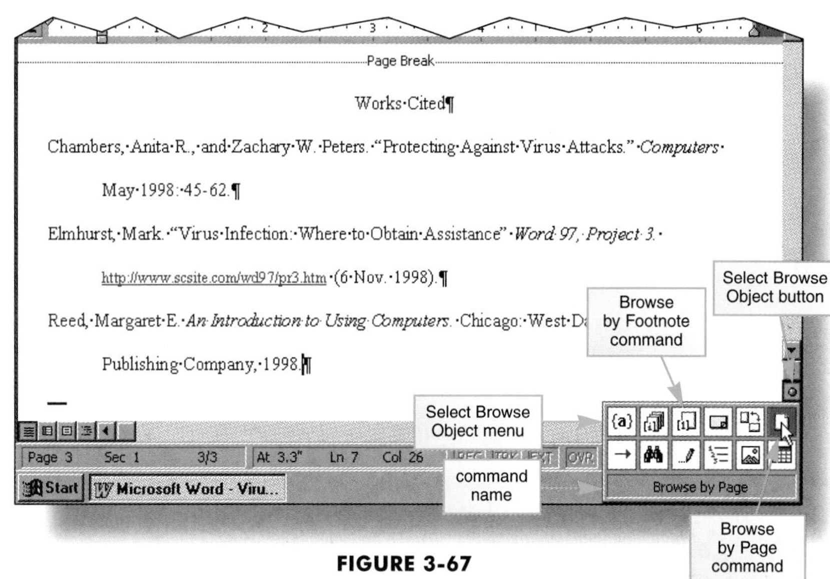

FIGURE 3-67

2 Click Browse by Page. Point to the Previous Page button on the vertical scroll bar.

Word closes the Select Browse Object menu (Figure 3-68). Depending on the command you select in the Select Browse Object menu, the function of the buttons above and below the Select Browse Object button on the vertical scroll bar changes. Because Browse by Page was selected, the buttons move to the previous or next page.

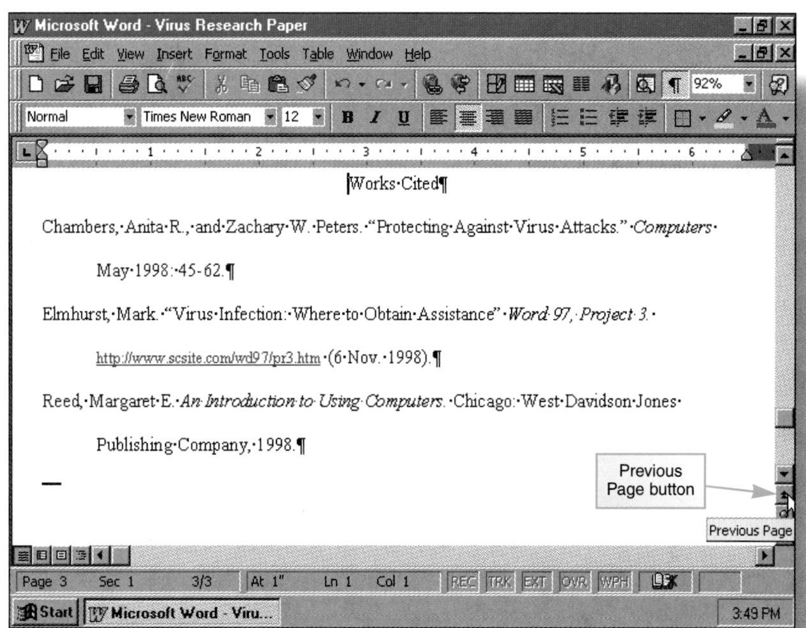

FIGURE 3-68

3 **Click the Previous Page button.**

Word places the top of page 2 (the previous page) at the top of the document window (Figure 3-69).

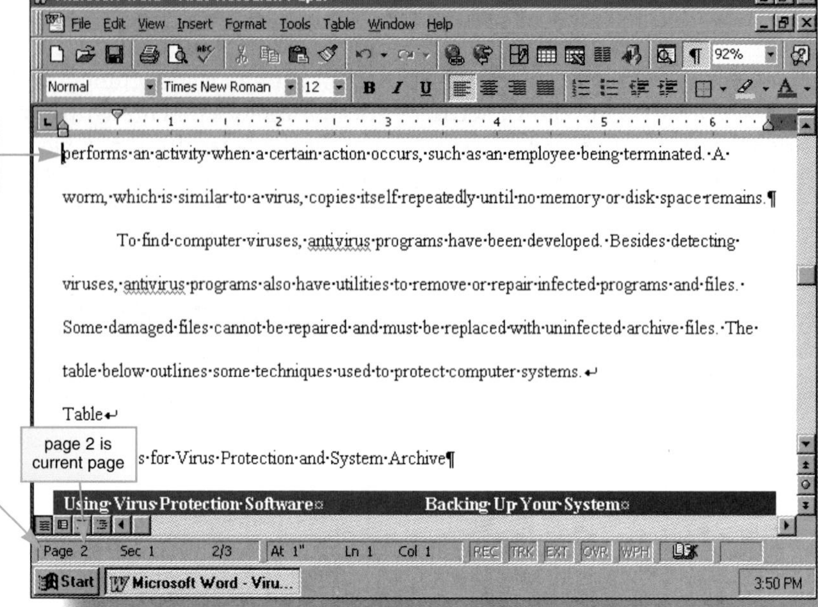

FIGURE 3-69

Other Ways

1. Double-click Page indicator on status bar, click Page in Go to what list box, type page number in Enter page number text box, click Go To button, click Close button
2. Click Select Browse Object button on vertical scroll bar, click Go To, and then proceed starting with click Page in Go to what list box as described in 1 above
3. On Edit menu click Go To, and then proceed starting with click Page in Go to what list box as described in 1 above
4. Press CTRL+G, and then proceed starting with click Page in Go to what list box as described in 1 above

Finding and Replacing Text

While proofreading the paper, notice that it contains the word, archive, more than once in the document (see Figure 3-70 below); and you would rather use the word, backup. Therefore, you must change all occurrences of the word, archive, to the word, backup. To do this, you can use Word's find and replace feature, which automatically locates each occurrence of a specified word or phrase and then replaces it with specified text as shown in these steps.

Steps To Find and Replace Text

1 **Click the Select Browse Object button on the vertical scroll bar. Point to Find.**

Word displays the Select Browse Object menu (Figure 3-70). The Find command is highlighted.

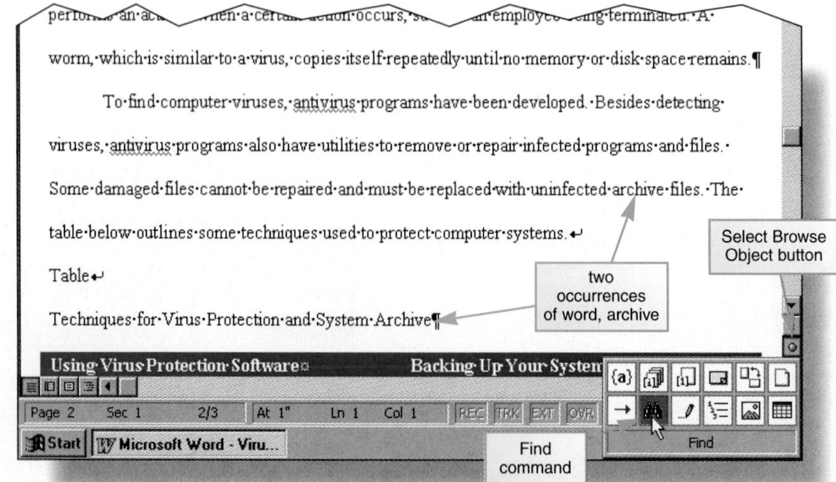

FIGURE 3-70

2 **Click Find. When the Find and Replace dialog box displays, click the Replace tab. Type** `archive` **in the Find what text box. Press the TAB key. Type** `backup` **in the Replace with text box. Point to the Replace All button.**

Word displays the Find and Replace dialog box (Figure 3-71). Clicking the Replace All button replaces all occurrences of the Find what text with the Replace with text.

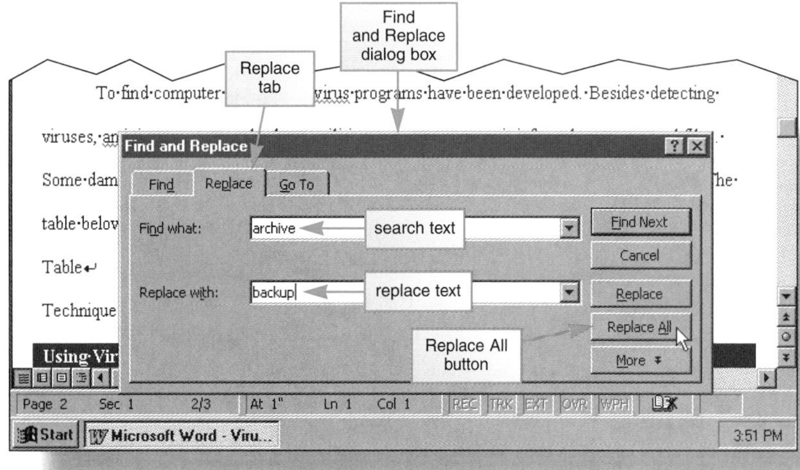

FIGURE 3-71

3 **Click the Replace All button.**

Word replaces all occurrences of the word, archive, with the word, backup, and then displays a Microsoft Word dialog box indicating the total number of replacements made (Figure 3-72).

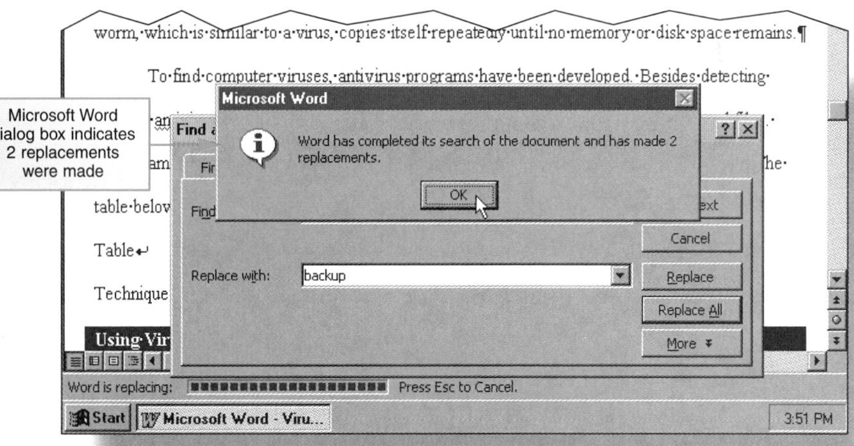

FIGURE 3-72

4 **Click the OK button in the Microsoft Word dialog box. Click the Close button in the Find and Replace dialog box.**

Word returns to the document window. The word, backup, now displays instead of the word, archive (Figure 3-73).

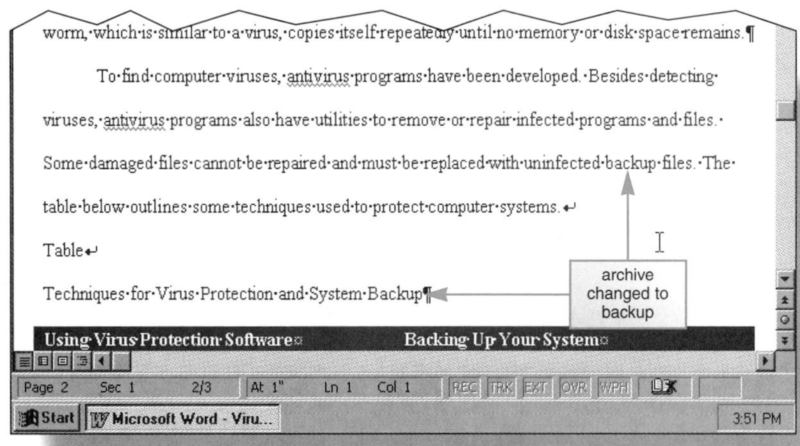

FIGURE 3-73

OtherWays

1. On Edit menu click Replace, type Find what text, type Replace with text, click Replace All button, click OK button, click Close button
2. Press CTRL+H, and then proceed starting with type Find what text as described in 1 above

In some cases, you may want to replace only certain occurrences of the text, not all of them. To instruct Word to confirm each change, click the Find Next button in the Find and Replace dialog box (Figure 3-71 on the previous page), instead of the Replace All button. When Word locates an occurrence of the text in the Find what text box, it pauses and waits for you to click either the Replace button or the Find Next button. Clicking the Replace button changes the text; clicking the Find Next button instructs Word to disregard the replacement and look for the next occurrence of the Find what text.

If you accidentally replace the wrong text, you can undo a replacement by clicking the Undo button on the Standard toolbar. If you used the Replace All button, Word undoes all replacements. If you used the Replace button, Word only undoes the most recent replacement.

Finding Text

Sometimes, you may want to only find text, instead of find and replace text. To search for just an occurrence of text, you would follow these steps.

More About Proofreading

When proofreading a paper, ask yourself these questions: Is the purpose clear? Does the title suggest the topic? Does the paper have an introduction, body, and conclusion? Is the thesis clear? Does each paragraph in the body relate to the thesis? Is the conclusion effective? Are all sources acknowledged?

TO FIND TEXT

Step 1: Click the Select Browse Object button on the vertical scroll bar.
Step 2: Click Find on the Select Browse Object menu.
Step 3: Type the text you want to locate in the Find what text box on the Find sheet.
Step 4: Click the Find Next button.
Step 5: To edit the text, click the Close button in the Find and Replace dialog box; to search for the next occurrence of the Find what text, click the Find Next button.

Using the Thesaurus

When writing papers, you may find that you used the same word in multiple locations or that a word you used was not quite appropriate. In these instances, you will want to look up a word similar in meaning to the duplicate or inappropriate word. These similar words are called **synonyms**. A book of synonyms is referred to as a **thesaurus**. Word provides its own thesaurus for your convenience. In this project, you need a synonym for the word, find, at the beginning of the fourth paragraph. Perform the following steps to use Word's thesaurus.

Steps To Use Word's Thesaurus

1. **Click the word for which you want to look up a synonym. Click Tools on the menu bar, point to Language on the Tools menu, and then point to Thesaurus on the Language submenu.**

The insertion point is positioned in the word, find, at the beginning of the fourth paragraph in the research paper (Figure 3-74).

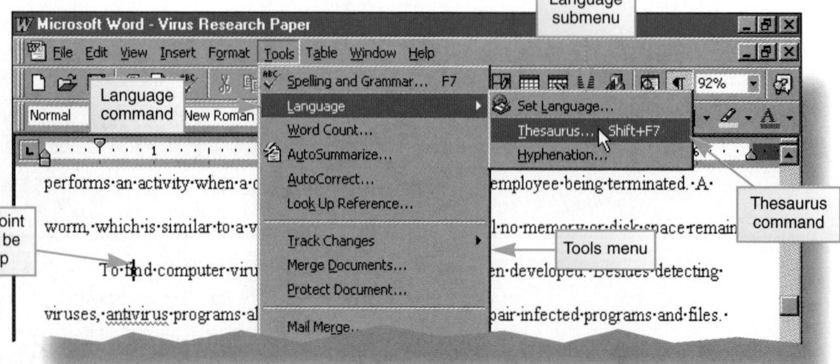

FIGURE 3-74

2 **Click Thesaurus. When the Thesaurus: English (United States) dialog box displays, click detect (verb) in the Meanings list box.**

Word displays the Thesaurus: English (United States) dialog box. The Meanings list box displays the different uses of the selected word, and the Replace with Synonym list box displays a variety of words with similar meanings. The Replace with Synonym list changes based on the meaning you select in the Meanings list.

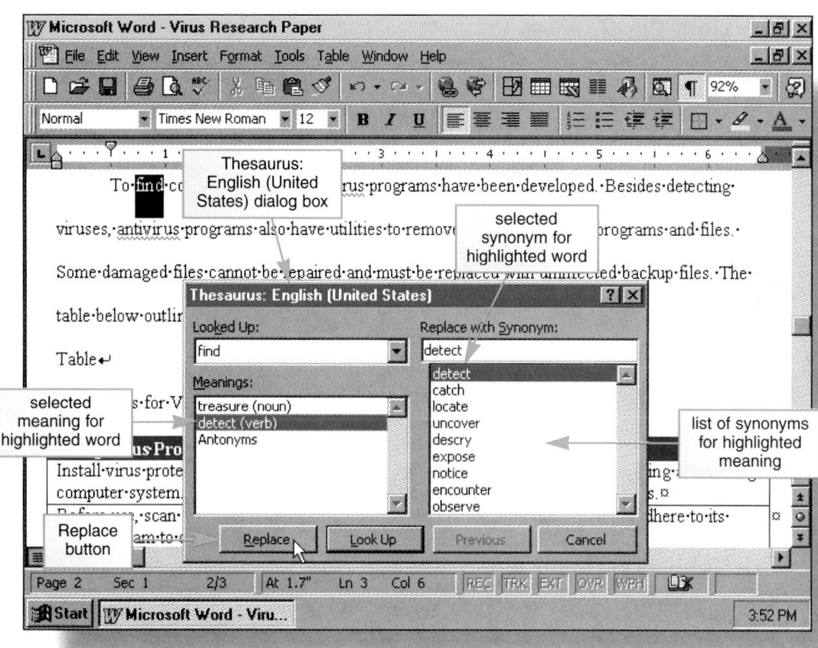

FIGURE 3-75

3 **Click the synonym you want (detect) and then point to the Replace button.**

The word, detect, is highlighted in the Replace with Synonym list (Figure 3-75).

4 **Click the Replace button.**

Word replaces the word, find, with detect and returns to the document window (Figure 3-76 below).

Other Ways

1. Press SHIFT+F7

Using Word Count

Often when you write papers, you are required to compose a paper with a specified number of words. The requirement for the research paper in this project was 500 words. For this reason, Word provides a command that displays the number of words, as well as the number of pages, characters, paragraphs, and lines in your document. Perform the following steps to use Word Count.

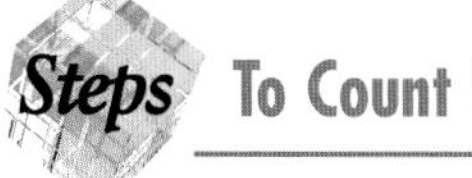

Steps To Count Words

1 **Click Tools on the menu bar and then point to Word Count (Figure 3-76).**

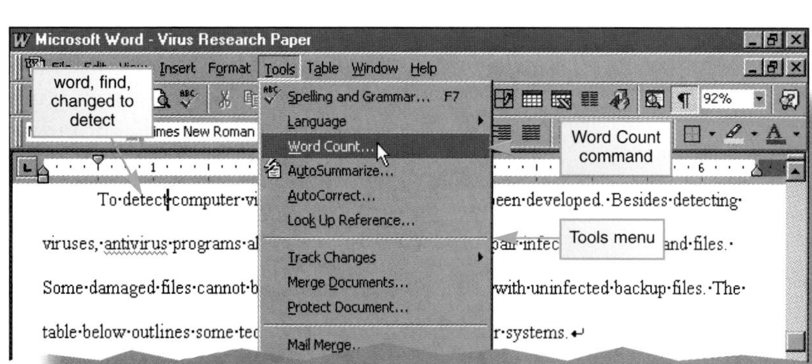

FIGURE 3-76

2 **Click Word Count. When the Word Count dialog box displays, if necessary, click Include footnotes and endnotes to select the check box.**

Word displays the Word Count dialog box (Figure 3-77). Word presents you with a variety of statistics on the current document, including number of pages, words, characters, paragraphs, and lines. You can choose to have note text included or not included in these statistics.

3 **Click Include footnotes and endnotes to deselect it. Click the Close button in the Word Count dialog box.**

Word deselects the Include footnotes and endnotes check box and then returns you to the document.

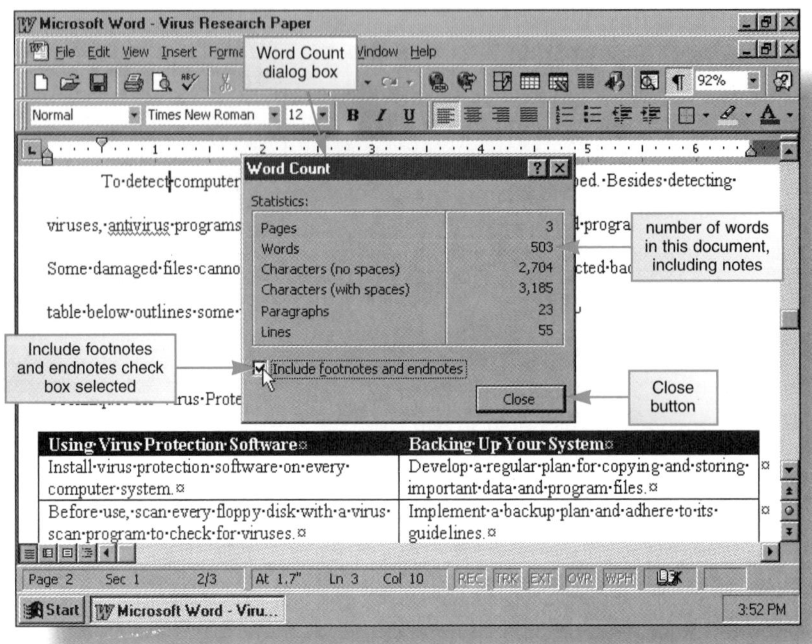

FIGURE 3-77

OtherWays

1. On File menu click Properties, click Statistics tab, click OK button

If you want statistics on only a section of your document, select the section before invoking the Word Count command.

You should change the zoom control back to 100% so the next person that uses Word will not have a reduced display.

TO ZOOM TO 100%

Step 1: Click the Zoom box arrow.
Step 2: Click 100% in the list of zoom percentages.

Word displays 100% in the Zoom box.

Checking Spelling, Saving Again, and Printing the Document

The document is now complete. After completing the document, you should check the spelling of the document by clicking the Spelling and Grammar button on the Standard toolbar. Because you have performed several tasks since the last save, you should save the research paper again by clicking the Save button on the Standard toolbar. Finally, you should print the research paper by clicking the Print button on the Standard toolbar. The completed research paper prints as shown in Figure 3-1 on page WD 3.5.

Navigating to a Hyperlink

Recall that one requirement of this research paper is that one of the works be a site on the Web. Your instructor, Professor J. Brown, has requested that you turn in a floppy disk with this research paper on it so he can verify information at the site. Perform the following steps to check your hyperlink.

To Navigate to a Hyperlink

1 **Display the third page of the research paper in the document window and then point to the hyperlink text.**

When you point to hyperlink text in a Word document, the mouse pointer shape changes to a pointing hand (Figure 3-78). To follow the link, click it.

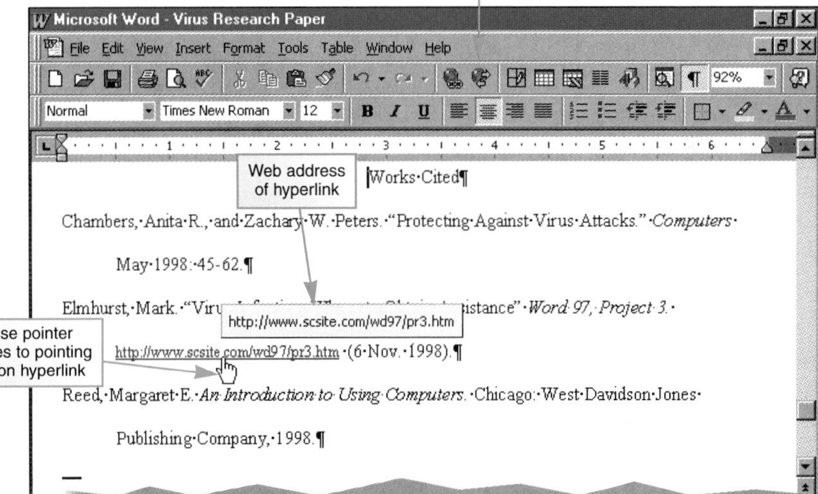

FIGURE 3-78

2 **Click the hyperlink text.**

If you currently are not connected to the Web, Word connects you using your default browser. After a few moments, the http://www.scsite.com/wd97/pr3.htm Web page displays (Figure 3-79).

3 **Close the browser window.**

The Word screen redisplays.

4 **Click the Web Toolbar button on the Standard toolbar to remove the Web toolbar.**

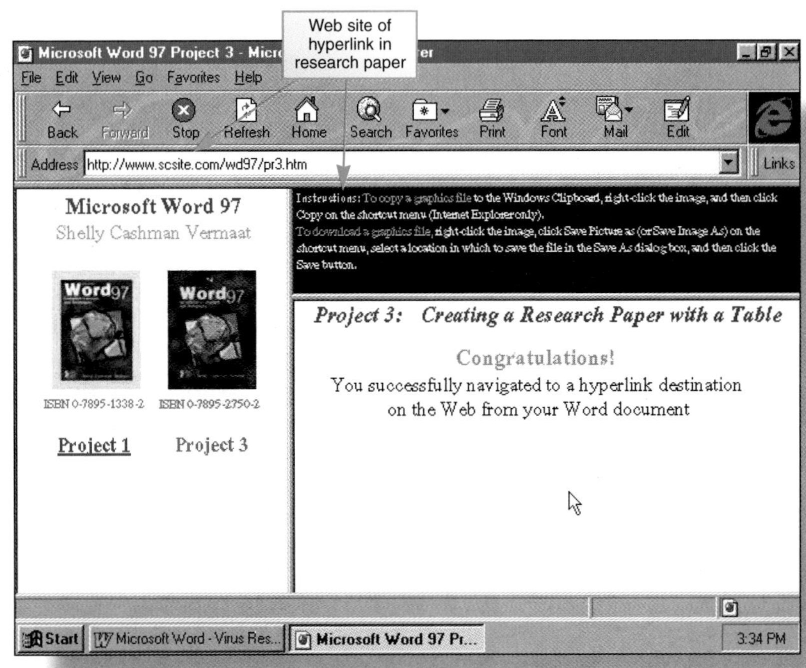

FIGURE 3-79

The final step in this project is to quit Word.

TO QUIT WORD

Step 1: Click the Close button in the Word window.

The Word window closes.

Project Summary

Project 3 introduced you to creating a research paper with a table using the MLA documentation style. You learned how to change margin settings, adjust line spacing, create headers with page numbers, and indent paragraphs. You learned how to use Word's AutoCorrect feature. Then, you added a footnote and created a table in the research paper. You alphabetized the works cited page by sorting its paragraphs and included a hyperlink to a Web page in one of the works. You learned how to browse through a Word document and find and replace text. Finally, you used Word's thesaurus to look up synonyms and saw how to display statistics about your document.

What You Should Know

Having completed this project, you now should be able to perform the following tasks:

- Add a Footnote (*WD 3.25*)
- AutoCorrect As You Type (*WD 3.22*)
- AutoFormat a Table (*WD 3.34*)
- Browse by Page (*WD 3.45*)
- Center a Paragraph before Typing (*WD 3.17*)
- Center the Title of the Works Cited Paragraph (*WD 3.40*)
- Change the Default Font Size (*WD 3.15*)
- Change the Default Margin Settings (*WD 3.8*)
- Count Words (*WD 3.49*)
- Create a Hanging Indent (*WD 3.40*)
- Create a Header (*WD 3.12*)
- Create a Hyperlink As You Type (*WD 3.42*)
- Create an AutoCorrect Entry (*WD 3.23*)
- Display Nonprinting Characters (*WD 3.7*)
- Double-Space a Document (*WD 3.10*)
- Enter Data into a Table (*WD 3.33*)
- Enter Name and Course Information (*WD 3.16*)
- Find and Replace Text (*WD 3.46*)
- Find Text (*WD 3.48*)
- First-Line Indent Paragraphs (*WD 3.18*)
- Insert a Blank Line above a Paragraph (*WD 3.37*)
- Insert an Empty Table (*WD 3.31*)
- Navigate to a Hyperlink (*WD 3.52*)
- Page Break Automatically (*WD 3.29*)
- Page Break Manually (*WD 3.38*)
- Quit Word (*WD 3.53*)
- Save a Document (*WD 3.18*)
- Select an Entire Table (*WD 3.36*)
- Sort Paragraphs (*WD 3.43*)
- Start Word (*WD 3.7*)
- Use Word's Thesaurus (*WD 3.48*)
- Zoom Page Width (*WD 3.21*)
- Zoom to 100% (*WD 3.50*)

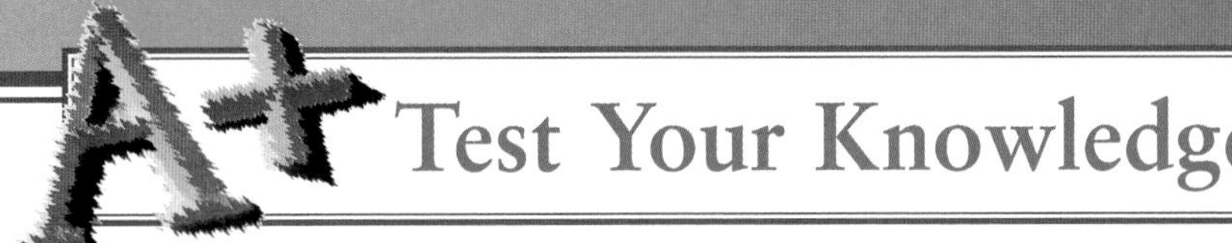

Test Your Knowledge

1 True/False

Instructions: Circle T if the statement is true or F if the statement is false.

T F 1. The MLA presents a popular documentation style used today for research papers.
T F 2. The MLA style uses the term works cited rather than bibliography.
T F 3. A footer is text you want to print at the bottom of each page in a document.
T F 4. Subscripted numbers are those that appear raised above other text in a document.
T F 5. An automatic page break displays on the screen as a single dotted horizontal line, separated by the words Page Break.
T F 6. A cell is the intersection of a row and a column in a Word table.
T F 7. To insert a tab character into a cell, press the TAB key.
T F 8. A hanging indent indents subsequent lines in the same paragraph one-half inch from the right margin.
T F 9. Word's thesaurus enables you to look up synonyms for a selected word.
T F 10. To jump to a hyperlink destination from a Word document, click the hyperlink text.

2 Multiple Choice

Instructions: Circle the correct response.

1. MLA stands for ____________.
   a. Modern Language Abbreviation
   b. Modern Language Association
   c. Modern Lexical Abbreviation
   d. Modern Lexical Association
2. How can you edit header text?
   a. switch to page layout view
   b. display the document in print preview
   c. click View on the menu bar and then click Header and Footer
   d. all of the above
3. The AutoCorrect feature automatically fixes misspelled words when you ____________ after entering the misspelled word.
   a. press the ESC key
   b. click the AutoCorrect button
   c. type a period
   d. press the SPACEBAR
4. If an AutoComplete tip displays on the screen, ____________ to instruct Word to place the text of the AutoComplete tip at the location of your typing.
   a. press the ENTER key
   b. press the SHIFT+ENTER keys
   c. click the AutoComplete button
   d. either b or c
5. A(n) ____________ occurs when the first line of a paragraph displays by itself at the bottom of a page.
   a. twin
   b. orphan
   c. sibling
   d. widow
6. A table with 7 rows and 4 columns is referred to as a(n) ____________ table.
   a. 28
   b. 11
   c. 7 × 4
   d. 4 × 7

(continued)

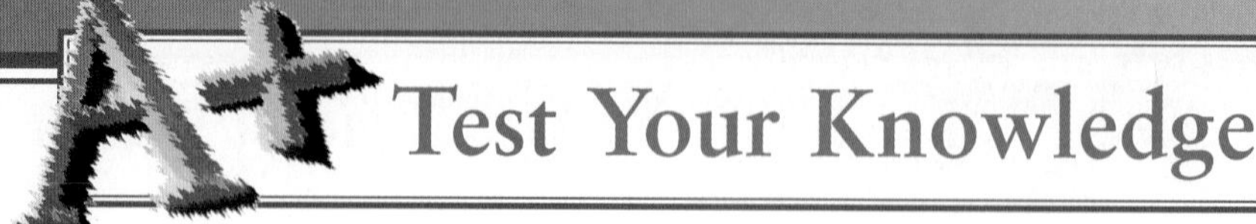

Test Your Knowledge

Multiple Choice *(continued)*

7. To insert a blank line above a paragraph, press the ____________ keys.
   a. CTRL+0 (zero) b. CTRL+B c. ALT+0 (zero) d. ALT+B
8. To move both the First Line Indent marker and Hanging Indent marker on the ruler at the same time, you ____________.
   a. drag the Left Indent marker
   b. select both markers and then drag
   c. right-drag the First Line Indent marker
   d. none of the above
9. A hyperlink is a shortcut that allows you to jump to ____________.
   a. another document on your computer
   b. another document on your network
   c. a page on the World Wide Web
   d. all of the above
10. The Select Browse Object button is located on the ____________.
   a. Standard toolbar
   b. Formatting toolbar
   c. vertical scroll bar
   d. horizontal scroll bar

3 Understanding the Ruler

Instructions: Answer the following questions concerning the ruler in Figure 3-80. The numbers in the figure correspond to the numbers of the questions below.

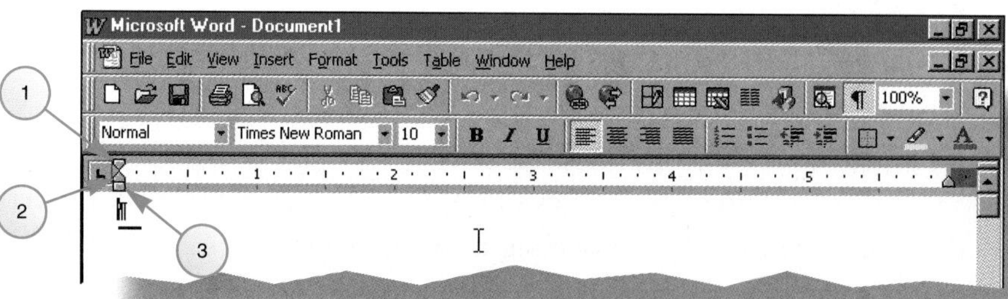

FIGURE 3-80

1. What is the name of the top triangle? What is the purpose of dragging this triangle?
2. What is the name of the bottom triangle? What is the purpose of dragging this triangle?
3. What is the name of the small square? What is the purpose of dragging this square?

4 Understanding the Note Pane

Instructions: In Figure 3-81, arrows point to major components of the note pane. Identify the various parts of the note pane in the spaces provided.

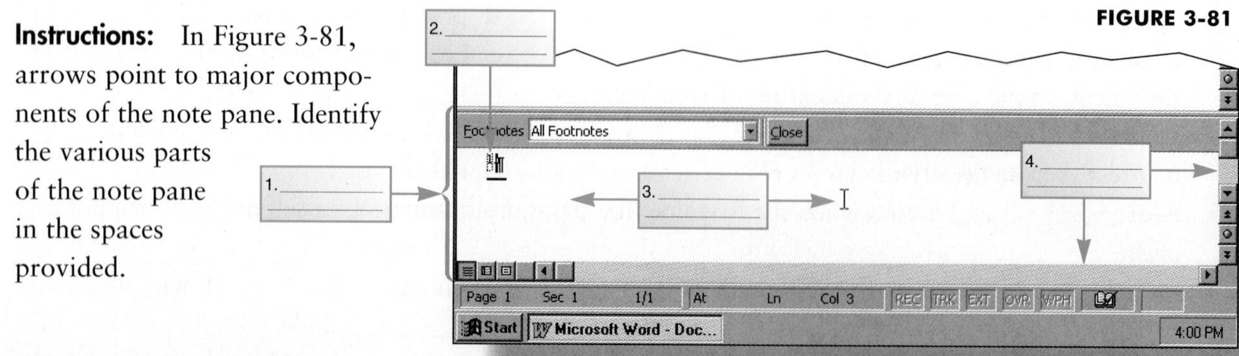

FIGURE 3-81

Use Help

1 Reviewing Project Activities

Instructions: Perform the following tasks using a computer.

1. Start Word.
2. If the Office Assistant is on your screen, click it to display its balloon. If the Office Assistant is not on your screen, click the Office Assistant button on the Standard toolbar.
3. Type `create a hyperlink` in the What would you like to do? text box. Click the Search button. Click the Create hyperlinks link. Read the information. Use the shortcut menu or Options button to print the information.
4. Click the Help Topics button to display the Help Topics: Microsoft Word dialog box. Click the Contents tab. Double-click the Working with Tables and Adding Borders book. Double-click the Parts of a table topic. Read and print the information.
5. Click the Help Topics button. Click the Index tab. Type `margins` and then double-click the overview topic. Double-click the Paragraph indenting vs. page margins topic. Read and print the information.
6. Click the Help Topics button. Click the Find tab. Type `header` and then double-click the Add page numbers topic. Read and print the information.
7. Close any open Help window(s) by clicking its Close button. Close the Office Assistant.

2 Expanding on the Basics

Instructions: Use Word Help to better understand the topics listed below. Answer the questions on your own paper or hand in the printed Help topic to your instructor.

1. In this project, you worked with a header. Use the Office Assistant to answer the following questions about headers and footers.
   a. What would cause the correct date, time, or other item to not appear in the header? When you locate the Help window containing this answer, the term, field, is used. What is a field?
   b. How do you create a unique header or footer for the first page of a document? When you locate the Help window containing the answer, the term, section, is used. What is a section?
   c. How do you delete a header or a footer?
2. In this project, you created a Word table. Use the Contents tab in the Help Topics: Microsoft Word dialog box to locate Help windows describing keys used for the following tasks: type and move around in a table and select items in a table. Print each of the two Help topics. Next, obtain answers to the following questions.
   a. How do you add a row to the end of a table? the middle of a table?
   b. How do you add a column to the right edge of a table? the middle of a table?
3. In this project, you inserted a hyperlink. Use the Index tab in the Help Topics: Microsoft Word dialog box to answer the following questions about hyperlinks.
   a. How do you change a hyperlink destination?
   b. How do you change existing hyperlink text?

(continued)

Expanding on the Basics *(continued)*

c. What is a Word publication?
d. Assume when you click a hyperlink, an error message displays. Identify three reasons the error message might display.

4. In this project, you created an AutoCorrect entry. Use the Find tab in the Help Topics: Microsoft Word dialog box to answer the following questions about AutoCorrect entries.
   a. How do you change the contents of an AutoCorrect entry?
   b. How do you delete an AutoCorrect entry?
   c. How can you prevent AutoCorrect from correcting abbreviations or capitalized text?
   d. How can you add an AutoCorrect entry during a spelling check?
5. Click the Web Toolbar button on the Standard toolbar to display the Web toolbar. Use the What's This? command on the Help menu to display ScreenTips for each button on the Web toolbar. Print each ScreenTip by right-clicking it, clicking Print Topic on the shortcut menu, and then clicking the OK button.

1 Working with a Table

Instructions: Start Word. Open the document, apply-3, from the Word folder on the Data Disk that accompanies this book. The document is a Word table that you are to edit and format. You may need to refer to your Use Help 2 responses for information on how to select items in the table and modify them. The revised table is shown in Figure 3-82.

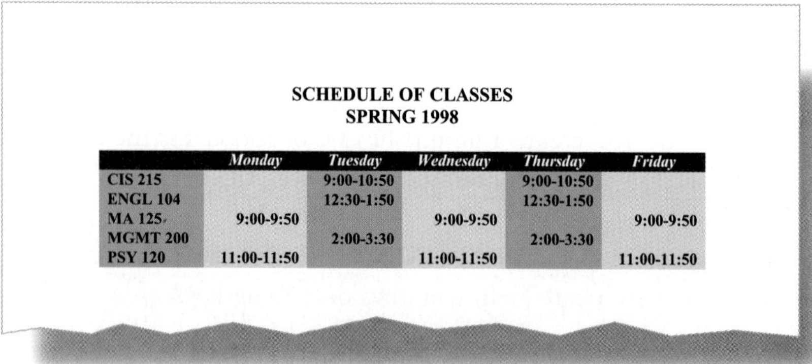

SCHEDULE OF CLASSES
SPRING 1998

	Monday	*Tuesday*	*Wednesday*	*Thursday*	*Friday*
CIS 215		9:00-10:50		9:00-10:50	
ENGL 104		12:30-1:50		12:30-1:50	
MA 125	9:00-9:50		9:00-9:50		9:00-9:50
MGMT 200		2:00-3:30		2:00-3:30	
PSY 120	11:00-11:50		11:00-11:50		11:00-11:50

FIGURE 3-82

Perform the following tasks:

1. Right-click the table and then click Table AutoFormat on the shortcut menu. Click Columns 2 in the Formats area of the Table AutoFormat dialog box. Be sure all of the check boxes in the Formats to apply area are checked. Also, be sure that only the Heading rows check box is checked in the Apply special formats to area; you may need to deselect First column. Click the OK button.

Apply Your Knowledge

2. Add a new row to the table for ENGL 104, which meets on Tuesdays and Thursdays from 12:30-1:50.
3. Delete the Saturday column by selecting it, right-clicking the selection, and then clicking Delete Columns on the shortcut menu. You do not have any Saturday classes scheduled.
4. Click in the table, click Table on the menu bar, and then click Select Table.
5. Click Table on the menu bar and then click Cell Height and Width. If necessary, click the Row tab, click Center in the Alignment area, and then click the OK button to center the table between the left and right margins.
6. With the table still selected, click Table on the menu bar, click Sort, and then click the OK button. Click anywhere to remove the highlight from the table.
7. Select the header row and then click the Italic button on the Formatting toolbar.
8. Select the cells containing the class times and then click the Align Right button on the Formatting toolbar.
9. Click File on the menu bar and then click Save As. Use the file name Revised Class Schedule and then save the document on your floppy disk.
10. Print the revised table.

In the Lab

1 Preparing a Research Paper with a Table

Problem: You are a college student currently enrolled in an introductory computer class. Your assignment is to prepare a short research paper (400-450 words) about Computer Security. The requirements are that the paper be prepared according to the MLA documentation style, contain a table, and have three references – one of which must be from the Internet (Figure 3-83 on the next two pages).

Instructions:

1. If necessary, click the Show/Hide ¶ button on the Standard toolbar. Change all margins to one inch. Adjust line spacing to double. Create a header to number pages. Change the font size of all characters to 12 point. Type the name and course information at the left margin. Center and type the title. First-line indent all paragraphs in the paper.
2. Type the body of the paper as shown in Figure 3-83a and Figure 3-83b. The table is formatted in the Grid 8 format with the all check boxes selected except Last row and Last column. At the end of the body of the research paper, press the ENTER key and insert a manual page break.
3. Create the works cited page (Figure 3-83c).
4. Check the spelling of the paper.

(continued)

Preparing a Research Paper with a Table *(continued)*

5. Save the document on a floppy disk with Computer Security Research Paper as the file name.
6. Print the research paper. Above the title of your printed research paper, hand write the number of words in the research paper.

West 1

Jonathan Paul West

Professor M. Carter

Information Systems 200

September 9, 1998

Computer Security

Many commercial software packages are designed with computer security features that control who can access the computer. These types of access controls use a process called identification and authentication. Identification verifies that the user is a valid user, and authentication verifies that the user is who he or she claims to be. Three common methods of authentication are remembered information, possessed objects, and biometric devices.

With remembered information, a user is required to enter a word or series of characters that match an entry in a security file in the computer. Most multiuser operating systems provide for a logon code, a user ID, and a password (all forms of remembered information) that all must be entered correctly before a user is allowed to use an application program. A logon code usually identifies the application, and a user ID identifies the user. A password usually is confidential, often known only by the user and the system administrator (Baker and Danville 29-47).

A possessed object is any item that a user must carry to gain access to the computer facility. Examples of possessed objects are badges, cards, and keys. Possessed objects often are used in conjunction with a personal identification number (PIN), which is a numeric password (Price 40-68).

A biometric device is one that verifies personal characteristics to authenticate a user. Examples of personal characteristics are fingerprints, voice pattern, signature, hand size, and

FIGURE 3-83a

In the Lab

West 2

retinal (eye) patterns. A biometric device usually translates a user's personal characteristics into a digital code that is compared to a digital code stored in the computer (Victors 22-85). If the digital code in the computer does not match the user's code, access is denied.

Each of these authentication techniques has advantages and disadvantages. The table below outlines the major advantage and disadvantage of each technique.

Table

Advantages and Disadvantages of Authentication Techniques

	Remembered Information	Possessed Object	Biometric Device
Advantages	Inexpensive	Relatively inexpensive	Virtually foolproof
Disadvantages	Can be forgotten or guessed by a perpetrator	Can be lost or forgotten	Expensive

A computer system should implement one or more of these authentication techniques to secure it from accidental or intentional misuse. In addition, the organization should review the techniques in place regularly to determine if they are still appropriate.

FIGURE 3-83b

West 3

Works Cited

Baker, Jamie D. and Cynthia I. Danville. "Security, Ethics, and Privacy." Computers and Society Journal Feb. 1998: 29-47.

Price, Karen E. "Identification and Authentication Controls." *Word 97, Project 3.* http://www.scsite.com/wd97/pr3.htm (31 Aug. 1998).

Victors, Michael R. The Computer Auditor. St. Louis: Green Valley Publishing Company, 1998.

FIGURE 3-83c

2 Preparing a Research Report with a Footnote and a Table

Problem: You are a college student currently enrolled in an English class. Your assignment is to prepare a short research paper in any area of interest to you. The only requirements are that the paper be presented according to the MLA documentation style, contain a table, and have three references, one of which must be from the Internet. You decide to prepare a paper comparing word processing software and desktop publishing software (Figure 3-84 on the next two pages).

(continued)

In the Lab

Preparing a Research Report with a Footnote and a Table *(continued)*

Reed 1

Sally Reed

Professor P. Harmon

English 204

December 9, 1998

Word Processing vs. Desktop Publishing

Many organizations distribute brochures and newsletters to promote their products and/or services. In the past, preparing these desktop publishing documents was best accomplished through outside agencies. In the 1980s, however, word processors began including graphics and different fonts as part of their standard software package (Larkin and Green, 8 Oct. 1998). That is, many word processors were emerging with desktop publishing capabilities.

Desktop publishing software (DTP) allows users to design and produce professional looking documents that contain both text and graphics. Examples of such documents include newsletters, marketing literature, technical manuals, and annual reports. The common thread among these packages is the ability to import graphic images, change fonts, draw lines, and display in WYSIWYG mode (What You See Is What You Get).

Graphic images can be imported from previously created art, called clip art. Clip art may be included with the software package being used or may be purchased.[1] Collections of clip art contain several hundred to several thousand images grouped by type, such as holidays, vehicles, or people. Input devices, called scanners, also can be used to import photographs and art into

[1] Winters found that nearly all of today's word processing software includes clip art, which can be enlarged, reduced, moved, and altered in other ways.

FIGURE 3-84a

Reed 2

DTP documents (Brown 14-35). Regardless of how it is accomplished, once the image has been imported into the document, it can be enlarged, reduced, rotated, or moved.

Many word processing software packages today include features that previously were considered to be the domain of desktop publishing software. Conversely, many recent releases of DTP software contain enhanced word processing capabilities. The table below outlines the DTP features in word processing packages and features not yet in most word processing packages.

Table

DTP Features

DTP Features in Word Processing Packages	Additional DTP Features in DTP Software
Alters typefaces, styles, and point sizes	Includes color libraries
Adjusts margins, alignment, and spacing	Creates master pages, larger page sizes, and page grids
Includes columns, tables, graphics, borders, and shading	Stacks and overlaps multiple objects on a page and traps objects

With each release of word processing and DTP software, the differences between the two will decrease and their similarities will increase.

FIGURE 3-84b

Instructions: Perform the following tasks:

1. Change all margin settings to one inch. Adjust line spacing to double. Create a header to number pages. Change the font size of all characters to 12 point. Type the name and course information at the left margin. Center and type the title. First-line indent all paragraphs in the paper.
2. Type the body of the paper as shown in Figure 3-84a and Figure 3-84b. The table is formatted in the Grid 8 format with the all check boxes selected except Last row and Last column. At the end of the body of the research paper, press the ENTER key once and insert a manual page break.
3. Create the works cited page. Enter the works cited shown below as separate paragraphs and then alphabetize the paragraphs.
   a. Larkin, Henry P., and Janice A. Green. "Word Processing." *Word 97, Project 3.* http://www.scsite.com/wd97/pr3.htm (8 Oct. 1998).
   b. Winters, Jill. "Word Processing Software Packages Today." *Microcomputer Journal* Nov. 1998: 58-66.
   c. Brown, Robert. *Introductory Computer Concepts and Techniques*. Boston: International Publishing Company, 1998.
4. Check the spelling of the paper. Use Word's thesaurus to change the word, domain, in the last paragraph to a word of your choice.
5. Save the document on a floppy disk with Word Processing Paper as the file name.
6. Print the research paper. Above the title of your printed research paper, hand write the number of words, including the footnote, in the research paper.

In the Lab

3 Composing a Research Report with a Table and Footnotes

Problem: You have drafted the notes shown in Figure 3-85. Your assignment is to prepare a short research paper based on these notes. You are to review the notes and then rearrange and reword. Embellish the paper as you deem necessary. Add a footnote elaborating on a personal experience you have had. Create a table listing examples of peripherals. Present the paper according to the MLA documentation style.

Instructions: Perform the following tasks:

1. If necessary, click the Show/Hide ¶ button on the Standard toolbar. Change all margin settings to one inch. Adjust line spacing to double. Create a header to number pages. Change the font size of all characters to 12 point. Type the name and course information at the left margin. Center and type the title. First-line indent all paragraphs in the paper.
2. Compose the body of the paper from the notes in Figure 3-85 . Be sure to include a footnote and a table as specified above. At the end of the body of the research paper, press the ENTER key once and insert a manual page break.
3. Create the works cited page from the listed sources. Be sure to alphabetize the works.
4. Check the spelling and grammar of the paper.
5. Save the document on a floppy disk with YourName Research Paper as the file name (where YourName is your last name).
6. Print the research paper. Above the title of your printed research paper, hand write the number of words, including the footnote, in the research paper.

The five major categories of computers are (1) personal computers, (2) servers, (3) minicomputers, (4) mainframe computers, and (5) supercomputers.

Personal computers also are called micros, PCs, or microcomputers. Examples include hand-held, palmtop, notebook, subnotebook, laptop, pen, desktop, tower, and workstation. Hand-held, palmtop, notebook, subnotebook, laptop, and pen computers are considered portable computers. Prices range from several hundred to several thousand dollars. Source: Personal Computers, a book published by Windy City Publishing Company in Chicago, 1998, pages 15-45, author Jane A. Polson.

A server supports a computer network. A network allows multiple users to share files, application software, and hardware. Small servers range from $5,000 to $20,000; larger servers can cost as much as $150,000. Source: "Serving Networks," an article in Network World, September 1998 issue, pages 135-148, author Peter S. Thorn.

Minicomputers are more powerful than PCs and can support multiple users performing different tasks. Originally, they were developed to perform specific tasks such as engineering calculations. Many businesses use them today for information processing requirements. Costs range from $15,000 to several hundred thousand dollars. Source: "Evaluating Computers," an article in Computer Monthly, August 1998 issue, pages 98-105, authors Karen D. Samuels and Benjamin R. Edwards.

A mainframe computer is a large system that can handle hundreds of users, store large amounts of data, and process transactions at a very high rate. They usually require a specialized environment with separate air conditioning and electrical power. Raised flooring often is built to accommodate the many cables connecting the system components. Prices range from several hundred thousand to several million dollars. Source: Web page article "Mainframe Issues" on Web page Word 97, Project 3 at site http://www.scsite.com/wd97/pr3.htm on September 4, 1998.

Supercomputers are the most powerful computers. They process hundreds of millions of instructions per second and are used for applications such as weather forecasting and space exploration. The cost is several million dollars. Same source as for minicomputers.

FIGURE 3-85

Cases and Places

The difficulty of these case studies varies: ◗ are the least difficult; ◗◗ are more difficult; and ◗◗◗ are the most difficult.

1 ◗ Having completed three projects with Word 97, you should be comfortable with its capabilities. To reinforce your knowledge of Word, write a research paper that discusses its components and features (such as spell checking, grammar checking, wizards, AutoCorrect, and so on). Use your textbook, Word Help, and any other resources available. Explain why you think the component or feature is important and then explain exactly how to perform the task in Word. Include at least two references. Use the concepts and techniques presented in this project to format the paper.

2 ◗ Windows is a graphical user interface (GUI), which claims to be a much more user-friendly environment that DOS. Write a brief research paper that discusses the features of Windows. Use your textbook, Windows Help, and any other resources available. For each feature you identify, discuss whether or not you feel this feature is user-friendly and state your reason(s). Include at least two references. Use the concepts and techniques presented in this project to format the paper.

3 ◗◗ This project required the MLA style of documentation in the preparation of the research paper. Another popular documentation style is by the American Psychological Association (APA). The MLA style generally is used in the humanities, whereas the APA style is preferred in the social sciences. Many differences exist between the two styles. Using the school library or other resources (such as the Internet), research the APA style. Then, prepare a brief research paper that compares and contrasts the two styles. Include at least one explanatory note and three references, one of which must be a Web site on the Internet. Use the concepts and techniques presented in this project to format the paper.

4 ◗◗ When you install Windows, two accessories are provided: a word processor and a text editor. Although Windows supplies these two programs, most users purchase a separate word processing package, such as Word, for creating documents. Try creating the research paper from this project in the Windows word processor and also the text editor. Use Windows Help or any other resources to assist you with these documents. Then, prepare a brief research paper comparing and contrasting Word 97 to the word processor and text editor supplied with Windows. Include at least one explanatory note and two references. Use the concepts and techniques presented in this project to format the paper.

Cases and Places

5 ▸▸ Microsoft Word was introduced in 1983. Since then, it has experienced many version changes and upgrades. Using a school library or other resources (such as the Internet), learn how Microsoft Word has evolved to the product it is today. Identify when and how the first word processors came to be. Then, prepare a brief research paper on the evolution of Microsoft Word since the beginning of word processors through today. Include at least one explanatory note and three references, one of which must be a Web site on the Internet. Use the concepts and techniques presented in this project to format the paper.

6 ▸▸▸ Many different word processing packages are on the market, e.g., Word, WordPerfect, and so on. Using a school library or other resources (such as the Internet), determine the top three word processing packages and their features. Contact two businesses and ask which word processor they use; find out what they like and dislike about their word processor. Then, prepare a brief research paper comparing and contrasting the three word processing packages. At the end of the paper, identify the one you feel is the best. Include at least two explanatory notes and three references, one of which must be a Web site on the Internet. Use the concepts and techniques presented in this project to format the paper.

7 ▸▸▸ When you purchase a personal computer, the price often includes some installed software. Sometimes, it is more economical to buy the package; however, you may not receive the exact software you desire. Visit or call two computer stores. Obtain package prices for their latest personal computers. Also, obtain prices of the hardware and software individually. Ask why they chose the software they did for the package deals. Then, prepare a brief research paper on computer package deals; discuss whether you would buy a package deal or not at the present time. Include at least two explanatory notes and three references. Use the concepts and techniques presented in this project to format the paper.

Creating Web Pages

INTEGRATION FEATURE

Case Perspective

Recall that in Project 2 Caroline Louise Schmidt created a resume (Figure 2-2 on page WD 2.6). Recently, Caroline has been *surfing the Internet* and has discovered that many people have their own personal Web pages with links to items such as resumes, schedules, and so on. These personal Web pages are very impressive. To make herself more attractive to a potential employer, Caroline has decided to create a personal Web page that contains a hyperlink to her resume. To do this, she will have to save her resume as an HTML file (Web page). She also plans to make her e-mail address a hyperlink to make it easy for a potential employer to send her a message.

To complete this Integration Feature, you will need the resume created in Project 2, so that you can save it as an HTML file and then use the resulting Web page as a hyperlink destination. (If you did not create the resume, see your instructor for a copy of it.)

Introduction

Word provides two techniques for creating Web pages. You can save any Word document as a **HyperText Markup Language (HTML)** file so that it can be posted on the Web and viewed by a Web browser, such as Internet Explorer. Or, you can start a new Web page by using a wizard or template.

If you have an existing Word document, you can convert it quickly to a Web page (HTML file). If you do not have an existing Word document to convert, you can create a new Web page by using the Web Page Wizard, which provides customized templates you can modify easily. In addition to these Web tools, Word has many other **Web page authoring** features. For example, you can include hyperlinks, sound, video, pictures, scrolling text, bullets, and horizontal lines on your Web pages.

Once complete, you want to make your Web page(s) available to others on your network, on an intranet, or on the World Wide Web. To post them on your network, simply save the Web page(s) and related files to the network server. If your company uses an **intranet**, which is a network that uses Internet technologies, you will have to copy your Web page(s) and related files to the Web server. To post your Web page(s) on the World Wide Web, you will need to locate an **Internet service provider (ISP)** that provides space for Web pages. Many ISPs allocate space for subscribers free of charge. What you need is an FTP (File Transfer Protocol) program so you can copy your Web page(s) and related files from your computer to your ISP's computer.

This Integration Feature illustrates saving the resume created in Project 2 as an HTML file (Figure 1c). Then, you use Word's Web Page Wizard to create a personal Web page (Figure 1a) that can be posted to a network, an intranet, or the World Wide Web (Figure 1b). The personal Web page contains a hyperlink to the resume (Figure 1c). It also contains a hyperlink to an e-mail address. When you click the e-mail address, Word opens your e-mail program automatically with the recipient's address already filled in (Figure 1d). You simply type your message and then click the Send button, which places the message in the Outbox or sends it if you are connected to an e-mail server.

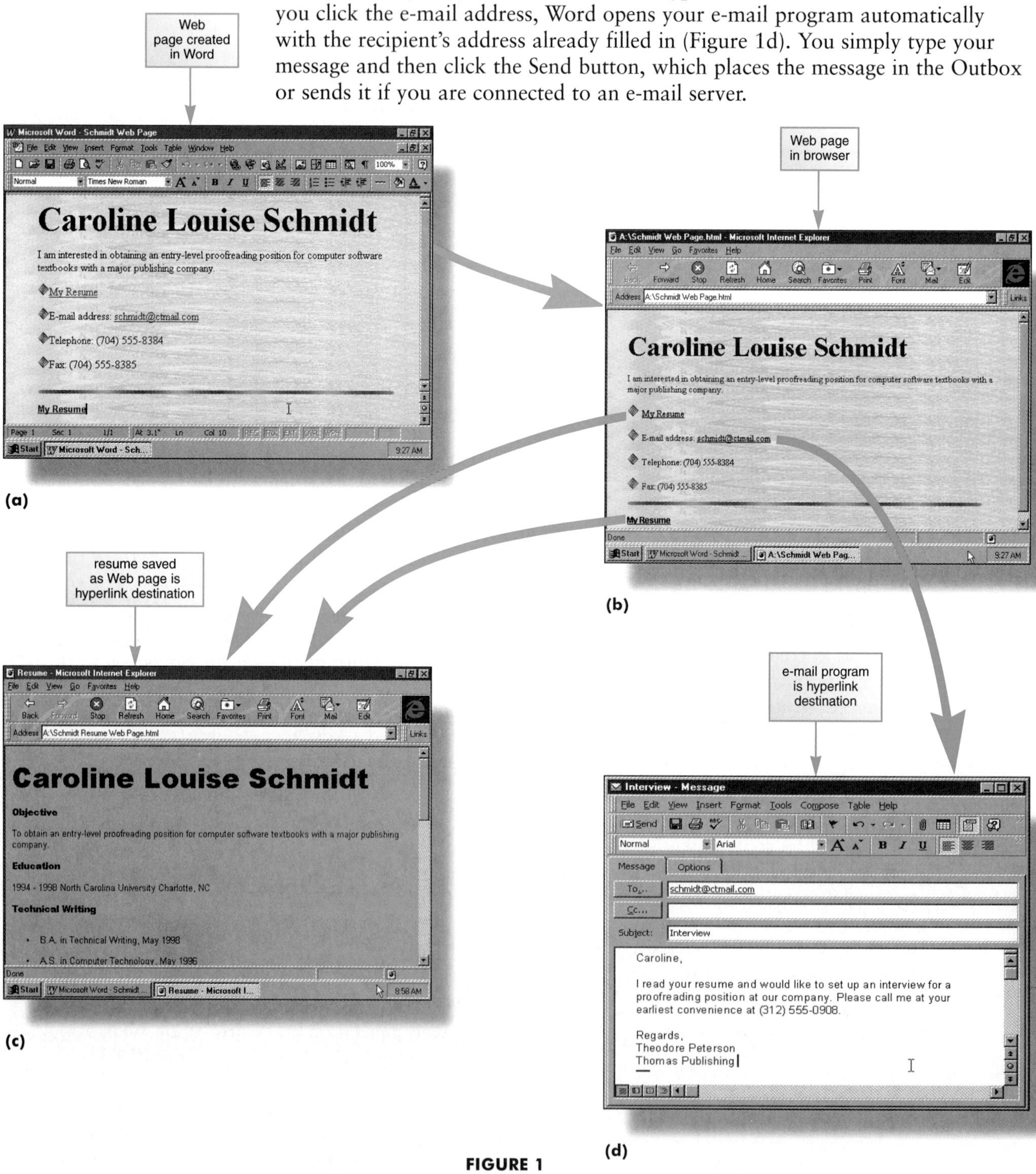

Web page created in Word

(a)

Web page in browser

(b)

resume saved as Web page is hyperlink destination

(c)

e-mail program is hyperlink destination

(d)

FIGURE 1

Saving a Word Document as a Web Page

Once you have created an existing Word document, you can save it easily as a HyperText Markup Language (HTML) file so it can be posted on the Web and viewed by a Web browser, such as Internet Explorer.

Some formatting in your Word document may not be supported by HTML. In this case, Word either changes the formatting or removes the text upon conversion. For example, certain table features are lost in the conversion. For this reason, it is recommended that you save the document as a Word file before converting it to HTML. In case you lose any information, you can reopen the original Word file and make the necessary adjustments.

Recall that the resume created in Project 2 contains a table. If you save the resume, as is, to an HTML format, the table will be removed (which is all the information below the heading). To preserve the table in the resume, you will convert the table to text; that is, remove the table formatting from the document. Then, you will save the revised resume as an HTML document.

Perform the following steps to convert the table in the Schmidt Resume to text.

More *About* Web Page Formatting

Formatting not supported by HTML is unavailable while you are authoring a Web page in Word. For example, you cannot emboss, shadow, or engrave characters; and you cannot change line spacing, margins, or set tabs. You can, however, apply bold, italic, underline, and adjust font sizes of characters.

To Convert a Table to Text

1 Start Word and then open the Schmidt Resume created in Project 2. (If you did not create the resume in Project 2, see your instructor for a copy of it.) If gridlines do not show on your resume's table, click Table on the menu bar, and then click Show Gridlines. Click anywhere in the table to position the insertion point in it. Click Table on the menu bar and then click Select Table. Click Table on the menu bar and then point to Convert Table to Text.

Word selects the table in the resume (Figure 2). Gridlines *are nonprinting characters that help you identify the rows and columns of a table. Your zoom percentage may differ from this figure.*

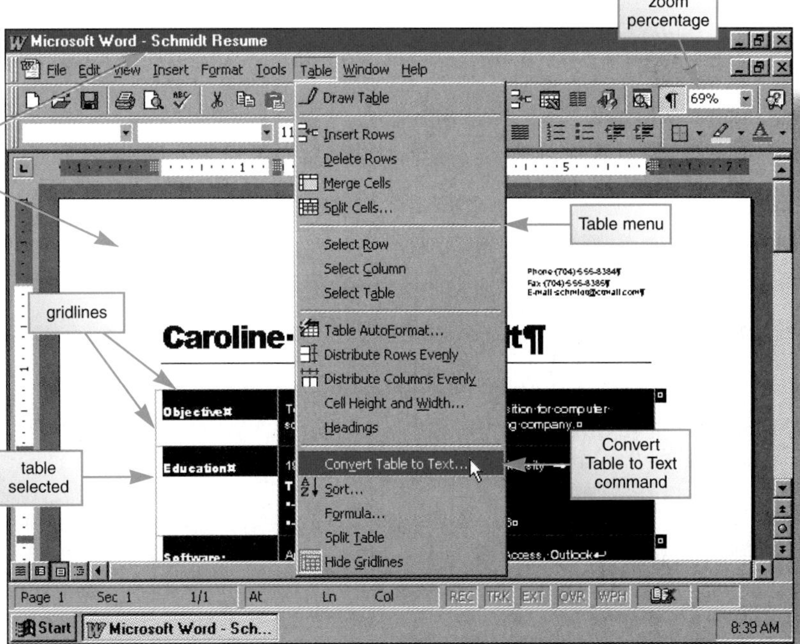

FIGURE 2

2 **Click Convert Table to Text. When the Convert Table To Text dialog box displays, click Paragraph marks.**

Word displays the Convert Table To Text dialog box (Figure 3). In this dialog box, you specify how Word should convert the columns to regular text; that is, every time a new column is encountered, what character should separate the text. Here you want each column to be treated as a new paragraph.

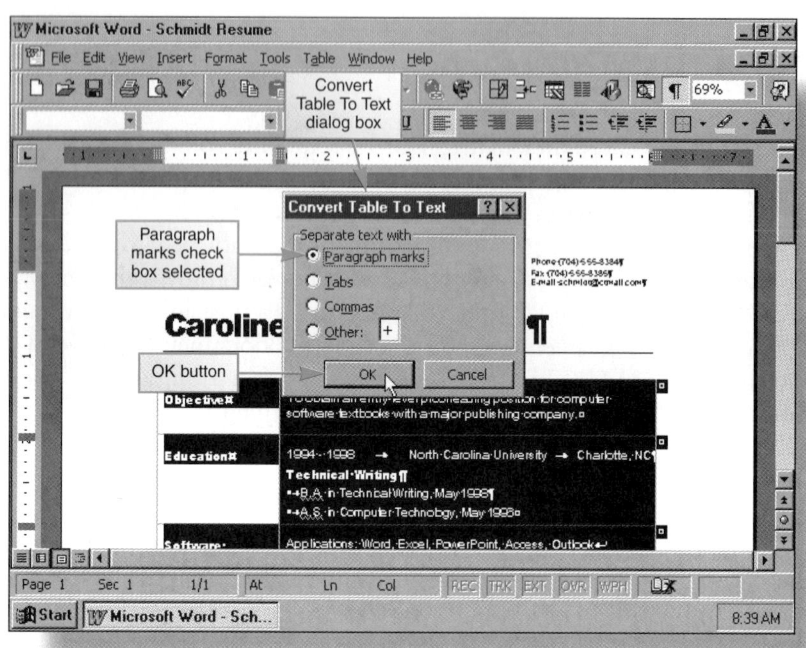

FIGURE 3

3 **Click the OK button. Click anywhere in the document to remove the highlight.**

Word converts the table in the resume to text (Figure 4 below). Notice the data originally in the second column of the table is formatted now as separate paragraphs in the resume.

The next step is to save the resume as a Web page.

To Save a Word Document as a Web Page

1 **Click File on the menu bar and then point to Save as HTML (Figure 4).**

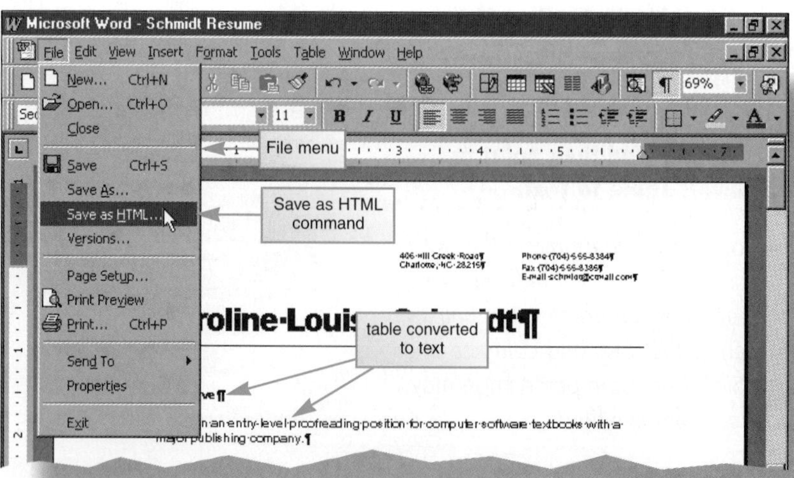

FIGURE 4

More About Web Page Paragraphs

Paragraphs created in Word automatically display a space before and after them on a Web page. Press CTRL+ENTER between paragraphs to eliminate the white space.

2 **Click Save as HTML. When the Save As HTML dialog box displays, type** `Schmidt Resume Web Page` **in the File name text box and then, if necessary, change the Save in drive to 3½ Floppy (A:). Point to the Save button in the Save As HTML dialog box.**

Word displays the Save As HTML dialog box (Figure 5).

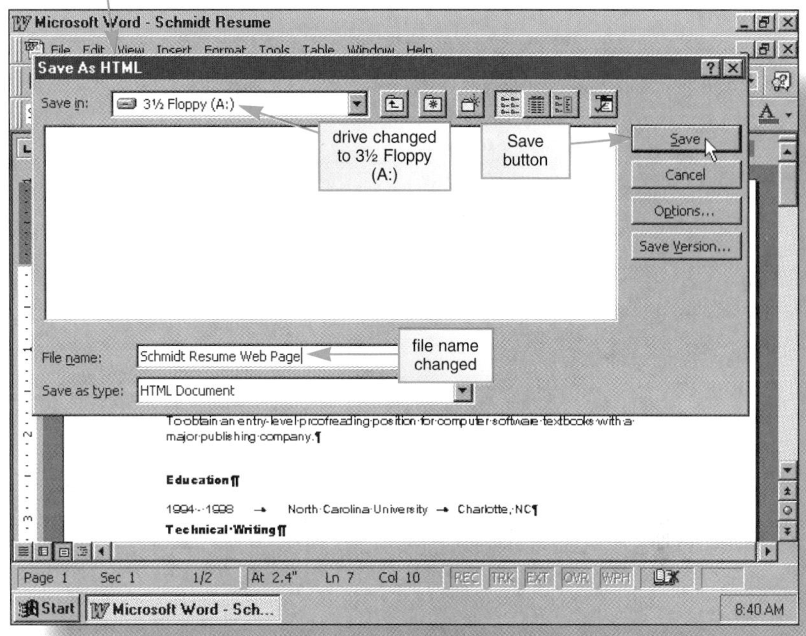

FIGURE 5

3 **Click the Save button. If Word displays a dialog box asking if you want to continue with the save, click the Yes button.**

Word closes the Schmidt Resume Word document and then reopens the file in HTML format (Figure 1-6 on the next page). Word also changes some of the toolbar buttons and menu commands to provide Web page authoring features. The resume displays on the Word screen similarly to how it will appear in a Web browser.

Recall that some of Word's formatting features are not supported by HTML; thus, your Web page may appear slightly different from the original Word document.

Viewing a Web Page Document

You may wish to view the Web page document in your default Web browser to see how it looks. Notice the Standard toolbar now has a **Web Page Preview button**. When you are working with a Web page, the buttons on the toolbars change to provide you with Web authoring features.

Perform the steps on the next page to view the Web page in your default browser.

More *About* HTML Source

If you wish to view the HTML source code associated with the Web page you have created, save the Web page in its current form, click View on the menu bar, and then click HTML Source. You can modify or print the HTML source. To return to the Web page, click the Exit HTML Source button on the Standard toolbar.

Steps To View an HTML File in a Browser

1 **Point to the Web Page Preview button on the Standard toolbar (Figure 6).**

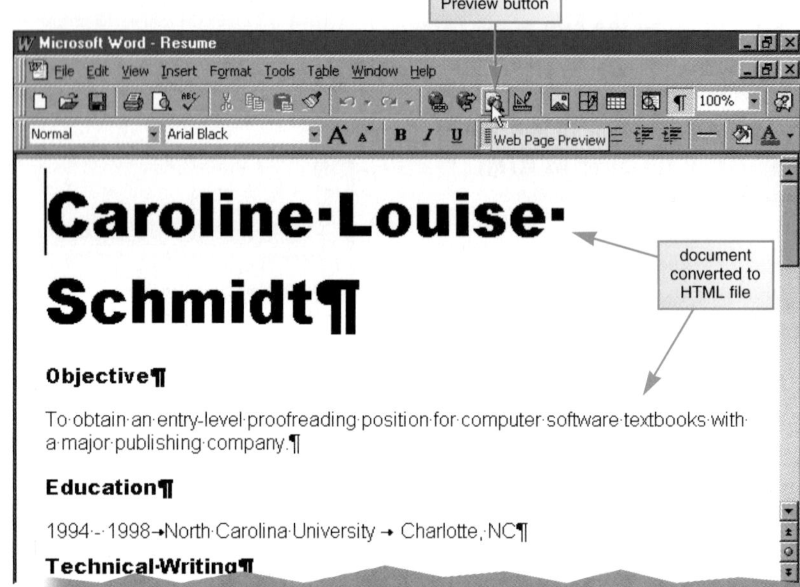

FIGURE 6

2 **Click the Web Page Preview button on the Standard toolbar.**

Word opens your Web browser in a separate window and displays the HTML file in the browser window (Figure 7).

3 **Close the Web browser window. When the Word window redisplays, close the Schmidt Resume Web page file by clicking the Close button at the right edge of the menu bar. Leave Word open for the next steps.**

The resume HTML files closes and the Word window redisplays.

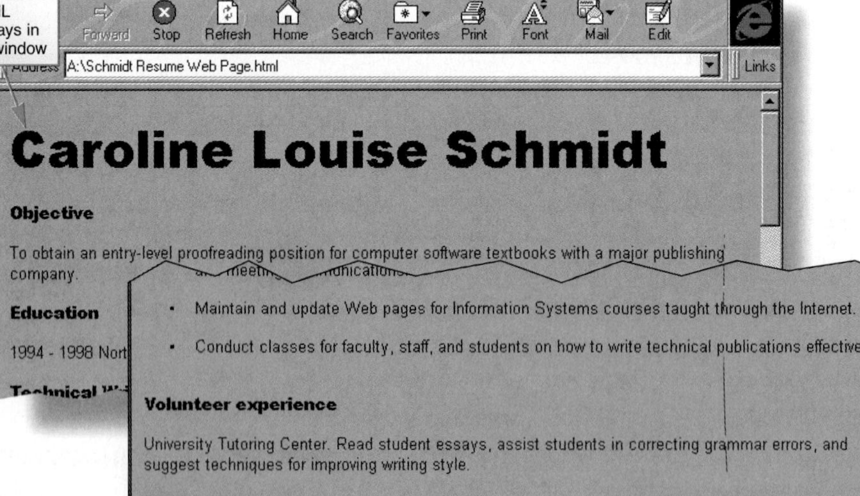

FIGURE 7

Other Ways

1. On File menu click Web Page Preview

Using Word's Web Page Wizard to Create a Web Page

In the previous section, you had an existing Word document you wanted to save as a Web page. Next, you want to create a brand new Web page. You can create a Web page from scratch using the Web page template or you can use the **Web Page Wizard**. Because this is your first experience creating a new Web page, you should use the Web Page Wizard as shown in the following steps.

To Create a Web Page with the Web Page Wizard

1 Click File on the menu bar and then click New. If necessary, click the Web Pages tab when the New dialog box first opens. Click the Web Page Wizard icon.

Office displays several icons on the Web Pages sheet (Figure 8). The Blank Web Page icon is a Web page template. The Web Page Wizard icon is selected.

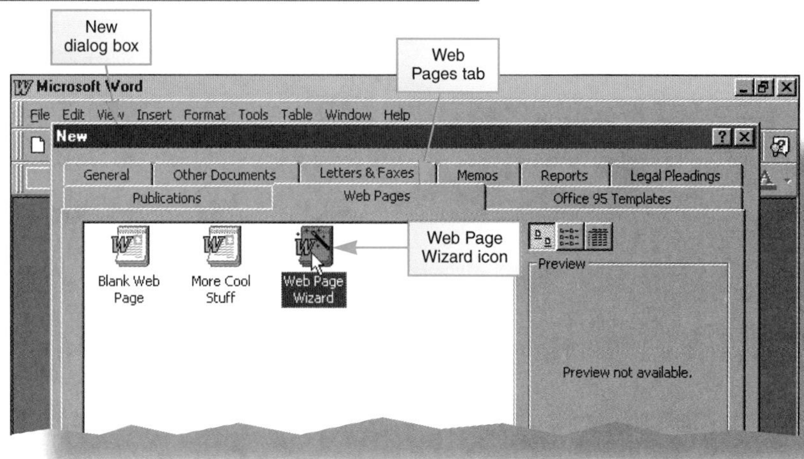

FIGURE 8

2 Click the OK button. When the Web Page Wizard dialog box displays, click Simple Layout, if necessary, and then point to the Next button.

After a few seconds, Word displays the first of two Web Page Wizard dialog boxes (Figure 9). This dialog box requests the type of Web page you wish to create. As you click the types in the list, the Web page in the background changes to reflect the selected type.

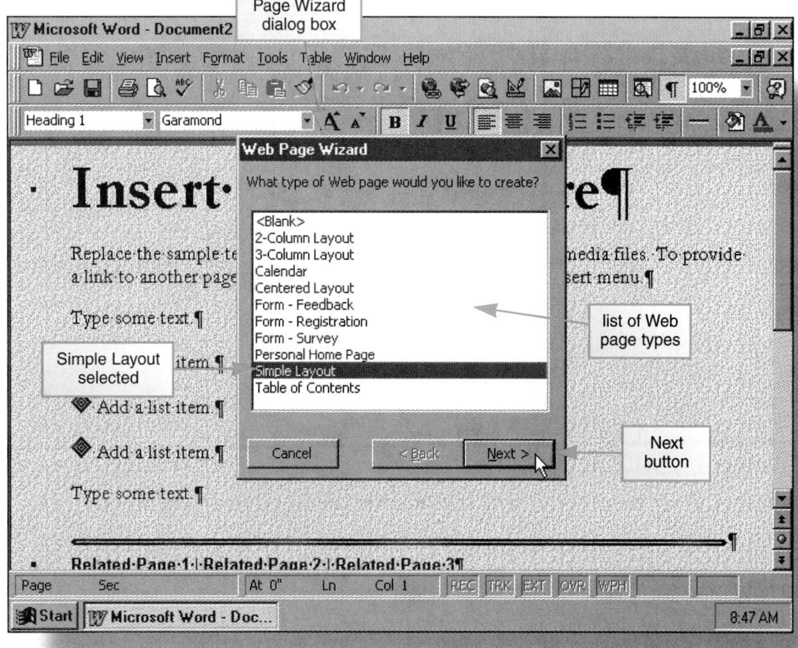

FIGURE 9

3 Click the Next button. When the next Web Page Wizard dialog box displays, click Contemporary, if necessary, and then point to the Finish button.

After a few seconds, Word displays the second, and final, Web Page Wizard dialog box (Figure 10). In this dialog box, you select the style of Web page you desire. As you click the styles in the list, the Web page in the background changes to reflect the selected style.

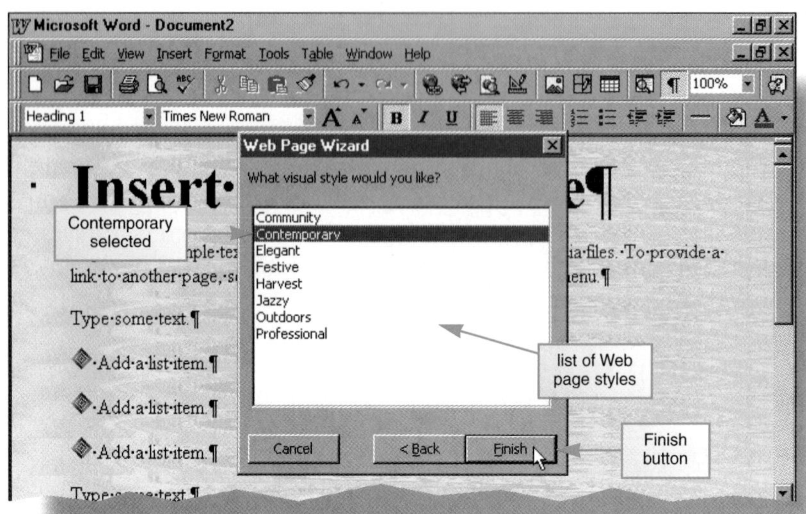

FIGURE 10

4 Click the Finish button.

Word creates a Web page layout for you (Figure 11). You are to personalize the Web page as indicated.

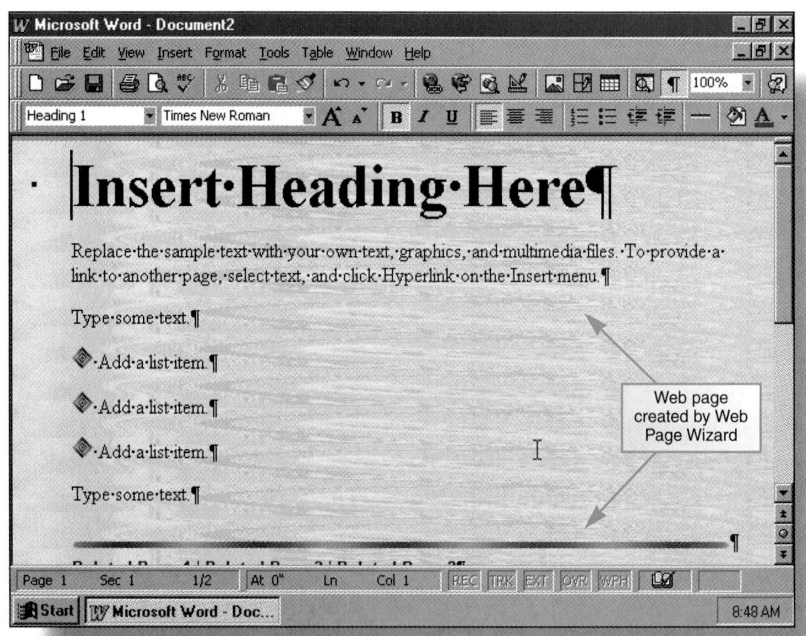

FIGURE 11

Other Ways

1. On Start menu click New Office Document, click Web Pages tab, double-click Web Page Wizard icon
2. Click Start a New Document button on Microsoft Office Shortcut Bar, click Web Pages tab, double-click Web Page Wizard icon

When you create a Web page using the Web Page Wizard, you can click the Back button in the second dialog box to change the Web page type, if you desire. To exit from the Web Page Wizard and return to the document window without creating the Web page, click the Cancel button in either of the Web Page Wizard dialog boxes.

Personalizing the Web Page with Hyperlinks

The next step is to personalize the Web page. First, you replace placeholder text with your own text. Next, you create hyperlinks, where necessary, to other documents, Web pages, or Internet sites. The following pages show how to personalize the Web page generated by the Web Page Wizard.

Recall from Project 3 that a **hyperlink** is colored and underlined text or a graphic that, when clicked, allows a user to jump easily and quickly to other documents, objects, or Web pages. If the AutoFormat As You Type feature is enabled, Word converts Internet and network paths to hyperlinks as you type them. In this Integration Feature, you want the e-mail address to be formatted as a hyperlink so that when someone clicks the e-mail address on your Web page, his or her e-mail program opens automatically with your e-mail address already filled in. Be sure this feature is enabled by clicking Tools on the menu bar, clicking AutoCorrect, clicking the AutoFormat As You Type tab, clicking Internet and network paths with hyperlinks, and then clicking the OK button.

Personalize the text on the Web page with e-mail address formatted as a hyperlink as described in the following steps.

More *About* Web Pages

Use horizontal lines to separate sections of a Web page. To add a horizontal line at the location of the insertion point, click Insert on the menu bar, click Horizontal Line, click desired style in the Style list or click the More button to select a different style, and then click the OK button. To insert additional lines with the same style, click the Horizontal Line button on the Formatting toolbar.

TO SELECT AND REPLACE TEXT

Step 1: Select the text, Insert Heading Here, and then type `Caroline Louise Schmidt` as the title.
Step 2: Select the paragraph below the title by triple-clicking it, and then type `I am interested in obtaining an entry-level proofreading position for computer software textbooks with a major publishing company.`
Step 3: Select the paragraph with the text, Type some text. Right-click the selection and then click Cut on the shortcut menu.
Step 4: Select the first bulleted item by dragging through the text, Add a list item. Type `My Resume` as the first item.
Step 5: Select the second bulleted item and then type `E-mail address: schmidt@ctmail.com` and then press the SPACEBAR to convert the e-mail address to a hyperlink.
Step 6: Select the third bulleted item and then type `Telephone: (704) 555-8384` and then press the ENTER key. Type `Fax: (704) 555-8385` as the fourth bulleted item.
Step 7: Select the paragraph below the bulleted list, Type some text. Right-click the selection and then click Cut on the shortcut menu.
Step 8: Select the text, | Related Page 2 | Related Page 3, at the bottom of the Web page. Right-click the selection and then click Cut on the shortcut menu.
Step 9: Select the words, Related Page 1, at the bottom of the Web page, and then type `My Resume` as the text.

The Web page is personalized (Figure 12 on the next page). Notice the e-mail address is formatted as a hyperlink. Word formats it automatically when you press the SPACEBAR *or the* ENTER *key after typing the address.*

More *About* Additional Resources

If you have access to the Web, you can download additional resources for Web page authoring. To download images, click Insert on the menu bar, point to Picture, and then click Browse Web Art Page. To download templates and other resources, click File on the menu bar, click New, click Web Pages tab, and then double-click More Cool Stuff.

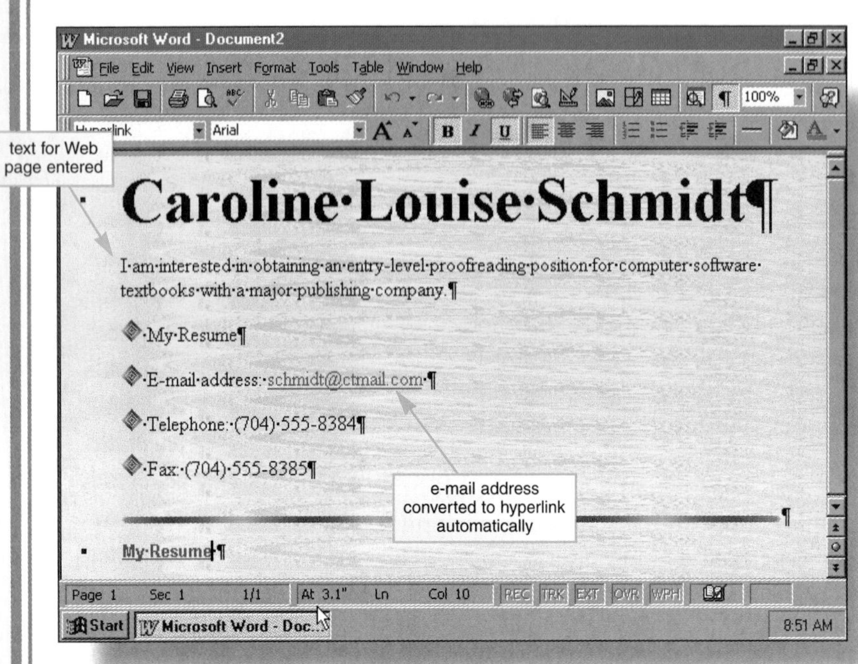

FIGURE 12

Save the Web page before proceeding to the next section.

TO SAVE THE WEB PAGE

Step 1: Insert your floppy disk into drive A.
Step 2: Click Save button on the Standard toolbar.
Step 3: Type the file name `Schmidt Web Page` in the File name text box. Do not press the ENTER key.
Step 4: If necessary, click the Save in box arrow and then click 3½ Floppy (A:).
Step 5: Click the Save button in the Save As dialog box.

Word saves the document on a floppy disk in drive A with the file name Schmidt Web Page.

Converting Text to a Hyperlink

In the previous example, the text you typed (the e-mail address) was an Internet or network path. Here, you want standard text (My Resume) to be a hyperlink. That is, when the user clicks My Resume, you want your resume page (Schmidt Web Page) to display on the screen. Perform the following steps to format existing text as a hyperlink.

Steps To Format Existing Text as a Hyperlink

1 Select the text in the first bulleted item, My Resume. Point to the Insert Hyperlink button on the Standard toolbar.

Word highlights the text, My Resume (Figure 13).

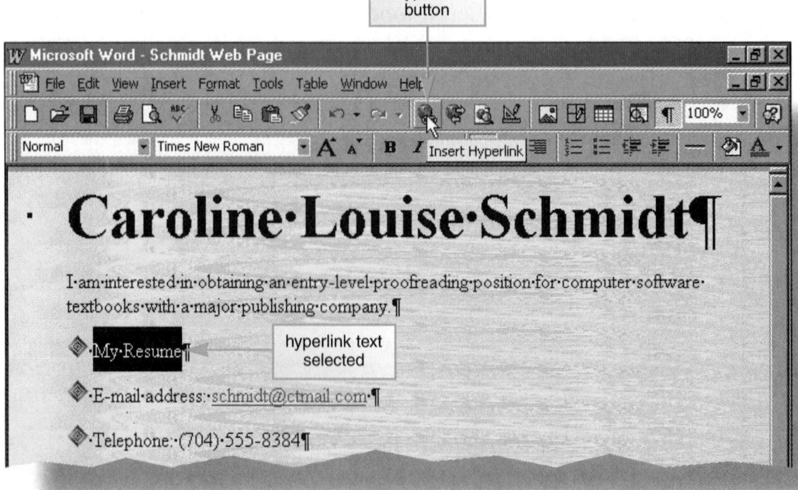

FIGURE 13

2 **Click the Insert Hyperlink button. Insert the disk with the Schmidt Resume Web Page into drive A. When the Insert Hyperlink dialog box displays, type** `a:Schmidt Resume Web Page.html` **and then point to the OK button.**

Word displays the Insert Hyperlink dialog box (Figure 14). If you are unable to remember the name of the Web page file, you can click the Browse button in this dialog box and find the desired file.

3 **Click the OK button.**

Word formats the selected text as a hyperlink (Figure 1a on page WDI 1.2).

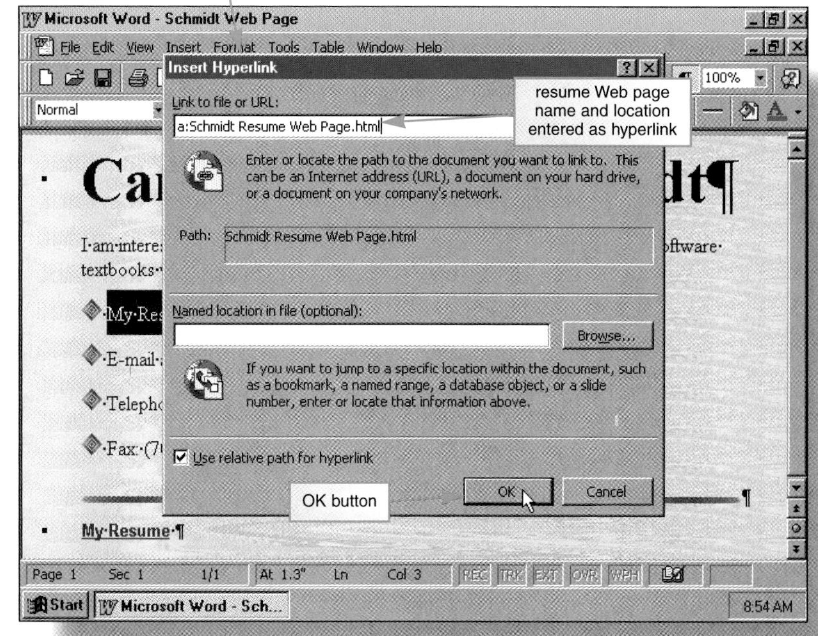

FIGURE 14

4 **Repeat Steps 1 through 3 for the words, My Resume, at the bottom of the Web page to format it as a hyperlink also.**

> ***Other* Ways**
> 1. Select text, right-click selected text, click Hyperlink on shortcut menu, type address in Insert Hyperlink dialog box, click OK button
> 2. Select text, on Insert menu click Hyperlink, type address in Insert Hyperlink dialog box, click OK button
> 3. Select text, press CTRL+K, type address in Insert Hyperlink dialog box, click OK button

The Web page now is complete. You should save it again by clicking the Save button on the Standard toolbar.

To test the links, click the Web Page Preview button on the Standard toolbar. When the Schmidt Web Page displays in your browser window (Figure 1b on page WDI 1.2), click the My Resume link to display the Schmidt Resume Web Page in your browser window (Figure 1c on page WDI 1.2). Then, click the Back button to return to the Schmidt Web Page. Click the e-mail address to open your e-mail program with the address, schmidt@ctmail.com entered in the recipient's address box (Figure 1d on page WDI 1.2). Close any open windows.

The next step is to make your Web pages (Schmidt Web Page and Schmidt Resume Web Page) available to others on your network, an intranet, or the World Wide Web. Talk to your instructor about how you should do this for your system.

Summary

This Integration Feature introduced you to creating a Web page by saving an existing Word document as an HTML file. You also created a new Web page by using the Web Page Wizard and then personalized this Web page with your own text. On the personal Web page, you created a hyperlink to the resume Web page and a hyperlink to your e-mail program.

In the Lab

1 Use Help

Instructions: Start Word. If the Office Assistant is on your screen, click it to display its balloon. If the Office Assistant is not on your screen, click the Office Assistant button on the Standard toolbar. Type `Web Page Wizard` in the What would you like to do? text box. Click the Search button. Click the Create a Web Page link. Read and print the information. Click the Help Topics button to display the Help Topics: Microsoft Word window. Double-click the Creating and Working with Web Pages book. Double-click the Creating Web Pages book. Double-click the Items you can add to Web pages topic. Read and print the topic. Close any open Help windows. Close the Office Assistant.

2 Creating a Web Page with a Hyperlink to a Resume Web Page

Problem: You created the resume shown in Figure 2-82 on page WD 2.58 in Project 2. You decide to create a personal Web Page with a link to the Peterson Resume. Thus, you also must save the resume as a Web page.

Instructions:

1. Open the Peterson Resume shown in Figure 2-82. (If you did not create the resume, see your instructor for a copy of it.) Convert its table to text. Then, save the resume as a Web page.
2. Create a personal Web page using the Web Page Wizard. Use the Simple Layout and the Harvest style. The personal Web page should contain the following information in this order: name; objective; the words, My Resume, as first bulleted item, e-mail address as second bulleted item, telephone number as third bulleted item, and fax number as fourth bulleted item; and the words, My Resume, again at the bottom of the Web page. See Figure 2-82 for this information.
3. Save the Web page and then format the two occurrences of My Resume as hyperlinks to the Peterson Resume Web Page. Save the Web page again. Test your Web page links.
4. Ask your instructor for instructions on how to post your Web pages so others may have access to them.

3 Creating a Web Page with Hyperlinks

Problem: You have decided to create your own personal Web page using the Personal Home Page type in the Web Page Wizard.

Instructions:

1. Create your own personal Web page using the Web Page Wizard. Use the Personal Home Page type and the style you like best.
2. Personalize the Web page as indicated on the template. For each bullet in the hot list section, enter a URL of a site on the Web that interests you.
3. Save the Web page. Test your Web page links.
4. Ask your instructor for instructions on how to post your Web page so others may have access to it.

PROJECT ONE

Creating a Worksheet and Embedded Chart

PROJECT TWO

Formulas, Formatting, Charts, and Web Queries

PROJECT THREE

What-If Analysis and Working with Large Worksheets

INTEGRATION FEATURE

Excel Worksheet to a Word Document

Microsoft Excel 97

Microsoft *Excel 97*

Creating a Worksheet and Embedded Chart

Objectives:

You will have mastered the material in this project when you can:

- Start Excel
- Describe the Excel worksheet
- Select a cell or range of cells
- Enter text and numbers
- Use the AutoSum button to sum a range of cells
- Copy a cell to a range of cells using the fill handle
- Change the size of the font in a cell
- Bold cell entries
- Center cell contents over a series of columns
- Apply the AutoFormat command to format a range
- Use the Name box to select a cell
- Create a 3-D Column chart using the Chart Wizard
- Save a workbook
- Print a worksheet
- Quit Excel
- Open a workbook
- Use the AutoCalculate area to determine totals
- Correct errors on a worksheet
- Use Office Assistant and other online Help tools to answer your questions

It's the Pits

Number-crunching notebooks are race cars' driving force

When six drivers first gathered in Chicago on Thanksgiving Day more than 100 years ago, little did they know they were pioneering the sport of auto racing. Two of them completed the 55-mile jaunt through foot-high snow, and the winner finished in 10 hours with an average speed of 5.5 miles per hour.

Since that first race, the sport has grown to a multibillion-dollar business. Stock car racing is the country's fastest growing professional sport. Drivers at the Indianapolis Motor Speedway, dash in 1,100-horsepower IndyCars at speeds averaging 150 mph and exceeding 235 mph.

To run a top racing team requires at least $10 million, with a crew that includes up to 200 people or more. While spectators may recognize drivers such as Michael Andretti and Jimmy Vasser, they may be less aware of the DAGs (Data Acquisition Geeks) — the engine engineers behind the scenes who gather data and scrutinize the results of calculations to optimize every facet of a race car's performance.

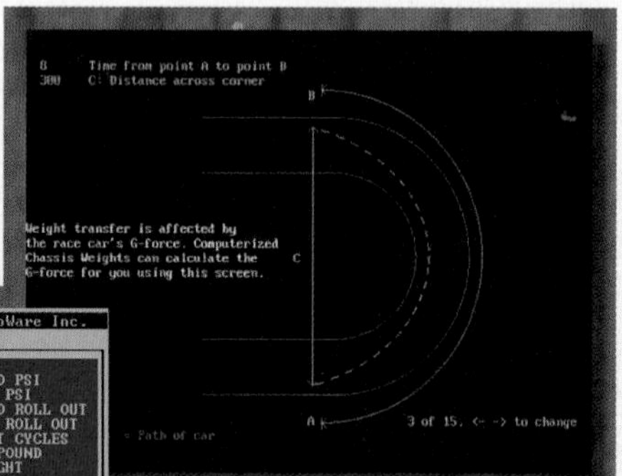

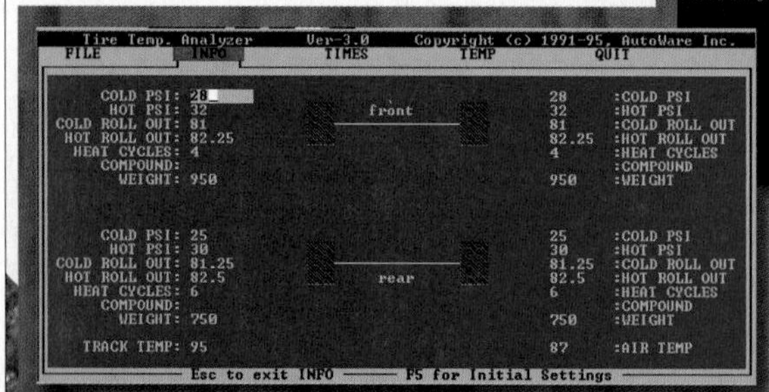

The DAGs perform their jobs with the assistance of notebook computers and data acquisition technology that can cost as much as $37,000. Sensors on various parts of the car collect readings on the suspension, G-force, wheel speed, fuel flow, brakes, tire temperatures, rpm, throttle position, and gear selection and send the data to sophisticated onboard control units, some of which can handle 100 analog and digital channels concurrently and have four megabytes of storage.

These onboard computers put each piece of data in a predefined area, or cell, of an electronic worksheet. This rectangular grid of columns and rows contains formulas that crunch the data. Then, the worksheet immediately displays vital information and graphs on the driver's digital instrument panel. Simultaneously, the processed data from the worksheet is beamed via telemetry to the DAGs' notebooks in the pits. The DAGs analyze the information and use headsets to instruct the driver to make adjustments, such as changing the stiffness of the suspension or modifying braking performance. The pit crew can analyze this output and make other modifications to the car when the driver comes into the pits, such as altering the tire air pressure to adapt to changing track conditions.

Other data acquisition systems use worksheets, such as those you will work with in Microsoft Excel, to perform pivotal functions. For example, one uses an infrared signal beamed at the start/finish line to trigger another onboard computer to perform lap counting and timing calculations. Another system analyzes chassis weights. This worksheet identifies handling problems and performs what-if analysis, such as what would happen if 40 pounds of lead were added in front of the rear axle. Another spreadsheet uses a fuel management strategy to determine when fuel stops should be made. Diagrams produced by the spreadsheet program precisely trace the driver's path on the track and superimpose color-coded parameters such as speed, braking effort, and throttle position.

Now that computer technology has become portable, powerful, and less expensive, the data acquisition systems are considered as much an essential part of a racer's equipment as the helmet and fireproof suit of the driver.

Microsoft
Excel 97

Creating a Worksheet and Embedded Chart

Case Perspective

The Computer Discount Company has experienced explosive growth since its inception a year ago. Thanks to the popularity of personal computers and the World Wide Web, the company has grown faster than anyone could have imagined — yet they still have little or no day-to-day accounting. As sales continue to grow, the management at Computer Discount finally has realized they need a better tracking system for daily sales. As a result, they have asked you to begin each day by preparing a worksheet that shows each previous day's sales.

In particular, they want to know the daily sales for the four key product groups (Computers, Monitors, Printers, and Software) by channel (Mail Order, Telephone, and Web). They want the totals by product group and by channel.

Your task is to develop a worksheet to show these daily sales. In addition, Kelly Montgomery, the president, also has asked you to create a graphical representation of the daily sales because she has little tolerance for lists of numbers.

What Is Microsoft Excel?

Microsoft Excel is a spreadsheet program that allows you to organize data, complete calculations, make decisions, graph data, develop professional-looking reports, convert Excel files for use on the Web, and access the Web. The three major parts of Excel are:

- **Worksheets** Worksheets allow you to enter, calculate, manipulate, and analyze data such as numbers and text. The term worksheet means the same as spreadsheet.
- **Charts** Charts pictorially represent data. Excel can draw a variety of two-dimensional and three-dimensional charts.
- **Databases** Databases manage data. For example, once you enter data onto a worksheet, Excel can sort the data, search for specific data, and select data that meets a criteria.

Project One – Computer Discount Daily Sales

From your meeting with Computer Discount's management, you have determined the following needs, source of data, calculations, and graph requirements.

Need: An easy-to-read worksheet (Figure 1-1) that shows Computer Discount's daily sales for each product group (Computers, Monitors, Printers, and Software) by channel (Mail Order, Telephone, and Web). The worksheet also includes total sales for each product group, each channel, and total company sales for the day.

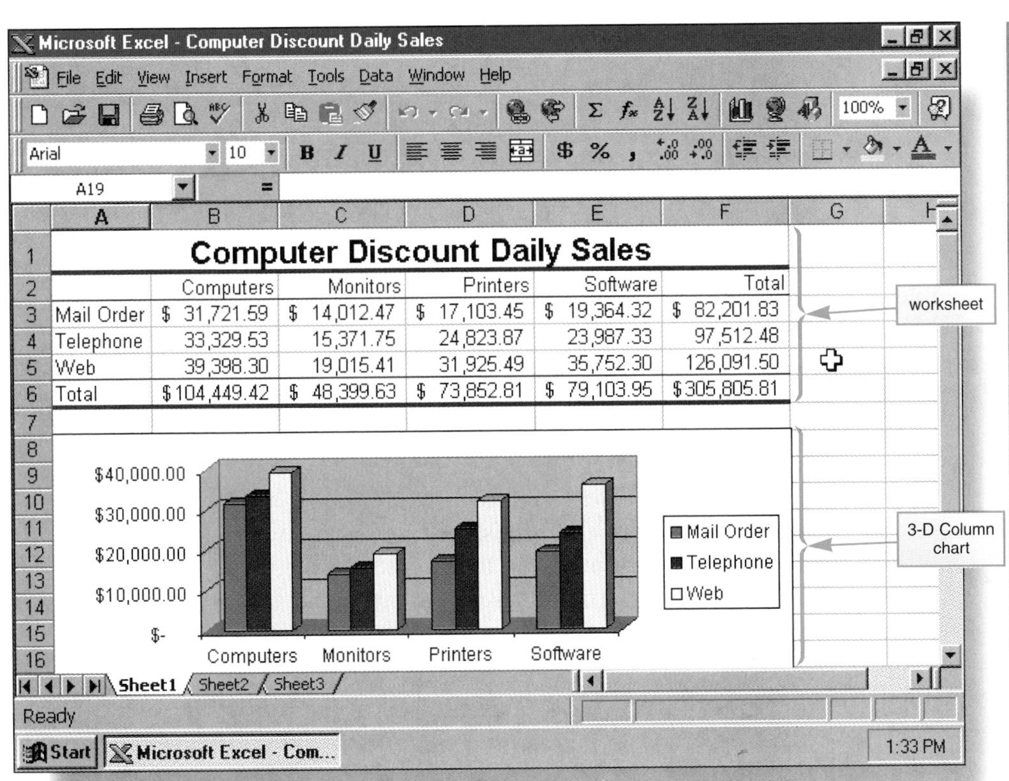

FIGURE 1-1

More About Excel's Ease, Power, and Web Capabilities

Because of Excel's shortcut menus, toolbars, what-if analysis tools, and Web queries, it is one of the easiest, and yet most powerful, worksheet packages available. Its easy-to-use formatting features allow you to produce professional-looking worksheets. Its powerful analytical features make it possible to answer complicated what-if questions with a few clicks of the mouse button. Its Web queries allow you to insert real-time data from Web sites into worksheets.

Source of Data: The data for the worksheet is available each morning from Emma Jo Winslow, Chief Financial Officer (CFO) of Computer Discount.

Calculations: You have determined that the following calculations must be made for the worksheet: (a) total daily sales for each of the four product groups; (b) total daily sales for each of the three sales channels; and (c) total company daily sales.

Graph Requirements: Beneath the worksheet, construct a 3-D Column chart that compares the three sales channels for each product group.

Preparation Steps

The preparation steps below and on the next page summarize how the worksheet and chart shown in Figure 1-1 will be developed in Project 1.

1. Start the Excel program.
2. Enter the worksheet title (Computer Discount Daily Sales), the column titles (Computers, Monitors, Printers, Software, and Total), and the row titles (Mail Order, Telephone, Web, and Total).
3. Enter the daily sales for each product group by sales channel.

More About Creating a Worksheet

The key to creating a useful worksheet is careful planning. Careful planning can reduce your effort significantly and result in a worksheet that is accurate, easy to read, flexible, and useful. When analyzing a problem and designing a worksheet solution, you should follow these steps: (1) define the problem, including need, source of data, calculations, charting and Web requirements; (2) design the worksheet; (3) enter the data and formulas; and (4) test the worksheet.

4. Calculate the daily sales for each product group, for each sales channel, and the total company daily sales.
5. Format the worksheet title (center it across the six columns, enlarge it, and make it bold).
6. Format the body of the worksheet (add underlines, display the numbers in dollars and cents).
7. Direct Excel to create the 3-D Column chart.
8. Save the workbook on a floppy disk.
9. Print the worksheet and 3-D Column chart.
10. Quit Excel.

The following pages contain a detailed explanation of these tasks.

Mouse Usage

In this book, the mouse is the primary way to communicate with Excel. You can perform six operations with a standard mouse: point, click, right-click, double-click, drag, and right-drag. If you have a **Microsoft IntelliMouse**, then you also have a wheel between the left and right buttons. This wheel can be used to perform three additional operations: rotate wheel, click wheel, or drag wheel.

Point means you move the mouse across a flat surface until the mouse pointer rests on the item of choice on the screen. As you move the mouse, the mouse pointer moves across the screen in the same direction. **Click** means you press and release the left mouse button. The terminology used in this book to direct you to point to a particular item and then click is, click the particular item. For example, click the Bold button means point to the Bold button and click.

Right-click means you press and release the right mouse button. As with the left mouse button, you normally will point to an item on the screen prior to right-clicking.

Double-click means you quickly press and release the left mouse button twice without moving the mouse. In most cases, you must point to an item before double-clicking. **Drag** means you point to an item, hold down the left mouse button, move the item to the desired location on the screen, and then release the left mouse button. **Right-drag** means you point to an item, hold down the right mouse button, move the item to the desired location, and then release the right mouse button.

If you have a Microsoft IntelliMouse, then you can use **rotate wheel** to view parts of the worksheet that are not visible. The wheel also can serve as a third button. When the wheel is used as a button, it is referred to as the **wheel button.** For example, dragging the wheel button causes some applications to scroll in the direction you drag.

The use of the mouse is an important skill when working with Microsoft Excel 97.

More *About* the Microsoft IntelliMouse™

The Microsoft IntelliMouse™ is the first major breakthrough in mouse technology since the advent of the mouse unit. The IntelliMouse has a wheel located between the two mouse buttons. You can scroll through worksheets quickly by rotating the wheel with your finger, rather than clicking the scroll arrows on the screen.

Starting Excel

To start Excel, Windows 95 must be running. Perform the following steps to start Excel.

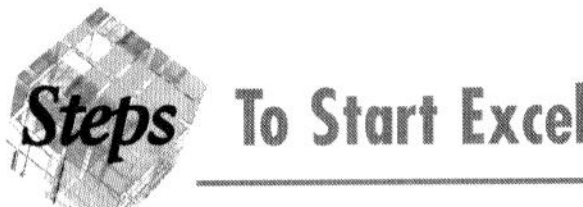

To Start Excel

1 **Click the Start button on the taskbar and then point to New Office Document (Figure 1-2).**

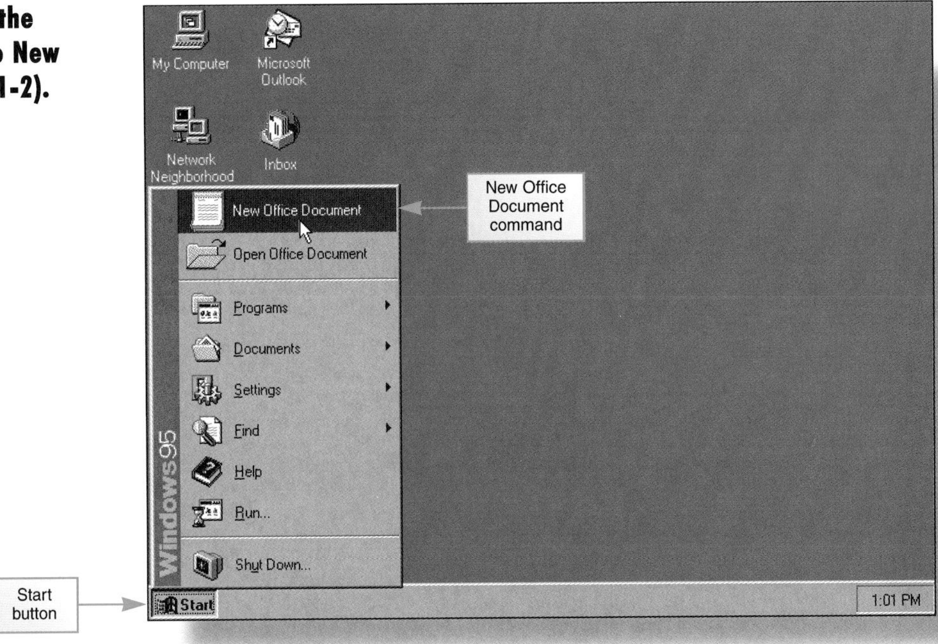

FIGURE 1-2

2 **Click New Office Document. If necessary, click the General tab in the New Office Document dialog box, and then point to the Blank Workbook icon (Figure 1-3).**

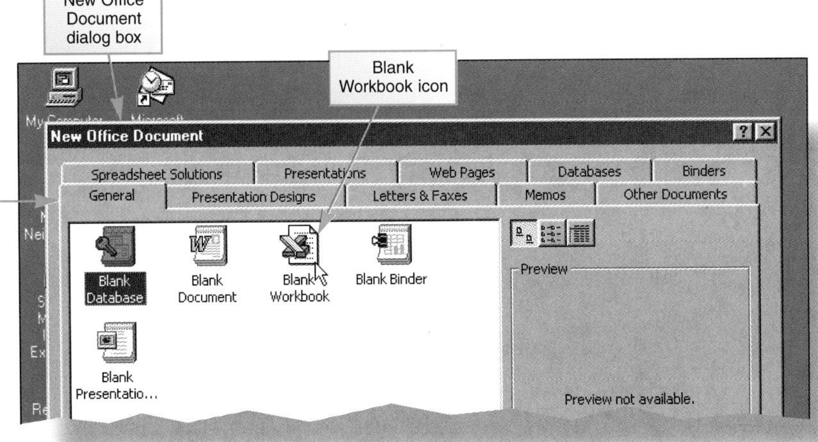

FIGURE 1-3

3 **Double-click the Blank Workbook icon. If necessary, enlarge the Excel window by double-clicking its title bar.**

Excel displays an empty workbook titled Book1 (Figure 1-4).

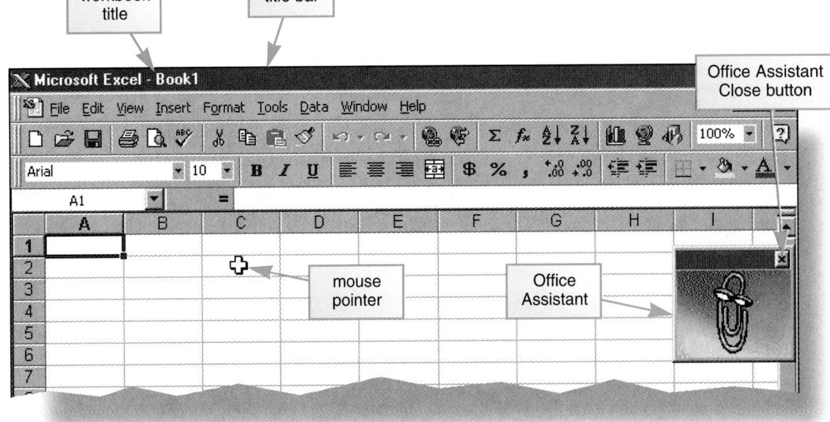

FIGURE 1-4

If the Office Assistant displays (Figure 1-4 on the previous page), click its Close button.

Excel closes the Office Assistant (Figure 1-5). The purpose of the Office Assistant will be discussed later in this project.

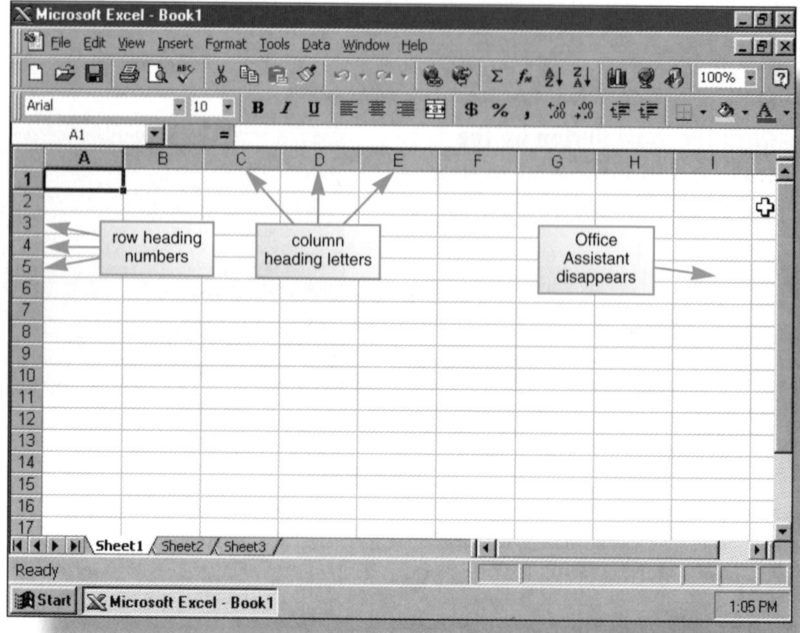

FIGURE 1-5

Other Ways

1. Right-click Start button, click Open, double-click New Office Document
2. On Microsoft Office Shortcut Bar, click Start a New Document button
3. On Start menu point to Programs, click Microsoft Excel

More About Office Assistant Tips

The Office Assistant keeps an eye on the way you work. If you complete a task and the Office Assistant knows a better, alternative way to carry out the task, it will add the alternative to its tips list. You can view the tips list by clicking the Office Assistant to display its balloon. Next, click the Tips button.

The Excel Window

The **Excel window** consists of a variety of features to help you work more efficiently. It contains a title bar, menu bar, toolbars, formula bar, the worksheet window, sheet tabs, scroll bars, and the status bar. Each of these Excel window features and their components are described in this section.

The Workbook

When Excel starts, it creates a new empty workbook, called Book1. The **workbook** (Figure 1-6) is like a notebook. Inside the workbook are sheets, called **worksheets**. Each sheet name appears on a **sheet tab** at the bottom of the workbook. For example, Sheet1 is the name of the active worksheet displayed in the workbook called Book1. If you click on the tab labeled Sheet2, Excel displays the Sheet2 worksheet. A new workbook opens with three worksheets. If necessary, you can add additional worksheets to a maximum of 255. This project will use only the Sheet1 worksheet. Later projects will use multiple worksheets in a workbook.

The Worksheet

The worksheet is organized into a rectangular grid containing columns (vertical) and rows (horizontal). A column letter above the grid, also called the column heading, identifies each **column**. A row number on the left side of the grid, also called the row heading, identifies each **row**. Nine complete columns (A through I) and seventeen complete rows (1 through 17) of the worksheet appear on the screen when the worksheet is maximized as shown in Figure 1-5.

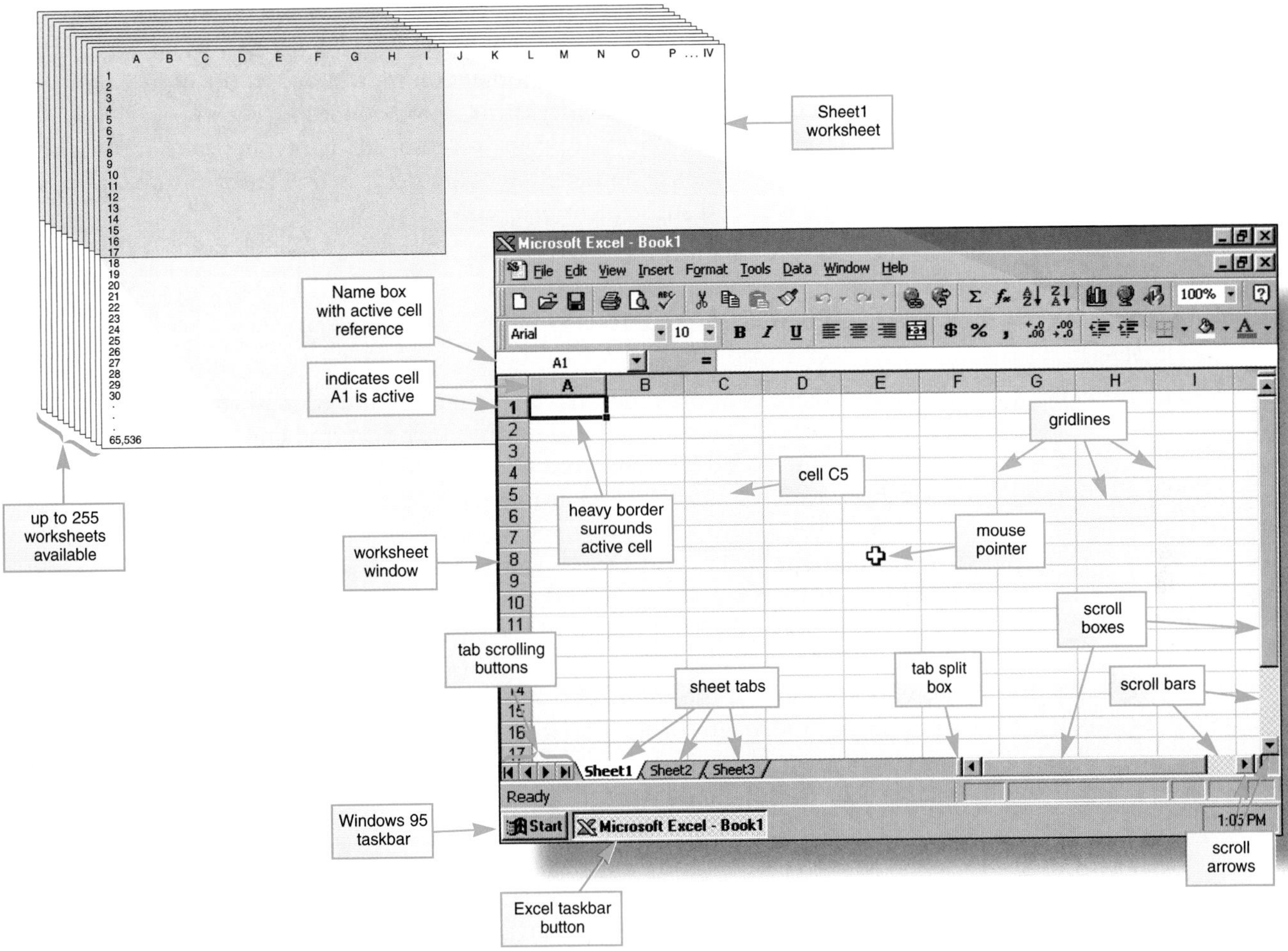

FIGURE 1-6

Cell, Active Cell, Gridlines, and Mouse Pointer

The intersection of each column and row is a **cell**. A cell is the basic unit of a worksheet into which you enter data. A cell is referred to by its unique address, or **cell reference**, which is the coordinates of the intersection of a column and a row. To identify a cell, specify the column letter first, followed by the row number. For example, cell reference C5 refers to the cell located at the intersection of column C and row 5 (Figure 1-6).

One cell on the worksheet, designated the **active cell**, is the one in which you can enter data. The active cell in Figure 1-6 is A1. Cell A1 is identified in three ways. First, a heavy border surrounds the cell; second, the **active cell reference** displays immediately above column A in the **Name box**; and third, the column heading A and row heading 1 "light up" so it is easy to see which cell is active (Figure 1-6).

The horizontal and vertical lines on the worksheet itself are called **gridlines**. Gridlines make it easier to see and identify each cell in the worksheet. If desired, you can turn the gridlines off so they do not display on the worksheet, but it is recommended that you leave them on.

The mouse pointer can change to one of more than 15 different shapes, such as an arrow, cross hair, or chart symbol, depending on the task you are performing in Excel and the mouse pointer's location on the screen.

The mouse pointer in Figure 1-6 on the previous page has the shape of a block plus sign. The mouse pointer displays as a **block plus sign** whenever it is located in a cell in the worksheet. Another common shape of the mouse pointer is the block arrow. The mouse pointer turns into the **block arrow** whenever you move it outside the worksheet or when you drag cell contents between rows or columns. The other mouse pointer shapes are described when they appear on the screen during this and subsequent projects.

More About the Worksheet Size and Window

256 columns and 65,536 rows make for a gigantic worksheet —so big, in fact, that you might imagine it takes up the entire wall of a large room. Your computer screen, by comparison, is like a small window which allows you to view only a small area of the worksheet at one time. While you can't see the entire worksheet, you can move the Excel window over the worksheet to view any part of it. To display the last row in a blank worksheet, press the END key and then press the DOWN ARROW key. Press CTRL+HOME to return to the top of the worksheet.

Worksheet Window

Each worksheet in a workbook has 256 columns and 65,536 rows for a total of 16,777,216 cells. The column headings begin with A and end with IV. The row headings begin with 1 and end with 65,536. Only a small fraction of the active worksheet displays on the screen at one time. You view the portion of the worksheet displayed on the screen through a **worksheet window** (Figure 1-6). Below and to the right of the worksheet window are **scroll bars**, **scroll arrows**, and **scroll boxes** which you can use to move the window around to view different parts of the active worksheet. To the right of the sheet tabs at the bottom of the screen is the **tab split box**. You can drag the tab split box (Figure 1-6) to increase or decrease the view of the sheet tabs. When you decrease the view of the sheet tabs, you increase the length of the horizontal scroll bar; and vice versa.

Menu Bar, Standard Toolbar, Formatting Toolbar, Formula Bar, Sheet and Scroll Tabs, and Status Bar

The menu bar, Standard toolbar, Formatting toolbar, and formula bar appear at the top of the screen just below the title bar (Figure 1-7). The sheet tabs, tab scrolling buttons, and the status bar appear at the bottom of the screen, above the Windows 95 taskbar.

More About Increasing the Size of Your Window

If you're distracted by all the buttons and bars on your screen, you can increase the number of rows and columns displayed by clicking Full Screen on the View menu. Excel immediately will hide the buttons and bars, thus increasing the size of your window. Excel also displays a small toolbar with the Full Screen button on it. Click the Full Screen button to return to the previous view.

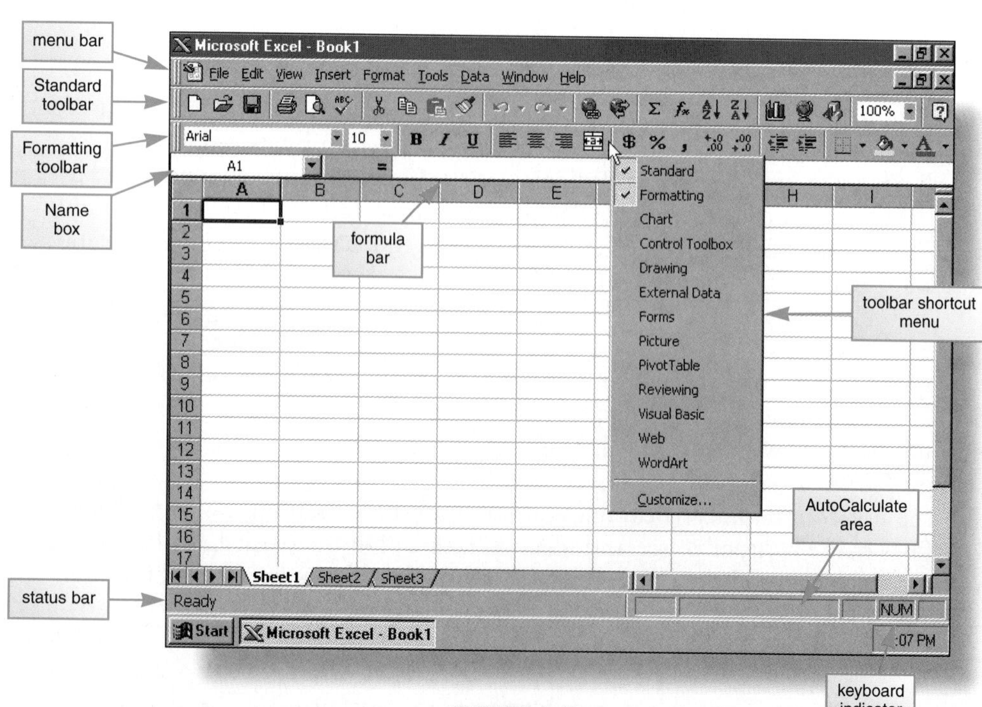

FIGURE 1-7

MENU BAR The **menu bar** is a special toolbar that includes the Excel menu names (Figure 1-7). The menu bar that displays when you start Excel is the **Worksheet menu bar.** Each menu name represents a menu of commands that you can use to retrieve, store, print, and manipulate data on the worksheet. When you point to a menu name on the menu bar, the area of the menu bar containing the name changes to a button. To display a menu, such as the **File menu**, click the menu name File on the menu bar. Once a menu displays, you can point to any command and its submenu displays.

The menu bar can change to include other menu names depending on the type of work you are doing in Excel. For example, if you are working with a chart sheet rather than a worksheet, the **Chart menu bar** will display with menu names that reflect charting command options.

More About Toolbars

If your toolbars have a different set of buttons, it probably means that a previous user changed the toolbars by using the Customize command on the shortcut menu to add or delete buttons (Figure 1-7). To reset the Standard or Formatting toolbars so they appear as shown in Figure 1-8, right-click any toolbar, click Customize, click the toolbar name to reset, click the Reset button, and click the OK button.

STANDARD TOOLBAR AND FORMATTING TOOLBAR The Standard toolbar and Formatting toolbar (Figure 1-7) contain buttons and list boxes that allow you to perform frequent tasks more quickly than when using the menu bar. For example, to print a worksheet, you click the Print button. Each button has a picture on the button face that helps you remember the button's function. Also, when you move the mouse pointer over a button or box, the name of the button or box appears below it. This is called a **ScreenTip.**

Figure 1-8 illustrates the Standard and Formatting toolbars and describes the functions of the buttons. Each of the buttons and list boxes will be explained in detail when they are used in the projects.

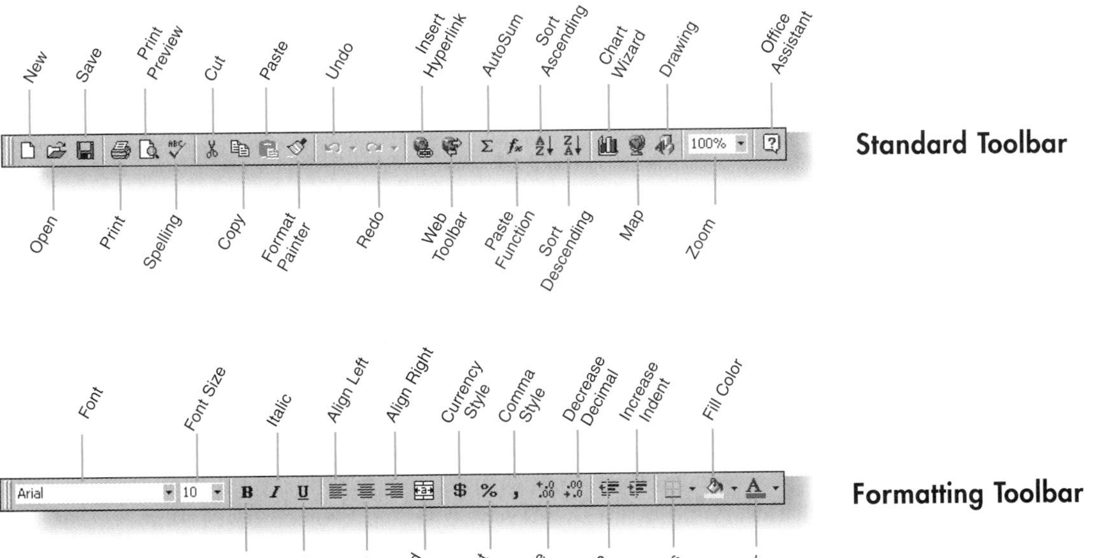

FIGURE 1-8

Excel has several additional toolbars you can activate by clicking View on the menu bar. You also can point to a toolbar, such as the Formatting toolbar, and then right-click to display a shortcut menu, which lists the toolbars available (Figure 1-7). A **shortcut menu** contains a list of commands or items to choose from that relate to the item you are pointing to when you right-click. Once a shortcut menu displays, you can click or right-click a command or item. The recessed check mark to the left of Standard and Formatting in the shortcut menu in Figure 1-7 indicates those toolbars are displaying on the screen.

More About Shortcut Menus

Shortcut menus display the more frequently used commands that relate to the object to which the mouse pointer is pointing. To display a shortcut menu, right-click the object. You also can display the shortcut menu by selecting the object and pressing SHIFT+F10. To hide a shortcut menu, click outside the shortcut menu or press the ESC key.

FORMULA BAR Below the Formatting toolbar is the **formula bar** (Figure 1-7 on page E 1.12). As you type, the data appears in the formula bar. Excel also displays the active cell reference on the left side of the formula bar in the Name box.

STATUS BAR Immediately above the Windows 95 taskbar at the bottom of the screen is the status bar. The **status bar** displays a brief description of the command selected (highlighted) in a menu, the function of the button the mouse pointer is pointing to, or the current activity (mode) in progress (Figure 1-7). **Mode indicators**, such as Enter and Ready, display on the status bar and specify the current mode of Excel. When the mode is Ready, Excel is ready to accept the next command or data entry. When the mode indicator reads Enter, Excel is in the process of accepting data through the keyboard into the active cell.

In the middle of the status bar is the AutoCalculate area. The **AutoCalculate area** can be used in place of a calculator to view the sum, average, or other types of totals of a group of numbers on the worksheet.

Keyboard indicators, such as NUM (Num Lock), show which keys are engaged. Keyboard indicators display on the right side of the status bar within the small rectangular boxes (Figure 1-7).

Selecting a Cell

To enter data into a cell, you first must select it. The easiest way to **select a cell** (make it active) is to use the mouse to move the block plus sign to the cell and click.

An alternative method is to use the **arrow keys** that are located just to the right of the typewriter keys on the keyboard. An arrow key selects the cell adjacent to the active cell in the direction of the arrow on the key.

You know a cell is selected (active) when a heavy border surrounds the cell and the active cell reference displays in the Name box on the left side of the formula bar.

More About Text

A text entry in a cell can contain from 1 to 32,767 characters. Text entries primarily are used to identify parts of the worksheet. Worksheet titles, column titles, and row titles are common text entries. There are applications, however, in which text entries are data that you dissect, string together, and manipulate using text functions.

Entering Text

In Excel, any set of characters containing a letter, hyphen (as in a telephone number), or space is considered **text**. Text is used to place titles on the worksheet, such as worksheet titles, column titles, and row titles. In Project 1 (Figure 1-9), the worksheet title centered in row 1, Computer Discount Daily Sales, identifies the worksheet. The column titles in row 2 (Computers, Monitors, Printers, Software, and Total) identify the data in each column. The row titles in column A (Mail Order, Telephone, Web, and Total) identify the data in each row.

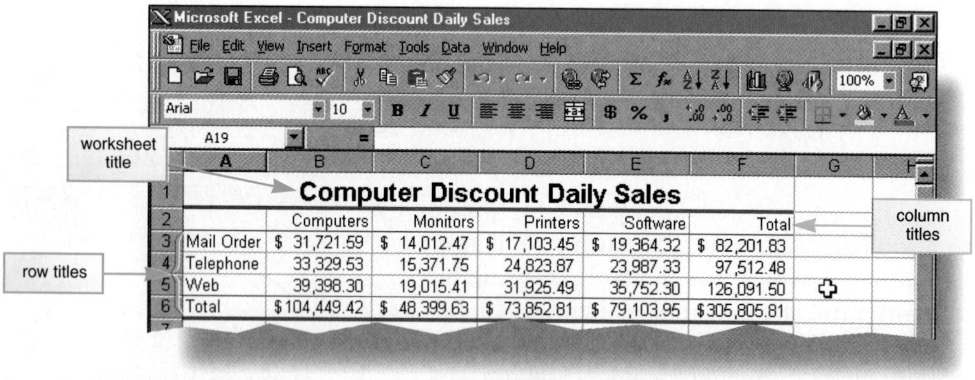

	Computers	Monitors	Printers	Software	Total
Mail Order	$ 31,721.59	$ 14,012.47	$ 17,103.45	$ 19,364.32	$ 82,201.83
Telephone	33,329.53	15,371.75	24,823.87	23,987.33	97,512.48
Web	39,398.30	19,015.41	31,925.49	35,752.30	126,091.50
Total	$104,449.42	$ 48,399.63	$ 73,852.81	$ 79,103.95	$305,805.81

FIGURE 1-9

Entering the Worksheet Title

The following steps show how to enter the worksheet title (Computer Discount Daily Sales) in cell A1. Later in this project, the worksheet title will be centered over the column titles as shown in Figure 1-9.

To Enter the Worksheet Title

Click cell A1.

Cell A1 becomes the active cell and a heavy border surrounds it (Figure 1-10).

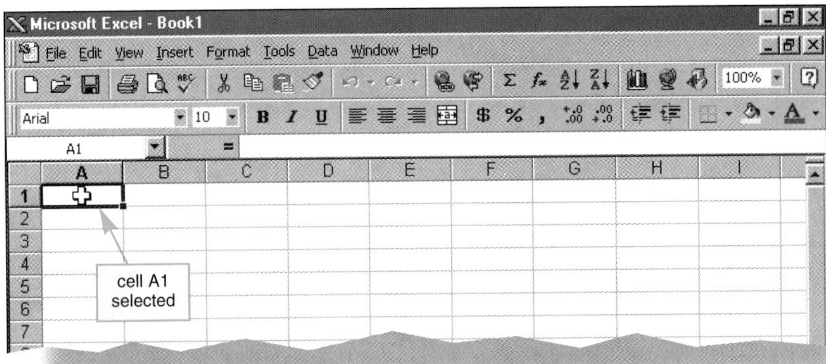

FIGURE 1-10

Type `Computer Discount Daily Sales` **in cell A1.**

When you type the first character, the mode indicator in the status bar changes from Ready to Enter and Excel displays three boxes in the formula bar: the **Cancel box**, *the* **Enter box**, *and the* **Edit Formula box** *(Figure 1-11). The entire title displays in the formula bar and the text also displays in cell A1 followed immediately by the insertion point. The* **insertion point** *is a blinking vertical line that indicates where the next character typed will appear.*

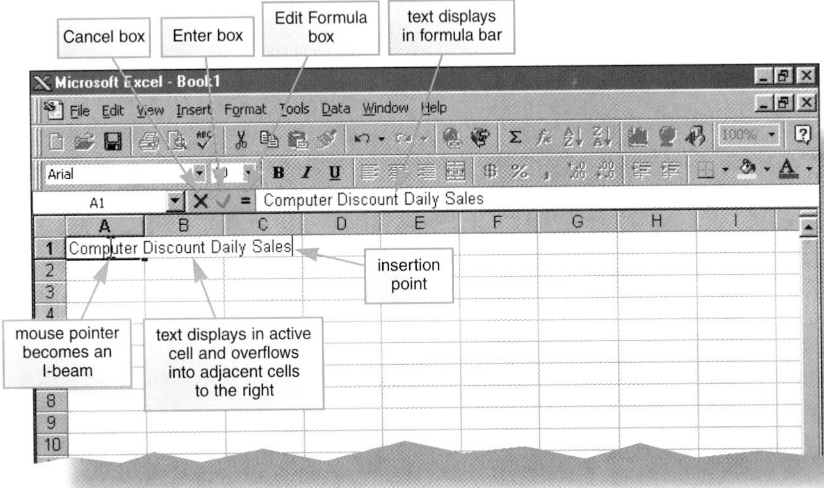

FIGURE 1-11

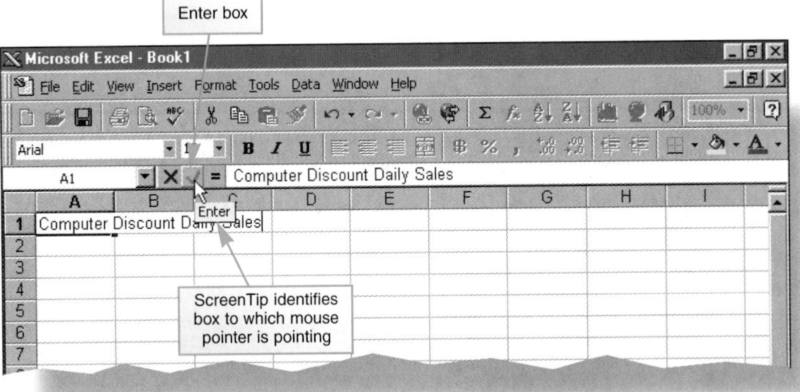

FIGURE 1-12

Click the Enter box to complete the entry.

Excel enters the worksheet title in cell A1 (Figure 1-13).

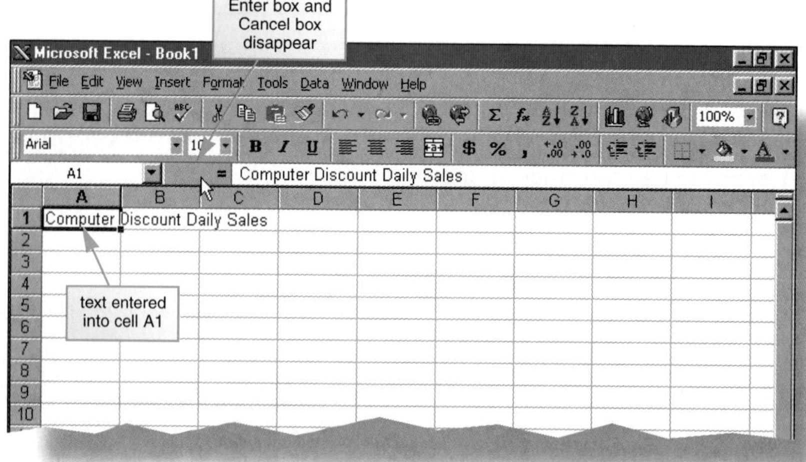

FIGURE 1-13

Other Ways

1. Click any cell other than active cell
2. Press ENTER
3. Press an arrow key
4. Press HOME, PAGE UP, PAGE DOWN, or END

When you complete a text entry into a cell, a series of events occurs. First, Excel positions the text left-aligned in the cell. **Left-aligned** means the cell entry is to the far left in the cell. Therefore, the C in the worksheet title, Computer Discount Daily Sales, begins in the leftmost position of cell A1.

Second, when the text is longer than the width of a column, Excel displays the overflow characters in adjacent cells to the right as long as these adjacent cells contain no data. In Figure 1-13, the width of cell A1 is approximately nine characters. The text entered consists of 26 characters. Therefore, Excel displays the overflow characters from cell A1 in cells B1 and C1, because these cells are empty. If cell B1 contained data, only the first nine characters in cell A1 would display on the worksheet. Excel would hide the overflow characters, but they still would remain stored in cell A1 and display in the formula bar whenever cell A1 was the active cell.

Third, when you complete an entry by clicking the Enter box, the cell in which the text is entered remains the active cell.

More About the ENTER key

Unless you are entering large amounts of data into a worksheet, you probably will want to set the ENTER key to complete an entry without changing the active cell location. If pressing the ENTER key changes the active cell location, you can change it by clicking Options on the Tools menu, clicking the Edit tab, clicking the Move Selection after Enter check box, and then clicking OK. If you want the ENTER key to change the active cell location, click the desired direction in the Move Selection after Enter list box and then click OK.

Correcting a Mistake While Typing

If you type the wrong letter and notice the error before clicking the Enter box or pressing the **ENTER key**, use the **BACKSPACE key** to erase all the characters back to and including the one that is wrong. To cancel the entire entry before entering it into the cell, click the Cancel box in the formula bar or press the **ESC key**. If you see an error in a cell, select the cell and retype the entry. Later in this project, additional error-correction techniques are covered.

AutoCorrect

The **AutoCorrect feature** of Excel works behind the scenes, correcting common mistakes when you complete a text entry in a cell. AutoCorrect makes three types of corrections for you:

1. Corrects two initial capital letters by changing the second letter to lowercase.
2. Capitalizes the first letter in the names of days.

3. Replaces commonly misspelled words with their correct spelling. For example, it will change the misspelled word *recieve* to *receive* when you press the ENTER key, click the Enter box, or press an arrow key to complete an entry. AutoCorrect will correct automatically the spelling of more than 400 words.

You can add misspelled words and their corresponding corrections to the AutoCorrect list and turn off any of the AutoCorrect features by clicking **AutoCorrect** on the **Tools menu**.

More *About* the AutoCorrect Feature

AutoCorrect is part of the IntelliSense™ technology that is built into Excel, which understands what you are trying to do and helps you do it. For example, Excel can correct common misspellings automatically. When you press the ENTER key, the corrected text is entered in the cell.

Entering Column Titles

To enter the column titles, select the appropriate cell and then enter the text, as described in the following steps.

To Enter Column Titles

1 Click cell B2.

Cell B2 becomes the active cell. The active cell reference in the Name box changes from A1 to B2 (Figure 1-14).

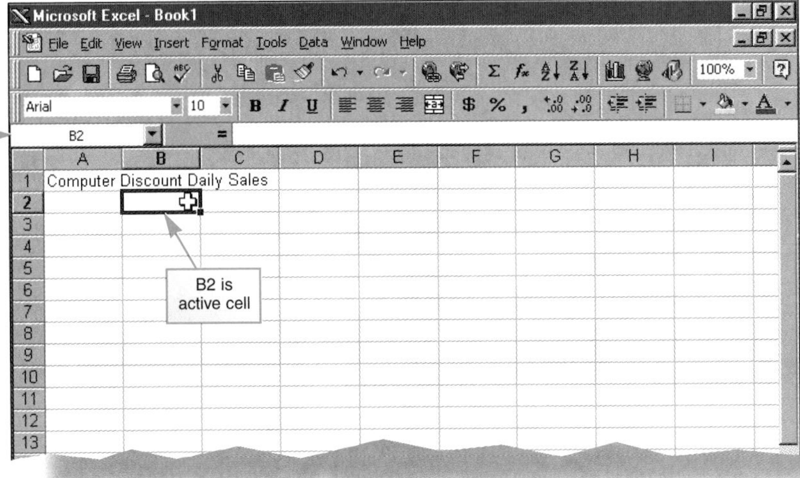

FIGURE 1-14

2 Type `Computers` **in cell B2.**

Excel displays Computers in the formula bar and in cell B2 (Figure 1-15).

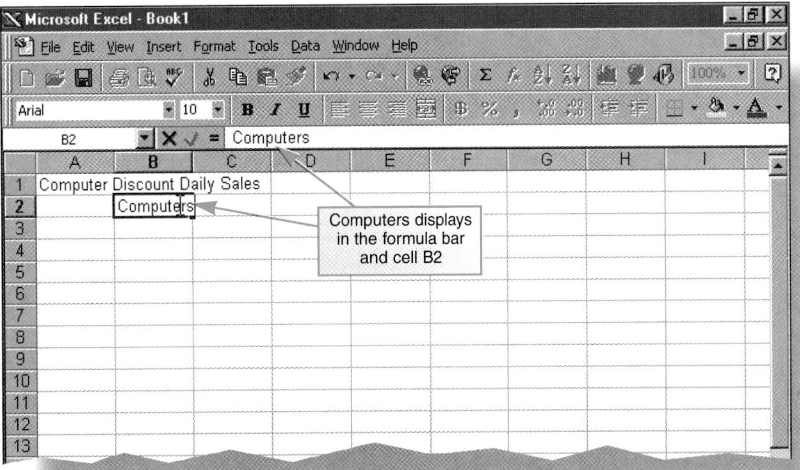

FIGURE 1-15

3 **Press the RIGHT ARROW key.**

Excel enters the column title, Computers, in cell B2 and makes cell C2 the active cell (Figure 1-16). When you press an arrow key to complete an entry, the adjacent cell in the direction of the arrow (up, down, left, or right) becomes the active cell.

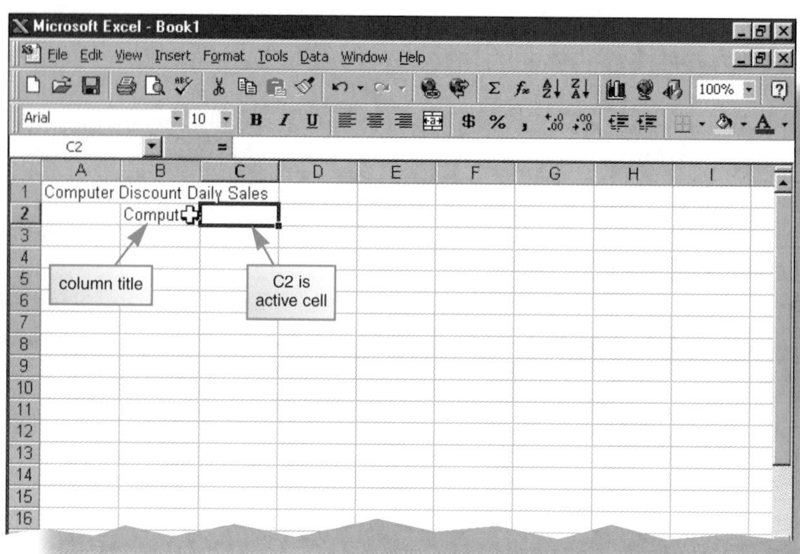

FIGURE 1-16

4 **Repeat Steps 2 and 3 for the remaining column titles in row 2. That is, enter `Monitors` in cell C2, `Printers` in cell D2, `Software` in cell E2, and `Total` in cell F2. Complete the last column title entry in cell F2 by clicking the Enter box or by pressing the ENTER key.**

The column titles display left-aligned as shown in Figure 1-17.

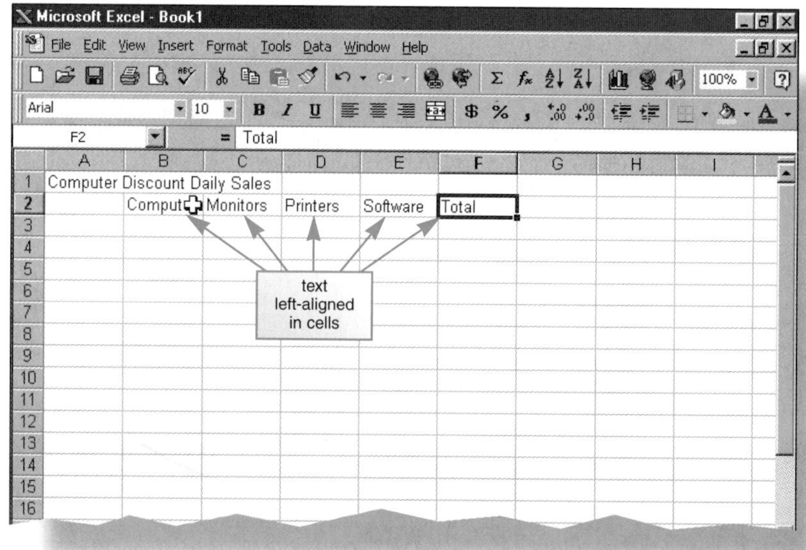

FIGURE 1-17

More About Entering Similar Data

When you type the first few letters of an entry in a cell, Excel can complete the entry for you, based on the entries already in that column. This is called the AutoComplete feature. If you want to pick an entry from a list of column entries, right-click on a cell in the column and then click Pick from List on the shortcut menu.

If the next entry is in an adjacent cell, use the arrow keys to complete the entry in a cell. If the next entry is in a non-adjacent cell, click the next cell in which you plan to enter data, or click the Enter box, or press the ENTER key and then click the appropriate cell for the next entry.

Entering Row Titles

The next step in developing the worksheet in Project 1 is to enter the row titles in column A. This process is similar to entering the column titles and is described in the following steps.

Steps To Enter Row Titles

1 Click cell A3.

Cell A3 becomes the active cell (Figure 1-18). The active cell reference in the Name box changes from F2 to A3.

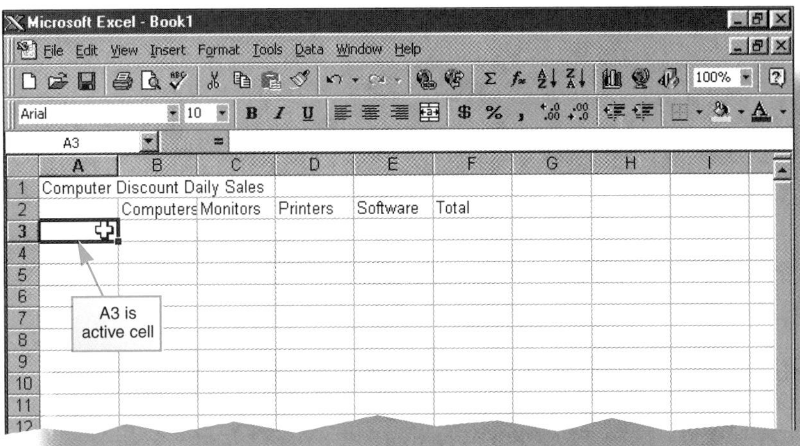

FIGURE 1-18

2 Type `Mail Order` **and then press the DOWN ARROW key.**

Excel enters the row title Mail Order in cell A3 and cell A4 becomes the active cell (Figure 1-19).

row title entered in cell A3

A4 is active cell

FIGURE 1-19

3 Repeat Step 2 for the remaining row titles in column A. Enter `Telephone` **in cell A4,** `Web` **in cell A5, and** `Total` **in cell A6. Complete the last row title in cell A6 by clicking the Enter box or by pressing the ENTER key.**

The row titles display as shown in Figure 1-20.

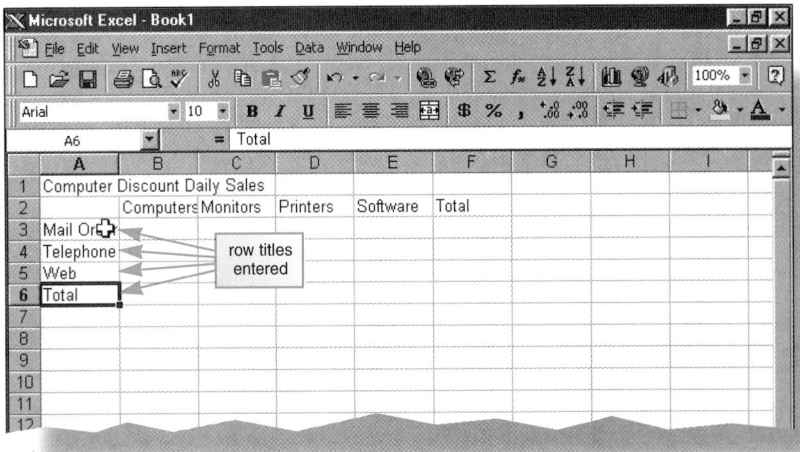

FIGURE 1-20

More About Entering Numbers as Text

There are times when you will want Excel to treat numbers, such as zip codes, as text. To enter a number as text, start the entry with an apostrophe (').

Entering Numbers

In Excel, you can enter numbers into cells to represent amounts. **Numbers** can include the digits zero through nine and any one of the following special characters:

+ - ( ) , / . $ % E e

If a cell entry contains any other keyboard character (including spaces), Excel interprets the entry as text and treats it accordingly. The use of the special characters is explained when they are used in a project.

In Project 1, the daily sales numbers obtained from Emma Jo Winslow, Chief Financial Officer (CFO) of Computer Discount, are summarized in Table 1-1.

These numbers, which represent daily sales for each of the channels and product groups, must be entered in rows 3, 4, and 5. The following steps illustrate how to enter these values one row at a time.

Table 1-1

	COMPUTERS	MONITORS	PRINTERS	SOFTWARE
MAIL ORDER	31,721.59	14,012.47	17,103.45	19,364.32
TELEPHONE	33,329.53	15,371.75	24,823.87	23,987.33
WEB	39,398.30	19,015.41	31,925.49	35,752.30

To Enter Numeric Data

1. **Click cell B3. Type** 31721.59 **and then press the RIGHT ARROW key.**

Excel enters the number 31721.59 in cell B3 and changes the active cell to cell C3 (Figure 1-21). The numbers are formatted with dollar signs and commas later in this project.

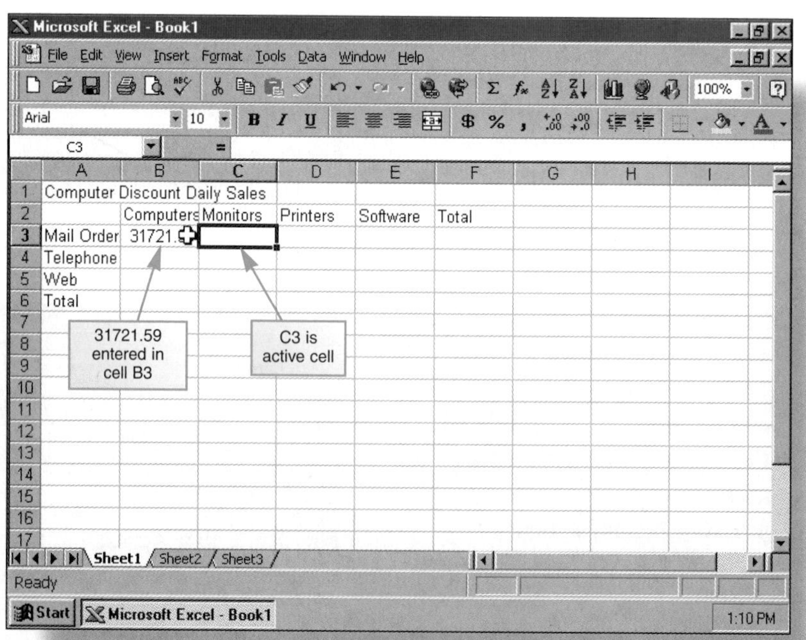

FIGURE 1-21

2 **Enter** 14012.47 **in cell C3,** 17103.45 **in cell D3, and** 19364.32 **in cell E3.**

Row 3 now contains the daily sales by mail order for the four product groups. The numbers in row 3 are right-aligned (Figure 1-22). ***Right-aligned*** *means Excel displays the cell entry to the far right in the cell.*

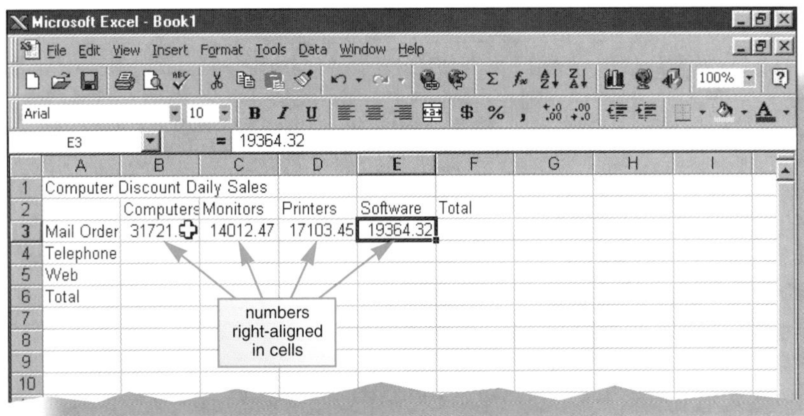

FIGURE 1-22

3 **Click cell B4. Enter the daily sales by Telephone for the four product groups (**33329.53 **for Computers,** 15371.75 **for Monitors,** 24823.87 **for Printers, and** 23987.33 **for Software) in row 4. Enter the daily sales by Web for the four product groups (**39398.30 **for Computers,** 19015.41 **for Monitors,** 31925.49 **for Printers, and** 35752.30 **for Software) in row 5.**

The daily sales by Telephone and Web display in rows 4 and 5 (Figure 1-23).

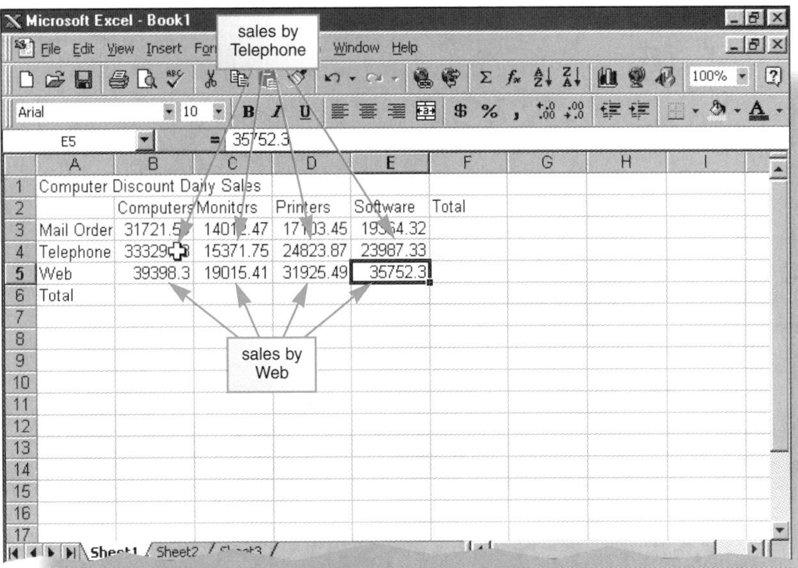

FIGURE 1-23

Steps 1 through 3 complete the numeric entries. You are not required to type dollar signs, commas, or trailing zeros. When you enter a number that has cents, however, you must add the decimal point and the numbers representing the cents when you enter the number. Later in this project, dollar signs, commas, and trailing zeros will be added to improve the appearance of the numbers.

The next section instructs Excel to calculate the totals in row 6 and in column F. Indeed, the capability of Excel to perform calculations is one of its major features.

More *About* Numbers

In Excel, a number can be between approximately -1×10^{308} and 1×10^{308}. To enter a number such as 93,000,000,000, you can type 93,000,000,000 or you can type 9.3E10, which stands for 9.3×10^{10}. If the cell is not wide enough to display a number, Excel displays it in Scientific format. If you enter a large number in a cell with an assigned format, Excel automatically increases the column width so the number displays properly.

Calculating a Sum

The next step in creating the daily sales worksheet is to determine the total daily sales for the Computers product group in column B. To calculate this value in cell B6, Excel must add the numbers in cells B3, B4, and B5. Excel's **SUM function** provides a convenient means to accomplish this task.

To use the SUM function, first you must identify the cell in which the sum will be stored after it is calculated. Then, you can use the **AutoSum button** on the Standard toolbar to enter the SUM function.

Although you can enter the SUM function in cell B6 through the keyboard as =SUM(B3:B5), the following steps illustrate how to use the AutoSum button to accomplish the same task.

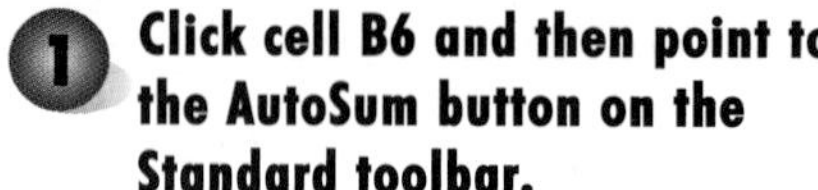

To Sum a Column of Numbers

1 Click cell B6 and then point to the AutoSum button on the Standard toolbar.

Cell B6 becomes the active cell (Figure 1-24).

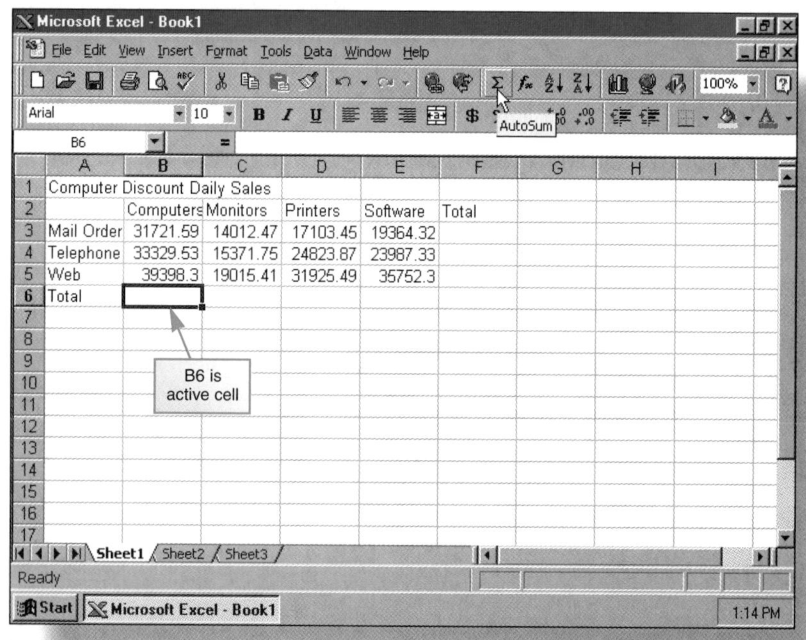

FIGURE 1-24

2 Click the AutoSum button.

Excel responds by displaying =SUM(B3:B5) in the formula bar and in the active cell B6 (Figure 1-25). The =SUM entry identifies the SUM function. The B3:B5 within parentheses following the function name SUM is Excel's way of identifying the cells B3, B4, and B5. Excel also surrounds the proposed cells to sum with a moving border, called a ***marquee****.*

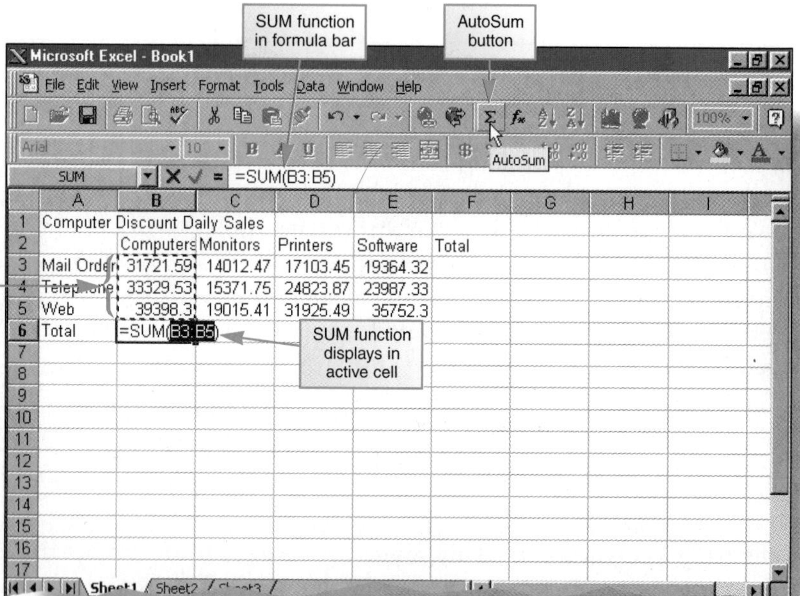

FIGURE 1-25

3 Click the AutoSum button a second time.

Excel enters the sum of the daily sales for Computers (104449.4 = 31721.59 + 33329.53 + 39398.3) in cell B6 (Figure 1-26). The SUM function assigned to cell B6 displays in the formula bar when B6 is the active cell.

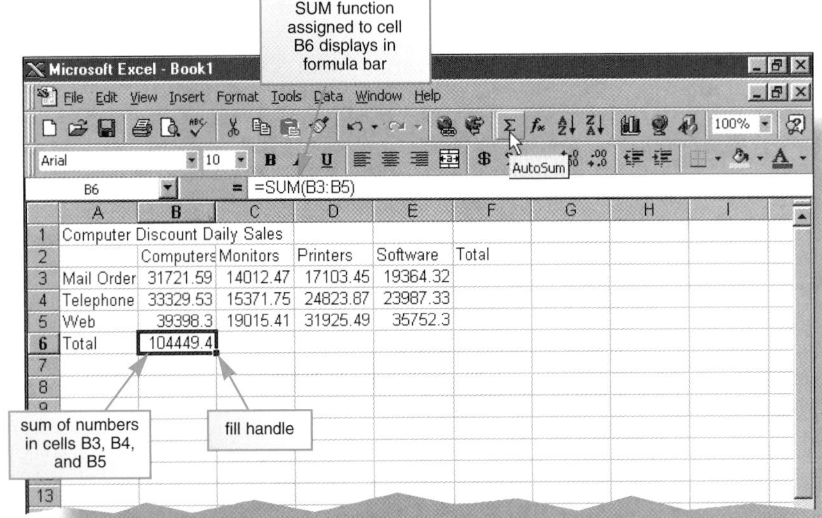

FIGURE 1-26

OtherWays

1. Press ALT+= twice
2. Click Edit Formula (=) box in formula bar, select Sum from Function list box, click OK button

When you enter the SUM function using the AutoSum button, Excel automatically selects what it considers to be your choice of the group of cells to sum. The group of cells B3, B4, and B5 is called a range. A **range** is a series of two or more adjacent cells in a column or row or a rectangular group of cells. Many Excel operations, such as summing numbers, take place on a range of cells.

When proposing the range to sum, Excel first looks for a range of cells with numbers above the active cell and then to the left. If Excel proposes the wrong range, you can drag through the correct range anytime prior to clicking the AutoSum button a second time. You also can enter the correct range by typing the beginning cell reference, a colon (:), and the ending cell reference.

When using the AutoSum button, you can click it once and then click the Enter box or press the ENTER key to complete the entry. Clicking the AutoSum button twice in succession, however, is the quickest way to enter the SUM function into a single cell.

Using the Fill Handle to Copy a Cell to Adjacent Cells

On the daily sales worksheet, Excel also must calculate the totals for Monitors in cell C6, Printers in cell D6, and for Software in cell E6. Table 1-2 illustrates the similarities between the entry in cell B6 and the entries required for the totals in cells C6, D6, and E6.

To place the SUM functions in cells C6, D6, and E6, you can follow the same steps shown in Figures 1-24 through 1-26. A second, more efficient method is to copy the SUM function from cell B6 to the range C6:E6. The cell being copied is called the **copy area**. The range of cells receiving the copy is called the **paste area**.

Table 1-2

CELL	SUM FUNCTION ENTRIES	REMARK
B6	=SUM(B3:B5)	Sums cells B3, B4, and B5
C6	=SUM(C3:C5)	Sums cells C3, C4, and C5
D6	=SUM(D3:D5)	Sums cells D3, D4, and D5
E6	=SUM(E3:E5)	Sums cells E3, E4, and E5

Notice from Table 1-2 on the previous page that although the SUM function entries are similar, they are not exact copies. The range in each SUM function entry to the right of cell B6 uses cell references that are one column to the right of the previous column. When you copy cell references, Excel adjusts them for each new position, resulting in the SUM function entries illustrated in Table 1-2. Each adjusted cell reference is called a **relative reference**.

The easiest way to copy the SUM formula from cell B6 to cells C6, D6, and E6 is to use the fill handle. The **fill handle** is the small black square located in the lower-right corner of the heavy border around the active cell (Figure 1-26 on the previous page). Perform the following steps to use the fill handle to copy cell B6 to the adjacent cells C6:E6.

Steps To Copy a Cell to Adjacent Cells in a Row

1 With cell B6 active, point to the fill handle.

The mouse pointer changes to a cross hair (Figure 1-27).

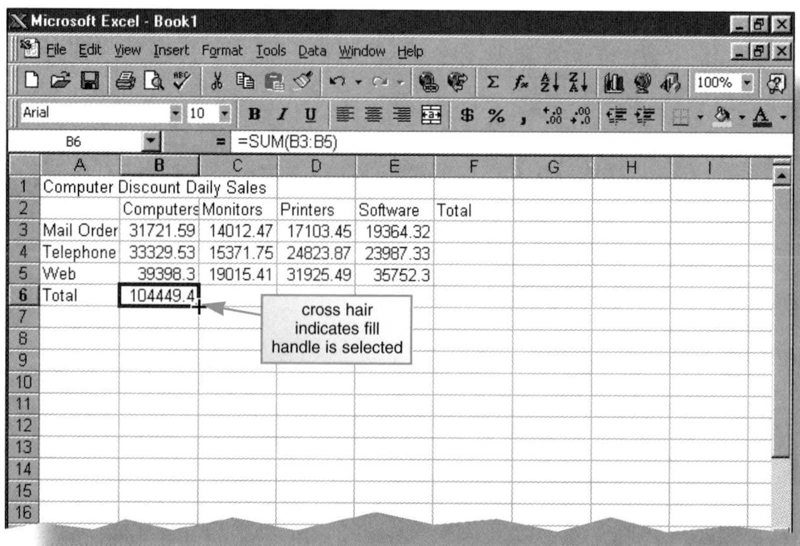

FIGURE 1-27

2 Drag the fill handle to select the paste area C6:E6.

Excel displays a shaded border around the paste area C6:E6 and the copy area B6 (Figure 1-28).

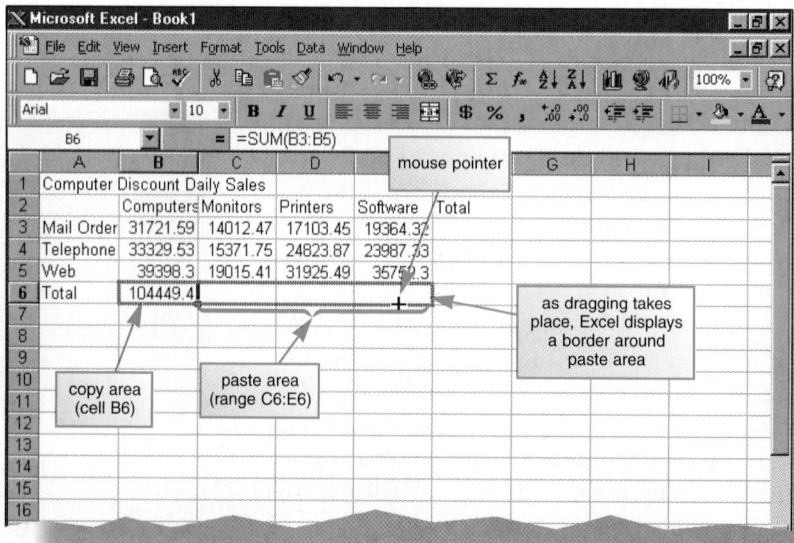

FIGURE 1-28

Release the left mouse button.

Excel copies the SUM function in cell B6 to the range C6:E6 (Figure 1-29). In addition, Excel calculates the sums and enters the results in cells C6, D6, and E6.

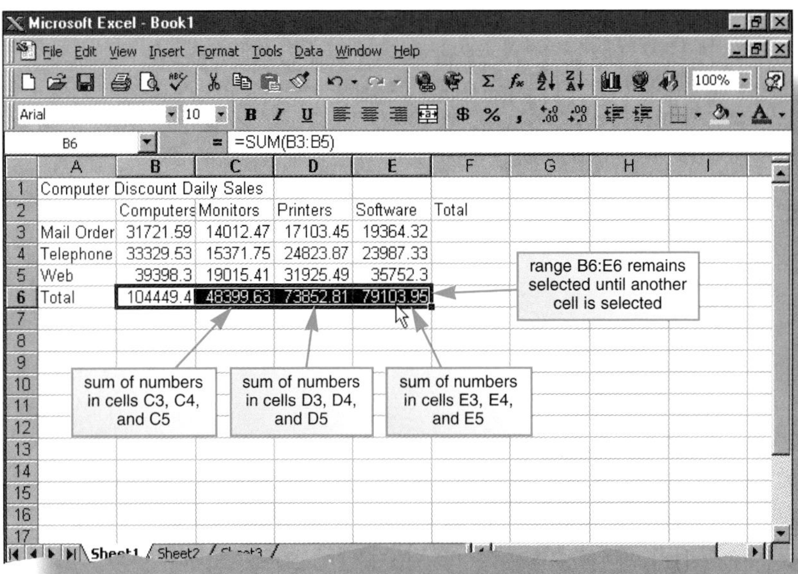

FIGURE 1-29

Determining Row Totals

The next step in building the daily sales worksheet is to determine totals for each sales channel and company total sales in column F. Use the SUM function in the same manner as you did when the daily sales by product group were totaled in row 6. In this example, however, all the rows will be totaled at the same time. The following steps illustrate this process.

More About Copying

Another way to copy a cell or range of cells is to select the copy area, point to the border of the copy area, and then, while holding down the CTRL key, drag the copy area to the paste area. If you drag without holding down the CTRL key, Excel moves the data, rather than copying it.

Steps To Determine Multiple Totals at the Same Time

1 Click cell F3.

Cell F3 becomes the active cell (Figure 1-30).

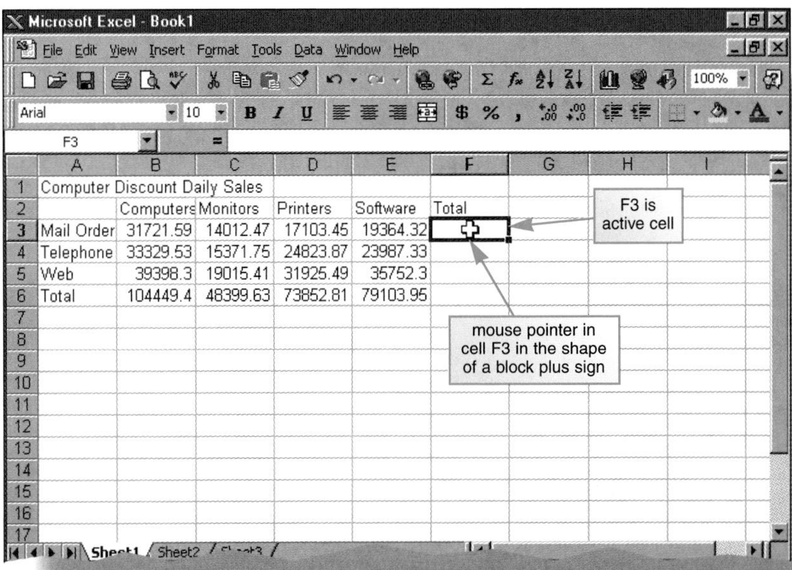

FIGURE 1-30

2 **With the mouse pointer in cell F3 and in the shape of a block plus sign, drag the mouse pointer down to cell F6.**

Excel highlights the range F3:F6 (Figure 1-31).

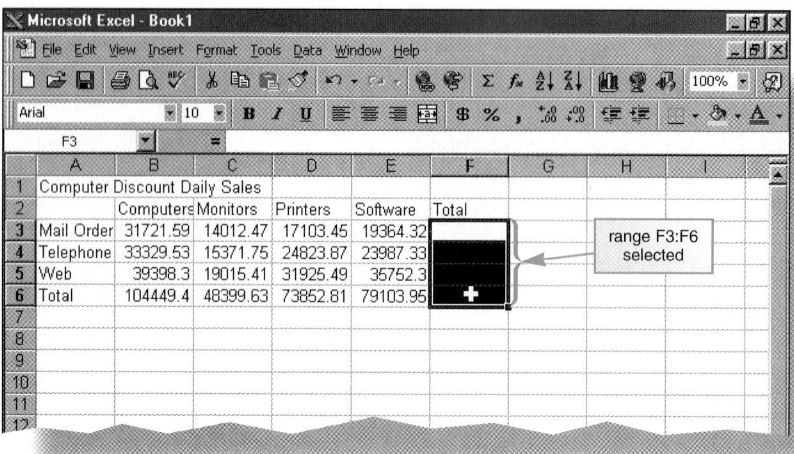

FIGURE 1-31

3 **Click the AutoSum button on the Standard toolbar.**

Excel assigns the functions =SUM(B3:E3) to cell F3, =SUM(B4:E4) to cell F4, =SUM(B5:E5) to cell F5, and =SUM(B6:E6) to cell F6, and then calculates and displays the sums in the respective cells (Figure 1-32).

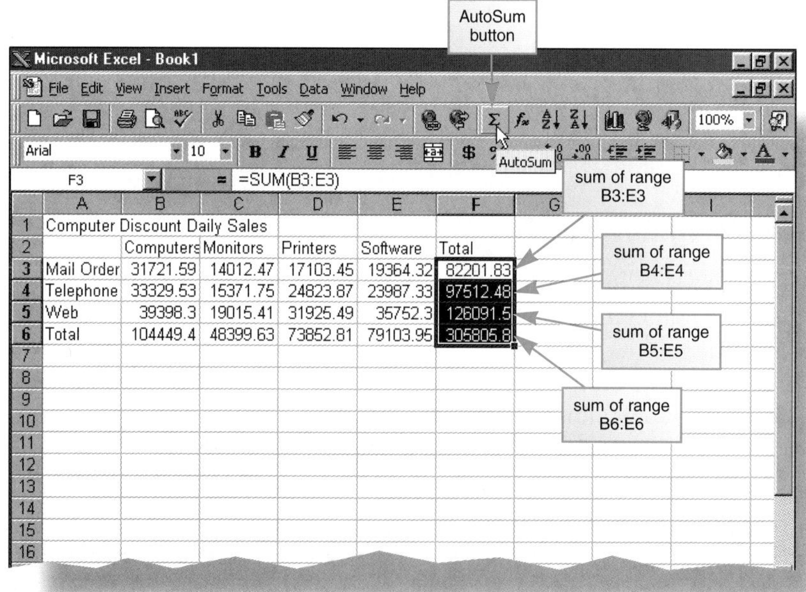

FIGURE 1-32

More About the AutoSum Button

A quick way to determine all the totals in row 6 and column F in Figure 1-32 at once is to select the range (B3:F6) and then click the AutoSum button. The range B3:F6 includes the numbers to sum plus an additional row (row 6) and an additional column (column F), in which the totals will display.

If each cell in the selected range is next to a row of numbers, Excel assigns the SUM function to each cell in the selected range when the AutoSum button is clicked. Thus, four SUM functions with different ranges were assigned to the selected range, one for each row. This same procedure could have been used earlier to sum the columns. That is, rather than selecting cell B6, clicking the AutoSum button twice, and then copying the SUM function to the range C6:E6, you could have selected the range B6:E6 and then clicked the AutoSum button once.

Formatting the Worksheet

The text, numeric entries, and functions for the worksheet now are complete. The next step is to format the worksheet. You **format** a worksheet to emphasize certain entries and make the worksheet easier to read and understand.

Figure 1-33a shows the worksheet before formatting. Figure 1-33b shows the worksheet after formatting. As you can see from the two figures, a worksheet that is formatted not only is easier to read, but also looks more professional.

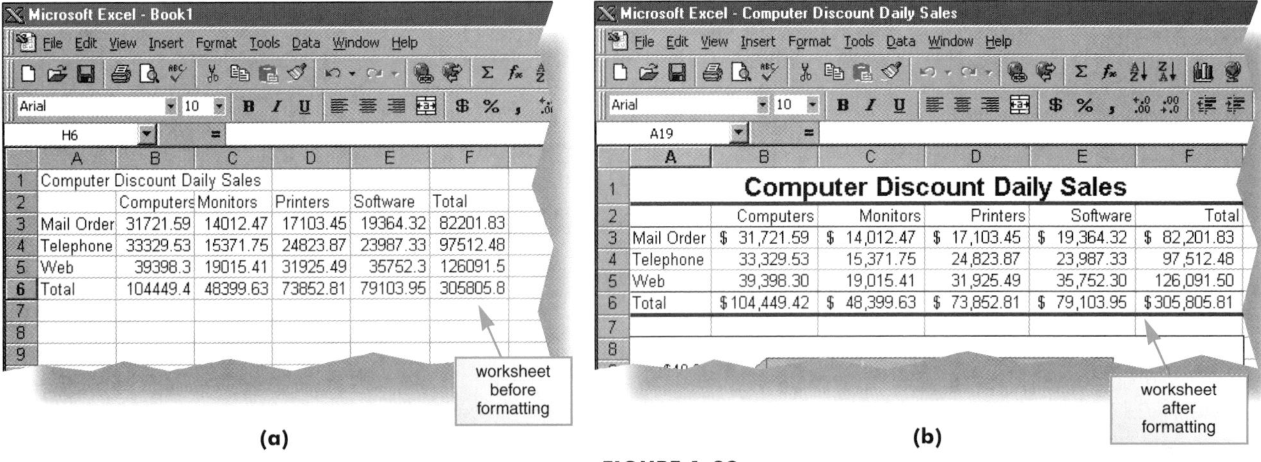

(a) (b)

FIGURE 1-33

To change the unformatted worksheet in Figure 1-33a to the formatted worksheet in Figure 1-33b, the following tasks must be completed:

1. Bold the worksheet title in cell A1.
2. Enlarge the worksheet title in cell A1.
3. Center the worksheet title in cell A1 across columns A through F.
4. Format the body of the worksheet. The body of the worksheet, range A2:F6, includes the column titles, row titles, and numbers. Formatting the body of the worksheet results in numbers represented in a dollars-and-cents format, dollar signs in the first row of numbers and the total row, underlines that emphasize portions of the worksheet, and modified column widths.

The process required to format the daily sales worksheet is explained in the remainder of this section. Although the format procedures will be carried out in the order described above, you should be aware that you can make these format changes in any order.

Fonts, Font Size, and Font Style

Characters that display on the screen are a specific shape, size, and style. The **font type** defines the appearance and shape of the letters, numbers, and special characters. The **font size** specifies the size of the characters on the screen. Font size is gauged by a measurement system called points. A single **point** is about 1/72 of one inch in height. Thus, a character with a **point size** of 10 is about 10/72 of one inch in height.

Font style indicates how the characters are formatted. Common font styles include regular, bold, underlined, or italicized.

When Excel begins, the default font type for the entire workbook is Arial with a size and style of 10-point regular. Excel allows you to change the font characteristics in a single cell, a range of cells, the entire worksheet, or the entire workbook.

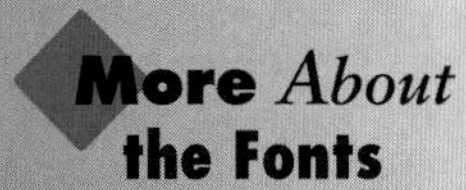

More *About* the Fonts

In general, use no more than two font types and font styles in a worksheet.

Bolding a Cell

You **bold** an entry in a cell to emphasize it or make it stand out from the rest of the worksheet. Perform the following steps to bold the worksheet title in cell A1.

To Bold a Cell

Click cell A1 and then point to the Bold button on the Formatting toolbar.

The ScreenTip displays immediately below the Bold button to identify the function of the button (Figure 1-34).

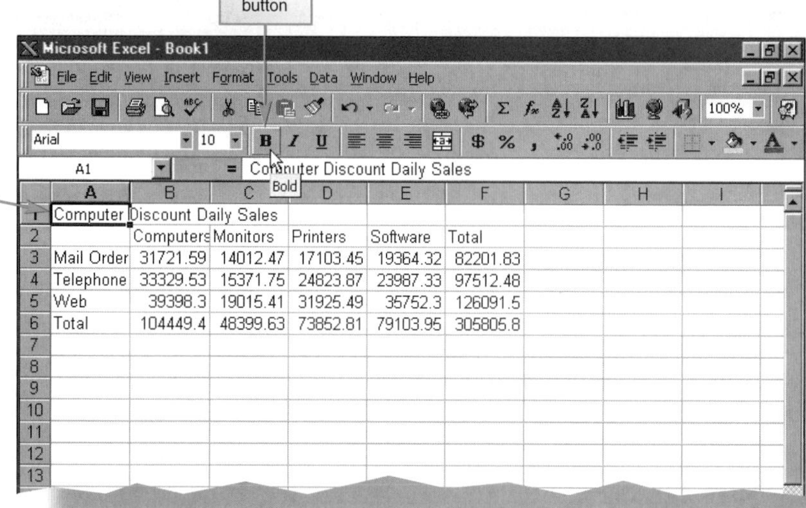

FIGURE 1-34

Click the Bold button.

Excel applies a bold format to the worksheet title Computer Discount Daily Sales (Figure 1-35).

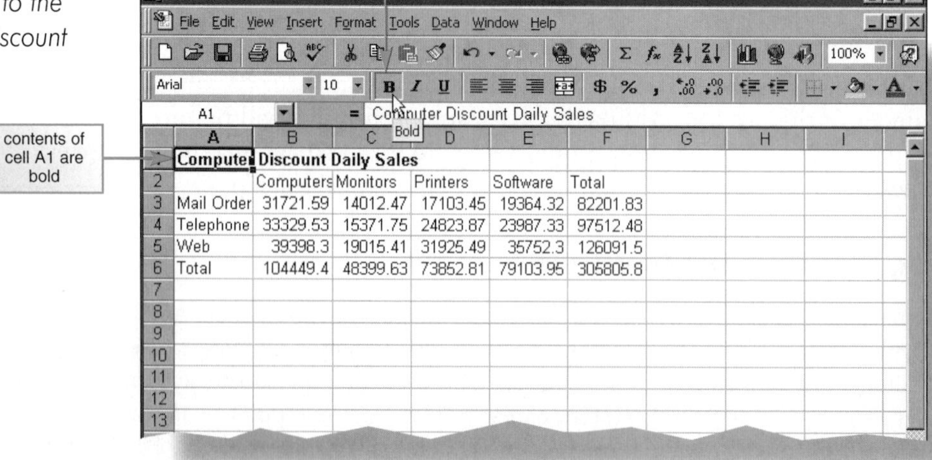

FIGURE 1-35

OtherWays

1. Press CTRL+B
2. Right-click cell, click Format Cells on shortcut menu, click Font tab, click Bold, click OK button
3. On Format menu click Cells, click Font tab, click Bold, click OK button

When the active cell is bold, the Bold button on the Formatting toolbar is recessed (Figure 1-35). Clicking the Bold button a second time removes the bold format.

Increasing the Font Size

Increasing the font size is the next step in formatting the worksheet title. You increase the font size of a cell so that the entry stands out and is easier to read.

To Increase the Font Size of a Cell Entry

1 **With cell A1 selected, click the Font Size box arrow on the Formatting toolbar and then point to 16 in the Font Size list box (Figure 1-36).**

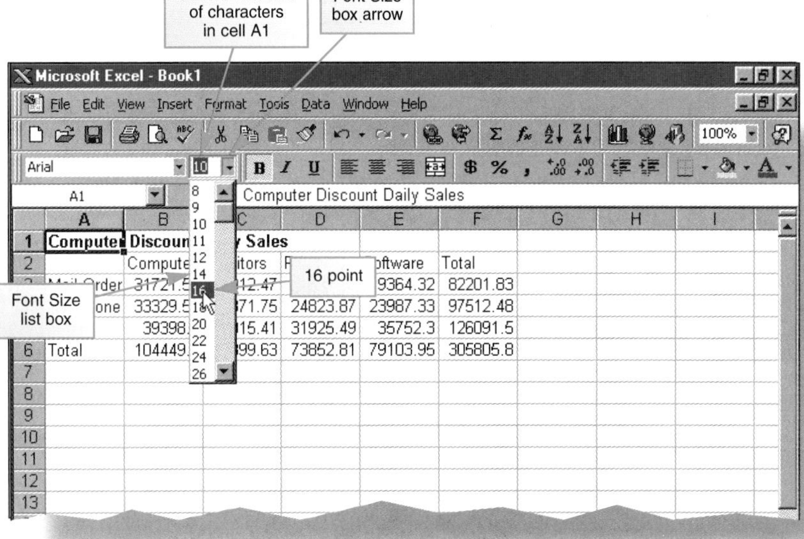

FIGURE 1-36

2 **Click 16.**

The characters in the worksheet title in cell A1 increase from 10 point to 16 point (Figure 1-37).

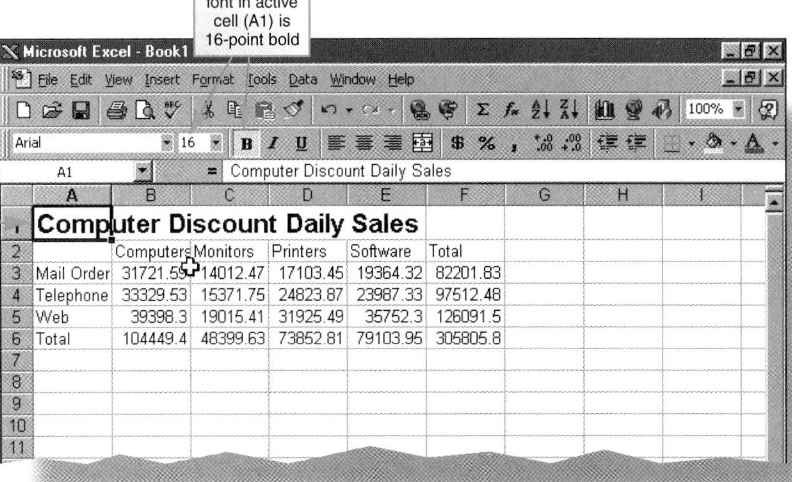

FIGURE 1-37

An alternative to clicking a font size in the Font Size list box is to type the font size in the Font Size box and press the ENTER key. With cell A1 selected (Figure 1-37), the Font Size box shows the new font size 16 and the recessed Bold button shows the active cell is bold.

Other Ways

1. Press CTRL+1, click Font tab, select font size, click OK button
2. Right-click cell, click Format Cells on shortcut menu, click Font tab, select font size, click OK button
3. On Format menu click Cells, click Font tab, select font size, click OK button

Centering the Worksheet Title Across Columns

The final step in formatting the worksheet title is to center it over columns A through F. Centering a worksheet title over the columns used in the body of the worksheet improves the worksheet's appearance.

To Center a Cell's Contents Across Columns

1 With cell A1 selected, drag the block plus sign to the rightmost cell (F1) of the range through which to center (A1:F1).

When you drag the mouse pointer through the range A1:F1, Excel highlights the cells (Figure 1-38).

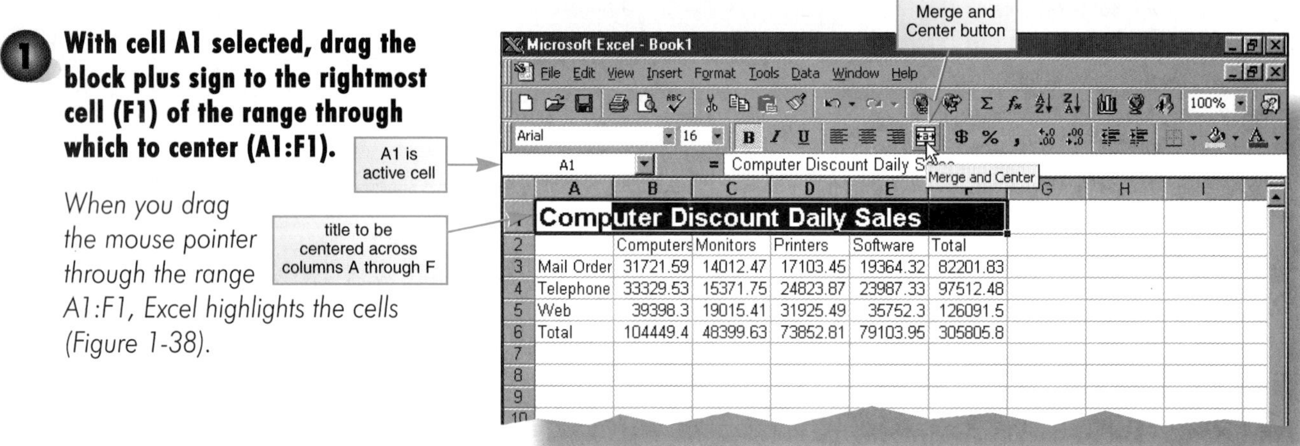

	A	B	C	D	E	F
1	Computer Discount Daily Sales					
2		Computers	Monitors	Printers	Software	Total
3	Mail Order	31721.59	14012.47	17103.45	19364.32	82201.83
4	Telephone	33329.53	15371.75	24823.87	23987.33	97512.48
5	Web	39398.3	19015.41	31925.49	35752.3	126091.5
6	Total	104449.4	48399.63	73852.81	79103.95	305805.8

FIGURE 1-38

2 Click the Merge and Center button on the Formatting toolbar.

Excel merges the cells A1 through F1 to create a new cell A1 and centers the contents of cell A1 across columns A through F (Figure 1-39).

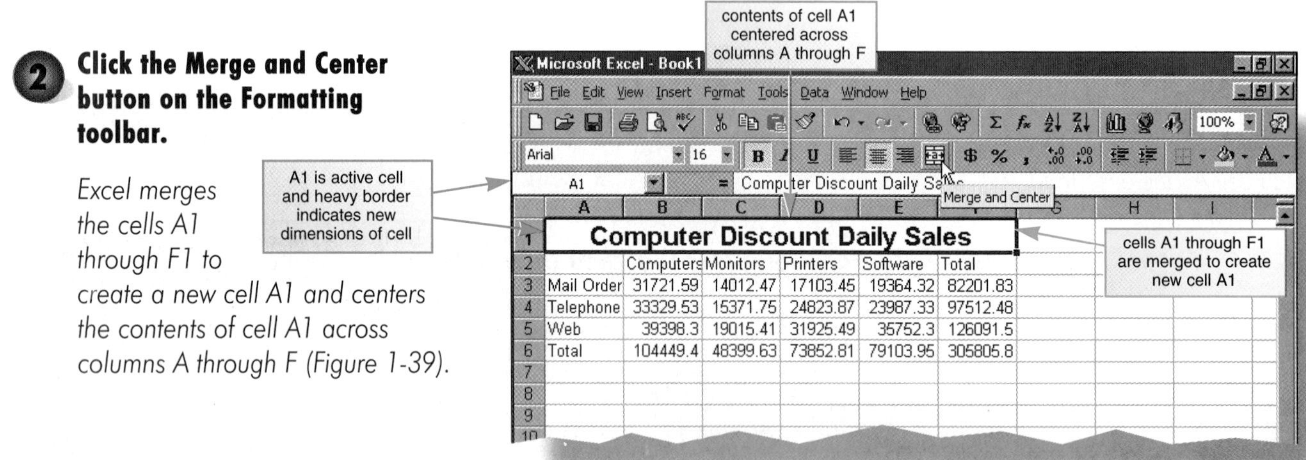

	A	B	C	D	E	F
1	Computer Discount Daily Sales					
2		Computers	Monitors	Printers	Software	Total
3	Mail Order	31721.59	14012.47	17103.45	19364.32	82201.83
4	Telephone	33329.53	15371.75	24823.87	23987.33	97512.48
5	Web	39398.3	19015.41	31925.49	35752.3	126091.5
6	Total	104449.4	48399.63	73852.81	79103.95	305805.8

FIGURE 1-39

Other Ways

1. Right-click cell, click Format Cells on shortcut menu, click Alignment tab, click Center Across Selection in Horizontal list box, click OK button
2. On Format menu click Cells, click Alignment tab, click Center Across Selection in Horizontal list box, click OK button

Excel not only centers the worksheet title, but also merges cells A1 through F1 into one cell, cell A1. Thus, the heavy border that defines the active cell in Figure 1-39 covers what was originally cells A1 through F1. For the Merge and Center button to work properly, all the cells except the leftmost cell in the range of cells must be empty.

Most formats assigned to a cell will display on the Formatting toolbar when the cell is selected. For example, the font type and font size display in their appropriate boxes. Recessed buttons indicate an assigned format. To determine if less frequently used formats are assigned to a cell, point to the cell and right-click. Next, click **Format Cells**, and then click each of the tabs in the **Format Cells dialog box**.

Using AutoFormat to Format the Body of a Worksheet

Excel has several customized format styles called table formats that allow you to format the body of the worksheet. The table formats can be used to give your worksheet a professional appearance. Follow these steps to format automatically the range A2:F6 in the daily sales worksheet using **AutoFormat** on the **Format menu**.

To Use AutoFormat to Format the Body of a Worksheet

1 Select cell A2, the upper-left corner cell of the rectangular range to format (Figure 1-40).

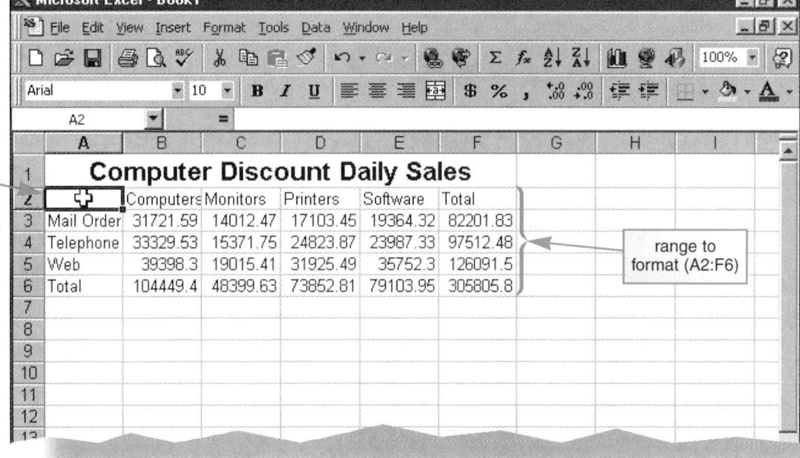

FIGURE 1-40

2 Drag the mouse pointer to cell F6, the lower-right corner cell of the range to format.

Excel highlights the range to format (Figure 1-41).

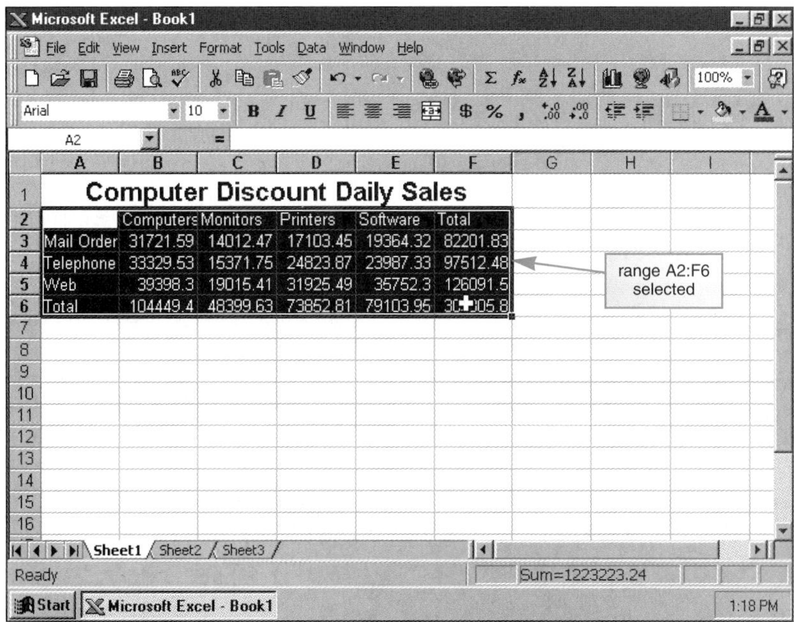

FIGURE 1-41

3 Click Format on the Worksheet menu bar and then point to AutoFormat.

The Format menu displays (Figure 1-42).

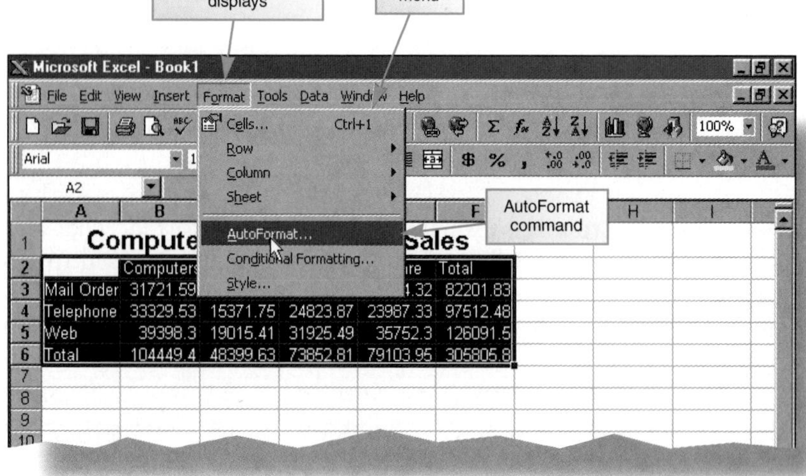

FIGURE 1-42

4 Click AutoFormat. Click Accounting 2 in the Table format list box. Point to the OK button.

Excel displays the AutoFormat dialog box (Figure 1-43). On the left side of the dialog box is the Table format list box with the Table format name, Accounting 2, highlighted. In the Sample area of the dialog box is a sample of the format that corresponds to the highlighted Table format name, Accounting 2.

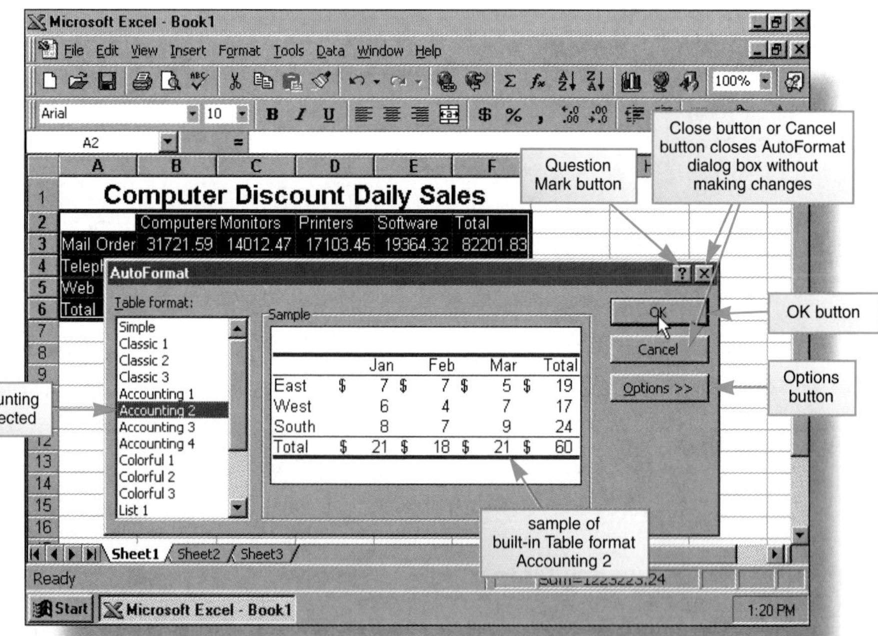

FIGURE 1-43

5 Click the OK button. Select cell A8 to deselect the range A2:F6.

Excel displays the worksheet with the range A2:F6 using the customized format, Accounting 2 (Figure 1-44).

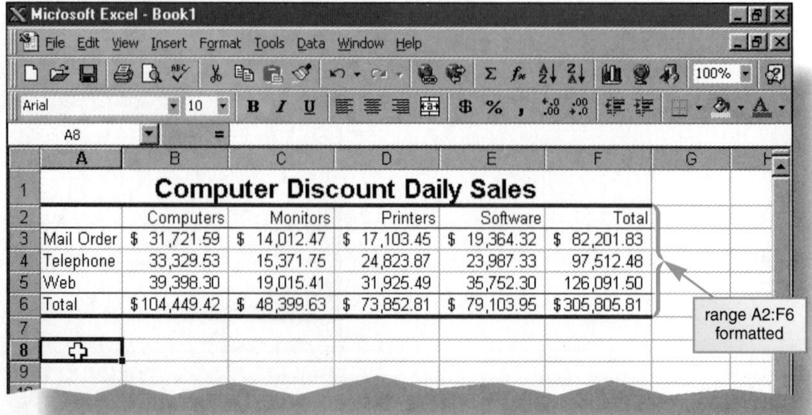

FIGURE 1-44

Excel provides 17 customized format styles from which to choose. Each format style has different characteristics. The format characteristics associated with the customized format, Accounting 2 (Figure 1-44), include right-alignment of column titles, numbers displayed as dollars and cents with comma separators, numbers aligned on the decimal point, dollar signs in the first row of numbers and in the total row, and top and bottom rows assigned borders. The width of column A also has been decreased so that the longest row title, Mail Order, just fits in the column.

The AutoFormat dialog box in Figure 1-43 includes five buttons. On the rightmost side of the title bar is the Close button. Use the **Close button** to terminate current activity without making changes. You also can use the **Cancel button**, immediately below the **OK button**, for this purpose. Use the **Question Mark button**, to obtain Help on any box or button located in the dialog box. The **Options button** allows you to select specific formats to assign as part of the customized format.

The worksheet now is complete. The next step is to chart the daily sales for the four product groups. To create the chart, you must select the cell in the upper-left corner of the range to chart. In this case, you must select cell A2 to make it the active cell. To select cell A2, you can move the mouse pointer to it and click. This is the procedure used in previous examples. You also can use the Name box to select a cell as described in the next section.

More *About*
Customizing the AutoFormat

The Options button on the right side of the AutoFormat dialog box in Figure 1-43 allows you to modify any of the formats associated with a customized format. If you assign two different customized formats to a range, Excel does not remove the assigned format from the range; it simply adds the second customized format to the first. Thus, if you decide to change a customized format, first select the range, click Clear on the Edit menu, and then click Formats on the submenu.

Using the Name Box to Select a Cell

The **Name box** is located on the left side of the formula bar. To select any cell, click the Name box and enter the cell reference of the cell you want to select. The following steps show how to select cell A2.

To Use the Name Box to Select a Cell

1 **Click the Name box in the formula bar. Type** a2 **in the Name box.**

Even though cell A8 is the active cell, the Name box displays the typed cell reference a2 (Figure 1-45).

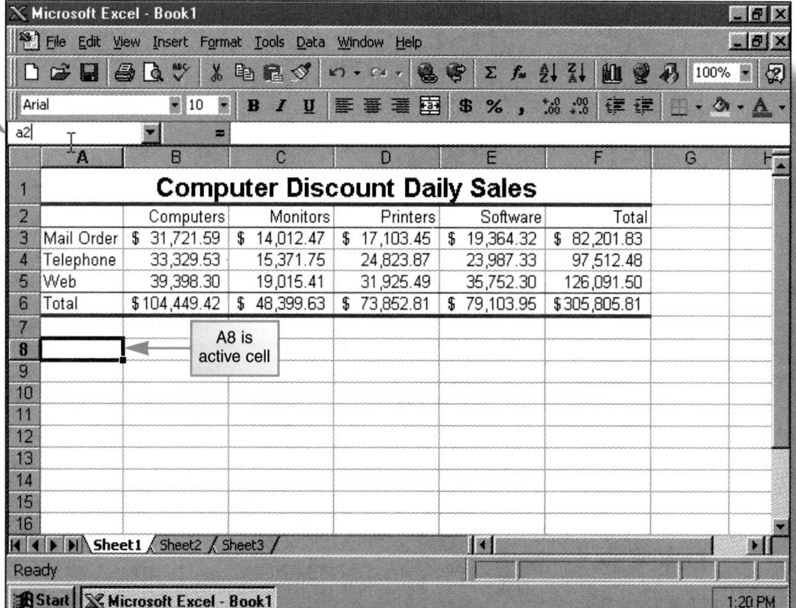

FIGURE 1-45

2 **Press the ENTER key.**

Excel changes the active cell from cell A8 to cell A2 (Figure 1-46).

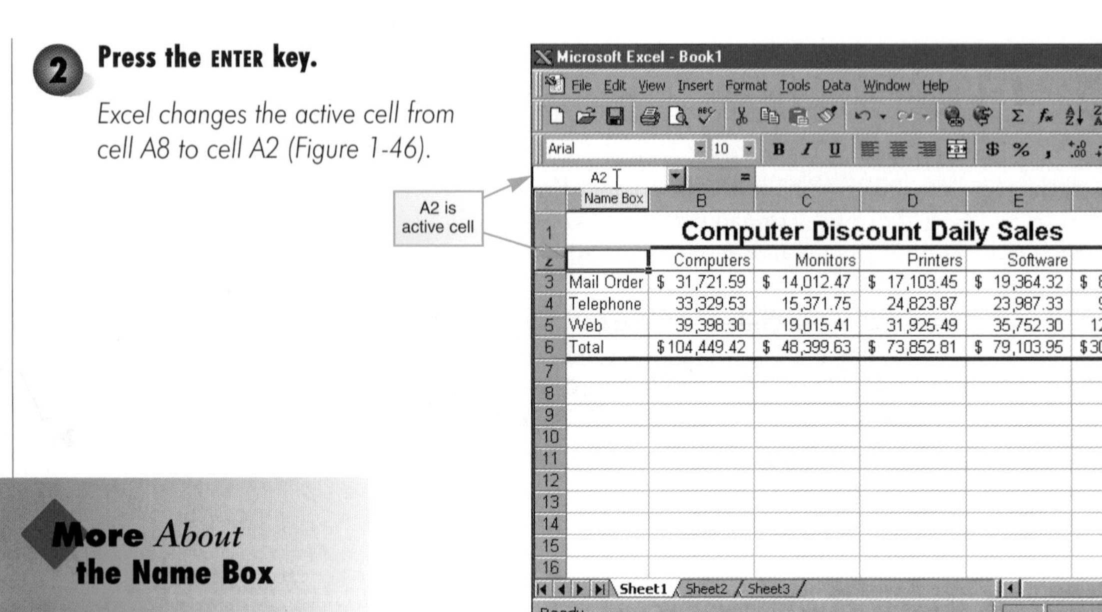

FIGURE 1-46

More *About* **the Name Box**

If you repeatedly select certain cells in a worksheet, consider naming the cells in the Name box. Select the cells one at a time and then type a name in the Name box for each, such as Company Total for cell F6 in Figure 1-45. Then, when you want to select one of the named cells, click the Name box arrow and then click the cell name in the Name box list box.

As you will see in later projects, besides using the Name box to select any cell in a worksheet, you also can use it to assign names to a cell or range of cells.

Excel supports several additional ways to select a cell, as summarized in Table 1-3.

Table 1-3

KEY, BOX, OR COMMAND	FUNCTION
ALT+PAGE DOWN	Selects the cell one window to the right and moves the window accordingly
ALT+PAGE UP	Selects the cell one window to the left and moves the window accordingly
ARROW	Selects the adjacent cell in the direction of the arrow on the key
CTRL+ARROW	Selects the border cell of the worksheet in combination with the arrow keys and moves the window accordingly. For example, to select the rightmost cell in the row that contains the active cell, press CTRL+RIGHT ARROW. You also can press the END key, release it, and then press the arrow key to accomplish the same task.
CTRL+HOME	Selects cell A1 or the cell one column and one row below and to the right of frozen titles and moves the window accordingly
Find command on Edit menu	Finds and selects a cell that contains specific contents that you enter in the Find dialog box. If necessary, Excel moves the window to display the cell. You can press SHIFT+F5 or CTRL+F to display the Find dialog box.
F5 or GoTo command on Edit menu	Selects the cell that corresponds to the cell reference you enter in the Go To dialog box and moves the window accordingly. You can press CTRL+G to display the Find dialog box.
HOME	Selects the cell at the beginning of the row that contains the active cell and moves the window accordingly
Name box	Selects the cell in the workbook that corresponds to the cell reference you enter in the Name box
PAGE DOWN	Selects the cell down one window from the active cell and moves the window accordingly
PAGE UP	Selects the cell up one window from the active cell and moves the window accordingly

Adding a 3-D Column Chart to the Worksheet

The 3-D Column chart drawn by Excel in this project is based on the data in the daily sales worksheet (Figure 1-47). It is called an **embedded chart** because it is drawn on the same worksheet as the data.

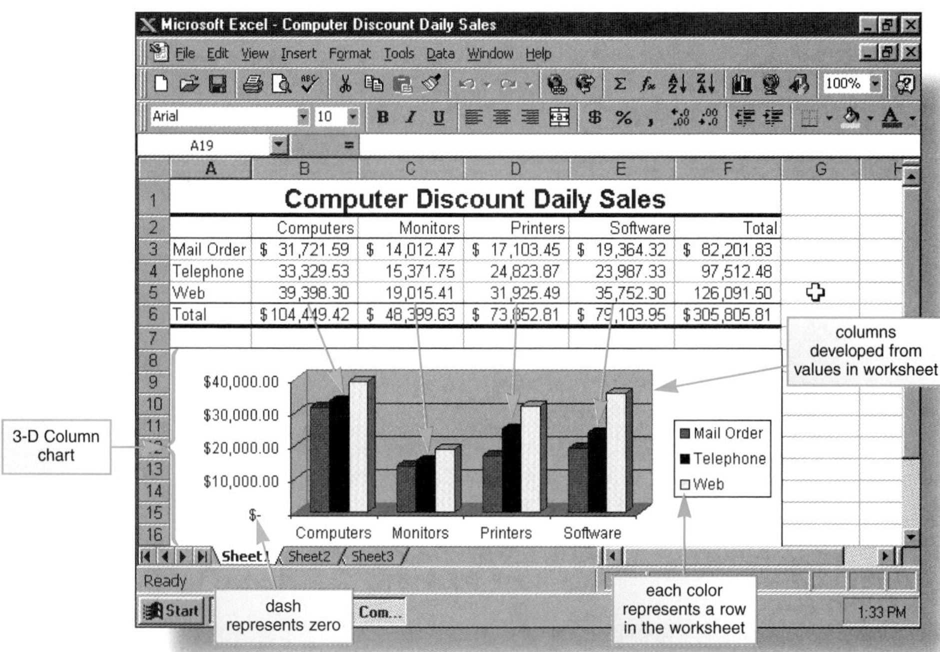

FIGURE 1-47

For the product Computers, the light blue column represents the sales by mail order ($31,721.59), the purple column represents the sales by Telephone ($33,329.53), and the light yellow column represents the sales by Web ($39,398.30). For the products Monitors, Printers, and Software, the columns follow the same color scheme to represent the comparable daily sales. The totals from the worksheet are not represented because the totals were not in the range specified for charting.

Excel derives the scale along the vertical axis (also called the **y-axis** or **value axis**) of the chart on the basis of the values in the worksheet. For example, no value in the range A2:E5 is less than zero or greater than $40,000.00. Excel also determines the $10,000.00 increments along the y-axis automatically. The format used by Excel for the numbers along the y-axis includes representing zero (0) with a dash (Figure 1-47).

To draw a chart like the one in Figure 1-47, select the range to chart, click the **Chart Wizard button** on the Standard toolbar, and select the type of chart. The area on the worksheet where the chart is drawn is called the **chart location**. In Figure 1-47, the chart is located immediately below the worksheet data.

Follow the detailed steps on the next page to draw a 3-D Column chart that compares the daily sales by channel for the four product groups.

To Add a 3-D Column Chart to the Worksheet

1 With cell A2 selected, position the block plus sign within the cell's border and drag the mouse pointer to the lower-right corner cell (cell E5) of the range to chart (A2:E5). Point to the Chart Wizard button on the Standard toolbar.

Excel highlights the range to chart (Figure 1-48).

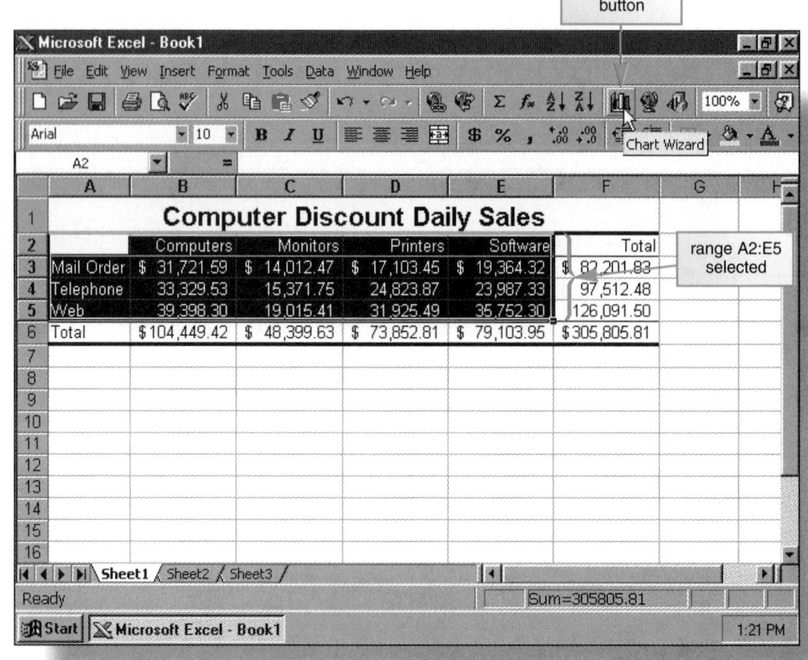

FIGURE 1-48

2 Click the Chart Wizard button.

The Chart Wizard – Step 1 of 4 – Chart Type dialog box displays.

3 With Column selected in the Chart type list, click the 3-D Column chart sub-type (column 1, row 2) in the Chart sub-type area. Point to the Finish button.

Column is highlighted in the Chart type list and 3-D Column is highlighted in the Chart sub-type area (Figure 1-49).

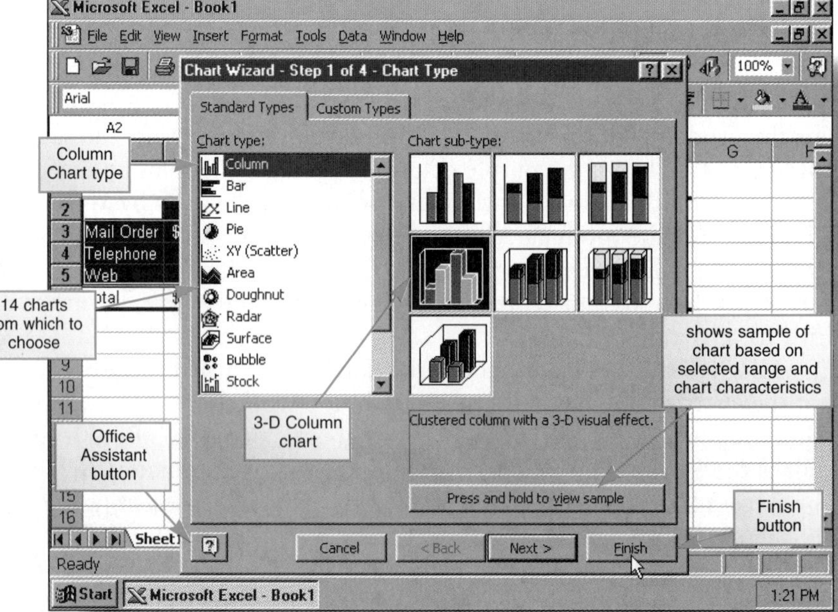

FIGURE 1-49

4 **Click the Finish button.**

Excel draws a 3-D Column chart comparing the daily sales of the four product groups by channel (Figure 1-50) and the Chart menu bar displays. The chart displays in the middle of the window in a ***selection rectangle****. The small* ***sizing handles*** *at the corners and along the sides of the selection rectangle indicate the chart is selected. When the chart is selected, you can drag the chart to any location on the worksheet. You also can resize the chart by dragging the sizing handles.*

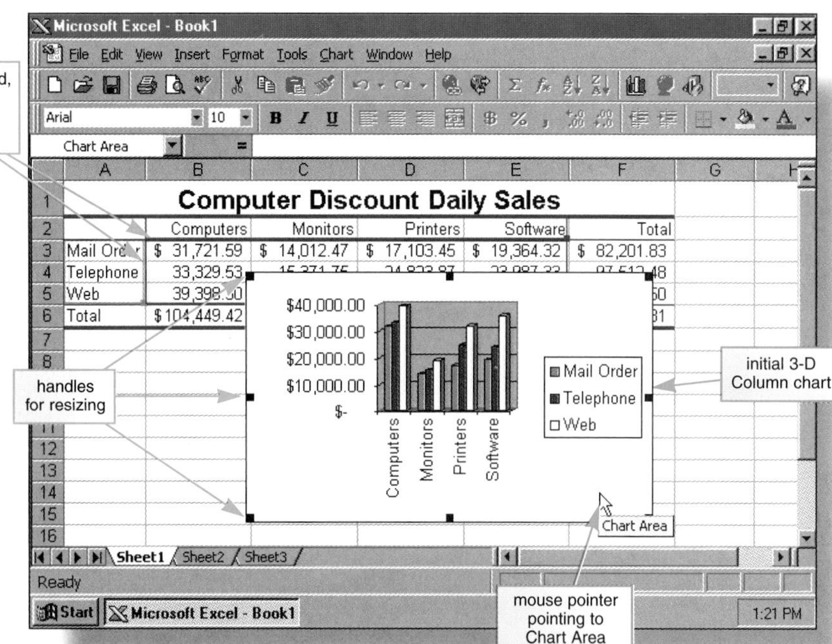

FIGURE 1-50

5 **Point to an open area in the lower-right section of the chart area so the ScreenTip, Chart Area, displays (Figure 1-50). Drag the chart down and to the left to position the upper-left corner of the dotted line rectangle over the upper-left corner of cell A8.**

Excel displays a dotted line rectangle showing the new chart location (Figure 1-51). As you drag the selected chart, the mouse pointer changes to a cross hair with four arrowheads.

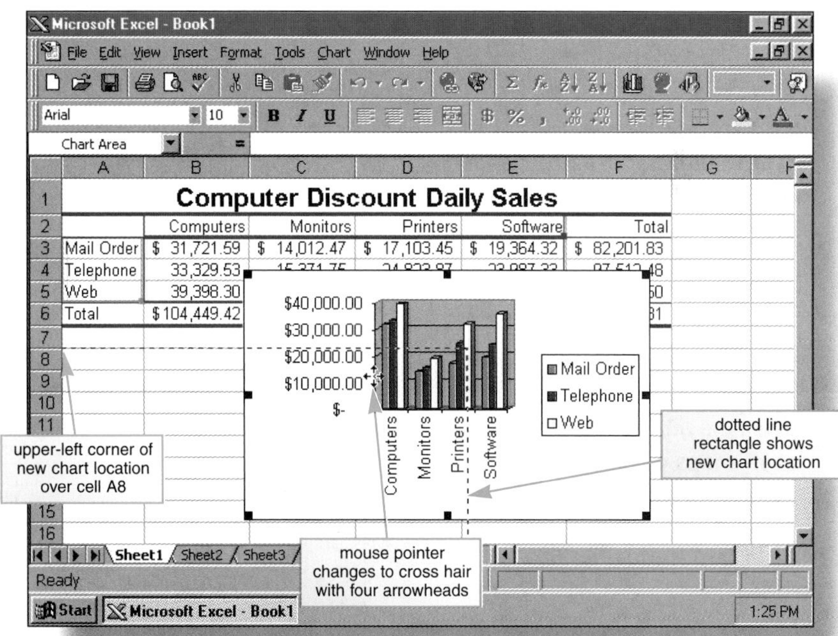

FIGURE 1-51

6 **Release the left mouse button. Point to the sizing handle in the middle of the lower border of the chart.**

The chart displays in a new location (Figure 1-52). The mouse pointer changes to a vertical line with two arrowheads.

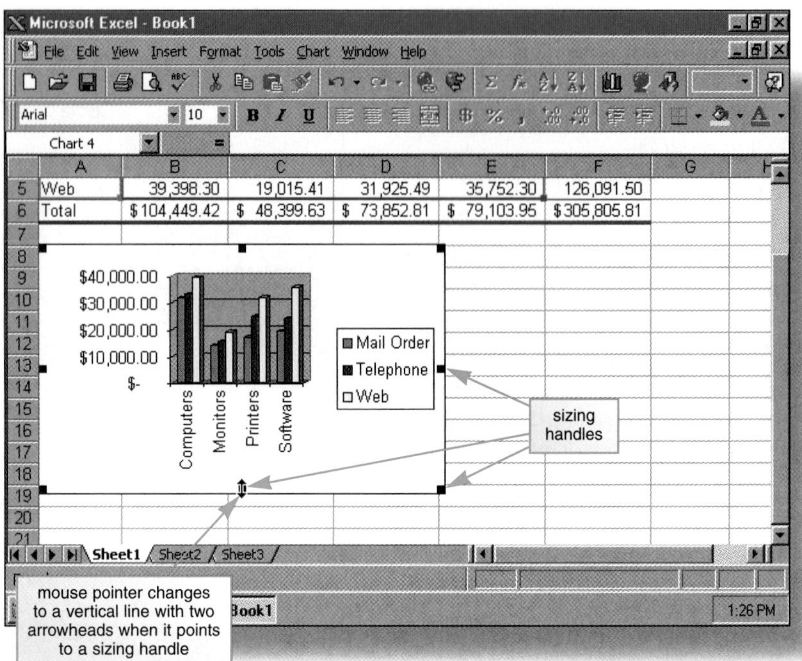

FIGURE 1-52

7 **While holding down the ALT key, drag the sizing handle to the bottom gridline of row 17. Release the left mouse button. While holding down the ALT key, drag the sizing handle in the middle of the right border of the chart location to the right gridline of column F.**

The dotted line shows the new chart location (Figure 1-53). Holding down the ALT key while you drag a chart ***snaps*** *(aligns) the new border to the worksheet gridlines.*

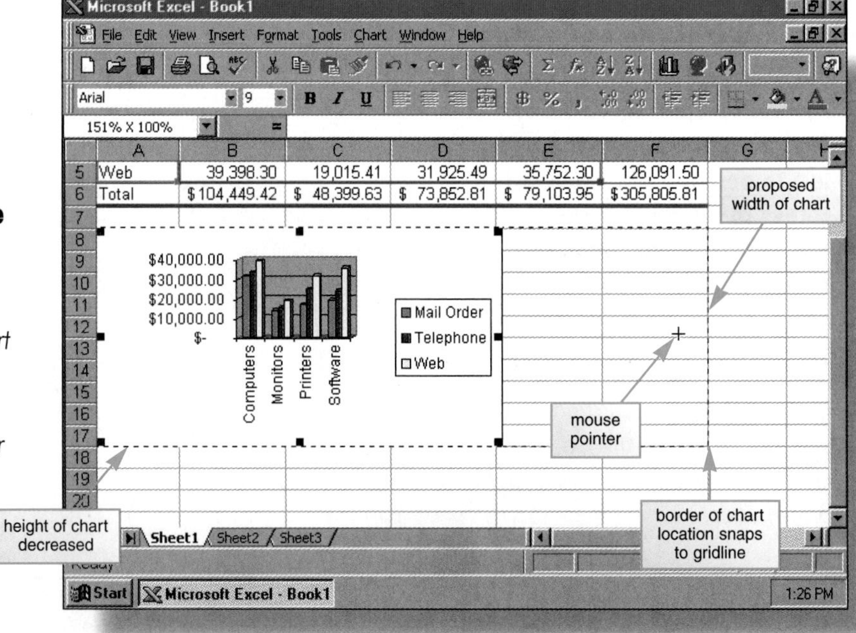

FIGURE 1-53

8 Release the left mouse button and then the ALT key. Select any cell outside the Chart Area to deselect the chart. Use the vertical scroll bar to scroll to the top of the worksheet.

The new chart location extends from the top of cell A8 to the bottom of cell F17 (Figure 1-54).

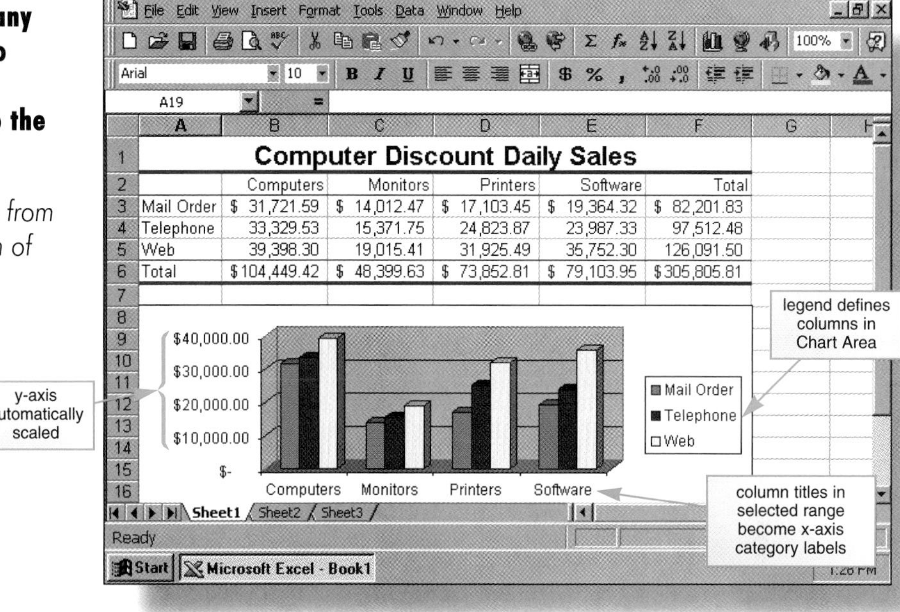

FIGURE 1-54

Other Ways

1. Select range, press F11
2. Select range, on Insert menu click Chart

The embedded 3-D Column chart in Figure 1-54 compares the three sales channels for each of the four product groups. It also allows you to compare daily sales between the product groups. Excel automatically selects the entries in the topmost row of the range (row 2) as the titles for the horizontal axis (also called the **x-axis** or **category axis**) and draws a column for each of the 12 cells in the range containing numbers. The small box to the right of the column chart in Figure 1-54 contains the legend. The **legend** identifies each bar in the chart. Excel automatically selects the leftmost column of the range (column A) as titles within the legend. As indicated earlier, it also automatically scales the y-axis on the basis of the magnitude of the numbers in the chart range.

Excel offers 14 different chart types (Figure 1-49 on page E 1.36). The **default chart type** is the chart Excel draws if you click the Finish button in the first Chart Wizard dialog box. When you install Excel on a computer, the default chart type is the 2-D (two-dimensional) Column chart.

More *About* Changing the Chart Type

Excel has 14 chart types from which to choose. You can change the embedded 3-D Column chart to another type by double-clicking the chart location. When a heavy gray border surrounds the chart location, right-click the chart and then click Chart Type on the shortcut menu. You also can use the shortcut menu to format the chart to make it look more professional. Subsequent projects will discuss changing charts, sizing charts, adding text to charts, and drawing a chart on a chart sheet.

Saving a Workbook

While you are building a workbook, the computer stores it in memory. If the computer is turned off or if you lose electrical power, the workbook is lost. Hence, you must save on a floppy disk any workbook that you will use later. A saved workbook is referred to as a **file** or **workbook**. The steps on the next page illustrate how to save a workbook on a floppy disk in drive A using the Save button on the Standard toolbar.

To Save a Workbook

1 **With a floppy disk in drive A, click the Save button on the Standard toolbar.**

Excel responds by displaying the Save As dialog box (Figure 1-55). The default Save in folder is My Documents, the default file name is Book1, and the file type is Microsoft Excel Workbook. The buttons next to the Save in box are used to select folders and change the display of file names and other information in the Save As dialog box.

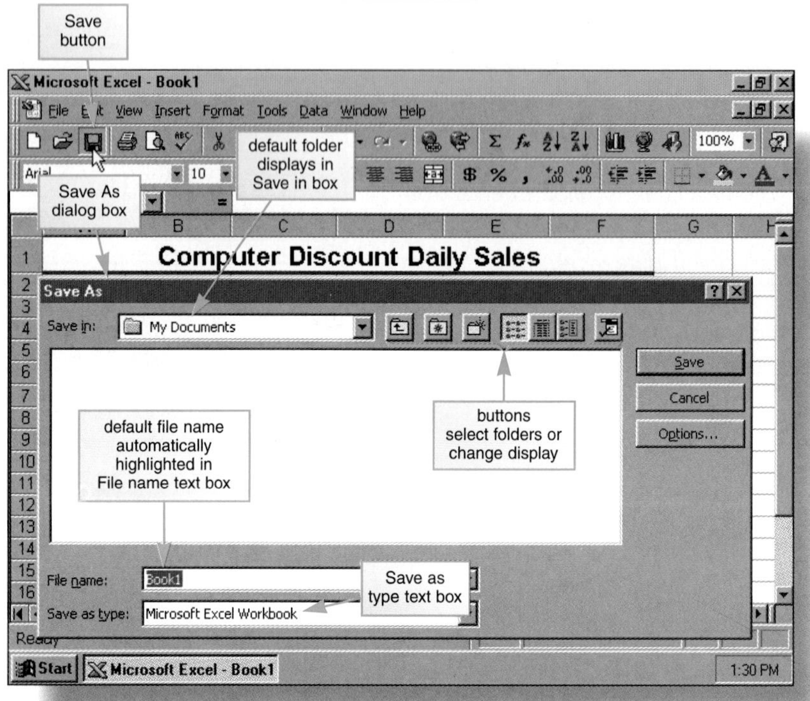

FIGURE 1-55

2 **Type** `Computer Discount Daily Sales` **in the File name text box.**

The file name Computer Discount Daily Sales replaces Book1 in the File name text box (Figure 1-56). A **file name** *can be up to 255 characters and can include spaces.*

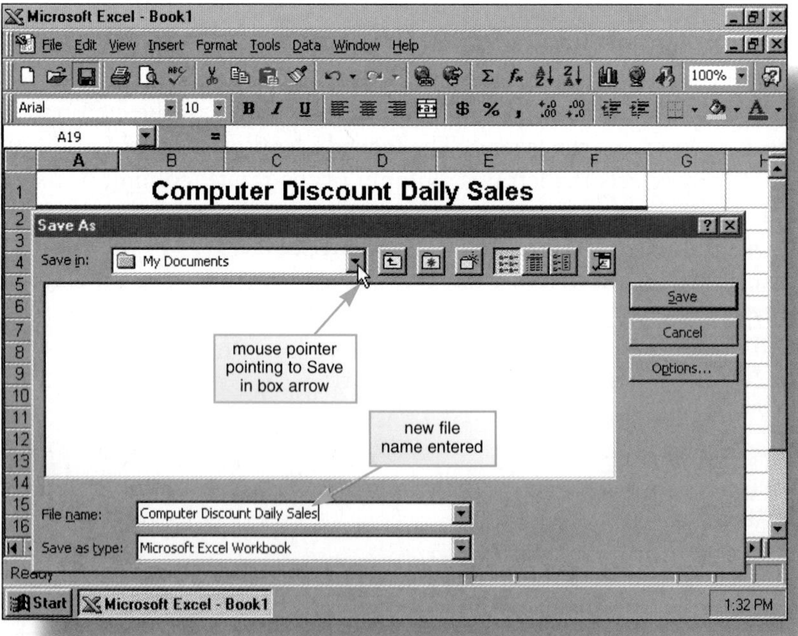

FIGURE 1-56

3 **Click the Save in box arrow and then point to 3½ Floppy (A:).**

A list of available drives and folders displays (Figure 1-57).

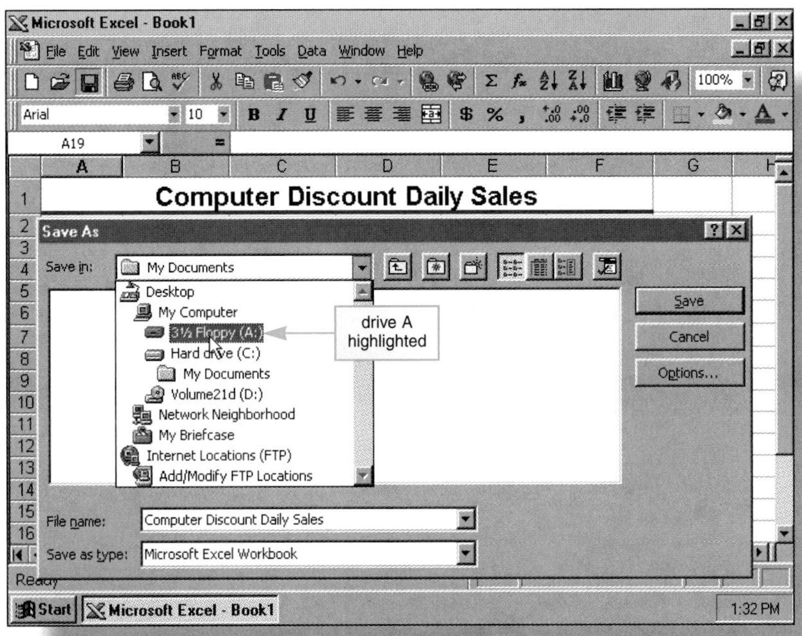

FIGURE 1-57

4 **Click 3½ Floppy (A:) and then point to the Save button.**

Drive A becomes the selected drive (Figure 1-58).

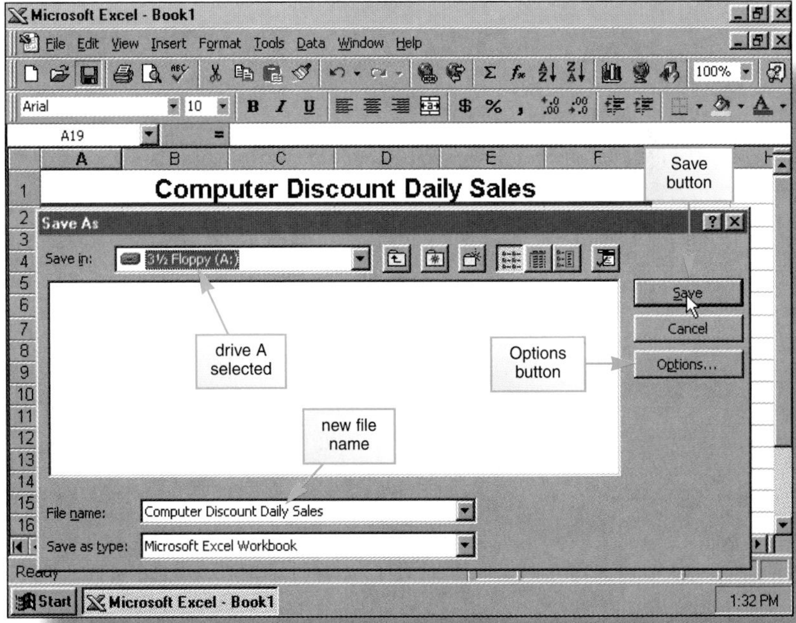

FIGURE 1-58

5 **Click the Save button.**

Excel saves the workbook on the floppy disk in drive A using the file name Computer Discount Daily Sales.xls. Excel automatically appends the extension .xls to the file name you entered in Step 2, which stands for Excel workbook. Although the Computer Discount Daily Sales workbook is saved on a floppy disk, it also remains in memory and displays on the screen (Figure 1-59). Notice the file name in the title bar.

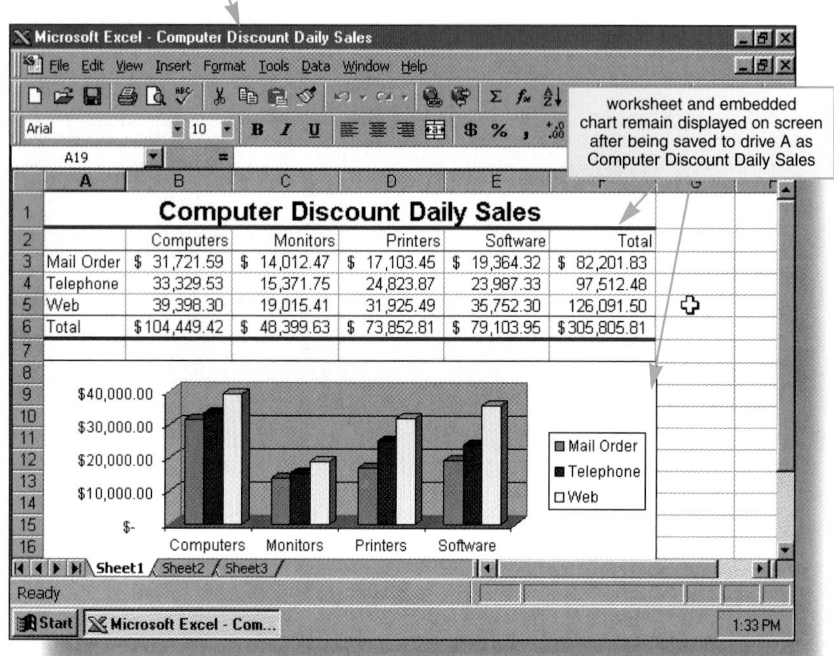

FIGURE 1-59

OtherWays

1. Press CTRL+S, type file name, select drive or folder, click OK button
2. Right-click document Control-menu icon on menu bar, click Save As on shortcut menu, type file name, select drive or folder, click OK button
3. On File menu click Save As, type file name, select drive or folder, click OK button

While Excel is saving the workbook, it momentarily changes the word Ready on the status bar to Saving. It also displays a horizontal bar on the status bar indicating the amount of the workbook saved. After the save operation is complete, Excel changes the name of the workbook in the title bar from Book1 to Computer Discount Daily Sales (Figure 1-59).

The **Options button** in the Save As dialog box (Figure 1-58 on the previous page), allows you to save a backup copy of the workbook or create a password to limit access to the workbook. Saving a **backup workbook** means that each time you save a workbook, Excel copies the current version of the workbook on disk to a file with the same name, but with a **.bak** extension. Thus, the second time you save a workbook, and each time thereafter, you will have two workbooks on disk with the same name, one with an extension of .xls and the other with an extension of .bak. In the case of a power failure or some other problem, use the backup version (.bak) to restore your work.

You also can use the Options button to assign a **password** to your workbook so others cannot open it. A password is case sensitive and can be up to 15 characters long. **Case sensitive** means Excel can differentiate between uppercase and lowercase letters. If you assign a password and forget the password, you cannot access the workbook.

The seven buttons at the top and to the right in the Save As dialog box (Figure 1-58) and their functions are summarized in Table 1-4.

More About Saving a Worksheet as a Web Page

Excel allows you to save a worksheet in HTML format so you can post it on the World Wide Web. Click Save as HTML on the File menu and follow the instructions in the Internet Assistant Wizard dialog box.

Table 1-4

BUTTON	BUTTON NAME	FUNCTION
	Up One Level	Displays contents of next level up folder
	Look In Favorites	Displays contents of Favorites folder
	Create New Folder	Creates new folder
	List	Displays file names in list format with no details
	Details	Displays file names in list format with details
	Properties	Displays properties of highlighted file
	Commands and Settings	Allows you to control settings, such as the sort order of file names

Printing the Worksheet

Once you have created the worksheet and saved it on disk, you might want to print it. A printed version of the worksheet is called a **hard copy** or **printout**.

You might want a printout for several reasons. First, to present the worksheet and chart to someone who does not have access to a computer, it must be in printed form. A printout, for example, can be handed out in a management meeting about daily sales. In addition, worksheets and charts often are kept for reference by persons other than those who prepare them. In many cases, worksheets and charts are printed and kept in binders for use by others. This section describes how to print a worksheet and an embedded chart.

More About Printing

Interested in saving trees? Rather than printing a worksheet over and over until it's right, you can preview the printout on your screen, make adjustments to the worksheet, and then print it only when it appears exactly as you want. The Print Preview button is immediately to the right of the Print button on the Standard toolbar. Clicking it displays an onscreen image of how the printout will appear. Each time you preview rather than print, you save paper destined for the wastepaper basket, which, in turn, saves trees.

Steps To Print a Worksheet

1 **Ready the printer according to the printer instructions. Point to the Print button on the Standard toolbar (Figure 1-60).**

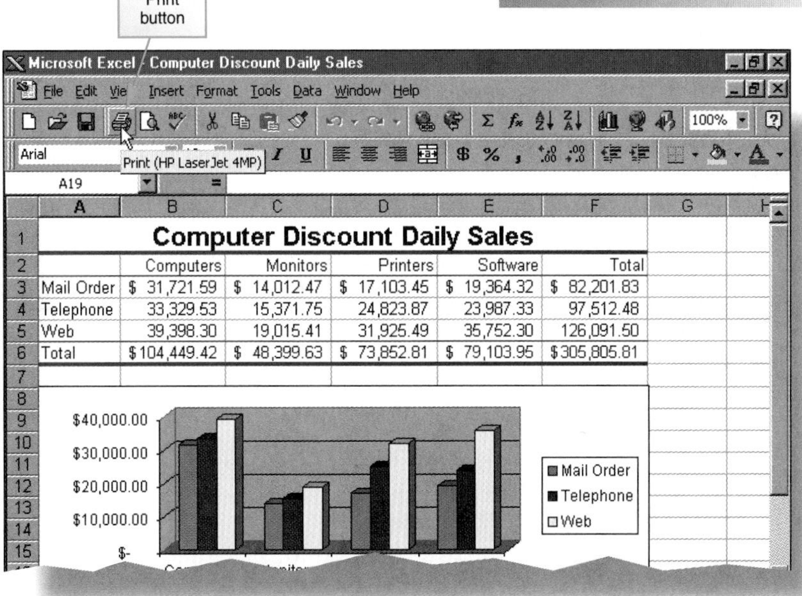

FIGURE 1-60

2 **Click the Print button.**

Excel displays the ***Printing dialog box*** *(Figure 1-61) that allows you to cancel the print job at any time while the system is sending the worksheet and chart image to the printer. Several seconds after the Printing dialog box disappears, the worksheet and chart begin printing on the printer.*

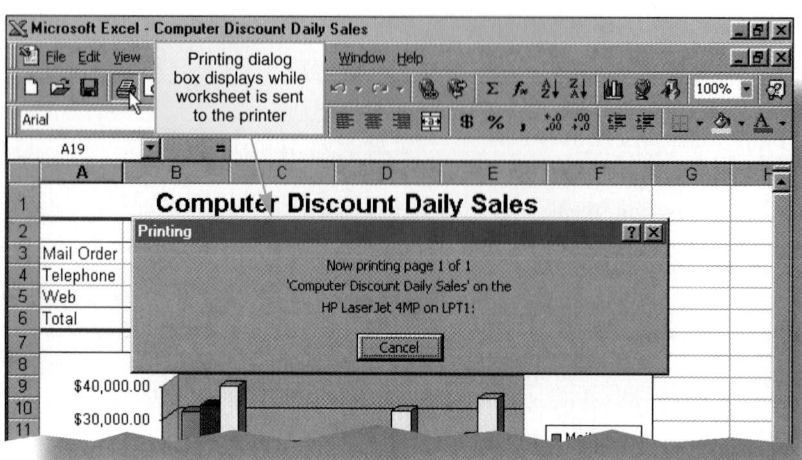

FIGURE 1-61

3 **When the printer stops printing the worksheet and the chart, retrieve the printout (Figure 1-62).**

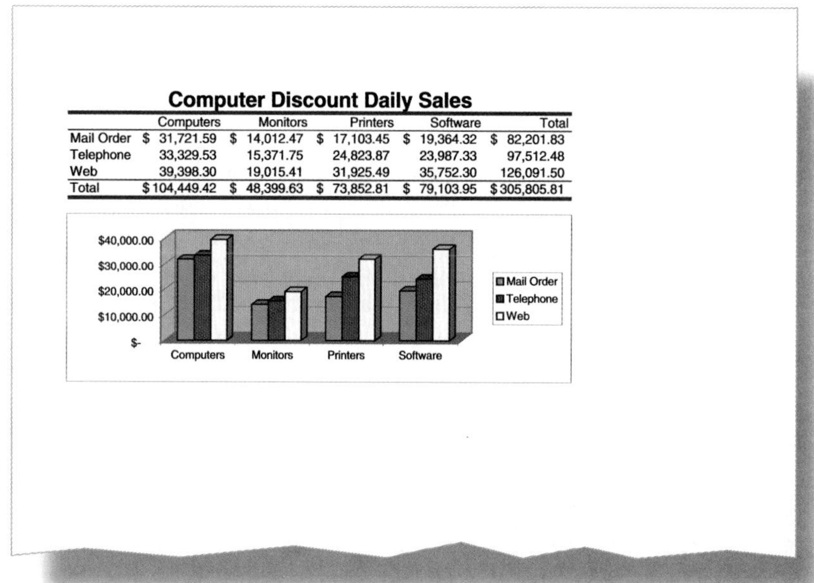

Computer Discount Daily Sales

	Computers	Monitors	Printers	Software	Total
Mail Order	$ 31,721.59	$ 14,012.47	$ 17,103.45	$ 19,364.32	$ 82,201.83
Telephone	33,329.53	15,371.75	24,823.87	23,987.33	97,512.48
Web	39,398.30	19,015.41	31,925.49	35,752.30	126,091.50
Total	$ 104,449.42	$ 48,399.63	$ 73,852.81	$ 79,103.95	$ 305,805.81

FIGURE 1-62

OtherWays

1. Press CTRL+P, click OK button
2. On File menu click Print, click OK button
3. Right-click document Control-menu icon on menu bar, click Print, click OK button

Prior to clicking the Print button, you can select which columns and rows in the worksheet to print. The range of cells you choose to print is called the **print area.** If you don't select a print area, as was the case in the previous set of steps, Excel automatically selects a print area on the basis of used cells. As you shall see in future projects, Excel has many different print options, such as allowing you to preview the printout on the screen to see if the printout is satisfactory prior to sending it to the printer. Several of these print options are discussed in Project 2.

Quitting Excel

After you build, save, and print the worksheet and chart, Project 1 is complete. To quit Excel, complete the following steps.

Steps To Quit Excel

1 Point to the Close button on the right side of the title bar (Figure 1-63).

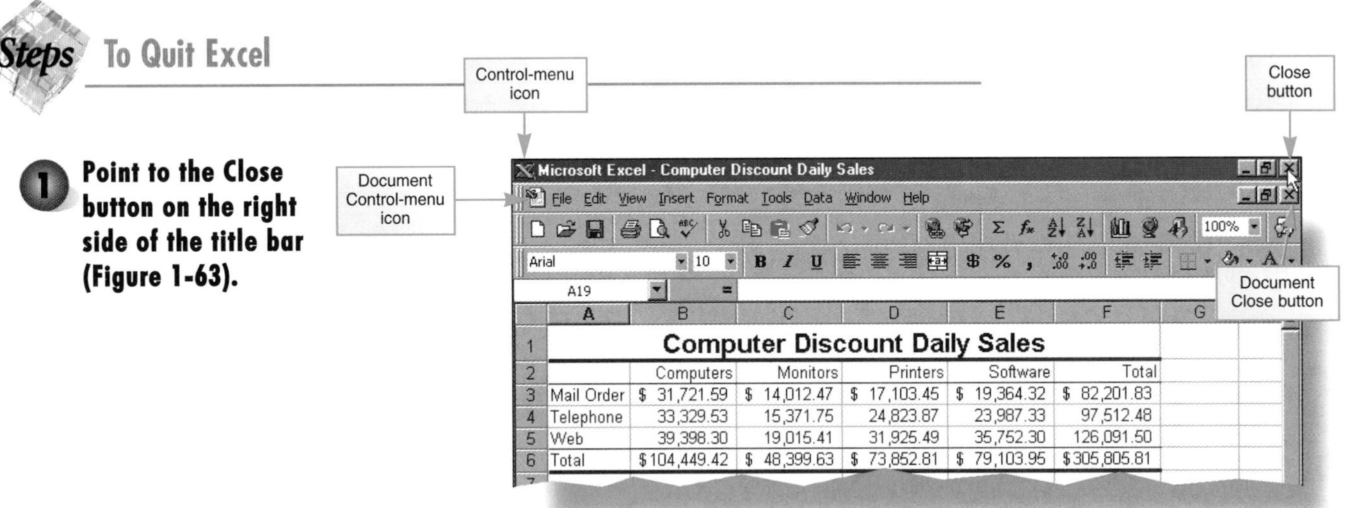

	Computers	Monitors	Printers	Software	Total
Mail Order	$ 31,721.59	$ 14,012.47	$ 17,103.45	$ 19,364.32	$ 82,201.83
Telephone	33,329.53	15,371.75	24,823.87	23,987.33	97,512.48
Web	39,398.30	19,015.41	31,925.49	35,752.30	126,091.50
Total	$104,449.42	$ 48,399.63	$ 73,852.81	$ 79,103.95	$305,805.81

FIGURE 1-63

2 Click the Close button.

If you made changes to the workbook, Microsoft Excel dialog box displays the question, Do you want to save the changes you made to 'Computer Discount Daily Sales.xls'? (Figure 1-64). Click the Yes button to save the changes before quitting Excel. Click the No button to quit Excel without saving the changes. Click the Cancel button to stop the Exit command and return to the worksheet.

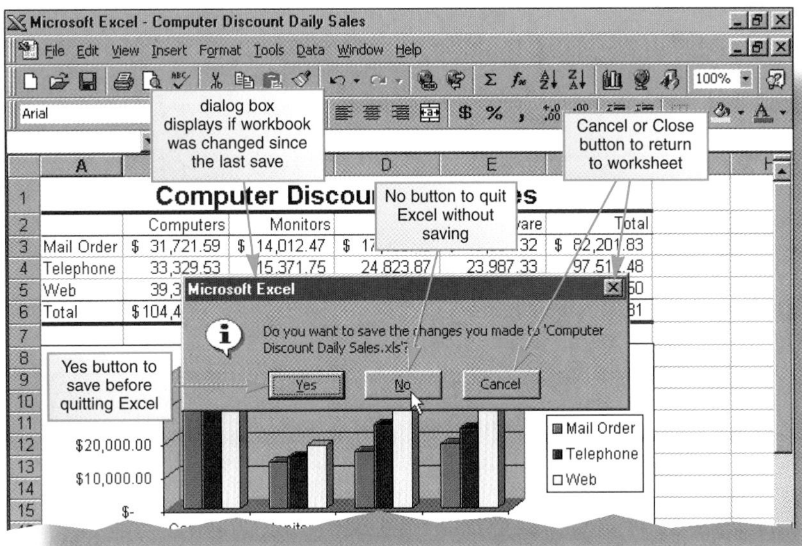

FIGURE 1-64

OtherWays

1. Double-click Control-menu icon
2. Right-click Microsoft Excel button on taskbar, click Close
3. On File menu click Exit

In Figure 1-63, you can see that two Close buttons and two Control-menu icons display. The Close button and Control-menu icon on the title bar close Excel. The Close button and Control-menu icon on the menu bar close the workbook.

Starting Excel and Opening a Workbook

Once you have created and saved a workbook, you often will have reason to retrieve it from a floppy disk. For example, you might want to review the calculations on the worksheet and enter additional or revised data to it. The steps on the next page assume Excel is not running.

To Start Excel and Open a Workbook

1. **With your floppy disk in drive A, click the Start button and then point to Open Office Document (Figure 1-65).**

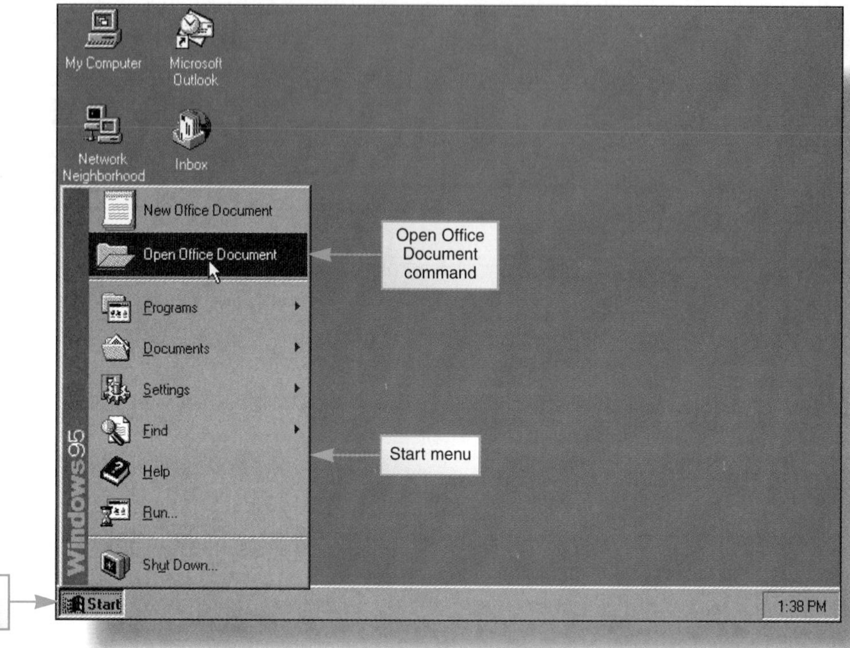

FIGURE 1-65

2. **Click Open Office Document. If necessary, click the Look in box arrow and then click 3½ Floppy (A:).**

The Open Office Document dialog box displays (Figure 1-66).

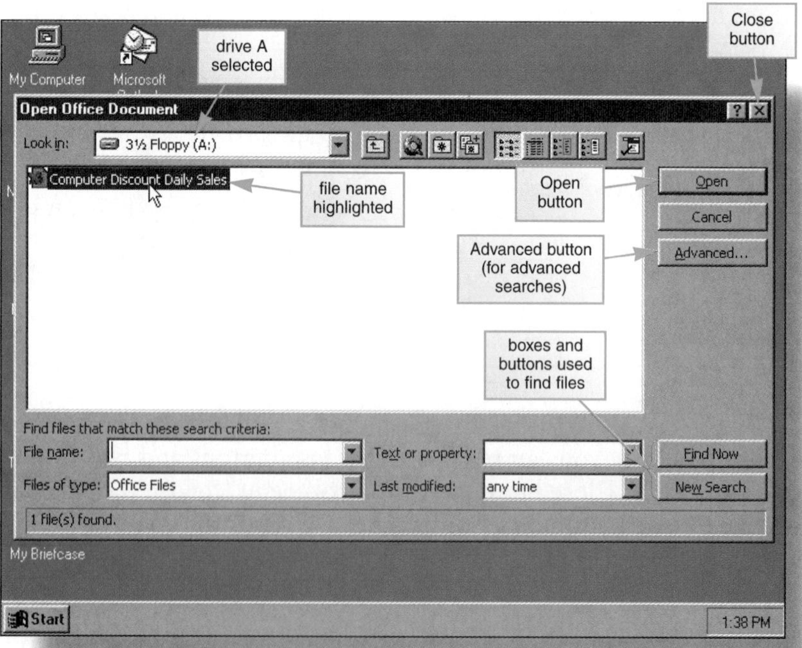

FIGURE 1-66

3 Double-click the file name Computer Discount Daily Sales.

Excel starts, opens the workbook Computer Discount Daily Sales.xls from drive A, and displays it on the screen (Figure 1-67). An alternative to double-clicking the file name is to click it and then click the Open button.

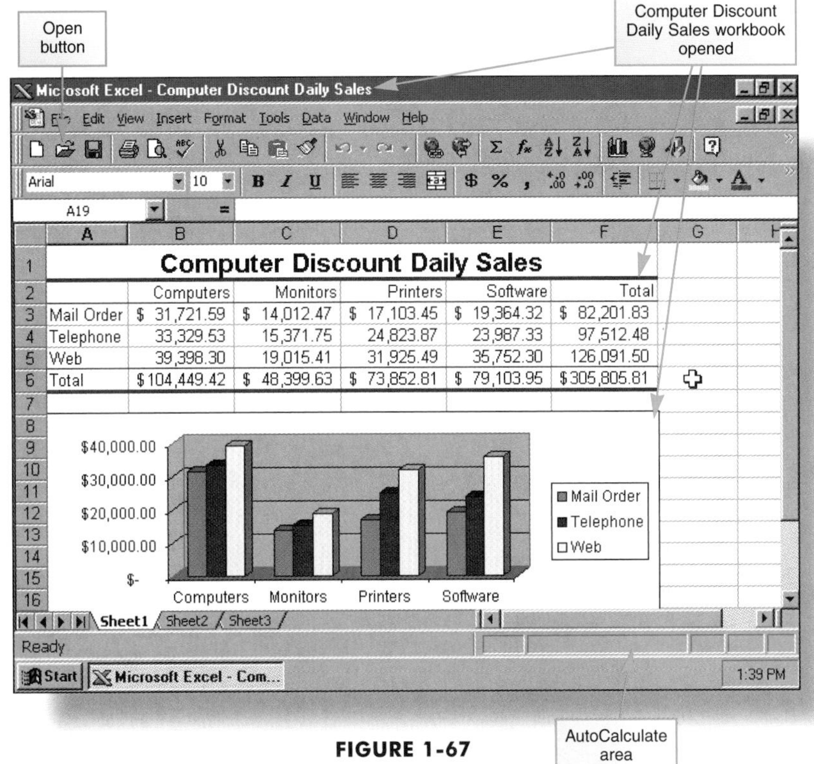

FIGURE 1-67

AutoCalculate

You easily can obtain a total, an average, or other information about the numbers in a range by using the AutoCalculate area on the status bar (Figure 1-67). All you need do is select the range of cells containing the numbers you want to check. Next, right-click the AutoCalculate area to display the shortcut menu (Figure 1-68 on the next page). The recessed check mark to the left of the active function (Sum) indicates that the sum of the selected range displays. The six function commands on the AutoCalculate shortcut menu are described in Table 1-5.

Table 1-5

COMMAND	FUNCTION
Average	**Displays the average of the numbers in the selected range**
Count	**Displays the number of nonblank cells in the selected range**
Count Nums	**Displays the number of cells containing numbers in the selected range**
Max	**Displays the greatest value in the selected range**
Min	**Displays the least value in the selected range**
Sum	**Displays the sum of the numbers in the selected range**

The steps on the next page show how to display the average daily sales by mail order.

More *About* Excel's Compatibility with Other Software Products

Do you have files that were created using another software package? Excel has the capability to save or open Lotus 1-2-3, Quattro Pro, or Microsoft Works files. It's easy. All you have to do is select the file type on the Save As or Open dialog boxes.

To Use the AutoCalculate Area to Determine an Average

Select the range B3:E3. Point to the AutoCalculate area on the status bar and then right-click.

As shown in Figure 1-68, the sum of the numbers in the range B3:E3 displays ($82,201.83) because Sum is active in the AutoCalculate area (you may see a total other than the Sum in your AutoCalculate area). The shortcut menu listing the various types of functions displays over the AutoCalculate area.

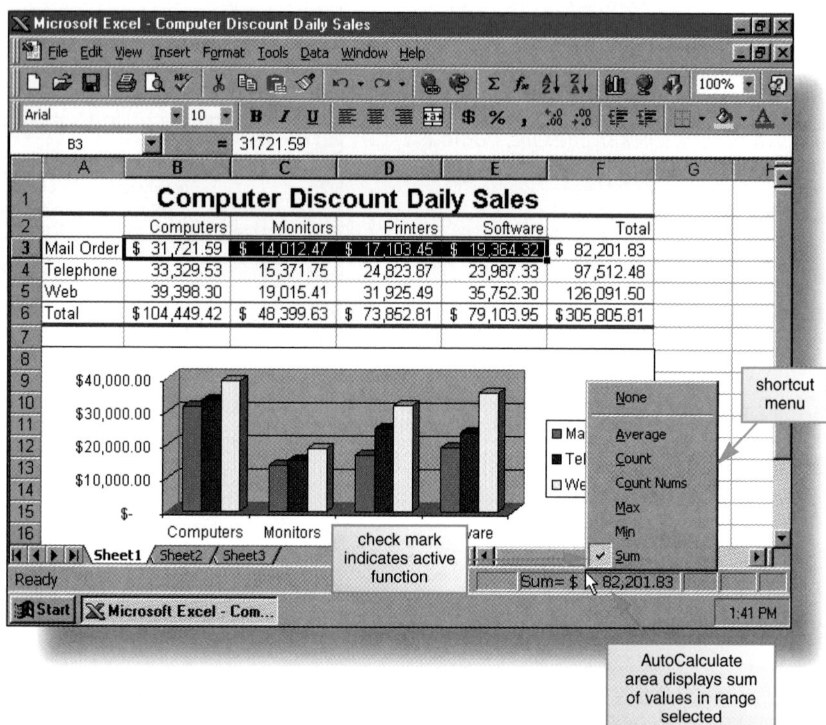

FIGURE 1-68

Click Average on the shortcut menu.

The average of the numbers in the range B3:E3 displays in the AutoCalculate area (Figure 1-69).

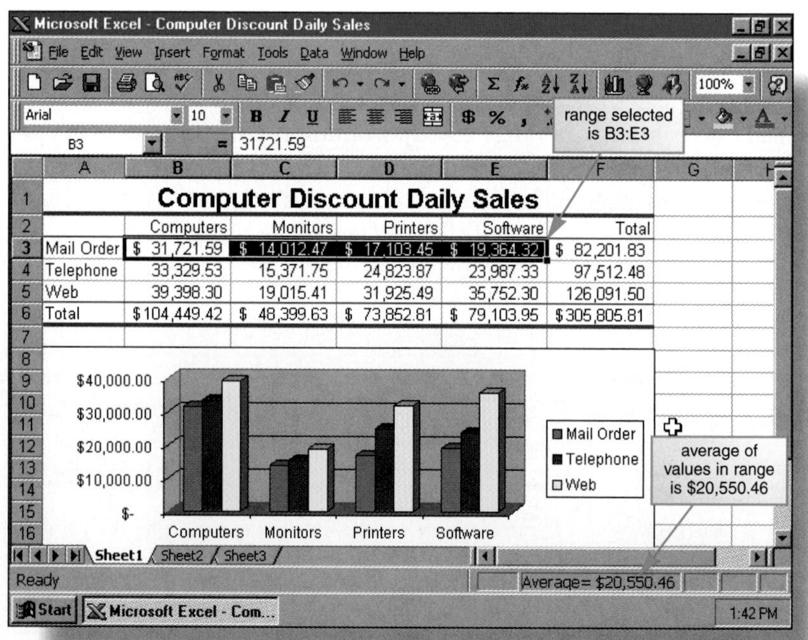

FIGURE 1-69

To change to any one of the other five functions for the range B3:E3, right-click the AutoCalculate area. Then click the desired function. Before continuing, change the total in the AutoCalculate area to Sum by pointing to the AutoCalculate area, right-clicking, and then clicking Sum on the shortcut menu.

Correcting Errors

You can correct errors on a worksheet using one of several methods. The one you choose will depend on the extent of the error and whether you notice it while typing the data or after you have entered the incorrect data into the cell.

More About Correcting Errors

Learning how to correct errors in a worksheet is critical to becoming proficient in Excel. Thus, carefully review this section on how to correct errors prior to entering data in a cell, how to perform in-cell editing, how to undo the last entry, and how to clear cells.

Correcting Errors Prior to Entering Data into a Cell

If you notice an error prior to entering data into a cell, use one of the following methods:

1. Press the BACKSPACE key to erase the portion in error and then type the correct characters; or
2. If the error is a major one, click the Cancel box or press the ESC key to erase the entire entry and then reenter the data from the beginning.

In-Cell Editing

If you find an error in the worksheet after entering the data, you can correct the error in one of two ways:

More About In-Cell Editing

An alternative to double-clicking the cell to edit is to select the cell and press F2.

1. If the entry is short, select the cell, retype the entry correctly, and click the Enter box or press the ENTER key. The new entry will replace the old entry.
2. If the entry in the cell is long and the errors are minor, the **Edit mode** may be a better choice. Use the Edit mode as described below.
   a. Double-click the cell containing the error. Excel switches to Edit mode, the active cell contents display in the formula bar, and a flashing insertion point displays in the active cell (Figure 1-70). This editing procedure is called **in-cell editing** because you can edit the contents directly in the cell. The active cell contents also display in the formula bar.

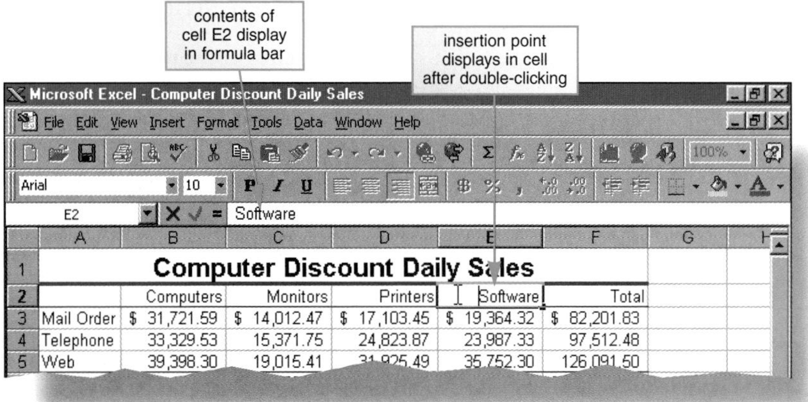

FIGURE 1-70

   b. Make your changes, as specified below.
      (1) To insert between two characters, place the insertion point between the two characters and begin typing. Excel inserts the new characters at the location of the insertion point.
      (2) To delete a character in the cell, move the insertion point to the left of the character you want to delete and press the **DELETE key**, or place the insertion point to the right of the character you want to delete and press the BACKSPACE key. You also can use the mouse to drag over the character or adjacent characters you want to delete and then press the DELETE key or click the **Cut button** on the Standard toolbar.

More About Editing the Contents of a Cell

Rather than using in-cell editing, you can select the cell and then click the formula bar to edit the contents.

When you are finished editing an entry, click the Enter box or press the ENTER key.

When Excel enters the Edit mode, the keyboard is usually in Insert mode. In **Insert mode**, as you type a character, Excel inserts the character and moves all characters to the right of the typed character one position to the right. You can change to Overtype mode by pressing the INSERT key. In **Overtype mode**, Excel overtypes the character to the right of the insertion point. The **INSERT key** toggles the keyboard between Insert mode and Overtype mode.

While in Edit mode, you may have reason to move the insertion point to various points in the cell, select portions of the data in the cell, or switch from inserting characters to overtyping characters. Table 1-6 summarizes the most common tasks used during in-cell editing.

Table 1-6

TASK	MOUSE	KEYBOARD
Move the insertion point to the beginning of data in a cell	Point to the left of the first character and click	Press HOME
Move the insertion point to the end of data in a cell	Point to the right of the last character and click	Press END
Move the insertion point anywhere in a cell	Point to the appropriate position and click the character	Press RIGHT ARROW or LEFT ARROW
Highlight one or more adjacent characters	Drag the mouse pointer through adjacent characters	Press SHIFT+RIGHT ARROW or SHIFT+LEFT ARROW
Select all data in a cell	Double-click the cell with the insertion point in the cell	
Delete selected characters	Click the Cut button on the Standard toolbar	Press DELETE
Toggle between Insert and Overtype modes		Press INSERT

Undoing the Last Entry

More About the Undo Button

The Undo button can undo far more complicated worksheet activities than just removing the latest entry from a cell. In fact, most commands can be undone if you click the Undo button before you make another entry or issue another command. You cannot undo a save or print, but, as a general rule, the Undo button can restore the worksheet data and settings to what they were the last time Excel was in Ready mode. With Excel 97, you have multiple-level undo and redo capabilities.

Excel provides the **Undo command** on the **Edit menu** and the **Undo button** on the Standard toolbar (Figure 1-71) that you can use to erase the most recent cell entry. Thus, if you enter incorrect data in a cell, click the Undo command or Undo button and Excel changes the cell contents to what they were prior to entering the incorrect data.

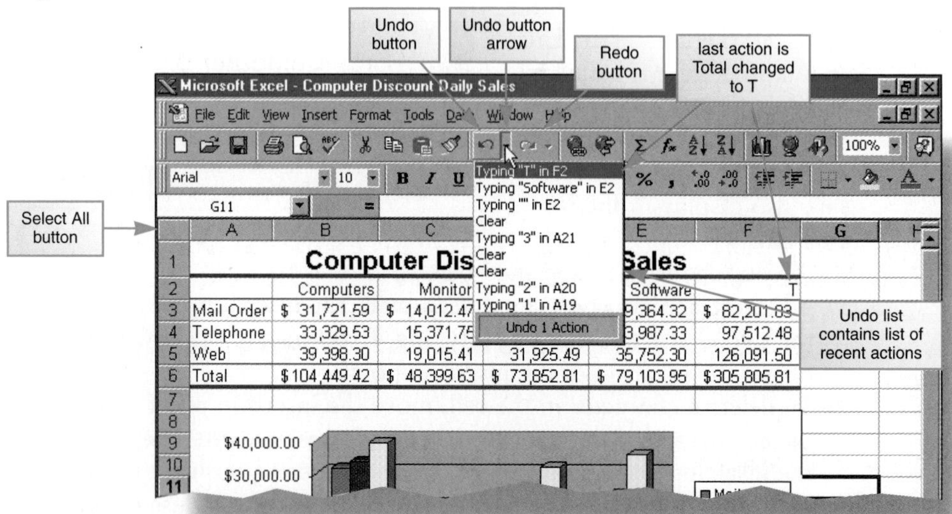

FIGURE 1-71

If Excel cannot undo an action, then the Undo button is inoperative. Excel remembers the last 16 actions you have completed. Thus, you can undo up to 16 previous actions by clicking the Undo box arrow to display the Undo list and clicking the action to be undone (Figure 1-71). You also can click Undo on the Edit menu rather than using the Undo button. If Excel cannot undo an action, then the words Can't Undo appear on the Edit menu in place of Undo.

Next to the Undo button on the Standard toolbar is the Redo button. The **Redo button** allows you to repeat previous actions. You also can click Redo on the Edit menu rather than using the Redo button.

Clearing a Cell or Range of Cells

If you enter data into the wrong cell or range of cells, you can erase or clear the data using one of several methods. **Never press the SPACEBAR to clear a cell.** Pressing the SPACEBAR enters a blank character. A blank character is text and is different from an empty cell, even though the cell may appear empty.

Excel provides three methods to clear the contents of a cell or a range of cells.

More *About* Clearing Formats

If you accidentally assign unwanted formats to a range of cells, you can use the Clear command on the Edit menu to delete the formats of a selected range. Doing so changes the format to normal. To view the characteristics of the normal format, click Style on the Format menu or press ALT+' (APOSTROPHE).

TO CLEAR CELL CONTENTS USING THE FILL HANDLE

Step 1: Select the cell or range of cells and point to the fill handle so the mouse pointer changes to a cross hair.
Step 2: Drag the fill handle back into the selected cell or range until a shadow covers the cell or cells you want to erase. Release the left mouse button.

TO CLEAR CELL CONTENTS USING THE SHORTCUT MENU

Step 1: Select the cell or range of cells to be cleared.
Step 2: Right-click the selection.
Step 3: Click Clear Contents.

TO CLEAR CELL CONTENTS USING THE DELETE KEY

Step 1: Select the cell or range of cells to be cleared.
Step 2: Press the DELETE key.

TO CLEAR CELL CONTENTS USING THE CLEAR COMMAND

Step 1: Select the cell or range of cells to be cleared.
Step 2: On the Edit menu, click Clear.
Step 3: Click All on the submenu.

You also can select a range of cells and click the Cut button on the Standard toolbar or click **Cut** on the Edit menu. Be aware, however, that the Cut button or Cut command not only deletes the contents from the range, but also copies the contents of the range to the Clipboard, thus erasing what was previously on the Clipboard.

Clearing the Entire Worksheet

Sometimes, everything goes wrong. If this happens, you may want to clear the worksheet entirely and start over. To clear the worksheet, follow the steps on the next page.

TO CLEAR THE ENTIRE WORKSHEET

Step 1: Click the Select All button (Figure 1-71 on page E 1.50).
Step 2: Press the DELETE key or click Clear on the Edit menu and then click All on the submenu.

The **Select All button** selects the entire worksheet. Instead of clicking the Select All button, you also can press CTRL+A. You also can clear an entire worksheet by clicking the worksheet's Close button or by clicking **Close** on the File menu. If you close the workbook, click the New button on the Standard toolbar or click **New** on the File menu to begin working on the next workbook.

More *About* **Global Activities**

Lotus 1-2-3 users may wonder how to carry out global activities in Excel, because there are no specific global commands. It's easy: simply click the Select All button or press CTRL+A before you issue a command, and the command will affect the entire worksheet.

TO DELETE AN EMDEDDED CHART

Step 1: Click the chart to select it.
Step 2: Press the DELETE key.

Excel Online Help

At any time while you are using Excel, you can answer your Excel questions by using **online Help**. Used properly, this form of online assistance can increase your productivity and reduce your frustrations by minimizing the time you spend learning how to use Excel. Table 1-7 summarizes the five categories of online Help available to you.

Table 1-7

TYPE	DESCRIPTION	ACTIVATE BY CLICKING
Office Assistant	Answers your questions, offers tips, and provides Help for a variety of Excel features.	Click the Office Assistant button on the Standard toolbar.
Contents sheet	Groups Help topics by general categories. Use when you know only the general category of the topic in question.	Click Contents and Index on the Help menu, and then click the Contents tab.
Index sheet	Similar to an index in a book; use when you know exactly what you want	Click Contents and Index on the Help menu, and then click the Index tab.
Find sheet	Searches the index for all phrases that include the term in question	Click Contents and Index on the Help menu, and then click the Find tab.
Question Mark button and What's This? command	Used to identify unfamiliar items on the screen	In a dialog box, click the Question Mark button and then click an item in the dialog box. Click What's This? on the Help menu, and then click an item on the screen.

The following sections show examples of each type of online Help described in Table 1-7.

Using the Office Assistant

The **Office Assistant** answers your questions and suggests more efficient ways to complete a task. With the Office Assistant active, for example, you can type a word or phrase in a text box and the Office Assistant provides immediate help on the subject. Also, as you create a worksheet, the Office Assistant accumulates tips that suggest more efficient ways to do the tasks you completed while building a worksheet, such as formatting, printing, and saving. This tip feature is part of the **IntelliSense technology** that is built into Excel, which understands what you are trying to do and suggests better ways to do it.

The following steps show how to use the Office Assistant to obtain information on copying data in a worksheet.

More About the Office Assistant

The Office Assistant unifies Excel Help, lets users ask questions in their own words, and interactively provides tips and suggestions to let users discover the power of Excel 97.

Steps To Obtain Help Using the Office Assistant

1 **If the Office Assistant is not on the screen, click the Office Assistant button on the Standard toolbar. If the Office Assistant is on the screen, click it. Type** copy **in the What would you like to do? text box in the Office Assistant balloon. Point to the Search button (Figure 1-72).**

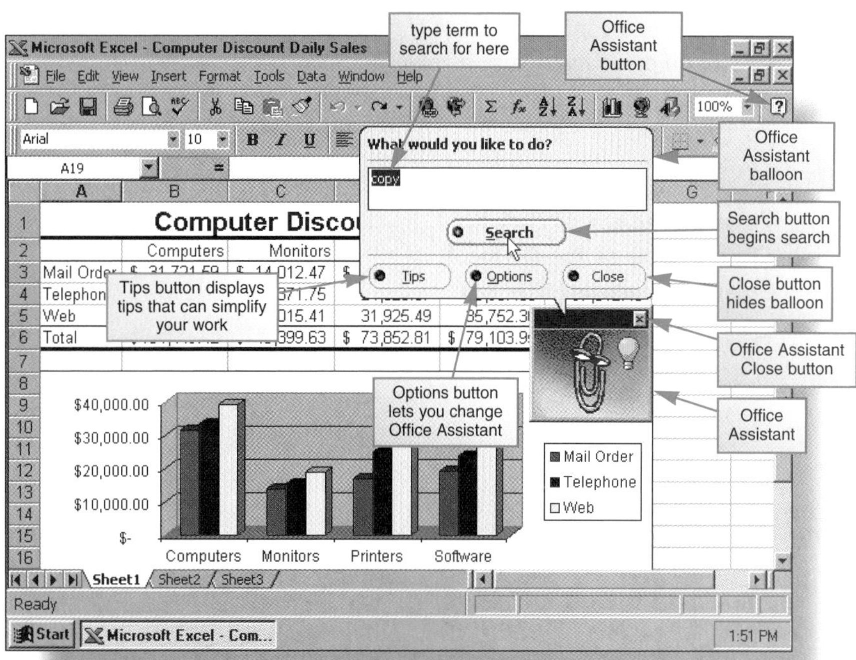

FIGURE 1-72

2 **Click the Search button. Point to the topic Move or copy cell data.**

The Office Assistant displays a list of topics relating to the word copy (Figure 1-73).

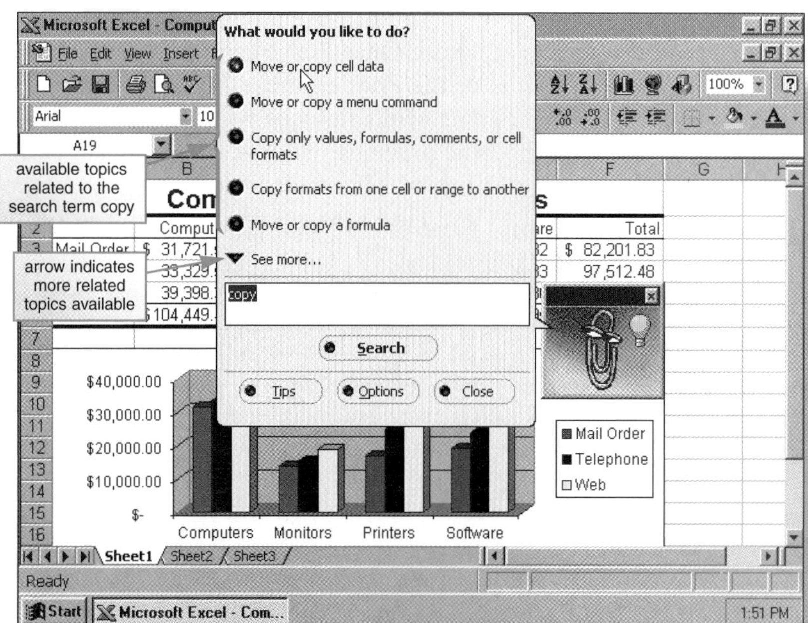

FIGURE 1-73

3 Click Move or copy cell data.

*The Office Assistant displays a Microsoft Excel Help window that provides Help information on moving or copying cell data (Figure 1-74). The icons (buttons), green underlined words, and the topics at the bottom of the window preceded by a button are **links** to topics related to moving and copying cell data. When you move the mouse pointer over a link, it changes to a pointing hand.*

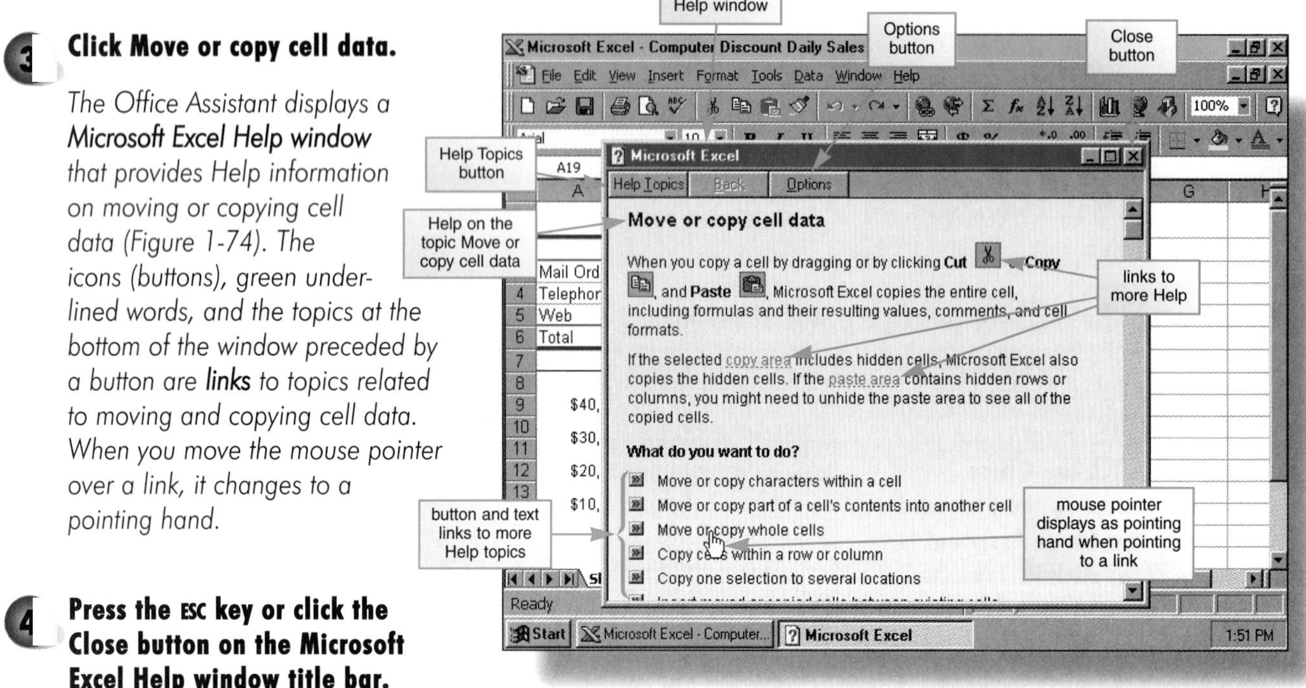

FIGURE 1-74

4 Press the ESC key or click the Close button on the Microsoft Excel Help window title bar.

The Microsoft Excel Help window closes and the worksheet again is active.

5 Click the Close button in the Office Assistant window.

The Office Assistant disappears from the screen.

OtherWays

1. To show Office Assistant, press F1 or on Help menu click Microsoft Excel Help
2. To hide Office Assistant, right-click the Office Assistant, click Hide Assistant on the shortcut menu

You can use the Office Assistant to search for Help on any topic concerning Excel. Once Help displays, you can read it, print it by clicking the **Options button** or the Print command on the shortcut menu, or display a related topic by clicking one of the links. If you display a related topic, click the **Back button** to return to the previous window. You also can click the **Help Topics button** to display the Help Topics: Microsoft Help dialog box and obtain help through the Contents, Index, and Find tabs, which are discussed further below.

Displaying Tips to Improve Your Work Habits

If you click the Office Assistant Tips button (Figure 1-72 on the previous page), Excel displays tips on how to work more efficiently. As you work through creating and editing a worksheet, Excel adds tips to the list. Once a tip displays, you can move backward or forward through the list of accumulated tips (Figure 1-75).

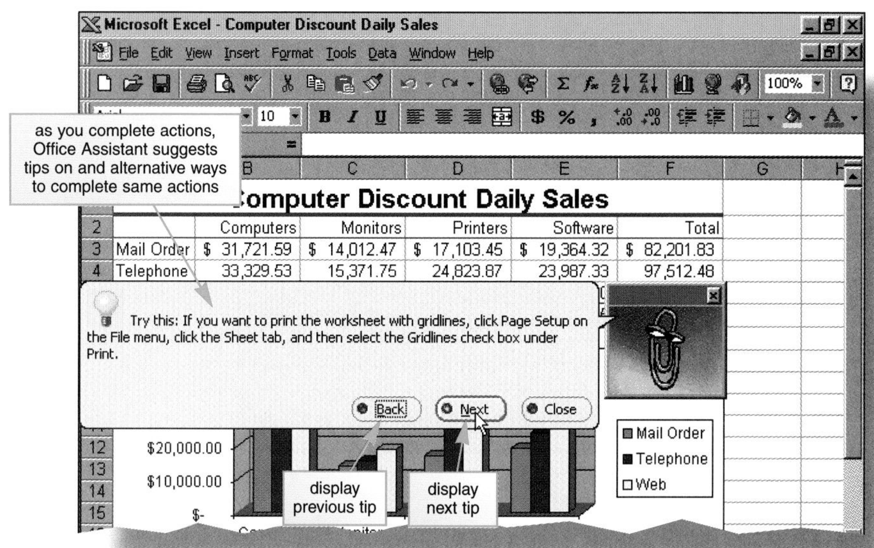

FIGURE 1-75

Office Assistant Shortcut Menu

When you right-click the Office Assistant window, a shortcut menu displays (Figure 1-76). This shortcut menu allows you to change the look and feel of Office Assistant. For example, you can hide the Office Assistant, display tips, change the way it works, choose a different Office Assistant, or view an animation of the current one. Most of these options also are available through the Options button that displays when you click the Office Assistant.

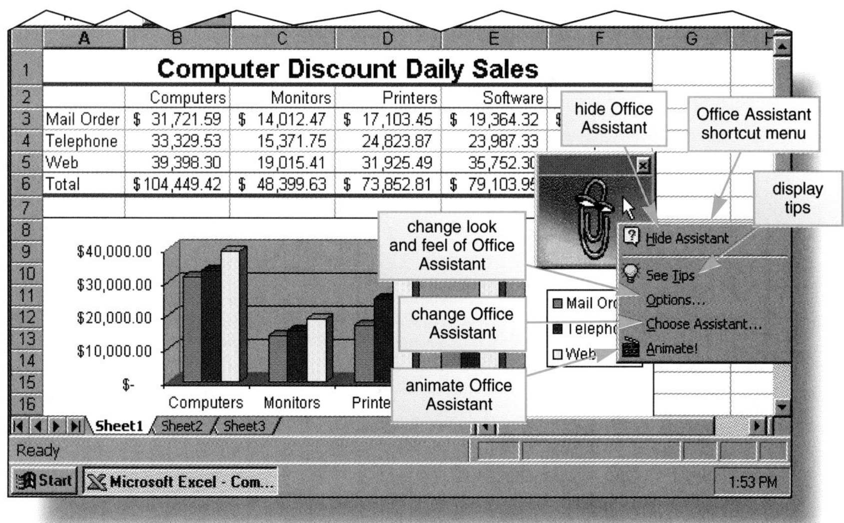

FIGURE 1-76

Using the Contents Sheet to Obtain Help

The **Contents sheet** in the **Help Topics: Microsoft Excel dialog box** helps when you know the general category of the topic in question, but not the specifics. The steps on the next page show how to use the Contents sheet in the Help Topics: Microsoft Excel dialog box to obtain information on editing the contents of cells.

More *About* the Contents Sheet

Use the Contents sheet in the same manner you would use a table of contents at the front of a textbook — simply browse through topics and subtopics to find the desired information.

To Obtain Help Using the Contents Sheet

1 Click Help on the Chart menu bar and then point to Contents and Index.

The Help menu displays (Figure 1-77).

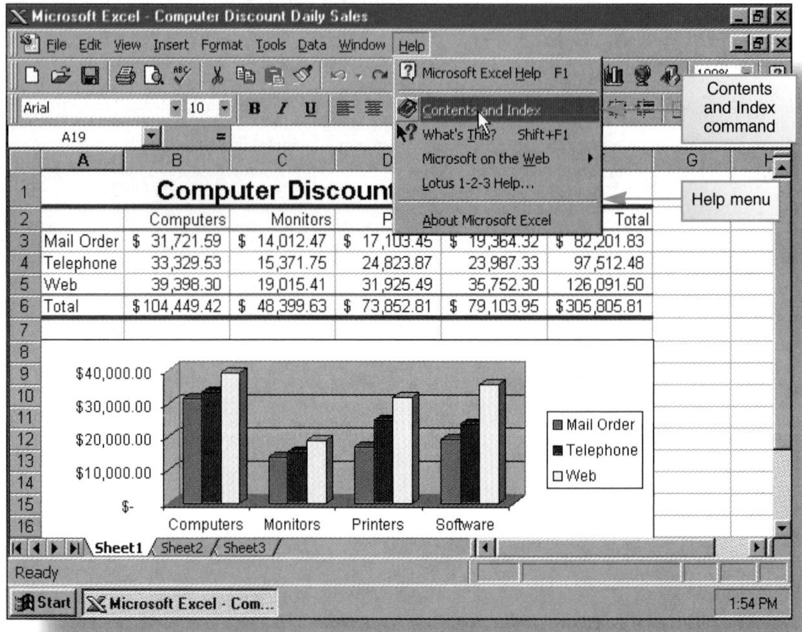

FIGURE 1-77

2 Click Contents and Index. Click the Contents tab. Double-click the Editing Worksheet Data book. Point to Edit cell contents.

The Help Topics: Microsoft Excel dialog box displays (Figure 1-78). The Contents sheet displays with the Editing Worksheet Data book open. Each topic on the Contents sheet (Figure 1-78) is preceded by a book icon or question mark icon. A ***book icon*** *indicates subtopics are available. A* ***question mark icon*** *means information on the topic will display if you double-click the title. Notice how the book icon opens when you double-click the book (or its title).*

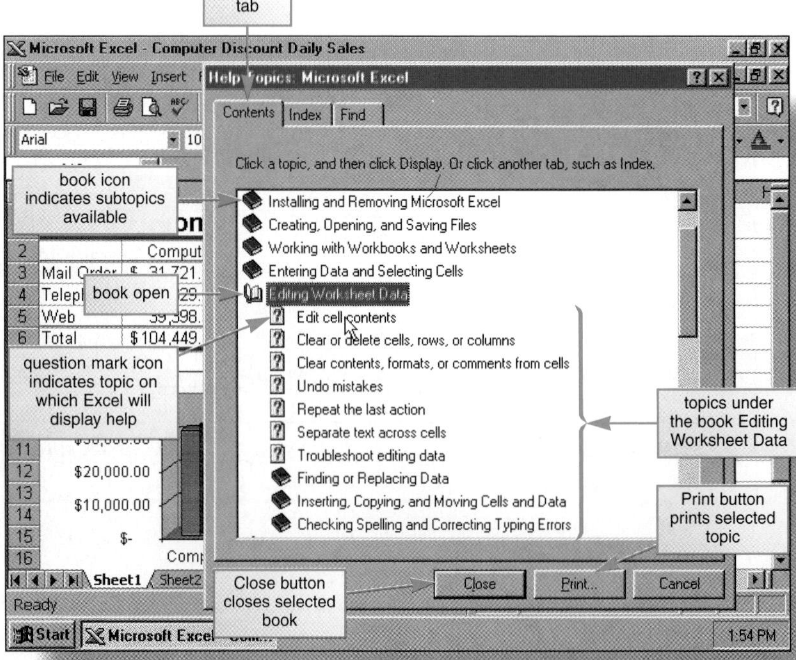

FIGURE 1-78

3 **Double-click Edit cell contents.**

A Microsoft Excel Help window displays describing the steps for editing a cell's contents (Figure 1-79).

4 **After reading the information, press the ESC key or click the Close button in the Microsoft Excel Help window.**

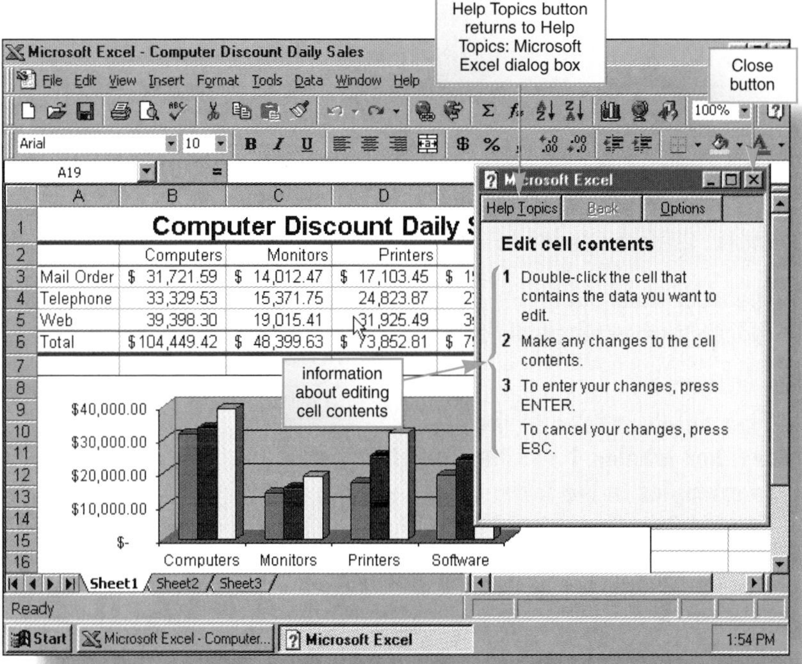

FIGURE 1-79

Rather than closing the Microsoft Excel window in Step 4, you can click the Help Topics button (Figure 1-79) to return to the Contents sheet (Figure 1-78). If you right-click in the Microsoft Excel Help window, a shortcut menu will display with several commands, such as Print Topic and Copy. You can use the Copy command to copy the online Help to your worksheet or a Word document.

Rather than double-clicking a topic in the Contents list box, you can click it and then use the buttons at the bottom of the dialog box to open a book, display information on a topic, print information on a topic, or close the dialog box.

Using the Index Sheet to Obtain Help

The next sheet in the Help Topics: Microsoft Excel dialog box is the Index sheet (Figure 1-80 on the next page). Like the index at the back of a textbook, the Index sheet helps when you know the first few letters of the term or the exact term you want to find.

The steps on the next page show how to obtain information on chart type examples by using the Index sheet and entering the term chart types.

If you have used a book's index to look up terms, then you will feel comfortable with the Index sheet. It works in much the same way, except that you type the term on which you want information, rather than paging through the index to find it.

To Obtain Help Using the Index Sheet

1 **Click Help on the Chart menu bar and then click Contents and Index. Click the Index tab.**

The Index sheet displays in the Help Topics: Microsoft Excel dialog box.

2 **Type** `chart types` **in the top text box labeled 1 and then point to examples in the lower box labeled 2.**

The term chart types is highlighted in the lower list box labeled 2 (Figure 1-80).

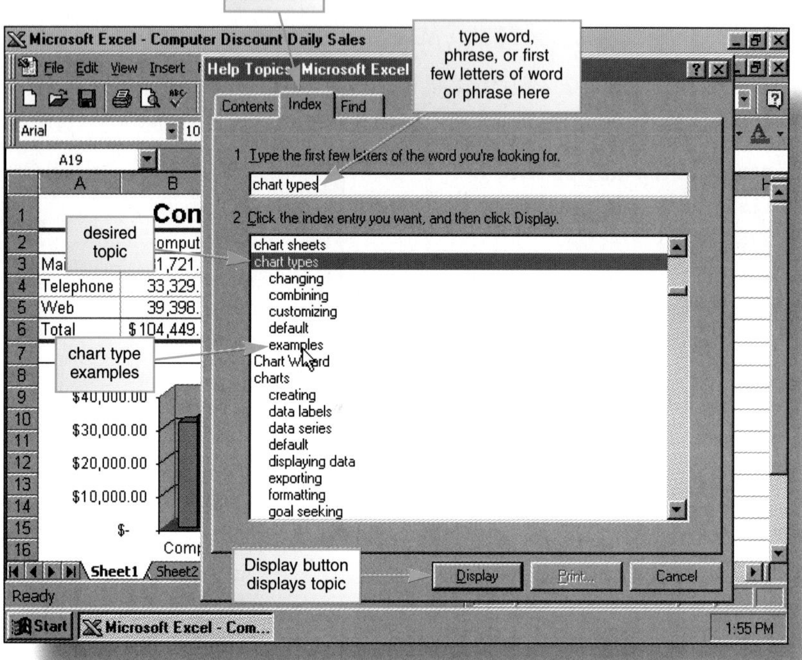

FIGURE 1-80

3 **Double-click examples in the lower list box labeled 2.**

Information describing column charts displays (Figure 1-81).

4 **Press the ESC key twice or click the Close button in the upper-right corner of the Microsoft Excel Help window to close it.**

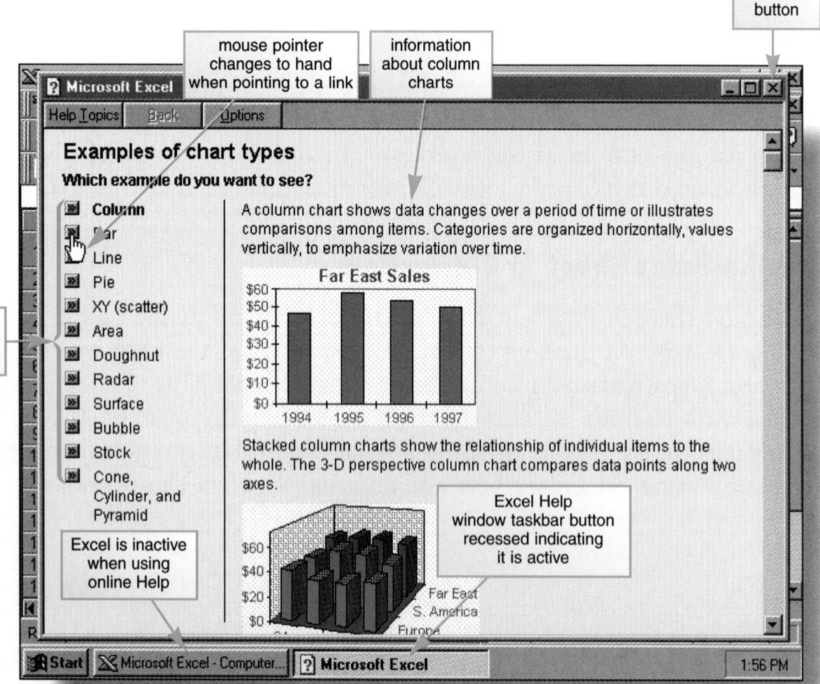

FIGURE 1-81

In Figure 1-81, you can click any of the 12 links on the left side of the screen to display information about the selected chart type.

Using the Find Sheet to Obtain Help

The third sheet in the Help Topics: Microsoft Excel dialog box is the Find sheet. The Find sheet will return a list of all topics pertaining to the word or phrase you type in the text box. You then can further select words to narrow your search.

The following steps show how to obtain help on creating a Web page from worksheet data.

More About the Find Sheet

Use the Find sheet when you know a word that is located somewhere in the term or phrase you want to look up.

Steps To Obtain Help Using the Find Sheet

1 Click Help on the Chart menu bar and then click Contents and Index. Click the Find tab.

The Find sheet displays in the Help Topics: Microsoft Excel dialog box.

2 Type web in the top text box labeled 1. In the lower box, point to Create a Web page from worksheet data or a chart.

The message below the lower list box indicates that 77 topics were found (Figure 1-82).

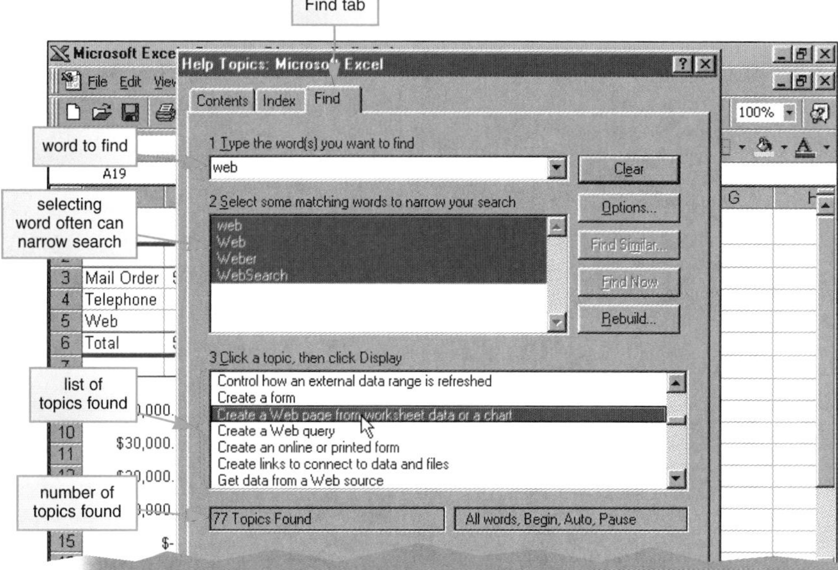

FIGURE 1-82

3 Double-click Create a Web page from worksheet data or a chart.

Information describing how to create a Web page from worksheet data or a chart displays (Figure 1-83).

4 Press the ESC key or click the Close button in the upper-right corner of the Microsoft Excel window to close it.

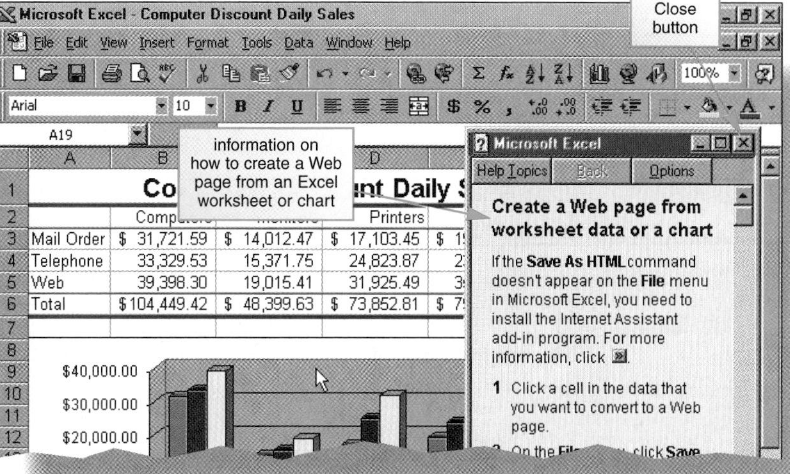

FIGURE 1-83

You can see from the previous steps that, like the Index sheet, the Find sheet allows you to enter a word or phrase. Instead of displaying an alphabetical listing, however, the Find sheet lists all the phrases that contain that word or phrase. You then can narrow your search by choosing the appropriate phrase.

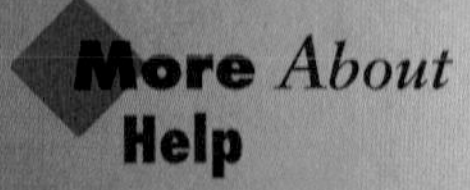

More About Help

The best way to familiarize yourself with the online Help features is to use them.

Obtaining Help and Other Information from the Web

To obtain Help and other information from the Web, point to Microsoft on the Web on the Help menu. A submenu of Web-related commands displays (Figure 1-84). If you click any command on the submenu, your system will start your browser program and connect to a corresponding Microsoft page on the World Wide Web. Use the commands on the Microsoft on the Web submenu to obtain up-to-date information on a variety of topics, including Help topics.

More About the What's This? Command

Both the Question Mark button on a dialog box and the What's This? command on the Help menu display ScreenTips, which provide an explanation of the item you click.

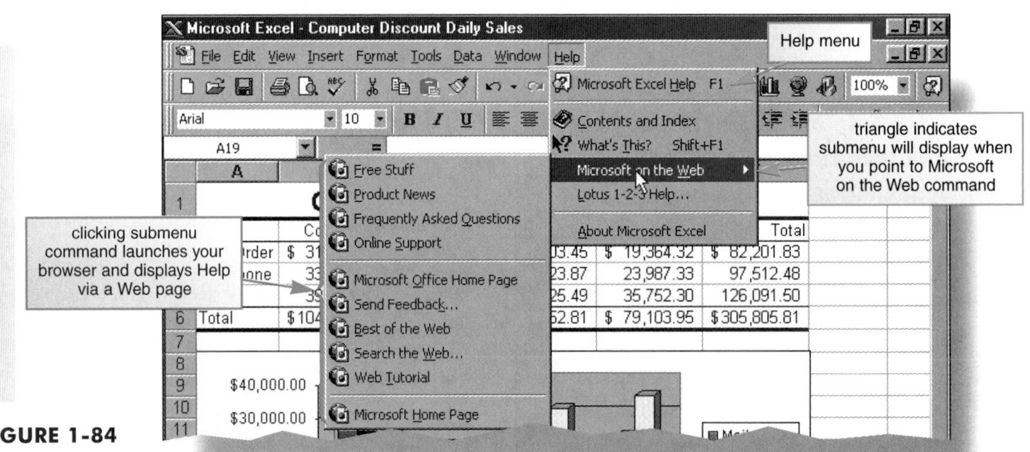

FIGURE 1-84

Using the Question Mark Button or What's This? Command to Define Items on the Screen

Use the Question Mark button in a dialog box or the What's This? command on the Help menu when you are not sure what an item on the screen is or what it does. Clicking the Question Mark button in a dialog box or the What's This? command on the Help menu causes the mouse pointer to change to an arrow with a question mark. Next, click any item on which you want more information. The information displays as a ScreenTip.

The **Question Mark button** displays in the upper-right corner of dialog boxes, next to the Close button. For example, in Figure 1-85, the AutoFormat dialog box is on the screen. If you click the Question Mark button, and then click anywhere in the Table format list box, an explanation of the Table format list box displays.

Whereas the Question Mark button is used to display ScreenTips concerning items in a dialog box, the **What's This? command** on the Help menu is used to display ScreenTips concerning items in the Excel window.

FIGURE 1-85

Quitting Excel

To quit Excel, complete the following steps.

TO QUIT EXCEL

Step 1: Click the Close button on the right side of the title bar.
Step 2: If the Microsoft Excel dialog box displays, click the No button.

More About Quitting Excel

Do not forget to remove your floppy disk from drive A after quitting Excel, especially if you are working in a laboratory environment. It's frustrating to leave your hard work behind for another user.

Project Summary

The worksheet created in this project (Figure 1-1 on page E 1.7) allows the management of the Computer Discount Company to examine the daily sales for the four main product groups. Furthermore, the 3-D Column chart should meet the needs of the president, Kelly Montgomery, who as you recall from the Case Perspective, has little tolerance for lists of numbers.

In creating the Computer Discount Daily Sales worksheet and chart in this project, you gained a broad knowledge about Excel. First, you were introduced to starting Excel. You learned about the Excel window and how to enter text and numbers to create a worksheet. You learned how to select a range and how to use the AutoSum button to sum numbers in a column or row. Using the fill handle, you learned how to copy a cell to adjacent cells.

Once the worksheet was built, you learned how to change the font size of the title, bold the title, and center the title over a range using buttons on the Formatting toolbar. Using the steps and techniques presented in the project, you formatted the body of the worksheet using the AutoFormat command, and you used the Chart Wizard to add a 3-D Column chart. After completing the worksheet, you saved the workbook on disk and printed the worksheet and chart. You learned how to edit data in cells. Finally, you learned how to use the different online Help tools to answer your questions.

What You Should Know

Having completed this project, you should be able to perform the following tasks:

- Add a 3-D Column Chart to the Worksheet *(E 1.36)*
- Bold a Cell *(E 1.28)*
- Center a Cell's Contents Across Columns *(E 1.30)*
- Clear Cell Contents Using the Clear Command *(E 1.51)*
- Clear Cell Contents Using the DELETE Key (E 1.51)
- Clear Cell Contents Using the Fill Handle *(E 1.51)*
- Clear Cell Contents Using the Shortcut Menu *(E 1.51)*
- Clear the Entire Worksheet *(E 1.52)*
- Copy a Cell to Adjacent Cells in a Row *(E 1.24)*
- Delete an Embedded Chart *(E 1.52)*
- Determine Multiple Totals at the Same Time *(E 1.25)*
- Enter Numeric Data *(E 1.20)*
- Enter Row Titles *(E 1.19)*
- Enter Column Titles *(E 1.17)*
- Enter the Worksheet Title *(E 1.15)*
- Increase the Font Size of a Cell Entry *(E 1.29)*
- Obtain Help Using the Contents Sheet *(E 1.56)*
- Obtain Help Using the Find Sheet *(E 1.59)*
- Obtain Help Using the Index Sheet *(E 1.58)*
- Obtain Help Using the Office Assistant *(E 1.53)*
- Print a Worksheet *(E 1.43)*
- Quit Excel *(E 1.45, E 1.61)*
- Save a Workbook *(E 1.40)*
- Start Excel *(E 1.9)*
- Start Excel and Open a Workbook *(E 1.46)*
- Sum a Column of Numbers *(E 1.22)*
- Use the AutoCalculate Area to Determine an Average *(E 1.48)*
- Use AutoFormat to Format the Body of a Worksheet *(E 1.31)*
- Use the Name Box to Select a Cell *(E 1.33)*

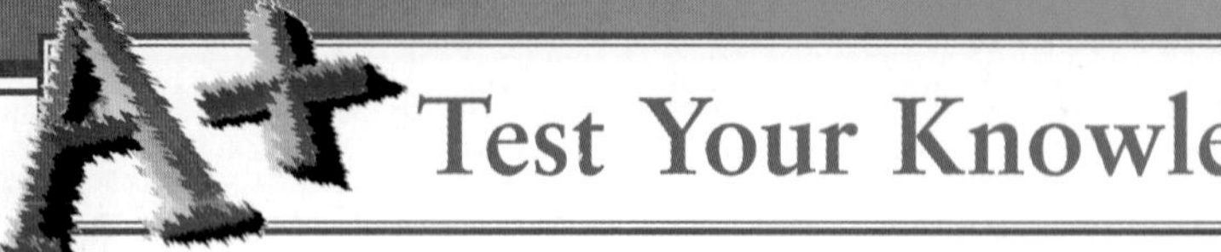

Test Your Knowledge

1 True/False

Instructions: Circle T if the statement is true or F is the statement is false.

T F 1. The column headings in an Excel worksheet begin with A and end with IV.

T F 2. You can use the AutoCalculate area to assign the SUM function to a cell.

T F 3. Press the ESC key to cancel a cell entry.

T F 4. To calculate the totals for multiple rows at the same time, highlight a range of cells with numbers, including a blank row below the range, and then click the AutoSum button.

T F 5. Hold down the CTRL key and drag the sizing handle to snap a chart border to the gridlines.

T F 6. Display the Office Assistant by clicking the What's This? command on the Help menu.

T F 7. The closed book icon on the Help window Contents sheet means subtopics are available.

T F 8. Double-click a toolbar to show its shortcut menu.

T F 9. Click the Question Mark button on a dialog box to display the Office Assistant.

T F 10. To clear the entire worksheet, click the Select All button and press the DELETE key.

2 Multiple Choice

Instructions: Circle the correct response.

1. You can edit text in a cell by __________.
   a. double-clicking the cell
   b. clicking the cell and pressing F2
   c. clicking the entry in the formula bar
   d. all of the above
2. Which button do you click to display ScreenTips in a dialog box?
   a. Office Assistant button
   b. Question Mark button
   c. Tips button
   d. none of the above
3. To display the __________ for a cell, right-click the cell.
   a. shortcut menu
   b. ScreenTip
   c. Office Assistant
   d. AutoCalculate function
4. The fill handle is located on the active __________ border.
   a. cell
   b. chart
   c. form
   d. dialog box
5. The __________ accumulates tips to suggest more efficient ways of completing a task.
   a. Help button
   b. Office Assistant
   c. Tip Wizard
   d. What's This? command
6. You can change the Office Assistant options by __________.
   a. double-clicking Office Assistant
   b. clicking Office Assistant
   c. right-clicking Office Assistant
   d. clicking Options on the Help menu
7. To quickly view the average of a range of cells, use the __________ feature.
   a. Formula
   b. AutoSum
   c. Function Wizard
   d. AutoCalculate

Test Your Knowledge

8. When you create a chart using the Chart Wizard, Excel draws the chart __________.
   a. in the middle of the window
   b. below the selected chart range
   c. on a new sheet
   d. to the right of the selected chart range
9. Hold down the __________ key and drag the sizing handle to snap a chart border to a gridline.
   a. SHIFT
   b. ALT
   c. CTRL
   d. none of the above
10. To quit Excel, click the __________.
    a. Close button on the title bar
    b. Control-menu icon on the menu bar
    c. Close command on the File menu
    d. all of the above

3 Understanding the Excel Worksheet

Instructions: In Figure 1-86, arrows point to components of the Excel window. Identify the various parts of the window in the spaces provided.

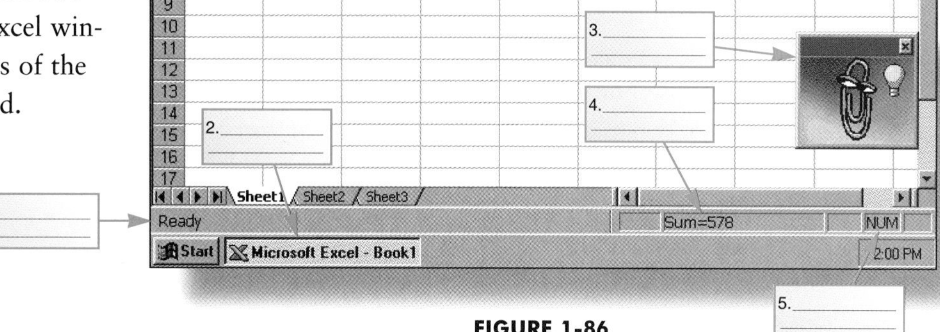

FIGURE 1-86

4 Understanding the Excel Toolbars and the AutoFormat Dialog Box

Instructions: In Figure 1-87, arrows point to buttons on the Standard and Formatting toolbars and in the AutoFormat dialog box. Identify the various buttons in the spaces provided.

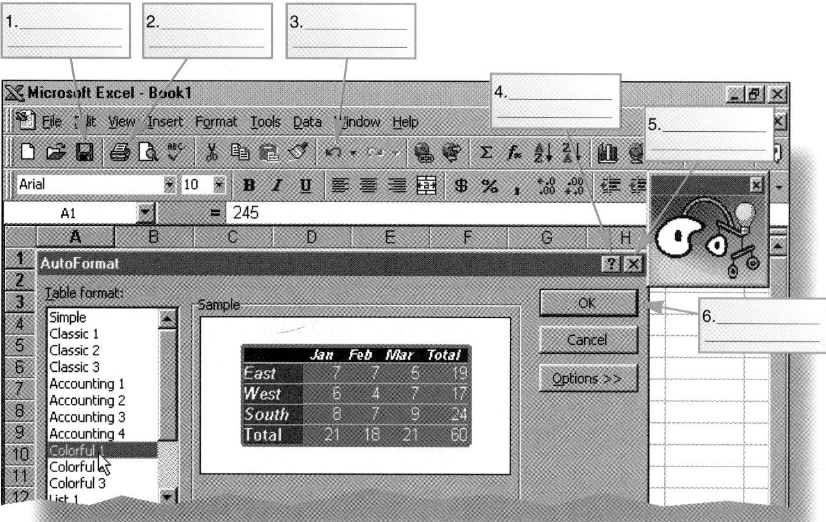

FIGURE 1-87

1 Reviewing Project Activities

Instructions: Perform the following tasks using a computer.

1. Start Excel.
2. If the Office Assistant is on your screen, click it to display the Office Assistant balloon. If the Office Assistant is not on your screen, then click the Office Assistant button on the Standard toolbar.
3. Click the Options button in the Office Assistant balloon. Click the Gallery tab and then click the Next button to view all the Office Assistants. Choose the Genius Assistant by clicking the OK button and then click the Options tab. Review the different options for the Office Assistant. Close the Office Assistant dialog box.
4. Click the Office Assistant and type `ranges` in the What would you like to do? text box. Click the Search button or press the ENTER key.
5. Click the See More link and then click the link About cell and range references.
6. Read the information. Use the shortcut menu or Options button to print the information. One at a time, click each of the three underlined green words (Figure 1-88) to display their ScreenTips. Print each definition that displays by right-clicking the ScreenTip and clicking Print Topic. Hand the printouts in to your instructor.
7. Click the Close button in the Microsoft Excel Help window.
8. Click the Office Assistant. Use the Options button and Gallery sheet to change the Office Assistant icon to Clippit.
9. Click Contents and Index on the Help menu. Click the Contents tab. Double-click the Entering Data and Selecting Cells book. Double-click the Selecting and Moving Around in a Workbook book. One at a time, double-click the first two topics under the Selecting and Moving Around in a Workbook book. Read and print the information. Click any underlined green words or other links and read the ScreenTips. Click the Help Topics button to return to the Contents sheet. Hand the printouts in to your instructor.

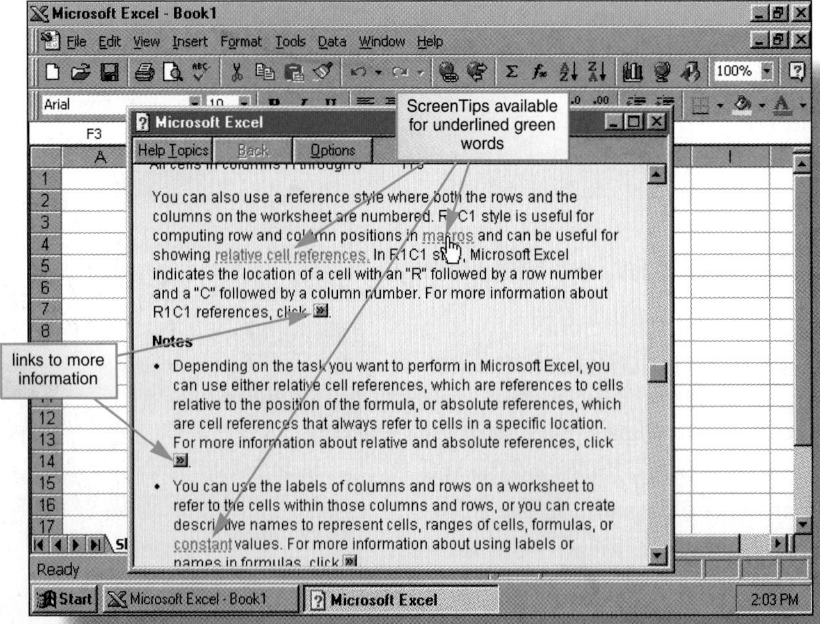

FIGURE 1-88

2 Expanding on the Basics

Instructions: Use Excel online Help to better understand the topics and answer the questions listed below. Answer the questions on your own paper, or hand in the printed Help information to your instructor.

1. Click the Office Assistant if it is on the screen or the Office Assistant button on the Standard toolbar to display the Office Assistant balloon. Search for the topic formatting a chart. Click the link About formatting charts. When the Microsoft Excel Help window displays (Figure 1-89), answer the following questions by clicking the links. Once you have answered the questions, close the Microsoft Excel Help window.
   a. What are three special options for different chart types? b. How do you apply number formats to an axis as you would on a worksheet? c. How do you format and rotate text on a chart?
2. Click Contents and Index on the Help menu. Click the Index tab. Type `align` in the top text box labeled 1. Double-click text in cells under aligning in the lower list box labeled 2. One at a time, double-click the four topics in the Topics Found dialog box. Read and print the information. Click the Help Topics button to return to the Contents sheet. Close the Microsoft Excel Help window. Hand the printouts in to your instructor.
3. Click Contents and Index on the Help menu. Click the Find tab. Type `help` in the top text box labeled 1. Double-click Help in the middle list box labeled 2. In the lower list box labeled 3, scroll down to and double-click Connect to Microsoft technical resources. Read through the information that displays. Use the links under Where do you want to go for technical information? to answer the following:
   a. What is the Microsoft Knowledge Base (KB)? Can you access the KB on the World Wide Web from the Help menu? If so, how?
   b. What is the Microsoft Software Library (MSL)? Can you access the MSL on the World Wide Web from the Help menu? If so, how?
   c. How can you get answers to your technical questions 24 hours a day from a touch tone phone? Give an example of what kind of information you can receive from this service.
4. Use the What's This? command on the Help menu to display ScreenTips for five of the buttons on the Standard and Formatting toolbars. Read and print the information. Hand the printouts in to your instructor.

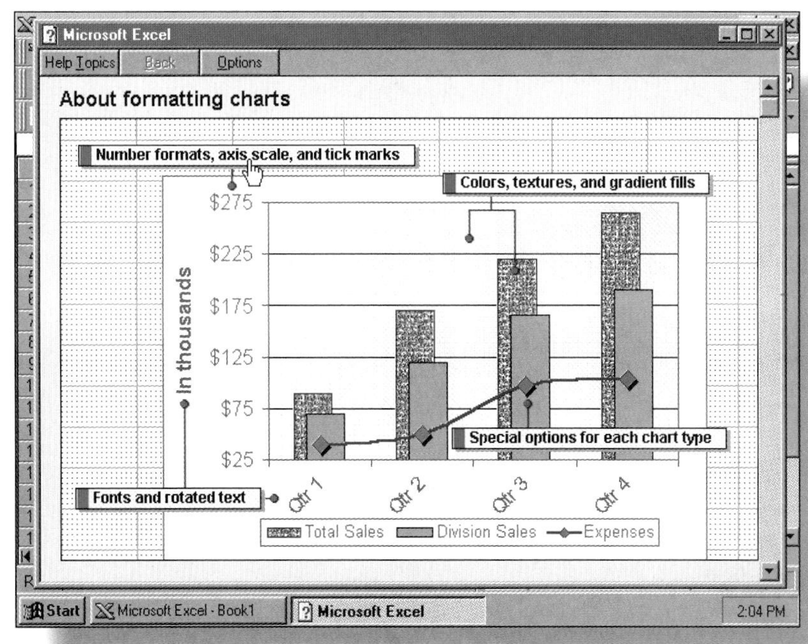

FIGURE 1-89

Apply Your Knowledge

CAUTION: To ensure you have enough disk space to save your files, it is recommended that you create a copy of the Data Disk that accompanies this book. Then, delete folders from the copy of the Data Disk that are not needed for the application you are working on. Do the following: (1) Insert the Data Disk in drive A; (2) start Explorer; (3) right-click the 3½ Floppy (A:) folder in the All Folders side of the window; (4) click Copy Disk; (5) click Start and OK as required; (6) insert a floppy disk when requested; (7) delete all folders on the floppy disk you created except the Excel folder; (8) remove the floppy disk from drive A and label it Excel Data Disk.

1 Changing Data in a Worksheet

Instructions: Start Excel. Open the workbook, Webmaster Software School, from the Excel folder on the Data Disk that accompanies this book. This worksheet is set up as an annual income statement (Figure 1-90).

	A	B	C	D	E	F
1	Income Statement for 1998					
2	Webmaster Software School					
3	INCOME:	Jan-April		May-Aug		Sept-Dec
4	Individual Tuition Revenue	$159.00		$5,400.00		$7,500.00
5	Corporate Tuition Revenue	5,000.00		30,000.00		30,000.00
6	Community College Revenue	1,000.00		25,000.00		30,000.00
7	TOTAL INCOME:	$6,159.00		$60,400.00		$67,500.00
8	EXPENSES:	Jan-April		May-Aug		Sept-Dec
9	Salaries	$32,400.00		$43,369.00		$43,369.00
10	Software	5,000.00		2,000.00		2,000.00
11	Classroom Rental	0.00		2,000.00		2,000.00
12	Hardware	24,999.00		1,000.00		1,000.00
13	TOTAL EXPENSES:	$62,399.00		$48,369.00		$48,369.00
14	NET PROFIT *(OR LOSS)*	($56,240.00)		$12,031.00		$19,131.00

FIGURE 1-90

1. Change the worksheet data as indicated in Table 1-8. As you edit the values in the cells, watch as Excel automatically updates the total incomes (B7, D7, and F7) and total expenses (B13, D13, and F13) to reflect the new amounts. Each of these values in these cells is based on the SUM function. As you enter a new value, Excel automatically recalculates the SUM function and updates the value displayed in the cell. After you successfully have made the changes listed in the table, the total incomes in cells B7, D7, and F7 should equal $6,359.00, $55,400.00, and $67,500.00, respectively. The total expenses in cells B13, D13, and F13 should equal $67,832.00, $50,369.00, and $48,369.00, respectively.
2. Save the workbook using the file name Web Page Design School.
3. Print the revised worksheet.

Table 1-8

CELL	CURRENT CELL CONTENTS	CHANGE CELL CONTENTS TO
A2	Webmaster Software School	Web Page Design School
B4	159.00	359.00
D5	30,000.00	25,000.00
D10	2,000.00	4,000.00
B11	0.00	1,000.00
B12	24,999.00	29,432.00

1 Creating and Modifying a Sales Analysis Worksheet

Problem: As the manager for Gulliver's Travel Bookstore, you want to analyze total sales for the different travel books by bookstore section. The sales figures are shown in Table 1-9.

Instructions: Perform the following tasks.

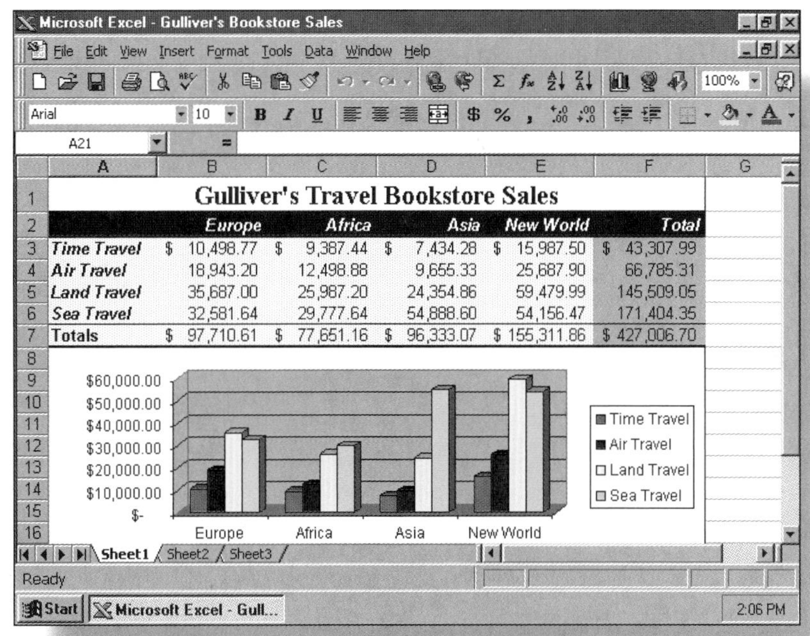

FIGURE 1-91

Table 1-9

	EUROPE	*AFRICA*	*ASIA*	*NEW WORLD*
TIME TRAVEL	**10,498.77**	**9,387.44**	**7,434.28**	**15,987.50**
AIR TRAVEL	**18,943.20**	**12,498.88**	**9,655.33**	**25,687.90**
LAND TRAVEL	**35,687.00**	**25,987.20**	**24,354.86**	**59,479.99**
SEA TRAVEL	**32,581.64**	**29,777.64**	**54,888.60**	**54,156.47**

1. Create the worksheet shown in Figure 1-91 using the title, sales amounts, and categories in Table 1-9.
2. Determine the totals for the types of travel, geographic locations, and store totals.
3. Format the worksheet title, Gulliver's Travel Bookstore, as 16-point Times New Roman, bold, centered over columns A through F.
4. Format the range A2:F7 using the AutoFormat command on the Format menu. Use the table format Colorful 2. Select the range B3:F3. Click the Currency Style button on the Formatting toolbar. Select the range B4:F6. Click the Comma Style button on the Formatting toolbar. Select the range B7:F7. Click the Currency Style button on the Formatting toolbar.
5. Select the range A2:E6 and use the Chart Wizard button on the Standard toolbar to draw a 3-D Column chart (Figure 1-91). Move the chart to the upper-left corner of cell A8 and then drag the lower-right corner of the chart location to cell F17.
6. Enter your name, course, laboratory assignment number, date, and instructor name in cells A19 through A23.
7. Save the worksheet using the file name Gulliver's Bookstore Sales.
8. Print the worksheet.

(continued)

Creating and Modifying a Sales Analysis Worksheet *(continued)*

9. Two corrections to the sales amounts need to be made. The corrected sales amounts are: $45,987.99 for Air Travel in Asia and $95,498.33 for Sea Travel in the New World. After you enter the corrections, the company totals should equal $132,665.73 in cell D7 and $196,653.72 in cell E7.
10. Print the modified worksheet. Close the workbook without saving the changes.

2 Creating a Quarterly Personal Budget

Problem: To estimate the funds you need to make it through the upcoming year, you decide to create a personal budget itemizing your quarterly expenses for the past year. The expenses you incurred are listed in Table 1-10.

Instructions: Perform the following tasks.

1. Create the worksheet shown in Figure 1-92 by entering the worksheet title, Quarterly Personal Budget, in cell B1 and using the expenses and category names in Table 1-10.
2. Use the AutoSum button and fill handle to determine the totals in row 9 and column F.
3. Change the worksheet title in cell B1 to 18-point bold. Center the worksheet title over columns B1 through F1.

Table 1-10

	JAN-MAR	APRIL-JUNE	JULY-SEPT	OCT-DEC
MORTGAGE	1500	1500	1500	1500
FOOD	900	950	950	1000
CAR & INS.	600	600	600	600
CLOTHES	567	433	200	459
UTILITIES	600	400	400	550
MISCELLANEOUS	149	121	159	349

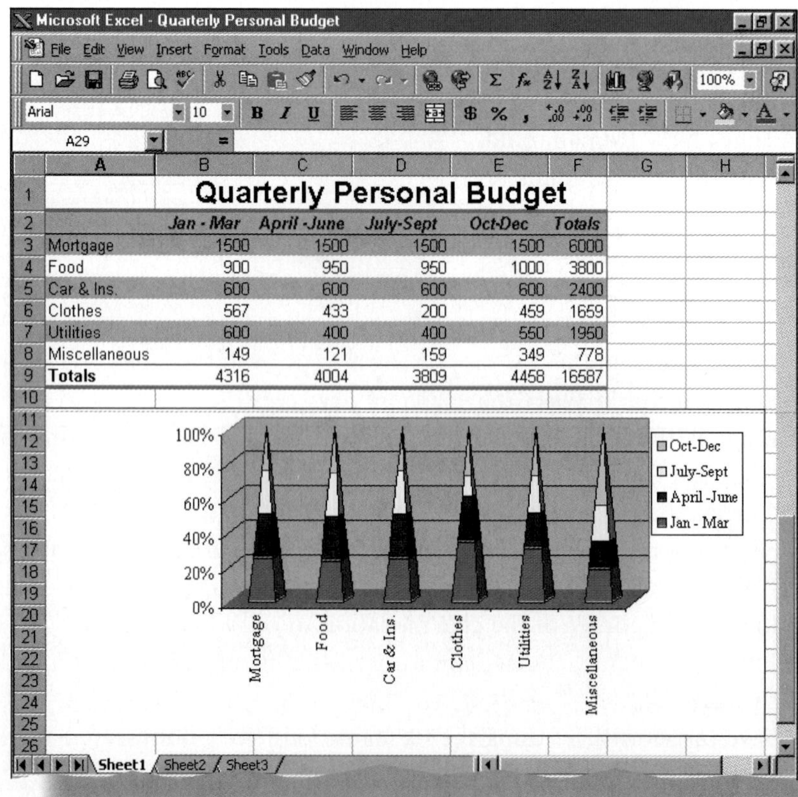

FIGURE 1-92

4. Use the AutoFormat command on the Format menu to format the range A2:F9. Use the table format List 1.
5. Use the Chart Wizard button to draw the 3-D Stacked Pyramid chart, as shown in Figure 1-92. Use the chart range A2:E8. Move the chart to the upper-left corner of cell A11. Hold down the ALT key and then drag the lower-right corner of the chart location to to cell H25.
6. Enter your name, course, laboratory assignment number, date, and instructor name in cells A27 through A32.
7. Save the workbook using the file name Quarterly Personal Budget.
8. Print the worksheet.
9. After talking with your banker, you decide to budget more for your last two mortgage payments. Make the following changes: Mortgage, July-Sept – 1700 and Mortgage, Oct-Dec – 1700. The new quarterly totals should now be 4009, and 4658, respectively. Print the worksheet with the revised data.
10. Close the workbook without saving the changes.

3 Analyzing College Expenses and Financial Resources

Problem: College expenses are skyrocketing and your resources are limited. To plan for the upcoming year, you have decided to organize your anticipated expenses and resources in a worksheet. The data required to prepare your worksheet is shown in Table 1-11.

Table 1-11

COLLEGE EXPENSES	*SEMESTER 1*	*SEMESTER 2*	*SUMMER*
ROOM & BOARD	2150	2150	950
TUITION & BOOKS	2125	2255	805
CLOTHES	250	210	190
ENTERTAINMENT	325	280	225
MISCELLANEOUS	200	200	375
FINANCIAL RESOURCES	*SEMESTER 1*	*SEMESTER 2*	*SUMMER*
SAVINGS	800	600	295
PARENTS	1750	1320	150
JOB	1000	1800	2000
FINANCIAL AID	1500	1375	100

Instructions: Using the numbers in Table 1-11, create the worksheet shown in Figure 1-93 on the next page. Enter the section titles, College Expenses and Financial Resources, in cells B1 and B10 respectively. Use the AutoSum button to calculate the totals in rows 8 and 16 and column E.

(continued)

Analyzing College Expenses and Financial Resources *(continued)*

To format the worksheet, use the table format Accounting 3 for the range A2:E8 and again for the range A11:E16. Center the section titles over columns B through E. Enter your name in cell A19 and your course, laboratory assignment number, date, and instructor name in cells A20 through A23.

Save the workbook using the file name College Expenses and Resources. Print the worksheet. Use the Office Assistant to learn how to print only a specific area of a worksheet and then print the selection A1:E8 of the worksheet.

Increment all summer expenses in column D by $100. Increment the financial aid for summer by $500. The totals in cells E8 and E16 should equal $13,190.00. Print the worksheet. Close the workbook without saving changes.

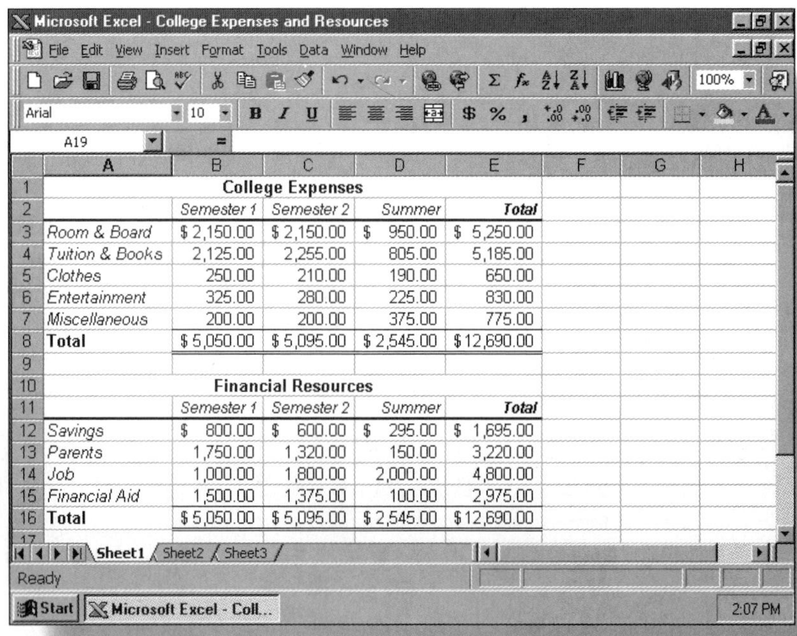

	A	B	C	D	E
1		College Expenses			
2		*Semester 1*	*Semester 2*	*Summer*	***Total***
3	*Room & Board*	$ 2,150.00	$ 2,150.00	$ 950.00	$ 5,250.00
4	*Tuition & Books*	2,125.00	2,255.00	805.00	5,185.00
5	*Clothes*	250.00	210.00	190.00	650.00
6	*Entertainment*	325.00	280.00	225.00	830.00
7	*Miscellaneous*	200.00	200.00	375.00	775.00
8	**Total**	$ 5,050.00	$ 5,095.00	$ 2,545.00	$12,690.00
9					
10		Financial Resources			
11		*Semester 1*	*Semester 2*	*Summer*	***Total***
12	*Savings*	$ 800.00	$ 600.00	$ 295.00	$ 1,695.00
13	*Parents*	1,750.00	1,320.00	150.00	3,220.00
14	*Job*	1,000.00	1,800.00	2,000.00	4,800.00
15	*Financial Aid*	1,500.00	1,375.00	100.00	2,975.00
16	**Total**	$ 5,050.00	$ 5,095.00	$ 2,545.00	$12,690.00

FIGURE 1-93

Cases and Places

The difficulty of these case studies varies: ◗ are the least difficult; ◗◗ are more difficult; and ◗◗◗ are the most difficult.

1 ◗ You just started as an assistant in an optometrist's office. Your employer, Dr. Mair, has asked you to prepare a worksheet to help him determine what age groups of patients are more likely to wear contacts than glasses. He has compiled some of the data, as shown in Table 1-12.

With this data, along with your employer's additional needs, design a worksheet to present the data in an easy-to-understand format. Use the concepts and techniques presented in this project to create the worksheet.

Table 1-12

AGES	21-30	31-40	41-50	51-60	61+	TOTALS
Glasses	44	51	56	62	65	278
Contacts	73	63	50	35	12	233
Totals	117	114	106	97	77	511

2 ◗ You are a teaching assistant for Professor Firewall. She is known around campus as the *gatekeeper of diplomas*, because her courses are so rigorous. Professor Firewall has asked you to take her grade ledger (Table 1-13), which shows her grade distributions for all her spring classes, and separate them into categories based on the class and the grade. She wants a worksheet and 3-D Column chart to make it easier to view the grades at a glance. Use the concepts and techniques presented in this project to create the worksheet and chart.

Table 1-13 Professor Firewall's Summary of Grades for the Spring Semester

GRADE	CS 210	CS 340	CS 360	CS 431
A	10	3	4	2
B	12	8	2	6
C	25	12	10	3
D	30	6	13	9
F	21	9	18	4

3 ◗◗ The Main Street Rib House restaurant is trying to decide whether it is feasible to open another restaurant in a neighboring community. The owner has asked you to develop a worksheet totaling all the revenue received in a week. The revenue by day is: Monday, $1,500.80; Tuesday, $1,220.09; Wednesday, $1,435.50; Thursday, $1,565.29; Friday, $2,556.32; and Saturday, $3,102.12. On Sunday the restaurant is closed. Create a 3-D Pie chart to illustrate revenue by day and total weekly revenue. Use the AutoCalculate area to find the average daily sales.

Cases and Places

4 ▶▶ The senior accountant at Great Expectations, a local cable company where you are a student consultant, has asked you to prepare a worksheet that can be used at the next annual stockholders' meeting. The worksheet is to compare the company's expenditures last year to its anticipated expenditures this year. Last year, the company spent $1,230,000 on staff salaries and benefits, $3,015,000 on equipment, $2,550,000 on programming, and $121,000 on building and grounds maintenance. This year, the company expects to spend $1,402,000 on staff salaries and benefits, $3,275,000 on equipment, $2,525,000 on programming, and $143,000 on building and grounds maintenance. Use the concepts and techniques presented in this project to prepare the worksheet. Include total expenditures for each category and for each year, and a column chart illustrating yearly expenditures. After completing the worksheet, prepare a second worksheet showing how this year's expenditures would be affected if the amount spent on staff salaries and benefits was changed to $1,504,000 (after hiring two new technicians) and the amount spent on equipment was changed to $3,550,000 (after purchasing four new utility trucks).

5 ▶▶▶ Each year, universities report an increase in the enrollment of undergraduate students 25 years or older, who often are referred to as non-traditional students. Visit your school's Office of the Registrar to determine the number of male and number of female undergraduate students under 25 years old, and the number of male and number of female undergraduate students 25 years or older for each of the last five years. From the data, create a worksheet and a 3-D Column chart to track the data obtained.

6 ▶▶▶ Athletic footwear stores must track carefully the sales of their different shoe brands so they can restock their inventory promptly. Visit an athletic shoe store and make a list of the different brands of running shoes. Find out how many of each brand was sold over the last three months. Using this information, create a worksheet showing the number of each brand sold each month, the total number of each brand sold over three months, and the total number of running shoes sold each month. Include a 3-D Column chart to illustrate your data.

7 ▶▶▶ Drugstores often advertise that they have the lowest prices. Make a list of seven items that can be purchased from any drugstore. Visit at least three drugstores and obtain a price for each of the items listed. Make sure your prices are for similar items. Using this data, together with the techniques presented in this project, create a worksheet showing the price of each individual item in the drugstore and the total price for all seven items in a particular drugstore. Include a 3-D Column chart to illustrate your data.

Microsoft *Excel 97*

Formulas, Formatting, Charts, and Web Queries

Objectives:

You will have mastered the material in this project when you can:

- Enter multiple lines of text in the same cell
- Enter a formula using the keyboard
- Enter formulas using Point mode
- Identify the arithmetic operators +, -, *, /, %, and ^
- Apply the AVERAGE, MAX, and MIN functions
- Determine a percentage
- Change the font of a cell
- Vary the font size of characters within a cell
- Color the characters and background of a cell
- Add borders to a range
- Format numbers using the Format Cells dialog box
- Align text in cells
- Change the width of a column and height of a row
- Check the spelling of a worksheet
- Create a 3-D Pie chart on a separate sheet
- Format chart items
- Rename sheets
- Preview how a printed copy of the worksheet will look
- Print multiple sheets
- Print a partial or complete worksheet
- Display and print the formulas version of a worksheet
- Print to fit
- Distinguish between portrait and landscape orientation
- Use a Web query to get real-time data from a Web site

Cyber Workout...

Takes Fitness to a Higher Level

Dust off that old rowing machine hidden in the back of your closet, and oil that bike hanging from the rafters of your garage. It's time to shape up — with the help of your cybertrainer.

Athletes and rising athletes alike can benefit from software designed to optimize a workout. These programs function by performing calculations on data you input, similarly to the way Excel performs calculations on formulas you enter, as you will learn in this project.

Most individuals exercise to lose weight, remain fit, and prevent heart disease. Few, however, can afford personal trainers or coaches to help develop workout plans or provide guidelines to prevent exhaustion or injury. Fitness and training software available commercially has bridged this gap by creating *virtual workouts*, allowing individuals to achieve maximum fitness through steady, regulated progress while increasing strength and endurance at a fixed pace.

Although the athletic community generally did not recognize computer-based training even 10 years ago, the notion of using a scientific approach in workouts is

Computer-Based Exercise Analysis
Track Your Training Efforts...
PROJECT FUTURE PERFORMANCE!

not new. Eastern bloc Olympic coaches used computers and sophisticated software prior to the Cold War to track their athletes' performances, particularly in the sports of swimming and running. By monitoring the athletes' training times, distances, and efforts, they could show trends mathematically and then use the results of these computations to help achieve amazing athletic successes.

Laboratories now use sophisticated, expensive athletic hardware and software to research specific medical topics, such as extensively analyzing the heart's performance during training with an electrocardiogram. Meanwhile, other less expensive and more generally useful software is available for the serious and occasional athlete. The spreadsheet programs insert data entered by the athlete into worksheets, perform calculations, and produce reports and graphs that track training efforts and project future performance.

One of the first programs, UltraCoach, was developed by a computer programmer for fellow triathletes. It was enhanced by a sports medicine physician who used his iron man triathlete experiences to input data and program actual swimming, biking, and running workouts based on training data. Today, this program has evolved into a sophisticated program using artificial intelligence that uses data downloaded from recordable heart rate monitors.

One of the newer heart rate monitors is the Polar XTrainer Plus. It consists of a one-piece chest transmitter that sends the direct electrical impulses of the heart wirelessly to the wrist receiver, which also functions as a sportswatch. The receiver can perform a myriad of functions, including calculating time spent at, below, and above the target heart rate zone. The target zone is how quickly that heart should beat when exercising based on individual fitness goals and the maximum and average heart rates during the entire workout. The receiver can store up to 67 hours of training performance data in an unlimited number of files that can be downloaded to a personal computer for advanced analysis by the Polar Training Advisor Software, UltraCoach, or other programs on the market.

These effective training tools suit the needs of most athletes at every fitness level. With a customized workout plan generated from calculations in your cybertraining software, you should be well on your way to pumping it up in style.

Microsoft
Excel 97

Formulas, Formatting, Charts, and Web Queries

Case Perspective

While in a high-school Economics class, Alex Hansen and four of his friends started *High-Tech Stock Club*, a stock club geared toward researching and investing in technology stocks. Every month, they invested $15 each, researched an assigned company, and came to the meetings with their buy and sell recommendations.

All are out of college, married, and have jobs around the country. They still invest as a group using e-mail and chat rooms on the Internet to conduct their meetings. They have increased their monthly contribution to $50.

Each month, Alex summarizes the month end financial status. The value of the club's portfolio, or group of investments, is almost $150,000. As a result, the members voted to buy trading software and Microsoft Office 97 for Alex. He plans to use the trading software to invest online to reduce the club's broker costs. With Office 97, he plans to create a worksheet summarizing the club's stock activities that he can e-mail to the members. He wants to use its Web query capabilities to access real-time stock quotes. Alex has asked you to show him how to create the workbook and access real-time stock quotes over the Internet using Office 97.

Introduction

In Project 1, you learned about entering data, summing values, how to make the worksheet easier to read, and how to draw a chart. You also learned about online Help and saving, printing, and loading a workbook from floppy disk into memory. This project continues to emphasize these topics and presents some new ones.

The new topics include formulas, changing fonts, adding color to both the characters in and the background of a cell, adding borders, formatting numbers, changing the widths of columns and heights of rows, spell checking, additional charting techniques, and alternative types of worksheet displays and printouts. One alternative display and printout shows the formulas rather than the values in the worksheet. When you display the formulas in the worksheet, you see exactly what text, data, formulas, and functions you have entered into it. Finally, this project covers Web queries to obtain real-time data from a Web site.

Project Two – High-Tech Stock Club

The summary notes from your meeting with Alex include the following: need, source of data, calculations, graph requirements, and Web requirements.

Need: An easy-to-read worksheet that summarizes the club's investments for each stock owned (Figure 2-1a on page E 2.6) is needed. For each stock, the worksheet is to include the name, symbol, date acquired, number of shares, initial price, initial cost, current price, current value, and gain/loss. Alex also has requested that the worksheet include totals and an average, maximum, and minimum for each of the calculations, and a total percentage gain/loss.

Source of Data: The data supplied by Alex includes the stock names, symbols, date acquired, number of shares, the initial price, and the current price. This data is shown in Table 2-1 on page E 2.8.

Calculations: The following calculations must be made for each of the stocks as shown in Figure 2-1a on the next page.

1. Initial Cost = Shares × Initial Price
2. Current Value = Shares × Current Price
3. Gain/Loss = Current Value – Initial Cost
4. Compute the totals for initial cost, current value, gain/loss.
5. Use the AVERAGE, MAX, and MIN functions to determine the average, highest, and lowest values for the number of shares, initial price per share, initial stock cost, current stock price, current stock value, and gain/loss for each stock.
6. Percentage Gain/Loss = $\frac{\text{Total Gain/Loss}}{\text{Total Initial Cost}}$

Graph Requirements: Draw a 3-D Pie chart (Figure 2-1b on the next page) that shows the contribution of each of the stocks to the total current value of the portfolio. Highlight the stock that makes the greatest contribution.

Web Requirements: Use the Web query feature of Excel to get real-time stock quotes for the stocks owned by the High-Tech Stock Club (Figure 2-1c on the next page).

More *About* Order of Operations

To make full use of Excel, it is important that you understand the order in which multiple operations in a formula are executed. Excel uses the same order as in algebra. That is, first all negations (-), then all percents (%), then all exponentiations (^), then all multiplications (*) and divisions (/) from left to right, and finally all additions (+) and subtractions (-) from left to right. Parentheses can be used to override the order of operations.

Preparation Steps

The preparation steps summarize how the worksheet, chart, and Web query shown in Figure 2-1 will be developed in Project 2. The following tasks will be completed in this project.

1. Start the Excel program.
2. Enter the worksheet title, column titles, row titles, and stock data.
3. Compute the initial cost, current value, and gain/loss for the first stock, Compaq.
4. Copy the formulas for the remaining stocks.
5. Use the AutoSum button to display the totals for initial cost, current value, and gain/loss.
6. Determine the average, highest, and lowest values for the shares, initial price, initial cost, current price, current value, and gain/loss.
7. Compute the percentage gain/loss.
8. Save an intermediate copy of the workbook.
9. Format the worksheet so it has a professional appearance and is easy to read.

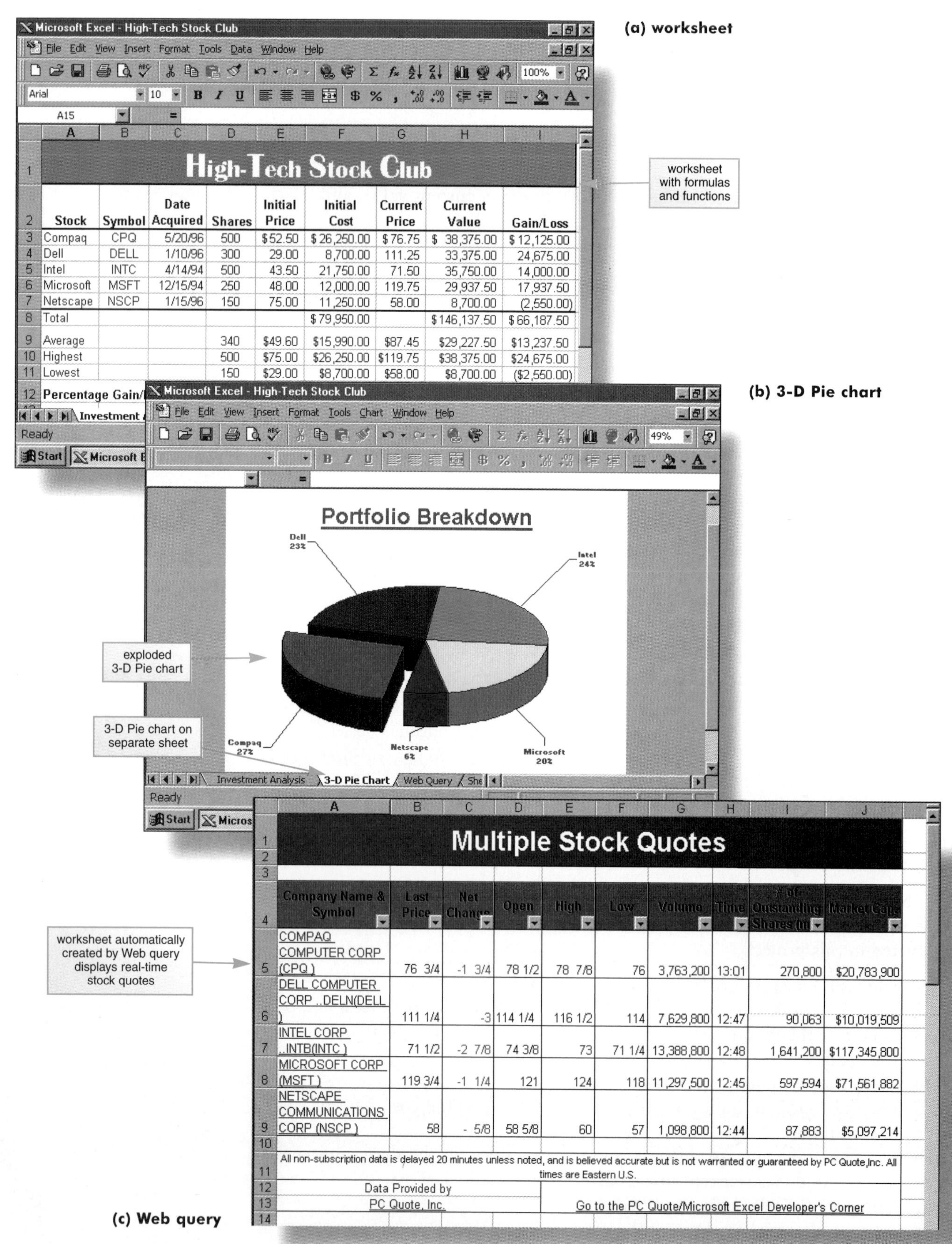
(a) worksheet
Microsoft Excel - High-Tech Stock Club
High-Tech Stock Club
worksheet with formulas and functions

Stock	Symbol	Date Acquired	Shares	Initial Price	Initial Cost	Current Price	Current Value	Gain/Loss
Compaq	CPQ	5/20/96	500	$52.50	$26,250.00	$76.75	$ 38,375.00	$12,125.00
Dell	DELL	1/10/96	300	29.00	8,700.00	111.25	33,375.00	24,675.00
Intel	INTC	4/14/94	500	43.50	21,750.00	71.50	35,750.00	14,000.00
Microsoft	MSFT	12/15/94	250	48.00	12,000.00	119.75	29,937.50	17,937.50
Netscape	NSCP	1/15/96	150	75.00	11,250.00	58.00	8,700.00	(2,550.00)
Total					$79,950.00		$146,137.50	$66,187.50
Average			340	$49.60	$15,990.00	$87.45	$29,227.50	$13,237.50
Highest			500	$75.00	$26,250.00	$119.75	$38,375.00	$24,675.00
Lowest			150	$29.00	$8,700.00	$58.00	$8,700.00	($2,550.00)
Percentage Gain/								

(b) 3-D Pie chart
Microsoft Excel - High-Tech Stock Club
Portfolio Breakdown
Dell 23%
Intel 24%
Compaq 27%
Netscape 6%
Microsoft 20%
exploded 3-D Pie chart
3-D Pie chart on separate sheet
Investment Analysis
3-D Pie Chart
Web Query

(c) Web query
Multiple Stock Quotes
worksheet automatically created by Web query displays real-time stock quotes

Company Name & Symbol	Last Price	Net Change	Open	High	Low	Volume	Time	# of Outstanding Shares (in	Market Cap
COMPAQ COMPUTER CORP (CPQ)	76 3/4	-1 3/4	78 1/2	78 7/8	76	3,763,200	13:01	270,800	$20,783,900
DELL COMPUTER CORP ..DELN(DELL)	111 1/4	-3	114 1/4	116 1/2	114	7,629,800	12:47	90,063	$10,019,509
INTEL CORP ..INTB(INTC)	71 1/2	-2 7/8	74 3/8	73	71 1/4	13,388,800	12:48	1,641,200	$117,345,800
MICROSOFT CORP (MSFT)	119 3/4	-1 1/4	121	124	118	11,297,500	12:45	597,594	$71,561,882
NETSCAPE COMMUNICATIONS CORP (NSCP)	58	- 5/8	58 5/8	60	57	1,098,800	12:44	87,883	$5,097,214

All non-subscription data is delayed 20 minutes unless noted, and is believed accurate but is not warranted or guaranteed by PC Quote,Inc. All times are Eastern U.S.
Data Provided by PC Quote, Inc.
Go to the PC Quote/Microsoft Excel Developer's Corner

FIGURE 2-1

10. Draw the 3-D Pie chart on a separate sheet (Figure 2-1b). Highlight the largest slice. Improve the readability of the pie chart by using colors to emphasize the chart title and pie slice labels.
11. Rename the sheets.
12. Save the workbook.
13. Preview and print the worksheet and 3-D Pie chart.
14. Print the formulas version of the worksheet so the formulas can be verified.
15. Use the Run Web Query command to display a worksheet with real-time stock quotes (Figure 2-1c).

The following pages contain a detailed explanation of these tasks.

Starting Excel

To start Excel, Windows 95 must be running. Perform the following steps to start Excel.

TO START EXCEL

Step 1: Click the Start button on the taskbar.
Step 2: Click New Office Document. If necessary, click the General tab in the New dialog box.
Step 3: Double-click the Blank Workbook icon.

An alternative to Steps 1 and 2 is to click the Start button, point to Programs, and click Microsoft Excel on the Programs submenu.

More *About* **Starting Excel**

An alternative way to start Excel when you want to open a workbook is to start Explorer, display the contents of the folder containing the workbook, and then double-click on the workbook name.

Entering the Titles and Numbers into the Worksheet

The worksheet title in Figure 2-1a is centered over columns A through I in row 1. Because the centered text first must be entered into the leftmost column of the area over which it is centered, it will be entered into cell A1.

TO ENTER THE WORKSHEET TITLE

Step 1: Select cell A1. Type `High-Tech Stock Club` in the cell.
Step 2: Press the DOWN ARROW key.

The worksheet title displays as shown in cell A1 of Figure 2-2 on page E 2.9.

The column headings in row 2 begin in cell A2 and extend through cell I2. As shown in Figure 2-1a, the column titles in row 2 include multiple lines of text. To start a new line in a cell, press ALT+ENTER after each line, except for the last line, which is completed by clicking the Enter box, pressing the ENTER key, or pressing one of the arrow keys. When you see ALT+ENTER in a step, while holding down the ALT key, press the ENTER key and then release both keys.

More *About* **Formatting a Worksheet**

With early spreadsheet packages, users often skipped rows to improve the appearance of the worksheet. With Excel it is not necessary to skip rows because you can increase the height of rows to add white space between information.

Table 2-1

STOCK	SYMBOL	DATE ACQUIRED	SHARES	INITIAL PRICE	CURRENT PRICE
Compaq	CPQ	5/20/96	500	$52.50	$76.75
Dell	DELL	1/10/96	300	29.00	111.25
Intel	INTC	4/14/94	500	43.50	71.50
Microsoft	MSFT	12/15/94	250	48.00	119.75
Netscape	NSCP	1/15/96	150	75.00	58.00

The stock names and total row titles in column A begin in cell A3 and continue down to cell A12. The stock club's investments, as submitted by Alex, are summarized in Table 2-1. These numbers are entered into rows 3 through 7. The steps required to enter the column titles, stock names and symbols, total row titles, and numbers as shown in Figure 2-2 are outlined in the remainder of this section.

More About Wrapping Text

If you have a long text entry, such as a paragraph, you can instruct Excel to wrap the text in a cell, rather than pressing ALT+ENTER to end a line. To wrap text, click Format Cells on the shortcut menu, click the Alignment tab, and click the Wrap Text check box. Excel will automatically increase the height of the cell so the additional lines will fit. However, if you want to control the contents of a line in a cell, rather than letting Excel wrap based on the width of a cell, then you must end a line with ALT+ENTER.

TO ENTER THE COLUMN TITLES

Step 1: With cell A2 active, type `Stock` and then press the RIGHT ARROW key.
Step 2: Type `Symbol` and then press the RIGHT ARROW key.
Step 3: Type `Date` and then press ALT+ENTER. Type `Acquired` and then press the RIGHT ARROW key.
Step 4: Type `Shares` and then press the RIGHT ARROW key.
Step 5: Type `Initial` and then press ALT+ENTER. Type `Price` and then press the RIGHT ARROW key.
Step 6: Type `Initial` and then press ALT+ENTER. Type `Cost` and then press the RIGHT ARROW key.
Step 7: Type `Current` and then press ALT+ENTER. Type `Price` and then press the RIGHT ARROW key.
Step 8: Type `Current` and then press ALT+ENTER. Type `Value` and then press the RIGHT ARROW key.
Step 9: Type `Gain/Loss` and then click cell A3.

The column titles display as shown in row 2 of Figure 2-2. When you press ALT+ENTER to add more lines to a cell, Excel automatically increases the height of the entire row.

More About Entering Numbers into a Range

An efficient way to enter a set of numbers into a range of cells, such as B3:C6 in Figure 2-2, is to select the range by dragging from cell B3 to cell C6 prior to entering the numbers. After initially selecting the range, cell B3 remains the active cell. Thus, type the value for cell B3 and press the ENTER key. Excel responds by entering the number and moving the active cell selection down one cell. When you enter the last value in the first column, Excel will move the active cell selection to the top of the next column and then proceed downward.

The stock data in Table 2-1 includes a date on which each stock was acquired. Excel considers a date to be a number and, therefore, displays it right-aligned in the cell. When you enter a date, Excel automatically formats the date so it resembles the way you entered it. For example, if you enter May 20, 1996, Excel displays it as 20-May-96. If you enter the same date in the format 5/20/96, then Excel displays it as 5/20/96. The following steps describe how to enter the stock data shown in Table 2-1.

TO ENTER THE STOCK DATA

Step 1: With cell A3 selected, type `Compaq` and then press the RIGHT ARROW key. Type `CPQ` and then press the RIGHT ARROW key.
Step 2: With cell C3 selected, type `5/20/96` and then press the RIGHT ARROW key. Type `500` and then press the RIGHT ARROW key.
Step 3: With cell E3 selected, type `52.5` and then press the RIGHT ARROW key twice. Type `76.75` and then press the ENTER key.
Step 4: Click cell A4. Enter the data for the four remaining stocks in rows 4 through 7.

The stock data displays in rows 3 through 7 as shown in Figure 2-2.

TO ENTER THE TOTAL ROW TITLES

Step 1: Click cell A8. Type `Total` and then press the DOWN ARROW key. Type `Average` and then press the DOWN ARROW key.

Step 2: With cell A10 selected, type `Highest` and then press the DOWN ARROW key. Type `Lowest` and then press the DOWN ARROW key.

Step 3: With cell A12 selected, type `Percentage Gain/Loss ====>` and then click cell F3.

The total row titles display as shown in Figure 2-2.

Microsoft Excel - Book1

File Edit View Insert Format Tools Data Window Help

Arial 10 | F3 | 100%

worksheet title

column titles on multiple lines within cell

	A	B	C	D	E	F	G	H	I
1	High-Tech Stock Club								
2	Stock	Symbol	Date Acquired	Shares	Initial Price	Initial Cost	Current Price	Current Value	Gain/Loss
3	Compaq	CPQ	5/20/96	500	52.5		76.75		
4	Dell	DELL	1/10/96	300	29		111.25		
5	Intel	INTC	4/14/94	500	43.5		71.5		
6	Microsoft	MSFT	12/15/94	250	48		119.75		
7	Netscape	NSCP	1/15/96	150	75		58		
8	Total								
9	Average								
10	Highest								
11	Lowest								
12	Percentage Gain/Loss ====>								

dates

numbers

FIGURE 2-2

Entering Formulas

The initial cost for each stock, which displays in column F, is equal to the number of shares in column D times the initial price in column E. Thus, the initial cost for Compaq in row 3 is obtained by multiplying 500 (cell D3) times 52.5 (cell E3).

One of the reasons Excel is such a valuable tool is that you can assign a **formula** to a cell and Excel will calculate the result. Consider, for example, what would happen if you had to multiply 500 × 52.5 and then enter the result, 26250, in cell F3 manually. Every time the values in cells D3 and E3 changed, you would have to recalculate the product and enter the new value in cell F3. By contrast, if you enter a formula in cell F3 to multiply the values in cells D3 and E3, Excel recalculates the product whenever new values are entered into those cells and displays the result in cell F3. Complete the following steps to enter the formula using the keyboard.

More *About* **Recalculation of Formulas**

Every time you enter a value into a cell in the worksheet, Excel recalculates all formulas. It makes no difference if there is one formula or hundreds of formulas in the worksheet. Excel recalculates the formulas instantaneously. This is one of the reasons why a spreadsheet package, such as Excel, is so powerful.

Steps To Enter a Formula Using the Keyboard

With cell F3 selected, type `=d3*e3` **in the cell.**

The formula displays in the formula bar and in cell F3 (Figure 2-3).

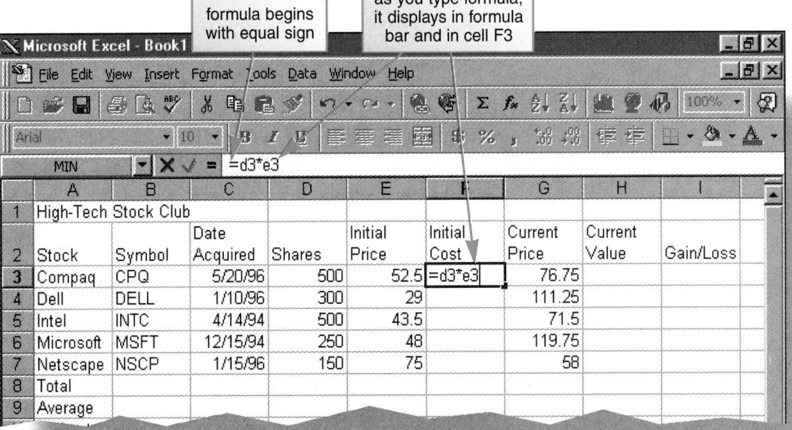

FIGURE 2-3

2 **Press the RIGHT ARROW key twice to select cell H3.**

Instead of displaying the formula in cell F3, Excel completes the arithmetic operation indicated by the formula and displays the result, 26250 (Figure 2-4).

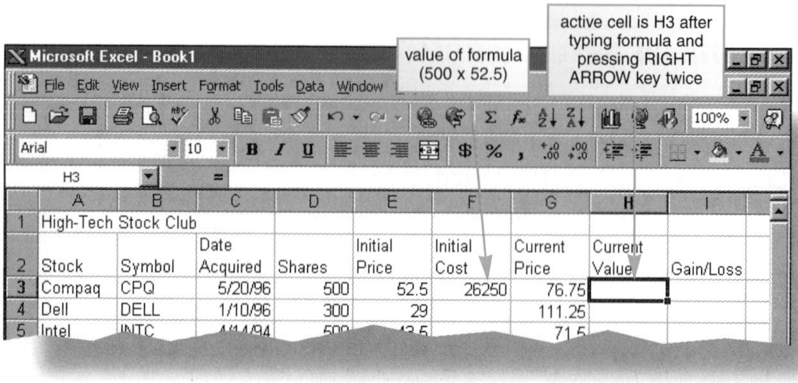

value of formula (500 x 52.5)

active cell is H3 after typing formula and pressing RIGHT ARROW key twice

	A	B	C	D	E	F	G	H	I
1	High-Tech Stock Club								
2	Stock	Symbol	Date Acquired	Shares	Initial Price	Initial Cost	Current Price	Current Value	Gain/Loss
3	Compaq	CPQ	5/20/96	500	52.5	26250	76.75		
4	Dell	DELL	1/10/96	300	29		111.25		
5	Intel	INTC					71.5		

FIGURE 2-4

More About Entering Formulas

Besides the equal sign (=), you can start a formula with a plus sign (+) or a minus sign (-). However, don't forget to start with one of these three characters or the formula will be interpreted by Excel as text.

The equal sign (=) preceding d3*e3 is an important part of the formula: it alerts Excel that you are entering a formula or function and not text. The asterisk (*) following d3 is the arithmetic operator, which directs Excel to perform the **multiplication operation**. Other valid Excel arithmetic operators include + (**addition**), – (**subtraction** or **negation**), / (**division**), % (**percentage**), and ^ (**exponentiation**).

You can enter the cell references in formulas in uppercase or lowercase, and you can add spaces before and after arithmetic operators to make the formulas easier to read. That is, =d3*e3 is the same as =d3 * e3, =D3 * e3, or =D3 * E3.

Order of Operations

More About Troubling Formulas

If Excel will not accept a formula, remove the equal sign from the left side and complete the entry as text. Later, after entering additional data or after you have determined the error, reinsert the equal sign.

When more than one operator is involved in a formula, Excel follows the same basic order of operations that you use in algebra. Moving from left to right in a formula, the **order of operations** is as follows: first negation (–), then all percentages (%), then all exponentiations (^), then all multiplications (*) and divisions (/), and, finally all additions (+) and subtractions (–). You can use **parentheses** to override the order of operations. For example, if Excel follows the order of operations, 10 * 6 – 3 equals 57. If you use parentheses, however, to change the formula to 10 * (6 – 3), the result is 30, because the parentheses instruct Excel to subtract 3 from 6 before multiplying by 10. Table 2-2 illustrates several examples of valid formulas and explains the order of operations.

Table 2-2

FORMULA	REMARK
=G6	Assigns the value in cell G6 to the active cell.
=4 + -5^2	Assigns the sum of 4 + 25 (or 29) to the active cell.
=3 * J4 or =J4 * 3 or =(3 * J4)	Assigns three times the contents of cell J4 to the active cell.
=25% * 12	Assigns the product of 0.25 times 12 (or 3) to the active cell.
=-J12 * S23	Assigns the negative value of the product of the values contained in cells J12 and S23 to the active cell.
=5 * (L14 – H3)	Assigns the product of five times the difference between the values contained in cells H3 and L14 to the active cell.
=D1 / X6 - A3 * A4 + A5 ^ A6	From left to right: first exponentiation (A5 ^ A6), then division (D1 / X6), then multiplication (A3 * A4), then subtraction (D1 / X6) - (A3 * A4), and finally addition (D1 / X6 - A3 * A4) + (A5 ^ A6). If cells D1 = 10, A3 = 6, A4 = 2, A5 = 5, A6 = 2, and X6 = 2, then Excel assigns the active cell the value 18 (10 / 2 - 6 * 2 + 5 ^ 2 = 18).

The first formula (=d3*e3) in the worksheet was entered into cell F3 using the keyboard. The next section shows you how to enter the formulas in cells H3 and I3 using the mouse to select cell references in a formula.

Entering Formulas Using Point Mode

In the worksheet shown in Figure 2-1a on page E 2.6, the current value of each stock displays in column H. The current value for Compaq in cell H3 is equal to the number of shares in cell D3 times the current price in cell G3. The gain/loss for Compaq in cell I3 is equal to the current value in cell H3 minus the initial cost in cell F3.

Instead of using the keyboard to enter the formulas =d3*g3 in cell H3 and =h3 – f3 in cell I3, you can use the mouse and Point mode to enter these last two formulas. **Point mode** allows you to select cells for use in a formula by using the mouse.

More *About* Using Point Mode

Point mode allows you to create formulas using the mouse. Rather than typing a cell reference in a formula, simply click a cell and Excel will append the corresponding cell reference at the location of the insertion point. You can also use the Customize command on the shortcut menu that displays when you right-click a toolbar to create a new toolbar made up of buttons that represent the operators. Thus, with Excel you can enter entire formulas without ever touching the keyboard.

To Enter Formulas Using Point Mode

1 With cell H3 selected, type = (an equal sign) to begin the formula and then click cell D3.

Excel surrounds cell D3 with a marquee and appends D3 to the equal sign (=) in cell H3 (Figure 2-5).

marquee surrounds selected cell D3

cell reference D3 appended to formula

FIGURE 2-5

2 Type * (an asterisk) and then click cell G3.

Excel surrounds cell G3 with a marquee and appends G3 to the asterisk (*) in cell H3 (Figure 2-6).

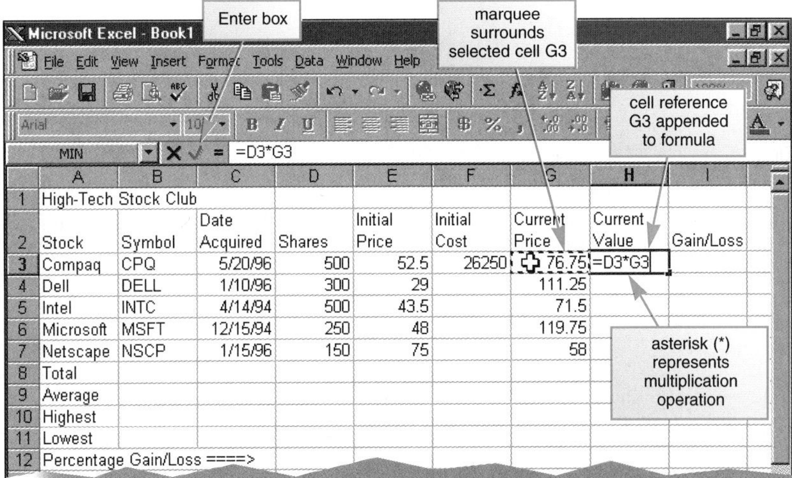

FIGURE 2-6

3 **Click the Enter box or press the ENTER key. Click cell I3.**

*Excel determines the product of =D3*G3 and displays the result, 38375, in cell H3 (Figure 2-7).*

4 **With cell I3 selected, type = (equal sign) and then click cell H3. Type - (minus sign) and then click cell F3.**

The formula =H3 – F3 displays in cell I3 and in the formula bar (Figure 2-7).

FIGURE 2-7

5 **Click the Enter box or press the ENTER key.**

The gain/loss for Compaq, 12125, displays in cell I3 (Figure 2-8).

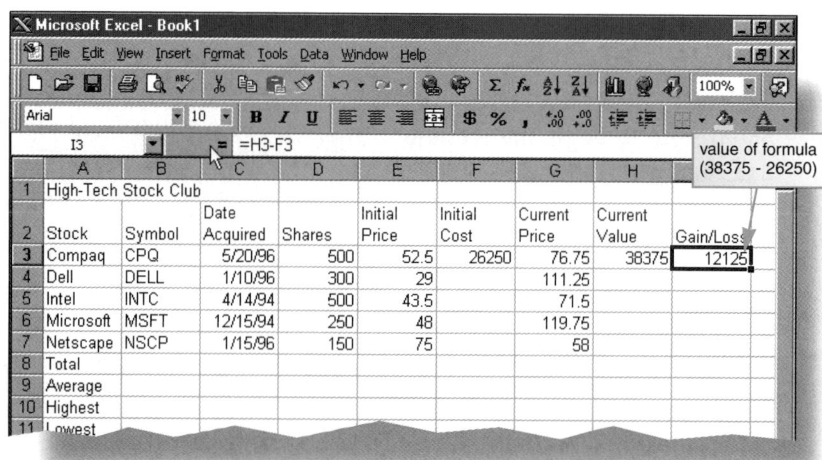

	A	B	C	D	E	F	G	H	I
1	High-Tech Stock Club								
2	Stock	Symbol	Date Acquired	Shares	Initial Price	Initial Cost	Current Price	Current Value	Gain/Loss
3	Compaq	CPQ	5/20/96	500	52.5	26250	76.75	38375	12125
4	Dell	DELL	1/10/96	300	29		111.25		
5	Intel	INTC	4/14/94	500	43.5		71.5		
6	Microsoft	MSFT	12/15/94	250	48		119.75		
7	Netscape	NSCP	1/15/96	150	75		58		
8	Total								
9	Average								
10	Highest								
11	Lowest								

FIGURE 2-8

More *About* **Range Finder**

Range Finder allows you to check to be sure a formula or chart is referencing the correct cell or range of cells. If you double-click a cell containing a formula or a chart, Excel will use colored frames to indicate the cells that are referenced in the formula. For example, if you double-click H3, Excel will draw colored frames around cells H3 and F3 because they are referenced in the formula. You can then point to the colored frame and move it to adjust the makeup of the formula or chart.

Depending on the length and complexity of the formula, using Point mode to enter formulas often is faster than using the keyboard. As shown later in the project, in some instances, you may want to combine the keyboard and mouse when entering a formula in a cell. You can use the keyboard to begin the formula, for example, and then use the mouse to select a range of cells.

Entering Formulas Using Natural Language

If the column titles in a worksheet are simple (no spaces and no multiple lines), then you can use them, rather than cell references, in formulas. For example, suppose you are creating a payroll worksheet in which the hours and rate columns are titled Hours and Rate, respectively. To determine the corresponding gross pay, you then could enter the formula, =hours*rate. When you enter a formula using the column or row titles, it is referred to as a **natural language formula**. See Test Your Knowledge Exercise 3 on page E 2.68 for additional examples.

Copying the Formulas Using the Fill Handle

The three formulas for Compaq in cells F3, H3, and I3 now are complete. You could enter the same three formulas one at a time for the four remaining stocks, Dell, Intel, Microsoft, and Netscape. An easier method of entering the formulas, however, is to select the formulas in row 3 and then use the fill handle to copy them through row 7. Perform the following steps to copy the formulas.

To Copy Formulas Using the Fill Handle

1 **Click cell F3 and then point to the fill handle. Drag the fill handle through cell F7 and hold down the left mouse button.**

A border surrounds the copy and paste areas (F3:F7) and the mouse pointer changes to a cross hair (Figure 2-9).

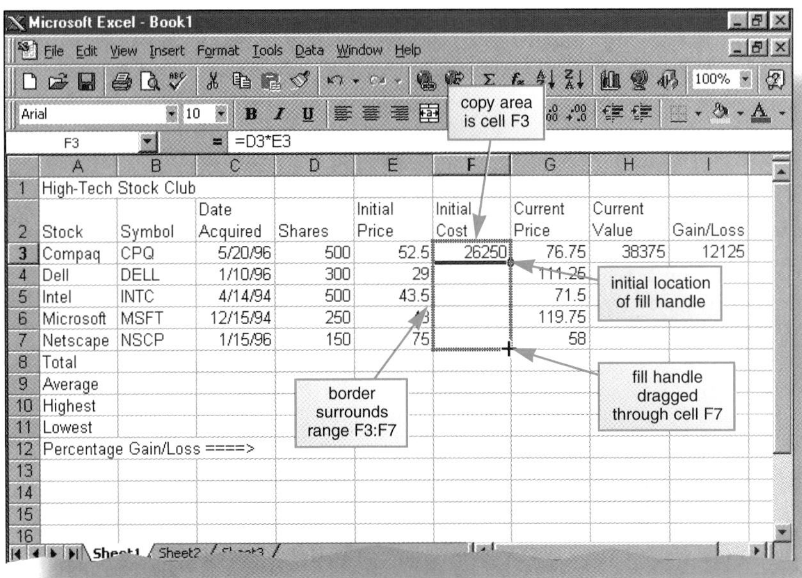

FIGURE 2-9

2 **Release the left mouse button.**

*Excel copies the formula =D3*E3 to the range F4:F7 and displays the initial costs for the remaining four stocks (Figure 2-10).*

3 **Select the range H3:I3 and then point to the fill handle.**

The range H3:I3 is highlighted (Figure 2-10).

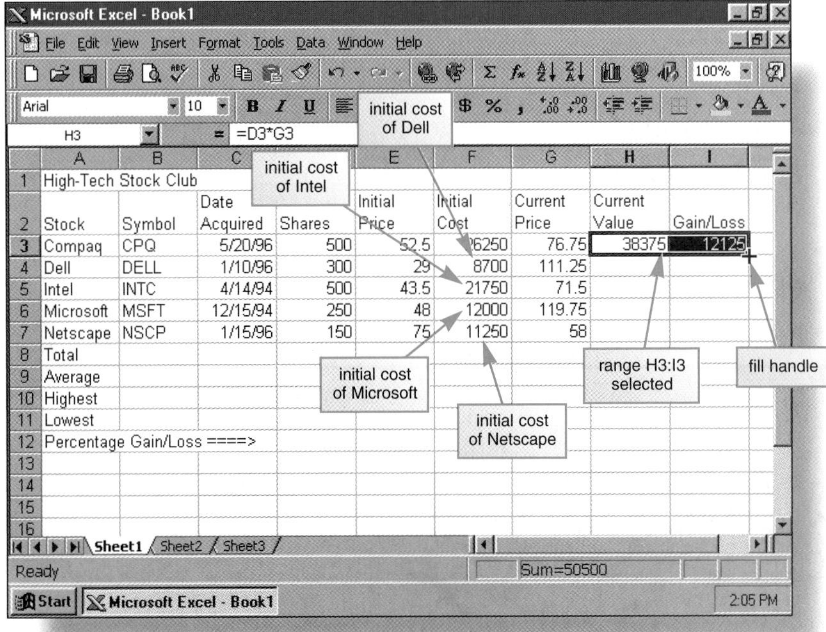

FIGURE 2-10

4 Drag the fill handle down through H7:I7.

*Excel copies the two formulas =D3*G3 in cell H3 and =H3-F3 in cell I3 to the range H4:I7 and displays the current value and gain/loss for the remaining four stocks (Figure 2-11).*

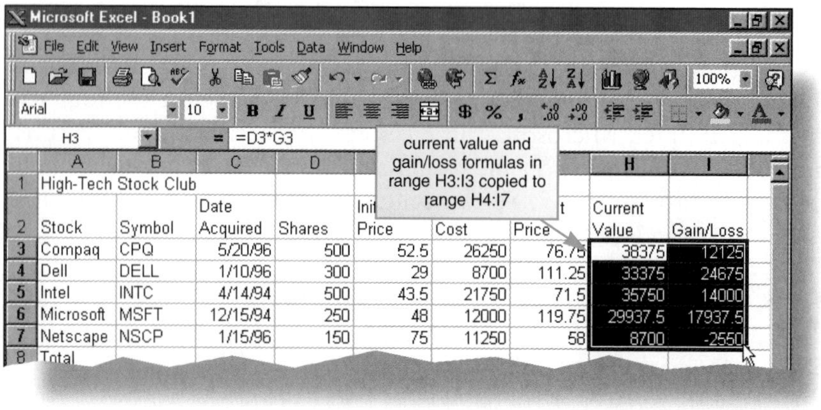

current value and gain/loss formulas in range H3:I3 copied to range H4:I7

FIGURE 2-11

OtherWays

1. Select copy area, right-click copy area, on shortcut menu click Copy, right-click paste area, on shortcut menu click Paste
2. Select copy area, on Standard toolbar click Copy button, select paste area, on Standard toolbar click Paste button
3. Select copy area, on Edit menu click Copy, select paste area, on Edit menu click Paste
4. Select copy area, press CTRL+C, select paste area, press CTRL+V

Recall that when you copy a formula, Excel adjusts the cell references so that the new formulas contain references corresponding to the new location and perform calculations using the appropriate values. Thus, if you copy downward, Excel adjusts the row portion of cell references. If you copy across, then Excel adjusts the column portion of cell references.

Determining the Totals Using the AutoSum Button

The next step is to determine the totals in row 8 for the following three columns: initial cost in column F, current value in column H, and gain/loss in column I. To determine the total initial cost in column F, you must sum cells F3 through F7. To do so, you can enter the function =sum(f3:f7) in cell F8, or you can select cell F8 and then click the AutoSum button on the Standard toolbar twice. Similar SUM functions or the AutoSum button can be used in cells H8 and I8 to determine total current value and total gain/loss, respectively.

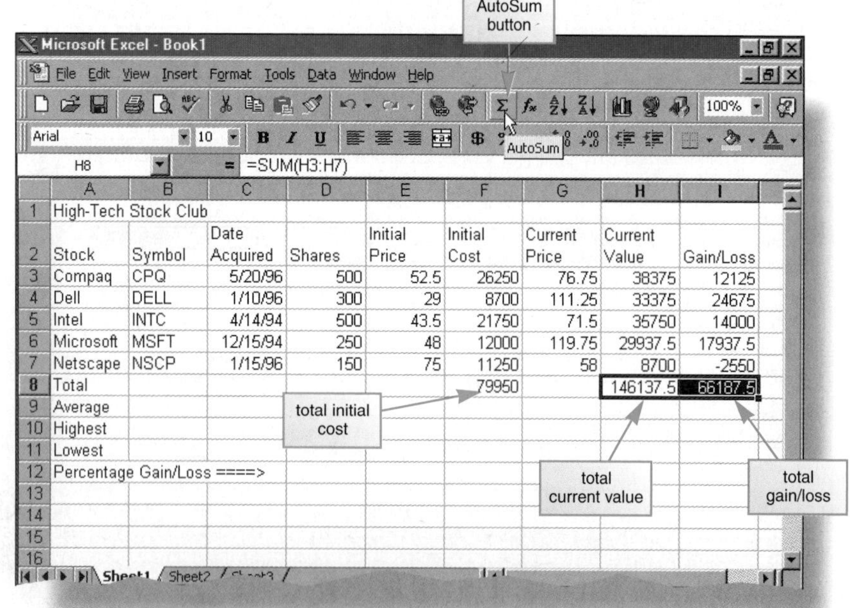

FIGURE 2-12

TO DETERMINE TOTALS USING THE AUTOSUM BUTTON

Step 1: Select cell F8. Click the AutoSum button twice. (Do not double-click.)

Step 2: Select the range H8:I8. Click the AutoSum button.

The three totals display in row 8 as shown in Figure 2-12.

Rather than using the AutoSum function to calculate column totals individually, you can select all three cells before clicking the AutoSum button to calculate all three column totals at one time. To select the nonadjacent range F8, H8, and I8, select cell F8, and then, while holding down the CTRL key, drag through the range H8:I8. Next, click the AutoSum button.

Using the AVERAGE, MAX, and MIN Functions

The next step in creating the High-Tech Stock Club worksheet is to compute the average, maximum value, and minimum value for the number of shares in column D. Once the values are determined, the entries can be copied across to the other columns. Excel includes prewritten formulas called **functions** to help you compute these statistics. A function takes a value or values, performs an operation, and returns a value or values. The values that you use with a function are called **arguments**. All functions begin with an equal sign and include the arguments in parentheses after the function name. For example, in the function =AVERAGE(D3:D7), the function name is AVERAGE and the argument is the range D3:D7.

With Excel, you can enter functions using one of three methods: (1) the keyboard or mouse; (2) the Edit Formula box and Function box; and (3) the Paste Function button. The method you choose will depend on whether you can recall the function name and required arguments. In the following pages, each of the three methods is used to calculate a different statistic: the keyboard and mouse are used to determine the average number of shares (cell D9); the Edit Formula box and Function box are used to determine the maximum number of shares (cell D10); and the Paste Function button is used to determine the minimum number of shares (cell D11).

More About Selecting a Range

If you dislike dragging to select a range, press F8 and use the arrow keys to select one corner of the range and then the cell diagonally opposite it in the proposed range. Make sure you press F8 to turn selection off after you are finished with the range or you will continue to select ranges.

Determining the Average of a Range of Numbers

To determine the average of the numbers in the range D3:D7, use the **AVERAGE function** as shown in the following steps.

To Determine the Average of a Range of Numbers Using the Keyboard and Mouse

1. **Select cell D9. Type** =average(**in the cell.**

   Excel displays the beginning of the AVERAGE function in the formula bar and in cell D9.

2. **Click cell D3, the first endpoint of the range to average. Drag through cell D7, the second endpoint of the range to average.**

   A marquee surrounds the range D3:D7. When you click cell D3, Excel appends cell D3 to the left parenthesis in the formula bar and surrounds cell D3 with a marquee. When you begin dragging, Excel appends a colon (:) and the cell reference of the cell where the mouse pointer is located to the function (Figure 2-13).

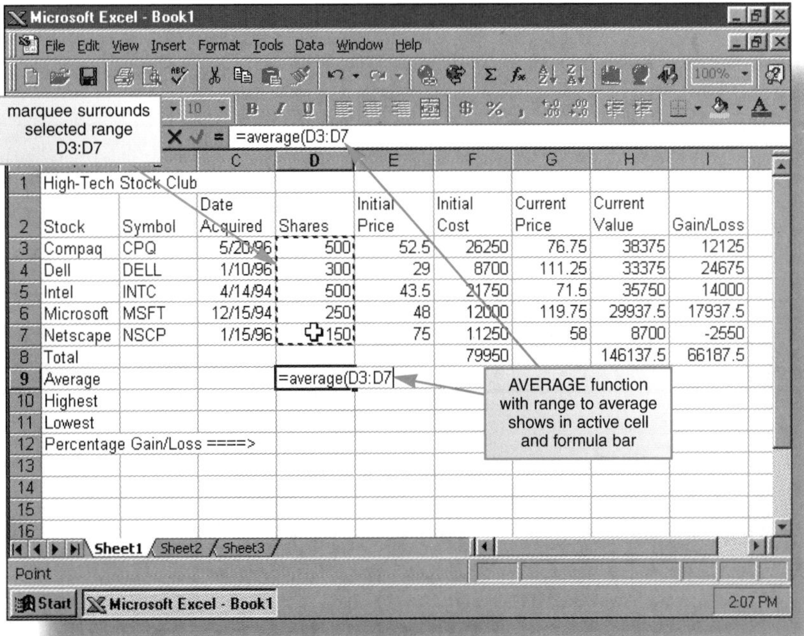

FIGURE 2-13

3 **Click the Enter box or press the ENTER key.**

Excel computes the average of the five numbers in the range D3:D7 and displays the result, 340, in cell D9 (Figure 2-14).

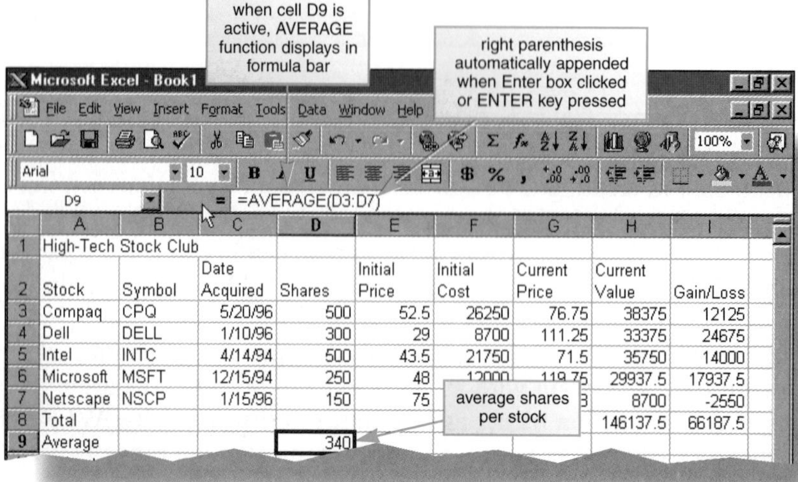

FIGURE 2-14

OtherWays

1. In formula bar click Edit Formula box, in Function box click AVERAGE
2. On Standard toolbar click Paste Function button, click AVERAGE function

The AVERAGE function requires that the range (the argument) be included within parentheses following the function name. Excel thus automatically appends the right parenthesis to complete the AVERAGE function when you click the Enter box or press the ENTER key. When you use the Point mode, as in the previous steps, you cannot use the arrow keys to complete the entry. While in Point mode, the arrow keys change the selected cell reference in the formula being created.

Determining the Highest Number in a Range of Numbers

The next step is to select cell D10 and determine the highest (maximum) number in the range D3:D7. Excel has a function called the **MAX function** that displays the highest value in a range. Although you could enter the MAX function using the keyboard and Point mode as you did in the previous steps, an alternative method to entering the function is to use the Edit Formula box and Function box.

To Determine the Highest Number in a Range of Numbers Using the Edit Formula Box and Function Box

1 **With cell D10 selected, click the Edit Formula box in the formula bar. Click the Function box arrow and then point to MAX.**

The Name box in the formula bar changes to the ***Function box****. The* ***Formula palette*** *displays immediately below the formula bar (Figure 2-15). An equal sign displays in the formula bar and active cell, D10.*

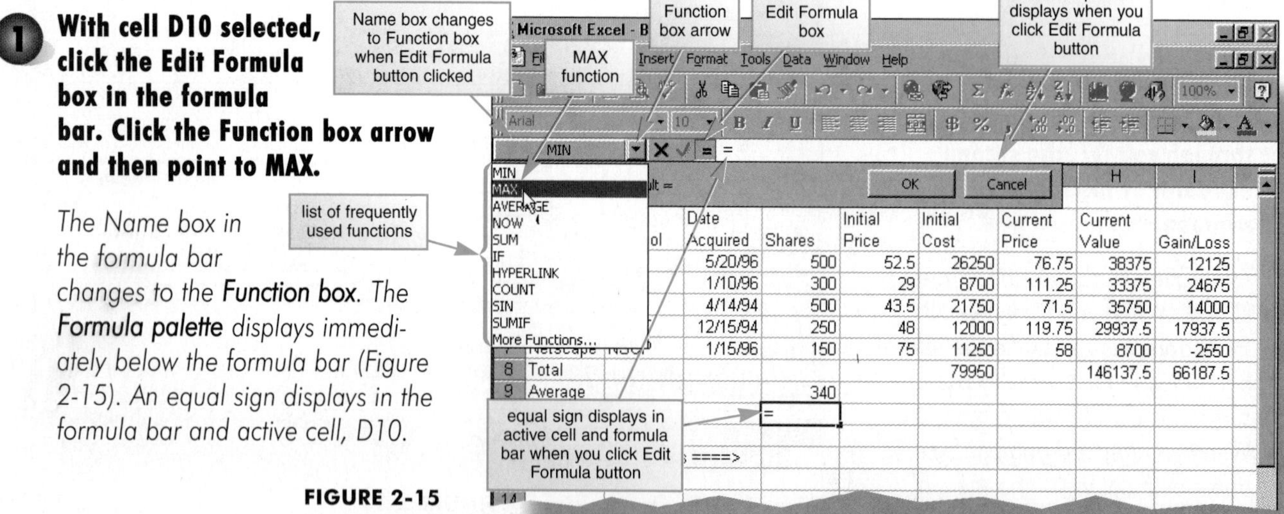

FIGURE 2-15

2 **Click MAX. When the Formula palette displays, type** d3:d7 **in the Number 1 text box. Point to the OK button.**

The MAX Formula palette displays with the range d3:d7 entered in the Number 1 text box (Figure 2-16). The completed MAX function displays in the formula bar and the end of the function displays in the active cell, D10.

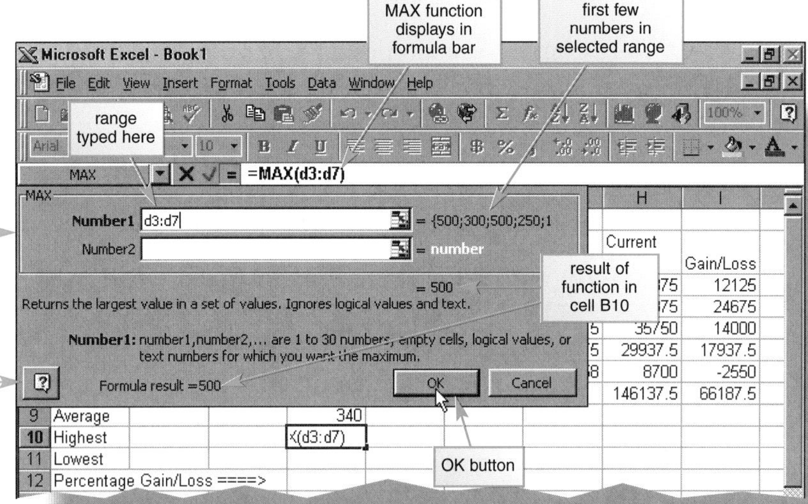

FIGURE 2-16

3 **Click the OK button.**

Excel determines that the highest value in the range D3:D7 is 500 (cell D3 and D5) and displays it in cell D10 (Figure 2-17).

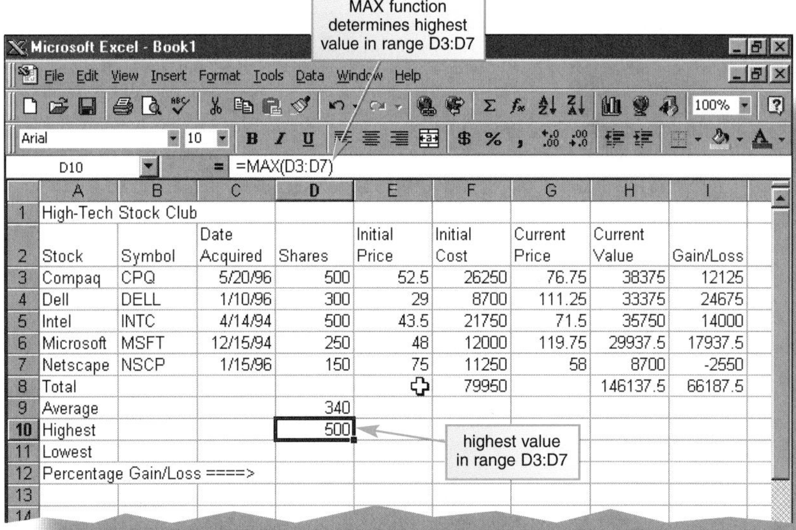

FIGURE 2-17

OtherWays

1. On Standard toolbar click Paste Function button, click MAX function
2. Type MAX function in cell

As shown in Figure 2-16, the Formula palette displays the value the MAX function will return to cell D10. It also lists the first few numbers in the selected range, next to the Number 1 text box.

In this example, rather than entering the MAX function, you easily could scan the range D3:D7, determine that the highest number of shares is 500, and enter the number as a constant in cell D10. The display would be the same as Figure 2-17. Because it contains a constant, cell D10 will continue to display 500, even if the values in the range D3:D7 change. If you use the MAX function, however, Excel will recalculate the highest value in the range D3:D7 each time a new value is entered into the worksheet. Manually determining the highest value in the range also would be more difficult if the club owned more stocks.

Determining the Lowest Number in a Range of Numbers

The next step is to enter the **MIN function** in cell D11 to determine the lowest (minimum) number in the range D3:D7. Although you could enter the MIN function using either of the methods used to enter the AVERAGE and MAX functions, the following steps show an alternative using Excel's **Paste Function** button on the Standard toolbar.

To Determine the Lowest Number in a Range of Numbers Using the Paste Function Button

1. Click cell D11. Click the Paste Function button on the Standard toolbar. When the Paste Function dialog box displays, click Statistical in the Function category list. Scroll down and click MIN in the Function name list. Point to the OK button.

Excel displays the Paste Function dialog box (Figure 2-18). Statistical and MIN are selected. An equal sign displays in the formula bar and in the active cell, D11.

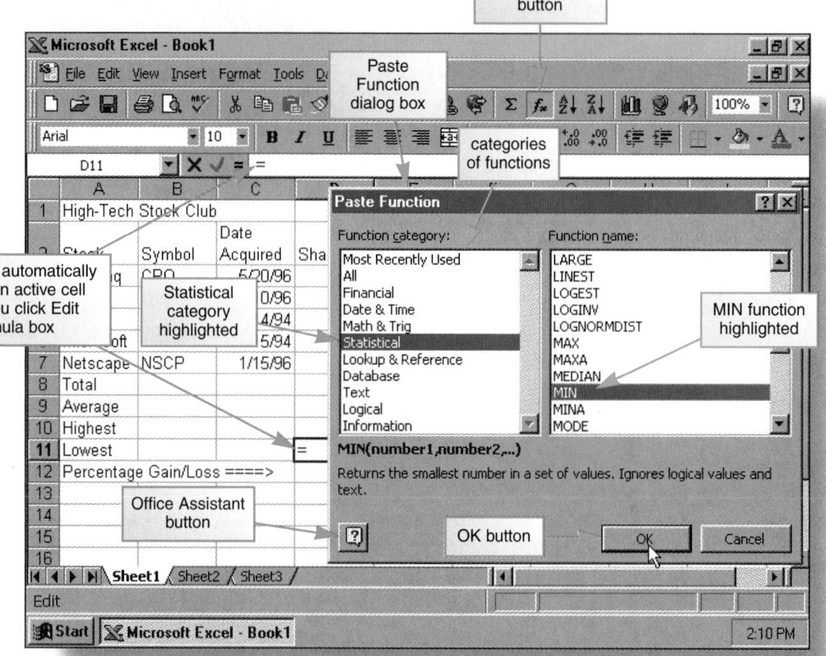

FIGURE 2-18

2. Click the OK button. When the MIN Formula palette displays, drag it to the bottom of the screen. Click cell D3 and then drag through cell D7.

The MIN Formula palette displays at the bottom of the screen (Figure 2-19). The range D3:D7 displays in the Number 1 text box. The desired MIN function displays in the formula bar and the end of it displays in the active cell, D11.

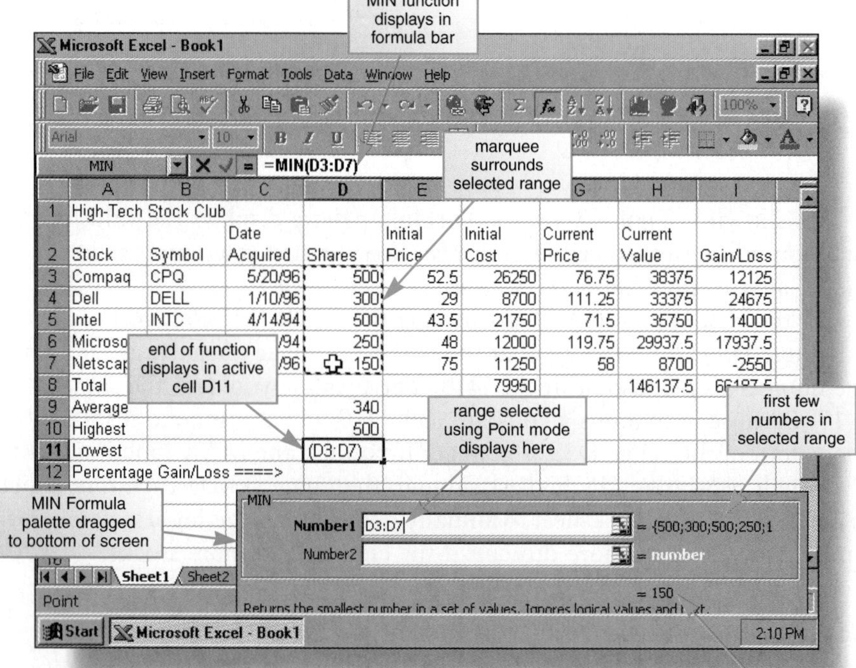

FIGURE 2-19

3 **Click the Enter box or press the ENTER key.**

Excel determines that the lowest value in the range D3:D7 is 150 and displays it in cell D11 (Figure 2-20).

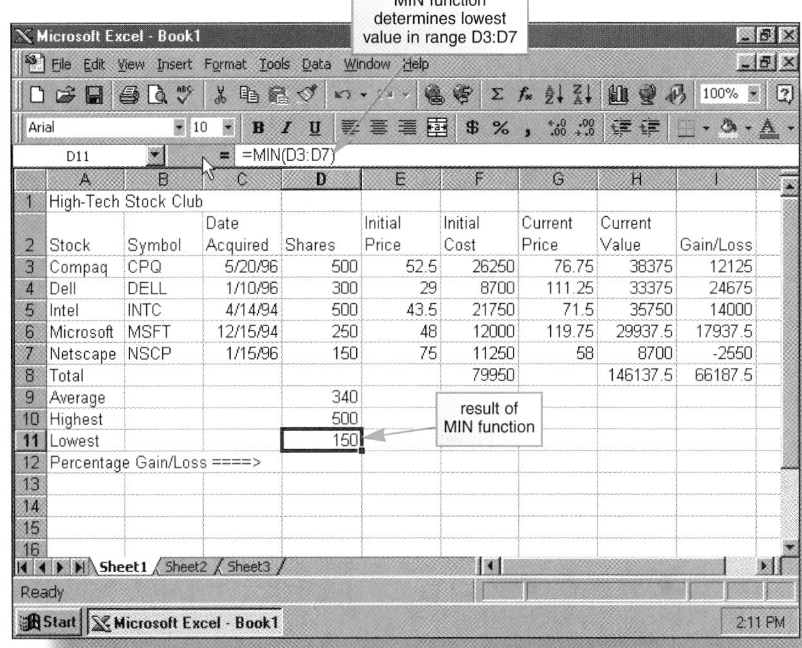

FIGURE 2-20

***Other*Ways**

1. In formula bar click Edit Formula box, in Function box click MIN function
2. Type MIN function in cell

You can see from the previous example that using the Paste Function button on the Standard toolbar allows you to enter a function into a cell easily without requiring you to memorize its name or the required arguments. Anytime you desire to enter a function, but cannot remember these, simply click the Paste Function button on the Standard toolbar, select the desired function, and enter the arguments in the Formula palette.

Thus far, you have learned to use the SUM, AVERAGE, MAX, and MIN functions. In addition to these four functions, Excel has more than 400 other functions that perform just about every type of calculation you can imagine. These functions are categorized as shown in the Function Category box in Figure 2-18.

To obtain a list and description of the available functions, click Contents and Index on the Help menu. When Excel displays the Help Topics: Microsoft Excel dialog box, click the Index tab and then type `functions` in the top text box labeled 1. Under functions in the lower list box labeled 2, double-click overview. One at a time, double-click each category. To obtain a printout of any topic, right-click the Help window and then click Print Topic on the shortcut menu. Click the Help Topics button to return to the Index sheet.

More *About* Excel's Add-Ins

Excel comes with add-ins that can simplify your work. Add-ins are installed during the installation process and activated through the Add-Ins command on the Tools menu. Some add-ins add commands to menus or controls to dialog boxes. Some of the more popular add-ins are View Manager (name and save frequently used worksheet locations), Analysis ToolPak (new function category), Engineering (engineering functions), Report Manager (additional printing capabilities), and Solver (linear and nonlinear optimization).

Copying the AVERAGE, MAX, and MIN Functions

The next step is to copy the AVERAGE, MAX, and MIN functions in the range D9:D11 to the range E9:I11. The fill handle again will be used to complete the copy.

To Copy a Range of Cells Across Columns to an Adjacent Range Using the Fill Handle

1. Select the range D9:D11. Drag the fill handle in the lower-right corner of the selected range through cell I11 and hold down the left mouse button.

Excel highlights the copy area (range D9:D11) and displays a border around the copy and paste areas (range D9:I11) (Figure 2-21).

border surrounds copy and paste area

mouse pointer

copy range D9:D11 selected

fill handle dragged to select paste area E9:I11

FIGURE 2-21

2. Release the left mouse button.

Excel copies the three functions to the range E9:I11 (Figure 2-22).

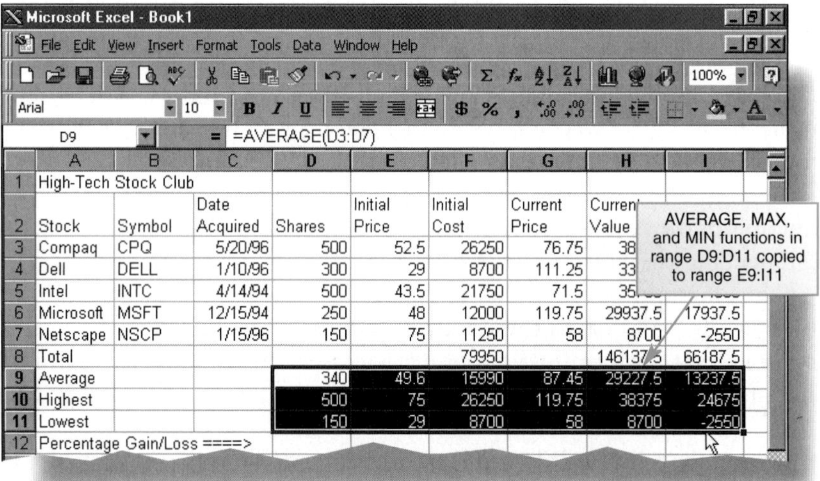

FIGURE 2-22

More About Ranges

If you are an experienced 1-2-3 user and find it difficult to change your ways, you can enter a range using two periods. For example, Excel interprets B5..B10 as B5:B10.

Again, remember that Excel adjusts the ranges in the copied functions so that each function refers to the column of numbers above it. Review the numbers in rows 9 through 11 in Figure 2-22. You should see that the functions in each column return the appropriate values, based on the numbers in rows 3 through 7 of that column.

Entering the Percentage Gain/Loss Formula

The last required entry is the formula that displays the percentage gain/loss in cell D12. The formula determines the percentage gain/loss by dividing the total gain/loss in cell I8 by the total initial cost in cell F8. After you enter the last entry in the worksheet, you also will want to save the worksheet to a floppy disk.

To Enter a Percentage Formula

1 **Click cell D12. Type = and then click cell I8. Type / and then click cell F8.**

The formula displays in the formula bar and in cell D12 (Figure 2-23). A marquee surrounds cell F8.

FIGURE 2-23

2 **Click the Enter box or press the ENTER key.**

Excel assigns the formula to cell D12 and displays the result of the formula (0.827861) in cell D12.

3 **Click the Save button on the Standard toolbar. Type** `High-Tech Stock Club` **in the File name text box. If necessary, change to 3½ Floppy (A:) in the Save in box. Click the Save button in the Save As dialog box.**

The file name in the title bar changes to High-Tech Stock Club (Figure 2-24).

FIGURE 2-24

This concludes entering the data and formulas into the worksheet. After Excel saves the file, the worksheet remains on the screen with the file name, High-Tech Stock Club, in the title bar. You immediately can continue with the next activity, which is applying formats to the worksheet to make it is easier to read.

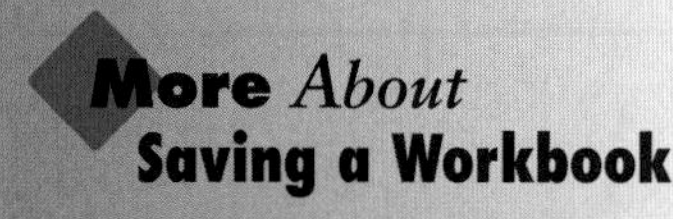

You should save your workbooks every 5 to 10 minutes so that if the system fails you can retrieve a copy without a major loss of work.

Applying Formats to the Text

Although the worksheet contains the appropriate data, formulas, and functions, the text and numbers need to be formatted to improve their appearance and readability.

In Project 1, you used the AutoFormat command to format the majority of the worksheet. This section describes how to change the unformatted worksheet in Figure 2-25a to the formatted worksheet in Figure 2-25b using the Formatting toolbar and Format Cells command.

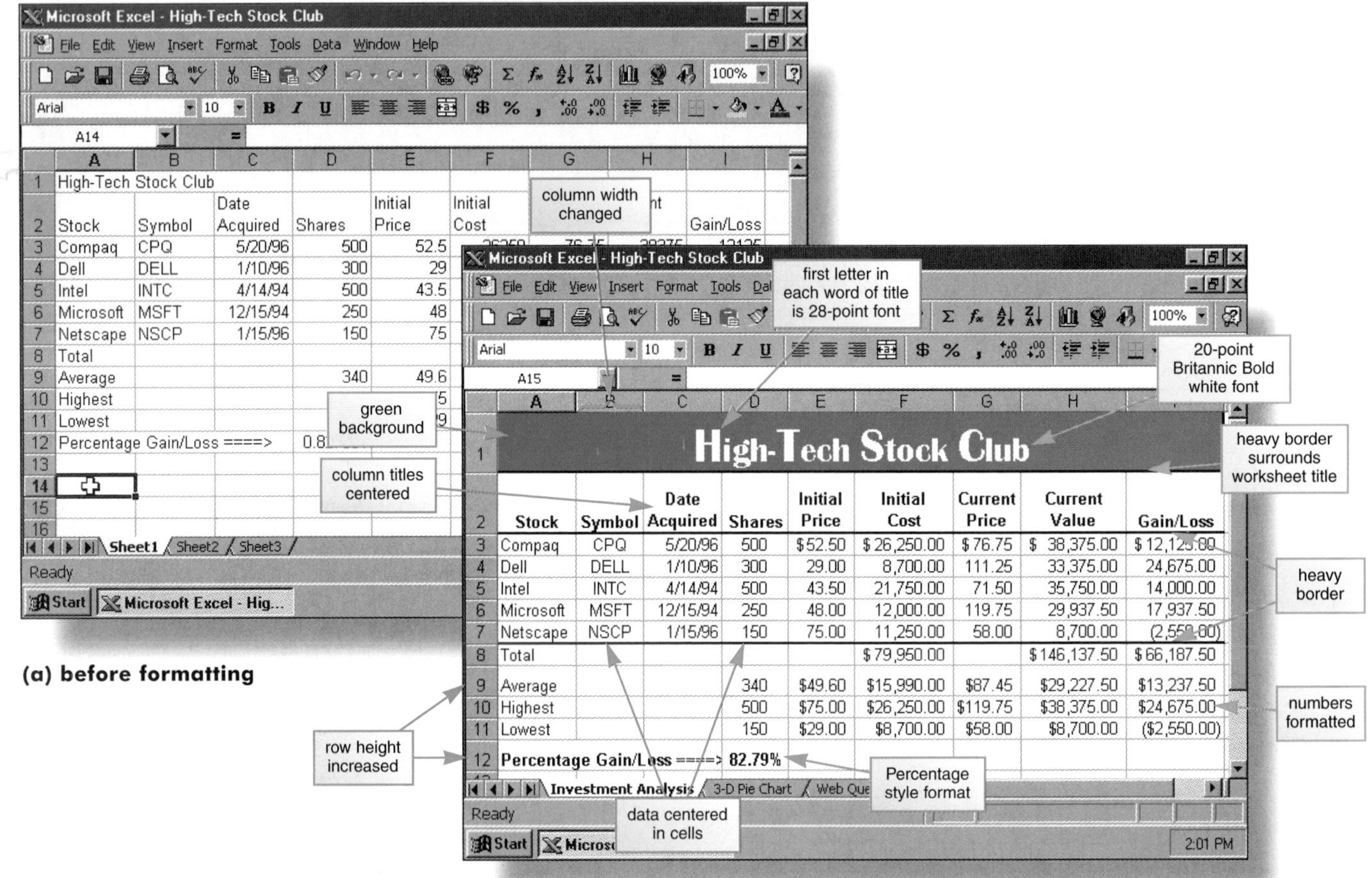

(a) before formatting

FIGURE 2-25

(b) after formatting

More *About* Choosing Colors

Knowing how people perceive colors helps you emphasize parts of your worksheet. Warmer colors (red and orange) tend to reach toward the reader. Cooler colors (blue, green, and violet) tend to pull away from the reader. Bright colors jump out of a dark background and are easiest to see. White or yellow text on a dark blue, green, purple, or black background is ideal.

The following outlines the type of formatting that is required in Project 2:

1. Worksheet title
   a. Font type — True Type (TT) Britannic Bold (or Impact if your system does not have TT Britannic Bold)
   b. Font size — 28 for first character in each word; 20 for subsequent characters
   c. Alignment — center across columns A through I
   d. Background color (range A1:I1) — green
   e. Font color — white
   f. Border — heavy border outline around A1:I1
2. Column titles
   a. Font style — bold
   b. Alignment — center
   c. Border — heavy bottom border
3. Data
   a. Alignment — center data in columns B and D
   b. Numbers in top row (row 3) — Currency style
   c. Numbers below top row (rows 4 through 7) — Comma style
   d. Border — heavy bottom border on row 7

4. Total line
   a. Numbers — Currency style
5. Function lines
   a. Numbers — Currency style in columns E through I
6. Percentage
   a. Numbers — Percentage style in cell D12
   b. Font style — bold
7. Column widths
   a. Columns B and G — 7.14 characters
   b. Columns D and E — 7.00 characters
   c. Remaining columns — best fit or default
8. Row heights
   a. Row 2 — 36.00 points
   b. Rows 9 and 12 — 18.00 points
   c. Remaining rows — best fit or default

Except for the Currency style assigned to the functions in rows 9 through 12, all of the above formats can be assigned to cells using buttons or boxes on the Formatting toolbar.

> **More *About***
> **Adding Colors and Borders**
>
> Colors and borders can change a boring worksheet into an interesting and easy-to-read worksheet. Colors and borders can also be used to make important information stand out.

Changing the Font and Centering the Worksheet Title

When developing presentation-quality worksheets, different fonts often are used in the same worksheet. Excel allows you to change the font of individual characters in a cell or all the characters in a cell, in a range of cells, or in the entire worksheet. To emphasize the worksheet title in cell A1, the font type, size, and style are changed and the worksheet title is centered as described in the following steps.

> **More *About***
> **Centering Across Columns**
>
> To deselect Center and Merge, right-click the cell, click Format Cells, click the Alignment tab, click the Merge cells check box, and click the OK button.

To Change Font and Center the Worksheet Title

1 **Click cell A1. Click the Font box arrow on the Formatting toolbar and then point to TT Britannic Bold (or TT Courier New if your system does not have TT Britannic Bold).**

The Font list box displays with TT Britannic Bold highlighted (Figure 2-26).

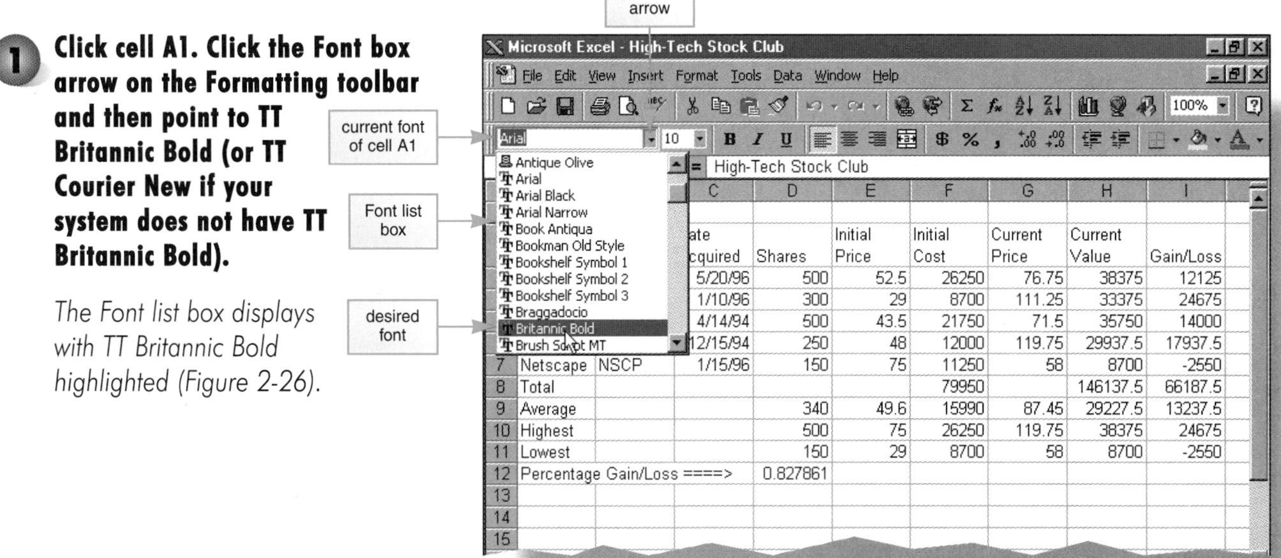

FIGURE 2-26

2 **Click TT Britannic Bold (or Impact). Click the Font Size box arrow on the Formatting toolbar and then point to 20.**

The characters in cell A1 display using TT Britannic Bold (or Impact). The font size 20 is highlighted in the Font Size list box (Figure 2-27).

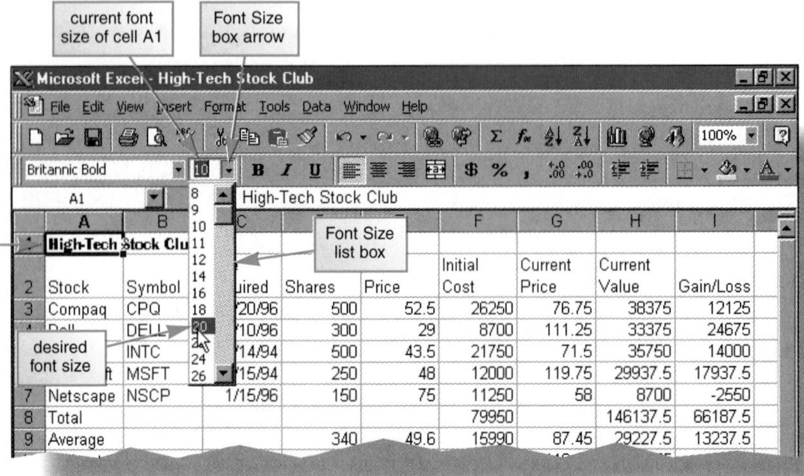

FIGURE 2-27

3 **Click 20. Double-click cell A1 to edit the cell contents. Drag through the first character H in the word, High, and then point to the Font Size box arrow.**

The text in cell A1 displays in 20-point Britannic Bold font. Excel automatically increases the height of row 1 so that the larger characters fit in the cells. This is called ***best fit****. Excel enters the Edit mode and the letter H in High is selected (Figure 2-28).*

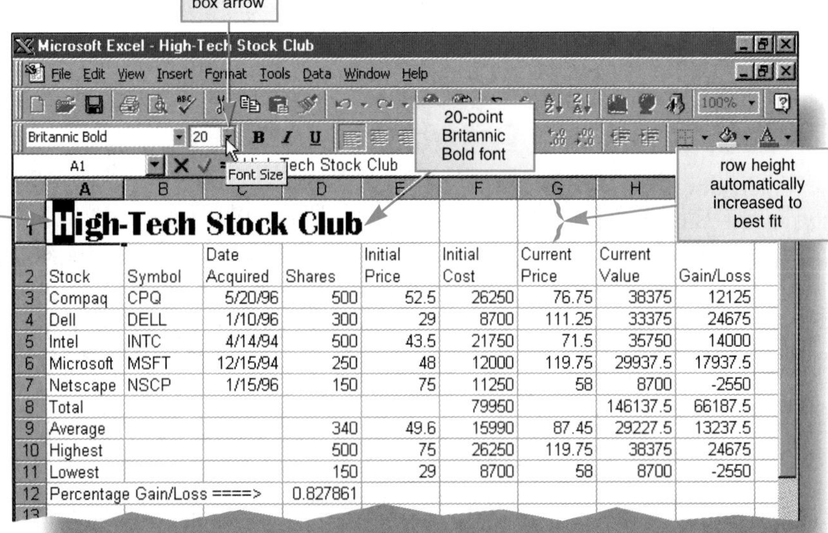

FIGURE 2-28

4 **Click the Font Size box arrow and then point to 28 (Figure 2-29).**

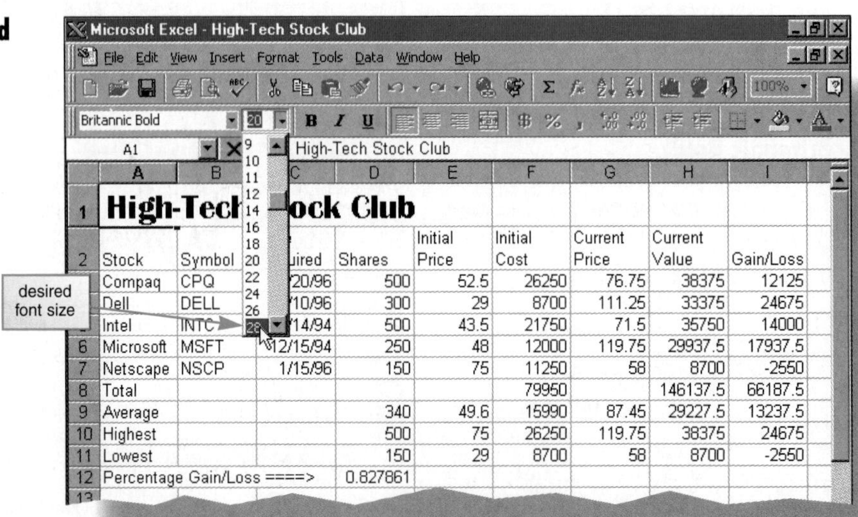

FIGURE 2-29

5 **Click 28. While in Edit mode, drag through the first letter of the remaining words in the worksheet title and then change their font size to 28.**

The first letter of each word in the worksheet title displays larger than the other characters (Figure 2-30).

letters H in High, T in Tech, S in Stock, and C in Club assigned 28 point

Microsoft Excel - High-Tech Stock Club

High-Tech Stock Club

	A	B	C	D	E	F	G	H	I
1	High-Tech Stock Club								
2	Stock	Symbol	Date Acquired	Shares	Initial Price	Initial Cost	Current Price	Current Value	Gain/Loss
3	Compaq	CPQ	5/20/96	500	52.5	26250	76.75	38375	12125
4	Dell	DELL	1/10/96	300	29	8700	111.25	33375	24675
5	Intel	INTC	4/14/94	500	43.5	21750	71.5	35750	14000
6	Microsoft	MSFT	12/15/94	250	48	12000	119.75	29937.5	17937.5
7	Netscape	NSCP	1/15/96	150	75	11250	58	8700	-2550
8	Total					79950		146137.5	66187.5
9	Average			340	49.6	15990	87.45	29227.5	13237.5
10	Highest			500	75	26250	119.75	38375	24675
11	Lowest			150	29	8700	58	8700	-2550

FIGURE 2-30

6 **Click the Enter box or press the ENTER key to complete editing the contents of cell A1. Select the range A1:I1. Click the Merge and Center button on the Formatting toolbar.**

Excel merges the cells A1 through I1 to create a new cell A1 and centers the worksheet title across columns A through I (Figure 2-31).

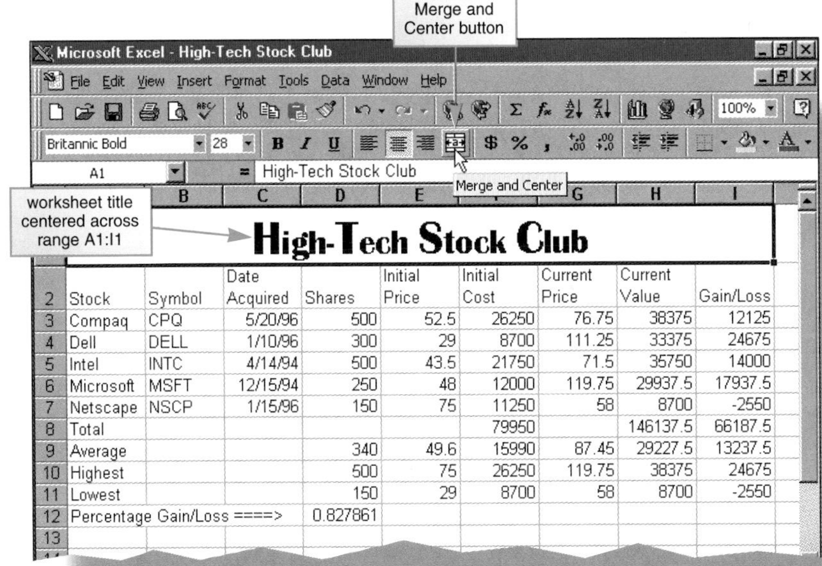

FIGURE 2-31

OtherWays

1. Right-click cell, click Format Cells, click Font tab, select font formats, click OK button
2. On Format menu click Cells, click Font tab, select font formats, click OK button
3. Press CTRL+1, click Font tab, select font formats, click OK button

You also can change a font type, size, or style at any time while the worksheet is active. Some Excel users prefer to change fonts before they enter any data. Others change the font while they are building the worksheet or after they have entered all the data.

Changing Worksheet Title Background and Font Colors and Applying an Outline Border

The final formats to be assigned to the worksheet title are the green background color, white font color, and heavy outline border (Figure 2-25b on page E 2.22). Perform the steps on the next page to complete the formatting of the worksheet title.

To Change the Background and Font Colors and Apply an Outline Border

1 With cell A1 selected, click the Fill Color button arrow on the Formatting toolbar and then point to the color green (column 4, row 2 on the Fill Color palette).

The Fill Color palette displays (Figure 2-32).

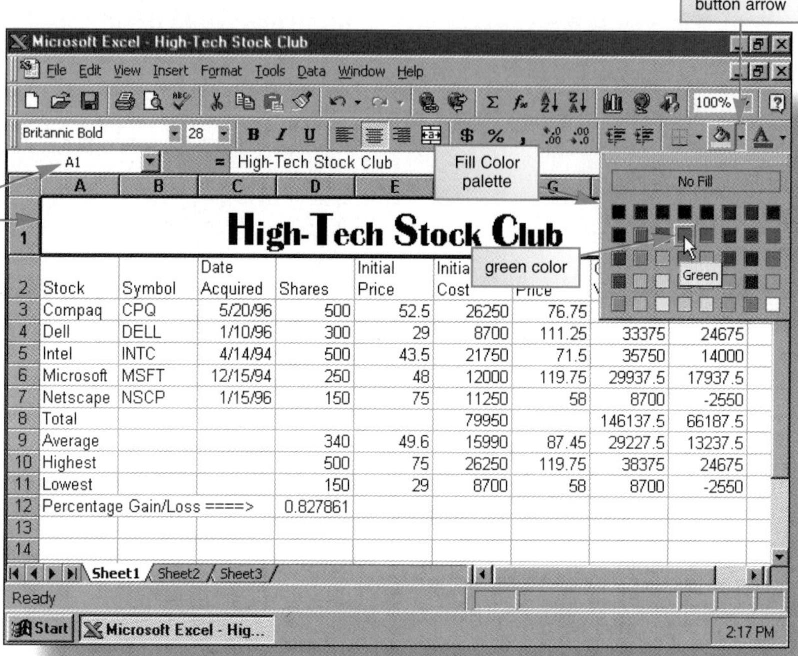

FIGURE 2-32

2 Click the color green. Click the Font Color button arrow on the Formatting toolbar. Point to the color white (column 8, row 5 on the Font Color palette).

The background color of cell A1 changes from white to green (Figure 2-33). The Font Color palette displays.

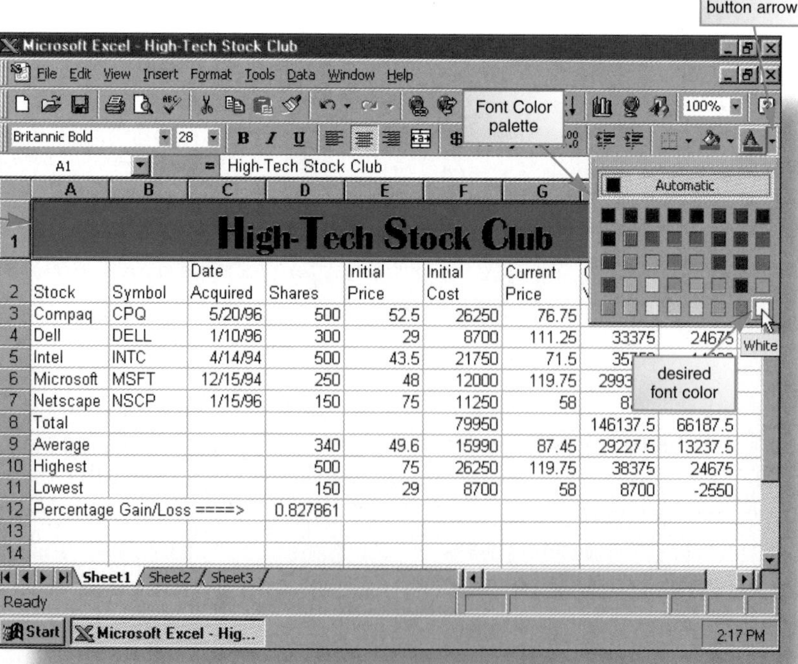

FIGURE 2-33

3 **Click the color white. Click the Borders button arrow on the Formatting toolbar and then point to the heavy outline border (column 4, row 3 on the Borders palette).**

The font in the worksheet title changes from black to white. The Borders palette displays (Figure 2-34).

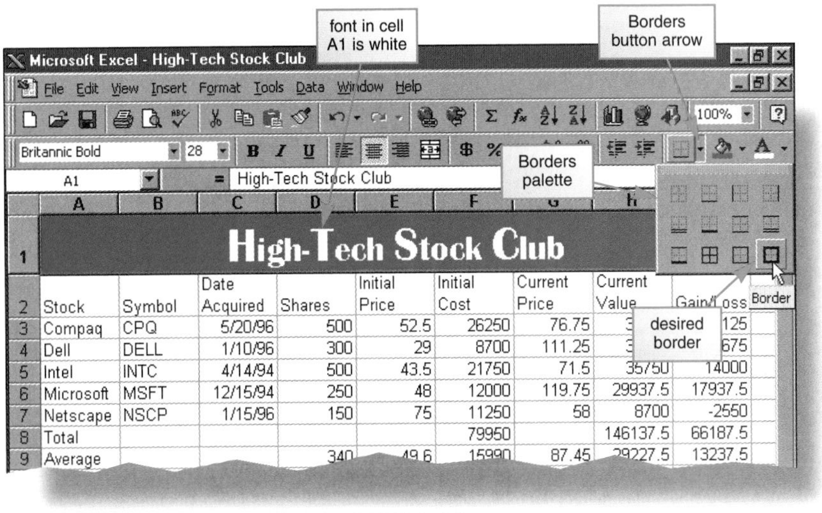

FIGURE 2-34

4 **Click the heavy outline border. Click cell A2.**

Excel displays a heavy outline border around cell A1 (Figure 2-35).

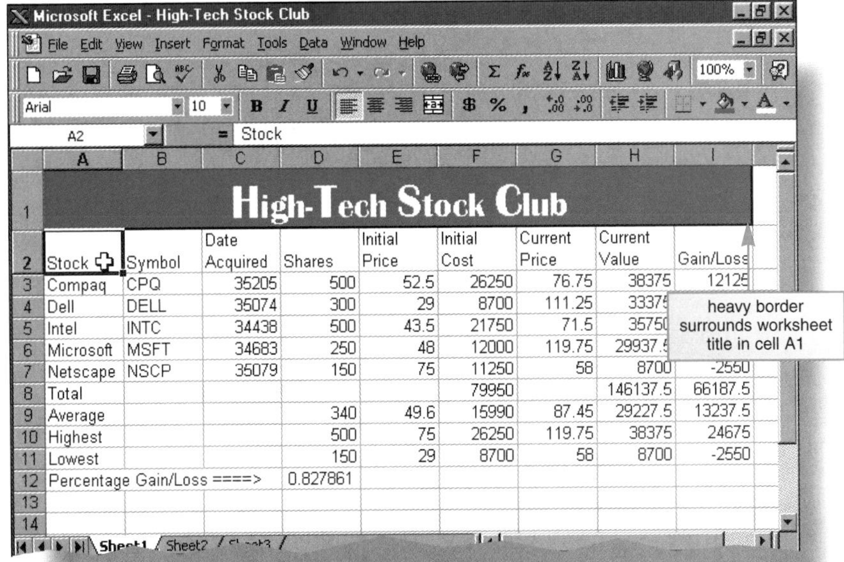

FIGURE 2-35

OtherWays

1. Right-click range, on shortcut menu click Format Cells, click Patterns tab, click desired background color, click OK button
2. On Format menu click Cells, click Patterns tab, click desired background color, click OK button
3. Right-click range, on shortcut menu click Format Cells, click Border tab, click desired style, click desired border, click OK button
4. On Format menu click Cells, click Border tab, click desired style, click desired border, click OK button

You can remove borders, such as the outline around the range A1:I1, by selecting the range and then pressing CTRL+SHIFT+_. You can remove a background color by selecting the range, clicking the Fill Color button arrow on the Formatting toolbar, and clicking No Fill on the Fill Color palette. The same technique allows you to change the font color back to Excel's default, except you use the Font Color button arrow and click Automatic.

Applying Formats to the Column Titles

According to Figure 2-25b on page E 2.22, the column titles are bold, centered, and have a heavy underline. The steps on the next page assign these formats to the column titles.

To Bold, Center, and Underline the Column Titles

1. **Select the range A2:I2. Click the Bold button on the Formatting toolbar. Click the Center button on the Formatting toolbar.**

   The column titles in row 2 are bold and centered.

2. **Click the Borders button arrow on the Formatting toolbar and then point to the heavy bottom border (column 2, row 2) on the Borders palette.**

   The Borders palette displays (Figure 2-36).

3. **Click the heavy bottom border. Select cell B3.**

   Excel adds a heavy bottom border to the range A2:I2.

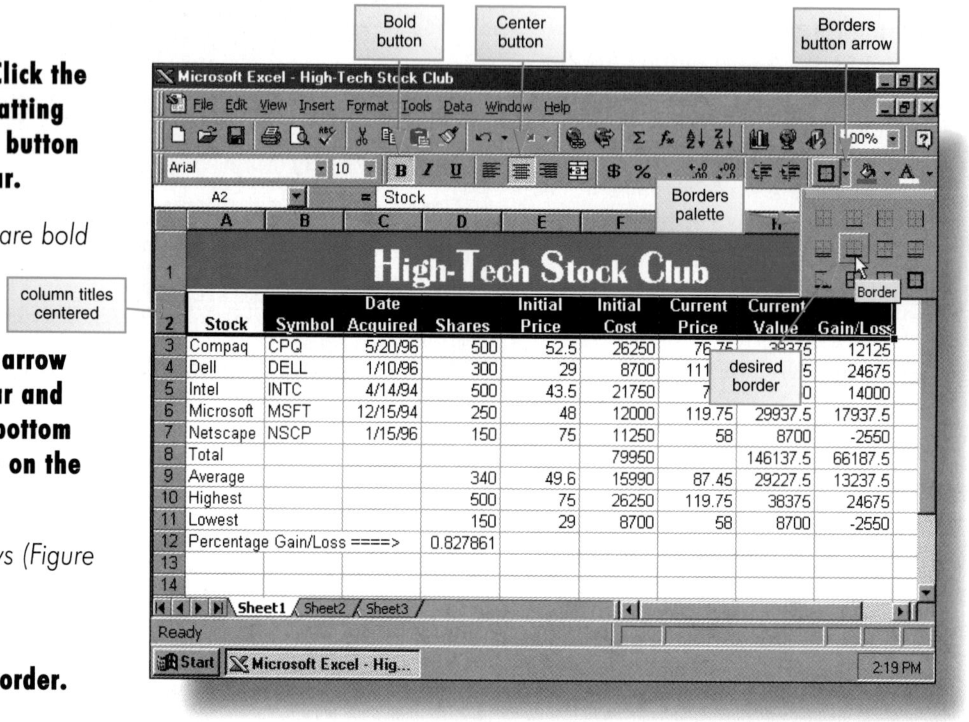

Bold button
Center button
Borders button arrow
Borders palette
column titles centered
desired border
Border

FIGURE 2-36

Other Ways

1. Right-click cell, click Format Cells, click Alignment tab, in Horizontal list box click Center, click Font tab, click Bold, click Border tab, click desired border, click OK button
2. On the Format menu click Cells, click Alignment tab, in Horizontal list box click Center, click Font tab, click Bold, click Border tab, click desired border, click OK button
3. Press CTRL+1, click Alignment tab, in Horizontal list box click Center, click Font tab, click Bold, click Border tab, click desired border, click OK button

You can align the contents of cells in several different ways. Left alignment, center alignment, and right alignment are the more frequently used alignments. In fact, these three alignments are used so often that Excel has Left Align, Center, and Right Align buttons on the Formatting toolbar. In addition to aligning the contents of a cell horizontally, you also can align the contents of a cell vertically. You even can rotate the contents of a cell to various angles.

You also can align text as you initially enter it in a cell, by including a special character at the beginning of the entry. An apostrophe (') instructs Excel to left-align the text. A caret (^) centers the text and a quotation mark (") right-aligns the text.

For more information on alignment, click Cells on the Format menu and then click the Alignment tab.

Applying Formats to the Numbers

With the column titles formatted, the next step is to format the data and total lines. If a cell entry is short, such as the stock symbols in column B or the number of shares in column D, centering the entries within their respective columns improves the appearance of the worksheet. The following steps center the data in columns B and D.

TO CENTER DATA IN CELLS

Step 1: Select the range B3:B7. Click the Center button on the Formatting toolbar.

Step 2: Select the range D3:D12. Click the Center button on the Formatting toolbar.

The stock symbols in column B and the shares in column D are centered (Figure 2-37).

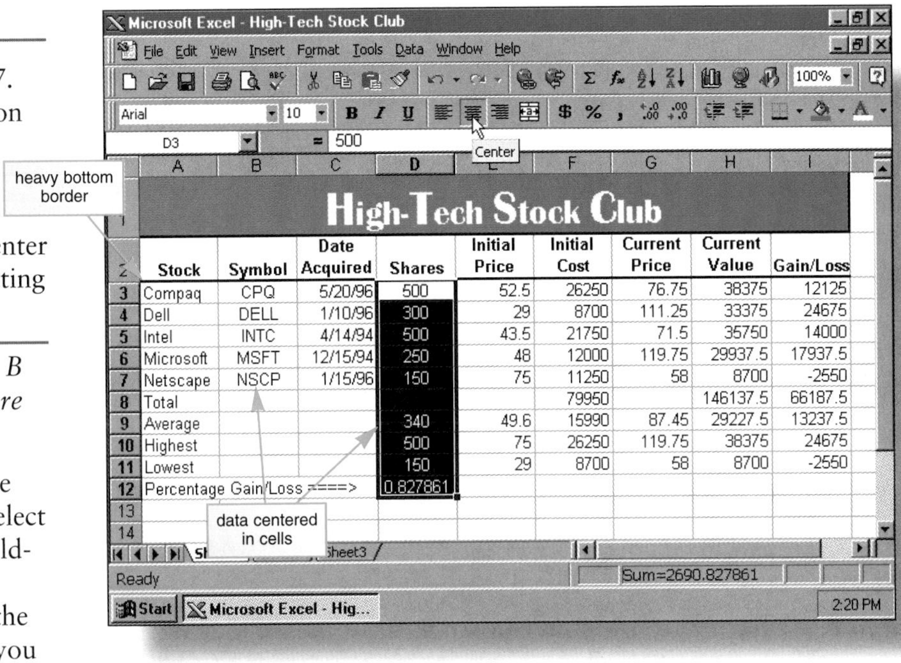

	A	B	C	D	E	F	G	H	I
1	High-Tech Stock Club								
2	Stock	Symbol	Date Acquired	Shares	Initial Price	Initial Cost	Current Price	Current Value	Gain/Loss
3	Compaq	CPQ	5/20/96	500	52.5	26250	76.75	38375	12125
4	Dell	DELL	1/10/96	300	29	8700	111.25	33375	24675
5	Intel	INTC	4/14/94	500	43.5	21750	71.5	35750	14000
6	Microsoft	MSFT	12/15/94	250	48	12000	119.75	29937.5	17937.5
7	Netscape	NSCP	1/15/96	150	75	11250	58	8700	-2550
8	Total					79950		146137.5	66187.5
9	Average			340	49.6	15990	87.45	29227.5	13237.5
10	Highest			500	75	26250	119.75	38375	24675
11	Lowest			150	29	8700	58	8700	-2550
12	Percentage Gain/Loss ====>			0.827861					

FIGURE 2-37

An alternative to centering the data one column at a time is to select the first range and then, while holding down the CTRL key, dragging through the second range. Once the nonadjacent ranges are selected, you can apply the format.

When using Excel, you can use the buttons on the Formatting toolbar to format numbers as dollar amounts, whole numbers with comma placement, and percentages. Customized formats can be assigned using the **Cells command** on the Format menu or the **Format Cells command** on the shortcut menu.

As shown in Figure 2-25b on page E 2.22, the worksheet is formatted to resemble an accounting report. For example, the first row of numbers (row 3) and the monetary totals (rows 8 through 12) display with dollar signs, while the remaining numbers (rows 4 through 7) do not. To display a dollar sign in a number, you should use the Currency style format.

The **Currency style format** displays a dollar sign to the left of the number, inserts a comma every three positions to the left of the decimal point, and displays numbers to the nearest cent (hundredths place). The **Currency Style button** on the Formatting toolbar will assign the desired Currency style format. When you use the Currency Style button, Excel displays a **fixed dollar sign** to the far left in the cell, often with spaces between it and the first digit. To assign a **floating dollar sign** that displays immediately to the left of the first digit with no spaces, you must use the Cells command on the Format menu or the Format Cells command on the shortcut menu. The project specifications call for a fixed dollar sign to be assigned to the numbers in rows 3 and 8, and a floating dollar sign to be assigned to the monetary totals in rows 9 through 11.

To display monetary amounts with commas and no dollar signs, you will want to use the Comma style format. The **Comma style format** inserts a comma every three positions to the left of the decimal point and displays numbers to the nearest hundredths (cents).

The remainder of this section describes how to format the numbers as shown in Figure 2-25b.

Formatting Numbers Using the Formatting Toolbar

The steps on the next page show how to assign formats using the Currency Style button and Comma Style button on the Formatting toolbar.

More *About* **Aligning and Rotating Text in Cells**

Besides aligning text horizontally in a cell, you can align text vertically (top, center, bottom, or justify). You can also rotate text. To align vertically or rotate the text, click Format Cells on the shortcut menu, click the Alignment tab, and then select the type of alignment you want.

More *About* **Formatting Numbers as You Enter Them**

You can format numbers when you enter them by entering a dollar sign ($), comma (,), or percent sign (%) as part of the number. For example, if you enter 1500, Excel displays 1500. However, if you enter $1500, Excel displays $1,500.

To Apply a Currency Style Format and Comma Style Format Using the Formatting Toolbar

1 **Select the range E3:I3. While holding down the CTRL key, select the nonadjacent range F8:I8. Point to the Currency Style button on the Formatting toolbar.**

The nonadjacent ranges display as shown in Figure 2-38.

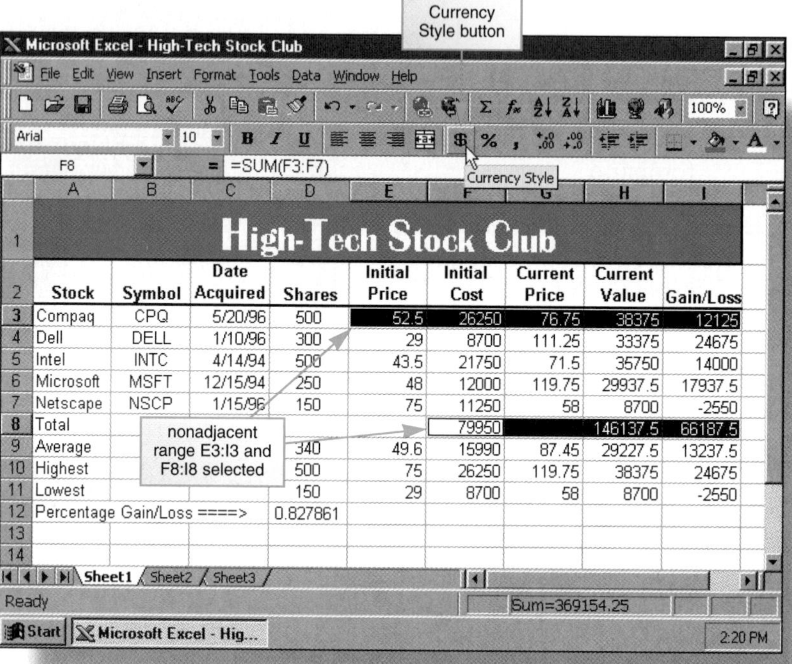

FIGURE 2-38

2 **Click the Currency Style button. Select the range E4:I7 and then point to the Comma Style button on the Formatting toolbar.**

Excel automatically increases the width of columns F, H, and I to best fit, so that the numbers assigned the Currency style format will fit in the cells (Figure 2-39). The right side of column I moves off the screen. The range E4:I7 is highlighted.

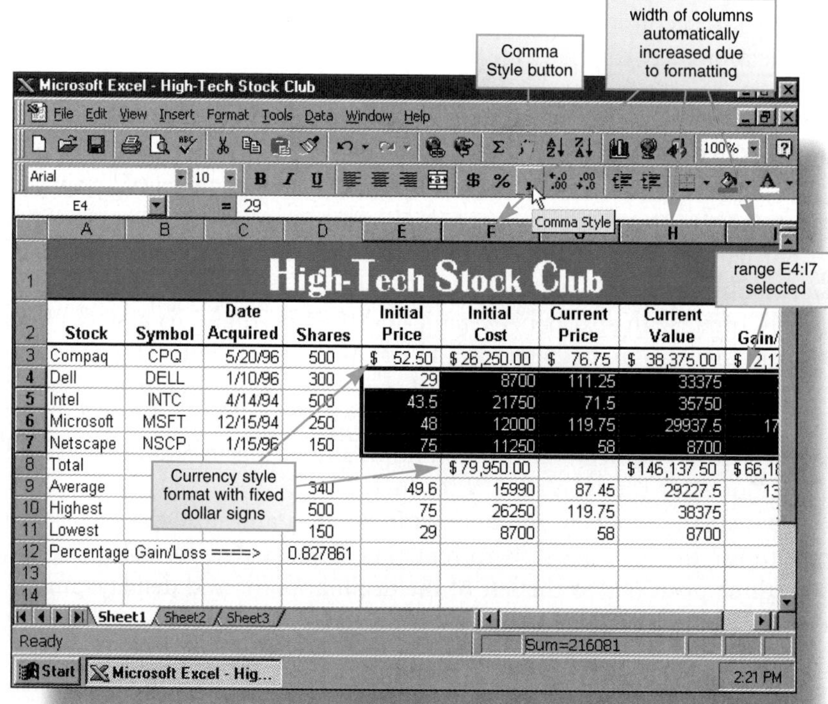

FIGURE 2-39

3 **Click the Comma Style button. Select the range A7:I7 and then click the Borders button on the Formatting toolbar. Click cell E9.**

Excel assigns the Comma style format to the range E4:I7 and a heavy bottom border to row 7 (Figure 2-40). The Borders button remains set to the heavy bottom border assigned to row 2. Thus, to assign the heavy bottom border to the range A7:I7, you simply click the Borders button.

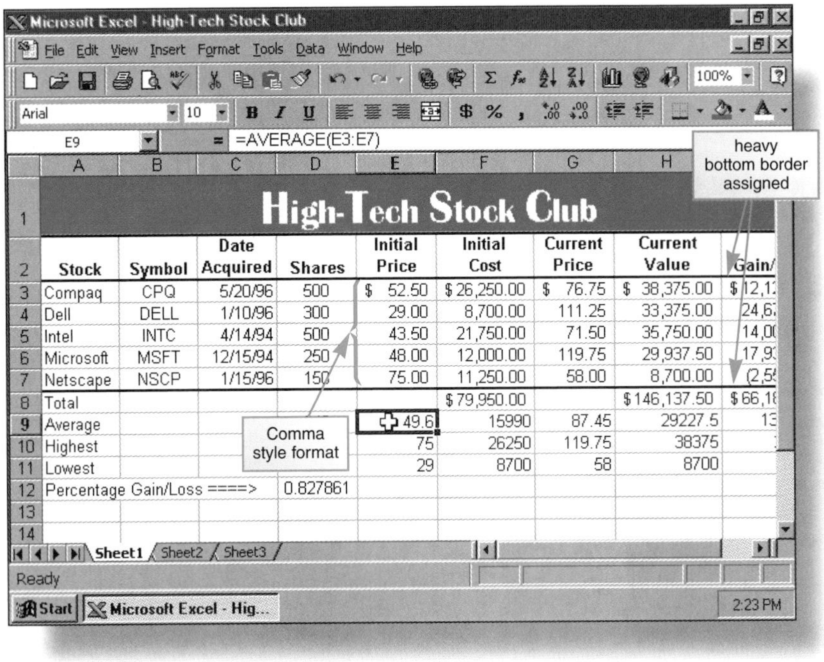

FIGURE 2-40

OtherWays

1. Right-click range, on shortcut menu click Format Cells, click Number tab, in Category list click Currency, click OK button
2. On Format menu click Cells, click Number tab, in Category list click Currency, click OK button

The Currency Style button assigns a fixed dollar sign to the numbers in the ranges E3:I3 and F8:I8. In each cell in these ranges, the dollar sign displays to the far left with spaces between it and the first digit in the cell. Excel automatically rounds a number to fit the selected format.

Formatting Numbers Using the Format Cells Command on the Shortcut Menu

Thus far, you have been introduced to two ways of formatting numbers in a worksheet. In Project 1, you formatted the numbers using the AutoFormat command on the Format menu. In the previous section, you were introduced to using the Formatting toolbar as a means of applying a format style. A third way to format numbers is to use the Cells command on the Format menu or the Format Cells command on the shortcut menu. Using either command allows you to display numbers in almost any format you want. The steps on the next page show you how to use the Format Cells command to apply the Currency style with a floating dollar sign to the totals in the range E9:I11.

More About Formatted Numbers in Calculations

The numbers you see on your screen may not be the same ones used in calculations. When a number has more decimal places than are showing on the screen because you formatted it, the actual number and not the displayed number is used in the computation.

To Apply a Currency Style with a Floating Dollar Sign Using the Format Cells Command

1 **Select the range E9:I11. Right-click the selected range. Point to Format Cells on the shortcut menu.**

The shortcut menu displays (Figure 2-41).

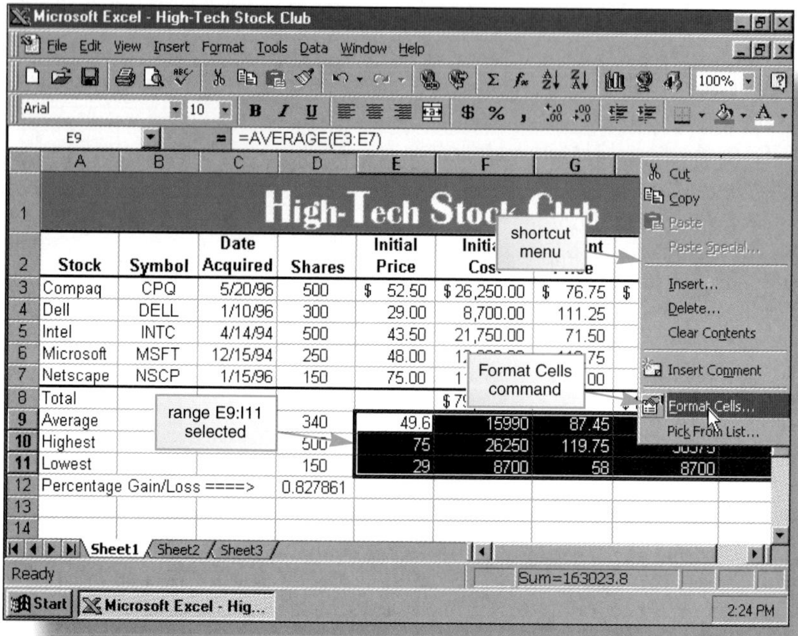

FIGURE 2-41

2 **Click Format Cells. Click the Number tab in the Format Cells dialog box. Click Currency in the Category list, click the third style ($1,234.10) in the Negative numbers list, and then point to the OK button.**

The Format Cells dialog box displays (Figure 2-42).

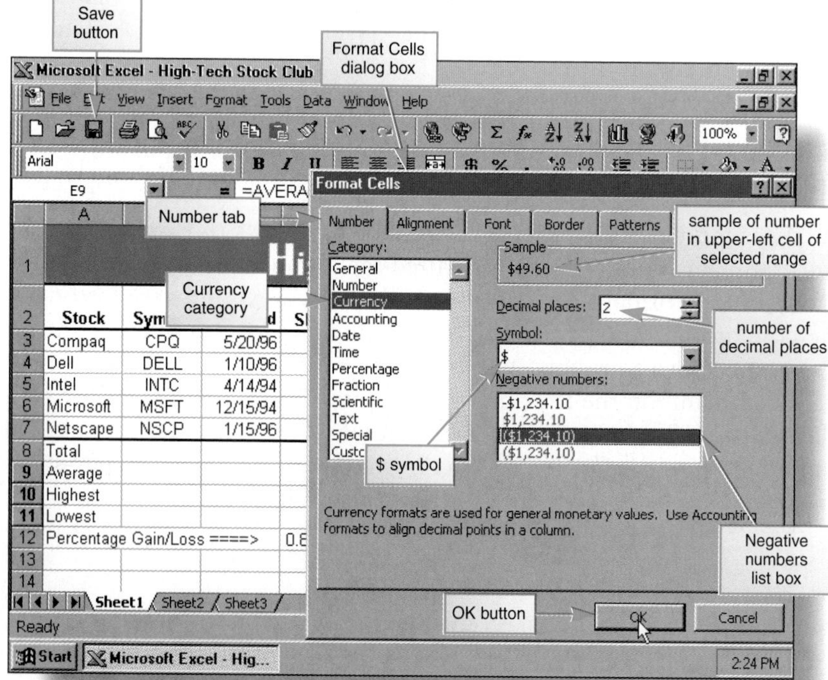

FIGURE 2-42

3 **Click the OK button. Click cell D12 to deselect the range E9:I11.**

The worksheet displays with the totals in rows 9 through 11 assigned the Currency style format with a floating dollar sign (Figure 2-43).

4 **Click the Save button on the Standard toolbar.**

formatting of cells causes Excel to increase column widths to best fit, which increases width of worksheet

D12 = =I8/F8

	A	B	C	D	E	F	G	H	I
1	High-Tech Stock Club								
2	Stock	Symbol	Date Acquired	Shares	Initial Price	Initial Cost	Current Price	Current Value	Gain/
3	Compaq	CPQ	5/20/96	500	$ 52.50	$ 26,250.00	$ 76.75	$ 38,375.00	$ 12,1
4	Dell	DELL	1/10/96	300	29.00	8,700.00	111.25	33,375.00	24,6
5	Intel	INTC	4/14/94	500	43.50	21,750.00	71.50	35,750.00	14,0
6	Microsoft	MSFT	12/15/94	250	48.00	12,000.00	119.75	29,937.50	17,9
7	Netscape	NSCP	1/15/96	150	75.00	11,250.00	58.00	8,700.00	(2,5
8	Total					$ 79,950.00		$ 146,137.50	$ 66,1
9	Average			340	$49.60	$15,990.00	$87.45	$29,227.50	$13,2
10	Highest			500	$75.00	$26,250.00	$119.75	$38,375.00	$24,6
11	Lowest			150	$29.00	$8,700.00	$58.00	$8,700.00	($2,5
12	Percentage Gain/Loss ====>			0.827861					

Currency style format with a floating dollar sign

negative numbers display surrounded by parentheses

Sheet1

Ready

Start | Microsoft Excel - Hig... | 2:26 PM

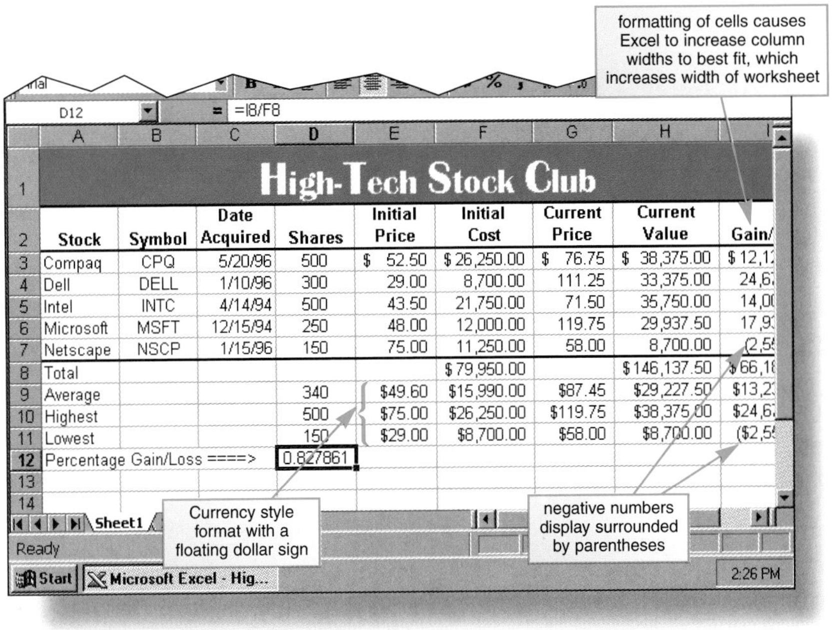

FIGURE 2-43

OtherWays

1. On Format menu click Cells, click Number tab, in Category list click Currency, select desired formats, click OK button
2. Press CTRL+SHIFT+$

Recall that a floating dollar sign always displays immediately to the left of the first digit and the fixed dollar sign always displays on the left side of the cell. Cell E3, for example, has a fixed dollar sign, while cell E9 has a floating dollar sign. Also recall that, while cells E3 and E9 both were assigned a Currency style format, the Currency style was assigned to cell E3 using the Currency Style button on the Formatting toolbar. The result is a fixed dollar sign. The Currency style was assigned to cell E9 using the Format Cells dialog box and the result is a floating dollar sign.

As shown in Figure 2-42, there are 12 categories of formats from which you can choose. Once you select a category, you can select the number of decimal places, whether or not a dollar sign should display, and how negative numbers should display.

Selecting the appropriate negative numbers format in Step 2 is important, because doing so adds a space to the right of the number (as do the Currency Style and Comma Style buttons). Some of the available negative numbers formats do not align the numbers in the worksheet on the decimal points. To verify this, click one of the formatted cells and then assign the Currency category with the negative numbers format (–$1,234.10) instead of ($1,234.10).

The negative number format selected in the previous set of steps displays in cell I11, which has a negative entry. The third selection in the Negative numbers list box (Figure 2-42) purposely was chosen to agree with the negative number format assigned to cell I7 using the Comma Style button.

More *About* **Painting Formats**

Painting is not an enviable chore. But in Excel, if you know how to paint you can save yourself time and effort when formatting a worksheet. For example, if you see a cell that has the format you want to assign to another cell or range of cells, click the cell with the desired format, click the Format Painter button on the Standard toolbar, and then click the cell or drag through the cells you want to paint.

Formatting Numbers Using the Percent Style Button and Increase Decimal Button

The last entry in the worksheet that needs to be formatted is the percentage gain/loss in cell D12. Currently, the number displays as a decimal fraction (0.827861). Follow the steps on the next page to change the format to the Percentage style with two decimal places. The last step bolds the percentage row title and number to make them stand out.

To Apply a Percentage Format

1 **With cell D12 selected, click the Percent Style button on the Formatting toolbar.**

The number in cell D12 (0.827861) displays as a whole percent (83%).

2 **Click the Increase Decimal button on the Formatting toolbar twice.**

The number in cell D12 (83%) displays with two decimal places (82.79%).

3 **Select the range A12:D12. Click the Bold button on the Formatting toolbar. Click cell D12.**

The entries in the range A12:D12 display in bold (Figure 2-44).

Bold button
Percent Style button
Increase Decimal button
Decrease Decimal button
font is bold
Percentage style format with two decimal places

Microsoft Excel - High-Tech Stock Club

D12 = =I8/F8

High-Tech Stock Club

Stock	Symbol	Date Acquired	Shares	Initial Price	Initial Cost	Current Price	Current Value	Gain/
Compaq	CPQ	5/20/96	500	$ 52.50	$26,250.00	$ 76.75	$ 38,375.00	$12,1
Dell	DELL	1/10/96	300	29.00	8,700.00	111.25	33,375.00	24,6
Intel	INTC	4/14/94	500	43.50	21,750.00	71.50	35,750.00	14,0
Microsoft	MSFT	12/15/94	250	48.00	12,000.00	119.75	29,937.50	17,9
Netscape	NSCP	1/15/96	150	75.00	11,250.00	58.00	8,700.00	(2,5
Total					$79,950.00		$146,137.50	$66,1
Average			340	$49.60	$15,990.00	$87.45	$29,227.50	$13,2
Highest			500	$75.00	$26,250.00	$119.75	$38,375.00	$24,6
Lowest			150	$29.00	$8,700.00	$58.00	$8,700.00	($2,5
Percentage Gain/Loss ====>			**82.79%**					

Sheet1 Sheet2 Sheet3
Ready
Start Microsoft Excel - Hig... 2:27 PM

FIGURE 2-44

OtherWays

1. Right-click range, on shortcut menu click Format Cells, click Number tab, in Category list click Percentage, select desired formats, click OK button
2. On Format menu click Cells, click Number tab, in Category list box click Percentage, select formats, click OK button
3. Press CTRL+SHIFT+%

The **Percent Style button** on the Formatting toolbar is used to display a value determined by multiplying the cell entry by 100, rounding the result to the nearest percent, and adding a percent sign. For example, when cell D12 is formatted using the Increase Decimal button, the value 0.827861 displays as 82.79%. While they do not display, Excel does maintain all the decimal places for computational purposes. Thus, if cell D12 is used in a formula, the value used for computational purposes is 0.827861.

The **Increase Decimal button** on the Formatting toolbar is used to display additional decimal places in a cell. Each time you click the Increase Decimal button, Excel adds a decimal place to the selected cell. The **Decrease Decimal button** removes a decimal place from the selected cell each time it is clicked.

With the number formatting complete, the next step is to change the column widths so the entire worksheet displays on the screen.

Changing the Widths of Columns and Heights of Rows

When Excel starts and the blank worksheet displays on the screen, all of the columns have a default width of 8.43 characters. A **character** is defined as a letter, number, symbol, or punctuation mark in 10-point TT Arial font, the default font used by Excel. An average of 8.43 characters in this font will fit in a cell. The default row height in a blank worksheet is 12.75 points. Recall from Project 1 that a point is equal to 1/72 of an inch. Thus, 12.75 points is equal to about one-sixth of an inch. You can change the width of the columns or height of the rows at any time to make the worksheet easier to read or to ensure that an entry displays properly in a cell.

More About Best Fit

Although Excel automatically increases the width of a column or the height of a row when you assign a format to a cell, it will not increase the column width or row height when a cell contains a formula and you change the value of a cell that is referenced in the formula. For example, if you change the number of shares in cell D3 from 500 to 10,0000, Excel will recalculate the formulas and display number signs (#) for the initial cost and gain/loss because the results of the formulas have more digits than can fit in the cell. You can fix the problem by double-clicking the right boundary of the column heading to change to best fit.

Changing the Widths of Columns

When changing the column width, you can set the width manually or you can instruct Excel to size the column to best fit. Best fit means that the width of the column will be increased or decreased so the widest entry will fit in the column. When the format you assign to a cell causes the entry to exceed the width of a column, Excel automatically changes the column width to best fit. This happened earlier when the Currency style format was used (Figure 2-39 on page E 2.30). To set a column width to best fit, double-click the right boundary of the column heading.

Sometimes, you may prefer more or less white space in a column than best fit provides. Excel thus allows you to manually change column widths. In the case of Project 2, for example, sizing every column to best fit will not allow the entire worksheet to display on the screen at one time. To ensure the entire High-Tech Stock Club worksheet displays at one time, the following changes will be made to the column widths: column B from 8.43 to 7.14; columns D and E from 8.43 to 7.00; and column G from best fit to 7.14. Complete the following steps to change the widths of columns B, D, E, and G.

Steps To Change the Width of a Column by Dragging

1 Point to the boundary on the right side of the column B heading above row 1. Drag to the left until the ScreenTip, Width: 7.14, displays.

The mouse pointer becomes a split double arrow. A dotted line shows the proposed right border of column B and the ScreenTip, Width: 7.14, displays (Figure 2-45).

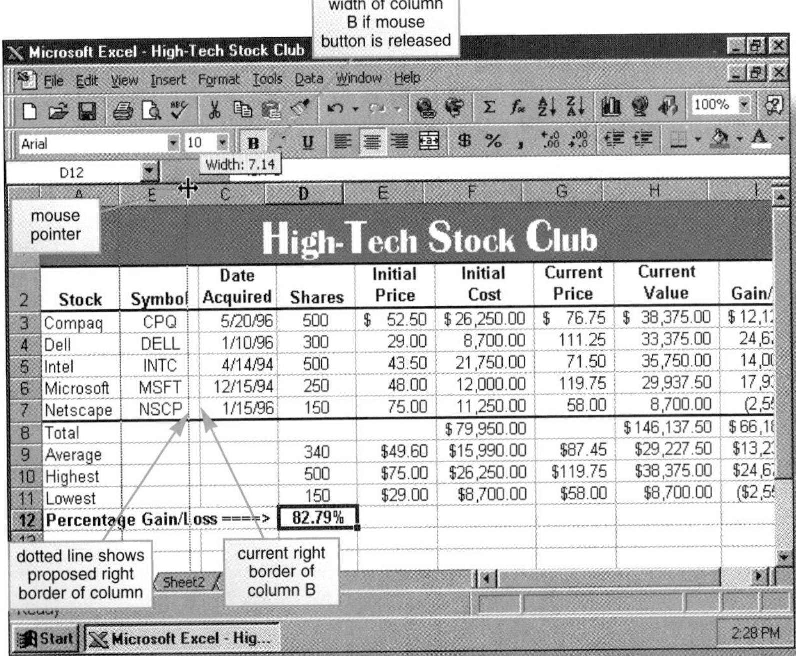

FIGURE 2-45

2 **Release the mouse button. Point to the boundary on the right side of the column D heading. Drag to the left until the ScreenTip, Width: 7.00, displays.**

A dotted line shows the proposed right border of column D and the ScreenTip, Width: 7.00, displays (Figure 2-46).

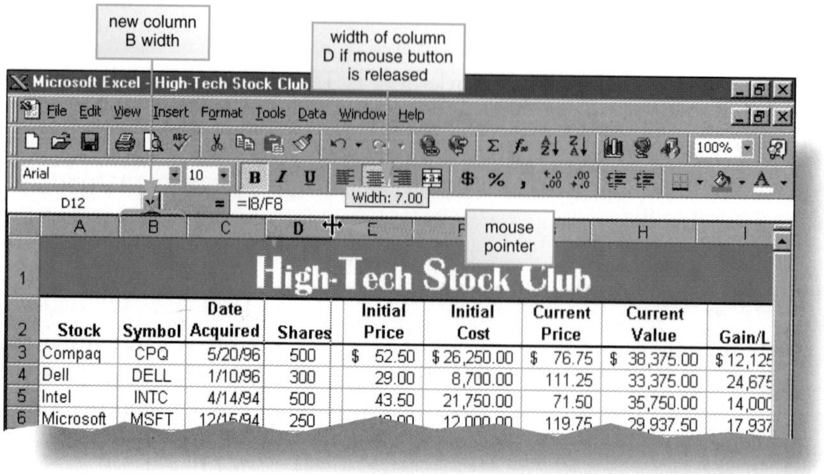

FIGURE 2-46

3 **Release the mouse button. Point to the boundary on the right side of the column E heading. Drag to the left until the ScreenTip, Width: 7.00, displays.**

A dotted line shows the proposed right border of column E and the ScreenTip, Width: 7.00 displays (Figure 2-47).

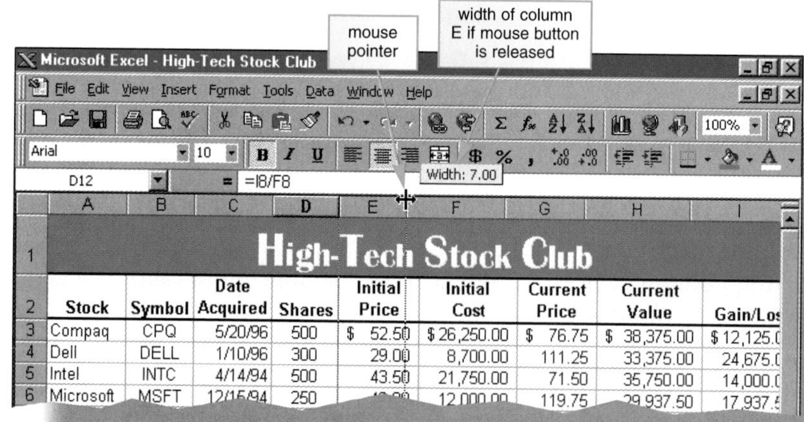

FIGURE 2-47

4 **Release the mouse button. Point to the boundary on the right side of the column G heading. Drag to the left until the ScreenTip, Width: 7.14, displays.**

A dotted line shows the proposed right border of column G and the ScreenTip, Width: 7.14, displays (Figure 2-48).

5 **Release the mouse button.**

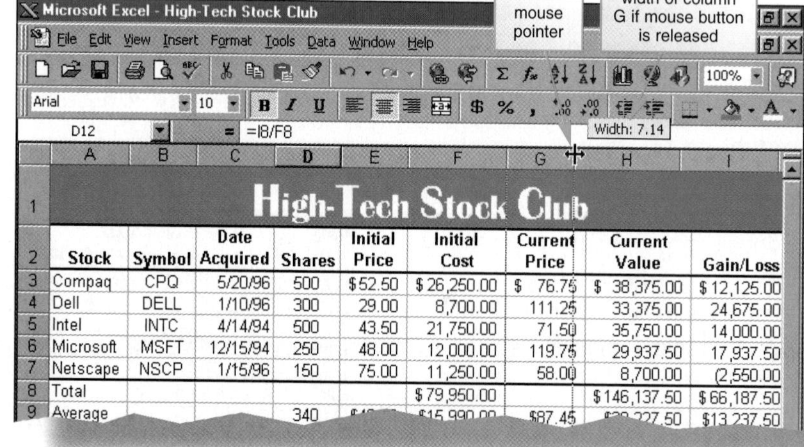

FIGURE 2-48

Other Ways

1. Right-click column heading, click Column Width, enter desired column width, click OK button
2. Select cell or range of cells, on Format menu click Column, click Width, enter desired column width, click OK button

Slightly decreasing the width of the four columns by dragging allows the entire worksheet to display on the screen (Figure 2-49).

If you want to increase or decrease the column width significantly, you can use the Column Width command on the shortcut menu to change a column's width. To use this command, however, you must select one or more entire columns. You select entire columns by dragging through the column headings. If the worksheet title had not been centered across columns A through I earlier, then in Steps 2 and 3 you could have selected columns D and E by dragging through their column headings and changed their width to 7.00 in one step. Excel, however, does not allow you to select columns that contain a merged cell.

A column width can vary from zero (0) to 255 characters. If you decrease the column width to zero, the column is hidden. **Hiding** is a technique you can use to hide data that might not be relevant to a particular report or sensitive data that you do not want others to see. When you print a worksheet, hidden columns do not print. To display a hidden column, position the mouse pointer to the left of the column heading boundary where the hidden column is located and then drag to the right.

More *About* Hidden Columns

It often gets frustrating trying to use the mouse to unhide a range of columns. An alternative is to unhide columns using the keyboard. First select the columns to the right and left of the hidden ones and then press CTRL+SHIFT+). To use the keyboard to hide a range of columns, press CTRL+0.

Changing the Heights of Rows

When you increase the font size of a cell entry, such as the title in cell A1, Excel automatically increases the row height to best fit so the characters display properly. Recall that Excel also did this when you entered multiple lines in a cell in row 2.

You also can manually increase or decrease the height of a row to improve the appearance of the worksheet. Recall that the height of row 2 was increased automatically from the default row height of 12.75 points to 26.25 points when multiple lines were entered into cells in row 2. The following steps show how to increase the height of row 2 from 26.25 points to 36.00 points and to manually increase the heights of row 8 and 11 from the default 12.75 points to 18.00 points using the mouse. Perform the following steps to change the heights of rows by dragging.

Steps To Change the Height of a Row by Dragging

1 Point to the boundary below row heading 2. Drag down until the ScreenTip, Height: 36.00, displays.

The mouse pointer changes to a split double arrow (Figure 2-49). The distance between the dotted line and the top of row 2 indicates the proposed row height for row 2.

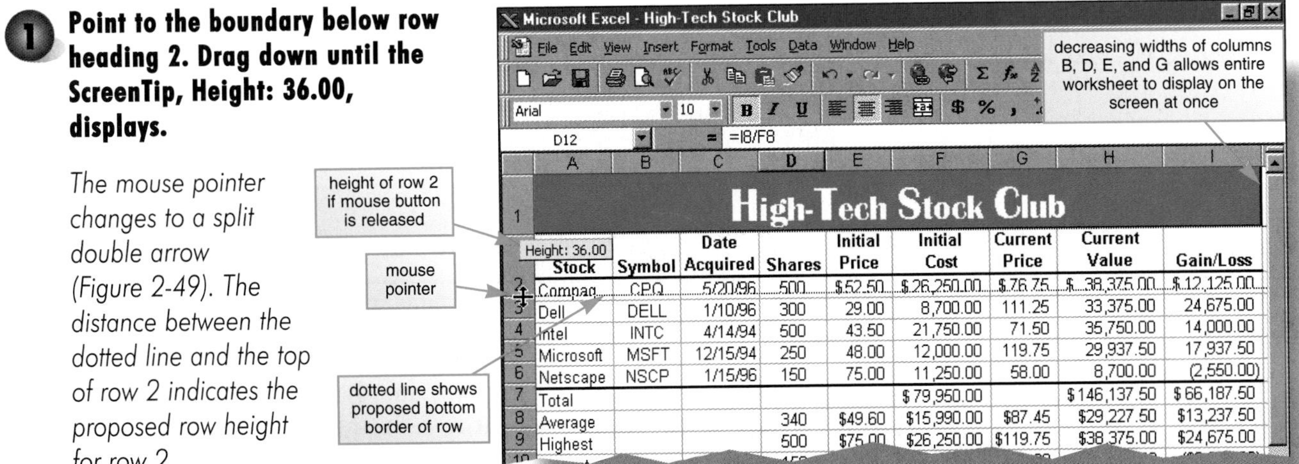

FIGURE 2-49

2 **Release the mouse button. Click row heading 9 to select row 9. While holding down the CTRL key, click the row heading 12 to select row 12. With both rows selected, point to the boundary below row heading 12. Drag down until the ScreenTip, Height: 18.00, displays.**

Excel displays a horizontal dotted line (Figure 2-50). The distance between the dotted line and the top of row 12 indicates the proposed row height for rows 9 and 12.

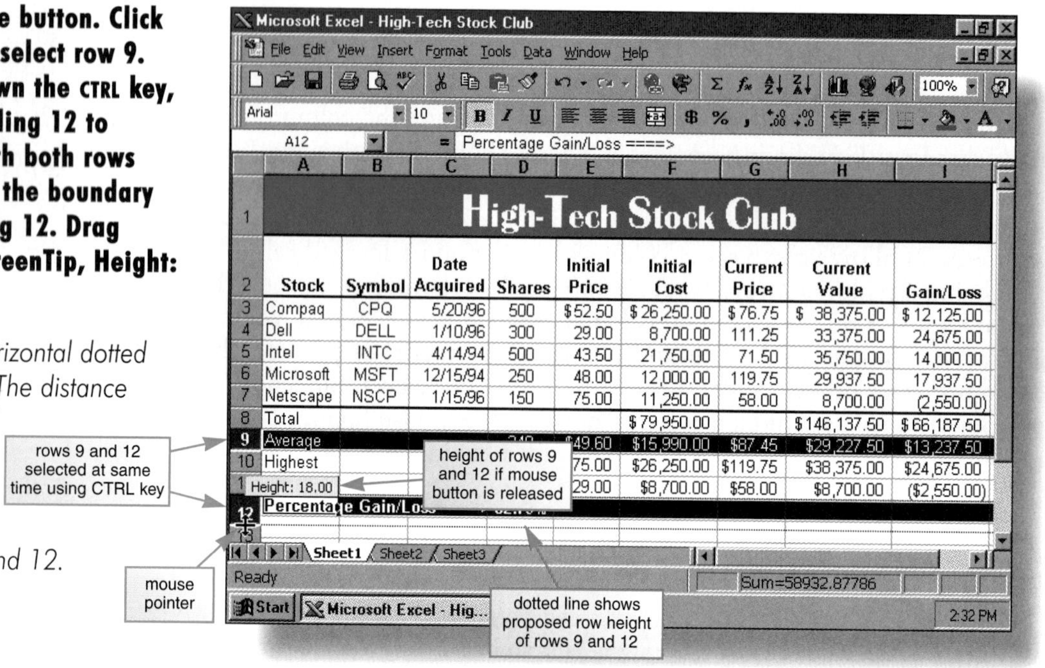

rows 9 and 12 selected at same time using CTRL key
Height: 18.00
height of rows 9 and 12 if mouse button is released
mouse pointer
dotted line shows proposed row height of rows 9 and 12

FIGURE 2-50

3 **Release the mouse button. Click cell A15.**

The High-Tech Stock Club worksheet displays with the new row heights (Figure 2-51).

4 **Click the Save button on the Standard toolbar.**

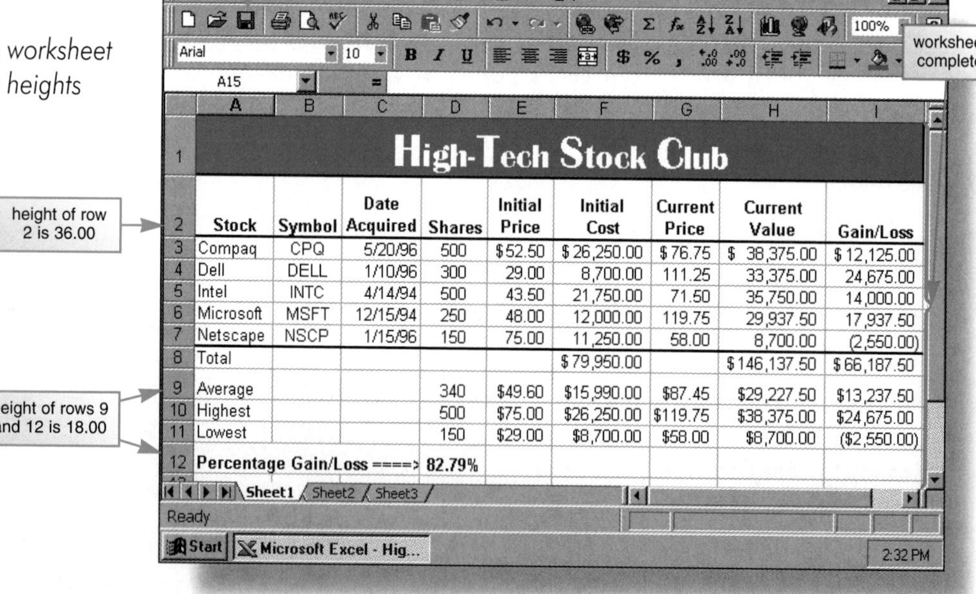

FIGURE 2-51

Other Ways

1. Right-click row heading or drag through multiple row headings and right-click, click Row Height, enter desired row height, click OK button
2. Select cell or range of cells in column, on Format menu click Row, click Height, enter desired row height, click OK button

The row height can vary between zero (0) and 409 points. As with column widths, when you decrease the row height to zero, the row is hidden. To display a hidden row, position the mouse pointer just below the row heading boundary where the row is hidden and then drag down. To set a row height to best fit, double-click the bottom boundary of the row heading.

The task of formatting the spreadsheet is complete. The next step is to check the spelling of the worksheet.

More About
Hidden Rows

You can use the keyboard to unhide a range of rows. First select the rows immediately above and below the hidden ones and press CTRL+SHIFT+(. To use the keyboard to hide a range of rows, press CTRL+9.

Checking Spelling

Excel has a spell checker you can use to check the worksheet for spelling errors. The spell checker looks for spelling errors by comparing words on the worksheet against words contained in its standard dictionary. If you often use specialized terms that are not in the standard dictionary, you may want to add them to a custom dictionary using the Spelling dialog box.

When the spell checker finds a word that is not in either dictionary, it displays the word in the Spelling dialog box. You then can correct it if it is misspelled.

You start the spell checker by clicking the Spelling button on the Standard toolbar. To illustrate how Excel responds to a misspelled word, the word, Stock, in cell A2 is purposely misspelled as the word, Stpck, as shown in Figure 2-52.

Steps To Check Spelling in the Worksheet

1. **Select cell A2 and enter** `Stpck` **to misspell the word Stock. Select cell A1. Click the Spelling button on the Standard toolbar. When the spell checker stops on High-Tech, click the Ignore button. When the spell checker stops on cell A2, click the word Stock in the Suggestions list.**

The spell checker starts checking the spelling of the text in the worksheet, beginning with the active cell (cell A1). It continues checking to the right and down row by row. When the spell checker comes across the misspelled word, Stpck, the Spelling dialog box displays (Figure 2-52).

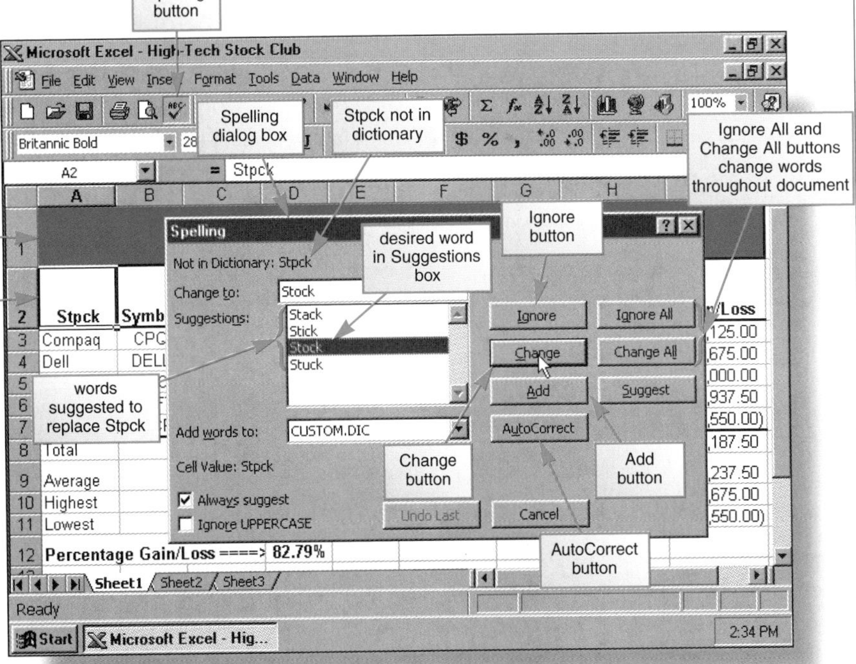

FIGURE 2-52

2 **Click the Change button. As the spell checker checks the remainder of the worksheet, click the Ignore and Change buttons as needed.**

The spell checker changes the misspelled word, Stpck, to the correct word, Stock, and continues spell checking the worksheet. When the spell checker is finished, it displays the Microsoft Excel dialog box with a message indicating that the spell check is complete for the entire sheet (Figure 2-53).

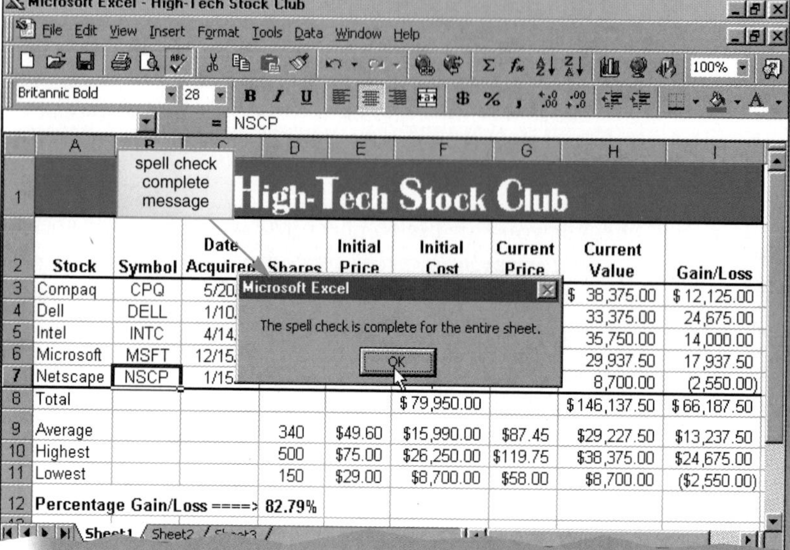

FIGURE 2-53

3 **Click the OK button.**

OtherWays

1. On Tools menu click Spelling
2. Press F7

When the spell checker identifies that a cell contains a word not in its standard or custom dictionary, it selects that cell as the active cell and displays the Spelling dialog box. The Spelling dialog box (Figure 2-52) lists the word not in the dictionary, a suggested correction, and a list of alternative suggestions. If you agree with the suggested correction in the **Change To box**, click the **Change button**. To change the word throughout the worksheet, click the **Change All button**.

If one of the words in the **Suggestions list** is correct, click the correct word in the Suggestions list and then click the Change button, or double-click the word in the Suggestions list. If none of the suggestions is correct, type the correct word in the Change to box and then click the Change button. To skip correcting the word, click the **Ignore button**. To have Excel ignore the word for the remainder of the worksheet, click the **Ignore All button**.

Consider these additional points regarding the spell checker:

- To check the spelling of the text in a single cell, double-click the cell to make the formula bar active and then click the Spelling button on the Standard toolbar.
- If you select a single cell so that the formula bar is not active and then start the spell checker, Excel checks the entire worksheet, including notes and embedded charts.
- If you select a range of cells before starting the spell checker, Excel checks only the spelling of the words in the selected range.
- To check the spelling of a chart, select the chart and then start the spell checker.
- To check the spelling of all the sheets in a workbook, click Select All Sheets on the sheet tab shortcut menu and then start the spell checker. To display the sheet tab shortcut menu, right-click the sheet tab.
- If you select a cell other than cell A1 before you start the spell checker, a dialog box will display when the spell checker reaches the end of the worksheet, asking if you want to continue checking at the beginning.

More About Checking Spelling

Always take the time to check the spelling of a worksheet before submitting it to your supervisor. Nothing deflates an impression more than a professional-looking report with misspelled words.

- To add words to the dictionary, click the **Add button** in the Spelling dialog box (Figure 2-52 on page E 2.39) when Excel identifies the word as not in the dictionary.
- Click the **AutoCorrect button** (Figure 2-52) to add the misspelled word and the correct version of the word to the AutoCorrect list. For example, suppose you misspell the word, do, as the word, dox. When the Spelling dialog box displays the correct word, do, in the Change to box, click the AutoCorrect button. Then, anytime in the future that you type the word dox, Excel will change it to the word do.

Saving the Workbook a Second Time Using the Same File Name

Earlier in this project, you saved an intermediate version of the workbook using the file name, High-Tech Stock Club. To save the workbook a second time using the same file name, click the Save button on the Standard toolbar. Excel automatically stores the latest version of the workbook using the same file name, High-Tech Stock Club. When you save a workbook a second time using the same file name, Excel will not display the Save As dialog box as it does the first time you save the workbook. You also can click **Save** on the File menu or press SHIFT+F12 or CTRL+S to save a workbook a second time using the same file name.

If you want to save the workbook using a new name or to a different drive, click **Save As** on the File menu. Some Excel users, for example, use the Save button to save the latest version of the workbook to the default drive. Then, they use the Save As command to save a copy to another drive.

More *About* **Saving**

If you want to save the workbook under a new name, click the Save As command on the File menu. Some Excel users feel better if they save workbooks to two different drives. They use the Save button on the Standard toolbar to save the latest version of the workbook to the default drive. Then, they use the Save As command to save a second copy to another drive.

Adding a 3-D Pie Chart to the Workbook

The next step in the project is to draw the 3-D Pie chart on a separate sheet, as shown in Figure 2-54. A **pie chart** is used to show the relationship or proportion of parts to a whole. Each slice (or wedge) of the pie shows what percent that slice contributes to the total (100%). The 3-D Pie chart in Figure 2-54 shows the contribution of each stock to the total value of the club's portfolio. The pie chart makes it easy to see that Compaq represents the largest part of the total value.

Unlike the 3-D Column chart in Project 1, the 3-D Pie chart in Figure 2-54 is not embedded in the worksheet. This pie chart was created on a separate sheet called a **chart sheet**.

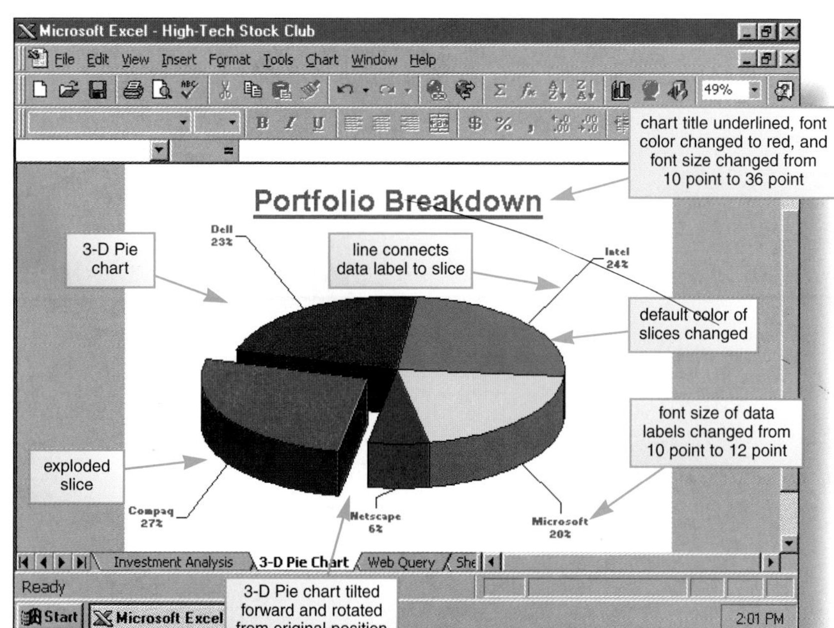

FIGURE 2-54

More About Charting

Line chart, bar chart, pie chart – which chart will best describe my worksheet data? For answers, click Contents and Index on the Help menu. Click the Contents tab. Double-click the Working with Charts book. Double-click the Changing the Type of a Chart book. Double-click the Examples of chart types link and click each chart type.

The ranges in the worksheet to chart are the nonadjacent ranges A3:A7 and H3:H7 (Figure 2-55). The stock names in the range A3:A7 will identify the slices; these entries are called **category names**. The range H3:H7 contains the data that determines the size of the slices in the pie; these entries are called the **data series.** Because there are five stocks, the 3-D Pie chart contains five slices.

This project also calls for emphasizing the stock with the greatest contribution to the total value (Compaq) by offsetting its slice from the main portion. A pie chart with one or more slices offset is called an **exploded pie chart.**

As shown in Figure 2-54 on the previous page, the default 3-D Pie chart also has been enhanced by rotating and tilting the pie forward, changing the colors of the slices, and modifying the chart title and labels that identify the slices.

Drawing the 3-D Pie Chart

To draw the 3-D Pie chart on a separate chart sheet, select the nonadjacent ranges and then click the Chart Wizard button. Once the chart is created, you can format it as shown in Figure 2-54 by completing the following steps:

1. Chart title — change to 36-point Arial, red, underlined font.
2. Slice labels — change to 12-point Arial, red font and drag them away from the slices they represent.
3. Slices – change the colors of the slices.
4. Explode the Compaq slice.
5. Rotate and tilt the pie chart to display the Compaq slice more prominently.

Steps To Draw a 3-D Pie Chart

1 Select the range A3:A7. While holding down the CTRL key, select the range H3:H7. Point to the Chart Wizard button on the Standard toolbar.

The nonadjacent ranges are selected (Figure 2-55).

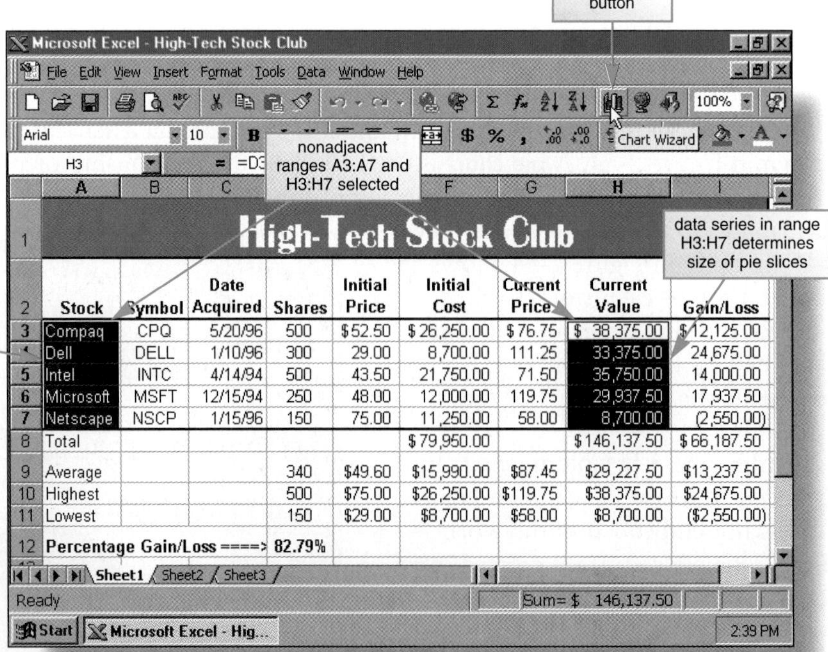

FIGURE 2-55

2 **Click the Chart Wizard button. When the Chart Wizard – Step 1 of 4 – Chart Type dialog box displays, click Pie in the Chart type list and then click the 3-D Pie chart (column 2, row 1) in the Chart sub-type box. Point to the Next button.**

Excel displays the Chart Wizard – Step 1 of 4 – Chart Type dialog box, which allows you to select one of the fourteen types of charts available in Excel (Figure 2-56).

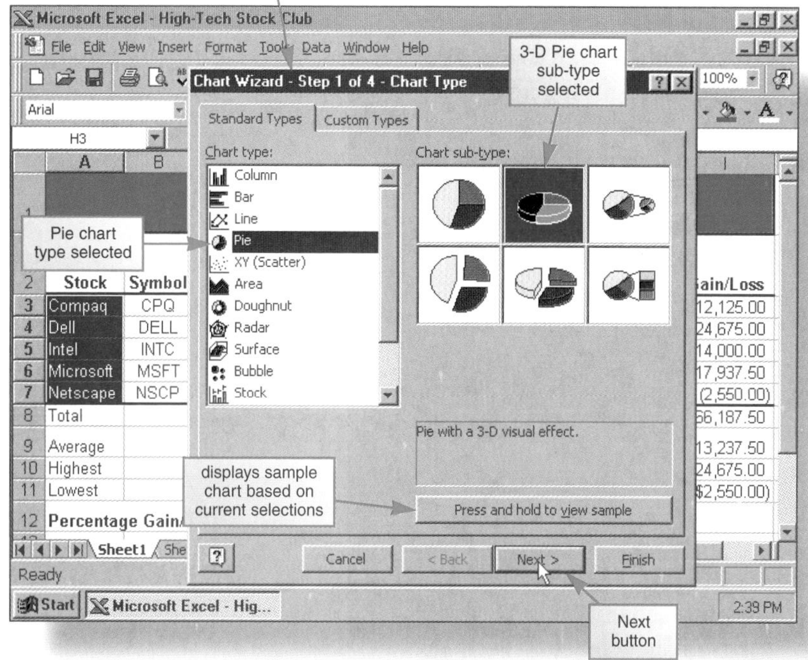

FIGURE 2-56

3 **Click the Next button.**

The Chart Wizard – Step 2 of 4 – Chart Source Data dialog box displays, showing a sample of the 3-D Pie chart and the chart data range (Figure 2-57).

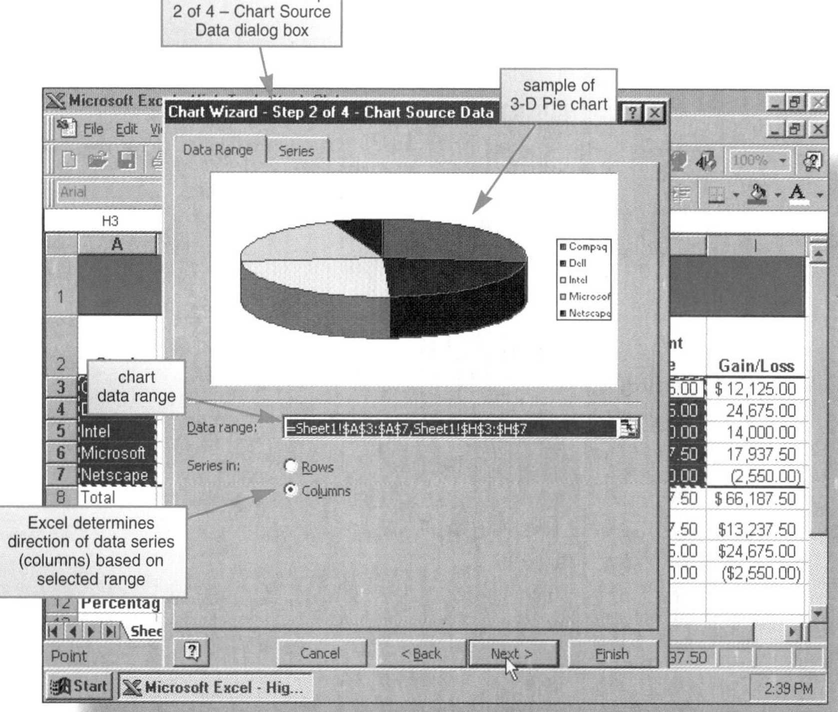

FIGURE 2-57

4 **Click the Next button. When the Chart Wizard – Step 3 of 4 – Chart Options dialog box displays, type** `Portfolio Breakdown` **in the Chart title box. Point to the Legend tab.**

Excel redraws the sample 3-D Pie chart with the chart title, Portfolio Breakdown (Figure 2-58).

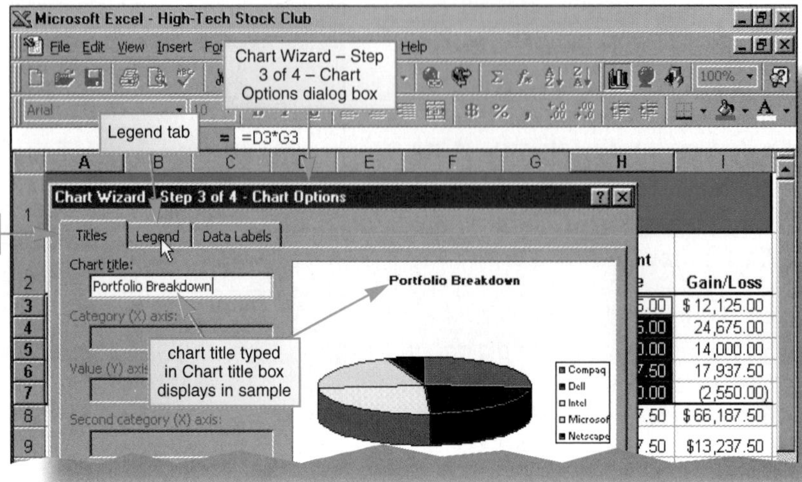

FIGURE 2-58

5 **Click the Legend tab and then click the Show legend check box to remove the check mark. Point to the Data Labels tab.**

The Legend tab displays. Excel redraws the sample 3-D Pie chart without the legend. (Figure 2-59).

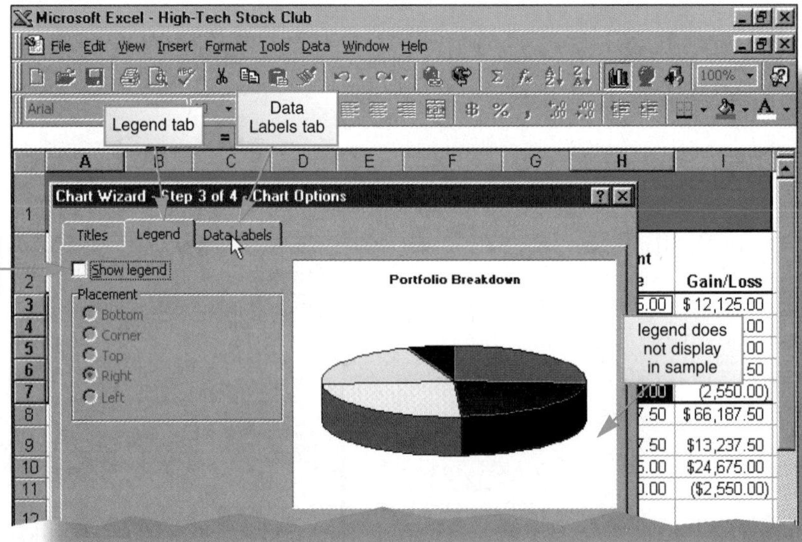

FIGURE 2-59

6 **Click the Data Labels tab. Click the Show label and percent option button in the Data labels area. Point to the Next button.**

The Data Labels sheet displays. Excel redraws the sample 3-D Pie chart with data labels and percents (Figure 2-60).

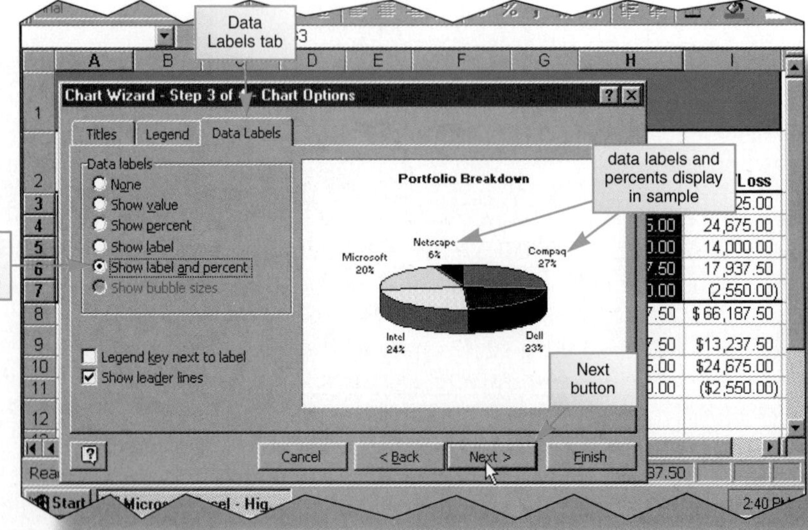

FIGURE 2-60

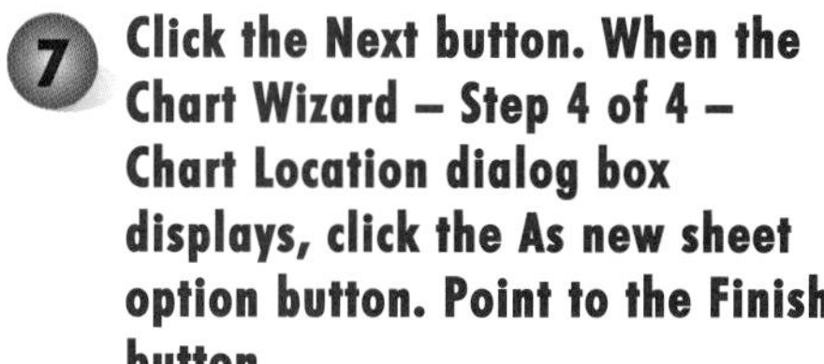

7 Click the Next button. When the Chart Wizard – Step 4 of 4 – Chart Location dialog box displays, click the As new sheet option button. Point to the Finish button.

The Chart Wizard – Step 4 of 4 – Chart Location dialog box gives you two chart location options: to draw the chart on a new sheet in the workbook or to draw it as an object in a worksheet as you did in Project 1 (Figure 2-61). You also can change the name of the chart sheet in this dialog box.

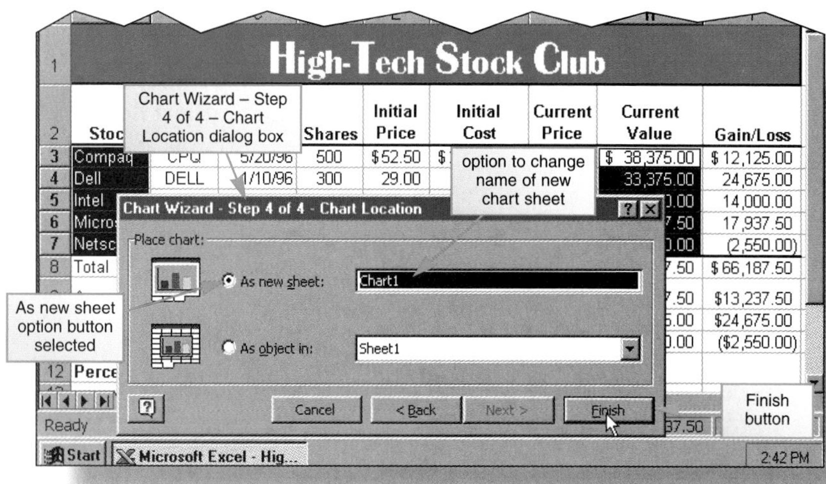

FIGURE 2-61

8 Click the Finish button.

Excel draws the 3-D Pie chart on a separate chart sheet in the High-Tech Stock Club workbook (Figure 2-62).

9 Click the Save button on the Standard toolbar.

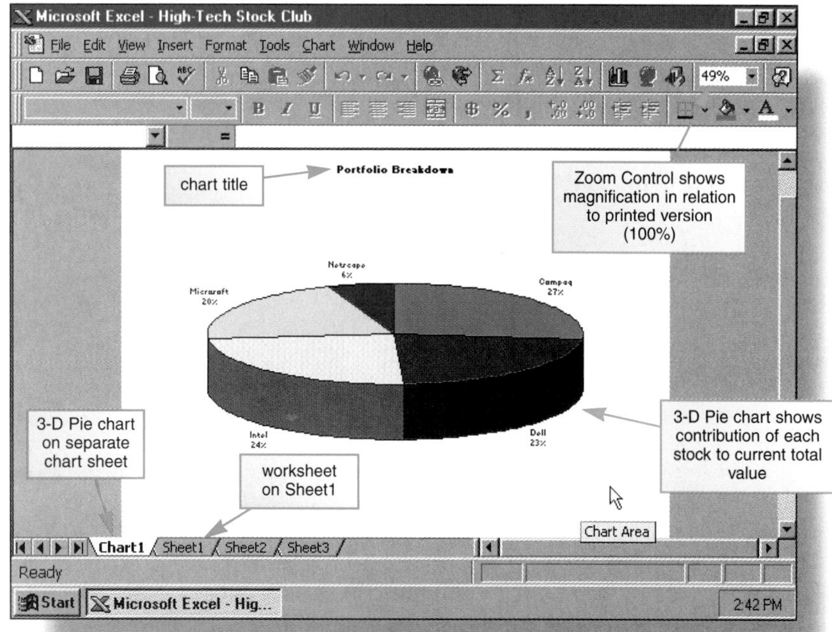

FIGURE 2-62

OtherWays

1. Select range to chart and then press F11

Each slice of the 3-D Pie chart in Figure 2-62 represents one of the five stocks – Compaq, Dell, Intel, Microsoft, and Netscape. The names of the stocks and the percent contribution to the total value display outside the slices. The chart title, Portfolio Breakdown, displays immediately above the 3-D Pie chart.

Excel determines the direction of the data series range (down a column or across a row) on the basis of the selected range. Because the selection for the 3-D Pie chart is down the worksheet (ranges A3:A7 and H3:H7), Excel automatically selects the Series in Columns option button as shown in Figure 2-57 on page E 2.43.

In any of the four Chart Wizard dialog boxes (Figure 2-56 through Figure 2-61 on pages E 2.43 through E 2.45), you can click the Back button to return to the previous Chart Wizard dialog box. You also can click the Finish button in any of the dialog boxes to create the chart with the options selected thus far.

Formatting the Chart Title and Chart Labels

The next step is to format the chart title and labels that identify the slices. Before you can format a **chart item**, such as the chart title or labels, you must select it. Once a chart item is selected, you can format it using the Formatting toolbar, shortcut menu, special keys, or the Format menu. In the following sections, you will use the Formatting toolbar to format chart items much like you formatted the cell entries earlier in this project. Complete the following steps to format the chart title and labels.

To Format the Chart Title and Labels

1. **Click the chart title. Click the Font Size box arrow on the Formatting toolbar and then click 36. Click the Underline button on the Formatting toolbar. Click the Font Color button arrow on the Formatting toolbar and then point to red (column 1, row 3 on the Font Color palette).**

   Excel displays a box with handles around the chart title, increases the font size of the chart title, and underlines the chart title (Figure 2-63). The Font Color palette displays.

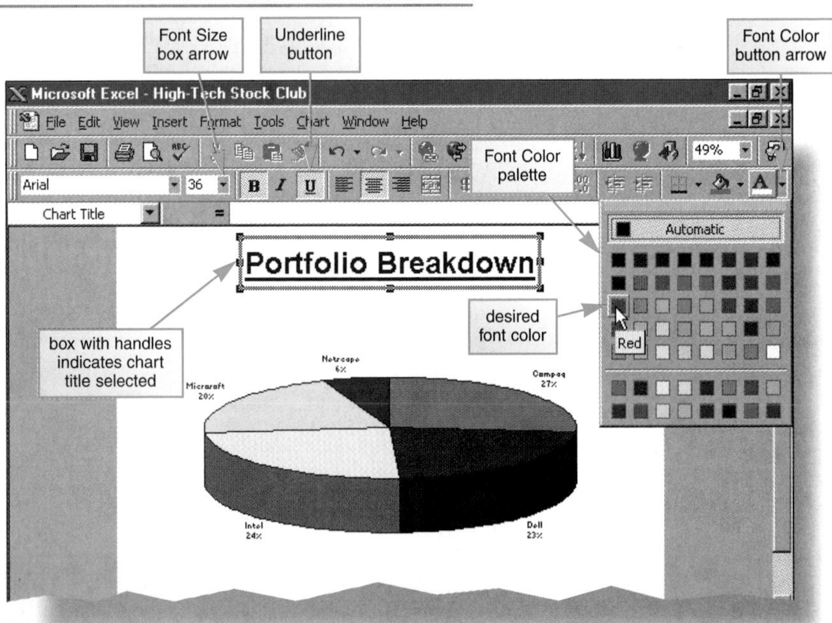

FIGURE 2-63

2. **Click the color red. Right-click one of the five data labels that identify the slices. Click the Font Size box arrow on the Formatting toolbar and then click 12. Click the Bold button on the Formatting toolbar. Click the Font Color button on the Formatting toolbar.**

   The chart title and data labels display in red as shown in Figure 2-64. The data labels are selected.

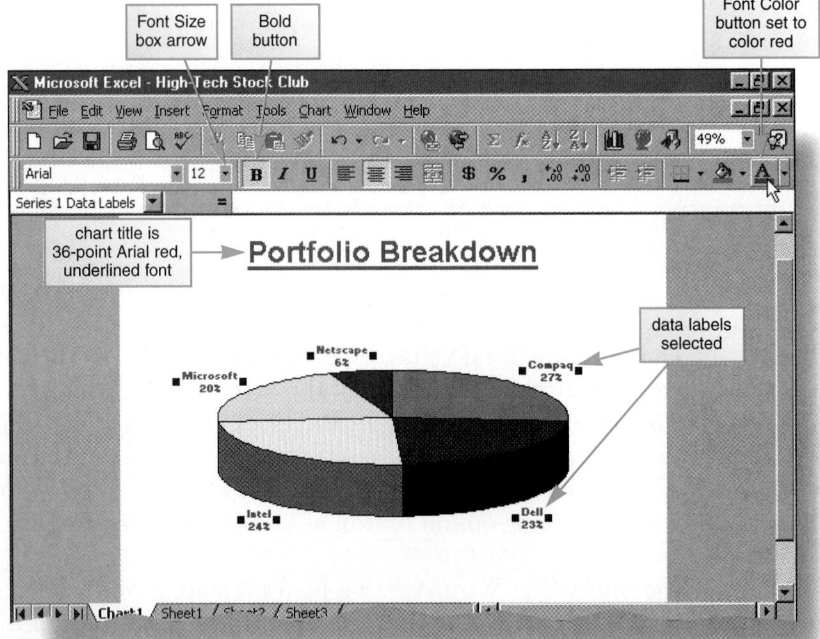

FIGURE 2-64

3 **One at a time, drag each data label away from the slice it represents so the data labels appear as shown in Figure 2-65.**

The data labels are moved away from each slice. Excel draws thin **leader lines** *that connect each data label to its corresponding slice. If the leader lines do not display, click Chart Options on the Chart menu and click the Show leader lines option button.*

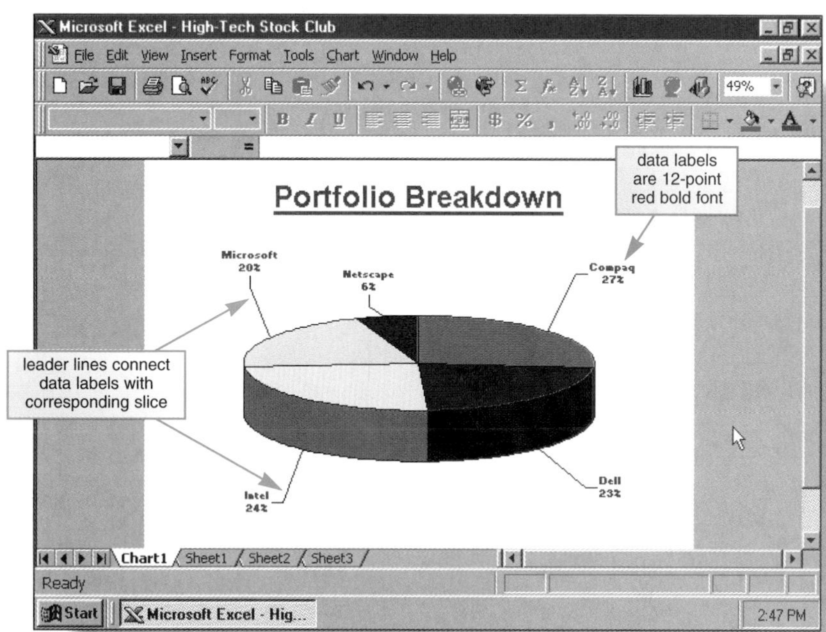

FIGURE 2-65

OtherWays

1. Right-click title or labels, click Format Title or click Format Data Labels
2. Press CTRL+B to bold
3. Press CTRL+U to underline

If you compare Figure 2-65 to Figure 2-62 on page E 2.45, you can see that the labels and chart title are easier to read and make the chart sheet look more professional.

As shown in Figure 2-65, when you drag a data label away from the 3-D Pie chart, Excel draws thin lines, called leader lines, to connect the labels to the corresponding slices. You also can select and format individual labels by clicking a specific data label after all the data labels have been selected. Making an individual data label larger or a different color, for example, helps you emphasize a small or large slice in a pie chart.

Changing the Colors of the Slices

The next step is to change the colors of the slices of the pie. The colors shown in Figure 2-66 on the next page are the default colors Excel uses when you first create a pie chart. Project 2 requires that the colors be changed to those shown in Figure 2-54 on page E 2.41. To change the colors of the slices, select them one at a time and use the Fill Color button on the Formatting toolbar as shown in the steps on the next page.

More About Clicking

A few Excel formatting activities, especially with charts, require you to click the object twice before selecting a format. Clicking an object twice is not the same as double-clicking. With double-clicking, the clicking sequence is rapid. When you are asked to click an object twice, pause before clicking a second time.

To Change the Colors of the Pie Slices

1 **Click the Compaq slice twice, once to select all the slices and once to select the individual slice. (Do not double-click.) Click the Fill Color button arrow on the Formatting toolbar and then point to the color red (column 1, row 3 on the Fill Color palette).**

Excel displays resizing handles around the Compaq slice and the Fill Color palette displays (Figure 2-66).

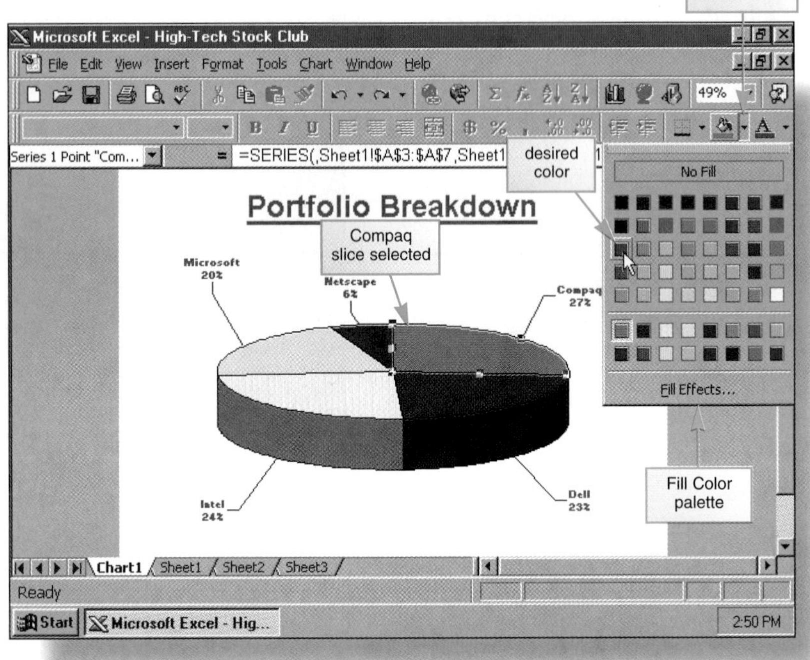

FIGURE 2-66

2 **Click the color red.**

Excel changes the Compaq slice to the color red.

3 **One at a time, click the remaining slices and then use the Fill Color palette to change each slice to the following colors: Netscape – blue (column 6, row 2); Microsoft – yellow (column 3, row 4); Intel – green (column 4, row 2); Dell – plum (column 7, row 4). Click outside the chart area.**

The pie chart displays as shown in Figure 2-67.

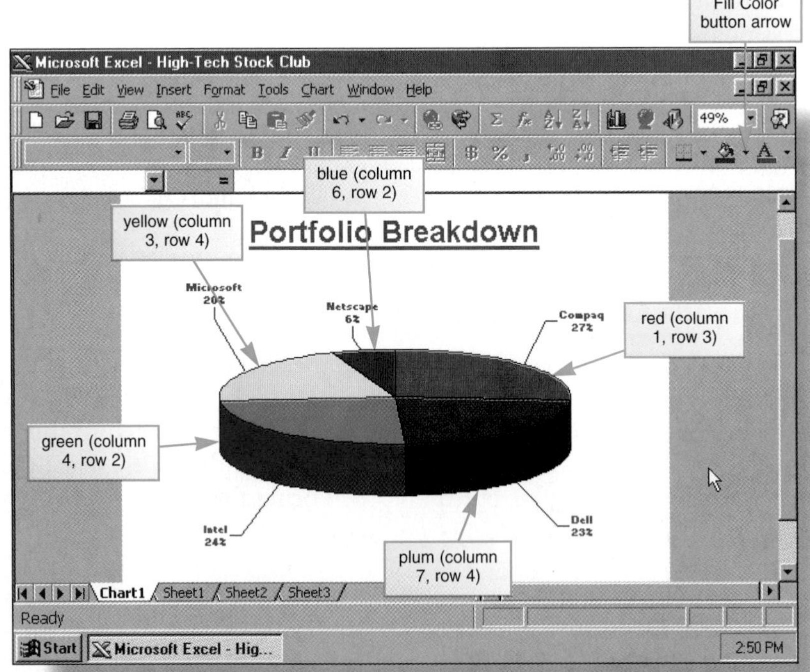

FIGURE 2-67

*Other*Ways

1. Right-click selected slice, on shortcut menu click Format Data Point, click Patterns tab, click color, click OK button
2. On Format menu click Selected Data Point, click Patterns tab, click color, click OK button

Exploding the 3-D Pie Chart

The next step is to emphasize the slice representing Compaq by offsetting, or **exploding**, it from the rest of the slices. Of the five stocks, Compaq represents the greatest profit contributor in the portfolio; by exploding it, you can make this slice stand out from the rest. Perform the following steps to explode a slice of the 3-D Pie chart.

Steps To Explode the 3-D Pie Chart

1. **Click the slice labeled Compaq twice. (Do not double-click.)**

   Excel displays resizing handles around the Compaq slice.

2. **Drag the slice to the desired position and then release the left mouse button.**

   Excel redraws the 3-D Pie chart with the Compaq slice offset from the rest of the slices (Figure 2-68).

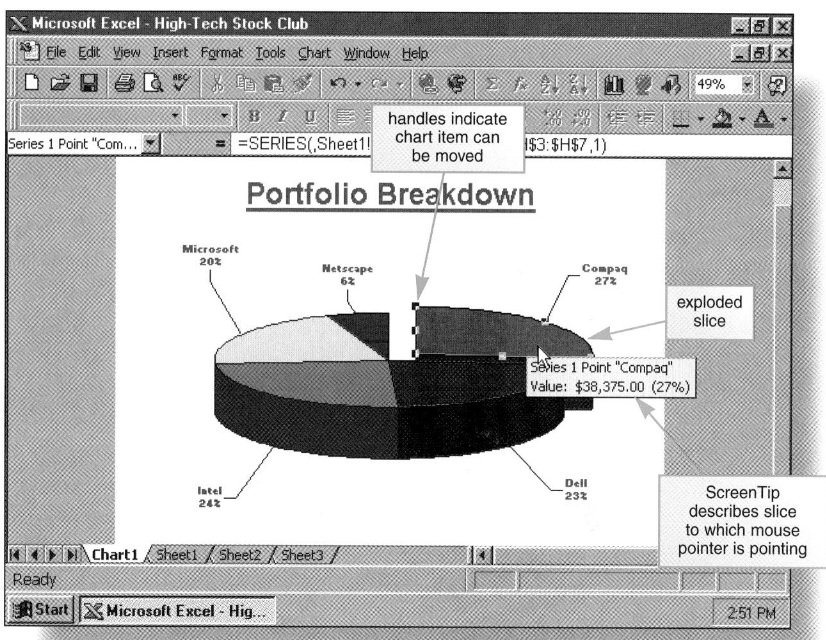

FIGURE 2-68

You can offset as many slices as you want, but remember that the reason for offsetting a slice is to emphasize it. Offsetting multiple slices tends to reduce the impact on the reader.

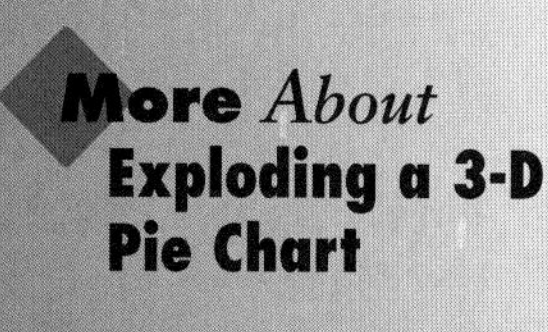

More *About* **Exploding a 3-D Pie Chart**

If you click the 3-D Pie Chart so that all the slices are selected, you can drag one of the slices to explode all of the slices.

Rotating and Tilting the 3-D Pie Chart

With a three-dimensional chart, you can change the view to better display the section of the chart you are trying to emphasize. Excel allows you to control the rotation angle, elevation, perspective, height, and angle of the axes by using the **3-D View command** on the Chart menu.

To obtain a better view of the offset Compaq slice, you can rotate the 3-D Pie chart 190^0 to the left. The rotation angle of the 3-D Pie chart is defined by the line that divides the Compaq and Netscape slices. When Excel initially draws a pie chart, it always points one of the dividing lines between two slices to twelve o'clock (or zero degrees). Besides rotating the 3-D Pie chart, the steps on the next page also change, or tilt, the elevation so the 3-D Pie chart is at less of an angle to the viewer.

To Rotate and Tilt the 3-D Pie Chart

1 **With the Compaq slice selected, click Chart on the menu bar and point to 3-D View.**

The Chart menu displays as shown in Figure 2-69.

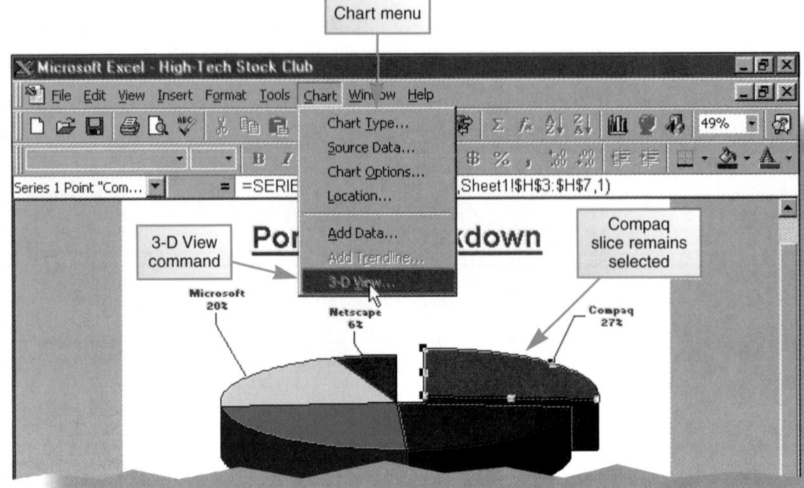

FIGURE 2-69

2 **Click 3-D View. When the 3-D View dialog box displays, click the Up Arrow button in the 3-D View dialog box until 25 displays in the Elevation box.**

The ***3-D View dialog box*** *displays (Figure 2-70). A sample of the 3-D Pie chart displays in the dialog box. The result of increasing the elevation of the 3-D Pie chart is to tilt it forward.*

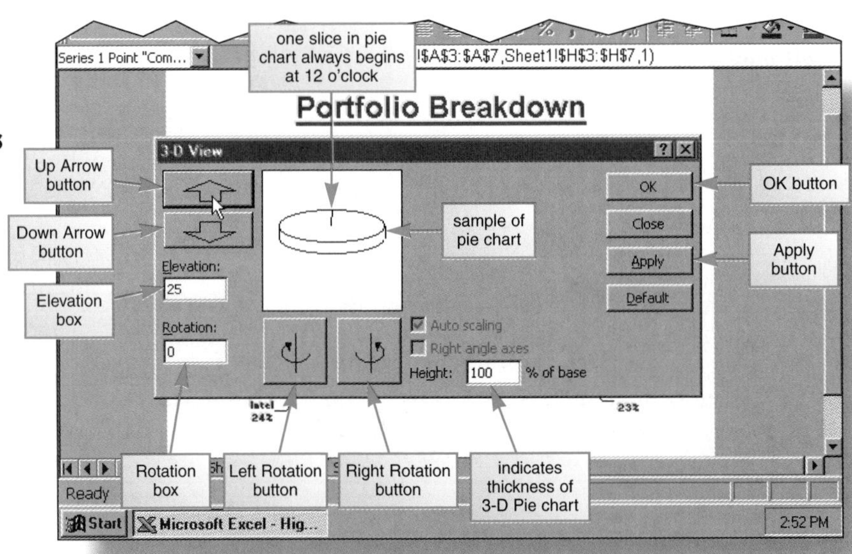

FIGURE 2-70

3 **Rotate the pie chart by clicking the Right Rotation button until the Rotation box displays 190.**

The new rotation setting (190) displays in the ***Rotation box*** *as shown in Figure 2-71. A sample of the rotated pie chart displays in the dialog box.*

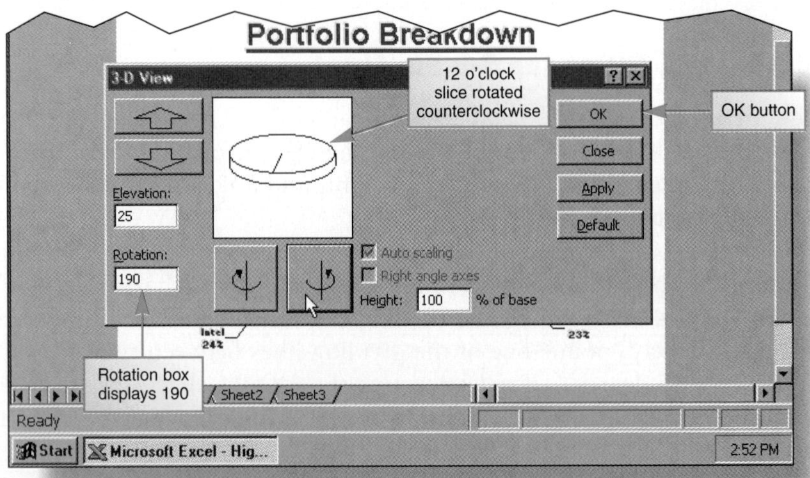

FIGURE 2-71

4 **Click the OK button.**

Excel displays the 3-D Pie chart tilted forward and rotated to the left, which makes the space between the Compaq slice and the main portion of the pie more prominent (Figure 2-72).

5 **Click the Save button on the Standard toolbar.**

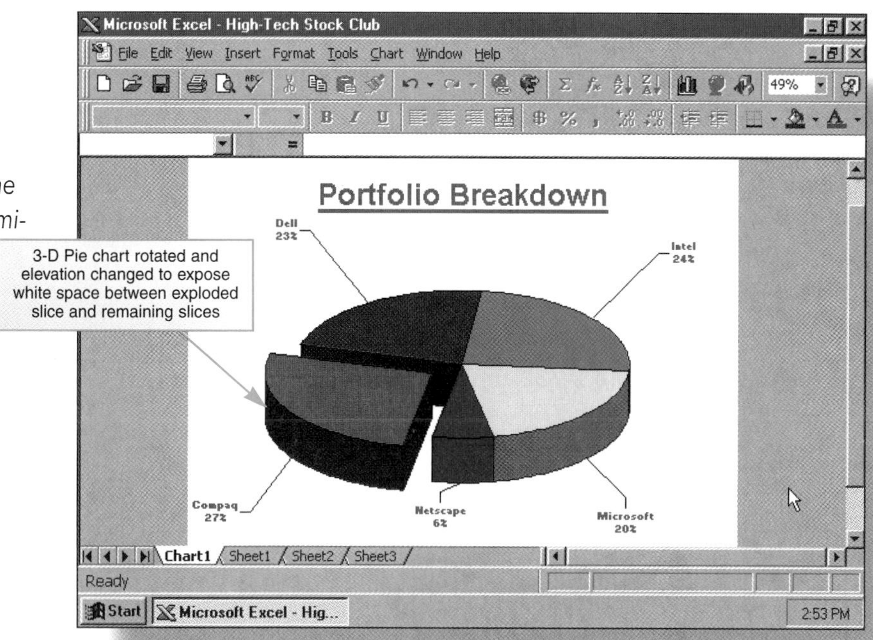

FIGURE 2-72

Compare Figure 2-72 to Figure 2-68 on page E 2.49. The offset of the Compaq slice is more noticeable in Figure 2-72 because the pie chart has been tilted and rotated to expose the white space between the Compaq slice and the main portion of the 3-D Pie chart.

In addition to controlling the rotation angle and elevation, you also can control the thickness of the 3-D Pie chart by entering a percent smaller or larger than the default 100% in the Height box (Figure 2-70).

The 3-D Pie chart is complete. The next step is to change the names of the sheets and reorder the sheets so the worksheet is first, followed by the chart. If you look at the sheet tabs below the pie chart in Figure 2-72, you will see that Sheet1, which contains the worksheet, follows the sheet labeled Chart1.

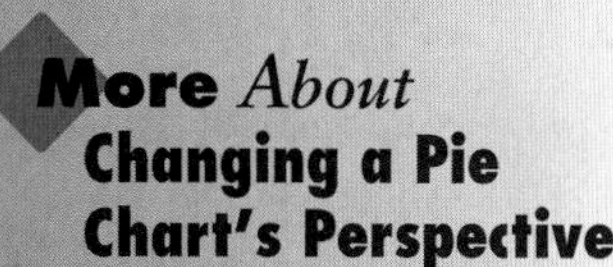

More About
Changing a Pie Chart's Perspective

You can increase or decrease the base height (thickness) of the pie chart by changing the height to base ratio in the Format 3-D View dialog box.

Changing the Sheet Names and Rearranging the Order of the Sheets

At the bottom of the screen (Figure 2-72) are the tabs that allow you to display any sheet in the workbook. Excel assigns the default names to the worksheets, such as Sheet1, Sheet2, and so on. When you draw a chart on a separate sheet, Excel assigns the default name Chart1 to the chart sheet, unless you change the sheet name in the last dialog box displayed by the Chart Wizard (Figure 2-61 on page E 2.45). To change the name of a sheet, double-click the sheet tab and then enter the new name. The steps on the next page show you how to rename sheets by double-clicking the sheet tabs and how to reorder the sheets so the worksheet comes before the chart sheet.

More About
Sheet Tabs

To move from sheet to sheet in a workbook, you click the sheet tabs at the bottom of the window. The name of the active sheet is always bold on a white background. Through the shortcut menu, you can rename the sheets, reorder the sheets, add and delete sheets, and move or copy sheets within a workbook or to another workbook.

To Rename the Sheets and Rearrange the Order of the Sheets

1 **Double-click the tab labeled Chart1 in the lower-left corner of the window. Type** `3-D Pie Chart` **as the new tab label and then press the ENTER key.**

The tab label changes from Chart1 to 3-D Pie Chart (Figure 2-73).

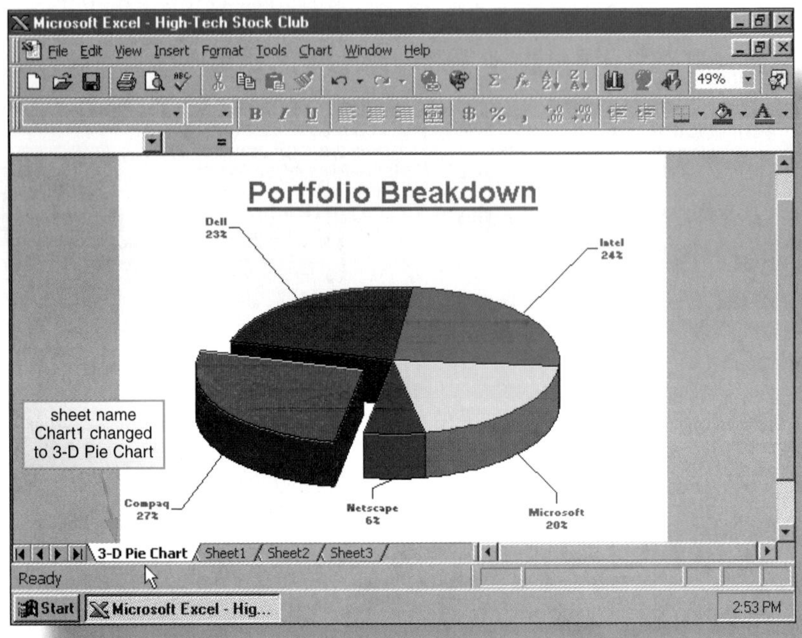

FIGURE 2-73

2 **Double-click the tab labeled Sheet1 in the lower-left corner of the window. Type** `Investment Analysis` **as the tab label and then press the ENTER key. Drag the Investment Analysis tab to the left and hold.**

The tab label changes from Sheet1 to Investment Analysis (Figure 2-74). The mouse pointer changes to an arrow with a document icon as you drag the tab.

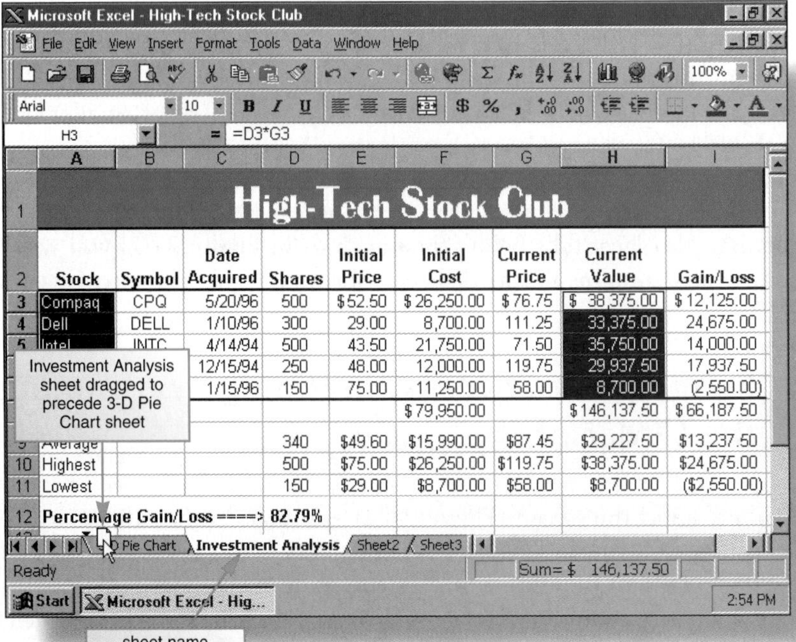

FIGURE 2-74

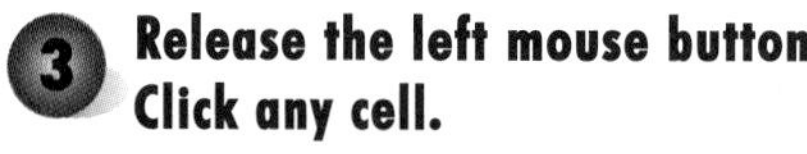

3 Release the left mouse button. Click any cell.

Excel reorders the sheets so the Investment Analysis worksheet is the first sheet in the workbook (Figure 2-75).

4 Click the Save button on the Standard toolbar.

Microsoft Excel - High-Tech Stock Club

	A	B	C	D	E	F	G	H	I
1	High-Tech Stock Club								
2	Stock	Symbol	Date Acquired	Shares	Initial Price	Initial Cost	Current Price	Current Value	Gain/Loss
3	Compaq	CPQ	5/20/96	500	$52.50	$ 26,250.00	$76.75	$ 38,375.00	$ 12,125.00
4	Dell	DELL	1/10/96	300	29.00	8,700.00	111.25	33,375.00	24,675.00
5	Intel	INTC	4/14/94	500	43.50	21,750.00	71.50	35,750.00	14,000.00
6	Microsoft	MSFT	12/15/94	250	48.00	12,000.00	119.75	29,937.50	17,937.50
7			1/15/96	150	75.00	11,250.00	58.00	8,700.00	(2,550.00)
8						$ 79,950.00		$ 146,137.50	$ 66,187.50
9				340	$49.60	$15,990.00	$87.45	$29,227.50	$13,237.50
10	Highest			500	$75.00	$26,250.00	$119.75	$38,375.00	$24,675.00
11	Lowest			150	$29.00	$8,700.00	$58.00	$8,700.00	($2,550.00)
12	Percentage Gain/Loss ====>			82.79%					

FIGURE 2-75

OtherWays

1. To rename, right-click sheet tab, click Rename
2. To move, right-click sheet tab, click Move or Copy
3. To move, on the Edit menu click Move or Copy
4. Right-click tab scrollling buttons, on shortcut menu click desired sheet

Sheet names can be up to 31 characters (including spaces) in length. Longer sheet names, however, mean that fewer tabs will display. To display more sheet tabs, you can drag the **tab split box** (Figure 2-75) to the right. This will reduce the size of the scroll bar at the bottom of the screen. Double-click the tab split box to reset it to its normal position.

You also can use the **tab scrolling buttons** to the left of the sheet tabs (Figure 2-75) to move between sheets. The leftmost and rightmost scroll buttons move to the first or last sheet in the workbook. The two middle scroll buttons move one sheet to the left or right.

Previewing and Printing Selected Sheets in a Workbook

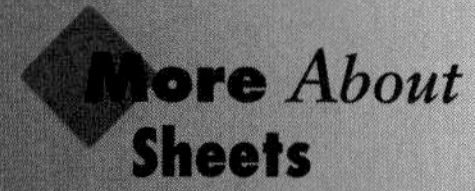

More About Sheets

You can use the keyboard to move from sheet to sheet in a workbook. Press CRTL+PGUP to move to the next sheet. Press CRTL+PGDN to move to the previous sheet.

In Project 1, you printed the worksheet without previewing it on the screen. By previewing the worksheet, you see exactly how it will look without generating a printout, or hard copy. Previewing a worksheet using the **Print Preview command** or **Print Preview button** on the Standard toolbar can save time, paper, and the frustration of waiting for a printout only to discover it is not what you want.

The Print Preview command, as well as the Print command, will preview or print only selected sheets. You know a sheet is selected when the sheet tab at the bottom of the screen is white. Thus, in Figure 2-75, the Investment Analysis sheet is selected, but the 3-D Pie Chart sheet is not. To select additional adjacent sheets, hold down the SHIFT key and then click the sheet tab of the last sheet you wish to select. This will select all sheets between the active sheet and the one clicked. To select a nonadjacent sheet, hold down the CTRL key and then select the desired sheet tab.

To Preview Selected Sheets in a Workbook

1. **While holding down the SHIFT key, click the 3-D Pie Chart sheet tab. Point to the Print Preview button on the Standard toolbar.**

Both the worksheet and the chart sheet are selected (Figure 2-76).

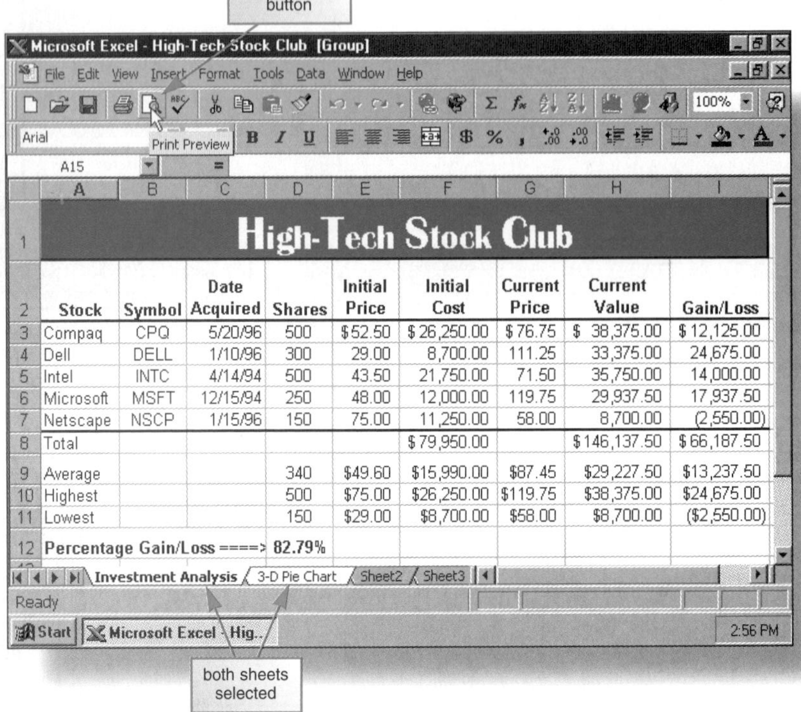

FIGURE 2-76

2. **Click the Print Preview button on the Standard toolbar.**

Excel displays a preview of the worksheet in the preview window and the mouse pointer changes to a magnifying glass (Figure 2-77). The word [Group] in the title bar indicates that multiple sheets are selected.

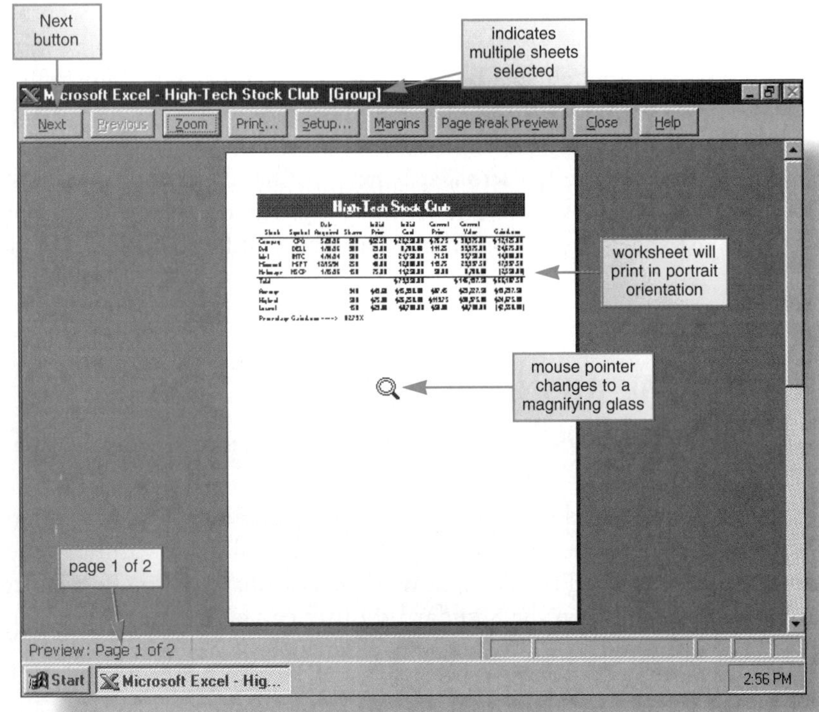

FIGURE 2-77

3 **Click the Next button to display a preview of the chart.**

A preview of the 3-D Pie chart displays (Figure 2-78).

4 **Click the Close button in the Preview window to return to the workbook.**

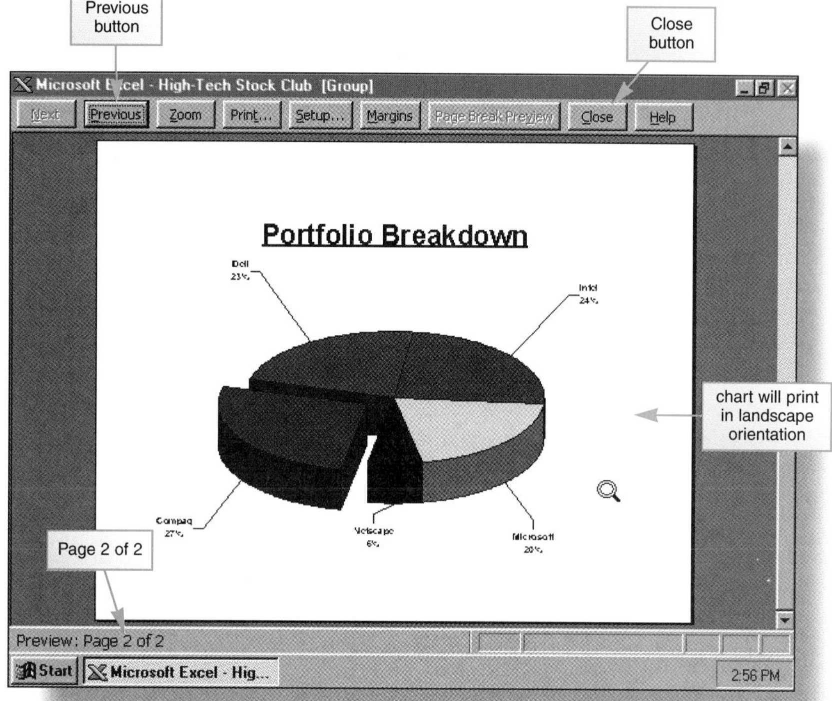

FIGURE 2-78

OtherWays

1. Right-click menu, click Page Setup, click Print Preview button
2. On File menu click Print Preview
3. On File menu click Page Setup, click Print Preview button
4. On File menu click Print, click Entire Workbook, click Preview button

Excel displays several buttons at the top of the Preview window (Figure 2-78). The functions of these buttons are summarized in Table 2-3.

Rather than click the Next and Previous buttons to move from page to page as described in Table 2-3, you also can press the PAGE UP and PAGE DOWN keys. You also can click the page in the Preview window when the mouse pointer is a magnifying glass to carry out the function of the Zoom button.

Printing Selected Sheets in a Workbook

Although you could have printed the two selected sheets from the Preview window, the steps on the next page show how to print them using the Print button on the Standard toolbar.

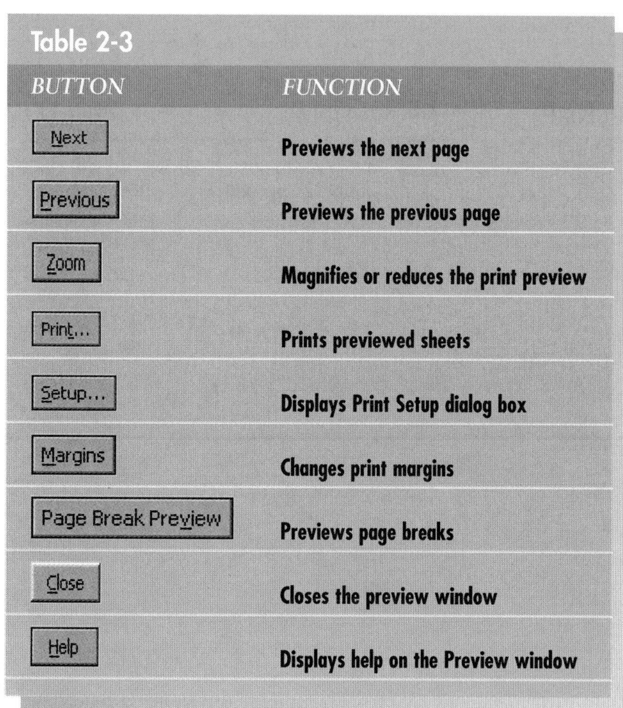

Table 2-3

BUTTON	FUNCTION
Next	Previews the next page
Previous	Previews the previous page
Zoom	Magnifies or reduces the print preview
Print...	Prints previewed sheets
Setup...	Displays Print Setup dialog box
Margins	Changes print margins
Page Break Preview	Previews page breaks
Close	Closes the preview window
Help	Displays help on the Preview window

More About Print Preview

A popular button in the Preview window (Figure 2-78) is the Margins button. The Margins button allows you to drag the top, bottom, left, and right margins to center a worksheet or add room to fit a wide or long worksheet on a page. You can even change the column widths.

To Print Selected Sheets in a Workbook

1. **Click the Investment Analysis sheet tab. If both sheets are not selected, while holding down the SHIFT key, click the inactive sheet tab.**

2. **Point to the Print button on the Standard toolbar (Figure 2-79).**

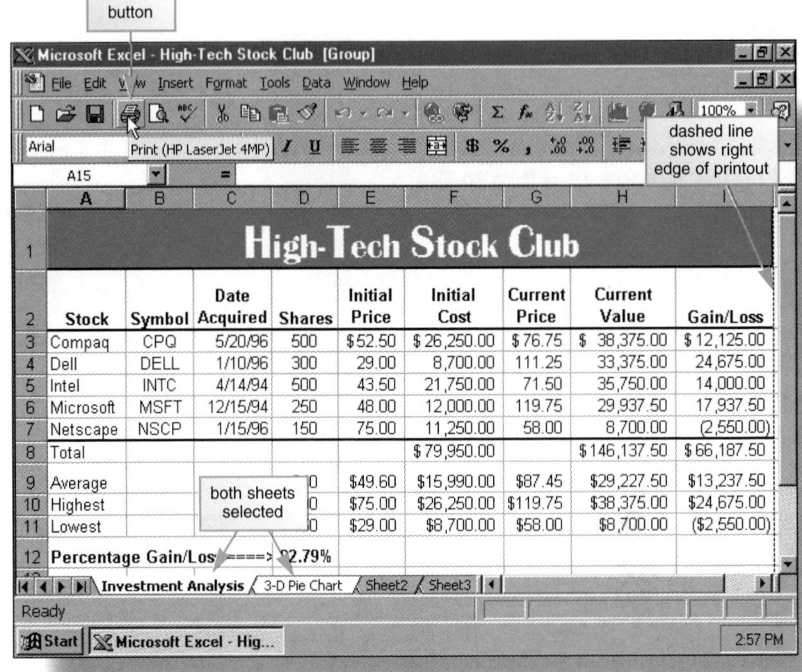

	A	B	C	D	E	F	G	H	I
1	High-Tech Stock Club								
2	Stock	Symbol	Date Acquired	Shares	Initial Price	Initial Cost	Current Price	Current Value	Gain/Loss
3	Compaq	CPQ	5/20/96	500	$52.50	$26,250.00	$76.75	$ 38,375.00	$12,125.00
4	Dell	DELL	1/10/96	300	29.00	8,700.00	111.25	33,375.00	24,675.00
5	Intel	INTC	4/14/94	500	43.50	21,750.00	71.50	35,750.00	14,000.00
6	Microsoft	MSFT	12/15/94	250	48.00	12,000.00	119.75	29,937.50	17,937.50
7	Netscape	NSCP	1/15/96	150	75.00	11,250.00	58.00	8,700.00	(2,550.00)
8	Total					$79,950.00		$146,137.50	$66,187.50
9	Average			0	$49.60	$15,990.00	$87.45	$29,227.50	$13,237.50
10	Highest			0	$75.00	$26,250.00	$119.75	$38,375.00	$24,675.00
11	Lowest			0	$29.00	$8,700.00	$58.00	$8,700.00	($2,550.00)
12	Percentage Gain/Loss ====>		2.79%						

FIGURE 2-79

3. **Click the Print button.**

   Excel prints the worksheet (Figure 2-80a) and the 3-D Pie chart on the printer (Figure 2-80b).

4. **While holding down the SHIFT key, click the Investment Analysis tab to deselect the 3-D Pie chart sheet.**

portrait orientation

High-Tech Stock Club

Stock	Symbol	Date Acquired	Shares	Initial Price	Initial Cost	Current Price	Current Value	Gain/Loss
Compaq	CPQ	5/20/96	500	$52.50	$26,250.00	$76.75	$ 38,375.00	$12,125.00
Dell	DELL	1/10/96	300	29.00	8,700.00	111.25	33,375.00	24,675.00
Intel	INTC	4/14/94	500	43.50	21,750.00	71.50	35,750.00	14,000.00
Microsoft	MSFT	12/15/94	250	48.00	12,000.00	119.75	29,937.50	17,937.50
Netscape	NSCP	1/15/96	150	75.00	11,250.00	58.00	8,700.00	(2,550.00)
Total					$79,950.00		$146,137.50	$66,187.50
Average			340	$49.60	$15,990.00	$87.45	$29,227.50	$13,237.50
Highest			500	$75.00	$26,250.00	$119.75	$38,375.00	$24,675.00
Lowest			150	$29.00	$8,700.00	$58.00	$8,700.00	($2,550.00)

Percentage Gain/Loss ====> 82.79%

FIGURE 2-80a

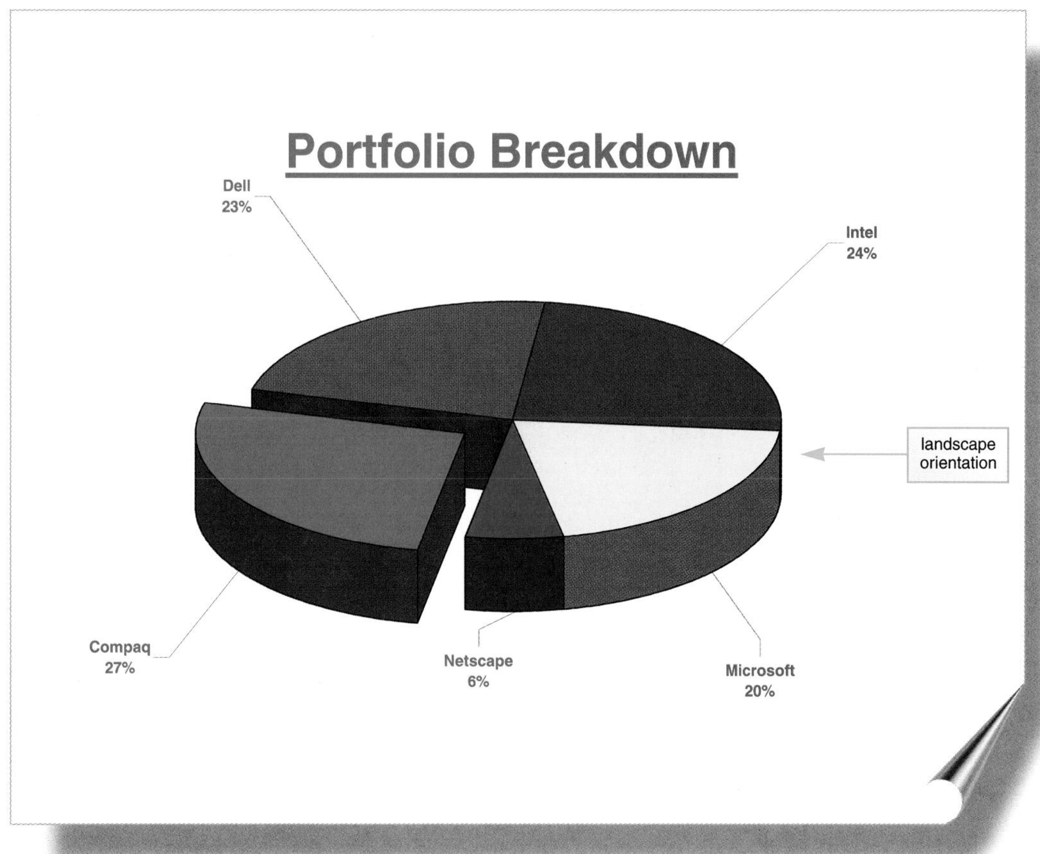

FIGURE 2-80b

OtherWays

1. Right-click tab, click Select All Sheets, click Print button
2. On File menu click Print, click Entire workbook option, click OK button

In Step 4, you also could have right-clicked the Investment Analysis tab and then clicked Ungroup Sheets to deselect the 3-D Pie Chart sheet.

As shown in Figures 2-80a and 2-80b, the worksheet is printed in portrait orientation and the chart is printed in landscape orientation. **Portrait orientation** means the printout is printed across the width of the page. **Landscape orientation** means the printout is printed across the length of the page. For any chart created on a separate sheet, Excel automatically sets it to print in landscape orientation.

Printing a Section of the Worksheet

You might not always want to print the entire worksheet. You can print portions of the worksheet by selecting the range of cells to print and then click the **Selection option button** in the **Print what area** on the Print dialog box. The steps on the next page show how to print the range A2:F7.

More About Printing

A dark font on a dark background, such as a red font on a blue background, will not print properly on a black and white printer. For black and white printing, use a light colored font on a dark background and a dark font on a light colored background.

To Print a Section of the Worksheet

1 Select the range A2:F7. Click Print on the File menu. Click the Selection option button in the Print what area in the Print dialog box. Point to the OK button.

Excel displays the Print dialog box (Figure 2-81). Because the Selection option button is selected, Excel will print only the selected range.

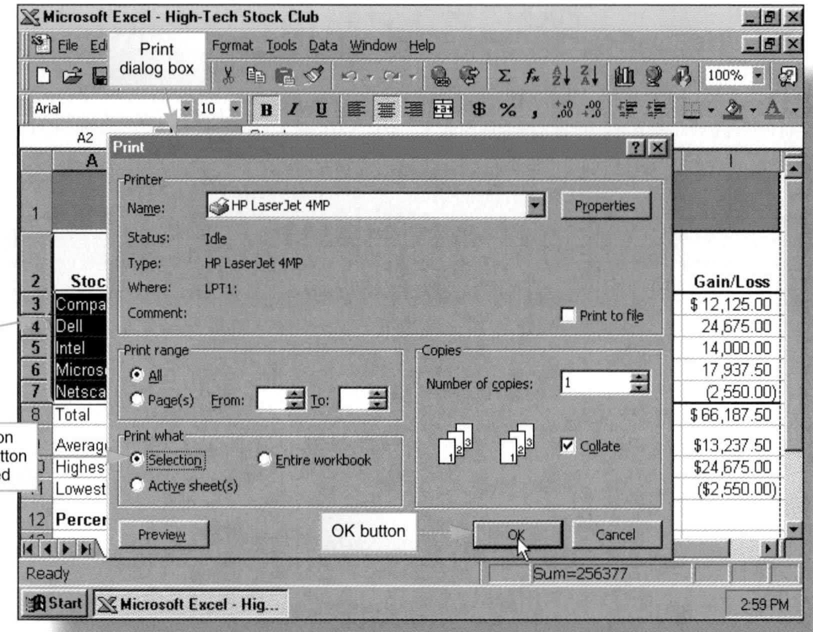

FIGURE 2-81

2 Click the OK button.

Excel prints the selected range of the worksheet on the printer (Figure 2-82).

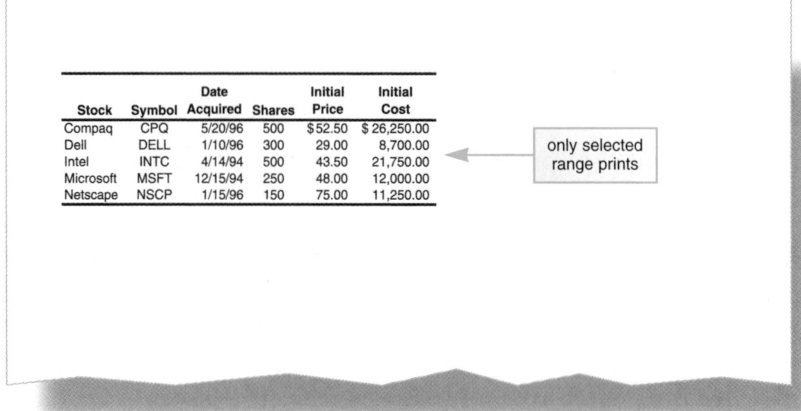

Stock	Symbol	Date Acquired	Shares	Initial Price	Initial Cost
Compaq	CPQ	5/20/96	500	$52.50	$ 26,250.00
Dell	DELL	1/10/96	300	29.00	8,700.00
Intel	INTC	4/14/94	500	43.50	21,750.00
Microsoft	MSFT	12/15/94	250	48.00	12,000.00
Netscape	NSCP	1/15/96	150	75.00	11,250.00

FIGURE 2-82

OtherWays

1. On File menu click Print Area, click Set Print Area, on Standard toolbar click Print button, on File menu click Print Area, click Clear Print Area

There are three option buttons in the Print what area in the Print dialog box (Figure 2-81). As shown in the previous steps, the Selection option button instructs Excel to print the selected range. The **Active sheet(s) option button** instructs Excel to print the active sheet (the one displaying on the screen) or the selected sheets. Finally, the **Entire workbook option button** instructs Excel to print all the sheets in the workbook. Selecting the Entire workbook option button is an alternative to selecting tabs by holding down the SHIFT or CTRL keys and then clicking tabs to make the sheets active. The Active sheets option is the default.

Displaying and Printing the Formulas in the Worksheet

Thus far, you have been working with the **values version** of the worksheet, which shows the results of the formulas you have entered, rather than the actual formulas. Excel also allows you to display and print the **formulas version** of the worksheet, which displays the actual formulas you have entered, rather than the resulting values. You can toggle between the values version and formulas version by pressing CTRL+` (left single quotation mark to the left of the number 1 key).

The formulas version is useful for debugging a worksheet. **Debugging** is the process of finding and correcting errors in the worksheet. Because the formula version displays and prints formulas and functions, rather than the results, it makes it easier to see if any mistakes were made in the formulas.

When you change from the values version to the formulas version, Excel increases the width of the columns so the formulas and text do not overflow into adjacent cells on the right. The formulas version of the worksheet thus is usually significantly wider than the values version. To fit the wide printout on one page, you can use landscape orientation and the **Fit to option** on the Page tab in the Page Setup dialog box. To change from the values version to the formulas version of the worksheet and print the formulas on one page, perform the following steps.

More *About* **Values versus Formulas**

When completing class assignments, do not enter numbers in cells that require formulas. Most instructors require their students to hand in both the values version and formulas version of the worksheet. The formulas version verifies that you entered formulas, rather than numbers, in formula-based cells.

To Display the Formulas in the Worksheet and Fit the Printout on One Page

1 **Press CTRL+` (left single quotation mark to the left of the number 1 key). Scroll to the right so column I displays.**

Excel changes the display of the worksheet from values to formulas (Figure 2-83). The formulas in the worksheet display showing unformatted numbers, formulas, and functions that were assigned to the cells. Excel automatically increases the column widths.

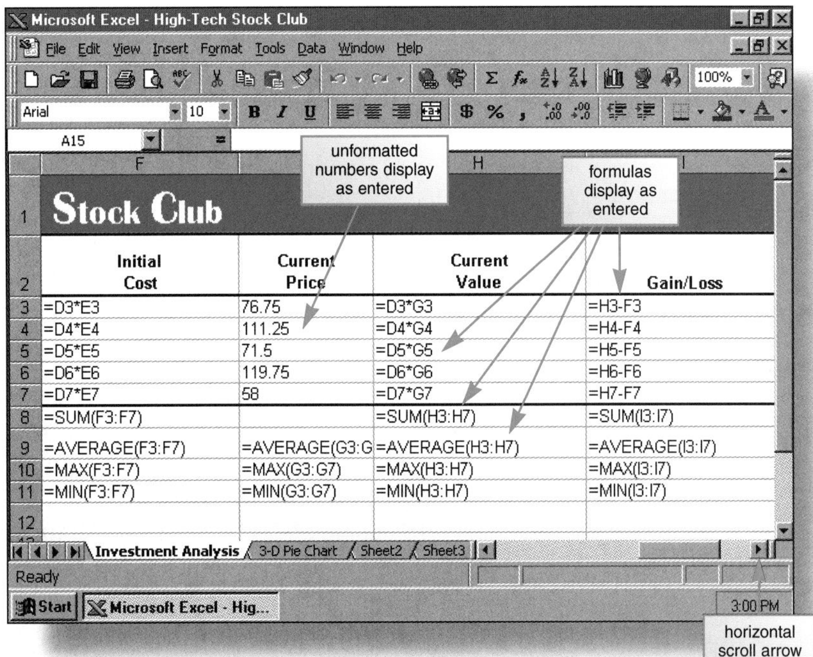

FIGURE 2-83

2 Click Page Setup on the File menu. When the Page Setup dialog box displays, click the Page tab, click the Landscape option, and click the Fit to option button so the wide worksheet prints on one page in landscape orientation. Point to the Print button.

Excel displays the Page Setup dialog box with the Landscape and Fit to option buttons selected (Figure 2-84).

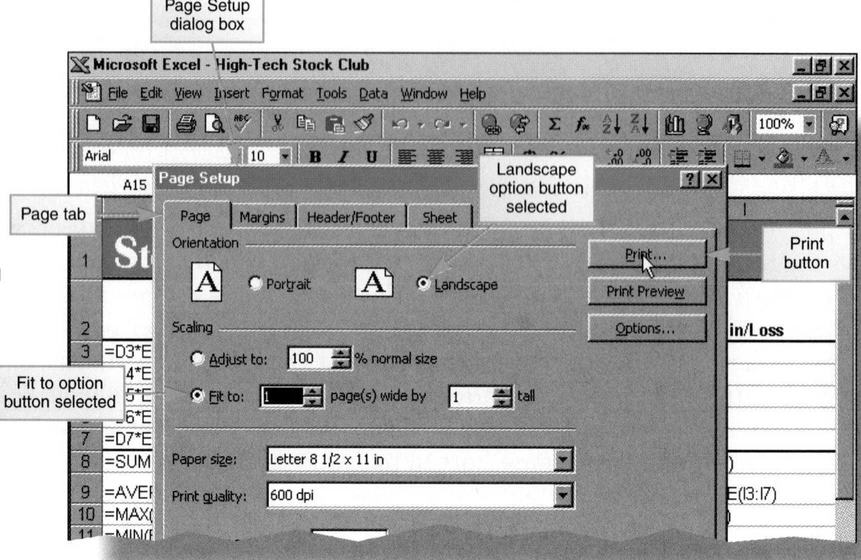

FIGURE 2-84

3 Click the Print button in the Page Setup dialog box. When the Print dialog box displays, click the OK button. When you are done viewing and printing the formulas version, press CTRL+` to display the values version.

Excel prints the formulas in the worksheet on one page in landscape orientation (Figure 2-85).

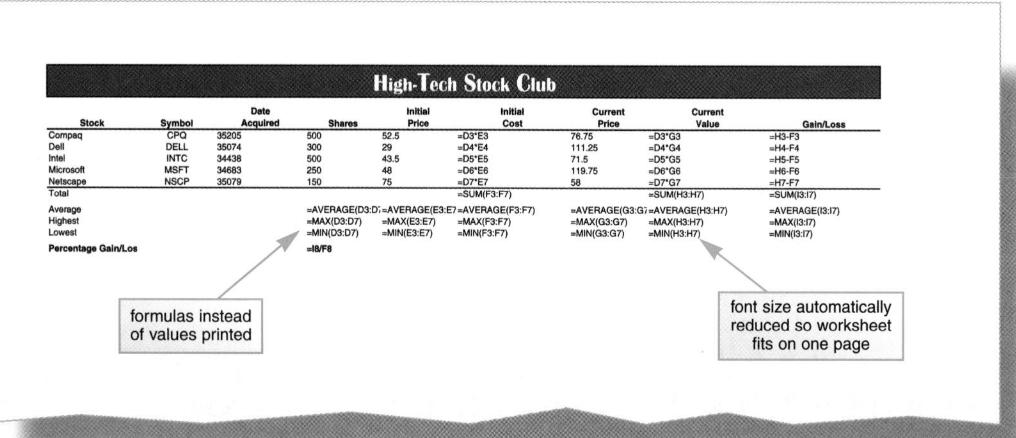

High-Tech Stock Club

Stock	Symbol	Date Acquired	Shares	Initial Price	Initial Cost	Current Price	Current Value	Gain/Loss
Compaq	CPQ	35205	500	52.5	=D3*E3	76.75	=D3*G3	=H3-F3
Dell	DELL	35074	300	29	=D4*E4	111.25	=D4*G4	=H4-F4
Intel	INTC	34438	500	43.5	=D5*E5	71.5	=D5*G5	=H5-F5
Microsoft	MSFT	34683	250	48	=D6*E6	119.75	=D6*G6	=H6-F6
Netscape	NSCP	35079	150	75	=D7*E7	58	=D7*G7	=H7-F7
Total					=SUM(F3:F7)		=SUM(H3:H7)	=SUM(I3:I7)
Average			=AVERAGE(D3:D7	=AVERAGE(E3:E7	=AVERAGE(F3:F7)	=AVERAGE(G3:G7	=AVERAGE(H3:H7)	=AVERAGE(I3:I7)
Highest			=MAX(D3:D7)	=MAX(E3:E7)	=MAX(F3:F7)	=MAX(G3:G7)	=MAX(H3:H7)	=MAX(I3:I7)
Lowest			=MIN(D3:D7)	=MIN(E3:E7)	=MIN(F3:F7)	=MIN(G3:G7)	=MIN(H3:H7)	=MIN(I3:I7)
Percentage Gain/Los			=I8/F8					

FIGURE 2-85

Although the formulas version of the worksheet was printed in the previous example, you can see from Figure 2-83 on the previous page that the display on the screen also can be used for debugging the worksheet.

As shown in Figure 2-79 on page E 2.56, a dashed line displays on the screen to represent the right edge of the printed worksheet. If the entries in a worksheet extend past this dashed line, the printout will be made up of multiple pages. If you prefer to print the worksheet on one page, click the Fit to option button in the Page Setup dialog box (Figure 2-84) before you print. The Fit to option was used to print the formulas version of the Investment Analysis worksheet, for example, so it would fit on one page.

Changing the Print Scaling Option Back to 100%

Depending on your printer driver, you may have to change the Print Scaling option back to 100% after using the Fit to option. Complete the following steps to reset the Print Scaling option so future worksheets print at 100%, instead of being squeezed on one page.

TO CHANGE THE PRINT SCALING OPTION BACK TO 100%

Step 1: Click Page Setup on the File menu.
Step 2: Click the Page tab in the Page Setup dialog box. Click the Adjust to option in the Scaling area.
Step 3: If necessary, type `100` in the Adjust to box.
Step 4: Click the OK button.

The Adjust to box allows you to specify the percentage of reduction or enlargement in the printout of a worksheet. The default percentage is 100%. When you click the Fit to option, this percentage automatically changes to the percentage required to fit the printout on one page.

More *About*
Fit To Option

Do not take the Fit To option lightly. Most applications involve worksheets that extend well beyond the 8½" by 11" page. However, most users want the information on one page, at least with respect to the width of the worksheet. Thus, the Fit To option is a common choice among Excel users.

Getting External Data from a Web Source Using a Web Query

One of the major features of Excel 97 is its capability to obtain external data from sites on the World Wide Web. To get external data from a World Wide Web site, you must have access to the Internet. You then can run a **Web query** to retrieve data stored on the World Wide Web site. When you run a Web query, Excel returns the external data in the form of a worksheet. As described in Table 2-4, there are four Web queries available when you first install Excel. Three of the four Web queries available relate to investment and stock market activities.

Table 2-4

QUERY	EXTERNAL DATA RETURNED
Detailed Stock Quote by PC Quote, Inc	Data for a specific stock of your choice
Dow Jones Stocks by PC Quote, Inc	Data for the 30 stocks that make up the Dow Jones Industrial Average
Get More Web Queries	Download additional Web queries
Multiple Stock Quotes by PC Quote, Inc	Data for up to 20 stocks of your choice

The data returned by the stock-related Web queries is real-time in the sense that it is no more than 20 minutes old during the business day. The steps on the next page show how to get the most recent stock quotes for the five stocks owned by the High-Tech Stock Club — Compaq, Dell, Intel, Microsoft, and Netscape. Although you can have a Web query return data to a blank workbook, the following steps have the data returned to a blank worksheet in the High-Tech Stock Club workbook.

More *About*
Integrating the Web and Office Applications

The most significant feature of Office 97 is the addition of Internet tools within the applications. Besides the valuable Web queries presented here, you can easily save workbooks as HTML files (Web pages), and insert hyperlinks and e-mail addresses in workbooks.

To Get External Data from a Web Source Using a Web Query

1 **With the High-Tech Stock Club workbook open, click the Sheet2 tab at the bottom of the screen. Click cell A1.**

2 **On the Data menu, point to Get External Data and then point to Run Web Query on the Get External Data submenu.**

The Get External Data submenu displays as shown in Figure 2-86.

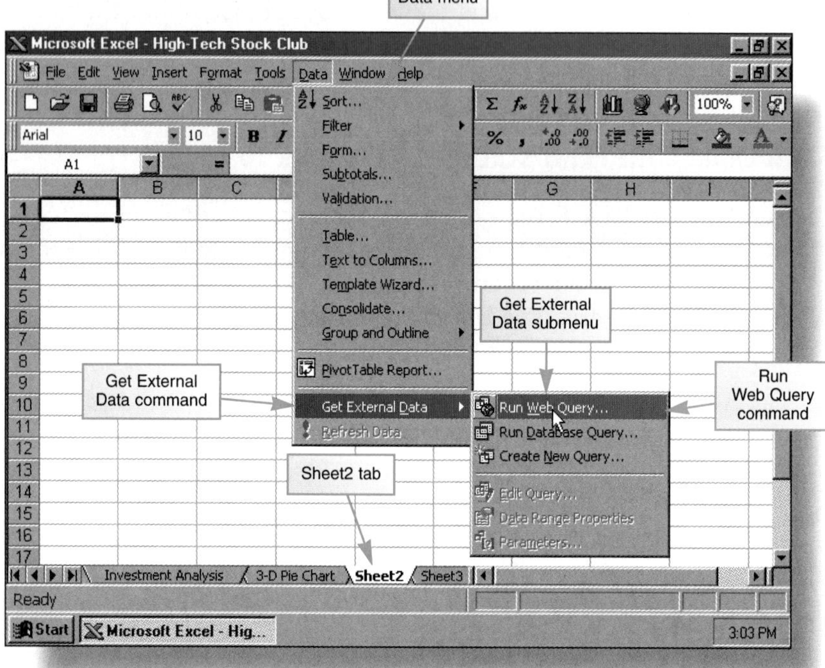

FIGURE 2-86

3 **Click Run Web Query. When the Run Query dialog box displays, click Multiple Stock Quotes by PC Quote, Inc. Point to the Get Data button.**

The Run Query dialog box displays (Figure 2-87). If your display is different, ask your instructor for the folder location of the Web queries.

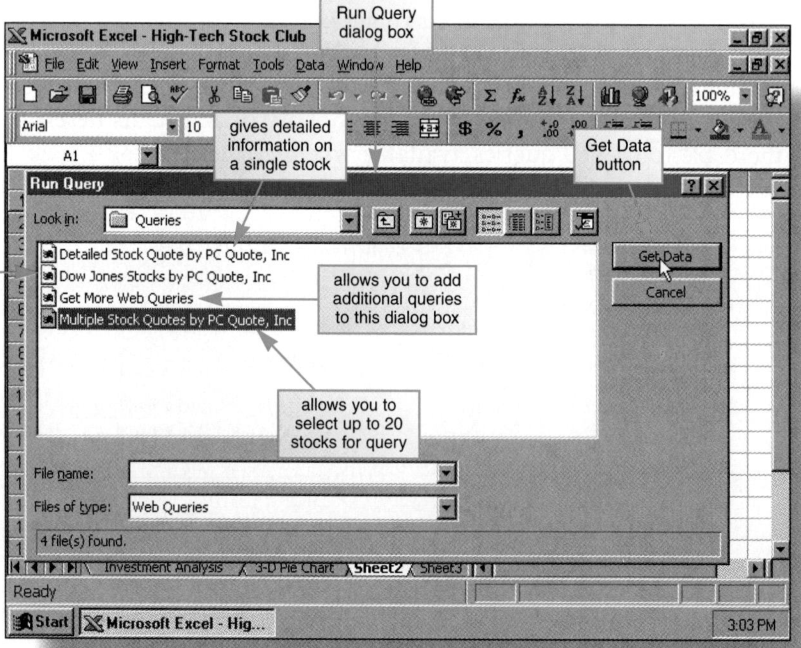

FIGURE 2-87

4 **Click the Get Data button. When the Returning External Data to Microsoft Excel dialog box displays, click the Existing worksheet option button, if necessary, to select it. Point to the OK button.**

*The **Returning External Data to Microsoft Excel dialog box** displays (Figure 2-88). The Existing worksheet option button is selected and the active cell A1 displays in the Existing worksheet box, meaning that the external data will be returned to a range starting with cell A1.*

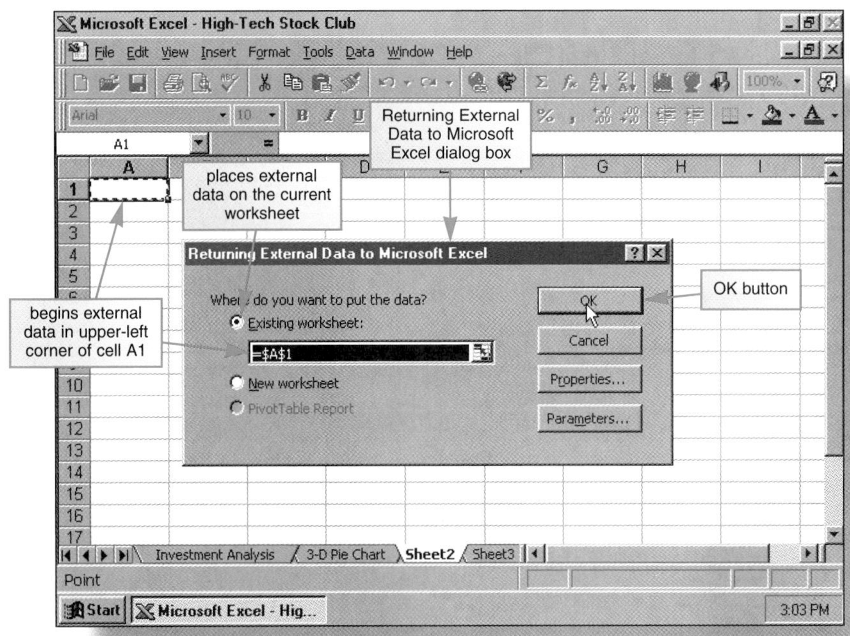

FIGURE 2-88

5 **Click the OK button. When the Enter Parameter Value dialog box displays, type the stock symbols** `cpq dell intc msft nscp` **in the box. Click the Use this value/reference for future refreshes check box to select it. Point to the OK button.**

*The **Enter Parameter Value dialog box** displays (Figure 2-89). You can enter up to 20 stock symbols separated by spaces.*

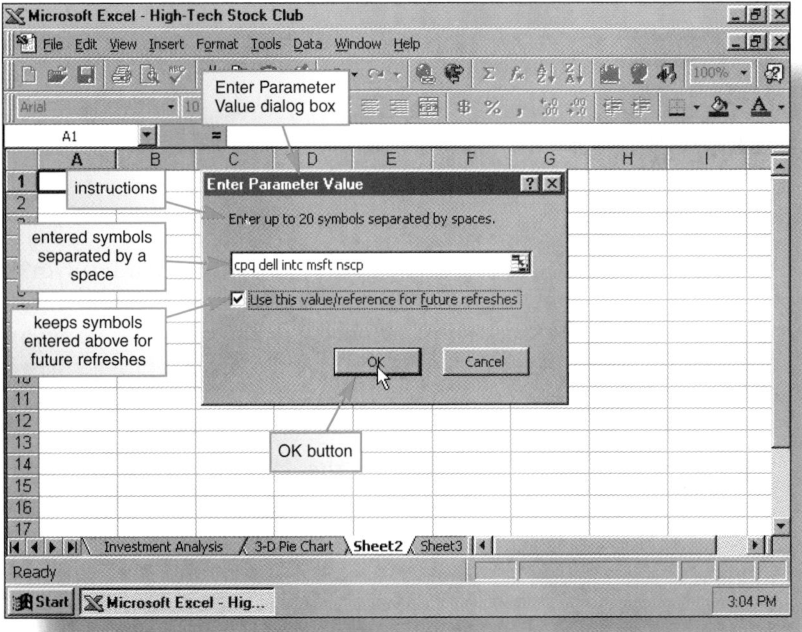

FIGURE 2-89

6 **Click the OK button. Double-click the Sheet2 tab and then type** `Web Query` **as the sheet name. Press the ENTER key.**

If you are using a modem, Excel will display a dialog box that connects you to the Internet via your provider. If you are directly connected to the Internet through a network, the dialog box does not display. Once your computer connects to the Internet, a message displays to inform you that Excel is getting external data. A small spinning globe displays on the status bar to indicate that the query is running. After a short period, Excel displays a new worksheet with the desired data (Figure 2-90).

FIGURE 2-90

Click the Save button on the Standard toolbar.

As shown in Figure 2-90, Excel displays the data returned from the Web query in an organized, formatted worksheet, which has a worksheet title, column titles, and a row of data for each stock symbol entered. Other than the first column, which contains the stock name and stock symbol, you have no control over the remaining columns of data returned. The latest price of each stock displays in column B.

Once the worksheet displays, you can refresh the data as often as you want. To refresh the data for all the stocks, click the **Refresh All button** on the **External Data toolbar** (Figure 2-91). Because the Use this value/reference for future refreshes check box was clicked (Figure 2-89 on the previous page), Excel will continue to use the same stock symbols each time it refreshes. You can change the symbols by clicking the **Query Parameters button** on the External Data toolbar. You also can refresh one stock at a time by clicking the cell with the company name and symbol in column A and then clicking the **Refresh Data button** on the External Data toolbar.

More *About* Refreshing Data

If you clicked the Use this value/reference for future refreshes check box (Figure 2-89) when you first created the Multiple Stock Quotes worksheet and you want to refresh with new stock symbols, click the Query Parameters button on the External Data toolbar and enter the new stock symbols. If the toolbar is hidden, right-click the worksheet and click Parameters.

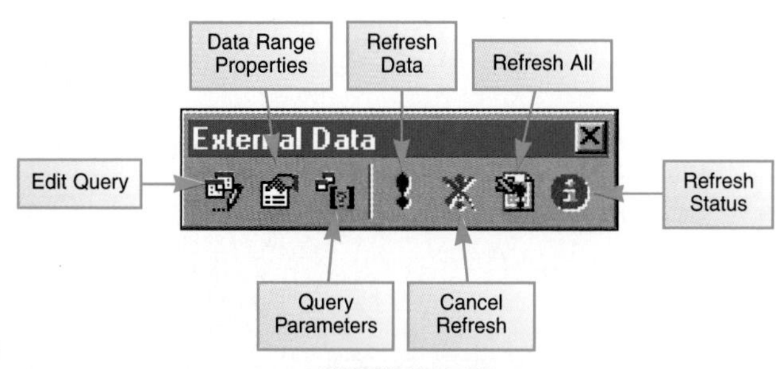

FIGURE 2-91

If the External Data toolbar does not display, right-click any toolbar and then click External Data. You also can invoke any Web query command by right-clicking the worksheet to display a shortcut menu.

The down arrows that display in the lower-right corner of the cells containing the column titles (row 4) are called **AutoFilter arrows**; they allow you to display only those stocks that meet the selected criteria. For example, if you click the AutoFilter arrow in cell A4 and then click INTEL CORP in the list box, Excel will hide all the stocks except for Intel.

This section gives you an idea of the potential of Web queries by having you use just one of Excel's many available Web queries. To reinforce the topics covered here, work through In the Lab 3 at the end of this project.

More *About* Web Queries

Most Excel specialists that do Web queries use the worksheet returned from the Web query as an engine that supplies data to another worksheet in the workbook. Through the use of 3-D cell references, you can create a worksheet similar to the High-Tech Stock Club, which feeds the Web query stock symbols and gets refreshed stock prices in return.

Quitting Excel

After completing the worksheet, 3-D Pie chart, and Web query, you can quit Excel by performing the following steps.

TO QUIT EXCEL

Step 1: Click the Investment Analysis tab.
Step 2: Click the Close button on the upper-right corner of the title bar.
Step 3: When the Microsoft Excel dialog box displays, click the Yes button.

Project Summary

The worksheet, 3-D Pie chart, and Web query (Figure 2-1 on page E 2.6) you created for Alex Hansen will serve his purpose well. The worksheet, which he plans to e-mail to the club members, contains valuable information in an easy to read format. The 3-D Pie chart dramatically shows the contribution of each stock to the current value of the club's portfolio. Finally, the Web query allows Alex to obtain the latest stock prices to keep the workbook as up-to-date as possible.

In creating the High-Tech Stock Club workbook, you learned how to enter formulas, calculate an average, find the highest and lowest numbers in a range, change fonts, draw borders, format numbers, and change column widths and row heights. You learned how to create a 3-D Pie chart on a separate chart sheet, format the pie chart, rename sheet tabs, preview a worksheet, print a workbook, print a section of a worksheet and display and print the formulas in the worksheet using the Fit to option. You also learned how to complete a Web query and generate a worksheet using external data obtained from the World Wide Web.

What You Should Know

Having completed this project, you now should be able to perform the following tasks:

- Apply a Currency Style Format and Comma Style Format Using the Formatting Toolbar *(E 2.30)*
- Apply a Currency Style with a Floating Dollar Sign Using the Format Cells Command *(E 2.32)*
- Apply a Percentage Format *(E 2.34)*
- Bold, Center, and Underline the Column Titles *(E 2.28)*
- Center Data in Cells *(E 2.29)*
- Change the Background and Font Colors and Apply an Outline Border *(E 2.26)*
- Change the Colors of the Pie Slices *(E 2.48)*
- Change the Font and Center the Worksheet Title *(E 2.23)*
- Change the Height of a Row by Dragging *(E 2.37)*
- Change the Print Scaling Option Back to 100% *(E 2.61)*
- Change the Width of a Column by Dragging *(E 2.35)*
- Check Spelling in the Worksheet *(E 2.39)*
- Copy a Range of Cells Across Columns to an Adjacent Range Using the Fill Handle *(E 2.20)*
- Copy Formulas Using the Fill Handle *(E 2.13)*
- Determine the Average of a Range of Numbers Using the Keyboard and Mouse *(E 2.15)*
- Determine the Highest Number in a Range of Numbers Using the Edit Formula Box and Function Box *(E 2.16)*
- Determine the Lowest Number in a Range of Numbers Using the Paste Function Button *(E 2.18)*
- Determine Totals Using the AutoSum Button *(E 2.14)*
- Display the Formulas in the Worksheet and Fit the Printout on One Page *(E 2.59)*
- Draw a 3-D Pie Chart *(E 2.42)*
- Enter a Formula Using the Keyboard *(E 2.9)*
- Enter a Percentage Formula *(E 2.21)*
- Enter Formulas Using Point Mode *(E 2.11)*
- Enter the Column Titles *(E 2.8)*
- Enter the Stock Data *(E 2.8)*
- Enter the Total Row Titles *(E 2.9)*
- Enter the Worksheet Title *(E 2.7)*
- Explode the 3-D Pie Chart *(E 2.49)*
- Format the Chart Title and Labels *(E 2.46)*
- Get External Data from a Web Source Using a Web Query *(E 2.62)*
- Preview Selected Sheets in a Workbook *(E 2.54)*
- Print a Section of the Worksheet *(E 2.58)*
- Print Selected Sheets in a Workbook *(E 2.56)*
- Quit Excel *(E 2.65)*
- Rename the Sheets and Rearrange the Order of the Sheets *(E 2.52)*
- Rotate and Tilt the 3-D Pie Chart *(E 2.50)*
- Start Excel *(E 2.7)*

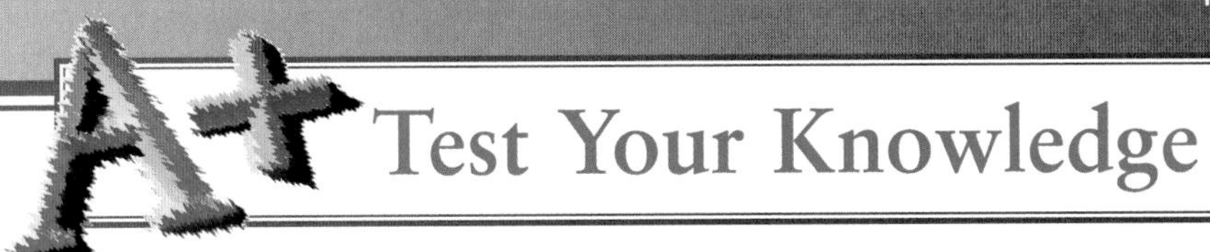

Test Your Knowledge

1 True/False

Instructions: Circle T if the statement is true or F if the statement is false.

T F 1. To assign a Currency style format with a floating dollar sign to the selected range, click the Currency Style button on the Formatting toolbar.

T F 2. The minimum row height is zero.

T F 3. If you enter the formula =10 * 3 into a cell, the number 30 displays in the cell.

T F 4. In the formula =4 * 6 – 8, the subtraction operation (–) is completed before the multiplication operation (*).

T F 5. The formulas =A4 * d3, =a4 * d3, and =A4*D3 result in the same value being assigned to the active cell.

T F 6. You can assign a function to a cell by typing it in the formula bar, clicking the Edit Formula box in the formula bar, and selecting a function from the Function box, or by clicking the Paste Function button on the Standard toolbar.

T F 7. If you use Point mode to enter a formula or select a range, you must press the ENTER key to complete the entry.

T F 8. If the function =MAX(A5:A8) assigns a value of 32 to cell H10, and cell H10 then is copied to cell I10, cell I10 may or may not equal 32.

T F 9. To run a Web query, click Consolidate on the Data menu.

T F 10. The Formula palette displays when you click the Edit Formula box in the formula bar.

2 Multiple Choice

Instructions: Circle the correct response.

1. If the following arithmetic operations all are found in a formula with no parentheses, which one is completed last?
   a. +
   b. *
   c. /
   d. ^
2. To alert Excel that you are entering a formula and not text, type a(n) __________ preceding the formula.
   a. ampersand (&)
   b. equal sign (=)
   c. number sign (#)
   d. asterisk (*)
3. When you copy a formula with relative cell references down a row, __________.
   a. the row references change in the formula
   b. the column references change in the formula
   c. no references are changed in the formula
   d. the cell reference of the formula remains the same

(continued)

Test Your Knowledge

Multiple Choice *(continued)*

4. The mouse pointer changes to a(n) __________ when you point to the boundary of a column heading or row heading.
   a. magnifying glass
   b. arrow
   c. cross hair
   d. plus sign with two arrowheads
5. The maximum height of a row is __________ points.
   a. 356
   b. 409
   c. 255
   d. 31
6. When Excel starts and a blank worksheet displays, the columns have a default width of __________ and the rows have a default height of __________.
   a. 8.43 characters, 12.75 points
   b. 12.75 characters, 8.43 points
   c. 9.43 characters, 15.00 points
   d. 15.00 characters, 9.43 points
7. When Excel automatically sets the width of a column based on the widest entry in the column, it is called __________.
   a. custom fit
   b. choice fit
   c. best fit
   d. close fit
8. The __________ version of the worksheet displays the results of the formulas entered into its cells.
   a. formulas
   b. displayed
   c. formatted
   d. values
9. A sheet tab name can be up to __________ characters in length.
   a. 31
   b. 255
   c. 12
   d. 48
10. To change the elevation of a selected pie chart, click __________ on the Chart menu.
    a. Format Data Series
    b. 3-D View
    c. Format 3-D Pie Group
    d. Chart Type

3 Entering Formulas

Instructions: Using the values in the worksheet in Figure 2-92, write the formula that accomplishes the task for each of the following items and then compute the value assigned to the specified cell.

Microsoft Excel - Book1

	A	B	C	D	E
1					
2					
3	Base	12	0	9	1
4	Height	1	6	1	15
5	Length	3	10	7	8
6	Width	5	2	13	11
7	Volume	4	21	6	2

FIGURE 2-92

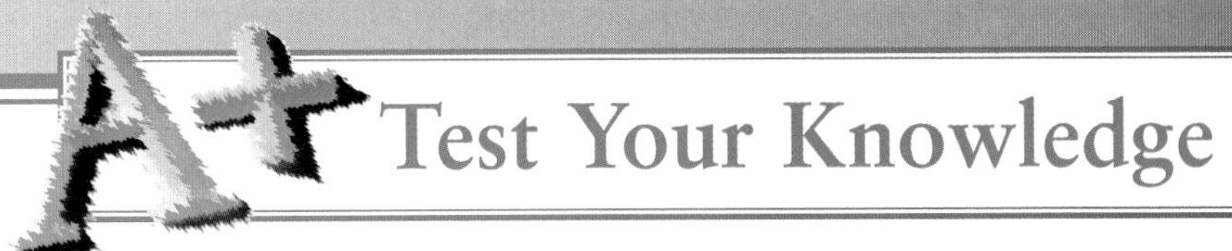

1. Use the natural language method of entering a formula as described on page E 2.12 to assign cell B8 the product of cells B3, B4, and B5.
   Formula: ____________________ Result: ____________________
2. Assign cell C8 the result of adding cells C3 and C5 and then dividing the sum by cell C6.
   Formula: ____________________ Result: ____________________
3. Assign cell C9 the sum of the range D3:E4 minus the value in cell E6.
   Formula: ____________________ Result: ____________________
4. Assign cell E8 three times the product of cells E6 and cell E7.
   Formula: ____________________ Result: ____________________
5. Assign cell F3 the sum of the range of cells B3:E3 minus the product of cells B6 and B7.
   Formula: ____________________ Result: ____________________
6. Assign cell B9 the result of cell B7 minus cell D4 raised to cell B5.
   Formula: ____________________ Result: ____________________
7. Assign cell E9 the expression (A ^ 3 - 4 * B * C) / (2 * B) where the value of A is in cell D7, the value of B is in cell D6, and the value of C is in cell D3. Show the result to four decimal places.
   Formula: ____________________ Result: ____________________

4 Understanding Formulas

Instructions: Figure 2-93 displays the formulas version of a worksheet. In the spaces provided, indicate the numeric value assigned to the cells if the numbers display instead of the formulas.

1. D1 ____________________
2. D2 ____________________
3. D3 ____________________
4. A4 ____________________
5. B4 ____________________
6. C4 ____________________

Microsoft Excel - Book1

	A	B	C	D
1	12	5	9	=C1+A1*B1
2	2	3	4	=(A3-A1)^A2
3	32	15	11	=A1+C1*A2/B2-B3
4	=C2	=SUM(B1:B3)	=(10+B3)*50%	

FIGURE 2-93

Use Help

1 Reviewing Project Activities

Instructions: Perform the following tasks using a computer.

1. Start Excel. Click Contents and Index on the Help menu. Click the Contents tab. Double-click the Creating Formulas and Auditing Workbooks book.
2. Double-click the Entering Formulas book. One at a time, double-click each of the ten links in the Entering Formulas book. Read and print the information for each link. To print the information, click the Print Topic command on the shortcut menu. To return to the previous dialog box, click the Help Topics button. Hand in the printouts to your instructor.
3. Repeat Step 2 for the Using Functions book. Print six of the thirteen links.
4. If the Help Topics: Microsoft Excel dialog box is not on the screen, click Contents and Index on the Help menu. Click the Find tab. Type `row height` in the top text box labeled 1. Double-click Change row height in the lower list box labeled 3. Read and print the information. Click the Close button to close the Microsoft Excel Help window. Hand in the printout to your instructor.
5. Click the Office Assistant button on the Standard toolbar. Type `how do i format numbers` in the Office Assistant balloon. Click the Search button. Click the button labeled Number formatting. One at a time, click the three links. Print the information for each link by using the Print Topic command on the shortcut menu. Hand in the printouts to your instructor.

2 Expanding on the Basics

Instructions: Use Excel online Help and the Office Assistant to better understand the topics listed below. Begin numbers 1 and 2 by clicking Contents and Index on the Help menu. If you are unable to print the Help information, then answer the questions on your own paper.

1. Click the Contents tab. Double-click the book titled, Using Microsoft Excel with the Internet, Your Intranet, or a Local Web. Double-click the book titled, Working with Files on the Web. Double-click the link titled, Get data from a Web source. Read the information and then click the button in step 4 for more information. Print the linked topic, click the Back button, and then print the topic, Get data from a Web source. Click the Close button. Hand in the printouts to your instructor.
2. Click the Find tab and then type `web` in the text box labeled 1. In the lower list box labeled 3, scroll down and double-click the topic, What's new with Microsoft Excel on the Web? Read and print the information. Hand in the printout to your instructor.
3. Use the Office Assistant to answer the question, How do I use Web queries? Click the button labeled, About creating a PivotTable from an external data source. Read and print the information and then click the Help Topics button. Click the Index tab and then type `web` in the text box labeled 1. Double-click queries in the list box labeled 2 and then double-click the topic, Create a Web query, in the Topics Found dialog box. Read the information and then print it. Hand in the printouts to your instructor.

Apply Your Knowledge

1 Changing the Appearance of a Pie Chart

Instructions: Start Excel. Open the workbook Featherbed Factory Cost Analysis from the Excel folder on the Data Disk that accompanies this book. Perform the following tasks to change the appearance of the 3-D Pie chart that accompanies the worksheet to make it look like Figure 2-94.

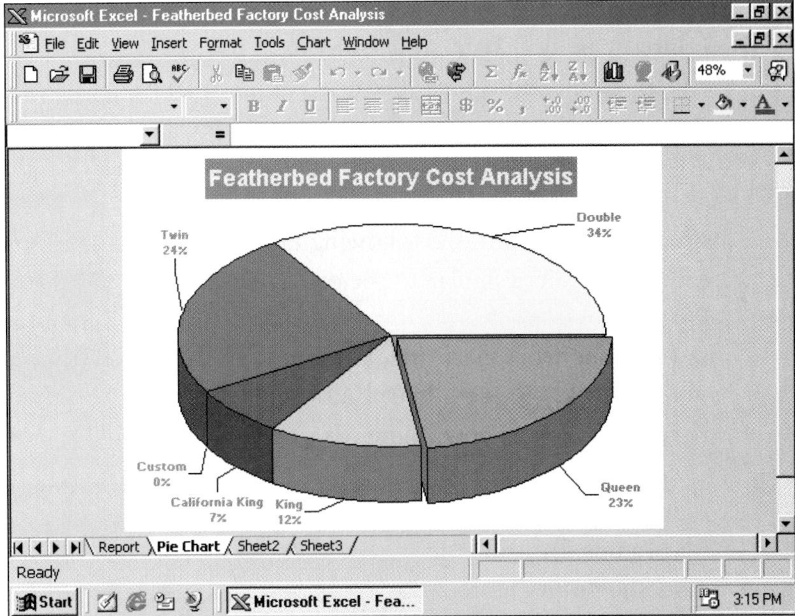

FIGURE 2-94

1. Double-click the Chart1 tab in the lower-left corner of the window. Change the sheet name to Pie Chart. Drag the sheet named Report to the left of the sheet named Pie Chart. Click the Pie Chart tab to display the 3-D Pie chart.
2. Click the 3-D Pie chart title and then change the font to 28 point, silver (column 2, row 5 on the Font Color palette). Change the chart title background to blue-gray (column 7, row 2 on the Fill Color palette).
3. Click one of the data labels that identify the slices. Change the font to 14 point, blue-gray, bold.
4. With the Queen slice selected, click 3-D View on the Chart menu. Change the elevation to 30° and the rotation to 240°.
5. Click the Queen slice twice. (Do not double-click.) Drag it away from the other slices. One at a time, drag the data labels away from their slices so the 3-D Pie chart displays as shown in Figure 2-94. See Step 3 on page E 2.47 if the leader lines do not show.
6. If the Queen slice is not selected, click it twice. (Do not double-click.) Change the color of the slice to coral (column 6, row 6 on the Fill Color palette). Change the colors of the Double and Twin slices as shown in Figure 2-94.
7. Print the 3-D Pie chart. Save the workbook using the file name Featherbed Factory Cost Analysis 2.
8. Click the Report tab. Change the Quantity On Hand (column F) for Twin to 19, Double to 27, and Queen to 26. After the changes, the total cost in cell G9 should be $9,734.81. Click the Pie Chart tab. Notice how the size of the slices changed to reflect the new entries. While holding down the CTRL key, click the Report tab. Preview and print the selected sheets. Close the workbook without saving the changes.

In the Lab

1 Security Lock & Key Weekly Payroll Worksheet

Problem: The Security Lock & Key Company has hired you as a work-study student in its software applications area. Because you took an Excel course in college, the Assistant Manager has asked you to prepare a weekly payroll report for the six employees listed in Table 2-5.

Table 2-5

EMPLOYEE	*RATE*	*HOURS*	*DEPENDENTS*
Scotch, Ben	25.00	40.25	3
Collings, Demi	17.50	53	2
Locken, Viola	27.75	36	4
Carr, Wessley	19.50	43.5	1
Bolte, Ernst	21.50	15	3
Christy, Rupert	15.65	25	4

Instructions: Perform the following tasks to create a worksheet similar to the one in Figure 2-95.

1. Enter the worksheet title, Security Lock & Key Weekly Payroll, in cell A1. Enter the column titles in row 2, the row titles in column A, and the data from Table 2-5 in columns B through D as shown in Figure 2-95.
2. Use the following formulas to determine the gross pay, federal tax, state tax, and net pay:
   a. Gross Pay = Rate*Hours (*Hint*: Assign cell E3 the formula =B3*C3 for the first employee and then copy the formula in cell E3 to the range E4:E8 for the remaining employees.)
   b. Federal Tax = 20% * (Gross Pay – Dependents * 38.46)
   c. State Tax = 3.2% * Gross Pay
   d. Net Pay = Gross Pay – (Federal Tax + State Tax)
3. Calculate totals for hours, gross pay, federal tax, state tax, and net pay in row 9.
4. Use the appropriate functions to determine the average, highest, and lowest values of each column in rows 10 through 12.
5. Bold the worksheet title.
6. Use buttons on the Formatting toolbar to assign the Comma style with two decimal places to the range B3:H12.

	A	B	C	D	E	F	G	H
1	**Security Lock & Key Weekly Payroll**							
2	*Employee*	*Rate*	*Hours*	*Dep.*	*Gross Pay*	*Fed. Tax*	*State Tax*	*Net Pay*
3	Scotch, Ben	25.00	40.25	3.00	1,006.25	178.17	32.20	795.88
4	Collings, Demi	17.50	53.00	2.00	927.50	170.12	29.68	727.70
5	Locken, Viola	27.75	36.00	4.00	999.00	169.03	31.97	798.00
6	Carr, Wessley	19.50	43.50	1.00	848.25	161.96	27.14	659.15
7	Bolte, Ernst	21.50	15.00	3.00	322.50	41.42	10.32	270.76
8	Christy, Rupert	15.65	25.00	4.00	391.25	47.48	12.52	331.25
9	*Totals*		212.75		4,494.75	768.19	143.83	3,582.73
10	*Average*	21.15	35.46	2.83	749.13	128.03	23.97	597.12
11	*Highest*	27.75	53.00	4.00	1,006.25	178.17	32.20	798.00
12	*Lowest*	15.65	15.00	1.00	322.50	41.42	10.32	270.76
13								
14								

FIGURE 2-95

7. Bold, italicize, and assign a heavy bottom border to the range A2:H2. Right-align the column titles in the range B2:H2.
8. Italicize the range A9:A12. Assign a top border and double line bottom border to the range A9:H9.
9. Change the width of column A to 15.00 characters. If necessary, change the widths of columns B through H to best fit. Change the height of rows 2 and 10 to 24.00 points.
10. Enter your name, course, laboratory assignment number (Lab 2-1), date, and instructor name in the range A14:A18.
11. Save the workbook using the file name Security Lock & Key.
12. Preview and then print the worksheet.
13. Press CTRL+` to change the display from the values version to the formulas version. Print the formulas version of the worksheet using the Fit to option on the Page tab in the Page Setup dialog box. After the printer is finished, press CTRL+` to reset the worksheet to display the values version. Reset the Scaling option to 100% by clicking Adjust to option button on the Page tab in the Page Setup dialog box and then setting the percent value to 100%.
14. Increase the number of hours worked for each employee by 10.25 hours. The total net pay in cell H9 should equal $4,581.69. If necessary, increase the width of column F to best fit to view the new federal tax total. Preview and print the worksheet with the new values. Close the workbook without saving the changes.

2 Esther's Music Emporium Monthly Accounts Receivable Balance Sheet

Problem: You were recently hired as a part-time assistant in the Accounting department of Esther's Music Emporium, a popular music store that sells new and used compact discs. You have been asked to use Excel to generate a report that summarizes the monthly accounts receivable balance. A graphic breakdown of the data also is desired. The customer accounts receivable data in Table 2-6 is available for test purposes.

Table 2-6

CUSTOMER NUMBER	NAME	BEGINNING BALANCE	PURCHASES	PAYMENTS	CREDITS
2325	Jordan, Van	325.51	83.50	250.00	0.00
5521	Crite, Deyna	56.02	122.85	10.00	25.75
1011	Simp, Bart	225.32	27.15	15.00	12.63
6528	Rose, Mel	455.25	210.66	100.00	175.22
3496	Benz, Bill	62.50	45.31	00.00	33.74

Instructions Part 1: Create a worksheet similar to the one shown in Figure 2-96 on the next page. Include all six items in Table 2-6 in the report, plus a service charge and a new balance for each customer. (Assume no negative unpaid monthly balances.)

(continued)

Esther's Music Emporium Monthly Accounts Receivable Balance Sheet *(continued)*

Perform the following tasks.

1. Click the Select All button (to the left of column heading A) and then click the Bold button to bold the entire worksheet.
2. Assign the worksheet title, Esther's Music Emporium, to cell A1. Assign the worksheet subtitle, Monthly Accounts Receivable, to cell A2.
3. Enter the column titles in the range A3:H3 as shown in Figure 2-96. Change the width of column A to 9.57. Change the widths of columns B through H to best fit.

Microsoft Excel - Esther's Music

	A	B	C	D	E	F	G	H
1	Esther's Music Emporium							
2	Monthly Accounts Receivable							
3	*Customer Number*	*Customer Name*	*Beginning Balance*	*Purchases*	*Payments*	*Credits*	*Service Charge*	*New Balance*
4	2325	Jordan, Van	$325.51	$83.50	$250.00	$0.00	$1.70	$160.71
5	5521	Crite, Deyna	56.02	122.85	10.00	25.75	0.46	143.58
6	1011	Simp, Bart	225.32	27.15	15.00	12.63	4.45	229.29
7	6528	Rose, Mel	455.25	210.66	100.00	175.22	4.05	394.74
8	3496	Benz, Bill	62.50	45.31	0.00	33.74	0.65	74.72
9	*Totals*		$1,124.60	$489.47	$375.00	$247.34	$11.30	$1,003.03
10	*Highest*		$455.25	$210.66	$250.00	$175.22	$4.45	$394.74
11	*Lowest*		$56.02	$27.15	$0.00	$0.00	$0.46	$74.72
12								

Accounts Receivable / 3-D Pie Chart / Sheet2 / Sheet3

FIGURE 2-96

4. Enter the customer numbers and row titles in column A. Enter the customer numbers as text, rather than numbers. To enter the customer numbers as text, begin each entry with an apostrophe ('). Enter the remaining data in Table 2-6.
5. Use the following formulas to determine the monthly service charge in column G and the new balance in column H for each account:
   a. Service Charge = 2.25% * (Beginning Balance – Payments – Credits)
   b. New Balance = Beginning Balance + Purchases – Payments – Credits + Service Charge
6. Calculate totals for beginning balance, purchases, payments, credits, service charge, and new balance in row 9.
7. Assign cell C10 the appropriate function to calculate the maximum value in the range C4:C8. Copy cell C10 to the range D10:H10.
8. Assign cell C11 the appropriate function to calculate the minimum value in the range C4:C8. Copy cell C11 to the range D11:H11.
9. Change the worksheet title in cell A1 to 28-point CG Times font. Format the worksheet subtitle in cell A2 to 16-point CG Times font. Change the first letter of each word in the subtitle to 24-point font. Center the worksheet titles in cells A1 and A2 across the range A1:H2. Change the heights of rows 1 through 3 and row 10 to 27.75. Add a heavy outline to the range A1:H2 using the Borders button on the Formatting toolbar.

10. Select the range A1:H2 and then change the background color to violet (column 7, row 3 of the Fill Color palette). Change the font color in the range A1:H2 to light yellow (column 3, row 5 of the Font Color palette).
11. Italicize the column titles in row 3. Use the Borders button to add a heavy bottom border to the column titles in row 3. Center the column titles in row 3. Italicize the titles in rows 9, 10, and 11. Use the Borders button to add a single top border and double line bottom border to the range A9:H9 (column 4, row 2 on the Borders palette).
12. Use the Format Cells command on the shortcut menu to assign the Currency style with a floating dollar sign to row 4 and rows 9 through 11. Use the same command to assign the Comma style (currency with no dollar sign) to the range C5:H8. The Format Cells command is preferred over the Comma Style button because the worksheet specifications call for displaying zero as 0.00 rather than as a dash (-), as shown in Figure 2-96.
13. Change the widths of columns B through H again to best fit, if necessary.
14. Rename the sheet Accounts Receivable.
15. Enter your name, course, laboratory assignment number (LAB2-2), date, and instructor name in the range A13:A17.
16. Save the workbook using the file name Esther's Music.
17. Preview and then print the worksheet. Print the range A3:C9.
18. Press CTRL+` to change the display from the values version to the formulas version and then print the worksheet to fit on one page in landscape orientation. After the printer is finished, press CTRL+` to reset the worksheet to display the values version. Reset the Scaling option to 100% by clicking the Adjust to option button on the Page tab in the Page Setup dialog box and then setting the percent value to 100%.

Instructions Part 2: Draw the 3-D Pie chart showing the contribution of each customer to the total new balance as shown in Figure 2-97. Select the nonadjacent chart ranges B4:B8 and H4:H8. The category names in the range B4:B8 will identify the slices, while the data series in the range H4:H8 will determine the size of the slices. Click the Chart Wizard button on the Standard toolbar. Draw the 3-D Pie chart on a new chart sheet. Use the 3-D Pie chart sub-type (column 2, row 1). Add the chart title Contributions to Accounts Receivable. Remove the legend. Add data labels with percents to represent the slices.

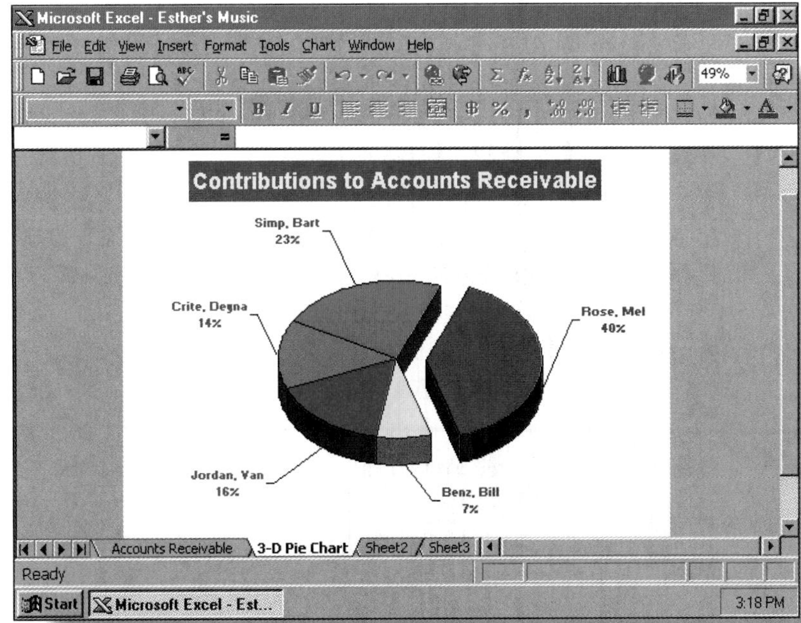

FIGURE 2-97

(continued)

Esther's Music Emporium Monthly Accounts Receivable Balance Sheet *(continued)*

Once the 3-D Pie chart displays, format the chart title to have a violet background and 28-point Arial, light yellow, bold font. Change the font of the data labels to 16-point Arial, violet, bold font. Drag the data labels away from the slices they represent. Change the colors of the slices to those shown in Figure 2-97. Explode the slice representing the greatest contribution. Select a slice and then use the 3-D View command on the Chart menu to change the chart rotation to 190° and elevation to 40°. Rename the Chart1 sheet 3-D Pie Chart. Rearrange the order of the sheets so the worksheet appears before the chart. Save the workbook using the same file name as in Part 1. Preview and print the chart.

Instructions Part 3: Change the following purchases: account number 2325 to $735.21; account number 6528 to $25.00. The total new balance in cell H9 should equal $1,469.08. Select both sheets. Preview and print the selected sheets. Close the workbook without saving the changes.

3 Online Web Queries

Problem: Nora Dame, president of Quasimodo, Inc., recently attended a Microsoft seminar and learned that Microsoft Excel can connect to the World Wide Web, download real-time stock data into a worksheet, and then refresh the data as often as needed. Because you have had courses in Excel and the Internet, she has hired you as a consultant to develop a stock analysis workbook. Her portfolio is listed in Table 2-7.

Table 2-7

COMPANY	STOCK SYMBOL
Corel Corp.	COSFF
Microsoft Corp.	MSFT
Netscape Corp.	NSCP
Yahoo Inc.	YHOO

Instructions Part 1: Open a new Excel workbook and then select cell A1. Perform the following steps to run a Web query to obtain multiple stock quotes, using the stock symbols in Table 2-7.

1. Point to Get External Data on the Data menu and then click Run Web Query.
2. Double-click Multiple Stock Quotes by PC Quote, Inc in the Run Query dialog box. If the Queries folder does not display, see your instructor for its location.
3. Click the OK button in the Returning External Data to Microsoft Excel dialog box.
4. When the Enter Parameter Value dialog box displays, enter the stock symbols in Table 2-7 into the text box, being sure to separate them by a space. Click the Use this value/reference for future refreshes check box and then click the OK button. The stock data returned by the Web query displays in a worksheet as shown in Figure 2-98. Because the stock data returned is real-time, the numbers on your worksheet may be different.
5. Enter your name, course, laboratory assignment number (Lab 2-3a), date, and instructor name in the range A15:A19.
6. Rename the sheet Multiple Stocks. Save the workbook using the file name Stocks Online. Preview and then print the worksheet in landscape orientation.

Instructions Part 2: Create a detailed stock quote for AT&T as shown in Figure 2-99.

1. With the workbook created in Part 1 open, click the Sheet2 tab. Point to Get External Data on the Data menu and then click Run Web Query.

Multiple Stock Quotes

Company Name & Symbol	Last Price	Net Change	Open	High	Low	Volume	Time	# of Outstanding Shares (m	Market Cap.
COREL CORPORATION (COSFF)	7 3/8	0	7 3/8	7 3/8	7 3/16	53,300	15:53		$
MICROSOFT CORP (MSFT)	81 5/8	-1	83 1/8	83 1/8	80 3/4	6,802,400	16:01	1,195,188	$97,557,221
NETSCAPE COMMUNICATIONS CORP (NSCP)	55 1/2	-1 3/8	56 3/4	57 1/2	54 3/4	1,197,800	16:00	87,883	$4,877,507
YAHOO INC (YHOO)	17 1/2	1/2	17	17 1/2	16 3/4	107,500	16:00	26,504	$463,820

All non-subscription data is delayed 20 minutes unless noted, and is believed accurate but is not warranted or guaranteed by PC Quote,Inc. All times are Eastern U.S.

Data Provided by PC Quote, Inc. | Go to the PC Quote/Microsoft Excel Developer's Corner

FIGURE 2-98

2. Double-click Detailed Stock Quote by PC Quote, Inc in the Run Query dialog box.
3. Click the OK button in the Returning External Data to Microsoft Excel dialog box, starting the data in cell A1 of the existing worksheet.
4. When the Enter Parameter Value dialog box displays, enter the symbol T (for the company AT&T) in the list box. Do not click the Use this value/reference for future refreshes check box. Click the OK button.
5. The Web query returns the worksheet shown in Figure 2-99. The worksheet contains data that stock experts use to determine if they should buy or sell this company's stock.

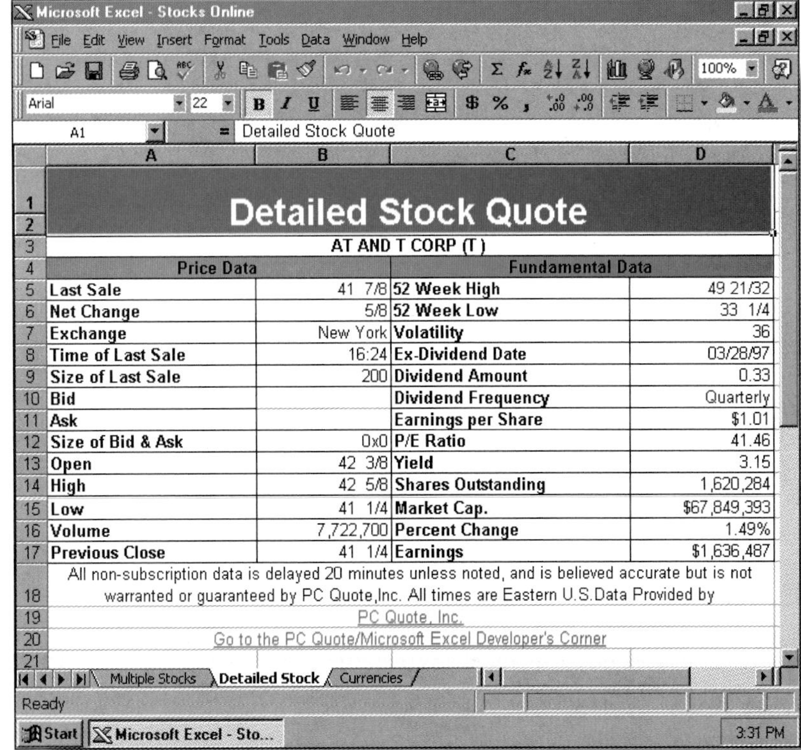

Detailed Stock Quote

AT AND T CORP (T)

Price Data		Fundamental Data	
Last Sale	41 7/8	52 Week High	49 21/32
Net Change	5/8	52 Week Low	33 1/4
Exchange	New York	Volatility	36
Time of Last Sale	16:24	Ex-Dividend Date	03/28/97
Size of Last Sale	200	Dividend Amount	0.33
Bid		Dividend Frequency	Quarterly
Ask		Earnings per Share	$1.01
Size of Bid & Ask	0x0	P/E Ratio	41.46
Open	42 3/8	Yield	3.15
High	42 5/8	Shares Outstanding	1,620,284
Low	41 1/4	Market Cap.	$67,849,393
Volume	7,722,700	Percent Change	1.49%
Previous Close	41 1/4	Earnings	$1,636,487

All non-subscription data is delayed 20 minutes unless noted, and is believed accurate but is not warranted or guaranteed by PC Quote,Inc. All times are Eastern U.S.Data Provided by PC Quote, Inc.

Go to the PC Quote/Microsoft Excel Developer's Corner

FIGURE 2-99

(continued)

Online Web Queries *(continued)*

6. Enter your name, course, laboratory assignment number (Lab 2-3b), date, and instructor name in the range A24:A28.
7. Rename the sheet Detailed Stock. Save the workbook. Preview and then print the worksheet.

Instructions Part 3: Create a worksheet showing the latest currency exchange rates. The Web query for exchange rates is not one of the four queries available in the Queries folder by default. Thus, you must download it from the World Wide Web to your computer system before you can use it. Because the downloading process creates a table of Web queries on the active worksheet, a new workbook will be opened to accept the table. Once you select a Web query from the table and save it to disk, you can delete the workbook with the table and return to the Stocks Online workbook to complete the query. You will need a floppy disk for this exercise.

Perform the following.

1. With the workbook created in Parts 1 and 2 open, open a new workbook using the New command on the File menu.
2. Point to Get External Data on the Data menu, and then click Run Web Query. Double-click Get More Web Queries in the Run Query dialog box.
3. Click the OK button in the Returning External Data to Microsoft Excel dialog box, starting the data in cell A1 of the existing worksheet.
4. When the Get More Web Queries worksheet appears, scroll down and click the link CNN Currencies under Currencies and Exchange Rates. Your Web browser displays. When prompted, select the Save it to disk option. When the Save As dialog box displays, save the Web query, CNNfn_Currencies, to your floppy disk.
5. Close your Web browser. Use the Exit command on the File menu to close the new workbook without saving.
6. With the Stocks Online workbook active, click the Sheet3 tab. Click cell A1. Point to Get External Data on the Data menu and then click Run Web Query.
7. When the Run Web Query dialog box displays, click the Look in box arrow and then click 3½ Floppy (A:). Double-click CNNfn_Currencies.
8. Click the OK button in the Returning External Data to Microsoft Excel dialog box, starting the data in cell A1 of the existing worksheet. The Web query returns the worksheet shown in Figure 2-100 (scroll down so row 13 is at the top of your screen). The data may be different on your worksheet.
9. Double-click the Sheet3 tab in the Stocks Online workbook and then rename the sheet Currencies.
10 Enter your name, course, laboratory assignment number (Lab 2-3c), date, and instructor name below the entries in column A, in separate but adjacent cells.
11. After viewing the Currencies worksheet, preview and print it. Click the Multiple Stocks tab and then save the workbook.

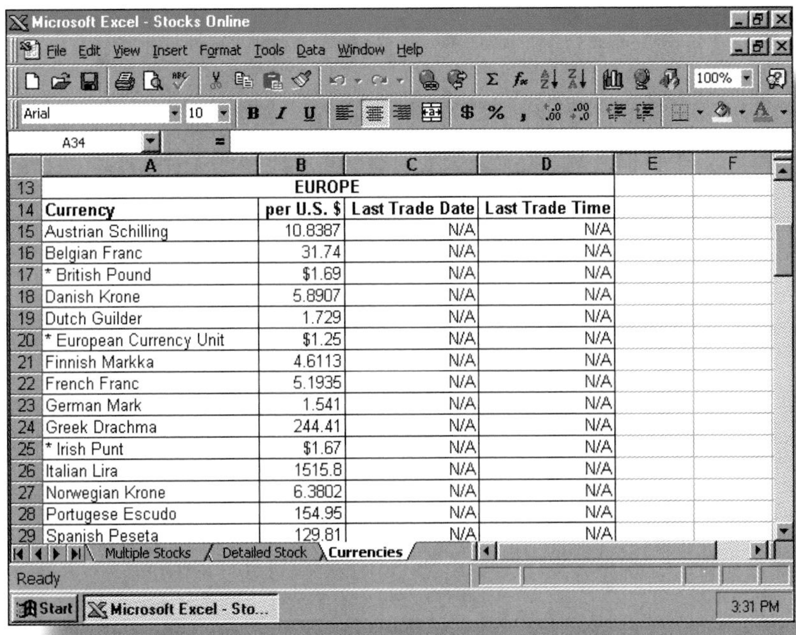

Currency	EUROPE per U.S. $	Last Trade Date	Last Trade Time
Austrian Schilling	10.8387	N/A	N/A
Belgian Franc	31.74	N/A	N/A
* British Pound	$1.69	N/A	N/A
Danish Krone	5.8907	N/A	N/A
Dutch Guilder	1.729	N/A	N/A
* European Currency Unit	$1.25	N/A	N/A
Finnish Markka	4.6113	N/A	N/A
French Franc	5.1935	N/A	N/A
German Mark	1.541	N/A	N/A
Greek Drachma	244.41	N/A	N/A
* Irish Punt	$1.67	N/A	N/A
Italian Lira	1515.8	N/A	N/A
Norwegian Krone	6.3802	N/A	N/A
Portugese Escudo	154.95	N/A	N/A
Spanish Peseta	129.81	N/A	N/A

FIGURE 2-100

Instructions Part 4: Refresh the data. To update the sheets, make sure the Stocks Online workbook is open and then do the following.

1. If the External Data toolbar is not showing, right-click any toolbar and then click External Data. Click the Refresh All button on the External Data toolbar. When the Enter Parameter Value dialog box displays, type `T` for AT&T and then click the OK button. Select all three sheets. Preview and print the updated selected worksheets.
2. Click the Detailed Stock sheet and then click the Refresh Data button. When the Enter Parameter Value dialog box displays, type `HDI` (for the company Harley Davidson Inc.) in the text box and then click the OK button. Print the Detailed Stock sheet with the new values. Save the workbook and then quit Excel.

Cases and Places

200 MHz

The difficulty of these case studies varies: ◗ are the least difficult; ◗◗ are more difficult; and ◗◗◗ are the most difficult.

1 ◗ Homes4U Realty has hired you to work with their prospective clients. Your job is to help prequalify the clients and determine a proposed monthly mortgage payment. Homes4U has a standard questionnaire clients fill out, but you discovered a mortgage calculator query that looks much more professional and requires less time.

Start Excel and open a new workbook. Type `Prequalifying Worksheet` in cell A1 and type `for Mr. & Mrs. Aarvis Bendix` in cell A2. Open a new workbook and then run a Web query to return the Get More Web Queries worksheet. Retrieve and save the CNNfn_Mortgage_Calculator Web query to floppy disk. Close the workbook without saving your changes. Click cell A4 and then run the CNNfn_Mortgage_Calculator Web query. Use the information in Table 2-8 to fill in the value boxes, clicking the Use this value/reference for future refreshes check box where indicated. Mr. and Mrs. Bendix want their After-tax PITI (Payment, Interest, Taxes, Insurance) payment to be around $750.00. Use the Refresh Data button to input the following data: Price – $110,000; Percent to Borrow – 60%; Interest Rate – 10%. Use the concepts and techniques presented in this project to create and format the worksheet titles and borders in rows 1 and 2.

Table 2-8

ITEM	*USE FOR FUTURE VALUE*	*REFRESHES*
Price	**$120,000**	**no**
Closing Costs	**3%**	**yes**
Percent to Borrow	**75%**	**no**
Days to End of Month	**0**	**yes**
Interest Rate	**10.75%**	**no**
Real Estate Tax Rate	**1.5%**	**yes**
Discount Points	**1%**	**yes**
Homeowner's Dues	**0**	**yes**
Amortization	**30 yrs.**	**yes**
Months to Escrow	**6**	**yes**
Seller's Contribution	**0**	**yes**
Federal Tax Bracket	**28%**	**yes**
Monthly Income	**$3500**	**yes**
Monthly Debt	**$1100**	**yes**
Earnest Money Deposit	**$500**	**yes**
Prepaid Closing Costs	**$250**	**yes**

Cases and Places

2 ◗ In order to determine the effectiveness of their endangered species recovery plan, the Fish and Wildlife Department traps and releases red wolves in selected areas and records how many are pregnant. To obtain a representative sample, the department tries to trap approximately 20% of the population. Use the following formula to determine the total red wolf population if the state is divided into 1,000 sections. The following data was collected from five sections:

Section 1: 35 wolves caught, 15 pregnant, one out of every six dies annually (17%);
Section 2: 22 wolves caught, 5 pregnant, one out of every five dies annually (20%);
Section 3: 45 wolves caught, 12 pregnant, one out of every four dies annually (25%);
Section 4: 28 wolves caught, 16 pregnant, one out of every ten dies annually (10%);
Section 5: 59 wolves caught, 22 pregnant, one out of every three dies annually (33%).

Use the following formula to determine the number of red wolves in a section:

Wolves in a Section = 5 * (Total Catch + Pregnant Wolves) – 5 * Annual Deaths * (Total Catch + Pregnant Wolves)

You have been asked to create a worksheet and pie chart using the data provided to determine an estimated red wolf population for the state. Use the concepts and techniques presented in this project to create and format the worksheet and chart.

3 ◗ You are shopping for a vehicle to get you to and from school. After a long search, you finally have it narrowed down to two vehicles. One is a $4,000 truck, the other is a $3,700 two-door coupe. The trade-in value of your car is $850.00. The car dealership is offering a three-year payment plan at 11% interest on the balance. You want to know the total amount you will owe for each vehicle, which can be determined with the following formula:

Amount = (Cost of Vehicle – Trade-in) x (1 + Interest Rate / 12) ^ (Years x 12)

Create a worksheet with the information about each vehicle and then use the formula to calculate the total amount of each. Use the concepts and techniques used in this project to format the worksheet.

4 ◗◗ Frugal Fleet Rental is a company that rents prop planes and Lear jets for commercial use. The rental charge is based on the formula f = 1000d + 8.5m, where f is the rental fee, d is the number of days the airplane is rented, and m is the flight miles. Over the last two weeks three prop planes and one Lear jet were rented. The prop planes rented were as follows: Lazy Sue, rented for three days with a total of 648 flight miles; Top Hat, rented one day with a total of 1280 flight miles; and Hawkeye, rented for four days with a total of 3267 flight miles. The Lear jet, named Fast One, was rented for two days with a total of 900 flight miles. Use the formula and these figures to develop a worksheet showing the number of days each airplane was rented, the flight miles for each airplane, the revenue generated by each airplane, and the percentage of the company's total revenue for these three rentals. Include totals, averages, maximum, and minimum where appropriate. Create a suitable chart on a different sheet to compare the income from each plane.

Cases and Places

5 ▶▶▶ Mortgage companies often use a formula to determine the highest selling price prospective customers can afford when purchasing a house. Visit a local mortgage company to discover how it analyzes the financial status of its clients. Use the company's formulas to create a worksheet based on estimates of your future income to determine the most expensive house you could afford now, and in five, ten, fifteen, twenty, and twenty-five years. Assuming you can make a 10% down payment, calculate the amount of money you would have to put down on each house and the amount you would need to borrow. Use the Run Web Query command and compare the figures obtained by the mortgage company's formula with the query results.

6 ▶▶▶ Pharmacists sometimes use a formula when mixing a prescription for a customer. Visit a local pharmacy and obtain the formulas for two different preparations. Use the formulas to create a worksheet showing the medication quantities for a child who is around 40 pounds, a child who is around 70 pounds, and an adult. Include a chart illustrating how the amount of medication varies based on weight factors.

7 ▶▶▶ Store owners occasionally use formulas to determine the selling price of an item based on that item's wholesale cost. Visit a store and obtain the formulas that are used to price items. Ask to see a list of the wholesale costs and then determine the cost of at least six individual items that are priced on the basis of the formula you are given. With this information, prepare a worksheet showing each item's wholesale cost, retail price, and the retailer's profit. Find the retail price and retailer's profit if the items were put on sale at a 10% discount. Show totals, averages, maximums, and minimums. Include a chart illustrating what part of the profit is represented by each item when all six items are sold.

Microsoft *Excel 97*

What-If Analysis and Working with Large Worksheets

Objectives:

You will have mastered the material in this project when you can:

- Rotate text in a cell
- Use the fill handle to create a series of month names
- Copy a cell's format to another cell using the Format Painter button
- Copy a range of cells to a nonadjacent paste area
- Freeze column and row titles
- Insert and delete cells
- Format numbers by entering them with a format symbol
- Use the NOW function to display the system date
- Format the system date
- Use the IF function to enter one value or another in a cell on the basis of a logical test
- Copy absolute cell references
- Italicize text
- Display and dock toolbars
- Add a drop shadow to a range of cells
- Create a 3-D Column chart on a separate chart sheet
- Format a 3-D Column chart
- Use the Zoom box to change the appearance of the worksheet
- View different parts of the worksheet through window panes
- Use Excel to answer what-if questions
- Use the Goal Seek command to analyze worksheet data

Here Comes the Money

Saying "I do" to Wedding Expense Planners Stops the Wedding Bell Blues

Unless your name is Elizabeth Taylor or Zsa Zsa Gabor, planning a wedding can be a daunting experience. Nearly two million couples marry each year and spend from $8,000 to $25,000 for their special day.

To ease the financial wedding bell blues, couples now are using electronic spreadsheet software, using capabilities similar to those found in Microsoft Excel, to budget their total wedding costs. From the bride's dress to the limousine fee, all budgeted and actual costs can be projected and tracked, complete with graphs depicting just how much cash is being outlaid in specific categories.

My Wedding Companion and WedPlan 96 use intuitive Microsoft Windows interfaces and organize the wedding tasks from a main menu. My Wedding Companion was created *out of necessity* by software developer/newlywed Robert Lam. "I couldn't find a decent wedding program to help us plan our wedding, so I decided to write one myself," he says. "I didn't want future couples to experience some of the headaches that we experienced when planning our wedding."

Both packages come complete with modules to maintain the guest list, print mailing labels, and organize the reception seating. But perhaps most useful to purse-string-conscious newlyweds-to-be is the budgeting component. All wedding-related expenses are organized in categories such as attire, transportation, stationery, reception, and honeymoon. Some of these groups are subdivided, such as flowers being broken down into bouquets, ceremony, corsages, and reception.

The couple begins the planning process by entering basic data, such as the wedding date, attendants' names, and budget estimate. If the future bride and groom have a maximum total expenditure figure, they can enter how much they want to spend for each item in the multipage worksheet and adjust these numbers until the estimated budget approximates the maximum figure. For example, initially they may want to spend $1,000 for the bride's attire, but after estimating her dress at $900, a headpiece at $75, accessories at $80, and shoes at $70, they realize a more realistic budget is $1,125 and decide to cut back on the flowers for the reception by $125. As they determine actual costs and make deposits, they enter these figures and let the worksheet compute the balance due for each item, subtotals in each category, and a running total of all actual costs.

At any point in this budgeting process, My Wedding Companion can produce graphs to depict more accurately where the money is flowing and how much more is needed. For instance, if the couple is concerned about running over budget, graphs of the actual and budgeted costs can show where the extra costs are incurred.

With the high wedding consultant cost of 15 percent commission on the total price of the affair, these new worksheet *wedding consultants in a box* can be quite a savings at a price less that $50 each. Considering all the plans to be made and arrangements to be confirmed, they may rescue some nerves and save the couple the added stress of an already assiduous experience. Then, off to the honeymoon to relax!

Microsoft
Excel 97

What-If Analysis and Working with Large Worksheets

Case Perspective

Home Network Computers is the premier provider of a new category of computers called the network computer (NetPC). NetPCs allow you to use basic application software and surf the Web, and yet cost much less than more powerful PCs. Each June and December, the chief financial officer (CFO) of Home Network Computers, Kelly Rite, submits a plan to the board of directors to show projected net sales, expenses, and income for the next six months.

Last June, Kelly used pencil, paper, and a calculator to complete the report and draw a 3-D Column chart. When she presented her report, the directors asked for the effect on the projected net income if the department expense allocations were changed.

While the directors waited impatiently, Kelly took several minutes to calculate the answers. Once she changed the projected expenses, the 3-D Column chart no longer matched the projections and thus was meaningless. Kelly now wants to use a computer and electronic spreadsheet to address what-if questions. As lead spreadsheet specialist for Home Network Computers, you are to meet with Kelly, determine her needs, and create the spreadsheet and chart.

Introduction

This project introduces you to techniques that will enhance your abilities to create worksheets and draw charts. You will learn about other methods for entering values in cells and formatting these values. You also will learn how to use absolute cell references and how to use the IF function to assign a value to a cell based on a logical test.

In the previous projects, you learned how to use the Standard and Formatting toolbars. Excel has several other toolbars that can make your work easier. One such toolbar is the **Drawing toolbar**, which allows you to draw shapes and arrows, and add drop shadows to cells you want to emphasize.

Worksheets normally are much larger than those created in the previous projects, often extending beyond the size of the window. Because you cannot see the entire worksheet on screen at one time, working with a large worksheet can be difficult. For this reason, Excel provides several commands that allow you to change the display on the screen so that you can view critical parts of a large worksheet at one time. One command lets you freeze the row and column titles so that they always display on screen. Another command splits the worksheet into separate window panes so you can view different parts of a worksheet.

From your work in Projects 1 and 2, you are aware of how easily charts can be created. This project covers additional charting techniques that allow you to convey your message in a dramatic pictorial fashion.

More About the Ultimate What-If Analysis Tool

The ability of Excel to instantaneously answer what-if questions is the single most important reason why millions of business people use this software. Just a few short years ago, what-if questions of any complexity could be answered only by large, expensive computers programmed by highly-paid computer professionals. And then you might have to wait days for the turnaround. Excel and its equivalents give the non-computer professional the capability to get complex, business-related questions answered quickly and economically.

When you set up a worksheet, you should use as many cell references in formulas as possible, rather than constant values. The cell references in a formula often are called assumptions. **Assumptions** are cells whose values you can change to determine new values for formulas. This project emphasizes the use of assumptions and introduces you to answering what-if questions such as, What if you decrease the advertising expenses assumption (cell B16 in Figure 3-1a) by 1% — how would the decrease affect the projected six-month net income (cell H13 in Figure 3-1a)? Being able to quickly analyze the effect of changing values in a worksheet is an important skill in making business decisions.

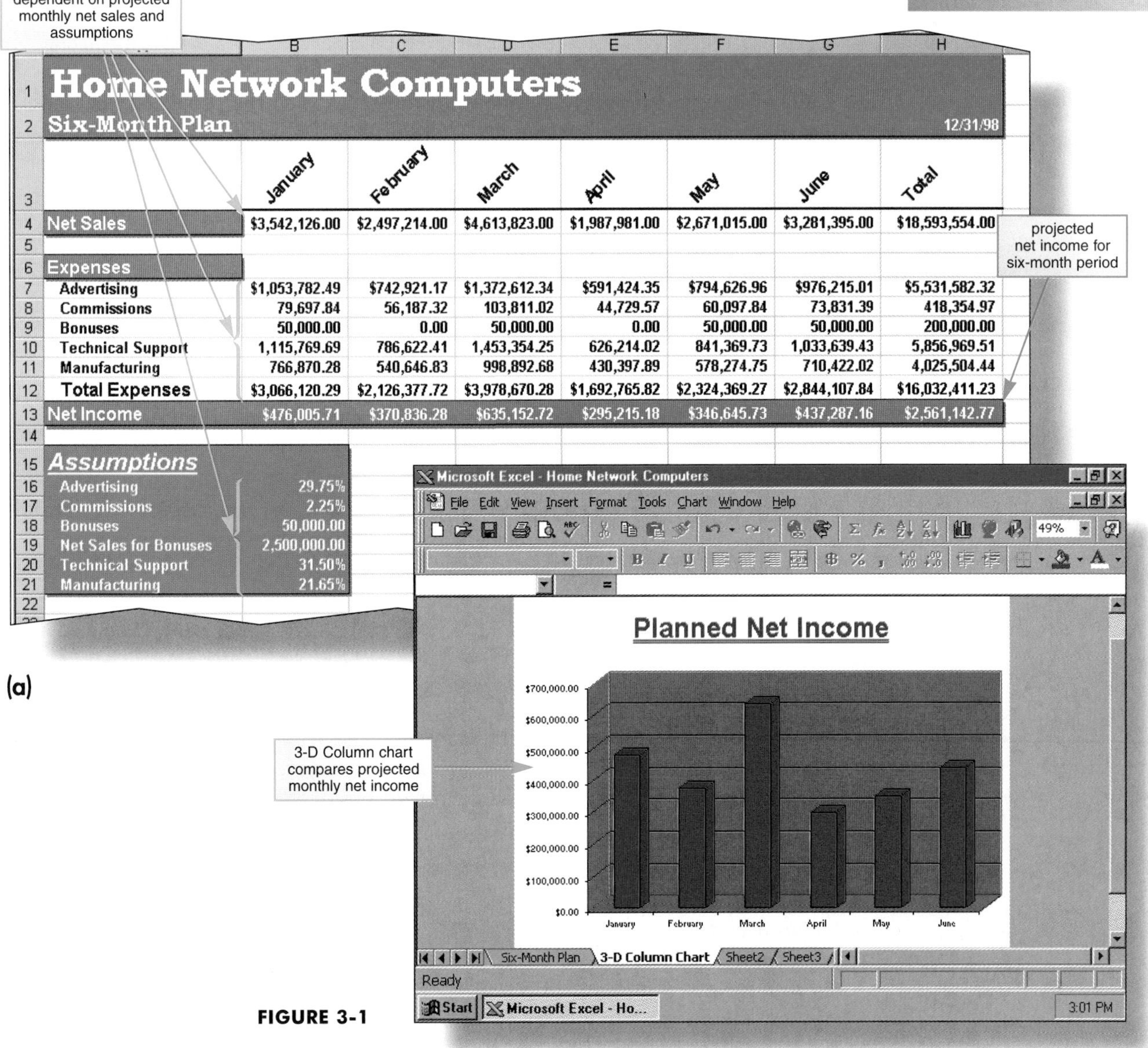

	January	February	March	April	May	June	Total
Net Sales	$3,542,126.00	$2,497,214.00	$4,613,823.00	$1,987,981.00	$2,671,015.00	$3,281,395.00	$18,593,554.00
Expenses							
Advertising	$1,053,782.49	$742,921.17	$1,372,612.34	$591,424.35	$794,626.96	$976,215.01	$5,531,582.32
Commissions	79,697.84	56,187.32	103,811.02	44,729.57	60,097.84	73,831.39	418,354.97
Bonuses	50,000.00	0.00	50,000.00	0.00	50,000.00	50,000.00	200,000.00
Technical Support	1,115,769.69	786,622.41	1,453,354.25	626,214.02	841,369.73	1,033,639.43	5,856,969.51
Manufacturing	766,870.28	540,646.83	998,892.68	430,397.89	578,274.75	710,422.02	4,025,504.44
Total Expenses	$3,066,120.29	$2,126,377.72	$3,978,670.28	$1,692,765.82	$2,324,369.27	$2,844,107.84	$16,032,411.23
Net Income	$476,005.71	$370,836.28	$635,152.72	$295,215.18	$346,645.73	$437,287.16	$2,561,142.77

Assumptions	
Advertising	29.75%
Commissions	2.25%
Bonuses	50,000.00
Net Sales for Bonuses	2,500,000.00
Technical Support	31.50%
Manufacturing	21.65%

FIGURE 3-1

Project Three – Home Network Computers Six-Month Plan

You took the following notes about the required worksheet and chart in your meeting with the CFO, Kelly Rite.

Need: A worksheet (Figure 3-1a on the previous page) and 3-D Column chart (Figure 3-1b on the previous page) are required. The worksheet is to show Home Network Computers' projected monthly net sales, expenses, and net income for a six-month period. The 3-D Column chart is to compare the projected monthly net incomes.

Source of Data: The projected monthly net sales (row 4 of Figure 3-1a) and the six assumptions (range B16:B21) that are used to determine the projected monthly expenses are available from Kelly.

Calculations: Each of the projected monthly expenses in the range B7:G11 of Figure 3-1a — advertising, commissions, bonuses, technical support, and manufacturing — is determined by taking an assumed percentage of the corresponding projected monthly net sales in row 4. The assumptions in the range B16:B21 are as follows:

1. The projected monthly advertising expenses are 29.75% of the projected net sales.
2. The projected monthly commissions are 2.25% of the projected net sales.
3. The projected monthly bonuses are $50,000.00, if the projected monthly net sales exceeds the net sales needed for bonuses to be awarded. The net sales for bonuses value is in cell B19 ($2,500,000.00).
4. The projected monthly technical support expenses are 31.50% of the projected sales.
5. The projected monthly manufacturing expenses are 21.65% of the projected sales.

The projected total monthly expenses in row 12 of Figure 3-1a are the sum of the corresponding projected monthly expenses in rows 7 through 11. The projected monthly net income in row 13 is equal to the corresponding projected monthly net sales minus the projected monthly total expenses.

Because the projected expenses in rows 7 through 11 are dependent on the assumptions in the range B16:B21 of Figure 3-1a, you can use the what-if capability of Excel to determine the impact of changing these assumptions on the projected monthly total expenses in row 12.

Graph Requirements: A 3-D Column chart on a separate sheet (Figure 3-1b) that compares the contribution of each month to the projected net income for the six-month period.

More *About* Recalculation

Each time you enter a value in a cell, Excel automatically recalculates all formulas in the workbook. If a workbook has many formulas, you can grow impatient waiting for the recalculation to take place, even though it seldom takes more than a few seconds with hundreds of formulas in a workbook. You can switch Excel to manual recalculation by clicking Options on the Tools menu, clicking the Calculation tab, and then clicking the Manual option button. You press F9 to recalculate when Excel is in the manual recalculation mode.

More *About* Worksheet Errors

Studies have shown that over 25% of all business worksheets have errors. You can ensure correctness by using the Auditing command on the Tools menu. The Auditing command indicates relationships among formulas.

Preparation Steps

The following tasks will be completed in this project to create the worksheet and chart shown in Figures 3-1a and b.

1. Start the Excel program.
2. Bold all cells in the worksheet.
3. Enter the worksheet titles, column titles, and row titles. Increase the column widths.
4. Save the workbook.
5. Enter the assumptions in the range B16:B21.
6. Enter the projected net sales for each of the six months in row 4.
7. Display the system date in cell H2.

8. Enter the formulas that determine the monthly projected expenses and monthly projected net income in the range B7:G13. Determine the totals in column H.
9. Format the worksheet so it appears as shown in Figure 3-1a on page E 3.5.
10. Create the 3-D Column chart that compares the monthly net incomes using the nonadjacent selection of ranges B3:G3 and B13:G13.
11. Format the 3-D Column chart.
12. Check spelling, preview, print, and save the workbook.
13. Use the Zoom box on the Standard toolbar to change the magnification of the worksheet and chart.
14. Divide the window into panes.
15. Analyze the data in the worksheet by changing the assumptions in the range B16:B21 and by goal seeking.

The following sections contain a detailed explanation of each of these steps.

Starting Excel

To start Excel, Windows 95 must be running. Perform the following steps to start Excel.

TO START EXCEL

Step 1: Click the Start button on the taskbar.
Step 2: Click New Office Document. If necessary, click the General tab in the New dialog box.
Step 3: Double-click the Blank Workbook icon.

An alternative to Steps 1 and 2 is to click the Start button, point to Programs, and click Microsoft Excel on the Programs submenu.

Changing the Font of the Entire Worksheet to Bold

The first step is to change the font of the entire worksheet to bold so all entries will be emphasized.

Bolding the entire worksheet makes it easier for people to read. An alternative is to increase the font size of the entire worksheet to 12- or 14-point.

TO BOLD THE FONT OF THE ENTIRE WORKSHEET

Step 1: Click the Select All button immediately above row heading 1 and to the left of column heading A.
Step 2: Click the Bold button on the Formatting toolbar.

No immediate change takes place on the screen. As you enter text and numbers into the worksheet, however, Excel will display them in bold.

Entering the Worksheet Titles

The worksheet contains two titles, one in cell A1, and another in cell A2. In the previous projects, titles were centered over the worksheet. With large worksheets that extend beyond the size of a window, it is best to enter titles in the upper-left corner as shown in Figure 3-1a.

TO ENTER THE WORKSHEET TITLES

Step 1: Select cell A1 and type `Home Network Computers` to enter the title.
Step 2: Select cell A2 and type `Six-Month Plan` to enter the second title.
Step 3: Select cell B3.

Excel responds by displaying the worksheet titles in cells A1 and A2 in bold (Figure 3-2).

More *About* **Rotating the Text**

If you enter 90° in the Degrees box on the Alignment tab in the Format Cells dialog box, the text will display vertically and read from bottom to top in the cell. You can rotate the text clockwise by entering a number between –1° and –90°. If you enter –90°, the text will display vertically and read from top to bottom in the cell.

Rotating Text and Using the Fill Handle to Create a Series

One of the new features of Excel 97 is the ability to **rotate text** in a cell. When you first enter text, its angle is zero degrees (0°), and it reads from left to right in a cell. You can rotate the text counterclockwise by entering a number between 1° and 90° on the Alignment sheet in the Format Cells dialog box. An example of rotating the text is shown in the next set of steps.

In Projects 1 and 2, you used the fill handle to copy a cell or a range of cells to adjacent cells. You also can use the fill handle to create a series of numbers, dates, or month names automatically. Perform the following steps to enter the month name, January, in cell B3, format cell B3 (including rotating the text), and then enter the remaining month names in the range C3:G3 using the fill handle (see Figure 3-6 on page E3.10).

To Rotate Text and Use the Fill Handle to Create a Series of Month Names

1 **With cell B3 active, type** `January` **and then click the Enter box or press the ENTER key. On the Formatting toolbar, click the Font Size box arrow and then click 11 in the Font Size list box. Click the Borders button arrow and then click the heavy bottom border on the Borders palette. Right-click cell B3.**

The text, January, displays in cell B3 using the assigned formats (Figure 3-2). The shortcut menu displays.

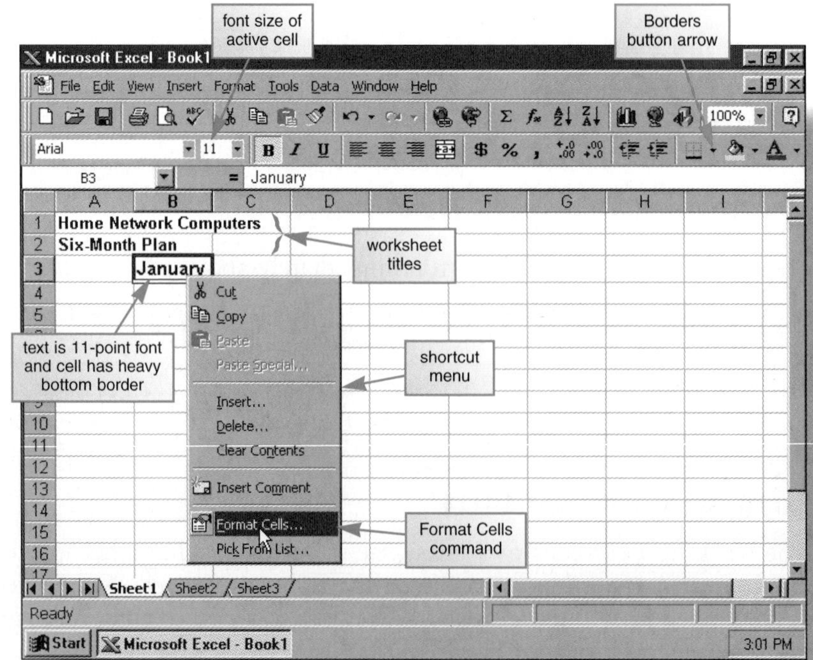

FIGURE 3-2

2 **Click Format Cells on the shortcut menu. When the Format Cells dialog box displays, click the Alignment tab. Click the 45° point in the Orientation area and point to the OK button.**

*The **Alignment sheet** in the Format Cells dialog box displays. The **Text hand** in the **Orientation area** points to the 45° point and 45 displays in the **Degrees box** (Figure 3-3).*

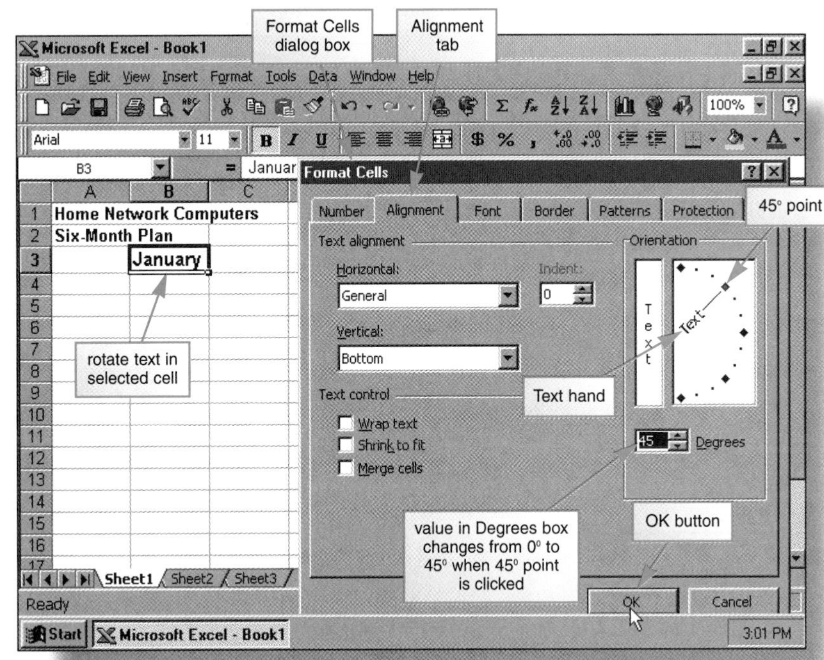

FIGURE 3-3

3 **Click the OK button. Point to the fill handle on the lower-left edge of cell B3.**

The text, January, in cell B3 displays at a 45° angle (Figure 3-4). Excel automatically increases the height of row 3 to best fit to display the rotated text. The mouse pointer changes to a cross hair.

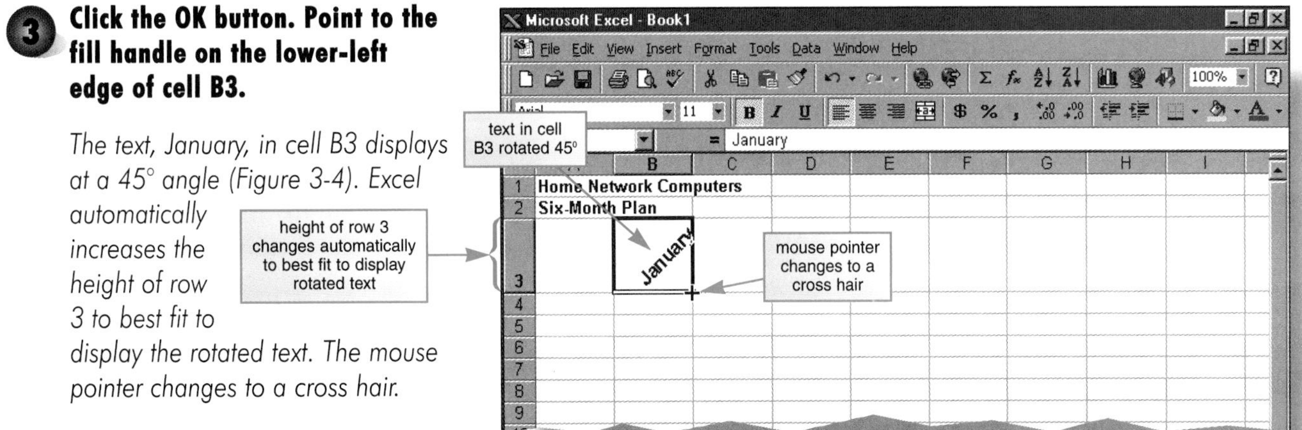

FIGURE 3-4

4 **Drag the fill handle to the right to select the range C3:G3.**

Excel displays a light border that surrounds the selected range (Figure 3-5).

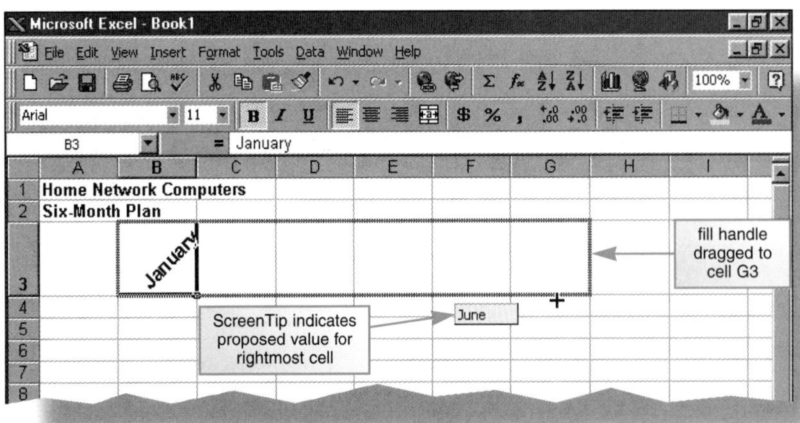

FIGURE 3-5

5 Release the mouse button.

Using January in cell B3 as the basis, Excel creates the month name series February through June in the range C3:G3 (Figure 3-6). The formats assigned to cell B3 earlier in Step 1 (11-point font, heavy bottom border, text rotated 45°) are copied to the range C3:G3.

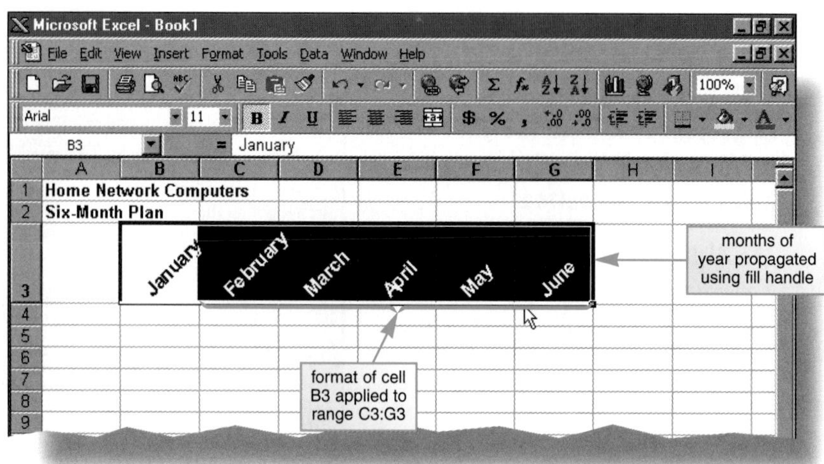

FIGURE 3-6

Other Ways

1. Enter first month in cell, right-drag fill handle to select range, on shortcut menu click Fill Months

Besides creating a series of values, the fill handle also copies the format of cell B3 (11-point font, heavy bottom border, text rotated 45°) to the range C3:G3. Notice that Excel rotates all of the titles in the series. As with any format style, you can rotate the text in a range of cells by first selecting the range and then changing the rotation on the Alignment sheet. Thus, the series of month names first could have been created in row 3 and then rotated as a group.

You can use the fill handle to create longer series than the one shown in Figure 3-6. If you drag the fill handle past cell G3 in Step 2, Excel continues to increment the months and logically will repeat January, February, and so on, if you extend the range far enough to the right.

You also can create different types of series using the fill handle. Table 3-1 illustrates several examples. Notice in Examples 4 through 7 in Table 3-1 that, if you use the fill handle to create a series of numbers or non-sequential months, you must enter the first item in the series in one cell and the second item in the series in an adjacent cell. You then select both cells and drag the fill handle through the paste area.

Table 3-1

EXAMPLE	CONTENTS OF CELL(S) COPIED USING THE FILL HANDLE	NEXT THREE VALUES OF EXTENDED SERIES
1	8:00	9:00, 10:00, 11:00
2	Qtr2	Qtr3, Qtr4, Qtr1
3	Quarter 1	Quarter 2, Quarter 3, Quarter 4
4	Jul-98, Oct-98	Jan-98, Apr-98, Jul-98
5	2000, 2001	2002, 2003, 2004
6	1, 2	3, 4, 5
7	300, 295	290, 285, 280
8	Mon	Tue, Wed, Thur
9	Wednesday	Thursday, Friday, Saturday
10	1st Part	2nd Part, 3rd Part, 4th Part
11	-9, -11	-13, -15, -17

More *About* **the Fill Handle**

To use the fill handle to copy a potential series initiator, like the word January, to a paste area, hold down the CTRL key while you drag.

Copying a Cell's Format Using the Format Painter Button

Because it is not part of the series, the last column title, Total, must be entered separately in cell H3 and formatted to match the other column titles. Imagine how many steps it would take, however, to assign the formatting of the other column titles to this cell — first, you have to change the font to 11 point, then add a heavy bottom border, and finally, rotate the text 45°. Using the **Format Painter button** on the Standard toolbar, however, you can format a cell quickly by copying a cell's format to another cell. The following steps enter the column title, Total, in cell H3 and format the cell using the Format Painter button.

More About the Format Painter Button

Double-click, rather than click, the Format Painter button to copy the formats to non-adjacent ranges and then drag through the ranges. Click the Format Painter button to deactivate it.

Steps To Copy a Cell's Format Using the Format Painter Button

1 **Select cell H3. Type** `Total` **and then press the LEFT ARROW key.**

2 **With cell G3 selected, click the Format Painter button on the Standard toolbar. Move the mouse pointer over cell H3.**

The mouse pointer changes to a block plus sign with a paint brush (Figure 3-7).

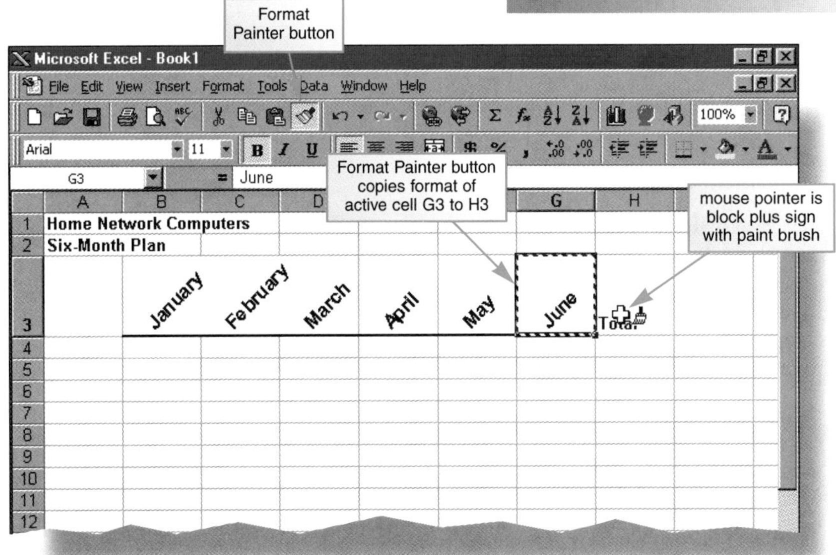

FIGURE 3-7

3 **Click cell H3 to assign the format of cell G3 to cell H3. Click cell A4.**

Cell H3 is assigned the same format (11-point font, heavy bottom border, text rotated 45°) as cell G3 (Figure 3-8).

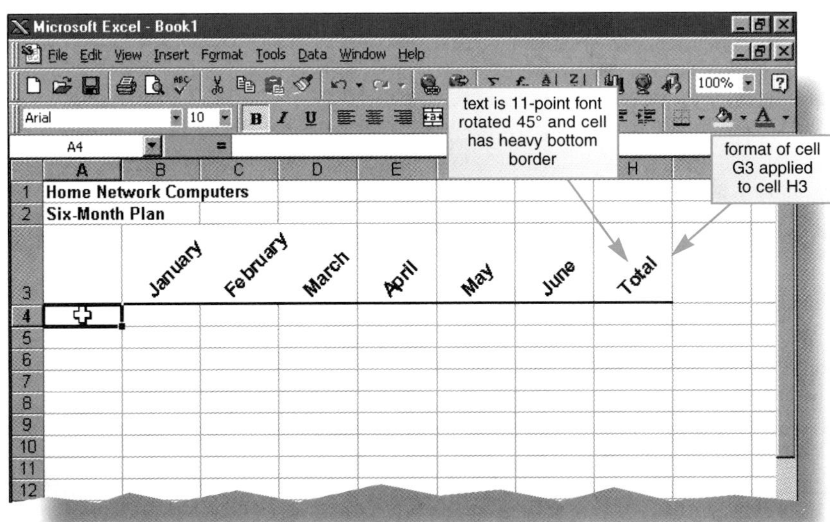

FIGURE 3-8

Other Ways

1. On Standard toolbar click Copy button, select paste area, on Edit menu click Paste Special, click Formats, click OK button

The Format Painter button also can be used to copy the formats of a cell to a range or to copy one range to another range. To copy formats to a range of cells, select the cell or range with the desired format, click the Format Painter button on the Standard toolbar, and then drag through the range to which you want to paste the formats.

More About Changing Column Widths

You can use the CTRL key to select nonadjacent columns before increasing the column width or assigning a common format.

Increasing the Column Widths and Entering Row Titles

In Project 2, the column widths were increased after the values were entered into the worksheet. Sometimes, you may want to increase the column widths before you enter the values and then, if necessary, adjust them later. The following steps increase the column widths and add the row titles in column A to Assumptions in cell A15.

Steps To Increase Column Widths and Enter Row Titles

1 Move the mouse pointer to the boundary between column heading A and column heading B, so the mouse pointer changes to a split double arrow. Drag the mouse pointer to the right until the ScreenTip displays, Width: 25.00.

The distance between the left edge of column A and the vertical dotted line below the mouse pointer shows the proposed column width. The ScreenTip, displays, Width: 25.00 (Figure 3-9).

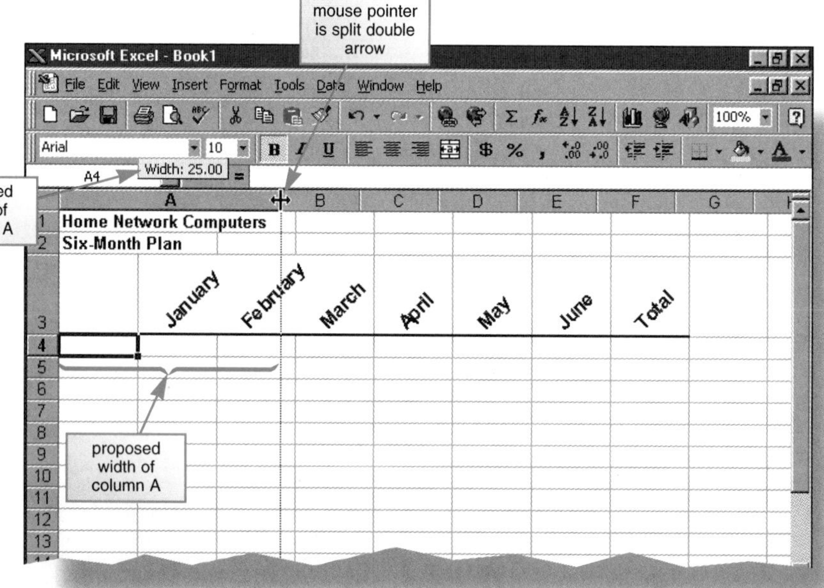

FIGURE 3-9

2 Release the mouse button. Click column heading B and drag through column heading G to select columns B through G. Move the mouse pointer to the boundary between column headings B and C and then drag the mouse to the right until the ScreenTip displays, Width: 13.00.

The distance between the left edge of column B and the vertical line below the mouse pointer shows the proposed width of columns B through G. Width: 13.00 displays in the ScreenTip (Figure 3-10).

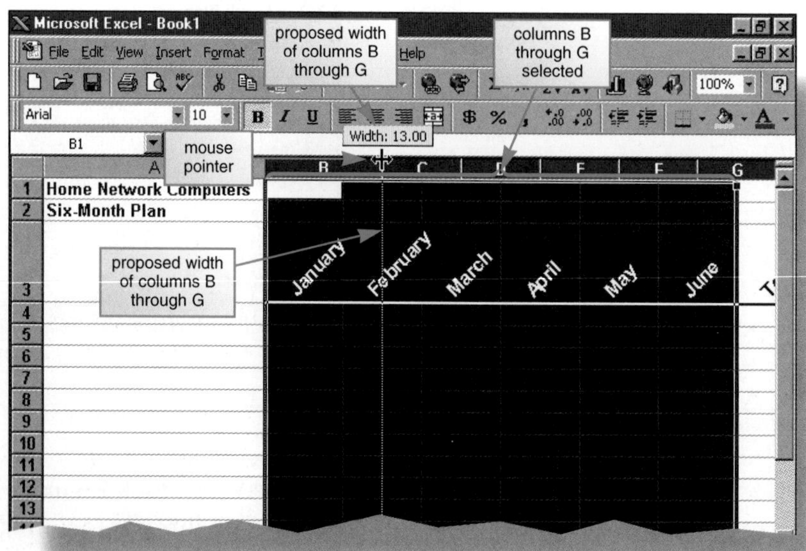

FIGURE 3-10

3 **Release the mouse button. Use the technique described in Step 1 to increase the width of column H to 15.00.**

4 **Enter** Net Sales **in cell A4,** Expenses **in cell A6,** Advertising **in cell A7, and** Commissions **in cell A8. Enter** Bonuses **in cell A9,** Technical Support **in cell A10,** Manufacturing **in cell A11,** Total Expenses **in cell A12,** Net Income **in cell A13, and** Assumptions **in cell A15.**

5 **Select the range A7:A12. Click the Increase Indent button on the Formatting toolbar. Click cell A16.**

The row titles display as shown in Figure 3-11.

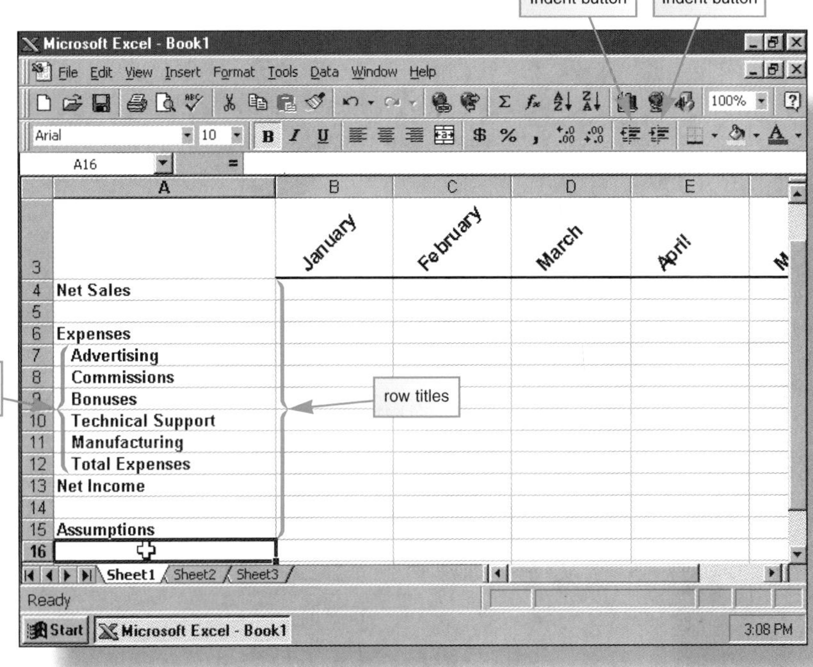

FIGURE 3-11

OtherWays

1. On the Alignment sheet in the Format cells dialog box click Left (Indent), enter number of spaces to indent in Indent box, click OK button

The **Increase Indent button** indents the contents of a cell to the right by three spaces each time you click it. The **Decrease Indent button** decreases the indent by three spaces each time you click it.

Copying a Range of Cells to a Nonadjacent Paste Area

As shown in Figure 3-1a on page E 3.5, the row titles in the Assumptions table in the range A16:A21 are the same as the row titles in the range A7:A11, with the exception of the additional entry in cell A19. Hence, you can create the Assumptions table row titles by copying the range A7:A11 to the range A16:A20 and inserting the additional entry in cell A19. Notice that the range to copy (range A7:A11) is not adjacent to the paste area (range A16:A20). In the first two projects, you used the fill handle to copy a range of cells to an adjacent paste area. To copy a range of cells to a nonadjacent paste area, however, you cannot use the fill handle.

A more versatile method of copying a cell or range of cells is to use the Copy button and Paste button on the Standard toolbar. You can use these two buttons to copy a range of cells to an adjacent or nonadjacent paste area.

When you click the **Copy button**, it copies the contents and format of the selected range and places the copy on the Clipboard, replacing the Clipboard's contents. The **Copy command** on the Edit menu or shortcut menu works the same as the Copy button.

More About Copying

If you have a range of cells in another workbook that you want to copy into the current workbook, open the source workbook, select the range, and then click the Copy button to place the range of cells on the Clipboard. Next, activate the destination workbook by clicking its file name on the Window menu. Finally, select the paste area and click the Paste button.

The **Paste button** copies the contents of the Clipboard to the paste area. The **Paste command** on the Edit menu or shortcut menu works the same as the Paste button. When you are copying the Clipboard contents to more than one nonadjacent cell or range, use the Paste button. When you are copying to a single cell or range, complete the copy by pressing the ENTER key.

To Copy a Range of Cells to a Nonadjacent Paste Area

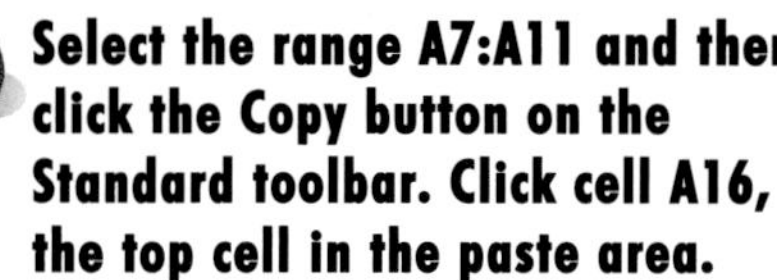

1. **Select the range A7:A11 and then click the Copy button on the Standard toolbar. Click cell A16, the top cell in the paste area.**

Excel surrounds the range A7:A11 with a marquee when you click the Copy button (Figure 3-12). Excel also copies the values and formats of the range A7:A11 onto the Clipboard.

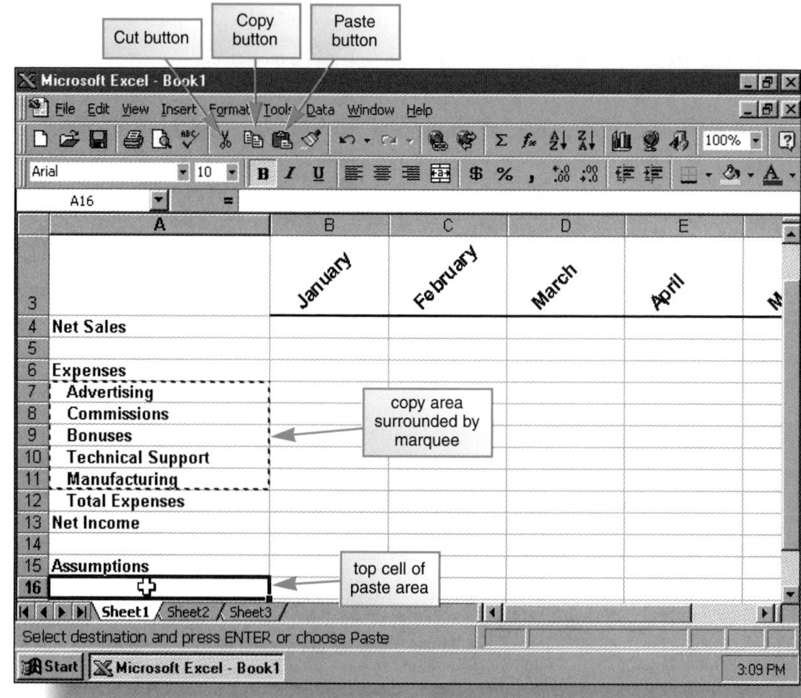

FIGURE 3-12

2. **Press the ENTER key to complete the copy.**

Excel copies the contents of the Clipboard (range A7:A11) to the paste area A16:A20 (Figure 3-13).

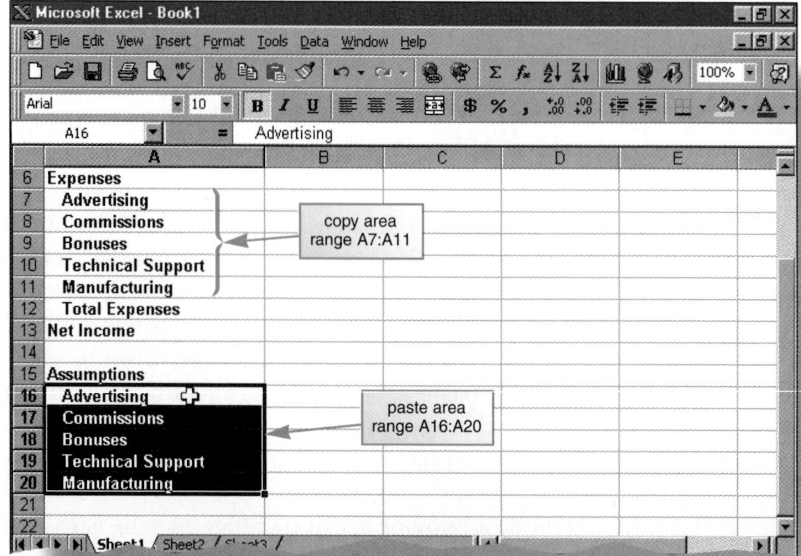

FIGURE 3-13

OtherWays

1. Select copy area, while holding down CTRL key drag copy area to paste area
2. Right-click copy area, on shortcut menu click Copy, right-click paste area on shortcut menu, click Paste
3. Select copy area, on Edit menu click Copy, select paste area, on Edit menu click Paste
4. Select copy area, press CTRL+C, select paste area, press CTRL+V

In Step 1 and Figure 3-12, you can see that you are not required to highlight the entire paste area (range A16:A20) before pressing the ENTER key to complete the copy. Because the paste area is exactly the same size as the range you are copying, you have to select only the top left cell of the paste area. In the case of a single column range such as A16:A20, the top cell of the paste area (cell A16) also is the upper-left cell of the paste area.

When you complete a copy, the values and formats in the paste area are replaced with the values and formats on the Clipboard. Any data contained in the paste area prior to the copy and paste is lost. If you accidentally delete valuable data, immediately click the Undo button on the Standard toolbar or click the **Undo Paste command** on the Edit menu to undo the paste.

When you press the ENTER key to complete a copy, the contents on the Clipboard are erased. When you paste using the Paste button or the Paste command on the Edit menu or shortcut menu, the contents of the Clipboard remain available for additional copying. Hence, if you plan to copy the cells to more than one paste area, click the Paste button or click Paste on the Edit menu or shortcut menu instead of pressing the ENTER key. Then, select the next paste area and invoke the Paste command again. If you paste using the Paste button or the Paste command on the Edit menu or shortcut menu, the marquee remains around the copied range to remind you that this range is still on the Clipboard. To remove the marquee, press the ESC key.

More *About* Moving Cells versus Copying Cells

You may hear someone say, "move it or copy it, it is all the same." No, it is not the same! When you move cells, the original location is blanked and the format is reset to the default. When you copy cells, the copy area remains intact. In short, copy cells to duplicate and move cells to rearrange.

Using Drag and Drop to Move or Copy Cells

You also can use the mouse to move or copy cells. First, you select the copy area and point to the border of the cell or range. You know you are pointing to the border of the cell or range when the mouse pointer changes to a block arrow. To move the selected cell or cells, drag the selection to its new location. To copy a selection, hold down the CTRL key while dragging the selection to its new location and then release the CTRL key. Be sure to release the mouse button before you release the CTRL key. Using the mouse to move or copy cells is called **drag and drop**.

Another way to move cells is to select them, click the Cut button on the Standard toolbar (Figure 3-12), select the new area, and then click the Paste button on the Standard toolbar or press the ENTER key. You also can use the **Cut command** on the Edit menu or shortcut menu.

More *About* Dragging and Dropping

If the mouse pointer does not change to an arrow when you point to the border of the range to copy, then the Drag and Drop option is turned off. To turn it on, click Options on the Tools menu, click the Edit tab, then click the Allow Cell Drag and Drop check box.

Inserting and Deleting Cells in a Worksheet

At any time while the worksheet is on the screen, you can insert cells to enter new data or delete cells to remove unwanted data. You can insert or delete individual cells, a range of cells, entire rows, entire columns, or entire worksheets.

Inserting Rows

The **Rows command** on the Insert menu or the **Insert command** on the shortcut menu allows you to insert rows between rows that already contain data. In the Assumptions table at the bottom of the worksheet, a row must be inserted between rows 18 and 19 so the Net Sales for Bonuses assumption can be added (see Figure 3-1a on page E 3.5). The steps on the next page show how to accomplish the task of inserting a new row into the worksheet.

To Insert Rows

1 Right-click row heading 19.

Row 19 is selected, and the shortcut menu displays (Figure 3-14).

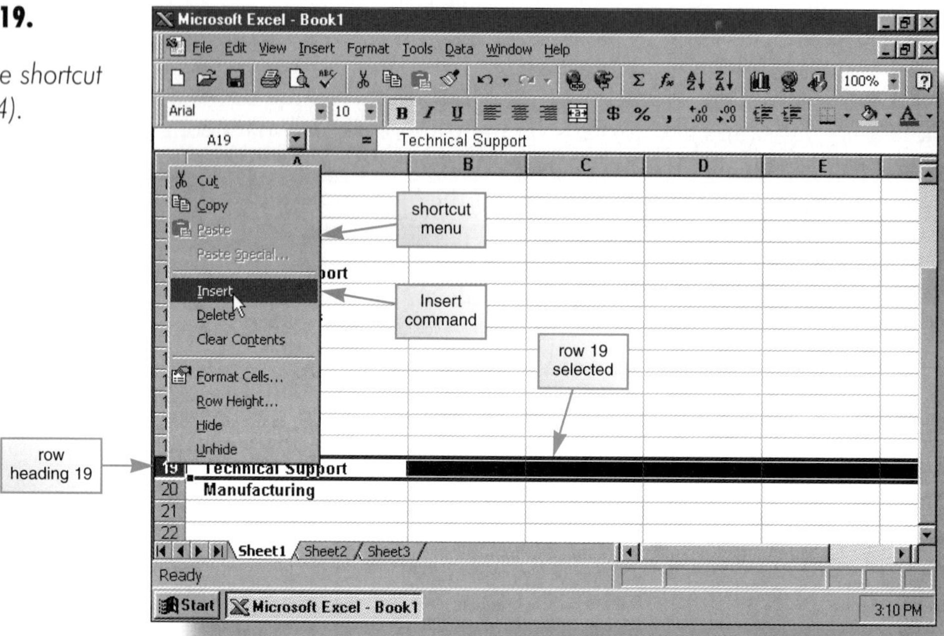

FIGURE 3-14

2 Click Insert on the shortcut menu. Click cell A19.

Excel inserts a new row by shifting down all rows below and including row 19, the one originally selected (Figure 3-15).

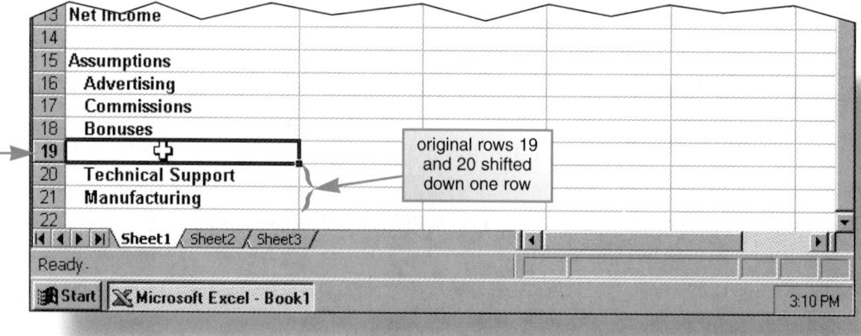

FIGURE 3-15

Other Ways

1. On Insert menu click Rows
2. Press CTRL+SHIFT+PLUS SIGN, click Entire Row, click OK button

If the rows that are shifted down include any formulas, Excel adjusts the cell references to the new locations. Thus, if a formula in the worksheet references a cell in row 19 before the insert, then the cell reference in the formula is adjusted to row 20 after the insert.

The primary difference between the Insert command on the shortcut menu and the Rows command on the Insert menu is this: The Insert command on the shortcut menu requires that you select an entire row (or rows) in order to insert a row (or rows). The Rows command on the Insert menu requires that you select a single cell in a row to insert one row or a range of cells to insert multiple rows. Inserted rows duplicate the format (including colors) of the row above them.

Inserting Columns

You insert columns into a worksheet in the same way you insert rows. To insert columns, begin your column selection immediately to the right of where you want Excel to insert the new blank columns. Select the number of columns you want to insert. Next, click the **Columns command** on the Insert menu or click Insert on the shortcut menu. Again, the primary difference between these two commands is this: The Columns command on the Insert menu requires that you select a single cell in a column to insert one column or a range of cells to insert multiple columns. The Insert command on the shortcut menu, however, requires that you select an entire column (or columns) to insert a column (or columns). Inserted columns duplicate the format (including colors) of the column to their left.

Inserting Individual Cells or a Range of Cells

The Insert command on the shortcut menu or the Cells command on the Insert menu allows you to insert a single cell or a range of cells. You should be aware that if you shift a single cell or a range of cells, however, they no longer may be lined up with their associated cells. To ensure that the values in the worksheet do not get out of order, it is recommended that you insert only entire rows or entire columns.

More *About* Moving and Inserting

You can move and insert between existing cells by holding down the SHIFT key while you drag the selection to the gridline where you want to insert. You can also copy and insert by holding down the CTRL and SHIFT keys while you drag the selection to the desired gridline.

Deleting Columns and Rows

The Delete command on the Edit menu or shortcut menu removes cells (including the data and format) from the worksheet. Deleting cells is not the same as clearing cells. The Clear command, which was described earlier in Project 1 on page E 1.51, clears the data from the cells, but the cells remain in the worksheet. The Delete command removes the cells from the worksheet and shifts the remaining rows up (when you delete rows) or shifts the remaining columns to the left (when you delete columns). If formulas located in other cells reference cells in the deleted row or column, Excel does not adjust these cell references. Excel displays the error message **#REF!** in those cells to indicate a cell reference error. For example, if cell A7 contains the formula =A4+A5 and you delete row 5, then Excel assigns the formula =A4+#REF! to cell A6 (originally cell A7) and displays the error message #REF! in cell A6.

Deleting Individual Cells or a Range of Cells

Although Excel allows you to delete an individual cell or range of cells, you should be aware that if you shift a cell or range of cells on the worksheet, they no longer may be lined up with their associated cells. For this reason, it is recommended that you delete only entire rows or entire columns.

More *About* Undoing Mistakes

Inserting, copying, deleting, and moving have the potential to render a worksheet useless. Carefully review these actions before going on to the next task. If you are not sure the action is correct, click the Undo button on the Standard toolbar.

Entering Numbers with a Format Symbol

The next step in creating the Six-Month Plan worksheet is to enter the row title, Net Sales for Bonuses, in cell A19 and enter the assumption values in the range B16:B21. You can enter the assumption numbers with decimal places and then format them later, as you did in Projects 1 and 2, or you can enter them with format symbols. When you enter a number with a **format symbol**, Excel immediately

Table 3-2

FORMAT SYMBOL	TYPED IN FORMULA BAR	DISPLAYS IN CELL	COMPARABLE FORMAT
,	3,541	3,541	Comma (0)
	5,621.8	5,621.80	Comma (2)
$	$221	$221	Currency (0)
	$1243.88	$1,243.88	Currency (2)
	$21,965.4	$21,965.40	Currency (2)
%	12%	12%	Percent (0)
	37.3%	37.30%	Percent (2)
	9.01%	9.01%	Percent (2)

displays the number with the assigned format. Valid format symbols include the dollar sign ($), comma (,), and percent sign (%). If the number entered is a whole number, then it displays without any decimal places.

If the number entered with a format symbol has one or more decimal places, then Excel displays the number with two decimal places. Table 3-2 illustrates several examples of numbers entered with format symbols. The number in parentheses in column 4 indicates the number of decimal places.

The following steps describe how to complete the entries in the Assumptions table and save an intermediate version of the workbook.

To Enter a Number with a Format Symbol

1. **Click cell A19 and enter** `Net Sales for Bonuses` **in the cell.**

2. **Enter** `29.75%` **in cell B16,** `2.25%` **in cell B17,** `50,000.00` **in cell B18,** `2,500,000.00` **in cell B19,** `31.50%` **in cell B20, and** `21.65%` **in cell B21.**

   The entries display in a format based on the format symbols entered with the numbers (Figure 3-16).

3. **With a floppy disk in drive A, click the Save button on the Standard toolbar. Type the file name** `Home Computer Networks` **in the File name text box. Click the Save in box arrow and then click 3½ Floppy (A:). Click the Save button in the Save As dialog box.**

   The workbook name in the title bar changes from Book1 to Home Network Computers.

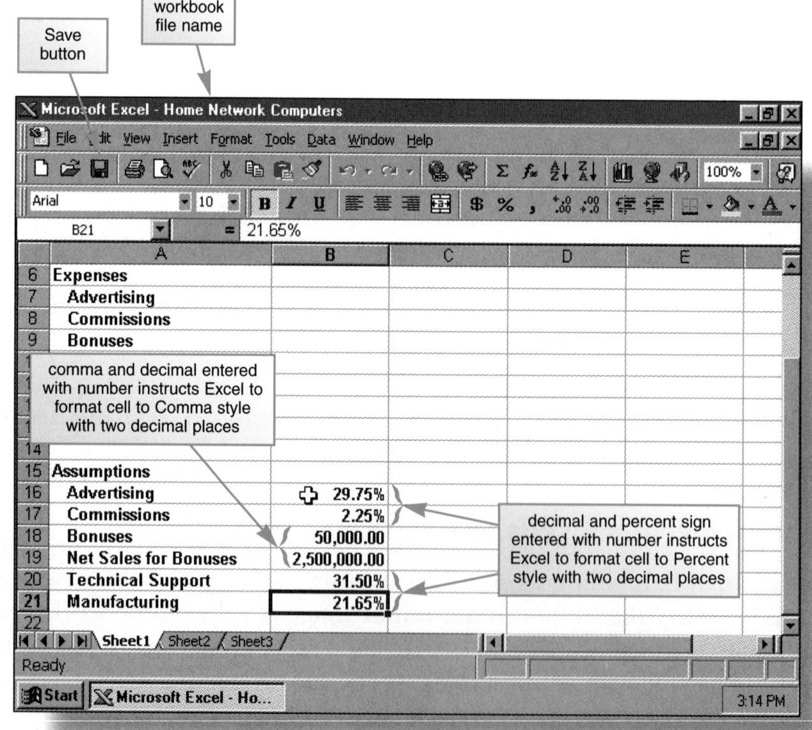

FIGURE 3-16

OtherWays

1. Enter numbers without format symbols, on shortcut menu click Format Cells
2. Enter numbers without format symbols, on Format menu click Cells

Freezing Worksheet Titles

Freezing worksheet titles is a useful technique for viewing large worksheets that extend beyond the window. For example, when you scroll down or to the right, the column titles in row 3 and the row titles in column A that define the numbers no longer display on the screen. This makes it difficult to remember what the numbers represent. To alleviate this problem, Excel allows you to freeze the titles so they display on the screen no matter how far down or to the right you scroll.

Complete the following steps to freeze the worksheet title and column titles in rows 1, 2, and 3, and the row titles in column A using the **Freeze Panes command** on the **Window menu**.

More About Freezing Titles

If you want to freeze only column headings, select the appropriate cell in column A before you click Freeze Panes on the Window menu. If you want to freeze only row titles, then select the appropriate cell in row 1. To freeze both column and row titles, select the cell that is the intersection of the column and row titles.

Steps To Freeze Column and Row Titles

1 **Click cell B4, the cell below the column headings you want to freeze and to the right of the row titles you want to freeze. Click Window on the menu bar and then point to Freeze Panes (Figure 3-17).**

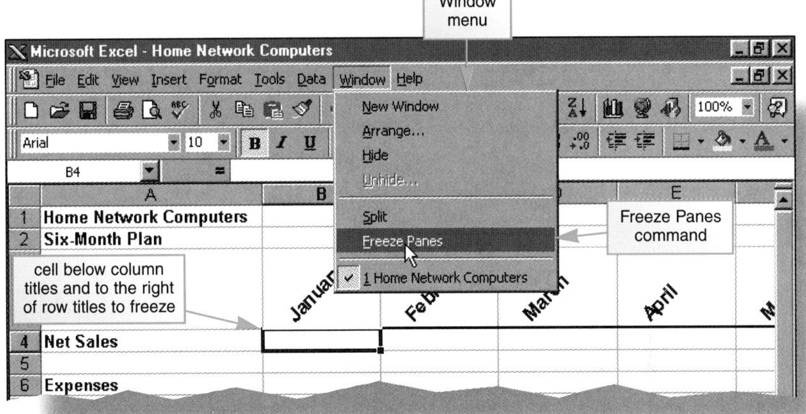

FIGURE 3-17

2 **Click Freeze Panes.**

Excel splits the window into two parts. The right border of column A changes to a thin black line indicating the split between the frozen row titles in column A and the rest of the worksheet. The bottom border of row 3 changes to a thin black line indicating the split between the frozen column titles in rows 1 through 3 and the rest of the worksheet (Figure 3-18).

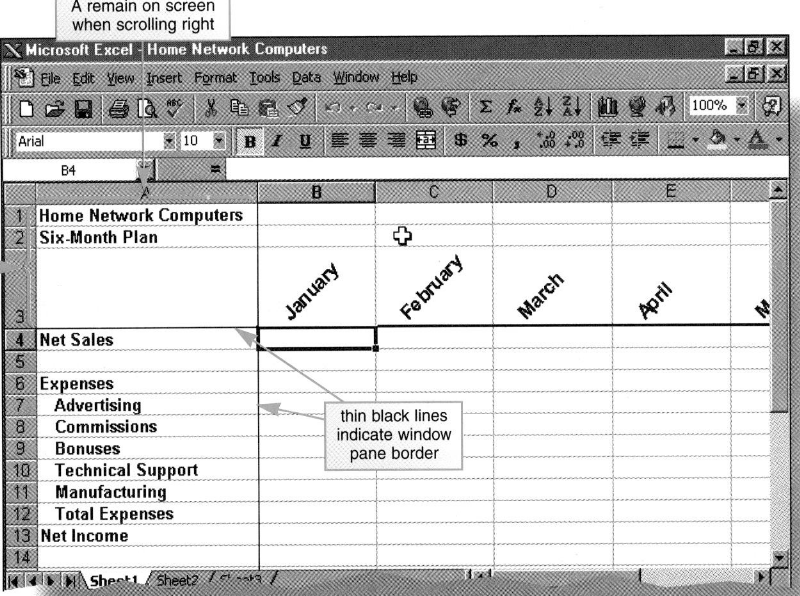

FIGURE 3-18

Once frozen, the row titles in column A will remain on the screen even when you scroll to the right to display column G.

The titles remain frozen until you unfreeze them. You unfreeze the titles by clicking the **Unfreeze Panes command** on the Window menu. Later steps in this project show you how to use the Unfreeze Panes command.

Entering the Projected Sales

The next step is to enter the projected monthly net sales and projected six-month total net sales in row 4. Enter these numbers without any format symbols as shown in the following steps.

TO ENTER THE PROJECTED SALES

Step 1: Enter `3542126` in cell B4, `2497214` in cell C4, `4613823` in cell D4, `1987981` in cell E4, `2671015` in cell F4, `3281395` in cell G4.

Step 2: Click cell H4 and then click the AutoSum button on the Standard toolbar twice.

The projected six-month total net sales displays in cell H4 (Figure 3-19). Notice that columns B, C, and D have scrolled off the screen, but column A remains because it was frozen earlier.

More About Verifying Formulas

Always verify the ranges used in a formula or function by double-clicking the cell. Excel will verify the ranges by drawing outlines around the cells referenced in the formula or function.

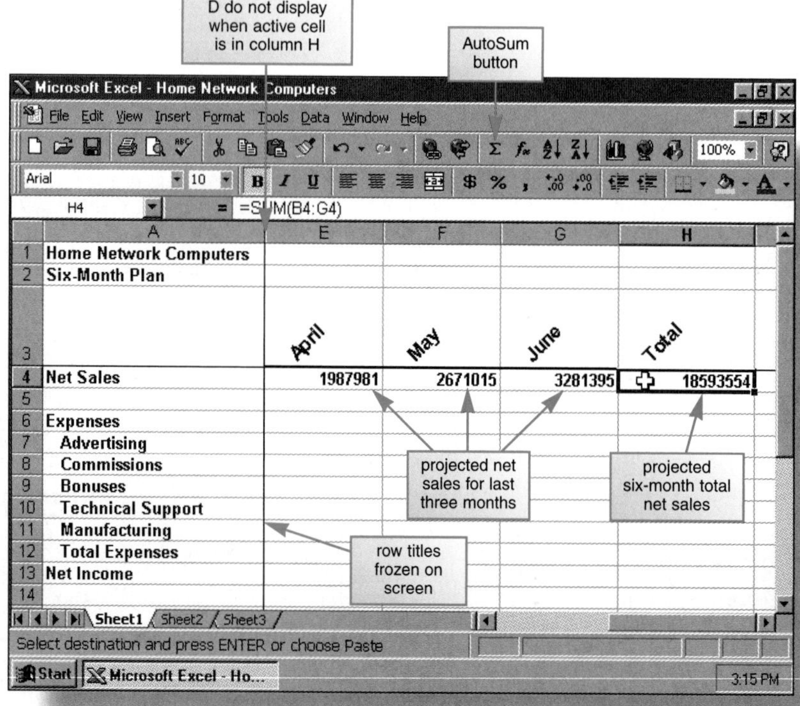

FIGURE 3-19

Displaying the System Date

The worksheet in Figure 3-1a on page E 3.5 includes a date stamp in cell H2. A **date stamp** shows the system date of which your computer keeps track. If the computer's system date is set to the current date, which normally it is, then the date stamp is equivalent to the current date.

In information processing, a report often is meaningless without a date stamp. For example, if Kelly took a printout of the worksheet to the board of directors meeting, the date stamp would show when the six-month projections were made.

To enter the system date in a cell in the worksheet, use the **NOW function**. The NOW function is one of 14 date functions available in Excel. When assigned to a cell, the NOW function returns a number which corresponds to the date and time for the days January 1, 1900 through December 31, 9999. Excel automatically formats the date stamp to the date and time format, m/d/yy h:mm, where the first m is the month, d is the day of the month, yy is the last two digits of the year, h is the hour of the day, and mm is the minutes past the hour.

The following steps show how to enter the NOW function and change the format from m/d/yy h:mm to m/d/yy, where m is the month number, d is the day of the month, and yy are the last two digits of the year.

More About Dates

How many days have you been alive? Enter today's date (i.e., 3/29/98) in cell A1. Next, enter your birthdate (i.e., 6/22/78) in cell A2. Select cell A3 and enter the formula =A1 - A2. Format cell A3 to the General style. Cell A3 will display the number of days you have been alive.

Steps To Enter and Format the System Date

1. **Click cell H2 and then click the Paste Function button on the Standard toolbar.**

2. **Click Date & Time in the Function category list box and then click NOW in the Function name list box. Point to the OK button.**

The Paste Function dialog box displays (Figure 3-20).

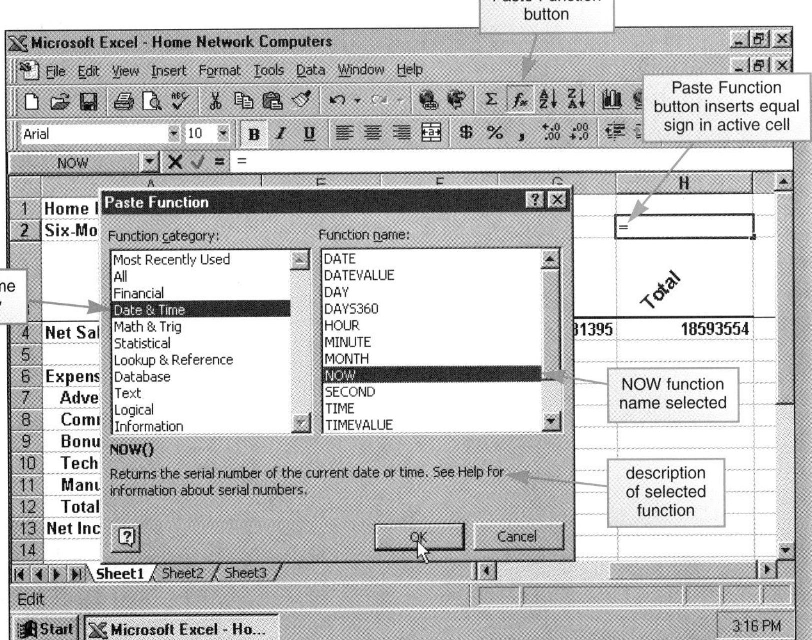

FIGURE 3-20

3 **Click the OK button When the NOW Formula palette displays, click the OK button. Right-click cell H2.**

Excel displays the system date and time in cell H2 using the default date and time format m/d/yy h:mm. The date on your computer may be different. The shortcut menu displays (Figure 3-21).

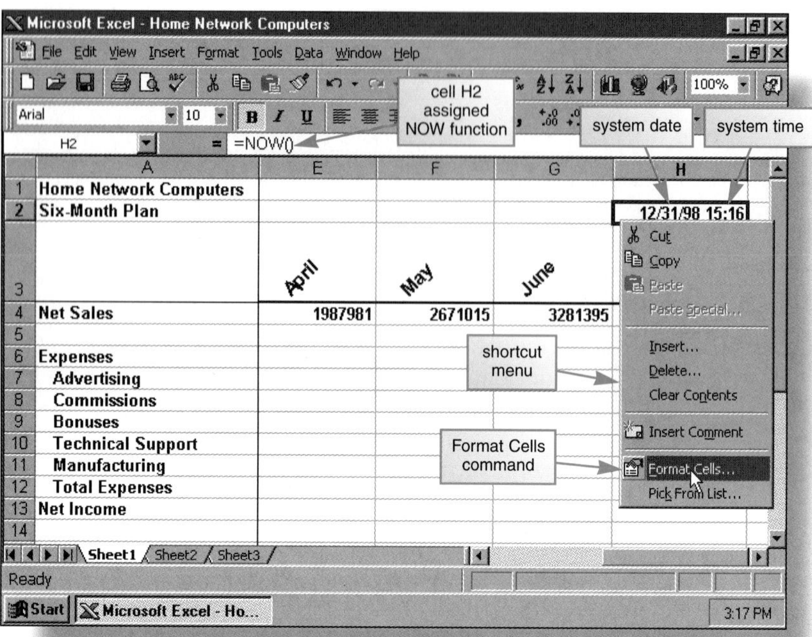

FIGURE 3-21

4 **Click Format Cells on the shortcut menu and then click the Number tab in the Format Cells dialog box. Click Date in the Category list box and then click 3/4/97 in the Type list box. Point to the OK button.**

Excel displays the Format Cells dialog box with Date and 3/4/97 (m/d/yy) highlighted (Figure 3-22).

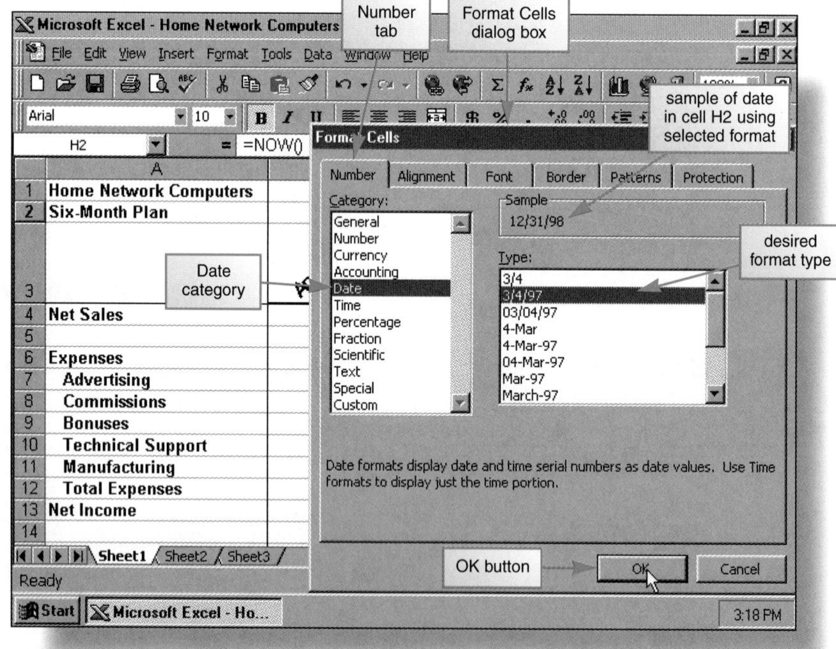

FIGURE 3-22

Click the OK button.

Excel displays the date in the form m/d/yy (Figure 3-23). Again, the date on your computer may be different.

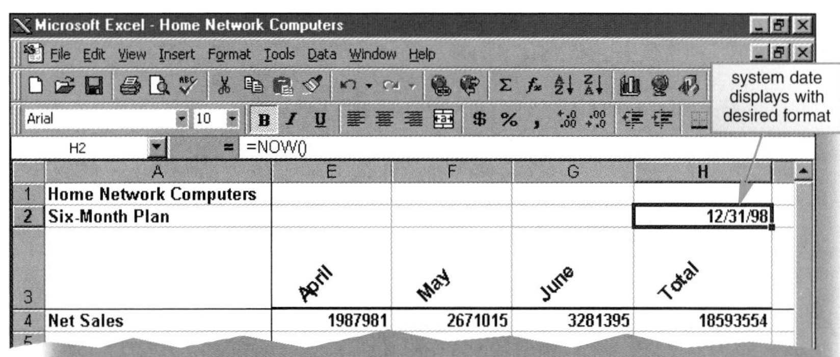

FIGURE 3-23

OtherWays

1. On Insert menu click Function, click Date & Time, click NOW, click OK button twice
2. Press CTRL+; (not a volatile date)
3. Press CTRL+SHIFT+# to format date to day-month-year

In Figure 3-23, the date displays right-aligned in the cell because Excel treats a date as a number. If you assign the **General format** (Excel's default format for numbers) to the date, the date displays as a number. For example, if the system time and date is 12:00 noon on January 21, 1998 and the cell containing the NOW function is assigned the General format, then Excel displays the following number in the cell:

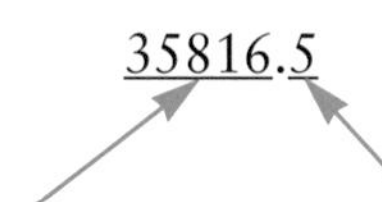

More About Date and Time

You can enter any date or time into a cell in a variety of formats such as 3/5/9, Feb-95, and 8:45 PM, and Excel will consider the entry to be a date. Excel automatically formats the entry in the same Date or Time style you enter it.

The whole number portion of the number (35816) represents the number of days since December 31, 1899. The decimal portion (.5) represents the time of day (12:00 noon). To assign the General format to a cell, click General in the Category list box in the Format Cells dialog box.

Absolute Versus Relative Addressing

The next step is to enter the formulas that calculate the projected monthly expenses in the range B7:G13 (Figure 3-1a on page E 3.5). The projected monthly expenses are based on the projected monthly net sales in row 4 and the assumptions in the range B16:B21. The formulas for each column are the same, except for the reference to monthly net sales in row 4, which varies according to the month (B4 for January, C4 for February, and so on). Thus, the formulas can be entered for January in column B and copied to columns C through G. The formulas for determining the projected January expenses and net income are shown in Table 3-3.

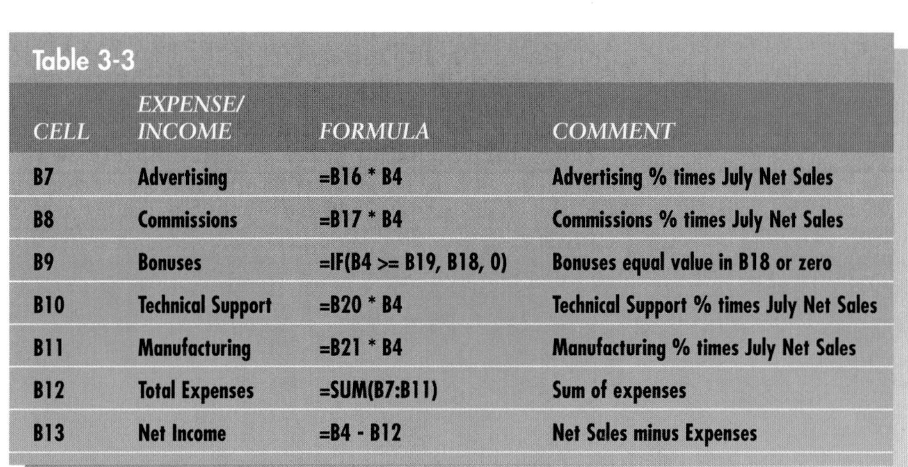

Table 3-3

CELL	EXPENSE/ INCOME	FORMULA	COMMENT
B7	Advertising	=B16 * B4	Advertising % times July Net Sales
B8	Commissions	=B17 * B4	Commissions % times July Net Sales
B9	Bonuses	=IF(B4 >= B19, B18, 0)	Bonuses equal value in B18 or zero
B10	Technical Support	=B20 * B4	Technical Support % times July Net Sales
B11	Manufacturing	=B21 * B4	Manufacturing % times July Net Sales
B12	Total Expenses	=SUM(B7:B11)	Sum of expenses
B13	Net Income	=B4 - B12	Net Sales minus Expenses

More *About* **Entering Fractions**

The forward slash (/) has multiple uses. For example, dates are often entered using the forward slash. In formulas, the forward slash represents division. What about fractions? To enter a fraction, such as ½, type .5 or 0 1/2 (i.e., type zero, followed by a space, followed by the number 1, followed by a forward slash, followed by the number 2). If you type 1/2, Excel will store the value in the cell as the date January 2.

If you enter the formulas from Table 3-3 on the previous page in column B of the worksheet and then copy them to columns C through G, Excel will adjust the cell references for each column automatically. Thus, after the copy, the February advertising expense in cell C7 would be =C16*C4. While the cell reference C4 (February Net Sales) is correct, the cell reference C16 references an empty cell. The formula for cell C7 should read =B16*C4 rather than =C16*C4. In this instance, you need a way to keep a cell reference in a formula the same when it is copied.

To keep a cell reference constant when it copies a formula or function, Excel uses a technique called **absolute referencing.** To specify an absolute reference in a formula, enter a dollar sign ($) before any column letters or row numbers you want to keep constant in formulas you plan to copy. For example, $B$16 is an absolute reference, while B16 is a relative reference. Both reference the same cell. The difference shows when they are copied. A formula using the absolute reference $B$16 instructs Excel to keep the cell reference B16 constant (absolute) as it copies the formula to a new location. A formula using the relative cell reference B16 instructs Excel to adjust the cell reference as it copies. Table 3-4 gives some additional examples of absolute references. A cell reference with only one dollar sign before either the column or the row is called a **mixed cell reference.**

More *About* **Absolute Referencing**

Absolute referencing is one of the most difficult worksheet concepts to understand. One point to keep in mind is that there is only one command, the Copy command, that is affected by an absolute cell reference. An absolute cell reference instructs Excel to keep the same cell reference as it copies a formula from one cell to another.

Table 3-4

CELL REFERENCE	*MEANING*
$B$16	Both column and row references remain the same when you copy this cell reference because they are absolute.
B$16	This cell reference is mixed. The column reference changes when you copy this cell reference to another column because it is relative. The row reference does not change because it is absolute.
$B16	This cell reference is mixed. The row reference changes when you copy this cell reference to another row because it is relative. The column reference does not change because it is absolute.
B16	Both column and row references are relative. When copied to another row and column, both the row and column in the cell reference are adjusted to reflect the new location.

Entering the January Advertising and Commissions Formulas

The following steps show how to enter the Advertising formula (=$B$16*B4) in cell B7 and the Commissions formula (=$B$17*B4) in cell B8 for the month of January using Point mode. To enter an absolute reference, you can type the $ or you can place the insertion point in or to the right of the cell reference you want to change to absolute and press F4.

To Enter Formulas Containing Absolute Cell References

1 Click cell B7 and then click the Edit Formula box in the Formula bar to begin a formula. Click cell B16. Press F4 to change B16 to an absolute reference in the formula. Type an asterisk (*) and then click cell B4.

*The formula =$B$16*B4 displays in cell B7 and in the formula bar. The formula result displays in the Formula palette (Figure 3-24).*

FIGURE 3-24

2 Click the OK button to complete the entry in cell B7. Click cell B8, click the Edit Formula box in the formula bar, and then click cell B17. Press F4 to change B17 to an absolute reference in the formula. Type an asterisk (*) and then click cell B4. Click the OK button.

Excel displays the results of the projected January advertising expense formula (1053782.485) in cell B7 and the projected January commissions expense formula (79697.835) in cell B8 (Figure 3-25).

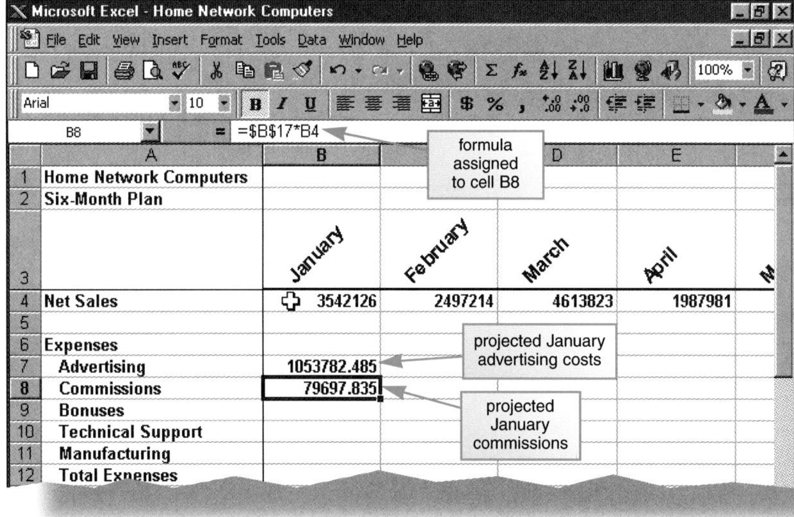

FIGURE 3-25

OtherWays

1. Enter formulas using keyboard

Making Decisions – The IF Function

If the projected January net sales in cell B4 is greater than or equal to the net sales for bonuses in cell B19, then the projected January bonuses in cell B9 is equal to the amount in cell B18 (50,000.00); otherwise, cell B9 is equal to zero. One way to assign the projected monthly bonuses in row 9 is to check each month individually to see if the projected net sales in row 4 equal or exceed the net sales for bonuses amount in cell B19 and, if so, then to enter 50,000 in row 9 for the corresponding month. Because the data in the worksheet changes each time you prepare the report or adjust the figures, however, you will find it preferable to have Excel assign the projected monthly bonus to the entries in the appropriate cells automatically. To do so, you need a formula or function in cell B9 that displays 50,000 or 0 (zero), depending on whether the projected January net sales in cell B4 is greater than or equal to or less than the number in cell B19.

Excel has the **IF function** that is useful when the value you want to assign to a cell is dependent on a logical test. A **logical test** is made up of two expressions and a relational operator. Each expression can be a cell reference, a number, text, a function, or a formula. A **comparison operator** is one of the following: > (greater than), < (less than), = (equal to), >= (greater than or equal to), <= (less than or equal to), or <> (not equal to). For example, assume you assign cell B9 the IF function:

=IF(B4>=$B$19,$B$18,0)

logical_test value_if_true value_if_false

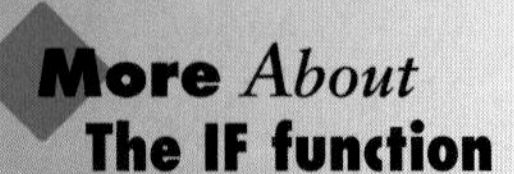

More *About*
The IF function

Assume you want to assign the formula =F4*G6 to the active cell, but display an empty cell (blank) when the formula is equal to zero. Try this: enter =IF(F4*G6 = 0, " ", F4*G6) into the cell. This IF function assigns the blank between the quotation marks to the cell when F4*G6 is equal to zero; otherwise, it assigns the formula to the cell.

If the projected January net sales in cell B4 is greater than or equal to the value in cell B19, then the value in cell B18, 50,000, displays in cell B9. If the projected January sales in cell B4 is less than the value in cell B19, then cell B9 displays a zero.

The general form of the IF function is:

=IF(logical_test, value_if_true, value_if_false)

The argument, value-if-true, is the value you want displayed in the cell when the logical test is true. The argument, value-if-false, is the value you want displayed in the cell when the logical test is false.

Table 3-5 lists the valid relational operators, their meaning, and examples of their use in IF functions.

Table 3-5

RELATIONAL OPERATOR	*MEANING*	*EXAMPLE*
=	Equal to	=IF(D25 = L17, C12 - F3, H5 + T3)
<	Less than	=IF(K57 * V5 < 214, $X$21, Y23 - 8)
>	Greater than	=IF(=SUM(T4:T9) > 300, 1, 0)
>=	Greater than or equal to	=IF(N15 >= $T$4, J4 * L5, 8)
<=	Less than or equal to	=IF(I5 + K5 <= 10, $J$21, 12 * K4)
<>	Not equal to	=IF(Y4 <> H$5, "Yes", "No")

The following steps assign the IF function =IF(B4>=$B$19,$B$18,0) to cell B9. This function will determine whether or not the worksheet assigns bonuses for January.

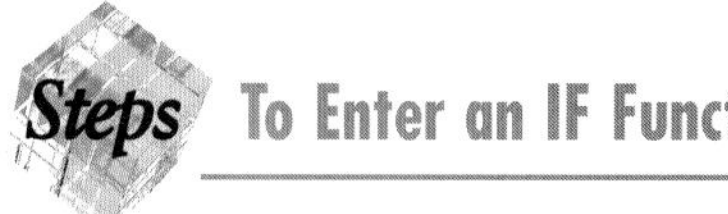

To Enter an IF Function

1 **Click cell B9, and then type** `=if(b4>=$b$19,$b$18,0` **in the cell. Click the Edit Formula box in the formula bar to display the IF Formula palette to view the function arguments.**

Excel displays the IF Formula palette that shows the logical_test, value_if_true, and value_if_false (Figure 3-26). The IF Formula palette also shows the results of each part of the IF function and the value that will be assigned to the cell based on the logical test.

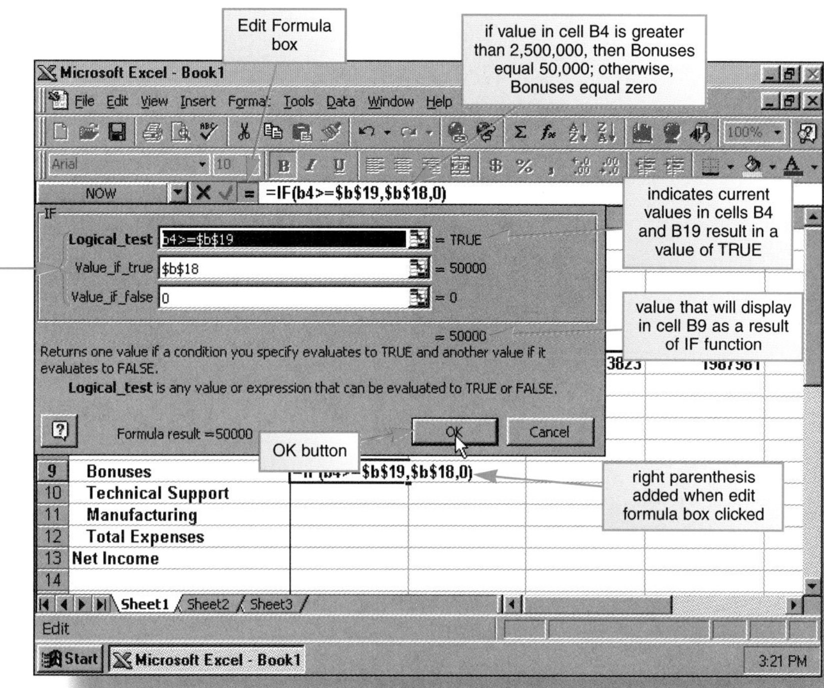

FIGURE 3-26

2 **Click the OK button.**

Excel displays 50000 in cell B9 because the value in cell B4 (3542126) is greater than or equal to the value in cell B19 (2,500,000.00) (Figure 3-27). Recall that it is not necessary to type the closing parenthesis when you enter a function.

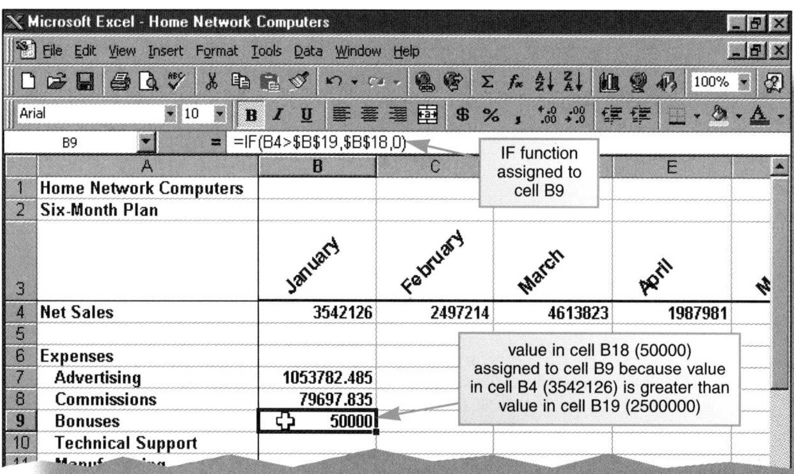

FIGURE 3-27

OtherWays

1. On Standard toolbar click Paste Function button, click Logical category, click IF

In Step 1, you could have clicked the Enter box or pressed the ENTER key to complete the entry rather than clicking the Edit Formula box. The Edit Formula box was clicked so you could see the IF function arguments on the Formula palette before assigning the function to cell B9.

The value that Excel displays in cell B9 depends on the values assigned to cells B4, B18, and B19. For example, if the projected sales in cell B4 is reduced below 2,500,000.00, then the IF function in cell B9 will change the display to zero. Increasing the net sales for bonuses in cell B19 has the same effect.

Entering the Remaining Projected Expense and Net Income Formulas for January

The projected January technical support expense in cell B10 is equal to the technical support assumption in cell B20 (31.50%) times the projected January net sales in cell B4. Likewise, the projected January manufacturing expenses in cell B11 is equal to the manufacturing assumption in cell B21 (21.65%) times the projected January net sales. The projected total expenses for January in cell B12 is equal to the sum of the January expenses in the range B7:B11. The projected January net income in cell B13 is equal to the projected January net sales in cell B4 minus the projected total January expenses in cell B12. The following steps enter the four formulas into the worksheet.

More About Freezing Formula Values

You can freeze the value of a formula by replacing the formula with the frozen value. Do the following: (1) click the cell with the formula; (2) press F2 or click in the formula bar; (3) press F9 to display the value in the formula bar; (4) click the Enter box or press the ENTER key.

TO ENTER THE REMAINING PROJECTED EXPENSE AND NET INCOME FORMULAS FOR JANUARY

Step 1: Click cell B10. Type `=$b$20*b4` and then press the DOWN ARROW key.
Step 2: Type `=$b$21*b4` and then press the DOWN ARROW key.
Step 3: Click the AutoSum button on the Standard toolbar twice.
Step 4: Click cell B13. Type `=b4-b12` and then click the Enter box or press the ENTER key.

The projected January technical support, manufacturing, total expenses, and net income display in cells B10, B11, B12, and B13, respectively (Figure 3-28a).

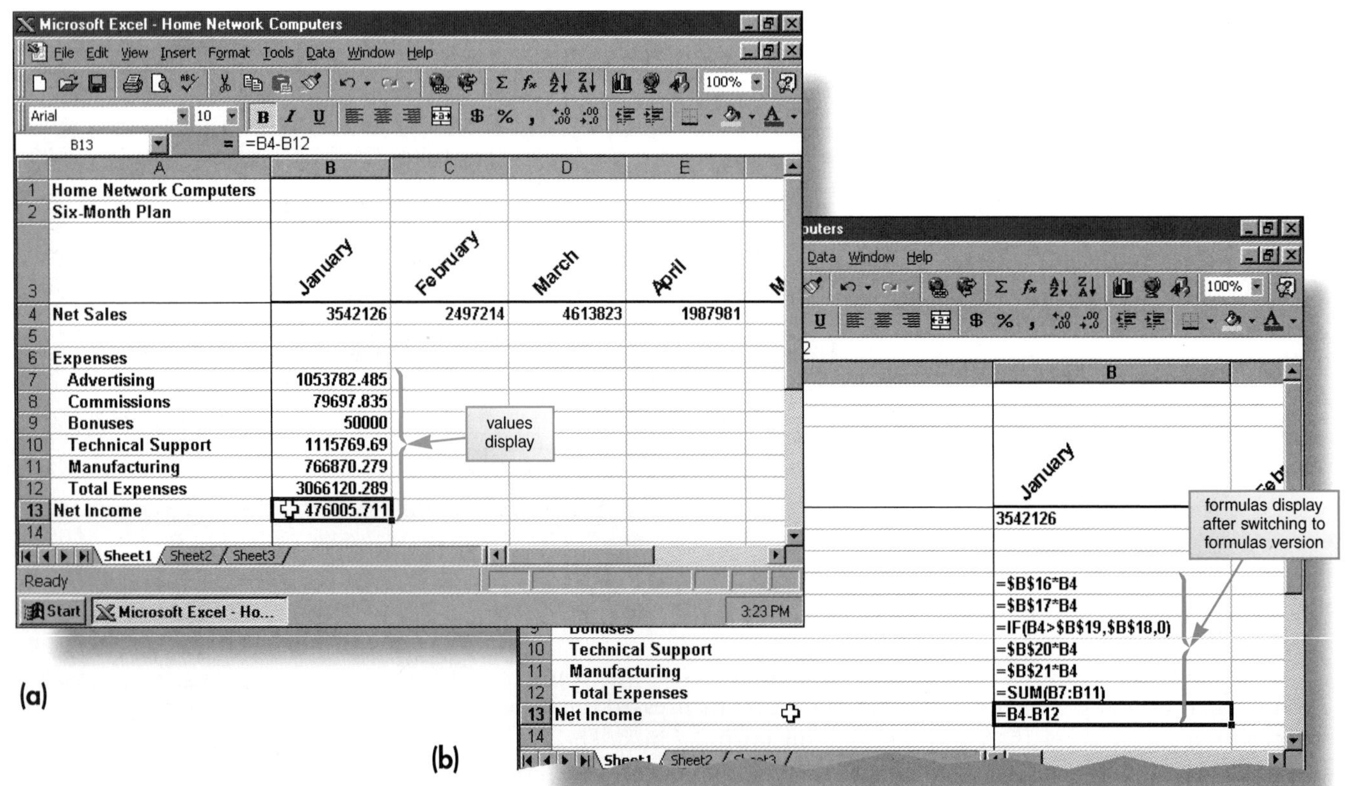

FIGURE 3-28

You can view the formulas in the worksheet by pressing CTRL+`. The display changes from Figure 3-28a to Figure 3-28b. Press CTRL+` to display the values again.

Copying the January Projected Expenses and Totals Formulas to the Other Months

To copy the projected expenses and totals for January to the other five months, complete the following steps using the fill handle.

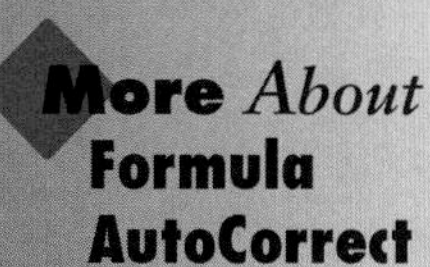

More About Formula AutoCorrect

When you enter a formula, Excel automatically checks for and corrects the 15 most common formula building errors, including double operators, double parentheses and transposed cell references.

To Copy the January Projected Expenses and Totals Using the Fill Handle

1. **Select the range B7:B13. Point to the fill handle near the lower-right corner of cell B13.**

   The range B7:B13 is selected and the mouse pointer changes to a cross hair (Figure 3-29).

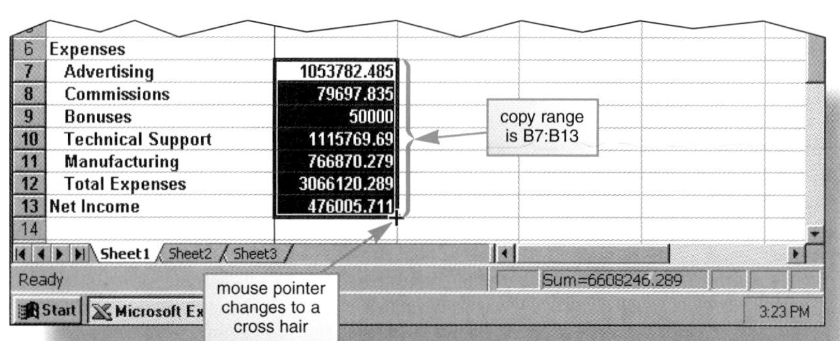

FIGURE 3-29

2. **Drag the fill handle to select the paste area C7:G13.**

   Excel copies the formulas in the range B7:B13 to the paste area C7:G13. The last three columns of the paste area (columns E through G) display as shown in Figure 3-30.

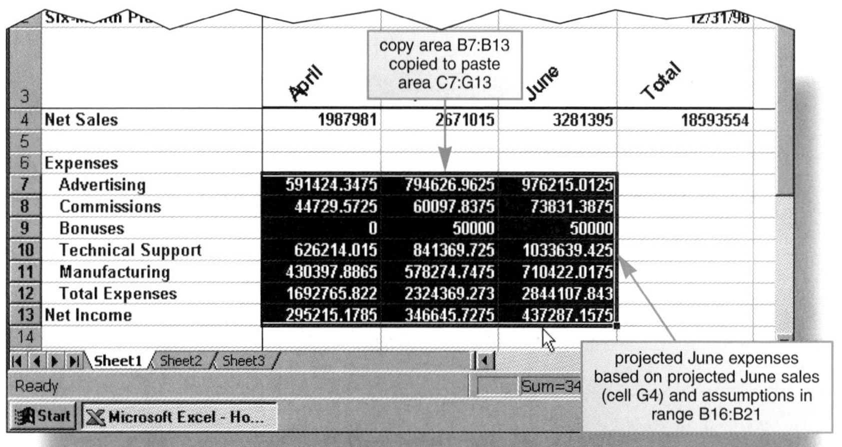

FIGURE 3-30

Determining the Projected Total Expenses by Category and Total Net Income

Follow the steps below to determine the total projected expenses by category and total net income in the range H7:H13.

TO DETERMINE THE PROJECTED TOTAL EXPENSES BY CATEGORY AND TOTAL NET INCOME

Step 1: Select the range H7:H13.
Step 2: Click the AutoSum button on the Standard toolbar.

The projected total expenses by category and total net income display in the range H7:H13 (Figure 3-31 on the next page).

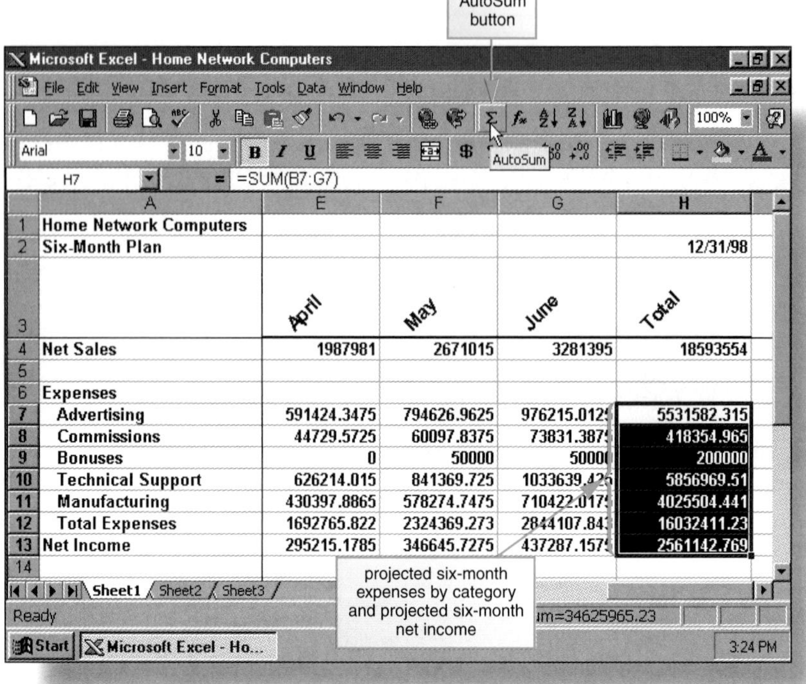

FIGURE 3-31

Unfreezing Worksheet Titles and Saving the Workbook

All the text, data, and formulas have been entered into the worksheet. The next step is to improve the appearance of the worksheet. Before modifying the worksheet's appearance, complete the following steps to unfreeze the titles and save the workbook under its current file name, Home Network Computers.

TO UNFREEZE THE WORKSHEET TITLES AND SAVE THE WORKBOOK

Step 1: Click cell B4 to clear the range selection from the previous steps.
Step 2: Click Window on the menu bar and then point to Unfreeze Panes (Figure 3-32).
Step 3: Click Unfreeze Panes.
Step 4: Click the Save button on the Standard toolbar.

Excel unfreezes the titles so that column A scrolls off the screen when you scroll to the right and the first three rows scroll off the screen when you scroll down. The latest changes to the workbook are saved to disk.

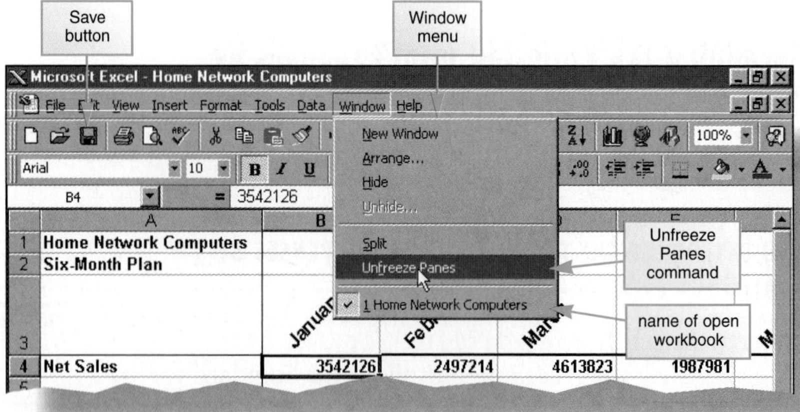

FIGURE 3-32

Formatting the Worksheet

The worksheet in Figure 3-32 determines the projected monthly expenses and net incomes for the six-month period. Its appearance is uninteresting, however, even though some minimal formatting was done earlier. This section will complete the formatting of the worksheet to make the numbers easier to read and to emphasize the titles, assumptions, categories, and totals (Figure 3-33).

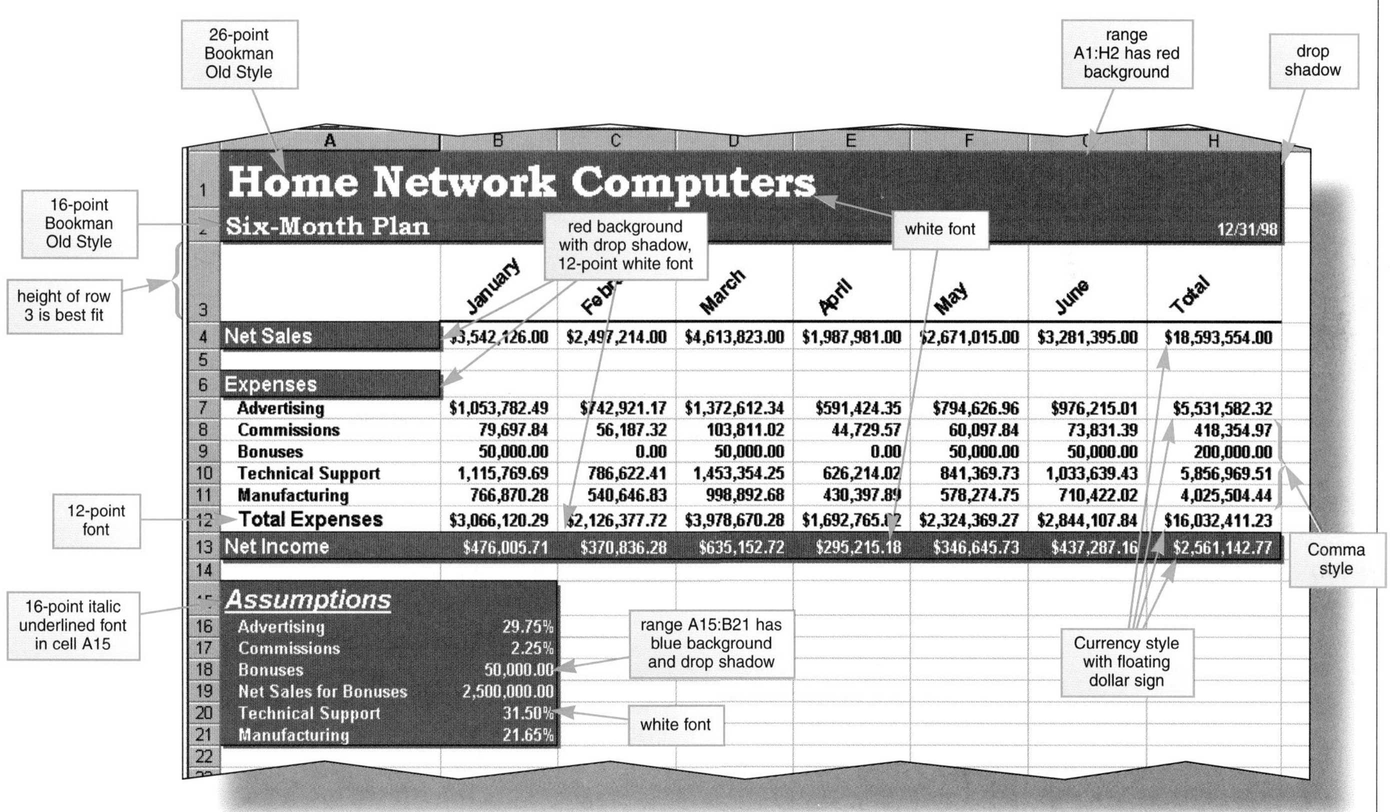

	A	B	C	D	E	F	G	H
1	Home Network Computers							
2	Six-Month Plan							12/31/98
3		January	Febr	March	April	May	June	Total
4	Net Sales	$3,542,126.00	$2,497,214.00	$4,613,823.00	$1,987,981.00	$2,671,015.00	$3,281,395.00	$18,593,554.00
5								
6	Expenses							
7	Advertising	$1,053,782.49	$742,921.17	$1,372,612.34	$591,424.35	$794,626.96	$976,215.01	$5,531,582.32
8	Commissions	79,697.84	56,187.32	103,811.02	44,729.57	60,097.84	73,831.39	418,354.97
9	Bonuses	50,000.00	0.00	50,000.00	0.00	50,000.00	50,000.00	200,000.00
10	Technical Support	1,115,769.69	786,622.41	1,453,354.25	626,214.02	841,369.73	1,033,639.43	5,856,969.51
11	Manufacturing	766,870.28	540,646.83	998,892.68	430,397.89	578,274.75	710,422.02	4,025,504.44
12	Total Expenses	$3,066,120.29	$2,126,377.72	$3,978,670.28	$1,692,765.[illegible]	$2,324,369.27	$2,844,107.84	$16,032,411.23
13	Net Income	$476,005.71	$370,836.28	$635,152.72	$295,215.18	$346,645.73	$437,287.16	$2,561,142.77
14								
15	Assumptions							
16	Advertising	29.75%						
17	Commissions	2.25%						
18	Bonuses	50,000.00						
19	Net Sales for Bonuses	2,500,000.00						
20	Technical Support	31.50%						
21	Manufacturing	21.65%						

FIGURE 3-33

Formatting the Numbers

First, format the projected monthly net sales and expenses as follows:

1. Assign the Currency style with a floating dollar sign to rows 4, 7, 12, and 13.
2. Assign a customized Comma style to rows 8 through 11.

To assign a Currency style with a floating dollar sign, you must use the Format Cells command rather than the Currency Style button on the Formatting toolbar, which assigns a fixed dollar sign. The Comma style also must be assigned using the Format Cells command, because the Comma Style button on the Formatting toolbar displays a dash (-) when a cell has a value of zero. The specifications for this worksheet call for displaying a value of zero as 0.00 (see cell E9 in Figure 3-33), rather than as a dash. To create a Comma style using the Format Cells command, you must assign a Numbers style with a 1,000 separator. The steps on the next page format the numbers in rows 4 and 7 through 13.

To Assign Formats to the Projected Net Sales, Expenses, and Net Income

1 **Select the range B4:H4. While holding down the CTRL key, select the nonadjacent ranges B7:H7 and B12:H13. Release the CTRL key. Right-click the selected range and then point to Format Cells.**

The selected range is highlighted and the shortcut menu displays as shown in Figure 3-34.

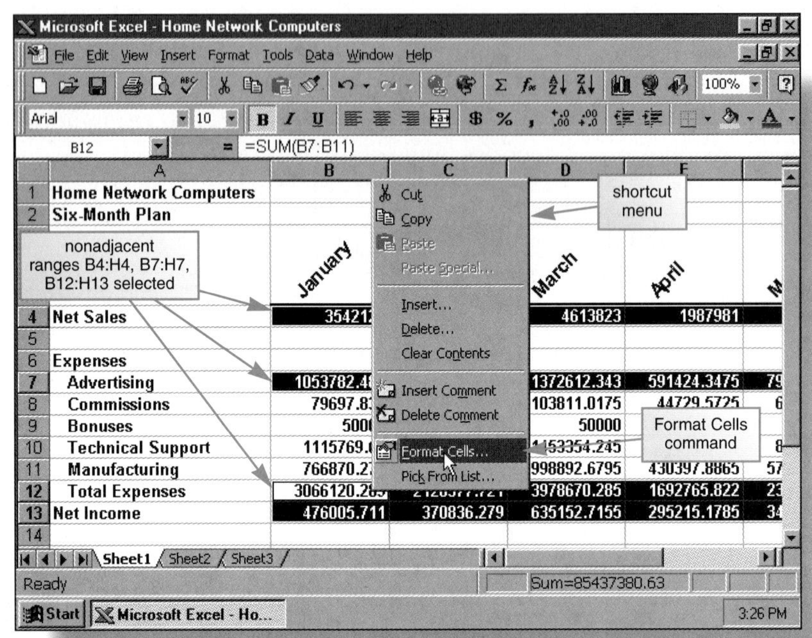

FIGURE 3-34

2 **Click Format Cells. When the Format Cells dialog box displays, click the Number tab, click Currency in the Category list box, select two decimal places in the Decimal places box, click $ in the Symbol list box to ensure a dollar sign displays, and click ($1,234.10) in the Negative numbers list box. Point to the OK button.**

The cell format settings display on the Number sheet in the Format Cells dialog box as shown in Figure 3-35.

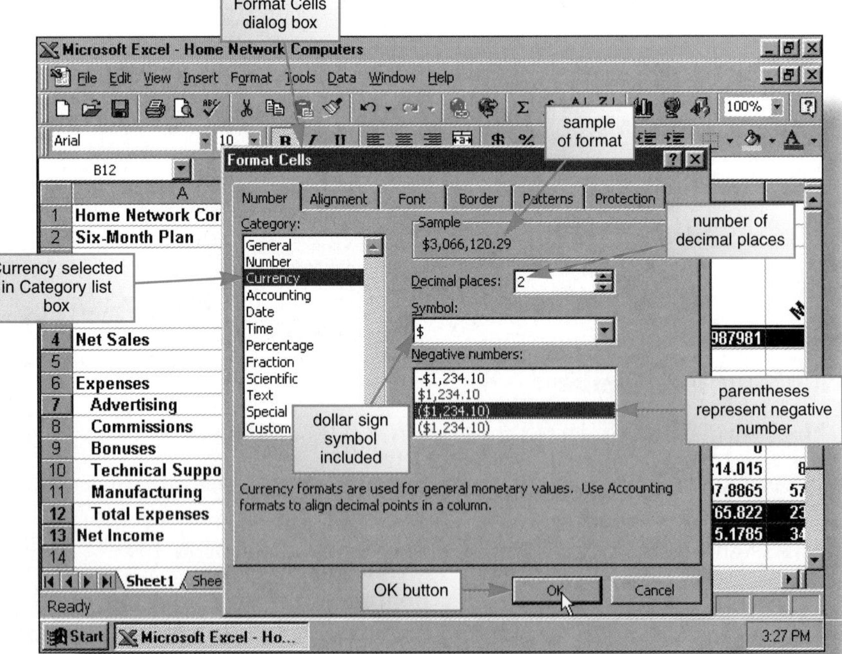

FIGURE 3-35

3 **Click the OK button.**

4 **Select the range B8:H11. Right-click the selected range. Click Format Cells on the shortcut menu. Click Currency in the Category list box, click 2 in the Decimal places box, click None in the Symbol list box so a dollar sign does not display, click (1,234.10) in the Negative numbers list box.**

The format settings display on the Number sheet in the Format Cells dialog box as shown in Figure 3-36.

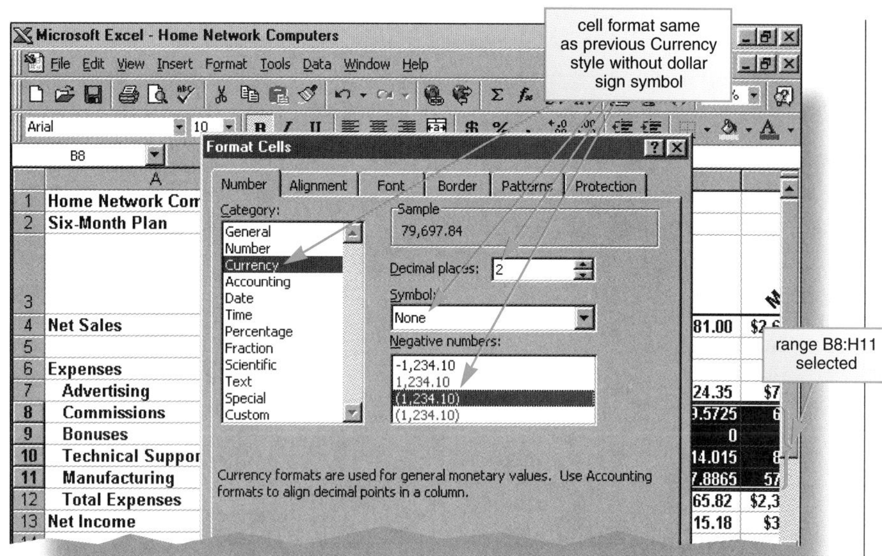

FIGURE 3-36

5 **Click the OK button.**

The cell formats display as shown in Figure 3-37.

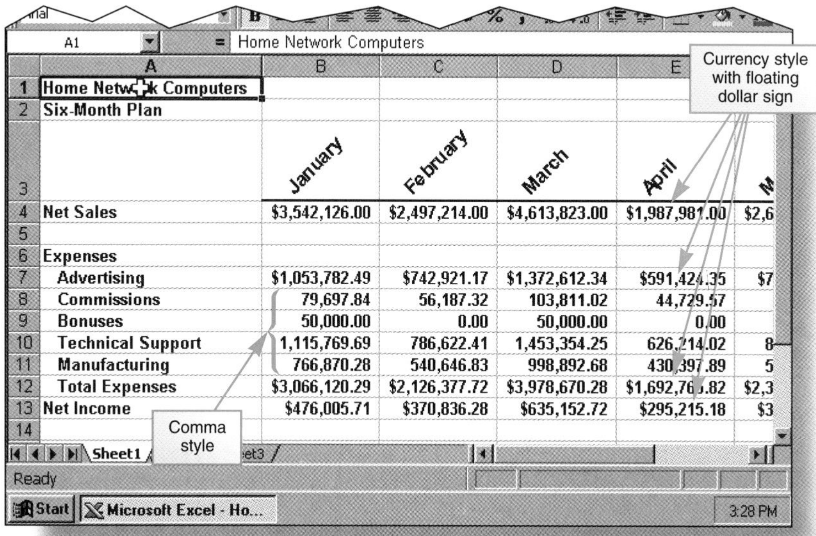

FIGURE 3-37

Instead of selecting Currency in the Category list box in Step 4 (Figure 3-36), you could have selected Accounting to generate the same format. You should review the formats available under each category title. Thousands of combinations of format styles can be created using the options in the Format Cells dialog box.

The next step is to format the titles at the top of the worksheet.

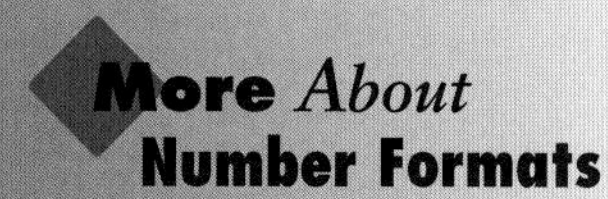

To view all the number formats available with Excel, click Custom in the Category list box on the Number tab in the Format Cells dialog box.

Formatting the Worksheet Titles

To emphasize the worksheet titles in cells A1 and A2, the font type, size, and color are changed as described in the steps on the next page.

To Format the Worksheet Titles

1 **Select the range A1:A2. Click the Font box arrow on the Formatting toolbar. Scroll down and point to Bookman Old Style (or a similar font).**

The Font list displays (Figure 3-38).

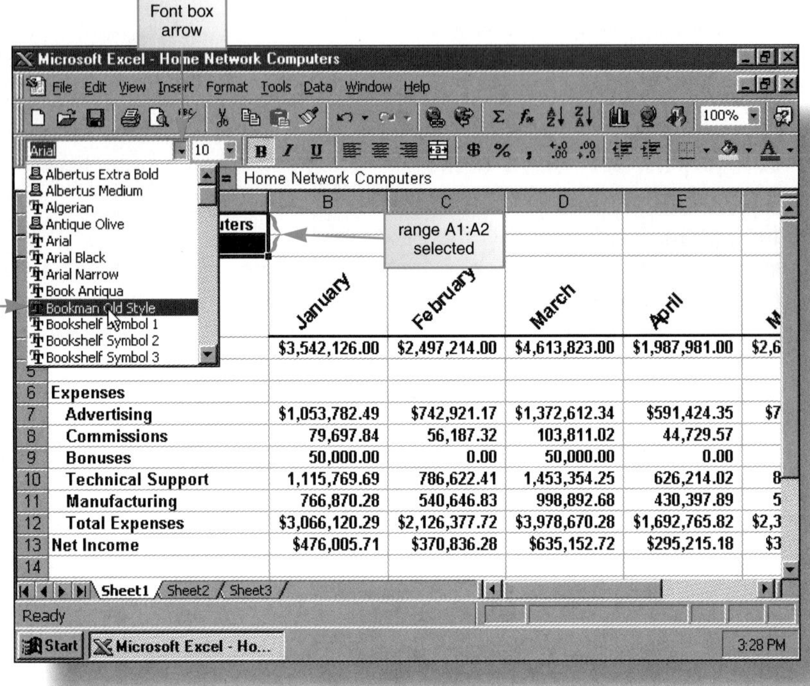

FIGURE 3-38

2 **Click Bookman Old Style. Click cell A1. Click the Font Size box arrow on the Formatting toolbar and then click 26 in the Font Size list box. Click cell A2. Click the Font Size box arrow on the Formatting toolbar and then click 16 in the Font Size list box.**

The titles in the range A1:A2 display (Figure 3-39).

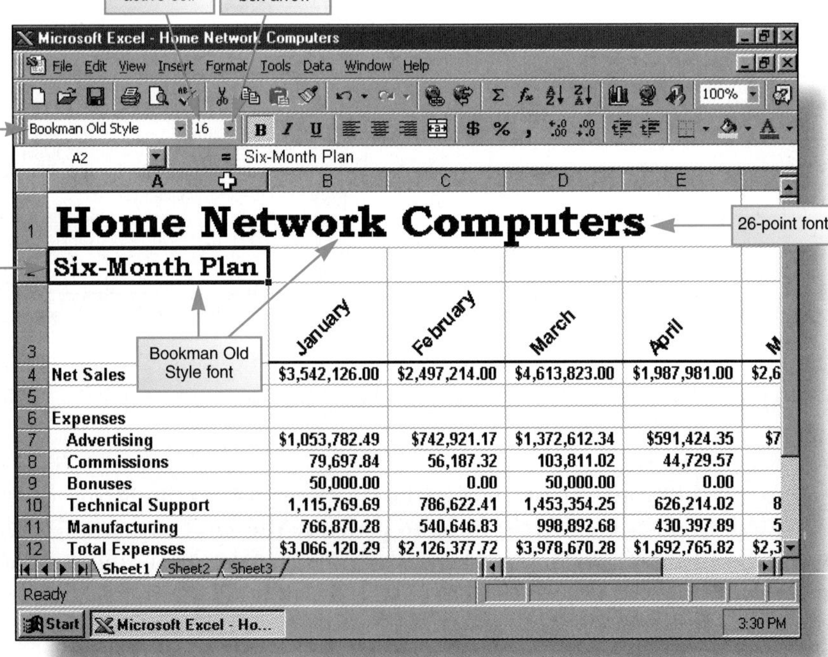

FIGURE 3-39

Select the range A1:H2. Click the Fill Color button arrow on the Formatting toolbar. Click red (column 1, row 3 on the Fill Color palette). Click the Font Color button arrow on the Formatting toolbar. Point to white (column 8, row 5 on the Font Color palette).

Excel assigns a red background to the selected range and the Font Color palette displays as shown in Figure 3-40.

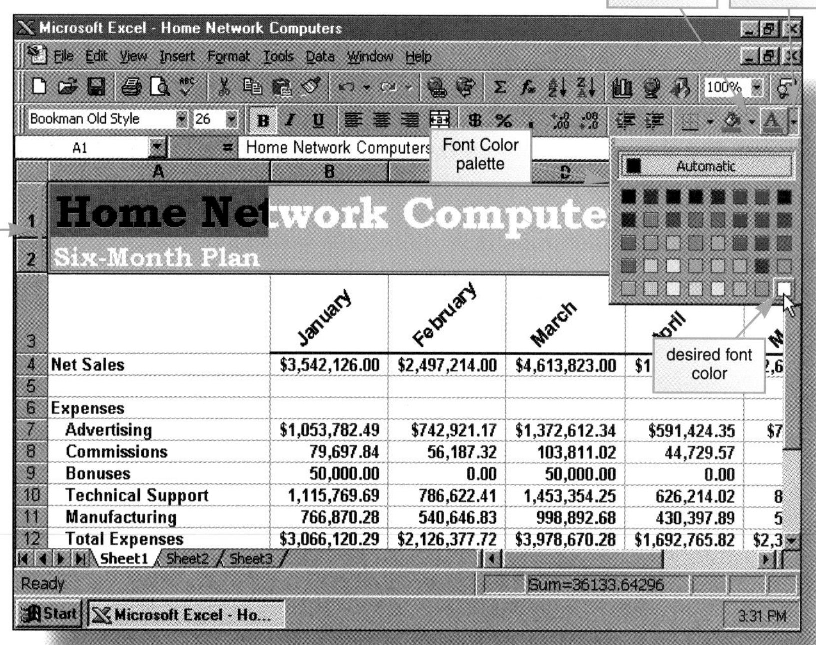

FIGURE 3-40

4 Click white.

Excel changes the color of the font in the range A1:H2 from black to white (see Figure 3-33 on page E 3.31).

OtherWays

1. Right-click range, click Format Cells, click Patterns tab to color background or click Font tab to color font

The next step is to add a drop shadow to the selected range A1:H2 using the Drawing toolbar. First, the Drawing toolbar must display on the screen. The following section describes how to display and dock an inactive (hidden) toolbar.

Displaying the Drawing Toolbar

Excel has more than 200 toolbar buttons, most of which display on 13 built-in toolbars. Two of these 13 built-in toolbars are the Standard toolbar and Formatting toolbar, which usually display at the top of the screen. Another built-in toolbar is the Drawing toolbar. The **Drawing toolbar** provides tools that can simplify adding lines, boxes, and other geometric figures to a worksheet. You also can create customized toolbars containing the buttons that you use often.

You can use the shortcut menu or the Toolbars command on the View menu to display or hide any one of the 13 toolbars. The Drawing toolbar also can be displayed or hidden by clicking the Drawing button on the Standard toolbar. Perform the steps on the next page to display the Drawing toolbar.

More About Color Palettes

If your Color palette has fewer colors than shown on the Color palette in Figure 3-40, then your system is using a different Color palette setting. The figures in this book were created using High Color (16 bit). To check your Color palette setting, minimize all applications, right-click the desktop, click Properties, click the Settings tab, and locate the Color palette box. If you change the settings, you must restart Windows 95.

More About Buttons

You can think of buttons as being assigned macros that execute whenever they are clicked.

To Display the Drawing Toolbar

1 Click the Drawing button on the Standard toolbar.

The Drawing toolbar displays (Figure 3-41). Excel displays the Drawing toolbar on the screen in the same location and with the same shape as it displayed the last time it was used.

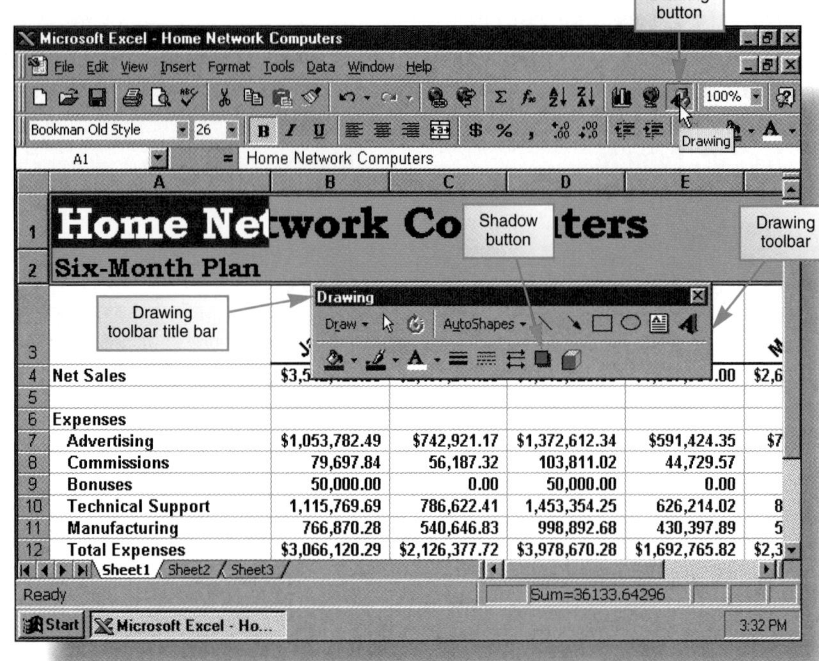

FIGURE 3-41

OtherWays

1. Right-click Standard or Formatting toolbar, click Drawing
2. On View menu point to Toolbars, click Drawing

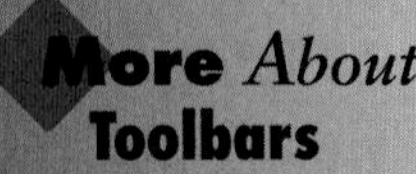

More About Toolbars

You can create your own toolbar and assemble the buttons you want on it by using the Customize command on the shortcut menu that displays when you right-click a toolbar.

Moving and Docking a Toolbar

The Drawing toolbar in Figure 3-41 is called a **floating toolbar** because it displays in its own window with a title bar and can be moved anywhere in the Excel window. You move the toolbar by pointing to the toolbar title bar or to a blank area within the toolbar window (not on a button) and then dragging the toolbar to its new location. As with any window, you also can resize the toolbar by dragging the toolbar window borders. To hide a floating toolbar, click the Close button on the toolbar title bar.

Sometimes a floating toolbar gets in the way no matter where you move it or how you resize it. Hiding the toolbar is one solution. At times, however, you will want to keep the toolbar available for use. For this reason, Excel allows you to position toolbars on the edge of its window. If you drag the toolbar close to the edge of the window, Excel positions the toolbar in a **toolbar dock**.

Excel has four toolbar docks, one on each of the four sides of the window. You can add as many toolbars to a dock as you want. However, each time you dock a toolbar, the Excel window slightly decreases in size to compensate for the room taken up by the toolbar. The following steps show how to dock the Drawing toolbar at the bottom of the screen below the scroll bar.

To Dock a Toolbar at the Bottom of the Screen

1. **Point to the Drawing toolbar title bar or to a blank area in the Drawing toolbar.**

2. **Drag the Drawing toolbar over the status bar at the bottom of the screen.**

   Excel docks the Drawing toolbar at the bottom of the screen (Figure 3-42).

Excel window shrinks when toolbar docked

Drawing toolbar docked horizontally across bottom of window

FIGURE 3-42

Compare Figure 3-42 to Figure 3-41. Excel automatically resizes the Drawing toolbar to fit across the window and between the scroll bar and status bar. Also notice that the heavy window border that surrounded the floating toolbar has changed to a light border. To move a toolbar to any of the other three docks, drag the toolbar from its current position to the desired side of the window.

Adding a Drop Shadow to the Title Area

With the Drawing toolbar docked at the bottom of the screen, the next step is to add the drop shadow to the range A1:H2.

To Add a Drop Shadow

1. **With the range A1:H2 selected, click the Shadow button on the Drawing toolbar. Point to the button titled Shadow Style 14 (column 2, row 4 on the Shadow palette).**

   Excel displays a palette of drop shadows with varying shadow depths (Figure 3-43).

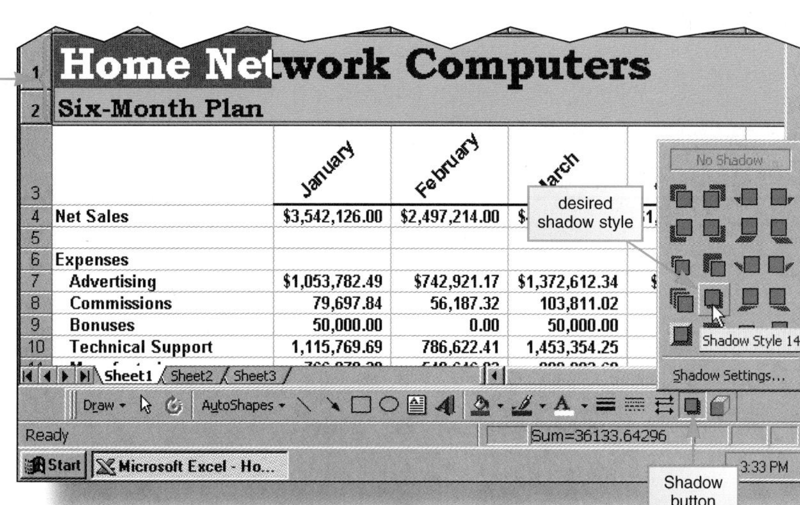

FIGURE 3-43

Click the Shadow Style 14 button. Click cell A5.

Excel adds a drop shadow to the range A1:H2 (Figure 3-44).

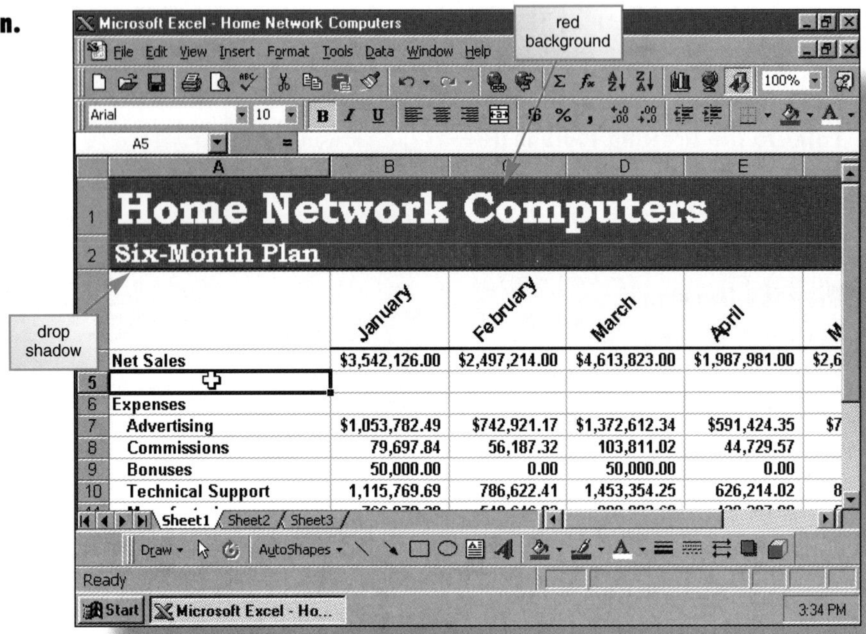

FIGURE 3-44

More About Drop Shadows

To remove an unwanted drop shadow, click it so the handles appear on the drop shadow, and then press the DELETE key. Also, a drop shadow is a shape and not a format. Thus, if you used the Format Painter button to apply formats from a range with a drop shadow, then the drop shadow will not be copied.

When you add a drop shadow to a range of cells, Excel also selects the drop shadow and surrounds it with black handles. To deselect the drop shadow, select any cell, as you did in Step 2 above.

Formatting the Category Row Titles and Net Income Row

The specifications in Figure 3-33 on page E 3.31 require a font size of 12 in cells A4, A6, A12, and A13. Cells A4, A6, and the range A13:H13 also must be assigned the same background color, font color, and drop shadow as those assigned to the worksheet titles in the range A1:H2. In Figure 3-45 you will notice that the last background and font colors selected and assigned to the worksheet titles display on the Fill Color and Font Color buttons on the Formatting toolbar. This means that, after you select a range to format, you simply click the Fill Color button to assign the red background to the range and click the Font Color button to assign the color white to the font in the range.

The following steps change the font size in cells A4, A6, A12, and A13; and then add the red background color, white font color, and drop shadows to cells A4, A6, and the range A13:H13.

More About Nonadjacent Ranges

One of the more difficult tasks to learn is selecting nonadjacent ranges. To complete this task, do not hold down the CTRL key when you select the first range because Excel will consider the current active cell to be the first selection. Once the first range is selected, hold down the CTRL key and drag through the ranges. If a desired range is not in the window, use the scroll arrows to move the window over the range. It is not necessary to hold down the CTRL key while you move the window.

To Change Font Size, Add Background and Font Colors, and Add Drop Shadows to Nonadjacent Selections

1. **Click cell A4. While holding down the CTRL key, click cells A6, A12, and A13. Click the Font Size box arrow on the Formatting toolbar and then click 12 in the Font Size list box.**

   The font size in cells A4, A6, A12, and A13 changes to 12 point.

2. **Click cell A4. While holding down the CTRL key, click cell A6 and then select the range A13:H13. Click the Fill Color button on the Formatting toolbar to assign the red background color to the nonadjacent range. Click the Font Color button on the Formatting toolbar to change the font of the selected range to white. Click the Shadow button on the Drawing toolbar and point to the Shadow Style 14 button.**

   The nonadjacent ranges are selected and the background and font colors are changed (Figure 3-45).

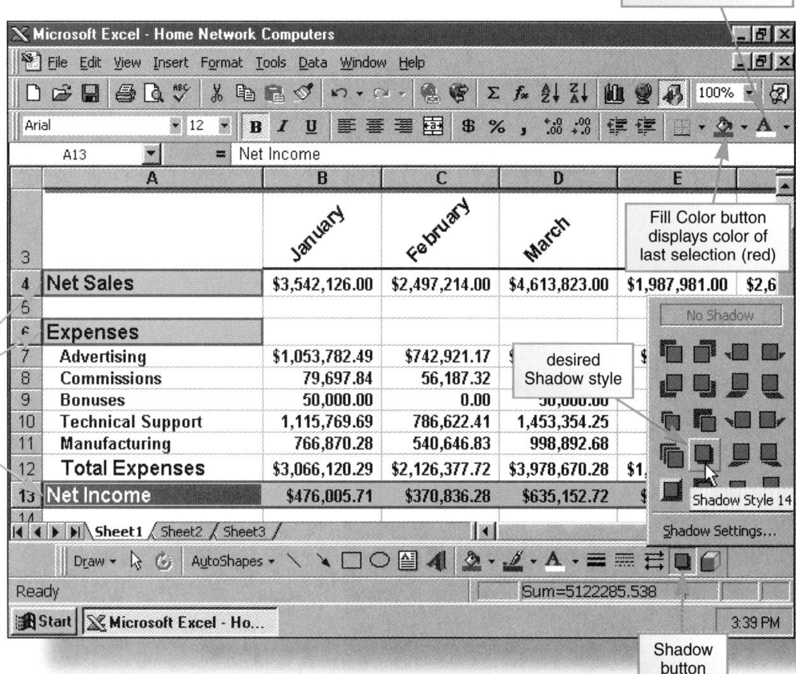

FIGURE 3-45

3. **Click the Shadow Style 14 button.**

   Excel adds a drop shadow to cells A4, A6, and the range A13:H13 (Figure 3-46).

4. **Click cell A5.**

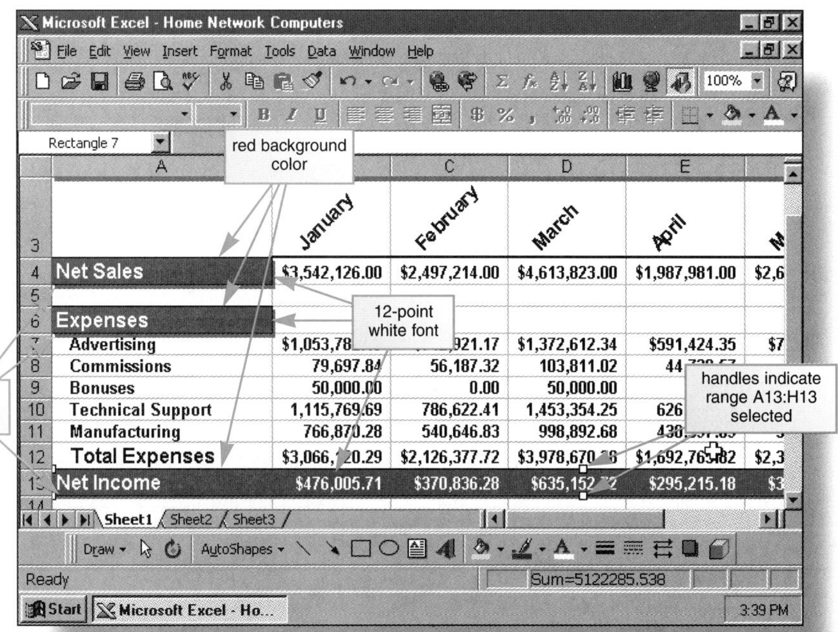

FIGURE 3-46

An alternative to formatting all three areas at once is to select each one separately and apply the formats.

Formatting the Assumptions Table

The last step to improving the appearance of the worksheet is to format the Assumptions table in the range A15:B21. The specifications in Figure 3-33 on page E 3.31 require a 16-point italic underlined font for the title in cell A15. The range A15:B21 has a red background color with a white font and a drop shadow surrounds it. The following steps format the Assumptions table.

To Format the Assumptions Table

1. **Click cell A15. Click the Font Size box arrow on the Formatting toolbar and then click 16. Click the Italic button and then the Underline button on the Formatting toolbar. Select the range A15:B21. Click the Fill Color button arrow on the Formatting toolbar. Point to blue (column 6, row 2 on the Fill Color palette).**

   The table heading Assumptions displays with the new formats. The range A15:B21 is selected and the Fill Color palette displays (Figure 3-47).

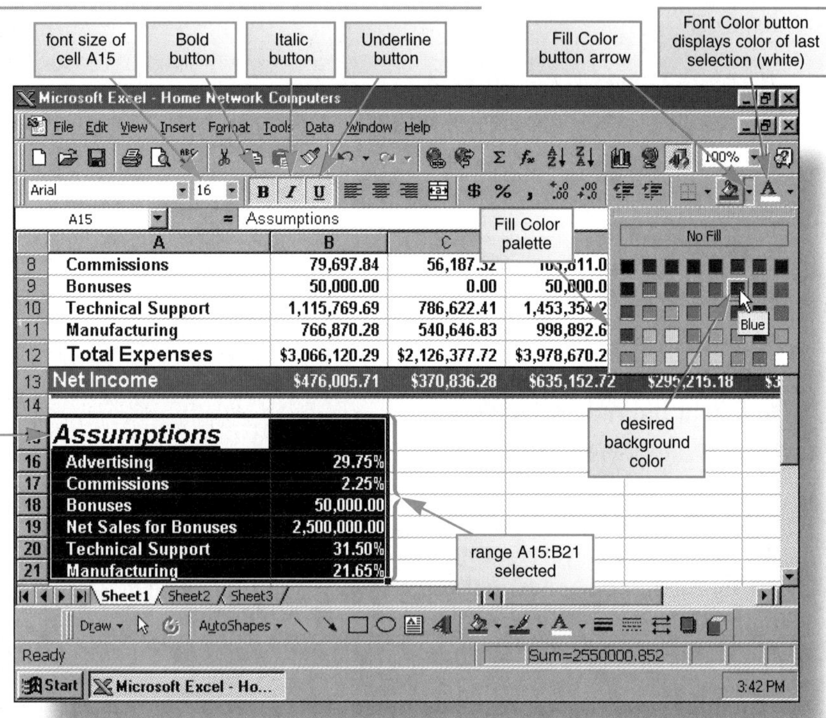

FIGURE 3-47

2. **Click blue on the Fill Color palette. Click the Font Color button on the Formatting toolbar. Click the Shadow button on the Drawing toolbar. Click the Shadow Style 14 button on the Shadow palette. Select cell D21.**

   The Assumptions table displays as shown in Figure 3-48.

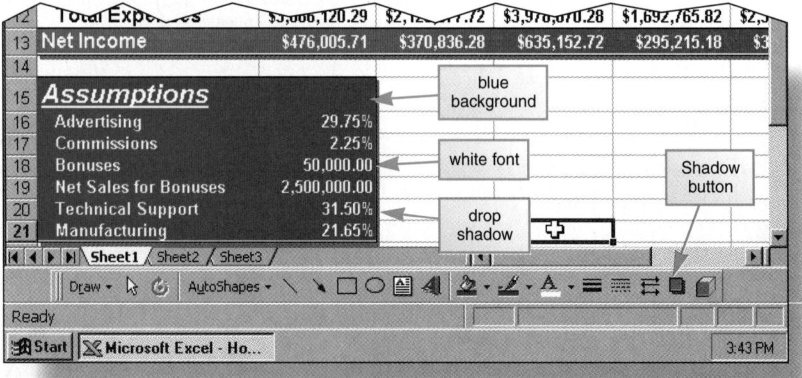

FIGURE 3-48

When you assign the **italic** font style to a cell, Excel slants the characters slightly to the right as shown in cell A15 in Figure 3-48.

Hiding a Toolbar

As shown in the first step below, you can hide the Drawing toolbar by clicking the Drawing button on the Standard toolbar. The second step saves the workbook.

Steps To Hide the Drawing Toolbar

1. **Click the Drawing button on the Standard toolbar.**

   The Drawing toolbar no longer displays on the screen (Figure 3-49).

2. **Click the Save button on the Standard toobar.**

Drawing button

Microsoft Excel - Home Network Computers

	A	B	C	D	E
8	Commissions	79,697.84	56,187.32	103,811.02	44,729.57
9	Bonuses	50,000.00	0.00	50,000.00	0.00
10	Technical Support	1,115,769.69	786,622.41	1,453,354.25	626,214.02
11	Manufacturing	766,870.28	540,646.83	998,892.68	430,397.89
12	Total Expenses	$3,066,120.29	$2,126,377.72	$3,978,670.28	$1,692,765.82
13	Net Income	$476,005.71	$370,836.28	$635,152.72	$295,215.18
15	Assumptions				
16	Advertising	29.75%			
17	Commissions	2.25%			
18	Bonuses	50,000.00			
19	Net Sales for Bonuses	2,500,000.00			
20	Technical Support	31.50%			
21	Manufacturing	21.65%			

Drawing toolbar no longer displays

FIGURE 3-49

OtherWays

1. Right-click toolbar, on shortcut menu click toolbar name
2. On View menu click Toolbars, click toolbar name

The worksheet is complete. The next step is to create the 3-D Column chart for the Six-Month Plan.

Creating a 3-D Column Chart on a Chart Sheet

A 3-D Column chart is used to show trends and comparisons. Each column emphasizes the magnitude of the value it represents. The 3-D Column chart in Figure 3-50 compares the projected net income for each of the six months. The 3-D Column chart makes it easy to see that March has the greatest projected net income, over $600,000.00.

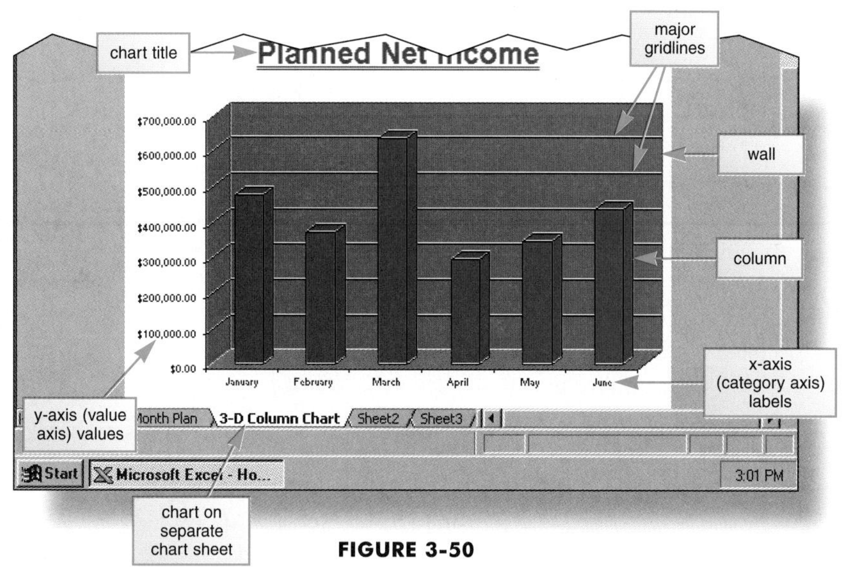

FIGURE 3-50

Drawing the 3-D Column Chart

The ranges of the worksheet to chart are B3:G3 and B13:G13 (Figure 3-51). The month names in the range B3:G3 are used as column labels and display at the bottom of the 3-D Column chart. These month names are called **category names.** The range B13:G13 contains the data that determines the magnitude of the columns. The values in this range are called the **data series.** Because six category names and six numbers are included in the range to chart, the 3-D Column chart contains six columns.

The following steps illustrate how to create a 3-D Column chart on a separate chart sheet.

To Draw a 3-D Column Chart on a Chart Sheet

1. **Select the range B3:G3. Hold down the CTRL key and select the nonadjacent range B13:G13. Click the Chart Wizard button on the Standard toolbar. Click Column in the Chart type list box. Click the 3-D Column chart (column 1, row 2) in the Chart sub-type area. Point to the Next button.**

   Excel displays the Chart Wizard – Step 1 of 4 – Chart Type dialog box with the selections highlighted (Figure 3-51).

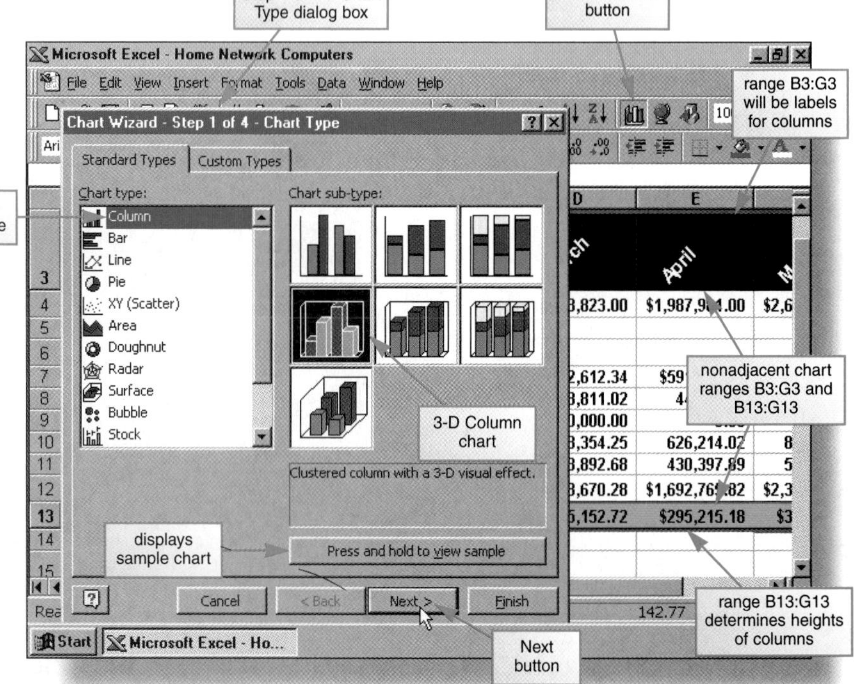

FIGURE 3-51

2. **Click the Next button.**

   Excel displays the Chart Wizard – Step 2 of 4 – Chart Source Data dialog box showing a sample of the 3-D Column chart (Figure 3-52). The range to chart, called the data range, displays below the sample chart. If necessary, you can change the range.

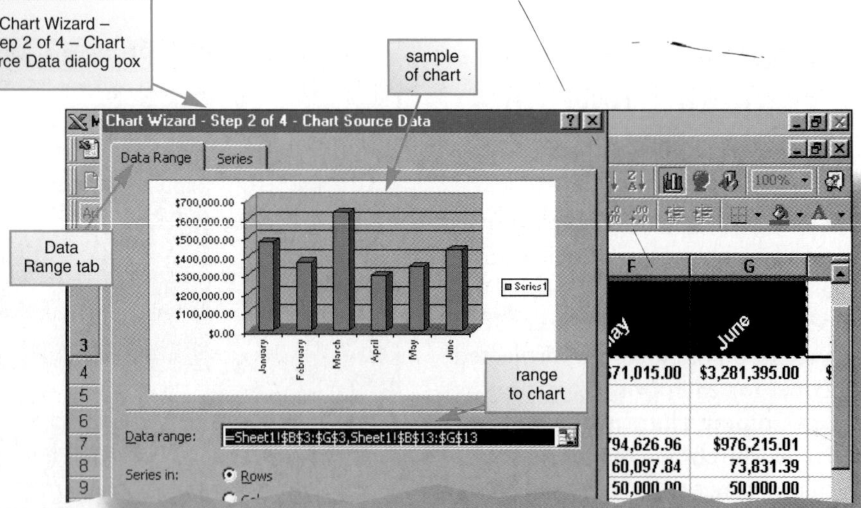

FIGURE 3-52

3 **Click the Next button. Click the Chart title text box and then type** `Planned Net Income` **as the chart title. Point to the Legend tab.**

The Chart Wizard – Step 3 of 4 – Chart Options dialog box displays (Figure 3-53). After you type the chart title, Excel redraws the sample chart with the chart title included. Because the chart includes only one series, the legend to the right in the sample chart adds little value and thus will be removed in the next step.

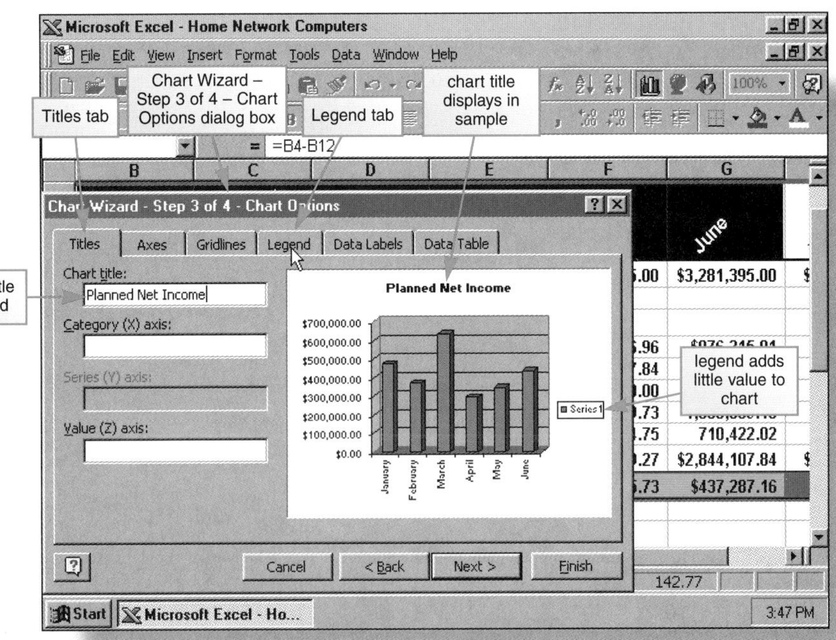

FIGURE 3-53

4 **Click the Legend tab. Click Show legend. Point to the Next button.**

The legend disappears from the sample chart (Figure 3-54).

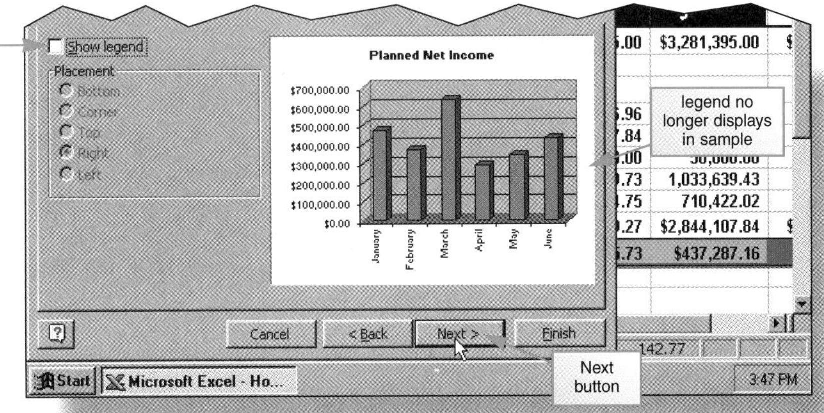

FIGURE 3-54

5 **Click the Next button. Click As new sheet. Point to the Finish button.**

The Chart Wizard – Step 4 of 4 – Chart Location dialog box displays. This dialog box gives you the option to draw the chart on a separate chart sheet in the workbook or to draw the chart on the same sheet as the worksheet (Figure 3-55). You also can rename the proposed chart sheet or the worksheet.

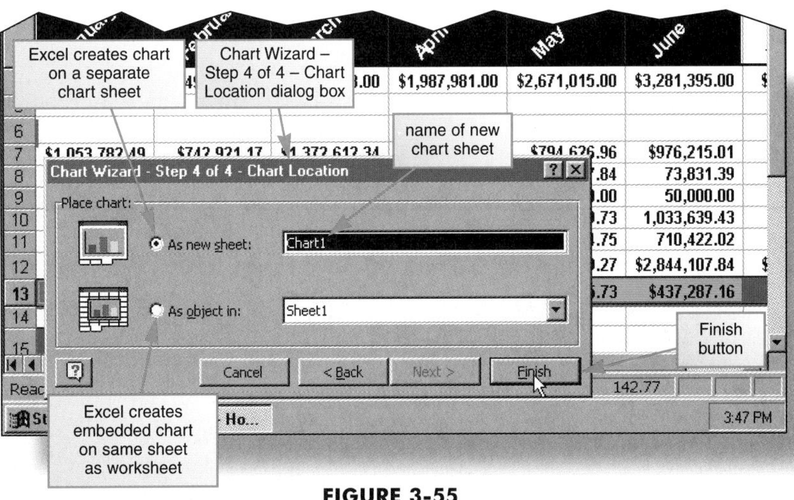

FIGURE 3-55

6 **Click the Finish button.**

Excel displays the 3-D Column chart on a separate chart sheet (Figure 3-56).

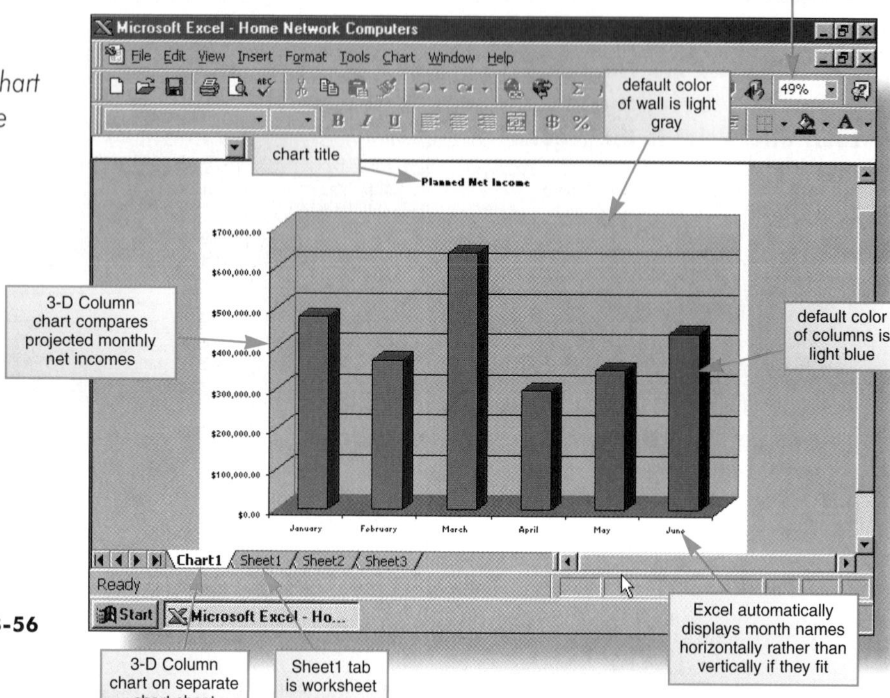

FIGURE 3-56

More *About* the Zoom Control Box

The chart size in Figure 3-56 is only 49% of the actual printed size. If you want to increase the size on the screen, click the Zoom Control box arrow on the Standard toolbar and click one of the larger percents.

More *About* the X-Axis Labels

If the labels along the x-axis display vertically (see sample chart in Figure 3-54) rather than horizontally (Figure 3-56), reduce their font size by right-clicking one of the labels and clicking Format Axis. What you see on the screen on a chart sheet is reduced by over 50% of the printed version.

Each column in the chart in Figure 3-56 represents one of the last six months of the year. The names of the months (range B3:G3) display on the x-axis below the corresponding columns. Excel automatically determines the values along the y-axis (the vertical line to the left of the columns) based on the highest and lowest projected net incomes in the range B13:G13 of the worksheet.

If you compare the sample chart in Figure 3-54 on the previous page and the chart in Figure 3-56, you will notice that Excel automatically displays the month names horizontally when they will fit, rather than vertically as shown in Figure 3-54.

Enhancing the 3-D Column Chart

To enhance the 3-D Column chart in Figure 3-56 so it looks like the one in Figure 3-50 on page E 3.41, the following changes must be made:

1. Chart title — change to 36-point blue, double underlined font
2. Columns — change color to blue
3. Wall — change color to red
4. Data labels on axes — increase font size to 12 point

Perform the following steps to enhance the 3-D Column chart.

Steps To Enhance the 3-D Column Chart

1 Right-click the chart title. Point to Format Chart Title on the shortcut menu.

A gray border with black handles surrounds the chart title, and Excel displays a shortcut menu (Figure 3-57).

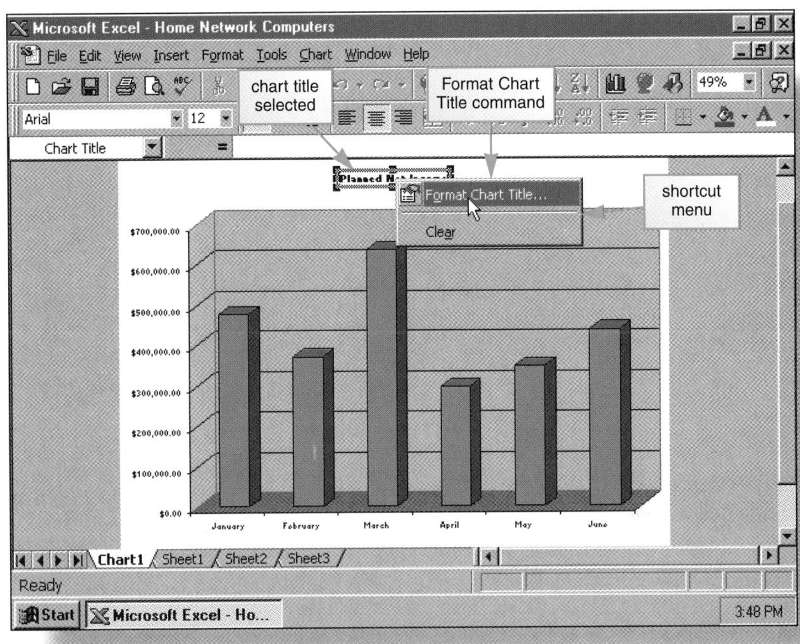

FIGURE 3-57

2 Click Format Chart Title on the shortcut menu. When the Format Chart Title dialog box displays, click the Font tab. Click 36 in the Size list. Click the Underline box arrow and then click Double in the Underline list. Click the Color box arrow and click blue (column 6, row 2 on the Color palette). Point to the OK button.

The Format Chart Title dialog box displays as shown in Figure 3-58.

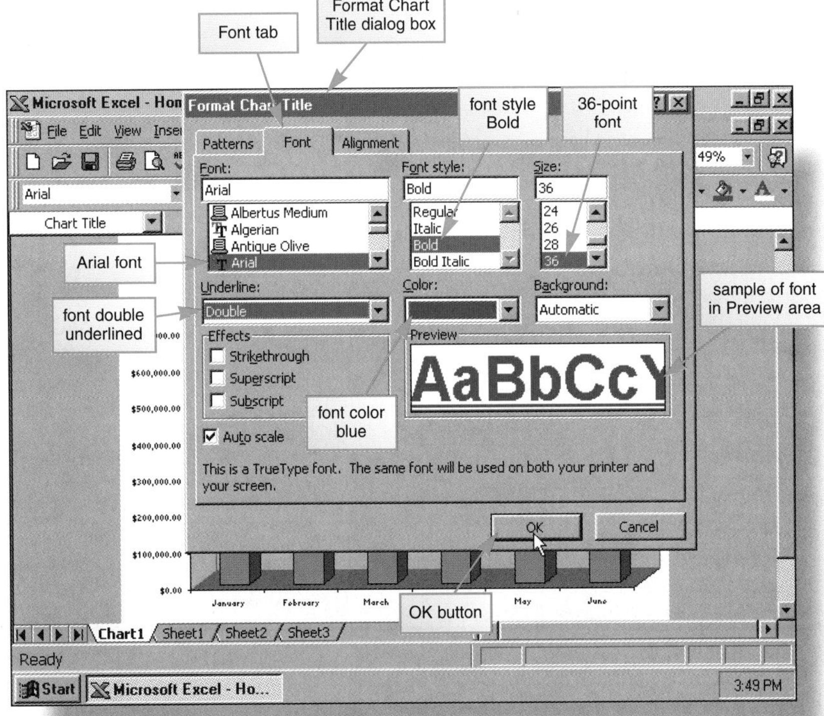

FIGURE 3-58

3 **Click the OK button. Click one of the six columns in the chart. Click the Fill Color button on the Formatting toolbar.**

Excel displays the formatted chart title. Handles display on the corner points of the six columns to indicate that they are selected. The color of the columns changes to blue (Figure 3-59).

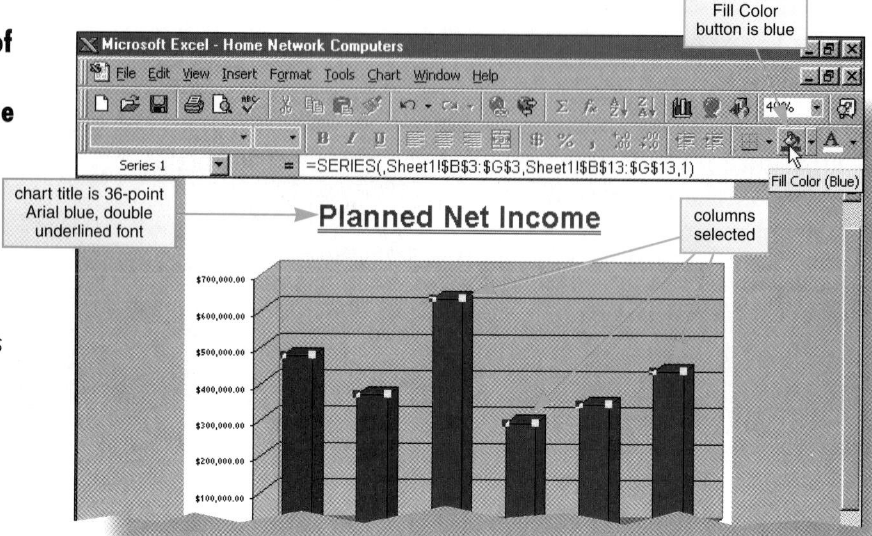

FIGURE 3-59

4 **Click the wall (not the gridlines) behind the columns. Click the Fill Color button arrow on the Formatting toolbar and point to red (column 1, row 3 on the Fill Color palette).**

Handles surround the wall behind the columns and the Fill Color palette displays (Figure 3-60).

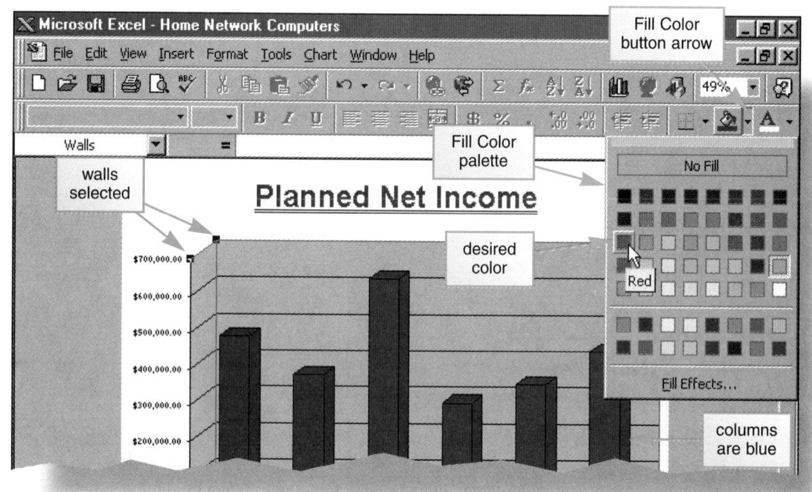

FIGURE 3-60

5 **Click red on the Fill Color palette. Click one of the labels on the y-axis. Click the Font size box arrow on the Formatting toolbar. Point to 12 in the Font Size list.**

The color of the walls behind the columns changes to red. The y-axis has handles on its endpoints. The Font Size list displays (Figure 3-61).

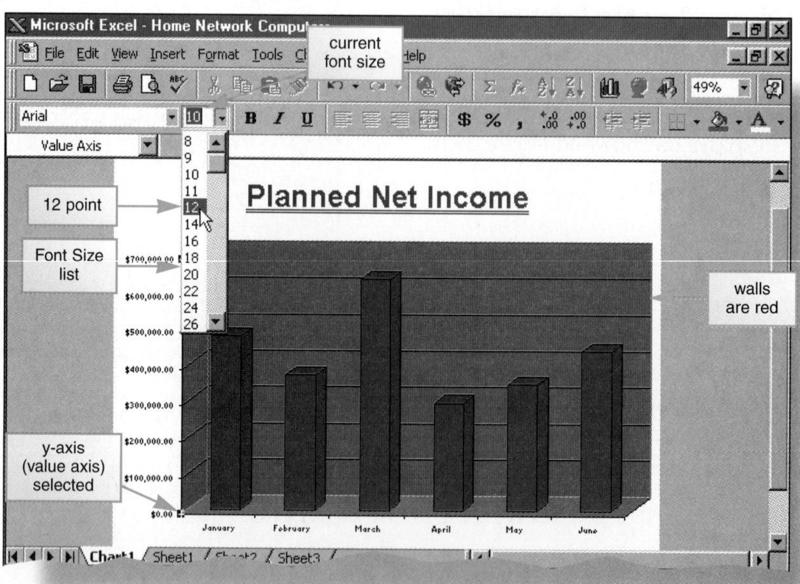

FIGURE 3-61

6 **Click 12 in the Font Size list. Click one of the month names on the x-axis. Click the Font Size box arrow on the Formatting toolbar. Click 12 in the Font Size list.**

The enhanced 3-D Column chart displays (Figure 3-62).

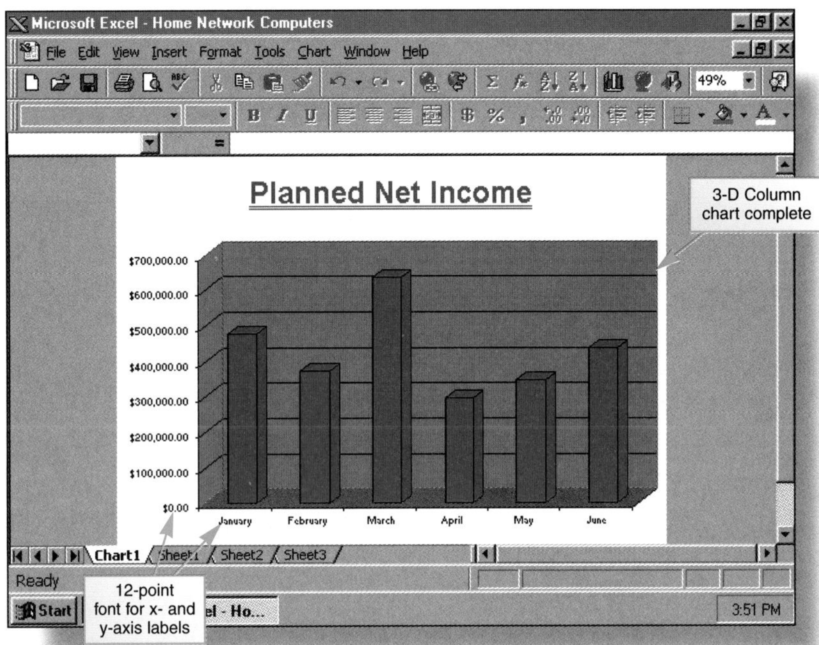

FIGURE 3-62

Compare the chart in Figure 3-56 on page E 3.44 to the one in Figure 3-62 and notice that the chart title stands out after being formatted. Unfortunately, the chart area itself is smaller, because Excel must decrease the size of the chart area to make room for the larger font.

Displaying the Magnitude of a Column in the Chart

If you point to a column, Excel displays the magnitude of the column in a ScreenTip as shown in Figure 3-63. The ScreenTip displays the value used to determine the value represented by the column to which the mouse is pointing.

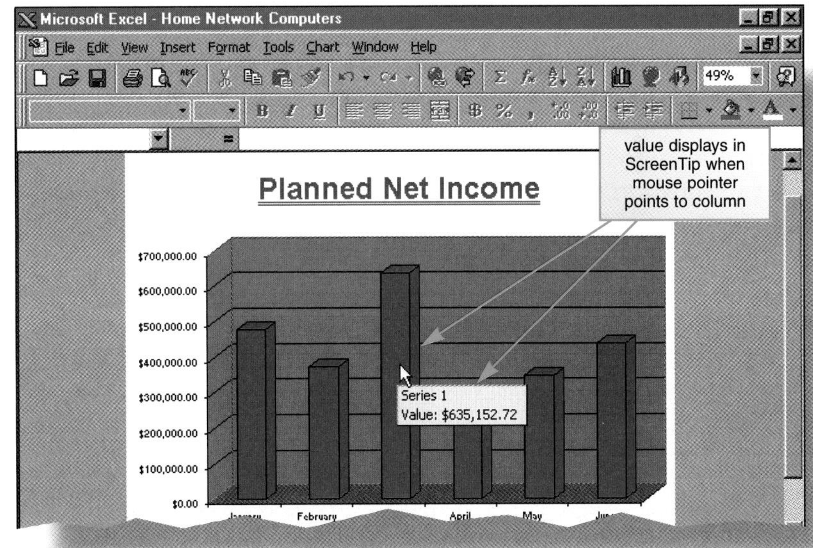

FIGURE 3-63

Changing the Name of the Sheets and Rearranging the Order of the Sheets

The final step in creating the Six-Month Plan worksheet and 3-D Column chart in Project 3 is to change the names of the sheets as shown at the bottom of the screen. The following steps show you how to rename the sheets and reorder the sheets so the worksheet comes before the chart sheet.

More About Charting

Press the ESC key to deselect a chart item.

To Rename the Sheets and Rearrange the Order of the Sheets

1 Double-click the tab labeled Chart1 at the bottom of the screen. Type `3-D Column Chart` **as the new tab label.**

The label on the Chart1 tab changes to 3-D Column Chart, and the insertion point displays after the label (Figure 3-64).

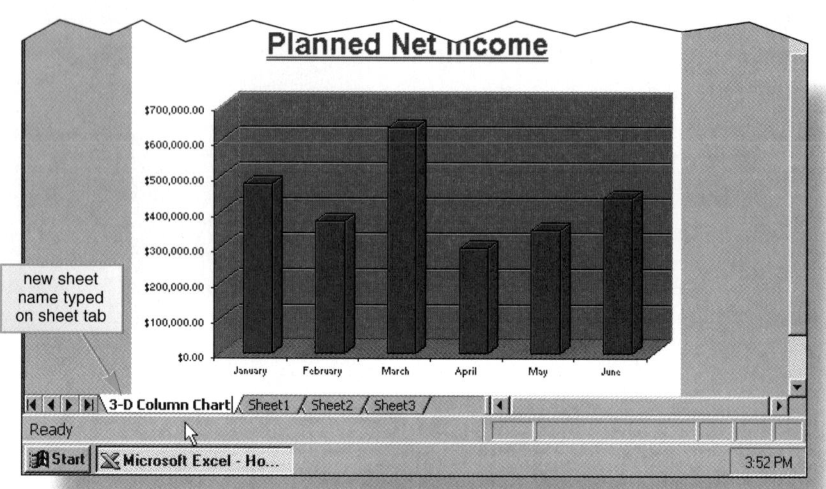

FIGURE 3-64

2 Press the ENTER key. Double-click the tab labeled Sheet1 at the bottom of the screen. Type `Six-Month Plan` **as the new tab label and then press the ENTER key. Drag the Six-Month Plan tab to the left in front of the 3-D Column Chart tab. Click cell A25 and then scroll to the top of the worksheet.**

Excel rearranges the sequence of the sheets and displays the worksheet (Figure 3-65).

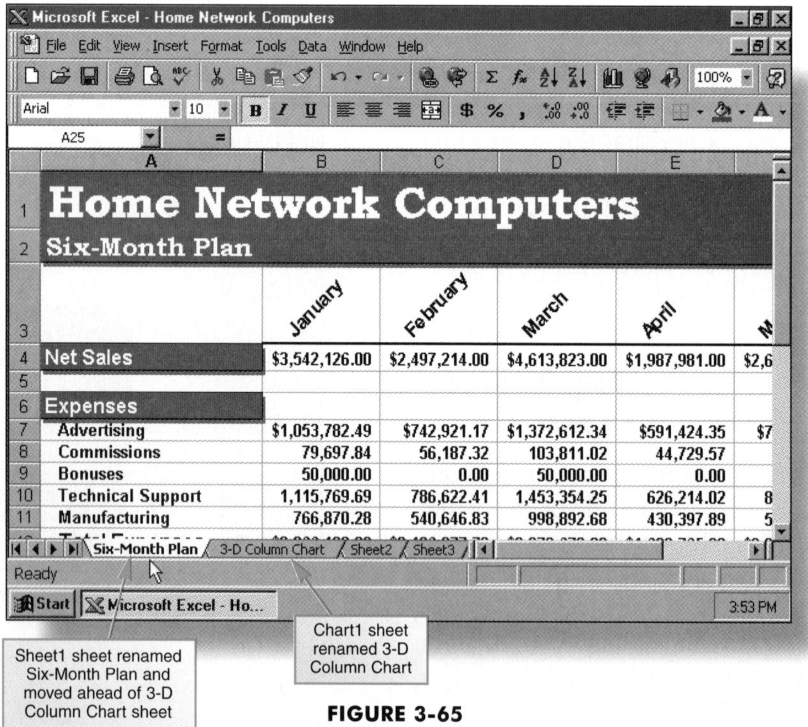

FIGURE 3-65

OtherWays

1. To move a sheet, right-click sheet, click Move or Copy

Checking Spelling, Saving, Previewing, and Printing the Workbook

With the workbook complete, the next series of steps is to check spelling, save, preview, and print the workbook. Each series of steps concludes with saving the workbook to ensure that the latest changes are saved on disk.

Checking Spelling in Multiple Sheets

The spelling checker checks the spelling in only the selected sheets. Thus, before checking the spelling, hold down the CTRL key and click the 3-D Column Chart tab as described in the following steps.

TO CHECK SPELLING IN MULTIPLE SHEETS

Step 1: With the Six-Month Plan sheet active, hold down the CTRL key and click the 3-D Column Chart tab.
Step 2: Click the Spelling button on the Standard toolbar. Correct any errors.
Step 3: Click the Save button on the Standard toolbar.

Previewing and Printing the Workbook

With the worksheet and chart complete, the next step is to preview and print them. Recall that Excel only previews and prints selected sheets. Also, because the worksheet is too wide to print in portrait orientation, you must change the orientation to landscape.

TO PREVIEW AND PRINT THE WORKBOOK IN LANDSCAPE ORIENTATION

Step 1: If both sheets are not selected, select the inactive one by holding down the CTRL key and clicking the tab of the inactive sheet.
Step 2: Click Page Setup on the File menu. Click the Page tab, click the Landscape option button, and click the OK button.
Step 3: Click the Print Preview button on the Standard toolbar. When you are finished previewing, click the Close button.
Step 4: Ready the printer.
Step 5: Click the Print button on the Standard toolbar.
Step 6: Right-click the Six-Month Plan tab. Click Ungroup Sheets on the shortcut menu to deselect the 3-D Column Chart tab.
Step 7: Click the Save button on the Standard toolbar.

The worksheet and 3-D Column chart print as shown in Figures 3-66a and b on the next page.

Changing the View of the Worksheet

With Excel, you easily can change the view of the worksheet. For example, you can magnify or shrink the worksheet on the screen. You also can view different parts of the worksheet through **window panes**.

Shrinking and Magnifying the View of a Worksheet or Chart

You can magnify (zoom in) or shrink (zoom out) the display of a worksheet or chart by using the **Zoom box** on the Standard toolbar. When you magnify a worksheet, the characters on the screen become large and fewer columns and rows display. Alternatively, when you shrink a worksheet, more columns and rows display. Magnifying or shrinking a worksheet affects only the view; it does not change the window size or printout of the worksheet or chart. Perform the steps on page E 3.51 to shrink and magnify the view of the worksheet.

More About Highlighting

You can use the Text Box button on the Drawing toolbar to add text to highlight parts of a worksheet or chart.

More About Checking Spelling

Unless a range of cells or an object is selected when you check spelling, Excel checks the selected worksheet, including all cell values, cell comments, embedded charts, text boxes, buttons, and headers and footers.

More About Zooming

You can enter any number between 10 and 400 in the Zoom Control box on the Standard toolbar.

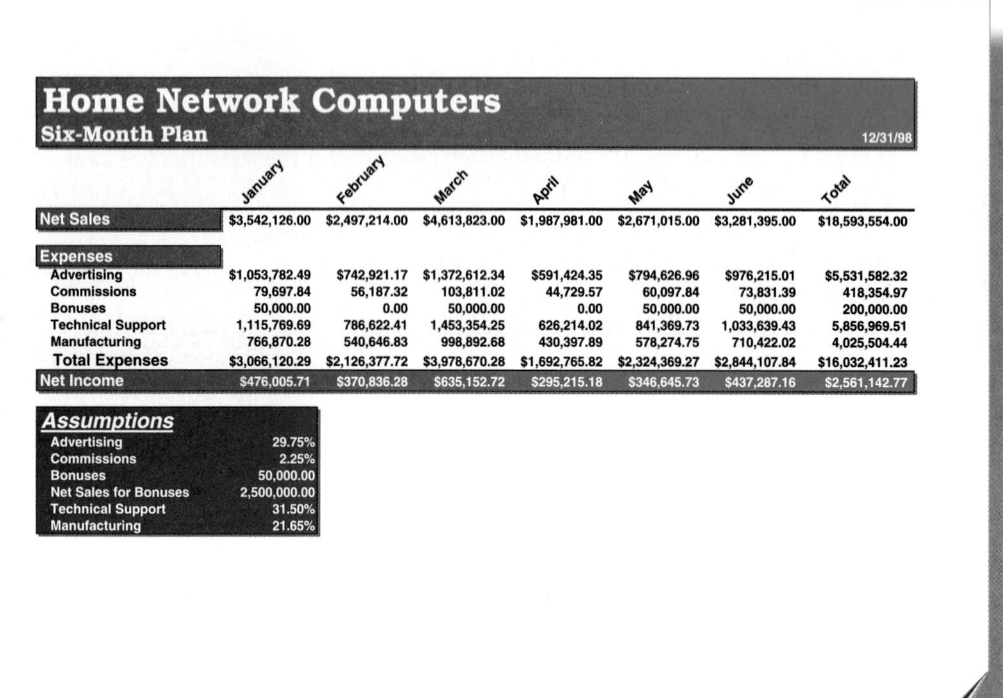

Home Network Computers
Six-Month Plan 12/31/98

	January	February	March	April	May	June	Total
Net Sales	$3,542,126.00	$2,497,214.00	$4,613,823.00	$1,987,981.00	$2,671,015.00	$3,281,395.00	$18,593,554.00
Expenses							
Advertising	$1,053,782.49	$742,921.17	$1,372,612.34	$591,424.35	$794,626.96	$976,215.01	$5,531,582.32
Commissions	79,697.84	56,187.32	103,811.02	44,729.57	60,097.84	73,831.39	418,354.97
Bonuses	50,000.00	0.00	50,000.00	0.00	50,000.00	50,000.00	200,000.00
Technical Support	1,115,769.69	786,622.41	1,453,354.25	626,214.02	841,369.73	1,033,639.43	5,856,969.51
Manufacturing	766,870.28	540,646.83	998,892.68	430,397.89	578,274.75	710,422.02	4,025,504.44
Total Expenses	$3,066,120.29	$2,126,377.72	$3,978,670.28	$1,692,765.82	$2,324,369.27	$2,844,107.84	$16,032,411.23
Net Income	$476,005.71	$370,836.28	$635,152.72	$295,215.18	$346,645.73	$437,287.16	$2,561,142.77

Assumptions	
Advertising	29.75%
Commissions	2.25%
Bonuses	50,000.00
Net Sales for Bonuses	2,500,000.00
Technical Support	31.50%
Manufacturing	21.65%

(a)

(b)

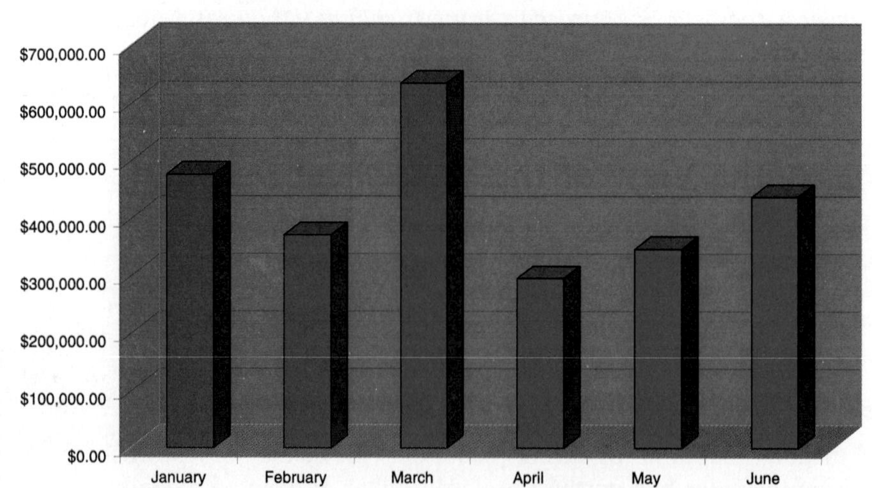

landscape orientation

FIGURE 3-66

To Shrink and Magnify the Display of a Worksheet or Chart

1 Click the Zoom box arrow on the Standard toolbar. Point to 50% in the Zoom list.

A list of percentages displays (Figure 3-67).

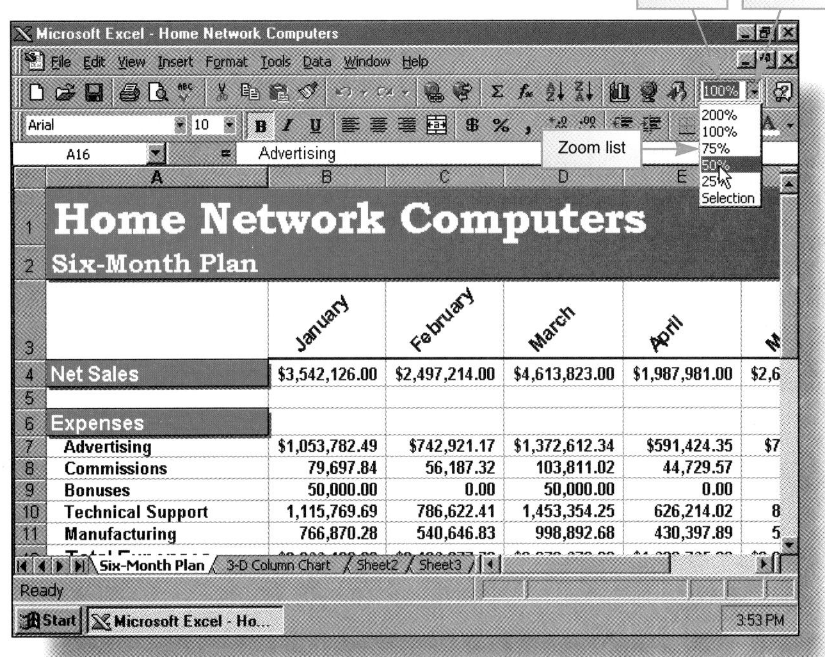

FIGURE 3-67

2 Click 50%.

Excel shrinks the display of the worksheet to 50% of its normal display (Figure 3-68). With the worksheet zoomed out to 50%, you can see more rows and columns than you did at 100% magnification. Most of the numbers, however, display as a series of number signs (#) because the columns are not wide enough to display the formatted numbers.

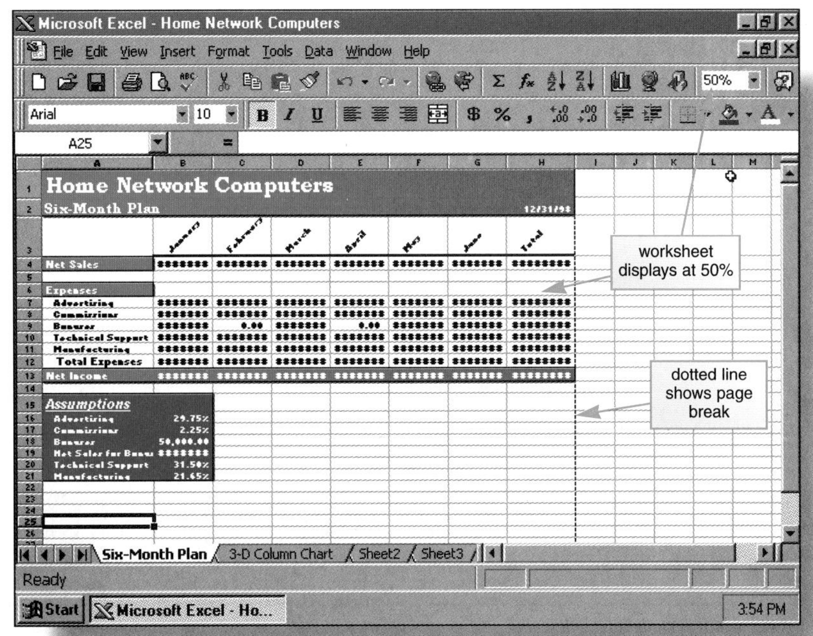

FIGURE 3-68

3 **Click the Zoom box arrow on the Standard toolbar and then click 100%.**

Excel returns to the default display of 100%.

4 **Click the 3-D Column Chart tab at the bottom of the screen. Click the Zoom box arrow on the Standard toolbar and then click 100%.**

Excel changes the magnification of the chart from 49% (see Figure 3-64 on page E 3.48) to 100% (Figure 3-69). The chart displays at the same size as the printout of the chart.

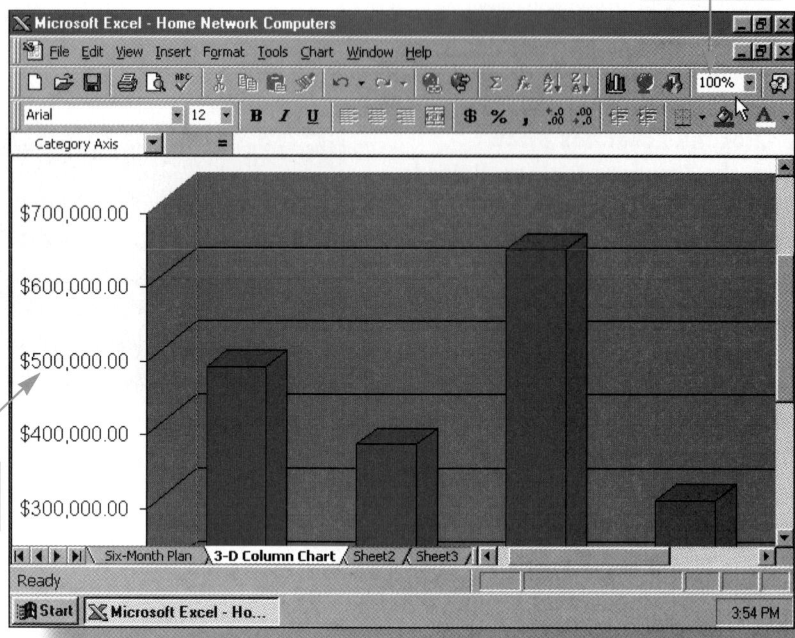

FIGURE 3-69

5 **Enter** 49 **in the Zoom box to return the chart to its original magnification.**

OtherWays

1. On View menu click Zoom, click desired percent magnification, click OK button
2. Type desired percent magnification in Zoom box

Excel normally displays a chart at approximately 50% magnification so that the entire chart displays on the screen. By changing the magnification to 100%, you can see only a part of the chart, but at a magnification that corresponds with the chart's size on a printout. Excel allows you to enter a percent magnification in the Zoom box between 10 and 200 for worksheets and chart sheets.

Splitting the Window into Panes

Previously in this project, you used the Freeze Panes command to freeze worksheet titles on a large worksheet so they always would display on the screen. When working with a large worksheet, you also can split the window into two or four window panes to view different parts of the worksheet at the same time. To split the window into four panes, select the cell where you want the four panes to intersect. Next, click the **Split command** on the Window menu. Follow the steps below to split the window into four panes.

To Split a Window into Four Panes

1 **Click the Six-Month Plan tab. Click cell D5, the intersection of the four proposed panes. Click Window on the menu bar and then point to Split.**

The Window menu displays as shown in Figure 3-70.

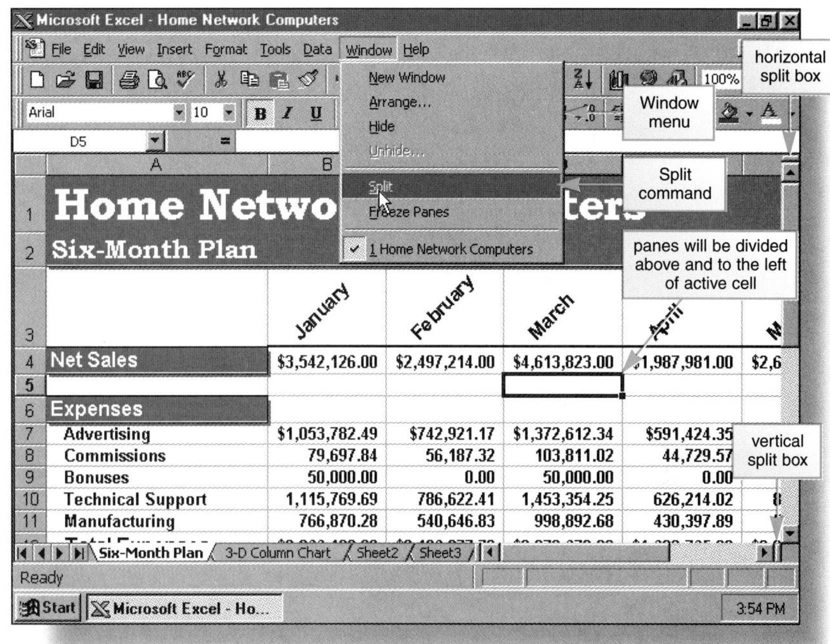

FIGURE 3-70

2 **Click Split on the Window menu. Use the scroll arrows to display the four corners of the worksheet.**

Excel divides the window into four panes, and the four corners of the worksheet display (Figure 3-71).

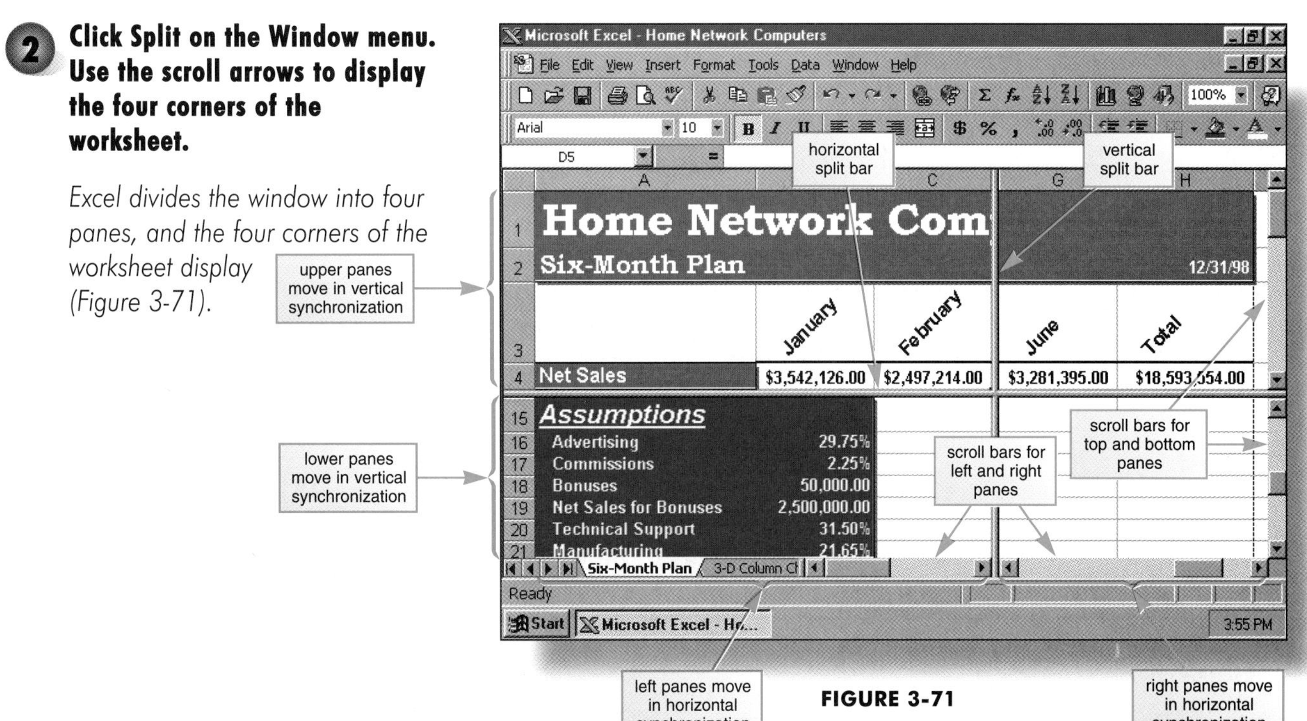

FIGURE 3-71

Other **Ways**

1. Drag horizontal split box and vertical split box to desired locations

More About Splitting a Window

If you want to split the window into two panes, rather than four, drag the vertical split box or horizontal split box (Figure 3-72) to the desired location.

The four panes in Figure 3-71 on the previous page are used to display the following: (1) the upper-left pane displays the range A1:C4; (2) the upper-right pane displays the range G1:H4; (3) the lower-left pane displays A15:C21; and (4) the lower-right pane displays the range G15:H21.

The vertical bar going up and down the middle of the window is called the **vertical split bar**. The horizontal bar going across the middle of the window is called the **horizontal split bar**. If you use the scroll bars below the window and to the right of the window to scroll the window, you will see that the panes split by the horizontal split bar scroll together vertically. The panes split by the vertical split bar scroll together horizontally. To resize the panes, drag either split bar to the desired location in the window.

You can change the values of cells in any of the four panes. Any change you make in one pane also takes effect in the other panes.

To remove one of the split bars from the window, drag the split box to the edge of the window or double-click the split bar. Follow these steps to remove both split bars.

TO REMOVE THE FOUR PANES FROM THE WINDOW

Step 1: Position the mouse pointer at the intersection of the horizontal and vertical split bars.
Step 2: Double-click the split four-headed arrow.

Excel removes the four panes from the window.

What-If Analysis

More About What-If Analysis

Besides manually changing assumptions in a worksheet, Excel has additional methods for answering what-if questions, including Goal Seeking, Solver, Pivot Tables, Scenario Manager, and the Analysis ToolPak.

The automatic recalculation feature of Excel is a powerful tool that can be used to analyze worksheet data. Recall from the Case Perspective on page E 3.4 the problem Kelly Rite had when members of the board of directors suggested she change her assumptions to generate new projections. Because she had to calculate these values manually, it took her several minutes. The recalculations then rendered her chart useless.

Using Excel to scrutinize the impact of changing values in cells that are referenced by a formula in another cell is called **what-if analysis** or **sensitivity analysis.** Excel not only recalculates all formulas in a worksheet when new data is entered, but also redraws any associated charts.

In Project 3, the projected monthly expenses and net incomes in the range A7:G13 are dependent on the assumptions in the range B16:B21. Thus, if you change any of the assumption values, Excel immediately recalculates the projected monthly expenses in rows 7 through 12 and the projected monthly net incomes in row 13. Finally, because the projected monthly net incomes in row 13 change, Excel redraws the 3-D Column chart which is based on these numbers.

A what-if question for the worksheet in Project 3 might be, What if the first three assumptions in the Assumptions table are changed as follows: Advertising 29.75% to 25.00%; Commissions 2.25% to 1.25%; Bonuses $50,000.00 to $10,000.00 — how would these changes affect the projected six-month net income in cell H13? To answer a question like this, you need to change only the first three values in the Assumptions table. Excel immediately recalculates the worksheet and redraws the 3-D Column chart to answer the question regarding the projected six-month net income in cell H13.

The following steps change the first three assumptions as indicated in the previous paragraph and determine the new projected six-month net income in cell H13. To ensure that the Assumptions table and the projected six-month net income in cell H13 show on the screen at the same time, the following steps also divide the window into two vertical panes.

Steps To Analyze Data in a Worksheet by Changing Values

1 Use the vertical scroll bar to move the window so cell A4 is in the upper-left corner of the screen.

2 Drag the vertical split box from the lower-right corner of the screen so that the vertical split bar is positioned immediately to the right of column D. Use the right scroll arrow to display the totals in column H in the right pane.

Excel divides the window into two vertical panes and shows the totals in column H in the pane on the right side of the window (Figure 3-72).

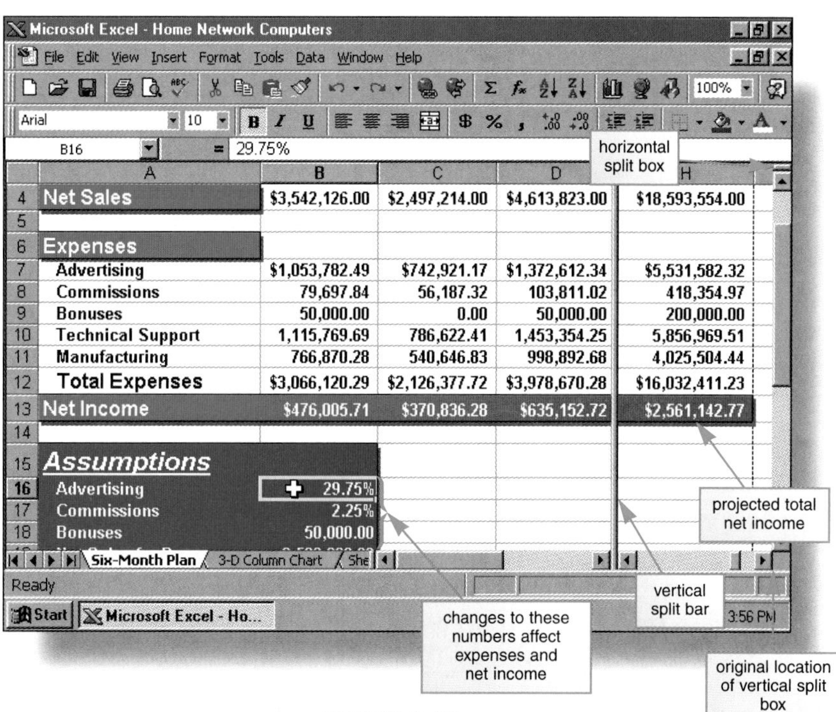

FIGURE 3-72

3 Enter 25 **in cell B16,** 1.25 **in cell B17, and** 10000 **in cell B18.**

Excel immediately recalculates all the formulas in the worksheet, including the projected six-month net income in cell H13 (Figure 3-73).

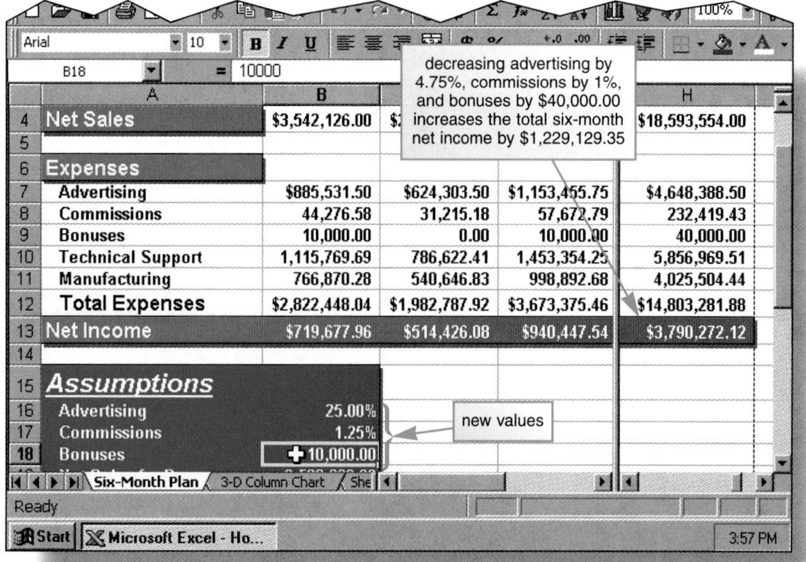

FIGURE 3-73

Each time you enter a new percent expense, Excel recalculates the worksheet. This process usually takes less than one second, depending on how many calculations must be performed and the speed of your computer. Compare the projected six-month net incomes in Figures 3-72 and 3-73 on the previous page. By changing the values of the three assumptions (Figure 3-73), the projected six-month net income in cell H13 increases from $2,561,142.77 to $3,790,272.12. This translates into an increase of $1,229,129.35 in the projected net income for the six-month period.

More *About* **Undo**

The Undo button is ideal for returning the worksheet to its original state after you have changed the value of a cell to answer a what-if question. Excel maintains a history of changes from which you can select. Click the Undo button arrow to view the history.

Goal Seeking

If you know the result you want a formula to produce, you can use goal seeking to determine the value of a cell on which the formula depends. The following example closes and reopens Home Network Computers and uses the Goal Seek command on the Tools menu to determine what projected advertising percentage in cell B16 will yield a projected six-month net income of $4,000,000.00 in cell H13.

Steps To Goal Seek

1. **Close the Home Network Computers workbook without saving changes. Click the Open button on the Standard toolbar and then reopen Home Network Computers.**

2. **Drag the vertical split box to the right of column D. Click cell H13, the cell that contains the projected six-month net income. Click Tools on the menu bar and then point to Goal Seek.**

   The vertical split bar displays to the right of column D, and the Tools menu displays (Figure 3-74).

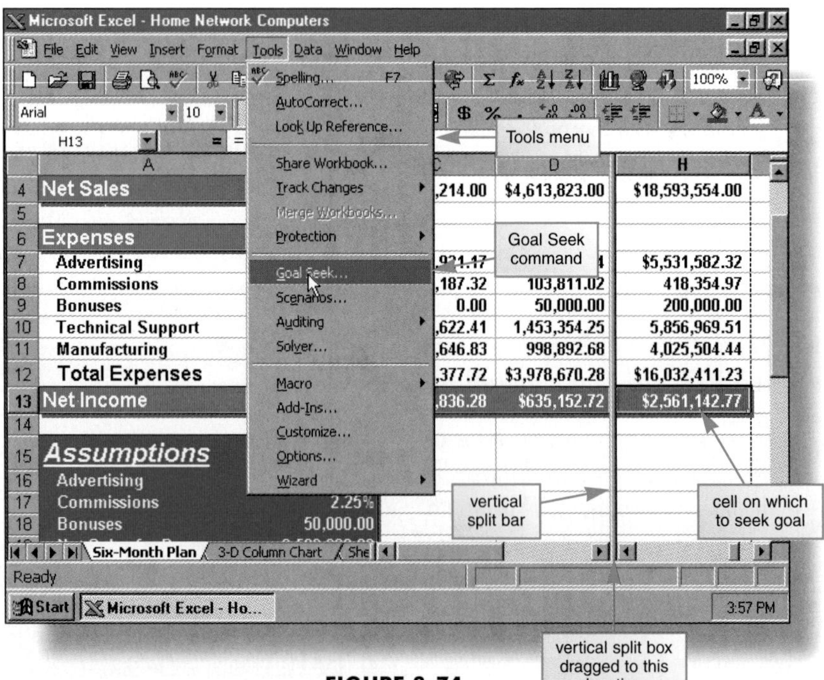

FIGURE 3-74

3 **Click Goal Seek.**

The Goal Seek dialog box displays. The Set cell text box is assigned the cell reference of the active cell in the worksheet (cell H13) automatically.

4 **Click the To value text box. Type** 4,000,000 **and click the By changing cell text box. Click cell B16 on the worksheet.**

The Goal Seek dialog box displays as shown in Figure 3-75. A marquee displays around cell B16.

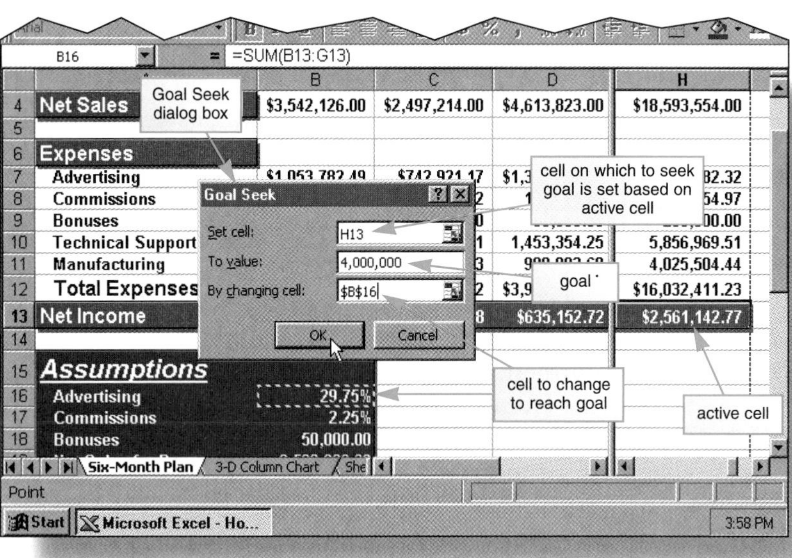

FIGURE 3-75

5 **Click the OK button. When the Goal Seek Status dialog box displays, click the OK button.**

Excel immediately changes cell H13 from $2,561,142.77 to the desired value of $4,000,000.00. More importantly, Excel changes the advertising assumption in cell B16 from 29.75% to 22.01% (Figure 3-76).

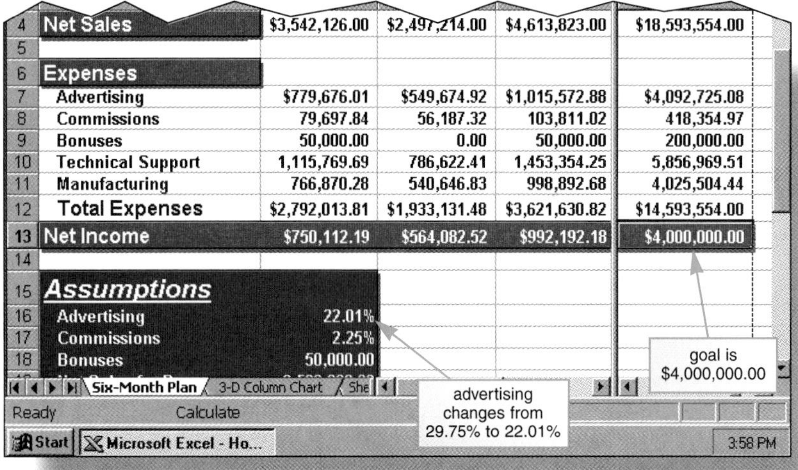

FIGURE 3-76

Goal seeking assumes you can change the value of only one cell referenced directly or indirectly. In this example, to change the projected six-month net income in cell H13 to $4,000,000.00, the advertising percentage in cell B16 must decrease by 7.74% from 29.75% to 22.01%.

You can see from this goal seeking example that the cell to change (cell B16) does not have to be referenced directly in the formula or function. For example, the projected six-month net income in cell H13 is calculated by the function =SUM(B13:G13). Cell B16, the advertising assumption, is not referenced in the function. Instead, cell B16 is referenced in the formulas in rows 7 through 12, on which the projected monthly net incomes in row 13 are based. Excel is able to goal seek on the projected six-month net income by varying the advertising assumption.

More *About* **Goal Seeking**

Goal seeking is a methodology in which you know what answer you want a formula in a cell to be, but you do not know the value to place in a cell that is involved in the formula. You can goal seek by changing the value in a cell that is indirectly used in the formula as illustrated in Figure 3-76.

Quitting Excel

To quit Excel, complete the steps on the next page.

TO QUIT EXCEL

Step 1: Click the Close button on the right side of the title bar.
Step 2: If the Microsoft Excel dialog box displays, click the No button.

Project Summary

With the worksheet and chart developed in this project, the CFO of Home Network Computers, Kelly Rite, easily can respond to any what-if questions the board members ask the next time she presents her Six-Month Plan. Questions that took several minutes to answer with paper and pencil now can be answered in a few seconds. Furthermore, computational errors are less likely to occur.

In creating the Home Network Computers workbook, you learned how to work with large worksheets that extend beyond the window and how to use the fill handle to create a series. You learned to display hidden toolbars, dock a toolbar at the bottom of the screen, and hide an active toolbar. You learned about the difference between absolute cell references and relative cell references and how to use the IF function. You also learned how to freeze titles, change the magnification of the worksheet, display different parts of the worksheets through panes, and improve the appearance of a chart. Finally, this project introduced you to using Excel to do what-if analyses by changing values in cells and goal seeking.

What You Should Know

Having completed this project, you now should be able to perform the following tasks:

Test Your Knowledge

1 True/False

Instructions: Circle T if the statement is true or F if the statement is false.

T F 1. If you enter 101 in cell A1 and 103 in cell A2, select the range A1:A2, and then drag the fill handle down to cell A8, Excel assigns cell A8 the value 103.

T F 2. To copy the text, Monday, in cell B1 to all the cells in the range C1:G1, drag the fill handle from cell B1 to cell G1 while holding down the CTRL key.

T F 3. You can paste an item that was copied to the Clipboard by pressing the ENTER key.

T F 4. There are three toolbar docks in an Excel window.

T F 5. You can dock as many toolbars as you want at a toolbar dock.

T F 6. You can seek answers to at most three cells using the Goal Seek command.

T F 7. A worksheet that has been saved with format changes will maintain the format changes when the worksheet is opened again.

T F 8. You can split a window into a maximum of four panes.

T F 9. F61 is an absolute reference, and $F$61 is a relative reference.

T F 10. If you assign the IF function =IF(B2>B3,25,1) to cell B12, and cells B2 and B3 are equal to 5000, then Excel displays the value 25 in cell B12.

2 Multiple Choice

Instructions: Circle the correct response.

1. If you assign the value 42 to cell E5, the value 11 to cell F5, and cell G5 contains the function =IF(E5>4*F5,"Deductions","No deductions"), then cell G5 displays the message, __________.
   a. Deductions
   b. No deductions
   c. #REF!
   d. F5
2. When you are drawing a chart using the Chart Wizard dialog box, click the __________ button to instruct Excel to draw the chart with the options thus far selected.
   a. Next
   b. Cancel
   c. Back
   d. Finish
3. Use the __________ function key to change a cell reference in the formula bar to an absolute reference.
   a. F5
   b. F2
   c. F6
   d. F4

(continued)

A+ Test Your Knowledge

Multiple Choice *(continued)*

4. You can use the Split command to split a window into __________.
   a. two horizontal panes
   b. two vertical panes
   c. four panes
   d. all of the above
5. If cell A2 contains the label, Qtr 1, and you select cell A2 and then drag the fill handle to the right, then cell B2 will contain the label __________.
   a. Qtr 1
   b. Qtr 2
   c. Qtr 3
   d. #REF!
6. When copying a range of cells using the drag and drop method, you first point to the border of the selected range so that the mouse pointer changes to a(n) __________.
   a. cross hair
   b. arrow
   c. block plus sign
   d. split double arrow
7. The horizontal and vertical split boxes are located __________.
   a. on the Standard toolbar
   b. on the status bar
   c. next to the scroll arrows
   d. in the Name box
8. When you insert a column in a worksheet, Excel __________ at the insertion point.
   a. copies over the existing column
   b. shifts the existing columns up
   c. shifts the existing columns down
   d. shifts the existing columns to the right
9. You can use the Shadow button on the __________ toolbar to add a drop shadow to a cell.
   a. Standard
   b. Drawing
   c. Formatting
   d. Chart
10. Which toolbar can be displayed or hidden by clicking a button on the Standard toolbar?
    a. Standard
    b. Drawing
    c. Formatting
    d. Chart

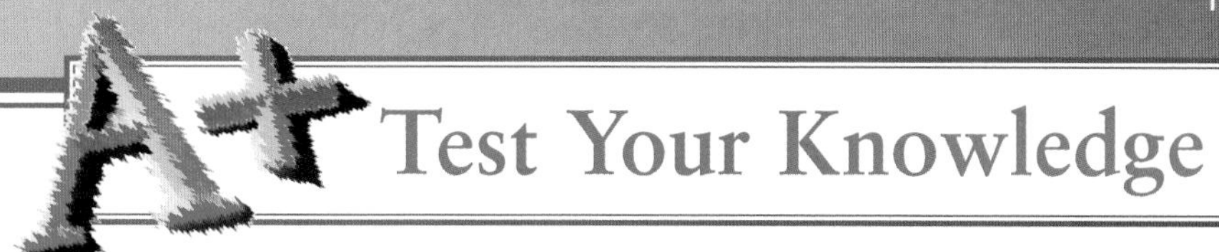

3 Understanding the Insert and Delete Commands and the IF Function

Instructions: Fill in the correct answers.

1. Assume you want to insert four rows between rows 8 and 9.
   a. Select rows ____________________ through ____________________.
   b. On the shortcut menu, click ____________________.
2. You have data in rows 1 through 6. Assume you want to delete rows 2 through 4.
   a. Select rows ____________________ through ____________________.
   b. On the shortcut menu, click ____________________.
   c. In which row would the data that was in row 6 be located? ____________________
3. Which command on the shortcut menu causes the #REF! error message to display in cells with formulas that reference the affected range? ____________________
4. Determine the truth value (true or false) of the following logical tests, given the following cell values: A1 = 125; B4 = 300; D6 = 4; G2 = 40; and H3 = 10. Enter true or false.
   a. D6 = G2 Truth value: ____________________
   b. A1 < B4 Truth value: ____________________
   c. G2 * 20 / H3 * 5 <> B4 Truth value: ____________________
   d. B4 / H3 <> G2 - D6 Truth value: ____________________
   e. A1 > G2 * D6 - 20 Truth value: ____________________
   f. B4 >= G2 * H3 Truth value: ____________________
   g. A1 + B4 <= 2 * (A1 + 25) Truth value: ____________________
   h. G2 + H3 = 2 * (A1 / 5) Truth value: ____________________
5. Cell A10 is the active cell. Write a function for cell A10 that assigns the value of cell A5 to cell A10 if the value in cell A2 is greater than the value in cell A3; otherwise the function assigns zero (0) to cell A10.
   Function: ____
6. Cell A1 is the active cell. Write a function for cell A1 that assigns the value Approved if the value in cell D20 is two times greater than the value in cell D34; otherwise the function assigns the value Not Approved.
   Function: ____
7. A nested IF function is an IF function that contains another IF function in the value_if_true or value_if_false arguments. For example,
   =IF(B1 = "ID","Region 1", IF(B1 = "WA", "Region 2", "Not Applicable"))
   is a valid nested IF function. Start Excel and enter this IF function in cell C1 and then use the fill handle to copy the function down through cell C7. Enter the following data in the cells in the range B1:B7 and then write down the results in cells C1 through C7 for each set. Set 1: B1 = ID; B2 = ID; B3 = CA; B4 = OR; B5 = UT; B6 = ID; B7 = ID. Set 2: B1= NV; B2 = WA; B3 = ID; B4 = WA; B5 = WA; B6 = ID; B7 = MT.

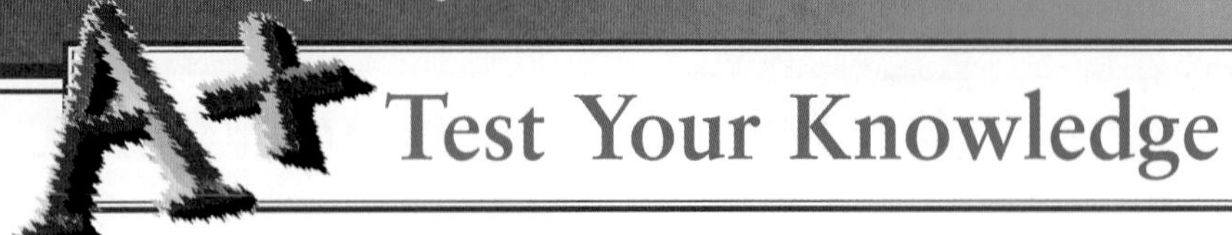

4 Understanding Relative, Absolute, and Mixed Cell References

Instructions: Fill in the correct answers. Use Figure 3-77 for problems 2 through 5.

1. Write cell B6 as a relative reference, absolute reference, mixed reference with the row varying, and mixed reference with the column varying.
   Relative reference: ________________
   Mixed, row varying: ________________
   Absolute reference: ________________
   Mixed, column varying: ________________

Microsoft Excel - Figure 3-77

	A	B	C	D	E	F	G	H	I
1									
2			6	4	2				
3									
4		4	3	1	4		32	32	
5		2	6	5	8		52	104	
6		7	2	9	1		72	18	
7		3	1	2	6		24	36	
8									
9			72	102	114				
10									
11			72	68	38				
12									

FIGURE 3-77

2. Write the formula for cell C9 that multiplies cell C2 times the sum of cells C4 through C7. Write the formula so that when it is copied to cells D9 and E9, cell C2 remains absolute. Verify your formula by checking it with the values found in cells C9, D9, and E9 in Figure 3-77.
   Formula for cell C9: ________________________
3. Write the formula for cell G4 that multiplies cell E4 times the sum of cells B4, C4, and D4. Write the formula so that when it is copied to cells G5, G6, and G7, cell E4 remains absolute. Verify your formula by checking it with the values found in cells G4 through G7 in Figure 3-77.
   Formula for cell G4: ________________________
4. Write the formula for cell C11 that multiplies cell C2 times the sum of cells C4 through C7. Write the formula so that when it is copied to cells D11 and E11, Excel adjusts all the cell references according to the new location. Verify your formula by checking it with the values found in cells C11, D11, and E11 in Figure 3-77.
   Formula for cell C11: ________________________
5. Write the formula for cell H4 that multiplies cell E4 times the sum of cells B4, C4, and D4. Write the formula so that when it is copied to cells H5, H6, and H7, Excel adjusts all the cell addresses according to the new location. Verify your formula by checking it with the values found in cells H4 through H7 in Figure 3-77.
   Formula for cell H4: ________________________

Use Help

1 Reviewing Project Activities

Instructions: Perform the following tasks using a computer. When you have completed the exercise, hand in your printouts to your instructor.

1. Start Excel. Click Contents and Index on the Help menu.
2. Click the Contents tab. Double-click the Creating Formulas and Auditing Workbooks book. Double-click the Using References book. Double-click the topic, The difference between relative and absolute references. Read and print the information.
3. Click the Help Topics button to return to the Help Topics: Microsoft Excel dialog box. Click the Index tab. Type `column chart` in the top text box labeled 1 and then click the Display button. Click the topic, Create a chart in the Topics Found dialog box, and then click the Display button. One at a time, click each link under What do you want to do? For each linked topic, read and print the information. Click the Back button to return to the links under What do you want to do?. Click the Help Topics button to return to the Help Topics: Microsoft Excel dialog box.
4. With the Help Topics: Microsoft Excel dialog box on the screen, click the Find tab. Type `if` in the top text box labeled 1. Click IF in the middle list box labeled 2, double-click IF in the bottom list box labeled 3. Read and print the information on the IF function. Close the Microsoft Excel Help window.

2 Expanding on the Basics

Instructions: Begin each of the following by either clicking Contents and Index on the Help menu or by clicking the Office Assistant button on the Standard toolbar. If you are unable to print the Help information, then answer the questions on your own paper. Hand in your printouts and answers to your instructor.

1. Use the Office Assistant to search for the topic, data tables. Click the button labeled, Create a one-variable data table. Read and print the information. Click the Close button to close the Microsoft Excel Help window. Click the Office Assistant and click the Search button. Click the button labeled, Create a two-variable data table. Read and print the information. Close the Microsoft Excel Help window.
2. Use the Find tab in the Help Topics: Microsoft Excel dialog box to display and then print one subtopic for the following topics: (a) type `freeze` for freezing row and column titles, (b) type `split` for splitting a window to view two parts of a worksheet at one time, (c) type `comparison` for calculation and comparison operators, and (d) type `abramowitz` for more information and a bibliography.
3. Use the Office Assistant to answer the question, How do I fill in a series of numbers? Print the information and answer the following related questions on your own paper: (a) What types of series can Excel fill in? (b) How do I fill in a series of months? (c) How do I fill in a series for growth trend? (d) How do I create a custom AutoFill list?

Apply Your Knowledge

1 Creating a Series

Instructions: Start Excel. Open the workbook, Create Series, from the Excel folder on the Data Disk that accompanies this book. The worksheet (Figure 3-78) contains the initial values for eight different series.

Use the fill handle on one column at a time to propagate the eight different series through row 17, as shown in Figure 3-79. For example, in column A, select cell A3 and drag the fill handle down to cell A17. In column D, select the range D3:D4 and drag the fill handle down to cell D17. Your final results for these columns should be 11:00 PM in cell A17 and 28-Feb-99 in cell D17. Save the worksheet using the file name, Create Series 2. Print the worksheet.

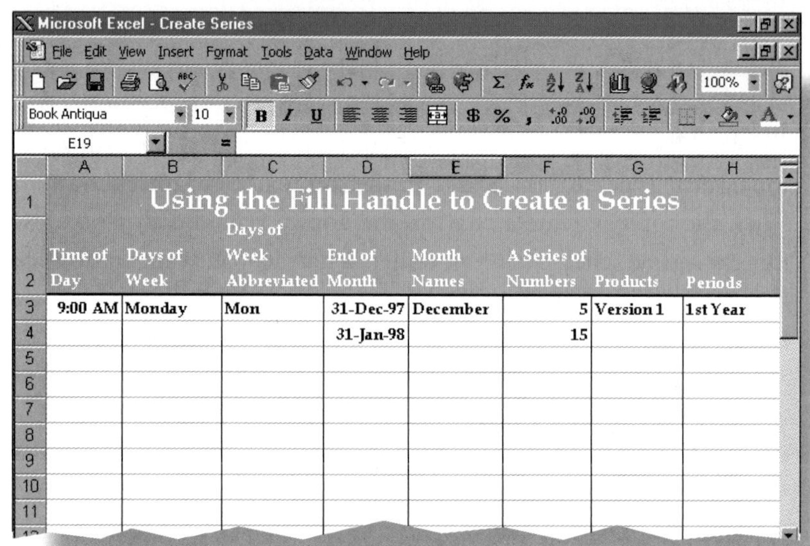

	A	B	C	D	E	F	G	H
2	Time of Day	Days of Week	Days of Week Abbreviated	End of Month	Month Names	A Series of Numbers	Products	Periods
3	9:00 AM	Monday	Mon	31-Dec-97	December	5	Version 1	1st Year
4				31-Jan-98		15		

FIGURE 3-78

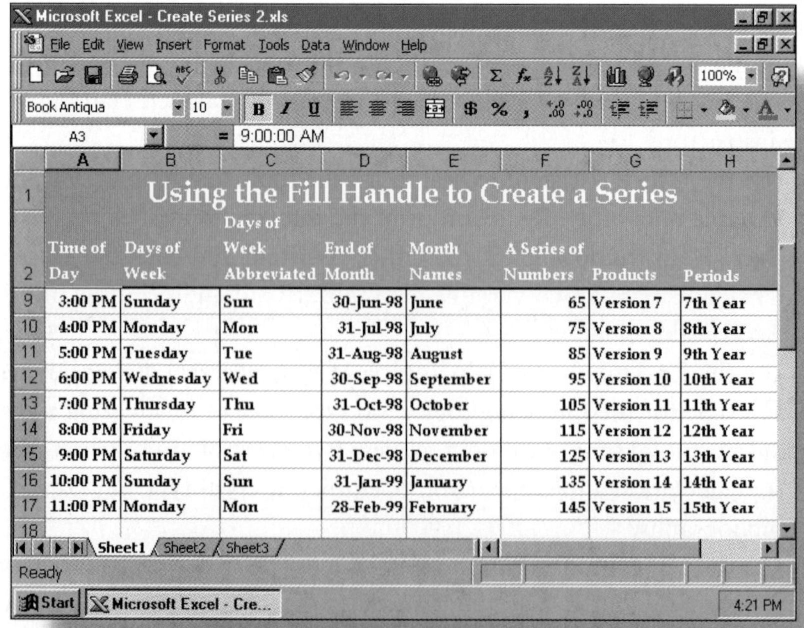

	A	B	C	D	E	F	G	H
2	Time of Day	Days of Week	Days of Week Abbreviated	End of Month	Month Names	A Series of Numbers	Products	Periods
9	3:00 PM	Sunday	Sun	30-Jun-98	June	65	Version 7	7th Year
10	4:00 PM	Monday	Mon	31-Jul-98	July	75	Version 8	8th Year
11	5:00 PM	Tuesday	Tue	31-Aug-98	August	85	Version 9	9th Year
12	6:00 PM	Wednesday	Wed	30-Sep-98	September	95	Version 10	10th Year
13	7:00 PM	Thursday	Thu	31-Oct-98	October	105	Version 11	11th Year
14	8:00 PM	Friday	Fri	30-Nov-98	November	115	Version 12	12th Year
15	9:00 PM	Saturday	Sat	31-Dec-98	December	125	Version 13	13th Year
16	10:00 PM	Sunday	Sun	31-Jan-99	January	135	Version 14	14th Year
17	11:00 PM	Monday	Mon	28-Feb-99	February	145	Version 15	15th Year

FIGURE 3-79

1 World Wide Web Bookstore Five-Year Projected Financial Statement

Problem: You are a work-study student at the World Wide Web Bookstore. The owner, Mrs. Tellurian, knows you learned Excel in college and has asked you to build a five-year Projected Financial Statement worksheet, based on figures available from 1997 (Figure 3-80).

Table 3-6

ASSUMPTIONS	
Units Sold 1997	**7835**
Unit Cost	**5.50**
Annual Sales Growth	**15%**
Annual Price Decrease	**5%**
Margin	**60%**

	A	B	C	D	E	F
1	World Wide Web Bookstore					
2	Five-Year Projected Financial Statement					1/2/98
3		1998	1999	2000	2001	2002
4	Net Sales	107,731	117,696	128,583	140,477	153,471
5	Cost of Goods Sold	43,093	47,079	51,433	56,191	61,389
6	Gross Margin	64,639	70,618	77,150	84,286	92,083
7	Expenses					
8	Advertising	17,160	18,654	20,287	22,072	24,021
9	Rent	10,800	11,880	13,068	14,375	15,812
10	Salaries	19,392	21,185	23,145	25,286	27,625
11	Supplies	1,616	1,765	1,929	2,107	2,302
12	Other Expenses	4,800	18,000	6,000	7,200	9,600
13	Total Expenses	53,767	71,485	64,429	71,039	79,360
14						
15	Income Before Taxes	10,871	(867)	12,721	13,247	12,723
16	Income Taxes	5,436	0	6,360	6,623	6,361
17	Net Income	5,436	(867)	6,360	6,623	6,361
18						
19	Assumptions					
20	Units Sold 1997	7,835				
21	Unit Cost	5.50				
22	Annual Sales Growth	15%				
23	Annual Price Decrease	5%				
24	Margin	60%				

FIGURE 3-80

Instructions Part 1: Do the following to create the worksheet in Figure 3-80.

1. Use the Select All button and Bold button to bold the entire worksheet. Enter the worksheet titles in cells A1 and A2. Enter the system date in cell F2 using the NOW function. Format the date to the 3/4/98 style.
2. Enter the five column titles 1998 through 2002 in the range B3:F3. Begin each year with an apostrophe so that the years are entered as text. Text headings are required for the charting in Part 2. Italicize cell B3 and rotate its contents 45°. Use the Format Painter button to copy the format assigned to cell B3 to the range C3:F3.
3. Enter the row titles in the range A4:A24. Change the font size in cells A7, A13, A15, and A17 to 12 point. Change the font size in cell A19 to 14 point and underline the characters in the cell. Add a heavy bottom border to the range A3:F3.

(continued)

World Wide Web Bookstore Five-Year Projected Financial Statement *(continued)*

4. Change the following column widths: A = 23.43; B through F = 11.00. Change the heights of rows 7, 13, 15, 16, and 17 to 24.00.
5. Enter the assumptions values in Table 3-6 in the range B20:B24. Use format symbols.
6. Assign the Comma style format with no decimal places to the range B4:F17.
7. Complete the following entries:
   a. 1998 Net Sales (cell B4) = Units Sold 1997 * (Unit Cost / (1 – Margin)) or =B20 * (B21 / (1 – B24))
   b. 1999 Net Sales (cell C4) = 1998 Net Sales * (1 + Annual Sales Growth) * (1 – Annual Price Decrease) or =B4 * (1 + $B$22) * (1 – $B$23)
   c. Copy cell C4 to range D4:F4.
   d. 1998 Cost of Goods Sold (cell B5) = 1998 Net Sales – (1998 Net Sales * Margin) or =B4 – (1 * $B$24)
   e. Copy cell B5 to range C5:F5.
   f. 1998 Gross Margin (cell B6) = 1998 Net Sales – 1998 Cost of Goods Sold or =B4 – B5
   g. Copy cell B6 to range C6:F6.
   h. 1998 Advertising (cell B8) = 1000 + 15% * 1998 Net Sales or =1000 + 15% * B4
   i. Copy cell B8 to C8:F8.
   j. 1998 Rent (cell B9) = 10800
   k. 1999 Rent (cell C9) = 1998 Rent + 10% * 1998 Rent or =B9 + (10% * B9)
   l. Copy cell C9 to range D9:F9.
   m. 1998 Salaries (cell B10) = 18% * 1998 Net Sales or =18% * B4
   n. Copy cell B10 to range C10:F10.
   o. 1998 Supplies (cell B11) = 1.5% * 1998 Net Sales or =1.5% * B4
   p. Copy cell B11 to range C11:F11.
   q. Other expenses: 1998 = $4,800; 1999 = $18,000; 2000 = $6,000; 2001 = $7,200; 2002 = $9,600
   r. 1998 Total Expenses (cell B13) = SUM(B8:B12)
   s. Copy cell B13 to range C13:F13.
   t. 1998 Income Before Taxes (cell B15) = 1998 Gross Margin – 1998 Total Expenses or =B6 – B13
   u. Copy cell B15 to range C15:F15.
   v. 1998 Income Taxes (cell B16): If 1998 Income Before Taxes is less than zero, then 1998 Income Taxes equal zero; otherwise 1998 Income Taxes equal 50% * 1998 Income Before Taxes or =IF(B15 < 0, 0, 50% * B15)
   w. Copy cell B16 to range C16:F16.
   x. 1998 Net Income (cell B17) = 1998 Income Before Taxes – 1998 Income Taxes or =B15 – B16
   y. Copy cell B17 to range C17:F17.
8. Change the font in cell A1 to 26-point Book Antiqua (or a similar font). Change the font in cell A2 to 16-point Book Antiqua (or a similar font). Change the font in cell F2 to 10-point Century Gothic (or a similar font). Change the background and font colors and add drop shadows as shown in Figure 3-80.

9. Enter your name, course, laboratory assignment (Lab 3-1), date, and instructor name in the range A27:A31. Save the workbook using the file name, WWW Bookstore.
10. Preview and print the worksheet. Preview and print the formulas version (CTRL+`) of the worksheet in landscape orientation using the Fit to option button in the Page Setup dialog box. After printing the formulas version, reset the print scaling to 100%. Press CTRL+` to display the values version of the worksheet. Save the workbook again.

Instructions Part 2: Draw a 3-D Column chart (Figure 3-81) that compares the projected net incomes for the years 1998 through 2002. Use the nonadjacent ranges B3:F3 and B17:F17. Add the chart title and format it as shown in Figure 3-81. Rename and rearrange the sheets as shown in Figure 3-81. Save the workbook using the same file name as defined in Part 1. Print both sheets.

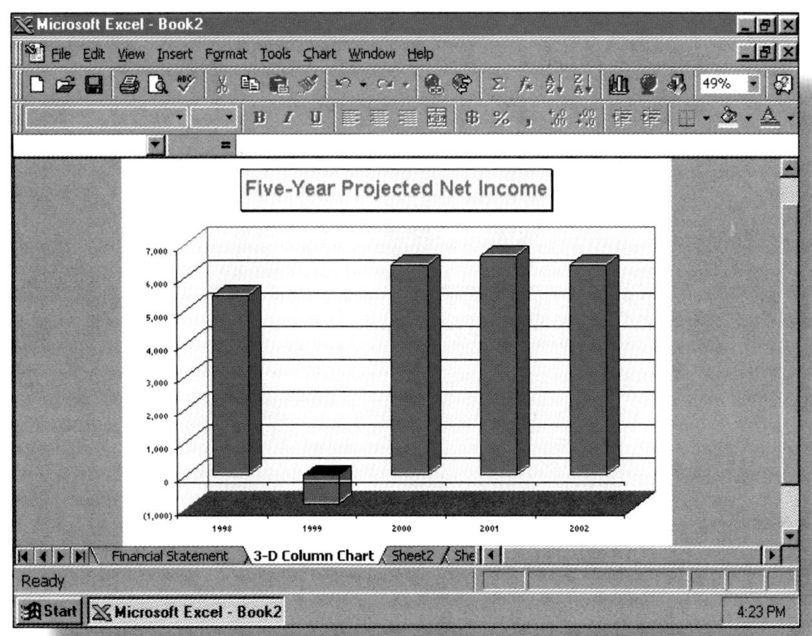

FIGURE 3-81

Instructions Part 3: If the 3-D Column chart is on the screen, click the Financial Statement tab to display the worksheet. Divide the window into two panes by dragging the horizontal split bar between rows 6 and 7. Use the scroll bars to display both the top and bottom of the worksheet.

Using the numbers in columns 2 and 3 of Table 3-7, analyze the effect of changing the annual sales growth (cell B22) and annual price decrease (cell B23) on the annual net incomes in row 17. The resulting answers are in column 4 of Table 3-7. Print both the worksheet and chart for each case.

Table 3-7

CASE	ANNUAL SALES GROWTH	ANNUAL PRICE DECREASE	2002 RESULTING NET INCOME
1	7%	2%	$3,401
2	12%	-3%	$11,120
3	20%	5%	$9,993

Close the workbook without saving it, and then reopen it. Use the Goal Seek command to determine a margin (cell B24) that would result in nearly tripling Mrs. Tellurian's net income in 2002 to $18,927 in cell F17. You should end up with a margin in cell B24 of 68%. After you complete the goal seeking, print only the worksheet. Do not save the workbook with the latest changes.

2 Modifying the Security Lock & Key Weekly Payroll Worksheet

Problem: Your supervisor in the Payroll department has asked you to modify the payroll workbook developed in Exercise 2 of the Project 2 In the Lab section on page E 2.72, so that it displays as shown in Figure 3-82. If you did not complete this exercise, ask your instructor for a copy of the Security Lock & Key workbook.

	A	B	C	D	E	F	G	H	I	J	K
1	Security Lock & Key										
2	Weekly Payroll Report For Week Ending						12/4/98				
3	Employee	YTD Soc. Sec.	Rate	Hours	Dep.	Gross Pay	Soc. Sec.	Medicare	Fed. Tax	State Tax	Net Pay
4	Scotch, Ben	4,012.20	25.00	40.25	3	1,009.38	42.80	14.64	178.80	32.30	740.84
5	Collings, Demi	3,447.60	17.50	53.00	2	1,041.25	64.56	15.10	192.87	33.32	735.41
6	Locken, Viola	4,055.00	27.75	36.00	4	999.00	0.00	14.49	169.03	31.97	783.51
7	Carr, Wessley	3,745.40	19.50	43.50	1	882.38	54.71	12.79	168.78	28.24	617.85
8	Bolte, Ernst	3,974.00	21.50	25.00	5	537.50	33.33	7.79	69.04	17.20	410.14
9	Chin, Huang Le	3,825.50	22.25	40.00	3	890.00	55.18	12.91	154.92	28.48	638.51
10	Lasarga, Mario	3,254.00	16.35	35.75	7	584.51	36.24	8.48	63.06	18.70	458.03
11	*Totals*	26,313.70		273.50		5,944.01	286.81	86.19	996.50	190.21	4,384.30
12											
13	***Assumptions***										
14	Social Security Tax		6.20%								
15	Medicare Tax		1.45%								
16	Maximum Social Security		$4,055.00								

FIGURE 3-82

The major modifications requested by your supervisor include reformatting the worksheet and adding computations of time and a half for hours worked greater than 40, no federal tax if the federal tax is greater than the gross pay, and Social Security and Medicare deductions. The Security Lock & Key workbook, as created in Project 2, is shown in Figure 2-95 on page E 2.72.

Instructions Part 1: Open the workbook, Security Lock & Key, created in Project 2. Perform the following tasks:

1. Use the Select All button and the Clear command on the Edit menu to clear all formats.
2. Bold the entire worksheet. Delete rows 10 through 12. Insert a row above row 2. Modify the worksheet title in cell A1 so it appears as shown in Figure 3-82. Enter the worksheet subtitle, Weekly Payroll Report For Week Ending, in cell A2.
3. Insert a new column between columns A and B. Title the new column B, YTD Soc. Sec. Insert two new columns between columns F and G. Enter the new column G title, Soc. Sec., in cell G3. Title column H in cell H3 Medicare. Assign the NOW function to cell G2 and format it to 3/4/98. Freeze the titles in column A and rows 1 through 3.
4. Change the column widths and row heights as follows: A = 14.00; B = 13.00; C = 9.00; D = 7.00; E = 5.00; F through K = 9.71; and row 3 = 18.00. Right-align the column titles in the range B3:K3.
5. Delete row 9 (Christy, Rupert). Change Ernst Bolte's hours worked to 25 and number of dependents to 5.
6. In row B, enter the YTD Social Security values listed in Table 3-8.
7. Insert two new rows immediately above the Totals row. Add the new employee data as listed in Table 3-9.

Table 3-8

NAME	YTD SOC. SEC.
Scotch, Ben	4,012.20
Collings, Demi	3,447.60
Locken, Viola	4,055.00
Carr, Wessley	3,745.40
Bolte, Ernst	3,974.00

Table 3-9

EMPLOYEE	YTD SOC. SEC.	RATE	HOURS	DEPENDENTS
Chin, Huang Le	3,825.50	22.25	40	3
Lasarga, Mario	3,254.00	16.35	35.75	7

8. Use the Format Cells dialog box to assign a Comma style and two decimal places to the ranges B4:D11 and F4:K11. Center-align the range E4:E10.
9. Enter the Assumptions table in the range A13:C16 and format it as shown in Figure 3-82 (opposite). Place the titles in column A and the numbers in column C.
10. Change the formulas to determine the gross pay in column F and the federal tax in column H.
    a. In cell F4, enter an IF function that applies the following logic:
       If Hours <= 40, then Gross Pay = Rate * Hours, otherwise Gross Pay = Rate * Hours + 0.5 * Rate * (Hours – 40)
    b. Copy the IF function in cell F4 to the range F5:F10.
    c. In cell I4, enter the IF function that applies the following logic:
       If (Gross Pay – Dependents * 38.46) > 0, then Federal Tax = 20% * (Gross Pay – Dependents * 38.46), otherwise Federal Tax = 0
    d. Copy the IF function in cell I4 to the range I5:I10.
11. An employee pays Social Security tax only if his or her YTD Social Security is less than the maximum Social Security in cell C16. Use the following logic to determine the Social Security tax for Ben Scotch in cell G4:
    If Soc. Sec. Tax * Gross Pay + YTD Soc. Sec. > Maximum Soc. Sec., then Maximum Soc. Sec. – YTD Soc. Sec., otherwise Soc. Sec. Tax * Gross Pay
12. Make sure references to the values in the Assumptions table are absolute and then copy the IF function to the range G5:G10.
13. In cell H4, enter the following formula and then copy it to the range H5:H10:
    Medicare = Medicare Tax * Gross Pay
14. Copy the state tax (=0.032 * Gross Pay) in cell J4 to the range J5:J10.
15. In cell K4, enter the following formula and copy it to the range K5:K10:
    = Gross Pay – (Soc. Sec. + Medicare + Fed. Tax + State Tax)
16. Determine any new totals as shown in row 11 of Figure 3-82.
17. Enter your name, course, laboratory assignment (Lab 3-2), date, and instructor name in the range A18:A22.
18. Unfreeze the titles. Save the workbook using the file name, Security Lock & Key 2.

(continued)

Modifying the Security Lock & Key Weekly Payroll Worksheet *(continued)*

19. Use the Zoom box on the Standard toolbar to change the view of the worksheet. One by one, select all the percents in the Zoom list. When you are done, return the worksheet to 100% magnification.
20. Preview the worksheet. If number signs display in place of numbers in any columns, adjust the column widths. Print the worksheet in landscape orientation. Save the worksheet using the same file name.
21. Preview and print the formulas version (CTRL+`) in landscape orientation using the Fit to option button in the Page Setup dialog box. Close the worksheet without saving the latest changes.

Instructions Part 2: Open the workbook, Security Lock & Key 2. Using the range A4:A10 (category names) and the range K4:K10 (data series), draw a Doughnut chart (column 1, row 1 in Chart sub-type area) with the labels inside each piece (select the Show label and percent on Data Labels tab) as shown in Figure 3-83. Add a chart title, Weekly Net Pay, and format it appropriately. Rename the Chart1 sheet to Doughnut Chart and the Sheet1 sheet to Payroll. Rearrange the sheets so the Payroll sheet is to the left of the Doughnut Chart sheet. Save the workbook using the same file name as in Part 1. Preview and print both sheets.

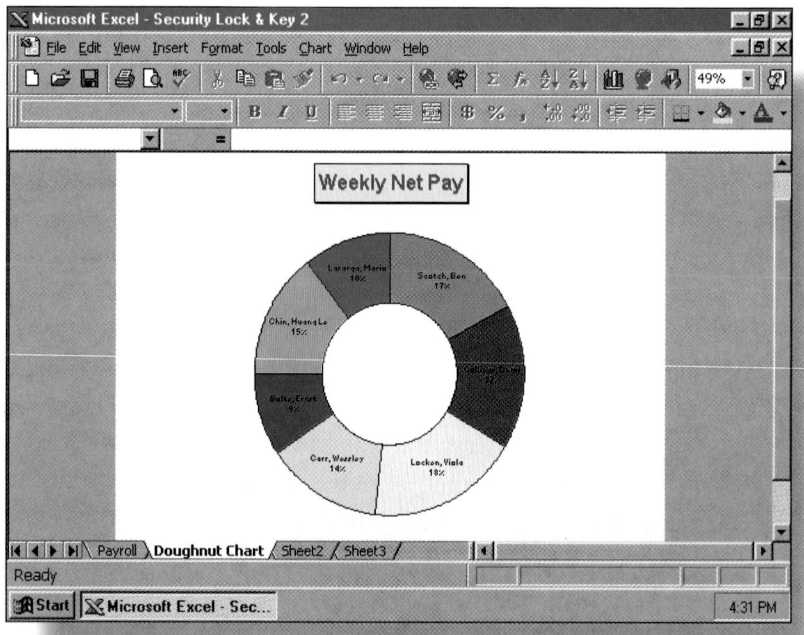

FIGURE 3-83

Instructions Part 3: If the Doughnut chart is on the screen, click the Payroll tab to display the worksheet.

Using the numbers in the Table 3-10, analyze the effect of changing the Social Security tax in cell C14 and the Medicare tax in cell C15. Print the worksheet for each case. The first case should result in a total Social Security tax in cell G11 of $337.97. The second case should result in a total Social Security tax of $436.36.

Table 3-10

CASE	SOCIAL SECURITY TAX	MEDICARE TAX
1	7.5%	2.25%
2	10%	3%

3 Solar Works, Inc. Projected Quarterly Report

Problem: You are employed as a spreadsheet specialist at Solar Works, Inc., a leading manufacturer of solar energy products. The company utilizes assumptions based on past business practice to plan for the coming quarter. You have been asked to create a worksheet similar to the one shown in Figure 3-84.

Instructions Part 1: Do the following to create the worksheet shown in Figure 3-84.

1. Bold the entire worksheet. Enter the worksheet titles in cells A1, A2, and A3. Use your own initials in cell A3. Enter the NOW function in cell E3 and format it to 4-Mar. Enter July in cell B4. With cell B4 selected, italicize and rotate the text 45°. Use the fill handle to create the month series in row 4. Enter Total in cell E4 and use the Format Painter button on the Standard toolbar to format it the same as cell D4. Add a heavy bottom border to the range A4:E4. Enter the row titles down through Assumptions in cell A20. Copy the row titles in the range A11:A15 to the range A21:A25.
2. Click the Select All button and then change the width of all the columns to 13.71. Change the widths of column A to 18.29 and column E to 14.86. Check the height of row 4 to ensure it is 60.00.

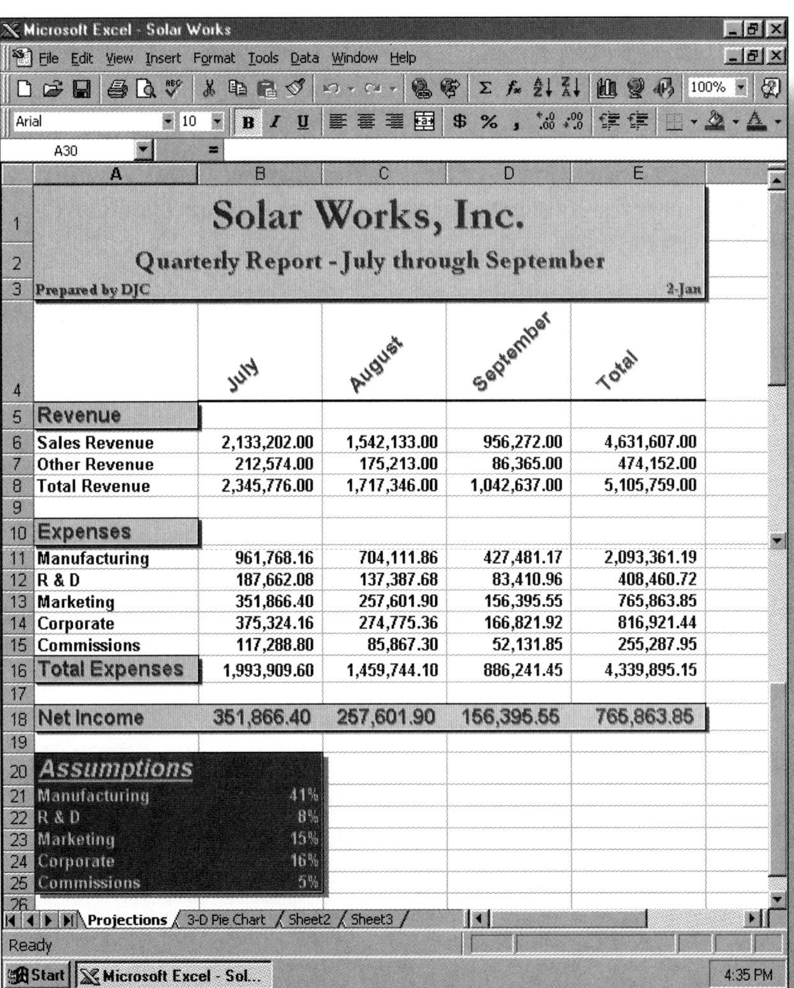

FIGURE 3-84

Table 3-11

	JULY	AUGUST	SEPTEMBER
Sales Revenue	2,133,202.00	1,542,133.00	956,272.00
Other Revenue	212,574.00	175,213.00	86,365.00

(continued)

Solar Works, Inc. Projected Quarterly Report *(continued)*

3. Enter the Assumptions values in the range B21:B25.
4. Using the values in Table 3-11 on the previous page, enter the sales revenue and other revenue in the range B6:D7. Determine the totals in the range E6:E7 and in the range B8:E8.
5. Each of the expense categories in the range B11:D15 is determined by multiplying the total monthly revenue by the corresponding assumption in the Assumptions table (range A20:B25). For example, the Manufacturing expense in cell B11 is equal to cell B21 times cell B8, or =B21 * B8. Once the formulas are assigned to the range B11:B15, they can be copied to the range C11:D15. For the copy to work properly, however, you must make any references to the Assumptions table absolute. Thus, enter the following formulas in the designated cells: B11 = $B$21 * B8; B12 = $B$22 * B8; B13 = $B$23 * B8; B14 = $B$24 * B8; B15 = $B$25 * B8.
6. Use the SUM function to determine all the totals. The net income in row 18 is equal to the total revenue for each month (row 8) minus the total expenses for each month (row 16).
7. Format the worksheet so it resembles Figure 3-84. Use Garamond font (or a similar font) in the range A1:E3.
8. Enter your name, course, laboratory assignment (Lab 3-3), date, and instructor name in the range A28:A32.
9. Save the workbook using the file name, Solar Works.
10. Print the worksheet. Preview and print the formulas version (CTRL+`) in landscape orientation using the Fit to option button in the Page Setup dialog box. Press CTRL+` to display the values version of the worksheet. Save the workbook again.

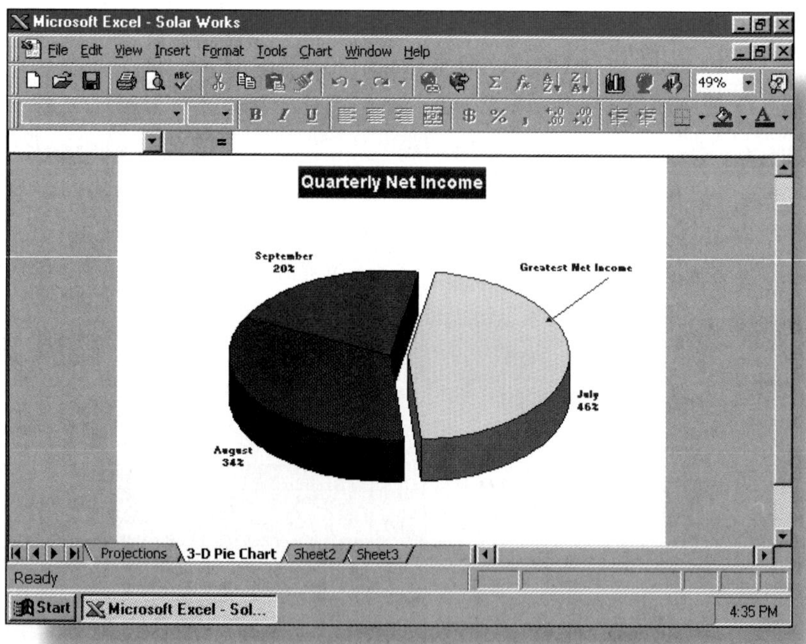

FIGURE 3-85

In the Lab

Instructions Part 2: Draw a 3-D Pie chart (Figure 3-85, opposite) that shows the monthly contribution to the quarterly net income. That is, chart the nonadjacent ranges B4:D4 (category names) and B18:D18 (data series). Do the following to the Pie chart:

1. Add the chart title and format it as shown in Figure 3-85.
2. Explode the July slice.
3. Select a slice and use the 3-D View command on the shortcut menu to change the elevation to 30° and the rotation to 10°.
4. Change the color of the slices as shown in Figure 3-85.
5. Use Help to step you through adding a text box with the phrase Greatest Net Income and an arrow pointing to the July slice. Format the text box and arrow as shown in Figure 3-85.
6. Rename the sheets as follows: Chart1 to 3-D Pie Chart; Sheet1 to Projections. Rearrange the sheets so the Projections sheet is to the left of the 3-D Pie Chart sheet.
7. Save the workbook and print both sheets.

Instructions Part 3: If the 3-D Pie chart is on the screen, click the Projections tab to display the worksheet. Using the numbers in the Table 3-12, analyze the effect of changing the assumptions in rows 21 through 25 on the quarterly net income in cell E18. Print the worksheet for each case.

You should end with the following quarterly net incomes in cell E18: Case 1 = 867,979.03; Case 2 = 357,403.13; Case 3 = 51,057.59.

Close the Solar Works workbook without saving it and then reopen it. Use the Goal Seek command to determine the marketing percentage (cell B23) that would result in a quarterly net income of $255,287.95 in cell E18. You should end up with a marketing percentage of 25%. Print only the worksheet. Close the Solar Works workbook without saving it.

Table 3-12

	CASE 1	CASE 2	CASE 3
Manufacturing	38%	40%	43%
R & D	9%	10%	14%
Marketing	16%	17%	18%
Corporate	14%	18%	19%
Commissions	6%	8%	5%

Cases and Places

The difficulty of these case studies varies: ◗ are the least difficult; ◗◗ are more difficult; ◗◗◗ are the most difficult.

1 ◗ The Penny Loafer is a free paper that is published once weekly. For $3.00 you can place an advertisement to buy or sell just about anything.

The paper relies completely on the advertising of local businesses for its revenue. You have been asked to prepare a worksheet, based on the figures provided by your manager (Figure 3-86). Include a chart that illustrates the net incomes. The paper's senior-level managers hope to increase private advertising revenues by 3% per month, thus bringing in $3,893.40 in April; $4,134.00 in May; and $4,447.20 in June. Expanding the paper's service area, however, will increase Marketing by 5%, Payroll by 3%, and Production Costs by 11%. Use the concepts and techniques presented in this project to create and format the worksheets.

Revenues:	April	May	June
Private Ads	3,780.00	3,900.00	4,080.00
Real Estate Ads	4,265.21	4,724.25	4,838.40
Business Ads	953.65	1,082.00	1,221.02
Expenses:			
Marketing	15%		
Payroll	38%		
Production Costs	16%		

FIGURE 3-86

Cases and Places

2 ▶ Web World is an Internet service provider for your community. They want to install lines to provide a local access number for Jeffers, a neighboring town. You have been hired to perform a feasibility study using the information provided as shown in Figure 3-87. The owners of Web World want to know how many years it will take to pay for the equipment upgrades and start showing a profit from the new venture.

	Year 1
Population	24,000
Customers	480
Revenue	10,080
Profit	-141,244
Assumptions	
Initial Cost	151,324
New Customers Each Year	2%
Population Increase	0.25%
Monthly Service Fee	21

FIGURE 3-87

The following formulas are supplied for Year 1:

Customers = Population x 2%
Revenue = Customers x Monthly Service Fee
Profit or Loss = Revenue - Upgrade Cost

The following formulas are supplied for Year 2:

Population = Year 1 Population x Population Increase + Year 1 Population (Example: =$B$3*$B$13+B3)
Customers = Year 2 Population x 2% + Year 1 Customers
Revenue = Year 2 Customers x Monthly Service Fee
Profit or Loss = Year 1 + Year 2 Revenue - Upgrade Cost (Example: =SUM($B$5:C5)-$B$11)

Create a worksheet for Web World that tracks Population, Customers, Revenue, and Profits or Losses over the next six years.

3 ▶▶ Melissa, a friend of yours, is trying to figure out how much money she will need to ask her parents for each year while she is attending college. She has asked you to help her design a worksheet that will itemize her school and living costs. She then wants to list her grant, scholarship, and work-study income and compare the totals. Melissa is not planning to attend the summer semester. Her grants provide her with $12,000.00 per year, scholarships are $3,000.00 per year, and work-study is a maximum of $1,300.00 per year. In addition, Melissa's grandparents have promised to send her a gift of 10% of the tuition for every semester she maintains a B average. Melissa foresees no problem maintaining a B average every semester.

Melissa's tuition is $12,000.00 and room and board costs are $4,000.00 per year. She spends $1,000.00 per year on books and supplies and estimates she will need $1,000.00 per year for miscellaneous items.

Melissa wants the worksheet to reflect her income and costs for each semester. She also wants two separate worksheets for goal seeking. First, Melissa wants to know how she will be affected if her tuition goes up next year to $13,200.00 as rumored. She also wants to prepare for the increase in book prices that will take effect in the second semester of the current year. She has heard that the cost of books and supplies will increase the second semester about 12%. Use the concepts and techniques presented in this project to create and format the worksheets.

Cases and Places

4 ▸▸ Your uncle, who owns Ben's Card Shop, finds that he sells the most cards during special occasions. Last year, he sold 2,300 Valentine's Day cards, 1,200 Easter cards, 1,400 Mother's Day cards, 1,100 Father's Day cards, 750 Graduation cards, 300 Halloween cards, and 600 Christmas cards. He also sold 475 boxed sets of Valentines and 250 boxed sets of Christmas cards. Uncle Ben has heard that you are a bit of a financial whiz, and he wants you to create a worksheet that will help him order enough special occasion cards each year.

Uncle Ben wants to take into account that the population of his town (8,500 last year) increases by about 150 people per year and that about 8% of the town population shops in his store. He also wants a separate worksheet to show his additional stock needs if he increases his patronage by 2% per year through advertising.

5 ▸▸▸ Every once in a while you buy a lottery ticket. This time, however, it paid off — you won! Immediately after you won, you sought the advice of an investment counselor, who is using your winnings to purchase stock for you. She has kept your stock in two major categories: Leisure Products (10,000 shares in Harley Davidson, 4,000 shares in Bell Sports, and 1,000 shares in Coleman Industries), and Internet Software and Services (5,000 shares in Spyglass, 3,000 shares in Yahoo, and 2,000 shares in FTP Software). Your investment counselor has assured you that, over the next 5 years, the Leisure stocks will return an average of 8% per year and the Internet stocks will return an average of 11% per year. Using the latest stock prices, create a worksheet that organizes your stock portfolio and projects its annual worth for the next five years. Group the companies by major categories and include a total for each category.

6 ▸▸▸ Keeping a balanced budget is important for everyone — from college students to chief executive officers (CEOs) in corporate America. Teachers, professors, and other instructors — who often earn far less than they are worth — also have to keep budgets. Interview one of your instructors and then create and format a worksheet that reflects his or her monthly budget throughout the year. Show all available income sources. Include monthly expenditures such as food, entertainment, mortgage or rent, travel and auto maintenance, etc. Include a row for miscellaneous expenses, like medical or dental insurance payments. Ascertain the money remaining each month; this amount will become part or all of the money available for the subsequent month. Perform at least one what-if analysis to examine the effect of changing one or more of the values in the worksheet.

7 ▸▸▸ Subcontractors, who are considered to be self-employed, must manage their income and expenses carefully in order to be profitable. They also must pay estimated taxes based on their income. Talk to a subcontractor (for example, carpenter, painter, landscaper, construction worker, or writer) and create a worksheet reflecting his or her profits over the past six months. Attempt to determine what percentage of the worker's income was spent on business-related expenses. Also find out about any occasional expenses and include these in the worksheet. With this information, and the subcontractor's income for the last six months, determine the expenses and profit each month. Include at least one chart that illustrates an aspect of your worksheet you feel is significant — perhaps monthly profits or the total money applied to each business-related expense.

Linking an Excel Worksheet to a Word Document

Case Perspective

Jacob D. Webb is Vice President of Sales for Corporate Intranets, a medium-size company that installs intranets for business, industry, and government agencies. Each week, Jacob sends out a memorandum to all district sales managers showing the previous week's daily sales by office. He currently uses Word to produce the memorandum, which includes a table of the daily sales. The wording in the memorandum remains nearly constant week to week. The table of daily sales changes significantly each week.

Jacob recently attended a seminar sponsored by Microsoft and learned of Office 97's Object Linking and Embedding (OLE) capabilities. He now wants to use Word to create the basic memorandum and then link a worksheet showing the week's daily sales to the memorandum. Using this technique, Jacob could update the worksheet simply by opening the memorandum in Word. Once he updates the week's daily sales in the worksheet linked to the memorandum, he can e-mail, print and mail, or save the memorandum as a Web page for review using a Web browser.

Introduction

With Microsoft Office 97 you can incorporate parts of documents or entire documents, called **objects**, from one application into another application. For example, you can copy a worksheet created in Excel into a document created in Word (Figure 1 on the next page). In this case, the Excel worksheet is called the **source document** (copied from) and the Word document is called the **destination document** (copied to). You can copy objects between applications in one of three ways: (1) copy and paste; (2) copy and embed; and (3) copy and link.

All the Microsoft Office applications allow you to use these three methods to copy objects between applications. The first method uses the Copy and Paste buttons. The latter two use the Paste Special command on the Edit menu and are referred to as **Object Linking and Embedding**, or **OLE**. Table 1 on page EI 1.3 summarizes the differences among the three methods.

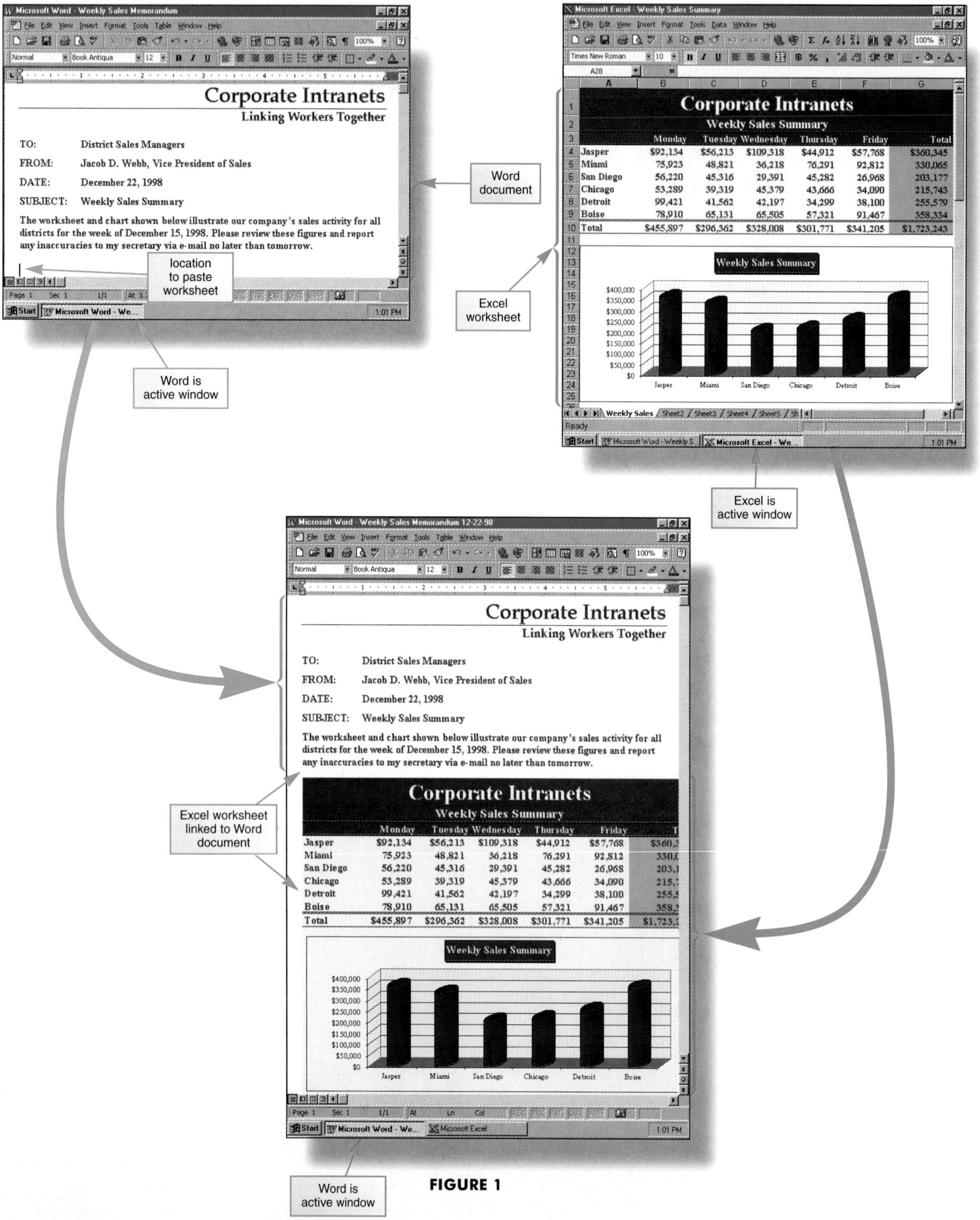

Microsoft Word - Weekly Sales Memorandum

Corporate Intranets

Linking Workers Together

TO: District Sales Managers

FROM: Jacob D. Webb, Vice President of Sales

DATE: December 22, 1998

SUBJECT: Weekly Sales Summary

The worksheet and chart shown below illustrate our company's sales activity for all districts for the week of December 15, 1998. Please review these figures and report any inaccuracies to my secretary via e-mail no later than tomorrow.

location to paste worksheet

Word document

Word is active window

Microsoft Excel - Weekly Sales Summary

Corporate Intranets

Weekly Sales Summary

	Monday	Tuesday	Wednesday	Thursday	Friday	Total
Jasper	$92,134	$56,213	$109,318	$44,912	$57,768	$360,345
Miami	75,923	48,821	36,218	76,291	92,812	330,065
San Diego	56,220	45,316	29,391	45,282	26,968	203,177
Chicago	53,289	39,319	45,379	43,666	34,090	215,743
Detroit	99,421	41,562	42,197	34,299	38,100	255,579
Boise	78,910	65,131	65,505	57,321	91,467	358,334
Total	$455,897	$296,362	$328,008	$301,771	$341,205	$1,723,243

Weekly Sales Summary

Jasper Miami San Diego Chicago Detroit Boise

Excel worksheet

Excel is active window

Microsoft Word - Weekly Sales Memorandum 12-22-98

Corporate Intranets

Linking Workers Together

TO: District Sales Managers

FROM: Jacob D. Webb, Vice President of Sales

DATE: December 22, 1998

SUBJECT: Weekly Sales Summary

The worksheet and chart shown below illustrate our company's sales activity for all districts for the week of December 15, 1998. Please review these figures and report any inaccuracies to my secretary via e-mail no later than tomorrow.

Excel worksheet linked to Word document

Word is active window

FIGURE 1

Table 1

METHOD	CHARACTERISTICS
Copy and paste	The source document becomes part of the destination document. An object may be edited, but the editing features are limited to those of the destination application. An Excel worksheet becomes a Word table. If changes are made to values in the Word table, any original Excel formulas are not recalculated.
Copy and embed	The source document becomes part of the destination document. An object may be edited in the destination document using source editing features. The Excel worksheet remains a worksheet in Word. If changes are made to values in the worksheet with Word active, Excel formulas will be recalculated. If you change the worksheet in Excel, however, these changes will not display in the Word document the next time you open it.
Copy and link	The source document does not become part of the destination document, even though it appears to be a part. Instead, a link is established between the two documents, so that when you open the Word document, the worksheet displays within the document, as though it were a part of it. When you attempt to edit a linked worksheet in Word, the system activates Excel. If you change the worksheet in Excel, the changes also will display in the Word document the next time you open it.

Copy and link is preferred over the other two methods if an object is likely to change and you want to make sure the object reflects the changes in the source document or if an object is large, such as a video clip or sound clip. Because the weekly sales worksheet for Corporate Intranets will change weekly, the copy and link method is the best method to use.

Opening a Word Document and an Excel Workbook

Both the Word document (Weekly Sales Memorandum) and the Excel workbook (Weekly Sales Summary) are in the Excel folder on the Data Disk that accompanies this book. The first step in linking the Excel worksheet to the Word document is to open the document in Word and the workbook in Excel as shown in the following steps.

More About Office 97

Because you can use OLE among Word, Excel, Access, PowerPoint, and Outlook, Office 97 can be viewed as one large integrated software package, rather than separate applications.

To Open a Word Document and an Excel Workbook

1 Insert the Data Disk that accompanies this book in drive A. Click the Start button. Click Open Office Document on the Start menu. Click the Look in box arrow, click 3½ Floppy (A:), and then click the Excel folder. Double-click the file name, Weekly Sales Memorandum.

The Weekly Sales Memorandum document displays (Figure 2).

FIGURE 2

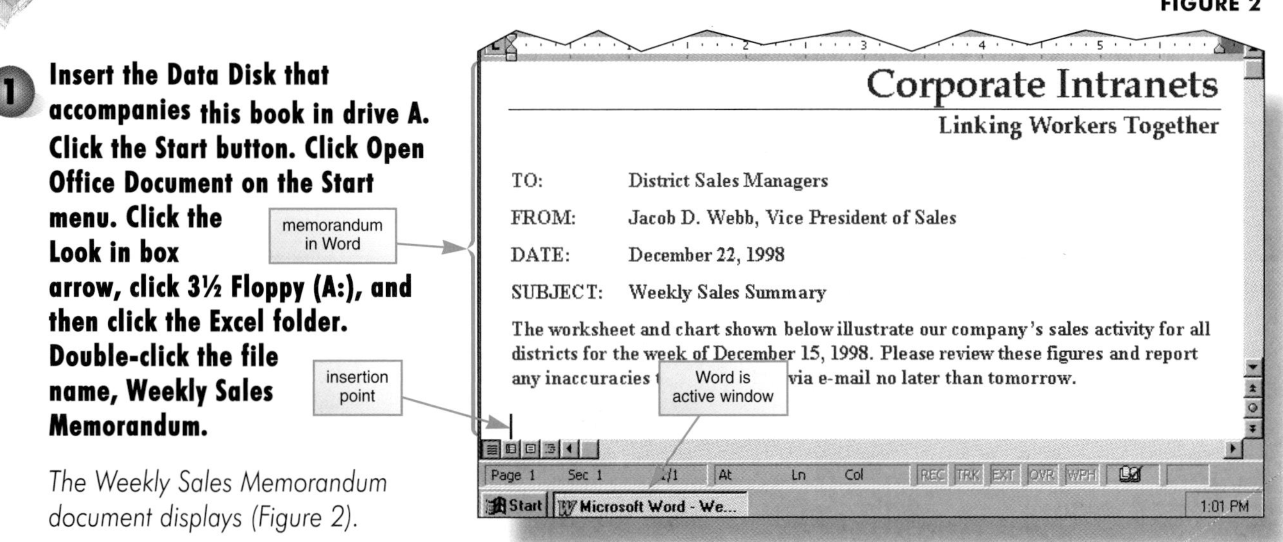

2 **Click the Start button. Click Open Office Document on the Start menu. Click the Look in box arrow, click 3½ Floppy (A:), and then click the Excel folder. Double-click the file name, Weekly Sales Summary.**

Excel becomes active and the Weekly Sales Summary workbook displays (Figure 3). At this point, Word is inactive, but still is in memory. Excel is the active window as shown on the taskbar.

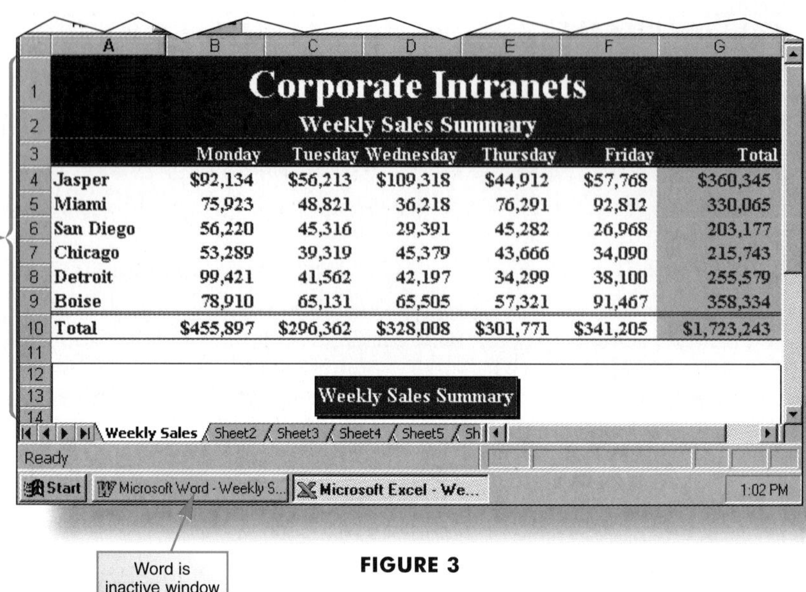

FIGURE 3

With both Word and Excel running and in memory, you can switch between the applications by clicking the appropriate button to the right of the Start button on the taskbar.

Linking an Excel Worksheet to a Word Document

With both applications running, the next step is to link the Excel worksheet to the Word document as shown in the following steps.

To Link the Excel Worksheet to the Word Document

With the Excel window active, select the range A1:G25. Click the Copy button to copy the selected range to the Clipboard.

A marquee surrounds the range A1:G25 indicating it has been copied to the Clipboard (Figure 4).

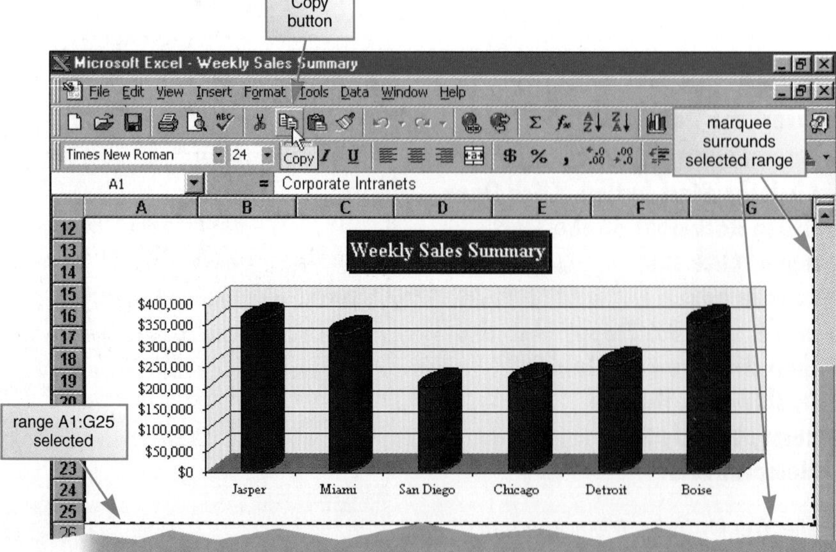

FIGURE 4

2 **Click the Microsoft Word button on the taskbar to activate the Word window. Move the insertion point to the bottom of the document to position the insertion point where you want the worksheet to display in the document. Click Edit on the menu bar and then point to Paste Special.**

The Weekly Sales Memorandum document and the Edit menu display on the screen. The insertion point blinks at the bottom of the document (Figure 5).

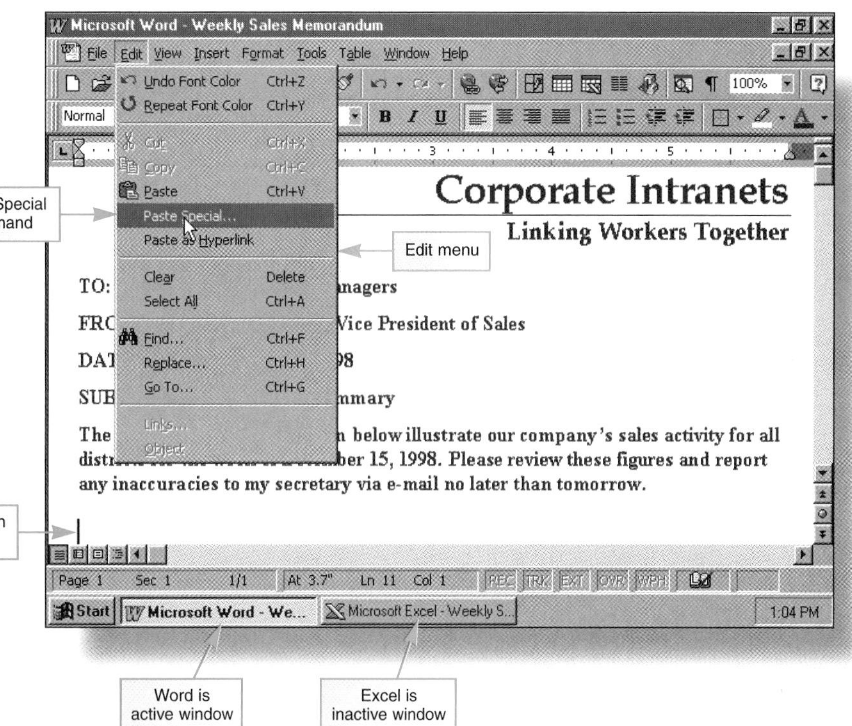

FIGURE 5

3 **Click Paste Special. When the Paste Special dialog box displays, click the Paste link option button, click Microsoft Excel Worksheet Object in the As list box, and click the Float over text check box to deselect it. Point to the OK button.**

The Paste Special dialog box displays as shown in Figure 6. Deselecting the Float over text check box instructs Excel to paste the worksheet in the document beginning at the location of the insertion point.

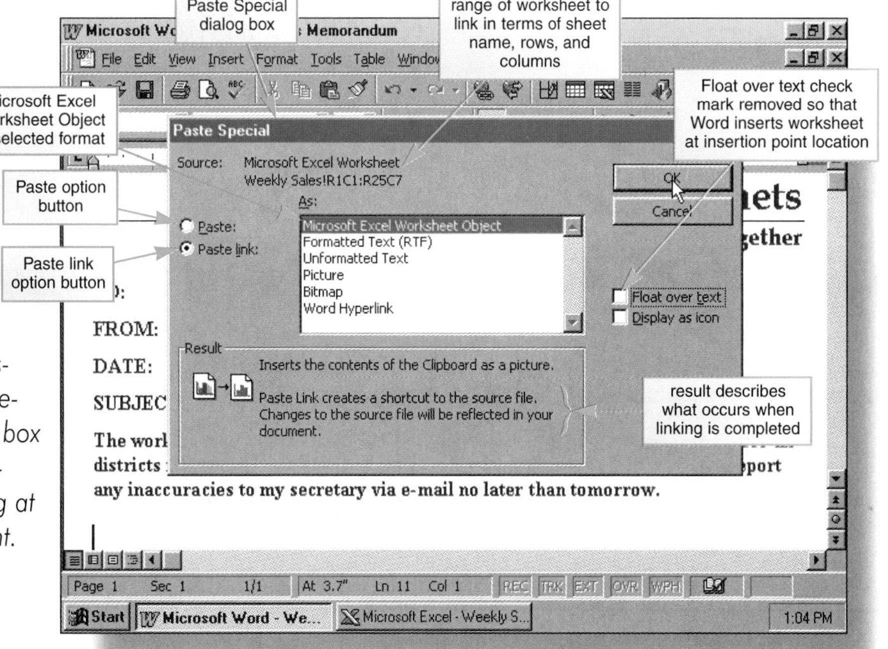

FIGURE 6

4 Click the OK button.

The range A1:G25 of the Excel worksheet displays in the Word document, beginning at the location of the insertion point (Figure 7).

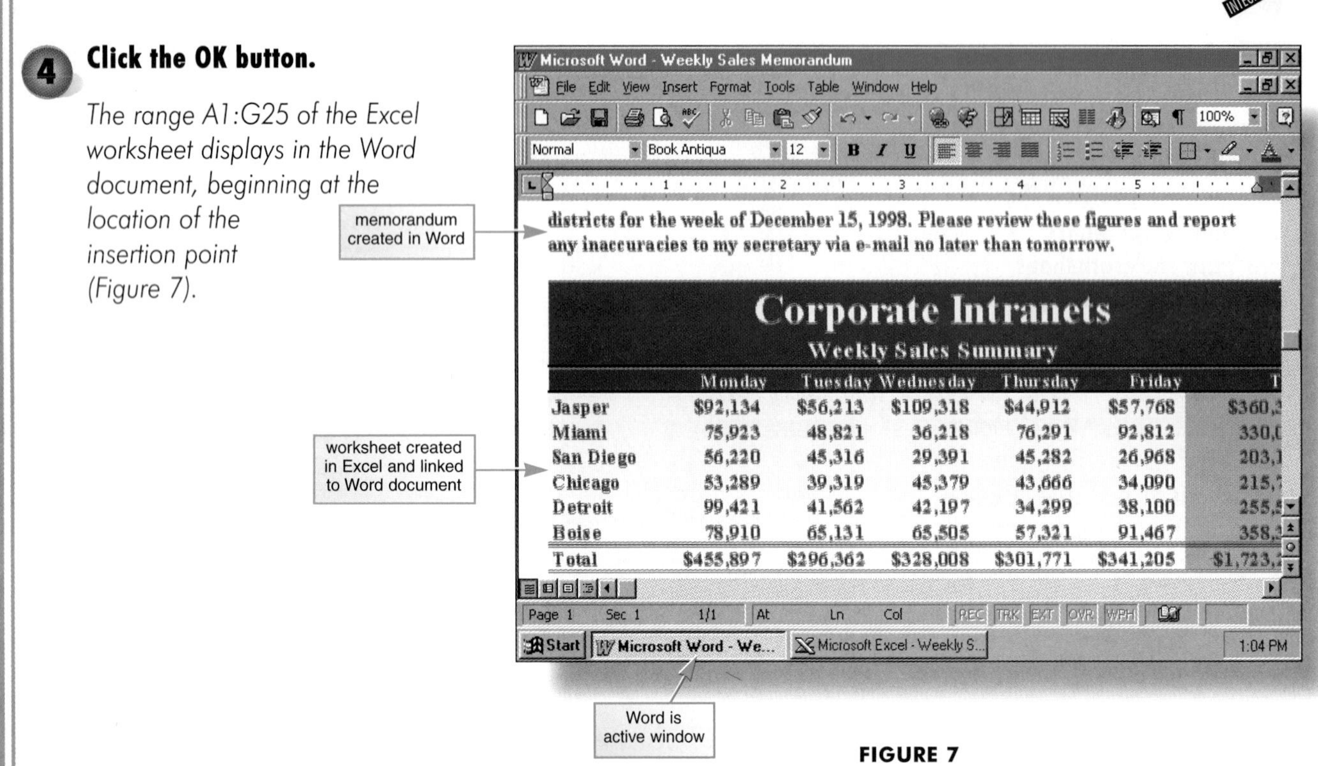

	Monday	Tuesday	Wednesday	Thursday	Friday
Jasper	$92,134	$56,213	$109,318	$44,912	$57,768
Miami	75,923	48,821	36,218	76,291	92,812
San Diego	56,220	45,316	29,391	45,282	26,968
Chicago	53,289	39,319	45,379	43,666	34,090
Detroit	99,421	41,562	42,197	34,299	38,100
Boise	78,910	65,131	65,505	57,321	91,467
Total	$455,897	$296,362	$328,008	$301,771	$341,205

FIGURE 7

The Excel worksheet now is linked to the Word document. If you save the Word document and reopen it, the worksheet will display exactly as it does in Figure 7. If you want to delete the worksheet, simply click the worksheet in the Word document and then press the DELETE key. The next section shows how to print and save the memorandum with the linked worksheet.

More *About* OLE

If you want to have more than one object at a time available for OLE, you can store objects to embed on the desktop, rather than using the Clipboard. When you use this technique, the objects are called **scrap**. To accomplish this task, part of the desktop must be visible behind the window of the source application. Next, right-drag the object from the source application onto the desktop. Once on the desktop, Windows displays the object as an icon. When the shortcut menu displays, click Create Scrap Here. Next, activate the destination document and drag the scrap from the desktop onto the destination document and drop it where you want it inserted. To delete a scrap from the desktop, right-click it and then click Delete.

Printing and Saving the Word Document with the Linked Worksheet

To print and save the Word document and linked Excel worksheet as a single document, complete the steps on the next page.

Steps To Print and Save the Word Document with the Linked Worksheet

1 **With the Word window active, click the Print button on the Standard toolbar.**

The memorandum and the worksheet print as one document as shown in Figure 8.

2 **Click Save As on the File menu. Type the file name** `Weekly Sales Memorandum 12-22-98` **in the File name text box. If necessary, click the Save in box arrow, click 3½ Floppy (A:), and then click the Excel folder. Click the Save button.**

Excel saves the Word document to your floppy disk using the file name, Weekly Sales Memorandum 12-22-98. Although the worksheet is not part of the saved file, the saved file does contain a link to the workbook, Weekly Sales Summary, and information about the Excel worksheet range to display in the Word document.

document with linked worksheet and chart printed as one entity

Corporate Intranets
Linking Workers Together

TO: District Sales Managers
FROM: Jacob D. Webb, Vice President of Sales
DATE: December 22, 1998
SUBJECT: Weekly Sales Summary

The worksheet and chart shown below illustrate our company's sales activity for all districts for the week of December 15, 1998. Please review these figures and report any inaccuracies to my secretary via e-mail no later than tomorrow.

Corporate Intranets
Weekly Sales Summary

	Monday	Tuesday	Wednesday	Thursday	Friday	Total
Jasper	$92,134	$56,213	$109,318	$44,912	$57,768	$360,345
Miami	75,923	48,821	36,218	76,291	92,812	330,065
San Diego	56,220	45,316	29,391	45,282	26,968	203,177
Chicago	53,289	39,319	45,379	43,666	34,090	215,743
Detroit	99,421	41,562	42,197	34,299	38,100	255,579
Boise	78,910	65,131	65,505	57,321	91,467	358,334
Total	$455,897	$296,362	$328,008	$301,771	$341,205	$1,723,243

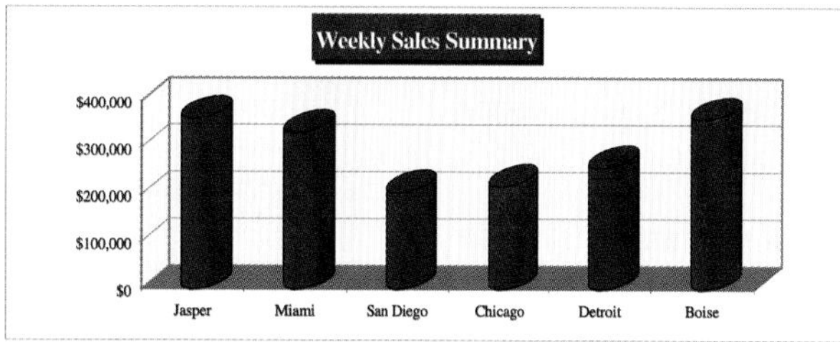

FIGURE 8

If you exit both applications and reopen Weekly Sales Memorandum 12-22-98, the worksheet will display in the document even though Excel is not running. Because it supports object linking and embedding (OLE), Word is able to display the linked portion of the Excel workbook. The next section describes what happens when you attempt to edit the linked worksheet while Word is active.

Editing the Linked Worksheet

When a worksheet is linked to a Word document, you can edit any of the cells in the worksheet. To edit the worksheet, double-click it. If Excel is running in memory, the system will switch to Excel and display the linked workbook. If Excel is not running, the system will start Excel and display the linked workbook. The following steps show how to change the Thursday sales for the San Diego office in cell E6 from 45,282 to 3,000.

Steps To Edit the Linked Worksheet

1 With the Word window active and the Weekly Sales Memorandum 12-22-98 document active, double-click the worksheet.

Windows switches from Word to Excel and displays the original workbook, Weekly Sales Summary.

2 Click cell E6 and enter 3000 **in the cell.**

Excel recalculates all formulas in the workbook (Figure 9) and redraws the 3-D Column chart.

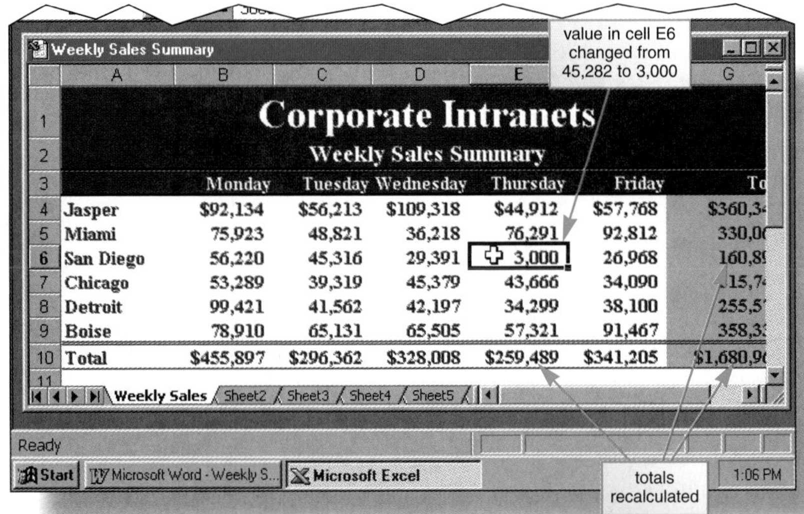

	Monday	Tuesday	Wednesday	Thursday	Friday
Jasper	$92,134	$56,213	$109,318	$44,912	$57,768
Miami	75,923	48,821	36,218	76,291	92,812
San Diego	56,220	45,316	29,391	3,000	26,968
Chicago	53,289	39,319	45,379	43,666	34,090
Detroit	99,421	41,562	42,197	34,299	38,100
Boise	78,910	65,131	65,505	57,321	91,467
Total	$455,897	$296,362	$328,008	$259,489	$341,205

FIGURE 9

3 Click the Microsoft Word button on the taskbar.

The Word window becomes active. The Thursday sales amount for the San Diego office is the newly entered 3,000. New totals display for Thursday sales (cell E10), San Diego sales (cell G6), and the Total sales (cell G10) for the company (Figure 10).

4 Quit both applications without saving the changes.

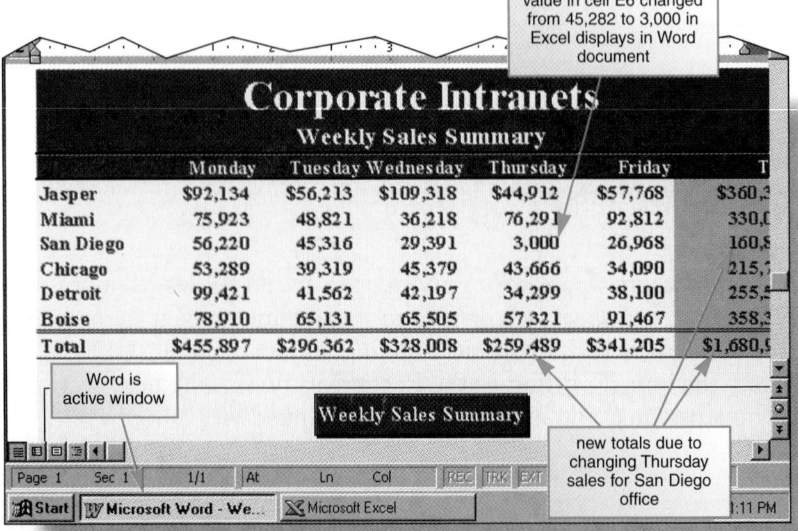

	Monday	Tuesday	Wednesday	Thursday	Friday
Jasper	$92,134	$56,213	$109,318	$44,912	$57,768
Miami	75,923	48,821	36,218	76,291	92,812
San Diego	56,220	45,316	29,391	3,000	26,968
Chicago	53,289	39,319	45,379	43,666	34,090
Detroit	99,421	41,562	42,197	34,299	38,100
Boise	78,910	65,131	65,505	57,321	91,467
Total	$455,897	$296,362	$328,008	$259,489	$341,205

FIGURE 10

As you can see from the previous steps, you double-click a linked object if you want to edit it. Windows will activate the source application and display the workbook or document from which the object came. You then can edit the object and return to the destination application. Any changes made to the object will appear in the destination document.

If you want the edited changes to the linked workbook to be permanent, you must save the workbook, Weekly Sales Summary, before quitting Excel.

Summary

With the Excel worksheet linked to the Word document, Jacob D. Webb, the Vice President of Sales, now can open the Word document each week, double-click the worksheet, and change the daily sales amounts. He then can e-mail the Word document, print and mail it, or save the Word document in HTML format and make it available for viewing on the company's intranet.

This Integration Feature introduced you to linking one document to another. When you link an object to a document and save it, only the link to the object is saved with the document. You edit a linked object by double-clicking it. The system activates the application and opens the source document file from which the object came.

If you change any part of the object and then return to the destination document, the updated object will display.

What You Should Know

Having completed this Integration Feature, you now should be able to perform the following tasks:

- Edit the Linked Worksheet *(EI 1.8)*
- Link the Excel Worksheet to the Word Document *(EI 1.4)*
- Open a Word Document and an Excel Workbook *(EI 1.5)*
- Print and Save the Word Document with the Linked Worksheet *(EI 1.7)*

1 Using Help

Instructions: Start Excel. Click Contents and Index on the Help menu. Click the Contents tab. Double-click the Sharing Information and Graphics Between Applications book. Double-click the Exchanging Data Between Microsoft Excel, Word, and PowerPoint book. Double-click the topic, Share Information Between Office Programs. Read and print the information. Click the Help Topics button. Double-click the topic, Copy Microsoft Excel data to Word or PowerPoint. Click each of the links at the bottom of the window and print the information. Use the Back buton to return to the previous Help window. Hand in the printouts to your instructor.

In the Lab

2 Linking an Excel Worksheet to a Word Document

Problem: Your manager, Ms. Julie Strong, at Pearl Gates Fencing, sends out a monthly memo with expense figures to the regional managers. You have been asked to simplify her task by linking the monthly expense worksheet to a memo.

Instructions: Perform the following tasks.

1. One at a time, open the Word document, Monthly Expense Memo, and the Excel workbook, Monthly Expense Summary, from the Excel folder on the Data Disk that accompanies this book.
2. Link the worksheet range A1:E17 at the bottom of the Monthly Expense Memo document. To link, click the Paste link option button, select Microsoft Excel Worksheet Object in the As list box, and clear the Float over text check box in the Paste Special dialog box.
3. Print and then save the document as Monthly Expense Memo 7-1-98.
4. Double-click the worksheet and increase each of the nine expense amounts by $200. Activate the Word window and print the memorandum with the new values. Close the document and workbook without saving.

3 Embedding a Word Document into an Excel Worksheet

Problem: Your supervisor, Ms. Julie Strong, at Pearl Gates Fencing, has asked you to embed the Word document into the Excel workbook, rather than linking the Excel workbook to the Word document as was done in Exercise 2.

Instructions: Complete the following tasks.

1. One at a time, open the Word document, Monthly Expense Memo, and the Excel workbook, Monthly Expense Summary from the Excel folder on the Data Disk that accompanies this book.
2. With the Excel window active, click the Monthly Office Expenses tab. Insert 17 rows above row 1 and then select cell A1. Activate the Word document and copy the entire document. Embed the Word document at the top of the Monthly Office Expenses worksheet. To embed, click the Paste option button on the Paste Special dialog box, select Microsoft Word Document Object in the As list box, and clear the Float over text check box.
3. Print the Monthly Office Expenses worksheet and then save the workbook as Monthly Expense with Memo 7-1-98.
4. With the Excel window active, double-click the embedded document and delete the first sentence. Activate the Excel window and print the worksheet with the new memo. Close the workbook and document without saving.

Microsoft Access 97

PROJECT ONE

CREATING A DATABASE USING DESIGN AND DATASHEET VIEWS

PROJECT TWO

QUERYING A DATABASE USING THE SELECT QUERY WINDOW

PROJECT THREE

MAINTAINING A DATABASE USING THE DESIGN AND UPDATE FEATURES OF ACCESS

INTEGRATION FEATURE

INTEGRATING EXCEL WORKSHEET DATA INTO AN ACCESS DATABASE

Microsoft Access 97

Creating a Database Using Design and Datasheet Views

Objectives:

You will have mastered the material in this project when you can:

- Describe databases and database management systems
- Start Access
- Describe the features of the Access screen
- Create a database
- Create a table
- Define the fields in a table
- Open a table
- Add records to an empty table
- Close a table
- Close a database and quit Access
- Open a database
- Add records to a nonempty table
- Print the contents of a table
- Use a form to view data
- Create a custom report
- Use Microsoft Access Help
- Design a database to eliminate redundancy

Selections Collections One of a Kind

Anthology of Data and Other Priceless Keepsakes

Seventy-four years after his death, the skeleton of an obscure, but wealthy English scientist was disinterred and taken across the Atlantic to lie with honor in the institution his money had founded — in a nation he had never seen! His final resting place, known as the "nation's attic," is now home to a fabulous array of artifacts that number in excess of 140 million. When James Smithson left his fortune to the United States to found the Smithsonian Institution, he doubtless never imagined how successful his eccentric bequest would become.

Among its incredible collections, the Smithsonian displays such rarities as the 45.5-karat Hope Diamond, Judy Garland's ruby slippers from *The Wizard of Oz*, Charles Lindbergh's *Spirit of Saint Louis*, the original Star-Spangled Banner, and the wood-encased prototype of the first Apple computer. Managing so many objects is no easy matter for the Smithsonian, which relies on computer databases to inventory and categorize its priceless collections and track the constant stream of donated articles.

Millions flock to see this eclectic display every year, partly from curiosity but also because collecting seems to be a common human fascination. Bootjacks, tintypes, inkwells, Elvis memorabilia, snuffboxes, ceramic dragons, tea cozies, and meerschaum pipes are among the thousands of articles that people collect. At the Southern California Exposition in Del Mar, California, even a collection of "Shoes without Mates — Found Beside the Freeway" was exhibited one year.

Compared to the Smithsonian's needs, most private collections do not require extensive databases. Yet, even in a modest book or music library, databases are convenient for locating an item or providing backup for tax purposes. As a collection expands, however, the need for a sophisticated database management system (DBMS), such as Microsoft Access 97, becomes increasingly important.

One of the more extensive applications of databases in today's world is that of gathering collections of names, addresses, and individual data, that then are used for such purposes as companies selling to or servicing clients, charities soliciting donations, politicians seeking support, or the U.S. government keeping tabs on Medicare benefits.

Whether you collect Pickard China or priceless paintings or just need to keep track of your friends and clients, Microsoft Access 97 provides the means to create your own information collection that can organize data on any subject quickly and easily. The Access Table Wizard helps you choose fields from a variety of predefined tables such as business contacts, household inventory, or medical records. If you want to create your own table, Access guides you each step of the process With its graphical user interface (GUI), you will find it easy to store, retrieve, and change data.

How favorable for the world that James Smithson did not squander his fortune collecting echoes like the hapless millionaire in Mark Twain's story, "The Canvasser's Tale." Even Access 97, with all its power, might have trouble managing echoes that talk back for fifteen minutes or others that speak only German.

Microsoft
Access 97

Creating a Database Using Design and Datasheet Views

Case Perspective

Pilotech Services is a new company offering a variety of technical services to its clients. Such services can include assistance with hardware and software problems, special backup services, archiving services, and so on. Each client is assigned to a specific technician at Pilotech. Services are billed at the technician's hourly billing rate. The management of Pilotech Services needs to maintain data on its technicians as well as its clients. By placing the data in a database, managed by a database management system such as Access, Pilotech ensures that its data is current and accurate. Using Access, managers are able to produce a variety of useful reports. In addition, they need to be able to ask questions concerning the data in the database and obtain answers to these questions easily and rapidly.

Introduction

Creating, storing, sorting, and retrieving data are important tasks. In their personal lives, many people keep a variety of records such as names, addresses, and telephone numbers of friends and business associates, records of investments, records of expenses for tax purposes, and so on. These records must be arranged for quick access. Businesses also must be able to store and access information quickly and easily. Personnel and inventory records, payroll information, client records, order data, and accounts receivable information all are crucial and must be available readily.

The term **database** describes a collection of data organized in a manner that allows access, retrieval, and use of that data. A database management system, such as Access, allows you to use a computer to create a database; add, change, and delete data in the database; sort the data in the database; retrieve data in the database; and create forms and reports using the data in the database.

In Access, a database consists of a collection of tables. Figure 1-1 shows a sample database for Pilotech Services. It consists of two tables. The Client table contains information about Pilotech's clients. The Technician table contains information about the technicians to whom these clients are assigned.

The rows in the tables are called **records**. A record contains information about a given person, product, or event. A row in the Client table, for example, contains information about a specific client.

fields

clients of technician Joanna Levin

Client table

CLIENT NUMBER	NAME	ADDRESS	CITY	STATE	ZIP CODE	BILLED	PAID	TECH NUMBER
AM53	Ashton-Mills	216 Rivard	Grattan	MA	58120	$215.50	$155.00	11
AS62	Alton-Scripps	722 Fisher	Empire	MA	58216	$425.00	$435.00	12
BL26	Blake Suppliers	5752 Maumee	Grattan	MA	58120	$129.50	$0.00	12
DE76	D & E Grocery	464 Linnell	Marshall	VT	52018	$385.75	$300.00	17
GR56	Grant Cleaners	737 Allard	Portage	NH	59130	$215.00	$165.00	11
GU21	Grand Union	247 Fuller	Grattan	MA	58120	$128.50	$0.00	12
JE77	Jones Electric	57 Giddings	Marshall	VT	52018	$0.00	$0.00	12
MI26	Morland Int.	665 Whittier	Frankfort	MA	56152	$212.50	$223.25	11
SA56	Sawyer Inc.	31 Lafayette	Empire	MA	58216	$352.50	$250.00	17
SI82	Simpson Ind.	752 Cadieux	Fernwood	MA	57412	$154.00	$0.00	12

records

Technician table

TECH NUMBER	LAST NAME	FIRST NAME	ADDRESS	CITY	STATE	ZIP CODE	HOURLY RATE	YTD EARNINGS
11	Levin	Joanna	26 Cottonwood	Carlton	MA	59712	$25.00	$6,245.00
12	Rogers	Brad	7972 Marsden	Kaleva	VT	57253	$30.00	$7,143.30
17	Rodriguez	Maria	263 Topsfield	Hudson	MA	57240	$35.00	$7,745.50

technician Joanna Levin

FIGURE 1-1

The columns in the tables are called fields. A **field** contains a specific piece of information within a record. In the Client table, for example, the fourth field, City, contains the city where the client is located.

The first field in the Client table is the Client Number. This is a code assigned by Pilotech to each client. Like many organizations, Pilotech calls it a *number* although it actually contains letters. The client numbers have a special format. They consist of two uppercase letters followed by a two-digit number.

These numbers are unique; that is, no two clients will be assigned the same number. Such a field can be used as a **unique identifier**. This simply means that a given client number will appear only in a single record in the table. Only one record exists, for example, in which the client number is BL26. A unique identifier also is called a **primary key**. Thus, the Client Number field is the primary key for the Client table.

The next eight fields in the Client table include the Name, Address, City, State, Zip Code, Billed, Paid, and Tech Number. The Billed field contains the amount billed to the client. The Paid field contains the amount the client already has paid.

For example, Client AM53 is Ashton-Mills. It is located at 216 Rivard in Grattan, Massachusetts. The zip code is 58120. The client has been billed $215.50 and already has paid $155.00 of this amount.

Each client is assigned to a single technician. The last field in the Client table, Tech Number, gives the number of the client's technician.

The first field in the Technician table, Tech Number, is the number assigned by Pilotech to each technician. These numbers are unique, so Tech Number is the primary key of the Technician table.

The other fields in the Technician table are Last Name, First Name, Address, City, State, Zip Code, Hourly Rate, and YTD Earnings. The Hourly Rate field gives the technician's hourly billing rate, and the YTD Earnings field contains the total amount that has been billed by the technician for the technician's services so far this year.

For example, Technician 11 is Joanna Levin. She lives at 26 Cottonwood in Carlton, Massachusetts. Her zip code is 59712. Her hourly billing rate is $25.00 and her YTD earnings are $6,245.00.

The tech number appears in both the Client table and the Technician table. It is used to relate clients and technicians. For example, in the Client table, you see that the tech number for client AM53 is 11. To find the name of this technician, look for the row in the Technician table that contains 11 in the Tech Number field. Once you have found it, you know the client is assigned to Joanna Levin. To find all the clients assigned to Joanna Levin, look through the Client table for all the clients that contain 11 in the Tech Number field. Her clients are AM53 (Ashton-Mills), GR56 (Grant Cleaners), and MI26 (Morland, Int.).

Project One — Pilotech Services Database

Together with the management of Pilotech Services, you have determined that the data that must be maintained in the database is the data shown in Figure 1-1 on page A 1.7. You first must create the database and the tables it contains. In the process, you must define the fields included in the two tables, as well as the type of data each field will contain. You then must add the appropriate records to the tables. You also must print the contents of the tables. Finally, you must create a report with the Client Number, Name, Billed, and Paid fields for each client of Pilotech Services. Other reports and requirements for the database at Pilotech Services will be addressed with the Pilotech Services management in the future.

What Is Microsoft Access?

Microsoft Access is a powerful database management system (DBMS) that functions in the Windows environment and allows you to create and process data in a database. To illustrate the use of Access, this book presents a series of projects.

The projects use the Client and Technician tables. In Project 1, the two tables that comprise the database are created and the appropriate records are added to them. The project also uses a form to display the data in the tables. In addition, the project presents steps and techniques to prepare and print a custom report that represents the data in the database.

Overview of Project Steps

The database preparation steps give you an overview of how the database consisting of the Client table and the Technician table shown in Figure 1-1 on page A 1.7 will be constructed. The following tasks will be completed in this project.

1. Start Access.
2. Create a database called Pilotech Services.
3. Create the Client table by defining its fields.
4. Save the Client table in the database called Pilotech Services.
5. Add data records to the Client table.
6. Print the contents of the Client table.
7. Create the Technician table, save it, and add data records to it.
8. Create a form to display data in the Client table.
9. Create and print a report that presents the data in the Client table.

The following pages contain a detailed explanation of each of these steps.

More About Creating a Database

In some DBMSs, every table, query, form, or report is stored in a separate file. This is not the case in Access, in which a database is stored in a single file on disk. The file contains all the tables, queries, forms, reports, and programs that you create for this database.

Mouse Usage

In this book, the mouse is the primary way to communicate with Access. You can perform six operations with a mouse: point, click, right-click, double-click, drag, and right-drag. If you have a **Microsoft IntelliMouse™**, then you also have a wheel between the left and right buttons. This wheel can be used to perform three additional operations: rotate wheel, click wheel, or drag wheel.

Point means you move the mouse across a flat surface until the mouse pointer rests on the item of choice on the screen. As you move the mouse, the mouse pointer moves across the screen in the same direction. **Click** means you press and release the left mouse button. The terminology used in this book to direct you to point to a particular item and then click is, click the particular item. For example, click the Primary Key button on the toolbar, means point to the Primary Key button on the toolbar and then click.

Right-click means you press and release the right mouse button. As with the left mouse button, you normally will point to an item on the screen prior to right-clicking. Right-clicking produces a **shortcut menu**, which is a menu of the more frequently used commands that relate to the portion of the screen to which you are pointing. You then can select one of these commands by pointing to it and clicking the left mouse button.

Double-click means you quickly press and release the left mouse button twice without moving the mouse. In most cases, you must point to an item before double-clicking. **Drag** means you point to an item, hold down the left mouse button, move the item to the desired location on the screen and then release the left mouse button. **Right-drag** means you point to an item, hold down the right mouse button, move the item to the desired location and then release the right mouse button.

If you have a Microsoft IntelliMouse™, then you can use **rotate wheel** to view parts of a table that are not visible. The wheel also can serve as a third button. When the wheel is used as a button, it is referred to as the **wheel button**. For example, dragging the wheel button causes some applications to scroll in the direction you drag.

The use of the mouse is an important skill when working with Microsoft Access 97.

Starting Access and Creating a New Database

To start Access, Windows 95 must be running. Perform the following steps to start Access and create a new database.

To Start Access

1 **Place a formatted floppy disk in drive A, click the Start button, and point to New Office Document near the top of the Start menu.**

The Start menu displays (Figure 1-2).

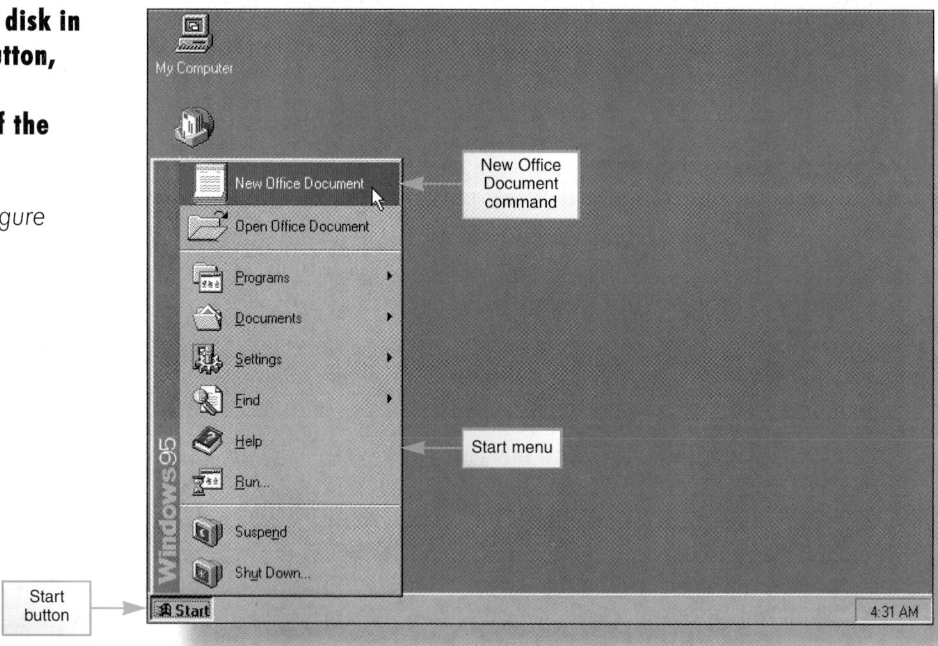

FIGURE 1-2

2 **Click New Office Document. If the General tab is not selected, that is, if it does not display in front of the other tabs, click the General tab. Make sure the Blank Database icon is selected and then point to the OK button.**

The New Office Document dialog box displays (Figure 1-3). The Blank Database icon is selected.

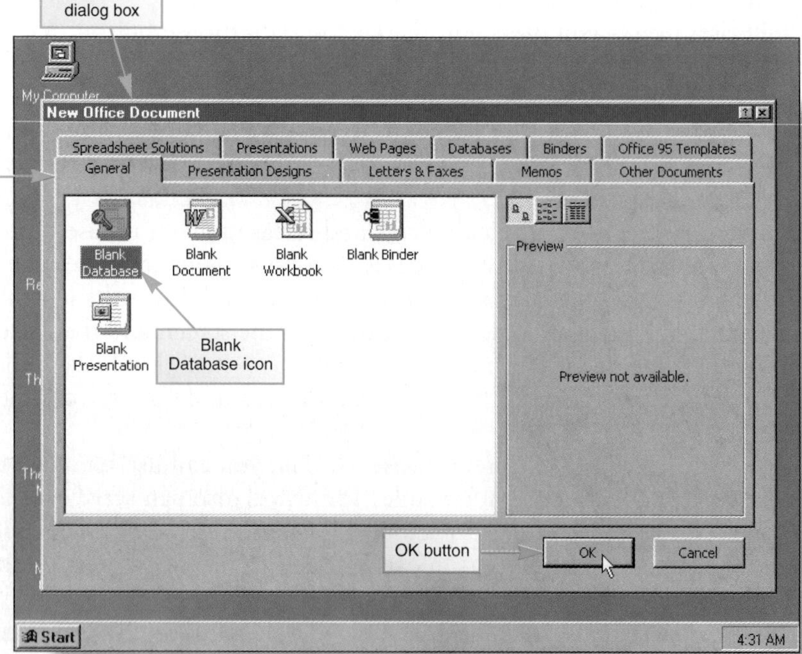

FIGURE 1-3

3 **Click the OK button and then point to the Save in box arrow.**

The File New Database dialog box displays (Figure 1-4).

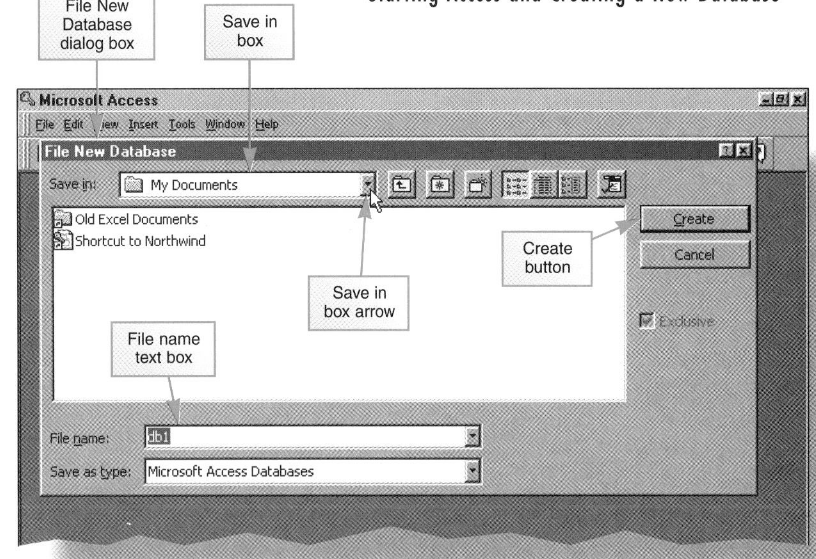

FIGURE 1-4

4 **Click the Save in box arrow and then point to 3½ Floppy (A:).**

The Save in list box displays (Figure 1-5).

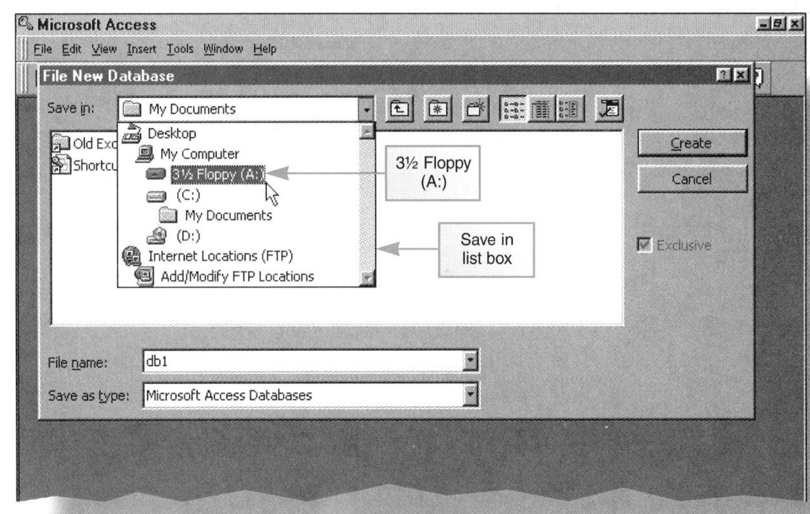

FIGURE 1-5

5 **Click 3½ Floppy (A:).**

The Save in box contains 3½ Floppy (A:) (Figure 1-6).

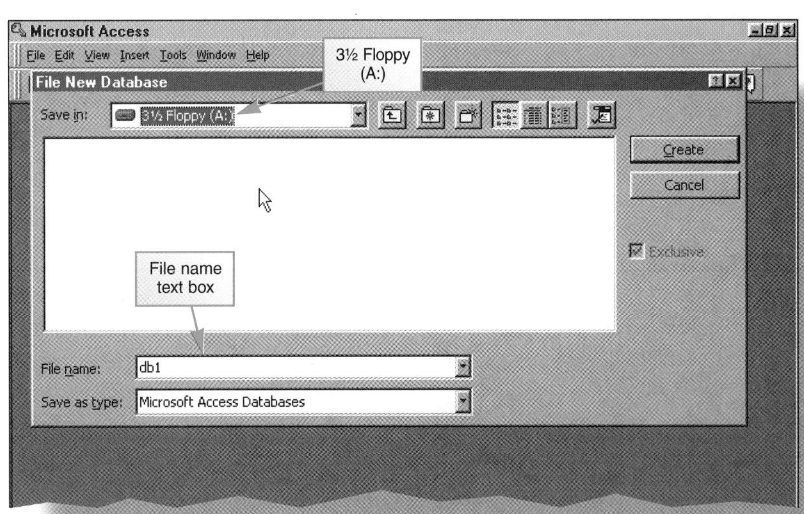

FIGURE 1-6

6 **Click in the File name text box. Repeatedly press the BACKSPACE key to delete db1 and then type** `Pilotech Services` **as the file name. Point to the Create button.**

The file name is changed to Pilotech Services (Figure 1-7).

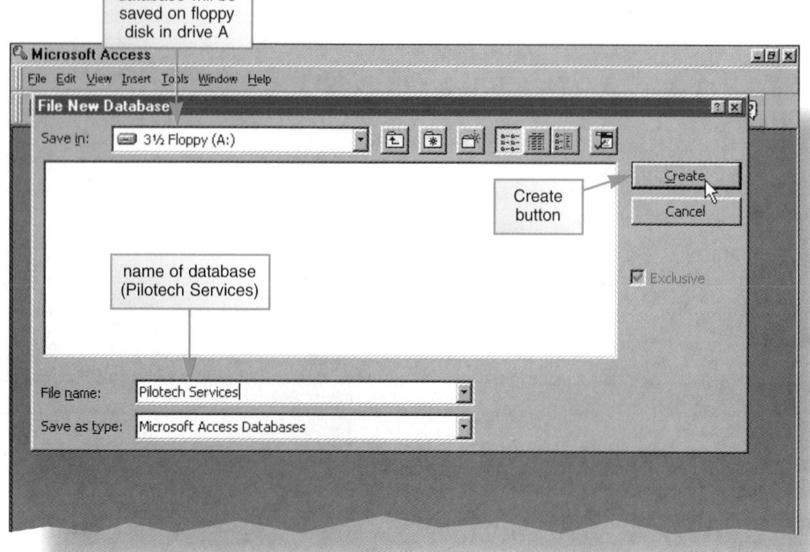

FIGURE 1-7

7 **Click the Create button to create the database.**

The Pilotech Services database is created. The Pilotech Services : Database window displays on the desktop (Figure 1-8). The **Office Assistant***, a tool you can use to obtain help while working with Microsoft Access may display. (You will see how to use the Office Assistant later in this project.)*

8 **If the Office Assistant displays, click the Close button for the Office Assistant.**

The Office Assistant no longer displays.

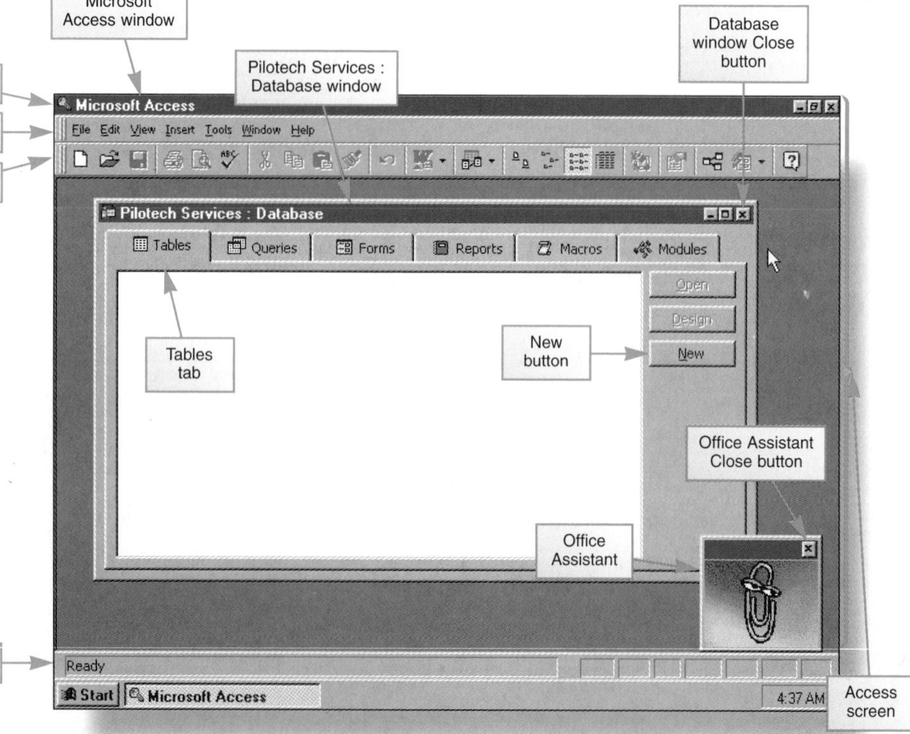

FIGURE 1-8

OtherWays

1. Right-click Start button, click Open, double-click New Office Document
2. On Office shortcut bar click Start a New Document button
3. On the Start menu click Programs, click Microsoft Access

The Access Desktop and the Database Window

The first bar on the desktop (Figure 1-8) is the **title bar**. It displays the title of the product, Microsoft Access. The button on the right is the **Close button**. Clicking the Close button closes the window.

The second bar is the **menu bar**. It contains a list of menus. You select a menu from the menu bar by clicking the menu name.

The third bar is the **toolbar**. The toolbar contains buttons that allow you to perform certain tasks more quickly than using the menu bar. Each button contains a picture, or **icon**, depicting its function. The specific buttons on the toolbar will vary, depending on the task on which you are working.

The **taskbar** at the bottom of the screen displays the Start button, any active windows, and the current time.

Immediately above the Windows 95 taskbar is the **status bar** (Figure 1-8). It contains special information that is appropriate for the task on which you are working. Currently, it contains the word, Ready, which means Access is ready to accept commands.

The **Database window**, referred to in Figure 1-8 as the Pilotech Services : Database window, is a special window that allows you to access easily and rapidly a variety of objects such as tables, queries, forms, and reports. To do so, you will use the various components of the window.

More About Toolbars

Normally, the correct Access toolbar automatically will display. If it does not, click View on the menu bar, and then click Toolbars. Select the toolbar for the activity in which you are engaged and then click the Close button.

Creating a Table

An Access database consists of a collection of tables. Once you have created the database, you must create each of the tables within it. In this project, for example, you must create both the Client and Technician tables shown in Figure 1-1 on page A 1.7.

To create a table, you describe the **structure** of the table to Access by describing the fields within the table. For each field, you indicate the following:

1. **Field name** — Each field in the table must have a unique name. In the Client table (Figure 1-9 on page A 1.14), for example, the field names are Client Number, Name, Address, City, State, Zip Code, Billed, Paid, and Tech Number.
2. **Data type** — Data type indicates to Access the type of data the field will contain. Some fields can contain only numbers. Others, such as Billed and Paid, can contain numbers and dollar signs. Still others, such as Name, and Address, can contain letters.
3. **Description** — Access allows you to enter a detailed description of the field.

You also can assign field widths to text fields (fields whose data type is Text). This indicates the maximum number of characters that can be stored in the field. If you do not assign a width to such a field, Access assumes the width is 50.

You also must indicate which field or fields make up the **primary key**; that is, the unique identifier, for the table. In the sample database, the Client Number field is the primary key of the Client table and the Tech Number field is the primary key of the Technician table.

The rules for field names are:

1. Names can be up to 64 characters in length.
2. Names can contain letters, digits, and spaces, as well as most of the punctuation symbols.
3. Names cannot contain periods, exclamation points (!), or square brackets ([ ]).
4. The same name cannot be used for two different fields in the same table.

More About Creating a Table

Access includes **Table Wizards** that can guide you through the table-creation process by suggesting some commonly used tables and fields. If you already know the fields you need, however, it usually is easier to simply create the table yourself.

Structure of Client table

FIELD NAME	DATA TYPE	FIELD SIZE	PRIMARY KEY?	DESCRIPTION
Client Number	Text	4	Yes	Client Number (Primary Key)
Name	Text	20		Client Name
Address	Text	15		Street Address
City	Text	15		City
State	Text	2		State (Two-Character Abbreviation)
Zip Code	Text	5		Zip Code (Five-Character Version)
Billed	Currency			Current Billed Amount
Paid	Currency			Current Paid Amount
Tech Number	Text	2		Number of Client's Technician

Data for Client table

CLIENT NUMBER	NAME	ADDRESS	CITY	STATE	ZIP CODE	BILLED	PAID	TECH NUMBER
AM53	Ashton-Mills	216 Rivard	Grattan	MA	58120	$215.50	$155.00	11
AS62	Alton-Scripps	722 Fisher	Empire	MA	58216	$425.00	$435.00	12
BL26	Blake Suppliers	5752 Maumee	Grattan	MA	58120	$129.50	$0.00	12
DE76	D & E Grocery	464 Linnell	Marshall	VT	52018	$385.75	$300.00	17
GR56	Grant Cleaners	737 Allard	Portage	NH	59130	$215.00	$165.00	11
GU21	Grand Union	247 Fuller	Grattan	MA	58120	$128.50	$0.00	12
JE77	Jones Electric	57 Giddings	Marshall	VT	52018	$0.00	$0.00	12
MI26	Morland Int.	665 Whittier	Frankfort	MA	56152	$212.50	$223.25	11
SA56	Sawyer Inc.	31 Lafayette	Empire	MA	58216	$352.50	$250.00	17
SI82	Simpson Ind.	752 Cadieux	Fernwood	MA	57412	$154.00	$0.00	12

FIGURE 1-9

More *About*
Data Types

Different database management systems have different available data types. Even data types that are essentially the same can have different names. The Access Text data type, for example, is referred to as Character in some systems and Alpha in others.

Each field has a **data type.** This indicates the type of data that can be stored in the field. The data types you will use in this project are:

1. **Text** — The field can contain any characters.
2. **Number** — The field can contain only numbers. The numbers can be either positive or negative. Fields are assigned this type so they can be used in arithmetic operations. Fields that contain numbers but will not be used for arithmetic operations usually are assigned a data type of Text. The Tech Number field, for example, is a text field because the Tech Numbers will not be involved in any arithmetic.
3. **Currency** — The field can contain only dollar amounts. The values will be displayed with dollar signs, commas, decimal points, and with two digits following the decimal point. Like numeric fields, you can use currency fields in arithmetic operations. Access assigns a size to currency fields automatically.

The field names, data types, field widths, primary key information, and descriptions for the Client table are shown in Figure 1-9. With this information, you are ready to begin creating the table. To create the table, use the following steps.

Steps To Create a Table

1 Click the New button in the Pilotech Services : Database window (see Figure 1-8 on page A 1.12). Point to Design View.

The New Table dialog box displays (Figure 1-10).

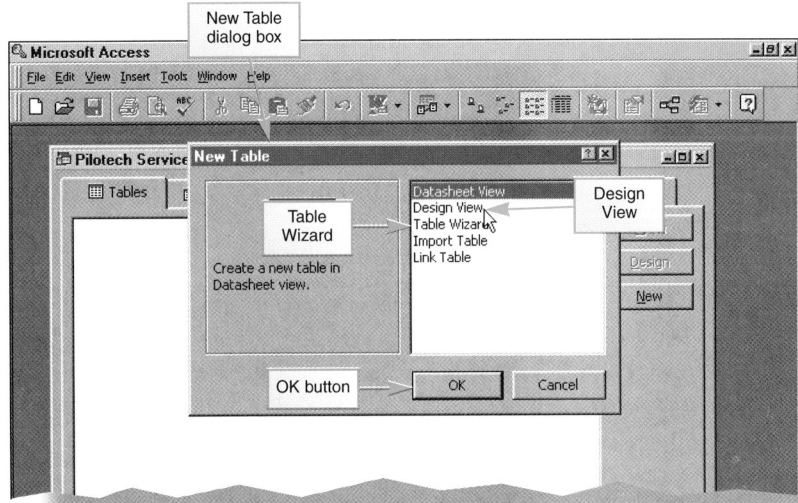

FIGURE 1-10

2 Click Design View and then click the OK button.

The Table1 : Table window displays (Figure 1-11).

3 Click the Maximize button for the Table1 : Table window.

A maximized Table1 : Table window displays.

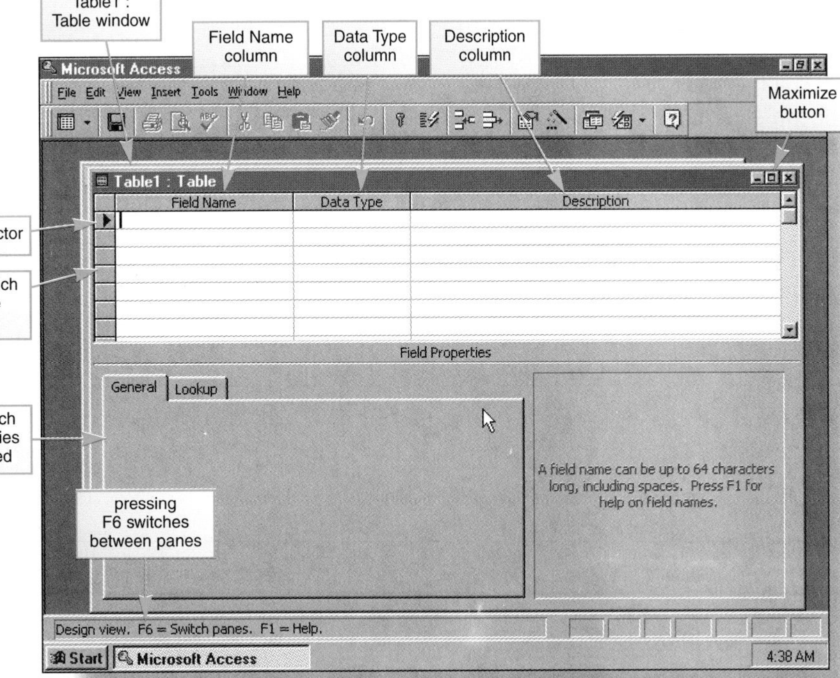

FIGURE 1-11

OtherWays

1. Click New Object button arrow on toolbar, click Table
2. On Insert menu click Table
3. Press ALT+N

Defining the Fields

The next step in creating the table is to define the fields by specifying the required details in the Table window. To do so, make entries in the Field Name, Data Type, and Description columns. Enter additional information in the Field Properties box in the lower portion of the Table window. To do so, press the F6 key to move from the upper **pane** (portion of the screen), the one where you define the fields, to the lower pane, the one where you define field properties. Enter the appropriate field size and then press the F6 key to return to the upper pane. As you define the fields, the **row selector** (Figure 1-11 on page A 1.15) indicates the field you currently are describing. It is positioned on the first field, indicating Access is ready for you to enter the name of the first field in the Field Name column.

Perform the following steps to define the fields in the table.

To Define the Fields in a Table

1 Type `Client Number` **(the name of the first field) in the Field Name column and press the TAB key.**

The words, Client Number, display in the Field Name column and the insertion point advances to the Data Type column, indicating you can enter the data type (Figure 1-12). The word, Text, one of the possible data types, currently displays. The arrow indicates a list of data types is available by clicking the arrow.

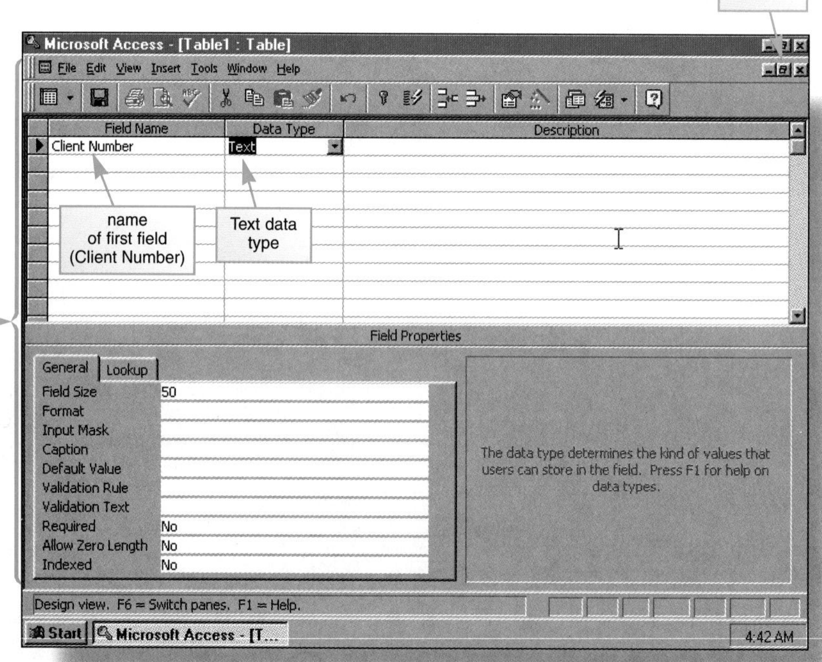

FIGURE 1-12

2 **Because Text is the correct data type, press the TAB key to move the insertion point to the Description column, type** `Client Number (Primary Key)` **as the description and then point to the Primary Key button on the toolbar.**

A ScreenTip, which is a description of the button, displays partially obscuring the description of the first field (Figure 1-13).

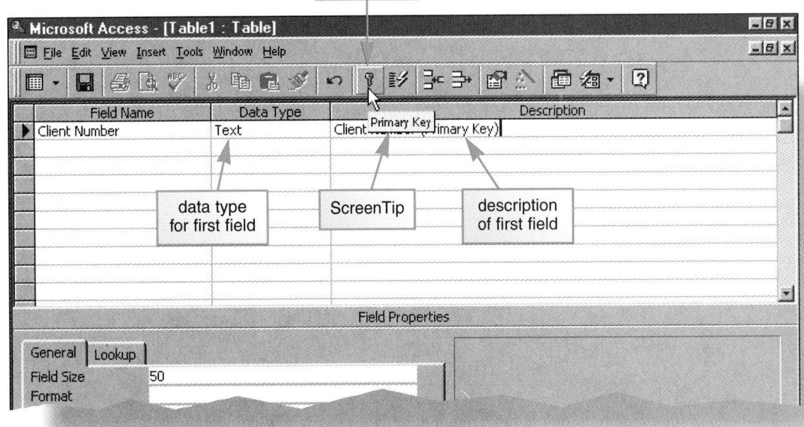

FIGURE 1-13

3 **Click the Primary Key button to make Client Number the primary key and then press the F6 key to move the insertion point to the Field Size text box.**

*The Client Number field is the primary key as indicated by the key symbol that displays in the row selector (Figure 1-14). The **row selector** is a small box or bar that, when clicked, selects the entire row. The current entry in the Field Size text box (50) is selected.*

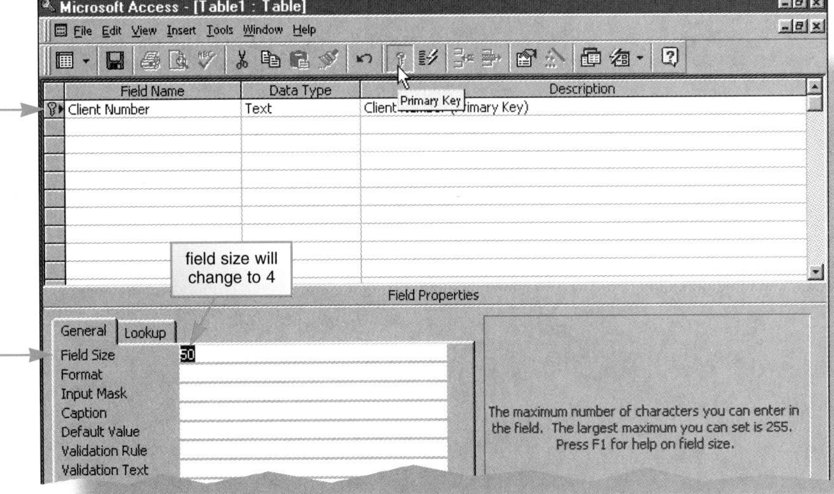

FIGURE 1-14

4 **Type** 4 **as the size of the Client Number field. Press the F6 key to return to the Description column for the Client Number field and then press the TAB key to move to the Field Name column in the second row.**

The row selector moves to the second row just below the field name Client Number (Figure 1-15).

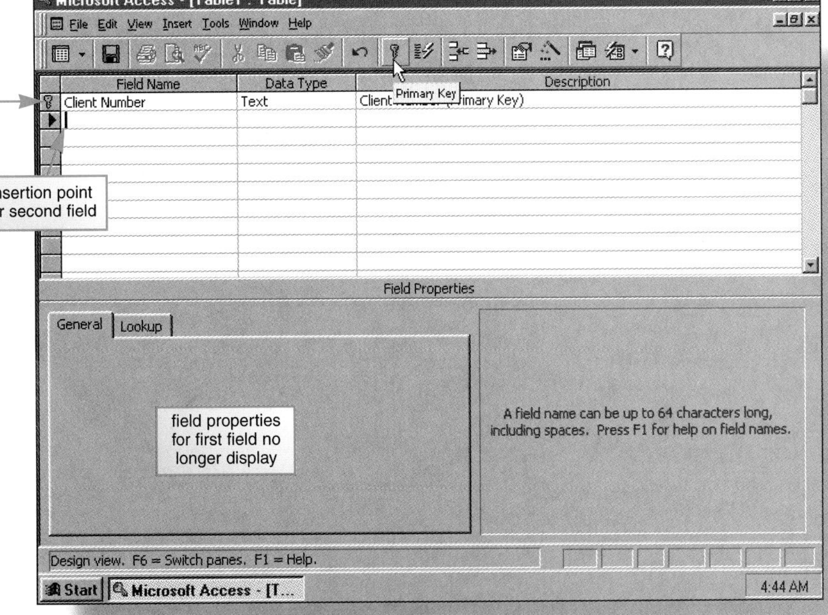

FIGURE 1-15

5 **Use the techniques illustrated in Steps 1 through 4 to make the entries from the Client table structure shown in Figure 1-9 on page A 1.14 up through and including the name of the Billed field. You will not need to click the Primary Key button for any of these fields. Click the Data Type column arrow and then point to the Currency data type.**

The additional fields are entered (Figure 1-16). A list of available data types displays in the Data Type column for the Billed field.

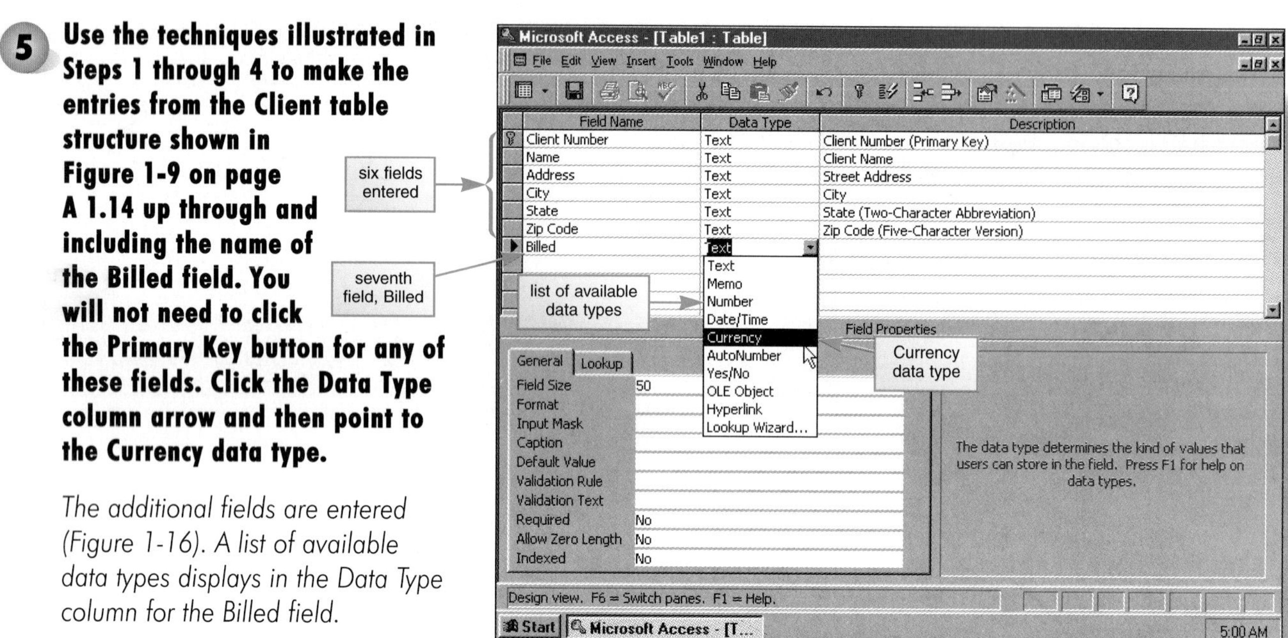

FIGURE 1-16

6 **Click the Currency data type and then press the TAB key. Make the remaining entries from the Client table structure shown in Figure 1-9.**

The fields are all entered (Figure 1-17)

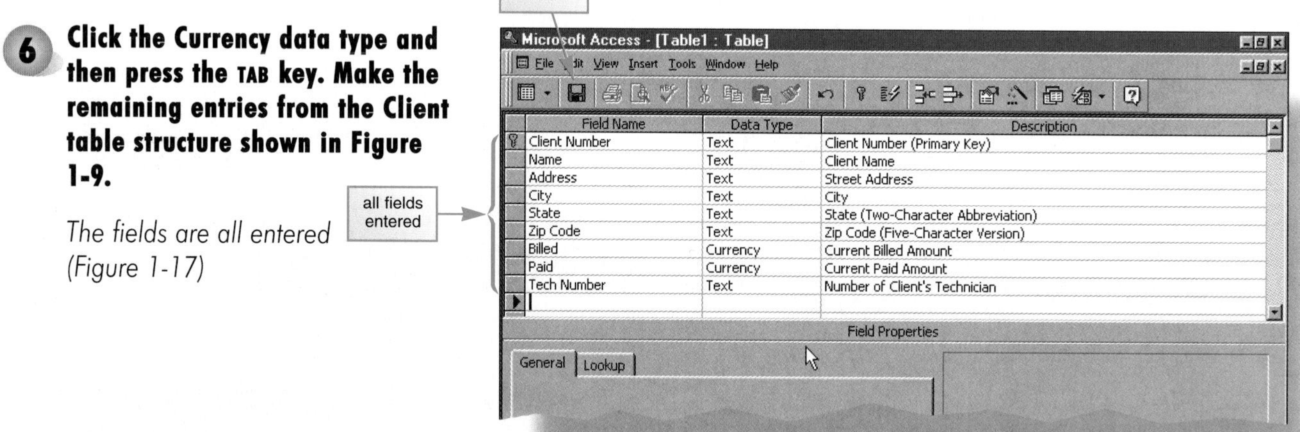

FIGURE 1-17

Correcting Errors in the Structure

When creating a table, check the entries carefully to ensure they are correct. If you make a mistake and discover it before you press the TAB key, you can correct the error by repeatedly pressing the BACKSPACE key until the incorrect characters are removed. Then, type the correct characters. If you do not discover a mistake until later, you can click the entry, type the correct value and then press the ENTER key.

If you accidentally add an extra field to the structure, select the field, by clicking the leftmost column on the row that contains the field to be deleted. Once you have selected the field, press the DELETE key. This will remove the field from the structure.

If you forget a field, select the field that will follow the field you wish to add, click Insert on the menu bar and then click Rows. The remaining fields move down one row, making room for the missing field. Make the entries for the new field in the usual manner.

If you made the wrong field a primary key field, click the correct primary key entry for the field and then click the Primary Key button on the toolbar.

As an alternative to these steps, you may want to start over. To do so, click the Close button for the Table1 : Table window and then click No. The original desktop displays and you can repeat the process you used earlier.

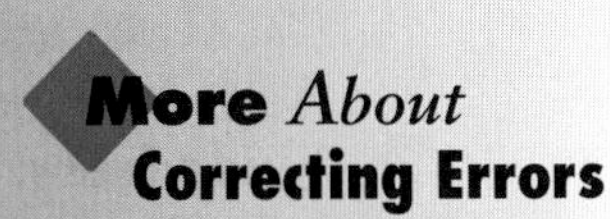

More About Correcting Errors

Even after you have entered data, it still is possible to correct errors in the structure. Access will make all the necessary adjustments to the structure of the table as well as to the data within it. (It is simplest to make the correction, however, before any data is entered.)

Saving a Table

The Client table structure now is complete. The final step is to **save the table** within the database. At this time, you should give the table a name.

Table names are from one to 64 characters in length and can contain letters, numbers, and spaces. The two table names in this project are Client and Technician.

To save the table, complete the following steps.

To Save a Table

1 **Click the Save button on the toolbar (see Figure 1-17). Type** `Client` **as the name of the table in the Table Name text box and then point to the OK button.**

The Save As dialog box displays (Figure 1-18). The name of the table displays in the Table Name text box.

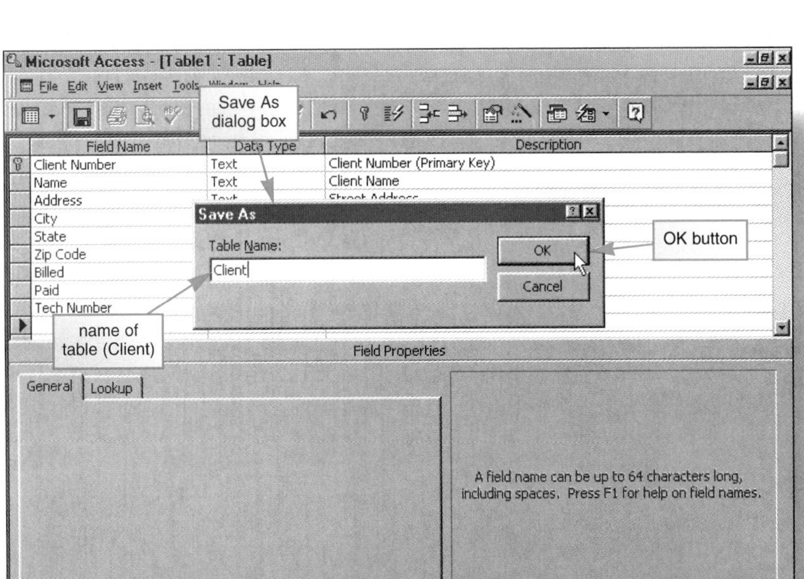

FIGURE 1-18

2 **Click the OK button and then point to the Close button for the Client : Table window.**

The Table is saved on the floppy disk in drive A. The name of the table is now Client as indicated in the title bar (Figure 1-19).

3 **Click the Close button for the Client : Table window. (Be sure not to click the Close button on the first line, because this would close Microsoft Access.)**

The Client : Table window no longer displays.

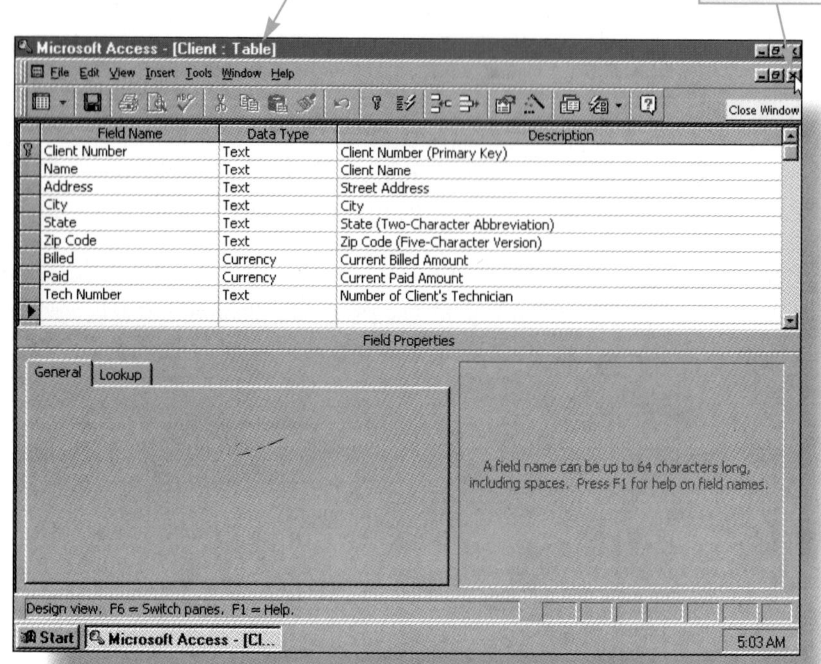

FIGURE 1-19

OtherWays

1. On File menu, click Save
2. Press CTRL+S

Adding Records to a Table

More About Adding Records

As soon as you have entered or modified a record and moved to another record, the original record is saved. This is different from other tools. The rows entered in a spreadsheet, for example, are not saved until the entire spreadsheet is saved.

Creating a table by building the structure and saving the table is the first step in a two-step process. The second step is to **add records** to the table. To add records to a table, the table must be open. To **open a table**, right-click the table in the Database window and then click Open on the shortcut menu. The table displays in Datasheet view. In **Datasheet view**, the table is represented as a collection of rows and columns called a **datasheet**. It looks very much like the tables shown in Figure 1-1 on page A 1.7.

You often add records in phases. You may, for example, not have enough time to add all the records in one session. To illustrate this process, this project begins by adding the first two records in the Client table (Figure 1-20). The remaining records are added later.

Client table (first 2 records)

CLIENT NUMBER	NAME	ADDRESS	CITY	STATE	ZIP CODE	BILLED	PAID	TECH NUMBER
AM53	Ashton-Mills	216 Rivard	Grattan	MA	58120	$215.50	$155.00	11
AS62	Alton-Scripps	722 Fisher	Empire	MA	58216	$425.00	$435.00	12

FIGURE 1-20

To open the Client table and then add records, use the following steps.

Steps To Add Records to a Table

1 Right-click the Client table in the Pilotech Services : Database window and then point to Open on the shortcut menu.

The shortcut menu for the Client table displays (Figure 1-21). The Pilotech Services : Database window is maximized because the previous window, the Client : Table window, was maximized. (If you wanted to restore the Database window to its original size, you would click the window's Restore button.)

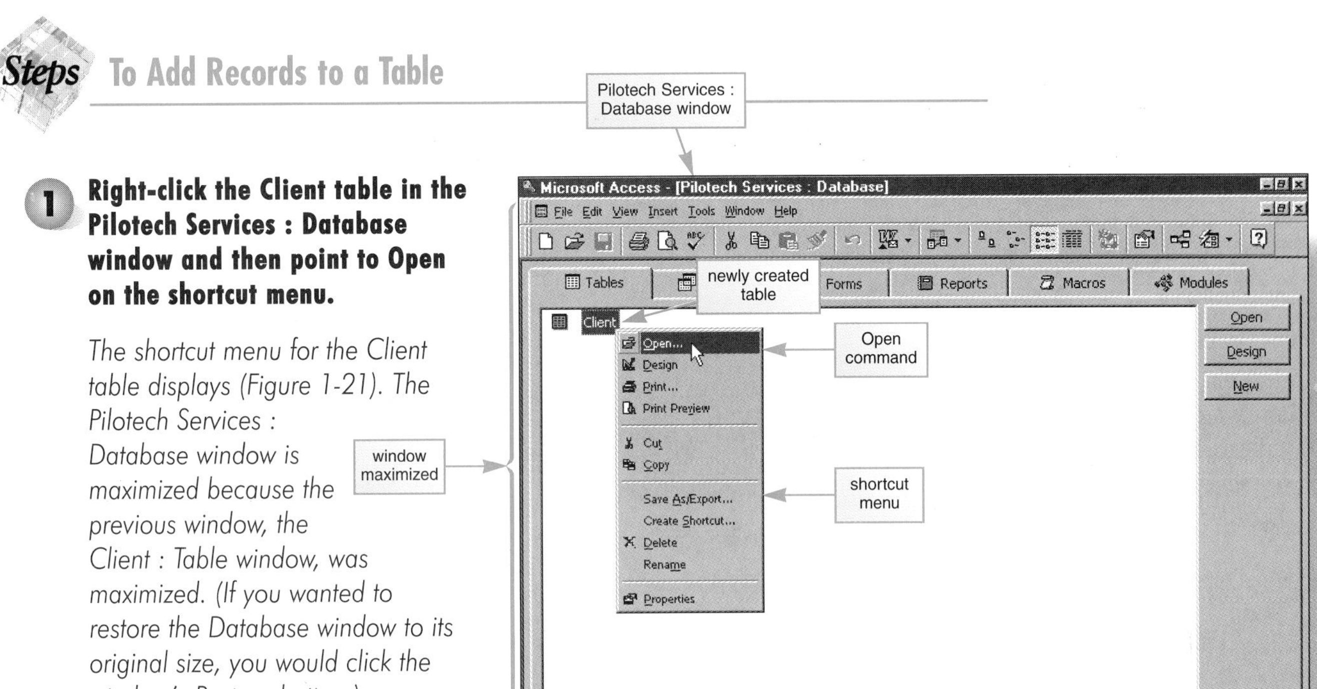

FIGURE 1-21

2 Click Open on the shortcut menu.

The Client : Table window displays (Figure 1-22). The window contains the Datasheet view for the Client table. The ***record selector*** *is positioned on the first record. The status bar at the bottom of the window also indicates that the record selector is positioned on record 1.*

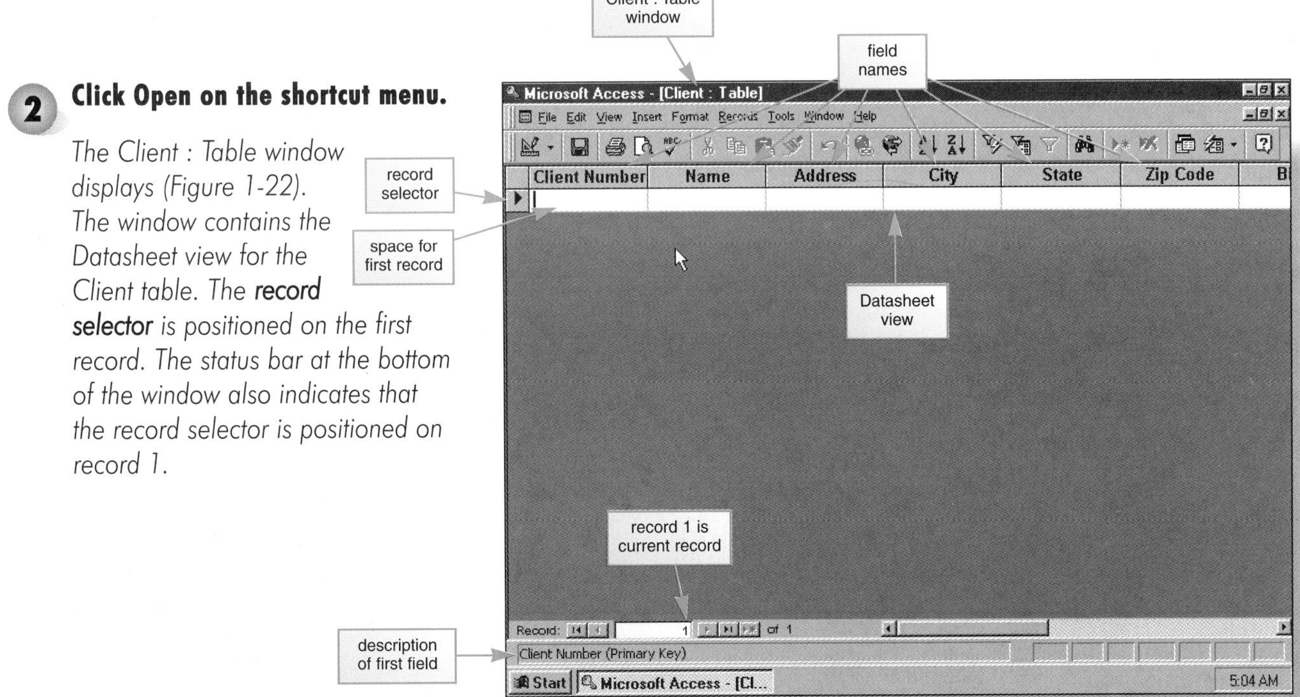

FIGURE 1-22

3 **If your window is not already maximized, click the Maximize button to maximize the window containing the table. Type** `AM53` **as the first Client Number, as shown in Figure 1-20 on page A 1.20. Be sure you type the letters in uppercase, because that is the way they are to be entered in the database.**

The Client Number is entered, but the insertion point is still in the Client Number field (Figure 1-23).

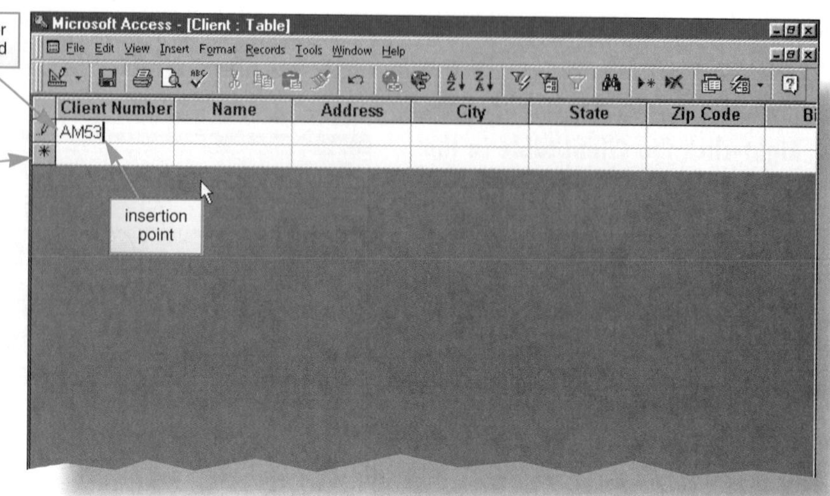

FIGURE 1-23

4 **Press the TAB key to complete the entry for the Client Number field. Type** `Ashton-Mills` **as the name and then press the TAB key. Type** `216 Rivard` **as the address and then press the TAB key. Type** `Grattan` **as the city and then press the TAB key. Type** `MA` **as the state name and then press the TAB key. Type** `58120` **as the zip code.**

The Name, Address, City, and State fields are entered. The data for the Zip Code field displays on the screen (Figure 1-24), but the entry is not complete because you have not yet pressed the TAB key.

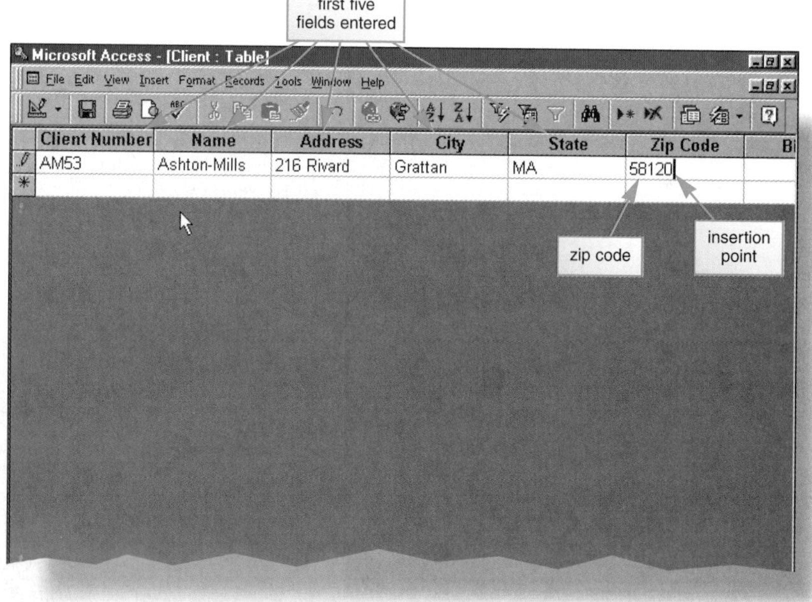

FIGURE 1-24

5 **Press the TAB key.**

The fields shift to the left (Figure 1-25). The Billed field displays.

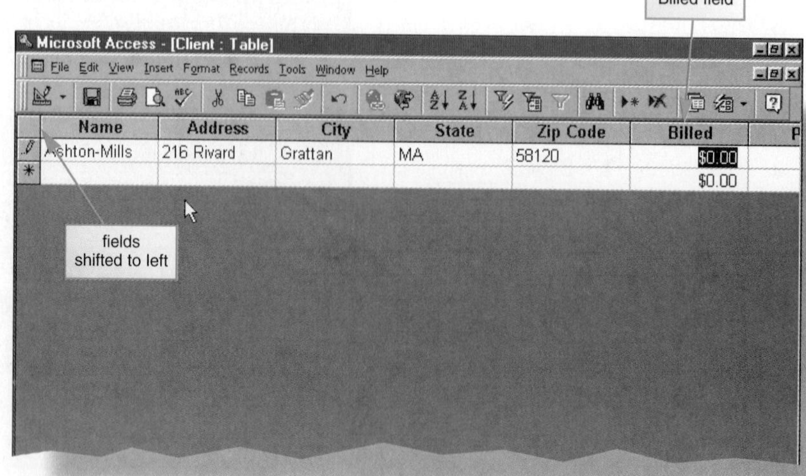

FIGURE 1-25

6 **Type** `215.50` **as the billed amount and then press the TAB key. (You do not need to type dollar signs or commas. In addition, if the digits to the right of the decimal point were both zeros, you would not need to type the decimal point.) Type** `155` **as the paid amount and then press the TAB key. Type** `11` **as the Tech Number to complete the record.**

The fields have shifted to the left (Figure 1-26). The Billed and Paid values display with dollar signs and decimal points. The value for the Tech Number has been entered, but the insertion point still is positioned on the field.

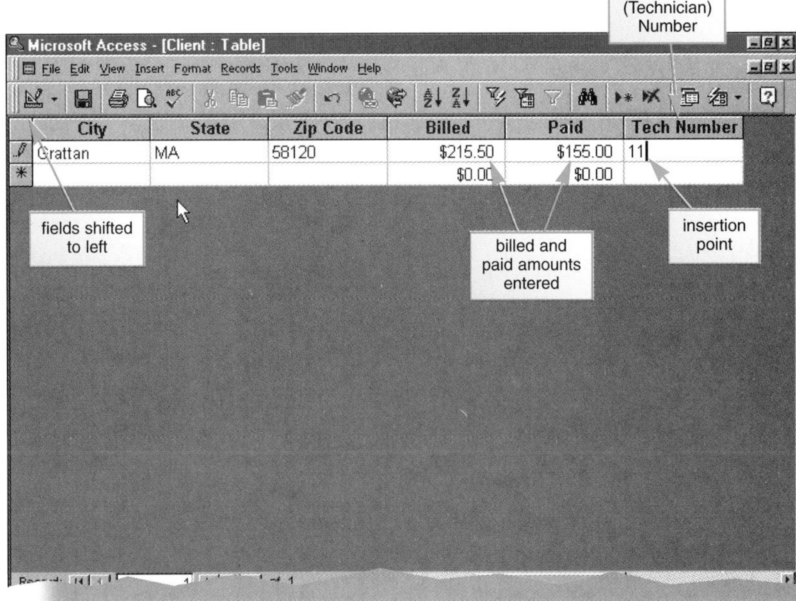

FIGURE 1-26

7 **Press the TAB key.**

The fields shift back to the right, the record is saved, and the insertion point moves to the Client Number on the second row (Figure 1-27).

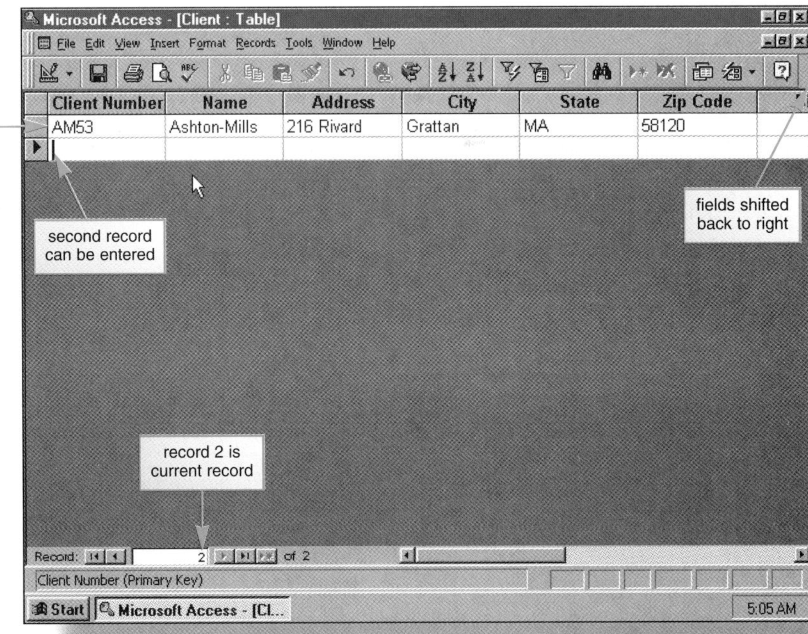

FIGURE 1-27

8 **Use the techniques shown in Steps 3 through 7 to add the data for the second record in Figure 1-20 on page A 1.20.**

The second record is added and the insertion point moves to the Client Number on the third row (Figure 1-28).

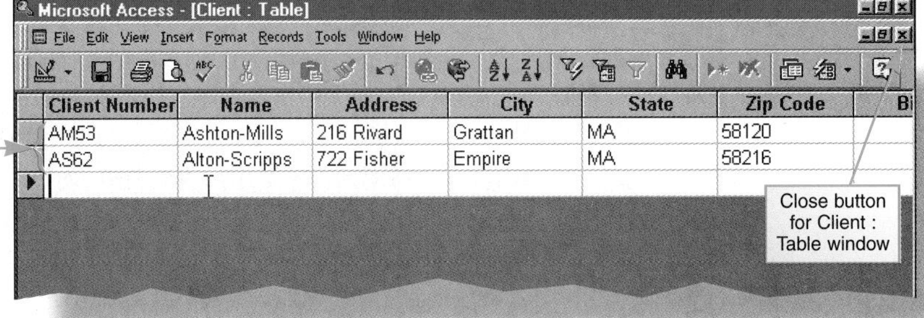

FIGURE 1-28

Closing a Table and a Database and Quitting Access

It is a good idea to close a table as soon as you have finished working with it. It keeps the screen from getting cluttered and prevents you from making accidental changes to the data in the table. If you no longer will work with the database, you should close the database as well. With the creation of the Client table complete, you can quit Access at this point.

Perform the following steps to close the table and the database and then quit Access.

To Close a Table and Database and Quit Access

1. **Click the Close button for the Client : Table window (see Figure 1-28 on page A 1.23).**

   The datasheet for the Client table no longer displays (Figure 1-29).

2. **Click the Close button for the Pilotech Services : Database window (see Figure 1-29).**

   The Pilotech Services : Database window no longer displays.

3. **Click the Close button for the Microsoft Access window.**

   The Microsoft Access window no longer displays.

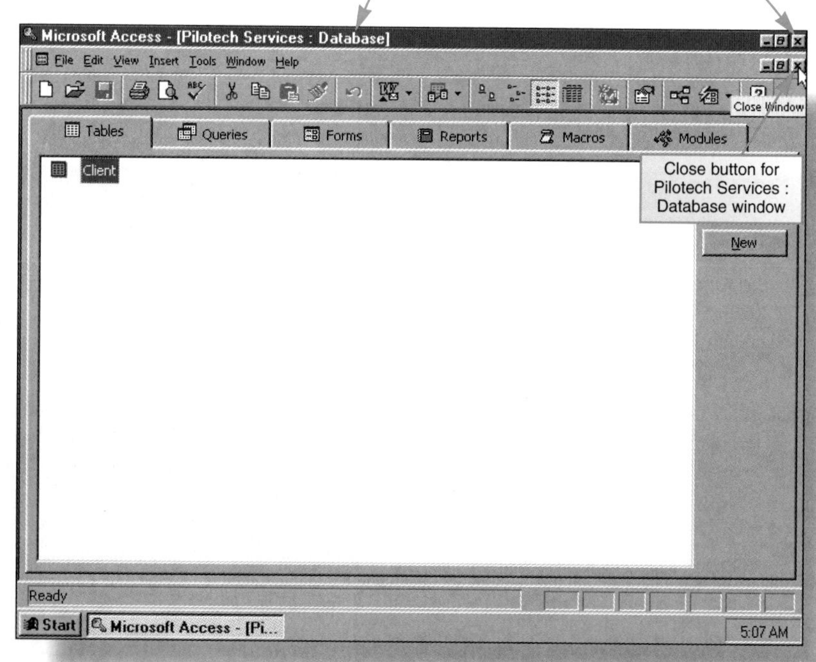

FIGURE 1-29

Other Ways

1. Double-click Control-menu icon on title bar for window
2. On File menu click Close

Opening a Database

To work with any of the tables, reports, or forms in a database, the database must be open. To open a database from the Windows 95 desktop, click Open Office Document on the Start menu by performing the following steps. (The Other Ways box indicates ways to open a database from within Access.)

To Open a Database

1 **Click the Start button and then point to Open Office Document on the Start menu (Figure 1-30).**

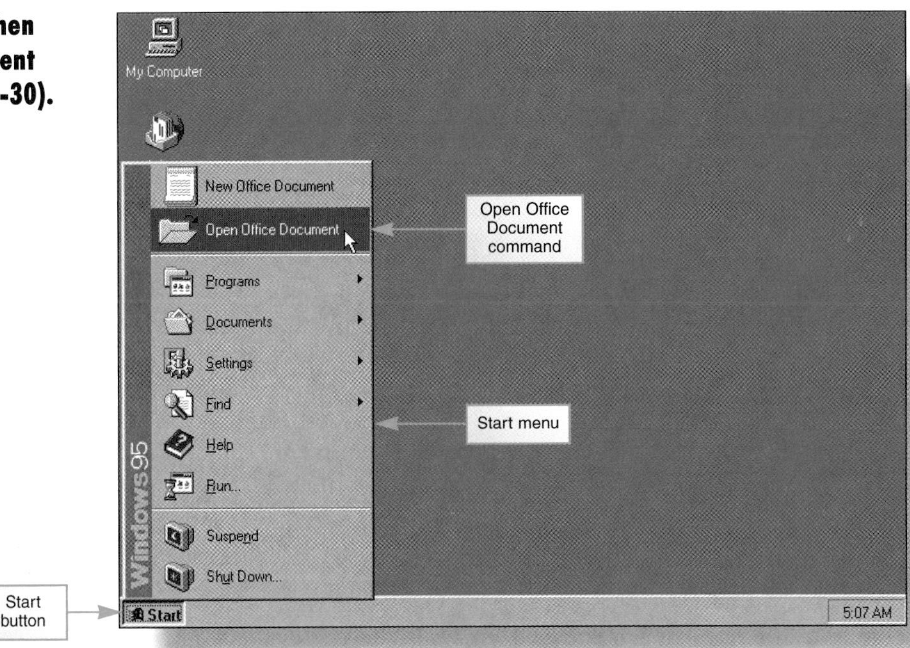

FIGURE 1-30

2 **Click Open Office Document. If necessary, click the Look in box arrow and then click 3½ Floppy (A:) in the Look in list box. If it is not already selected, click the Pilotech Services database name. Point to the Open button.**

The Open Office Document dialog box displays (Figure 1-31). The 3½ Floppy (A:) folder displays in the Look in box and the files on the floppy disk in drive A display. Your list may be different.

3 **Click the Open button.**

The database opens and the Pilotech Services : Database window displays.

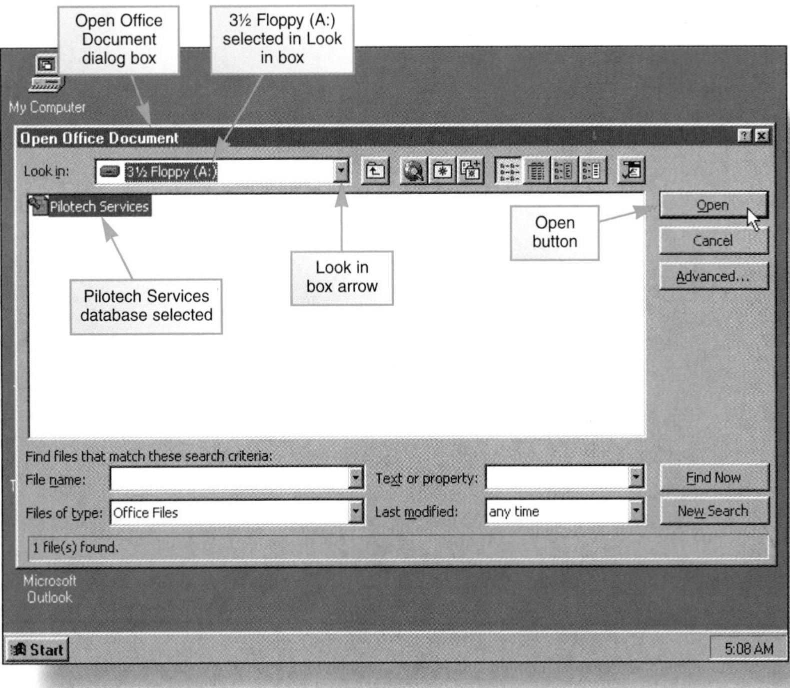

FIGURE 1-31

Other Ways

1. Click Open Database button on toolbar
2. On File menu click Open Database
3. Press CTRL+O

Adding Additional Records

You can add records to a table that already contains data using a process almost identical to that used to add records to an empty table. The only difference is that you place the insertion point after the last data record before you enter the additional data. To do so, use the **Navigation buttons** found near the lower-left corner of the screen. The purpose of each of the Navigation buttons is described in Table 1-1.

Table 1-1

BUTTON	PURPOSE
First Record	Moves to the first record in the table
Previous Record	Moves to the previous record
Next Record	Moves to the next record
Last Record	Moves to the last record in the table
New Record	Moves past the last record in the table to a position for a new record

Complete the following steps to add the remaining records (Figure 1-32) to the Client table.

Client table (last 8 records)

CLIENT NUMBER	NAME	ADDRESS	CITY	STATE	ZIP CODE	BILLED	PAID	TECH NUMBER
BL26	Blake Suppliers	5752 Maumee	Grattan	MA	58120	$129.50	$0.00	12
DE76	D & E Grocery	464 Linnell	Marshall	VT	52018	$385.75	$300.00	17
GR56	Grant Cleaners	737 Allard	Portage	NH	59130	$215.00	$165.00	11
GU21	Grand Union	247 Fuller	Grattan	MA	58120	$128.50	$0.00	12
JE77	Jones Electric	57 Giddings	Marshall	VT	52018	$0.00	$0.00	12
MI26	Morland Int.	665 Whittier	Frankfort	MA	56152	$212.50	$223.25	11
SA56	Sawyer Inc.	31 Lafayette	Empire	MA	58216	$352.50	$250.00	17
SI82	Simpson Ind.	752 Cadieux	Fernwood	MA	57412	$154.00	$0.00	12

FIGURE 1-32

Steps To Add Additional Records to a Table

1 **Right-click the Client table selected in the Pilotech Services : Database window and then click Open on the shortcut menu.**

2 **When the Client table displays, maximize the window by clicking the Maximize button. Point to the New Record button.**

The datasheet displays (Figure 1-33).

Client : Table window

two records currently in table

Microsoft Access - [Client : Table]

Client Number	Name	Address	City	State	Zip Code
AM53	Ashton-Mills	216 Rivard	Grattan	MA	58120
AS62	Alton-Scripps	722 Fisher	Empire	MA	58216

Next Record button

First Record button

New Record button

Navigation buttons

Previous Record button

Last Record button

FIGURE 1-33

3 **Click the New Record button.**

Access places the insertion point in position to enter a new record (Figure 1-34).

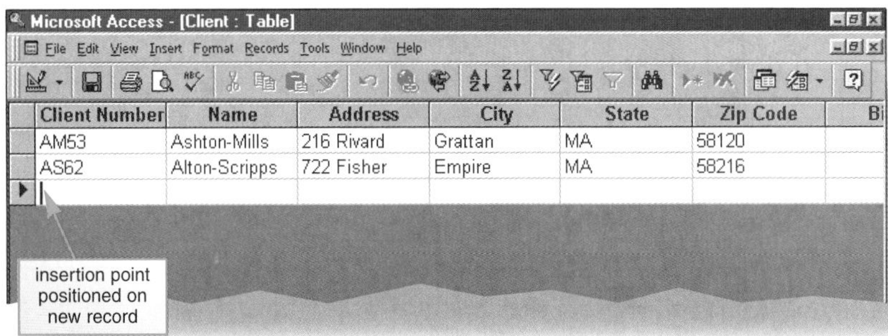

Microsoft Access - [Client : Table]

Client Number	Name	Address	City	State	Zip Code
AM53	Ashton-Mills	216 Rivard	Grattan	MA	58120
AS62	Alton-Scripps	722 Fisher	Empire	MA	58216

FIGURE 1-34

4 **Add the remaining records from Figure 1-32 using the same techniques you used to add the first two records. Point to the Close button.**

The additional records are added (Figure 1-35).

all ten records entered

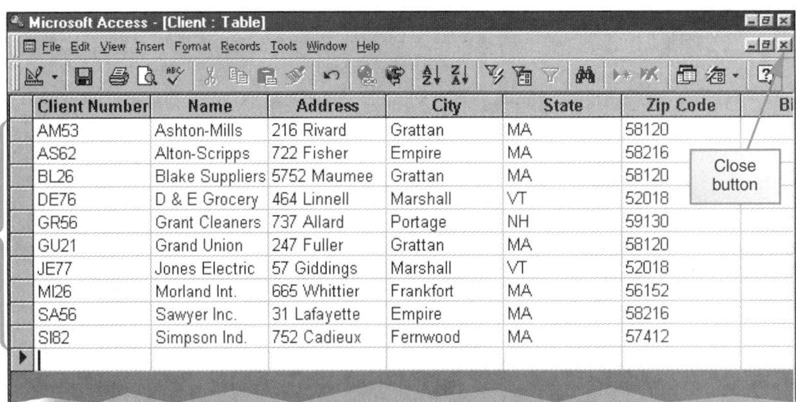

Microsoft Access - [Client : Table]

Client Number	Name	Address	City	State	Zip Code
AM53	Ashton-Mills	216 Rivard	Grattan	MA	58120
AS62	Alton-Scripps	722 Fisher	Empire	MA	58216
BL26	Blake Suppliers	5752 Maumee	Grattan	MA	58120
DE76	D & E Grocery	464 Linnell	Marshall	VT	52018
GR56	Grant Cleaners	737 Allard	Portage	NH	59130
GU21	Grand Union	247 Fuller	Grattan	MA	58120
JE77	Jones Electric	57 Giddings	Marshall	VT	52018
MI26	Morland Int.	665 Whittier	Frankfort	MA	56152
SA56	Sawyer Inc.	31 Lafayette	Empire	MA	58216
SI82	Simpson Ind.	752 Cadieux	Fernwood	MA	57412

5 **Close the window containing the table by clicking its Close button.**

FIGURE 1-35

OtherWays

1. Click New Record button on toolbar
2. On Insert menu click New Record

Correcting Errors in the Data

Check your entries carefully to ensure they are correct. If you make a mistake and discover it before you press the TAB key, correct it by pressing the BACKSPACE key until the incorrect characters are removed and then typing the correct characters.

If you discover an incorrect entry later, correct the error by clicking the incorrect entry and then making the appropriate correction. If the record you must correct is not on the screen, use the Navigation buttons (Next Record, Previous Record, and so on) to move to it. If the field you want to correct is not visible on the screen, use the horizontal scroll bar along the bottom of the screen to shift all the fields until the one you want displays. Then make the correction.

If you add an extra record accidentally, select the record by clicking the **record selector** that immediately precedes the record. Then, press the DELETE key. This will remove the record from the table. If you forget a record, add it using the same procedure as for all the other records. Access will place it in the correct location in the table automatically.

If you cannot determine how to correct the data, you are, in effect, stuck on the record. Access neither allows you to move to any other record until you have made the correction, nor allows you to close the table. If you encounter this situation, simply press the ESC key. Pressing the ESC key will remove from the screen the record you are trying to add. You then can move to any other record, close the table, or take any other action you desire.

Previewing and Printing the Contents of a Table

More *About* **Printing the Contents of a Table**

You can change the paper size, paper source, or the printer that will be used to print the report. To change any of these, select the Page sheet of the Page Setup dialog box, click the appropriate down arrow, and then select the desired option.

When working with a database, you often will need to **print** a copy of the table contents. Figure 1-36 shows a printed copy of the contents of the Client table. (Yours may look slightly different, depending on your printer.) Because the Client table is wider substantially than the screen, it also will be wider than the normal printed page in portrait orientation. **Portrait orientation** means the printout is across the width of the page. **Landscape orientation** means the printout is across the length of the page. Thus, to print the wide database table, use landscape orientation. If you are printing the contents of a table that fits on the screen, you will not need landscape orientation. A convenient way to change to landscape orientation is to **preview** what the printed copy will look like by using Print Preview. This allows you to determine whether landscape orientation is necessary and, if it is, to change easily the orientation to landscape. In addition, you also can use Print Preview to determine whether any adjustments are necessary to the page margins.

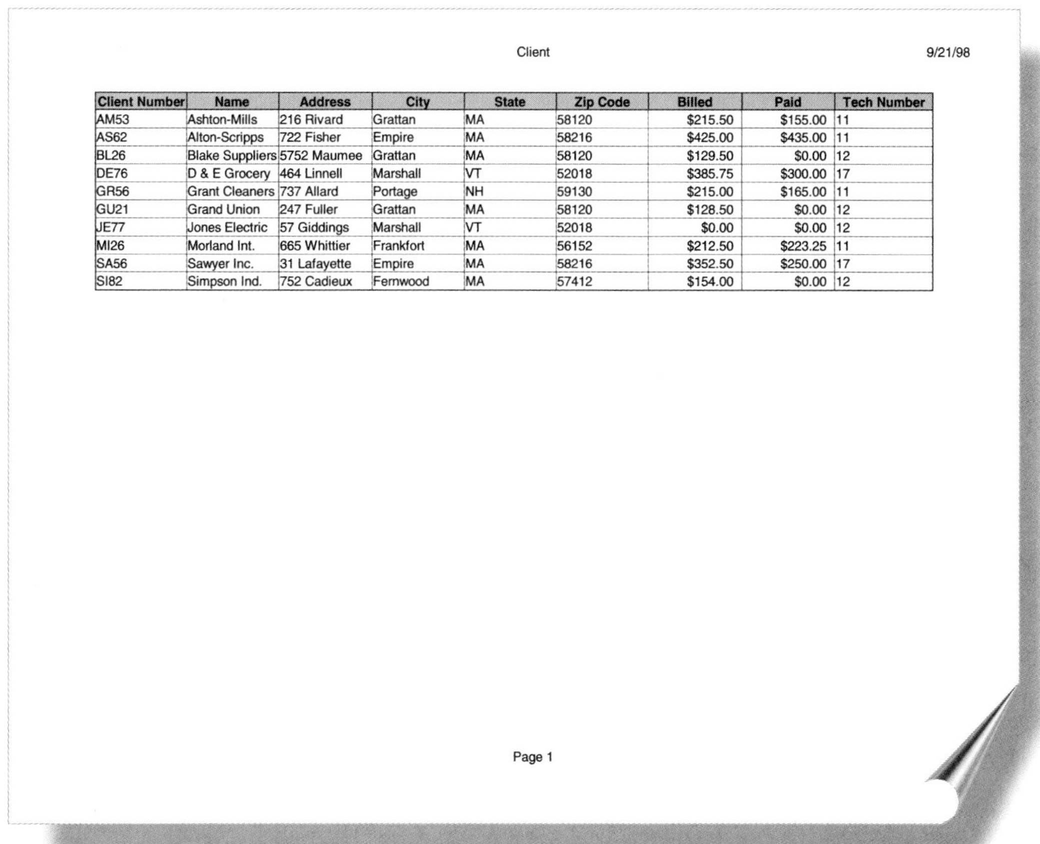

Client 9/21/98

Client Number	Name	Address	City	State	Zip Code	Billed	Paid	Tech Number
AM53	Ashton-Mills	216 Rivard	Grattan	MA	58120	$215.50	$155.00	11
AS62	Alton-Scripps	722 Fisher	Empire	MA	58216	$425.00	$435.00	11
BL26	Blake Suppliers	5752 Maumee	Grattan	MA	58120	$129.50	$0.00	12
DE76	D & E Grocery	464 Linnell	Marshall	VT	52018	$385.75	$300.00	17
GR56	Grant Cleaners	737 Allard	Portage	NH	59130	$215.00	$165.00	11
GU21	Grand Union	247 Fuller	Grattan	MA	58120	$128.50	$0.00	12
JE77	Jones Electric	57 Giddings	Marshall	VT	52018	$0.00	$0.00	12
MI26	Morland Int.	665 Whittier	Frankfort	MA	56152	$212.50	$223.25	11
SA56	Sawyer Inc.	31 Lafayette	Empire	MA	58216	$352.50	$250.00	17
SI82	Simpson Ind.	752 Cadieux	Fernwood	MA	57412	$154.00	$0.00	12

Page 1

FIGURE 1-36

Perform the following steps to use Print Preview to preview and then print the Client table.

To Preview and Print the Contents of a Table

1 Right-click the Client table and then point to Print Preview on the shortcut menu.

The shortcut menu for the Client table displays (Figure 1-37).

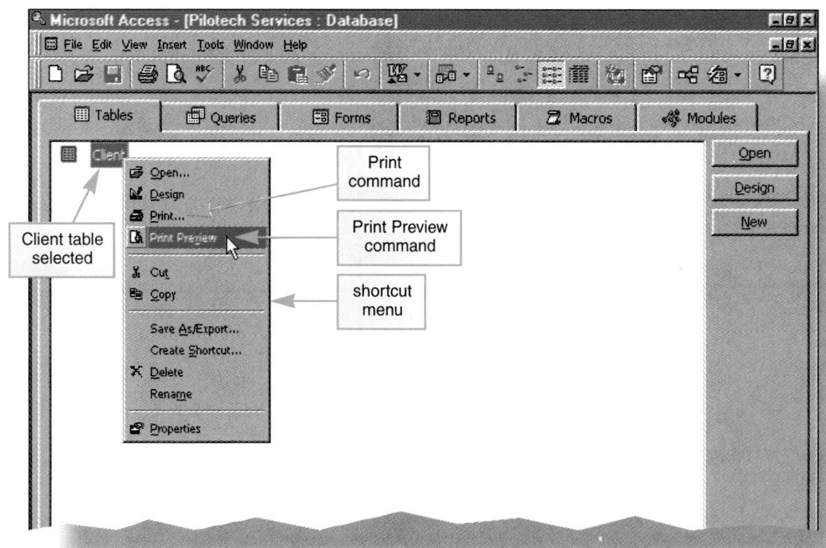

FIGURE 1-37

2 Click Print Preview on the shortcut menu. Point anywhere in the upper-right portion of the report.

The preview of the report displays (Figure 1-38).

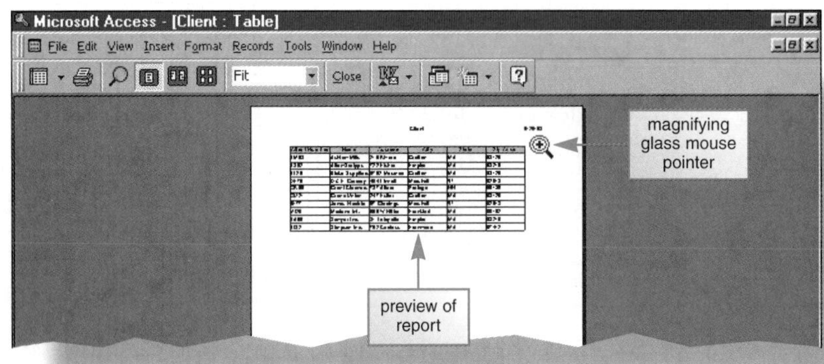

FIGURE 1-38

3 Click the magnifying glass mouse pointer in the approximate position shown in Figure 1-38.

The portion surrounding the mouse pointer is magnified (Figure 1-39). The last field that displays is the Zip Code field. The Billed, Paid, and Tech Number fields do not display. To display the additional fields, you will need to switch to landscape orientation.

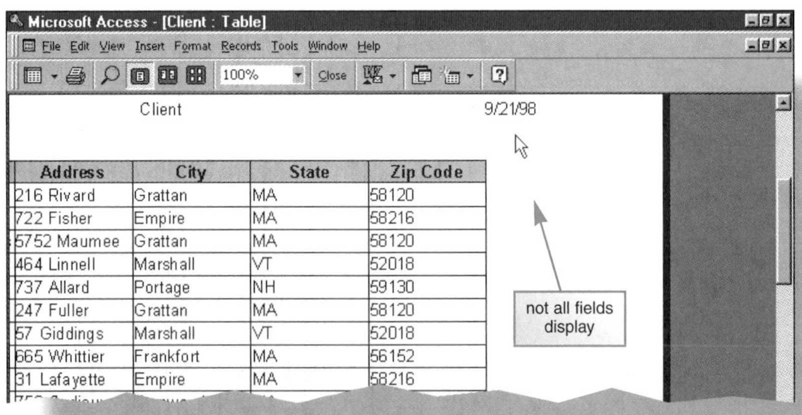

FIGURE 1-39

4 Click File on the menu bar and then point to Page Setup.

The File menu displays (Figure 1-40).

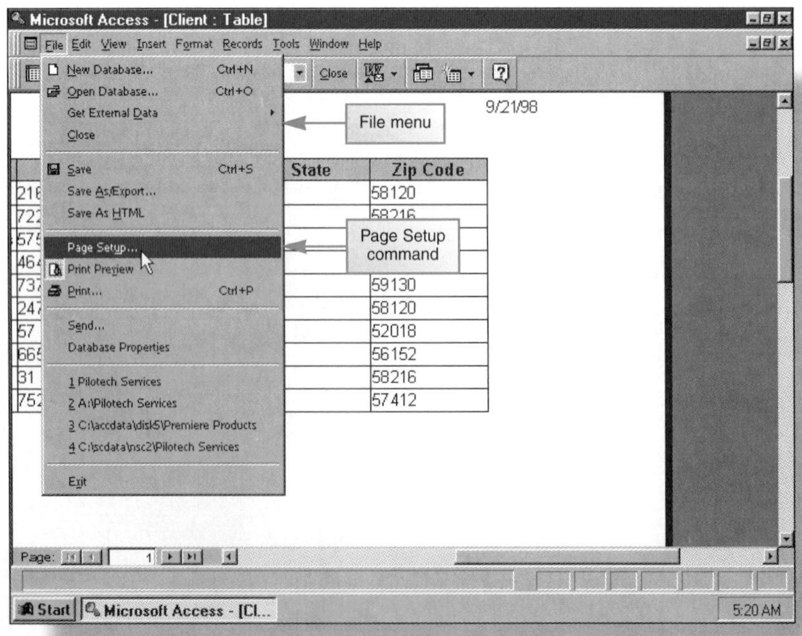

FIGURE 1-40

5 **Click Page Setup and then point to the Page tab.**

The Page Setup dialog box displays (Figure 1-41).

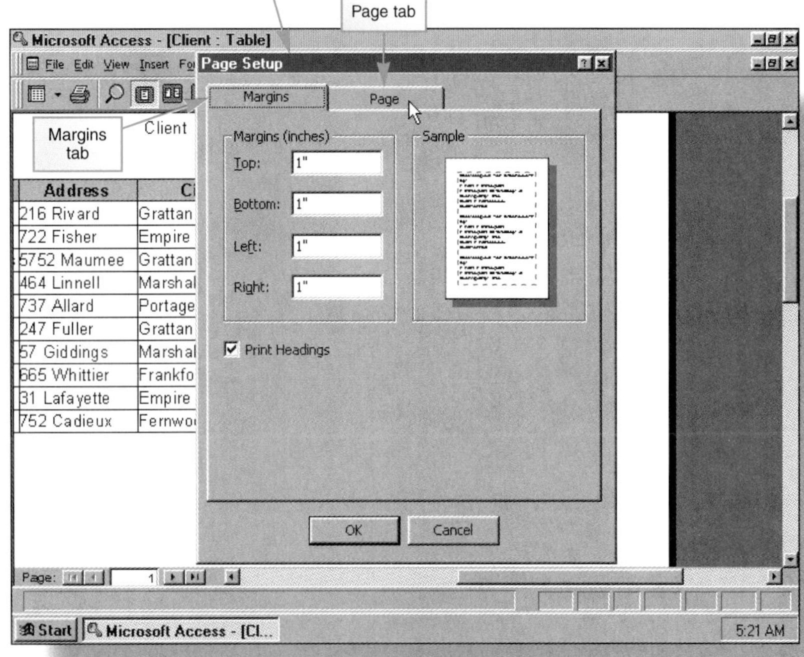

FIGURE 1-41

6 **Click the Page tab and then point to Landscape.**

*The Page sheet displays (Figure 1-42). The Portrait option button currently is selected. (**Option button** refers to the round button that indicates choices in a dialog box. When the corresponding option is selected, the button contains within it a solid circle. Clicking an option button selects it, and deselects all others.)*

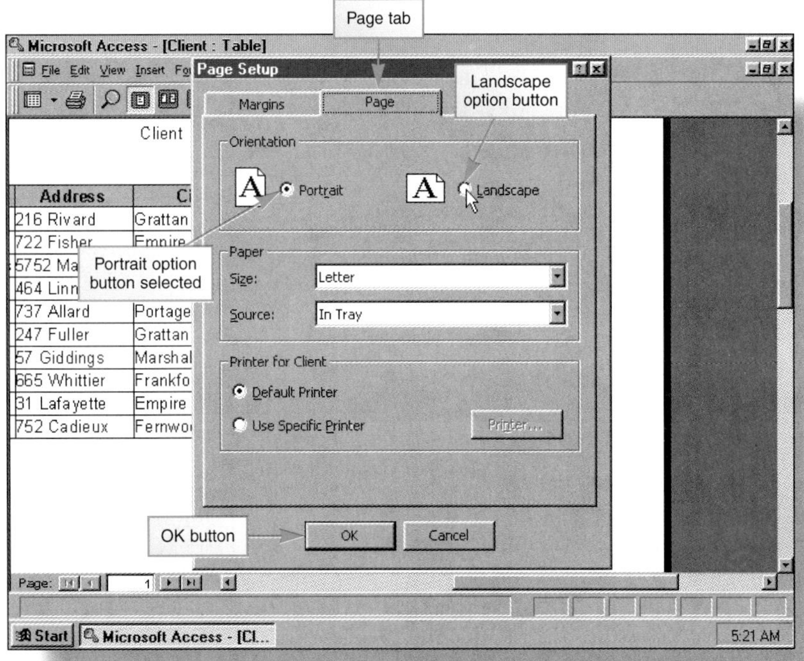

FIGURE 1-42

7 Click Landscape and then click the OK button. Click the mouse pointer to view the entire report.

The orientation is changed to landscape as shown by the report that displays on the screen (Figure 1-43). The characters in the report are so small that it is difficult to determine whether all fields currently display. To zoom in on a portion of the report, click the desired portion of the report.

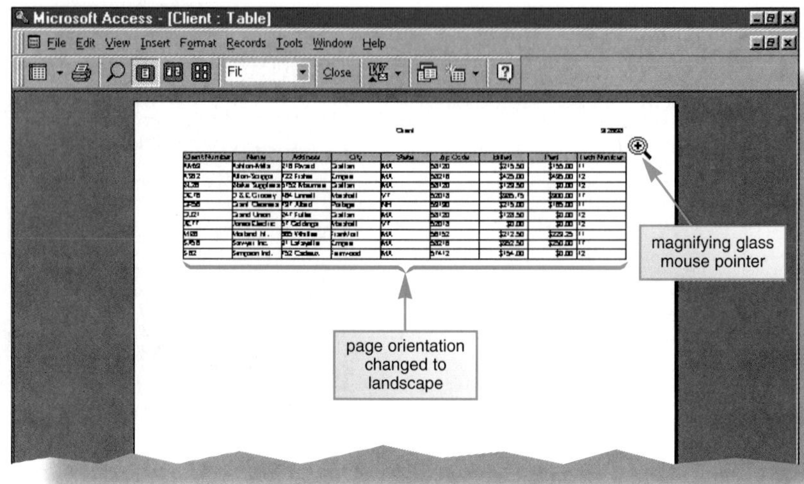

FIGURE 1-43

8 Click the magnifying glass mouse pointer in the approximate position shown in Figure 1-43.

The portion surrounding the mouse pointer is magnified (Figure 1-44). The last field that displays is the Tech Number field, so all fields currently display. If they did not, you could decrease the left and right margins, the amount of space left by Access on the left and right edges of the report.

9 Click the Print button to print the report. Click the Close button when the report has been printed to close the Print Preview window.

The Preview window no longer displays.

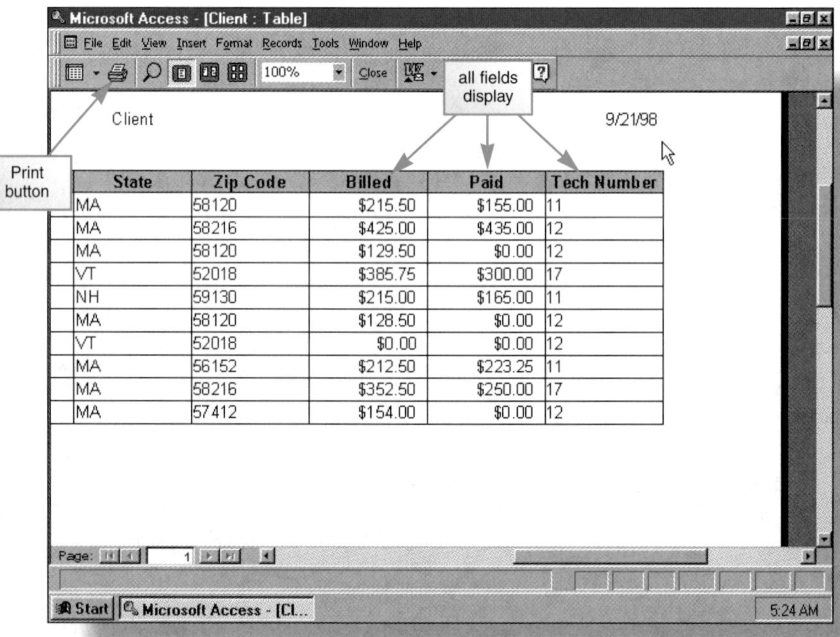

State	Zip Code	Billed	Paid	Tech Number
MA	58120	$215.50	$155.00	11
MA	58216	$425.00	$435.00	12
MA	58120	$129.50	$0.00	12
VT	52018	$385.75	$300.00	17
NH	59130	$215.00	$165.00	11
MA	58120	$128.50	$0.00	12
VT	52018	$0.00	$0.00	12
MA	56152	$212.50	$223.25	11
MA	58216	$352.50	$250.00	17
MA	57412	$154.00	$0.00	12

FIGURE 1-44

Other Ways

1. On File menu click Print Preview to preview
2. On File menu click Print to print
3. Press CTRL+P to print

Creating Additional Tables

A database typically consists of more than one table. The sample database contains two, the Client table and the Technician table. You need to repeat the process of creating a table and adding records for each table in the database. In the sample database, you need to create and add records to the Technician table. The structure and data for the table are given in Figure 1-45. The steps to create the table follow.

Structure of Technician table

FIELD NAME	DATA TYPE	FIELD SIZE	PRIMARY KEY?	DESCRIPTION
Tech Number	Text	2	Yes	Technician Number (Primary Key)
Last Name	Text	10		Last Name of Technician
First Name	Text	8		First Name of Technician
Address	Text	15		Street Address
City	Text	15		City
State	Text	2		State (Two-Character Abbreviation)
Zip Code	Text	5		Zip Code (Five-Character Version)
Hourly Rate	Currency			Hourly Rate of Technician
YTD Earnings	Currency			YTD Earnings of Technician

Data for Technician table

TECH NUMBER	LAST NAME	FIRST NAME	ADDRESS	CITY	STATE	ZIP CODE	HOURLY RATE	YTD EARNINGS
11	Levin	Joanna	26 Cottonwood	Carlton	MA	59712	$25.00	$6,245.00
12	Rogers	Brad	7972 Marsden	Kaleva	VT	57253	$30.00	$7,143.30
17	Rodriguez	Maria	263 Topsfield	Hudson	MA	57240	$35.00	$7,745.50

FIGURE 1-45

To Create an Additional Table

1 **Make sure the Pilotech Services database is open. Point to the New button.**

The Pilotech Services : Database window displays (Figure 1-46). If you recently maximized another window, this window also will be maximized as shown in the figure. If not, it will appear in its normal size.

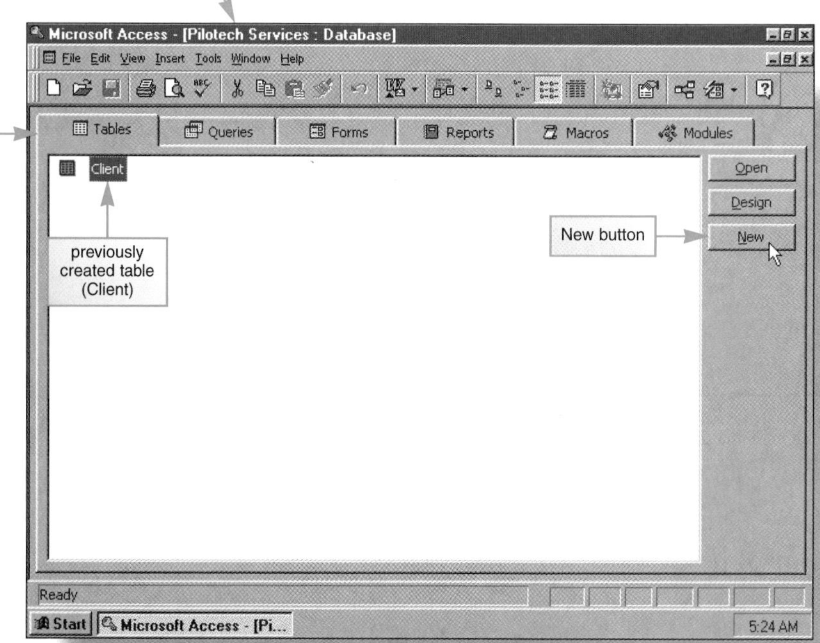

FIGURE 1-46

2 **Click the New button, click Design View in the New Table dialog box, click the OK button and then enter the data for the fields for the Technician table from Figure 1-45 on page A 1.33. Be sure to click the Primary Key button when you enter the Tech Number field. Point to the Save button on the toolbar.**

The entries display (Figure 1-47).

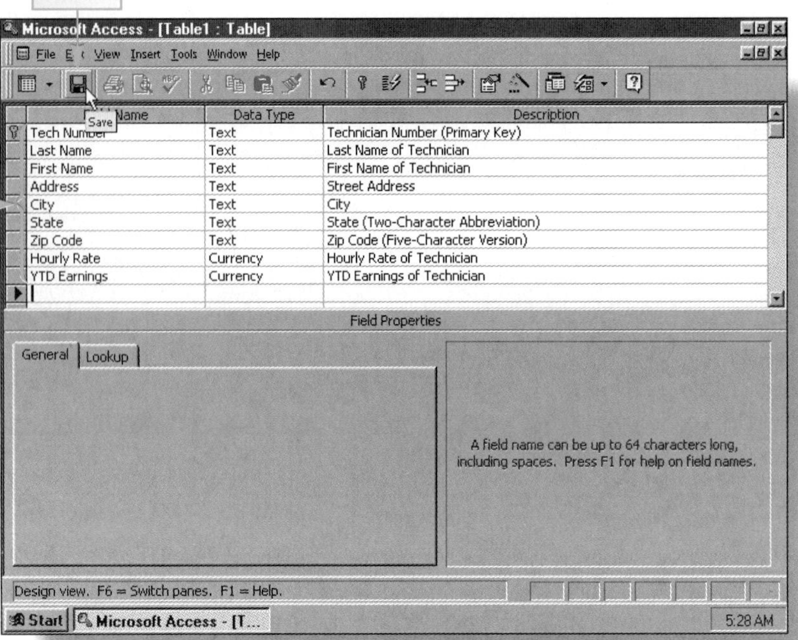

FIGURE 1-47

3 **Click the Save button, type** `Technician` **as the name of the table, and click the OK button. Click the Close button to close the Table window.**

The table is saved in the Pilotech Services database. The Table window no longer displays.

Adding Records to the Additional Table

Now that you have created the Technician table, use the following steps to add records to it.

To Add Records to an Additional Table

1 **Right-click the Technician table and point to Open on the shortcut menu.**

The shortcut menu for the Technician table displays (Figure 1-48).

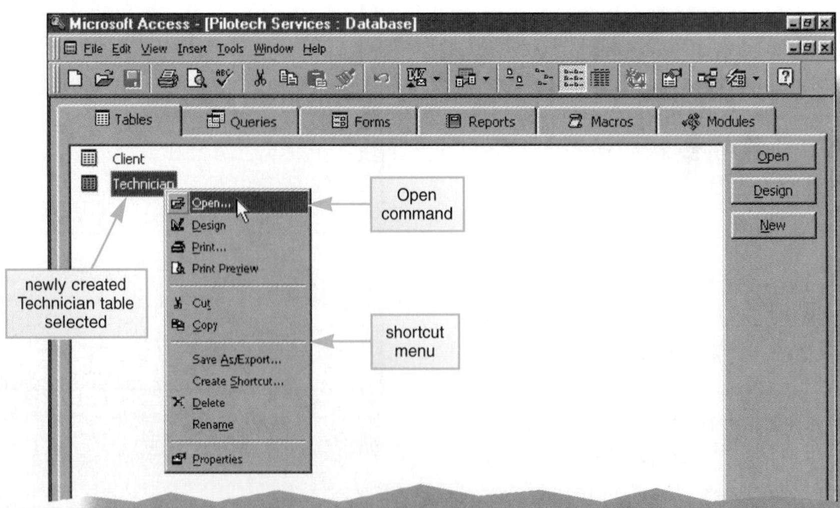

FIGURE 1-48

2 **Click the Yes button and then point to the OK button.**

The Save As dialog box displays (Figure 1-54). The name of the table (Client) becomes the name of the form automatically. This name can be replaced with any name.

3 **Click the OK button in the Save As dialog box.**

The form is saved as part of the database and is removed from the screen. The Pilotech Services : Database window again displays.

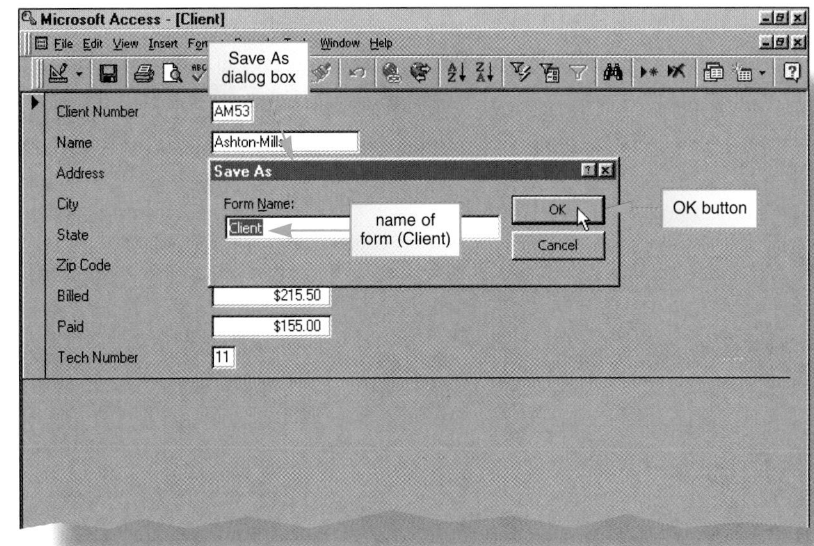

FIGURE 1-54

OtherWays

1. Double-click Control-menu icon on title bar for window
2. On File menu, click Close

Opening the Saved Form

Once you have saved a form, you can use it at any time in the future by opening it. **Opening a form** is similar to opening a table; that is, make sure the form to be opened is selected, right-click, and then click Open on the shortcut menu. Before opening the form, however, the Forms tab, rather than the Tables tab, must be selected.

Perform the following steps to open the Client form.

Steps To Open a Form

1 **With the Pilotech Services database open and the Database window on the screen, point to the Forms tab (Figure 1-55).**

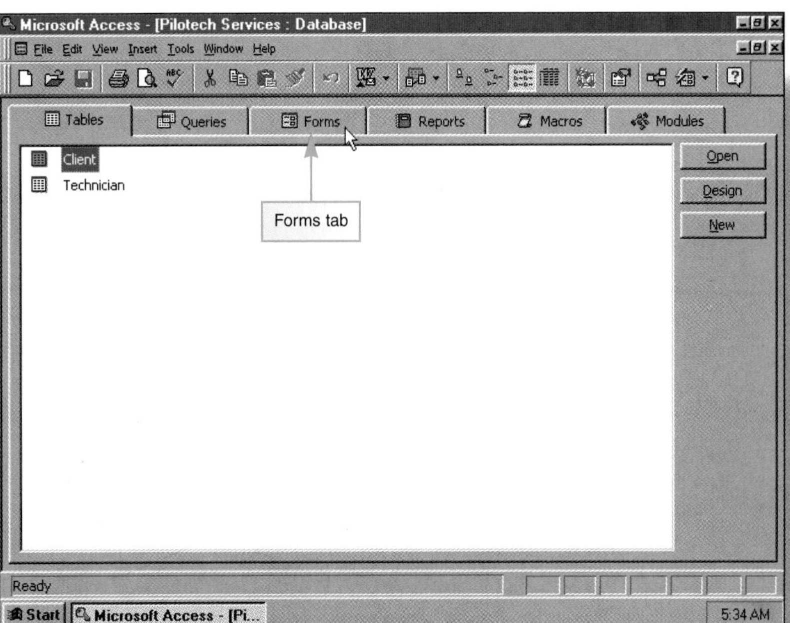

FIGURE 1-55

2 **Click the Forms tab, right-click the Client form and then point to Open on the shortcut menu.**

The Forms sheet is selected and the list of available forms displays (Figure 1-56). Currently, the Client form is the only form. The shortcut menu for the Client form displays.

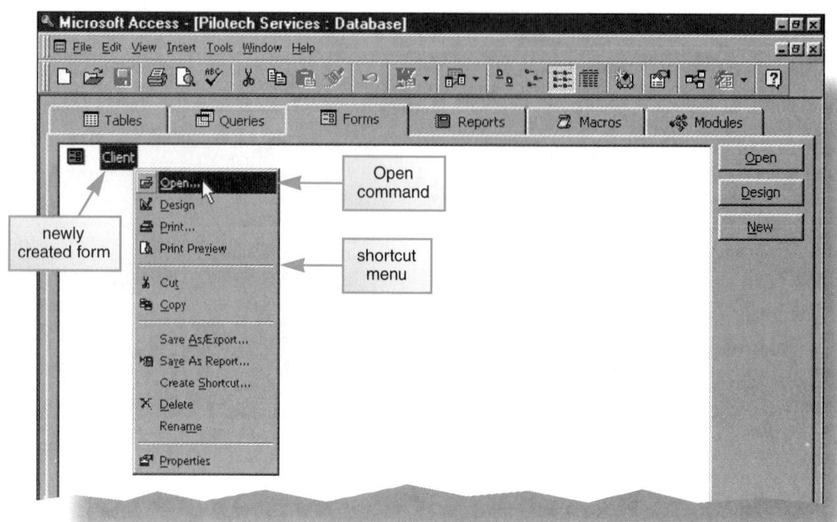

FIGURE 1-56

3 **Click Open on the shortcut menu.**

The Client form displays (Figure 1-57).

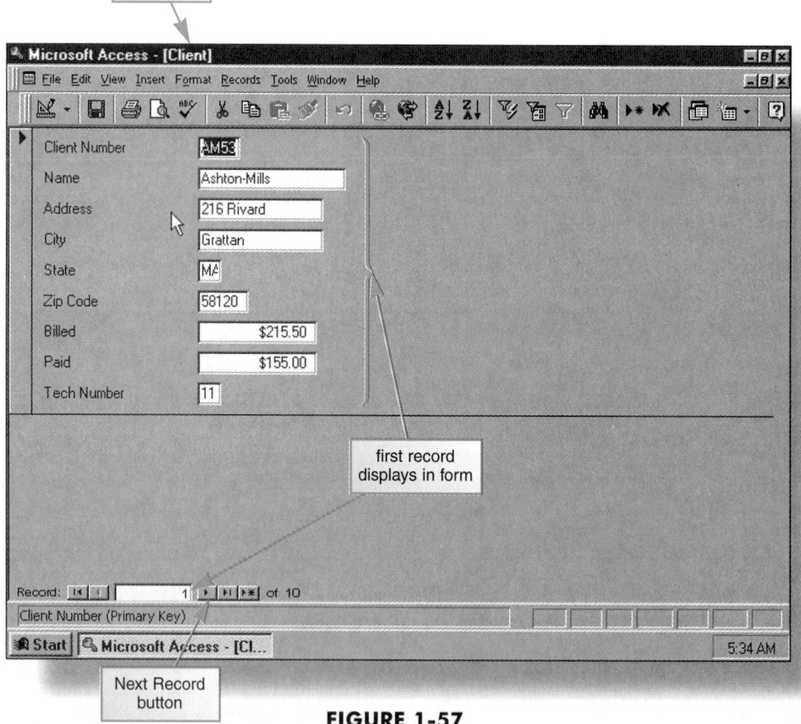

FIGURE 1-57

***Other*Ways**

1. Click Forms tab, double-click desired Form
2. Click desired form, click Open button
3. Press ALT+O

Using the Form

You can **use the form** just as you used Datasheet view. You use the Navigation buttons to move between records. You can add new records or change existing ones. To delete the record displayed on the screen, after selecting the record by clicking its record selector, press the DELETE key. Thus, you can perform database operations using either Form view or Datasheet view.

Because you can see only one record at a time in Form view, to see a different record, such as the fifth record, use the Navigation buttons to move to it. To move from record to record in Form view, perform the following step.

To Use a Form

1 Click the Next Record button four times.

The fifth record displays on the form (Figure 1-58).

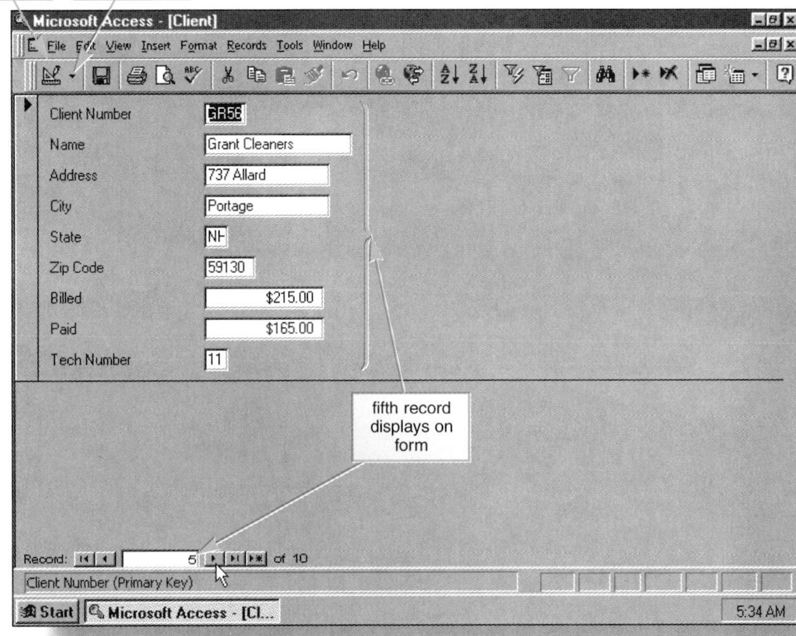

FIGURE 1-58

Switching Between Form View and Datasheet View

In some cases, once you have seen a record in Form view, you will want to move to Datasheet view to again see a collection of records. To do so, click the Form View button arrow on the toolbar and then click Datasheet View in the list that displays.

Perform the following steps to switch from Form view to Datasheet view.

To Switch from Form View to Datasheet View

1 Click the View button arrow on the toolbar (see Figure 1-58) and then point to Datasheet View.

The list of available views displays (Figure 1-59).

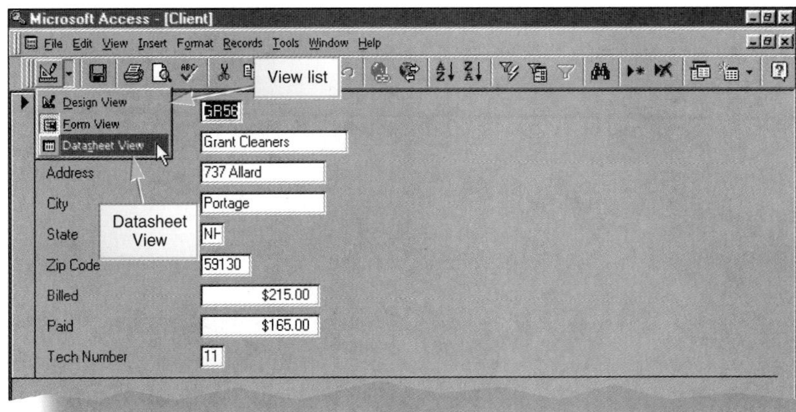

FIGURE 1-59

2 Click Datasheet View.

The table displays in Datasheet view (Figure 1-60). The record selector is positioned on the fifth record.

3 Close the Client window by clicking its Close button.

The datasheet no longer displays.

Close button

Microsoft Access - [Client]

File Edit View Insert Format Records Tools Window Help

Client Number	Name	Address	City	State	Zip Code
AM53	Ashton-Mills	216 Rivard	Grattan	MA	58120
AS62	Alton-Scripps	722 Fisher	Empire	MA	58216
BL26	Blake Suppliers	5752 Maumee	Grattan	MA	58120
DE76	D & E Grocery	464 Linnell	Marshall	VT	52018
GR56	Grant Cleaners	737 Allard	Portage	NH	59130
GU21	Grand Union	247 Fuller	Grattan	MA	58120
JE77	Jones Electric	57 Giddings	Marshall	VT	52018
MI26	Morland Int.	665 Whittier	Frankfort	MA	56152
SA56	Sawyer Inc.	31 Lafayette	Empire	MA	58216
SI82	Simpson Ind.	752 Cadieux	Fernwood	MA	57412

fifth record is current record

Datasheet view

Record: 5 of 10

Client Number (Primary Key)

Start | Microsoft Access - [Cl... | 5:35 AM

FIGURE 1-60

OtherWays

1. On View menu click Datasheet View

Creating a Report

Earlier in this project, you printed a table using the Print button. The report you produced was shown in Figure 1-36 on page A 1.29. While this type of report presented the data in an organized manner, it was not very flexible. It included all the fields, but in precisely the same order in which they occurred in the table. A way to change the title was not presented; it remained Client.

In this section, you will **create the report** shown in Figure 1-61. This report features significant differences from the one in Figure 1-36. The portion at the top of the report in Figure 1-61, called a **page header**, contains a custom title. The contents of this page header appear at the top of each page. The **detail lines**, which are the lines that are printed for each record, contain only those fields you specify.

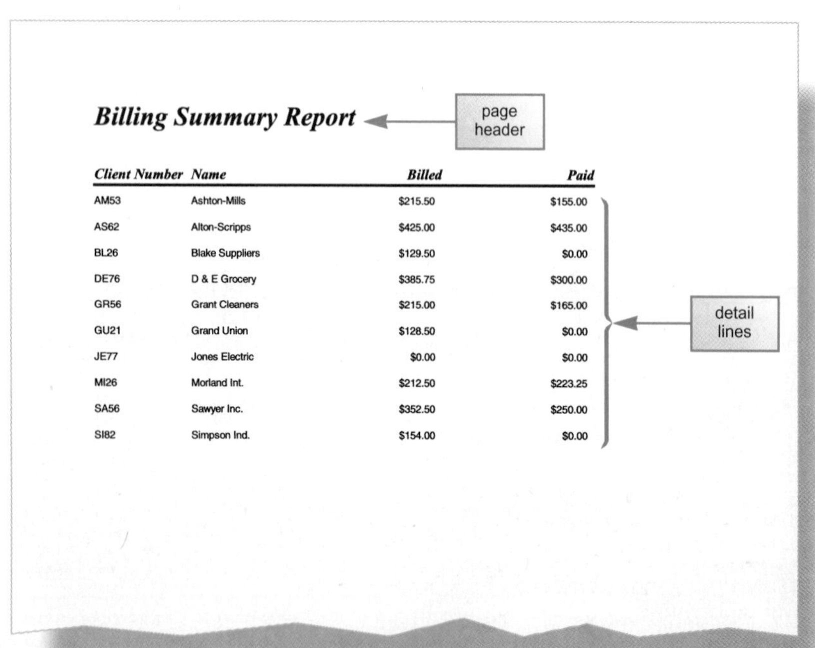

Billing Summary Report

Client Number	*Name*	*Billed*	*Paid*
AM53	Ashton-Mills	$215.50	$155.00
AS62	Alton-Scripps	$425.00	$435.00
BL26	Blake Suppliers	$129.50	$0.00
DE76	D & E Grocery	$385.75	$300.00
GR56	Grant Cleaners	$215.00	$165.00
GU21	Grand Union	$128.50	$0.00
JE77	Jones Electric	$0.00	$0.00
MI26	Morland Int.	$212.50	$223.25
SA56	Sawyer Inc.	$352.50	$250.00
SI82	Simpson Ind.	$154.00	$0.00

FIGURE 1-61

Perform the following steps to create the report in Figure 1-61.

To Create a Report

1 **Click the Tables tab. Make sure the Client table is selected. Click the New Object: AutoForm button arrow on the toolbar.**

The list of available objects displays (Figure 1-62).

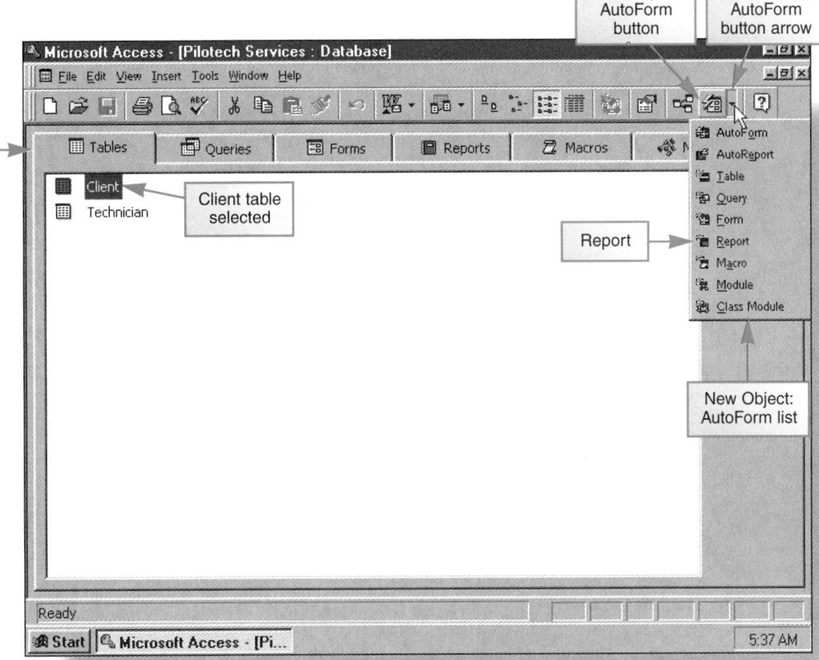

FIGURE 1-62

2 **Click Report and then point to Report Wizard.**

The New Report dialog box displays (Figure 1-63).

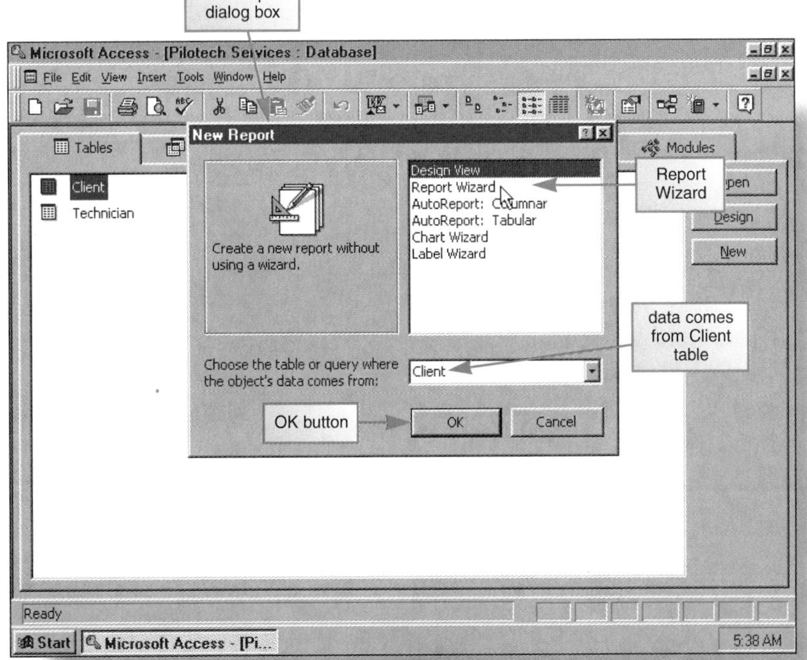

FIGURE 1-63

3 **Click Report Wizard and then click the OK button. Point to the Add Field button.**

The Report Wizard dialog box displays (Figure 1-64).

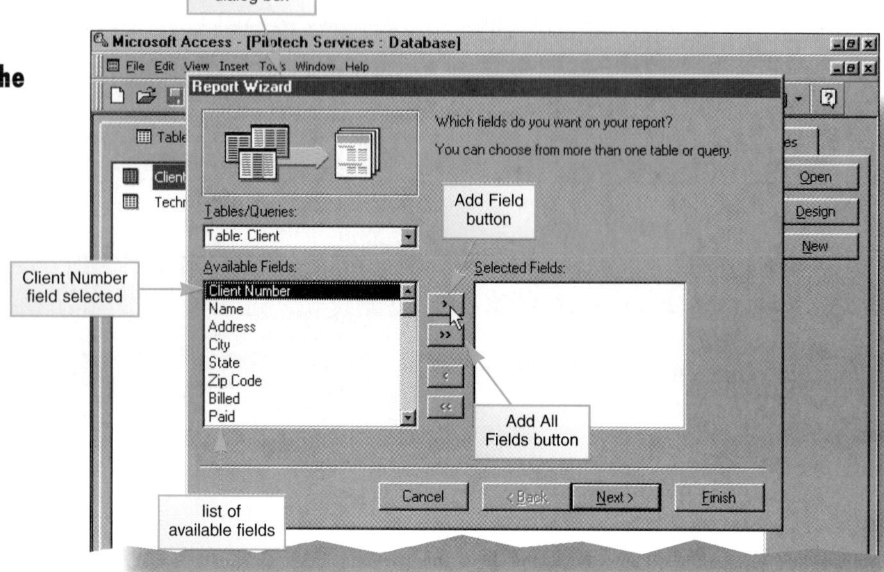

FIGURE 1-64

OtherWays

1. On Insert menu click Report
2. Click Reports tab, click New

Selecting the Fields for the Report

To select a field for the report; that is, to indicate the field that is to be included in the report, click the field in the Available Fields list box. Next, click the Add Field button. This will move the field from the Available Fields list box to the Selected Fields list box, thus including the field in the report. If you wanted to select all fields, a shortcut is available simply by clicking the Add All Fields button.

To select the Client Number, Name, Billed, and Paid fields for the report, perform the following steps.

Steps To Select the Fields for a Report

1 **Click the Add Field button to add the Client Number field. Add the Name field by clicking it and then clicking the Add Field button. Add the Billed and Paid fields just as you added the Client Number and Name fields.**

The fields for the report display in the Selected Fields list box (Figure 1-65).

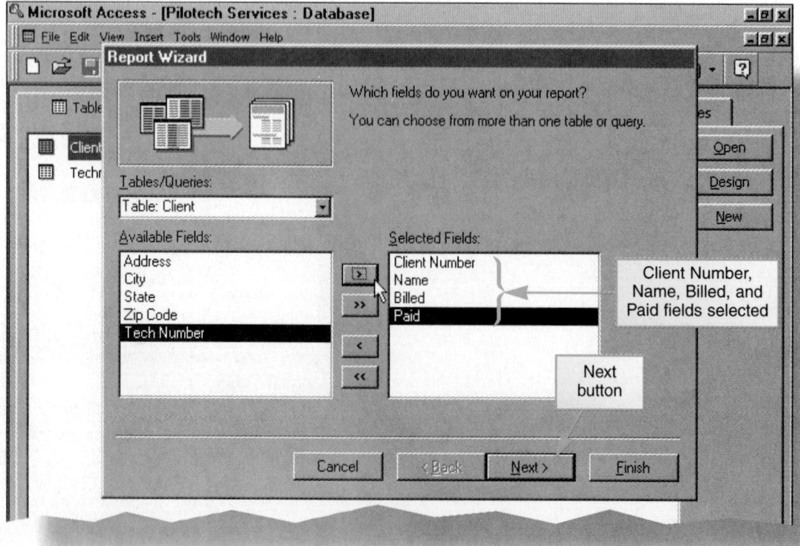

FIGURE 1-65

2 **Click the Next button.**

The Report Wizard dialog box displays (Figure 1-66).

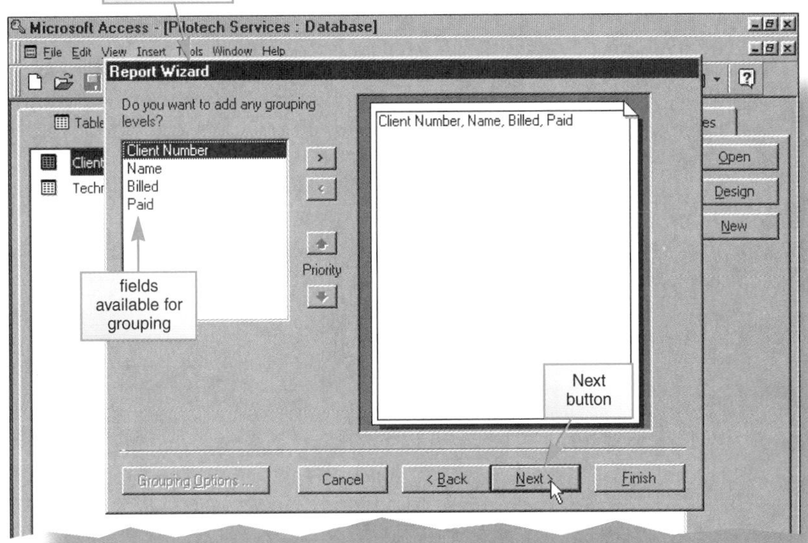

FIGURE 1-66

OtherWays

1. Double-click field

Completing the Report

Several additional steps are involved in completing the report. With the exception of changing the title, the Access selections are acceptable, so you simply will click the Next button.

Perform the following steps to complete the report.

To Complete a Report

1 **Because you will not specify any grouping, click the Next button in the Report Wizard dialog box (see Figure 1-66). Click the Next button a second time because you will not need to make changes on the screen that follows.**

The Report Wizard dialog box displays (Figure 1-67). In this dialog box, you can change the layout or orientation of the report.

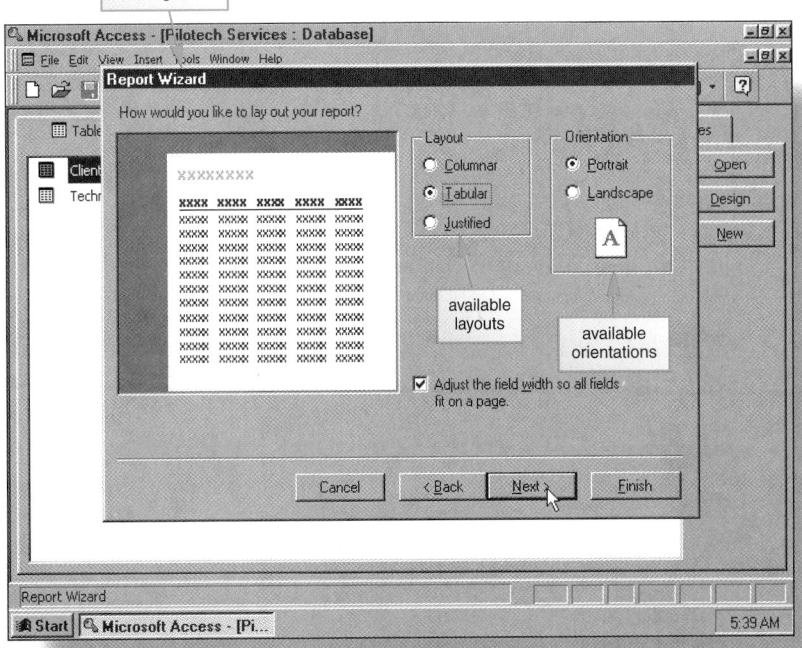

FIGURE 1-67

2 Make sure that Tabular is selected as the layout and Portrait is selected as the orientation and then click the Next button.

The Report Wizard dialog box displays (Figure 1-68). In this dialog box, you can select a style for the report.

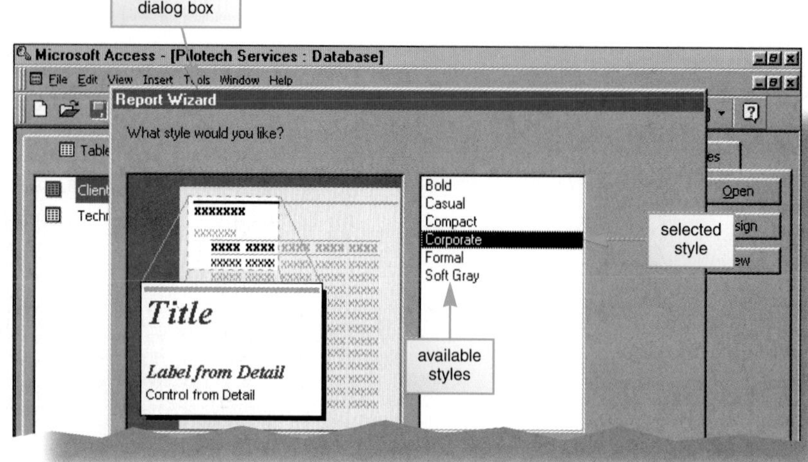

FIGURE 1-68

3 Be sure that the Corporate style is selected and then click the Next button.

The Report Wizard dialog box displays (Figure 1-69). In this dialog box, you can specify a title for the report.

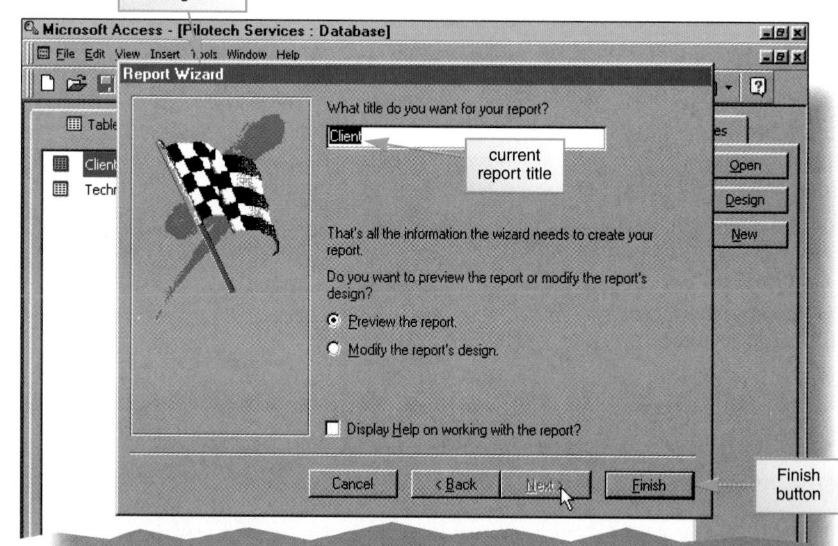

FIGURE 1-69

4 Type `Billing Summary Report` **as the new title and then click the Finish button.**

A preview of the report displays (Figure 1-70). Yours may look slightly different, depending on your printer.

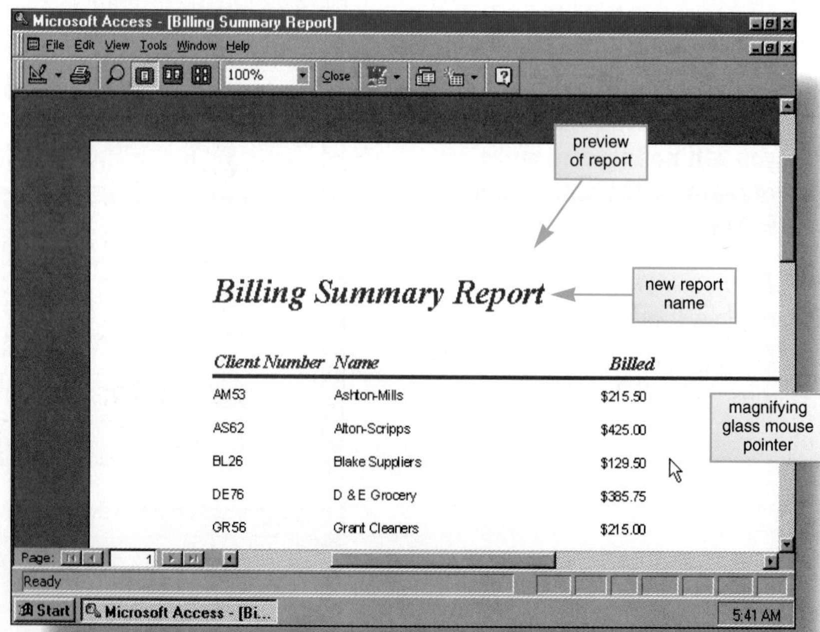

FIGURE 1-70

5 **Click anywhere within the report to see the entire report.**

The entire report displays (Figure 1-71).

6 **Close the report by clicking the Close button for the Billing Summary Report window.**

The report no longer displays. It has been saved automatically using the name Billing Summary Report.

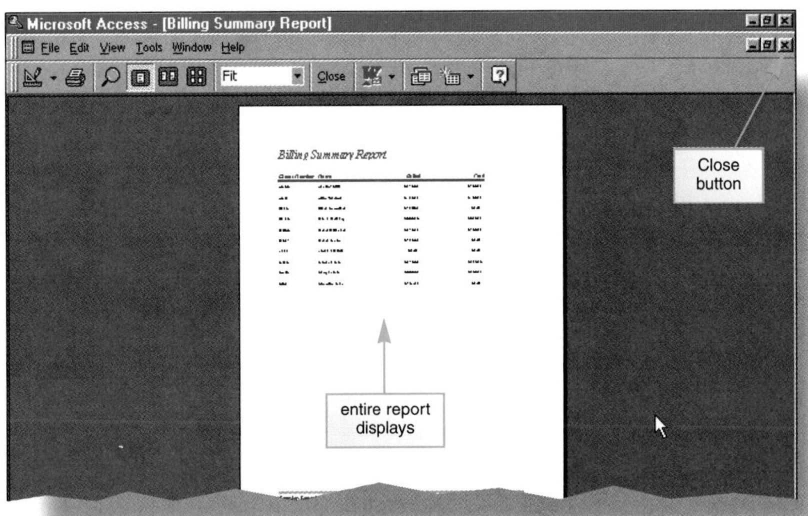

FIGURE 1-71

Printing the Report

To print a report from the Database window, first make sure the report displays. Then, you can click Print on the shortcut menu to print the report or Print Preview on the shortcut menu to see a preview of the report on the screen.

Perform the following steps to print the report.

More About Reports

Custom reports represent one of the most important ways of presenting the data in a database. Reports can incorporate data from multiple tables and can be formatted in a wide variety of ways. The ability to create sophisticated custom reports is one of the major benefits of a DBMS like Access.

To Print a Report

1 **Click the Reports tab in the Database window, right-click the Billing Summary Report and then point to Print on the shortcut menu.**

The shortcut menu for the Billing Summary Report displays (Figure 1-72).

2 **Click Print on the shortcut menu.**

The report prints. It should look similar to the one shown in Figure 1-61 on page A 1.40.

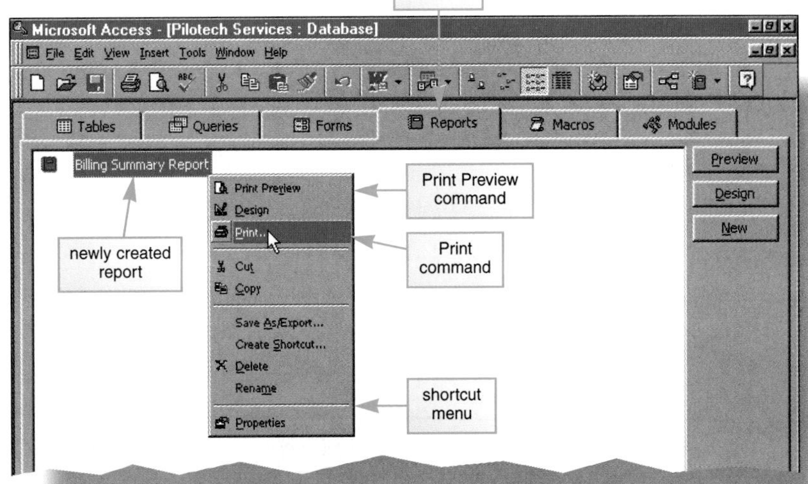

FIGURE 1-72

OtherWays

1. On File menu click Print Preview to preview
2. On File menu click Print to print
3. Press CTRL+P to print

Closing the Database

Once you have finished working with a database, you should close it. The following step closes the database by closing its Database window.

TO CLOSE A DATABASE

Step 1: Click the Close button for the Pilotech Services : Database window.

Microsoft Access Help

At any time while you are working with Microsoft Access, you can answer your questions by using Access Help. Used properly, this form of online assistance can increase your productivity and reduce your frustrations by minimizing the time you spend learning how to use Access. Table 1-2 summarizes the categories of Access Help available to you.

Table 1-2

TYPE	DESCRIPTION	ACTIVATE BY
Office Assistant	Answers your questions, offers tips, and provides Help for a variety of Access features	Clicking Office Assistant button on the toolbar
Contents sheet	Groups Help topics by general categories; use when you know only the general category of the topic in question	Clicking Contents and Index on the Help menu, then clicking the Contents tab
Index sheet	Similar to an index in a book; use when you know exactly what you want	Clicking Contents and Index on the Help menu, then clicking the Index tab
Find sheet	Searches the index for all phrases that include the term in question	Clicking Contents and Index on the Help menu, then clicking the Find tab
Question Mark button and What's This? command	Identify unfamiliar items on the screen	Clicking the Question Mark button, then clicking an item in a dialog box; clicking What's This? on the Help menu, then clicking an item on the screen

The following sections show examples of each type of online Help described in Table 1-2.

Using the Office Assistant

The **Office Assistant** answers your questions and suggests more efficient ways to complete a task. With the Office Assistant active, for example, you can type a word or phrase in a text box and the Office Assistant will provide immediate Help on the subject. In addition, as you perform a task, the Office Assistant accumulates tips that suggest more efficient ways to complete the task. This tip feature is part of the **IntelliSense™ technology** built into Access, which understands what you are trying to do and suggests better ways to do it.

The following steps show how to use the Office Assistant to obtain information on creating a table.

To Obtain Help Using the Office Assistant

1 **If the Office Assistant is not on the screen, click the Office Assistant button on the toolbar. If the Office Assistant is on the screen, click it. Type** `create` **in the What would you like to do? text box and then point to the Search button (Figure 1-73).**

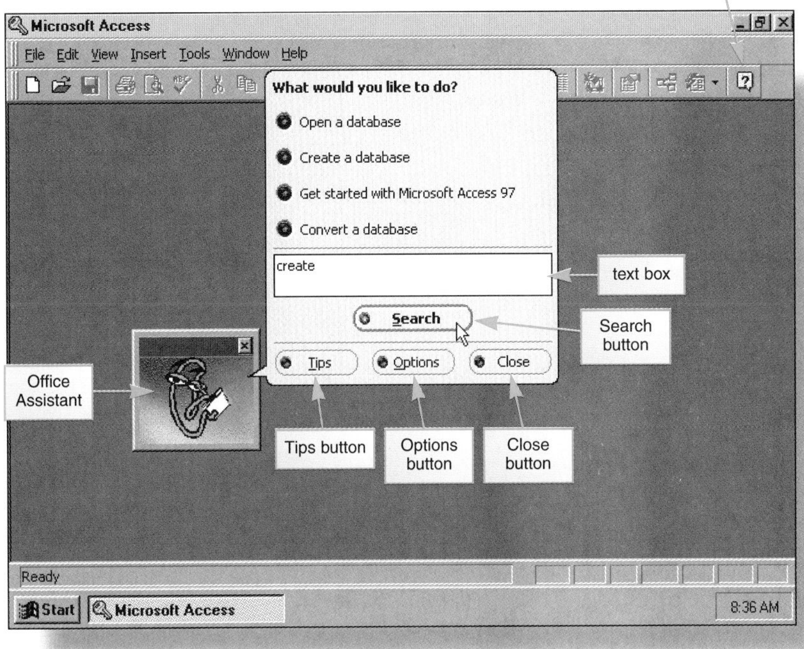

FIGURE 1-73

2 **Click the Search button and then point to Create a table.**

The Office Assistant displays a list of topics relating to the word create (Figure 1-74).

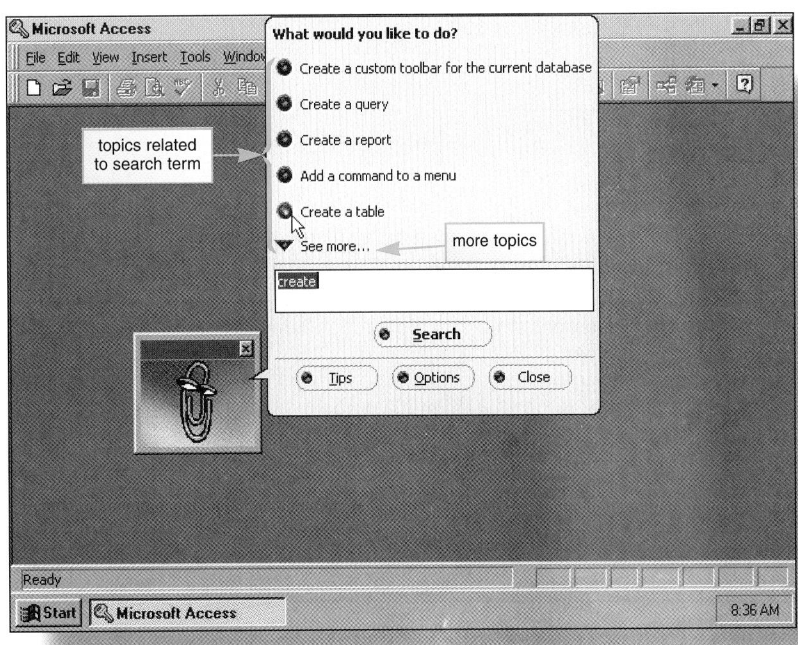

FIGURE 1-74

3 **Click Create a table.**

*The Office Assistant displays the Microsoft Access 97 window with Help on creating a table (Figure 1-75). The underlined words in green and the topics at the bottom of the window preceded by a button are **links** to topics related to creating a table. When you move the mouse pointer over a link, it changes to a pointing hand.*

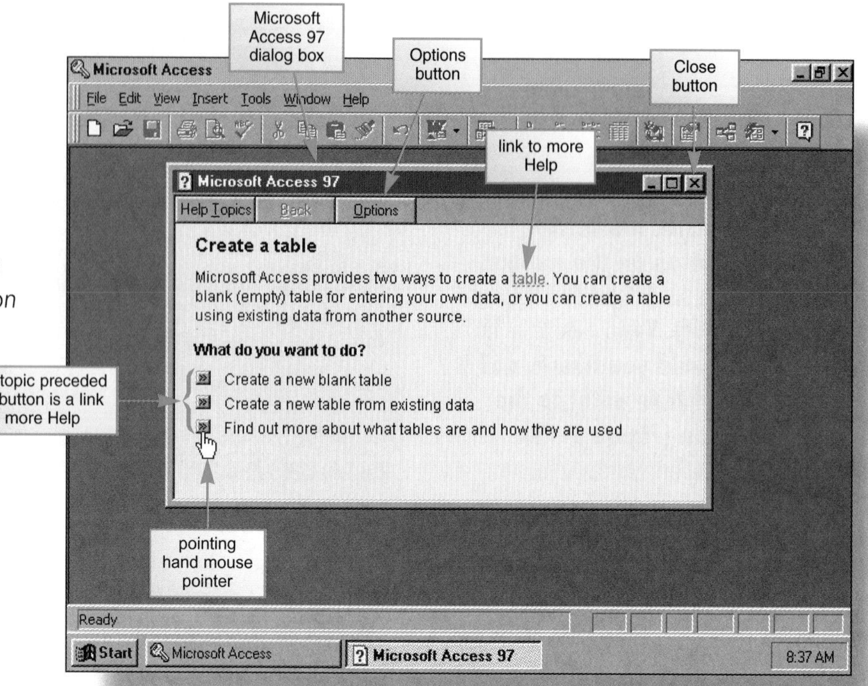

FIGURE 1-75

4 **Click the Close button on the Microsoft Access 97 title bar.**

The Microsoft Access 97 window disappears and control returns to the desktop.

5 **Click the Close button on the title bar of the Office Assistant window.**

The Office Assistant disappears from the screen.

OtherWays

1. To show Office Assistant, press F1 key or on Help menu click Microsoft Access Help
2. To hide Office Assistant, click Office Assistant button on toolbar or click Hide Assistant on shortcut menu

You can use the Office Assistant to search for Help on any topic concerning Access. Once Help displays, you can read it, print it via the **Options button** or shortcut menu, or click one of the links to display a related topic. If you display a related topic, click the **Back button** to return to the previous screen. You also can click the **Help Topics button** to obtain Help through the Contents, Index, and Find tabs.

When you right-click the Office Assistant window, a shortcut menu displays (Figure 1-76). It allows you to change the look and feel of the Office Assistant. For example, you can hide the Office Assistant, display tips, change the way it works, change the icon representing the Office Assistant, or view animation of the Office Assistant. These options also are available through the Options button that displays when you click the Office Assistant.

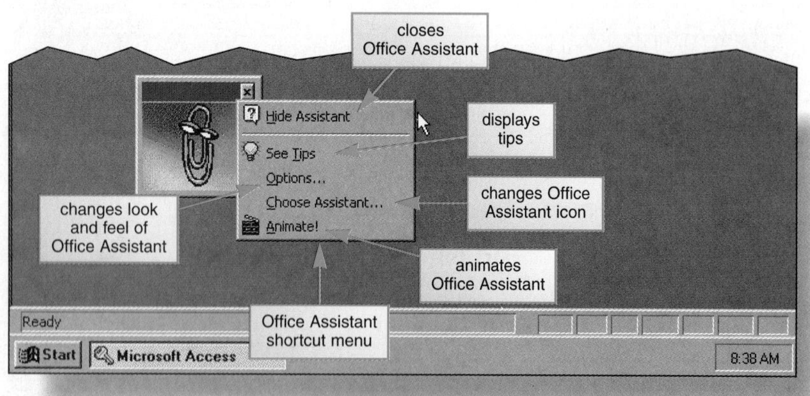

FIGURE 1-76

Using the Contents Sheet to Obtain Help

The Contents sheet in the Help Topics dialog box offers you assistance when you know the general category of the topic in question, but not the specifics. The following steps show how to use the Contents sheet in the Help Topics: Microsoft Access 97 dialog box to obtain information on adding or editing data.

Steps To Obtain Help Using the Contents Sheet

1 Click Help on the menu bar and then point to Contents and Index.

The Help menu displays (Figure 1-77).

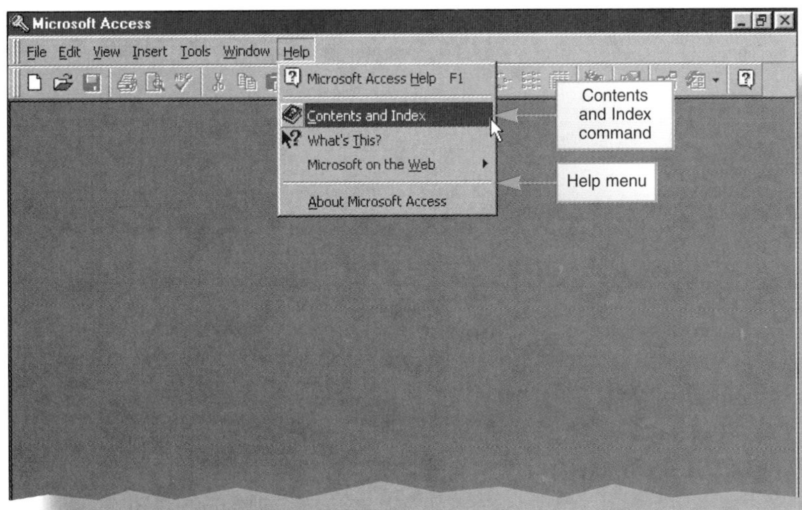

FIGURE 1-77

2 Click Contents and Index. Click the Contents tab. Double-click the Working with Data book. Point to the Adding or Editing Data book.

The Help Topics: Microsoft Access 97 dialog box displays (Figure 1-78). The Contents sheet displays with the Working with Data book open.

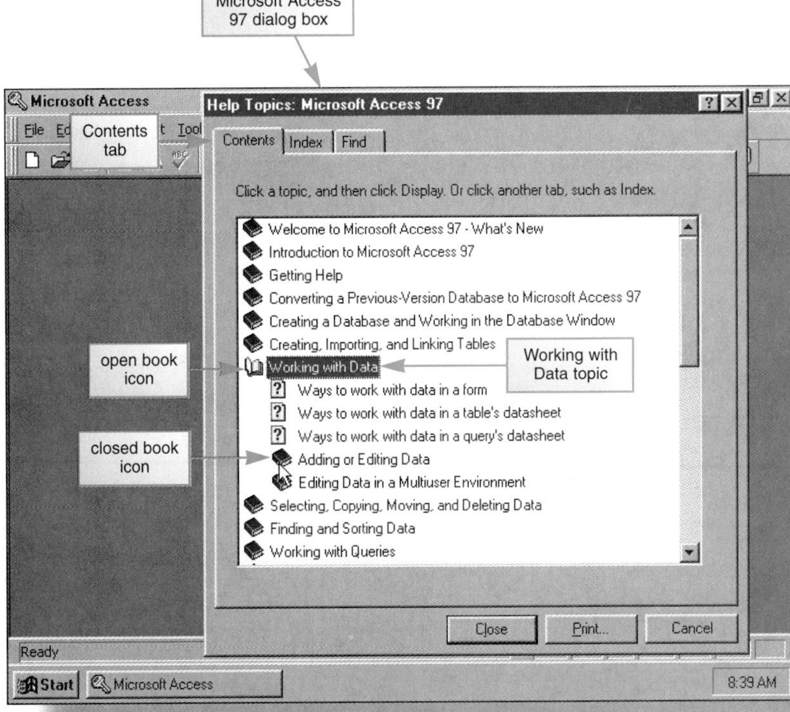

FIGURE 1-78

3 Double-click the Adding or Editing Data book.

The Adding or Editing Data book is open with a list of topics (Figure 1-79).

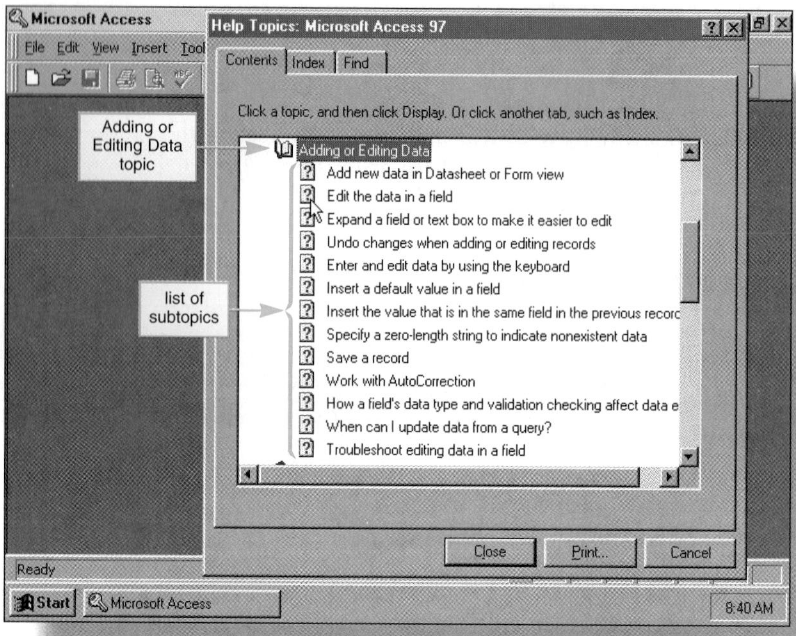

FIGURE 1-79

4 Double-click the topic, Edit the data in a field, listed below the open book Adding or Editing Data.

A Microsoft Access 97 window displays describing the steps for editing the data in a field (Figure 1-80).

5 After reading the information, click the Close button in the Microsoft Access 97 window.

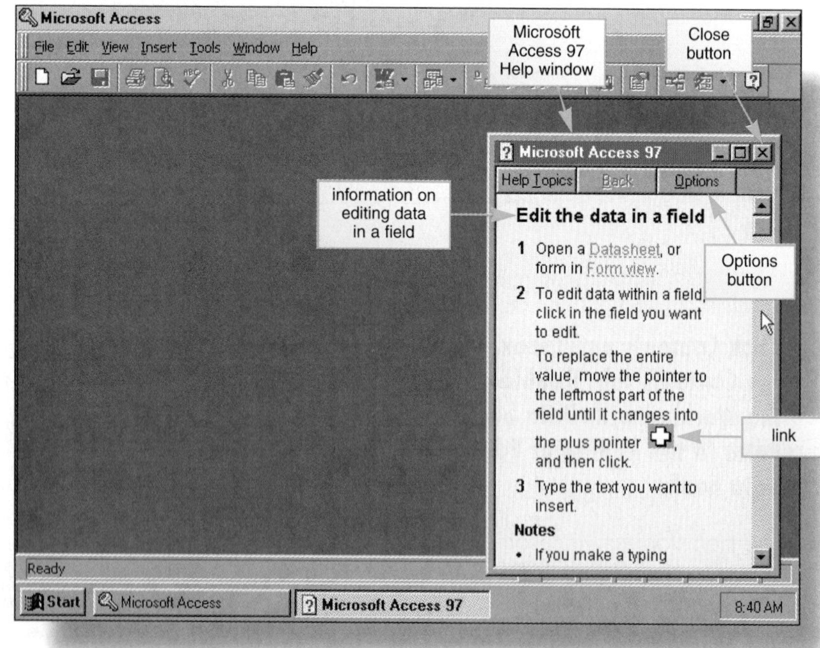

FIGURE 1-80

Instead of closing the Microsoft Access 97 window in Step 5, you can click Help Topics in Figure 1-80 to return to the Contents sheet (Figure 1-79). If you right-click in the Microsoft Access 97 window, a shortcut menu will display with several commands, such as Print Topic and Copy. You can use the Copy command to copy the Help information to a Word document.

Each topic on the Contents sheet (Figure 1-79) is preceded by a book icon or question mark icon. A **book icon** indicates subtopics are available. A **question mark icon** means information will display on the topic if you double-click the title. Notice how the book icon opens when you double-click the book (or its title).

Rather than double-clicking a topic in the list box, you can click it and then use the buttons in the dialog box to open a book, display information on a topic, or print information on a topic.

Using the Index Sheet to Obtain Help

The next sheet in the Help Topics: Microsoft Access 97 dialog box is the Index sheet. Use the Index sheet when you know the term you want to find or at least the first few letters of the term. Use the Index sheet in the same manner you would use an index at the back of a textbook.

The following steps show how to obtain information on primary keys by using the Index sheet and entering the letters, pri, the first three letters of primary.

Steps To Obtain Help Using the Index Sheet

1 Click Help on the menu bar and then click Contents and Index. Click the Index tab.

The Index sheet displays in the Help Topics: Microsoft Access 97 dialog box.

2 Type `pri` **in the top text box labeled 1.**

The words, primary keys, display in the lower list box labeled 2 (Figure 1-81). Several index entries relating to primary keys are in the list.

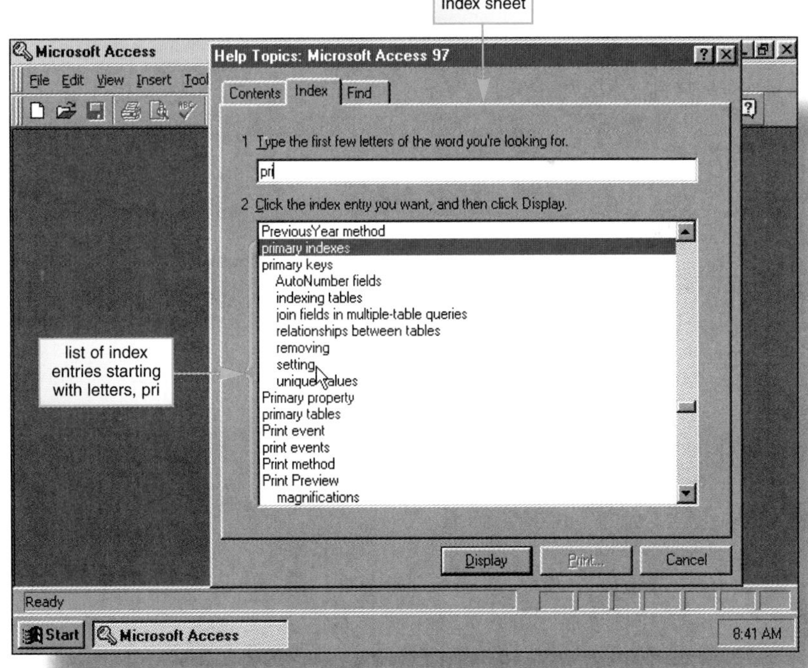

FIGURE 1-81

3 **Double-click the index entry, setting, under primary keys. Double-click Set or change the primary key in the Topics Found dialog box.**

Information on setting or changing the primary key displays in the Microsoft Access 97 window (Figure 1-82).

4 **Click the Close button in the upper-right corner of the Microsoft Access 97 window to close it.**

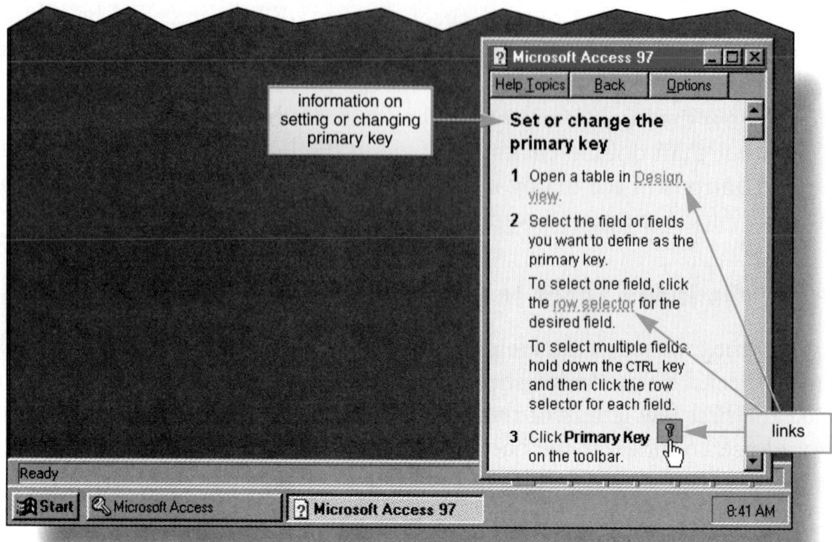

FIGURE 1-82

Using the Find Sheet to Obtain Help

The third sheet in the Help Topics: Microsoft Access 97 dialog box is the Find sheet. The Find sheet will return a list of all topics pertaining to the word or phrase you type in the text box. You then can further select words to narrow your search.

The following steps show how to obtain information on connecting database applications to the Internet.

To Obtain Help Using the Find Sheet

1 **Click Help on the menu bar and then click Contents and Index. Click the Find tab.**

The Find sheet displays in the Help Topics: Microsoft Access dialog box.

2 **Type** web **in the top text box labeled 1. Click Web in the middle list box labeled 2. Click the down arrow on the scroll bar in the lower list box labeled 3. Point to New Internet Features for Developers.**

The message box indicates that 69 topics were found (Figure 1-83).

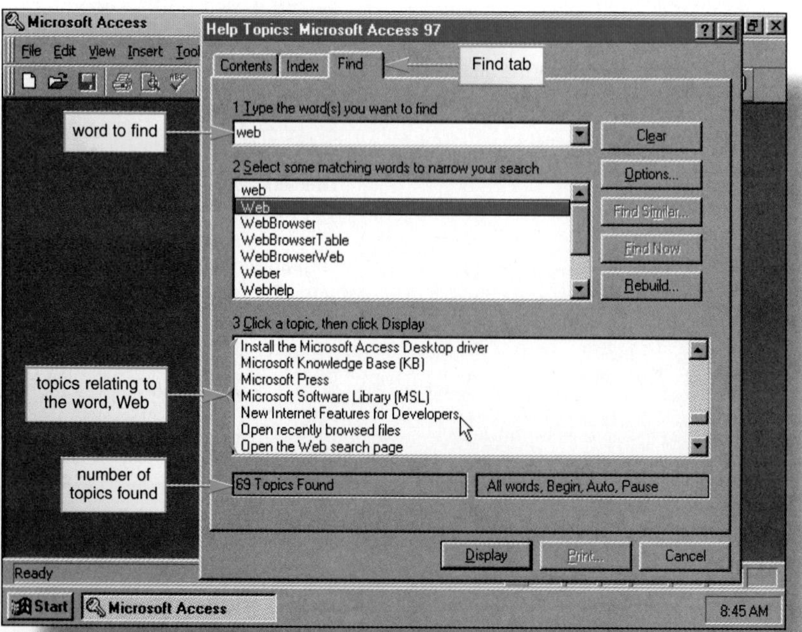

FIGURE 1-83

3 Double-click New Internet Features for Developers.

Information describing new Internet features displays (Figure 1-84).

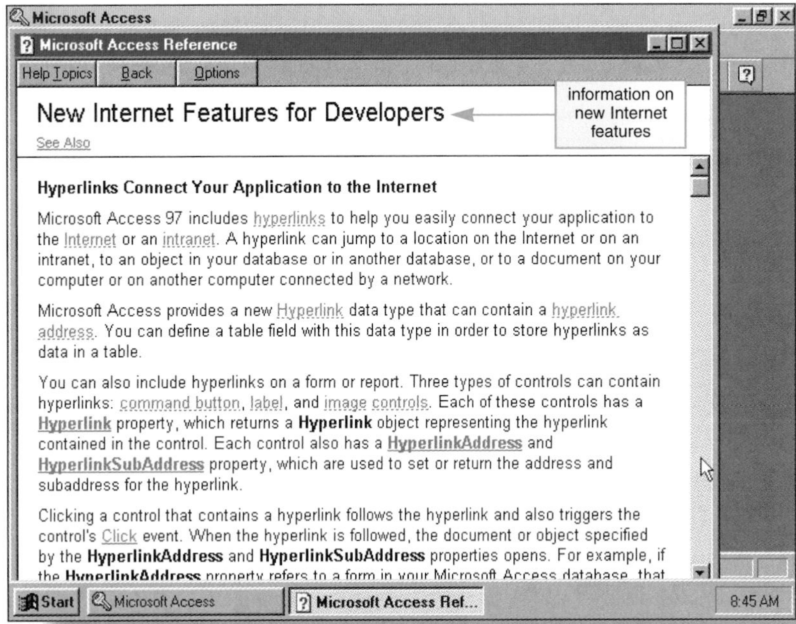

FIGURE 1-84

You can see from the previous steps that the Find sheet allows you to enter a word similarly to the Index sheet, but instead of displaying an alphabetical listing, the Find sheet lists all the words or phrases that include the word you entered. You then can click the appropriate words or phrases to narrow your search.

Obtaining Web Information

To obtain Web-related information, you can use the Microsoft on the Web command on the Help menu. A submenu of Web-related commands displays (Figure 1-85). If you click any command on the submenu, your system will launch your browser and connect to a corresponding page on the World Wide Web. Use the commands on the Microsoft on the Web submenu to obtain up-to-date information on a variety of topics.

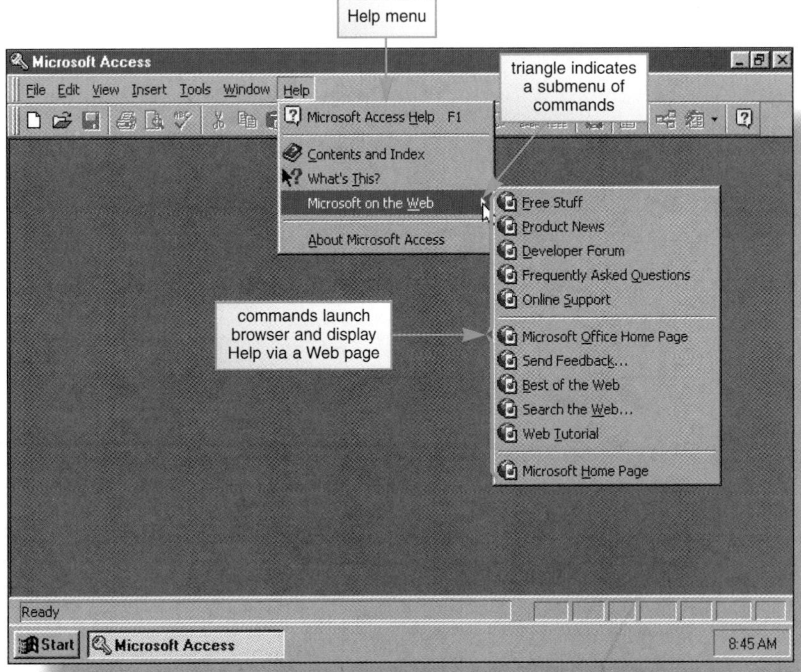

FIGURE 1-85

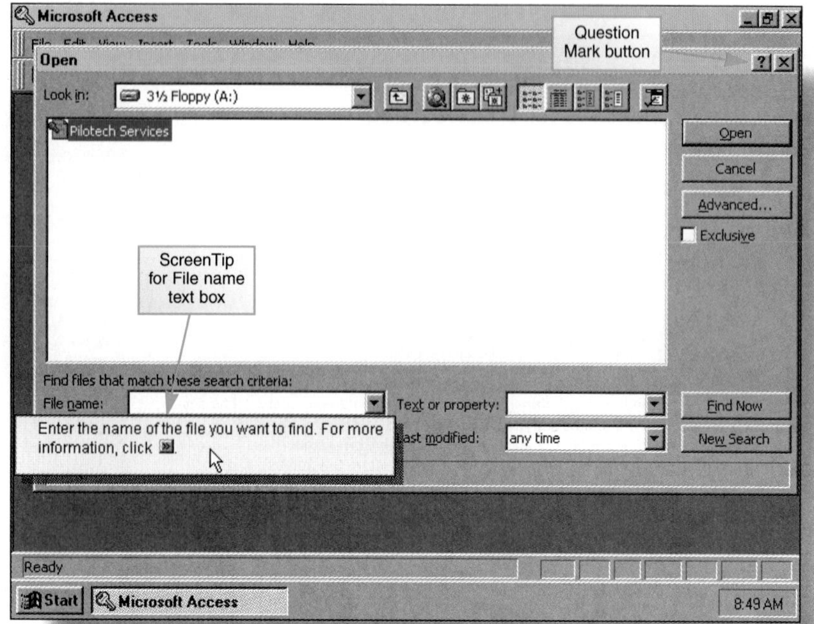

FIGURE 1-86

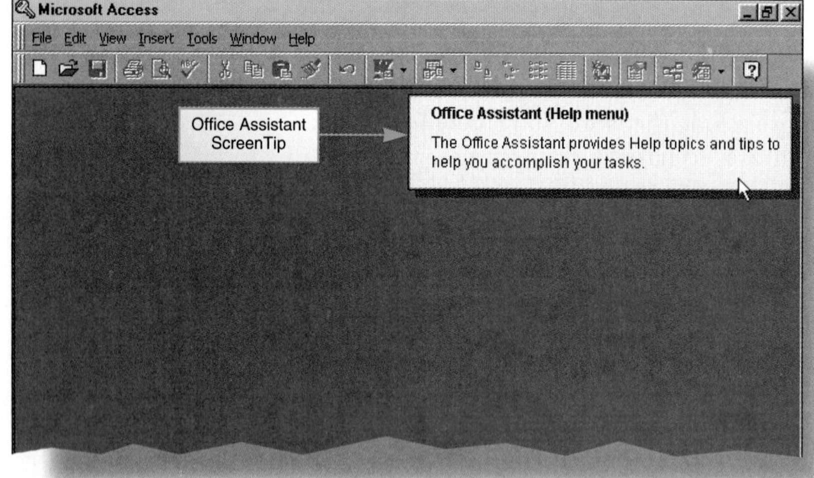

FIGURE 1-87

Using the Question Mark Button or Help Button to Define Items on the Screen

Use the Question Mark button or What's This? command on the Help menu when you are not sure of an item on the screen or its function. Click either button and the mouse pointer changes to an arrow and a question mark. Next, click any item on which you want more information. The information displayed is called a **ScreenTip**.

The **Question Mark button** displays in the upper-right corner of dialog boxes, next to the Close button. For example, in Figure 1-86, the Open dialog box is on the screen. If you click the Question Mark button and then click anywhere in the File name text box, an explanation of the File name text box displays.

Whereas the Question Mark button is used to display ScreenTips concerning items in a dialog box, the **What's This? command** on the Help menu is used to display ScreenTips concerning items on the Access window. Once you click What's This?, you can move the arrow and question mark pointer to any menu name, button, or cell, and click to display a ScreenTip. For example, clicking the Office Assistant button displays the ScreenTip shown in Figure 1-87. Click anywhere in the window to close the ScreenTip.

More *About* Database Design

There is a special technique for identifying and eliminating redundancy, called **normalization**. For a description and illustration of this technique, see *Concepts of Database Management*, by Pratt and Adamski (CTI, 1997). The text also includes a complete database design method.

Designing a Database

Database design refers to the arrangement of data into tables and fields. In the example in this project, the design is specified, but in many cases, you will have to determine the design based on what you want the system to accomplish.

With large, complex databases, the database design process can be extensive. Major sections of advanced database textbooks are devoted to this topic. Often, however, you should be able to design a database effectively by keeping one simple principle in mind: Design to remove redundancy. **Redundancy** means storing the same fact in more than one place.

To illustrate, you need to maintain the following information shown in Figure 1-88. In the figure, all the data is contained in a single table. Notice that the data for a given Technician (number, name, address, and so on) occurs on more than one record.

Client table

CLIENT NUMBER	NAME	ADDRESS	CITY	STATE	ZIP CODE	BILLED	PAID	TECH NUMBER	LAST NAME	FIRST NAME	ADDRESS	CITY	STATE	ZIP CODE	HOURLY RATE	YTD EARNINGS
AM53	Ashton-Mills	216 Rivard	Grattan	MA	58120	$215.50	$155.00	11	Levin	Joanna	26 Cottonwood	Carlton	MA	59712	$25.00	$6,245.00
AS62	Alton-Scripps	722 Fisher	Empire	MA	58216	$425.00	$435.00	12	Rogers	Brad	7972 Marsden	Kaleva	VT	57253	$30.00	$7,143.30
BL26	Blake Suppliers	5752 Maumee	Grattan	MA	58120	$129.50	$5,000.00	12	Rogers	Brad	7972 Marsden	Kaleva	VT	57253	$30.00	$7,143.30
DE76	D & E Grocery	464 Linnell	Marshall	VT	52018	$385.75	$300.00	17	Rodriguez	Maria	263 Topsfield	Hudson	MA	57240	$35.00	$7,745.50
GR56	Grant Cleaners	737 Allard	Portage	NH	59130	$215.00	$165.00	11	Levin	Joanna	26 Cottonwood	Carlton	MA	59712	$25.00	$6,245.00
GU21	Grand Union	247 Fuller	Grattan	MA	58120	$128.50	$0.00	12	Rogers	Brad	7972 Marsden	Kaleva	VT	57253	$30.00	$7,143.30
JE77	Jones Electric	57 Giddings	Marshall	VT	52018	$0.00	$0.00	12	Rogers	Brad	7972 Marsden	Kaleva	VT	57253	$30.00	$7,143.30
MI26	Morland Int.	665 Whittier	Frankfort	MA	56152	$212.50	$223.25	11	Levin	Joanna	26 Cottonwood	Carlton	MA	59712	$25.00	$6,245.00
SA56	Sawyer Inc.	31 Lafayette	Empire	MA	58216	$352.50	$250.00	17	Rodriguez	Maria	263 Topsfield	Hudson	MA	57240	$35.00	$7,745.50
SI82	Simpson Ind.	752 Cadieux	Fernwood	MA	57412	$154.00	$0.00	12	Rogers	Brad	7972 Marsden	Kaleva	VT	57253	$30.00	$7,143.30

duplicate technician names

FIGURE 1-88

Storing this data on multiple records is an example of redundancy, which causes several problems:

1. Redundancy wastes space on the disk. The address of Technician 11 (Joanna Levin), for example, should be stored only once. Storing this fact several times is wasteful.
2. Redundancy makes updating the database more difficult. If, for example, Joanna Levin moves, her address would need to be changed in several different places.
3. A possibility of inconsistent data exists. Suppose, for example, that you change the address of Joanna Levin on client GR56's record to 146 Valley, but do not change it on client AM53's record. In both cases, the Tech Number is 11, but the addresses are different. In other words, the data is inconsistent.

The solution to the problem is to place the redundant data in a separate table, one in which the data will no longer be redundant. If, for example, you place the data for technicians in a separate table (Figure 1-89), the data for each technician will appear only once.

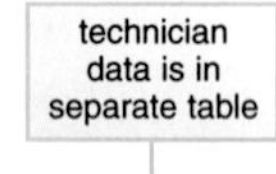

Technician table

TECH NUMBER	LAST NAME	FIRST NAME	ADDRESS	CITY	STATE	ZIP CODE	HOURLY RATE	YTD EARNINGS
11	Levin	Joanna	26 Cottonwood	Carlton	MA	59712	$25.00	$6,245.00
12	Rogers	Brad	7972 Marsden	Kaleva	VT	57253	$30.00	$7,143.30
17	Rodriguez	Maria	263 Topsfield	Hudson	MA	57240	$35.00	$7,745.50

Client table

CLIENT NUMBER	NAME	ADDRESS	CITY	STATE	ZIP CODE	BILLED	PAID	TECH NUMBER
AM53	Ashton-Mills	216 Rivard	Grattan	MA	58120	$215.50	$155.00	11
AS62	Alton-Scripps	722 Fisher	Empire	MA	58216	$425.00	$435.00	12
BL26	Blake Suppliers	5752 Maumee	Grattan	MA	58120	$129.50	$0.00	12
DE76	D & E Grocery	464 Linnell	Marshall	VT	52018	$385.75	$300.00	17
GR56	Grant Cleaners	737 Allard	Portage	NH	59130	$215.00	$165.00	11
GU21	Grand Union	247 Fuller	Grattan	MA	58120	$128.50	$0.00	12
JE77	Jones Electric	57 Giddings	Marshall	VT	52018	$0.00	$0.00	12
MI26	Morland Int.	665 Whittier	Frankfort	MA	56152	$212.50	$223.25	11
SA56	Sawyer Inc.	31 Lafayette	Empire	MA	58216	$352.50	$250.00	17
SI82	Simpson Ind.	752 Cadieux	Fernwood	MA	57412	$154.00	$0.00	12

FIGURE 1-89

Notice that you need to have the Tech Number in both tables. Without it, no way exists to tell which technician is associated with which client. All the other technician data, however, was removed from the Client table and placed in the Technician table. This new arrangement corrects the problems of redundancy in the following ways:

1. Because the data for each technician is stored only once, space is not wasted.
2. Changing the address of a technician is easy. You have only to change one row in the Technician table.
3. Because the data for a technician is stored only once, inconsistent data cannot occur.

Designing to omit redundancy will help you to produce good and valid database designs.

Project Summary

Project 1 introduced you to starting Access and creating a database. You created the database that will be used by Pilotech Services. Within the Pilotech Services database, you created the Client and Technician tables by defining the fields within them. You then added records to these tables. Once you created the tables, you printed the contents of the tables. You also used a form to view the data in the table. Finally, you used the Report Wizard to create a report containing the Client Number, Name, Billed, and Paid fields for each client of Pilotech Services.

What You Should Know

Having completed this project, you now should be able to perform the following tasks:

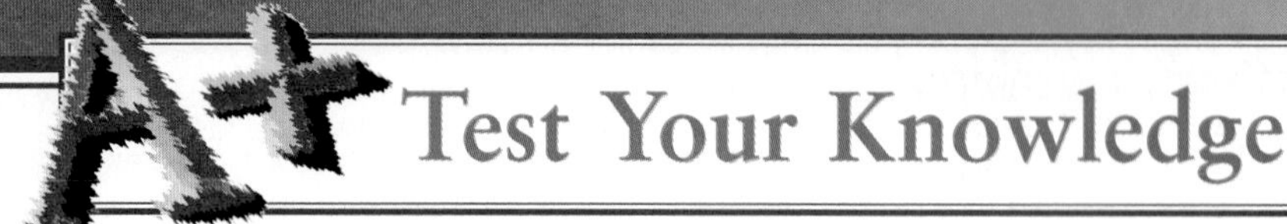

Test Your Knowledge

1 True/False

Instructions: Circle T if the statement is true or F if the statement is false.

T F 1. A field contains information about a given person, product, or event.
T F 2. An Access database consists of a collection of tables.
T F 3. If you do not assign a width to a text field, Access assumes the width is 25.
T F 4. You can use the TAB key to move to the next field in a record in Datasheet view.
T F 5. Field names can be no more than 64 characters in length and can include numeric digits.
T F 6. The only field type available for fields that must be used in arithmetic operations is number.
T F 7. To delete a record from a table, select the record and then press the DELETE key.
T F 8. To add a field to a table structure, select the field that will follow the field you want to add, click Insert on the menu bar and then click Rows.
T F 9. To add records to a table that already contains data, open the table and then click the Append Record button.
T F 10. Controlling redundancy results in an increase in consistency.

2 Multiple Choice

Instructions: Circle the correct response.

1. A database is __________.
   a. the same as a file
   b. a collection of data organized in a manner that allows access, retrieval, and use of that data
   c. a software product
   d. none of the above
2. Which of the following is not a benefit of controlling redundancy?
   a. greater consistency is maintained
   b. less space is occupied
   c. update is easier
   d. all of the above are benefits
3. A field that uniquely identifies a particular record in a table is called a __________.
   a. secondary key
   b. foreign key
   c. principal key
   d. primary key
4. Access is a(n) __________.
   a. application software package
   b. DBMS
   c. database
   d. both a and b

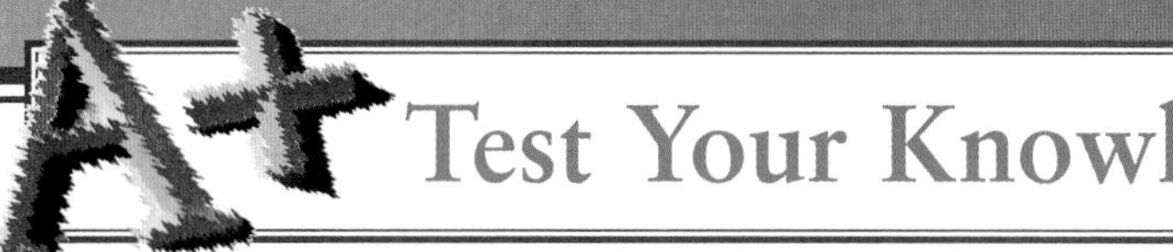

Test Your Knowledge

5. To add a record to a table that already contains data, open the table and click the __________ button.
   a. Add Record
   b. New Record
   c. Append Record
   d. Insert Record
6. A record in Access is composed of a __________.
   a. series of databases
   b. series of files
   c. series of records
   d. series of fields
7. To make a field the primary key for a table, select the field and then click the __________ button on the toolbar.
   a. Unique Key
   b. Single Key
   c. First Key
   d. Primary Key
8. To remove a field from a table structure, select the field and then press the __________ key(s).
   a. DELETE
   b. CTRL+D
   c. CTRL+DELETE
   d. CTRL+Y
9. To change to landscape orientation to print a table, on the File menu, click __________.
   a. Print Preview
   b. Page Setup
   c. Print
   d. Print Settings
10. To move from the upper pane, the one where you define fields, in the Table window to the lower pane, the one where you define field properties, press the __________ key.
   a. F3
   b. F4
   c. F6
   d. F7

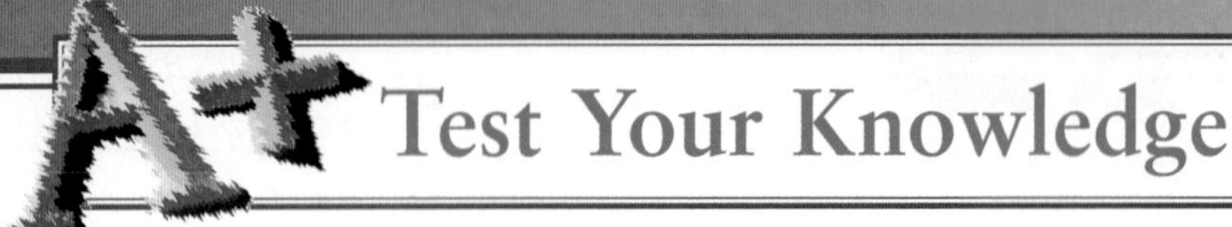

3 Understanding Access Windows

Instructions: In Figure 1-90, arrows point to the major components of an Access window. In the spaces provided, indicate the purpose of each of these components.

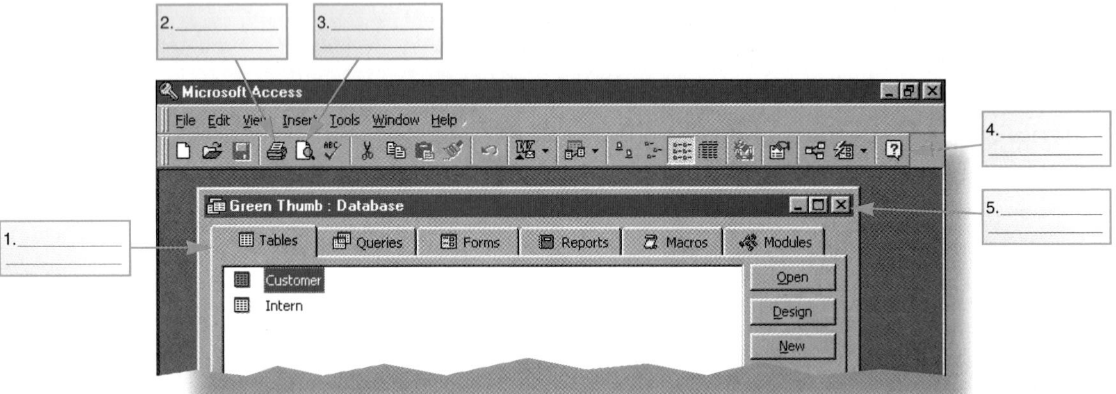

FIGURE 1-90

4 Understanding the Table Window in Datasheet View

Instructions: On the form in Figure 1-91, arrows point to the major components of a Table window in Datasheet view. In the spaces provided, indicate the purpose of each of these components.

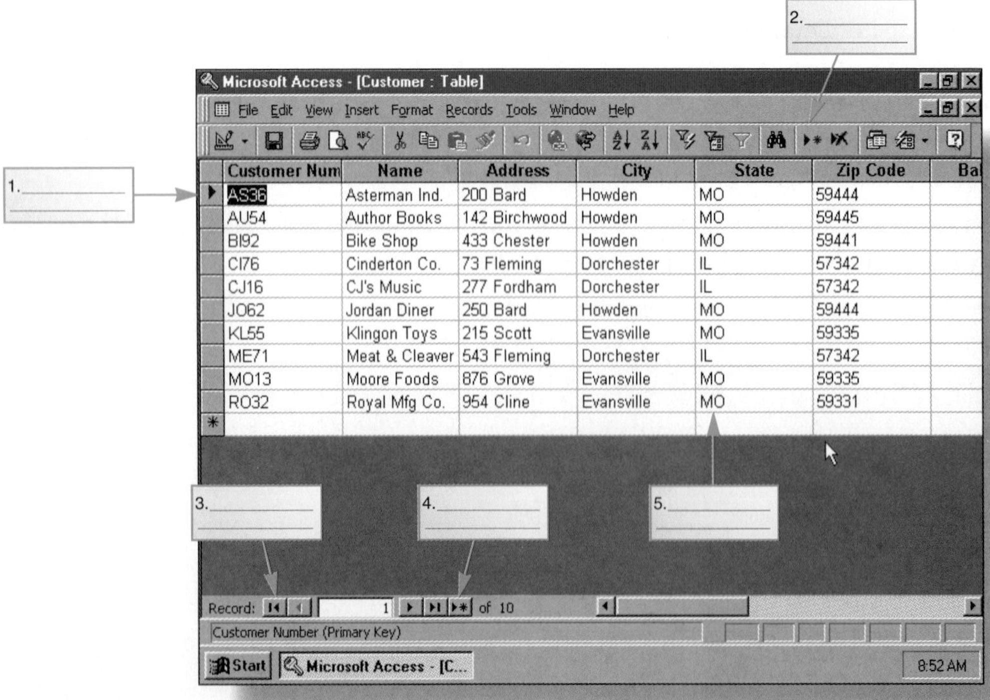

FIGURE 1-91

Use Help

1 Reviewing Project Activities

Instructions: Perform the following tasks using a computer.

1. Start Access.
2. If the Office Assistant is on your screen, then click it to display its balloon. If the Office Assistant is not on your screen, then click the Office Assistant button on the toolbar.
3. Click the Office Assistant and type `data types` in the What would you like to do? text box. Click the Search button.
4. Click What data type should I use for a field in my table?. Read the Help information. Use the shortcut menu or Options button to print the information. Hand in the printout to your instructor.
5. Click the Help Topics button. Click the Index tab. Type `Datasheet` in the top text box labeled 1 and then double-click entering and editing data under Datasheet view in the list box labeled 2. Double-click Delete a record in Datasheet or Form view in the Topics Found dialog box. When the Help information displays, read it. Use the shortcut menu or Options button to print the information. Hand in the printout to your instructor. Click the Help Topics button to return to the Help Topics: Microsoft Access 97 dialog box.
6. Click the Find tab. Type `preview` in the top text box labeled 1. Click Previewing in the list box abeled 2. Double-click Preview a report in the list box labeled 3. When the Microsoft Access 97 window displays, read it and use the shortcut menu or Options button to print the information. Click the Preview all the data in the report page by page button in the Help window. Print the Help information. Hand in the printouts to your instructor. Click the Close button.

2 Expanding on the Basics

Instructions: Use Access Help to better understand the topics listed below. If you are unable to print the Help information, then answer the question on your own paper.

1. Using the Working with Data book on the Contents sheet in the Help Topics: Microsoft Access 97 dialog box, answer the following questions:
   a. When does Access save the data in a record?
   b. How can you save the data in a record while you are editing it?
2. Using the words, shortcut keys, and the Index tab in the Help Topics: Microsoft Access 97 dialog box, display and print the shortcut keys to use in Datasheet view and Form view. Then, answer the following questions:
   a. Which key or combination keys add a new record?
   b. Which key or combination keys delete the current record?
   c. Which key or combination keys save changes to the current record?

(continued)

Use Help

Expanding on the Basics *(continued)*

d. Which key or combination keys undo changes in the current field?
e. Which key or combination keys insert the value from the same field in the previous record?

3. Use the Find sheet in the Help Topics: Microsoft Access 97 dialog box to display and print information about automatically correcting two capital letters in a row.
4. Use the Office Assistant to display and print information about backing up a database.

Apply Your Knowledge

CAUTION: To ensure you have enough disk space to save your files, it is recommended that you create a copy of the Data Disk that accompanies this book. Then, delete folders from the copy of the Data Disk that are not needed for the application you are working on. Do the following: (1) Insert the Data Disk in drive A; (2) start Explorer; (3) right-click the 3½ Floppy (A:) folder in the All Folders side of the window; (4) click Copy Disk; (5) click Start and OK as required; (6) insert a floppy disk when requested; (7) delete all folders on the floppy disk you created except the Access folder; (8) remove the floppy disk from drive A and label it Access Data Disk.

1 Changing Data and Creating Reports

Instructions: Start Access and open the Green Thumb document from the Access folder on the Data Disk that accompanies this book. Green Thumb is a small company that was started by two graduates of the horticulture program at the local college. It provides plants and plant care to local businesses. Green Thumb designs indoor landscapes and does regular maintenance, for example, watering, fertilizing, and pruning. The company employs horticulture students who do internships with the company. Green Thumb has a database that keeps track of its interns and customers. The database has two tables. The Customer table contains data on the customers who use Green Thumb's services. The Intern table contains data on the students employed by Green Thumb. The structure and data are shown for the Customer table in Figure 1-92 below and at the top of the next page and for the Intern table in Figure 1-93.

Structure of Customer table

FIELD NAME	DATA TYPE	FIELD SIZE	PRIMARY KEY?	DESCRIPTION
Customer Number	Text	4	Yes	Customer Number (Primary Key)
Name	Text	20		Customer Name
Address	Text	15		Street Address
City	Text	15		City
State	Text	2		State (Two-Character Abbreviation)
Zip Code	Text	5		Zip Code (Five-Character Version)
Balance	Currency			Amount Owed by Customer
Intern Id	Text	3		Id of Customer's Intern

Apply Your Knowledge

Data for Customer table

CUSTOMER NUMBER	NAME	ADDRESS	CITY	STATE	ZIP CODE	BALANCE	INTERN ID
AS36	Asterman Ind.	200 Bard	Howden	MO	59444	$85.00	102
AU54	Author Books	142 Birchwood	Howden	MO	59445	$50.00	109
BI92	Bike Shop	433 Chester	Howden	MO	59441	$40.00	109
CI76	Cinderton Co.	73 Fleming	Dorchester	IL	57342	$0.00	113
CJ16	CJ's Music	277 Fordham	Dorchester	IL	57342	$105.00	102
JO62	Jordan Diner	250 Bard	Howden	MO	59444	$74.00	109
KL55	Klingon Toys	215 Scott	Evansville	MO	59335	$115.00	109
ME71	Meat & Cleaver	543 Fleming	Dorchester	IL	57342	$138.00	102
MO13	Moore Foods	876 Grove	Evansville	MO	59335	$0.00	113
RO32	Royal Mfg Co.	954 Cline	Evansville	MO	59331	$93.00	109

FIGURE 1-92

Structure of Intern table

FIELD NAME	DATA TYPE	FIELD SIZE	PRIMARY KEY?	DESCRIPTION
Intern Id	Text	3	Yes	Intern Identification Number (Primary Key)
Last Name	Text	10		Last Name of Intern
First Name	Text	8		First Name of Intern
Address	Text	15		Street Address
City	Text	15		City
State	Text	2		State (Two-Character Abbreviation)
Zip Code	Text	5		Zip Code (Five-Character Version)
Pay Rate	Currency			Hourly Pay Rate

Data for Intern table

INTERN ID	LAST NAME	FIRST NAME	ADDRESS	CITY	STATE	ZIP CODE	PAY RATE
102	Dang	Chou	764 Clay	Howden	MO	59444	$7.50
109	Hyde	Michelle	65 Parkwood	Dorchester	IL	57342	$7.75
113	Lopez	Javier	345 Norton	Howden	MO	59444	$7.65

FIGURE 1-93

(continued)

Apply Your Knowledge

Changing Data and Creating Reports *(continued)*

Perform the following tasks.

1. Open the Intern table in Datasheet view and add the following record to the table:

105	Eckels	Lois	24 Riley	Evansville	MO	59335	7.40

   Close the Intern table.
2. Open the Intern table again. Notice that the record you just added has been moved. It is no longer at the end of the table. The records are in order by the primary key, Intern Id.
3. Print the Intern table.
4. Open the Customer table.
5. Change the Intern Id for customer KL55 to 105.
6. Print the Customer table.
7. Create the report shown in Figure 1-94 for the Customer table.

Balance Due Report

Customer Number	*Name*	*Balance*
AS36	Asterman Ind.	$85.00
AU54	Author Books	$50.00
BI92	Bike Shop	$40.00
CI76	Cinderton Co.	$0.00
CJ16	CJ's Music	$105.00
JO62	Jordan Diner	$74.00
KL55	Klingon Toys	$115.00
ME71	Meat & Cleaver	$138.00
MO13	Moore Foods	$0.00
RO32	Royal Mfg Co.	$93.00

FIGURE 1-94

8. Print the report.

1 Creating the Museum Mercantile Database

Problem: The County Museum runs a small gift shop, Museum Mercantile, that is staffed by volunteers. The museum purchases products from vendors that specialize in handcrafted products and vintage merchandise. The director of the museum has asked you to create and update a database that volunteers can use. The database consists of two tables. The Product table contains information on items available for sale. The Vendor table contains information on the vendors.

Instructions: Perform the following tasks.

1. Create a new database in which to store all the objects related to the gift shop data. Call the database Museum Mercantile.
2. Create the Product table using the structure shown in Figure 1-95. Use the name Product for the table.

Structure of Product table

FIELD NAME	DATA TYPE	FIELD SIZE	PRIMARY KEY?	DESCRIPTION
Product Id	Text	4	Yes	Product Id Number (Primary Key)
Description	Text	25		Description of Product
On Hand	Number	Long Integer		Number of Units On Hand
Cost	Currency			Cost of Product
Selling Price	Currency			Selling Price of Product
Vendor Code	Text	2		Code of Product Vendor

Data for Product table

PRODUCT ID	DESCRIPTION	ON HAND	COST	SELLING PRICE	VENDOR CODE
CH04	Chess Set	11	$26.75	$28.90	WW
DI24	Dinosaurs	14	$3.75	$4.95	MS
GL18	Globe	2	$27.50	$29.95	MS
JG01	Jigsaw Puzzle	3	$5.40	$6.95	MS
PC03	Pick Up Sticks	5	$8.50	$10.95	WW
ST23	Stationery	8	$3.95	$5.00	AR
TD05	Tiddly Winks	6	$13.75	$15.95	WW
WI10	Wizard Cards	10	$7.50	$9.95	MS
WL34	Wildlife Posters	15	$2.50	$2.95	AR
YO12	Wooden YoYo	9	$1.60	$1.95	WW

FIGURE 1-95

(continued)

Creating the Museum Mercantile Database *(continued)*

3. Add the data shown in Figure 1-95 to the Product table.
4. Print the Product table.
5. Create the Vendor table using the structure shown in Figure 1-96. Use the name Vendor for the table.

Structure of Vendor table

FIELD NAME	DATA TYPE	FIELD SIZE	PRIMARY KEY?	DESCRIPTION
Vendor Code	Text	2	Yes	Vendor Code (Primary Key)
Name	Text	20		Name of Vendor
Address	Text	15		Street Address
City	Text	15		City
State	Text	2		State (Two-Character Abbreviation)
Zip Code	Text	5		Zip Code (Five-Character Version)
Telephone Number	Text	12		Telephone Number (999-999-9999 Version)

Data for Vendor table

VENDOR CODE	NAME	ADDRESS	CITY	STATE	ZIP CODE	TELEPHONE NUMBER
AR	Artisan's Co-op	3540 Grand	Hancock	WI	69780	414-555-7865
MS	Museum Stores	134 Union	Delana	SD	41345	605-555-3498
WW	Woodworkers	655 Clive	Great Falls	WV	34567	304-555-4532

FIGURE 1-96

6. Add the data shown in Figure 1-96 to the Vendor table.
7. Print the Vendor table.
8. Create a form for the Product table. Use the name Product for the form.
9. Create and print the report shown in Figure 1-97 for the Product table.

Inventory Report

Product Id	*Description*	*On Hand*	*Cost*
WI10	Wizard Cards	10	$7.50
PC03	Pick Up Sticks	5	$8.50
WL34	Wildlife Posters	15	$2.50
TD05	Tiddly Winks	6	$13.75
ST23	Stationery	8	$3.95
JG01	Jigsaw Puzzle	3	$5.40
YO12	Wooden YoYo	9	$1.60
DI24	Dinosaurs	14	$3.75
GL18	Globe	2	$27.50
CH04	Chess Set	11	$26.75

FIGURE 1-97

2 Creating the City Telephone System Database

Problem: The city government maintains its own internal telephone system. Each user is billed separately for monthly charges and all the bills for a department are sent to the department manager. The telephone manager has asked you to create and update a database that the city government can use as a telephone tracking system. The database consists of two tables. The User table contains information on the individuals with telephone accounts. The Department table contains information on the department in which the individual works.

Instructions: Perform the following tasks.

1. Create a new database in which to store all the objects related to the telephone system data. Call the database City Telephone System.
2. Create the User table using the structure shown in Figure 1-98. Use the name User for the table.

Structure of User table

FIELD NAME	DATA TYPE	FIELD SIZE	PRIMARY KEY?	DESCRIPTION
User Id	Text	4	Yes	User Id Number (Primary Key)
Last Name	Text	14		Last Name of User
First Name	Text	10		First Name of User
Phone Ext	Text	4		Telephone Extension (9999 Version)
Office	Text	3		Office Location (Room Number)
Basic Charge	Currency			Basic Service Charge (per Month)
Extra Charges	Currency			Extra Charges for Special Services and Long Distance Calls (per Month)
Dept Code	Text	3		Code of User's Department

Data for User table

USER ID	LAST NAME	FIRST NAME	PHONE EXT	OFFICE	BASIC CHARGE	EXTRA CHARGES	DEPT CODE
T129	Bishop	Fred	3383	212	$10.00	$22.00	ITD
T238	Chan	Rose	3495	220	$13.00	$29.95	ITD
T347	Febo	Javier	4267	323	$10.00	$7.75	HRS
T451	Ginras	Mary	3156	444	$17.00	$52.85	APV
T536	Hanneman	William	3578	317	$13.00	$18.75	HRS
T645	Johnsen	Paul	4445	234	$21.00	$7.75	ITD
T759	Kim	Lei	3068	310	$10.00	$13.55	ENG
T780	Mentor	Melissa	3418	525	$17.00	$73.95	PLN
T851	Sanchez	Alfredo	3134	438	$11.00	$6.25	APV
T888	TenClink	Brian	3414	521	$10.00	$37.45	PLN

FIGURE 1-98
(continued)

In the Lab

Creating the City Telephone System Database *(continued)*

3. Add the data shown in Figure 1-98 to the User table.
4. Print the User table.
5. Create the Department table using the structure shown in Figure 1-99. Use the name Department for the table.

Structure of Department table

FIELD NAME	DATA TYPE	FIELD SIZE	PRIMARY KEY?	DESCRIPTION
Dept Code	Text	3	Yes	Department Code (Primary Key)
Dept Name	Text	14		Name of Department
First Name	Text	8		First Name of Department Manager
Last Name	Text	12		Last Name of Department Manager

Data for Department table

DEPT CODE	DEPT NAME	FIRST NAME	LAST NAME
APV	Assessment	Joyce	Murphy
ENG	Engineering	Darnell	James
HRS	Housing	Billie	Buchanan
ITD	Income Tax	Maria	Fuentes
PLN	Planning	Joseph	Lippman

FIGURE 1-99

6. Add the data shown in Figure 1-99 to the Department table.
7. Print the Department table.
8. Create a form for the User table. Use the name User for the form.
9. Use the form you created to add the following two new city employees to the User table.

T087	Anders	Jane	3923	531	$10.00	$0.00	PLN
T832	Reison	Jason	3803	312	$13.00	$0.00	ENG

10. Create and print the report shown in Figure 1-100 for the User table. When the Report Wizard asks, What Sort Order do you want for your records?, click the Last Name field.

Telephone List

Last Name	First Name	Phone Ext	Office	Dept Code
Anders	Jane	3923	531	PLN
Bishop	Fred	3383	212	ITD
Chan	Rose	3495	220	ITD
Febo	Javier	4267	323	HRS
Ginras	Mary	3156	444	APV
Hanneman	William	3578	317	HRS
Johnsen	Paul	4445	234	ITD
Kim	Lei	3068	310	ENG
Mentor	Melissa	3418	525	PLN
Reison	Jason	3803	312	ENG
Sanchez	Alfredo	3134	438	APV
TenClink	Brian	3414	521	PLN

FIGURE 1-100

3 Creating the City Scene Database

Problem: The *City Scene* is a local arts magazine that relies on advertising to help finance its operations. Local firms buy advertising from ad representatives who work for the magazine. Ad representatives receive a commission based on the advertising revenues they generate. The managing editor of the magazine has asked you to create and update a database that will keep track of the advertising accounts and ad representatives. The database consists of two tables. The Advertiser table contains information on the organizations that advertise in the magazine. The Ad Rep table contains information on the representative assigned to the advertising account.

Instructions: Perform the following tasks.

1. Create a new database in which to store all the objects related to the advertising data. Call the database City Scene.
2. Create the Advertiser table using the structure shown in Figure 1-101 on the next page. Use the name Advertiser for the table.
3. Add the data shown in Figure 1-101 to the Advertiser table.

(continued)

Creating the City Scene Database *(continued)*

Structure of Advertiser table

FIELD NAME	DATA TYPE	FIELD SIZE	PRIMARY KEY?	DESCRIPTION
Advertiser Number	Text	4	Yes	Advertiser Number (Primary Key)
Name	Text	20		Name of Advertiser
Address	Text	15		Street Address
City	Text	15		City
State	Text	2		State (Two-Character Abbreviation)
Zip Code	Text	5		Zip Code (Five-Character Version)
Balance	Currency			Amount Currently Owed
Amount Paid	Currency			Amount Paid Year-to-Date
Ad Rep Number	Text	2		Number of Advertising Representative

Data for Advertiser table

ADVERTISER NUMBER	NAME	ADDRESS	CITY	STATE	ZIP CODE	BALANCE	AMOUNT PAID	AD REP NUMBER
A226	Alden Books	74 Benton	Fernwood	WA	91191	$60.00	$535.00	16
B101	Bud's Diner	384 Carter	Crestview	OR	92332	$155.00	$795.00	19
C047	Chip and Putt	1 Golfview	Crestview	OR	92330	$0.00	$345.00	19
C134	Clover Clothes	62 Adams	New Castle	WA	91234	$100.00	$835.00	22
D216	Dogs 'n Draft	3 Riverview	Crestview	OR	92330	$260.00	$485.00	16
F345	Fast Freddie's	507 Oakley	Fernwood	WA	91191	$0.00	$775.00	19
G080	Green Thumb	619 Lincoln	New Castle	WA	91234	$185.00	$825.00	19
L189	Lighthouse Inc.	1 Riverview	Crestview	OR	92330	$35.00	$150.00	16
N034	New Releases	107 Main	Fernwood	WA	91191	$435.00	$500.00	22
S010	Skates R You	67 Adams	New Castle	WA	91234	$85.00	$235.00	16

FIGURE 1-101

4. Print the Advertiser table.
5. Create the Ad Rep table using the structure shown in Figure 1-102. Use the name Ad Rep for the table. Be sure to change the field size for the Comm Rate field to Double.
6. Add the data shown in Figure 1-102 to the Ad Rep table.

In the Lab

Structure of Ad Rep table

FIELD NAME	DATA TYPE	FIELD SIZE	PRIMARY KEY?	DESCRIPTION
Ad Rep Number	Text	2	Yes	Advertising Rep Number (Primary Key)
Last Name	Text	10		Last Name of Advertising Rep
First Name	Text	8		First Name of Advertising Rep
Address	Text	15		Street Address
City	Text	15		City
State	Text	2		State (Two-Character Abbreviation)
Zip Code	Text	5		Zip Code (Five-Character Version)
Comm Rate	Number	Double		Commision Rate on Advertising Sales
Compensation	Currency			Year-to-Date Total Compensation

Data for Ad Rep table

AD REP NUMBER	LAST NAME	FIRST NAME	ADDRESS	CITY	STATE	ZIP CODE	COMM RATE	COMPENSATION
16	Hammond	Anne	75 Bartow	New Castle	WA	91234	0.08	$6,000.00
19	Morales	Louis	67 Shawmont	Fernwood	WA	91191	0.07	$5,750.00
22	Rodgers	Elaine	43 Manderly	Crestview	OR	92332	0.08	$6,500.00

FIGURE 1-102

7. Print the Ad Rep table.
8. Create a form for the Advertiser table. Use the name Advertiser for the form.
9. Open the form you created and change the address for Advertiser Number B101 to 384 Gartern.
10. Change to Datasheet view and delete the record for Advertiser Number F345.
11. Print the Advertiser table.
12. Create and print the report shown in Figure 1-103 on the next page for the Advertiser table.

(continued)

Creating the City Scene Database *(continued)*

Status Report

Advertiser Number	*Name*	*Balance*	*Amount Paid*
A226	Alden Books	$60.00	$535.00
B101	Bud's Diner	$155.00	$795.00
C047	Chip and Putt	$0.00	$345.00
C134	Clover Clothes	$100.00	$835.00
D216	Dogs 'n Draft	$260.00	$485.00
G080	Green Thumb	$185.00	$825.00
L189	Lighthouse Inc.	$35.00	$150.00
N034	New Releases	$435.00	$500.00
S010	Skates R You	$85.00	$235.00

Monday, September 21, 1998 *Page 1 of 1*

FIGURE 1-103

Cases and Places

The difficulty of these case studies varies: ◗ are the least difficult; ◗◗ are more difficult; and ◗◗◗ are the most difficult.

1 ◗ For years, the students at your school have complained about the inequities of the book buy-back policy. Student government finally has decided to do something about it by organizing a used textbook cooperative. As a member of student government, you create a system whereby students can locate other students who have used a particular book in a previous semester and want to sell it to another student. Student government advertises the plan on its Web page and receives the responses shown in Figure 1-104.

Create a database to store the file related to the textbooks. Then create a table, enter the data from Figure 1-104, and print the table.

BOOK TITLE	AUTHOR	COURSE USED	PRICE	SELLER'S NAME	TELEPHONE	CONDITION (E=EXCELLENT, G=GOOD, P=POOR)
Sociology Today	Munroe	Soc 101	$14	Joe Van	555-7632	G
Creative Writing	Swan & Shell	Eng 150	$18	Mary Nordman	555-9421	E
Reach for the Stars	Alvarez	Ast 210	$23	John Mott	555-9981	E
Creative Writing	Swan & Shell	Eng 150	$15	Peter Rudd	555-9156	E
Ethics for Today's Society	Garrison & Pierce	Phi 310	$20	Sandi Radle	555-7636	P
Sociology Today	Munroe	Soc 101	$17	Daniel Lewis	555-0873	E
Understanding Psychology	Navarone	Psy 101	$22	Karen Sing	555-9802	P
Electronic Circuitry	Carlson	Egr 255	$37	Karen Sing	555-9802	G
Nutrition for Our Souls	Francis	Nrs 330	$18	Dave Corsi	555-2384	E
Geriatric Nursing	Dyer	Nrs 265	$36	Mary Healy	555-9932	E

FIGURE 1-104

Cases and Places

2 ◗ You have decided to start a meal delivery service. As a first step, you consult the telephone directory for the numbers of local restaurants to make reservations and to order food for carry out and delivery. You have decided to create a database to store these numbers along with other pertinent data about the establishment, such as address, hours of operation, type of food, and days when specials are offered. You gather the information shown in Figure 1-105.

Create a database to store the file related to the restaurants. Then create a table, enter the data from Figure 1-105, and print the table.

NAME	TELEPHONE	ADDRESS	OPEN	CLOSE	FOOD TYPE	SPECIALS	CARRYOUT	DELIVERY
Noto's	(714) 555-2339	223 N. Jackson	11:00 a.m.	11:00 p.m.	Japanese	Wednesday	Yes	No
Ole Taco	(714) 555-5444	3294 E. Devon	4:00 p.m.	10:00 p.m.	Mexican	Monday	Yes	No
Red Rose	(714) 555-8001	1632 W. Clark	3:00 p.m.	1:00 a.m.	Indian	Friday	No	No
Pan Pacific	(714) 555-2470	3140 W. Halsted	11:00 a.m.	4:00 a.m.	Korean	Thursday	Yes	No
New Crete	(714) 555-9337	1805 W. Broadway	3:30 p.m.	10:00 p.m.	Greek	Monday	Yes	No
Texas Diner	(714) 555-1673	2200 E. Lawrence	4:30 p.m.	1:00 a.m.	American	Thursday	Yes	Yes
Little Venice	(714) 555-8632	13 N. Devon	11:30 a.m.	2:00 a.m.	Italian	Wednesday	Yes	No
Curry and More	(714) 555-3377	1027 E. Wells	5:00 p.m.	2:00 a.m.	Indian	Thursday	Yes	No
Napoli's Pizza	(714) 555-6168	787 N. Monroe	10:30 a.m.	3:00 a.m.	Italian	Tuesday	Yes	Yes
House of China	(714) 555-7373	1939 W. Michigan	11:00 a.m.	11:00 p.m.	Chinese	Wednesday	Yes	No

FIGURE 1-105

3 ◗◗ A local nursing home has a variety of classic movies on videocassette. You are a volunteer at the home and the director of volunteers has asked you to create an inventory of the movies. One afternoon, you sort through the boxes and list each movie's name, leading actors, year produced, and original running time. You also assign a rating system of one to four stars. You create the following list: *The Little Princess*, starring Shirley Temple and Richard Greene, 1939, 94 minutes, three stars; *North by Northwest*, Cary Grant and Eva Marie Saint, 1959, 136 minutes, four stars; *Of Mice and Men*, Burgess Meredith and Lon Chaney Jr., 1939, 107 minutes, four stars; *The Quiet Man*, John Wayne and Maureen O'Hara, 1952, 129 minutes, four stars; *On the Waterfront*, Marlon Brando and Eva Marie Saint, 1954, 108 minutes, four stars; *Pardon My Sarong*, Bud Abbott and Lou Costello, 1942, 84 minutes, three stars; *Ride 'em Cowboy*, Bud Abbott and Lou Costello, 1942, 82 minutes, two stars; *You Can't Take It With You*, Jean Arthur and Lionel Barrymore, 1938, 127 minutes, three stars; *The Undefeated*, John Wayne and Rock Hudson, 1969, 119 minutes, two stars; and *Operation Pacific*, John Wayne and Patricia Neal, 1951, 109 minutes, three stars. Using this information, create a database to store the file related to these movies. Then create a table, enter the data, and print the table.

Cases and Places

4 ▶▶ You are taking a nutrition class this semester, and your instructor has assigned you a research project on the relationship between heart disease and meat. Heart disease is one of the leading killers of adults in this country. With this knowledge, the meat industry has aggressively tried to deliver products that are low in fat and yet high in nutrients. The American Heart Association states that lean meat can be part of a healthy diet, as long as the meat is served in moderation. Three cooked ounces of lean cuts of beef have various nutritional contents. Eye of round has 140 calories, top round steak has 150 calories, tip round roast has 160 calories, sirloin steak has 170 calories, and top loin and tenderloin steaks both have 180 calories. Regarding fat content, eye of round and top round steak have four fat grams in three ounces, tip round roast and sirloin both have six grams, top loin steak has eight grams, and tenderloin steak has the most with nine grams. Cholesterol also varies, with eye of round the lowest at 60 milligrams in three ounces, top loin with 65 mg, top round, tip round, and tenderloin with 70 mg, and sirloin the highest with 75 mg. Create a database to store the file related to the nutritional content of meat. Then create a table, enter the data, and print the table.

5 ▶▶▶ As any comparison shopper knows, food and drug store prices can vary dramatically from one store to another. Make a list of six specific items you purchase frequently from area stores in the four categories of dairy (for example, milk, yogurt, butter, sour cream, cottage cheese), snacks (for example, pretzels, soda, granola bars, raisins, rice cakes), cosmetics/toiletries (for example, deodorant, bath soap, toothpaste, shampoo, contact lens solution), and kitchen supplies (for example, paper towels, dish washing detergent, scouring pads, trash bags, sandwich bags). List the size or weight of each item. Then, visit a local convenience store, grocery store, and discount store to compare prices. Be certain you obtain prices on identical products. Then create a table, enter the data you obtained in each category, and print the table.

6 ▶▶▶ Because you do not live on campus, you do not have easy access to a campus directory. When you do locate the book, usually you cannot find the information you need. Consequently, you have decided to create your own database containing the pertinent information. Obtain important names, telephone numbers, and room numbers of campus offices that you frequent. Start by organizing the data in the categories of faculty, administration, and services. In the faculty category, list your adviser and your instructors from this semester. In the administration category, list the registrar, the dean of your area, and the financial aid director. In the services category, list the bookstore, campus police station, daycare services, and library reference desk. Add other pertinent data to any of the categories. Then create a table, enter the data you obtained, and print the table.

Cases and Places

7 ▶▶▶ Your accounting professor has given every student in the class a hypothetical $1,000. Your assignment is to research Individual Retirement Accounts (IRAs). Visit or call a total of five local banks, credit unions, or savings and loan associations. Make a list of the current interest rates for an IRA opened with $1,000, minimum investment amount, total amount earned by the time you turn age 65, annual fees, and amount you would be penalized if you withdrew the money in two years. Using this information, create a database and enter the data showing the types of financial institutions (bank, savings and loan, or credit union), names of the financial institutions, their addresses and telephone numbers, interest rates, annual fees, total values of the IRAs by age 65, amount of interest earned in this time, and amount you would be penalized if you withdrew the money in two years. Print this table, and then create and print a bar graph indicating the amount of interest you would earn and the total value of your IRA at age 65 for each financial institution.

Microsoft *Access 97*

Querying a Database Using the Select Query Window

You will have mastered the material in this project when you can:

- State the purpose of queries
- Create a new query
- Use a query to display all records and all fields
- Run a query
- Print the answer to a query
- Close a query
- Clear a query
- Use a query to display selected fields
- Use character data in criteria in a query
- Use wildcards in criteria
- Use numeric data in criteria
- Use comparison operators
- Use compound criteria involving AND
- Use compound criteria involving OR
- Sort the answer to a query
- Join tables in a query
- Restrict the records in a join
- Use computed fields in a query
- Calculate statistics in a query
- Use grouping with statistics
- Save a query
- Use a saved query

In Pursuit of the Money Trail

At a bullfight in Madrid during the 1960s, thousands of Spaniards rose from their seats cheering, "El Fugitivo," when they spotted David Janssen in the crowd. Star of the world-popular television series, *The Fugitive*, Janssen portrayed Dr. Richard Kimble, a man unjustly accused of murdering his wife, a crime actually committed by Fred Johnson — a one-armed man. The series aired from 1963 to 1967. Each episode featured Dr. Richard Kimble with his feigned, humble smile and moody, sideways leer engaged in a weekly search to clear his name and escape the clutches of determined, but technologically challenged, Inspector Gerard. In those days before massive worldwide databases shared by law enforcement officials everywhere, the doctor had a much better chance of eluding capture.

Such evasion still is possible in the 1990s, but much more difficult, owing to the fact that virtually all human activity in the modern world creates an economic event of some kind. When a retail clerk swipes your credit card through a reader, not only is the purchase approved according to your credit availability, but the information is recorded and classified for billing purposes and for future research analysis. Similar actions occur when your check shoots around the track of a check verifier.

Credit card and checking account activity have become the two primary sources of information about people. Using these sources to trap tax evaders, the Internal Revenue Service monitors spending activity in order to calculate *imputed* income, and likewise, private and law enforcement investigators routinely use such data to construct personality profiles. Social Security numbers and Driver License numbers, originally based on the economics of pensions and automobile ownership, also aid in collecting data. As we move to so-called *cyberdollars* — money on a debit card — *all* transactions made in the new cash will be recorded.

Usually, if a person tries to disappear it's because of some illegal activity, but occasionally, the law itself needs to hide people, as in the Federal Witness Protection Program. Ironically, this is becoming more difficult because the very tools developed by law enforcement also can be used by the bad guys!

These same databases are used to research new consumer products, streamline mail delivery, supply better foods and medicines, and improve education, among the dozens of beneficial uses. Without databases, activities that we take for granted — utilities, insurance, airline reservations, food services — and a host of other vital functions would be impossible.

Microsoft Access 97 gives you the power to build your own personal or business databases that are every bit as effective as the gigantic repositories maintained by governments and larger companies. Using Access query capabilities and an extensive set of statistical functions, the tasks of retrieving and analyzing data are simplified substantially.

You may not be an aspiring Charlie Chan or Sherlock Holmes, but when it comes to tracking down answers, Access can be the perfect detective.

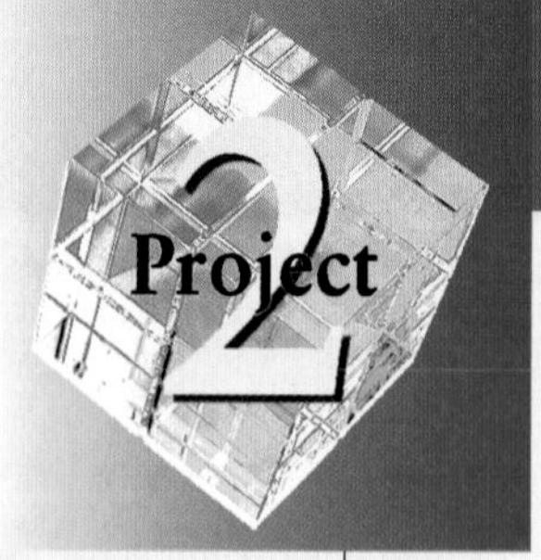

Microsoft
Access 97

Querying a Database Using the Select Query Window

Case Perspective

Now that Pilotech Services has created a database with client and technician data, the management and staff of the organization hope to gain the benefits they expected when they set up the database. One of the more important benefits is the capability of easily asking questions concerning the data in the database and rapidly obtaining the answers. Among the questions they want answered are the following:

1. What are the billed and paid amounts for client DE76?
2. Which clients' names begin with Gr?
3. Which clients are located in Grattan?
4. What is the outstanding amount (amount billed minus amount paid) for each client?
5. Which clients of technician 12 have been billed more than $300?

Introduction

A database management system such as Access offers many useful features, among them the capability of answering questions such as those posed by the management of Pilotech Services (Figure 2-1). The answers to these questions, and many more, are found in the database, and Access can find the answers quickly. When you pose a question to Access, or any other database management system, the question is called a query. A **query** is simply a question represented in a way that Access can understand.

Thus, to find the answer to a question, you first create a corresponding query using the techniques illustrated in this project. Once you have created the query, you instruct Access to **run the query**; that is, to perform the steps necessary to obtain the answer. When finished, Access will display the answer to your question in the format shown at the bottom of Figure 2-1.

Project Two — Querying the Pilotech Services Database

You must obtain answers to the questions posed by the management of Pilotech Services. These include the questions shown in Figure 2-1, as well as any other questions that management deems important.

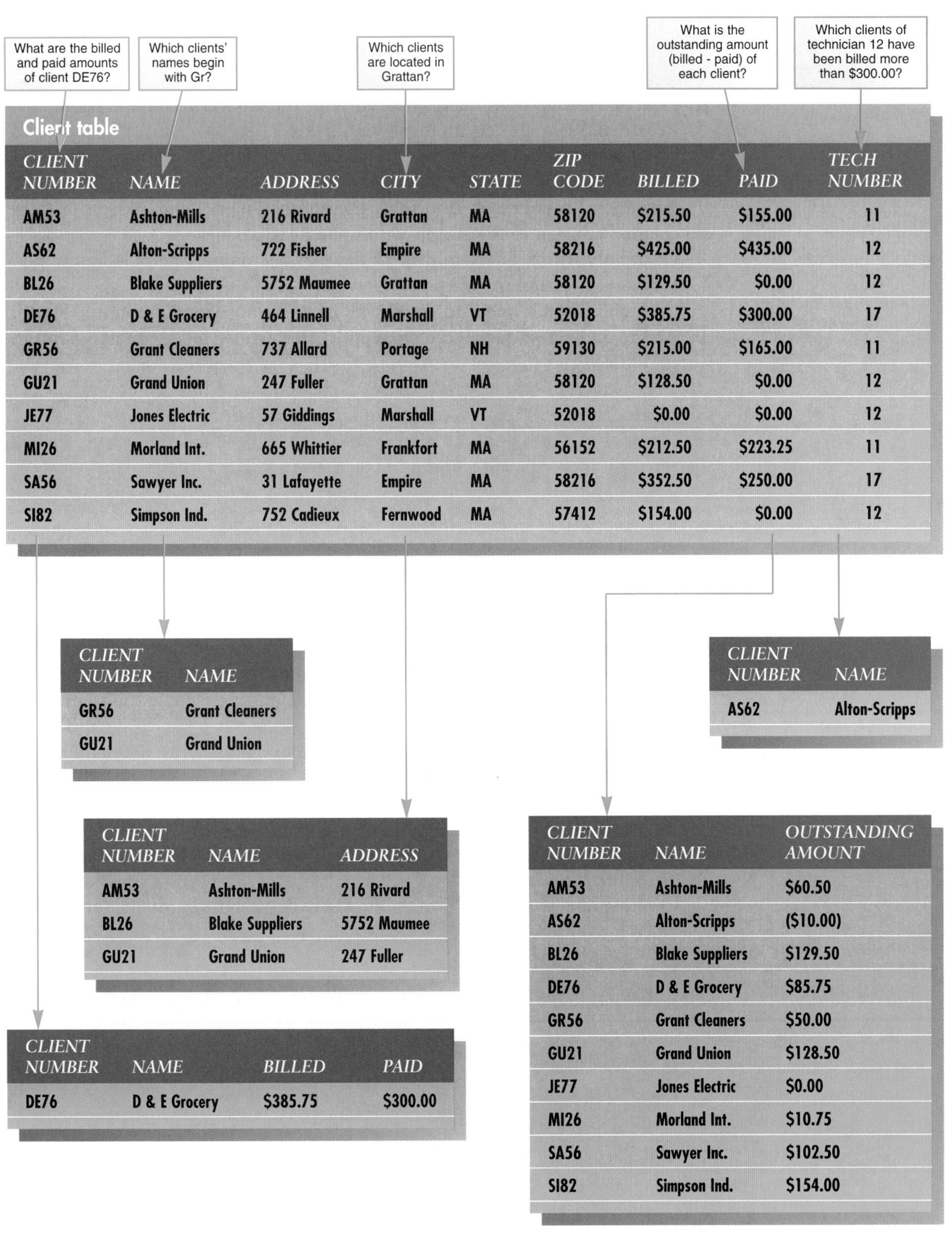

Client table

CLIENT NUMBER	NAME	ADDRESS	CITY	STATE	ZIP CODE	BILLED	PAID	TECH NUMBER
AM53	Ashton-Mills	216 Rivard	Grattan	MA	58120	$215.50	$155.00	11
AS62	Alton-Scripps	722 Fisher	Empire	MA	58216	$425.00	$435.00	12
BL26	Blake Suppliers	5752 Maumee	Grattan	MA	58120	$129.50	$0.00	12
DE76	D & E Grocery	464 Linnell	Marshall	VT	52018	$385.75	$300.00	17
GR56	Grant Cleaners	737 Allard	Portage	NH	59130	$215.00	$165.00	11
GU21	Grand Union	247 Fuller	Grattan	MA	58120	$128.50	$0.00	12
JE77	Jones Electric	57 Giddings	Marshall	VT	52018	$0.00	$0.00	12
MI26	Morland Int.	665 Whittier	Frankfort	MA	56152	$212.50	$223.25	11
SA56	Sawyer Inc.	31 Lafayette	Empire	MA	58216	$352.50	$250.00	17
SI82	Simpson Ind.	752 Cadieux	Fernwood	MA	57412	$154.00	$0.00	12

CLIENT NUMBER	NAME
GR56	Grant Cleaners
GU21	Grand Union

CLIENT NUMBER	NAME
AS62	Alton-Scripps

CLIENT NUMBER	NAME	ADDRESS
AM53	Ashton-Mills	216 Rivard
BL26	Blake Suppliers	5752 Maumee
GU21	Grand Union	247 Fuller

CLIENT NUMBER	NAME	OUTSTANDING AMOUNT
AM53	Ashton-Mills	$60.50
AS62	Alton-Scripps	($10.00)
BL26	Blake Suppliers	$129.50
DE76	D & E Grocery	$85.75
GR56	Grant Cleaners	$50.00
GU21	Grand Union	$128.50
JE77	Jones Electric	$0.00
MI26	Morland Int.	$10.75
SA56	Sawyer Inc.	$102.50
SI82	Simpson Ind.	$154.00

CLIENT NUMBER	NAME	BILLED	PAID
DE76	D & E Grocery	$385.75	$300.00

FIGURE 2-1

Overview of Project Steps

The project steps give you an overview of how the Pilotech Services database will be queried. The following tasks will be completed in this project.

1. Start Access and open the Pilotech Services database.
2. Create a new query
3. Create and run a query to display the client number, name, and technician number for all clients.
4. Print the results of a query; that is, print the answer to the question.
5. Create and run a query to display all fields.
6. Create and run a query to display the client number, name, billed amount, and paid amount of client DE76.
7. Create and run a query to display the number, name, and address of those clients with names that begin with the letters Gr.
8. Create and run a query to display the number, name, and billed amounts for clients located in Grattan.
9. Create and run a query to display all clients whose paid amount is $0.00.
10. Create and run a query to display all clients whose billed amount is more than $300.
11. Create and run a query to display all clients whose billed amount is greater than $300 and whose technician is technician 12.
12. Create and run a query to display all clients whose billed amount is more than $300 or whose technician is technician 12.
13. Create and run a query to display the cities in which the clients are located in alphabetical order.
14. Create and run a query to display the number, name, technician number, and billed amount for all clients sorted by descending billed amount within technician number.
15. Create and run a query to display the client number, name, technician number, technician's last name, and technician's first name for all clients.
16. Create and run a query to display the client number, name, technician number, technician's last name, and technician's first name for all clients whose billed amount is more than $300.
17. Create and run a query to display the number, name, and outstanding amount (billed amount minus paid amount) for all clients.
18. Create and run a query to calculate the average billed amount for all clients.
19. Create and run a query to calculate the average billed amount for clients of technician 12.
20. Create and run a query to calculate the average billed amount for clients of each technician.
21. Save a query for future use.

The following pages contain a detailed explanation of each of these steps.

Opening the Database

Before creating queries, first you must open the database. The following steps summarize the procedure to complete this task.

TO OPEN A DATABASE

Step 1: Click the Start button.
Step 2: Click Open Office Document and then click 3½ Floppy (A:) in the Look in list box. Make sure the database called Pilotech Services is selected.
Step 3: Click the Open button. If the Tables tab is not already selected, click the Tables tab.

The database is open and the Pilotech Services : Database window displays.

Creating a New Query

You **create a query** by making entries in a special window called a **Select Query window**. Once the database is open, the first step in creating a query is to select the table for which you are creating a query in the Database window. Next, using the New Object: AutoForm button, you will design the new query. The Select Query window will display. It typically is easier to work with the Select Query window if it is maximized. Thus, as a standard practice, maximize the Select Query window as soon as you have created it.

Perform the following steps to begin the creation of a query.

More *About* **Queries: Query Languages**

Prior to the advent of query languages in the mid 1970s, obtaining answers to questions concerning data in a database was very difficult, requiring that someone write lengthy (several hundred line) programs in languages like COBOL. Query languages made it easy to obtain answers to such questions.

To Create a Query

1 **With the Pilotech Services database open, the Tables tab selected, and the Client table selected, click the New Object: AutoForm button arrow on the toolbar.**

The list of available objects displays (Figure 2-2).

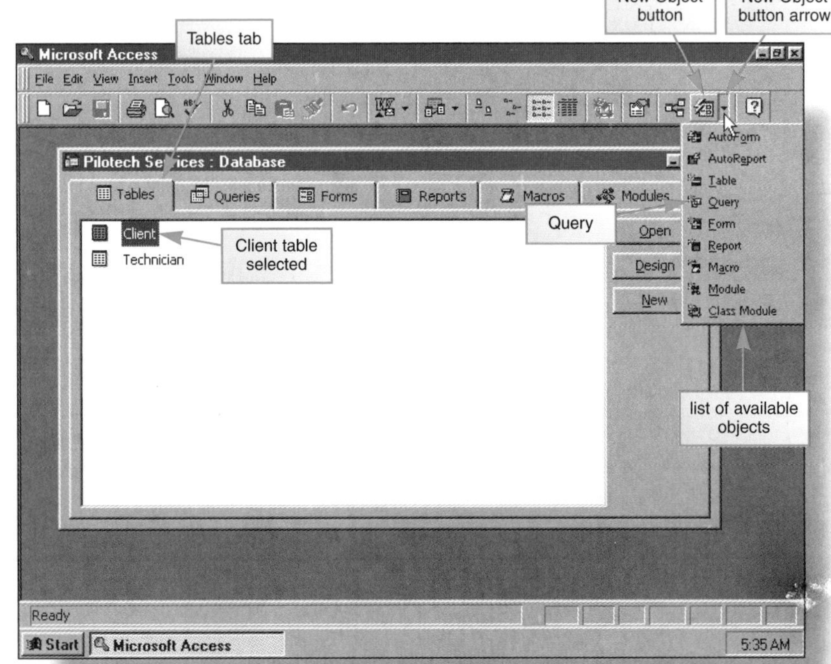

FIGURE 2-2

2 **Click Query.**

The New Query dialog box displays (Figure 2-3).

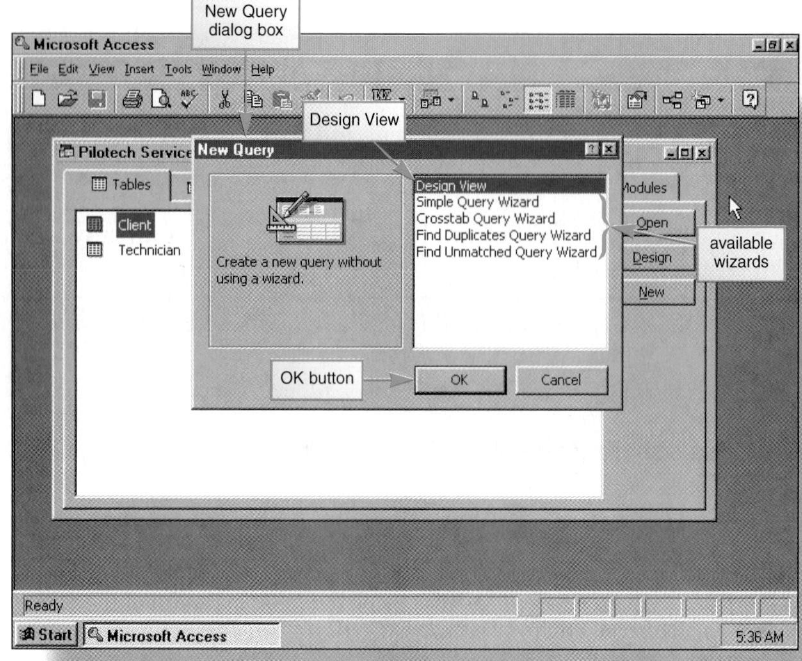

FIGURE 2-3

3 **With Design View selected, click the OK button.**

The Query1 : Select Query window displays (Figure 2-4).

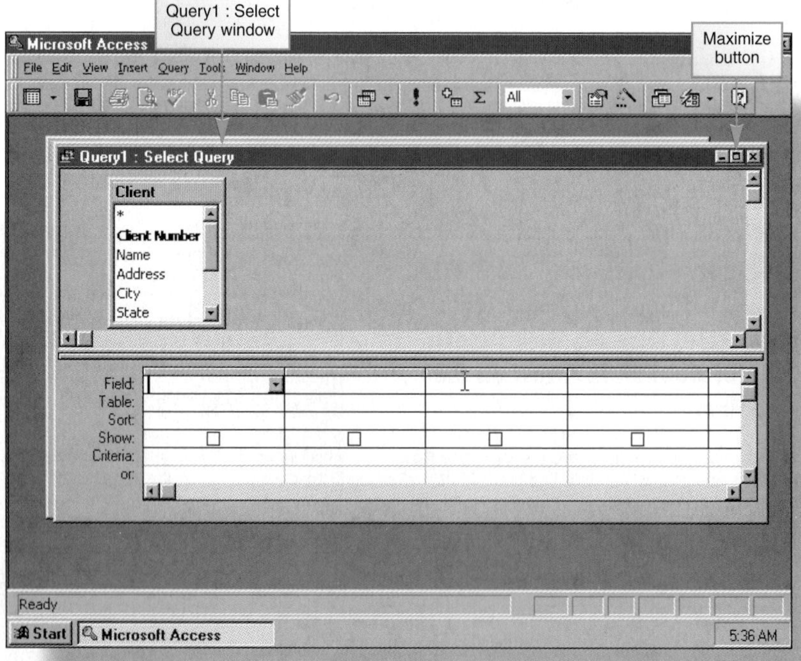

FIGURE 2-4

4 **Maximize the Query1 : Select Query window by clicking its Maximize button, and then point to the dividing line that separates the upper and lower panes of the window. The mouse pointer will change shape to a two-headed arrow with a horizontal bar.**

The Query1 : Select Query window is maximized (Figure 2-5). The upper pane of the window contains a field list for the Client table. The lower pane contains the **design grid**, *which is the area where you specify fields to be included, sort order, and the criteria the records you are looking for must satisfy.*

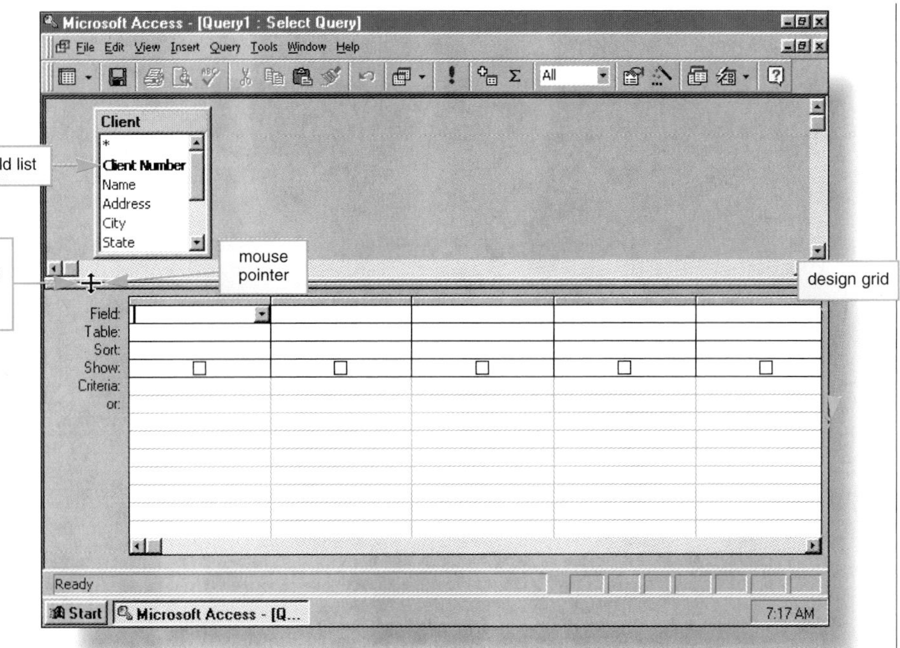

FIGURE 2-5

5 **Drag the line down to the approximate position shown in Figure 2-6 and then move the mouse pointer to the lower edge of the field list box so it changes shape to a two-headed arrow as shown in the figure.**

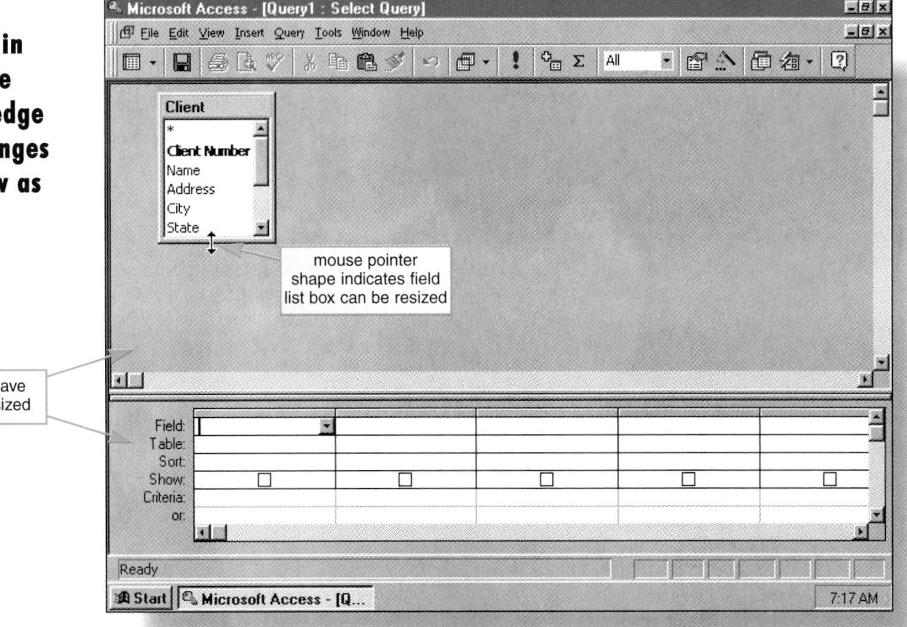

FIGURE 2-6

6 Drag the lower edge of the box down far enough so that all fields in the Client table are visible.

All fields in the Client table display (Figure 2-7).

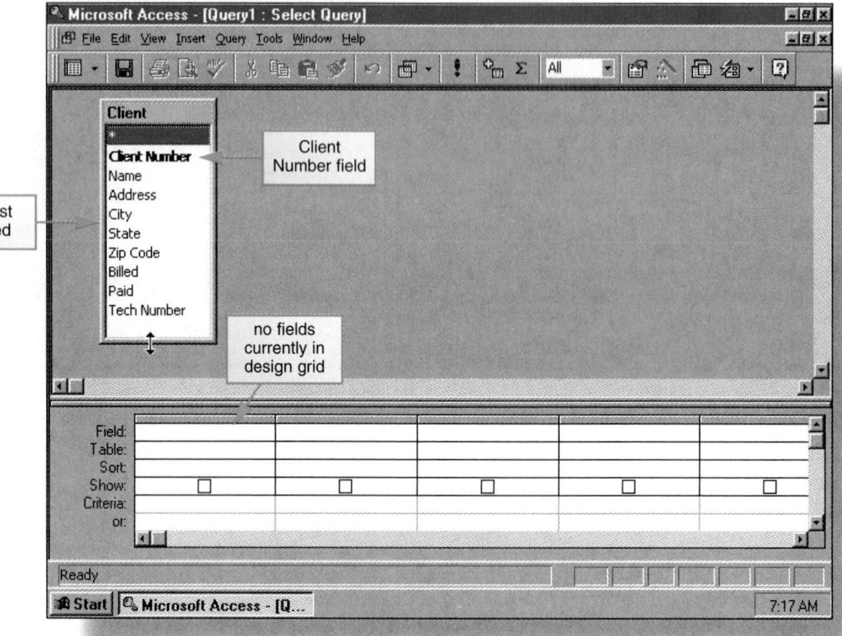

FIGURE 2-7

OtherWays

1. Click Queries tab, click New
2. On Insert menu click Query

Using the Select Query Window

Once you have created a new Select Query window, you are ready to create the actual query by making entries in the design grid in the lower pane of the window. You enter the names of the fields you want included in the Field row in the grid. You also can enter criteria, such as, client number must be DE76, in the Criteria row of the grid. When you do so, only the record or records that match the criterion will be included in the answer.

Displaying Selected Fields in a Query

More About Queries: Query-by-Example

Query-by-Example, often referred to as QBE, was a query language first proposed in the mid 1970s. In this approach, users asked questions by filling in a table on the screen. The approach to queries taken by several DBMSs is based on Query-by-Example.

Only the fields that appear in the design grid will be included in the results of the query. Thus, to display only certain fields, place only these fields in the grid, and no others. If you place the wrong field in the grid inadvertently, click Edit on the menu bar and then click Delete to remove it. Alternatively, you could click Clear Grid to clear the entire design grid and then start over.

The following steps create a query to show the client number, name, and technician number for all clients by including only those fields in the design grid.

Steps To Include Fields in the Design Grid

1 **Make sure you have a maximized Query1 : Select Query window containing a field list for the Client table in the upper pane of the window and an empty design grid in the lower pane (see Figure 2-7).**

2 **Double-click the Client Number field to include the Client Number field in the query.**

The Client Number is included as the first field in the design grid (Figure 2-8).

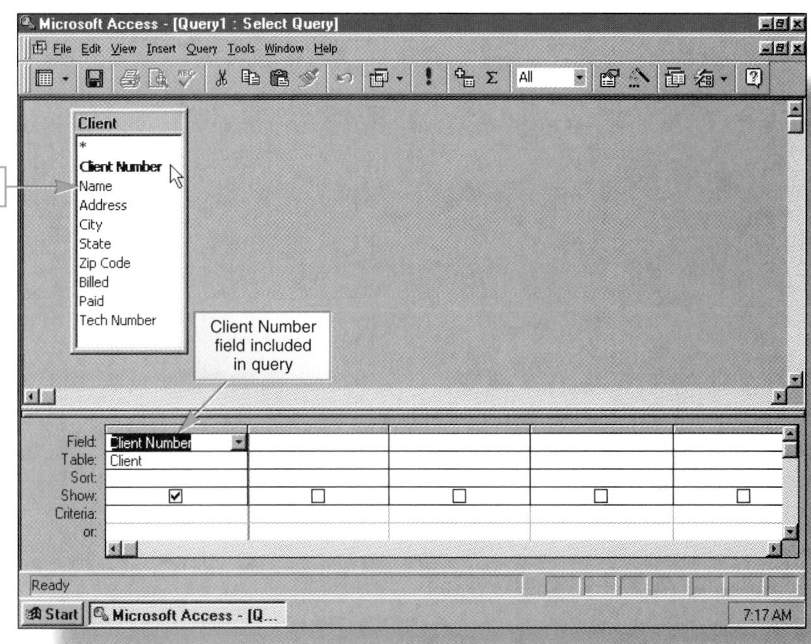

FIGURE 2-8

3 **Double-click the Name field to include it in the query. Include the Tech Number field using the same technique.**

The Client Number, Name, and Tech Number fields are included in the query (Figure 2-9).

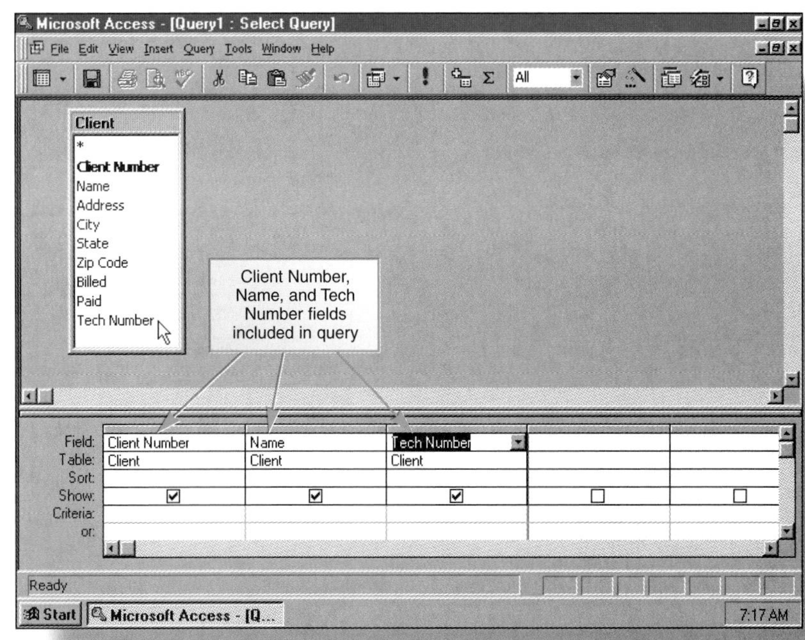

FIGURE 2-9

Other Ways

1. Drag field from list box to grid
2. Click column in grid, click arrow, click field

More About Queries: SQL

The most widespread of all the query languages is a language called SQL. In SQL, users type commands like SELECT BILLED FROM CLIENT WHERE CITY = "Marshall" to find the billed amounts of all clients who live in Marshall.

Running a Query

Once you have created the query, you need to **run the query** to produce the results. To do so, click the Run button. Access then will perform the steps necessary to obtain and display the answer. The set of records that makes up the answer will be displayed in Datasheet view. Although it looks like a table that is stored on your disk, it really is not. The records are constructed from data in the existing Client table. If you were to change the data in the Client table and then rerun this same query, the results would reflect the changes.

Steps To Run the Query

1 **Point to the Run button on the toolbar (Figure 2-10).**

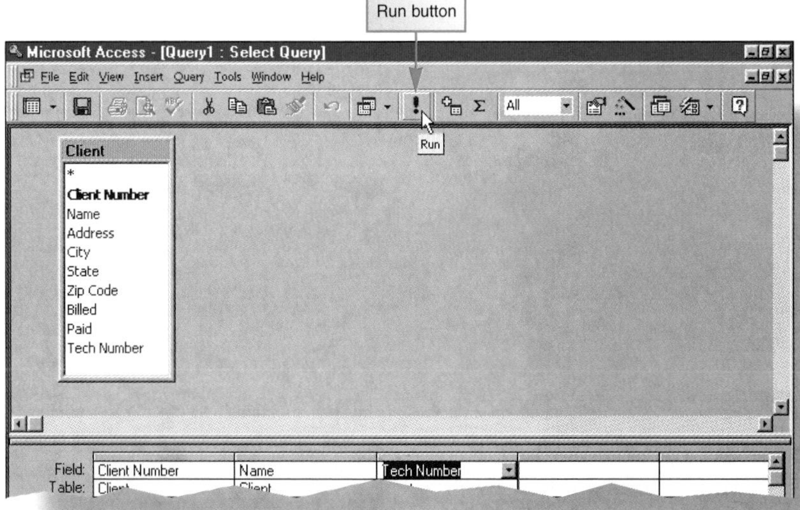

FIGURE 2-10

2 **Click the Run button.**

The query is executed and the results display (Figure 2-11). If you do not move the mouse pointer at all after clicking the Run button, the ScreenTip for the Sort Ascending button will display as shown in the figure. This ScreenTip may obscure a portion of the first record. (Because only three fields exist in this query, the first record is not obscured by a button's ScreenTip.) As a general practice, it is a good idea to move the mouse pointer as soon as you have run a query, so it no longer points to the toolbar.

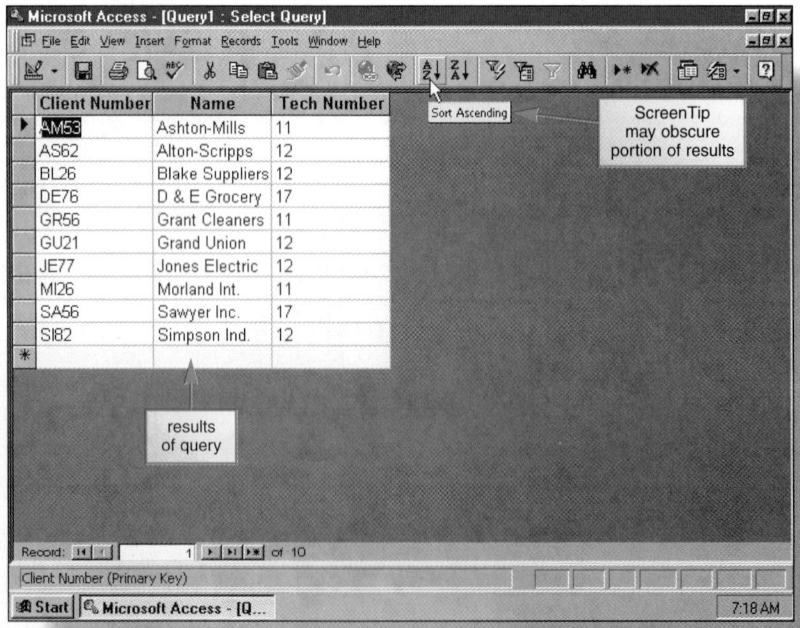

FIGURE 2-11

3 **Move the mouse pointer to a position that is outside of the data and is not on the toolbar.**

The data displays without obstruction (Figure 2-12). Notice that an extra blank row, marking the end of the table, displays at the end of the results.

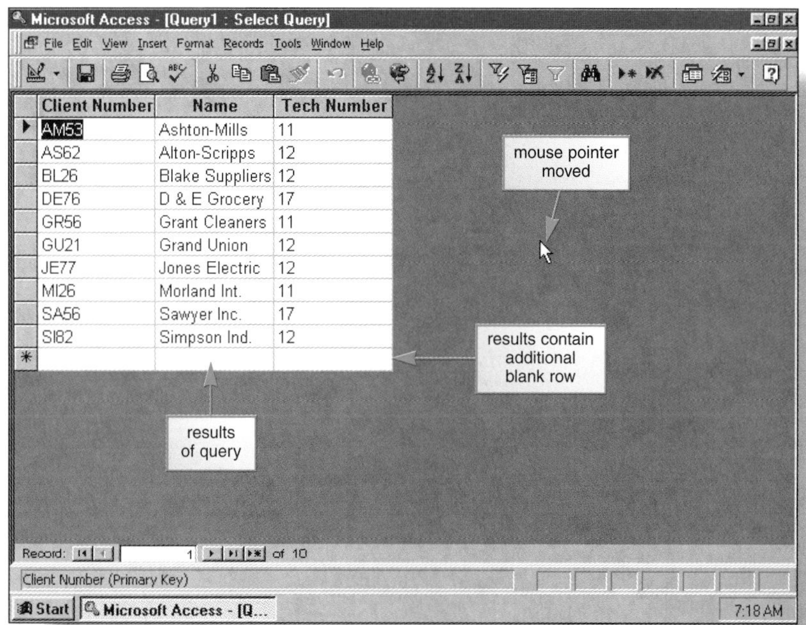

FIGURE 2-12

1. On Query menu click Run

In all future examples, after running a query, move the mouse pointer so the table displays without obstruction.

Printing the Results of a Query

To print the results of a query, use the same techniques you learned in Project 1 to print the data in the table. Complete the following steps to print the query results that currently display on the screen.

TO PRINT THE RESULTS OF A QUERY

Step 1: Ready the printer and then point to the Print button on the toolbar (Figure 2-13).
Step 2: Click the Print button.

The results print.

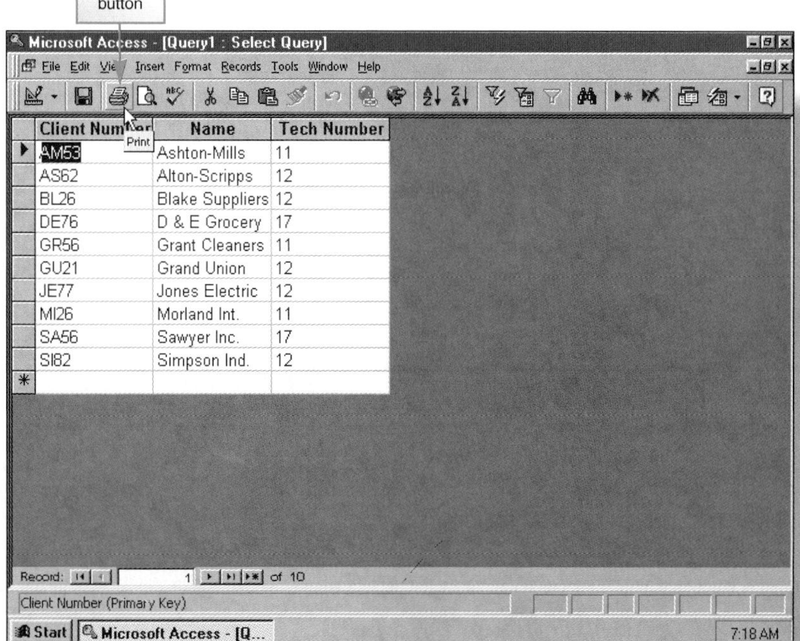

FIGURE 2-13

If the results of a query require landscape orientation, switch to landscape orientation before you click the Print button as indicated in Project 1 on page A 1.29.

Returning to the Select Query Window

You can examine the results of a query on your screen to see the answer to your question. You can scroll through the records, if necessary, just as you scroll through the records of any other table. You also can print a copy of the table. In any case, once you are finished working with the results, you can return to the Select Query window to ask another question. To do so, click the View button arrow on the toolbar as shown in the following steps.

To Return to the Select Query Window

1 Point to the View button arrow on the toolbar (Figure 2-14).

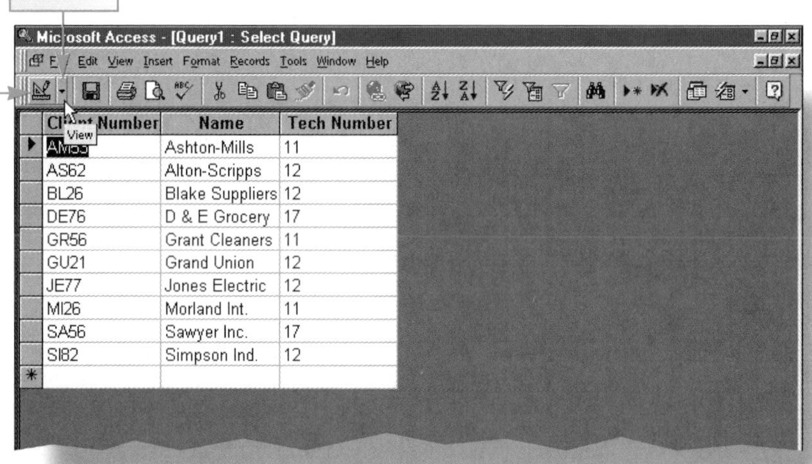

FIGURE 2-14

2 Click the View button arrow. Point to Design View.

The Query View list displays (Figure 2-15).

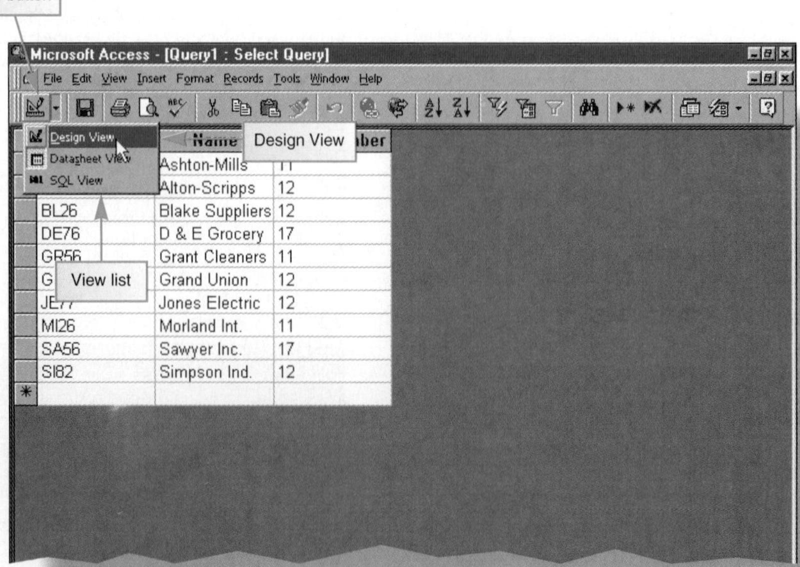

FIGURE 2-15

3 **Click Design View.**

The Query1 : Select Query window displays (Figure 2-16).

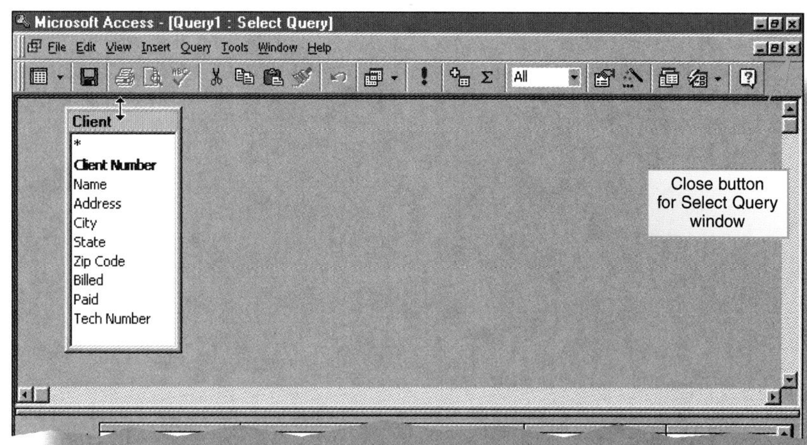

FIGURE 2-16

OtherWays

1. On View menu click Design View

Closing a Query

To **close a query**, close the Select Query window. When you do so, Access displays the Microsoft dialog box asking if you want to save your query for future use. If you think you will need to create the same exact query often, you should save the query. For now, you will not save any queries. You will see how to save them later in the project. The following steps close a query without saving it.

To Close the Query

1 **Click the Close button for the Query1 : Select Query window (Figure 2-16).**

The Microsoft Access dialog box displays (Figure 2-17). Clicking the Yes button saves the query and clicking the No button closes the query without saving.

2 **Click the No button in the Microsoft Access dialog box.**

The Query1 : Select Query window is removed from the desktop.

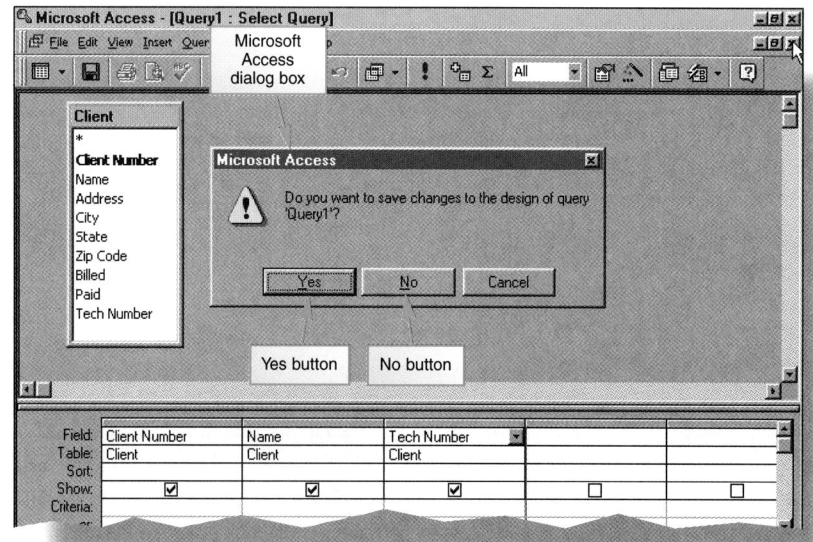

FIGURE 2-17

OtherWays

1. Double-click Control-menu icon
2. On File menu click Close

Including All Fields in a Query

If you want to **include all fields** in a query, you could select each field individually. A more simplified way exists to include fields, however. By selecting the **asterisk (*)** that appears in the field list, you are indicating that all fields are to be included. Complete the following steps to use the asterisk to include all fields.

Steps To Include All Fields in a Query

1 **Be sure you have a maximized Query1 : Select Query window containing a field list for the Client table in the upper pane of the window and an empty design grid in the lower pane. (See Steps 1 through 6 on pages A 2.7 through A 2.10 to create the query and resize the window.) Point to the asterisk at the top of the field list box.**

A maximized Query1 : Select Query window displays (Figure 2-18). The two panes of the window have been resized.

asterisk

FIGURE 2-18

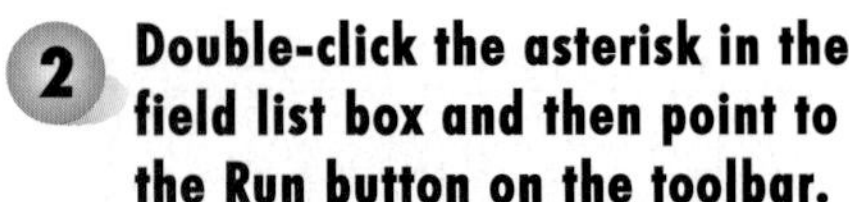

2 **Double-click the asterisk in the field list box and then point to the Run button on the toolbar.**

The table name, Client, followed by an asterisk is added to the design grid (Figure 2-19), indicating all fields are included.

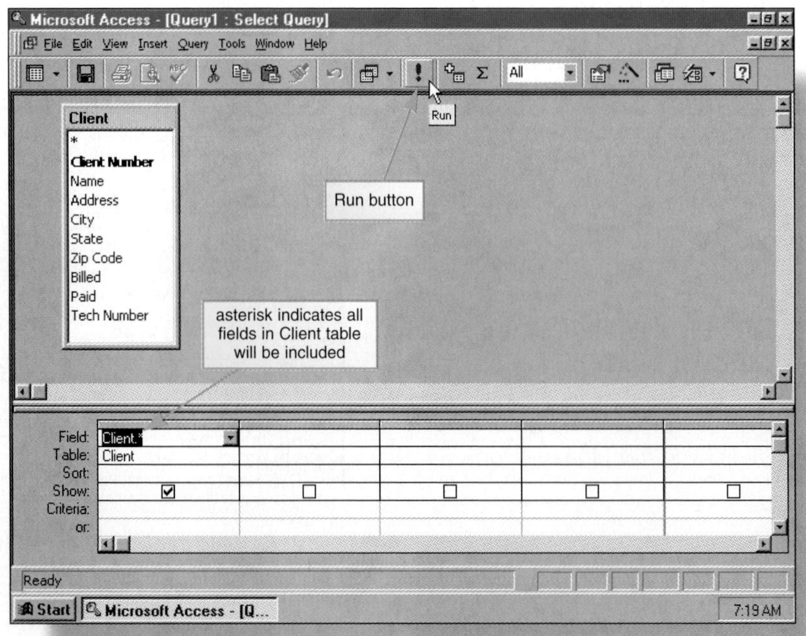

FIGURE 2-19

3 Click the Run button.

The results display and all fields in the Client table are included (Figure 2-20).

4 Click the View button arrow on the toolbar. Click Design View to return to the Query1 : Select Query window.

The datasheet is replaced by the Query1 : Select Query window.

Microsoft Access - [Query1 : Select Query]

all fields included

View button

Client Number	Name	Address	City	State	Zip Code
AM53	Ashton-Mills	216 Rivard	Grattan	MA	58120
AS62	Alton-Scripps	722 Fisher	Empire	MA	58216
BL26	Blake Suppliers	5752 Maumee	Grattan	MA	58120
DE76	D & E Grocery	464 Linnell	Marshall	VT	52018
GR56	Grant Cleaners	737 Allard	Portage	NH	59130
GU21	Grand Union	247 Fuller	Grattan	MA	58120
JE77	Jones Electric	57 Giddings	Marshall	VT	52018
MI26	Morland Int.	665 Whittier	Frankfort	MA	56152
SA56	Sawyer Inc.	31 Lafayette	Empire	MA	58216
SI82	Simpson Ind.	752 Cadieux	Fernwood	MA	57412

FIGURE 2-20

OtherWays

1. Drag asterisk from list box to grid
2. Click column in grid, click arrow, click asterisk

Clearing the Design Grid

If you make mistakes as you are creating a query, you can fix each one individually. Alternatively, you simply may want to **clear the query**; that is, clear out the entries in the design grid and start over. One way to clear out the entries is to close the Select Query window and then start a new query just as you did earlier. A simpler approach, however, is to click Clear Grid on the Edit menu.

Steps To Clear a Query

1 Click Edit on the menu bar.

The Edit menu displays (Figure 2-21).

2 Click Clear Grid.

Access clears the design grid so you can enter your next query.

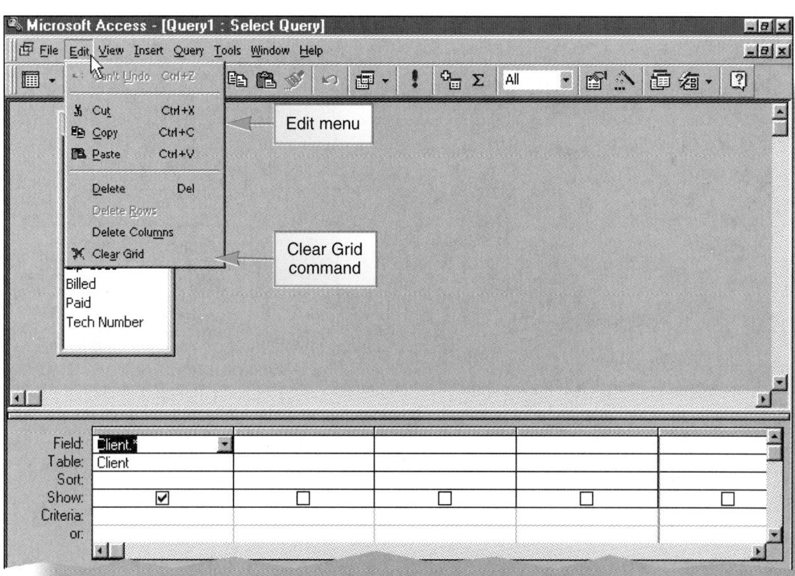

FIGURE 2-21

Entering Criteria

When you use queries, usually you are looking for those records that satisfy some criterion. You might want the name, billed, and paid amounts of the client whose number is DE76, for example, or of those clients whose names start with the letters, Gr. To **enter criteria**, enter them on the Criteria row in the design grid below the field name to which the criterion applies. For example, to indicate that the client number must be DE76, you would type DE76 in the Criteria row below the Client Number field. You first must add the Client Number field to the design grid before you can enter the criterion.

The next examples illustrate the types of criteria that are available.

More *About* **Using Text Data in Criteria**

Some database systems require that text data must be enclosed in quotation marks. For example, to find customers in Michigan, "MI" would be entered as the criterion for the State field. In Access this is not necessary, because Access will insert the quotation marks automatically.

Using Text Data in Criteria

To use **text data** (data in a field whose type is text) in criteria, simply type the text in the Criteria row below the corresponding field name. The following steps query the Client table and display the client number, name, billed amount, and paid amount of client DE76.

Steps To Use Text Data in a Criterion

1 One by one, double-click the Client Number, Name, Billed, and Paid fields to add them to the query. Point to the Criteria entry for the first field in the design grid.

The Client Number, Name, Billed, and Paid fields are added to the design grid (Figure 2-22). The mouse pointer on the Criteria entry for the first field (Client Number) has changed shape to an I-beam.

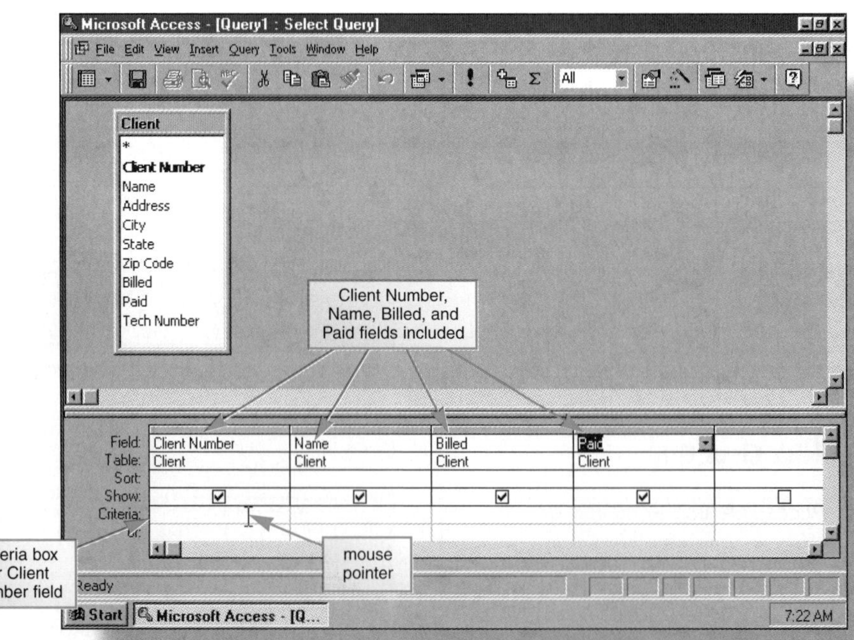

FIGURE 2-22

2 **Click the criteria entry, type** DE76 **as the criteria for the Client Number field.**

The criteria is entered (Figure 2-23).

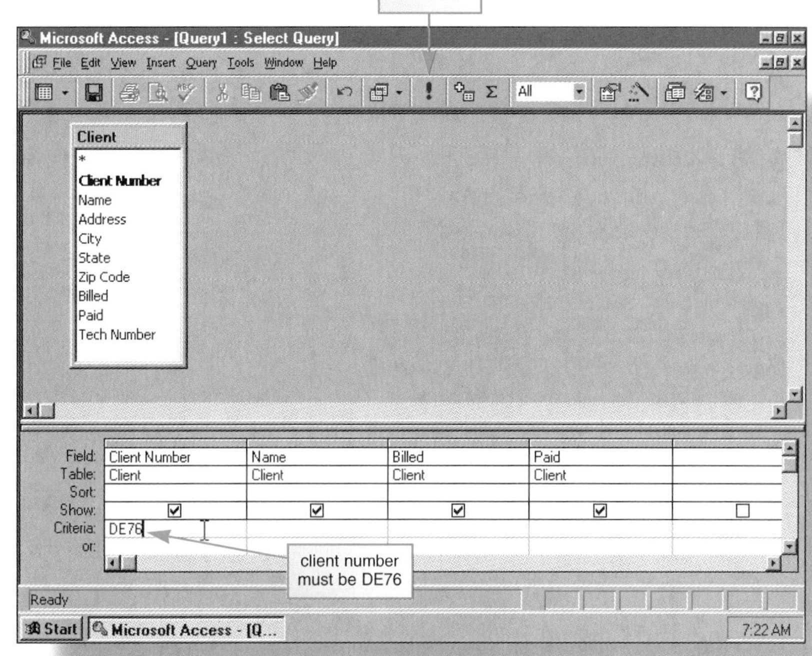

FIGURE 2-23

3 **Run the query by clicking the Run button.**

The results display (Figure 2-24). Only client DE76 is included. (The extra blank row contains $0.00 in the Billed and Paid fields. Unlike text fields, which are left blank, number and currency fields in the extra row contain 0. Because the Billed and Paid fields are currency fields, the values display as $0.00.)

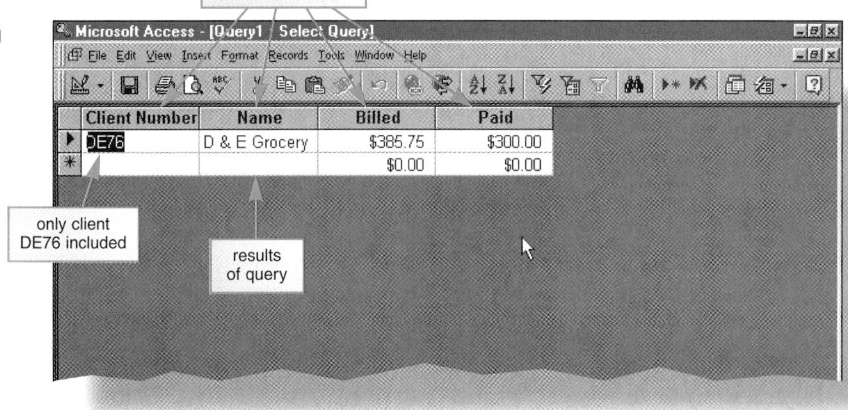

FIGURE 2-24

Using Wildcards

Two special wildcards are available in Microsoft Access. **Wildcards** are symbols that represent any character or combination of characters. The first of the two wildcards, the **asterisk (*)**, represents any collection of characters. Thus Gr* represents the letters, Gr, followed by any collection of characters. The other wildcard symbol is the **question mark (?)**, which represents any individual character. Thus t?m represents the letter, T, followed by any single character followed by the letter, m, such as Tim or Tom.

The steps on the next page use a wildcard to find the number, name, and address of those clients whose names begin with Gr. Because you do not know how many characters will follow the Gr, the asterisk is appropriate.

To Use a Wildcard

1 **Click the View button on the toolbar to return to the Query1 : Select Query window. Click the Criteria row under the Client Number field and then use the DELETE or BACKSPACE key to delete the current entry (DE76). Click the Criteria row under the Name field. Type** `LIKE Gr*` **as the entry.**

The criteria is entered (Figure 2-25).

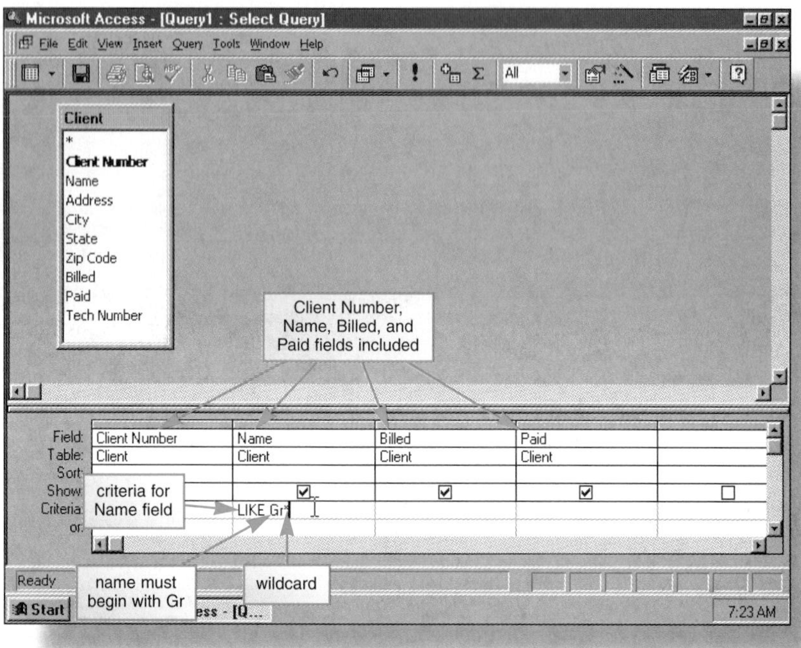

FIGURE 2-25

2 **Click the Run button on the toolbar.**

The results display (Figure 2-26). Only the clients whose names start with Gr are included.

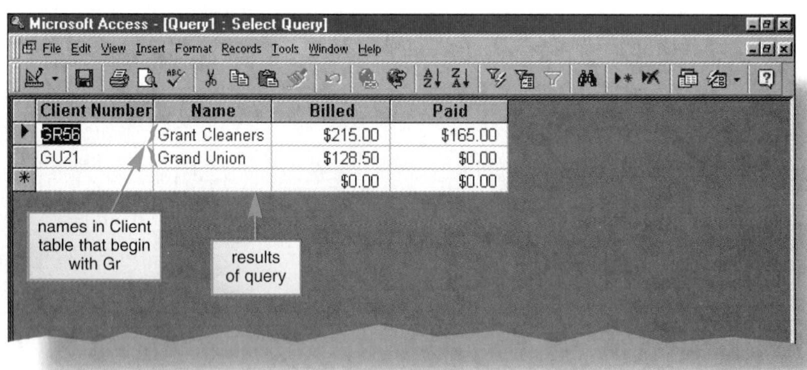

FIGURE 2-26

Criteria for a Field Not in the Result

In some cases, you may have criteria for a particular field that should not appear in the results of the query. For example, you may wish to see the client number, name, address, and billed amounts for all clients located in Grattan. The criteria involves the City field, which is not one of the fields to be included in the results.

To enter a criterion for the City field, it must be included in the design grid. Normally, this also would mean it would appear in the results. To prevent this from happening, remove the check mark from its **Show check box** in the Show row of the grid. The following steps illustrate the process by displaying the client number, name, and billed amounts for clients located in Grattan.

To Use Criteria for a Field Not Included in the Results

1 Click the View button on the toolbar to return to the Query1 : Select Query window. On the Edit menu, click Clear Grid.

Access clears the design grid so you can enter the next query.

2 Include the Client Number, Name, Address, Billed, and City fields in the query. Type `Grattan` **as the criteria for the City field and then point to the City field's Show check box.**

The fields are included in the grid, and the criteria for the City field is entered (Figure 2-27). The space between the left scroll arrow and the scroll box indicates that fields are off the leftmost edge of the grid. In this case, the first field, Client Number, currently does not display. Clicking the left scroll arrow would move the scroll box to the left, shift the fields currently in the grid to the right, and cause the Client Number field to display.

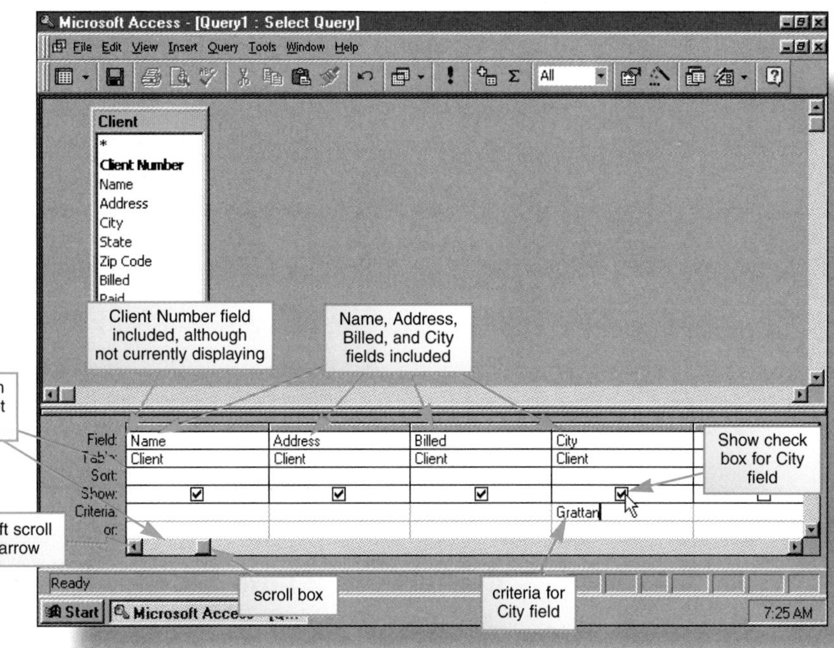

FIGURE 2-27

3 Click the Show check box to remove the check mark.

The check mark is removed from the Show check box for the City field (Figure 2-28), indicating it will not show in the result. Access has added quotation marks before and after Grattan automatically.

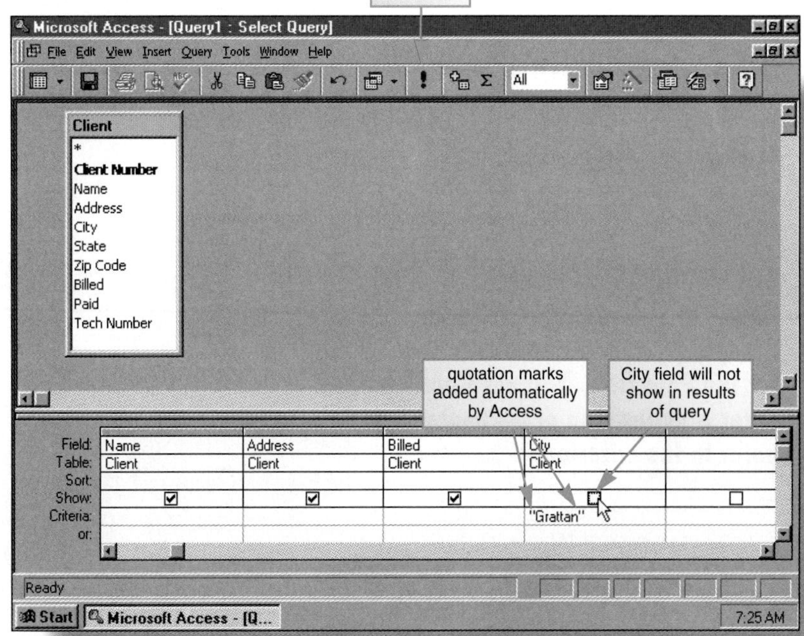

FIGURE 2-28

4 **Click the Run button on the toolbar.**

The results display (Figure 2-29). The City field does not appear. The only clients included are those located in Grattan.

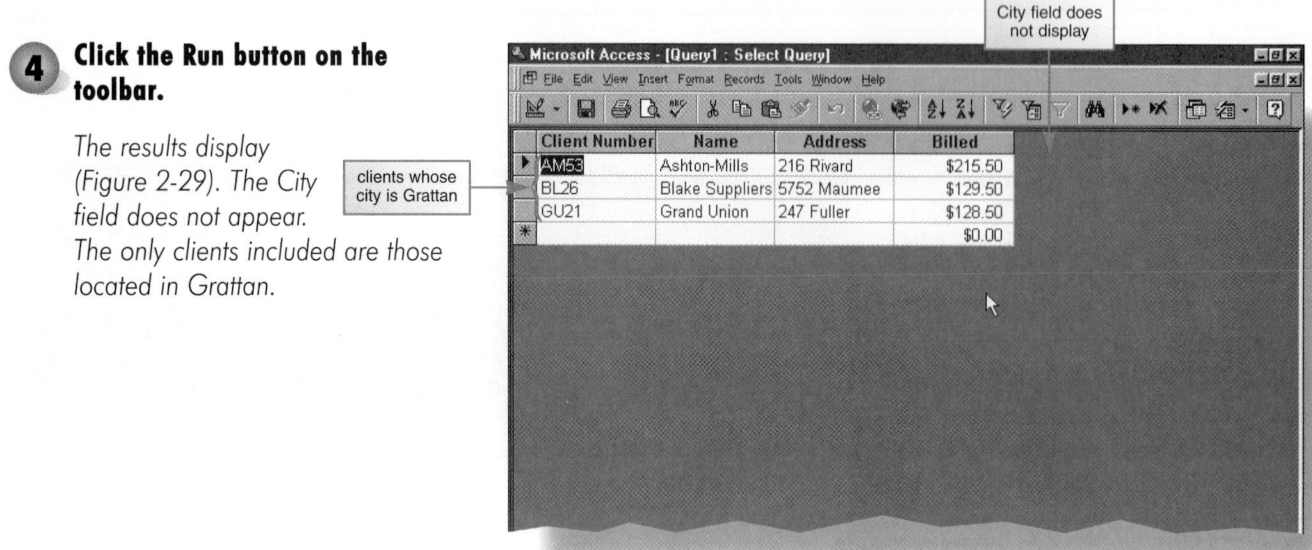

FIGURE 2-29

Using Numeric Data in Criteria

To enter a number in a criterion, type the number without any dollar signs or commas. Complete the following steps to display all clients whose paid amount is $0.00. To do so, you will need to type a zero as the criterion for the Paid field.

Steps To Use a Number in a Criterion

1 **Click the View button on the toolbar to return to the Query1 : Select Query window. On the Edit menu, click Clear Grid. Click the left scroll arrow so no space exists between the scroll arrow and the scroll box.**

Access clears the design grid so you can enter the next query.

2 **Include the Client Number, Name, Billed, and Paid fields in the query. Type** 0 **as the criterion for the Paid field. You need not enter a dollar sign or decimal point in the criterion.**

The fields are selected and the criterion is entered (Figure 2-30).

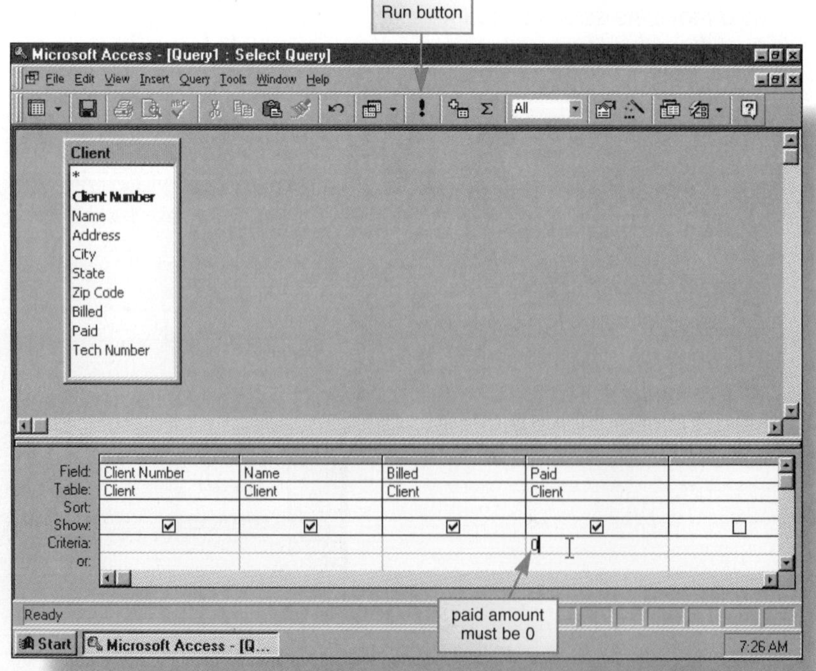

FIGURE 2-30

3 **Click the Run button on the toolbar.**

The results display (Figure 2-31). Only those clients that have a paid amount of $0.00 are included.

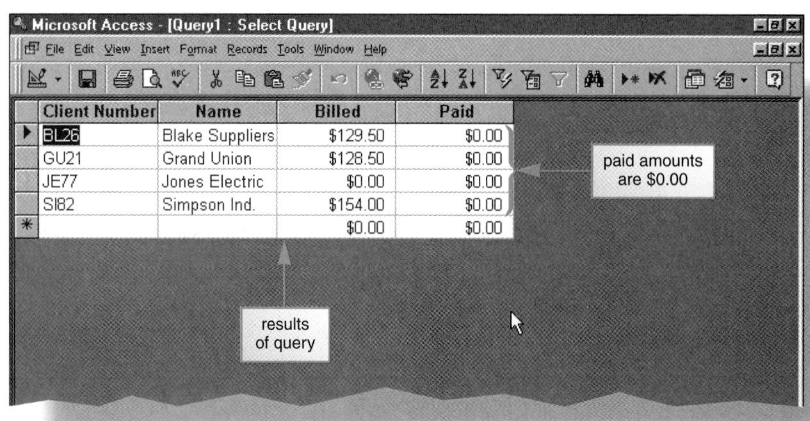

FIGURE 2-31

Using Comparison Operators

Unless you specify otherwise, Access assumes that the criteria you enter involve equality (exact matches). In the last query, for example, you were requesting those clients whose paid amount is equal to 0. If you want something other than an exact match, you must enter the appropriate **comparison operator**. The comparison operators are > (greater than), < (less than), >= (greater than or equal to), <= (less than or equal to), and NOT (not equal to).

Perform the following steps to use the > operator to find all clients whose billed amount is greater than $300.

Steps To Use a Comparison Operator in a Criterion

1 **Click the View button on the toolbar to return to the Query1 : Select Query window. On the Edit menu, click Clear Grid.**

Access clears the design grid so you can enter the next query.

2 **Include the Client Number, Name, Billed, and Paid fields in the query. Type** >300 **as the criterion for the Billed field.**

The fields are selected and the criterion is entered (Figure 2-32).

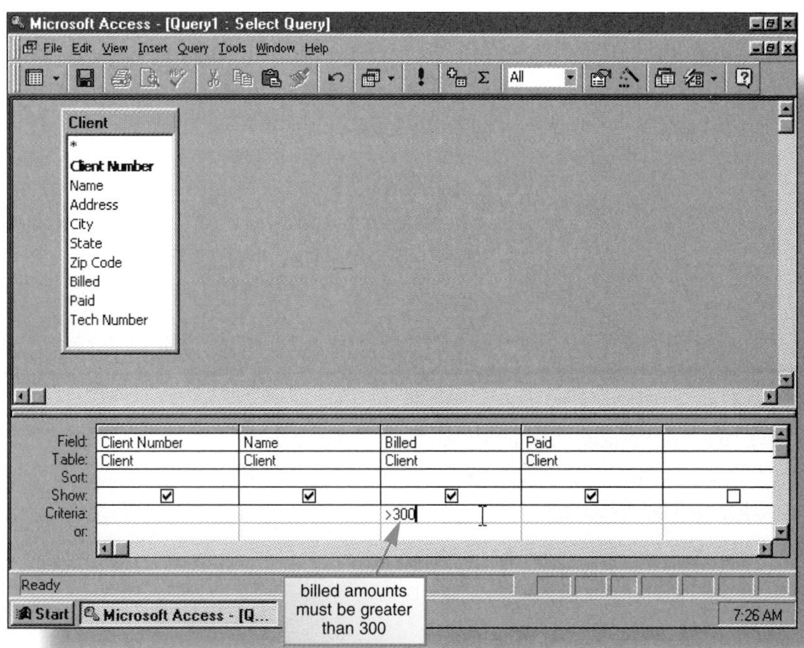

FIGURE 2-32

3 Click the Run button on the toolbar.

The results display (Figure 2-33). Only those clients that have a billed amount more than $300 are included.

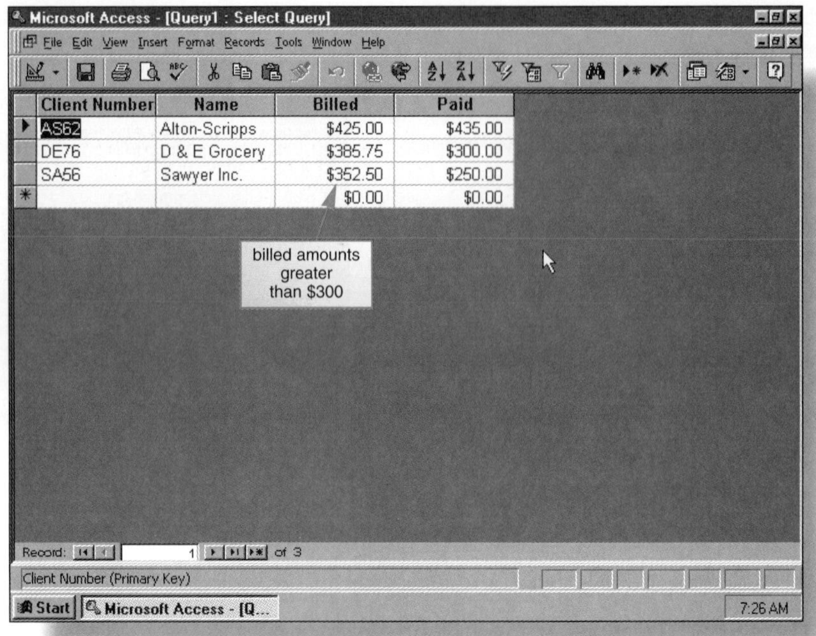

FIGURE 2-33

Using Compound Criteria

More About Compound Criteria

Access to compound criteria is precisely the approach that was proposed for Query-by-Example. (Placing criteria on the same lines indicates they are connected by the word AND. Placing criteria on separate lines indicates they are connected by the word OR.)

Often you will have more than one criterion that the data for which you are searching must satisfy. This type of criterion is called a **compound criterion**. Two types of compound criteria exist.

In **AND criterion**, each individual criterion must be true in order for the compound criterion to be true. For example, an AND criterion would allow you to find those clients that have a billed amount greater than $300 and whose technician is technician 12.

Conversely, **OR criterion** is true provided either individual criterion is true. An OR criterion would allow you to find those clients that have a billed amount greater than $300 or whose technician is technician 12. In this case, any client whose billed amount is greater than $300 would be included in the answer whether or not the client's technician is technician 12. Likewise, any client whose technician is technician 12 would be included whether or not the client had a billed amount greater than $300.

To combine criteria with AND, place the criteria on the same line. Perform the following steps to use an AND criterion to find those clients whose billed amount is greater than $300 and whose technician is technician 12.

Steps To Use a Compound Criterion Involving AND

1. **Click the View button on the toolbar to return to the Query1 : Select Query window. On the Edit menu, click Clear Grid.**

   Access clears the design grid so you can enter the next query.

2. **Include the Client Number, Name, Billed, Paid, and Tech Number fields in the query.**

3. **Click the Criteria entry for the Billed field, and then type** >300 **as a criterion for the Billed field. Click the Criteria entry for the Tech Number field and then type** 12 **as the criterion for the Tech Number field.**

   The fields shift to the left (Figure 2-34). Criteria have been entered for the Billed and Tech Number fields.

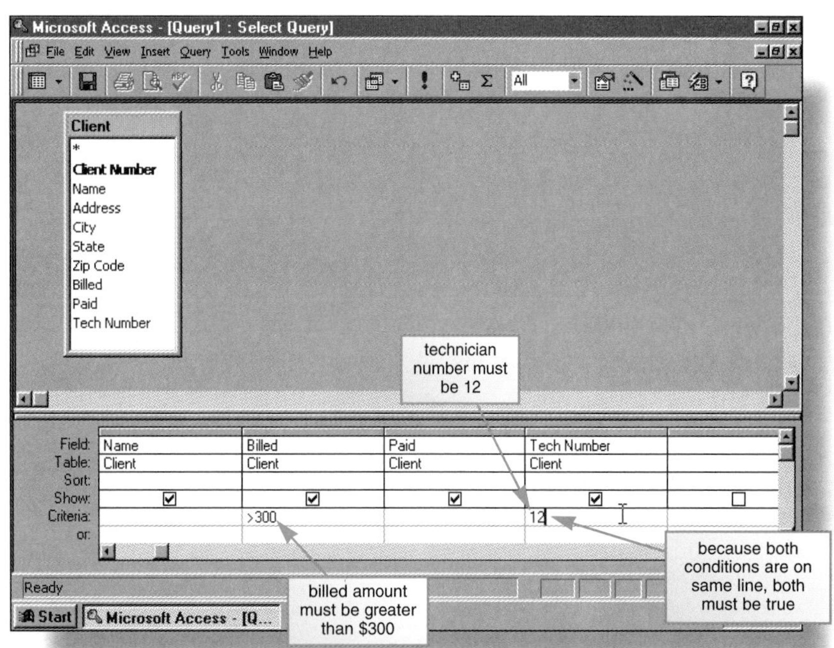

FIGURE 2-34

4. **Click the Run button on the toolbar.**

   The results display (Figure 2-35). Only the single client whose billed amount is greater than $300.00 and whose technician number is 12 is included.

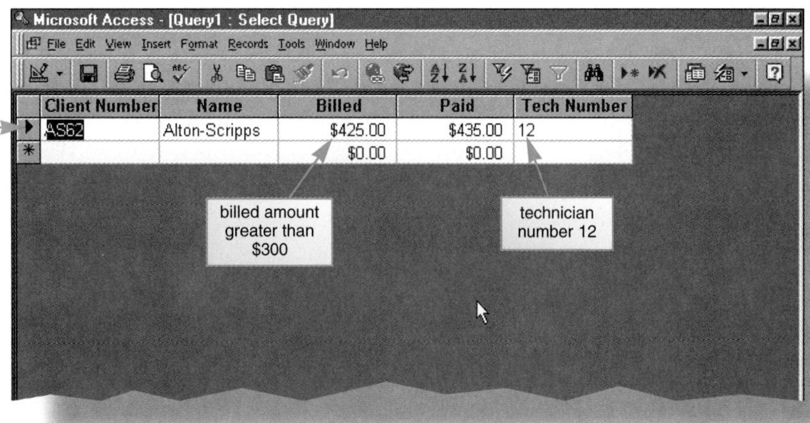

FIGURE 2-35

To combine criteria with OR, the criteria must go on separate lines in the Criteria area of the grid. The steps on the next page use an OR criterion to find those clients whose billed amount is more than $300.00 or whose technician is technician 12 (or both).

To Use a Compound Criterion Involving OR

1 **Click the View button on the toolbar to return to the Query1 : Select Query window.**

2 **Click the Criteria entry for the Tech Number field. Use the BACKSPACE key to delete the entry ("12"). Click the or entry (below Criteria) for the Tech Number field and then type** 12 **as the entry.**

The criteria are entered for the Billed and Tech Number fields on different lines (Figure 2-36).

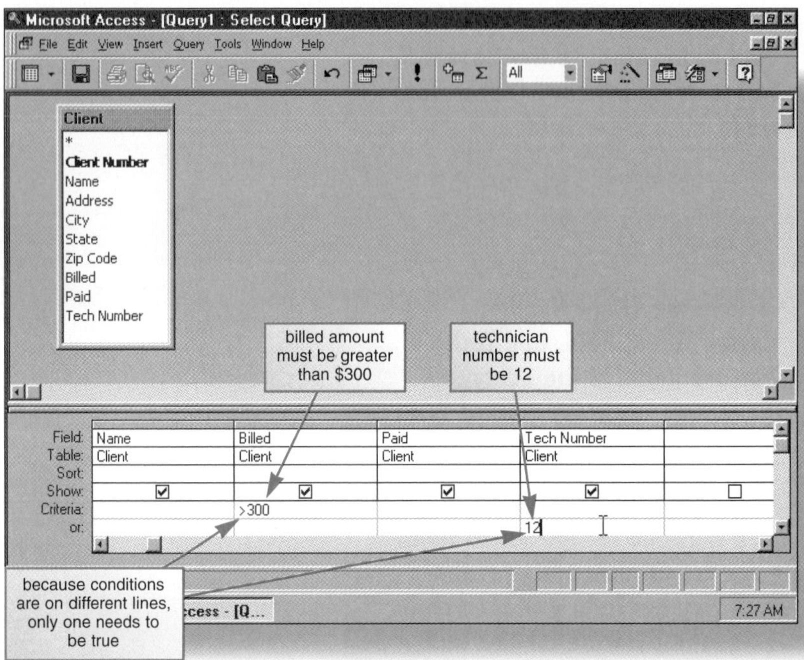

FIGURE 2-36

3 **Click the Run button on the toolbar.**

The results display (Figure 2-37). Only those clients whose billed amount is more than $300.00 or whose technician number is 12 are included.

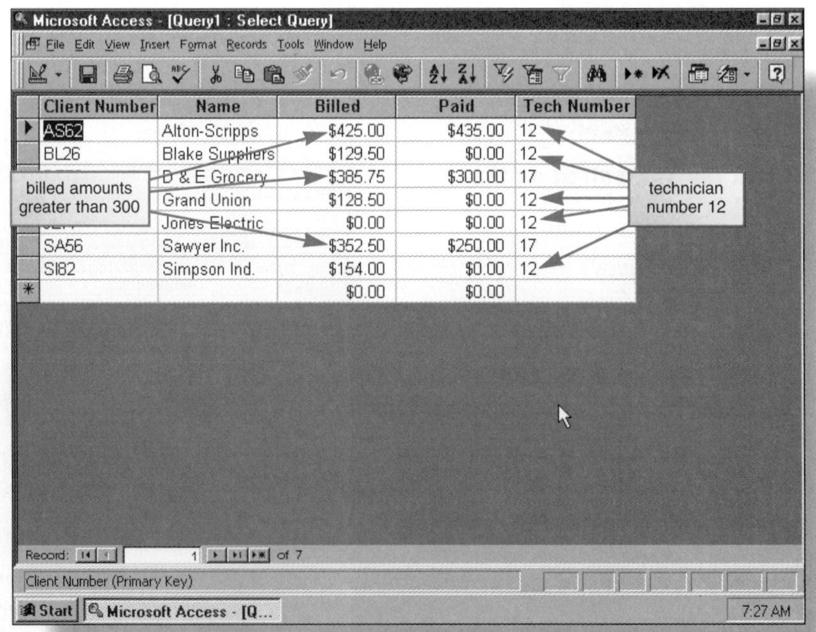

FIGURE 2-37

Sorting Data in a Query

In some queries, the order in which the records are displayed really does not matter. All you need be concerned about are the records that appear in the results. It does not matter which one is first or which one is last.

In other queries, however, the order can be very important. You may want to see the cities in which clients are located and would like them arranged alphabetically. Perhaps you want to see the clients listed by technician number. Further, within all the clients of any given technician, you would like them to be listed by billed amount.

To order the records in the answer to a query in a particular way, you **sort** the records. The field or fields on which the records are sorted is called the **sort key**. If you are sorting on more than one field (such as sorting by billed amount within technician number), the more important field (Tech Number) is called the **major key** (also called the **primary sort key**) and the less important field (Billed) is called the **minor key** (also called the **secondary sort key**).

To sort in Microsoft Access, specify the sort order in the Sort line of the design grid below the field that is the sort key. If you specify more than one sort key, the sort key on the left will be the major sort key and the one on the right will be the minor key.

The following steps sort the cities in the Client table.

More *About* Sorting Data in a Query

When sorting data in a query, the records in the underlying tables (the tables on which the query is based) are not actually rearranged. Instead, the DBMS will determine the most efficient method of simply displaying the records in the requested order. The records in the underlying tables remain in their original order.

To Sort Data in a Query

1 **Click the View button on the toolbar to return to the Query1 : Select Query window. On the Edit menu, click Clear Grid. Click the left scroll arrow so no space exists between the scroll arrow and the scroll box.**

2 **Include the City field in the design grid. Click the Sort row below the City field, and then click the down arrow that appears.**

The City field is included (Figure 2-38). A list of available sort orders displays.

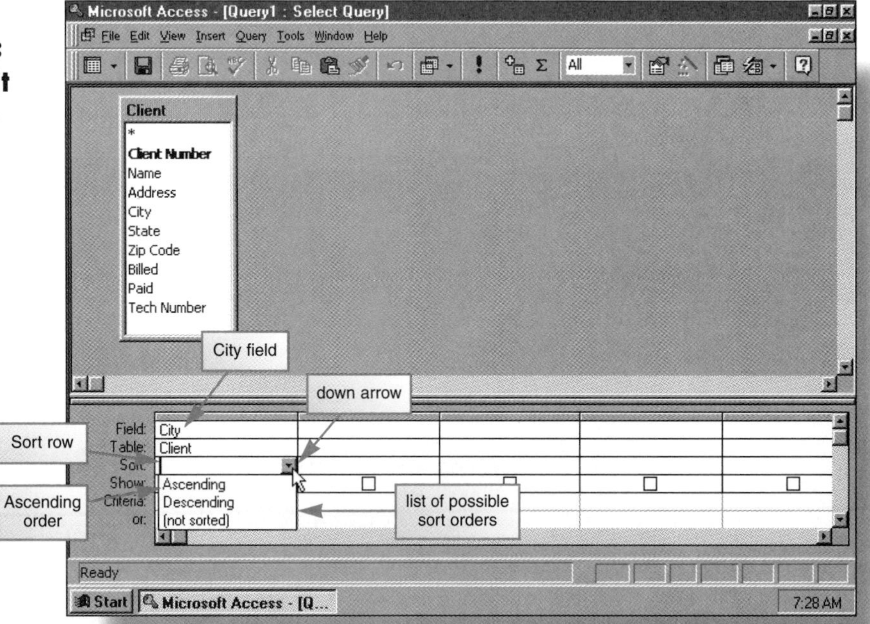

FIGURE 2-38

3 **Click Ascending.**

Ascending is selected as the order (Figure 2-39).

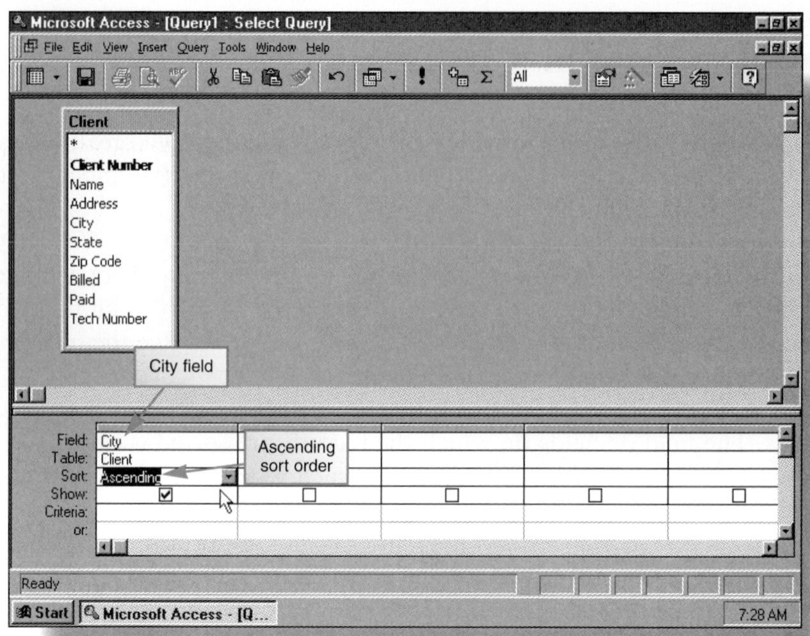

FIGURE 2-39

4 **Run the query by clicking the Run button on the toolbar.**

The results contain the cities from the Client table (Figure 2-40). The cities display in alphabetical order. Duplicates, that is, identical rows, are included.

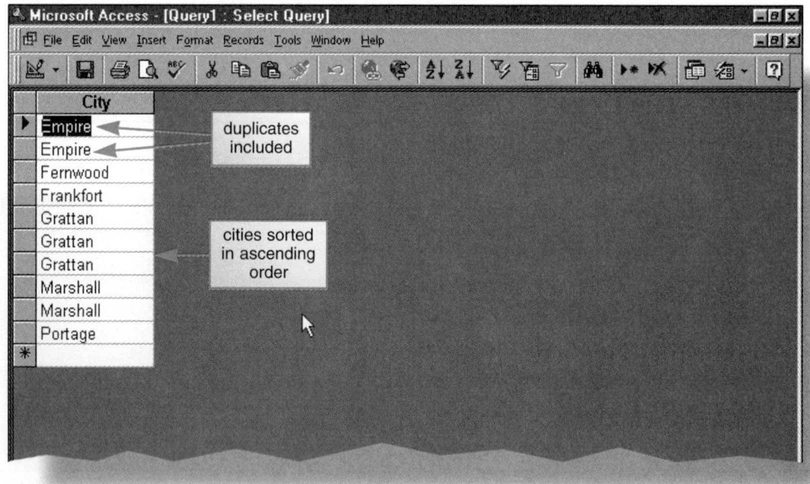

FIGURE 2-40

Sorting on Multiple Keys

The next example lists the number, name, technician number, and billed amount for all clients. The data is to be sorted by descending billed amount (high to low) within technician number, which means that the Tech Number field is the major key and the Billed field is the minor key. It also means that the Billed field should be sorted in descending order.

The following steps accomplish this sorting by specifying the Tech Number and Billed fields as sort keys and by selecting Descending as the sort order for the Billed field.

To Sort on Multiple Keys

1. **Click the View button on the toolbar to return to the Query1 : Select Query window. On the Edit menu, click Clear Grid.**

2. **Include the Client Number, Name, Tech Number, and Billed fields in the query in this order. Select Ascending as the sort order for the Tech Number field and Descending as the sort order for the Billed field (Figure 2-41).**

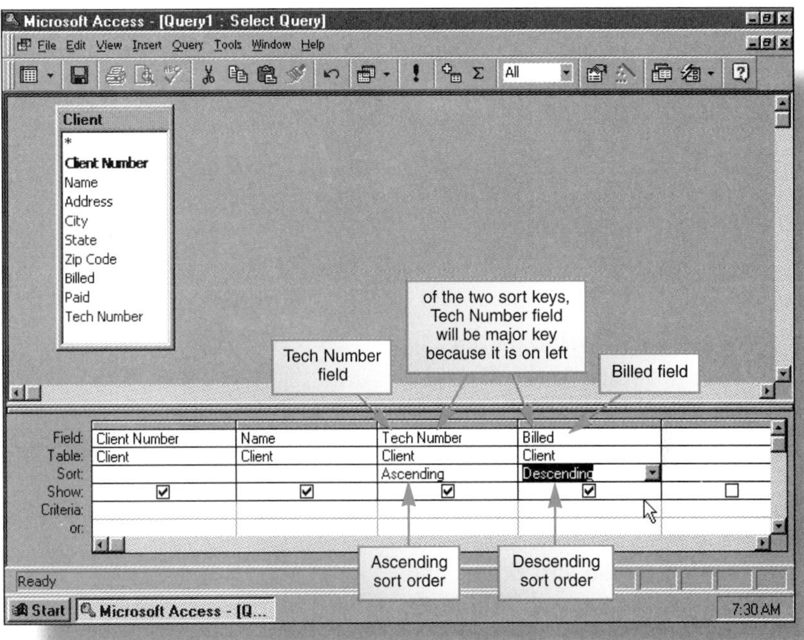

FIGURE 2-41

3. **Run the query.**

The results display (Figure 2-42). The clients are sorted by technician number. Within the collection of clients having the same technician, the clients are sorted by descending billed amount.

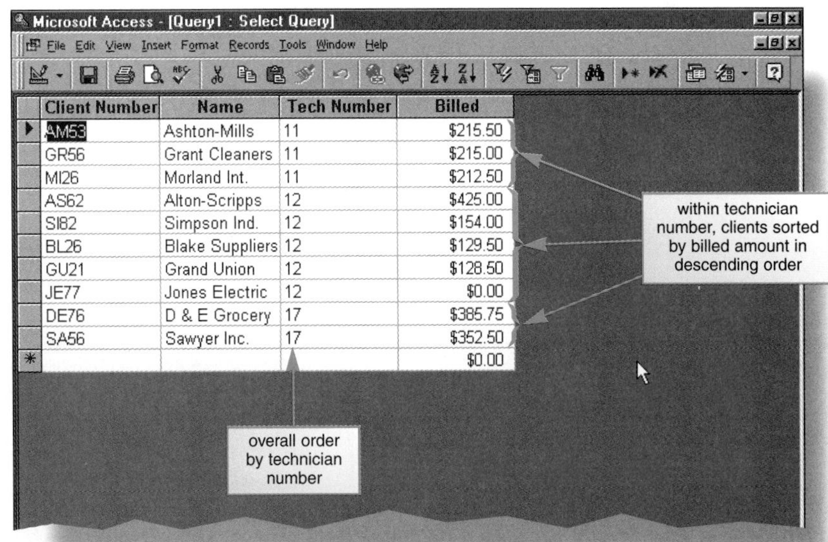

Client Number	Name	Tech Number	Billed
AM53	Ashton-Mills	11	$215.50
GR56	Grant Cleaners	11	$215.00
MI26	Morland Int.	11	$212.50
AS62	Alton-Scripps	12	$425.00
SI82	Simpson Ind.	12	$154.00
BL26	Blake Suppliers	12	$129.50
GU21	Grand Union	12	$128.50
JE77	Jones Electric	12	$0.00
DE76	D & E Grocery	17	$385.75
SA56	Sawyer Inc.	17	$352.50
			$0.00

FIGURE 2-42

It is important to remember that the major sort key must appear to the left of the minor sort key in the design grid. If you attempted to sort by billed amount within technician number, but placed the Billed field to the left of the Tech Number field, your results would be incorrect.

Omitting Duplicates

As you saw earlier, when you sort data, duplicates are included. In Figure 2-40 on page A 2.28, for example, Empire appeared twice, Grattan appeared three times, and Marshall appeared twice. If you do not want duplicates included, use the Properties command and specify Unique Values Only. Perform the following steps to produce a sorted list of the cities in the Client table in which each city is listed only once.

Steps To Omit Duplicates

1. **Click the View button on the toolbar to return to the Query1 : Select Query window. On the Edit menu, click Clear Grid.**

2. **Include the City field, click Ascending as the sort order, and right-click the second field in the design grid (the empty field following City).**

   The shortcut menu displays (Figure 2-43).

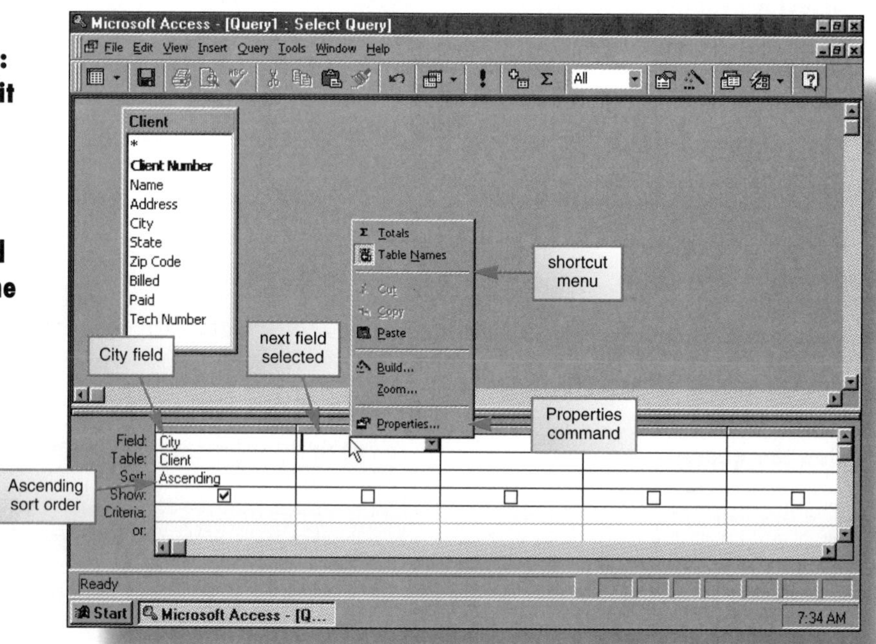

FIGURE 2-43

3. **Click Properties on the shortcut menu.**

   The Query Properties sheet displays (Figure 2-44).

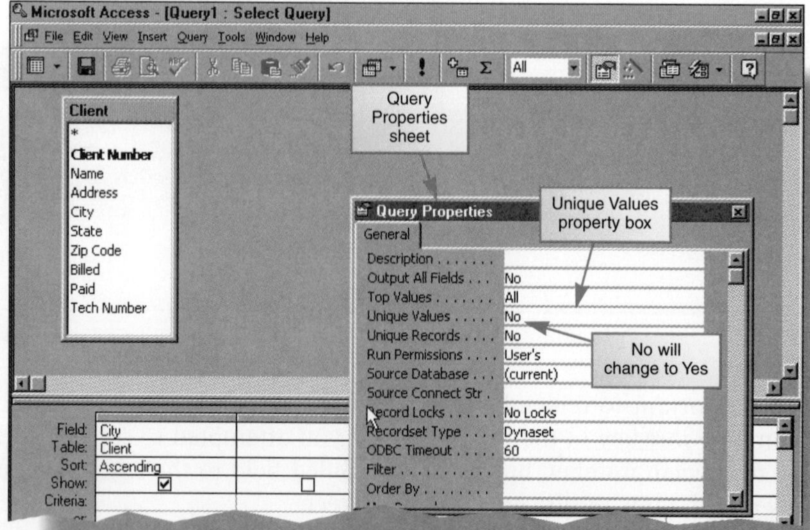

FIGURE 2-44

4 **Click the Unique Values property box, and then click the down arrow that displays to produce a list of available choices for Unique Values (Figure 2-45).**

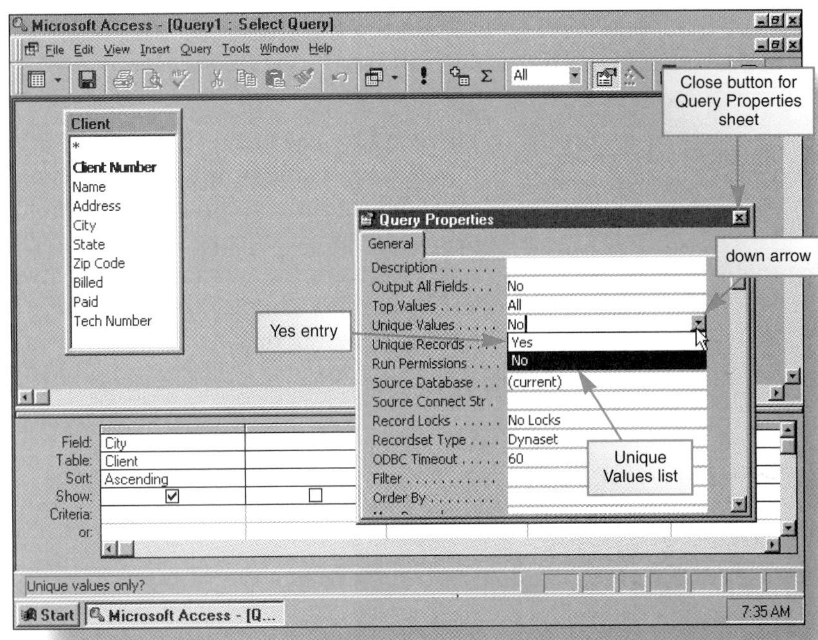

FIGURE 2-45

5 **Click Yes, and then close the Query Properties sheet by clicking its Close button. Run the query.**

The results display (Figure 2-46). The cities are sorted alphabetically. Each city is included only once.

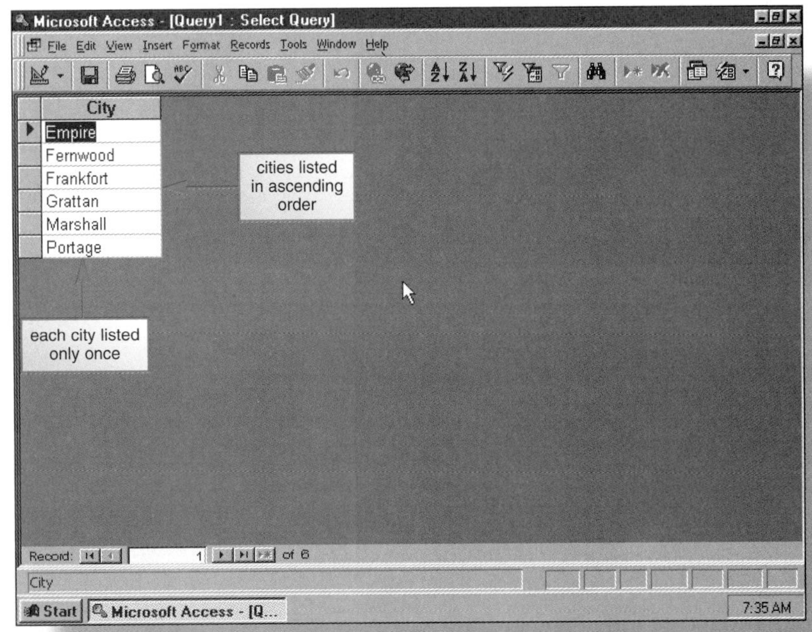

FIGURE 2-46

OtherWays

1. Click Properties button on toolbar
2. On View menu click Properties

More *About* **Joining Tables**

One of the key features that distinguishes database management systems from file systems is the ability to join tables, that is, to create queries that draw data from two or more tables. Several types of joins are available. The most common type, the one illustrated in the text, formally is called the natural join.

Joining Tables

Pilotech Services needs to list the number and name of each client along with the number and name of the client's technician. The client's name is in the Client table, whereas the technician's name is in the Technician table. Thus, this query cannot be satisfied using a single table. You need to **join** the tables; that is, to find records in the two tables that have identical values in matching fields (Figure 2-47). In this example, you need to find records in the Client table and the Technician table that have the same value in the Tech Number fields.

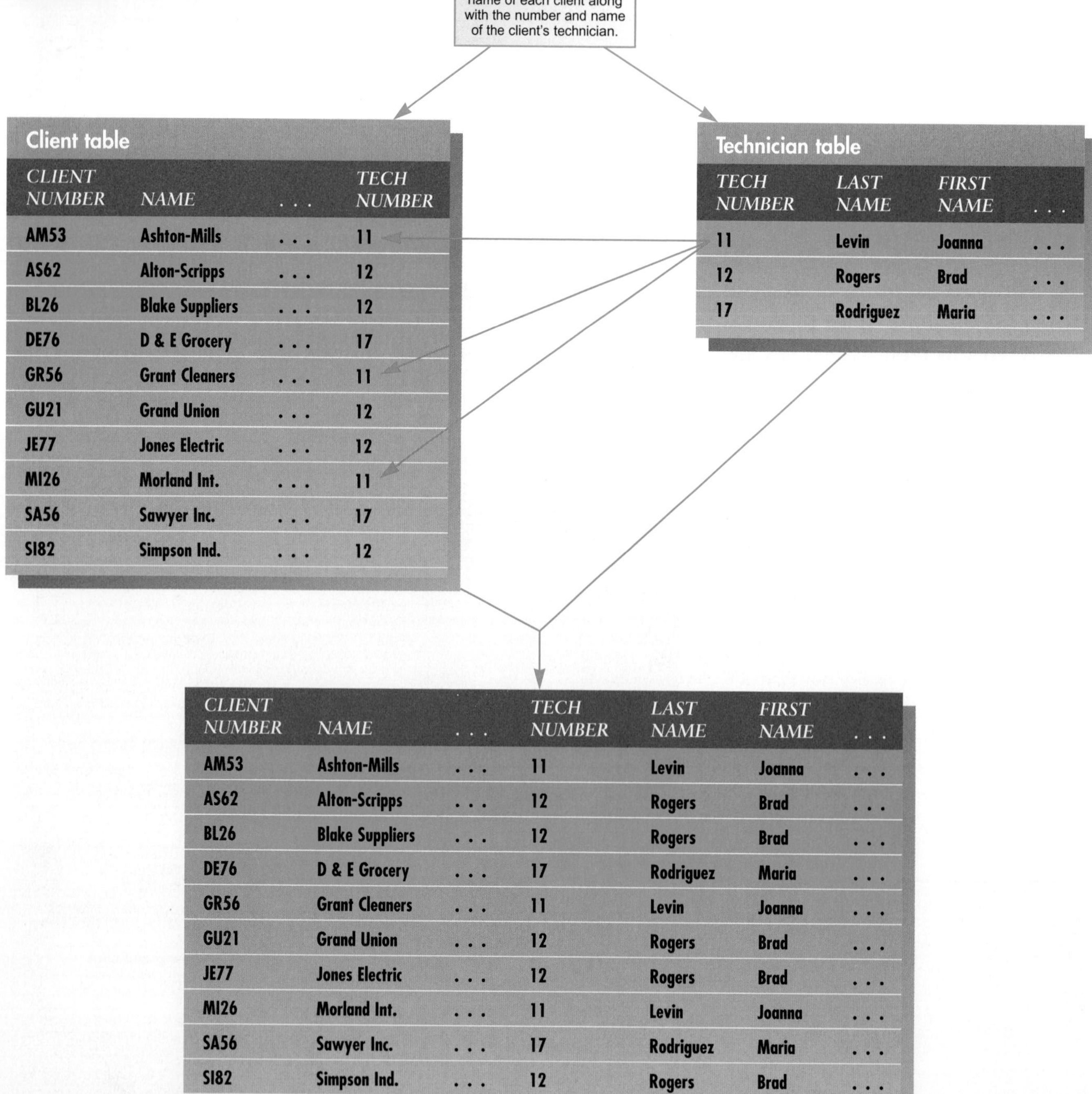

Client table

CLIENT NUMBER	NAME	. . .	TECH NUMBER
AM53	Ashton-Mills	. . .	11
AS62	Alton-Scripps	. . .	12
BL26	Blake Suppliers	. . .	12
DE76	D & E Grocery	. . .	17
GR56	Grant Cleaners	. . .	11
GU21	Grand Union	. . .	12
JE77	Jones Electric	. . .	12
MI26	Morland Int.	. . .	11
SA56	Sawyer Inc.	. . .	17
SI82	Simpson Ind.	. . .	12

Technician table

TECH NUMBER	LAST NAME	FIRST NAME	. . .
11	Levin	Joanna	. . .
12	Rogers	Brad	. . .
17	Rodriguez	Maria	. . .

CLIENT NUMBER	NAME	. . .	TECH NUMBER	LAST NAME	FIRST NAME	. . .
AM53	Ashton-Mills	. . .	11	Levin	Joanna	. . .
AS62	Alton-Scripps	. . .	12	Rogers	Brad	. . .
BL26	Blake Suppliers	. . .	12	Rogers	Brad	. . .
DE76	D & E Grocery	. . .	17	Rodriguez	Maria	. . .
GR56	Grant Cleaners	. . .	11	Levin	Joanna	. . .
GU21	Grand Union	. . .	12	Rogers	Brad	. . .
JE77	Jones Electric	. . .	12	Rogers	Brad	. . .
MI26	Morland Int.	. . .	11	Levin	Joanna	. . .
SA56	Sawyer Inc.	. . .	17	Rodriguez	Maria	. . .
SI82	Simpson Ind.	. . .	12	Rogers	Brad	. . .

FIGURE 2-47

To join tables in Access, first you bring field lists for both tables to the upper pane of the Select Query window. Access will draw a line, called a **join line**, between matching fields in the two tables indicating that the tables are related. You then can select fields from either table. Access will join the tables automatically.

The first step is to add an additional table to the query as illustrated in the following steps, which add the Technician table.

Steps To Join Tables

1 **Click the View button on the toolbar to return to the Query1 : Select Query window. On the Edit menu, click Clear Grid.**

2 **Right-click any open area in the upper pane of the Query1 : Select Query window.**

The shortcut menu displays (Figure 2-48).

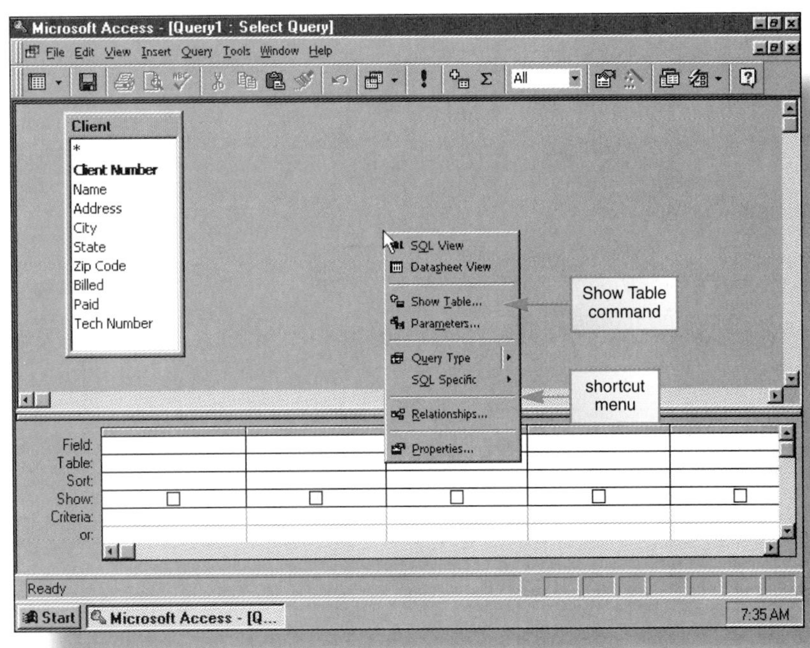

FIGURE 2-48

3 **Click Show Table on the shortcut menu.**

The Show Table dialog box displays (Figure 2-49).

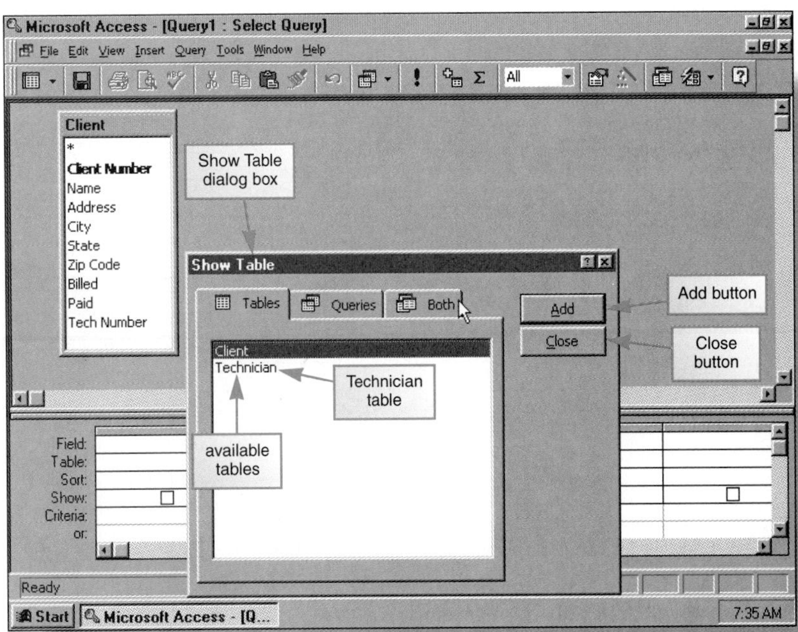

FIGURE 2-49

4 **Click Technician to select the Technician table, and then click the Add button. Close the Show Table dialog box by clicking the Close button. Expand the size of the field list so all the fields in the Technician table display.**

A field list for the Technician table displays (Figure 2-50). It has been enlarged so all the technician fields are visible. A join line appears joining the Tech Number fields in the two field lists. The join line indicates how the tables are related; that is, linked through the matching fields. (If you fail to give the matching fields the same name, Access will not insert the line. You can insert it manually, however, by clicking one of the two matching fields and dragging the mouse pointer to the other matching field.)

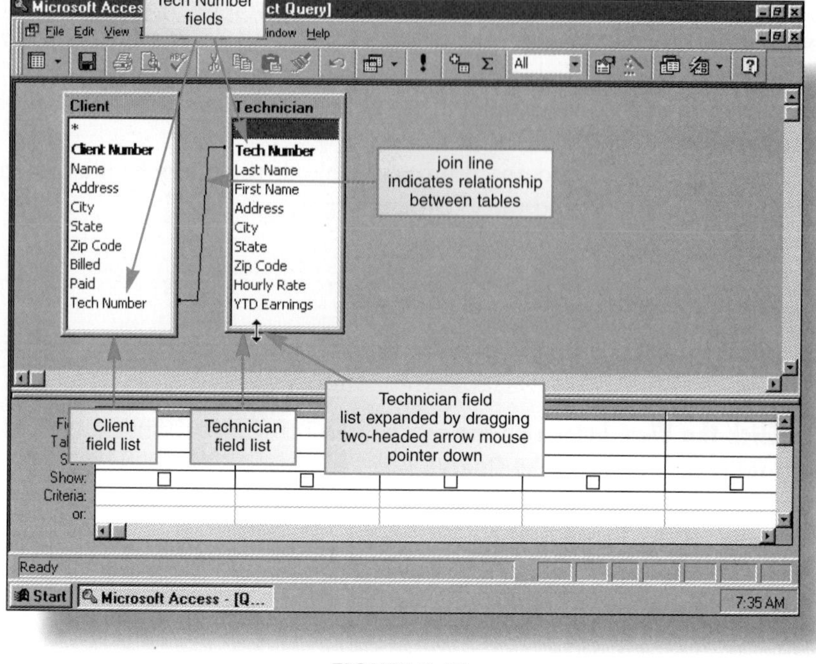

FIGURE 2-50

5 **Include the Client Number, Name, and Tech Number fields from the Client table and the Last Name and First Name fields from the Technician table.**

The fields from both tables are selected (Figure 2-51).

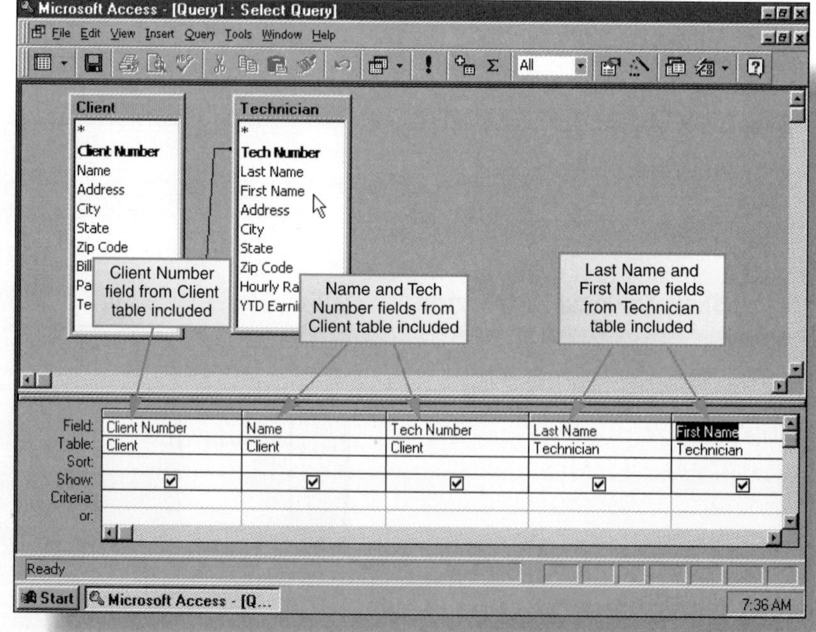

FIGURE 2-51

6 **Run the query.**

The results display (Figure 2-52). They contain data from the Client table as well as data from the Technician table.

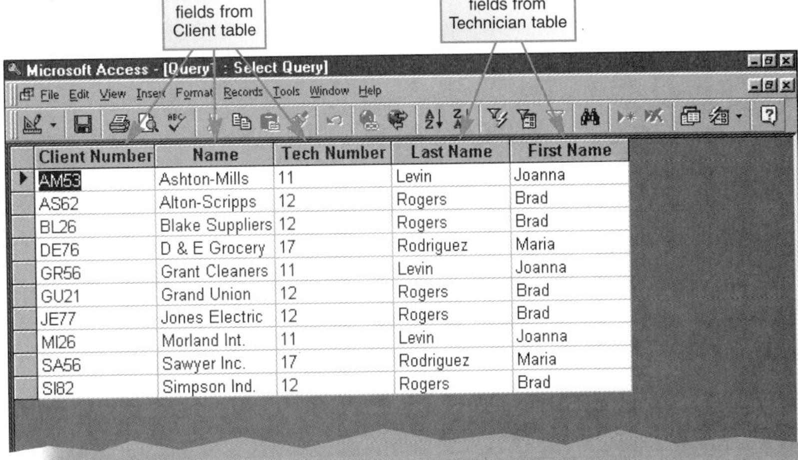

FIGURE 2-52

OtherWays

1. Click Show Table button on toolbar
2. On Query menu click Show Table

Restricting Records in a Join

Sometimes you will want to join tables, but you will not want to include all possible records. In such cases, you will relate the tables and include fields just as you did before. You also will include criteria. For example, to include the same fields as in the previous query, but only those clients whose billed amount is more than $300, you will make the same entries as before and then also type >300 as a criterion for the Billed field.

The following steps modify the query from the previous example to restrict the records that will be included in the join.

Steps To Restrict the Records in a Join

1 **Click the View button on the toolbar to return to the Query1 : Select Query window. Add the Billed field to the query. If necessary, scroll the fields to the left so the Billed field displays in the design grid. Type** >300 **as the criterion for the Billed field and then click the Show check box for the Billed field to remove the check mark.**

The Billed field displays in the design grid (Figure 2-53). A criterion is entered for the Billed field and the Show check box is empty, indicating that the field will not display in the results of the query.

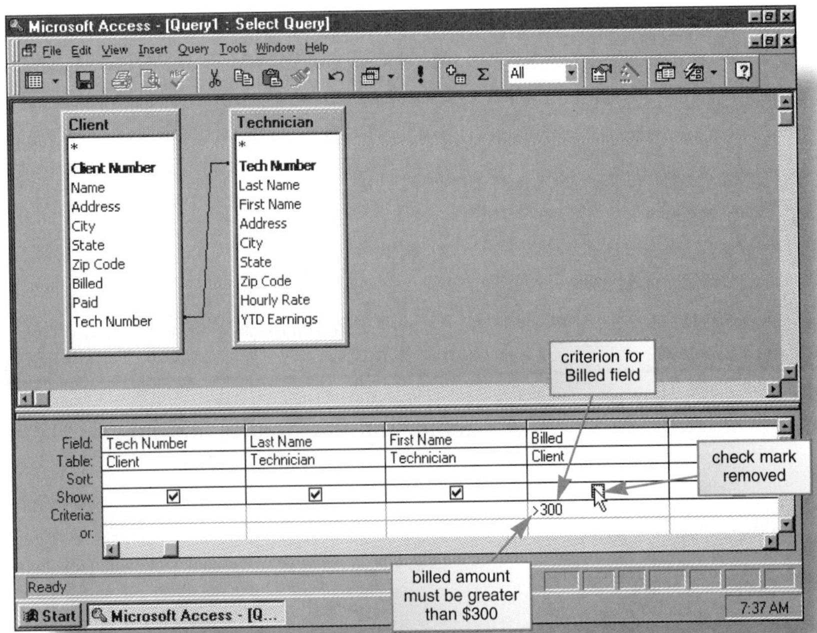

FIGURE 2-53

Run the query.

The results display (Figure 2-54). Only those clients with a billed amount greater than $300 appear in the result. The Billed field does not display.

clients with billed amount greater than $300

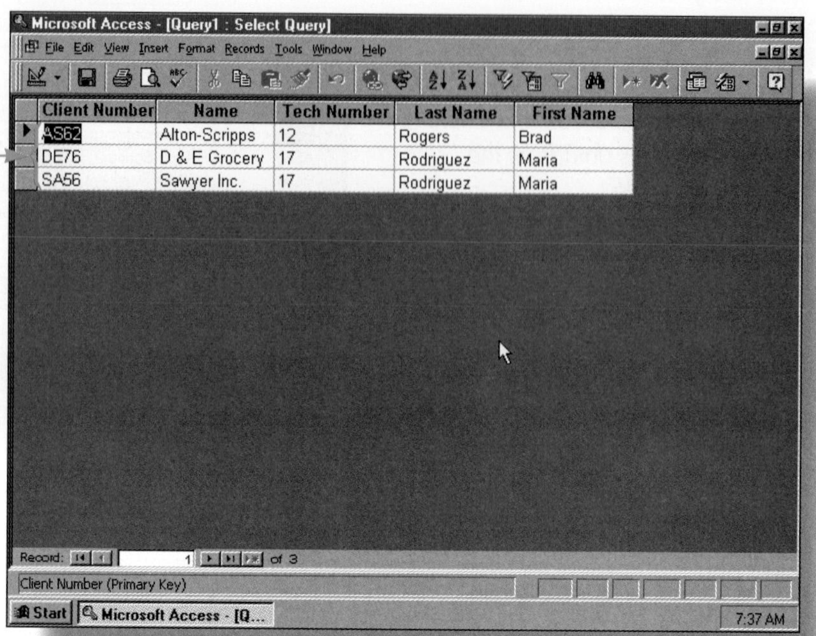

FIGURE 2-54

Using Computed Fields in a Query

More About Computed Fields

Because it is easy to compute values in a query, there is no need to store computed fields, also called calculated fields, in a database. There is no need, for example, to store the client amount (the billed amount minus the paid amount), because it can be calculated whenever it is required.

It is important to Pilotech Services to know the outstanding amount for each client; that is, the amount billed to the client minus the amount the client already has paid. This poses a problem because the Client table does not include a field for outstanding amount. You can compute it, however, because the outstanding amount is equal to the billed amount minus the paid amount. Such a field is called a **computed field**.

To include computed fields in queries, you enter a name for the computed field, a colon, and then the expression in one of the columns in the Field row. For the outstanding amount, for example, you will type Outstanding Amount:[Billed]-[Paid]. You can type this directly into the Field row. You will not be able to see the entire entry, however, because the Field row is not large enough. The preferred way is to select the column in the Field row, right-click to display the shortcut menu, and then click Zoom. The Zoom dialog box displays where you can type the expression.

You are not restricted to subtraction in computations. You can use addition (+), multiplication (*), or division (/). In addition, you can include parentheses in your computations to indicate which computations should be done first.

Perform the following steps to use a computed field to display the number, name, and outstanding amount of all clients.

Steps To Use a Computed Field in a Query

1 **Click the View button on the toolbar to return to the Query1 : Select Query window. Right-click any field in the Technician table field list.**

The shortcut menu displays (Figure 2-55).

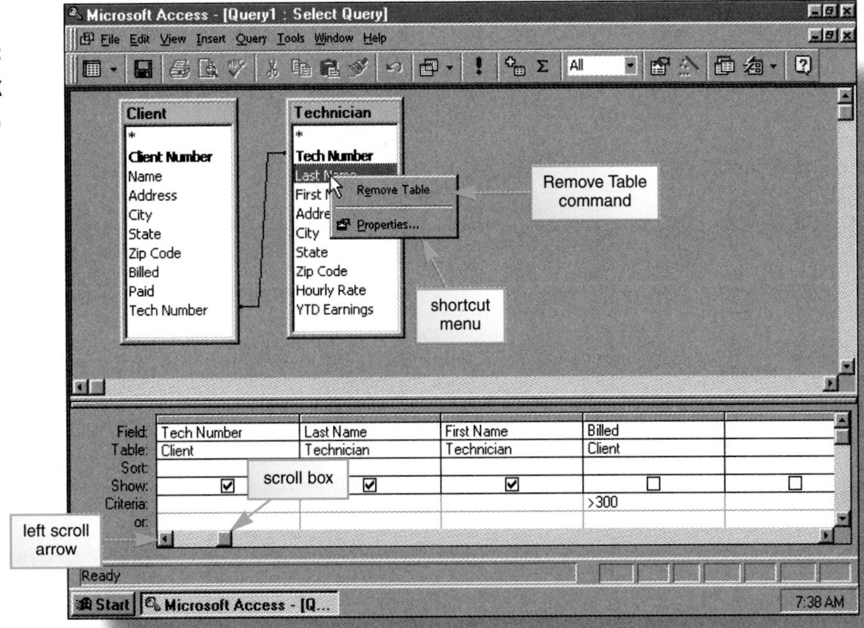

FIGURE 2-55

2 **Click Remove Table to remove the Technician table from the Query1 : Select Query window. On the Edit menu, click Clear Grid. Click the left scroll arrow so no space exists between the scroll arrow and the scroll box.**

3 **Include the Client Number and Name fields. Right-click the Field row in the third column in the design grid and then click Zoom on the shortcut menu. Type** `Outstanding Amount:[Billed]-[Paid]` **in the Zoom dialog box that displays.**

The Zoom dialog box displays (Figure 2-56). The expression you typed displays within the dialog box.

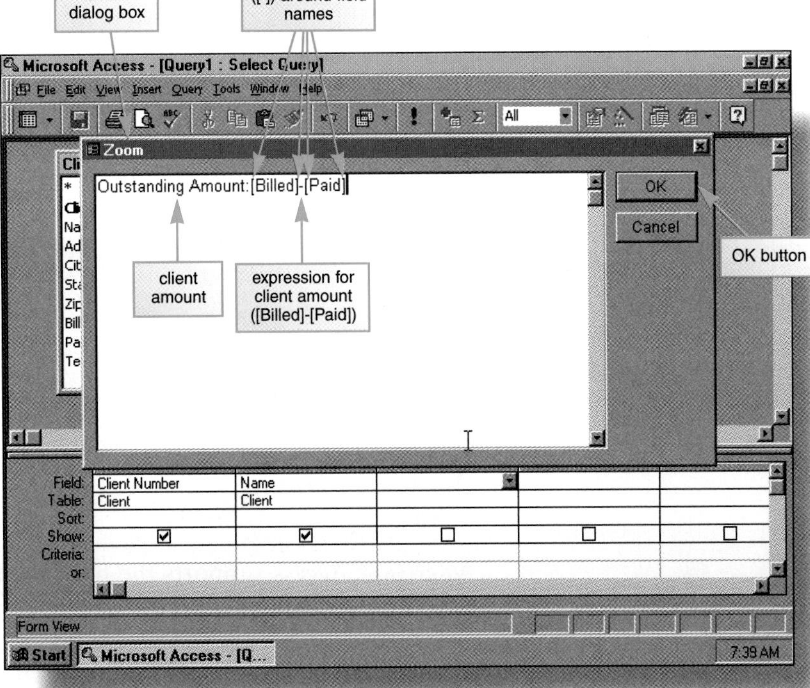

FIGURE 2-56

4 **Click the OK button.**

The Zoom dialog box no longer displays (Figure 2-57). A portion of the expression you entered displays in the third field within the design grid.

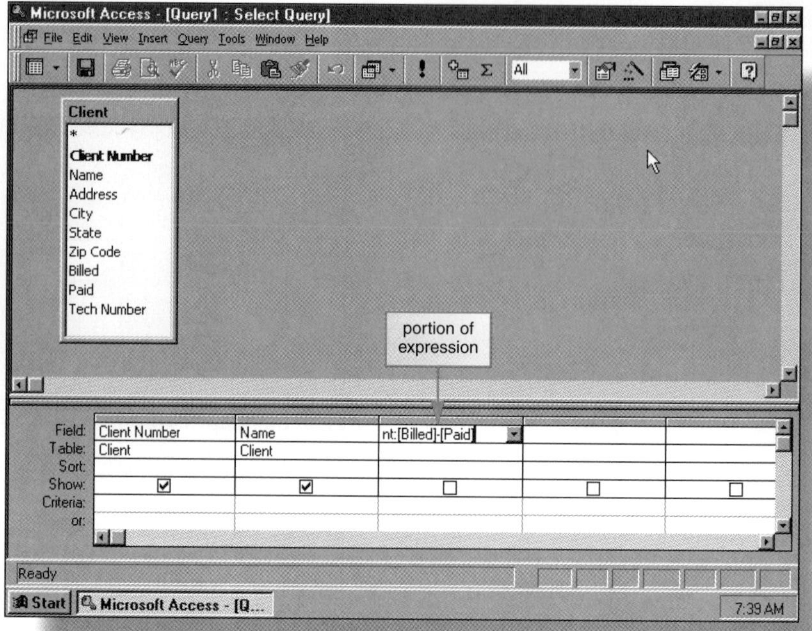

FIGURE 2-57

5 **Run the query.**

The results display (Figure 2-58). Microsoft Access has calculated and displayed the client amounts. The parentheses around $10.00 and $10.75 indicate they are negative numbers; that is, the clients possibly paid more than the amount that was billed.

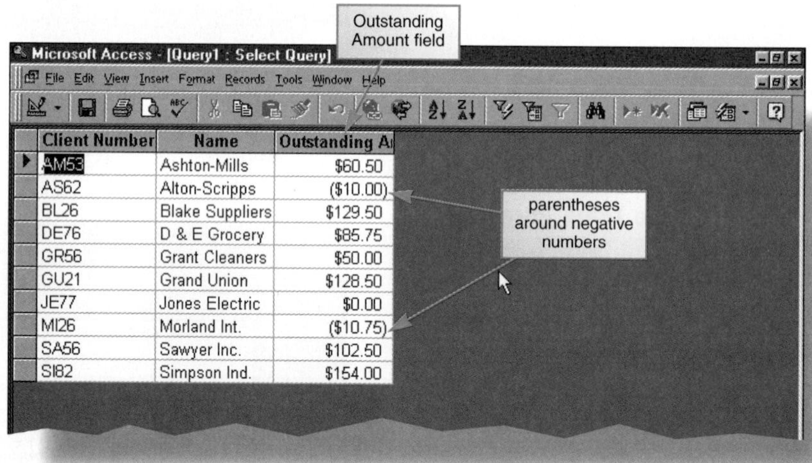

FIGURE 2-58

OtherWays

1. Press SHIFT+F2

Calculating Statistics

Microsoft Access supports the built-in **statistics**: COUNT, SUM, AVG (average), MAX (largest value), MIN (smallest value), STDEV (standard deviation), VAR (variance), FIRST, and LAST. To use any of these in a query, you include it in the Total row in the design grid. The Total row routinely does not appear in the grid. To include it, right-click the grid, and then click Totals on the shortcut menu.

The following example illustrates how you use these functions by calculating the average billed amount for all clients.

More About Calculating Statistics

Virtually all database management systems support the basic set of statistical calculations: sum, average, count, maximum, and minimum as part of their query feature. Some systems, including Access, add several more, such as standard deviation, variance, first, and last.

To Calculate Statistics

1 **Click the View button on the toolbar to return to the Query1 : Select Query window. On the Edit menu, click Clear Grid.**

2 **Right-click the grid.**

The shortcut menu displays (Figure 2-59).

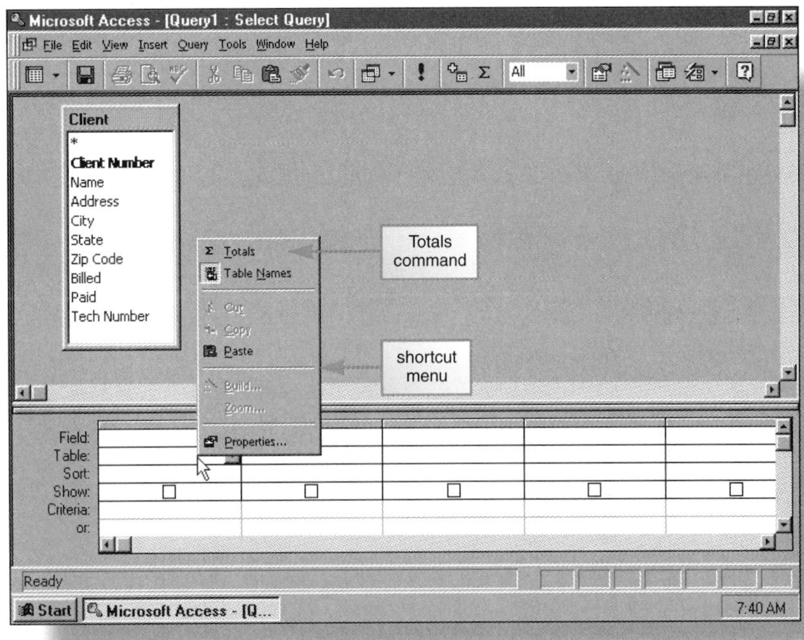

FIGURE 2-59

3 **Click Totals on the shortcut menu and then include the Billed field. Point to the Total row in the Billed column.**

The Total row now is included in the design grid (Figure 2-60). The Billed field is included, and the entry in the Total row is Group By. The mouse pointer, which has changed shape to an I-beam, is positioned on the Total row under the Billed field.

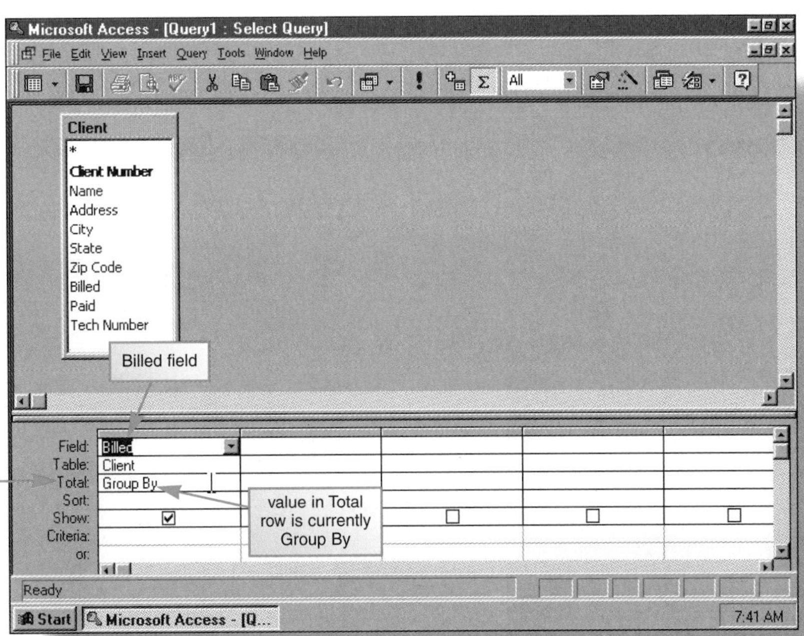

FIGURE 2-60

4 **Click the Total row in the Billed column, and then click the arrow that displays.**

The list of available selections displays (Figure 2-61).

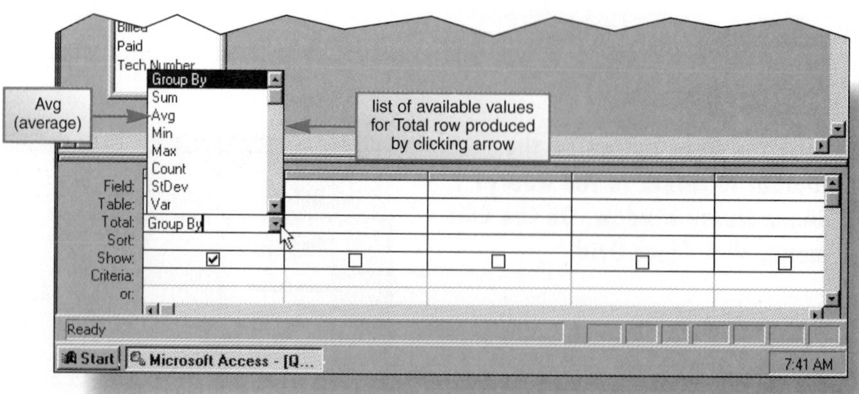

FIGURE 2-61

5 **Click Avg.**

Avg is selected (Figure 2-62).

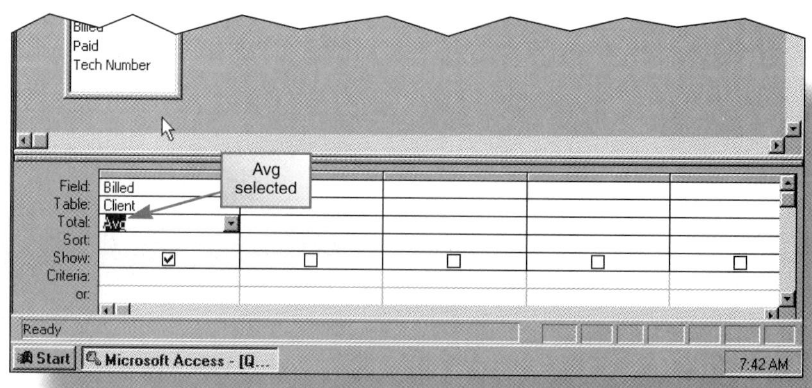

FIGURE 2-62

6 **Run the query.**

The result displays (Figure 2-63), showing the average billed amount for all clients.

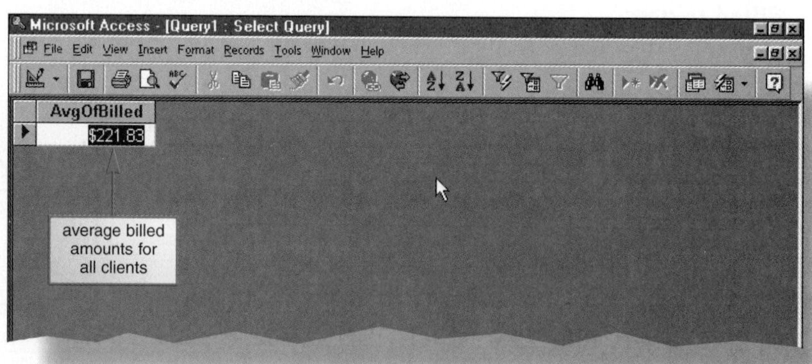

FIGURE 2-63

OtherWays

1. Click Totals button on toolbar
2. On View menu click Totals

Using Criteria in Calculating Statistics

Sometimes calculating statistics for all the records in the table is appropriate. In other cases, however, you will need to calculate the statistics for only those records that satisfy certain criteria. To enter a criterion in a field, first you select Where as the entry in the Total row for the field and then enter the criterion in the Criteria row. The following steps use this technique to calculate the average billed amount for clients of technician 12.

To Use Criteria in Calculating Statistics

1 **Click the View button on the toolbar to return to the Query1 : Select Query window.**

2 **Include the Tech Number field in the design grid. Next, produce the list of available options for the Total entry just as you did when you selected Avg for the Billed field. Use the vertical scroll bar to move through the options until the word, Where, displays.**

The list of available selections displays (Figure 2-64). The Group By entry in the Tech Number field may not be highlighted on your screen depending where you clicked in the Total row.

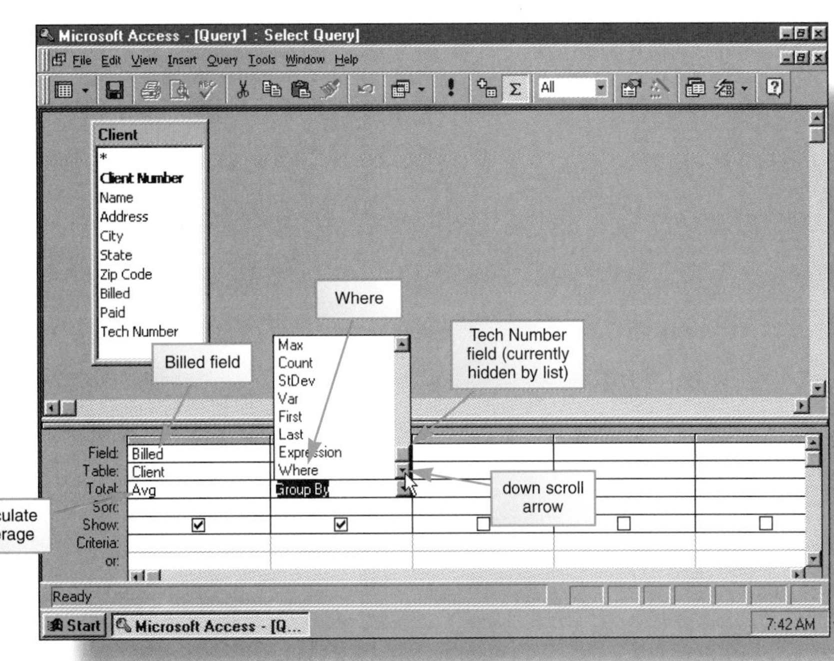

FIGURE 2-64

3 **Click Where. Then, type** 12 **as criterion for the Tech Number field.**

Where is selected as the entry in the Total row for the Tech Number field (Figure 2-65) and 12 is entered as the Criteria.

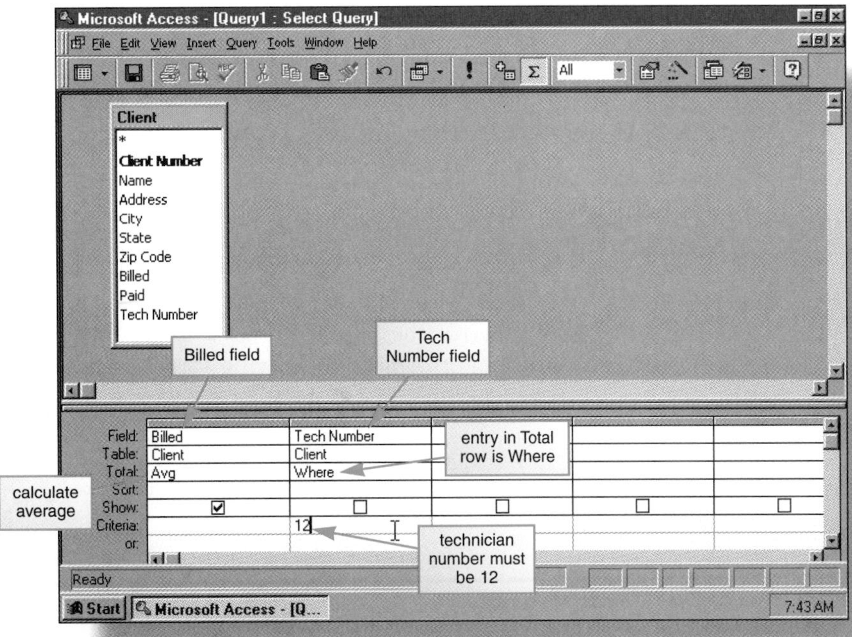

FIGURE 2-65

Run the query.

The result displays (Figure 2-66), giving the average billed amount for clients of technician 12.

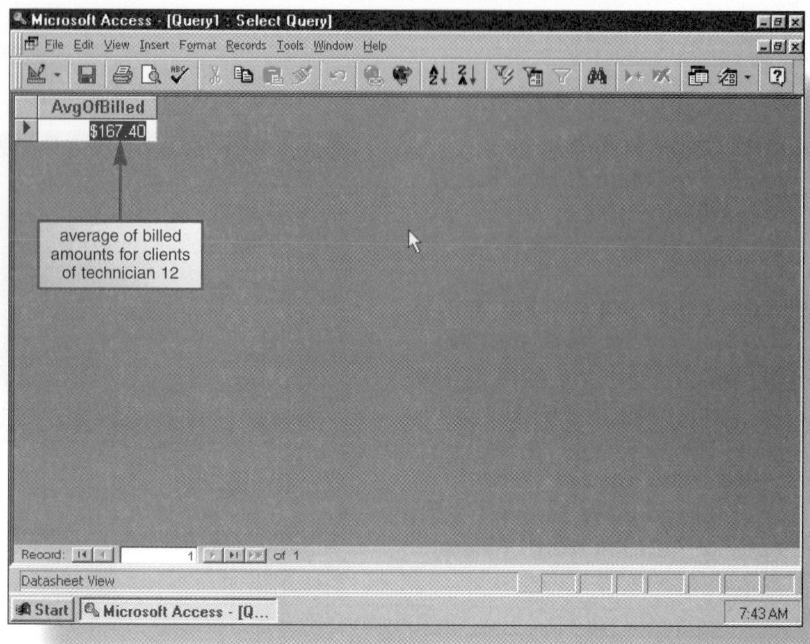

FIGURE 2-66

Grouping

Another way statistics often are used is in combination with grouping, in which statistics are calculated for groups of records. You may, for example, need to calculate the average billed amount for the clients of each technician. You will want the average for the clients of technician 11, the average for clients of technician 12, and so on.

Grouping means creating groups of records that share some common characteristic. In grouping by Tech Number, for example, the clients of technician 11 would form one group, the clients of technician 12 would be a second, and the clients of technician 17 form a third. The calculations then are made for each group. To indicate grouping in Access, select Group By as the entry in the Total row for the field to be used for grouping.

Perform the following steps to calculate the average billed amount for clients of each technician.

To Use Grouping

1 **Click the View button on the toolbar to return to the Query1 : Select Query window. On the Edit menu, click Clear Grid.**

2 **Include the Tech Number field. Include the Billed field, and then click Avg as the calculation.**

The Tech Number and Billed fields are included (Figure 2-67). The Total entry for the Tech Number field currently is Group By, which is correct; thus, it was not changed.

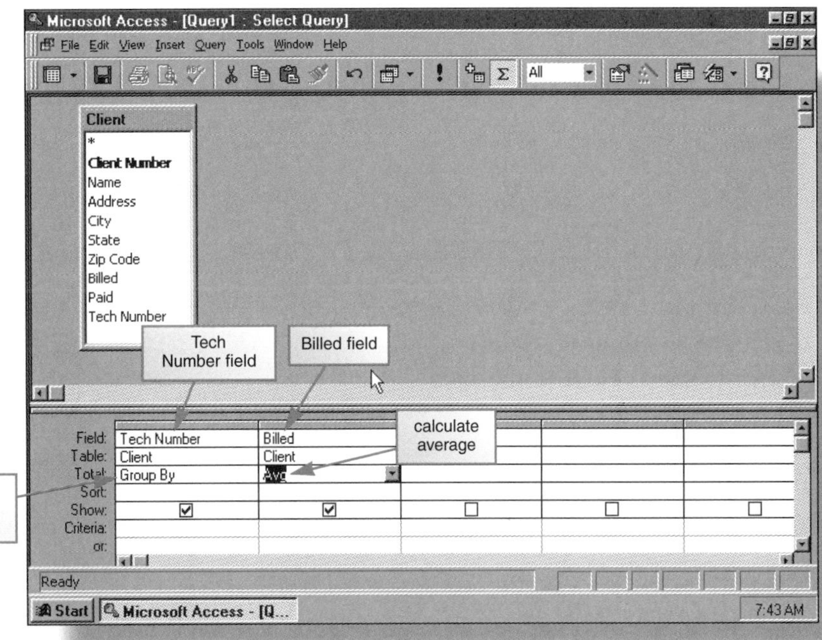

FIGURE 2-67

3 **Run the query.**

The result displays (Figure 2-68), showing each technician's number along with the average billed amount for the clients of that technician.

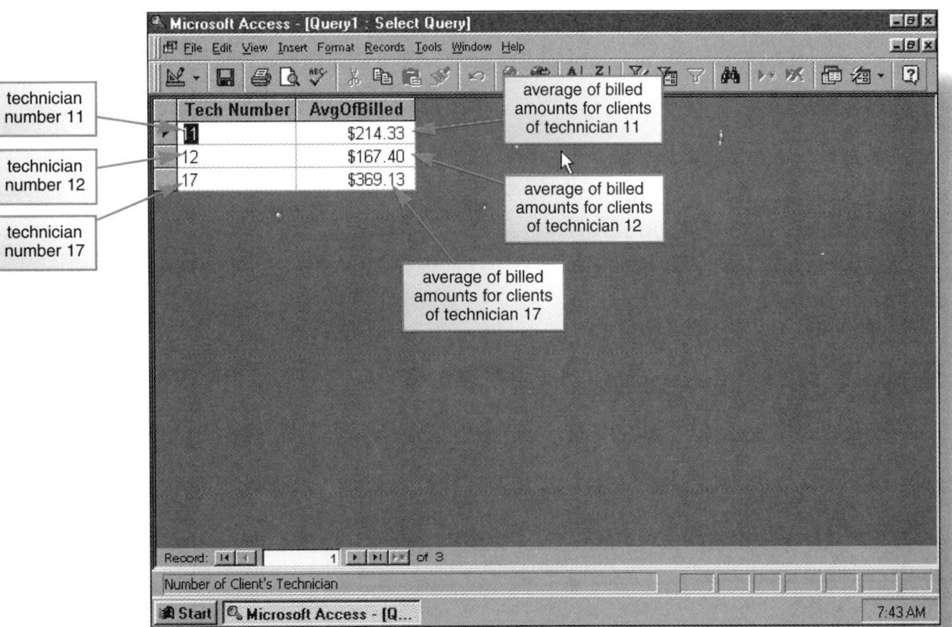

FIGURE 2-68

Saving a Query

In many cases, you will construct a query you will want to use again. By **saving the query**, you will eliminate the need to repeat all your entries. The following steps illustrate the process by saving the query you just have created and assigning it the name Average Billed Amount by Technician.

To Save a Query

1. **Return to the Query1 : Select Query window. Point to the Save button (Figure 2-69).**

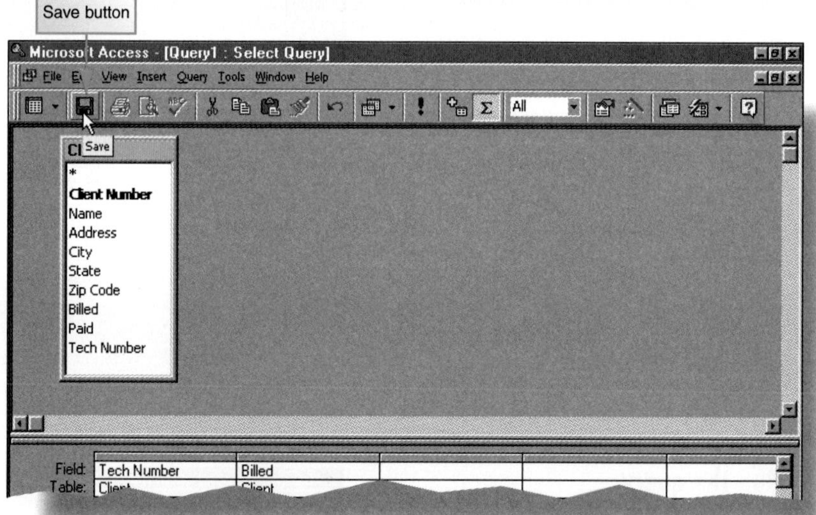

FIGURE 2-69

2. **Click the Save button. Type** `Average Billed Amount by Technician` **and then point to the OK button.**

   The Save As dialog box displays with the query name you typed (Figure 2-70).

3. **Click the OK button to save the query, and then close the query by clicking the Query window's Close button.**

   Access saves the query and closes the Query1 : Select Query window.

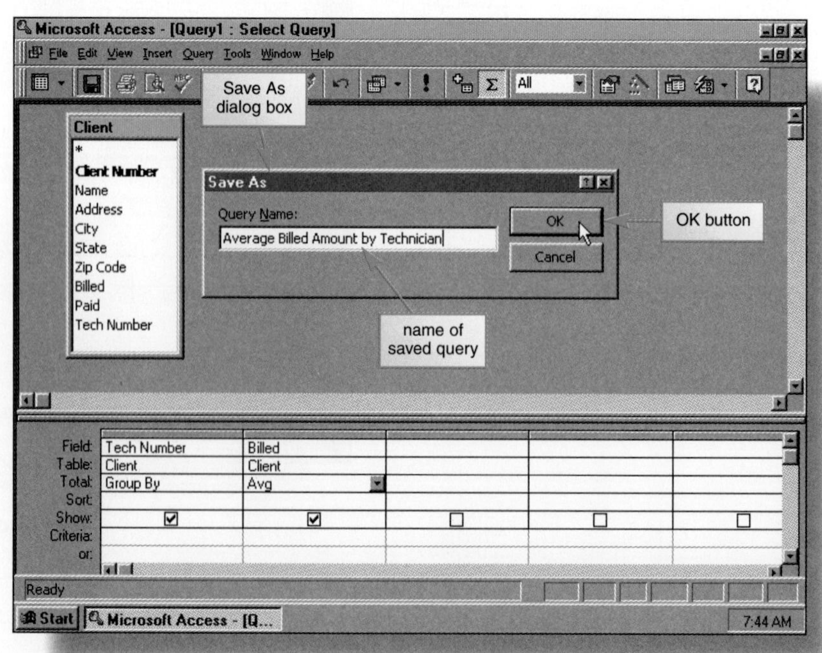

FIGURE 2-70

Other Ways

1. On File menu click Save
2. Press CTRL+S

Once you have saved a query, you can use it at any time in the future by opening it. To open a saved query, click the Queries tab in the Database window, right-click the query, and then click Open on the shortcut menu (Figure 2-71).

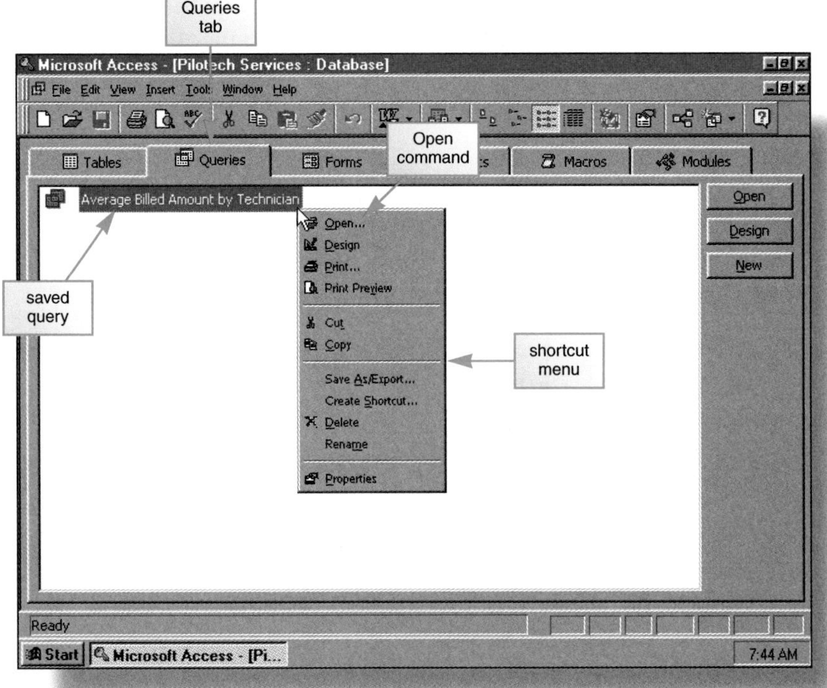

FIGURE 2-71

The query is run against the current database. Thus, if changes have been made to the data since the last time you ran it, the results of the query may be different.

Closing a Database

The following step closes the database by closing its Database window.

TO CLOSE A DATABASE

Step 1: Click the Close button for the Pilotech Services : Database window.

More *About* **Saved Queries**

Forms and reports can be based on either tables or saved queries. To create a report or form based on a query, click the Query tab, select the query, click the New Object button arrow, and then click the appropriate command (Report or Form). From that point on the process is the same as for a table.

Project Summary

Project 2 introduced you to querying a database using Access. You created and ran queries for Pilotech Services. You used various types of criteria in these queries. You joined tables in some of the queries. Some Pilotech Services queries used calculated fields and statistics. Finally, you saved one of the queries for future use.

What You Should Know

Having completed this project, you now should be able to perform the following tasks:

- Calculate Statistics *(A 2.39)*
- Clear a Query *(A 2.17)*
- Close a Database *(A 2.45)*
- Close the Query *(A 2.15)*
- Create a Query *(A 2.7)*
- Include All Fields in a Query *(A 2.16)*
- Include Fields in the Design Grid *(A 2.11)*
- Join Tables *(A 2.33)*
- Omit Duplicates *(A 2.30)*
- Open a Database *(A 2.7)*
- Print the Results of a Query *(A 2.13)*
- Restrict the Records in a Join *(A 2.35)*
- Return to the Select Query Window *(A 2.14)*
- Run the Query *(A 2.12)*
- Save a Query *(A 2.44)*
- Sort Data in a Query *(A 2.27)*
- Sort on Multiple Keys *(A 2.29)*
- Use a Comparison Operator in a Criterion *(A 2.23)*
- Use a Compound Criterion Involving AND *(A 2.25)*
- Use a Compound Criterion Involving OR *(A 2.26)*
- Use a Computed Field in a Query *(A 2.37)*
- Use a Number in a Criterion *(A 2.22)*
- Use a Wildcard *(A 2.20)*
- Use Criteria for a Field Not Included in the Results *(A 2.21)*
- Use Criteria in Calculating Statistics *(A 2.41)*
- Use Grouping *(A 2.43)*
- Use Text Data in a Criterion *(A 2.18)*

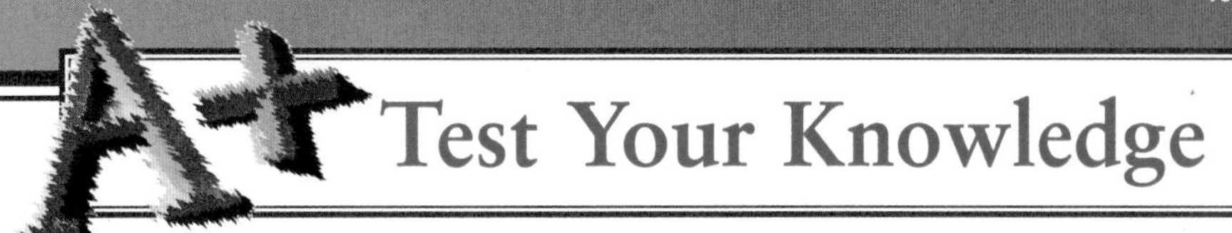

Test Your Knowledge

1 True/False

Instructions: Circle T if the statement is true or F if the statement is false.

T F 1. To include all the fields in a record in a query, click the word ALL that appears at the top of the field list.

T F 2. To create a compound criterion using OR, enter each criterion on a separate line.

T F 3. To create a compound criterion using AND, type the word, INTERSECT, before the second criterion.

T F 4. To create a criterion involving Equals, you do not need to type the equal sign (=).

T F 5. When you enter a criteria for a particular field, that field must appear in the results of the query.

T F 6. To find all clients whose billed amount is $100 or more, type >=100 as the criterion for the Billed field.

T F 7. To clear all the entries in a design grid, on the Query menu, click Clear Grid.

T F 8. When you sort a query on more than one key, the major sort key must appear to the right of the minor sort key.

T F 9. To omit duplicates from a query, use the Properties command and specify Unique Values Only.

T F 10. The wildcard symbols available for use in a query are ? and *.

2 Multiple Choice

Instructions: Circle the correct response.

1. To list only certain records in a table, use a(n) ____________.
   a. list
   b. answer
   c. question
   d. query
2. To find all clients whose billed amount is $100 or more, type ____________ as the criteria for the Billed field.
   a. >= $100.00
   b. >=100
   c. =>$100.00
   d. =>100
3. To clear all the entries in a design grid, on the ____________ menu, click Clear Grid.
   a. Edit
   b. File
   c. Query
   d. View

(continued)

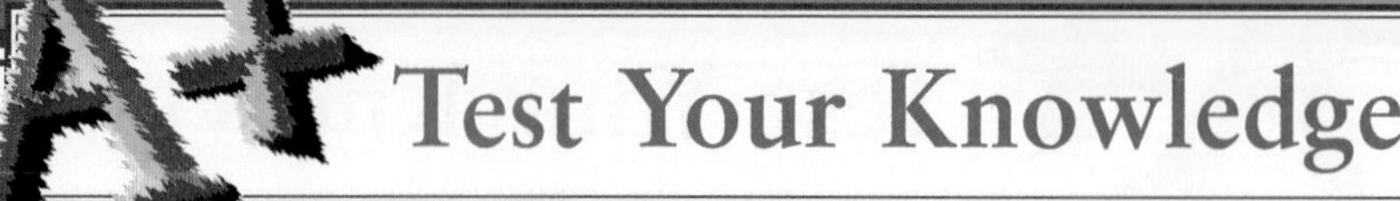

Test Your Knowledge

Multiple Choice *(continued)*

4. The wildcard symbols available for use in a query are the __________ and the __________.
   a. double period (..), asterisk (*)
   b. question mark (?), asterisk (*)
   c. double period (..), at symbol (@)
   d. question mark (?), ampersand (&)
5. Equal to (=), less than (<), and greater than (>) are examples of __________.
   a. criteria
   b. values
   c. comparison operators
   d. compound criteria
6. When two or more criteria are connected with AND or OR, the result is called a __________.
   a. simple criterion
   b. pattern criterion
   c. character criterion
   d. compound criterion
7. To add an additional table to a query, click __________ on the shortcut menu for the Select Query window.
   a. Join Table
   b. Show Table
   c. Add Table
   d. Include Table
8. Use a query to __________ tables; that is, find records in two tables that have identical values in matching fields.
   a. merge
   b. match
   c. combine
   d. join
9. To remove a table from a query, right-click any field in the field list for the table and then click __________ on the shortcut menu.
   a. Remove Table
   b. Delete Table
   c. Clear Table
   d. Erase Table
10. To add a Total row to a design grid, click __________ on the shortcut menu for the Select Query window.
    a. Aggregates
    b. Functions
    c. Statistics
    d. Totals

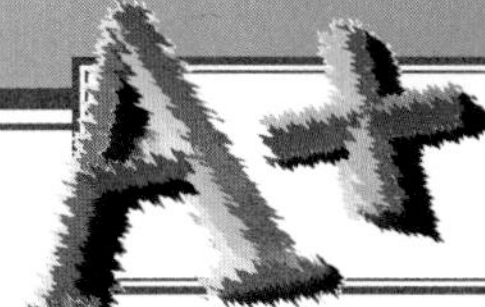

Test Your Knowledge

3 Understanding the Select Query Window

Instructions: In Figure 2-72, arrows point to the major components of the Select Query window. Identify the various parts of the Query window in the spaces provided.

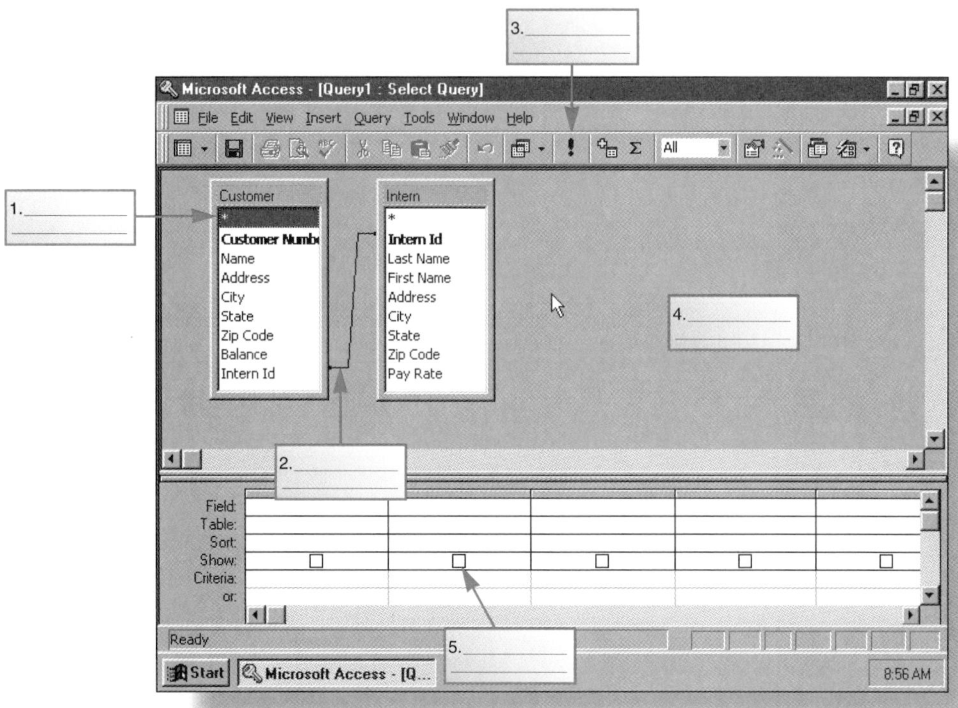

FIGURE 2-72

4 Understanding Statistics

Instructions: Figure 2-73 on the next page shows a created query using statistics for the Customer table and Figure 2-74 on the next page lists the contents of the Customer table. List the answer to this query in the spaces provided.

(continued)

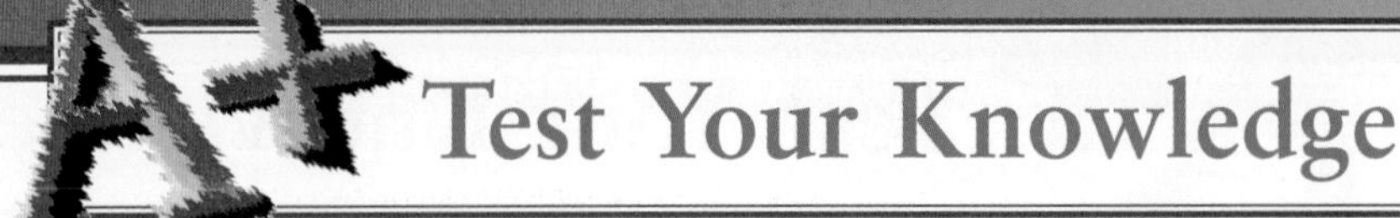

Test Your Knowledge

Understanding Statistics *(continued)*

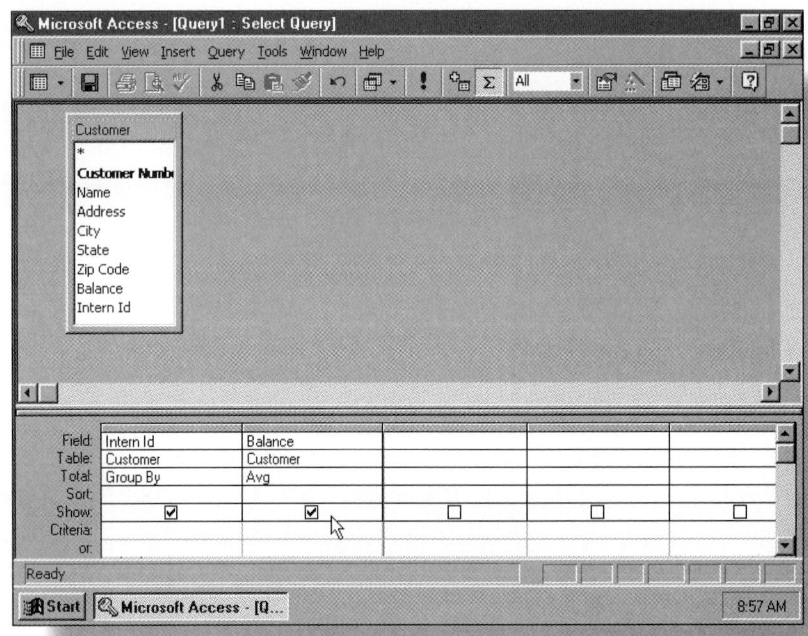

FIGURE 2-73

Data for Customer table

CUSTOMER NUMBER	NAME	ADDRESS	CITY	STATE	ZIP CODE	BALANCE	INTERN ID
AS36	Asterman Ind.	200 Bard	Howden	MO	59444	$85.00	102
AU54	Author Books	142 Birchwood	Howden	MO	59445	$50.00	109
BI92	Bike Shop	433 Chester	Howden	MO	59441	$40.00	109
CI76	Cinderton Co.	73 Fleming	Dorchester	IL	57342	$0.00	113
CJ16	CJ's Music	277 Fordham	Dorchester	IL	57342	$105.00	102
JO62	Jordan Diner	250 Bard	Howden	MO	59444	$74.00	109
KL55	Klingon Toys	215 Scott	Evansville	MO	59335	$115.00	105
ME71	Meat & Cleaver	543 Fleming	Dorchester	IL	57342	$138.00	102
MO13	Moore Foods	876 Grove	Evansville	MO	59335	$0.00	113
RO32	Royal Mfg Co.	954 Cline	Evansville	MO	59331	$93.00	109

FIGURE 2-74

Use Help

1 Reviewing Project Activities

Instructions: Perform the following tasks using a computer.

1. Start Access.
2. If the Office Assistant is on your screen, then click it to display its balloon. If the Office Assistant is not on your screen, click the Office Assistant button on the toolbar.
3. Type `working with queries` in the What would you like to do? text box. Click the Search button. Click Queries: What they are and how they work.
4. Read the Help information. Use the page number links in the upper-left corner of the screen to move to the next Help windows. A total of three Help windows will display. When you finish reading the Help information, click the Close button.
5. Click the Office Assistant. Type `perform calculations in a query` in the What would you like to do? text box. Click the Search button. Click Ways to perform calculations in queries. Read and print the Help information. Hand in the printout to your instructor. Click the Help Topics button.
6. If necessary, click the Index tab. Type `wildcard` in the top text box labeled 1, and then double-click wildcard characters in the list box labeled 2. Double-click the Search for partial or matching values using wildcard characters topics. When the Help information displays, read it. Next, right-click within the box, and then click Print Topic. Hand in the printout to your instructor. Click the Help Topics button to return to the Help Topics: Microsoft Access 97 dialog box.
7. Click the Find tab. Type `sorting` in the top text box labeled 1. Double-click The records the query retrieves are in the wrong order in the bottom box labeled 3. When the Help information displays, read it, ready the printer, right-click, and click Print Topic. Hand in the printout to your instructor. Click the Close button.

2 Expanding on the Basics

Instructions: Use Access Help to learn about the topics listed below. If you cannot print the Help information, then answer the question on your own paper.

1. Using the Office Assistant, answer the following questions:
   a. How do you insert a field between other fields in the design grid of a query?
   b. How do you remove a field from the design grid?
   c. How do you change a field name in a query?
   d. When you use the asterisk (*) to select all fields, how do you specify criteria for fields?
   e. How do you insert a Criteria row in the design grid?
2. Using the word, format, and the Find sheet in the Help Topics: Microsoft Access 97 dialog box, display and print information on defining the data display format for a field in query Design view. Then, answer the following questions:
   a. How can you display a field's property sheet using the menu bar?
   b. How do the Regional Settings on the Windows Control Panel affect the formats in a query?
3. Using the word, OR, and the Index sheet in the Help Topics: Microsoft Access 97 dialog box, display and then print information about ways to use multiple criteria in a query. Then answer the following questions:
   a. How do you enter criteria to OR two values in one field?
   b. How do you enter criteria to AND two values in one field?
   c. How do you enter criteria to OR and AND in three fields?
4. Use the Office Assistant to display and print information on searching for a range of values.

Apply Your Knowledge

1 Querying the Green Thumb Database

Instructions: Start Access. Open the Green Thumb database from the Access folder on the Data Disk that accompanies this book. Perform the following tasks.

1. Create a new query for the Customer table.
2. Add the Customer Number, Name, and Balance fields to the design grid as shown in Figure 2-75.
3. Restrict retrieval to only those records where the balance is greater than $100.
4. Run the query and print the results.
5. Return to the Select Query window and clear the grid.
6. Add the Customer Number, Name, City, Balance, and Intern Id fields to the design grid.
7. Restrict retrieval to only those records where the Intern Id is either 109 or 113.
8. Sort the records in order by Balance (descending) within City (ascending).
9. Run the query and print the results.
10. Return to the Select Query window and clear the grid.
11. Join the Customer and Intern tables. Add the Customer Number, Name, and Intern Id fields from the Customer table and the Last Name and First Name fields from the Intern table.
12. Sort the records in ascending order by Intern Id.
13. Run the query and print the results.

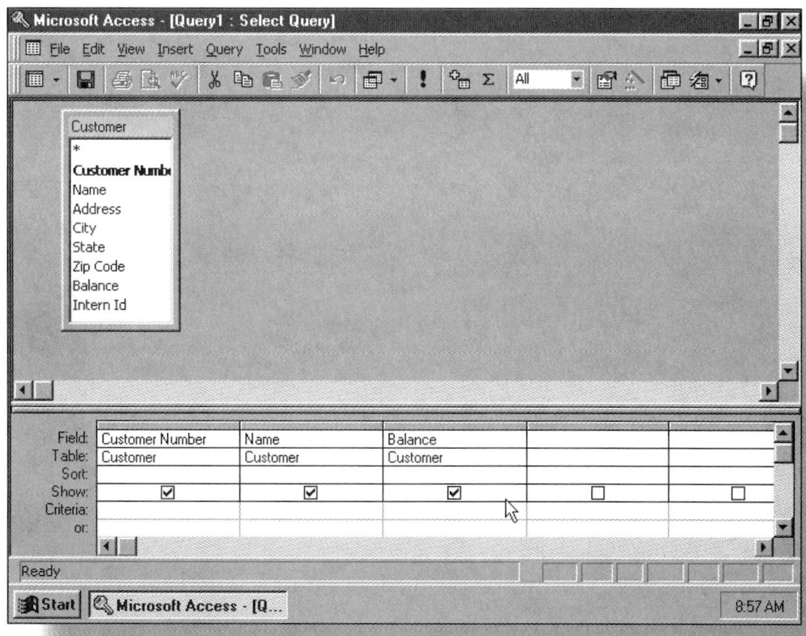

FIGURE 2-75

1 Querying the Museum Mercantile Database

Problem: The volunteers who staff Museum Mercantile have determined a number of questions they want the database management system to answer. You must obtain answers to the questions posed by the volunteers.

Instructions: Use the database created in the In the Lab 1 of Project 1 for this assignment. Perform the following tasks.

1. Open the Museum Mercantile database and create a new query for the Product table.
2. Display and print the Product Id, Description, and Selling Price for all records in the table as shown in Figure 2-76.
3. Display all fields and print all the records in the table.
4. Display and print the Product Id, Description, Cost, and Vendor Code for all products where the Vendor Code is MS.
5. Display and print the Product Id and Description for all products where the Description begins with the letters, Wi.
6. Display and print the Product Id, Description, and Vendor Code for all products that cost more than $20.
7. Display and print the Product Id and Description for all products that have a Selling Price of $5 or less.
8. Display and print all fields for those products that cost more than $10 and where the number of units on hand is less than 10.
9. Display and print all fields for those products that have a Vendor Code of WW or have a Selling Price less than $10.
10. Join the Product table and the Vendor table. Display the Product Id, Description, Cost, Name, and Telephone Number fields. Run the query and print the results.
11. Restrict the records retrieved in task 10 above to only those products where the number of units on hand is less than 10. Display and print the results.
12. Remove the Vendor table and clear the design grid.
13. Include the Product Id and Description in the design grid. Compute the on-hand value (on hand * cost) for all records in the table. Display and print the results.
14. Display and print the average selling price of all products.
15. Display and print the average selling price of products grouped by Vendor Code.
16. Join the Product and Vendor tables. Include the Vendor Code and Name fields from the Vendor table. Include the Product Id, Description, Cost, and On Hand fields from the Product table. Save the query as Vendors and Products. Run the query and print the results.

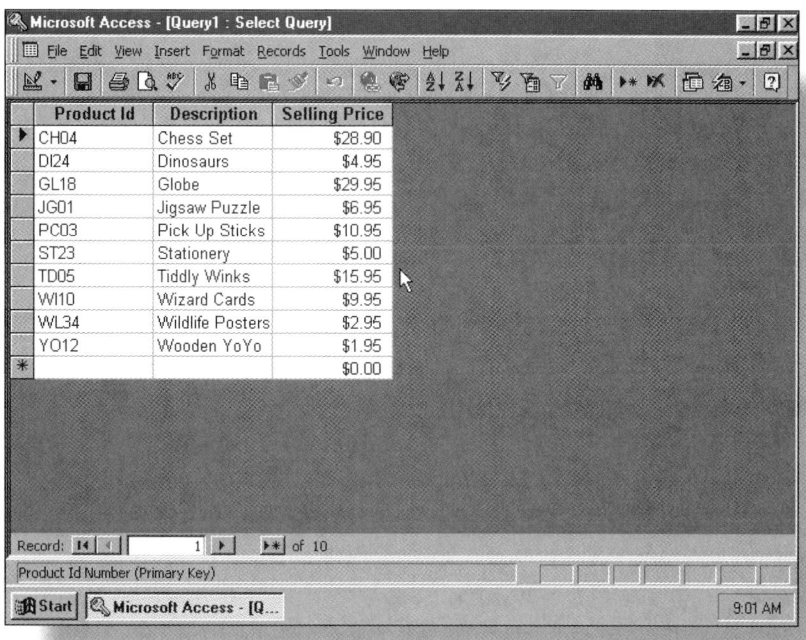

Product Id	Description	Selling Price
CH04	Chess Set	$28.90
DI24	Dinosaurs	$4.95
GL18	Globe	$29.95
JG01	Jigsaw Puzzle	$6.95
PC03	Pick Up Sticks	$10.95
ST23	Stationery	$5.00
TD05	Tiddly Winks	$15.95
WI10	Wizard Cards	$9.95
WL34	Wildlife Posters	$2.95
YO12	Wooden YoYo	$1.95
		$0.00

FIGURE 2-76

2 Querying the City Telephone System Database

Problem: The telephone manager has determined a number of questions that she wants the database management system to answer. You must obtain answers to the questions posed by the telephone manager.

Instructions: Use the database created in the In the Lab 2 of Project 1 for this assignment. Perform the following tasks.

1. Open the City Telephone System database and create a new query for the User table.
2. Display and print the User Id, Last Name, First Name, Phone Ext, and Office for all the records in the table as shown in Figure 2-77 on the next page.
3. Display all fields and print all the records in the table.
4. Display and print the User Id, First Name, Last Name, Basic Charge, and Extra Charges for all users in the department with the code of PLN.
5. Display and print the User Id, First Name, Last Name, and Phone Ext for all users whose basic charge is $13 per month.
6. Display and print the User Id, First Name, Last Name, and Extra Charges for all users in the department with a code ITD who have Extra Charges greater than $20. List the records in descending order by Extra Charges.

(continued)

Querying the City Telephone System Database *(continued)*

7. Display and print the User Id, First Name, Last Name, and Extra Charges for all users who have extra charges greater than $25 and are in either the Assessment (APV) or Planning (PLN) department. (*Hint*: Use information from Use Help 2 on page A 2.52 to solve this problem.)
8. Display and print the Basic Charge in ascending order. List each Basic Charge only once.
9. Join the User table and the Department table. Display and print the User Id, Last Name, First Name, Basic Charge, Extra Charges, and Name of the department.
10. Restrict the records retrieved in task 10 above to only those users who have extra charges greater than $20.
11. Remove the Department table and clear the design grid.
12. Include the User Id, First Name, Last Name, Basic Charge, and Extra Charges fields in the design grid. Compute the total bill for each user (Basic Charge + Extra Charges). Display and print the results.
13. Display and print the average extra charges.
14. Display and print the highest extra charge.
15. Display and print the total extra charges for each department.
16. Join the User and Department tables. Include the Department Name, User Id, Last Name, First Name, Phone Ext, Basic Charge, and Extra Charges fields. Save the query as Departments and Users. Run the query and print the results.

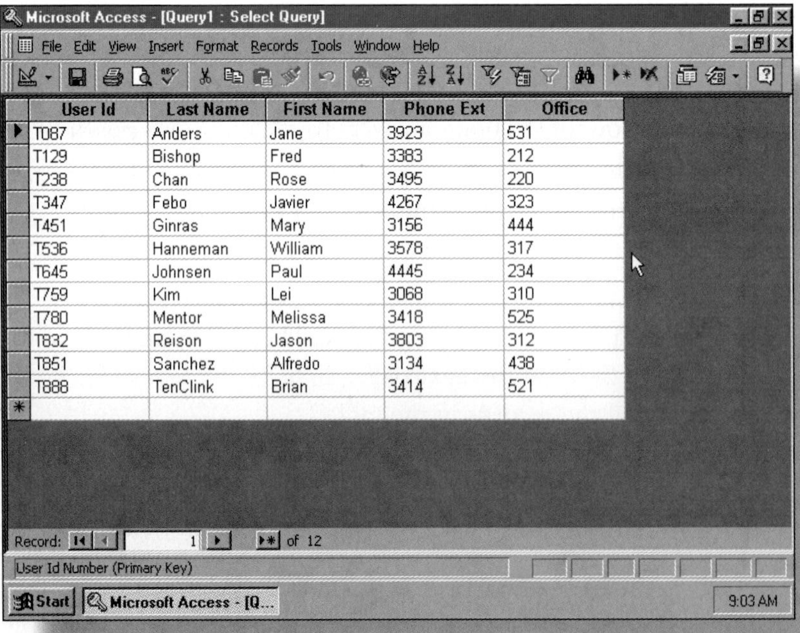

User Id	Last Name	First Name	Phone Ext	Office
T087	Anders	Jane	3923	531
T129	Bishop	Fred	3383	212
T238	Chan	Rose	3495	220
T347	Febo	Javier	4267	323
T451	Ginras	Mary	3156	444
T536	Hanneman	William	3578	317
T645	Johnsen	Paul	4445	234
T759	Kim	Lei	3068	310
T780	Mentor	Melissa	3418	525
T832	Reison	Jason	3803	312
T851	Sanchez	Alfredo	3134	438
T888	TenClink	Brian	3414	521

FIGURE 2-77

In the Lab

3 Querying the City Scene Database

Problem: The managing editor of the *City Scene* magazine has determined a number of questions that he wants the database management system to answer. You must obtain answers to the questions posed by the managing editor.

Instructions: Use the database created in the In the Lab 3 of Project 1 for this assignment. Perform the following tasks.

1. Open the City Scene database and create a new query for the Advertiser table.
2. Display and print the Advertiser Number, Name, Balance, and Amount Paid for all the records in the table as shown in Figure 2-78 on the next page.
3. Display and print the Advertiser Number, Name, and Balance for all advertisers where the Ad Rep Number is 19.
4. Display and print the Advertiser Number, Name, and Balance for all advertisers where the Balance is greater than $100.
5. Display and print the Advertiser Number, Name, and Amount Paid for all advertisers where the Ad Rep Number is 16 and the Amount Paid is greater than $250.
6. Display and print the Advertiser Number and Name of all advertisers where the Name begins with C.
7. Display and print the Advertiser Number, Name, and Balance for all advertisers where the Ad Rep Number is 19 or the Balance is less than $100.
8. Include the Advertiser Number, Name, City, and State in the design grid. Sort the records in ascending order by City within State. Display and print the results. The City field should display in the result to the left of the State field. (*Hint*: Use information from Use Help 1 on page A 2.51.)
9. Display and print the cities in ascending order. Each city should display only once.
10. Display and print the Advertiser Number, Name, Balance, and Amount Paid fields from the Advertiser table and the First Name, Last Name, and Comm Rate fields from the Ad Rep table.
11. Restrict the records retrieved in task 10 above to only those advertisers that are in WA. Display and print the results.
12. Clear the design grid and add the Last Name, First Name, and Comm Rate fields from the Ad Rep table to the grid. Add the Amount Paid field from the Advertiser table. Compute the Commission (Amount Paid * Comm Rate) for the Ad Rep table. Sort the records in ascending order by Last Name and format Commission as currency. (*Hint*: Use information from Use Help 2 on page A 2.52 to solve this problem.) Run the query and print the results.
13. Display and print the following statistics: the total balance and amount paid for all advertisers; the total balance for advertisers of ad rep 16; and the total amount paid for each ad rep.
14. Display and print the Ad Rep Number, Last Name, First Name, Advertiser Number, Name, Balance, and Amount Paid. Save the query as Ad Reps and Advertisers.

(continued)

Querying the City Scene Database *(continued)*

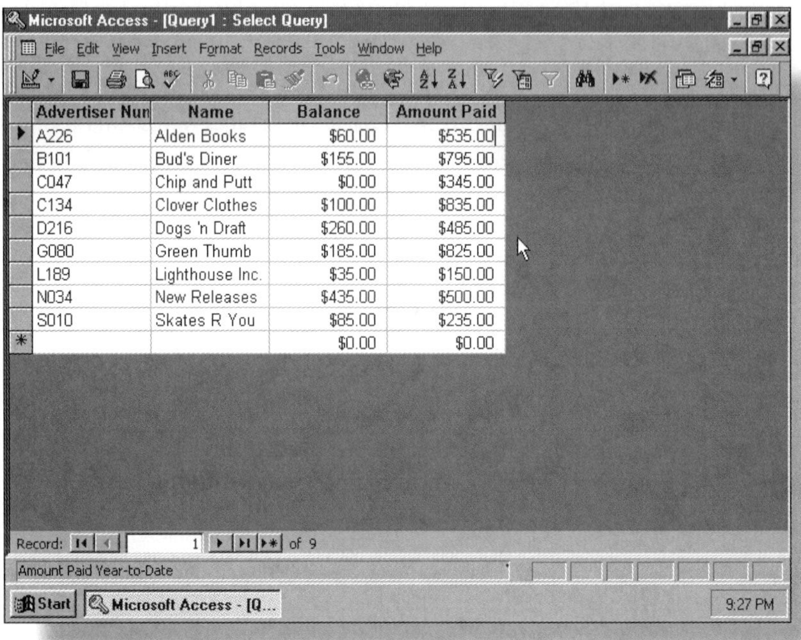

Advertiser Num	Name	Balance	Amount Paid
A226	Alden Books	$60.00	$535.00
B101	Bud's Diner	$155.00	$795.00
C047	Chip and Putt	$0.00	$345.00
C134	Clover Clothes	$100.00	$835.00
D216	Dogs 'n Draft	$260.00	$485.00
G080	Green Thumb	$185.00	$825.00
L189	Lighthouse Inc.	$35.00	$150.00
N034	New Releases	$435.00	$500.00
S010	Skates R You	$85.00	$235.00
*		$0.00	$0.00

FIGURE 2-78

The difficulty of these case studies varies: ◗ are the least difficult; ◗◗ are more difficult; and ◗◗◗ are the most difficult.

1 ◗ Use the textbook database created in Case Study 1 of Project 1 for this assignment. Perform the following: (a) The textbook cooperative receives a call asking if anyone is selling a book for Eng 150. Display and print the sellers' names and telephone numbers and their asking prices for books available for that course. (b) Karen Sing asks which books she has submitted. Display and print the titles, authors, and courses of her books. (c) Several nursing students call to ask which textbooks from that department are available. Display and print the titles, authors, and courses of the nursing books. (d) Display and print the titles, authors, and prices of books listed for less than $20. (e) Display and print the titles and course numbers for books in excellent condition.

Cases and Places

2 ◗ Use the restaurant database created in Case Study 2 of Project 1 for this assignment. You decide to survey the campus community to get some marketing ideas for your meal delivery service. You want to know the students' restaurant habits. Perform the following: (a) It is 10:30 p.m. and a student has a craving for pizza. Display and print the names and telephone numbers of all Italian restaurants open that will deliver the order. (b) Students are cramming for an exam at 2:00 a.m. and would settle for any type of food. Display and print the names, telephone numbers, addresses, and closing times of all restaurants that are open. (c) A student's last class on Wednesday ends at 3:50 p.m., and he wants to pick up some food to take home to eat before he leaves for work. Display and print the names, addresses, and opening times of all restaurants that open before 5:00 p.m. (d) Payday for student employees is Friday, and they are short on cash at midweek. Display and print the names, addresses, telephone numbers, and food types of all restaurants that have specials on Wednesday or Thursday. (e) A group of students decides to meet for lunch. Display and print the names, addresses, telephone numbers, and opening times of all restaurants that open before noon.

3 ◗◗ Use the movie collection database created in Case Study 3 of Project 1 for this assignment. Perform the following: (a) Display and print the movie titles in ascending order, along with the two actors and year produced. (b) You have less than two hours to show a movie to the nursing home residents. Display and print the movie titles and running times that would fit this time constraint. (c) Display and print the movie titles starring John Wayne. (d) Display and print the movie titles starring Jean Arthur. (e) The nursing home is having a comedy night. Display and print the movies starring Abbott and Costello. (f) Display and print the movie titles and leading actors of films rated more than two stars. (g) It's Grandparents' Weekend at the nursing home. Display and print the movies produced in the 1930s and 1940s.

4 ◗◗ The American Heart Association recommends a maximum of two, three-ounce cooked servings of lean meat, or six ounces total daily. A three-ounce serving is the size of a woman's palm. Use the nutritional content database created in Case Study 4 of Project 1 for this assignment. Perform the following: (a) Display and print the cuts of beef with less than 70 milligrams of cholesterol in one, three-ounce serving. (b) Display and print the cuts of beef with more than 160 calories in a three-ounce serving. (c) For your research project, you are to consume less than 20 grams of fat daily. During the day, you have eaten food with a total fat gram content of 15. Display and print the cuts of beef that would be within the project's requirements.

Cases and Places

5 ▶▶▶ Use the product comparison database created in Case Study 5 of Project 1 for this assignment. Display and print the following: (a) The six specific items in ascending order, along with sizes and prices for the dairy items at the convenience, grocery, and discount stores. (b) The six specific items in ascending order, along with sizes and prices for the snack items at the convenience, grocery, and discount stores. (c) The six specific items in ascending order, along with sizes and prices for the cosmetics/toiletries items at the convenience, grocery, and discount stores. (d) The six specific items in ascending order, along with sizes and prices for the kitchen supplies items at the convenience, grocery, and discount stores.

6 ▶▶▶ Use the campus directory database created in Case Study 6 of Project 1 for this assignment. Display and print the following: (a) The names of your instructors in ascending order, along with their telephone numbers and room numbers. (b) The names of the administrators in ascending order, along with their telephone numbers and room numbers. (c) The services in ascending order, including telephone numbers and room numbers.

7 ▶▶▶ Use the financial institutions database created in Case Study 7 of Project 1 for this assignment. Display and print the following: (a) The names of the financial institutions and total values of the IRAs at age 65 in descending order. (b) The names and telephone numbers of the financial institutions and total amounts of interest earned at age 65 in descending order. (c) The average value of the IRAs at age 65. (d) The average interest rates for the banks, savings and loans, and credit unions. (e) The name, address, and interest rate of the financial institution with the highest interest rate. (f) The name, telephone number, and interest rate of the financial institution with the lowest interest rate. (g) The names of the financial institutions and penalties for early withdrawal in two years in ascending order. (h) The names of the financial institutions and annual fees in descending order.

Microsoft *Access 97*

Maintaining a Database Using the Design and Update Features of Access

Objectives

You will have mastered the material in this project when you can:

- Add records to a table
- Locate records
- Change the contents of records in a table
- Delete records from a table
- Restructure a table
- Change field characteristics
- Add a field
- Save the changes to the structure
- Update the contents of a single field
- Make changes to groups of records
- Delete groups of records
- Specify a required field
- Specify a range
- Specify a default value
- Specify legal values
- Specify a format
- Update a table with validation rules
- Specify referential integrity
- Order records
- Create single-field and multiple-field indexes

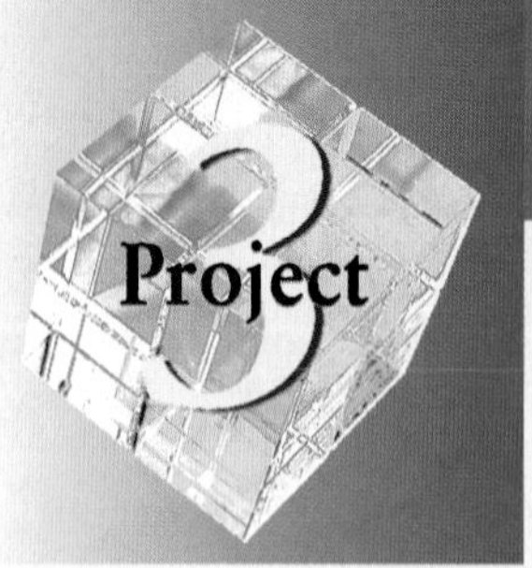

Enterprise to Earth: *The View Is Superb!*

When you hear the name *Enterprise,* what comes to mind? A Federation starship? The aircraft carrier that became the most decorated American ship of World War II? A business venture?

On June 18, 1861, the first electronic message from the skies flashed down from 500 feet above Washington, DC via telegraph wire to President Lincoln, sent by the intrepid Dr. Thaddeus S.C. Lowe from the hot air balloon *Enterprise.* Lowe went on to organize the Federal Balloon Corps, providing the first aerial fire control for Union artillery during the Civil War. The Confederacy soon emulated this feat, but alas! the Federals captured one Confederate balloon — made of silk dresses contributed by dozens of patriotic Southern ladies — before it ever flew.

Since 1783, when Benjamin Franklin watched the Montgolfier brothers of France send their hot air balloon aloft, innovators and daredevils alike have built and flown hundreds of different designs for balloons and dirigibles. Count von Zeppelin of Germany took the science to its highest form with enormous hydrogen-filled dirigibles carrying wealthy passengers on luxury cruises from Germany to America, Rio de Janeiro, Tokyo, Siberia, and other exotic destinations. This form of air service came to an abrupt halt on May 6, 1937, when the 803-foot monster dirigible *Hindenburg* ignited at Lakehurst, New Jersey and seven million cubic feet of gas erupted like Vesuvius. In thirty-two seconds, the mighty lord of the air was gone.

That spectacular disaster, however, did not end the interest in lighter-than-air vessels. From convoy escorts and barrage balloons during World War II, lighter-than-air craft have evolved into commercial and pleasure vehicles. After glimpsing the world through the Goodyear blimp's television camera, one can readily imagine the excitement of scudding through the heavens dangling beneath a hot air balloon, while exchanging wedding vows over California's Napa Valley or watching gazelles and wildebeests bounding across the Serengeti Plain.

A captivating subject, the exploits of pioneers who went aloft in sometimes-crazy contraptions are but a few of the billions of facts that historians, encylopedists, and librarians spend their lifetimes collecting and preserving. In the monumental task of managing ever-accumulating mountains of historical data, computer databases are indispensable.

Maintaining such important archives is an essential, on-going operation. Modern revision tools, such as those provided by Microsoft Access 97, have streamlined the business of updating or restructuring databases significantly. Unlike past programs, which could require hours to add or delete a field, the design and update features found in Access allow you to make global changes to your own databases in just minutes.

Although warp speed is great when doing updates, think how much fun it would have been to accompany Phileas Fogg in his balloon on the leisurely first leg of his trip *Around the World in Eighty Days*. Now, that's flying!

Microsoft
Access 97

Maintaining a Database Using the Design and Update Features of Access

Case Perspective

Pilotech Services has created a database and loaded it with client and technician data. The management and staff have received many benefits from the database, including the ability to ask a variety of questions concerning the data in the database. They now face the task of keeping the database up to date. They must add new records as they take on new clients and technicians. They must make changes to existing records to reflect additional billings, payments, changes of address, and so on. Pilotech Services also found that it needed to change the structure of the database in two specific ways. The management decided the database needed to categorize the clients by type (regular, non-profit, and educational organization) and so they needed to add a Client Type field to the Client table. They found the Name field was too short to contain the name of one of the clients. They also determined they could improve the efficiency of certain types of database processing and found that to do so, they needed to create indexes, which are similar to indexes found in the back of books.

Introduction

Once a database has been created and loaded with data, it must be maintained. **Maintaining the database** means modifying the data to keep it up to date, such as adding new records, changing the data for existing records, and deleting records. **Updating** can include **mass updates** or **mass deletions**; that is, updates to, or deletions of, many records at the same time.

In addition to adding, changing, and deleting records, maintenance of a database periodically can involve the need to **restructure** the database; that is, to change the database structure. This can include adding new fields to a table, changing the characteristics of existing fields, and removing existing fields. It also can involve the creation of **indexes**, which are similar to indexes found in the back of books and which are used to improve the efficiency of certain operations.

Figure 3-1 summarizes some of the various types of activities involved in maintaining a database.

Project Three — Maintaining the Pilotech Services Database

You are to make the changes to the data in the Pilotech Services database as requested by the management of

Pilotech Services. You also must restructure the database to meet the current needs of Pilotech. This includes adding an additional field as well as increasing the width of one of the existing fields. You also must modify the structure of the database in a way that prevents users from entering invalid data. Finally, management is concerned that some operations, for example, those involving sorting the data, are taking longer than they would like. You are to create indexes to attempt to address this problem.

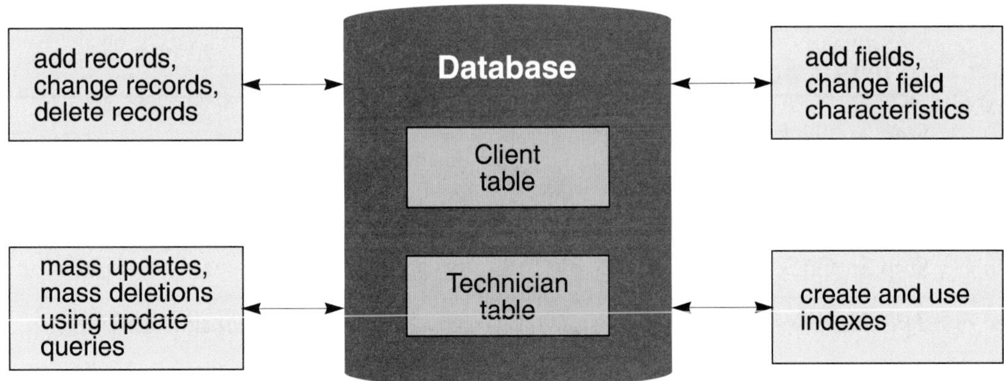

FIGURE 3-1

Overview of Project Steps

These steps give you an overview of how the Pilotech Services database will be maintained. The following tasks will be completed in this project.

1. Start Access and open the Pilotech Services database.
2. Use a form to add a new record to the Client table.
3. Locate the record for client GU21 and then change the name of the client.
4. Delete the record for client BL26.
5. Increase the width of the Name field to accommodate a client name that will not fit in the current structure.
6. Add a field for client category (called Client Type) to the Client table.
7. Change the name of client GU21 (the one that previously would not fit).
8. Resize the columns in Datasheet view.
9. Use an update query to set all the values in the Client Type field initially to REG, which is the most common client category.
10. Use a delete query to delete all clients in zip code 52018.

11. Create a validation rule to make the Name field a required field.
12. Create a validation rule to ensure that only values between $0.00 and $800.00 may be entered in the Billed field.
13. Specify that REG is to be the default value for the Client Type field.
14. Create a validation rule to ensure that only the values of REG, NPR, or EDU may be entered in the Client Type field.
15. Specify that any letters entered in the Client Number field are to be converted automatically to uppercase.
16. Specify referential integrity between the Client and Technician tables.
17. Use the Sort buttons to sort records in the database.
18. Create and use indexes to improve performance.

Opening the Database

Before carrying out the steps in this project, first you must open the database. To do so, perform the following steps.

TO OPEN A DATABASE

Step 1: Click the Start button.
Step 2: Click Open Office Document and then click 3½ Floppy (A:) in the Look in list box. If necessary, click the Pilotech Services database name.
Step 3: Click the Open button.

The database opens and the Pilotech Services : Database window displays.

Adding, Changing, and Deleting

Keeping the data in a database up to date requires three tasks: adding new records, changing the data in existing records, and deleting existing records.

Adding Records

In Project 1, you added records to a database using Datasheet view; that is, as you were adding records, the records were displayed on the screen in the form of a datasheet, or table. When you need to add additional records, you can use the same techniques.

In Project 1, you used a form to view records. This is called **Form view**. You also can use Form view to update the data in a table. To add new records, change existing records, or delete records, you will use the same techniques you used in Datasheet view. To add a record to the Client table with a form, for example, use the following steps. These steps use the Client form you created in Project 1.

To Use a Form to Add Records

1 **With the Pilotech Services database open, point to the Forms tab (Figure 3-2).**

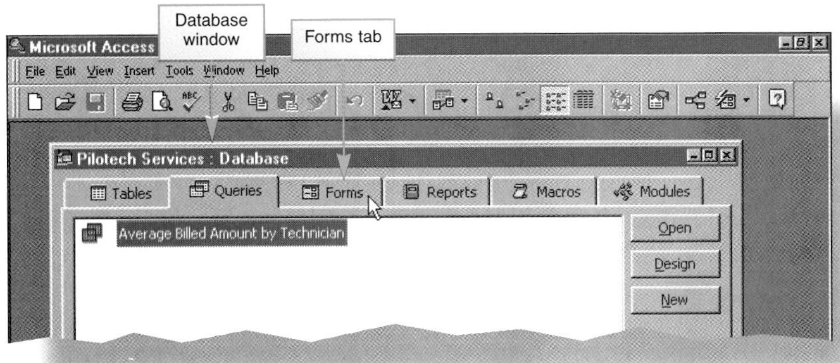

FIGURE 3-2

2 **Click the Forms tab. Right-click Client.**

The shortcut menu displays (Figure 3-3).

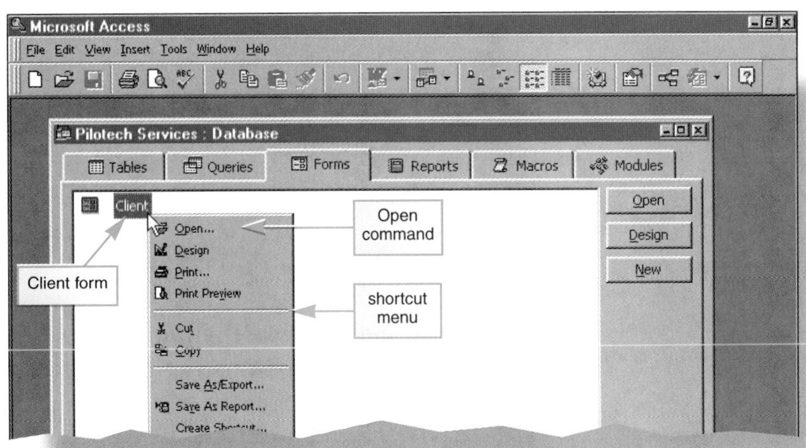

FIGURE 3-3

3 **Click Open on the shortcut menu.**

The form for the Client table displays (Figure 3-4).

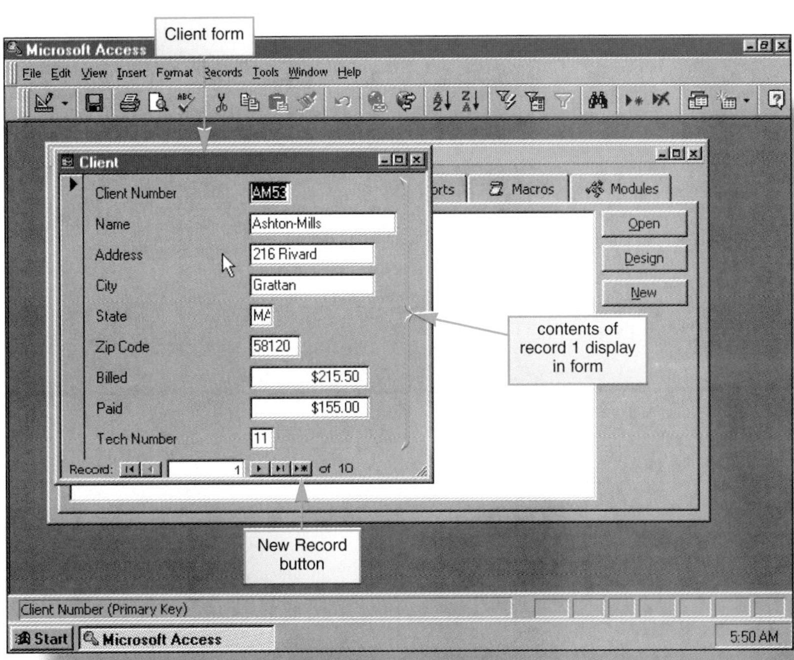

FIGURE 3-4

4 **Click the New Record button.**

The contents of the form are erased in preparation for a new record.

5 **Type the data for the new record as shown in Figure 3-5. Press the TAB key after typing the data in each field, except after typing the final field (Tech Number).**

The record appears as shown in Figure 3-5.

6 **Press the TAB key.**

The record now is added to the Client table and the contents of the form erased.

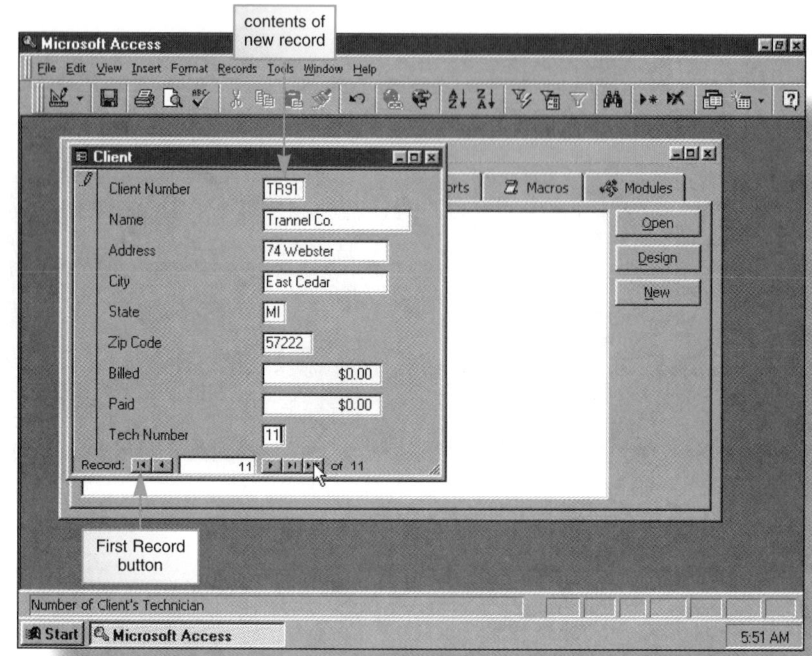

FIGURE 3-5

OtherWays

1. Click Forms tab, click form object, click Open button
2. Click Forms tab, double-click form object

More About Searching for a Record

When you are searching for a record, your current position in the database is immaterial if you click the Find First button. The position will change to the first record that satisfies the condition. Your current position is important if you click the Find Next button, because the search then will begin at the current position.

Searching for a Record

In the database environment, **searching** means looking for records that satisfy some criteria. Looking for the client whose number is GU21 is an example of searching. The queries in Project 2 also were examples of searching. Access had to locate those records that satisfied the criteria.

A need for searching also exists when using Form view or Datasheet view. To update client GU21, for example, first you need to find the client. In a small table, repeatedly pressing the Next Record button until client GU21 is on the screen may not be particularly difficult. In a large table with many records, however, this would be extremely cumbersome. You need a way to be able to go directly to a record just by giving the value in some field. This is the function of the **Find button** on the toolbar. Before clicking the Find button, select the field for the search.

Perform the following steps to move to the first record in the file, select the Client Number field, and then use the Find button to search for the client whose number is GU21.

To Search for a Record

1 Make sure the Client table is open and the form for the Client table is on the screen. Click the First Record button (see Figure 3-5) to display the first record. If the Client Number field is not currently selected, select it by clicking the field name. Point to the Find button on the toolbar.

The first record displays in the form (Figure 3-6).

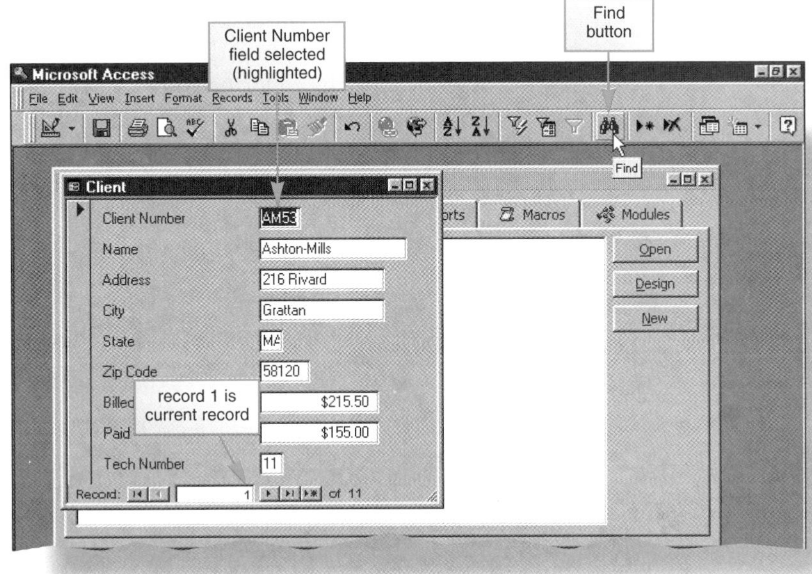

FIGURE 3-6

2 Click the Find button. Type GU21 **in the Find What text box.**

The Find in field: 'Client Number' dialog box displays (Figure 3-7). The Find What text box contains the entry, GU21.

3 Click the Find First button and then click the Close button.

Access locates the record for client GU21.

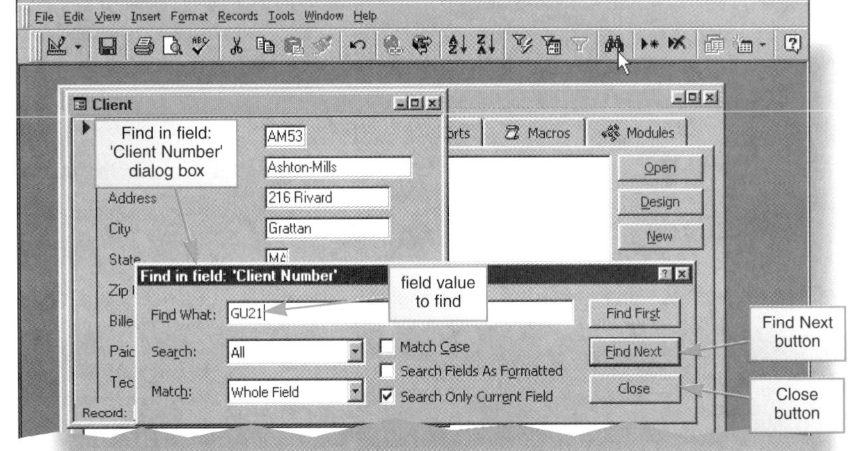

FIGURE 3-7

OtherWays

1. On Edit menu click Find
2. Press CTRL+F

In some cases, after locating a record that satisfies a criterion, you might need to find the next record that satisfies the same criterion. For example, if you have just found the first client whose technician number is 11, you then may want to find the second such client, then the third, and so on. To do so, repeat the same process. You will not need to retype the value, however.

More About Changing the Contents of a Record

When you are changing the value in a field, clicking within the field will produce an insertion point. Clicking the name of the field will select the entire field. The new entry typed then will completely replace the previous entry.

Changing the Contents of a Record

After locating the record to be changed, select the field to be changed by clicking the field. You also can repeatedly press the TAB key. Then make the appropriate changes. Clicking the field name automatically produces an insertion point in the field name text box. If you use the TAB key, you will need to press F2 to produce an insertion point.

Normally, Access is in Insert mode, so the characters typed will be inserted at the appropriate position. To change to Overtype mode, press the INSERT key. The letters, OVR, will display near the bottom right edge of the status bar. To return to Insert mode, press the INSERT key. In **Insert mode**, if the data in the field completely fills the field, no additional characters can be inserted. In this case, increase the size of the field before inserting the characters. You will see how to do this later in the project.

Complete the following steps to use Form view to change the name of client GU21 to Grand Union Supply by inserting the word, Supply, at the end of the name. Sufficient room exists in the field to make this change.

Steps To Update the Contents of a Field

1. **Position the mouse pointer in the Name field text box for client GU21 after the word, Union.**

   The mouse pointer shape is an I-beam (Figure 3-8).

2. **Click to produce an insertion point, press the SPACEBAR to insert a space and then type** `Supply` **to correct the name.**

   The name is now Grand Union Supply.

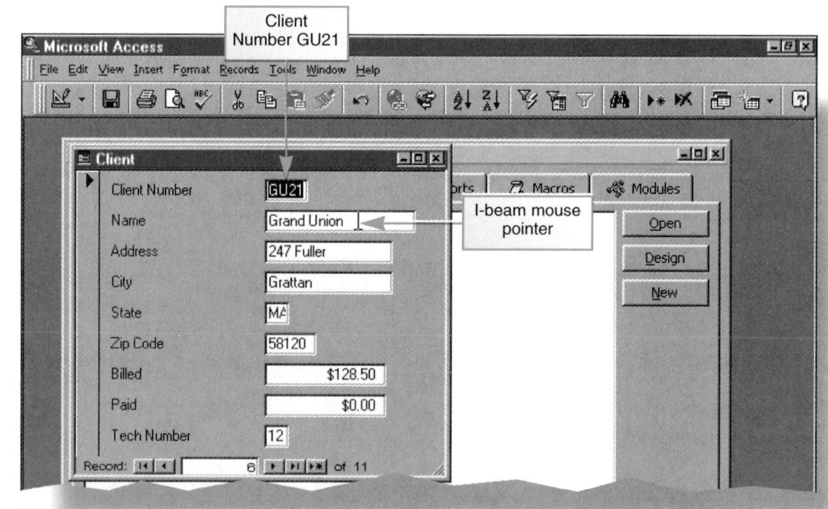

FIGURE 3-8

Switching Between Views

Sometimes, after working in Form view where you can see all fields, but only one record, it would be helpful to see several records at a time. To do so, switch to Datasheet view by clicking the View button arrow and then clicking Datasheet View. Perform the following steps to switch from Form view to Datasheet view.

Steps To Switch from Form View to Datasheet View

1. **Point to the View button arrow on the toolbar (Figure 3-9).**

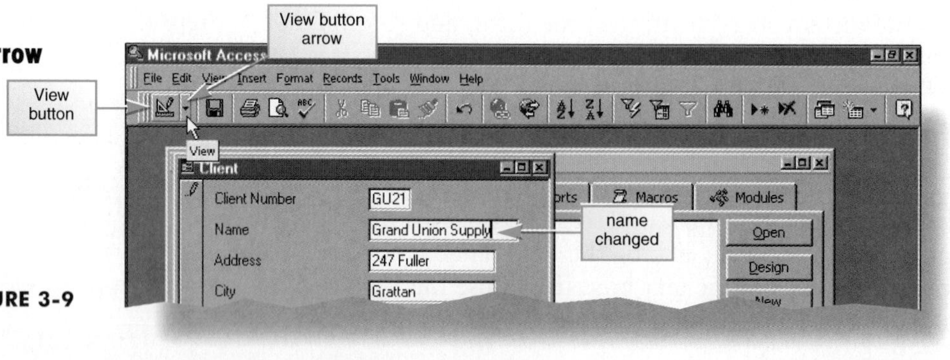

FIGURE 3-9

2 **Click the View button arrow. Point to Datasheet View.**

The View list displays (Figure 3-10).

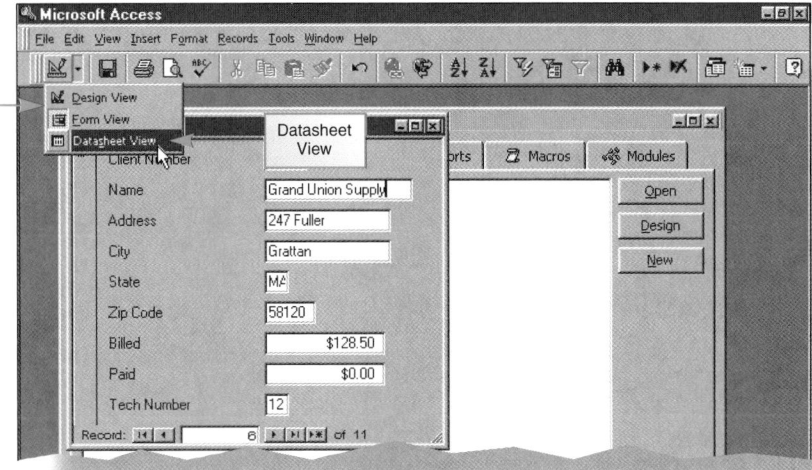

FIGURE 3-10

3 **Click Datasheet View, and then maximize the window containing the datasheet.**

The datasheet displays (Figure 3-11). The position in the table is maintained. The current record selector points to client GU21, the client that displayed on the screen in Form view. The Name field, the field in which the insertion point is displayed, is selected.

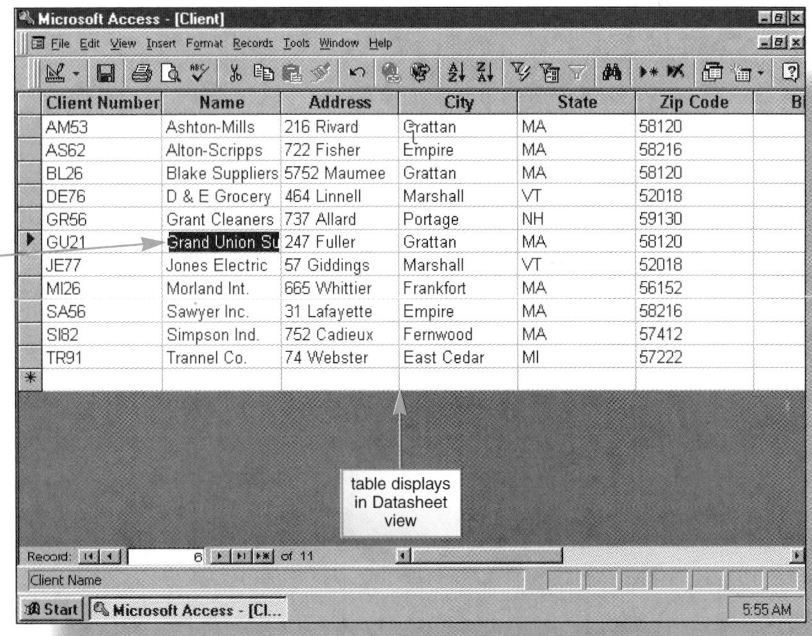

FIGURE 3-11

Other Ways

1. On View menu click Datasheet View

If you wanted to return to Form view, you would use the same process. The only difference is that you would click Form View rather than Datasheet View.

Deleting Records

When records are no longer needed, **delete the records** (remove them) from the table. If, for example, client BL26 has moved its offices to a city that is not served by Pilotech and already has settled its final bill, that client's record should be deleted. To delete a record, first locate it and then press the DELETE key. Complete the steps on the next page to delete client BL26.

More About the View Button

You can use the View button to transfer easily between viewing the form, called Form view, and viewing the design of the form, called Design view. To move to Datasheet view, you *must* click the down arrow, and then click Datasheet view in the list that displays.

Steps To Delete a Record

1. **With the datasheet for the Client table on the screen, position the mouse pointer on the record selector of the record in which the client number is BL26 (Figure 3-12).**

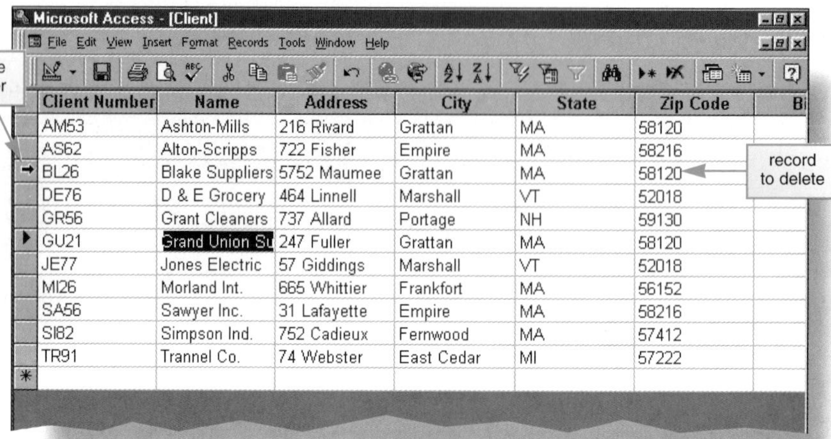

FIGURE 3-12

2. **Click the record selector to select the record, and then press the DELETE key to delete the record.**

The Microsoft Access dialog box displays (Figure 3-13). The message indicates that one record will be deleted.

3. **Click the Yes button to complete the deletion. Close the window containing the table by clicking its Close button.**

The record is deleted and the table disappears from the screen.

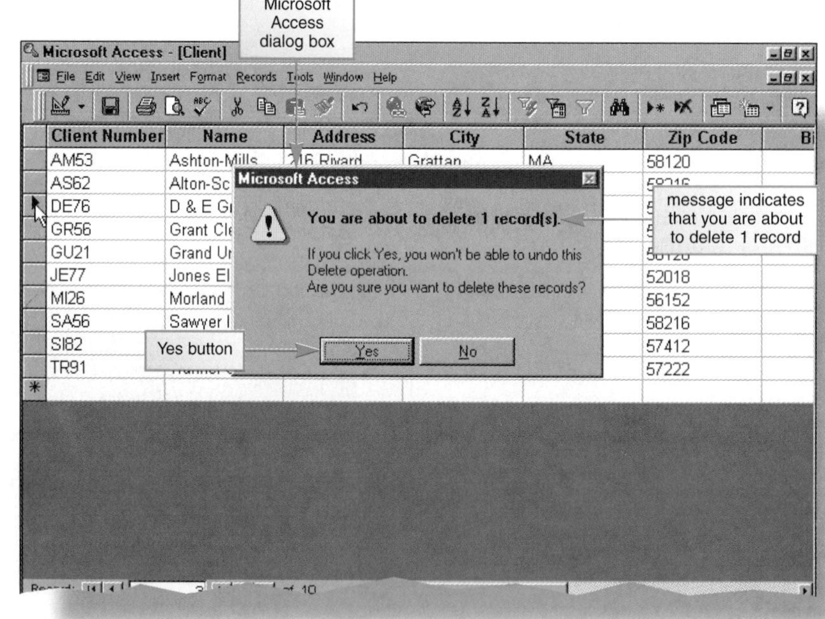

FIGURE 3-13

Other Ways

1. Click record to delete, click Delete Record button on toolbar
2. Click record to delete, on Edit menu click Delete Record

Changing the Structure

When you initially create a database, you define its **structure**; that is, you indicate the names, types, and sizes of all the fields. In many cases, the structure you first defined will not continue to be appropriate as you use the database. A variety of reasons exist why the structure of a table might need to change. Changes in the needs of users of the database may require additional fields to be added. In the Client table, for example, if it is important to store a code indicating the client type of a client, you need to add such a field.

Characteristics of a given field might need to change. For example, the client Grand Union Supply's name is stored incorrectly in the database. It actually should be Grand Union Supply, Inc. The Name field is not large enough, however, to hold the correct name. To accommodate this change, you need to increase the width of the Name field.

It may be that a field currently in the table no longer is necessary. If no one ever uses a particular field, it is not needed in the table. Because it is occupying space and serving no useful purpose, it should be removed from the table. You also would need to delete the field from any forms, reports, or queries that include it.

To make any of these changes, click Design on the shortcut menu.

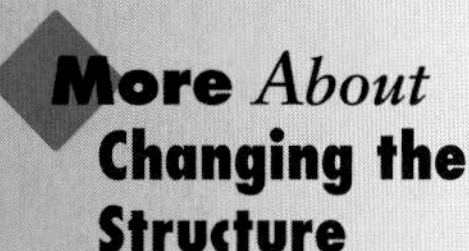

More About Changing the Structure

A major advantage of using a full-featured database management system is the ease with which you can change the structure of the tables that make up the database. In a nondatabase environment, changes to the structure can be very cumbersome, requiring difficult and time-consuming changes to many programs.

Changing the Size of a Field

The following steps change the size of the Name field from 20 to 25 to accommodate the change of name from Grand Union Supply to Grand Union Supply, Inc.

Steps To Change the Size of a Field

1 **With the Database window on the screen, click the Tables tab and then right-click Client.**

The shortcut menu displays (Figure 3-14).

FIGURE 3-14

2 **Click Design on the shortcut menu and then point to the row selector for the Name field.**

The Client : Table window displays (Figure 3-15).

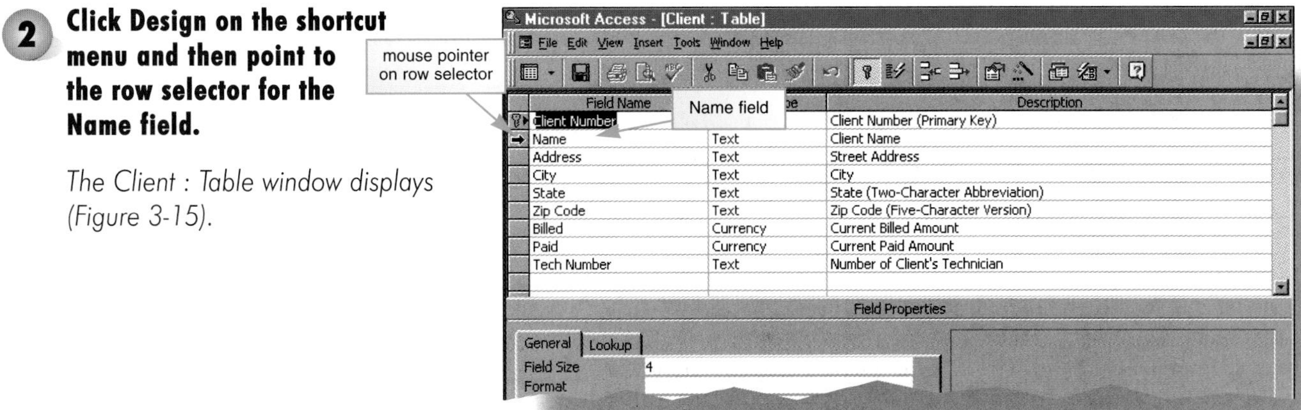

FIGURE 3-15

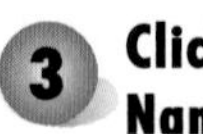

Click the row selector for the Name field.

The Name field is selected (Figure 3-16).

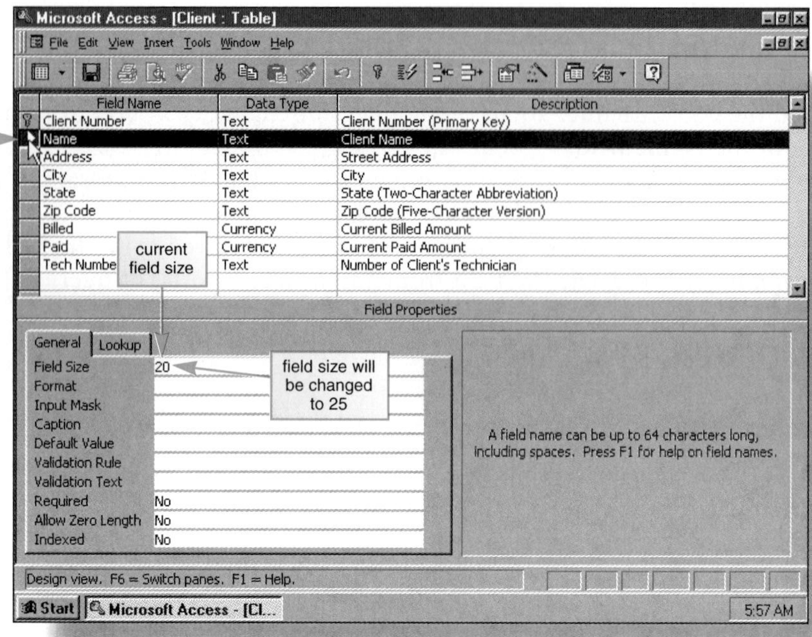

FIGURE 3-16

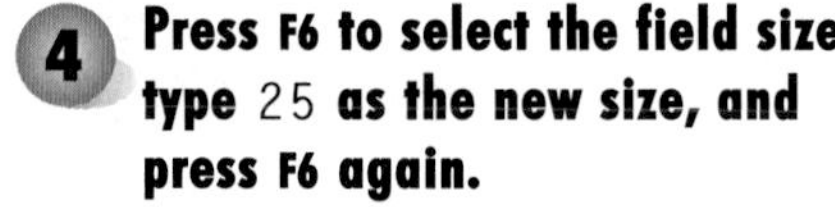

Press F6 to select the field size, type 25 as the new size, and press F6 again.

The size is changed (Figure 3-17).

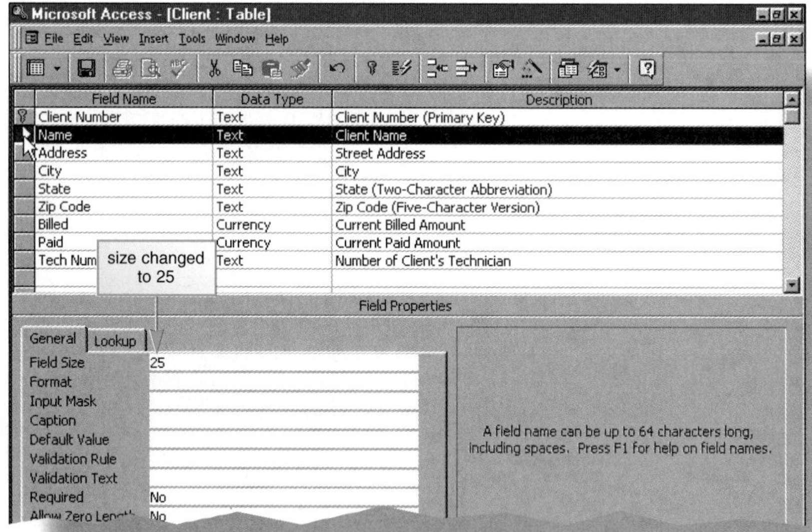

FIGURE 3-17

More *About* Adding a New Field

Tables frequently need to be expanded to include additional fields for a variety of reasons. Users needs can change. The field may have been omitted by mistake when the table was first created. Government regulations may change in such a way that the organization needs to maintain additional information.

Adding a New Field

The following steps add a new field, called Client Type, to the table. This field is used to indicate the type of client. The possible entries in this field are REG (regular client), NPR (nonprofit organization), and EDU (educational institution). The new field will follow the Zip Code in the list of fields; that is, it will be the seventh field in the restructured table. The current seventh field (Billed) will become the eighth field, Paid will become the ninth field, and so on. Complete the following steps to add the field.

Steps To Add a Field to a Table

1 **Point to the row selector for the Billed field (Figure 3-18).**

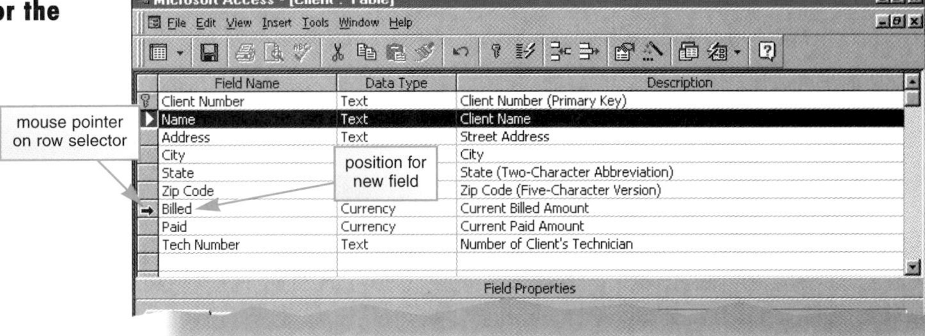

FIGURE 3-18

2 **Click the row selector for the Billed field and then press the INSERT key to insert a blank row.**

A blank row displays in the position for the new field (Figure 3-19).

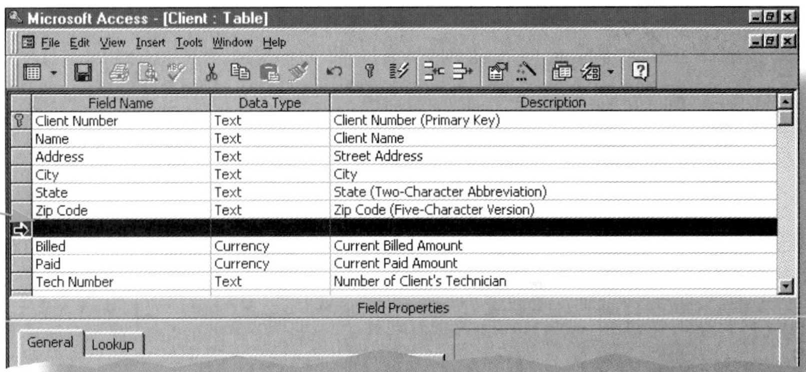

FIGURE 3-19

3 **Click the Field Name column for the new field. Type** `Client Type` **(field name) and then press the TAB key. Select the Text data type by pressing the TAB key. Type** `Client Type (REG, NPR, or EDU)` **as the description. Press F6 to move to the Field Size text box, type** `3` **(the size of the Client Type field), and press F6 again.**

The entries for the new field are complete (Figure 3-20).

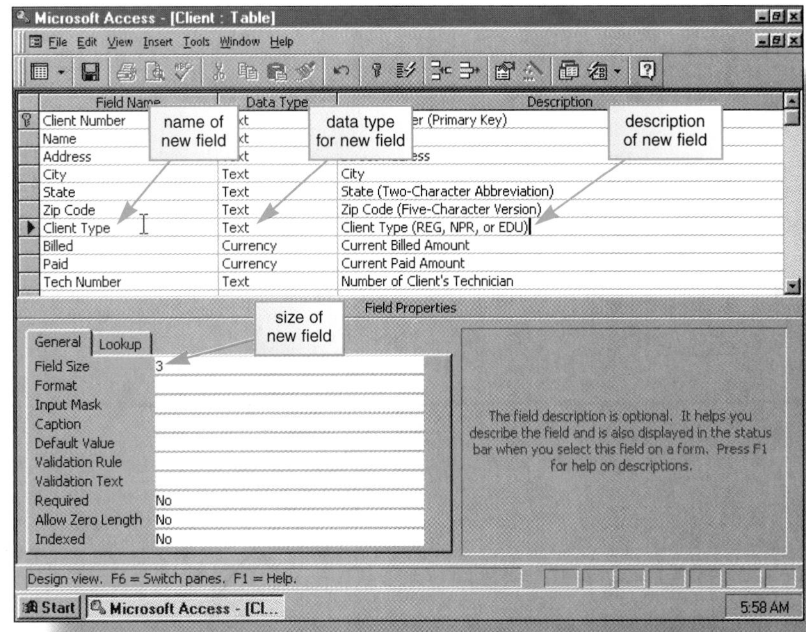

FIGURE 3-20

4 **Close the Client : Table window by clicking its Close button.**

The Microsoft Access dialog box displays (Figure 3-21).

5 **Click the Yes button to save the changes.**

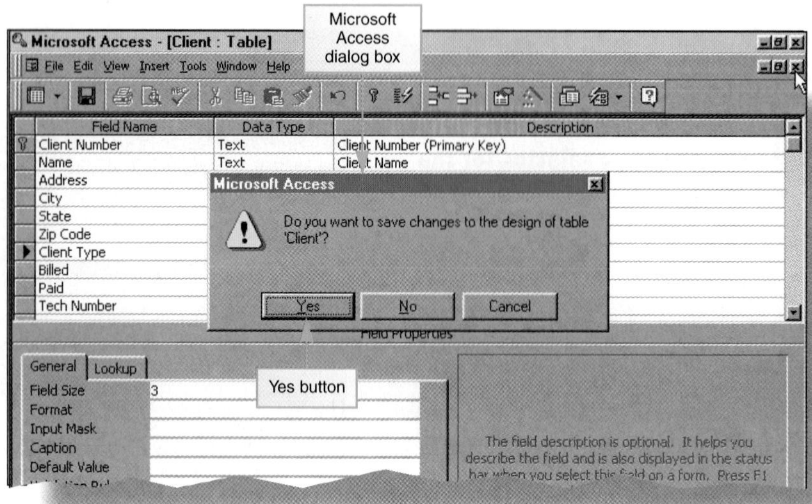

FIGURE 3-21

Other Ways

1. Click row selector below where new field is to be added, click Insert Rows button on toolbar
2. Click row selector below where new field is to be added, on Insert menu click Rows

Updating the Restructured Database

Changes to the structure are available immediately. The Name field is longer, although it does not appear that way on the screen, and the new Client Type field is included.

To make a change to a single field, such as changing the name from Grand Union Supply to Grand Union Supply, Inc., click the field to be changed, and then type the new value. If the record to be changed is not on the screen, use the Navigation buttons (Next Record, Previous Record) to move to it. If the field to be corrected simply is not visible on the screen, use the horizontal scroll bar along the bottom of the screen to shift all the fields until the correct one displays. Then make the change.

Perform the following steps to change the name of Grand Union Supply to Grand Union Supply, Inc.

Steps To Update the Contents of a Field

1 **Right-click Client.**

The shortcut menu displays (Figure 3-22).

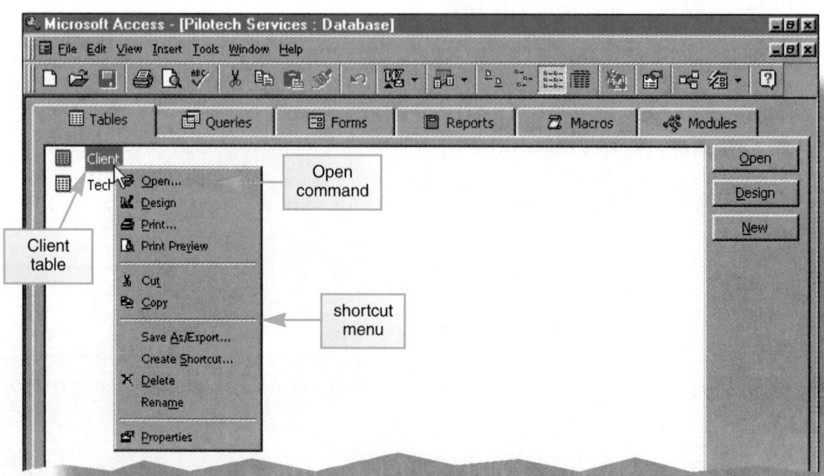

FIGURE 3-22

2 **Click Open on the shortcut menu. Position the I-beam mouse pointer to the right of the u of Grand Union Supply (client GU21).**

The datasheet displays (Figure 3-23).

3 **Click in the field, use the RIGHT ARROW key to move to the end of the name, and then type** , Inc. **as the addition to the name.**

The name is changed from Grand Union Supply to Grand Union Supply, Inc.

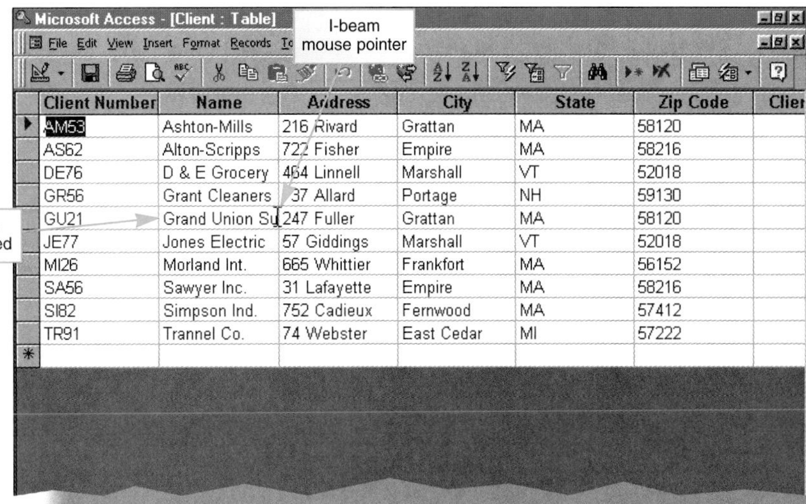

FIGURE 3-23

Resizing Columns

The default column sizes provided by Access do not always allow all the data in the field to display. You can correct this problem by **resizing the column** (changing its size) in the datasheet. In some instances, you actually may want to reduce the size of a column. The City field, for example, is short enough that it does not require all the space on the screen that is allotted to it.

Both types of changes are made the same way. Position the mouse pointer on the right boundary of the column's **field selector** (the line in the column heading immediately to the right of the name of the column to be resized). The mouse pointer will change to a two-headed arrow with a vertical bar. You then can drag the line to resize the column. In addition, you can double-click in the line, in which case Access will determine the best size for the column.

The following steps illustrate the process for resizing the Name column to the size that best fits the data.

More *About* Updating a Restructured Database

After changing the structure in a nondatabase environment, it can take several hours before the new structure is available for use. Computer jobs to change the structure often would run overnight or even over a weekend. Having the changes available immediately is a major benefit to using a system like Access.

Steps To Resize a Column

1 **Point to the right boundary of the field selector for the Name field (Figure 3-24).**

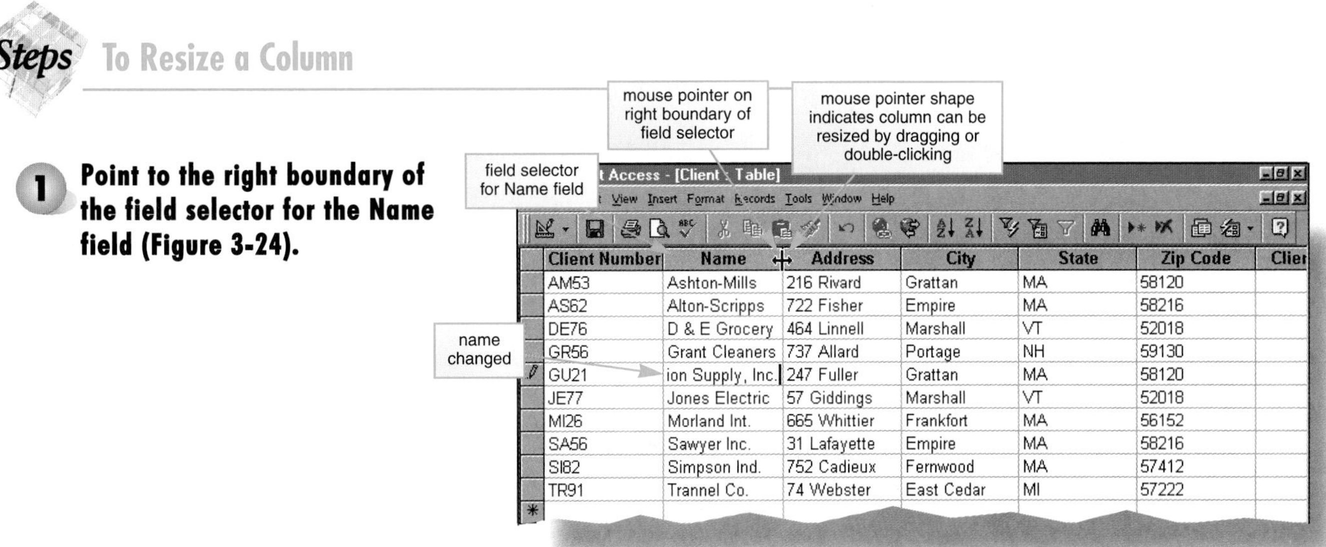

FIGURE 3-24

2 **Double-click the right boundary of the field selector for the Name field.**

The Name column has been resized (Figure 3-25).

Client Number	Name	Address	City	State	Zip Code
AM53	Ashton-Mills	216 Rivard	Grattan	MA	58120
AS62	Alton-Scripps	722 Fisher	Empire	MA	58216
DE76	D & E Grocery	464 Linnell	Marshall	VT	52018
GR56	Grant Cleaners	737 Allard	Portage	NH	59130
GU21	Grand Union Supply, Inc.	247 Fuller	Grattan	MA	58120
JE77	Jones Electric	57 Giddings	Marshall	VT	52018
MI26	Morland Int.	665 Whittier	Frankfort	MA	56152
SA56	Sawyer Inc.	31 Lafayette	Empire	MA	58216
SI82	Simpson Ind.	752 Cadieux	Fernwood	MA	57412
TR91	Trannel Co.	74 Webster	East Cedar	MI	57222

FIGURE 3-25

3 **Use the same technique to resize the Address, City, State, Zip Code, and Client Type columns to best fit the data.**

The columns have been resized (Figure 3-26).

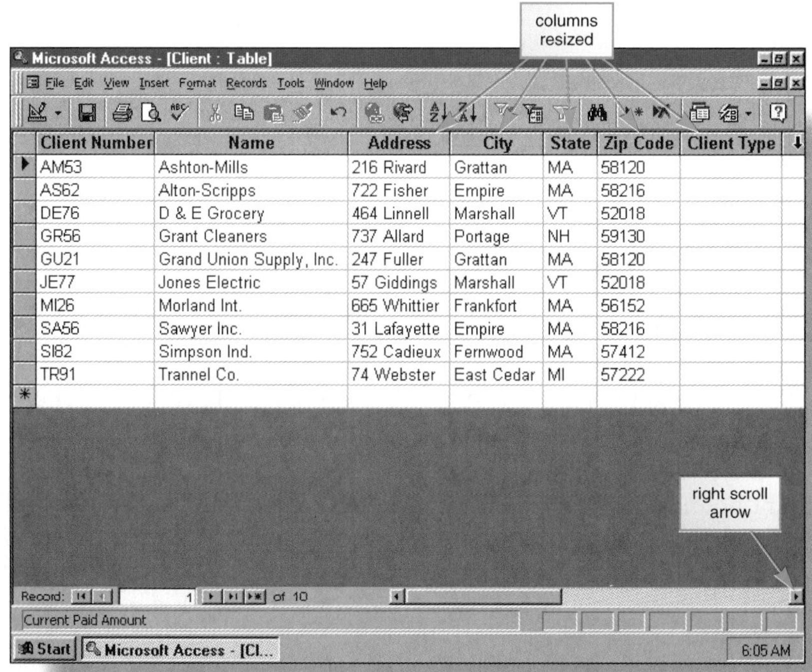

Client Number	Name	Address	City	State	Zip Code	Client Type
AM53	Ashton-Mills	216 Rivard	Grattan	MA	58120	
AS62	Alton-Scripps	722 Fisher	Empire	MA	58216	
DE76	D & E Grocery	464 Linnell	Marshall	VT	52018	
GR56	Grant Cleaners	737 Allard	Portage	NH	59130	
GU21	Grand Union Supply, Inc.	247 Fuller	Grattan	MA	58120	
JE77	Jones Electric	57 Giddings	Marshall	VT	52018	
MI26	Morland Int.	665 Whittier	Frankfort	MA	56152	
SA56	Sawyer Inc.	31 Lafayette	Empire	MA	58216	
SI82	Simpson Ind.	752 Cadieux	Fernwood	MA	57412	
TR91	Trannel Co.	74 Webster	East Cedar	MI	57222	

FIGURE 3-26

4 **Click the right scroll arrow to display the Billed, Paid, and Tech Number columns, and then resize the columns to best fit the data.**

All the columns have been resized (Figure 3-27).

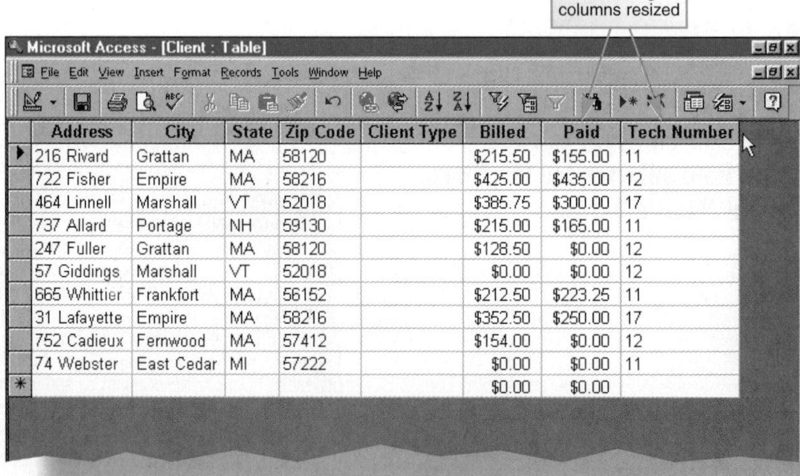

Address	City	State	Zip Code	Client Type	Billed	Paid	Tech Number
216 Rivard	Grattan	MA	58120		$215.50	$155.00	11
722 Fisher	Empire	MA	58216		$425.00	$435.00	12
464 Linnell	Marshall	VT	52018		$385.75	$300.00	17
737 Allard	Portage	NH	59130		$215.00	$165.00	11
247 Fuller	Grattan	MA	58120		$128.50	$0.00	12
57 Giddings	Marshall	VT	52018		$0.00	$0.00	12
665 Whittier	Frankfort	MA	56152		$212.50	$223.25	11
31 Lafayette	Empire	MA	58216		$352.50	$250.00	17
752 Cadieux	Fernwood	MA	57412		$154.00	$0.00	12
74 Webster	East Cedar	MI	57222		$0.00	$0.00	11
					$0.00	$0.00	

FIGURE 3-27

5 **Close the Client : Table window by clicking its Close button.**

The Microsoft Access dialog box displays (Figure 3-28).

6 **Click the Yes button.**

The change is saved. The next time the datasheet displays, the columns will have the new widths.

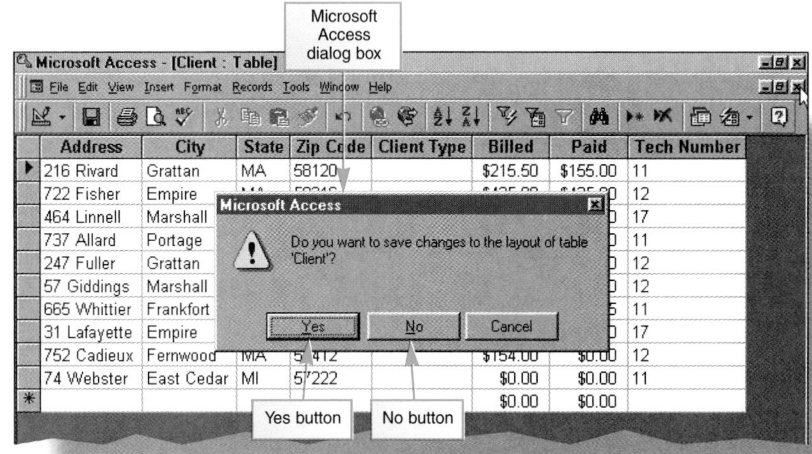

FIGURE 3-28

OtherWays

1. On Format menu click Column Width, click Best Fit

Using an Update Query

The Client Type field is blank on every record. One approach to entering the information for the field would be to step through the entire table, assigning each record its appropriate value. If most of the clients have the same type, a simpler approach is available.

Suppose, for example, that more clients are type REG. Initially, you can set all the values to REG. To accomplish this quickly and easily, you use a special type of query called an **update query**. Later, you can change the type for the nonprofit and educational clients.

The process for creating an update query begins the same as the process for creating the queries in Project 2. After selecting the table for the query, right-click any open area of the upper pane, click Query Type on the shortcut menu, and then click Update Query on the menu of available query types. An extra row, Update To:, displays in the design grid. Use this additional row to indicate the way the data will be updated. If a criterion is entered, then only those records that satisfy the criterion will be updated.

Perform the following steps to change the value in the Client Type field to REG for all the records. Because all records are to be updated, no criteria will be entered.

More About Resizing Columns

After you have changed the size of a field, the forms you have created will not reflect your changes. If you used the AutoForm command, you can change the field sizes by simply recreating the form. To do so, right-click the form, click Delete, and create the form as you did in Project 1.

Steps To Use an Update Query to Update All Records

1 **With the Client table selected, click the New Object: AutoForm button arrow on the toolbar.**

The New Object list displays (Figure 3-29).

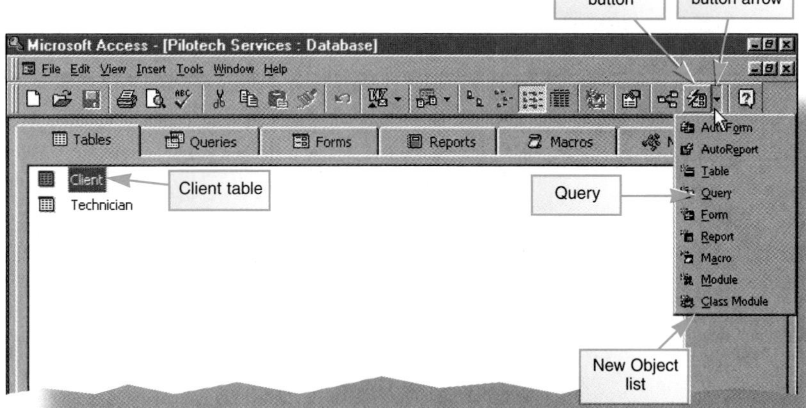

FIGURE 3-29

2 **Click Query.**

The New Query dialog box displays (Figure 3-30). Design View is selected.

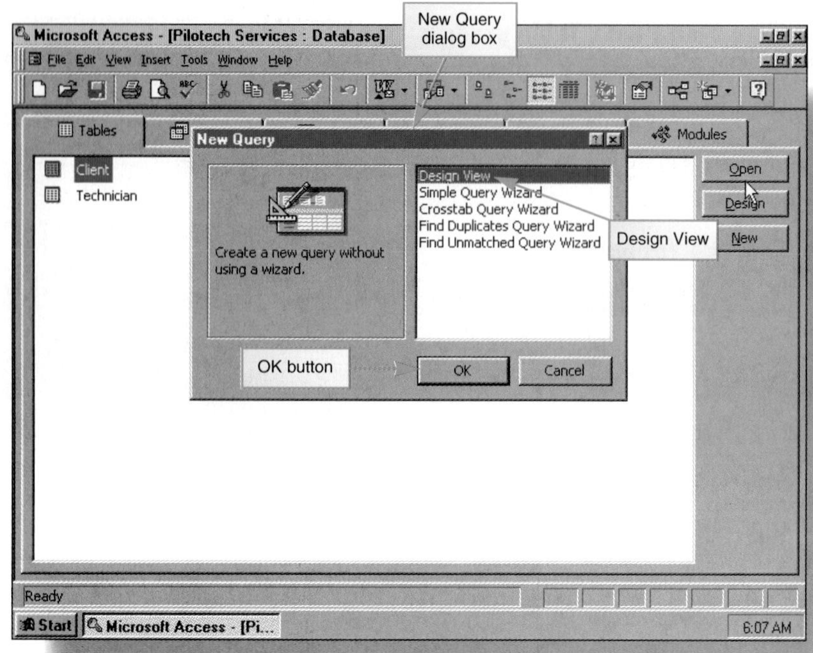

FIGURE 3-30

3 **Click the OK button, and be sure the Query1 : Select Query window is maximized. Resize the upper and lower panes of the window as well as the Client field list so all fields in the Client table field list display (see page A 2.9 in Project 2). Right-click the upper pane and point to Query Type on the shortcut menu.**

The shortcut menu displays (Figure 3-31). The Query Type submenu displays the available query types.

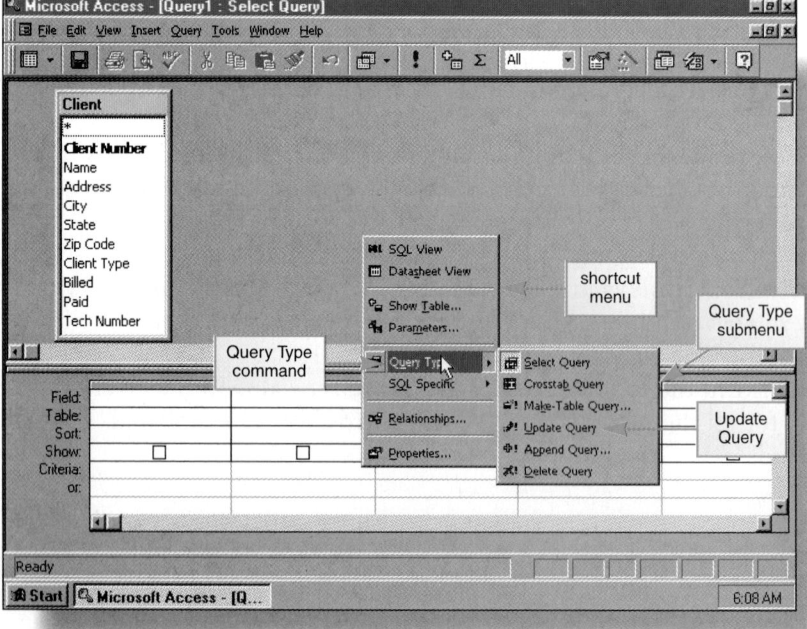

4 **Click Update Query on the submenu, double-click the Client Type field to select the field, click the Update To text box in the first column of the design grid, and type** `REG` **as the new value.**

The Client Type field is selected (Figure 3-32). In an Update Query, the Update To row displays in the design grid. The value to which the field is to be changed is entered as REG. Because no criteria are entered, the Client Type value on every row will be changed to REG.

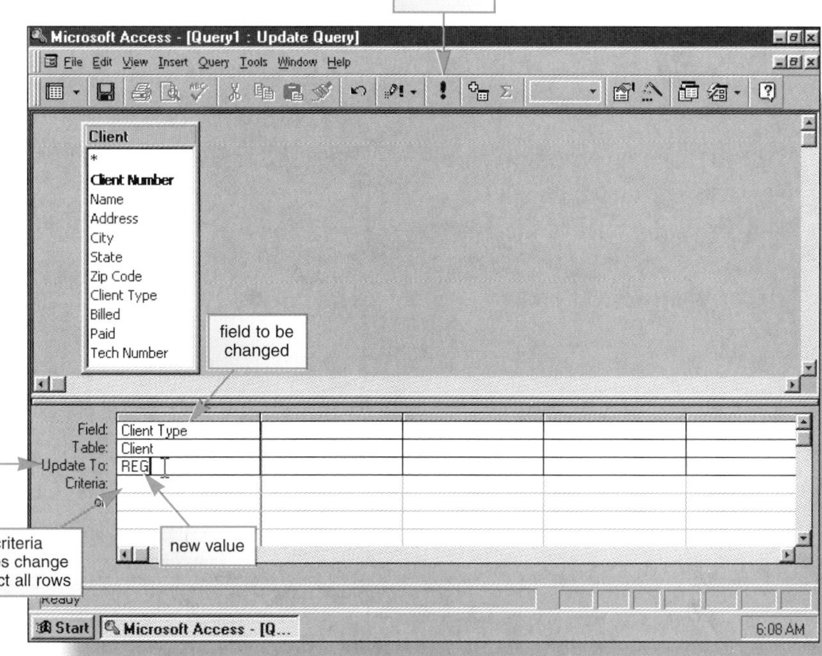

FIGURE 3-32

5 **Click the Run button on the toolbar.**

The Microsoft Access dialog box displays (Figure 3-33). The message indicates that 10 rows will be updated by the query.

6 **Click the Yes button.**

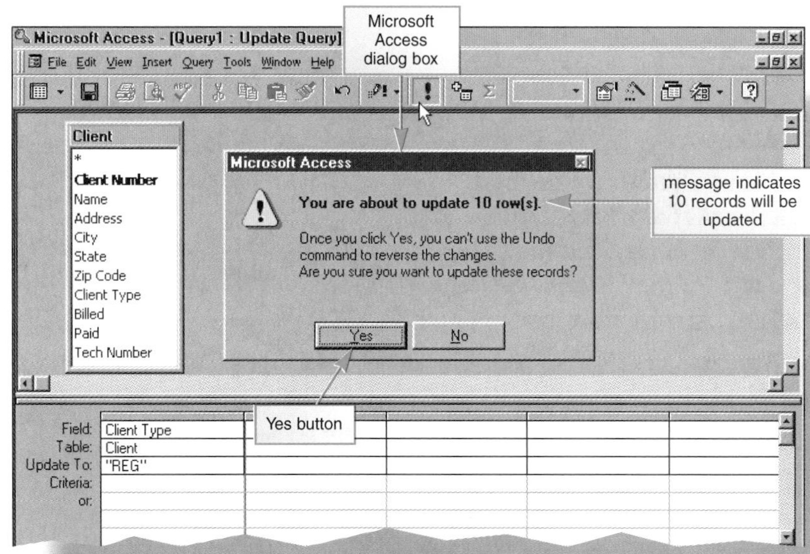

FIGURE 3-33

OtherWays

1. Click Query Type button arrow on toolbar, click Update Query
2. On Query menu click Update Query

Using a Delete Query to Delete a Group of Records

In some cases, you may need to delete several records at a time. If, for example, all clients in a particular zip code are to be serviced by another firm, the clients with this zip code can be deleted from the Pilotech Services database. Rather than deleting these clients individually, which could be very cumbersome, you can delete them in one operation by using a **delete query**, which is a query that will delete all the records satisfying the criteria entered in the query.

Perform the steps on the next page to use a delete query to delete all clients whose zip code is 52018.

To Use a Delete Query to Delete a Group of Records

1. **Clear the grid by clicking Edit on the menu bar and then clicking Clear Grid. Right-click the upper pane and then point to Query Type on the shortcut menu.**

   The shortcut menu displays (Figure 3-34). The Query Type submenu displays the available query types.

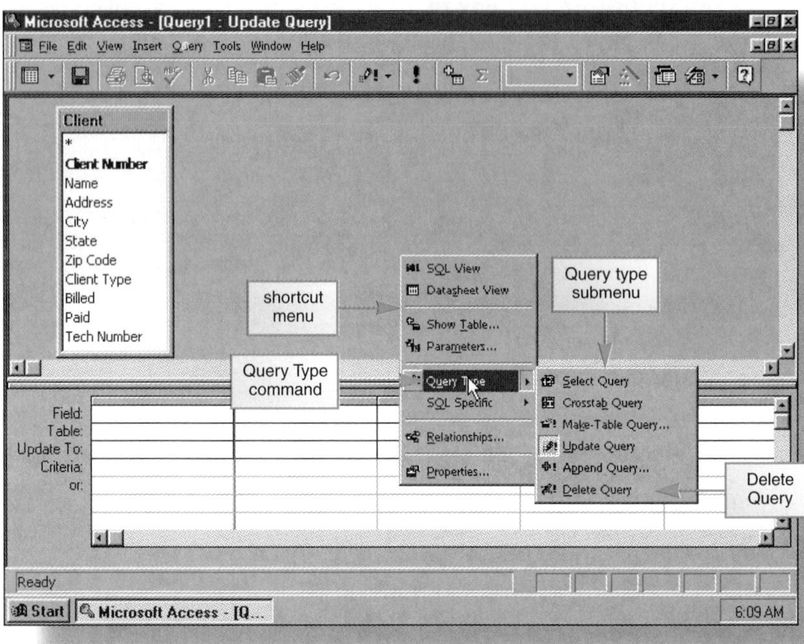

FIGURE 3-34

2. **Click Delete Query on the submenu, double-click the Zip Code field to select the field, and click the Criteria box. Type** `52018` **as the criterion.**

   The criterion is entered in the Zip Code column (Figure 3-35). In a Delete Query, the Delete row displays in the design grid.

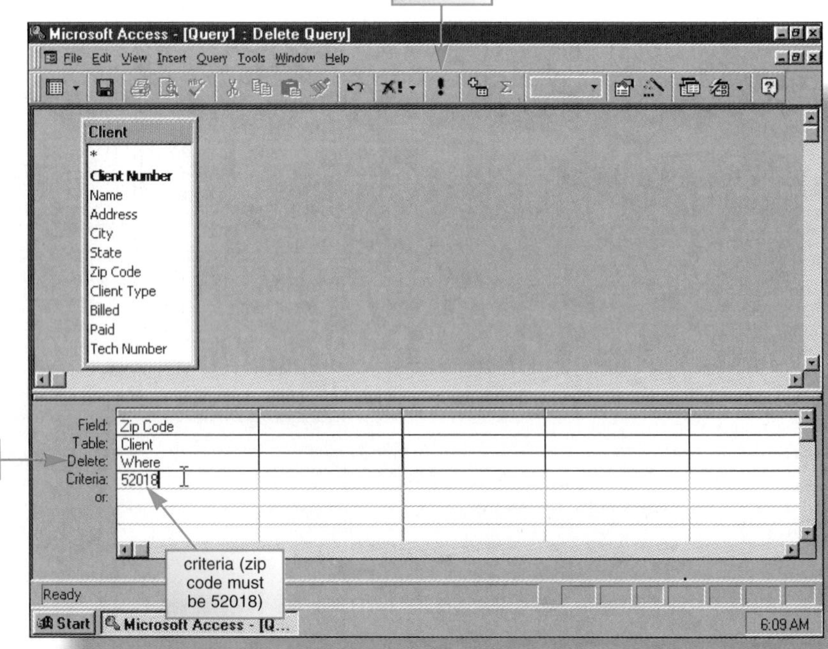

FIGURE 3-35

3 Run the query.

The Microsoft Access dialog box displays (Figure 3-36). The message indicates the query will delete 2 rows (records).

4 Click the Yes button. Close the Query window. Do not save the query.

The two clients with zip code 52018 have been removed from the table.

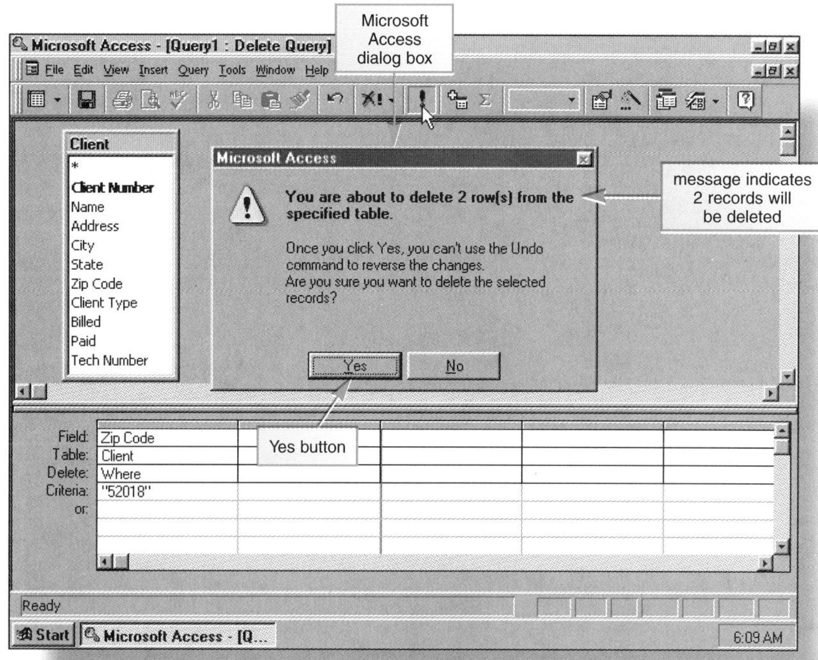

FIGURE 3-36

OtherWays

1. Click Query Type button arrow on toolbar, click Delete Query
2. On Query menu click Delete Query

Creating Validation Rules

Up to this point in this book, you have created, loaded, queried, and updated a database. Nothing done so far, however, ensures that users enter only valid data. This section explains how to create **validation rules**; that is, rules that the data entered by a user must follow. As you will see, Access will prevent users from entering data that does not follow the rules. The steps also specify **validation text**, which is the message that will be displayed if a user violates the validation rule.

Validation rules can indicate a **required field**, a field in which the user actually must enter data. For example, by making the Name field a required field, a user actually must enter a name (that is, the field cannot be blank). Validation rules can make sure a user's entry lies within a certain **range of values**; for example, that the values in the Billed field are between $0.00 and $800.00. They can specify a **default value**; that is, a value that Access will display on the screen in a particular field before the user begins adding a record. To make data entry of client numbers more convenient, you also can have lowercase letters converted automatically to uppercase letters. Finally, validation rules can specify a collection of acceptable values; for example, that the only legitimate entries for the Client Type field are REG, NPR, and EDU.

Specifying a Required Field

To specify that a field is to be required, change the value in the Required text box from No to Yes. The steps on the next page specify that the Name field is to be a required field.

More About Update Queries

Any full-featured database management system will offer some mechanism for updating multiple records at a time, that is, for making the same change to all the records that satisfy some criterion. Some systems, including Access, accomplish this through the query tool by providing a special type of query for this purpose.

More About Delete Queries

Any full-featured database management system will offer some mechanism for deleting multiple records at a time, that is, for deleting all the records that satisfy some criterion. Some systems, including Access, accomplish this through the query tool by providing a special type of query for this purpose.

To Specify a Required Field

1 **With the Database window on the screen and the Tables tab selected, right-click Client.**

The shortcut menu displays.

2 **Click Design on the shortcut menu, and then select the Name field by clicking its row selector. Point to the Required text box.**

The Client : Table window displays (Figure 3-37). The Name field is selected.

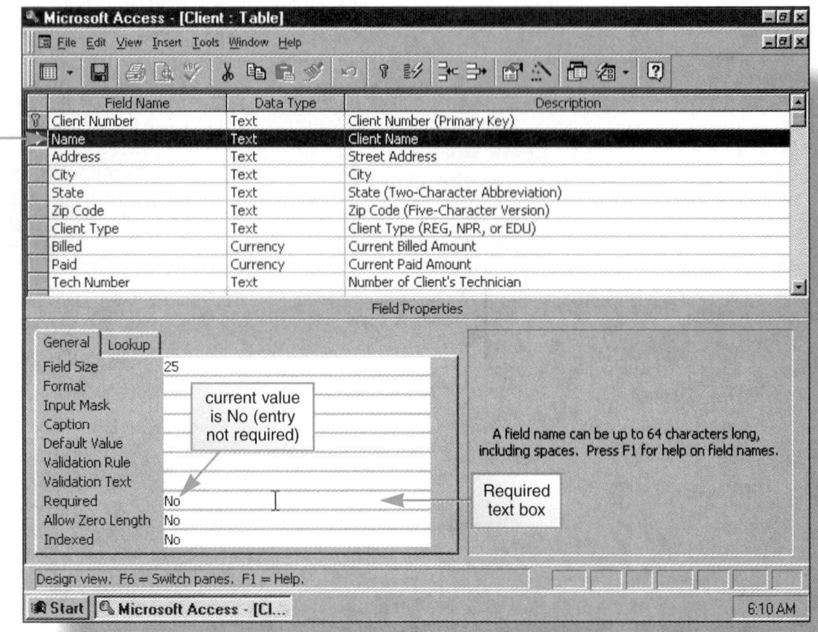

FIGURE 3-37

3 **Click the Required text box in the Field Properties area, and then click the down arrow that displays. Click Yes in the list.**

The value in the Required text box changes to Yes (Figure 3-38). It now is required that the user enter data into the Name field when adding a record.

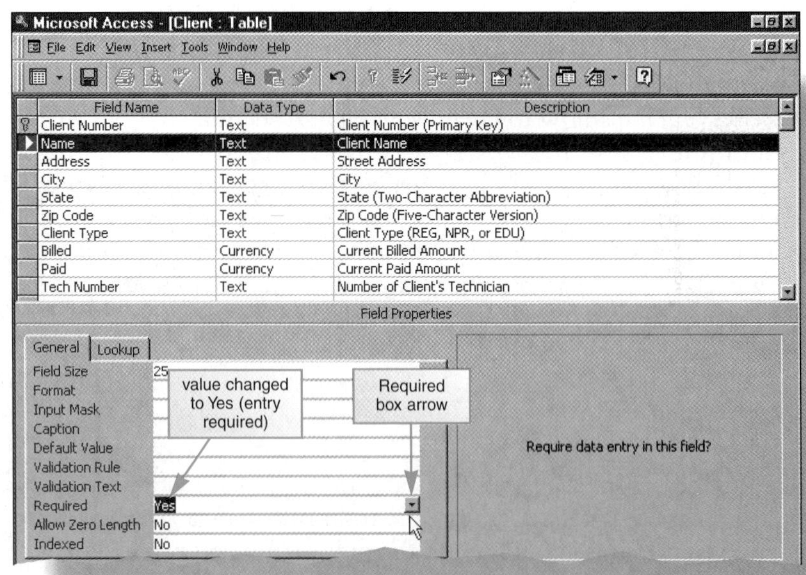

FIGURE 3-38

Specifying a Range

The following step specifies that entries in the Billed field must be between $0.00 and $800.00. To indicate this range, you will enter a condition that specifies that the billed amount must be both >= 0 (greater than or equal to zero) and <= 800 (less than or equal to 800).

To Specify a Range

1 **Select the Billed field by clicking its row selector. Click the Validation Rule text box to produce an insertion point, and then type** `>=0 and <=800` **as the rule. Click the Validation Text text box to produce an insertion point, and then type** `Must be between $0.00 and $800.00` **as the text. You must type all the text, including the dollar signs in this text box.**

The validation rule and text are entered (Figure 3-39).

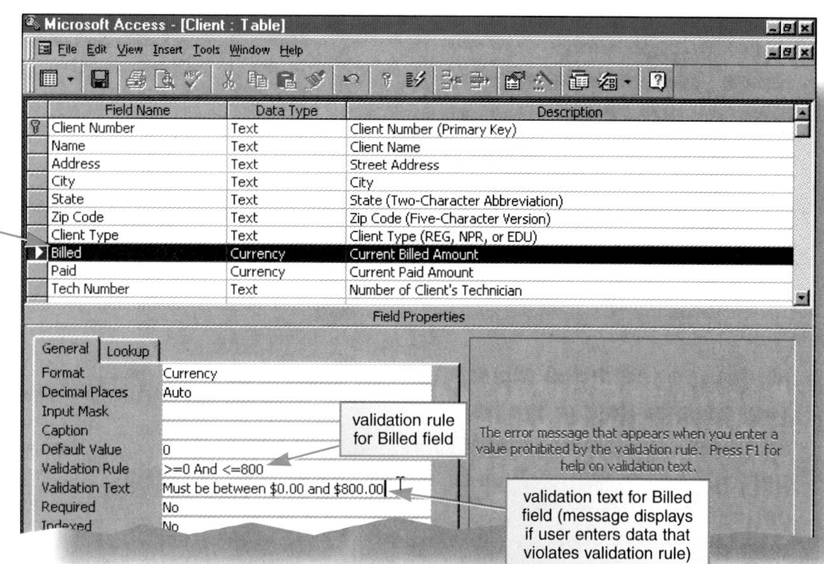

FIGURE 3-39

Users now will be prohibited from entering a billed amount that is either less than $0.00 or greater than $800.00 when they add records or change the value in the Billed field.

Specifying a Default Value

To specify a default value, enter the value in the Default Value text box. The following step specifies REG as the default value for the Client Type field. This simply means that if users do not enter a client type, the type will be REG.

To Specify a Default Value

1 **Select the Client Type field. Click the Default Value text box and then type** `=REG` **as the value.**

The Client Type field is selected. The default value is entered in the Default Value text box (Figure 3-40).

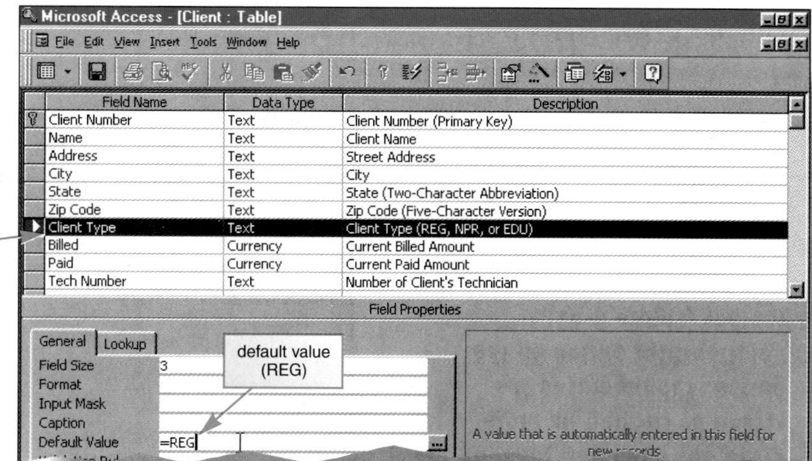

FIGURE 3-40

From this point on, if users do not make an entry in the Client Type field when adding records, Access will set the value to REG.

Specifying a Collection of Legal Values

The only **legal values** for the Client Type field are REG, NPR, and EDU. An appropriate validation rule for this field can direct Access to reject any entry other than these three possibilities. Perform the following step to specify the legal values for the Client Type field.

To Specify a Collection of Legal Values

1. **Make sure the Client Type field is selected. Click the Validation Rule text box and then type** `=REG or =NPR or =EDU` **as the validation rule. Click the Validation Text text box and then type** `Must be REG, NPR, or EDU` **as the validation text.**

The Client Type field is selected. The validation rule and text have been entered (Figure 3-41). In the Validation Rule text box, Access automatically inserted quotation marks around the REG, NPR, and EDU values and changed the lowercase letter, o, to uppercase in the word, or.

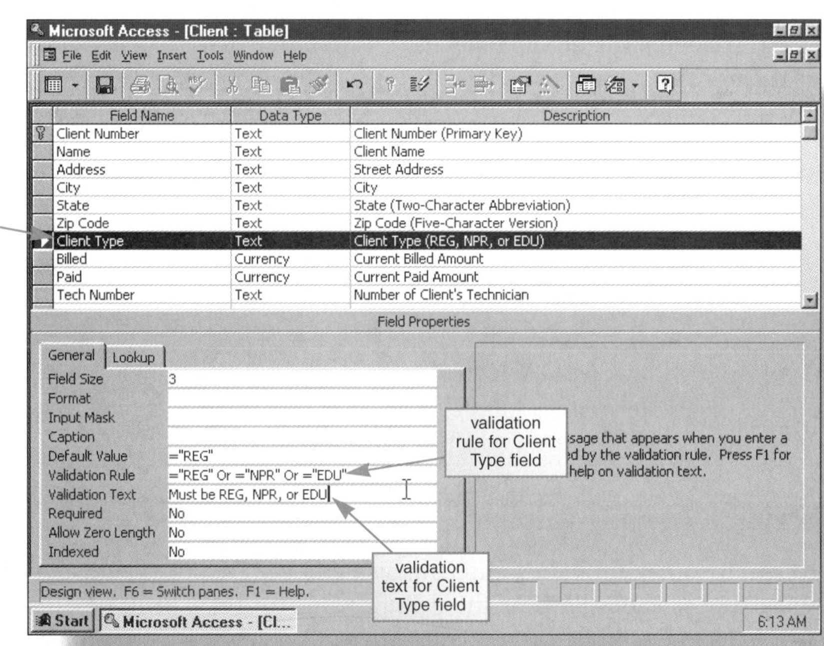

FIGURE 3-41

Users now will be allowed to enter only REG, NPR, or EDU in the Client Type field when they add records or make changes to this field.

Using a Format

To affect the way data is entered in a field, you can use a **format**. To use a format, you enter a special symbol, called a **format symbol**, in the field's Format text box. The following step specifies a format for the Client Number field in the Client table. The format symbol used in the example is >, which causes Access to convert lowercase letters automatically to uppercase. The format symbol < would cause Access to convert uppercase letters automatically to lowercase.

Index on Name

NAME	RECORD NUMBER
Alton-Scripps	2
Ashton-Mills	1
Grand Union Supply, Inc.	4
Grant Cleaners	3
Morland Int.	5
Sawyer Inc.	6
Simpson Ind.	7
Trannel Co.	8

Client table

RECORD NUMBER	CLIENT NUMBER	NAME	ADDRESS	CITY	STATE	ZIP CODE	. . .
1	AM53	Ashton-Mills	216 Rivard	Grattan	MA	58120	. . .
2	AS62	Alton-Scripps	722 Fisher	Empire	MA	58216	. . .
3	GR56	Grant Cleaners	737 Allard	Portage	NH	59130	. . .
4	GU21	Grand Union Supply, Inc.	247 Fuller	Grattan	MA	58120	. . .
5	MI26	Morland Int.	665 Whittier	Frankfort	MA	56152	. . .
6	SA56	Sawyer Inc.	31 Lafayette	Empire	MA	58216	. . .
7	SI82	Simpson Ind.	752 Cadieux	Fernwood	MA	57412	. . .
8	TR91	Trannel Co.	74 Webster	East Cedar	MI	57222	. . .

FIGURE 3-66

Each name occurs in the index along with the number of the record on which the corresponding client is located. Further, the names appear in the index in alphabetical order. If Access were to use this index to find the record on which the name is Grant Cleaners, for example, it could scan rapidly the names in the index to find Grant Cleaners. Once it did, it would determine the corresponding record number (3) and then go immediately to record 3 in the Client table, thus finding this client more quickly than if it had to look through the entire Client table one record at a time. Indexes make the process of retrieving records very fast and efficient.

Because no two clients happen to have the same name, the Record Number column contains only single values. This may not always be the case. Consider the index on the Zip Code field shown in Figure 3-67 on the next page. In this index, the Record Number column contains several values, namely all the records on which the corresponding zip code appears. The first row, for example, indicates that zip code 56152 is found only on record 5; whereas, the fourth row indicates that zip code 58120 is found on records 1 and 4. If Access were to use this index to find all clients in zip code 58120, it could scan rapidly the zip codes in the index to find 58120. Once it did, it would determine the corresponding record numbers (1 and 4) and then go immediately to these records. It would not have to examine any other records in the Client table.

Index on Zip Code

ZIP CODE	RECORD NUMBERS
56152	5
57222	8
57412	7
58120	1, 4
58216	2, 6
59130	3

Client table

RECORD NUMBER	CLIENT NUMBER	NAME	ADDRESS	CITY	STATE	ZIP CODE	. . .
1	AM53	Ashton-Mills	216 Rivard	Grattan	MA	58120	. . .
2	AS62	Alton-Scripps	722 Fisher	Empire	MA	58216	. . .
3	GR56	Grant Cleaners	737 Allard	Portage	NH	59130	. . .
4	GU21	Grand Union Supply, Inc.	247 Fuller	Grattan	MA	58120	. . .
5	MI26	Morland Int.	665 Whittier	Frankfort	MA	56152	. . .
6	SA56	Sawyer Inc.	31 Lafayette	Empire	MA	58216	. . .
7	SI82	Simpson Ind.	752 Cadieux	Fernwood	MA	57412	. . .
8	TR91	Trannel Co.	74 Webster	East Cedar	MI	57222	. . .

FIGURE 3-67

Another benefit of indexes is that they provide an efficient way to order records. That is, if the records are to appear in a certain order, Access can use an index instead of physically having to rearrange the records in the database file. Physically rearranging the records in a different order, which is called **sorting**, can be a very time-consuming process.

To see how indexes can be used for alphabetizing records, look at the record numbers in the index (Figure 3-66 on the previous page) and suppose you used these to list all clients. That is, simply follow down the Record Number column, listing the corresponding clients. In this example, first you would list the client on record 2 (Alton-Scripps), then the client on record 1 (Ashton-Mills), then the client on record 4 (Grand Union Supply, Inc.), and so on. The clients would be listed alphabetically by name without actually sorting the table.

To gain the benefits from an index, you first must create one. Access automatically creates an index on the primary key as well as some other special fields. If, as is the case with both the Client and Technician tables, a table contains a field called Zip Code, for example, Access will create an index for it automatically. You must create any other indexes you feel you need, indicating the field or fields on which the index is to be built.

Although the index key usually will be a single field, it can be a combination of fields. For example, you might want to sort records by Billed within Tech Number. In other words, the records are ordered by a combination of fields: Tech Number and Billed. An index can be used for this purpose by using a combination of fields for the index key. In this case, you must assign a name to the index. It is a good idea to assign a name that represents the combination of fields. For example, an index whose key is the combination of Tech Number and Billed, might be called Techbill.

How Does Access Use an Index?

Access creates an index whenever you request that it do so. It takes care of all the work in setting up and maintaining the index. In addition, it will use the index automatically.

If you request that data be sorted in a particular order and Access determines that an index is available that it can use to make the process efficient, it will do so. If no index is available, it still will sort the data in the order you requested; it will just take longer.

Similarly, if you request that Access locate a particular record that has a certain value in a particular field, Access will use an index if an appropriate one exists. If not, it will have to examine each record until it finds the one you want.

In both cases, the added efficiency provided by an index will not be readily apparent in tables that have only a few records. As you add more records to your tables, however, the difference can be dramatic. Even with only fifty to one hundred records, you will notice a difference. You can imagine how dramatic the difference would be in a table with fifty thousand records.

When Should You Create an Index?

An index improves efficiency for sorting and finding records. On the other hand, indexes occupy space on your disk. They also require Access to do extra work. Access must maintain all the indexes that have been created up to date. Thus, both advantages and disadvantages exist to using indexes. Consequently, the decision as to which indexes to create is an important one. The following guidelines should help you in this process.

Create an index on a field (or combination of fields) if one or more of the following conditions are present:

1. The field is the primary key of the table (Access will create this index automatically)
2. The field is the foreign key in a relationship you have created (Access also will create this index automatically when you specify the relationship)
3. You frequently will need your data to be sorted on the field
4. You frequently will need to locate a record based on a value in this field

Because Access handles 1 and 2 automatically, you need only to concern yourself about 3 and 4. If you think you will need to see client data arranged in order of billed amounts, for example, you should create an index on the Billed field. If you think you will need to see the data arranged by billed within technician number, you should create an index on the combination of the Tech Number field and the Billed field. Similarly, if you think you will need to find a client given the client's name, you should create an index on the Name field.

Creating Single-Field Indexes

A **single-field index** is an index whose key is a single field. In this case, the index key is to be the Name field. In creating an index, you need to indicate whether to allow duplicates in the index key; that is, two records that have the same value. For example, in the index for the Name field, if duplicates are not allowed, Access would not allow the addition of a client whose name is the same as the name of a client already in the database. In the index for the Name field, duplicates will be allowed. Perform the following steps to create a single-field index.

To Create a Single-Field Index

1. **Right-click Client.**

   The shortcut menu displays.

2. **Click Design on the shortcut menu, and then, if necessary, maximize the Client : Table window. Click the row selector to select the Name field. Point to the Indexed text box.**

   A maximized Client : Table window displays (Figure 3-68). The Name field is selected.

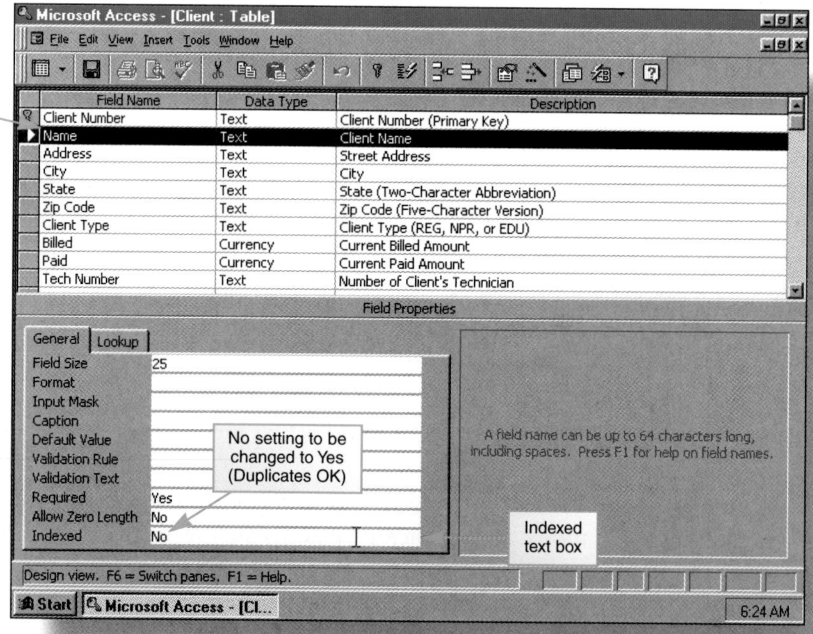

FIGURE 3-68

3 **Click the Indexed text box in the Field Properties pane. Click the down arrow that displays.**

The Indexed list displays (Figure 3-69). The settings are No (no index), Yes (Duplicates OK) (create an index and allow duplicates), and Yes (No Duplicates) (create an index but reject (do not allow) duplicates).

4 **Click Yes (Duplicates OK).**

The index on the Name field now will be created and is ready for use as soon as you save your work.

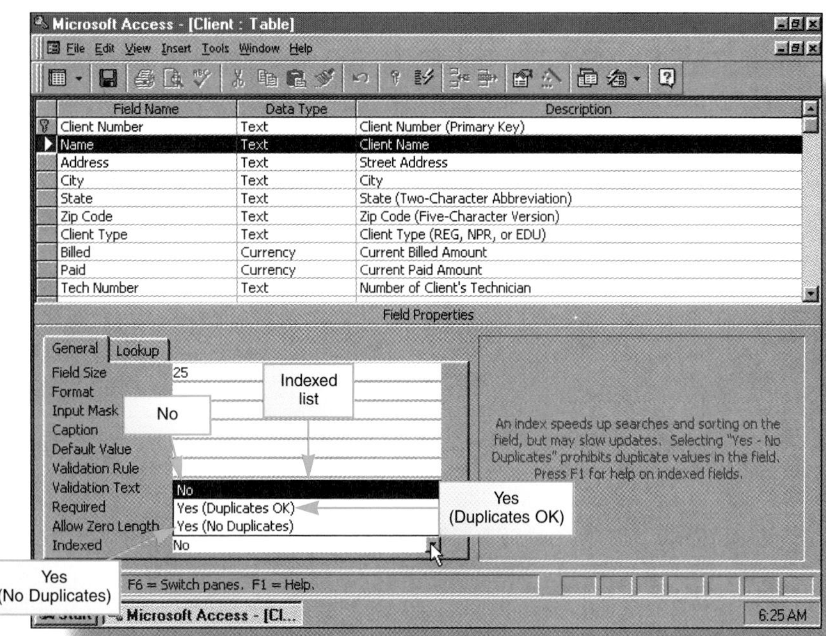

FIGURE 3-69

Creating Multiple-Field Indexes

Creating **multiple-field indexes**, that is, indexes whose key is a combination of fields, involves a different process from creating single-field indexes. To create multiple-field indexes, you will use the **Indexes button** on the toolbar, enter a name for the index, and then enter the combination of fields that make up the index key. The following steps create a multiple-field index with the name Techbill. The key will be the combination of the Tech Number field and the Billed field.

To Create a Multiple-Field Index

1 **Point to the Indexes button on the toolbar (Figure 3-70).**

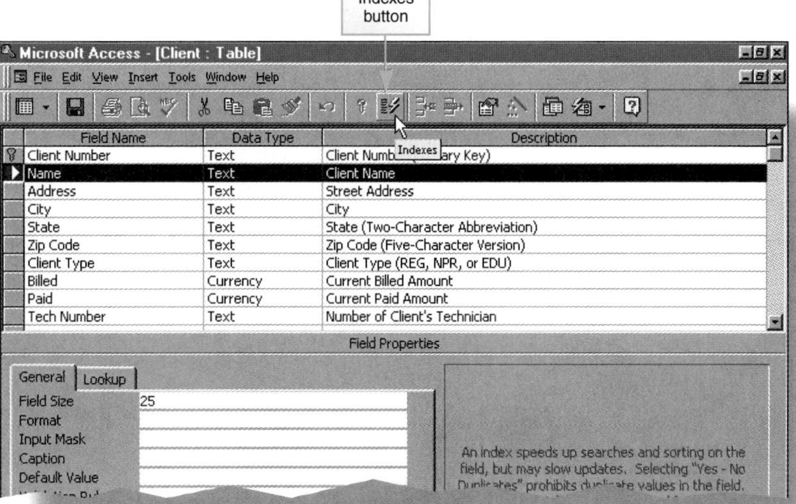

FIGURE 3-70

2 **Click the Indexes button. Click the blank row (the row following Name) in the Index Name column. Type** `Techbill` **as the index name, and then press the TAB key. Point to the down arrow.**

The Indexes: Client dialog box displays. It shows the indexes that already have been created and allows you to create additional indexes (Figure 3-71). The index name has been entered as Techbill. An insertion point displays in the Field Name column. The index on Client Number is the primary index and was created automatically by Access. The index on Name is the one just created. Access created other indexes (Paid and Zip Code) automatically. In this dialog box, you can create additional indexes.

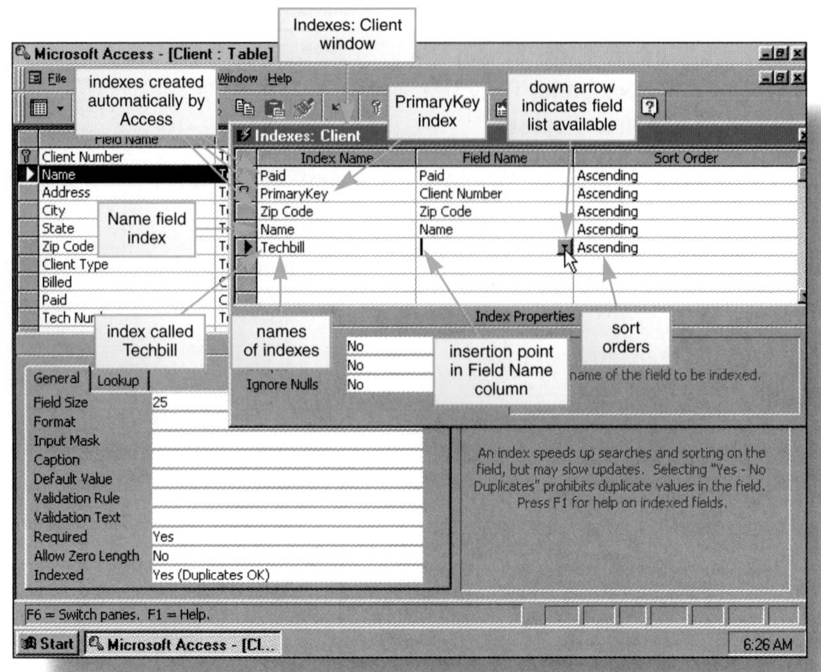

FIGURE 3-71

3 **Click the down arrow in the Field Name column to produce a list box of fields in the Client table, scroll down the list, and select Tech Number. Press the TAB key three times to move to the Field Name column on the following row. Select the Billed field in the same manner as the Tech Number field.**

Tech Number and Billed are selected as the two fields for the Techbill index (Figure 3-72). The absence of an index name on the row containing the Billed field indicates that it is part of the previous index, Techbill.

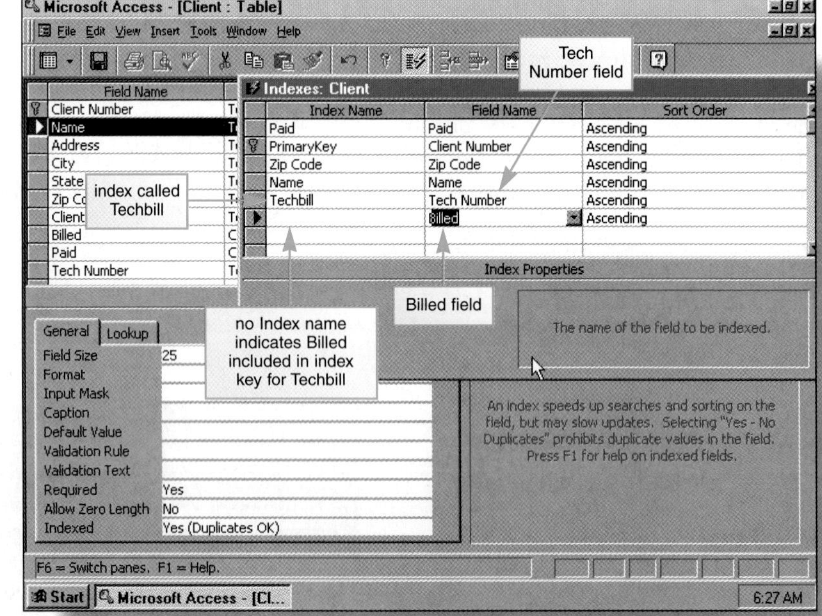

FIGURE 3-72

4 **Close the Indexes: Client dialog box by clicking its Close button, and then close the Client : Table window by clicking its Close button. When the Microsoft Access dialog box displays, click the Yes button to save your changes.**

The indexes are created and the Database window displays.

Other Ways

1. On View menu click Indexes

Closing the Database

The following step closes the database by closing its Database window.

TO CLOSE A DATABASE

Step 1: Click the Close button for the Pilotech Services : Database window.

The database closes.

The indexes now have been created. Access will use them automatically whenever possible to improve efficiency of ordering or finding records. Access also will maintain them automatically. That is, whenever the data in the Client table is changed, Access will make appropriate changes in the indexes automatically.

Project Summary

Project 3 covered the issues involved in maintaining a database. You used Form view to add a record to the Pilotech Services database and searched for a record satisfying a criterion. You changed and deleted records. You changed the structure of the Client table in the Pilotech Services database, created validation rules, and specified referential integrity between the Client and the Technician tables by creating relationships. You made mass changes to the Client table. Finally, you created indexes to improve performance.

What You Should Know

Having completed this project, you now should be able to perform the following tasks:

- Add a Field to a Table *(A 3.15)*
- Change the Size of a Field *(A 3.13)*
- Close a Database *(A 3.45)*
- Create a Multiple-Field Index *(A 3.43)*
- Create a Single-Field Index *(A 3.42)*
- Delete a Record *(A 3.12)*
- Make Individual Changes *(A 3.30)*
- Open a Database *(A 3.6)*
- Resize a Column *(A 3.17)*
- Save the Validation Rules, Default Values, and Formats *(A 3.27)*
- Search for a Record *(A 3.9)*
- Specify a Collection of Legal Values *(A 3.26)*
- Specify a Default Value *(A 3.25)*
- Specify a Format *(A 3.27)*
- Specify a Range *(A 3.25)*
- Specify a Required Field *(A 3.24)*
- Specify Referential Integrity *(A 3.32)*
- Switch from Form View to Datasheet View *(A 3.10)*
- Update the Contents of a Field *(A 3.10, A 3.16)*
- Use a Delete Query to Delete a Group of Records *(A 3.22)*
- Use a Form to Add Records *(A 3.7)*
- Use an Update Query to Update All Records *(A 3.19)*
- Use the Sort Ascending Button to Order Records *(A 3.35)*
- Use the Sort Ascending Button to Order Records on Multiple Fields *(A 3.37)*

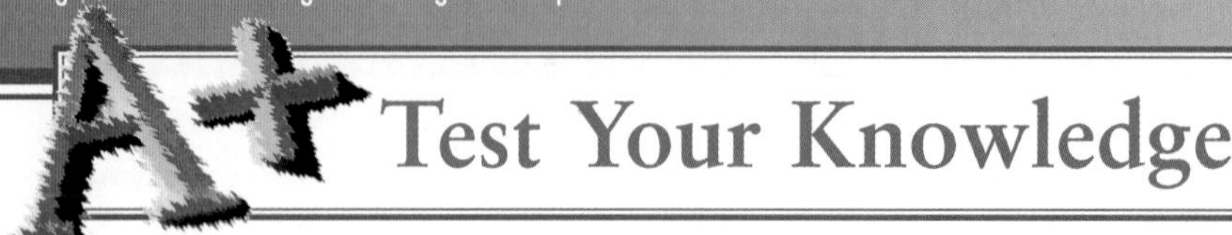

Test Your Knowledge

1 True/False

Instructions: Circle T if the statement is true or F if the statement is false.

T F 1. Access sorts records automatically by the primary index.

T F 2. Indexes provide an efficient alternative to sorting.

T F 3. To force all letters in a field to display as uppercase, use the ! symbol in the Format text box.

T F 4. You can add and change records using Datasheet view, but you can only delete records using Form view.

T F 5. To change the order in which records appear in a table, click the Order Records Ascending or Order Records Descending button on the toolbar.

T F 6. To delete a record from a table, click the record selector for the record, and then press the DELETE key.

T F 7. To delete a group of records that satisfy a criteria, use a query.

T F 8. A secondary key is a field in one table whose values are required to match a primary key of another table.

T F 9. The property that the value in a foreign key must match that of another table's primary key is called referential integrity.

T F 10. To specify referential integrity, click the Relationships button on the toolbar.

2 Multiple Choice

Instructions: Circle the correct response.

1. Indexes __________.
   a. allow rapid retrieval of tables
   b. allow rapid retrieval of records
   c. provide an efficient alternative to sorting
   d. both b and c
2. To create a multiple-field index, click the __________ button on the toolbar in the Table Design window.
   a. Secondary Index
   b. Create Secondary Indexes
   c. Indexes
   d. Create Indexes
3. __________ rules are rules that the data entered by a user must follow.
   a. Data
   b. Validation
   c. Integrity
   d. Edit

Test Your Knowledge

4. To search for a specific record in a table, select the field to search and then click the __________ button on the toolbar.
   a. Search
   b. Locate
   c. Find
   d. Query
5. To force all letters in a field to display as uppercase, use the __________ symbol in the Format text box.
   a. ?
   b. >
   c. !
   d. &
6. A(n) __________ key is a field in one table whose values are required to match a primary key of another table.
   a. secondary
   b. auxiliary
   c. foreign
   d. matching
7. The property that the value in a foreign key must match that of another table's primary key is called __________ integrity.
   a. entity
   b. interrelation
   c. relationship
   d. referential
8. To delete a record from a table, click the record selector for the record, and then press the __________ key(s).
   a. CTRL+DELETE
   b. DELETE
   c. CTRL+D
   d. CTRL+U
9. To specify referential integrity, click the __________ button on the toolbar.
   a. Referential Integrity
   b. Relationships
   c. Integrity
   d. Primary Key
10. To add a field to a table structure, select the field below where you would like the new field inserted and then press the __________ key(s).
    a. CTRL+N
    b. CTRL+I
    c. ALT+INSERT
    d. INSERT

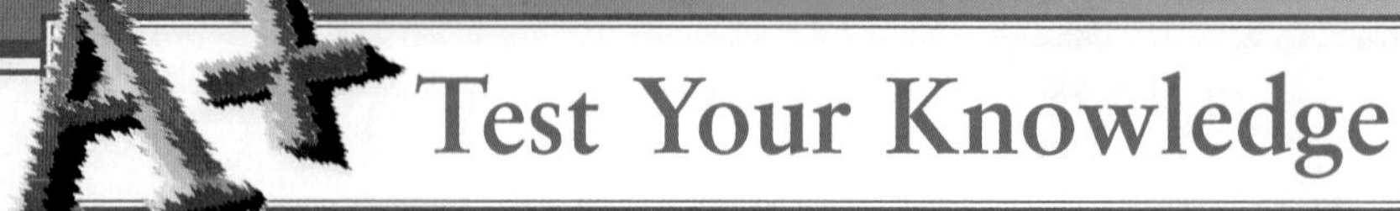

3 Adding, Changing, and Deleting Records

Instructions: Figure 3-73 shows the first record in the Customer table in Form view. Use this figure to help explain how to perform the following tasks in Form view. Write your answers on your own paper.

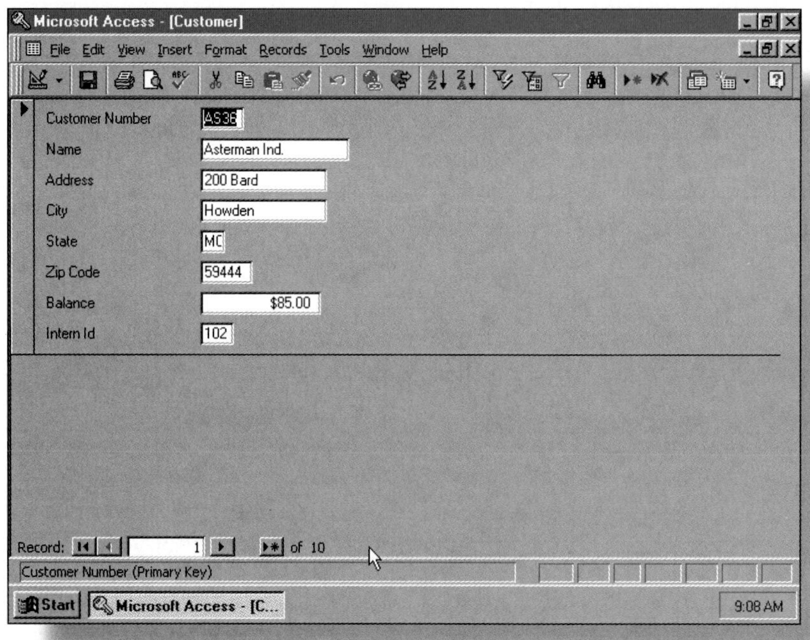

FIGURE 3-73

1. Change the Address from 200 Bard to 200 Bardsen.
2. Add a new record to the Customer table.
3. Locate the record that contains the value ME71 in the Customer Number field.
4. Switch to Datasheet view.
5. In Datasheet view, delete the record where the Customer Number is ME71.

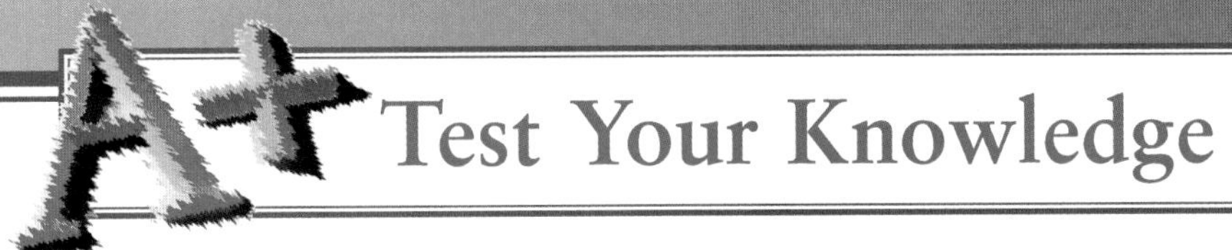

4 Understanding Validation Rules and Indexes

Instructions: Figure 3-74 shows the Intern table in Design view. Use this figure to help explain how to create the following validation rules and indexes. For each question, assume that the proper field already has been selected. Write your answers on your own paper.

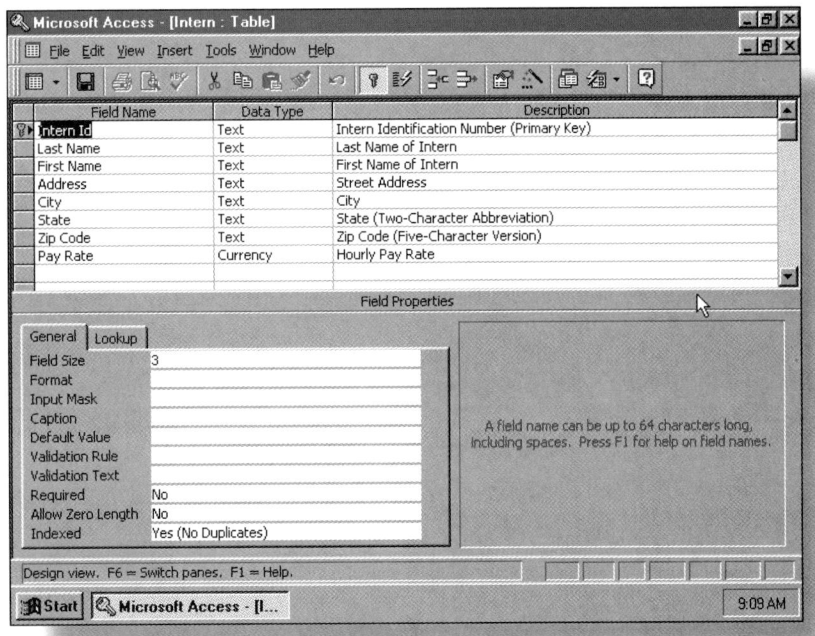

FIGURE 3-74

1. Make the Last Name field a required field.
2. Specify a default value of $7.25 for the Pay Rate field.
3. Specify that any value entered in the Pay Rate field must be greater than or equal to $7.25 and less than or equal to $10.00.
4. Create an index on the Last Name field that allows duplicates.

Use Help

1 Reviewing Project Activities

Instructions: Perform the following tasks using a computer.

1. Start Access.
2. If the Office Assistant is on your screen, then click it to display its balloon. If the Office Assistant is not on your screen, click the Office Assistant button on the toolbar.
3. Type `find records` in the What would you like to do? text box. Click the Search button. Click Find data. Read the Help information and then click The Find dialog box link under Which method do you want to use to find data?
4. Read the Help information on finding specific occurrences of a value in a field. Next, right-click within the box, and then click Print Topic. Hand in the printout to your instructor. Click the Help Topics button to return to the Help Topics: Microsoft Access 97 dialog box.
5. Click the Index tab. Type `sort` in the top text box labeled 1 and then double-click tables under sorting data in the list box labeled 2. Double-click Ways to work with data in a table's datasheet in the Topics Found dialog box. Click each of the links and read the Help information. When you are finished, click the Help Topics button to return to the Help Topics: Microsoft Access 97 dialog box.
6. Click the Find tab. Type `validation` in the top text box labeled 1. Click Validation in the list box labeled 2. Double-click Define validation rules to control what values can be entered into a field in the bottom box labeled 3. When the Help information displays, read it, ready the printer, right-click, and click Print Topic. Hand in the printout to your instructor. Click the Close button in the Microsoft Access 97 Help window.
7. Click the Office Assistant to display its balloon. Type `indexes` in the What would you like to do? text box. Click the Search button. Click Create an index to find and sort records faster. Read and print the Help information. Hand in the printout to your instructor.

Use Help

2 Expanding the Basics

Instructions: Use Access Help to learn about the topics listed below. If you are unable to print the Help information, then answer the question on your own paper.

1. Using the Creating, Importing, and Linking Tables book on the Contents sheet in the Help Topics: Microsoft Access 97 dialog box, answer the following questions:
   a. How do you delete an index?
   b. You cannot create indexes on fields of certain data types. What are these data types?
   c. What is the maximum number of fields in a multiple-field index?
   d. How can you create a primary key that includes more than one field?
2. Using the word, update, and the Index sheet in the Help Topics: Microsoft Access 97 dialog box, display and print information on update queries. Then, answer the following questions:
   a. How can you see a list of records that will be updated?
   b. How can you stop a query after you start it?
3. Use the Find sheet in the Help Topics: Microsoft Access 97 dialog box to display and then print information about replacing specific occurrences of a value in a field. Then answer the following questions:
   a. What are the advantages of using the Replace command instead of an update query?
   b. What is a null value?
4. Use the Office Assistant to display and print information on defining a custom data display format for a field.

Apply Your Knowledge

1 Maintaining the Green Thumb Database

Instructions: Start Access. Open the Green Thumb database from the Access folder on the Data Disk that accompanies this book. Perform the following tasks.

1. Open the Customer table in Design view as shown in Figure 3-75.

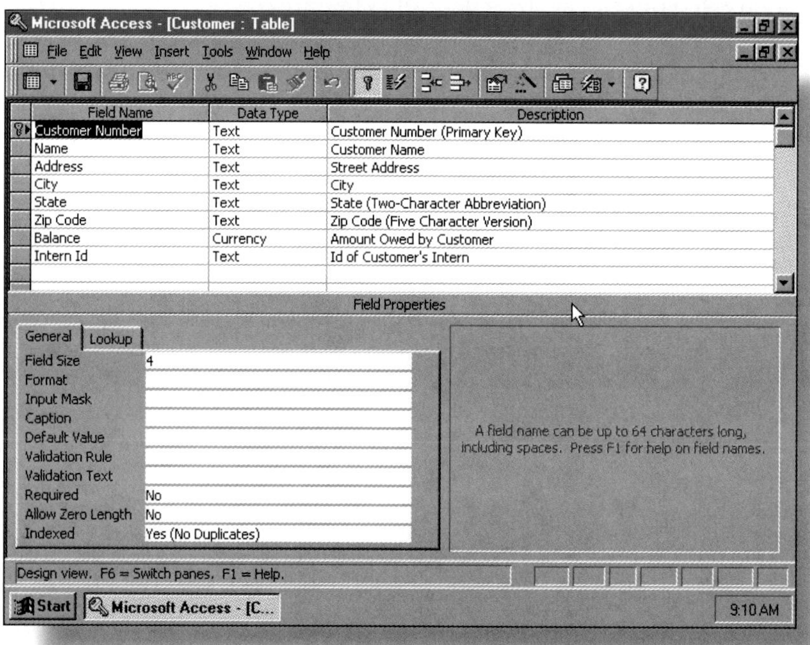

FIGURE 3-75

Apply Your Knowledge

2. Increase the size of the Name field to 25.
3. Format the Customer Number field so any lowercase letters display in uppercase.
4. Make the Name field a required field.
5. Specify that Balance amounts must be greater than or equal to $0.00 and less than or equal to $150.00. Include validation text.
6. Create an index that allows duplicates for the Name field.
7. Save the changes to the structure.
8. Open the Customer table in Datasheet view.
9. Change the name of Customer Number CJ16 to CJ's Music and Videos.
10. Resize the Name column so the complete name for customer CJ16 displays. Resize the City, State, Zip Code, Balance, and Intern Id columns to the best size.
11. Close the table and click Yes to save the changes to the layout of the table.
12. Print the table.
13. Open the Customer table and delete the record of Customer Number ME71.
14. Print the table.
15. Sort the data in ascending order by Zip Code within State.
16. Print the table. Close the table. If you are asked to save changes to the design of the table, click the No button.
17. Establish referential integrity between the Intern table (the one table) and the Customer table (the many table).

1 Maintaining the Museum Mercantile Database

Problem: The Museum Mercantile volunteers would like to make some changes to the database structure. They need to increase the size of the Description field and add an additional index. Because several different individuals update the data, the volunteers also would like to add some validation rules to the database. Finally, some new products must be added to the database.

Instructions: Use the database created in the In the Lab 1 of Project 1 for this assignment. Perform the following tasks.

1. Open the Museum Mercantile database and open the Product table in Design view as shown in Figure 3-76.
2. Create an index for the Description field. Be sure to allow duplicates.
3. Create and save the following validation rules for the Product table. List the steps involved on your own paper.
   a. Make the Description field a required field.
   b. Ensure that any lowercase letters entered in the Product Id field are converted to uppercase.
   c. Specify that the on hand units must be between 0 and 100. Include validation text.

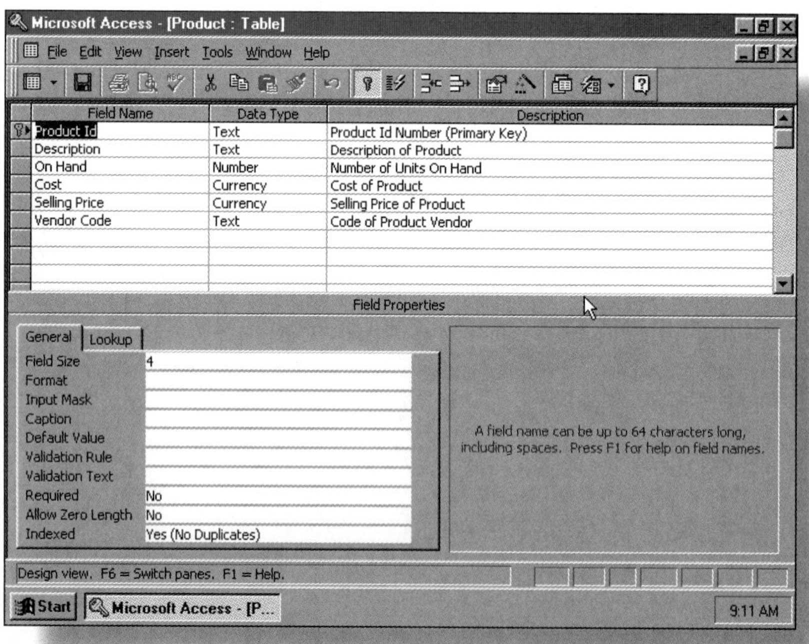

FIGURE 3-76

4. Save the changes.
5. Open the Product form you created in Project 1, and then add the following record to the Product table:

MN04	Mancala	4	$17.50	$21.95	WW

6. Switch to Datasheet view and sort the records in ascending order by Description.
7. Print the table. Close the table. If you are asked to save changes to the design of the table, click the No button.
8. Create a new query for the Product table.
9. Using a query, delete all records in the Product table where the Description starts with the letter T. (*Hint*: Use information from Use Help Exercise 2 to solve this problem.) Close the query without saving it.
10. Print the Product table.
11. Open the Vendor table in Design view, change the field width of the Name field to 22, and save the change.
12. Open the Vendor table in Datasheet view, and then change the name on the third record to Woodcrafters Guild. Resize the column so the complete name displays.
13. Print the table. Save the change to the layout of the table.
14. Specify referential integrity between the Vendor table (the one table) and the Product table (the many table). List the steps involved on your own paper.

2 Maintaining the City Telephone System Database

Problem: The manager of the City Telephone System would like to make some changes to the database structure. Another field must be added to the database, and the size of the First Name field must be increased. Because several different individuals update the data, the manager also would like to add some validation rules to the database. Finally, some additions and deletions are to be made to the database.

Instructions: Use the database created in the In the Lab 2 of Project 1 for this assignment. Perform the following tasks.

1. Open the City Telephone System database and open the User table in Design view as shown in Figure 3-77.

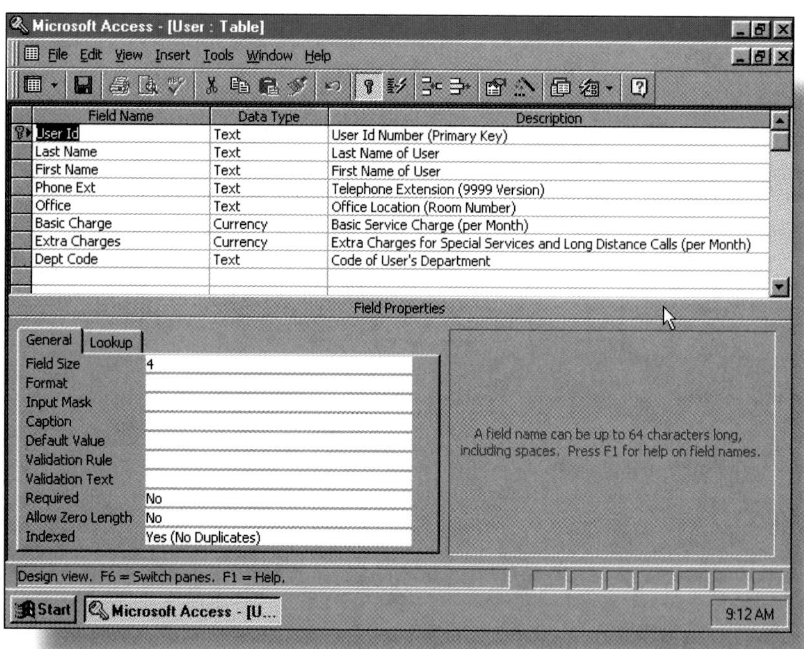

FIGURE 3-77

In the Lab

2. Create an index for the Last Name field. Be sure to allow duplicates.
3. Create an index on the combination of the Dept Code and Last Name fields. Name the index Deptname.
4. Change the field width of the First Name field to 15.
5. Save these changes and display the User table in Datasheet view.
6. Change the first name for User Id T451 to Mary Catherine.
7. Print the table.
8. Sort the records in ascending order by Dept Code.
9. Print the table. Close the table. If you are asked to save changes to the design of the table, click the No button.
10. Open the User table in Design view, and then add a Phone Code field to the User table. Define the field as Text with a width of 3. Insert the Phone Code field after the Extra Charges field. This field will contain data on whether the type of telephone is a regular single-line telephone (REG), multi-line telephone (MLT), or portable telephone (POR). Save the changes to the User table.
11. Create a new query for the User table.
12. Using this query, change all the entries in the Phone Code column to REG. This will be the status of most telephones. Do not save the query.
13. Print the table.
14. Open the User table in Design view and create the following validation rules for the User table. List the steps involved on your own paper.
    a. Make First Name and Last Name required fields.
    b. Specify the legal values, REG, MLT, and POR for the Phone Code field. Include validation text.
    c. Ensure that any letters entered in the User Id field are converted to uppercase.
    d. Specify a default value of $10.00 for the Basic Charge field.
15. Save the changes.
16. You can use either Form view or Datasheet view to add records to a table. To use Form view, you must replace the form you created in Project 1 with a form that includes the new field, Phone Code. With the User table selected, click the New Object: AutoForm button arrow on the toolbar. Click AutoForm. Use this form that contains the phone code to add the following record:

T890	Tartar	Joan	4655	240	$10.00	$0.00	REG	HRS

(continued)

Maintaining the City Telephone System Database *(continued)*

17. Close the form. Click the Yes button when asked if you want to save the form. Save the form as User. Click the Yes button when asked if you want to replace the User form you created in Project 1.
18. Open the User form and then locate the users with User Ids T645 and T759. Change the Phone Code for each record to MLT. Locate the user with User Id T888 and change the Phone Code to POR.
19. Switch to Datasheet view and print the table in order by last name. Close the table. If you are asked to save changes to the design of the table, click the No button.
20. Create a new query for the User table.
21. Using a query, delete all records in the User table where the Dept Code is ENG.
22. Close the query without saving it.
23. Print the User table.
24. Specify referential integrity between the Department table (the one table) and the User table (the many table). List the steps involved on your own paper.

3 Maintaining the City Scene Database

Problem: The managing editor has determined that some changes must be made to the database structure. Another field must be added and the size of the Name field must be increased. Because several different individuals update the data, the editor also would like to add some validation rules to the database. Finally, some additions and deletions are required to the database.

Instructions: Use the database created in the In the Lab 3 of Project 1 for this assignment. Perform the following tasks.

1. Open the City Scene database and open the Advertiser table in Design view as shown in Figure 3-78.
2. Create an index for the Name field. Be sure to allow duplicates. Create an index on the combination of the State and Zip Code fields. Name the index Statezip. Save these changes.

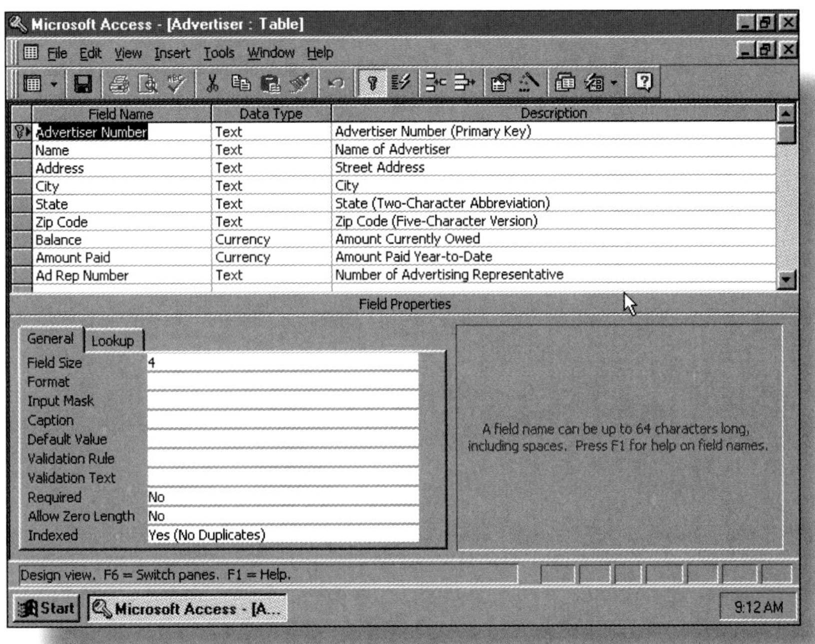

FIGURE 3-78

3. Display the Advertiser table in Datasheet view and order the records by Zip Code within State.
4. Print the table. Close the table. If you are asked to save changes to the design of the table, click the No button.
5. Change the field width of the Name field to 25.
6. Add the field, Ad Type, to the Advertiser table. Define the field as Text with a width of 3. Insert the Ad Type field after the Zip Code field. This field will contain data on the type of advertising account. Advertisers are classified as retail (RET), service (SER), and dining (DIN).
7. Save these changes and display the Advertiser table in Datasheet view.
8. Change the name of account C134 to Baker & Clover Clothes.
9. Resize the Name column to fit the changed entry. Decrease the width of the remaining columns.
10. Print the table. If necessary, change the margins so the table prints on one page in landscape orientation. Close the table. Save the layout changes to the table.
11. Using a query, change all the entries in the Ad Type column to RET. This will be the type of most accounts. Do not save the query.
12. Open the Advertiser table and order the records by name. Print the table. Close the table. If you are asked to save changes to the design of the table, click the No button.

(continued)

Maintaining the City Scene Database (continued)

13. Create the following validation rules for the Advertiser table and save the changes to the table. List the steps involved on your own paper.
    a. Make Name a required field.
    b. Specify the legal values RET, SER, and DIN for the Ad Type field. Include validation text.
    c. Ensure that any letters entered in the Advertiser Number and State fields are converted to uppercase.
    d. Specify that Balance must be between $0.00 and $450.00. Include validation text.
14. You can use either Form view or Datasheet view to add records to a table. To use Form view, you must replace the form you created in Project 1 with a form that includes the new field, Ad Type. With the Advertiser table selected, click the New Object: AutoForm button arrow on the toolbar. Click AutoForm. Use this form that contains Ad Type to add the following record:

M121	Shoe Salon	113 Main	Fernwood	WA	91191	RET	$50.00	$0.00	22

15. Close the form. Click the Yes button when asked if you want to save the form. Save the form as Advertiser. Click the Yes button when asked if you want to replace the Advertiser form you created in Project 1.
16. Open the Advertiser form and locate the advertisers with Advertiser Numbers B101, and D216 and then change the Ad Type for each record to DIN. Change the Ad Type for advertisers C047 and G080 to SER.
17. Change to Datasheet view and print the table.
18. Using a query, delete all records in the table where the account has the Ad Type of SER and is located in the state of OR. Do not save the query.
19. Print the Advertiser table. Specify referential integrity between the Ad Rep table (the one table) and the Advertiser table (the many table). List the steps involved on your own paper.

Cases and Places

The difficulty of these case studies varies: ◗ are the least difficult; ◗◗ are more difficult; and ◗◗◗ are the most difficult.

1 ◗ Use the textbook database created in Case Study 1 of Project 1 for this assignment. Execute each of these tasks and then print the results: (a) Mary Healy has dropped the price of her textbook from $36 to $30. (b) John Mott has sold his book, so you can delete his record from your database. (c) Sandi Radle informs you she gave you the wrong course number for her textbook. It is used in Phi 210 instead of Phi 310. (d) You decide to sell the computer book you are using in this class for $35. It is in good condition. (e) The Psychology department has changed textbooks in the introductory course for the upcoming semester. Delete the books listed for Psy 101. (f) Dave Corsi's book is in good condition. (g) Peter Rudd has changed his telephone number to 555-1782.

2 ◗ Use the restaurant database created in Case Study 2 of Project 1 for this assignment. Execute each of these tasks and then print the results: (a) Ye Old Cafe now occupies the location formerly occupied by Curry and More, which has gone out of business. Ye Old Cafe serves Continental cuisine, is open from 6:00 a.m. to 9:00 p.m., and has carryout but no delivery service. Its telephone number is (714) 555-3628. You like the all-you-can-eat special on Wednesday. (b) Ole Taco now offers delivery service. (c) New Crete now opens at 11:00 a.m. and closes at 11:00 p.m. (d) Little Venice has moved to 532 S. Madison. (e) Texas Diner has changed its special from Thursday to Friday. (f) Red Rose now offers carryout service.

3 ◗◗ Use the movie collection database created in Case Study 3 of Project 1 for this assignment. Add five of your favorite movie titles to the table. Print the entire table sorted by movie title in ascending order.

4 ◗◗ Use the nutritional content database created in Case Study 4 of Project 1 for this assignment. Execute each of these tasks and then print the results: (a) Other meat also can be considered lean. For example, pork tenderloin has the same calories and fat as eye of round and has 65 mg of cholesterol. Top pork loin chop and center chop both have 170 calories, 7 grams of fat, and 70 mg of cholesterol. Boneless ham is one of the most nutritional meats, with 125 calories, 4 grams of fat, and 45 mg of cholesterol. Lamb loin chop has 180 calories, 8 grams of fat, and 80 mg of cholesterol, and whole leg of lamb has 160 calories, 7 grams of fat, and 75 mg of cholesterol. Add these cuts of meat to the database. (b) Display and print the cuts of meat with less than 70 milligrams of cholesterol in a three-ounce serving. (c) Display and print the cuts of meat with more than 160 calories in a three-ounce serving. (d) Your nutrition instructor wants you to experiment by consuming less than 20 grams of fat daily. During the day, you have eaten food with a total fat gram content of 15. Display and print the cuts of meat that would be within the experiment guidelines.

Cases and Places

5 ▶▶▶ Use the product comparison database you created in Case Study 5 of Project 1 for this assignment. Often generic items are available for products on your shopping list. During your next shopping trip, locate any generic items that you could substitute for the 24 items in the table. Create a new field in the table and add the generic prices. Then, print the six items in each of the four categories in ascending order, along with the sizes and prices.

6 ▶▶▶ You have found the campus directory database you created in Case Study 6 of Project 1 to be invaluable. You have been handwriting additional names and telephone numbers and making changes to the printout, and now you want to update the table. Add a new category called departmental coordinators, and add the names, telephone numbers, and room numbers of departmental coordinators you call. In the faculty category, list your favorite instructors from previous semesters. Add your current instructors' office hours to the table. In the administration category, add data for the president and vice president of the school. In the services category, add the library circulation desk, athletic office, and theatre box office data. Print the entire table. Then print the instructors' names in ascending order, along with their telephone numbers, office hours, and office room numbers. Create a similar printout for the administrators and for the departmental coordinators. Finally, print the services in ascending order, including telephone numbers and room numbers.

7 ▶▶▶ Many national brokers offer IRAs. Call three of these brokerage companies and obtain the same information for investing $1,000 that you needed to complete Case Study 7 of Project 1 in the financial institutions database. Add these records to the table. Then, display and print the following: (a) The names of all the financial institutions in the table and total values of the IRAs at age 65 in descending order. (b) The names and telephone numbers of the financial institutions and total amounts of interest earned at age 65 in descending order. (c) The average value of the IRAs at age 65. (d) The average interest rates for the banks, savings and loans, credit unions, and brokerage companies. (e) The name, address, and interest rate of the financial institution with the highest interest rate. (f) The name, telephone number, and interest rate of the financial institution with the lowest interest rate. (g) The names of the financial institutions and penalties for early withdrawal in two years in ascending order. (h) The names of the financial institutions and annual fees in ascending order.

Integrating Excel Worksheet Data into an Access Database

INTEGRATION FEATURE

Case Perspective

Tamalex Industries has used Excel to automate a variety of tasks for several years. Employees at Tamalex have created several useful worksheets that have simplified their work. Along with the worksheets, they have created attractive charts for visual representation of the data.

When Tamalex decided it needed to maintain employee data, the familiarity with Excel led to the decision to maintain the data as an Excel worksheet. This worked well for a while. Then, they began to question whether Excel was the best choice. Their counterparts at other companies indicated that they were using Access to maintain employee data. Access had worked well for them. As the structure of their data became more complex, Access easily adapted to the increased complexity. They appreciated the power of the query and reporting features in Access. Finally, officials at Tamalex decided that they should follow the lead of the other companies. The company decided to convert its data from Excel to Access.

Introduction

It is not uncommon for people to use an application for some specific purpose, only to find later that another application may be better suited. For example, a company such as Tamalex Industries initially might keep data in an Excel worksheet, only to discover later that the data would be better maintained in an Access database. Some common reasons for using a database instead of a worksheet are:

1. The worksheet contains a great deal of redundant data. As discussed in Project 1 on pages A 1.54 through A 1.56, databases can be designed to eliminate redundant data.
2. The worksheet would need to be larger than Excel can handle. Excel has a limit of 16,384 rows. In Access, no such limit exists.
3. The data to be maintained consists of multiple interrelated items. For example, Pilotech Services needed to maintain data on two items, clients and technicians, and these items are interrelated. A client has a single technician and each technician services several clients. The Pilotech Services database is a very simple one. Databases easily can contain 30 or more interrelated items.
4. You want to use the extremely powerful query and report capabilities of Microsoft Access.

More About Converting Data: Worksheets

It is possible to convert a single worksheet within a Microsoft Excel multiple-worksheet workbook to an Access table. With other spreadsheet packages, however, you first must save the worksheet as an individual file and then convert the individual file.

Regardless of the reasons for making the change from a worksheet to a database, it is important to be able to make the change easily. In the not-too-distant past, converting data from one tool to another often could be a very difficult, time-consuming task. Fortunately, an easy way of converting data from Excel to Access is available.

Figures 1 and 2 illustrate the conversion process. The type of worksheet that can be converted is one in which the data is stored as a **list**, that is, a labeled series of rows in which each row contains the same type of data. For example, in the worksheet in Figure 1, the first row contains the labels, which are entries indicating the type of data found in the column. The entry in the first column, for example, is SS Number, indicating that all the other values in the column are Social Security numbers. The entry in the second column is Last Name, indicating that all the other values in the column are last names. Other than the first row, which contains the labels, all the rows contain precisely the same type of data: a Social Security number in the first column, a last name in the second column, a first name in the third column, and so on.

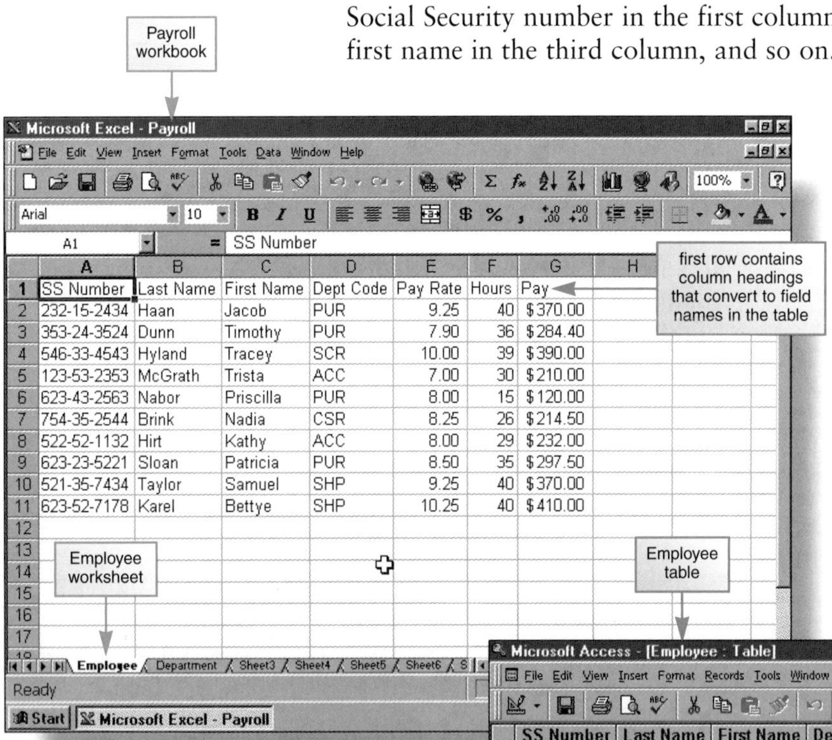

Payroll workbook

Microsoft Excel - Payroll

	A	B	C	D	E	F	G
1	SS Number	Last Name	First Name	Dept Code	Pay Rate	Hours	Pay
2	232-15-2434	Haan	Jacob	PUR	9.25	40	$370.00
3	353-24-3524	Dunn	Timothy	PUR	7.90	36	$284.40
4	546-33-4543	Hyland	Tracey	SCR	10.00	39	$390.00
5	123-53-2353	McGrath	Trista	ACC	7.00	30	$210.00
6	623-43-2563	Nabor	Priscilla	PUR	8.00	15	$120.00
7	754-35-2544	Brink	Nadia	CSR	8.25	26	$214.50
8	522-52-1132	Hirt	Kathy	ACC	8.00	29	$232.00
9	623-23-5221	Sloan	Patricia	PUR	8.50	35	$297.50
10	521-35-7434	Taylor	Samuel	SHP	9.25	40	$370.00
11	623-52-7178	Karel	Bettye	SHP	10.25	40	$410.00

first row contains column headings that convert to field names in the table

Employee worksheet

Employee table

FIGURE 1

Microsoft Access - [Employee : Table]

SS Number	Last Name	First Name	Dept Code	Pay Rate	Hours	Pay
123-53-2353	McGrath	Trista	ACC	$7.00	30	$210.00
232-15-2434	Haan	Jacob	PUR	$9.25	40	$370.00
353-24-3524	Dunn	Timothy	PUR	$7.90	36	$284.40
521-35-7434	Taylor	Samuel	SHP	$9.25	40	$370.00
522-52-1132	Hirt	Kathy	ACC	$8.00	29	$232.00
546-33-4543	Hyland	Tracey	SCR	$10.00	39	$390.00
623-23-5221	Sloan	Patricia	PUR	$8.50	35	$297.50
623-43-2563	Nabor	Priscilla	PUR	$8.00	15	$120.00
623-52-7178	Karel	Bettye	SHP	$10.25	40	$410.00
754-35-2544	Brink	Nadia	CSR	$8.25	26	$214.50

rows sorted by SS Number, because it is the primary key

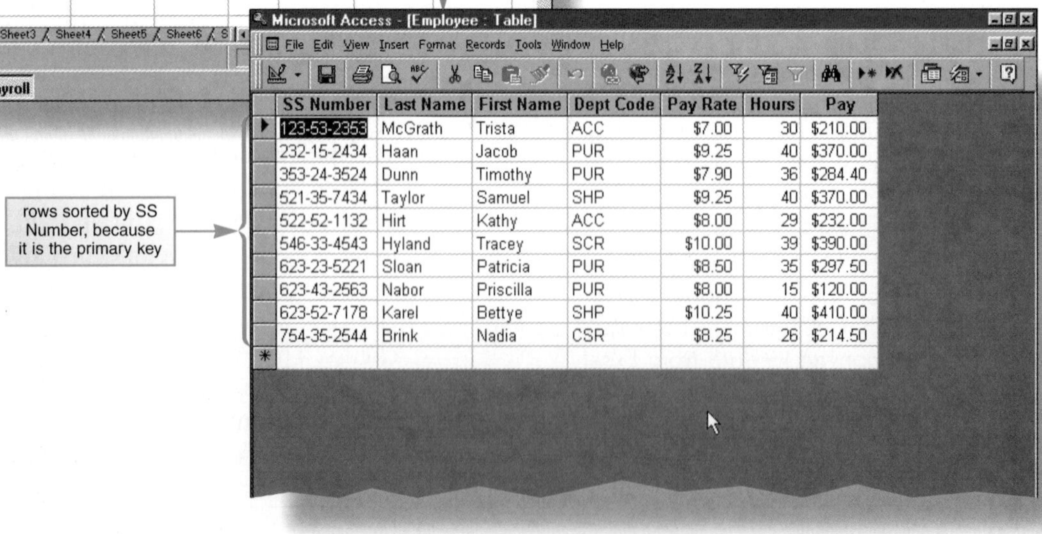

FIGURE 2

As the figures illustrate, the worksheet, shown in Figure 1, is converted to a database table, shown in Figure 2. The columns in the worksheet become the fields. The column headings in the first row of the worksheet become the field names. The rows of the worksheet, other than the first row, which contains the labels, become the records in the table. In the process, each field will be assigned the data type that seems the most reasonable, given the data currently in the worksheet.

The conversion process uses the **Import Spreadsheet Wizard**. The wizard takes you through some basic steps, asking a few simple questions. Once you have answered the questions, the wizard will perform the conversion.

More *About* Converting Data: Databases

It is possible to convert data from objects other than spreadsheets to a database. You can also convert data from one database management system to another. Access, for example, provides tools for easily converting data from such database systems as dBASE III, dBASE IV, and Paradox.

Creating an Access Database

Before converting the data, you need to create the database that will contain the data. Perform the following steps to create the Tamalex Industries database.

TO CREATE A NEW DATABASE

Step 1: Click the Start button and then click New Office Document on the Start menu.
Step 2: Click the General tab, make sure the Blank Database icon is selected, and then click the OK button.
Step 3: Click the Save in box arrow and then click 3½ Floppy (A:).
Step 4: Type `Tamalex Industries` as the file name and then click the Create button.

Converting an Excel Worksheet to an Access Database

To convert the data, you will use the Import Spreadsheet Wizard. In the process, you will indicate that the first row contains the column headings. These column headings then will become the field names in the Access table. In addition, you will indicate the primary key for the table. As part of the process, you can choose not to include all the fields from the worksheet in the resulting table. You should be aware that some of the steps on the next page might take a significant amount of time for Access to execute.

More *About* Converting Data: Other Formats

It is possible to convert data to a database from a variety of special file formats, including delimited and fixed-width text files. If you cannot convert directly from another spreadsheet or database directly to Access, you often can convert to one of these special formats and then convert the resulting file to Access.

Steps To Convert an Excel Worksheet to an Access Database

1. **With the Tamalex Industries database open, click File on the menu bar and then click Get External Data. Point to Import.**

   The submenu of commands for getting external data displays (Figure 3).

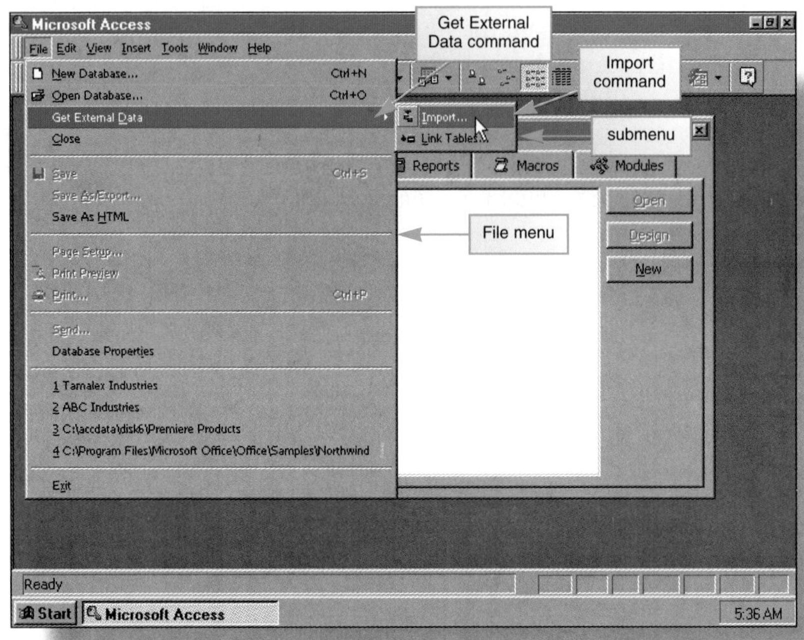

FIGURE 3

2. **Click Import. Click the Files of type box arrow in the Import dialog box and then click Microsoft Excel. Click 3½ Floppy (A:) in the Look in list box, and then select the Access folder. Make sure the Payroll workbook is selected and then click the Import button.**

   The Import Spreadsheet Wizard dialog box displays (Figure 4). It displays the list of worksheets in the Payroll workbook.

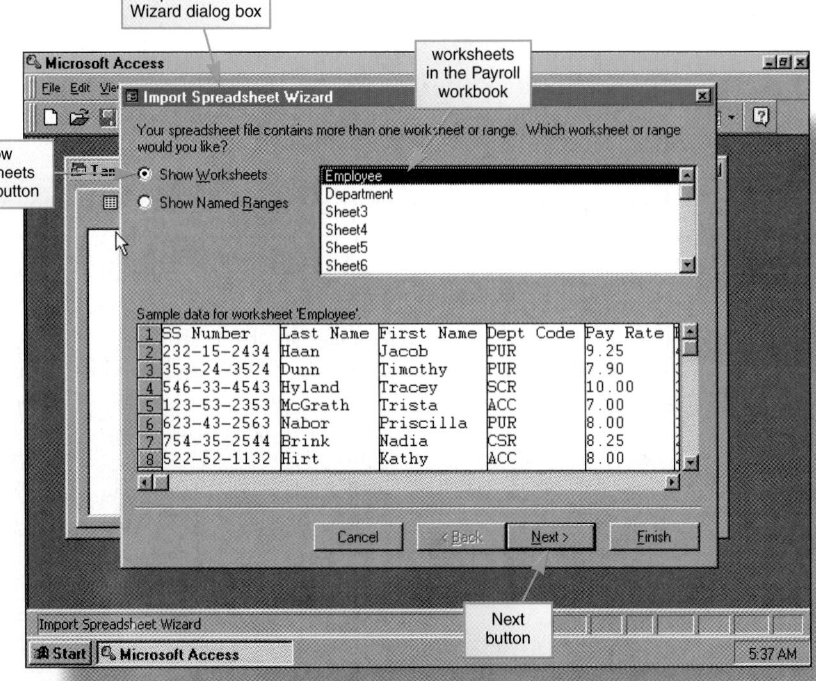

FIGURE 4

3 **Be sure the Employee worksheet is selected and then click the Next button.**

The Import Spreadsheet Wizard dialog box displays (Figure 5). It displays a portion of the worksheet that is being converted. In this dialog box, you indicate that the first row of the worksheet contains the column headings. The wizard uses these values as the field names in the Access table.

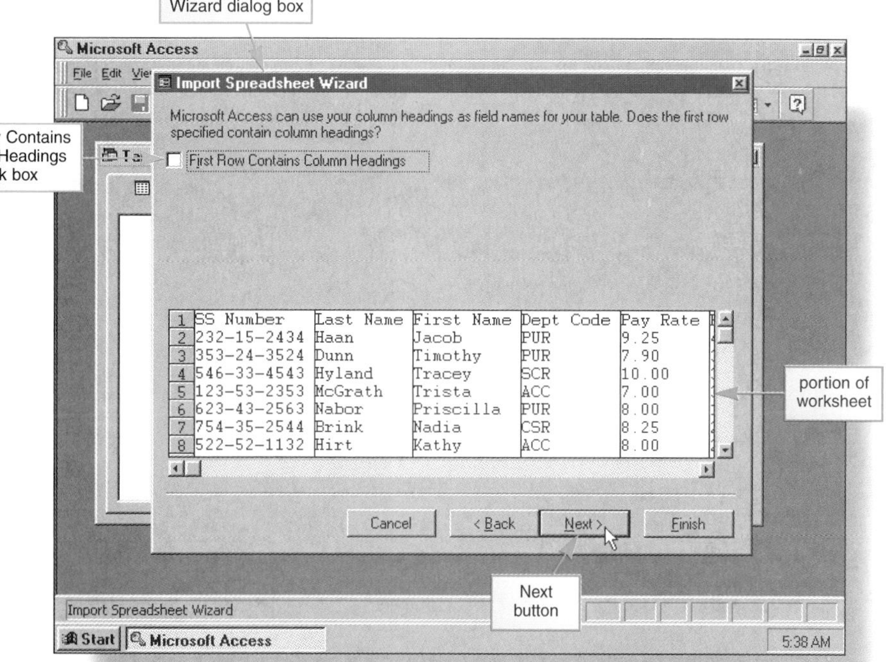

1	SS Number	Last Name	First Name	Dept Code	Pay Rate
2	232-15-2434	Haan	Jacob	PUR	9.25
3	353-24-3524	Dunn	Timothy	PUR	7.90
4	546-33-4543	Hyland	Tracey	SCR	10.00
5	123-53-2353	McGrath	Trista	ACC	7.00
6	623-43-2563	Nabor	Priscilla	PUR	8.00
7	754-35-2544	Brink	Nadia	CSR	8.25
8	522-52-1132	Hirt	Kathy	ACC	8.00

FIGURE 5

4 **Click First Row Contains Column Headings and then click the Next button.**

The Import Spreadsheet Wizard dialog box displays asking whether the data is to be placed in a new table or in an existing table (Figure 6).

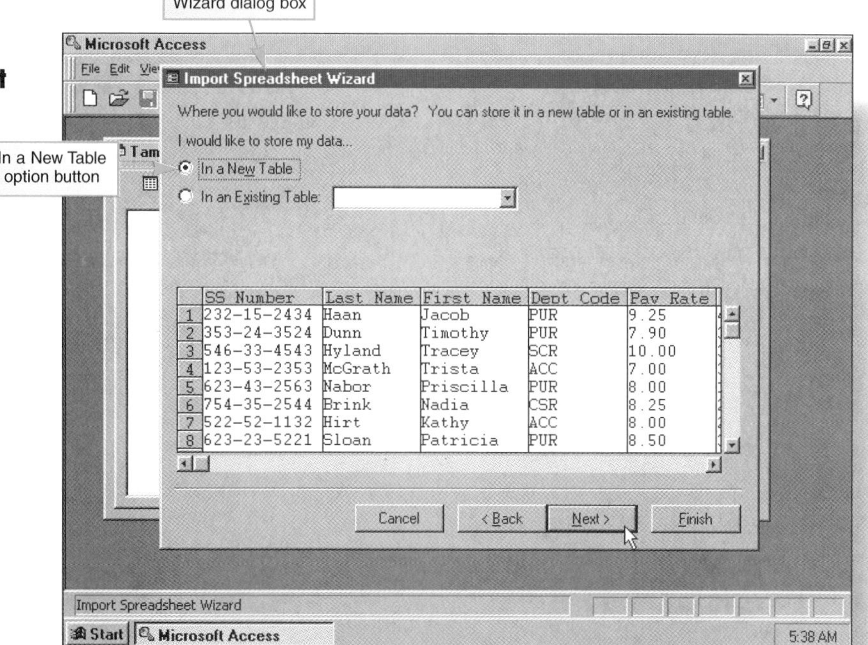

	SS Number	Last Name	First Name	Dept Code	Pay Rate
1	232-15-2434	Haan	Jacob	PUR	9.25
2	353-24-3524	Dunn	Timothy	PUR	7.90
3	546-33-4543	Hyland	Tracey	SCR	10.00
4	123-53-2353	McGrath	Trista	ACC	7.00
5	623-43-2563	Nabor	Priscilla	PUR	8.00
6	754-35-2544	Brink	Nadia	CSR	8.25
7	522-52-1132	Hirt	Kathy	ACC	8.00
8	623-23-5221	Sloan	Patricia	PUR	8.50

FIGURE 6

5 Be sure that In a New Table is selected and then click the Next button.

The Import Spreadsheet Wizard dialog box displays giving you the opportunity to specify field options (Figure 7). You can specify that indexes are to be created for certain fields. You also can specify that certain fields should not be included in the Access table.

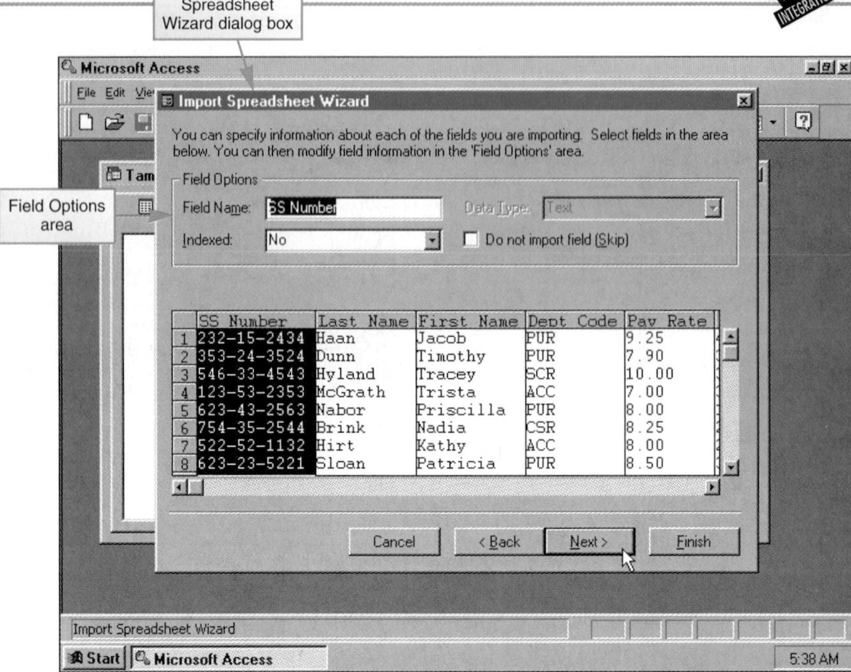

FIGURE 7

6 Click the Next button.

The Import Spreadsheet Wizard dialog box displays (Figure 8). In this dialog box, you indicate the primary key of the Access table. You can allow Access to add a special field to serve as the primary key as illustrated in the figure. You can choose an existing field to serve as the primary key. You also can indicate no primary key. Most of the time, one of the existing fields will serve as the primary key. In this worksheet, for example, the SS Number serves as the primary key.

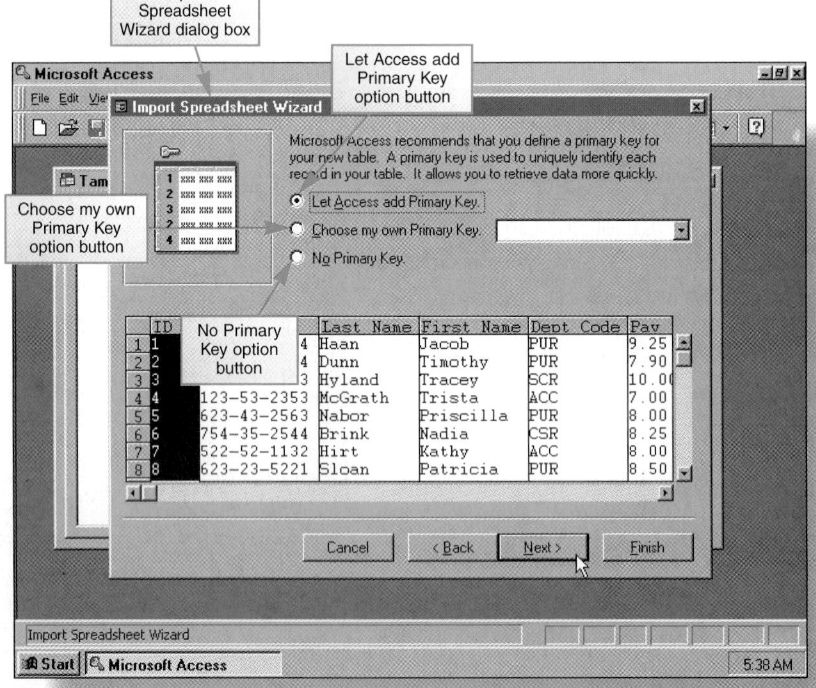

FIGURE 8

7 Click Choose my own Primary Key.

The SS Number field, which is the correct field, will be the primary key. If some other field were to be the primary key, you could click the down arrow and select the other field from the list of available fields.

8 Click the Next button. Be sure Employee displays in the Import to Table text box.

The Import Spreadsheet Wizard dialog box displays (Figure 9). The name of the table will be Employee.

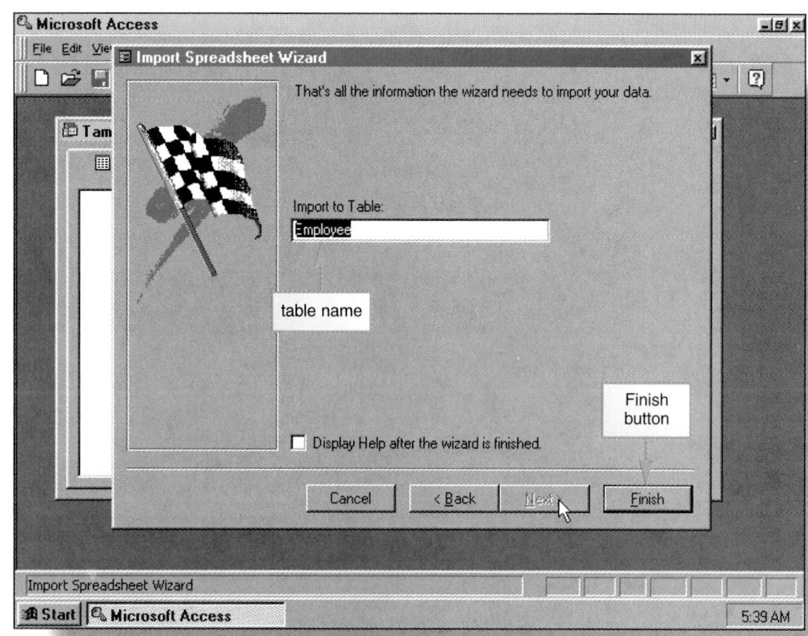

FIGURE 9

9 Click the Finish button.

The worksheet will be converted into an Access table. When the process is completed, the Import Spreadsheet Wizard dialog box will display (Figure 10).

10 Click the OK button.

The table now has been created (see Figure 2 on page AI 1.2).

11 Close Access.

The Employee table has been created in the Tamalex Industries database.

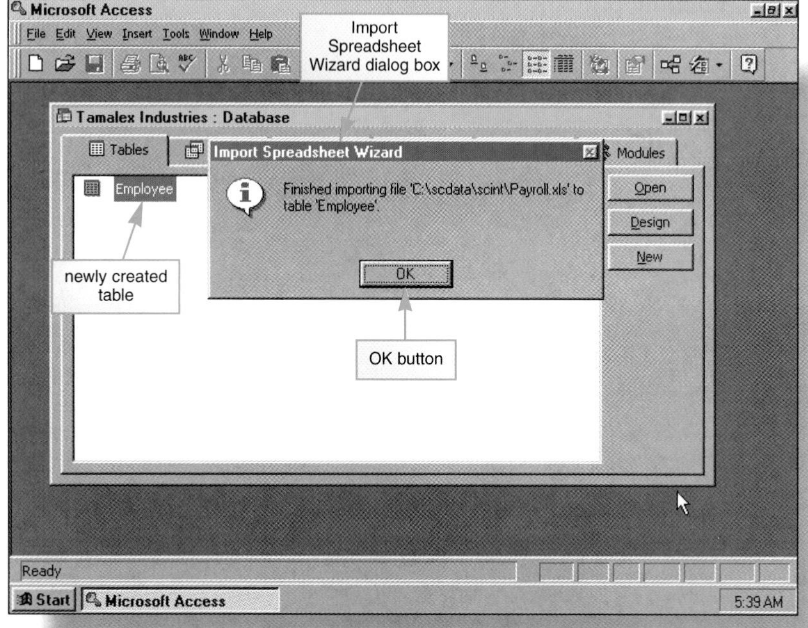

FIGURE 10

Using the Access Table

Once the Access version of the table has been created, you can treat it as you would any other table. After first opening the database containing the table, you can open the table in Datasheet view (Figure 2 on page AI 1.2). You can make changes to the data. You can create queries that use the data in the table.

By clicking Design on the table's shortcut menu, you can view the table's structure and make any necessary changes to the structure. The changes may include changing field sizes and types, creating indexes, or adding additional fields. To accomplish any of these tasks, use the same steps you used in Project 3. In the Employee table shown in Figure 2, for example, the data type for the Pay Rate field has been changed to Currency and the columns have all been resized to best fit the data.

Summary

The Integration Feature covered the process of integrating an Excel worksheet into an Access database. To convert a worksheet to an Access table, you learned to use the Import Spreadsheet Wizard. Working with the wizard, you identified the first row of the worksheet as the row containing the column headings and you indicated the primary key. The wizard then created the table for you and placed it in a new database.

What You Should Know

Having completed this Integration Feature, you now should be able to perform the following tasks:

- Convert an Excel Worksheet to an Access Database *(AI 1.4)*
- Create a New Database *(AI 1.3)*

In the Lab

1 Use Help

Instructions: Perform the following tasks using a computer.

1. Start Access.
2. If the Office Assistant is on your screen, then click it to display its balloon. If the Office Assistant is not on your screen, click the Office Assistant button on the toolbar.
3. Type `spreadsheets` in the What would you like to do? text box. Click the Search button. Click Import or link data from a spreadsheet. When the Help information displays, read it. Next, right-click within the box, and then click Print Topic. Hand in the printout to your instructor. Click the Help Topics button to return to the Help Topics: Microsoft Access 97 dialog box.
4. Click the Index tab. Type `troubleshooting` in the top text box labeled 1 and then double-click troubleshooting imported and linked data in the list box labeled 2. Double-click Troubleshoot text or spreadsheet import errors in the Topics Found dialog box. When the Help information displays, click the first link and read the information. Next, right-click within the box and click Print Topic. Click the Back button and then click the second link. Read and print the information. Hand in the printouts to your instructor.

2 Converting the Inventory Worksheet

Problem: The Tennis Is Everything Catalog Company has been using Excel to keep track of its inventory. Employees at Tennis Is Everything use several worksheets to reorder products, keep track of carrying costs, and graph trends in buying. The company is expanding rapidly and branching out into other sports-related products. They now need to maintain additional data and would like to produce reports and queries that are more sophisticated. The company management has asked you to convert its inventory data to an Access database.

Instructions: Perform the following tasks.

1. Create a new database in which to store all the objects related to the inventory data. Call the database Tennis Is Everything.
2. Open the Inventory workbook in the Access folder on the Data Disk that accompanies this book. Import the Product worksheet into Access.
3. Use Product as the name of the Access table and Product Number as the primary key.
4. Open and print the Product table shown in Figure 11 on the next page.

(continued)

In the Lab

Converting the Inventory Worksheet *(continued)*

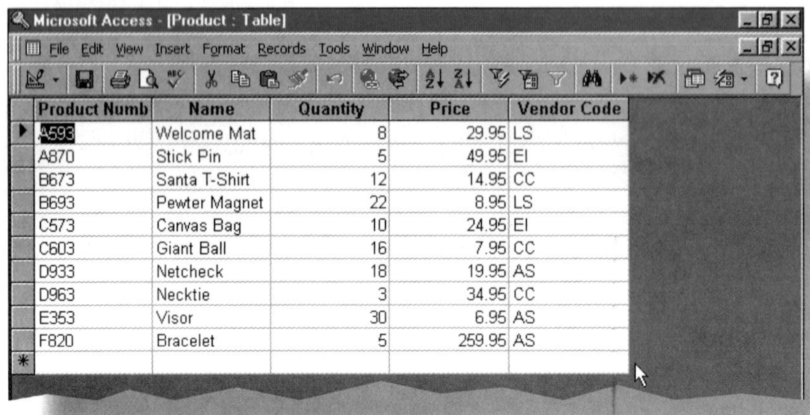

Microsoft Access - [Product : Table]

Product Numb	Name	Quantity	Price	Vendor Code
A593	Welcome Mat	8	29.95	LS
A870	Stick Pin	5	49.95	EI
B673	Santa T-Shirt	12	14.95	CC
B693	Pewter Magnet	22	8.95	LS
C573	Canvas Bag	10	24.95	EI
C603	Giant Ball	16	7.95	CC
D933	Netcheck	18	19.95	AS
D963	Necktie	3	34.95	CC
E353	Visor	30	6.95	AS
F820	Bracelet	5	259.95	AS

FIGURE 11

3 Converting the Customer Worksheet

Problem: Midwest Computer Supply has been using Excel to keep track of its customer data. Employees at Midwest Computer Supply use several worksheets to maintain information on inventory as well as customers. The company realizes that customer data would be better handled in Access. A Midwest employee created a database to store the data but has not yet imported the data. The company management has asked you to complete the conversion of its customer data to an Access database.

Instructions: Perform the following tasks.

1. Open the Midwest Computer Supply database in the Access folder on the Data Disk that accompanies this book.
2. Open the Sales workbook in the Access folder on the Data Disk that accompanies this book. Import the Customer worksheet into Access.
3. Append the worksheet data to the Customer table that already exists in the Midwest Computer Supply database. *(Hint:* Use Help on the previous page can help you solve this problem.)
4. Open the Customer table, resize the columns, and print the table shown in Figure 12.

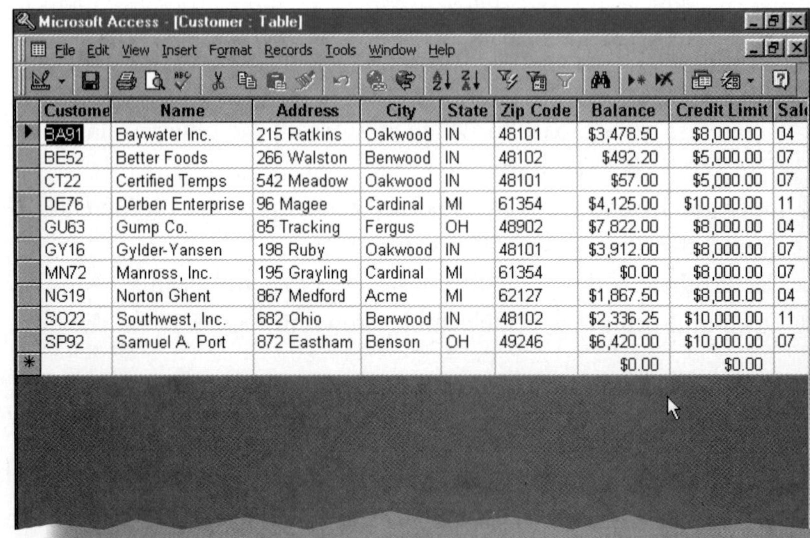

Microsoft Access - [Customer : Table]

Custome	Name	Address	City	State	Zip Code	Balance	Credit Limit	Sal
BA91	Baywater Inc.	215 Ratkins	Oakwood	IN	48101	$3,478.50	$8,000.00	04
BE52	Better Foods	266 Walston	Benwood	IN	48102	$492.20	$5,000.00	07
CT22	Certified Temps	542 Meadow	Oakwood	IN	48101	$57.00	$5,000.00	07
DE76	Derben Enterprise	96 Magee	Cardinal	MI	61354	$4,125.00	$10,000.00	11
GU63	Gump Co.	85 Tracking	Fergus	OH	48902	$7,822.00	$8,000.00	04
GY16	Gylder-Yansen	198 Ruby	Oakwood	IN	48101	$3,912.00	$8,000.00	07
MN72	Manross, Inc.	195 Grayling	Cardinal	MI	61354	$0.00	$8,000.00	07
NG19	Norton Ghent	867 Medford	Acme	MI	62127	$1,867.50	$8,000.00	04
SO22	Southwest, Inc.	682 Ohio	Benwood	IN	48102	$2,336.25	$10,000.00	11
SP92	Samuel A. Port	872 Eastham	Benson	OH	49246	$6,420.00	$10,000.00	07
						$0.00	$0.00	

FIGURE 12

PROJECT ONE

Using a Design Template and Style Checker to Create a Presentation

PROJECT TWO

Using Outline View and Clip Art to Create an Electronic Slide Show

INTEGRATION FEATURE

Importing Clip Art from the Microsoft Clip Gallery Live Web Site

Microsoft PowerPoint 97

Microsoft *PowerPoint 97*

Using a Design Template and Style Checker to Create a Presentation

Objectives:

You will have mastered the material in this project when you can:

- Start a new PowerPoint document
- Describe the PowerPoint window
- Select a design template
- Create a title slide
- Change the font size of selected text
- Italicize selected text
- Save a presentation
- Add a new slide
- Demote a bulleted paragraph
- Promote a bulleted paragraph
- View a presentation in slide show view
- Quit PowerPoint
- Open a presentation
- Use Style Checker to identify spelling, visual clarity, case, and end punctuation inconsistencies
- Edit a presentation
- Change line spacing on the slide master
- Display a presentation in black and white
- Print a presentation in black and white
- Use online Help

A THoUsaNd aND OnE WaYs tO MaKE a HiT

What if your very life depended on your ability to make a captivating presentation? This was the predicament faced by Princess Scheherazade, the fabled storyteller to whom we owe the tales of the *Arabian Nights*. Married to King Schahriar, who beheaded each new bride after the wedding night, she beguiled him with a continuing story so fabulous and intriguing, that each night he spared her life, so she might relate the next installment. Thus, she successfully staved off the king's sword for a thousand and one nights, when at last, he granted her a permanent stay of execution, a tribute to her powers of presentation.

Fortunately, in today's world, the stakes usually are not that high. Yet, the skill to present an argument or a concept in the most dynamic and pleasing way possible may spell the difference between huge success or severe failure. Salespeople the world over know the truth in this, as do politicians seeking election, scientists pursuing funding for a project, or any of countless situations where the ability to persuade is the key to victory.

In some ways, modern requirements are more demanding than in Scheherazade's time. Today, mere words are not enough. Because audiences have developed a taste for multimedia, they demand both aural and graphical ingredients in presentations. This means that appearance is just as important as the words — you not only have to "talk the talk," you have to "walk the walk." The presentation of food in commercials is an excellent example. Food stylists, who are a special breed of presenters, prepare food especially for displays, photographs, or films, *styling* the product to fit the message. And for many people, the presentation of food in restaurants — from the chef's artistic arrangement of food on a plate to the waiter's proud delivery to the table — is just as important as the cuisine.

Conversely, the wrong image can confuse or distort one's message. Many familiar instances exist in literature and movies: *The Hunchback of Notre Dame*, Yoda in *Star Wars*, *Rain Man*, *Powder*, *Mask*, *Forrest Gump*, and *The Elephant Man*, where appearances obscure the understanding of true worth.

Now, Microsoft's PowerPoint 97 makes it easier than ever to deliver your presentation with panache while ensuring your audience understands the true value of your message. Whether you are a new user or just in a hurry, templates give you ready-made patterns, and the AutoLayout feature provides shortcuts for maintaining your design. With PowerPoints's Style Checker, you analyze visual clarity and consistency, and then you can make your presentation sizzle with clip art and multimedia effects.

So, before you plunge into that next persuasive effort, take a cue from the Princess Scheherazade. Leave them thirsting for more — with help from PowerPoint.

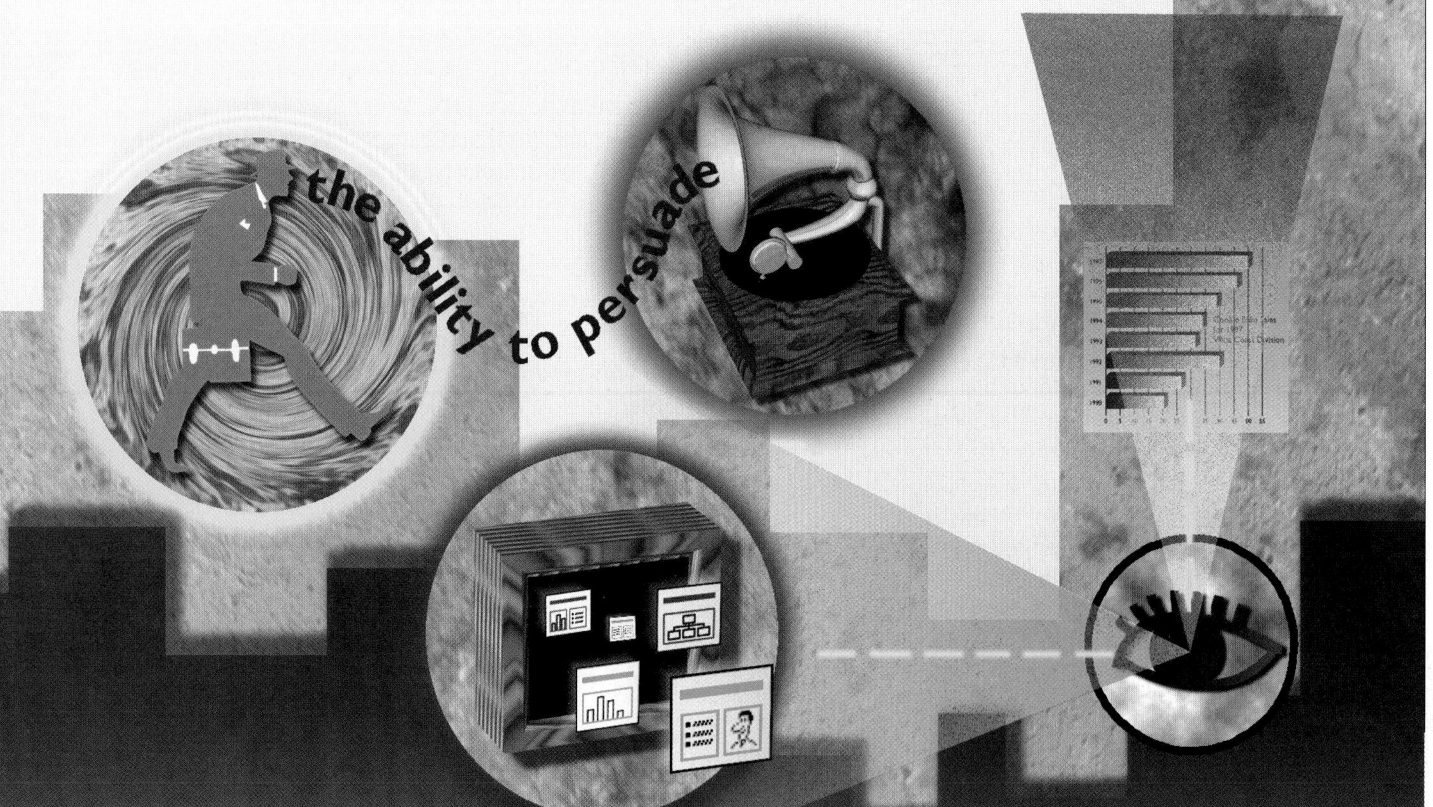

Microsoft
PowerPoint 97

Using a Design Template and Style Checker to Create a Presentation

Case Perspective

Everyday, more and more people are connecting to the Internet via the World Wide Web. The World Wide Web, often called the Web, is a collection of hypertext links that creates an interconnected network of links within the Internet. The most popular method of accessing the World Wide Web is a graphical software program called a browser. A person having a browser, and the proper hardware and communications requirements, easily can explore a wealth of information on the Internet. But what exactly are those requirements?

Elizabeth McGiver is a World Wide Web expert. She has prepared a short presentation to explain the requirements for connecting to the World Wide Web. Her presentation identifies the minimum hardware and software requirements for connecting to the World Wide Web as well as options for Internet service providers. Ms. McGiver selected a design template to create a consistent look throughout the presentation. To make the presentation more appealing, she adjusted paragraph spacing. In the event that the location in which she speaks does not have the equipment necessary to conduct an electronic presentation, she prepared a copy of the presentation on transparency film to use with an overhead projector.

What Is PowerPoint?

Microsoft PowerPoint is a complete presentation graphics program that allows you to produce professional-looking presentations. PowerPoint gives you the flexibility to make informal presentations using overhead transparencies (Figure 1-1a), make electronic presentations using a projection device attached to a personal computer (Figure 1-1b), make formal presentations using 35mm slides (Figure 1-1c), or take advantage of the World Wide Web and run virtual presentations on the Internet (Figure 1-1d). Additionally, PowerPoint can create paper printouts, outlines, speaker notes, and audience handouts.

PowerPoint contains several features to simplify creating a presentation. For example, you can instruct PowerPoint to create a predesigned presentation, and then you can modify the presentation to fulfill your requirements. You quickly can format a presentation using one of the professionally designed presentation design templates. To make your presentation more impressive, you can add tables, graphs, pictures, video, sound, and, animation effects. You can be certain your presentation meets specific design criteria by using Style Checker to locate inconsistencies in spelling, visual clarity, uppercase and lowercase usage, and end punctuation.

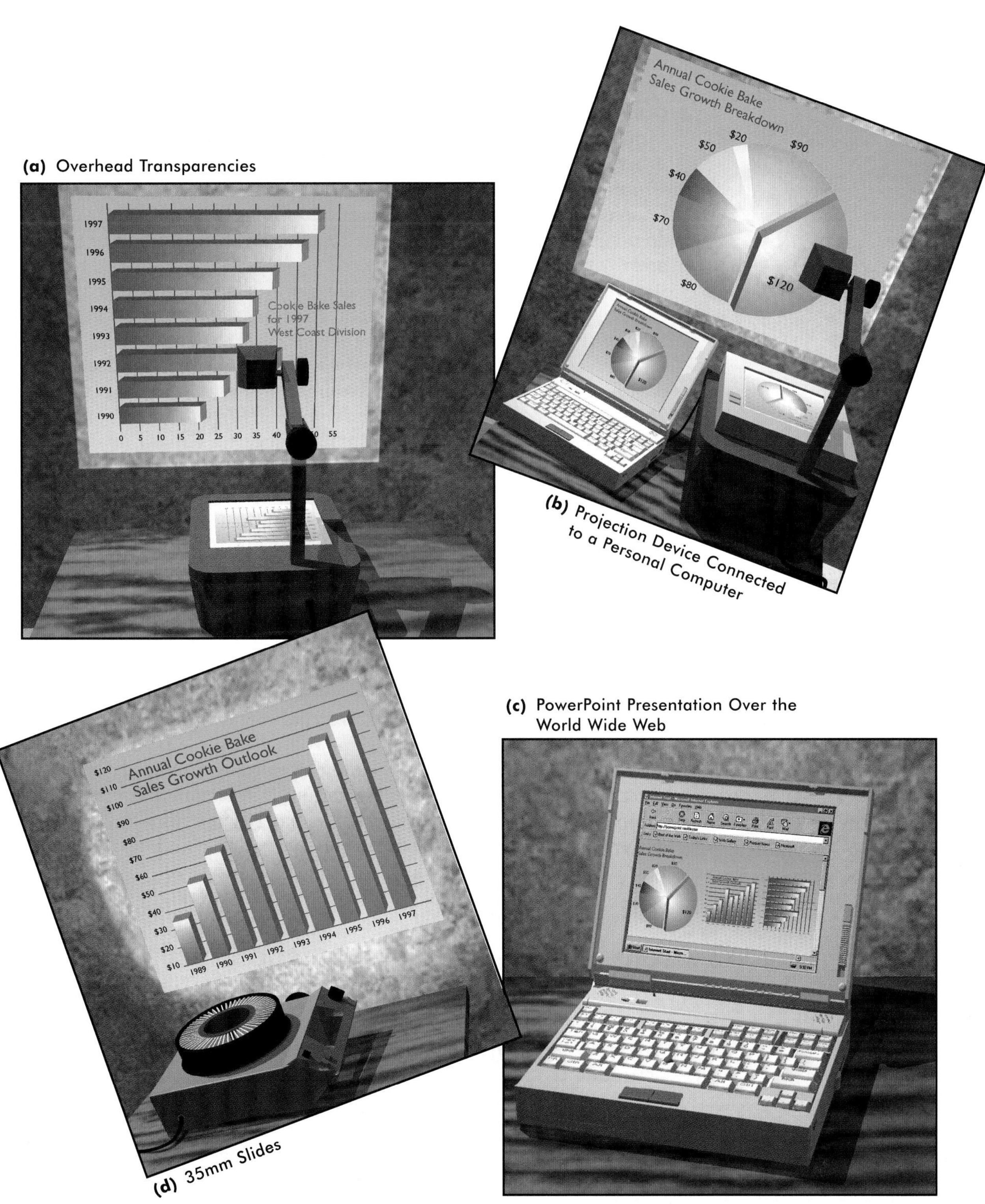
(a) Overhead Transparencies
Cookie Bake Sales
for 1997
West Coast Division
(b) Projection Device Connected to a Personal Computer
Annual Cookie Bake
Sales Growth Breakdown
$20
$50
$90
$40
$70
$80
$120
(c) PowerPoint Presentation Over the World Wide Web
Annual Cookie Bake
Sales Growth Outlook
(d) 35mm Slides

FIGURE 1-1

More *About* **Electronic Presentations**

Use an electronic presentation for any size audience. The choice of projection device depends on the number of people in the audience. Be certain you test the system before you deliver the presentation.

For example, you can instruct PowerPoint to restrict the number of bulleted items on a slide or limit the number of words in each paragraph. Additional PowerPoint features include the following:

- **Word processing** — allows you to create bulleted lists, combine words and images, find and replace text, and use multiple fonts and type sizes. Using its IntelliSense features, PowerPoint can perform tasks such as checking spelling and formatting text – *all while you are typing.*
- **Outlining** — allows you quickly to create your presentation using an outline format. You also can import outlines from Microsoft Word or other word processing programs.
- **Graphing** — allows you to create and insert charts into your presentations. Graph formats include two-dimensional (2-D) graphs: area, bar, column, combination, line, pie, xy (scatter); and three-dimensional (3-D) graphs: area, bar, column, line, and pie.
- **Drawing** — allows you to create diagrams using shapes such as arcs, arrows, cubes, rectangles, stars, and triangles. Drawing also allows you to modify shapes without redrawing.
- **Clip art** — allows you to insert artwork into your presentation without creating it yourself. You can find hundreds of graphic images in the Microsoft Clip Gallery, or you can import art from other applications. With the **AutoClipArt feature**, PowerPoint can suggest a clip art image appropriate for your presentation.
- **Multimedia effects** — adds interest and keeps your audience attentive by adding effects, such as sound and video, to your presentations. PowerPoint 97 allows you to create interactive multimedia presentations that can be placed on the World Wide Web.
- **Wizards** — a tutorial approach for quickly and efficiently creating a presentation. PowerPoint wizards make it easy to create quality presentations by prompting you for specific content criteria. For example, the **AutoContent Wizard** prompts you for what are you going to talk about and the type of presentation you are going to give, such as recommending a strategy or selling a product. When giving a presentation away from the computer, on which it was created, it is important you take all the necessary files. The **Pack and Go Wizard** helps you bundle everything you need, including any objects associated with that presentation. If you cannot confirm that the computer on which you are presenting has PowerPoint, you also can pack **PowerPoint Viewer**, a program that allows you to run, but not edit, a PowerPoint presentation.

More *About* **35mm Slides**

35mm slides are best for formal presentations made to any size audience and are highly recommended when audience size exceeds 50 people. 35mm slide presentations are best-suited for a non-interactive presentation because the room is dark.

Project One – Unlocking the Internet

This book presents a series of projects using PowerPoint to produce slides similar to those you would develop in an academic or business environment. Project 1 uses PowerPoint to create the presentation shown in Figure 1-2. The objective is to produce a presentation, called Unlocking the Internet, to be presented using an overhead projector. As an introduction to PowerPoint, this project steps you through the most common type of presentation, a bulleted list. A **bulleted list** is a list of paragraphs, each preceded by a bullet. A **bullet** is a symbol (usually a heavy dot (•)) that precedes text when the text warrants special emphasis. The first of the four slides is called the title slide. The **title slide** introduces the presentation to the audience.

(a)

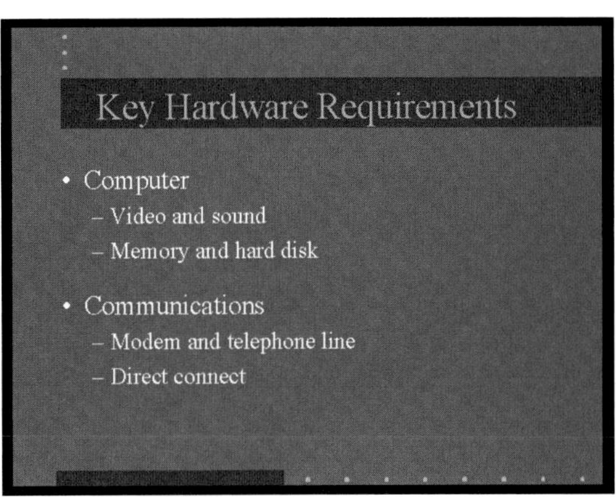

(b)

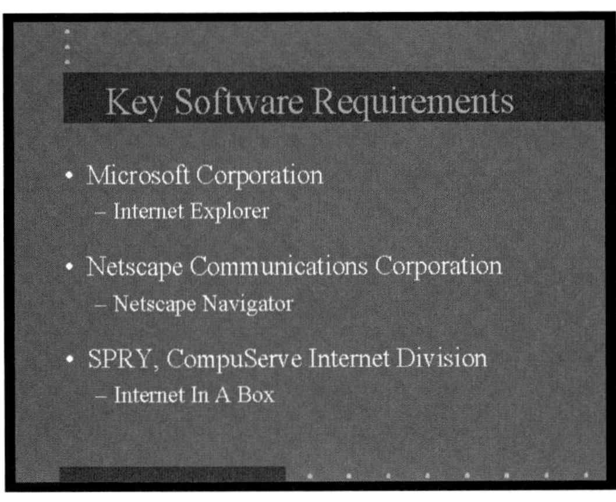

(c)

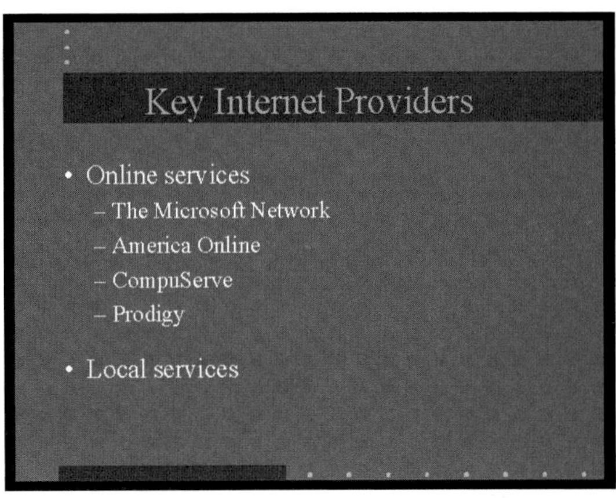

(d)

FIGURE 1-2

Mouse Usage

In this book, the mouse is used as the primary way to communicate with PowerPoint. You can perform seven operations with a standard mouse: point, click, right-click, double-click, triple-click, drag, and right-drag. If you have a **Microsoft IntelliMouse**, then you also have a wheel between the left and right buttons. This wheel can be used to perform three additional operations: rotate wheel, click wheel, or drag wheel.

Point means you move the mouse across a flat surface until the mouse pointer rests on the item of choice on the screen. As you move the mouse, the mouse pointer moves across the screen in the same direction. **Click** means you press and release the left mouse button. The terminology used in this book to direct you to point to a particular item and then click is, Click the particular item. For example, Click the Bold button means point to the Bold button and click.

Right-click means you press and release the right mouse button. As with the left mouse button, you normally will point to an item on the screen prior to right-clicking.

More *About* Presentation Graphics

Presentation graphics help people *see* what they *hear*. People remember:

- 10% of what they *read*
- 20% of what they *hear*
- 30% of what they *see*
- 70% of what they *see* and *hear*

More *About* **Presentation Design**

Identify the purpose of the presentation. Is it to sell an idea or product, report results of a study, or educate the audience? Whatever the purpose, your goal is to capture the attention of the audience and to explain the data or concept in a manner that is easy to understand.

Double-click means you quickly press and release the left mouse button twice without moving the mouse. In most cases, you must point to an item before double-clicking. In this book, **triple-clicking** in a text object selects the entire paragraph. **Drag** means you point to an item, hold down the left mouse button, move the item to the desired location on the screen, and then release the left mouse button. **Right-drag** means you point to an item, hold down the right mouse button, move the item to the desired location, and then release the right mouse button.

If you have a Microsoft IntelliMouse, then you can use **rotate wheel** to view parts of the presentation that are not visible. The wheel also can serve as a third button. When the wheel is used as a button, it is referred to as the **wheel button**. For example, dragging the wheel button causes some applications to scroll in the direction you drag.

The use of the mouse is an important skill when working with Microsoft PowerPoint 97.

Slide Preparation Steps

The preparation steps summarize how the slide presentation shown in Figure 1-2 on the previous page will be developed in Project 1. The following tasks will be completed in this project.

1. Start a new Office document.
2. Select a design template.
3. Create a title slide.
4. Save the presentation on a floppy disk.
5. Create three multi-level bulleted lists.
6. Save the presentation again.
7. Quit PowerPoint.
8. Open the presentation as a Microsoft Office document.
9. Style check the presentation.
10. Edit the presentation.
11. Print the presentation.
12. Quit PowerPoint.

The following pages contain a detailed explanation of these tasks.

More *About* **Design Templates**

When deciding on a design template, choose one designed to display light colored text on a medium to dark background. Light text on a dark background provides a stronger contrast than light text on a light background.

Starting a Presentation as a New Office Document

A PowerPoint document is called a **presentation**. The quickest way to begin a new presentation is to use the **Start button** on the **taskbar** at the bottom of your screen. When you click the Start button, the **Start menu** displays several commands for simplifying tasks in Windows 95. When Microsoft Office 97 is installed, the Start menu displays two commands: New Office Document and Open Office Document. You use the **New Office Document** command to designate the type of Office document you are creating. Then, you specify the design template or wizard on which you wish to base your document. A **design template** provides consistency in design and color throughout the entire presentation. The design template determines the color scheme, font and font size, and layout of your presentation. Then PowerPoint starts and the specified template or wizard displays. The Open Office Document command is discussed later in this project. Perform the steps on the following pages to start a new presentation, or ask your instructor how to start PowerPoint on your system.

To Start a New Presentation

1 **Point to the Start button on the taskbar at the lower-left corner of the desktop.**

When you position the mouse pointer on the Start button, it displays as a left pointing block arrow and a ScreenTip displays, Click here to begin (Figure 1-3). Your computer system displays the time on the clock at the right end of the taskbar.

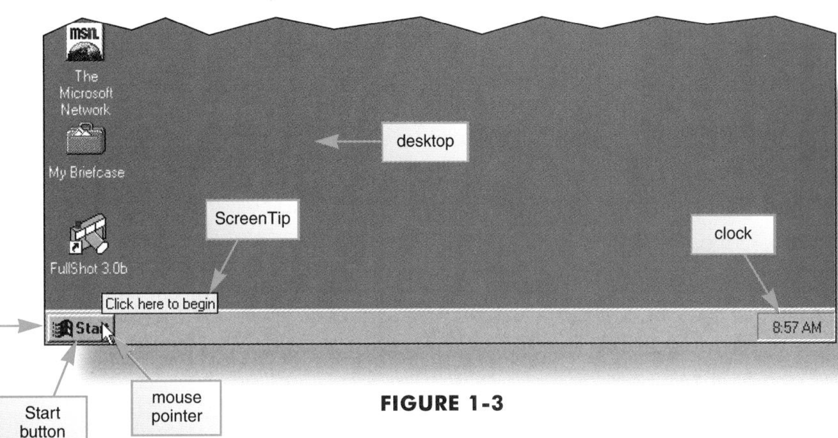

FIGURE 1-3

2 **Click the Start button. When the Windows 95 Start menu displays, point to New Office Document.**

The Windows 95 Start menu displays the names of several programs. The mouse pointer points to New Office Document (Figure 1-4). When the mouse pointer points to a name on the menu, the name is highlighted.

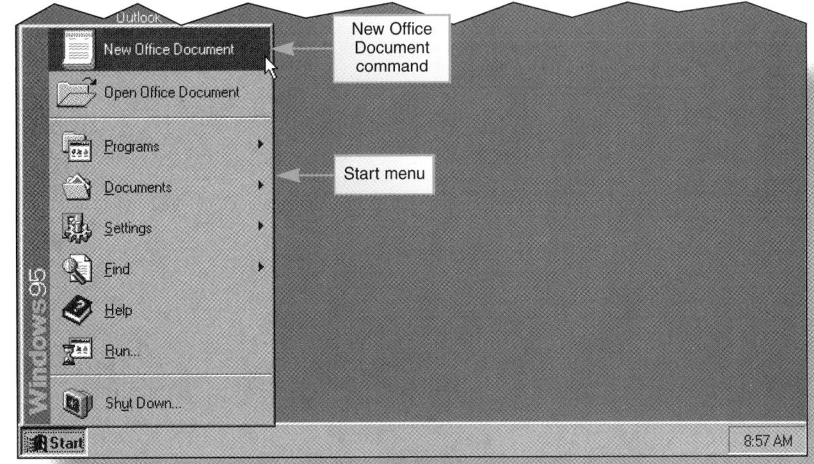

FIGURE 1-4

3 **Click New Office Document. When the New Office Document dialog box displays, point to the Presentatio . . . tab.**

The New Office Document dialog box automatically displays the General sheet and the mouse pointer points to the Presentatio . . . (Presentation Designs) tab (Figure 1-5). Depending on your installation, your computer may display a Presentation Designs tab or a Designs tab.

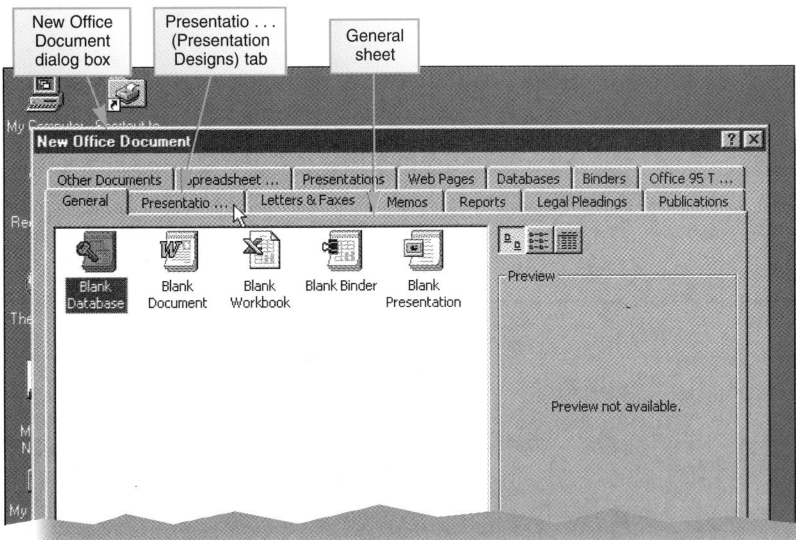

FIGURE 1-5

4 Click the Presentatio . . . tab. When the Presentatio . . . sheet displays, point to Contempo. . . (Contemporary).

The Presentatio . . . sheet displays the names and icons for several design templates (Figure 1-6). The Preview box displays a message about how to see a preview of a presentation design template. The OK button currently is dimmed, which means it is not available because a design template icon has not been selected. The Cancel button is available, however, as indicated by the black text on the button. The Cancel button is used to close the New Office Document dialog box and return to the desktop or return to the window from which you started.

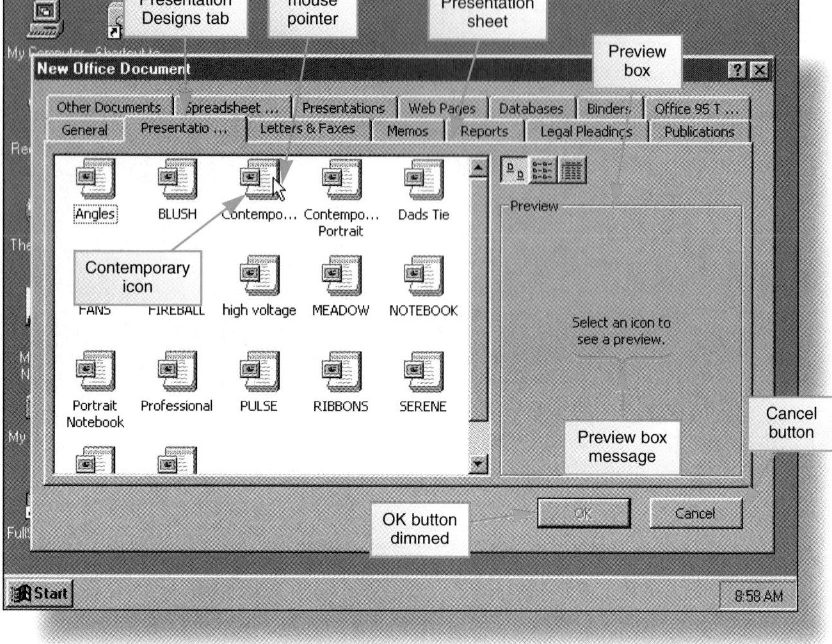

FIGURE 1-6

5 Click Contempo. . ..

The Contempo. . . design template icon is highlighted and a thumbnail view of the design template displays in the Preview box (Figure 1-7). The OK button now is available as indicated by the black text on the button.

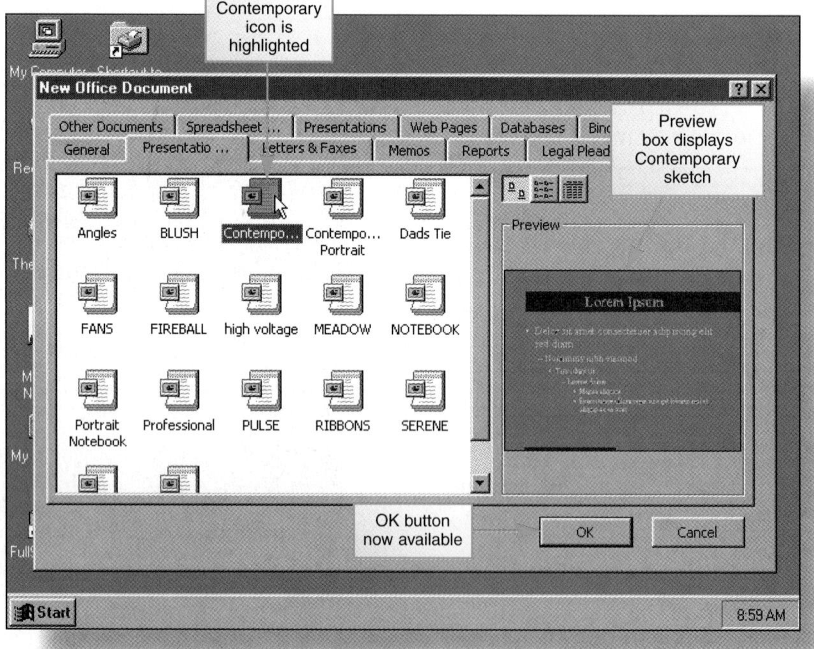

FIGURE 1-7

6 **Double-click Contempo. . .. When the Office Assistant displays, point to the Close button on the Office Assistant.**

Double-clicking the Contemporary design template icon indicates that you are applying a PowerPoint design template. As a result, PowerPoint starts and displays the New Slide dialog box, the Common Tasks toolbar, and the Office Assistant (Figure 1-8). The Office Assistant displays if it was active during the last computer session or when Microsoft Office 97 starts for the first time. You learn how to use the Office Assistant later in this project. Microsoft PowerPoint displays as a button on the taskbar at the bottom of the screen.

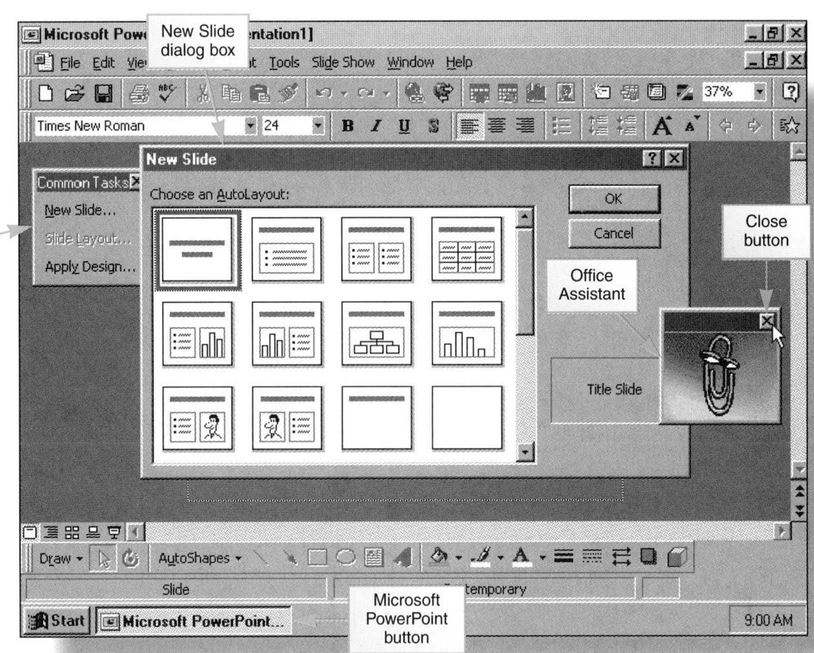

FIGURE 1-8

7 **Click the Close button and then point to the OK button in the New Slide dialog box.**

The Office Assistant closes. A frame displays around the Title Slide AutoLayout to indicate it is selected (Figure 1-9). The name of the selected AutoLayout displays on the lower-right corner of the New Slide dialog box.

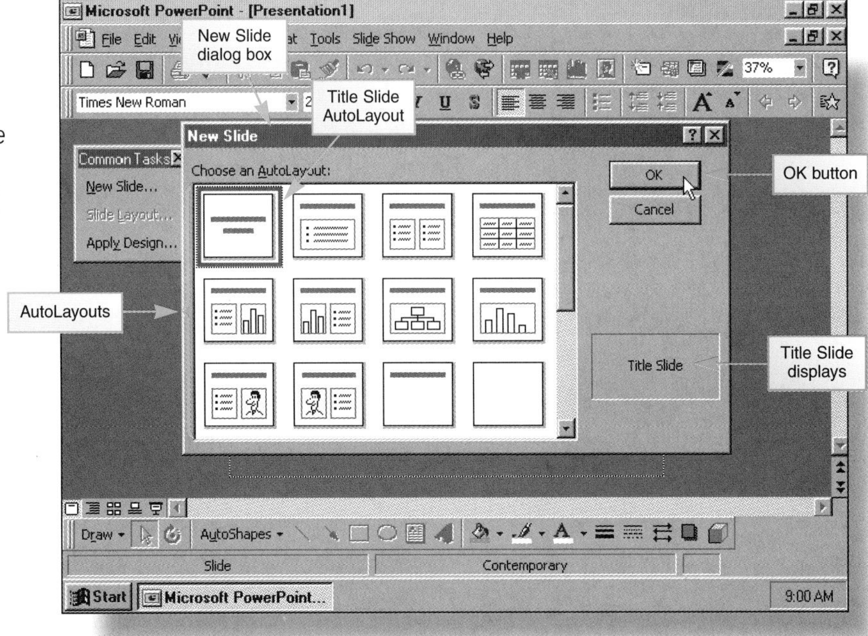

FIGURE 1-9

8 **Click the OK button.**

PowerPoint displays the Title Slide AutoLayout and the Contemporary design template on Slide 1 (Figure 1-10). The title bar identifies this as a Microsoft PowerPoint presentation currently titled Presentation1. The status bar displays information about the current slide, such as the slide number and the current design template.

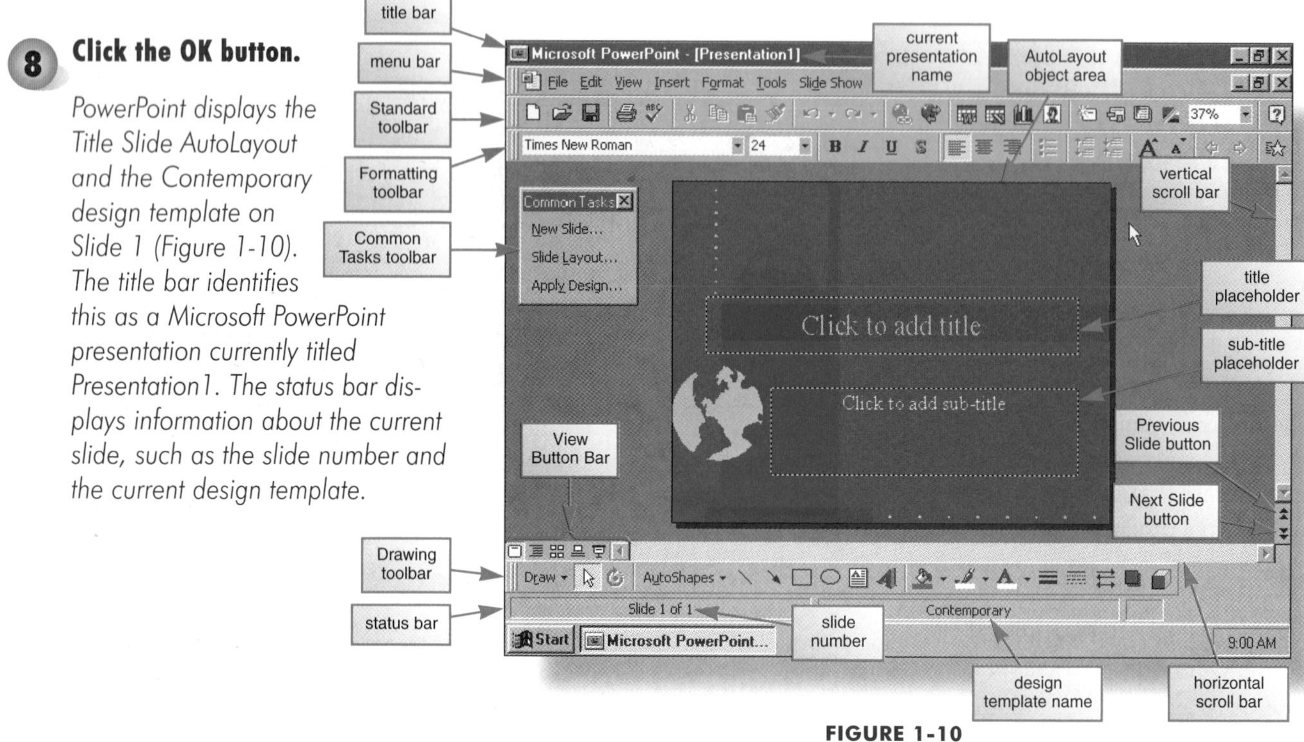

FIGURE 1-10

As an alternative to double-clicking the Contemporary design template in Step 6, you can click the OK button to apply the selected design template. The Office Assistant, closed in Step 7, is discussed later in this project.

More *About* **The PowerPoint Window**

To drag and drop objects quickly between two presentations, display both presentations in one PowerPoint window. To display two presentations in one PowerPoint window, open both presentations, click the Restore button on the presentation title bar of one of the presentations, and drag the presentation window border to size the window to fill one-half the PowerPoint window. Repeat the process for the second presentation window.

The PowerPoint Window

The basic unit of a PowerPoint presentation is a **slide**. **Objects** are the building blocks for a PowerPoint slide. A slide contains one or many objects, such as a title, text, graphics, tables, charts, and drawings. In PowerPoint, you have the option of using the PowerPoint default settings or establishing your own. A **default setting** is a particular value for a variable that is assigned initially by PowerPoint and remains in effect unless canceled or overridden by the user. These settings control the placement of objects, the color scheme, the transition between slides, and other slide attributes. **Attributes** are the properties or characteristics of an object. For example, if you underline the title of a slide, the title is the object and the underline is the attribute. When you start PowerPoint, the default **slide layout** is **landscape orientation**, in which the slide width is greater than its height. In landscape orientation, the slide size is preset to 10 inches wide and 7.5 inches high. The slide layout can be changed to **portrait orientation**, so that the slide height is greater than its width, by clicking Page Setup on the File menu. In portrait orientation, the slide height is 10 inches and its width is 7.5 inches.

PowerPoint Views

PowerPoint has five views: slide view, outline view, slide sorter view, notes page view, and slide show view. A **view** is the mode in which the presentation displays on the screen. You may use any or all views when creating your presentation, but you can use only one at a time. Change views by clicking one of the view buttons found on the **View Button Bar** at the bottom of the PowerPoint screen (Figure 1-10). The PowerPoint window display is dependent on the view. Some views are graphical while others are textual.

Table 1-1 identifies the view buttons and provides an explanation of each view.

Table 1-1

BUTTON	BUTTON NAME	FUNCTION
	Slide View	Displays a single slide as it appears in your presentation. Use slide view to create or edit a presentation. Slide view also is used to incorporate text and graphic objects and to create line-by-line progressive disclosure, called build effects.
	Outline View	Displays a presentation in an outline format showing slide titles and text. It is best used for organizing and developing the content of your presentation.
	Slide Sorter View	Displays miniature versions of all slides in your presentation. You then can copy, cut, paste, or otherwise change slide position to modify your presentation. Slide sorter view also is used to add slide transitions.
	Notes Page View	Displays the current notes page. Notes page view allows you to create speaker's notes to use when you give your presentation. Each notes page corresponds to a slide and includes a reduced slide image.
	Slide Show View	Displays your slides as an electronic presentation on the full screen of your computer's monitor. Looking much like a slide projector display, you can see the effect of transitions, build effects, and slide timings.

PowerPoint Window in Slide View

The PowerPoint window in slide view contains: the title bar; the menu bar; the status bar; the toolbars: Standard, Formatting, Drawing, and Common Tasks; the AutoLayout object area; the mouse pointer; the scroll bars; and the View Button Bar.

TITLE BAR The **title bar** (Figure 1-10) displays the name of the current PowerPoint document. Until you save your presentation, PowerPoint assigns the default name Presentation1.

MENU BAR The **menu bar** (Figure 1-10) displays the PowerPoint menu names. Each menu name represents a list of commands that allows you to retrieve, store, print, and change objects in your presentation. To display a menu, such as the File menu, click File (the name) on the menu bar.

STATUS BAR Located at the bottom of the PowerPoint window, the **status bar** consists of a message area and a presentation design template identifier (Figure 1-10). Most of the time, the current slide number and the total number of slides in the presentation display in the message area. For example, in Figure 1-10, the message area displays Slide 1 of 1. Slide 1 is the current slide, and of 1 indicates there is only one slide in the presentation.

SCROLL BARS The **vertical scroll bar** (Figure 1-10), located on the right side of the PowerPoint window, allows you to move forward or backward through your presentation. Clicking the **Next Slide button** (Figure 1-10), located on the vertical scroll bar, advances to the next slide in the presentation. Clicking the **Previous Slide button** (Figure 1-10), located on the vertical scroll bar, backs up to the slide preceding the current slide.

The **horizontal scroll bar** (Figure 1-10 on page PP 1.14), located on the bottom of the PowerPoint window, allows you to display a portion of the window when the entire window does not fit on the screen.

It should be noted that in slide view, both the vertical and horizontal scroll bar actions are dependent on the **Zoom** settings. You control how large or small a document displays on the PowerPoint window by zooming in or out. If you are in slide view and Zoom is set such that the entire slide is not visible in the Slide window, clicking the up arrow on the vertical scroll bar displays the next portion of your slide, not the previous slide. Recall that to go to the previous slide, click the Previous Slide button. To go to the next slide, click the Next Slide button.

AUTOLAYOUT OBJECT AREA The **AutoLayout object area** (Figure 1-10) is a collection of placeholders for the title, text, clip art, graphs, tables, and media clips (video and sound). These placeholders display when you create a new slide. You can change the AutoLayout any time during the creation of your presentation by clicking the Slide Layout button on the Common Tasks toolbar and then selecting a different slide layout.

PLACEHOLDERS Surrounded by a dashed line, **placeholders** are the empty objects on a new slide. Depending on the AutoLayout selected, placeholders will display for the title, text, graphs, tables, organization charts, media clips, and clip art. Once you place contents in a placeholder, the placeholder becomes an object. For example, text typed in a placeholder becomes a text object.

More *About* Zoom

Increase the Zoom setting when working with small objects to better see details, such as when modifying a graphic. Decrease the Zoom setting to work with large objects.

TITLE PLACEHOLDER Surrounded by a dashed line, the **title placeholder** is the empty title object on a new slide (Figure 1-10). Text typed in the title placeholder becomes the **title object**.

SUB-TITLE PLACEHOLDER Surrounded by a dashed line, the **sub-title placeholder** is the empty sub-title object that displays below the title placeholder on a title slide (Figure 1-10).

MOUSE POINTER The **mouse pointer** can become one of several different shapes depending on the task you are performing in PowerPoint and the pointer's location on the screen. The different shapes are discussed when they display in subsequent projects. The mouse pointer in Figure 1-10 has the shape of a left-pointing block arrow.

More *About* Toolbars

Hiding a toolbar that you no longer need increases the Zoom setting and displays a larger PowerPoint view. To hide a toolbar, right-click any toolbar and then click the check mark next to the name of the toolbar you wish to hide.

TOOLBARS PowerPoint **toolbars** consist of buttons that allow you to perform tasks more quickly than when using the menu bar. For example, to save a presentation, click the Save button on the Standard toolbar. Each button face has a graphical representation that helps you remember its function. Figures 1-11 through 1-14 illustrate the buttons on each of the four toolbars that display when you start PowerPoint and display a slide in slide view. They are the Standard toolbar, the Formatting toolbar, the Drawing toolbar, and the Common Tasks toolbar. Each button is explained in detail when it is used.

PowerPoint has several additional toolbars you can display by clicking View on the menu bar. You also can display a toolbar by pointing to a toolbar and right-clicking to display a shortcut menu, which lists the available toolbars. A **shortcut menu** contains a list of commands or items that relate to the item to which you are pointing when you right-click.

PowerPoint allows you to customize all toolbars and to add the toolbar buttons you use most often. In the same manner, you can remove those toolbar buttons you do not use. To customize a toolbar, click Tools on the menu bar, and then click Customize to modify the toolbar to meet your requirements. Another way to customize a toolbar is to click View on the menu bar, click Toolbars, click Customize, and then make changes in the Customize dialog box to fulfill your requirements.

STANDARD TOOLBAR The **Standard toolbar** (Figure 1-11) contains the tools to execute the more common commands found on the menu bar, such as Open, Print, Save, Copy, Cut, Paste, and many more. The Standard toolbar contains a button for setting Zoom. Recall that you control how large or small a document displays in the PowerPoint window with the Zoom list.

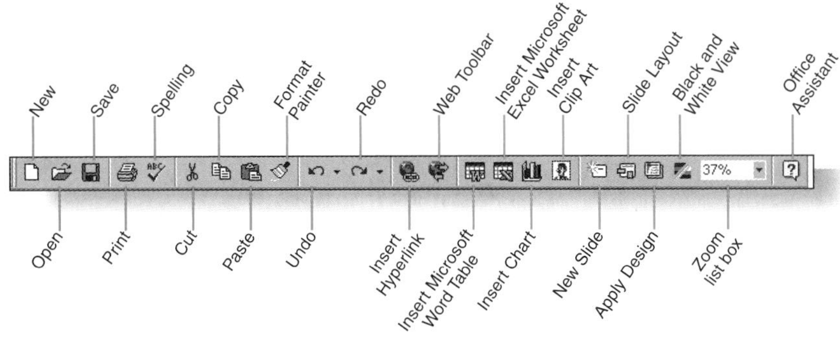

FIGURE 1-11

FORMATTING TOOLBAR The **Formatting toolbar** (Figure 1-12) contains the tools for changing text attributes. The Formatting toolbar allows you to quickly change font, font size, and alignment. It also contains tools to bold, italicize, underline, shadow, color, and bullet text. The five **attribute buttons, Bold, Italic, Underline, Shadow**, and **Bullets**, are on/off switches, or toggles. Click the button once to turn the attribute on; then click it again to turn the attribute off.

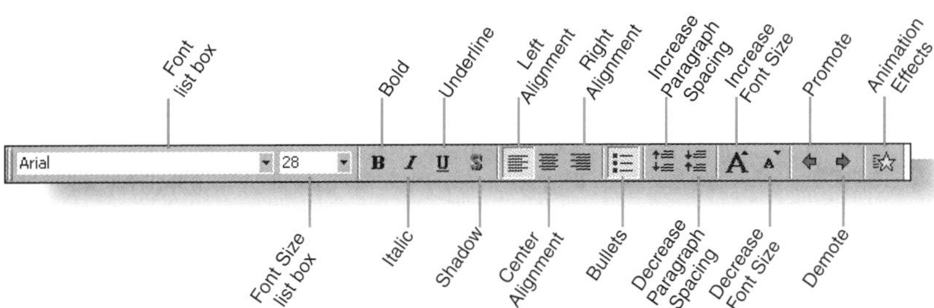

FIGURE 1-12

DRAWING TOOLBAR The **Drawing toolbar** (Figure 1-13) is a collection of tools for drawing objects such as lines, circles, and boxes. The Drawing toolbar also contains tools to edit the objects once you have drawn them. For example, you can change the color of an object with the **Fill Color button**, or rotate an object by clicking the **Free Rotate** button.

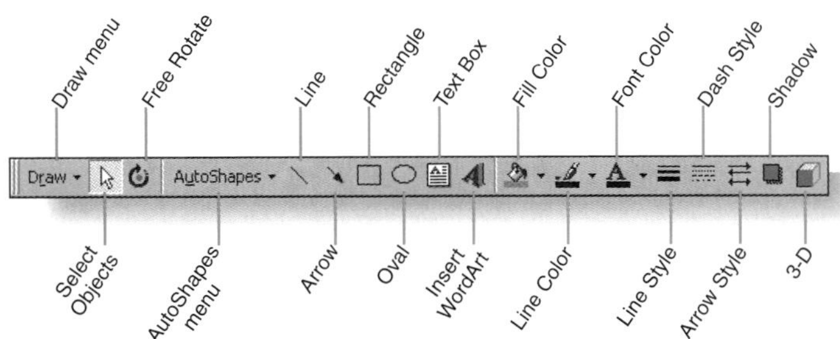

FIGURE 1-13

COMMON TASKS TOOLBAR The **Common Tasks toolbar** (Figure 1-14) contains the three more frequently used commands; **New Slide button, Slide Layout button**, and the **Apply Design button**.

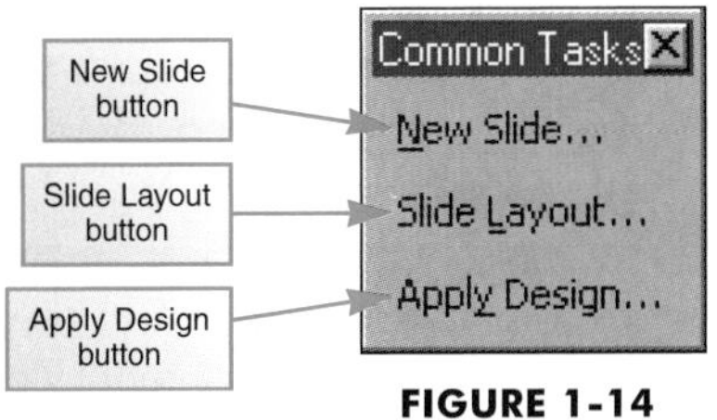

FIGURE 1-14

More *About* **Presentation Design**

The audience determines the level of detail you place on one slide. Before you create your presentation, determine who is likely to attend. Design your presentation around the amount of detail the audience wants to see. Remember, you want to keep their attention, not bore them with details.

Creating a Title Slide

The purpose of a title slide is to introduce the presentation to the audience. PowerPoint assumes the first slide in a new presentation is the title slide. With the exception of a blank slide, PowerPoint also assumes every new slide has a title. To make creating your presentation easier, any text you type after a new slide displays becomes the title object. In other words, you do not have to first select the title placeholder before typing the title text. The AutoLayout for the title slide has a title placeholder near the middle of the window and a sub-title placeholder directly below the title placeholder (Figure 1-15).

Entering the Presentation Title

The presentation title for Project 1 is Unlocking the Internet. Type the presentation title in the title placeholder on the title slide. Perform the following step to create the title slide for this project.

Steps To Enter the Presentation Title

1 **Type** `Unlocking the Internet` **in the title placeholder. Do not press the ENTER key.**

The title text, Unlocking the Internet, displays in the title text box (Figure 1-15). The recessed Center Alignment button indicates the title text is center-aligned in the title text box. When you type the first character, the selection rectangle, a slashed outline, displays around the title box. A blinking vertical line (|), called the ***insertion point****, indicates where the next character will display.*

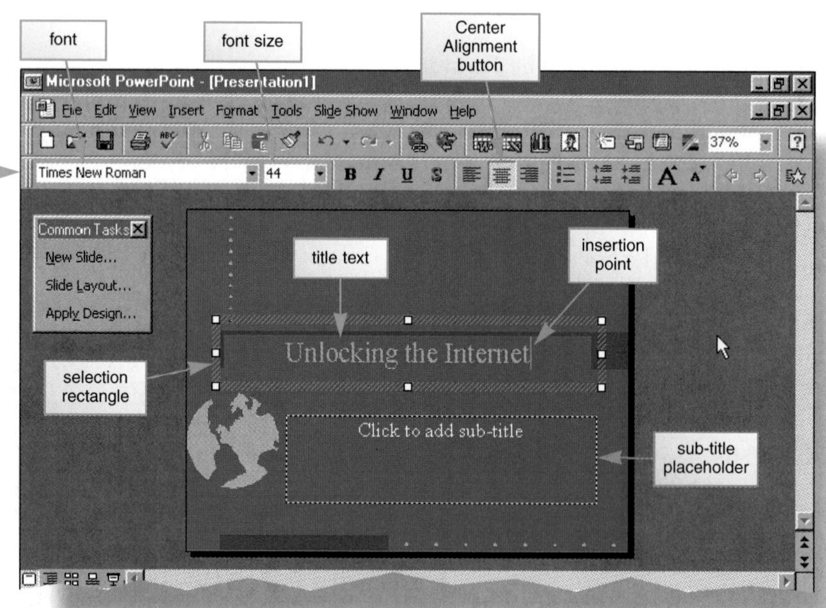

FIGURE 1-15

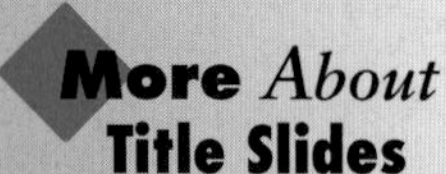

More *About* **Title Slides**

To identify a new section in a long presentation, insert a title slide with the name of the new section.

Notice that you do not press the ENTER key after the word Internet. If you press the ENTER key after typing the title, PowerPoint creates a new paragraph. A **paragraph** is a segment of text with the same format that begins when you press the ENTER key and ends when you press the ENTER key again. Pressing the ENTER key creates a new line in a new paragraph. Therefore, do not press the ENTER key unless you want to create a two-paragraph title. Additionally, PowerPoint **line wraps** text that exceeds the width of the placeholder. For example, if the slide title was, Experiencing the World Wide Web, it would exceed the width of the title placeholder and display on two lines.

The title is centered in the window because the Contemporary design template alignment attribute is centered. The Center Alignment button is recessed on the Formatting toolbar in Figure 1-15.

Correcting a Mistake When Typing

If you type the wrong letter and notice the error before pressing the ENTER key, press the BACKSPACE key to erase all the characters back to and including the one that is incorrect. If you mistakenly press the ENTER key after entering the title and the insertion point is on the new line, simply press the BACKSPACE key to return the insertion point to the right of the letter t in the word Internet.

When you first install PowerPoint, the default setting allows you to reverse up to the last 20 changes by clicking the **Undo button** on the Standard toolbar. The ScreenTip that displays when you point to the Undo button changes to indicate the type of change just made. For example, if you type text in the title placeholder and then point to the Undo button, the ScreenTip that displays is Undo Typing. For clarity, when referencing the Undo button in this project, the name displaying in the ScreenTip is referenced. Another way to reverse changes is to click the Undo command on the Edit menu. Like the Undo button, the Undo command name reflects the last type of change made to the presentation.

You can reapply a change that you reversed with the Undo button by clicking the Redo button on the Standard toolbar. Clicking the **Redo button** reverses the last undo action. The ScreenTip name reflects the type of reversal last preformed.

More About Undo

The number of times you can click the Undo button to reverse changes can be modified. To increase or decrease the number of undos, click Tools on the menu bar, click Options, and then click the Edit tab. Use the up and down arrows in the Maximum number of undos box to change the number of undos. The maximum number of undos is 150; the minimum number is 3.

Entering the Presentation Subtitle

The next step in creating the title slide is to enter the subtitle text into the sub-title placeholder. Complete the steps below to enter the presentation subtitle.

Steps To Enter the Presentation Subtitle

1. **Click the label, Click to add sub-title, located inside the sub-title placeholder.**

The insertion point is in the sub-title text box (Figure 1-16). The mouse pointer changes to an I-beam. The I-beam mouse pointer indicates the mouse is in a text placeholder. The selection rectangle indicates the sub-title placeholder is selected.

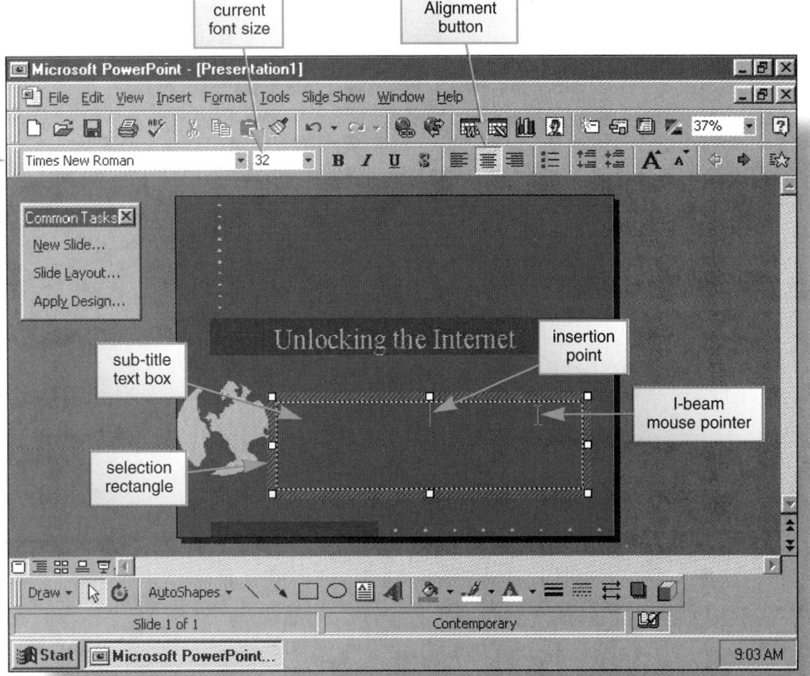

FIGURE 1-16

2 **Type** World Wide Web Requirements **and press the ENTER key. Type** Presented by: **and press the ENTER key. Type** Elizabeth McGiver **but do not press the ENTER key.**

The text displays in the sub-title object as shown in Figure 1-17. The insertion point displays after the letter r in McGiver.

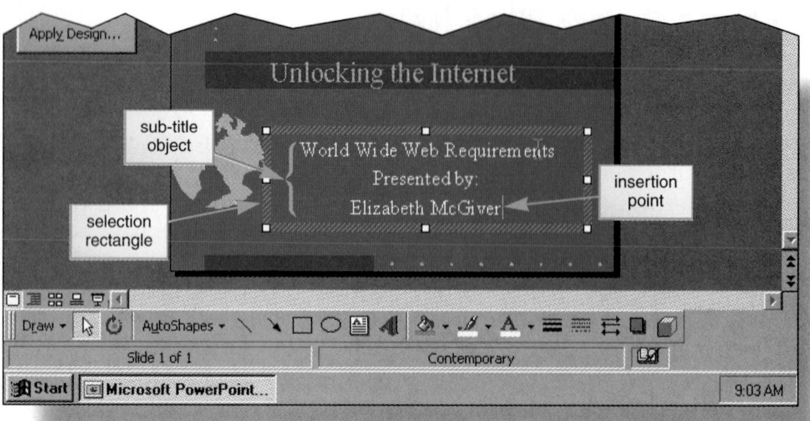

FIGURE 1-17

The previous section created a title slide using an AutoLayout for the title slide. PowerPoint displayed the title slide layout because you created a new presentation. You entered text in the title placeholder without selecting the title placeholder because PowerPoint assumes every slide has a title. You could, however, click the title placeholder to select it and then type your title. In general, to type text in any text placeholder, click the text placeholder and begin typing. You also added a subtitle that identifies the presenter. While this is not required, it often is useful information for the audience.

More *About* **Text Attributes**

Be consistent with color and text attributes. Use bold and italics sparingly for emphasis. Use no more than three type fonts and styles.

Text Attributes

This presentation is using the Contemporary design template that you selected from the Presentation sheet. Each design template has its own text attributes. A **text attribute** is a characteristic of the text, such as font, font size, font style, or text color. You can adjust text attributes any time before, during, or after you type the text. Recall that a design template determines the color scheme, font and font size, and layout of your presentation. Most of the time, you use the design template's text attributes and color scheme. There are times when you wish to change the way your presentation looks, however, and still keep a particular design template. PowerPoint gives you that flexibility. You can use the design template you wish and change the text color, text font size, text font, and text font style. Table 1-2 explains the different text attributes available in PowerPoint.

The next two sections explain how to change the font size and text font style attributes.

Table 1-2

ATTRIBUTE	DESCRIPTION
Font	Defines the appearance and shape of letters, numbers, and special characters.
Text color	Defines the color of text. Displaying text in color requires a color monitor. Printing text in color requires a color printer or plotter.
Font size	Specifies the size of characters on the screen. Character size is gauged by a measurement system called points. A single point is about 1/72 of an inch in height. Thus, a character with a point size of eighteen is about 18/72 (or 1/4) of an inch in height.
Text font style	Defines text characteristics. Text font styles include plain, italic, bold, shadowed, and underlined. Text may have one or more font styles at a time.
Subscript	Defines the placement of a character in relationship to another. A subscript character displays or prints slightly below and immediately to one side of another character.
Superscript	Defines the placement of a character in relationship to another. A superscript character displays or prints above and immediately to one side of another character.

Changing the Font Size

The Contemporary design template default font size is 32 points for body text and 44 points for title text. A point is 1/72 of an inch in height. Thus, a character with a point size of 44 is about 44/72 (or 11/18) of an inch in height. Slide 1 requires you to decrease the font size for the paragraph, Presented by:. Perform the following steps to decrease font size.

More About Presentation Design

Uppercase letters are less distinct, and therefore, more difficult to read than lowercase letters. For emphasis, it is acceptable to use all uppercase letters in short titles. Capitalize only the first letter in all words in long titles, except for short articles, unless the article is the first word in the title.

Steps To Decrease Font Size

1 Triple-click the paragraph, Presented by:, in the sub-title object.

The paragraph, Presented by:, is highlighted (Figure 1-18).

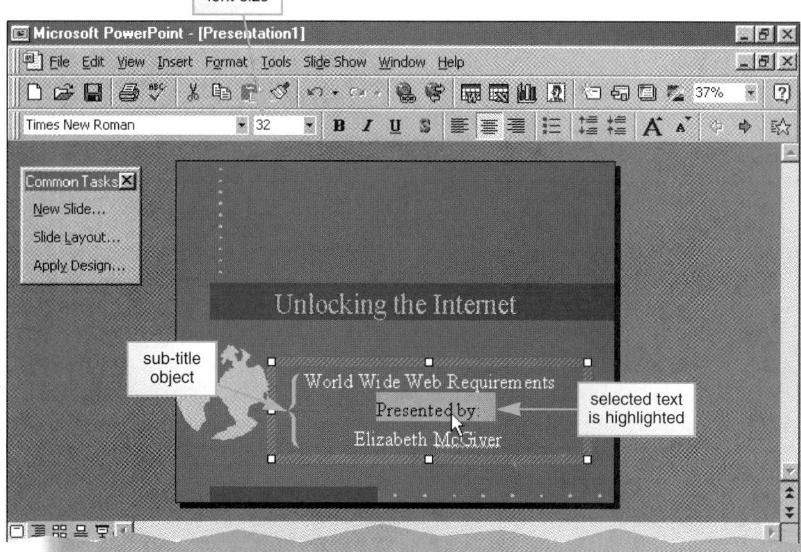

FIGURE 1-18

2 With Presented by: highlighted, point to the Decrease Font Size button on the Formatting toolbar.

*When you point to a button on a toolbar, PowerPoint displays a ScreenTip. A **ScreenTip** contains the name of the tool to which you are pointing. When pointing to the **Decrease Font Size button**, the ScreenTip displays the words, Decrease Font Size (Figure 1-19).*

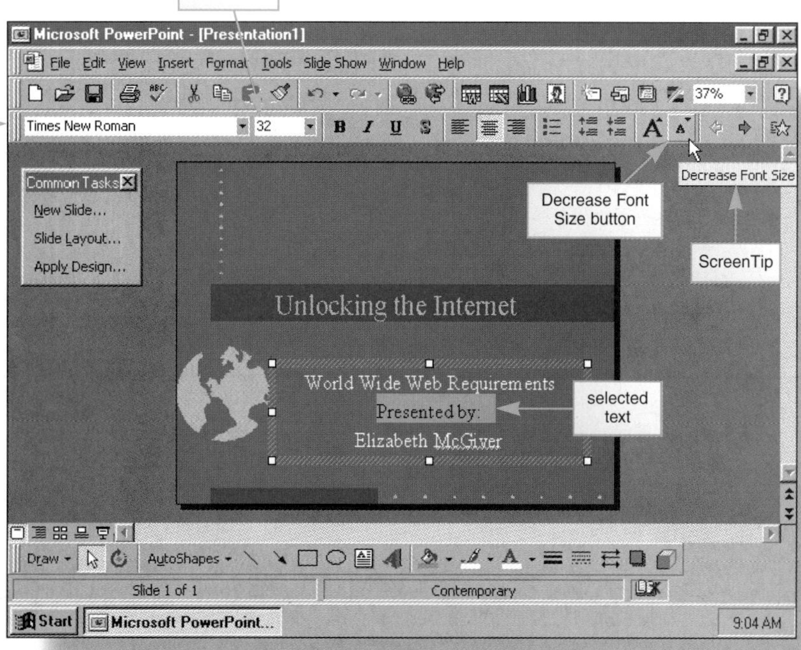

FIGURE 1-19

3 **Click the Decrease Font Size button twice so that 24 displays in the Font Size list box on the Formatting toolbar.**

The paragraph, Presented by:, reduces to 24 points (Figure 1-20). The **Font Size list box** *displays the new font size as 24.*

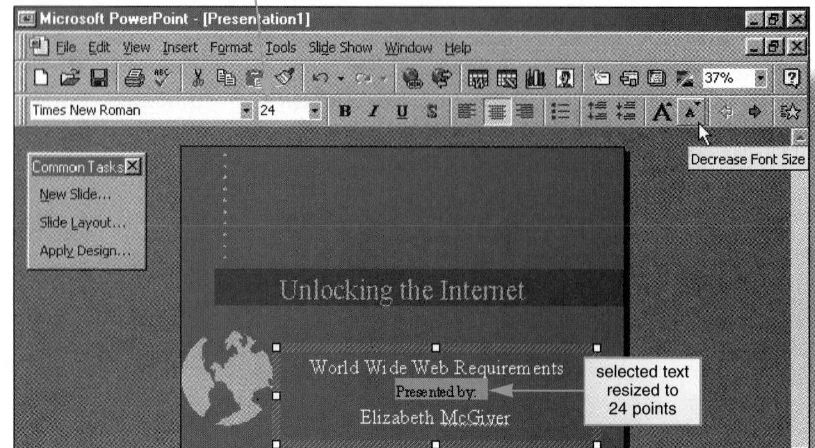

FIGURE 1-20

Other Ways

1. Right-click selected text, click Font on shortcut menu, click new font size in Size list box
2. Click Font Size arrow on Formatting toolbar, click one of listed font sizes, or click Font Size list box on Formatting toolbar, type font size between 1 and 4000
3. On Format menu click Font, click new font size in Size list box

If you need to increase the font size, click the **Increase Font Size button**, located immediately to the left of the Decrease Font Size button on the Formatting toolbar.

Changing the Style of Text to Italic

Text font styles include plain, italic, bold, shadowed, and underlined. PowerPoint allows you to use one or more text font styles in your presentation. Perform the following steps to add emphasis to the title slide by changing plain text to italic text.

Steps To Change the Text Font Style to Italic

1 **With the paragraph, Presented by:, highlighted, click the Italic button on the Formatting toolbar.**

The text is italicized and the **Italic button** *is recessed (Figure 1-21).*

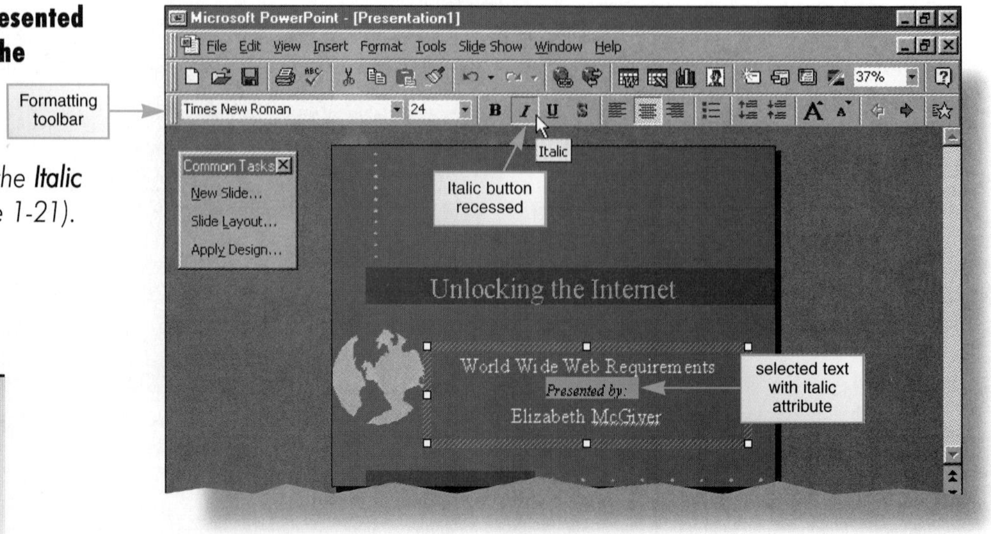

Formatting toolbar

Italic

Italic button recessed

selected text with italic attribute

FIGURE 1-21

Other Ways

1. Right-click selected text, click Font on shortcut menu, click Italic in Font style list box
2. On Format menu click Font, click Italic in Font style list box
3. Press CTRL+I

To remove italics from text, select the italicized text and then click the Italic button. As a result, the Italic button is not recessed and the text does not have the italic font style.

More About Saving

Before you make extreme changes to your presentation, save a copy of it with a different file name using the Save As command on the File menu. This way, if you decide you do not like the new version, you still will have a copy of the original presentation.

Saving a Presentation to a Floppy Disk

While you are building your presentation, the computer stores it in main memory. It is important to save your presentation frequently because, if the computer is turned off or you lose electrical power, the presentation is lost. Another reason to save your work is that if you run out of lab time before completing your project, you may finish the project later without having to start over. You must, therefore, save any presentation you will use later. Before you continue with Project 1, save the work completed thus far. Perform the following steps to save a presentation to a floppy disk using the Save button on the Standard toolbar.

Steps To Save a Presentation to a Floppy Disk

1 **Insert a formatted floppy disk in drive A. Then click the Save button on the Standard toolbar.**

The Save dialog displays (Figure 1-22). The insertion point displays in the File name list box. The default folder, My Documents, displays in the Save in list box. Presentation displays in the Save as type list box. The Save button is dimmed (not available) because you have not yet entered a name in the File name list box. The Cancel button is available, as indicated by the black text on the button. Clicking the Cancel button closes the Save dialog box and returns to the PowerPoint window.

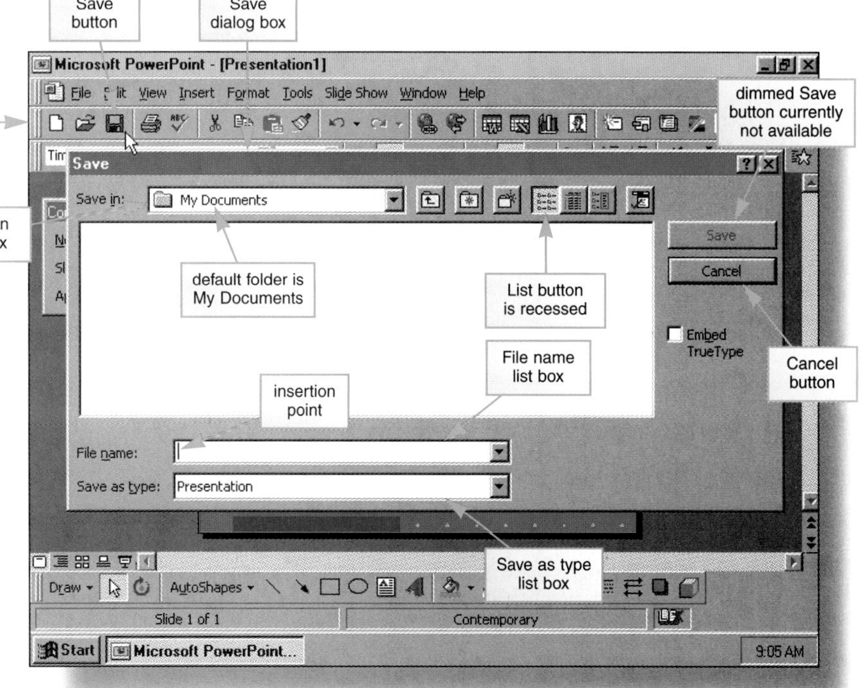

FIGURE 1-22

2 **Type** `Unlocking the Internet` **in the File name list box. Do not press the ENTER key after typing the file name.**

The name, Unlocking the Internet, displays in the File name list box (Figure 1-23). The black text on the Save button indicates it is available.

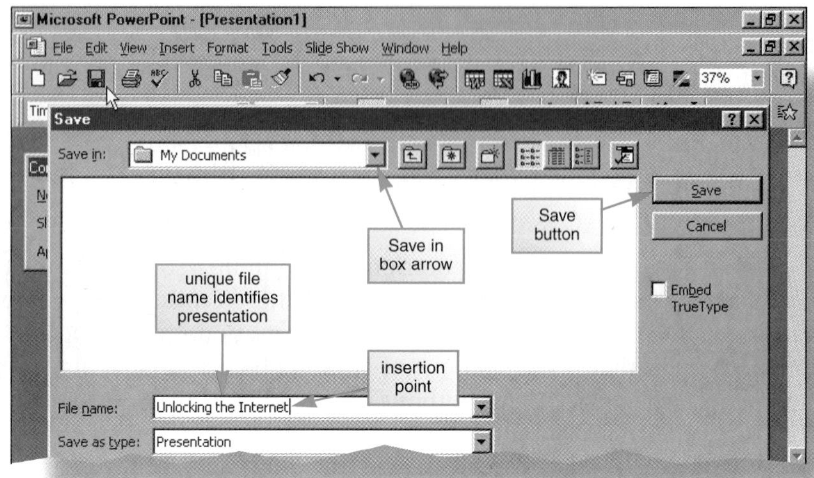

FIGURE 1-23

3 **Click the Save in box arrow. Point to 3½ Floppy (A:) in the Save in list.**

The Save in list displays a list of locations to which you can save your presentation (Figure 1-24). Your list may look different depending on the configuration of your system. 3½ Floppy (A:) is highlighted.

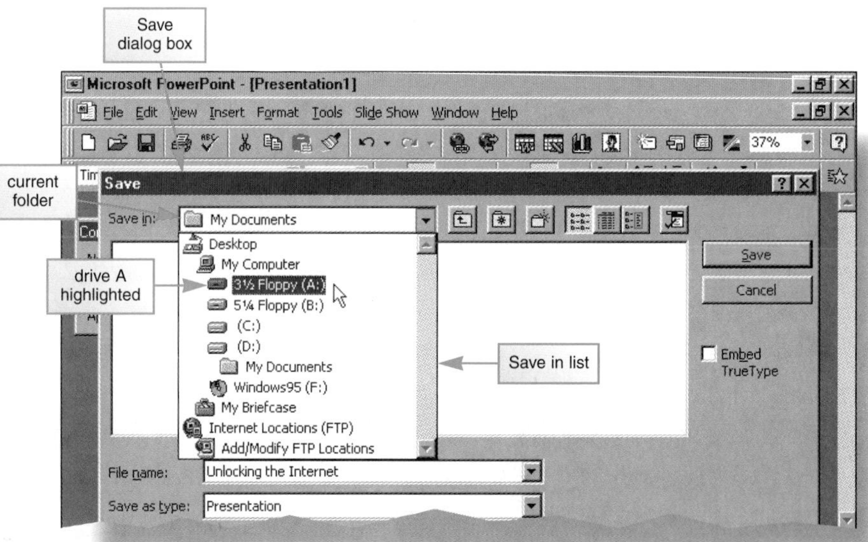

FIGURE 1-24

4 **Click 3½ Floppy (A:). Then point to the Save button.**

Drive A becomes the current drive (Figure 1-25).

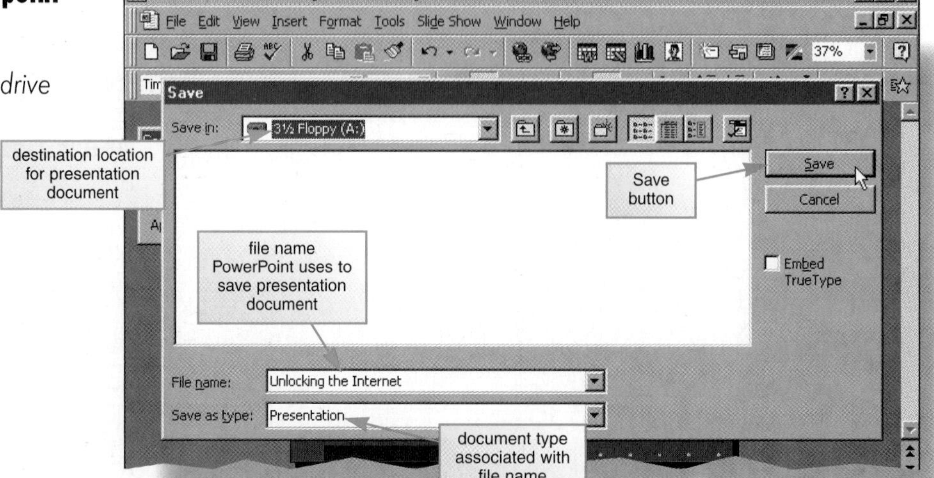

FIGURE 1-25

Click the Save button.

PowerPoint saves the presentation to your floppy disk in drive A. Slide 1 displays in slide view. The title bar displays the file name used to save the presentation, Unlocking the Internet (Figure 1-26).

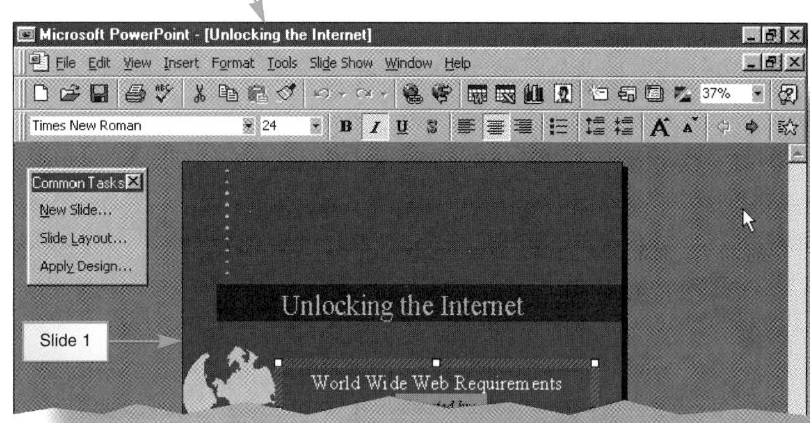

FIGURE 1-26

OtherWays

1. On File menu click Save
2. Press CTRL+S or press SHIFT+F12

PowerPoint automatically appends to the file name, Unlocking the Internet, the extension **.ppt**, which stands for **P**ower**P**oin**t**. Although the presentation, Unlocking the Internet, is saved on a floppy disk, it also remains in main memory and displays on the screen.

It is a good practice to save periodically while you are working on a project. By doing so, you protect yourself from losing all the work you have done since the last time you saved.

Adding a New Slide to a Presentation

The title slide for your presentation is created. The next step is to add the first bulleted list slide in Project 1. Clicking the New Slide button on the Common Tasks toolbar adds a slide into the presentation immediately after the current slide. Usually when you create your presentation, you are adding slides with text, graphics, or charts. When you add a new slide, PowerPoint displays a dialog box for you to choose one of the AutoLayouts. These AutoLayouts have placeholders for various objects, such as a title, text, graphics, graphs, and charts. Some placeholders provide access to other PowerPoint objects by allowing you to double-click the placeholder. Figure 1-27 displays the 24 different AutoLayouts available in PowerPoint. More information about using AutoLayout placeholders to add graphics follows in subsequent projects. Perform the steps on the next page to add a new slide using the Bulleted List AutoLayout.

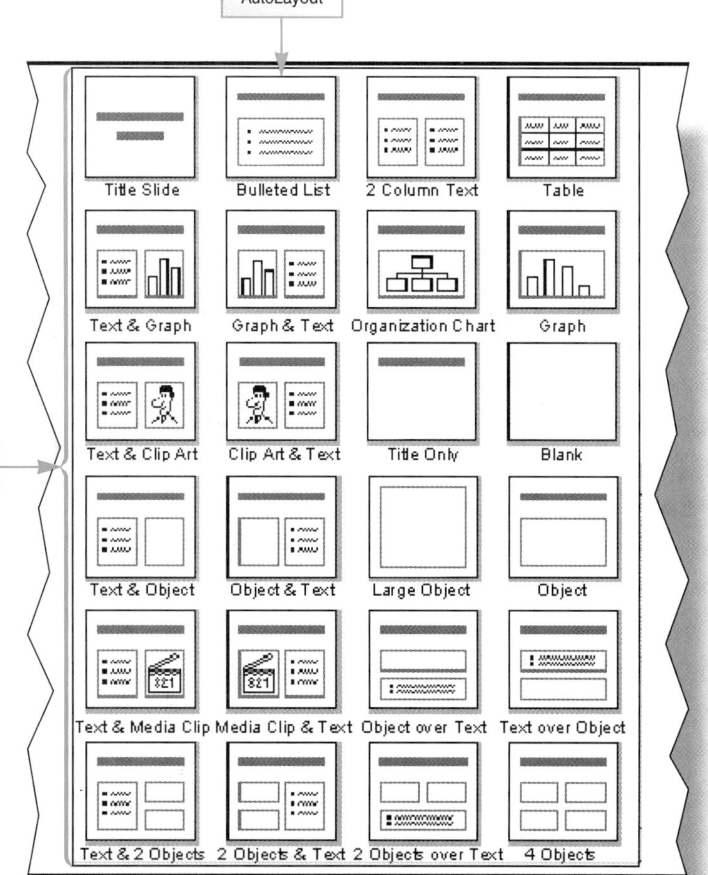

FIGURE 1-27

Steps To Add a New Slide Using the Bulleted List AutoLayout

1 Point to the New Slide button on the Common Tasks toolbar (Figure 1-28).

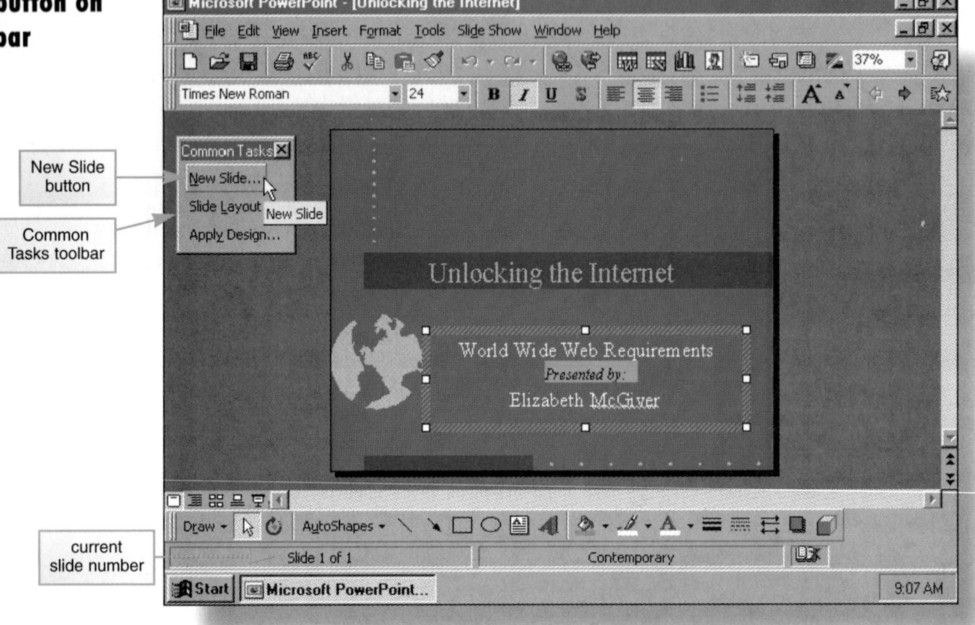

FIGURE 1-28

2 Click the New Slide button. When the New Slide dialog box displays, point to the OK button.

The New Slide dialog box displays (Figure 1-29). The Bulleted List AutoLayout is selected and the AutoLayout title, Bulleted List, displays at the bottom-right corner of the New Slide dialog box.

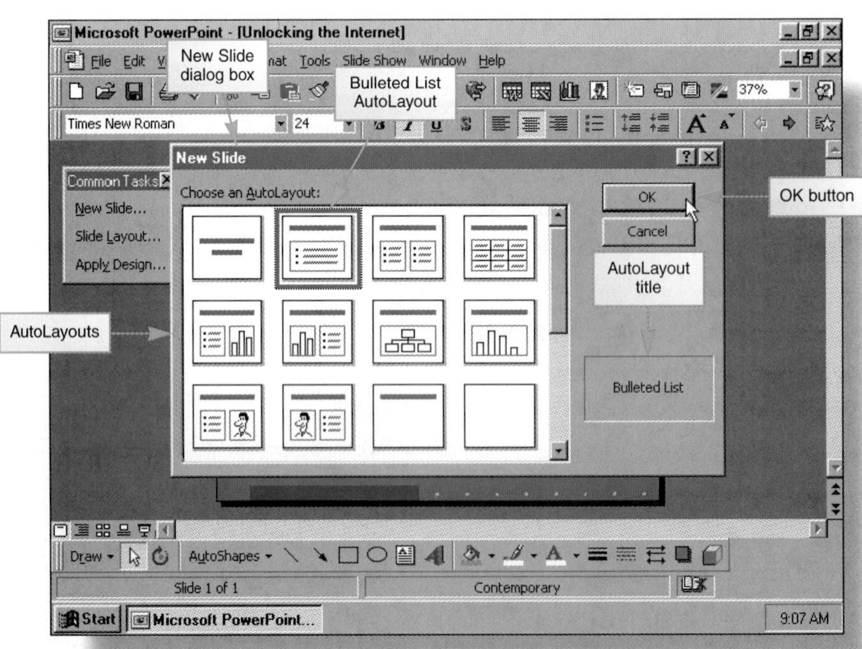

FIGURE 1-29

3 Click the OK button.

Slide 2 displays, keeping the attributes of the Contemporary design template (Figure 1-30). Slide 2 of 2 displays on the status bar.

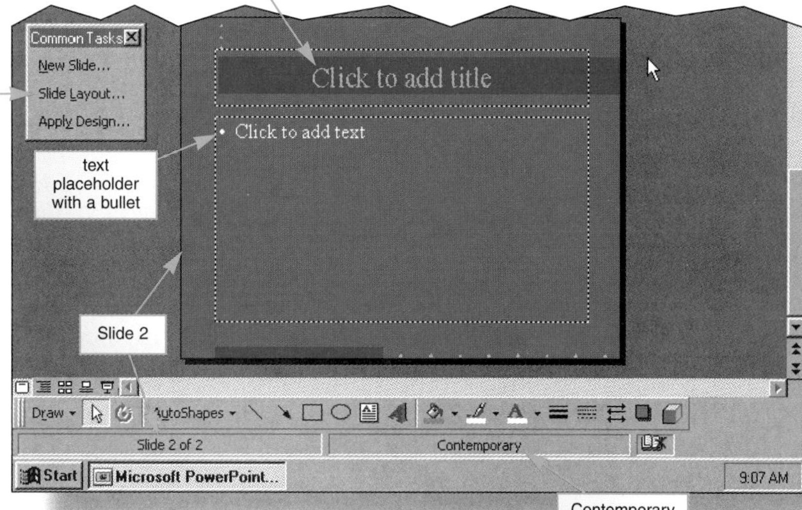

FIGURE 1-30

OtherWays

1. Click New Slide button on Standard toolbar
2. On Insert menu click New Slide
3. Press CTRL+M

Because you selected the Bulleted List AutoLayout, PowerPoint displays Slide 2 with a title placeholder and a text placeholder with a bullet. You can change the layout for a slide at any time during the creation of your presentation by clicking the Slide Layout button on the Common Tasks toolbar and then double-clicking the AutoLayout of your choice.

Creating a Bulleted List Slide

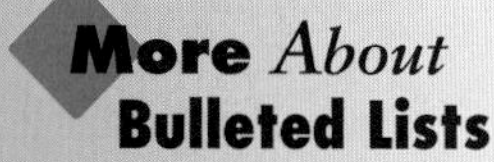

More *About* Bulleted Lists

Short lines of text are easier to read than long lines.

The bulleted list slides in Figure 1-2 on page PP 1.9, contain more than one level of bulleted text. A slide with more than one level of bulleted text is called a **multi-level bulleted list slide**. A **level** is a position within a structure, such as an outline, that indicates a magnitude of importance. PowerPoint allows for five paragraph levels. Each paragraph level has an associated bullet. The bullet font is dependent on the design template. Figure 1-31 identifies the five paragraph levels and the bullet fonts for the Contemporary design template. Beginning with the Second level, each paragraph indents to the right of the preceding level.

An indented paragraph is said to be **demoted**, or pushed down to a lower level. For example, if you demote a First level paragraph, it becomes a Second level paragraph. This lower-level paragraph is a subset of the higher-level paragraph. It usually contains information that supports the topic in the paragraph immediately above it. You demote a paragraph by clicking the **Demote button** on the Formatting toolbar.

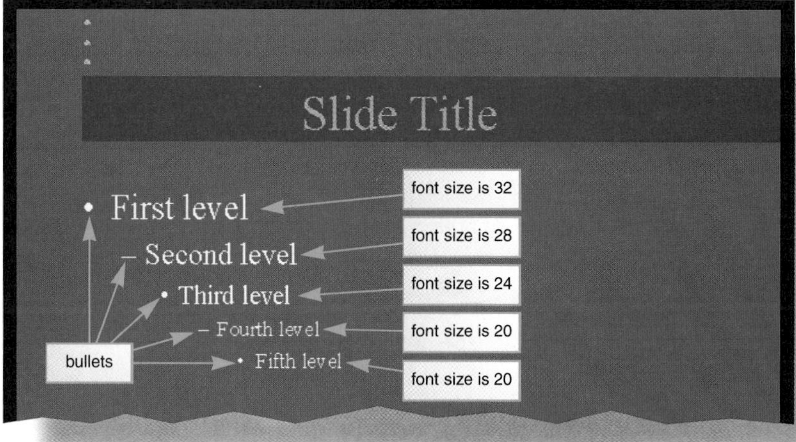

FIGURE 1-31

When you want to raise a paragraph from a lower level to a higher level, you **promote** the paragraph by clicking the **Promote button** on the Formatting toolbar.

Creating a multi-level bulleted list slide requires several steps. Initially, you enter a slide title. Next, you select a text placeholder. Then you type the text for the multi-level bulleted list, demoting and promoting paragraphs as needed. The next several sections explain how to add a multi-level bulleted list slide.

Entering a Slide Title

PowerPoint assumes every new slide has a title. Any text you type after a new slide displays becomes the title object. The title for Slide 2 is Key Hardware Requirements. Perform the following step to enter this title.

Steps To Enter a Slide Title

1. **Type** `Key Hardware Requirements` **in the title placeholder. Do not press the ENTER key.**

The title, Key Hardware Requirements, displays in the title object (Figure 1-32). The insertion point displays after the s in Requirements.

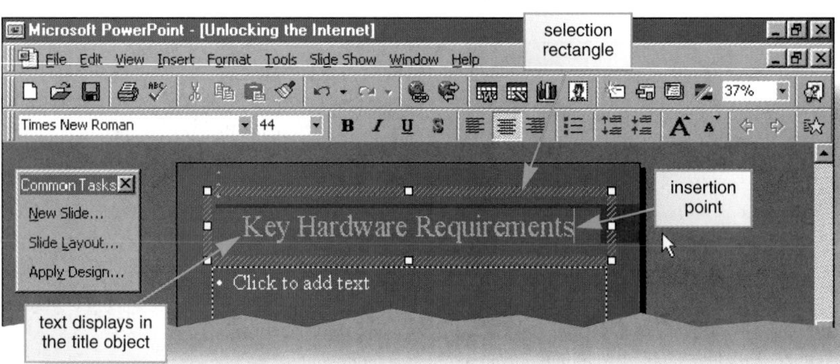

FIGURE 1-32

Selecting a Text Placeholder

Before you can type text into the text placeholder, you first must select it. Perform the following step to select the text placeholder on Slide 2.

Steps To Select a Text Placeholder

1. **Click the bulleted paragraph labeled, Click to add text.**

The insertion point displays immediately after the bullet on Slide 2 (Figure 1-33). The Bullets button is recessed.

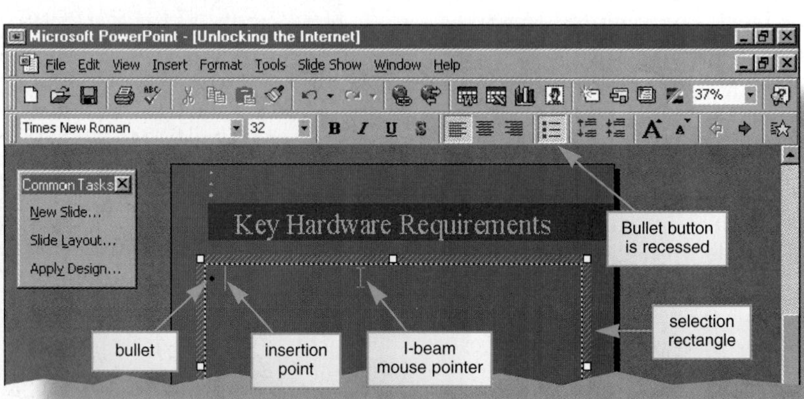

FIGURE 1-33

Other Ways

1. Press CTRL+ENTER

Typing a Multi-level Bulleted List

Recall that a bulleted list is a list of paragraphs, each of which is preceded by a bullet. Also recall that a paragraph is a segment of text ended by pressing the ENTER key. The next step is to type the multi-level bulleted list, which consists of the six entries shown in Figure 1-2 on page PP 1.9. Perform the following steps to type a multi-level bulleted list.

More About Presentation Design

Keep to one concept per slide. Highlight the subject rather than presenting a page of text. Limit your slide to five to seven words per line and five to seven lines per slide. Do not clutter; use empty space effectively.

To Type a Multi-level Bulleted List

1 **Type** `Computer` **and press the ENTER key.**

The paragraph, Computer, displays. The font size is 32. The insertion point displays after the second bullet (Figure 1-34). When you press the ENTER key, the word processing feature of PowerPoint marks the end of one paragraph and begins a new paragraph. Because you are using the Bulleted List AutoLayout, PowerPoint places a bullet in front of the new paragraph.

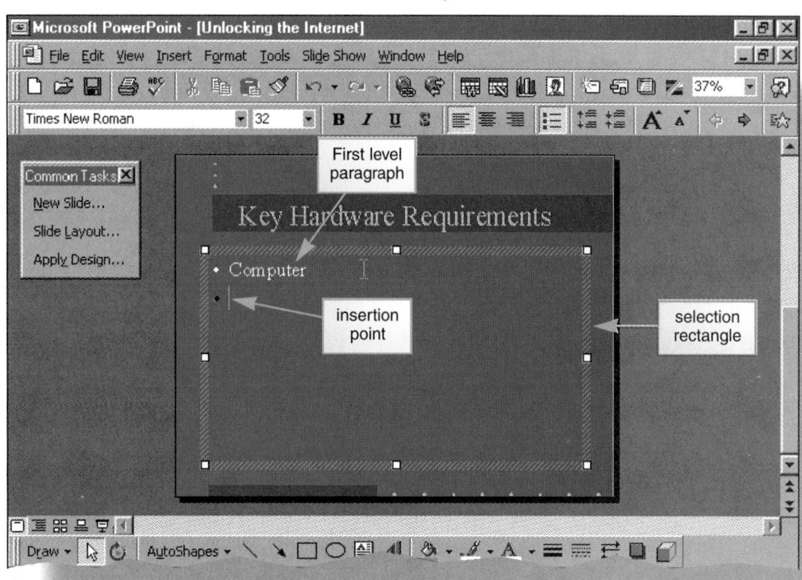

FIGURE 1-34

2 **Point to the Demote button on the Formatting toolbar (Figure 1-35).**

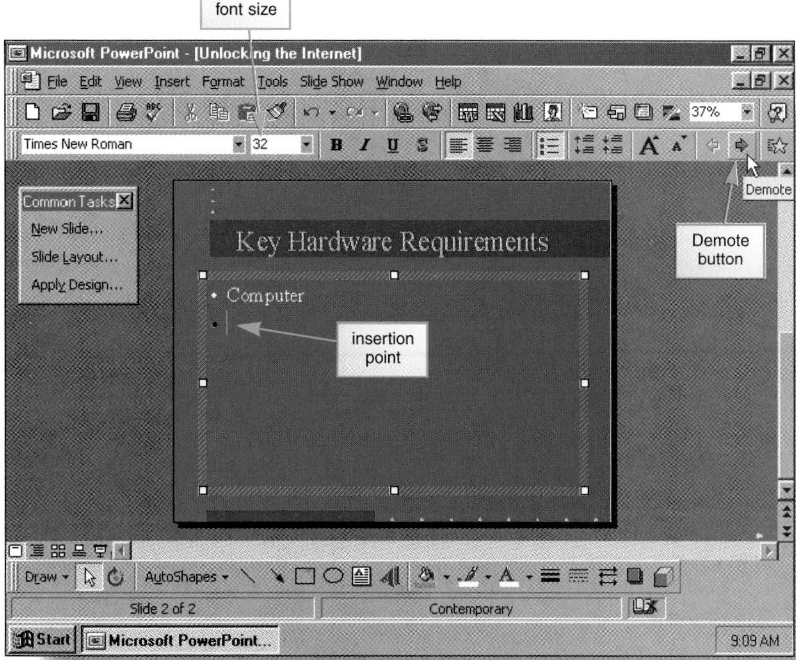

FIGURE 1-35

3 **Click the Demote button.**

The second paragraph indents under the first and becomes a Second level paragraph (Figure 1-36). Notice the bullet in front of the second paragraph changes from a dot to a dash and the font size for the demoted paragraph is now 28. The insertion point displays after the dash.

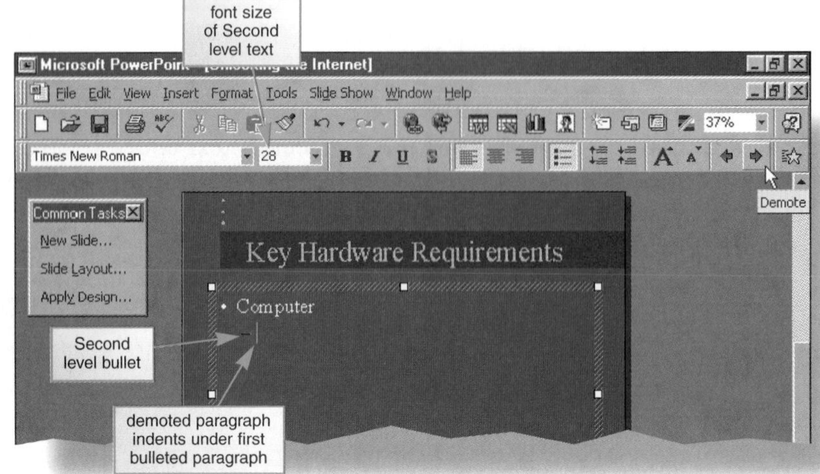

FIGURE 1-36

4 **Type** `Video and sound` **and press the ENTER key. Type** `Memory and hard disk` **and then press the ENTER key.**

Two new Second level paragraphs display with dash bullets (Figure 1-37). When you press the ENTER key, PowerPoint adds a new paragraph at the same level as the previous paragraph.

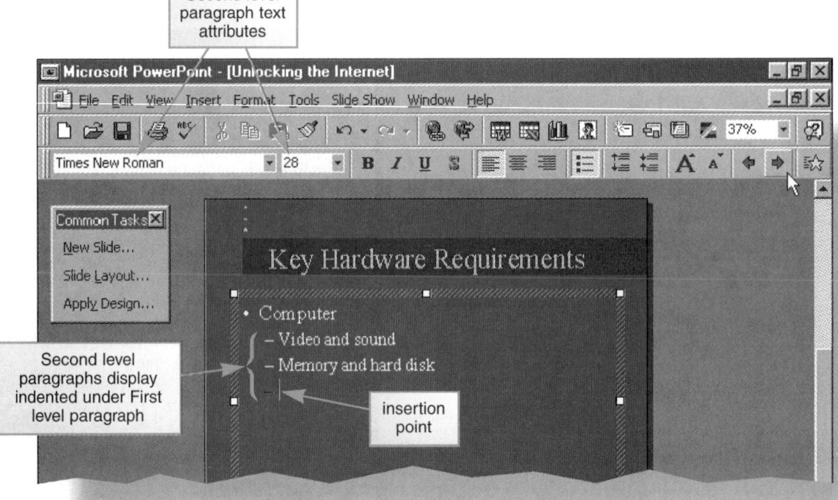

FIGURE 1-37

5 **Point to the Promote button on the Formatting toolbar (Figure 1-38).**

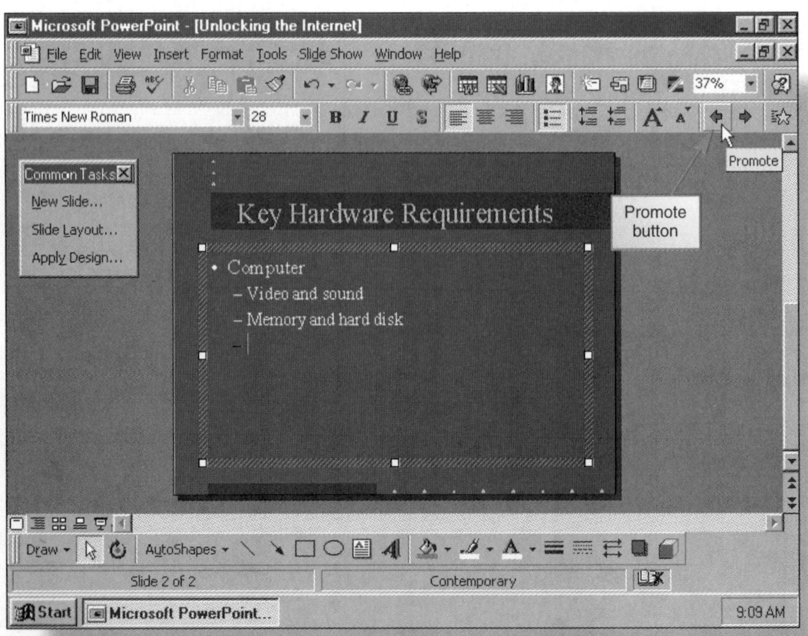

FIGURE 1-38

6 **Click the Promote button.**

The Second level paragraph becomes a First level paragraph (Figure 1-39). Notice the bullet in front of the new paragraph changes from a dash to a dot and the font size for the promoted paragraph is 32. The insertion point displays after the dot bullet.

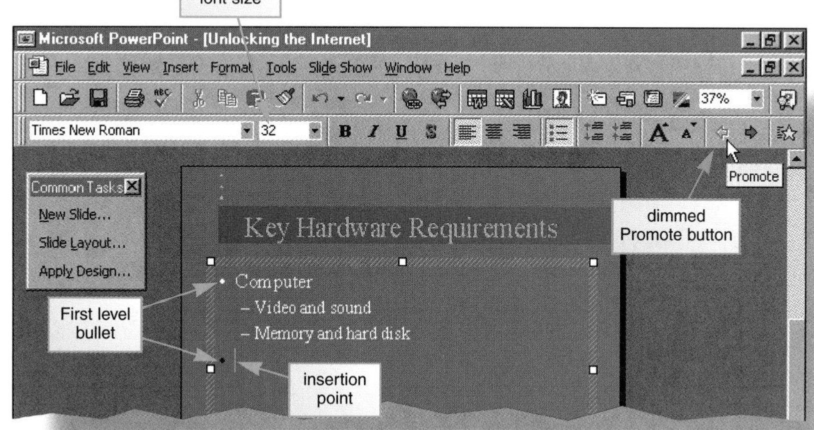

FIGURE 1-39

Perform the following steps to complete the text for Slide 2.

TO TYPE THE REMAINING TEXT FOR SLIDE 2

Step 1: Type `Communications` and press the ENTER key.
Step 2: Click the Demote button.
Step 3: Type `Modem and telephone line` and press the ENTER key.
Step 4: Type `Direct connect` and do not press the ENTER key.

The insertion point displays after the t in connect (Figure 1-40).

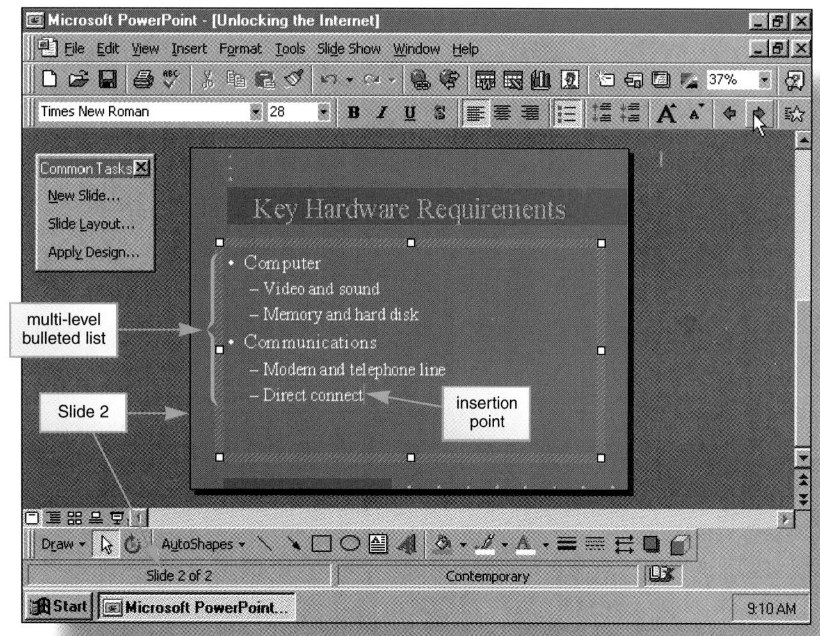

FIGURE 1-40

Notice that you did not press the ENTER key after typing the last paragraph in Step 4. If you press the ENTER key, a new bullet displays after the last entry on this slide. To remove an extra bullet, press the BACKSPACE key.

Adding a New Slide with the Same AutoLayout

When you add a new slide to a presentation and want to keep the same AutoLayout used on the previous slide, PowerPoint gives you a shortcut. Instead of clicking the New Slide button and clicking an AutoLayout in the New Slide dialog box, you can press and hold down the SHIFT key and click the New Slide button. Perform the step on the next page to add a new slide (Slide 3) and keep the Bulleted List AutoLayout used on the previous slide.

More About Presentation Design

Two acronyms pertain directly to presentation design:
- KIS (Keep It Simple)
- CCC (Clutter Creates Confusion)

To Add a New Slide with the Same AutoLayout

1 Press and hold down the SHIFT key. Click the New Slide button on the Common Tasks toolbar. Then release the SHIFT key.

Slide 3 displays the Bulleted List AutoLayout (Figure 1-41). Slide 3 of 3 displays on the status bar.

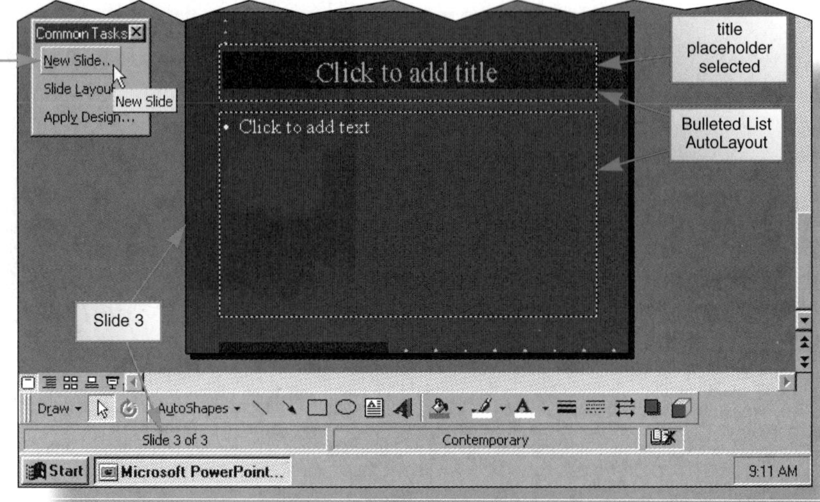

FIGURE 1-41

OtherWays

1. Press SHIFT+CTRL+M

Slide 3 is added to the presentation. Perform the following steps to add text to Slide 3 and create a multi-level bulleted list.

TO CREATE SLIDE 3

Step 1: Type `Key Software Requirements` in the title placeholder.
Step 2: Click the text placeholder.
Step 3: Type `Microsoft Corporation` and press the ENTER key.
Step 4: Click the Demote button. Type `Internet Explorer` and press the ENTER key.
Step 5: Click the Promote button. Type `Netscape Communications Corporation` and press the ENTER key.
Step 6: Click the Demote button. Type `Netscape Navigator` and press the ENTER key.
Step 7: Click the Promote button. Type `SPRY, CompuServe Internet Division` and press the ENTER key.
Step 8: Click the Demote button. Type `Internet In A Box` but do not press the ENTER key.

Slide 3 displays as shown in Figure 1-42.

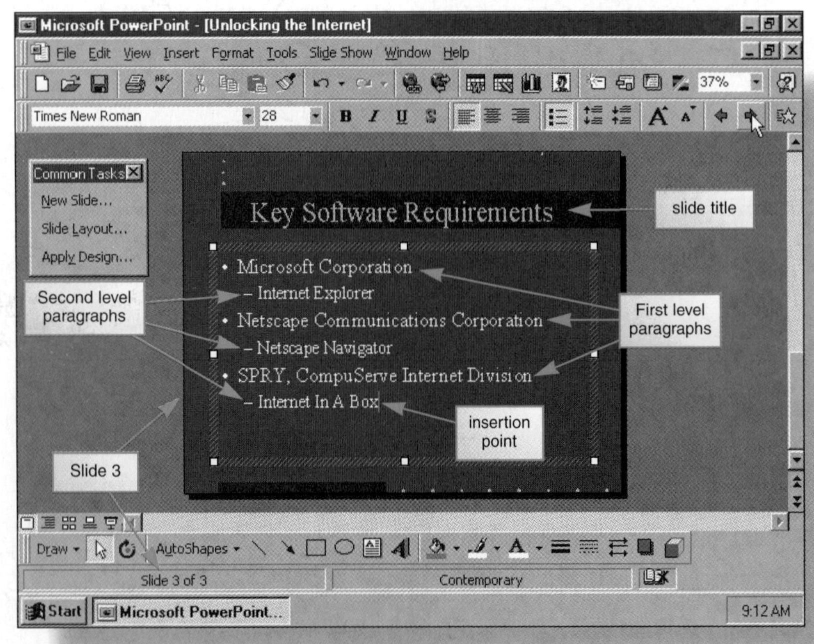

FIGURE 1-42

Slide 4 is the last slide in this presentation. It, too, is a multi-level bulleted list. Perform the following steps to create Slide 4.

TO CREATE SLIDE 4

Step 1: Press and hold down the SHIFT key and click the New Slide button on the Common Tasks toolbar. Release the SHIFT key.
Step 2: Type `Key Internet Providers` in the title placeholder.
Step 3: Click the text placeholder.
Step 4: Type `Online services` and press the ENTER key.
Step 5: Click the Demote button. Type `The Microsoft Network` and press the ENTER key.
Step 6: Type `America Online` and press the ENTER key.
Step 7: Type `CompuServe` and press the ENTER key.
Step 8: Type `Prodigy` and press the ENTER key.
Step 9: Click the Promote button. Type `Local services` but do not press the ENTER key.

The slide title and text object display as shown in Figure 1-43.

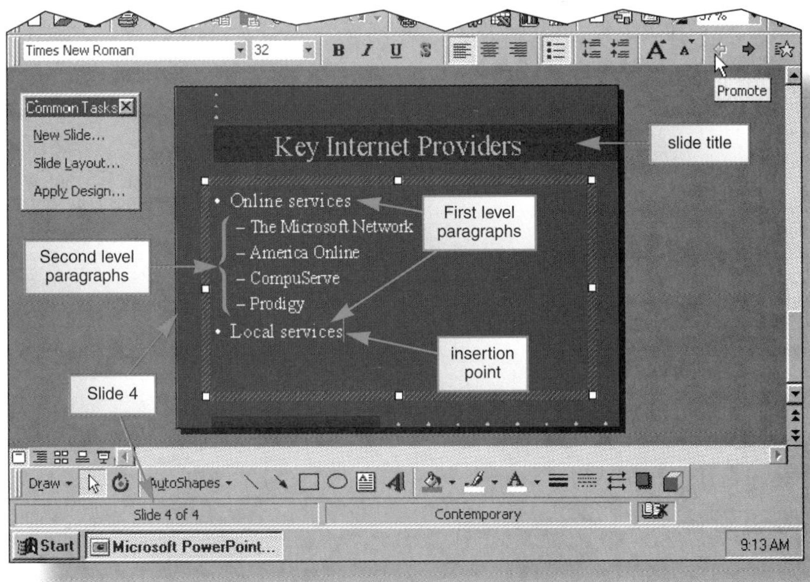

FIGURE 1-43

All slides for the Unlocking the Internet presentation are created. This presentation consists of a title slide and three multi-level bulleted list slides.

Saving a Presentation with the Same File Name

Saving frequently never can be overemphasized. When you first saved the presentation, you clicked the Save button on the Standard toolbar and the Save dialog box displayed. When you want to save the changes made to the presentation after your last save, you again click the Save button. This time, however, the Save dialog box does not display because PowerPoint updates the document called Unlocking the Internet.ppt on your floppy disk. Perform the steps on the next page to save the presentation again.

Protect yourself by making a second copy of a presentation prior to making several edits. On the File menu, click Save As, then save the presentation with a new name. Make your changes to the original file. When satisfied you no longer need the second file, delete it.

TO SAVE A PRESENTATION WITH THE SAME FILE NAME

Step 1: Be sure your floppy disk is in drive A.
Step 2: Click the Save button on the Standard toolbar.

PowerPoint overwrites the old Unlocking the Internet.ppt document on the floppy disk in drive A with the revised presentation document, Unlocking the Internet.ppt. Slide 4 displays in the PowerPoint window.

Moving to Another Slide in Slide View

When creating or editing a presentation in slide view, you often want to display a slide other than the current one. Dragging the vertical scroll bar box up or down moves you through your presentation. The box on the vertical scroll bar is called the **scroll box** and is shown in Figure 1-44. When you drag the scroll box, the **slide indicator** displays the number and the title of the slide you are about to display. Releasing the mouse button displays the slide.

Using the Vertical Scroll Bar to Move to Another Slide

Before continuing with Project 1, you want to display the title slide. Perform the following steps to move from Slide 4 to the Slide 1 using the vertical scroll bar.

Steps To Use the Vertical Scroll Bar to Move to Another Slide

1. **Position the mouse pointer on the scroll box. Press and hold down the left mouse button.**

Slide: 4 of 4 Key Internet Providers, displays in the slide indicator (Figure 1-44).

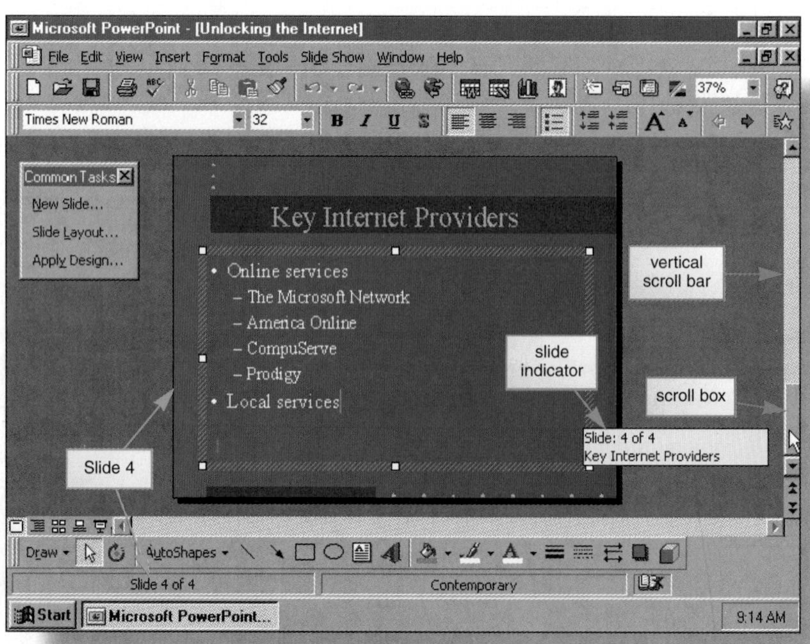

FIGURE 1-44

2 **Drag the scroll box up the vertical scroll bar until Slide: 1 of 4 Unlocking the Internet displays in the slide indicator.**

Slide: 1 of 4 Unlocking the Internet, displays in the slide indicator. Slide 4 still displays in the PowerPoint window (Figure 1-45).

3 **Release the left mouse button.**

Slide 1, titled Unlocking the Internet, displays in the PowerPoint window.

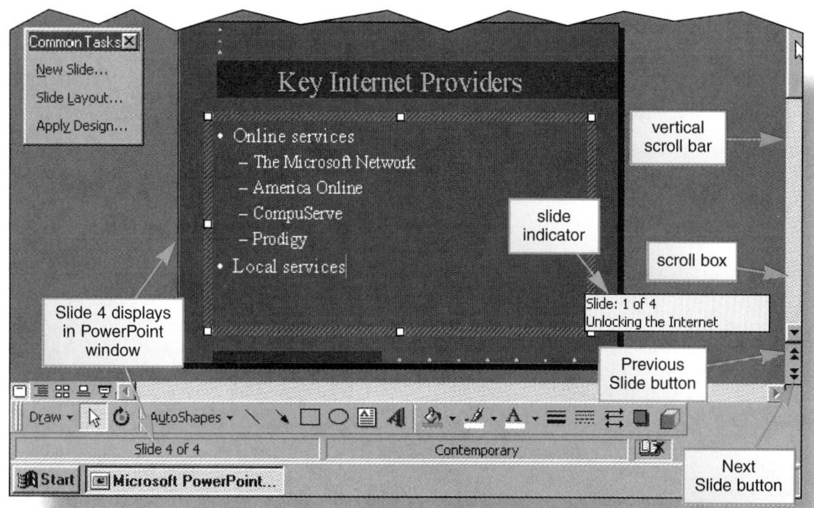

FIGURE 1-45

OtherWays

1. Click Next Slide button on vertical scroll bar to move forward one slide, or click Previous Slide button on vertical scroll bar to move back one slide
2. Press PAGE DOWN to move forward one slide, or press PAGE UP to move back one slide

Viewing the Presentation Using Slide Show

The **Slide Show button**, located at the bottom left of the PowerPoint window, allows you to display your presentation electronically using a computer. The computer acts like a slide projector, displaying each slide on a full screen. The full screen slide hides the toolbars, menus, and other PowerPoint window elements.

Starting Slide Show View

Slide show view begins when you click the Slide Show button. PowerPoint then displays the current slide on the full screen without any of the PowerPoint window objects, such as the menu bar or toolbars. Perform the following steps to start slide show view.

Steps To Start Slide Show View

1 **Point to the Slide Show button on the View Button Bar.**

The Slide View button is recessed because you are still in slide view (Figure 1-46).

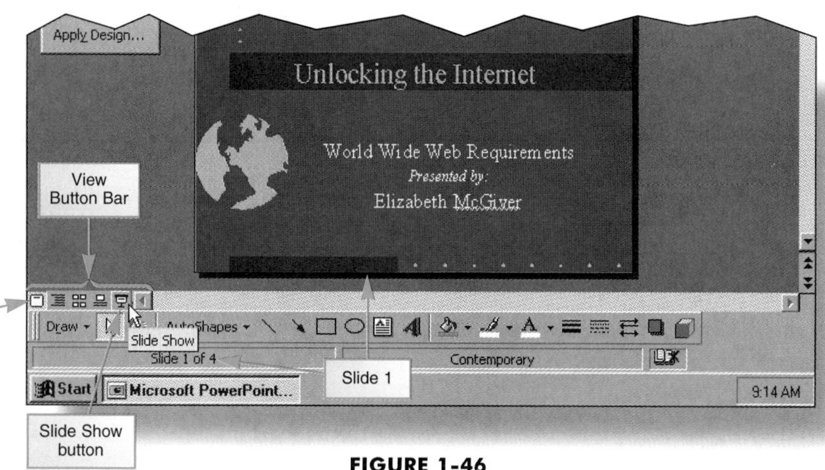

FIGURE 1-46

2 Click the Slide Show button.

The title slide fills the screen (Figure 1-47). The PowerPoint window is hidden.

FIGURE 1-47

OtherWays

1. On View menu click Slide Show

Advancing through a Slide Show Manually

After you begin slide show view, you can move forward or backward through your slides. PowerPoint allows you to advance through your slides manually or automatically. Automatic advancing is discussed in a later project. Perform the step below to manually move through your slides.

Steps To Manually Move Through Slides in a Slide Show

1 Click each slide until the last slide of the presentation, Slide 4, Key Internet Providers, displays.

Each slide in your presentation displays on the screen, one slide at a time. Each time you click the mouse button, the next slide displays (Figure 1-48).

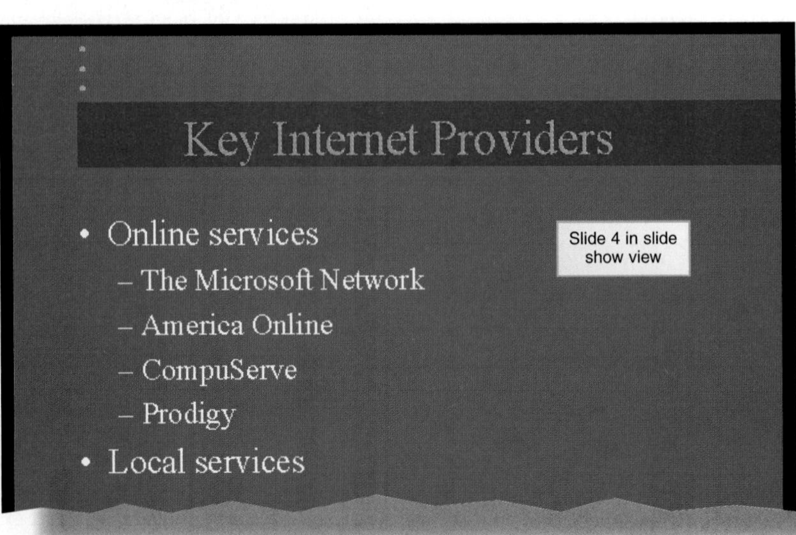

FIGURE 1-48

OtherWays

1. Press PAGE DOWN to advance one slide at a time, or press PAGE UP to go backward one slide at a time

Displaying the Popup Menu in Slide Show View

Slide show view has a shortcut menu, called **Popup Menu**, that displays when you right-click a slide in slide show view. The Popup Menu contains commands to assist you during a slide show. For example, clicking the **Next command** moves you to the next slide. Clicking the **Previous command** moves you to the previous slide. You can jump to any slide in your presentation by clicking the **Go command** and then clicking Slide Navigator. The **Slide Navigator dialog box** contains a list of the slides in your presentation. Jump to the requested slide by double-clicking the name of that slide.

Additional Popup Menu commands allow you to create a list of action items during a slide show, change the mouse pointer from an arrow to a pen, blacken the screen, and end the slide show. Popup Menu commands are discussed in subsequent projects. Perform the following step to display the Slide Show View Popup Menu.

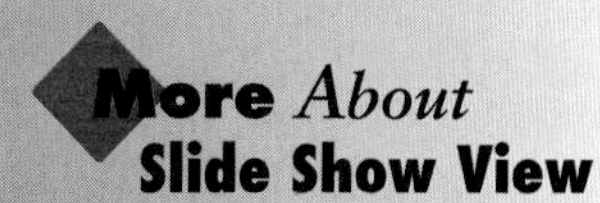

More About Slide Show View

The Pen command on the Popup Menu changes the mouse pointer into a pen used to mark on the slides. The effect is similar to electronic whiteboards used by TV sports announcers explaining plays. Markings are not saved with the presentation.

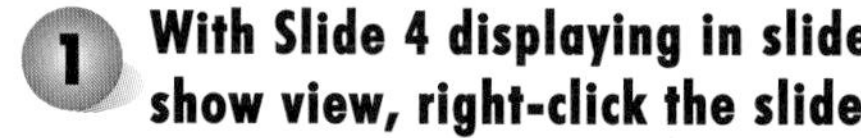

To Display the Slide Show View Popup Menu

1 With Slide 4 displaying in slide show view, right-click the slide.

The Popup Menu displays on Slide 4 (Figure 1-49). Your screen may look different because the Popup Menu displays near the location of the mouse pointer at the time you right-click.

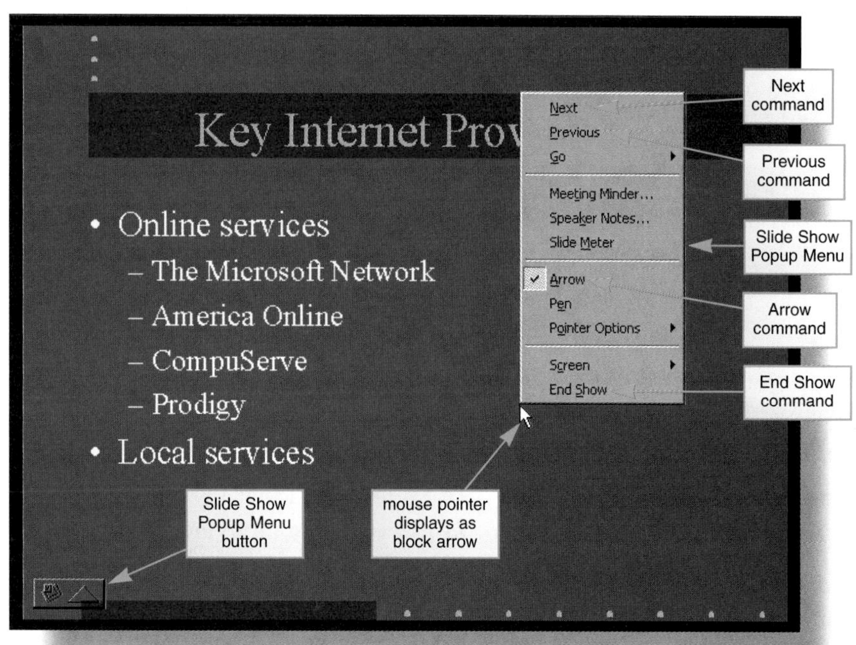

FIGURE 1-49

OtherWays

1. Move mouse pointer during slide show to display Popup Menu button, and then click Popup Menu button

Some presenters prefer to right-click to move backward through a slide show. Because PowerPoint allows you to display the Slide Show View Popup Menu by clicking the Slide Show View Popup Menu button, you can turn off the option setting that displays the Popup menu when you right-click. To turn off the Popup menu on right mouse click option on the Tools menu, click Options, click the View tab to display the View sheet, click Popup menu on right mouse click to remove the check, and then click the OK button. After turning off the Popup menu on right mouse click option setting, you can right-click to move backward, one slide at a time, in slide show view.

Using the Popup Menu to End a Slide Show

The **End Show command** on the Popup Menu exits slide show view and returns to the view you were in when you clicked the Slide Show button. Perform the following step to end slide show view.

To Use the Popup Menu to End a Slide Show

Click End Show on the Popup Menu.

PowerPoint exits slide show view and displays the slide last displayed in slide show view, which in this instance, is Slide 4 (Figure 1-50).

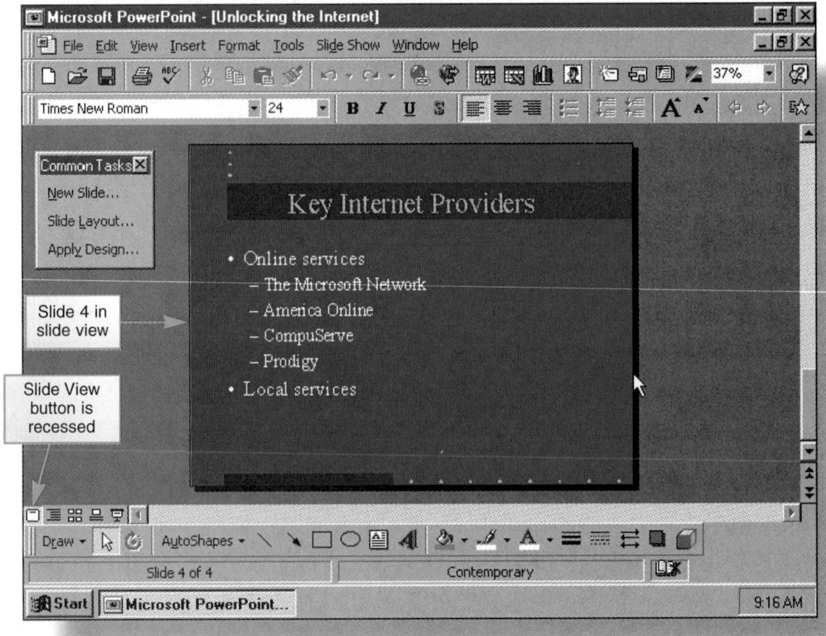

FIGURE 1-50

Other Ways

1. Click last slide in presentation to return to slide at which you began slide show view
2. Press ESC to display slide last viewed in slide show view

Slide show view is excellent for rehearsing a presentation. You can start slide show view from any view: slide view, outline view, slide sorter view, or notes page view.

Quitting PowerPoint

The Unlocking the Internet presentation now is complete. When you quit PowerPoint, PowerPoint prompts you to save any changes made to the presentation since the last save, closes all PowerPoint windows, and then quits PowerPoint. Closing PowerPoint returns control to the desktop. Perform the following steps to quit PowerPoint.

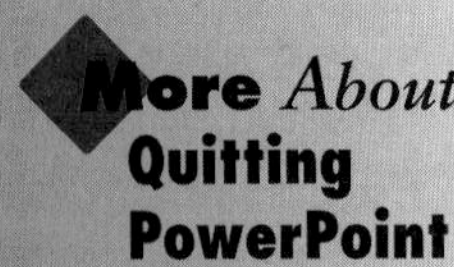

More About Quitting PowerPoint

If you notice your computer system is performing more slowly than normal, close all unnecessary applications. This releases memory held by those open applications and should improve your system's performance.

Steps To Quit PowerPoint

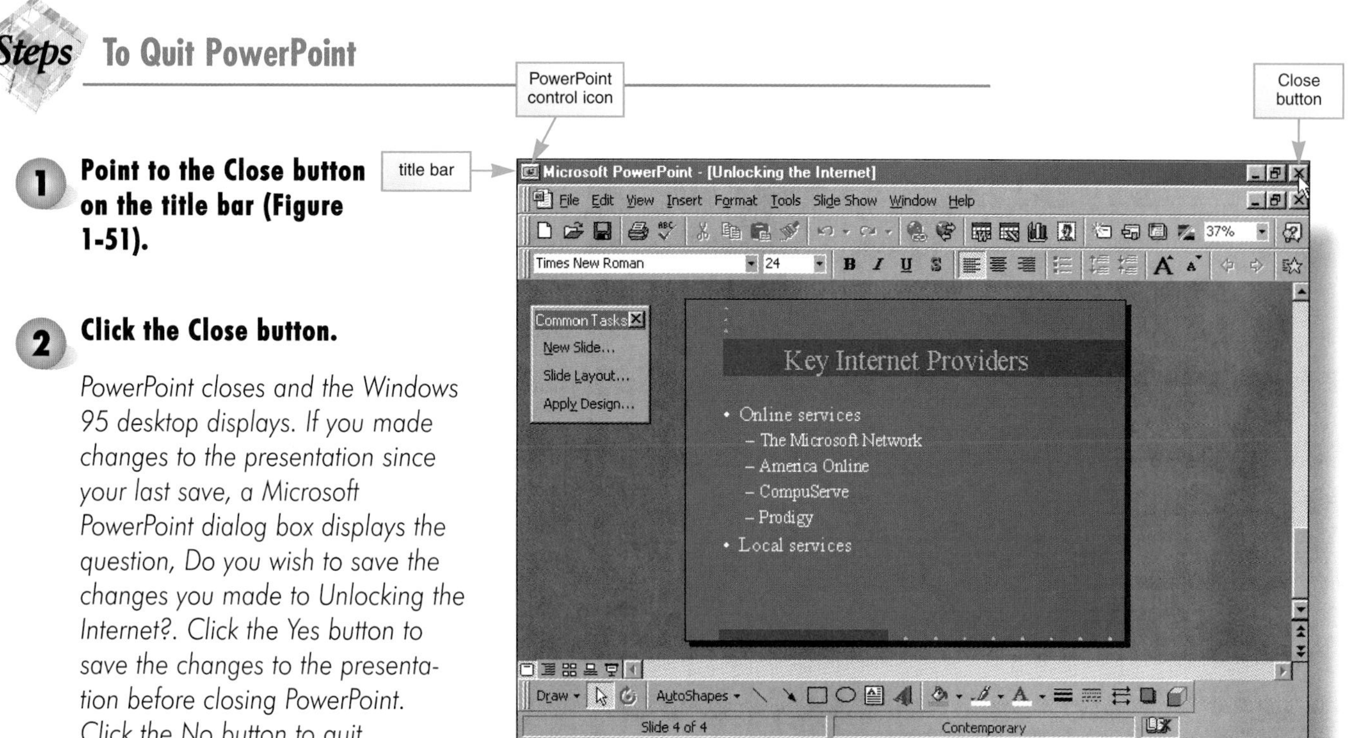

FIGURE 1-51

1. **Point to the Close button on the title bar (Figure 1-51).**

2. **Click the Close button.**

   PowerPoint closes and the Windows 95 desktop displays. If you made changes to the presentation since your last save, a Microsoft PowerPoint dialog box displays the question, Do you wish to save the changes you made to Unlocking the Internet?. Click the Yes button to save the changes to the presentation before closing PowerPoint. Click the No button to quit PowerPoint without saving the changes. Click the Cancel button to terminate the Close command and return to the presentation.

Other Ways

1. On title bar double-click PowerPoint control icon; or on title bar, click PowerPoint control icon, click Close
2. On File menu click Exit
3. Press CTRL+Q or press ALT+F4

Opening a Presentation

Earlier, you saved the presentation on a floppy disk using the file name, Unlocking the Internet.ppt. Once you create and save a presentation, you may need to retrieve it from the floppy disk to make changes. For example, you may want to replace the design template or modify some text. Recall that a presentation is a PowerPoint document. Use the **Open Office Document command** to open an existing presentation.

More About Opening Presentations

PowerPoint allows you to open more than one presentation at a time. To display another open presentation, click Window on the menu bar and then click the desired presentation.

Opening an Existing Presentation

Ensure that the floppy disk used to save Unlocking the Internet.ppt is in drive A. Then perform the steps on the next page to open the Unlocking the Internet presentation using the Open Office Document command on the Start menu.

To Open an Existing Presentation

1 Click the Start button on the taskbar and point to Open Office Document.

The Windows 95 Start menu displays (Figure 1-52). Open Office Document is highlighted.

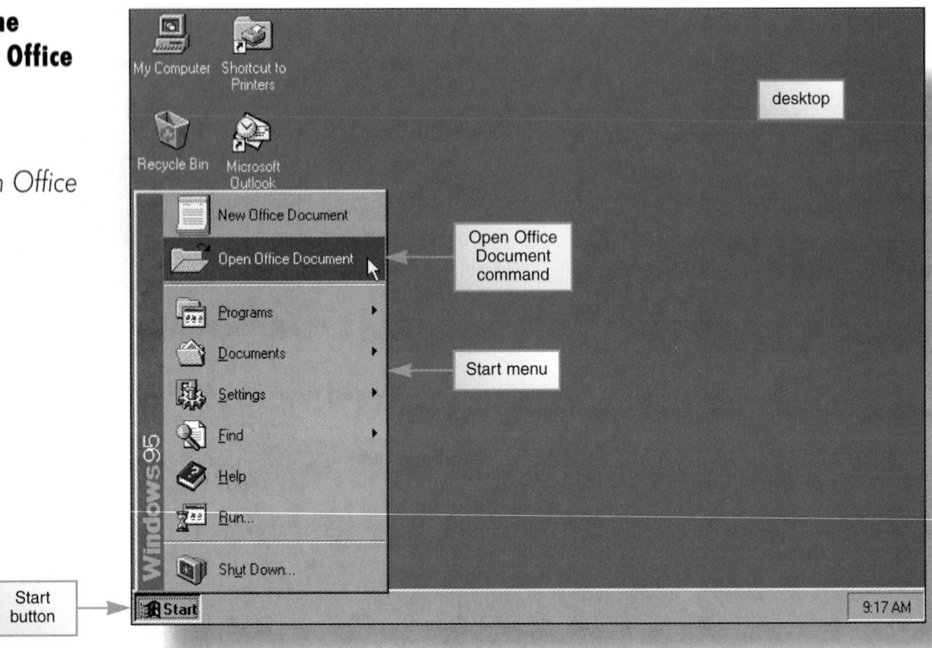

FIGURE 1-52

2 Click Open Office Document. When the Open Office Document dialog box displays, click the Look in box arrow and then click 3½ Floppy (A:) (see Figures 1-23 and 1-24 on page PP 1.24 to review this process).

The Open Office Document dialog box displays (Figure 1-53). A list of existing files on drive A displays because your floppy disk is in drive A. Notice that Office Files displays in the Files of type list box. The file, Unlocking the Internet, is highlighted. Your list of existing files may be different depending on the files saved on your floppy disk.

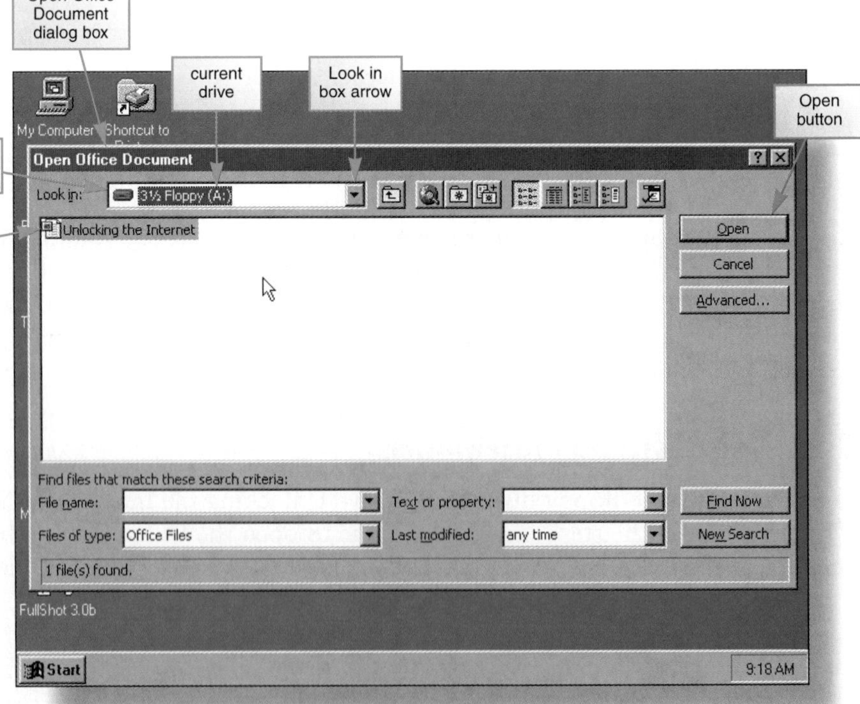

FIGURE 1-53

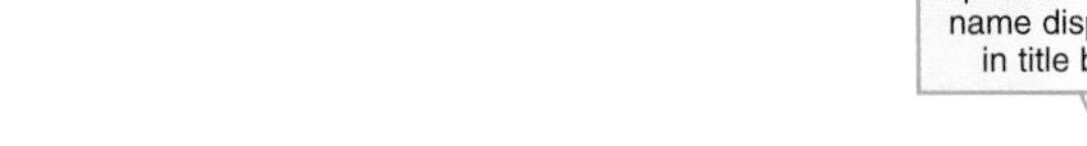

3 Double-click Unlocking the Internet.

PowerPoint starts and opens Unlocking the Internet.ppt from drive A into main memory and displays the first slide on the screen (Figure 1-54). The presentation displays in slide view because PowerPoint opens presentations in the same view in which they were saved.

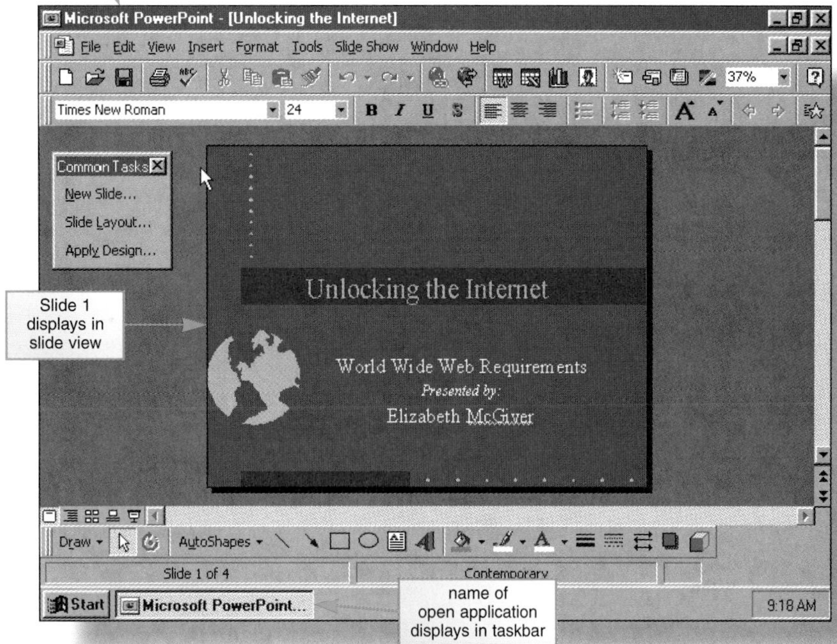

FIGURE 1-54

OtherWays

1. Click Open a Document button on Microsoft Office Shortcut Bar, click folder or drive name in Look in list, double-click document name
2. On Start menu click Documents, click document name

When an application is open, its name displays on a button on the taskbar. The **active application** is the one displaying in the foreground of the desktop. That application's corresponding button on the taskbar displays recessed.

When more than one application is open, you can switch between applications by clicking the button labeled with the name of the application to which you want to switch.

Checking a Presentation for Visual Clarity, Consistency, and Style

After you create a presentation, you should proofread it for errors. Typical errors include spelling errors, punctuation errors, and design errors. PowerPoint has a tool, called **Style Checker**, that helps you identify errors in your presentation. When you start Style Checker, the Style Checker dialog box displays three check boxes: Spelling, Visual clarity, and Case and end punctuation. A check mark in a check box instructs Style Checker to look for that particular type of inconsistency. For example, a check mark in the Spelling check box causes Style Checker to check the presentation for spelling errors. Table 1-3 identifies the purpose of each check box in the Style Checker dialog box.

Table 1-3

CHECK BOX	PURPOSE
Spelling	Checks the presentation for spelling errors.
Visual clarity	Checks the presentation for appropriate font usage and for legibility of slide titles and body text.
Case and end punctuation	Checks the presentation for consistency of capitalization and end punctuation in slide titles and body text.

PowerPoint checks your presentation for spelling errors using a standard dictionary contained in the Microsoft Office group. This dictionary is shared with the other Microsoft Office applications such as Word and Excel. A **custom dictionary** is available if you want to add special words such as proper names, cities, and acronyms. When checking a presentation for spelling errors, PowerPoint opens the standard dictionary and the custom dictionary file, if one exists. When a word displays in the Spelling dialog box, you perform one of the actions listed in Table 1-4.

Table 1-4

ACTION	DESCRIPTION
Manually correct the word	Retype the word with the proper spelling in the Change to box and then click Change. PowerPoint continues checking the rest of the presentation.
Ignore the word	Click Ignore when the word is spelled correctly but not found in the dictionaries. PowerPoint continues checking the rest of the presentation.
Ignore all occurrences of the word	Click Ignore All when the word is spelled correctly but not found in the dictionaries. PowerPoint ignores all occurrences of the word and continues checking the rest of the presentation.
Select a different spelling	Click the proper spelling of the word from the list in the Suggestions box. Click Change. PowerPoint corrects the word and continues checking the rest of the presentation.
Change all occurrences of the misspelling to a different spelling	Click the proper spelling of the word from the list in the Suggestions box. Click Change All. PowerPoint changes all occurrences of the misspelled word and continues checking the rest of the presentation.
Add a word to the custom dictionary	Click Add. PowerPoint opens the custom dictionary, adds the word, and continues checking the rest of the presentation.
View alternative spellings	Click Suggest. PowerPoint lists suggested spellings. Click the correct word from the Suggestions box or type the proper spelling. Then click Change. PowerPoint continues checking the rest of the presentation.
Add spelling error to AutoCorrect list	Click AutoCorrect. PowerPoint adds the spelling error and its correction to the AutoCorrect list. Any future misspelling of the word is corrected automatically as you type.

The standard dictionary contains commonly used English words. It does not, however, contain proper names, abbreviations, technical terms, poetic contractions, or antiquated terms. PowerPoint treats words not found in the dictionaries as misspellings.

Starting Style Checker

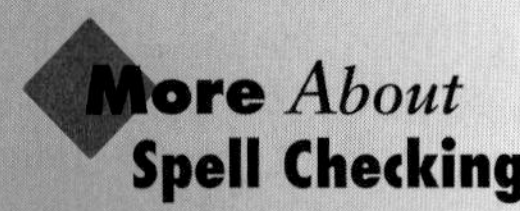

More *About* Spell Checking

To check a presentation for spelling errors without also checking the presentation for style errors, click the Spelling button on the Standard toolbar.

Start Style Checker by clicking the Style Checker command on the Tools menu. Perform the following steps to start Style Checker.

To Start Style Checker

1 Click Tools on the menu bar, and then point to Style Checker (Figure 1-55).

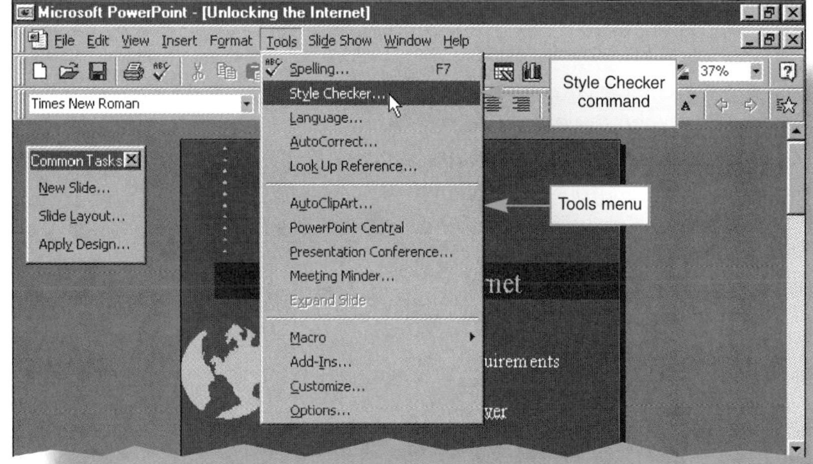

FIGURE 1-55

2 Click Style Checker. When the Style Checker dialog box displays, click Case and end punctuation, and then point to the Start button.

The Style Checker dialog box displays (Figure 1-56). Check marks display in the check box in front of Spelling and in front of Visual clarity. The check box in front of Case and end punctuation is blank to prevent Style Checker from automatically changing the capitalization of the company names in this presentation.

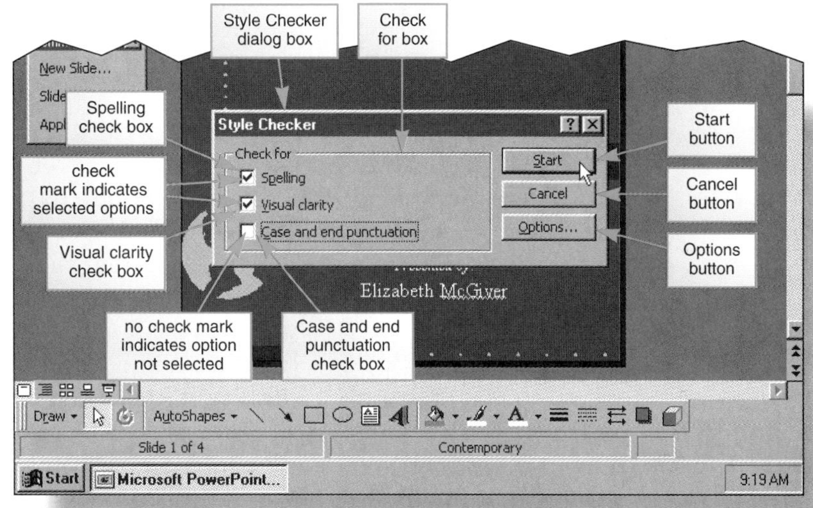

FIGURE 1-56

3 Click the Start button.

PowerPoint launches the spelling feature and displays the Spelling dialog box (Figure 1-57). McGiver displays in the Not in dictionary box. Depending on your custom dictionary, McGiver may not be recognized as a misspelled word.

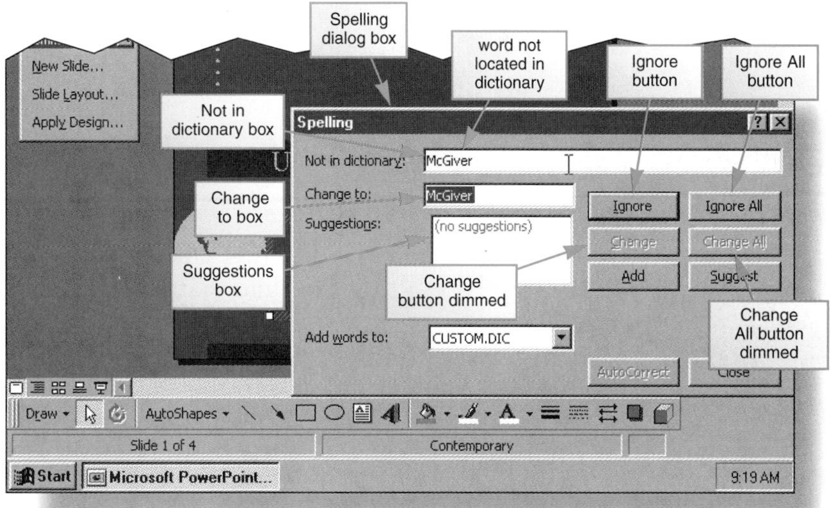

FIGURE 1-57

Click the Ignore button.

PowerPoint ignores the word McGiver and continues searching for additional misspelled words. PowerPoint may stop on additional words depending on your typing accuracy. When PowerPoint has checked all slides for misspellings, it checks for style errors and displays the Microsoft PowerPoint dialog box (Figure 1-58).

Click the OK button.

PowerPoint closes Style Checker and returns to the current slide, Slide 1, or to the slide where a misspelled word occurred.

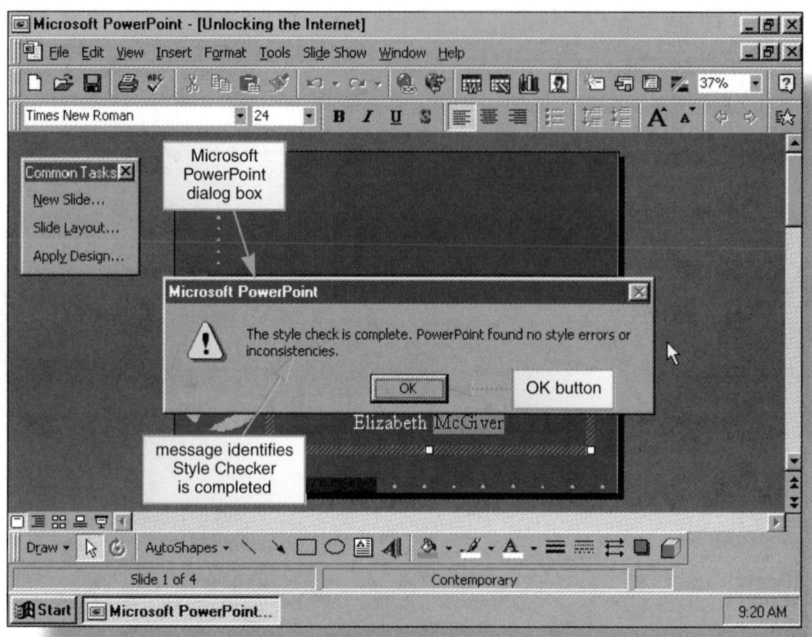

FIGURE 1-58

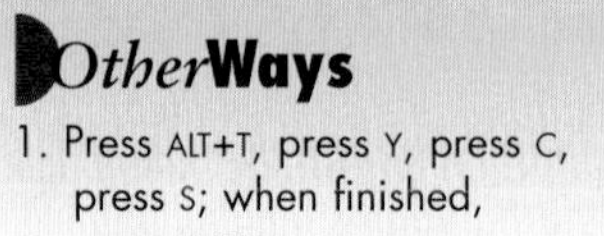

OtherWays

1. Press ALT+T, press Y, press C, press S; when finished, press ENTER

If Style Checker identifies an error, it displays a message indicating the slide number on which the error occurred. If you have punctuation errors, you can click one of the buttons to ignore or change them. If you want to stop Style Checker and return to the current slide, click the Cancel button.

If Style Checker identifies visual clarity inconsistencies, it displays them in the Style Checker Summary dialog box. Write the slide number and the message on a sheet of paper. Then display the slide and correct the inconsistencies.

The Style Checker dialog box contains an **Options button** (Figure 1-56 on the previous page), which when clicked, displays the Style Checker Options dialog box. The **Style Checker Options dialog box** has two tabbed sheets: Case and End Punctuation, and Visual Clarity. Each tabbed sheet has several options that can be changed to suit your design specifications. Table 1-5 identifies each option available in Style Checker and each default setting.

Table 1-5

OPTION	SETTING
CASE	
Slide title style	Title Case
Body text style	Sentence case.
END PUNCTUATION	
Slide title periods	Remove
Body text periods	Remove
VISUAL CLARITY	
Number of fonts should not exceed	3
Title text size should be at least	36
Body text size should be at least	24
Number of bullets should not exceed	6
Number of lines per title should not exceed	2
Number of lines per bullet should not exceed	2
Check for title and placeholder text off slide	Checked on

Correcting Errors

After creating a presentation and running Style Checker, you may find that you must make changes. Changes may be required because a slide contains an error, the scope of the presentation shifts, or Style Checker found a style inconsistency. This section explains the types of errors that commonly occur when creating a presentation.

Types of Corrections Made to Presentations

There usually are three types of corrections to text in a presentation: additions, deletions, and replacements.

- **Additions** — are necessary when you omit text from a slide and need to add it later. You may need to insert text in the form of a sentence, word, or single character. For example, you may want to add the rest of the presenter's first name on your title slide.
- **Deletions** — are required when text on a slide is incorrect or is no longer relevant to the presentation. For example, Style Checker identified too many bullets on Slide 3. Therefore, you may want to remove one of the bulleted paragraphs.
- **Replacements** — are needed when you want to revise the text in your presentation. For example, you may want to substitute the word, their, for the word, there.

Editing text in PowerPoint is basically the same as editing text in a word processing package. The following sections illustrate the most common changes made to text in a presentation.

Deleting Text

There are three methods for deleting text. One is to use the BACKSPACE key to remove text just typed. The second is to position the insertion point to the left of the text you wish to delete and then press the DELETE key. The third method is to drag through the text you wish to delete and press the DELETE key. (Use the third method when deleting large sections of text.)

Replacing Text into an Existing Slide

When you need to correct a word or phrase, you can replace the text by selecting the text to be replaced and then typing the new text. As soon as you press any key on the keyboard, the highlighted text is deleted and the new text displays.

PowerPoint inserts text to the left of the insertion point. The text to the right of the insertion point moves to the right (and shifts downward if necessary) to accommodate the added text.

Changing Line Spacing

The bulleted lists on Slides 2, 3, and 4 look crowded; yet, there is ample blank space that could be used to separate the paragraphs. You can adjust the spacing on each slide, but when several slides need to be changed, you should change the slide master. Each PowerPoint component (slides, title slides, audience handouts, and speaker's notes) has a **master**, which controls its appearance. Slides have two masters, title master and slide master. The **title master** controls the appearance of the title slide. The **slide master** controls the appearance of the other slides in your presentation.

More *About* Line Spacing

Resist the temptation to regard blank space on a slide as wasted space. Blank space, added for directing the attention of the audience to specific text or graphics, is called white space. White space is a powerful design tool. Used effectively, white space improves audience attention.

Each design template has a specially designed slide master; so if you select a design template, but want to change one of its components, you can override that component by changing the slide master. Any change to the slide master results in changing every slide in the presentation, except the title slide. For example, if you change the line spacing to .5 inches before each paragraph on the slide master, each slide (except the title slide) changes line spacing after each paragraph to .5 inches. The slide master components more frequently changed are listed in Table 1-6.

Table 1-6

COMPONENT	DESCRIPTION
Font	Defines the appearance and shape of letters, numbers, and special characters.
Font size	Specifies the size of the characters on the screen. Character size is gauged by a measurement system called points. A single point is about 1/72 of an inch in height. Thus, a character with a point size of eighteen is about 18/72 of an inch in height.
Text font style	Text font styles include plain, italic, bold, shadowed, and underlined. Text may have more than one font style at a time.
Text position	Position of text in a paragraph is left-aligned, right-aligned, centered, or justified. Justified text is proportionally spaced across the object.
Color scheme	A coordinated set of eight colors designed to complement each other. Color schemes consist of background color, line and text color, shadow color, title text color, object fill color, and three different accent colors.
Background items	Any object other than the title object or text object. Typical items include borders and graphics – such as a company logo, page number, date, and time.
Slide number	Inserts the special symbol used to print the slide number.
Date	Inserts the special symbol used to print the date the presentation was printed.
Time	Inserts the special symbol used to print the time the presentation was printed.

Additionally, each view has its own master. You can access the master by holding down the SHIFT key while clicking the appropriate view button. For example, holding down the SHIFT key and clicking the Slide View button displays the slide master. To exit a master, click the view button to which you wish to return. To return to slide view, for example, click the Slide View button.

Displaying the Slide Master

Before you can change line spacing on the slide master, you first must display it. Perform the following steps to display the slide master.

To Display the Slide Master

1 **Drag the scroll box to display Slide 2. Press and hold down the SHIFT key and then point to the Slide View button.**

When you hold down the SHIFT key, the ScreenTip displays Slide Master (Figure 1-59).

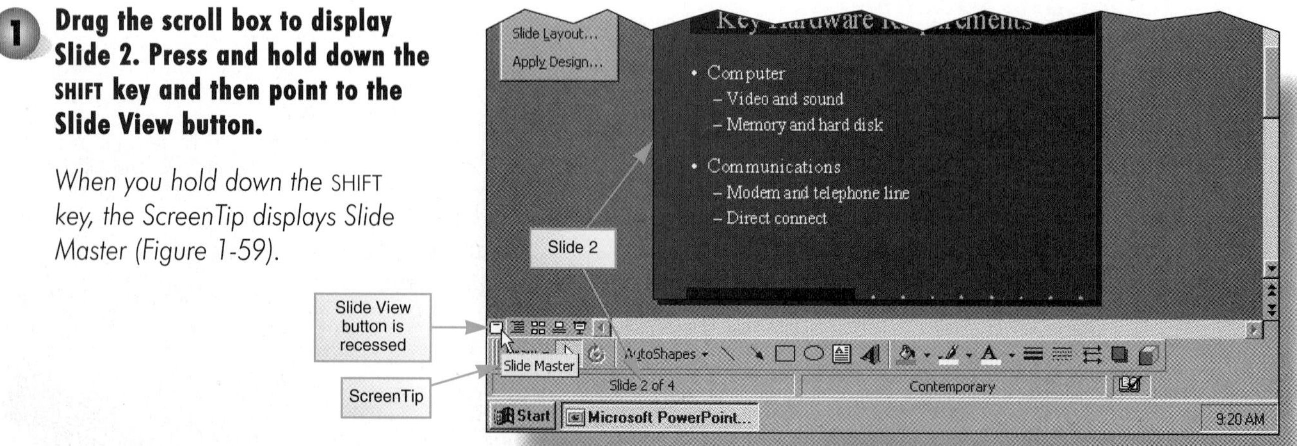

FIGURE 1-59

2 **While holding down the SHIFT key, click the Slide Master button. Then release the SHIFT key.**

The slide master displays (Figure 1-60). The Master toolbar displays. The Common Tasks toolbar changes to display a Master Layout button, which replaces the Slide Layout button in slide master.

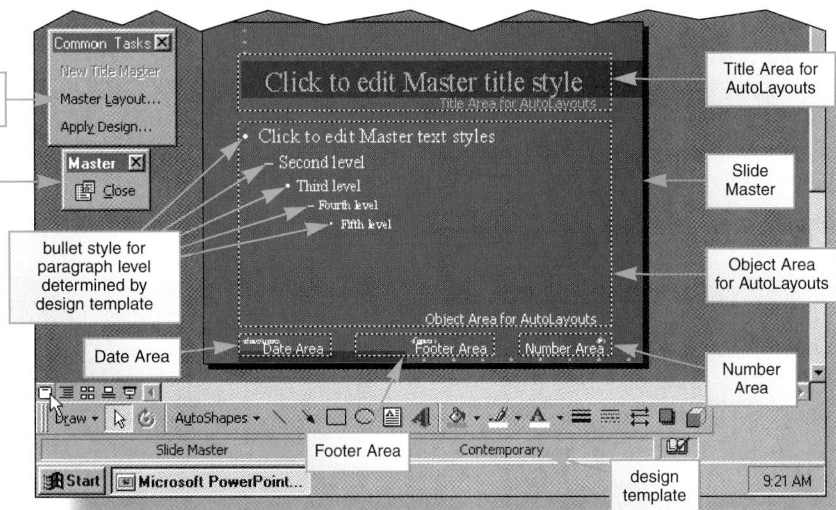

FIGURE 1-60

OtherWays

1. On View menu click Master, click Slide Master

Changing Line Spacing on the Slide Master

Change line spacing by clicking the Line Spacing command on the Format menu. When you click the **Line Spacing command**, the Line Spacing dialog box displays. The Line Spacing dialog box contains three boxes, Line spacing, Before paragraph, and After paragraph, which allow you to adjust line spacing within a paragraph, before a paragraph, and after a paragraph, respectively.

In this project, you change the number in the amount of space box to increase the amount of space that displays before every paragraph, except the first paragraph, on every slide. For example, increasing the amount of space box to 0.75 lines increases the amount of space that displays before each paragraph. The first paragraph on every slide, however, does not change because of its position in the text placeholder. Perform the following steps to change the line spacing.

Steps To Change Line Spacing on the Slide Master

1 **Click the bulleted paragraph labeled, Click to edit Master text styles.**

The insertion point displays at the point you clicked (Figure 1-61). The text object area is selected.

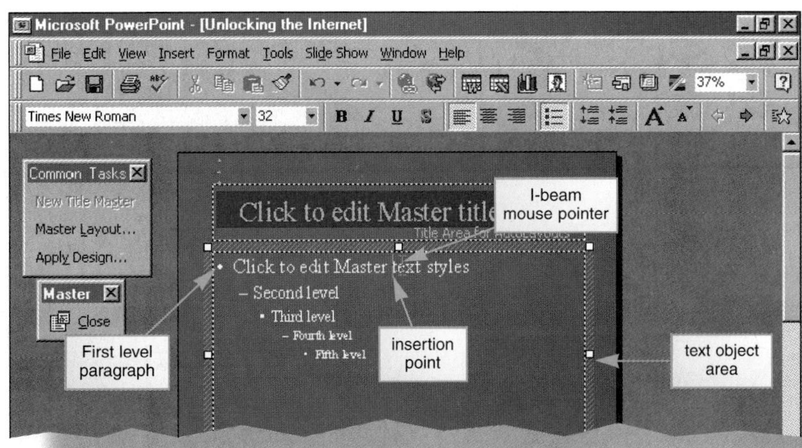

FIGURE 1-61

2 **Click Format on the menu bar and then point to Line Spacing (Figure 1-62).**

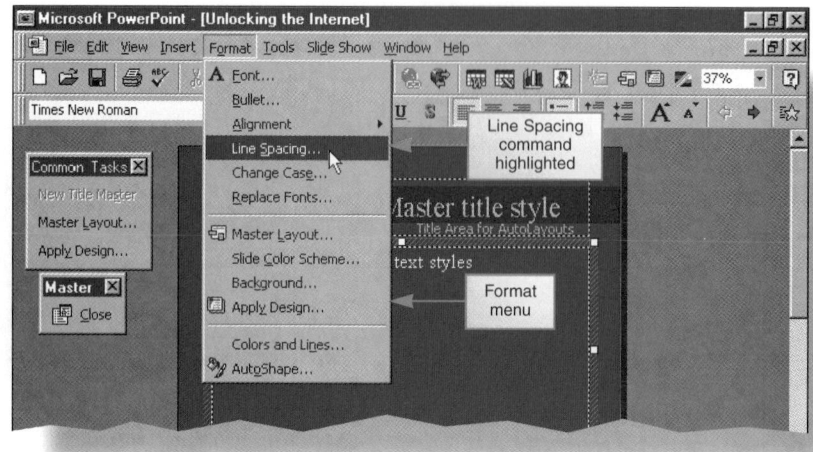

FIGURE 1-62

3 **Click Line Spacing.**

PowerPoint displays the Line Spacing dialog box (Figure 1-63). The default Before paragraph line spacing is set at 0.2 Lines.

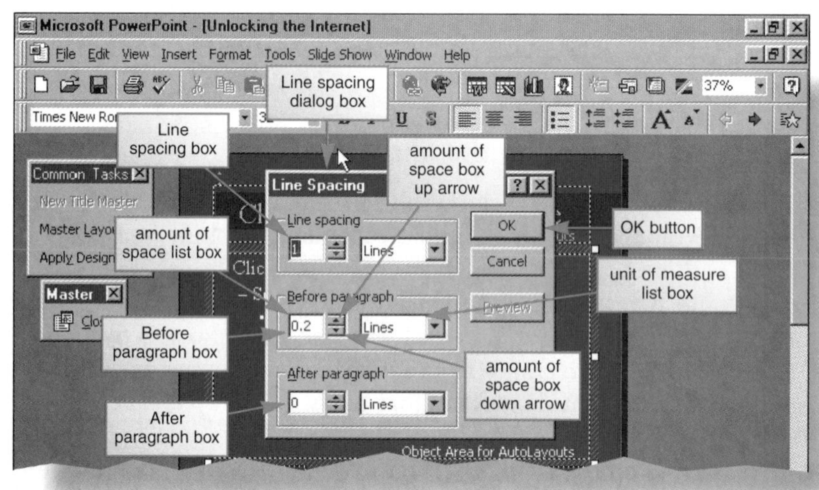

FIGURE 1-63

4 **Double-click the amount of space list box in the Before paragraph box. Then type** .75 **in the box.**

The amount of space list box displays 0.75 (Figure 1-64). The Preview button is available after a change is made in the Line Spacing dialog box.

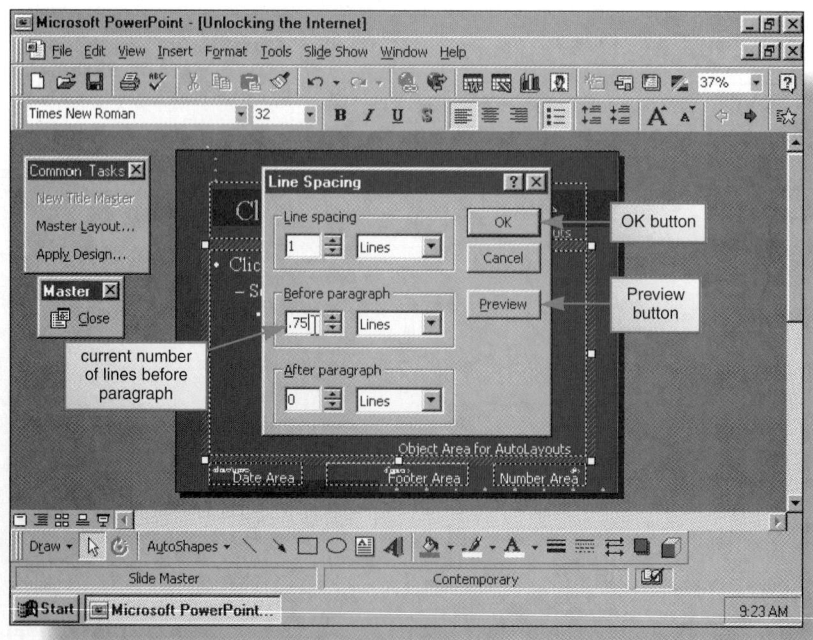

FIGURE 1-64

5 **Click the OK button.**

The slide master text placeholder displays the new line spacing (Figure 1-65). Depending on the video drivers installed, the spacing on your screen may appear slightly different than this figure.

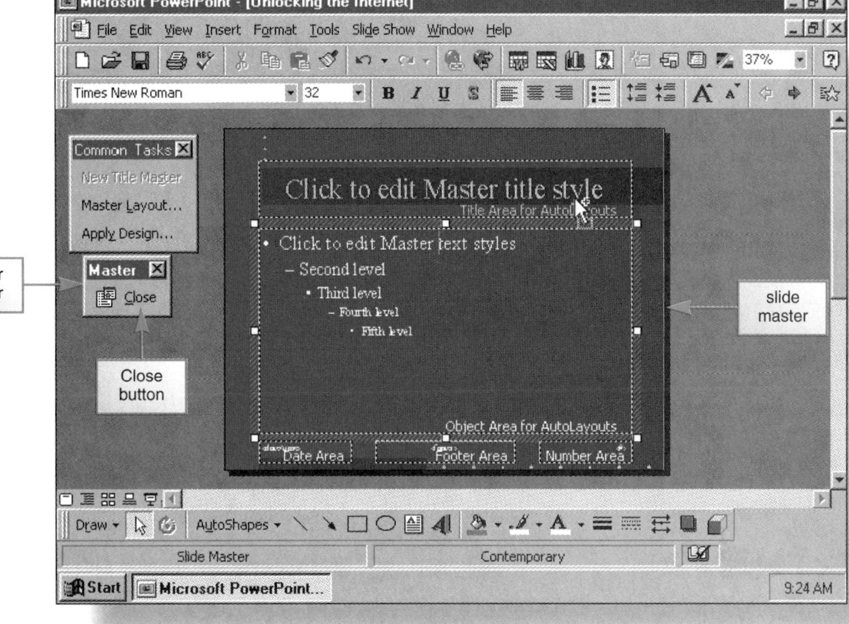

FIGURE 1-65

6 **Click the Close button on the Master toolbar to return to slide view.**

Slide 2 displays with the Before paragraph line spacing set to 0.75 lines (Figure 1-66).

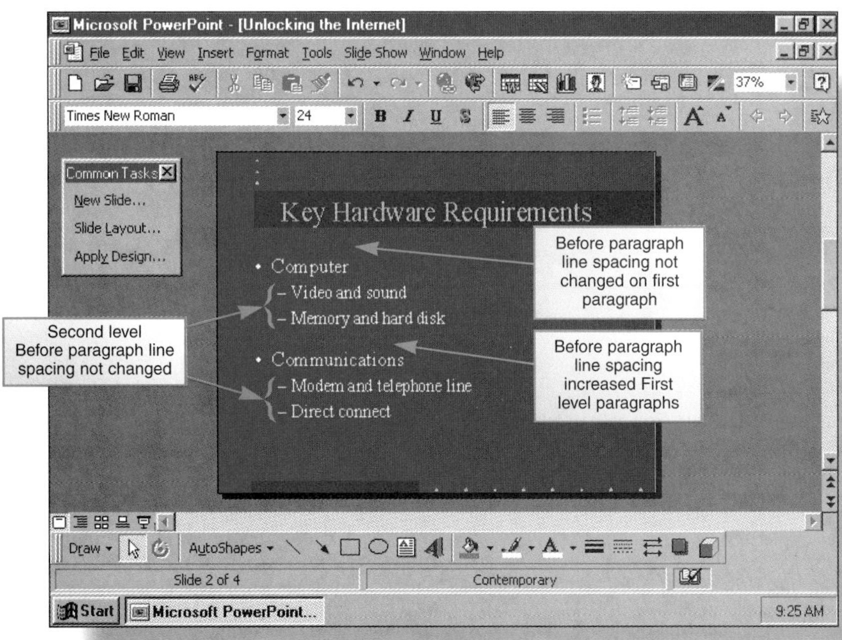

FIGURE 1-66

To display line spacing changes without making them permanent, click the Preview button in the Line Spacing dialog box. If you want to close the Line Spacing dialog box without applying the changes, click the Cancel button.

Before paragraph line spacing is controlled by establishing the number of units before a paragraph. Units are either lines or points; lines are the default unit. Points may be selected by clicking the down arrow next to the Before paragraph box (Figure 1-64 on page PP 1.48). Recall from page PP 1.20 that a single point is about 1/72 of an inch in height.

The Line spacing box and the After paragraph box each contain an amount of space list box and a unit of measure list box. To change the amount of space displaying between paragraphs, click the amount of space box up arrow or down arrow in the Line spacing box. To change the amount of space displaying after a paragraph, click the amount of space box up arrow or down arrow in the After paragraph box. To change the unit of measure from Lines to Points in either the Line spacing box or the After paragraph box, click the down arrow next to the unit of measure list box and then click Points.

The placeholder at the top of the slide master (Figure 1-65 on the previous page) is used to edit the Master title style. The large placeholder under the Master title placeholder is used to edit the Master text styles. Here you make changes to the various bullet levels. Changes can be made to line spacing, bullet font, text and line color, alignment, and text shadow. It is also the object area for AutoLayouts.

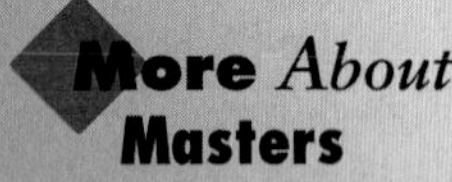

To modify the attributes of the slide master or title master, display the master, and then use the buttons on the Formatting toolbar. To override a master attribute, change the attribute directly on a slide. For example, to italicize text not italicized on a master, select the text object and click the Italic button.

Displaying a Presentation in Black and White

This project explains how to print a presentation for the purpose of making transparencies. The **Black and White View button** allows you to display the presentation in black and white before you print. Table 1-7 identifies how PowerPoint objects display in black and white.

Table 1-7

OBJECT	APPEARANCE IN BLACK AND WHITE VIEW
Text	Black
Text shadows	Hidden
Embossing	Hidden
Fills	Grayscale
Frame	Black
Pattern fills	Grayscale
Lines	Black
Object shadows	Grayscale
Bitmaps	Grayscale
Slide backgrounds	White

Perform the following steps to display the presentation in black and white.

To Display a Presentation in Black and White

1 Point to the Black and White View button on the Standard toolbar (Figure 1-67).

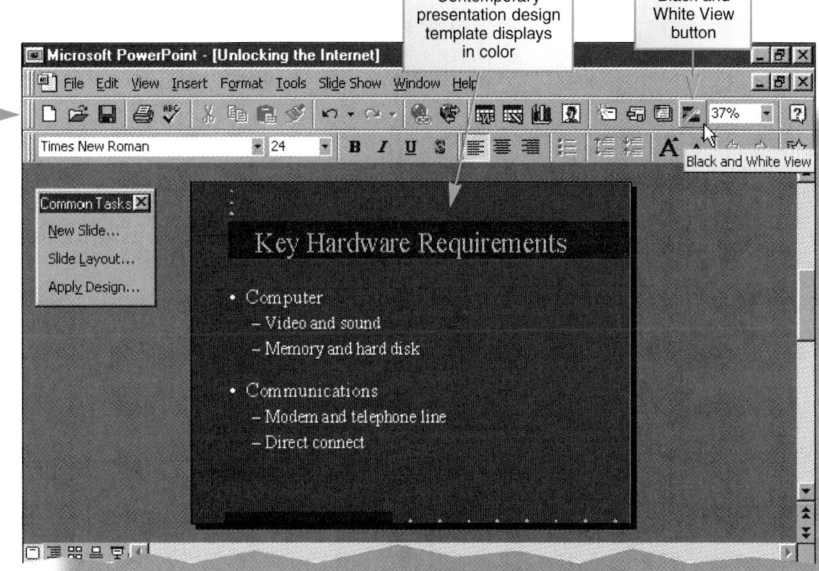

FIGURE 1-67

2 Click the Black and White View button.

The presentation displays in black and white (Figure 1-68). The Black and White View button is recessed. The Color box displays a miniature of the current slide in color.

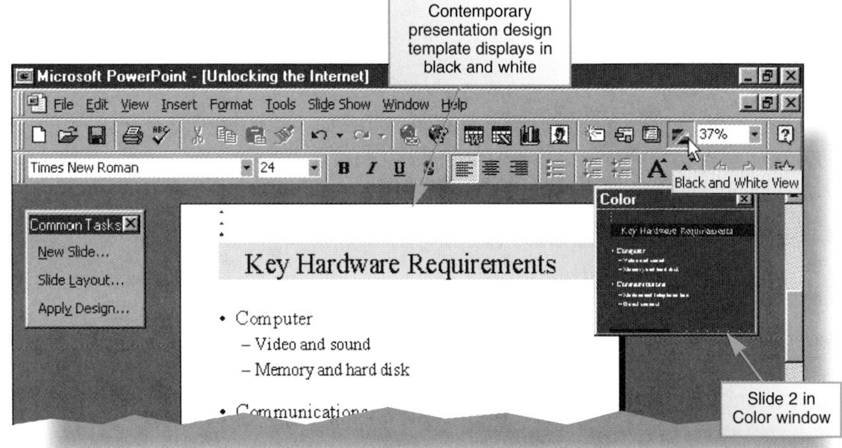

FIGURE 1-68

OtherWays

1. On View menu click Black and White

To return to the color view of the presentation, click the Black and White View button again.

Printing a Presentation

After you create a presentation, you often want to print it. A printed version of the presentation is called a **hard copy**, or **printout**. The first printing of the presentation is called a **rough draft**. The rough draft allows you to proofread the presentation to check for errors and readability. After correcting errors, you print the final copy of your presentation.

Saving Before Printing

Prior to printing your presentation, you should save your work in the event you experience difficulties with the printer. You occasionally may encounter system problems that can be resolved only by restarting the computer. In such an instance, you will need to reopen your presentation. As a precaution, always save your presentation before you print. Perform the following steps to save the presentation before printing.

TO SAVE A PRESENTATION BEFORE PRINTING

Step 1: Verify that your floppy disk is in drive A.
Step 2: Click the Save button on the Standard toolbar.

All changes made after your last save now are saved on a floppy disk.

Printing the Presentation

After saving the presentation, you are ready to print. Because you are in slide view, clicking the **Print button** on the Standard toolbar causes PowerPoint to print all slides in the presentation. Additionally, because you currently are viewing the presentation in black and white, the slides print in black and white, even if you have a color printer. Perform the following steps to print the presentation slides.

To Print a Presentation

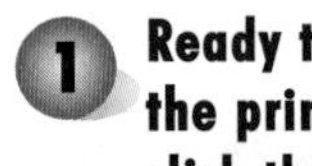

Ready the printer according to the printer instructions. Then, click the Print button on the Standard toolbar.

The mouse pointer momentarily changes to an hourglass. An animated printer icon displays on the status bar identifying which slide is being prepared (Figure 1-69). The printer icon, on the status bar, indicates there is a print job processing. After several moments, the presentation begins printing on the printer. When the presentation is finished printing, the printer icon on the status bar no longer displays.

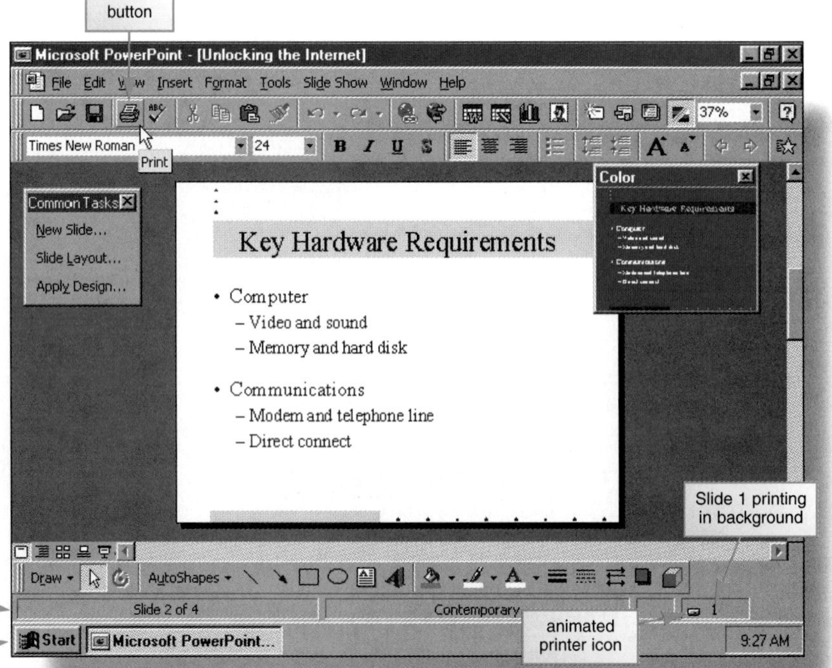

FIGURE 1-69

2 **When the printer stops, retrieve the printouts of the slides.**

The presentation, Unlocking the Internet, prints on four pages (Figure 1-70).

(d)

(c)

(b)

(a)

FIGURE 1-70

OtherWays

1. On File menu click Print
2. Press CTRL+P or press CTRL+SHIFT+F12

More *About* **Online Help**

Prior versions of PowerPoint used to come with a thick manual. Most beginners had difficulty determining where to find the information they wanted. The extensive online Help shipped with PowerPoint replaces the manual and simplifies the process of finding helpful information.

Double-clicking the animated printer icon on the status bar cancels the printing process.

Making a Transparency

This project requires you to make overhead transparencies. You make transparencies using one of several devices. One device is a printer attached to your computer, such as an ink-jet printer or a laser printer. Transparencies produced on a printer may be in black and white or color, depending on the printer. Another device is a photocopier. A third device is a thermal copier. A thermal copier transfers a carbonaceous substance, like toner from a photocopier, from a paper master to an acetate film. Because each of the three devices requires a special transparency film, check the user's manual for the film requirement of your specific device, or ask your instructor.

PowerPoint Help

You can get assistance anytime while you are working in PowerPoint using online Help. When used effectively, online Help can increase your productivity and reduce the amount of time you spend learning how to use PowerPoint. Table 1-8 summarizes the five categories of online Help.

The following sections show examples of each of the online Help described in Table 1-8.

Table 1-8

HELP CATEGORY	SUMMARY	HOW TO START
Office Assistant	Answers your questions, offers tips, and provides help for a variety of PowerPoint features.	Click the Office Assistant button on the Standard toolbar.
Contents sheet	Groups Help topics by general categories. Use when you know, in general, what you want.	Click the Help menu, click Contents and Index, then click the Contents tab.
Index sheet	Alphabetical list of Help topics. Similar to an index in a book. Use when you know exactly what you want. For example, "adding footers."	Click the Help menu, click Contents and Index, then click the Index tab.
Find sheet	Searches the index for all phrases that include the term you specify. For example, "bullets."	Click the Help menu, click Contents and Index, then click the Find tab.
Question mark button	Provides an explanation of objects on the screen.	In a dialog box, click the Question mark button and then click a dialog box object. Click What's This? on the Help menu, then click an item on the screen.

Using Office Assistant

The **Office Assistant** answers your questions and suggests more efficient ways to complete a task. With the Office Assistant active, for example, you can type a word or phrase in a text box and the Office Assistant will provide immediate help on the subject. Also, as you create a presentation, the Office Assistant accumulates tips that suggest more efficient ways to complete the task you did in building a presentation, such as applying a design template, decreasing font size, printing, and saving. This tip feature is part of the IntelliSense technology that is built into PowerPoint, which understands what you are trying to do and suggests better ways to do it.

The following steps show how to use the Office Assistant to obtain information on footers in a presentation.

To Obtain Help Using the Office Assistant

1. **If the Office Assistant is not on the screen, click the Office Assistant button on the Standard toolbar. If the Office Assistant is on the screen, click it. Type** `footer` **in the What would you like to do? box and then point to the Search button (Figure 1-71).**

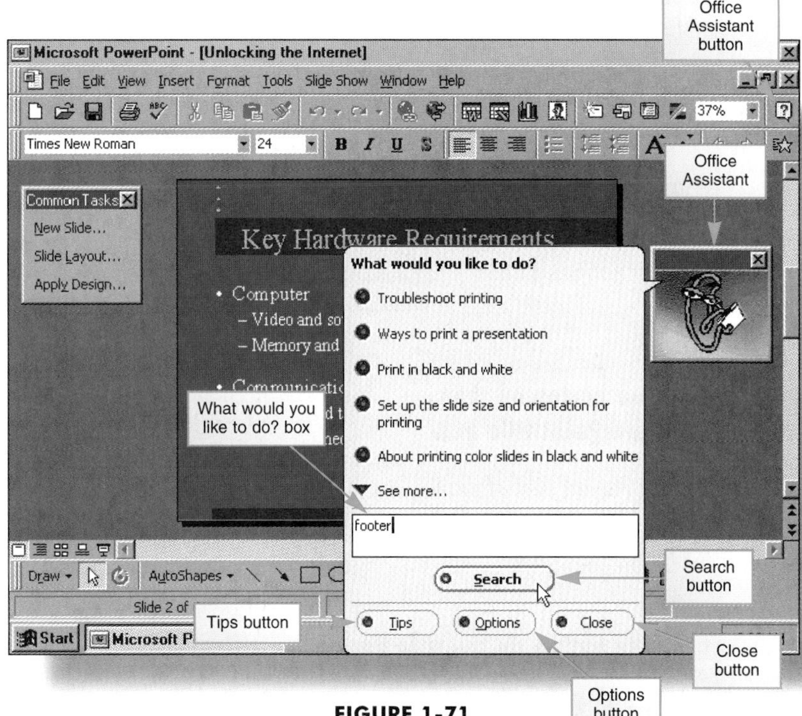

FIGURE 1-71

2. **Click the Search button and then point to the topic, Add or change the date, time, slide number, or footer text.**

The Office Assistant displays a list of topics relating to the word footer (Figure 1-72).

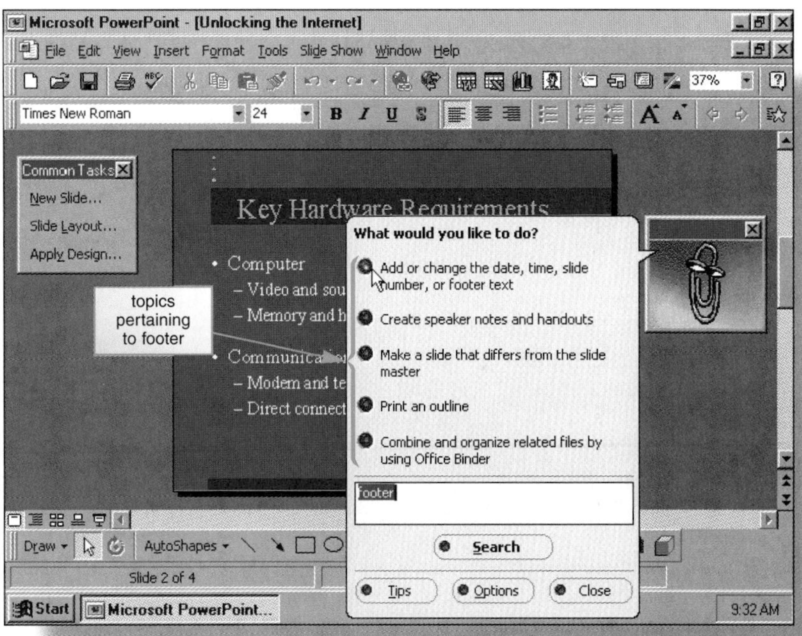

FIGURE 1-72

3 Click Add or change the date, time, slide number, or footer text.

The Office Assistant displays the Microsoft PowerPoint window with Add or change the date, time, slide number, or footer text (Figure 1-73). The topics at the bottom of the window, preceded by a button, are ***links*** *to topics related to Add or change the date, time, slide number, or footer text. When you move the mouse pointer over a link, it changes to a hand.*

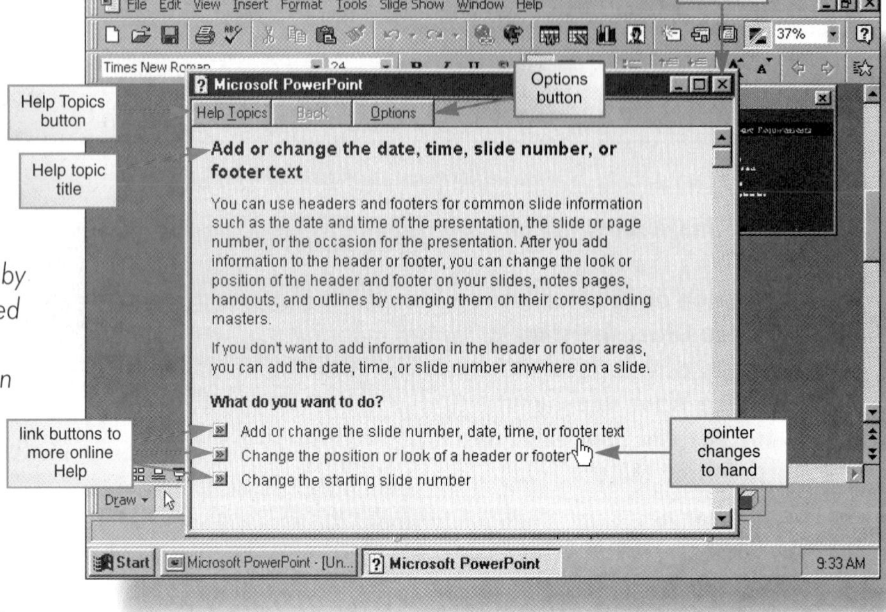

FIGURE 1-73

4 Click the Close button on the Microsoft PowerPoint title bar.

The Microsoft PowerPoint window no longer displays and control returns to the presentation.

5 Click the Close button on the title bar of the Office Assistant window.

The Office Assistant closes and no longer displays on the screen.

Other Ways

1. To show the Office Assistant, press F1 or on Help menu click Microsoft PowerPoint Help
2. To hide the Office Assistant, click the Office Assistant button on the Standard toolbar or on shortcut menu click Hide Assistant

You can use the Office Assistant to search for online Help on any topic concerning PowerPoint. Once Help displays, you can read it, print it using the **Options button** or shortcut menu, or click one of the links to display a related topic. If you display a related topic, click the **Back button** to return to the previous screen. You also can click the **Help Topics button** to obtain Help through the Contents, Index, and Find tabs.

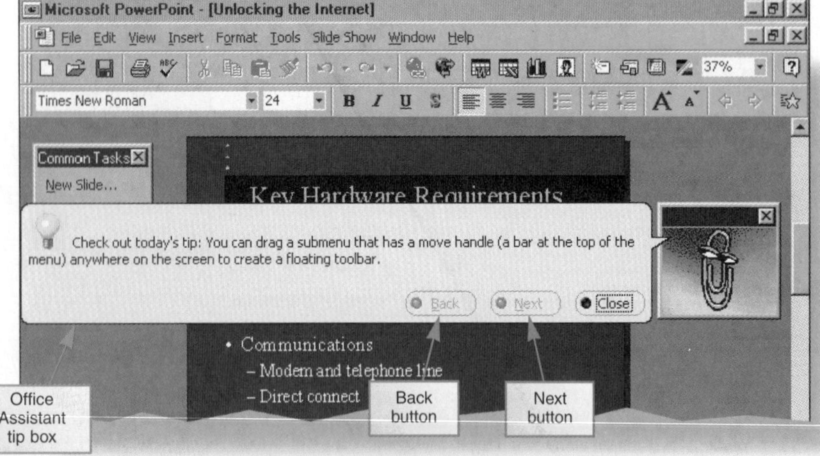

FIGURE 1-74

DISPLAYING TIPS If you click the Office Assistant Tips button (Figure 1-71 on the previous page), PowerPoint displays tips on how to work more efficiently. As you create and edit a presentation, PowerPoint adds tips to the list. Once a tip displays, you can move backward or forward through the list of accumulated tips (Figure 1-74). When you finish reading the tips, click the Close button to return to the presentation.

OFFICE ASSISTANT SHORTCUT MENU When you right-click the Office Assistant window, a shortcut menu displays (Figure 1-75). It allows you to change the look and feel of Office Assistant. You can hide the Office Assistant, display tips, change the way it works, change the icon representing the Office Assistant, or view the animation of the Office Assistant. These options also are available through the Options button that displays when you click the Office Assistant. Click Hide Assistant on the shortcut menu to remove the Office Assistant from the screen.

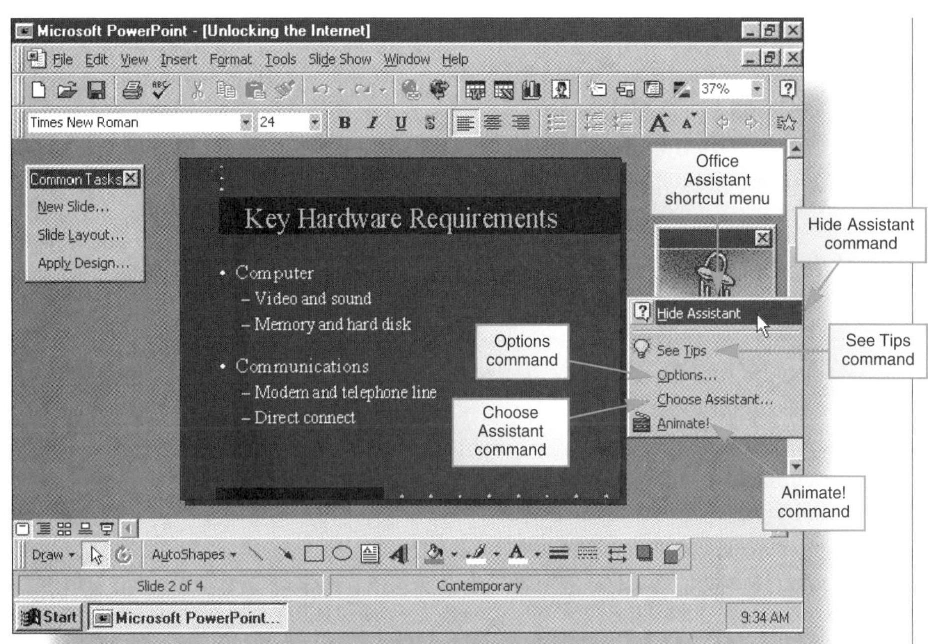

FIGURE 1-75

Using the Contents Sheet to Obtain Help

The **Contents sheet** in the Help Topics dialog box assists you in finding online Help about a specific subject. Use the Contents sheet in the same manner you use the table of contents in a book. Perform the following steps to use the Contents sheet to obtain Help on using the slide master to change the appearance of your presentation.

To Obtain Help Using the Contents Sheet

Click Help on the menu bar and then point to Contents and Index.

The Help menu displays (Figure 1-76).

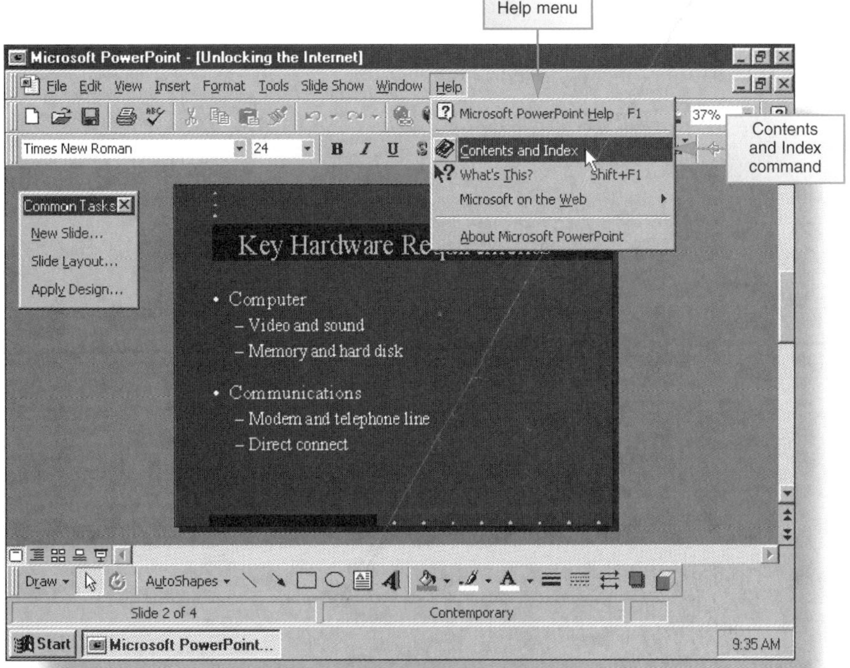

FIGURE 1-76

2 **Click Contents and Index. Click the Contents tab. Double-click Creating the Look of Your Presentation. Point to Ways to give my presentation a consistent look.**

The Help Topics: Microsoft PowerPoint dialog box displays (Figure 1-77). The Contents sheet displays with the Creating the Look of Your Presentation book open. An icon precedes each entry in the list. A book icon indicates there are subtopics. A question mark icon indicates information will display when the title is double-clicked.

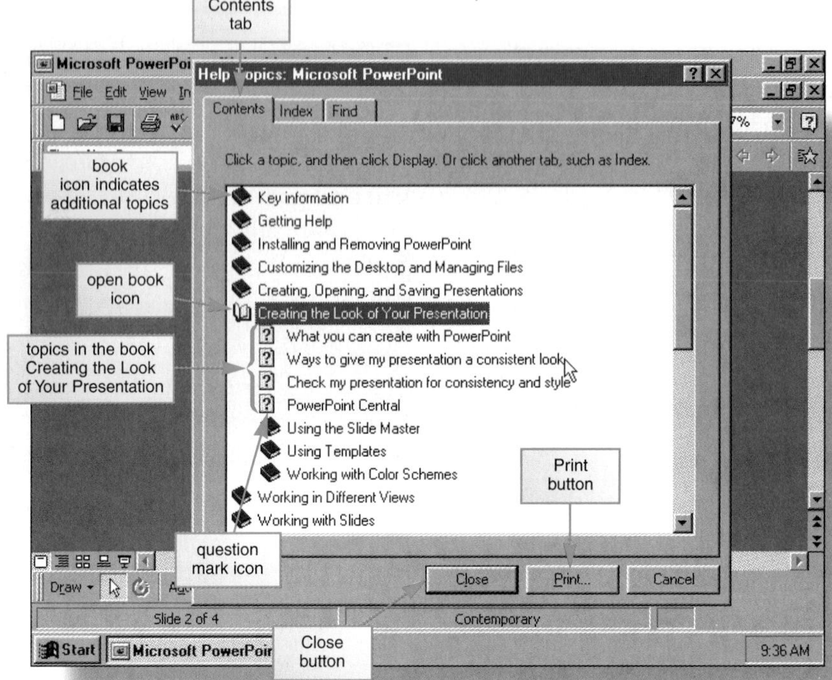

FIGURE 1-77

3 **Double-click the topic labeled Ways to give my presentation a consistent look.**

A Microsoft PowerPoint window displays information about Ways to give my presentation a consistent look (Figure 1-78).

4 **After reading the information, click the Close button on the Microsoft PowerPoint window.**

The Microsoft PowerPoint window closes.

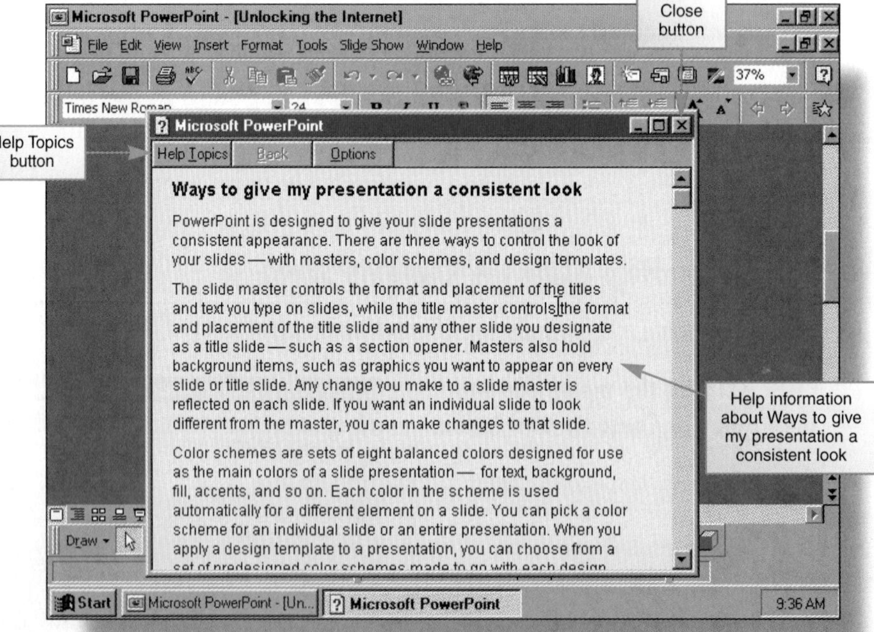

FIGURE 1-78

Other Ways

1. Press F1

As an alternative to double-clicking the topic name in the list, you can click it and then use the buttons at the bottom of the Microsoft PowerPoint window to display information about a topic or print information about a topic (Figure 1-78). Additionally, you can print information about a topic by pointing to the Help window, right-clicking, and then clicking Print Topic; or by clicking the Options button at the top of the Microsoft PowerPoint window, and then clicking Print Topic (Figure 1-78). To close or cancel the Microsoft PowerPoint window, click the Close button to return to PowerPoint, or click the Help Topics button to return to the Contents sheet.

Using the Index Sheet to Obtain Help

Use the Index sheet in the Help Topics: Microsoft PowerPoint dialog box when you know the term about which you are seeking Help. You can locate the term you are looking for by typing part or all of the word, or you can scroll through the alphabetical list and click the term. You use the Index sheet in the same manner you use an index at the back of a book.

Many of the online Help windows display jump boxes, which, when clicked, display a ScreenTip with information about that topic. For example, if you want to know how to create an interactive presentation to send on the World Wide Web, PowerPoint displays a window that contains three jump boxes. When you click one of the jump boxes, such as Start an interactive action, PowerPoint displays a ScreenTip that contains a detailed explanation of how to start an interactive action. Perform the following steps to obtain information about creating an interactive presentation that then could be sent on the World Wide Web.

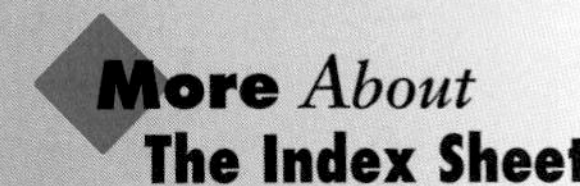

The Index sheet works the same as the index in a book. However, instead of looking through a list of printed topics, you simply type the name of the topic. PowerPoint then searches for your information.

To Obtain Help Using the Index Sheet

1 Click Help on the menu bar. Click Contents and Index. If necessary, click the Index tab to display the Index sheet.

The Help Topics: Microsoft PowerPoint dialog box displays.

2 Type `Web` **in the box labeled 1. Click Web in the box labeled 2.**

The term Web is highlighted in the box labeled 2 (Figure 1-79).

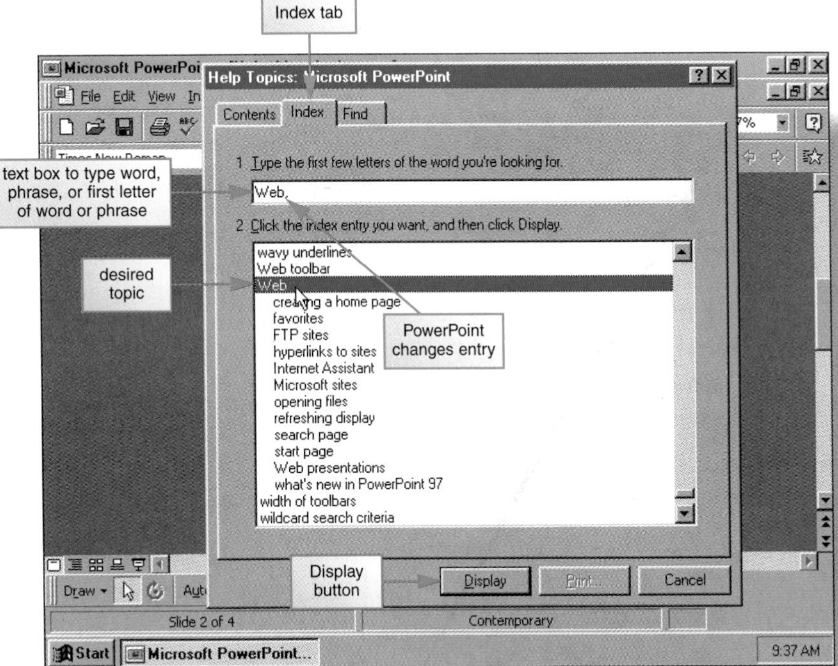

FIGURE 1-79

3 Click the Display button.

PowerPoint displays the Topics Found window (Figure 1-80). The About creating interactive presentation topic is highlighted.

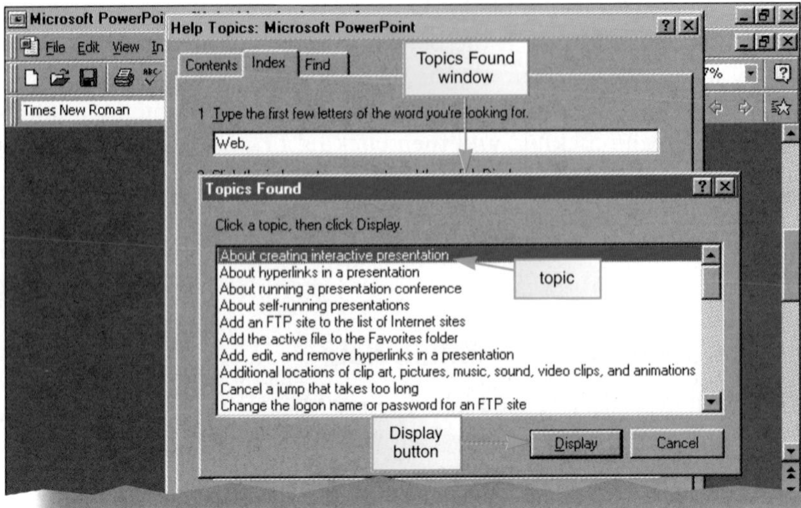

FIGURE 1-80

4 Click the Display button in the Topics Found window. When the About creating interactive presentations Microsoft PowerPoint window displays, click Start an interactive action.

PowerPoint displays a Microsoft PowerPoint window containing jump boxes that point to specific items on a slide. When you click the jump box labeled Start an interactive action, a ScreenTip displays containing information about starting an interactive action (Figure 1-81).

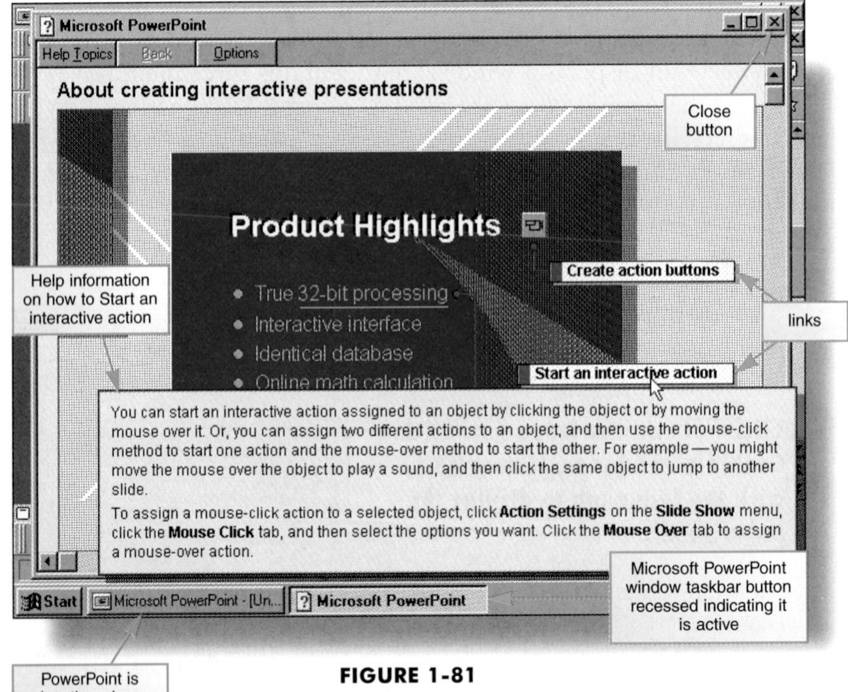

FIGURE 1-81

5 After reading the information, click anywhere outside the ScreenTip to close it. Click the Close button in the upper-right corner of the Microsoft PowerPoint window to close it.

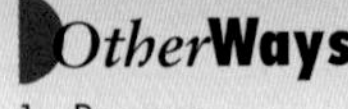

1. Press F1

Using the Find Sheet to Obtain Help

The Find sheet in the Help Topics: Microsoft PowerPoint dialog box locates the word or phrase you want. Use the Find sheet when you wish to find information about a term or a word contained within a phrase. The Find sheet displays a list of all topics pertaining to the specified term or phrase. You then can narrow your search by selecting words or phrases from the list. Perform the following steps to obtain information about changing the distance between bullets and text.

To Obtain Help Using the Find Sheet

1 Click the Help button on the menu bar, and then click Contents and Index.

The Help Topics: Microsoft PowerPoint dialog box displays.

2 If necessary, click the Find tab. Type `bulleted` **in the box labeled 1. Then point to the topic in the box labeled 3, Add, change, or remove a bullet.**

Seven of the eight topics found that contain the word, bulleted, display in the box labeled 3. The topic, Add, change, or remove a bullet, is highlighted (Figure 1-82).

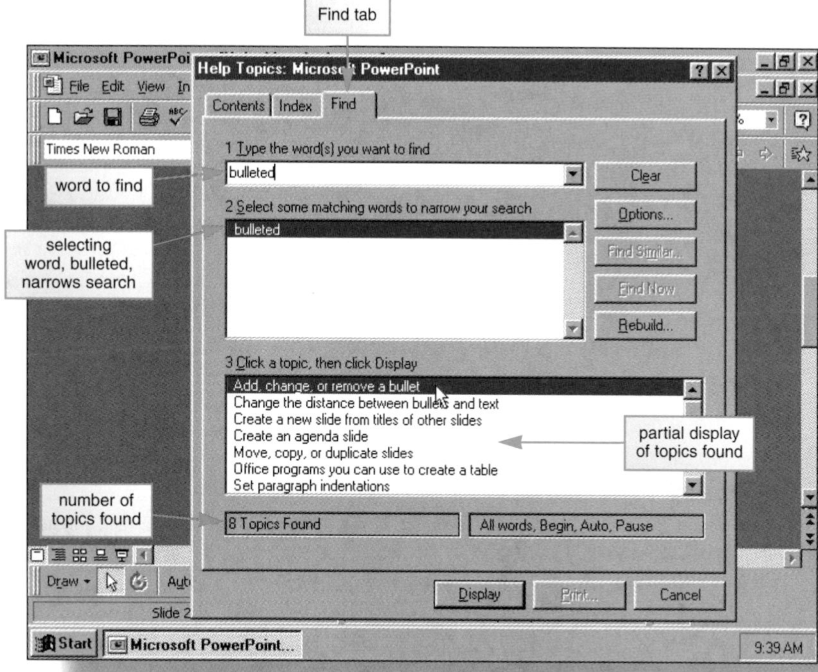

FIGURE 1-82

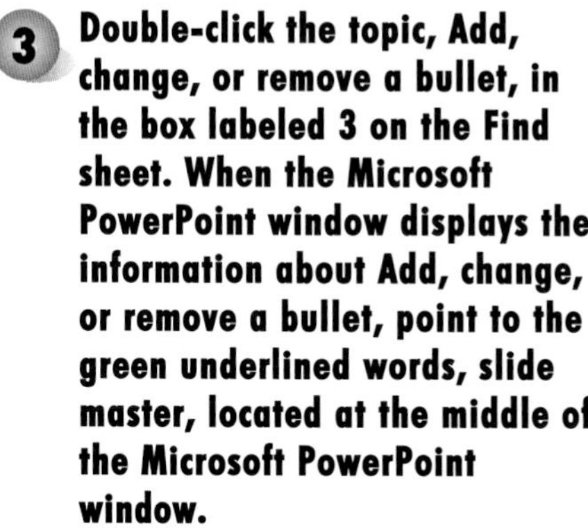

3 Double-click the topic, Add, change, or remove a bullet, in the box labeled 3 on the Find sheet. When the Microsoft PowerPoint window displays the information about Add, change, or remove a bullet, point to the green underlined words, slide master, located at the middle of the Microsoft PowerPoint window.

A Microsoft PowerPoint window displays information about changing the distance between bullets and text. The green underlined text at the middle of the Microsoft PowerPoint window identifies a jump to additional information (Figure 1-83).

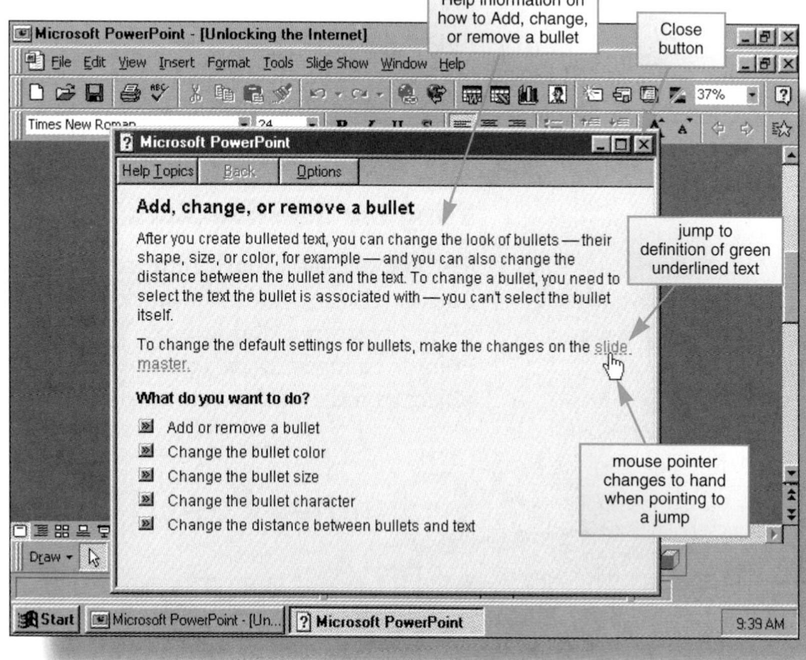

FIGURE 1-83

4 Click slide master.

Clicking the green underlined text displays a ScreenTip (Figure 1-84). The ScreenTip provides additional information about the word (often a definition).

5 Read the ScreenTip, and then click the Close button on the Microsoft PowerPoint window two times.

Clicking the Close button once closes the ScreenTip. Clicking the Close button a second time closes the Microsoft PowerPoint window and returns to PowerPoint.

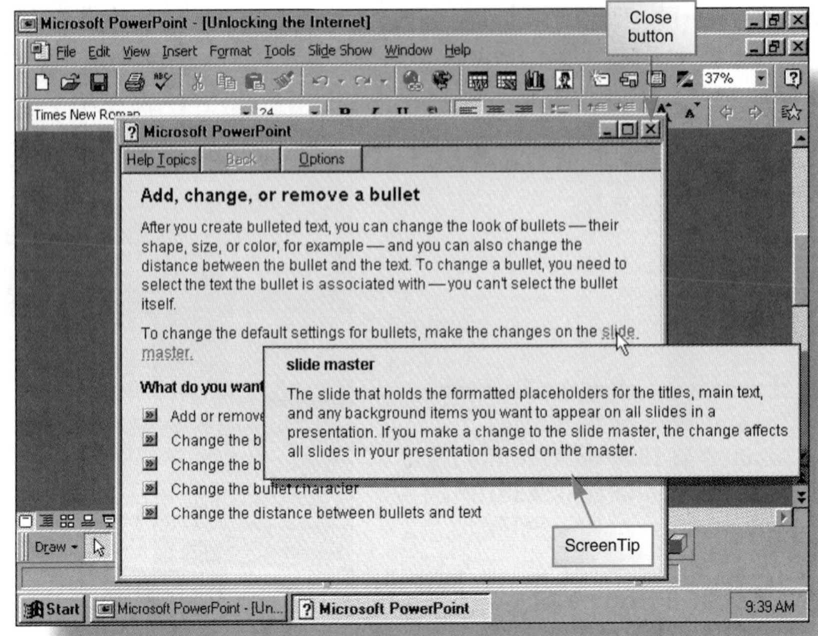

FIGURE 1-84

Other Ways

1. Press F1

You may specify more than one word in the box labeled 1 (Figure 1-82 on the previous page) if you separate the words with a space. If you specify words in uppercase letters, then only uppercase occurrences of the words (within the Help Topics) are found. If you specify words in lowercase letters, however, both uppercase and lowercase occurrences of the words are found. Search options can be changed by clicking the Options button on the Find sheet.

More About The Question Mark Button and Help Button

The Question Mark button in a dialog box and the Help button on the Standard toolbar display ScreenTips that provide a brief explanation of the object clicked when the pointer displays as an arrow with a question mark.

Using the Question Mark Button to Obtain Online Help

The question mark button (Figure 1-82) is similar to the Office Assistant button. Use the question mark button when you are not certain about the purpose of an object in a dialog box. When you click the question mark button, the mouse pointer changes to an arrow with a question mark. Then, when you click an object in a dialog box, a ScreenTip displays.

Quitting PowerPoint

Project 1 is complete. The final task is to close the presentation and PowerPoint. Perform the following steps to quit PowerPoint.

TO QUIT POWERPOINT

Step 1: Click the Close button on the title bar.
Step 2: If prompted to save the presentation before closing PowerPoint, click the Yes button in the Microsoft PowerPoint dialog box.

Project Summary

Project 1 introduced you to starting PowerPoint and creating a multi-level bulleted list presentation. You learned about PowerPoint design templates, objects, and attributes. This project illustrated how to create an interesting introduction to a presentation by changing the text font style to italic and decreasing font size on the title slide. Completing these tasks, you saved your presentation. Then, you created three multi-level bulleted list slides to explain the necessary requirements for connecting to the World Wide Web. Next, you learned how to view the presentation in slide show view. After which, you learned how to quit PowerPoint and how to open an existing presentation. Using Style Checker, you learned how to look for spelling errors and identify inconsistencies in design specifications. Using the slide master, you quickly adjusted the Before paragraph line spacing on every slide to make better use of white space. You learned how to display the presentation in black and white. Then, you learned how to print hard copies of your slides in order to make overhead transparencies. Finally, you learned how to use PowerPoint online Help.

What You Should Know

Having completed this project, you should be able to perform the following tasks:

- Add a New Slide Using the Bulleted List AutoLayout *(PP 1.26)*
- Add a New Slide with the Same AutoLayout *(PP 1.32)*
- Change Line Spacing on the Slide Master *(PP 1.47)*
- Change the Text Font Style to Italic *(PP 1.22)*
- Create Slide 3 *(PP 1.32)*
- Create Slide 4 *(PP 1.33)*
- Decrease Font Size *(PP 1.21)*
- Display a Presentation in Black and White *(PP 1.51)*
- Display the Slide Master *(PP 1.46)*
- Display the Slide Show View Popup Menu *(PP 1.37)*
- Enter a Slide Title *(PP 1.28)*
- Enter the Presentation Subtitle *(PP 1.19)*
- Enter the Presentation Title *(PP 1.18)*
- Manually Move Through Slides in a Slide Show *(PP 1.36)*
- Obtain Help Using the Contents Sheet *(PP 1.57)*
- Obtain Help Using the Find Sheet *(PP 1.61)*
- Obtain Help Using the Index Sheet *(PP 1.59)*
- Obtain Help Using the Office Assistant *(PP 1.55)*
- Open an Existing Presentation *(PP 1.40)*
- Print a Presentation *(PP 1.52)*
- Quit PowerPoint *(PP 1.39, 1.62)*
- Save a Presentation Before Printing *(PP 1.52)*
- Save a Presentation to a Floppy Disk *(PP 1.23)*
- Save a Presentation with the Same File Name *(PP 1.34)*
- Select a Text Placeholder *(PP 1.28)*
- Start a New Presentation *(PP 1.11)*
- Start Slide Show View *(PP 1.35)*
- Start Style Checker *(PP 1.43)*
- Type a Multi-level Bulleted List *(PP 1.29)*
- Type the Remaining Text for Slide 2 *(PP 1.31)*
- Use the Popup Menu to End a Slide Show *(PP 1.38)*
- Use the Vertical Scroll Bar to Move to Another Slide *(PP 1.34)*

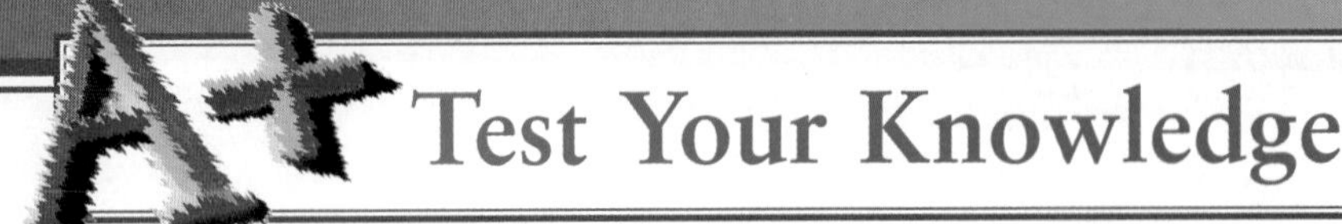

Test Your Knowledge

1 True/False

Instructions: Circle T if the statement is true or F if the statement is false.

T F 1. PowerPoint presentations can be run on a World Wide Web page.
T F 2. A wizard is a tutorial approach for quickly and efficiently creating a presentation.
T F 3. A PowerPoint document is called a slide show.
T F 4. A slide is the basic unit of a PowerPoint presentation.
T F 5. The name of the current presentation displays on the status bar.
T F 6. Toolbars consist of buttons that access commonly used PowerPoint tools.
T F 7. In PowerPoint, the Formatting toolbar contains tools for changing attributes of drawing objects.
T F 8. Press and hold down the SHIFT key and click the New Slide button to add a new slide to a presentation with the same AutoLayout as the current slide.
T F 9. PowerPoint assumes that every slide has a title.
T F 10. The slide indicator shows only the slide number.

2 Multiple Choice

Instructions: Circle the correct response.

1. When the mouse pointer is pointing to a button, it has the shape of a(n) ______________.
   a. hand b. hourglass c. I-beam d. left-pointing block arrow
2. ______________ displays your slides as an electronic presentation on the full screen of your computer's monitor, looking much like a slide projector display.
   a. Slide view b. Outline view c. Slide sorter view d. Slide show view
3. ______________ are the properties or characteristics of an object.
   a. Wizards b. Color schemes c. Attributes d. Design templates
4. Before you italicize a paragraph, you first must ______________.
   a. underscore the paragraph to be formatted
   b. position the mouse pointer beside the first character in the paragraph to be formatted
   c. highlight the paragraph to be formatted
   d. highlight the first word in the paragraph to be formatted
5. PowerPoint automatically appends the extension ______________ to a file name when you save a presentation.
   a. .DOC b. .PPT c. .TXT d. .XLS
6. When you exit PowerPoint, ______________.
   a. the presentation remains in memory
   b. the presentation is erased from the floppy disk
   c. control is returned to the desktop
   d. the presentation is saved automatically to a floppy disk

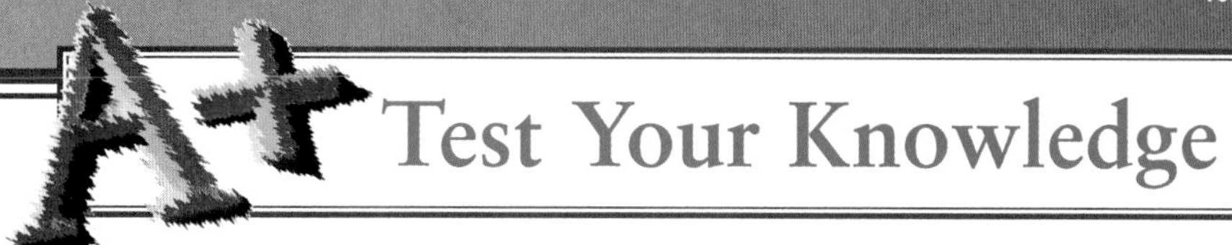

Test Your Knowledge

7. If you add objects to the slide master, they display on ______________.
   a. every slide
   b. every slide except the title slide
   c. the slide master
   d. both b and c
8. Press the ______________ key to remove characters to the right of the insertion point.
   a. BACKSPACE
   b. DELETE
   c. INSERT
   d. both a and b
9. To display online Help information that suggests more efficient ways to complete a task, use the ______________.
   a. Office Assistant
   b. Contents sheet
   c. Find sheet
   d. Index sheet
10. To close a presentation and quit PowerPoint, click the Close button on the ______________.
    a. menu bar
    b. title bar
    c. Standard toolbar
    d. Common Tasks toolbar

3 Understanding the PowerPoint Window

Instructions: In Figure 1-85, arrows point to the major components of the PowerPoint window. Identify the various parts of the window in the spaces provided.

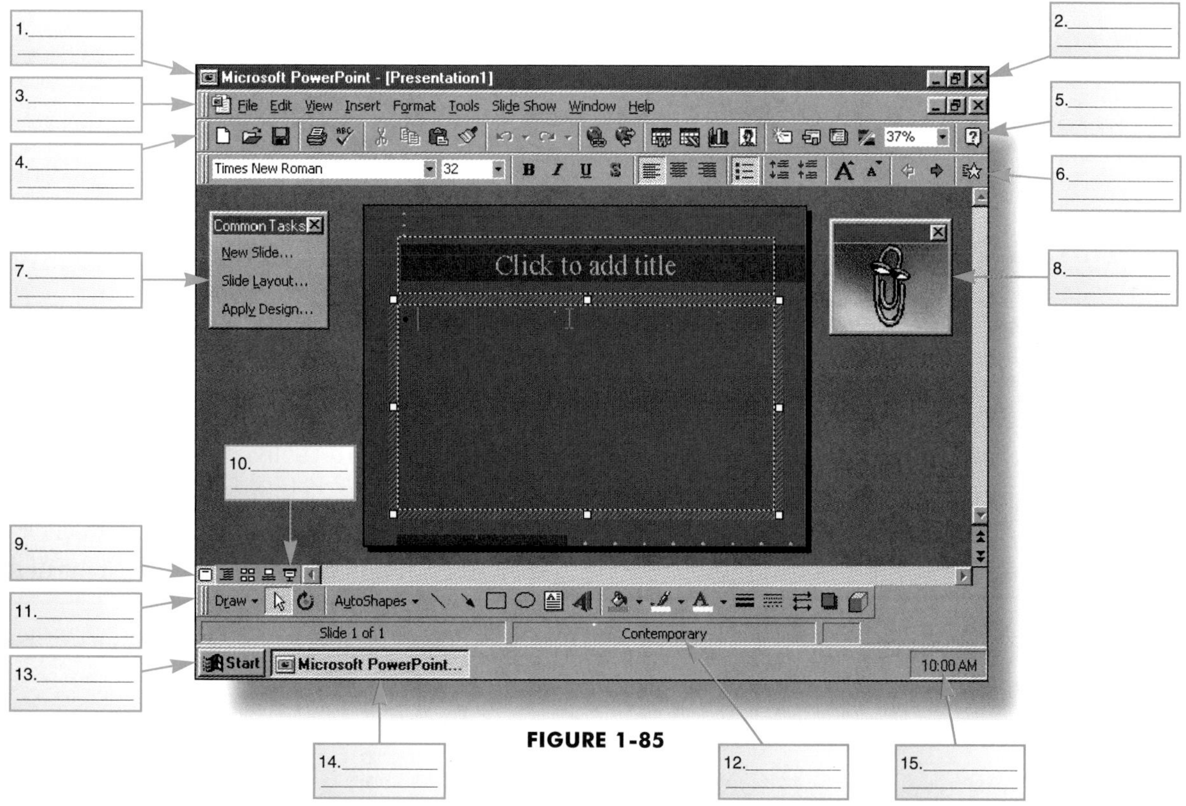

FIGURE 1-85

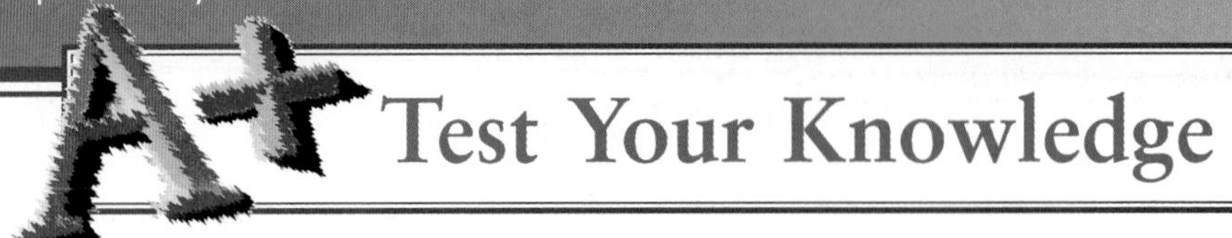

4 Understanding the PowerPoint Toolbars

Instructions: In Figure 1-86, arrows point to several buttons on the Standard and Formatting toolbars. Identify the buttons in the spaces provided.

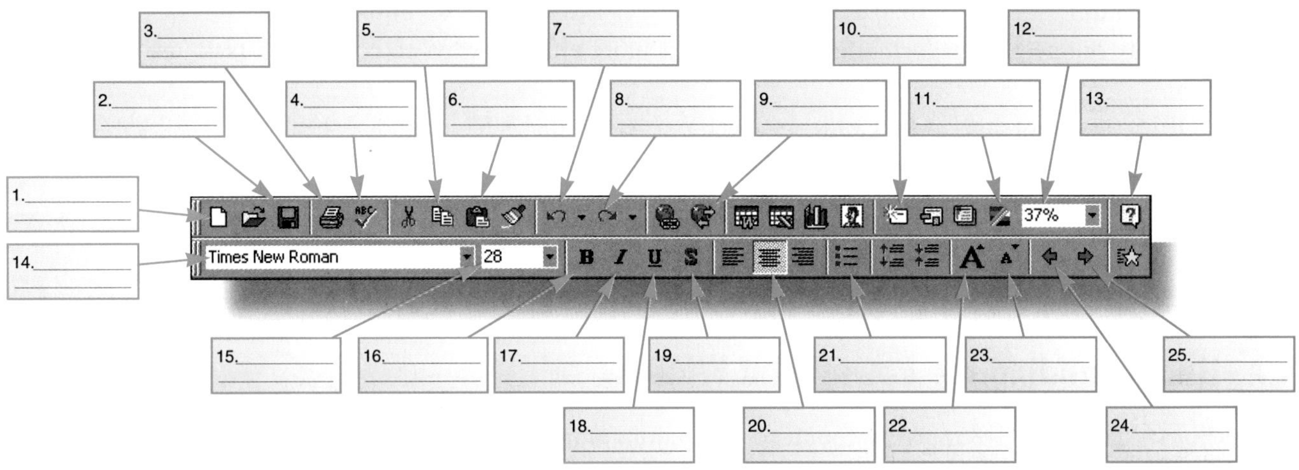

FIGURE 1-86

1 Reviewing Project Activities

Instructions: Perform the following tasks using a computer.

1. Start PowerPoint.
2. If the Office Assistant is on your screen, click it to display its balloon. If the Office Assistant is not on your screen, then click the Office Assistant button on the Standard toolbar.
3. Click Options in the Office Assistant balloon. Click the Gallery tab. Click the Next button to view each of the Office Assistants. Click the Back button to go to the Clippit Assistant and then click the Options tab. Review the different options for the Office Assistant. Close the Office Assistant dialog box.
4. Click the Office Assistant and type `slide master` in the What would you like to do? text box. Click the Search button.

Use Help

5. Click the link, Make a slide that differs from the slide master.
6. Read the information. Right-click the Help window to display a shortcut menu. Click Print Topic to print the information. Click the underlined green words, color scheme. Print the definition that displays by right-clicking the ScreenTip and then clicking Print Topic. Submit the printouts to your instructor.
7. Click the Close button in the Help window.
8. Click Help on the menu bar. Click Contents and Index. Click the Contents tab. Double-click Working with Slides. Double-click Make a new slide. Read and print the information. Click the Help Topics button to return the Contents sheet. Double-click Move, copy, or duplicate slides. Read and print the information. Click, read, and print the Help information for each of the three jumps at the bottom of the Help window. Submit the printouts to your instructor.

2 Expanding on the Basics

Instructions: Use PowerPoint online Help to better understand the topics listed below. Answer the questions on your own paper or submit the printed Help topic to your instructor.

1. Click the Office Assistant or the Office Assistant button on the Standard toolbar to display the Office Assistant balloon. Search for the topic, spelling. Click the link, Check spelling. When the Help window displays, answer the following questions by clicking the links. Close the Help window.
   a. How do you check spelling as you type? b. How do you check spelling at anytime? c. How do you temporarily hide spelling errors?
2. Click Contents and Index on the Help menu. Click the Index tab. Type `line spacing` in the top text box labeled 1. Use the Index sheet to display and print the answers to the following questions.
   a. How do you change the After paragraph line spacing? b. How do you change the amount of space within a paragraph?
3. Use the Find sheet in the Help Topics: Microsoft PowerPoint dialog box to display and then print information about keyboard shortcuts. Answer the following questions.
   a. Which key, or combination of keys, do you press to copy selected text? b. Which key, or combination of keys, do you press to move to the end of a line of text? c. Which key, or combination of keys, do you press to display a shortcut menu relevant to the selected object? d. Which key, or combination of keys, do you press to update the files listed in the Open or Save As dialog box? e. Which keys do you press to advance to the next slide during the running of a slide show?
4. Use the Find sheet in the Help Topics: Microsoft PowerPoint dialog box to display and then print the information about slide masters.
   a. How do you make a slide that is different from the slide master? b. What happens to a slide when its master changes? c. How do you make a slide with a different title or text format than the master?

Apply Your Knowledge

CAUTION: To ensure you have enough disk space to save your files, it is recommended that you create a copy of the Data Disk that accompanies this book. Then, delete folders from the copy of the Data Disk that are not needed for the application you are working on. Do the following: (1) Insert the Data Disk in drive A; (2) start Explorer; (3) right-click the 3½ Floppy (A:) folder in the All Folders side of the window; (4) click Copy Disk; (5) click Start and OK as required; (6) insert a floppy disk when requested; (7) delete all folders on the floppy disk you created except the PowerPoint folder; (8) remove the floppy disk from drive A and label it PowerPoint Data Disk.

1 Formatting a Multi-level Slide

Instructions: Start PowerPoint. Open the presentation Apply-1 from the PowerPoint folder on the Data Disk that accompanies this book. This slide lists features of a proposed insurance option. Perform the following tasks to change the slide so it looks like the one in Figure 1-87.

1. Press and hold down the SHIFT key, and then click the Slide View button to display the slide master. Click the paragraph, Click to edit Master text styles. Click Format on the menu bar and then click Line Spacing. Increase the Before paragraph line spacing to 0.6 lines. Click the OK button. Then click the Close button on the Master toolbar to return to slide view.
2. Select the title text. Click the Bold button on the Formatting toolbar.
3. Select the No paperwork paragraph. Click the Underline button on the Formatting toolbar.
4. Click the paragraph, Annual check-up, and then click the Demote button on the Formatting toolbar.
5. Click the paragraph, No out-of-pocket expense, and then click the Demote button on the Formatting toolbar.
6. Click File on the menu bar and then click Save As. Type `Preferred Provider Option` in the File name list box. If drive A is not already displaying in the Save in list box, click the Save in box arrow, and click drive A. Then, click the Save button.
7. Click the Black and White View button on the Standard toolbar to display the presentation in black and white.
8. Click the Print button on the Standard toolbar.
9. Click the Close button on the menu bar to exit PowerPoint.
10. Submit the printout to your instructor.

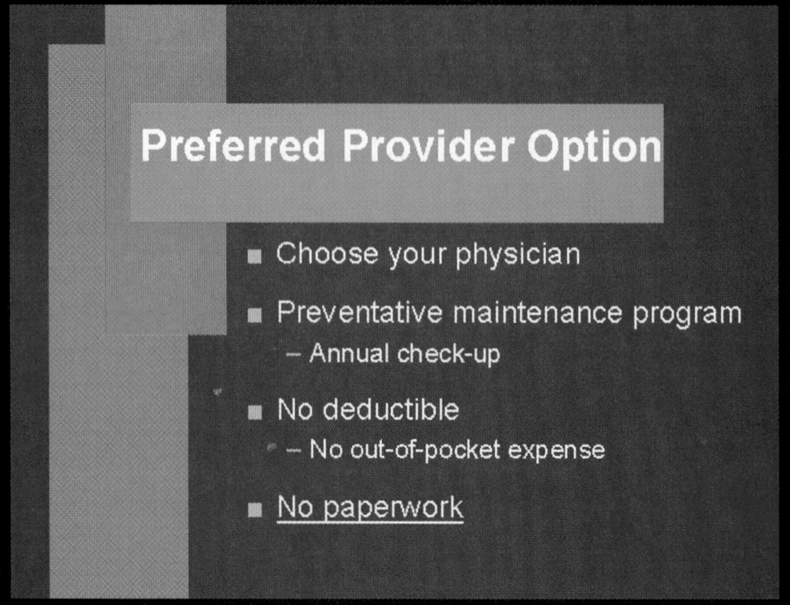

FIGURE 1-87

1 Designing and Creating a Presentation

Problem: You are the Director for the Career Development Center at Hammond College. You have been asked to speak as a guest lecturer in an undergraduate communications class. The course instructor suggests you discuss strategies for finding the right job. To prepare for the class, you create the presentation shown in Figure 1-88.

Instructions: Perform the following tasks.

1. Create a new presentation using the high voltage design template.
2. Using the typewritten notes illustrated in Figure 1-89, create the title slide shown in Figure 1-88 using your name in place of Leland Zoladz. Decrease the font size of the paragraph, Presented by:, to 24. Decrease the font size of the paragraphs, Director, Career Development, and Hammond College, to 28.
3. Using the typewritten notes in Figure 1-89, create the three bulleted list slides shown in Figure 1-88.
4. Click the Spelling button on the Standard toolbar. Correct any errors.
5. Save the presentation on a floppy disk using the file name, Finding the Right Job.
6. Display the presentation in black and white.
7. Print the black and white presentation. Quit PowerPoint.

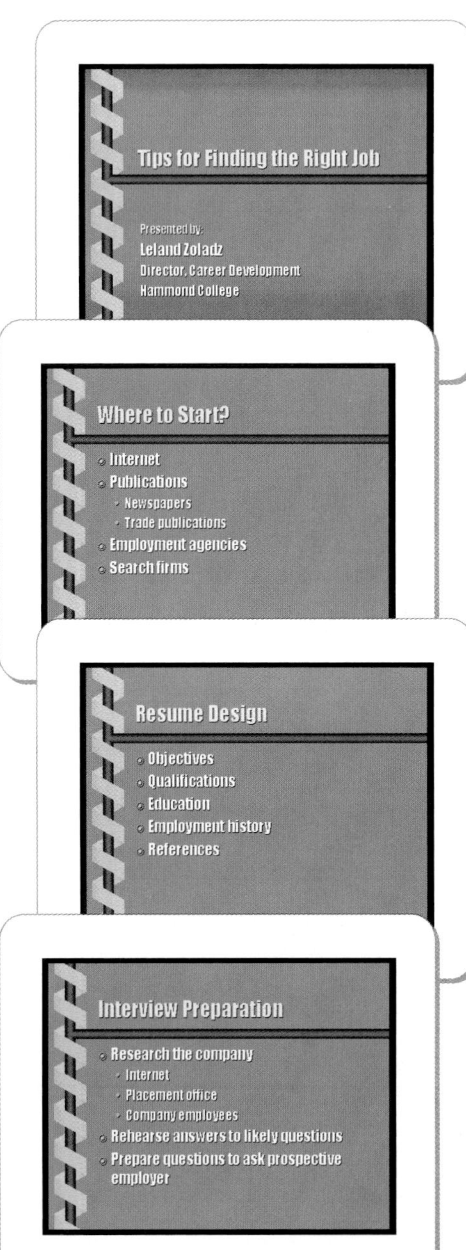

FIGURE 1-88

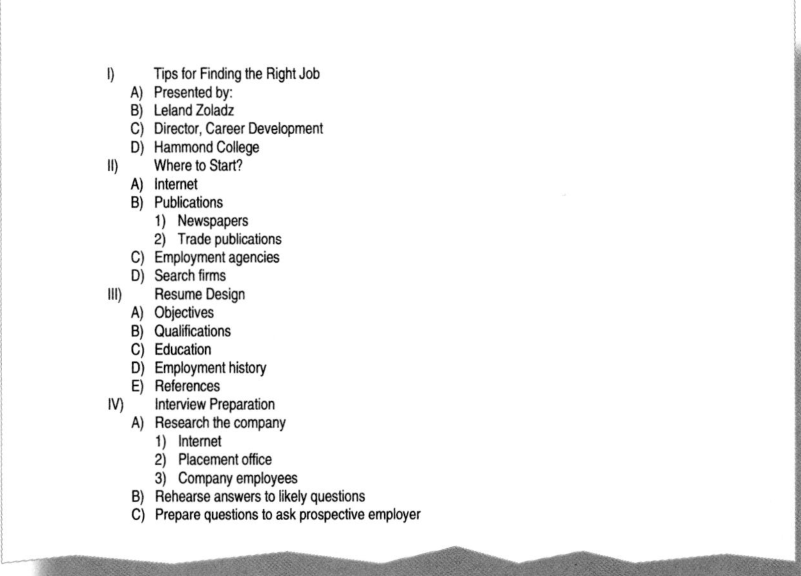
I) Tips for Finding the Right Job
A) Presented by:
B) Leland Zoladz
C) Director, Career Development
D) Hammond College
II) Where to Start?
A) Internet
B) Publications
1) Newspapers
2) Trade publications
C) Employment agencies
D) Search firms
III) Resume Design
A) Objectives
B) Qualifications
C) Education
D) Employment history
E) References
IV) Interview Preparation
A) Research the company
1) Internet
2) Placement office
3) Company employees
B) Rehearse answers to likely questions
C) Prepare questions to ask prospective employer

FIGURE 1-89

2 Modifying Masters to Override Design Template Attributes

Problem: You are the Festival Coordinator for the Annual Lakeview Autumn Festival. To promote this year's festival, you design a brief presentation. You select a design template but decide to modify it. *Hint*: Use Help to solve this problem.

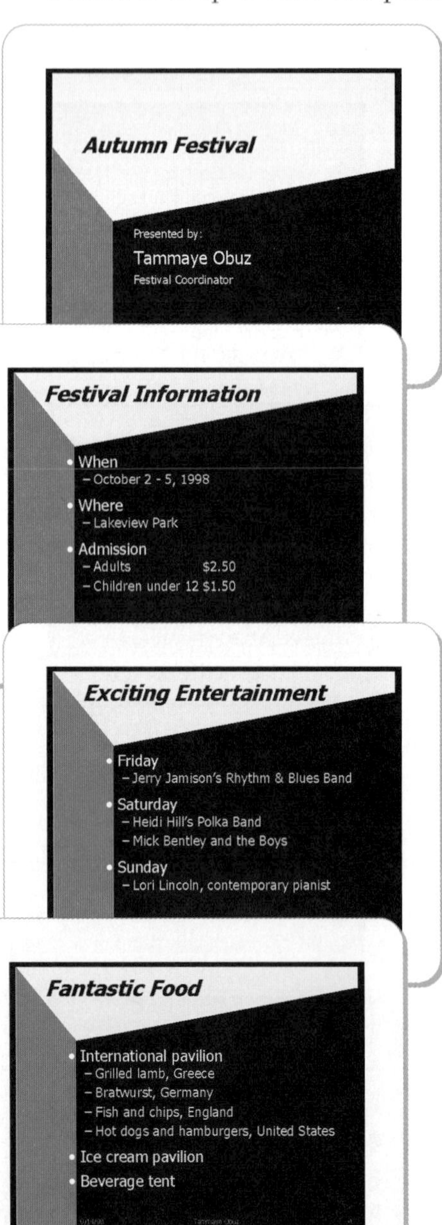

FIGURE 1-91

Instructions: Perform the following tasks.

1. Create a new presentation using the Angles design template.
2. Using the notes in Figure 1-90, create the title slide shown in Figure 1-91, using your name in place of Tammaye Obuz. Decrease the font size of the paragraphs, Presented by:, and Festival Coordinator, to 24. Increase the font size of your name to 36.
3. Using the notes in Figure 1-90, create the three multi-level bulleted list slides shown in Figure 1-91.
4. Display the slide master. Click the paragraph, Click to edit Master title style. Click the Bold button, the Shadow button, and the Italic button on the Formatting toolbar.
5. Click the paragraph, Click to edit Master text styles. On the Format menu, click Line Spacing, and then increase the Before paragraph line spacing to 0.3 lines. Click the paragraph, Second level. On the Format menu, click Line Spacing, and then increase the After paragraph spacing to 0.15 lines.

I) Autumn Festival
  A) Presented by:
  B) Tammaye Obuz
  C) Festival Coordinator
II) Festival Information
  A) When
    1) October 2 - 5, 1998
  B) Where
    1) Lakeview Park
  C) Admission
    1) Adults $2.50
    2) Children under 12 $1.50
III) Exciting Entertainment
  A) Friday
    1) Jerry Jamison's Rhythm & Blues Band
  B) Saturday
    1) Heidi Hill's Polka Band
    2) Mick Bentley and the Boys
  C) Sunday
    1) Lori Lincoln, contemporary pianist
IV) Fantastic Food
  A) International pavilion
    1) Grilled lamb, Greece
    2) Bratwurst, Germany
    3) Fish and chips, England
    4) Hot dogs and hamburgers, United States
  B) Ice cream pavilion
  C) Beverage tent

FIGURE 1-90

6. Drag the scroll box to display the title master. Click the paragraph, Click to edit Master title style. If necessary, click the Bold, Shadow, and Italic buttons on the Formatting toolbar.
7. Return to slide view. On the View menu, click Header and Footer. If necessary, click the Slide tab. Add the date (so it updates automatically), a slide number, and your name to the footer. Display the footer on all slides.
8. Drag the scroll box to display Slide 1. Click the Slide Show button to start slide show view. Then click to display each slide.
9. Save the presentation on a floppy disk using the file name, Autumn Festival. Display and print the presentation in black and white. Quit PowerPoint.

3 Creating a Training Presentation

Problem: You are the marketing manager for International Diamond and Jewels, a large jewelry wholesaler. Several people on your sales staff have requested presentation training. You decide to create a short presentation to emphasize the importance of rehearsing a presentation. *Hint*: Use Help to solve this problem.

Instructions: Using the list in Figure 1-92, design and create a presentation. The presentation must include a title slide and three bulleted list slides. Perform the following tasks.

1. Create a new presentation using the Whirlpool design template.
2. Create a title slide titled, Perfect Presentations. Include a subtitle, using your name in place of Roberto Cruz. Decrease the font size for paragraphs Presented by:, Marketing Manager, and International Diamond and Jewels to 24. Increase the font size of your name to 36. Italicize the paragraph, Presented by:.
3. Using Figure 1-92, create three multi-level bulleted list slides. On Slide 2, use numbers instead of bullets for the three Practice paragraphs.
4. Adjust Before paragraph and After paragraph line spacing to utilize the available white space.
5. Insert a footer on every slide except the title slide that includes the current date, your name, and the slide number.
6. View the presentation in slide show view to look for errors. Correct any errors.
7. Check the presentation for spelling errors.
8. Save the presentation to a floppy disk with the file name, Perfect Presentations. Print the presentation slides in black and white. Quit PowerPoint.

```
I)    Perfect Presentations
   A) Presented by:
   B) Roberto Cruz
   C) Marketing Manager
   D) International Diamond and Jewels
II)   Practice Makes Perfect
   A) Secrets for a successful presentation
              1. Practice
              2. Practice
              3. Practice
III) Why Practice?
   A) Increase confidence
   B) Develop rhythm
      1) Pause for emphasis
   C) Improve articulation
      1) Vary pitch and inflection
   D) Identify problems
IV)   How To Practice
   A) Speak out loud
      1) Make a recording
      2) Look into a mirror
      3) Find a live audience
   B) Visit presentation site
      1) Inspect equipment
      2) Check environment
```

FIGURE 1-92

Cases and Places

The difficulty of these case studies varies: ◗ are the least difficult; ◗◗ are more difficult; and ◗◗◗ are the most difficult.

1 ◗ Maria Hernandez, coordinator for the Lincoln Elementary Fun Fair, has contacted Fun Fair Specialties to assist the school with this year's fun fair. Before finalizing plans, Ms. Hernandez needs approval from the parent-teacher association. She has prepared the notes in Figure 1-93 for a presentation that will be delivered at the next parent-teacher association meeting.

Ms. Hernandez has asked you to prepare a title slide and three additional slides that can be used on an overhead projector. Use the concepts and techniques introduced in this project to create the presentation.

Lincoln Elementary Fun Fair
Saturday, February 7, 1998
10:00 A.M. to 3:00 P.M.

Parent-Teacher Booths
- *Bake sale*
- *Clown face painting*
- *Jelly bean contest*
  - *Winner gets container of jelly beans*
- *Raffle ticket sales*
  - *Donated prizes*

Fun Fair Specialties Booths
- *Dunk the principal*
  - *Teacher volunteers welcome*
- *Fishing pond*
- *Balloon animals*

Fun Fair Goals
- *Repair audio-visual equipment*
- *Purchase five tumbling mats*
- *Install telephone line for Internet access in library*

FIGURE 1-93

2 ◗ Jackie Jacowski, a food technology instructor from Technology Tech High School, is delivering a presentation on how to make dinner in minutes. She has written out her recipe for baked pasta (Figure 1-94).

With this recipe, Mrs. Jacowski has asked you to prepare four slides that can be used on an overhead projector. She wants the title slide to introduce her and the recipe. Use the concepts and techniques introduced in this project to create the presentation.

Baked Pasta

Preparation
- *Cook ground meat in large skillet.*
  - *Drain fat from meat.*
- *Add cooked pasta, spaghetti sauce, and parmesan cheese.*
  - *Stir mixture.*
  - *Pour into 13 x 9 inch baking dish.*
- *Sprinkle shredded mozzarella cheese over pasta mixture.*

Ingredients
- *1 pound ground beef or ground turkey*
- *5 cups cooked pasta*
- *1 30 oz. jar of spaghetti sauce*
- *1/2 cup grated parmesan cheese*
- *1 8 oz. package shredded mozzarella cheese*

Baking and Serving
- *Put baking dish with pasta into oven.*
- *Bake 20 minutes at 375° Fahrenheit.*
  - *Remove from oven.*
- *Serving Suggestion:*
  - *Serve with tossed green salad and garlic bread.*

FIGURE 1-94

Cases and Places

3 ▶▶ Party-Time is a store that specializes in parties. The consultants are trained to help clients in every aspect of party planning. Clients can stop by the store and pick up party favors; streamers; noise makers; and decorations for walls and windows. Party-Time also carries a complete line of paper and plastic items, such as plates, napkins, table-clothes, dinnerware, and serving utensils. Many clients consult Party-Time to help plan bridal showers, graduation receptions, and business meetings. The store is located in Logan's Mall, 621 West Logan Street, Thunder Bay, Ontario. For more information call 555-9979. Using the techniques presented in this project, prepare a title slide and three bulleted list slides to be used on an overhead projector.

4 ▶▶ After many months of hard work, you and your partner, Lydia Statton, finally open Paws Inn, an animal boarding resort. Your research found most pet owners want a home-like atmosphere for their furry friends. Pet owners want reassurance that their pet is treated with respect and cared for by compassionate, attentive individuals. All staff members are associate members of the Hillside Humane Society and have pets of their own. Paws Inn offers five living room suites, complete with pet couches, and five bedroom suites with day beds. For pets needing an outdoors atmosphere, cabins are available. Cabins include an enclosed exercise run, accessible through a door-gate. Additional Paws Inn facilities include an exercise area, a wading pool, and a grooming salon. A dietitian is available for special meal requirements. Veterinarian services are available 24 hours a day. Reservations are recommended. Paws Inn is located at 2144 Deer Creek Road, Hillside, New Hampshire. The telephone number is 555-PAWS. Using the concepts and techniques presented in this project, prepare a title slide and three bulleted list slides to be used on an overhead projector.

5 ▶▶▶ Many companies allow employees to work at home rather than commute to a central office. Some companies require the employee to present a work-at-home proposal to management before authorizing the work-at-home request. Research home-based offices using the Internet or a local library. Determine what is needed for the typical home-based office as well as the working environment. Using the concepts and techniques presented in this project, prepare a presentation to report your findings. Create a title slide and at least three additional slides that can be used with an overhead projector.

6 ▶▶▶ Credit card debt looms over millions of people everyday. Occasionally, people run out of money before all their financial obligations can be met. Financial planners write articles and often speak on television and radio about how to best handle this type of financial crisis. Contact a financial planner or a financial institution. Interview a financial consultant about what to do in a financial emergency and how to prevent a financial crisis in the future. Using the concepts and techniques presented in this project, prepare a presentation to report your findings. Create a title slide and at least three additional slides that can be used with an overhead projector

Cases and Places

7 ▶▶▶ Proper nutrition and exercise are necessary for a healthy body. But nutritionists often disagree on the daily requirements. Research the Internet for recommended daily portions for fruits, vegetables, grains, meats, dairy, and fats. Use more than one source to determine the daily requirements. Then, using the concepts and techniques presented in this project, prepare a presentation to report your findings. Create a title slide and at least three additional slides that can be used with an overhead projector.

Microsoft *PowerPoint 97*

Using Outline View and Clip Art to Create an Electronic Slide Show

Objectives:

You will have mastered the material in this project when you can:

- Create a presentation in outline view
- Describe the PowerPoint window in outline view
- Insert a blank line in a bulleted list
- Change the slide layout
- Move text between objects
- Insert clip art from Microsoft Clip Gallery 3.0
- Change clip art size
- Add a header and footer to outline pages
- Add slide transition effects
- Animate text
- Animate clip art
- Print a presentation outline
- Change printing options

Unsinkable: *Molly Brown and You!*

On the clear, cold night of April 14, 1912, in the North Atlantic, the Titanic — called *unsinkable* by her builders — struck an iceberg, ripping a mortal 300-foot hole in her hull, well below the water line. In just under three hours, the remorseless sea claimed fifteen hundred lives as the Titanic plunged into the dark abyss. Only a few remember the names of those ill-fated passengers, but most know of heroic Molly Brown, immortalized on Broadway and in the subsequent movie, who refused to go down with the ship. This disaster also gave rise to the saying, "Tip of the iceberg," which now is universally understood as a metaphor describing any endeavor where the majority of the work or information is hidden. Figuratively, this term has found expression in other ways, such as that attributed to Vince Lombardi, "Spectacular success is preceded by unspectacular preparation."

This certainly is true for all major entertainment events. To present a three-hour opera, an opera company books the stars a year or more in advance, creates sets that take hundreds of hours to build, and conducts hours of rehearsals. A circus that opens with a grand parade, then proceeds with two hours of performances in three rings takes thousands of hours in costume preparation, rigging, and animal training, not to mention lifetimes of dedication from acrobats and aerialists. A two-hour movie may have been in studio development for two years, plus another six months or more in shooting.

Plays, concerts, televised sporting events, Academy Awards, political conventions, and many other productions share a common thread: for even a chance at success, careful preparation is mandatory. In today's academic, scientific, and business arenas, the requirements are equally exacting. Often, the same people who demand top-notch operas, concerts, football games, and movies are decision-makers who sit for presentations in Melbourne, London, Toronto, and Atlanta. They are accustomed to the best and expect the best in business presentations, too.

Until recently, preparing a slide presentation was not a job for the faint-hearted. Writing and artwork were separate tasks, usually performed by specialists, then integrated by a graphics production company — at great expense. Changes were slow to make and costly. Relatively short presentations required days, even weeks of preparation.

Microsoft's PowerPoint 97 has changed all this by removing the mechanical impediments to producing slide shows, letting you concentrate on the creative content. With Pick a Look and AutoContent Wizards, you can use ready-made formats and speedily produce outstanding presentations. Build effects, clip art, drawings, graphs, logos, and a wide range of background, color, and style selections allow you to spice your message to suit the most sophisticated tastes.

At your next presentation, aided by PowerPoint, you, too, can be like the Titanic's Molly Brown: unsinkable.

Microsoft PowerPoint 97

Using Outline View and Clip Art to Create an Electronic Slide Show

Case Perspective

Voyager Travel Tours is a travel agency promoting two new vacation packages. They are focusing on college students who want a great spring break vacation at a terrific price. After contacting several schools to learn how to reach the student community, your boss, Mr. Suarez, is asked if he would like to set up a booth at a spring break vacation fair. He accepts the offer. The vacation fair, however, is the day after tomorrow. To allow Mr. Suarez to finalize his travel arrangements, he asks you to put together a short electronic presentation. The purpose of the presentation is to entice students to buy one of the two vacation packages.

Voyager Travel Tour's marketing department supplies you with an outline to use in creating the presentation. The outline contains promotional information about the two new vacation packages — the Stargazer and the Castaway. You decide to call them Break Away Bargains.

To persuade students to buy one of the Break Away Bargains, you choose a design template with tropical colors. Then, to make the presentation more exciting, you add pictures and apply animation effects.

Creating a Presentation from an Outline

At some time during either your academic or business life, you probably will make a presentation. Most academic presentations are informative — providing detailed information about some topic. Business presentations, however, are usually sales presentations, such as selling a proposal or a product to a client, convincing management to approve a new project, or persuading the board of directors to accept the new fiscal budget. As an alternative to creating your presentation in slide view, as you did in Project 1, PowerPoint provides an outlining feature to help you organize your thoughts. When the outline is complete, it becomes the foundation for your presentation.

You create a presentation outline in outline view. When you create an outline, you type all of the text at one time, as if you were typing an outline on a sheet of paper. This is different than slide view where you type text as you create each individual slide. PowerPoint creates the presentation as you type the outline by evaluating the outline structure. Regardless of the view in which you build a presentation, PowerPoint automatically creates the views discussed in Project 1, such as slide view.

The first step in creating a presentation in outline view is to type a title for the outline. The **outline title** is the subject of the presentation and later becomes the presentation title slide. Then you type the remainder of the outline, indenting appropriately to establish a structure or hierarchy. Once the outline is complete, you make your presentation more persuasive by adding graphics. This project uses outlining to create the presentation and clip art graphics to visually support the text.

Project Two – Break Away Bargains

Project 2 uses PowerPoint to create the six-slide Break Away Bargains presentation shown in Figure 2-1. You create the presentation from the outline in Figure 2-2 on the next page.

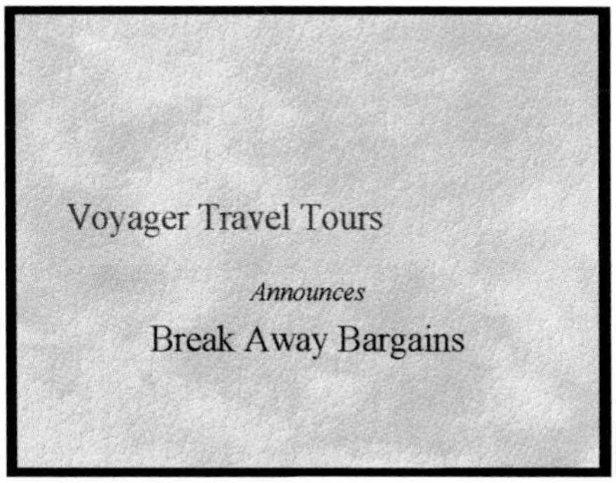

Voyager Travel Tours

Announces

Break Away Bargains

FIGURE 2-1a

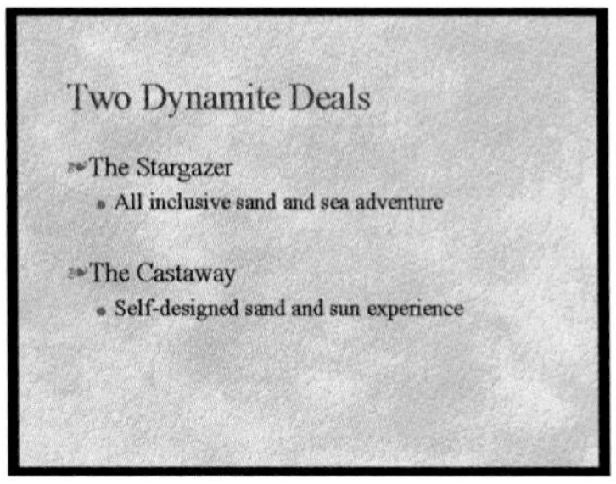

Two Dynamite Deals

- The Stargazer
  - All inclusive sand and sea adventure
- The Castaway
  - Self-designed sand and sun experience

FIGURE 2-1b

The Stargazer

- One incredible low price includes:
  - Round-trip airfare
  - Five-day cruise and two-day beach party
  - Sumptuous gourmet cuisine
  - Fabulous entertainment

FIGURE 2-1c

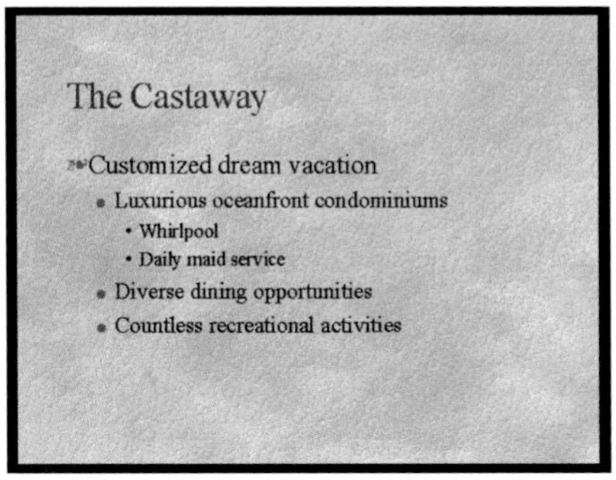

The Castaway

- Customized dream vacation
  - Luxurious oceanfront condominiums
    - Whirlpool
    - Daily maid service
  - Diverse dining opportunities
  - Countless recreational activities

FIGURE 2-1d

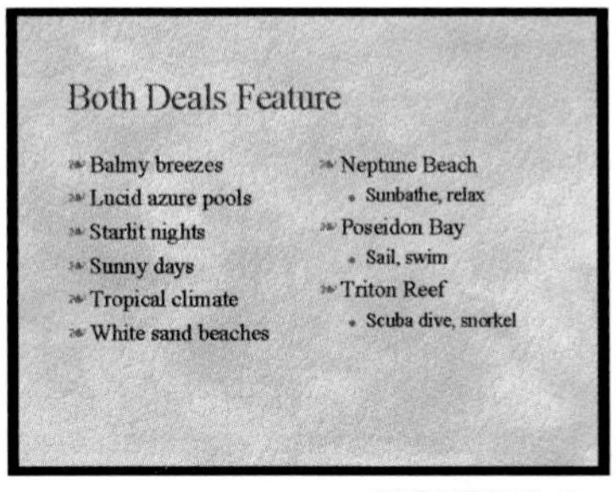

Both Deals Feature

- Balmy breezes
- Lucid azure pools
- Starlit nights
- Sunny days
- Tropical climate
- White sand beaches
- Neptune Beach
  - Sunbathe, relax
- Poseidon Bay
  - Sail, swim
- Triton Reef
  - Scuba dive, snorkel

FIGURE 2-1e

Time Is Running Out

- Contact Student Activities Office
  - Detter Hall, Room 225
  - Ext. 2772
- Call Voyager Travel Tours
  - 555-AWAY

FIGURE 2-1f

More About Electronic Slide Show

Preparing an electronic slide show has several advantages. For example, you can add multimedia effects, such as sound and video, as well as animate text and graphics. You can add slide transitions and build text objects to control the pace of the presentation. Most important is the ability to make last minute changes.

More About Presentation Design

When designing a presentation, create your conclusion, or closing, first. Then design the rest of the presentation to reach the conclusion. This causes you to focus on the objectives of the presentation.

I. Voyager Travel Tours
  A. Announces
  B. Break Away Bargains
II. Two Dynamite Deals
  A. The Stargazer
    1. All inclusive sand and sea adventure
  B. The Castaway
    1. Self-designed sand and sun experience
III. The Stargazer
  A. One incredible low price includes:
    1. Round-trip airfare
    2. Five day cruise and two day beach party
    3. Sumptuous gourmet cuisine
    4. Fabulous entertainment
IV. The Castaway
  A. Customized dream vacation
    1. Luxurious oceanfront condominiums
      a) Whirlpool
      b) Daily maid service
    2. Diverse dining opportunities
    3. Countless recreational activities
V. Both Deals Feature
  A. Balmy breezes
  B. Lucid azure pools
  C. Starlit nights
  D. Sunny days
  E. Tropical climate
  F. White sand beaches
  G. Neptune Beach
    1. Sunbathe, relax
  H. Poseidon Bay
    1. Sail, swim
  I. Triton Reef
    1. Scuba dive, snorkel
VI. Time Is Running Out
  A. Contact Student Activities Office
    1. Detter Hall, Room 225
    2. Ext. 2772
  B. Call Voyager Travel Tours
    1. 555-AWAY

FIGURE 2-2

Presentation Preparation Steps

The preparation steps summarize how the slide presentation shown in Figure 2-1 on the previous page will be developed in Project 2. The following tasks will be completed in this project.

1. Start a new document and apply a design template.
2. Create a presentation in outline view.
3. Save the presentation.
4. Insert a blank line in the bulleted list on Slide 2.
5. Change the slide layout on Slide 5 to 2 Column Text and move text from the left column to the right column.
6. Change the slide layout on Slide 6 to Clip Art Text and insert a clip art picture into a clip art placeholder.
7. Insert clip art into Slide 3 and then move and reduce the size of the clip art picture.
8. Add header and footer text to the outline pages.
9. Add slide transition effects.

10. Add text and clip art animation effects.
11. Save the presentation.
12. Print the presentation outline and slides.
13. Quit PowerPoint.

The following pages contain a detailed explanation of these tasks.

> **More About Design Templates**
>
> You can build a presentation with the default design template and later select a different one. When you change design templates, PowerPoint automatically updates color scheme, font attributes, and location of slide objects on every slide in the presentation.

Starting a New Presentation

Project 1 introduced you to starting a presentation document and applying a design template. The following steps summarize how to start a new presentation, apply a design template, and choose an AutoLayout. For a more detailed explanation, see pages PP 1.10 through PP 1.14 in Project 1. Perform the following steps to start a new presentation.

TO START A NEW PRESENTATION

Step 1: Click the Start button on the taskbar.
Step 2: Click New Office Document.
Step 3: Click the Presentation Designs tab. (Depending on your installation, the tab may display as Presentatio ... .) When the Presentation Designs sheet displays, scroll down the list of design templates until SERENE displays.
Step 4: Double-click SERENE.
Step 5: When the New Slide dialog box displays, click the OK button.
Step 6: If the Office Assistant displays, click the Office Assistant Close button.

PowerPoint displays the Title Slide AutoLayout and the Serene design template on Slide 1 in slide view (Figure 2-3).

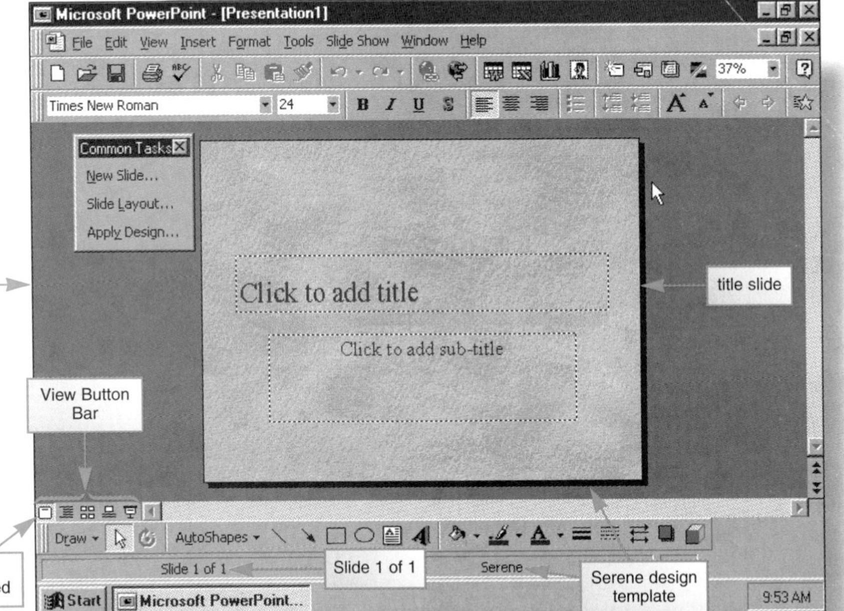

FIGURE 2-3

Using Outline View

Outline view provides a quick, easy way to create a presentation. Outlining allows you to organize your thoughts in a structured format. An outline uses indentation to establish a hierarchy, which denotes levels of importance to the main topic. An **outline** is a summary of thoughts, presented as headings and subheadings, often used as a preliminary draft when you create a presentation.

More About Presentation Design

The key to a successful presentation is organization. Begin by jotting down your ideas. Next, look over your list and decide on three or four major topics. Then group the remaining ideas around the major topics selecting ideas that support the major topics and leaving out those that do not.

In outline view, title text displays at the left side of the window along with a slide icon and a slide number. Body text is indented under the title text. Graphic objects, such as pictures, graphs, or tables, do not display in outline view. When a slide contains a graphic object, the slide icon next to the slide title displays with a small graphic on it. The slide icon is blank when a slide does not contain graphics. The attributes for text in outline view are the same as in slide view except for color and paragraph style. PowerPoint displays the current slide in **Color View.** This allows you to see how the current slide will look in slide view and slide show view while you continue to work in outline view.

PowerPoint limits the number of heading levels to six. The first heading level is the slide title and is not indented. The remaining five heading levels are the same as the five indent levels in slide view. Recall from Project 1 that PowerPoint allows for five indent levels and that each indent level has an associated bullet.

The outline begins with a title on **heading level 1**. The title is the main topic of the slide. Text supporting the main topic begins on **heading level 2** and indents under heading level 1. **Heading level 3** indents under heading level 2 and contains text to support heading level 2. **Heading level 4, heading level 5,** and **heading level 6** indent under heading level 3, heading level 4, and heading level 5, respectively. Use heading levels 4, 5, and 6 as required. They generally are used for very detailed scientific and engineering presentations. Business and sales presentations usually focus on summary information and use heading level 1, heading level 2, and heading level 3.

PowerPoint initially displays in slide view when you start a new presentation. Change from slide view to outline view by clicking the Outline View button on the View Button Bar. Perform the following steps to change the view from slide view to outline view.

Steps To Change the View to Outline View

1 Point to the Outline View button located on the View Button Bar at the lower-left corner of the Microsoft PowerPoint window (Figure 2-4).

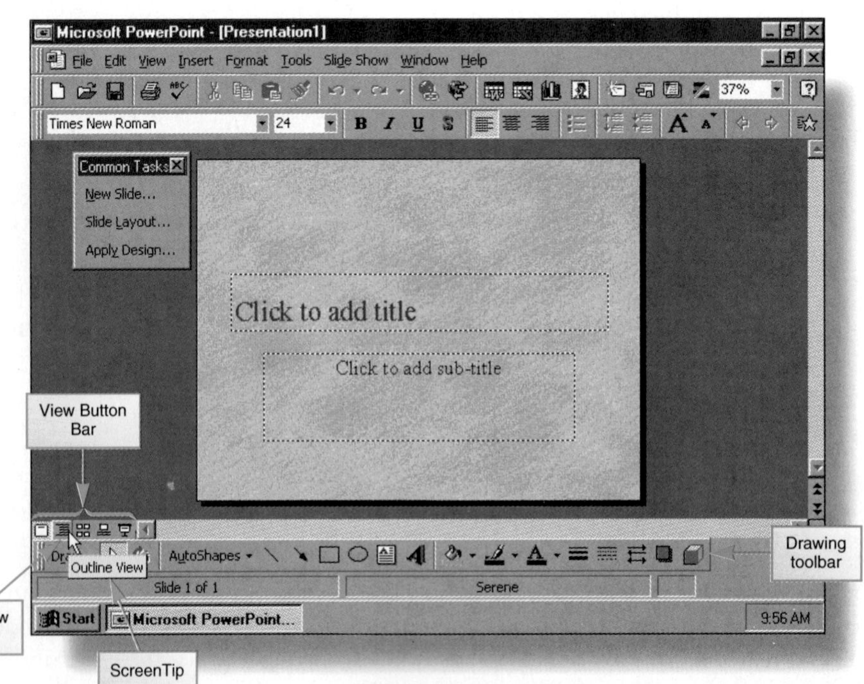

FIGURE 2-4

2 Click the Outline View button. If necessary, drag the Common Tasks toolbar to the right side of the Microsoft PowerPoint window as shown in Figure 2-5.

PowerPoint displays in outline view (Figure 2-5). PowerPoint displays the color view of Slide 1 in the Color View window.

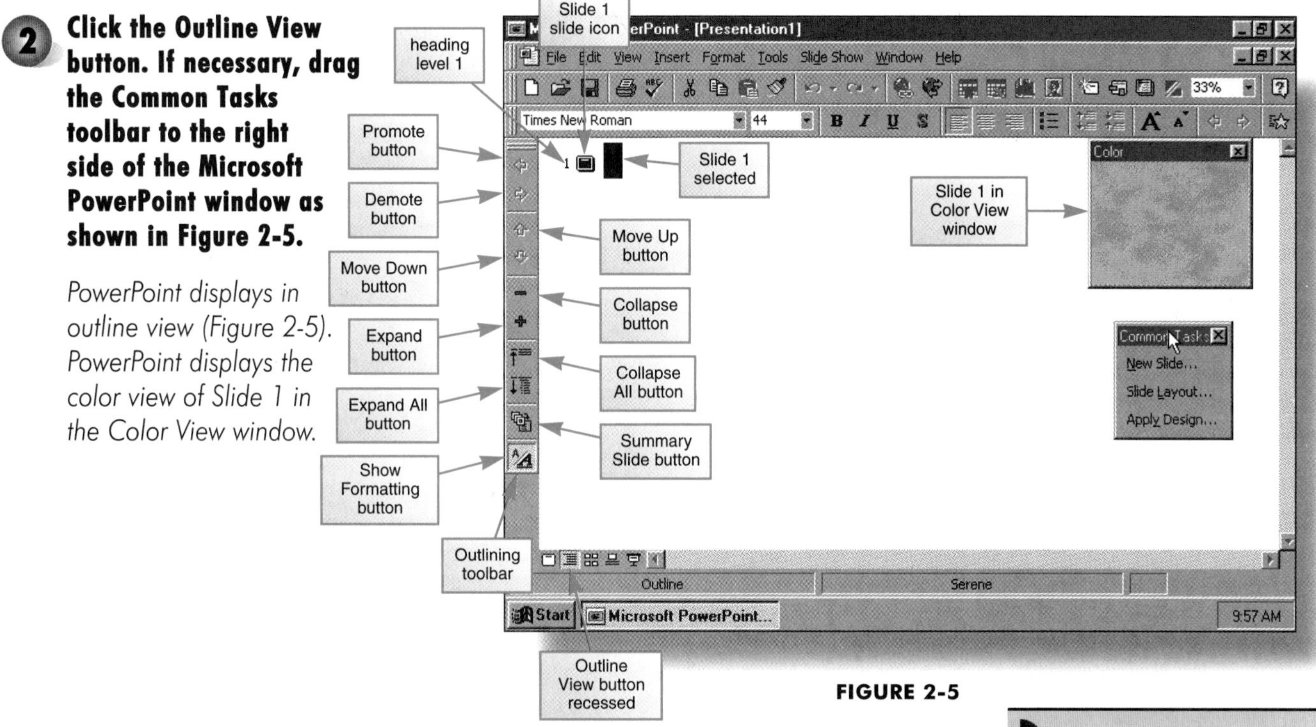

FIGURE 2-5

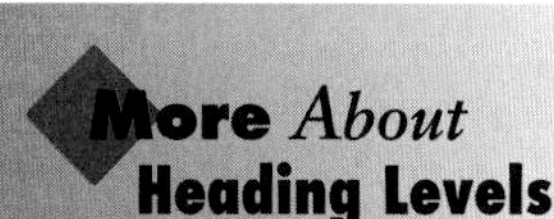

OtherWays

1. On View menu click Outline
2. Press ALT+V, press O

You can create and edit your presentation in outline view. Outline view also makes it easy to sequence slides and to relocate title text and body text from one slide to another. In addition to typing text to create a new presentation in outline view, PowerPoint can produce slides from an outline created in Microsoft Word or another word processor, if you save the outline as an RTF file or as a plain text file. The file extension **RTF** stands for **R**ich **T**ext **F**ormat.

The PowerPoint Window in Outline View

The PowerPoint window in outline view differs from the window in slide view because the Outlining toolbar displays but the Drawing toolbar does not (Figures 2-4 and 2-5). Table 2-1 on the next page describes the buttons on the Outlining toolbar.

More *About* Heading Levels

You may overwhelm the audience if a slide contains too much detail and requires more than six heading levels with which to explain the topic. Decompose large topics into two or more subtopics. Then, create a new slide for each group of subtopics.

Table 2-1

BUTTON	BUTTON NAME	DESCRIPTION
	Promote	The Promote button moves the selected paragraph up one level in the outline hierarchy each time you click the button. Promoting a paragraph outdents or moves it to the left until your reach heading level 1.
	Demote	The Demote button moves the selected paragraph down one level in the outline hierarchy each time you click the button. Demoting a paragraph indents or moves it to the right. You only can demote down to heading level 6.
	Move Up	The Move Up button moves selected text above the preceding displayed paragraph while maintaining its hierarchical heading level and text style. The selected text changes position with the paragraph located above it.
	Move Down	The Move Down button moves selected text below the following displayed paragraph while maintaining its hierarchical heading level and text style. The selected text changes position with the paragraph located below it.
	Collapse	The Collapse button hides all heading levels except the title of the selected slide. The button is useful when you want to collapse one slide in your outline. Hidden text displays as a gray line.
	Expand	The Expand button displays all heading levels and text for the selected slide. The button is useful when you want to expand one slide in your outline.
	Collapse All	The Collapse All button hides all heading levels to show only the slide titles of the entire presentation. This button is useful when you are looking at the organization of your presentation and do not care to see the details. Hidden text displays as gray lines below the title.
	Expand All	Expands all heading levels to display the slide title and text for all slides.
	Summary Slide	Creates a bulleted list slide from the titles of the slides selected in slide sorter view or outline view, and then inserts that slide in front of the first selected slide.
	Show Formatting	The Show Formatting button is a toggle that displays or hides the text attributes. This is useful when you want to work with plain text as opposed to working with bolded, italicized, or underlined text. When printing your outline, plain text often speeds up the printing process.

Creating a Presentation in Outline View

Outline view enables you to view title and body text, add and delete slides, **drag and drop** slide text, drag and drop slides to change slide order, promote and demote text, save a presentation, print an outline, print slides, copy and paste slides or text to and from other presentations, apply a design template, and import an outline.

Developing a presentation in outline view is quick because you type the text for all slides on one screen. Once you type the outline, the presentation fundamentally is complete. If you choose, you then can go to slide view to enhance your presentation with graphics.

More *About* **Creating Presentations in Outline View**

A method some presenters use to create a presentation is to create a list of the main topics for a presentation in outline view. Developing the list of main topics generates all presentation slides because each topic becomes the title for a slide. The presenter then completes each slide with relevant subtopics.

Creating a Title Slide in Outline View

Recall from Project 1 that the title slide introduces the presentation to the audience. In addition to introducing the presentation, Project 2 uses the title slide to capture the attention of the audience by using a design template with tropical colors. Remember that Voyager Travel Tours is trying to sell vacation packages. They want the audience to focus on getting away to a warm, tropical climate for an exciting vacation; consequently, they use an appropriate design template. Perform the following steps to create a title slide in outline view.

Steps To Create a Title Slide in Outline View

1 Type `Voyager Travel Tours` **and press the ENTER key.**

Voyager Travel Tours displays as the title for Slide 1 and is called heading level 1. A slide icon displays to the left of each slide title. The font for heading level 1 is Times New Roman and the font size is 44 points. In outline view, the default Zoom setting is 33% of the actual slide size. Depending on the ***resolution*** *of your computer monitor (the number of pixels displaying per unit of measurement, such as a centimeter or an inch), your Zoom setting may be different. Pressing the ENTER key moves the insertion point to the next line and maintains the same heading level. The insertion point, therefore, is in position for typing the title for Slide 2 (Figure 2-6).*

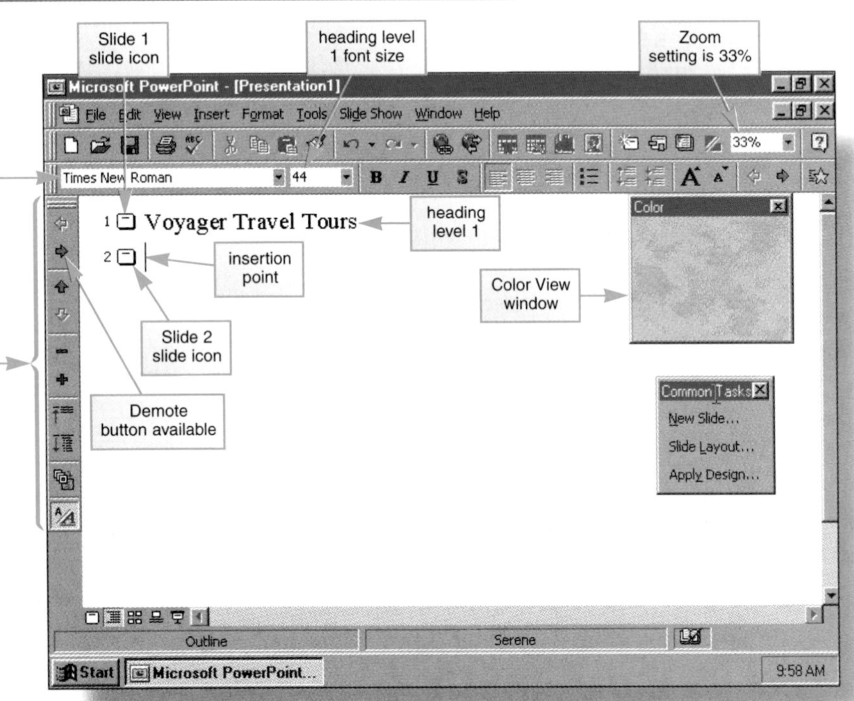

FIGURE 2-6

2 Point to the Demote button on the Outlining toolbar.

The Demote ScreenTip displays (Figure 2-7).

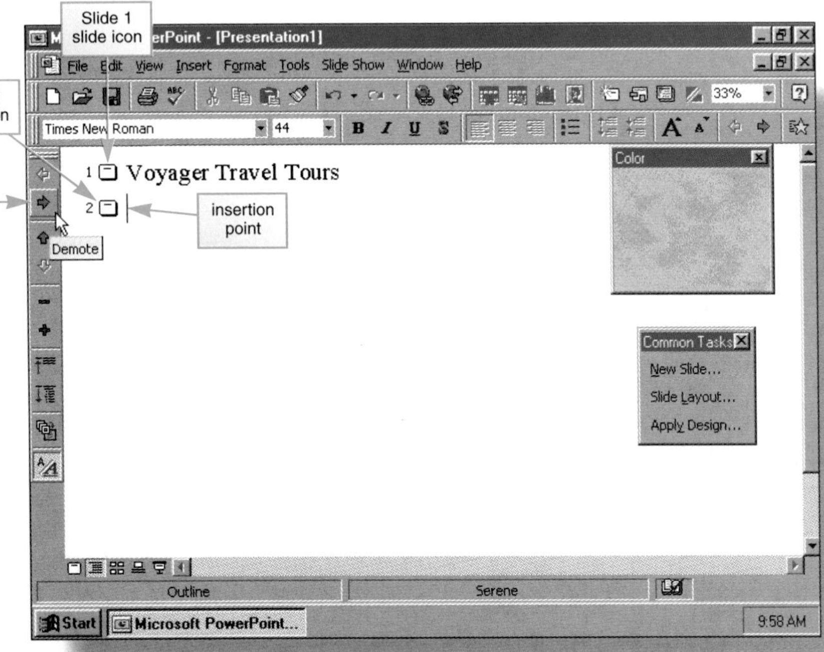

FIGURE 2-7

3 **Click the Demote button. Type** Announces **and press the ENTER key. Type** Break Away Bargains **and press the ENTER key.**

The Slide 2 slide icon does not display (Figure 2-8). The paragraphs, Announces and Break Away Bargains, are subtitles on the title slide (Slide 1) and demote to heading level 2. Heading level 2 is indented to the right under heading level 1. The heading level 2 font is Times New Roman and the heading level 2 font size is 32 points.

heading level 2 font size

heading level 2 font

Demote button available

title slide title text (heading level 1)

title slide subtitle text (heading level 2)

insertion point

Slide 1 slide icon (title slide)

text displays in Color View window

FIGURE 2-8

OtherWays

1. Type title text, press ENTER, on Formatting toolbar, click Demote button, type subtitle text, press ENTER
2. Type title text, press ENTER, press TAB, type subtitle text, press ENTER

The title slide text for the Voyager Travel Tours presentation is complete. The next section explains how to add a slide in outline view.

Adding a Slide in Outline View

Recall from Project 1 that when you add a new slide, PowerPoint defaults to the Bulleted List AutoLayout layout. This is true in outline view as well. One way to add a new slide in outline view is to promote a paragraph to heading level 1 by clicking the Promote button until the insertion point or the paragraph displays at heading level 1. A slide icon displays when the insertion point or paragraph reaches heading level 1. Perform the following steps to add a slide in outline view.

Steps To Add a Slide in Outline View

1 **Point to the Promote button on the Outlining toolbar.**

The insertion point still is positioned at heading level 2 (Figure 2-9).

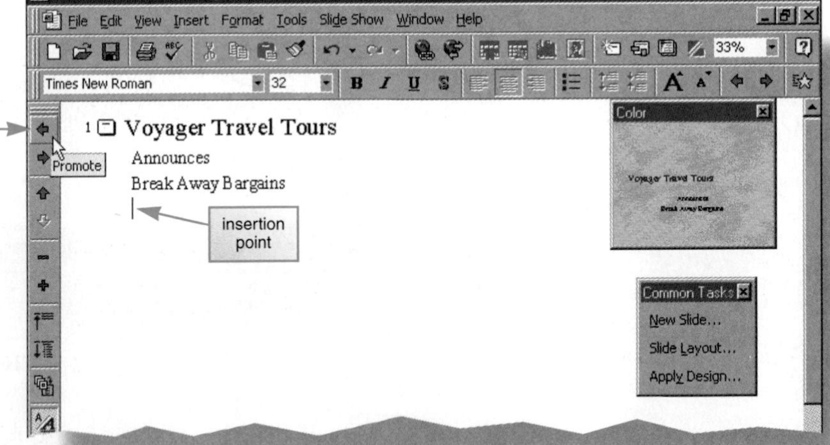

FIGURE 2-9

2 **Click the Promote button.**

The Slide 2 slide icon displays indicating a new slide is added to the presentation (Figure 2-10). The insertion point is in position to type the title for Slide 2 at heading level 1.

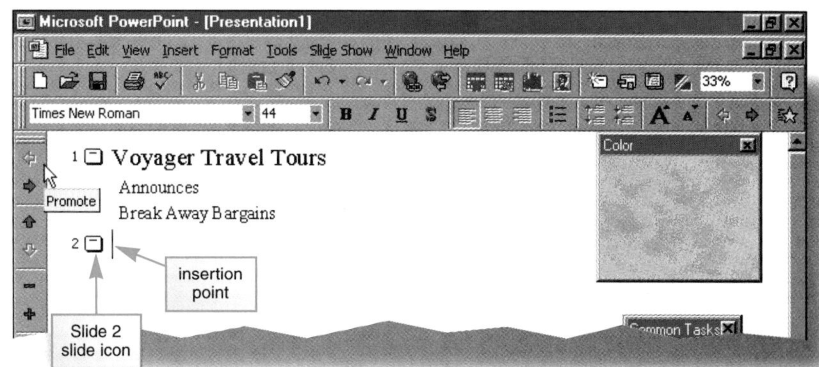

FIGURE 2-10

OtherWays

1. On Standard toolbar, click New Slide button, click OK button in New Slide dialog box
2. On Insert menu click New Slide, click OK button in New Slide dialog box
3. Press ALT+I, press N, press ENTER
4. Press CTRL+M, press ENTER
5. Press and hold SHIFT, press TAB until paragraph or insertion point displays at heading level 1, release TAB

After you add a slide, you are ready to type the slide text. The next section explains how to create a multi-level bulleted list slide in outline view.

Creating Multi-level Bulleted List Slides in Outline View

To create a multi-level bulleted list slide, you demote or promote the insertion point to the appropriate heading level and then type the paragraph text. Recall from Project 1 that when you demote a paragraph, PowerPoint adds a bullet to the left of each heading level. Depending on the design template, each heading level has a different bullet font. Also recall that the design template determines font attributes, including the bullet font.

Slide 2 is the first **informational slide** for Project 2. Slide 2 introduces the main topic — two vacation packages offered by Voyager Travel Tours. Each vacation package displays as heading level 2, and each **supportive paragraph** displays as heading level 3. The following steps explain how to create a multi-level bulleted list slide in outline view.

Steps To Create a Multi-level Bulleted List Slide in Outline View

1 **Type** `Two Dynamite Deals` **and press the ENTER key. Then click the Demote button to demote to heading level 2.**

The title for Slide 2, Two Dynamite Deals, displays and the insertion point is in position to type the first bulleted paragraph (Figure 2-11). A leaf shaped bullet displays to the left of the insertion point.

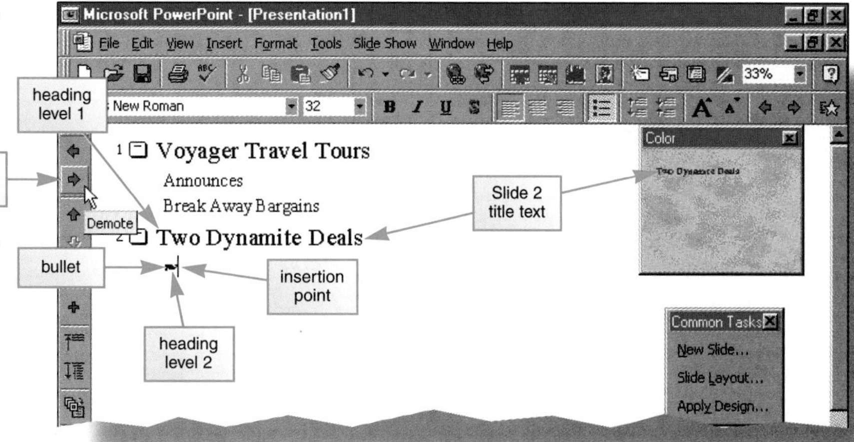

FIGURE 2-11

2 **Type** `The Stargazer` **and press the ENTER key. Then click the Demote button to demote to heading level 3.**

Slide 2 displays three heading levels: the title, Two Dynamite Deals, on heading level 1, the bulleted paragraph, The Stargazer, on heading level 2, and the insertion point on heading level 3 (Figure 2-12). The bullet for heading level 2 is a leaf. The bullet for heading level 3 is a dot.

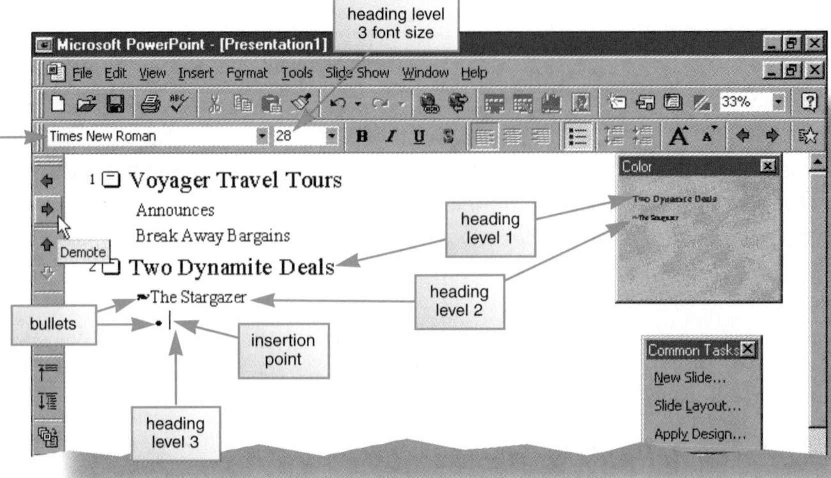

FIGURE 2-12

3 **Type** `All inclusive sand and sea adventure` **and press the ENTER key. Then click the Promote button.**

Pressing the ENTER key begins a new paragraph at the same heading level as the previous paragraph. Clicking the Promote button moves the insertion point left and elevates the paragraph from heading level 3 to heading level 2 (Figure 2-13).

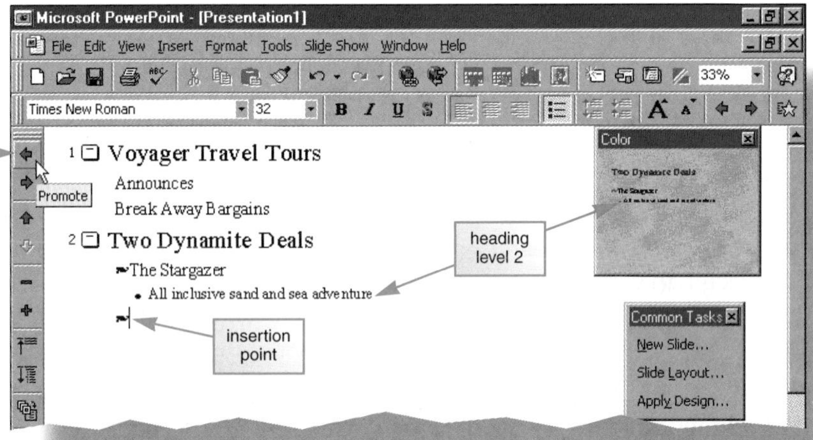

FIGURE 2-13

4 **Type** `The Castaway` **and press the ENTER key. Click the Demote button. Type** `Self-designed sand and sun experience` **and press the ENTER key (Figure 2-14).**

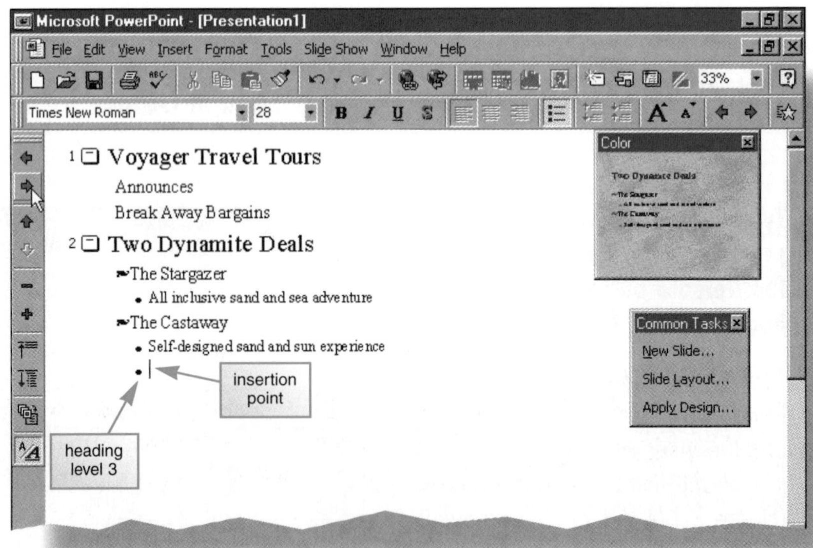

FIGURE 2-14

Creating a Subordinate Slide

When developing your presentation, begin with a main topic and follow with **subordinate slides**, slides to support the main topic. Placing all your information on one slide may overwhelm your audience. Decompose your presentation, therefore, into several slides with three to six bullets per slide or per object. The following steps explain how to create a subordinate slide that further explains the vacation package, The Stargazer, first introduced on Slide 2. This new slide, Slide 3, provides additional information that supports the first heading level 2 on Slide 2. Later in this project, you create another subordinate slide to support the second heading level 2 on Slide 2, The Castaway.

More About Outline View

When working in outline view, many people prefer to use keyboard keys instead of toolbar buttons. This way their hands never leave the keyboard and their typing is finished quickly. For example, instead of clicking the Demote button to demote text, press the TAB key.

TO CREATE A SUBORDINATE SLIDE

Step 1: Click the Promote button two times so that Slide 3 is added to the end of the presentation.
Step 2: Type `The Stargazer` and press the ENTER key.
Step 3: Click the Demote button to demote to heading level 2.
Step 4: Type `One incredible low price includes:` and press the ENTER key.
Step 5: Click the Demote button to demote to heading level 3.
Step 6: Type `Round-trip airfare` and press the ENTER key.
Step 7: Type `Five-day cruise and two-day beach party` and press the ENTER key.
Step 8: Type `Sumptuous gourmet cuisine` and press the ENTER key.
Step 9: Type `Fabulous entertainment` and press the ENTER key.

The screen displays as shown in Figure 2-15.

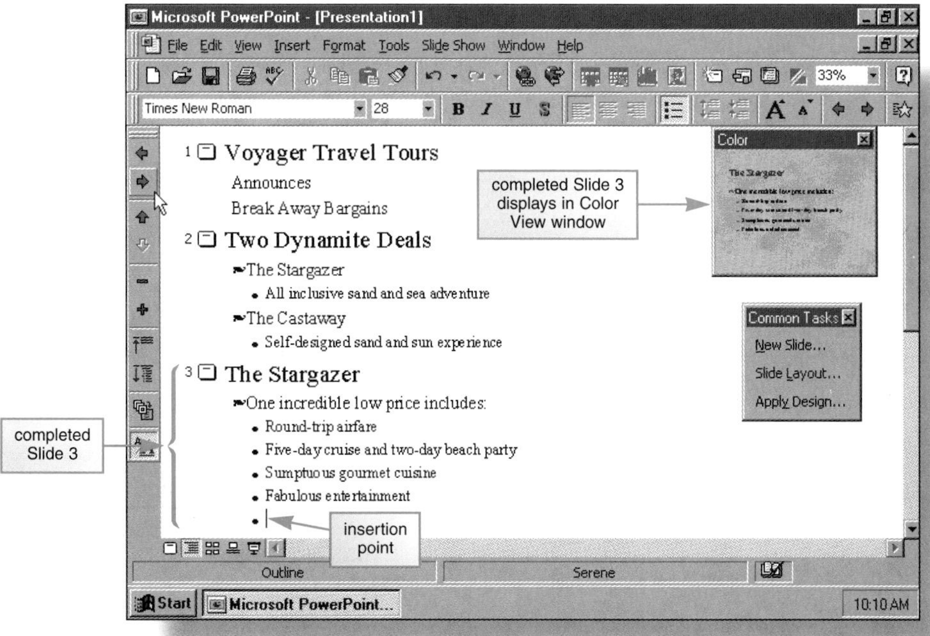

FIGURE 2-15

More About Subordinate Slides

When reviewing a presentation, look for slides containing more information than the audience can quickly grasp. When a slide gets complicated, simplify the presentation by clicking the Expand Slide command on the Tools menu. This generates a new slide for each bulleted item on the original slide.

More *About* **Subordinate Slides**

Subordinate items must directly support the main topic under which they are placed. This means that they must be less important in meaning while being logically related. Indentation identifies levels of importance. The more important the item, the closer it displays to the left margin.

Creating a Second Subordinate Slide

The next step is to create the slide that supports The Castaway, which is the second heading level 2 on Slide 2. Perform the following steps to create this subordinate slide.

TO CREATE A SECOND SUBORDINATE SLIDE

Step 1: Click the Promote button two times so that Slide 4 is added to the end of the presentation. Type `The Castaway` and press the ENTER key.
Step 2: Click the Demote button to demote to heading level 2. Type `Customized dream vacation` and press the ENTER key.
Step 3: Click the Demote button to demote to heading level 3. Type `Luxurious oceanfront condominiums` and press the ENTER key.
Step 4: Click the Demote button to demote to heading level 4. Type `Whirlpool` and press the ENTER key. Type `Daily maid service` and press the ENTER key.
Step 5: Click the Promote button to promote to heading level 3. Type `Diverse dining opportunities` and press the ENTER key. Type `Countless recreational activities` and press the ENTER key.

The screen displays as shown in Figure 2-16.

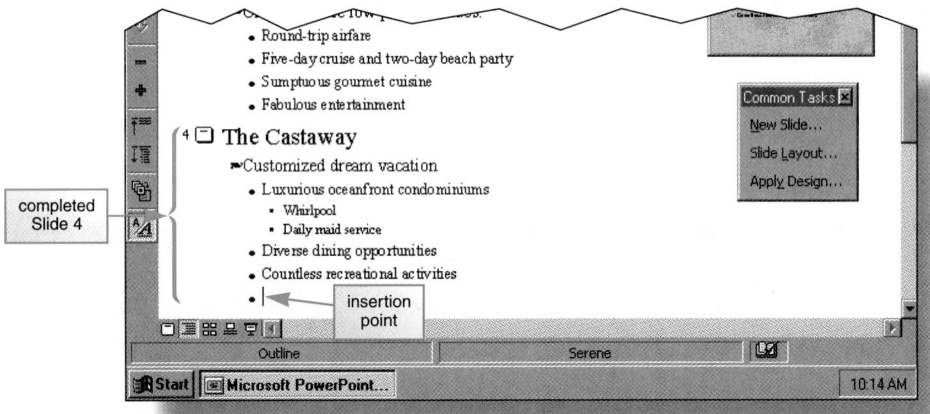

FIGURE 2-16

Creating a Slide with Multiple Text Objects in Outline View

All of the slides you have created to this point consist of a title object and one text object. Occasionally, you need to provide the audience with a long list of items. If you use the Bulleted List slide layout, Style Checker will identify the slide as having too many bullets. Recall from Project 1 that Style Checker checks a presentation for spelling, visual clarity, case, and end punctuation. One of the design standards Style Checker looks for is too many bullets in an object.

In order to create a slide with more than six bulleted paragraphs and still comply with design standards, break the list into two or more objects. When you divide the text into multiple objects, each object complies with PowerPoint's default settings for visual clarity in Style Checker, as long as the number of bullets per object is less than or equal to six. Six is the default setting for the number of bullets per object.

Because you are creating the presentation in outline view, type the text for this slide as a bulleted list. Later in this project, you convert the bulleted list slide into a multiple object slide by changing views, changing slide layout, and moving some of the text from the bulleted list to another object. Perform the following steps to create a slide with multiple text objects in outline view.

TO CREATE A SLIDE WITH MULTIPLE TEXT OBJECTS IN OUTLINE VIEW

Step 1: Click the Promote button two times so that Slide 5 is added to the end of the presentation. Type `Both Deals Feature` as the slide title and press the ENTER key.

Step 2: Click the Demote button to demote to heading level 2. Type `Balmy breezes` and press the ENTER key. Type `Lucid azure pools` and press the ENTER key. Type `Starlit nights` and press the ENTER key. Type `Sunny days` and press the ENTER key. Type `Tropical climate` and press the ENTER key. Type `White sand beaches` and press the ENTER key. Type `Neptune Beach` and press the ENTER key.

Step 3: Click the Demote button to demote to heading level 3. Type `Sunbathe, relax` and press the ENTER key.

Step 4: Click the Promote button to promote to heading level 2. Type `Poseidon Bay` and press the ENTER key.

Step 5: Click the Demote button to demote to heading level 3. Type `Sail, swim` and press the ENTER key.

Step 6: Click the Promote button to promote to heading level 2. Type `Triton Reef` and press the ENTER key.

Step 7: Click the Demote button to demote to heading level 3. Type `Scuba dive, snorkel` and press the ENTER key.

The screen displays as shown in Figure 2-17.

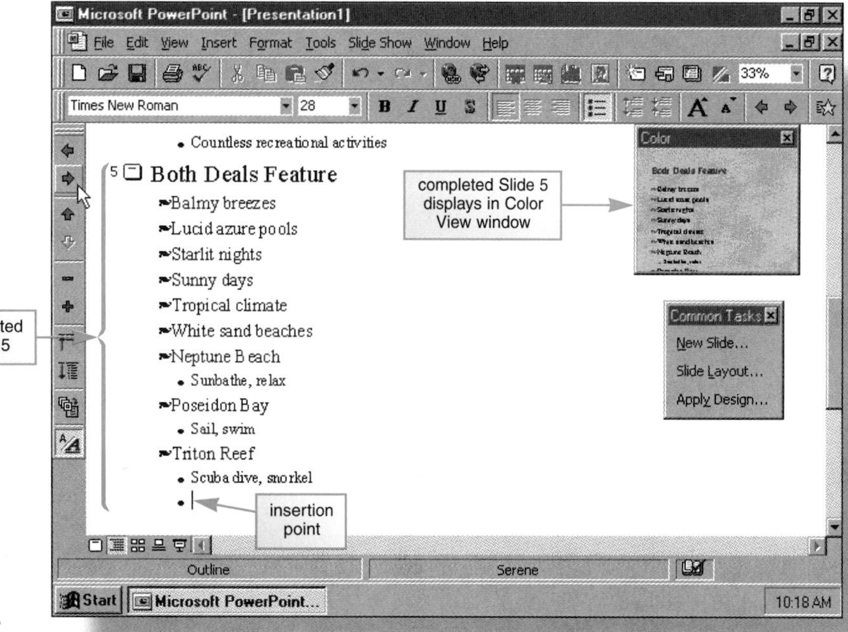

FIGURE 2-17

Creating a Closing Slide in Outline View

The last slide in your presentation is the closing slide. A **closing slide** gracefully ends a presentation. Often used during a question and answer session, the closing slide usually remains on the screen to reinforce the message delivered during the presentation. Professional speakers design the closing slide with one or more of the methods on the next page.

1. List important information. Tell the audience what to do next.
2. Provide a memorable illustration or example to make a point.
3. Appeal to emotions. Remind the audience to take action or accept responsibility.
4. Summarize the main points of the presentation.
5. Cite a quotation that directly relates to the main points of the presentation. This is most effective if the presentation started with a quotation.

The closing slide in this project combines listing important information and providing an illustration. Because Voyager Travel Tours wants students to buy one of the tropical island vacations, they combine telling students what to do next with providing a list of telephone numbers on the Serene design template. Perform the following steps to create this closing slide.

More About Closing Slides

Keep the closing slide brief. It should be a conclusion, not a complete restatement of the entire presentation. Remember that the audience is ready to leave, so keep your closing slide simple.

TO CREATE A CLOSING SLIDE IN OUTLINE VIEW

Step 1: Click the Promote button two times so that Slide 6 is added to the end of the presentation. Type `Time Is Running Out` as the slide title and press the ENTER key.

Step 2: Click the Demote button to demote to heading level 2. Type `Contact Student Activities Office` and press the ENTER key.

Step 3: Click the Demote button to demote to heading level 3. Type `Detter Hall, Room 225` and press the ENTER key. Type `Ext. 2772` and press the ENTER key.

Step 4: Click the Promote button to promote to heading level 2. Type `Call Voyager Travel Tours` and press the ENTER key.

Step 5: Click the Demote button to demote to heading level 3. Type `555-AWAY` but do not press the ENTER key.

Slide 6 displays as shown in Figure 2-18.

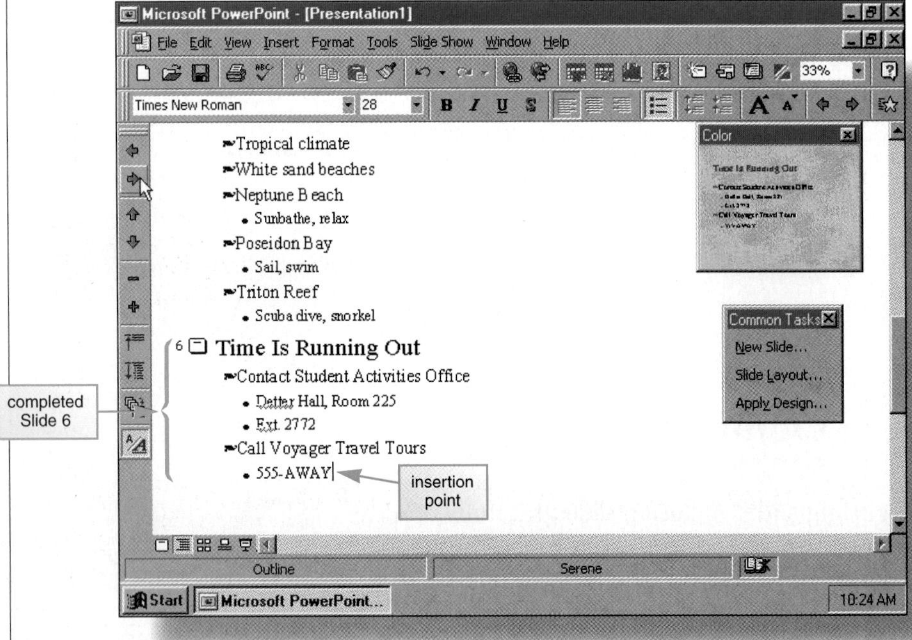

FIGURE 2-18

The outline now is complete and the presentation should be saved. The next section explains how to save the presentation.

Saving a Presentation

Recall from Project 1 that it is wise to frequently save your presentation. Because you have created all the text for your presentation, you should save your presentation now. For a detailed explanation of the following summarized steps, refer to pages PP 1.23 through PP 1.25 in Project 1.

TO SAVE A PRESENTATION

Step 1: Insert a formatted floppy disk in drive A and then click the Save button on the Standard toolbar.
Step 2: Type `Break Away Bargains` in the File name box. Do not press the ENTER key.
Step 3: Click the Save in box arrow. Click 3½ Floppy (A:) in the Save in list.
Step 4: Click the Save button.

The presentation is saved to drive A under the file name Break Away Bargains. The file name displays in the title bar.

Reviewing a Presentation in Slide Sorter View

In Project 1, you displayed slides in slide show view to evaluate the presentation. Slide show view, however, restricts your evaluation to one slide at a time. Outline view is best for quickly reviewing all the text for a presentation. Recall from Project 1 that slide sorter view allows you to look at several slides at one time, which is why it is the best view to use to evaluate a presentation for content, organization, and overall appearance. Perform the following step to change from outline view to slide sorter view.

To Change the View to Slide Sorter View

1 Click the Slide Sorter View button on the View Button Bar at the bottom of the PowerPoint window.

PowerPoint displays the presentation in slide sorter view (Figure 2-19). Slide 6 is selected because it was the current slide in outline view.

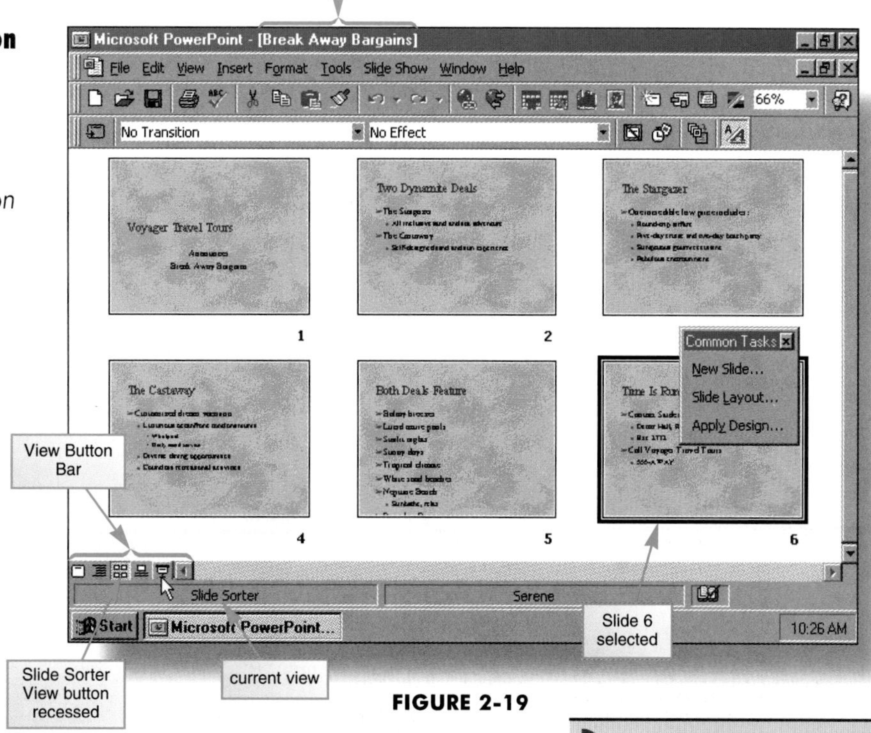

FIGURE 2-19

Other Ways

1. On View menu click Slide Sorter
2. Press ALT+V, press D

Because there are only six slides in this presentation and the Zoom setting is 66%, you can review all slides in one window. Notice that all slides have a significant amount of white space and that the text on Slide 5 exceeds the length of the slide. These observations indicate a need to adjust line spacing to make better use of the slide. Recall that Slide 5 will be corrected by changing the slide layout to one that displays text in two text objects. Additionally, the presentation lacks excitement. To make the presentation more interesting, you may wish to add graphics, such as clip art. The next several sections explain how to improve the presentation by adding a blank line in a bulleted list, changing slide layouts, and adding clip art.

Adding a Blank Line to a Bulleted List

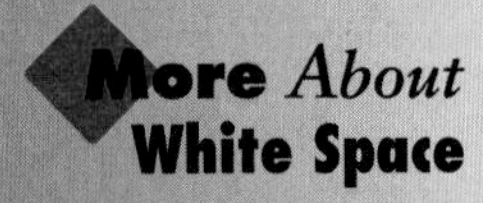

More *About* **White Space**

Do not crowd a slide with text. White space allows the reader's eye to relax and then focus on the next line of text. Balance text, graphics, and white space to create an appealing slide.

The first improvement to this presentation is adding a blank line to Slide 2. In order to increase white space between paragraphs, add a blank line after the heading level 3 paragraph, All inclusive sand and sea adventure. Recall that a paragraph begins when you press the ENTER key and ends when you again press the ENTER key. Also recall that PowerPoint adds a bullet in front of every new paragraph in a bulleted list. Thus, to create a blank line in a bulleted list, you also must remove the bullet.

You can make changes to text in both slide view and outline view. It is best, however, to change the view to slide view when making changes that impact white space so that you can see the result of editing the text object. Perform the following steps to change the view to slide view.

Steps To Change the View to Slide View

1 Point to the slide miniature of Slide 2 (Figure 2-20).

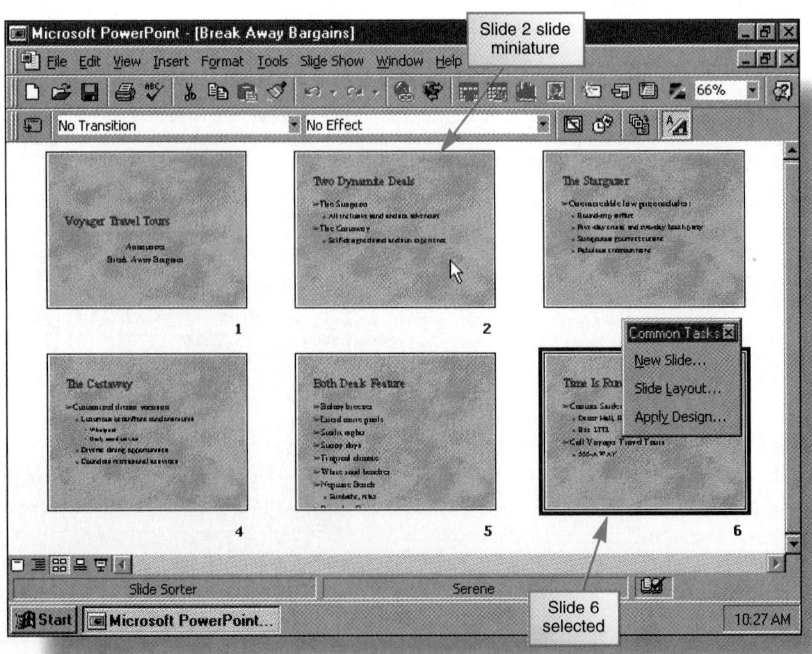

FIGURE 2-20

2 **Double-click the Slide 2 slide miniature.**

Slide 2 displays in slide view (Figure 2-21). The Slide View button is recessed on the View Button Bar.

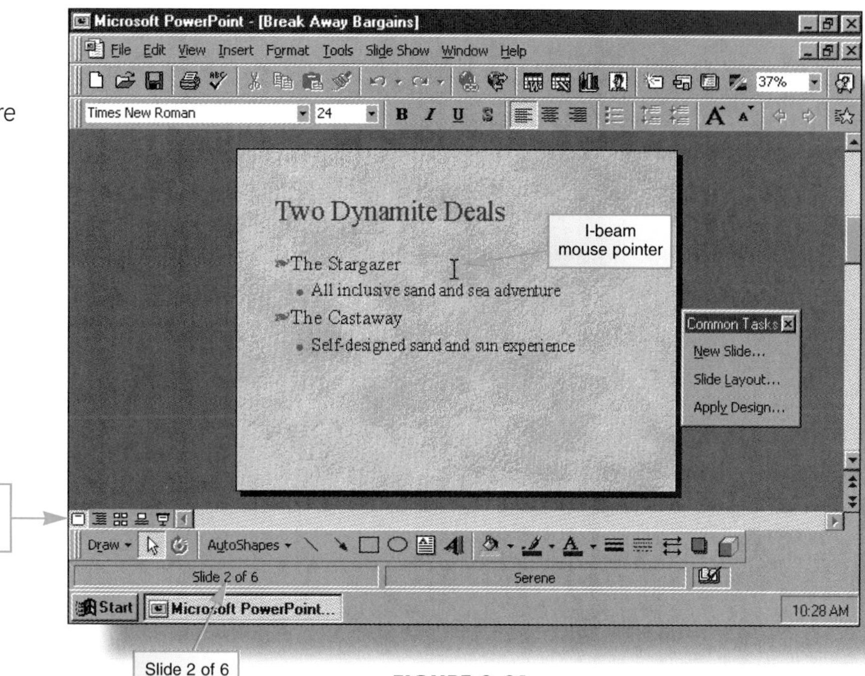

FIGURE 2-21

OtherWays

1. On View menu click Slide
2. Press ALT+V, press S

The next section explains how to add a blank line to Slide 2.

Adding a Blank Line to Slide 2

Now that Slide 2 displays in slide view, you are ready to add a blank line after the paragraph, All inclusive sand and sea adventure. Perform the following steps to add a blank line.

Steps To Add a Blank Line

1 **Position the I-beam mouse pointer to the right of the second letter e in the word adventure in the paragraph All inclusive sand and sea adventure. Then click the left mouse button.**

PowerPoint selects the text object and positions the insertion point after the second e in the word, adventure (Figure 2-22). The mouse pointer displays as an I-beam when located in a text object.

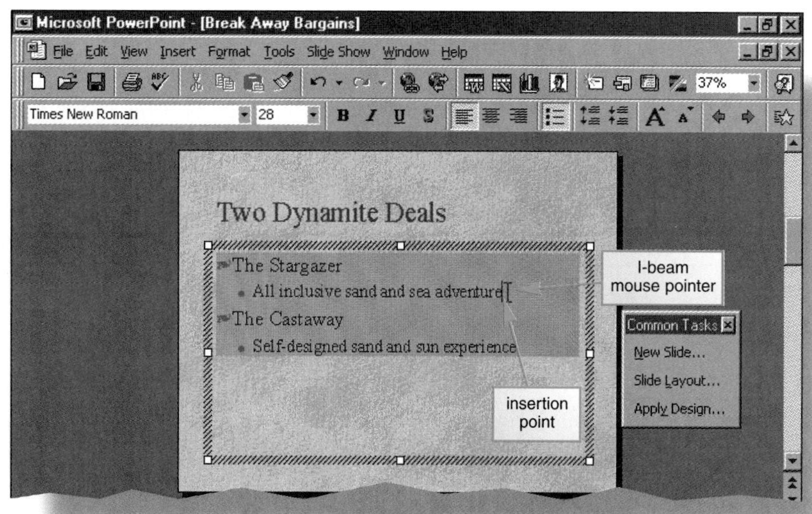

FIGURE 2-22

2 Press the ENTER key.

PowerPoint inserts a new paragraph (Figure 2-23). The new paragraph has the same attributes as the previous paragraph. The Bullets button is recessed on the Formatting toolbar.

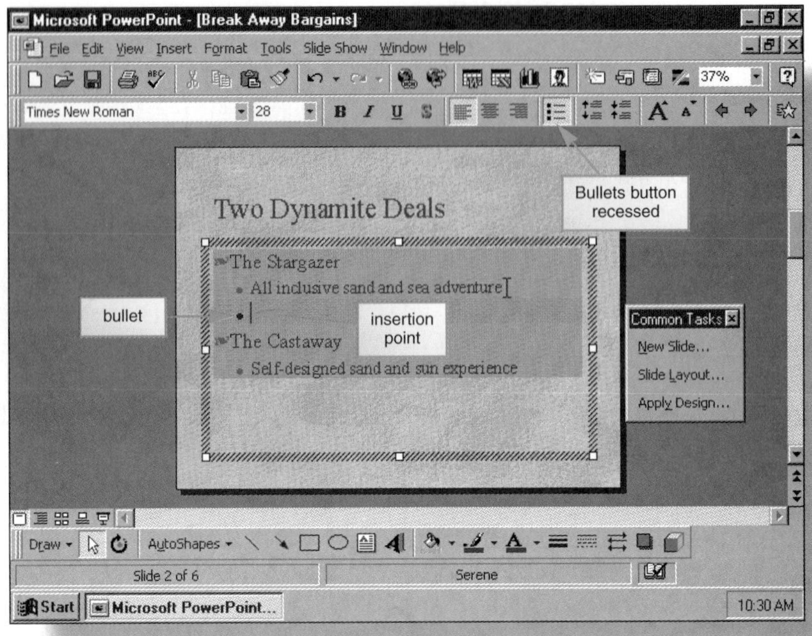

FIGURE 2-23

3 Click the Bullets button to remove the bullet.

The line displays blank because the bullet does not display (Figure 2-24). The Bullets button is not recessed.

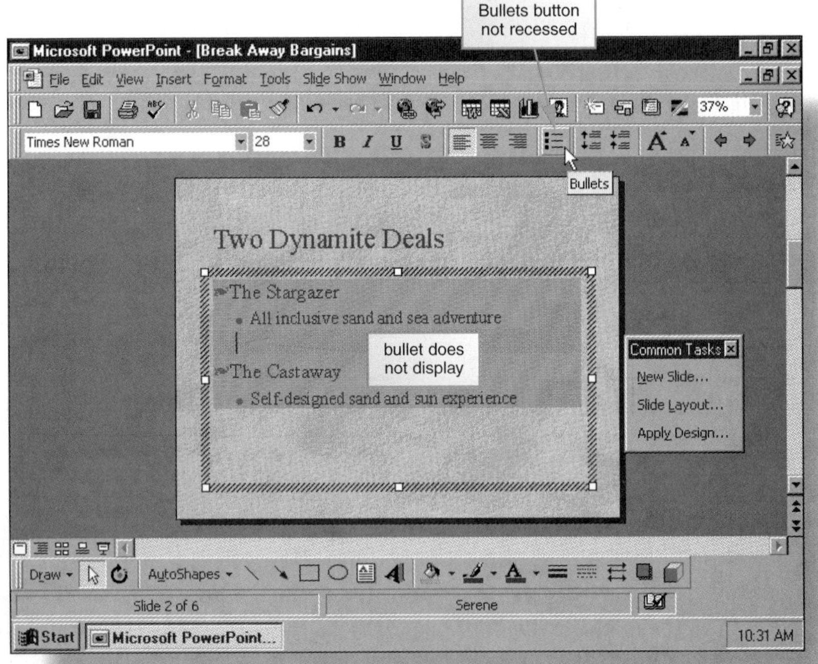

FIGURE 2-24

Positioning the insertion point at the end of a paragraph and then pressing the ENTER key two times also creates a blank paragraph. The bullet, however, displays dimmed on the screen and the Bullets button displays recessed on the Formatting toolbar. If you click a paragraph other than the blank paragraph, the bullet does not display. Additionally, the dimmed bullet does not display when you run the presentation in slide show view.

To display a bullet on a selected paragraph, click the Bullets button on the Formatting toolbar.

Changing Slide Layout

Recall from Project 1 that when you add a new slide, PowerPoint displays the New Slide dialog box from which you choose one of the slide AutoLayouts. After creating a slide, you can change its layout by clicking the **Slide Layout button** on the Common Tasks toolbar. The Slide Layout dialog box then displays. Like the AutoLayout dialog box, the Slide Layout dialog box allows you to choose one of the 24 different slide layouts.

When you change the layout of a slide, PowerPoint retains the text and graphics and repositions them into the appropriate placeholders. Using slide layouts eliminates the need to resize objects because PowerPoint automatically sizes the object to fit the placeholder.

To keep your presentation interesting, PowerPoint includes several slide layouts to combine text with nontext objects, such as clip art. The placement of the text, in relationship to the nontext object, depends on the slide layout. The nontext object placeholder may be to the right or left of the text, above the text, or below the text. Additionally, some slide layouts are constructed with two nontext object placeholders. Refer to Project 1 for a list of the available slide layouts (Figure 1-27 on PP 1.25). The following steps explain how to change the slide layout from a bulleted list to two columns of text.

More About Slide Layout

Vary your slide layouts to keep a presentation from becoming monotonous. Choose layouts designed for one text object, multiple text objects, graphs, tables, and clip art. While varying slide layouts increases audience attention, be careful to maintain a common theme throughout the presentation by using a design template or color scheme.

To Change Slide Layout

1 Drag the scroll box on the vertical scroll bar to display Slide 5 (Figure 2-25).

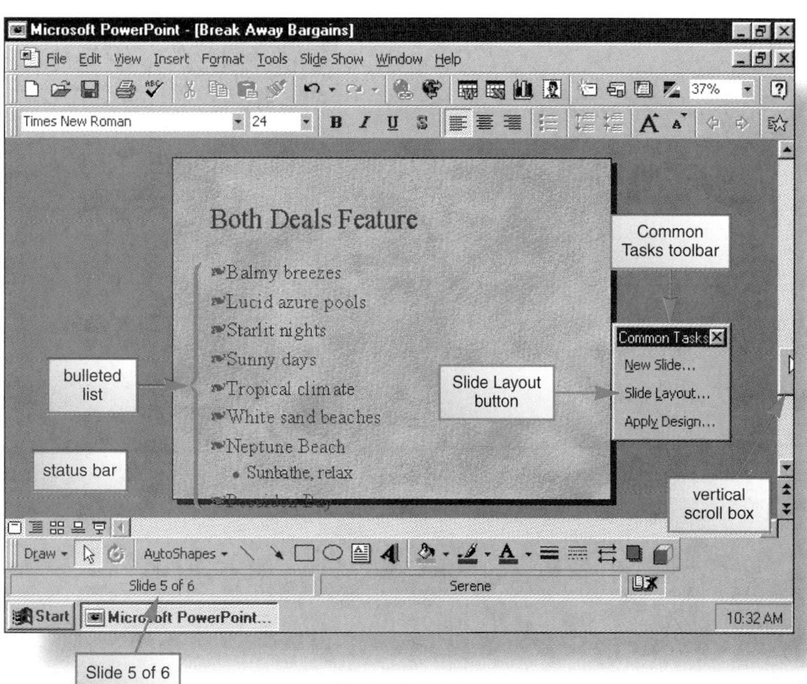

FIGURE 2-25

2 **Click the Slide Layout button on the Common Tasks toolbar. When the Slide Layout dialog box displays, click the 2 Column Text slide layout located in row one, column three.**

The Slide Layout dialog box displays (Figure 2-26). The 2 Column Text slide layout is selected. When you click a slide layout, its name displays in the box at the lower-right corner of the Slide Layout dialog box.

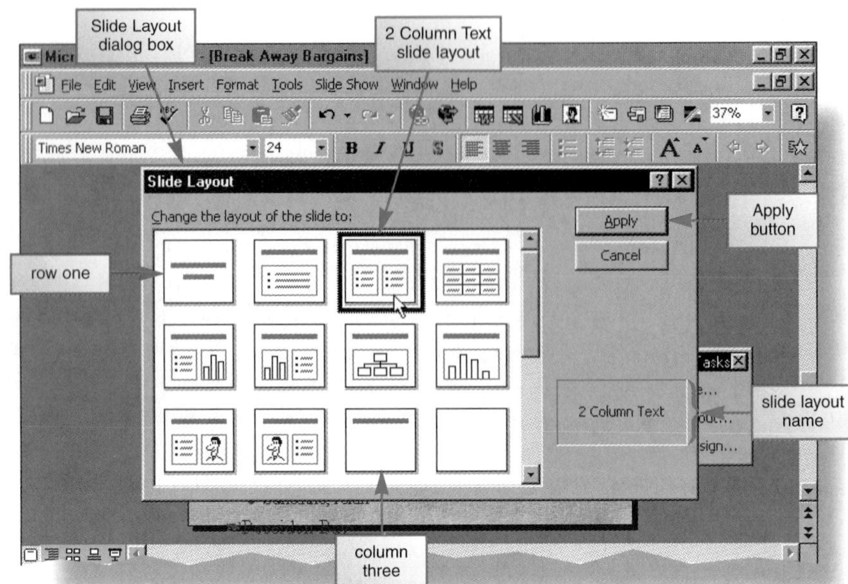

FIGURE 2-26

3 **Click the Apply button.**

Slide 5 displays the bulleted list in the left column text object (Figure 2-27). The right column text placeholder displays the message, Click to add text.

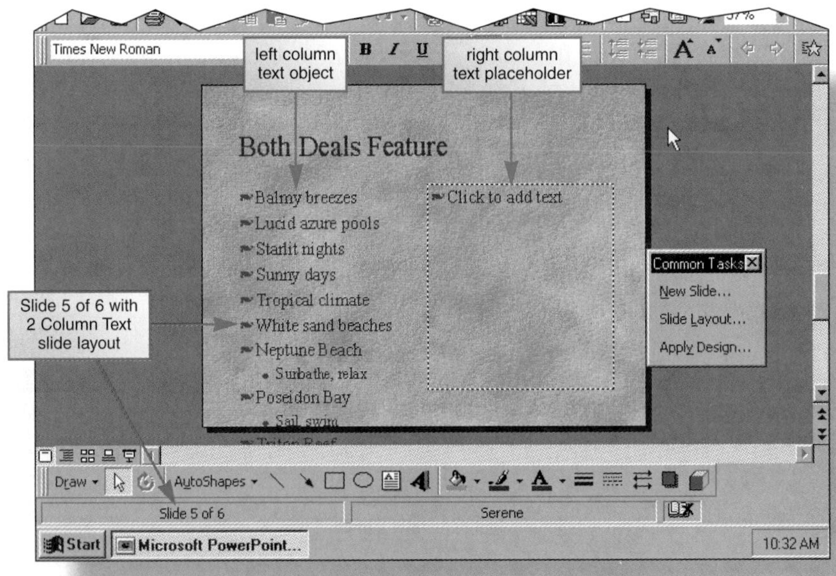

FIGURE 2-27

OtherWays

1. On Common Tasks toolbar click Slide Layout, double-click desired slide layout
2. On Format menu click Slide Layout, double-click desired slide layout
3. Press ALT+L, press arrow keys to select desired slide layout, press ENTER
4. Press ALT+O, press L, press arrow keys to select desired slide layout, press ENTER

The text in the left column of Slide 5 is too lengthy to fit into the text object. The next section explains how to move the text at the bottom of the left column to the top of the right column text placeholder.

Moving Text

Because the bulleted list on Slide 5 contains more paragraphs than will fit in the left column text object, select a portion of the list and move it to the right column text placeholder. Perform the following steps to select a portion of the text in the left column and then move it to the right column.

To Move Text

1 **Position the I-beam mouse pointer immediately to the left of the N in Neptune. Drag to the right and down so that the last six bulleted paragraphs are selected. If necessary, click the vertical scroll bar down arrow to display all the bulleted items.**

The six bulleted paragraphs, Neptune Beach, Sunbathe, relax; Poseidon Bay, Sail, swim; and Triton Reef, Scuba dive, snorkel are selected (Figure 2-28).

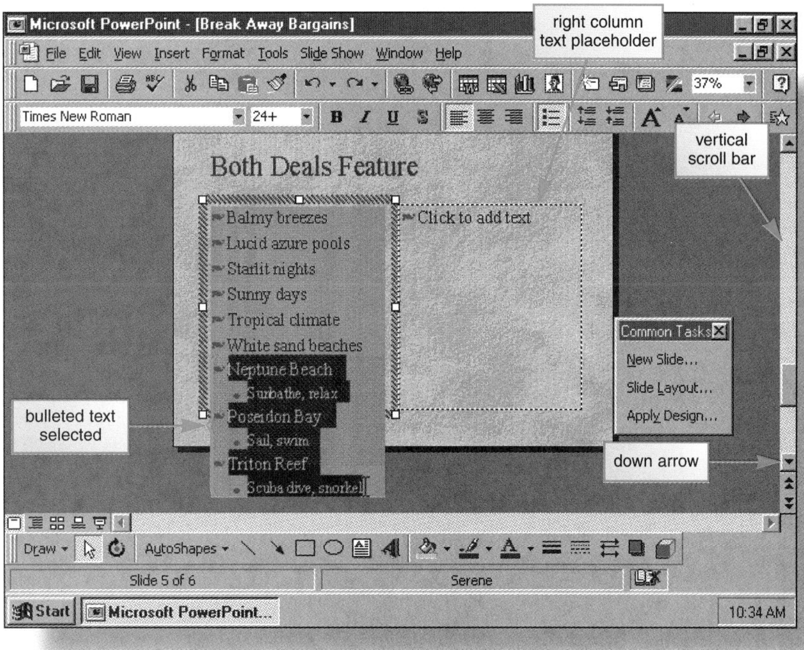

FIGURE 2-28

2 **Point to the selected text. If the mouse pointer displays as a four-headed arrow, move the mouse pointer to the right of the bullets so that it is positioned over the text. Then drag the selected text to the right column text placeholder.**

As you drag the text, the mouse pointer displays as a block arrow with a small dotted box around the arrow shaft. The six selected paragraphs are moved to the right column text placeholder (Figure 2-29). When you insert text into a text placeholder, it becomes a text object.

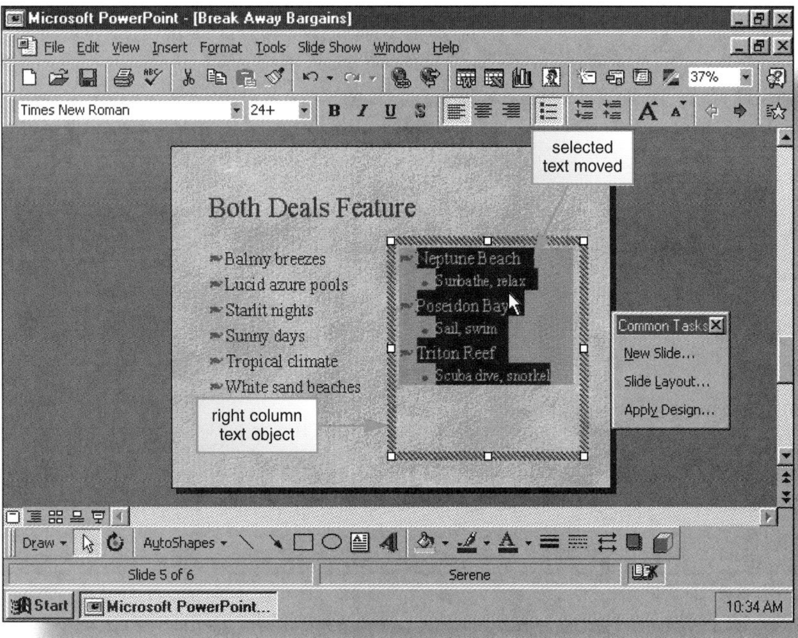

FIGURE 2-29

Other Ways

1. Right-click selected text, click Cut, right-click new text location, click Paste
2. Select text, click Cut button, click new text location, click Paste button

Because Slide 5 contains two bulleted text objects, it now complies with the default Style Checker design rules of no more than six bullets per object.

Adding Clip Art to a Slide

Clip art offers a quick way to add professional-looking graphic images to your presentation without creating the images yourself. One clip art source is the Microsoft Clip Gallery 3.0. **Microsoft Clip Gallery 3.0** is a tool that accompanies Microsoft Office 97 that allows you to insert clip art, pictures, audio clips, and video clips to a presentation. It contains a wide variety of clip art images and is shared with other Microsoft Office applications. Microsoft Clip Gallery 3.0 combines topic-related clip art images into categories, such as Animals, Household, and People at Work.

Table 2-2 gives you an idea of the organization of Microsoft Clip Gallery 3.0 that accompanies PowerPoint. The table contains four of the categories from Microsoft Clip Gallery 3.0 and keywords of the clip art contained therein. Clip art images have one or more keywords that associate an image with various entities, activities, labels, and emotions. In most instances, the keyword does not contain the name of the physical object. For example, an image of a magnifying glass in the Academic category has keywords of Focus Investigation Identify Small. As a result, you may find it necessary to scroll through several categories to find an appropriate picture.

Table 2-2

CATEGORY	*CLIP ART KEYWORDS*
Academic	**Reward Accomplishment, Reward Accomplishment Milestone Guarantee, Focus Investigation Identify Small, Leadership Information Test Communication Listen Dictate**
Cartoons	**Anger Demanding, Stress Frustration Anger Chaos, Reward Agreeable, Success Victory Accomplishment Result Invincible Milestone Superior**
Gestures	**Success Impress, Harmony Trust Compromise Consensus Guarantee Synergy, Trust Protect, Success Invincible, Failure**
Transportation	**Performance Fast Sports Car, War Battle Powerful Battleship Navigate, Performance Fast War Battle Plane, Performance Ship Navigate, Priority Traffic Light**

Depending on the installation of Microsoft Clip Gallery 3.0 on your computer, you may not have the clip art pictures used in this project. Contact your instructor if you are missing clip art when you perform the following steps.

Using AutoLayouts to Add Clip Art

PowerPoint simplifies adding clip art to a slide by providing AutoLayouts designed specifically for clip art. Recall from Project 1 that an AutoLayout is a collection of placeholders for the title, text, clip art, graphs, tables, and media clips. A clip art placeholder contains instructions to open Microsoft Clip Gallery 3.0. Double-clicking the clip art placeholder activates the instructions. When you use an AutoLayout placeholder to add an object to a slide, such as clip art, PowerPoint automatically sizes the object to fit the placeholder. If the object is in landscape orientation, PowerPoint sizes it to the width of the placeholder. If the object is in portrait orientation, PowerPoint sizes it to the height of the placeholder.

Adding clip art to Slide 6 requires two steps. First, change the slide layout to Clip Art & Text. Then insert clip art into the clip art placeholder. The next two sections explain how to add clip art into an AutoLayout placeholder.

More *About* **Clip Art**

Humor and interest are just two of several reasons to add clip art to your presentation. People have limited attention spans. A carefully placed humorous clip art image can spark attention and interest. When interest is high, it greatly increases the chance that your concept or idea will be remembered.

Changing Slide Layout to Clip Art & Text

Before you insert clip art into an AutoLayout placeholder, you first must select one of the slide layouts that includes a clip art placeholder. The clip art placeholder on the left side of Slide 6 will hold clip art. Perform the following steps to change the slide layout to Clip Art & Text.

Steps To Change the Slide Layout to Clip Art & Text

1 **Drag the scroll box on the vertical scroll bar to display Slide 6 (Figure 2-30).**

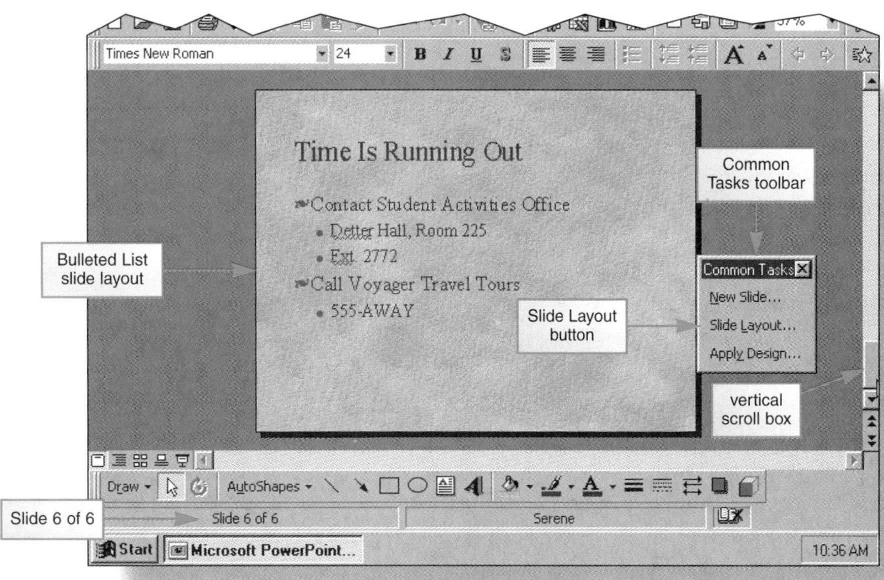

FIGURE 2-30

2 **Click the Slide Layout button on the Common Tasks toolbar. When the Slide Layout dialog box displays, click the Clip Art & Text slide layout located in row three, column two. Then point to the Apply button.**

The Clip Art & Text slide layout is selected in the Slide Layout dialog box (Figure 2-31).

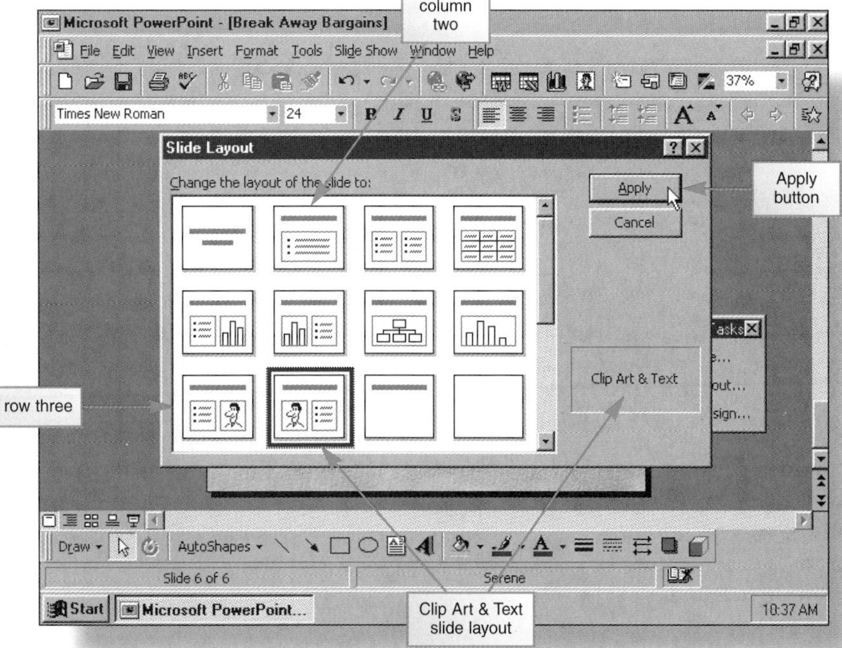

FIGURE 2-31

3 Click the Apply button.

Slide 6 displays the Clip Art & Text slide layout (Figure 2-32). PowerPoint moves the text object and automatically resizes the text to fit the object.

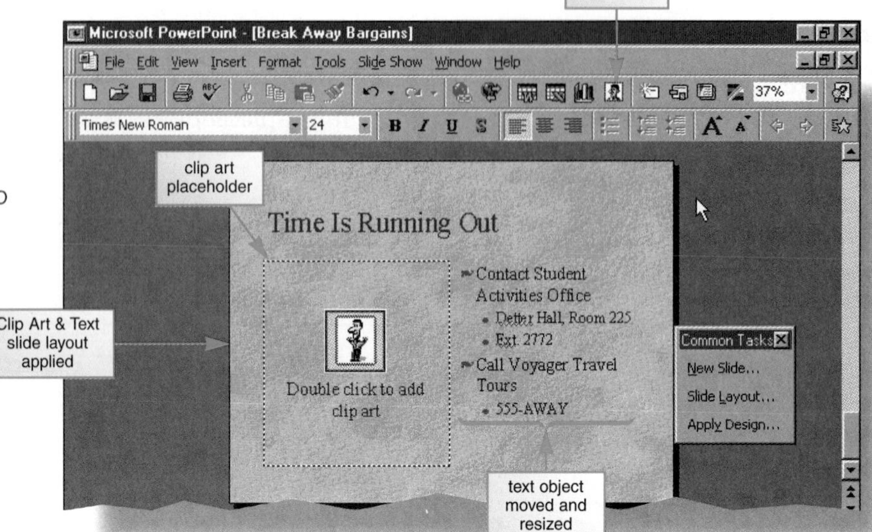

FIGURE 2-32

Other Ways

1. Right-click slide anywhere except text or object placeholders, click Slide Layout, double-click Clip Art & Text slide layout
2. Press ALT+L, press arrow keys to select Clip Art & Text slide layout, press ENTER
3. Press ALT+O, press L, press arrow keys to select Clip Art & Text slide layout, press ENTER

You can use an AutoLayout placeholder to insert clip art even if the AutoLayout does not have a clip art placeholder. For example, to insert clip art into the object placeholder of the Object AutoLayout, click the placeholder to select it, click the Insert Clip Art button on the Standard toolbar, and then select a clip art picture.

Inserting Clip Art into a Clip Art Placeholder

Now that the Clip Art & Text placeholder is applied to Slide 6, you insert clip art into the clip art placeholder. Perform the following steps to insert clip art to the clip art placeholder on Slide 6.

Steps To Insert Clip Art into a Clip Art Placeholder

1 Position the mouse pointer anywhere within the clip art placeholder.

The mouse pointer is positioned inside the clip art placeholder (Figure 2-33). The mouse pointer becomes a four-headed arrow. It is not necessary to point to the picture inside the placeholder.

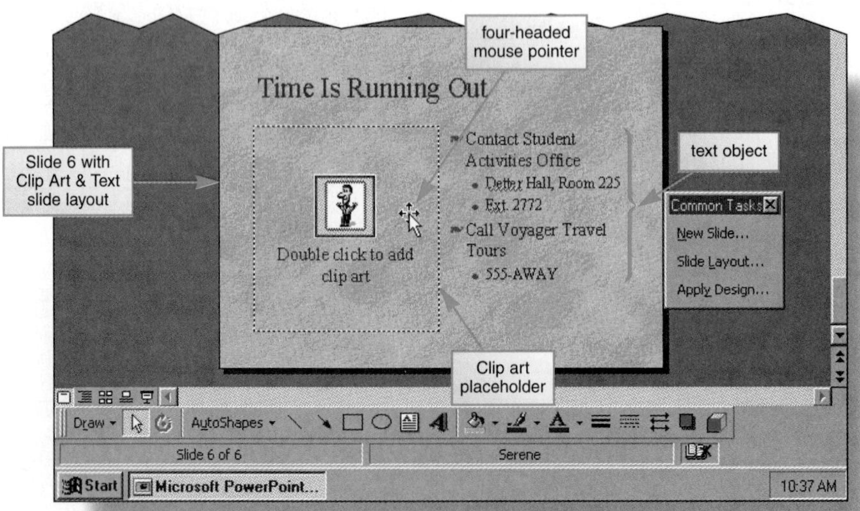

FIGURE 2-33

2 **Double-click the clip art placeholder on the left side of Slide 6.**

PowerPoint displays the Microsoft Clip Gallery 3.0 dialog box (Figure 2-34). The Clip Art list box displays clip art images by category. When you open Microsoft Clip Gallery 3.0, All Categories is the selected category on the Clip Art sheet. The selected clip art image in this figure is a diploma. Your selected image may be different depending on the clip art installed on your computer.

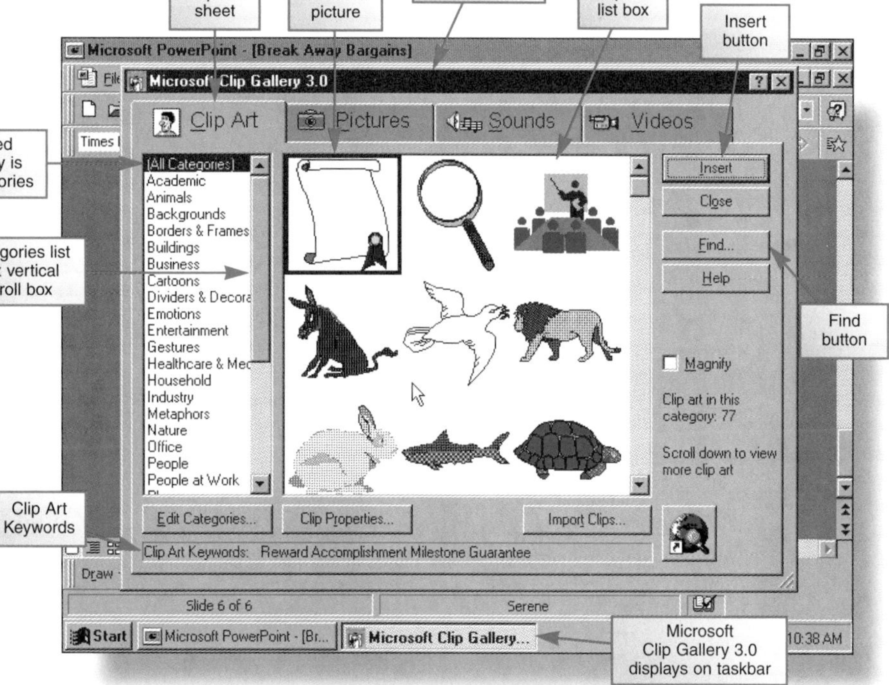

FIGURE 2-34

3 **Click the Find button.**

The Find Clip dialog box displays three boxes in which you enter clip art search criteria (Figure 2-35). The Keywords text box is selected and contains the keyword, All Keywords. Use the Keywords text box to find clip art when you know one of the words associated with the clip art image. Use the File name containing text box when you know the name of the file containing the desired clip art image. Use the Clip type list box when you want to find clip art saved in a specific format.

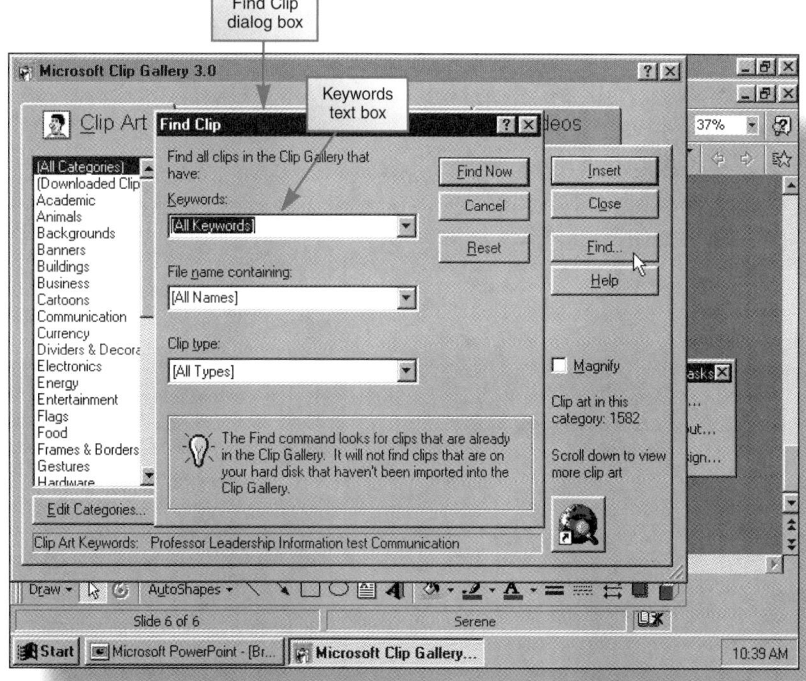

FIGURE 2-35

4 **Type** `time` **in the Keywords text box and point to the Find Now button.**

The Keywords text box contains time (Figure 2-36). You do not need to type the full keyword because the Find feature of Microsoft Clip Gallery 3.0 searches for all pictures containing the consecutive letters typed in the Keywords text box. The Find Now button initiates the clip art search. The Reset button resets the Keywords, File name containing, and Clip type boxes. Click the Reset button when you wish to begin a new search.

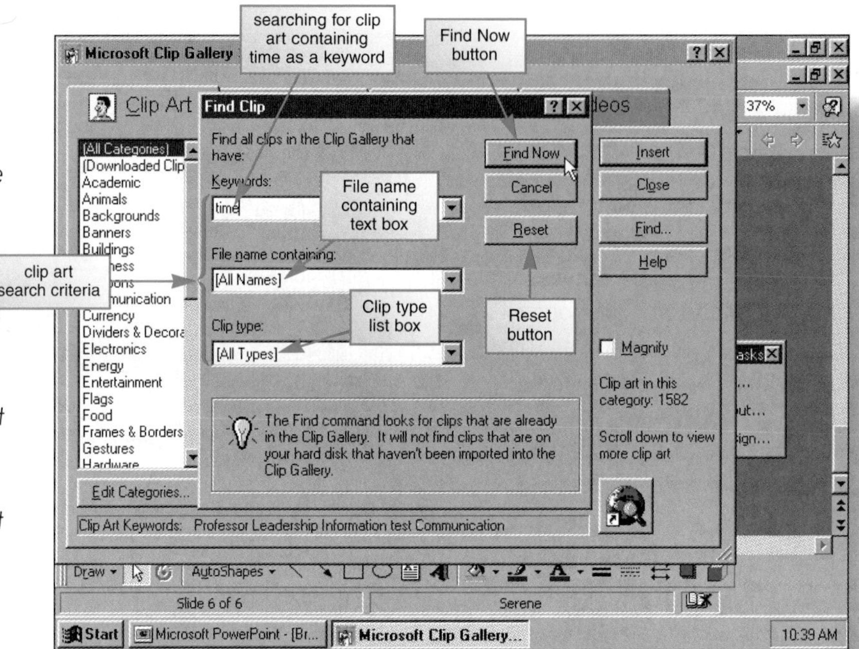

FIGURE 2-36

5 **Click the Find Now button. If necessary, scroll to display the clip art with the keywords, Timeline Schedule Clock Wait Procrastinate. Click the clock clip art to select it.**

The Microsoft Clip Gallery searches for all pictures that contain time in the keywords. All pictures that contain the keyword display in the Pictures box (Figure 2-37). The picture of a clock is selected. The selected category changes to Results of Last Find. Timeline Schedule Clock Wait Procrastinate displays at the bottom of the Microsoft Clip Gallery 3.0 dialog box as the keywords of the selected picture. Your selected picture may be different depending on the clip art installed on your computer.

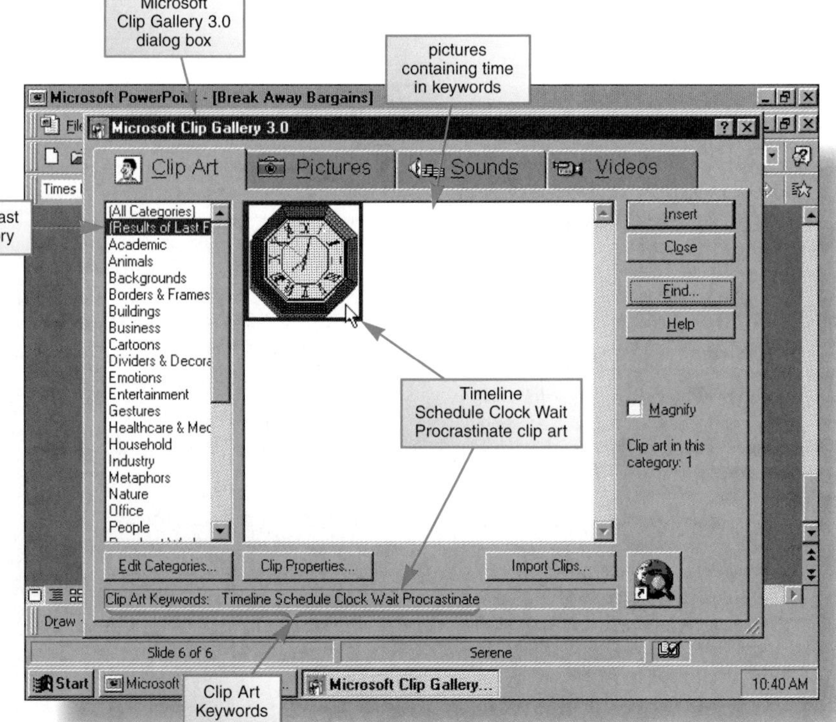

FIGURE 2-37

Click the Insert button.

The selected picture is inserted into the clip art placeholder on Slide 6 (Figure 2-38). PowerPoint automatically sizes the picture to best fit the placeholder. In this instance, the picture is taller than it is wide (portrait orientation), so PowerPoint sizes the picture to fit the height of the placeholder. When a picture is in landscape orientation, PowerPoint sizes the picture to fit the width of the placeholder.

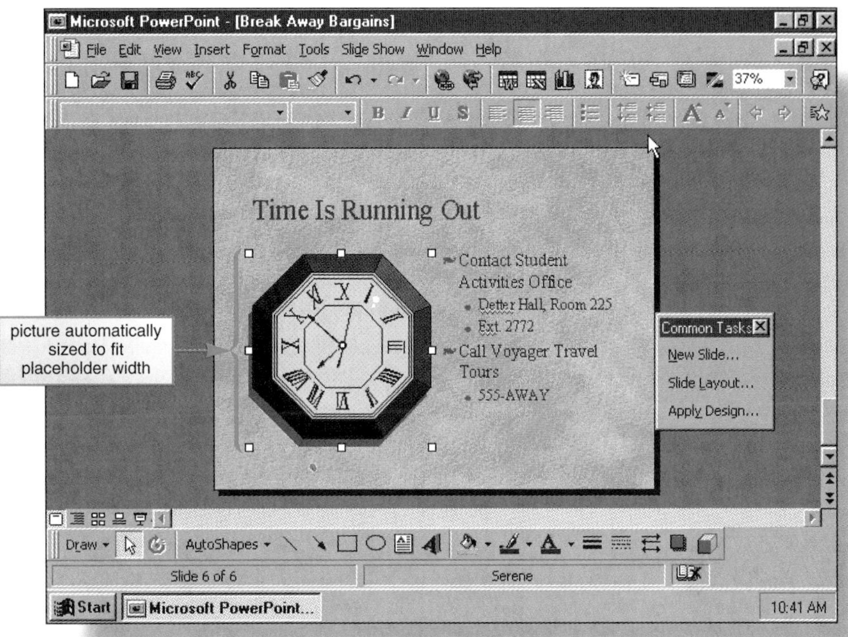

FIGURE 2-38

In addition to the clip art images in Microsoft Clip Gallery 3.0, other sources for clip art include retailers specializing in computer software, the Internet, bulletin board systems, and online information systems. Some popular online information systems are The Microsoft Network, America Online, CompuServe, and Prodigy. A **bulletin board system** is a computer system that allows users to communicate with each other and share files. Microsoft has created a special page on their World Wide Web site where you can add new clips to the Clip Gallery.

Besides clip art, you can insert pictures into your presentation. These may include scanned photographs, line art, and artwork from compact discs. To insert a picture into a presentation, the picture must be saved in a format that PowerPoint can recognize. Table 2-3 identifies some of the formats PowerPoint recognizes.

PowerPoint converts pictures saved in the formats listed in Table 2-3 by using filters. These filters are shipped with the PowerPoint installation software and must be installed before PowerPoint can properly convert files.

Table 2-3

FORMAT	*FILE EXTENSION*
AutoCAD Format 2-D	***.dxf**
Computer Graphics Metafile	***.cgm**
CorelDRAW	***.cdr**
Encapsulated PostScript	***.eps**
Graphics Interchange Format	***.gif**
JPEG File Interchange Format	***.jpg**
Kodak Photo CD	***.pcd**
Macintosh PICT	***.pct**
Micrografx Designer/Draw	***.drw**
PC Paintbrush	***.pcx**
Portable Network Graphics	***.png**
Tagged Image File Format	***.tif**
Targa	***.tga**
Windows Bitmaps	***.bmp, .rle, .dib**
Windows Enhanced Metafile	***.emf**
Windows Metafile	***.wmf**
WordPerfect Graphics	***.wpg**

More About Clip Art

Clip art serves a purpose in a presentation – it conveys a message. Clip art should contribute to the understandability of the slide. It should not be used decoratively. Before adding clip art to a presentation, ask yourself: "Does the clip art convey a message or support the slide topic?" If the answer is yes, put the clip art on the slide.

Inserting Clip Art on a Slide without a Clip Art Placeholder

PowerPoint does not require you to use an AutoLayout containing a clip art placeholder to add clip art to a slide. You can insert clip art on any slide regardless of its slide layout. On Slide 3, you are adding a picture of a sailboat to illustrate the type of sailing vessel used in The Stargazer vacation package. Recall that the slide layout on Slide 3 is the Bulleted List slide layout. Because the Bulleted List AutoLayout does not contain a clip art placeholder, you click the Insert Clip Art button on the Standard toolbar to start Microsoft Clip Gallery 3.0. The picture for which you are searching is a sailing ship. Its keywords are Performance Ship Navigate. Perform the following steps to insert the picture of a ship on a slide that does not have a clip art placeholder.

TO INSERT CLIP ART ON A SLIDE WITHOUT A CLIP ART PLACEHOLDER

Step 1: Drag the scroll box on the vertical scroll bar until Slide 3, titled The Stargazer, displays in the slide indicator.

Step 2: Click the Insert Clip Art button on the Standard toolbar (Figure 2-32 on page PP 2.28).

Step 3: Click the Find button. When the Find Clip dialog box displays, type `navigate` in the Keywords text box. Click the Find Now button.

Step 4: If necessary, when the Microsoft Clip Gallery 3.0 dialog box displays the results, click the down arrow on the Pictures box scroll bar until the sailboat displays. If the sailboat is not installed on your computer, see your instructor for an appropriate replacement picture.

Step 5: Double-click the picture of the sailboat that has the keywords Performance Ship Navigate.

The sailboat displays on Slide 3 (Figure 2-39). A selection box indicates the clip art is selected.

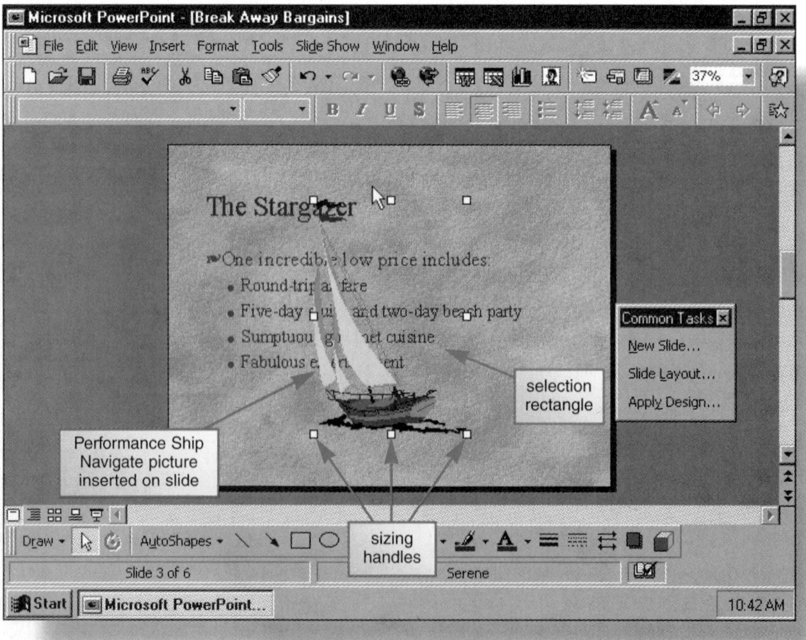

FIGURE 2-39

Moving Clip Art

More About Clip Art

When used appropriately, clip art reduces misconceptions. If a presentation consists of words alone, the audience creates its own mental picture. The mental picture created may be different from the concept you are trying to convey. The audience better understands the concept when a graphic is included.

After you insert clip art on a slide, you may want to reposition it. The picture of the sailboat on Slide 3 overlays the bulleted list. Moving the picture to the lower-right corner of the slide places the sailboat away from the text. Because you want to align the sailboat mast under the letter b in the word beach on the second heading level 2, you first move the picture and then change its size. You change the size of the sailboat later in this project. Perform the steps below to move the sailboat to the lower-right corner of the slide.

To Move Clip Art

1. **If the picture of the sailboat is not already selected, use the mouse pointer to point to the sailboat and then click.**

2. **Press and hold down the left mouse button. Drag the picture of the sailboat past the bottom of the slide and then to the right until the top-left corner of the dotted box aligns below the b in beach. Release the left mouse button.**

   When you drag an object, a dotted box displays. The dotted box indicates the new position of the object. When you release the left mouse button, the picture of the sailboat displays in the new location (Figure 2-40). Sizing handles appear at the corners and along the edges of the selection box.

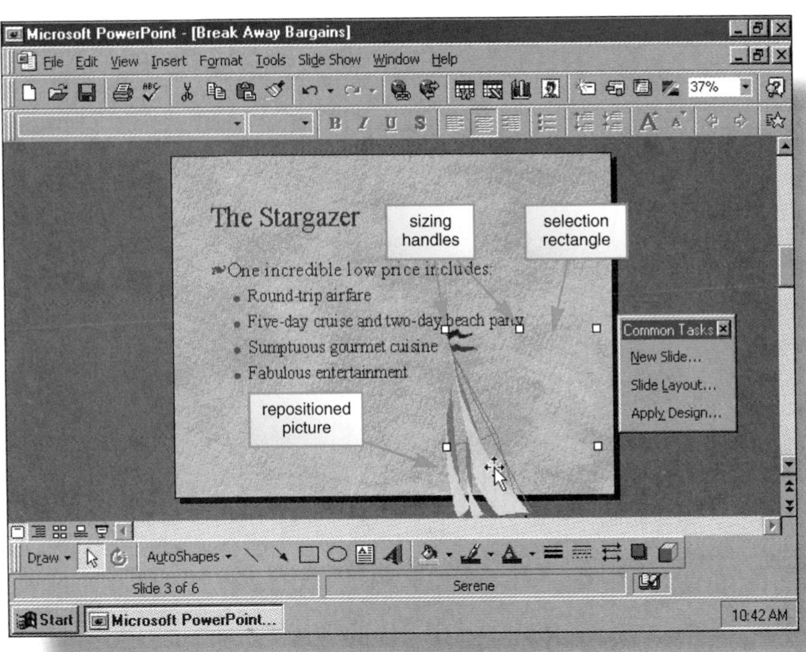

FIGURE 2-40

Other Ways

1. Select clip art, press arrow keys to move to new position

Changing the Size of Clip Art

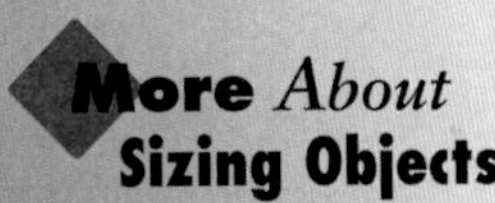

More About Sizing Objects

The Preview button in the Format Picture dialog box allows you to check the object's new size without applying it. When you want to make an object bigger, increase the number in the Height box or the Width box. To make an object smaller, decrease the number.

Sometimes it is necessary to change the size of clip art. For example, on Slide 3, the sailboat displays off the slide. In order to make the picture fit onto the slide, you reduce its size. To change the size of a clip art picture by an exact percentage, use the **Format Picture command**. The Format Picture dialog box contains five sheets with several options for formatting a picture. The **Size sheet** contains options for changing the size of a picture. You either enter the exact height and width in the Size and rotate area, or enter the height and width as a percentage of the original picture in the Scale area. When the **Lock aspect ratio check box** displays a check mark, the height and width settings change to maintain the aspect ratio of the original picture. **Aspect ratio** is the relationship between the height and width of an object. For example, a picture 3 inches high by 5 inches wide scaled to fifty percent would become 1½ inches high by 2½ inches wide. Perform the following steps to reduce the size of the sailboat.

To Change the Size of Clip Art

1 **Right-click the sailboat picture. When the shortcut menu displays, point to Format Picture (Figure 2-41).**

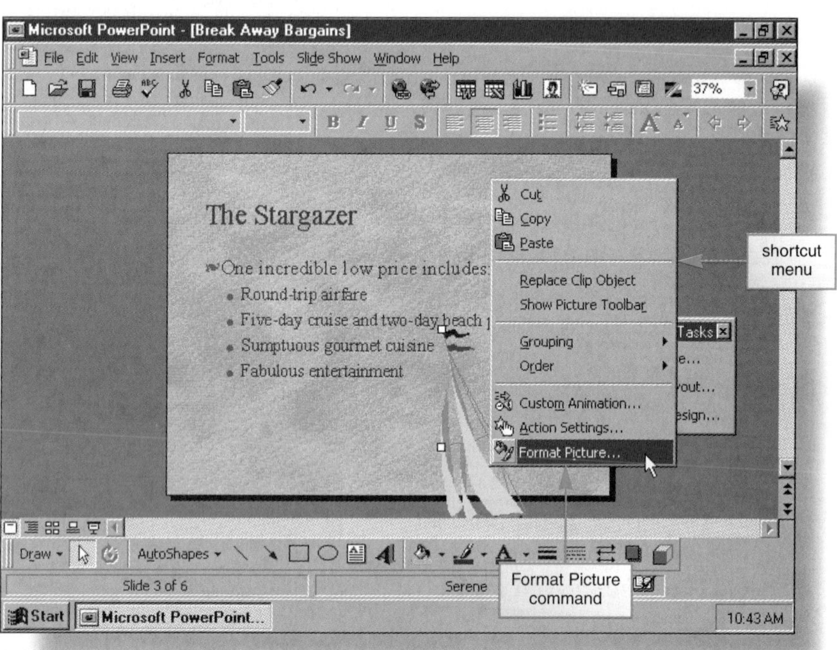

FIGURE 2-41

2 **Click Format Picture. If necessary, when the Format Picture dialog box displays, click the Size tab.**

The Format Picture dialog box displays the Size sheet (Figure 2-42). The Height and Width text boxes in the Scale area display the current percentage of the sailboat picture, 100. Check marks display in the Lock aspect ratio and Relative to original picture size check boxes.

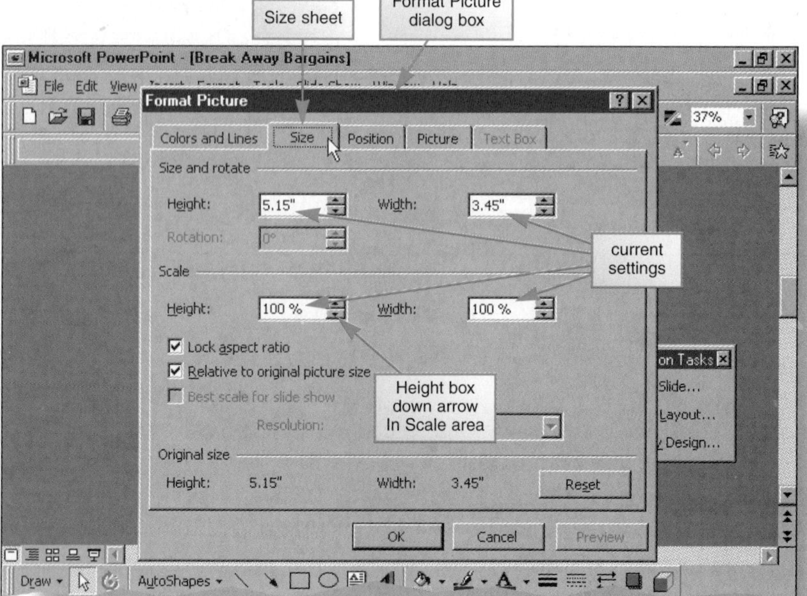

FIGURE 2-42

3 Click the Height box down arrow in the Scale area until 70 displays. Then point to the OK button.

Both the Height and Width text boxes in the Scale area display 70% (Figure 2-43). PowerPoint automatically changes the Height and Width text boxes in the Size and rotate area to reflect changes in the Scale area.

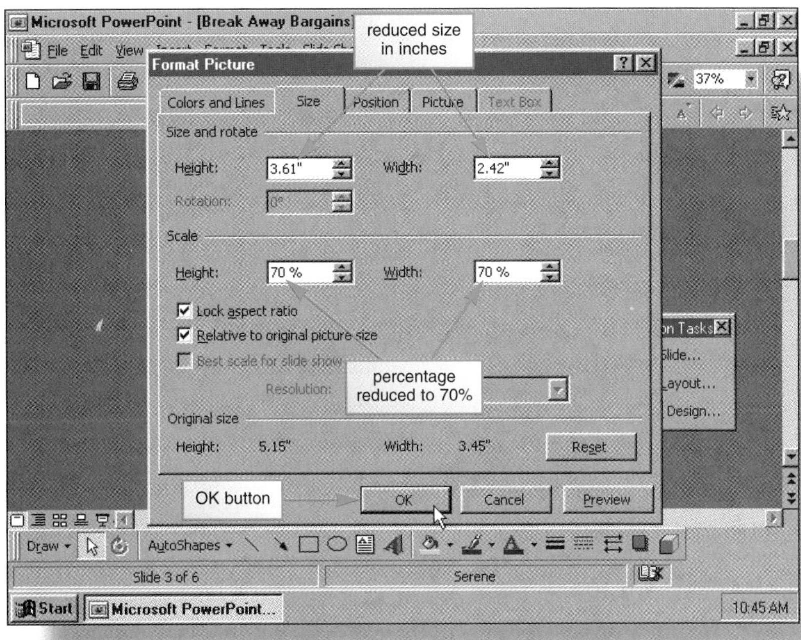

FIGURE 2-43

4 Click the OK button.

PowerPoint displays the reduced sailboat picture and closes the Format Picture dialog box (Figure 2-44).

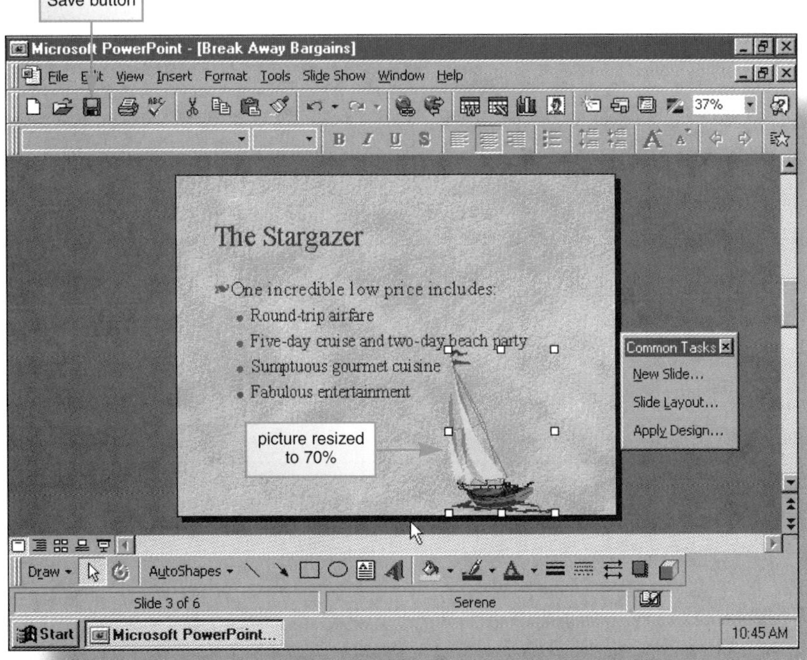

FIGURE 2-44

*Other*Ways

1. Click clip art object, on Format menu click Picture, click Size tab, click Height box up or down arrows in Scale area, click OK
2. Press ALT+O, press I, press arrow keys to select Size tab, press TAB to select Height text box in Scale area, press up or down arrow keys to increase or decrease size, press ENTER

More About Headers and Footers

Consider placing footers on slides that are used for making overhead transparencies. A slide number and presentation name help keep the presentation organized. The slide number can be a great time saver in the event you drop your transparencies.

Saving the Presentation Again

To preserve the work completed this far, save the presentation again.

TO SAVE A PRESENTATION

Step 1: Click the Save button on the Standard toolbar.

The changes made to the presentation after the previous save are saved to a floppy disk.

A default setting in PowerPoint allows for **fast saves**, which saves only the changes made since the last time you saved. If you want to **full save** a copy of the complete presentation, on the menu bar click Tools, click Options on the Tools menu, click the Save tab and then remove the check mark in the Allow fast saves check box by clicking the check box. Then click the OK button.

Adding a Header and Footer to Outline Pages

A printout of the presentation outline often is used as an audience handout. Distributing a copy of the outline provides the audience with paper on which to write notes or comments. Another benefit of distributing a copy of the outline is to help the audience see the text on the slides when lighting is poor or the room is too large. To help identify the source of the printed outline, add a descriptive header and footer.

Using the Notes and Handouts Sheet to Add Headers and Footers

Add headers and footers to outline pages by clicking the Notes and Handouts sheet in the Header and Footer dialog box and entering the information you wish to print. Perform the following steps to add the current date, a header, the page number, and a footer to the printed outline.

To Use the Notes and Handouts Sheet to Add Headers and Footers

1 Click View on the menu bar. Point to Header and Footer (Figure 2-45).

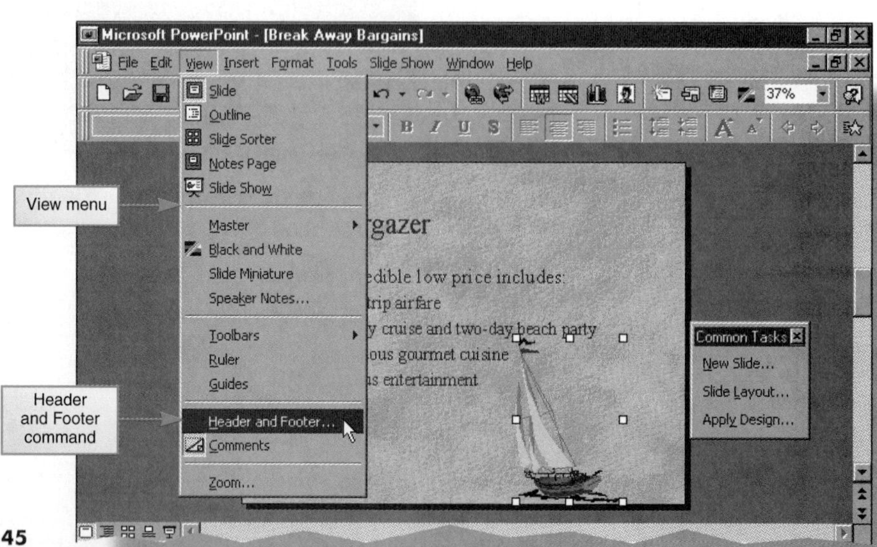

FIGURE 2-45

2 **Click Header and Footer. If necessary, click the Notes and Handouts tab.**

The Header and Footer dialog box displays the Notes and Handouts sheet (Figure 2-46). Check marks display in the Date and time, Header, Page number, and Footer check boxes. The Fixed option button is selected.

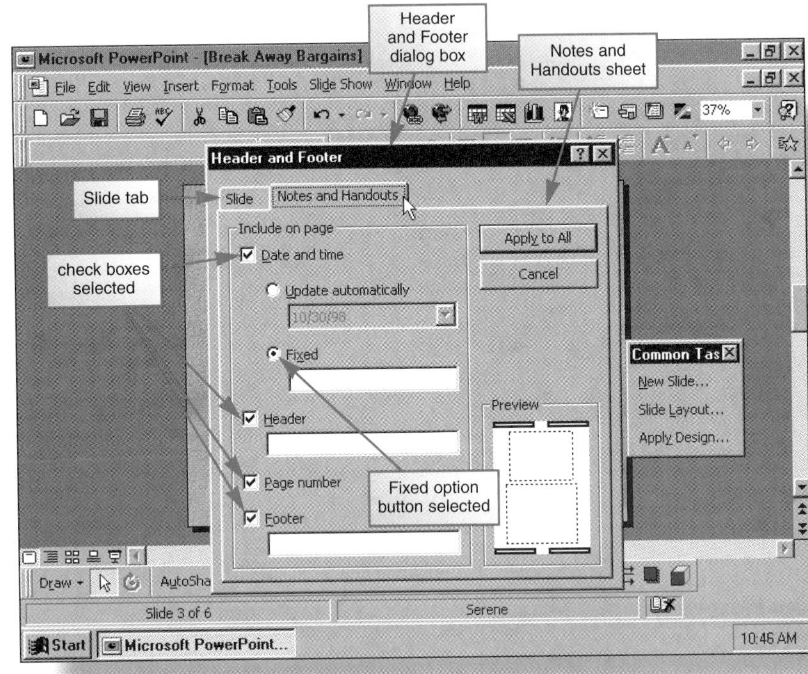

FIGURE 2-46

3 **Click the Update automatically option button. Click the Header text box. Type** `Break Away Bargains` **in the Header text box. Type** `Voyager Travel Tours` **in the Footer text box. Then point to the Apply to All button (Figure 2-47).**

4 **Click the Apply to All button.**

PowerPoint applies the header and footer text to the outline, closes the Header and Footer dialog box, and displays Slide 3. You cannot see header and footer text until you print the outline.

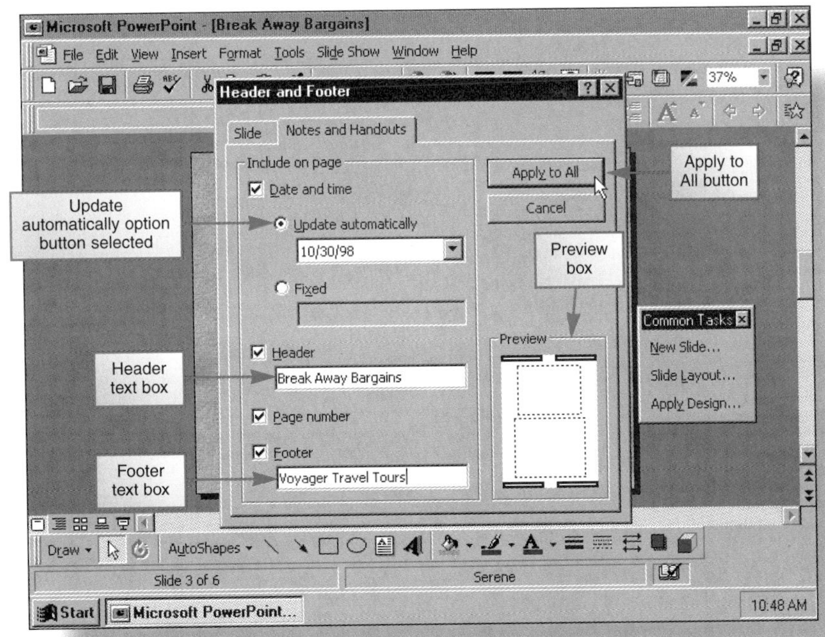

FIGURE 2-47

Checking the Presentation for Spelling and Style Errors

Now that the individual slide changes have been made, you should run Style Checker to identify errors in your presentation. Recall from Project 1 that Style Checker identifies possible errors in spelling, visual clarity, case, and end punctuation. Perform the following steps to run Style Checker.

TO RUN STYLE CHECKER

Step 1: Click Tools on the menu bar.
Step 2: Click Style Checker.
Step 3: When the Style Checker dialog box displays, click the Case and end punctuation check box.
Step 4: Click the Start button.
Step 5: Correct spelling errors and ignore correct spellings of words not located in the standard dictionary.
Step 6: If Style Checker lists visual clarity inconsistencies in the Style Checker Summary dialog box, write the slide number and the message on a sheet of paper.
Step 7: When the Microsoft PowerPoint dialog box displays, press the OK button.

PowerPoint closes Style Checker and displays the slide containing the last word not in the dictionaries, Slide 6 (Figure 2-48). Ext., the abbreviation for extension, is not found in the standard dictionary and therefore displays highlighted.

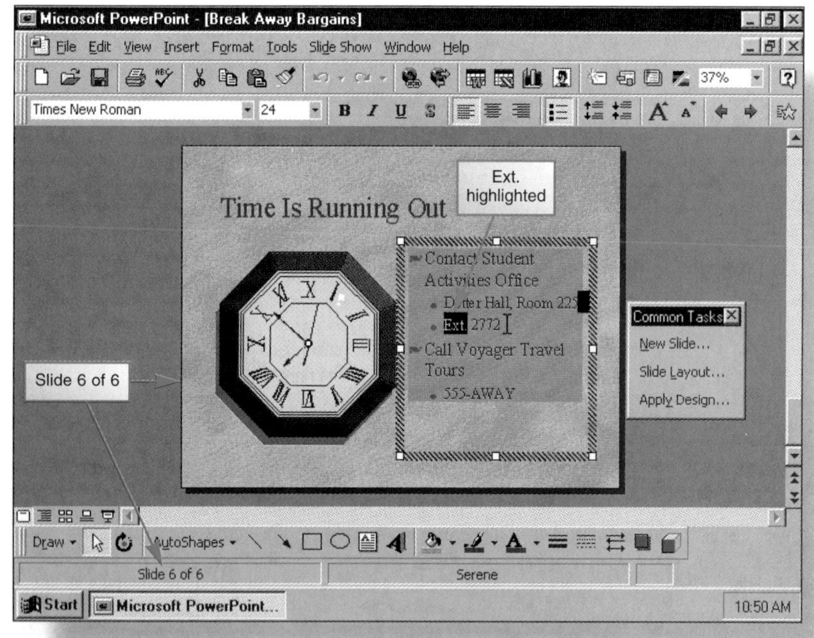

FIGURE 2-48

This presentation contains no visual clarity inconsistencies. If Style Checker identifies visual clarity inconsistencies, review the steps for correcting the identified slide. Then make the appropriate corrections. For more information about Style Checker, see page PP 1.41 in Project 1.

ore *About* **Animation**

To keep your audience from reading ahead while making a point related to the current item on your slide, use animation effects to build the slide.

Adding Animation Effects

PowerPoint provides many animation effects to make your slide show presentation look professional. In this project you use slide transition and custom animation. **Slide transition effects** define special effects for progressing from one slide to the next in a slide show. **Custom animation effects** define animation, sound effects, and timing for objects on a slide. The following pages discuss each of these animation effects in detail.

Adding Slide Transitions to a Slide Show

PowerPoint allows you to control the way you advance from one slide to the next by adding slide transitions to an on-screen slide show. Slide transitions are visual effects that display when you move one slide off the screen and bring the next one on. PowerPoint has 46 different slide transitions. The name of the slide transition characterizes the visual effect that displays. For example, the slide transition effect, Split Vertical In, displays the next slide by covering the previous slide with two vertical boxes moving toward the center of the screen until the two boxes meet. The effect is similar to closing draw drapes over a window.

PowerPoint requires you to select at least one slide before applying slide transition effects. In this presentation, you apply slide transition effects to all slides except the title slide. Because Slide 6 already is selected, you must select Slides 2 through 5. The technique used to select more than one slide is the **SHIFT+click technique**. To perform the SHIFT+click technique, press and hold down the SHIFT key as you click each slide. After you click the slides to which you want to add animation effects, release the SHIFT key.

In the Break Away Bargains presentation, you wish to display the Box Out slide transition effect between slides. That is, all slides begin stacked on top of one another, like a deck of cards. As you click the mouse to view the next slide, the new slide enters the screen by starting at the center of the slide and exploding out toward the edges of the slide while maintaining a box shape. Perform the following steps to apply the Box Out slide transition effect to the Break Away Bargains presentation.

More About Slide Transition

Resist the temptation to use several slide transition effects within a presentation. Too many different slide transition effects will cause the audience to focus on the visual effects and not your topic. A general presentation design rule is to limit the number of slide transition effects to two.

Steps To Add Slide Transitions to a Slide Show

1 Click the Slide Sorter View button on the View Button Bar at the bottom of the Microsoft PowerPoint – [Break Away Bargains] screen.

PowerPoint displays the presentation in slide sorter view (Figure 2-49). Slide 6 is selected. Slide 6 currently does not have a slide transition effect as noted in the Slide Transition Effects list box on the Slide Sorter toolbar.

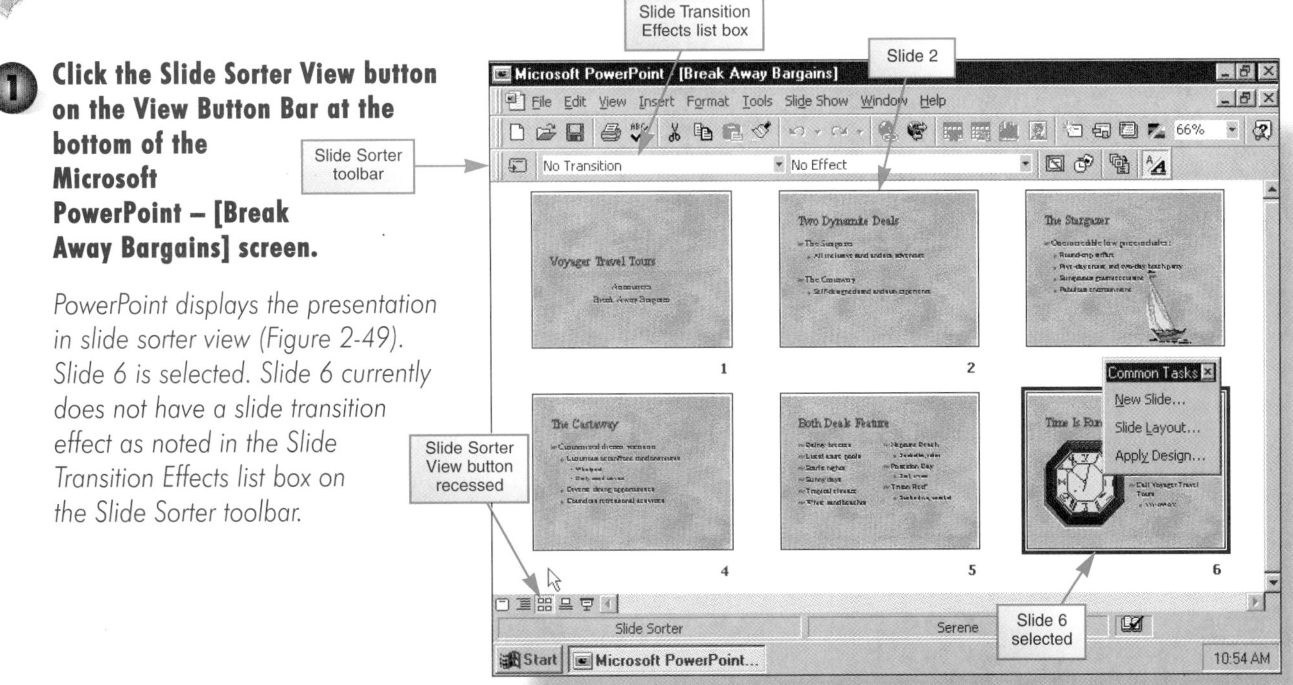

FIGURE 2-49

2 **Press and hold down the SHIFT key and click Slide 2, Slide 3, Slide 4, and Slide 5. Release the SHIFT key.**

Slides 2 through 6 are selected, as indicated by the heavy border around each slide (Figure 2-50).

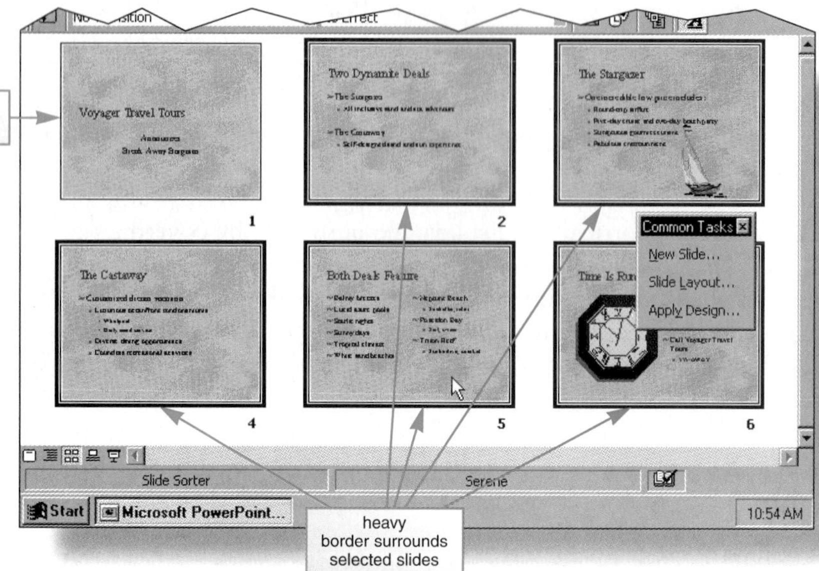

FIGURE 2-50

3 **Point to Slide 5 and right-click. When a shortcut menu displays, point to Slide Transition (Figure 2-51).**

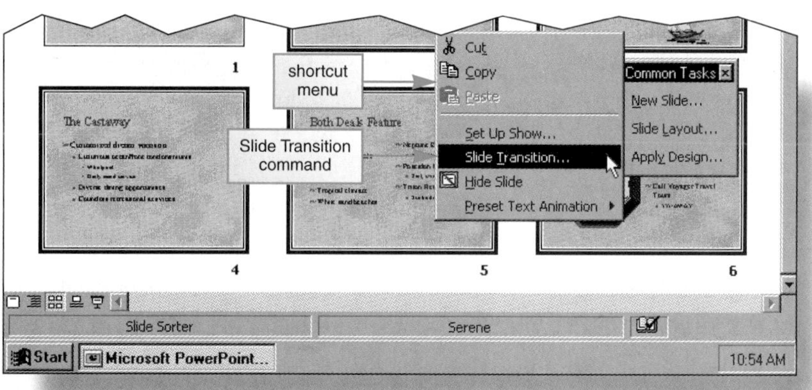

FIGURE 2-51

4 **Click Slide Transition. When the Slide Transition dialog box displays, click the Effect box arrow and point to Box Out.**

The Slide Transition dialog box displays (Figure 2-52). The Effect list displays available slide transition effects.

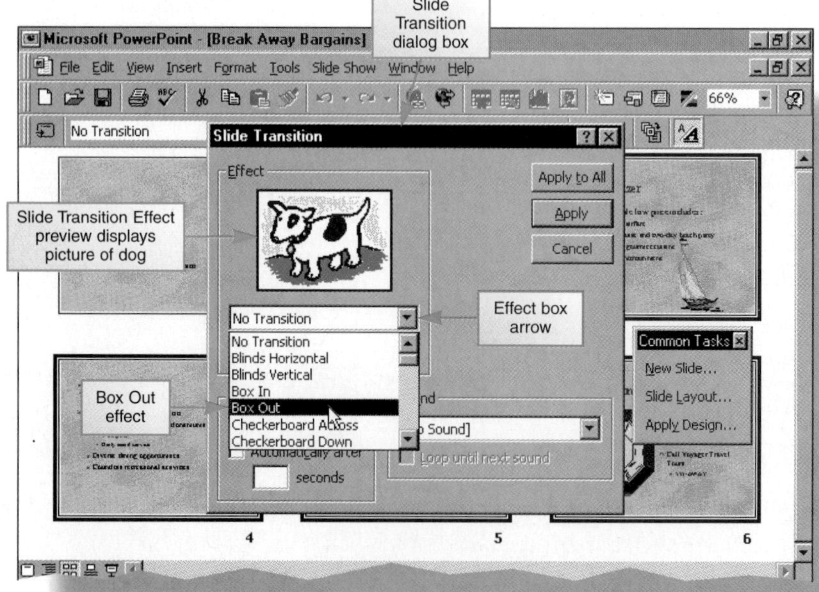

FIGURE 2-52

5 Click Box Out.

The Slide Transition Effect preview demonstrates the Box Out effect (Figure 2-53). To see the demonstration again, click the picture in the Slide Transition Effect preview.

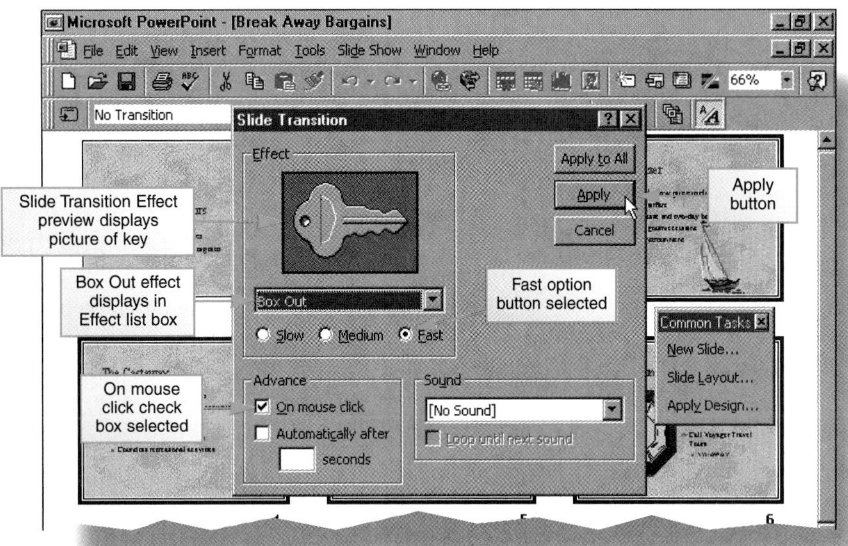

FIGURE 2-53

6 Click the Apply button.

PowerPoint displays the presentation in slide sorter view (Figure 2-54). A slide transition icon displays under each selected slide, which indicates that slide transition effects have been added to those slides. The current slide transition effect, Box Out, displays in the Slide Transition Effects box.

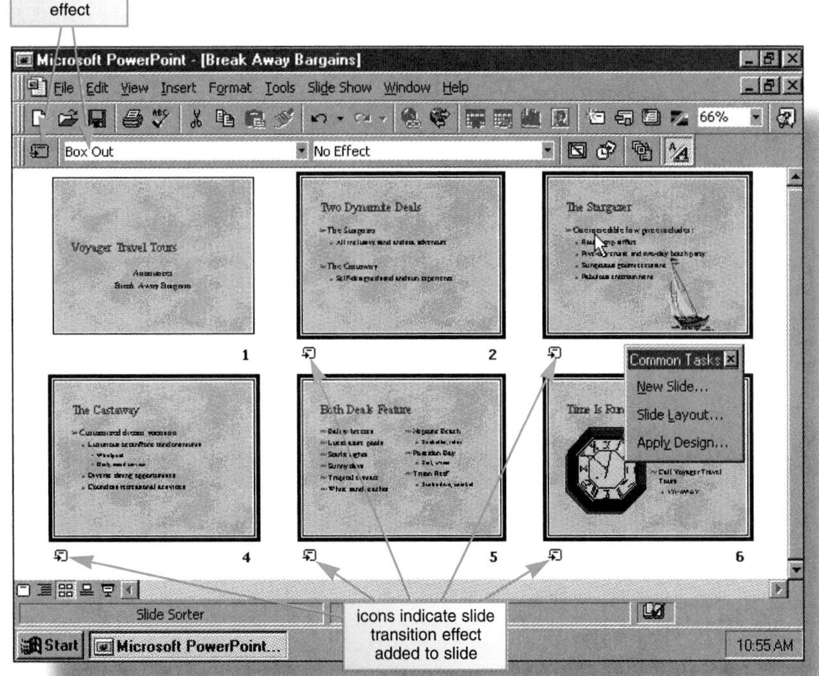

FIGURE 2-54

OtherWays

1. Select slides, right-click selected slide, click Slide Transition, click Effect box arrow, select slide transition effect, click Apply button
2. Select slides, on Slide Show menu click Slide Transition, click Effect box arrow, select slide transition effect, click Apply button

To apply slide transition effects to every slide in the presentation, select a slide, choose the desired slide transition effect and then click the Apply to All button in the Slide Transition dialog box.

To remove slide transition effects when displaying the presentation in slide sorter view, select the slides to which slide transition effects are applied, right-click one of the selected slides, click the Effect box arrow, select No Transition, and then click the Apply button.

Slide Sorter Toolbar

PowerPoint provides you with multiple methods for accomplishing most tasks. Generally, the fastest method is to right-click to display a shortcut menu. Another frequently used method is to click a toolbar button. For example, you can apply slide transition effects by clicking the Slide Transition Effects list box on the Slide Sorter toolbar.

The Slide Sorter toolbar displays only when you are in slide sorter view. It displays beneath the Standard toolbar, in place of the Formatting toolbar. The Slide Sorter toolbar contains tools to help you quickly add animation effects to your slide show. Table 2-4 explains the function of the buttons and boxes on the Slide Sorter toolbar.

Table 2-4

BUTTON/BOX	BUTTON/BOX NAME	FUNCTION
	Slide Transition	Displays the Slide Transition dialog box, which lists special effects used for slide changes during a slide show.
Box Out	Slide Transition Effects	Displays a list of slide transition effects. Selecting a slide transltion effect from the list applies it to the selected slide(s) and demonstrates it in the preview box.
	Text Preset Animation	Displays a list of text animation effects.
	Hide Slide	Excludes a slide from the presentation without deleting it.
	Rehearse Timings	Runs your slide show in rehearsal mode, in which you can set or change the timing of your electronic slide show.
	Summary Slide	Creates a bulleted list slide from the titles of the slides selected in slide sorter view or outline view, and then inserts that slide in front of the first selected slide.
	Show Formatting	Displays or hides character formatting attributes in outline view. In slide sorter view, switches between showing all text and graphics on each slide and displaying titles only.

More *About* **Custom Animation Effects**

The After animation list box contains eight colors and four commands controlling what happens after animation effects display. By default, Don't Dim is selected. To change the color of the previous bulleted text, click one of the eight listed colors from the applied design template. To display additional colors, click More Colors. To hide text as soon as its animation effect displays, click Hide after Animation. To hide text when you click the mouse, click Hide on Next Mouse click.

The Box Out slide transition effect has been applied to the presentation. The next step in creating this slide show is to add animation effects to individual slides.

Applying Animation Effects to Bulleted Slides

Animation effects can be applied to text as well as to objects, such as clip art. When you apply animation effects to bulleted text, you progressively disclose each bulleted paragraph. As a result, you build the slide, paragraph by paragraph during the running of a slide show to control the flow of information. PowerPoint has 55 custom animation effects and the capability to dim the paragraphs already displaying on the slide when the new paragraph is displayed.

The next step is to apply the Zoom In From Screen Center animation effect to Slides 2, 3, 4, 5, and 6 in the Break Away Bargains presentation. All slides, except the title slide will have the Zoom In From Screen Center animation effect. Recall from Project 1, that when you need to make a change that affects all slides, make the change to the slide master. Perform the following steps to apply animation effects to the bulleted paragraphs in this presentation.

More About Animating Objects

Used sparingly, animated objects add interest to a presentation. Overused animated objects are distracting and minimize the message of the presentation.

To Use the Slide Master to Apply Animation Effects to All Bulleted Slides

1 Press and hold down the SHIFT key and then click the Slide Master button on the View Button Bar.

The slide master displays. If necessary, drag the Master toolbar onto the screen as shown in Figure 2-55.

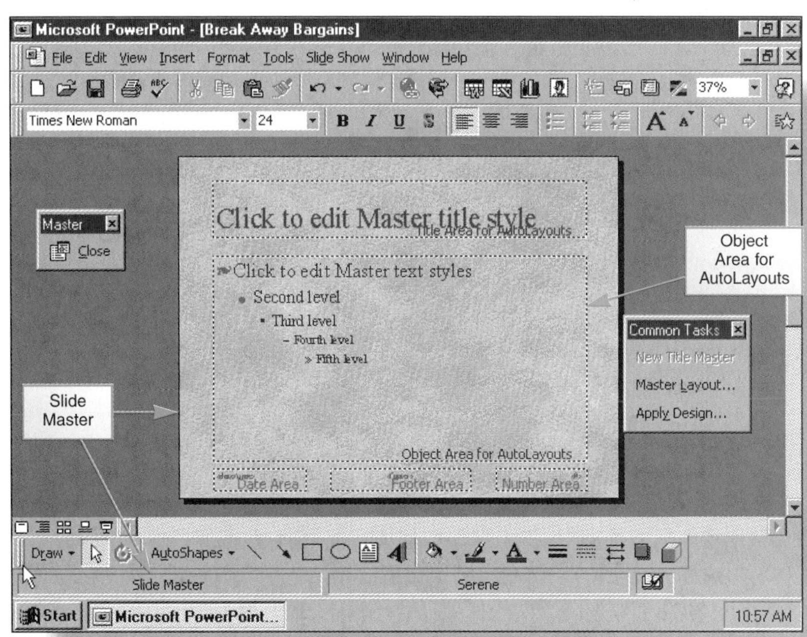

FIGURE 2-55

2 Right-click the slide master. When a shortcut menu displays, point to Custom Animation (Figure 2-56).

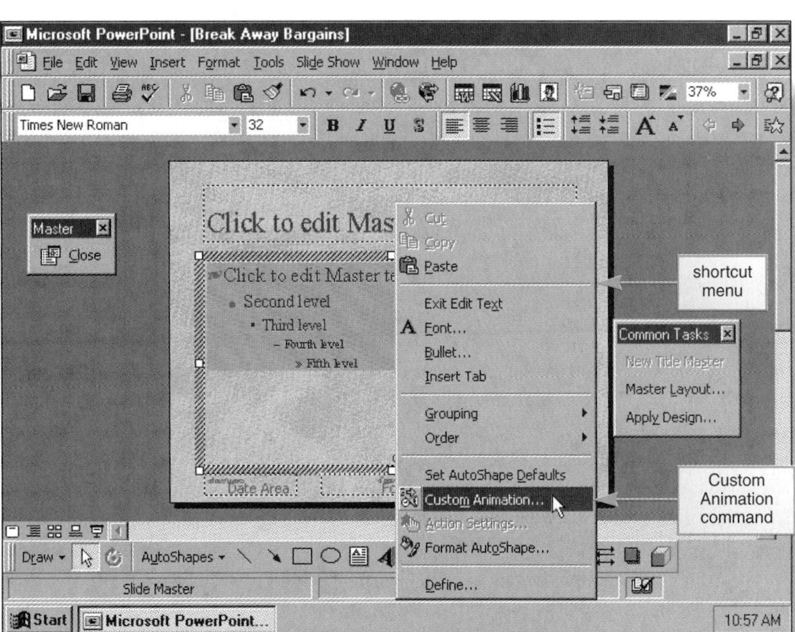

FIGURE 2-56

3 Click Custom Animation. If necessary, when the Custom Animation dialog box displays, click the Effects tab.

The Custom Animation dialog box displays (Figure 2-57).

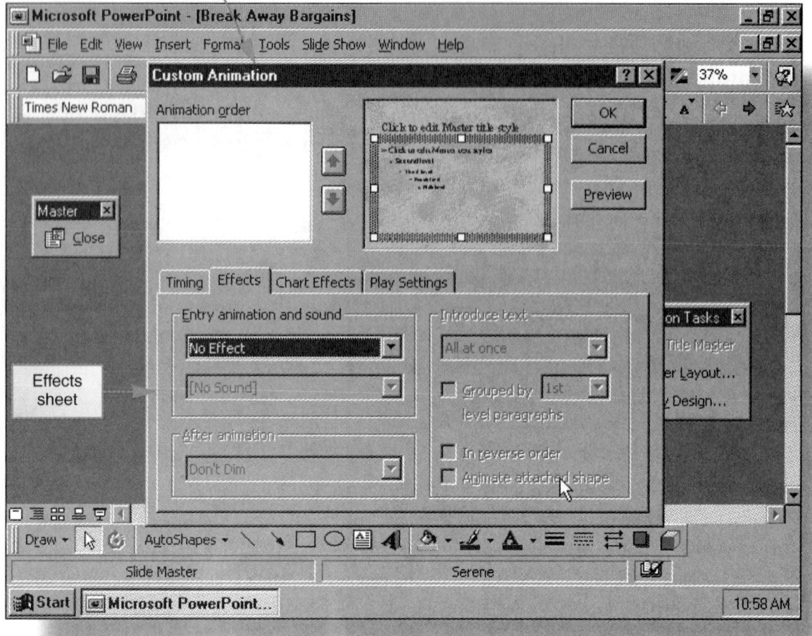

FIGURE 2-57

4 Click the Entry animation and sound box arrow. Scroll down the list until Zoom In From Screen Center displays. Then point to Zoom In From Screen Center (Figure 2-58).

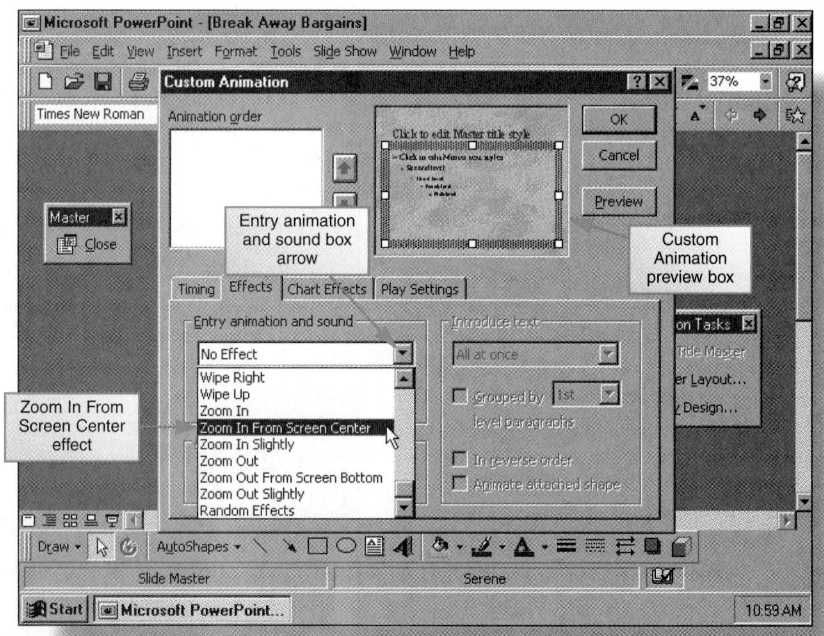

FIGURE 2-58

5 **Click Zoom In From Screen Center. Then point to the Grouped by level paragraphs box arrow.**

The Entry animation and sound list box displays Zoom In From Screen Center (Figure 2-59). A check mark displays in the Grouped by level paragraphs list box.

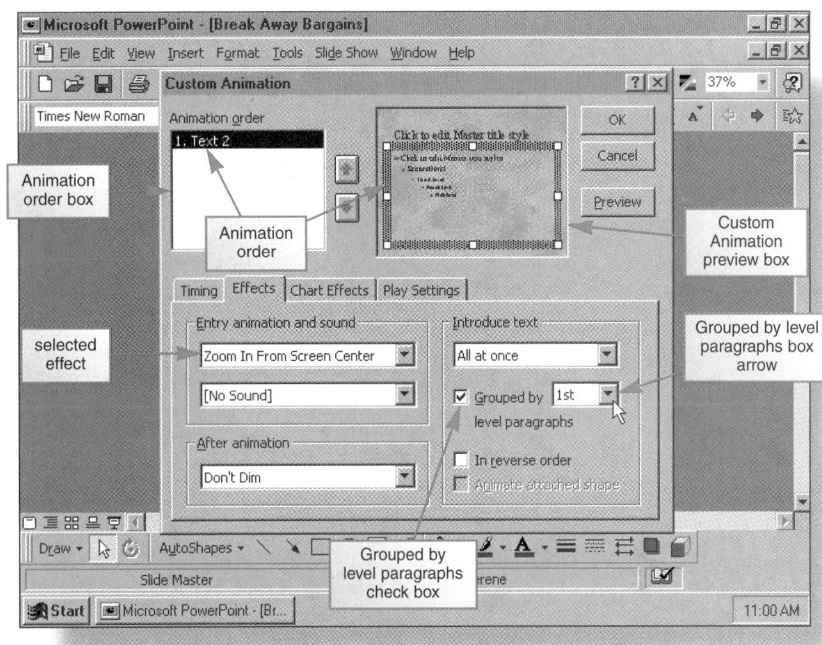

FIGURE 2-59

6 **Click the Grouped by level paragraphs box arrow and then point to 3rd.**

3rd is highlighted in the Grouped by level paragraphs list (Figure 2-60).

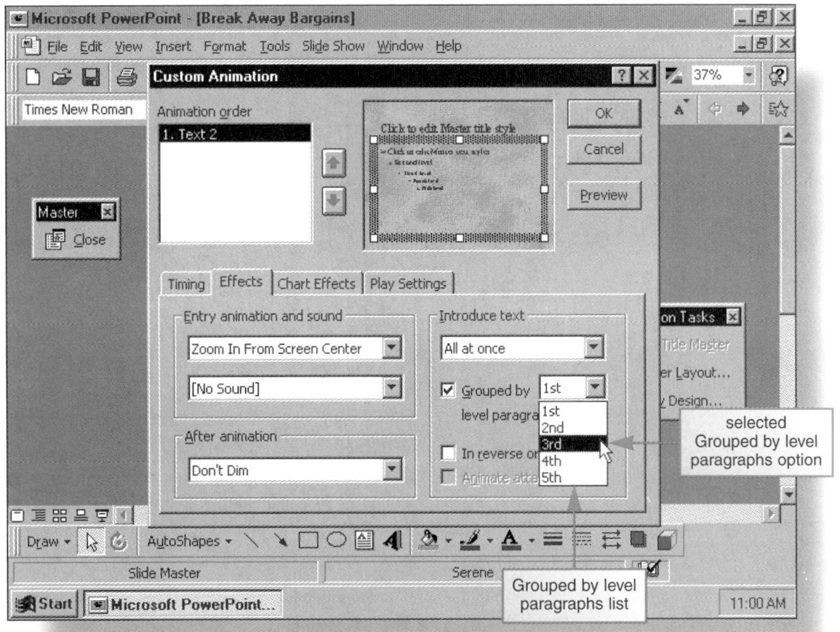

FIGURE 2-60

7 **Click 3rd and then click the OK button.**

PowerPoint applies the animation effects to the slide master, closes the Custom Animation dialog box, and then displays the slide master (Figure 2-61).

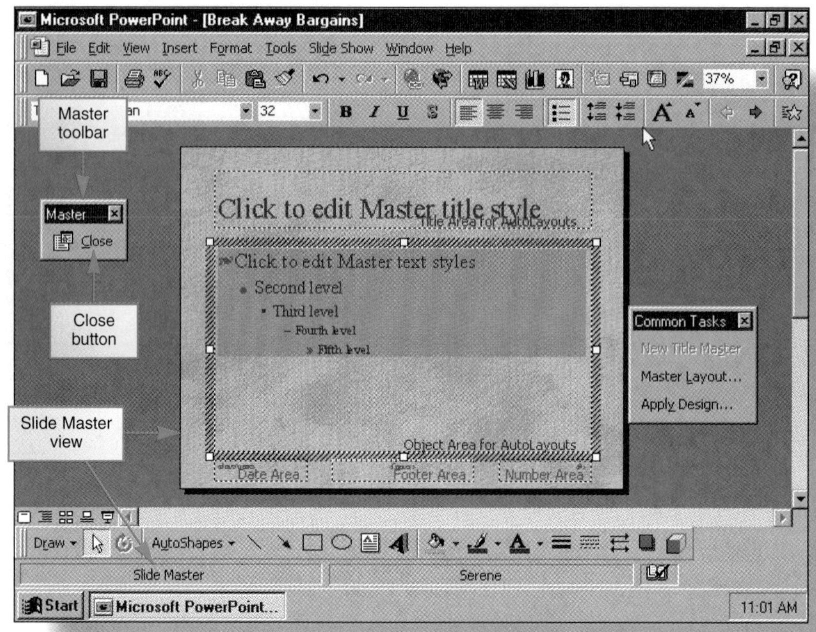

FIGURE 2-61

8 **Click the Close button on the Master toolbar.**

PowerPoint closes the slide master and returns to slide sorter view (Figure 2-62).

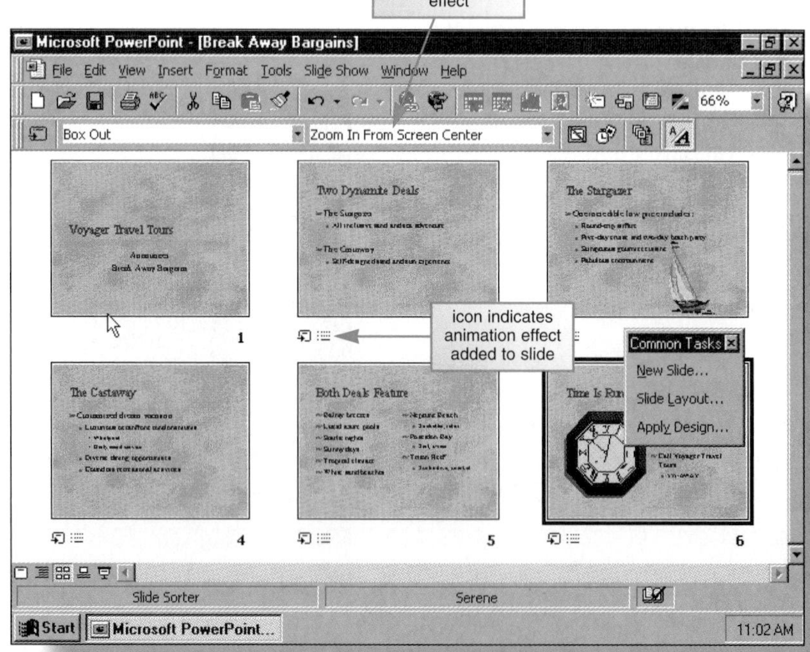

FIGURE 2-62

OtherWays

1. On View menu point to Master, click Slide Master, on Slide Show menu click Custom Animation, click Effects tab, click Entry animation and sound box arrow, click an animation effect, click Grouped by level paragraphs box arrow, click appropriate paragraph level, click OK

The Zoom In From Screen Center animation effect displays for each bulleted paragraph on paragraph level 1, 2, or 3 on Slides 2 through 6 during the running of an electronic slide show.

To remove animation effects from the slide master, press and hold down the SHIFT key, click the Slide View button, release the SHIFT key, right-click the slide master, click Custom Animation, click the Entry animation and sound box arrow, click No effect in the Entry animation and sound list, click the OK button, and then click the Close button on the Master toolbar.

Animating Clip Art Objects

Animating a clip art object takes several steps. First display the slide containing the clip art in slide view (Slide 3 in this project). Then select the clip art object and display the Custom Animation dialog box. Next, select the animation effect. Finally, apply the animation effect as described in the following sections.

Displaying a Slide in Slide View

PowerPoint requires you to display a slide in slide view before adding animation effects to clip art. Before continuing with the animation of the sailboat on Slide 3, display the slide in slide view as described in the following step.

TO DISPLAY A SLIDE IN SLIDE VIEW

Step 1: Double-click Slide 3.

Slide 3 displays in slide view.

With Slide 3 displaying in slide view, you are ready to animate the sailboat clip art as explained in the next section.

Animating Clip Art

PowerPoint allows you to animate clip art by selecting an animation effect from a list. Because Slide 3 features The Stargazer vacation package, you want to emphasize the slow, gentle cruise by displaying the sailboat slowly across the bottom of the slide. Perform the steps on the next page to add the Crawl From Right animation effect to the sailboat on Slide 3.

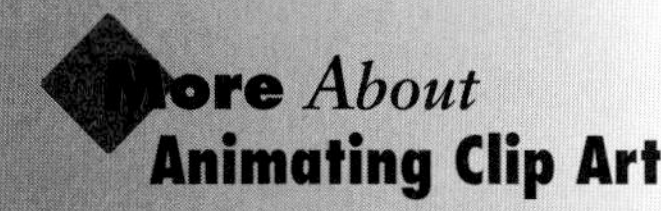

When animating a clip art object, consider adding sound effects to communicate a concept. Select an appropriate sound from the list in the Entry animation and sound list box on the Effects sheet in the Custom Animation dialog box.

To Animate Clip Art

1 Right-click the sailboat clip art object and then click Custom Animation on the shortcut menu. If necessary, click the Effects tab.

The Custom Animation dialog box displays (Figure 2-63). The sailboat is selected in the preview box. Text 2, the bulleted list on Slide 3, is listed in the Animation order box because of the text animation applied to the slide master earlier in this project.

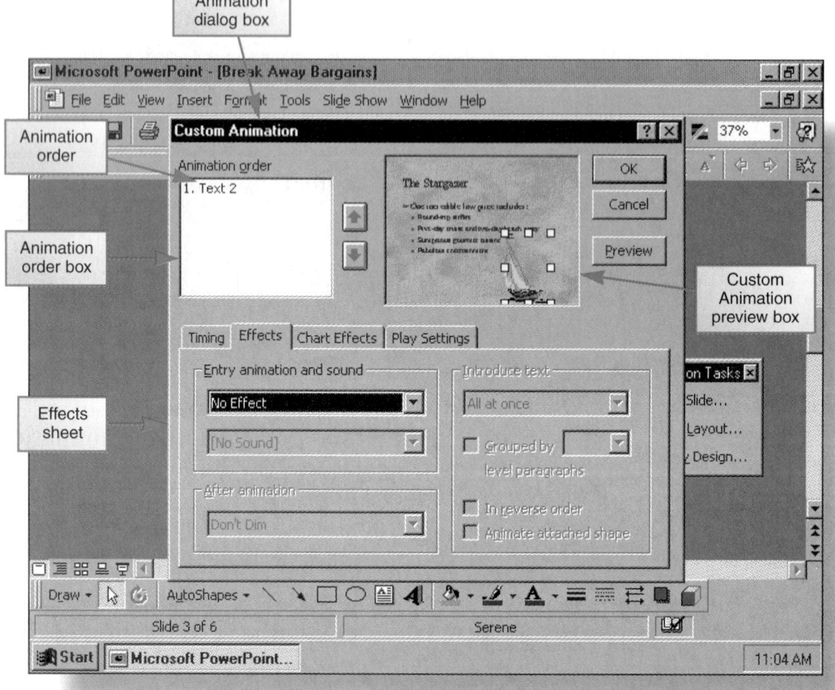

FIGURE 2-63

2 Click the Entry animation and sound box arrow. Scroll down the list until Crawl From Right displays and then point to Crawl From Right (Figure 2-64).

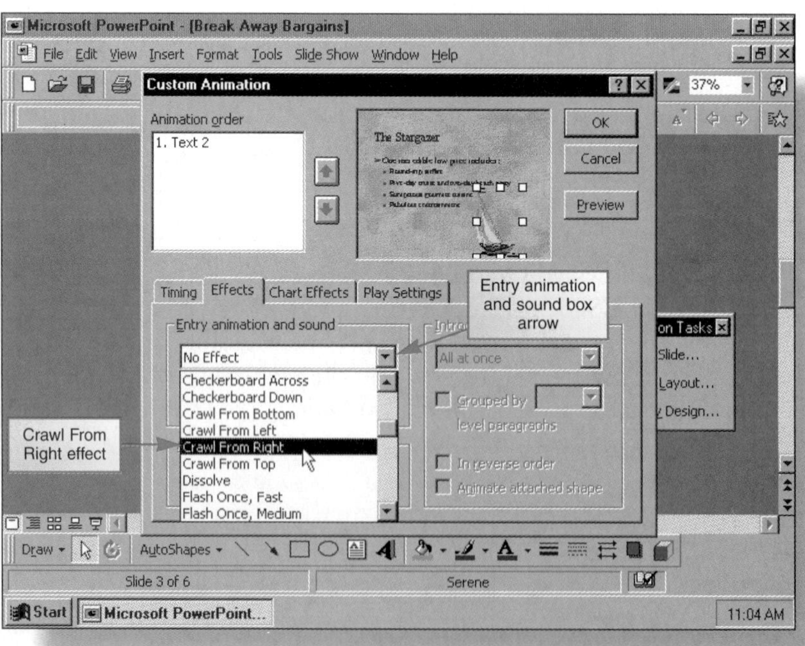

FIGURE 2-64

3 **Click Crawl From Right and then point to the OK button.**

Crawl From Right displays in the Entry animation and sound list box (Figure 2-65). Object 3, the sailboat, displays as number 2 in the Animation order box.

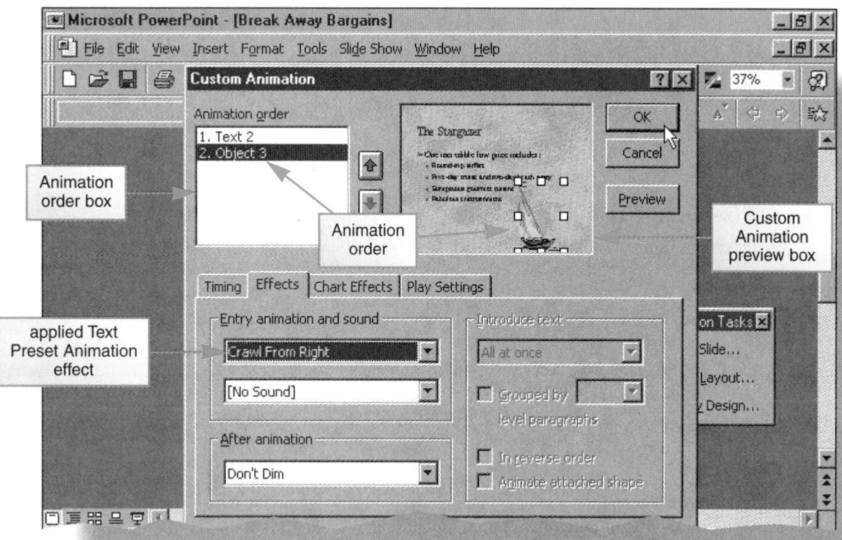

FIGURE 2-65

4 **Click the OK button.**

PowerPoint applies Crawl From Right animation effects to the clip art and closes the Custom Animation dialog box (Figure 2-66). Slide 3 displays in slide view.

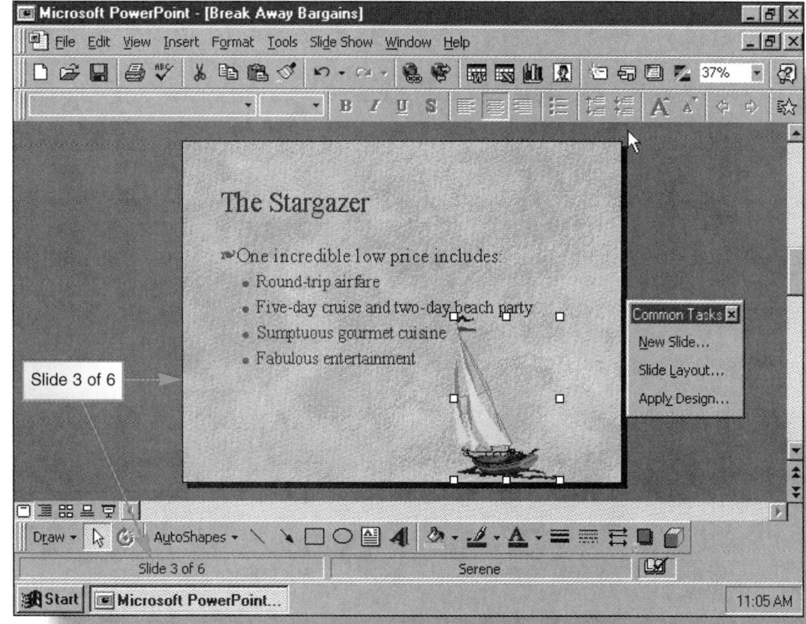

FIGURE 2-66

During the running of the slide show, the sailboat slowly will move across the bottom of the slide as if it was sailing across water. The sailboat will begin moving from the right side of the slide and stop at the position at which it was placed when you inserted the sailboat onto Slide 3.

OtherWays

1. Click clip art, on Slide Show menu click Custom Animation, click Effects tab, click Entry animation and sound box arrow, click desired animation effect, click OK
2. Press TAB until clip art is selected, press ALT+D, press M, press right arrow key to select Effects tab, press down arrow until desired animation effect selected, press ENTER

More About Animating a Title Slide

Choose title slide animation effects carefully. Choose traditional effects, such as Fly From Left, when addressing a serious topic. Choose flashy, fun animation effects, such as Spiral, for lighter, less serious topics.

Formatting and Animating a Title Slide

The title slide of every presentation should seize the attention of the audience. In order to excite the audience with the Break Away Bargains presentation, you want to intensify the subtitle object on the title slide. First, you italicize the word Announces and then increase the size of the words in the subtitle, Break Away Bargains. Finally, you add animation effects to the subtitle.

The first step is to display Slide 1 and then format the title slide subtitle. Perform the following steps to format the subtitle object on Slide 1.

TO CHANGE TEXT FONT STYLE TO ITALIC AND INCREASE FONT SIZE

Step 1: Drag the vertical scroll box to display Slide 1.
Step 2: Double-click the word, Announces, and then click the Italic button on the Formatting toolbar.
Step 3: Triple-click the paragraph, Break Away Bargains.
Step 4: Click the Increase Font Size button three times until 44 displays in the Font Size list box on the Formatting toolbar.

The formatted subtitle on Slide 1 displays (Figure 2-67). The word, Announces, displays the italic font style and the paragraph, Break Away Bargains, displays in font size 44.

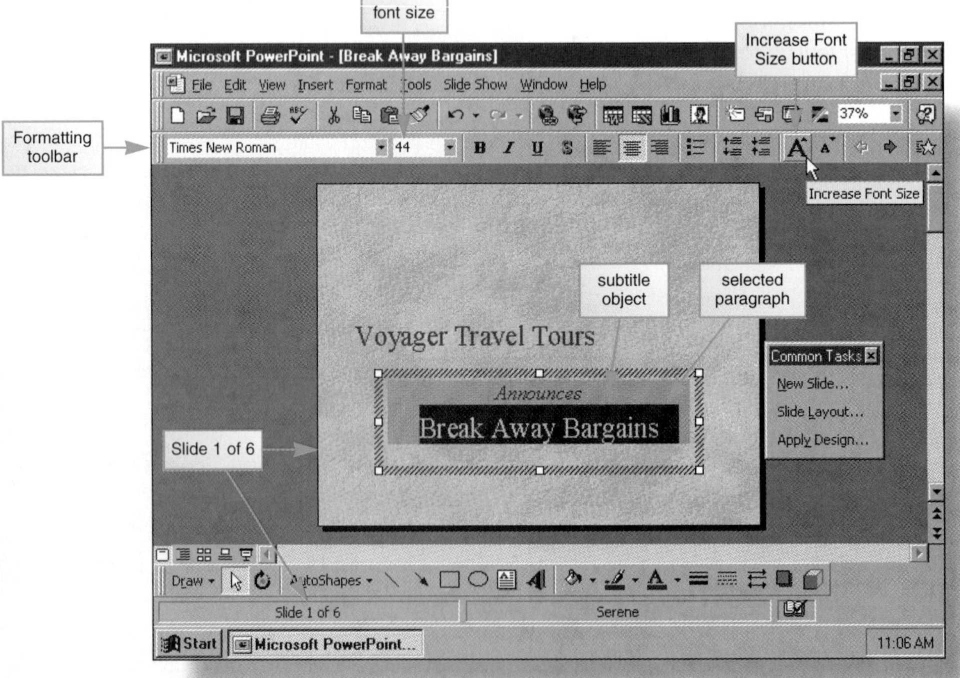

FIGURE 2-67

The next step is to apply the Spiral animation effect to the subtitle text. Perform the following steps to animate the paragraphs in the subtitle object on Slide 1.

TO ANIMATE TEXT

Step 1: Right-click the subtitle object and then click Custom Animation on the shortcut menu.
Step 2: If necessary, click the Effects tab in the Custom Animation dialog box.
Step 3: Click the Entry animation and sound box arrow.
Step 4: Scroll down the list until Spiral displays and then click Spiral.
Step 5: Click the OK button.

The subtitle object, Text 2, displays in the Animation order box and is selected in the preview box. Spiral displays in the Entry animation and sound list box. By default, the subtitle text is grouped by first level paragraphs. PowerPoint applies the animation effect, closes the Custom Animation dialog box, and then displays Slide 1.

Animation effects are complete for this presentation. You now are ready to review the presentation in slide show view.

Saving the Presentation Again

The presentation is complete. Save the finished presentation to a floppy disk before running the slide show.

TO SAVE A PRESENTATION TO A FLOPPY DISK

Step 1: Click the Save button on the Standard toolbar.

PowerPoint saves the presentation to your floppy disk by saving the changes made to the presentation since the last save.

More About Electronic Slide Shows

Before presenting to an audience, install and run your slide show on the computer you will be using. This gives you the opportunity to correct any problems so your presentation runs without any surprises.

Running an Animated Slide Show

Project 1 introduced you to using slide show view to look at your presentation one slide at a time. This project introduces you to running a slide show with slide transition effects and text and object animation effects. When you run a slide show with slide transition effects, PowerPoint displays the slide transition effect when you click the mouse button to advance to the next slide. When a slide has text animation effects, each paragraph level displays as determined by the animation settings. Animated clip art objects display the selected animation effect in the sequence established in the Custom Animation dialog box. Perform the steps on the next page to run the animated Break Away Bargains slide show.

More About Electronic Slide Shows

PowerPoint comes with an application called PowerPoint Viewer that allows you to run an electronic slide show without installing PowerPoint. Microsoft has licensed PowerPoint Viewer to distribute freely because PowerPoint Viewer runs only the existing presentation. To download a copy of PowerPoint Viewer, click Help on the menu bar, point to Microsoft on the Web, and click Free Stuff, or visit www.microsoft.com/powerpoint/internet/viewer/default.htm on the Web.

Steps To Run an Animated Slide Show

1. **With Slide 1 displaying, click the Slide Show button on the View Button Bar. When Slide 1 displays in slide show view, click the slide anywhere except on the Popup Menu buttons.**

PowerPoint first displays the Serene design template and then displays the title slide title object, Voyager Travel Tours (Figure 2-68). Recall the Popup Menu buttons display when you move the mouse pointer during a slide show.

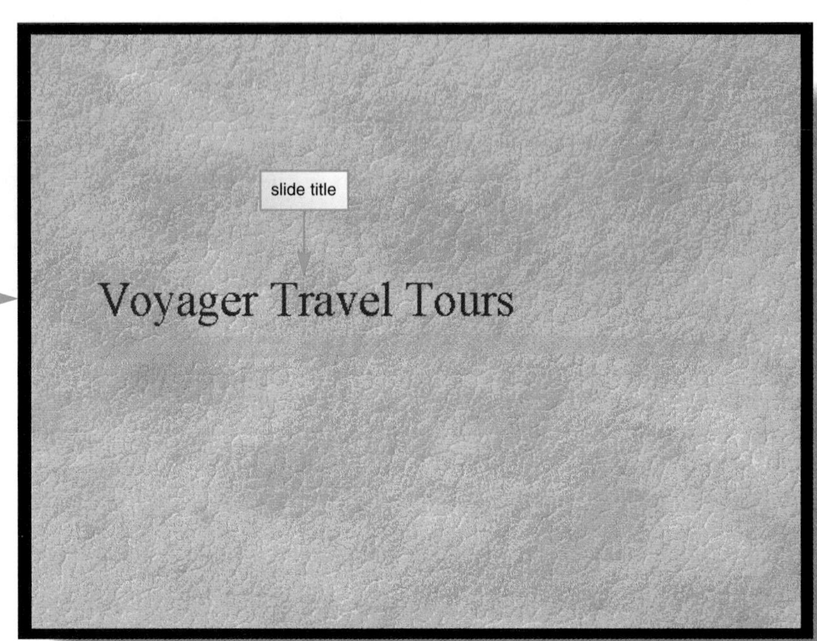

FIGURE 2-68

2. **Click the slide anywhere except on the Popup Menu buttons.**

PowerPoint displays the first heading level 1 subtitle paragraph using the Spiral animation effect (Figure 2-69).

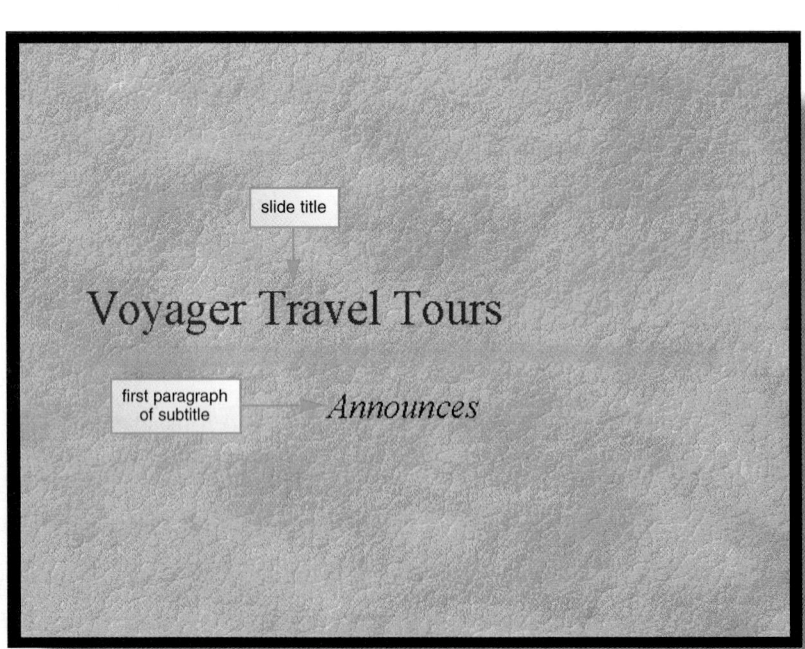

FIGURE 2-69

3 Click the slide anywhere except on the Popup Menu buttons.

PowerPoint displays the second heading level 1 subtitle paragraph beneath the first heading level 1 subtitle paragraph. PowerPoint again uses the Spiral animation effect (Figure 2-70).

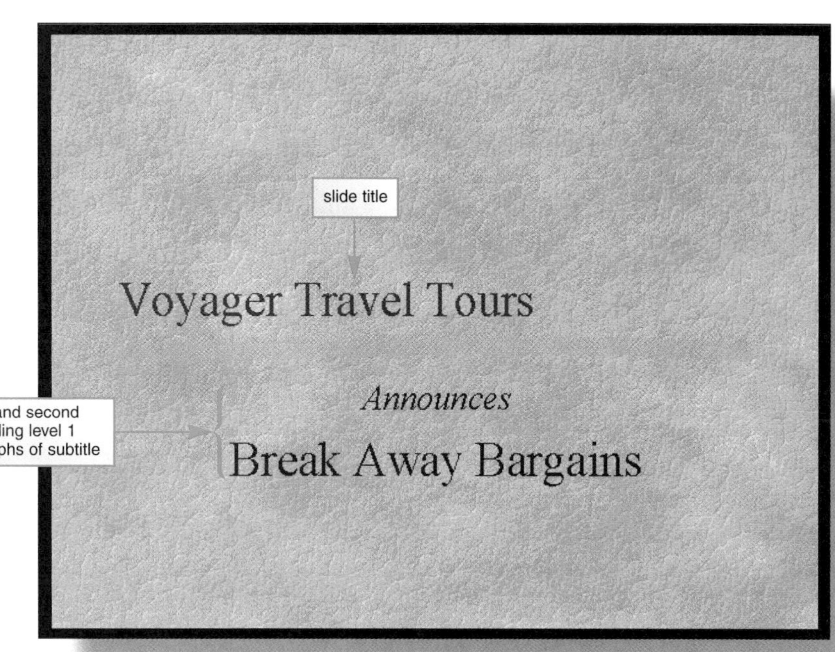

FIGURE 2-70

4 Click the slide anywhere except on the Popup Menu buttons. Continue clicking to finish running the slide show and return to slide sorter view.

Each time a new slide displays, PowerPoint first displays the Box Out slide transition effect and then displays only the slide title. Then, PowerPoint builds each slide based on the animation settings. When you click the slide after the last paragraph displays on the last slide of the presentation, PowerPoint exits slide show view and returns to slide sorter view.

OtherWays

1. On Slide Show menu click View Show, click slide until slide show ends
2. Press ALT+D, press V, press ENTER until slide show ends

Now that the presentation is complete and you have tested the animation effects, the last step is to print the presentation outline and slides.

Printing in Outline View

When you click the Print button on the Standard toolbar, PowerPoint prints a hard copy of the presentation component last selected in the Print what box in the Print dialog box. To be certain to print the component you want, such as the presentation outline, use the Print command located on the File menu. When the Print dialog box displays, you can select the appropriate presentation component in the Print what box. The next two sections explain how to use the Print command to print the presentation outline and the presentation slides.

Printing an Outline

During the development of a lengthy presentation, it often is easier to review your outline in print rather than on-screen. Printing your outline also is useful for audience handouts or when your supervisor or instructor wants to review your subject matter before you fully develop your presentation.

Recall that the Print dialog box displays print options. When you wish to print your outline, select Outline View in the Print what list located in the Print dialog box. The outline, however, prints as last viewed in outline view. This means that you must select the Zoom setting to display the outline text as you wish it to print. If you are uncertain of the Zoom setting, you should return to outline view and review it prior to printing. Perform the following steps to print an outline from slide view.

Steps To Print an Outline

1 Ready the printer according to the printer manufacturer's instructions. Click File on the menu bar and then point to Print.

The File menu displays (Figure 2-71).

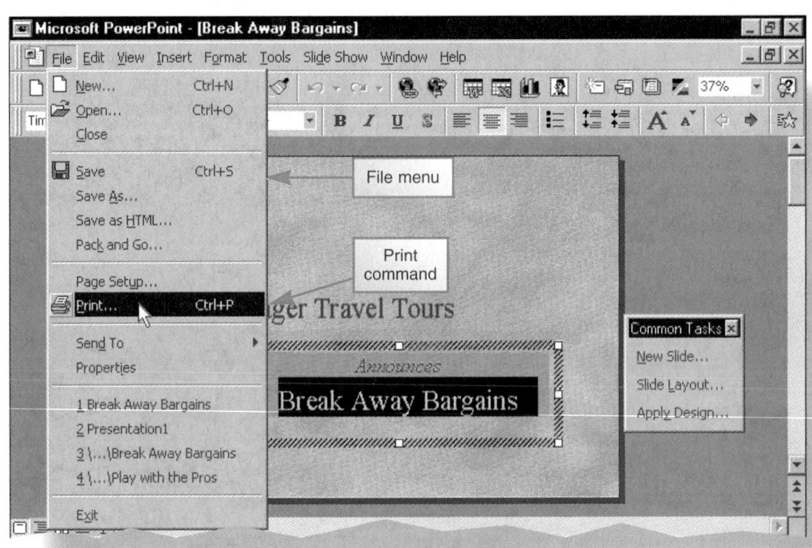

FIGURE 2-71

2 Click Print.

The Print dialog box displays (Figure 2-72).

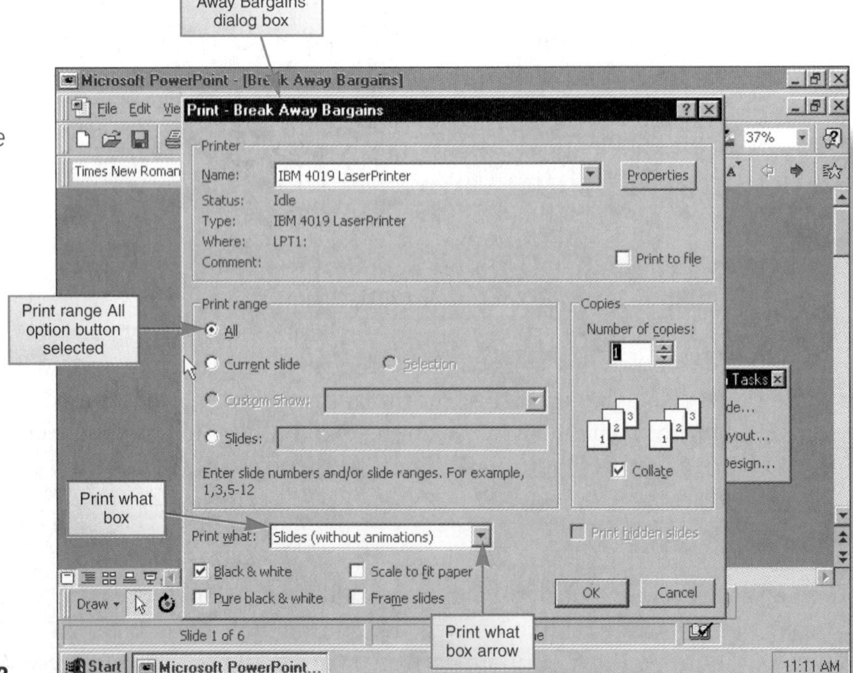

FIGURE 2-72

3 **Click the Print what box arrow and then point to Outline View.**

Outline View displays highlighted in the Print what list (Figure 2-73).

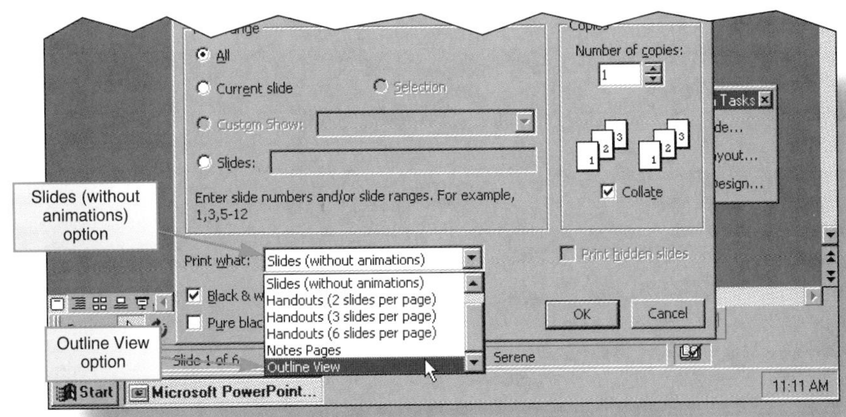

FIGURE 2-73

4 **Click Outline View and then point to the OK button (Figure 2-74).**

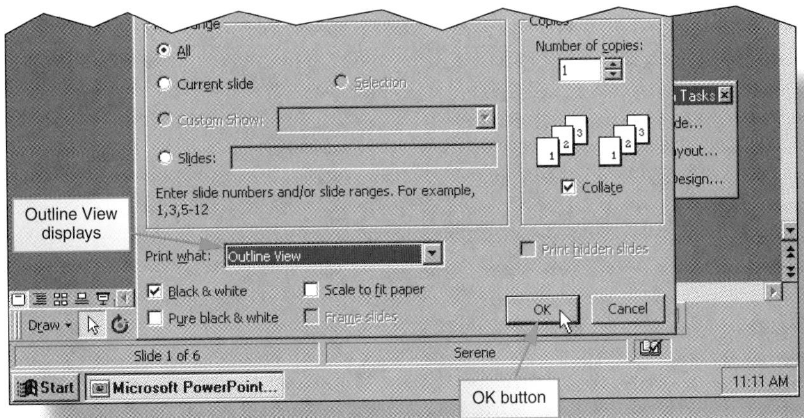

FIGURE 2-74

5 **Click the OK button.**

PowerPoint momentarily displays a message in the Print Status dialog box explaining that the outline is printing as last viewed (Figure 2-75). To cancel the print request, click the Cancel button.

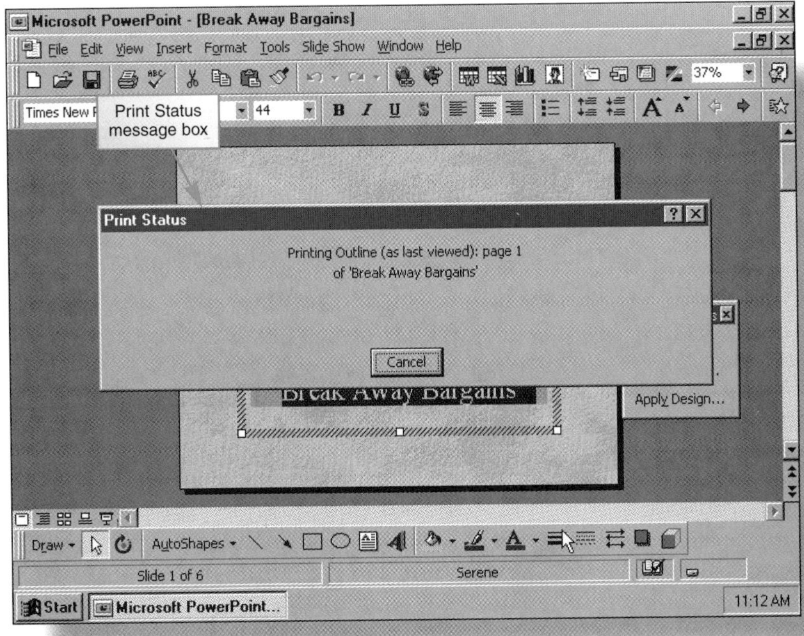

FIGURE 2-75

6 **When the printer stops, retrieve the printout of the outline (Figure 2-76).**

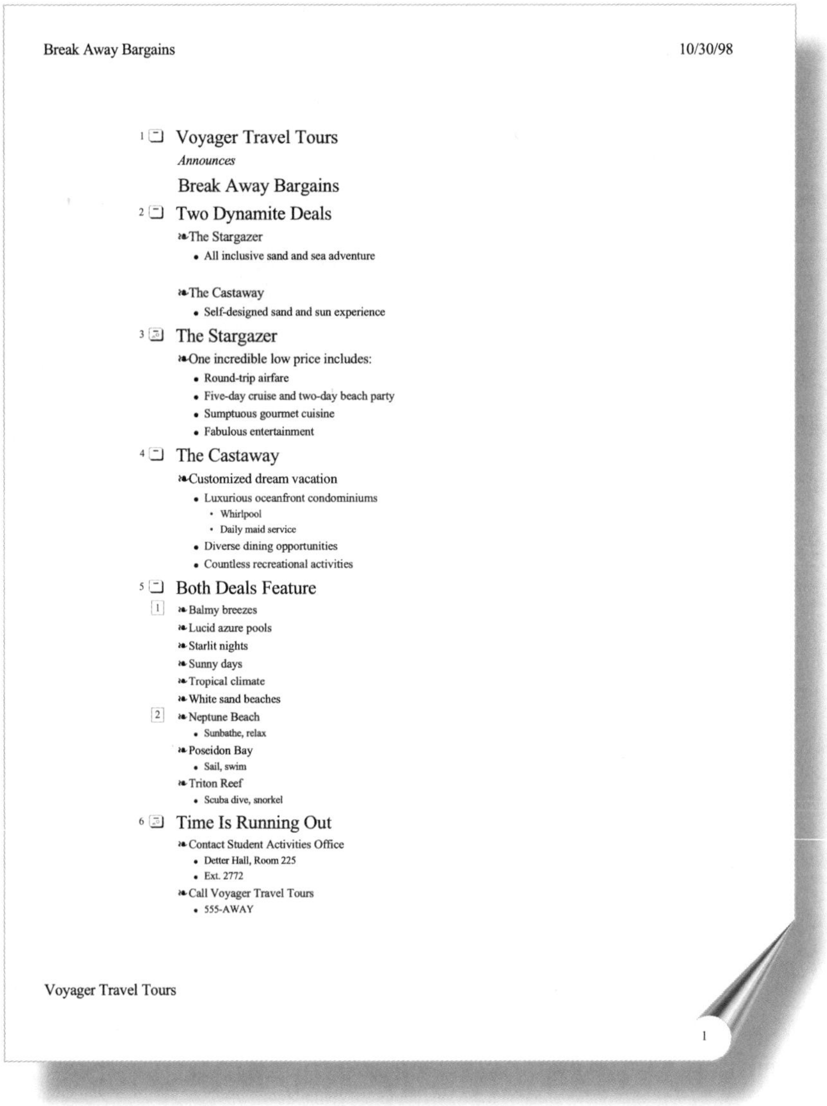

Break Away Bargains 10/30/98

1 Voyager Travel Tours
Announces
Break Away Bargains
2 Two Dynamite Deals
- The Stargazer
  - All inclusive sand and sea adventure
- The Castaway
  - Self-designed sand and sun experience

3 The Stargazer
- One incredible low price includes:
  - Round-trip airfare
  - Five-day cruise and two-day beach party
  - Sumptuous gourmet cuisine
  - Fabulous entertainment

4 The Castaway
- Customized dream vacation
  - Luxurious oceanfront condominiums
    - Whirlpool
    - Daily maid service
  - Diverse dining opportunities
  - Countless recreational activities

5 Both Deals Feature
1
- Balmy breezes
- Lucid azure pools
- Starlit nights
- Sunny days
- Tropical climate
- White sand beaches

2
- Neptune Beach
  - Sunbathe, relax
- Poseidon Bay
  - Sail, swim
- Triton Reef
  - Scuba dive, snorkel

6 Time Is Running Out
- Contact Student Activities Office
  - Detter Hall, Room 225
  - Ext. 2772
- Call Voyager Travel Tours
  - 555-AWAY

Voyager Travel Tours

1

FIGURE 2-76

*Other***Ways**

1. Press ALT+F, press P, press TAB, press W, press down arrow until Outline View selected, press ENTER, press ENTER

You may select the Print command from the File menu while in any view except slide show view.

Printing Presentation Slides

After correcting errors, you will want to print a final copy of your presentation. If you made any changes to your presentation since your last save, be sure to save your presentation before you print.

Perform the following steps to print the presentation.

TO PRINT PRESENTATION SLIDES

Step 1: Ready the printer according to the printer manufacturer's instructions.
Step 2: Click File on the menu bar and then click Print.
Step 3: When the Print dialog box displays, click the Print what box arrow.
Step 4: Click Slides (without animations).
Step 5: Click the OK button. When the printer stops, retrieve the slide printouts.

The printouts should look like the slides in Figure 2-77.

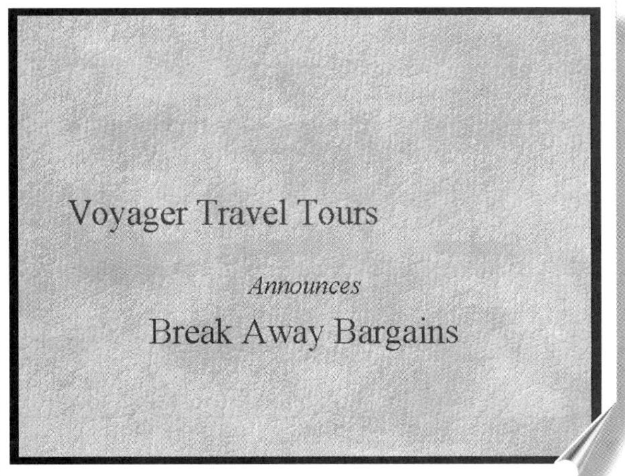

FIGURE 2-77a

Two Dynamite Deals
The Stargazer
All inclusive sand and sea adventure
The Castaway
Self-designed sand and sun experience

FIGURE 2-77b

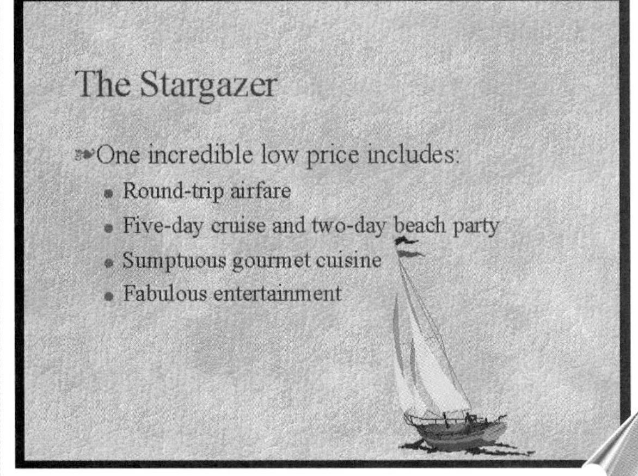

FIGURE 2-77c

The Castaway
Customized dream vacation
Luxurious oceanfront condominiums
Whirlpool
Daily maid service
Diverse dining opportunities
Countless recreational activities

FIGURE 2-77d

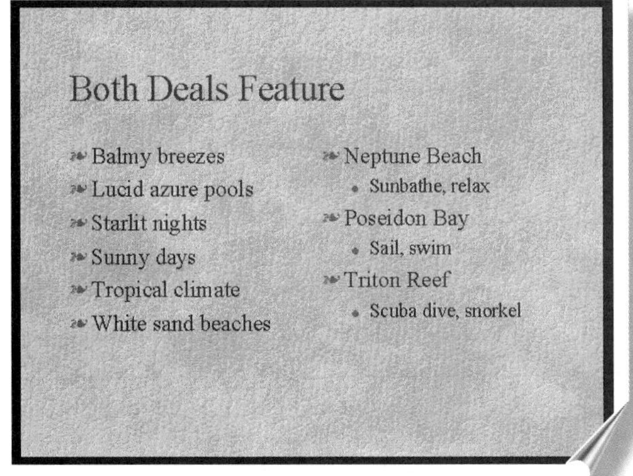

FIGURE 2-77e

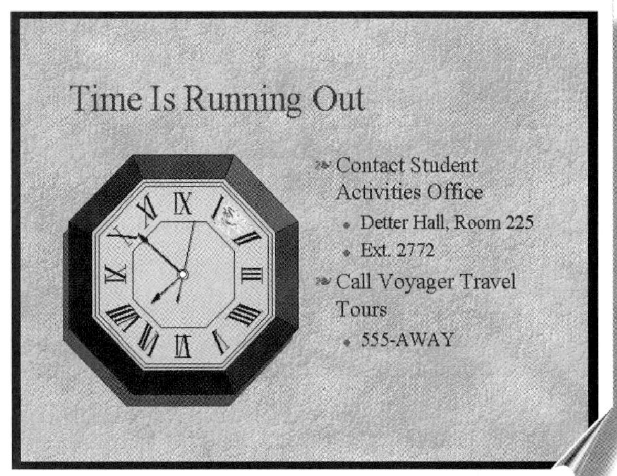

FIGURE 2-77f

The Print what list in the Print dialog box contains options for printing two, three, or six slide images per page. These options are labeled as Handouts (2 slides per page), Handouts (3 slides per page), and Handouts (6 slides per page). Printing handouts is useful for reviewing a presentation because you print several slides on one page. Additionally, many businesses distribute handouts of the slide show before a presentation so the attendees can refer to a copy.

Saving and Quitting PowerPoint

If you made any changes to your presentation since your last save, you should save it again before quitting PowerPoint. For more details on quitting PowerPoint, refer to page PP 1.38 in Project 1. Perform the following steps to save changes to the presentation and quit PowerPoint.

TO SAVE CHANGES AND QUIT POWERPOINT

Step 1: Click the Close button on the title bar.
Step 2: If prompted, click the Yes button in the Microsoft PowerPoint dialog box.

PowerPoint saves any changes made to the presentation since the last save and then quits PowerPoint.

Project Summary

Project 2 introduced you to outline view, clip art, and animation effects. You created a slide presentation in outline view where you entered all the text in the form of an outline. You arranged the text using the Promote and Demote buttons. Once your outline was complete, you changed slide layouts and added clip art to a clip art placeholder. After adding clip art to another slide without using a clip art placeholder, you moved and sized the picture. You added slide transition effects and text animation effects. Then you applied animation effects to clip art. You learned how to run an animated slide show demonstrating slide transition and animation effects. Finally, you printed the presentation outline and slides using the Print command.

What You Should Know

Having completed this project, you now should be able to perform the following tasks:

- Add a Blank Line *(PP 2.21)*
- Add a Slide in Outline View *(PP 2.12)*
- Add Slide Transitions to a Slide Show *(PP 2.39)*
- Animate Clip Art *(PP 2.48)*
- Animate Text *(PP 2.51)*
- Change Slide Layout *(PP 2.23)*
- Change the Size of Clip Art *(PP 2.34)*
- Change the Slide Layout to Clip Art & Text *(PP 2.27)*
- Change the View to Outline View *(PP 2.8)*
- Change the View to Slide Sorter View *(PP 2.19)*
- Change the View to Slide View *(PP 2.20)*
- Change Text Font Style to Italic and Increase Font Size *(PP 2.50)*
- Create a Closing Slide in Outline View *(PP 2.18)*
- Create a Multi-level Bulleted List Slide in Outline View *(PP 2.13)*
- Create a Second Subordinate Slide *(PP 2.16)*
- Create a Slide with Multiple Text Objects in Outline View *(PP 2.17)*
- Create a Subordinate Slide *(PP 2.15)*
- Create a Title Slide in Outline View *(PP 2.11)*
- Display a Slide in Slide View *(PP 2.47)*
- Insert Clip Art into a Clip Art Placeholder *(PP 2.28)*
- Insert Clip Art on a Slide without a Clip Art Placeholder *(PP 2.32)*
- Move Clip Art *(PP 2.33)*
- Move Text *(PP 2.25)*
- Print an Outline *(PP 2.54)*
- Print Presentation Slides *(PP 2.56)*
- Run an Animated Slide Show *(PP 2.52)*
- Run Style Checker *(PP 2.38)*
- Save a Presentation *(PP 2.19, 2.36)*
- Save a Presentation to a Floppy Disk *(PP 2.51)*
- Save Changes and Quit PowerPoint *(PP 2.58)*
- Start a New Presentation *(PP 2.7)*
- Use the Notes and Handouts Sheet to Add Headers and Footers *(PP 2.36)*
- Use the Slide Master to Apply Animation Effects to All Bulleted Slides *(PP 2.43)*

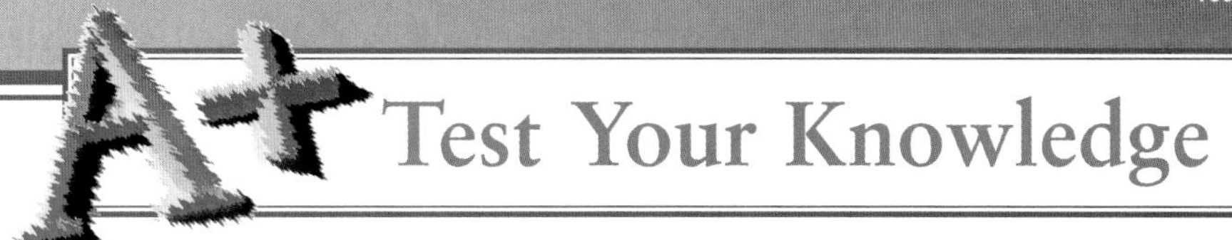

Test Your Knowledge

1 True/False

Instructions: Circle T if the statement is true or F if the statement is false.

T F 1. An outline is a summary of thoughts presented as headings, subheadings, and pictures.
T F 2. Graphic objects, such as pictures, graphs, and tables, do not display in outline view.
T F 3. When in outline view, Microsoft PowerPoint displays the current slide in black-and-white view so you can see how the slide will look in both slide view and slide show view.
T F 4. Each time you click the Demote button the selected paragraph moves down one level in the outline hierarchy.
T F 5. Resolution is the number of pixels per unit of measurement displaying on your computer monitor.
T F 6. The slide that gracefully ends a presentation is the ending slide.
T F 7. Microsoft Clip Gallery 3.0 accompanies Microsoft Office 97 and is a tool that allows you to insert clip art, pictures, audio clips, and video clips into Microsoft Office documents.
T F 8. Right-clicking a clip art placeholder activates instructions to open the Microsoft Clip Gallery 3.0.
T F 9. PowerPoint inserts clip art only into clip art placeholders.
T F 10. Double-clicking a slide miniature in slide sorter view displays that slide in slide view.

2 Multiple Choice

Instructions: Circle the correct response.

1. Outline view provides a quick, easy way to ______________.
   a. add animation effects
   b. create a presentation
   c. insert clip art
   d. display slide miniatures
2. An outline ______________.
   a. is a summary of thoughts
   b. uses indentation to establish a hierarchy to denote levels of importance
   c. allows you to organize your thoughts in a structured format
   d. all of the above
3. When viewing a presentation in outline view, you know which slides contain graphic objects because ______________.
   a. slide icons display blank when a slide contains graphics
   b. all graphics display in outline view
   c. slide icons display a small graphic when a slide contains graphics
   d. none of the above

(continued)

A+ Test Your Knowledge

Multiple Choice *(continued)*

4. In PowerPoint, a presentation outline begins with a title on ______________.
   a. heading level 0
   b. heading level 1
   c. heading level 2
   d. none of the above
5. Clicking the ______________ button moves selected text above the preceding displayed paragraph while maintaining its hierarchical heading level and text style.
   a. Promote
   b. Demote
   c. Move Up
   d. Move Down
6. Microsoft Clip Gallery 3.0 ______________.
   a. is shared with PowerPoint and other Microsoft Office 97 applications
   b. combines topic-related images into categories
   c. is a tool that allows you to insert clip art, pictures, audio clips, and video clips into a presentation
   d. all of the above
7. The relationship between the height and width of an object is its ______________.
   a. height-to-width ratio
   b. aspect ratio
   c. size
   d. scale
8. The animation effect that displays when one slide moves off the screen and another slide displays on the screen is ______________.
   a. custom animation
   b. clip art animation
   c. text animation
   d. slide transition
9. The default PowerPoint setting that allows for saving only the changes made to a presentation since the last save is called a(n) ______________.
   a. intermediate save
   b. full save
   c. fast save
   d. all of the above
10. Clicking the Print button on the Standard toolbar when displaying the presentation in outline view instructs PowerPoint to print the presentation in ______________.
    a. outline view
    b. slide view
    c. slide sorter view
    d. the view last printed

Test Your Knowledge

3 Understanding a Microsoft PowerPoint Window in Outline View

Instructions: Arrows in Figure 2-78 point to the major components of a Microsoft PowerPoint window in outline view. Identify the various parts of the window in the spaces provided.

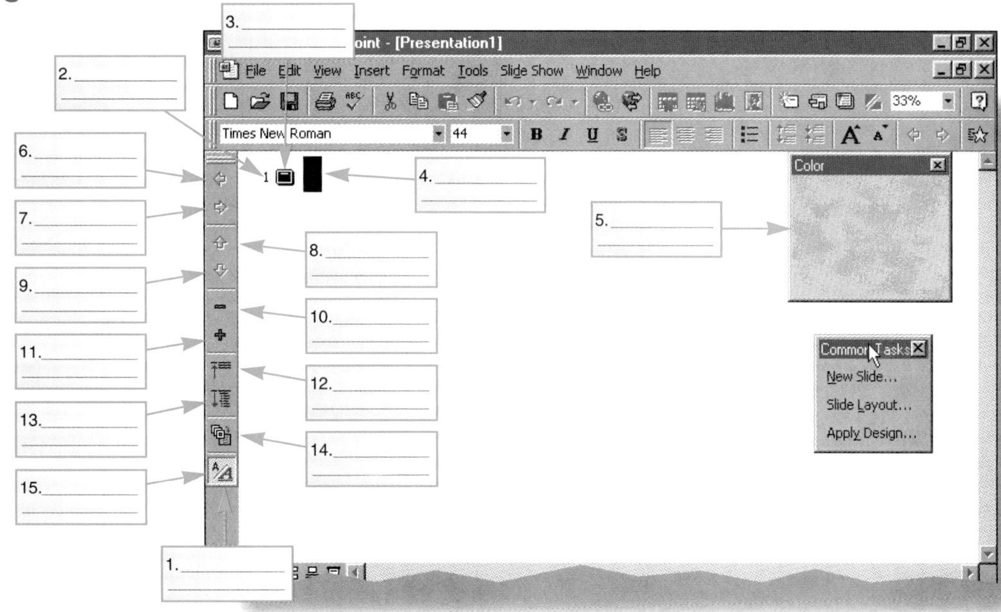

FIGURE 2-78

4 Understanding the Custom Animation Dialog Box

Instructions: In Figure 2-79, arrows point to several of the components in the Custom Animation dialog box. Identify the various parts of the dialog box in the spaces provided.

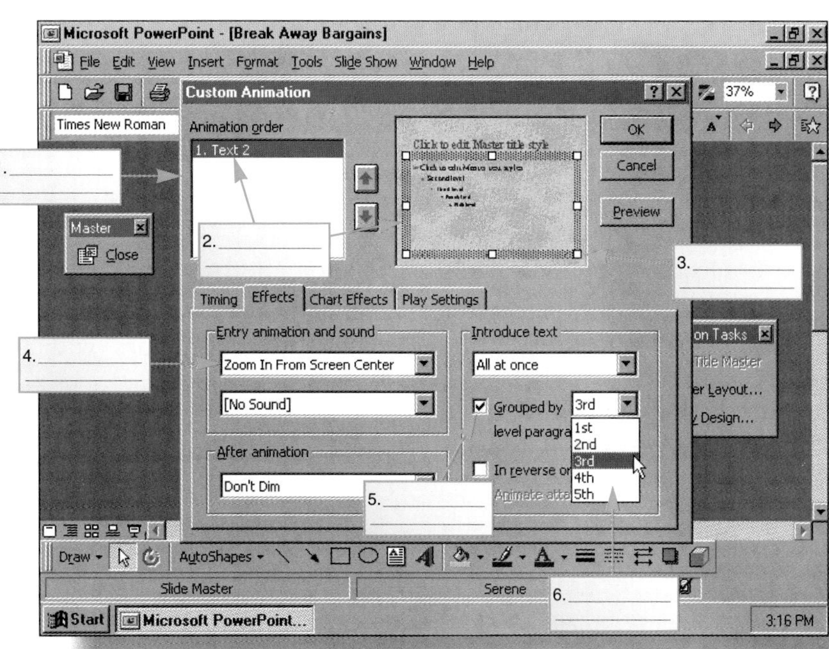

FIGURE 2-79

Use Help

1 Learning More about PowerPoint

Instructions: Perform the following tasks using a computer.

1. If PowerPoint is not started already, start a new PowerPoint presentation and select any AutoLayout. If necessary, click the Office Assistant to display the What would you like to do? box.
2. Type `outline view` in the What would you like to do? text box and then click the Search button. Click the topic Ways to organize my content in outline view. When the Microsoft PowerPoint window displays, read the information, right-click within the dialog box, and click Print Topic. When the Print dialog box displays, click the OK button. Click the Help Topics button to return to the Help Topics: Microsoft PowerPoint dialog box. If necessary, click the Find tab.
3. Type `outline` in box 1. Double-click the Change the order of slides in a presentation topic displayed in box 3. When the Microsoft PowerPoint window displays, read and print the information. Click the Help Topics button to return to the Help Topics: Microsoft PowerPoint dialog box.
4. Scroll the topics listed in box 3 to display File formats for saving presentations. Double-click File formats for saving presentations. When the Microsoft PowerPoint window displays, read and print the information. Click the Close button to exit Help. Submit the printouts to your instructor.

2 Expanding on the Basics

Instructions: Use PowerPoint online Help to better understand the topics listed below. Begin each of the following by clicking the Office Assistant button on the Standard toolbar. If you cannot print the Help information, answer the question on a separate piece of paper.

1. When in outline view, how do you change the color of a bullet for all slides in a presentation?
2. How do you change the bullet character from a dot to an open file folder?
3. How do you add a period to the end of every paragraph in a list?
4. How do you replace one clip art picture in a slide with another picture?
5. How do you build a slide with a clip art image that appears to fly onto the slide?
6. How do you add sound to animation effects?
7. How do you change the order animated objects display on a slide?
8. What happens when you print slides using the Slides (with animations) option?

Apply Your Knowledge

1 Intensifying a Presentation by Applying a Design Template, Changing Slide Layout, Inserting Clip Art, and Applying Animation Effects

Instructions: Start PowerPoint. Open the presentation, Apply-2, from the PowerPoint folder on the Data Disk that accompanies this book. Perform the following tasks to change the presentation to look like Figure 2-80 on the next page.

1. Apply the Blush design template. Add the current date, slide number, and your name to the footer. Display the footer on all slides and on notes and handouts.
2. On Slide 1, insert one blank paragraph after the November 14, 1998 paragraph. Insert the runner clip art image shown in Figure 2-80 that has the keywords, Victory Performance Fast Invincible. Scale the clip art to 65% using the Format Picture command. Drag the runner clip art image to align the upper-left corner of the dotted box below the letter o in the word Triathlon, as shown in Figure 2-80. Apply the Zoom In From Screen Center custom animation effect to the clip art. Italicize the paragraph, Sponsored by:, and then decrease the font size to 24 points.
3. Go to Slide 3. Change the slide layout to 2 Column Text. Move the six male categories to the right column placeholder.
4. Go to Slide 4. Change the slide layout to Text & Clip Art. Insert the trophy clip art image shown in Figure 2-80 that has the keywords, Goal Success Reward Accomplishment Impress Trophy. Change the size of the trophy clip art image to 105%. Change the line spacing for the heading level 1 bullets to 0.75 lines before each paragraph.
5. Go to Slide 5. Change the slide layout to Clip Art & Text. Insert the directional post clip art image shown in Figure 2-80 that has the keywords, Direction Alternative Solution. Change the line spacing for the heading level 1 bullets to 1 line before each paragraph.
6. Add the Box Out slide transition effect to all slides except the title slide.
7. Save the presentation to a floppy disk using the file name, Southwestern Triathlon.
8. Print the presentation in black and white. Print the presentation outline.
9. Quit PowerPoint.

(continued)

Apply Your Knowledge

Intensifying a Presentation by Applying a Design Template, Changing Slide Layout, Inserting Clip Art, and Applying Animation Effects *(continued)*

FIGURE 2-80a

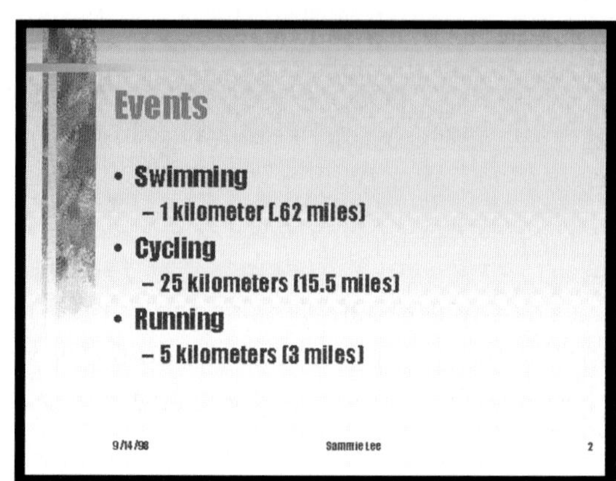

FIGURE 2-80b

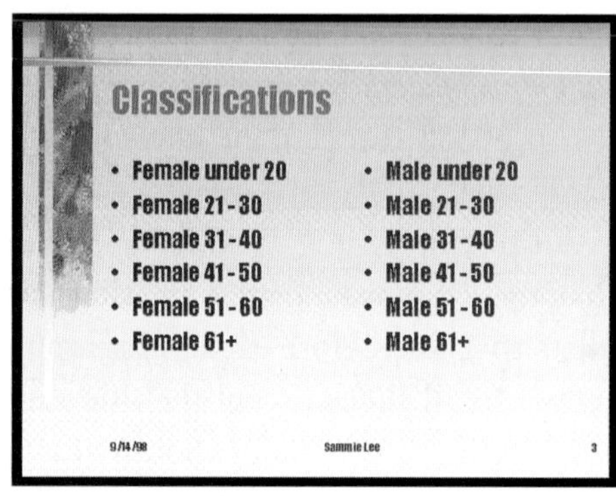

FIGURE 2-80c

FIGURE 2-80d

FIGURE 2-80e

1 Adding Clip Art and Animation Effects to a Presentation Created in Outline View

Problem: You are enrolled in Psychology 401. Your professor assigns a research paper and requires you to present your findings during a five-minute presentation. Your topic is positive mental attitude. You create the outline shown in Figure 2-81 to prepare your presentation. You use the outline to create the slide show shown in Figure 2-82 on the next page. Because of your research findings, you create a unique closing slide.

Instructions: Perform the following tasks.

1. Create a new presentation using the high voltage design template.
2. Using the outline shown in Figure 2-81, create the title slide shown in Figure 2-82. Use your name instead of the name Chelsea Ihalainen. Increase the font size of your name to 36 points.
3. Using the outline in Figure 2-81, create the three bulleted list slides shown in Figure 2-82.
4. Change the slide layout on Slide 2 to Clip Art & Text. Using the clip art placeholder, insert the clip art shown in Figure 2-82 that has the keywords, Success Victory Accomplishment Result Invincible Milestone Superior. Increase the bulleted list font size to 36 points.

1) Positive Mental Attitude
   a) Chelsea Ihalainen
   b) Psychology 401
2) Positive Attitude Characteristics
   a) Cheerful
   b) Considerate
   c) Courteous
   d) Friendly
   e) Neat
   f) Thoughtful
3) How to Improve Your Attitude
   a) Associate with positive people
   b) Speak well of others
   c) Isolate negative thoughts
   d) Treat others with respect
   e) Forgive and forge on
4) Attitude is Everything. . .
   a) Anything is possible with a positive attitude

FIGURE 2-81

5. Change the slide layout on Slide 3 to Text & Clip Art. Using the clip art placeholder, insert the clip art shown in Figure 2-82 that has the keywords, Consensus Cooperate Guarantee Synergy Agreeable. Increase the bulleted list line spacing to 0.4 lines before each paragraph.
6. On Slide 4, change the font size of Anything is possible with a positive attitude, to italic, 72 points. Center the bulleted text and then remove the bullet.
7. Add the slide number and your name to the slide footer. Display the footer on all slides. Add your name to the outline header and your school's name to the outline footer.

(continued)

Adding Clip Art and Animation Effects to a Presentation Created in Outline View *(continued)*

8. Apply the Strips Right-Down slide transition effect to all slides. Apply the Wipe Right custom animation effect to all heading level 1 paragraphs on Slide 2 and Slide 3.
9. Check the presentation for errors.
10. Save the presentation on a floppy disk using the file name, Positive Attitude.
11. Print the presentation outline. Print the black and white presentation.
12. Quit PowerPoint.

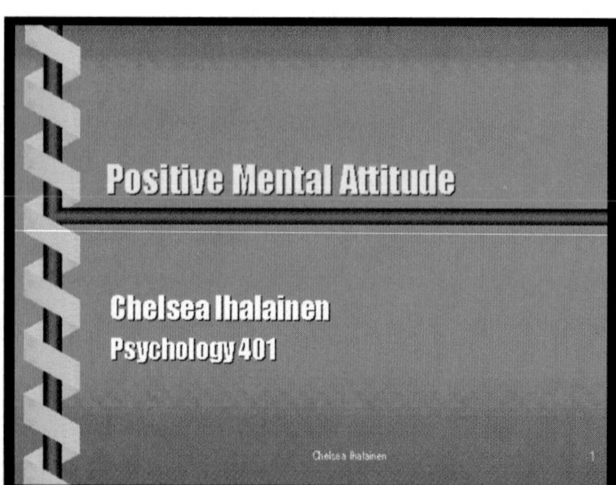

FIGURE 2-82a

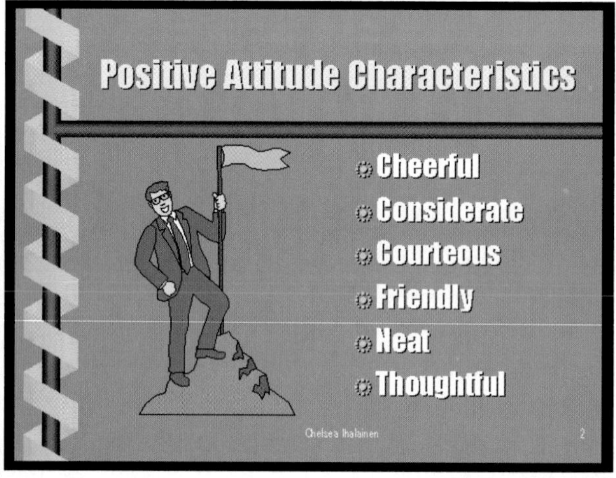

FIGURE 2-82b

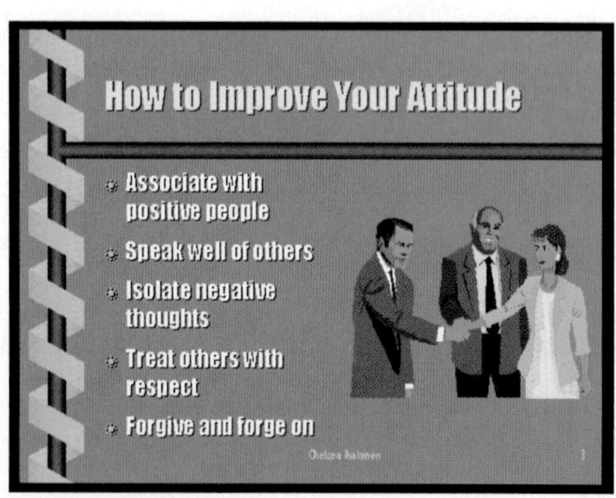

FIGURE 2-82c

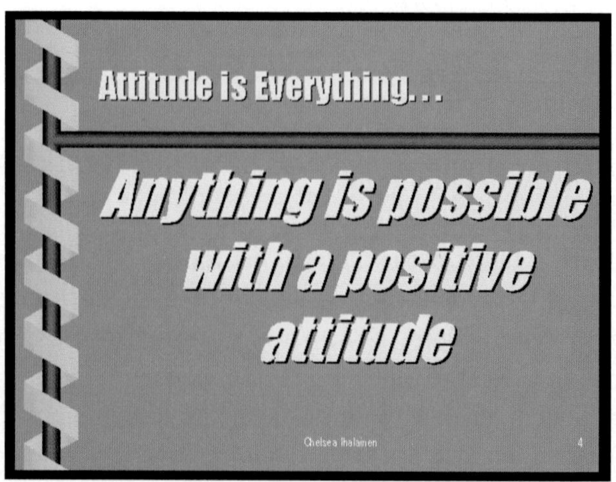

FIGURE 2-82d

FIGURE 2-82

In the Lab

2 Animating a Slide Show

Problem: You are the marketing director for Clarity Health Products, a manufacturer of vitamins and other nutritional supplements. Experience tells you that sales are related directly to the quality of the sales presentation. Sales quotas are higher than last year and you want to make sure your sales staff understands the importance of practicing the delivery of a presentation. After much research, you prepare the outline shown in Figure 2-83. When you practice your presentation, you decide to add animation effects to the slide show. The completed slide show is shown in Figure 2-84.

Instructions: Perform the following tasks. *Hint*: Use Help to solve this problem.

1. Create a new presentation using the Ribbons design template and the outline shown in Figure 2-83.
2. On the title slide, use your name instead of the name Anna Douglas. Decrease the font size of Presented by: to 20 points. Decrease the font size of Marketing Director and Clarity Health Products to 24 points.
3. On Slide 2, increase the font size of the heading level 1 bullets to 36 points and heading level 2 bullets to 32 points. Increase the line spacing for heading level 2 bullets to 0.75 lines before each paragraph. Using Figure 2-84 as a reference, insert the clip art that has the keyword, Leadership. Scale the clip art to 95% and drag it to the lower-right corner of the slide as shown in Figure 2-84.
4. On Slide 3, insert the clip art shown in Figure 2-84 that has the keywords, Surprise Incomprehensible Incredible. Scale the clip art to 90%. Drag the clip art to the right side of the slide.

I. Polishing Your Presentation
    A. Presented by:
    B. Anna Douglas
    C. Marketing Director
    D. Clarity Health Products
II. Practice Makes Perfect
    A. Three key factors for a successful presentation
        1. Practice
        2. Practice
        3. Practice
III. Why Practice?
    A. Increase confidence
    B. Develop rhythm
        1. Pause for emphasis
    C. Improve articulation
        1. Vary pitch and inflection
    D. Establish timings
    E. Identify problems
IV. How To Practice
    A. Speak out loud
        1. Make a recording
            a) Video
            b) Audio
        2. Look into a mirror
        3. Find a live audience
            a) Friend or co-worker
            b) Group or team
    B. Go to delivery site
        1. Inspect equipment
            a) Audio-visual
            b) Lectern
        2. Check environment
            a) Noise
            b) Lighting
            c) Room temperature
V. Practice Makes Perfect

FIGURE 2-83

(continued)

Animating a Slide Show *(continued)*

5. On Slide 4, change the slide layout to 2 Column Text. Drag the text into the right column placeholder so your slide looks like Slide 4 in Figure 2-84. Increase the line spacing to 0.5 lines before each paragraph.
6. On Slide 5, change the slide layout to Object. Insert the clip art that has the keywords, Target Incredible.
7. Add the current date, slide number, and your name to the slide footer. Display the footer on all slides. Include the current date and your name on the outline header. Include Clarity Health Products and the page number on the outline footer.
8. Apply the Strips Right-Up slide transition effect to all slides. Apply the Fly From Bottom custom animation effect to bulleted text on Slides 1 through 4. Introduce text grouped by 3rd level paragraphs.
9. Animate the clip art on Slide 2 using the Fly From Bottom-Right custom animation effect so it displays immediately after the slide title when you run the slide show. Animate clip art on Slide 5 using the Zoom In From Screen Center custom animation effect.
10. Save the presentation on a floppy disk using the file name, Polishing Your Presentation.
11. Print the presentation outline. Print the presentation slides without animations in black and white.
12. Quit PowerPoint.

FIGURE 2-84a

FIGURE 2-84b

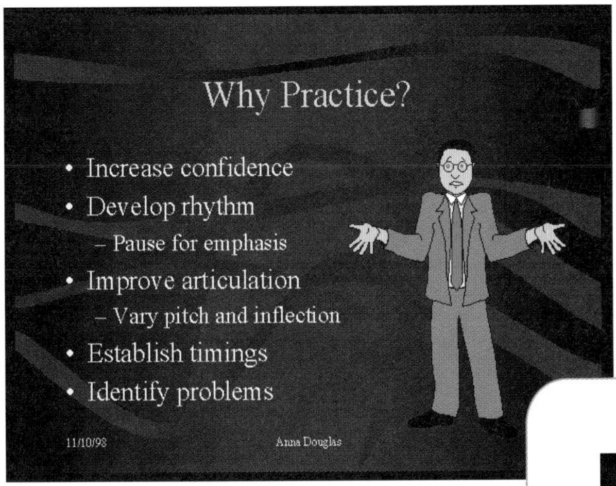

Why Practice?

- Increase confidence
- Develop rhythm
  - Pause for emphasis
- Improve articulation
  - Vary pitch and inflection
- Establish timings
- Identify problems

11/10/98 Anna Douglas

FIGURE 2-84c

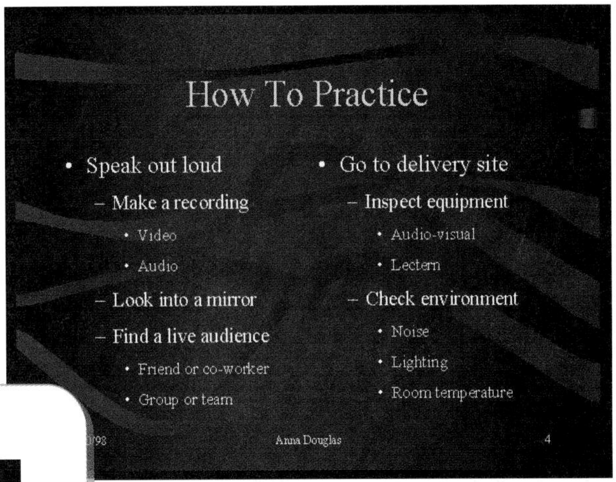

How To Practice

- Speak out loud
  - Make a recording
    - Video
    - Audio
  - Look into a mirror
  - Find a live audience
    - Friend or co-worker
    - Group or team
- Go to delivery site
  - Inspect equipment
    - Audio-visual
    - Lectern
  - Check environment
    - Noise
    - Lighting
    - Room temperature

/98 Anna Douglas 4

FIGURE 2-84d

FIGURE 2-84e

3 Creating a Presentation in Outline View, Inserting and Moving Clip Art, and Applying Slide Transition and Animation Effects

Problem: You are Maurice Barber, the Director of Career Development and Placement at Mercedes Valley College. A local middle school principal has asked you to speak to his eighth grade students about career opportunities. You create the presentation using the outline shown in Figure 2-85. You then refine the presentation using clip art, slide transitions, and animation effects to create the slide show shown in Figure 2-86. *Hint*: Use Help to solve this problem.

Instructions: Perform the following tasks.

1. Create a new presentation using the Zesty design template and the outline in Figure 2-85.
2. On the title slide, animate the subtitle with the Zoom In From Screen Center custom animation effect.
3. Use Figure 2-86 as a reference. Change the slide layout on Slide 2 to Clip Art & Text. Then insert clip art that has the keywords, Opportunity Knocks. Increase line spacing to 1 line before paragraph on heading level 1.
4. Change the slide layout on Slide 3 to Clip Art & Text. Insert clip art that has the keywords, Focus Investigation Diagnose.
5. On Slide 4, insert the clip art that has the keywords, Surprise Incomprehensible Incredible. Scale the clip art to 75%. Move the clip art to the right edge of the slide as shown in Figure 2-86.
6. Add the slide number and your name to the slide footer. Display the footer on all slides. Display your name to the outline header, and the page number, and the name of the school, Mercedes Valley College, to the outline footer.
7. Check the presentation for spelling errors.

I. Future Considerations
  A. What Will You Be When You Grow Up?
II. What Is In Your Future?
  A. Education
    1. College
    2. Technical School
    3. Apprenticeship
  B. Work
    1. On the job training
III. Investigate Options
  A. Engineer
  B. Entertainer
  C. Florist
  D. Machinist
  E. Nurse
  F. Programmer
  G. Teacher
  H. Veterinarian
IV. How Do You Choose?
  A. Consider likes and dislikes
    1. Reading and writing
    2. Working with people
    3. Working with animals
    4. Working with computers
    5. Working with your hands

FIGURE 2-85

In the Lab

8. Apply the Box In slide transition effect to all slides. Apply the Strips Right-Down custom animation effect to all 2nd level paragraphs on Slides 2 through 4. Apply the Peek From Left custom animation effect to clip art on Slide 3 and then change animation order so the clip art displays before the bulleted text.
9. Save the presentation on a floppy disk using the file name, Future Considerations.
10. Run the electronic slide show.
11. Print the presentation outline. Print the presentation slides without animations in black and white.
12. Quit PowerPoint.

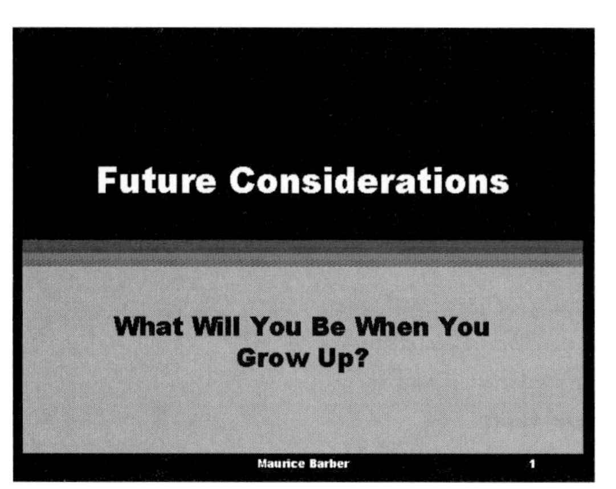

FIGURE 2-86a

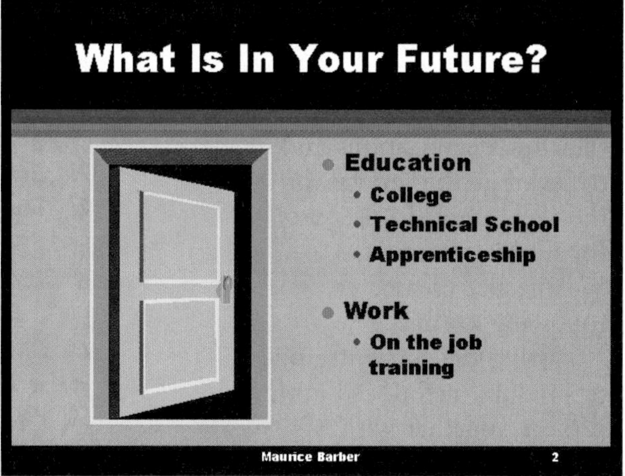

FIGURE 2-86b

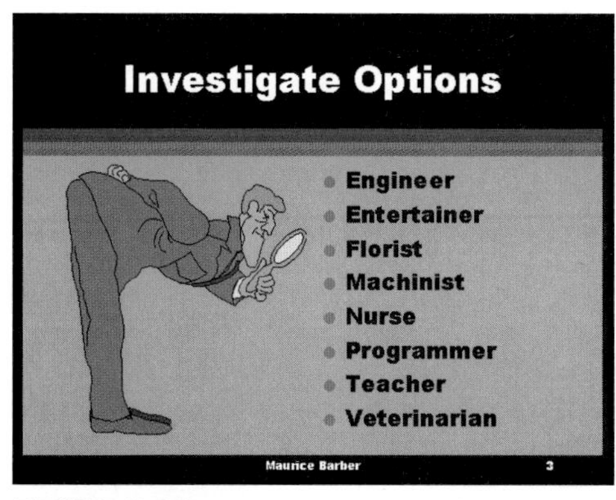

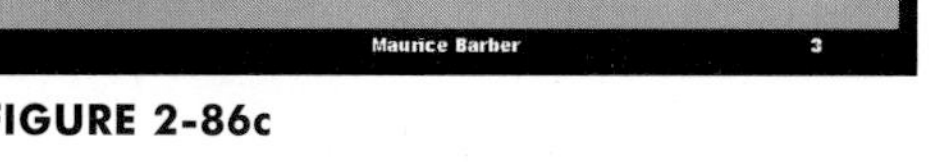

FIGURE 2-86c

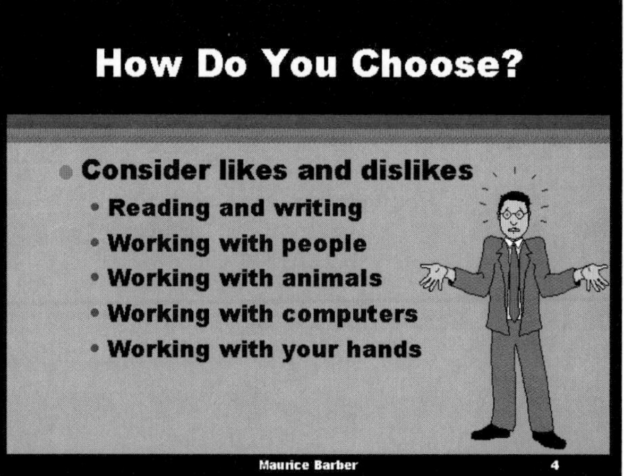

FIGURE 2-86d

Cases and Places

The difficulty of these case studies varies: ◗ are the least difficult; ◗◗ are more difficult; and ◗◗◗ are the most difficult.

1 ◗ AAA Accounting and Tax Consultants is a privately owned accounting firm. Marshall Weatherbee, president of the firm, is one of several Certified Public Accountants conducting short presentations at a financial planning seminar. The purpose of the seminar is to inform people about their financial options and to promote the services of the presenters. To prepare for the presentation, Mr. Weatherbee created the following outline.

Using the concepts and techniques introduced in this project, together with Mr. Weatherbee's outline, develop slides for an electronic slide show. Include clip art and animation effects to add interest. Print the outline so that it can be distributed to the audience at the conclusion of the presentation.

I. AAA Accounting and Tax Consultants
   A. We listen to you and work as a team to meet your financial goals.
   B. Marshall Weatherbee, President
II. Prepare for Retirement, Now
   A. Follow 20/80 rule for current income
      1. Live on 20%
      2. Save 80%
   B. Eliminate all debt
   C. Establish financial plan
III. Financial Plan
   A. Establish monthly budget
   B. Develop investment strategy
      1. High-risk investments
      2. Low-risk investments
      3. Savings
   C. Consult with certified financial planner
IV. AAA Accounting and Tax Consultants
   A. Comprehensive financial planning
      1. Financial and estate
      2. Retirement
      3. Education
      4. Investments
      5. Insurance
   B. Additional services
      1. Tax strategies
      2. Tax preparation
      3. Tax audit representation
      4. Debt reduction strategies
      5. Business planning

FIGURE 2-87

Cases and Places

2 ◗ First Class Limousine advertises their services at bridal fairs, county fairs, and business conventions. Next week is the 1998 Stone Mountain bridal fair. You have been asked to create a professional-looking presentation from the outline developed by the company owner, Margo Quinn.

Using the concepts and techniques introduced in this project along with the following outline, create an electronic presentation for First Class Limousine. Include appropriate clip art and animation effects. Ms. Quinn would like a printed outline that can be distributed to the audience at the conclusion of the presentation.

I. First Class Limousine
  A. The ultimate in luxury, comfort, and affordability
  B. A special ride for your special day
II. Affordable Packages
  A. Debutante
    1. Luxury transportation at reasonable rates
  B. Princess
    1. Pampered conveyance in style
  C. Royalty
    1. A once-in-a-lifetime adventure
III. Debutante
  A. The basic package includes:
    1. Six passenger sedan
    2. Courteous, licensed driver
    3. Soft drinks
IV. Princess
  A. The most popular package offers:
    1. Eight passenger luxury sedan
    2. Courteous, licensed driver in chauffeur's cap
    3. Refreshments
      a) Soft drinks and hors d'oeuvres
    4. Twelve-speaker CD sound system
V. Royalty
  A. The aristocratic package features:
    1. Ten or twelve passenger stretch limousine
    2. Courteous, licensed driver in top hat and tails
    3. Refreshments
      a) Soft drinks and hors d'oeuvres
      b) Lobster salad or prime rib sandwiches
    4. Live music
      a) Concert violinist performs customized selection of songs
VI. Luxury Limousines
  A. New 6, 8, and 12 passenger sedans
  B. TV, VCR, and mood lights
  C. Beverages
  D. Glass and privacy partitions
  E. Cellular telephone
VII. Travel First Class Limousine
  A. Telephone
    1. 555-LIMO
  B. Ask about our FREE hour special

FIGURE 2-88

Cases and Places

3 ▶▶ Diver Dan's Dive Shop sells equipment for SCUBA divers. SCUBA is the acronym for Self-Contained Underwater Breathing Apparatus. Dan, the store's owner, is frequently asked for information about three SCUBA certification programs, PATI, NAUI, and YMCA. Each program has different teaching approaches and certification standards. Dan wants you to create a presentation that compares and contrasts the three programs. He also wants the presentation to be animated and include clip art. Research the three certification programs and then using the concepts and techniques introduced in this project, create the presentation. Create handouts from the presentation outline.

4 ▶▶ Goals are often divided into four categories: spiritual, family, career, and self. A 1973 Yale University economics study concluded that three-percent of the 1953 Yale graduating class had written goals and defined a plan with which to reach them. Twenty years later, the same three-percent had achieved a net worth greater than the rest of the entire class combined. Using the techniques introduced in the project, create a presentation about yourself. Provide a brief biography. Develop a list of your goals. Under each goal category, identify two or more goals. One goal should be a short-term goal, something that will take less than a year to achieve. Another goal would be a long-term goal, something that will take longer than one year to achieve. Include appropriate clip art and animation effects.

5 ▶▶▶ In addition to Microsoft PowerPoint, other presentation graphics software packages include Persuasion, Compel, Freelance Graphics, and Harvard Graphics. Visit a software vendor and try one of these or another presentation graphics package. Using current computer magazines or other resources, learn more about the package you tested. Based on what you have discovered, together with the concepts and techniques introduced in this project, prepare a presentation comparing and contrasting the package you tested against Microsoft PowerPoint. Contrast the capabilities, strengths, weaknesses, ease of use, and cost of each package. End by noting which package you prefer and your reasons why. Enhance the presentation with clip art and custom animation. Print the outline of the presentation.

6 ▶▶▶ Recent economic changes have forced many organizations to alter their business focus from manufacturing to service. To be successful, service-oriented businesses must be able to clearly and convincingly explain how they can benefit prospective clients. Visit a local business that provides a service and learn all you can about the service and the people to whom it is being offered. Using the results of your visit, along with the concepts and techniques introduced in this project, prepare a presentation promoting the company's services. Embellish the presentation with clip art and custom animation effects. Print the presentation and the presentation outline.

7 ▶▶▶ Are people born with great leadership skills, or do ordinary people develop into great leaders? Leadership expert and author, John Maxwell, states in his book, *The Success Journey*; "Success is not a destination thing, it is a daily thing." Go to the library or use the World Wide Web to research some of the world's great leaders. What qualities do they share? Why are these people considered to be great leaders? Using the results of your research, together with the concepts and techniques introduced in this project, prepare a presentation about leadership. Feature one of the leaders you researched. Enhance the presentation with clip art and custom animation.

Importing Clip Art from the Microsoft Clip Gallery Live Web Site

Case Perspective

Because of the success of the Break Away Bargains promotion, Mr. Hayes, your boss at Voyager Travel Tours, decides to run the promotion at several schools. After reviewing the presentation, you suggest he replace the clock clip art on Slide 6 to something more persuasive, like a sun, radiating sun rays into the audience. Mr. Hayes agrees and asks you to find a picture of a sun. You look at Microsoft Clip Gallery 3.0, but don't find clip art that you like. Knowing that World Wide Web access was built into Microsoft Clip Gallery 3.0, you decide to browse the Microsoft Clip Gallery Live Web site for clip art. You find several sun clip art images on the Web. You decide to open the clip art into the Microsoft Clip Gallery 3.0 and then insert it into Slide 6.

Your suggestion to Mr. Hayes is to animate the sun to make sure the audience remembers it when they leave the presentation. You decide the best animation effect for the sun is Swivel.

Introduction

As you become more experienced with PowerPoint, you realize that Microsoft Clip Gallery 3.0 has a limited amount of clip art. There are times when you cannot locate an appropriate clip art image in Microsoft Clip Gallery 3.0, or other times when you just want something different. Microsoft, fortunately, created a source for additional clip art, called Microsoft Clip Gallery Live, which is conveniently located on the World Wide Web. To make accessing the Web site easy, Microsoft added a button to the Microsoft Clip Gallery 3.0 dialog box, which, when clicked, connects you directly to the Microsoft Clip Gallery Live start page (Figure 1 on the next page).

In this integration feature, you modify the presentation created in Project 2 by replacing the clock clip art on Slide 6 with clip art from the Web as shown in Figure 2 on the next page.

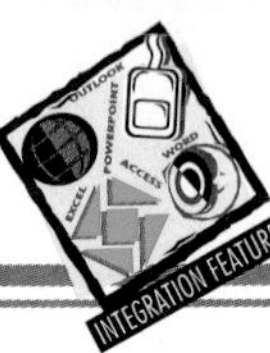

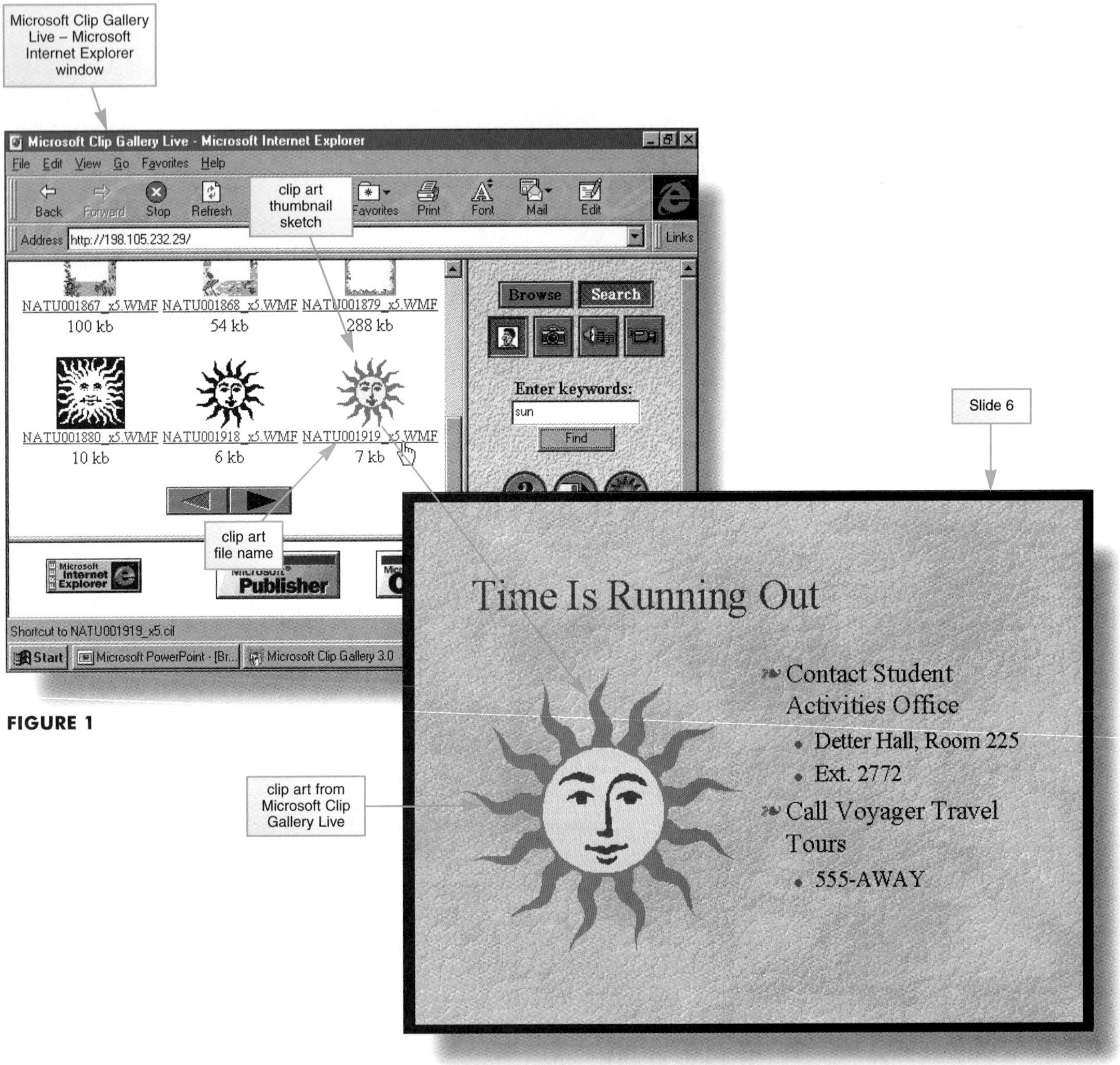
Microsoft Clip Gallery Live – Microsoft Internet Explorer window
Microsoft Clip Gallery Live - Microsoft Internet Explorer
clip art thumbnail sketch
Address http://198.105.232.29/
NATU001867_x5.WMF 100 kb
NATU001868_x5.WMF 54 kb
NATU001879_x5.WMF 288 kb
NATU001880_x5.WMF 10 kb
NATU001918_x5.WMF 6 kb
NATU001919_x5.WMF 7 kb
Browse
Search
Enter keywords:
sun
Find
clip art file name
Shortcut to NATU001919_x5.cil
Slide 6
Time Is Running Out
Contact Student Activities Office
Detter Hall, Room 225
Ext. 2772
Call Voyager Travel Tours
555-AWAY
clip art from Microsoft Clip Gallery Live

FIGURE 1

FIGURE 2

Opening an Existing Presentation and Saving it with a New File Name

Because you are replacing clip art in the Break Away Bargains presentation created in Project 2, the first step is to open the presentation. To ensure that the original Break Away Bargains presentation remains intact, you save the presentation with a new name: Break Away Bargains Sun. Then, you connect to the World Wide Web and import clip art. The following pages illustrate these steps.

Opening an Existing Presentation

Before making changes to the clip art in the Break Away Bargains presentation, you first must open it. Perform the following steps to open the Break Away Bargains presentation.

TO OPEN AN EXISTING PRESENTATION

Step 1: Insert your floppy disk into drive A that contains the Break Away Bargains presentation created in Project 2.
Step 2: Click the Start button on the taskbar. Click Open Office Document. Click 3½ Floppy (A:) in the Look in list box.
Step 3: Double-click the presentation, Break Away Bargains.

PowerPoint opens and displays the presentation in the view in which it was last saved. Project 2 last saved the presentation in slide view.

More *About* Custom Slide Shows

When you need slightly different presentations for separate audiences, consider creating a custom slide show instead of several individual presentations. A custom slide show allows you to group slides common to all audiences with slides unique to an individual audience. For details on creating a custom slide show, see Create a custom show in PowerPoint online Help.

Saving a Presentation with a New File Name

Because you want to preserve the original Break Away Bargains presentation, you save the open presentation with a new file name. Then, you make the changes to the new presentation. Essentially, you are making a duplicate copy of a file. Perform the following steps to save the Break Away Bargains presentation with a new file name using the Save As command.

TO SAVE A PRESENTATION WITH A NEW FILE NAME

Step 1: Click File on the menu bar. Click Save As.
Step 2: Type `Break Away Bargains Sun` in the File name text box.
Step 3: Click the Save button.

The Break Away Bargains presentation is saved with the file name Break Away Bargains Sun. The new file name displays in the title bar.

Moving to Another Slide

When creating or editing your presentation, you often want to display a slide other than the current one. Dragging the vertical scroll bar box up or down displays the slide indicator. Recall the slide indicator displays the slide number and title of the slide you are about to display. Once you see the number of the slide you wish to display, release the left mouse button. Perform the step on the next page to move to Slide 6 using the vertical scroll box.

Steps To Move to Another Slide

1 **Drag the vertical scroll bar down until Slide: 6 of 6 Time Is Running Out displays in the slide indicator.**

Slide 6 displays (Figure 3).

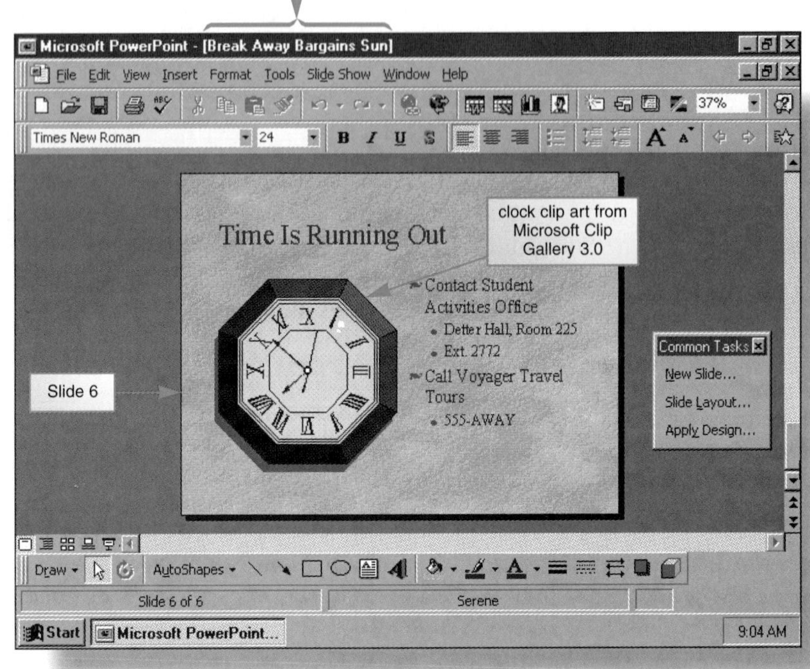

FIGURE 3

Importing Clip Art from Microsoft Clip Gallery Live on the World Wide Web

More *About* **Clip Art Web Sites**

Searching the World Wide Web for sources of clip art can supplement clip art available in the Microsoft Clip Gallery or the Microsoft Clip Gallery Live Web site. Use one of the search engines to search for public domain clip art. Search for the following keywords: clip art and clip+art.

Recall from Project 2 that one source for additional clip art images is the World Wide Web. Many companies provide clip art images on the Web; some free of cost, some charge a fee. Microsoft maintains a Web site called **Microsoft Clip Gallery Live** that contains files for clip art, photographs, sounds, and videos.

Because Microsoft Clip Gallery 3.0 has a limited amount of clip art, you sometimes cannot find an image that best enhances your slide. At those times, you may want to connect to the Microsoft Clip Gallery Live Web site to search for additional clip art files. To use the Microsoft Clip Gallery Live Web site you must have access to the World Wide Web and Web browser software. You access the World Wide Web through an **Internet service provider**, called an **ISP**. This project, for example, uses **The Microsoft Network** to access the Web and uses **Microsoft Internet Explorer** for the Web browser. If you do not have an ISP, your instructor will provide the clip art file used in this project.

To simplify connecting to the Microsoft Clip Gallery Live Web site, the Microsoft Clip Gallery 3.0 dialog box contains a **Connect to Web for additional clips** button. When you click the Connect to Web for additional clips button, a network Sign In window displays. Depending on your ISP, the Sign In window will vary.

Opening Microsoft Clip Gallery 3.0

A clip art image on a slide maintains a **link** to Microsoft Clip Gallery 3.0. When you double-click a clip art image, Microsoft Clip Gallery 3.0 opens and the Clip Art sheet displays. In this project you want to replace the clock clip art image on Slide 6 with an image of the sun to improve the closing slide. A picture of the sun reinforces the warm tropical vacations of the Break Away Bargains promotion.

Perform the following step to open Microsoft Clip Gallery 3.0.

To Open Microsoft Clip Gallery 3.0

1. **Double-click the clock clip art image on Slide 6.**

Microsoft Clip Gallery 3.0 opens and displays the Clip Art sheet (Figure 4).

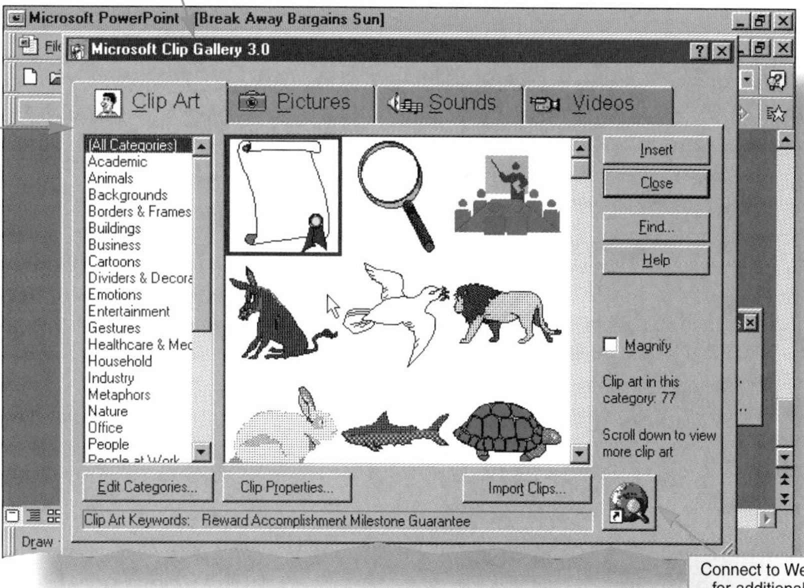

FIGURE 4

Connecting to the Microsoft Clip Gallery Live World Wide Web Site

When you are ready to access clip art in Microsoft Clip Gallery Live, you click the Connect to Web for additional clips button. A Sign In window for your ISP displays if you are required to identify yourself with a name and password. Some schools by-pass this window because of the school's Web connection setup. See your instructor for your school's requirements. If you are connecting to the Web at a location other than school, you must know the ISP's sign in requirements.

Once you connect to the Web, the Microsoft Clip Gallery Live start page displays. A **start page** is a specially designed page that serves as a starting point for a Web site.

Perform the step on the next page to connect to the World Wide Web and display the Microsoft Clip Gallery Live start page.

More About Connecting to Microsoft Clip Gallery Live

To connect to the Microsoft Clip Gallery Live Web page using a browser other than Internet Explorer, such as Netscape, start the browser and type http://www.microsoft.com/clipgallerylive in the Location text box, and then press the ENTER key.

Steps To Connect to the Microsoft Clip Gallery Live World Wide Web Site

1 Click the Connect to Web for additional clips button in the Microsoft Clip Gallery 3.0 dialog box. Connect to the World Wide Web as required by your browser software and ISP. When the Microsoft Clip Gallery Live start page displays, read the End-User License Agreement for Microsoft Software. Click the Accept button.

If you are using a modem, Microsoft Clip Gallery 3.0 displays a dialog box that connects you to the World Wide Web via your ISP. If you are directly connected to the World Wide Web through a computer network, the dialog box does not display. Once connected to the World Wide Web, the Microsoft Clip Gallery Live start page displays the End-User License Agreement. When you click the Accept button, the End-User License Agreement area no longer displays. The area now displays buttons to locate clip art, photo, sound, and video clips (Figure 5). The Browse button and the Clip Art button are recessed indicating the current mode is set to browse the Clip Art category listed in the Select a category text box. Underlined text is a hypertext link to other Web pages.

Microsoft Internet Explorer window
status indicator
Browse button is recessed
current Web page address
clip art button
Search button
Select a category text box
hypertext link
Microsoft PowerPoint – [Break Away Bargains Sun] button
Microsoft Clip Gallery 3.0 button
Microsoft Internet Explorer button is recessed
ISP icon

FIGURE 5

> **More About Searching Microsoft Clip Gallery Live**
>
> You can search the Microsoft Clip Gallery Live for more than just clip art. To search for pictures, sound, or video files, click the corresponding media button in the Microsoft Clip Gallery Live window, select a category in the Select a category list box, and then click the Go button.

Searching for Microsoft Clip Gallery Live Clip Art

Microsoft Clip Gallery Live is similar to Microsoft Clip Gallery 3.0 in that you can search for clip art by keywords. This project is looking for a clip art image of the sun, so you want to search Microsoft Clip Gallery Live using the keyword, sun. Perform the following steps to search for clip art in Microsoft Clip Gallery Live.

Steps To Search for Microsoft Clip Gallery Live Clip Art

1 **Click the Search button. Click the Enter keywords text box. Type** sun **in the Enter keywords text box. Point to the Find button.**

When you click the Search button, the Enter keywords text box replaces the Select a category text box (Figure 6).

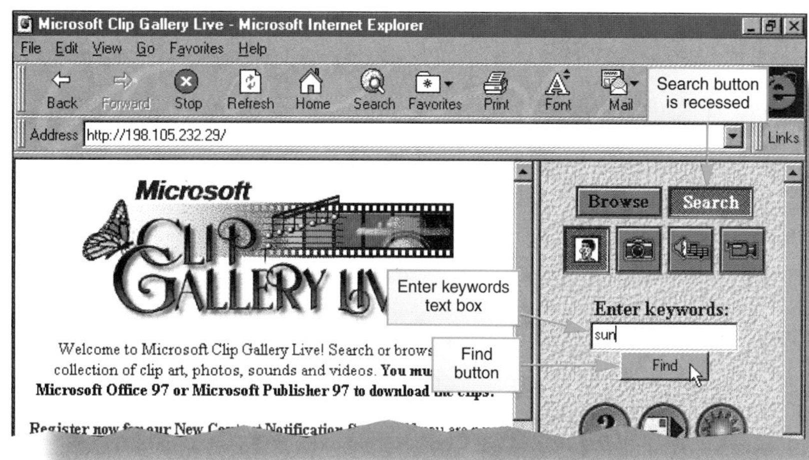

FIGURE 6

2 **Click the Find button.**

After a few moments, the result of the search displays in the left side of the page (Figure 7). Search status displays at the top of the area, such as the number of images that match the search criteria. Below the search status information is the number of images that display in this page. The underlined text below each image is its file name and a hypertext link used to import the image. The number below the file name is the file size.

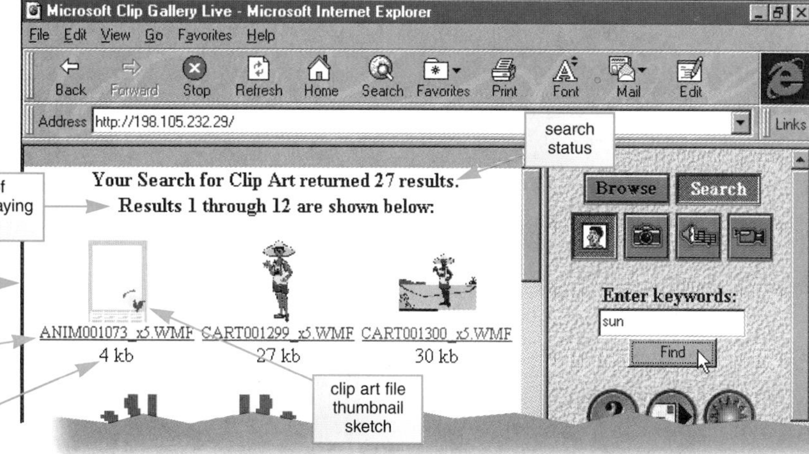

FIGURE 7

3 **Scroll down the search results area until the orange and yellow sun with the file name NATU001919_x5.WMF displays. Then point to the file name hypertext link NATU001919_x5.WMF (Figure 8).**

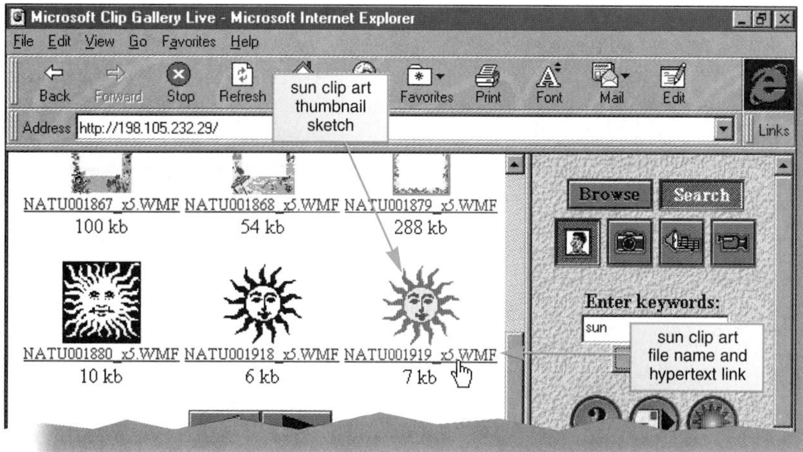

FIGURE 8

4 **Click NATU001919_x5. When the Internet Explorer dialog box displays, click the Open it option button. Then click the OK button.**

Microsoft Internet Explorer displays a dialog box cautioning that viruses could be transmitted when this file is sent to your computer. The Open it option button is selected. By default, a check mark displays in the Always ask before opening this type of file check box. The file extension for the clip art file is cil, which stands for Clip Gallery Download Package. The NATU001919_x5.WMF file is added to the Microsoft Clip Gallery 3.0 in the Downloaded Clips category (Figure 9). Keywords for this clip art display at the bottom of the Clip Art sheet.

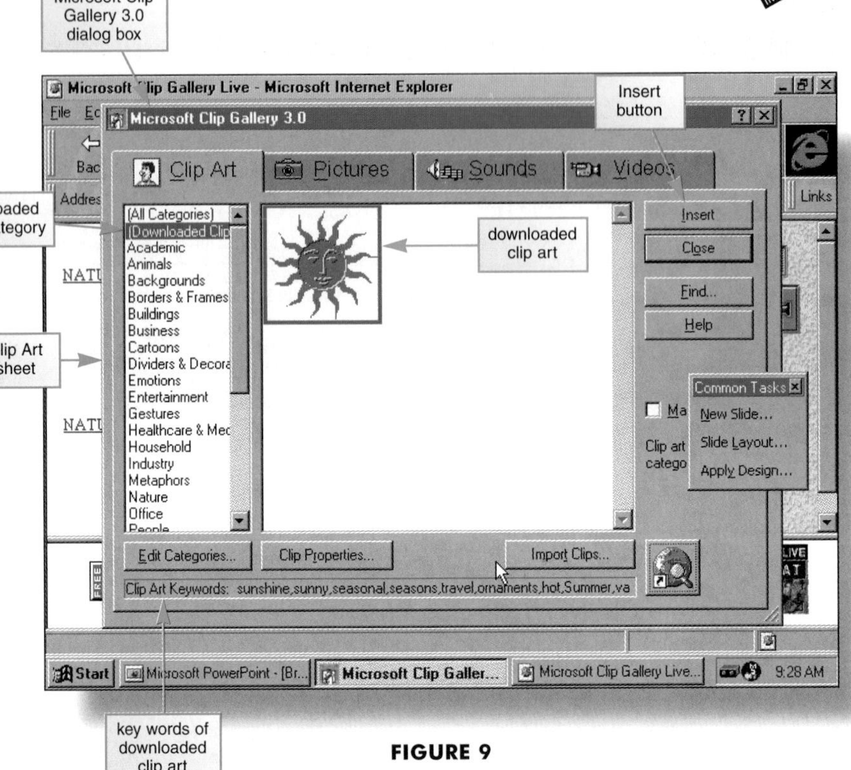

FIGURE 9

5 **Click the Insert button.**

The clip art displays on Slide 6 and replaces the clock clip art (Figure 10). Microsoft Clip Gallery Live still is open and you still are connected to the ISP.

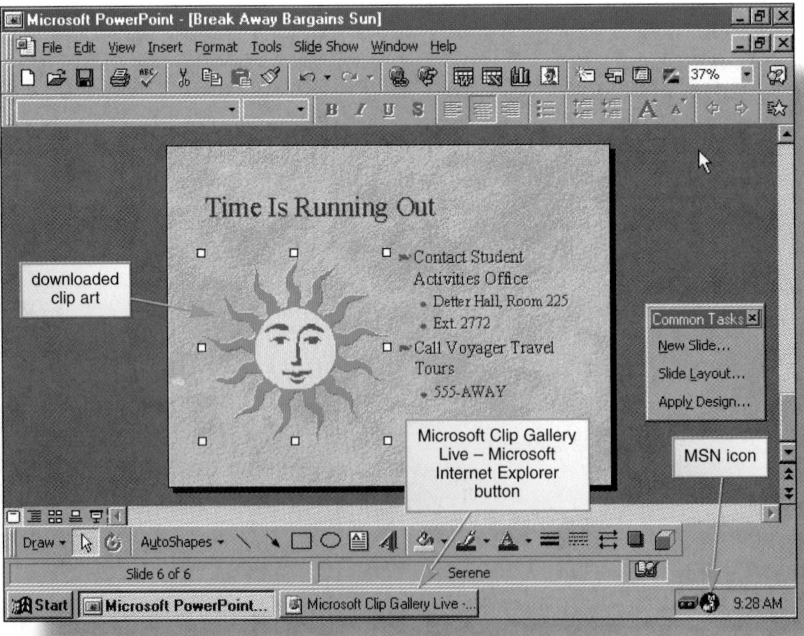

FIGURE 10

If you click the Save it to disk option button in the Internet Explorer dialog box in Step 4 above, you download the file to disk. If you save clip art to disk, you must double-click the file name in Explore to decompress the file and insert it into the Microsoft Clip Gallery 3.0.

More About Microsoft Clip Gallery Live

Click the Hot Clips button in the Microsoft Clip Gallery Live Web page to open a sample of the latest clip art images available for the selected media type, such as clip art. Microsoft updates this Web site regularly.

Quitting a Web Session

Once you have downloaded your clip art, you want to quit your Web session. Because Windows 95 displays buttons on the taskbar for each open application, you quickly can quit an application by right-clicking an application button and then clicking the Close button on the shortcut menu. Perform the following steps to quit your current Web session.

TO QUIT A WEB SESSION

Step 1: Right-click the Microsoft Clip Gallery Live – Microsoft Internet Explorer button on the taskbar. If you are not using Microsoft Internet Explorer, right-click the button for your browser.
Step 2: Click Close on the shortcut menu.
Step 3: When The Microsoft Network dialog box displays, click the Yes button to disconnect. If you are using a different ISP, click the Yes button to disconnect.

The browser software closes and the ISP connection is terminated.

Adding Animation Effects

To draw attention to the sun clip art on Slide 6, you apply animation effects. In this project you add the Swivel custom animation effect as described in the following steps.

More About Animation Effects

Animation effects help direct the eyes to follow an object. The goal is to assist the audience in understanding the content supported by the graphic object. The more efficiently you control the eye movement of the audience, the more effective the presentation.

TO ANIMATE CLIP ART

Step 1: Right-click the sun clip art object and then click Custom Animation on the shortcut menu. If necessary, click the Effects tab.
Step 2: Click the Entry animation and sound box arrow. Drag the Entry animation and sound list scroll box until Swivel displays.
Step 3: Click Swivel.
Step 4: Click the OK button.

PowerPoint applies Swivel animation effects to the sun clip art and closes the Custom Animation dialog box.

Saving the Presentation

The changes to the presentation are complete. Perform the following step to save the finished presentation to a floppy disk before running the slide show.

TO SAVE A PRESENTATION

Step 1: Click the Save button on the Standard toolbar.

PowerPoint saves the presentation by saving the changes made to the presentation since the last save.

Running an Animated Slide Show

To verify that the presentation looks like expected, run the presentation in slide show view. Perform the following steps to run the revised Break Away Bargains Sun slide show.

TO RUN AN ANIMATED SLIDE SHOW

Step 1: Drag the vertical scroll bar to display Slide: 1 of 6 Voyager Travel Tours.
Step 2: Click the Slide Show button on the View Button Bar. When Slide 1 displays in slide show view, click the slide anywhere except on the Popup Menu buttons.
Step 3: Continue clicking the slides to finish running the slide show and return to slide view.

The presentation displays the animation effects in slide show view and returns to slide view when finished.

Now that the presentation is complete, the last step is to print the presentation slides.

Printing Presentation Slides

Perform the following steps to print the revised presentation.

TO PRINT PRESENTATION SLIDES

Step 1: Click File on the menu bar and then click Print.
Step 2: When the Print dialog box displays, click the Print what box arrow.
Step 3: Click Slides (without animations) and then click the OK button.

Quitting PowerPoint

The changes to this presentation are saved. The last step is to quit PowerPoint. Perform the following steps to quit PowerPoint.

TO QUIT POWERPOINT

Step 1: Click the Close button on the title bar.
Step 2: If the Microsoft PowerPoint dialog box displays, click the Yes button to save changes made since the last save.

PowerPoint closes.

Project Summary

This integration feature introduced importing clip art to Microsoft Clip Gallery 3.0 from Microsoft Clip Gallery Live on the World Wide Web. You began by opening an existing presentation, Break Away Bargains, and then saving the presentation with a new file name. Next you opened Microsoft Clip Gallery 3.0 by double-clicking the clip art on Slide 6. You then accessed the Microsoft Clip Gallery Live start page on the World Wide Web by clicking the Connect to Web for additional clips button. Once connected to the Microsoft Clip Gallery Live start page, you searched for clip art with the keyword, sun. Then you imported the clip art file to the Microsoft Clip Gallery 3.0 by downloading the file from the Web page. To insert the sun clip art into Slide 6, you double-clicked the imported clip art. You then quit the Web session by closing the browser software and disconnecting from the ISP. Next you applied the Swivel animation effect to the sun clip art. Finally, you saved the presentation, ran the presentation in slide show view to check for continuity, printed the presentation slides, and quit PowerPoint.

What You Should Know

Having completed this project, you now should be able to perform the following tasks:

- Animate Clip Art *(PPI 1.10)*
- Connect to the Microsoft Clip Gallery Live World Wide Web Site *(PPI 1.6)*
- Move to Another Slide *(PPI 1.4)*
- Open an Existing Presentation *(PPI 1.3)*
- Open Microsoft Clip Gallery 3.0 *(PPI 1.5)*
- Print Presentation Slides *(PPI 1.11)*
- Quit a Web Session *(PPI 1.9)*
- Quit PowerPoint *(PPI 1.11)*
- Run an Animated Slide Show *(PPI 1.10)*
- Save a Presentation *(PPI 1.10)*
- Save a Presentation with a New File Name *(PPI 1.3)*
- Search for Microsoft Clip Gallery Live Clip Art *(PPI 1.7)*

1 Using Help

Instructions: Perform the following tasks using a computer.

1. Open an existing presentation. Click Office Assistant. Type `web` in the What would you like to do? box. Click the Search button. Click Presentations on the Internet. Click the hypertext link, Internet. Read and print the information. Read and print the other seven hypertext links on this Microsoft PowerPoint Help window. Click the Help Topics button.
2. Click the Index tab. Type `internet` in box 1. Double-click Microsoft Web sites in box 2. Double-click Additional locations of clip art, pictures, music, sound, video clips, and animations.
   Read and print the online Help information. Click the Help Topics button.

(continued)

In the Lab

In the Lab 1 *(continued)*

3. Double-click Microsoft Web sites. Double-click Connect to Microsoft technical resources. Read and print the online Help information. Click the hypertext link for Microsoft Knowledge Base (KB). Read and print the information. Click the hypertext link for Microsoft Software Library (MSL). Read and print the information.
4. Click the Close button. Click the Office Assistant Close button. Quit PowerPoint.

2 Importing Clip Art

Problem: You are the manager of Holiday Getaways travel agency. You need to find a piece of clip art for a sports-lover vacation presentation you are developing. In order to open easily Microsoft Clip Gallery 3.0 and search the Web for clip art, you create a one slide presentation using the Text & Clip Art AutoLayout. You then search the Web for appropriate clip art and download it into your slide.

Instructions: Open the presentation Sports Holiday from the PowerPoint folder on the Data Disk that accompanies this book. Perform the following tasks.

1. Double-click the clip art placeholder. Click the Connect to Web for additional clips button. After connecting to the Microsoft Internet Explorer and the World Wide Web, click the Accept button, if necessary. Click the Search button. Type `sports` in the Enter keywords text box and then click the Find button.
2. Download one of the clip art files listed in the results area of the Microsoft Clip Gallery Live page. Double-click the downloaded clip art when it displays in the Microsoft Clip Gallery 3.0.
3. Disconnect from the Web.
4. Add your name in the slide footer.
5. Save the presentation as Play with the Pros. Print the slide in black and white. Quit PowerPoint.

3 Importing and Animating Clip Art

Problem: The marketing manager at Mega-Money Management, Mr. Money, conducts financial seminars at which he displays graphics to illustrate his topic. He recently learned that you could create a PowerPoint presentation and include graphics from the World Wide Web. He asks you to create a PowerPoint presentation and find clip art for his upcoming debt reduction seminar.

Instructions: Perform the following tasks.

1. Open the presentation Debt from the PowerPoint folder on the Data Disk that accompanies this book.
2. Insert clip art into the clip art placeholder on Slide 2 by searching Microsoft Clip Gallery Live for clip art with the keyword, dollars. Import the file, BUSI001193_x5.WMF to Microsoft Clip Gallery 3.0. Disconnect from the Web.
3. Animate the clip art with the Zoom In Slightly animation effect.
4. Add your name in the footer on all slides.
5. Save the presentation as Debt Reduction. Print the presentation in black and white. Quit PowerPoint.

Microsoft Outlook 97

▶ **PROJECT ONE**

Desktop Information Management Using Outlook

Objectives:

You will have mastered the material in this project when you can:

- Describe and define desktop information management (DIM)
- Start Outlook
- Understand the elements of the Outlook Bar
- Open the Calendar folder
- Describe the components of the Calendar – Microsoft Outlook window
- Create a personal subfolder
- Enter one-time and recurring appointments
- Use the Date Navigator to move to different days
- Use natural language phrases to enter appointment dates and times
- Move and edit appointments
- Create an event
- Display the calendar in Day, Week, and Month views
- Print the calendar in Daily, Weekly, and Monthly Styles
- Create and print a task list
- Create and print a contact list
- Import and export personal subfolders
- Delete personal subfolders from the hard disk
- Quit Outlook

The Information Explosion

Help or Hindrance?

Can you imagine Cro-Magnon man riding his wheel using a cell phone to check his office's computer for e-mail messages and appointment changes?

Absurd? Not really. Although electronic devices are from this millennium, even prehistoric man was concerned with timekeeping and calendars.

More than 20,000 years ago, ice-age hunters in Europe scratched lines and gouged holes in sticks and bones, possibly counting the days between phases of the moon. More than 4,000 years ago in England, Stonehenge's alignments show its purposes apparently included the determination of seasonal or celestial events. The Egyptians devised a 365-day calendar that seems to have begun in 4236 B.C. — the earliest recorded year in history.

As far back as six thousand years ago, great Middle Eastern and North African civilizations introduced clock making. About 1500 B.C., sundials, the first portable timepieces, were designed, which led to the development of horology, or the science of measuring time.

Currently, we find the ever-expanding need to develop newer methods to organize and manage time

more effectively. Computer users today have no shortage of tools that combine the capabilities of accessing information and communications using e-mail, voice mail, facsimile, meetings, telephone, newsletters, reports, planners, browsers, and custom groupware.

Today, tremendous quantities of electronic and paper communications bombard us. This vast sea of information does not necessarily improve productivity; unless efficiently organized, it actually may hamper our ability to get things done.

A major impact of electronic information transmission has been to decrease the amount of time it takes to send information. We now send business correspondence instantly through cyberspace rather than the U.S. Postal Service. This global electronic network is remaking daily life and forces individuals to prioritize their tasks.

Although e-mail has reduced paper quantity, managing the paper and electronic communications that cross our desktops still is a staggering task. Microsoft Outlook 97 has been designed to answer the problem of electronic information overload. A desktop information management (DIM) system, Outlook is a central location from which you can create, view, and organize all of your information. The data is stored in folders. A Shortcut stores the folder location and allows you to open it quickly using buttons on the Outlook Bar.

From Inbox, you can read and send e-mail messages. Calendar provides the tools to create appointments, plan meetings and events, and review tasks. Using Contacts, you are able to store names, addresses, and other data about your business and personal contacts. Tasks simplifies to-do lists and allows you to organize assignments. Journal presents a review of your work history. Notes is an area where you can formulate ideas and save reminders. With this integration, you eliminate the need for weekly planners, daily pocket calendars, sticky notes, and task lists. With its Internet browsing capabilities, Outlook also acts as a Web Address Book and allows you to store, manage, and navigate favorite sites.

Perhaps in the historic archives of the next millennium, our civilization's desktop information management systems will seem as obsolete as the Aztec calendar stone. Until then, however, the organization, efficiency, and timesavings they give to the information explosion of today are indeed a blessing.

Microsoft
Outlook 97

Desktop Information Management Using Outlook

Case Perspective

Bert Montgomery works a sales route for Dixon Office Supply Products. The company has given Bert a new laptop computer with Microsoft Office 97. His boss, Mr. Fredrick, wants Bert to learn the new software and has offered to pay for classes at Central College. Bert completed an associate degree in business, but he has decided to accept the offer and get his bachelor's degree in business administration.

Central College is a commuter college with 8,000 students, offering a variety of degree programs. Because many of the students have part-time jobs, Central College schedules sections of the more popular courses in the morning, evenings, and weekends.

Mr. Fredrick agreed to let Bert cut back on his work hours so he could register for 12 credit hours. Bert joined the National Managers Association (NMA) and is looking forward to meeting other students at the monthly afternoon meetings. With morning classes, busy afternoons of sales calls, and NMA meetings to attend, Bert needs to get organized. Microsoft Outlook 97 is just what he needs to do the job.

What Is Microsoft Outlook?

Microsoft Outlook, an application contained in Microsoft Office 97, is a powerful **desktop information management** (**DIM**) program that assists you in organizing your busy schedule, keeping track of your files, and communicating with others. All the information you used to track in a weekly planner or daily pocket calendar now can be stored on your computer and easily organized using a DIM. DIMs such as Outlook provide a way for individuals and workgroups to organize, find, view, and share information easily. Managers who have to juggle many people's calendars now are using DIMs to eliminate phone tag and constant reshuffling of schedules.

Outlook, the newest member of the Office 97 software suite, is the focal point for tighter integration between Office 97 applications. You can create files in Word, Excel, Access, and PowerPoint and use them in your Outlook folder or attach them to an e-mail message. Outlook also makes it easy to share data between applications. For instance, your contact list can become the data source for a Word mail merge or you can use Word as your editor for e-mail messages. With Outlook's Inbox and Calendar folders, you easily can update, print, and fax your schedule to anyone, anywhere.

Project One — Bert Montgomery's DIM System

In Project 1 you will learn the basic features of Outlook by creating and printing a calendar of classes and appointments, a task list for a given day, and a contact list. Figure 1-1 outlines the creation process.

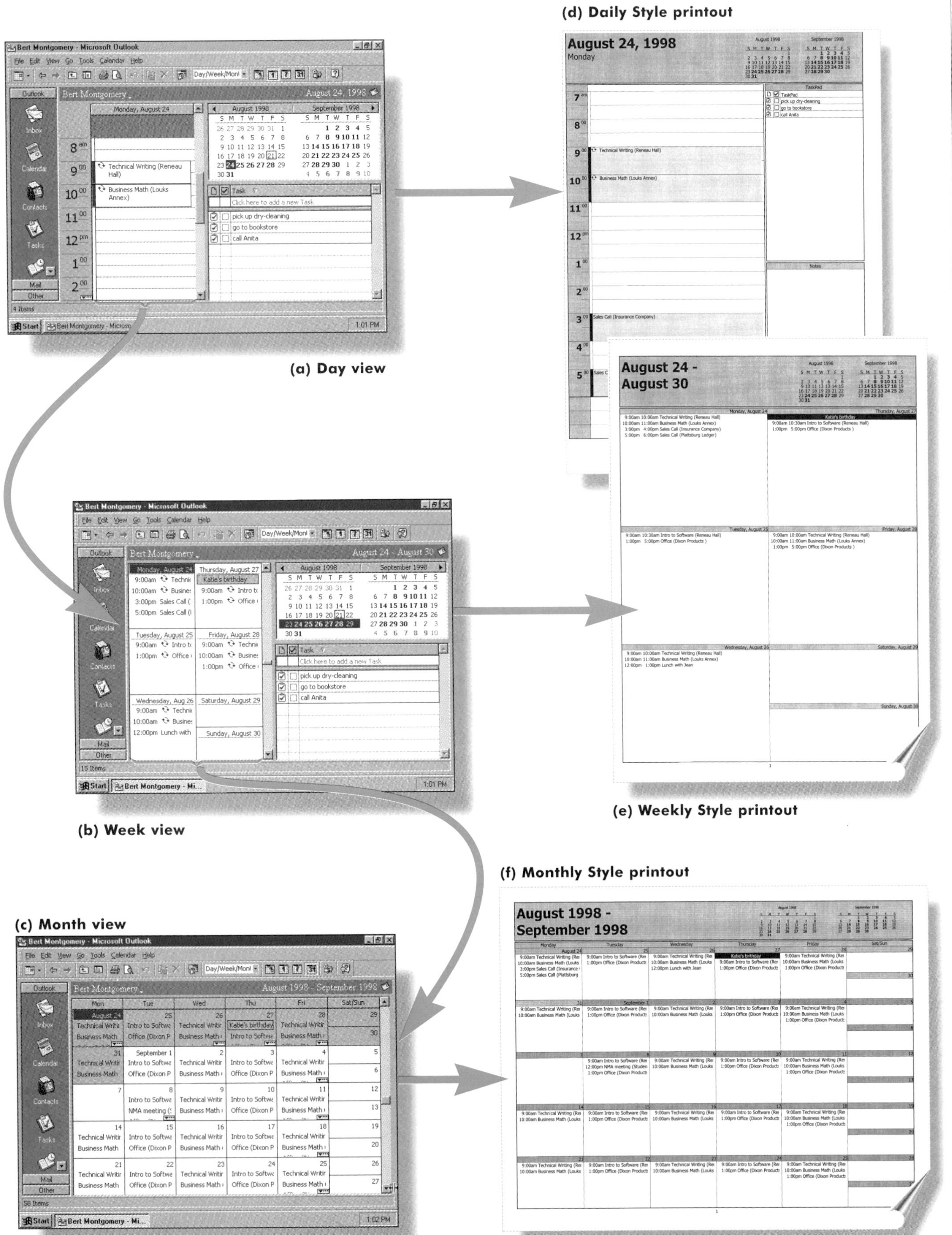
(a) Day view
(b) Week view
(c) Month view
(d) Daily Style printout
(e) Weekly Style printout
(f) Monthly Style printout

FIGURE 1-1

Preparation Steps

The preparation steps below provide an overview of how the calendar shown in Figures 1-1a through 1-1f on the previous page will be developed. The following tasks will be completed in this project:

1. Start Outlook.
2. Open the Calendar folder.
3. Create Bert Montgomery's personal subfolder in the Calendar folder.
4. Enter Bert Montgomery's sales calls for the first week of school.
5. Enter Bert Montgomery's class schedule for the semester.
6. Create and print a task list of things to do on the first day of classes.
7. Print a copy of the calendar in Daily, Weekly, and Monthly Styles.
8. Create and print a contact list of Bert Montgomery's clients at work.
9. Export personal subfolders to a floppy disk.
10. Delete personal subfolders.
11. Import the personal subfolders from a floppy disk.
12. Quit Outlook.

The following pages contain a detailed explanation of these tasks.

Starting Outlook

With Windows 95 running, perform the following steps to start Outlook.

Steps To Start Outlook

1 Click the Start button on the taskbar. Point to Programs on the Start menu and then point to Microsoft Outlook on the Programs submenu.

2 Click Microsoft Outlook. If the Office Assistant displays, click its Close button.

After a few seconds, Outlook displays the Inbox folder in the Inbox – Microsoft Outlook window (Figure 1-2).

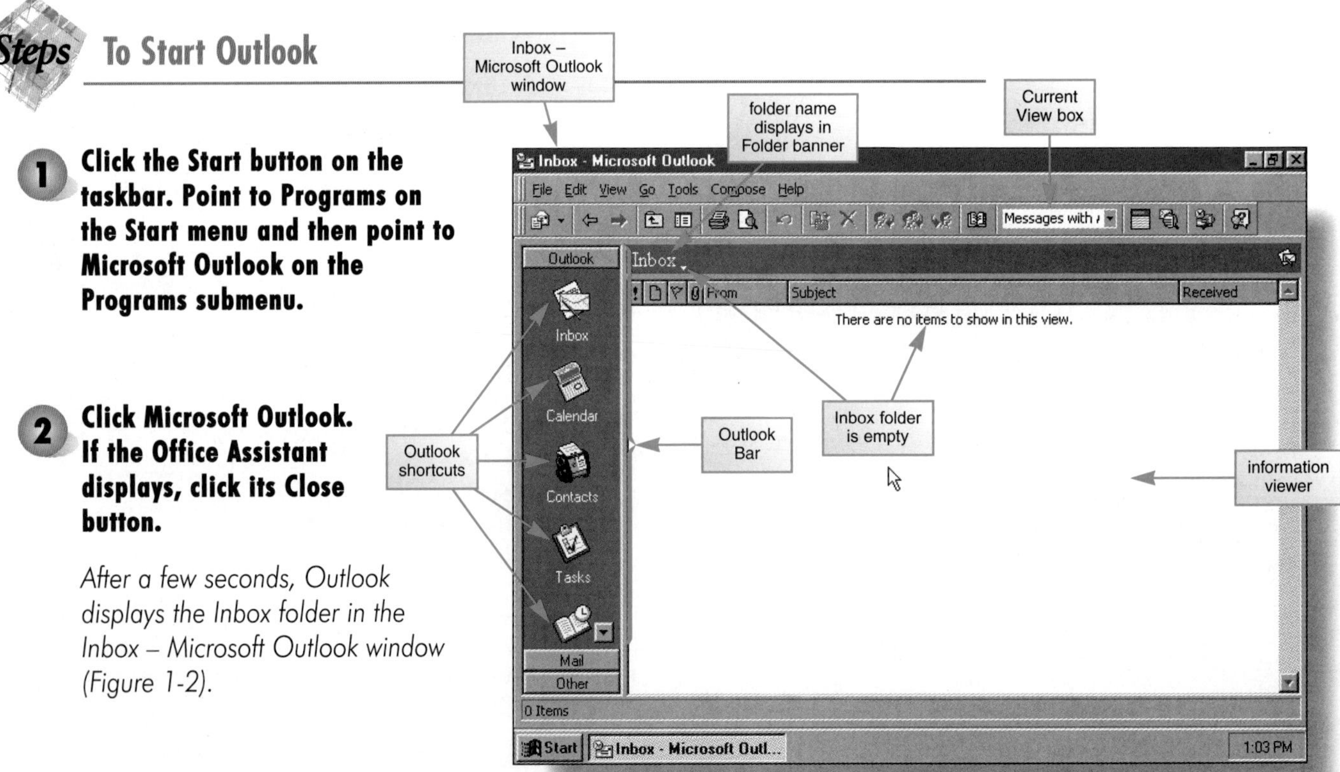

FIGURE 1-2

Outlook is organized around types of **items**, such as mail messages, appointments, contacts, journal entries, tasks, and notes. Items of the same type are stored in the same Outlook **folder**. For example, all appointments are stored in the Calendar folder and all tasks are stored in the Tasks folder. When you open a folder, the items in the selected folder display in the **information viewer**, as shown in Figure 1-2. To change the way items display in the information viewer, you can select a different view using the **Current View box**.

Opening the Calendar Folder

To begin entering items in Bert Montgomery's calendar, you must open the Calendar folder. Perform the following steps to open the Calendar folder.

Steps To Open the Calendar Folder

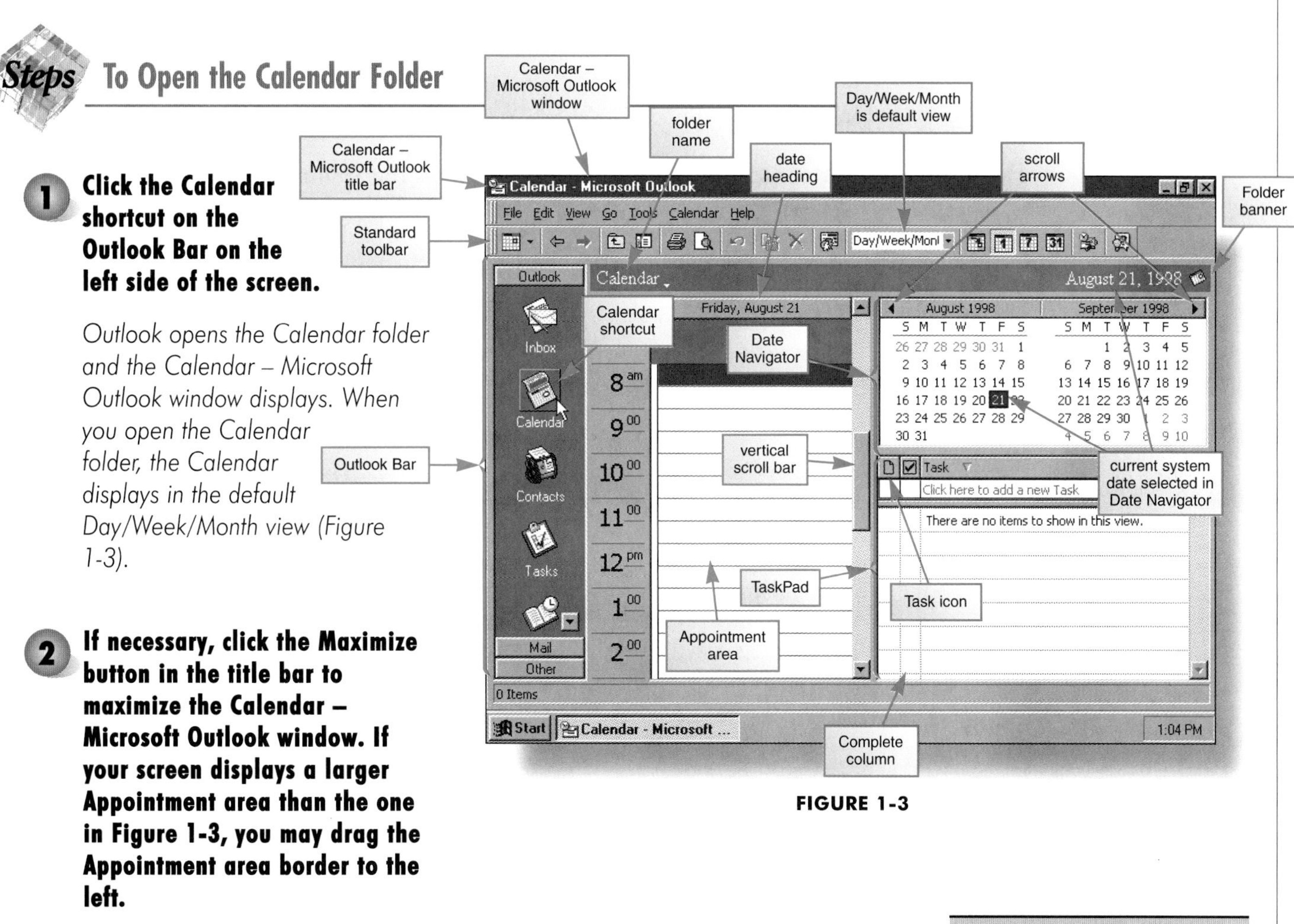

FIGURE 1-3

1. **Click the Calendar shortcut on the Outlook Bar on the left side of the screen.**

   Outlook opens the Calendar folder and the Calendar – Microsoft Outlook window displays. When you open the Calendar folder, the Calendar displays in the default Day/Week/Month view (Figure 1-3).

2. **If necessary, click the Maximize button in the title bar to maximize the Calendar – Microsoft Outlook window. If your screen displays a larger Appointment area than the one in Figure 1-3, you may drag the Appointment area border to the left.**

Other Ways

1. On Go menu click Calendar
2. Press ALT+G, press C

The Calendar – Microsoft Outlook Window

The **Calendar – Microsoft Outlook window** (Figure 1-3 on the previous page) includes a variety of features to help you work more efficiently. It contains many elements similar to the windows in other applications, as well as some which are unique to Outlook. The main elements of the Calendar – Microsoft Outlook window are the Outlook Bar, the Standard toolbar, the Folder banner, the Date Navigator, the Appointment area, and the TaskPad. The information viewer of the Calendar – Microsoft Outlook window is made up of the last three elements.

OUTLOOK BAR On the left side of the Calendar – Microsoft Outlook window is a vertical bar called the **Outlook Bar** (Figure 1-4). The Outlook Bar contains shortcuts representing the standard applications that are part of Microsoft Outlook. The Outlook Bar is divided into groups to help organize your information. The standard Outlook group includes shortcuts to folders for your Inbox, Calendar, Contacts, Tasks, Journal, Notes, and Deleted Items. When you click a shortcut, Outlook opens the folder.

The Outlook Bar

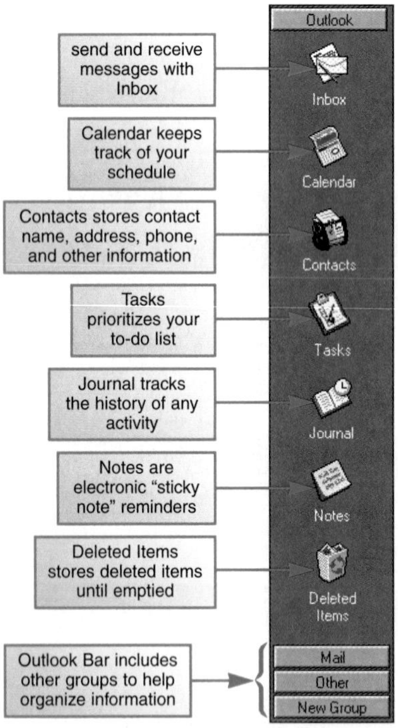

Outlook
send and receive messages with Inbox
Inbox
Calendar keeps track of your schedule
Calendar
Contacts stores contact name, address, phone, and other information
Contacts
Tasks prioritizes your to-do list
Tasks
Journal tracks the history of any activity
Journal
Notes are electronic "sticky note" reminders
Notes
Deleted Items stores deleted items until emptied
Deleted Items
Outlook Bar includes other groups to help organize information
Mail
Other
New Group

FIGURE 1-4

STANDARD TOOLBAR Figure 1-5 shows the Standard toolbar in the Calendar – Microsoft Outlook window and each button's function. Each button can be clicked to perform a frequently used task, such as creating a new appointment, printing, or changing the current view.

FOLDER BANNER The **Folder banner** (Figure 1-3) is the horizontal bar just below the Standard toolbar. The name of the active folder displays on the left side of the Folder banner; an icon for the active folder displays on the right. When you click the folder name, the Folder List showing available folders and subfolders displays.

DATE NAVIGATOR The **Date Navigator** (Figure 1-3) includes two monthly calendars (the current month and the previous or following month) and scroll arrows. When you click the scroll arrows to move to a new date, Calendar displays the name of the month, week, or day in the current view in the Appointment area. The current system date has a square around it in the Date Navigator. Dates displayed in bold in the Date Navigator indicate days for which you have scheduled an item.

APPOINTMENT AREA The **Appointment area** (Figure 1-3) contains a date heading and time slots for the current view. The date currently selected in the Date Navigator displays in the date heading. By default, workday time slots are set from 8:00 am to 5:00 pm and display with a white background. Time slots outside this period are shaded. A vertical scroll bar allows you to move backward and forward through the time slots.

The Standard Toolbar

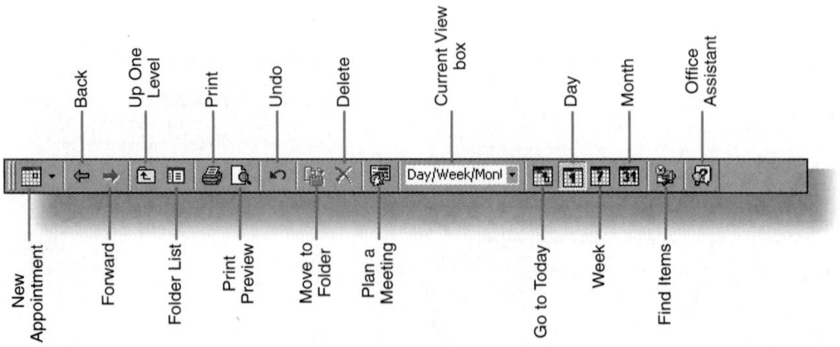

Back
Up One Level
Print
Undo
Delete
Current View box
Day
Month
Office Assistant
Day/Week/Mont
New Appointment
Forward
Folder List
Print Preview
Move to Folder
Plan a Meeting
Go to Today
Week
Find Items

FIGURE 1-5

As you schedule items such as appointments, meetings, or events, they display in the Appointment area. An **appointment** is an activity that does not involve other resources or people. A **meeting**, by contrast, is an appointment to which other resources or people are invited. You can use Outlook's Calendar to schedule several people to attend a meeting or only one person to attend an appointment (like a class). An **event** is an activity that lasts 24 hours or longer, such as a seminar, birthday, or vacation. Scheduled events do not occupy time slots in the Appointment area; instead, they display in a banner below the date heading.

TASKPAD The **TaskPad** (Figure 1-3) displays below the Date Navigator. **Tasks** are personal or work-related duties you want to track through completion. The TaskPad displays your tasks and their status. You can change the way tasks appear by clicking TaskPad View on the View menu or add details to a task by double-clicking the **Task icon**. When a task is complete, you can select the check box in the **Complete column**.

More *About* Folders

All the files on your computer are available through Outlook Bar folders. To view or open any of the files on your computer as well as on any network drive you are connected to, click the Other group on the Outlook Bar, and then click My Computer. You can view files as icons, in a table, or in a timeline.

Creating a Personal Subfolder in the Calendar Folder

One advantage of using Outlook's Calendar application is its capability to schedule multiple people and resources, as well as individual users. If you were the only person using Outlook on a computer, you could enter appointments and events directly into the main Calendar folder. In many office and school situations, however, several people share a computer and thus need to create separate folders in which to store appointments and events. With Outlook you can create personal subfolders in which to store your personal calendar and other files. You then can save the subfolders to the hard disk or a floppy disk. If you are working on a networked computer, check with your instructor or database manager for the policy on creating and saving subfolders. In this project you should substitute your name in place of Bert Montgomery as you create the personal subfolders. Perform the following steps to create a personal subfolder to store Bert Montgomery's calendar.

More *About* Opening Calendars

If you have access permission, you can open another user's calendar and make appointments, check free times, schedule meetings, check or copy contacts, or just about anything you could do with your own personal schedule. This feature is particularly useful if you are required to schedule meetings or events that depend on other people's schedules.

Steps To Create a Personal Subfolder in the Calendar Folder

1 **Right-click the folder name Calendar in the Folder banner. Point to Create Subfolder on the shortcut menu.**

Outlook displays a shortcut menu of tasks associated with the Calendar folder (Figure 1-6).

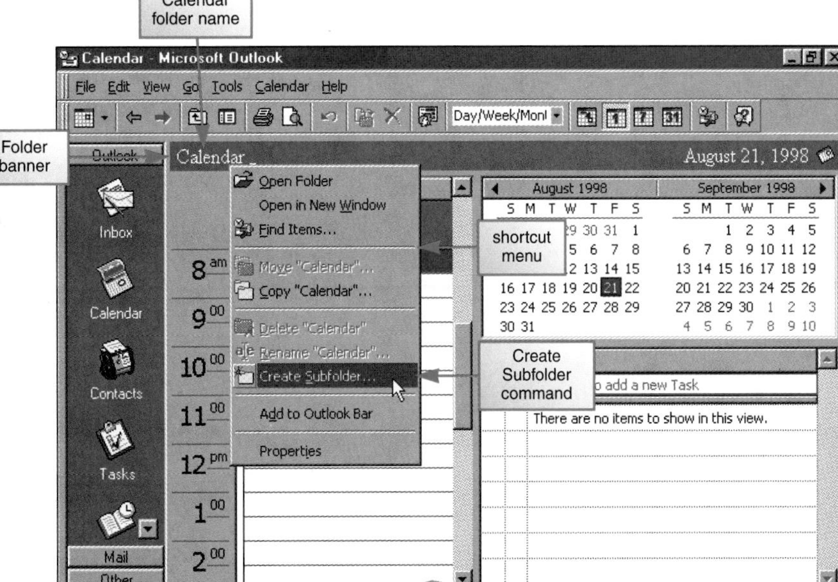

FIGURE 1-6

2 **Click Create Subfolder. Type** `Bert Montgomery` **in the Name text box. If necessary, click the Create a shortcut to this folder in the Outlook Bar check box at the bottom of the dialog box to remove the check mark. Point to the OK button.**

The Create New Folder dialog box displays. It contains a text box for the folder name, a list box to indicate what type of items the folder contains, and a list of folders and subfolders. It also includes a text box in which you can enter a brief description and a check box that allows you to create a shortcut to the folder in the Outlook Bar (Figure 1-7).

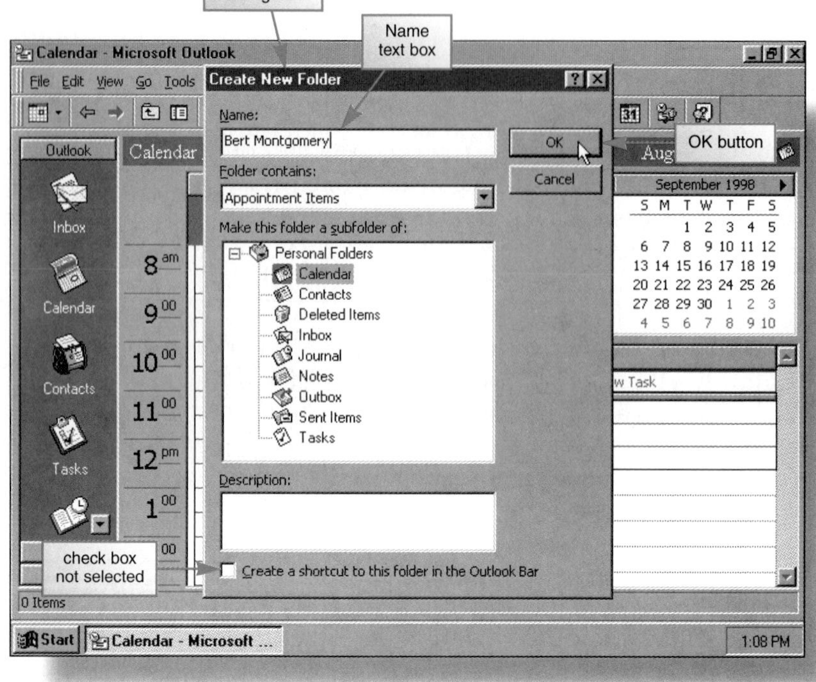

FIGURE 1-7

3 **Click the OK button. Click the folder name Calendar in the Folder banner to display the Folder List. Click the plus sign (+) to the left of the Calendar icon.**

The Folder List displays, showing a list of available folders and subfolders. The plus sign changes to a minus sign (-) and the new subfolder icon and name display (Figure 1-8).

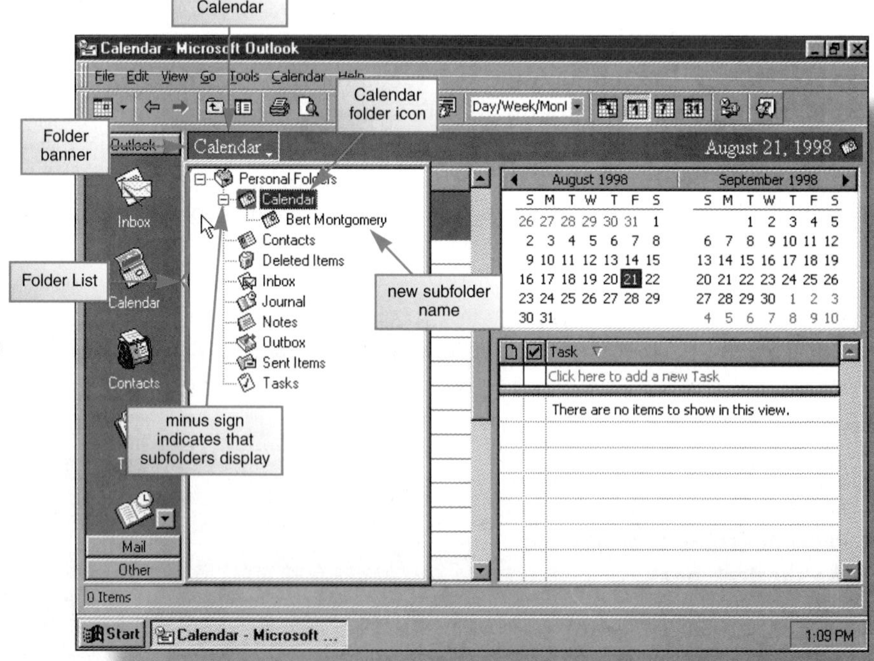

FIGURE 1-8

4 **Click the Bert Montgomery subfolder.**

The Bert Montgomery subfolder displays (Figure 1-9). The subfolder name displays on the Outlook title bar, in the Folder banner, and on the taskbar button. To change your display to match Figure 1-9, click the scroll arrows in the Date Navigator to display August and September 1998 and then click Friday, August 21.

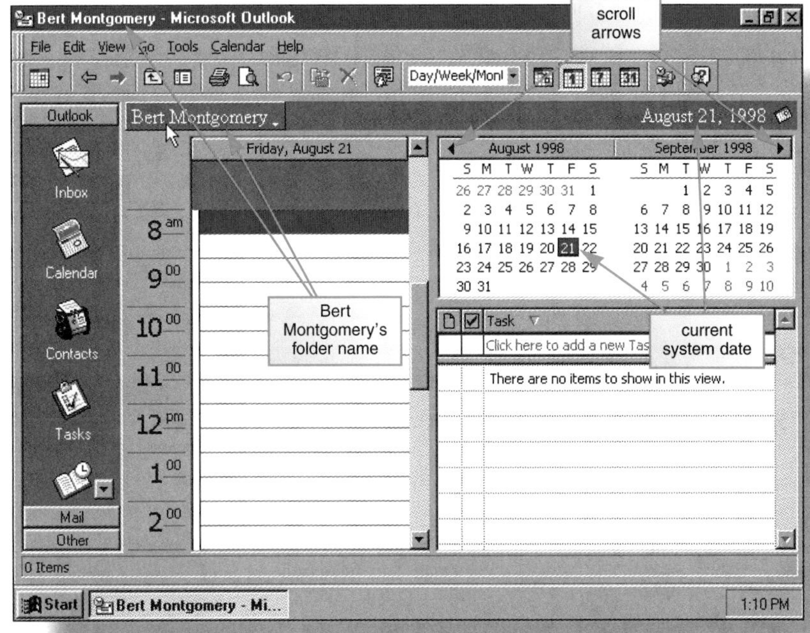

FIGURE 1-9

Other**Ways**

1. On File menu click Folder, click Create Subfolder
2. Press CTRL+SHIFT+E

Now that Bert Montgomery's personal subfolder is open, you can begin entering items into his schedule.

Entering Appointments Using the Appointment Area

Calendar lets you schedule appointments, meetings, and events for yourself as well as for others who have given you permission to open their subfolders. Businesses will find that scheduling resources and people is easy to do with Outlook's Calendar application.

The next section describes how to enter appointments from Table 1-1 into Bert Montgomery's personal subfolder, starting with appointments for August 24, 1998. As shown in Table 1-1, classes and office hours are recurring appointments; sales calls and lunch are one-time appointments.

If you need to enter an appointment into a time slot that is not visible in the current view, use the vertical scroll bar to bring the time slot into view. Once an appointment is entered, you can perform ordinary editing actions. Perform the steps on the next page to enter appointments using the Appointment area.

Table 1-1

TIME	APPOINTMENT	OCCURRENCE
9:00 am - 10:00 am	Technical Writing (Reneau Hall)	Every Monday, Wednesday, Friday
10:00 am - 11:00 am	Business Math (Louks Annex)	Every Monday, Wednesday, Friday
12:00 pm - 1:00 pm	Lunch with Jean	Monday, August 24, 1998
2:00 pm - 3:00 pm	Sales Call (Missouri Electric)	Monday, August 24, 1998
3:00 pm - 4:00 pm	Sales Call (Insurance Company)	Monday, August 24, 1998
4:00 pm - 5:00 pm	Sales Call (Plattsburg Ledger)	Monday August 24, 1998
9:00 am - 10:30 am	Intro to Software (Reneau Hall)	Every Tuesday, Thursday
1:00 pm - 5:00 pm	Office (Dixon Products)	Every Tuesday, Thursday, Friday

Steps To Enter Appointments Using the Appointment Area

1 **Click Monday, August 24, 1998 in the Date Navigator to display it in the Appointment area. Drag through the 9:00 am - 10:00 am time slot.**

The 9:00 am - 10:00 am time slot is highlighted (Figure 1-10).

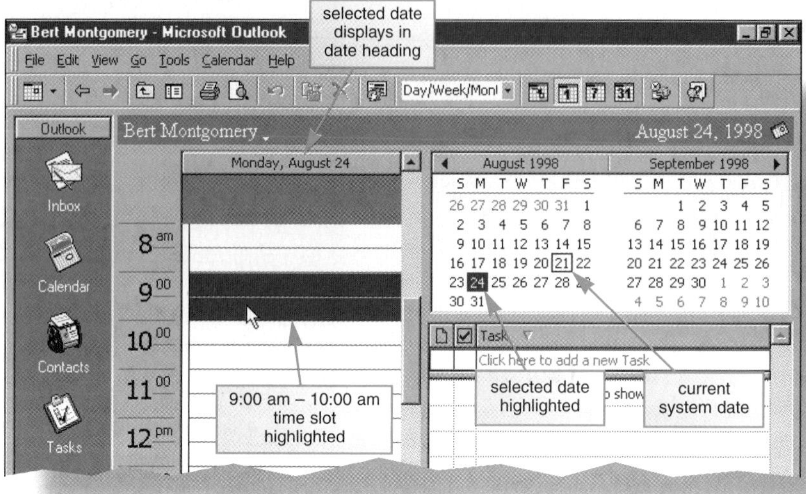

FIGURE 1-10

2 **Type** `Technical Writing` **to enter the first appointment.**

As soon as you begin typing the highlighted time slot changes to a text box with blue top and bottom borders.

3 **Drag through the 10:00 am - 11:00 am time slot. Type** `Business Math` **to enter the second appointment. Drag through the 12:00 pm - 1:00 pm time slot. Type** `Lunch with Jean` **to enter the third appointment and then press ENTER.**

The three appointments display in the Appointment area (Figure 1-11).

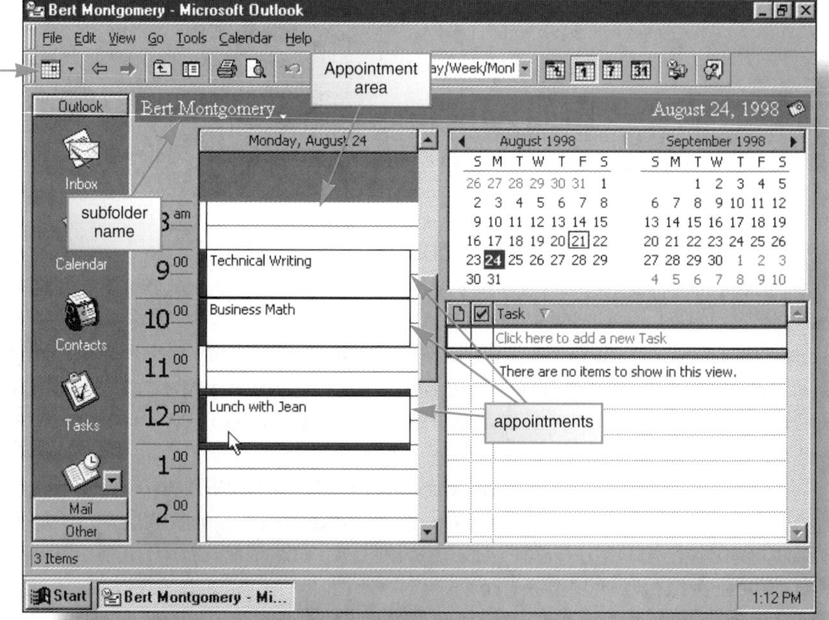

FIGURE 1-11

If you make a mistake while typing and notice the error before clicking outside the appointment time slot or pressing ENTER, use the BACKSPACE key to erase all the characters back to and including the error. To cancel the entire entry before clicking outside the appointment time slot or pressing ENTER, press the ESC key. If you see an error in an appointment after you click outside the appointment or press ENTER, click the appointment and retype the entry. Later in this project, additional editing techniques are covered.

Entering Appointments Using the Appointment Window

Appointments either can be typed directly into the Appointment area as shown in the previous section, or they can be entered by using the **Appointment window**. Using the Appointment window is a slightly more involved process, but it allows you to specify more details about the appointment. The following steps describe how to enter appointments using the Appointment window.

To Enter Appointments Using the Appointment Window

1. **Drag through the 2:00 pm - 3:00 pm time slot and then click the New Appointment button on the Standard toolbar.**

   The Untitled – Appointment window displays with the insertion point in the Subject text box on the Appointment tab (Figure 1-12).

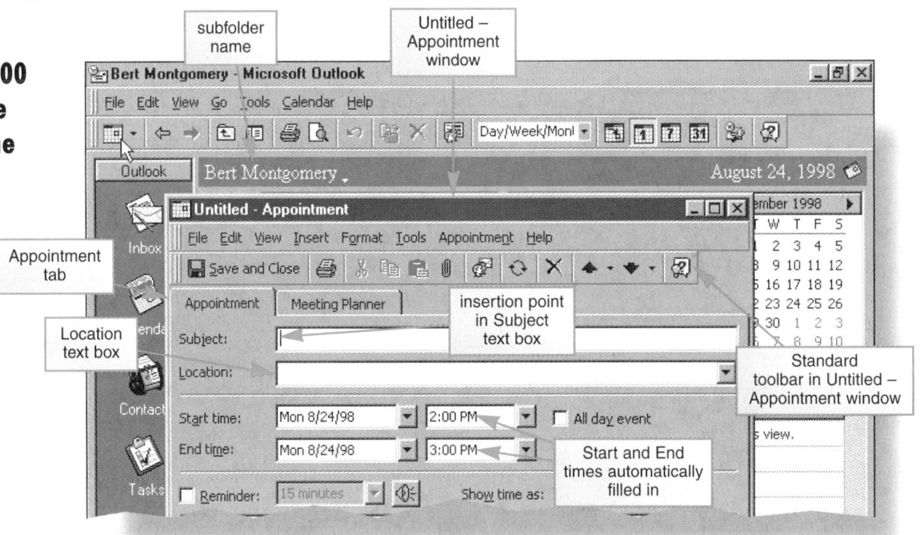

FIGURE 1-12

2. **Type** `Sales Call` **in the Subject text box and then press TAB to move the insertion point to the Location text box. Type** `Missouri Electric` **in the Location text box and then point to the Save and Close button.**

   Both the subject and location of the appointment are entered into the appropriate text boxes. Once entered, the appointment subject displays in the Appointment window title bar and on the taskbar (Figure 1-13).

3. **Click the Save and Close button.**

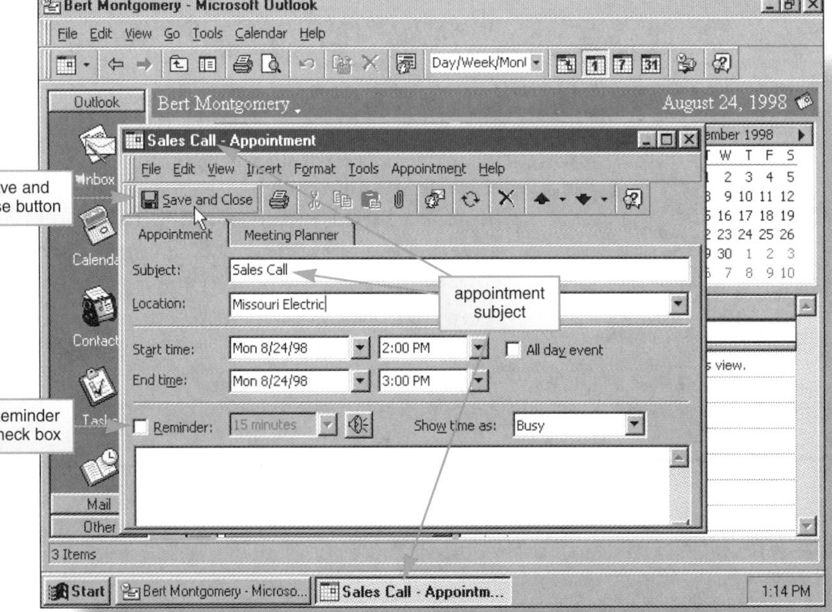

FIGURE 1-13

4 **Drag through the 3:00 pm – 4:00 pm time slot and then click the New Appointment button. Type** `Sales Call` **in the Subject text box and** `Insurance Company` **in the Location text box. Click the Save and Close button. Drag through the 4:00 pm – 5:00 pm time slot and then click the New Appointment button. Type** `Sales Call` **in the Subject text box and** `Plattsburg Ledger` **in the Location text box. Click the Save and Close button.**

The schedule for Monday, August 24, 1998 displays in the Appointment area with the three new sales calls entered (Figure 1-14).

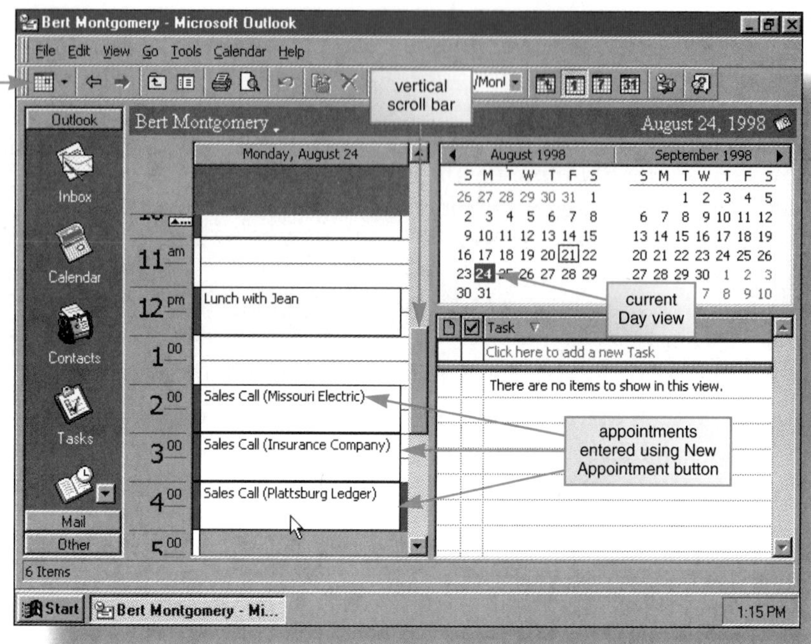

FIGURE 1-14

Other Ways

1. Double-click time slot
2. Right-click time slot, on shortcut menu click New Appointment
3. On menu bar click Calendar, click New Appointment
4. Press CTRL+N

Selecting the Reminder check box in Figure 1-13 instructs your computer to play a reminder sound before the appointment time. A bell icon, called the **Reminder symbol**, displays next to appointments with reminders. You can press TAB to move through the fields in the Appointment window, or you can click any text or list box in which you wish to make a change. Normal editing techniques also can be used to make changes.

Recurring Appointments

Many appointments are **recurring**, or occur at regular intervals. For example, a company meeting held every Friday from 1:00 pm to 3:00 pm is a recurring meeting. In this project, Bert Montgomery's college classes and office hours occur at regular weekly intervals. Typing in these recurring appointments for each occasion would be extremely time-consuming. By designating an appointment as recurring, you only need to enter the appointment once and then specify the days on which it occurs. Perform the following steps to set recurring appointments.

More *About* Appointments

You can specify how others view your calendar by designating the time an appointment takes as busy, free, tentative, or out of office. You also can mark appointments as private, thereby preventing them from being seen by other users who have access to your calendar. Use the private check box in the bottom-right corner of the Appointment window. Once marked as private, a key symbol displays next to the text, indicating the information is private or "locked." This feature can be applied to appointments, tasks, meetings, or contacts.

To Set Recurring Appointments

1 With Monday, August 24, 1998 displayed, use the vertical scroll bar to display the Technical Writing appointment in the Appointment area. Double-click the Technical Writing appointment.

The Technical Writing – Appointment window opens.

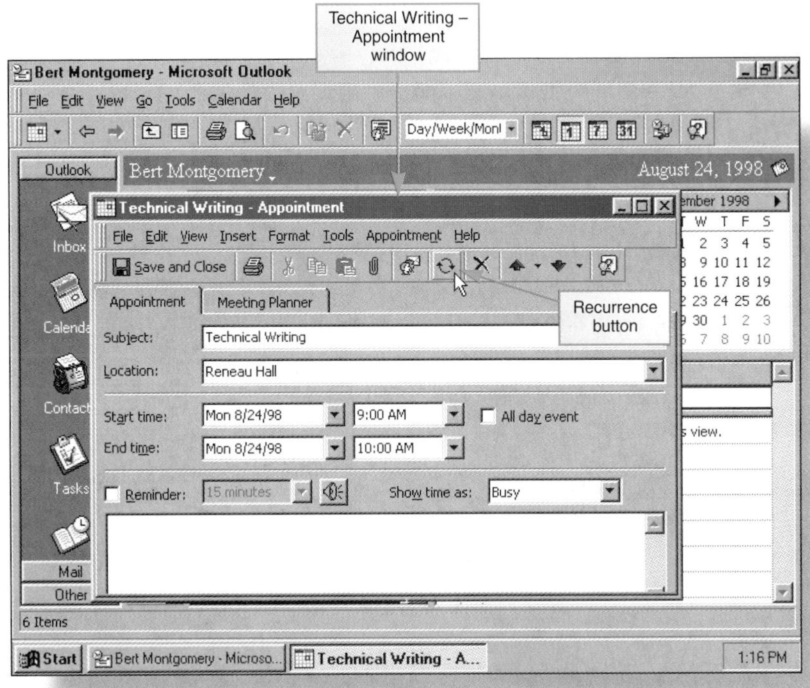

FIGURE 1-15

2 Type `Reneau Hall` **in the Location text box. Point to the Recurrence button, as shown in Figure 1-15.**

The symbol on the Recurrence button will become the **Recurrence symbol** *that displays beside the appointment in the Appointment area.*

3 Click the Recurrence button. Click the Wednesday and Friday check boxes to select the days this appointment will recur. Click the End after option button. Because this class meets 3 times a week for 15 weeks (45 times), type `45` **in the End after text box to change the number of occurrences from 10 to 45. Point to the OK button.**

The Appointment Recurrence dialog box displays (Figure 1-16). The Technical Writing appointment is set to recur on Mondays, Wednesdays, and Fridays and end after 45 occurrences.

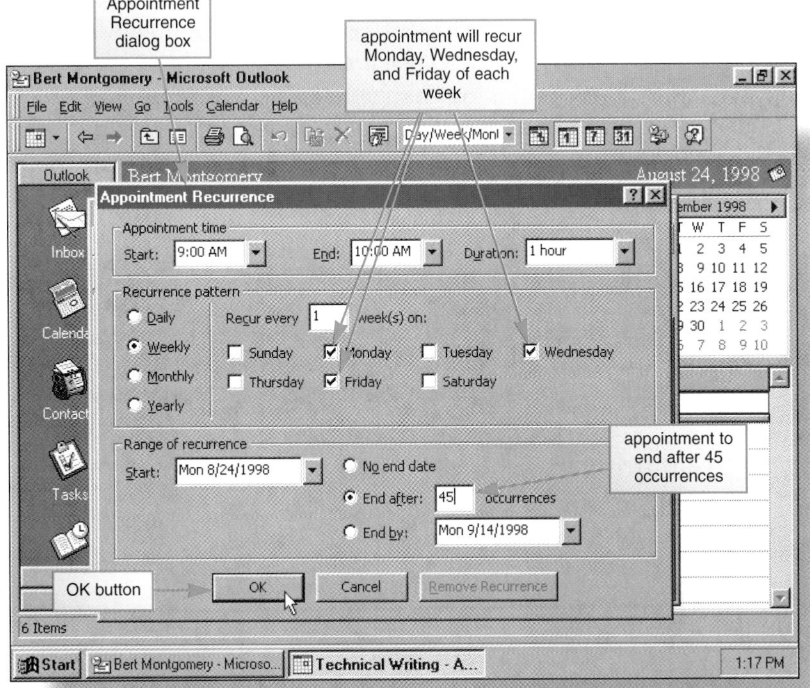

FIGURE 1-16

4 **Click the OK button. When the Technical Writing – Recurring Appointment window displays, click the Save and Close button.**

5 **Repeat Steps 1 through 5 to make the Business Math appointment a recurring appointment that meets at the location, Louks Annex. This class also has 45 occurrences, meeting Mondays, Wednesdays, and Fridays. See Table 1-1 on page O 1.11.**

The Monday, August 24, 1998 schedule is complete (Figure 1-17). A Recurrence symbol displays beside each recurring appointment.

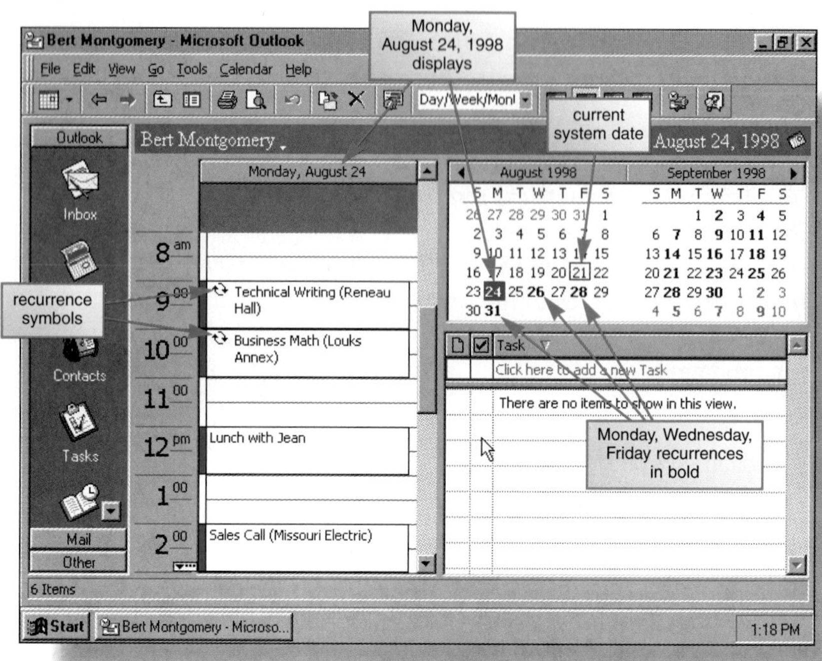

FIGURE 1-17

Other Ways

1. On Calendar menu click New Recurring Appointment
2. Press ALT+C, press N, press CTRL+G

When you are creating appointments, the Date Navigator serves several purposes. Recurring appointments are assigned to their appropriate dates automatically. You can see at a glance if appointments have been assigned to a date, because it displays in bold in the Date Navigator (Figure 1-17). These features can be changed using the Format View command in the View menu.

The Date Navigator also allows you to move to and display a specific date in the Appointment area so you can enter appointments. This technique of moving through your calendar is demonstrated in the next section.

More *About* the Recurring Icon

You can apply a Recurring icon to appointments, events, meetings, and tasks. Double-click the item to open its dialog window and click the Recurrence button.

Moving to the Next Day in the Calendar

Now that the Monday schedule is complete, the next step is to enter appointments for Tuesday. To do so, Tuesday must display in the Appointment area. The following step shows how to move to the next day using the Date Navigator.

More *About* Moving a Recurring Appointment

If the appointment is recurring, only the selected instance of the appointment is moved. To move all instances of an appointment, open the appointment, click Recurrence on the Appointment menu, and then change the recurrence pattern.

To Move to the Next Day in the Appointment Area

1 Click Tuesday, August 25, 1998 in the Date Navigator.

Tuesday, August 25, 1998 displays in the Appointment area (Figure 1-18).

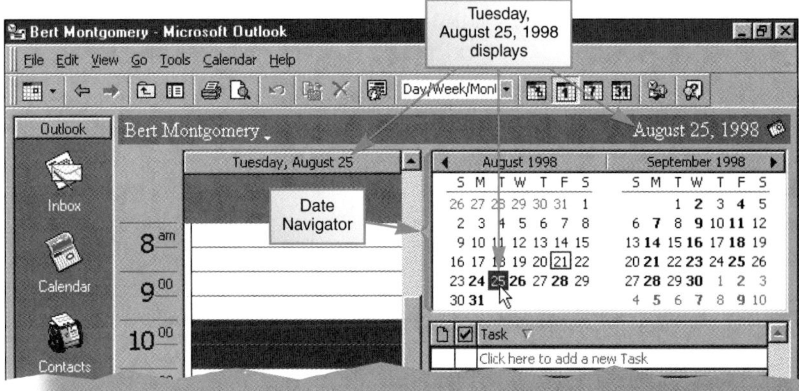

FIGURE 1-18

OtherWays

1. On Go menu click Go to Date
2. Right-click Appointment area, on shortcut menu click Go to Date
3. Press CTRL+G, enter date

The following steps describe how to finish entering the recurring appointments.

TO COMPLETE THE RECURRING APPOINTMENTS

Step 1: With Tuesday, August 25, 1998 displayed in the Appointment area, double-click the 9:00 am time slot. In the Subject text box, type `Intro to Software` and press TAB. In the Location text box, type `Reneau Hall` and then click the End time time box arrow. Click 10:30 am (1.5 hours). Click the Recurrence button. When the Appointment Recurrence dialog box displays, click the Thursday check box and then click the End after option button. Type `30` in the End after text box. Click the OK button. When the Intro to Software – Recurring Appointment window displays, click the Save and Close button.

Step 2: Double-click the 1:00 pm time slot. In the Subject text box, enter `Office` and press TAB. In the Location text box, enter `Dixon Products` and then click the End time time box arrow. Scroll down to click 5:00 PM (4 hours). Click the Recurrence button. In the Appointment Recurrence dialog box, click the Thursday and Friday check boxes. If necessary, click the No end date option button to select it, because this recurring appointment has no end date. Click the OK button. When the Office – Recurring Appointment window appears, click the Save and Close button.

The schedule for Tuesday, August 25, 1998 displays (Figure 1-19).

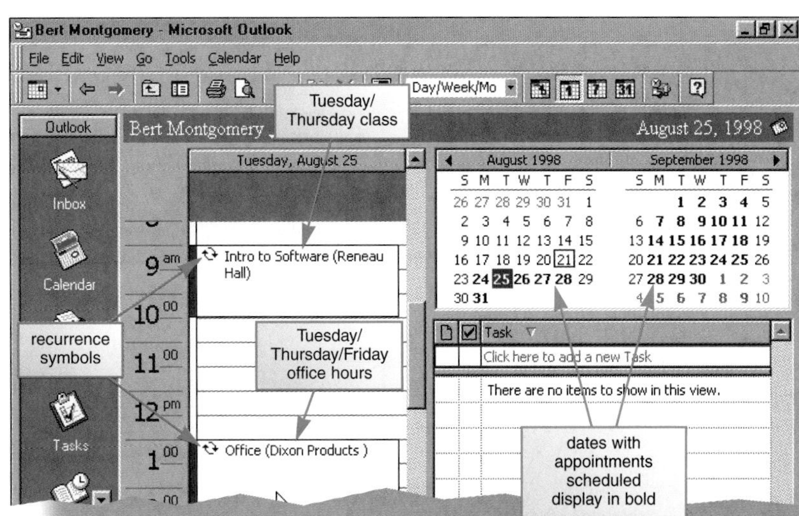

FIGURE 1-19

> **More About**
> **AutoDate Functionality**
>
> Outlook converts the description you type into a number format for you. For example, if you type one week from today in a date field, Outlook shows the numbers that represent the correct month, day, and year. You can enter dates spelled out or abbreviated, times spelled out, descriptions of times and dates (e.g., tomorrow at midnight), or holidays that fall on the same date every year. If you type something in a date or time field and later change your mind, you can delete the entry or type none.

When you designate an appointment as recurring, Outlook provides three options for the range of recurrence. An appointment can be set to occur a certain number of times or up to a certain date. If the recurring appointment is on-going, like office hours, you can specify no end date using the No end date option button.

An appointment can be set as recurring when you first enter the appointment, or, if you decide to make a one-time appointment recurring later, you easily can double-click the appointment and then click the Recurrence button. Recurring appointments also can be edited to add new days, omit certain days, or change other recurrence details. Editing recurring appointments will be covered in more detail later in the project.

Using Natural Language Phrases to Enter Appointment Dates and Times

Thus far, you have entered dates and times in the Appointment window using standard numerical entries. Outlook's **AutoDate function**, however, lets you specify appointment dates and times using natural language phrases. For example, you can enter phrases such as next Tuesday, two weeks from yesterday, or midnight, and Outlook will calculate the correct date.

In this example, the student chapter of the National Managers Association (NMA) will meet for lunch at the Student Union, two weeks from Tuesday, August 25, 1998. The following steps describe how to enter appointment dates and times using natural language phrases.

To Enter Appointment Dates and Times Using Natural Language Phrases

1 **With Tuesday, August 25, 1998 displayed in the Appointment area, click the New Appointment button on the Standard toolbar.**

2 **Type** `NMA meeting` **in the Subject text box and then press TAB. Type** `Student Union` **in the Location text box and then press TAB.**

The appointment information is entered in the Appointment window. Tues 8/25/98 is highlighted in the Start time date list box (Figure 1-20).

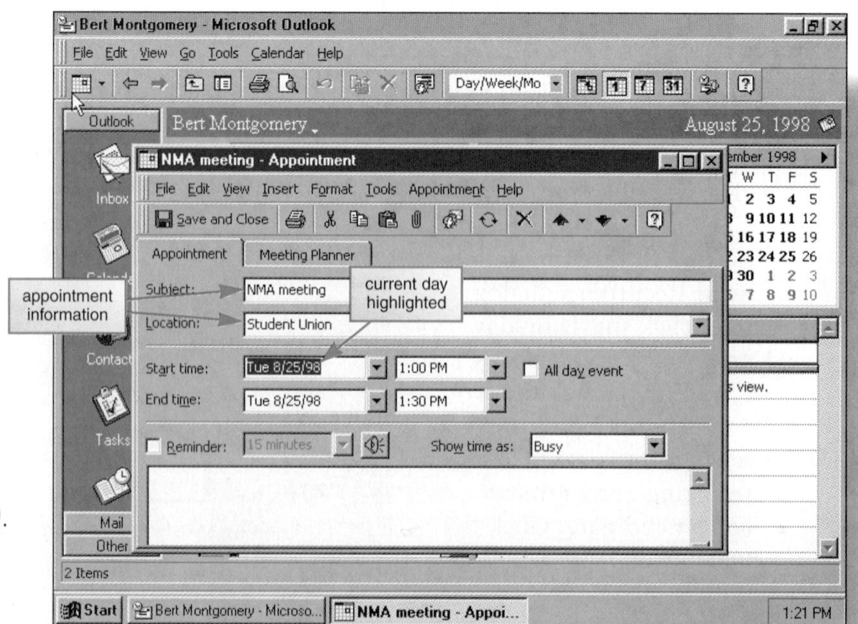

FIGURE 1-20

3 **Type** `in two weeks` **in the Start time date list box. Press TAB. Type** `noon` **in the Start time time list box.**

Outlook automatically converts the phrase, in two weeks, into the date, Tues 9/8/98, The appropriate date in both the Start time date and End time date list boxes (Figure 1-21).

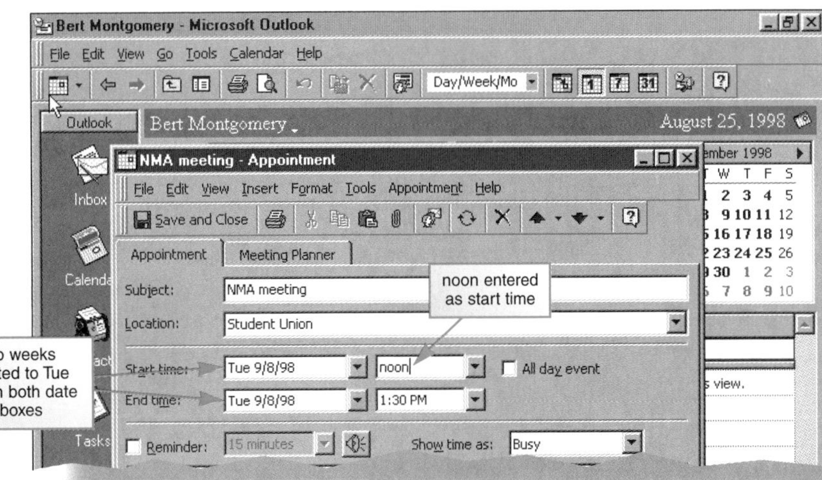

FIGURE 1-21

4 **Press TAB.**

Outlook automatically converts the word, noon, to 12:00 pm and sets the appointment end time for 12:30 pm (Figure 1-22). Outlook sets appointments for 30 minutes unless you drag through a longer time slot in the Appointment area before clicking the New Appointment button or change the default setting.

5 **Click the Save and Close button.**

The NMA meeting – Appointment window closes and Tuesday, August 25, 1998 displays in the Appointment area. The NMA meeting is added to the calendar on Tuesday, September 8, 1998.

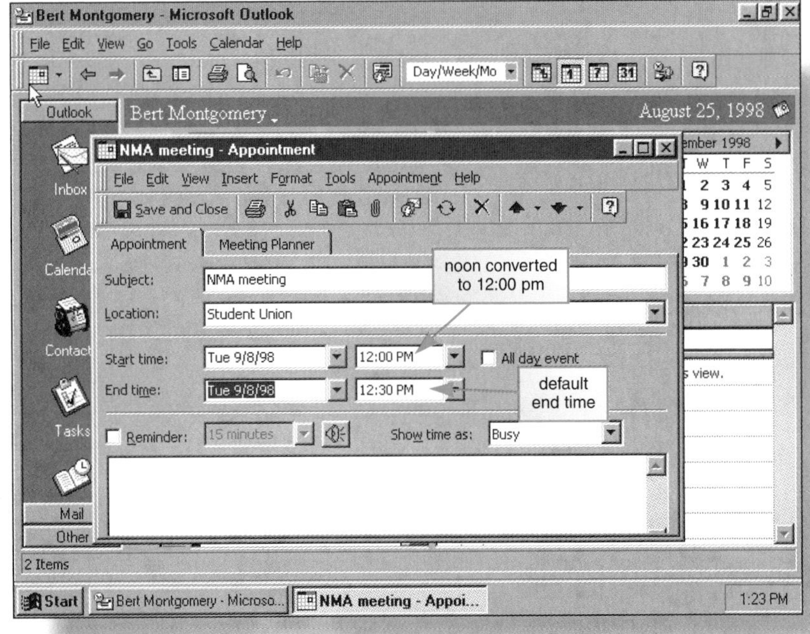

FIGURE 1-22

In addition to natural language phrases, Outlook can convert abbreviations and ordinal numbers into complete words and dates. For example, you can type Feb instead of February or the first of September instead of 9/1. Outlook's Calendar application also will convert words like yesterday, tomorrow, and the names of holidays that occur only once each year, such as Halloween.

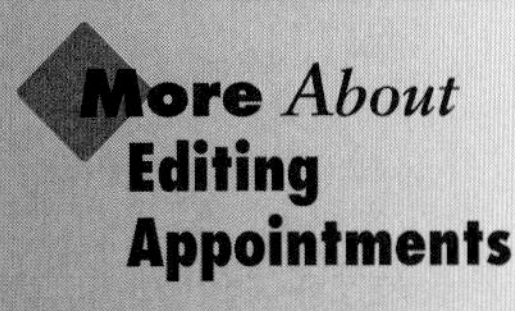

More ***About*** **Editing Appointments**

If you cannot remember when an appointment is, on the Tools menu, click Find Items. In the Look for box, click Appointments and meetings. You then may search for any word or subject.

Editing Appointments

Because schedules often need to be rearranged and juggled, Outlook provides several different ways of editing appointments. You can edit the subject and location of an appointment by clicking the appointment and editing the information directly in the Appointment area, or you can double-click the appointment and make corrections using the Appointment window.

Deleting Appointments

Appointments sometimes are canceled and must be deleted from the schedule. For example, the schedule created thus far in this project contains appointments on Monday, September 7, 1998. Because September 7 is Labor Day, however, no classes will meet and the scheduled appointments need to be deleted. The following steps describe how to delete an appointment from the schedule.

To Delete an Appointment

1 **Click Monday, September 7, 1998 in the Date Navigator. Click the first appointment to be deleted, Technical Writing, and then point to the Delete button on the Standard toolbar (Figure 1-23).**

Monday, September 7, 1998 displays in the Appointment area. The blue top and bottom borders indicate the Technical Writing appointment is selected.

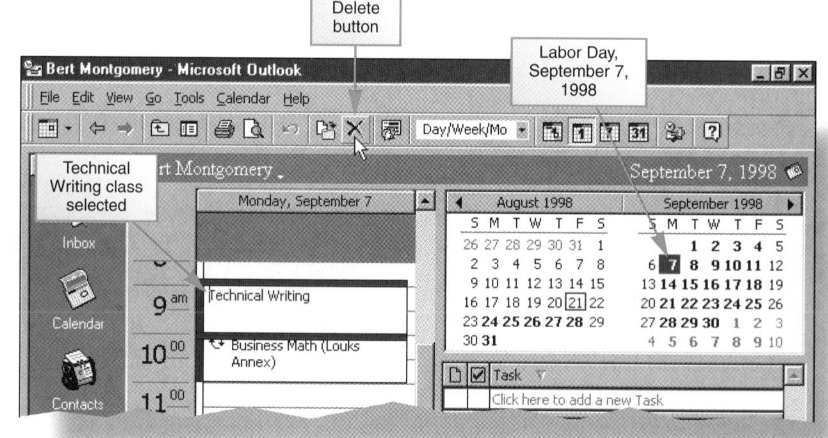

FIGURE 1-23

2 **Click the Delete button. When the Confirm Delete dialog box appears, point to the OK button.**

Because the appointment you have selected to delete is a recurring appointment, a Confirm Delete dialog box displays, asking if you want to delete all occurrences of the recurring appointment or just this one (Figure 1-24). The Delete this one option button is selected automatically.

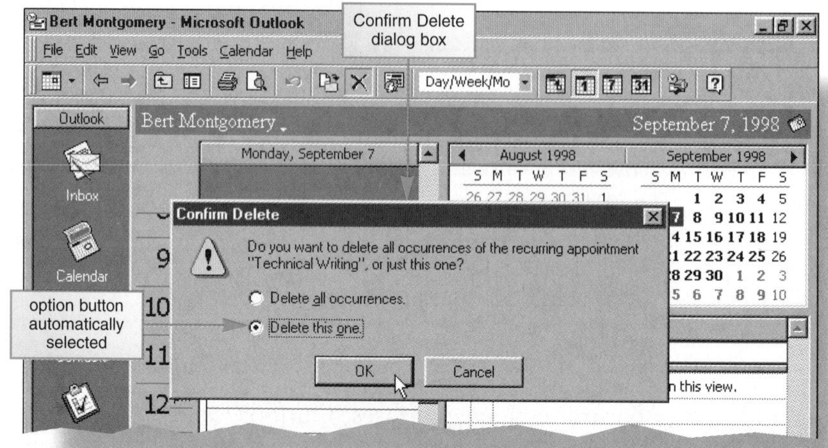

FIGURE 1-24

3 **Click the OK button.**

The Technical Writing appointment is deleted from Monday, September 7, 1998. All other occurrences of the appointment remain in the schedule.

4 **Repeat Steps 1 through 3 to delete the Business Math appointment from Monday, September 7, 1998.**

OtherWays

1. Right-click appointment to be deleted, on shortcut menu click Delete
2. Click blue left border of appointment, press DELETE

You also can delete appointments using the DELETE key. First, select the entire appointment by clicking the blue left border and then press the DELETE key. If you do not select the entire appointment, pressing the DELETE key (or the BACKSPACE key) will not delete the entry; it will only delete individual characters of the appointment subject. Even if you delete all the characters, the time slot remains active and any symbols remain in place.

Moving Appointments to a New Time

More About Moving Appointments

You can send an appointment to a co-worker. Right-click the appointment and choose Forward on the shortcut menu.

Outlook also provides several ways to move appointments. Suppose for instance, that Plattsburg Ledger called to reschedule the 4:00 pm appointment on Monday, August 24, 1998 to 5:00 pm on the same day. Instead of deleting and then retyping the appointment in the new time slot, you simply can drag it to the new time slot. The following steps describe how to move an appointment to a new time.

Steps To Move an Appointment to a New Time

1. **Click Monday, August 24, 1998 in the Date Navigator. Use the vertical scroll bar to display the 4:00 pm – 5:00 pm time slot. Position the mouse pointer on the blue left border of the appointment.**

   The mouse pointer changes to a four-headed arrow, as shown in Figure 1-25.

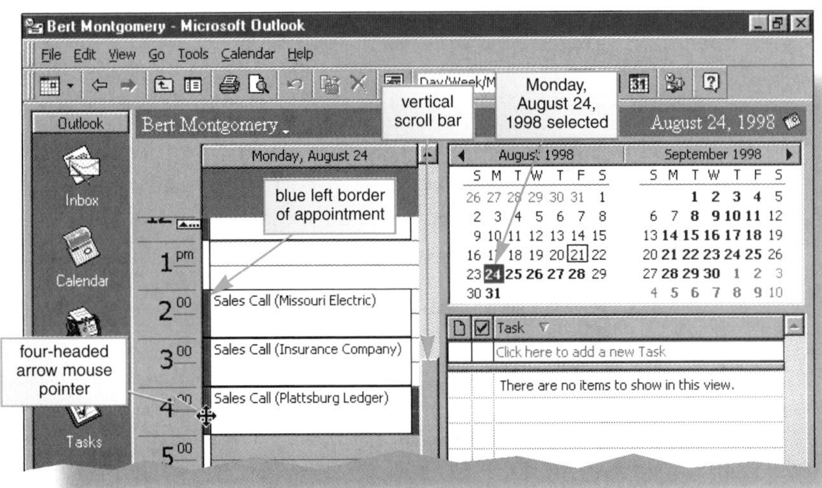

FIGURE 1-25

2. **Drag the appointment down to the 5:00 pm – 6:00 pm time slot.**

   *As you drag the appointment, the mouse pointer changes to a pointer with a small dotted box below it. This is called the **drag icon** (Figure 1-26). A blue left border remains in the previous 4:00 pm – 5:00 pm time slot, while top, bottom, and left blue borders around the 5:00 pm – 6:00 pm time slot indicate the new time slot in which the appointment will be placed.*

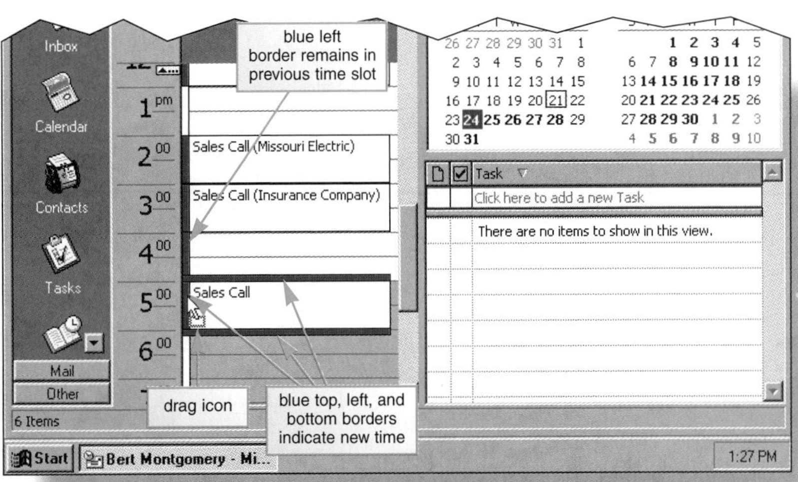

FIGURE 1-26

3 **Release the mouse button to drop the appointment in the new time slot.**

The appointment is placed in the 5:00 pm – 6:00 pm time slot (Figure 1-27). Outlook automatically allows adequate time for the moved appointment, in this case, one hour.

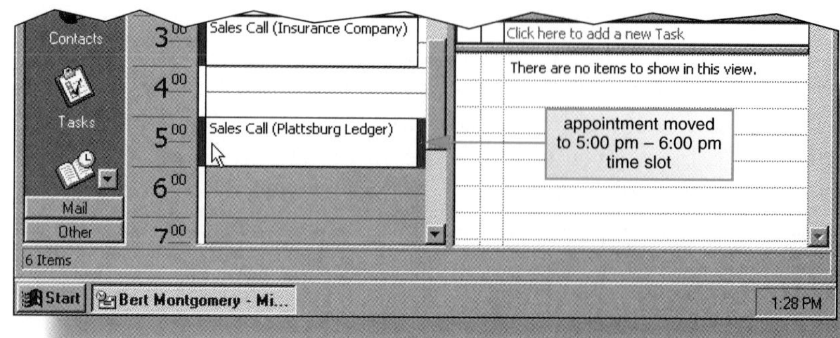

FIGURE 1-27

OtherWays

1. Double-click appointment, edit time in Start time and End time time list boxes
2. Click left border of appointment, press CTRL+X, click new time slot, press CTRL+V

You can move an appointment to a new time using the Appointment window as well. Simply type a different time in the Start time time or End time time list box or click one of the time box arrows and choose a different time from the list. You also can use the natural language phrases in the time box, which Outlook will convert to the appropriate times.

Moving Appointments to a New Date

If an appointment is being moved to a new date but remaining in the same time slot, you simply can drag the appointment to the new date in the Date Navigator. Using this method allows you quickly and easily to move an appointment to a new date, as shown in the following steps.

Steps To Move an Appointment to a New Date

1 **Click Monday, August 24, 1998 in the Date Navigator. Click the blue left border of the Lunch with Jean appointment to select it. Drag the appointment from the Appointment area to Wednesday, August 26, 1998.**

As you drag outside the Appointment area, the mouse pointer changes to the drag icon. A thick black border displays around Wednesday, August 26, 1998 in the Date Navigator (Figure 1-28).

2 **Release the left mouse button.**

The appointment moves from Monday, August 24, 1998 to Wednesday, August 26, 1998.

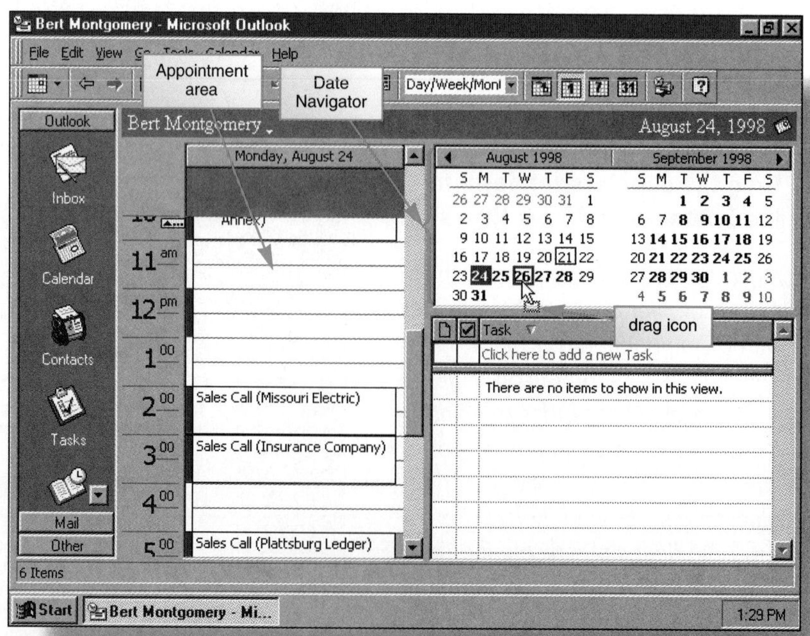

FIGURE 1-28

Outlook provides several ways to move appointments to new dates in addition to the drag and drop method used in the previous steps. Appointments can be moved to new dates by making changes in the Appointment window or by using the cut and paste method discussed in the following section.

OtherWays

1. Double-click appointment, edit date in Start time date list box in Appointment window
2. Click left border of appointment, press CTRL+X, click new date in Date Navigator, click new time slot in Appointment area, press CTRL+V

Moving an Appointment to a New Month

If an appointment is being moved to a month not displayed in the Date Navigator, you simply cannot drag an appointment to a date that is not displayed. You can, however, cut and paste the appointment to a new date.

When you cut an item in other Office 97 applications, the item that you cut disappears from the screen. In Outlook, the item remains on the screen until you paste it to another location.

Missouri Electric is adequately stocked with supplies until October. You need to move the appointment to October 5, 1998. The following steps describe how to move an appointment to a new month using the cut and paste method.

Steps To Move an Appointment to a New Month

1. **Click Monday, August 24, 1998 in the Date Navigator. Click the blue left border of the Missouri Electric appointment to select it. Click Edit on the menu bar and then point to Cut.**

   The Edit menu displays (Figure 1-29).

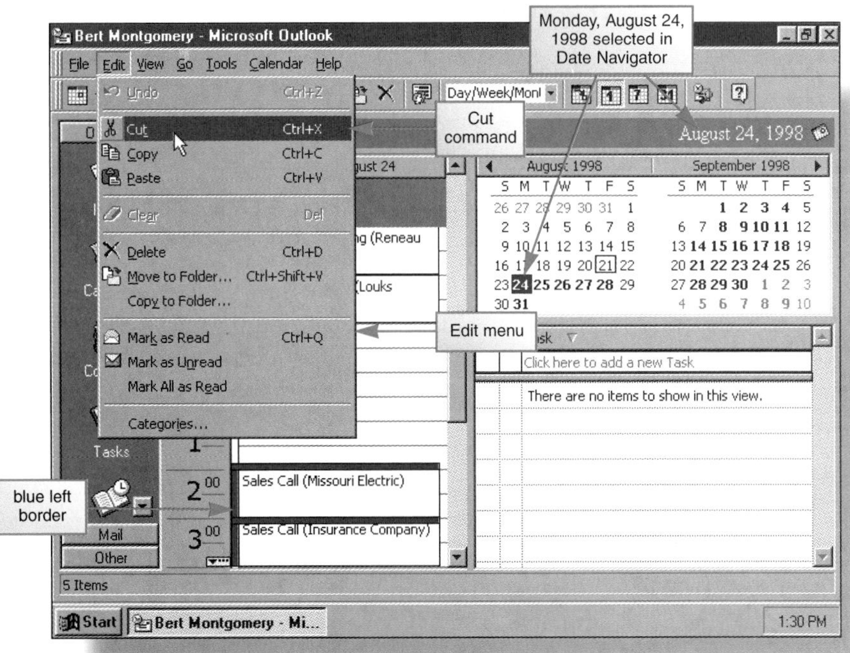

FIGURE 1-29

2 Click Cut on the Edit menu.

The appointment is copied to the Clipboard. The appointment does not disappear, as you would expect. The appointment stays on the screen in its original location until you paste it somewhere else.

3 Click the right scroll arrow in the Date Navigator to display October 1998. Click Monday, October 5, 1998.

Outlook displays Monday, October 5, 1998 in the Appointment area. The time slot of the sales call with Missouri Electric is highlighted (Figure 1-30).

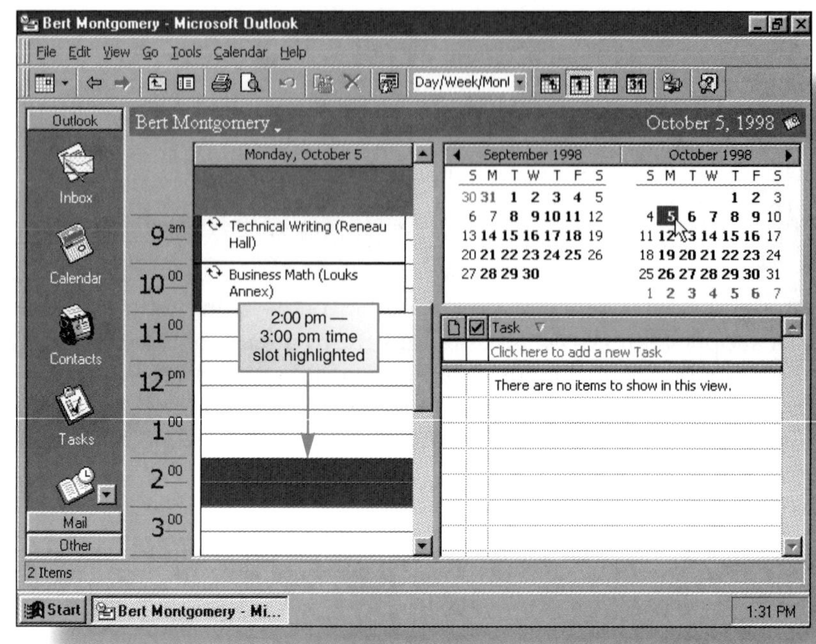

FIGURE 1-30

4 On the Edit menu, click Paste.

The appointment now appears in the 2:00 pm – 3:00 pm time slot in the Appointment area for Monday, October 5, 1998 (Figure 1-31).

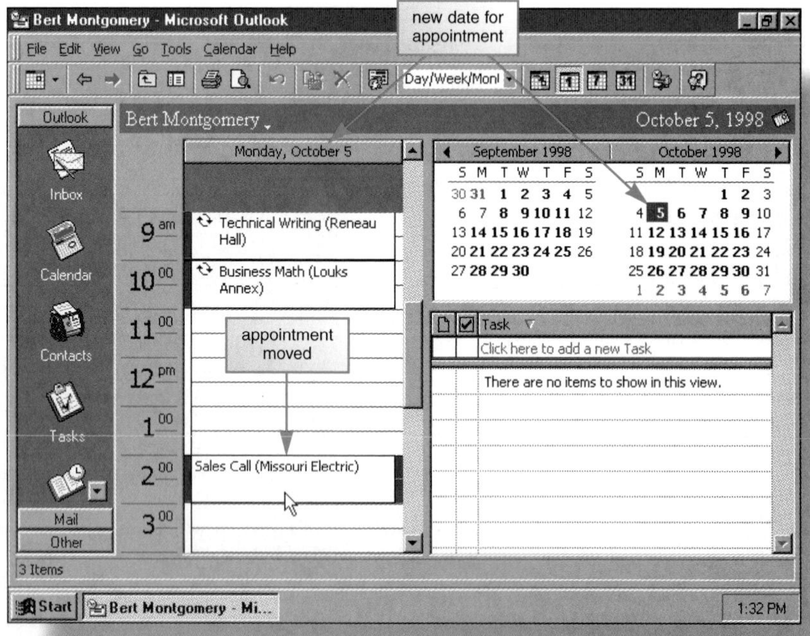

FIGURE 1-31

The method you use to move an appointment depends on its new date. In general, if an appointment is being moved to a new time on the same day or if the appointment is being moved to a day that is visible in the Date Navigator, use the drag and drop method. If the appointment is being moved to a month that is not visible in the Date Navigator, use the cut and paste method.

Creating an Event

Outlook's Calendar folder allows you to keep track of important events, which are activities that last 24 hours or longer. Examples of events include birthdays, conferences, weddings, vacations, holidays, and so on; they can be one time or recurring. Events differ from appointments in that they do not display in individual time slots in the Appointment area. Instead, when you schedule an event, its description displays in a small **banner** below the date heading. You can change the details of the event to indicate whether you will be free, busy, or out of the office during the event. The following steps show how to enter a birthday as an event.

More About Locations

As you enter appointments or events with specific locations, the locations automatically are accumulated in a list, accessible through the arrow to the right of the Location text box. Frequently used locations can be selected from this list, thus saving you typing time.

To Create an Event

1. **Click the left scroll arrow to display August 1998 in the Date Navigator. Click Thursday, August 27, 1998.**

2. **Double-click the date heading at the top of the Appointment area. When the Untitled – Event window displays, type** `Katie's Birthday` **in the Subject text box. Point to the Save and Close button (Figure 1-32).**

   The Untitled – Event window displays. Double-clicking the date heading indicates that you want to schedule an all day event. The All day event check box thus is selected by default.

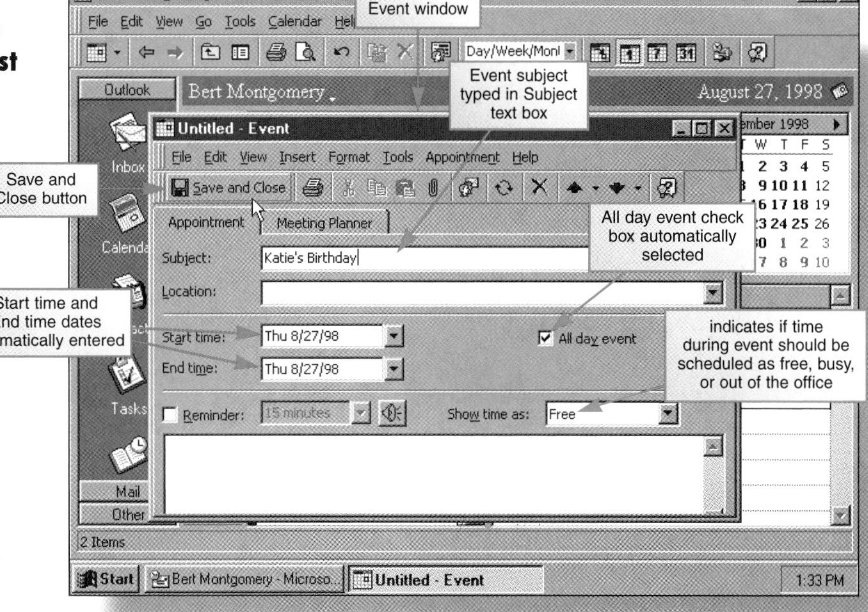

FIGURE 1-32

Click the Save and Close button.

The Event subject displays in a banner below the date heading (Figure 1-33).

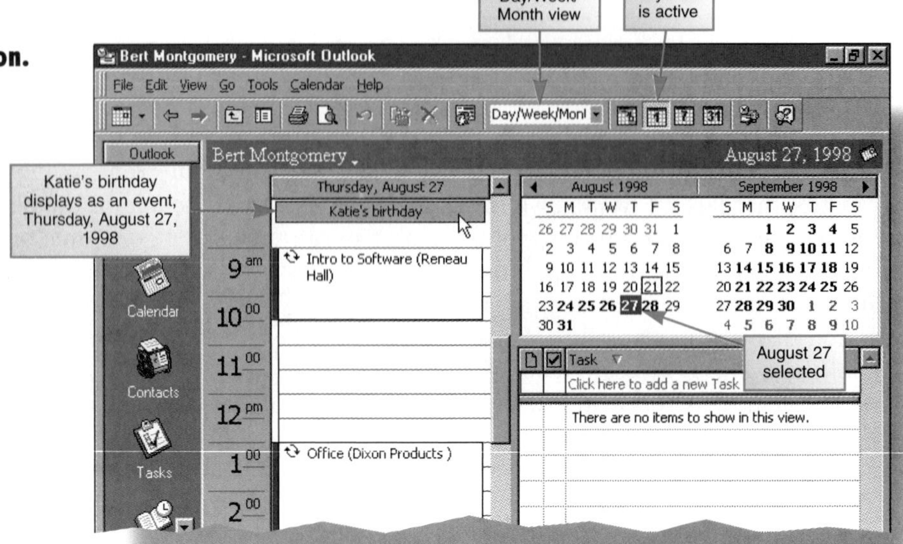

FIGURE 1-33

OtherWays

1. On Calendar menu click New event
2. Right-click Appointment area, on shortcut menu click New event
3. Press CTRL+N, click All day event check box

You could use the same steps to enter holidays as annual events; however, Outlook has a folder of typical holidays for various countries that can be added to your calendar automatically. To do this, click Options on the Tools menu and then click the Add Holidays button on the Calendar tab.

Now that the schedule is complete, you are ready to display the Calendar in various views.

Displaying the Calendar in Week and Month Views

The default view type of the Calendar folder is the Day/Week/Month view. While in Day/Week/Month view, Outlook can display calendars in three different views: Day, Week, and Month. Thus far in the project, you have used only the Day view, which is indicated by the recessed Day button on the Standard toolbar while Day/Week/Month view displays in the Current View box.

Now that the schedule is complete, you can see what it looks like displayed in Week or Month view. Although the screen displays quite differently in Week and Month views, you can perform the same tasks as in Day view: appointments and events can be added, edited, or deleted, and reminders can be set and removed.

Week View

The advantage of displaying a calendar in **Week view** is that you can see how many appointments are scheduled for any given week. In Week view, the seven days of the selected week display in the Appointment area. The five days of the work week (Monday through Friday) display in individual frames, while Saturday and Sunday share a single frame. The following step describes how to display the calendar in Week view.

Steps To Change to Week View

1 Click Wednesday, September 9, 1998 in the Date Navigator and then click the Week button on the Standard toolbar.

The calendar displays in Week view (Figure 1-34). Note that Day/Week/Month displays in the Current View box and the Week button is recessed.

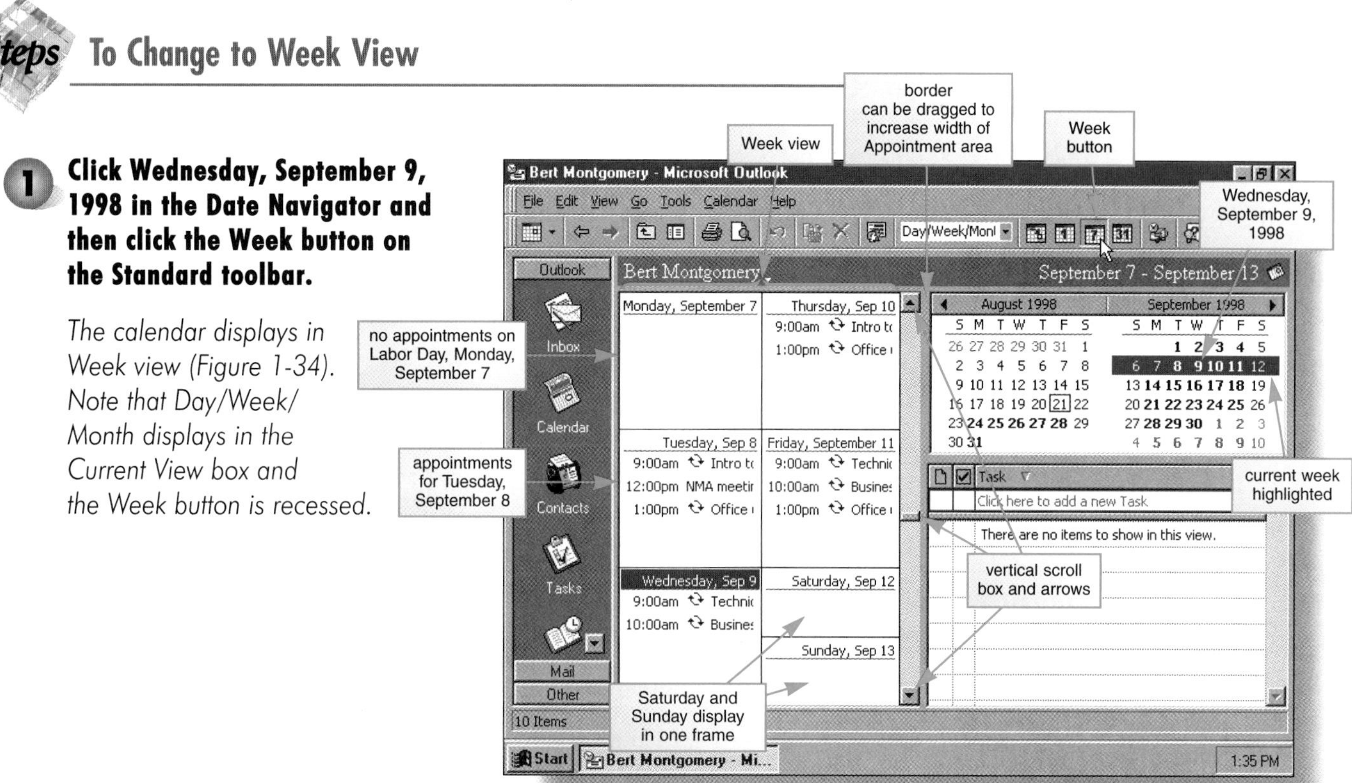

FIGURE 1-34

OtherWays

1. On View menu click Week
2. Press ALT+V press W

The vertical scroll box and arrows allow you to move backward or forward one week at a time. As in Day view, you can double-click an appointment to view and edit appointment details. As shown in Figure 1-35 on the next page, some appointments may be too long to display horizontally in the Appointment area. Dragging the border of the Appointment area to the right will increase its width so that more of the appointments display. The rest of the Week view is adjusted accordingly to display a single month in the Date Navigator and a more narrow TaskPad. If a day has too many items to display vertically, Outlook will display a down arrow in the bottom right-hand corner of the day frame. Clicking the down arrow returns the calendar to Day view so you can view the rest of the appointments for the day.

Month View

The **Month view** resembles a standard monthly calendar page and displays your schedule for an entire month. Appointments are listed in each date frame in the calendar. The steps on the next page show how to display your calendar in Month view.

More About the Current View Box

The Current View box on the Standard toolbar has several settings to customize the view of your calendar. They include Day/Week/Month, Active Appointments, Events, Annual Events, Recurring Appointments, and By Category.

To Change to Month View

1 Click the Month button on the Standard toolbar.

The calendar displays in Month view (Figure 1-35). Several days contain more appointments than can be displayed in the allotted space; these days have a down arrow in the bottom right-hand corner.

2 Click the down arrow in Friday, September 11, 1998 to return to Day view.

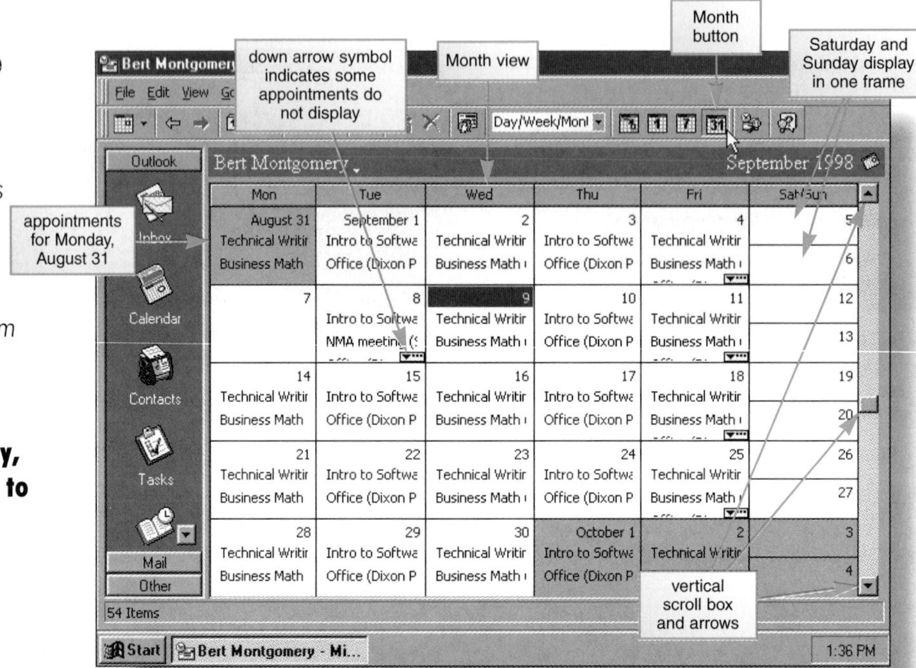

FIGURE 1-35

OtherWays

1. On View menu click Month
2. Press ALT+V, press M

You can use the vertical scroll box and arrows to move the Month view forward and backward one week at a time. As you drag the vertical scroll box, Outlook displays the first day of the week in a ScreenTip beside the scroll box. As with Day and Week views, you can add, edit or delete appointments in Month view. Because the appointments are considerably abbreviated in Month view, however, it is easier to switch back to Day view to make changes.

Creating a Task List Using the TaskPad

Now that you have organized your daily appointments, you may want to use the **TaskPad** in the Calendar window to organize the many duties and projects you work on each day. The TaskPad, which displays in the bottom right section of the Calendar window, allows you to create a **task list** of items you wish to track through completion. **Tasks** can be simple to do items, daily reminders, assignments with due dates, or business responsibilities. In this project you will enter single-user tasks that occur once, but you can use Outlook to create a Tasks folder for recurring tasks, group tasks, and assigned or forwarded tasks. Perform the following steps to create a task list using the TaskPad.

More *About* **Tasks**

A task is any personal or work-related duty or errand you keep in your Outlook task list to track through completion. A task can occur once or repeatedly (a recurring task). You can add a task to the Outlook task list for a document you are working on in Word. For example, if you have a note to yourself that you need to review a document by a certain date, you can open the document, and, from Word, add the document review as a task in your Outlook task list. From Outlook, you can assign tasks to other people and track the progress of tasks as they are completed.

Steps To Create a Task List Using the TaskPad

1. **Click Monday, August 24, 1998 in the Date Navigator.**

   The TaskPad displays in the bottom right section of the window. The TaskPad is divided into two main sections, a ***New task area*** *and the task list.*

2. **In the New task area, click the box labeled Click here to add a new task. When the area changes to a text box, type** `go to bookstore` **in the text box (Figure 1-36).**

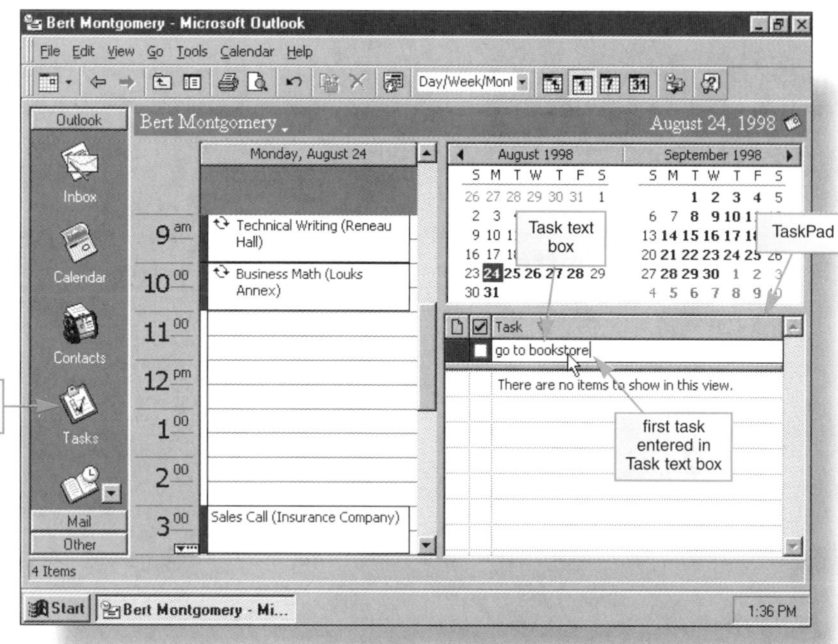

FIGURE 1-36

3. **Press ENTER.**

   The task is added to the TaskPad (Figure 1-37). The insertion point remains active in the Task text box so you can enter the next task.

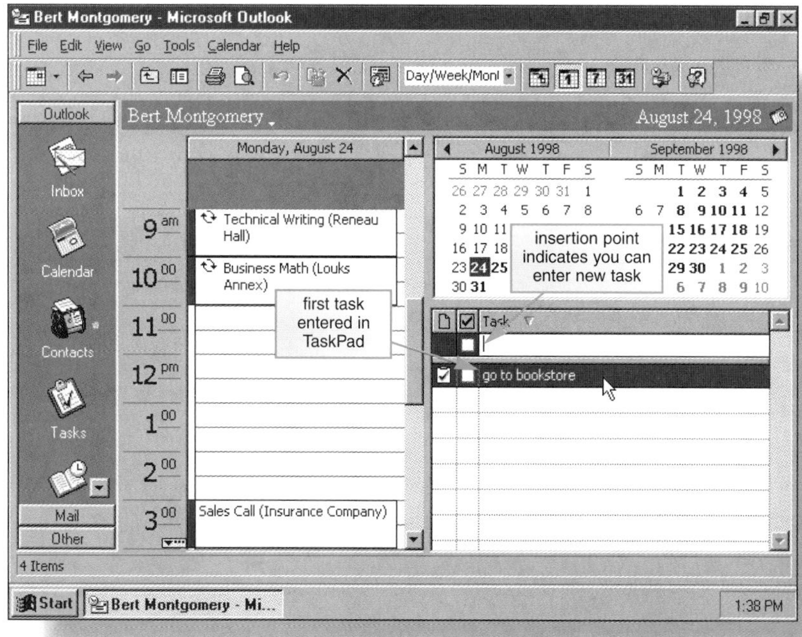

FIGURE 1–37

4 **Type** `call Anita` **in the text box and press ENTER. Type** `pick up dry-cleaning` **in the text box and press ENTER.**

As each task is entered, the previous task moves down the list. The insertion point is active in the text box.

5 **Click outside the TaskPad to finish entering new tasks.**

Your TaskPad now should look like the one in Figure 1-38.

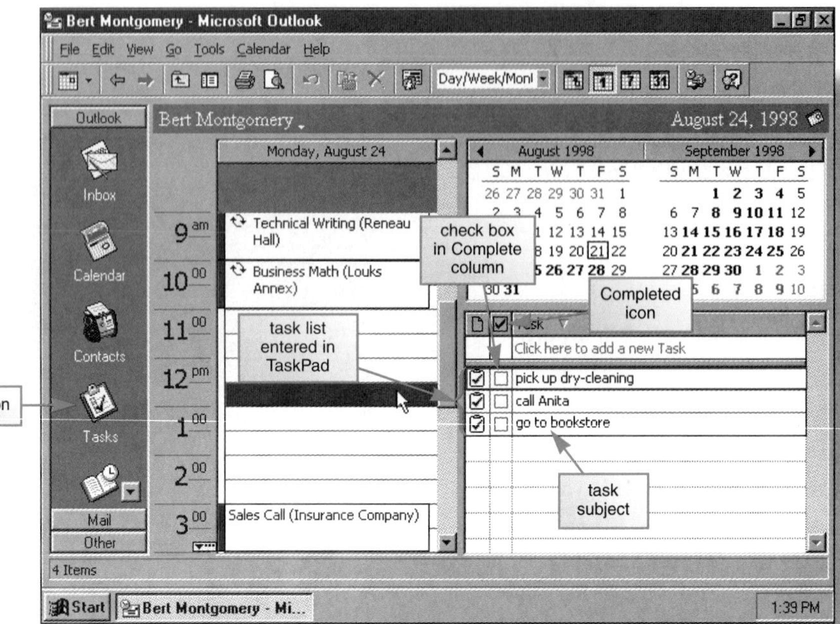

FIGURE 1-38

OtherWays

1. On File menu click New, click Task
2. Click New Appointment button arrow, click Task
3. Press CTRL+SHIFT+K
4. On Outlook Bar click Tasks, click New Task button

To add details to task, such as due date, status, and priority, you can double-click the **Task icon** to open a Task window.

When a task is complete, click the check box in the Complete column to the left of the task's subject. A check mark called a **Completed icon** will display in the Complete column and a line will be placed through the task indicating it is complete. To delete a task from the TaskPad entirely, select the task and then click the Delete button on the Standard toolbar.

If you have lots of tasks on various days or if you assign tasks to others, it is advisable to create a personal Tasks subfolder for your task list, as you did for your calendar. This also is true if you are working in a lab situation or on a shared computer.

re *About* Editing Tasks

You can drag any task from the TaskPad to a time slot in the appointment area, thereby making the task an appointment.

Printing a Calendar

You can print all or part of your calendar in a number of different layouts or **print styles.** The following section describes how to print the calendar you created in Daily, Weekly, and Monthly Styles.

Daily Style

A printout of a single day of the calendar, called the **Daily Style**, shows the day's appointments, tasks, and a two-month calendar. Follow the steps to print the calendar in Daily Style.

To Print the Calendar in Daily Style

1 **Ready the printer. Click Monday, August 24, 1998 in the Date Navigator and then click the Print button on the Standard toolbar. Point to the OK button.**

The Print dialog box displays (Figure 1-39). Because the Appointment window was in Day view when you clicked the Print button, Daily Style is selected in the Print style list by default.

2 **With Daily Style selected in the Print style list, click the OK button.**

The daily schedule of appointments for Monday, August 24, 1998 prints on the printer. The printout should appear as shown in Figure 1-1d on page O 1.5.

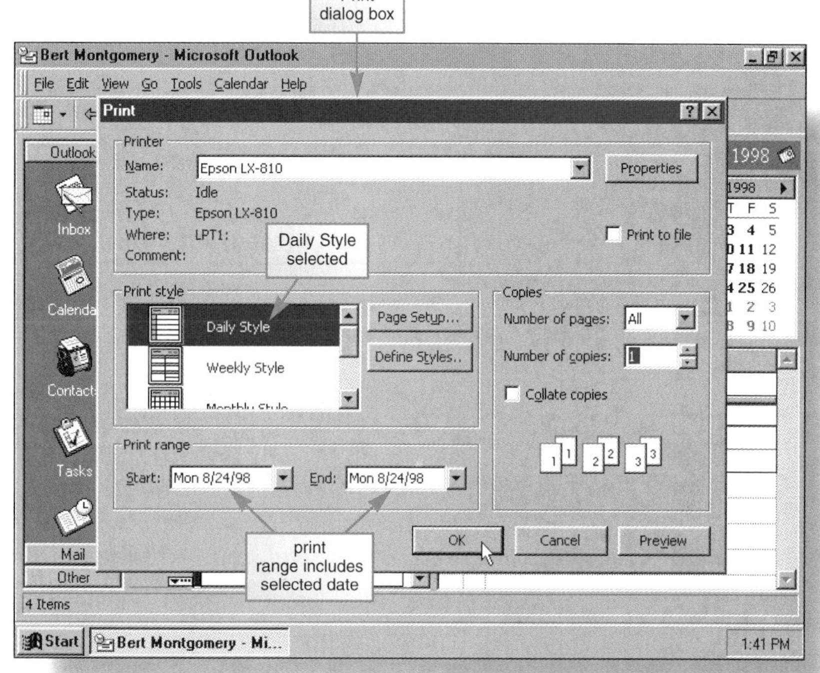

FIGURE 1-39

*Other*Ways

1. On File menu click Print
2. Press CTRL+P

The Daily Style printout includes features from the Day view of the Calendar, including appointments, events, tasks, and notes. Dates with appointments are bolded in the two-month calendar. Page numbers and current system dates appear at the bottom of the page. The Page Setup button in the Print dialog box allows you to modify the style to include or omit various features.

More About Printing

You can use the Page Setup dialog box to change the margins, orientation, or paper size of the paper on which your calendar prints.

Weekly Style

To print a calendar in the Weekly Style, you can click the Print button while viewing the calendar in Week view or select the Weekly Style in the Print dialog box, as shown in the following step.

TO PRINT THE CALENDAR IN WEEKLY STYLE

Step 1: Ready the printer. With Monday, August 24, 1998 selected in the Date Navigator, click the Print button on the Standard toolbar. Click Weekly Style in the Print style list and then click the OK button.

The calendar for the week of Monday, August 24, 1998 through Sunday, August 30, 1998 prints on the printer as shown in Figure 1-1e on page O 1.5.

Depending on how many appointments you have, you may choose to print the weekly calendar on one or two pages. To change the number of pages in the printout, click the Page Setup button in the Print dialog box. Tasks and notes also can be added to the printout.

Monthly Style

The following step prints the calendar in Monthly Style.

TO PRINT THE CALENDAR IN MONTHLY STYLE

Step 1: Ready the printer. With Monday, August 24, 1998 selected in the Date Navigator, click the Print button on the Standard toolbar. Click Monthly Style in the Print style list and then click the OK button.

The calendar for the month of August 1998 prints on the printer. As shown in Figure 1-1f on page O 1.5, selecting Monthly Style prints the calendar in landscape orientation. Some appointments are truncated due to lack of space. The Monthly Style of printout is intended to show the larger picture rather than the detail of a Daily Style printout.

Another useful print style is Tri-fold Style, which prints a daily appointment list, a task list, and a calendar for the week. Styles and setups can be saved using the Define Styles button in the Print dialog box.

Printing the Task List

If you want to print just the task list, you first must open the Tasks folder. The following steps describe how to print the task list by itself.

TO PRINT THE TASK LIST

Step 1: Click the Tasks shortcut in the Outlook Bar. The task list you entered in the TaskPad displays.
Step 2: Click the Print button on the Standard toolbar. When the Print Dialog box displays, click OK.

The task list prints as shown (Figure 1-40).

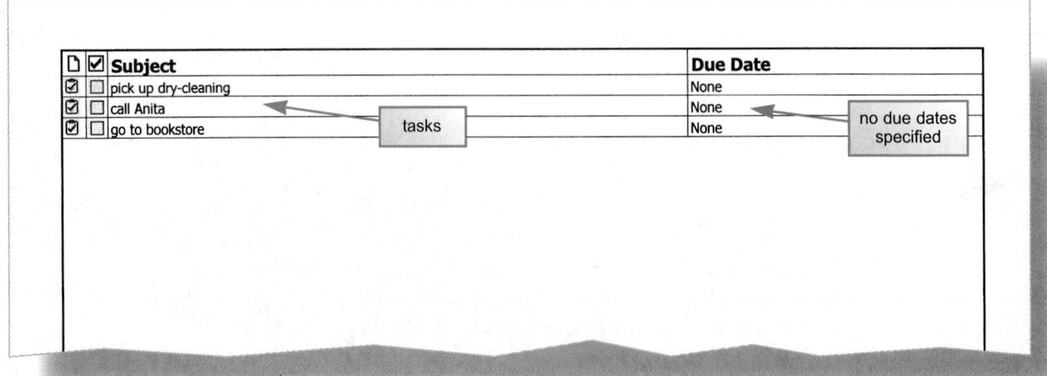

FIGURE 1-40

Contacts

Contacts are people with whom you communicate for business or personal reasons. To help him organize information about his contacts, Bert keeps their names, addresses, and telephone numbers in a business card holder and in his address book. With Outlook you can create and maintain important contact information in a **contact list**, which is stored in the Contacts folder. Your contact list is like an electronic address book that allows you to store names, addresses, e-mail addresses, and more. Once the information has been entered, you can retrieve, sort, edit, organize, or print your contact list.

When you open the Contacts folder, information about each contact displays on an address card in the default Address Card view. Each address card includes fields such as name, address, telephone numbers, as well as e-mail and Web page addresses. You may choose which fields display on the cards using the View menu.

In addition to organizing your contacts, Outlook's Contacts can serve many other functions. For example, you can use Contacts quickly to assign a task, send a message, or schedule a meeting with a contact. You even can use your contact list as an e-mail address book or as a database for a mail merge using Microsoft Word 97. You even can log on to the Internet through Contacts by clicking a contact's Web page address. If you click your contact's e-mail address, an addressed message box comes up — ready for you to use.

Although his address book works fine, Bert thinks he could communicate more efficiently if he entered his clients into a contact list. The following sections describe how to create and print a contact list containing the contacts shown in Table 1-2.

Table 1-2

NAME	ADDRESS	TELEPHONE	COMPANY
Nancy Goolsby	123 Main Street, Plattsburg, MO 64477	(816) 555-1317	Plattsburg Ledger
Nate Thomas	2312 Oak, Plattsburg, MO 64477	(816) 555-2468	Insurance Office
Carl Fredrick	355 Belt Highway, St. Joseph, MO 64650	(816) 555-3579	Dixon Products
Marsha Elana	197 Jessie James Ave., St. Joseph, MO 64650	(816) 555-0864	Missouri Electric

Creating a Personal Subfolder in the Contacts Folder

The first step in creating the contact list is creating a personal subfolder. If you are the only person working on your computer, you could store the contact list in Outlook's Contacts folder. Bert, however, shares his computer with co-workers and students and thus wants to store his contact list in a subfolder.

More *About* **the Internet**

When you type an Internet Web page address or e-mail address in the text box of a Contact window, Outlook creates a hyperlink for you from the text. If you are connected to an Internet browser (such as Microsoft Internet Explorer), you can click the hyperlink to go quickly to the destination or send your e-mail message.

Steps To Create a Personal Subfolder in the Contacts Folder

1. **Click the Contacts shortcut in the Outlook Bar. When the Contacts folder opens, right-click the Folder banner and click Create Subfolder.**

   The Contacts – Microsoft Outlook window displays, and the Create New Folder dialog box opens (Figure 1-41).

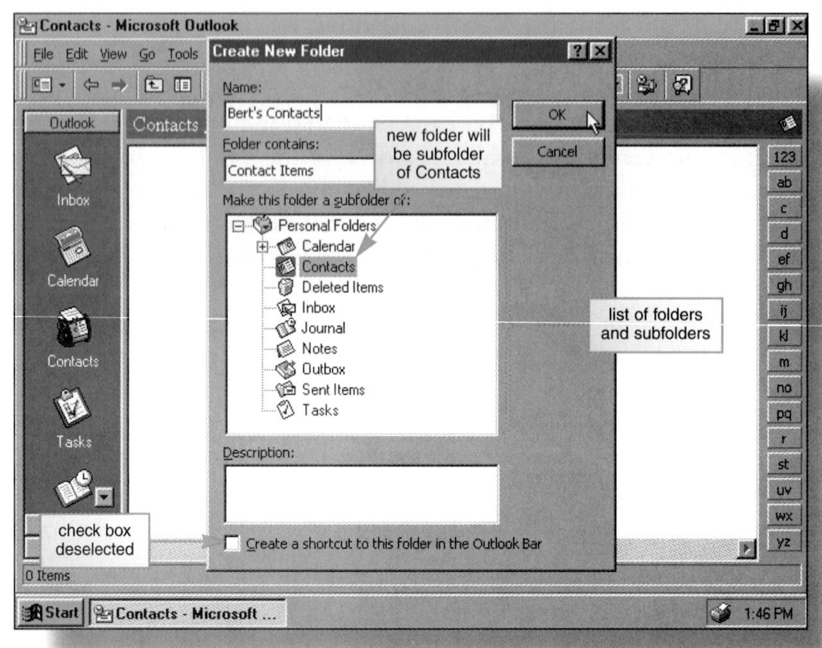

FIGURE 1-41

2. **Type** `Bert's Contacts` **in the Name text box. If necessary, click the Create a shortcut to this folder in the Outlook Bar check box to deselect it. Point to the OK button.**

   The name of the new subfolder, Bert's Contacts, displays in the Name text box. Outlook will make it a subfolder of the Contacts folder.

3. **Click the OK button. Click the folder name Contacts in the Folder banner. When the Folder List displays, click the plus sign (+) to the left of the Contacts icon and then click Bert's Contacts subfolder.**

   The Bert's Contacts – Microsoft Outlook window displays. Because you have not entered any contacts, a message displays as shown in Figure 1-42.

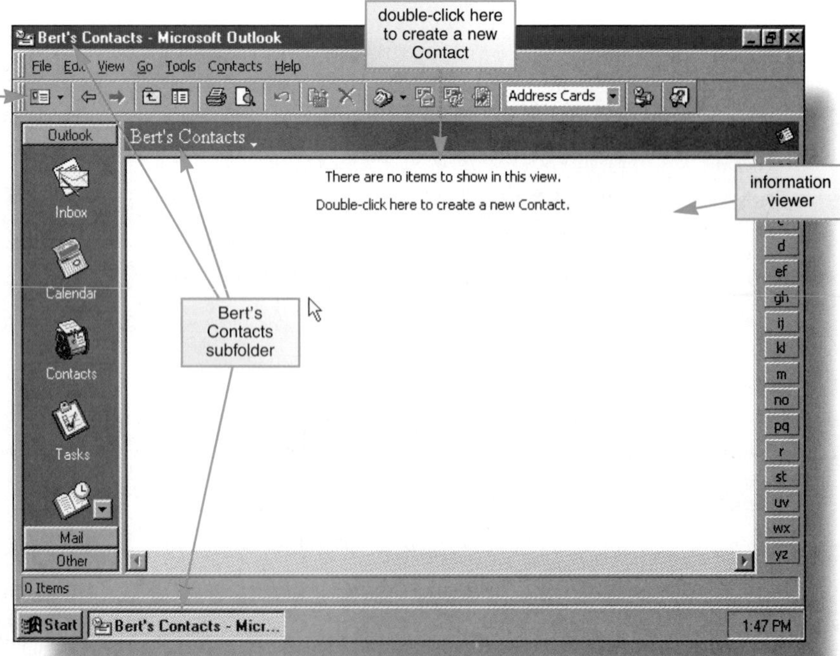

FIGURE 1-42

Other Ways

1. On File menu click Folder, click Create Subfolder
2. Press CTRL+SHIFT+E

Now that you have a subfolder in which to store the contact list, you can enter the contact names and other pertinent information.

Creating a Contact List

The following steps describe how to enter the data in Table 1-2 on page O 1.33 in the contact list.

To Create a Contact List

1. **Double-click the text, Double-click here to create a new Contact, in the information viewer, as shown in Figure 1-42.**

   The Untitled – Contact window displays. This window allows you to enter general contact information.

2. **Type** `Nancy Goolsby` **in the Full Name text box. Click the Company text box.**

   Notice that Outlook automatically fills in the File as text box, last name first (Figure 1-43). The Untitled – Contact window changes to the Nancy Goolsby – Contact window.

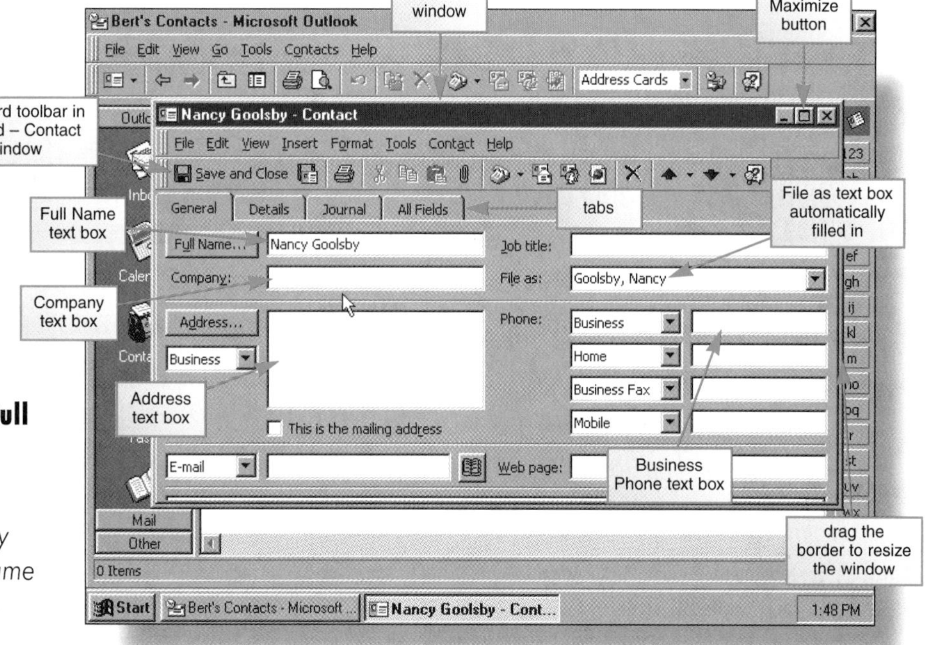

FIGURE 1-43

3. **Type** `Plattsburg Ledger` **in the Company text box. Click the Address text box. In the Address text box, type** `123 Main Street` **and then press ENTER. Type** `Plattsburg, MO 64477` **and then click the Business Phone text box.**

4. **Type** `(816) 555-1317` **in the Business Phone text box. If necessary, click the Maximize button or drag the border of the window to the right until the entire telephone number displays. Point to the Save and Close button.**

   The completed fields in the Nancy Goolsby – Contact window display as shown in Figure 1-44.

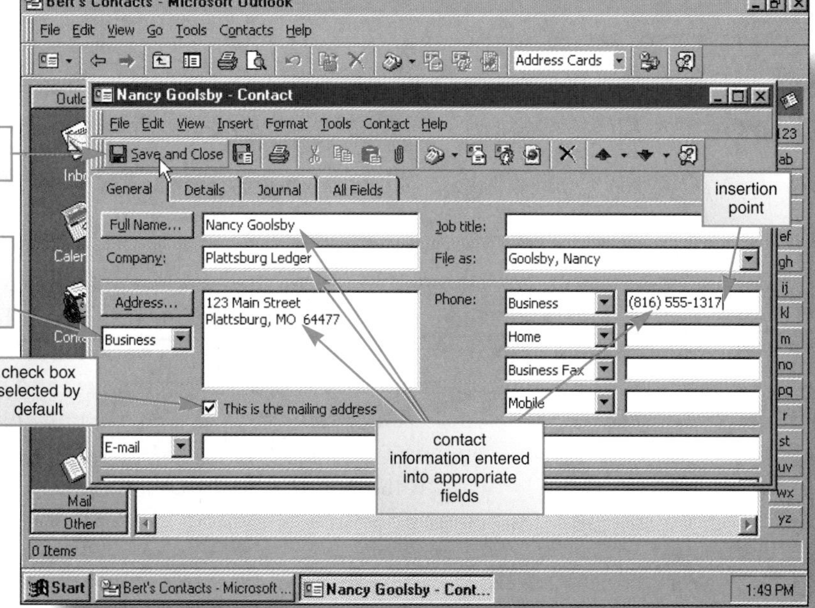

FIGURE 1-44

5 Click the Save and Close button.

Outlook returns to the Bert's Contacts – Microsoft Outlook window. Because Address Cards is the current view, Nancy Goolsby's contact information displays in an address card (Figure 1-45).

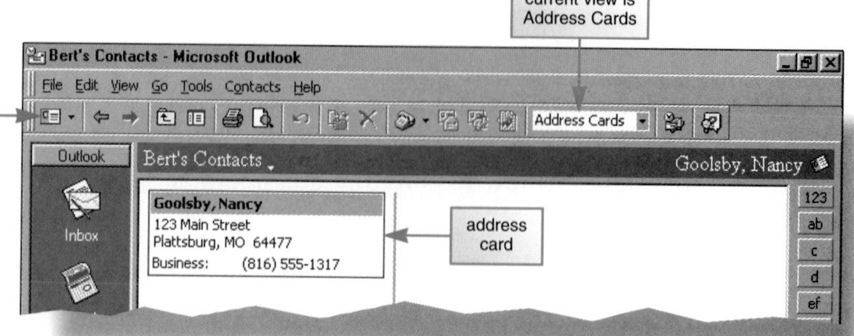

FIGURE 1-45

6 Click the New Contact button. Repeat Steps 2 through 5 to enter the three remaining contacts in Table 1-2 on page O 1.33.

When complete, the contact list should look like Figure 1-46. Outlook automatically lists the contacts in alphabetical order. The phrase on the right side of the Folder banner, Ela – Tho, indicates the range of contacts currently displayed (Elana to Thomas).

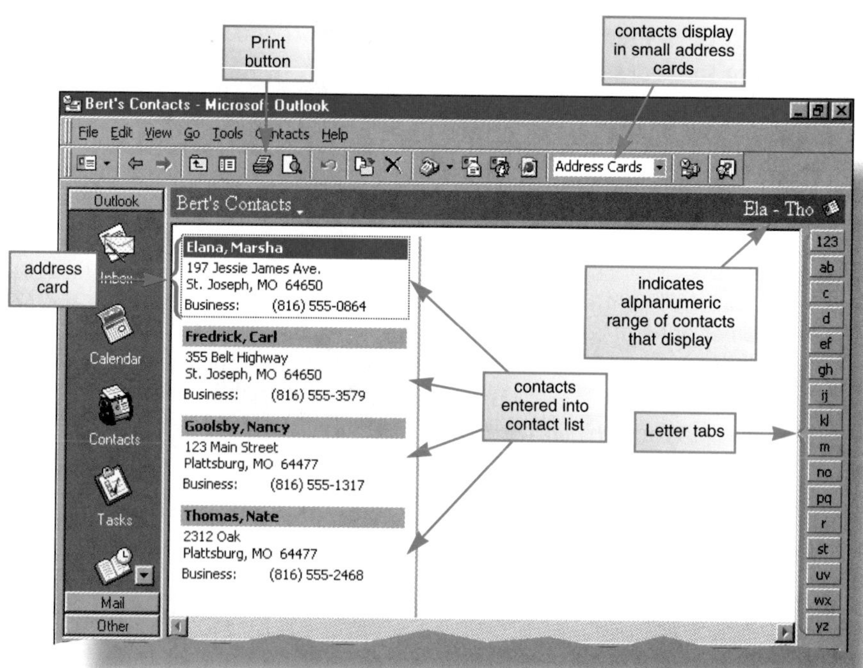

FIGURE 1-46

OtherWays

1. On Contacts menu click New Contact
2. With Contacts folder displayed, press CTRL+N

Because this contact list is very short, all the names display on screen. With longer lists, however, you quickly can locate a specific contact by clicking the Letter tab on the right side of the Microsoft Outlook – Contacts window (Figure 1-46).

Once the contact list is complete, it can be viewed, edited, or updated at any time. You can make some changes by typing inside the card itself. To display and edit all the information for a contact, double-click the address card to display the Contact window. You can use this window to enter information about a contact, such as e-mail and Web page addresses. Up to 18 different telephone numbers also can be stored for each contact and categorized by location and type (business, home, fax, mobile, pager, and so on). Clicking the Details tab allows you to enter the contact's department, manager's name, nickname, and even their birthday.

To further help you manage your contacts, you can categorize and sort the contact list in any number of ways. For example, you can group contacts into categories such as Key Customer, Business, Hot Contact, or even Ideas, Competition, or Strategies. Or, you can create your own categories to group contacts by company, department, a particular project, a specific class, and so on. You also can sort by any part of the address, for example, to sort by postal code for bulk mailings.

Although the Contacts folder displays in Address Cards view by default (Figure 1-46), several other views are available. Clicking the Current View box arrow on the Standard toolbar lets you choose views such as Detailed Address Cards, Phone List, By Category, By Company, and By Location.

Printing the Contact List

Printing the contact list is an easy way to obtain a listing of people you frequently contact. The printed list can be used for business mailings, invitations to social gatherings, or even a telephone or Christmas card list. The following step describes how to print the contact.

TO PRINT THE CONTACT LIST

Step 1: Ready the printer. Click the Print button on the Standard toolbar. When the Print dialog box displays, click OK.

The printed contact list should look like Figure 1-47.

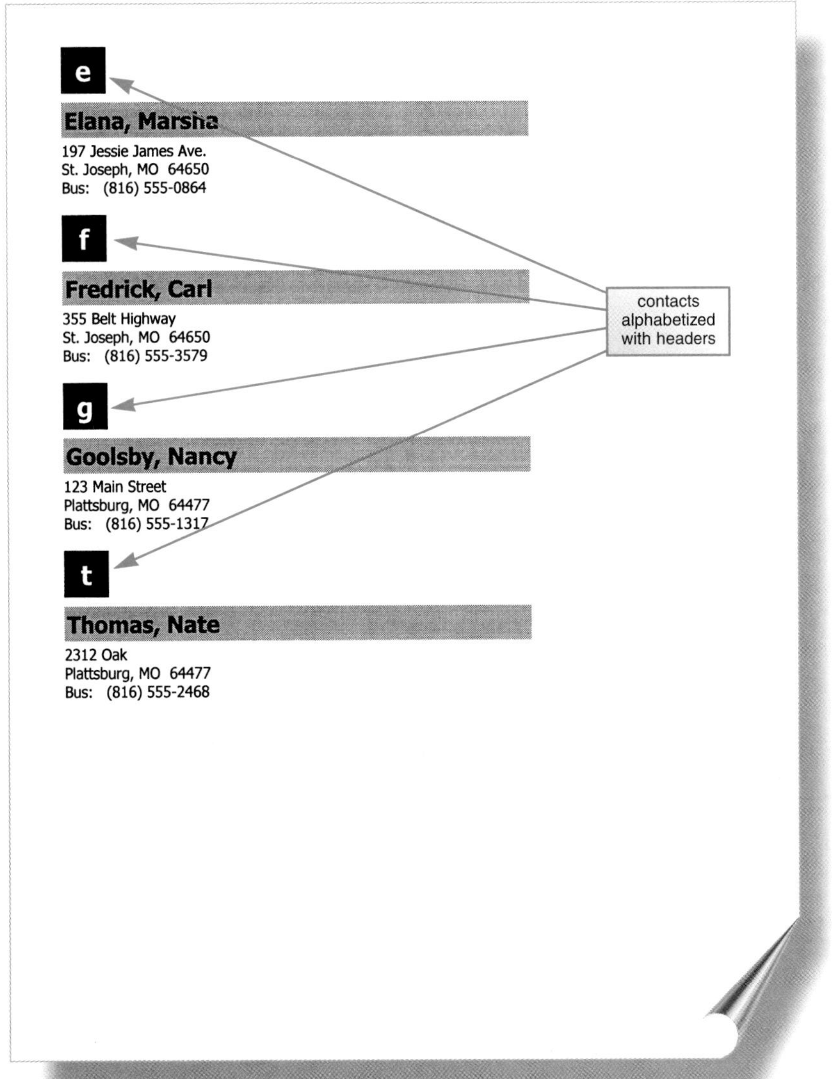

FIGURE 1-47

You can customize your printout by changing the Print style in the Print dialog box. These styles let you choose from a variety of fields, along with choices for paper orientation and size.

More About Saving

Each appointment, event, meeting, and task is saved as a separate file on your disk, and therefore can be edited, moved, copied, or deleted. Saving these items together as a group is accomplished through the Import and Export Wizard.

Exporting Subfolders

You now are ready to save the calendar and contact list on a floppy disk. Saving your work on a floppy disk allows you to take your schedule with you to another computer or to merge your contacts as a mailing list into another computer's word processor.

With many application software packages, you can save a single file, such as a letter or spreadsheet, directly to a floppy disk. With Outlook, however, each appointment, task, or contact is a file in itself. Thus, rather than saving numerous individual files, Outlook uses an Import and Export Wizard to guide you through the process of saving an entire subfolder. Transferring a subfolder to a floppy disk is called **exporting**. Moving a subfolder back to a computer is called **importing**. You can import and export subfolders from any Outlook application. Outlook then saves the subfolder on a floppy disk, adding the extension **.pst**.

Because you have just finished creating Bert Montgomery's contact list, you will export Bert's Contacts subfolder first. The following steps show how to export subfolders to a floppy disk.

Steps To Export Subfolders to a Floppy Disk

1 Insert a floppy disk in your floppy disk drive. On the File menu, click Import and Export. If the Office Assistant displays, click its Close button. Point to Export to a personal folder file (.pst) in the Choose an action to perform list.

The Import and Export Wizard dialog box displays (Figure 1-48). You can choose to perform one of six import and export options available with Outlook.

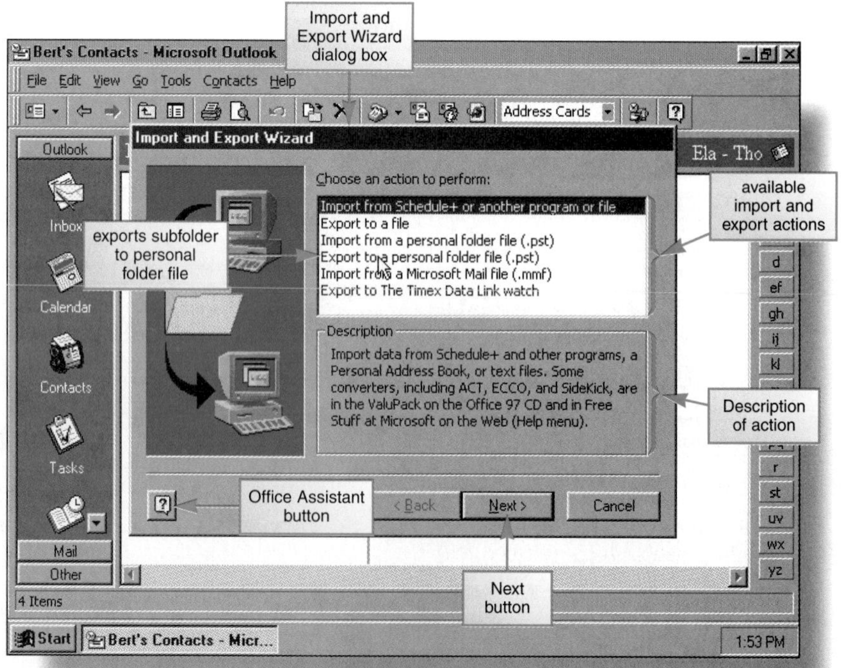

FIGURE 1-48

2 **Click Export to a personal folder file (.pst) and then click Next. If necessary, click the plus sign (+) to the left of the Contacts icon in the Folder List. Click Bert's Contacts subfolder.**

The Export Personal Folders dialog box displays (Figure 1-49). Bert's Contacts subfolder is selected as the folder from which to export.

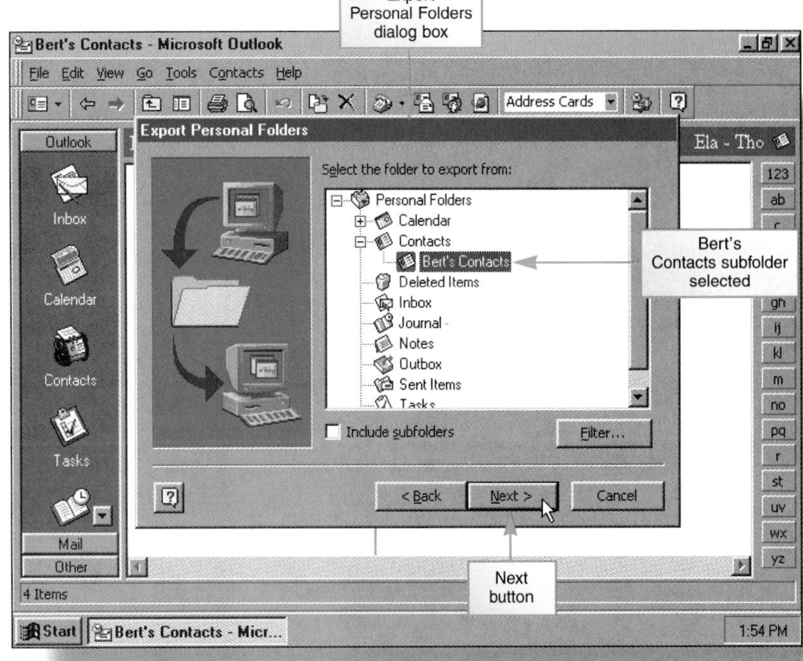

FIGURE 1-49

3 **Click the Next button. Type** `a:\Bert's Contacts` **in the Save exported file as text box. (If your floppy drive is not labeled A, type the drive letter accordingly.) Point to Finish.**

The last screen of the Import and Export Wizard, displays (Figure 1-50). The subfolder will be exported to drive A and saved as Bert's Contacts. Outlook will add the extension .pst to the saved folder.

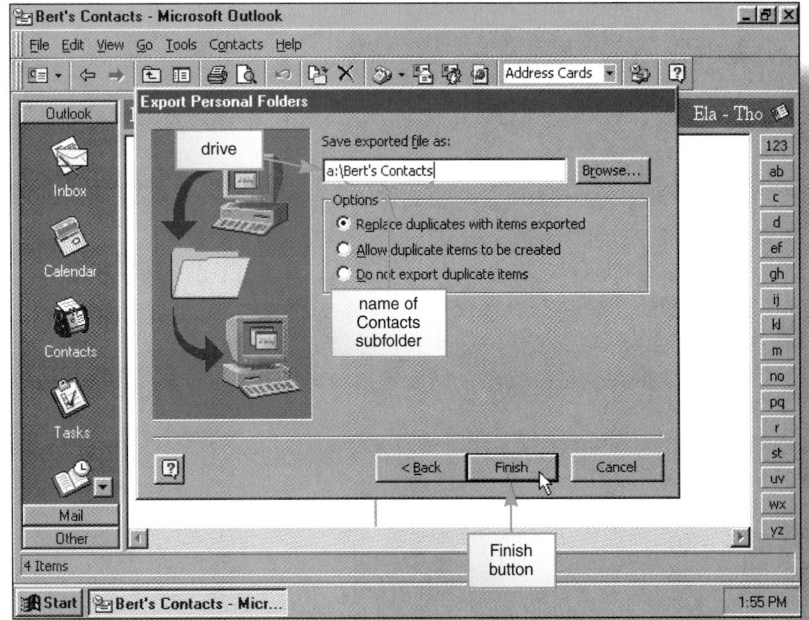

FIGURE 1-50

4 **Click Finish.**

The Export – Personal Folder dialog box displays as Outlook exports the folder. The subfolder is saved on your floppy disk.

5 **To export a Calendar subfolder, repeat Steps 1 through 4. You do not have to open the Calendar folder to export the subfolder. Instead, when the Export Personal Folders dialog box displays, click the plus sign (+) next to the Calendar icon and then click the Bert Montgomery subfolder. Save the exported file on a floppy disk as Bert Montgomery.**

More About Buttons

The Folder List button on the Standard toolbar is a quick way to view all the folders in Outlook. It displays in a resizable pane between the Outlook Bar and the Appointment area. You press it again to remove the display. Next to the Folder List button is the Up One Level button. When clicked, it automatically displays the parent folder in the Folder List hierarchy.

You can export subfolders to a personal folder file, which only can be viewed in Outlook, or save them as another file type, such as a text file, which then can be imported into other programs. Importing and exporting folders allows you to share Outlook items easily. For example, you might import a company Calendar subfolder to publicize a company meeting, a group Contacts subfolder to make information about the people who work on a project available to everyone, or a team Tasks subfolder to help everyone track work on a project.

Deleting Subfolders

The Bert's Contacts and Bert Montgomery subfolders now have been exported to a floppy disk. A copy of each still is present on the hard disk of your computer, however, and displays in Outlook's Folder List. To delete a subfolder from the computer entirely, you must use the Delete command. Perform the following steps to delete a personal subfolder.

To Delete a Personal Subfolder

1 **Click the Calendar shortcut in the Outlook Bar. Click the Folder List button on the Standard toolbar. If necessary, drag the right border of the Folder List window until you see the entire list.**

2 **If necessary, click the plus sign (+) to the left of the Calendar icon. Right-click the Bert Montgomery subfolder. On the shortcut menu, point to Delete "Bert Montgomery" (Figure 1-51).**

3 **Click Delete "Bert Montgomery". Repeat Steps 1 through 3 to delete the Bert's Contacts subfolder. When you have finished, click the Folder List button to close the Folder List.**

The folders no longer display in the Folder list.

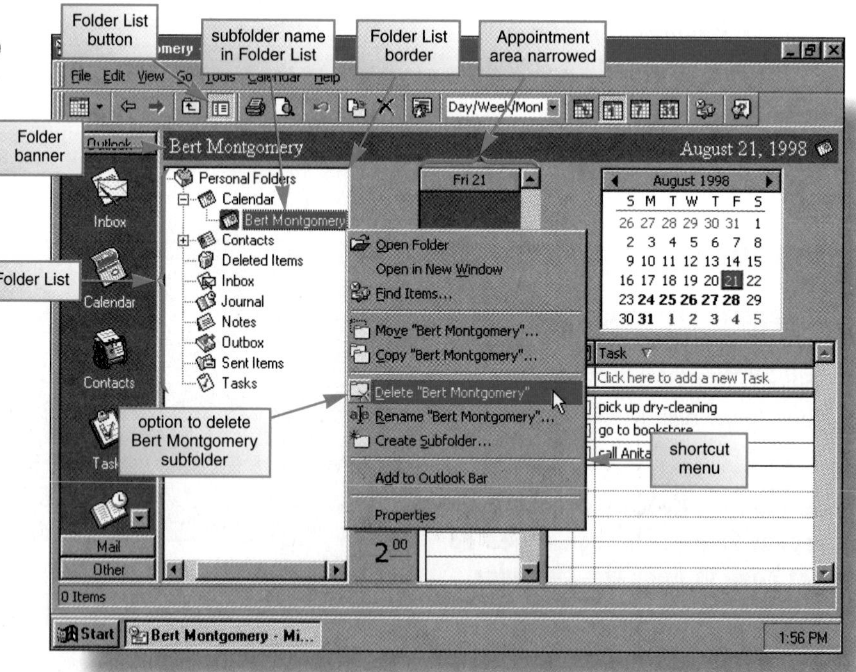

FIGURE 1-51

Other Ways

1. Click Folder List button, click subfolder name, click delete on Standard toolbar
2. On Folder banner, right-click folder name, click delete

Outlook sends the deleted subfolders to a special folder called Deleted Items. If you accidentally delete a subfolder without first exporting it to a floppy disk, you still can open the subfolder by double-clicking it in the Folder List. (You may have to click the plus sign (+) next to the Deleted Items folder to display the subfolder.) Once you are sure you no longer need the subfolder, right-click the subfolder in the Folder List and click Delete on the shortcut menu. Deleting a subfolder from the Deleted Items folder permanently removes it from the hard disk. You can delete subfolders only; Outlook's main application folders, such as Calendar and Contacts, cannot be deleted.

Thus far in Project 1 you have created a schedule, a task list, and a contact list and exported your personal subfolders to a floppy disk. Once you have created and exported a subfolder, you often will have reason to retrieve or import it from the disk. For example, you might want to revise your office hours, add exam dates to your schedule, or use your schedule on a different computer. To do so, you must import or retrieve the subfolder from the floppy disk.

Importing Subfolders

More About Importing

You can import other contact lists through the Import and Export Wizard on the File menu. The Wizard allows you to copy information that exists in other applications to Outlook.

Earlier, you exported the Calendar subfolder containing appointment and event files to a floppy disk. The following steps illustrate how to import the same Calendar subfolder from the floppy disk. To import a subfolder, Outlook must be running. You then can import any type of subfolder from any application within Outlook.

Steps To Import a Subfolder

1. **Insert a floppy disk in your floppy disk drive. Click the Calendar shortcut in the Outlook Bar. Click Import and Export on the File menu.**

   The Import and Export Wizard dialog box displays.

2. **Click Import from a personal folder file (.pst) and then click Next. Type** `a:\Bert Montgomery.pst` **in the File to import text box or click the Browse button to access your floppy drive and select the Bert Montgomery subfolder. Point to Next.**

   The drive, subfolder name, and extension for the subfolder you wish to import display in the Name text box (Figure 1-52).

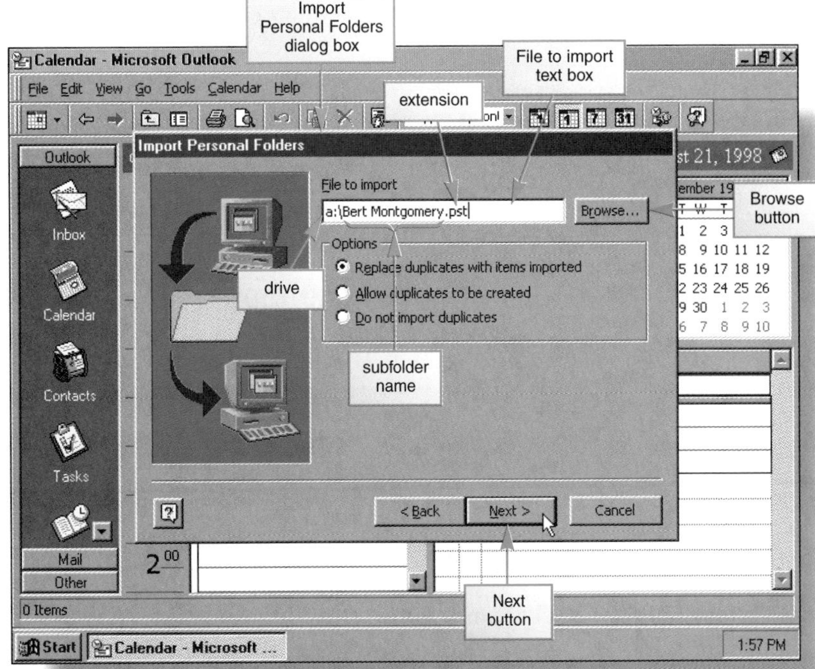

FIGURE 1-52

3 **Click Next. When the Import Personal Folders dialog box displays, click Calendar in the Select the folder to import from list. Point to Finish.**

The last screen of the Import and Export Wizard displays, allowing you to choose the Outlook application to which you wish to import (Figure 1-53).

4 **Click Finish.**

The Import – Personal Folder dialog box displays and then closes when the process is complete. The subfolder is imported into Outlook as a subfolder of Calendar.

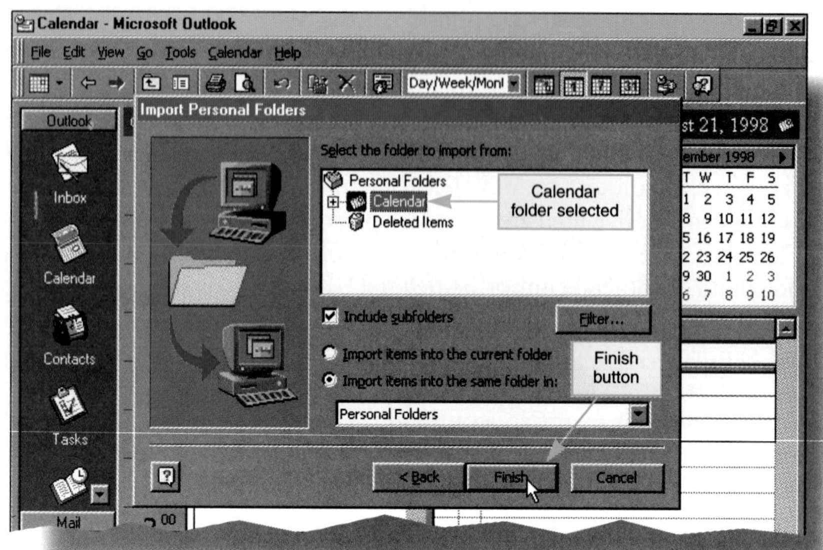

FIGURE 1-53

The Calendar subfolder now is available for you to open, edit, and print as described earlier in this project. When you have finished making changes, you can again export your subfolder and delete the subfolder from the hard disk. In addition to Outlook subfolders, Outlook's Import and Export Wizard allows you to import a Personal Address Book with contact names, addresses, and phone numbers, or bring in existing information from other programs, such as Microsoft Mail or Schedule+.

Quitting Outlook

The project now is complete and you are ready to quit Outlook. The following step describes how to quit Outlook.

TO QUIT OUTLOOK

Step 1: Click the Close button on the Outlook title bar.

A dialog box displays, instructing you to please wait while Microsoft Outlook exits. Outlook closes and the Windows 95 desktop displays.

Project Summary

Bert Montgomery's class and work schedule, including sales calls and lunch appointments, are entered in his calendar and saved in a personal subfolder. In this project you learned about desktop information management by using Outlook to create a personal schedule, task list, and a contact list. You learned how to enter appointments, create recurring appointments, move appointments to new dates, schedule events, and view and print your calendar in different views and print styles. You created a task list to serve as a reminder of tasks to be completed. You also created and printed a contact list. Finally, you exported your personal subfolders to a floppy disk and later imported the subfolders for further updating.

What You Should Know

Having completed this project, you should be able to perform the following tasks:

- Change to Month View *(O 1.28)*
- Change to Week View *(O 1.27)*
- Complete the Recurring Appointments *(O 1.17)*
- Create an Event *(O 1.25)*
- Create a Contact List *(O 1.35)*
- Create a Personal Subfolder in the Calendar Folder *(O 1.9)*
- Create a Personal Subfolder in the Contacts Folder *(O 1.34)*
- Create a Task List Using the TaskPad *(O 1.29)*
- Delete an Appointment *(O 1.20)*
- Delete a Personal Subfolder *(O 1.40)*
- Enter Appointment Dates and Times Using Natural Language Phrases *(O 1.18)*
- Enter Appointments Using the Appointment Window *(O 1.13)*
- Enter Appointments Using the Appointment Area *(O 1.12)*
- Export Subfolders to a Floppy Disk *(O 1.38)*
- Import a Subfolder *(O 1.41)*
- Move an Appointment to a New Date *(O 1.22)*
- Move an Appointment to a New Month *(O 1.23)*
- Move an Appointment to a New Time *(O 1.21)*
- Move to the Next Day in the Appointment Area *(O 1.17)*
- Open the Calendar Folder *(O 1.7)*
- Print the Contact List *(O 1.37)*
- Print the Calendar in Daily Style *(O 1.31)*
- Print the Calendar in Monthly Style *(O 1.32)*
- Print the Calendar in Weekly Style *(O 1.31)*
- Print the Task List *(O 1.32)*
- Quit Outlook *(O 1.42)*
- Set Recurring Appointments *(O 1.15)*
- Start Outlook *(O 1.6)*

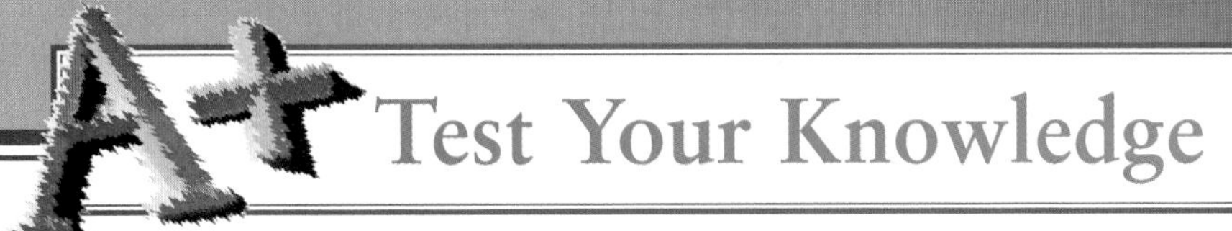

1 True/False

Instructions: Circle T if the statement is true or F if the statement is false.

T F 1. If you share your computer with other users, it is best to create a personal subfolder for each application in Outlook, rather than use the main application folders.
T F 2. Outlook cannot share its data with other programs.
T F 3. Appointments and events display in the Date Navigator.
T F 4. Appointments can be moved to a new date by dragging them to the Date Navigator.
T F 5. The difference between events and appointments is that other people and resources are invited to events.
T F 6. Holidays must be entered as events, one by one.
T F 7. By default, contacts display in rows and columns on the screen, like a spreadsheet.
T F 8. Outlook's Calendar folder cannot be deleted.
T F 9. A contact list can include e-mail and Web page addresses.
T F 10. Exporting a personal subfolder to a floppy disk will delete it from the hard disk.

Test Your Knowledge

2 Multiple Choice

Instructions: Circle the correct response.

1. DIM stands for __________.
   a. Desktop Information Management
   b. Desktop Interface Management
   c. Desktop Informative Manipulation
   d. Definition of Internet Management
2. Which of the following is *not* an application folder that is part of Outlook?
   a. Calendar b. Schedule c. Tasks d. Contacts
3. With Outlook, you can __________.
   a. merge a contact list into a form letter
   b. assign tasks to others
   c. use Word as your e-mail editor
   d. all of the above
4. The Folder banner in Calendar contains the __________.
   a. user's name, appointment date and time
   b. folder names of all Outlook folders
   c. open folder name, selected date, and folder icon
   d. Date Navigator and scroll arrows
5. In Calendar, if you need to schedule more than one person or resource, you enter a new __________.
   a. event b. task c. meeting d. appointment
6. Which of the following phrases will *not* work as a start time for an appointment?
   a. Next Friday
   b. Two weeks from yesterday
   c. Every Tuesday
   d. Tomorrow
7. A recurring appointment __________.
   a. can occur weekly
   b. only can occur a maximum of ten times
   c. can occur on several days at different times
   d. cannot be deleted
8. The best way to move an appointment from March to June is to __________.
   a. click the New Month button
   b. drag the appointment using the Date Navigator
   c. cut and paste the appointment
   d. none of the above
9. You can do all the following using the Contact window except __________.
   a. perform a global search and replace
   b. dial your contact's telephone number
   c. keep track of your contact's birthday
   d. change which fields display on each card
10. By default, a(n) __________ is assigned to each appointment typed in the Appointment window.
    a. appointment icon b. recurring icon c. reminder icon d. none of the above

Use Help

1 Reviewing Project Activities

Instructions: Use Outlook Help and a computer to perform the following tasks.

1. Start Outlook. Open the Calendar folder. With any view of the calendar displayed, click Help on the menu bar. Click Contents and Index. If necessary, click the Contents tab. Double-click the Using Calendar book icon.
2. Double-click the topic, What is Calendar? Click the Events Tip. Read the information that displays and then right-click the information box. On the shortcut menu, click Print Topic. Move the mouse pointer around the screen. To what shape does the mouse pointer change when positioned over a Tip? Read and print each Tip. Write your name at the top of each printout and hand them in to your instructor.
3. Click the Help Topics button to return to the Help Topics: Microsoft Outlook window. Click the Index tab. Type `Appointments` in the text box and then click the Display button. Double-click the topic, All about appointments, meetings, and events. Read and print the information. Close the Help window. Hand the printout in to your instructor.
4. Click the Office Assistant button on the Standard toolbar. Type `How do I add holidays to my calendar?` in the text box. Click Search. When the list of topics displays, click Add holidays for a country to my Calendar. Read and print the information. Write your name on the printout and hand it in to your instructor.

In the Lab

1 Creating a Schedule

Problem: You are a junior student at a university. In addition to carrying a full class load this semester, you are on a committee to organize a fall food drive for the community food pantry and are a member of the university's gymnastic team. You also hold a part-time job in the Financial Aid Office. Using Outlook's Calendar, you are to create a schedule for your Fall semester that begins Monday, August 24, 1998.

Instructions: Perform the following tasks.

1. Create a personal Calendar subfolder called My Schedule. Using the information in Table 1-3 on the next page, enter each of the classes as a recurring appointment.
2. Add your Financial Aid Office work hours to the schedule as a recurring appointment occurring Tuesday and Thursday from 1:00 pm – 4:30 pm.
3. Schedule your Food Drive Committee meetings on the next three Thursdays from 7:00 pm – 8:00 pm.

(continued)

In the Lab

Creating a Schedule *(continued)*

4. Because of Homecoming, all classes for Thursday, October 1, 1998 have been canceled. Delete the single occurrence of these appointments, but not all recurring instances.
5. Add gymnastics practice to the schedule on every Monday, Wednesday, and Friday from 2:00 pm – 5:00 pm. Also add your Saturday gymnastic meets on September 12, 19, 26, and October 3. A meet takes up most of the day and should be scheduled as a one-time event.
6. Print a copy of your calendar in Weekly Style for the week of Monday, September 14, 1998 to Sunday, September 20, 1998.
7. Export your subfolder to a floppy disk and then delete it from the hard disk.

Table 1-3

CLASS	DAYS	TIME
Philosophy of Government	M, W, F	8:00 am - 8:50 am
Advanced Data Processing	M, W, F	9:00 am - 9:50 am
Calculus	T, TH	8:00 am - 9:30 am
History of the Americas	M, W, F	10:00 am - 10:50 am
Contemporary Poetry	M, W, F	11:00 am - 11:50 am
Political Conflicts	T, TH	10:00 am - 11:30 am

2 Creating a Contact List

Problem: You are the volunteer campaign chairman of a friend's campaign for state senate. Many people have pledged their support by donating money or other services. At the end of the campaign, you would like to personally contact and thank each donor for their support. To do so, you need to create and maintain a list of the donors' names, addresses, telephone numbers, and type of donation.

Instructions: Create a personal Contacts subfolder in which to store a contact list containing the donors listed in Table 1-4. In the Contact window, enter their donation in the Job Title field. Add the Job Title field to Address Cards view using the Show Fields on the View menu. When the list is complete, export the subfolder to a floppy disk and then delete it from the hard disk.

Table 1-4

NAME	ADDRESS	TELEPHONE	DONATION
Dennis Orell	2123 Broadway	555-1225	Money
Jonathan Arthur	3234 Gary Owen	555-2404	Telephone Support
Charles Lewis	4345 Park Lane	555-1217	Money
Ann Schulke	5456 Melton Rd.	555-0987	Catering
Stacy Hooton	6567 Mildred Ln.	555-4444	Transportation
Michael Tingler	7678 Marsh St.	555-1324	Advertising

3 Creating a Calendar and a Task List

Problem: You are the owner of a small hardware store. Your company has experienced rapid growth during the last several months, and with winter approaching, you need to change seasonal stock. As the owner, you also have administrative duties to perform, such as staff meetings, payroll, advertising, and sales campaigns. To make your schedule even more hectic, you also are a member of a reserve unit which meets for a full day at the end of each month. You need to create a schedule of appointments, as well as a task list, to help you keep track of your various jobs and responsibilities each day.

In the Lab

Instructions: Perform the following tasks.

1. Create a personal Calendar subfolder called Bay Hardware Company.
2. Enter the appointments in the calendar, using the information listed in Table 1-5.
3. Create a task list containing the following tasks:
   a. Call Bernita to confirm Lykin's Lab visit
   b. Bring After-action Report on last field maneuvers to drill
   c. Call to set meeting to look over new line of hand trucks
   d. Sign contract to renew accounting firm agreement
4. Change the Monthly Reserve drill appointment to an all day event.
5. Print the calendar for the week of Monday, October 26, 1998 to Sunday, November 1, 1998.
6. Export the personal subfolder to a floppy disk and then delete it from the hard disk.

Table 1-5

DESCRIPTION	*DATE*	*TIME*
Manager's meeting	**Oct. 26**	**8:00 am - 11:30 am**
Plan ads for Fall Closeout Sale	**Oct. 27**	**8:00 am - 11:30 am**
Payroll Verification	**Oct. 28**	**8:00 am - 3:00 pm**
Meet with Duffy on new store plans	**Oct. 29**	**7:00 am - 11:30 am**
Meet at Lykin's Lab about new appliances	**Oct. 30**	**7:30 am - 4:00 pm**
Tour stores	**Oct. 26, 27, 29, 30**	**1:00 pm - 4:00 pm**
Monthly Reserve drill	**Oct. 31**	**6:00 am - 4:00 pm**

Cases and Places

The difficulty of these case studies varies: ◗ are the least difficult, ◗◗ are more difficult; and ◗◗◗ are the most difficult.

1 ◗ You are the secretary for a university academic office. Part of your job is to let students know when advising hours are during registration periods. You are responsible for posting advising hours for the five professors in your department. Professor Ayers keeps hours on Monday, Wednesday, and Friday from 12:00 pm – 3:30 pm. Professor Bartlett is in from 8:00 am – 10:00 am on Monday, Tuesday, and Wednesday. Professor Cerillo is in on Tuesday and Thursday from 12:00 pm – 4:00 pm. Professor Diaz is in on Tuesday and Thursday from 8:00 am – 11:30 am. Professor Ellis is available every Monday and Tuesday from 5:00 pm – 8:00 pm. Registration starts in two weeks, and students have begun to request advising hours for the professors. Create a calendar showing when each professor has advising hours.

Cases and Places

2 ◗ You have secured a part-time position in the Computer Center. As part of your duties, you are in charge of printing a weekly schedule of lab hours which shows when the lab is reserved for classes and when it is free for student use. From Monday through Saturday, the lab opens at 8:00 am and closes at 10:00 pm. Sunday hours are 12:00 pm – 6:00 pm. Classes are held in the lab from 10:00 am – 12:00 pm every weekday, and from 2:00 pm – 4:00 pm Monday and Wednesday.

3 ◗◗ Create your own schedule for the next month. Include a task list. Include your classes, if you are a student, and any business or social obligations for the next few weeks. To save time, remember to schedule recurring appointments when possible.

4 ◗◗ You are the manager of Java Joe's, a small coffee shop. As manager, you are responsible for scheduling the employees' work hours. The coffee shop is open from 6:00 am – 6:00 pm on Monday through Saturday and from 7:00 am – 4:00 pm on Sundays. In addition to yourself and two full-time workers who work forty hours each week, you have seven part-time employees. Each employee has been guaranteed between twelve and twenty hours of work each week. Choose fictional names and create a schedule showing the hours for each employee. Use a seven-day work week.

5 ◗◗ Create a contact list containing your friends, family, classmates, co-workers, or business contacts. Be certain you include the name, home address, and telephone number of the contact at the very least. If you use business contacts, you also should include a business address and telephone number. If any of your contacts have e-mail addresses, include those. For friends, list their birthday and spouse's name, if any, using the Details tab.

6 ◗◗ You are a volunteer at the county library. Part of your job includes scheduling reservations for the library's large Community Conference Room, which is used by various local groups. Three groups meet before 12:00 pm each weekday: the Preschoolers' Craft Fair, Toddler Hour, and Children's Story Time. From 3:30 pm – 5:00 pm each weekday, the After School Club meets. The room's evening reservations include the Neighborhood Watch Committee, which meets twice each week from 7:00 pm – 9:00 pm, and the Good Reads book discussion group and the Friends of the Library, which meet once each week for two hours. Based on this information, create and print a monthly schedule showing the reservations for the conference room.

7 ◗◗◗ You have secured a job with an international paper company, and your first assignment is to make the main telephone and address file available to everyone in the firm. The file, which currently is kept in a three-ring binder, contains names, addresses, telephone numbers, e-mail addresses and Web sites of your company's many subsidiaries and vendors. You decide to create a contact list using Outlook so everyone can access the same information and automatically dial and send e-mail and access Web sites. Create a contact list that includes at least the names, addresses, and Web sites of seven paper companies. Make up some fictional company names and addresses or look up paper companies on the Web using one of the Internet search engines. Create a Contacts subfolder in which to store the contact list.

Office 97 Integration

PROJECT ONE

Introduction to Integrating Office 97 Applications

Office 97 Integration

Introduction to Integrating Office 97 Applications

Objectives:

You will have mastered the material in this project when you can:

- Create a 3-D cell reference in Excel
- Refresh data in a Web query
- Embed an Excel chart into a Word document
- Change the size of an embedded object
- Embed an Excel worksheet into a Word document
- Print an Access report without opening the document
- Send an open document as a file attachment in an e-mail message
- Create an e-mail message
- Attach a file as a file attachment in an e-mail message
- Print an e-mail message

The Cutting Edge

Personalized Business Practice

Moletas. To hear it, one may think of a new Italian dish being prepared as the feature of the day. To Richard Nella, owner of Nella Cutlery Inc., it represents a fourth-generation trade.

Moletas, or knife grinders, emanated from a region in Valle Rendena in the Brenta Dolomites in Italy. The village and its grinder trade date back prior to the year 1000.

Knives are considered by many to be the oldest tool and knife making the core technology that makes all other technologies possible. Knife makers and grinders today are a living repository for a knowledge and tradition that spans millennia. Moletas are not content simply to carry on that tradition, but seek to improve it, passing on a more vibrant and robust trade to succeeding generations.

One such improvement made at Nella Cutlery was to customize programs designed for the customer's operation.

Pinzolo
Venice
Florence
Italy

Trade Demands

These programs increase efficiency while reducing costs. How? By bringing the computer and the World Wide Web into the knife grinding trade.

Nella Cutlery provides complete service and sales for professional food preparation equipment, machines, and tools and manufactures many related products. To do so, the company relies on vendors that encompass the globe. Nella uses the word processing, database, worksheet, Web query, and desktop information management capabilities of Microsoft Office 97 to integrate its operation.

To start the price, quote, or bid or check on availability/ship date, the customer receives a personalized letter along with a price list. To check on the current price of a product and its exchange to U.S. dollars, Nella developed an Excel worksheet with 3-D references and a Web query worksheet. The worksheet describes the products, prices, and available quantities. The Web query worksheet can be refreshed anytime. The vendors update their prices and product availability daily. A Web site that converts international currency to U.S. dollars refreshes any price to the current U.S. value.

Once the pricing and availability are confirmed, a personalized letter, generated with Word, is sent to the customer. The letter contains the pertinent worksheet information and an embedded Excel chart on product information. A list of customers and their e-mail and telephone numbers are kept in an Access database.

The nature of the food preparation trade requires speedy response. Any customer with Internet and e-mail capabilities will have the price, availability, and/or quote letter sent via Outlook's e-mail program. The company also uses Outlook to produce daily task lists and delivery schedules for each driver. Using Office's integrated features, Nella Cutlery provides real-time, friendly, and personalized customer service.

It has been years since Rich Nella's ancestors pushed their moläs (pushcarts) with their mounted grindstones. Today, technology has replaced the moläs, but the service and dedication brought to the trade by his ancestors four generations ago continues.

Office 97
Integration

Introduction to Integrating Office 97 Applications

Case Perspective

Alex Hansen, permanent treasurer for High-Tech Stock Club, recently started using Microsoft Office 97 for many club-related functions, such as keeping track of club investments and writing monthly reports to club members. Each month, Alex summarizes the club's end-of-month financial status. Using Office Help, Alex discovered an easy way to update his Investment Analysis worksheet using a Web query.

Alex is preparing the end-of-month report for November. He already has prepared the Analysis Worksheet, 3-D Pie Chart, and Web Query worksheets in Microsoft Excel; the draft for his report in Microsoft Word; and updated the club membership report in Microsoft Access. Alex will run the Web query, insert the Analysis worksheet and 3-D Pie Chart into his monthly report and then e-mail the monthly report and the updated membership report to all club members using Microsoft Outlook.

Because Alex has never inserted an Excel chart or worksheet into a Word document or attached a file in an e-mail message, he has asked for your assistance.

Introduction

From your meeting with Alex Hansen, you have identified the documents necessary to complete the monthly reporting system.

Documents: The documents required for the monthly reporting system were created on Alex Hansen's personal computer and saved on a floppy disk. They are described below:

1. The stock investment information is maintained in the Excel High-Tech Stock Club workbook on the Investment Analysis worksheet.
2. The 3-D Pie chart graphically illustrating the stock club's portfolio breakdown by stock is contained in the Excel High-Tech Stock Club workbook on the 3-D Pie Chart sheet.
3. The Web Query used to update the current prices on the Investment Analysis worksheet is contained in the Excel High-Tech Stock Club workbook on the Web Query sheet. Refreshing the Web Query requires access to the World Wide Web (Figure 1-1d on page I 1.8).
4. The updated club members' e-mail and telephone report, High-Tech Stock Club E-mail and Telephone Directory (Figure 1-1f on page I 1.8) is used to address the monthly e-mail message and was created from data contained in the Access High-Tech Membership database in the Club Members table (Figure 1-1g on page I 1.8).

5. The final Monthly Report will be created by modifying the Monthly Report draft previously created by Alex.

Output: The monthly reporting system produces the following:

1. The Excel High-Tech Stock Club Latest Quotes workbook includes the Investment Analysis worksheet that contains 3-D references to the current stock prices contained on the Web Query sheet (Figure 1-1a on page I 1.8); the updated 3-D Pie chart illustrating the club's portfolio breakdown by stock company (Figure 1- 1b on page I 1.8); and the Web query worksheet containing the latest stock quotes (Figure 1-1c on page I .7).
2. The Word Monthly Report that shows club members the club's current investments at the close of business on the last day of the month. This report contains the embedded Investment Analysis worksheet and the embedded 3-D Pie Chart (Figure 1-1e on page I 1.9).
3. The printout of the Access report, E-mail & Telephone List (Figure 1-1f on page I 1.8), to address an e-mail message to club members.
4. An Outlook e-mail message containing two file attachments; the Monthly Report document created in Word and the Access High-Tech Membership database containing the updated E-mail & Telephone List report (Figure 1-1h on page I 1.9). Sending the e-mail message to club members requires access to the Internet (Figure 1-1d on page I 1.8).

More *About* Integrating Applications

The advantage of using an integrated set of applications, such as Microsoft Office 97, is the capability to share information between applications. The Object Linking and Embedding features of Office 97 simplifies the integration process. A chart created in Excel, for example, can be included in both a Word document and a PowerPoint presentation.

Integration Project — High-Tech Stock Club Monthly Reporting System

Many business-type applications, such as the one described in the Case Perspective, require worksheet data from another worksheet in a workbook. The three-dimensional capabilities of Excel make it easy for you to complete this type of application. Worksheet data for individual stock quotes can be maintained on a separate worksheet in the workbook. Using the tab at the bottom of the Excel window, you can move from worksheet to worksheet. In addition, Excel has the capability of referencing cells found on different worksheets, which allows you to summarize easily worksheet data. The process of summarizing worksheet data found on multiple worksheets is called **consolidation**.

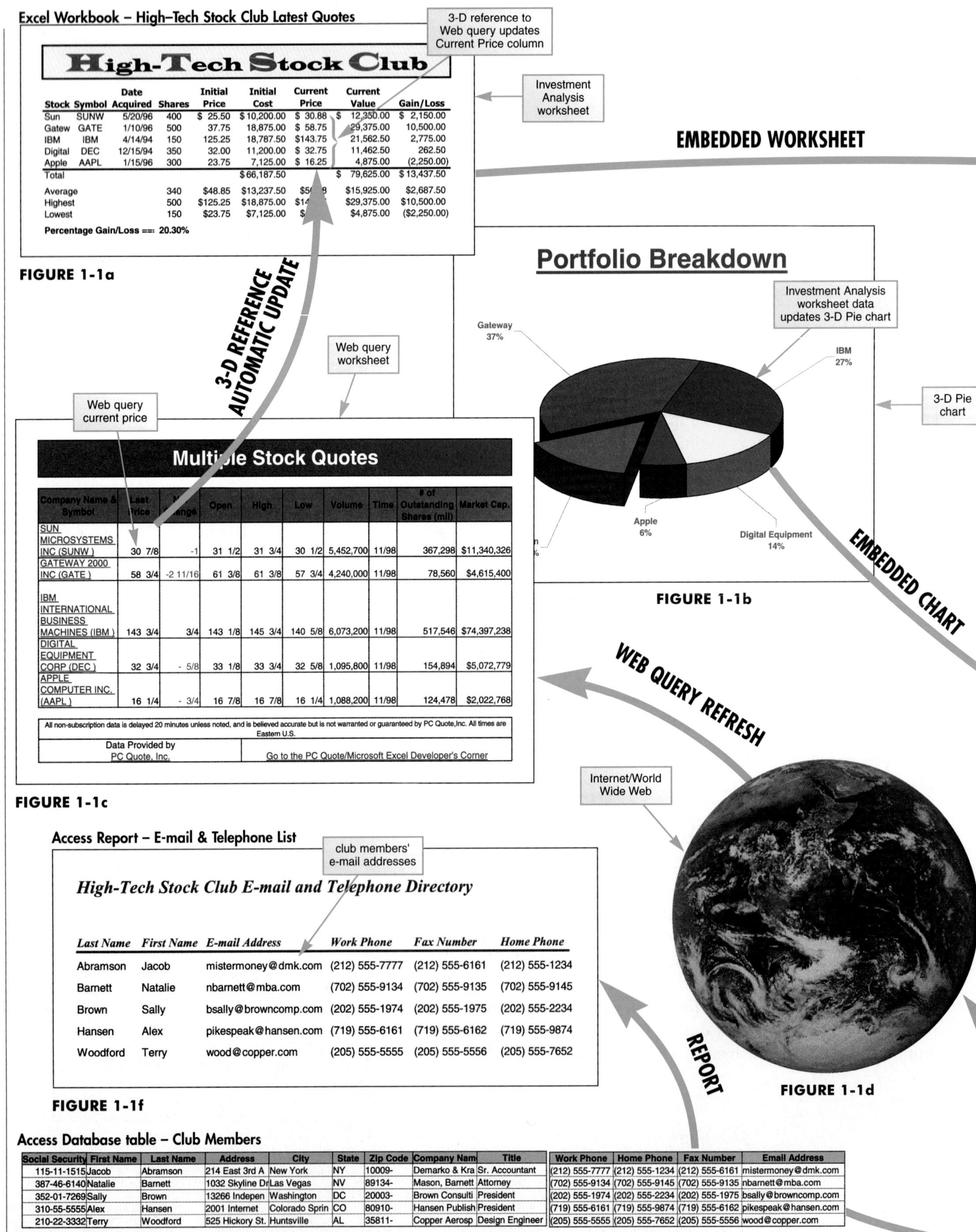

FIGURE 1-1a

FIGURE 1-1b

FIGURE 1-1c

FIGURE 1-1d

FIGURE 1-1f

FIGURE 1-1g

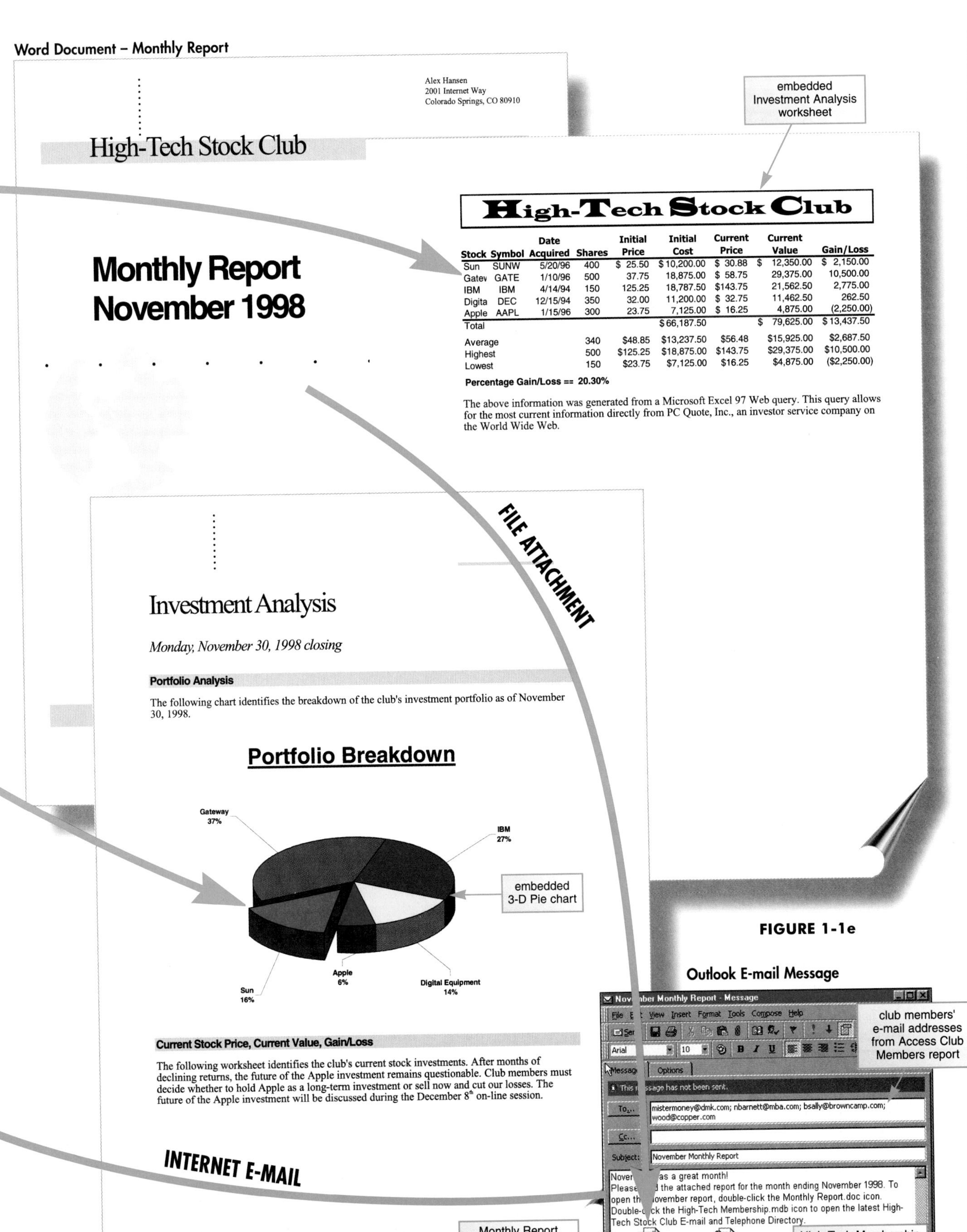

Alex Hansen
2001 Internet Way
Colorado Springs, CO 80910

High-Tech Stock Club

Monthly Report
November 1998

High-Tech Stock Club

Stock	Symbol	Date Acquired	Shares	Initial Price	Initial Cost	Current Price	Current Value	Gain/Loss
Sun	SUNW	5/20/96	400	$ 25.50	$ 10,200.00	$ 30.88	$ 12,350.00	$ 2,150.00
Gatev	GATE	1/10/96	500	37.75	18,875.00	$ 58.75	29,375.00	10,500.00
IBM	IBM	4/14/94	150	125.25	18,787.50	$143.75	21,562.50	2,775.00
Digita	DEC	12/15/94	350	32.00	11,200.00	$ 32.75	11,462.50	262.50
Apple	AAPL	1/15/96	300	23.75	7,125.00	$ 16.25	4,875.00	(2,250.00)
Total					$ 66,187.50		$ 79,625.00	$ 13,437.50
Average			340	$48.85	$13,237.50	$56.48	$15,925.00	$2,687.50
Highest			500	$125.25	$18,875.00	$143.75	$29,375.00	$10,500.00
Lowest			150	$23.75	$7,125.00	$16.25	$4,875.00	($2,250.00)

Percentage Gain/Loss == 20.30%

The above information was generated from a Microsoft Excel 97 Web query. This query allows for the most current information directly from PC Quote, Inc., an investor service company on the World Wide Web.

Investment Analysis

Monday, November 30, 1998 closing

Portfolio Analysis

The following chart identifies the breakdown of the club's investment portfolio as of November 30, 1998.

Portfolio Breakdown

Gateway 37%
IBM 27%
Digital Equipment 14%
Apple 6%
Sun 16%

Current Stock Price, Current Value, Gain/Loss

The following worksheet identifies the club's current stock investments. After months of declining returns, the future of the Apple investment remains questionable. Club members must decide whether to hold Apple as a long-term investment or sell now and cut our losses. The future of the Apple investment will be discussed during the December 8th on-line session.

FILE ATTACHMENT

FIGURE 1-1h

Reporting System Preparation Steps

The preparation steps summarize how to develop the monthly reporting system shown in Figures 1-1a through 1-1h on pages I 1.8 and I 1.9. The following tasks will be completed in this project.

1. Create a 3-D cell reference in an Excel worksheet.
2. Refresh data in a Web query.
3. Embed an Excel chart into a Word document.
4. Change the size of an embedded object.
5. Embed an Excel worksheet into a Word document.
6. Print an Access report without opening the document.
7. Quit Access.
8. Send an open document as a file attachment in an e-mail message.
9. Create an e-mail message using Outlook.
10. Attach a file to an e-mail message.
11. Print an e-mail message.
12. Quit Outlook.
13. Quit Word.
14. Quit Excel.

The following pages contain a detailed explanation of these tasks.

Opening an Excel Workbook

Before creating 3-D cell references in the High-Tech Stock Club Analysis worksheet, you first must open the workbook. Perform the following steps to complete this task.

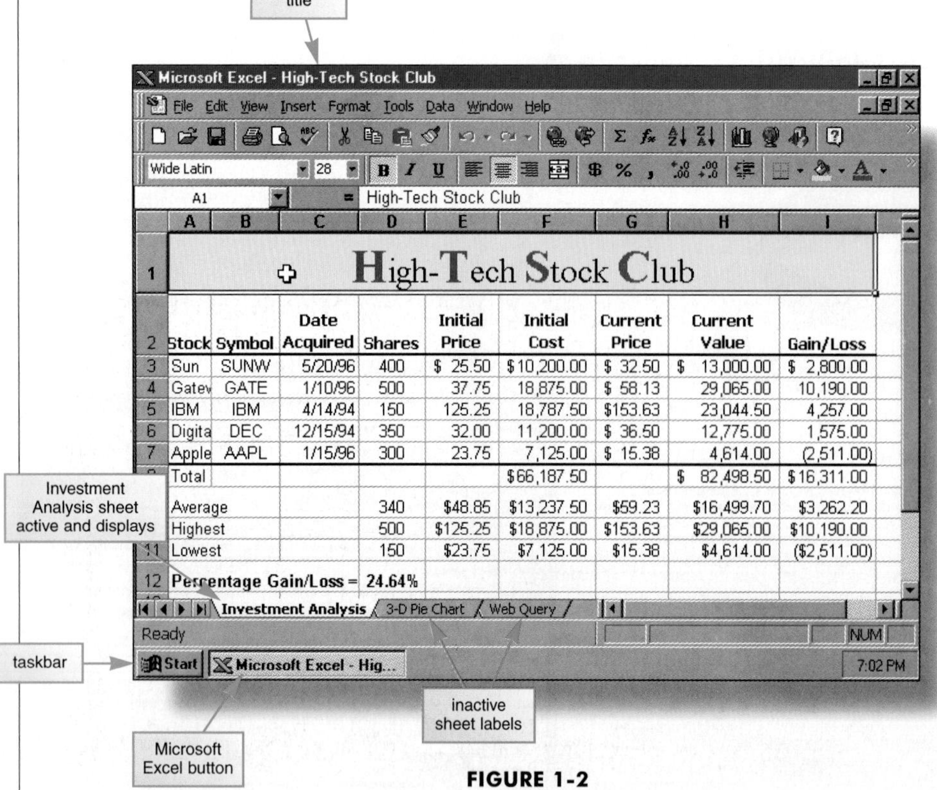

FIGURE 1-2

TO OPEN AN EXCEL WORKBOOK

Step 1: Click the Start button on the taskbar. Click Open Office Document.

Step 2: Click the Look in box arrow and then click 3½ Floppy (A:).

Step 3: Double-click High-Tech Stock Club.

*The High-Tech Stock Club workbook opens and the Investment Analysis worksheet displays (Figure 1-2). The bolded label on a worksheet tab identifies the **active worksheet**. The 3-D Pie Chart and Web Query worksheets are inactive, therefore, the sheet labels are not bolded. The Microsoft Excel – High-Tech Stock Club button displays on the taskbar.*

Creating a 3-D Reference

To reference cells on other sheets in a workbook, you use the sheet name, which also is called the **sheet reference**. For example, you refer to cell B5 on the Web Query sheet in the following format:

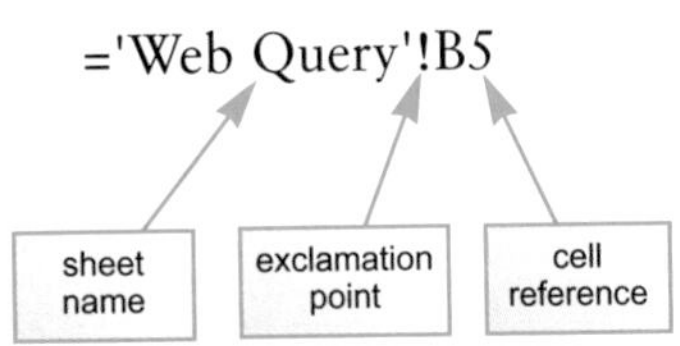

More About 3-D References

You can use a 3-D reference to refer to cells on other worksheets to create a formula. Use the following functions to create the formula: SUM, AVERAGE, AVERAGEA, COUNT, COUNTA, MAX, MAXA, MIN, MINA, PRODUCT, STDEV, STDEVA, STDEVP, STDEVPA, VAR, VARA, VARP, and VARPA.

One way to copy the value in cell B5 on the Web Query worksheet to cell G3 on the Investment Analysis worksheet would be to enter ='Web Query'!B5 into cell G3. **Single quotation marks** around the sheet name Web Query are required because the name includes spaces.

A more efficient way to copy the value of cell B5 is to select cell B5, type an equal sign (=), click the Web Query worksheet tab, click cell G3, and then click the Enter box in the formula bar. You can enter a sheet reference by typing it or by clicking the sheet tab to activate it. When you click the sheet tab, Excel automatically adds the name of the sheet followed by an exclamation point at the insertion point in the formula bar and activates the sheet. Next, click or drag through the cells you want to reference on the sheet. Referring to cells on two or more sheets in a workbook is called a **3-D reference.**

A sheet reference, such as 'Web Query'!, is always absolute. Unlike a relative cell reference, however, the sheet reference will remain constant when you copy formulas. In this project, you create a 3-D reference in cell G3 on the Investment Analysis worksheet and then copy that formula to the cells for the remaining stock prices.

Perform the following steps to create a 3-D reference.

To Create a 3-D Reference

1 **Click cell G3 to select it. Type = in cell G3.**

Cell G3 is the active cell and displays an equal sign (Figure 1-3). An equal sign also displays in the formula bar.

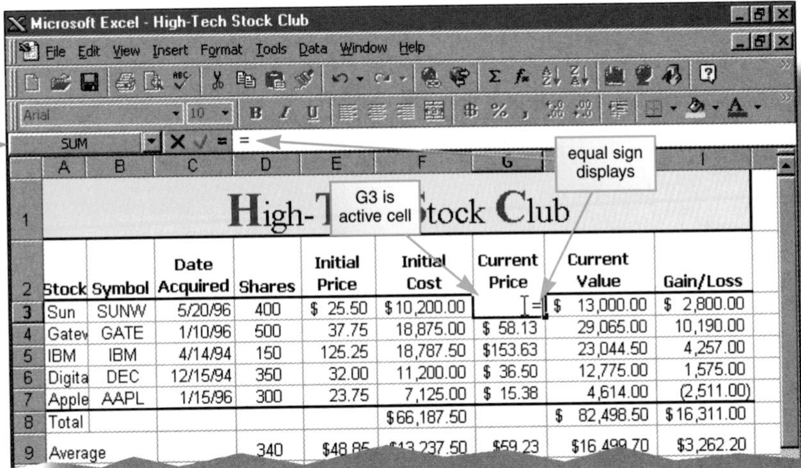

FIGURE 1-3

2 **Click the Web Query tab at the bottom of the worksheet window.**

The Web Query worksheet is the active worksheet as indicated by the bold sheet label (Figure 1-4). The sheet name, Web Query, displays in single quotation marks in the formula bar. The exclamation point displays after the sheet name. The Investment Analysis worksheet is selected but not currently active, as indicated by the sheet label not being bolded on a white tab.

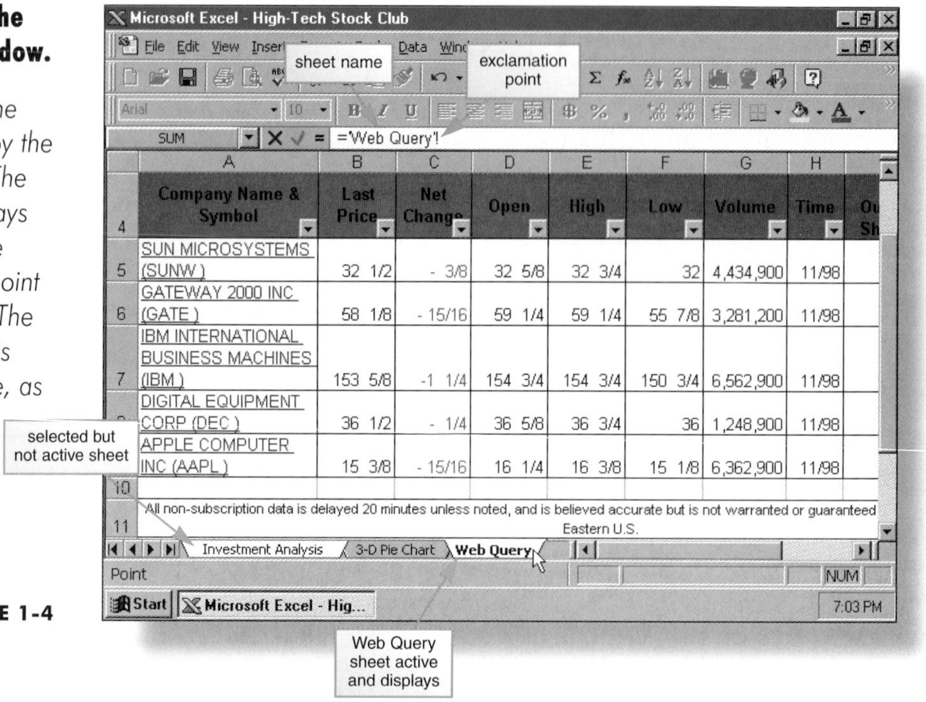

sheet name
exclamation point
selected but not active sheet
Web Query sheet active and displays

FIGURE 1-4

3 **Click cell B5.**

Cell B5 is selected (Figure 1-5). The reference to cell B5 is added to the formula in the formula bar.

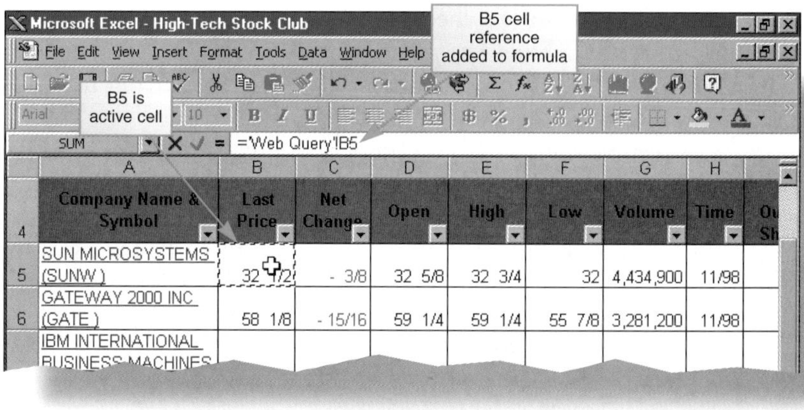

B5 cell reference added to formula
B5 is active cell

FIGURE 1-5

4 **Point to the Enter box in the formula bar (Figure 1-6).**

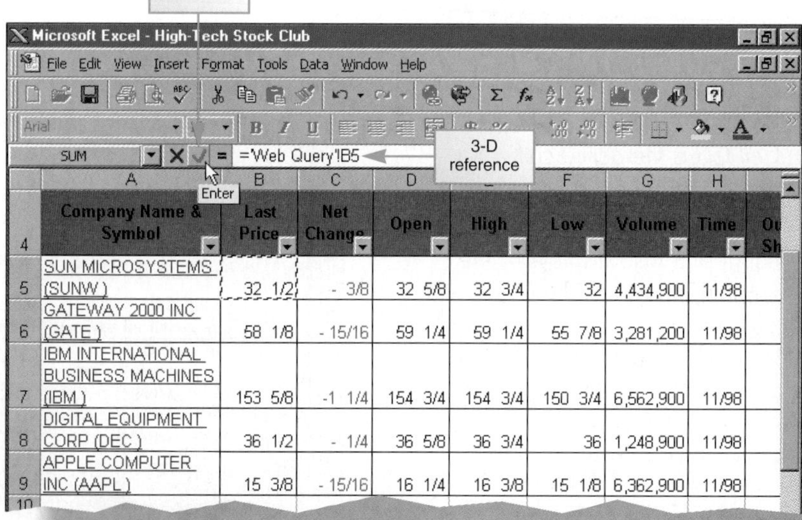

FIGURE 1-6

5 **Click the Enter box.**

The Investment Analysis worksheet displays and the 3-D reference replaces the value in cell G3 (Figure 1-7). The formula bar displays the 3-D reference. The current stock price displays as a fraction.

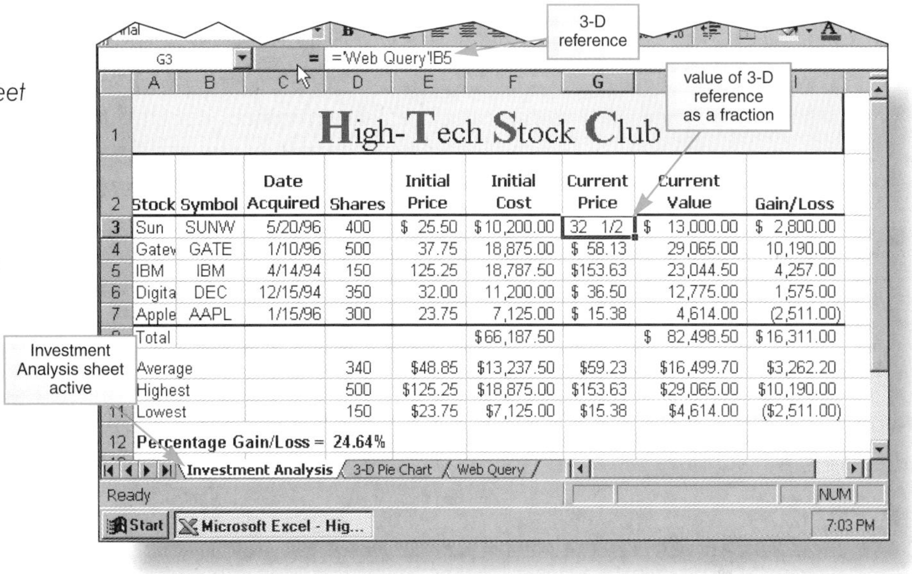

FIGURE 1-7

OtherWays

1. Display worksheet receiving 3-D reference, press arrow keys to select cell, type =, press CTRL+PAGE DOWN to display referenced worksheet, press arrow keys to select referenced cell, press ENTER

The above example referenced one cell on one sheet. If you are spanning multiple sheets, click the first sheet, select the cell or range of cells, and then press and hold down the SHIFT key and click the last sheet. Excel will include the cell or range on the two sheets and all the sheets between. It also will add a colon between the first sheet and the last sheet referenced.

Applying Currency Style to a Cell

Entering the 3-D reference in cell G3 changed the format to the fraction format previously applied to cell B5 on the Web Query sheet. To convert the fractional value to a monetary value, you must change the format to Currency Style as explained in the following step.

Steps To Apply Currency Style to a Cell

1 **With cell G3 selected, click the Currency Style button on the Formatting toolbar.**

Excel applies the Currency Style format to cell G3 (Figure 1-8).

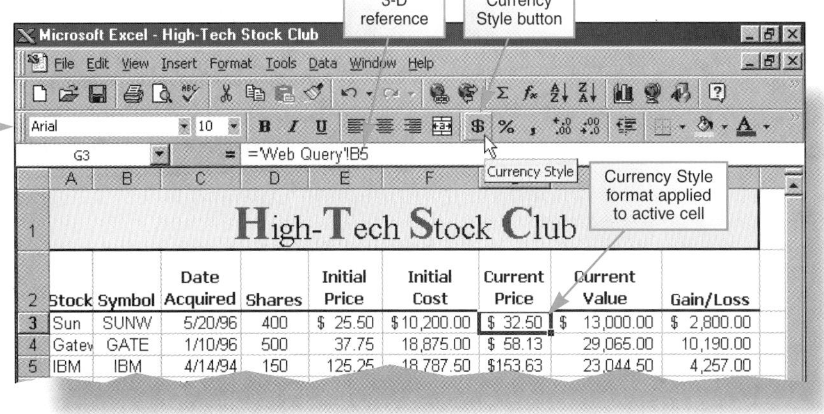

FIGURE 1-8

OtherWays

1. Right-click cell, click Format Cells on shortcut menu, click Number tab, click Currency in Category box, click OK button
2. Select cell, on Format menu click Cells, click Number tab, click Currency in Category box, click OK button

Copying a 3-D Reference to Other Cells

To copy a 3-D reference to another cell or cells, drag the fill handle of the cell containing the 3-D reference. Recall that the **fill handle** is the small black square at the lower-right corner of the active cell or selection. Dragging the fill handle to copy a 3-D reference copies the *absolute* address of the 3-D sheet reference and the *relative* address of the cell reference. For example, the 3-D reference of cell G3 is Web Query!B5. Dragging the fill handle to cell G6 copies the 3-D reference as 'Web Query'!B6, keeping the absolute sheet reference, Web Query, but changing the relative cell reference to B6 to reflect the position of the cell below the original cell on the Web Query, B5.

Perform the following step to copy the 3-D reference to the other cells in the Current Price column for the remaining four stocks.

Steps To Copy a 3-D Reference

1 With cell G3 active, drag the fill handle down through cell G7.

Excel copies the formula in cell G3 to cells G4, G5, G6, and G7 (Figure 1-9). Excel retains the format of cell G3, Currency Style.

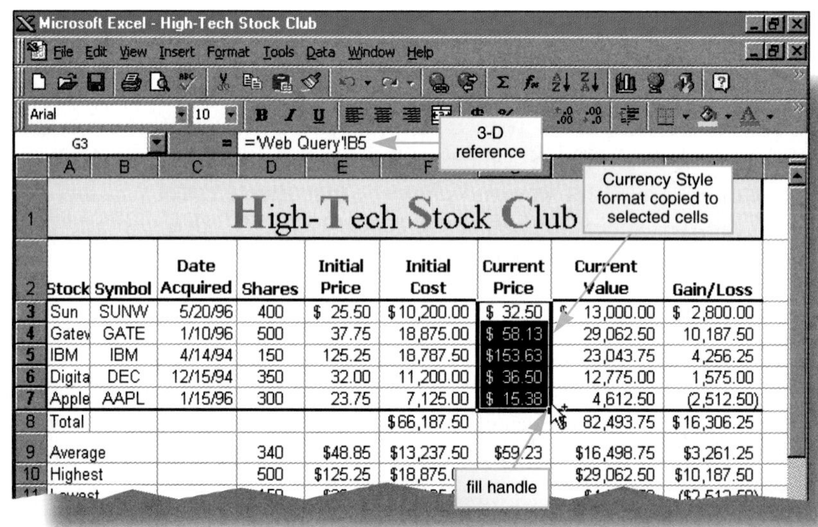

FIGURE 1-9

OtherWays

1. Right-click cell, click Copy, right-click cells receiving copy, click Paste
2. Press CTRL+C, press and hold SHIFT+arrow keys to select cells receiving copy, press CTRL+V

Saving a Workbook with a New File Name

Because you modified an existing workbook, you should save the changes with a new file name. This creates a new file without destroying the original. Perform the following steps to save the High-Tech Stock Club workbook as High-Tech Stock Club Latest Quotes.

TO SAVE A WORKBOOK WITH A NEW FILE NAME

Step 1: Click File on the menu bar and then click Save As.
Step 2: When the Save As dialog box displays type `High-Tech Stock Club Latest Quotes` in the File name text box.
Step 3: Click the Save button.

Excel saves the workbook with the file name, High-Tech Stock Club Latest Quotes. The file name displays in the workbook title bar.

All required changes to the High-Tech Stock Club Latest Quotes are complete. The next step in preparing the end-of-month report is to update the Web Query worksheet, which then updates the Investment Analysis worksheet and the 3-D Pie Chart.

Refreshing External Data from a Web Source Using a Web Query

The 3-D reference is a link to the prices on the Web Query worksheet. Refreshing the data in the Web Query retrieves the current stock prices and displays them on the Web Query worksheet. Because of the 3-D references entered in the Investment Analysis worksheet, the Investment Analysis worksheet is updated automatically with the stock prices updated on the Web Query worksheet. Additionally, because the 3-D Pie Chart graphically displays the breakdown of the current investment portfolio, the Pie chart also is updated when you refresh the Web Query data.

When you run the Web Query, Excel uses the built-in Internet features of Microsoft Office 97 to connect automatically to the World Wide Web and update the Web Query worksheet. Once the Web query is created, you can run the update anytime you want current stock information. The format of the Web query is controlled by PC Quote, Inc., the company that supplies the stock information. Stock information supplied to nonsubscribers of PC Quote, Inc. is delayed 20 minutes. For more current information, click the hyperlink at the bottom of the Web Query worksheet to contact PC Quote, Inc. about subscription information.

Perform the following steps to run the Web query and update the stock prices on the Web Query worksheet and the Investment Analysis worksheet.

More *About* Web Queries

A Web query functions like an engine driving the process of connecting to the Internet and automatically updating a worksheet. Excel includes sample Web queries that you can modify by changing the HTML code. You can find these sample Web queries in the Queries folder of Microsoft Office.

Steps To Refresh Data in a Web Query

1 **Click the Web Query tab to display the Web Query worksheet.**

The Web Query worksheet and External Data toolbar display (Figure 1-10).

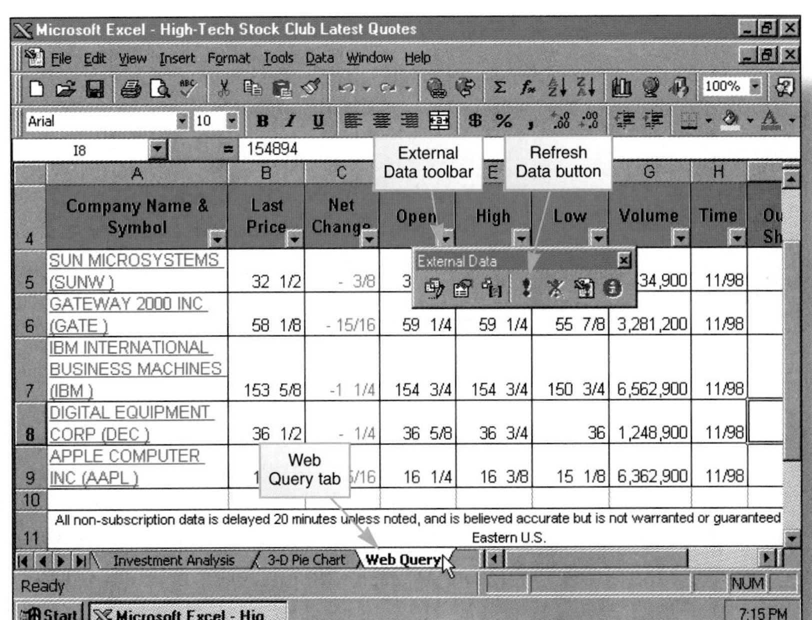

FIGURE 1-10

2 Click the Refresh Data button on the External Data toolbar.

If you are using a modem, Excel will display a dialog box that connects you to the Internet via your Internet service provider. If you connect directly to the Internet through a network, the dialog box does not display. Once connected to the World Wide Web, a message displays informing you that Excel is getting external data. After a short period, Excel displays the updated worksheet (Figure 1-11). Your screen may display differently because each time you refresh data in a Web query, the values are updated according to current stock prices.

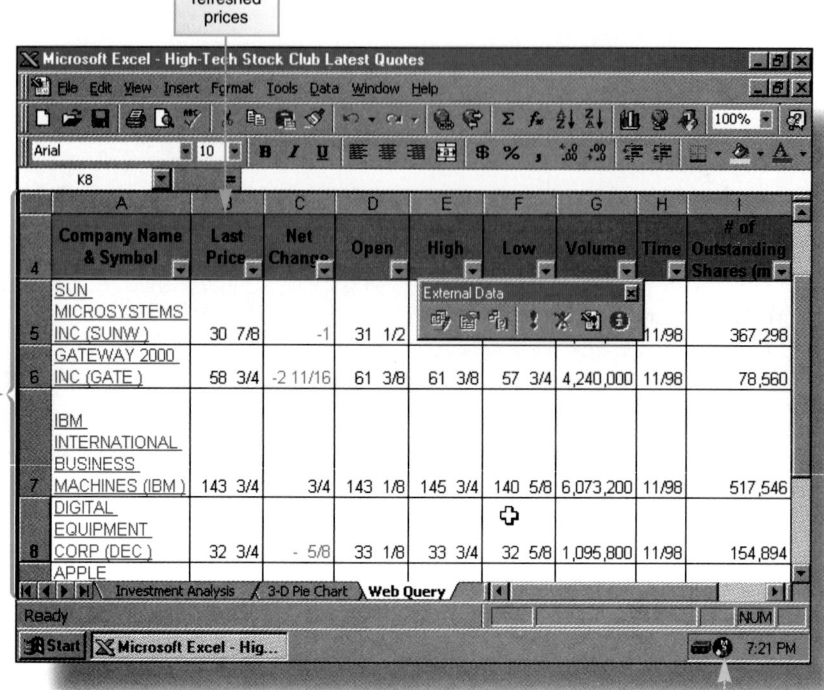

FIGURE 1-11

3 Right-click the browser icon next to the current time on the taskbar. When the shortcut menu displays, click Sign Out. When the dialog box prompting you to disconnect from your browser program displays, click the Yes button.

The browser disconnects from the World Wide Web.

OtherWays

1. Display Web Query worksheet, press ALT+D, press R

More About Linking and Embedding

Link rather than embed when you have an object that is to be placed in several destination documents. Also, link when you want to update the destination file when the source document changes. Embed when the object is not likely to change.

Once the worksheet displays, you can refresh the data as often as you want. You refresh the data for all the stocks by clicking the Refresh Data button on the External Data toolbar. Because Use this value/reference for future references is the default setting Excel will continue to use the same stock symbols each time it refreshes. You can change the symbols by clicking the **Query Parameters button** in the External Data toolbar. You also can refresh one stock at a time by clicking the cell with a stock symbol in column A.

Embedding an Excel Chart and a Worksheet into a Word Document

Before you can embed an object into a document, you first must open the document. Perform the following steps to complete this task.

TO OPEN A WORD DOCUMENT

Step 1: Click the Start button on the taskbar. Click Open Office Document.
Step 2: Click the Look in box arrow and then click 3½ Floppy (A:).
Step 3: Double-click Monthly Report Draft.

Microsoft Word opens and the Monthly Report Draft document cover page displays in Page Layout view (Figure 1-12). The Microsoft Word – Monthly Report Draft button displays on the taskbar.

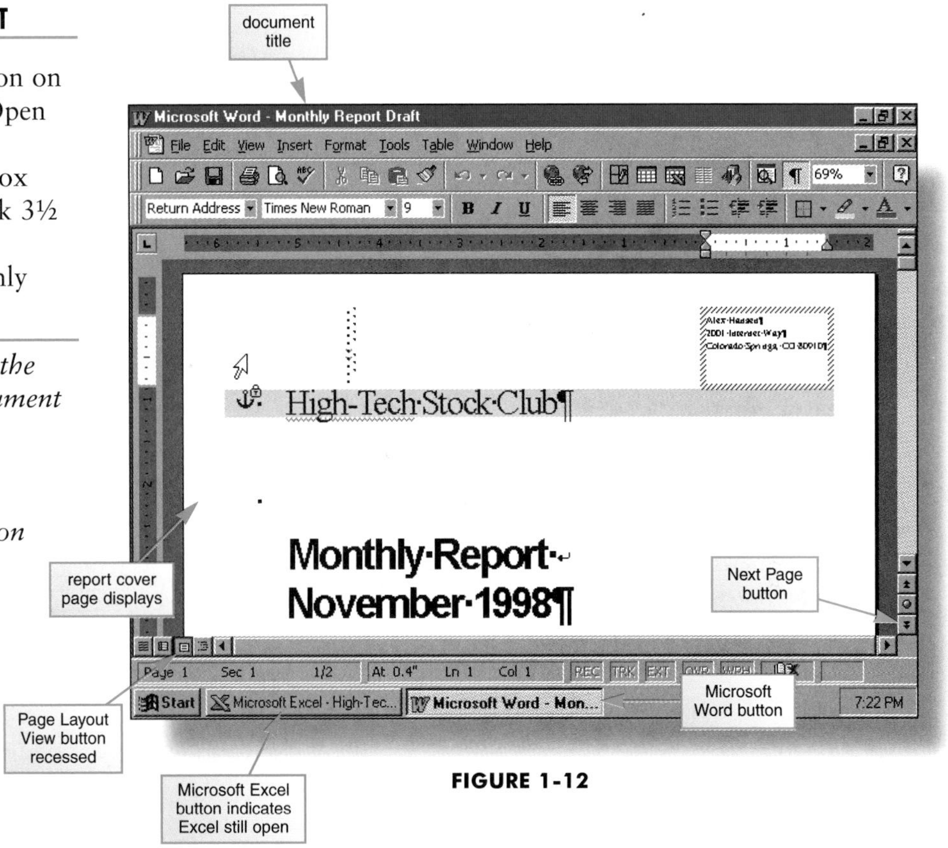

document title
report cover page displays
Next Page button
Page Layout View button recessed
Microsoft Word button
Microsoft Excel button indicates Excel still open

FIGURE 1-12

Embedding an Excel Chart into a Word Document

This project uses the **Object Linking and Embedding (OLE)** feature of Microsoft Office to insert an Excel chart and worksheet into a Word document. OLE allows you to incorporate parts of a document or entire documents from one application into another. You will complete the monthly report in this project, by opening the Monthly Report Draft document from the Data Disk that accompanies this book and then embedding the 3-D Pie Chart and the Investment Analysis worksheet from the High-Tech Stock Club workbook.

The Pie chart and worksheet in Excel are called **source objects** and the Monthly Report Draft document is the **destination file**. Once an object is embedded, it becomes part of the destination file. This project illustrates using the **Paste Special command** on the Edit menu to embed the Excel objects. The Paste Special command inserts an object into Word, but still recognizes the **source program**, the program in which the object was created. When you double-click an embedded object, such as the Investment Analysis worksheet, the source program opens and allows you to make changes. In this example, Excel is the source program.

The next two sections explain how to embed an Excel chart and worksheet into a Word document. The first section explains embedding a chart into a Word document. Perform the steps on the next page to embed the Excel 3-D Pie Chart into the Word Monthly Report Draft.

Double-click an embedded object to edit it. When you double-click an embedded object, the source program starts and opens the source object. You then can edit the object. Save the object before quitting the source program.

To Embed an Excel Chart into a Word Document

1 Click the Next Page button on the vertical scroll bar, and then click the blank line following the paragraph ending November 30, 1998.

Page 2 displays (Figure 1-13). The insertion point displays at the beginning of the blank line.

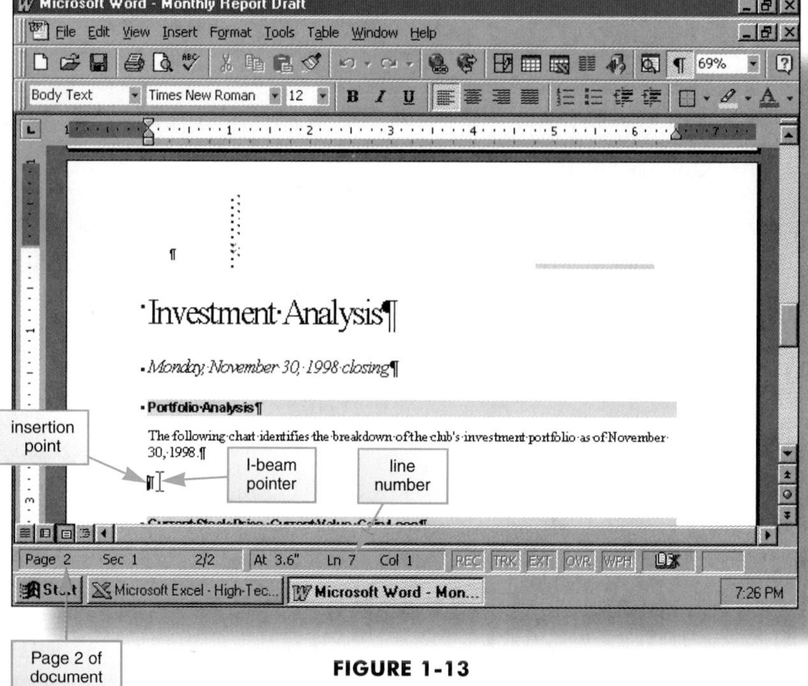

FIGURE 1-13

2 Click the Microsoft Excel – High-Tech Stock Club Latest Quotes button on the taskbar. Click the 3-D Pie Chart tab.

The 3-D Pie Chart is active and displays (Figure 1-14).

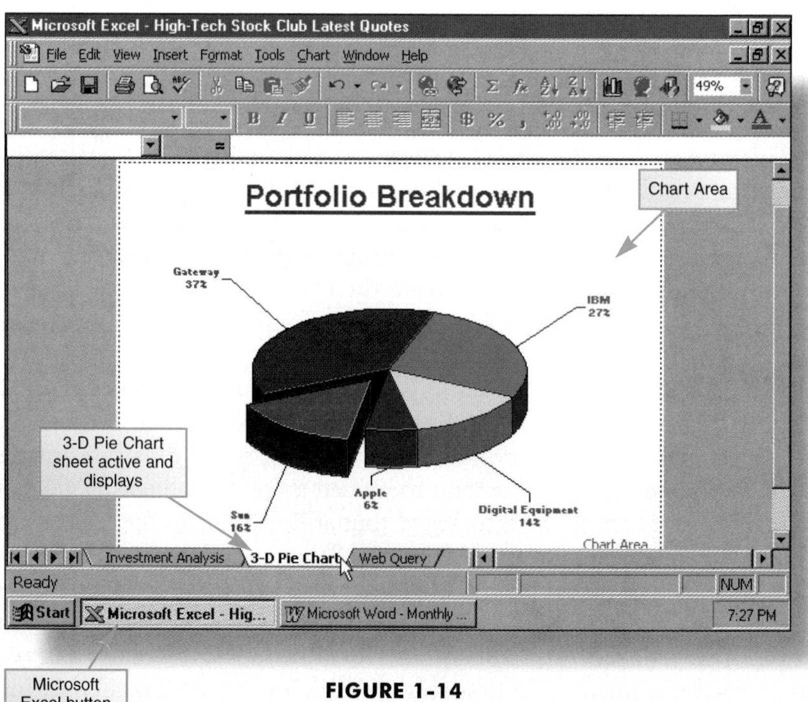

FIGURE 1-14

Project Summary

This project introduced you to integrating Microsoft Office applications. You started this project by creating a three-dimensional reference in an existing Excel worksheet, which changes the cell value each time a Web query is updated. You learned how to get external data using built-in Web features by connecting to the World Wide Web. You embedded and sized an Excel Pie chart into a Word document. You also embedded an Excel worksheet into a Word document. Then, you printed an Access database report that you later used to address an Outlook e-mail message. Using Word, you activated Outlook to send the open Word file as a file attachment in an e-mail message. Then you learned how to insert a file as a file attachment in an e-mail message. Finally, you learned how to print an e-mail message in Outlook.

What You Should Know

Having completed this project, you now should be able to perform the following tasks:

- Apply Currency Style to a Cell (*I 1.13*)
- Change the Size of an Embedded Object (*I 1.21*)
- Copy a 3-D Reference (*I 1.14*)
- Create a 3-D Reference (*I 1.11*)
- Embed an Excel Chart into a Word Document (*I 1.18*)
- Embed an Excel Worksheet into a Word Document (*I 1.23*)
- Insert an Access File into an E-mail Message (*I 1.30*)
- Open a Word Document (*I 1.17*)
- Open an Access Database (*I 1.25*)
- Open an Excel Workbook (*I 1.10*)
- Print an Access Report (*I 1.26*)
- Print an Outlook Message (*I 1.31*)
- Quit Access (*I 1.26*)
- Quit Excel (*I 1.32*)
- Quit Outlook (*I 1.32*)
- Quit Word (*I 1.32*)
- Refresh Data in a Web Query (*I 1.15*)
- Save a Word Document with a New File Name (*I 1.25*)
- Save a Workbook with a New File Name (*I 1.14*)
- Send an E-mail Message from Word (*I 1.27*)

Test Your Knowledge

1 True/False

Instructions: Circle T if the statement is true or F if the statement is false.

T F 1. In Excel, the process of summarizing worksheet data on multiple worksheets is called consolidation.

T F 2. In Excel, a sheet reference that refers to cells on two or more sheets in a workbook is called a 2-D reference.

T F 3. In Excel, a sheet reference, such as 'Web Query'! is always relative.

T F 4. To save a file with a new file name, click the Save button on the Standard toolbar.

T F 5. In Excel, to change stock symbols in an existing Web Source Web Query, click the Query Parameters button.

T F 6. In Access, you can preview a report before you print it.

T F 7. Office has integrated mailing features in Word, which enable you to send a document while still viewing it in the Word window.

T F 8. It is possible to attach a file to an e-mail message while in Outlook.

T F 9. When you click the Send button on the Send Mail toolbar in Outlook, the e-mail message moves to the Outbox, where it resides until sent over the Web.

T F 10. To quit an Office application, click its Close button on the taskbar.

2 Multiple Choice

Instructions: Circle the correct response.

1. If an Excel sheet name contains spaces, then ____________ must surround the sheet reference.
   a. parentheses (( ))
   b. brackets ([ ])
   c. single quotation marks (')
   d. double quotation marks (")
2. To create an Excel sheet reference that spans multiple sheets, click the first sheet, select the cell or range of cells, press and hold the ____________ key, and then click the last sheet.
   a. CTRL
   b. SHIFT
   c. ALT
   d. TAB
3. If an Excel sheet reference spans multiple sheets, a(n) ____________ displays between the first sheet and the last sheet referenced.
   a. colon (:)
   b. semicolon (;)
   c. exclamation point (!)
   d. single quotation mark (')

Test Your Knowledge

4. Given the following cell reference, 'Web Query'!C10, Web Query is ___________ and C10 is ___________.
   a. absolute, absolute
   b. absolute, relative
   c. relative, absolute
   d. relative, relative
5. OLE stands for ___________.
   a. Office Linking Environment
   b. Office Linking and Embedding
   c. Object Linking Environment
   d. Object Linking and Embedding
6. Once an object is embedded, it becomes part of the ___________.
   a. source object
   b. destination file
   c. source program
   d. both a and c
7. In the Format Object dialog box, the height-to-width ratio is called ___________ ratio.
   a. size and rotate
   b. original size
   c. aspect
   d. scale
8. If the Word window is open and you want to send the current file as an attachment to an e-mail message, you can use Word's ___________ feature.
   a. Send To Mail Recipient
   b. Attach Document
   c. Include File
   d. E-mail Attachment
9. In the e-mail address, bsally@browncamp.com, the right side of the address (browncamp.com) is called the ___________.
   a. destination
   b. source
   c. domain
   d. mailbox
10. When you insert a file into an e-mail message, ___________ displays in the message.
    a. the file's content
    b. an icon representing the file
    c. a command button representing the file
    d. both a and b

Test Your Knowledge

3 Understanding 3-D References

Instructions: Answer the questions 1 through 3 about this sheet reference: ='Latest Stock Quotes'!D10. Then, answer question 4.

1. Why do single quotation marks surround the sheet name? ______________________________
2. Is the sheet name absolute or relative? ______________________________
3. Is the cell reference absolute or relative? ______________________________
4. Write the sheet reference that would sum the contents of cells B2 through B5 on Sheet1 and Sheet2. ______________________________

4 Understanding the Paste Special Dialog Box

Instructions: Answer the following questions about Figure 1-38.

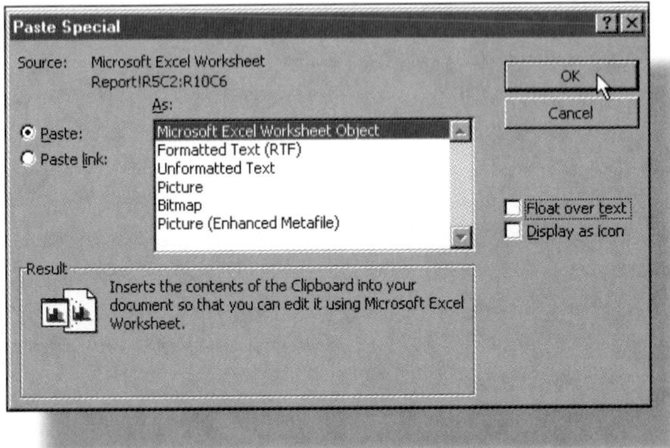

FIGURE 1-38

1. The contents of which Excel sheet are being pasted into the Word document? ______________________________
2. Which rows and columns are being pasted? ______________________________
3. Why is the Float over text check box cleared? ______________________________
4. Explain the difference between Paste and Paste link. ______________________________

Use Help

1 Reviewing Project Activities

Instructions: Perform the following tasks using a computer.

1. Start Excel. If the Office Assistant is on your screen, click it to display its balloon. If the Office Assistant is not on your screen, click the Office Assistant button on the Standard toolbar. Type `consolidate data` in the What would you like to do? text box. Click the Search button. Click the Consolidate data link. Read the information. Use the shortcut menu or Options button to print the information.
2. Click the Help Topics button to display the Help Topics: Microsoft Excel dialog box. Click the Index tab. Type `web` in the top text box labeled 1 and then double-click the queries topic. Double-click the Get data from a Web source topic. Read and print the information. Close any open Help window(s). Close the Office Assistant. Close Excel.
3. Start Word. Click Help on the menu bar and then click Contents and Index. Click the Find tab. Type `paste special` and then double-click the Create an embedded object from an existing Microsoft Excel worksheet or chart topic. Read and print the information. Close any open Help window(s). Close Word.
4. Start Outlook. Click Help on the menu bar and then click Contents and Index. Click the Contents tab. Double-click the Organizing and Viewing Items in Outlook book. Scroll to and then double-click the Inserting Items and Files into Outlook Items book. Double-click the Ways to share information in Outlook topic. Read and print the information. Close any open Help window(s). Close Outlook.

Use Help

2 Expanding on the Basics

Instructions: Use Word, Excel, and Outlook Help to better understand the topics listed below. Answer the questions on your own paper or hand in the printed Help topic to your instructor.

1. In this project, you embedded an Excel object into a Word document. Use Word Help to answer the following questions about linking and embedding objects into Word documents.
   a. How do you insert the contents of an Access table or query into an existing Word document?
   b. How do you link a single PowerPoint slide to a Word document?
   c. How do you embed a single PowerPoint slide to a Word document?
   d. Differentiate between linking and embedding objects.
2. In this project, you embedded an Excel chart into a Word document. Use Excel Help to answer these questions about sharing data in Excel.
   a. How do you embed an Excel chart into a PowerPoint presentation?
   b. How do you copy a Word table onto an Excel worksheet?
   c. When you double-click an embedded or linked object in Excel, a "cannot edit" error message displays. What would cause this to occur?
3. In this project, you inserted objects into an Outlook message. Use Outlook Help to answer the following questions about Outlook.
   a. How do you sign messages automatically with AutoSignature?
   b. How do you turn Word on as your e-mail editor?
   c. As you are typing your message, some of the text displays blue and underlined. What would cause this to occur?

Apply Your Knowledge

1 Embedding a PowerPoint Slide into a Word Document

Instructions: As shown in Figures 1-39 and 1-40 on the next page, you are to create a PowerPoint slide containing the new lab room rules for your school. Next, you create a memo in Word using the Professional Memo template and embed the PowerPoint slide into the Word document so all faculty are aware of the new lab room rules. You may need to refer to your Use Help 2 responses for information on how to embed a PowerPoint slide into a Word document. Perform the following tasks.

1. Start PowerPoint. Click Blank presentation in the PowerPoint dialog box and then click the OK button. Click the Clip Art & Text AutoLayout in the New Slide dialog box and then click the OK button. Click the title placeholder, type `ATTENTION!` and then press the ENTER key. Type `Lab Room Rules` and then double-click the clip art placeholder. When the Microsoft Clip Gallery displays, click the Communication category and then double-click the Information Communication clip art to insert it into the slide. Click the text object. Type `No food` and then press the ENTER key. Type `No drinks` and then press the ENTER key. Type `No smoking` and then press the ENTER key. Type `No cellular phones` and then press the ENTER key. Type `No headsets` and then press the ENTER key. Type `No radios` and then press the SHIFT+ENTER keys twice. Type `THANK YOU!` as the last line of text. Save the presentation with the name Lab Room Rules Slide. Print the slide. Leave PowerPoint open.
2. Start Word. Click File on the menu bar and then click New. Click the Memos tab in the New dialog box, and then double-click Memo Wizard. Use the following information when the Memo Wizard requests it: (a) Style: Professional; (b) Title: Interoffice Memo; (c) Date: 8/24/98; (d) From: Ms. Williams; (e) Subject: Lab Room Rules; (f) To: All Faculty; (g) Cc: File (h) no distribution list; (i) enter your initials as typist's initials; and (j) clear all check boxes in Header/Footer panel.
3. When the completed memo displays in the document window, click the placeholder text, Click here and type your memo text, and then type `The sign below has been posted in all lab rooms.` and then press the ENTER key. If necessary, close the Office Assistant.
4. Switch to PowerPoint by clicking its button on the taskbar. Click the Slide Sorter View button at the bottom of the PowerPoint window. With Slide 1 selected, click the Copy button on the Standard toolbar.
5. Switch to Word by clicking its button on the taskbar. Be sure the insertion point is positioned on the paragraph mark below the text in the memo. Click Edit on the menu bar and then click Paste Special. When the Paste Special dialog box displays, click Paste, click Microsoft PowerPoint Slide Object, and click Float over text to clear the check box. Click the OK button to embed the slide into the Word document.
6. Save the Word document with the name Lab Room Rules Memo. Print the memo. Close Word. Close PowerPoint.

(continued)

Apply Your Knowledge

Embedding a PowerPoint Slide into a Word Document *(continued)*

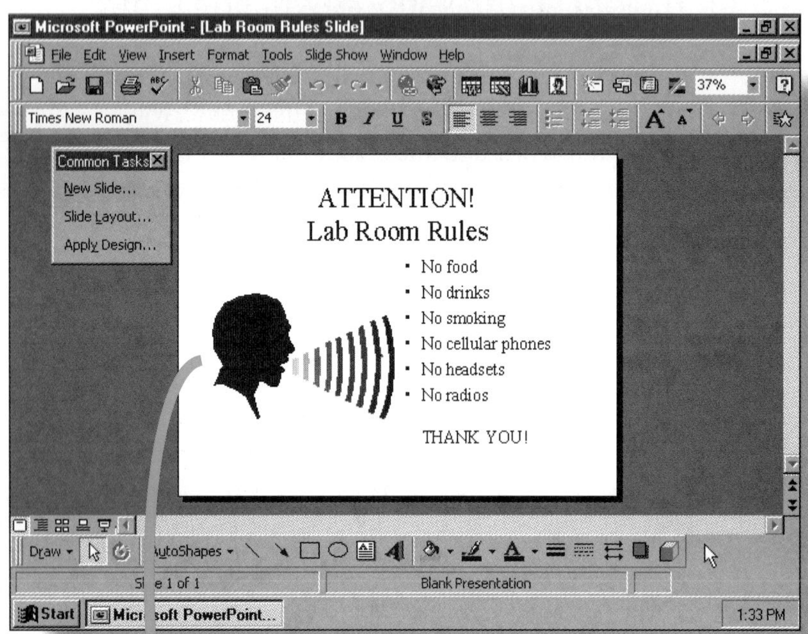

FIGURE 1-39

Interoffice Memo

Date: 8/24/98

To: All Faculty

Cc: File

From: Ms. Williams

Re: Lab Room Rules

The sign below has been posted in all lab rooms.

ATTENTION!
Lab Room Rules

- No food
- No drinks
- No smoking
- No cellular phones
- No headsets
- No radios

THANK YOU!

FIGURE 1-40

In the Lab

1 Creating a Word Document with an Embedded Excel Worksheet and Chart

Problem: As president of United Cable Company, you have created a preliminary five-year plan for your company as a worksheet in Excel (Figure 1-41 on the next page). You also charted the total revenues, total costs, and profit after tax columns (Figure 1-42 on the next page). Then, you created a memo in Word informing your vice presidents of the next staff meeting date and time. In the memo, you embedded the worksheet and chart (Figure 1-43 on the next page) so your vice presidents could review them before the staff meeting.

Instructions:

1. Start Excel. Rename the Sheet1 tab to Report and the Sheet2 tab to Bar Chart. Create the worksheet shown in Figure 1-41 on the Report sheet. Enter the numbers in the Total Revenue and Total Costs rows. Compute the remaining rows as follows: Profit Before Tax = Total Revenue – Total Costs; Tax = .49 * Profit Before Tax; and Profit After Tax = Profit Before Tax – Tax. Use the following formatting guidelines: (a) 10-point Arial font unless otherwise specified; (b) title: 26-point Bookman Old Style white, bold font with violet background color; (c) subtitle: 14-point bold; (d) column headings: 12-point white, bold font with violet background color; and (e) row titles: bold with gray 25% background color. Save the workbook using United Cable Five Year Plan as the file name. Print the worksheet.
2. Use the Chart Wizard to create the Bar chart shown in Figure 1-42 on the Bar Chart sheet. Chart the five years of data for the Total Revenue row, Total Costs row, and the Profit After Tax row. Use the following when requested: (a) Chart type: Bar; (b) Chart sub-type: Clustered bar with a 3-D visual effect; (c) chart title: United Cable Company; (d) Category (X) axis: Year; and (e) Value (Z) axis: (in thousands). Save the workbook again. Print the Bar chart. Leave Excel open.
3. Start Word. Create a memo using the Memo Wizard. Use the following information when the Memo Wizard requests it: (a) Style: Professional; (b) Title: Interoffice Memo; (c) Date: 10/6/98; (d) From: Carl R. Brosner; (e) Subject: Staff Meeting; (f) To: Vice Presidents; (g) Cc: File; (h) no distribution list; (i) clear all check boxes in the Closing Fields panel; and (j) clear all check boxes in Header/Footer panel.
4. When the completed memo displays in the document window, change the placeholder text to the verbiage shown in Figure 1-43 and then press the ENTER key.
5. Embed the Excel worksheet into the Word memo. That is, switch to Excel, select the worksheet, copy the worksheet to the Clipboard, switch to Word, and use the Paste Special dialog box in Word to embed the Excel Worksheet Object. Be sure the Float over text check box is cleared in the Paste Special dialog box.
6. Embed the Excel chart into the Word memo. Click the Center button on the Formatting toolbar to center the chart.
7. Spell check the memo. Save the memo using United Cable Memo as the file name. Print the memo.

(continued)

Creating a Word Document with an Embedded Excel Worksheet and Chart *(continued)*

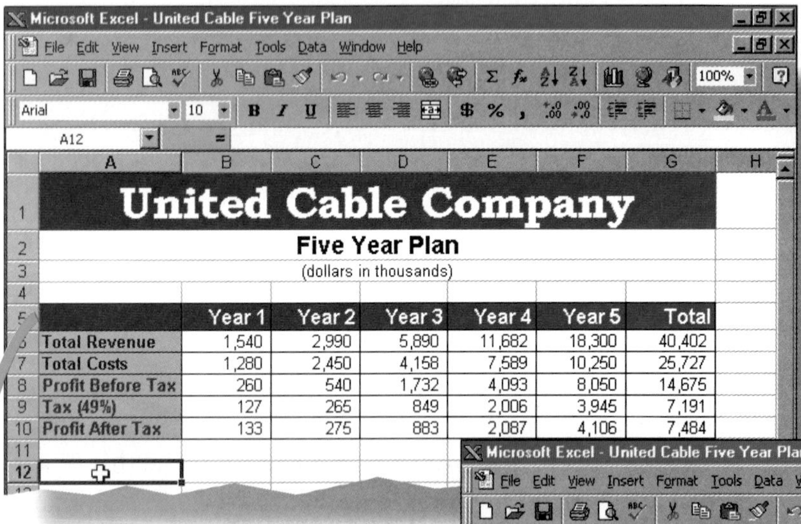

Microsoft Excel - United Cable Five Year Plan

United Cable Company

Five Year Plan

(dollars in thousands)

	Year 1	Year 2	Year 3	Year 4	Year 5	Total
Total Revenue	1,540	2,990	5,890	11,682	18,300	40,402
Total Costs	1,280	2,450	4,158	7,589	10,250	25,727
Profit Before Tax	260	540	1,732	4,093	8,050	14,675
Tax (49%)	127	265	849	2,006	3,945	7,191
Profit After Tax	133	275	883	2,087	4,106	7,484

FIGURE 1-41

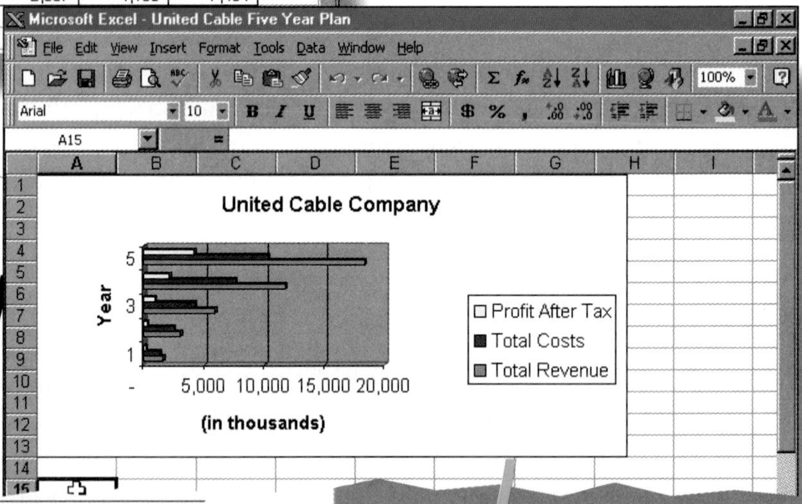

Microsoft Excel - United Cable Five Year Plan

United Cable Company

Year: 5, 3, 1

-, 5,000, 10,000, 15,000, 20,000

(in thousands)

Profit After Tax
Total Costs
Total Revenue

FIGURE 1-42

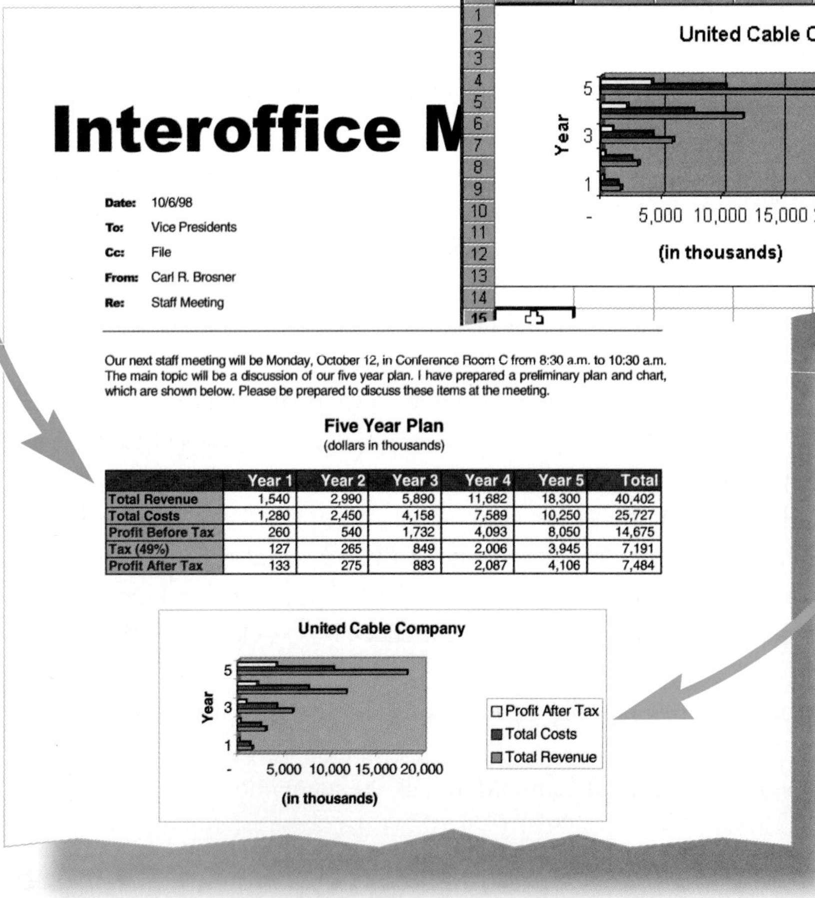

Interoffice Memo

Date: 10/6/98

To: Vice Presidents

Cc: File

From: Carl R. Brosner

Re: Staff Meeting

Our next staff meeting will be Monday, October 12, in Conference Room C from 8:30 a.m. to 10:30 a.m. The main topic will be a discussion of our five year plan. I have prepared a preliminary plan and chart, which are shown below. Please be prepared to discuss these items at the meeting.

Five Year Plan

(dollars in thousands)

	Year 1	Year 2	Year 3	Year 4	Year 5	Total
Total Revenue	1,540	2,990	5,890	11,682	18,300	40,402
Total Costs	1,280	2,450	4,158	7,589	10,250	25,727
Profit Before Tax	260	540	1,732	4,093	8,050	14,675
Tax (49%)	127	265	849	2,006	3,945	7,191
Profit After Tax	133	275	883	2,087	4,106	7,484

United Cable Company

Year: 5, 3, 1

-, 5,000, 10,000, 15,000, 20,000

(in thousands)

Profit After Tax
Total Costs
Total Revenue

FIGURE 1-43

2 Attaching an Excel Workbook with a Web Query to an Outlook Message

Problem: Jon Williams, president of Cool Wheels Auto Club, has heard that Microsoft Excel can connect to the World Wide Web, download real-time stock data into a worksheet, and then refresh the data as often as needed (see Figure 1-1c on page I 1.8). Because you are a member of the Cool Wheels Auto Club and have had experience with Excel, he has asked you to assist him in developing a stock workbook that contains a worksheet of stock data (Figure 1-44 on the next page), a chart of the data (Figure 1-45 on the next page), and the Web query. Then, he would like to send the entire workbook to all Cool Wheels Auto Club members via e-mail (Figure 1-46 on the next page).

Instructions:

1. Start Excel. Rename the Sheet1 tab to Report, the Sheet2 tab to Column Chart, and the Sheet 3 tab to Web Query. On the Web Query sheet, run the Web query to obtain multiple stock quotes using these symbols: C, F, GM, HMC, and TOYOY. For detailed instructions on how to create this type of Web query, refer to pages E 2.61 through E 2.64 in Project 2 of Excel.
2. Create the worksheet shown in Figure 1-44 on the Report sheet. Do not enter the numbers in the Open, High, Low, and Close columns. Instead, use 3-D referencing to point to the Web Query page. For example, the formula in cell C6 is ='Web Query'!D9 because the Open price for Chrysler is listed in cell D9 on the Web Query page. Then, use the following formatting guidelines: (a) 10-point Arial font unless otherwise specified; (b) title: 24-point Braggadocio indigo, bold font with light turquoise background color; (c) subtitle: 12-point light yellow bold font with blue-gray background color; (d) column headings: white font with blue-gray background color; (e) Chrysler, General Motors, and Toyota Motor Corporation rows: light turquoise background color; and (f) Ford Motor Company and Honda Motor Company rows: light yellow background color. Save the workbook using Cool Wheels Stock Analysis as the file name. Print the worksheet.
3. Use the Chart Wizard to create the Column chart shown in Figure 1-45 on the Column Chart sheet. Chart the Symbol and Close columns. Use the following when requested: (a) Chart type: Column; (b) Chart sub-type: Clustered column with a 3-D visual effect; and (c) Chart title: Auto Manufacturer Stock Analysis. Save the workbook again. Print the Column chart. Close Excel.
4. Start Outlook. Click the New Mail Message button to open the Message window. Enter the message shown in Figure 1-46. Use the Insert File button to insert the Cool Wheels Stock Analysis Excel file into the message as shown in Figure 1-46. Save the message. Print the message.

(continued)

Attaching an Excel Workbook with a Web Query to an Outlook Message *(continued)*

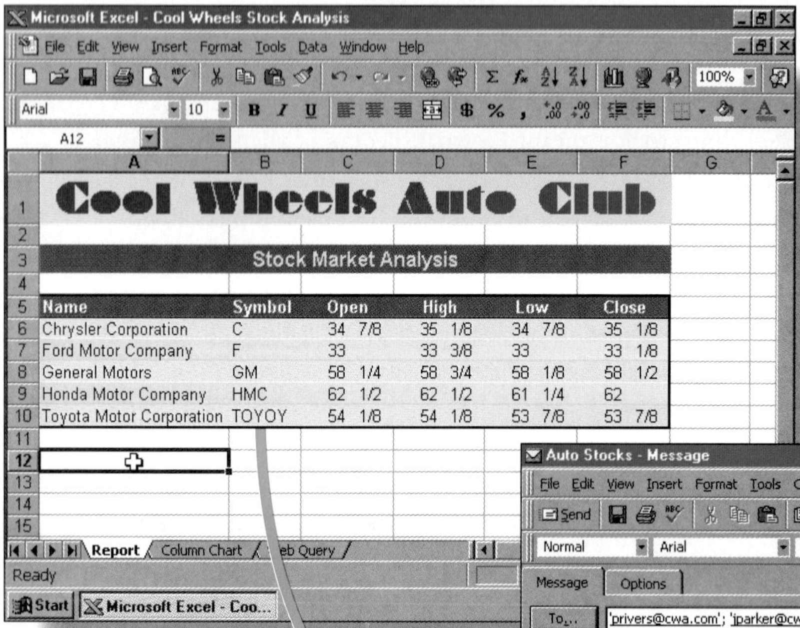

Microsoft Excel - Cool Wheels Stock Analysis

Cool Wheels Auto Club

Stock Market Analysis

Name	Symbol	Open	High	Low	Close
Chrysler Corporation	C	34 7/8	35 1/8	34 7/8	35 1/8
Ford Motor Company	F	33	33 3/8	33	33 1/8
General Motors	GM	58 1/4	58 3/4	58 1/8	58 1/2
Honda Motor Company	HMC	62 1/2	62 1/2	61 1/4	62
Toyota Motor Corporation	TOYOY	54 1/8	54 1/8	53 7/8	53 7/8

Report / Column Chart / Web Query

FIGURE 1-44

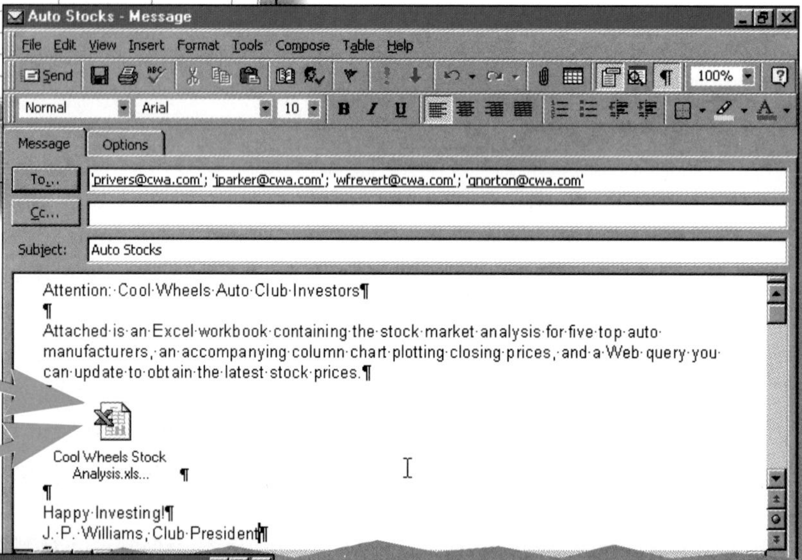

Auto Stocks - Message

To... 'privers@cwa.com'; 'jparker@cwa.com'; 'wfrevert@cwa.com'; 'gnorton@cwa.com'

Cc...

Subject: Auto Stocks

Attention: Cool Wheels Auto Club Investors

Attached is an Excel workbook containing the stock market analysis for five top auto manufacturers, an accompanying column chart plotting closing prices, and a Web query you can update to obtain the latest stock prices.

Cool Wheels Stock Analysis.xls...

Happy Investing!
J. P. Williams, Club President

FIGURE 1-46

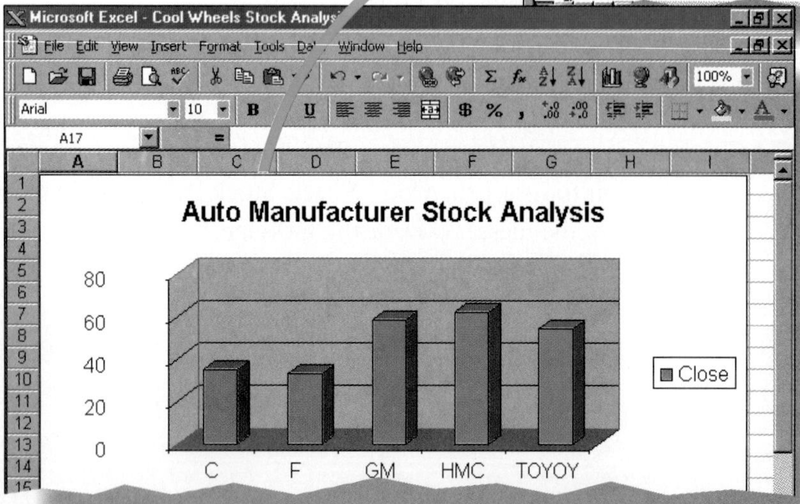

Microsoft Excel - Cool Wheels Stock Analysis

Auto Manufacturer Stock Analysis

80
60
40
20
0
C F GM HMC TOYOY
Close

FIGURE 1-45

3 Embedding an Excel Worksheet to an Outlook Message

Problem: As marketing specialist for Secure Securities, you are responsible for e-mail distributions of up-to-date securities' prices to all your investors. You plan to create a Web query of U.S. Treasury Bills and U.S. Treasury Notes and Bonds (Figure 1-47 on the next page). Once you create a worksheet of this stock data (Figure 1-48 on the next page), you plan to include the worksheet in an e-mail message to all investors (Figure 1-49 on the next page).

Instructions:

1. Start Excel. Rename the Sheet1 tab to Report and the Sheet2 tab to Web Query. On the Web Query sheet, run the Web query to obtain CNN Interest Rates. If the CNNfn_Interest_Rates Web query is not in your Run Web Query dialog box, then double-click Get More Web Queries to display the Get More Web Queries worksheet; scroll down and click the link CNN Interest Rates under the Consumer heading; save the query on disk and then run the Web query (Figure 1-47).
2. Create the worksheet shown in Figure 1-48 on the Report sheet of the workbook. Do not enter the numbers in the Price rows. Instead, use 3-D referencing to point to the Web Query page. For example, the formula in cell C7 is ='Web Query'!B9 because the price of 3-month Treasury bills is listed in cell B9 on the Web Query page. Then, use the following formatting guidelines: (a) 12-point Arial bold font unless otherwise specified; (b) title: 26-point Algerian light green, bold font with green background color; (c) subtitle and price rows: green bold font with light green background color; and (d) column headings: light green bold italic font with green background color. Save the workbook using Secure Securities as the file name. Print the worksheet. Leave Excel open.
3. Start Outlook. Click the New Mail Message button to open the Message window. Enter the message shown in Figure 1-49. To embed the Excel worksheet data into the Outlook message, switch to Excel, select the worksheet, copy the worksheet to the Clipboard, switch to Outlook, and use the Paste Special command in Word to embed the Excel Worksheet Object. Be sure the Float over text check box is cleared in the Paste Special dialog box. Save the message. Print the message. Close Outlook. Close Excel.

(continued)

Embedding an Excel Worksheet to an Outlook Message *(continued)*

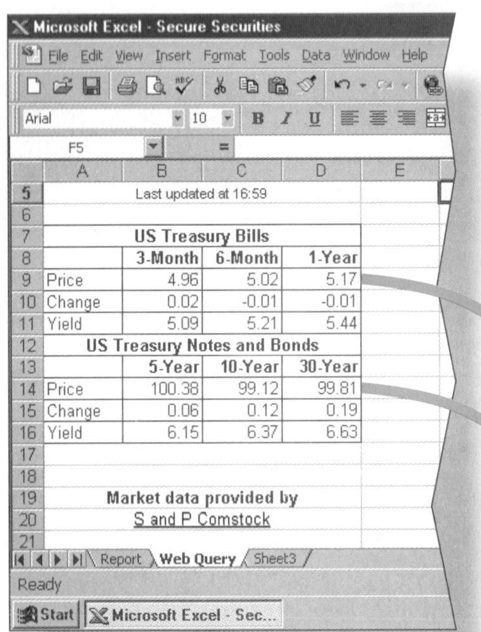

FIGURE 1-47

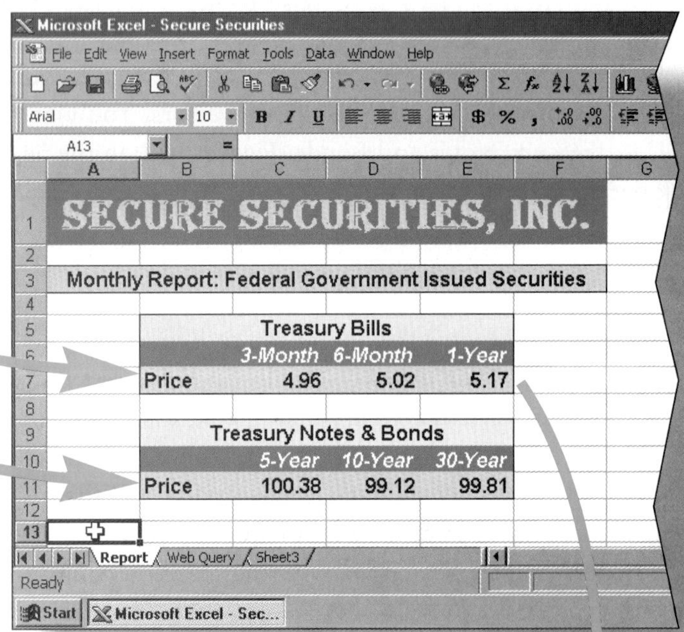

FIGURE 1-48

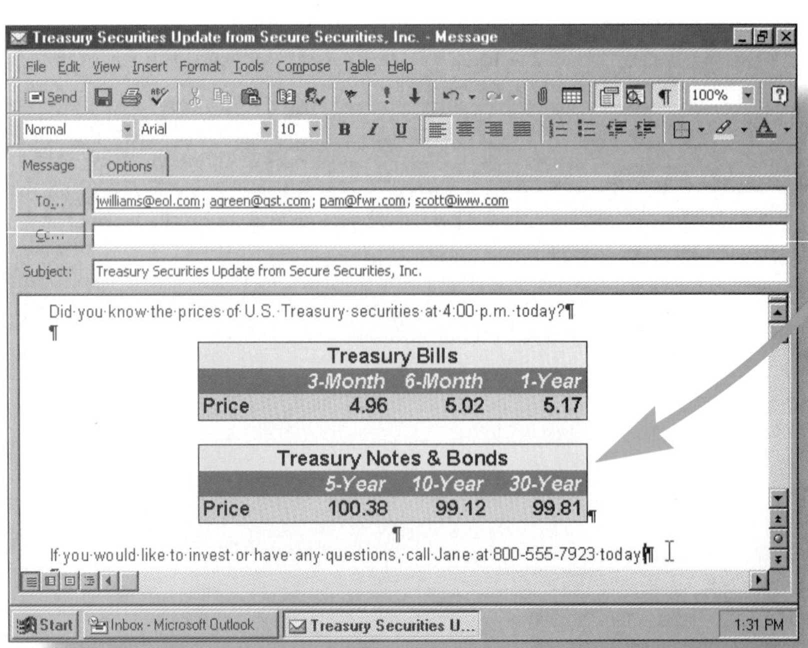

FIGURE 1-49

Cases and Places

The difficulty of these case studies varies: ◗ are the least difficult; ◗◗ are more difficult; and ◗◗◗ are the most difficult.

1 ◗ You are membership director of the Fitness Counts health club, which has three membership plans. The Gold plan is good for a single membership, has an initial fee of $100 and a monthly charge of $25, and provides the member with unlimited access to club facilities. The Silver plan also is good for a single membership, has an initial fee of $35 and a monthly charge of $10, and restricts the member's admittance to non-prime-time hours. The Family plan is good for an entire family membership, has an initial fee of $250 and a monthly charge of $50, and provides each family member with unlimited access to club facilities. Create a worksheet in Excel that summarizes each of these plans. Compose a memo to the general public that embeds the Excel worksheet; the goal of the memo is to gain new members.

2 ◗ For your own information, you want to compare the costs of the various Internet service providers (ISPs). Take a poll of 10 students in your class that have e-mail addresses and determine the following: the name of their Internet service provider, the monthly fee they pay their ISP, how often they send e-mail (daily, weekly, monthly, never), how often they access the Internet (daily, weekly, monthly, never), and their rating of the ISP's service (excellent, good, average, poor). Create an Excel worksheet summarizing your data and a chart of the monthly fees paid to ISPs. Then, write a memo in Word to your fellow students identifying the top two ISPs according to cost; embed the Excel chart in the memo.

3 ◗◗ As investment broker for Securities Plus, you want to provide your clients with the latest value of their portfolios. So, each month you send every client his or her current portfolio summary via e-mail. Obtain the ticker symbols of five companies in an area of interest to you. Do not use any companies presented in this project. Then, run a Web query to obtain multiple stock quotes. Create a worksheet similar to the one in this project. Use 3-D references for the prices. Create a Pie chart of the portfolio breakdown. Compose an e-mail message to your client informing him or her of the current value of the portfolio; attach the Excel workbook file to the e-mail message.

Cases and Places

4 ▸▸ As chairperson of the Promotions committee for your Finance Club, you are responsible for distributing valuable information to the club members. You notice that Excel has a Web query called DBC Best Credit Cards, which lists the issuing institution, the telephone number, the interest rate, the fee, and the number of interest-free days for 10 to 15 companies. You decide this is extremely useful information. After running the Web query, create a worksheet that nicely organizes this information using 3-D references to the Web Query sheet. Then, create a memo to your club members that includes the Excel worksheet as an embedded object. If you do not have the DBC Best Credit Cards Web query, you will need to download it from the Get More Web Queries worksheet (see In the Lab 3 Instruction 1 for more detailed information on downloading Web queries).

5 ▸▸▸ As a member of the Student Government Association for your school, you are delivering a five-minute presentation about the current student body at your school. Obtain statistics and interesting facts on your school's student body, e.g., percentage of male/female; number of freshman, sophomore, junior, senior students; ratio of part-time vs. full-time students; age ranges; and so on. Create an Excel worksheet summarizing your findings. Create an Excel chart for one of the interesting statistics. Create a PowerPoint slide show containing at least seven slides, one of which is the title slide and one is a closing slide. Embed the Excel chart into one of the PowerPoint slides.

6 ▸▸▸ As a loan officer at Rivers Finance Company, you notice that Excel has a Web query called CNN Mortgage Calculator under the Consumer heading. You decide to investigate this Web query. If you do not have the CNN Mortgage Calculator Web query, you will need to download it from the Get More Web Queries worksheet (see In the Lab 3 Instruction 1 for more detailed information on downloading Web queries). Run the Web query and summarize the results in an Excel worksheet. Then, write an e-mail message to your colleagues that explains how to use the Web query. Include your workbook as an attached file so your colleagues can open it and run the Web query.

7 ▸▸▸ In your English Composition class, you have been assigned the task of preparing a 1,200-word research paper that compares and contrasts complete computer systems for home use on the market today. You are to discuss prices, equipment included, software included, and so on for each system studied. For your references, you obtain information from four computer stores: one via the telephone, one in the newspaper or magazine, one in person that you visit, and one on the Internet. Your paper is to summarize data on the systems in an Excel worksheet. Include the Excel worksheet and at least one Excel chart of the data in your research paper. Use the documentation style assigned by your instructor.

OFFICE 2000 SPECIAL FEATURE

Office 2000 Preview

Approximately every two years, Microsoft Corporation introduces a new version of Office. The newest version is Office 2000, which was released in June 1999.

The majority of tools and techniques you learned for use with Office 97 work in Office 2000. Some differences in the menu bar and the toolbars, however, change the user interface. Microsoft also has added new application programs to Office 2000, and has increased your ability to create and manage interactive World Wide Web pages. The purpose of this section is to introduce you to some of the new features of Office 2000 so you can transfer your knowledge of Office 97 to your use of Office 2000.

Office 2000 User Interface

The user interface changes for Office 2000 include adaptive menus, smart toolbars, and the Office 2000 Help system. These changes will enable you to work more quickly, easily, and efficiently than in Office 97. Each of these changes is discussed in the following sections.

Adaptive Menus

Office 2000 applications use **adaptive menus**, where only basic commands display on the **short menu** when you click the menu name on the menu bar (Figure 1).

To see the remaining commands on the menu, point to or click the **double arrow bar**. If selected on your computer, you also can wait approximately five seconds and the **full menu** will display automatically (Figure 2).

Click a command on the menu the same as Office 97. If you click a command that does not display on the short menu, that command is promoted to the menu so it displays the next time you display the menu. For example, if you click the Change Case command on the Word 2000 Format menu shown in Figure 2, the next time you display the Format menu, the Change Case command will show on the menu (Figure 3).

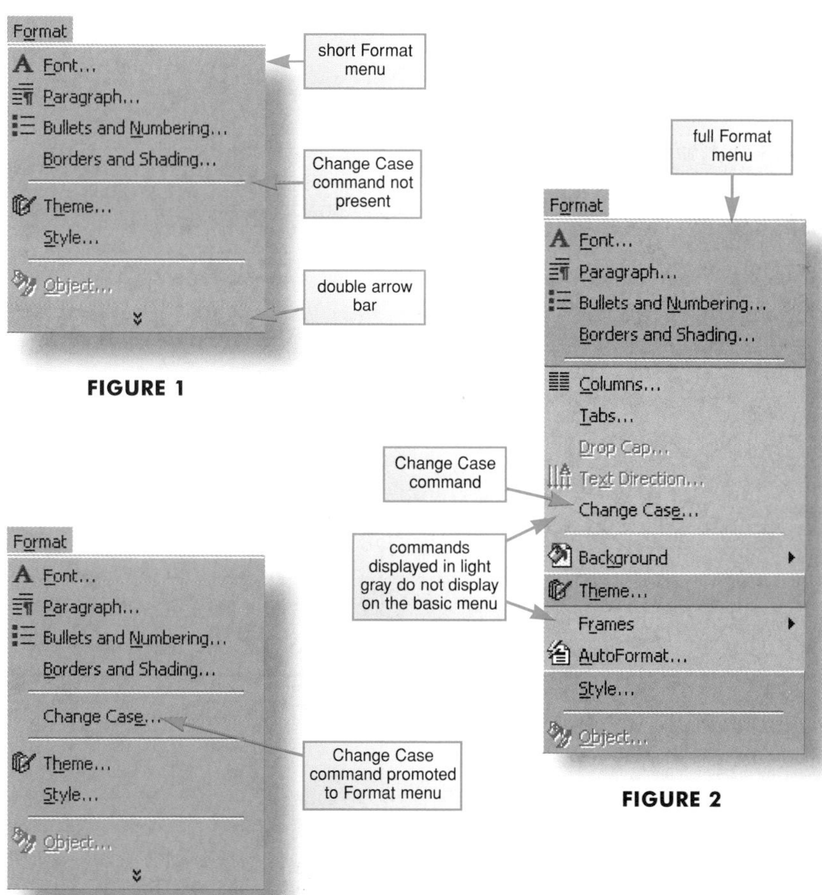

FIGURE 1

FIGURE 2

FIGURE 3

Smart Toolbars

In Office 2000, the Standard toolbar and the Formatting toolbar share a single row (Figure 4).

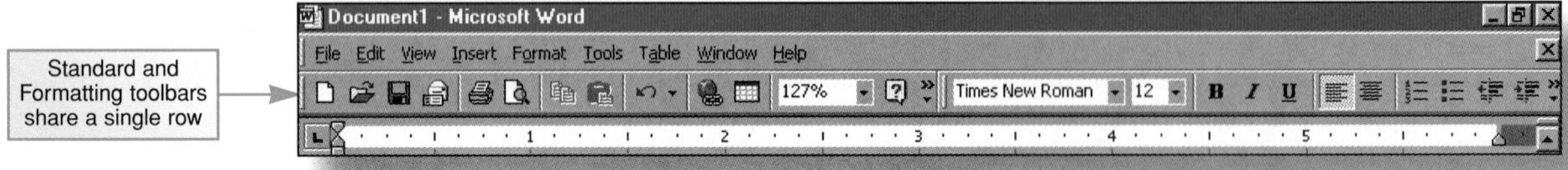

FIGURE 4

By default in Word 2000, the Standard toolbar and the Formatting toolbar each consume roughly half of the toolbar row. To use a button that is hidden on the Formatting toolbar, such as the Align Right button, complete the following steps.

To Use the Hidden Align Right Button on the Formatting Toolbar

1 Place the insertion point in a paragraph. Click the More Buttons button on the right of the Formatting toolbar.

The More Buttons menu displays (Figure 5). You can click any of the buttons on the menu to use that command.

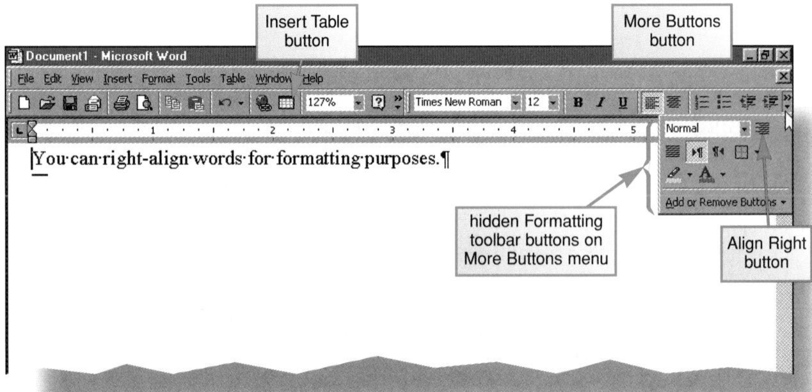

FIGURE 5

2 Click the Align Right button on the More Buttons menu.

Word 2000 right-aligns the selected paragraph (Figure 6). The Align Right button is promoted to the Formatting toolbar. The rightmost button on the Standard toolbar (the Insert Table button) is demoted from the toolbar row to make room. Using this same technique, you can use hidden buttons on the Standard toolbar and all other Office 2000 toolbars.

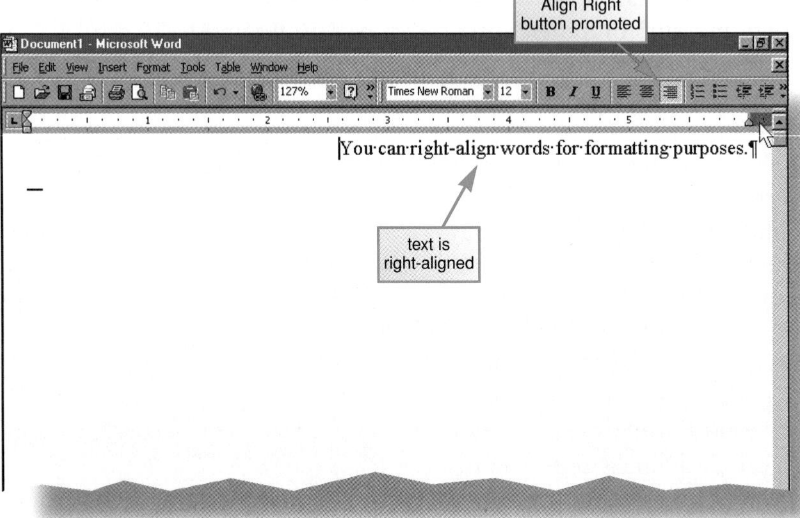

FIGURE 6

OFFICE 2000 SPECIAL FEATURE

Displaying the Entire Formatting Toolbar

You can display the entire Formatting toolbar in order to access all the buttons on the toolbar by completing the following steps.

Steps To Display the Entire Formatting Toolbar

1 Place the mouse pointer on the move handle for the Formatting toolbar.

The mouse pointer changes to a four-headed arrow (Figure 7).

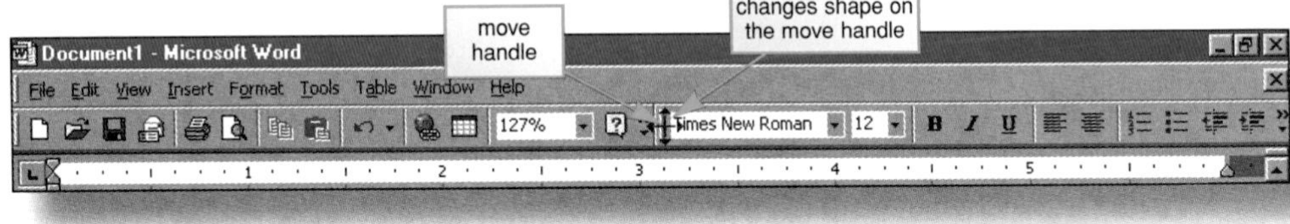

FIGURE 7

2 Double-click the move handle.

The entire Formatting toolbar displays and most of the buttons on the Standard toolbar are hidden (Figure 8).

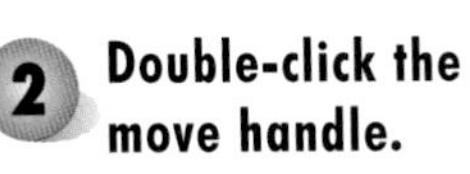

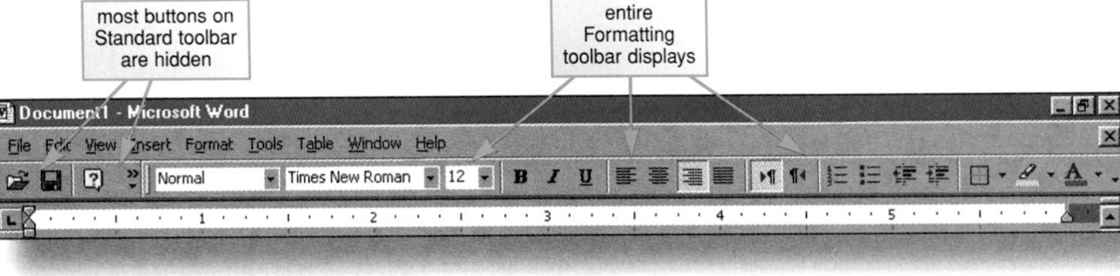

FIGURE 8

To redisplay the entire Standard toolbar, double-click the move handle at the left of the Standard toolbar. You also can drag toolbar move handles to show more or less of the toolbar.

Collect and Paste

In Office 2000, you can collect up to twelve different items from any Office 2000 application on the Office Clipboard by cutting or copying. If you have more than one item on the Office Clipboard, the **Clipboard toolbar** displays. You can paste any or all of the items on the Office Clipboard into another location or another document or file. Figure 9 shows the Clipboard toolbar containing three Word and two Excel items.

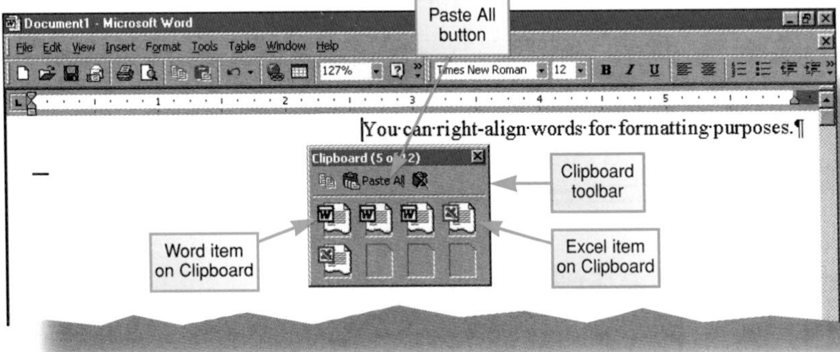

FIGURE 9

To paste any of the items on the Office Clipboard into a document or file, place the insertion point where you want the item to appear and then click the icon for the item on the Office Clipboard. To paste all the items on the Office Clipboard at one location, place the insertion point where you want the items and then click the Paste All button on the Clipboard toolbar.

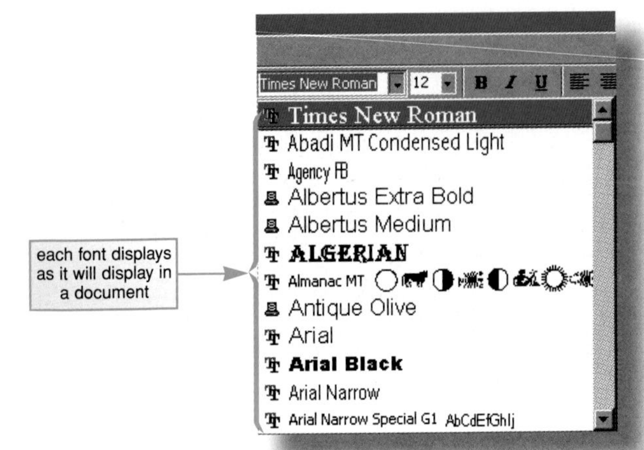

FIGURE 10

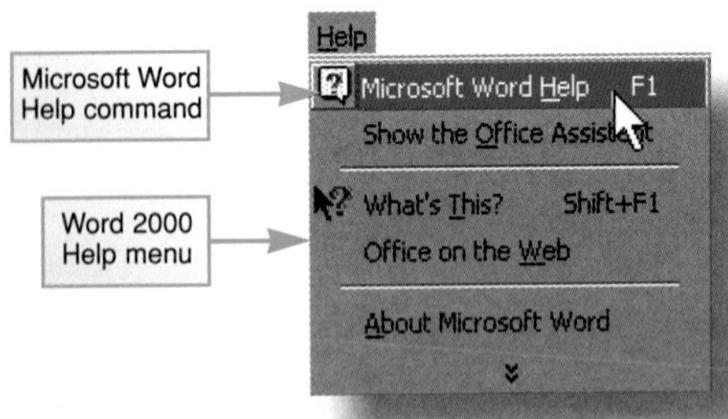

FIGURE 11

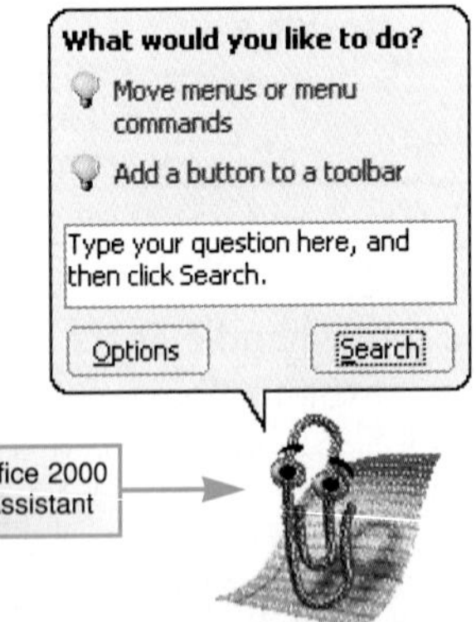

FIGURE 12

Font Style in the Font List Box

When you display the **Font list box**, each font style displays as it will display in the document itself (Figure 10).

Help Menu

The Help menu and Office Assistant function somewhat differently in Office 2000 than they do in Office 97. The Help menu displays in Figure 11.

The Help menu contains the Microsoft Word Help command the same as Office 97, but the Contents and Index command does not appear on the Help menu. By default, when you click the Microsoft Word Help command, the Office Assistant will display (Figure 12).

Once you have opened the Office Assistant, the icon remains on the screen. To use it again, click the icon.

To hide the Office Assistant so the icon does not display on your screen, click Help on the menu bar and then click Hide the Office Assistant. The icon will disappear.

In Office 2000, unlike Office 97, you can turn off the Office Assistant so it does not display when you click the Microsoft Word Help command on the Help menu. The following steps demonstrate this process.

Steps To Turn Off the Office Assistant

1 Right-click the Office Assistant icon on your screen.

The shortcut menu for the Office Assistant displays (Figure 13).

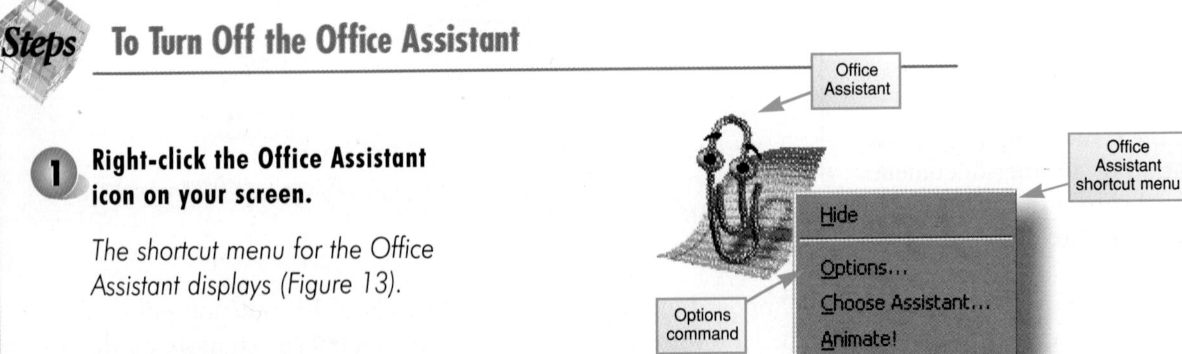

FIGURE 13

OFFICE 2000 SPECIAL FEATURE

2 Click Options on the Office Assistant shortcut menu.

The Office Assistant dialog box displays with the Options sheet selected (Figure 14). The Use the Office Assistant check box contains a check mark.

3 Click Use the Office Assistant so it does not contain a check mark. Then, click the OK button in the Office Assistant dialog box.

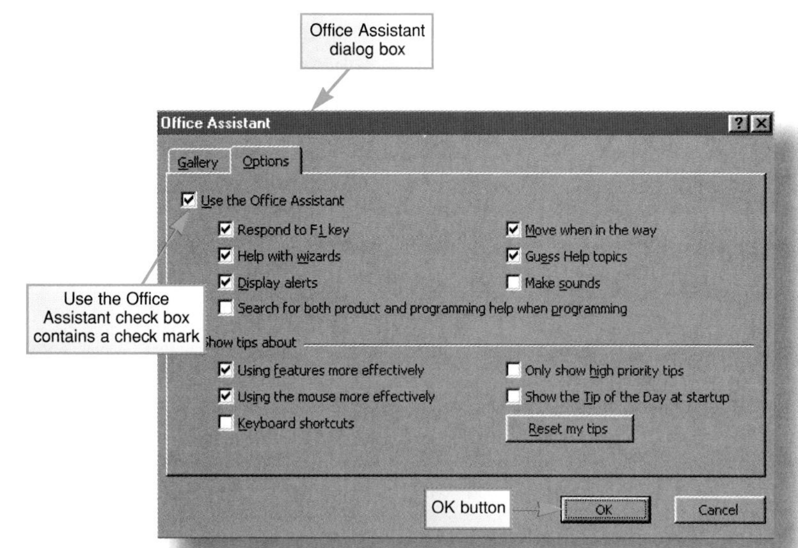

FIGURE 14

When you have turned off the Office Assistant, clicking the Microsoft Word Help command on the Help menu will display the Microsoft Word Help window (Figure 15).

You can use this window in much the same way you learned for the Contents and Index command in Office 97, except that the Answer Wizard sheet allows you to ask a question using your own words.

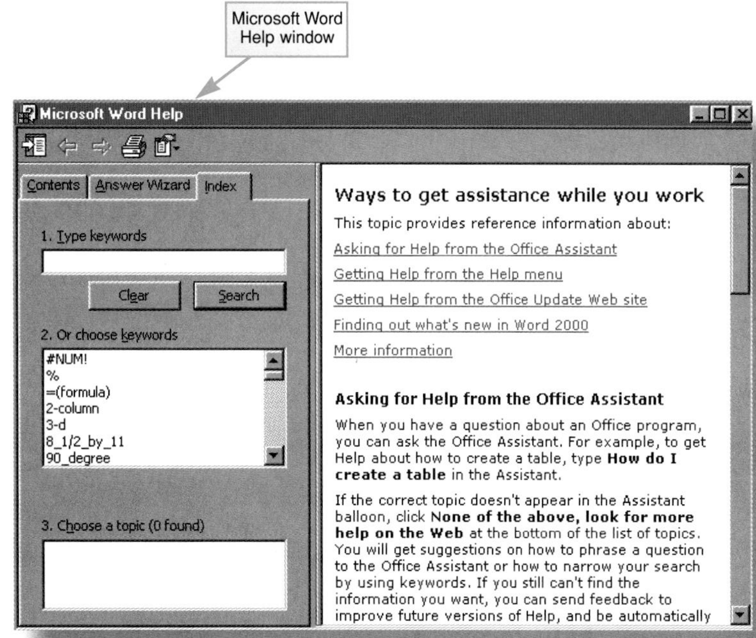

FIGURE 15

Individual Applications

The section on the following pages discusses differences for each Office 2000 application.

Word 2000

The following changes are contained in Word 2000.

CLICK-N-TYPE When you display a document in either Web Layout View or Print Layout View, you can double-click any portion of the document not containing text and begin entering text or graphics at that point (Figure 16).

FLOATING TABLES You can place a table anywhere in a Word 2000 document. The easiest way to accomplish this is to use the **Draw Table command** on the Table menu. If you place the table within text, the text will wrap around the table (Figure 17).

SYNONYMS ON SHORTCUT MENU When you place the insertion point within a word and then right-click, Word 2000 displays a shortcut menu that contains the Synonyms command. If you point to the **Synonyms command**, a submenu containing synonyms displays (Figure 18). To replace the word with a synonym, click the synonym on the submenu.

OTHER CHANGES Within the Word dialog boxes and menus, certain commands have been moved, renamed, or revised. As you use Word 2000, you can use your experience with Office 97 to interpret and use these revisions. If you have any questions, always remember you can use Word 2000 Help.

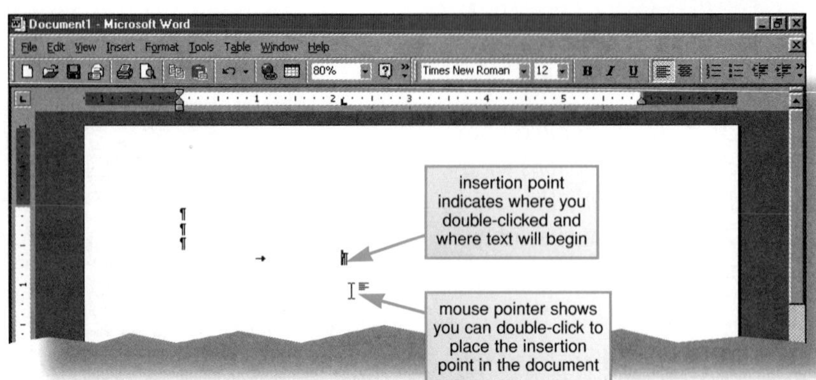

FIGURE 16

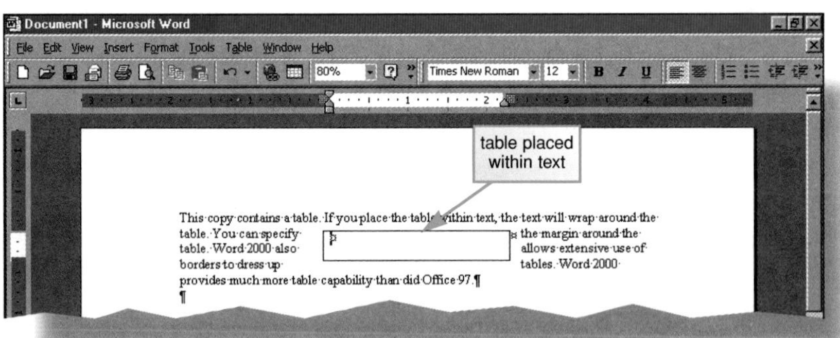

FIGURE 17

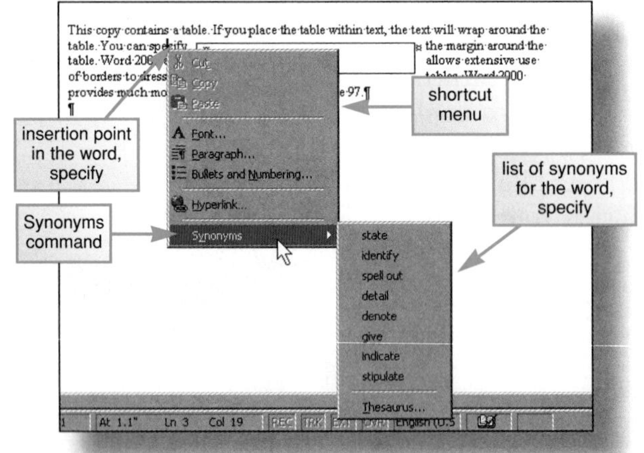

FIGURE 18

Excel 2000

SEE-THROUGH VIEW (SELECTED RANGE HAS BLUE BACKGROUND) Excel 2000 displays a selected range with a blue background (Figure 19).

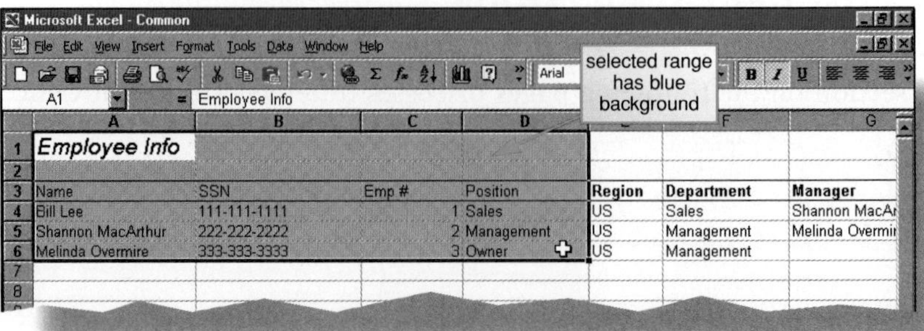

FIGURE 19

Access 2000

The major change in Access 2000 regarding the interface is the Database window, where the different objects that can display are shown on the left in the **Objects bar** (Figure 20).

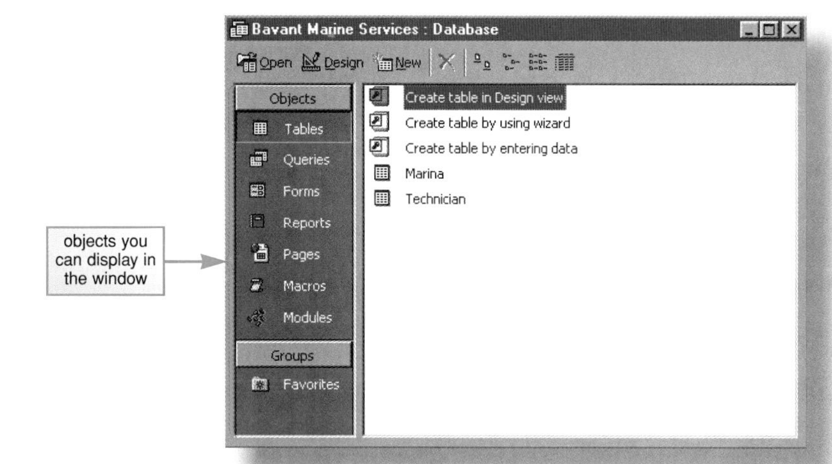

FIGURE 20

PowerPoint 2000

A major change in PowerPoint 2000 is the **tri-pane view** when you work on a presentation (Figure 21).

On the left, the PowerPoint presentation is shown in Outline view. The upper-right of the tri-pane view shows the actual slide you develop. The window on the bottom displays any notes you make as you develop the presentation.

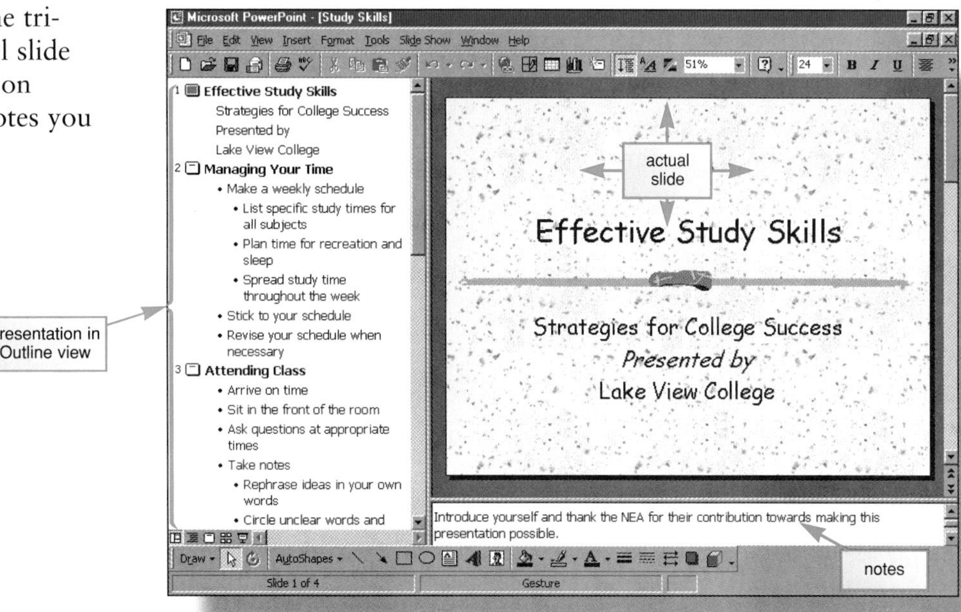

FIGURE 21

Using the World Wide Web

A fundamental premise of Office 2000 is that the World Wide Web will be a major way for computer users to communicate, whether individually, within workgroups, or within large corporations. This means that not only should people be able to view Web pages in their browsers, they also should be able to create pages easily on a Web site for use by others, either on the Internet or on an intranet. All Office 2000 applications allow users to post pages to a Web site by making all documents and files display perfectly either in the application format (.doc, .xls, etc.) or in HTML.

Web View

In any Office 2000 application except Access, you can view the document or file you are creating as an HTML page by clicking **Web Page Preview** on the File menu (Figure 22).

The page or file will display in your browser.

You can save the document or file as a Web page by clicking **Save as Web Page** on the File menu (see Figure 22). The Save As dialog box that displays is shown in Figure 23.

The Save as type is Web Page, which means the page will be saved in the HTML format and then can be displayed in a Web browser.

In addition, the Save in list box contains an FTP Locations entry, which identifies one or more servers that contain Web sites on which you can directly store the page.

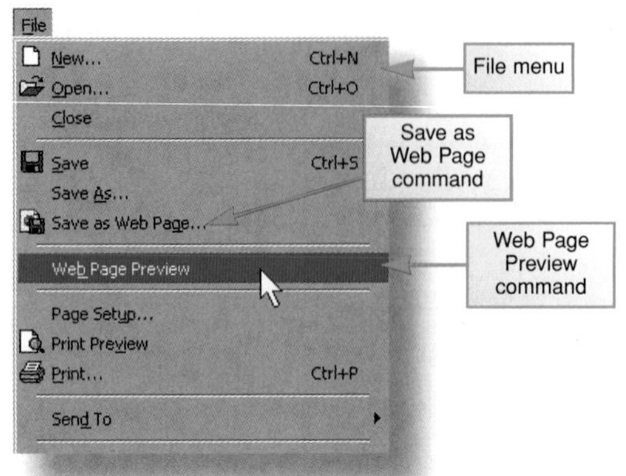

FIGURE 22

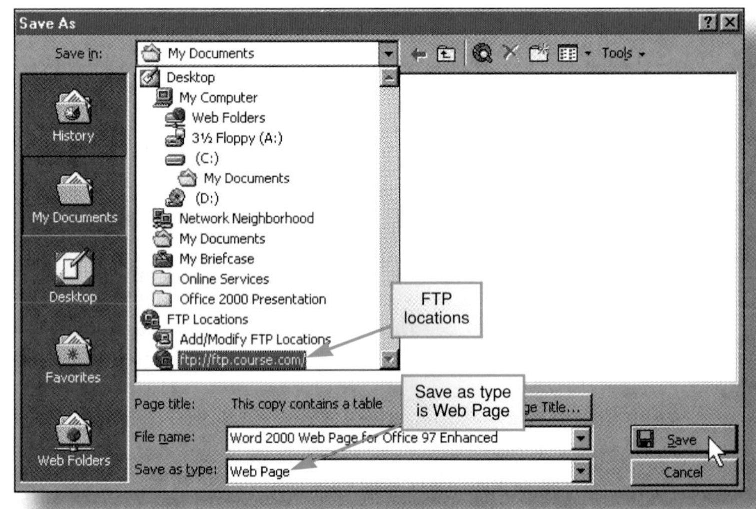

FIGURE 23

Office 2000 Programs and Editions

Microsoft added the following programs to Office 2000.

PUBLISHER 2000 Publisher 2000 is a desktop publishing program that allows you to create a myriad of documents from professionally designed templates.

FRONTPAGE 2000 FrontPage 2000 is a Web design and Web management application. You can create Web pages and also control one or more Web sites from within the FrontPage program.

PHOTODRAW 2000 PhotoDraw 2000 allows you to create drawings and to modify drawings and photographs. Its primary function is to provide an easy-to-use photo editor for graphics you might use in Web pages.

Table 1 to the right summarizes each of the editions of Office 2000 and the application programs found in each version.

Office 2000 offers a multitude of changes when compared to Office 97. Whether or not you should use Office 2000 as opposed to Office 97 will depend on your needs and your computer's capabilities.

Table 1 Summary of Office Editions

EDITION	PROGRAMS
Standard	Word, Excel, PowerPoint, Outlook
Small Business	Word, Excel, Outlook, Publisher
Professional	Word, Excel, Access, PowerPoint, Outlook, Publisher
Premium	Word, Excel, Access, PowerPoint, Outlook, Publisher, FrontPage, PhotoDraw

Word 97 Enhanced Exercises

Word 97 Project 1 Laboratory Exercises

For a sample result of an exercise, visit www.scsite.com/off97enh/labs.htm.

1 Camper for Sale

Your neighbor is selling his 19 foot Travel Trailer. Because you are a marketing major, he has asked you to prepare an announcement that he can post at various locations around town. He has a picture of the camper that he would like you to place in the announcement. Use the following text and picture: headline – Camper for Sale; a picture of a camper is located at this Web site: www.scsite.com/wd97/pr1.htm; body title – 19' Mallard Travel Trailer; paragraph text – Enjoy the great outdoors with all the comforts of home. Equipped with shower, microwave, stove, heater, and air conditioner, this unit comfortably sleeps two adults and three children.; first bulleted item – Small enough to pull with a full-sized car or minivan; second bulleted item – Very clean; excellent condition; asking $8,500; last line – Call 555-1010 for more information. Use the following fonts: headline – 36-point Arial Black font; body title – 36-point Times New Roman bold font; all other text – 22-point Times New Roman font. Resize the graphic so the announcement fits on a single page. Use the concepts and techniques presented in Word Project 1 to create and format this announcement.

2 Downtown Apartments

You work as a computer specialist at Reed Property Management. Your manager has assigned you the task of preparing an announcement to mail to potential customers in several suburbs. The announcement should contain a graphic of high-rise buildings. Use the following text and picture: headline – Downtown Apartments; a picture of high-rise buildings is located in the Buildings category of the Clip Gallery; body title – Reed Property Management; paragraph text – Looking for a spacious downtown apartment? Let the qualified experts at Reed Property Management help you find that perfect apartment.; first bulleted item – For an appointment or more information, e-mail us at reed@star.com or call 555-4141; second bulleted item – Appointments available seven days a week; last line – Visit us on the Web at www.reed.com. Use the following fonts: headline – 28-point Arial Black font; body title – 26-point Times New Roman bold font; all other text – 20-point Times New Roman font. Resize the graphic so the announcement fits on a single page. Use the concepts and techniques presented in Word Project 1 to create and format this announcement.

3 Sports Car

A co-worker is selling her sports car. Because of your extensive computer experience, she has asked you to prepare an announcement that she can post on the office bulletin boards. She has a photograph of the car for the announcement. Use the following text and picture: headline – For Sale; a picture of a sports car is located at this Web site: www.scsite.com/wd97/pr1.htm; body title – 1969 XKE Jaguar; paragraph text – This beautiful black California sports car has had only one owner. Must see. It is a 2+2, four speed, 4.2 liter with factory air conditioning, power steering, and power brakes.; first bulleted item – Nice clean car with only 68,000 miles; second bulleted item – Appraised at $18,000; last line – Call 555-1476 for more information. Use the following fonts: headline – 72-point Arial Black font; body title – 48-point Times New Roman bold font; all other text – 22-point Times New Roman font. Resize the graphic so the announcement fits on a single page. Use the concepts and techniques presented in Word Project 1 to create and format this announcement.

Word 97 Project 2 Laboratory Exercises

For a sample result of an exercise, visit www.scsite.com/off97enh/labs.htm.

1 Kimberly Ann Winters Resume

Because you are majoring in Computer Technology, your friend, Kim, has asked you to assist her in preparing her resume. Use the concepts and techniques presented in Word Project 2, along with the following information, to create and format the resume.

Kim's full name is Kimberly Ann Winters, and she lives at 114 Cedar Street in Mokena, Illinois, 60448. Her telephone is (708) 555-3356, her fax is (708) 555-3357, and her e-mail address is winters@town.net. Her objective is to obtain a position at a commercial radio station.

She attended Illinois University in Chicago, Illinois, from 1997 to 2001 and obtained her B.A. in Radio and Television in May 2001 with a major in Broadcasting. Relevant courses she took included Introduction to Mass Media, Mass Communication, Electronic Media, Radio Production, Television Production, Broadcast Journalism, Communication Law, Radio and Television Writing, Advertising, Public Relations, Voice Diction, and Group Discussions.

Kim received the following awards while in college: 2000 – 2001 Outstanding Senior; 1st Place – 1999 Radio Script Writing Contest; Dean's list, six semesters; and 1997 – 2001 Scholarship, Public Radio Association. She worked from 1998 to 2001 at Illinois University as a Student Assistant for the College Radio Station performing the following tasks: established guidelines for music, served as an on-air disc jockey, conducted on-air talk shows, and managed operations of the music library.

Her interests and activities included the following: Phi Beta Alpha Honorary Society; Public Radio Association, Student Chapter Vice President; The Broadcasting Club, Member; and Student Government Association, Vice President. Kim speaks the following languages: English, fluent; Spanish, fluent; and French, working knowledge. Her hobbies include camping and photography.

2 Kimberly Ann Winters Cover Letter

Your friend Kim would like to prepare a cover letter for her resume. She has asked you to assist her with composing the letter using a Word template. Use the concepts and techniques presented in Word Project 2, along with the following information, to create and format the cover letter.

For the return address, Kim's complete name is Kimberly Ann Winters, and she lives at 114 Cedar Street in Mokena, Illinois 60448. Use today's date and the following inside address: Mr. Terry Allen, WJJX Radio, 142 Fourteenth Street in Chicago, Illinois 60606.

Below the salutation, the text of the cover letter is as follows: first paragraph – I am responding to the advertisement for a disc jockey that appeared in Sunday's edition of the *Chicago Times*. I have enclosed my resume highlighting my background and feel I can be a valuable asset to WJJX Radio.; second paragraph – Through my part-time work at the university for the College Radio Station, I have first-hand experience as a disc jockey. My course of study at Illinois University has focused heavily on radio broadcasting. As shown in the following table, I have obtained exceptional grades in broadcasting and communications courses.; first row of table – GPA for Broadcasting Courses 4.0/4.0; second row – GPA for Communications Courses 3.8/4.0; third row – Overall GPA – 3.9/4.0; last paragraph – Given my extensive course work and experience, I feel I can be a definite asset to your organization. I look forward to hearing from you to schedule an interview and to discuss my career opportunities with WJJX Radio.

WORD EXERCISES

Word 97 Project 3 Laboratory Exercises

For a sample result of an exercise, visit www.scsite.com/off97enh/labs.htm.

1 Letter Perfect

This week's assignment in your introductory computer class is to prepare a short research paper about the evolution of word processing. The paper must be presented according to the MLA documentation style, contain a table, one footnote (explanatory note) and have two references. Use the concepts and techniques presented in Word Project 3, along with the following information, to create and format the research paper.

Use the title, Letter Perfect, for the research paper. The first and second paragraphs of your research paper are the same text as the first and second paragraphs of the article on pages WD 1.4 and WD 1.5 in your textbook.

Begin the third paragraph by typing this sentence, `In today's digital age, letters are created by the computer, and an abundance of font styles are available.` Then, continue the paragraph with the text from the fifth paragraph of the article (page WD 1.5). Type these two sentences to the end of this paragraph: `For example, two popular fonts are Arial and Times New Roman. The following table outlines these fonts in a variety of font styles.`

Use Fonts and Font Styles as the table title. Table W-1 shows the data for the table. Be sure to format the cells as shown. For example, the Bold in the Arial row should be the Arial font in bold.

Use the last paragraph on page WD 1.5 as the text in the last paragraph of your research paper with the following change. Type the last sentence so it reads, `As you work through Word, recall that the letters you type are descendants of the footprints left by our printing forefathers.`

You should use this textbook and the www.scsite.com/wd97/pr3.htm Web site as your references. Reflecting on a personal experience, write an explanatory note as a footnote where you deem appropriate in the research paper.

Table W-1 Letter Perfect Table Data

Arial	**Bold**	Underlined	*Italicized*
Times New Roman	**Bold**	Underlined	*Italicized*

2 MLA or APA

Your English composition instructor has assigned a research paper on documentation styles. The paper must be presented according to the MLA documentation style, contain a table, one footnote (explanatory note) and have two references. Use the concepts and techniques presented in Word Project 3, along with the following information, to create and format the research paper.

Use the title, MLA or APA, for the research paper. The first paragraph of your research paper is the same text as the first paragraph of the article on pages WD 3.2 and WD 3.3 in your textbook. Type the following text for the second paragraph, `Depending on the course you are taking and the type of document that is assigned, your method of presenting these sources will vary. In academia, three major style systems for writers of research and scientific papers generally are recognized. Your instructors likely will direct you to the required style and appropriate handbooks as assignments are given. Two popular styles are the Modern Language Association (MLA) style and the American Psychological Association (APA) style. The third style is the number system used by writers in the applied sciences. The following table presents the MLA and APA documentation styles.`

Table W-2 shows the data for the table. The table title is Popular Documentation Styles. Use the fifth paragraph of the article on page WD 3.3 as the text in the last paragraph of your research paper.

You should use this textbook and the www.scsite.com/wd97/pr3.htm Web site as your references. Reflecting on a personal experience, write an explanatory note as a footnote where you deem appropriate in the research paper.

Table W-2 MLA or APA Table Data

MLA STYLE	APA STYLE
Used by humanities fields	Used in the social sciences
Explained in the *MLA Handbook for Writers of Research Papers*	Explained in the *Publication Manual of the American Psychological Association*

EXCEL EXERCISES

Excel 97 Enhanced Exercises

Excel 97 Project 1 Laboratory Exercises

For a sample result of an exercise, visit www.scsite.com/off97enh/labs.htm.

1 Kylie's Pet Shop 1st Qtr Sales

John Kylie has hired you to create a quarterly sales report from the data in Table E-1 that shows totals for each store location, each pet category, and the entire company. Mr. Kylie also would like a Clustered column with a 3-D visual effect chart that compares the pet category sales within each store location. Use the title of this exercise as the worksheet title. Change the worksheet title to 18-point bold font. Merge and center the title across columns A through F. Use the AutoFormat command to format the body to the Accounting 2 type. Draw the chart in the range A9:F16. Save the workbook using the title of this exercise. Hand in a printout of the worksheet.

Table E-1 Kylie's Pet Shop 1st Qtr Sales Data

	MIAMI	CHICAGO	SAN JOSE	NASHVILLE
Fish	$15,123.43	$22,734.00	$23,198.75	$9,141.00
Hamsters	8,526.50	13,582.40	17,340.75	20,965.25
Dogs	34,204.50	19,444.50	29,975.43	19,456.23
Cats	7,436.25	9,657.43	7,634.90	9,087.50

2 Terry's Tunes Weekly Sales Report

You work as a spreadsheet specialist for Terry's Tunes. Your manager has assigned you the task of developing a weekly sales report that shows sales of CDs, cassettes, and videos by city from the data in Table E-2. The report should contain totals for each city, each product category, and the entire company. Your manager also would like a Stacked column with a cylindrical shape chart that compares the product category sales within each city. Use the title of this exercise as the worksheet title. Use Terry's Tunes as the worksheet title in cell A1. Change it to 20-point bold font. Use Weekly Sales Report as the worksheet subtitle in cell A2. Change it to 14-point bold font. One at a time, merge and center both titles across columns A through G. Use the AutoFormat command to format the body to the Accounting 3 type. Draw the chart in the range A9:G22. Save the workbook using the title of this exercise. Hand in a printout of the worksheet.

Table E-2 Terry's Tunes Weekly Sales Data

	ST. LOUIS	GARY	TOLEDO	DAYTONA	PEORIA
CDs	$49,127.35	$64,110.55	$52,546.00	$39,623.50	$53,134.56
Cassettes	25,450.00	20,659.40	26,342.56	33,761.45	21,098.45
Videos	53,289.50	44,198.00	25,194.25	34,312.35	31,657.15

EXCEL EXERCISES

Excel 97 Project 2 Laboratory Exercises

For a sample result of an exercise, visit www.scsite.com/off97enh/labs.htm.

1 Envirosystems Sales Analysis

You are a spreadsheet specialist for Envirosystems. Your supervisor has requested that you create a worksheet that shows the sales by salesperson. The data and the format of the report she wants, including the totals, are shown in Figure E-1. The formulas in Figure E-1 are as follows: Formula A = Sales Amount – Sales Return; Formula B = Net Sales – Sales Quota; and Formula C = Total Net Sales / Total Sales Quota.

The specifications also require a 3-D Column chart (column 1, row 2 in the Chart sub-type area) created on a separate sheet. Use the concepts and techniques developed in Excel Project 2 to create and format the worksheet and 3-D Column chart. Save the workbook using the title of this exercise. Hand in a printout of the values version (including the Pie chart) and formulas version of the worksheet (see page E 2.59). Change Ali Kaffari's sales amount to $2,000,000. The % of Quota Sold should be equal to 111.53%. Hand in a printout of the modified worksheet and 3-D Column chart.

Envirosystems Sales Analysis					
SALES REP NAME	SALES AMOUNT	SALES RETURN	NET SALES	SALES QUOTA	ABOVE QUOTA VALUE
Jose Ortega	$2,125,007	$120,250	Formula A	$2,000,000	Formula B
Latonya Boyd	1,452,675	359,000		1,000,000	
Zhu Rongjee	4,268,350	922,100		3,000,000	
Ali Kaffari	1,256,350	213,500		1,000,000	
Nipul Bhatia	3,960,000	430,000		3,545,000	
Total	—	—	—	—	—
Average	—	—	—	—	
% of Quota Sold	Formula C				

FIGURE E-1

2 Ahab's Pool and Patio Profit Potential

Mr. Ahab hired you as a student intern to develop worksheets for his Pool and Patio business. Highest on his priority list is a Profit Potential worksheet. The data and the format of the report he wants are shown in Figure E-2 on the next page. Also include a sum, average, highest, and lowest for each column. The formulas in Figure E-2 are as follows:

Formula A = Units on Hand * Average Unit Cost Formula C = Units on Hand * Average Unit Price
Formula B = Average Unit Cost * (1 / (1 - .65)) Formula D = Total Value – Total Cost

Mr. Ahab also wants a 3-D Pie chart similar to the one shown in Figure 2-54 on page E 2.41. Use the concepts and techniques developed in Excel Project 2 to create and format the worksheet and chart. Save the workbook using the title of this exercise. Hand in a printout of the values version (including the Pie chart) and formulas version of the worksheet (see page E 2.59). Mr. Ahab just received a shipment of 2,000 additional Gliders. Change the Units on Hand to 2,667 and hand in a printout of the worksheet and Pie chart. The additional inventory yields a total profit potential of $1,929,434.46.

(continued)

Ahab's Pool and Patio Profit Potential *(continued)*

Ahab's Pool and Patio Profit Potential						
ITEM	UNITS ON HAND	AVERAGE UNIT COST	TOTAL COST	AVERAGE UNIT PRICE	TOTAL VALUE	PROFIT POTENTIAL
8' Table	2,325	$129.45	Formula A	Formula B	Formula C	Formula D
Swivel Chair	2,875	62.50	↓	↓	↓	↓
Lounge Chair	1,935	42.95	↓	↓	↓	↓
Glider	667	125.75	↓	↓	↓	↓
Umbrella	1,616	86.50	↓	↓	↓	↓
Total	—		—		—	—

FIGURE E-2

Excel 97 Project 3 Laboratory Exercises

For a sample result of an exercise, visit www.scsite.com/off97enh/labs.htm.

1 Newton's Apple Orchard Quarterly Growth

You are a project leader in the Information Technology department at Newton's Apple Orchard Corporation. The planning committee has requested a workbook that shows quarterly growth based on Qtr 1 sales and growth data. The data and general layout of the worksheet, including the totals, are shown in Figure E-3. Enter the following formulas for Qtr 1 in the locations shown in Figure E-3 and then copy them to the remaining quarters:

Formula A = Qtr 1 Revenue
Formula B = IF(Qtr Growth Rate < 0, Revenue * (Qtr Cost Rate + Extra), Revenue * Qtr Cost Rate)
Formula C = Revenue – Cost
The total profit for the four quarters should equal $5,874,696.98.

The planning committee also wants an embedded (on the same sheet with the data) 3-D Pie chart (column 2, row 1 in the Chart sub-type area) showing the profit contribution of each quarter to the total profit. The specifications also call for exploding Qtr 4 in the 3-D Pie chart. Use the concepts and techniques developed in the first three projects to create and format the worksheet and 3-D Pie chart.

Save the workbook using the title of this exercise. Hand in a printout of the values version and formulas version of the worksheet (see page E 2.59). Use the Goal Seek command to determine the Qtr 1 Revenue (first value in the Assumptions area) that will generate a total profit of $7,000,000.00. You should end up with a Qtr 1 Revenue of $3,286,683.22. Hand in a printout of the modified worksheet and 3-D Pie chart.

Newton's Apple Orchard Quarterly Growth					
	QTR 1	QTR 2	QTR 3	QTR 4	TOTAL
Revenue	Formula A →			→	—
Cost	Formula B →			→	—
Profit	Formula C →			→	—
Assumptions					
Qtr 1 Revenue	$2,758,324.00				
Qtr Growth Rate	0.00%	-2.00%	3.00%	4.25%	
Qtr Cost Rate	46.00%	42.00%	56.00%	43.00%	
Extra	1.75%	2.30%	1.15%	2.90%	

FIGURE E-3

Access 97 Enhanced Exercises

Access 97 Project 1 Laboratory Exercises

For a sample result of an exercise, visit www.scsite.com/off97enh/labs.htm.

1 Creating the Gadget Gizmos Database

Gadget Gizmos, a local manufacturing company, has asked you to create and update a database that will keep track of salaried employees. The owner provides you with the data shown in Figure A-1.

Create a database called Gadget Gizmos in which to store the employee data. The primary key of the Employee table is Employee Number. Use Text data type for Employee Number (4), Last Name (15), First Name (10), Job Title (20) and Dept Code (2). The number in parentheses indicates the size of the text field. Use Currency data type for Salary. The primary key for the Department table is Dept Code. Use Text data type for both Dept Code (2) and Dept Name (18). Add the data shown in Figure A-1 to the database. Print the Employee table and the Department table. Create and print a report for the Employee table. Name the report, Salary Report. The report should include the employee's last name, first name, job title, and salary. Sort the report in ascending order by last name.

Data for Employee table

EMPLOYEE NUMBER	LAST NAME	FIRST NAME	JOB TITLE	SALARY	DEPT CODE
0031	Fitzpatrick	Luke	Materials Manager	$42,500.00	04
0043	Radel	Nancy	Buyer	$37,250.00	04
0056	McCoy	Mark	Cost Accountant	$29,900.00	01
0067	Peng	Ung	Benefits Analyst	$33,500.00	02
0078	Alvarez	Elvira	Expediter	$28,500.00	04
0230	Sampers	Gene	Shift Supervisor	$28,000.00	03
0233	Gerriston	Chandra	Economist	$35,000.00	01
0344	Novelli	Laura	Director	$43,000.00	02
0440	Evans	Michael	Trainer	$38,500.00	02
0551	Pierson	Kim	Quality Assurance	$31,000.00	03

Data for Department table

DEPT CODE	DEPT NAME
01	Finance
02	Human Resources
03	Manufacturing
04	Purchasing

FIGURE A-1

2 Creating the Silent Auction Database

A local charity is organizing a fund-raiser that will include a silent auction. A silent auction is one in which the attendees have a specified amount of time to bid (in writing) on items or services donated by businesses. The charity has asked you to create a database to keep track of the donated goods and services as well as the businesses that donate them. The charity already has received some donations and provides you with the data shown in Figure A-2 on the next page.

Create a database called Silent Auction in which to store the auction items. The primary key of the Item table is Item Number. Use text data type for Item Number (3), Description (30), and Donor Number (2). The number in parentheses indicates the size of the text field. Use Currency data type for Item Value and Minimum Bid. The primary key for the Donor table is Donor Number. Use Text data type for Donor Number (2), Name (25), Address (15), City (15), State (2), Zip Code (5), and Telephone Number (12). Add the data shown in Figure A-2 to the database. Print the Item table and the Donor table. Create and print a report for the Item table that includes the description, item value, and minimum bid. Name the report, Silent Auction Items. Sort the report in ascending order by description.

(continued)

Creating the Silent Auction Database *(continued)*

Data for Item table

ITEM NUMBER	DESCRIPTION	ITEM VALUE	MINIMUM BID	DONOR NUMBER
B08	Birdhouse	$30.00	$8.00	04
B12	Beauty Makeover	$75.00	$10.00	03
C01	Crystal Vase	$35.00	$5.00	03
C03	Cookware Set	$120.00	$30.00	03
D05	Dinner for 2	$60.00	$20.00	01
F04	Fresh Floral Arrangement	$40.00	$10.00	02
F06	Silk Floral Arrangement	$60.00	$15.00	02
G11	Gourmet Basket	$90.00	$50.00	01
Q02	Log Cabin Quilt	$250.00	$100.00	04
Q04	Quilted Wall Hanging	$110.00	$80.00	04

Data for Donor table

DONOR NUMBER	NAME	ADDRESS	CITY	STATE	ZIP CODE	TELEPHONE NUMBER
01	Stone Kitchens	215 Watkins	Oakdale	MN	48101	610-555-6543
02	Ole Florist	266 Ralston	Allanson	ND	48102	520-555-9876
03	Atwater's Dept Store	542 Prairie	Oakdale	MN	48101	610-555-7890
04	Bea's Handcrafts	96 Prospect	Bishop	ND	48103	520-555-1298

FIGURE A-2

Access 97 Project 2 Laboratory Exercises

For a sample result of an exercise, visit www.scsite.com/off97enh/labs.htm.

1 Querying the Gadget Gizmos Database

Now that you have entered the data for the Gadget Gizmos database, the owner has several questions to pose to the database. Use the database to answer the following: (a) The employees in the Purchasing department have not had training on using company e-mail. Display and print the first name, last name, and job title of all employees who work in the Purchasing department. (b) The organization chart for Gadget Gizmos needs to be updated. Display and print the job titles in ascending order. List the job titles only once. (c) Employees who are paid less than $30,000 and work in the Manufacturing department are eligible for a bonus equal to 4% of their annual salary. Display and print the first name, last name, salary, and bonus amount for these eligible employees. (d) The owner would like an updated department list. Display and print the department name, first name, last name, job title, and salary. Sort the output in order by salary (descending) within department name (ascending.)

2 Calculating Statistics for the Gadget Gizmos Database

Gadget Gizmos has been asked to provide salary data for a national manufacturing survey. Use the database to answer the following: (a) What is the average salary of all employees? (b) What is the highest salary? (c) What is the lowest salary? (d) What is the total salary of all employees? (e) What is the average salary by department?

ACCESS EXERCISES

3 Querying the Silent Auction Database

Now that you have entered the silent auction data, the charity volunteers have several questions they would like answered. Use the database to answer the following: (a) Display and print the description, item value, and minimum bid of all items that are some type of floral arrangement (*Hint:* Use wildcards to solve this problem.) (b) Display and print the item number, description, and minimum bid of all items that have a value greater than $100. (c) Display and print the donor name, item number, description and item value of all items. (d) Display and print the item number, item value, and minimum bid of all items with a minimum bid of $10 or less. (e) Display and print the item number, description, and item value of all donated items. Sort the output in order by description (ascending) within item value (descending). (*Hint:* Use Help to solve this problem.)

Access 97 Project 3 Laboratory Exercises

For a sample result of an exercise, visit www.scsite.com/off97enh/labs.htm.

1 Updating the Gadget Gizmos Database

Gadget Gizmos has had several personnel changes in the past few weeks and the database must be updated. In some cases, the table structure must be changed before the data can be updated. For example, the last name field is not large enough for Nancy Radel's married name. Execute each of these tasks: (a) Nancy Radel recently married and is now known as Nancy Radel-Machajewski. (b) Monica Sales has joined the company as a cost accountant in the Finance department. Monica's starting salary is $32,000. Her employee number is 0671. (c) Michael Evans is no longer employed by the company. (d) Elvira Alvarez has been promoted to Buyer at a salary of $30,000. Resize the columns in the Employee table to best fit the data. Print the updated Employee table.

2 Improving the Gadget Gizmos Database

Because the Gadget Gizmos database contains salary information, the owner wants to be sure that all data entered in the database is accurate. He also wants to improve the efficiency of the database by creating some additional indexes. The owner has asked you to do the following: (a) The company frequently needs to display employee data in order by last name within department code. Create an index to help with this task. (b) The Employee Number and Dept Code fields were defined as text. This is correct but the owner wants to be sure that only numbers are entered in these fields. (*Hint:* Use Help and search for input mask to solve this problem.) (c) The Employee table should include the Dept Code for only those departments in the Department table. (d) No employee makes less than $15,000 or more than $55,000.

3 Updating the Silent Auction Database

The charity organization would like to add another field to the database. They would like to know whether the donated item is a good or a service. Create a text field to store this information. Name the field, Item Type (3) and place it after the Description field. The field has the value GDS if the item is a good and SER if the item is a service. Currently, the only items in the database that are service items are items B12 and D05. The charity has received another item from Atwater's Dept Store. The store is donating a leather briefcase (item number L01) worth $95. The minimum bid is $45. Atwater's also has informed you that item C01 is really a crystal bud vase. Bea's Handcrafts has withdrawn the quilted wall hanging and replaced it with a baby quilt. The item number, item value, and minimum bid remain the same. Resize the columns in the Item table to best fit the data. Print the Item table.

PowerPoint 97 Enhanced Exercises

PowerPoint 97 Project 1 Laboratory Exercises

For a sample result of an exercise, visit www.scsite.com/off97enh/labs.htm.

1 North County Car Club

As chairperson of the Promotions committee for the North County Car Club, you are responsible for designing a presentation for the summer road rally. Use the data in Table P-1 to create a slide show presentation. Choose an appropriate design template. Be sure to include a title slide. Adjust line spacing if necessary. Save the presentation with the name of this exercise. Print the presentation slides.

2 Hammond State University

Hammond State University is a comprehensive university dedicated to serving the professional, cultural, and general educational needs of the citizens of Western Arizona. As the assistant director of admissions, you have been asked to give a presentation highlighting Hammond State University. Create a presentation from the data in Table P-2. Choose an appropriate design template. Include a title slide and four bulleted list slides. Select interesting slide layouts and adjust line spacing as necessary. Check for spelling errors. Save the presentation with the name of this exercise. Print the presentation slides.

PowerPoint 97 Project 2 Laboratory Exercises

For a sample result of an exercise, visit www.scsite.com/off97enh/labs.htm.

1 Smith, Jones, and Jones New Employee Orientation

Employees in the law firm of Smith, Jones, and Jones often are required to entertain clients. As a member of the new employee orientation team, you have been assigned the role of etiquette trainer. Use the outline in Figure P-1 to create an electronic presentation for the next orientation to identify important etiquette topics. Select an appropriate design template. Introduce the presentation with a title slide. Include clip art and animation effects. Display the presentation title in the outline header and the company name in the outline footer. Save the presentation using the title, Everyday Manners. Print the slides without animations and the presentation outline.

2 Mercy Memorial Hospital

Due to the increased need for organ and tissue donors, the hospital nursing staff suggests that you create a presentation to educate patients and their family members about organ donation. Select a design template and create an electronic slide show using the data in Table P-3. Introduce the presentation with a title slide that includes your name as the developer. Use the row headings in Table P-3 to create Slide 2. Modify the slide layouts. Choose appropriate clip art and add animation effects. Include interesting slide transitions. Adjust line spacing where necessary. Display the presentation title in the outline header and the hospital's name in the outline footer. Save the presentation using the name, Mercy Memorial Hospital. Print the slides without animations. Also, print the presentation outline.

POWERPOINT EXERCISES

Table P-1 North County Car Club Data

North County Car Club Summer Road Rally	Rally Information
	• Central High School parking lot
	• Registration 4:00 p.m.
	• Tech 4:30 - 5:30 p.m.
	  • Inspections
	• 1st car off at 6:01 p.m.
	  • 1 minute intervals between cars
	• Awards ceremony at end of rally

North County Car Club Summer Road Rally
• Car Club of America
  • 10th Annual Summer Road Rally
• Approximately 130 miles
  • Paved and dirt roads
  • Road course 15 minutes before departure
• Scoring: T. S. D.
  • Time - Speed - Distance
	Prizes
	• First place $1,000
	• Second place $500
	• Third place $250
	• Fourth place $150
	• Fifth place $100

Table P-2 Hammond State University Data

Hammond State Highlights
• Academic programs
• Supportive environment
• Advantages and benefits
• Partners with the region
	Supportive Environment
	• Hospitable atmosphere for students
	  • Diverse career goals and ethnic backgrounds
	  • Old and young
	  • Both sexes
	  • All races
	• Faculty and staff reflecting cultural diversity
	• Academic consideration of cultural differences
	• Affirmative action hiring and student recruiting

• Academic Programs
• Certificates
  • Post Baccalaureate
  • Technical Proficiency
• Degrees
  • Associate
  • Baccalaureate
  • Master
	Advantages and Benefits
	• Primary emphasis on educational activities
	• Pre-college course work
	• Reasonable in-state tuition rates
	• State support paying for two-thirds of the cost of education
	• Financial aid
	• Strong student support services
	• Flexible courses, scheduling, and sites

I. **Everyday Manners**
  A. Thoughtfulness
    1. Concern for those around you
  B. Updated Golden Rule
    1. Treat people like you want to be treated
  C. Please and thank you
II. **Things to Avoid**
  A. Staring at people
  B. Speaking loudly
  C. Making personal or lewd remarks
  D. Discussing private affairs
  E. Personal grooming
III. **Ladies and Gentlemen**
  A. Walking
    1. Man next to street
  B. Seating
    1. Everyone offers seat to elderly or ill
    2. Man may offer seat to woman
      a) Woman may refuse
  C. Opening doors
    1. Car door
      a) Man opens woman's door
    2. Open door
      a) Man steps aside allowing woman to pass
    3. Closed door
      a) Man opens and holds for woman
      b) Courteous person holds for person following
IV. **Public Display of Affection**
  A. Lovers
    1. Keep passion private
      a) Embarrassing to witness
  B. Friends
    1. Long-time acquaintance
      a) Handshake
        (1) Casual kiss on cheek or light hug
    2. New acquaintance
      a) Handshake
V. **Dining**
  A. Follow action of hostess when in doubt
  B. Place napkin in lap
    1. Not in collar, belt, or between shirt buttons
  C. Begin eating when hostess begins
  D. Use dining implement farthest from plate
  E. Chew with closed mouth

FIGURE P-1

Table P-3 Organ Donation Data

Commonly Asked Questions About Organ Donation	
Who Can Be an Organ/	Almost anyone from birth to age 75. Tissue Donor? In general, anyone wishing to donate. Some age limitations may apply for specific organs and tissues. Children under 18 can donate with parental consent.
What Can Be Donated?	Organs - Kidneys, Heart, Lungs, Pancreas: Tissues - Corneas, Skin, Heart Valves, Tendons.
Can I Sell My Organs?	No! Federal law prohibits the sale of organs or tissues. All anatomical donations are an extraordinary gift... a gift of life!
How Do I Become a	Discuss your wishes with your family. Donor? At the time of death, the family is asked to give permission for your donation. Complete and sign a donor card or complete the donor card on the back of your driver's license.

MOUS CERTIFICATION

Appendix A MOUS Certification Program

MOUS Certification Program

The Microsoft Office User Specialist (MOUS) Certification program provides a framework for measuring your proficiency with the Microsoft Office 97 applications, such as Word 97, Excel 97, Access 97, and PowerPoint 97. Three levels of certification are available — Master, Expert, and Proficient. The three levels of certification are described in Table A-1.

Table A-1 Three Levels of MOUS Certification

LEVEL	DESCRIPTION	REQUIREMENTS	CREDENTIAL AWARDED
Master	Indicates that you have a comprehensive understanding of Microsoft Office 97	Pass all FOUR of the required exams: Microsoft Word 97 Expert Microsoft Excel 97 Expert Microsoft Access 97 Expert Microsoft PowerPoint 97 Expert	Candidates will be awarded one certificate for passing all four of the required Expert exams: Microsoft Office User Specialist: Microsoft Office 97 Master
Expert	Indicates that you have a comprehensive understanding of the advanced features in a specific Microsoft Office 97 application	Pass any ONE of the Expert exams: Microsoft Word 97 Expert Microsoft Excel 97 Expert Microsoft Access 97 Expert Microsoft PowerPoint 97 Expert	Candidates will be awarded one certificate for each of the Expert exams they have passed: Microsoft Office User Specialist: Microsoft Word 97 Expert Microsoft Office User Specialist: Microsoft Excel 97 Expert Microsoft Office User Specialist: Microsoft Access 97 Expert Microsoft Office User Specialist: Microsoft PowerPoint 97 Expert
Proficient	Indicates that you have a comprehensive understanding of the core features in a specific Microsoft Office 97 application	Pass any ONE of the Proficient exams: Microsoft Word 97 Proficient Microsoft Excel 97 Proficient	Candidates will be awarded one certificate for each of the Proficient exams they have passed: Microsoft Office User Specialist: Microsoft Word 97 Proficient Microsoft Office User Specialist: Microsoft Excel 97 Proficient

Why Should You Get Certified?

Being a Microsoft Office User Specialist provides a valuable industry credential — proof that you have the Office 97 applications skills required by employers. By passing one or more MOUS certification exams, you demonstrate your proficiency in a given Office application to employers. With nearly 80 million copies of Office in use around the world, Microsoft is targeting Office certification to a wide variety of companies. These companies include temporary employment agencies that want to prove the expertise of their workers, large corporations looking for a way to measure the skill set of employees, and training companies and educational institutions seeking Microsoft Office teachers with appropriate credentials.

MOUS CERTIFICATION

The MOUS Exams

You pay $50 to $100 each time you take an exam, whether you pass or fail. The fee varies among testing centers. The Expert exams, which you can take up to 60 minutes to complete, consist of between 40 and 60 tasks that you perform online. The tasks require you to use the application just as you would in doing your job. The Proficient exams have fewer tasks, and you will have slightly less time to complete them. The tasks you will perform differ on the two types of exams.

How Can You Prepare for the MOUS Exams?

After taking an instructor-led course on Microsoft Office 97 using this textbook, the best way to prepare for the MOUS exams is to step through the Microsoft Office User Specialist Certification map (also called a MOUS map) on the next page. Each application includes its complete map. The map lists the exact activities you will be responsible for on the exams and the page numbers where you can get more information from this book. It is recommended that you look up the activities in Help and print the information as another reference as you prepare for the exams. You also should visit the Shelly Cashman Series MOUS Web page (Figure A-1 on the next page) for exam-taking tips.

Some of the activities in the MOUS map refer to the Shelly Cashman Series textbook, *Microsoft Office 97: Advanced Concepts and Techniques,* which is a continuation of this textbook.

How to Find an Authorized Testing Center

You can locate a testing center by calling 1-800-933-4493 in North America or visiting the Shelly Cashman Series MOUS Web page at www.scsite.com/off97/cert.htm and then clicking the Locate an Authorized Testing Center Near You link. This Web page allows you to look for testing centers around the world.

Shelly Cashman Series MOUS Web Page

The Shelly Cashman Series MOUS Web page (Figure A-1) contains more than fifteen Web pages you can visit to obtain additional information on the MOUS Certification Program. The Web page (www.scsite.com/off97/cert.htm) includes links to general information on certification, choosing an application for certification, preparing for the certification exam, and taking and passing the certification exam.

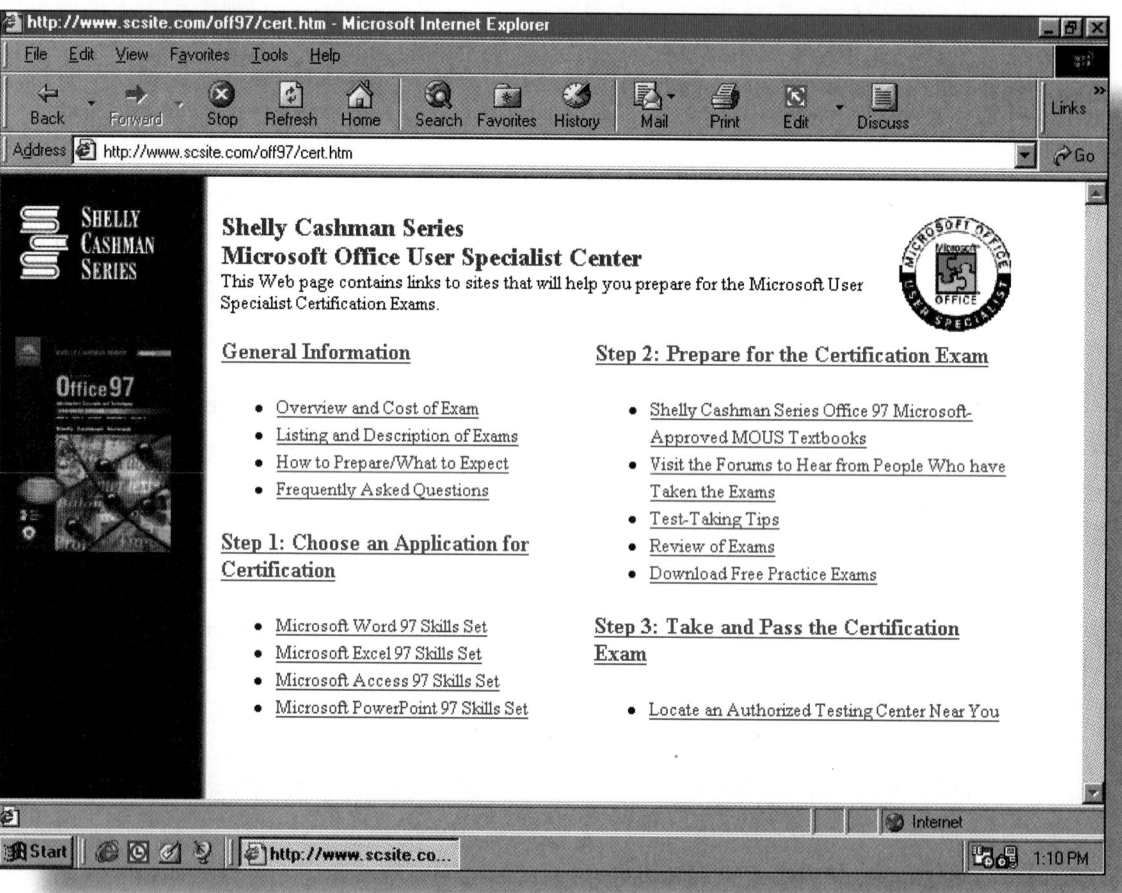

FIGURE A-1

MOUS CERTIFICATION

MOUS Certification Map

The tables on the following pages list the skill sets and activities you should be familiar with if you plan to take one of the Microsoft Office User Specialist Certification examinations. Each activity is accompanied by page numbers on which the activity is illustrated in the book.

Microsoft Word 97 Proficient User Skill Sets and Activities

Table A-1 lists the skill sets and activities you should be familiar with if you plan to take the Microsoft Word 97 Proficient examination. Red page numbers mean that the activity is demonstrated in the companion textbook *Microsoft Office 97: Advanced Concepts and Techniques* (ISBN 0-7895-1335-8).

Table A-1 Word 97 MOUS Skills and Activities

SKILL SETS	ACTIVITIES	PAGE NUMBERS
Process text	Cut, copy, insert, and move text	WD 1.52, WD 2.40
	Add bullets and numbering	WD 1.23, WD 2.20, WD 4.48
	Use the Undo and Repeat commands	WD 1.53, WD 2.42, see Help
	Use the Overtype mode	WD 1.53
Format characters	Apply font styles (Bold, Italic)	WD 1.34, WD 1.38, WD 2.37
	Use all underline options	WD 1.29, WD 1.36, WD 2.38
	Use effects (subscript, superscript, strikethrough, small caps, and outline)	WD 1.29, WD 2.38, WD 3.26
	Select and change fonts and font size (automatically and manually)	WD 1.14, WD 1.31, WD 2.24
Place and align text	Use hyphenation (non-breaking and soft hyphens)	WD 2.20
	Align text (Center, Left, Right, and Justified)	WD 1.30, WD 3.16, WD 6.17
	Set margins	WD 3.7, WD 4.11, WD 6.8
	Insert page breaks	WD 3.29, WD 3.38
	Align text vertically	WD 2.43, WD 4.34
	Set line spacing options	WD 2.16, WD 3.9, WD 3.35
	Insert date and time	WD 5.23, WD 5.25
	Prepare envelopes and labels	WD 5.41, WD 5.46
Use paragraph formatting and tab setting options	Use Tabs command (Center, Decimal, Left, and Right)	WD 2.42, WD 4.32, WD 6.11
	Set tabs with leaders	WD 4.34
	Use indentation options (Left, Right, First Line, and Hanging Indent)	WD 2.43, WD 3.18, WD 3.40
Use page numbers, headers and footers, and sections	Create and modify page numbers	WD 3.12, WD 4.52
	Create and modify headers and footers	WD 3.12, WD 4.51, WD 5.7
	Create sections with formatting that differs from other sections	WD 4.27, WD 4.51, WD 6.14
	Alternate headers and footers	See Help
Use styles and templates	Create and apply styles	WD 2.15, 2.30, WD 4.26
	Edit styles	WD 5.21, WD 6.7
	Use a template	WD 2.28
	Create a fax	WD 2.13, WD 2.61

Table A-1 Word 97 MOUS Skills and Activities *(cont.)*

SKILL SETS	ACTIVITIES	PAGE NUMBERS
Edit text	Find and replace text	WD 3.46
	Find specific text (Go To)	WD 3.48
	Navigate through a document	WD 1.22, WD 1.35, WD 3.45
	Set AutoCorrect exceptions	WD 3.21, WD 3.23
	Create and apply frequently used text	WD 2.34, WD 2.38, WD 3.23
Generate an outline	Create an outline	See Help
	Modify an outline	See Help
Create documents for use on Internet/ intranet	Save as HTML	WDI 1.4
	Create a hyperlink	WD 3.41, WDI 1.10
	Browse through files	WD 3.51, WDI 1.11
Use writing tools	Use the Spelling command	WD 1.20, WD 2.46
	Use the Grammar command	WD 1.17, WD 1.64
	Use the Thesaurus command	WD 3.48
Use columns	Key and edit text in columns	WD 6.17, WD 6.28
	Revise column structure	WD 6.15, WD 6.27, WD 6.34
	Delete and move columns	WD 6.14
Create tables	Create and format tables	WD 2.23, WD 3.30, WD 4.36
	Add borders and shading to tables	WD 3.34, WD 4.35
	Revise tables	WD 3.32, WDI 1.3, WD 4.43
	Modify table structure (merge cells, change height and width)	WD 3.34, WD 3.56, WD 4.40
	Rotate text in a table	WD 4.45
Manage files	Locate and open an existing document	WD 1.50, WD 4.29
	Save a document with the same name	WD 1.46, WD 2.48, WD 3.50
	Save a document with a different name	WD 1.25, WD 1.47, WD 4.30
	Create a subdirectory	See Help
	Save documents as HTML	WDI 1.4
Use draw	Create and modify lines and objects	WD 6.46
	Create and modify 3D shapes	WDI 2.3, WDI 2.5, WDI 2.8
Print documents and envelopes	Use print preview	WD 2.25
	Print a document	WD 1.47, WD 2.14, WD 2.30
	Print envelopes and labels	WD 5.41, WD 5.46

MOUS CERTIFICATION

Microsoft Excel 97 Proficient User Skill Sets and Activities

Table A-2 lists the skill sets and activities you should be familiar with if you plan to take the Microsoft Excel 97 Proficient examination. Red page numbers mean that the activity is demonstrated in the companion textbook *Microsoft Office 97: Advanced Concepts and Techniques* (ISBN 0-7895-1335-8).

Table A-2 Excel 97 MOUS Skills and Activities

SKILL SETS	ACTIVITIES	PAGE NUMBERS
Create workbooks	Open electronic workbooks	E 1.46
	Enter text	E 1.14, E 2. 7, E 3.7
	Enter numbers	E 1.20, E 2.8, E 3.17
	Enter formulas	E 2.9, E 2.21, E 5.11
	Save workbooks	E 1.39, E 2.41
	Close workbooks	E 1.45, E 2.65, E 4.25
Modify workbooks	Delete cell contents	E 1.49, E 1.51, E 5.20
	Delete worksheets	E 1.51
	Revise text	E 1.49, E 1.57, E 6.31
	Revise numbers	E 1.49, E 3.55, E 4.29
	Rotate text	E 3.8
	Indent text	E 3.13
	Revise formulas	E 1.49
	Copy data	E 1.23, E 3.13, E 3.29
	Move data	E 1.25, E 3.15, E 3.15
	Insert rows and columns	E 3.15, E 3.17
	Modify rows and columns	E 2.34, E 3.12
	Delete rows and columns	E 3.17
	Use relative references	E 1.24, E 3.23
	Use absolute references	E 3.23
	Use mixed references	E 3.23, E 4.32
	Sort data	E 6.14
Print workbooks	Preview and print worksheets	E 1.43, E 2.53, E 4.46
	Print the screen	E 2.58
	Print ranges	E 2.57, E 6.14
	Print headers and footers	E 4.43
Format worksheets	Modify cell size and alignment	E 1.30, E 2.29
	Apply general number formats	E 2.28, E 3.21, E 4.21
	Apply font formats	E 1.27, E 2.21, E 3.10
	Apply outlines	E 2.27, E 4.20, E 5.9
Create and apply range names	Create and name ranges	E 1.23, E 5.12, E 6.9
	Clear and format ranges	E 1.51, E 2.22
	Copy and move ranges	E 2.20, E 3.13
Use functions	Use AVERAGE function	E 2.15
	Use MIN function	E 2.17
	Use MAX function	E 2.16
	Use worksheet functions	E 1.21, E 2.15, E 2.19
Use draw	Create lines and objects	E 3.35, E 3.40, E 3.73
	Modify lines and objects	E 3.37
	Create 3D shapes	E 3.35, E 4.38
	Modify 3D shapes	E 4.40
Use charts	Create charts	E 1.35, E 2.41, E 3.41
	Modify charts	E 1.37, E 2.46, E 3.44
	Preview and print charts	E 1.43, E 2.53, E 3.49
Save spreadsheets as HTML documents	Save spreadsheets as HTML documents	E 1.42, E 1.59, E 4.48

MOUS CERTIFICATION

Microsoft Access 97 Expert User Skill Sets and Activities

Table A-3 lists the skill sets and activities you should be familiar with if you plan to take the Microsoft Access 97 Expert examination. Red page numbers mean that the activity is demonstrated in the companion textbook *Microsoft Office 97: Advanced Concepts and Techniques* (ISBN 0-7895-1335-8).

Table A-3 Access 97 MOUS Skills and Activities

SKILL SETS	ACTIVITIES	PAGE NUMBERS
Create a database	Plan a database	A 1.6, A 1.13, A 1.54
	Create a table	A 1.13, A 1.32, A 5.7
	Enter data into a table	A 1.20, A 1.27, A 1.34
	Modify data in a table	A 3.9, A 3.16, A 3.19
	Enter data into a form	A 3.6, A 3.10
	Navigate through a table	A 1.26, A 1.38, A 3.16
	Delete data from a table	A 3.11, A 3.21, A 3.23
Use forms	Create a simple form	A 1.35, A 4.32
	Modify a form	A 4.33, A 5.23
	Create controls on a form	A 4.36, A 6.17, A 6.24
	Modify controls	A 4.38, A 5.28, A 6.29
	Add a record using a form	A 3.6, A 3.10
	Show related records on a form	A 5.18, A 5.40
Modify a database	Open a database	A 1.24, A 2.7
	Modify field properties	A 3.23
	Modify field layout	A 3.12, A 3.14, A 3.17
	Modify the presentation of a database	A 3.17, A 5.12, A 6.36
View information	Present information in a chart	See Help
	View information in a form	A 4.46, A 5.40, A 6.13
	View multiple records	A 2.13, A 2.22, A 3.10
	Switch between views	A 3.10, A 4.16
Organize information	Sort data on single fields	A 2.27, A 3.35, A 3.40
	Sort data on multiple fields	A 2.27, A 3.36
Locate information	Find a specific record	A 2.18, A 3.8, A 3.38
	Create a simple query	A 2.7, A 2.16
	Create a query with multiple criteria	A 2.18
	Add filters (selection and form)	See Help
	Remove filters	See Help
Refine results of a query	Add fields to a query	A 2.10, A 2.16, A 2.37
	Remove fields from a query	A 2.17, A 2.21, A 2.37
	Sort a query	A 2.27, A 6.30
	Join tables in a query	A 2.32
	Remove joins in a query	A 2.37
	Save a query	A 2.44
Analyze data	Build summary queries	A 2.38
	Calculate fields	A 2.36
	Set crosstab queries	See Help

Table A-3 Access 97 MOUS Skills and Activities *(cont.)*

SKILL SETS	ACTIVITIES	PAGE NUMBERS
Create subforms	Identify appropriate use for subforms	A 5.18
	Add a record with a main form	A 3.6, A 5.40
	Add records with subforms	A 5.40
	Merge two tables into a form	A 5.18
Build a relational database	Identify relationships	A 1.54, A 2.32, A 3.31, A 5.18
	Relate tables	A 2.32, A 3.31
Integrate information from other applications	Import data	AI 1.3
	Link data	AI 2.4
	Add pictures to records	A 5.13, A 5.30
Utilize Web capability	Create hyperlinks	A 5.8, A 5.15, A 5.40
	Build order forms for Internet use	A 4.48
Maintain data integrity	Identify criteria for data integrity	A 3.23
	Validate text	A 3.23, A 3.28
	Set required properties	A 3.23
	Set validation rules	A 3.23
	Set look up fields	See Help
	Use expressions in calculated controls	A 4.36
Build a form for other users	Title a form	A 4.42
	Modify form design	A 4.33, A 5.23
	Improve accuracy in forms	A 4.38, A 4.47, A 6.24
	Enhance design of a form	A 4.33, A 5.23, A 6.17
Produce reports	Create a report	A 1.40, A 4.11, A 4.21
	Modify a report	A 4.15, A 4.25
	Label a report	A 4.16, A 4.30, A 4.42
	Customize headers and footers	A 4.27, A 4.29
	Make a calculation on a report	A 4.11
	Group data in a report	A 4.20
	Sort data in a report	A 3.38, A 4.21
	Add custom pages	A 4.20, A 4.49
Print	Print a report	A 4.20, A 6.13
	Print a form	A 4.57
	Print a result of a query	A 2.13

MOUS CERTIFICATION

Microsoft PowerPoint 97 Expert User Skill Sets and Activities

Table A-4 lists the skill sets and activities you should be familiar with if you plan to take the Microsoft PowerPoint 97 Expert examination. Red page numbers mean that the activity is demonstrated in the companion textbook *Microsoft Office 97: Advanced Concepts and Techniques* (ISBN 0-7895-1335-8).

Table A-4 PowerPoint 97 MOUS Skills and Activities

SKILL SETS	ACTIVITIES	PAGE NUMBERS
Create a presentation	Start a new presentation	PP 1.10, PP 2.7, PP 4.12
	Create from a template	PP 1.11, PP 2.7, PP 4.9
	Create from an outline	PP 2.10, PP 3.8
	Create from an existing presentation	PPI 1.3, PP 4.7
	Delete slides	PP 4.33
Add textual information	Enter text in slide and outline view	PP 1.18, PP 1.28, PP 2.11
	Enter bulleted information	PP 1.27, PP 2.11, PP 4.47
	Change the text alignment	PP 1.29, PP 2.13, PP 2.23
Add visual elements	Add formatting	PP 1.20, PP 1.46, PP 2.50
	Build a graph	PP 1.8, PP 4.37
	Draw an object	PP 4.13, PP 4.15
	Rotate and fill an object	PP 4.16, PP 4.20, PP 4.23
	Scale and size an object	PP 2.33, PP 3.45, PP 3.50
	Add a table	PP 4.25
	Add shapes	PP 4.34
	Animate objects	PP 2.38, PP 2.47, PPI 1.9
	Add transitions	PP 2.39, PP 3.59, PP 4.52
	Add an organizational chart	PP 3.27
	Set custom options	PP 1.37, PP 1.44, PP 2.36
	Check styles	PP 1.41, PP 1.43, PP 2.38
Bring in data from other sources	Add clip art	PP 2.26, PPI 1.5, PP 3.54
	Insert an Excel chart	PP 3.18
	Import text from Word	PP 3.9
	Add scanned images	PP 3.15, PP 3.49, PP 4.48
	Add sound and movie	PP 1.8, PP 4.57
	Export an outline to Word	PP 3.13
Modify a presentation	Change the sequence of a slide	PP 2.10, PP 4.6
	Find and replace text	PP 4.46
	Modify the slide master	PP 1.46, PP 1.47, PP 4.27
	Modify sequence in outline mode	PP 2.10
	Change tabs	PP 4.13
	Change fonts	PP 1.20, PP 4.9, PP 4.43
	Change the alignment of text	PP 1.29, PP 2.11, PP 2.24
Prepare for distribution	Spell check	PP 1.41, PP 2.38, PP 4.59
	Add speaker notes	PP 2.57, PP 4.59
	Set automatic slide timing	PP 4.54, PP 4.57
Customize a presentation	Create a custom background	PP 3.13, PP 4.11
	Customize a color scheme	PP 3.53, PP 4.9, PP 4.11
	Customize clip art and other objects	PP 2.33, PP 3.56, PP 3.58
	Recolor and edit objects	PP 3.21, PP 3.42, PP 4.31
	Apply a template from another presentation	PP 1.10, PP 2.7, PP 4.8
	Add links to other slides within the presentation	PP 4.34, PP 4.53, PPI 2.5
	Hide slides	PP 4.52
Deliver presentations	Start a slide show on any slide	PP 1.35, PP 2.51, PP 2.52
	Use onscreen navigation tools	PP 1.37, PPI 2.6, PPI 2.8
	Generate meeting notes	PP 4.59
	Electronically incorporate meeting feedback	PP 4.8
	Print slides in a variety of formats	PP 1.51, PP 2.53, PP 3.60
	Print color presentations	PP 1.51, PPI 1.10, PP 3.60
	Export to overhead	PP 1.54
	Export to 35mm slides	PP 1.6, PP 1.8
	Present with Presentation conferencing	PP 4.54
	Save presentation for use on another computer	PP 1.23, PP 2.19, PP 4.7
	Save for Internet	PPI 2.2

QUICK REFERENCE

Appendix B Quick Reference Summary

Microsoft Office 97 Quick Reference

In the Microsoft Office 97 applications, you can accomplish a task in a number of ways. The following five tables (one each for Word, Excel, Access, PowerPoint, and Outlook) provide a quick reference to each task presented in this textbook. You can invoke the commands listed in the Menu Bar and Shortcut Menu columns using either the mouse or keyboard.

Table B-1 Word 97 Quick Reference

TASK	PAGE NO.	MOUSE	MENU BAR	SHORTCUT MENU	KEYBOARD SHORTCUT
AutoCorrect Entry, Create	WD 3.23		Tools | AutoCorrect | AutoCorrect tab		
AutoText Entry, Create	WD 2.34		Insert | AutoText | New		
AutoText Entry, Insert	WD 2.38		Insert | AutoText		F3
Blank Line Above Paragraph	WD 2.16		Format | Paragraph | Indents and Spacing tab	Paragraph | Indents and Spacing tab	CTRL+0
Bold	WD 1.34	Bold button on Formatting toolbar	Format | Font | Font tab	Font | Font tab	CTRL+B
Bulleted List	WD 1.23	Bullets button on Formatting toolbar	Format | Bullets and Numbering | Bulleted tab	Bullets and Numbering | Bulleted tab	* and then space followed by text, then ENTER
Capitalize Letters	WD 2.38		Format | Font | Font tab	Font | Font tab	CTRL+SHIFT+A
Center	WD 1.30	Center button on Formatting toolbar	Format | Paragraph | Indents and Spacing tab	Paragraph | Indents and Spacing tab	CTRL+E
Close All Documents	WD 2.50		SHIFT+File | Close All		
Close Document	WD 1.54	Close button on menu bar	File | Close		CTRL+W
Convert Table to Text	WDI 1.3		Table | Convert Table to Text		
Count Words	WD 3.49		Tools | Word Count		
Delete Text	WD 1.53	Cut button on Standard toolbar	Edit | Cut	Cut	DELETE
Double-Space Text	WD 3.10		Format | Paragraph | Indents and Spacing tab	Paragraph | Indents and Spacing tab	CTRL+2
Find	WD 3.48	Select Browse Object button on vertical scroll bar	Edit | Find		CTRL+F
Find and Replace	WD 3.46	Select Browse Object button on vertical scroll bar	Edit | Replace		CTRL+H
First-Line Indent	WD 3.18	Drag First Line Indent marker on ruler	Format | Paragraph | Indents and Spacing tab	Paragraph | Indents and Spacing tab	
Font	WD 1.33	Font button on Formatting toolbar	Format | Font | Font tab	Font | Font tab	CTRL+SHIFT+F
Font Size	WD 1.14	Font Size box arrow on Formatting toolbar	Format | Font | Font tab	Format | Font | Font tab | Font | Font tab	CTRL+SHIFT+P
Footnote, Create	WD 3.25		Insert | Footnote		
Footnote, Edit	WD 3.28	Double-click note reference mark in document window	View | Footnotes		
Formatting, Remove	WD 2.38		Format | Font | Font tab	Font | Font tab	CTRL+SPACEBAR
Go To	WD 3.45	Select Browse Object button on vertical scroll bar	Edit | Go To		CTRL+G
Hanging Indent	WD 3.40	Drag Hanging Indent marker on ruler	Format | Paragraph | Indents and Spacing tab	Paragraph | Indents and Spacing tab	CTRL+T
Header	WD 3.12	In page layout view, double-click header area	View | Header and Footer		
Help	WD 1.54	Office Assistant button on Standard toolbar	Help | Microsoft Word Help		F1
Hyperlink	WD 3.42	Insert Hyperlink button on Standard toolbar			Web address then SPACEBAR or ENTER
Italicize	WD 1.38	Italic button on Formatting toolbar	Format | Font | Font tab	Font | Font tab	CTRL+I
Left Margin	WD 2.43	Left Indent marker on ruler	Format | Paragraph | Indents and Spacing tab	Paragraph | Indents and Spacing tab	
Left-Align	WD 3.40	Align Left button on Formatting toolbar	Format | Paragraph | Indents and Spacing tab	Paragraph | Indents and Spacing tab	CTRL+L
Margins	WD 3.7	In page layout view, drag margin boundary	File | Page Setup | Margins tab		
Move	WD 2.41	Drag and drop	Edit | Cut; Edit | Paste		CTRL+X; CTRL+V
Nonprinting Characters	WD 1.18	Show/Hide ¶ button on Standard toolbar	Tools | Options | View tab		CTRL+SHIFT+*

(continued)

QUICK REFERENCE

Table B-1 Word 97 Quick Reference *(continued)*

TASK	PAGE NO.	MOUSE	MENU BAR	SHORTCUT MENU	KEYBOARD SHORTCUT
Numbered List	WD 1.25	Numbering button on Formatting toolbar	Format | Bullets and Numbering | Numbered tab	Bullets and Numbering | Numbered tab	1. and then space followed by text, then ENTER
Open Document	WD 1.51	Open button on Standard toolbar	File | Open		CTRL+O
Orphan	WD 3.30		Format | Paragraph | Line and Page Breaks tab	Paragraph | Line and Page Breaks tab	
Page Break	WD 3.38		Insert | Break		CTRL+ENTER
Page Numbers	WD 3.12	Insert Page Number button on Header and Footer toolbar	Insert | Page Numbers		
Picture	WD 1.40		Insert | Picture | From File		
Print Document	WD 1.47	Print button on Standard toolbar	File | Print		CTRL+P
Print Preview	WD 2.25	Print Preview button on Standard toolbar	File | Print Preview		CTRL+F2
Quit Word	WD 1.49	Close button on title bar	File | Exit		ALT+F4
Redo Action	WD 1.53	Redo button on Standard toolbar	Edit | Redo		
Resize Graphic	WD 1.40	Drag sizing handle	Format|Picture | Size tab		
Right-Align	WD 3.13	Align Right button on Formatting toolbar	Format | Paragraph | Indents and Spacing tab	Paragraph | Indents and Spacing tab	CTRL+R
Ruler, Show or Hide	WD 1.13		View | Ruler		
Save as Web Page	WDI 1.4		File | Save as HTML		
Save Document – New Name	WD 1.47		File | Save As		
Save Document – Same Name	WD 1.25	Save button on Standard toolbar	File | Save		CTRL+S
Select Document	WD 2.41	Point to left and triple-click	Edit | Select All		CTRL+A
Select Graphic	WD 2.41	Click graphic			
Select Group of Words	WD 1.37	Drag through words			CTRL+SHIFT+ RIGHT ARROW
Select Line	WD 1.31	Point to left and click			SHIFT+DOWN ARROW
Select Multiple Paragraphs	WD 1.29	Point to left and drag down			CTRL+SHIFT+ DOWN ARROW
Select Paragraph	WD 2.36	Triple-click paragraph			
Select Sentence	WD 2.40	CTRL+click			CTRL+SHIFT+ RIGHT ARROW
Select Table	WD 2.23	Drag through table	Table | Select Table		ALT+5
Select Word	WD 1.35	Double-click word			CTRL+SHIFT+ RIGHT ARROW
Sort Paragraphs	WD 3.43		Table | Sort		
Spelling Check as You Type	WD 1.20	Double-click Spelling and Grammar Status icon on status bar		correct word	
Spelling Check At Once	WD 2.46	Spelling and Grammar button on Standard toolbar	Tools | Spelling and Grammar	Spelling	F7
Subscript	WD 2.38		Format | Font | Font tab	Font | Font tab	CTRL+=
Superscript	WD 2.38		Format | Font | Font tab	Font | Font tab	CTRL+SHIFT+PLUS SIGN
Switch to Open Document	WD 2.49		Window | document name		
Table AutoFormat	WD 3.34		Table | Table AutoFormat	Table AutoFormat	
Table, Create	WD 3.30	Insert Table button on Standard toolbar	Table | Insert Table		
Template	WD 2.28		File | New		
Thesaurus	WD 3.48		Tools | Language | Thesaurus		SHIFT+F7
Underline	WD 1.36	Underline button on Formatting toolbar	Format | Font | Font tab	Font | Font tab	CTRL+U
Undo Action	WD 1.53	Undo button on Standard toolbar	Edit | Undo		CTRL+Z
Web Page, View	WDI 1.5	Web Page Preview button on Standard toolbar	File | Web Page Preview		
Widow	WD 3.30		Format | Paragraph | Line and Page Breaks tab	Paragraph | Line and Page Breaks tab	
Wizard	WD 2.27		File | New		
Zoom Document	WD 2.31	Zoom box arrow on Formatting toolbar	View | Zoom		

QUICK REFERENCE

Table B-2 Excel 97 Quick Reference

TASK	PAGE NO.	MOUSE	MENU BAR	SHORTCUT MENU	KEYBOARD SHORTCUT
AutoFormat	E 1.31		Format I AutoFormat		
AutoSum	E 1.22	AutoSum button on Standard toolbar	Insert I Function		ALT+=
Bold	E 1.28	Bold button on Formatting toolbar	Format I Cells I Font tab	Format Cells I Font tab	CTRL+B
Borders	E 2.28	Borders button on Formatting toolbar	Format I Cells I Border tab	Format Cells I Border tab	CTRL+1 I B
Center	E 2.29	Center button on Formatting toolbar	Format I Cells I Alignment tab	Format Cells I Alignment tab	CTRL+1 I A
Center Across Columns	E 1.30	Merge and Center button on Formatting toolbar	Format I Cells I Alignment tab	Format Cells I Alignment tab	CTRL+1 I A
Chart	E 2.41	ChartWizard button on Standard toolbar	Insert I Chart		F11
Clear Cell	E 1.51	Drag fill handle back	Edit I Clear I All	Clear Contents	DELETE
Close Workbook	E 1.45	Close button on menu bar	File I Close		CTRL+W
Color Background	E 2.26	Fill Color button on Formatting toolbar	Format I Cells I Patterns tab	Format Cells I Patterns tab	CTRL+1 I P
Column Width	E 2.35	Drag column heading boundary	Format I Column	Column Height	
Comma Style Format	E 2.32	Percent Style button on Formatting toolbar	Format I Cells I Number tab I Accounting	Format Cells I Number tab I Accounting	CTRL+1 I N
Copy and Paste	E 3.13	Copy button and Paste button on Standard toolbar	Edit I Copy; Edit I Paste	Copy to copy I Paste to paste	CTRL+C; CTRL+V
Currency Style Format	E 3.32	Percent Style button on Formatting toolbar	Format I Cells I Number tab I Currency	Format Cells I Number tab I Accounting	CTRL+1 I N
Date	E 3.21	Paste Function button on Standard toolbar	Insert I Function		CTRL+;
Decimal Place, Decrease	E 2.33	Decrease Decimal button on Formatting toolbar	Format I Cells I Number tab I Currency	Format Cells I Number tab I Currency	CTRL+1 I N
Decimal Place, Increase	E 2.33	Increase Decimal button on Formatting toolbar	Format I Cells I Number tab I Currency	Format Cells I Number tab I Currency	CTRL+1 I N
Delete Rows or Columns	E 3.17		Edit I Delete	Delete	DELETE
Drop Shadow	E 3.37	Shadow button on Drawing toolbar			
Embed	EI 1.3		Edit I Copy; Edit I Paste Special		
Fit to Print	E 2.61		File I Page Setup I Page tab		
Font Color	E 2.26	Font Color button on Formatting toolbar	Format I Cells I Font tab	Format Cells I Font tab	CTRL+1 I F
Font Size	E 1.29	Font Size box arrow on Formatting toolbar	Format I Cells I Font tab	Format Cells I Font tab	CTRL+1 I F
Font Type	E 2.23	Font box on Formatting toolbar	Format I Cells I Font tab	Format Cells I Font tab	CTRL+1 I F
Formula Palette	E 2.16	Edit Formula box in formula bar	Insert I Function		CTRL+A after you type function name
Formulas Version	E 2.59		Tools I Options I View I Formulas		CTRL+`
Freeze Worksheet Titles	E 3.19		Windows I Freeze Panes		
Function	E 2.15	Paste Function button on Standard toolbar	Insert I Function		SHIFT+F3
Go To	E 1.34	Click cell	Edit I Go To		F5
Goal Seek	E 3.56		Tools I Goal Seek		
Help	E 1.52	Office Assistant button on Standard toolbar	Help I Microsoft Excel Help		F1
Hide Column	E 2.37	Drag column heading boundary	Format I Column	Column Height	CTRL+SHIFT+)
Hide Row	E 2.39	Drag row heading boundary	Format I Row	Row Height	CTRL+SHIFT+(
Insert Rows or Columns	E 3.15		Insert I Rows or Insert I Columns	Insert	
Italicize	E 3.40	Italicize button on Formatting toolbar	Format I Cells I Font tab	Format Cells I Font tab	CTRL+I
Link	EI 1.3		Edit I Copy; Edit I Paste Special		
Move	E 3.15	Point to border and drag	Edit I Cut; Edit I Paste		CTRL+X; CTRL+V
New Workbook	E 1.52	New button on Standard toolbar	File I New		CTRL+N
Open Workbook	E 1.45	Open button on Standard toolbar	File I Open		CTRL+O
Percent Style Format	E 2.33	Percent Style button on Formatting toolbar	Format I Cells I Number tab I Percentage	Format Cells I Number tab I Percentage	CTRL+1 I N
Preview Worksheet	E 2.53	Print Preview button on Standard toolbar	File I Print Preview		
Print Worksheet	E 2.53	Print button on Standard toolbar	File I Print		CTRL+P
Quit Excel	E1.44	Close button on title bar	File I Exit		ALT+F4

(continued)

Table B-2 Excel 97 Quick Reference *(continued)*

TASK	PAGE NO.	MOUSE	MENU BAR	SHORTCUT MENU	KEYBOARD SHORTCUT
Redo	E 1.51	Redo button on Standard toolbar	Edit | Redo		
Remove Splits	E 3.52	Double-click split bar	Window | Split		
Rename Sheet Tab	E 2.51	Double-click sheet tab		Rename	
Rotate Text	E 3.8		Format | Cells | Alignment tab	Format Cells | Alignment tab	
Row Height	E 2.37	Drag row heading boundary	Format | Row	Row Height	
Save Workbook	E 1.39	Save button on Standard toolbar	File | Save As		CTRL+S or F12
Select All of Worksheet	E 1.52	Select All button on worksheet			CTRL+A
Select Sheets	E 2.56	SHIFT and click tab		Select All Sheets	
Series	E 3.10	Drag fill handle	Edit | Fill | Series		
Shortcut Menu	E 2.32	Right-click			SHIFT+F10
Spell Check	E 2.39	Spelling button on Standard toolbar	Tools | Spelling		F7
Split Window into Panes	E 3.52	Drag vertical or horizontal split box	Window | Split		
Stock Quotes	E 2.61		Data | Get External Data | Run Web Query		
Toolbar, Show or Hide	E 1.12	Right-click toolbar	View | Toolbars		
Underline	E 3.40	Underline button on Formatting toolbar	Format | Cells | Font tab	Format Cells | Font tab	CTRL+U
Undo	E 1.50	Undo button on Standard toolbar	Edit | Undo		CTRL+Z
Unfreeze Worksheet Titles	E 3.30		Windows | Unfreeze Panes		
Zoom	E 3.49	Zoom box on Standard toolbar	View | Zoom		

Table B-3 Access 97 Quick Reference

TASK	PAGE NO.	MOUSE	MENU BAR	SHORTCUT MENU	KEYBOARD SHORTCUT
Add Field	A 3.15	Insert Rows button	Insert | Rows	Insert Rows	INSERT
Add Record	A 1.21, A1.34	New Record button	Insert | New Record	New Record	
Add Table to Query	A 2.33	Show Table button	Query | Show Table	Show Table	
Calculate Statistics	A 2.39	Totals button	View | Totals	Totals	
Change Group of Records	A 3.19	Query Type arrow | Update Query	Query | Update Query	Query Type | Update Query	
Clear Query	A 2.17		Edit | Clear Grid		
Close Database	A 1.46	Close button	File | Close		
Close Form	A 1.36	Close button	File | Close		
Close Query	A 2.15	Close button	File | Close		
Close Table	A 1.24	Close button	File | Close		
Convert Worksheet to Table	AI 1.4		File | Get External Data | Import		
Create Computed Field	A 2.37			Zoom	SHIFT+F2
Create Database	A 1.10	Start button | New Office Document	File | New Database		CTRL+N
Create Form	A 1.35	Forms tab | New button	Insert | Form		
Create Index	A 3.42	Indexes button	View | Indexes		
Create Query	A 2.7	Queries tab | New button	Insert | Query		
Create Report	A 1.41	Reports tab | New button	Insert | Report		
Create Table	A 1.15	Tables tab | New button	Insert | Table		
Default Value	A 3.25	Default Value box			
Delete Field	A 1.18	Delete Rows button	Edit | Delete Rows	Delete Rows	DELETE
Delete Group of Records	A 3.22	Query Type arrow | Delete Query	Query | Delete Query	Query Type | Delete Query	
Delete Record	A 3.11	Delete Record button	Edit | Delete Record	Delete Record	DELETE
Exclude Duplicates	A 2.30	Properties button	View | Properties | Unique Values Only	Properties | Unique Values Only	
Exclude Field from Query Results	A 2.21	Show check box			
Field Size	A3.13	Field Size text box			
Field Type	A 1.16	Data Type arrow | appropriate type			Appropriate letter
Format	A 3.27	Format box			
Help	A 1.49	Office Assistant button	Help | Microsoft Access Help		F1
Include All Fields in Query	A 2.16	Double-click asterisk			

QUICK REFERENCE

Table B-3 Access 97 Quick Reference *(continued)*

TASK	PAGE NO.	MOUSE	MENU BAR	SHORTCUT MENU	KEYBOARD SHORTCUT
Include Field in Query	A 2.11	Double-click field in field list box			
Key Field	A 1.17	Set Primary Key button	Edit I Primary Key	Primary Key	
Move to First Record	A 1.26	First Record button			CTRL+UP ARROW
Move to Last Record	A 1.26	Last Record button			CTRL+DOWN ARROW
Move to Next Record	A 1.26	Next Record button			DOWN ARROW
Move to Previous Record	A 1.26	Previous Record button			UP ARROW
Open Database	A 1.25	Open button	File I Open Database		CTRL+O
Open Form	A 3.7	Forms tab I Open button		Open	Use arrow keys to move highlight to name, then press ENTER key
Open Table	A 1.20	Tables tab I Open button		Open	Use arrow keys to move highlight to name, then press ENTER key
Order Records	A 3.35	Sort Ascending or Sort Descending button	Records I Sort I Sort Ascending or Sort Descending	Sort Ascending or Sort Descending	
Preview Table	A 1.28	Print Preview button	File I Print Preview	Print Preview	
Print Report	A 1.45	Print button	File I Print	Print	CTRL+P
Print Results of Query	A 2.13	Print button	File I Print	Print	CTRL+P
Print Table	A 1.25	Print button	File I Print	Print	CTRL+P
Quit Access	A 1.24	Close button	File I Exit		ALT+F4
Relationships (Referential Integrity)	A 3.32	Relationships button	Tools I Relationships		
Resize Column	A 3.17	Drag right edge of column			
Restructure Table	A 3.12	Tables tab I Design button		Design	Use arrow keys to move highlight to name, then press ENTER key
Return to Select Query Window	A 2.14	View button	View I Design View		
Run Query	A 2.12	Run button	Query I Run		
Save Form	A 1.36	Save button	File I Save		CTRL+S
Save Query	A 2.44	Save button	File I Save		CTRL+S
Save Table	A 1.19	Save button	File I Save		CTRL+S
Search for Record	A 3.9	Find button	Edit I Find		CTRL+F
Select Fields for Report	A 1.42	Add Field button or Add All Fields button			
Sort Data in Query	A 2.27	Sort row I arrow I type of sort			
Switch Between Form and Datasheet Views	A 1.39	View button	View I Datasheet View		
Use AND Criterion	A 2.25				Place criteria on same line
Use OR Criterion	A 2.26				Place criteria on separate lines
Validation Rule	A 3.23	Validation Rule box			
Validation Text	A 3.23	Validation Text box			

Table B-4 PowerPoint 97 Quick Reference

TASK	PAGE NO.	MOUSE	MENU BAR	SHORTCUT MENU	KEYBOARD SHORTCUT
Apply Design	PP 3.12	Apply Design button	Format | Apply Design | template file	Apply Design	ALT+O | Y
Change Fill Color	PP 4.16	Fill Color button and then click color sample	Format | Colors and Lines | Fill | color sample	Format AutoShape | Colors and Lines tab sheet/Fill color	ALT+O | N | TAB | DOWN ARROW
Change Slide Layout	PP 2.23	Slide Layout button	Format | Slide Layout | slide layout	Slide Layout | slide layout	ALT+O | L | Arrow keys
Change Text Color	PP 4.10	Text Color button and color sample	Format | Font | Color | color sample	Font | Color	ALT+O | F | ALT+C | DOWN ARROW
Check Spelling	PP 1.41	Spelling button on Standard toolbar	Tools | Spelling		F7
Decrease Font Size	PP 1.21	Decrease Font Size button on Formatting toolbar	Format | Font | size	Font | Size	CTRL+SHIFT+<
Demote a Paragraph	PP 1.29	Demote button on Formatting toolbar			TAB or ALT+SHIFT+ RIGHT ARROW
Help	PP 1.54	Office Assistant button on Standard toolbar	Help | Microsoft PowerPoint Help		F1
Increase Font Size	PP 2.50	Increase Font Size button on Formatting toolbar	Format | Font | size	Font | Size	CTRL+SHIFT+>
Italicize Text	PP 1.22	Italic button on Formatting toolbar	Format | Font | Font style | Italic	Font | Font Style	CTRL+I
Move a Paragraph Down	PP 2.10	Move Down button on Outline toolbar			ALT+SHIFT+DOWN ARROW
Move a Paragraph Up	PP 2.10	Move Up button on Outline toolbar			ALT+SHIFT+UP ARROW
New Slide	PP 1.26	New Slide button on Common Tasks toolbar	Insert | New Slide		CTRL+M
Next Slide	PP 1.34	Next Slide button on vertical scroll bar			PAGE DOWN
Open a Presentation	PP 1.40	Open button on Standard toolbar	File | Open		CTRL+O
Previous Slide	PP 1.15	Previous Slide button			PAGE UP
Print a Presentation	PP 1.51	Print button on Standard toolbar	File | Print		CTRL+P
Promote a Paragraph	PP 1.28	Promote button on Formatting toolbar			SHIFT+TAB or ALT+SHIFT+LEFT ARROW
Quit PowerPoint	PP 1.39	Double-click Control icon on title bar	File | Exit		ALT+F4
Redo button	PP 1.19	Redo button on Standard toolbar	Edit | Repeat		CTRL+Y or ALT+E | R
Save a Presentation	PP 1.33	Save button on Standard toolbar	File | Save		CTRL+S
Slide Show	PP 1.35	Slide Show button on View Button Bar	View | Slide Show		ALT+V | W
Undo button	PP 1.19	Undo button on Standard toolbar	Edit | Undo		CTRL+Z or ALT+E | U

Table B-5 Outlook 97 Quick Reference

TASK	PAGE NO.	MOUSE	MENU BAR	SHORTCUT MENU	KEYBOARD SHORTCUT
Appointment	O 1.12	New Appointment button on Standard toolbar	File | New | Appointment	New Appointment	CTRL+SHIFT+A or DELETE
Contact List	O 1.35	New Contact button on Standard toolbar	File | New | Contact	New Contact	CTRL+SHIFT+C
Delete Appointment	O 1.20	Delete button on Standard toolbar	Edit | Delete	Delete	CTRL+D or DELETE
Delete Subfolder	O 1.40	Delete button on Standard toolbar	File | Folder | Delete	Delete	CTRL+D or DELETE
Display Day	O 1.27	Day button on Standard toolbar	View | Day		ALT+1
Display Month	O 1.27	Month button on Standard toolbar	View | Month		ALT+=
Display Week	O 1.27	Week button on Standard toolbar	View | Week		ALT+MINUS SIGN
Event	O 1.25		Calendar | Event	New Event	
Help	O 1.45	Office Assistant button on Standard toolbar	Help | Microsoft Outlook Help		F1
Export Subfolder	O 1.38		File | Import and Export		
Import Subfolder	O 1.41		File | Import and Export		
Move Appointment	O 1.21		Edit | Cut; Edit | Paste		CTRL+X; CTRL+V
Move to New Date	O 1.17	Date Navigator	Go | Go to Date	Go to Date	CTRL+G
Open Calendar	O 1.3	Calendar Shortcut on Outlook bar	Go | Calendar		
Print Calendar	O 1.30	Print button on Standard toolbar	File | Print		CTRL+P
Print Contact List	O 1.37	Print button on Standard toolbar	File | Print		CTRL+P
Quit Outlook	O 1.42	Close button on title bar	File | Exit		ALT+F4
Recurring Appointment	O 1.14	Recurrence button on Standard toolbar	Appointment | Recurrence	New Recurring Appointment	CTRL+G
Save Appointment	O 1.13	Save and Close button on Standard toolbar	File | Save		CTRL+S
Subfolder	O 1.6		File | Folder | Create New Subfolder	Create Subfolder	CTRL+SHIFT+E
Task	O 1.28	New Task button on Standard toolbar	File | New | Task	New Task	CTRL+SHIFT+K

Index